MW00659335

FOUNDATION PRESS EDITORIAL BOARD

SAUL LEVMORE
DIRECTING EDITOR
William B. Graham Distinguished Service Professor of Law and
Former Dean of the Law School
University of Chicago

GUY-URIEL E. CHARLES
Charles J. Ogletree Jr. Professor of Law
Harvard Law School

NORA FREEMAN ENGSTROM
Ernest W. McFarland Professor of Law
Stanford Law School

DANIEL A. FARBER
Sho Sato Professor of Law
University of California at Berkeley

HEATHER K. GERKEN
Dean and the Sol & Lillian Goldman Professor of Law
Yale University

SAMUEL ISSACHAROFF
Bonnie and Richard Reiss Professor of Constitutional Law
New York University

HAROLD HONGJU KOH
Sterling Professor of International Law and
Former Dean of the Law School
Yale University

THOMAS W. MERRILL
Charles Evans Hughes Professor of Law
Columbia University

HILLARY A. SALE
Agnes Williams Sesquicentennial Professor of Law
Associate Dean for Strategy, and Professor of Management
Georgetown University

UNIVERSITY CASEBOOK SERIES®

FEDERAL CONSTITUTIONAL LAW

NIKOLAS BOWIE
Harvard Law School

FOUNDATION PRESS

The publisher is not engaged in rendering legal or other professional advice, and this publication is not a substitute for the advice of an attorney. If you require legal or other expert advice, you should seek the services of a competent attorney or other professional.

University Casebook Series is a trademark registered in the U.S. Patent and Trademark Office.

© 2022 LEG, Inc. d/b/a West Academic
444 Cedar Street, Suite 700
St. Paul, MN 55101
1-877-888-1330

Printed in the United States of America

ISBN: 978-1-64708-583-4

PREFACE

This is a casebook about the most fundamental document in American law, the United States Constitution. In a little under 8000 words, the document establishes a government—the federal government of the United States of America—organizes it into three major branches, explains what each branch has the power to do, and imposes limits on those powers. The document also explains the relationship between the federal government and other governments—states, tribes, and foreign nations among them. At times, it imposes limits on the powers of those other governments as well.

The Constitution does all this in the name of "We the People," written in a format meant to be accessible to anyone. That is, anyone can compare the activities of their governments with the values codified in the Constitution. Anyone can then ask themselves whether the governments are advancing or compromising those values. Anyone, in other words, can practice constitutional law. And that remains true today.

This casebook reviews each clause of the unamended Constitution—along with the amendments enacted after the Civil War—to understand how people have practiced federal constitutional law in the centuries since the Constitution's ratification. In that time, the Constitution's words have provided the vocabulary for virtually every major political controversy this country has ever debated. We will read about slavery, war, and the prosecution of political dissidents; about capitalism, regulation, and the displacement of Native tribes; about secession, martial law, and equal citizenship; about the right to vote, white supremacy, and empire; about unions, child labor, and the rights of the accused; about Communism, eugenics, and immigration; about desegregation, states' rights, and sexual equality; about gerrymandering, apportionment, and the War on Drugs; about impeachment, economic inequality, and sexual orientation; about abortion, religious liberty, and incarceration; and about climate change, tribal sovereignty, and concentration camps. Debates over all of these issues have inevitably turned over whether Congress, the president, the judiciary, or a government officer has the power to act in a certain way—or whether, instead, the Constitution limits that power. Although the 8000 words of the Constitution rarely resolve these debates one way or another, interpretations of those words have opened and closed the range of permissible outcomes, shaping the political landscape in which we live.

The structure of this casebook hews closely to the structure of the Federal Constitution. Beginning with the Preamble and continuing with Article I, Section 1, the casebook asks fifty essential questions about what the words of the Constitution mean. What makes these questions "essential" is not only that the answers to them continue to be debated, but also that the process of pursuing the questions will help you understand the deep interpretive and ideological issues at the heart of constitutional law.

This casebook would not have been possible without an incredible resource produced and updated by the Congressional Research Service and other editors since 1911: *The Constitution of the United States of America: Analysis and Interpretation* (Michael J. Garcia, Gaitlain Devereaux Lewis, Andrew Nolan, Meghan Totten, Ashley Tyson eds., 2017). What began as a modest list of U.S. Supreme Court constitutional decisions now describes and summarizes almost 6000 cases organized by the clause of the Constitution they interpret. This "Annotated Constitution" is available to the public online: www.gpo.gov/constitution annotated. It is an excellent reference guide, even though it does not provide excerpts from cases, the historical context in which cases were decided, or other notes and questions that would make it suitable for teaching and understanding constitutional law.

I used the Annotated Constitution as a template and initial source of cases for this casebook. Putting the two works side-by-side, the many ways in which I was inspired by its organization and analysis should be readily apparent. Without access to such a comprehensive accounting of Supreme Court cases, I never would have attempted to organize and write my own materials for teaching a first-year class on constitutional law.

In writing this casebook, I was also inspired by many fantastic works of legal history that have put interpretations of the Constitution in historical context. I think it is impossible to understand any interpretation of a constitutional clause—whether in a judicial opinion or on Twitter—without an appreciation for what linguists call "diachrony" and "synchrony." The first term refers to the historical evolution of the interpretation: the many previous decisions, events, people, and cultural developments that made the interpretation intelligible and persuasive. The second refers to the immediate context in which the interpretation was formed: the partisan and ideological lenses through with the authors of the interpretation and the parties to the controversy would have understood the interpretation. This casebook takes the position that both types of context are necessary to understand constitutional interpretations.

The materials in this casebook emphasize judicial opinions. One reason for this is because many people today accept the Supreme Court's announcement in *Cooper v. Aaron* that "the federal judiciary is supreme in the exposition of the law of the Constitution." 358 U.S. 1, 18 (1958). A more important reason is convenience. Judicial opinions typically frame competing sides of constitutional debates in fewer pages than the many other places in which the Constitution is interpreted, including floor debates in Congress, memo traffic in the executive branch, op-eds in the press, and articles in law reviews. But as I emphasize in section 3.2, just because this casebook emphasizes judicial opinions does not mean that the judiciary interprets the Constitution any better than elected politicians or members of the public.

That said, even judges provide limited information about the historical and political context in which they make decisions. Only rarely do courts clearly express the assumptions and normative values they hope to promote with their interpretations; indeed, those assumptions and values are often clear only in retrospect. To make these assumptions and values clear to a twenty-first century reader with limited knowledge of American history, the casebook includes background descriptions of the historical context behind all of the excerpted cases and other primary material. The excerpts themselves typically exclude the author's own description of the factual or procedural background of its interpretation. They also typically exclude the author's citations to precedents that the casebook did not previously identify in the background description.

I am deeply grateful to my wife and daughter, whose patience allowed me to complete the first version of this casebook while also teaching a full course load. Rachel Keeler and Sheila Sybrant were truly invaluable in bringing this casebook to fruition—as collaborators, copyeditors, proofreaders, and more. I also received outstanding research and editing assistance from a fabulous team of law students at Harvard Law School: Jackson Beard, Zachary Cohen, Raisa Cramer, Madeleine DeMeules, Sophi Guzzo, Connor Haaland, Devon Himelman, Meredith Manda, Daniel Polonsky, Norah Rast, and Emma Shirey.

NIKOLAS BOWIE

February 2022

SUMMARY OF CONTENTS

PART TWO. THE EXECUTIVE BRANCH

TABLE OF CONTENTS

TABLE OF CASES

The principal cases are in bold type.

UNIVERSITY CASEBOOK SERIES®

FEDERAL CONSTITUTIONAL LAW

PREAMBLE

CHAPTER 1

WHY IS THERE A CONSTITUTION?

PREAMBLE: We the People of the United States, in Order to form a more perfect Union, establish Justice, insure domestic Tranquility, provide for the common defence, promote the general Welfare, and secure the Blessings of Liberty to ourselves and our Posterity, do ordain and establish this Constitution for the United States of America.

1.1 PREDECESSORS TO THE CONSTITUTION

The U.S. Constitution was drafted in 1787—more than two hundred years after British settlers began colonizing North America and eleven years after their descendants declared independence from Great Britain. Those two centuries of colonial settlement, revolution, and their aftermath heavily influenced why the Constitution was written and what it said. Before turning to the Constitution's text, therefore, we'll start this casebook with a brief historical overview of some of the events and documents that significantly inspired the creation of the Constitution.

English colonization and empire

North America was home to millions of people when the first English subjects arrived in the 1580s. Along the Atlantic coast, dozens of tribes like the Wampanoag and Powhatan thrived in well-established political communities. *See* David Treuer, *The Heartbeat of Wounded Knee* 39 (2019). Yet when English entrepreneurs began establishing temporary fishing colonies nearby, they brought with them diseases and an ideology of domination. Through wars, coercive diplomacy, and near-genocidal practices, the English and other Europeans upended preexisting political arrangements in North America and displaced smaller tribes into protective confederacies, such as the Cherokee, Seminole, and Sioux. *Id.* at 46. Over the next two hundred years, a steady stream of European colonists decimated the Native population and claimed much of the land as their own. *See* Russell Thornton, *American Indian Holocaust and Survival: A Population History since 1492*, at 133 (1990).

Most of the first English colonies in North America were founded by large corporations, such as the Virginia Company and the Massachusetts Bay Company. *See* Nikolas Bowie, *Why the Constitution Was Written Down*, 71 Stan. L. Rev. 1397, 1407 (2019). These seventeenth-century corporations were structured similarly to modern corporations: they were profit-making enterprises run by chief executives and boards of directors annually elected by shareholders. *Id.* at 1416. They also had corporate charters that outlined in detail how their corporate governments should be organized, what they had the power to do, and what they were prohibited from doing. *Id.* In contrast with England, whose "constitution" referred to the written and unwritten arrangement of laws and customs that *constituted*, or organized, the British government, colonists in Massachusetts began referring to their own charter as a "Charter Constitution" that collected the most important of these laws and customs in one place. *Id.* at 1404. These charters would provide the most important source of material for the U.S. and state constitutions after independence; in fact, Rhode Island and Connecticut would govern themselves according to their corporate charters until the nineteenth century. *Id.* at 1498.

These early corporate colonies were eventually followed by proprietary colonies claimed by individual owners and royal colonies claimed by the British Crown. The leaders of most of these colonies hoped to profit religiously, politically, and financially. Between 1619 and 1808, commercial traders kidnapped millions of people from Africa, of whom approximately 460,000 arrived alive to work in bondage in Massachusetts, Georgia, and the eleven colonies in between. *See* David Hacker, *From "20. and Odd" to 10 Million: The Growth of the Slave Population in the United States*, 41 Slavery & Abolition 840, 847 (2020). By 1770, approximately a fifth of the two million people living in the British North American colonies were enslaved. *Id.*

That same year, most white people living in British North America considered themselves British subjects, loyal to the British Crown, who happened to live outside the British Isles. Many educated colonists were familiar with British history, followed its politics, and practiced its law. In particular, the English Civil War (1642–1651) and the Glorious Revolution (1688–1689) were widely revered for their principle that no man, not even the British monarch, could violate England's unwritten "constitution." *See* Bowie, *supra*, at 1462–64. Published speeches of John Wilkes, Edmund Burke, and other British politicians were popular in the American colonies for their defenses of the British constitution and its "rights of Englishmen," which included written rights listed in the English Bill of Rights (1689) and unwritten rights such as the right not to be taxed without representation in Great Britain's Parliament. Also popular were legal compilations such as Sir William Blackstone's *Commentaries of the Laws of England* (1765–1769), which summarized the state of English law for contemporary learners. All of these British sources would become part of American historical, political, and legal thought when the U.S. and state constitutions were drafted.

First Continental Congress

In 1770, the major difference between a white British subject in London and one in Boston was that the Londoner might be permitted to elect a member of Parliament while the Bostonian could, if qualified, elect only a member of the Massachusetts colonial legislature. This difference eventually presented a problem for the colonists, some of whom argued that the British Parliament had no power to legislate for Boston, just as the Massachusetts legislature had no power to legislate for London. They argued, in other words, that Parliament was the local legislature for the British Isles, not a superior legislature that could override Massachusetts's charter or laws. *See* Gordon S. Wood, *The Creation of the American Republic* 177–79 (1998).

This legal argument about Parliament's overseas jurisdiction spread alongside various forms of social unrest among Indians, debtors, merchants, women, and enslaved people. *See* Woody Holton, *Liberty Is Sweet* 155–62 (2021). It ultimately helped spark a continent-wide resistance movement to a series of laws passed by Parliament in the 1760s and early 1770s in which Parliament asserted the power to tax the internal affairs of the colonies. When a group of Bostonians, "dressed in the Indian manner," dumped tea into Boston Harbor to protest one such tax in 1773, Parliament retaliated by passing an act to nullify Massachusetts's charter. *See* Robert Middlekauff, *The Glorious Cause* 232–33 (2007). It also sent soldiers to occupy Boston and enforce British exercises of jurisdiction. *Id.*

These parliamentary responses led colonial legislatures up and down the continent to send representatives to confer in Philadelphia, then British North America's largest city, at the First Continental Congress. *Id.* at 242. In 1774, this Continental Congress issued the Declaration and Resolves, in which the delegates argued that Parliament's actions violated a list of colonial rights derived from "the immutable laws of nature, the principles of the English constitution, and the several charters or compacts." 1 *Journals of the Continental Congress* 63–73 (Worthington Chauncey Ford ed., 1905). The full text of this declaration included many rights that would be incorporated into the U.S. Constitution, but its basic message was captured in the fourth resolution: "That the foundation of English liberty, and of all free government, is a right in the people to participate in their legislative council"—a right that gave the colonists "a free and exclusive power of legislation in their several provincial legislatures, where their right of representation can alone be preserved. . . ." *Id.* at 68.

The First Continental Congress, which met for only a few weeks, also established one of the first continent-wide political organizations: the Continental Association, which organized an economic boycott of British goods until Parliament respected the Continental Congress's declaration of rights. *See id.* at 75–81. The Continental Congress's declaration and boycott didn't resolve tensions with Parliament, however. In 1775, war broke out in Lexington, Massachusetts.

Second Continental Congress and Declaration of Independence

Colonial legislatures responded to the war by sending delegates to the Second Continental Congress in Philadelphia, which continued meeting in modified forms for the next decade.

The Second Continental Congress's first order of business was giving advice to Massachusetts colonists on how they should govern themselves while at war with their colony's governor, a British general appointed by the Crown. The Continental Congress proposed that Massachusetts modify its seventeenth-century charter for use as a constitution. *See* 2 *id.* at 83–84.

Shortly afterward, as other colonial legislatures sought the Continental Congress's advice, the Continental Congress recommended that the legislatures "call a full and free representation of the people, and that the representatives, if they think it necessary, establish such a form of government, as, in their judgment, will best produce the happiness of the people, and most effectually secure peace and good order in the province." 3 *id.* at 319. In early 1776, the wartime governments of New Hampshire and South Carolina followed this advice by enacting "constitutions" to govern their colonies "until an accommodation of the unhappy differences between Great Britain and America can be obtained." S.C. Const. of 1776, *reprinted in* 6 *The Federal and State Constitutions* 3243 (Francis Newton Thorpe ed., 1909). As in Massachusetts, these constitutions were modeled on preexisting colonial charters. They generally established powerful elected legislatures, weak or nonexistent governors, and bills of rights that would be enforceable by politics and the oaths of public officials not to violate them.

As war continued through July 1776, the Second Continental Congress voted to declare the colonies' independence. The resulting Declaration of Independence explained the reasons for the colonies' separation from Great Britain:

> We hold these truths to be self-evident, that all men are created equal, that they are endowed by their Creator with certain unalienable Rights, that among these are Life, Liberty and the pursuit of Happiness.—That to secure these rights, Governments are instituted among Men, deriving their just powers from the consent of the governed,—That whenever any Form of Government becomes destructive of these ends, it is the Right of the People to alter or to abolish it, and to institute new Government, laying its foundation on such principles and organizing its powers in such form, as to them shall seem most likely to effect their Safety and Happiness.

4 *Journals of the Continental Congress*, *supra*, at 510–11. Although this famous sentence didn't make any new law for the colonies, it established a basic principle that the independent states would be bound by an ideal of political equality. *See* Danielle Allen, *Our Declaration* 178–82 (2014).

After continuing with a list of specific grievances, the Declaration of Independence concluded with an announcement that the colonies were now "FREE AND INDEPENDENT STATES" with "full Power to levy War, conclude Peace, contract Alliances, establish Commerce, and do all other Acts and Things which INDEPENDENT STATES may of right do." *Id.* at 514. In other words, the colonies now considered themselves thirteen sovereigns that each had the same powers that, say, France or Spain possessed under international law. Although these new sovereigns called themselves "United States," they used the term *united* much in the same way that the "United Nations" would decades later.

The Declaration of Independence precipitated another wave of state constitution-making: within nine months of July 1776, every wartime government enacted or proclaimed some written document to serve as its "Constitution or Form of Government." *See* Bowie, *supra*, at 1497–98. Most of these constitutions continued the pattern of establishing legislatures with nearly unlimited powers. But some of them, notably Pennsylvania and Virginia, included declarations of rights that the legislature was instructed not to violate, such as the "freedom of speech." *See, e.g.*, Pa. Const. of 1776, *reprinted in* 5 *The Federal and State Constitutions*, *supra*, at 3081. In 1778, residents of Massachusetts initiated another method of limiting the power of legislatures when they demanded a constitution that could be ratified or amended only by a popular referendum. *See* Bowie, *supra*, at 1500–01. During a popularly elected "convention," John Adams and other delegates coauthored a new constitution that significantly weakened the legislature by creating a government with three separate branches: a legislature, an independent executive, and an independent judiciary. Voters ratified this constitution in 1780. With amendments, it remains the oldest currently active written constitution. *Id.*

Articles of Confederation

Meanwhile, the thirteen independent states continued to send delegates to the Second Continental Congress as they waged a war for independence with Great Britain. In 1777, the Continental Congress proposed a plan to better provide for the states' "common defense, the security of their liberties, and their mutual and general welfare"—a plan that became known as the "Articles of Confederation and Perpetual Union." Articles of Confederation, art. III. Like NATO or the European Union today, the Articles of Confederation functioned as more of a treaty among separate sovereigns than as a replacement for state governments. Article II specifically declared that "each state retains its sovereignty, freedom, and independence." *Id.* art. II. But the Articles of Confederation effectively became the first constitution for a new, central government: a "Confederacy" titled "The United States of America." *Id.* art. I.

Effective in 1778, the Articles of Confederation replaced the informally organized Continental Congress with a new Confederation

Congress. Like its predecessor, the Confederation Congress was a unicameral legislature in which each state received a single vote regardless of the state's population or the number of delegates it sent. *Id.* art. V. Unlike the Continental Congress, the authority of the Confederation Congress was limited to a list of powers "expressly delegated" by the Articles. *Id.* art. II. Specifically, the Articles empowered the Confederation Congress to engage in war, enter treaties, borrow and spend money, and sit as a supreme court to resolve disputes between the states. *Id.* art. IX. Exercising any of these powers required the votes of nine state delegations. *Id.*

These limited powers made sense for a military alliance whose main role was to coordinate the activities of states at war with a common enemy. Exercising these powers, the Confederation Congress successfully maintained a Continental Army; negotiated alliances with France, Spain, and the Netherlands; and oversaw victory in the American War of Independence. *See* Middlekauff, *supra*, at 624–25. But even before the war drew to a close with the 1783 Treaty of Paris, weaknesses in the Articles became readily apparent. *See* Michael J. Klarman, *The Framers' Coup: The Making of the United States Constitution* 14–15 (2016).

The main problem was that the Articles didn't expressly delegate to the Confederation Congress any power to impose taxes. *Id.* If the federal government needed money, the Confederation Congress could either take out a loan or submit requisitions to the states. But the Articles didn't give the Confederation Congress any power to enforce these requisitions. States therefore ignored the federal government's requests. Between 1781 and 1786, the Confederation Congress collected only $2.4 million of the $15.7 million it had requisitioned. 30 *Journals of the Continental Congress*, *supra*, at 44–46.

A second problem was that the Articles didn't give the Confederation Congress power to create federal courts of general jurisdiction. *See* Klarman, *supra*, at 21–22. When the Confederation Congress negotiated treaties, it had to rely on state governments to uphold each treaty's promises. This turned out to be politically unfeasible. The Treaty of Paris, for example, required U.S. citizens to repay British creditors and to return lands confiscated from British loyalists. But state legislatures were not all that motivated to require their citizens to return property to a defeated enemy. Instead, they enacted debt-relief legislation and printed paper money to accommodate veterans and farmers who had no gold or silver after the war. As popular as these programs were domestically, they made the United States' treaties less credible, prompting Great Britain in particular to renege on its own treaty obligations. *See id.* at 48.

The Confederation Congress's reliance on the states might have been more palatable had the Articles given it the power to regulate foreign or interstate commerce. But when Great Britain retaliated for violations of the Treaty of Paris by requiring all shipping from Britain to enter America on British ships, the Confederation Congress had no power to respond. Instead, states responded individually—competing with one another in the process. *See id.* at 22–23. For example, when New York enacted a retaliatory tariff on goods imported on British ships, Connecticut and New Jersey responded by welcoming British ships to its nearby ports for free. New York, in turn, taxed goods imported into New York from Connecticut and New Jersey unless the importer could prove that the goods had never been on British ships. Connecticut and New Jersey retaliated with a trade war. *See id.* at 23–24.

Efforts to strengthen the Confederation Congress

All in all, the Confederation Congress emerged from the Revolutionary War with significant debts and without basic powers to repay them or to prevent trade disputes among the states. In 1783 and 1784, the Confederation Congress therefore proposed amendments to the Articles that would give it powers to collect certain taxes and to regulate foreign commerce. But the Articles of Confederation declared that the Articles' terms

> shall be inviolably observed by every State, and the Union shall be perpetual; nor shall any alteration at any time hereafter be made in any of them; unless such alteration be agreed to in a Congress of the United States, and be afterwards confirmed by the legislatures of every State.

Id. art. XIII. In other words, an amendment to the Articles required the unanimous consent of every state. However, each amendment proposed and agreed upon by twelve states was vetoed by either Rhode Island or New York. *See* Klarman, *supra*, at 42–47.

By January 1786, the Virginia legislature had had enough. It invited delegates from other states to meet in Annapolis, Maryland,

> to take into consideration the trade of the United States; to examine the relative situations and trade of the said States; to consider how far a uniform system in their commercial regulations may be necessary to their common interest and their permanent harmony; and to report to the several States, such an act relative to this great object, as when unanimously ratified by them, will enable the United States in Congress, effectually to provide for the same.

Documents Illustrative of the Formation of the Union of the American States, H. Doc. No. 69-398, at 38 (1927).

Despite widespread agreement among state legislatures that the Articles needed to be revised, many legislators raised objections about sending delegates to a convention whose legality was suspect. The Articles of Confederation provided that only the Confederation Congress—not some convention—could propose amendments. The

Articles also provided that the Articles' terms were to be "inviolably observed." Enough legislators believed that the Annapolis Convention was unconstitutional that only five state delegations attended. Klarman, *supra*, at 108–09.

The Annapolis Convention met anyway in September 1786, where the delegates present unanimously agreed that the "important defects in the system of the Federal Government" warranted radical reform. H. Doc. No. 69-398, at 42. Alexander Hamilton of New York, James Madison of Virginia, and other delegates renewed their call for a convention, asking every state to send delegates to meet in Philadelphia in May 1787 to form "a plan for supplying such defects." *Id.*

This planned second convention looked like it would be as doomed to fail as the Annapolis Convention, but public opinion was swayed by a popular uprising in Massachusetts. *See* Klarman, *supra*, at 124. In late 1786, indebted farmers in the western half of the state rose to arms and closed several county courts by force. Massachusetts had been one of the few states in the 1780s that had attempted to raise taxes and fully enforce debts, and the farmers, led by Daniel Shays, demanded relief. Many of the farmers were veterans whom the Confederation Congress had never paid in full—and the Confederation Congress continued to lack the resources to assist them. The Confederation Congress also lacked the resources to fund an army to oppose them, highlighting for many observers the inherent weaknesses of the Articles of Confederation. Although wealthy Massachusetts creditors ultimately raised a privately funded militia to suppress the rebellion, the event terrified their prosperous peers in other states. *Id.* at 88–93.

Shays' Rebellion, as it became known, was the breaking point for conservatives who had resisted calls to give the Confederation Congress more power to tax, to enforce debts, to end trade wars, and to suppress insurrections. Even the Confederation Congress admitted in February 1787 "that there are defects in the present Confederation." H. Doc. No. 69-398, at 46. When the New York legislature petitioned the Confederation Congress to approve the proposed Philadelphia Convention and to confer some legitimacy on the proceedings, the Confederation Congress authorized a convention

> for the sole and express purpose of revising the Articles of Confederation and reporting to Congress and the several legislatures such alterations and provisions therein as shall[,] when agreed to in Congress and confirmed by the states[,] render the federal constitution adequate to the exigencies of Government & the preservation of the Union.

Id. at 46.

1.2 THE CONSTITUTIONAL CONVENTION

Beginning in May 1787, fifty-five delegates arrived at the Philadelphia Convention from every state but Rhode Island. Most of them were the wealthiest or most prominent men from their home states, and virtually all were fervent nationalists. Almost half, twenty-five, owned slaves. George Washington even brought three of his more than two hundred slaves to the convention. Michael J. Klarman, *The Framers' Coup: The Making of the United States Constitution* 263–64 (2016). The delegates agreed to keep the proceedings confidential—making it difficult for historians to know the full extent of their deliberations. (Most of the deliberations we know of came from notes taken by individual delegates, particularly James Madison. But Madison, aware of his historical legacy, spent the rest of his life modifying his notes to make the debates appear more consistent with his later views as a member of Congress and as president. *See* Mary Sarah Bilder, *Madison's Hand: Revising the Constitutional Convention* (2015).)

Nevertheless, the basic outline of how the convention proceeded is relatively uncontested. On May 29, the Virginia delegates who had originally called for the convention led off the substantive discussion by proposing fifteen resolutions for a new plan of government. *See* Klarman, *supra*, at 133–34. As Madison later explained, the delegation wanted to preserve the "republican principle" in which representatives would govern by majority rule. *See The Federalist No. 10* (James Madison). But the delegation also wanted to create a strong, national government whose structure would protect the contracts and property rights of wealthy minorities. *See* Klarman, *supra*, at 129. Unlike the Articles of Confederation—in which the legislative, executive, and judicial powers were all vested in a unicameral Congress—the Virginia plan called for a new government with three separate branches and a bicameral legislature that had the power to veto state legislation. Already, this plan was a radical departure from the Confederation Congress's instructions to simply "revis[e] the Articles of Confederation." But the plan effectively set the agenda for the remainder of the summer. *See* Klarman, *supra*, at 138.

The convention debated the Virginia plan from May to July 5, at which point the delegates reached an impasse. Virginia was, by far, the most populous state at the time, and its delegates wanted the number of representatives in both Houses of Congress to reflect each state's population, including enslaved people who couldn't vote. *See id.* at 183–92. But the delegates from smaller states, led by New Jersey, wanted each state to have an equal vote—as in the Confederation Congress. *See id.* As delegates on both sides threatened to walk out, the convention reached a compromise that (1) gave each state an equal vote in the Senate, (2) gave each state one representative in the House for every 40,000 people, (3) counted only three-fifths of enslaved people for purposes of a state's House representation, and (4) made the House responsible for originating revenue bills. This so-called Great Compromise was the most contentious issue of the entire convention. *See id.* at 193–204.

Another subject of lengthy debate included the Virginians' proposal to give the federal government the power to veto state legislation. *See id.* at 158–61. This was rejected in favor of the Supremacy Clause, which declared federal law the "supreme Law of the land . . ., any Thing in the Constitution or Laws of any State to the Contrary notwithstanding." U.S. Const. art. VI.

The three-fifths compromise was also repeatedly debated throughout the convention, as some delegates complained that the Constitution should not reward states for maintaining slavery. *See* Klarman, *supra*, at 269–71. These complaining delegates were able to win only two explicit concessions: Congress would have the power to abolish the transatlantic slave trade (but only after 1808), and three-fifths of enslaved people would count not only for purposes of a state's representation in the House but also for purposes of "direct Taxes." U.S. Const. art. I, § 2. Yet these antislavery delegates ended up losing more than they won. The Three-Fifths Clause would prove to be a vital source of southern states' political power within the federal government. And the convention later adopted the Fugitive Slave Clause, which required all states to return "fugitives" from slavery back to their putative owners. *Id.* art. IV, § 2.

A final major source of debate was the composition and powers of the executive and judicial branches. Many delegates wanted the executive branch to be independent of the legislative branch, but nearly every delegate feared that uneducated voters would be unable to wisely elect a chief executive. *See* Klarman, *supra*, at 229–33. After initially placing the power in Congress, the convention eventually adopted a complicated system that became known as the Electoral College, in which state legislatures could determine for themselves how presidential electors would be apportioned. *See id.* Similar debates about the independence, power, and number of the judiciary resulted in a spartan article outlining the judicial branch's powers. The convention left it to Congress to decide which of these powers to assign to the Supreme Court and whether to create inferior federal courts at all. *See id.* at 164–69.

1.3 RATIFICATION

When the Constitutional Convention ended on September 17, 1787, the delegates submitted their draft constitution to the Confederation Congress. The document was controversial. *See* Pauline Maier, *Ratification*, at *ix* (2010). Where the Confederation Congress had instructed the delegates to report amendments to the Articles of Confederation, the delegates had instead reported a new Constitution. *Id.* at 29. And although the Articles of Confederation required amendments to receive the consent of thirteen state legislatures, only twelve states sent delegates to the convention, whose Constitution said it would take effect with the approval of only nine state "conventions." *See* U.S. Const. art. VII. Nevertheless, after a week of debate, the Confederation Congress authorized the state legislatures to assemble conventions and debate the proposed Constitution. 33 *Journals of the Continental Congress* 549 (Worthington Chauncey Ford ed., 1905).

Almost immediately, newspapers in every state began printing anonymous essays attacking the proposed Constitution. *See* Maier, *supra*, at 72–76. They argued that the Constitutional Convention was illegal, that the Constitution fatally lacked a bill of rights to protect individuals from abuse, and that the federal government created by the Constitution would displace the existing state governments. *Id.* In particular, they objected that the Constitution empowered Congress to impose "direct Taxes," pass all "necessary and proper laws," and preempt contrary state laws: a recipe for an all-powerful government. *Id.* at 81.

Supporters of the Constitution, calling themselves "Federalists," denounced these critics as "Antifederalists." *See id.* at xiv–xv. Conceding that the Constitution was not a perfect document, the Federalists argued that it was the best constitution under the circumstances and, more importantly, far superior to the unsustainable Articles of Confederation. One of the most comprehensive defenses of the Constitution was a series of eighty-five anonymous essays published in New York newspapers by Alexander Hamilton, James Madison, and John Jay. Although these essays had limited circulation outside of New York, they would later be compiled in a book, *The Federalist*, and celebrated as the most authoritative contemporary interpretation of the Constitution. *See id.* at 83–85. *The Federalist* not only defended each clause of the Constitution to a skeptical audience but also addressed principles underlying the Constitution, such as the doctrine of enumerated powers, the separation of powers, and federalism.

In general, supporters of the Constitution tended to be like Hamilton: wealthy, educated, urban, eastern, northern, and young. Opponents tended to be indebted, less educated, rural, western, southern, and older. But these patterns were not dispositive. Virginia's planter aristocracy, for example, was evenly divided between supporters (such as Madison and George Washington) and opponents (such as Patrick Henry and George Mason). *See id.* at 225–27.

When states elected representatives to participate in ratification conventions, Federalists dominated small states like Connecticut, Delaware, Georgia, and New Jersey, all of which voted overwhelmingly to support ratification. But opponents of the Constitution constituted majorities of most other state conventions. In Pennsylvania, Federalists successfully pushed through a ratification vote only after rushing the elections for the state convention and limiting debate. *Id.* at 59–69. Outraged Antifederalists, complaining that they had been railroaded, sent letters to allies in other states warning them of the need to organize. By the time Massachusetts held its convention the following year, influential Antifederalists such as Samuel Adams and John Hancock precluded the convention from supporting the Constitution outright. Rather, they agreed to support to Constitution only after proposing a list of amendments, which included a bill of rights and a clause limiting Congress's powers only to those "expressly" enumerated by the Constitution. *Id.* at 191–208. Although this compromise was enough to get Massachusetts to ratify the Constitution, enough Antifederalists were elected in the New Hampshire and North Carolina conventions to force them to adjourn. *Id.* at 216–23. Meanwhile, the Constitution was approved in Maryland and South Carolina, but in closely contested conventions.

By the time the Virginia and New York conventions met in the summer of 1788, only eight states had ratified the Constitution—one short of the nine required by Article VII. Antifederalist delegates were majorities in both conventions, including by a two-to-one ratio in New York. But by this point in the process, with eight states behind the Constitution, the debate over ratification had shifted from whether the Constitution was a good document to whether New York and Virginia should hold themselves out of the Union while the first Congress made important decisions such as where to place the nation's capital. *Id.* at 377. Enough delegates in both conventions were sufficiently afraid of the Union's collapse that even Antifederalists grudgingly supported ratification. But both conventions also proposed extensive lists of amendments—over one hundred—that they expected the first Congress to address. *Id.* at 396–97.

On September 13, 1788, after New Hampshire, Virginia, and New York voted to ratify the Constitution, the Confederation Congress passed a resolution to put the Constitution into operation on March 4, 1789. George Washington took the first presidential oath of office in New York City on April 30, 1789. The new government consisted of eleven states. North Carolina and Rhode Island waited to see the amendments proposed by Congress.

1.4 THE BILL OF RIGHTS

George Washington's inauguration didn't end the initial development of the Constitution. Four of the ratifying states—Massachusetts, New Hampshire, New York, and Virginia—had expressly called for dozens of amendments, including the addition of a bill of rights.

Even though James Madison resisted these calls while he was a Federalist participant in the ratification debates, he soon changed his mind about the usefulness of a bill of rights. *See* 5 *The Writings of James Madison* 319 (G. Hunt ed., 1904). This was likely because in the 1788–1789 elections, the Virginia legislature denied him a seat in the first

Senate primarily because of his opposition to a bill of rights. And when Madison ran for a House seat instead, rumors about his opposition to a bill of rights threatened to undermine his candidacy. *See* Michael J. Klarman, *The Framers' Coup: The Making of the United States Constitution* 547 (2016).

Article V of the Constitution specified that two-thirds of each house of Congress could propose amendments and send them to the states for ratification by three-quarters of the state legislatures. After being elected to the first House of Representatives, Madison embraced this task immediately, proposing seventeen amendments to the House in June 1789. *See id.* at 572–77. Surprisingly, much of the debate over the amendments turned not on their merits but on the procedural question of whether amendments should be incorporated directly into the text of the Constitution or whether they should be added as successive articles. *See* Jonathan Gienapp, *The Second Creation* 179 (2018). Congress ultimately decided that the amendments should be tacked on to the end of the Constitution, submitting twelve new articles for the states' approval.

Many Antifederalists were outraged that Congress's proposed amendments didn't come close to the structural demands of the state conventions that called for them. For example, where Massachusetts had called for an amendment that would limit Congress's powers to those "expressly delegated" by the Constitution, Congress proposed only that "[t]he powers not delegated to the United States by the Constitution, nor prohibited by it to the States, are reserved to the States respectively, or to the people." *See* U.S. Const., amend. X. Virginia, similarly, had demanded a supermajority vote before Congress could regulate foreign commerce. Congress ignored this demand. *See* Klarman, *supra,* at 618–19. But the proposed amendments—along with threats of coercion and trade sanctions by the federal government—persuaded North Carolina and Rhode Island to join the Union. *See id.* at 513–29. By 1791, ten of the twelve amendments proposed by Congress were ratified. Today, these first ten amendments are commonly called the Bill of Rights.

1.5 CONSTITUTIONAL DOCUMENTS

For reference, the Articles of Confederation, Constitution, and Bill of Rights and later amendments to the Constitution are included below.

1.5.1

The Articles of Confederation and Perpetual Union

1777 (effective 1778)

To all to whom these Presents shall come, we, the undersigned Delegates of the States affixed to our Names send greeting. Whereas the Delegates of the United States of America in Congress assembled did on the fifteenth day of November in the year of our Lord One Thousand Seven Hundred and Seventy seven, and in the

Second Year of the Independence of America agree to certain articles of Confederation and perpetual Union between the States of Newhampshire, Massachusetts-bay, Rhodeisland and Providence Plantations, Connecticut, New York, New Jersey, Pennsylvania, Delaware, Maryland, Virginia, North Carolina, South Carolina, and Georgia in the Words following, viz. "Articles of Confederation and perpetual Union between the States of Newhampshire, Massachusetts-bay, Rhodeisland and Providence Plantations, Connecticut, New York, New Jersey, Pennsylvania, Delaware, Maryland, Virginia, North Carolina, South Carolina, and Georgia."

ARTICLE I. The Stile of this confederacy shall be, "The United States of America."

ARTICLE II. Each state retains its sovereignty, freedom and independence, and every Power, Jurisdiction and right, which is not by this confederation expressly delegated to the United States, in Congress assembled.

ARTICLE III. The said states hereby severally enter into a firm league of friendship with each other, for their common defence, the security of their Liberties, and their mutual and general welfare, binding themselves to assist each other, against all force offered to, or attacks made upon them, or any of them, on account of religion, sovereignty, trade, or any other pretence whatever.

ARTICLE IV. The better to secure and perpetuate mutual friendship and intercourse among the people of the different states in this union, the free inhabitants of each of these states, paupers, vagabonds and fugitives from Justice excepted, shall be entitled to all privileges and immunities of free citizens in the several states; and the people of each state shall have free ingress and regress to and from any other state, and shall enjoy therein all the privileges of trade and commerce, subject to the same duties, impositions and restrictions as the inhabitants thereof respectively, provided that such restrictions shall not extend so far as to prevent the removal of property imported into any state, to any other State of which the Owner is an inhabitant; provided also that no imposition, duties or restriction shall be laid by any state, on the property of the united states, or either of them.

If any Person guilty of, or charged with, treason, felony, or other high misdemeanor in any state, shall flee from Justice, and be found in any of the united states, he shall upon demand of the Governor or executive power of the state from which he fled, be delivered up, and removed to the state having jurisdiction of his offence.

Full faith and credit shall be given in each of these states to the records, acts and judicial proceedings of the courts and magistrates of every other state.

ARTICLE V. For the more convenient management of the general interests of the united states, delegates shall be annually appointed in such manner as the legislature of each state shall direct, to meet in Congress on the first Monday in November, in every year, with a power reserved to each state to recall its delegates, or any of them, at any time within the year, and to send others in their stead, for the remainder of the Year.

No State shall be represented in Congress by less than two, nor by more than seven Members; and no person shall be capable of being delegate for more than three years, in any term of six years; nor shall any person, being a delegate, be capable of holding any office under the united states, for which he, or another for his benefit receives any salary, fees or emolument of any kind.

Each State shall maintain its own delegates in a meeting of the states, and while they act as members of the committee of the states.

In determining questions in the united states, in Congress assembled, each state shall have one vote.

Freedom of speech and debate in Congress shall not be impeached or questioned in any Court, or place out of Congress, and the members of congress shall be protected in their persons from arrests and imprisonments, during the time of their going to and from, and attendance on congress, except for treason, felony, or breach of the peace.

ARTICLE VI. No State, without the Consent of the united States, in congress assembled, shall send any embassy to, or receive any embassy from, or enter into any conferrence, agreement, alliance, or treaty, with any King prince or state; nor shall any person holding any office of profit or trust under the united states, or any of them, accept of any present, emolument, office, or title of any kind whatever, from any king, prince, or foreign state; nor shall the united states, in congress assembled, or any of them, grant any title of nobility.

No two or more states shall enter into any treaty, confederation, or alliance whatever between them, without the consent of the united states, in congress assembled, specifying accurately the purposes for which the same is to be entered into, and how long it shall continue.

No State shall lay any imposts or duties, which may interfere with any stipulations in treaties, entered into by the united States in congress assembled, with any king, prince, or State, in pursuance of any treaties already proposed by congress, to the courts of France and Spain.

No vessels of war shall be kept up in time of peace, by any state, except such number only, as shall be deemed necessary by the united states, in congress assembled, for the defence of such state, or its trade; nor shall any body of forces be kept up, by any state, in time of peace, except such number only as, in the judgment of the united states, in congress assembled, shall be deemed requisite to garrison the forts necessary for the defence of such state; but every state shall always keep up a well regulated and disciplined militia, sufficiently armed and accounted, and shall provide and constantly have ready for use, in public stores, a due number of field pieces and tents, and a proper quantity of arms, ammunition, and camp equipage.

No State shall engage in any war without the consent of the united States in congress assembled, unless such State be actually invaded by enemies, or shall have received certain advice of a resolution being formed by some nation of Indians to invade such State, and the danger is so imminent as not to admit of a delay till the united states in congress assembled, can be consulted: nor shall any state grant commissions to any ships or vessels of war, nor letters of marque or reprisal, except it be after a declaration of war by the united states in congress assembled, and then only against the kingdom or State, and the subjects thereof, against which war has been so declared, and under such regulations as shall be established by the united states in congress assembled, unless such state be infested by pirates, in which case vessels of war may be fitted out for that occasion, and kept so long as the danger shall continue, or until the united states in congress assembled shall determine otherwise.

ARTICLE VII. When land forces are raised by any state, for the common defence, all officers of or under the rank of colonel, shall be appointed by the legislature of each state respectively by whom such forces shall be raised, or in such manner as such state shall direct, and all vacancies shall be filled up by the state which first made appointment.

ARTICLE VIII. All charges of war, and all other expenses that shall be incurred for the common defence or general welfare, and allowed by the united states in congress assembled, shall be defrayed out of a common treasury, which shall be supplied by the several states, in proportion to the value of all land within each state, granted to or surveyed for any Person, as such land and the buildings and improvements thereon shall be estimated, according to such mode as the united states, in congress assembled, shall, from time to time, direct and appoint. The taxes for paying that proportion shall be laid and levied by the authority and direction of the legislatures of the several states within the time agreed upon by the united states in congress assembled.

ARTICLE IX. The united states, in congress assembled, shall have the sole and exclusive right and power of determining on peace and war, except in the cases mentioned in the sixth article—of sending and receiving ambassadors—entering into treaties and alliances, provided that no treaty of commerce shall be made, whereby the legislative power of the respective states shall be restrained from imposing such imposts and duties on foreigners, as their own people are subjected to, or from prohibiting the exportation or importation of any species of goods or commodities whatsoever—of establishing rules for deciding, in all cases, what captures on land or water shall be legal, and in what manner prizes taken by land or naval forces in the service of the united Sates, shall be divided or appropriated—of granting letters of marque and reprisal in times of peace—appointing courts for the trial of piracies and felonies committed on the high seas; and establishing courts; for receiving and determining finally appeals in all cases of captures; provided that no member of congress shall be appointed a judge of any of the said courts.

The united states, in congress assembled, shall also be the last resort on appeal, in all disputes and differences now subsisting, or that hereafter may arise between two or more states concerning boundary, jurisdiction, or any other cause whatever; which authority shall always be exercised in the manner following. Whenever the legislative or executive authority, or lawful agent of any state in controversy with another, shall present a petition to congress, stating the matter in question, and praying for a hearing, notice thereof shall be given, by order of congress, to the legislative or executive authority of the other state in controversy, and a day assigned for the appearance of the parties by their lawful agents, who shall then be directed to appoint, by joint consent, commissioners or judges to constitute a court for hearing and determining the matter in question: but if they cannot agree, congress shall name three persons out of each of the united states, and from the list of such persons each party shall alternately strike out one, the petitioners beginning, until the number shall be reduced to thirteen; and from that number not less than seven, nor more than nine names, as congress shall direct, shall, in the presence of congress, be drawn out by lot, and the persons whose names shall be so drawn, or any five of them, shall be commissioners or judges, to hear and finally determine the controversy, so always as a major part of the judges, who shall hear the cause, shall agree in the determination: and if either party shall neglect to attend at the day appointed, without showing reasons which congress shall judge sufficient, or being present, shall refuse to strike, the congress shall proceed to nominate three persons out of each State, and the secretary of congress shall strike in behalf of such party absent or refusing; and the judgment and sentence of the court, to be appointed in the manner before prescribed, shall be final and conclusive; and if any of the parties shall refuse to submit to the authority of such court, or to appear or defend their claim or cause, the court shall nevertheless proceed to pronounce sentence, or judgment, which shall in like manner be final and decisive; the judgment or sentence and other proceedings being in either case transmitted to congress, and lodged among the acts of congress, for the security of the parties concerned: provided that every commissioner, before he sits in judgment, shall take an oath to be administered by one of the judges of the supreme or superior court of the State where the cause shall be tried, "well and truly to hear and determine the matter in question, according to the best of his judgment, without favour, affection, or hope of reward: "provided, also, that no State shall be deprived of territory for the benefit of the united states.

All controversies concerning the private right of soil claimed under different grants of two or more states, whose jurisdictions as they may respect such lands, and the states which passed such grants are adjusted, the said grants or either of them being at the same time claimed to have originated antecedent to such settlement of jurisdiction, shall, on the petition of either party to the congress of the united states, be finally determined, as near as may be, in the same manner as is before prescribed for deciding disputes respecting territorial jurisdiction between different states.

The united states, in congress assembled, shall also have the sole and exclusive right and power of regulating the alloy and value of coin struck by their own authority, or by that of the respective states—fixing the standard of weights and measures throughout the united states—regulating the trade and managing all affairs with the Indians, not members of any of the states; provided that the legislative right of any state, within its own limits, be not infringed or violated—establishing and regulating post-offices from one state to another, throughout all the united states, and exacting such postage on the papers passing through the same, as may be requisite to defray the expenses of the said office—appointing all officers of the land forces in the service of the united States, excepting regimental officers—appointing all the officers of the naval forces, and commissioning all officers whatever in the service of the united states; making rules for the government and regulation of the said land and naval forces, and directing their operations.

The united States, in congress assembled, shall have authority to appoint a committee, to sit in the recess of congress, to be denominated, "A Committee of the States," and to consist of one delegate from each State; and to appoint such other committees and civil officers as may be necessary for managing the general affairs of the united states under their direction—to appoint one of their number to preside; provided that no person be allowed to serve in the office of president more than one year in any term of three years; to ascertain the necessary sums of money to be raised for the service of the united states, and to appropriate and apply the same for defraying the public expenses; to borrow money or emit bills on the credit of the united states, transmitting every half year to the respective states an account of the sums of money so borrowed or emitted,—to build and equip a navy—to agree upon the number of land forces, and to make requisitions from each state for its quota, in proportion to the number of white inhabitants in such state, which requisition shall be binding; and thereupon the legislature of each state shall appoint the regimental officers, raise the men, and clothe, arm, and equip them, in a soldier-like manner, at the expense of the united states; and the officers and men so clothed, armed, and equipped, shall march to the place appointed, and within the time agreed on by the united states, in congress assembled; but if the united states, in congress assembled, shall, on consideration of circumstances, judge proper that any state should not raise men, or should raise a smaller number than its quota, and that any other state should raise a greater number of men than the quota thereof, such extra number shall be raised, officered, clothed, armed, and equipped in the same manner as the quota of such state, unless the legislature of such state shall judge that such extra number cannot be safely spared out of the same, in which case they shall raise, officer, clothe, arm, and equip, as many of such extra number as they judge can be safely spared. And the officers and men so clothed, armed, and equipped, shall march to the place appointed, and within the time agreed on by the united states in congress assembled.

The united states, in congress assembled, shall never engage in a war, nor grant letters of marque and reprisal in time of peace, nor enter into any treaties or alliances, nor coin money, nor regulate the value thereof nor ascertain the sums and expenses necessary for the defence and welfare of the united states, or any of them, nor emit bills, nor borrow money on the credit of the united states, nor appropriate money, nor agree upon the number of vessels of war to be built or purchased, or the number of land or sea forces to be raised, nor appoint a commander in chief of the army or navy, unless nine states assent to the same, nor shall a question on any other point, except for adjourning from day to day, be determined, unless by the votes of a majority of the united states in congress assembled.

The congress of the united states shall have power to adjourn to any time within the year, and to any place within the united states, so that no period of adjournment be for a longer duration than the space of six Months, and shall publish the Journal of their proceedings monthly, except such parts thereof relating to treaties, alliances, or military operations, as in their judgment require secrecy; and the yeas and nays of the delegates of each State, on any question, shall be entered on the Journal, when it is desired by any delegate; and the delegates of a State, or any of them, at his or their request, shall be furnished with a transcript of the said Journal, except such parts as are above excepted, to lay before the legislatures of the several states.

ARTICLE X. The committee of the states, or any nine of them, shall be authorized to execute, in the recess of congress, such of the powers of congress as the united states, in congress assembled, by the consent of nine states, shall, from time to time, think expedient to vest them with; provided that no power be delegated to the said committee, for the exercise of which, by the articles of confederation, the voice of nine states, in the congress of the united states assembled, is requisite.

ARTICLE XI. Canada acceding to this confederation, and joining in the measures of the united states, shall be admitted into, and entitled to all the advantages of this union: but no other colony shall be admitted into the same, unless such admission be agreed to by nine states.

ARTICLE XII. All bills of credit emitted, monies borrowed, and debts contracted by or under the authority of congress, before the assembling of the united states, in pursuance of the present confederation, shall be deemed and considered as a charge against the united States, for payment and satisfaction whereof the said united states and the public faith are hereby solemnly pledged.

ARTICLE XIII. Every State shall abide by the determinations of the united states, in congress assembled, on all questions which by this confederation are submitted to them. And the Articles of this confederation shall be inviolably observed by every state, and the union shall be perpetual; nor shall any alteration at any time hereafter be made in any of them, unless such alteration be agreed to in a congress of the united states, and be afterwards confirmed by the legislatures of every state.

And Whereas it hath pleased the Great Governor of the World to incline the hearts of the legislatures we respectively represent in congress, to approve of, and to authorize us to ratify the said articles of confederation and perpetual union, Know Ye, that we, the undersigned delegates, by virtue of the power and authority to us given for that purpose, do, by these presents, in the name and in behalf of our respective constituents, fully and entirely ratify and confirm each and every of the said articles of confederation and perpetual union, and all and singular the matters and things therein contained. And we do further solemnly plight and engage the faith of our respective constituents, that they shall abide by the determinations of the united states in congress assembled, on all questions, which by the said confederation are submitted to them. And that the articles thereof shall be inviolably observed by the states we respectively represent, and that the union shall be perpetual. In Witness whereof, we have hereunto set our hands, in Congress. Done at Philadelphia, in the State of Pennsylvania, the ninth Day of July, in the Year of our Lord one Thousand seven Hundred and Seventy eight, and in the third year of the Independence of America.

1.5.2

The Constitution of the United States

1787 (ratified 1788)

We the People of the United States, in Order to form a more perfect Union, establish Justice, insure domestic Tranquility, provide for the common defence, promote the general Welfare, and secure the Blessings of Liberty to ourselves and our Posterity, do ordain and establish this Constitution for the United States of America.

ARTICLE I, SECTION 1. All legislative Powers herein granted shall be vested in a Congress of the United States, which shall consist of a Senate and House of Representatives.

SECTION 2. The House of Representatives shall be composed of Members chosen every second Year by the People of the several States, and the Electors in each State shall have the Qualifications requisite for Electors of the most numerous Branch of the State Legislature.

No Person shall be a Representative who shall not have attained to the Age of twenty five Years, and been seven Years a Citizen of the United States, and who shall not, when elected, be an Inhabitant of that State in which he shall be chosen.

Representatives and direct Taxes shall be apportioned among the several States which may be included within this Union, according to their respective Numbers, which shall be determined by adding to the whole Number of free Persons, including those bound to Service for a Term of Years, and excluding Indians not taxed, three fifths of all other Persons. The actual Enumeration shall be made within three Years after the first Meeting of the Congress of the United States, and within every subsequent Term of ten Years, in such Manner as they shall by Law direct. The Number of Representatives shall not exceed one for every thirty Thousand, but each State shall have at Least one Representative; and until such enumeration shall be made, the State of New Hampshire shall be entitled to chuse three, Massachusetts eight, Rhode-Island and Providence Plantations one, Connecticut five, New-York six, New Jersey four, Pennsylvania eight, Delaware one, Maryland six, Virginia ten, North Carolina five, South Carolina five, and Georgia three.

When vacancies happen in the Representation from any State, the Executive Authority thereof shall issue Writs of Election to fill such Vacancies.

The House of Representatives shall chuse their Speaker and other Officers; and shall have the sole Power of Impeachment.

SECTION 3. The Senate of the United States shall be composed of two Senators from each State, chosen by the Legislature thereof, for six Years; and each Senator shall have one Vote.

Immediately after they shall be assembled in Consequence of the first Election, they shall be divided as equally as may be into three Classes. The Seats of the Senators of the first Class shall be vacated at the Expiration of the second Year, of the second Class at the Expiration of the fourth Year, and of the third Class at the Expiration of the sixth Year, so that one third may be chosen every second Year; and if Vacancies happen by Resignation, or otherwise, during the Recess of the Legislature of any State, the Executive thereof may make temporary Appointments until the next Meeting of the Legislature, which shall then fill such Vacancies.

No Person shall be a Senator who shall not have attained to the Age of thirty Years, and been nine Years a Citizen of the United States, and who shall not, when elected, be an Inhabitant of that State for which he shall be chosen.

The Vice President of the United States shall be President of the Senate, but shall have no Vote, unless they be equally divided.

The Senate shall chuse their other Officers, and also a President pro tempore, in the Absence of the Vice President, or when he shall exercise the Office of President of the United States.

The Senate shall have the sole Power to try all Impeachments. When sitting for that Purpose, they shall be on Oath or Affirmation. When the President of the United States is tried, the Chief Justice shall preside: And no Person shall be convicted without the Concurrence of two thirds of the Members present.

Judgment in Cases of Impeachment shall not extend further than to removal from Office, and disqualification to hold and enjoy any Office of honor, Trust or Profit under the United States: but the Party convicted shall nevertheless be liable and subject to Indictment, Trial, Judgment and Punishment, according to Law.

SECTION 4. The Times, Places and Manner of holding Elections for Senators and Representatives, shall be prescribed in each State by the Legislature thereof; but the Congress may at any time by Law make or alter such Regulations, except as to the Places of chusing Senators.

The Congress shall assemble at least once in every Year, and such Meeting shall be on the first Monday in December, unless they shall by Law appoint a different Day.

SECTION 5. Each House shall be the Judge of the Elections, Returns and Qualifications of its own Members, and a Majority of each shall constitute a Quorum to do Business; but a smaller Number may adjourn from day to day, and may be authorized to compel the Attendance of absent Members, in such Manner, and under such Penalties as each House may provide.

Each House may determine the Rules of its Proceedings, punish its Members for disorderly Behaviour, and, with the Concurrence of two thirds, expel a Member.

Each House shall keep a Journal of its Proceedings, and from time to time publish the same, excepting such Parts as may in their Judgment require Secrecy; and the Yeas and Nays of the Members of either House on any question shall, at the Desire of one fifth of those Present, be entered on the Journal.

Neither House, during the Session of Congress, shall, without the Consent of the other, adjourn for more than three days, nor to any other Place than that in which the two Houses shall be sitting.

SECTION 6. The Senators and Representatives shall receive a Compensation for their Services, to be ascertained by Law, and paid out of the Treasury of the United States. They shall in all Cases, except Treason, Felony and Breach of the Peace, be privileged from Arrest during their Attendance at the Session of their respective Houses, and in going to and returning from the same; and for any Speech or Debate in either House, they shall not be questioned in any other Place.

No Senator or Representative shall, during the Time for which he was elected, be appointed to any civil Office under the Authority of the United States, which shall have been created, or the Emoluments whereof shall have been encreased during such time; and no Person holding any Office under the United States, shall be a Member of either House during his Continuance in Office.

SECTION 7. All Bills for raising Revenue shall originate in the House of Representatives; but the Senate may propose or concur with Amendments as on other Bills.

Every Bill which shall have passed the House of Representatives and the Senate, shall, before it become a Law, be presented to the President of the United States; If he approve he shall sign it, but if not he shall return it, with his Objections to that House in which it shall have originated, who shall enter the Objections at large on their Journal, and proceed to reconsider it. If after such Reconsideration two thirds of that House shall agree to pass the Bill, it shall be sent, together with the Objections, to the other House, by which it shall likewise be reconsidered, and if approved by two thirds of that House, it shall become a Law. But in all such Cases the Votes of both Houses shall be determined by yeas and Nays, and the Names of the Persons voting for and against the Bill shall be entered on the Journal of each House respectively. If any Bill shall not be returned by the President within ten Days (Sundays excepted) after it shall have been presented to him, the Same shall be a Law, in like Manner as if he had signed it, unless the Congress by their Adjournment prevent its Return, in which Case it shall not be a Law.

Every Order, Resolution, or Vote to which the Concurrence of the Senate and House of Representatives may be necessary (except on a question of Adjournment) shall be presented to the President of the United States; and before the Same shall take Effect, shall be approved by him, or being disapproved by him, shall be repassed by two thirds of the Senate and House of Representatives, according to the Rules and Limitations prescribed in the Case of a Bill.

SECTION 8. The Congress shall have Power To lay and collect Taxes, Duties, Imposts and Excises, to pay the Debts and provide for the common Defence and general Welfare of the United States; but all Duties, Imposts and Excises shall be uniform throughout the United States;

To borrow Money on the credit of the United States;

To regulate Commerce with foreign Nations, and among the several States, and with the Indian Tribes;

To establish an uniform Rule of Naturalization, and uniform Laws on the subject of Bankruptcies throughout the United States;

To coin Money, regulate the Value thereof, and of foreign Coin, and fix the Standard of Weights and Measures;

To provide for the Punishment of counterfeiting the Securities and current Coin of the United States;

To establish Post Offices and post Roads;

To promote the Progress of Science and useful Arts, by securing for limited Times to Authors and Inventors the exclusive Right to their respective Writings and Discoveries;

To constitute Tribunals inferior to the supreme Court;

To define and punish Piracies and Felonies committed on the high Seas, and Offences against the Law of Nations;

To declare War, grant Letters of Marque and Reprisal, and make Rules concerning Captures on Land and Water;

To raise and support Armies, but no Appropriation of Money to that Use shall be for a longer Term than two Years;

To provide and maintain a Navy;

To make Rules for the Government and Regulation of the land and naval Forces;

To provide for calling forth the Militia to execute the Laws of the Union, suppress Insurrections and repel Invasions;

To provide for organizing, arming, and disciplining, the Militia, and for governing such Part of them as may be employed in the Service of the United States, reserving to the States respectively, the Appointment of the Officers, and the Authority of training the Militia according to the discipline prescribed by Congress;

To exercise exclusive Legislation in all Cases whatsoever, over such District (not exceeding ten Miles square) as may, by Cession of particular States, and the Acceptance of Congress, become the Seat of the Government of the United States, and to exercise like Authority over all Places purchased by the Consent of the Legislature of the State in which the Same shall be, for the Erection of Forts, Magazines, Arsenals, dock-Yards, and other needful Buildings;—And

To make all Laws which shall be necessary and proper for carrying into Execution the foregoing Powers, and all other Powers vested by this Constitution in the Government of the United States, or in any Department or Officer thereof.

SECTION 9. The Migration or Importation of such Persons as any of the States now existing shall think proper to admit, shall not be prohibited by the Congress prior to the Year one thousand eight hundred and eight, but a Tax or duty may be imposed on such Importation, not exceeding ten dollars for each Person.

The Privilege of the Writ of Habeas Corpus shall not be suspended, unless when in Cases of Rebellion or Invasion the public Safety may require it.

No Bill of Attainder or ex post facto Law shall be passed.

No Capitation, or other direct, Tax shall be laid, unless in Proportion to the Census or enumeration herein before directed to be taken.

No Tax or Duty shall be laid on Articles exported from any State.

No Preference shall be given by any Regulation of Commerce or Revenue to the Ports of one State over those of another: nor shall Vessels bound to, or from, one State, be obliged to enter, clear, or pay Duties in another.

No Money shall be drawn from the Treasury, but in Consequence of Appropriations made by Law; and a regular Statement and Account of the Receipts and Expenditures of all public Money shall be published from time to time.

No Title of Nobility shall be granted by the United States: And no Person holding any Office of Profit or Trust under them, shall, without the Consent of the

Congress, accept of any present, Emolument, Office, or Title, of any kind whatever, from any King, Prince, or foreign State.

SECTION 10. No State shall enter into any Treaty, Alliance, or Confederation; grant Letters of Marque and Reprisal; coin Money; emit Bills of Credit; make any Thing but gold and silver Coin a Tender in Payment of Debts; pass any Bill of Attainder, ex post facto Law, or Law impairing the Obligation of Contracts, or grant any Title of Nobility.

No State shall, without the Consent of the Congress, lay any Imposts or Duties on Imports or Exports, except what may be absolutely necessary for executing it's inspection Laws: and the net Produce of all Duties and Imposts, laid by any State on Imports or Exports, shall be for the Use of the Treasury of the United States; and all such Laws shall be subject to the Revision and Controul of the Congress.

No State shall, without the Consent of Congress, lay any Duty of Tonnage, keep Troops, or Ships of War in time of Peace, enter into any Agreement or Compact with another State, or with a foreign Power, or engage in War, unless actually invaded, or in such imminent Danger as will not admit of delay.

ARTICLE II, SECTION 1. The executive Power shall be vested in a President of the United States of America. He shall hold his Office during the Term of four Years, and, together with the Vice President, chosen for the same Term, be elected, as follows

executive-President

Each State shall appoint, in such Manner as the Legislature thereof may direct, a Number of Electors, equal to the whole Number of Senators and Representatives to which the State may be entitled in the Congress: but no Senator or Representative, or Person holding an Office of Trust or Profit under the United States, shall be appointed an Elector.

The Electors shall meet in their respective States, and vote by Ballot for two Persons, of whom one at least shall not be an Inhabitant of the same State with themselves. And they shall make a List of all the Persons voted for, and of the Number of Votes for each; which List they shall sign and certify, and transmit sealed to the Seat of the Government of the United States, directed to the President of the Senate. The President of the Senate shall, in the Presence of the Senate and House of Representatives, open all the Certificates, and the Votes shall then be counted. The Person having the greatest Number of Votes shall be the President, if such Number be a Majority of the whole Number of Electors appointed; and if there be more than one who have such Majority, and have an equal Number of Votes, then the House of Representatives shall immediately chuse by Ballot one of them for President; and if no Person have a Majority, then from the five highest on the List the said House shall in like Manner chuse the President. But in chusing the President, the Votes shall be taken by States, the Representation from each State having one Vote; A quorum for this Purpose shall consist of a Member or Members from two thirds of the States, and a Majority of all the States shall be necessary to a Choice. In every Case, after the Choice of the President, the Person having the greatest Number of Votes of the Electors shall be the Vice President. But if there should remain two or more who have equal Votes, the Senate shall chuse from them by Ballot the Vice President.

The Congress may determine the Time of chusing the Electors, and the Day on which they shall give their Votes; which Day shall be the same throughout the United States.

No Person except a natural born Citizen, or a Citizen of the United States, at the time of the Adoption of this Constitution, shall be eligible to the Office of President;

neither shall any Person be eligible to that Office who shall not have attained to the Age of thirty five Years, and been fourteen Years a Resident within the United States.

In Case of the Removal of the President from Office, or of his Death, Resignation, or Inability to discharge the Powers and Duties of the said Office, the Same shall devolve on the Vice President, and the Congress may by Law provide for the Case of Removal, Death, Resignation or Inability, both of the President and Vice President, declaring what Officer shall then act as President, and such Officer shall act accordingly, until the Disability be removed, or a President shall be elected.

The President shall, at stated Times, receive for his Services, a Compensation, which shall neither be encreased nor diminished during the Period for which he shall have been elected, and he shall not receive within that Period any other Emolument from the United States, or any of them.

Before he enter on the Execution of his Office, he shall take the following Oath or Affirmation:—"I do solemnly swear (or affirm) that I will faithfully execute the Office of President of the United States, and will to the best of my Ability, preserve, protect and defend the Constitution of the United States."

SECTION 2. The President shall be Commander in Chief of the Army and Navy of the United States, and of the Militia of the several States, when called into the actual Service of the United States; he may require the Opinion, in writing, of the principal Officer in each of the executive Departments, upon any Subject relating to the Duties of their respective Offices, and he shall have Power to grant Reprieves and Pardons for Offences against the United States, except in Cases of Impeachment.

He shall have Power, by and with the Advice and Consent of the Senate, to make Treaties, provided two thirds of the Senators present concur; and he shall nominate, and by and with the Advice and Consent of the Senate, shall appoint Ambassadors, other public Ministers and Consuls, Judges of the supreme Court, and all other Officers of the United States, whose Appointments are not herein otherwise provided for, and which shall be established by Law: but the Congress may by Law vest the Appointment of such inferior Officers, as they think proper, in the President alone, in the Courts of Law, or in the Heads of Departments.

The President shall have Power to fill up all Vacancies that may happen during the Recess of the Senate, by granting Commissions which shall expire at the End of their next Session.

SECTION 3. He shall from time to time give to the Congress Information of the State of the Union, and recommend to their Consideration such Measures as he shall judge necessary and expedient; he may, on extraordinary Occasions, convene both Houses, or either of them, and in Case of Disagreement between them, with Respect to the Time of Adjournment, he may adjourn them to such Time as he shall think proper; he shall receive Ambassadors and other public Ministers; he shall take Care that the Laws be faithfully executed, and shall Commission all the Officers of the United States.

SECTION 4. The President, Vice President and all civil Officers of the United States, shall be removed from Office on Impeachment for, and Conviction of, Treason, Bribery, or other high Crimes and Misdemeanors.

ARTICLE III, SECTION 1. The judicial Power of the United States, shall be vested in one supreme Court, and in such inferior Courts as the Congress may from time to time ordain and establish. The Judges, both of the supreme and inferior Courts, shall hold their Offices during good Behaviour, and shall, at stated Times, receive for their

Services, a Compensation, which shall not be diminished during their Continuance in Office.

SECTION 2. The judicial Power shall extend to all Cases, in Law and Equity, arising under this Constitution, the Laws of the United States, and Treaties made, or which shall be made, under their Authority;—to all Cases affecting Ambassadors, other public Ministers and Consuls;—to all Cases of admiralty and maritime Jurisdiction;—to Controversies to which the United States shall be a Party;—to Controversies between two or more States;—between a State and Citizens of another State,—between Citizens of different States,—between Citizens of the same State claiming Lands under Grants of different States, and between a State, or the Citizens thereof, and foreign States, Citizens or Subjects.

In all Cases affecting Ambassadors, other public Ministers and Consuls, and those in which a State shall be Party, the supreme Court shall have original Jurisdiction. In all the other Cases before mentioned, the supreme Court shall have appellate Jurisdiction, both as to Law and Fact, with such Exceptions, and under such Regulations as the Congress shall make.

The Trial of all Crimes, except in Cases of Impeachment, shall be by Jury; and such Trial shall be held in the State where the said Crimes shall have been committed; but when not committed within any State, the Trial shall be at such Place or Places as the Congress may by Law have directed.

SECTION 3. Treason against the United States, shall consist only in levying War against them, or in adhering to their Enemies, giving them Aid and Comfort. No Person shall be convicted of Treason unless on the Testimony of two Witnesses to the same overt Act, or on Confession in open Court.

The Congress shall have Power to declare the Punishment of Treason, but no Attainder of Treason shall work Corruption of Blood, or Forfeiture except during the Life of the Person attainted.

ARTICLE IV, SECTION 1. Full Faith and Credit shall be given in each State to the public Acts, Records, and judicial Proceedings of every other State. And the Congress may by general Laws prescribe the Manner in which such Acts, Records and Proceedings shall be proved, and the Effect thereof.

Full Faith & Credit

SECTION 2. The Citizens of each State shall be entitled to all Privileges and Immunities of Citizens in the several States.

Privileges & immunitics

A Person charged in any State with Treason, Felony, or other Crime, who shall flee from Justice, and be found in another State, shall on Demand of the executive Authority of the State from which he fled, be delivered up, to be removed to the State having Jurisdiction of the Crime.

extradite

No Person held to Service or Labour in one State, under the Laws thereof, escaping into another, shall, in Consequence of any Law or Regulation therein, be discharged from such Service or Labour, but shall be delivered up on Claim of the Party to whom such Service or Labour may be due.

Return slaves

SECTION 3. New States may be admitted by the Congress into this Union; but no new State shall be formed or erected within the Jurisdiction of any other State; nor any State be formed by the Junction of two or more States, or Parts of States, without the Consent of the Legislatures of the States concerned as well as of the Congress.

The Congress shall have Power to dispose of and make all needful Rules and Regulations respecting the Territory or other Property belonging to the United

States; and nothing in this Constitution shall be so construed as to Prejudice any Claims of the United States, or of any particular State.

SECTION 4. The United States shall guarantee to every State in this Union a Republican Form of Government, and shall protect each of them against Invasion; and on Application of the Legislature, or of the Executive (when the Legislature cannot be convened), against domestic Violence.

ARTICLE V. The Congress, whenever two thirds of both Houses shall deem it necessary, shall propose Amendments to this Constitution, or, on the Application of the Legislatures of two thirds of the several States, shall call a Convention for proposing Amendments, which, in either Case, shall be valid to all Intents and Purposes, as Part of this Constitution, when ratified by the Legislatures of three fourths of the several States, or by Conventions in three fourths thereof, as the one or the other Mode of Ratification may be proposed by the Congress; Provided that no Amendment which may be made prior to the Year One thousand eight hundred and eight shall in any Manner affect the first and fourth Clauses in the Ninth Section of the first Article; and that no State, without its Consent, shall be deprived of its equal Suffrage in the Senate.

ARTICLE VI. All Debts contracted and Engagements entered into, before the Adoption of this Constitution, shall be as valid against the United States under this Constitution, as under the Confederation.

This Constitution, and the Laws of the United States which shall be made in Pursuance thereof; and all Treaties made, or which shall be made, under the Authority of the United States, shall be the supreme Law of the Land; and the Judges in every State shall be bound thereby, any Thing in the Constitution or Laws of any State to the Contrary notwithstanding.

The Senators and Representatives before mentioned, and the Members of the several State Legislatures, and all executive and judicial Officers, both of the United States and of the several States, shall be bound by Oath or Affirmation, to support this Constitution; but no religious Test shall ever be required as a Qualification to any Office or public Trust under the United States.

ARTICLE VII. The Ratification of the Conventions of nine States, shall be sufficient for the Establishment of this Constitution between the States so ratifying the Same.

The Word, "the," being interlined between the seventh and eighth Lines of the first Page, The Word "Thirty" being partly written on an Erazure in the fifteenth Line of the first Page, The Words "is tried" being interlined between the thirty second and thirty third Lines of the first Page and the Word "the" being interlined between the forty third and forty fourth Lines of the second Page.

Attest William Jackson Secretary

done in Convention by the Unanimous Consent of the States present the Seventeenth Day of September in the Year of our Lord one thousand seven hundred and Eighty seven and of the Independance of the United States of America the Twelfth In witness whereof We have hereunto subscribed our Names,

G°. Washington

Presidt and deputy from Virginia

1.5.3

The Bill of Rights and Later Amendments

ratified 1791–1992

FIRST AMENDMENT (1791). Congress shall make no law respecting an establishment of religion, or prohibiting the free exercise thereof; or abridging the freedom of speech, or of the press; or the right of the people peaceably to assemble, and to petition the Government for a redress of grievances.

SECOND AMENDMENT (1791). A well regulated Militia, being necessary to the security of a free State, the right of the people to keep and bear Arms, shall not be infringed.

THIRD AMENDMENT (1791). No Soldier shall, in time of peace be quartered in any house, without the consent of the Owner, nor in time of war, but in a manner to be prescribed by law.

FOURTH AMENDMENT (1791). The right of the people to be secure in their persons, houses, papers, and effects, against unreasonable searches and seizures, shall not be violated, and no Warrants shall issue, but upon probable cause, supported by Oath or affirmation, and particularly describing the place to be searched, and the persons or things to be seized.

FIFTH AMENDMENT (1791). No person shall be held to answer for a capital, or otherwise infamous crime, unless on a presentment or indictment of a Grand Jury, except in cases arising in the land or naval forces, or in the Militia, when in actual service in time of War or public danger; nor shall any person be subject for the same offence to be twice put in jeopardy of life or limb; nor shall be compelled in any criminal case to be a witness against himself, nor be deprived of life, liberty, or property, without due process of law; nor shall private property be taken for public use, without just compensation.

SIXTH AMENDMENT (1791). In all criminal prosecutions, the accused shall enjoy the right to a speedy and public trial, by an impartial jury of the State and district wherein the crime shall have been committed, which district shall have been previously ascertained by law, and to be informed of the nature and cause of the accusation; to be confronted with the witnesses against him; to have compulsory process for obtaining witnesses in his favor, and to have the Assistance of Counsel for his defence.

SEVENTH AMENDMENT (1791). In suits at common law, where the value in controversy shall exceed twenty dollars, the right of trial by jury shall be preserved, and no fact tried by a jury, shall be otherwise re-examined in any Court of the United States, than according to the rules of the common law.

EIGHTH AMENDMENT (1791). Excessive bail shall not be required, nor excessive fines imposed, nor cruel and unusual punishments inflicted.

NINTH AMENDMENT (1791). The enumeration in the Constitution, of certain rights, shall not be construed to deny or disparage others retained by the people.

TENTH AMENDMENT (1791). The powers not delegated to the United States by the Constitution, nor prohibited by it to the States, are reserved to the States respectively, or to the people.

ELEVENTH AMENDMENT (1795). The Judicial power of the United States shall not be construed to extend to any suit in law or equity, commenced or prosecuted against one of the United States by Citizens of another State, or by Citizens or Subjects of any Foreign State.

TWELFTH AMENDMENT (1804). The Electors shall meet in their respective states and vote by ballot for President and Vice-President, one of whom, at least, shall not be an inhabitant of the same state with themselves; they shall name in their ballots the person voted for as President, and in distinct ballots the person voted for as Vice-President, and they shall make distinct lists of all persons voted for as President, and of all persons voted for as Vice-President, and of the number of votes for each, which lists they shall sign and certify, and transmit sealed to the seat of the government of the United States, directed to the President of the Senate;—the President of the Senate shall, in the presence of the Senate and House of Representatives, open all the certificates and the votes shall then be counted;—The person having the greatest number of votes for President, shall be the President, if such number be a majority of the whole number of Electors appointed; and if no person have such majority, then from the persons having the highest numbers not exceeding three on the list of those voted for as President, the House of Representatives shall choose immediately, by ballot, the President. But in choosing the President, the votes shall be taken by states, the representation from each state having one vote; a quorum for this purpose shall consist of a member or members from two-thirds of the states, and a majority of all the states shall be necessary to a choice. And if the House of Representatives shall not choose a President whenever the right of choice shall devolve upon them, before the fourth day of March next following, then the Vice-President shall act as President, as in case of the death or other constitutional disability of the President.—The person having the greatest number of votes as Vice-President, shall be the Vice-President, if such number be a majority of the whole number of Electors appointed, and if no person have a majority, then from the two highest numbers on the list, the Senate shall choose the Vice-President; a quorum for the purpose shall consist of two-thirds of the whole number of Senators, and a majority of the whole number shall be necessary to a choice. But no person constitutionally ineligible to the office of President shall be eligible to that of Vice-President of the United States.

THIRTEENTH AMENDMENT (1865), SECTION 1. Neither slavery nor involuntary servitude, except as a punishment for crime whereof the party shall have been duly convicted, shall exist within the United States, or any place subject to their jurisdiction.

SECTION 2. Congress shall have power to enforce this article by appropriate legislation.

FOURTEENTH AMENDMENT (1868), SECTION 1. All persons born or naturalized in the United States, and subject to the jurisdiction thereof, are citizens of the United States and of the State wherein they reside. No State shall make or enforce any law which shall abridge the privileges or immunities of citizens of the United States; nor shall any State deprive any person of life, liberty, or property, without due process of law; nor deny to any person within its jurisdiction the equal protection of the laws.

SECTION 2. Representatives shall be apportioned among the several States according to their respective numbers, counting the whole number of persons in each State, excluding Indians not taxed. But when the right to vote at any election for the choice of electors for President and Vice-President of the United States, Representatives in Congress, the Executive and Judicial officers of a State, or the members of the Legislature thereof, is denied to any of the male inhabitants of such State, being twenty-one years of age,* and citizens of the United States, or in any way abridged, except for participation in rebellion, or other crime, the basis of representation therein shall be reduced in the proportion which the number of such male citizens shall bear to the whole number of male citizens twenty-one years of age in such State.

SECTION 3. No person shall be a Senator or Representative in Congress, or elector of President and Vice-President, or hold any office, civil or military, under the United States, or under any State, who, having previously taken an oath, as a member of Congress, or as an officer of the United States, or as a member of any State legislature, or as an executive or judicial officer of any State, to support the Constitution of the United States, shall have engaged in insurrection or rebellion against the same, or given aid or comfort to the enemies thereof. But Congress may by a vote of two-thirds of each House, remove such disability.

SECTION 4. The validity of the public debt of the United States, authorized by law, including debts incurred for payment of pensions and bounties for services in suppressing insurrection or rebellion, shall not be questioned. But neither the United States nor any State shall assume or pay any debt or obligation incurred in aid of insurrection or rebellion against the United States, or any claim for the loss or emancipation of any slave; but all such debts, obligations and claims shall be held illegal and void.

SECTION 5. The Congress shall have the power to enforce, by appropriate legislation, the provisions of this article.

FIFTEENTH AMENDMENT (1870), SECTION 1. The right of citizens of the United States to vote shall not be denied or abridged by the United States or by any State on account of race, color, or previous condition of servitude—

SECTION 2. The Congress shall have the power to enforce this article by appropriate legislation.

SIXTEENTH AMENDMENT (1913). The Congress shall have power to lay and collect taxes on incomes, from whatever source derived, without apportionment among the several States, and without regard to any census or enumeration.

SEVENTEENTH AMENDMENT (1913). The Senate of the United States shall be composed of two Senators from each State, elected by the people thereof, for six years; and each Senator shall have one vote. The electors in each State shall have the qualifications requisite for electors of the most numerous branch of the State legislatures.

When vacancies happen in the representation of any State in the Senate, the executive authority of such State shall issue writs of election to fill such vacancies: Provided, That the legislature of any State may empower the executive thereof to make temporary appointments until the people fill the vacancies by election as the legislature may direct.

This amendment shall not be so construed as to affect the election or term of any Senator chosen before it becomes valid as part of the Constitution.

EIGHTEENTH AMENDMENT (1919), SECTION 1. After one year from the ratification of this article the manufacture, sale, or transportation of intoxicating liquors within, the importation thereof into, or the exportation thereof from the United States and all territory subject to the jurisdiction thereof for beverage purposes is hereby prohibited.

SECTION 2. The Congress and the several States shall have concurrent power to enforce this article by appropriate legislation.

SECTION 3. This article shall be inoperative unless it shall have been ratified as an amendment to the Constitution by the legislatures of the several States, as provided in the Constitution, within seven years from the date of the submission hereof to the States by the Congress.

NINETEENTH AMENDMENT (1920). The right of citizens of the United States to vote shall not be denied or abridged by the United States or by any State on account of sex.

Congress shall have power to enforce this article by appropriate legislation.

TWENTIETH AMENDMENT (1933), SECTION 1. The terms of the President and the Vice President shall end at noon on the 20th day of January, and the terms of Senators and Representatives at noon on the 3d day of January, of the years in which such terms would have ended if this article had not been ratified; and the terms of their successors shall then begin.

SECTION 2. The Congress shall assemble at least once in every year, and such meeting shall begin at noon on the 3d day of January, unless they shall by law appoint a different day.

SECTION 3. If, at the time fixed for the beginning of the term of the President, the President elect shall have died, the Vice President elect shall become President. If a President shall not have been chosen before the time fixed for the beginning of his term, or if the President elect shall have failed to qualify, then the Vice President elect shall act as President until a President shall have qualified; and the Congress may by law provide for the case wherein neither a President elect nor a Vice President elect shall have qualified, declaring who shall then act as President, or the manner in which one who is to act shall be selected, and such person shall act accordingly until a President or Vice President shall have qualified.

SECTION 4. The Congress may by law provide for the case of the death of any of the persons from whom the House of Representatives may choose a President whenever the right of choice shall have devolved upon them, and for the case of the death of any of the persons from whom the Senate may choose a Vice President whenever the right of choice shall have devolved upon them.

SECTION 5. Sections 1 and 2 shall take effect on the 15th day of October following the ratification of this article.

SECTION 6. This article shall be inoperative unless it shall have been ratified as an amendment to the Constitution by the legislatures of three-fourths of the several States within seven years from the date of its submission.

TWENTY-FIRST AMENDMENT (1933), SECTION 1. The eighteenth article of amendment to the Constitution of the United States is hereby repealed.

SECTION 2. The transportation or importation into any State, Territory, or possession of the United States for delivery or use therein of intoxicating liquors, in violation of the laws thereof, is hereby prohibited.

SECTION 3. This article shall be inoperative unless it shall have been ratified as an amendment to the Constitution by conventions in the several States, as provided in the Constitution, within seven years from the date of the submission hereof to the States by the Congress.

TWENTY-SECOND AMENDMENT (1951), SECTION 1. No person shall be elected to the office of the President more than twice, and no person who has held the office of President, or acted as President, for more than two years of a term to which some other person was elected President shall be elected to the office of the President more than once. But this Article shall not apply to any person holding the office of President when this Article was proposed by the Congress, and shall not prevent any person who may be holding the office of President, or acting as President, during the term within which this Article becomes operative from holding the office of President or acting as President during the remainder of such term.

SECTION 2. This article shall be inoperative unless it shall have been ratified as an amendment to the Constitution by the legislatures of three-fourths of the several States within seven years from the date of its submission to the States by the Congress.

TWENTY-THIRD AMENDMENT (1961), SECTION 1. The District constituting the seat of Government of the United States shall appoint in such manner as the Congress may direct:

A number of electors of President and Vice President equal to the whole number of Senators and Representatives in Congress to which the District would be entitled if it were a State, but in no event more than the least populous State; they shall be in addition to those appointed by the States, but they shall be considered, for the purposes of the election of President and Vice President, to be electors appointed by a State; and they shall meet in the District and perform such duties as provided by the twelfth article of amendment.

SECTION 2. The Congress shall have power to enforce this article by appropriate legislation.

TWENTY-FOURTH AMENDMENT (1964), SECTION 1. The right of citizens of the United States to vote in any primary or other election for President or Vice President, for electors for President or Vice President, or for Senator or Representative in Congress, shall not be denied or abridged by the United States or any State by reason of failure to pay any poll tax or other tax.

SECTION 2. The Congress shall have power to enforce this article by appropriate legislation.

TWENTY-FIFTH AMENDMENT (1967), SECTION 1. In case of the removal of the President from office or of his death or resignation, the Vice President shall become President.

SECTION 2. Whenever there is a vacancy in the office of the Vice President, the President shall nominate a Vice President who shall take office upon confirmation by a majority vote of both Houses of Congress.

SECTION 3. Whenever the President transmits to the President pro tempore of the Senate and the Speaker of the House of Representatives his written declaration that he is unable to discharge the powers and duties of his office, and until he transmits to them a written declaration to the contrary, such powers and duties shall be discharged by the Vice President as Acting President.

SECTION 4. Whenever the Vice President and a majority of either the principal officers of the executive departments or of such other body as Congress may by law provide, transmit to the President pro tempore of the Senate and the Speaker of the House of Representatives their written declaration that the President is unable to discharge the powers and duties of his office, the Vice President shall immediately assume the powers and duties of the office as Acting President.

Thereafter, when the President transmits to the President pro tempore of the Senate and the Speaker of the House of Representatives his written declaration that no inability exists, he shall resume the powers and duties of his office unless the Vice President and a majority of either the principal officers of the executive department or of such other body as Congress may by law provide, transmit within four days to the President pro tempore of the Senate and the Speaker of the House of Representatives their written declaration that the President is unable to discharge the powers and duties of his office. Thereupon Congress shall decide the issue, assembling within forty-eight hours for that purpose if not in session. If the Congress, within twenty-one days after receipt of the latter written declaration, or, if Congress is not in session, within twenty-one days after Congress is required to assemble, determines by two-thirds vote of both Houses that the President is unable to discharge the powers and duties of his office, the Vice President shall continue to discharge the same as Acting President; otherwise, the President shall resume the powers and duties of his office.

TWENTY-SIXTH AMENDMENT (1971), SECTION 1. The right of citizens of the United States, who are eighteen years of age or older, to vote shall not be denied or abridged by the United States or by any State on account of age.

SECTION 2. The Congress shall have power to enforce this article by appropriate legislation.

TWENTY-SEVENTH AMENDMENT (1992). No law, varying the compensation for the services of the Senators and Representatives, shall take effect, until an election of Representatives shall have intervened.

PART ONE

THE LEGISLATIVE BRANCH

CHAPTER 2

WHAT ARE THE "LEGISLATIVE POWERS," AND WHAT IS THEIR EFFECT ON STATE LAW?

ARTICLE I, SECTION 1: All legislative Powers herein granted shall be vested in a Congress of the United States, which shall consist of a Senate and House of Representatives.

ARTICLE I, SECTION 8, CLAUSE 1: The Congress shall have Power To lay and collect Taxes, Duties, Imposts and Excises, to pay the Debts and provide for the common Defence and general Welfare of the United States; . . .

> **CLAUSE 2:** To borrow Money on the credit of the United States;
>
> **CLAUSE 3:** To regulate Commerce with foreign Nations, and among the several States, and with the Indian Tribes; . . .—And
>
> **CLAUSE 18:** To make all Laws which shall be necessary and proper for carrying into Execution the foregoing Powers, and all other Powers vested by this Constitution in the Government of the United States, or in any Department or Officer thereof.

ARTICLE VI, PARAGRAPH 2: This Constitution, and the Laws of the United States which shall be made in Pursuance thereof; and all Treaties made, or which shall be made, under the Authority of the United States, shall be the supreme Law of the Land; and the Judges in every State shall be bound thereby, any Thing in the Constitution or Laws of any State to the Contrary notwithstanding.

TENTH AMENDMENT (1791): The powers not delegated to the United States by the Constitution, nor prohibited by it to the States, are reserved to the States respectively, or to the people.

2.1 IMPLIED POWERS AND FEDERAL SUPREMACY

The U.S. Constitution is organized into a preamble, seven "articles," and twenty-seven amendments, each of which has a different focus. Article I describes the federal and state "legislative Powers." Article II describes the federal "executive Power." Article III describes the federal "judicial Power." Article IV describes relationships between the states. Article V describes how the Constitution may be amended. Article VI describes the relationship between federal and state law. Article VII describes the process for ratifying the Constitution. The amendments, finally, generally describe limits on how the federal or state governments may exercise power.

In general, this casebook will examine each article and amendment, one section or clause at a time, drawing from other articles and amendments only as needed to understand a particular clause. That said, the first clause of the first article—"All legislative Powers herein granted shall be vested in a Congress of the United States . . ."—is the sort of clause that is difficult to understand without jumping around the document. Nevertheless, the first clause is an appropriate place to begin because identifying what those legislative powers are is perhaps the most foundational and extensively debated question in U.S. constitutional law.

So let's dive right in and ask the all-important question: What are the "legislative Powers" referred to in this opening sentence? The answer, at first blush, is simple: they are whatever powers are "herein granted" by the rest of the Constitution. For example, Article I, Section 8, includes eighteen clauses that together enumerate a list of over eighteen specific powers granted to Congress, beginning with Clause 1: "Congress shall have Power To lay and collect Taxes."

herein granted seems to limit but then cl. 18

One reasonable interpretation of *legislative Powers herein granted*, then, is that Congress may do what the Constitution specifies—like lay and collect taxes—but nothing else.

This intuitive interpretation, however, is complicated by the final clause in that list from Article I, Section 8: "Congress shall have Power . . . To make all Laws which shall be necessary and proper for carrying into Execution the foregoing Powers, and all other Powers vested by this Constitution in the Government of the United States. . . ." This clause, called the Necessary and Proper Clause or the Elastic Clause, appears to give Congress additional implied powers that are not expressly specified in the Constitution's text—that is, whatever powers are "necessary and proper" to execute an enumerated power.

Also complicating the interpretation is the Tenth Amendment. When James Madison drafted the amendment as a member of the first Congress in 1789, he modeled his text on Article II of the Articles of Confederation, which stated, "Each state retains its sovereignty, freedom, and independence, and every power, jurisdiction, and right, which is not by this Confederation expressly delegated to the United States, in Congress assembled." Madison, however, removed the word *expressly*, so his amendment read, "The powers not delegated to the United States by the Constitution, nor prohibited by it to the States, are reserved to the States respectively, or to the people." *See* 1 *Annals of Congress* 767–68 (1789). During the 1789 debate over the amendment, several members of the first Congress noticed Madison's modification and tried to add the word *expressly* before the word *delegated* so that the new amendment would emphasize that Congress's powers were limited to the express delegations of the Constitution. But these proposals were defeated in both the House and the Senate, and the Tenth Amendment was ratified without the word *expressly*. *See* U.S. Const. amend. X.

All of this makes it difficult to accept the intuitive interpretation that the legislative powers are limited to those expressly enumerated in the Constitution. Yet any other interpretation presents its own difficulties: If the legislative powers include implied powers, does that mean that Congress can do anything it considers necessary and proper?

Why bother including enumerated powers like the power to lay and collect taxes if Congress isn't limited to those powers?

The stakes for resolving these difficulties couldn't be higher. The Constitution contains no express language authorizing Congress to acquire new territory, enact criminal laws, regulate working conditions, create interstate highways, regulate health insurance, create immigration laws, offer education loans, or maintain a nuclear weapons system. Congress's ability to do any of these things depends on how to interpret the scope of its legislative powers—an issue that first arose almost immediately after the Constitution got off the ground.

scope?

2.1.1

Opinions on the National Bank

1791 (*reprinted in The Federalist* 651 (Paul Leicester Ford ed., 1898))

In the winter of 1789, George Washington was months into his first term as president, and the United States was still carrying a massive, $54 million dollar debt from the Revolutionary War. *See* Alexander Hamilton, *Report Relative to a Provision for the Support of Public Credit* (Jan. 9, 1790), *in* 6 *Papers of Alexander Hamilton* 65, 86 (Harold C. Syrett ed., 1962). Individual states were also deeply in debt: they collectively owed $25 million. *Id.* These were enormous sums at a time when the federal government could hope to earn only about $4 million annually from tariffs and other taxes. *Id.* at 137. Washington therefore asked his Secretary of the Treasury, Alexander Hamilton, to develop a plan to help Congress and the states reduce the debt.

Hamilton proposed a complicated plan in which the federal government would assume the state debts and pay them off over a long period. *See id.* at 78. At the center of his plan was a proposal for Congress to charter a national bank. *See* Alexander Hamilton, *Second Report on the Further Provision Necessary for Establishing Public Credit* (Dec. 13, 1790), *in* 6 *Papers of Alexander Hamilton*, *supra*, at 305. Rather than treat the debt as a burden that needed to be paid off immediately, a bank could hold onto the debt and use it to grow the economy, stabilize the currency, and increase the country's tax base.

Unfortunately for Hamilton, nothing in the Constitution expressly gave Congress the power to charter a bank. In fact, as Hamilton was aware from personal experience, the Constitutional Convention specifically rejected a proposal to give Congress the power to charter corporations. *See* 2 *The Records of the Federal Convention of 1787*, at 615–16 (Max Farrand ed., 1911). Hamilton needed a legal strategy. He had previously observed that when the Constitution gave Congress legislative power, it not only enumerated specific powers like the power to tax, but also authorized Congress to enact whatever laws were "necessary and proper" for carrying those enumerated powers into execution. *See The Federalist No. 33*, at 205–06 (Alexander Hamilton)

(Jacob E. Cooke ed., 1961) (quoting U.S. Const. art. I, § 8, cl. 18). It was therefore arguable that Congress had the *implied power* to charter a bank, because such a bank was "necessary and proper" for executing Congress's powers to tax, borrow money, and regulate commerce.

In 1790, Hamilton proposed his national bank plan to Congress, where his theory of implied powers was contentiously debated. Over the objections of members who argued that the federal government had no power to charter corporations, Congress passed a bill adopting Hamilton's plan in full. *See* Jonathan Gienapp, *The Second Creation* 202–47 (2018).

Because of his own concerns about the constitutionality of implied powers, however, Washington asked his cabinet whether he should sign or veto the bill. Washington's secretary of state, Thomas Jefferson, wrote a stinging criticism of the bill's constitutionality, which called for Hamilton's response.

■ SECRETARY OF STATE THOMAS JEFFERSON[1]

[I] consider the foundation of the Constitution as laid on this ground: That "all powers not delegated to the United States, by the Constitution, nor prohibited by it to the States, are reserved to the States or to the people." To take a single step beyond the boundaries thus specially drawn around the powers of Congress, is to take possession of a boundless field of power, no longer susceptible of any definition.

The incorporation of a bank, and the powers assumed by this bill, have not, in my opinion, been delegated to the United States, by the Constitution. . . .

They are not among the powers specially enumerated: for these are: 1. A power to lay taxes for the purpose of paying the debts of the United States; but no debt is paid by this bill, nor any tax laid. . . .

2. "To borrow money." But this bill neither borrows money nor ensures the borrowing of it. The proprietors of the bank will be just as free as any other money holders, to lend or not to lend their money to the public. . . .

3. To "regulate commerce with foreign nations, and among the States, and with the Indian tribes." To erect a bank, and to regulate commerce, are very different acts. He who erects a bank, creates a subject of commerce in its bills, so does he who makes a bushel of wheat, or digs a dollar out of the mines; yet neither of these persons regulates commerce thereby. To make a thing which may be bought and sold, is not to prescribe regulations for buying and selling. Besides, if this was an exercise of the power of regulating commerce, it would be void, as extending as much to the internal commerce of every State, as to its external. For the power given to Congress by the Constitution does not extend to the internal regulation of the commerce of a State, (that is to say of the commerce between citizen and citizen,) which remain exclusively with its own legislature; but to its external commerce only, that is to say, its commerce with another State, or with foreign nations, or with the Indian tribes. . . .

---

1 **As You Read, Consider:** The beginning of this section lists several of the specific powers that Article I gives Congress, including the powers to "borrow Money" and "regulate Commerce." Why doesn't Thomas Jefferson think that any of these powers justifies the bank bill? Does Alexander Hamilton disagree?

What does Jefferson worry will happen if Congress can establish a bank or enact any other legislation it considers "necessary and proper"? Does Hamilton address his concern?

Nor are they within either of the general phrases, which are the two following:

1. To lay taxes to provide for the general welfare of the United States, that is to say, "to lay taxes for *the purpose of* providing for the general welfare." For the laying of taxes is the *power*, and the general welfare the *purpose* for which the power is to be exercised. They are not to lay taxes *ad libitum for any purpose they please*; but only *to pay the debts or provide for the welfare of the Union*. In like manner, they are not *to do anything they please* to provide for the general welfare, but only to *lay taxes* for that purpose. To consider the latter phrase, not as describing the purpose of the first, but as giving a distinct and independent power to do any act they please, which might be for the good of the Union, would render all the preceding and subsequent enumerations of power completely useless. It would reduce the whole instrument to a single phrase, that of instituting a Congress with power to do whatever would be for the good of the United States; and, as they would be the sole judges of the good or evil, it would be also a power to do whatever evil they please. . . .

Certainly no such universal power was meant to be given [members of Congress]. [The Constitution] was intended to lace them up straitly within the enumerated powers, and those without which, as means, these powers could not be carried into effect. It is known that the very power now proposed *as a means* was rejected as *an end* by the Convention which formed the Constitution. A proposition was made to them to authorize Congress to open canals, and an amendatory one to empower them to incorporate. But the whole was rejected, and one of the reasons for rejection urged in debate was, that then they would have a power to erect a bank, which would render the great cities, where there were prejudices and jealousies on the subject, adverse to the reception of the Constitution.

2. The second general phrase is, "to make all laws *necessary* and proper for carrying into execution the enumerated powers." But they can all be carried into execution without a bank. A bank therefore is not *necessary*, and consequently not authorized by this phrase.

It has been urged that a bank will give great facility or convenience in the collection of taxes, Suppose this were true: yet the Constitution allows only the means which are "*necessary*," not those which are merely "convenient" for effecting the enumerated powers. If such a latitude of construction be allowed to this phrase as to give any non-enumerated power, it will go to everyone, for there is not one which ingenuity may not torture into a *convenience* in some instance *or other*, to *some one* of so long a list of enumerated powers. It would swallow up all the delegated powers, and reduce the whole to one power, as before observed. Therefore it was that the Constitution restrained them to the *necessary* means, that is to say, to those means without which the grant of power would be nugatory. . . .

The negative of the President is the shield provided by the Constitution to protect against the invasions of the legislature: . . . The present is the case of a right remaining exclusively with the States, and consequently one of those intended by the Constitution to be placed under its protection. . . .

■ SECRETARY OF THE TREASURY ALEXANDER HAMILTON

In entering upon the argument, it ought to be premised that the objections of the Secretary of State . . . are founded on a general denial of the authority of the United States to erect corporations. . . .

The first of these arguments is, that the foundation of the Constitution is laid on this ground: "That all powers not delegated to the United States by the Constitution, nor prohibited to it by the States, are reserved for the States, or to the people." Whence it is meant to be inferred, that Congress can in no case exercise any power not included in those not enumerated in the Constitution. And it is affirmed, that the power of erecting a corporation is not included in any of the enumerated powers.

The main proposition here laid down, in its true signification is not to be questioned. It is nothing more than a consequence of this republican maxim, that all government is a delegation of power. But how much is delegated in each case, is a question of fact, to be made out by fair reasoning and construction, upon the particular provisions of the Constitution, taking as guides the general principles and general ends of governments.

It is not denied that there are implied as well as express powers, and that the former are as effectually delegated as the latter. . . . It will not be doubted, that if the United States should make a conquest of any of the territories of its neighbors, they would possess sovereign jurisdiction over the conquered territory. This would be rather a result, from the whole mass of the powers of the government, and from the nature of political society, than a consequence of either of the powers specially enumerated.

But be this as it may, it furnishes a striking illustration of the general doctrine contended for; it shows an extensive case in which a power of erecting corporations is either implied in or would result from, some or all of the powers vested in the national government. The jurisdiction acquired over such conquered country would certainly be competent to any species of legislation.

To return: It is conceded that implied powers are to be considered as delegated equally with express ones. Then it follows, that as a power of erecting a corporation may as well be implied as any other thing, it may as well be employed as an instrument or mean of carrying into execution any of the specified powers, as any other instrument or mean whatever. The only question must be in this, as in every other case, whether the mean to be employed or in this instance, the corporation to be erected, has a natural relation to any of the acknowledged objects or lawful ends of the government. Thus a corporation may not be erected by Congress for superintending the police of the city of Philadelphia, because they are not authorized to regulate the police of that city. But one may be erected in relation to the collection of taxes, or to the trade with foreign countries, or to the trade between the States, or with the Indian tribes; because it is the province of the federal government to regulate those objects, and because it is incident to a general sovereign or legislative power to regulate a thing, to employ all the means which relate to its regulation to the best and greatest advantage.

A strange fallacy seems to have crept into the manner of thinking and reasoning upon the subject. . . . An incorporation seems to have been regarded as some great independent substantive thing; as a political end of peculiar magnitude and moment; whereas it is truly to be considered as a quality, capacity, or mean to an end. Thus a mercantile company is formed, with a certain capital, for the purpose of carrying on a particular branch of business. Here the business to be prosecuted is the end. The association, in order to form the requisite capital, is the primary mean. Suppose that an incorporation were added to this, it would only be to add a new quality to that association, to give it an artificial capacity, by which it would be enabled to prosecute the business with more safety and convenience. . . .

To this mode of reasoning respecting the right of employing all the means requisite to the execution of the specified powers of the government, it is objected, that none but necessary and proper means are to be employed; and the Secretary of State maintains, that no means are to be considered as necessary but those without which the grant of the power would be nugatory. . . .

It is essential to the being of the national government, that so erroneous a conception of the meaning of the word necessary should be exploded.

It is certain that neither the grammatical nor popular sense of the term requires that construction. According to both, necessary often means no more than needful, requisite, incidental, useful, or conducive to. It is a common mode of expression to say, that it is necessary for a government or a person to do this or that thing, when nothing more is intended or understood, than that the interests of the government or person require, or will be promoted by, the doing of this or that thing. The imagination can be at no loss for exemplifications of the use of the word in this sense. And it is the true one in which it is to be understood as used in the Constitution. The whole turn of the clause containing it indicates, that it was the intent of the Convention, by that clause, to give a liberal latitude to the exercise of the specified powers. . . .

To understand the word as the Secretary of State does, would be to depart from its obvious and popular sense, and to give it a restrictive operation, an idea never before entertained. It would be to give it the same force as if the word absolutely or indispensably had been prefixed to it.

Such a construction would beget endless uncertainty and embarrassment. The cases must be palpable and extreme, in which it could be pronounced, with certainty, that a measure was absolutely necessary, or one, without which, the exercise of a given power would be nugatory. There are few measures of any government which would stand so severe a test. To insist upon it, would be to make the criterion of the exercise of any implied power, a case of extreme necessity; which is rather a rule to justify the overleaping of the bounds of constitutional authority, than to govern the ordinary exercise of it. . . .

The degree in which a measure is necessary, can never be a test of the legal right to adopt it. . . . The relation between the measure and the end; between the nature of the mean employed toward the execution of a power, and the object of that power must be the criterion of constitutionality, not the more or less of necessity or utility.

The practice of the government is against the rule of construction advocated by the Secretary of State. Of this, the Act concerning lighthouses, beacons, buoys, and public piers, is a decisive example.[2] This, doubtless, must be referred to the powers of regulating trade, and is fairly relative to it. But it cannot be affirmed that the exercise of that power in this instance was strictly necessity or that the power itself would be nugatory, with out that of regulating establishments of this nature.

This restrictive interpretation of the word necessary is also contrary to this sound maxim of construction, namely, that the powers contained in a constitution of government, especially those which concern the general administration of the affairs of a country, its finances, trade, defense, etc., ought to be construed liberally in advancement of the public good. This rule does not depend on the particular form of a government, or on the particular demarcation of the boundaries of its powers, but on the nature and object of government itself. The means by which national exigencies are to be provided for, national inconveniences obviated, national prosperity promoted, are of such infinite variety, extent, and complexity, that there must of necessity be great latitude of discretion in the selection and application of those means. Hence, consequently, the necessity and propriety of exercising the authorities intrusted to a government on principles of liberal construction. . . .

---

[2] **Note:** Hamilton here is referring to the ninth statute passed by the first Congress, an uncontroversial law that established lighthouses. Act of Aug. 7, 1789, ch. 9, 1 Stat. 53.

But while on the one hand the construction of the Secretary of State is deemed inadmissible, it will not be contended, on the other, that the clause in question gives any new or independent power. But it gives an explicit sanction to the doctrine of implied powers, and is equivalent to an admission of the proposition that the government, as to its specified powers and objects, has plenary and sovereign authority, in some cases paramount to the States; in others, co-ordinate with it. For such is the plain import of the declaration, that it may pass all laws necessary and proper to carry into execution those powers.

It is no valid objection to the doctrine to say, that it is calculated to extend the power of the government throughout the entire sphere of State legislation. The same thing has been said, and may be said, with regard to every exercise of power by implication or construction. The moment the literal meaning is departed from, there is a chance of error and abuse. And yet an adherence to the letter of its powers would at once arrest the motions of government. It is not only agreed, on all hands, that the exercise of constructive powers is indispensable, but every act which has been passed, is more or less an exemplification of it. . . .

The truth is, that difficulties on this point are inherent in the nature of the Federal Constitution; . . . there will be cases clearly within the power of the national government; others, clearly without its powers; and a third class, which will leave room for controversy and difference of opinion, and concerning which a reasonable latitude of judgment must be allowed.

But the doctrine which is contended for . . . does not affirm that the national government is sovereign in all respects, but that it is sovereign to a certain extent; that is, to the extent of the objects of its specified powers. It leaves, therefore, a criterion of what is constitutional, and of what is not so. This criterion is the end, to which the measure relates as a mean. If the end be clearly comprehended within any of the specified powers, and if the measure have an obvious relation to that end, and is not forbidden by any particular provision of the Constitution, it may safely be deemed to come within the compass of the national authority.[3]

2.1.2

McCulloch v. Maryland

17 U.S. (4 Wheat.) 316 (1819)

Hamilton's argument carried the day; in 1791, Washington signed the bill, which chartered the Bank of the United States for a twenty-year term. During its tenure, the bank successfully put the United States on a path toward paying off its war debt. Yet the bank remained unpopular with Jefferson and his supporters, catalyzing the political division of the country into Democratic-Republicans, led by Jefferson, and Federalists, led by Washington and Hamilton.

Despite the bank's financial success, Democratic-Republicans continued to assail the bank over the next twenty years on constitutional and political grounds. Although the bank was chartered by Congress, private individuals operated it on behalf of private shareholders. Just as many large corporations today are reviled for contributing to economic

---

[3] **Question:** Under Hamilton's interpretation of the Necessary and Proper Clause, can you think of any law that would be beyond Congress's power to enact?

inequality, the bank was criticized as a monopoly that favored financial speculators over farmers.

In 1811, the year the bank's charter was due to expire, Democratic-Republicans controlled Congress and allowed the charter to lapse. *See* Adam Winkler, *We the Corporations* 68–70 (2018). The timing was unlucky: the United States went to war with the United Kingdom in 1812, and the country had a difficult time financing the war without a national bank to sell bonds, issue legal tender, or manage the national debt. *Id.* at 70.

The Democratic-Republican Congress eventually created a Second Bank of the United States in 1816. *See* Eric Lomazoff, *Reconstructing the National Bank Controversy* 113 (2018). Members who remained skeptical of the Necessary and Proper Clause argued instead that they were exercising Congress's power to "coin Money." *Id.* But this second bank remained unpopular, particularly in states like Maryland that were seriously indebted by the War of 1812. In 1818, Maryland passed a law levying a $15,000 tax on any bank that operated in the state without the state legislature's permission. *See id.* at 121–28. Soon afterward, the state sued James William McCulloch, the cashier of the Maryland branch of the Second Bank of the United States, demanding that he pay the tax. *Id.*

McCulloch refused on the ground that the Maryland law was unconstitutional. Instead of relying on the Coinage Clause, McCulloch revived Hamilton's argument from three decades earlier: the Necessary and Proper Clause gave Congress the legislative power to charter the Second Bank. *Id.* at 4–5. The Maryland law, McCulloch continued, conflicted with the federal law because a tax on the Second Bank made it more difficult for the bank to accomplish the important purposes that Congress set out for it. Under Article VI of the Constitution, federal law is "the supreme Law of the Land; and the Judges in every State shall be bound thereby, any Thing in the Constitution or Laws of any State to the Contrary notwithstanding." McCulloch argued that this Supremacy Clause prohibited Maryland from taxing the bank.

The Supreme Court that heard McCulloch's case, *McCulloch v. Maryland*, 17 U.S. (4 Wheat.) 316 (1819), was led by Chief Justice John Marshall, a towering figure in American law. During his thirty-four years as chief justice, Marshall wrote hundreds of opinions, usually unanimous, that interpreted many of the clauses in the Constitution for the first time. Appointed to the court by President John Adams in 1801, Marshall considered himself a political protégé of Washington, Hamilton, and other Federalists. In fact, Marshall so admired Washington and Hamilton that in 1805 he wrote a five-volume biography of the first president, in which he praised Hamilton's argument in support of the bank. 5 John Marshall, *The Life of George Washington* 295–99 (1805).

In 1819, Marshall was in a position to consider the Jefferson-Hamilton debate anew, not as a biographer but as a justice. As you'll see, he divided his opinion into two questions:

(1) Does Congress have the power to incorporate a bank?

(2) If so, is the federally chartered bank immune from state taxes?

His opinion answered yes to both.

■ MARSHALL, C.J., delivered the opinion of the Court.[4]

In the case now to be determined, the defendant, a sovereign state, denies the obligation of a law enacted by the legislature of the Union, and the plaintiff, on his part, contests the validity of an act which has been passed by the legislature of that state. The constitution of our country, in its most interesting and vital parts, is to be considered; the conflicting powers of the government of the Union and of its members, as marked in that constitution, are to be discussed; and an opinion given, which may essentially influence the great operations of the government. . . .

[I]

The first question made in the cause is—has congress power to incorporate a bank? It has been truly said, that this can scarcely be considered as an open question, entirely unprejudiced by the former proceedings of the nation respecting it. The principle now contested was introduced at a very early period of our history, has been recognised by many successive legislatures, and has been acted upon by the judicial department, in cases of peculiar delicacy, as a law of undoubted obligation. . . .[5] balance of power & precedent

The power now contested was exercised by the first congress elected under the present constitution. The bill for incorporating the Bank of the United States did not steal upon an unsuspecting legislature, and pass unobserved. Its principle was completely understood, and was opposed with equal zeal and ability. After being resisted, first, in the fair and open field of debate, and afterwards, in the executive cabinet, with as much persevering talent as any measure has ever experienced, and being supported by arguments which convinced minds as pure and as intelligent as this country can boast, it became a law. The original act was permitted to expire; but a short experience of the embarrassments to which the refusal to revive it exposed the government, convinced those who were most prejudiced against the measure of its necessity, and induced the passage of the present law. It would require no ordinary share of intrepidity, to assert that a measure adopted under these circumstances, was a bold and plain usurpation, to which the constitution gave no countenance. . . .

In discussing this question, the counsel for the state of Maryland have deemed it of some importance, in the construction of the constitution, to consider that instrument, not as emanating from the people, but as the act of sovereign and independent states. The powers of the general government, it has been said, are

---

[4] **As You Read, Consider:** When the Supreme Court faces a constitutional question, the justices typically balance a variety of conflicting principles to come up with a new rule. Sometimes the justices are explicit about which principles are guiding them; sometimes the principles are implied. Consider the list of principles in section 3.3, several of which appear in this opinion (and will be highlighted in the footnotes). Which of these principles do you find most persuasive?

[5] **Question:** The first question Chief Justice John Marshall asks is whether Congress has the power to incorporate a bank. He begins his answer by discussing a principle of settled practice: it matters whether the other branches have already recognized this power. Why is this principle relevant to the main question before the Court?

delegated by the states, who alone are truly sovereign; and must be exercised in subordination to the states, who alone possess supreme dominion. It would be difficult to sustain this proposition. The convention which framed the constitution was indeed elected by the state legislatures. But the instrument, when it came from their hands, was a mere proposal, without obligation, or pretensions to it. It was reported to the then existing congress of the United States, with a request that it might "be submitted to a convention of delegates, chosen in each state by the people thereof, under the recommendation of its legislature, for their assent and ratification." This mode of proceeding was adopted; and by the convention, by congress, and by the state legislatures, the instrument was submitted to the people. They acted upon it in the only manner in which they can act safely, effectively and wisely, on such a subject, by assembling in convention. It is true, they assembled in their several states—and where else should they have assembled? No political dreamer was ever wild enough to think of breaking down the lines which separate the states, and of compounding the American people into one common mass. Of consequence, when they act, they act in their states. But the measures they adopt do not, on that account, cease to be the measures of the people themselves, or become the measures of the state governments.

From these conventions, the constitution derives its whole authority. The government proceeds directly from the people; is "ordained and established," in the name of the people; and is declared to be ordained, "in order to form a more perfect union, establish justice, insure domestic tranquillity, and secure the blessings of liberty to themselves and to their posterity." The assent of the states, in their sovereign capacity, is implied, in calling a convention, and thus submitting that instrument to the people. But the people were at perfect liberty to accept, or reject it; and their act was final. It required not the affirmance, and could not be negatived, by the state governments. The constitution, when thus adopted, was of complete obligation, and bound the state sovereignties. . . .[6]

This government is acknowledged by all, to be one of enumerated powers. The principle, that it can exercise only the powers granted to it, would seem too apparent, to have required to be enforced by all those arguments, which its enlightened friends, while it was depending before the people, found it necessary to urge; that principle is now universally admitted. But the question respecting the extent of the powers actually granted, is perpetually arising, and will probably continue to arise, so long as our system shall exist. In discussing these questions, the conflicting powers of the general and state governments must be brought into view, and the supremacy of their respective laws, when they are in opposition, must be settled.

If any one proposition could command the universal assent of mankind, we might expect it would be this—that the government of the Union, though limited in its powers, is supreme within its sphere of action. This would seem to result, necessarily, from its nature. It is the government of all; its powers are delegated by all; it represents all, and acts for all. Though any one state may be willing to control its operations, no state is willing to allow others to control them. The nation, on those subjects on which it can act, must necessarily bind its component parts. But this question is not left to mere reason: the people have, in express terms, decided it, by saying, "this constitution, and the laws of the United States, which shall be made in pursuance thereof," "shall be the supreme law of the land," and by requiring that the members of the state legislatures, and the officers of the executive and judicial departments of

[6] **Questions:** In answering the question of whether Congress can charter a bank, Marshall turns to a principle of *popular sovereignty*: it matters whether the Constitution was ratified by the states or by the people. Why is this principle relevant to the main question before the Court? Should it matter more or less than the principle of settled practice?

the states, shall take the oath of fidelity to it. The government of the United States, then, though limited in its powers, is supreme; and its laws, when made in pursuance of the constitution, form the supreme law of the land, "anything in the constitution or laws of any state to the contrary notwithstanding."[7]

Among the enumerated powers, we do not find that of establishing a bank or creating a corporation. But there is no phrase in the instrument which, like the articles of confederation, excludes incidental or implied powers; and which requires that everything granted shall be expressly and minutely described. Even the 10th amendment, which was framed for the purpose of quieting the excessive jealousies which had been excited, omits the word "expressly," and declares only, that the powers "not delegated to the United States, nor prohibited to the states, are reserved to the states or to the people;" thus, leaving the question, whether the particular power which may become the subject of contest, has been delegated to the one government, or prohibited to the other, to depend on a fair construction of the whole instrument. The men who drew and adopted this amendment had experienced the embarrassments resulting from the insertion of this word in the articles of confederation, and probably omitted it, to avoid those embarrassments. A constitution, to contain an accurate detail of all the subdivisions of which its great powers will admit, and of all the means by which they may be carried into execution, would partake of the prolixity of a legal code, and could scarcely be embraced by the human mind. It would, probably, never be understood by the public. Its nature, therefore, requires, that only its great outlines should be marked, its important objects designated, and the minor ingredients which compose those objects, be deduced from the nature of the objects themselves. That this idea was entertained by the framers of the American constitution, is not only to be inferred from the nature of the instrument, but from the language. Why else were some of the limitations, found in the 9th section of the 1st article, introduced? It is also, in some degree, warranted, by their having omitted to use any restrictive term which might prevent its receiving a fair and just interpretation. In considering this question, then, we must never forget that it is a constitution we are expounding.

Although, among the enumerated powers of government, we do not find the word "bank" or "incorporation," we find the great powers, to lay and collect taxes; to borrow money; to regulate commerce; to declare and conduct a war; and to raise and support armies and navies.[8] The sword and the purse, all the external relations, and no inconsiderable portion of the industry of the nation, are intrusted to its government. It can never be pretended, that these vast powers draw after them others of inferior importance, merely because they are inferior. Such an idea can never be advanced. But it may with great reason be contended, that a government, intrusted with such

---

7 **Questions:** Marshall here defines the stakes of the question before the Court: if Congress has the power to charter a bank, then the law incorporating the bank "shall be the supreme law of the land." This language will be highly relevant to the second half of his opinion.

For now, in the next several paragraphs, he turns to a principle of *text*: it matters how readers understand the Constitution's text. In answering whether Congress can charter a bank, should this principle be more or less relevant than the other principles Marshall has considered? Does the text support McCulloch, Maryland, neither, or both?

8 **Questions:** Marshall appears to concede that nothing in the text of the Constitution explicitly empowers Congress to charter a bank. Yet he considers this concession alongside a principle of *purpose*: it matters what the Constitution was drafted and ratified to do. Does this principle cut in favor of McCulloch or Maryland?

In discussing the purposes of the Constitution, Marshall also draws on some policy principles, including a principle of *empire* or *conquest*: it matters whether the federal government has sufficient power to raise and march armies "from the Atlantic to the Pacific." Why is this principle relevant to the main question before the Court? How would you weigh this principle against the other principles Marshall has discussed?

ample powers, on the due execution of which the happiness and prosperity of the nation so vitally depends, must also be intrusted with ample means for their execution. The power being given, it is the interest of the nation to facilitate its execution. It can never be their interest, and cannot be presumed to have been their intention, to clog and embarrass its execution, by withholding the most appropriate means. Throughout this vast republic, from the St. Croix to the Gulf of Mexico, from the Atlantic to the Pacific, revenue is to be collected and expended, armies are to be marched and supported. The exigencies of the nation may require, that the treasure raised in the north should be transported to the south, that raised in the east, conveyed to the west, or that this order should be reversed. Is that construction of the constitution to be preferred, which would render these operations difficult, hazardous and expensive? Can we adopt that construction (unless the words imperiously require it), which would impute to the framers of that instrument, when granting these powers for the public good, the intention of impeding their exercise, by withholding a choice of means? If, indeed, such be the mandate of the constitution, we have only to obey; but that instrument does not profess to enumerate the means by which the powers it confers may be executed; nor does it prohibit the creation of a corporation, if the existence of such a being be essential, to the beneficial exercise of those powers. It is, then, the subject of fair inquiry, how far such means may be employed.

Means approach — broad construction of nec & proper — broad!

It is not denied, that the powers given to the government imply the ordinary means of execution. That, for example, of raising revenue, and applying it to national purposes, is admitted to imply the power of conveying money from place to place, as the exigencies of the nation may require, and of employing the usual means of conveyance. But it is denied, that the government has its choice of means; or, that it may employ the most convenient means, if, to employ them, it be necessary to erect a corporation. On what foundation does this argument rest? On this alone: the power of creating a corporation, is one appertaining to sovereignty, and is not expressly conferred on congress. This is true. But all legislative powers appertain to sovereignty. . . .

In America, the powers of sovereignty are divided between the government of the Union, and those of the states. They are each sovereign, with respect to the objects committed to it, and neither sovereign, with respect to the objects committed to the other. . . . The power of creating a corporation, though appertaining to sovereignty, is not, like the power of making war, or levying taxes, or of regulating commerce, a great substantive and independent power, which cannot be implied as incidental to other powers, or used as a means of executing them. It is never the end for which other powers are exercised, but a means by which other objects are accomplished. No contributions are made to charity, for the sake of an incorporation, but a corporation is created to administer the charity; no seminary of learning is instituted, in order to be incorporated, but the corporate character is conferred to subserve the purposes of education. No city was ever built, with the sole object of being incorporated, but is incorporated as affording the best means of being well governed. The power of creating a corporation is never used for its own sake, but for the purpose of effecting something else. No sufficient reason is, therefore, perceived, why it may not pass as incidental to those powers which are expressly given, if it be a direct mode of executing them.

But the constitution of the United States has not left the right of congress to employ the necessary means, for the execution of the powers conferred on the government, to general reasoning. To its enumeration of powers is added, that of making "all laws which shall be necessary and proper, for carrying into execution the foregoing powers, and all other powers vested by this constitution, in the government of the United States, or in any department thereof."[9] The counsel for the state of Maryland have urged various arguments, to prove that this clause, though, in terms, a grant of power, is not so, in effect; but is really restrictive of the general right, which might otherwise be implied, of selecting means for executing the enumerated powers. . . . Congress is not empowered by it to make all laws, which may have relation to the powers conferred on the government, but such only as may be "necessary and proper" for carrying them into execution. The word "necessary" is considered as controlling the whole sentence, and as limiting the right to pass laws for the execution of the granted powers, to such as are indispensable, and without which the power would be nugatory. That it excludes the choice of means, and leaves to congress, in each case, that only which is most direct and simple.

Is it true, that this is the sense in which the word "necessary" is always used? Does it always import an absolute physical necessity, so strong, that one thing to which another may be termed necessary, cannot exist without that other? We think it does not. If reference be had to its use, in the common affairs of the world, or in approved authors, we find that it frequently imports no more than that one thing is convenient, or useful, or essential to another. To employ the means necessary to an end, is generally understood as employing any means calculated to produce the end, and not as being confined to those single means, without which the end would be entirely unattainable. Such is the character of human language, that no word conveys to the mind, in all situations, one single definite idea; and nothing is more common than to use words in a figurative sense. Almost all compositions contain words, which, taken in their rigorous sense, would convey a meaning different from that which is obviously intended. It is essential to just construction, that many words which import something excessive, should be understood in a more mitigated sense—in that sense which common usage justifies. The word "necessary" is of this description. It has not a fixed character, peculiar to itself. It admits of all degrees of comparison; and is often connected with other words, which increase or diminish the impression the mind receives of the urgency it imports. A thing may be necessary, very necessary, absolutely or indispensably necessary. To no mind would the same idea be conveyed by these several phrases. The comment on the word is well illustrated by the passage cited at the bar, from the 10th section of the 1st article of the constitution. It is, we think, impossible to compare the sentence which prohibits a state from laying "imposts, or duties on imports or exports, except what may be absolutely necessary for executing its inspection laws," with that which authorizes congress "to make all laws which shall be necessary and proper for carrying into execution" the powers of the general government, without feeling a conviction, that the convention understood itself to change materially the meaning of the word "necessary," by prefixing the word "absolutely." This word, then, like others, is used in various senses; and, in its construction, the subject, the context, the intention of the person using them, are all to be taken into view.

Let this be done in the case under consideration. The subject is the execution of those great powers on which the welfare of a nation essentially depends. It must have been the intention of those who gave these powers, to insure, so far as human prudence could insure, their beneficial execution. This could not be done, by confiding the choice of means to such narrow limits as not to leave it in the power of congress to adopt any which might be appropriate, and which were conducive to the end. This provision is made in a constitution, intended to endure for ages to come, and consequently, to be adapted to the various crises of human affairs. To have

---

9 **Question:** Here, Marshall returns to the principle of text and observes that one of Congress's listed powers is the power to make "necessary and proper" laws. Does this text support McCulloch or Maryland? Do you agree with Marshall's answer?

prescribed the means by which government should, in all future time, execute its powers, would have been to change, entirely, the character of the instrument, and give it the properties of a legal code. It would have been an unwise attempt to provide, by immutable rules, for exigencies which, if foreseen at all, must have been seen dimly, and which can be best provided for as they occur. To have declared, that the best means shall not be used, but those alone, without which the power given would be nugatory, would have been to deprive the legislature of the capacity to avail itself of experience, to exercise its reason, and to accommodate its legislation to circumstances. If we apply this principle of construction to any of the powers of the government, we shall find it so pernicious in its operation that we shall be compelled to discard it. . . .[10]

Take, for example, the power "to establish post-offices and post-roads." This power is executed, by the single act of making the establishment. But, from this has been inferred the power and duty of carrying the mail along the post-road, from one post-office to another. And from this implied power, has again been inferred the right to punish those who steal letters from the post-office, or rob the mail. It may be said, with some plausibility, that the right to carry the mail, and to punish those who rob it, is not indispensably necessary to the establishment of a post-office and post-road. This right is indeed essential to the beneficial exercise of the power, but not indispensably necessary to its existence. So, of the punishment of the crimes of stealing or falsifying a record or process of a court of the United States, or of perjury in such court. To punish these offences, is certainly conducive to the due administration of justice. But courts may exist, and may decide the causes brought before them, though such crimes escape punishment.

The baneful influence of this narrow construction on all the operations of the government, and the absolute impracticability of maintaining it, without rendering the government incompetent to its great objects, might be illustrated by numerous examples drawn from the constitution, and from our laws. . . . This clause, as construed by the state of Maryland, would abridge, and almost annihilate, this useful and necessary right of the legislature to select its means. . . . We think so for the following reasons: 1st. The clause is placed among the powers of congress, not among the limitations on those powers. 2d. Its terms purport to enlarge, not to diminish the powers vested in the government. It purports to be an additional power, not a restriction on those already granted. No reason has been, or can be assigned, for thus concealing an intention to narrow the discretion of the national legislature, under words which purport to enlarge it. . . . If no other motive for its insertion can be suggested, a sufficient one is found in the desire to remove all doubts respecting the right to legislate on that vast mass of incidental powers which must be involved in the constitution, if that instrument be not a splendid bauble.

We admit, as all must admit, that the powers of the government are limited, and that its limits are not to be transcended, But we think the sound construction of the constitution must allow to the national legislature that discretion, with respect to the means by which the powers it confers are to be carried into execution, which will enable that body to perform the high duties assigned to it, in the manner most beneficial to the people. Let the end be legitimate, let it be within the scope of the constitution, and all means which are appropriate, which are plainly adapted to that

---

[10] **Questions:** Marshall finally invokes a principle of *governmental efficacy*: it matters that the federal government has sufficient power to meet the needs of its constituents. How should this principle weigh in relation to the other principles Marshall has considered? What about principles that Marshall does not appear to sympathize with, such as a principle of *federalism*: it matters that power isn't concentrated in the federal government?

end, which are not prohibited, but consist with the letter and spirit of the constitution, are constitutional.[11]

That a corporation must be considered as a means not less usual, not of higher dignity, not more requiring a particular specification than other means, has been sufficiently proved. . . . Had it been intended to grant this power, as one which should be distinct and independent, to be exercised in any case whatever, it would have found a place among the enumerated powers of the government. But being considered merely as a means, to be employed only for the purpose of carrying into execution the given powers, there could be no motive for particularly mentioning it. . . .

After the most deliberate consideration, it is the unanimous and decided opinion of this court, that the act to incorporate the Bank of the United States is a law made in pursuance of the constitution, and is a part of the supreme law of the land. . . .

[II]

It being the opinion of the court, that the act incorporating the bank is constitutional; and that the power of establishing a branch in the state of Maryland might be properly exercised by the bank itself, we proceed to inquire—

Whether the state of Maryland may, without violating the constitution, tax that branch?[12] That the power of taxation is one of vital importance; that it is retained by the states; that it is not abridged by the grant of a similar power to the government of the Union; that it is to be concurrently exercised by the two governments—are truths which have never been denied. But such is the paramount character of the constitution, that its capacity to withdraw any subject from the action of even this power, is admitted. The states are expressly forbidden to lay any duties on imports or exports, except what may be absolutely necessary for executing their inspection laws. If the obligation of this prohibition must be conceded—if it may restrain a state from the exercise of its taxing power on imports and exports—the same paramount character would seem to restrain, as it certainly may restrain, a state from such other exercise of this power, as is in its nature incompatible with, and repugnant to, the constitutional laws of the Union. . . .

On this ground, the counsel for the bank place its claim to be exempted from the power of a state to tax its operations. There is no express provision for the case, but the claim has been sustained on a principle which so entirely pervades the constitution . . . as to be incapable of being separated from it, without rending it into shreds. This great principle is, that the constitution and the laws made in pursuance thereof are supreme; that they control the constitution and laws of the respective states, and cannot be controlled by them. From this, which may be almost termed an axiom, other propositions are deduced as corollaries, on the truth or error of which, and on their application to this case, the cause has been supposed to depend. These

---

[11] **Question:** After weighing various principles of text, purpose, policy, conquest, and governmental efficacy—among others—Marshall announces a new *rule*: Congress can enact any law if it is an "appropriate" means of serving a "legitimate" end. Do you agree that this rule follows from the principles he discussed (or failed to discuss)?

[12] **Question:** Marshall has concluded that Congress had the power to charter the bank, and he now considers whether the Constitution permits Maryland to tax the bank. Maryland is not arguing that states, like Congress, must point to the powers listed in Article I before they can act. Rather, Maryland is arguing that before the Constitution created the federal government, states had the power to tax everything within their borders, and that Maryland's ratification of the Constitution didn't eliminate that power.

Here, Marshall's first response invokes a principle of *federal supremacy*: it matters that "the constitution and laws made in pursuance thereof are supreme." From where does he draw this principle?

are, 1st. That a power to create implies a power to preserve: 2d. That a power to destroy, if wielded by a different hand, is hostile to, and incompatible with these powers to create and to preserve: 3d. That where this repugnancy exists, that authority which is supreme must control, not yield to that over which it is supreme. . . .

The power of congress to create, and of course, to continue, the bank, was the subject of the preceding part of this opinion; and is no longer to be considered as questionable. That the power of taxing it by the states may be exercised so as to destroy it, is too obvious to be denied. But taxation is said to be an absolute power, which acknowledges no other limits than those expressly prescribed in the constitution and like sovereign power of every other description, is intrusted to the discretion of those who use it. But the very terms of this argument admit, that the sovereignty of the state, in the article of taxation itself, is subordinate to, and may be controlled by the constitution of the United States. How far it has been controlled by that instrument, must be a question of construction. In making this construction, no principle, not declared, can be admissible, which would defeat the legitimate operations of a supreme government. It is of the very essence of supremacy, to remove all obstacles to its action within its own sphere, and so to modify every power vested in subordinate governments, as to exempt its own operations from their own influence. This effect need not be stated in terms. It is so involved in the declaration of supremacy, so necessarily implied in it, that the expression of it could not make it more certain. We must, therefore, keep it in view, while construing the constitution.

The argument on the part of the state of Maryland, is, not that the states may directly resist a law of congress, but that they may exercise their acknowledged powers upon it, and that the constitution leaves them, this right, in the confidence that they will not abuse it. . . . It is admitted, that the power of taxing the people and their property, is essential to the very existence of government, and may be legitimately exercised on the objects to which it is applicable, to the utmost extent to which the government may choose to carry it. The only security against the abuse of this power, is found, in the structure of the government itself. In imposing a tax, the legislature acts upon its constituents. This is, in general, a sufficient security against erroneous and oppressive taxation.[13]

The people of a state, therefore, give to their government a right of taxing themselves and their property, and as the exigencies of government cannot be limited, they prescribe no limits to the exercise of this right, resting confidently on the interest of the legislator, and on the influence of the constituent over their representative, to guard them against its abuse. But the means employed by the government of the Union have no such security, nor is the right of a state to tax them sustained by the same theory. Those means are not given by the people of a particular state, not given by the constituents of the legislature, which claim the right to tax them, but by the people of all the states. They are given by all, for the benefit of all—and upon theory, should be subjected to that government only which belongs to all.

It may be objected to this definition, that the power of taxation is not confined to the people and property of a state. It may be exercised upon every object brought within its jurisdiction. This is true, But to what source do we trace this right? It is obvious, that it is an incident of sovereignty, and is co-extensive with that to which it is an incident. All subjects over which the sovereign power of a state extends, are objects of taxation; but those over which it does not extend, are, upon the soundest

[13] **Question:** In these final paragraphs, Marshall considers Maryland's argument that the authors of the Constitution trusted the states to exercise within their borders their traditionally sovereign power "in the confidence that they will not abuse it." What principles does Marshall invoke to reject this argument? Are you persuaded?

principles, exempt from taxation. This proposition may almost be pronounced self-evident.

The sovereignty of a state extends to everything which exists by its own authority, or is introduced by its permission; but does it extend to those means which are employed by congress to carry into execution powers conferred on that body by the people of the United States? We think it demonstrable, that it does not. Those powers are not given by the people of a single state. They are given by the people of the United States, to a government whose laws, made in pursuance of the constitution, are declared to be supreme. Consequently, the people of a single state cannot confer a sovereignty which will extend over them.

If we measure the power of taxation residing in a state, by the extent of sovereignty which the people of a single state possess, and can confer on its government, we have an intelligible standard, applicable to every case to which the power may be applied. We have a principle which leaves the power of taxing the people and property of a state unimpaired; which leaves to a state the command of all its resources, and which places beyond its reach, all those powers which are conferred by the people of the United States on the government of the Union, and all those means which are given for the purpose of carrying those powers into execution. We have a principle which is safe for the states, and safe for the Union. . . .

But, waiving this theory for the present, let us resume the inquiry, whether this power can be exercised by the respective states, consistently with a fair construction of the constitution? That the power to tax involves the power to destroy; that the power to destroy may defeat and render useless the power to create; that there is a plain repugnance in conferring on one government a power to control the constitutional measures of another, which other, with respect to those very measures, is declared to be supreme over that which exerts the control, are propositions not to be denied. But . . . [i]f we apply the principle for which the state of Maryland contends, to the constitution, generally, we shall find it capable of changing totally the character of that instrument. We shall find it capable of arresting all the measures of the government, and of prostrating it at the foot of the states. The American people have declared their constitution and the laws made in pursuance thereof, to be supreme; but this principle would transfer the supremacy, in fact, to the states. If the states may tax one instrument, employed by the government in the execution of its powers, they may tax any and every other instrument. They may tax the mail; they may tax the mint; they may tax patent-rights; they may tax the papers of the custom-house; they may tax judicial process; they may tax all the means employed by the government, to an excess which would defeat all the ends of government. This was not intended by the American people. They did not design to make their government dependent on the states. . . .

fed power to create > state power to destroy

It has also been insisted, that, as the power of taxation in the general and state governments is acknowledged to be concurrent, every argument which would sustain the right of the general government to tax banks chartered by the states, will equally sustain the right of the states to tax banks chartered by the general government. But the two cases are not on the same reason. The people of all the states have created the general government, and have conferred upon it the general power of taxation. The people of all the states, and the states themselves, are represented in congress, and, by their representatives, exercise this power. When they tax the chartered institutions of the states, they tax their constituents; and these taxes must be uniform. But when a state taxes the operations of the government of the United States, it acts upon institutions created, not by their own constituents, but by people over whom they claim no control. It acts upon the measures of a government created by others as well as themselves, for the benefit of others in common with themselves. The difference is that which always exists, and always must exist, between the action of the whole on a part, and the action of a part on the whole—between the laws of a government declared to be supreme, and those of a government which, when in opposition to those laws, is not supreme. . . .

The court has bestowed on this subject its most deliberate consideration. The result is a conviction that the states have no power, by taxation or otherwise, to retard, impede, burden, or in any manner control, the operations of the constitutional laws enacted by congress to carry into execution the powers vested in the general government. . . . We are unanimously of opinion, that the law passed by the legislature of Maryland, imposing a tax on the Bank of the United States, is unconstitutional and void.[14]

2.2 INTERGOVERNMENTAL IMMUNITY

McCulloch v. Maryland, 17 U.S. (4 Wheat.) 316 (1819), remains the most important Supreme Court precedent for identifying when Congress can exercise an implied power and when its valid exercises of power preempt contrary state laws. But in answering these two questions, the case raised a third question: When can a person claim he or she is immune from state taxes or regulations because of a federal law? For example, is it constitutional for a state to apply its generally applicable income tax to federal postal carriers? Can a state police officer pull over a federal judicial clerk for speeding? Or are all federal employees and contractors immune from state laws?

For a century after *McCulloch*, the Supreme Court struck down all state laws that directly or indirectly made it costlier for the federal government to operate. *See, e.g.*, *Panhandle Oil Co. v. Mississippi ex rel. Knox*, 277 U.S. 218, 221–22 (1928). For example, in *Johnson v. Maryland*, 254 U.S. 51 (1920), the Court prohibited Maryland from arresting a postal worker who refused to obtain a driver's license from the state. *Id.* at 56–57. Conceding that Congress might not wish to immunize federal agents from *all* state laws, the Court nevertheless held that postal workers might not be able to do their federal jobs if states could test and regulate them. It cited a recent precedent to observe that "even the most unquestionable and most universally applicable of state laws, such as those concerning murder, will not be allowed to control the conduct of a marshal of the United States acting under and in pursuance of the laws of the United States." *Id.* (citing *Ex parte Neagle*, 135 U.S. 1 (1890)). *But see United States v. Kirby*, 74 U.S. (7 Wall.) 482, 487 (1869) (holding that

---

14 **Question:** Consider two contemporary versions of Maryland's argument. First, imagine that the federal government dispatches soldiers to Oregon, where they arrest protestors who the soldiers claim are threatening a federal courthouse. Do the principles that Marshall has invoked in *McCulloch* persuade you that the Oregon state police should not be allowed to arrest the soldiers for violating the state's anti-kidnapping laws? fed property belongs to all

Second, imagine that the federal government dispatches federal physicians to provide abortions, vaccines, and other medical care to people in Texas. Do the principles in *McCulloch* persuade you that the Texas state police should not be able to arrest the physicians for violating any contrary laws the state has enacted? TX has soveirengty over the people of TX and can enforce laws not in conflict w/fed laws

Are there any principles that you would find relevant in answering these questions that Marshall's opinion failed to consider?

a specific federal statute did not prohibit a state from arresting a postal worker for murder).

The Court announced a new default rule in two decisions in the 1930s. *See Graves v. New York ex rel. O'Keefe*, 306 U.S. 466, 479–80 (1939); *James v. Dravo Contracting Co.*, 302 U.S. 134, 161 (1937). While reaffirming Congress's power to immunize federal agents from state taxes and regulations, the Court put the burden on Congress to do so clearly. *See Graves*, 306 U.S. at 478–80. The Court therefore held that it would presume that Congress did not oppose nondiscriminatory state taxes, like an income tax, that incidentally burdened federal agents. *Id.* If Congress disagreed, it could always pass a law expressly preempting these sorts of state taxes. *Id.*

Since then, the Court has generally presumed that Congress would want to preempt a state tax or regulation only if the state law directly regulates the United States, if it discriminates against the federal government, or if it conflicts with a valid federal law that specifically immunizes the person or entity from state interference. *See, e.g., Davis v. Mich. Dep't of Treasury*, 489 U.S. 803, 810–14 (1989); *South Carolina v. Baker*, 485 U.S. 505, 523 (1988). For more on preemption, see section 11.2.

CHAPTER 3

WHO GETS TO DECIDE WHETHER A LEGISLATIVE POWER IS VALIDLY EXERCISED?

ARTICLE I, SECTION 1: All legislative Powers herein granted shall be vested in a Congress of the United States, which shall consist of a Senate and House of Representatives.

ARTICLE II, SECTION 1, CLAUSE 8: Before [the President] enter on the Execution of his Office, he shall take the following Oath or Affirmation:—"I do solemnly swear (or affirm) that I will faithfully execute the Office of President of the United States, and will to the best of my Ability, preserve, protect and defend the Constitution of the United States."

ARTICLE II, SECTION 2, CLAUSE 2: [The President] shall nominate, and by and with the Advice and Consent of the Senate, shall appoint . . . Judges of the supreme Court, and all other Officers of the United States. . . .

ARTICLE II, SECTION 3: He shall . . . Commission all the Officers of the United States.

ARTICLE III, SECTION 1: The judicial Power of the United States, shall be vested in one supreme Court, and in such inferior Courts as the Congress may from time to time ordain and establish.

ARTICLE III, SECTION 2, CLAUSE 1: The judicial Power shall extend to all Cases, in Law and Equity, arising under this Constitution. . . .

> **CLAUSE 2:** In all Cases affecting Ambassadors, other public Ministers and Consuls, and those in which a State shall be Party, the supreme Court shall have original Jurisdiction. In all the other Cases before mentioned, the supreme Court shall have appellate Jurisdiction, both as to Law and Fact, with such Exceptions, and under such Regulations as the Congress shall make.

ARTICLE VI, PARAGRAPH 2: This Constitution, and the Laws of the United States which shall be made in Pursuance thereof; and all Treaties made, or which shall be made, under the Authority of the United States, shall be the supreme Law of the Land; and the Judges in every State shall be bound thereby, any Thing in the Constitution or Laws of any State to the Contrary notwithstanding.

> **PARAGRAPH 3:** The Senators and Representatives before mentioned, and the Members of the several State Legislatures, and all executive and judicial Officers, both of the United States and of the several States, shall be bound by Oath or Affirmation, to support this Constitution. . . .

3.1 JUDICIAL REVIEW

Although *McCulloch v. Maryland*, 17 U.S. (4 Wheat.) 316 (1819), held that Congress had the constitutional power to charter a national bank, the Supreme Court didn't provide the last word on the dispute. The Second Bank of the United States, like the first, had been chartered for only a twenty-year term. In 1832, as the bank's 1836 expiration date approached, its supporters in Congress passed a bill to renew the charter four years early. But the president in 1832, Andrew Jackson, was a vehement critic of the bank's constitutionality. He vetoed the bank bill, writing that "the powers and privileges possessed by the existing bank are unauthorized by the Constitution, subversive of the rights of the States, and dangerous to the liberties of the people." 8 Reg. Deb. app. 73–74 (1832).

Jackson recognized, of course, that the Supreme Court had upheld the bank's constitutionality in *McCulloch*. But he argued that the Court "ought not to control the co-ordinate authorities of this Government." *Id.* at 76. Rather, "[t]he Congress, the Executive, and the Court must each for itself be guided by its own opinion of the Constitution." *Id.* To Jackson, it was important that he and every other public officer had taken "an oath to support the Constitution"—an oath that made it

> as much the duty of the House of Representatives, of the Senate, and of the President to decide upon the constitutionality of any bill or resolution which may be presented to them for passage or approval as it is of the supreme judges when it may be brought before them for judicial decision.

Id. Although he said he respected the Supreme Court, he argued that its opinions had "no more authority over Congress than the opinion of Congress has over the judges, and on that point the President is independent of both." *Id.* He concluded that "the authority of the Supreme Court must not, therefore, be permitted to control the Congress or the Executive when acting in their legislative capacities, but to have only such influence as the force of their reasoning may deserve." *Id.* Disagreeing with the Supreme Court's reasoning in *McCulloch*, he killed the national bank, which remained dead until it was revived in modified form as the Federal Reserve System in 1913.

Jackson's veto message in 1832 illustrates what many political figures in the early nineteenth century believed: although the Supreme Court undoubtedly had the power to interpret the Constitution, it was not the only institution with that power, nor were its interpretations supreme. Rather, the president, members of Congress, state legislators, and ordinary citizens also claimed the power to interpret the Constitution's words and decide for themselves whether one of Congress's legislative powers had been validly exercised. *See* Larry Kramer, *The People Themselves* 200–02 (2004). Even Supreme Court justices adhered to a version of this view. In *McCulloch*, Chief Justice John Marshall emphasized that his interpretation of Congress's powers had been earlier advanced "by the first congress . . ., in the fair and open field of debate, and afterwards, in the executive cabinet, with as much persevering talent as any measure has ever experienced." 17 U.S. (4 Wheat.) at 401–02.

Nevertheless, early in the Supreme Court's history, Marshall made a pitch for why the Supreme Court should have the last word on deciding the scope of Congress's legislative powers. Like *McCulloch*, this pitch arose at the tail end of a quarrel begun in the 1790s by Thomas Jefferson and Alexander Hamilton.

3.1.1

Resolutions on the Constitutionality of the Alien and Sedition Acts

1798–99 (4 *the debates . . . on the adoption of the federal constitution* 540 (Jonathan Elliot ed., 1836))

In 1793, after losing the battle over the national bank, Jefferson so detested Hamilton that he resigned from President George Washington's administration and formed an informal political party in opposition to the administration's policies. In 1796, Jefferson and his Democratic-Republicans narrowly lost the next presidential election to Vice President John Adams, a member of Hamilton's proadministration Federalist Party. The main issue that divided the two parties was whether to support revolutionary France in its war with Great Britain. Jefferson wanted to, while Hamilton and Adams did not.

The issue erupted early in the Adams administration when three U.S. diplomats to France—including a young John Marshall—were told by three French diplomats that the French would negotiate with them only if they paid a bribe. *See* James Morton Smith, *Freedom's Fetters: The Alien and Sedition Laws and American Civil Liberties* 3–5 (1956). Marshall wrote to Adams that he and the other U.S. diplomats had been so insulted by the French diplomats, whom he called *X*, *Y*, and *Z*, that he and his colleagues were returning to America. The "XYZ Affair" galvanized public support behind war with France. Marshall in particular became so admired for his morality that he was eventually elected to a seat in Congress as a Federalist from Virginia, before serving as Adams's secretary of state. *Id.*

Before Marshall took his seat, Congress responded to the XYZ Affair by authorizing expenditures toward an undeclared war between the United States and France. It also passed four laws, known as the Alien and Sedition Acts of 1798, that gave the president the power to arrest certain foreigners and to prosecute newspaper publishers who printed defamatory articles about his administration. *See* Acts of Jun. 18–Jul. 6, chs. 54, 58, 66, 74, 1 Stat. 566–596.

These acts scandalized Jefferson and his fellow Virginian, James Madison. Together, they wrote two scathing criticisms of the constitutionality of the Alien and Sedition Acts. Out of fear that they might be prosecuted under these very laws if they published their complaints individually, Jefferson and Madison urged the legislatures of Virginia and Kentucky to issue their criticisms as resolutions.

On the merits, which we'll discuss in a later section on immigration (10.3), Madison's Virginia Resolution argued that the Alien and Sedition Acts were unconstitutional because Congress's legislative powers did not include the power to regulate immigration or to abridge the freedom of the press. But the most notable question that the Virginia Resolution answered was who should decide whether the Alien and Sedition Acts are constitutional: Should it be the Supreme Court or the individual states? Madison's answer prompted the legislature of Massachusetts, Adams's home state, to issue a response.

THE VIRGINIA RESOLUTION[1]

In the House of Delegates, Friday, *December 21, 1798.*

Resolved, . . . That this Assembly doth explicitly and peremptorily declare, that it views the powers of the federal government as resulting from the compact to which the states are parties, as limited by the plain sense and intention of the instrument constituting that compact, as no further valid than they are authorized by the grants enumerated in that compact; and that, in case of a deliberate, palpable, and dangerous exercise of other powers, not granted by the said compact, the states, who are parties thereto, have the right, and are in duty bound, to interpose, for arresting the progress of the evil, and for maintaining, within their respective limits, the authorities, rights and liberties, appertaining to them. . . .

States have say on constitutionality

That the General Assembly doth particularly PROTEST against the palpable and alarming infractions of the Constitution, in the two late cases of the "Alien and Sedition Acts" passed at the last session of Congress; the first of which exercises a power no where delegated to the federal government, . . . and the other of which acts exercises, in like manner, a power not delegated by the constitution, but on the contrary, expressly and positively forbidden by one of the amendments. . . .

That the good people of this commonwealth . . . doth solemnly appeal to the like dispositions in the other states, in confidence that they will concur with this commonwealth in declaring, as it does hereby declare, that the acts aforesaid are unconstitutional; and that the necessary and proper measures will be taken *by each,* for coöperating with this state, in maintaining unimpaired the authorities, rights, and liberties, reserved to the states respectively, or to the people.

ANSWER OF MASSACHUSETTS

In Senate, *February 9, 1799.*

The legislature of Massachusetts, having taken into serious consideration the resolutions of the state of Virginia . . ., deem it their duty solemnly to declare that, while they hold sacred the principle, that consent of the people is the only pure source of just and legitimate power, they cannot admit the right of the state legislatures to denounce the administration of that government to which the people themselves, by a solemn compact, have exclusively committed their national concerns. . . . [T]he

---

1 **As You Read, Consider:** It is one thing to announce that you think a federal law is unconstitutional. It is quite another for you to announce that your view should prevail even when Congress, the president, and federal courts all disagree with it. Are you persuaded by Virginia's defense of its power to decide the constitutionality of a federal law?

Massachusetts responds that only federal courts should decide constitutional questions. Does Massachusetts reach this conclusion by drawing from the Constitution's text or from some other principle?

decision of all cases in law and equity arising under the Constitution of the United States, and the construction of all laws made in pursuance thereof, are exclusively vested by the people in the judicial courts of the United States.

[T]he people, in that solemn compact which is declared to be the supreme law of the land, have not constituted the state legislatures the judges of the acts or measures of the federal government, but have confided to them the power of proposing such amendments of the Constitution as shall appear to them necessary. . . .

[Should] Virginia persist in the assumption of the right to declare the acts of the national government unconstitutional, and . . . oppose successfully her force and will to those of the nation, the Constitution would be reduced to a mere cipher, to the form and pageantry of authority, without the energy of power; every act of the federal government which thwarted the views or checked the ambitious projects of a particular state, or of its leading and influential members, would be the object of opposition . . .; while the people, convulsed and confused by the conflict between two hostile jurisdictions, enjoying the protection of neither, would be wearied into a submission to some bold leader, who would establish himself on the ruins of both.

And, lastly, [we] feel a strong conviction, that the several United States are connected by a common interest, which ought to render their union indissoluble. . . .

3.1.2

Marbury v. Madison

5 U.S. (1 Cranch) 137 (1803)

When the Massachusetts legislature wrote that "the construction of all laws . . . [is] exclusively vested by the people in the judicial courts of the United States," it was not quoting the U.S. Constitution. Nothing in the Constitution, in fact, expressly gave any federal court or branch of government the general power to review existing federal or state laws. During the Constitutional Convention, Madison had proposed giving Congress the power to veto any unconstitutional state law. But this proposal was voted down in favor of giving Congress a more limited power of "Revision and Control" over state tariffs. U.S. Const. art. I, § 10, cl. 2. In addition, although the Supremacy Clause made the U.S. Constitution, federal law, and federal treaties "the supreme Law of the Land," it left enforcement to state judges: "the Judges in every State shall be bound thereby." U.S. Const. art. VI, ¶ 2. And while many delegates discussed "judicial review"—the principle that courts could review whether one law was consistent with some more supreme law—they never formally voted on whether to condone or repudiate this principle. *See, e.g.*, 1 *The Records of the Federal Convention of 1787*, at 97–98, 109 (Max Farrand ed., 1911); 2 *id.* at 28, 73–93, 430, 440. All the Constitution said about the judiciary's power was that "the judicial Power of the United States, shall be vested in one supreme Court, and in such inferior Courts as the Congress may from time to time ordain and establish." U.S. Const. art. III, § 1. This was hardly a ringing endorsement of the Massachusetts legislature's view that only federal courts could construe the constitutionality of federal laws.

Cts have final say

will there be judicial review?

Nevertheless, the principle of judicial review had become well established by 1799. During the colonial period, ministers of the British Crown had exercised the power to review laws passed by colonial legislatures and had declared laws void if they conflicted with a colonial charter, Crown policies, or an act of Parliament. *See generally* Mary Sarah Bilder, *The Corporate Origins of Judicial Review*, 116 Yale L.J. 502 (2006). After independence, state courts occasionally reviewed the constitutionality of state laws under state constitutions, with some judges declaring the laws "contrary to the plain declaration of the constitution; and therefore void." *Commonwealth v. Caton*, 8 Va. (4 Call.) 5, 7 (1782); *see, e.g., Trevett v. Weeden* (R.I. 1786); *Ten Pound Act Cases* (N.H. Inferior Ct. Com. Pl. 1786); *Bayard v. Singleton*, 1 N.C. 5 (Super. Ct. Law & Eq. 1787); *State v. Parkhurst*, 9 N.J.L. (4 Halst.) 427 (1802). And during the ratification debates, Madison, Hamilton, and other advocates of a strong federal government argued that federal courts would ensure that the state and federal governments would respect the Constitution's limits. *See, e.g.*, 2 Jonathan Elliot, *Debates in the Several State Conventions on the Adoption of the Federal Constitution* 131, 196–97, 348, 362, 445–46, 478 (1836); *The Federalist No. 39*, at 256 (James Madison) (Jacob E. Cooke ed., 1961); *id. No. 44*, at 305 (James Madison); *id. No. 78*, at 524 (Alexander Hamilton); *id. No. 81*, at 541 (Alexander Hamilton). For example, during the Virginia ratifying convention in 1788, then-delegate John Marshall declared that if Congress "were to make a law not warranted by any of the powers enumerated, it would be considered by the judge as an infringement of the Constitution which they are to guard." 3 Elliot, *supra*, at 553–54. The judge would have to consider the law "void," Marshall added, because "[t]here is no other body that can afford such a protection." *Id.*

Even the first Congress appears to have accepted the principle of judicial review. In the Judiciary Act of 1789, which created the federal court system, Congress authorized the Supreme Court to review the final judgment of any state court "where is drawn in question the validity of a treaty or statute of, or an authority exercised under the United States, and the decision is against their validity." 1 Stat. 85 (1789). In 1796, the Supreme Court applied this statute in a case brought against then-advocate John Marshall (the man was everywhere). The decision, *Ware v. Hylton*, 3 U.S. (3 Dall.) 199 (1796), invalidated a Virginia law for being inconsistent with the 1783 Treaty of Paris. *See Calder v. Bull*, 3 U.S. (3 Dall.) 386 (1798) (upholding a state law challenged for violating the Ex Post Facto Clause of Article I, Section 10).

Only once before 1799 had the Supreme Court declared a *federal* law unconstitutional, however. In 1792, Congress passed the Invalid Pensions Act, 1 Stat. 243, which required federal circuit courts to hear testimony from injured Revolutionary War veterans. The law required circuit court judges to recommend to the secretary of war whether the veterans were entitled to receive pensions for their injuries, but it did not order the secretary of war to accept the judges' recommendations. In an unpublished opinion, the Supreme Court objected to this advisory role that the Invalid Pensions Act required judges to fill, writing that "the power proposed to be conferred on the Circuit Courts of the United States by the act of 1792 was not judicial power within the meaning of the Constitution, and was, therefore, unconstitutional." *United States v. Yale Todd* (1794), *reprinted in United States v. Ferreira*, 52 U.S. (13 How.) 40 (1851); *see also Hayburn's Case*, 2 U.S. (2 Dall.) 409 (1792). But the Court didn't elaborate on this point, and it certainly did not hold, as the Massachusetts legislature argued, that only federal courts could determine the constitutionality of federal laws.

In any event, when the federal courts first confronted the Alien and Sedition Acts of 1798, they ignored the Virginia legislature's objections and enforced the acts' terms with gusto. The Adams administration vigorously prosecuted Democratic-Republican newspaper publishers for their criticisms of its policies. Federalist judges even developed reputations as partisans in the cases they oversaw. These blatantly political prosecutions proved to be deeply unpopular. When Adams ran for reelection in 1800, his Federalist Party was demolished by Jefferson's Democratic-Republicans.

Despite losing the White House and Congress in the November elections, the lame-duck Federalist Party still retained control of the federal government for four months, until March 4. (Inauguration day would not be moved up to January 20 until 1933.) The Federalists tried to make the most of their remaining power by packing the federal courts. *See* Richard Brookhiser, *John Marshall* 71–72 (2018).

In December 1800, Chief Justice Oliver Ellsworth retired, allowing President Adams to quickly nominate a replacement. He chose John Marshall, his then-secretary of state, to serve as the fourth chief justice. *See* Brookhiser, *supra*, at 74. In February 1801, as the Federalist-controlled Senate confirmed Marshall as chief justice, it also passed the Judiciary Act of 1801, ch. 4, 2 Stat. 89. This statute created sixteen new federal judgeships and empowered the new judges to hear all appeals from federal trial courts. Later in February, the Federalist Congress also passed the District of Columbia Organic Act of 1801, ch. 15, 2 Stat. 103, which created several dozen magistrate judgeships—then called *justices of the peace*—for the District. These two laws permitted Adams to appoint dozens of new federal judges in the few days remaining before the Democratic-Republicans arrived in the nation's capital. *See generally* Brookhiser, *supra*, at 81–82.

Adams and the Senate filled the last days of Adams's administration by nominating, confirming, and signing the commissions of as many judges as possible. *Id.* Even though Marshall had already taken the oath of office for his new job, he continued to serve as Adams's secretary of state. That role gave him two administrative responsibilities that would prove extremely important. First, he had to apply the "Great Seal of the

United States" to the commissions signed by Adams—providing evidence that his signature was valid. Second, he had to deliver the commissions to the newly confirmed judges before they could begin hearing disputes. As the clock struck midnight on March 4, however, some of the commissions were still sitting in Marshall's office: signed, sealed, and undelivered. Marshall's replacement as secretary of state was Madison, and Madison immediately ordered the deliveries to stop. *Id.* at 82–88.

One of the halted commissions bore the name of William Marbury, a Federalist partisan who had been confirmed and commissioned as a D.C. justice of the peace the previous day. When he didn't receive the commission that entitled him to take his office, Marbury demanded that Secretary of State Madison act. Madison refused, prompting Marbury to petition the Supreme Court for a writ of mandamus. A writ is a court order, and *mandamus* is Latin for *we command*. What Marbury wanted was a court order that commanded a government official, Madison, to do what the law required. Marbury premised his request on Section 13 of the Judiciary Act of 1789, ch. 20, 1 Stat. 73, 80–81, which stated, "The Supreme Court . . . shall have power to issue . . . writs of mandamus, in cases warranted by the principles and usages of law, to any courts appointed, or persons holding office, under the authority of the United States." Marbury and his lawyers wanted the Court to rebuke Madison, thus proving that the new administration was acting illegally. When the Court asked Madison to show cause why the writ shouldn't be issued, Madison didn't show up—apparently rejecting the Court's authority to hear the petition. Brookhiser, *supra*, at 88–89.

As the petition was pending, President Jefferson and the Democratic-Republican Congress sought to purge the judiciary of Federalists whom they regarded as illegitimate. Even though Article III states that federal judges "shall hold their Offices during good Behaviour," the Democratic-Republican Congress repealed the Judiciary Act of 1801, terminating the offices of the sixteen newly appointed circuit judges. *See* Judiciary Act of 1802, ch. 31, 2 Stat. 156. The repeal act also ordered the Supreme Court to next reconvene not in October 1802 but in February 1803. This had the effect of insulating both the repeal act and Marbury's petition from immediate Supreme Court review.

Then, a week before the Court was scheduled to hear arguments in Marbury's case, Jefferson requested that the House of Representatives impeach a federal district judge, John Pickering, for drinking and delivering biased statements while in office. Although Pickering was widely regarded even by Federalists as an embarrassment, Jefferson's move was seen as the opening shot in a campaign to purge Federalists from the judiciary. *See* Lynn W. Turner, *The Impeachment of John Pickering*, 54 Am. Hist. Rev. 485, 487–91 (1949). In fact, only one year later, the House would impeach Justice Samuel Chase, an ardent Federalist, for his public criticisms of the 1802 repeal act.

It was in this context that the Supreme Court decided *Marbury v. Madison*, 5 U.S. (1 Cranch) 137 (1803), perhaps the most famous case in U.S. history. Once again, Madison didn't show up to argue his position—essentially daring the Court to issue a provocative order with which the Jefferson administration had no intention of complying.

■ MR. CHIEF JUSTICE MARSHALL delivered the opinion of the Court.[2]

At the last term . . ., a rule was granted in this case, requiring the secretary of state to show cause why a mandamus should not issue, directing him to deliver to William Marbury his commission as a justice of the peace for the county of Washington, in the district of Columbia.

No cause has been shown, and the present motion is for a mandamus. The peculiar delicacy of this case, the novelty of some of its circumstances, and the real difficulty attending the points which occur in it, require a complete exposition of the principles on which the opinion to be given by the court is founded. . . .

In the order in which the court has viewed this subject, the following questions have been considered and decided.[3]

1st. Has the applicant a right to the commission he demands?

2dly. If he has a right, and that right has been violated, do the laws of his country afford him a remedy?

3dly. If they do afford him a remedy, is it a mandamus issuing from this court?

[Question 1: Has Madison violated the law?]

The first object of inquiry is,

1st. Has the applicant a right to the commission he demands?

His right originates in an act of congress passed in February, 1801, concerning the district of Columbia . . ., [which] enacts, "that there shall be appointed in and for each of the said counties, such number of discreet persons to be justices of the peace as the president of the United States shall, from time to time, think expedient, to continue in office for five years."

It appears, from the affidavits, that in compliance with this law, a commission for William Marbury, as a justice of peace for the county of Washington, was signed by John Adams, then President of the United States; after which the seal of the United States was affixed to it; but the commission has never reached the person for whom it was made out.

In order to determine whether he is entitled to this commission, it becomes necessary to inquire whether he has been appointed to the office. For if he has been appointed, the law continues him in office for five years, and he is entitled to the

---

[2] **As You Read, Consider:** *Marbury v. Madison* is famous for announcing the principle of "judicial review," the idea that the Supreme Court can review the constitutionality of federal laws and decline to enforce those it considers unconstitutional. The opinion is also famously confusing. Which federal law does the Marbury Court actually review? Does it enforce the law or not?

[3] **Note:** Chief Justice John Marshall begins his opinion by posing three questions:

(1) Has Secretary of State James Madison violated the law by withholding William Marbury's commission?

(2) If so, can a federal court provide a legal remedy for Madison's lawbreaking?

(3) If so, is the appropriate legal remedy the writ of mandamus that Marbury has asked for?

Marshall's answer to question (3) is what makes this opinion famous, but he takes his time getting there.

possession of those evidences of office, which, being completed, became his property.

The 2d section of the 2d article of the constitution declares, that "the president shall nominate, and, by and with the advice and consent of the senate, shall appoint, ambassadors, other public ministers and consuls, and all other officers of the United States, whose appointments are not otherwise provided for."[4]

The 3d section declares, that "he shall commission all the officers of the United States."

An act of congress directs the secretary of state to keep the seal of the United States, "to make out and record, and affix the said seal to all civil commissions to officers of the United States, to be appointed by the president, by and with the consent of the senate, or by the president alone; provided, that the said seal shall not be affixed to any commission before the same shall have been signed by the President of the United States."

These are the clauses of the constitution and laws of the United States, which affect this part of the case.

They seem to contemplate three distinct operations:

1st. The nomination. This is the sole act of the president, and is completely voluntary.

2d. The appointment. This is also the act of the president, and is also a voluntary act, though it can only be performed by and with the advice and consent of the senate.

3d. The commission. To grant a commission to a person appointed, might, perhaps, be deemed a duty enjoined by the constitution. "He shall," says that instrument, "commission all the officers of the United States." . . .

This is an appointment made by the president, by and with the advice and consent of the senate, and is evidenced by no act but the commission itself. In such a case, therefore, the commission and the appointment seem inseparable; it being almost impossible to show an appointment otherwise than by proving the existence of a commission. . . .

The commission being signed, the subsequent duty of the secretary of state is prescribed by law, and not to be guided by the will of the president. He is to affix the seal of the United States to the commission, and is to record it.

This is not a proceeding which may be varied, if the judgment of the executive shall suggest one more eligible; but is a precise course accurately marked out by law, and is to be strictly pursued. It is the duty of the secretary of state to conform to the law, and in this he is an officer of the United States, bound to obey the laws. He acts, in this respect, . . . under the authority of law, and not by the instructions of the president. It is a ministerial act which the law enjoins on a particular officer for a particular purpose. . . .

It is, therefore, decidedly the opinion of the court, that when a commission has been signed by the president, the appointment is made; and that the commission is complete when the seal of the United States has been affixed to it by the secretary of state. . . . It has conferred legal rights which cannot be resumed. . . .

---

[4] **Note:** Marshall here is quoting language from Article II of the Constitution that describes the appointment process. Before a person may hold federal office, the president must first nominate the person (if Senate confirmation is required) and give the person a written commission. The Appointments Clause will be discussed in more detail later in the book (section 27.1).

The discretion of the executive is to be exercised until the appointment has been made. But having once made the appointment, his power over the office is terminated in all cases, where by law the officer is not removable by him. The right to the office is then in the person appointed, and he has the absolute, unconditional power of accepting or rejecting it.[5]

Mr. Marbury, then, since his commission was signed by the president, and sealed by the secretary of state, was appointed; and as the law creating the office, gave the officer a right to hold for five years, independent of the executive, the appointment was not revocable, but vested in the officer legal rights, which are protected by the laws of his country.

To withhold his commission, therefore, is an act deemed by the court not warranted by law, but violative of a vested legal right.

[Question 2: Can a court provide a remedy for Madison's lawbreaking?]

This brings us to the second inquiry; which is,

2dly. If he has a right, and that right has been violated, do the laws of his country afford him a remedy?

The very essence of civil liberty certainly consists in the right of every individual to claim the protection of the laws, whenever he receives an injury. One of the first duties of government is to afford that protection. In Great Britain the king himself is sued in the respectful form of a petition, and he never fails to comply with the judgment of his court.

In the 3d vol. of his Commentaries, p. 23. Blackstone states two cases in which a remedy is afforded by mere operation of law.[6]

"In all other cases," he says, "it is a general and indisputable rule, that where there is a legal right, there is also a legal remedy by suit, or action at law, when ever that right is invaded." . . .

The government of the United States has been emphatically termed a government of laws, and not of men. It will certainly cease to deserve this high appellation, if the laws furnish no remedy for the violation of a vested legal right.

If this obloquy is to be cast on the jurisprudence of our country, it must arise from the peculiar character of the case.[7]

It behoves us[,] then[,] to enquire whether there be in its composition any ingredient which shall exempt it from legal investigation, or exclude the injured party from legal redress. . . . Is it in the nature of the transaction? Is the act of delivering or withholding a commission to be considered as a mere political act, belonging to the executive department alone, for the performance of which entire confidence is

---

[5] **Note:** This language is confusing, but Marshall here answers the first question: Yes, Madison has broken the law by withholding Marbury's commission. Although there are plenty of times during the appointment process when an executive officer has discretion not to act—after all, a president might nominate a person and later withdraw the nomination—in this case, the appointment has been finalized.

[6] **Note:** Marshall is quoting William Blackstone (1723–1780), a famous English judge whose *Commentaries* books are frequently cited as a restatement of English law in the 1760s.

[7] **Question:** Marshall is making the point that while every injury deserves a remedy, there are some injuries for which a *legal* remedy would be inappropriate. For example, a person might be "injured" when a president decides not to nominate that person for a cabinet position; but that's a *political* injury that only the president could remedy, not a legal injury that a court could remedy. How does Marshall know when he's facing a *political* question as opposed to a *legal* question?

placed by our constitution in the supreme executive; and for any misconduct respecting which, the injured individual has no remedy[?]

That there may be such cases is not to be questioned; but that every act of duty, to be performed in any of the great departments of government, constitutes such a case, is not to be admitted.

By the act concerning invalids, passed in June, 1794, vol. 3. p. 112, the secretary at war is ordered to place on the pension list all persons whose names are contained in a report previously made by him to congress. If he should refuse to do so, would the wounded veteran be without remedy? Is it to be contended that where the law in precise terms, directs the performance of an act, in which an individual is interested, the law is incapable of securing obedience to its mandate? Is it on account of the character of the person against whom the complaint is made? Is it to be contended that the heads of departments are not amenable to the laws of their country?

Whatever the practice on particular occasions may be, the theory of this principle will certainly never be maintained. No act of the legislature confers so extraordinary a privilege, nor can it derive countenance from the doctrines of the common law. . . .

It follows, then, that the question, whether the legality of an act of the head of a department be examinable in a court of justice or not, must always depend on the nature of that act.

If some acts be examinable, and others not, there must be some rule of law to guide the court in the exercise of its jurisdiction.

In some instances there may be difficulty in applying the rule to particular cases; but there cannot, it is believed, be much difficulty in laying down the rule.

By the constitution of the United States, the president is invested with certain important political powers, in the exercise of which he is to use his own discretion, and is accountable only to his country in his political character and to his own conscience. To aid him in the performance of these duties, he is authorized to appoint certain officers, who act by his authority, and in conformity with his orders.

In such cases, their acts are his acts; and whatever opinion may be entertained of the manner in which executive discretion may be used, still there exists, and can exist, no power to control that discretion. The subjects are political. They respect the nation, not individual rights, and being intrusted to the executive, the decision of the executive is conclusive. . . .

But when the legislature proceeds to impose on that officer other duties: when he is directed peremptorily to perform certain acts; when the rights of individuals are dependent on the performance of those acts; he is so far the officer of the law; is amenable to the laws for his conduct; and cannot at his discretion sport away the vested rights of others.

The conclusion from this reasoning is, that where the heads of departments are the political or confidential agents of the executive, merely to execute the will of the president, or rather to act in cases in which the executive possesses a constitutional or legal discretion, nothing can be more perfectly clear than that their acts are only politically examinable. But where a specific duty is assigned by law, and individual rights depend upon the performance of that duty, it seems equally clear that the individual who considers himself injured, has a right to resort to the laws of his country for a remedy.

If this be the rule, let us inquire how it applies to the case under the consideration of the court.

The power of nominating to the senate, and the power of appointing the person nominated, are political powers, to be exercised by the president according to his own discretion. When he has made an appointment, he has exercised his whole power, and his discretion has been completely applied to the case. If, by law, the officer be removable at the will of the president, then a new appointment may be immediately made, and the rights of the officer are terminated. But as a fact which has existed cannot be made never to have existed, the appointment cannot be annihilated; and, consequently, if the officer is by law not removable at the will of the president, the rights he has acquired are protected by the law, and are not resumable by the president. They cannot be extinguished by executive authority, and he has the privilege of asserting them in like manner as if they had been derived from any other source.

The question whether a right has vested or not, is, in its nature, judicial, and must be tried by the judicial authority. If, for example, Mr. Marbury had taken the oaths of a magistrate, and proceeded to act as one; in consequence of which a suit had been instituted against him, in which his defence had depended on his being a magistrate, the validity of his appointment must have been determined by judicial authority.

So, if he conceives that, by virtue of his appointment, he has a legal right either to the commission which has been made out for him, or to a copy of that commission, it is equally a question examinable in a court, and the decision of the court upon it must depend on the opinion entertained of his appointment.

That question has been discussed, and the opinion is, that the latest point of time which can be taken as that at which the appointment was complete, and evidenced, was when, after the signature of the president, the seal of the United States was affixed to the commission.[8]

It is, then, the opinion of the court,

1st. That by signing the commission of Mr. Marbury, the President of the United States appointed him a justice of peace for the county of Washington, in the district of Columbia; and that the seal of the United States, affixed thereto by the secretary of state, is conclusive testimony of the verity of the signature, and of the completion of the appointment; and that the appointment conferred on him a legal right to the office for the space of five years.

2dly. That, having this legal title to the office, he has a consequent right to the commission; a refusal to deliver which is a plain violation of that right, for which the laws of his country afford him a remedy.

[Question 3: Did Marbury request an appropriate legal remedy?]

It remains to be inquired whether,

3dly. He is entitled to the remedy for which he applies. This depends on,

1st. The nature of the writ applied for; and,

2dly. The power of this court.

1st. The nature of the writ.

Blackstone, in the 3d volume of his Commentaries, page 110, defines a mandamus to be "a command issuing in the king's name from the court of king's bench, and directed to any person, corporation, or inferior court of judicature within

[8] **Note:** Marshall here answers the second question: Yes, this is a legal question, not a political question, and therefore a federal court should be able to provide a legal remedy for Madison's lawbreaking.

the king's dominions, requiring them to do some particular thing therein specified, which appertains to their office and duty, and which the court of king's bench has previously determined, or at least supposes, to be consonant to right and justice." . . .

This writ, if awarded, would be directed to an officer of government, and its mandate to him would be [consistent with] the words of Blackstone. . . .

This, then, is a plain case for a mandamus, either to deliver the commission, or a copy of it from the record; and it only remains to be inquired,[9]

[2dly.] Whether it can issue from this court.

The act to establish the judicial courts of the United States authorizes the supreme court "to issue writs of mandamus, in cases warranted by the principles and usages of law, to any courts appointed, or persons holding office, under the authority of the United States."

The secretary of state, being a person holding an office under the authority of the United States, is precisely within the letter of the description; and if this court is not authorized to issue a writ of mandamus to such an officer, it must be because the law is unconstitutional, and therefore absolutely incapable of conferring the authority, and assigning the duties which its words purport to confer and assign.

The constitution vests the whole judicial power of the United States in one supreme court, and such inferior courts as congress shall, from time to time, ordain and establish. This power is expressly extended to all cases arising under the laws of the United States; and, consequently, in some form, may be exercised over the present case; because the right claimed is given by a law of the United States.

In the distribution of this power it is declared that "the supreme court shall have original jurisdiction in all cases affecting ambassadors, other public ministers and consuls, and those in which a state shall be a party. In all other cases, the supreme court shall have appellate jurisdiction."[10]

It has been insisted, at the bar, that as the original grant of jurisdiction, to the supreme and inferior courts, is general, and the clause, assigning original jurisdiction to the supreme court, contains no negative or restrictive words, the power remains to the legislature, to assign original jurisdiction to that court in other cases than those specified in the article which has been recited; provided those cases belong to the judicial power of the United States.[11]

If it had been intended to leave it in the discretion of the legislature to apportion the judicial power between the supreme and inferior courts according to the will of that body, it would certainly have been useless to have proceeded further than to

---

9 **Question:** This is the beginning of the section that makes *Marbury* famous. Marshall is asking: A writ of mandamus looks like the appropriate legal remedy for Marbury's situation, but does the Supreme Court have the power to issue such a writ? It looks like the Judiciary Act of 1789 says that the Court can "issue writs of mandamus." Does that conclude the issue?

10 **Note:** Marshall here is quoting Article III, which describes the jurisdiction of the Supreme Court. *Original jurisdiction* refers to the power of a court to issue orders deciding a dispute. *Appellate jurisdiction* refers to the power of a court to issue orders with respect to disputes already decided by an inferior court with original jurisdiction.

11 **Question:** We're finally at the constitutional question! Given Marbury's legal injury, he is entitled to a legal remedy: a "writ of mandamus" requiring Madison to hand over his commission. A federal statute says that federal courts can issue writs of mandamus. But rather than asking a federal trial court to issue the writ, Marbury has gone first to the Supreme Court, invoking its original jurisdiction. Article III of the Constitution says the Supreme Court can exercise original jurisdiction only over cases involving "Ambassadors" or a "State." Marbury is neither. So would it be consistent with the Constitution for the Supreme Court to apply the statute in Marbury's case?

have defined the judicial power, and the tribunals in which it should be vested. The subsequent part of the section is mere surplusage, is entirely without meaning, if such is to be the construction. If congress remains at liberty to give this court appellate jurisdiction, where the constitution has declared their jurisdiction shall be original; and original jurisdiction where the constitution has declared it shall be appellate; the distribution of jurisdiction, made in the constitution, is form without substance.

Affirmative words are often, in their operation, negative of other objects than those affirmed; and in this case, a negative or exclusive sense must be given to them, or they have no operation at all.

It cannot be presumed that any clause in the constitution is intended to be without effect; and, therefore, such a construction is inadmissible, unless the words require it. . . .

When an instrument organizing fundamentally a judicial system, divides it into one supreme, and so many inferior courts as the legislature may ordain and establish; then enumerates its powers, and proceeds so far to distribute them, as to define the jurisdiction of the supreme court by declaring the cases in which it shall take original jurisdiction, and that in others it shall take appellate jurisdiction; the plain import of the words seems to be, that in one class of cases its jurisdiction is original, and not appellate; in the other it is appellate, and not original. If any other construction would render the clause inoperative, that is an additional reason for rejecting such other construction, and for adhering to their obvious meaning.

To enable this court, then, to issue a mandamus, it must be shown to be an exercise of appellate jurisdiction, or to be necessary to enable them to exercise appellate jurisdiction.

It has been stated at the bar that the appellate jurisdiction may be exercised in a variety of forms, and that if it be the will of the legislature that a mandamus should be used for that purpose, that will must be obeyed. This is true, yet the jurisdiction must be appellate, not original.

It is the essential criterion of appellate jurisdiction, that it revises and corrects the proceedings in a cause already instituted, and does not create that cause. Although, therefore, a mandamus may be directed to courts, yet to issue such a writ to an officer for the delivery of a paper, is in effect the same as to sustain an original action for that paper, and, therefore, seems not to belong to appellate, but to original jurisdiction. Neither is it necessary in such a case as this, to enable the court to exercise its appellate jurisdiction.

The authority, therefore, given to the supreme court, by the act establishing the judicial courts of the United States, to issue writs of mandamus to public officers, appears not to be warranted by the constitution; and it becomes necessary to inquire whether a jurisdiction so conferred can be exercised.

The question, whether an act, repugnant to the constitution, can become the law of the land, is a question deeply interesting to the United States; but, happily, not of an intricacy proportioned to its interest. It seems only necessary to recognise certain principles, supposed to have been long and well established, to decide it.[12]

That the people have an original right to establish, for their future government, such principles as, in their opinion, shall most conduce to their own happiness is the basis on which the whole American fabric has been erected. The exercise of this

---

[12] **Note:** Marshall's answer to the above question—the federal statute is unconstitutional—raises the famous question that *Marbury* has since become remembered for: What should the Supreme Court do when it is asked to apply a statute that it considers "repugnant to the [C]onstitution"?

original right is a very great exertion; nor can it, nor ought it, to be frequently repeated. The principles, therefore, so established, are deemed fundamental. And as the authority from which they proceed is supreme, and can seldom act, they are designed to be permanent.

This original and supreme will organizes the government, and assigns to different departments their respective powers. It may either stop here, or establish certain limits not to be transcended by those departments.

The government of the United States is of the latter description. The powers of the legislature are defined and limited; and that those limits may not be mistaken, or forgotten, the constitution is written. To what purpose are powers limited, and to what purpose is that limitation committed to writing, if these limits may, at any time, be passed by those intended to be restrained? The distinction between a government with limited and unlimited powers is abolished, if those limits do not confine the persons on whom they are imposed, and if acts prohibited and acts allowed, are of equal obligation. It is a proposition too plain to be contested, that the constitution controls any legislative act repugnant to it; or, that the legislature may alter the constitution by an ordinary act.

Between these alternatives there is no middle ground. The constitution is either a superior paramount law, unchangeable by ordinary means, or it is on a level with ordinary legislative acts, and, like other acts, is alterable when the legislature shall please to alter it.

If the former part of the alternative be true, then a legislative act contrary to the constitution is not law: if the latter part be true, then written constitutions are absurd attempts, on the part of the people, to limit a power in its own nature illimitable.

Certainly all those who have framed written constitutions contemplate them as forming the fundamental and paramount law of the nation, and, consequently, the theory of every such government must be, that an act of the legislature, repugnant to the constitution, is void.

This theory is essentially attached to a written constitution, and, is consequently, to be considered, by this court, as one of the fundamental principles of our society. It is not therefore to be lost sight of in the further consideration of this subject.

If an act of the legislature, repugnant to the constitution, is void, does it, notwithstanding its invalidity, bind the courts, and oblige them to give it effect? Or, in other words, though it be not law, does it constitute a rule as operative as if it was a law? This would be to overthrow in fact what was established in theory; and would seem, at first view, an absurdity too gross to be insisted on. It shall, however, receive a more attentive consideration.

It is emphatically the province and duty of the judicial department to say what the law is. Those who apply the rule to particular cases, must of necessity expound and interpret that rule. If two laws conflict with each other, the courts must decide on the operation of each.[13]

---

13 **Questions:** The last several paragraphs of *Marbury* are an "emphatic" defense of the Supreme Court's power to decline to enforce a law that it considers repugnant to the Constitution. Its rationale makes the most sense when everyone agrees that a statute is unconstitutional. But imagine a situation in which Congress and the president think that a law is constitutional and only the Supreme Court disagrees. Does *Marbury* offer any explanation for why the Supreme Court is better equipped to determine a law's constitutionality than the legislature that passed the law, the executive who signed it, or the states and people subjected to it?

Another way of framing this question is to imagine that *Marbury* had held that it is "emphatically the province and duty of the judicial department to apply the statutes passed by

So if a law be in opposition to the constitution; if both the law and the constitution apply to a particular case, so that the court must either decide that case conformably to the law, disregarding the constitution; or conformably to the constitution, disregarding the law; the court must determine which of these conflicting rules governs the case. This is of the very essence of judicial duty.

If, then, the courts are to regard the constitution, and the constitution is superior to any ordinary act of the legislature, the constitution, and not such ordinary act, must govern the case to which they both apply.

Those, then, who controvert the principle that the constitution is to be considered, in court, as a paramount law, are reduced to the necessity of maintaining that courts must close their eyes on the constitution, and see only the law.

This doctrine would subvert the very foundation of all written constitutions. It would declare that an act which, according to the principles and theory of our government, is entirely void, is yet, in practice, completely obligatory. It would declare that if the legislature shall do what is expressly forbidden, such act, notwithstanding the express prohibition, is in reality effectual. It would be giving to the legislature a practical and real omnipotence, with the same breath which professes to restrict their powers within narrow limits. It is prescribing limits, and declaring that those limits may be passed at pleasure.

That it thus reduces to nothing what we have deemed the greatest improvement on political institutions, a written constitution, would of itself be sufficient, in America, where written constitutions have been viewed with so much reverence, for rejecting the construction. But the peculiar expressions of the constitution of the United States furnish additional arguments in favour of its rejection. . . .

It is declared that "no tax or duty shall be laid on articles exported from any state." Suppose a duty on the export of cotton, of tobacco, or of flour; and a suit instituted to recover it. Ought judgment to be rendered in such a case? [O]ught the judges to close their eyes on the constitution, and only see the law[?]

The constitution declares "that no bill of attainder or ex post facto law shall be passed."

If, however, such a bill should be passed, and a person should be prosecuted under it; must the court condemn to death those victims whom the constitution endeavours to preserve?

"No person," says the constitution, "shall be convicted of treason unless on the testimony of two witnesses to the same overt act, or on confession in open court."

Here the language of the constitution is addressed especially to the courts. It prescribes, directly for them, a rule of evidence not to be departed from. If the legislature should change that rule, and declare one witness, or a confession out of court, sufficient for conviction, must the constitutional principle yield to the legislative act?

From these, and many other selections which might be made, it is apparent, that the framers of the constitution contemplated that instrument as a rule for the government of courts, as well as of the legislature. . . . Why otherwise does it direct the judges to take an oath to support it? This oath certainly applies in an especial manner, to their conduct in their official character. How immoral to impose it on them, if they were to be used as the instruments, and the knowing instruments, for violating what they swear to support!

Congress and signed by the president. It is not the role of the judiciary to second-guess the other branches." What, if anything, would have been objectionable about such a holding?

The oath of office, too, imposed by the legislature, is completely demonstrative of the legislative opinion on this subject. It is in these words: "I do solemnly swear that I will administer justice without respect to persons, and do equal right to the poor and to the rich; and that I will faithfully and impartially discharge all the duties incumbent on me as, according to the best of my abilities and understanding, agreeably to the constitution and laws of the United States."

Why does a judge swear to discharge his duties agreeably to the constitution of the United States, if that constitution forms no rule for his government? if it is closed upon him, and cannot be inspected by him?

If such be the real state of things, this is worse than solemn mockery. To prescribe, or, to take this oath, becomes equally a crime.

It is also not entirely unworthy of observation, that in declaring what shall be the supreme law of the land, the constitution itself is first mentioned; and not the laws of the United States generally, but those only which shall be made in pursuance of the constitution, have that rank.

Thus, the particular phraseology of the constitution of the United States confirms and strengthens the principle, supposed to be essential to all written constitutions, that a law repugnant to the constitution is void; and that courts, as well as other departments, are bound by that instrument.

3.2 LEGISLATIVE REVIEW, EXECUTIVE REVIEW, AND STATE REVIEW

The Supreme Court's decision in *Marbury v. Madison*, 5 U.S. (1 Cranch) 137 (1803), was a defeat for William Marbury, a Federalist, and a victory for James Madison, a Democratic-Republican: Marbury never received his commission. But contemporaries could easily see that Marbury's case was a pawn sacrificed in a larger war against the Democratic-Republicans in the White House and Congress. Chief Justice John Marshall had been able to roundly criticize the Jefferson administration for breaking the law without having to rely on the administration to enforce a controversial order. More importantly, the Marshall Court emerged from *Marbury* with a strong assertion of its power to review more controversial legislation in the future—a power it continued to exercise in cases like *Fletcher v. Peck*, 10 U.S. (6 Cranch) 87 (1810), the first case to declare a state law unconstitutional. For the remainder of his two-term administration, President Thomas Jefferson complained that the defeated Federalist Party had turned the judiciary into a fortress from which it could continue to strengthen the federal government's power over the states. The first case we read, *McCulloch v. Maryland*, 17 U.S. (4 Wheat.) 316 (1819), is a good illustration of what Jefferson feared.

But as a twentieth-century critic of judicial review has observed, *Marbury* "begged the question-in-chief, which was not whether an act repugnant to the Constitution could stand, but who should be empowered to decide that the act is repugnant." Alexander Bickel, *The Least Dangerous Branch* 3 (1962). The real question, which *Marbury* didn't address, was whether federal courts were better able to determine when a law conflicts with the Constitution than the legislature that passed the law, the executive that signed it, or the states and ordinary people subjected to it. As a historical matter, this question persisted for decades after *Marbury*.

State review versus judicial review pre-Civil War

The question first principally arose in the 1810s, when the Virginia Supreme Court decided several cases in which it held that it had final, unreviewable authority to determine the constitutionality of state laws. The court based its reasoning on the Supremacy Clause, which made the Constitution and federal law "the supreme Law of the Land" but made "the Judges in every State" responsible for interpreting it. *See* U.S. Const. art. VI, ¶ 2. After each of these Virginia cases, the Marshall Court asserted its own power to review the state supreme court's decision and order the state court to accept its own interpretation of the Constitution. The Supreme Court explained that any other rule could lead to a divided nation in which the Constitution meant different things in different states. *See Martin v. Hunter's Lessee*, 14 U.S. (1 Wheat.) 304 (1816) (holding the Supreme Court could review and reverse state-court interpretations of federal law); *Cohens v. Virginia*, 19 U.S. (6 Wheat.) 264 (1821) (holding the Supreme Court could review and reverse state-court criminal proceedings in which the defendants based their defense on federal law).

A few decades later, as the supreme courts of northern states began declaring the Fugitive Slave Act of 1850 unconstitutional, the Court reiterated that the principle of uniformity demanded that it have the last word on the constitutionality of state and federal laws. *See Ableman v. Booth*, 62 U.S. (21 How.) 506 (1859).

Nevertheless, the Supreme Court's decisions were not universally accepted. Early in the Court's history, in one of its first decisions, the Court held that Alexander Chisholm, a citizen of South Carolina, could sue the State of Georgia in federal court despite the state's claim of immunity. *See Chisholm v. Georgia*, 2 U.S. (2 Dall.) 419 (1793). Even though the decision was justified by the text of Article III, the decision was repudiated two years later with the passage and ratification of the Eleventh Amendment, which we'll discuss in section 35.1.

State review versus executive review

Not every situation presented a case or controversy for the Supreme Court to review. In 1828, for example, a political crisis erupted between South Carolina and the federal government when the legislature of South Carolina threatened to violently resist a system of federal tariffs that it believed was unconstitutional. *See* Robert Elder, *Calhoun: American Heretic* 241–44 (2021). John C. Calhoun, the sitting vice president and an ardent defender of slavery, supported the legislature. *Id.* at 244–50. In an essay and resolution he anonymously authored on behalf of the legislature, Calhoun asserted that the state had "the power, by its veto, or right of interposition, to arrest the encroachment" of a federal government that was violating its constitutional limits. *The South Carolina Exposition and Protest* (1828), *in Union and Liberty: The Political Philosophy of John C. Calhoun* 311 (Ross M. Lence ed., 1992).

Anticipating the argument that only the Supreme Court could interpret the constitutionality of federal laws, Calhoun argued that the Union was a "constitutional compact" that divided all power between the federal government and the states. *Id.* at 343. "[I]t would seem impossible to deny to the States the right of deciding on the infractions of their powers, and the proper remedy to be applied for their correction," he explained. *Id.* at 348. "In fact, to divide power, and to give to one of the parties the exclusive right of judging of the portion allotted to each, is, in reality, not to divide it at all." *Id.* Calhoun continued by adding that "to reserve such exclusive right to the General Government (it matters not by what department) to be exercised, is to convert it, in fact, into a great consolidated government, with unlimited powers, and to divest the States, in reality, of all their rights." *Id.* In other words, while Calhoun accepted the idea that federal courts might have the power to review legislation, giving federal courts the *exclusive* power of review seemed like letting burglars police their own conduct.

In later speeches, Calhoun would add that constitutional questions should be resolved by a "concurrent majority" of both the federal government and conventions specifically called by state legislatures. *See* Elder, *supra*, at 388–90. Just as the president could veto legislation, Calhoun argued that state conventions could wield the threat of resistance or secession to nullify unconstitutional actions of the federal government. *Id.* at 482–90.

These protests by Calhoun on behalf of South Carolina were part of a proxy battle over slavery: he was keen to defend the state's exclusive power over slavery from any federal interference. *See* Elder, *supra*, at 245–46. However, they provoked a stinging rebuke from President Andrew Jackson, another slaveholder, who criticized "the strange position that any one State may not only declare an act of Congress void, but prohibit its execution . . . [and] be bound by no other of its laws than those it may choose to consider as constitutional." President Andrew Jackson, Proclamation on Nullification, 11 Stat. 771, 772 (1832).

Jackson argued that "the power to annul a law of the United States, assumed by one State," was "*incompatible with the existence of the Union, contradicted expressly by the letter of the Constitution, unauthorized by its spirit, inconsistent with every principle on which It was founded, and destructive of the great object for which it was formed.*" *Id.* at 773. He added that if South Carolina persisted in threatening to violently oppose the enforcement of the federal tariffs, he would ask Congress to authorize him to send the military into Charleston Harbor. South Carolina soon relented—at least until 1860.

In December 1860, South Carolina finally took Calhoun's arguments to their logical conclusion and held a state convention to secede from the Union. The convention explained its decision to secede by arguing that "an increasing hostility on the part of the non-slaveholding States to the institution of slavery, has led to a disregard of their obligations, and the laws of the General Government have ceased to effect the objects of the Constitution." *Journal of the Convention of the People of South Carolina* 461 (R. W. Gibbes, Columbia, S.C. 1862).

Executive review versus judicial review

Although Jackson refused to accept the idea that a state could nullify a federal law, he also refused to accept the idea that only the Supreme Court could evaluate that law's constitutionality. For example, as discussed above, in 1832 he vetoed the Second Bank of the United States as unconstitutional despite the contrary decision in *McCulloch*.

Jackson was not the only president to oppose judicial supremacy. In his 1861 inaugural address, President Abraham Lincoln dedicated several minutes to criticizing the Supreme Court's recent decision in *Dred Scott v. Sandford*, 60 U.S. (19 How.) 393 (1857), in which the Court held that Congress had no power to restrict slavery in federal territories:

> I do not forget the position assumed by some that constitutional questions are to be decided by the Supreme Court, nor do I deny that such decisions must be binding in any case upon the parties to a suit as to the object of that suit, while they are also entitled to very high respect and consideration in all parallel cases by all other departments of the Government. . . . At the same time, the candid citizen must confess that if the policy of the Government upon vital questions affecting the whole people is to be irrevocably fixed by decisions of the Supreme Court, the instant they are made in ordinary litigation between parties in personal actions the people will have ceased to be their own rulers, having to that extent practically resigned their Government into the hands of that eminent tribunal.

First Inaugural Address (1861), *in* 6 *The Life and Works of Abraham Lincoln* 133 (Marion Mills Miller ed., 1907).

Lincoln's argument against judicial supremacy is today often identified with James Bradley Thayer, a professor at Harvard Law School in the late nineteenth century. In a famous 1893 article, Thayer argued that the question posed by judicial supremacy was not whether a statute that violates the Constitution was valid, but whether the Supreme Court should enforce a statute when the president and a majority of Congress think the statute constitutional but a majority of the justices disagree. *See* James B. Thayer, *The Origin and Scope of the American Doctrine of Constitutional Law*, 7 Harv. L. Rev. 129, 150 (1893). Thayer observed that most constitutional questions are ambiguous. When members of Congress debate whether a proposed bill is constitutional, they necessarily attempt to interpret the Constitution with a "combination of a lawyer's rigor with a statesman's breadth of view." *Id.* at 138. And given that Congress has the "primary authority to interpret" the scope of its legislative power—an authority that it exercises every time it passes a statute—Thayer argued that Congress should be "entitled to a corresponding respect" by the Supreme Court. *Id.* at 136.

For Thayer, it was fine for members of Congress to vote against a bill that they believed was unconstitutional. It was also fine for a president to veto a bill for the same reason. But for a federal judge to consider the constitutionality of an enacted statute without regard for the judgments of the other two branches was inappropriate lawmaking. *Id.* at 137–38. "Whoever hath an absolute authority to interpret any written or spoken laws, it is he who is truly the lawgiver, to all intents and purposes, and not the person who first wrote or spoke them," Thayer quipped, quoting a famous contemporary judge, Oliver Wendell Holmes. *Id.* at 152. Thayer argued that federal judges should adopt a deferential attitude toward the constitutionality of statutes, asking only whether it was completely irrational for the legislators to conclude that a law was constitutional. *Id.* at 151.

State review versus judicial review post-Civil War

Notably, while Thayer objected to the Supreme Court's claim of interpretive supremacy with respect to *federal* statutes, he did not raise the same objection when the Supreme Court reviewed *state* statutes. Instead, he argued that it involved a completely "different matter":

> Fundamentally, it involves the allotment of power between the two governments,—where the line is to be drawn. True, the judiciary is still debating whether a legislature has transgressed its limit; but the departments are not co-ordinate, and the limit is at a different point. The judiciary now speaks as representing a paramount constitution and government, whose duty it is, in all its departments, to allow to that constitution nothing less than its just and true interpretation; and having fixed this, to guard it against any inroads from without.

Id. at 154–55.

Thayer's distinction between *judicial* supremacy (which he opposed) and *federal* supremacy (which he supported) reflected not only an abstract theory of federalism but also the experience of Southern secession during and after the Civil War. The war repudiated the attempts by South Carolina and other states to nullify federal legislation. Yet during the Reconstruction era that followed, white politicians in the South continued to resist federal civil rights laws and reject the idea that the Supreme Court's interpretations of the Constitution were supreme. Virginia, for example, refused to respect the mandate of the Supreme Court regarding the legitimacy of the Confederate government, despite the Supreme Court's repeated attempts to make it comply. *See, e.g., Williams v. Bruffy*, 102 U.S. 248 (1880).

This form of explicit Southern resistance reappeared in the 1950s. Virginia politicians in Richmond and in Congress led a campaign of Massive Resistance against the Supreme Court's decision in *Brown v. Board of Education* (*Brown I*), 347 U.S. 483 (1954), which held that state laws segregating schools were unconstitutional. After the *Brown* decision, several Virginia counties shut down their public schools for all children rather than desegregate them. The state legislature even passed legislation that formally satisfied *Brown*'s mandate without desegregating the state's schools. Nineteen senators and eighty-two representatives from southern states applauded these actions. In the Southern Manifesto, these politicians agreed that "the decision of the Supreme Court in the school cases" was an "unwarranted exercise of power by the court, contrary to the Constitution." 102 Cong. Rec. 4459 (1956).

Supreme Court's assertion of power in Cooper

All of this led the Supreme Court to issue a decisive opinion, *Cooper v. Aaron*, 358 U.S. 1 (1958), asserting its role as the supreme expositor of the Constitution. Although *Cooper* was issued as an assertion of *federal* supremacy, it gave the Court an excuse to affirm its understanding of *judicial* supremacy as well.

Cooper stemmed from a desegregation case in Arkansas. In the days after *Brown*, in 1954, the school board of Little Rock, Arkansas, began developing a plan to desegregate its public-school system. In 1957, however, a violent crowd and armed members of the Arkansas National Guard barred nine black students attempting to enter Central High School. The school board, led by William Cooper, responded by delaying the implementation of its desegregation plan, complaining that "[t]he legislative, executive, and judicial departments of the state government opposed the desegregation of Little Rock schools by enacting laws, calling out troops, making statements vilifying federal law and federal courts, and failing to utilize state law enforcement agencies and judicial processes to maintain public peace." *Cooper*, 358 U.S. at 15. But the parents of John Aaron and the other black children complained that the state should not be permitted to resist the Supreme Court's constitutional interpretation.

In *Cooper*, the Supreme Court unanimously agreed with the black children. Answering "the premise of the actions of the Governor and Legislature that they are not bound by our holding in the *Brown* case," the Court explained that their position had been repudiated by the Supremacy Clause and *Marbury*. *Id.* at 17. "In 1803, Chief Justice Marshall, speaking for a unanimous Court, referring to the Constitution as 'the fundamental and paramount law of the nation,' declared . . . the basic principle that the federal judiciary is supreme in the exposition of the law of the Constitution," the Court wrote in *Cooper*. *Id.* at 18. "[T]hat principle has ever since been respected by this Court and the Country as a permanent and indispensable feature of our constitutional system." *Id.* It followed, the Court explained, that the interpretation of the Constitution "enunciated by this Court in the *Brown* case is the supreme law of the land, and Art. VI of the Constitution makes it of binding effect on the States 'any Thing in the Constitution or Laws of any State to the Contrary notwithstanding.' " *Id.*

Like President Jackson, the *Cooper* Court thought it significant that "[e]very state legislator and executive and judicial officer is solemnly committed by oath taken pursuant to Art. VI, cl. 3, 'to support this Constitution.' " *Id.* But unlike Jackson, the Court declared that this oath imposed an obligation on other officers to respect the Court's interpretations of the Constitution rather than to make their own. "No state legislator or executive or judicial officer can war against the Constitution without violating his undertaking to support it," the Court concluded. *Id.* "A Governor who asserts a power to nullify a federal court order is similarly restrained." *Id.* at 18–19.

Cooper in modern-day America

Today, it seems apparent that most public officials agree with the *Cooper* Court. In 2012, when President Barack Obama said it would be "an unprecedented, extraordinary step" for the Supreme Court to strike down the Affordable Care Act—"a law that was passed by a strong majority of a democratically elected Congress"—a snarky panel of the U.S. Court of Appeals for the Fifth Circuit asked the administration to write a letter explaining his statement. *See* Devin Dwyer, *Federal Judge Demands Obama Explain "Obamacare" Statements*, ABC News, Apr. 4, 2012. Eric Holder, the attorney general, responded that "[t]he power of the courts to review the constitutionality of legislation is beyond dispute. The Supreme Court resolved this question in *Marbury v. Madison*, 1 Cranch 137, 177–78 (1803)." *See* Letter from Eric Holder, Att'y Gen., to Judge Jerry E. Smith et al. (Apr. 5, 2012). The attorney general added that "the Executive Branch has often urged courts to respect the legislative judgments of Congress, . . . a coequal branch of government whose Members take the same oath [judges] do to uphold the Constitution of the United States." *Id.* But unlike some of the president's predecessors, Holder did not contend that the president's power to interpret the Constitution was equal to that of the courts. *See id.*

Moreover, in 2015, when a Kentucky county clerk named Kim Davis refused to issue same-sex marriage licenses after the Supreme Court's decision in *Obergefell v. Hodges*, 576 U.S. 644 (2015), she was held in contempt of court and jailed. "It cannot be defensibly argued that the holder of the Rowan County clerk's office . . . may decline to act in conformity with the United States Constitution," the U.S. Court of

Appeals for the Sixth Circuit wrote. *Miller v. Davis*, 2015 WL 10692640 (6th Cir. 2015).

Similarly, the chief justice of the Supreme Court of Alabama, Roy Moore, was suspended from the bench after he ordered probate judges in the state not to issue marriage licenses contrary to then-existing Alabama law. *See* Roy Moore, Administrative Order of the Chief Justice of the Alabama Supreme Court (2016). Such an order, if challenged, would likely have been declared unconstitutional.

3.3 METHODS OF CONSTITUTIONAL INTERPRETATION

As the preface to this casebook observed, the materials in this book emphasize judicial opinions. Yet judges do not interpret the Constitution any better or any differently than do politicians or ordinary people. Everyone, generally speaking, applies similar methods for making difficult decisions or interpreting ambiguous documents. This section's discussion of the process of constitutional interpretation is adapted from Mitchell Berman, *Our Principled Constitution*, 166 U. Pa. L. Rev. 1325 (2018). It also draws insights from David E. Pozen & Adam M. Samaha, *Anti-Modalities*, 119 Mich. L. Rev. 729 (2021), Mark Tushnet, *Taking Back the Constitution* (2020), and Philip Bobbitt, *Constitutional Interpretation* (1991).

A metaphor illustrates the process of how judges, politicians, and other interpreters typically approach constitutional interpretation. Imagine Lady Justice, the personification of legal decision-making. She is typically depicted as a blindfolded woman holding "the scales of justice," a balance scale whose two sides represent competing perspectives on a legal dilemma. Imagine that she is standing on a beach littered with stones. Some of the stones are massive boulders. Others are tiny pebbles. Each of these stones represents a different *legal principle*, or argument that something matters or has force.

The process of constitutional interpretation is, in practice, often a question of collecting relevant stones, weighing the stones on the scales of justice, and announcing a new *constitutional rule* based on whichever side of the scales carries more weight. For example, in *McCulloch v. Maryland*, 17 U.S. (4 Wheat.) 316 (1819), Chief Justice John Marshall confronted the question of whether Congress had the power to establish a bank. His opinion gathered a half dozen legal principles, some weightier than others, in support of the bank:

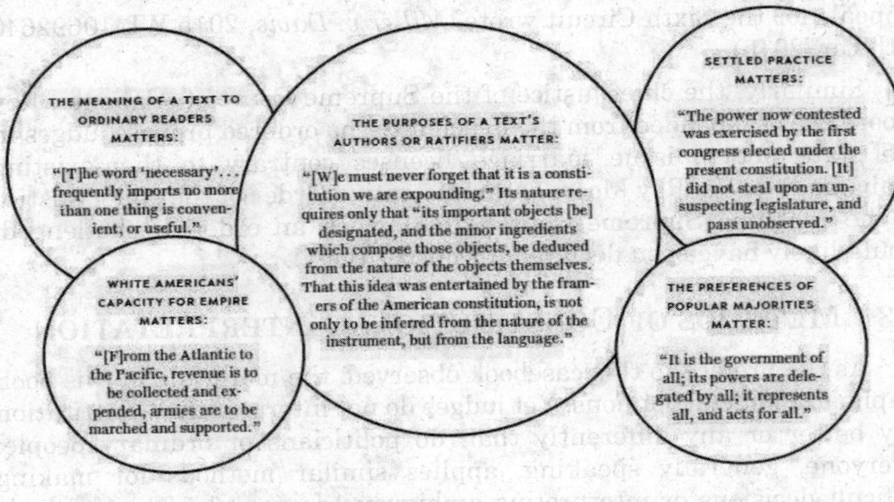

The opinion also considered a number of legal principles that supported a contrary rule—a rule against Congress's power to establish a bank:

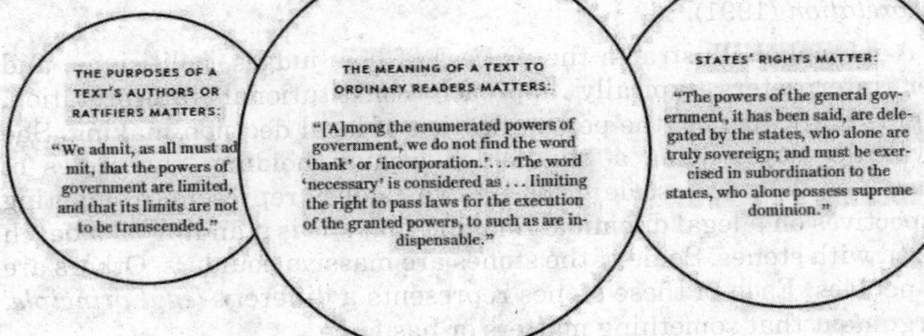

The opinion then effectively weighed these competing principles against one another before announcing a new rule: the Constitution allows Congress to employ "all means which are appropriate" to enforce one of its enumerated powers. *Id.* at 421.

Of course, this is simply a metaphor: Marshall did not expressly weigh individual principles against one another. Nor could such principles be objectively measured. As with any political decision, deciding upon the best interpretation of the Constitution is a subjective matter for which different principles can weigh differently for different people at different times. But the metaphor illustrates how developing constitutional rules involves balancing a variety of considerations. It is usually not simply a matter of reading and applying the words of a text. That said, there are some principles, including text-based principles, that often appear as decisive considerations in Supreme Court opinions. *See generally* Berman, *supra*, at 1386–90 (proposing this framework of principles and listing many of the following examples).

Principles of text

In recent years, many justices argue that the most decisive and weighty legal principle for them is that THE MEANING OF A TEXT TO ORDINARY READERS MATTERS. To return to the metaphor of the stony beach, text-based principles are often treated as massive boulders that can outweigh many other competing principles.

The dominant approach on the current Supreme Court is *textualist*—that is, guided by the definitions, diction, syntax, and structure of the Constitution's words. On a theoretical level, this approach has been justified on the ground that judges do not *make* constitutional law but rather *interpret* the Constitution. Therefore, judges should apply the Constitution based on what they think its words would mean to an ordinary reader rather than what they think is good policy. *See generally* Antonin Scalia & Bryan A. Garner, *Reading Law* (2012). A contrary approach, its advocates maintain, would make constitutional interpreters more like lawmakers than like judges. These advocates fall on both the right and left; as Justice Elena Kagan famously observed while speaking at Harvard Law School in 2015, "we're all textualists now." Harvard L. Sch., *The Antonin Scalia Lecture Series*, YouTube (Nov. 25, 2015).

Yet the meaning of text can change over time. *Originalists* on the Court—Clarence Thomas, Neil Gorsuch, and Amy Coney Barrett—frame their favored principle as THE MEANING OF A TEXT TO ORDINARY READERS *AT THE TIME OF ENACTMENT* MATTERS. The originalists' focus on the eighteenth century (for most of the Constitution) and the mid-nineteenth century (for the Reconstruction amendments) often leads them to take interpretive positions at odds with how recent, nonoriginalist Supreme Court opinions subsequently interpreted the Constitution's terms. The basic justification for originalism is that the Constitution and its amendments derive their legitimacy from the people who originally ratified them: because ratification is what makes a constitutional term the law, judges have a responsibility to interpret that law as its ratifiers would have understood it, rather than to allow other considerations to change the law's meaning.

Originalists are often contrasted with *living constitutionalists*, who frame the principle as THE MEANING OF A TEXT TO ORDINARY READERS *TODAY* MATTERS. This articulation of the principle reflects how language evolves, with old terms incorporating new meanings that can appear more just and relevant than older meanings. As Justice Anthony Kennedy wrote in *Obergefell v. Hodges*, a term like *equal* can mean one thing in 1787 or 1868 and something very different in 2015 as "new insights and societal understandings can reveal unjustified inequality within our most fundamental institutions that once passed unnoticed and unchallenged." 576 U.S. 644, 647 (2015).

Principles of purpose

Textualism is often contrasted with purposivism, an interpretive approach guided by the principle that THE PURPOSES OF THE DRAFTERS OR RATIFIERS OF A TEXT MATTER. In his 2005 book Active Liberty, Justice Stephen Breyer explained his position that the Constitution is full of broad, abstract terms—freedom of speech, judicial power, etc.—that are often ambiguous and rarely self-defining. Interpreting these terms often requires judges to put down their dictionaries and look to other sources to figure out why the terms are there. The goal of this approach is to understand not just what a term means but also why it was included in the Constitution and what broader principles it might stand for.

Despite the theoretical distinctions between textualism and purposivism, they can look the same in practice. For example, textualists like Justice Clarence Thomas and purposivists like Breyer both might have reason to read *The Federalist* as part of their constitutional interpretations: Thomas to understand what a word or phrase meant in its ordinary sense at the time it was written, and Breyer to understand what sort of problem that word or phrase was intended to solve. In addition, the Constitution has many structural features—notably federalism, the separation of powers, implied powers, and judicial review—that self-described textualists accept, even though the textual hooks for these features are ambiguous or nonexistent.

Principles of judicial precedent

Although Supreme Court justices often say that the text or purpose of the Constitution should always be decisive, there are hundreds of historical examples in which these principles have been explicitly outweighed by a variety of other principles. In particular, the text and history of a provision are often outweighed by how that provision has been interpreted by prior Supreme Court precedents.

For example, a literal interpretation of the Equal Protection Clause's text—"No state shall . . . deny to any person within its jurisdiction the equal protection of the laws," U.S. Const. amend. XIV, § 1—might suggest that all laws that treat people unequally must be struck down. But over time, successive Supreme Court opinions have developed a series of rules known as the "rational-basis test," "intermediate scrutiny," and "strict scrutiny"; and it has applied those rules to defer to the legislature with respect to most classifications, while being less deferential with respect to "suspect" classifications and those that infringe on a "fundamental right." As a result, most equal-protection cases today hinge on which doctrinal rule the Court has applied to similar cases in the past, as opposed to what the text or history of the Equal

Protection Clause would say. *See* David A. Strauss, *Foreword—Does the Constitution Mean What It Says?*, 129 Harv. L. Rev. 1, 3 (2015).

This principle is often described as *stare decisis*: PREVIOUS DECISIONS OF THE SUPREME COURT MATTER. Despite the importance of this principle, no justice has a fully consistent take on when the Court must apply a previously decided rule or when it should discard it. Ever since *Pollock v. Farmers' Loan & Trust Co.*, 158 U.S. 601 (1895), when the Court attempted to correct "a century of error" regarding the constitutionality of the federal income tax, *id.* at 690 (Brown, J., dissenting), the Court has overruled more than two hundred of its previous decisions.

Principles of historical practice

In addition to deferring to historical judicial opinions, the Supreme Court also often defers to historical interpretations of Congress, the executive branch, and the states. This principle of *settled practice* declares that IT MATTERS THAT AN EXERCISE OF POWER HAS BEEN ACCEPTED AND PROVEN TO BE WORKABLE.

In *McCulloch*, for example, Marshall emphasized that Congress's power to establish a bank was not a new idea in 1819: the power had been "introduced at a very early period of our history" and had been debated by President George Washington's cabinet "with as much persevering talent as any measure has ever experienced." 17 U.S. (4 Wheat.) 316, 401 (1819). After the bank later expired, "a short experience of the embarrassments to which the refusal to revive it exposed the government, convinced those who were most prejudiced against the measure of its necessity." *Id.* at 402. Neither of these points was an idle musing by Marshall: they reflected an important premise that when presidents and members of Congress interpret the Constitution, they combine "a lawyer's rigor with a statesman's breadth of view." James Bradley Thayer, *The American Doctrine of Constitutional Law* 12 (1893).

As we will see, this sort of deference to historical practice is very common when a constitutional provision reaches the Supreme Court for the first time. It is also common in cases involving the president's powers under Article II. More recently, the Court has often invoked what law professor Leah Litman criticizes as a principle of *antinovelty*: IT IS SUSPICIOUS WHEN A PARTICULAR POWER HAS ONLY RECENTLY BEEN EXERCISED FOR THE FIRST TIME. *See* Leah M. Litman, *Debunking Antinovelty*, 66 Duke L.J. 1407, 1411–12 (2017). The Court has recently used this principle to invalidate novel legislative responses to novel problems, such as the creative governing structure of a consumer-protection agency established in response to the 2008 financial crisis. *See Seila Law LLC v. CFPB*, 140 S. Ct. 2183, 2201 (2020).

Principles of policy, moral reasoning, and partisanship

Principles of text, purpose, and precedent all represent attempts to avoid describing interpretive decisions using the more familiar vocabulary of policy arguments. Policy arguments—the sorts of arguments you might consider in deciding whether to vote for a particular politician—are often denigrated by judges as "political" or "legislating from the bench." But policy arguments are unavoidable: "Every decision with even a sliver of discretion reflects, on some level, the preferences and predilections of the decisionmaker." Pozen & Samaha, *supra*, at 747. Moreover, there is nothing rare or inappropriate about policy arguments; they are easily visible in most judicial opinions, even as judges say they are guided by politically neutral considerations.

Principles of policy take a variety of forms, including THE PEOPLE WHO WILL BENEFIT FROM THIS DECISION MATTER, or IT MATTERS THAT THE SOCIOECONOMIC BENEFITS OF THIS RULE OUTWEIGH THE COSTS. For example, the Court in *Parents Involved in Community Schools v. Seattle School District No. 1* explicitly recognized the perceived (and allegedly negative) consequences of upholding the use of race-conscious policies to desegregate public schools, noting that doing so would "contribut[e] to an escalation of racial hostility and conflict." 551 U.S. 701, 746 (2007).

Closely related to principles of policy are principles of moral reasoning, or judgments about what is ethical or substantively just. Many people believe that DISTRIBUTIVE JUSTICE MATTERS, or THE TEACHINGS OF THE BIBLE MATTER, or IT MATTERS THAT POOR PEOPLE CAN LIVE WITH DIGNITY, or IT MATTERS WHETHER A RULE IS GOOD FOR THE DEVELOPMENT OF FREE-MARKET CAPITALISM. Even when a judge declines to invoke moral reasoning explicitly, such reasoning is often essential for understanding the text or purpose of a constitutional provision. Indeed, constitutional rules often take the form of moral precepts. In the late nineteenth century, for example, the Court invoked a principle of moral reasoning—laissez-faire liberalism—to hold that the Fourteenth Amendment's protection of "due process" prohibited governments from regulating activities that did not directly endanger the health, morals, or safety of others. *See, e.g.*, *Mugler v. Kansas*, 123 U.S. 623, 660 (1887). This rule was a restatement of contemporary liberal orthodoxy, in contrast with egalitarian principles that the Court derisively referred to as "the doctrines of the commune." *Id.*

Although principles of policy and moral reasoning appear frequently in judicial opinions, the justices tend to be most scornful of *partisanship*: IT MATTERS WHETHER SOMETHING IS GOOD FOR PEOPLE POLITICALLY AFFILIATED WITH ME. That is, the justices appear to find it embarrassing when their policy considerations and moral arguments are the same as those advanced by the Republican or Democratic parties that appointed them to the bench. *See, e.g.*, Stephen Breyer, *The Authority of the Court and the Peril of Politics* 55, 63 (2021). But a judge's so-called judicial philosophy is often highly correlated with what ordinary people would call a political philosophy. Republican politicians and the judges they appoint often use their official power to oppose reproductive rights, affirmative action programs, and business regulations. *See, e.g.*, Eugene Robinson, *Amy Coney Barrett Wants Us to Believe the Supreme Court Isn't Partisan. Good Luck with That*, Wash. Post (Sep. 13, 2021). By the same token, Democratic politicians and the judges they appoint tend to support progressive goals. Indeed, given the ambiguities of text and purpose in most constitutional provisions, it is difficult to imagine a coherent judicial philosophy that did not take contemporary principles of policy and moral reasoning into account. Partisan alignments are therefore predictable.

Principles of white supremacy

One of the most historically significant policy principles—one that has routinely guided or outweighed principles based in text, democracy, and historical practice—is white supremacy. Illustrative is a series of Supreme Court decisions issued after 1898, when the United States seized Puerto Rico, the Philippines, and other islands from Spain. When litigants argued that American officials were violating established constitutional rights in these new, insular territories, the Court responded that the "uncivilized parts" of the territories "were wholly unfitted to exercise" these rights. *Dorr v. United States*, 195 U.S. 138, 145 (1904). This principle of *imperialism* maintained that IT MATTERS THAT WHITE AMERICANS HAVE SUFFICIENT POWER OR AUTONOMY TO DOMINATE "INFERIOR" FOREIGN POPULATIONS.

White supremacy appears even more often in cases involving the domestic subordination of black people, particularly in the context of slavery, Jim Crow, and mass incarceration. For decades, when the Supreme Court first interpreted Congress's power to "regulate Commerce . . . among the several States," U.S. Const. art. I, § 8, cl. 3, it developed rules to ensure that the federal government would not interfere with state laws protecting commerce in enslaved people. *See, e.g.*, *Groves v. Slaughter*, 40 U.S. (15 Pet.) 449 (1841). Even after the United States abolished slavery and ratified the Fourteenth Amendment to protect the civil rights of freed people, the Court crafted rules that permitted a racial apartheid system while invalidating labor protections and redistributive laws. More recently, the Court has minimized the power of state legislatures and federal courts to desegregate schools, hold police officers accountable, or otherwise redress societal racial discrimination. A common thread behind these cases is that IT MATTERS THAT WHITE AMERICANS HAVE SUFFICIENT POWER OR AUTONOMY TO DOMINATE "INFERIOR" DOMESTIC POPULATIONS.

Principles of the distribution of power

Several of the most well-known principles that the Supreme Court invokes to interpret the Constitution relate to the distribution and dispersal of power. This very casebook is organized around three of these principles: *federalism, the separation of powers*, and *individual rights*.

The first of these principles, *federalism*, concerns the federal government's relationship with the states. Even though the term does not appear in the text of the Constitution, the Supreme Court has repeatedly treated federalism as if it were an implied limit on Congress's powers—particularly since Reconstruction, when Congress allegedly ignored federalism to reconstruct the southern states as multiracial democracies. The Court has explained that the independence and autonomy of states are "indispensable" to "our complex system." *Collector v. Day*, 78 U.S. 113, 125 (1870). "By denying any one government complete jurisdiction over all the concerns of public life, federalism protects the liberty of the individual from arbitrary power." *Bond v. United States*, 564 U.S. 211, 222 (2011). Applying this principle, IT MATTERS THAT STATES POSSESS SUFFICIENT AUTONOMY TO DISPERSE POWER OR SERVE AS EFFECTIVE LOCAL GOVERNMENTS.

The *separation of powers* principle concerns the relationship between Congress, the executive branch, and the federal judiciary. *Separation of powers*, another term that does not appear in the text of the Constitution, is the principle that IT MATTERS THAT POWER IS NOT UNDULY CONCENTRATED. The Court has invalidated laws and other government actions based on this principle. As we will see, this principle has evolved steadily from an eighteenth-century description of a good way to structure governments into a freestanding limit on a statute's ability to regulate the executive or judicial branch.

Finally, the principle of *individual rights* is often invoked to defend liberty, autonomy, equality, dignity, and legality.

These three principles are typically contrasted with *governmental efficacy*: the principle that IT MATTERS THAT GOVERNMENT HAS SUFFICIENT POWER TO MEET THE CHANGING NEEDS OF ITS CONSTITUENTS. During the coronavirus pandemic, for example, when litigants attacked the constitutionality of mask mandates and lockdown requirements, governments responded with the principle that they had a compelling interest in protecting all constituents, even if this meant sacrificing individual autonomy.

Principles of popular sovereignty and democracy

Closely related to the principle of *governmental efficacy* is the principle of *majoritarianism*, an argument that THE PREFERENCES OF POPULAR MAJORITIES MATTER. When judges invalidate legislation on constitutional grounds, they also necessarily declare that the elected representatives of a political community misinterpreted the Constitution. These sorts of decisions can, over time, harm the Court's claim to interpretive supremacy. As the Court explained in a famous abortion decision, *Planned Parenthood of Southeastern Pennsylvania v. Casey*, the Court draws its power not from its ability to coerce the other branches into listening to it, but from "its legitimacy, a product of substance and perception that shows itself in the people's acceptance of the Judiciary as fit to determine what the Nation's law means and to declare what it demands." 505 U.S. 833, 865 (1992). Because the people might no longer accept the Court's conclusions if it repeatedly invalidated legislation for unprincipled reasons, the Court has emphasized that it should generally be deferential to the preferences of popular majorities unless the unconstitutionality of the majorities' actions is "beyond dispute." *Id.*

Similar to the idea of *majoritarianism* is *popular opinion*: IT MATTERS WHAT PEOPLE WILL THINK. Although judicial opinions rarely appeal explicitly to popular opinion, the best explanation for many decisions is that members of the Court were worried about how the public might react to a contrary ruling. In fact, when the justices speak privately in conference, they often explicitly invoke this principle among themselves. *See, e.g.*, *The Supreme Court in Conference* 648 (Del Dickson ed., 2001) (reprinting conference notes in *Brown v. Board of Education* (*Brown I*), 347 U.S. 483 (1954), in which the justices worried about the "serious and drastic" effects of outlawing racial segregation). The Court has also surveyed the practices of the majority of states in reaching certain conclusions. *See, e.g.*, *Timbs v. Indiana*, 139 S. Ct. 682, 689 (2019) (declaring excessive state and local fines unconstitutional after relying in part on the existence of many state constitutional provisions banning such fines).

Majoritarianism can sometimes conflict with a principle of *political process*—that is, IT MATTERS THAT THE POLITICAL PROCESS ALLOWS CONSTITUENTS TO FREELY EXERCISE THEIR POWER TO RULE. As in *McCulloch*, this principle is often linked to the Constitution's preamble, whose opening words, *We the People*, establish that the Constitution's ultimate source of authority is *all* of the people, not a select group of monarchs or oligarchs. The most famous exponent of this principle is the late law professor John Hart Ely, whose 1980 book, *Democracy and Distrust*, argued that judicial review of legislation was justified only to the extent that it facilitated or reinforced the ability of political minorities to protect themselves through the political process. Ely tied his argument to a remarkable footnote in an otherwise unremarkable case, *United States v. Carolene Products Co.*, 304 U.S. 144 (1938). In footnote four, the Supreme Court declared that it would defer to legislatures regarding the constitutionality of most legislation except where a law "restricts those political processes which can ordinarily be expected to bring about repeal of undesirable legislation" or where "prejudice against discrete and insular minorities . . . curtail[s] the operation of those political processes ordinarily to be relied upon to protect minorities." *Carolene Prods.*, 304 U.S. at 152–53 n.4.

Closely related to Ely's political-process principle is a principle of *democracy* or *political equality*: IT MATTERS THAT ALL PEOPLE ARE

TREATED AS POLITICAL EQUALS WITH THE SAME POWER TO MAKE POLITICAL DECISIONS. In contrast with Ely, who argued that the judicial review of any law could be justifiable if the decision enhanced the political process, adherents of political equality reject the idea that judges are superior to politicians or voters at distinguishing between good and bad laws. *See, e.g.*, Ryan Doerfler & Samuel Moyn, *Democratizing the Supreme Court*, 109 Calif. L. Rev. 1703, 1743–44 (2021). Instead, following Abraham Lincoln and James Bradley Thayer—discussed in the previous section (3.2)—advocates of political equality argue that judicial supremacy is incompatible with a government in which ordinary people, not judges, make the most important decisions. *See, e.g.*, Nikolas Bowie, *Antidemocracy*, 135 Harv. L. Rev. 160, 174–75 (2021).

Advocates of this version of political equality typically reject judicial supremacy in favor of judicial deference to federal legislation. But unlike advocates of majoritarianism, they do not all reject *federal* supremacy or call for judicial deference to *state* legislation. *Id.* at 203. There are many circumstances in which the federal government and state governments have disagreed about the constitutionality of a law. Examples include *McCulloch v. Maryland*, 17 U.S. (4 Wheat.) 316 (1819), or Congress's civil rights legislation in the 1870s and 1960s. There are also many federal laws that instruct federal courts to review the constitutionality of state laws, as will be discussed in section 21.1. To the extent Congress is at least as democratic as state legislatures, then when federal courts enforce federal laws to invalidate contrary state laws, their actions may democratically enforce the will of one legislature against another. *See* Bowie, *supra*, at 203.

Principles of liberty

Although majoritarianism sometimes conflicts with popular sovereignty, it often conflicts with individual rights. In particular, IT MATTERS THAT ALL PEOPLE MAY PURSUE HAPPINESS AS THEY CONCEIVE OF IT, FREE FROM ARBITRARY RESTRAINTS OR UNNECESSARY DEMANDS FOR CONFORMITY TO MAJORITARIAN NORMS. This general principle of *liberty*, *autonomy*, or *the pursuit of happiness* pervades the Supreme Court's interpretation of the Fourteenth Amendment. Constitutional rules concerning property rights, reproductive rights, privacy, marriage, family relationships, bodily autonomy, and suicide all are illustrations of this principle.

Principles of equality and dignity

In addition to protecting "liberty," the Fourteenth Amendment also prohibits states from denying people "the equal protection of the laws." Two major principles have emerged as arguments for how to define this language.

First, one principle holds that IT MATTERS THAT THE GOVERNMENT RARELY MAKES DISTINCTIONS ON THE BASIS OF RACE OR OTHER SUSPECT

CLASSIFICATIONS. This principle is often associated with Justice John Marshall Harlan's dissent in *Plessy v. Ferguson*, in which he argued that racial segregation was unconstitutional because "[o]ur Constitution is color-blind, and neither knows nor tolerates classes among citizens." 163 U.S. 537, 559 (1896) (Harlan, J., dissenting). The principle of colorblindness was repeatedly invoked a half century later, when the Supreme Court began invalidating segregation laws. It has also been invoked more recently to invalidate *desegregation* laws. For example, in a 2007 decision, the Supreme Court struck down two race-conscious programs to desegregate public schools because "[t]he way to stop discrimination on the basis of race is to stop discriminating on the basis of race." *Parents Involved*, 551 U.S. at 748.

Today, the colorblindness principle is often contrasted with a principle that THE INHERENT AND EQUAL DIGNITY OF ALL PEOPLE—AND THE LEGACY OF SLAVERY, JIM CROW, MASS INCARCERATION, AND OTHER INJUSTICES—ALL MATTER. This principle could be described as an *antisubordination* principle because it argues that colorblindness ignores or perpetuates subordination, specifically antiblack racism. One justice recently articulated this principle when she argued "[t]he way to stop discrimination on the basis of race is to speak openly and candidly on the subject of race, and to apply the Constitution with eyes open to the unfortunate effects of centuries of racial discrimination." *Schuette v. Coal. to Defend Affirmative Action*, 572 U.S. 291, 381 (2014) (Sotomayor, J., dissenting).

Principles of legality

The Court also has invoked many process-based principles designed to prevent the government from arbitrarily or unfairly depriving people of their life, liberty, or property. For example, in interpreting the Constitution's prohibitions on ex post facto laws and bills of attainder, the Court has emphasized the *legality* principle: IT MATTERS THAT LAWS OPERATE PROSPECTIVELY, GENERALLY, AND IMPARTIALLY. Relatedly, in *Marbury v. Madison*, 5 U.S. (1 Cranch) 137 (1803), the Court invoked and defended the *redressability* principle: IT MATTERS THAT THERE IS A REMEDY FOR THE VIOLATION OF A RIGHT.

Principles of compromise

Finally, there have been occasions when members of the Court have engaged in *log-rolling*, a principle that might be described as REACHING COMPROMISES WITH COLLEAGUES MATTERS. This sort of principle is commonplace: every majority decision requires multiple interpreters to reach some form of consensus, even if the ultimate outcome is not what any single individual would have wanted. Yet there is also a strong norm against vote-trading and other practices that would "pose a special threat to the good-faith search for constitutional meaning." Pozen & Samaha, *supra*, at 764–66. In this respect, principles of compromise can often seem taboo. When a journalist reported that Chief Justice John Roberts may have cooperated with two liberal justices in *NFIB v. Sebelius*, 567 U.S. 519 (2012), to uphold one section of the Affordable Care Act while invalidating another, the reported horse-trading generated controversy. Pozen & Samaha, *supra*, at 765.

The principles and their fluidity

This list of principles is not comprehensive. *See* Berman, *supra*, at 1386 (describing the list of principles on which this list was based as "a highly abbreviated first pass at 30,000 feet"). This list also does not reflect the relative weight of each principle. The weight of principles can vary by person: for some interpreters, text-based principles might always weigh more than equality-based principles. For others, democracy-based principles might weigh the most. Similarly, the weight of principles might change over time: the principles of colorblindness and antisubordination are far more widely acknowledged today than they were decades ago.

However, the list does reflect how constitutional interpretation involves moral and subjective judgment instead of the rote skill of reading the words of a page and applying them to new fact patterns. As you read the cases in this casebook, consider which principles you find personally persuasive and how they relate to your own sense of justice.

3.4 POLITICAL QUESTIONS

In the centuries since *Marbury v. Madison*, 5 U.S. (1 Cranch) 137 (1803), the Supreme Court has reviewed the constitutionality of a federal law in approximately thirteen hundred cases. It has invalidated the law about a quarter of the time. Keith E. Whittington, *Judicial Review of Congress Database* (May 2019), https://scholar.princeton.edu/kewhitt/judicial-review-congress-database. Although these numbers help to illustrate how central and "supreme" of a role the Court now plays in checking and balancing the other branches, the Court has never claimed for itself the power to review the constitutionality of *all* government action. Instead, it has preserved an important exception to its ability to review government action—an exception known as the "political question" doctrine.

Marbury and unreviewable government actions

The doctrine derives its name from the section of *Marbury* in which Chief Justice John Marshall explained that some government actions are unreviewable by a court. "By the constitution of the United States," he wrote, "the president is invested with certain important political powers, in the exercise of which he is to use his own discretion, and is accountable only to his country in his political character and to his own conscience." *Marbury*, 5 U.S. (1 Cranch) at 165. Even if someone felt harmed by the manner in which the president exercised these powers, Marshall maintained, "still there exists, and can exist, no power to control that discretion. The subjects are political. They respect the nation, not individual rights, and being intrusted to the executive, the decision of the executive is conclusive. . . ." *Id.*

Marshall didn't provide many examples of what he meant by *political powers*, but the idea is intuitive. Imagine President Adams has a choice of whom to nominate to fill a Supreme Court vacancy: John Marshall or William Marbury. The president, exercising his discretion, chooses Marshall. Could Marbury sue, claiming that the president should have chosen him? No, the *Marbury* Court explained, because the president's choice doesn't present a *judicial* question that can be resolved by applying the law to the facts. Rather, it presents a *political* question that can be resolved only by evaluating different candidates and policy considerations—something the president should do instead of a court.

The *Marbury* Court distinguished this sort of political discretion (which the Court could not review) from the law that obligated James Madison to deliver to Marbury his commission (which the Court could review).

Political discretion: War and foreign affairs

In the years since *Marbury*, the Court has maintained this distinction, particularly in the context of war and foreign affairs. In *Martin v. Mott*, 25 U.S. (12 Wheat.) 19 (1827), for example, a soldier objected to a president's decision to call out the militia, claiming that there was no insurrection or invasion that warranted it. The Court rejected the soldier's argument, explaining that only the president, not a court, could review whether an emergency called for a military response. *Id.* at 29–31.

Even when the Court does review executive action, it often defers to the political branches on matters of war or foreign affairs. *See, e.g.*, *Trump v. Hawaii*, 138 S. Ct. 2392 (2018).

Deference to state in Luther v. Borden

The political question doctrine isn't limited to actions by the executive branch. In fact, the most famous political question case of the nineteenth century involved a state. In 1776, as most states adopted new constitutions after declaring independence, the legislature of Rhode Island declared that it would retain the same corporate charter that had governed it since 1663. This charter was progressive for the 1660s but became very conservative by the 1840s as neighboring states lowered or eliminated property qualifications for the right to vote. In 1841, a group of democratic activists drafted a new constitution, submitted it for ratification, announced that it had been ratified, and proceeded to organize a new state government under the new constitution. This activist government, led by Thomas Wilson Dorr, met alongside the preexisting charter government for six weeks in 1842. *See* Erik J. Chaput, *The People's Martyr: Thomas Wilson Dorr and His 1842 Rhode Island Rebellion* 57–69 (2013).

Tensions between the activist government and charter government were so high that the state threatened to descend into civil war. In an attempt to quash the so-called Dorr Rebellion, leaders of the charter government declared martial law and ordered the state militia to arrest leaders of the activist government. *Id.* at 173. When Luther Borden, a member of the militia, broke into the house of Martin Luther, one of the activists, Luther resisted. Luther ultimately sued Borden for trespass, claiming that Borden had been following the orders of an illegitimate government. *Id.* at 192–93.

By the time the Supreme Court heard *Luther v. Borden*, 48 U.S. (7 How.) 1 (1849), the charter government had compromised with the activists and agreed upon a new, more moderate constitution. Nevertheless, Luther pressed the Court to resolve whether the charter government that ordered his arrest in 1842 was so unrepresentative that it violated the Guarantee Clause in Article IV, Section 4, which read, "The United States shall guarantee to every State in this Union a Republican Form of Government, and shall protect each of them against Invasion." The Court responded: "We decline." *Id.* at 47. Citing examples in which courts deferred to the other branches in determining who was the ruler of a foreign state, Chief Justice Roger Taney explained that courts lack the institutional capacity to determine, in the abstract, whether a particular government is supported by a majority of the population or whether the qualifications for voters are appropriate. *Id.* at 42–44. Under the Guarantee Clause, he reasoned that "it rests with Congress to decide what government is the established one in a State. For as the United States guarantee to each State a republican government, Congress must necessarily decide what government is established in the State before it can determine whether it is republican or not." *Id.* at 42. Taney observed that Congress was also better positioned than the Court to enforce the Guarantee Clause by excluding any senators and representatives from a state that failed to be adequately republican. Accordingly, the Court concluded that while the people of every state have the right to change their form of government,

> whether they have changed it or not by abolishing an old government and establishing a new one in its place is a question to be settled by the political power. And when that power has decided, the courts are bound to take notice of its decision, and to follow it.

Id. at 47.

Marbury *and* Luther*: Continuing basis of political question doctrine*

Marbury and *Luther* remained the Court's main expositions of the political question doctrine until the mid-twentieth century. At that time, as we will read in a later section (22.3), the doctrine resurfaced in challenges to state regulations of elections. Today, the Court typically relies on the following factors to determine whether a question is political:

> Prominent on the surface of any case held to involve a political question is found [1] a textually demonstrable constitutional commitment of the issue to a coordinate political department; or [2] a lack of judicially discoverable and manageable standards for resolving it; or [3] the impossibility of deciding without an initial policy determination of a kind clearly for nonjudicial discretion; or [4] the impossibility of a court's undertaking independent resolution without expressing lack of the respect due coordinate branches of government; or [5] an unusual need for unquestioning adherence to a political decision already made; or [6] the potentiality of embarrassment from multifarious pronouncements by various departments on one question.
>
> Unless one of these formulations is inextricable from the case at bar, there should be no dismissal for nonjusticiability on the ground of a political question's presence. The doctrine of which we treat is one of "political questions," not one of "political cases." . . . The cases we have reviewed show the necessity for discriminating inquiry into the precise facts and posture of the particular case, and the impossibility of resolution by any semantic cataloguing.

Baker v. Carr, 369 U.S. 186, 217–18 (1962).

CHAPTER 4

HOW MUST FEDERAL TAXES BE APPORTIONED?

ARTICLE I, SECTION 2, CLAUSE 3: Representatives and direct Taxes shall be apportioned among the several States which may be included within this Union, according to their respective Numbers, which shall be determined by adding to the whole Number of free Persons, including those bound to Service for a Term of Years, and excluding Indians not taxed, three fifths of all other Persons.

ARTICLE I, SECTION 8, CLAUSE 1: The Congress shall have Power To lay and collect Taxes, Duties, Imposts and Excises, to pay the Debts and provide for the common Defence and general Welfare of the United States; but all Duties, Imposts and Excises shall be uniform throughout the United States;

ARTICLE I, SECTION 9, CLAUSE 4: No Capitation, or other direct, Tax shall be laid, unless in Proportion to the Census or Enumeration herein before directed to be taken.

THE SIXTEENTH AMENDMENT (1913): The Congress shall have power to lay and collect taxes on incomes, from whatever source derived, without apportionment among the several States, and without regard to any census or enumeration.

4.1 DIRECT VERSUS INDIRECT TAXES

Article I, Section 1, references the "legislative Powers herein granted" to Congress—most of which are listed in Article I, Section 8. First on the list is the power to "lay and collect Taxes, Duties, Imposts, and Excises." As discussed in the preamble to this casebook (section 1.1), one of the principal reasons why the Constitutional Convention met in 1787 was that the Confederation Congress lacked the power to tax anyone. Under the Articles of Confederation, Congress's sole source of revenue was its power to ask for funds from "the several states, in proportion to the value of all land within each state." Articles of Confederation of 1781, art. VIII. But states regularly failed to comply with Congress's requests, sending it less than one-fifth of the $15.7 million it requested between 1781 and 1786. *See* 30 *Journals of the Continental Congress* 44–46 (John C. Fitzpatrick ed., 1934). And both times Congress requested an amendment to the Articles that would authorize it to collect *imposts*, or taxes on imports, the amendment was vetoed by a single state. The power to tax was, accordingly, on the front of the convention delegates' minds.

The taxing power was added early in the convention and, given Congress's recent history, was relatively uncontroversial. The delegates were eager to give Congress wide latitude to enact taxes on "exports & imports & on [the] consumption" of property. 1 *Records of the Federal Convention of 1787*, at 592 (Max Farrand ed., 1911). As long as Congress levied this sort of "indirect" tax on how people transferred or used their property, the only explicit requirement that the Constitution imposed was that the tax had to be "uniform throughout the United States." U.S. Const. art. I, § 8, cl. 1.

Many of the delegates feared, however, that Congress might broadly interpret this grant of taxing power as permission to levy a tax not just on the transfer or use of property but also on the property itself. This was a particularly serious difficulty for the many delegates who enslaved people. *See* Michael J. Klarman, *The Framers' Coup: The Making of the United States Constitution* 275–76 (2016). To see why, consider what would happen if Congress attempted to levy a direct tax on slave owners for each person they enslaved. Some states, like Virginia, had many enslaved people in 1787; other states, like Massachusetts, had few. If representatives from free states eventually controlled Congress, then they could enact this sort of "slave tax" without fear of taxing their northern constituents. If the tax was high enough, Congress could even exercise its taxing power to abolish slavery completely.

To protect slave owners from this sort of prohibitive tax, the convention introduced a major obstacle to direct taxes: an apportionment requirement. The final version of the Constitution declared that all "direct Taxes shall be apportioned among the several States which may be included within this Union, according to their respective Numbers." U.S. Const. art. I, § 2, cl. 3. In other words, if Congress wanted to impose a direct tax on enslaved people, it would have to structure the tax so that taxpayers in Massachusetts would pay exactly the same amount, per capita, as taxpayers in Virginia. If one slave owner lived in Massachusetts, he would owe as much as all the slave owners in Virginia—an exorbitant burden that would make the tax itself impossible for Massachusetts representatives to support.

The apportionment requirement proved to be a workable compromise in part because northern delegates linked it to the Three-Fifths Clause, which we will discuss in more detail in a later section on elections (section 22.1). Beyond a tax on enslaved people, however, it was not clear what else counted as a "direct" tax. For example, no one at the convention responded when Rufus King of Massachusetts asked, "[W]hat was the precise meaning of *direct* taxation?" 2 *Records of the Federal Convention of 1787*, *supra*, at 350.

Nevertheless, during the ratification debates, the fact that the Constitution specifically empowered Congress to collect not only imposts but also undefined "direct Taxes" proved to be a lightning rod. Despite the procedural obstacle of apportionment, Antifederalists warned that Congress would tax all real estate and personal property, leaving the states with nothing to fund their own governments. James Madison later wrote that "the opposition to the federal constitution is in my opinion reduced to a single point, the power of direct taxation." Letter from James Madison to George Washington (Dec. 5, 1789), *in* 4 *The Papers of George Washington* 367–69 (Dorothy Twohig ed., 1993).

4.1.1

Hylton v. United States

3 U.S. (3 Dall.) 171 (1796)

The first time the Supreme Court ever reviewed the constitutionality of a law passed by Congress—years before *Marbury v. Madison*, 5 U.S. (1 Cranch) 137 (1803)—involved an attempt to determine what the Constitution meant by *direct Taxes*. In *Hylton v. United States*, 3 U.S. (3 Dall.) 171 (1796), the Court considered whether a law imposing a tax on carriages was constitutional. In 1794, Congress passed and President George Washington signed "An Act laying duties upon Carriages," which required anyone in the United States who owned a "coach," "chariot," "phaeton," or "carriage" to pay up to $10 per vehicle per year. Ch. 45, 1 Stat. 373, 373–74 (1794). Daniel Hylton, a prominent Virginia merchant backed by former Antifederalists, refused to pay the tax on the 125 carriages he claimed to own. Hylton's lawyers argued that the carriage tax was a "direct" tax on his property that had not been "apportioned among the several States," as Article I, Sections 2 and 9, required. *Hylton*, 3 U.S. (3 Dall.) at 173.

To defend the law's constitutionality, the United States employed Alexander Hamilton, who had recently resigned as secretary of the Treasury. For three hours, Hamilton argued before the Supreme Court that it made no sense to apportion a tax on carriages among the states. *See* 8 Alexander Hamilton, *The Works of Alexander Hamilton* 378 (Henry Cabot Lodge ed., 1904). What would such a tax even look like, Hamilton asked, when not every state had the same number of carriages? He urged the Court to instead treat the tax as an "indirect" excise, or a tax on the manufacture, use, or sale of property. *Id.* at 379. Hamilton argued that the only limit the Constitution imposed on excise taxes was the requirement in Article I, Section 8, that they "shall be uniform throughout the United States," which this tax was. *Id.* at 383.

The Court voted to uphold the law after each justice issued his own individual opinion, the typical practice before John Marshall joined the Court in 1801.

THE COURT DELIVERED THEIR OPINIONS SERIATIM. . . .[1]

■ CHASE, JUSTICE.

I am inclined to think, that a tax on carriages is not a direct tax, within the letter, or meaning, of the Constitution.

---

[1] **As You Read, Consider:** The debate in *Hylton v. United States* is whether a federal tax on carriages is "direct" or "indirect." If direct, then Article I, Section 2, would require the tax to be "apportioned among the several States," such that New York taxpayers would pay the same amount, per capita, as Delaware taxpayers—even if New York contained far more carriages. If indirect, then Article I, Section 8, would require the tax merely to be "uniform throughout the United States," such that the tax in New York, Delaware, and everywhere else would be the same $10 per carriage per year. Because the uniformity requirement is far easier to satisfy than the apportionment requirement, calling a tax *direct* is a death sentence for most federal taxes. (State taxes, by the way, are not subject to these odd rules.) What rules do

The great object of the Constitution was, to give Congress a power to lay taxes, adequate to the exigencies of government; but they were to observe two rules in imposing them, namely, the rule of uniformity, when they laid duties, imposts, or excises[, Art. I § 8, cl. 1]; and the rule of apportionment, according to the census, when they laid any direct tax[, Art. I § 9, cl. 4]. . . . Three kinds of taxes, to wit, duties, imposts, and excises by the first rule, and capitation, or other direct taxes, by the second rule. . . .

The Constitution evidently contemplated no taxes as direct taxes, but only such as Congress could lay in proportion to the census. The rule of apportionment is only to be adopted in such cases where it can reasonably apply; and the subject taxed, must ever determine the application of the rule.

If it is proposed to tax any specific article by the rule of apportionment, and it would evidently create great inequality and injustice, it is unreasonable to say, that the Constitution intended such tax should be laid by that rule.

It appears to me, that a tax on carriages cannot be laid by the rule of apportionment, without very great inequality and injustice. For example: Suppose two States, equal in census, to pay 80,000 dollars each, by a tax on carriages, of 8 dollars on every carriage; and in one State there are 100 carriages, and in the other 1000. The owners of carriages in one State, would pay ten times the tax of owners in the other. *A* in one State, would pay for his carriage 8 dollars, but *B* in the other state, would pay for his carriage, 80 dollars. . . .

I am inclined to think, but of this I do not give a judicial opinion, that the direct taxes contemplated by the Constitution, are only two, to wit, a capitation, or poll tax, simply, without regard to property, profession, or any other circumstances; and a tax on LAND.—I doubt whether a tax, by a general assessment of personal property, within the United States, is included within the term direct tax. . . .

■ PATERSON, JUSTICE.

Whether direct taxes, in the sense of the Constitution, comprehend any other tax than a capitation tax, and tax on land, is a questionable point. . . . The provision was made in favor of the southern States. They possessed a large number of slaves; they had extensive tracts of territory, thinly settled, and not very productive. A majority of the states had but few slaves, and several of them a limited territory, well settled, and in a high state of cultivation. The southern states, if no provision had been introduced in the Constitution, would have been wholly at the mercy of the other states. Congress in such case, might tax slaves, at discretion or arbitrarily, and land in every part of the Union after the same rate or measure: so much a head in the first instance, and so much an acre in the second. To guard them against imposition in these particulars, was the reason of introducing the clause in the Constitution, which directs that representatives and direct taxes shall be apportioned among the states, according to their respective numbers. . . .

A tax on carriages, if apportioned, would be oppressive and pernicious. How would it work? In some states there are many carriages, and in others but few. Shall the whole sum fall on one or two individuals in a state, who may happen to own and possess carriages? The thing would be absurd, and inequitable. . . . The rule of uniformity, on the contrary, implies certainty, and leaves nothing to the will and

members of the Supreme Court introduce to determine whether a tax is direct or indirect? What principles underlie these rules?

pleasure of the assessor. In such case, the object and the sum coincide, the rule and the thing unite, and of course there can be no imposition. . . .[2]

4.1.2

Pollock v. Farmers' Loan & Trust Co.

157 U.S. 429 (1895), *aff'd on reh'g*, 158 U.S. 601 (1895)

Despite the fear among southerners during and after the Constitutional Convention that Congress might abuse its power of direct taxation, Congress tended not to engage in direct taxation—at least not in the manner envisioned by *Hylton*. For the seventy years from 1790 through 1860, the federal government received the vast majority of its revenue—at least 85 percent—from imposts and customs duties collected at the nation's ports. *See* Cong. Rsch. Serv., *U.S. Federal Government Revenues: 1790 to the Present* 3–4 (2006). In 1811, for example, it collected only $2,000 from internal revenue—roughly one-hundredth of 1 percent of total federal revenues. *Id.* at 3.

These dynamics changed after the Civil War, the cost of which required the federal government to raise vastly more revenue than it could collect from trade alone. In the 1860s, Congress established the predecessor to the Internal Revenue Service; introduced a series of excise taxes on whiskey, tobacco, and other items; and created the country's first income tax. *Id.* at 4–5; *see, e.g.*, Act of Aug. 5, 1861, ch. 45, 12 Stat. 292; Act of June 30, 1864, ch. 173, 13 Stat. 223. The Supreme Court sustained all of these taxes, relying on *Hylton* for the premise that every tax that applies nationwide is a valid "indirect" and "uniform" excise tax unless it taxes land or people. *See, e.g.*, *Veazie Bank v. Fenno*, 75 U.S. (8 Wall.) 533, 546–47 (1869) (upholding a federal tax on state bank notes); *Scholey v. Rew*, 90 U.S. (23 Wall.) 331, 342–43 (1875) (upholding an inheritance tax); *Springer v. United States*, 102 U.S. 586, 602 (1881) (upholding an income tax). By the end of the war, the revenue from excise and income taxes accounted for close to 40 percent of the federal government's budget. *See* Cong. Rsch. Serv., *supra*, at 2–5.

Although Congress abolished the income tax after the Civil War ended, the tax remained a popular idea among social reformers, who saw it as a far more progressive alternative to impost and excise taxes on food, clothing, and other items that the rich and poor paid for equally. *See* Ajay K. Mehrotra, *"More Mighty than the Waves of the Sea": Toilers, Tariffs, and the Income Tax Movement, 1880–1913*, 45 Lab. Hist. 165, 165–66 (2004). In the 1892 presidential elections, the Populist Party became the first third party in a generation to win electoral votes after campaigning on a platform of redistributing wealth to the poor with policies such as a graduated income tax. The Democratic Party, eager to court Populist

[2] **Questions:** Consider a modern version of *Hylton*'s annual carriage tax: an annual tax on the possession of firearms. How might a court today decide how that tax should be apportioned? Are there any differences between this tax and the one challenged in *Hylton*?

voters, passed a milder version of this income tax in 1894. The Revenue Act of 1894 imposed a 2 percent tax on all incomes over $4,000, including those from securities and corporate profits. § 27, 28 Stat. 509, 553.

New York lawyers who opposed the tax contrived a suit in which Charles Pollock, a shareholder of Farmers' Loan & Trust Co., sued his bank after it announced that it would (reluctantly) pay the tax. In oral arguments, they harshly criticized the tax as a communist attack on private property. They also claimed that, despite *Hylton* and the century of precedent that followed it, the income tax was a direct tax.

The Supreme Court, surprisingly, agreed. The case, *Pollock v. Farmers' Loan & Trust Co.*, 157 U.S. 429 (1895), *aff'd on reh'g*, 158 U.S. 601 (1895), reargued over two separate sessions, was one of the first to overrule a precedent.

■ MR. CHIEF JUSTICE FULLER delivered the opinion of the Court.[3]

[T]he Constitution provides that representatives and direct taxes shall be apportioned among the several States according to numbers, and that no direct tax shall be laid except according to the enumeration provided for; and also that all duties, imposts and excises shall be uniform throughout the United States.

The men who framed and adopted that instrument had just emerged from the struggle for independence whose rallying cry had been that "taxation and representation go together." . . . The principle was that the consent of those who were expected to pay it was essential to the validity of any tax. . . .

The [question in this case] is whether a tax on the rents or income of real estate is a direct tax within the meaning of the Constitution. Ordinarily all taxes paid primarily by persons who can shift the burden upon some one else, or who are under no legal compulsion to pay them, are considered indirect taxes; but a tax upon property holders in respect of their estates, whether real or personal, or of the income yielded by such estates, and the payment of which cannot be avoided, are direct taxes. . . .

[For nearly twenty pages, the Court describes the history of the American Revolution; colonists' opposition to parliamentary taxation; the weaknesses of the Articles of Confederation; discussions of direct and indirect taxation by Adam Smith and other eighteenth-century economists; the Constitutional Convention and the addition of "direct Taxes" to the Constitution; the ratification debates; *Hylton v. United States*; and, finally, the century of precedent since *Hylton*.]

From the [foundation of taxation in America since 1776—including the American Revolution, the work of nineteenth-century economists like Adam Smith, the Constitutional Convention, and the century of precedent since *Hylton v. United States*—] it is apparent: 1. That the distinction between direct and indirect taxation was well understood by the framers of the Constitution and those who adopted it. 2. That under the state systems of taxation all taxes on real estate or personal property or the rents or income thereof were regarded as direct taxes. 3. That the rules of apportionment and of uniformity were adopted in view of that distinction and those

[3] **As You Read, Consider:** *Pollock v. Farmers' Loan & Trust Co.* was decided a century after *Hylton v. United States* first considered how to distinguish a direct tax from an indirect tax. What does the Court make of *Hylton* and the long-standing precedent that taxes on the use of property are indirect?

Members of the *Hylton* Court observed that the apportionment requirement was introduced to protect slavery. According to the *Pollock* Court, what modern evils does the apportionment requirement protect against?

systems. 4. That whether the tax on carriages was direct or indirect was disputed, but the tax was sustained as a tax on the use and an excise. 5. That the original expectation was that the power of direct taxation would be exercised only in extraordinary exigencies, and down to August 15, 1894, this expectation has been realized. The act of that date was passed in a time of profound peace, and if we assume that no special exigency called for unusual legislation, and that resort to this mode of taxation is to become an ordinary and usual means of supply, that fact furnishes an additional reason for circumspection and care in disposing of the case. . . .

Doubtless the doctrine of *stare decisis* is a salutary one, and to be adhered to on all proper occasions, but it only arises in respect of decisions directly upon the points in issue. . . . Manifestly, as this court is clothed with the power, and entrusted with the duty, to maintain the fundamental law of the Constitution, the discharge of that duty requires it not to extend any decision upon a constitutional question if it is convinced that error in principle might supervene. . . .

The requirement of the Constitution is that no direct tax shall be laid otherwise than by apportionment—the prohibition is not against direct taxes on land, from which the implication is sought to be drawn that indirect taxes on land would be constitutional, but it is against all direct taxes—and it is admitted that a tax on real estate is a direct tax. Unless, therefore, a tax upon rents or income issuing out of lands is intrinsically so different from a tax on the land itself that it belongs to a wholly different class of taxes, such taxes must be regarded as falling within the same category as a tax on real estate [in its own name]. The name of the tax is unimportant. The real question is, is there any basis upon which to rest the contention that real estate belongs to one of the two great classes of taxes, and the rent or income which is the incident of its ownership belongs to the other? We are unable to perceive any ground for the alleged distinction. An annual tax upon the annual value or annual user of real estate appears to us the same in substance as an annual tax on the real estate, which would be paid out of the rent or income. This law taxes the income received from land and the growth or produce of the land. Mr. Justice Paterson observed in *Hylton's case*, "land, independently of its produce, is of no value;" and certainly had no thought that direct taxes were confined to unproductive land. . . .

Nothing can be clearer than that what the Constitution intended to guard against was the exercise by the general government of the power of directly taxing persons and property within any State through a majority made up from the other States. It is true that the effect of requiring direct taxes to be apportioned among the States in proportion to their population is necessarily that the amount of taxes on the individual taxpayer in a State having the taxable subject-matter to a larger extent in proportion to its population than another State has, would be less than in such other State, but this inequality must be held to have been contemplated, and was manifestly designed to operate to restrain the exercise of the power of direct taxation to extraordinary emergencies, and to prevent an attack upon accumulated property by mere force of numbers.

It is not doubted that property owners ought to contribute in just measure to the expenses of the government. As to the States and their municipalities, this is reached largely through the imposition of direct taxes. As to the Federal government, it is attained in part through excises and indirect taxes upon luxuries and consumption generally, to which direct taxation may be added to the extent the rule of apportionment allows. And through one mode or the other, the entire wealth of the country, real and personal, may be made, as it should be, to contribute to the common defence and general welfare.

But the acceptance of the rule of apportionment was one of the compromises which made the adoption of the Constitution possible, and secured the creation of that dual form of government, so elastic and so strong, which has thus far survived in unabated vigor. If, by calling a tax indirect when it is essentially direct, the rule of protection could be frittered away, one of the great landmarks defining the boundary between the Nation and the States of which it is composed, would have disappeared, and with it one of the bulwarks of private rights and private property.

We are of opinion that the law in question, so far as it levies a tax on the rents or income of real estate, is in violation of the Constitution, and is invalid. . . .[4]

■ MR. JUSTICE WHITE, with whom concurred MR. JUSTICE HARLAN, dissenting.

[T]he result of the opinion of the court just announced is to overthrow a long and consistent line of decisions, and to deny to the legislative department of the government the possession of a power conceded to it by universal consensus for one hundred years, and which has been recognized by repeated adjudications of this court. . . .

In considering whether we are to regard an income tax as "direct" or otherwise, it will, in my opinion, serve no useful purpose, at this late period of our political history, to seek to ascertain the meaning of the word "direct" in the Constitution by resorting to the theoretical opinions on taxation found in the writings of some economists prior to the adoption of the Constitution or since. . . . [W]hatever may have been the value of their opinions as to the economic sense of the word "direct," they cannot now afford any criterion for determining its meaning in the Constitution, inasmuch as an authoritative and conclusive construction has been given to that term, as there used by an interpretation adopted shortly after the formation of the Constitution by the legislative department of the government, and approved by the Executive; by the adoption of that interpretation from that time to the present without question, and its exemplification and enforcement in many legislative enactments, and its acceptance by the authoritative text-writers on the Constitution; by the sanction of that interpretation, in a decision of this court rendered shortly after the Constitution was adopted; and finally by the repeated reiteration and affirmance of that interpretation, so that it has become imbedded in our jurisprudence, and therefore may be considered almost a part of the written Constitution itself. . . .

[It is nevertheless] argued that "a century of error" should furnish no obstacle to the reversal, by this court, of a continuous line of decisions interpreting the constitutional meaning of that word, if such decisions be considered wrong. . . . It is, I submit, greatly to be deplored that, after more than one hundred years of our national existence, after the government has withstood the strain of foreign wars and the dread

[4] **Questions:** During and after the 2020 Democratic presidential primary, Senators Elizabeth Warren and Bernie Sanders each proposed a "wealth tax" to pay for redistributive programs such as providing universal childcare and expanding Medicare to cover every American. Warren's plan, for example, proposed a 2 percent tax on the assets of Americans whose net worth is more than $50 million. *See* Jim Tankersley, *Warren Revives Plan for a Wealth Tax*, N.Y. Times, Mar. 1, 2021, at B3. Is such a wealth tax direct or indirect? How might the *Hylton* and *Pollock* Courts have answered this question?

An ongoing debate persists over the constitutionality of a wealth tax. On one side are scholars like Daniel Hemel and Rebecca Kysar, who doubt its constitutionality. A wealth tax, they say, would apply to real estate, making it a direct tax under *Pollock* that would need to be apportioned. *See* Daniel Hemel & Rebecca Kysar, *The Big Problem with Wealth Taxes*, N.Y. Times, Nov. 7, 2019. On the other side are scholars like Dawn Johnsen and Walter Dellinger, who defend the constitutionality of such a tax. They argue that even after *Pollock*, it would not be difficult for Congress to structure a wealth tax so that it is an indirect tax rather than a direct tax. What might they have in mind? *See* Dawn Johnsen & Walter Dellinger, *The Constitutionality of a National Wealth Tax*, 93 Ind. L.J. 111 (2018); Bruce Ackerman, *Taxation and the Constitution*, 99 Colum. L. Rev. 1 (1999).

ordeal of civil strife, and its people have become united and powerful, this court should consider itself compelled to go back to a long repudiated and rejected theory of the Constitution, by which the government is deprived of an inherent attribute of its being, a necessary power of taxation.

■ MR. JUSTICE BROWN, dissenting.

[B]y resuscitating an argument that was exploded in the *Hylton* case, and has lain practically dormant for a hundred years, [the Court] is made to do duty in nullifying, not this law alone, but every similar law that is not based upon an impossible theory of apportionment. Even the spectre of socialism is conjured up to frighten Congress from laying taxes upon the people in proportion to their ability to pay them. It is certainly a strange commentary upon the Constitution of the United States and upon a democratic government that Congress has no power to lay a tax which is one of the main sources of revenue of nearly every civilized State. It is a confession of feebleness in which I find myself wholly unable to join. . . .

4.2 SHIFT TO INDIRECT TAXES AND INCOME TAXES

As soon as it was announced, *Pollock v. Farmers' Loan & Trust Co.*, 157 U.S. 429 (1895) became one of the most controversial opinions in the Supreme Court's history. Populists and progressives criticized it not only because it made it effectively impossible for Congress to collect an income tax but also because of its cavalier attitude toward overruling precedent.

The loud and sustained opposition to *Pollock* likely influenced the Court's decision to reevaluate its distinction between direct and indirect taxes and move immediately back toward the rule of *Hylton v. United States*, 3 U.S. (3 Dall.) 171 (1796). In *Knowlton v. Moore*, the Court upheld an inheritance tax as an indirect tax despite the fact that it obviously taxed the decedent's estate. 178 U.S. 41, 83 (1900). Instead of holding that all taxes on property are direct taxes, as *Pollock* implied, the Court offered a new rule: direct taxes are "taxes imposed on property, real or personal, *as* such, because of its ownership and possession," whereas indirect taxes are taxes on the manufacture, use, or "transmission or receipt" of property. *Id.* at 47. As it is possible to characterize nearly any tax on property as a tax on the manufacture, use, transmission, or receipt of it, the Court subsequently resumed upholding every tax it encountered as an indirect tax. *See, e.g., Spreckels Sugar Refin. Co. v. McClain*, 192 U.S. 397, 413 (1904) (upholding a tax on a sugar company's income as an indirect tax on the business of refining sugar); *Flint v. Stone Tracy Co.*, 220 U.S. 107, 150 (1911) (upholding a tax on a corporation's income as an indirect tax on the privilege of doing business as a corporation); *N.Y. Tr. Co. v. Eisner*, 256 U.S. 345, 349 (1921) (upholding an estate tax as an indirect tax on the transfer of property).

The specific holding of *Pollock* itself was overruled by the Sixteenth Amendment, ratified in 1913, which declared that "[t]he Congress shall have power to lay and collect taxes on incomes, from whatever source derived, without apportionment among the several States, and without regard to any census or enumeration." But by the time the amendment was ratified, *Pollock* was already a dead letter. *See Brushaber v. Union*

Pac. R.R., 240 U.S. 1, 18–19 (1916). Since 1913, apportionment challenges to taxes have mainly focused on whether, say, corporate dividends count as taxable "income." *See, e.g.*, *Bowers v. Kerbaugh-Empire Co.*, 271 U.S. 170, 174 (1926) (*income* refers to the "gain derived from capital, from labor, or from both combined," inclusive of the "profit gained through sale or conversion of capital").

CHAPTER 5

WHAT IS THE SCOPE OF CONGRESS'S POWER TO TAX?

ARTICLE I, SECTION 8, CLAUSE 1: The Congress shall have Power To lay and collect Taxes, Duties, Imposts and Excises, to pay the Debts and provide for the common Defence and general Welfare of the United States; but all Duties, Imposts and Excises shall be uniform throughout the United States; . . .—And

> **CLAUSE 18:** To make all Laws which shall be necessary and proper for carrying into Execution the foregoing Powers, and all other Powers vested by this Constitution in the Government of the United States, or in any Department or Officer thereof.

ARTICLE I, SECTION 9, CLAUSE 1: The Migration or Importation of such Persons as any of the States now existing shall think proper to admit, shall not be prohibited by the Congress prior to the Year one thousand eight hundred and eight, but a Tax or duty may be imposed on such Importation, not exceeding ten dollars for each Person.

> **CLAUSE 5:** No Tax or Duty shall be laid on Articles exported from any State.

TENTH AMENDMENT (1791): The powers not delegated to the United States by the Constitution, nor prohibited by it to the States, are reserved to the States respectively, or to the people.

5.1 THE UNIFORMITY REQUIREMENT

Neither *Hylton v. United States*, 3 U.S. (3 Dall.) 171 (1796), nor *Pollock v. Farmers' Loan & Trust Co.*, 157 U.S. 429 (1895), *aff'd on reh'g*, 158 U.S. 601 (1895), was about whether Congress had the power to collect certain taxes. Rather, what was at stake was whether the taxes before the Supreme Court were (1) direct taxes, subject to the apportionment requirement of Article I, Sections 2 and 9; or (2) indirect taxes, subject to the requirement of Article I, Section 8, that "all Duties, Imposts and Excises shall be uniform throughout the United States." Whereas apportioning excise and income taxes under the first requirement is difficult, if not impossible, meeting the second requirement is usually straightforward in most cases. To satisfy the uniformity requirement, the Court has explained, it is enough for a tax to apply across the entire United States—even if it disproportionately affects certain populations.

For example, in the *Head Money Cases*, 112 U.S. 580 (1884), a transportation company challenged a customs duty on immigrant ships, claiming that it applied only to states like New York that took in the vast majority of immigrants. The Court disagreed, holding that the tax satisfied the uniformity requirement because it "operates with the same force and effect in every place where the subject of it is found." *Head Money Cases*, 112 U.S. at 594. The Court rhetorically asked, "Is the tax on tobacco void because in many of the states no tobacco is raised or manufactured?" *Id.* The Court thought the question too obvious to answer—even though, throughout the nineteenth century, southern and northern politicians criticized the legality of various tariffs because they unequally benefited one region of the country over another.

The Court has similarly upheld against uniformity challenges progressive taxes that tax wealthier taxpayers at higher rates. *Knowlton v. Moore*, 178 U.S. 41, 107–08 (1900). And in *United States v. Ptasynski*, 462 U.S. 74 (1983), the Court upheld a tax that exempted crude oil produced from wells located north of the Arctic Circle—an exemption that applied only to Alaska. The Court explained that Congress has wide latitude to frame taxes in geographic terms, but, where it does so, the Court "will examine the classification closely to see if there is actual geographic discrimination." *Ptasynski*, 462 U.S. at 85. If the Court finds no purpose to discriminate against particular states, it will uphold the law.

5.2 LIMITS ON TAXING THE SLAVE TRADE AND EXPORTS

Even if a tax is indirect and uniform, Article I, Section 9, prohibits Congress from laying any tax "on Articles exported from any State." This prohibition was demanded by southern delegates to the Constitutional Convention because the vast majority of the South's wealth was derived from exporting the tobacco and rice harvested by enslaved people. *See* Michael J. Klarman, *The Framers' Coup: The Making of the United States Constitution* 279–82 (2016).

Yet where the Constitution erected several obstacles to protect the property of slave owners, most of the delegates distinguished *slavery* from the *slave trade*. Even many southern delegates considered it barbaric to kidnap Africans and transport them in bondage to the Americas. *Id.* Moreover, slavery was an economic market, and importing additional enslaved people into the United States reduced the relative value of the enslaved people that the delegates owned. This was particularly true in the Upper South states such as Virginia, in which enslaved people had far longer life expectancies than those in South Carolina or Georgia, whose economies depended on importing as many enslaved people as possible. *See id.* at 287. As a consequence, when the convention raised the possibility of abolishing the slave trade, the delegates from South Carolina and Georgia not only resisted the possibility but also threatened to walk out if such a provision were enacted. *Id.* at 262–64, 301–02. The compromises that the convention reached included (1) prohibiting Congress from taxing exports and (2) prohibiting Congress from abolishing the foreign slave trade before 1808, but (3) permitting Congress to impose a $10-per-person tax on slave importers. *See Dred Scott v. Sandford*, 60 U.S. (19 How.) 393, 411, 536–37 (1857) (recounting these compromises as evidence that the delegates believed black people had no rights that deserved their respect).

In the centuries since the convention, the Supreme Court has interpreted the prohibition on export taxes narrowly. For example, in 1868, after Congress imposed a tax on all tobacco—including tobacco intended for exportation—the Supreme Court upheld the tax. It explained that the prohibition on export taxes "has reference to the imposition of duties on goods by reason or because of their exportation, or intended exportation, or while they are being exported," but did not apply to general taxes, "laid on all property alike," that happened to apply to goods being exported. *Turpin v. Burgess*, 117 U.S. 504, 507 (1886).

But the Court has struck a few taxes that discriminate against exports or that have the effect of applying only to exports. For example, in *United States v. U.S. Shoe Corp.*, a unanimous Court struck down a "harbor maintenance tax" that required shippers to pay a uniform charge on all commercial cargo shipped through the country's ports. 523 U.S. 360, 363 (1998). Justice Ruth Bader Ginsburg, writing for the majority, suggested that despite the tax's name, it was based on the value of exported goods as opposed to, say, the cost to the government of actually maintaining the harbor. *Id.* at 367.

5.3 LIMITS ON TAXING STATE PROPERTY

Recall *McCulloch v. Maryland*, 17 U.S. (4 Wheat.) 316 (1819), in which the Supreme Court struck down Maryland's attempt to tax the Second Bank of the United States. "[T]he power to tax involves the power to destroy," Chief Justice John Marshall wrote, and the Supremacy Clause of Article VI, which makes federal law supreme to state law, prohibited states from attempting to obstruct Congress's valid exercises of power. *McCulloch*, 17 U.S. (4 Wheat.) at 431. But is the reverse true? Could Congress, say, tax the Bank of Maryland?

Shortly after the Civil War, the Court first answered yes in one case—and then no in another. A major effect of the Civil War had been the dramatic expansion of the federal government. Before the war, virtually all regulation, internal taxation, infrastructure projects, and public administration had been conducted by state and local governments, as opposed to the federal government. But to preserve the Union, Congress had conscripted an army, issued its own paper currency, and passed an income tax. After defeating the Confederacy, the federal government required southern states to ratify the Thirteenth Amendment and abolish slavery. But many southern states followed their ratification with laws that reintroduced slavery in all but name. Congress responded to this southern intransigence by proposing dramatic innovations, including the Fourteenth and Fifteenth Amendments, while also passing the Reconstruction Acts, which put southern states under the administration of military governors. It was in this context—an increasingly powerful federal government threatening to upend previous federal-state relations—that the Court decided *Veazie*

Bank v. Fenno, 75 U.S. (8 Wall.) 533 (1869), and *Collector v. Day*, 78 U.S. (11 Wall.) 113 (1871).

The first case, *Veazie Bank*, concerned the constitutionality of an 1866 tax that Congress passed to facilitate its paper currency. At the time, most Americans paid for purchases using notes issued by state-chartered banks, which a bearer could redeem, like a check, for gold or silver coins. To help finance its war debt, Congress wanted Americans to pay for purchases instead using its newly established federal currency—greenbacks. To eliminate its state-bank competition, Congress imposed a steep, 10 percent tax on all banknotes issued by state-chartered banks, making them too expensive for anyone to use. Veazie Bank, a bank chartered by Maine, challenged this tax as "excessive." *Veazie Bank*, 75 U.S. (8 Wall.) at 548.

Although the Supreme Court agreed that the purpose of the tax was to destroy state banknotes, the Court held that the case was controlled by *McCulloch*. "[I]n the exercise of undisputed constitutional powers, undertaken to provide a currency for the whole country, it cannot be questioned that Congress may, constitutionally, secure the benefit of it to the people by appropriate legislation," the Court wrote. *Id.* at 549. Just as Maryland once had to give way to federal policy, Maine and other states had to allow their corporations to be taxed. In this respect, Congress's power to ban state-sponsored currency was no different from its power to ban, say, counterfeit currency. "Without this power, indeed, its attempts to secure a sound and uniform currency for the country must be futile." *Id.*

5.3.1

Collector v. Day

78 U.S. (11 Wall.) 113 (1871)

The *Veazie Bank* decision immediately raised the prospect that Congress might attempt to tax other state institutions out of existence. In the context of Reconstruction, this was not a hypothetical idea. Many conservative white people, including the business-friendly justices on the Supreme Court, grew increasingly concerned about Congress's novel exercises of power to protect multiracial democracy. *See* W. E. B. Du Bois, *Black Reconstruction in America* 690 (1935). Perhaps for this reason, the Supreme Court dramatically reined in *Veazie Bank* two years later.

At issue in *Collector v. Day*, 78 U.S. (11 Wall.) 113 (1871), was the income tax that Congress had passed during the Civil War. A state judge in Massachusetts, J. M. Day, refused to pay it. He argued that any federal tax on state officers violated the Tenth Amendment, which states, "The powers not delegated to the United States by the Constitution, nor prohibited by it to the States, are reserved to the States respectively, or to the people." Lawyers for the collector of internal revenue responded that the power to tax *was* delegated to Congress in Article I, Section 8.

For the first time, the Supreme Court held that the Constitution not only gave Congress implied *powers* but also imposed implied *limitations*.

■ MR. JUSTICE NELSON delivered the opinion of the Court.[1]

The case presents the question whether or not it is competent for Congress, under the Constitution of the United States, to impose a tax upon the salary of a judicial officer of a State? . . .

It is conceded in the case of *McCulloch v. Maryland*, that the power of taxation by the States was not abridged by the grant of a similar power to the government of the Union; that it was retained by the States, and that the power is to be concurrently exercised by the two governments; and also that there is no express constitutional prohibition upon the States against taxing the means or instrumentalities of the general government. But, it was held, and, we agree properly held, to be prohibited by necessary implication; otherwise, the States might impose taxation to an extent that would impair, if not wholly defeat, the operations of the Federal authorities when acting in their appropriate sphere. . . .

It is a familiar rule of construction of the Constitution of the Union, that the sovereign powers vested in the State governments by their respective constitutions, remained unaltered and unimpaired, except so far as they were granted to the government of the United States. That the intention of the framers of the Constitution in this respect might not be misunderstood, this rule of interpretation is expressly declared in the tenth article of the amendments, namely: "The powers not delegated to the United States are reserved to the States respectively, or, to the people." The government of the United States, therefore, can claim no powers which are not granted to it by the Constitution, and the powers actually granted must be such as are expressly given, or given by necessary implication.

The general government, and the States, although both exist within the same territorial limits, are separate and distinct sovereignties, acting separately and independently of each other, within their respective spheres. The former in its appropriate sphere is supreme; but the States within the limits of their powers not granted, or, in the language of the tenth amendment, "reserved," are as independent of the general government as that government within its sphere is independent of the States. . . .

The relations existing between the two governments are well stated by the present Chief Justice in the case of *Lane County v. Oregon*. "Both the States and the United States," he observed, "existed before the Constitution. The people, through that instrument, established a more perfect union, by substituting a National government, acting with ample powers directly upon the citizens, instead of the Confederate government, which acted with powers greatly restricted, only upon the States. But, in many of the articles of the Constitution, the necessary existence of the States, and within their proper spheres, the independent authority of the States, are distinctly recognized. To them nearly the whole charge of interior regulation is committed or left; to them, and to the people, all powers, not expressly delegated to the National government, are reserved." Upon looking into the Constitution it will be found that but a few of the articles in that instrument could be carried into practical effect without the existence of the States.

Two of the great departments of the government, the executive and legislative, depend upon the exercise of the powers, or upon the people of the States. The

---

[1] **As You Read, Consider:** According to the *Collector* Court, the Constitution imposes implied limitations on Congress's enumerated powers, including its power to tax. Where do these limitations come from? Why does the Court consider them necessary?

Constitution guarantees to the States a republican form of government, and protects each against invasion or domestic violence. Such being the separate and independent condition of the States in our complex system, as recognized by the Constitution, and the existence of which is so indispensable, that, without them, the general government itself would disappear from the family of nations, it would seem to follow, as a reasonable, if not a necessary consequence, that the means and instrumentalities employed for carrying on the operations of their governments, for preserving their existence, and fulfilling the high and responsible duties assigned to them in the Constitution, should be left free and unimpaired, should not be liable to be crippled, much less defeated by the taxing power of another government, which power acknowledges no limits but the will of the legislative body imposing the tax. And, more especially, those means and instrumentalities which are the creation of their sovereign and reserved rights, one of which is the establishment of the judicial department, and the appointment of officers to administer their laws. Without this power, and the exercise of it, we risk nothing in saying that no one of the States under the form of government guaranteed by the Constitution could long preserve its existence. A despotic government might. . . . It is, therefore, one of the sovereign powers vested in the States by their constitutions, which remained unaltered and unimpaired, and in respect to which the State is as independent of the general government as that government is independent of the States.

The supremacy of the general government, therefore, so much relied on in the argument of the counsel for the plaintiff in error, in respect to the question before us, cannot be maintained. The two governments are upon an equality, and the question is whether the power "to lay and collect taxes" enables the general government to tax the salary of a judicial officer of the State, which officer is a means or instrumentality employed to carry into execution one of its most important functions, the administration of the laws, and which concerns the exercise of a right reserved to the States?

We do not say the mere circumstance of the establishment of the judicial department, and the appointment of officers to administer the laws, being among the reserved powers of the State, disables the general government from levying the tax, as that depends upon the express power "to lay and collect taxes," but it shows that it is an original inherent power never parted with, and, in respect to which, the supremacy of that government does not exist, and is of no importance in determining the question. . . .

It is admitted that there is no express provision in the Constitution that prohibits the general government from taxing the means and instrumentalities of the States, nor is there any prohibiting the States from taxing the means and instrumentalities of that government. In both cases the exemption rests upon necessary implication, and is upheld by the great law of self-preservation; as any government, whose means employed in conducting its operations, if subject to the control of another and distinct government, can exist only at the mercy of that government. Of what avail are these means if another power may tax them at discretion?

But we are referred to the *Veazie Bank v. Fenno*, in support of this power of taxation. That case furnishes a strong illustration of the position taken by the Chief Justice in *McCulloch v. Maryland*, namely, "That the power to tax involves the power to destroy."

The power involved was one which had been exercised by the States since the foundation of the government, and had been, after the lapse of three-quarters of a century, annihilated from excessive taxation by the general government, just as the judicial office in the present case might be, if subject, at all, to taxation by that government. But, notwithstanding the sanction of this taxation by a majority of the court, it is conceded, in the opinion, that "the reserved rights of the States, such as the right to pass laws; to give effect to laws through executive action; to administer justice through the courts, and to employ all necessary agencies for legitimate purposes of State government, are not proper subjects of the taxing power of Congress." This concession covers the case before us, and adds the authority of this court in support of the doctrine which we have endeavored to maintain.[2]

NOTE: AFTERMATH OF *COLLECTOR*

The explicit holding of *Collector* is no longer good law. As with *Pollock v. Farmers' Loan & Trust Co.*, 157 U.S. 429 (1895), *aff'd on reh'g*, 158 U.S. 601 (1895), the Supreme Court followed its decision over the next few decades by steadily limiting state-officer immunity from federal taxation until it was nonexistent. In 1939, the Court explicitly overruled *Collector* in *Graves v. New York ex rel. O'Keefe*, holding that Congress *does* have the power to impose generally applicable taxes, such as an income tax, on state officers, agencies, and property. 306 U.S. 466, 486 (1939).

The Supreme Court summarized the current state of the law in *South Carolina v. Baker*:

> In sum, then, under current intergovernmental tax immunity doctrine the States can never tax the United States directly but can tax any private parties with whom it does business, even though the financial burden falls on the United States, as long as the tax does not discriminate against the United States or those with whom it deals. . . . The rule with respect to state tax immunity is essentially the same, except that at least some nondiscriminatory federal taxes can be collected directly from the States even though a parallel state tax could not be collected directly from the Federal Government.

485 U.S. 505, 523 (1988) (citations omitted). In other words, the federal government may not pass a tax that applies only to states, but states and their officials are required to pay nondiscriminatory federal taxes.

So if *Collector* is no longer good law in its particulars, why read it? The answer is that it illustrates what is now the Supreme Court's most important method of limiting the federal government's power, sometimes called *states' rights* or *reserved powers*. Regardless of the terminology, this implied limitation is the idea that even if one of Congress's enumerated powers might literally be read to authorize a certain action, the Supreme Court will invalidate it if it interferes with the sovereignty that states originally possessed under the Articles of Confederation. According to the *Collector* Court, the Tenth Amendment demonstrated that states didn't forfeit all of their sovereign powers when they ratified the Constitution; rather, they "reserved" some of them. In an effort to cabin the Reconstruction Congress's ability to regulate the states, the Court held that the Tenth Amendment implies that Congress and the states coexist in mutually exclusive spheres,

---

[2] **Question:** Is there a meaningful difference, in your view, between a federal tax that applies only to state officers and one that applies generally to everyone, including state officers and agencies?

each with unlimited power within its own sphere but no power outside of it. As we will see, all of these ideas will resurface again and again when discussing each of Congress's powers.

5.4 LIMITS ON TAXES FOR THE PURPOSE OF REGULATION

The principal reason why the Constitutional Convention gave Congress the power to tax was to raise revenue. But as the delegates recognized in their debates over whether Congress could tax slavery or the slave trade, taxes always have the secondary effect of regulating the thing taxed. "[T]he power to tax involves the power to destroy" only because a tax can be so onerous that no one can afford to use the taxed product. *See McCulloch v. Maryland*, 17 U.S. (4 Wheat.) 316, 431 (1819). The second statute passed by the first Congress even explained as much, declaring that a tax on imported goods was necessary "for the support of government, for the discharge of the debts of the United States, and the encouragement and protection of manufactures." Tariff Act of 1789, ch. 2, 1 Stat. 24.

Despite this pedigree, federal taxes passed for the purpose of regulating the *domestic* affairs of the United States have long been controversial. Before the Civil War, if Congress had ever attempted to exercise such a power, southerners would have feared that a North-controlled Congress might one day impose a prohibitive tax on the sale or transfer of enslaved people. Unsurprisingly, therefore, it was not until after the North won the Civil War that the Supreme Court weighed in and expressly upheld Congress's power to impose taxes for the express purpose of domestic regulation.

The *Veazie Bank v. Fenno* decision, 75 U.S. (8 Wall.) 533 (1869), was one of the first Supreme Court opinions to consider and expressly uphold Congress's power to impose a tax for the purpose of prohibiting the thing taxed—state banknotes—rather than for the purpose of raising revenue.

Similarly, in the *License Tax Cases*, 72 U.S. (5 Wall.) 462 (1867), the Court established that Congress could use the taxing power to regulate entire industries. The *License Tax Cases* involved a Civil War law in which Congress required anyone who wished to sell lottery tickets or liquor—anywhere in the nation—to first pay for a "license" from the United States. Several retailers who were fined for failing to obtain one of these licenses complained that the Constitution gave Congress no enumerated power to regulate lotteries or liquor sales. But the Court held that the granting of a license "must be regarded as nothing more than a mere form of imposing a tax, and of implying nothing except that the licensee shall be subject to no penalties under national law if he pays it." *The License Tax Cases*, 72 U.S. at 471. Even though it was obvious that Congress could one day charge thousands of dollars for a license—effectively banning liquor and lottery sales nationwide—the Court wrote that "we cannot say that there is anything contrary to the Constitution in these provisions of the recent or existing internal revenue acts relating to licenses." *Id.* at 472.

Congress followed these two decisions by steadily increasing its use of the taxing power to regulate domestic products. For example, when Congress passed laws regulating the packaging of food, drugs, and cigarettes, it justified its regulations on the ground that the newly required packaging facilitated the collection of taxes. Initially, the Supreme Court agreed. *See, e.g., United States v. Doremus*, 249 U.S. 86, 94–95 (1919). But in 1922, the Court imposed its first limit on Congress's power to regulate using the taxing power.

5.4.1

Bailey v. Drexel Furniture Co. (The Child Labor Tax Case)

259 U.S. 20 (1922)

Throughout nineteenth-century America, children worked. Enslaved children worked in fields, poor children worked in mines and factories, and even well-off children in the Northeast worked in textile mills. But by 1910, when over two million children under the age of fifteen worked in industrial jobs for wages, social reformers increasingly criticized the practice of child labor for harming children and depriving them of an education. A major obstacle that these reformers faced was that child labor tended to be significantly cheaper than adult labor. This meant that when some state legislatures began prohibiting child labor, the owners of textile mills, meatpacking houses, and canneries often found it cheaper to move their production to other states—especially those in the South—rather than comply with the bans. *See* Hugh D. Hindman, *Child Labor: An American History* 58 (2002).

The collective-action problem caused by some states banning child labor while other states refused to do so led the opponents of child labor to turn to Congress. As we will see later in this course (section 8.2), when Congress first attempted to ban child labor in 1916, it relied on the Commerce Clause to prohibit goods made by children from crossing state lines. *See* Keating-Owen Child Labor Act of 1916, Pub. L. No. 64–249, 39 Stat. 675. This law was struck down in *Hammer v. Dagenhart*, in which the Supreme Court held that the Commerce Clause didn't permit Congress to regulate manufacturing. 247 U.S. 251, 272 (1918). So Congress tried again with the Child Labor Tax Law of 1919, Pub. L. No. 65–254, 40 Stat. 1138, this time imposing a 10 percent excise tax on the profits of specified businesses that employed child labor. When J. W. Bailey, the collector of internal revenue, attempted to collect the tax from the Drexel Furniture Company of North Carolina, the Drexel Furniture Co. responded with this lawsuit, *Bailey v. Drexel Furniture Co.* (*The Child Labor Tax Case*), 258 U.S. 20 (1922).

The Court determined that the Child Labor Tax Act of 1919 was as unconstitutional as its predecessor.[3]

■ MR. CHIEF JUSTICE TAFT delivered the opinion of the Court.

This case presents the question of the constitutional validity of the Child Labor Tax Law. . . . The law is attacked on the ground that it is a regulation of the employment of child labor in the States—an exclusively state function under the Federal Constitution and within the reservations of the Tenth Amendment. It is defended on the ground that it is a mere excise tax levied by the Congress of the United States under its broad power of taxation conferred by § 8, Article I, of the Federal Constitution. We must construe the law and interpret the intent and meaning of Congress from the language of the act. The words are to be given their ordinary meaning unless the context shows that they are differently used. Does this law impose a tax with only that incidental restraint and regulation which a tax must inevitably involve? Or does it regulate by the use of the so-called tax as a penalty? If a tax, it is clearly an excise. If it were an excise on a commodity or other thing of value we might not be permitted under previous decisions of this court to infer solely from its heavy burden that the act intends a prohibition instead of a tax. But this act is more. It provides a heavy exaction for a departure from a detailed and specified course of conduct in business. That course of business is that employers shall employ in mines and quarries, children of an age greater than sixteen years; in mills and factories, children of an age greater than fourteen years, and shall prevent children of less than sixteen years in mills and factories from working more than eight hours a day or six days in the week. If an employer departs from this prescribed course of business, he is to pay to the Government one-tenth of his entire net income in the business for a full year. The amount is not to be proportioned in any degree to the extent or frequency of the departures, but is to be paid by the employer in full measure whether he employs five hundred children for a year, or employs only one for a day. Moreover, if he does not know the child is within the named age limit, he is not to pay; that is to say, it is only where he knowingly departs from the prescribed course that payment is to be exacted. Scienter is associated with penalties not with taxes. The employer's factory is to be subject to inspection at any time not only by the taxing officers of the Treasury, the Department normally charged with the collection of taxes, but also by the Secretary of Labor and his subordinates whose normal function is the advancement and protection of the welfare of the workers. In the light of these features of the act, a court must be blind not to see that the so-called tax is imposed to stop the employment of children within the age limits prescribed. Its prohibitory and regulatory effect and purpose are palpable. All others can see and understand this. How can we properly shut our minds to it?

It is the high duty and function of this court in cases regularly brought to its bar to decline to recognize or enforce seeming laws of Congress, dealing with subjects not entrusted to Congress but left or committed by the supreme law of the land to the control of the States. We can not avoid the duty even though it require us to refuse to give effect to legislation designed to promote the highest good. The good sought in unconstitutional legislation is an insidious feature because it leads citizens and legislators of good purpose to promote it without thought of the serious breach it will make in the ark of our covenant or the harm which will come from breaking down recognized standards. In the maintenance of local self government, on the one hand,

[3] **As You Read, Consider:** Like *Collector v. Day*, the *Bailey v. Drexel Furniture Co.* Court introduces a new implied limit on Congress's power to tax: exercises of the taxing power must levy genuine *taxes*, not *penalties*. What principles does the Court invoke in defense of this distinction? Does the Court offer a test to distinguish a tax from a penalty?

and the national power, on the other, our country has been able to endure and prosper for near a century and a half.

Out of a proper respect for the acts of a coordinate branch of the Government, this court has gone far to sustain taxing acts as such, even though there has been ground for suspecting from the weight of the tax it was intended to destroy its subject. But, in the act before us, the presumption of validity cannot prevail, because the proof of the contrary is found on the very face of its provisions. Grant the validity of this law, and all that Congress would need to do, hereafter, in seeking to take over to its control any one of the great number of subjects of public interest, jurisdiction of which the States have never parted with, and which are reserved to them by the Tenth Amendment, would be to enact a detailed measure of complete regulation of the subject and enforce it by a so-called tax upon departures from it. To give such magic to the word "tax" would be to break down all constitutional limitation of the powers of Congress and completely wipe out the sovereignty of the States.

The difference between a tax and a penalty is sometimes difficult to define and yet the consequences of the distinction in the required method of their collection often are important. Where the sovereign enacting the law has power to impose both tax and penalty the difference between revenue production and mere regulation may be immaterial, but not so when one sovereign can impose a tax only, and the power of regulation rests in another. Taxes are occasionally imposed in the discretion of the legislature on proper subjects with the primary motive of obtaining revenue from them and with the incidental motive of discouraging them by making their continuance onerous. They do not lose their character as taxes because of the incidental motive. But there comes a time in the extension of the penalizing features of the so-called tax when it loses its character as such and becomes a mere penalty with the characteristics of regulation and punishment. Such is the case in the law before us. Although Congress does not invalidate the contract of employment or expressly declare that the employment within the mentioned ages is illegal, it does exhibit its intent practically to achieve the latter result by adopting the criteria of wrongdoing and imposing its principal consequence on those who transgress its standard. . . .[4]

5.4.2

National Federation of Independent Business (NFIB) v. Sebelius

567 U.S. 519 (2012)

The Supreme Court in *Drexel Furniture* was clearly annoyed that Congress had attempted to evade its holding in *Hammer* by turning to another constitutional source of power. In later, less politically charged cases, the Court returned to its pre-*Drexel Furniture* pattern of upholding taxes that had been passed with the express purpose of regulation. *See, e.g., United States v. Sanchez*, 340 U.S. 42 (1950) (regulatory tax on marijuana); *Sonzinsky v. United States*, 300 U.S. 506, 513 (1937) (regulatory tax on sawed-off shotguns).

The next time the Court faced a case directly analogous to *Drexel Furniture* was after the passage of the Patient Protection and Affordable

[4] **Questions:** Applying the logic of *Drexel Furniture*, at what point does a law stop becoming a "tax" and start becoming a "penalty"? Suppose the Child Labor Tax Law had imposed only a five-person excise tax? Or a 1 percent tax? Same result?

Care Act of 2010, Pub. L. No. 111–148, 124 Stat. 119, the signature legislative achievement of President Barack Obama. As with the Child Labor Tax Law, the Affordable Care Act was the product of a long campaign to enlist the federal government in tackling a nationwide problem: one in six Americans in 2010 lacked health insurance. In debates over how to shrink this fraction and cover everyone, the president and Congress decided to require private health insurers to provide affordable coverage to all Americans, even people with preexisting health conditions. But health insurers complained that this requirement would make their business unprofitable, as people with preexisting conditions were more likely than most Americans to need expensive care. The insurers asked Congress to balance this burden on their business by also requiring relatively healthy people to purchase private health insurance. Congress agreed, requiring health insurers to cover everyone but also requiring that everyone "shall" purchase health insurance. 26 U.S.C. § 5000A(a). This latter requirement was commonly called the *individual mandate*.

Congress enforced the mandate by requiring Americans who failed to purchase health insurance to make a "[s]hared [r]esponsibility [p]ayment" to the Internal Revenue Service as part of their annual taxes. *Id.* § 5000A(g)(1). This payment, which the Affordable Care Act called a *penalty*, was calculated based on the person's tax status, household income, and the average annual premium that the person would have paid for private health insurance. *Id.*

Although some states, notably Massachusetts, had enacted similar individual mandates, critics of the Affordable Care Act argued that Congress had no equivalent power to require people to purchase health insurance—or broccoli or anything else. *See* James B. Stewart, *How Broccoli Landed on Supreme Court Menu*, N.Y. Times, Jun. 14, 2021, at A1. As with the challengers to Congress's child-labor bans a century earlier, these critics focused their attention on the Commerce Clause, treating Congress's taxing power as a secondary concern. After the president signed the act, twenty-six states and the National Federation of Independent Business, a trade association, sued Kathleen Sebelius, the secretary of health and human services. Their cases reached the Supreme Court.

Over three days of oral argument, only a few minutes were dedicated to whether the individual mandate could be construed as a tax. One likely explanation is that when Obama publicly defended the individual mandate, he refused to call it a "tax" because of that word's negative political connotations.

Initially in *National Federation of Business (NFIB) v. Sebelius*, 567 U.S. 519 (2012), five of the nine justices, including Chief Justice John Roberts, thought that the individual mandate was unconstitutional. But in the course of writing an opinion striking down the law, Roberts changed his mind. *See* Joan Biskupic, *The Chief* 238–39 (2019). The chief justice's Taxing Clause analysis is excerpted below (we will consider his Commerce Clause analysis later in this casebook (section 9.3)).[5]

■ CHIEF JUSTICE ROBERTS announced the judgment of the Court and delivered the opinion of the Court with respect to Parts I, II, and III-C. . . .

[I]n our federal system, the National Government possesses only limited powers; the States and the people retain the remainder. Nearly two centuries ago, Chief Justice Marshall observed that "the question respecting the extent of the powers actually granted" to the Federal Government "is perpetually arising, and will probably continue to arise, as long as our system shall exist." *McCulloch v. Maryland*, 4 Wheat. 316, 405 (1819). In this case we must again determine whether the Constitution grants Congress powers it now asserts, but which many States and individuals believe it does not possess. Resolving this controversy requires us to examine both the limits of the Government's power, and our own limited role in policing those boundaries. . . .

The Federal Government has expanded dramatically over the past two centuries, but it still must show that a constitutional grant of power authorizes each of its actions. . . . This case concerns two powers that the Constitution [grants] the Federal Government, but which must be read carefully to avoid creating a general federal authority akin to the police power. The Constitution authorizes Congress to "regulate Commerce with foreign Nations, and among the several States, and with the Indian Tribes." Art. I, § 8, cl. 3. . . . Congress may also "lay and collect Taxes, Duties, Imposts and Excises, to pay the Debts and provide for the common Defence and general Welfare of the United States." U. S. Const., Art. I, § 8, cl. 1. . . .

The Government advances two theories for the proposition that Congress had constitutional authority to enact the individual mandate. First, the Government argues that Congress had the power to enact the mandate under the Commerce Clause. Under that theory, Congress may order individuals to buy health insurance because the failure to do so affects interstate commerce, and could undercut the Affordable Care Act's other reforms. Second, the Government argues that if the commerce power does not support the mandate, we should nonetheless uphold it as an exercise of Congress's power to tax. According to the Government, even if Congress lacks the power to direct individuals to buy insurance, the only effect of the individual mandate is to raise taxes on those who do not do so, and thus the law may be upheld as a tax. . . .

The most straightforward reading of the mandate is that it commands individuals to purchase insurance. After all, it states that individuals "shall" maintain health insurance. 26 U.S.C. § 5000A(a). Congress thought it could enact such a command under the Commerce Clause, and the Government primarily defended the law on that basis. But, for the reasons explained above, the Commerce Clause does not give Congress that power. Under our precedent, it is therefore necessary to ask whether the Government's alternative reading of the statute—that it only imposes a tax on those without insurance—is a reasonable one.[6]

---

[5] **As You Read, Consider:** In *Bailey v. Drexel Furniture Co.*, Congress described its law as a tax, not a penalty. Here, however, Congress describes its individual mandate as a penalty, not a tax. What does Chief Justice John Roberts make of Congress's "choice of label"?

Drexel Furniture offered an informal test for distinguishing a tax from a penalty. Does Roberts faithfully apply the same test, or does he modify it?

In light of *Hylton v. United States* and *Pollock v. Farmers' Loan & Trust Co.*, does the individual mandate impose a direct tax subject to apportionment or an indirect tax subject to uniformity?

[6] **Note:** The Court's discussion of the Commerce Clause is excerpted in section 9.3.

Under the mandate, if an individual does not maintain health insurance, the only consequence is that he must make an additional payment to the IRS when he pays his taxes. See § 5000A(b). That, according to the Government, means the mandate can be regarded as establishing a condition—not owning health insurance—that triggers a tax—the required payment to the IRS. Under that theory, the mandate is not a legal command to buy insurance. Rather, it makes going without insurance just another thing the Government taxes, like buying gasoline or earning income. And if the mandate is in effect just a tax hike on certain taxpayers who do not have health insurance, it may be within Congress's constitutional power to tax.

The question is not whether that is the most natural interpretation of the mandate, but only whether it is a "fairly possible" one. *Crowell v. Benson*, 285 U.S. 22, 62 (1932). As we have explained, "every reasonable construction must be resorted to, in order to save a statute from unconstitutionality." *Hooper v. California*, 155 U.S. 648, 657 (1895). The Government asks us to interpret the mandate as imposing a tax, if it would otherwise violate the Constitution. Granting the Act the full measure of deference owed to federal statutes, it can be so read, for the reasons set forth below.

C

The exaction the Affordable Care Act imposes on those without health insurance looks like a tax in many respects. The "[s]hared responsibility payment," as the statute entitles it, is paid into the Treasury by "taxpayer[s]" when they file their tax returns. 26 U.S.C. § 5000A(b). It does not apply to individuals who do not pay federal income taxes because their household income is less than the filing threshold in the Internal Revenue Code. § 5000A(e)(2). For taxpayers who do owe the payment, its amount is determined by such familiar factors as taxable income, number of dependents, and joint filing status. §§ 5000A(b)(3), (c)(2), (c)(4). The requirement to pay is found in the Internal Revenue Code and enforced by the IRS, which—as we previously explained—must assess and collect it "in the same manner as taxes." *Supra*, at 2583–2584. This process yields the essential feature of any tax: it produces at least some revenue for the Government. *United States v. Kahriger*, 345 U.S. 22, 28, n. 4 (1953). Indeed, the payment is expected to raise about $4 billion per year by 2017.

It is of course true that the Act describes the payment as a "penalty," not a "tax." But [that label] does not determine whether the payment may be viewed as an exercise of Congress's taxing power. . . . Our precedent reflects this: In 1922, we decided [a challenge] to the "Child Labor Tax." . . . [W]e held that [an] exaction, although labeled a tax, was not in fact authorized by Congress's taxing power. *Drexel Furniture*, 259 U.S., at 38. That constitutional question was not controlled by Congress's choice of label.

We have similarly held that exactions not labeled taxes nonetheless were authorized by Congress's power to tax. In the *License Tax Cases*, for example, we held that federal licenses to sell liquor and lottery tickets—for which the licensee had to pay a fee—could be sustained as exercises of the taxing power. 5 Wall., at 471. . . . We thus ask whether the shared responsibility payment falls within Congress's taxing power, "[d]isregarding the designation of the exaction, and viewing its substance and application." *United States v. Constantine*, 296 U.S. 287, 294 (1935). . . .

Our cases confirm this functional approach. For example, in *Drexel Furniture*, we focused on three practical characteristics of the so-called tax on employing child laborers that convinced us the "tax" was actually a penalty. First, the tax imposed an exceedingly heavy burden—10 percent of a company's net income—on those who employed children, no matter how small their infraction. Second, it imposed that exaction only on those who knowingly employed underage laborers. Such scienter requirements are typical of punitive statutes, because Congress often wishes to punish only those who intentionally break the law. Third, this "tax" was enforced in part by the Department of Labor, an agency responsible for punishing violations of labor laws, not collecting revenue. . . .

The same analysis here suggests that the shared responsibility payment may for constitutional purposes be considered a tax, not a penalty: First, for most Americans the amount due will be far less than the price of insurance, and, by statute, it can never be more. It may often be a reasonable financial decision to make the payment rather than purchase insurance, unlike the "prohibitory" financial punishment in *Drexel Furniture*. Second, the individual mandate contains no scienter requirement. Third, the payment is collected solely by the IRS through the normal means of taxation—except that the Service is *not* allowed to use those means most suggestive of a punitive sanction, such as criminal prosecution. See § 5000A(g)(2). The reasons the Court in *Drexel Furniture* held that what was called a "tax" there was a penalty support the conclusion that what is called a "penalty" here may be viewed as a tax.

None of this is to say that the payment is not intended to affect individual conduct. Although the payment will raise considerable revenue, it is plainly designed to expand health insurance coverage. But taxes that seek to influence conduct are nothing new. Some of our earliest federal taxes sought to deter the purchase of imported manufactured goods in order to foster the growth of domestic industry. Today, federal and state taxes can compose more than half the retail price of cigarettes, not just to raise more money, but to encourage people to quit smoking. And we have upheld such obviously regulatory measures as taxes on selling marijuana and sawed-off shotguns. See *United States v. Sanchez*, 340 U.S. 42, 44–45 (1950); *Sonzinsky v. United States*, 300 U.S. 506 (1937). Indeed, "[e]very tax is in some measure regulatory. To some extent it interposes an economic impediment to the activity taxed as compared with others not taxed." *Sonzinsky*, *supra*, at 513. That § 5000A seeks to shape decisions about whether to buy health insurance does not mean that it cannot be a valid exercise of the taxing power.

In distinguishing penalties from taxes, this Court has explained that "if the concept of penalty means anything, it means punishment for an unlawful act or omission." *United States v. Reorganized CF & I Fabricators of Utah, Inc.*, 518 U.S. 213, 224 (1996). While the individual mandate clearly aims to induce the purchase of health insurance, it need not be read to declare that failing to do so is unlawful. Neither the Act nor any other law attaches negative legal consequences to not buying health insurance, beyond requiring a payment to the IRS. The Government agrees with that reading, confirming that if someone chooses to pay rather than obtain health insurance, they have fully complied with the law.

Indeed, it is estimated that four million people each year will choose to pay the IRS rather than buy insurance. We would expect Congress to be troubled by that prospect if such conduct were unlawful. That Congress apparently regards such extensive failure to comply with the mandate as tolerable suggests that Congress did not think it was creating four million outlaws. It suggests instead that the shared responsibility payment merely imposes a tax citizens may lawfully choose to pay in lieu of buying health insurance. . . .

The joint dissenters argue that we cannot uphold § 5000A as a tax because Congress did not "frame" it as such. *Post*, at 2650–2651. In effect, they contend that even if the Constitution permits Congress to do exactly what we interpret this statute to do, the law must be struck down because Congress used the wrong labels. An example may help illustrate why labels should not control here. Suppose Congress enacted a statute providing that every taxpayer who owns a house without energy efficient windows must pay $50 to the IRS. The amount due is adjusted based on factors such as taxable income and joint filing status, and is paid along with the taxpayer's income tax return. Those whose income is below the filing threshold need not pay. The required payment is not called a "tax," a "penalty," or anything else. No one would doubt that this law imposed a tax, and was within Congress's power to tax. That conclusion should not change simply because Congress used the word "penalty" to describe the payment. Interpreting such a law to be a tax would hardly "[i]mpos[e] a tax through judicial legislation." *Post*, at 2655. Rather, it would give practical effect to the Legislature's enactment. . . .

Even if the taxing power enables Congress to impose a tax on not obtaining health insurance, any tax must still comply with other requirements in the Constitution. Plaintiffs argue that the shared responsibility payment does not do so, citing Article I, § 9, clause 4. That clause provides: "No Capitation, or other direct, Tax shall be laid, unless in Proportion to the Census or Enumeration herein before directed to be taken." This requirement means that any "direct Tax" must be apportioned so that each State pays in proportion to its population. According to the plaintiffs, if the individual mandate imposes a tax, it is a direct tax, and it is unconstitutional because Congress made no effort to apportion it among the States.

Even when the Direct Tax Clause was written it was unclear what else, other than a capitation (also known as a "head tax" or a "poll tax"), might be a direct tax. Soon after the framing, Congress passed a tax on ownership of carriages, over James Madison's objection that it was an unapportioned direct tax. This Court upheld the tax, in part reasoning that apportioning such a tax would make little sense, because it would have required taxing carriage owners at dramatically different rates depending on how many carriages were in their home State. See *Hylton v. United States*, 3 Dall. 171, 174 (1796) (opinion of Chase, J.). The Court was unanimous, and those Justices who wrote opinions either directly asserted or strongly suggested that only two forms of taxation were direct: capitations and land taxes. See *id.*, at 175; *id.*, at 177 (opinion of Paterson, J.). . . .

That narrow view of what a direct tax might be persisted for a century. . . . In 1895, we expanded our interpretation to include taxes on personal property and income from personal property, in the course of striking down aspects of the federal income tax. *Pollock v. Farmers' Loan & Trust Co.*, 158 U.S. 601, 618 (1895). That result was overturned by the Sixteenth Amendment, although we continued to consider taxes on personal property to be direct taxes. See *Eisner v. Macomber*, 252 U.S. 189, 218–219 (1920).

A tax on going without health insurance does not fall within any recognized category of direct tax. It is not a capitation. Capitations are taxes paid by every person, "without regard to property, profession, or *any other circumstance*." *Hylton*, *supra*, at 175 (opinion of Chase, J.) (emphasis altered). The whole point of the shared responsibility payment is that it is triggered by specific circumstances—earning a certain amount of income but not obtaining health insurance. The payment is also plainly not a tax on the ownership of land or personal property. The shared responsibility payment is thus not a direct tax that must be apportioned among the several States.

There may, however, be a more fundamental objection to a tax on those who lack health insurance. Even if only a tax, the payment under § 5000A(b) remains a burden that the Federal Government imposes for an omission, not an act. . . .

Three considerations allay this concern. First, and most importantly, it is abundantly clear the Constitution does not guarantee that individuals may avoid taxation through inactivity. A capitation, after all, is a tax that everyone must pay simply for existing, and capitations are expressly contemplated by the Constitution. The Court today holds that our Constitution protects us from federal regulation under the Commerce Clause so long as we abstain from the regulated activity. But from its creation, the Constitution has made no such promise with respect to taxes. See Letter from Benjamin Franklin to M. Le Roy (Nov. 13, 1789) ("Our new Constitution is now established . . . but in this world nothing can be said to be certain, except death and taxes"). . . .

Second, Congress's ability to use its taxing power to influence conduct is not without limits. A few of our cases policed these limits aggressively, invalidating punitive exactions obviously designed to regulate behavior otherwise regarded at the time as beyond federal authority. See, *e.g., Drexel Furniture*, 259 U.S. 20. . . . [We] maintained that "there comes a time in the extension of the penalizing features of the so-called tax when it loses its character as such and becomes a mere penalty with the characteristics of regulation and punishment.". . .

Third, although the breadth of Congress's power to tax is greater than its power to regulate commerce, the taxing power does not give Congress the same degree of control over individual behavior. . . . Congress's authority under the taxing power is limited to requiring an individual to pay money into the Federal Treasury, no more. If a tax is properly paid, the Government has no power to compel or punish individuals subject to it. We do not make light of the severe burden that taxation—especially taxation motivated by a regulatory purpose—can impose. But imposition of a tax nonetheless leaves an individual with a lawful choice to do or not do a certain act, so long as he is willing to pay a tax levied on that choice.

The Affordable Care Act's requirement that certain individuals pay a financial penalty for not obtaining health insurance may reasonably be characterized as a tax. Because the Constitution permits such a tax, it is not our role to forbid it, or to pass upon its wisdom or fairness.[7]

---

[7] **Questions:** In 2017, a Republican-controlled Congress passed the Tax Cuts and Jobs Act of 2017, Pub. L. No. 115–97, 131 Stat. 2054, in which it set the Affordable Care Act's "shared responsibility payment" at zero dollars. Is a tax that does not produce any revenue still a tax? *See California v. Texas*, 141 S. Ct. 2104, 2113 (2021) (dismissing a challenge to the amended Affordable Care Act on procedural grounds without answering this question).

CHAPTER 6

WHAT IS THE SCOPE OF CONGRESS'S POWER TO SPEND FOR THE GENERAL WELFARE?

ARTICLE I, SECTION 8, CLAUSE 1: The Congress shall have Power To lay and collect Taxes, Duties, Imposts and Excises, to pay the Debts and provide for the common Defence and general Welfare of the United States; but all Duties, Imposts and Excises shall be uniform throughout the United States; . . .—And

> **CLAUSE 18:** To make all Laws which shall be necessary and proper for carrying into Execution the foregoing Powers, and all other Powers vested by this Constitution in the Government of the United States, or in any Department or Officer thereof.

ARTICLE I, SECTION 9, CLAUSE 7: No Money shall be drawn from the Treasury, but in Consequence of Appropriations made by Law; and a regular Statement and Account of the Receipts and Expenditures of all public Money shall be published from time to time.

TENTH AMENDMENT (1791): The powers not delegated to the United States by the Constitution, nor prohibited by it to the States, are reserved to the States respectively, or to the people.

ELEVENTH AMENDMENT (1795): The Judicial power of the United States shall not be construed to extend to any suit in law or equity, commenced or prosecuted against one of the United States by Citizens of another State, or by Citizens or Subjects of any Foreign State.

tax
gen welfare
nec & proper
law decides spending
states rights
Jurisdiction

6.1 SPENDING AS AN INDEPENDENT POWER

There are at least two ways to read the opening sentence of Article I, Section 8, which gives Congress "Power To lay and collect Taxes, Duties, Imposts and Excises, to pay the Debts and provide for the common Defence and general Welfare of the United States." A broad reading interprets this sentence to give Congress three powers: Congress can (1) collect taxes, (2) pay debts, *and* (3) provide for the common defense and general welfare. A narrow reading interprets this sentence to give Congress only one power: Congress can (1) collect taxes *only for the purpose of* paying debts and providing for the common defense and general welfare.

broad & narrow reading

The difference between these two interpretations is significant, particularly for Congress's power to spend money. The broad reading treats the power to "provide for the . . . general Welfare" as an independent power, allowing Congress to spend money on any project anywhere in the country. The narrow reading, by contrast, denies that this sentence empowers Congress to spend money. For adherents of this interpretation, Congress may spend money only when necessary and proper to exercise one of its enumerated powers, such as the power to "establish Post Offices and post Roads."

The drafting history of this sentence at the Constitutional Convention doesn't clear up the ambiguity between the broad and narrow interpretations. Early drafts of the sentence gave Congress a power to lay and collect taxes but said nothing further. *See* 2 *The Records of the Federal Convention of 1787*, at 305 (Max Farrand ed., 1911). The final version of the sentence was added by a committee of style on which Alexander Hamilton and James Madison sat as members. *Id.* at 497.

Yet, after the convention, Hamilton and Madison offered opposite interpretations of the sentence, with Hamilton supporting the broad reading and Madison the narrow one. In *The Federalist No. 30*, for example, Hamilton explained that the Constitution empowered Congress to provide "for the support of the national civil list; for the payment of the national debts contracted, or that may be contracted; and, in general, for all those matters which will call for disbursements out of the national treasury." *The Federalist No. 30*, at 188 (Alexander Hamilton) (Jacob E. Cooke ed., 1961). He added in *The Federalist No. 34* that "the objects that will require a Federal provision in respect to revenue . . . are altogether unlimited," and it would "be the extreme of folly" to attempt to predict what the federal government might need to spend money on in the remote future. *The Federalist No. 34*, at 210–11 (Alexander Hamilton) (Jacob E. Cooke ed., 1961). But only six essays later, in *The Federalist No. 41*, Madison considered it "an absurdity" that Congress possessed "an unlimited power of providing for the common defense and general welfare." *The Federalist No. 41*, at 278 (James Madison) (Jacob E. Cooke ed., 1961). Instead, he argued that the sentence merely gave context for how Congress could exercise the rest of its enumerated powers listed in Article I, Section 8.

Hamilton and Madison never resolved their competing interpretations of this *general welfare* language. As secretary of the Treasury, Hamilton urged Congress to appropriate money for the construction of internal improvements and to provide subsidies for important industries. Over the country's first few decades, Congress complied, spending money to support fisheries, paying $15 million for the purchase of the Louisiana Territory, and authorizing the construction of a national road to connect Cumberland, Maryland, to Ohio. *See* Act of Feb. 16, 1792, ch. 6, 1 Stat. 229 (fisheries); Act of Oct. 31, 1803, ch. 1, 2 Stat. 245 (Louisiana); Act of Mar. 29, 1806, ch. 19, 2 Stat. 357 (road). But when Madison became president in 1809, he expressed doubt that any clause of the Constitution gave Congress the power to spend money on subsidies or construction.

6.1.1

President Madison's Veto of the Bonus Bill

Mar. 3, 1817 (*The Papers of James Madison* (Library of Congress))

On the final day of his administration, Madison delivered the following veto message, excerpted in its entirety. The veto rejected a bill that would have used dividends and other "bonuses" from the Second Bank of the United States to pay for infrastructure in the newly acquired Louisiana Territory.

■ TO THE HOUSE OF REPRESENTATIVES OF THE UNITED STATES:[1]

Having considered the bill this day presented to me entitled "An act to set apart and pledge certain funds for internal improvements," and which sets apart and pledges funds "for constructing roads and canals, and improving the navigation of water courses, in order to facilitate, promote, and give security to internal commerce among the several States, and to render more easy and less expensive the means and provisions for the common defense," I am constrained by the insuperable difficulty I feel in reconciling the bill with the Constitution of the United States to return it with that objection to the House of Representatives, in which it originated.

The legislative powers vested in Congress are specified and enumerated in the eighth section of the first article of the Constitution, and it does not appear that the power proposed to be exercised by the bill is among the enumerated powers, or that it falls by any just interpretation within the power to make laws necessary and proper for carrying into execution those or other powers vested by the Constitution in the Government of the United States.

"The power to regulate commerce among the several States" can not include a power to construct roads and canals, and to improve the navigation of water courses in order to facilitate, promote, and secure such a commerce without a latitude of construction departing from the ordinary import of the terms strengthened by the known inconveniences which doubtless led to the grant of this remedial power to Congress.

To refer the power in question to the clause "to provide for the common defense and general welfare" would be contrary to the established and consistent rules of interpretation, as rendering the special and careful enumeration of powers which follow the clause nugatory and improper. Such a view of the Constitution would have the effect of giving to Congress a general power of legislation instead of the defined and limited one hitherto understood to belong to them, the terms "common defense and general welfare" embracing every object and act within the purview of a legislative trust. It would have the effect of subjecting both the Constitution and laws of the several States in all cases not specifically exempted to be superseded by laws of Congress, it being expressly declared "that the Constitution of the United States and laws made in pursuance thereof shall be the supreme law of the land, and the judges of every State shall be bound thereby, anything in the constitution or laws of any State to the contrary notwithstanding." Such a view of the Constitution, finally, would have the effect of excluding the judicial authority of the United States from its participation in guarding the boundary between the legislative powers of the General and the State Governments, inasmuch as questions relating to the general welfare,

---

[1] **As You Read, Consider:** Who does President James Madison think would be harmed by a broad interpretation of the *general welfare* language?

When, if ever, does he think it appropriate for Congress to spend money?

being questions of policy and expediency, are unsusceptible of judicial cognizance and decision.

A restriction of the power "to provide for the common defense and general welfare" to cases which are to be provided for by the expenditure of money would still leave within the legislative power of Congress all the great and most important measures of Government, money being the ordinary and necessary means of carrying them into execution.

If a general power to construct roads and canals, and to improve the navigation of water courses, with the train of powers incident thereto, be not possessed by Congress, the assent of the States in the mode provided in the bill can not confer the power. The only cases in which the consent and cession of particular States can extend the power of Congress are those specified and provided for in the Constitution.

I am not unaware of the great importance of roads and canals and the improved navigation of water courses, and that a power in the National Legislature to provide for them might be exercised with signal advantage to the general prosperity. But seeing that such a power is not expressly given by the Constitution, and believing that it can not be deduced from any part of it without an inadmissible latitude of construction and a reliance on insufficient precedents; believing also that the permanent success of the Constitution depends on a definite partition of powers between the General and the State Governments, and that no adequate landmarks would be left by the constructive extension of the powers of Congress as proposed in the bill, I have no option but to withhold my signature from it, and to cherishing the hope that its beneficial objects may be attained by a resort for the necessary powers to the same wisdom and virtue in the nation which established the Constitution in its actual form and providently marked out in the instrument itself a safe and practicable mode of improving it as experience might suggest.

6.1.2
United States v. Butler

297 U.S. 1 (1936)

Even after Madison stepped down from the presidency, his narrow reading of Congress's spending power dogged supporters of Hamilton's broad interpretation. Two years later, in *McCulloch v. Maryland*, Chief Justice John Marshall alluded to Madison's argument by suggesting in dicta that Congress's power "to establish post-offices and post-roads" might authorize it to construct roads. 17 U.S. (4 Wheat.) 316, 417 (1819). But in 1822, President James Monroe vetoed a road-construction bill similar to the one that Madison had vetoed, explaining that the power to establish post roads meant only that Congress could designate existing roads as good for travel by postal carriers. *See* 2 *A Compilation of the Messages and Papers of the Presidents, 1789–1907*, at 142–43 (James D. Richardson ed., 1908). Similarly, in 1830, when Kentucky politician Henry Clay pushed Congress to subsidize the construction of another major road, President Andrew Jackson vetoed the bill. The president quoted Madison's earlier veto message and argued that "[i]f it be the wish of the people that the construction of roads and canals should be conducted by the Federal Government, it is not only highly expedient, but indispensably necessary, that a previous amendment of the Constitution . . . should be made." *Id.* at 491–92.

Some of the opposition to a broad reading of the General Welfare Clause was motivated by the fear that a powerful federal government might interfere with slavery. Politicians in South Carolina and other Southern states argued that if the clause permitted Congress to build roads or pass tariffs, then the clause might also permit Congress to purchase the freedom of enslaved people or even to declare that abolition was within the "general welfare." *See* Robert Elder, *Calhoun* 232–34 (2021). Before the Civil War, it therefore remained an open question whether Congress could spend money to construct internal improvements or whether its spending power was merely incidental to other enumerated powers. *Compare, e.g., Searight v. Stokes*, 44 U.S. (3 How.) 151, 166 (1845) (suggesting that Congress could compact with states regarding the use and upkeep of a post road), *with United States v. R.R. Bridge Co.*, 27 F. Cas. 686, 689 (C.C.N.D. Ill. 1855) (No. 16,114) (McLean, J.) (holding that Congress could designate existing roads as postal roads but that it lacked the power to construct them).

After the post-Civil War amendments abolished slavery, by contrast, the Supreme Court began to explicitly hold that Congress could use its Article I powers to construct internal improvements. *See, e.g., California v. Cent. Pac. R.R. Co.*, 127 U.S. 1, 39 (1888) (permitting Congress to charter railroads); *Kohl v. United States*, 91 U.S. 367, 372 (1876) (permitting Congress to exercise the power of eminent domain). However, the Court never expressly weighed in on the scope of Congress's spending power until the 1930s, when extreme times called for extreme measures.

On October 24, 1929, the New York Stock Exchange witnessed the beginning of the worst stock market crash in U.S. history, plunging economies around the world into the Great Depression. Three years later, as U.S. unemployment levels rose from 4 percent to 25 percent, Franklin D. Roosevelt campaigned for the presidency on a platform of providing a "New Deal" for the American people. *See* Ira Katznelson, *Fear Itself: The New Deal and the Origins of Our Time* 487 (2013). Roosevelt won in a landslide. Upon taking office, he spent the first one hundred days of his administration issuing and pushing Congress to enact dozens of potential solutions to the Great Depression. Most of these early New Deal programs were experimental and quickly drafted. Three of them—the suspension of the gold standard; the National Industrial Relations Act of 1933, Pub. L. No. 73–67, 48 Stat. 195; and the Agricultural Adjustment Act of 1933, Pub. L. No. 73–10, 48 Stat. 31—would become the subjects of major Supreme Court cases about the scope of Congress's powers.

The first of these that we'll consider, the Agricultural Adjustment Act, was designed to raise farm prices by limiting production. The statute provided that any farmer who agreed to reduce production of a specified commodity would receive a "benefit payment" from the federal government. 48 Stat. at 35. The revenue for this payment, in turn, came from an excise tax levied on the person who first processed that commodity. William Butler, a cotton processor, objected to paying this processing tax on the ground that the entire statute was unconstitutional. Before the Supreme Court, he invoked Madison's old argument that Congress's power to tax and spend didn't include the power to subsidize private farmers.

In *United States v. Butler*, 297 U.S. 1 (1936), the Court found Butler's arguments persuasive.

■ MR. JUSTICE ROBERTS delivered the opinion of the Court.[2]

In this case we must determine whether certain provisions of the Agricultural Adjustment Act, 1933, conflict with the Federal Constitution. . . .

The Government asserts that even if the respondents may question the propriety of the appropriation embodied in the statute their attack must fail because Article I, § 8 of the Constitution authorizes the contemplated expenditure of the funds raised by the tax. This contention presents the great and the controlling question in the case. We approach its decision with a sense of our grave responsibility to render judgment in accordance with the principles established for the governance of all three branches of the Government. . . .

Article I, § 8, of the Constitution vests sundry powers in the Congress. . . . The clause thought to authorize the legislation,—the first,—confers upon the Congress power "to lay and collect Taxes, Duties, Imposts and Excises, to pay the Debts and provide for the common Defence and general Welfare of the United States. . . ." It is not contended that this provision grants power to regulate agricultural production upon the theory that such legislation would promote the general welfare. The Government concedes that the phrase "to provide for the general welfare" qualifies the power "to lay and collect taxes." The view that the clause grants power to provide for the general welfare, independently of the taxing power, has never been authoritatively accepted. Mr. Justice Story points out that if it were adopted "it is obvious that under color of the generality of the words, to 'provide for the common defence and general welfare,' the government of the United States is, in reality, a government of general and unlimited powers, notwithstanding the subsequent enumeration of specific powers." The true construction undoubtedly is that the only thing granted is the power to tax for the purpose of providing funds for payment of the nation's debts and making provision for the general welfare.

Nevertheless the Government asserts that warrant is found in this clause for the adoption of the Agricultural Adjustment Act. The argument is that Congress may appropriate and authorize the spending of moneys for the "general welfare"; that the phrase should be liberally construed to cover anything conducive to national welfare; that decision as to what will promote such welfare rests with Congress alone, and the courts may not review its determination; and finally that the appropriation under attack was in fact for the general welfare of the United States.

The Congress is expressly empowered to lay taxes to provide for the general welfare. Funds in the Treasury as a result of taxation may be expended only through appropriation. (Art. I, § 9, cl. 7.) They can never accomplish the objects for which they were collected unless the power to appropriate is as broad as the power to tax.

---

2 **As You Read, Consider:** Does Justice Owen Roberts agree with James Madison's narrow interpretation of the *general welfare* language, or does he agree with Alexander Hamilton's broad interpretation?

Does he think that the broad interpretation would give Congress an unlimited power, or does he think something in the Constitution would impose limits?

The necessary implication from the terms of the grant is that the public funds may be appropriated "to provide for the general welfare of the United States." These words cannot be meaningless, else they would not have been used. The conclusion must be that they were intended to limit and define the granted power to raise and to expend money. How shall they be construed to effectuate the intent of the instrument?

Since the foundation of the Nation sharp differences of opinion have persisted as to the true interpretation of the phrase. Madison asserted it amounted to no more than a reference to the other powers enumerated in the subsequent clauses of the same section; that, as the United States is a government of limited and enumerated powers, the grant of power to tax and spend for the general national welfare must be confined to the enumerated legislative fields committed to the Congress. In this view the phrase is mere tautology, for taxation and appropriation are or may be necessary incidents of the exercise of any of the enumerated legislative powers. Hamilton, on the other hand, maintained the clause confers a power separate and distinct from those later enumerated, is not restricted in meaning by the grant of them, and Congress consequently has a substantive power to tax and to appropriate, limited only by the requirement that it shall be exercised to provide for the general welfare of the United States. Each contention has had the support of those whose views are entitled to weight. This court has noticed the question, but has never found it necessary to decide which is the true construction. Mr. Justice Story, in his Commentaries, espouses the Hamiltonian position. We shall not review the writings of public men and commentators or discuss the legislative practice. Study of all these leads us to conclude that the reading advocated by Mr. Justice Story is the correct one. While, therefore, the power to tax is not unlimited, its confines are set in the clause which confers it, and not in those of § 8 which bestow and define the legislative powers of the Congress. It results that the power of Congress to authorize expenditure of public moneys for public purposes is not limited by the direct grants of legislative power found in the Constitution.

But the adoption of the broader construction leaves the power to spend subject to limitations. . . . That the qualifying phrase ["for the common Defence and general Welfare"] must be given effect all advocates of broad construction admit. . . . As elsewhere throughout the Constitution the section in question lays down principles which control the use of the power, and does not attempt meticulous or detailed directions. . . .

We are not now required to ascertain the scope of the phrase "general welfare of the United States" or to determine whether an appropriation in aid of agriculture falls within it. Wholly apart from that question, another principle embedded in our Constitution prohibits the enforcement of the Agricultural Adjustment Act. The act invades the reserved rights of the states. It is a statutory plan to regulate and control agricultural production, a matter beyond the powers delegated to the federal government. The tax, the appropriation of the funds raised, and the direction for their disbursement, are but parts of the plan. They are but means to an unconstitutional end.[3]

---

[3] **Note:** The analysis in these paragraphs is confusing.

To understand what Roberts is getting at, imagine that Congress considered two bills in 1933 when it wanted to prevent farmers from producing excess cotton. The first bill, a hypothetical "compulsory" bill, would have ordered certain farmers not to produce cotton. Under then-existing precedent, such a bill would have been unconstitutional: nothing in the Constitution permitted Congress to compel farmers not to produce cotton.

Now consider the bill that Congress actually passed. The Agricultural Adjustment Act accomplished the same purpose as the hypothetical bill by paying certain farmers a massive subsidy not to produce cotton. The subsidy was intended to be so large that no farmer would

From the accepted doctrine that the United States is a government of delegated powers, it follows that those not expressly granted, or reasonably to be implied from such as are conferred, are reserved to the states or to the people. To forestall any suggestion to the contrary, the Tenth Amendment was adopted. The same proposition, otherwise stated, is that powers not granted are prohibited. None to regulate agricultural production is given, and therefore legislation by Congress for that purpose is forbidden. . . .

The Government asserts that whatever might be said against the validity of the plan if compulsory, it is constitutionally sound because the end is accomplished by voluntary cooperation. There are two sufficient answers to the contention. The regulation is not in fact voluntary. The farmer, of course, may refuse to comply, but the price of such refusal is the loss of benefits. The amount offered is intended to be sufficient to exert pressure on him to agree to the proposed regulation. The power to confer or withhold unlimited benefits is the power to coerce or destroy. If the cotton grower elects not to accept the benefits, he will receive less for his crops; those who receive payments will be able to undersell him. The result may well be financial ruin. . . . This is coercion by economic pressure. The asserted power of choice is illusory. . . .[4]

We are not here concerned with a conditional appropriation of money, nor with a provision that if certain conditions are not complied with the appropriation shall no longer be available. By the Agricultural Adjustment Act the amount of the tax is appropriated to be expended only in payment under contracts whereby the parties bind themselves to regulation by the Federal Government. There is an obvious difference between a statute stating the conditions upon which moneys shall be expended and one effective only upon assumption of a contractual obligation to submit to a regulation which otherwise could not be enforced. Many examples pointing the distinction might be cited. We are referred to appropriations in aid of education, and it is said that no one has doubted the power of Congress to stipulate the sort of education for which money shall be expended. But an appropriation to an educational institution which by its terms is to become available only if the beneficiary enters into a contract to teach doctrines subversive of the Constitution is clearly bad. An affirmance of the authority of Congress so to condition the expenditure of an appropriation would tend to nullify all constitutional limitations upon legislative power. . . .

Congress has no power to enforce its commands on the farmer to the ends sought by the Agricultural Adjustment Act. It must follow that it may not indirectly accomplish those ends by taxing and spending to purchase compliance. The Constitution and the entire plan of our government negative any such use of the power to tax and to spend as the act undertakes to authorize. It does not help to declare that local conditions throughout the nation have created a situation of national concern; for this is but to say that whenever there is a widespread similarity of local conditions, Congress may ignore constitutional limitations upon its own powers and usurp those reserved to the states. If, in lieu of compulsory regulation of subjects within the states' reserved jurisdiction, which is prohibited, the Congress could invoke the taxing and spending power as a means to accomplish the same end, clause 1 of § 8 of Article I would become the instrument for total subversion of the governmental powers reserved to the individual states. . . .

---

refuse it. Roberts explains here: If the hypothetical compulsory bill was unconstitutional, the "coercion" present in this real bill also must be "means to an unconstitutional end."

4 **Questions:** What constitutes "coercion by economic pressure"? Under the Court's rule, what constitutional options are available for Congress to get cotton farmers to produce less cotton?

Hamilton himself, the leading advocate of broad interpretation of the power to tax and to appropriate for the general welfare, never suggested that any power granted by the Constitution could be used for the destruction of local self-government in the states. Story countenances no such doctrine. It seems never to have occurred to them, or to those who have agreed with them, that the general welfare of the United States, (which has aptly been termed "an indestructible Union, composed of indestructible States,") might be served by obliterating the constituent members of the Union. But to this fatal conclusion the doctrine contended for would inevitably lead. And its sole premise is that, though the makers of the Constitution, in erecting the federal government, intended sedulously to limit and define its powers, so as to reserve to the states and the people sovereign power, to be wielded by the states and their citizens and not to be invaded by the United States, they nevertheless by a single clause gave power to the Congress to tear down the barriers, to invade the states' jurisdiction, and to become a parliament of the whole people, subject to no restrictions save such as are self-imposed. The argument when seen in its true character and in the light of its inevitable results must be rejected. . . .

6.2 CONDITIONAL SPENDING

United States v. Butler, 297 U.S. 1 (1936), is a confusing decision, one that drives in one direction and, in the middle of the opinion, pops a U-turn and heads the other way. In the first half, the Supreme Court decisively embraced Alexander Hamilton's interpretation of what has since become known as the Spending Clause or General Welfare Clause: Congress may constitutionally spend federal revenue on virtually any subject as long as that subject is intended to serve the common defense or general welfare. But in the second half of the decision, the Court declared that even if agriculture were an acceptable subject for federal spending, Congress may not engage in "coercion by economic pressure" and condition its spending in such a way that accomplishes a result that Congress could not accomplish directly. *Butler*, 297 U.S. at 71.

In the years since *Butler*, this implied limit on conditional expenditures has become the main source of litigation surrounding the Spending Clause. It took some time, however, for *Butler*'s implied limit to be enforced again.

Grants and conditions in Steward Machine Co.

Butler was one of several controversial Supreme Court decisions in President Franklin D. Roosevelt's first term that struck down New Deal and state responses to the Great Depression. By the time the decision was announced in 1936, the press and even the Roosevelt administration were castigating the justices as "The Nine Old Men" who were substituting their nineteenth-century economic theories for those of modern, democratic majorities. Jeff Shesol, *Supreme Power* 4 (2011).

In the presidential elections that fall, Roosevelt was reelected with the highest share of the popular vote in over a century. Roosevelt followed this win in February 1937 with a proposal to "pack" the Supreme Court by replacing six justices over the age of seventy with his own appointments. *Id.* at 304. Although the president's court-packing plan was very unpopular, he was popular enough that it looked likely to pass a hostile Congress.

Then, in May 1937, the Supreme Court announced a series of decisions that both upheld New Deal programs and reversed recent precedents regarding the Spending Clause, the Commerce Clause, and the Due Process Clause of the Fourteenth Amendment. Justice Owen Roberts, the author of *Butler*, was the swing voter in these decisions. The press later called his change of mind "the switch in time that saved nine" because the Court's 1937 decisions sapped the court-packing plan of its momentum. *See id.* at 429.

One of these 1937 decisions—*Steward Machine Co. v. Davis*, 301 U.S. 548 (1937)—upheld the Social Security Act of 1935, Pub. L. No. 74–271, 49 Stat. 620, from a similar challenge to that in *Butler*. The subject of *Steward Machine Co.* was a controversial spending condition included in the Social Security Act. In general, the statute taxed employers and spent the revenue on providing people with unemployment insurance. But if a state enacted its own unemployment-compensation law, then the Social Security Act would effectively pay the state and reduce the tax for local employers by 90 percent. Opponents of the law derided these conditional benefits as "weapons of coercion," claiming that their end was "to drive the state Legislatures under the whip of economic pressure into the enactment of unemployment compensation laws at the bidding of the central government." *Steward Machine Co.*, 301 U.S. at 587.

But the *Steward Machine Co.* Court resisted the comparison between these conditions and the grants it had just struck down as "coercion by economic pressure" in *Butler*. Where the grants in *Butler* "were coupled with coercive contracts, unlawful in their aim and oppressive in their consequences," the Court explained, the Social Security Act's conditions were mild enough that "the state is free at pleasure to disregard or to fulfill [them]." *Id.* at 592, 595. Although the Court declined to "fix the outermost line" after which "inducement or persuasion [goes] beyond the bounds of power," it held that none of the conditions on federal grants were coercive, and the federal government could use its spending power to indirectly regulate subjects outside of Congress's enumerated powers. Id. at 591; *see also Helvering v. Davis*, 301 U.S. 619, 640–41 (1937) (upholding the Social Security Act's old-age benefits).

Explosion of "conditional" laws

Steward Machine Co. opened a door that Congress immediately blazed through. Soon, Congress enacted hundreds of "grant-in-aid" laws in which it made federal funds available to states or individuals in exchange for the beneficiaries' acceptance of conditions. Many of these laws were modeled after the Smith-Lever Act of 1914, Pub. L. No. 63–95, 38 Stat. 372—alluded to approvingly in *Butler*—in which Congress gave money to states for developing their land-grant universities. Significantly, the Smith-Lever Act also required the receiving states to enact their own specified programs and to match a proportion of the federal grants with their own funds.

Later examples of this sort of legislation included Title VI of the Civil Rights Act of 1964, Pub. L. No. 88–352, 78 Stat. 241, Title IX of the Education Amendments of 1972, Pub. L. No. 92–318, 86 Stat. 235, and Title V of the Rehabilitation Act of 1973, Pub. L. No. 93–112, 87 Stat. 355—all of which conditioned the receipt of federal funds on the recipient's agreement to abide by federal antidiscrimination law. In reviewing these sorts of laws, the Supreme Court favorably used the term *cooperative federalism*. *King v. Smith*, 392 U.S. 309, 316 (1968) (interpreting the Aid to Families with Dependent Children program). The Court also broadly upheld Congress's power to condition the receipt of federal funds on a beneficiary's compliance with certain directives. *See, e.g.*, *Oklahoma v. U.S. Civ. Serv. Comm'n*, 330 U.S. 127, 143–44 (1947) (upholding the Hatch Act's prohibition on political activity by any government beneficiary of federal funds).

Implied limits once again

Beginning in the 1980s, however, the Supreme Court under Chief Justice Warren Burger began to resuscitate *Butler*'s implied limits on the spending power.

In *Pennhurst State School & Hospital v. Halderman*, 451 U.S. 1 (1981), the Court declined to apply a federal antidiscrimination law to a state hospital because the text of the law did not make it obvious that, in accepting federal funds, the state had agreed to abide by the law's restrictions. "Congress must express clearly its intent to impose conditions on the grant of federal funds so that the States can knowingly decide whether or not to accept those funds," the Court wrote. *Halderman*, 451 U.S. at 3.

Six years later, the Court distilled its post-*Butler* precedent to serve up a multifactor test for when Congress exceeds its limits.

6.2.1

South Dakota v. Dole

483 U.S. 203 (1987)

In 1919, Nebraska became the thirty-sixth state to ratify the Eighteenth Amendment, giving Congress the express power to prohibit the production and sale of alcohol. But Prohibition proved to be a failed experiment. Only fourteen years later, the Twenty-First Amendment repealed the Eighteenth Amendment. Along with repeal, Congress lost the power to regulate directly the intrastate sale of alcohol. *See United States v. Chambers*, 291 U.S. 217, 222 (1934).

Despite this loss of power, in 1984, as part of a movement to raise the nationwide drinking age, Congress enacted the National Minimum Drinking Age Act. The act withheld federal highway funds from any state that failed to raise its drinking age to twenty-one. Pub. L. No. 98–363, 98 Stat. 435, 437. South Dakota, one of thirty-four states with a lower drinking age (nineteen), sued Elizabeth Dole, the secretary of transportation, claiming, as in *Butler*, that Congress could not use its spending power to achieve a result that it could not constitutionally direct.

Although the Court in *South Dakota v. Dole*, 483 U.S. 203 (1987), recognized that the spending power is not unlimited, it applied a multifactor test to conclude that Congress did not exceed its power in this case.

■ CHIEF JUSTICE REHNQUIST delivered the opinion of the Court.[5]

[T]he Constitution empowers Congress to "lay and collect Taxes, Duties, Imposts, and Excises, to pay the Debts and provide for the common Defence and general Welfare of the United States." Art. I, § 8, cl. 1. Incident to this power, Congress may attach conditions on the receipt of federal funds, and has repeatedly employed the power "to further broad policy objectives by conditioning receipt of federal moneys upon compliance by the recipient with federal statutory and administrative directives." *Fullilove v. Klutznick*, 448 U. S. 448, 474 (1980) (opinion of Burger, C. J.). See *Oklahoma v. Civil Service Comm'n*, 330 U. S. 127, 143–144 (1947); *Steward Machine Co. v. Davis*, 301 U. S. 548 (1937). The breadth of this power was made clear in *United States v. Butler*, 297 U. S. 1, 66 (1936), where the Court, resolving a longstanding debate over the scope of the Spending Clause, determined that "the power of Congress to authorize expenditure of public moneys for public purposes is not limited by the direct grants of legislative power found in the Constitution." Thus, objectives not thought to be within Article I's "enumerated legislative fields," *id.*, at 65, may nevertheless be attained through the use of the spending power and the conditional grant of federal funds.

The spending power is of course not unlimited, *Pennhurst State School and Hospital v. Halderman*, 451 U. S. 1 (1981), but is instead subject to several general restrictions articulated in our cases. The first of these limitations is derived from the language of the Constitution itself: the exercise of the spending power must be in pursuit of "the general welfare." See *Helvering v. Davis*, 301 U. S. 619, 640–641 (1937); *United States v. Butler*, *supra*, at 65. In considering whether a particular expenditure is intended to serve general public purposes, courts should defer substantially to the judgment of Congress. Second, we have required that if Congress desires to condition the States' receipt of federal funds, it "must do so unambiguously . . ., enabl[ing] the States to exercise their choice knowingly, cognizant of the consequences of their participation." *Pennhurst State School and Hospital v. Halderman*, *supra*, at 17. Third, our cases have suggested (without significant elaboration) that conditions on federal grants might be illegitimate if they are unrelated "to the federal interest in particular national projects or programs." *Massachusetts v. United States*, 435 U. S. 444, 461 (1978) (plurality opinion). Finally, we have noted

---

[5] **As You Read, Consider:** Chief Justice William Rehnquist announces a list of implied limits on Congress's power to spend money. Where in the Constitution do these limits come from? If they are not based in text, what other principles do they serve?

that other constitutional provisions may provide an independent bar to the conditional grant of federal funds. *King v. Smith*, 392 U. S. 309, 333, n. 34 (1968).[6]

South Dakota does not seriously claim that § 158 is inconsistent with any of the first three restrictions mentioned above. We can readily conclude that the provision is designed to serve the general welfare, especially in light of the fact that "the concept of welfare or the opposite is shaped by Congress. . . ." *Helvering v. Davis*, *supra*, at 645. Congress found that the differing drinking ages in the States created particular incentives for young persons to combine their desire to drink with their ability to drive, and that this interstate problem required a national solution. The means it chose to address this dangerous situation were reasonably calculated to advance the general welfare. The conditions upon which States receive the funds, moreover, could not be more clearly stated by Congress. See 23 U. S. C. § 158. And the State itself, rather than challenging the germaneness of the condition to federal purposes, admits that it "has never contended that the congressional action was . . . unrelated to a national concern in the absence of the Twenty-first Amendment." Brief for Petitioner 52. Indeed, the condition imposed by Congress is directly related to one of the main purposes for which highway funds are expended—safe interstate travel. See 23 U. S. C. § 101(b). This goal of the interstate highway system had been frustrated by varying drinking ages among the States. A Presidential commission appointed to study alcohol-related accidents and fatalities on the Nation's highways concluded that the lack of uniformity in the States' drinking ages created "an incentive to drink and drive" because "young persons commut[e] to border States where the drinking age is lower." Presidential Commission on Drunk Driving, Final Report 11 (1983). By enacting § 158, Congress conditioned the receipt of federal funds in a way reasonably calculated to address this particular impediment to a purpose for which the funds are expended.

The remaining question about the validity of § 158—and the basic point of disagreement between the parties—is whether the Twenty-first Amendment constitutes an "independent constitutional bar" to the conditional grant of federal funds. Petitioner, relying on its view that the Twenty-first Amendment prohibits *direct* regulation of drinking ages by Congress, asserts that "Congress may not use the spending power to regulate that which it is prohibited from regulating directly under the Twenty-first Amendment." Brief for Petitioner 52–53. But our cases show that this "independent constitutional bar" limitation on the spending power is not of the kind petitioner suggests. *United States v. Butler*, *supra*, at 66, for example, established that the constitutional limitations on Congress when exercising its spending power are less exacting than those on its authority to regulate directly.

We have also held that a perceived Tenth Amendment limitation on congressional regulation of state affairs did not concomitantly limit the range of conditions legitimately placed on federal grants. In *Oklahoma v. Civil Service Comm'n*, 330 U. S. 127 (1947), the Court considered the validity of the Hatch Act insofar as it was applied to political activities of state officials whose employment was financed in whole or in part with federal funds.[7] The State contended that an order under this provision to withhold certain federal funds unless a state official was removed invaded its sovereignty in violation of the Tenth Amendment. Though finding that "the United States is not concerned with, and has no power to regulate, local political activities

---

[6] **Question:** Among the four limits listed in the previous paragraph, which do you think is most likely to invalidate a law that conditions federal funds on a state's agreement to do something?

[7] **Note:** The Hatch Act of 1939, Pub. L. No. 76–252, 53 Stat. 1147, prohibits federal employees and state officials paid with federal funds from engaging in political campaign activities.

as such of state officials," the Court nevertheless held that the Federal Government "does have power to fix the terms upon which its money allotments to states shall be disbursed." *Id.*, at 143. The Court found no violation of the State's sovereignty because the State could, and did, adopt "the 'simple expedient' of not yielding to what she urges is federal coercion. The offer of benefits to a state by the United States dependent upon cooperation by the state with federal plans, assumedly for the general welfare, is not unusual." *Id.*, at 143–144 (citation omitted). . . .

These cases establish that the "independent constitutional bar" limitation on the spending power is not, as petitioner suggests, a prohibition on the indirect achievement of objectives which Congress is not empowered to achieve directly. Instead, we think that the language in our earlier opinions stands for the unexceptionable proposition that the power may not be used to induce the States to engage in activities that would themselves be unconstitutional. Thus, for example, a grant of federal funds conditioned on invidiously discriminatory state action or the infliction of cruel and unusual punishment would be an illegitimate exercise of the Congress' broad spending power. But no such claim can be or is made here. Were South Dakota to succumb to the blandishments offered by Congress and raise its drinking age to 21, the State's action in so doing would not violate the constitutional rights of anyone.

Our decisions have recognized that in some circumstances the financial inducement offered by Congress might be so coercive as to pass the point at which "pressure turns into compulsion." *Steward Machine Co. v. Davis*, *supra*, at 590. Here, however, Congress has directed only that a State desiring to establish a minimum drinking age lower than 21 lose a relatively small percentage of certain federal highway funds. Petitioner contends that the coercive nature of this program is evident from the degree of success it has achieved. We cannot conclude, however, that a conditional grant of federal money of this sort is unconstitutional simply by reason of its success in achieving the congressional objective.[8]

When we consider, for a moment, that all South Dakota would lose if she adheres to her chosen course as to a suitable minimum drinking age is 5% of the funds otherwise obtainable under specified highway grant programs, the argument as to coercion is shown to be more rhetoric than fact. . . . Here Congress has offered relatively mild encouragement to the States to enact higher minimum drinking ages than they would otherwise choose. But the enactment of such laws remains the prerogative of the States not merely in theory but in fact. Even if Congress might lack the power to impose a national minimum drinking age directly, we conclude that encouragement to state action found in § 158 is a valid use of the spending power. . . .[9]

---

[8] **Question:** Does this paragraph introduce a fifth limit in addition to the four limits described earlier, or does it offer an application of one of those earlier limits?

[9] **Questions:** Note the inducement that Congress has offered in this case: lower your drinking age or lose 5 percent of federal highway funds. Does the Court suggest at what point "pressure turns into compulsion"? Fifty percent?

6.2.2

National Federation of Independent Business (NFIB) v. Sebelius

567 U.S. 519 (2012)

This case again. The legal opponents of the Affordable Care Act of 2010 challenged two distinct provisions of the law.

The first provision was the "individual mandate," in which Congress required most Americans to purchase health insurance or pay a penalty. We just talked about that in the section detailing the limits on Congress's taxing power for the purpose of regulation (section 5.4).

The second provision was commonly called the *Medicaid expansion*. It involved Congress's spending power, and *National Federation of Independent Business (NFIB) v. Sebelius*, 567 U.S. 519 (2012), describes the situation.

In contrast with the Court's ruling with regard to the first provision, the Court agreed with the National Federation of Independent Business and states with regard to the second provision, i.e., that the provision's conditions were coercive. Although this part of the chief justice's opinion was joined by only two justices, its conclusion was reached by four other justices—Antonin Scalia, Anthony Kennedy, Clarence Thomas, and Samuel Alito—making it the holding of the Court.

■ CHIEF JUSTICE ROBERTS . . . delivered . . . an opinion with respect to Part IV, in which JUSTICE BREYER and JUSTICE KAGAN join. . . .[10]

The second provision of the Affordable Care Act directly challenged here is the Medicaid expansion. Enacted in 1965, Medicaid offers federal funding to States to assist pregnant women, children, needy families, the blind, the elderly, and the disabled in obtaining medical care. See 42 U.S.C. § 1396a(a)(10). In order to receive that funding, States must comply with federal criteria governing matters such as who receives care and what services are provided at what cost. By 1982 every State had chosen to participate in Medicaid. Federal funds received through the Medicaid program have become a substantial part of state budgets, now constituting over 10 percent of most States' total revenue.

The Affordable Care Act expands the scope of the Medicaid program and increases the number of individuals the States must cover. For example, the Act requires state programs to provide Medicaid coverage to adults with incomes up to 133 percent of the federal poverty level, whereas many States now cover adults with children only if their income is considerably lower, and do not cover childless adults at all. See § 1396a(a). The Act increases federal funding to cover the States' costs in expanding Medicaid coverage, although States will bear a portion of the costs on their own. § 1396d(y)(1). If a State does not comply with the Act's new coverage

---

10 **As You Read, Consider:** What is the federal funding at issue in this case? What conditions did Congress place on this funding?

Which of the limits identified in *South Dakota v. Dole* are relevant in this case?

What principle does Chief Justice John Roberts say he is protecting when the Court sets limits on Congress's ability to set conditions on federal funds?

requirements, it may lose not only the federal funding for those requirements, but all of its federal Medicaid funds. § 1396c. . . .

Along with their challenge to the individual mandate, the state plaintiffs in the Eleventh Circuit argued that the Medicaid expansion exceeds Congress's constitutional powers . . . under the Spending Clause. . . .

[IV]

The Spending Clause grants Congress the power "to pay the Debts and provide for the . . . general Welfare of the United States." U.S. Const., Art. I, § 8, cl. 1. We have long recognized that Congress may use this power to grant federal funds to the States, and may condition such a grant upon the States "taking certain actions that Congress could not require them to take." Such measures "encourage a State to regulate in a particular way, [and] influenc[e] a State's policy choices." The conditions imposed by Congress ensure that the funds are used by the States to "provide for the . . . general Welfare" in the manner Congress intended.

At the same time, our cases have recognized limits on Congress's power under the Spending Clause to secure state compliance with federal objectives. "We have repeatedly characterized . . . Spending Clause legislation as 'much in the nature of a contract.' " *Pennhurst State School and Hospital v. Halderman*, 451 U.S. 1, 17 (1981). The legitimacy of Congress's exercise of the spending power "thus rests on whether the State voluntarily and knowingly accepts the terms of the 'contract.' " *Pennhurst, supra*, at 17. Respecting this limitation is critical to ensuring that Spending Clause legislation does not undermine the status of the States as independent sovereigns in our federal system. That system "rests on what might at first seem a counter-intuitive insight, that 'freedom is enhanced by the creation of two governments, not one.' " For this reason, "the Constitution has never been understood to confer upon Congress the ability to require the States to govern according to Congress' instructions." Otherwise the two-government system established by the Framers would give way to a system that vests power in one central government, and individual liberty would suffer.

That insight has led this Court to strike down federal legislation that commandeers a State's legislative or administrative apparatus for federal purposes. It has also led us to scrutinize Spending Clause legislation to ensure that Congress is not using financial inducements to exert a "power akin to undue influence." *Steward Machine Co. v. Davis*, 301 U.S. 548, 590 (1937). Congress may use its spending power to create incentives for States to act in accordance with federal policies. But when "pressure turns into compulsion," *ibid.*, the legislation runs contrary to our system of federalism. "[T]he Constitution simply does not give Congress the authority to require the States to regulate." That is true whether Congress directly commands a State to regulate or indirectly coerces a State to adopt a federal regulatory system as its own.

Permitting the Federal Government to force the States to implement a federal program would threaten the political accountability key to our federal system. "[W]here the Federal Government directs the States to regulate, it may be state officials who will bear the brunt of public disapproval, while the federal officials who devised the regulatory program may remain insulated from the electoral ramifications of their decision." Spending Clause programs do not pose this danger when a State has a legitimate choice whether to accept the federal conditions in exchange for federal funds. In such a situation, state officials can fairly be held politically accountable for choosing to accept or refuse the federal offer. But when the State has no choice, the Federal Government can achieve its objectives without accountability. . . . Indeed, this danger is heightened when Congress acts under the

Spending Clause, because Congress can use that power to implement federal policy it could not impose directly under its enumerated powers.

We addressed such concerns in *Steward Machine*. That case involved a federal tax on employers that was abated if the businesses paid into a state unemployment plan that met certain federally specified conditions. An employer sued, alleging that the tax was impermissibly "driv[ing] the state legislatures under the whip of economic pressure into the enactment of unemployment compensation laws at the bidding of the central government." 301 U.S., at 587. . . . In rejecting the argument that the federal law was a "weapon[ ] of coercion, destroying or impairing the autonomy of the states," the Court noted that there was no reason to suppose that the State in that case acted other than through "her unfettered will." *Id.*, at 586, 590. Indeed, the State itself did "not offer a suggestion that in passing the unemployment law she was affected by duress." *Id.*, at 589.

As our decision in *Steward Machine* confirms, Congress may attach appropriate conditions to federal taxing and spending programs to preserve its control over the use of federal funds. In the typical case we look to the States to defend their prerogatives by adopting "the simple expedient of not yielding" to federal blandishments when they do not want to embrace the federal policies as their own. *Massachusetts v. Mellon*, 262 U.S. 447, 482 (1923). The States are separate and independent sovereigns. Sometimes they have to act like it.

The States, however, argue that the Medicaid expansion is far from the typical case. They object that Congress has "crossed the line distinguishing encouragement from coercion," in the way it has structured the funding: Instead of simply refusing to grant the new funds to States that will not accept the new conditions, Congress has also threatened to withhold those States' existing Medicaid funds. The States claim that this threat serves no purpose other than to force unwilling States to sign up for the dramatic expansion in health care coverage effected by the Act.

Given the nature of the threat and the programs at issue here, we must agree. We have upheld Congress's authority to condition the receipt of funds on the States' complying with restrictions on the use of those funds, because that is the means by which Congress ensures that the funds are spent according to its view of the "general Welfare." Conditions that do not here govern the use of the funds, however, cannot be justified on that basis. When, for example, such conditions take the form of threats to terminate other significant independent grants, the conditions are properly viewed as a means of pressuring the States to accept policy changes.

In *South Dakota v. Dole*, we considered a challenge to a federal law that threatened to withhold five percent of a State's federal highway funds if the State did not raise its drinking age to 21. The Court found that the condition was "directly related to one of the main purposes for which highway funds are expended—safe interstate travel." 483 U.S., at 208. At the same time, the condition was not a restriction on how the highway funds—set aside for specific highway improvement and maintenance efforts—were to be used.

We accordingly asked whether "the financial inducement offered by Congress" was "so coercive as to pass the point at which 'pressure turns into compulsion.' " *Id.*, at 211. By "financial inducement" the Court meant the threat of losing five percent of highway funds; no new money was offered to the States to raise their drinking ages. We found that the inducement was not impermissibly coercive, because Congress was offering only "relatively mild encouragement to the States." *Dole*, 483 U.S., at 211. We observed that "all South Dakota would lose if she adheres to her chosen course as to a suitable minimum drinking age is 5%" of her highway funds. *Ibid.* In fact, the federal funds at stake constituted less than half of one percent of South

Dakota's budget at the time. In consequence, "we conclude[d] that [the] encouragement to state action [was] a valid use of the spending power." *Dole*, 483 U.S., at 212. Whether to accept the drinking age change "remain[ed] the prerogative of the States not merely in theory but in fact." Id., at 211–212.

In this case, the financial "inducement" Congress has chosen is much more than "relatively mild encouragement"—it is a gun to the head. Section 1396c of the Medicaid Act provides that if a State's Medicaid plan does not comply with the Act's requirements, the Secretary of Health and Human Services may declare that "further payments will not be made to the State." 42 U.S.C. § 1396c. A State that opts out of the Affordable Care Act's expansion in health care coverage thus stands to lose not merely "a relatively small percentage" of its existing Medicaid funding, but all of it. *Dole, supra*, at 211. Medicaid spending accounts for over 20 percent of the average State's total budget, with federal funds covering 50 to 83 percent of those costs. See Nat. Assn. of State Budget Officers, Fiscal Year 2010 State Expenditure Report, p. 11, Table 5 (2011). The Federal Government estimates that it will pay out approximately $3.3 trillion between 2010 and 2019 in order to cover the costs of pre-expansion Medicaid. Brief for United States 10, n. 6. In addition, the States have developed intricate statutory and administrative regimes over the course of many decades to implement their objectives under existing Medicaid. It is easy to see how the *Dole* Court could conclude that the threatened loss of less than half of one percent of South Dakota's budget left that State with a "prerogative" to reject Congress's desired policy, "not merely in theory but in fact." 483 U.S., at 211–212. The threatened loss of over 10 percent of a State's overall budget, in contrast, is economic dragooning that leaves the States with no real option but to acquiesce in the Medicaid expansion.[11]

Justice GINSBURG claims that *Dole* is distinguishable because here "Congress has not threatened to withhold funds earmarked for any other program." *Post*, at 2634. But that begs the question: The States contend that the expansion is in reality a new program and that Congress is forcing them to accept it by threatening the funds for the existing Medicaid program. We cannot agree that existing Medicaid and the expansion dictated by the Affordable Care Act are all one program simply because "Congress styled" them as such. *Post*, at 2635. If the expansion is not properly viewed as a modification of the existing Medicaid program, Congress's decision to so title it is irrelevant.

Here, the Government claims that the Medicaid expansion is properly viewed merely as a modification of the existing program because the States agreed that Congress could change the terms of Medicaid when they signed on in the first place. The Government observes that the Social Security Act, which includes the original Medicaid provisions, contains a clause expressly reserving "[t]he right to alter, amend, or repeal any provision" of that statute. 42 U.S.C. § 1304. So it does. But "if Congress intends to impose a condition on the grant of federal moneys, it must do so unambiguously." *Pennhurst*, 451 U.S., at 17. A State confronted with statutory language reserving the right to "alter" or "amend" the pertinent provisions of the Social Security Act might reasonably assume that Congress was entitled to make adjustments to the Medicaid program as it developed. Congress has in fact done so, sometimes conditioning only the new funding, other times both old and new. See, e.g., Social Security Amendments of 1972, 86 Stat. 1381 (extending Medicaid eligibility, but partly conditioning only the new funding); Omnibus Budget

---

[11] **Question:** Roberts here distinguishes the level of federal funding threatened by the Affordable Care Act ("over 10 percent of a State's overall budget") from that at stake in *Dole* ("less than half of one percent of South Dakota's budget"). At what point does Congress's financial inducement cross the line from "relatively mild encouragement" to a "gun to the head"?

Reconciliation Act of 1990, 104 Stat. 1388 (extending eligibility, and conditioning old and new funds).

The Medicaid expansion, however, accomplishes a shift in kind, not merely degree. The original program was designed to cover medical services for four particular categories of the needy: the disabled, the blind, the elderly, and needy families with dependent children. See 42 U.S.C. § 1396a(a)(10). Previous amendments to Medicaid eligibility merely altered and expanded the boundaries of these categories. Under the Affordable Care Act, Medicaid is transformed into a program to meet the health care needs of the entire nonelderly population with income below 133 percent of the poverty level. It is no longer a program to care for the neediest among us, but rather an element of a comprehensive national plan to provide universal health insurance coverage.[12]

Indeed, the manner in which the expansion is structured indicates that while Congress may have styled the expansion a mere alteration of existing Medicaid, it recognized it was enlisting the States in a new health care program. Congress created a separate funding provision to cover the costs of providing services to any person made newly eligible by the expansion. While Congress pays 50 to 83 percent of the costs of covering individuals currently enrolled in Medicaid, once the expansion is fully implemented Congress will pay 90 percent of the costs for newly eligible persons. The conditions on use of the different funds are also distinct. Congress mandated that newly eligible persons receive a level of coverage that is less comprehensive than the traditional Medicaid benefit package. § 1396a(k)(1).

As we have explained, "[t]hough Congress' power to legislate under the spending power is broad, it does not include surprising participating States with post-acceptance or 'retroactive' conditions." *Pennhurst, supra,* at 25. A State could hardly anticipate that Congress's reservation of the right to "alter" or "amend" the Medicaid program included the power to transform it so dramatically. . . .

The Court in *Steward Machine* did not attempt to "fix the outermost line" where persuasion gives way to coercion. 301 U.S., at 591. The Court found it "[e]nough for present purposes that wherever the line may be, this statute is within it." *Ibid.* We have no need to fix a line either. It is enough for today that wherever that line may be, this statute is surely beyond it. Congress may not simply "conscript state [agencies] into the national bureaucratic army," and that is what it is attempting to do with the Medicaid expansion. . . .

Nothing in our opinion precludes Congress from offering funds under the Affordable Care Act to expand the availability of health care, and requiring that States accepting such funds comply with the conditions on their use. What Congress is not free to do is to penalize States that choose not to participate in that new program by taking away their existing Medicaid funding. Section 1396c gives the Secretary of

---

[12] **Questions:** Suppose Medicaid did not exist before 2010 but rather was created by the Affordable Care Act. Had the act specified that states could receive billions of dollars in federal grants—the equivalent of "over 10 percent of a State's overall budget"—if they agreed to the terms of this brand-new program, would the situation present the same risk of coercion as in this case, where Roberts fears that Congress was changing the terms of a preexisting program to accomplish "a shift in kind, not merely degree"? If your answer to the above question is "no, the risk of coercion is higher when Congress changes the conditions of an existing program rather than when it sets the conditions of a new program," can you explain precisely what the difference is?

Most federal appropriations must be renewed by statute every year as part of the annual budget process. Why shouldn't each new appropriation bill count as creating a new program with new conditions? Another way to ask this question: Would the situation be as coercive if Congress had passed a statute ending the Medicaid program in December 2009, months before Congress started the program over in 2010?

Health and Human Services the authority to do just that. It allows her to withhold all "further [Medicaid] payments . . . to the State" if she determines that the State is out of compliance with any Medicaid requirement, including those contained in the expansion. 42 U.S.C. § 1396c. In light of the Court's holding, the Secretary cannot apply § 1396c to withdraw existing Medicaid funds for failure to comply with the requirements set out in the expansion. That fully remedies the constitutional violation we have identified. . . .[13]

NOTE: CONDITIONAL SPENDING AFTER NFIB

South Dakota v. Dole, 483 U.S. 203 (1987), outlined five implied limits on Congress's spending power: (1) exercises of the power must be in pursuit of the general welfare, (2) conditions must be unambiguous, (3) conditions must be related to a federal interest in a particular program, (4) conditions must not induce recipients to violate the Constitution, and (5) conditions must not be coercive. While *Dole* addressed the fourth prong, *NFIB* addressed the fifth. But all of the conditions can arise in litigation.

For example, when President Donald Trump took office in 2017, he immediately attempted to use Congress's spending power to punish "sanctuary jurisdictions." *See, e.g.*, Exec. Order No. 13768 (Jan. 25, 2017). His administration defined *sanctuary jurisdiction* as a state or local government that interfered with certain communications between federal immigration officials and local law enforcement. *See* 8 U.S.C. § 1373. In July 2017, Attorney General Jeff Sessions announced that if he determined that a state or local government was a sanctuary jurisdiction, he would withhold federal grants appropriated for that jurisdiction's criminal justice programs. The statute governing those grants required state and local governments to certify that they would comply with "all other applicable Federal laws." 34 U.S.C. § 10153(a).

Various states and local governments sued the Trump administration to challenge its withholding of federal grants. Among other claims, these governments argued that if any statute authorized the attorney general's conduct, the statute necessarily violated several implied limits of the Spending Clause. In particular, the attorney general's new conditions were unrelated to the receipt of criminal justice funds, no statute unambiguously specified that states would lose federal funding if they adopted particular immigration policies, and the overall effect was unduly coercive. *See* Toni M. Massaro & Shefali Milczarek-Desai, *Constitutional Cities: Sanctuary Jurisdictions, Local Voice, and Individual Liberty*, 50 Colum. Hum. Rts. L. Rev. 1, 32–33 (2018). Most courts of appeals agreed with the challengers. *See, e.g.*, *City of Chicago v. Barr*, 961 F.3d 882 (7th Cir. 2020); *City of Los Angeles*

---

[13] **Questions:** What is it, exactly, about this spending condition that the Court finds unconstitutionally coercive? Is it that the condition is attached to a large amount of federal money, changes the terms of participation in an entrenched cooperative program, or ties together separate programs into a package deal? One scholar thinks that all of the above are required before the Court will strike down such a condition. See Samuel R. Bagenstos, *The Anti-Leveraging Principle and the Spending Clause After* NFIB, 101 Geo. L.J. 861 (2013).

If you were a member of Congress interested in using the Spending Clause to persuade states to adopt a particular program (for example, you wanted states to adopt mail-in voting laws or laws to make it easier to purchase firearms), how would you craft the legislation to satisfy this opinion?

v. Barr, 941 F.3d 931 (9th Cir. 2019); *City of Philadelphia v. Att'y Gen.*, 916 F.3d 276 (3d Cir. 2019); *City of Chicago v. Sessions*, 888 F.3d 272 (7th Cir. 2018).

In 2020, however, the U.S. Court of Appeals for the Second Circuit created a circuit split by upholding the attorney general's funding conditions as applied to New York. *See New York v. Dep't of Just.*, 951 F.3d 84 (2d Cir. 2020). After finding that the attorney general's conduct was authorized by statute, the Second Circuit held that "[t]his case is much more akin to *Dole* than to *NFIB*." *Id.* at 116. The court found that states used federal criminal justice grants for "the prosecution, incarceration, or release of aliens," making the two programs related. *Id.* at 119. The court also found that the statute unambiguously required states to comply with all other applicable federal laws. Finally, the court emphasized that "New York's anticipated 2017 [grant] award is $8,879,161, a significant amount of money to be sure, but one representing less than 0.1% of the State's annual $152.3 billion budget, a smaller percentage loss even than that in *Dole*." *Id.*

New York petitioned the Supreme Court for a writ of certiorari in December 2020, but the petition was dismissed after President Joe Biden's inauguration. Assuming for the sake of argument that Congress has allowed the attorney general to withhold criminal justice grants from states that interfered in communications between federal immigration officials and local law enforcement, what information would you need to determine whether to side with the Second Circuit or the Third, Seventh, and Ninth Circuits?

6.3 CONGRESSIONAL EXCLUSIVITY

As we will see when we reach Article II, there are some powers that the Constitution splits between Congress and the president. Congress may "declare War," for example, but the president is "Commander in Chief." The Spending Clause, however, is not one of these splitable powers. Article I, Section 9, Clause 7, puts the spending power exclusively in Congress's hands, declaring, "No Money shall be drawn from the Treasury, but in Consequence of Appropriations made by Law; and a regular Statement and Account of the Receipts and Expenditures of all public Money shall be published from time to time."

In practice, this congressional exclusivity means two things. First, no one in the executive branch, not even the president, may spend money from the federal Treasury without a statute first appropriating it. An executive official may not, unilaterally, incur a debt that binds the United States to pay someone money absent a statute authorizing the action., *Off. of Pers. Mgmt. v. Richmond*, 496 U.S. 414, 424 (1990). Nor may the president use the pardon power to return a criminal fine that has already been paid to the government. *Knote v. United States*, 95 U.S. 149, 154 (1877). Several courts of appeals relied on this congressional exclusivity to invalidate the spending conditions that the Donald Trump administration imposed on sanctuary jurisdictions. These courts reasoned that no statute clearly authorized the attorney general to withhold federal grants that had already been appropriated by Congress. *See, e.g.*, *City of Chicago v. Sessions*, 888 F.3d 272, 286–87 (7th Cir. 2018).

Second, congressional exclusivity also means that when Congress and the executive branch disagree about how money should be paid, Congress wins. If Congress passes a law prohibiting the president from giving someone money, *Hart v. United States*, 118 U.S. 62, 67 (1886), or requiring the president to give someone money, *United States v. Price*, 116 U.S. 43, 44 (1885), the president must obey. That said, Congress may, of course, award lump sums of money to agencies or officials and allow them to use their own discretion to determine how to spend the money. *Cincinnati Soap Co. v. United States*, 301 U.S. 308, 322 (1937).

CHAPTER 7

WHAT IS THE SCOPE OF CONGRESS'S OTHER FINANCIAL POWERS?

ARTICLE I, SECTION 8, CLAUSE 1: The Congress shall have Power To lay and collect Taxes, Duties, Imposts and Excises, to pay the Debts and provide for the common Defence and general Welfare of the United States; but all Duties, Imposts and Excises shall be uniform throughout the United States; . . .—And

CLAUSE 2: To borrow Money on the credit of the United States;

CLAUSE 3: To regulate Commerce with foreign Nations, and among the several States, and with the Indian Tribes;

CLAUSE 4: To establish . . . uniform Laws on the subject of Bankruptcies throughout the United States;

CLAUSE 5: To coin Money, regulate the Value thereof, and of foreign Coin, and fix the Standard of Weights and Measures;

CLAUSE 6: To provide for the Punishment of counterfeiting the Securities and current Coin of the United States;

CLAUSE 8: To promote the Progress of Science and useful Arts, by securing for limited Times to Authors and Inventors the exclusive Right to their respective Writings and Discoveries . . .;—And

CLAUSE 18: To make all Laws which shall be necessary and proper for carrying into Execution the foregoing Powers, and all other Powers vested by this Constitution in the Government of the United States, or in any Department or Officer thereof.

ARTICLE VI, PARAGRAPH 1: All debts contracted . . ., before the adoption of this Constitution, shall be as valid against the United States under this Constitution, as under the Confederation.

7.1 THE POWER TO REGULATE FINANCE, REVENUE, AND THE CURRENCY

The Taxing Clause and Spending Clause are two of several clauses in Article I, Section 8, that relate to money, along with the Borrowing Clause, the Commerce Clause, the Coinage Clause, the Weights and Measures Clause, the Bankruptcy Clause, and the Necessary and Proper Clause. Since *McCulloch v. Maryland*, 17 U.S. (4 Wheat.) 316 (1819), when the Supreme Court first interpreted these clauses to grant Congress sufficient power to charter a national bank, the Court has considered them collectively as a "solid constitutional foundation" for Congress's exercises of financial regulation. *Knox v. Lee* (*The Legal Tender Cases*), 79 U.S. (12 Wall.) 457, 625 (1871). The clauses reinforce one another, giving Congress near plenary authority "over the revenue and the currency of the country." *Id.* at 537.

On the basis of these clauses, the Court has repeatedly upheld Congress's power to charter national banks and other financial institutions and to circulate notes, bonds, and other tax-exempt securities. *See, e.g., McCulloch*, 17 U.S. (4 Wheat.) at 354; *Smith v. Kan. City Title Co.*, 255 U.S. 180, 208 (1921). The Court has also allowed Congress to issue its own paper currency and to make the paper "legal tender"—that is, to require creditors to accept the currency instead of gold or silver as payment for all debts. *The Legal Tender Cases*, 79 U.S. at 544–46. Furthermore, the Court has upheld Congress's power to promote the national currency by regulating state banks, prohibiting certain types of securities, and making it a crime to counterfeit or deface federal securities. *See, e.g., Veazie Bank v. Fenno*, 75 U.S. (8 Wall.) 533, 548 (1869); *United States v. Marigold*, 50 U.S. (9 How.) 560, 568 (1850).

Extraordinary measures for extraordinary times

Congress's financial powers were tested when the Great Depression and ensuing financial panic threatened the collapse of banks.

When President Franklin D. Roosevelt took the oath of office in March 1932, the U.S. dollar was tied to the gold standard, meaning that anyone could take a dollar to a bank and exchange it for a fixed amount of gold. But Roosevelt was elected in the middle of the Great Depression, when financial panic was so widespread that people around the country were withdrawing their entire savings from banks, leaving the banks without enough gold for everyone. To restore confidence in the banking system, the president declared a nationwide "bank holiday," shutting all banks for four days. He also issued an executive order requiring anyone possessing gold coins, bullion, or certificates to surrender their gold to the federal government in exchange for a fixed price of $21 dollars per ounce—an order that suspended the fluctuating gold standard and gave the government plenty of gold to distribute to the failing banks. Furthermore, he also asked Congress to cancel clauses in all public and private contracts that gave anyone the option of receiving payment in gold. By the end of the week, Congress ratified his orders with the Emergency Banking Act, Pub. L. No. 73–1, 48 Stat. 1; and H.R.J. Res. 192, Pub. Res. No. 10, 48 Stat. 112.

The plan worked. Americans, on the whole, were reassured that their bank deposits would be honored; and when the nation's banks reopened, people began returning their withdrawn savings to their banks, averting a crisis.

Gold Clause Cases

But the plan also infuriated creditors whose gold reserves and contracts were now worth less than when the country had been on the gold standard. In dozens of lawsuits, many of these creditors claimed that the federal government had no power to repudiate the gold clauses of private contracts, to suspend the gold standard and compel the surrender of gold, or to repudiate the gold clauses of its own contracts.

By 1935, the Supreme Court had three cases before it, each presenting one of these challenges. The *Gold Clause Cases* of 1935, perhaps the most dramatic Supreme Court cases touching on Congress's extensive financial powers, addressed the constitutionality of Roosevelt's actions during his first week in office. *See Norman v. Balt. & Ohio R.R.*, 294 U.S. 240 (1935); *Nortz v. United States*, 294 U.S. 317 (1935); *Perry v. United States*, 294 U.S. 330 (1935).

The Court appeared ready to invalidate the government's actions. The president was so worried that he drafted an incendiary speech in which he planned to defy the Court's orders. *See* Jeff Shesol, *Supreme Power: Franklin Roosevelt vs. the Supreme Court* 99–100 (2011). The speech never needed to be delivered because the Court upheld Congress's powers in two of the cases; and although it rejected Congress's powers in the third case, the issue was moot because the Court dismissed the case.

Affirmation of abrogation of gold clauses in private contracts

In *Norman v. Baltimore & Ohio Railroad*, 294 U.S. 240 (1935), the first of the three cases, the Court upheld Congress's abrogation of gold clauses in private contracts. It held that Congress had validly exercised its "broad and comprehensive national authority over the subjects of revenue, finance and currency." *Norman*, 294 U.S. at 303. This authority, the Court explained, "is derived from the aggregate of the powers granted to the Congress" and included the power " 'to provide a sound and uniform currency for the country' and to 'secure the benefit of it to the people by appropriate legislation.' " *Id.* at 303–04. The Court added that "by virtue of this national power, there attaches to the ownership of gold and silver those limitations which public policy may require by reason of their quality as legal tender and as a medium of exchange." *Id.* at 304. So even if Congress's abrogation of the private gold clauses " 'were justly chargeable with impairing contract obligations, they would not, for that reason, be forbidden.' . . . [C]ontracts must be understood as having been made in reference to the possible exercise of the rightful authority of the government, and . . . no obligation of a contract 'can extend to the defeat' of that authority." *Id.* at 305.

Affirmation of forced exchange of gold for set price[1]

In the second case, *Nortz v. United States*, 294 U.S. 317 (1935), the Supreme Court also upheld Congress's power to compel people to deliver

[1] **Note:** Money is often described by what it does: it functions mainly as the medium of exchange and mode of payment in a society. Some scholars, however, have taken a "constitutional approach" that characterizes what money is: a tool of governance with a deliberate design. Christine Desan, for example, has suggested that the clauses allocating to

their gold to the government in exchange for a set price. Congress "has complete authority to regulate the currency system of the country," the Court wrote, which included the powers to prohibit the exportation of gold, regulate its use, and define its quality "as a legal tender and as a medium of exchange." *Nortz*, 294 U.S. at 328, 330. Even though the worldwide price of gold had risen from $21/ounce in 1932 to $33/ounce by 1934, the Court explained that no one has an inherent right to buy and sell on a world market. Congress had the power to restrict the currency market available to the plaintiff and fix the price of gold at $21/ounce.

Rejection of repudiation of gold clauses in government contracts

It was not until the third case, *Perry v. United States*, 294 U.S. 330 (1935), that the Court imposed any limitations on Congress's financial powers. That case involved the owner of a 1918 gold bond, John Perry, to whom the federal government promised to pay $10,000 worth of "gold coin of the [1918] standard of value" in 1934. *Perry*, 294 U.S. at 347. By 1934, that promise was worth roughly $17,000 in gold coin on the world market. But the federal government refused to honor the gold clause, offering Perry only $10,000 in paper currency. In *Perry*, the Court harshly criticized the government's change of terms. It held that the government's repudiation of its own contract exceeded Congress's Article I power "[t]o borrow Money on the credit of the United States."

The Court in *Perry* was careful to distinguish the federal government's acknowledged power over the currency from its asserted power to "disregard the obligations of the Government at its discretion." *Id.* at 350. If Congress possessed such a power, the Court explained, then "when the Government borrows money, the credit of the United States is an illusory pledge." *Id.* The Court rejected this possibility:

> By virtue of the power to borrow money "on the credit of the United States," the Congress is authorized to pledge that credit as an assurance of payment as stipulated, as the highest assurance the government can give, its plighted faith. To say that the Congress may withdraw or ignore that pledge, is to assume that the Constitution contemplates a vain promise; a pledge having no other sanction than the pleasure and convenience of the pledgor. This Court has given no sanction to such a conception of the obligations of our government.

Id. at 351.

The Court nevertheless dismissed Perry's challenge on a technicality. After attempting to figure out what damages Perry might be owed for the government's breach, the Court concluded that any

---

Congress authority over money helped shape the modern system of American capitalism, reflecting deliberate choices about how we work and what we produce, what wealth looks like and how we distribute it, and who gets credit and who doesn't. *See* Christine Desan, *The Constitutional Approach to Money: Monetary Design and the Production of the Modern World*, *in Money Talks: Explaining How Money Really Works* (Nina Bandelj et al. eds., 2017).

amount over $10,000 would unjustly enrich Perry relative to his peers who, instead of holding a gold bond, had once held actual gold but who had been required to surrender it to the government. The Court held that Perry had therefore failed to plead actual damages. The Court achieved what Chief Justice John Marshall had done in *Marbury v. Madison*, 5 U.S. (1 Cranch) 137 (1803): it criticized the government for violating the Constitution but issued no orders that it knew it would be unable to enforce.

7.2 THE POWER TO PROVIDE A UNIFORM RULE OF BANKRUPTCY

Article I, Section 8, is full of powers that the delegates to the Constitutional Convention believed should be wielded at the national level instead of the state level. One of these is Congress's power to "establish . . . uniform Laws on the subject of Bankruptcies throughout the United States." A course in bankruptcy law will cover at length the laws that Congress has passed pursuant to this clause. As a matter of constitutional law, by contrast, the Bankruptcy Clause has presented just two doctrinal questions.

Beneficiaries of a federal bankruptcy law

The first question is this: Who is entitled to benefit from a federal bankruptcy law?

Under long-standing British precedent, bankruptcy was a type of mercantile insurance for bad luck: if a ship carrying all of a trader's goods sank through no fault of the trader, then a creditor could ask a court to equitably split what the trader could salvage. *See Adams v. Storey*, 1 F. Cas. 141, 142 (C.C.D.N.Y. 1817) (No. 66).

When Congress passed the first federal bankruptcy statute, by contrast, it included not only traders but also bankers, brokers, and underwriters. Act of Apr. 4, 1800, ch. 19, 2 Stat. 19 (1800). Moreover, Congress later allowed the debtor, not just the creditor, to initiate bankruptcy proceedings—converting it into a method by which debtors could resolve outstanding debts of all kinds.

For a long time, it was questionable whether Congress had the power to extend bankruptcy law past its British moorings. But in a series of cases in the early twentieth century, the Supreme Court held that Congress had broad authority to extend bankruptcy law beyond traders. *See*, e.g., *Hanover Nat'l Bank v. Moyses*, 186 U.S. 181, 186 (1902).

Constitutional limits on Congress's bankruptcy power

The second question is this: What limits does the Constitution place on Congress's exercise of its bankruptcy power?

Early on, in cases similar to the *Gold Clause Cases*, the Court held that Congress has the power to impair existing contracts by authorizing one of the parties to default on its promises. *In re Klein*, 42 U.S. (1 How.) 277 (1843); *Hanover Nat'l Bank*, 186 U.S. at 188. It also held that bankruptcy courts were allowed to recognize and apply state laws without violating the requirement that federal bankruptcy law be "uniform." *Stellwagen v. Clum*, 245 U.S. 605, 613 (1918). But during the Great Depression, when Congress extended federal bankruptcy law to include local governments, the Supreme Court held that the Tenth Amendment prohibited Congress from subjecting the fiscal affairs of a state's subdivision to the control of a federal bankruptcy court. *Ashton v. Cameron Cnty. Water Improvement Dist. No. 1*, 298 U.S. 513, 531 (1936).

In response to these decisions, Congress modified the bankruptcy code to require states to consent before one of its municipalities could be eligible for bankruptcy. In *United States v. Bekins*, 304 U.S. 27, 53–54 (1938), the Supreme Court upheld the new statute.

7.3 THE POWER TO REGULATE COPYRIGHTS AND PATENTS

Article I, Section 8, Clause 8, also gives Congress significant powers to regulate intellectual property. As with bankruptcy, most of the details of this subject will be discussed in an intellectual property, copyright, patent law, or trademarks and competition course. But there are some basic questions presented by the clauses of the Constitution themselves.

Copyrights

Congress's power "[t]o promote the Progress of Science and useful Arts, by securing for limited Times to Authors and Inventors the exclusive Right to their respective Writings and Discoveries," has been interpreted to give Congress the power to protect copyrights—that is, the exclusive right of an author to publish a writing for a limited time.

One of the first copyright cases involved two of the reporters responsible for printing the Supreme Court's early opinions: Henry Wheaton (Wheat.) and Richard Peters (Pet.). The two men disagreed about whether Wheaton had the sole right to publish his compilation of the Supreme Court's opinions absent any statute protecting this right. The Court answered no because only Congress could "secur[e]" the exclusive right protected by this clause. *Wheaton v. Peters*, 33 U.S. (8 Pet.) 591, 642 (1834).

In later copyright cases, the Court has generally deferred to Congress's judgment about who is an author and what kinds of writings qualify for protection. *See, e.g.*, *Stevens v. Gladding*, 58 U.S. (17 How.) 447, 452–53 (1855) (owner of a printing press copperplate is not the author of the map produced by the plate); *Kalem Co. v. Harper Bros.*, 222 U.S. 55, 62 (1911) (silent films can be "Writings").

Patents

Clause 8 also gives Congress the "exclusive Right" of an "Inventor" to its "Discoveries" for a "limited Time"—that is, the power to award patents.

In 1793, Congress required the government to award patents only after evaluating whether an invention was "new and useful." Act of Feb. 21, 1793, ch. 11, 1 Stat. 318, 319. Later cases have treated these concepts as constitutional requirements. *See, e.g., Funk Bros. Seed Co. v. Kalo Inoculant Co.*, 333 U.S. 127, 130 (1948) (the discovery of a previously unknown law of nature can be patentable only if it comes "from the application of the law of nature to a new and useful end").

The Court has added that, to be patentable, an invention must display "more ingenuity . . . than the work of a mechanic skilled in the art," *Sinclair & Carroll Co. v. Interchem. Corp.*, 325 U.S. 327, 330 (1945)—a requirement later codified as "non-obvious." 35 U.S.C. § 103.

Limits of the Patent and Copyright Clause

There are a few occasions in which the Court has disagreed with Congress about the limits imposed by the Patent and Copyright Clause.

First, because the clause requires anything protected "[t]o promote the Progress of Science and useful Arts," the Court voided Congress's first attempts to protect *trademarks*—that is, the features of an item in commerce that distinguish one company's merchandise from that of another company. *See Trade-Mark Cases*, 100 U.S. 82 (1879). "The ordinary trade-mark," the Court wrote, "has no necessary relation to invention or discovery." *Id.* at 94. It was not until the 1940s that the Court upheld Congress's power to regulate trademarks—but as an exercise of its power to regulate interstate commerce, not as an exercise of its power to promote the progress of science and useful arts. *See* Lanham Act of 1946, Pub. L. No. 79–489, 60 Stat. 427 (protecting trademarks that have a "use in commerce").

Second, because the clause extends protection only for "limited Times," the Court has held that Congress may not extend patents or copyrights forever. Writings and inventions must, at some point, enter the public domain. *See Golan v. Holder*, 565 U.S. 302, 317 (2012). (That said, in *Eldred v. Ashcroft*, 537 U.S. 186 (2003), the Court upheld the Copyright Term Extension Act of 1998, which effectively extended the copyright term of Disney characters such as Mickey Mouse until at least 2024.)

Third, and finally, because the protection that the clause grants is an "exclusive Right," the Court has held that Congress may not reserve for itself the power to infringe on the patents or copyrights that it protects. Rather, it must pay just compensation to use a copyright or patent, just like everyone else. *James v. Campbell*, 104 U.S. 356, 358 (1882).

CHAPTER 8

WHAT IS THE HISTORICAL SCOPE OF CONGRESS'S POWER TO REGULATE COMMERCE?

ARTICLE I, SECTION 8, CLAUSE 3: The Congress shall have Power . . . To regulate Commerce with foreign Nations, and among the several States . . .;—And

> **CLAUSE 18:** To make all Laws which shall be necessary and proper for carrying into Execution the foregoing Powers, and all other Powers vested by this Constitution in the Government of the United States, or in any Department or Officer thereof.

TENTH AMENDMENT (1791): The powers not delegated to the United States by the Constitution, nor prohibited by it to the States, are reserved to the States respectively, or to the people.

8.1 REGULATION OF THE CHANNELS AND INSTRUMENTALITIES OF COMMERCE

One of the most widely shared criticisms of the Articles of Confederation was that the Articles failed to give Congress any power to regulate foreign or domestic commerce. When Congress signed treaties with foreign countries, it had no power to enforce the United States' promises—leading to reprisals by Great Britain and France. States individually responded to foreign trade disputes with their own protective legislation—leading to reprisals by other states. As previously discussed (section 1.1), when New York imposed port fees and tonnage duties on British ships in retaliation for British trade restrictions, Connecticut and New Jersey took advantage of the situation by opening up their own free ports. And when New York responded by taxing goods coming in from those two states, Connecticut and New Jersey escalated the trade war with their own taxes and suspensions of trade with New York. One member of Congress at the time warned that it was only "the restraining hand of Congress (weak as it is) that prevents New Jersey and Connecticut from entering the lists very seriously with New York and bloodshed would very quickly be the consequence." Michael J. Klarman, *The Framers' Coup: The Making of the United States Constitution* 23–24 (2016).

In 1786, when the Virginia legislature first called for a constitutional convention, it invited delegates "to take into consideration the trade of the United States" and "to consider how far a uniform system in their commercial regulations may be necessary to their common interest and their permanent harmony." *See* 2 *The Records of the Federal Convention of 1787*, at 374 (Max Farrand ed., 1911). It therefore isn't surprising that the eventual product of this invitation gave Congress the power "[t]o regulate Commerce with foreign Nations, and among the several States." *Id.*

Commerce Clause and a supermajority

Even so, the Commerce Clause was controversial from its inception. Southern delegates, including some from Virginia, worried that a North-controlled Congress might regulate commerce to prohibit the importation of enslaved people, make southern exports more expensive, or require southern exports to sail on expensive American ships instead of the far more common European ships. *Id.* Understanding the wide-reaching possibilities of commercial regulations, George Mason of Virginia proposed requiring a two-thirds supermajority before Congress could exercise the Commerce Clause. *Id.* at 633. Although this proposal was rejected in favor of a twenty-year ban on prohibiting the importation of enslaved people, one of the amendments proposed by the ratifying conventions in Virginia and other southern states was a supermajority requirement for any "law regulating commerce." 10 *Documentary History of the Ratification of the Constitution* 1554 (John P. Kaminski et al. eds., 1993).

Embargo Act of 1807 and regulation of commerce

As predicted by the southern delegates, the first major dispute over Congress's exercise of the Commerce Clause concerned its regulation of international trade. But the most vocal opponents of the regulation, ironically, were northerners opposed to a law signed by a Virginian, President Thomas Jefferson. The law was a response to European politics. Between the French Revolution in 1789 and the Battle of Waterloo in 1815, France and Great Britain were engaged in near-constant war with one another. The United States adopted a policy of neutrality—but French and British ships seized U.S. ships and impressed U.S. sailors into their navies. An exasperated Congress finally passed the Embargo Act of 1807, which prohibited the departure of any ship from the United States to any foreign port "except vessels under the immediate direction of the President." 2 Stat. 451. This law—which was signed by Jefferson—outraged New Englanders, who dominated American shipping and feared that the embargo would threaten their livelihoods. They also complained that the power to regulate commerce did not include the power to prohibit it. As a rebellious Massachusetts legislature later resolved, "[a] power to regulate Commerce is abused, when employed to destroy it; and a manifest and voluntary abuse of power sanctions the right of resistance, as much as a direct and palpable usurpation." *State Documents on Federal Relations* 69 (Herman V. Ames ed., 1911).

In the first case to consider the question of whether Congress had the power to prohibit commerce, *United States v. The William*, 28 F. Cas.

614 (D. Mass. 1808), a federal district court upheld the Embargo Act. "Power to regulate, it is said, cannot be understood to give a power to annihilate," the court wrote. *The William*, F. Cas. at 621. But even the law's opponents agreed "that partial prohibitions are authorized by the expression." *Id.* Otherwise, the power to regulate would be meaningless, as regulations inherently prohibit whatever activities fail to comply with the regulation. Accepting this, the court recharacterized the question as "How shall the degree, or extent, of the prohibition be adjusted?" *Id.* And the answer, the court ruled, should not be provided by Massachusetts or by a federal court but "by the discretion of the national government, to whom the subject appears to be committed." *Id.*

The court bolstered its conclusion with an analogy, writing that the term *regulate* must be interpreted broadly because the term *commerce* had already been interpreted more broadly than a dictionary would suggest. *See id.*; Samuel Johnson, *A Dictionary of the English Language* 417–18 (London, W. Strahan 1755) (defining *commerce* as "Intercourse . . .; trade; traffick"). *Commerce*, the court explained, "does not necessarily include shipping or navigation; much less does it include the fisheries. Yet it never has been contended, that they are not the proper objects of national regulation; and several acts of congress have been made respecting them." *Id.* The court added:

> It may be replied, that these are incidents to commerce, and intimately connected with it; and that congress, in legislating respecting them, act under the authority, given them by the constitution, to make all laws necessary and proper, for carrying, into execution the enumerated powers. Let this be admitted; and are they not at liberty, also, to consider the present prohibitory system, as necessary and proper to an eventual beneficial regulation? . . . I see nothing to prohibit or restrain the measure.

Id.

8.1.1

Gibbons v. Ogden

22 U.S. (9 Wheat.) 1 (1824)

As with Congress's power to charter a national bank, it took decades before the issue of Congress's power to regulate commerce first reached the Supreme Court. This time, the issue wasn't a war between two nations but between two neighbors.

In nineteenth-century New Jersey, few people hated each other more than Aaron Ogden and Thomas Gibbons. Both men lived within a half mile of each other and began their relationship as partners in a ferry service from the Staten Island area to Manhattan. But they soon developed a rivalry that went well beyond business. In 1816, Ogden involved himself in a dispute between Gibbons and members of Gibbons's family. When Gibbons tried to get Ogden kicked off the ferry pier that they shared, Ogden had Gibbons arrested for nonpayment of a check. Gibbons responded by walking up to Ogden's house with a horsewhip, announcing, "I pronounce your conduct *rascally*." *See* T.J. Stiles, *The First Tycoon* 43 (2009). Ogden fled out the back before again having Gibbons arrested—this time for the crime of attempting to duel. *Id.*

The thing that made this neighborly dispute the stuff of constitutional law was that Ogden also happened to be New Jersey's governor. Ogden ran for governor because he wanted to replace his fleet of sailboat ferries with a new, safer invention: the steamboat. But decades earlier, before the invention of steamboats had even been perfected, the New York legislature granted a monopoly on all steamboat traffic to Robert R. Livingston, the coauthor of the Declaration of Independence and the powerful chancellor of New York's highest court. Governor Ogden used his state's resources to challenge New York's claims to the waters it shared with New Jersey. By 1815, New York paid him off by giving him a license to run his own steamboat between Elizabethtown, New Jersey, and New York. *Id.* at 42.

So when Gibbons wanted revenge for Ogden's refusal to duel him, he decided to directly compete with Ogden's steamboat license. On the advice of former duelist and vice president Aaron Burr, Gibbons purchased a federal license under the Coasting Act of 1793, which provided "[t]hat ships or vessels . . . having a license in force, . . . and no others, shall be deemed ships or vessels of the United States, entitled to the privileges of ships or vessels employed in the coasting trade or fisheries." Coasting Act, ch. 8, 1 Stat. 305. Although this license said nothing about ferries, Gibbons then purchased his own steamboats and hired a 25-year-old ferry captain from Staten Island, Cornelius Vanderbilt, to pilot them back and forth across New York Harbor. Even after a New York court ordered Gibbons and Vanderbilt not to interfere with Ogden's monopoly, the two men undercut Ogden's prices, dodged process servers, and survived attempts to sink their ships. Finally, a desperate Ogden secured an injunction against his competitors, which Gibbons appealed to the Supreme Court. *See* Stiles, *supra*, at 43–63.

In *Gibbons v. Ogden*, 22 U.S. (9 Wheat.) 1 (1824), Gibbons's lawyer, Daniel Webster, argued before the Court that New York's monopoly was invalid because the Commerce Clause gave Congress exclusive authority to regulate "Commerce . . . among the several States." Moreover, he added, Gibbons had a federal license to operate his ferry, with which, like the bank in *McCulloch v. Maryland*, 17 U.S. (4 Wheat.) 316 (1819), the state could not interfere. Ogden's lawyer responded that the Commerce Clause was a grant of power to Congress, not a restraint on what a state like New York could regulate. He dismissed the license as irrelevant given that the Coasting Act said nothing about state ferry regulations.

Chief Justice John Marshall, for his part, used the occasion as an excuse to weigh in on the long-standing debate about the meaning of the terms *regulate* and *commerce*, determining that *commerce* included navigation and that federal law thus preempted New York's regulation.

■ MR. CHIEF JUSTICE MARSHALL delivered the opinion of the Court . . .:[1]

The appellant[, Gibbons,] contends that this decree is erroneous, because the laws which purport to give the exclusive privilege [to Ogden], are repugnant to the constitution and laws of the United States.

They are said to be repugnant . . . To that clause in the constitution which authorizes Congress to regulate commerce. . . .

[The Constitution] contains an enumeration of powers expressly granted by the people to their government. It has been said, that these powers ought to be construed strictly. But why ought they to be so construed? Is there one sentence in the constitution which gives countenance to this rule? In the last of the enumerated powers, that which grants, expressly, the means for carrying all others into execution, Congress is authorized "to make all laws which shall be necessary and proper" for the purpose. But this limitation on the means which may be used, is not extended to the powers which are conferred; nor is there one sentence in the constitution, which has been pointed out by the gentlemen of the bar, or which we have been able to discern, that prescribes this rule. We do not, therefore, think ourselves justified in adopting it. . . . As men, whose intentions require no concealment, generally employ the words which most directly and aptly express the ideas they intend to convey, the enlightened patriots who framed our constitution, and the people who adopted it, must be understood to have employed words in their natural sense, and to have intended what they have said. If, from the imperfection of human language, there should be serious doubts respecting the extent of any given power, it is a well settled rule, that the objects for which it was given, especially when those objects are expressed in the instrument itself, should have great influence in the construction. . . . The grant . . . is an investment of power for the general advantage, in the hands of agents selected for that purpose; which power can never be exercised by the people themselves, but must be placed in the hands of agents, or lie dormant. We know of no rule for construing the extent of such powers, other than is given by the language of the instrument which confers them, taken in connexion with the purposes for which they were conferred.

The words are, "Congress shall have power to regulate commerce with foreign nations, and among the several States and with the Indian tribes."

The subject to be regulated is commerce; and our constitution being, as was aptly said at the bar, one of enumeration, and not of definition, to ascertain the extent of the power, it becomes necessary to settle the meaning of the word. The counsel for the appellee would limit it to traffic, to buying and selling, or the interchange of commodities, and do not admit that it comprehends navigation. This would restrict a

---

[1] **As You Read, Consider:** The basic question here is whether New York's monopoly is preempted by the federal Coasting Act. In all cases involving preemption, the Court asks the same questions that it asked in *McCulloch v. Maryland*: First, is the federal conduct at issue constitutional? If so, does the state conduct present an obstacle to the federal government's purposes?

In answering the first question, Chief Justice John Marshall interprets the Commerce Clause, which gives Congress the power to (1) "regulate" (2) "Commerce" (3) "among the several States." How does Marshall define each of these three terms?

In light of Marshall's definition of the Commerce Clause, does he think that the Coasting Act is a valid exercise of the Commerce Clause?

If so, does Marshall think that New York's monopoly presents an obstacle to the purposes behind the Coasting Act? Does he think that New York could ever regulate "Commerce . . . among the several States"?

general term, applicable to many objects, to one of its significations. Commerce, undoubtedly, is traffic, but it is something more: it is intercourse. It describes the commercial intercourse between nations, and parts of nations, in all its branches, and is regulated by prescribing rules for carrying on that intercourse. The mind can scarcely conceive a system for regulating commerce between nations, which shall exclude all laws concerning navigation, which shall be silent on the admission of the vessels of the one nation into the ports of the other, and be confined to prescribing rules for the conduct of individuals, in the actual employment of buying and selling, or of barter.

If commerce does not include navigation, the government of the Union has no direct power over that subject, and can make no law prescribing what shall constitute American vessels, or requiring that they shall be navigated by American seamen. Yet this power has been exercised from the commencement of the government, has been exercised with the consent of all, and has been understood by all to be a commercial regulation. All America understands, and has uniformly understood, the word "commerce," to comprehend navigation. It was so understood, and must have been so understood, when the constitution was framed. The power over commerce, including navigation, was one of the primary objects for which the people of America adopted their government, and must have been contemplated in forming it. The convention must have used the word in that sense, because all have understood it in that sense; and the attempt to restrict it comes too late. . . .

The universally acknowledged power of the government to impose embargoes, must also be considered as showing, that all America is united in that construction which comprehends navigation in the word commerce. Gentlemen have said, in argument, that this is a branch of the war-making power, and that an embargo is an instrument of war, not a regulation of trade.

That it may be, and often is, used as an instrument of war, cannot be denied. . . . But . . . [t]hey are sometimes resorted to without a view to war, and with a single view to commerce. In such case an embargo is no more a war measure, than a merchantman is a ship of war, because both are vessels which navigate the ocean with sails and seamen.

When Congress imposed that embargo which for a time, engaged the attention of every man in the United States, the avowed object of the law was, the protection of commerce, and the avoiding of war.[2] By its friends and its enemies it was treated as a commercial, not as a war measure. The preserving earnestness and zeal with which it was opposed, in a part of our country which supposed its interests to be vitally affected by the act, cannot be forgotten. A want of acuteness in discovering objections to a measure to which they felt the most deep rooted hostility, will not be imputed to those who were arrayed in opposition to this. Yet they never suspected that navigation was no branch of trade, and was, therefore, not comprehended in the power to regulate commerce. They did, indeed, contest the constitutionality of the act, but, on a principle which admits the construction for which the appellant contends. They denied that the particular law in question was made in pursuance of the constitution, not because the power could not act directly on vessels, but because a perpetual embargo was the annihilation, and not the regulation of commerce. In terms, they admitted the applicability of the words used in the constitution to vessels;

---

[2] **Note:** Here, Marshall is referring to the controversial Embargo Act of 1807, which prohibited the departure of any ship from the United States to any foreign port "except vessels under the immediate direction of the President." Embargo Act, ch. 5, 2 Stat. 451. The act was an attempt by Thomas Jefferson's supporters to keep the United States out of the Napoleonic Wars. The act was criticized by New England merchants as unconstitutional on the ground that it *prohibited* commerce rather than regulating it.

and that, in a case which produced a degree and an extent of excitement, calculated to draw forth every principle on which legitimate resistance could be sustained. No example could more strongly illustrate the universal understanding of the American people on this subject.

The word used in the constitution, then, comprehends, and has been always understood to comprehend, navigation within its meaning; and a power to regulate navigation, is as expressly granted, as if that term had been added to the word "commerce."[3]

To what commerce does this power extend? The constitution informs us, to commerce "with foreign nations, and among the several States, and with the Indian tribes."

It has, we believe, been universally admitted, that these words comprehend every species of commercial intercourse between the United States and foreign nations. No sort of trade can be carried on between this country and any other, to which this power does not extend. It has been truly said, that commerce, as the word is used in the constitution, is a unit, every part of which is indicated by the term.

If this be the admitted meaning of the word, in its application to foreign nations, it must carry the same meaning throughout the sentence, and remain a unit, unless there be some plain intelligible cause which alters it.

The subject to which the power is next applied, is to commerce "among the several States." The word "among" means intermingled with. A thing which is among others, is intermingled with them. Commerce among the States, cannot stop at the external boundary line of each State, but may be introduced into the interior.

It is not intended to say that these words comprehend that commerce, which is completely internal, which is carried on between man and man in a State, or between different parts of the same State, and which does not extend to or affect other States. Such a power would be inconvenient, and is certainly unnecessary.

Comprehensive as the word "among" is, it may very properly be restricted to that commerce which concerns more States than one. The phrase is not one which would probably have been selected to indicate the completely interior traffic of a State, because it is not an apt phrase for that purpose; and the enumeration of the particular classes of commerce, to which the power was to be extended, would not have been made, had the intention been to extend the power to every description. The enumeration presupposes something not enumerated; and that something, if we regard the language or the subject of the sentence, must be the exclusively internal commerce of a State. The genius and character of the whole government seem to be, that its action is to be applied to all the external concerns of the nation, and to those internal concerns which affect the States generally; but not to those which are completely within a particular State, which do not affect other States, and with which it is not necessary to interfere, for the purpose of executing some of the general powers of the government. The completely internal commerce of a State, then, may be considered as reserved for the State itself.

But, in regulating commerce with foreign nations, the power of Congress does not stop at the jurisdictional lines of the several States. It would be a very useless power, if it could not pass those lines. The commerce of the United States with foreign nations, is that of the whole United States. Every district has a right to participate in

---

[3] **Question:** Marshall has defined the term *commerce* and is moving on to ask whether Congress's power to regulate commerce includes the power to regulate ferry traffic between New York and New Jersey. Specifically, if New York claims that its monopoly is enforced only within its own maritime borders, can Congress reach the monopoly via its power to regulate commerce among the several states?

it. The deep streams which penetrate our country in every direction, pass through the interior of almost every State in the Union, and furnish the means of exercising this right. If Congress has the power to regulate it, that power must be exercised whenever the subject exists. If it exists within the States, if a foreign voyage may commence or terminate at a port within a State, then the power of Congress may be exercised within a State.

This principle is, if possible, still more clear, when applied to commerce "among the several States." They either join each other, in which case they are separated by a mathematical line, or they are remote from each other, in which case other States lie between them. What is commerce "among" them; and how is it to be conducted? Can a trading expedition between two adjoining States, commence and terminate outside of each? And if the trading intercourse be between two States remote from each other, must it not commence in one, terminate in the other, and probably pass through a third? Commerce among the States must, of necessity, be commerce with the States. . . . The power of Congress, then, whatever it may be, must be exercised within the territorial jurisdiction of the several States. The sense of the nation on this subject, is unequivocally manifested by the provisions made in the laws for transporting goods, by land, between Baltimore and Providence, between New-York and Philadelphia, and between Philadelphia and Baltimore.[4]

We are now arrived at the inquiry—What is this power?

It is the power to regulate; that is, to prescribe the rule by which commerce is to be governed. This power, like all others vested in Congress, is complete in itself, may be exercised to its utmost extent, and acknowledges no limitations, other than are prescribed in the constitution. . . . If, as has always been understood, the sovereignty of Congress, though limited to specified objects, is plenary as to those objects, the power over commerce with foreign nations, and among the several States, is vested in Congress as absolutely as it would be in a single government, having in its constitution the same restrictions on the exercise of the power as are found in the constitution of the United States. The wisdom and the discretion of Congress, their identity with the people, and the influence which their constituents possess at elections, are, in this, as in many other instances, as that, for example, of declaring war, the sole restraints on which they have relied, to secure them from its abuse. They are the restraints on which the people must often rely solely, in all representative governments.

The power of Congress, then, comprehends navigation, within the limits of every State in the Union; so far as that navigation may be, in any manner, connected with "commerce with foreign nations, or among the several States, or with the Indian tribes." It may, of consequence, pass the jurisdictional line of New-York, and act upon the very waters to which the prohibition now under consideration applies.

But it has been urged with great earnestness, that, although the power of Congress to regulate commerce with foreign nations, and among the several States, be co-extensive with the subject itself, and have no other limits than are prescribed in the constitution, yet the States may severally exercise the same power, within their respective jurisdictions. In support of this argument, it is said, that they possessed it as an inseparable attribute of sovereignty, before the formation of the constitution, and still retain it, except so far as they have surrendered it by that instrument; that this principle results from the nature of the government, and is secured by the tenth

---

4 **Question:** Marshall has defined the phrase *commerce among the several states* and is now asking what is meant by Congress's power to "regulate" this commerce. Specifically, could anything prevent Congress from declaring that New York cannot enforce a monopoly on ferry traffic from New Jersey?

navigation is part of commerce

commerce between states

Commerce between states includes things within one state

supremacy

amendment; that an affirmative grant of power is not exclusive, unless in its own nature it be such that the continued exercise of it by the former possessor is inconsistent with the grant, and that this is not of that description.[5]

The appellant, conceding these postulates, except the last, contends, that full power to regulate a particular subject, implies the whole power, and leaves no residuum; that a grant of the whole is incompatible with the existence of a right in another to any part of it. . . .

The grant of the power to lay and collect taxes is, like the power to regulate commerce, made in general terms, and has never been understood to interfere with the exercise of the same power by the States; and hence has been drawn an argument which has been applied to the question under consideration. But the two grants are not, it is conceived, similar in their terms or their nature. Although many of the powers formerly exercised by the States, are transferred to the government of the Union, yet the State governments remain, and constitute a most important part of our system. The power of taxation is indispensable to their existence, and is a power which, in its own nature, is capable of residing in, and being exercised by, different authorities at the same time. We are accustomed to see it placed, for different purposes, in different hands. Taxation is the simple operation of taking small portions from a perpetually accumulating mass, susceptible of almost infinite division; and a power in one to take what is necessary for certain purposes, is not, in its nature, incompatible with a power in another to take what is necessary for other purposes. Congress is authorized to lay and collect taxes, &c. to pay the debts, and provide for the common defence and general welfare of the United States. This does not interfere with the power of the States to tax for the support of their own governments; nor is the exercise of that power by the States, an exercise of any portion of the power that is granted to the United States. In imposing taxes for State purposes, they are not doing what Congress is empowered to do. Congress is not empowered to tax for those purposes which are within the exclusive province of the States. When, then, each government exercises the power of taxation, neither is exercising the power of the other. But, when a State proceeds to regulate commerce with foreign nations, or among the several States, it is exercising the very power that is granted to Congress, and is doing the very thing which Congress is authorized to do. There is no analogy, then, between the power of taxation and the power of regulating commerce.[6]

In discussing the question, whether this power is still in the States, in the case under consideration, we may dismiss from it the inquiry, whether it is surrendered by the mere grant to Congress, or is retained until Congress shall exercise the power. We may dismiss that inquiry, because it has been exercised, and the regulations which Congress deemed it proper to make, are now in full operation.[7] The sole

---

[5] **Questions:** Marshall is now considering something of an aside: imagine that Congress has the power to regulate ferry traffic between New York and New Jersey, but it has not passed any legislation to do so. In this situation, can New York regulate interstate ferry traffic? In other words, when the Constitution grants Congress the power to regulate commerce among the several states, is that an *exclusive* grant of power that states cannot exercise themselves?

[6] **Question:** Marshall is tackling this exclusivity question by first noting that some powers, like taxation, are not exclusive. That is, despite the Constitution's grant of the taxing power to Congress, there is no question that states can tax items that Congress has not yet taxed. Is there a difference between taxing something and regulating it?

[7] **Question:** Here, Marshall complicates the inquiry of whether the Commerce Clause is an exclusive grant of power to Congress by observing that, in this case, the question is not whether New York could *ever* regulate interstate commerce but whether New York can do so after Congress has passed the Coasting Act. The basic question remains the same: Can New York regulate commerce among the several states, or does that power exclusively belong to Congress?

question is, can a State regulate commerce with foreign nations and among the States, while Congress is regulating it?

The counsel for the respondent answer this question in the affirmative, and rely very much on the restrictions in the 10th section, [which say, "No State shall, without the Consent of the Congress, lay any Imposts or Duties on Imports or Exports, *except what may be absolutely necessary for executing [its] inspection Laws.*" (emphasis added)]. They say, very truly, that [States always have the power to execute their inspection laws no matter what Congress does]. . . . [T]he inspection laws are said to be regulations of commerce, and are certainly recognised in the constitution, as being passed in the exercise of a power remaining with the States.

That inspection laws may have a remote and considerable influence on commerce, will not be denied; but that a power to regulate commerce is the source from which the right to pass them is derived, cannot be admitted. The object of inspection laws, is to improve the quality of articles produced by the labour of a country; to fit them for exportation; or, it may be, for domestic use. They act upon the subject before it becomes an article of foreign commerce, or of commerce among the States, and prepare it for that purpose. They form a portion of that immense mass of legislation, which embraces every thing within the territory of a State, not surrendered to the general government: all which can be most advantageously exercised by the States themselves. Inspection laws, quarantine laws, health laws of every description, as well as laws for regulating the internal commerce of a State, and those which respect turnpike roads, ferries, &c., are component parts of this mass.

No direct general power over these objects is granted to Congress; and, consequently, they remain subject to State legislation. If the legislative power of the Union can reach them, it must be for national purposes; it must be where the power is expressly given for a special purpose, or is clearly incidental to some power which is expressly given. It is obvious, that the government of the Union, in the exercise of its express powers, that, for example, of regulating commerce with foreign nations and among the States, may use means that may also be employed by a State, in the exercise of its acknowledged powers; that, for example, of regulating commerce within the State. If Congress license vessels to sail from one port to another, in the same State, the act is supposed to be, necessarily, incidental to the power expressly granted to Congress, and implies no claim of a direct power to regulate the purely internal commerce of a State, or to act directly on its system of police. So, if a State, in passing laws on subjects acknowledged to be within its control, and with a view to those subjects, shall adopt a measure of the same character with one which Congress may adopt, it does not derive its authority from the particular power which has been granted, but from some other, which remains with the State, and may be executed by the same means. All experience shows, that the same measures, or measures scarcely distinguishable from each other, may flow from distinct powers; but this does not prove that the powers themselves are identical. Although the means used in their execution may sometimes approach each other so nearly as to be confounded, there are other situations in which they are sufficiently distinct to establish their individuality.

In our complex system, presenting the rare and difficult scheme of one general government, whose action extends over the whole, but which possesses only certain enumerated powers; and of numerous State governments, which retain and exercise all powers not delegated to the Union, contests respecting power must arise. Were it even otherwise, the measures taken by the respective governments to execute their acknowledged powers, would often be of the same description, and might,

---

New York's first answer to this question is that states can always regulate certain aspects of interstate commerce. As evidence, the state cites Article I, Section 10, which allows states to enact "inspection Laws" absent the consent of Congress. Does Marshall buy this answer?

sometimes, interfere. This, however, does not prove that the one is exercising, or has a right to exercise, the powers of the other. . . .[8]

Since, however, in exercising the power of regulating their own purely internal affairs, whether of trading or police, the States may sometimes enact laws, the validity of which depends on their interfering with, and being contrary to, an act of Congress passed in pursuance of the constitution, the Court will enter upon the inquiry, whether the laws of New-York, as expounded by the highest tribunal of that State, have, in their application to this case, come into collision with an act of Congress, and deprived a citizen of a right to which that act entitles him. Should this collision exist, it will be immaterial whether those laws were passed in virtue of a concurrent power "to regulate commerce with foreign nations and among the several States," or, in virtue of a power to regulate their domestic trade and police. In one case and the other, the acts of New-York must yield to the law of Congress; and the decision sustaining the privilege they confer, against a right given by a law of the Union, must be erroneous.

This opinion has been frequently expressed in this Court, and is founded, as well on the nature of the government as on the words of the constitution. In argument, however, it has been contended, that if a law passed by a State, in the exercise of its acknowledged sovereignty, comes into conflict with a law passed by Congress in pursuance of the constitution, they affect the subject, and each other, like equal opposing powers.

But the framers of our constitution foresaw this state of things, and provided for it, by declaring the supremacy not only of itself, but of the laws made in pursuance of it. The nullity of any act inconsistent with the constitution, is produced by the declaration, that the constitution is the supreme law. The appropriate application of that part of the clause which confers the same supremacy on laws and treaties, is to such acts of the State Legislatures as do not transcend their powers, but, though enacted in the execution of acknowledged State powers, interfere with, or are contrary to the laws of Congress, made in pursuance of the constitution, or some treaty made under the authority of the United States. In every such case, the act of Congress, or the treaty, is supreme; and the law of the State, though enacted in the exercise of powers not controverted, must yield to it.[9]

In pursuing this inquiry at the bar, it has been said, that the constitution does not confer the right of intercourse between State and State. That right derives its source from those laws whose authority is acknowledged by civilized man throughout the world. This is true. The constitution found it an existing right, and gave to Congress the power to regulate it. In the exercise of this power, Congress has passed "an act for enrolling or licensing ships or vessels to be employed in the coasting trade

---

[8] **Note:** Here, Marshall is making an important argument about how to interpret the Constitution. Because the Constitution delegates certain powers to Congress and reserves all nondelegated powers to the states or to the people, he is arguing that states cannot exercise powers that have been delegated to Congress *and* that Congress cannot exercise power reserved to states. A major implication from this argument is that all regulations are a zero-sum game: either Congress has the power to regulate something, or states have the power.

It follows from Marshall's argument that where Congress's power to regulate interstate commerce ends, there begins what he calls the states' "power to regulate their domestic trade and police." This latter power has become known as the *police power*.

In keeping with this argument, later Commerce Clause cases will ask whether certain regulations (e.g., a law prohibiting child labor) are best understood as regulations of interstate commerce (that only Congress has the power to enact) or as regulations of domestic trade and police (that only states have the power to enact). This doctrine of "dual sovereignty" is similar to the implied limits discussed in the tax case *Collector v. Day* (see section 5.3).

[9] **Note:** The final questions that Marshall considers are whether the Coasting Act is a regulation of commerce among the several states and whether New York's ferry monopoly presents an obstacle to the federal government's purposes.

and fisheries, and for regulating the same." The counsel for the respondent contend, that this act does not give the right to sail from port to port, but confines itself to regulating a pre-existing right, so far only as to confer certain privileges on enrolled and licensed vessels in its exercise.

It will at once occur, that, when a Legislature attaches certain privileges and exemptions to the exercise of a right over which its control is absolute, the law must imply a power to exercise the right. The privileges are gone, if the right itself be annihilated. It would be contrary to all reason, and to the course of human affairs, to say that a State is unable to strip a vessel of the particular privileges attendant on the exercise of a right, and yet may annul the right itself; that the State of New-York cannot prevent an enrolled and licensed vessel, proceeding from Elizabethtown, in New-Jersey, to New-York, from enjoying, in her course, and on her entrance into port, all the privileges conferred by the act of Congress; but can shut her up in her own port, and prohibit altogether her entering the waters and ports of another State. To the Court it seems very clear, that the whole act on the subject of the coasting trade, according to those principles which govern the construction of statutes, implies, unequivocally, an authority to licensed vessels to carry on the coasting trade. . . .

But, if the license be a permit to carry on the coasting trade, the respondent denies that these boats were engaged in that trade, or that the decree under consideration has restrained them from prosecuting it. The boats of the appellant were, we are told, employed in the transportation of passengers; and this is no part of that commerce which Congress may regulate.[10]

If, as our whole course of legislation on this subject shows, the power of Congress has been universally understood in America, to comprehend navigation, it is a very persuasive, if not a conclusive argument, to prove that the construction is correct; and, if it be correct, no clear distinction is perceived between the power to regulate vessels employed in transporting men for hire, and property for hire. The subject is transferred to Congress, and no exception to the grant can be admitted, which is not proved by the words or the nature of the thing. A coasting vessel employed in the transportation of passengers, is as much a portion of the American marine, as one employed in the transportation of a cargo; and no reason is perceived why such vessel should be withdrawn from the regulating power of that government, which has been thought best fitted for the purpose generally. . . .

If we refer to the constitution, the inference to be drawn from it is rather against the distinction. The section which restrains Congress from prohibiting the migration or importation of such persons as any of the States may think proper to admit, until the year 1808, has always been considered as an exception from the power to regulate commerce, and certainly seems to class migration with importation.[11] Migration applies as appropriately to voluntary, as importation does to involuntary, arrivals; and, so far as an exception from a power proves its existence, this section proves that the power to regulate commerce applies equally to the regulation of

---

[10] **Note:** In the previous paragraph, Marshall concluded that the ferry monopoly interferes with the federal Coasting Act. But, here, New York argues that the Coasting Act is not a regulation of commerce because *passengers*, as opposed to *goods*, are not articles of commerce. This argument had been made by opponents of federal immigration restrictions since the 1790s.

[11] **Note:** Here, Marshall is citing a provision of Article I, Section 9, that prohibits Congress from banning the transatlantic slave trade before 1808. He is making the observation that if enslaved people can be articles of commerce, why not ferry passengers? It is worth noting that when Congress abolished the transatlantic slave trade in 1808, it invoked not the Commerce Clause but rather the clause that empowers Congress to "define and punish Piracies and Felonies committed on the high Seas, and Offences against the law of nations." U.S. Const. art. I, § 8, cl. 10; see 16 Annals of Cong. 271 (1807).

vessels employed in transporting men, who pass from place to place voluntarily, and to those who pass involuntarily.

If the power reside in Congress, as a portion of the general grant to regulate commerce, then acts applying that power to vessels generally, must be construed as comprehending all vessels. . . . If, then, it were even true, that [two of Gibbons's ferries,] the *Bellona* and the *Stoudinger*[,] were employed exclusively in the conveyance of passengers between New-York and New-Jersey, it would not follow that this occupation did not constitute a part of the coasting trade of the United States, and was not protected by the license annexed to the answer. . . .

The Court is aware that, in stating the train of reasoning by which we have been conducted to this result, much time has been consumed in the attempt to demonstrate propositions which may have been thought axioms. It is felt that the tediousness inseparable from the endeavour to prove that which is already clear, is imputable to a considerable part of this opinion. But it was unavoidable. The conclusion to which we have come, depends on a chain of principles which it was necessary to preserve unbroken; and, although some of them were thought nearly self-evident, the magnitude of the question, the weight of character belonging to those from whose judgment we dissent, and the argument at the bar, demanded that we should assume nothing.[12]

Powerful and ingenious minds, taking, as postulates, that the powers expressly granted to the government of the Union, are to be contracted by construction, into the narrowest possible compass, and that the original powers of the States are retained, if any possible construction will retain them, may, by a course of well digested, but refined and metaphysical reasoning, founded on these premises, explain away the constitution of our country, and leave it, a magnificent structure, indeed, to look at, but totally unfit for use. They may so entangle and perplex the understanding, as to obscure principles, which were before thought quite plain, and induce doubts where, if the mind were to pursue its own course, none would be perceived. In such a case, it is peculiarly necessary to recur to safe and fundamental principles to sustain those principles, and, when sustained, to make them the tests of the arguments to be examined.

NOTE: DUAL FEDERALISM AND THE NEGATIVE COMMERCE CLAUSE

The holding of *Gibbons* is straightforward and analogous to *McCulloch*: New York's monopoly was preempted by the federal Coasting Act of 1793. But to reach this holding, Marshall wrote that it was "unavoidable" for the Court first to determine (1) what is meant by the term *commerce*, (2) what is meant by the term *among the several States*, (3) what is meant by the term *regulate*, (4) whether the power granted by the Commerce Clause is exclusive to Congress or can be exercised by the states as well, (5) whether the Coasting Act is a valid exercise of the Commerce Clause, and (6) whether New York's monopoly interferes with the Coasting Act. *Gibbons*, 22 U.S. at 222.

For the first century after *Gibbons*, Marshall's answer to question 4 was the most significant. In his analysis of "the immense mass of legislation,

---

[12] **Questions:** Here, Marshall apologizes to you, the reader, for answering the basic question at issue in this case—Can New York enforce its ferry monopoly?—only after boarding a lengthy "train of reasoning." Did you pick up what the answer to the question is? Can New York enforce its monopoly?

which embraces every thing within the territory of a State, not surrendered to the general government," the chief justice reasoned that the Constitution divides all legislation into two separate spheres. *Id.* at 203. One sphere, Marshall wrote, is occupied exclusively by the federal government: only Congress may exercise the powers in Article I, Section 8, such as passing a law regulating commerce among the states. The other sphere is occupied exclusively by the states: states draw their power not from the U.S. Constitution but from their own constitutions, and they can do everything that Congress is not empowered to do, including the passage of "[i]nspection laws, quarantine laws, health laws of every description, as well as laws for regulating the internal commerce of a State." *Id.* These two spheres are not *geographically* separated, the chief justice wrote: the federal sphere often operates entirely within one state's borders, as when Congress regulates the "deep streams" of a state in a manner "clearly incidental" to its power to regulate foreign commerce. *Id.* at 195, 205. But the two spheres are *conceptually* separated: if the Constitution gives a power to Congress, the Constitution withholds that same power from a state—even if the power ends up "[lying] dormant" because Congress fails to pass any relevant laws. *Id.* at 189.

This theory of the Constitution would later be called *dual federalism*: the federal government and states are each preeminent in their own spheres but powerless to operate in the other's sphere. *See* Edward S. Corwin, *The Twilight of the Supreme Court* 10–51 (1934). Applying this theory, the Supreme Court over the course of the nineteenth century categorized all legislation as belonging to *either* the state sphere *or* the federal sphere *but not both*. In practice, this theory had a profound effect on how the Court reviewed the constitutionality of both federal and state laws. If, for example, the Court reviewed a federal minimum-wage law and determined that the law was a valid exercise of the Commerce Clause, then by implication a state could not pass its own minimum-wage law. Giving Congress the power would deny it to the states. And if the Court reviewed a state law regulating a railroad's ticket prices and determined that the law was valid, then by the same implication Congress could *not* regulate that railroad's ticket prices in the same way. Giving the power to the states would deny it to Congress.

State police powers. One consequence of the dual federalism doctrine was that the Supreme Court closely scrutinized Congress's attempts to regulate interstate commerce to determine whether the thing that Congress was regulating was part of the federal sphere or whether it more properly belonged to what the *Gibbons* Court called a state's "system of police," 22 U.S. at 204—or what now is referred to as a state's "police powers." For example, in *United States v. Dewitt*, the Court struck down a federal law prohibiting the sale of dangerous "illuminating oils" because there was no connection between that prohibition and interstate commerce. 76 U.S. (9 Wall.) 41, 44 (1869). The Constitution's "express grant of power to regulate commerce among the states has always been understood as limited by its terms," the Court explained. *Id.* at 44. "As a police regulation, relating exclusively to the internal trade of the State," such a prohibition was something only the state could enact if the state's own constitution allowed. *Id.* at 45.

Negative Commerce Clause. The inverse consequence of this doctrine was the development of the Negative Commerce Clause (also called the Dormant Commerce Clause): the theory that states may never pass laws that regulate interstate commerce—at least without Congress's permission. Even if a state law regulating interstate commerce doesn't conflict with any federal law, the Court reasoned, the power is always exclusive to the federal government. *See, e.g., Groves v. Slaughter*, 40 U.S. (15 Pet.) 449 (1841) (discussing but not deciding whether Mississippi's prohibition on the importation of enslaved people from other states violated the Commerce Clause); *Passenger Cases*, 48 U.S. (7 How.) 283 (1849) (striking down New York and Massachusetts immigration regulations in light of the Commerce Clause).

We will discuss the Negative Commerce Clause later in the course when we focus on states (section 37.2). For now, just know that while we're currently focusing on federal law, the overwhelming majority of Commerce Clause litigation in the nineteenth century challenged state laws, which were far more common. *See* Ezra Prentice & John Egan, *The Commerce Clause of the Federal Constitution* 14 (1898).

NOTE: WHAT COUNTS AS "COMMERCE"

Marshall concluded in *Gibbons* that the term *commerce* definitely includes "navigation" and likely includes much more.

Channels of commerce. On the basis of this conclusion, the Court had no difficulty concluding that Congress (and, by implication, not states) had the exclusive power to regulate all navigable waters and streams that could be accessed by multiple states. *Gilman v. City of Philadelphia*, 70 U.S. (3 Wall.) 713 (1866). The Court also held that as part of its regulatory authority, Congress could authorize the construction of bridges across navigable rivers, *Pennsylvania v. Wheeling & Belmont Bridge Co.*, 59 U.S. (18 How.) 421 (1855); and improve interstate streams by constructing dams to sell excess waterpower, *United States v. Chandler-Dunbar Co.*, 229 U.S. 53 (1913).

Instrumentalities of commerce. Soon, the Court extended these precedents to other forms of navigation. For example, in the late nineteenth century, the Court upheld Congress's powers to construct railways, to charter corporations for that purpose, to vest those corporations with the power of eminent domain, and to exempt those corporations from state taxes. *See, e.g., Thomson v. Pacific R.R.*, 76 U.S. (9 Wall.) 579 (1870); *California v. Pac. R.R. Co.* (*Pacific Ry. Cases*), 127 U.S. 1 (1888); *Cherokee Nation v. S. Kan. Ry.*, 135 U.S. 641 (1890); *Luxton v. N. River Bridge Co.*, 153 U.S. 525 (1894). Even though railroads did not exist in 1789, when the Commerce Clause was written, the Court held that the Commerce Clause applies to all "instrumentalities of commerce, . . . from the horse with its rider to the stage-coach, from the sailing-vessel to the steamboat, from the coach and the steamboat to the railroad, and from the railroad to the telegraph." *Pensacola Tel. Co. v. W. Union Tel. Co.*, 96 U.S. 1 (1878). In 1894, the Court upheld the

Interstate Commerce Act, 24 Stat. 379 (1887), in which Congress created the Interstate Commerce Commission, one of the first federal agencies, and authorized it to regulate the rates charged by interstate railroads for cargo and passengers. *ICC v. Brimson*, 154 U.S. 447 (1894). By the early twentieth century, Congress had developed a completely integrated regulatory system over motor, railroad, and water carriers, and over telecommunications systems that had just been invented. *See, e.g.*, Act of Sep. 18, 1940, Pub. L. No. 76–785, 54 Stat. 898.

People and goods in commerce. During this period, the Court also concluded that *commerce* refers not just to the channels of commerce (e.g., rivers) and the instrumentalities of commerce (e.g., boats) but also to the people and goods in commerce (e.g., ferry passengers and cargo). As with its other Commerce Clause precedents, this conclusion was first developed in *Gibbons*, when Marshall noted that "no clear distinction is perceived between the power to regulate vessels employed in transporting men for hire, and property for hire." *Gibbons*, 22 U.S. at 215. Although the chief justice was talking about regulating boats as opposed to the people or property that the boats carried, he cited Congress's acknowledged power to prohibit the slave trade as evidence that its power to regulate commerce likely included the power to regulate the transportation of particular people or property. Accordingly, in the years after *Gibbons*, the Court generally indicated that Congress's power to regulate interstate commerce includes the power to regulate the people and goods that travel in interstate or foreign commerce. For example, in *Reid v. Colorado*, the Court approvingly discussed a federal law that prohibited knowingly transporting diseased livestock from one state to another. 187 U.S. 137, 150 (1902).

Lottery Case. The first case to directly consider whether Congress could prohibit the interstate transportation of people or goods concerned an "evil of vast proportions": the Louisiana State Lottery. *See* 12 *A Compilation of the Messages and Papers of the Presidents* 5515 (James D. Richardson ed., 1897) (message of President Benjamin Harrison). In 1890, as now, the lottery supplied a healthy percentage of Louisiana's budget. But in a message to Congress, President Benjamin Harrison warned that Louisiana was advertising and selling its lottery tickets nationwide, which "debauched and defrauded" the people of neighboring states; led to "the robbery of the poor and the widespread corruption of public and private morals"; and was a "prostitution of an agency," the U.S. Postal Service, "only intended to serve the purpose of a legitimate trade and a decent social intercourse." 21 Cong. Rec. 7916 (1890). Congress eventually responded with An Act for the Suppression of Lottery Traffic, 28 Stat. 963 (1895), which made it a criminal offense for any person to mail or carry a lottery ticket from one state to another. It was one of only a handful of federal criminal offenses at the time.

After three rounds of oral arguments, a closely divided Supreme Court in the *Lottery Case*, 188 U.S. 321 (1903), upheld the federal prosecution of an express company that carried a lottery ticket among its freight across state lines. On behalf of a 5–4 majority, Justice John Marshall Harlan explained "that lottery tickets are subjects of traffic and therefore are subjects of commerce, and the regulation of the carriage of such tickets from State to

State, . . . is a regulation of commerce among the several States." *Lottery Case*, 188 U.S. at 354. In response to the four dissenters who argued that the power to regulate did not include the power to prohibit or criminally punish, Harlan quoted from the conclusion in *Gibbons* that all regulations inherently prohibit some conduct, and the Constitution gives Congress "plenary" discretion to decide how far its regulation should go. *Id.* at 356. "If a State, when considering legislation for the suppression of lotteries within its own limits, may properly take into view the evils that inhere in the raising of money, in that mode," Harlan asked, "why may not Congress, invested with the power to regulate commerce among the several States, provide that such commerce shall not be polluted by the carrying of lottery tickets from one State to another?" *Id.* He called lotteries a "widespread pestilence" that "infests the whole community" and declared that Congress had to have the power to "protect the commerce which concerns all the states." *Id.* at 356–57. Although Harlan recognized the possibility that Congress might, in the future, "arbitrarily exclude from commerce" articles and commodities that properly belonged to state control, he responded that "the possible abuse of a power is not an argument against its existence." *Id.* at 362–63. He added, "It will be time enough to consider the constitutionality of such legislation when we must do so." *Id.* at 362.

The *Lottery Case* was a watershed decision that immediately led Congress to enact more criminal offenses, beginning a trend that has resulted in the current federal criminal code of thousands of crimes scattered over tens of thousands of pages. Most of these early offenses were upheld on the same lines as in the *Lottery Case*. For example, in *Hoke v. United States*, 227 U.S. 308 (1913), the Court upheld the White-Slave Traffic Act of 1910, 36 Stat. 825a, which made it a crime to transport women (of any race) across state lines for the purpose of prostitution. In *Caminetti v. United States*, 242 U.S. 470 (1917), the Court upheld the application of the statute to the transportation of a woman across state lines for noncommercial sexual purposes—a definition that allowed racist prosecutors to convict Jack Johnson, the heavyweight boxing champion and a black man, for traveling with a white girlfriend. *See* Geoffrey C. Ward, *Unforgivable Blackness: The Rise and Fall of Jack Johnson* 304–39 (2004). In *Cleveland v. United States*, 329 U.S. 14 (1946), the Court upheld a similar act that prohibited the transportation of plural wives across state lines. And in *United States v. Simpson*, 252 U.S. 465, 466 (1920), the Court upheld an act prohibiting the interstate transportation of whiskey for personal consumption.

8.2 REGULATION OF INTRASTATE ECONOMIC ACTIVITIES THAT AFFECT INTERSTATE COMMERCE

The Commerce Clause cases of the late nineteenth century mainly considered federal laws that regulated people and items crossing state lines, whether over navigable waters, railroads, or telegraphs. In these contexts, the Court could almost take for granted that Congress had satisfied the Article I requirement that it regulate commerce only "among the several States." But despite these broad precedents, the Court did not conclude that everything that affects multiple states counts as interstate commerce. Rather, on the basis of the dual federalism theory articulated in *Gibbons v. Ogden*, 22 U.S. (9 Wheat.) 1 (1824), it attempted to carefully distinguish intrastate activities, which only states could regulate, from interstate activities, which only Congress could regulate.

Negative Commerce Clause cases

This distinction first emerged in Negative Commerce Clause cases reviewing the constitutionality of state laws. When residents challenged Iowa's regulation of interstate manufacturing companies and Virginia's regulation of interstate insurance transactions, the Court upheld the state laws on the theory that manufacturing goods and selling insurance were not the same thing as engaging in "Commerce . . . among the several States." *See Paul v. Virginia*, 75 U.S. (8 Wall.) 168, 183 (1869); *Kidd v. Pearson*, 128 U.S. 1, 22–23 (1888). Even though these activities certainly affected other states, the Court didn't think it appropriate to prohibit states from regulating them. "There must be a point of time when [intrastate goods or activities] cease to be governed exclusively by the domestic law and begin to be governed and protected by the national law of commercial regulation," the Court wrote in the related case of *Coe v. Errol*, but "that moment [is when] they commence their final movement from the State of their origin to that of their destination." 116 U.S. 517, 525 (1886).

By implication of the dual federalism theory, allowing states to regulate insurance and manufacturing as part of their police powers meant that Congress lacked the power to regulate them as interstate commerce.

Sherman Antitrust Act, interstate commerce, and dual federalism

The Court made this implication explicit in *United States v. E.C. Knight Co.*, 156 U.S. 1 (1895), one of the first cases brought under the Sherman Antitrust Act of 1890, 26 Stat. 209.

The Sherman Act broadly prohibited "every contract, combination . . ., or conspiracy, in restraint of trade or commerce *among the several States.*" *E.C. Knight Co.*, 156 U.S. at 22 (emphasis in original). In *E.C. Knight Co.*, federal prosecutors charged the American Sugar Refining Company with violating this language by attempting to monopolize the sugar refining industry. The prosecutors acknowledged that, under the Court's precedent, sugar refining was a type of intrastate manufacturing that could be regulated only by a state's police power. But they explained that a monopoly over sugar is a monopoly over a "necessary of life, . . . the enjoyment of which by a large part of the population of the United States interstate commerce is indispensable." *Id.* at 11–12.

The Court declared that this supposed connection between sugar manufacturing and interstate commerce was too attenuated. "Commerce [follows] manufacture, and is not a part of it," the Court explained. *Id.* at 12. While Congress might be able to regulate the interstate sale or transfer of sugar after it had been refined, it couldn't touch the sugar until it started moving.

Moreover, the Court reasoned that if it treated manufacturing as an appropriate subject of federal regulation "whenever interstate or international commerce may be ultimately affected," then under the theory of dual federalism, states would no longer be able to regulate most manufacturers. *Id.* at 13. The Court wrote:

> It is vital that the independence of the commercial power and of the police power, and the delimitation between them, however sometimes perplexing, should always be recognized and observed, for while the one furnishes the strongest bond of union, the other is essential to the preservation of the autonomy of the States as required by our dual form of government.

Id.

Antitrust and direct versus indirect effect on interstate commerce

In subsequent Sherman Act cases, the Court upheld prosecutions only where the alleged conspiracy *directly* restrained intercourse and traffic among the states, not where it *indirectly* did so by restraining only intrastate activity. For example, in *Addyston Pipe & Steel Co. v. United States*, the Court upheld a prosecution of pipe makers who sought to monopolize not only the manufacture of pipes but also the "sale or exchange of the manufactured commodity among the states." 175 U.S. 211, 241 (1899). And in *Swift & Co. v. United States*, the Court upheld a prosecution of a conspiracy to monopolize the "current of commerce" created "[w]hen cattle are sent for sale from a place in one State, with the expectation that they will end their transit, after purchase, in another, and when in effect they do so." 196 U.S. 375, 398 (1905).

Railroads and direct versus indirect effect on interstate commerce

In contexts outside of antitrust, the Court similarly allowed Congress to regulate intrastate activities that directly affected interstate commerce but not intrastate activities that merely indirectly affected it.

For example, in the *Employers' Liability Cases*, the Supreme Court struck down the Employers' Liability Act of 1906, ch. 3073, 34 Stat. 232, which required railroad companies operating in multiple states to provide compensation to "any of its officers, agents, or employees" injured on the job. *Employers' Liability Cases*, 207 U.S. 463, 498 (1908). This statute applied even to local employees who never left the state, but federal lawyers argued that every employee of an interstate railroad, even someone who never moves, necessarily affects interstate commerce. The Court dismissively declared that this argument

> would extend the power of Congress to every conceivable subject, however inherently local[;] would obliterate all the limitations of power imposed by the Constitution[;] and would destroy the authority of the States as to all conceivable matters which from the beginning have been, and must continue to be, under their control so long as the Constitution endures.

Id. at 502–03.

After the decision, Congress modified the statute to apply only to employees actually engaged in interstate or foreign commerce. 35 Stat. 65 (1908). With this limitation, the Court had no difficulty upholding the new law. *See Second Emps.' Liab. Cases*, 223 U.S. 1 (1912).

Relatedly, in *Southern Railway v. United States*, 222 U.S. 20 (1911), the Court upheld a federal statute that required air brakes on intrastate trains that used tracks shared by trains in interstate commerce. Unlike railroad employees who operated within a single state, the Court explained, unsafe local trains could directly affect interstate commerce by crashing into an interstate train that ran on the same tracks.

And in *Houston, East & West Texas Railway Company v. United States*, 234 U.S. 342 (1914)—also known as the *Shreveport Rate Case*—the Court upheld a law that gave the Interstate Commerce Commission the power to regulate the rates of railroads that operated entirely within one state, if the commission found that the regulation was needed to prevent the intrastate railroad from having a competitive advantage over interstate lines. The Court explained that the "essence" of the Commerce Clause was to prevent interstate trade from being "destroyed or impeded by the rivalries of local governments. The purpose was to make impossible the recurrence of the evils which had overwhelmed the Confederation and to provide the necessary basis of national unity." *Shreveport Rate Case*, 234 U.S. at 350.

8.2.1

Hammer v. Dagenhart

247 U.S. 251 (1918)

By 1916, the Supreme Court had thus announced two rules for interpreting the Commerce Clause that were simple in theory but could be difficult to apply in practice. In the line of cases emanating from the *Lottery Case*, 188 U.S. 321 (1903), the Court held that Congress had plenary authority to regulate waterways, railways, and other channels of interstate commerce, as well as the vehicles, goods, and people that used them to cross state lines. And in the *E.C. Knight* line of cases, the Court held that Congress had the power to regulate intrastate activities that directly affected interstate commerce, including activities that put interstate concerns at a competitive disadvantage.

Both of these lines came crashing together when Congress first attempted to prohibit the use of child labor in 1916 in the Keating-Owen Child Labor Act, 39 Stat. 675 (1916). As a reminder, back in the section on the limits of Congress's taxing power for the purposes of regulation (section 5.4), we discussed Congress's *second* attempt to regulate child labor when it passed the Child Labor Tax Law—a statute that the Court struck down as a "penalty" in *Bailey v. Drexel Furniture Co.* (*The Child Labor Tax Case*), 259 U.S. 20 (1922). The outcome of this first attempt should therefore come as no surprise.

Congress's first law, passed as an exercise of the Commerce Clause, declared that "no producer, manufacturer, or dealer shall ship or deliver for shipment in interstate or foreign commerce any article or commodity . . . [from a place in which] children under the age of fourteen years [worked]." Keating-Owen Child Labor Act, 39 Stat. at 675. Congress had good reason to think that this law was valid: not only did it regulate articles of interstate commerce, as in the *Lottery Case*, but it also equalized the competitive disadvantage faced by businesses in states that regulated child labor compared to businesses in states that did not, as in *E.C. Knight*.

But after a North Carolina father, Roland H. Dagenhart, sued a U.S. attorney to block the enforcement of this law, the Supreme Court in *Hammer v. Dagenhart*, 247 U.S. 251 (1918), announced new limits on its previous lines of cases.

■ MR. JUSTICE DAY delivered the opinion of the Court.[13]

[T]he controlling question for decision is: Is it within the authority of Congress in regulating commerce among the States to prohibit the transportation in interstate commerce of manufactured goods, the product of a factory in which, within thirty days prior to their removal therefrom, children under the age of fourteen have been employed or permitted to work . . .?

The power essential to the passage of this act, the Government contends, is found in the commerce clause of the Constitution which authorizes Congress to regulate commerce with foreign nations and among the States.

In *Gibbons v. Ogden*, 9 Wheat. 1, Chief Justice Marshall, speaking for this court, and defining the extent and nature of the commerce power, said, "It is the power to regulate; that is, to prescribe the rule by which commerce is to be governed." In other words, the power is one to control the means by which commerce is carried on, which is directly the contrary of the assumed right to forbid commerce from moving and thus destroy it as to particular commodities. But it is insisted that adjudged cases in this court establish the doctrine that the power to regulate given to Congress incidentally includes the authority to prohibit the movement of ordinary commodities and therefore that the subject is not open for discussion. The cases demonstrate the contrary. They rest upon the character of the particular subjects dealt with and the fact that the scope

[13] **As You Read, Consider:** How does the theory of dual federalism articulated in *Gibbons v. Ogden* shape the decision in this case? Assume that no member of the Supreme Court was a fan of child labor. Why might a majority of the Court nevertheless be worried about allowing Congress to regulate it?

of governmental authority, state or national, possessed over them is such that the authority to prohibit is as to them but the exertion of the power to regulate.[14]

The first of these cases is *Champion v. Ames*, 188 U.S. 321, the so-called *Lottery Case*, in which it was held that Congress might pass a law having the effect to keep the channels of commerce free from use in the transportation of tickets used in the promotion of lottery schemes. In *Hipolite Egg Co. v. United States*, 220 U.S. 45, this court sustained the power of Congress to pass the Pure Food and Drug Act which prohibited the introduction into the States by means of interstate commerce of impure foods and drugs. In *Hoke v. United States*, 227 U.S. 308, this court sustained the constitutionality of the so-called "White Slave Traffic Act" whereby the transportation of a woman in interstate commerce for the purpose of prostitution was forbidden. . . . In *Caminetti v. United States*, 242 U.S. 470, we held that Congress might prohibit the transportation of women in interstate commerce for the purposes of debauchery and kindred purposes. In *Clark Distilling Co. v. Western Maryland Ry. Co.*, 242 U.S. 311, the power of Congress over the transportation of intoxicating liquors was sustained. . . .

In each of these instances the use of interstate transportation was necessary to the accomplishment of harmful results. In other words, although the power over interstate transportation was to regulate, that could only be accomplished by prohibiting the use of the facilities of interstate commerce to effect the evil intended.

This element is wanting in the present case. The thing intended to be accomplished by this statute is the denial of the facilities of interstate commerce to those manufacturers in the States who employ children within the prohibited ages. The act in its effect does not regulate transportation among the States, but aims to standardize the ages at which children may be employed in mining and manufacturing within the States. The goods shipped are of themselves harmless. The act permits them to be freely shipped after thirty days from the time of their removal from the factory. When offered for shipment, and before transportation begins, the labor of their production is over, and the mere fact that they were intended for interstate commerce transportation does not make their production subject to federal control under the commerce power.

drawing the line

Commerce "consists of intercourse and traffic . . . and includes the transportation of persons and property, as well as the purchase, sale and exchange of commodities." The making of goods and the mining of coal are not commerce, nor does the fact that these things are to be afterwards shipped or used in interstate commerce, make their production a part thereof.[15]

Over interstate transportation, or its incidents, the regulatory power of Congress is ample, but the production of articles, intended for interstate commerce, is a matter of local regulation.

"When the commerce begins is determined, not by the character of the commodity, nor by the intention of the owner to transfer it to another state for sale, nor by his preparation of it for transportation, but by its actual delivery to a common

---

[14] **Question:** The opinions in the line of cases being discussed here all stand for the principle that Congress's power to regulate interstate commerce includes the power to ban certain articles from traveling in interstate commerce. In this case, Congress has banned goods manufactured with child labor from traveling in interstate commerce. Does this line of cases therefore control?

[15] **Question:** It can be difficult for a twenty-first-century reader to understand the distinction that the Supreme Court was making a century ago. But, as in *Gibbons*, Justice William Day argues that there is a border between regulations that fall exclusively within Congress's power to regulate interstate commerce and regulations that fall exclusively within the states' police power. Where does Day think that border lies in this case?

carrier for transportation, or the actual commencement of its transfer to another state." This principle has been recognized often in this court. *Coe v. Errol*, 116 U.S. 517. If it were otherwise, all manufacture intended for interstate shipment would be brought under federal control to the practical exclusion of the authority of the States, a result certainly not contemplated by the framers of the Constitution when they vested in Congress the authority to regulate commerce among the States. *Kidd v. Pearson*, 128 U.S. 1, 21.

It is further contended that the authority of Congress may be exerted to control interstate commerce in the shipment of child-made goods because of the effect of the circulation of such goods in other States where the evil of this class of labor has been recognized by local legislation, and the right to thus employ child labor has been more rigorously restrained than in the State of production. In other words, that the unfair competition, thus engendered, may be controlled by closing the channels of interstate commerce to manufacturers in those States where the local laws do not meet what Congress deems to be the more just standard of other States.

There is no power vested in Congress to require the States to exercise their police power so as to prevent possible unfair competition. Many causes may cooperate to give one State, by reason of local laws or conditions, an economic advantage over others. The Commerce Clause was not intended to give to Congress a general authority to equalize such conditions. In some of the States laws have been passed fixing minimum wages for women, in others the local law regulates the hours of labor of women in various employments. Business done in such States may be at an economic disadvantage when compared with States which have no such regulations; surely, this fact does not give Congress the power to deny transportation in interstate commerce to those who carry on business where the hours of labor and the rate of compensation for women have not been fixed by a standard in use in other States and approved by Congress.

The grant of power to Congress over the subject of interstate commerce was to enable it to regulate such commerce, and not to give it authority to control the States in their exercise of the police power over local trade and manufacture.

The grant of authority over a purely federal matter was not intended to destroy the local power always existing and carefully reserved to the States in the Tenth Amendment to the Constitution.

Police regulations relating to the internal trade and affairs of the States have been uniformly recognized as within such control. . . . In the judgment which established the broad power of Congress over interstate commerce, Chief Justice Marshall said (9 Wheat. 203): "They [inspection laws] act upon the subject before it becomes an article of foreign commerce, or of commerce among the states, and prepare it for that purpose. They form a portion of that immense mass of legislation, which embraces everything within the territory of a state, not surrendered to the general government; all which can be most advantageously exercised by the states themselves. Inspection laws, quarantine laws, health laws of every description, as well as laws for regulating the internal commerce of a state, and those which respect turnpike-roads, ferries, &c., are component parts of this mass." . . .

That there should be limitations upon the right to employ children in mines and factories in the interest of their own and the public welfare, all will admit. . . . It may be desirable that such laws be uniform, but our Federal Government is one of enumerated powers; "this principle," declared Chief Justice Marshall in *McCulloch v. Maryland*, 4 Wheat. 316, "is universally admitted."

A statute must be judged by its natural and reasonable effect. . . . To sustain this statute would not be in our judgment a recognition of the lawful exertion of congressional authority over interstate commerce, but would sanction an invasion by the federal power of the control of a matter purely local in its character, and over which no authority has been delegated to Congress in conferring the power to regulate commerce among the States. . . . We have neither authority nor disposition to question the motives of Congress in enacting this legislation. . . . In our view the necessary effect of this act is, by means of a prohibition against the movement in interstate commerce of ordinary commercial commodities, to regulate the hours of labor of children in factories and mines within the States, a purely state authority. . . . The far reaching result of upholding the act cannot be more plainly indicated than by pointing out that if Congress can thus regulate matters entrusted to local authority by prohibition of the movement of commodities in interstate commerce, all freedom of commerce will be at an end, and the power of the States over local matters may be eliminated, and thus our system of government be practically destroyed.[16]

NOTE: AFTERMATH OF *HAMMER*

As we've seen already, Congress responded to *Hammer* by attempting to accomplish the same goal using the taxing power. When the Supreme Court struck down that attempt as well, progressive social reformers were incensed—as were moderate members of Congress. In June 1924, Congress submitted to the states a proposed constitutional amendment, Section 1 of which declared, "The Congress shall have power to limit, regulate, and prohibit the labor of persons under 18 years of age." But ratification was slow. By 1937, only twenty-eight of the needed thirty-six states had ratified the amendment.

The Supreme Court nevertheless may have been chastened by the proposed amendment: for twelve years after *Hammer*, it acted as though the case did not exist.

For example, the *Hammer* Court had interpreted the *Lottery Case* line of cases narrowly, reading them as holding that Congress could regulate goods or people that crossed state lines only when they were inherently dangerous or immoral. Under that interpretation, the goods produced by child laborers didn't qualify as articles of interstate commerce even if the child labor that produced them was dangerous and immoral. Yet after *Hammer*, in *Brooks v. United States*, 267 U.S. 432 (1925), the Court upheld the National Motor Vehicle Theft Act, 41 Stat. 324, which prohibited crossing state lines with a vehicle that had once been stolen. As in earlier cases, the Court didn't focus on whether the vehicle itself was dangerous or immoral (only the theft that "produced" the stolen vehicle was immoral). Rather, the Court simply declared that a vehicle was an article of interstate commerce. *See also, e.g.*, *Thornton v. United States*, 271 U.S. 414 (1926) (upholding the prohibition of taking certain cattle across state lines).

Similarly, the *Hammer* Court had ignored the *E.C. Knight Co.* line of cases when holding that Congress had no power to regulate intrastate activities even when necessary to protect interstate activities from being

16 **Questions:** One way of making the Supreme Court's opinion here more intuitive is to imagine that Congress had passed a law *requiring* the use of child labor. Under the logic of this opinion, could Congress preempt state laws that banned the employment of children in factories or coal mines? What principle could possibly distinguish commerce from manufacturing or mining?

competitively disadvantaged. "The Commerce Clause was not intended to give to Congress a general authority to equalize such conditions," the Court wrote. But in *Board of Trade v. Olsen*, 262 U.S. 1 (1923), the Court held that Congress could regulate a commodity exchange in order to protect interstate buyers of grain from being competitively disadvantaged by local sales for speculative "futures contracts." Turning to precedents in the *E.C. Knight Co.* line, the Court authorized the regulation of intrastate activities where "interstate commerce would be directly impaired and weakened by the unrestrained" local activity. *Olsen*, 262 U.S. at 37.

The Court's response to the Great Depression, however, proved to observers that *Hammer* still had heft.

8.2.2

A.L.A. Schechter Poultry Corp. v. United States

295 U.S. 495 (1935)

As discussed previously (sections 6.1, 7.1), President Franklin D. Roosevelt signed dozens of bills into law in his first one hundred days in the White House, three of which were headline pieces of legislation. The Agricultural Adjustment Act of 1933 paid farmers not to produce crops (although it was struck down as coercive spending legislation in *United States v. Butler*, 297 U.S. 1 (1936)). The Emergency Banking Act of 1933 suspended the gold standard and abrogated all gold clauses in private and public contracts (although it was harshly criticized for repudiating the nation's debt in *Perry v. United States*, 294 U.S. 330 (1935)). These were major pieces of legislation, but they paled in comparison to the third law, the National Industrial Recovery Act (NIRA) of 1933, Pub. L. No. 73–67, 48 Stat. 195. The centerpiece of the first New Deal, the NIRA was enacted on the premise that the Great Depression was caused by overproduction and unfair and unnecessary competition. The act gave workers the right to collectively bargain; gave businesses the right to collaborate in forming "industrial codes" of fair prices, wages, and standards; and gave the president the power to sign these business-drafted codes into law. It was scheduled to last for two years.

Because businesses themselves were entrusted with establishing industrial codes, much of the NIRA depended on their voluntary support. In the first several months after the NIRA was enacted, the logo for the agency it created—a blue eagle with the phrase "We Do Our Part"—was on store windows, in newspaper advertisements, and everywhere else. But many NIRA regulations were shoddily drafted, hastily reviewed, and sloppily enforced. By 1935, the law was deeply unpopular and headed toward its expiration without hope of renewal.

The law never made it to its natural expiration date, however. In *A.L.A. Schechter Poultry Corp. v. United States*, 295 U.S. 495 (1935), the Supreme Court sent the NIRA to its deathbed early.

The case involved the A.L.A. Schechter Poultry Corporation, which operated the largest wholesale poultry slaughterhouse in Brooklyn. At the time, New York City was the largest live-poultry market in the United States; and the Schechter Corporation did well, earning more than $1 million per year processing more than 30,000 pounds of chicken per week from other states. When the city's poultry slaughterhouses adopted the Live Poultry Code under the NIRA, however, the Schechter brothers, who operated the company, persistently failed to follow the code's requirements regarding selling diseased poultry, selling below cost, and paying workers a minimum wage. For example, the code had a "straight killing" rule that required wholesale slaughterhouses to sell buyers an entire coop of chickens after those unfit for human consumption were removed. But the Schechters allowed white sellers to buy chickens individually—selling the unfit chickens "on Fridays to the colored trade." Transcript of Record at 531, *United States v. Schechter*, 8 F. Supp. 136 (E.D.N.Y. 1934).

Federal prosecutors convicted the Schechter brothers and their company of violating the code. They also argued that the code was properly promulgated under the NIRA and that the NIRA, as applied, was a proper exercise of the Commerce Clause. An appellate court agreed, writing, "The practice of selective killing, rather than straight killing, resulted in price cutting, and a lowering of prices received by the farmers and the interstate shippers." *United States v. A.L.A. Schechter Poultry Corp.*, 76 F.2d 617, 619 (2d Cir. 1935).

But the Supreme Court reversed, striking down the NIRA on several grounds. The following excerpt picks up where the Court begins reviewing the codes under the *E.C. Knight* line of Commerce Clause cases.

■ MR. CHIEF JUSTICE HUGHES delivered the opinion of the Court.[17]

This aspect of the case presents the question whether the particular provisions of the Live Poultry Code, which the defendants were convicted for violating and for having conspired to violate, were within the regulating power of Congress. These provisions relate to the hours and wages of those employed by defendants in their slaughterhouses in Brooklyn and to the sales there made to retail dealers and butchers.

(1) Were these transactions *"in"* interstate commerce? Much is made of the fact that almost all the poultry coming to New York is sent there from other States. But the code provisions, as here applied, do not concern the transportation of the poultry from other States to New York, or the transactions of the commission men or others to whom it is consigned, or the sales made by such consignees to defendants.

---

17 **As You Read, Consider:** There is no question in this case that Congress could regulate the conditions by which chickens traveled in interstate commerce. But the NIRA regulations take effect after the chickens have been unloaded from trucks and before they have been sold. At what point does the Court think that Congress's exclusive power over the chickens stops and the states' exclusive power over the chickens begins?

As in *Hammer v. Dagenhart*, assume that Chief Justice Charles Evans Hughes does not like unfair wages or unhealthy food practices. Why might he still be worried about this federal regulation?

When defendants had made their purchases, . . . the poultry was trucked to their slaughterhouses in Brooklyn for local disposition. The interstate transactions in relation to that poultry then ended. Defendants held the poultry at their slaughterhouse markets for slaughter and local sale to retail dealers and butchers who in turn sold directly to consumers. Neither the slaughtering nor the sales by defendants were transactions in interstate commerce.

The undisputed facts thus afford no warrant for the argument that the poultry handled by defendants at their slaughterhouse markets was in a *"current"* or *"flow"* of interstate commerce and was thus subject to congressional regulation. The mere fact that there may be a constant flow of commodities into a State does not mean that the flow continues after the property has arrived and has become commingled with the mass of property within the State and is there held solely for local disposition and use. So far as the poultry here in question is concerned, the flow in interstate commerce had ceased. The poultry had come to a permanent rest within the State. It was not held, used, or sold by defendants in relation to any further transactions in interstate commerce and was not destined for transportation to other States. Hence, decisions which deal with a stream of interstate commerce—where goods come to rest within a State temporarily and are later to go forward in interstate commerce—and with the regulations of transactions involved in that practical continuity of movement, are not applicable here. See *Swift & Co. v. United States*, 196 U.S. 375, 387, 388; *Chicago Board of Trade v. Olsen*, 262 U.S. 1, 35.

(2) Did the defendants' transactions directly *"affect"* interstate commerce so as to be subject to federal regulation? The power of Congress extends not only to the regulation of transactions which are part of interstate commerce, but to the protection of that commerce from injury. It matters not that the injury may be due to the conduct of those engaged in intrastate operations. Thus, Congress may protect the safety of those employed in interstate transportation "no matter what may be the source of the dangers which threaten it." *Southern Ry. Co. v. United States*, 222 U.S. 20, 27. We said in *Second Employers' Liability Cases*, 223 U.S. 1, 51, that it is the "effect upon interstate commerce," not "the source of the injury," which is "the criterion of congressional power." We have held that, in dealing with common carriers engaged in both interstate and intrastate commerce, the dominant authority of Congress necessarily embraces the right to control their intrastate operations in all matters having such a close and substantial relation to interstate traffic that the control is essential or appropriate to secure the freedom of that traffic from interference or unjust discrimination and to promote the efficiency of the interstate service. The *Shreveport Case*, 234 U.S. 342, 351, 352. And combinations and conspiracies to restrain interstate commerce, or to monopolize any part of it, are none the less within the reach of the Anti-Trust Act because the conspirators seek to attain their end by means of intrastate activities. . . .

The instant case is not of that sort. . . . Defendants have been convicted, not upon direct charges of injury to interstate commerce or of interference with persons engaged in that commerce, but of violations of certain provisions of the Live Poultry Code and of conspiracy to commit these violations. Interstate commerce is brought in only upon the charge that violations of these provisions—as to hours and wages of employees and local sales—*"affected"* interstate commerce.

In determining how far the federal government may go in controlling intrastate transactions upon the ground that they "affect" interstate commerce, there is a necessary and well-established distinction between direct and indirect effects.[18] The

[18] **Questions:** Hughes here draws a distinction between "direct" and "indirect" effects on interstate commerce. Does he offer any hints regarding how to draw the line between them in future cases?

precise line can be drawn only as individual cases arise, but the distinction is clear in principle. Direct effects are illustrated by the railroad cases we have cited, as *e.g.*, the effect of failure to use prescribed safety appliances on railroads which are the highways of both interstate and intrastate commerce, injury to an employee engaged in interstate transportation by the negligence of an employee engaged in an intrastate movement, the fixing of rates for intrastate transportation which unjustly discriminate against interstate commerce. But where the effect of intrastate transactions upon interstate commerce is merely indirect, such transactions remain within the domain of state power. If the commerce clause were construed to reach all enterprises and transactions which could be said to have an indirect effect upon interstate commerce, the federal authority would embrace practically all the activities of the people and the authority of the State over its domestic concerns would exist only by sufferance of the federal government. . . .

NOTE: DIRECT VERSUS INDIRECT EFFECTS ON COMMERCE

A.L.A. Schechter was not the only case in Roosevelt's first term that struck down one of Roosevelt's New Deal laws under the Commerce Clause. In *Railroad Retirement Board v. Alton Railroad*, 295 U.S. 330 (1935), the Court struck down as too indirect the Railroad Retirement Act of 1934, 48 Stat. 1283, which ordered the early but pensioned retirement of elderly employees of interstate carriers. And in *Carter v. Carter Coal Co.*, 298 U.S. 238 (1936), the Court similarly struck down as too indirect the Bituminous Coal Conservation Act of 1935, 49 Stat. 991, which regulated the wages and hours of workers engaged in the mining of coal sold in interstate commerce.

8.2.3

United States v. Darby Lumber Co.

312 U.S. 100 (1941)

As we read in the section on conditional spending (section 6.2), Roosevelt responded to cases like *A.L.A. Schechter* with a proposal to pack the Supreme Court with six young New Deal supporters. In the spring of 1937, the Court responded by upholding the second round of New Deal legislation: the "switch in time that saved nine" (see section 6.2).

Only two years after writing the opinion in *A.L.A. Schechter*, Chief Justice Charles Evans Hughes signed on to a radically different opinion in *NLRB v. Jones & Laughlin Steel Corp.*, 301 U.S. 1 (1937). In *Jones & Laughlin*, after the NLRB penalized the Jones & Laughlin Steel Corporation for unfairly discriminating against unionized steel workers, a 5–4 majority upheld the constitutionality of the National Labor Relations Act of 1935, 49 Stat. 449, a law that began with the finding that "[t]he denial by employers of the right of employees to organize and the refusal by employers to accept the procedure of collective bargaining

---

As in *Hammer*, suppose that Congress had declared that the Great Depression had been caused by too much regulation, and therefore anyone who worked in a slaughterhouse in which chickens came from out of state could not collectively bargain or be subject to a state's minimum-wage or labor protections. Same outcome as in *A.L.A. Schechter Poultry Corp. v. United States*?

lead to strikes and other forms of industrial strife or unrest, which have the intent or the necessary effect of burdening or obstructing commerce." *Jones & Laughlin*, 301 U.S. at 24 n.2. Based on that finding, the law guaranteed the right of all employees to collectively bargain and also gave the National Labor Relations Board (NLRB) the power to prohibit any employer from interfering with that right in a manner affecting interstate commerce. The law represented an audacious expansion of the "affecting interstate . . . commerce" theory rejected in *A.L.A. Schechter*, 295 U.S. at 545–46.

Importantly, the *Jones & Laughlin* Court interpreted *A.L.A. Schechter*'s "stream of . . . commerce" argument in a remarkably broad way. The Court noted that the Pennsylvania company was the fourth-largest producer of steel in the United States—"a completely integrated enterprise," with mines in Michigan and Minnesota, limestone properties in West Virginia, warehouses and fabricating shops in six states, and railroads and steam barges connecting them like "arteries" through a single body. *Jones & Laughlin*, 301 U.S. at 26–27. Because of this integration, the government urged the Court to hold that the steel workers were engaged in a "flow" or "stream of commerce." *Id.* at 35–36. The Court may have agreed, but in a stunning paragraph, it announced that this theory of the Commerce Clause was too narrow:

> We do not find it necessary to determine whether these features of defendant's business dispose of the asserted analogy to the "stream of commerce" cases. The instances in which that metaphor has been used are but particular, and not exclusive, illustrations of the protective power which the Government invokes in support of the present Act. The congressional authority to protect interstate commerce from burdens and obstructions is not limited to transactions which can be deemed to be an essential part of a "flow" of interstate or foreign commerce. Burdens and obstructions may be due to injurious action springing from other sources. The fundamental principle is that the power to regulate commerce is the power to enact "all appropriate legislation" for "its protection and advancement"; to adopt measures "to promote its growth and insure its safety"; "to foster, protect, control and restrain." *Second Employers' Liability Cases*, *supra*, p. 47. That power is plenary and may be exerted to protect interstate commerce "no matter what the source of the dangers which threaten it." *Second Employers' Liability Cases*, p. 51; *Schechter Corp.* v. *United States*, *supra*. Although activities may be intrastate in character when separately considered, if they have such a close and substantial relation to interstate commerce that their control is essential or appropriate to protect that commerce from burdens and obstructions, Congress cannot be denied the power to exercise that control. *Schechter Corp.* v. *United States*, *supra*.

> Undoubtedly the scope of this power must be considered in the light of our dual system of government and may not be extended so as to embrace effects upon interstate commerce so indirect and remote that to embrace them, in view of our complex society, would effectually obliterate the distinction between what is national and what is local and create a completely centralized government. *Id.* The question is necessarily one of degree. As the Court said in *Chicago Board of Trade* v. *Olsen, supra*, p. 37, repeating what had been said in *Stafford* v. *Wallace, supra:* "Whatever amounts to more or less constant practice, and threatens to obstruct or unduly to burden the freedom of interstate commerce is within the regulatory power of Congress under the commerce clause and it is primarily for Congress to consider and decide the fact of the danger and meet it.

Id. at 36–37.

Needless to say, this was quite the about-face for the author of *A.L.A. Schechter*. With a theory of the Commerce Clause that allowed Congress to regulate virtually anything that burdens or obstructs interstate commerce, the Court upheld the statute's application to steel workers engaged in manufacturing.

Congress quickly took advantage of the Supreme Court's newfound deference to commercial regulations by passing new versions of laws that the Court had previously struck down. For example, Congress passed the Fair Labor Standards Act of 1938, Pub. L. No. 75–718, 52 Stat. 1060, which, among other things, prohibited "oppressive child labor." 52 Stat. at 1067. The law also specified federal minimum-wage and maximum-hour requirements for employees "engaged in commerce or the production of goods in commerce." *Id.* at 1062–63. Section 15 made it unlawful to knowingly transport goods in interstate commerce that had been produced in violation of the law, and also prohibited certain employers from violating the wage and hour requirements.

By the time the Supreme Court reviewed the Fair Labor Standards Act in 1941 in *United States v. Darby Lumber Co.*, 312 U.S. 100 (1941), Roosevelt had appointed six of the nine justices. The case involved the Darby Lumber Company, a Georgia corporation that refused to comply with the minimum-wage and maximum-hour requirements for its employees. When federal regulators suspended the transportation of Darby's lumber, the company complained that, under *Hammer*, Congress had no power to regulate benign goods in interstate commerce as a means of regulating how those goods had been manufactured. The company also argued that Congress had no power to regulate the wages or hours of employees engaged in manufacturing.

The Court considered these claims separately, ruling that Congress did, in fact, have the power to do both.

■ MR. JUSTICE STONE delivered the opinion of the Court.[19]

The prohibition of shipment of the proscribed goods in interstate commerce. Section 15(a)(1) prohibits, and the indictment charges, the shipment in interstate commerce, of goods produced for interstate commerce by employees whose wages and hours of employment do not conform to the requirements of the Act. . . . [T]he only question arising under the commerce clause with respect to such shipments is whether Congress has the constitutional power to prohibit them.

While manufacture is not of itself interstate commerce, the shipment of manufactured goods interstate is such commerce and the prohibition of such shipment by Congress is indubitably a regulation of the commerce. The power to regulate commerce is the power "to prescribe the rule by which commerce is governed." *Gibbons v. Ogden*, 9 Wheat. 1, 196. It extends not only to those regulations which aid, foster and protect the commerce, but embraces those which prohibit it. *Reid v. Colorado*, 187 U.S. 137; *Lottery Case*, 188 U.S. 321; *Hoke v. United States*, 227 U.S. 308. It is conceded that the power of Congress to prohibit transportation in interstate commerce includes noxious articles, *Lottery Case, supra*; cf. *Hoke v. United States, supra*; stolen articles, *Brooks v. United States*, 267 U.S. 432; kidnapped persons, *Gooch v. United States*, 297 U.S. 124, and articles such as intoxicating liquor or convict made goods, traffic in which is forbidden or restricted by the laws of the state of destination.

But it is said that the present prohibition falls within the scope of none of these categories; that while the prohibition is nominally a regulation of the commerce its motive or purpose is regulation of wages and hours of persons engaged in manufacture, the control of which has been reserved to the states and upon which Georgia and some of the states of destination have placed no restriction; that the effect of the present statute is not to exclude the proscribed articles from interstate commerce . . . but instead, under the guise of a regulation of interstate commerce, it undertakes to regulate wages and hours within the state contrary to the policy of the state which has elected to leave them unregulated.

The power of Congress over interstate commerce "is complete in itself, may be exercised to its utmost extent, and acknowledges no limitations other than are prescribed in the Constitution." *Gibbons v. Ogden, supra*, 196. That power can neither be enlarged nor diminished by the exercise or non-exercise of state power. Congress, following its own conception of public policy concerning the restrictions which may appropriately be imposed on interstate commerce, is free to exclude from the commerce articles whose use in the states for which they are destined it may conceive to be injurious to the public health, morals or welfare, even though the state has not sought to regulate their use. *Reid v. Colorado, supra*; *Lottery Case, supra*; *Hoke v. United States, supra*.

Such regulation is not a forbidden invasion of state power merely because either its motive or its consequence is to restrict the use of articles of commerce within the states of destination; and is not prohibited unless by other Constitutional provisions. It is no objection to the assertion of the power to regulate interstate commerce that

---

[19] **As You Read, Consider:** An underlying assumption connecting *Hammer v. Dagenhart* and *A.L.A. Schechter Poultry Corp. v. United States* was that if Congress had the power to regulate intrastate activity like manufacturing, then a necessary consequence was that states lacked the power to regulate these same intrastate activities—regardless of whether Congress acted. How does Justice Harlan Stone address this assumption? Why isn't he as worried about ignoring this assumption as the previous Courts were?

its exercise is attended by the same incidents which attend the exercise of the police power of the states.[20]

The motive and purpose of the present regulation are plainly to make effective the Congressional conception of public policy that interstate commerce should not be made the instrument of competition in the distribution of goods produced under substandard labor conditions, which competition is injurious to the commerce and to the states from and to which the commerce flows. The motive and purpose of a regulation of interstate commerce are matters for the legislative judgment upon the exercise of which the Constitution places no restriction and over which the courts are given no control. *Sonzinsky v. United States*, 300 U.S. 506, 513 and cases cited. "The judicial cannot prescribe to the legislative department of the government limitations upon the exercise of its acknowledged power." *Veazie Bank v. Fenno*, 8 Wall. 533. Whatever their motive and purpose, regulations of commerce which do not infringe some constitutional prohibition are within the plenary power conferred on Congress by the Commerce Clause. Subject only to that limitation, presently to be considered, we conclude that the prohibition of the shipment interstate of goods produced under the forbidden substandard labor conditions is within the constitutional authority of Congress.

In the more than a century which has elapsed since the decision of *Gibbons v. Ogden*, these principles of constitutional interpretation have been so long and repeatedly recognized by this Court as applicable to the Commerce Clause, that there would be little occasion for repeating them now were it not for the decision of this Court twenty-two years ago in *Hammer v. Dagenhart*, 247 U.S. 251. In that case it was held by a bare majority of the Court . . . that Congress was without power to exclude the products of child labor from interstate commerce. The reasoning and conclusion of the Court's opinion there cannot be reconciled with the conclusion which we have reached, that the power of Congress under the Commerce Clause is plenary to exclude any article from interstate commerce subject only to the specific prohibitions of the Constitution.

Hammer v. Dagenhart has not been followed. The distinction on which the decision was rested that Congressional power to prohibit interstate commerce is limited to articles which in themselves have some harmful or deleterious property—a distinction which was novel when made and unsupported by any provision of the Constitution—has long since been abandoned. *Brooks v. United States, supra*. The thesis of the opinion that the motive of the prohibition or its effect to control in some measure the use or production within the states of the article thus excluded from the commerce can operate to deprive the regulation of its constitutional authority has long since ceased to have force. *Reid v. Colorado, supra*; *Lottery Case, supra*. . . .

The conclusion is inescapable that *Hammer v. Dagenhart*, was a departure from the principles which have prevailed in the interpretation of the Commerce Clause both before and since the decision and that such vitality, as a precedent, as it then had has long since been exhausted. It should be and now is overruled.

Validity of the wage and hour requirements. Section 15(a)(2) and §§ 6 and 7 require employers to conform to the wage and hour provisions with respect to all employees engaged in the production of goods for interstate commerce. As appellee's employees are not alleged to be "engaged in interstate commerce" the validity of the prohibition turns on the question whether the employment . . . of employees engaged

[20] **Questions:** Stone here is suggesting that Congress's power to regulate interstate commerce might overlap with the states' police power—a point that no previous decision held. What principle justifies this new approach toward Congress's power? Does it carry with it any dangers for state autonomy?

in the production of goods for interstate commerce is so related to the commerce and so affects it as to be within the reach of the power of Congress to regulate it. . . .

The power of Congress over interstate commerce is not confined to the regulation of commerce among the states. It extends to those activities intrastate which so affect interstate commerce or the exercise of the power of Congress over it as to make regulation of them appropriate means to the attainment of a legitimate end, the exercise of the granted power of Congress to regulate interstate commerce. See *McCulloch v. Maryland*, 4 Wheat. 316, 421.[21]

While this Court has many times found state regulation of interstate commerce, when uniformity of its regulation is of national concern, to be incompatible with the Commerce Clause even though Congress has not legislated on the subject, the Court has never implied such restraint on state control over matters intrastate not deemed to be regulations of interstate commerce or its instrumentalities even though they affect the commerce. In the absence of Congressional legislation on the subject state laws which are not regulations of the commerce itself or its instrumentalities are not forbidden even though they affect interstate commerce. *Kidd v. Pearson*, 128 U.S. 1.[22]

But it does not follow that Congress may not by appropriate legislation regulate intrastate activities where they have a substantial effect on interstate commerce. A recent example is the National Labor Relations Act for the regulation of employer and employee relations in industries in which strikes, induced by unfair labor practices named in the Act, tend to disturb or obstruct interstate commerce. See *National Labor Relations Board v. Jones & Laughlin Steel Corp.*, 301 U.S. 1, 38, 40. But long before the adoption of the National Labor Relations Act this Court had many times held that the power of Congress to regulate interstate commerce extends to the regulation through legislative action of activities intrastate which have a substantial effect on the commerce or the exercise of the Congressional power over it.

In such legislation Congress has sometimes left it to the courts to determine whether the intrastate activities have the prohibited effect on the commerce, as in the Sherman Act. It has sometimes left it to an administrative board or agency to determine whether the activities sought to be regulated or prohibited have such effect, as in the case of the Interstate Commerce Act, and the National Labor Relations Act. . . . And sometimes Congress itself has said that a particular activity affects the commerce, as it did in the present Act. . . . In passing on the validity of legislation of the class last mentioned the only function of courts is to determine whether the particular activity regulated or prohibited is within the reach of the federal power.

Congress, having by the present Act adopted the policy of excluding from interstate commerce all goods produced for the commerce which do not conform to the specified labor standards, it may choose the means reasonably adapted to the attainment of the permitted end, even though they involve control of intrastate activities. . . .[23] As we have said the evils aimed at by the Act are the spread of

---

[21] **Question:** *McCulloch v. Maryland* was a case about Congress's power under the Necessary and Proper Clause. What does it have to do with Congress's power to regulate commerce within a single state?

[22] **Question:** In *Gibbons v. Ogden*, Chief Justice John Marshall strongly suggested that even if Congress had not passed the Coasting Act, New York would lack the power to enforce its ferry monopoly because Congress's power to regulate interstate commerce is exclusive. Does this paragraph overrule *Gibbons*, or is it compatible with Gibbons?

[23] **Question:** The Court here announces a new test for evaluating Congress's power to regulate intrastate commerce—a test adapted from *McCulloch*. Imagine that a conservative Congress declared that any business that sells goods in interstate commerce may ignore all state minimum-wage, maximum-hour, or child-labor restrictions. Same result as in this case?

substandard labor conditions through the use of the facilities of interstate commerce for competition by the goods so produced with those produced under the prescribed or better labor conditions; and the consequent dislocation of the commerce itself caused by the impairment or destruction of local businesses by competition made effective through interstate commerce. The Act is thus directed at the suppression of a method or kind of competition in interstate commerce which it has in effect condemned as "unfair." . . . The Sherman Act and the National Labor Relations Act are familiar examples of the exertion of the commerce power to prohibit or control activities wholly intrastate because of their effect on interstate commerce.

The means adopted by § 15(a)(2) for the protection of interstate commerce by the suppression of the production of the condemned goods for interstate commerce is so related to the commerce and so affects it as to be within the reach of the commerce power. Congress, to attain its objective in the suppression of nationwide competition in interstate commerce by goods produced under substandard labor conditions, has made no distinction as to the volume or amount of shipments in the commerce or of production for commerce by any particular shipper or producer. It recognized that in present day industry, competition by a small part may affect the whole and that the total effect of the competition of many small producers may be great. See H. Rept. No. 2182, 75th Cong. 1st Sess., p. 7. The legislation aimed at a whole embraces all its parts. . . .

Our conclusion is unaffected by the Tenth Amendment which provides: "The powers not delegated to the United States by the Constitution, nor prohibited by it to the States, are reserved to the States respectively, or to the people." The amendment states but a truism that all is retained which has not been surrendered. There is nothing in the history of its adoption to suggest that it was more than declaratory of the relationship between the national and state governments as it had been established by the Constitution before the amendment or that its purpose was other than to allay fears that the new national government might seek to exercise powers not granted, and that the states might not be able to exercise fully their reserved powers.[24]

From the beginning and for many years the amendment has been construed as not depriving the national government of authority to resort to all means for the exercise of a granted power which are appropriate and plainly adapted to the permitted end. *McCulloch v. Maryland, supra*, 405, 406; *Lottery Case, supra*; see *United States v. The Brigantine William*, 28 Fed. Cas. No. 16,700, p. 622. Whatever doubts may have arisen of the soundness of that conclusion, they have been put at rest by the decisions under the Sherman Act and the National Labor Relations Act which we have cited. . . .

8.2.4

Wickard v. Filburn

317 U.S. 111 (1942)

Darby was a sweeping, unanimous decision, establishing the principles that continue to guide Congress's exercise of the Commerce Clause. But the high-water mark of the Commerce Clause arrived the

[24] **Questions:** We have already read several tax and commerce cases that cite the Tenth Amendment as a source of limits on Congress's power to tax or regulate commerce. Do those limits survive this description of the Tenth Amendment? Put bluntly, are there any limits on Congress's power to regulate commerce after this decision?

following year in a case involving the Agricultural Adjustment Act of 1938, as amended, 52 Stat. 31.

As discussed in the section on the spending power (section 6.1), Roosevelt believed that the main cause of low agricultural prices during the Great Depression was overproduction. To encourage farmers to stop producing too many crops, the 1933 version of the statute used financial inducements—which were struck down as coercive in *United States v. Butler*, 297 U. S. 1 (1936). By contrast, the 1938 version of the law, passed after the 1937 switch in time, authorized the secretary of agriculture simply to impose "marketing quotas" to control the amount of crops that every county in the country was allowed to produce for market. It also provided that anyone who produced more than his or her quota under a county's marketing quota could be penalized.

In 1940, representatives of the Department of Agriculture told Roscoe Filburn, a small farmer in Montgomery County, Ohio, that he was authorized by the statute to plant no more than 11.1 acres of wheat the following fall. Ignoring this warning, Filburn planted 23 acres of wheat and harvested an extra 239 bushels over his marketing quota. Filburn explained to curious department representatives that he had always raised wheat for his personal use, including as feed for his animals and as flour for his family. (A single bushel yields approximately forty-two pounds of white flour, or seventy loaves of bread.) To this, the representatives responded that the "marketing quota" extended to all crops, including crops destined for livestock or personal use; and if Filburn didn't want to be penalized, he had to store his extra wheat with them. Rather than turn over the wheat, Filburn sued the secretary of agriculture, Claude Wickard, to block the enforcement of the penalty against him. His case, *Wickard v. Filburn*, 317 U.S. 111 (1942), made its way to the Supreme Court, where his attorney, a former member of Congress from Ohio, argued that Congress had no power to regulate how much wheat a person could grow for his own use. By this point, Roosevelt had appointed or promoted all but one of the justices on the Court.

■ MR. JUSTICE JACKSON delivered the opinion of the Court. . . .[25]

[I]t is urged that under the Commerce Clause of the Constitution, Article I, § 8, clause 3, Congress does not possess the power it has in this instance sought to exercise. The question would merit little consideration since our decision in *United States v. Darby*, 312 U.S. 100, sustaining the federal power to regulate production of goods for commerce, except for the fact that this Act extends federal regulation to production not intended in any part for commerce but wholly for consumption on the farm. . . . Wheat produced on excess acreage is designated as "available for marketing" as so defined, and the penalty is imposed thereon. Penalties do not depend upon whether any part of the wheat, either within or without the quota, is sold or intended to be sold. The sum of this is that the Federal Government fixes a quota including all that the farmer may harvest for sale or for his own farm needs, and

[25] **As You Read, Consider:** Roscoe Filburn grew his own wheat on his own farm; these crops never entered commerce at all, much less interstate commerce. Why, then, can Congress regulate this production, according to the Court?

declares that wheat produced on excess acreage may neither be disposed of nor used except upon payment of the penalty, or except it is stored as required by the Act or delivered to the Secretary of Agriculture.

Appellee says that this is a regulation of production and consumption of wheat. Such activities are, he urges, beyond the reach of Congressional power under the Commerce Clause, since they are local in character, and their effects upon interstate commerce are at most "indirect." In answer the Government argues that the statute regulates neither production nor consumption, but only marketing; and, in the alternative, that if the Act does go beyond the regulation of marketing it is sustainable as a "necessary and proper" implementation of the power of Congress over interstate commerce.

The Government's concern lest the Act be held to be a regulation of production or consumption, rather than of marketing, is attributable to a few dicta and decisions of this Court which might be understood to lay it down that activities such as "production," "manufacturing," and "mining" are strictly "local" and, except in special circumstances which are not present here, cannot be regulated under the commerce power because their effects upon interstate commerce are, as matter of law, only "indirect." Even today, when this power has been held to have great latitude, there is no decision of this Court that such activities may be regulated where no part of the product is intended for interstate commerce or intermingled with the subjects thereof. We believe that a review of the course of decision under the Commerce Clause will make plain, however, that questions of the power of Congress are not to be decided by reference to any formula which would give controlling force to nomenclature such as "production" and "indirect" and foreclose consideration of the actual effects of the activity in question upon interstate commerce.

At the beginning Chief Justice Marshall described the federal commerce power with a breadth never yet exceeded. *Gibbons v. Ogden*, 9 Wheat. 1, 194–195. He made emphatic the embracing and penetrating nature of this power by warning that effective restraints on its exercise must proceed from political rather than from judicial processes. *Id.* at 197.

For nearly a century, however, decisions of this Court under the Commerce Clause dealt rarely with questions of what Congress might do in the exercise of its granted power under the Clause, and almost entirely with the permissibility of state activity which it was claimed discriminated against or burdened interstate commerce. During this period there was perhaps little occasion for the affirmative exercise of the commerce power, and the influence of the Clause on American life and law was a negative one, resulting almost wholly from its operation as a restraint upon the powers of the states. In discussion and decision the point of reference, instead of being what was "necessary and proper" to the exercise by Congress of its granted power, was often some concept of sovereignty thought to be implicit in the status of statehood. Certain activities such as "production," "manufacturing," and "mining" were occasionally said to be within the province of state governments and beyond the power of Congress under the Commerce Clause.

It was not until 1887, with the enactment of the Interstate Commerce Act, that the interstate commerce power began to exert positive influence in American law and life. This first important federal resort to the commerce power was followed in 1890 by the Sherman Anti-Trust Act and, thereafter, mainly after 1903, by many others. These statutes ushered in new phases of adjudication, which required the Court to approach the interpretation of the Commerce Clause in the light of an actual exercise by Congress of its power thereunder.

When it first dealt with this new legislation, the Court adhered to its earlier pronouncements, and allowed but little scope to the power of Congress. *United States v. Knight Co.*, 156 U.S. 1. These earlier pronouncements also played an important part in several of the five cases in which this Court later held that Acts of Congress under the Commerce Clause were in excess of its power.

Even while important opinions in this line of restrictive authority were being written, however, other cases called forth broader interpretations of the Commerce Clause destined to supersede the earlier ones, and to bring about a return to the principles first enunciated by Chief Justice Marshall in *Gibbons v. Ogden, supra*. . . .

The present Chief Justice has said in summary of the present state of the law: "The commerce power is not confined in its exercise to the regulation of commerce among the states. It extends to those activities intrastate which so affect interstate commerce, or the exertion of the power of Congress over it, as to make regulation of them appropriate means to the attainment of a legitimate end, the effective execution of the granted power to regulate interstate commerce. . . . The power of Congress over interstate commerce is plenary and complete in itself, may be exercised to its utmost extent, and acknowledges no limitations other than are prescribed in the Constitution. . . . It follows that no form of state activity can constitutionally thwart the regulatory power granted by the commerce clause to Congress. Hence the reach of that power extends to those intrastate activities which in a substantial way interfere with or obstruct the exercise of the granted power." *United States v. Wrightwood Dairy Co.*, 315 U.S. 110, 119.

Whether the subject of the regulation in question was "production," "consumption," or "marketing" is, therefore, not material for purposes of deciding the question of federal power before us. That an activity is of local character may help in a doubtful case to determine whether Congress intended to reach it. The same consideration might help in determining whether in the absence of Congressional action it would be permissible for the state to exert its power on the subject matter, even though in so doing it to some degree affected interstate commerce. But even if appellee's activity be local and though it may not be regarded as commerce, it may still, whatever its nature, be reached by Congress if it exerts a substantial economic effect on interstate commerce, and this irrespective of whether such effect is what might at some earlier time have been defined as "direct" or "indirect."[26]

The parties have stipulated a summary of the economics of the wheat industry. Commerce among the states in wheat is large and important. Although wheat is raised in every state but one, production in most states is not equal to consumption. Sixteen states on average have had a surplus of wheat above their own requirements for feed, seed, and food. Thirty-two states and the District of Columbia, where production has been below consumption, have looked to these surplus-producing states for their supply as well as for wheat for export and carry-over.

The wheat industry has been a problem industry for some years. Largely as a result of increased foreign production and import restrictions, annual exports of wheat and flour from the United States during the ten-year period ending in 1940 averaged less than 10 per cent of total production, while during the 1920's they averaged more than 25 per cent. The decline in the export trade has left a large surplus in production which, in connection with an abnormally large supply of wheat and other grains in recent years, caused congestion in a number of markets; tied up railroad cars; and caused elevators in some instances to turn away grains, and railroads to institute embargoes to prevent further congestion. . . .

---

[26] **Question:** Applying the language from this paragraph, can you imagine any law that would fall beyond Congress's power to regulate interstate commerce?

In the absence of regulation, the price of wheat in the United States would be much affected by world conditions. During 1941, producers who cooperated with the Agricultural Adjustment program received an average price on the farm of about $1.16 a bushel, as compared with the world market price of 40 cents a bushel. . . .

The maintenance by government regulation of a price for wheat undoubtedly can be accomplished as effectively by sustaining or increasing the demand as by limiting the supply. The effect of the statute before us is to restrict the amount which may be produced for market and the extent as well to which one may forestall resort to the market by producing to meet his own needs. That appellee's own contribution to the demand for wheat may be trivial by itself is not enough to remove him from the scope of federal regulation where, as here, his contribution, taken together with that of many others similarly situated, is far from trivial. *United States v. Darby*, *supra*, at 123.[27]

It is well established by decisions of this Court that the power to regulate commerce includes the power to regulate the prices at which commodities in that commerce are dealt in and practices affecting such prices. One of the primary purposes of the Act in question was to increase the market price of wheat, and to that end to limit the volume thereof that could affect the market. It can hardly be denied that a factor of such volume and variability as home-consumed wheat would have a substantial influence on price and market conditions. This may arise because being in marketable condition such wheat overhangs the market and, if induced by rising prices, tends to flow into the market and check price increases. But if we assume that it is never marketed, it supplies a need of the man who grew it which would otherwise be reflected by purchases in the open market. Home-grown wheat in this sense competes with wheat in commerce. The stimulation of commerce is a use of the regulatory function quite as definitely as prohibitions or restrictions thereon. This record leaves us in no doubt that Congress may properly have considered that wheat consumed on the farm where grown, if wholly outside the scheme of regulation, would have a substantial effect in defeating and obstructing its purpose to stimulate trade therein at increased prices.

It is said, however, that this Act, forcing some farmers into the market to buy what they could provide for themselves, is an unfair promotion of the markets and prices of specializing wheat growers. It is of the essence of regulation that it lays a restraining hand on the self-interest of the regulated and that advantages from the regulation commonly fall to others. The conflicts of economic interest between the regulated and those who advantage by it are wisely left under our system to resolution by the Congress under its more flexible and responsible legislative process. Such conflicts rarely lend themselves to judicial determination. And with the wisdom, workability, or fairness, of the plan of regulation we have nothing to do. . . .[28]

NOTE: *WICKARD* AND EXPANSION OF THE COMMERCE CLAUSE

The Supreme Court's interpretation of the Commerce Clause in *Jones & Laughlin*, *Darby*, and *Wickard* didn't come out of nowhere. An animating purpose of the Constitutional Convention had been to empower the federal government to resolve collective-action problems among the states, and the

---

27 **Question:** To be clear, after announcing that Congress can regulate intrastate activities that have a "substantial economic effect" on interstate commerce, Justice Robert Jackson conceded that Filburn's effect on interstate commerce is "trivial." Why, then, can Congress regulate it?

28 **Question:** If Congress can limit Filburn's ability to grow his own wheat, could Congress also require Filburn to purchase wheat on the open market?

Supreme Court had recognized as early as *Gibbons* that Congress's power to regulate interstate commerce could easily justify the regulation of intrastate activities. In this respect, the Court after 1937 appears correct that *E.C. Knight Co.*, *Hammer*, and *A.L.A. Schechter* were all attempts to impose artificial limits on the Commerce Clause's logic out of fear that it might permit the federal government to possess the same police powers as the states.

But *Wickard* nevertheless represented such an expansion of the Commerce Clause that the clause quickly became the basis for virtually all federal legislation. Over the next several decades, as litigants reminded the Court of limits once imposed by earlier precedents, the Court overruled them. For example, in *Paul v. Virginia*, 75 U.S. (8 Wall.) 168 (1869), the Court had held that insurance transactions are not commerce; but the Court overruled this conclusion in *United States v. South-Eastern Underwriters Ass'n*, 322 U.S. 533 (1944). Similarly, in the *Employers' Liability Cases*, 207 U.S. 463 (1908), the Court had rejected the government's argument that every employee of an interstate business necessarily affects interstate commerce; but in *Maryland v. Wirtz*, 392 U.S. 183 (1968), the Court overruled this conclusion, upholding an amendment to the Fair Labor Standards Act of 1938 that regulated the wages and hours of all employees of any enterprise engaged in commerce or the production of commerce.

CHAPTER 9

WHAT IS THE MODERN SCOPE OF CONGRESS'S POWER TO REGULATE COMMERCE?

ARTICLE I, SECTION 8, CLAUSE 3: The Congress shall have Power . . . To regulate Commerce with foreign Nations, and among the several States . . .;—And

> **CLAUSE 18:** To make all Laws which shall be necessary and proper for carrying into Execution the foregoing Powers, and all other Powers vested by this Constitution in the Government of the United States, or in any Department or Officer thereof.

TENTH AMENDMENT (1791): The powers not delegated to the United States by the Constitution, nor prohibited by it to the States, are reserved to the States respectively, or to the people.

Regulation of Commerce Within Three Areas of Law

Congress responded to the Supreme Court's 1937 "switch in time" (see section 6.2) by invoking the Commerce Clause to pass laws that previously had been constitutionally questionable. In particular, Congress transformed three areas of law: civil rights law, criminal law, and administrative law. These three areas are also areas in which the Court has imposed modern limits on the Commerce Clause in the spirit of *Hammer v. Dagenhart*, 247 U.S. 251 (1918), and other earlier cases.

9.1 CIVIL RIGHTS LAW

Early civil rights attempts

The history of federal civil rights legislation before 1937 was a history of disappointment. We will discuss the details in a later section on Congress's power to enforce the Reconstruction amendments (section 20.1).

The short version is that the end of the Civil War in 1865 brought with it high expectations that Congress would quickly eradicate the vestiges of slavery. *See* Eric Foner, *Reconstruction* 182–83 (2014). Between 1865 and 1876, a Republican-controlled Congress pressured states to ratify the Thirteenth, Fourteenth, and Fifteenth Amendments, which abolished slavery, guaranteed the equal citizenship of all people born in the United States, and prohibited states from abridging the right to vote on the basis of race. These amendments also gave Congress new enumerated powers "to enforce, by appropriate legislation, the provisions" of each amendment. U.S. Const. amend. XIV, § 5; *see id.*

amend. XIII, § 2; *id.* amend. XV, § 2. Invoking these amendments, Congress passed a series of civil rights laws that allowed multiracial democracy to exist in the United States for the first time. These laws made it an offense for people to deprive others of their constitutionally protected rights; prohibited racial discrimination by inns, common carriers, theaters, and other places of public amusement; and prohibited individual and state interference with a person's right to vote. *See, e.g.*, Civil Rights Act of 1875, ch. 114, 18 Stat. 335; Ku Klux Klan Act of 1871, ch. 22, 17 Stat. 13; Enforcement Act of 1871, ch. 99, 16 Stat. 433; Enforcement Act of 1870, ch. 114, 16 Stat. 140; Civil Rights Act of 1866, ch. 31, 14 Stat. 27.

This period of Reconstruction was short-lived, though. White insurrectionists throughout the South launched a violent counterrevolution. To prevent black majorities from electing Republican candidates, organizations like the Ku Klux Klan lynched black voters and terrorized their Republican supporters in southern states. The Democratic Party campaigned on a platform of "redeeming" the South in the name of white supremacy. *See* Eric Foner, *Reconstruction* 31 (2014). By 1875, it seized control over most southern states as well as the U.S. House of Representatives.

The Supreme Court bowed to these shifting political winds. After 1875, the Court held that, even after the ratification of the Reconstruction amendments, Congress had no power to confer the rights to vote or to hold office, *United States v. Reese*, 92 U.S. 214 (1875); to punish intrastate crimes like murder or assault, *United States v. Cruikshank*, 92 U.S. 542 (1875); *United States v. Harris*, 106 U.S. 629 (1883); or to prohibit "private" racial discrimination by individuals or private companies, *Civil Rights Cases*, 109 U.S. 3 (1883). As the Court wrote in the *Civil Rights Cases*, if Congress could "establish a code of municipal law regulative of all private rights between man and man in society[,] [it] would be to make Congress take the place of the State legislatures and to supersede them." 109 U.S. at 13.

In the twentieth century, Congress didn't come close to enacting another civil rights statute until the 1940s. Even then, bills were routinely blocked by southern-led filibusters in the Senate. *See, e.g.*, S. 101, 78th Cong. (1945).

Renewed civil rights attempts

In May 1954, however, the Supreme Court decided *Brown v. Board of Education* (*Brown I*), 347 U.S. 483 (1954), a monumental reinterpretation of the Fourteenth Amendment. The decision outlawed racial segregation in public schools and strongly suggested that all segregation was unconstitutional. The following year, black residents of Montgomery, Alabama, began protesting a segregated, privately run bus system by refusing to stand when the drivers instructed. Police arrested the protestors for trespassing, disturbing the peace, and otherwise violating local laws requiring segregation. Local residents, led by the twenty-six-year-old Reverend Martin Luther King Jr., responded by boycotting the bus system for over a year. They also successfully challenged the segregation laws in federal court.

Brown and the Montgomery bus boycott were early stirrings of a nationwide civil rights movement. The next decade witnessed "sit-ins," in which black people sat in white-only areas of restaurants and theaters; "freedom rides," in which black and white passengers rode interstate bus facilities; voter-registration drives, in which organizers attempted to help black residents pass impenetrable registration tests; integration campaigns, in which black students attempted to enroll in public schools and universities; and boycotts, in which protestors marched outside facilities that maintained segregation. These protests were met with violence, harassment, and arrests that sparked international condemnation. *See, e.g.,* Taylor Branch, *At Canaan's Edge: America in the King Years, 1965–68*, at 527 (2006).

The protests galvanized members of Congress. In 1957, supporters of federal civil rights legislation overcame a southern-led filibuster in the Senate for the first time since 1875. The Civil Rights Act of 1957, Pub. L. No. 85–315, 71 Stat. 634, created the Civil Rights Division of the Department of Justice. But all the division was empowered to do was seek injunctive relief to prevent state interference with the voting rights of citizens. A second act in 1960 made it slightly easier for the attorney general to register disenfranchised citizens if a court first found a "pattern or practice" of discrimination. Civil Rights Act of 1960, Pub. L. No. 86–449, 74 Stat. 86. Yet this act was also ignored. Publicly run schools, libraries, and parks remained segregated, as did privately run bus companies, libraries, hotels, restaurants, and movie theaters.

Civil Rights Act of 1964

Three years later, the 1963 March on Washington for Jobs and Freedom pressured President John F. Kennedy to propose a major civil rights bill to outlaw segregation in all of its forms. Kennedy's assassination prompted Congress to pass the bill one year later. The Civil Rights Act of 1964, Pub. L. No. 88–352, 78 Stat. 241, prohibited racial discrimination in voting, schools, and a variety of other contexts.

The Civil Rights Act of 1964 codified many of the same antidiscrimination provisions that the Supreme Court had declared beyond Congress's powers in the 1870s. The main difference was that in 1964, Congress based its authority to prohibit private segregation on the Commerce Clause instead of the Fourteenth Amendment. In particular, the law prohibited racial discrimination in "any place of public accommodation"—including any hotel, restaurant, theater, or retail establishment—"if its operations affect commerce, or if discrimination or segregation by it is supported by State action." 78 Stat. at 243. The statute defined *affect[ing] commerce* to include catering to interstate travelers or serving food, goods, or entertainment that had crossed state lines. *Id.*

9.1.1

Heart of Atlanta Motel v. United States

379 U.S. 241 (1964)

The first test case of the new Civil Rights Act concerned the Heart of Atlanta Motel in downtown Atlanta. The motel qualified as a place of public accommodation because it was readily accessible from Interstates 75 and 85, it advertised in national magazines and billboards, and 75 percent of its guests came from out of state. But its owner, Moreton Rolleston, passionately opposed integration. In his suit against the United States, *Heart of Atlanta Motel v. United States*, 379 U.S. 241 (1964), Rolleston argued that the Civil Rights Act exceeded Congress's power under the Commerce Clause. Without irony, he also argued that the act violated the Thirteenth Amendment's abolition of slavery because it forced him to involuntarily serve people whom he didn't want in his motel.

The Court was unconvinced by Rolleston's arguments.

■ MR. JUSTICE CLARK delivered the opinion of the Court.[1]

[T]he sole question posed is . . . the constitutionality of the Civil Rights Act of 1964 as applied to these facts. . . .

In light of our ground for decision, it might be well at the outset to discuss the *Civil Rights Cases*, 109 U. S. 3, which declared provisions of the Civil Rights Act of 1875 unconstitutional. 18 Stat. 335, 336. We think that decision inapposite, and without precedential value in determining the constitutionality of the present Act. Unlike Title II of the present legislation, the 1875 Act broadly proscribed discrimination in "inns, public conveyances on land or water, theaters, and other places of public amusement," without limiting the categories of affected businesses to those impinging upon interstate commerce. In contrast, the applicability of Title II is carefully limited to enterprises having a direct and substantial relation to the interstate flow of goods and people, except where state action is involved. Further, the fact that certain kinds of businesses may not in 1875 have been sufficiently involved in interstate commerce to warrant bringing them within the ambit of the commerce power is not necessarily dispositive of the same question today. Our populace had not reached its present mobility, nor were facilities, goods and services circulating as readily in interstate commerce as they are today. Although the principles which we apply today are those first formulated by Chief Justice Marshall in *Gibbons v. Ogden*, 9 Wheat. 1 (1824), the conditions of transportation and commerce have changed dramatically, and we must apply those principles to the present state of commerce. The sheer increase in

---

1 **As You Read, Consider:** In earlier opinions from the 1880s, the Supreme Court struck down a nearly identical antidiscrimination law as beyond Congress's power. Why is the Civil Rights Act of 1964 different?

In *United States v. Darby Lumber Co.*, *Wickard v. Filburn*, and other decisions from the 1940s, the Supreme Court announced that Congress could regulate intrastate activity that substantially affected interstate commerce. How, if at all, does the Heart of Atlanta Motel substantially affect interstate commerce? If only a handful of out-of-state guests stayed at the motel every year, could Congress still regulate it?

volume of interstate traffic alone would give discriminatory practices which inhibit travel a far larger impact upon the Nation's commerce than such practices had on the economy of another day. . . . We, therefore, conclude that the *Civil Rights Cases* have no relevance to the basis of decision here where the Act explicitly relies upon the commerce power, and where the record is filled with testimony of obstructions and restraints resulting from the discriminations found to be existing. We now pass to that phase of the case. . . .

While the Act as adopted carried no congressional findings the record of its passage through each house is replete with evidence of the burdens that discrimination by race or color places upon interstate commerce. This testimony included the fact that our people have become increasingly mobile with millions of people of all races traveling from State to State; that Negroes in particular have been the subject of discrimination in transient accommodations, having to travel great distances to secure the same; that often they have been unable to obtain accommodations and have had to call upon friends to put them up overnight, and that these conditions had become so acute as to require the listing of available lodging for Negroes in a special guidebook which was itself "dramatic testimony to the difficulties" Negroes encounter in travel. These exclusionary practices were found to be nationwide, the Under Secretary of Commerce testifying that there is "no question that this discrimination in the North still exists to a large degree" and in the West and Midwest as well. This testimony indicated a qualitative as well as quantitative effect on interstate travel by Negroes. The former was the obvious impairment of the Negro traveler's pleasure and convenience that resulted when he continually was uncertain of finding lodging. As for the latter, there was evidence that this uncertainty stemming from racial discrimination had the effect of discouraging travel on the part of a substantial portion of the Negro community. This was the conclusion not only of the Under Secretary of Commerce but also of the Administrator of the Federal Aviation Agency who wrote the Chairman of the Senate Commerce Committee that it was his "belief that air commerce is adversely affected by the denial to a substantial segment of the traveling public of adequate and desegregated public accommodations." We shall not burden this opinion with further details since the voluminous testimony presents overwhelming evidence that discrimination by hotels and motels impedes interstate travel. . . .

The power of Congress to deal with these obstructions depends on the meaning of the Commerce Clause. Its meaning was first enunciated 140 years ago by the great Chief Justice John Marshall in *Gibbons v. Ogden*, 9 Wheat. 1 (1824). . . . [T]he determinative test of the exercise of power by the Congress under the Commerce Clause is simply whether the activity sought to be regulated is "commerce which concerns more States than one" and has a real and substantial relation to the national interest. Let us now turn to this facet of the problem.

That the "intercourse" of which the Chief Justice spoke included the movement of persons through more States than one was settled as early as 1849, in the *Passenger Cases*, 7 How. 283, where Mr. Justice McLean stated: "That the transportation of passengers is a part of commerce is not now an open question." Again in 1913 Mr. Justice McKenna, speaking for the Court, said: "Commerce among the States, we have said, consists of intercourse and traffic between their citizens, and includes the transportation of persons and property." *Hoke v. United States*, 227 U. S. 308, 320. . . .

The same interest in protecting interstate commerce which led Congress to deal with segregation in interstate carriers and the white-slave traffic has prompted it to extend the exercise of its power to gambling, *Lottery Case*, 188 U. S. 321 (1903); to criminal enterprises, *Brooks v. United States*, 267 U. S. 432 (1925); to deceptive

Expansion

practices in the sale of products, *Federal Trade Comm'n v. Mandel Bros., Inc.*, 359 U. S. 385 (1959); to fraudulent security transactions, *Securities & Exchange Comm'n v. Ralston Purina Co.*, 346 U. S. 119 (1953); to misbranding of drugs, *Weeks v. United States*, 245 U. S. 618 (1918); to wages and hours, *United States v. Darby*, 312 U. S. 100 (1941); to members of labor unions, *Labor Board v. Jones & Laughlin Steel Corp.*, 301 U. S. 1 (1937); to crop control, *Wickard v. Filburn*, 317 U. S. 111 (1942); to discrimination against shippers, *United States v. Baltimore & Ohio R. Co.*, 333 U. S. 169 (1948); to the protection of small business from injurious price cutting, *Moore v. Mead's Fine Bread Co.*, 348 U. S. 115 (1954); to resale price maintenance, *Hudson Distributors, Inc. v. Eli Lilly & Co.*, 377 U. S. 386 (1964), *Schwegmann v. Calvert Distillers Corp.*, 341 U. S. 384 (1951); to professional football, *Radovich v. National Football League*, 352 U. S. 445 (1957); and to racial discrimination by owners and managers of terminal restaurants. *Boynton v. Virginia*, 364 U. S. 454 (1960).

That Congress was legislating against moral wrongs in many of these areas rendered its enactments no less valid. In framing Title II of this Act Congress was also dealing with what it considered a moral problem. But that fact does not detract from the overwhelming evidence of the disruptive effect that racial discrimination has had on commercial intercourse. It was this burden which empowered Congress to enact appropriate legislation, and, given this basis for the exercise of its power, Congress was not restricted by the fact that the particular obstruction to interstate commerce with which it was dealing was also deemed a moral and social wrong.

It is said that the operation of the motel here is of a purely local character. But, assuming this to be true, "[i]f it is interstate commerce that feels the pinch, it does not matter how local the operation which applies the squeeze." *United States v. Women's Sportswear Mfrs. Assn.*, 336 U. S. 460, 464 (1949). As Chief Justice Stone put it in *United States v. Darby*, *supra*: "The power of Congress over interstate commerce is not confined to the regulation of commerce among the states. It extends to those activities intrastate which so affect interstate commerce or the exercise of the power of Congress over it as to make regulation of them appropriate means to the attainment of a legitimate end, the exercise of the granted power of Congress to regulate interstate commerce."

Thus the power of Congress to promote interstate commerce also includes the power to regulate the local incidents thereof, including local activities in both the States of origin and destination, which might have a substantial and harmful effect upon that commerce. One need only examine the evidence which we have discussed above to see that Congress may—as it has—prohibit racial discrimination by motels serving travelers, however "local" their operations may appear. . . .

We find no merit in the remainder of appellant's contentions, including that of "involuntary servitude." [Thirty-two] States prohibit racial discrimination in public accommodations. These laws but codify the common-law innkeeper rule which long predated the Thirteenth Amendment. It is difficult to believe that the Amendment was intended to abrogate this principle. . . . We could not say that the requirements of the Act in this regard are in any way "akin to African slavery." *Butler v. Perry*, 240 U. S. 328, 332 (1916).[2]

We, therefore, conclude that the action of the Congress in the adoption of the Act as applied here to a motel which concedely serves interstate travelers is within the power granted it by the Commerce Clause of the Constitution, as interpreted by

[2] **Note:** Here, Justice Tom Clark is responding to the argument that forcing a motel to serve black customers violates the Thirteenth Amendment's prohibition of "involuntary servitude."

this Court for 140 years. It may be argued that Congress could have pursued other methods to eliminate the obstructions it found in interstate commerce caused by racial discrimination. But this is a matter of policy that rests entirely with the Congress not with the courts. How obstructions in commerce may be removed—what means are to be employed—is within the sound and exclusive discretion of the Congress. It is subject only to one caveat—that the means chosen by it must be reasonably adapted to the end permitted by the Constitution. We cannot say that its choice here was not so adapted. The Constitution requires no more.[3]

NOTE: AFTERMATH OF *HEART OF ATLANTA*

For Moreton Rolleston, *Heart of Atlanta* was a devastating decision. Rather than cater to black customers, he sold his motel, which was torn down and replaced by what is now the Hilton Atlanta. To satisfy a debt, Rolleston was later forced to sell his seventeen-acre suburban estate. In 2005, his estate was purchased by Tyler Perry—the black director of *Madea* fame—who replaced Rolleston's former home with his own mansion. "To have this property was such poetic justice," Perry said. *See* Rembert Browne, *The Brand Keeping Oprah in Business*, N.Y. Mag., Dec. 28, 2015.

For the rest of the country, *Heart of Atlanta* signaled that the Supreme Court would extend the Commerce Clause—and with it, the Civil Rights Act—as far as it could go.

McClung. The same day that the Court decided *Heart of Atlanta*, it also decided *Katzenbach v. McClung*, 379 U.S. 294 (1964). *McClung* upheld the Civil Rights Act's application to Ollie's Barbecue, a segregated restaurant in Birmingham, Alabama, that exclusively catered to a local clientele. Even though Ollie's did not serve many out-of-state customers, the *McClung* Court held that Ollie's was still subject to federal regulation under the Commerce Clause because it spent 46 percent of its 1963 food budget on meat that it bought from a local supplier who had procured it from outside the state:

> The record is replete with testimony . . . that discrimination in restaurants had a direct and highly restrictive effect upon interstate travel by Negroes. . . . It goes without saying that, viewed in isolation, the volume of food purchased by Ollie's Barbecue from sources supplied from out of state was insignificant when compared with the total foodstuffs moving in commerce. But, as our late Brother Jackson said for the Court in *Wickard v. Filburn*, 317 U. S. 111 (1942): "That appellee's own contribution to the demand for wheat may be trivial by itself is not enough to remove him from the scope of federal regulation where, as here, his

---

[3] **Questions:** As we will discuss later (section 20.1), a central purpose of the Fourteenth Amendment was to empower Congress to prohibit racial discrimination. Is it odd that the Court is upholding the Civil Rights Act under the Commerce Clause rather than under the Fourteenth Amendment?

To what extent does *Heart of Atlanta* extend the reach of prior Commerce Clause cases? In a globalized world, is there any context not subject to federal regulation under the Commerce Clause?

In answering the above questions, consider the cases discussed in the postcase note below: *Katzenbach v. McClung*, 379 U.S. 294 (1964) (Congress can regulate restaurant that serves meat delivered from out of state), and *Daniel v. Paul*, 395 U.S. 298 (1969) (Congress can regulate private club that serves hot dogs whose ingredients traveled from out of state).

> contribution, taken together with that of many others similarly situated, is far from trivial." We noted in *Heart of Atlanta Motel* that a number of witnesses attested to the fact that racial discrimination was not merely a state or regional problem, but was one of nationwide scope. Against this background, we must conclude that, while the focus of the legislation was on the individual restaurant's relation to interstate commerce, Congress appropriately considered the importance of that connection with the knowledge that the discrimination was but representative of many others throughout the country, the total incidence of which, if left unchecked, may well become far-reaching in its harm to commerce.

McClung, 375 U.S. at 299–301.

Daniel. Five years later, in *Daniel v. Paul*, 395 U.S. 298 (1969), the Supreme Court extended the Civil Rights Act to a facility whose relationship with interstate commerce was even less direct. The Lake Nixon Club was a swimming, boating, and dancing facility in Little Rock, Arkansas, that refused to admit black members. The Club operated a snack bar that sold hot dogs, hamburgers on buns, and sodas. The Court found it sufficient for the Commerce Clause that the "principal ingredients going into the bread were produced and processed in other States" and that "certain ingredients [of the soft drinks] were probably obtained . . . from out-of-State sources." *Daniel*, 395 U.S. at 305. Based on this finding, the Court concluded that "[t]here can be no serious doubt that a 'substantial portion of the food' served at the snack bar has moved in interstate commerce." *Id.* Under the terms of the Civil Rights Act, the Court added, "[t]he snack bar's status as a covered establishment automatically brings the entire Lake Nixon facility within the ambit of Title II." *Id.*

9.2 CRIMINAL LAW

Just as federal civil rights law was radically transformed by the Commerce Clause, so was federal criminal law.

Enumerated powers

Throughout the nineteenth century, Congress's power to enact criminal legislation was constitutionally suspect. The Constitution gives Congress only four powers that expressly mention punishment: the power to "provide for the Punishment of counterfeiting the Securities and current Coin of the United States"; to "define and punish Piracies and Felonies committed on the high Seas, and Offences against the Law of Nations"; to "declare the Punishment of Treason"; and to impeach civil officers for "high Crimes and Misdemeanors." But that's it. In the 1880s, the Supreme Court even held that Congress lacks a freestanding power to punish crimes such as murder and assault. *United States v. Harris*, 106 U.S. 629 (1883). Instead, the Court held that Congress's power to enact criminal laws could be justified only as a necessary and proper "incident" of an enumerated power. *See Cohens v. Virginia*, 19 U.S. (6 Wheat.) 264 (1821).

Due to this constitutional limitation, Congress passed relatively few criminal laws in the nineteenth century. And the Court upheld those laws only if it could connect them to one of Congress's enumerated powers. *See, e.g., Miller v. United States*, 78 U.S. (11 Wall.) 268, 305 (1871) (upholding Congress's power to "declare the Punishment of Treason"); *United States v. Smith*, 18 U.S. (5 Wheat.) 153, 160 (1820) (upholding Congress's power to "punish Piracies"). For instance, the Court interpreted the clause permitting Congress to "establish Post Offices and post Roads" to uphold laws and government actions that prohibited people from sending certain materials in the mail, interfering with the transmission of the mail, or using the mail to commit fraud. *See, e.g., In re Debs*, 158 U.S. 564 (1895); *Ex parte Jackson*, 96 U.S. 727 (1878). The Court interpreted the various financial clauses to allow Congress to punish financial crimes. *See, e.g., United States v. Marigold*, 50 U.S. (9 How.) 560 (1850). And the Court upheld laws protecting federal officers, such as laws punishing the bribery of federal officers or injuring someone in U.S. custody. *See, e.g., Logan v. United States*, 144 U.S. 263 (1892).

Commerce Clause and criminal laws

But the most important source of federal criminal laws became the Commerce Clause, particularly after the Supreme Court decided the *Lottery Case*, 188 U.S. 321 (1903). That decision upheld Congress's power to punish the interstate transportation of lottery tickets. Building off this precedent, later cases expansively suggested that the Commerce Clause permitted Congress to punish any crime as long as a person or thing crossed a state or national border. *See* William J. Stuntz, *The Collapse of American Criminal Justice* 167–79 (2011); *see, e.g., Hoke v. United States*, 227 U.S. 308 (1913) (upholding a law prohibiting the transportation of women for the purpose of prostitution); *Brooks v. United States*, 267 U.S. 432 (1925) (stolen autos); *Gooch v. United States*, 297 U.S. 124 (1936) (kidnapping).

As the Commerce Clause expanded in scope with the 1937 "switch in time" (see section 6.2), so did Congress's power to enact criminal laws. For example, in *Perez v. United States*, 402 U.S. 146 (1971), the Court upheld the federal prosecution of a "loan shark" for using the threat of violence as a method of collecting $1,000 from the owner of a local butcher shop. The Court explained that even if Perez's activity didn't affect interstate commerce, the prosecution was justified under *Wickard v. Filburn*, 317 U.S. 111 (1942), and *Heart of Atlanta Motel v. United States*, 379 U.S. 241 (1964), because loan-sharking was part of a "class of activities" that affects interstate commerce. *Perez*, 402 U.S. at 152–53. The Court applied identical reasoning in *Russell v. United States*, 471 U.S. 858 (1985), which allowed Congress to punish the arson of a two-unit apartment building on the theory that the rental of real estate is a class of activity that affects interstate commerce. Equally broad were *Barrett v. United States* and *Scarborough v. United States*, which upheld convictions under a statute that prohibited felons from receiving or possessing a firearm "in commerce." *Barrett*, 423 U.S. 212, 224–25 (1976); *Scarborough*, 431 U.S. 563, 577 (1977); *see also United States v. Bass*, 404 U.S. 336 (1971) (holding that the "in commerce" element was an essential feature of the law). The Court wrote that the crimes fell within the Commerce Clause as long as prosecutors could show that the guns had, at some point, traveled across state lines.

9.2.1

United States v. Lopez

514 U.S. 549 (1995)

By 1990, it had been a half century since the Supreme Court last struck down a statute under the Commerce Clause. That year, Congress passed the Gun-Free School Zones Act of 1990, which made it a federal offense for anyone to bring a firearm into a "school zone." Pub. L. No. 101–647, 104 Stat. 4789, 4844. Unlike previous gun laws, this law did not formally declare that the gun must have previously moved in commerce. Congress instead found that guns and schools both substantially affect interstate commerce.

Under this law, a San Antonio high school student, Alfonso Lopez, was federally prosecuted for bringing a handgun and five bullets to school in 1992. Lopez defended himself with the now-familiar complaint that the statute exceeded Congress's power under the Commerce Clause. The Supreme Court heard Lopez's argument on Election Day 1994—the same day Republicans won control of both houses of Congress for the first time in forty years.

In *United States v. Lopez*, 514 U.S. 549 (1995), a decision that many observers suspected was the beginning of a conservative backlash to the New Deal, the Court agreed with Lopez. *See* Mark Tushnet, *Living in a Constitutional Moment?:* Lopez *and Constitutional Theory*, 46 Case W. Res. L. Rev. 845, 845 (1996).

■ CHIEF JUSTICE REHNQUIST delivered the opinion of the Court.[4]

In the Gun-Free School Zones Act of 1990, Congress made it a federal offense "for any individual knowingly to possess a firearm at a place that the individual knows, or has reasonable cause to believe, is a school zone." 18 U. S. C. § 922(q)(1)(A). The Act neither regulates a commercial activity nor contains a requirement that the possession be connected in any way to interstate commerce. We hold that the Act

---

[4] **As You Read, Consider:** *United States v. Lopez* is today remembered as an attempt by a conservative Supreme Court to reintroduce limits on the Commerce Clause for the first time since 1937. Where do these limits come from? What normative principles do they advance?

What is the government's argument for why the Gun-Free School Zones Act implicates interstate commerce? Does Chief Justice William Rehnquist consider this argument empirically wrong or legally wrong?

exceeds the authority of Congress "[t]o regulate Commerce . . . among the several States. . . ." U. S. Const., Art. I, § 8, cl. 3. . . .

[Following a period of Commerce Clause cases from *Gibbons* through *Wickard* that highlighted a "framework of legal uncertainty,"] *Jones* & *Laughlin Steel*, *Darby*, and *Wickard* ushered in an era of Commerce Clause jurisprudence that greatly expanded the previously defined authority of Congress under that Clause. . . . But even these modern-era precedents which have expanded congressional power under the Commerce Clause confirm that this power is subject to outer limits. In *Jones* & *Laughlin Steel*, the Court warned that the scope of the interstate commerce power "must be considered in the light of our dual system of government and may not be extended so as to embrace effects upon interstate commerce so indirect and remote that to embrace them, in view of our complex society, would effectually obliterate the distinction between what is national and what is local and create a completely centralized government." 301 U. S., at 37. . . .

Consistent with this structure, we have identified three broad categories of activity that Congress may regulate under its commerce power. First, Congress may regulate the use of the channels of interstate commerce. See, e.g., *Darby*, 312 U.S., at 114; *Heart of Atlanta Motel*, *supra*, at 256 (" '[T]he authority of Congress to keep the channels of interstate commerce free from immoral and injurious uses has been frequently sustained, and is no longer open to question' "). Second, Congress is empowered to regulate and protect the instrumentalities of interstate commerce, or persons or things in interstate commerce, even though the threat may come only from intrastate activities. See, e.g., *Southern R. Co. v. United States*, 222 U.S. 20 (1911) (upholding amendments to Safety Appliance Act as applied to vehicles used in intrastate commerce); *Perez*, *supra*, at 150 ("[F]or example, the destruction of an aircraft (18 U. S. C. § 32), or . . . thefts from interstate shipments (18 U. S. C. § 659)"). Finally, Congress' commerce authority includes the power to regulate those activities having a substantial relation to interstate commerce, *Jones & Laughlin Steel*, 301 U. S., at 37, *i.e.*, those activities that substantially affect interstate commerce. . . .

We now turn to consider the power of Congress, in the light of this framework, to enact § 922(q). The first two categories of authority may be quickly disposed of: § 922(q) is not a regulation of the use of the channels of interstate commerce, nor is it an attempt to prohibit the interstate transportation of a commodity through the channels of commerce; nor can § 922(q) be justified as a regulation by which Congress has sought to protect an instrumentality of interstate commerce or a thing in interstate commerce. Thus, if § 922(q) is to be sustained, it must be under the third category as a regulation of an activity that substantially affects interstate commerce.

First, we have upheld a wide variety of congressional Acts regulating intrastate economic activity where we have concluded that the activity substantially affected interstate commerce. Examples include the regulation of intrastate coal mining; *Hodel*, *supra*, intrastate extortionate credit transactions, *Perez*, *supra*, restaurants utilizing substantial interstate supplies, *McClung*, *supra*, inns and hotels catering to interstate guests, *Heart of Atlanta Motel*, *supra*, and production and consumption of homegrown wheat, *Wickard v. Filburn*, 317 U. S. 111 (1942). These examples are by no means exhaustive, but the pattern is clear. Where economic activity substantially affects interstate commerce, legislation regulating that activity will be sustained.[5]

---

[5] **Question:** Rehnquist emphasizes here that the Commerce Clause does not reach *all* intrastate activities that substantially affect interstate commerce, but only intrastate activities

Even *Wickard*, which is perhaps the most far reaching example of Commerce Clause authority over intrastate activity, involved economic activity in a way that the possession of a gun in a school zone does not. . . .

Section 922(q) is a criminal statute that by its terms has nothing to do with "commerce" or any sort of economic enterprise, however broadly one might define those terms. Section 922(q) is not an essential part of a larger regulation of economic activity, in which the regulatory scheme could be undercut unless the intrastate activity were regulated. It cannot, therefore, be sustained under our cases upholding regulations of activities that arise out of or are connected with a commercial transaction, which viewed in the aggregate, substantially affects interstate commerce.

Second, § 922(q) contains no jurisdictional element which would ensure, through case-by-case inquiry, that the firearm possession in question affects interstate commerce. For example, in *United States v. Bass*, 404 U. S. 336 (1971), the Court interpreted former 18 U. S. C. § 1202(a), which made it a crime for a felon to "receiv[e], posses[s], or transpor[t] in commerce or affecting commerce . . . any firearm." 404 U. S., at 337. The Court interpreted the possession component of § 1202(a) to require an additional nexus to interstate commerce both because the statute was ambiguous and because "unless Congress conveys its purpose clearly, it will not be deemed to have significantly changed the federal-state balance." Id., at 349. The *Bass* Court set aside the conviction because, although the Government had demonstrated that Bass had possessed a firearm, it had failed "to show the requisite nexus with interstate commerce." Id., at 347. . . . Unlike the statute in *Bass*, § 922(q) has no express jurisdictional element which might limit its reach to a discrete set of firearm possessions that additionally have an explicit connection with or effect on interstate commerce. . . .[6]

The Government's essential contention, in fine, is that we may determine here that § 922(q) is valid because possession of a firearm in a local school zone does indeed substantially affect interstate commerce. Brief for United States 17. The Government argues that possession of a firearm in a school zone may result in violent crime and that violent crime can be expected to affect the functioning of the national economy in two ways. First, the costs of violent crime are substantial, and, through the mechanism of insurance, those costs are spread throughout the population. Second, violent crime reduces the willingness of individuals to travel to areas within the country that are perceived to be unsafe. Cf. *Heart of Atlanta Motel*, 379 U. S., at 253. The Government also argues that the presence of guns in schools poses a substantial threat to the educational process by threatening the learning environment. A handicapped educational process, in turn, will result in a less productive citizenry. That, in turn, would have an adverse effect on the Nation's economic well-being. As a result, the Government argues that Congress could rationally have concluded that § 922(q) substantially affects interstate commerce.

We pause to consider the implications of the Government's arguments. The Government admits, under its "costs of crime" reasoning, that Congress could regulate not only all violent crime, but all activities that might lead to violent crime, regardless of how tenuously they relate to interstate commerce. See Tr. of Oral Arg.

---

that are *economic* or *commercial*. Did *Wickard v. Filburn* and *Heart of Atlanta Motel v. United States* similarly emphasize economic/commercial intrastate activities, or is this limit new?

6 **Questions:** Does this section of *Lopez* advance a meaningful limit on the Commerce Clause or a mere warning for Congress to draft its laws more carefully? For example, suppose that instead of making it illegal to bring any firearm into a school zone, Congress had made it illegal to bring a firearm into a school zone *if the firearm had previously traveled in interstate commerce*. Would this hypothetical statute be constitutional under Rehnquist's analysis? If so, what principles does his analysis serve beyond mere formalism?

8–9. Similarly, under the Government's "national productivity" reasoning, Congress could regulate any activity that it found was related to the economic productivity of individual citizens: family law (including marriage, divorce, and child custody), for example. Under the theories that the Government presents in support of § 922(q), it is difficult to perceive any limitation on federal power, even in areas such as criminal law enforcement or education where States historically have been sovereign. Thus, if we were to accept the Government's arguments, we are hard pressed to posit any activity by an individual that Congress is without power to regulate. . . .

For instance, if Congress can, pursuant to its Commerce Clause power, regulate activities that adversely affect the learning environment, then, a fortiori, it also can regulate the educational process directly. Congress could determine that a school's curriculum has a "significant" effect on the extent of classroom learning. As a result, Congress could mandate a federal curriculum for local elementary and secondary schools because what is taught in local schools has a significant "effect on classroom learning," and that, in turn, has a substantial effect on interstate commerce. . . .[7]

We do not doubt that Congress has authority under the Commerce Clause to regulate numerous commercial activities that substantially affect interstate commerce and also affect the educational process. That authority, though broad, does not include the authority to regulate each and every aspect of local schools.

Admittedly, a determination whether an intrastate activity is commercial or noncommercial may in some cases result in legal uncertainty. But, so long as Congress' authority is limited to those powers enumerated in the Constitution, and so long as those enumerated powers are interpreted as having judicially enforceable outer limits, congressional legislation under the Commerce Clause always will engender "legal uncertainty.". . . The Constitution mandates this uncertainty by withholding from Congress a plenary police power that would authorize enactment of every type of legislation. See Art. I, § 8. Congress has operated within this framework of legal uncertainty ever since this Court determined that it was the Judiciary's duty "to say what the law is." *Marbury v. Madison*, 1 Cranch 137, 177 (1803) (Marshall, C. J.). Any possible benefit from eliminating this "legal uncertainty" would be at the expense of the Constitution's system of enumerated powers. . . .

The possession of a gun in a local school zone is in no sense an economic activity that might, through repetition elsewhere, substantially affect any sort of interstate commerce. Respondent was a local student at a local school; there is no indication that he had recently moved in interstate commerce, and there is no requirement that his possession of the firearm have any concrete tie to interstate commerce.

To uphold the Government's contentions here, we would have to pile inference upon inference in a manner that would bid fair to convert congressional authority under the Commerce Clause to a general police power of the sort retained by the States. Admittedly, some of our prior cases have taken long steps down that road, giving great deference to congressional action. The broad language in these opinions has suggested the possibility of additional expansion, but we decline here to proceed any further. To do so would require us to conclude that the Constitution's enumeration of powers does not presuppose something not enumerated, cf. *Gibbons v. Ogden*, *supra*, at 195, and that there never will be a distinction between what is truly national and what is truly local, cf. *Jones & Laughlin Steel*, *supra*, at 30. This we are unwilling to do.

---

[7] **Question:** The Court is treating these hypothetical federal statutes as obvious illustrations of excessive federal power. Precisely what is so bad about them?

■ JUSTICE BREYER, with whom JUSTICE STEVENS, JUSTICE SOUTER, and JUSTICE GINSBURG join, dissenting.

The issue in this case is whether the Commerce Clause authorizes Congress to enact a statute that makes it a crime to possess a gun in, or near, a school. In my view, the statute falls well within the scope of the commerce power as this Court has understood that power over the last half century.

In reaching this conclusion, I apply three basic principles of Commerce Clause interpretation. First, the power to "regulate Commerce . . . among the several States," U. S. Const., Art. I, § 8, cl. 3, encompasses the power to regulate local activities insofar as they significantly affect interstate commerce. See, e.g., *Gibbons v. Ogden*, 9 Wheat. 1, 194–195 (1824); *Wickard v. Filburn*, 317 U. S. 111, 125 (1942). . . .

Second, in determining whether a local activity will likely have a significant effect upon interstate commerce, a court must consider, not the effect of an individual act (a single instance of gun possession), but rather the cumulative effect of all similar instances (i.e., the effect of all guns possessed in or near schools). See, e.g., *Wickard, supra*, at 127–128. . . .

Third, the Constitution requires us to judge the connection between a regulated activity and interstate commerce, not directly, but at one remove. Courts must give Congress a degree of leeway in determining the existence of a significant factual connection between the regulated activity and interstate commerce—both because the Constitution delegates the commerce power directly to Congress and because the determination requires an empirical judgment of a kind that a legislature is more likely than a court to make with accuracy. . . .[8]

Applying these principles to the case at hand, we must ask whether Congress could have had a rational basis for finding a significant (or substantial) connection between gun-related school violence and interstate commerce. . . . Numerous reports and studies—generated both inside and outside government—make clear that Congress could reasonably have found the empirical connection that its law, implicitly or explicitly, asserts. . . . Education, although far more than a matter of economics, has long been inextricably intertwined with the Nation's economy. . . . Scholars estimate that nearly a quarter of America's economic growth in the early years of this century is traceable directly to increased schooling; that investment in "human capital" (through spending on education) exceeded investment in "physical capital" by a ratio of almost two to one; and that the economic returns to this investment in education exceeded the returns to conventional capital investment. . . .

The majority's holding—that § 922 falls outside the scope of the Commerce Clause—creates three serious legal problems. First, the majority's holding runs contrary to modern Supreme Court cases that have upheld congressional actions despite connections to interstate or foreign commerce that are less significant than the effect of school violence. [See *Perez v. United States* (loansharking), *Katzenbach v. McClung* (Ollie's Barbeque), *Daniel v. Paul* (Lake Nixon Club), and *Wickard v. Filburn* (wheat).]

The second legal problem the Court creates comes from its apparent belief that it can reconcile its holding with earlier cases by making a critical distinction between "commercial" and noncommercial "transaction[s]." That is to say, the Court believes the Constitution would distinguish between two local activities, each of which has an identical effect upon interstate commerce, if one, but not the other, is "commercial" in nature. As a general matter, this approach fails to heed this Court's earlier warning

[8] **Questions:** Under this test proposed by Justice Stephen Breyer, would there be any judicially enforceable limits on Congress's power to pass domestic legislation? Why might the absence of Article I limits be a bad thing?

not to turn "questions of the power of Congress" upon "formula[s]" that would give "controlling force to nomenclature such as 'production' and 'indirect' and foreclose consideration of the actual effects of the activity in question upon interstate commerce." *Wickard, supra*, at 120. See also *United States v. Darby*, 312 U. S. 100, 116–117 (1941) (overturning the Court's distinction between "production" and "commerce" in the child labor case, *Hammer v. Dagenhart*, 247 U. S. 251, 271–272 (1918) . . . . Moreover, the majority's test is not consistent with what the Court saw as the point of the cases that the majority now characterizes. Although the majority today attempts to categorize *Perez*, *McClung*, and *Wickard* as involving intrastate "economic activity," the Courts that decided each of those cases did not focus upon the economic nature of the activity regulated. Rather, they focused upon whether that activity affected interstate or foreign commerce. In fact, the *Wickard* Court expressly held that Filburn's consumption of homegrown wheat, "though it may not be regarded as commerce," could nevertheless be regulated—"whatever its nature"—so long as "it exerts a substantial economic effect on interstate commerce." *Wickard*, supra, at 125.

More importantly, if a distinction between commercial and noncommercial activities is to be made, this is not the case in which to make it. The majority clearly cannot intend such a distinction to focus narrowly on an act of gun possession standing by itself, for such a reading could not be reconciled with either the civil rights cases (*McClung* and *Daniel*) or *Perez*—in each of those cases the specific transaction (the race-based exclusion, the use of force) was not itself "commercial." And, if the majority instead means to distinguish generally among broad categories of activities, differentiating what is educational from what is commercial, then, as a practical matter, the line becomes almost impossible to draw. Schools that teach reading, writing, mathematics, and related basic skills serve both social and commercial purposes, and one cannot easily separate the one from the other. American industry itself has been, and is again, involved in teaching. When, and to what extent, does its involvement make education commercial? Does the number of vocational classes that train students directly for jobs make a difference? Does it matter if the school is public or private, nonprofit or profit seeking? Does it matter if a city or State adopts a voucher plan that pays private firms to run a school? Even if one were to ignore these practical questions, why should there be a theoretical distinction between education, when it significantly benefits commerce, and environmental pollution, when it causes economic harm?

Regardless, if there is a principled distinction that could work both here and in future cases, Congress (even in the absence of vocational classes, industry involvement, and private management) could rationally conclude that schools fall on the commercial side of the line. In 1990, the year Congress enacted the statute before us, primary and secondary schools spent $230 billion—that is, nearly a quarter of a trillion dollars—which accounts for a significant portion of our $5.5 trillion gross domestic product for that year. See Statistical Abstract 147, 442 (1993). . . . Certainly, Congress has often analyzed school expenditure as if it were a commercial investment, closely analyzing whether schools are efficient, whether they justify the significant resources they spend, and whether they can be restructured to achieve greater returns. Why could Congress, for Commerce Clause purposes, not consider schools as roughly analogous to commercial investments from which the Nation derives the benefit of an educated work force?[9]

[9] **Questions:** Applying the majority opinion in *Lopez*, could Congress regulate, say, the National Football League's concussion policy? *See* Margaret Greer, Note, *Concussion Crisis: Regulating the NFL's Concussion Policy Under the Commerce Clause*, 42 Hastings Const. L.Q.

NOTE: *LOPEZ*'S THREE-CATEGORY FRAMEWORK

The *Lopez* Court appeared to offer a clear, manageable, three-category framework for Congress's power under the Commerce Clause. Congress has virtually free rein to regulate all activities, intrastate and interstate, if necessary to (1) "regulate the use of the channels of interstate commerce" or (2) "protect the instrumentalities of interstate commerce"; but Congress is limited to regulating only "commercial" or "economic" activities if it wants to (3) regulate a class of intrastate "activities that substantially affect interstate commerce." *Lopez*, 514 U.S. at 558–59.

As Justice Stephen Breyer wrote in dissent, however, the *Lopez* Court's new commercial/economic distinction looked much like the direct-versus-indirect and manufacturing-versus-commerce distinctions of the pre-1937 Court. *Id.* at 627–28 (Breyer, J., dissenting). Moreover, the *Lopez* Court didn't offer any guidance about how to distinguish a commercial/economic intrastate activity from a noncommercial/noneconomic one. All it did was admit that "a determination whether an intrastate activity is commercial or noncommercial may in some cases result in legal uncertainty"—and leave it to future cases to figure out the difference. *Id.* at 566 (majority opinion).

9.2.3

Gonzales v. Raich

545 U.S. 1 (2005)

The Court's first chance came five years later in *United States v. Morrison*, 529 U.S. 598 (2000). The case involved the Violence Against Women Act of 1994, Pub. L. No. 103–322, 108 Stat. 1796, which authorized "victims of crimes of violence motivated by gender" to sue and collect damages from the people who injured them. 108 Stat. at 1941. Although Congress passed the law before *Lopez*, related congressional reports detailed findings that gender-motivated violence affects interstate commerce "by deterring potential victims from traveling interstate, from engaging in employment in interstate business, . . . [and] by diminishing national productivity, increasing medical and other costs." *Morrison*, 529 U.S. at 615. Applying this statute, a Virginia Tech student filed suit in federal court against a classmate, Antonio Morrison, for assaulting and raping her and bragging about it to other students. Morrison responded by attacking the law, arguing that rape and assault were noncommercial, intrastate activities that, after *Lopez*, Congress could not regulate under the Commerce Clause.

A 5–4 Court—with the same majority as in *Lopez*—agreed with Morrison. "Gender-motivated crimes of violence are not, in any sense of the phrase, economic activity," wrote Chief Justice William Rehnquist. *Id.* at 598. Although Congress had amassed "numerous findings regarding the serious impact that gender-motivated violence has on

---

187 (2014). Can you think of other examples that might straddle the line between commercial and noncommercial activity?

victims and their families," the Court dismissed these findings as "substantially weakened by the fact that they rely so heavily on a method of reasoning that we have already rejected as unworkable if we are to maintain the Constitution's enumeration of powers." *Id.* at 614–15. If Congress could regulate gender-motivated violence because of its aggregated effects on the economy, the Court wrote, "it would be able to regulate murder or any other type of violence since gender-motivated violence, as a subset of all violent crime, is certain to have lesser economic impacts than the larger class of which it is part." *Id.* at 615. "The Constitution requires a distinction between what is truly national and what is truly local," the Court concluded. "Indeed, we can think of no better example of the police power, which the Founders denied the National Government and reposed in the States, than the suppression of violent crime and vindication of its victims." *Id.* at 618.

In dissent, Justice David Souter reiterated Breyer's complaint that the commercial-versus-noncommercial distinction was an artificial and improper limit on the Commerce Clause.

Justices Souter and Breyer were in the majority the next time the Court considered whether an intrastate activity was commercial, in *Gonzales v. Raich*, 545 U.S. 1 (2005).

In 1996, California became the first state to legalize the use of marijuana for medical purposes, even though marijuana remained illegal in all contexts under the federal Controlled Substances Act of 1970, Pub. L. No. 91–513, 84 Stat. 1242. Diane Monson, a resident of California, received permission under the state's law to grow her own marijuana for medical use. In 2002, however, federal authorities raided Monson's home and destroyed her cannabis plants. Monson and another resident, Diane Raich, sued the U.S. attorney general, Alberto Gonzales, arguing that the personal medical use of marijuana was a noncommercial, intrastate activity that Congress lacked the power to regulate in light of *Lopez* and *Morrison*. Federal lawyers responded that the situation was indistinguishable from *Wickard*. They argued that growing marijuana was one instance of an inherently commercial "class of activities" given the nationwide black market for the drug. *Raich*, 545 U.S. at 17.

In *Raich*, the Supreme Court upheld the application of the Controlled Substances Act (CSA) to Raich and Monson.

■ JUSTICE STEVENS delivered the opinion of the Court.[10]

California is one of at least nine States that authorize the use of marijuana for medicinal purposes. The question presented in this case is whether the power vested in Congress by Article I, § 8, of the Constitution "[t]o make all Laws which shall be necessary and proper for carrying into Execution" its authority to "regulate Commerce with foreign Nations, and among the several States" includes the power to prohibit the local cultivation and use of marijuana in compliance with California law. . . .

---

[10] **As You Read, Consider:** *United States v. Lopez* narrowly cabined Congress's power under the Commerce Clause to regulate "noneconomic" activities that take place only within a single state. Does Justice John Paul Stevens repudiate this holding, or does he distinguish it?

Our case law firmly establishes Congress' power to regulate purely local activities that are part of an economic "class of activities" that have a substantial effect on interstate commerce. See, *e. g., Wickard* v. *Filburn,* 317 U. S. 111, 128–129 (1942). . . . We have never required Congress to legislate with scientific exactitude. When Congress decides that the " 'total incidence' " of a practice poses a threat to a national market, it may regulate the entire class. See *Perez,* 402 U. S., at 154–155. In this vein, we have reiterated that when "a general regulatory statute bears a substantial relation to commerce, the *de minimis* character of individual instances arising under that statute is of no consequence." *E. g., Lopez,* 514 U. S., at 558 (emphasis deleted).

Our decision in *Wickard,* 317 U. S. 111, is of particular relevance. In *Wickard,* we . . . [held] that Congress can regulate purely intrastate activity that is not itself "commercial," in that it is not produced for sale, if it concludes that failure to regulate that class of activity would undercut the regulation of the interstate market in that commodity.

The similarities between this case and *Wickard* are striking. Like the farmer in *Wickard,* respondents are cultivating, for home consumption, a fungible commodity for which there is an established, albeit illegal, interstate market. Just as the Agricultural Adjustment Act was designed "to control the volume [of wheat] moving in interstate and foreign commerce in order to avoid surpluses . . ." and consequently control the market price, *id.,* at 115, a primary purpose of the [Controlled Substances Act] is to control the supply and demand of controlled substances in both lawful and unlawful drug markets. In *Wickard,* we had no difficulty concluding that Congress had a rational basis for believing that, when viewed in the aggregate, leaving home-consumed wheat outside the regulatory scheme would have a substantial influence on price and market conditions. Here too, Congress had a rational basis for concluding that leaving home-consumed marijuana outside federal control would similarly affect price and market conditions. . . .

In assessing the scope of Congress' authority under the Commerce Clause, we stress that the task before us is a modest one. We need not determine whether respondents' activities, taken in the aggregate, substantially affect interstate commerce in fact, but only whether a "rational basis" exists for so concluding. *Lopez,* 514 U. S., at 557; *Heart of Atlanta Motel, Inc.* v. *United States,* 379 U. S. 241, 252–253 (1964). Given the enforcement difficulties that attend distinguishing between marijuana cultivated locally and marijuana grown elsewhere and concerns about diversion into illicit channels, we have no difficulty concluding that Congress had a rational basis for believing that failure to regulate the intrastate manufacture and possession of marijuana would leave a gaping hole in the CSA. Thus, as in *Wickard,* when it enacted comprehensive legislation to regulate the interstate market in a fungible commodity, Congress was acting well within its authority to "make all Laws which shall be necessary and proper" to "regulate Commerce . . . among the several States." U. S. Const., Art. I, § 8. That the regulation ensnares some purely intrastate activity is of no moment. As we have done many times before, we refuse to excise individual components of that larger scheme.[11]

IV

To support their contrary submission, respondents rely heavily on two of our more recent Commerce Clause cases. . . . Those two cases, of course, are *Lopez,*

[11] **Question:** Observe how Stevens doesn't rely only on the Commerce Clause to reach his conclusion that Congress can regulate the intrastate possession of marijuana. He also cites the Necessary and Proper Clause. To the extent the Necessary and Proper Clause permits Congress to regulate intrastate activities when Congress thinks such regulation is "necessary and proper" to regulate interstate commerce, why wasn't the regulation in *Lopez* also necessary and proper?

514 U. S. 549, and *Morrison,* 529 U. S. 598. As an initial matter, the statutory challenges at issue in those cases were markedly different from the challenge respondents pursue in the case at hand. Here, respondents ask us to excise individual applications of a concededly valid statutory scheme. In contrast, in both *Lopez* and *Morrison,* the parties asserted that a particular statute or provision fell outside Congress' commerce power in its entirety. This distinction is pivotal for we have often reiterated that "[w]here the class of activities is regulated and that class is within the reach of federal power, the courts have no power 'to excise, as trivial, individual instances' of the class." *Perez,* 402 U. S., at 154. . . .

[Moreover, unlike] those at issue in *Lopez* and *Morrison,* the activities regulated by the CSA are quintessentially economic. "Economics" refers to "the production, distribution, and consumption of commodities." Webster's Third New International Dictionary 720 (1966). The CSA is a statute that regulates the production, distribution, and consumption of commodities for which there is an established, and lucrative, interstate market. Prohibiting the intrastate possession or manufacture of an article of commerce is a rational (and commonly utilized) means of regulating commerce in that product. . . .[12]

■ JUSTICE SCALIA, concurring in the judgment. . . .[13]

Our cases show that the regulation of intrastate activities may be necessary to and proper for the regulation of interstate commerce in two general circumstances. Most directly, the commerce power permits Congress not only to devise rules for the governance of commerce between States but also to facilitate interstate commerce by eliminating potential obstructions, and to restrict it by eliminating potential stimulants. See *NLRB* v. *Jones & Laughlin Steel Corp.,* 301 U. S. 1, 36–37 (1937). That is why the Court has repeatedly sustained congressional legislation on the ground that the regulated activities had a substantial effect on interstate commerce. See, *e. g., Heart of Atlanta Motel, Inc.* v. *United States,* 379 U. S. 241, 258 (1964) (discrimination by hotels). . . .

This principle is not without limitation. In *Lopez* and *Morrison,* the Court—conscious of the potential of the "substantially affects" test to "obliterate the distinction between what is national and what is local," *Lopez, supra,* at 566–567—rejected the argument that Congress may regulate *noneconomic* activity based solely on the effect that it may have on interstate commerce through a remote chain of inferences. . . .

As we implicitly acknowledged in *Lopez,* however, Congress's authority to enact laws necessary and proper for the regulation of interstate commerce is not limited to laws directed against economic activities that have a substantial effect on interstate commerce. Though the conduct in *Lopez* was not economic, the Court nevertheless recognized that it could be regulated as "an essential part of a larger regulation of economic activity, in which the regulatory scheme could be undercut unless the intrastate activity were regulated." 514 U. S., at 561. . . .

Although this power "to make . . . regulation effective" commonly overlaps with the authority to regulate economic activities that substantially affect interstate commerce, and may in some cases have been confused with that authority, the two are distinct. The regulation of an intrastate activity may be essential to a

[12] **Question:** Stevens describes marijuana as a commodity and therefore an "article of commerce." But if the definition of "economics" is so broad, why wasn't the gun in *Lopez* also an article of commerce on the same principle?

[13] **Questions:** In contrast with Stevens, who dissented in *Lopez,* Justice Antonin Scalia joined the majority opinion in *Lopez.* He nevertheless concurs with Stevens in this case, also citing the Necessary and Proper Clause. From Scalia's perspective, when is a federal regulation of intrastate activity "necessary and proper" for regulating interstate commerce, and when does it go too far? Does his answer turn on the economic/noneconomic distinction of *Lopez*?

comprehensive regulation of interstate commerce even though the intrastate activity does not itself "substantially affect" interstate commerce. Moreover, as the passage from *Lopez* quoted above suggests, Congress may regulate even noneconomic local activity if that regulation is a necessary part of a more general regulation of interstate commerce. The relevant question is simply whether the means chosen are "reasonably adapted" to the attainment of a legitimate end under the commerce power. See *Darby, supra,* at 121. . . .

NOTE: THE FIRST TWO *LOPEZ* CATEGORIES

As noted above, *Lopez* divided Congress's power under the Commerce Clause into three categories: Congress may regulate (1) the use of the "channels of interstate commerce," (2) the "instrumentalities of interstate commerce," and (3) certain intrastate activities that "substantially affect interstate commerce." *Lopez*, *Morrison*, and *Raich* all addressed the third category. But the first two categories remain relatively unconstrained.

Accordingly, Congress continues to regulate highways, telecommunications, and other channels of commerce. *See, e.g.*, *Pierce Cnty. v. Guillen*, 537 U.S. 129 (2003) (prohibiting the use of highway data in federal or state court proceedings). And Congress continues to regulate guns, people, and other instrumentalities that have traveled in interstate commerce. *See, e.g.*, *United States v. Sullivan*, 332 U.S. 689 (1948) (upholding the regulation of a drug that had previously crossed state lines). Indeed, after *Lopez*, Congress fixed the Gun-Free School Zones Act simply by adding an element that the relevant firearm must have "moved in . . . interstate or foreign commerce." *See Luna Torres v. Lynch*, 578 U.S. 452 (2016) (observing that "most federal offenses" include a similar "jurisdictional element").

9.3 NECESSARY AND PROPER REGULATIONS

As the cases we have read so far repeatedly stress, Congress's power under the Commerce Clause is extensive. Yet even if it were possible to accurately trace the outer limits of the Commerce Clause, those limits would not fully define Congress's regulatory power. As the Court recognized in *Gonzales v. Raich*, 545 U.S. 1 (2005), Congress possesses the power not only to regulate commerce among the states but also to "make all Laws which shall be necessary and proper for carrying into Execution" its commercial regulations. U.S. Const. art. I, § 8, cl. 18. Ever since *McCulloch v. Maryland*, 17 U.S. (4 Wheat.) 316 (1819), the Court has interpreted the Necessary and Proper Clause to permit laws that go far beyond simple acts of commercial regulation.

Federal prisons are a good example of how the Necessary and Proper Clause has extended Congress's power under the Commerce Clause. As discussed in the previous section, most federal criminal laws today are exercises of Congress's Commerce Clause power. As a necessary and proper incident of this power, Congress has constructed federal prisons and created the Federal Bureau of Prisons to take custody of federally incarcerated people. As a necessary and proper incident of these creations, Congress has authorized the Bureau of Prisons to promulgate a host of regulations regarding how incarcerated people may communicate with the outside world, what they are allowed to eat, what kinds of clothes and provisions they are allowed to have, and so much more. These regulations can be personal, compulsory, and local, having nothing to do with interstate commerce. Yet, in the final analysis, all of these prison regulations trace their constitutional authority along a chain of necessary and proper incidents of the Commerce Clause.

9.3.1

United States v. Comstock

560 U.S. 126 (2010)

Just as *United States v. Lopez*, 514 U.S. 549 (1995), addressed limits on the Commerce Clause, the Court has also occasionally addressed limits on the Necessary and Proper Clause.

In 2010, a federal prisoner named Graydon Earl Comstock Jr. challenged a federal civil-commitment statute, which permitted the Department of Justice to hold him indefinitely beyond his criminal sentence as a "mentally ill, sexually dangerous federal prisoner." Act of Jul. 27, 2006, Pub. L. No. 109–248, 120 Stat. 620. Comstock argued that no enumerated power permitted Congress to pass this legislation and that Congress's power under the Necessary and Proper Clause was limited to laws only one degree removed from an enumerated power.

In rejecting his argument in *United States v. Comstock*, 560 U.S. 126 (2010), the Court developed a new, five-factor framework for evaluating the Necessary and Proper Clause.

■ JUSTICE BREYER delivered the opinion of the Court.[14]

A federal civil-commitment statute authorizes the Department of Justice to detain a mentally ill, sexually dangerous federal prisoner beyond the date the prisoner would otherwise be released. 18 U.S.C. § 4248. . . . The question presented is whether the Necessary and Proper Clause, Art. I, § 8, cl. 18, grants Congress authority sufficient to enact the statute before us. [W]e conclude that the Constitution grants Congress legislative power sufficient to enact § 4248. We base this conclusion on five considerations, taken together.

First, the Necessary and Proper Clause grants Congress broad authority to enact federal legislation. Nearly 200 years ago, this Court stated that the Federal "[G]overnment is acknowledged by all to be one of enumerated powers," *McCulloch*, 4 Wheat., at 405, which means that "[e]very law enacted by Congress must be based on one or more of" those powers, *United States v. Morrison,* 529 U.S. 598, 607 (2000). But, at the same time, "a government, entrusted with such" powers "must also be entrusted with ample means for their execution." *McCulloch*, 4 Wheat.,

---

[14] **As You Read, Consider:** Are the five factors discussed by Justice Stephen Breyer *limits* on Congress's power to enforce the Necessary and Proper Clause, or are they *descriptions* of Congress's power to enforce the Necessary and Proper Clause?

In arguing against the constitutionality of the civil-commitment statute, the petitioner proposed that Congress should not be allowed to pass any legislation that is more than one degree removed from an enumerated power. What principles would such a rule serve? Why does Breyer reject this rule?

at 408. Accordingly, the Necessary and Proper Clause makes clear that the Constitution's grants of specific federal legislative authority are accompanied by broad power to enact laws that are "convenient, or useful" or "conducive" to the authority's "beneficial exercise." . . .

We have since made clear that, in determining whether the Necessary and Proper Clause grants Congress the legislative authority to enact a particular federal statute, we look to see whether the statute constitutes a means that is rationally related to the implementation of a constitutionally enumerated power. See *Gonzales v. Raich*, 545 U.S. 1, 22 (2005) (holding that because "Congress had a rational basis" for concluding that a statute implements Commerce Clause power, the statute falls within the scope of congressional "authority to 'make all Laws which shall be necessary and proper' to 'regulate Commerce . . . among the several States' "); see also *United States v. Lopez*, 514 U.S. 549, 557 (1995). . . .

We have also recognized that . . . "[T]he Constitution . . . leaves to Congress a large discretion as to the means that may be employed in executing a given power." [*Lottery Case*, 188 U.S. 321, 355 (1903)]; *Morrison*, *supra*, at 607.

Thus, the Constitution, which nowhere speaks explicitly about the creation of federal crimes beyond those related to "counterfeiting," "[t]reason," or "Piracies and Felonies committed on the high Seas" or "against the Law of Nations," Art. I, § 8, cls. 6, 10; Art. III, § 3, nonetheless grants Congress broad authority to create such crimes. See *McCulloch*, 4 Wheat, at 416 ("All admit that the government may, legitimately, punish any violation of its laws; and yet, this is not among the enumerated powers of Congress"). And Congress routinely exercises its authority to enact criminal laws in furtherance of, for example, its enumerated powers to regulate interstate and foreign commerce, to enforce civil rights, to spend funds for the general welfare, to establish federal courts, to establish post offices, to regulate bankruptcy, to regulate naturalization, and so forth. Art. I, § 8, cls. 1, 3, 4, 7, 9; Amdts. 13–15. See, *e.g.*, *Lottery Case*, *supra* (upholding criminal statute enacted in furtherance of the Commerce Clause); *Ex parte Yarbrough*, 110 U.S. 651 (1884) (upholding Congress' authority to [criminalize] civil-rights violations); *Sabri*, *supra* (upholding criminal statute enacted in furtherance of the Spending Clause); *Jinks*, *supra*, at 462, n. 2 (describing perjury and witness tampering as federal crimes enacted in furtherance of the power to constitute federal tribunals; see also 18 U.S.C. § 1691 *et seq.* (postal crimes); § 151 *et seq.* (bankruptcy crimes); 8 U.S.C. §§ 1324–1328 (immigration crimes).

Similarly, Congress, in order to help ensure the enforcement of federal criminal laws enacted in furtherance of its enumerated powers, "can cause a prison to be erected at any place within the jurisdiction of the United States, and direct that all persons sentenced to imprisonment under the laws of the United States shall be confined there." *Ex parte Karstendick*, 93 U.S. 396, 400 (1876). Moreover, Congress, having established a prison system, can enact laws that seek to ensure that system's safe and responsible administration by, for example, requiring prisoners to receive medical care and educational training, see, *e.g.*, 18 U.S.C. §§ 4005–4006; § 4042(a)(3), and can also ensure the safety of the prisoners, prison workers and visitors, and those in surrounding communities by, for example, creating further criminal laws governing entry, exit, and smuggling, and by employing prison guards to ensure discipline and security, see, *e.g.*, § 1791 (prohibiting smuggling contraband); § 751 *et seq.* (prohibiting escape and abetting thereof); 28 CFR § 541.10 *et seq.* (2009) (inmate discipline).

Neither Congress' power to criminalize conduct, nor its power to imprison individuals who engage in that conduct, nor its power to enact laws governing prisons and prisoners, is explicitly mentioned in the Constitution. But Congress nonetheless possesses broad authority to do each of those things in the course of "carrying into Execution" the enumerated powers "vested by" the "Constitution in the Government of the United States," Art. I, § 8, cl. 18—authority granted by the Necessary and Proper Clause.

Second, the civil-commitment statute before us constitutes a modest addition to a set of federal prison-related mental-health statutes that have existed for many decades. We recognize that even a longstanding history of related federal action does not demonstrate a statute's constitutionality. A history of involvement, however, can nonetheless be "helpful in reviewing the substance of a congressional statutory scheme," *Gonzales*, 545 U.S., at 21, and, in particular, the reasonableness of the relation between the new statute and pre-existing federal interests. . . .

Third, Congress reasonably extended its longstanding civil-commitment system to cover mentally ill and sexually dangerous persons who are already in federal custody, even if doing so detains them beyond the termination of their criminal sentence. For one thing, the Federal Government is the custodian of its prisoners. As federal custodian, it has the constitutional power to act in order to protect nearby (and other) communities from the danger federal prisoners may pose. If a federal prisoner is infected with a communicable disease that threatens others, surely it would be "necessary and proper" for the Federal Government to take action, pursuant to its role as federal custodian, to refuse (at least until the threat diminishes) to release that individual among the general public, where he might infect others (even if not threatening an interstate epidemic, cf. Art. I, § 8, cl. 3). And if confinement of such an individual is a "necessary and proper" thing to do, then how could it not be similarly "necessary and proper" to confine an individual whose mental illness threatens others to the same degree? . . .

Fourth, the statute properly accounts for state interests. Respondents . . . contend that § 4248 violates the Tenth Amendment because it "invades the province of state sovereignty" in an area typically left to state control. See *Jackson v. Indiana*, 406 U.S. 715, 736 (1972) ("The States have traditionally exercised broad power to commit persons found to be mentally ill"). But the Tenth Amendment's text is clear: "The powers *not delegated to the United States* by the Constitution, nor prohibited by it to the States, are reserved to the States respectively, or to the people." The powers "delegated to the United States by the Constitution" include those specifically enumerated powers listed in Article I along with the implementation authority granted by the Necessary and Proper Clause. Virtually by definition, these powers are not powers that the Constitution "reserved to the States." See *Darby*, *supra*, at 123–124.

Nor does this statute invade state sovereignty or otherwise improperly limit the scope of "powers that remain with the States." To the contrary, it requires *accommodation* of state interests: The Attorney General must inform the State in which the federal prisoner "is domiciled or was tried" that he is detaining someone with respect to whom those States may wish to assert their authority, and he must encourage those States to assume custody of the individual. § 4248(d). He must also immediately "release" that person "to the appropriate official of" either State "if such State will assume [such] responsibility." *Ibid*. . . .

Fifth, the links between § 4248 and an enumerated Article I power are not too attenuated. Neither is the statutory provision too sweeping in its scope. Invoking the cautionary instruction that we may not "pile inference upon inference" in order to sustain congressional action under Article I, *Lopez*, 514 U.S., at 567, respondents argue that, when legislating pursuant to the Necessary and Proper Clause, Congress' authority can be no more than one step removed from a specifically enumerated power. See Brief for Respondents 21–22; Tr. of Oral Arg. 27–28. But this argument is irreconcilable with our precedents. . . . [A]s Chief Justice Marshall recognized in

McCulloch, "the power 'to establish post offices and post roads' . . . is executed by the single act of *making* the establishment. . . . [F]rom this has been inferred the power and duty of *carrying* the mail along the post road, from one post office to another. And, from this *implied* power, has *again* been inferred the right to *punish* those who steal letters from the post office, or rob the mail." 4 Wheat., at 417 (emphasis added). . . .

Indeed . . . [we cannot] point to a single specific enumerated power "that justifies a criminal defendant's arrest or conviction" in *all* cases because Congress relies on different enumerated powers (often, but not exclusively, its Commerce Clause power) to enact its various federal criminal statutes. But every such statute must itself be legitimately predicated on an enumerated power. And the same enumerated power that justifies the creation of a federal criminal statute, and that justifies the additional implied federal powers . . ., justifies civil commitment under § 4248 as well. Thus, we must reject respondents' argument that the Necessary and Proper Clause permits no more than a single step between an enumerated power and an Act of Congress. . . .

Taken together, these considerations lead us to conclude that the statute is a "necessary and proper" means of exercising the federal authority that permits Congress to create federal criminal laws, to punish their violation, to imprison violators, to provide appropriately for those imprisoned, and to maintain the security of those who are not imprisoned but who may be affected by the federal imprisonment of others. The Constitution consequently authorizes Congress to enact the statute. . . .[15]

9.3.2

National Federation of Independent Business (NFIB) v. Sebelius

567 U.S. 519 (2012)

The statute at issue in *Comstock* was a compulsory law passed pursuant to the Commerce Clause and the Necessary and Proper Clause: it required prisoners to remain in federal custody if they once violated a criminal regulation of interstate commerce. When Congress passed the Affordable Care Act of 2010, however, many people objected that Congress had no power to compel individuals to purchase private health insurance. We have already read about how the Court upheld the individual mandate as an exercise of the taxing power. But the thrust of the argument surrounding the mandate was as an exercise of the Commerce Clause or Necessary and Proper Clause.

To recap the purpose of the individual mandate: Congress wanted insurance companies to provide affordable insurance to everyone, including people with preexisting conditions. But insurance companies

[15] **Questions:** Is *Comstock*'s five-factor framework consistent with *McCulloch v. Maryland*? Recall that *McCulloch* declared that the Necessary and Proper Clause permitted Congress to pass any law that was "appropriate" and "plainly adapted" to a legitimate end. *McCulloch*, 17 U.S. (4 Wheat.) 316, 421 (1819).

After reading *Comstock*, can you think of any law that would be "too attenuated" for Congress to pass under the Commerce Clause and Necessary and Proper Clause? 560 U.S. at 146.

complained that this would raise their costs by requiring them to accept relatively unhealthy people without charging them relatively higher fees. So Congress mandated that all individuals, including relatively healthy individuals, must purchase health insurance or pay a penalty. Opponents of this mandate complained that if Congress could require people to purchase health insurance, Congress would have virtually unlimited power, including the power to make people buy broccoli. *See* James B. Stewart, *How Broccoli Landed on Supreme Court Menu*, N.Y. Times, June 13, 2012. But supporters explained that, under *Wickard v. Filburn*, 317 U.S. 111 (1942), and *Gonzales v. Raich*, 545 U.S. 1 (2005), Congress had a rational basis for deciding how to regulate people's personal decisions regarding when and how they would pay for the health care that they would inevitably need. Moreover, supporters maintained, the mandate was a necessary and proper part of a larger economic regulation of the health-care industry.

Writing only for himself but joined in the judgment by four dissenters, Chief Justice John Roberts in *National Federation of Independent Business (NFIB) v. Sebelius*, 567 U.S. 519 (2012), sided with the broccoli haters.

■ CHIEF JUSTICE ROBERTS announced . . . an opinion with respect to Parts III-A, III-B, and III-D.[16]

III-A

The Government's first argument is that the individual mandate is a valid exercise of Congress's power under the Commerce Clause and the Necessary and Proper Clause. . . .

[The Commerce Clause]

The Government contends that the individual mandate is within Congress's power because the failure to purchase insurance "has a substantial and deleterious effect on interstate commerce" by creating the cost-shifting problem. Brief for United States 34. The path of our Commerce Clause decisions has not always run smooth, see *United States v. Lopez*, 514 U.S. 549, 552–559 (1995), but it is now well established that Congress has broad authority under the Clause. We have recognized, for example, that "[t]he power of Congress over interstate commerce is not confined to the regulation of commerce among the states," but extends to activities that "have a substantial effect on interstate commerce." *United States v. Darby*, 312 U.S. 100, 118–119 (1941). Congress's power, moreover, is not limited to regulation of an activity that by itself substantially affects interstate commerce, but also extends to activities that do so only when aggregated with similar activities of others. See *Wickard*, 317 U.S., at 127–128.

Given its expansive scope, it is no surprise that Congress has employed the commerce power in a wide variety of ways to address the pressing needs of the time. But Congress has never attempted to rely on that power to compel individuals not

[16] **As You Read, Consider:** The first part of Chief Justice John Roberts's opinion discusses the difference between the power to *regulate* commerce and the power to *create* commerce. Is this a principled distinction? Why does it matter to Roberts?

The second part of Roberts's opinion interprets the Necessary and Proper Clause to contain implied limits. Is his interpretation consistent with *McCulloch v. Maryland* or *United States v. Comstock*, or is it new?

engaged in commerce to purchase an unwanted product. Legislative novelty is not necessarily fatal; there is a first time for everything. But sometimes "the most telling indication of [a] severe constitutional problem . . . is the lack of historical precedent" for Congress's action. At the very least, we should "pause to consider the implications of the Government's arguments" when confronted with such new conceptions of federal power. *Lopez, supra*, at 564.

The Constitution grants Congress the power to "*regulate* Commerce." Art. I, § 8, cl. 3 (emphasis added). The power to *regulate* commerce presupposes the existence of commercial activity to be regulated. If the power to "regulate" something included the power to create it, many of the provisions in the Constitution would be superfluous. For example, the Constitution gives Congress the power to "coin Money," in addition to the power to "regulate the Value thereof." *Id.*, cl. 5. And it gives Congress the power to "raise and support Armies" and to "provide and maintain a Navy," in addition to the power to "make Rules for the Government and Regulation of the land and naval Forces." *Id.*, cls. 12–14. If the power to regulate the armed forces or the value of money included the power to bring the subject of the regulation into existence, the specific grant of such powers would have been unnecessary. The language of the Constitution reflects the natural understanding that the power to regulate assumes there is already something to be regulated. See *Gibbons*, 9 Wheat., at 188 ("[T]he enlightened patriots who framed our constitution, and the people who adopted it, must be understood to have employed words in their natural sense, and to have intended what they have said").

Our precedent also reflects this understanding. As expansive as our cases construing the scope of the commerce power have been, they all have one thing in common: They uniformly describe the power as reaching "activity." It is nearly impossible to avoid the word when quoting them. See, *e.g., Lopez, supra*, at 560 ("Where economic activity substantially affects interstate commerce, legislation regulating that activity will be sustained"); *Perez*, 402 U.S., at 154; *Wickard, supra*, at 125; NLRB v. Jones & Laughlin Steel Corp., 301 U.S. 1 (1937).

The individual mandate, however, does not regulate existing commercial activity. It instead compels individuals to *become* active in commerce by purchasing a product, on the ground that their failure to do so affects interstate commerce. Construing the Commerce Clause to permit Congress to regulate individuals precisely *because* they are doing nothing would open a new and potentially vast domain to congressional authority. Every day individuals do not do an infinite number of things. In some cases they decide not to do something; in others they simply fail to do it. Allowing Congress to justify federal regulation by pointing to the effect of inaction on commerce would bring countless decisions an individual could *potentially* make within the scope of federal regulation, and—under the Government's theory—empower Congress to make those decisions for him.

Applying the Government's logic to the familiar case of *Wickard v. Filburn* shows how far that logic would carry us from the notion of a government of limited powers. In *Wickard*, the Court famously upheld a federal penalty imposed on a farmer for growing wheat for consumption on his own farm. 317 U.S., at 114–115. That amount of wheat caused the farmer to exceed his quota under a program designed to support the price of wheat by limiting supply. The Court rejected the farmer's argument that growing wheat for home consumption was beyond the reach of the commerce power. It did so on the ground that the farmer's decision to grow wheat for his own use allowed him to avoid purchasing wheat in the market. That decision, when considered in the aggregate along with similar decisions of others, would have had a substantial effect on the interstate market for wheat. *Id.*, at 127–129.

Wickard has long been regarded as "perhaps the most far reaching example of Commerce Clause authority over intrastate activity," *Lopez*, 514 U.S., at 560, but the Government's theory in this case would go much further. Under *Wickard* it is within Congress's power to regulate the market for wheat by supporting its price. But price can be supported by increasing demand as well as by decreasing supply. The aggregated decisions of some consumers not to purchase wheat have a substantial effect on the price of wheat, just as decisions not to purchase health insurance have on the price of insurance. Congress can therefore command that those not buying wheat do so, just as it argues here that it may command that those not buying health insurance do so. The farmer in *Wickard* was at least actively engaged in the production of wheat, and the Government could regulate that activity because of its effect on commerce. The Government's theory here would effectively override that limitation, by establishing that individuals may be regulated under the Commerce Clause whenever enough of them are not doing something the Government would have them do.

Indeed, the Government's logic would justify a mandatory purchase to solve almost any problem. To consider a different example in the health care market, many Americans do not eat a balanced diet. That group makes up a larger percentage of the total population than those without health insurance. The failure of that group to have a healthy diet increases health care costs, to a greater extent than the failure of the uninsured to purchase insurance. Those increased costs are borne in part by other Americans who must pay more, just as the uninsured shift costs to the insured. Congress addressed the insurance problem by ordering everyone to buy insurance. Under the Government's theory, Congress could address the diet problem by ordering everyone to buy vegetables.[17]

People, for reasons of their own, often fail to do things that would be good for them or good for society. Those failures—joined with the similar failures of others—can readily have a substantial effect on interstate commerce. Under the Government's logic, that authorizes Congress to use its commerce power to compel citizens to act as the Government would have them act.

That is not the country the Framers of our Constitution envisioned. James Madison explained that the Commerce Clause was "an addition which few oppose and from which no apprehensions are entertained." The Federalist No. 45, at 293. While Congress's authority under the Commerce Clause has of course expanded with the growth of the national economy, our cases have "always recognized that the power to regulate commerce, though broad indeed, has limits." *Maryland v. Wirtz*, 392 U.S. 183, 196 (1968). The Government's theory would erode those limits, permitting Congress to reach beyond the natural extent of its authority, "everywhere extending the sphere of its activity and drawing all power into its impetuous vortex." The Federalist No. 48, at 309 (J. Madison). Congress already enjoys vast power to regulate much of what we do. Accepting the Government's theory would give Congress the same license to regulate what we do not do, fundamentally changing the relation between the citizen and the Federal Government.

---

[17] **Questions:** Roberts here makes a powerful rhetorical move, emphasizing that if Congress had the power to create commerce, then Congress would have the power to force Americans to purchase vegetables. Precisely what is so dangerous about such a universe?

As you think about this question, consider that *National Federation of Independent Business (NFIB) v. Sebelius* and the Commerce Clause relate only to *Congress's* powers. Nothing about this opinion restricts what *states* can do. As an exercise of their police powers—whose source is found in state constitutions rather than the federal Constitution—states can compel people to purchase broccoli, auto insurance, and many other products. Is there a principled reason to prohibit Congress from passing such laws when states are able to do so?

To an economist, perhaps, there is no difference between activity and inactivity; both have measurable economic effects on commerce. But the distinction between doing something and doing nothing would not have been lost on the Framers, who were "practical statesmen," not metaphysical philosophers. As we have explained, "the framers of the Constitution were not mere visionaries, toying with speculations or theories, but practical men, dealing with the facts of political life as they understood them, putting into form the government they were creating, and prescribing in language clear and intelligible the powers that government was to take." The Framers gave Congress the power to *regulate* commerce, not to *compel* it, and for over 200 years both our decisions and Congress's actions have reflected this understanding. There is no reason to depart from that understanding now.

The Government sees things differently. It argues that because sickness and injury are unpredictable but unavoidable, "the uninsured as a class are active in the market for health care, which they regularly seek and obtain." Brief for United States 50. The individual mandate "merely regulates how individuals finance and pay for that active participation—requiring that they do so through insurance, rather than through attempted self-insurance with the back-stop of shifting costs to others." *Ibid.*

The Government repeats the phrase "active in the market for health care" throughout its brief, see *id.*, at 7, 18, 34, 50, but that concept has no constitutional significance. An individual who bought a car two years ago and may buy another in the future is not "active in the car market" in any pertinent sense. The phrase "active in the market" cannot obscure the fact that most of those regulated by the individual mandate are not currently engaged in any commercial activity involving health care, and that fact is fatal to the Government's effort to "regulate the uninsured as a class." *Id.*, at 42. Our precedents recognize Congress's power to regulate "class[es] of *activities*," *Gonzales v. Raich*, 545 U.S. 1, 17 (2005) (emphasis added), not classes of *individuals*, apart from any activity in which they are engaged, see, *e.g.*, *Perez*, 402 U.S., at 153.

The individual mandate's regulation of the uninsured as a class is, in fact, particularly divorced from any link to existing commercial activity. The mandate primarily affects healthy, often young adults who are less likely to need significant health care and have other priorities for spending their money. It is precisely because these individuals, as an actuarial class, incur relatively low health care costs that the mandate helps counter the effect of forcing insurance companies to cover others who impose greater costs than their premiums are allowed to reflect. If the individual mandate is targeted at a class, it is a class whose commercial inactivity rather than activity is its defining feature.

The Government, however, claims that this does not matter. The Government regards it as sufficient to trigger Congress's authority that almost all those who are uninsured will, at some unknown point in the future, engage in a health care transaction. Asserting that "[t]here is no temporal limitation in the Commerce Clause," the Government argues that because "[e]veryone subject to this regulation is in or will be in the health care market," they can be "regulated in advance." Tr. of Oral Arg. 109 (Mar. 27, 2012). . . .

[But e]veryone will likely participate in the markets for food, clothing, transportation, shelter, or energy; that does not authorize Congress to direct them to purchase particular products in those or other markets today. The Commerce Clause is not a general license to regulate an individual from cradle to grave, simply because he will predictably engage in particular transactions. Any police power to regulate individuals as such, as opposed to their activities, remains vested in the States.

The Government argues that the individual mandate can be sustained as a sort of exception to this rule, because health insurance is a unique product. According to the Government, upholding the individual mandate would not justify mandatory purchases of items such as cars or broccoli because, as the Government puts it, "[h]ealth insurance is not purchased for its own sake like a car or broccoli; it is a means of financing health-care consumption and covering universal risks." Reply Brief for United States 19. But cars and broccoli are no more purchased for their "own sake" than health insurance. They are purchased to cover the need for transportation and food. . . .

The individual mandate forces individuals into commerce precisely because they elected to refrain from commercial activity. Such a law cannot be sustained under a clause authorizing Congress to "regulate Commerce." . . . .

[The Necessary and Proper Clause]

The Government next contends that Congress has the power under the Necessary and Proper Clause to enact the individual mandate because the mandate is an "integral part of a comprehensive scheme of economic regulation"—the guaranteed-issue and community-rating insurance reforms. Brief for United States 24. Under this argument, it is not necessary to consider the effect that an individual's inactivity may have on interstate commerce; it is enough that Congress regulate commercial activity in a way that requires regulation of inactivity to be effective.

The power to "make all Laws which shall be necessary and proper for carrying into Execution" the powers enumerated in the Constitution, Art. I, § 8, cl. 18, vests Congress with authority to enact provisions "incidental to the [enumerated] power, and conducive to its beneficial exercise," *McCulloch*, 4 Wheat., at 418. Although the Clause gives Congress authority to "legislate on that vast mass of incidental powers which must be involved in the constitution," it does not license the exercise of any "great substantive and independent power[s]" beyond those specifically enumerated. *Id.*, at 411, 421. Instead, the Clause is "merely a declaration, for the removal of all uncertainty, that the means of carrying into execution those [powers] otherwise granted are included in the grant."[18]

As our jurisprudence under the Necessary and Proper Clause has developed, we have been very deferential to Congress's determination that a regulation is "necessary." We have thus upheld laws that are " 'convenient, or useful' or 'conducive' to the authority's 'beneficial exercise.' " *Comstock*, 560 U.S., at ___. But we have also carried out our responsibility to declare unconstitutional those laws that undermine the structure of government established by the Constitution. Such laws, which are not "consist[ent] with the letter and spirit of the constitution," *McCulloch*, *supra*, at 421, are not "*proper* [means] for carrying into Execution" Congress's enumerated powers. Rather, they are, "in the words of The Federalist, 'merely acts of usurpation' which 'deserve to be treated as such.' " The Federalist No. 33, at 204 (A. Hamilton).

Applying these principles, the individual mandate cannot be sustained under the Necessary and Proper Clause as an essential component of the insurance reforms. Each of our prior cases upholding laws under that Clause involved exercises of authority derivative of, and in service to, a granted power. For example, we have upheld provisions permitting continued confinement of those *already in federal custody* when they could not be safely released, *Comstock*, *supra*, at ___; criminalizing bribes involving organizations *receiving federal funds*, *Sabri v. United States*, 541 U.S. 600, 602, 605 (2004); and tolling state statutes of limitations while

[18] **Question:** Roberts here invokes the two major Necessary and Proper Clause opinions: *McCulloch* and *Comstock*. Is he *reinterpreting* those decisions or *reaffirming* them?

cases are *pending in federal court*, *Jinks v. Richland County*, 538 U.S. 456, 459, 462 (2003). The individual mandate, by contrast, vests Congress with the extraordinary ability to create the necessary predicate to the exercise of an enumerated power.

This is in no way an authority that is "narrow in scope," *Comstock, supra*, at ___, 130 S.Ct., at 1964, or "incidental" to the exercise of the commerce power, *McCulloch, supra*, at 418. Rather, such a conception of the Necessary and Proper Clause would work a substantial expansion of federal authority. No longer would Congress be limited to regulating under the Commerce Clause those who by some preexisting activity bring themselves within the sphere of federal regulation. Instead, Congress could reach beyond the natural limit of its authority and draw within its regulatory scope those who otherwise would be outside of it. Even if the individual mandate is "necessary" to the Act's insurance reforms, such an expansion of federal power is not a "proper" means for making those reforms effective.

The Government relies primarily on our decision in *Gonzales v. Raich*. In *Raich*, we considered "comprehensive legislation to regulate the interstate market" in marijuana. 545 U.S., at 22. Certain individuals sought an exemption from that regulation on the ground that they engaged in only intrastate possession and consumption. We denied any exemption, on the ground that marijuana is a fungible commodity, so that any marijuana could be readily diverted into the interstate market. Congress's attempt to regulate the interstate market for marijuana would therefore have been substantially undercut if it could not also regulate intrastate possession and consumption. *Id.*, at 19. Accordingly, we recognized that "Congress was acting well within its authority" under the Necessary and Proper Clause even though its "regulation ensnare[d] some purely intrastate activity." *Id.*, at 22; see also *Perez*, 402 U.S., at 154. *Raich* thus did not involve the exercise of any "great substantive and independent power," *McCulloch, supra*, at 411, of the sort at issue here. Instead, it concerned only the constitutionality of "individual *applications* of a concededly valid statutory scheme." *Raich, supra*, at 23, 125 S.Ct. 2195 (emphasis added).

Just as the individual mandate cannot be sustained as a law regulating the substantial effects of the failure to purchase health insurance, neither can it be upheld as a "necessary and proper" component of the insurance reforms. The commerce power thus does not authorize the mandate.[19]

NOTE: A "GREAT SUBSTANTIVE AND INDEPENDENT POWER"

In rejecting the federal government's argument that the individual mandate was necessary and proper for regulating the interstate healthcare market, Chief Justice John Roberts crafted a novel limit on the Necessary and Proper Clause: a law is not "proper" if it represents a "great substantive and independent power." 567 U.S. at 560–61. Roberts drew this language from *McCulloch v. Maryland*, 17 U.S. (4 Wheat.) 316 (1819), in which Chief Justice John Marshall affirmed the constitutionality of the Bank of United

[19] **Questions:** The search for a limiting principle animates much of the current debate over the scope of the Commerce Clause. In 2012, when *NFIB* was before the Supreme Court, both sides of the debate proposed rules that would allow Congress to regulate many activities but not all activities. *Compare* Jack Balkin, *The Limiting Principle*, Balkinization (Mar. 28, 2012) (identifying three limiting principles that could justify the Affordable Care Act's individual mandate), *with* Jonathan H. Adler, *The Search for a Limiting Principle for Federal Power: Collective Action Problems*, Volokh Conspiracy (May 29, 2012) (rejecting collective action problems as a sufficient limiting principle). Is such a limiting principle necessary? What is wrong with giving Congress unlimited discretion to determine when a law regulates interstate commerce?

States. Among other arguments in support of the bank, Marshall wrote that "[t]he power of creating a corporation . . . is not, like the power of making war, or levying taxes, or of regulating commerce, a great substantive and independent power, which cannot be implied as incidental to other powers, or used as a means of executing them." *Id.* at 411. Roberts interpreted the middle of this quote as frontier beyond which Congress could not cross using the Necessary and Proper Clause. He also implied that a law could not be proper if it compromised "essential attributes of state sovereignty" or created "the necessary predicate to the exercise of an enumerated power." *Id.* at 560.

Taken seriously, Roberts's interpretation of the Necessary and Proper Clause would limit a wide range of federal legislation that the Supreme Court has previously upheld. For example, as we will see in the next few sections (10.1–10.4), Congress has enacted laws governing immigration and deportation despite the absence of an enumerated immigration clause. Federal laws relating to war (section 13.4), foreign affairs (section 14.2), federal courts (15.2), Native tribes (17.2), and other domestic regulations also rely heavily on the Necessary and Proper Clause even though many of these laws could be described as exercising great substantive and independent powers.

Perhaps because the rule in *NFIB* could undermine so many existing federal laws, the Supreme Court has not applied *NFIB* to invalidate legislation in the decade since the decision. To the contrary, the Court has continued to interpret the Necessary and Proper Clause broadly even when states have objected that Congress was compromising their "state sovereignty." *See, e.g., PennEast Pipeline Co., LLC v. New Jersey*, 141 S. Ct. 2244, 2263 (2021). Illustrative is a 2021 decision, *PennEast*, in which New Jersey objected to a federal law that authorized private corporations to seize property belonging to the state. New Jersey complained that nothing in the Constitution explicitly gave the federal government the power of eminent domain, much less the authority to delegate that power to private corporations or the additional authority to exercise it against state-owned property. *Id.* at 2253–54. But in a majority opinion written by Roberts, the Court relied on century-old precedent to reaffirm Congress's "eminent domain power." *Id.* at 2255 (citing *Kohl v. United States*, 91 U.S. 367, 371–74 (1876)). Without mentioning the Necessary and Proper Clause, *NFIB*, or any enumerated power, Roberts wrote that Congress had the power to authorize private parties to seize state property. *Id.* Four dissenting justices objected that "the Constitution enumerates no stand-alone 'eminent-domain power' " and argued that the law at issue exceeded the scope of the Necessary and Proper Clause. *Id.* at 2267 (Barrett, J., dissenting).

CHAPTER 10

WHAT IS THE SCOPE OF CONGRESS'S POWER TO REGULATE IMMIGRATION?

ARTICLE I, SECTION 8, CLAUSE 3: The Congress shall have Power . . . To regulate Commerce with foreign Nations . . .;

> **CLAUSE 4:** To establish an uniform Rule of Naturalization . . .;—And
>
> **CLAUSE 18:** To make all Laws which shall be necessary and proper for carrying into Execution the foregoing Powers, and all other Powers vested by this Constitution in the Government of the United States, or in any Department or Officer thereof.

ARTICLE I, SECTION 9, CLAUSE 1: The Migration or Importation of such Persons as any of the States now existing shall think proper to admit, shall not be prohibited by the Congress prior to the Year one thousand eight hundred and eight, but a Tax or duty may be imposed on such Importation, not exceeding ten dollars for each Person.

TENTH AMENDMENT (1791): The powers not delegated to the United States by the Constitution, nor prohibited by it to the States, are reserved to the States respectively, or to the people.

10.1 THE POWER TO REGULATE FOREIGN COMMERCE

The Constitution doesn't give Congress an express power to regulate immigration. Instead, Article I gives Congress several other powers, the most relevant of which are the powers (1) to "regulate Commerce with foreign Nations" and (2) to "establish an uniform Rule of Naturalization." Article I of the Constitution also forbids Congress from prohibiting, before 1808, the "Migration or Importation of such Persons as any of the States now existing shall think proper to admit." Although this prohibition was a lightly concealed reference to the transatlantic slave trade, it provides an unmistakable implication that Congress has the power to prevent at least some people from entering the United States.

Before jumping into Congress's power over immigration, it is worth first considering what its enumerated powers allow it to do, beginning with Congress's power to regulate foreign commerce.

As discussed in the preamble (section 1.1), one of the widespread criticisms of the Articles of Confederation was that the Articles contained no mechanism by which the Confederation Congress could compel states to abide by the United States' treaty commitments with European powers. The Commerce Clause was designed not only to allow Congress to establish nationwide commercial regulations but also to ensure that the United States could maintain a uniform response in foreign trade disputes. Some of the first examples of federal commercial regulation—including the embargo at issue in *United States v. The William*, 28 F. Cas. 614 (D. Mass. 1808)—were regulations of *foreign* commerce as opposed to *interstate* commerce. In general, the Supreme Court has drawn no distinction between Congress's power to regulate interstate commerce as opposed to foreign commerce: "The power to regulate commerce among the several States is granted to Congress in the same clause, and by the same words, as the power to regulate commerce with foreign nations, and is coextensive with it." *License Cases*, 46 U.S. (5 How.) 504, 578 (1847).

At the very least, therefore, Congress's power to regulate foreign commerce includes the power to regulate the "channels" and "instrumentalities" of foreign commerce, *Gibbons v. Ogden*, 22 U.S. (9 Wheat.) 1, 91 (1824), as well as domestic activities that substantially affect foreign commerce. Just as Congress can prohibit certain people or goods from crossing state lines, it has at least the same power at the international border.

But the Court has also, at times, suggested that Congress's power over foreign commerce is even greater than its power over interstate commerce. Many of the limits that the Court has historically imposed on Congress's power to regulate interstate commerce—the distinctions between manufacturing and commerce, direct versus indirect taxation, economic versus noneconomic activity, and activity versus inactivity—have been offered for the sole purpose of protecting principles of federalism in which states exercise a general police power that Congress lacks. These principles are inapplicable, by contrast, when Congress legislates with respect to the international border or overseas. Accordingly, members of the Court have occasionally described Congress's power to regulate foreign commerce in sweeping terms.

For example, in the *Lottery Case*, the dissenters explained that the power to regulate interstate commerce "was intended to secure equality and freedom in commercial intercourse as between the States." 188 U.S. 321, 373 (1903). By contrast, the power to regulate foreign commerce "clothed Congress with that power over international commerce, pertaining to a sovereign nation in its intercourse with foreign nations, and subject, generally speaking, to no implied or reserved power in the States." *Id.* (Fuller, C.J., dissenting). The dissenters suggested that "[t]he laws which would be necessary and proper in the one case, would not be necessary or proper in the other." *Id.* Although no case has turned on this suggestion that Congress's power to regulate foreign commerce is greater than its power to regulate interstate commerce, the absence of federal restrictions when Congress legislates at the border or overseas is a theme that dominates the Court's appraisal of all federal foreign policy, as we will see when we discuss the power to exclude noncitizens (section 10.3), the war powers (section 13.1), and the president's power to conduct foreign affairs (section 32.1).

10.2 THE POWER TO ESTABLISH A UNIFORM RULE OF NATURALIZATION

Although *immigration* and *naturalization* are often treated as synonyms, they are very different. *Immigration* refers to the entry of people from other countries; *naturalization* refers to the process by which a person becomes a citizen. In giving Congress the power to establish "an uniform Rule of Naturalization," Article I, Section 8, Clause 4, of the Constitution provided that Congress could set the standards by which a person could become a citizen of the United States.

Naturalization laws

The first Congress passed such an act in 1790, providing that "any alien, being a free white person, who shall have resided within the limits and under the jurisdiction of the United States for the term of two years, may be admitted to become a citizen thereof." Act of Mar. 26, 1790, ch. 3, 1 Stat. 103. To apply, all the free white person had to do was prove to a state court "that he is a person of good character" and take an oath "to support the constitution of the United States." *Id.* After taking the oath, the person would be "considered as a citizen of the United States"—as would his or her minor children. *Id.* at 104. The 1790 statute also "considered as natural born citizens" any children of citizens "born beyond sea," as long as the father had once resided in the United States. *Id.*

Although later naturalization laws modified this procedure and lengthened the residency requirement to five years—*see, e.g.*, Act of Jan. 29, 1795, ch. 20, 1 Stat. 414—the 1790 law established a few important precedents. The first Congress apparently believed that, in enacting a "uniform" rule, it could nevertheless withhold citizenship from certain groups of people—namely, people who weren't white, free, or residents. Congress also, apparently, didn't see naturalization as something that only federal officials could administer: it left state courts in charge. In addition, the 1790 law said nothing about *state* citizenship, allowing states to continue their pre-1789 practice of determining for themselves who could become a citizen of, say, Massachusetts. (State citizenship continues to come up in federal litigation because Article III of the Constitution gives federal courts jurisdiction over controversies "between Citizens of different States.") Congress also extended citizenship to some but not all children of citizens born abroad.

Naturalization and discrimination

These precedents have long guided judicial interpretations of the Naturalization Clause—and discrimination against certain groups has been the result.

In *Dred Scott v. Sandford*, 60 U.S. (19 How.) 393 (1857), the Supreme Court cited the 1790 law's reference to white people as evidence that black people were constitutionally ineligible for federal or state citizenship. The law demonstrated to the Court that black people had always been "regarded as beings of an inferior order, . . . and so far inferior that they had no rights which the white man was bound to respect." *Dred Scott*, 60 U.S. (19 How.) at 407.

After the Civil War, Congress repudiated this particular holding by proposing the Fourteenth Amendment, Section 1 of which began, "All persons born or naturalized in the United States and subject to the jurisdiction thereof, are citizens of the United States and of the State wherein they reside." In 1870, Congress also expanded naturalization eligibility from "free white persons" alone to "aliens of African nativity and to persons of African descent." Act of July 14, 1870, ch. 254, 16 Stat. 254.

But Congress continued to exclude various groups from eligibility for citizenship. An 1882 law, for example, declared that "no State court or court of the United States shall admit Chinese to citizenship." Act of May 6, 1882, ch. 126, 22 Stat. 58. Later laws withheld naturalization from people who believed in anarchy or polygamy, Act of Mar. 3, 1903, ch. 1012, 32 Stat. 1213, and people "who can not speak the English language," Act of June 29, 1906, Pub. L. No. 59–338, 34 Stat. 596, 599 (1906). In the 1920s, immigrants from Japan and India challenged their status as "racially ineligible for citizenship," arguing that they were fair-skinned or scientifically Caucasian. But the Supreme Court rejected their arguments, interpreting the Naturalization Act's use of the term *white persons* as referring to the "popular meaning" of race "in accordance with the understanding of the common man." *United States v. Bhagat Singh Thind*, 261 U.S. 204, 208–09 (1923); *see Takao Ozawa v. United States*, 260 U.S. 178 (1922).

Denaturalization for those naturalized by descent

It was not until the Immigration and Nationality Act of 1952, Pub. L. No. 82–414, 66 Stat. 163, that Congress prohibited the denial of naturalization because of race, sex, or marital status. But Congress continued to deny naturalization for a number of other reasons, including membership in a communist organization or lack of "good moral character." Immigration and Nationality Act, 66 Stat. at 242. The 1952 statute also extended birthright citizenship to seven categories of people, from "(1) a person born in the United States" to "(7) a person born outside the geographical limits of the United States . . . of parents one of whom is an alien and the other a citizen of the United States." *Id.* at 235–36. But the law noted that people in category 7 could lose their citizenship if they failed to reside in the United States for at least five continuous years between their fourteenth and twenty-eighth birthdays. *Id.*

This loss-of-citizenship condition in category 7 became the subject of a Supreme Court case, *Rogers v. Bellei*, 401 U.S. 815 (1971). Aldo Mario Bellei, the Italian-born son of an Italian father and American mother, involuntarily lost his U.S. citizenship after failing to reside in the United States for five years before his twenty-eighth birthday. He sued the secretary of state, William Rogers, arguing that Congress lacked the unilateral power to revoke a person's citizenship. But in *Bellei*, the Court upheld the revocation of Bellei's citizenship on the ground that the Naturalization Clause permits Congress to impose reasonable conditions on eligibility for citizenship, even if those conditions are triggered after citizenship is granted. *Bellei*, 401 U.S. at 826–27.

The Court emphasized that Bellei was not born or naturalized in the United States and therefore was not guaranteed citizenship by Section 1 of the Fourteenth Amendment. Rather, he was claiming "naturalization by descent"—a privilege Congress first awarded in 1790 to some but not all children of citizens born abroad. *Id.* at 830–31. No one doubted, the Court maintained, that Congress could have chosen to withhold citizenship from Bellei until he lived in the United States for five years. Treating Congress's revocation as functionally identical to this hypothetical, the Court concluded "that it does not make good constitutional sense, or comport with logic, to say, on the one hand, that Congress may impose a condition precedent, with no constitutional complication, and yet be powerless to impose precisely the same condition subsequent." *Id.* at 834. Statutory citizenship, in other words, does not have to be "unconditional." *Id.* at 835.

Denaturalization for those born or naturalized in the United States

Bellei turned on the fact that the five-year residency requirement was one of several statutory conditions that made Bellei eligible for citizenship in the first place. In contexts where Congress has attempted to denaturalize citizens who were either born in the United States or who had satisfied all the conditions necessary to become naturalized, the Court has focused on other factors, eventually concluding that denaturalization in such cases can only occur when there was a material misrepresentation in the citizenship application.

Congress first attempted to denaturalize citizens in 1907, when it declared that any American woman who married a foreign citizen would have her U.S. citizenship held "in abeyance." Act of Mar. 2, 1907, Pub. L. No. 59–1903, 34 Stat. 1228. This statute had the effect of denaturalizing and disenfranchising thousands of women just as many were obtaining the right to vote for the first time. *See* Amanda Frost, *You Are Not American* 1–2 (2021). In *Mackenzie v. Hare*, 239 U.S. 299 (1915), a San Francisco suffragist named Ethel Coope Mackenzie challenged the law after she married a British man, lost her citizenship, and was subsequently denied the right to vote in California. But the Court upheld the statute on the basis of coverture, explaining that it was an "ancient principle of our jurisprudence" to "merge" the identity of husband and wife and to "give dominance to the husband." *Mackenzie*, 239 U.S. at 311; Frost, *supra*, at 2.

But in *Schneider v. Rusk*, 377 U.S. 163 (1964), and *Afroyim v. Rusk*, 387 U.S. 253 (1967), the Court reevaluated its precedents and held that Congress had no power to denaturalize a naturalized U.S. citizen. Instead, the Court held that Congress's power over naturalization is subject to the complete "control" of Section 1 of the Fourteenth Amendment, which declares that anyone born "or naturalized" in the United States is a citizen of the United States. "There is no indication in these words of a fleeting citizenship, good at the moment it is acquired but subject to destruction by the Government at any time," the Court wrote in *Afroyim*. 387 U.S. at 262. "Rather the Amendment can most reasonably be read as defining a citizenship which a citizen keeps unless he voluntarily relinquishes it." *Id.*

There is obvious tension between *Afroyim* and *Bellei*. The former all but declares that citizenship is permanent. The latter declares that naturalized citizenship can be granted subject to conditions—at least where the citizen was neither born nor naturalized in the United States. Although the Court has not attempted to resolve this tension, the *Afroyim* Court noted, in a footnote, that "naturalization unlawfully procured can be set aside." *Id.* at 267 n.23.

Invoking *Afroyim*'s footnote, the federal government has repeatedly applied a statute, 8 U.S.C. § 1451, that permits a person's naturalization to be "canceled" if the person included a material misrepresentation in the citizenship application. In 2016, President Barack Obama's administration invoked this statute as part of Operation Janus, a proposal to denaturalize dozens of citizens whom the administration argued were national security risks. *See* Amanda Frost, *Alienating Citizens*, 114 Nw. U. L. Rev. Online 241, 249–51 (2019). President Donald Trump dramatically expanded Operation Janus to investigate over 700,000 naturalized citizens, thousands of whom the administration prosecuted for naturalization fraud. *Id.* at 251–53. In one denaturalization case that reached the Supreme Court, Trump's deputy solicitor general argued that failing "to list the 'offense' of driving sixty miles an hour in a fifty-five-mile-per-hour zone would allow the government to denaturalize a citizen years later." *Id.* at 248. In *Maslenjak v. United States*, the Supreme Court appeared to accept that the federal government could denaturalize a citizen for a *material* misrepresentation that genuinely contributed to obtainment of citizenship. 137 S. Ct. 1918, 1924 (2017). However, the Court denied that such a trivial and unrelated offense as failing to disclose a speeding ticket qualified as material. *Id.* at 1924–27.

10.3 THE POWER TO EXCLUDE NONCITIZENS

Congress's enumerated powers to regulate foreign commerce and naturalize foreign immigrants form the basis of its implied power to regulate the entry and removal of noncitizens. Yet Congress's attempts to regulate immigration have been controversial from the beginning.

Alien Friends Act and lack of federal immigration restrictions

The first federal immigration law was the Alien Friends Act of 1798, ch. 58, 1 Stat. 570. Despite its friendly name, it was one of the four Alien and Sedition Acts signed by President John Adams in anticipation of hostilities with France. The law authorized the president "to *order* all such *aliens* as he shall judge dangerous to the peace and safety of the United States . . . to depart out of the territory of the United States." Alien Friends Act, 1 Stat. at 571.

This law drew the ire of James Madison, who wrote to Thomas Jefferson that "[t]he Alien bill proposed in the Senate is a monster that must for ever disgrace its parents." *See* 30 *The Papers of Thomas Jefferson* 358 (Barbara B. Oberg ed., 2003). On behalf of the Virginia legislature, Madison drafted the Virginia Resolutions of 1798, some of which were excerpted previously (section 3.1).The resolutions condemned the Alien Friends Act as a law that "exercises a power no where delegated to the federal government." 17 *The Papers of James Madison* 185, 189 (David B. Mattern et al. eds., 1991).

After its constitutionality was pilloried by protestors and members of Congress, the Alien Friends Act expired without ever being enforced. *See* 6 *The Papers of Thomas Jefferson, Retirement Series* 191 (J. Jefferson Looney ed., 2009). For the next seventy years, Congress passed no federal restrictions of immigration: people could enter or leave the country as easily as they could cross state lines. *See* Elliott Young, *Alien Nation* 10–12, 130 (2014). The only relevant laws that Congress passed were those registering and setting safety standards for passenger and coastal ships, like the federal statute at issue in *Gibbons v. Ogden*, 22 U.S. (9 Wheat.) 1 (1824).

The Supreme Court reinforced this absence of federal restrictions by interpreting the Commerce Clause narrowly to allow Congress to regulate *passengers*, as in *Gibbons*, but not *people who were not on a passenger ship*. *See New York v. Miln*, 36 U.S. (11 Pet.) 102, 136 (1837). This narrow definition ensured that Congress could not use the Commerce Clause to interfere with states' exclusive control over slavery. *See Groves v. Slaughter*, 40 U.S. (15 Pet.) 449, 505 (1841) (McLean, J., concurring). In fact, when Congress abolished the transatlantic slave trade in 1808, it relied not on the Commerce Clause but on its power to "define and punish Piracies and Felonies committed on the high Seas, and Offences against the law of nations." U.S. Const. art. I, § 8, cl. 10; *see* 16 Annals of Cong. 271 (1807). Congress ultimately declared that anyone convicted of participating in the transatlantic slave trade would be "adjudged a pirate." Act of May 15, 1820, ch. 66, §§ 4–5, 3 Stat. 600, 601.

State immigration laws

As Congress avoided restricting immigration, states passed their own immigration laws. New York and Massachusetts set the standard for coastal states by levying taxes on new immigrants and prohibiting poor, infirm, and other unwanted people from entering their borders. Hidetaka Hirota, *Expelling the Poor* 42–83 (2017). Meanwhile, states from Mississippi to Oregon set the standard for domestic borders by excluding black people from other states. *Id.* at 87. When these sorts of exclusionary laws reached the Supreme Court, the Court responded that the power to exclude was "not a regulation of commerce, but of police, and [therefore] . . . a power which rightfully belonged to the states." *Miln*, 36 U.S. (11 Pet.) at 132. In later cases, the Court reasoned that Congress's power to regulate foreign commerce extended to passengers while they were on their "voyage" to the United States—but Congress's power ended once the passengers' voyages ended, at which point the immigrants became subject to exclusive state control. *See Smith v. Turner* (*The Passenger Cases*), 48 U.S. 283, 445–49 (1849) (Catron, J.).

The issue of state immigration laws ramped up with the discovery of gold in California, which led to an explosion of Chinese immigration. Western railroad, mining, and manufacturing employers increasingly recruited laborers from China instead of from the eastern states. Chinese immigration sparked a firestorm of racism and xenophobia. *See* Erika Lee, *America for Americans* 75–79 (2019). Western states generally failed to protect the legal rights of Chinese workers, allowing employers to pay and treat them terribly. This practice undercut the wages of white workers, leading white labor leaders to demand the expulsion of Chinese immigrants from their communities. *See* Richard White, *Railroaded* 296 (2011). As white rioters in California, Oregon, and Washington burned homes of Chinese families, western politicians blamed the immigrants themselves for bringing criminals, prostitutes, and drugs into wholesome neighborhoods. *See* Charles J. McClain, *In Search of Equality* 9–42 (1996).

In the 1850s, California passed the first of many state laws that declared that any people "of the Chinese or Mongolian races, shall not be permitted to enter this state." 1858 Cal. Stat. 295; *see also People ex rel. Att'y Gen. v. Naglee*, 1 Cal. 232 (1850). When California adopted its current constitution in 1879, it even included an entire article on "The Chinese," full of sections that declared that the government would have "all necessary power . . . for the removal of Chinese." Cal. Const. of 1879, art. XIX, §§ 2–4.

Federal immigration restrictions

However, these state laws conflicted with a federal treaty in which the United States promised China that Chinese subjects could freely travel to the United States. *See* Burlingame-Seward Treaty of 1868, 6 U.S.T. 680, 682. State and federal courts also held that California's laws regulated immigrants during their voyages and were therefore regulations of foreign commerce—a power that only Congress could exercise. *See, e.g.*, *In re Ah Fong*, 1 F. Cas. 213, 214 (C.C.D. Cal. 1874) (No. 102); *People v. Downer*, 7 Cal. 169 (1857).

As anti-Chinese activists in California watched courts strike down their laws, they demanded that Congress pass the first-ever federal restrictions of immigration. With the Page Act of 1875, Congress authorized state officials to exclude any immigrants from "China, Japan, or any Oriental country" whom they believed were immigrating for "lewd and immoral purposes" or under a contract to perform labor. Page Act, ch. 141, 18 Stat. 477, 477.

Five years later, the United States renegotiated its treaty with China to permit Congress to suspend all new Chinese laborers for ten years. *See* Angell Treaty of 1880, 6 U.S.T. 685. Congress enforced this treaty with the Chinese Restriction Act of 1882, 22 Stat. 58. The act temporarily suspended "the coming of Chinese laborers to the United States" and required all other Chinese immigrants to carry a certificate of identification. Chinese Restriction Act, 22 Stat. at 59.

These federal anti-Chinese laws set an important precedent: Congress soon added to the list of excluded persons, including "any convict, lunatic, idiot, or any person unable to take care of himself or herself without becoming a public charge." Act of Aug. 3, 1882, ch. 376, 22 Stat. 214.

The laws also forced the Supreme Court to consider what, precisely, in the Constitution permitted Congress to regulate immigration. The Court quickly concluded that any law that "prescribes terms or conditions on which alone a vessel can discharge its passengers, is a regulation of commerce." *Henderson v. Mayor of the City of N.Y.*, 92 U.S. 259, 273 (1876). The Court therefore sustained Congress's power to exclude or regulate new immigrants as a "branch of foreign commerce which is involved in immigration." *Edye v. Robertson* (*The Head Money Cases*), 112 U.S. 580, 582 (1884).

10.3.1

Chae Chan Ping v. United States (The Chinese Exclusion Case)

130 U.S. 581 (1889)

In the wake of these decisions, anti-Chinese members of Congress began clamoring for even more restrictions on Chinese immigrants. Although the 1880 treaty with China and the Chinese Restriction Act of 1882 barred new Chinese laborers from entering the country, they guaranteed the right of Chinese laborers already living in the United States to obtain a certificate and travel back and forth between the United States and China. Xenophobic white voters in California complained that these certificates were easy to counterfeit, allowing any Chinese immigrants to fraudulently claim that they had previously lived in the United States. As California was a major swing state in the 1880s, President Grover Cleveland attempted to renegotiate the 1880 treaty and close this loophole.

Unfortunately for Cleveland, negotiations over the new treaty collapsed weeks before the 1888 presidential election. The president's allies in Congress quickly passed a new measure that abrogated the 1880 treaty and prohibited all Chinese laborers from entering the United States, regardless of whether they had a return certificate. Act of Oct. 1, 1888, ch. 1064, 25 Stat. 504.

One week later, federal port officials denied entry to Chae Chan Ping, a Chinese subject who was returning home to San Francisco after a trip to China. He argued that nothing in the Constitution, not even the Commerce Clause, permitted Congress to exclude immigrants permitted to enter the United States by previous laws and treaties.

When the Supreme Court considered Ping's case in *Chae Chan Ping v. United States* (*The Chinese Exclusion Case*), 130 U.S. 581 (1889), it had already decided that Congress's power to exclude immigrants was an application of the Commerce Clause. The only question before it was whether Chae's certificate gave him a right to reenter the United States that Congress could not violate.

The Supreme Court's answer to that specific question would eventually establish the framework by which the Court has come to evaluate the source of Congress's power to exclude immigrants.

■ MR. JUSTICE FIELD delivered the opinion of the Court.[1]

The appeal involves a consideration of the validity of the act of Congress of October 1, 1888, prohibiting Chinese laborers from entering the United States who had departed before its passage. . . .

The discovery of gold in California in 1848, as is well known, was followed by a large immigration thither from all parts of the world, attracted not only by the hope of gain from the mines, but from the great prices paid for all kinds of labor. The news of the discovery penetrated China, and laborers came from there in great numbers, a few with their own means, but by far the greater number under contract with employers, for whose benefit they worked. . . . Not being accompanied by families, except in rare instances, their expenses were small; and they were content with the simplest fare, such as would not suffice for our laborers and artisans. The competition between them and our people was for this reason altogether in their favor, and the consequent irritation, proportionately deep and bitter, was followed, in many cases, by open conflicts, to the great disturbance of the public peace.

The differences of race added greatly to the difficulties of the situation. . . . [T]hey remained strangers in the land, residing apart by themselves, and adhering to the customs and usages of their own country. It seemed impossible for them to

1 **As You Read, Consider:** The author of the *Chinese Exclusion Case*, Justice Stephen Field, had recently declared that "there is no such thing as a power of inherent sovereignty in the government of the United States." *Juilliard v. Greenman*, 110 U.S. 421, 467 (1884) (Field, J., dissenting). He wrote that the United States was "a government of delegated powers, supreme within its prescribed sphere but powerless outside of it. In this country, sovereignty resides in the people, and Congress can exercise no power which they have not, by their Constitution, entrusted to it." *Id.* Is this opinion consistent with his previously stated view?

assimilate with our people or to make any change in their habits or modes of living. As they grew in numbers each year the people of the coast saw, or believed they saw, in the facility of immigration, and in the crowded millions of China, where population presses upon the means of subsistence, great danger that at no distant day that portion of our country would be overrun by them unless prompt action was taken to restrict their immigration. The people there accordingly petitioned earnestly for protective legislation. . . .

So urgent and constant were the prayers for relief against existing and anticipated evils, both from the public authorities of the Pacific Coast and from private individuals, that Congress was impelled to act on the subject. . . . On the 6th of May, 1882, . . . [Congress suspended the coming of all new Chinese laborers to the United States but allowed Chinese laborers already in the United States to obtain a certificate, leave, and return].

To prevent the possibility of the policy of excluding Chinese laborers being evaded, the act of October 1, 1888, the validity of which is the subject of consideration in this case, was passed. . . . [It prohibits the entry of all Chinese laborers, even if they have a return certificate.]

The validity of this act, as already mentioned, is assailed, as . . . in violation of existing treaties between the United States and the government of China, and of rights vested in them under the laws of Congress. . . . A treaty, it is true, is in its nature a contract between nations. . . . [But if the treaty] relates to a subject within the power of Congress, it can be deemed in that particular only the equivalent of a legislative act, to be repealed or modified at the pleasure of Congress. In either case the last expression of the sovereign will must control [*see The Head Money Cases*, 112 U. S. 580 (1884)]. . . .

There being nothing in the treaties between China and the United States to impair the validity of the act of Congress of October 1, 1888, was it on any other ground beyond the competency of Congress to pass it? If so, it must be because it was not within the power of Congress to prohibit Chinese laborers who had at the time departed from the United States, or should subsequently depart, from returning to the United States. Those laborers are not citizens of the United States; they are aliens. That the government of the United States, through the action of the legislative department, can exclude aliens from its territory is a proposition which we do not think open to controversy. Jurisdiction over its own territory to that extent is an incident of every independent nation. It is a part of its independence. If it could not exclude aliens it would be to that extent subject to the control of another power. As said by this court in the case of *The Exchange*, 7 Cranch, 116, 136, speaking by Chief Justice Marshall: "The jurisdiction of the nation within its own territory is necessarily exclusive and absolute. It is susceptible of no limitation not imposed by itself. Any restriction upon it, deriving validity from an external source, would imply a diminution of its sovereignty to the extent of the restriction, and an investment of that sovereignty to the same extent in that power which could impose such restriction. All exceptions, therefore, to the full and complete power of a nation within its own territories, must be traced up to the consent of the nation itself. They can flow from no other legitimate source."[2]

---

[2] **Questions:** The next few paragraphs have become extremely important for the history of federal immigration law. What is Field saying here?

A narrow interpretation holds that Field is explaining why the Constitution's various enumerated powers—including the power to "regulate foreign commerce"—must give Congress the power to repeal Chae Chan Ping's certificate. Otherwise, the United States would not be a sovereign nation but would instead be "subject to the control of another power." Let's call this the "enumerated power" reading.

While under our Constitution and form of government the great mass of local matters is controlled by local authorities, the United States, in their relation to foreign countries and their subjects or citizens are one nation, invested with powers which belong to independent nations, the exercise of which can be invoked for the maintenance of its absolute independence and security throughout its entire territory. The powers to declare war, make treaties, suppress insurrection, repel invasion, regulate foreign commerce, secure republican governments to the States, and admit subjects of other nations to citizenship, are all sovereign powers, restricted in their exercise only by the Constitution itself and considerations of public policy and justice which control, more or less, the conduct of all civilized nations. . . .

The control of local matters being left to local authorities, and national matters being entrusted to the government of the Union, the problem of free institutions existing over a widely extended country, having different climates and varied interests, has been happily solved. For local interests the several States of the Union exist, but for national purposes, embracing our relations with foreign nations, we are but one people, one nation, one power.

To preserve its independence, and give security against foreign aggression and encroachment, is the highest duty of every nation, and to attain these ends nearly all other considerations are to be subordinated. It matters not in what form such aggression and encroachment come, whether from the foreign nation acting in its national character or from vast hordes of its people crowding in upon us. The government, possessing the powers which are to be exercised for protection and security, is clothed with authority to determine the occasion on which the powers shall be called forth; and its determination, so far as the subjects affected are concerned, are necessarily conclusive upon all its departments and officers. If, therefore, the government of the United States, through its legislative department, considers the presence of foreigners of a different race in this country, who will not assimilate with us, to be dangerous to its peace and security, their exclusion is not to be stayed because at the time there are no actual hostilities with the nation of which the foreigners are subjects. The existence of war would render the necessity of the proceeding only more obvious and pressing. The same necessity, in a less pressing degree, may arise when war does not exist, and the same authority which adjudges the necessity in one case must also determine it in the other. In both cases its determination is conclusive upon the judiciary. If the government of the country of which the foreigners excluded are subjects is dissatisfied with this action it can make complaint to the executive head of our government, or resort to any other measure which, in its judgment, its interests or dignity may demand; and there lies its only remedy. . . .

The exclusion of paupers, criminals and persons afflicted with incurable diseases, for which statutes have been passed, is only an application of the same power to particular classes of persons, whose presence is deemed injurious or a source of danger to the country.[3] As applied to them, there has never been any

---

A broad interpretation holds that Field is explaining that the power to exclude immigrants "is an incident of every independent nation" and that Congress would have the power to exclude immigrants even if nothing in the Constitution gave it that power. Let's call this the "sovereign power" reading.

Which reading is more persuasive? Is Field saying that the power to exclude is derived from one of the Constitution's enumerated powers or, instead, from the United States' status as a sovereign?

[3] **Note:** Here, Field is referring to the Page Act and other federal legislation that the Court had previously sustained as regulations of foreign commerce.

question as to the power to exclude them. The power is constantly exercised; its existence is involved in the right of self-preservation. . . .

The power of exclusion of foreigners being an incident of sovereignty belonging to the government of the United States, as a part of those sovereign powers delegated by the Constitution, the right to its exercise at any time when, in the judgment of the government, the interests of the country require it, cannot be granted away or restrained on behalf of any one.[4] The powers of government are delegated in trust to the United States, and are incapable of transfer to any other parties. They cannot be abandoned or surrendered. Nor can their exercise be hampered, when needed for the public good, by any considerations of private interest. The exercise of these public trusts is not the subject of barter or contract. Whatever license, therefore, Chinese laborers may have obtained, previous to the act of October 1, 1888, to return to the United States after their departure, is held at the will of the government, revocable at any time, at its pleasure. Whether a proper consideration by our government of its previous laws, or a proper respect for the nation whose subjects are affected by its action, ought to have qualified its inhibition and made it applicable only to persons departing from the country after the passage of the act, are not questions for judicial determination. If there be any just ground of complaint on the part of China, it must be made to the political department of our government, which is alone competent to act upon the subject. . . .

During the argument reference was made by counsel to the alien law of June 25, 1798, and to opinions expressed at the time by men of great ability and learning against its constitutionality. 1 Stat. 570, c. 58. We do not attach importance to those opinions in their bearing upon this case. The act vested in the President power to order all such aliens as he should judge dangerous to the peace and safety of the United States, or should have reasonable grounds to suspect were concerned in any treasonable or secret machination against the government, to depart out of the territory of the United States within such time as should be expressed in his order. There were other provisions also distinguishing it from the act under consideration. The act was passed during a period of great political excitement, and it was attacked and defended with great zeal and ability. It is enough, however, to say that it is entirely different from the act before us, and the validity of its provisions was never brought to the test of judicial decision in the courts of the United States.[5]

NOTE: EXERCISE OF SOVEREIGN POWER AFTER THE *CHINESE EXCLUSION CASE*

Read in context, the *Chinese Exclusion Case* was a relatively straightforward, if racist, opinion that affirmed Congress's power to legislate despite a contrary agreement not to. *See, e.g.*, *Constitutional Law—Chinese Exclusion Act—Treaty Rights*, 3 Harv. L. Rev. 136, 136 (1889) (describing the decision as a case about "Treaty Rights"). The opinion principally cited earlier decisions, like the *Head Money Cases*, in which the Supreme Court

---

[4] **Questions:** Again, what does Field mean here when he says that the power to exclude is "an incident of sovereignty . . . as a part of those sovereign powers delegated by the Constitution"? Is he adopting the enumerated power reading or the sovereign power reading? Put differently: If Congress were to enact an immigration regulation that would not be permissible under the Commerce Clause—say, a law compelling immigrants living in the United States to purchase health insurance-would it be constitutional?

[5] **Question:** Here, Field distinguishes the power to *exclude* immigrants from the power to *expel* immigrants. He writes that the Alien Friends Act of 1798, a deportation law, "is entirely different from the act before us." Does the *Chinese Exclusion Case* offer guidance for how the Court would evaluate the constitutionality of a federal deportation law?

affirmed Congress's power to exercise the Commerce Clause to regulate immigration. Justice Field's language also paraphrased cases in which the Court held that no contract could permanently deprive a sovereign of its delegated powers, as such a contract would render the sovereign subject to the control of a separate entity.

In invoking the term *sovereign*, Field did not intend to suggest that all sovereigns have an inherent power to exclude people. In the years before and after the *Chinese Exclusion Case*, he stridently declared that "[t]he government of the United States is one of limited and delegated powers. It takes nothing . . . by any supposed inherent sovereignty." *Fong Yue Ting v. United States*, 149 U.S. 698, 746–50 (1893) (Field, J., dissenting).

Since the early 1900s, however, Field's decision has been widely interpreted to suggest that "he believed . . . that every sovereign nation had inherent authority to exclude strangers from its territory." Adam B. Cox & Cristina M. Rodríguez, *The President and Immigration Law* 34 (2020). Even the Supreme Court began citing the *Chinese Exclusion Case* as if Congress's power to exclude immigrants were an unlimited power derived from its "sovereignty" and not, as Field had written, an exercise of "those sovereign powers delegated by the Constitution." *See, e.g.*, *United States ex rel. Knauff v. Shaughnessy*, 338 U.S. 537, 542 (1950). Applying this broad interpretation of the *Chinese Exclusion Case*, the *Knauff* Court suggested that when Congress legislated with respect to immigrants, it could pass laws derived from its "sovereignty," which would be unacceptable if Congress were forced to defend the laws under the Commerce Clause. *Id.*

Expansion of immigration restrictions. The *Chinese Exclusion Case* consequently opened the door for Congress to pass even more regulations regarding who was eligible to enter the country.

Congress first expanded the list of people ineligible to enter the country to include Chinese laborers, contract laborers, "persons likely to become a public charge," "persons who have been convicted of . . . [a] crime or misdemeanor involving moral turpitude," "polygamists, anarchists," "insane persons, epileptics," "persons afflicted with a loathsome or with a dangerous contagious disease," unaccompanied minors, and "prostitutes." *See* Immigration Act of 1907, Pub. L. No. 59–96, 34 Stat. 898, 898–99.

In 1924, Congress passed the Johnson-Reed Act, Pub. L. No. 68–139, 43 Stat. 153, which radically constricted the nation's ports of entry. For the first time, Congress restricted the total number of people who could immigrate to the United States from outside the Western Hemisphere (to 155,000 per year); it set individual quotas for each foreign nation, based on an estimate of how many descendants from that nation lived in the United States in 1890; and it excluded from immigration all Japanese, Indian, and other nonwhite and non-African people. Together, these changes had the effect of blocking legal immigration from everywhere except for the United Kingdom and Northern Europe (whose countries received high quotas), as well as Mexico, Central America, and South America (whose countries were unaffected by the law and could continue to send unlimited numbers of immigrants). Supporters of the law explained that the restrictions were justified by eugenics and other scientific concepts of the American "race" because it ranked European nations on a hierarchy of desirability while excluding people who were thought to be "backward" or unable to assimilate. *See* Mae M. Ngai, *Impossible Subjects* 22–25 (2004).

The Supreme Court sustained all of these various restrictions. An illustrative decision is *United States ex rel. Turner v. Williams*, in which the Court upheld Congress's power to exclude alleged anarchists:

> Repeated decisions of this court have determined that Congress has the power to exclude aliens from the United States; to prescribe the terms and conditions on which they may come in; to establish regulations for sending out of the country such aliens as have entered in violation of law, and to commit the enforcement of such conditions and regulations to executive officers. . . . Whether rested on the accepted principle of international law that every sovereign nation has the power, as inherent in sovereignty and essential to self-preservation, to forbid the entrance of foreigners within its dominions, or to admit them only in such cases and upon such conditions as it may see fit to prescribe; or on the power to regulate commerce with foreign nations, which includes the entrance of ships, the importation of goods, and the bringing of persons into the ports of the United States, the act before us is not open to constitutional objection.

194 U.S. 279, 289–90 (1904).

In keeping with this broad understanding of Congress's power, the Court reviewed various other exclusions with a wide degree of deference. For example, in the *Japanese Immigrant Case*, 189 U.S. 86 (1903), the Court upheld an 1891 statute that provided for the exclusion of people suspected of being inadmissible without judicial review. And in *Knauff* and *Shaughnessy v. United States ex rel. Mezei*, 345 U.S. 206 (1953), the Court held that it had no power to review the exclusion of a person based on confidential information that the government would not disclose.

Modern immigration regime. Congress established the modern immigration regime with the Immigration and Nationality (McCarran-Walter) Act of 1952, which retained the national origins formula of the 1924 law but abolished its racial restrictions. Pub. L. No. 82–414, 66 Stat. 163.

Far more sweeping was the Hart-Celler Act of 1965, Pub. L. No. 89–236, 79 Stat. 911, a civil rights measure that abolished the national origins formula, increased the total numeric limit on immigration, and gave every country in the world the same maximum limit of twenty thousand people. The 1965 law attempted to purge the white supremacy baked into the 1924 quota system by putting all countries on an "equal footing." *See* Ngai, *supra*, at 254–60. However, it applied numerical limits on countries in the Western Hemisphere for the first time—imposing the same per-country limit on immigration from Mexico as from much smaller or more distant countries, like Liechtenstein. The immediate result was the creation of a large number of "illegal" or "unauthorized aliens" from Central and South America, who had previously been allowed to cross the border freely. *Id.* In the long term, the higher limits on the total number of immigrants—and the authorization of large-scale immigration from Asia and Africa for the first time since 1924—led to a sharp growth in the nation's foreign-born population from 5.4 percent in 1960 to 13.6 percent in 2017, the highest since 14.7 percent in 1910. *See* Jynnah Radford & Luis Noe-Bustamante, *Facts on U.S. Immigrants*, Pew Rsch. Ctr. (June 3, 2019).

Although the 1952 and 1965 laws profoundly changed the nation's immigration policy, they have not affected the Supreme Court's deference to the federal government's power to exclude certain noncitizens. As the Court reiterated in *Kleindienst v. Mandel*, 408 U.S. 753 (1972), it will defer to immigration officials whenever they comply with federal law and offer "a facially legitimate and bona fide reason" for excluding someone. *See, e.g.*, *Sale v. Haitian Ctrs. Council*, 509 U.S. 155 (1993) (upholding the president's statutory authority to intercept noncitizens in international waters to prevent them from entering the United States).

Trump. The Supreme Court's deference to the federal government's "sovereign" power to exclude was vividly on display after President Donald Trump issued an executive order banning the entry of noncitizens from several Muslim-majority countries. As a presidential candidate, Trump had called for "a total and complete shutdown of Muslims entering the United States until our country's representatives can figure out what the hell is going on." Jenna Johnson, *Trump Calls for "Total and Complete Shutdown of Muslims Entering the United States,"* Wash. Post, Dec. 7, 2015. He repeated similar calls while in office. Michael D. Shear & Helene Cooper, *Trump Bars Refugees and Citizens of 7 Muslim Countries*, N.Y. Times, Jan. 27, 2017. When he issued a series of executive orders that appeared to impose such a shutdown of Muslims, a group of states sued. They argued that his orders were not authorized by any statute, nor could they be interpreted to satisfy the First Amendment's prohibition on religious discrimination.

In *Trump v. Hawaii*, 138 S. Ct. 2392 (2018), the Supreme Court disagreed. The Court first found that when Congress passed the Immigration and Naturalization Act, it gave the president virtually unlimited discretion to exclude anyone deemed a threat to American interests. The Court then concluded that the final version of the president's executive order was consistent with the First Amendment. Applying a deferential standard of review, the Court limited its scrutiny to "whether the policy is facially legitimate and bona fide"—that is, whether "it can reasonably be understood to result from a justification independent of unconstitutional grounds." *Trump*, 138 S. Ct. at 2420. Applying this deferential standard, the Court noted that the executive order was "expressly premised on legitimate purposes: preventing entry of nationals who cannot be adequately vetted and inducing other nations to improve their practices." *Id.* The Court therefore held that "because there is persuasive evidence that the entry suspension has a legitimate grounding in national security concerns, quite apart from any religious hostility, we must accept that independent justification." *Id.* at 2421.

Post-*Trump*. Since *Trump*, the Court has continued to apply extraordinary deference to Congress and the president when evaluating their powers to regulate immigrants at the nation's border. *See, e.g., Dep't of Homeland Sec. v. Thuraissigiam*, 140 S. Ct. 1959 (2020) (upholding federal immigration statute limiting habeas review in expedited removal proceedings). In one 2020 decision, the Court even announced, for the first time, that "it is long settled as a matter of American constitutional law that foreign citizens outside U.S. territory do not possess rights under the U.S. Constitution." *Agency for Int'l Dev. v. All. for Open Soc'y Int'l, Inc.*, 140 S. Ct. 2082, 2086 (2020) (citing, among other cases, *Turner*, 194 U.S. at 292).

10.4 THE POWER TO EXPEL NONCITIZENS

Exclusion is not the same thing as expulsion: the former denies someone entry into the country, while the latter deports people who are already here. Justice Stephen Field emphasized this distinction at the end of the *Chinese Exclusion Case*, 130 U.S. 581 (1889), distinguishing the exclusion law at issue from the infamous Alien Friends Act of 1798, ch. 58, 1 Stat. 570, a deportation law.

Nevertheless, in the wake of the *Chinese Exclusion Case*, Congress passed a law promising to deport all Chinese laborers living in the United States who could not obtain a certificate of legal residence with the supportive testimony of at least one white witness. *See* Act of May 5, 1892, ch. 60, 27 Stat. 25. Dissenters in Congress called the law "an act of barbarous legislation" that went "far beyond any bill that probably was ever introduced into the Congress of the United States." *See* 23 Cong. Rec. 3870–77 (1892). The idea of federal agents deporting immigrants reminded some members of the Fugitive Slave Act of 1850. *Id.*

Chinese American advocacy organizations were so convinced that the deportation law was unconstitutional that they urged Chinese laborers to defy the law. *See The Six Companies Will Fight*, N.Y. Times, Mar. 18, 1893, at 1. By the time the act took effect in 1893, over 85 percent of Chinese residents in the United States had refused to register. *See* H.R. Rep. No. 53–70, at 2 (1893). The advocacy organizations also hired an eminent team of Wall Street lawyers to initiate a test case. They recruited three Chinese residents of New York, including Fong Yue Ting, to either refuse to apply for a certificate of residence or to do so without a white witness.

In *Fong Yue Ting v. United States*, 149 U.S. 698 (1893), the Supreme Court upheld the deportation law. "The right of a nation to expel or deport foreigners . . . rests upon the same grounds [as in the *Chinese Exclusion Case*], and is as absolute and unqualified as the right to prohibit and prevent their entrance into the country," the Court wrote. *Fong Yue Ting*, 149 U.S. at 707. Quoting "leading commentators on the law of nations," the Court explained that the "right to exclude or to expel all aliens, or any class of aliens, absolutely or upon certain conditions, in war or in peace, [is] an inherent and inalienable right of every sovereign and independent nation, essential to its safety, its independence and its welfare." *Id.* at 711. The Constitution, the Court concluded, was consistent with this international consensus because it gave the federal government exclusive powers over "international relations," of which [t]he power to exclude or expel aliens" was a part. *Id.* As examples of these powers, the Court cited the Foreign Commerce Clause as well as the Necessary and Proper Clause. *Id.* at 712. As in the *Chinese Exclusion Case*, however, the *Fong Yue Ting* Court left it unclear whether Congress's power to deport immigrants was an application of its enumerated powers—like the Commerce Clause and Necessary and Proper Clause—or whether it was an "inherent and inalienable right of every sovereign."

Field, who wrote the majority opinion in the *Chinese Exclusion Case*, dissented in *Fong Yue Ting* on the ground that nothing in the Constitution permitted Congress to pass a deportation law. *See id.* at 757–58 (Field, J., dissenting). And decisions immediately following *Fong Yue Ting* refused to allow Congress to ignore the Sixth Amendment and criminally punish immigrants without a jury trial. *Wong Wing v. United States*, 163 U.S. 228, 237 (1896).

Yet, by 1913, the Court was citing *Fong Yue Ting* for the proposition that "[i]t is thoroughly established that Congress has power to order the deportation of aliens whose presence in the country it deems hurtful. . . . [D]eportation [is not] a punishment; it is simply a refusal by the Government to harbor persons whom it does not want." *Bugajewitz v. Adams*, 228 U.S. 585, 591 (1913); *see also Lapina v. Williams*, 232 U.S. 78, 82–83 (1914). Summarizing these decisions in 1916, the Senate Committee on Immigration reported that the Court had "emphatically and distinctly" upheld Congress's power to deport any "undesirable" immigrants it wanted—and at any time. S. Rep. No. 64–352, at 15 (1916). As Congress passed harsher deportation laws, the Court reiterated that "Congress has power to order at any time the deportation of aliens whose presence in the country it deems hurtful, and may do so by appropriate executive proceedings." Ng Fung Ho v. White, 259 U.S. 276, 278 (1922). To support this conclusion, the Court cited not the Constitution but earlier decisions like *Fong Yue Ting*.

After a nineteenth century in which judges and members of Congress rejected the premise that Congress could exercise powers inherent in sovereignty, the twentieth-century Court interpreted the Chinese exclusion cases as if they held that "[t]he right to expel aliens is a sovereign power, necessary to the safety of the country." *Mahler v. Eby*, 264 U.S. 32, 39 (1924) (citing *Fong Yue Ting*, 149 U.S. at 730).

CHAPTER 11

WHEN CAN A FEDERAL REGULATION AND A STATE REGULATION OF THE SAME SUBJECT COEXIST?

ARTICLE VI, PARAGRAPH 2: This Constitution, and the Laws of the United States which shall be made in Pursuance thereof; and all Treaties made, or which shall be made, under the Authority of the United States, shall be the supreme Law of the Land; and the Judges in every State shall be bound thereby, any Thing in the Constitution or Laws of any State to the Contrary notwithstanding.

TENTH AMENDMENT (1791): The powers not delegated to the United States by the Constitution, nor prohibited by it to the States, are reserved to the States respectively, or to the people.

11.1 THE RISE AND FALL OF DUAL FEDERALISM

Recall that in the Commerce Clause case of *Gibbons v. Ogden*, 22 U.S. (9 Wheat.) 1 (1824), Chief Justice John Marshall articulated the theory that became known as *dual federalism*: the federal government and states are each preeminent in their own spheres but powerless to act in the other's sphere. *See* Edward S. Corwin, *The Passing of Dual Federalism*, 36 Va. L. Rev. 1, 14–15 (1950). This theory was coined by political scientist Edward Corwin in 1950 to describe how the Supreme Court interpreted the Commerce Clause for generations earlier. As the Court explained in *Hammer v. Dagenhart*, one reason why Congress lacked any power to regulate child labor was because if Congress had such an authority, then it would "destroy the local power always existing and carefully reserved to the States." 247 U.S. 251, 274 (1918). Any given type of regulation could be exercised by Congress or by states—but not by both.

Rise of dual federalism

This theory of dual federalism was not unique to the Commerce Clause but applied to all domestic regulations. For example, in *Keller v. United States*, the Court considered a 1907 statute that made it a felony to "harbor in any house or other place, for the purpose of prostitution, or for any other immoral purpose, any alien woman or girl." 213 U.S. 138, 139 (1909) (quoting Act of Congress of Feb. 20, 1907, ch. 1134, 34 Stat. 898, 899). When federal prosecutors indicted a defendant for harboring a Hungarian woman, they defended the statute on the ground that Congress had plenary power to regulate "the conditions upon which an alien female may be permitted to remain in this country, and the grounds which warrant her exclusion." 213 U.S. at 147. But the *Keller* Court rejected the parallel between Congress's power to exclude or expel noncitizens, on the one hand, and Congress's power to regulate the domestic conduct of citizens, on the other. Even assuming that Congress could expel a noncitizen for engaging in certain conduct, the Court explained, that was not the same thing as prohibiting anyone from engaging in conduct that had no "general effect upon the importation and exclusion of aliens":

> [C]an it be within the power of Congress to control all the dealings of our citizens with resident aliens? If that be possible, the door is open to the assumption by the National Government of an almost unlimited body of legislation. By the census of 1900 the population of the United States between the oceans was in round numbers 76,000,000. Of these, 10,000,000 were of foreign birth, and 16,000,000 more were of foreign parentage. Doubtless some have become citizens by naturalization, but certainly scattered through the country there are millions of aliens. If the contention of the Government be sound, whatever may have been done in the past, however little this field of legislation may have been entered upon, the power of Congress is broad enough to take cognizance of all dealings of citizens with aliens. . . . In other words, an immense body of legislation, which heretofore has been recognized as peculiarly within the jurisdiction of the States, may be taken by Congress away from them. Although Congress has not largely entered into this field of legislation, it may do so, if it has the power. Then we should be brought face to face with such a change in the internal conditions of this country as was never dreamed of by the framers of the Constitution. While the acts of Congress are to be liberally construed in order to enable it to carry into effect the powers conferred, it is equally true that prohibitions and limitations upon those powers should also be fairly and reasonably enforced. To exaggerate in the one direction and restrict in the other will tend to substitute one consolidated government for the present Federal system.

Id. at 148–49.

Consistent with the *Keller* Court's view that domestic regulations were ordinarily the province of states, not the federal government, the Court initially upheld all sorts of state laws that regulated the conduct of noncitizens. These included laws that prohibited noncitizens from owning land. *See, e.g.*, *Terrace v. Thompson*, 263 U.S. 197 (1923). (As we will discuss later (section 48.4), these cases were overruled on Fourteenth Amendment grounds in the 1970s.)

Fall of dual federalism

This theory of dual federalism collapsed with the Court's 1937 "switch in time" (see section 6.2).

In *United States v. Darby Lumber Co.*, 312 U.S. 100 (1941), the Court expressly observed that even though Congress now had the power to set a nationwide standard of minimum wages and maximum hours, that did not mean that states automatically lacked the power to regulate the same thing. "In the absence of Congressional legislation on the subject state laws which are not regulations of the commerce itself or its instrumentalities are not forbidden even though they affect interstate commerce," the Court wrote. *Darby*, 312 U.S. at 119.

And even where Congress did legislate on the same subject as a state law, the mere existence of federal legislation on a subject did not necessarily displace all related state laws. After all, states presumably could set their own minimum wages higher than the wage set by Congress.

11.2 THE CONCURRENT POWER TO REGULATE NONCITIZENS DOMESTICALLY

The collapse of dual federalism with the "switch in time" in 1937 (see section 6.2) meant that the Supreme Court had to develop a new standard for determining when a state law could exist alongside a federal law on the same subject. On the one hand, the Supremacy Clause has provided a clear rule at least since *McCulloch v. Maryland*, 17 U.S. (4 Wheat.) 316 (1819): states may not interfere with the federal government. On the other hand, it is not obvious, even today, precisely *when* a state law interferes with a federal law. What if both laws have the same objective or are complementary? We will explore this issue, called *preemption*, in the context of immigrants living in the United States—a situation involving people who have long been regulated by both state and federal law.

11.2.1

Hines v. Davidowitz

312 U.S. 52 (1941)

In 1939, when World War II erupted in Europe, states and Congress both began considering war measures in case the United States entered the conflict. Many of these laws concerned immigrants, whom politicians feared might be disloyal.

One statute in Pennsylvania required every noncitizen in the state to register for and receive an "alien identification card." The law required noncitizens to carry their cards at all times and to show them whenever demanded by a police officer. In *Hines v. Davidowitz*, Bernard

Davidowitz, a Hungarian national who lived in Philadelphia, sued, objecting that this law "encroached upon legislative powers constitutionally vested in the federal government." 312 U.S. 52, 60 (1941).

While Davidowitz's case against the law was pending, Congress passed the Alien Registration Act of 1940, which provided that "it shall be the duty of every alien now or hereafter in the United States . . . to apply for registration and to be fingerprinted" by the federal Immigration and Naturalization Service. Pub. L. No. 76–670, 54 Stat. 670, 673–74. Permanent residents who registered would receive a green card demonstrating their legal status—the first example of what is now called the *green card* or *permanent resident card*. Even though it was physically possible for Davidowitz to comply with both the state and federal law, federal lawyers joined him in maintaining that Congress had "occupied the field" of immigrant registration, preempting the state law. *Davidowitz*, 312 U.S. at 78.

The *Davidowitz* Court determined that the two laws in this case could not coexist—and that the federal law preempted the state law.

■ MR. JUSTICE BLACK delivered the opinion of the Court.[1]

This case involves the validity of an Alien Registration Act adopted by the Commonwealth of Pennsylvania. . . . The Act, passed in 1939, requires every alien 18 years or over, with certain exceptions, to register once each year; provide such information as is required by the statute, plus any "other information and details" that the Department of Labor and Industry may direct; pay $1 as an annual registration fee; receive an alien identification card and carry it at all times; show the card whenever it may be demanded by any police officer or any agent of the Department of Labor and Industry; and exhibit the card as a condition precedent to registering a motor vehicle in his name or obtaining a license to operate one. . . . Nonexempt aliens who fail to register are subject to a fine of not more than $100 or imprisonment for not more than 60 days, or both. For failure to carry an identification card or for failure to show it upon proper demand, the punishment is a fine of not more than $10, or imprisonment for not more than 10 days, or both. . . .

[I]n 1940, . . . Congress enacted a federal Alien Registration Act. We must therefore pass upon the state Act in the light of the Congressional Act.

The federal Act provides for a single registration of aliens 14 years of age and over; detailed information specified by the Act, plus "such additional matters as may be prescribed by the Commissioner, with the approval of the Attorney General"; finger-printing of all registrants; and secrecy of the federal files, which can be "made available only to such persons or agencies as may be designated by the Commissioner, with the approval of the Attorney General." No requirement that aliens carry a registration card to be exhibited to police or others is embodied in the law, and only the wilful failure to register is made a criminal offense; punishment is fixed at a fine of not more than $1000, imprisonment for not more than 6 months, or both.

---

1 **As You Read, Consider:** Like *McCulloch v. Maryland* and *Gibbons v. Ogden*, this case discusses the question of "preemption," i.e., when a state law is incompatible with a federal law. What provision of the Constitution does Justice Hugo Black identify as the basis for preemption? What test does Black use to determine when a state law can coexist?

The basic subject of the state and federal laws is identical—registration of aliens as a distinct group. . . . Appellees' . . . contention is that the power to restrict, limit, regulate and register aliens as a distinct group is not an equal and continuously existing concurrent power of state and nation, but that even if the state can legislate on this subject at all, its power is subordinate to supreme national law. Appellees conclude that by its adoption of a comprehensive, integrated scheme for regulation of aliens—including its 1940 registration act—Congress has precluded state action like that taken by Pennsylvania. . . .

Obviously the answer to appellees' . . . question depends upon an analysis of the respective powers of state and national governments in the regulation of aliens as such, and a determination of whether Congress has, by its action, foreclosed enforcement of Pennsylvania's registration law.

First. That the supremacy of the national power in the general field of foreign affairs, including power over immigration, naturalization and deportation, is made clear by the Constitution, was pointed out by the authors of The Federalist in 1787, and has since been given continuous recognition by this Court. *E.g., Fong Yue Ting v. United States*, 149 U.S. 698, 711.[2] When the national government by treaty or statute has established rules and regulations touching the rights, privileges, obligations or burdens of aliens as such, the treaty or statute is the supreme law of the land. No state can add to or take from the force and effect of such treaty or statute, for Article VI of the Constitution provides that "This Constitution, and the Laws of the United States which shall be made in Pursuance thereof; and all Treaties made, or which shall be made, under the Authority of the United States, shall be the supreme Law of the Land; and the Judges in every State shall be bound thereby, any Thing in the Constitution or Laws of any State to the Contrary notwithstanding."[3] The Federal Government, representing, as it does the collective interests of the forty-eight states, is entrusted with full and exclusive responsibility for the conduct of affairs with foreign sovereignties. "For local interests the several States of the Union exist, but for national purposes, embracing our relations with foreign nations, we are but one people, one nation, one power." *Chinese Exclusion Case*, 130 U.S. 581, 606. Our system of government is such that the interest of the cities, counties and states, no less than the interest of the people of the whole nation, imperatively requires that federal power in the field affecting foreign relations be left entirely free from local interference. As Mr. Justice Miller well observed of a California statute burdening immigration: "If [the United States] should get into a difficulty which would lead to war, or to suspension of intercourse, would California alone suffer, or all the Union?"

One of the most important and delicate of all international relationships, recognized immemorially as a responsibility of government, has to do with the protection of the just rights of a country's own nationals when those nationals are in another country. Experience has shown that international controversies of the gravest moment, sometimes even leading to war, may arise from real or imagined wrongs to another's subjects inflicted, or permitted, by a government. This country, like other nations, has entered into numerous treaties of amity and commerce since its

---

2 **Note:** *Fong Yue Ting v. United States* was a follow-on decision to the *Chinese Exclusion Case*. Applying a similar analysis as the *Chinese Exclusion Case*, it was the first decision to uphold a federal deportation law. The law authorized the deportation of any Chinese laborer who could not obtain a certificate of legal residence with the supportive testimony of at least one white witness.

3 **Question:** Black here is referencing the Supremacy Clause of Article VI. In *McCulloch*, Chief Justice John Marshall invoked this clause to conclude that the Maryland tax could not be enforced because it was "contrary" to the federal law authorizing the Bank of the United States. 17 U.S. (4 Wheat.) 316, 437 (1819). Is the Pennsylvania registration requirement at issue in this case contrary to the federal registration requirement?

inception—treaties entered into under express constitutional authority, and binding upon the states as well as the nation. Among those treaties have been many which not only promised and guaranteed broad rights and privileges to aliens sojourning in our own territory, but secured reciprocal promises and guarantees for our own citizens while in other lands. And apart from treaty obligations, there has grown up in the field of international relations a body of customs defining with more or less certainty the duties owing by all nations to alien residents—duties which our State Department has often successfully insisted foreign nations must recognize as to our nationals abroad. In general, both treaties and international practices have been aimed at preventing injurious discriminations against aliens. . . .

Legal imposition of distinct, unusual and extraordinary burdens and obligations upon aliens—such as subjecting them alone, though perfectly law-abiding, to indiscriminate and repeated interception and interrogation by public officials—thus bears an inseparable relationship to the welfare and tranquility of all the states, and not merely to the welfare and tranquility of one. Laws imposing such burdens are not mere census requirements, and even though they may be immediately associated with the accomplishment of a local purpose, they provoke questions in the field of international affairs. And specialized regulation of the conduct of an alien before naturalization is a matter which Congress must consider in discharging its constitutional duty "To establish an Uniform Rule of Naturalization . . ." It cannot be doubted that both the state and the federal registration laws belong "to that class of laws which concern the exterior relation of this whole nation with other nations and governments." Consequently the regulation of aliens is so intimately blended and intertwined with responsibilities of the national government that where it acts, and the state also acts on the same subject, "the act of Congress, or the treaty, is supreme; and the law of the State, though enacted in the exercise of powers not controverted, must yield to it." And where the federal government, in the exercise of its superior authority in this field, has enacted a complete scheme of regulation and has therein provided a standard for the registration of aliens, states cannot, inconsistently with the purpose of Congress, conflict or interfere with, curtail or complement, the federal law, or enforce additional or auxiliary regulations.[4] There is not—and from the very nature of the problem there cannot be—any rigid formula or rule which can be used as a universal pattern to determine the meaning and purpose of every act of Congress. This Court, in considering the validity of state laws in the light of treaties or federal laws touching the same subject, has made use of the following expressions: conflicting; contrary to; occupying the field; repugnance; difference; irreconcilability; inconsistency; violation; curtailment; and interference. But none of these expressions provides and infallible constitutional test or an exclusive constitutional yardstick. In the final analysis, there can be no one crystal clear distinctly marked formula. Our primary function is to determine whether, under the circumstances of this particular case, Pennsylvania's law stands as an obstacle to the accomplishment and execution of the full purposes and objectives of Congress.[5] And in that determination, it is of importance that this legislation is in a field which affects international relations, the one aspect of our government that from the first has been most generally conceded imperatively to demand broad national authority. Any concurrent state power that may exist is restricted to the narrowest of limits; the state's power here is not bottomed on

---

[4] **Question:** Black writes that when the federal government has enacted a "complete scheme of regulation," states can neither "conflict" *nor* "complement" the federal law. How can a complementary state law be contrary to federal law for purposes of the Supremacy Clause?

[5] **Question:** Here, Black describes preemption as a question of whether a state law "stands as an obstacle to the accomplishment and execution of the full purposes and objectives of Congress." What evidence has he relied on to determine what Congress's purposes were when it passed its registration requirement?

the same broad base as is its power to tax. And it is also of importance that this legislation deals with the rights, liberties, and personal freedoms of human beings, and is in an entirely different category from state tax statutes or state pure food laws regulating the labels on cans.

Our conclusion is that appellee is correct in his contention that the power to restrict, limit, regulate, and register aliens as a distinct group is not an equal and continuously existing concurrent power of state and nation, but that whatever power a state may have is subordinate to supreme national law. We proceed therefore to an examination of Congressional enactments to ascertain whether or not Congress has acted in such manner that its action should preclude enforcement of Pennsylvania's law.

Second. For many years Congress has provided a broad and comprehensive plan describing the terms and conditions upon which aliens may enter this country, how they may acquire citizenship, and the manner in which they may be deported. Numerous treaties, in return for reciprocal promises from other governments, have pledged the solemn obligation of this nation to the end that aliens residing in our territory shall not be singled out for the imposition of discriminatory burdens. Our Constitution and our Civil Rights Act have guaranteed to aliens "the equal protection of the laws [which] is a pledge of the protection of equal laws." With a view to limiting prospective residents from foreign lands to those possessing the qualities deemed essential to good and useful citizenship in America, carefully defined qualifications are required to be met before aliens may enter our country. These qualifications include rigid requirements as to health, education, integrity, character, and adaptability to our institutions. Nor is the alien left free from the application of federal laws after entry and before naturalization. If during the time he is residing here he should be found guilty of conduct contrary to the rules and regulations laid down by Congress, he can be deported. At the time he enters the country, at the time he applies for permission to acquire the full status of citizenship, and during the intervening years, he can be subjected to searching investigations as to conduct and suitability for citizenship. And in 1940 Congress added to this comprehensive scheme a complete system for alien registration.

The nature of the power exerted by Congress, the object sought to be attained, and the character of the obligations imposed by the law, are all important in considering the question of whether supreme federal enactments preclude enforcement of state laws on the same subject. Opposition to laws permitting invasion of the personal liberties of law-abiding individuals, or singling out aliens as particularly dangerous and undesirable groups, is deep-seated in this country. Hostility to such legislation in America stems back to our colonial history, and champions of freedom for the individual have always vigorously opposed burdensome registration systems. The drastic requirements of the alien Acts of 1798 brought about a political upheaval in this country the repercussions from which have not even yet wholly subsided. So violent was the reaction to the 1798 laws that almost a century elapsed before a second registration act was passed. This second law, which required Chinese to register and carry identification cards with them at all times, was enacted May 5, 1892. An opponent of this legislation, speaking in the Senate of the requirement that cards be carried, said: "[The Chinese covered by the Act] are here ticket-of-leave men; precisely as, under the Australian law, a convict is allowed to go at large upon a ticket-of-leave, these people are to be allowed to go at large and earn their livelihood, but they must have their tickets-of-leave in their possession. . . . This inaugurates in our system of government a new departure; one, I believe never before practised, although it was suggested in conference that some such rules had been adopted in slavery times to secure the peace of society."

For many years bills have been regularly presented to every Congress providing for registration of aliens. Some of these bills proposed annual registration of aliens, issuance of identification cards containing information about and a photograph of the bearer, exhibition of the cards on demand, payment of an annual fee, and kindred requirements. Opposition to these bills was based upon charges that their requirements were at war with the fundamental principles of our free government, in that they would bring about unnecessary and irritating restrictions upon personal liberties of the individual, and would subject aliens to a system of indiscriminate questioning similar to the espionage systems existing in other lands.

When Congress passed the Alien Registration Act of 1940, many of the provisions which had been so severely criticized were not included. The Congressional purpose, as announced by the chairman of the Senate subcommittee which drafted the final bill, was to "work . . . the new provisions into the existing [immigration and naturalization] laws, so as to make a harmonious whole." That "harmonious whole" included the "Uniform Rule of Naturalization" the Constitution empowered the Congress to provide. And as a part of that "harmonious whole," under the federal Act aliens need not carry cards, and can only be punished for wilful failure to register. . . .

We have already adverted to the conditions which make the treatment of aliens, in whatever state they may be located, a matter of national moment. And whether or not registration of aliens is of such a nature that the Constitution permits only of one uniform national system, it cannot be denied that the Congress might validly conclude that such uniformity is desirable. The legislative history of the Act indicates that Congress was trying to steer a middle path, realizing that any registration requirement was a departure from our traditional policy of not treating aliens as a thing apart, but also feeling that the Nation as in need of the type of information to be secured. Having the constitutional authority so to do, it has provided a standard for alien registration in a single integrated and all-embracing system in order to obtain the information deemed to be desirable in connection with aliens. When it made this addition to its uniform naturalization and immigration laws, it plainly manifested a purpose to do so in such a way as to protect the personal liberties of law-abiding aliens through one uniform national registration system, and to leave them free from the possibility of inquisitorial practices and police surveillance that might not only affect our international relations but might also generate the very disloyalty which the law has intended guarding against. Under these circumstances, the Pennsylvania Act cannot be enforced. . . .[6]

11.2.2

Arizona v. United States

567 U.S. 387 (2012)

The *Davidowitz* Court determined whether the Pennsylvania law could coexist with the federal law by asking the following:

(1) Is the federal law a valid exercise of Congress's constitutional power?

[6] **Question:** Suppose Pennsylvania had instead enacted a criminal statute punishing all immigrants for failing to comply with the federal act. Do state laws that further Congress's express purposes prompt the same preemption concerns?

(2) Does the state law "stand[ ] as an obstacle to the accomplishment and execution of the full purposes and objectives of Congress"?

The second of these two questions is usually the tricky one in preemption cases because it requires figuring out two subordinate questions:

(2a) What are the "purposes and objectives of Congress"? (This is often a difficult assignment on its own.)

(2b) Is the state law in fact an obstacle to those objectives?

In the years since *Davidowitz*, the Court has approached the questions about Congress's objectives "much as [it] would any other [question] about statutory meaning, looking to the text and context of the law in question and guided by the traditional tools of statutory interpretation." *Va. Uranium, Inc. v. Warren*, 139 S. Ct. 1894, 1901 (2019). Sometimes these methods of statutory interpretation will persuade the Court that Congress did not intend to preempt any state law; other times the Court will conclude that Congress intended to exercise one of three categories of preemption.

The first category is "express preemption," where Congress expressly declares that certain state laws are obstacles to its objectives and are therefore preempted. Although figuring out Congress's objectives in these cases is relatively straightforward, determining whether a state law conflicts with those objectives remains a challenge. For example, in the Immigration Reform and Control Act of 1986 (IRCA), Congress made it unlawful for anyone to hire an "unauthorized alien." 8 U.S.C. § 1324a. The same section of the IRCA then declared, "The provisions of this section preempt any State or local law imposing civil or criminal sanctions (other than through licensing and similar laws) upon those who employ, or recruit or refer for a fee for employment, unauthorized aliens." *Id.* § 1324a(h)(2). In 2007, Arizona passed a law authorizing courts to suspend or revoke the licenses necessary to do business in the state if an employer hired an unauthorized alien in violation of federal law. The Chamber of Commerce and other organizations contended that this restrictive state law was expressly preempted by the IRCA. But in *Chamber of Commerce of the United States v. Whiting*, 563 U.S. 582 (2011), a 7–2 Court disagreed and upheld the Arizona law. "IRCA expressly preempts States from imposing 'civil or criminal sanctions' on those who employ unauthorized aliens, 'other than through licensing and similar laws,'" the Court explained. *Whiting*, 563 U.S. at 594–95. "The Arizona law, on its face, purports to impose sanctions through licensing laws." *Id.* The only question was whether a law permitting the revocation of a license counted as a "licensing law." The Court held that it did.

A second category is "conflict preemption," where Congress doesn't expressly declare which state laws are preempted but impliedly preempts any state laws that act as obstacles to the federal law's purposes ("obstacle preemption") or that make it impossible for a person to comply with both federal and state law ("impossibility preemption"). Either way, the state law conflicts with the federal law. For example, in 1973, the University of Maryland adopted a policy of allowing "in-state" residents to pay less for tuition than out-of-state residents. The policy added that people would be considered out-of-state residents if they lived in Maryland but held a "G-4 visa"—a nonimmigrant visa for employees of international organizations and members of their immediate families. But in *Toll v. Moreno*, 458 U.S. 1 (1982), the Supreme Court struck down the Maryland policy as preempted by the federal statute that created the G-4 visa program. Interpreting the text and legislative history of the Immigration and Nationality Act of 1952, the Court concluded that Congress intended to benefit G-4 visa holders and support the international organizations that employ them by allowing them to domicile in the United States and to work for their organizations without paying certain state and federal taxes. Given these purposes, the Court held:

> [W]e cannot conclude that Congress ever contemplated that a State, in the operation of a university, might impose discriminatory tuition charges and fees solely on account of the federal immigration classification. We therefore conclude that insofar as [the State] bars domiciled G-4 aliens (and their dependents) from acquiring in-state status, the University's policy violates the Supremacy Clause.

Moreno, 458 U.S. at 17.

The third category is "field preemption," another type of implied preemption where Congress enacts such a comprehensive regulatory scheme that its apparent purpose is to "occupy the field" and displace all state legislation, whether or not it is complementary. *Davidowitz*, which you just read, is an example of field preemption. Because Congress enacted such a "broad and comprehensive plan" and indicated that only "one uniform national system" was required, the Pennsylvania law presented an obstacle by its very existence, even though it was arguably complementary. *Davidowitz,* 312 U.S. at 69, 73. In subsequent immigration cases, the Court emphasized the comprehensive nature of federal immigration law to strike down California's prohibition on land ownership by Japanese immigrants, *Takahashi v. Fish & Game Comm'n*, 334 U.S. 410 (1948); and its later prohibition on the employment of "unauthorized aliens," *De Canas v. Bica*, 424 U.S. 351 (1976). California "can neither add to nor take from the conditions lawfully imposed by Congress upon admission, naturalization and residence of aliens in the United States or the several states," the *Takahashi* Court wrote. 334 U.S. at 419.

All three types of preemption became relevant in 2010, when the Republican-controlled legislature of Arizona attempted to deter unauthorized immigration from Mexico and Central America. Arizona's law, known as S.B. 1070, was widely seen as a repudiation of President Barack Obama, a Democrat. S.B. 1070 was expressly designed to enforce federal immigration law in ways that the Obama administration would not. It added a state penalty to businesses that hired workers in violation of federal law and also allowed local police to stop and arrest people suspected of violating federal immigration law. In *Arizona v. United States*, 567 U.S. 387 (2012), the Obama administration sued to enjoin Arizona's law, claiming that it was an obstacle to the federal government's enforcement of its own policies.

Both sides won and lost as the Court, in analyzing the law, upheld certain parts but struck down other parts as preempted by federal law.

■ JUSTICE KENNEDY delivered the opinion of the Court.[7]

To address pressing issues related to the large number of aliens within its borders who do not have a lawful right to be in this country, the State of Arizona in 2010 enacted a statute called the Support Our Law Enforcement and Safe Neighborhoods Act. The law is often referred to as S.B. 1070, the version introduced in the State Senate. . . . Its stated purpose is to "discourage and deter the unlawful entry and presence of aliens and economic activity by persons unlawfully present in the United States." . . . The question before the Court is whether federal law preempts and renders invalid four separate provisions of the state law. . . .

The United States filed this suit against Arizona, seeking to enjoin S.B. 1070 as preempted. Four provisions of the law are at issue here. Two create new state offenses. Section 3 makes failure to comply with federal alien-registration requirements a state misdemeanor. Section 5, in relevant part, makes it a misdemeanor for an unauthorized alien to seek or engage in work in the State; this provision is referred to as § 5(C). Two other provisions give specific arrest authority and investigative duties with respect to certain aliens to state and local law enforcement officers. Section 6 authorizes officers to arrest without a warrant a person "the officer has probable cause to believe . . . has committed any public offense that makes the person removable from the United States." Section 2(B) provides that officers who conduct a stop, detention, or arrest must in some circumstances make efforts to verify the person's immigration status with the Federal Government. . . .

II

The Government of the United States has broad, undoubted power over the subject of immigration and the status of aliens. *See Toll v. Moreno*, 458 U.S. 1 (1982). This authority rests, in part, on the National Government's constitutional power to "establish a uniform Rule of Naturalization," Art. I, § 8, cl. 4, and its inherent power as sovereign to control and conduct relations with foreign nations, *see Toll, supra*, at 10.[8]

The federal power to determine immigration policy is well settled. Immigration policy can affect trade, investment, tourism, and diplomatic relations for the entire

[7] **As You Read, Consider:** *Arizona* walks through the Court's typical approach to preemption. How does Justice Anthony Kennedy answer the following questions: (1) Is the federal law a valid exercise of Congress's constitutional powers? (2a) If so, what are the objectives of Congress? (2b) Is the state law an obstacle to those objectives?

[8] **Question:** Note, here, how Kennedy evaluates Congress's power to enact federal immigration laws, which have expanded considerably from the first federal exclusion laws evaluated in 1889. Does Kennedy rely on the same explanation as the *Chinese Exclusion Case* did?

Nation, as well as the perceptions and expectations of aliens in this country who seek the full protection of its laws. Perceived mistreatment of aliens in the United States may lead to harmful reciprocal treatment of American citizens abroad.

It is fundamental that foreign countries concerned about the status, safety, and security of their nationals in the United States must be able to confer and communicate on this subject with one national sovereign, not the 50 separate States. This Court has reaffirmed that "[o]ne of the most important and delicate of all international relationships . . . has to do with the protection of the just rights of a country's own nationals when those nationals are in another country." *Hines v. Davidowitz*, 312 U.S. 52 (1941).

Federal governance of immigration and alien status is extensive and complex. Congress has specified categories of aliens who may not be admitted to the United States. *See* 8 U.S.C. § 1182. Unlawful entry and unlawful reentry into the country are federal offenses. §§ 1325, 1326. Once here, aliens are required to register with the Federal Government and to carry proof of status on their person. *See* §§ 1301–1306. Failure to do so is a federal misdemeanor. §§ 1304(e), 1306(a). Federal law also authorizes States to deny noncitizens a range of public benefits, § 1622; and it imposes sanctions on employers who hire unauthorized workers, § 1324a.

Congress has specified which aliens may be removed from the United States and the procedures for doing so. Aliens may be removed if they were inadmissible at the time of entry, have been convicted of certain crimes, or meet other criteria set by federal law. *See* § 1227. Removal is a civil, not criminal, matter. A principal feature of the removal system is the broad discretion exercised by immigration officials. Federal officials, as an initial matter, must decide whether it makes sense to pursue removal at all. If removal proceedings commence, aliens may seek asylum and other discretionary relief allowing them to remain in the country or at least to leave without formal removal. *See* § 1229a(c)(4). . . .

Agencies in the Department of Homeland Security play a major role in enforcing the country's immigration laws. United States Customs and Border Protection (CBP) is responsible for determining the admissibility of aliens and securing the country's borders. . . . Immigration and Customs Enforcement (ICE), a second agency, "conducts criminal investigations involving the enforcement of immigration-related statutes." . . . ICE officers are responsible "for the identification, apprehension, and removal of illegal aliens from the United States." Hundreds of thousands of aliens are removed by the Federal Government every year. . . .

These concerns are the background for the formal legal analysis that follows. The issue is whether, under preemption principles, federal law permits Arizona to implement the state-law provisions in dispute.

III

Federalism, central to the constitutional design, adopts the principle that both the National and State Governments have elements of sovereignty the other is bound to respect. From the existence of two sovereigns follows the possibility that laws can be in conflict or at cross-purposes. The Supremacy Clause provides a clear rule that federal law "shall be the supreme Law of the Land; and the Judges in every State shall be bound thereby, any Thing in the Constitution or Laws of any state to the Contrary notwithstanding." Art. VI, cl. 2. Under this principle, Congress has the power to preempt state law. There is no doubt that Congress may withdraw specified powers from the States by enacting a statute containing an express preemption provision. *Chamber of Commerce of United States of America v. Whiting*, 563 U.S. 582 (2011).

State law must also give way to federal law in at least two other circumstances. First, the States are precluded from regulating conduct in a field that Congress, acting within its proper authority, has determined must be regulated by its exclusive governance. The intent to displace state law altogether can be inferred from a framework of regulation "so pervasive . . . that Congress left no room for the States to supplement it" or where there is a "federal interest . . . so dominant that the federal system will be assumed to preclude enforcement of state laws on the same subject."

Second, state laws are preempted when they conflict with federal law. This includes cases where "compliance with both federal and state regulations is a physical impossibility," and those instances where the challenged state law "stands as an obstacle to the accomplishment and execution of the full purposes and objectives of Congress," *Hines*, 312 U.S., at 67. . . . In preemption analysis, courts should assume that "the historic police powers of the States" are not superseded "unless that was the clear and manifest purpose of Congress."

The four challenged provisions of the state law each must be examined under these preemption principles.

IV

Section 3

Section 3 of S.B. 1070 creates a new state misdemeanor. . . . In effect, § 3 adds a state-law penalty for conduct proscribed by federal law. The United States contends that this state enforcement mechanism intrudes on the field of alien registration, a field in which Congress has left no room for States to regulate. . . . [We agree that the Federal Government has occupied the field of alien registration.] The federal statutory directives provide a full set of standards governing alien registration, including the punishment for noncompliance. . . . Federal law makes a single sovereign responsible for maintaining a comprehensive and unified system to keep track of aliens within the Nation's borders. If § 3 of the Arizona statute were valid, every State could give itself independent authority to prosecute federal registration violations, "diminish[ing] the [Federal Government]'s control over enforcement" and "detract[ing] from the 'integrated scheme of regulation' created by Congress." . . .

Section 5(C)

Unlike § 3, which replicates federal statutory requirements, § 5(C) enacts a state criminal prohibition where no federal counterpart exists. The provision makes it a state misdemeanor for "an unauthorized alien to knowingly apply for work, solicit work in a public place or perform work as an employee or independent contractor" in Arizona. The United States contends that the provision upsets the balance struck by the Immigration Reform and Control Act of 1986 (IRCA) and must be preempted as an obstacle to the federal plan of regulation and control. . . . [We agree] that Congress made a deliberate choice not to impose criminal penalties on aliens who seek, or engage in, unauthorized employment. . . . Although § 5(C) attempts to achieve one of the same goals as federal law—the deterrence of unlawful employment—it involves a conflict in the method of enforcement. The Court has recognized that a "[c]onflict in technique can be fully as disruptive to the system Congress erected as conflict in overt policy." The correct instruction to draw from the text, structure, and history of IRCA is that Congress decided it would be inappropriate to impose criminal penalties on aliens who seek or engage in unauthorized employment. It follows that a state law to the contrary is an obstacle to the regulatory system Congress chose. . . .

Section 6

Section 6 of S.B. 1070 provides that a state officer, "without a warrant, may arrest a person if the officer has probable cause to believe . . . [the person] has committed any public offense that makes [him] removable from the United States." The United States argues that arrests authorized by this statute would be an obstacle to the removal system Congress created.

[We again agree.] As a general rule, it is not a crime for a removable alien to remain present in the United States. If the police stop someone based on nothing more than possible removability, the usual predicate for an arrest is absent. When an alien is suspected of being removable, a federal official issues an administrative document called a "Notice to Appear." The form does not authorize an arrest. Instead, it gives the alien information about the proceedings, including the time and date of the removal hearing. If an alien fails to appear, an in absentia order may direct removal. . . .

Section 6 attempts to provide state officers even greater authority to arrest aliens on the basis of possible removability than Congress has given to trained federal immigration officers. Under state law, officers who believe an alien is removable by reason of some "public offense" would have the power to conduct an arrest on that basis regardless of whether a federal warrant has issued or the alien is likely to escape. . . . This is not the system Congress created. . . . By authorizing state officers to decide whether an alien should be detained for being removable, § 6 violates the principle that the removal process is entrusted to the discretion of the Federal Government. . . .

Section 2(B)

Section 2(B) of S.B. 1070 requires state officers to make a "reasonable attempt . . . to determine the immigration status" of any person they stop, detain, or arrest on some other legitimate basis if "reasonable suspicion exists that the person is an alien and is unlawfully present in the United States." The law also provides that "[a]ny person who is arrested shall have the person's immigration status determined before the person is released." The accepted way to perform these status checks is to contact ICE, which maintains a database of immigration records. . . .[9]

The United States and its amici contend that . . . the State's verification requirements pose an obstacle to the framework Congress put in place. The first concern is the mandatory nature of the status checks. The second is the possibility of prolonged detention while the checks are being performed. . . . Congress has done nothing to suggest it is inappropriate to communicate with ICE in these situations, however. Indeed, it has encouraged the sharing of information about possible immigration violations. . . . The federal scheme thus leaves room for a policy requiring state officials to contact ICE as a routine matter. However the law is interpreted, if § 2(B) only requires state officers to conduct a status check during the course of an authorized, lawful detention or after a detainee has been released, the provision likely would survive preemption. . . .

---

[9] **Questions:** The Court in these final paragraphs upholds section 2(B) while striking down S.B. 1070's other provisions. What distinguishes this section from the others?

Imagine that in response to the beginning of the coronavirus pandemic in 2020, Arizona enacted a law that required all prospective visitors to first gain permission from the state—essentially creating a state visa system. How might the Court have treated this law? Does the preemption analysis change when questions of national sovereignty are less salient? For one scholar's answer, see Kerry Abrams, *Plenary Power Preemption*, 99 Va. L. Rev. 601 (2013).

CHAPTER 12

What Are the Generally Applicable Limits on Congress's Powers to Regulate?

ARTICLE I, SECTION 9, CLAUSE 2: The Privilege of the Writ of Habeas Corpus shall not be suspended, unless when in Cases of Rebellion or Invasion the public Safety may require it.

CLAUSE 3: No Bill of Attainder or ex post facto Law shall be passed.

CLAUSE 6: No Preference shall be given by any Regulation of Commerce or Revenue to the Ports of one State over those of another: nor shall Vessels bound to, or from, one State, be obliged to enter, clear, or pay Duties in another.

CLAUSE 8: No Title of Nobility shall be granted by the United States: And no Person holding any Office of Profit or Trust under them, shall, without the Consent of the Congress, accept of any present, Emolument, Office, or Title, of any kind whatever, from any King, Prince, or foreign State.

ARTICLE III, SECTION 2, CLAUSE 3: The Trial of all Crimes, except in Cases of Impeachment, shall be by Jury; and such Trial shall be held in the State where the said Crimes shall have been committed; but when not committed within any State, the Trial shall be at such Place or Places as the Congress may by Law have directed.

FIRST AMENDMENT (1791): Congress shall make no law respecting an establishment of religion, or prohibiting the free exercise thereof; or abridging the freedom of speech, or of the press; or the right of the people peaceably to assemble, and to petition the Government for a redress of grievances.

SECOND AMENDMENT (1791): A well regulated Militia, being necessary to the security of a free State, the right of the people to keep and bear Arms, shall not be infringed.

THIRD AMENDMENT (1791): No Soldier shall, in time of peace be quartered in any house, without the consent of the Owner, nor in time of war, but in a manner to be prescribed by law.

FOURTH AMENDMENT (1791): The right of the people to be secure in their persons, houses, papers, and effects, against unreasonable searches and seizures, shall not be violated, and no Warrants shall issue, but upon probable cause, supported by Oath or affirmation, and particularly describing the place to be searched, and the persons or things to be seized.

FIFTH AMENDMENT (1791): No person shall be held to answer for a capital, or otherwise infamous crime, unless on a presentment or indictment of a Grand Jury, except in cases arising in the land or naval forces, or in the Militia, when in actual service in time of War or public danger; nor shall any person be subject for the same offence to be twice put in jeopardy of life or limb; nor shall be compelled in any criminal case to be a witness against himself, nor be deprived of life, liberty, or property, without due process of law; nor shall private property be taken for public use, without just compensation.

SIXTH AMENDMENT (1791): In all criminal prosecutions, the accused shall enjoy the right to a speedy and public trial, by an impartial jury of the State and district wherein the crime shall have been committed, which district shall have been previously ascertained by law, and to be informed of the nature and cause of the accusation; to be confronted with the witnesses against him; to have compulsory process for obtaining witnesses in his favor, and to have the Assistance of Counsel for his defence.

SEVENTH AMENDMENT (1791): In Suits at common law, where the value in controversy shall exceed twenty dollars, the right of trial by jury shall be preserved, and no fact tried by a jury, shall be otherwise re-examined in any Court of the United States, than according to the rules of the common law.

EIGHTH AMENDMENT (1791): Excessive bail shall not be required, nor excessive fines imposed, nor cruel and unusual punishments inflicted.

NINTH AMENDMENT (1791): The enumeration in the Constitution, of certain rights, shall not be construed to deny or disparage others retained by the people.

TENTH AMENDMENT (1791): The powers not delegated to the United States by the Constitution, nor prohibited by it to the States, are reserved to the States respectively, or to the people.

ELEVENTH AMENDMENT (1795): The Judicial power of the United States shall not be construed to extend to any suit in law or equity, commenced or prosecuted against one of the United States by Citizens of another State, or by Citizens or Subjects of any Foreign State.

THIRTEENTH AMENDMENT (1865), SECTION 1: Neither slavery nor involuntary servitude, except as a punishment for crime whereof the party shall have been duly convicted, shall exist within the United States, or any place subject to their jurisdiction.

FOURTEENTH AMENDMENT (1868), SECTION 1: All persons born or naturalized in the United States, and subject to the jurisdiction thereof, are citizens of the United States and of the State wherein they reside. . . .

> **SECTION 4:** The validity of the public debt of the United States, authorized by law, including debts incurred for payment of pensions and bounties for services in suppressing insurrection or rebellion, shall not be questioned.

FIFTEENTH AMENDMENT (1870), SECTION 1: The right of citizens of the United States to vote shall not be denied or abridged by the United States or by any State on account of race, color, or previous condition of servitude.

NINETEENTH AMENDMENT (1920), CLAUSE 1: The right of citizens of the United States to vote shall not be denied or abridged by the United States or by any State on account of sex.

TWENTY-FIRST AMENDMENT (1933), SECTION 2: The transportation or importation into any State, Territory, or possession of the United States for delivery or use therein of intoxicating liquors, in violation of the laws thereof, is hereby prohibited.

TWENTY-FOURTH AMENDMENT (1964), SECTION 1: The right of citizens of the United States to vote in any primary or other election for President or Vice President, for electors for President or Vice President, or for Senator or Representative in Congress, shall not be denied or abridged by the United States or any State by reason of failure to pay any poll tax or other tax.

TWENTY-SIXTH AMENDMENT (1971), SECTION 1: The right of citizens of the United States, who are eighteen years of age or older, to vote shall not be denied or abridged by the United States or by any State on account of age.

TWENTY-SEVENTH AMENDMENT (1992): No law, varying the compensation for the services of the Senators and Representatives, shall take effect, until an election of Representatives shall have intervened.

Three General Limits on Regulatory Powers

Previous sections of this casebook have discussed the extensive scope of some of Congress's enumerated powers. This scope has resisted many attempts by politicians and the Supreme Court to limit "Taxes" to revenues as opposed to penalties, to limit the "general Welfare" to a purpose of taxation as opposed to an independent spending power, to limit "Commerce" to trade as opposed to manufacturing, and to limit "Naturalization" to citizenship as opposed to immigration.

But defining the scope of Congress's enumerated powers is not the end of the story; not every law that levies a tax or regulates interstate commerce is valid. Later clauses of the Constitution contain independent limits on Congress's power that prohibit Congress from, say, passing any law "abridging the freedom of speech" or infringing "the right of the people to keep and bear Arms"—regardless of whether the law otherwise fits within the scope of Congress's taxing or regulatory power. The sections within question 12 (sections 12.1–12.3) will consider three of these general limits on Congress's powers: (1) implied limits within Article I, Section 8; (2) explicit limits within Article I, Section 9; and (3) the Bill of Rights.

12.1 THE ANTICOMMANDEERING DOCTRINE

The most important implied limit on Congress's exercise of its enumerated powers is the anticommandeering doctrine. This doctrine prescribes that, with several exceptions, Article I, Section 8, does not permit Congress to direct state legislatures or state officers to enforce federal law. The doctrine has a long, contentious history that dates back to the Constitutional Convention of 1787.

Supremacy Clause, preemption, and assertive action

In May 1787, the Virginia delegation opened the substantive debate at the Constitutional Convention with the Virginia Plan: a list of more than a dozen resolutions for a new, federal government to replace the Articles of Confederation. Most of these resolutions were incorporated into the final document. But one, championed by James Madison, was too controversial: a proposal for the federal government "to negative all laws passed by the several States, contravening, in the opinion of the national Legislature, the articles of union." 3 *The Records of the Federal Convention of 1787*, at 593 (Max Farrand ed., 1911).

Madison strenuously argued for the proposal throughout the summer of 1787, arguing that states would otherwise "pursue their particular interests in opposition to the general interest." Michael J. Klarman, *The Framers' Coup* 155 (2016). But opponents of the federal veto countered with their objections that the power might be used to "enslave the states"—or, even worse to many southern delegates, that it might be used to veto state legislation regarding slavery. *Id.* at 167–70. Eventually, the delegates reached a compromise that Congress could simply preempt state laws that it considered contrary to the federal Constitution rather than veto them. The Supremacy Clause of Article VI was the product of this compromise, declaring that the U.S. Constitution and federal law "shall be the supreme Law of the Land . . ., and the Judges in every State shall be bound thereby, any Thing in the Constitution or Laws of any State to the Contrary notwithstanding."

As discussed earlier (section 2.1), the Supremacy Clause has long allowed Congress to *preempt* state action. But it was immediately debated whether this clause, combined with Congress's Article I powers, also permitted Congress to *direct* or *prohibit* state action. During the ratification debates, it was not hard for anyone to imagine Congress exercising its Commerce Clause authority by ordering state legislatures to enact laws regulating interstate commerce, or exercising its Taxing Clause authority by ordering state administrators to collect federal taxes.

In *The Federalist*, Madison and Alexander Hamilton argued that the Constitution authorized Congress to do all of these things. "[T]he Legislatures, Courts and Magistrates of the respective members will be incorporated into the operations of the national government, *as far as its just and constitutional authority extends*; and will be rendered auxiliary to the enforcement of its laws," Hamilton wrote of the Supremacy Clause. *The Federalist No. 27*, at 175 (Alexander Hamilton) (Jacob E. Cooke ed., 1961). Madison added that "it is extremely probable that [in the collection of taxation and] other instances, particularly in the organization of the judicial power, the officers of the States will be clothed with the correspondent authority of the Union." *Id. No. 45*, at 313 (James Madison). These sorts of arguments drew fierce opposition from Antifederalists, who complained that if Congress could direct state action, "the individual states must very soon be annihilated." *The Anti-Federalist* 110 (Herbert J. Storing ed., 1985) (Brutus). But after the Constitution was ratified, Congress almost immediately began directing state officers, particularly state judges, to enforce federal law.

Laws ordering state officials to enforce federal law

Other sections of this casebook discuss major laws passed by the first few Congresses that ordered state officials to enforce federal law. For example, the Naturalization Act of 1790, ch. 3, 1 Stat. 103, required state courts to review applications for U.S. citizenship. The Carriage Tax Act of 1794, ch. 45, 1 Stat. 373, which the Supreme Court upheld in *Hylton v. United States,* 3 U.S. (3 Dall.) 171 (1796), required state courts to hear enforcement actions by federal tax commissioners. And the Alien Enemies Act of 1798 made it the "duty" of state courts "to cause [enemy] alien or aliens to be duly apprehended" and to "order such alien or aliens to be removed out of the territory of the United States." Alien Enemies Act, ch. 66, 1 Stat. 577, 577

Another law that was particularly influential in defining the scope of Congress's power to direct state officials was the Judiciary Act of 1789, ch. 20, 1 Stat. 73, which Congress passed as an exercise of its Article I power to "constitute Tribunals inferior to the supreme Court." Although the statute created federal trial courts, it gave state courts exclusive jurisdiction over cases arising under the Constitution or federal law. Over time, the Supreme Court made clear that Congress not only could authorize state courts to hear these claims but also could require state courts to do so.

In *Martin v. Hunter's Lessee,* for example, the Court quoted the Supremacy Clause's declaration that "the Judges in every State shall be bound [by federal law]" as evidence that state judges were obligated to hear federal claims and to enforce federal laws. 14 U.S. (1 Wheat.) 304, 340 (1816). Later, in a series of cases beginning with *Claflin v. Houseman*, 93 U.S. 130 (1876), the Court reiterated this obligation to hold that state courts could not, in ordinary circumstances, decline to hear a claim brought under federal law—even if the federal law contradicted the state's own policies. *See Testa v. Katt*, 330 U.S. 386 (1947) (federal criminal law); *Second Emps.' Liab. Cases*, 223 U.S. 1 (1912) (federal civil law). More recently, the Court has struck down attempts by state courts to avoid hearing federal civil rights claims against state officials. *See, e.g., Haywood v. Drown*, 556 U.S. 729, 740 (2009).

And in a related series of cases, the Court has long authorized federal courts to order state courts, state executive officials, and state legislatures to comply with the Court's own interpretations of federal and constitutional law. *See, e.g., Maine v. Thiboutot*, 448 U.S. 1 (1980) (upholding a federal law that authorized federal courts to enforce federal statutory obligations against state officials); *Cooper v. Aaron*, 358 U.S. 1 (1958) (requiring state officials to enforce the U.S. Constitution as interpreted by the U.S. Supreme Court); *Ex parte Young*, 209 U.S. 123 (1908) (prohibiting a state official from enforcing an unconstitutional law).

Court decision dialing back compliance mandates

Another influential early law was the Fugitive Slave Act of 1793, ch. 7, 1 Stat. 302, which authorized state officials to assist enslavers from other states in capturing and renditioning fugitives from slavery. The law became deeply unpopular in northern states, and it caused several northern jurists to question the constitutionality of federal laws that used states as instruments for enforcing federal policies. *See, e.g.*, 1 James Kent, *Commentaries on American Law* 396–404 (1826).

In *Prigg v. Pennsylvania*, the Supreme Court upheld the law—but warned that it was doubtful "whether state magistrates are *bound* to act under it," particularly if they were prohibited from doing so "by state legislation." 41 U.S. (16 Pet.) 539, 622 (1842) (emphasis added). Northern states, accordingly, followed *Prigg* by enacting so-called personal liberty laws that prohibited state officials from complying with the Fugitive Slave Act and its far harsher replacement in 1850. These laws led to a series of Supreme Court cases that prohibited states from deliberately interfering with federal policy but that allowed states not to comply with federal policy. *See, e.g.*, *Ableman v. Booth*, 62 U.S. (21 How.) 506, 526 (1859); *Moore v. Illinois*, 55 U.S. (14 How.) 13, 22 (1853); *Jones v. Van Zandt*, 46 U.S. (5 How.) 215, 229 (1847).

The personal liberty laws so angered politicians in southern states that when South Carolina seceded in 1860, its declaration of secession described the laws as its main evidence that the constitutional compact "has been deliberately broken and disregarded by the non-slaveholding States, and the consequence follows that South Carolina is released from her obligation." *Journal of the Convention of the People of South Carolina* 464 (R. W. Gibbes, Columbia, S.C. 1862).

Court decisions giving power to the states

After the Civil War began, the Court reiterated its point from *Prigg* in bolder terms, holding that Congress

> has no power to impose on a State officer, as such, any duty whatever, and compel him to perform it, for if it possessed this power, it might overload the officer with duties which would fill up all his time, and disable him from performing his obligations to the State, and might impose on him duties of a character incompatible with the rank and dignity to which he was elevated by the State.

Kentucky v. Dennison, 65 U.S. (24 How.) 66, 107–08 (1861). The Court continued, "It is true that Congress may authorize a particular State officer to perform a particular duty, but if he declines to do so, it does not follow that he may be coerced or punished for his refusal." *Id.* at 108.

This idea that Congress has no power to coerce state officials to enforce federal law (even if federal courts *do* have that power) continued after the Civil War. For example, in *Ashton v. Cameron County Water Improvement District*, 298 U.S. 513 (1936), the Court struck down a federal bankruptcy law that authorized municipalities to reorganize their debts. The Court explained, "If obligations of States or their political subdivisions may be subjected to the interference here attempted, they are no longer free to manage their own affairs; the will of Congress prevails over them." *Ashton*, 298 U.S. at 531. The Court only upheld a federal municipal bankruptcy law after Congress amended it to require the municipality's state to consent to the proceeding. *United States v. Bekins*, 304 U.S. 27, 49–54 (1938).

Similarly, after the 1937 "switch in time" (see section 6.2), as Congress became more assertive in its use of the Commerce Clause to regulate domestic affairs, states began to argue that Congress had no power to regulate the activities of their officers. At first, the Supreme Court rejected these claims, holding that Congress's power to regulate commerce extended to all activities that substantially affected interstate commerce, including activities of state officers and employees. *See, e.g.*, *California v. Taylor*, 353 U.S. 553 (1957) (regarding the applicability of the federal Railway Labor Act to state-owned railroads); *California v. United States*, 320 U.S. 577 (1944) (finding that Congress has the power to regulate the activities of state and municipal agencies). For example, in *Maryland v. Wirtz*, 392 U.S. 183 (1968), the Court upheld the constitutionality of applying the Fair Labor Standards Act of 1938, as amended, to the wages and hours of employees of state-operated schools and hospitals. In *Fry v. United States*, 421 U.S. 542 (1975), the Court extended this principle to uphold federal wage and salary controls on all state governmental employees.

But in *National League of Cities v. Usery*, the Court dramatically reversed course, overruled *Wirtz*, and struck down a federal wage and hour law "undoubtedly within the scope of the Commerce Clause" because it was "applied directly to the States and subdivisions of States as employers." 426 U.S. 833, 841 (1976). The Court explained that the Tenth Amendment embraced a theory of federalism that protected the "reserved" powers of states, including their sovereignty, from federal impairment. *Id.* at 841–45. "One undoubted attribute of state sovereignty," the Court continued, "is the State's power to determine the wages which shall be paid to those whom they employ in order to carry out their governmental functions, what hours those persons will work, and what compensation will be provided where these employees may be called upon to work overtime." *Id.* at 845. Such powers are "functions essential to [the] separate and independent existence" of the states, the Court concluded, and Congress had no power to take them away. *Id.* (quoting *Lane Cnty. v. Oregon*, 74 U.S. 71, 74 (1868)).

Court pendulum swinging again to the feds

Usery was not the first time the Court had held that an otherwise valid federal law could not apply to states or their employees. As we read in the section on the taxing power (section 5.3), in *Collector v. Day*, 78 U.S. (11 Wall.) 113 (1871), the Court held that Congress had no power to levy a tax upon the official salary of a state judge. The Court feared that Congress might otherwise have the power to destroy an essential governmental function of a state. But the Supreme Court eventually overruled *Collector* after determining that giving state employees immunity from federal taxes was unworkable. *Helvering v. Gerhardt*, 304 U.S. 405 (1938).

And just as *Collector*'s distinction eventually fell, so, too, did the distinction in *Usery*. In *Garcia v. San Antonio Metropolitan Transit Authority*, 469 U.S. 528 (1985), the Court considered a federal law that regulated San Antonio's operation of a mass-transit system. The district court, after considering the history of publicly and privately owned mass-transit systems, concluded that mass transit was a traditional, essential governmental "function" immunized from federal review by *Usery*. But the Supreme Court held that *Usery*'s distinction between essential governmental functions and nontraditional governmental functions was arbitrary:

> Our examination of this "function" standard applied in these and other cases over the last eight years now persuades us that the attempt to draw the boundaries of state regulatory immunity in terms of "traditional governmental function" is not only unworkable but is also inconsistent with established principles of federalism. . . .

Garcia, 469 U.S. at 531. For example, many mass-transit systems were twentieth-century inventions run by private companies—hardly a "traditional" governmental function. Yet, most mass-transit systems had since become essential state-run projects.

It was unclear to the *Garcia* Court why this industry-specific history should matter when determining the scope of Congress's powers. Rather than demand a judicially enforceable limit on generally applicable federal legislation, the Court concluded, states should look to the political process to protect them from any abuse of federal power. "[T]he principal means chosen by the Framers to ensure the role of States in the federal system lies in the structure of the Federal Government itself," the Court wrote. *Id.* at 550–51. States could participate in the Electoral College, and they could send representatives and senators to Congress. "[T]he principal and basic limit on the federal commerce power is that inherent in all congressional action—the built-in restraints that our system provides through state participation in federal governmental action." *Id.* at 556.

Garcia remains good law. It also influenced the Court to reevaluate some of its earlier decisions that had declared that Congress couldn't require state officials to enforce federal law. In *Puerto Rico v. Branstad*, 483 U.S. 219 (1987), the Court reevaluated a federal law passed to enforce the Extradition Clause of Article IV, Section 2, which reads:

> A Person charged in any State with Treason, Felony, or other Crime, who shall flee from Justice, and be found in another State, shall on demand of the executive Authority of the State from which he fled, be delivered up, to be removed to the State having Jurisdiction of the Crime.

Under the Court's antebellum precedents, particularly *Kentucky v. Dennison*, 65 U.S. (24 How.) 66 (1861), Congress had no power to require state governors to enforce any federal requirement. But in *Branstad*, the Court dismissed *Dennison* as "the product of another time." 483 U.S. at 230. It held that Congress could, in fact, require state, local, or territorial officials to extradite fugitives from justice. *Id.*

12.1.1

New York v. United States

505 U.S. 144 (1992)

As the Supreme Court entered the 1990s, when Congress's power to regulate interstate commerce remained at its peak post-*Wickard v. Filburn*, 317 U.S. 111 (1942), many conservative members of the Court continued to look for some limit on Congress's powers that would protect states from being run as agencies of the federal government.

They found one such limit in *Gregory v. Ashcroft*, 501 U.S. 452 (1991). There, the Court considered whether the federal Age Discrimination in Employment Act of 1967, Pub. L. No. 90–202, 81 Stat. 602, could constitutionally prohibit Missouri from imposing a mandatory retirement age on its state judges. The Court noted that "[c]ongressional interference with this decision of the people of Missouri, defining their constitutional officers, would upset the usual constitutional balance of federal and state powers." *Gregory*, 501 U.S. at 460. Rather than declare the law unconstitutional, however, the Court held that where "Congress intends to alter the usual constitutional balance between the States and the Federal Government, it must make its intention to do so unmistakably clear in the language of the statute." *Id.* (internal quotation marks omitted). The Court considered this "clear statement rule" less onerous than trying to award states immunity from certain regulations, but strong enough to acknowledge "that the States retain substantial sovereign powers under our constitutional scheme, powers with which Congress does not readily interfere." *Id.* at 461. Applying this rule, the Court concluded that Congress had not plainly stated that the federal age discrimination act should apply to state judges. *Id.* at 473.

In the following decision, *New York v. United States*, 505 U.S. 144 (1992), the Court resuscitated an even more important limit on Congress: the anticommandeering doctrine. The factual context of the case is best described by the Court itself.

■ JUSTICE O'CONNOR delivered the opinion of the Court.[1]

These cases implicate one of our Nation's newest problems of public policy, and perhaps our oldest question of constitutional law. The public policy issue involves the disposal of radioactive waste: In these cases, we address the constitutionality of three

---

1 **As You Read, Consider:** As the background notes before this decision describe, the Supreme Court has held since the 1840s that Congress has no power to compel states to enforce federal policy. Where in the Constitution does Justice Sandra Day O'Connor locate this limit?

provisions of the Low-Level Radioactive Waste Policy Amendments Act of 1985. The constitutional question is as old as the Constitution: it consists of discerning the proper division of authority between the Federal Government and the States. We conclude that, while Congress has substantial power under the Constitution to encourage the States to provide for the disposal of the radioactive waste generated within their borders, the Constitution does not confer upon Congress the ability simply to compel the States to do so. We therefore find that only two of the Act's three provisions at issue are consistent with the Constitution's allocation of power to the Federal Government. . . .

A

We live in a world full of low level radioactive waste. Radioactive material is present in luminous watch dials, smoke alarms, measurement devices, medical fluids, research materials, and the protective gear and construction materials used by workers at nuclear power plants. . . . The waste must be isolated from humans for long periods of time, often for hundreds of years. Millions of cubic feet of low level radioactive waste must be disposed of each year. . . . [But] since 1979, only three disposal sites—those in Nevada, Washington, and South Carolina—have been in operation. Waste generated in the rest of the country must be shipped to one of these three sites for disposal.

[In response to rules that would permit these "sited" States to exclude waste from 31 "unsited" States, Congress passed the legislation challenged here, the Low-Level Radioactive Waste Policy Amendments Act of 1985.]

In broad outline, the Act embodies a compromise among the sited and unsited States. The sited States agreed to extend for seven years the period in which they would accept low level radioactive waste from other States. In exchange, the unsited States agreed to end their reliance on the sited States by 1992. . . .

The Act provides three types of incentives to encourage the States to comply with their statutory obligation to provide for the disposal of waste generated within their borders. . . .

1. *Monetary incentives.* [The federal government would pay States that disposed of all low-level radioactive waste within their borders by 1993.]

2. *Access incentives*. The second type of incentive involves the denial of access to disposal sites. [Unsited States that failed to meet certain deadlines would have to pay sited States double or triple surcharges.]

3. *The take-title provision*. The third type of incentive is the most severe. The Act provides: "If a State (or, where applicable, a compact region) in which low-level radioactive waste is generated is unable to provide for the disposal of all such waste generated within such State or compact region by January 1, 1996, each State in which such waste is generated, upon the request of the generator or owner of the waste, shall take title to the waste, be obligated to take possession of the waste, and shall be liable for all damages directly or indirectly incurred by such generator or owner as a consequence of the failure of the State to take possession of the waste as soon after January 1, 1996, as the generator or owner notifies the State that the waste is available for shipment."

New York, a State whose residents generate a relatively large share of the Nation's low level radioactive waste, . . . complied with the Act's requirements by enacting legislation providing for the siting and financing of a disposal facility in New York. . . . [But the state and other petitioners claim] that the Act is inconsistent with the Tenth Amendment. . . .

[T]he task of ascertaining the constitutional line between federal and state power has given rise to many of th[is] Court's most difficult and celebrated cases. . . . These questions can be viewed in either of two ways. In some cases, the Court has inquired whether an Act of Congress is authorized by one of the powers delegated to Congress in Article I of the Constitution. *See, e.g., Perez v. United States*, 402 U.S. 146 (1971); *McCulloch v. Maryland*, 4 Wheat. 316 (1819). In other cases the Court has sought to determine whether an Act of Congress invades the province of state sovereignty reserved by the Tenth Amendment. *See, e.g., Garcia v. San Antonio Metropolitan Transit Authority*, 469 U.S. 528 (1985). In a case like these, involving the division of authority between federal and state governments, the two inquiries are mirror images of each other. If a power is delegated to Congress in the Constitution, the Tenth Amendment expressly disclaims any reservation of that power to the States; if a power is an attribute of state sovereignty reserved by the Tenth Amendment, it is necessarily a power the Constitution has not conferred on Congress.

It is in this sense that the Tenth Amendment "states but a truism that all is retained which has not been surrendered." *United States v. Darby*, 312 U.S. 100, 124 (1941). . . . This has been the Court's consistent understanding: "The States unquestionably do retai[n] a significant measure of sovereign authority . . . to the extent that the Constitution has not divested them of their original powers and transferred those powers to the Federal Government." *Garcia, supra*, at 549.[2]

Congress exercises its conferred powers subject to the limitations contained in the Constitution. Thus, for example, under the Commerce Clause, Congress may regulate publishers engaged in interstate commerce, but Congress is constrained in the exercise of that power by the First Amendment. The Tenth Amendment likewise restrains the power of Congress, but this limit is not derived from the text of the Tenth Amendment itself, which, as we have discussed, is essentially a tautology. Instead, the Tenth Amendment confirms that the power of the Federal Government is subject to limits that may, in a given instance, reserve power to the States. The Tenth Amendment thus directs us to determine, as in this case, whether an incident of state sovereignty is protected by a limitation on an Article I power. . . . Among the provisions of the Constitution that have been particularly important in this regard, three concern us here.

First, the Constitution allocates to Congress the power "[t]o regulate Commerce . . . among the several States." Art. I, § 8, cl. 3. . . . As interstate commerce has become ubiquitous, activities once considered purely local have come to have effects on the national economy, and have accordingly come within the scope of Congress' commerce power. *See, e. g., Katzenbach v. McClung*, 379 U.S. 294 (1964); *Wickard v. Filburn*, 317 U.S. 111 (1942).

Second, the Constitution authorizes Congress "to pay the Debts and provide for the . . . general Welfare of the United States." Art. I, § 8, cl. 1. . . . While the spending power is "subject to several general restrictions articulated in our cases," *South Dakota v. Dole*, 483 U.S. 203 (1987), these restrictions have not been so severe as to prevent the regulatory authority of Congress from generally keeping up with the growth of the federal budget.

The Court's broad construction of Congress' power under the Commerce and Spending Clauses has of course been guided, as it has with respect to Congress'

---

[2] **Questions:** Take careful note of O'Connor's description of the Tenth Amendment (which is not at all different from the Court's description in the Commerce Clause case of *United States v. Darby Lumber Co.*). Is she describing the Tenth Amendment as (1) a freestanding limit on Congress's powers or (2) an unenforceable implication that Article I does not give Congress the power to do everything? In other words, is it possible for Congress to enact a law that would be a valid exercise of the Commerce Clause but invalid because of the Tenth Amendment?

power generally, by the Constitution's Necessary and Proper Clause, which authorizes Congress "[t]o make all Laws which shall be necessary and proper for carrying into Execution the foregoing Powers." U.S. Const., Art. I, § 8, cl. 18. *See, e.g., Legal Tender Case,* 110 U S. 421, 449–450 (1884); *McCulloch v. Maryland,* 4 Wheat., at 411–421.

Finally, the Constitution provides that "the Laws of the United States . . . shall be the supreme Law of the Land . . . any Thing in the Constitution or Laws of any State to the Contrary notwithstanding." U.S. Const., Art. VI, cl. 2. As the Federal Government's willingness to exercise power within the confines of the Constitution has grown, the authority of the States has correspondingly diminished. . . .

In the end, just as a cup may be half empty or half full, it makes no difference whether one views the question at issue in these cases as one of ascertaining the limits of the power delegated to the Federal Government under the affirmative provisions of the Constitution or one of discerning the core of sovereignty retained by the States under the Tenth Amendment. Either way, we must determine whether any of the three challenged provisions of the Low-Level Radioactive Waste Policy Amendments Act of 1985 oversteps the boundary between federal and state authority. . . .

B

As an initial matter, Congress may not simply "commandee[r] the legislative processes of the States by directly compelling them to enact and enforce a federal regulatory program." *Hodel v. Va. Surface Mining & Reclamation Assn., Inc.*, 452 U.S. 264, 288 (1981). . . . While Congress has substantial powers to govern the Nation directly, including in areas of intimate concern to the States, the Constitution has never been understood to confer upon Congress the ability to require the States to govern according to Congress' instructions.[3]

Indeed, the question whether the Constitution should permit Congress to employ state governments as regulatory agencies was a topic of lively debate among the Framers. Under the Articles of Confederation, Congress lacked the authority in most respects to govern the people directly. . . . The inadequacy of this governmental structure was responsible in part for the Constitutional Convention. . . . The Convention generated a great number of proposals for the structure of the new Government, but two quickly took center stage. Under the Virginia Plan, . . . Congress would exercise legislative authority directly upon individuals, without employing the States as intermediaries. Under the New Jersey Plan, . . . Congress would continue to require the approval of the States before legislating, as it had under the Articles of Confederation. . . . One frequently expressed objection to the New Jersey Plan was that it might require the Federal Government to coerce the States into implementing legislation. As [a Virginian] explained the distinction, . . . "Coercion [is] *impracticable, expensive, cruel to individuals. . . . We must resort therefore to a national Legislation over individuals.*" . . .

In the end, the Convention opted for a Constitution in which Congress would exercise its legislative authority directly over individuals, rather than over States; for a variety of reasons, it rejected the New Jersey Plan in favor of the Virginia Plan. . . . In providing for a stronger central government, therefore, the Framers explicitly chose a Constitution that confers upon Congress the power to regulate individuals, not States. As we have seen, the Court has consistently respected this choice. We have always understood that, even where Congress has the authority under the

---

[3] **Question:** Based on her discussion of the Tenth Amendment in the previous section, where, precisely, in the Constitution does O'Connor believe that Congress is prohibited from commandeering states?

Constitution to pass laws requiring or prohibiting certain acts, it lacks the power directly to compel the States to require or prohibit those acts. The allocation of power contained in the Commerce Clause, for example, authorizes Congress to regulate interstate commerce directly; it does not authorize Congress to regulate state governments' regulation of interstate commerce. . . .[4]

This is not to say that Congress lacks the ability to encourage a State to regulate in a particular way, or that Congress may not hold out incentives to the States as a method of influencing a State's policy choices. . . . Two of these methods are of particular relevance here.

First, under Congress' spending power, "Congress may attach conditions on the receipt of federal funds." *South Dakota v. Dole*, 483 U. S., at 206. Such conditions must (among other requirements) bear some relationship to the purpose of the federal spending; otherwise, of course, the spending power could render academic the Constitution's other grants and limits of federal authority. . . .

Second, where Congress has the authority to regulate private activity under the Commerce Clause, we have recognized Congress' power to offer States the choice of regulating that activity according to federal standards or having state law pre-empted by federal regulation. This arrangement, which has been termed "a program of cooperative federalism," *Hodel*, *supra*, at 289, is replicated in numerous federal statutory schemes. . . .

By either of these methods, as by any other permissible method of encouraging a State to conform to federal policy choices, the residents of the State retain the ultimate decision as to whether or not the State will comply. If a State's citizens view federal policy as sufficiently contrary to local interests, they may elect to decline a federal grant. If state residents would prefer their government to devote its attention and resources to problems other than those deemed important by Congress, they may choose to have the Federal Government, rather than the State, bear the expense of a federally mandated regulatory program, and they may continue to supplement that program to the extent state law is not pre-empted. Where Congress encourages state regulation, rather than compelling it, state governments remain responsive to the local electorate's preferences; state officials remain accountable to the people. . . .

But where the Federal Government directs the States to regulate, it may be state officials who will bear the brunt of public disapproval, while the federal officials who devised the regulatory program may remain insulated from the electoral ramifications of their decision. Accountability is thus diminished when, due to federal coercion, elected state officials cannot regulate in accordance with the views of the local electorate in matters not preempted by federal regulation.

With these principles in mind, we turn to the three challenged provisions of the Low-Level Radioactive Waste Policy Amendments Act of 1985.

C

[We uphold the first two provisions as legitimate exercises of the Spending Clause and the Commerce Clause, but] [t]he take-title provision is of a different character. This third so-called "incentive" offers States, as an alternative to regulating pursuant to Congress' direction, the option of taking title to and possession of the low level radioactive waste generated within their borders and becoming liable for all damages waste generators suffer as a result of the States' failure to do so promptly. In this provision, Congress has crossed the line distinguishing encouragement from

---

4 **Question:** Based on this paragraph, does O'Connor believe that the federal law at issue here is a valid exercise of the Commerce Clause?

coercion. . . . The take-title provision offers state governments a "choice" of either accepting ownership of waste or regulating according to the instructions of Congress. Respondents do not claim that the Constitution would authorize Congress to impose either option as a freestanding requirement. On one hand, the Constitution would not permit Congress simply to transfer radioactive waste from generators to state governments. Such a forced transfer, standing alone, would in principle be no different than a congressionally compelled subsidy from state governments to radioactive waste producers. The same is true of the provision requiring the States to become liable for the generators' damages. Standing alone, this provision would be indistinguishable from an Act of Congress directing the States to assume the liabilities of certain state residents. Either type of federal action would "commandeer" state governments into the service of federal regulatory purposes, and would, for this reason, be inconsistent with the Constitution's division of authority between federal and state governments. On the other hand, the second alternative held out to state governments—regulating pursuant to Congress' direction—would, standing alone, present a simple command to state governments to implement legislation enacted by Congress. As we have seen, the Constitution does not empower Congress to subject state governments to this type of instruction. . . .

A choice between two unconstitutionally coercive regulatory techniques is no choice at all. Either way, "the Act commandeers the legislative processes of the States by directly compelling them to enact and enforce a federal regulatory program," an outcome that has never been understood to lie within the authority conferred upon Congress by the Constitution. . . .[5]

12.1.2

Printz v. United States

521 U.S. 898 (1997)

New York was controversial among left-leaning academics and lawyers, who harshly questioned where the anticommandeering doctrine came from. But even *New York* was significantly less controversial than its follow-on case, *Printz v. United States*, 521 U.S. 898 (1997).

Printz arose because of an assassination attempt on President Ronald Reagan in 1981. Although the president fully recovered, his press secretary, James Brady, was partially paralyzed for the remainder of his life. Brady became a lifelong advocate of gun control. A nonprofit organization he led pushed Congress and President Bill Clinton to enact the Brady Handgun Violence Prevention Act of 1993 (Brady Act), Pub. L. No. 103–159, 107 Stat. 1536.

The basic thrust of the law was the creation of a national instant background-check system by 1998. For the five years until then, the law temporarily imposed a five-day waiting period in states without instant background checks before a firearms dealer was allowed to sell or transfer a handgun to a prospective buyer. On the first day of this five-day waiting period, the law required the dealer to provide a local "chief

5 **Questions:** Can you imagine a revised Low-Level Radioactive Waste Policy Amendments Act that meets the constitutional standard articulated by the Court? What changes would you propose to accomplish the same result sought by the act (i.e., to encourage states to reduce waste production levels) while satisfying O'Connor's objections?

law enforcement officer" (CLEO) with information about the prospective buyer. Brady Act § 102(a)(1). It then required the officer to "make a reasonable effort to ascertain within five business days whether receipt or possession would be in violation of the law, including research in whatever state and local recordkeeping systems are available and in a national system designated by the Attorney General." *Id.* § 102(a)(2). If the officer determined that a prospective buyer was ineligible to receive a handgun, the statute required him to provide the would-be buyer with a written statement of the reasons for that determination. *Id.* § 102(a)(3). If the officer didn't find anything objectionable about the purchase, the law required the officer to destroy any records relating to the transfer. *Id.* § 102(a)(6).

The National Rifle Association (NRA) lobbied extensively against the Brady Act. After it passed, the NRA recruited nine CLEOs—including Sheriff Jay Printz of Ravalli County, Montana, and Sheriff Richard Mack of Graham County, Arizona—to sue the Clinton administration. They argued that forcing CLEOs to enforce federal law violated the anticommandeering doctrine announced in *New York*. The Clinton administration responded that *New York* was limited to attempts to coerce states to *legislate*, not attempts to make state officials *enforce* federal law. After all, for much of American history, the federal government had relied on state officers to enforce federal law.

The *Printz* Court found the NRA's arguments more compelling.

■ JUSTICE SCALIA delivered the opinion of the Court.[6]

The question presented in these cases is whether certain interim provisions of the Brady Handgun Violence Prevention Act, commanding state and local law enforcement officers to conduct background checks on prospective handgun purchasers and to perform certain related tasks, violate the Constitution. . . .

[I]t is apparent that the Brady Act purports to direct state law enforcement officers to participate, albeit only temporarily, in the administration of a federally enacted regulatory scheme. Regulated firearms dealers are required to forward Brady Forms not to a federal officer or employee, but to the CLEOs. . . . While the CLEOs are subjected to no federal requirement that they prevent the sales determined to be unlawful (it is perhaps assumed that their state-law duties will require prevention or apprehension), they are empowered to grant, in effect, waivers of the federally prescribed 5-day waiting period for handgun purchases by notifying the gun dealers that they have no reason to believe the transactions would be illegal.

Petitioners here object to being pressed into federal service, and contend that congressional action compelling state officers to execute federal laws is unconstitutional. Because there is no constitutional text speaking to this precise question, the answer to the CLEOs' challenge must be sought in historical understanding and practice, in the structure of the Constitution, and in the

---

[6] **As You Read, Consider:** Does Justice Antonin Scalia defend the anticommandeering doctrine by invoking the same principles that Justice Sandra Day O'Connor announced in *New York v. United States*, or does he offer a different perspective on the doctrine?

jurisprudence of this Court.[7] We treat those three sources, in that order, in this and the next two sections of this opinion.

Petitioners contend that compelled enlistment of state executive officers for the administration of federal programs is, until very recent years at least, unprecedented. The Government contends, to the contrary, that "the earliest Congresses enacted statutes that required the participation of state officials in the implementation of federal laws." . . . The Government observes that statutes enacted by the first Congresses required state courts to record applications for citizenship, to transmit abstracts of citizenship applications and other naturalization records to the Secretary of State, and to register aliens seeking naturalization and issue certificates of registry. It may well be, however, that these requirements applied only in States that authorized their courts to conduct naturalization proceedings. Other statutes of that era apparently or at least arguably required state courts to perform functions unrelated to naturalization, such as resolving controversies between a captain and the crew of his ship concerning the seaworthiness of the vessel, hearing the claims of slave owners who had apprehended fugitive slaves and issuing certificates authorizing the slave's forced removal to the State from which he had fled [*see* Fugitive Slave Act of 1793], taking proof of the claims of Canadian refugees who had assisted the United States during the Revolutionary War, and ordering the deportation of alien enemies in times of war. . . .

These early laws establish, at most, that the Constitution was originally understood to permit imposition of an obligation on state *judges* to enforce federal prescriptions, insofar as those prescriptions related to matters appropriate for the judicial power. That assumption [was made explicit by] the Supremacy Clause, Art. VI, cl. 2, [which] announced that "the Laws of the United States . . . shall be the supreme Law of the Land; and the Judges in every State shall be bound thereby." It is understandable why courts should have been viewed distinctively in this regard; unlike legislatures and executives, they applied the law of other sovereigns all the time. . . .[8]

For these reasons, we do not think the early statutes imposing obligations on state courts imply a power of Congress to impress the state executive into its service. Indeed, it can be argued that the numerousness of these statutes, contrasted with the utter lack of statutes imposing obligations on the States' executive (notwithstanding the attractiveness of that course to Congress), suggests an assumed *absence* of such power. . . .

The constitutional practice we have examined above tends to negate the existence of the congressional power asserted here, but is not conclusive. We turn next to consideration of the structure of the Constitution . . . .

It is incontestible that the Constitution established a system of "dual sovereignty." We have set forth the historical record in more detail elsewhere, *see New York v. United States*, 505 U. S., at 161–166, and need not repeat it here. It suffices to repeat the conclusion: "the Framers explicitly chose a Constitution that confers upon Congress the power to regulate individuals, not States." The great innovation of this design was that "our citizens would have two political capacities, one state and one federal, each protected from incursion by the other"—"a legal system unprecedented in form and design, establishing two orders of government, each with its own direct

---

7 **Question:** Scalia observes that "no constitutional text" speaks to the precise question at issue. As you read the rest of his opinion, would you say (1) that he thinks the Brady Act is not a valid regulation of interstate commerce or (2) that he thinks the Brady Act is a valid regulation of interstate commerce but violates some nontextual limit?

8 **Question:** Do you agree with Scalia that this distinction between state *judges* and state *executive officers/legislators* is a principled distinction?

relationship, its own privity, its own set of mutual rights and obligations to the people who sustain it and are governed by it." . . . This separation of the two spheres is one of the Constitution's structural protections of liberty. "Just as the separation and independence of the coordinate branches of the Federal Government serve to prevent the accumulation of excessive power in any one branch, a healthy balance of power between the States and the Federal Government will reduce the risk of tyranny and abuse from either front." . . .

Finally, and most conclusively in the present litigation, we turn to the prior jurisprudence of this Court. [In *New York v. United States* (1992), we held that the federal government] "may not compel the States to enact or administer a federal regulatory program."

The Government contends that *New York* is distinguishable on the following ground: Unlike the "take title" provisions invalidated there, the background-check provision of the Brady Act does not require state legislative or executive officials to make policy, but instead issues a final directive to state CLEOs. It is permissible, the Government asserts, for Congress to command state or local officials to assist in the implementation of federal law so long as "Congress itself devises a clear legislative solution that regulates private conduct" and requires state or local officers to provide only "limited, non-policymaking help in enforcing that law." "[T]he constitutional line is crossed only when Congress compels the States to make law in their sovereign capacities." . . .

gov arg

The Government purports to find support for its proffered distinction of *New York* in our decisio[n] in *Testa v. Katt*, 330 U.S. 386 (1947). . . . [But] *Testa* stands for the proposition that state courts cannot refuse to apply federal law—a conclusion mandated by the terms of the Supremacy Clause ("the Judges in every State shall be bound [by federal law]"). As we have suggested earlier, that says nothing about whether state executive officers must administer federal law. . . . We held in *New York* that Congress cannot compel the States to enact or enforce a federal regulatory program. Today we hold that Congress cannot circumvent that prohibition by conscripting the States' officers directly. The Federal Government may neither issue directives requiring the States to address particular problems, nor command the States' officers, or those of their political subdivisions, to administer or enforce a federal regulatory program. It matters not whether policymaking is involved, and no case-by-case weighing of the burdens or benefits is necessary; such commands are fundamentally incompatible with our constitutional system of dual sovereignty. . . .

dual sovereignty

■ JUSTICE STEVENS, with whom JUSTICE SOUTER, JUSTICE GINSBURG, and JUSTICE BREYER join, dissenting.

When Congress exercises the powers delegated to it by the Constitution, it may impose affirmative obligations on executive and judicial officers of state and local governments as well as ordinary citizens. This conclusion is firmly supported by the text of the Constitution, the early history of the Nation, decisions of this Court, and a correct understanding of the basic structure of the Federal Government.

These cases do not implicate the more difficult questions associated with congressional coercion of state legislatures addressed in *New York v. United States* (1992). . . . The question is whether Congress, acting on behalf of the people of the entire Nation, may require local law enforcement officers to perform certain duties during the interim needed for the development of a federal gun control program. It is remarkably similar to the question, heavily debated by the Framers of the Constitution, whether Congress could require state agents to collect federal taxes. Or the question whether Congress could impress state judges into federal service to entertain and decide cases that they would prefer to ignore.

Indeed, since the ultimate issue is one of power, we must consider its implications in times of national emergency. Matters such as the enlistment of air raid wardens, the administration of a military draft, the mass inoculation of children to forestall an epidemic, or perhaps the threat of an international terrorist, may require a national response before federal personnel can be made available to respond. If the Constitution empowers Congress and the President to make an appropriate response, is there anything in the Tenth Amendment, . . . that forbids the enlistment of state officers to make that response effective? More narrowly, what basis is there in any of those sources for concluding that it is the Members of this Court, rather than the elected representatives of the people, who should determine whether the Constitution contains the unwritten rule that the Court announces today? . . .[9]

12.1.3

Murphy v. National Collegiate Athletic Ass'n

138 S. Ct. 1461 (2018)

For over two decades, *Printz* was the Court's last word on the anticommandeering doctrine. When similar cases arose, the Court distinguished *New York* or *Printz* on various grounds. Most significantly, in *Reno v. Condon*, 528 U.S. 141 (2000), the Court upheld the Driver's Privacy Protection Act of 1994 (DPPA), Pub. L. No. 103–332, 108 Stat. 1796, which prohibited the disclosure of personal information contained in the records of state motor vehicle departments (DMVs). The Court distinguished *New York* and *Printz* as laws that applied to states alone, whereas the DPPA was a law of "general applicability" that applied to individuals as well as state DMVs. *Condon*, 528 U.S. at 151. In other words, Congress *may* direct state officers to abide by a federal law—but only when the federal law applies to *everyone*, states and individuals.

Nearly twenty years after *Condon*, when it appeared that *Printz* and *New York* may be dead letters, the Court in *Murphy v. National Collegiate Athletic Ass'n*, 138 S. Ct. 1461 (2018), applied the anticommandeering doctrine to a new type of federal statute: one that prohibited states from passing certain laws. This sort of statute presented a puzzle. On the one hand, as discussed previously (section 11.2), when a federal statute *preempts* a state law, it supersedes state law—effectively, but not directly, prohibiting a state from passing legislation on a particular issue. No one on the Court questioned Congress's power to continue to preempt state laws. On the other hand, as discussed in *New York* and *Printz*, majorities of the Court believed that Congress has no power to issue *direct orders* to a state legislature or its officers—at least as long as it is not also regulating private

[9] **Question:** The political valence of the anticommandeering doctrine has shifted since the left-leaning justices all dissented in 1997. During the administration of President Donald Trump, for example, many Democratic-run states and local governments refused to cooperate with the federal government's efforts to arrest, detain, and deport certain immigrants. Given all the ways that the federal government can induce states and local governments to enforce its policies—by withholding funds, for example, or by regulating private individuals and preempting contrary state laws—does the anticommandeering doctrine serve a principled function?

individuals. Yet, it is not always obvious when a law *preempts* a state law and when it *orders* a state not to pass certain laws.

In *Murphy*, Congress passed a law that prohibited states from authorizing sports gambling. The federal government's lawyers argued that the federal prohibition was a classic example of express preemption. But New Jersey, which wanted to legalize sports gambling, argued that the federal law fell within the *New York* and *Printz* anticommandeering doctrine because it applied only to states and directly ordered state legislatures not to pass certain laws.

The *Murphy* Court agreed with New Jersey.

■ JUSTICE ALITO delivered the opinion of the Court.[10]

The State of New Jersey wants to legalize sports gambling at casinos and horseracing tracks, but a federal law, the Professional and Amateur Sports Protection Act, generally makes it unlawful for a State to "authorize" sports gambling schemes. We must decide whether this provision is compatible with the system of "dual sovereignty" embodied in the Constitution. . . .

PASPA's most important provision, part of which is directly at issue in these cases, makes it "unlawful" for a State or any of its subdivisions "to sponsor, operate, advertise, promote, license, or authorize by law or compact . . . a lottery, sweepstakes, or other betting, gambling, or wagering scheme based . . . on" competitive sporting events. . . . PASPA does not make sports gambling a federal crime (and thus was not anticipated to impose a significant law enforcement burden on the Federal Government). Instead, PASPA allows the Attorney General, as well as professional and amateur sports organizations, to bring civil actions to enjoin violations. . . .

[Between 2011 and 2014, New Jersey passed two statutes, one of which repealed its ban on sports gambling.] The major professional sports leagues and the NCAA brought an action in federal court against the New Jersey Governor and other state officials (hereinafter New Jersey), seeking to enjoin the new law on the ground that it violated PASPA. In response, the State argued, among other things, that PASPA unconstitutionally infringed the State's sovereign authority to end its sports gambling ban.

In making this argument, the State relied primarily on two cases, *New York v. United States*, 505 U.S. 144 (1992), and *Printz v. United States*, 521 U.S. 898 (1997), in which we struck down federal laws based on what has been dubbed the "anticommandeering" principle. In *New York*, we held that a federal law unconstitutionally ordered the State to regulate in accordance with federal standards, and in *Printz*, we found that another federal statute unconstitutionally compelled state officers to enforce federal law.

Relying on these cases, New Jersey argued that PASPA is similarly flawed because it regulates a State's exercise of its lawmaking power by prohibiting it from modifying or repealing its laws prohibiting sports gambling. The plaintiffs countered that PASPA is critically different from the commandeering cases because it does not command the States to take any affirmative act. Without an affirmative federal

---

[10] **As You Read, Consider:** Where in the Constitution does Justice Samuel Alito locate the anticommandeering doctrine?

What test does he announce for how to distinguish a valid federal law that *preempts* state laws from an invalid federal law that commandeers state legislatures?

command to *do* something, the plaintiffs insisted, there can be no claim of commandeering. . . .

The anticommandeering doctrine may sound arcane, but it is simply the expression of a fundamental structural decision incorporated into the Constitution, *i.e.*, the decision to withhold from Congress the power to issue orders directly to the States. When the original States declared their independence, they claimed the powers inherent in sovereignty—in the words of the Declaration of Independence, the authority "to do all . . . Acts and Things which Independent States may of right do." The Constitution limited but did not abolish the sovereign powers of the States, which retained "a residuary and inviolable sovereignty." Thus, both the Federal Government and the States wield sovereign powers, and that is why our system of government is said to be one of "dual sovereignty."

The Constitution limits state sovereignty in several ways. It directly prohibits the States from exercising some attributes of sovereignty. See, *e.g.*, Art. I, § 10. Some grants of power to the Federal Government have been held to impose implicit restrictions on the States. And the Constitution indirectly restricts the States by granting certain legislative powers to Congress, see Art. I, § 8, while providing in the Supremacy Clause that federal law is the "supreme Law of the Land . . . any Thing in the Constitution or Laws of any State to the Contrary notwithstanding," Art. VI, cl. 2. This means that when federal and state law conflict, federal law prevails and state law is preempted.

The legislative powers granted to Congress are sizable, but they are not unlimited. The Constitution confers on Congress not plenary legislative power but only certain enumerated powers. Therefore, all other legislative power is reserved for the States, as the Tenth Amendment confirms. And conspicuously absent from the list of powers given to Congress is the power to issue direct orders to the governments of the States. The anticommandeering doctrine simply represents the recognition of this limit on congressional authority.[11]

Although the anticommandeering principle is simple and basic, it did not emerge in our cases until relatively recently, when Congress attempted in a few isolated instances to extend its authority in unprecedented ways. The pioneering case was *New York v. United States*, 505 U.S. 144 (1992), which concerned a federal law that required a State, under certain circumstances, either to "take title" to low-level radioactive waste or to "regulat[e] according to the instructions of Congress." *Id.* at 175. . . . [The Court held that] the provision was unconstitutional because "the Constitution does not empower Congress to subject state governments to this type of instruction." *Id.* at 176. . . .

Five years after *New York*, the Court applied the same principles to a federal statute requiring state and local law enforcement officers to perform background checks and related tasks in connection with applications for handgun licenses. *Printz*, 521 U.S. 898. Holding this provision unconstitutional, the Court put the point succinctly: "The Federal Government" may not "command the States' officers, or those of their political subdivisions, to administer or enforce a federal regulatory program." *Id.* at 935. This rule applies, *Printz* held, not only to state officers with policymaking responsibility but also to those assigned more mundane tasks. *Id.* at 929–930. . . .

---

[11] **Question:** Does Alito's discussion here suggest that the anticommandeering doctrine is a freestanding limit on Congress's power to regulate, or does he think that it is analogous to gaps in Congress's Article I powers, such as Congress's inability to regulate intrastate, noneconomic activity under the Commerce Clause?

Our opinions in *New York* and *Printz* explained why adherence to the anticommandeering principle is important. . . . First, the rule serves as "one of the Constitution's structural protections of liberty." *Printz, supra*, at 921. . . . Second, [it] promotes political accountability. . . . *See New York, supra*, at 168–169; *Printz, supra*, at 929–930. . . . Third, [it] prevents Congress from shifting the costs of regulation to the States. If Congress enacts a law and requires enforcement by the Executive Branch, it must appropriate the funds needed to administer the program. It is pressured to weigh the expected benefits of the program against its costs. But if Congress can compel the States to enact and enforce its program, Congress need not engage in any such analysis. . . .

The PASPA provision at issue here—prohibiting state authorization of sports gambling—violates the anticommandeering rule. That provision unequivocally dictates what a state legislature may and may not do. And this is true under either our interpretation or that advocated by respondents and the United States. In either event, state legislatures are put under the direct control of Congress. It is as if federal officers were installed in state legislative chambers and were armed with the authority to stop legislators from voting on any offending proposals. A more direct affront to state sovereignty is not easy to imagine.

Neither respondents nor the United States contends that Congress can compel a State to enact legislation, but they say that prohibiting a State from enacting new laws is another matter. Noting that the laws challenged in *New York* and *Printz* "told states what they must do instead of what they must not do," respondents contend that commandeering occurs "only when Congress goes beyond precluding state action and affirmatively commands it." . . . This distinction is empty. It was a matter of happenstance that the laws challenged in *New York* and *Printz* commanded "affirmative" action as opposed to imposing a prohibition. The basic principle—that Congress cannot issue direct orders to state legislatures—applies in either event. . . .

Respondents and the United States [also] defend the anti-authorization prohibition on the ground that it constitutes a valid preemption provision, but it is no such thing. Preemption is based on the Supremacy Clause, and that Clause is not an independent grant of legislative power to Congress. Instead, it simply provides "a rule of decision." It specifies that federal law is supreme in case of a conflict with state law. Therefore, in order for the PASPA provision to preempt state law, it must satisfy two requirements. First, it must represent the exercise of a power conferred on Congress by the Constitution; pointing to the Supremacy Clause will not do. Second, since the Constitution "confers upon Congress the power to regulate individuals, not States," *New York*, the PASPA provision at issue must be best read as one that regulates private actors.

Our cases have identified three different types of preemption—"conflict," "express," and "field"—but all of them work in the same way: Congress enacts a law that imposes restrictions or confers rights on private actors; a state law confers rights or imposes restrictions that conflict with the federal law; and therefore the federal law takes precedence and the state law is preempted.

This mechanism is shown most clearly in cases involving "conflict preemption." A recent example is *Mutual Pharmaceutical Co. v. Bartlett* (2013). In that case, a federal law enacted under the Commerce Clause regulated manufacturers of generic drugs, prohibiting them from altering either the composition or labeling approved by the Food and Drug Administration. A State's tort law, however, effectively required a manufacturer to supplement the warnings included in the FDA-approved label. We held that the state law was preempted because it imposed a duty that was inconsistent—*i.e.*, in conflict—with federal law.

"Express preemption" operates in essentially the same way, but this is often obscured by the language used by Congress in framing preemption provisions. The provision at issue in *Morales v. Trans World Airlines, Inc.* (1992) is illustrative. The Airline Deregulation Act of 1978 lifted prior federal regulations of airlines, and "[t]o ensure that the States would not undo federal deregulation with regulation of their own," the Act provided that "no State or political subdivision thereof . . . shall enact or enforce any law, rule, regulation, standard, or other provision having the force and effect of law relating to rates, routes, or services of any [covered] air carrier." This language might appear to operate directly on the States, but it is a mistake to be confused by the way in which a preemption provision is phrased. . . . [If] we look beyond the phrasing employed in the Airline Deregulation Act's preemption provision, it is clear that this provision operates just like any other federal law with preemptive effect. It confers on private entities (i.e., covered carriers) a federal right to engage in certain conduct subject only to certain (federal) constraints.

"Field preemption" operates in the same way. Field preemption occurs when federal law occupies a "field" of regulation "so comprehensively that it has left no room for supplementary state legislation." *R. J. Reynolds Tobacco Co. v. Durham County* (1986). In describing field preemption, we have sometimes used the same sort of shorthand employed by Congress in express preemption provisions. But in substance, field preemption does not involve congressional commands to the States. Instead, like all other forms of preemption, it concerns a clash between a constitutional exercise of Congress's legislative power and conflicting state law. . . .

In sum, regardless of the language sometimes used by Congress and this Court, every form of preemption is based on a federal law that regulates the conduct of private actors, not the States.

Once this is understood, it is clear that the PASPA provision prohibiting state authorization of sports gambling is not a preemption provision because there is no way in which this provision can be understood as a regulation of private actors. It certainly does not confer any federal rights on private actors interested in conducting sports gambling operations. . . . Nor does it impose any federal restrictions on private actors. If a private citizen or company started a sports gambling operation, either with or without state authorization, [PASPA] would not be violated and would not provide any ground for a civil action by the Attorney General or any other party. Thus, there is simply no way to understand the provision prohibiting state authorization as anything other than a direct command to the States. And that is exactly what the anticommandeering rule does not allow. . . .[12]

NOTE: ANTICOMMANDEERING DOCTRINE AND ITS MANY EXCEPTIONS

No one on the *Murphy* Court objected to the anticommandeering doctrine—not even Justices Stephen Breyer and Ruth Bader Ginsburg, who both dissented in *Printz*. Yet the anticommandeering doctrine remains controversial, in part because it is riddled with exceptions. Congress may not require state legislatures to enforce federal law, as in *New York*—but it may require state judges to enforce federal law, as in *Testa v. Katt*, 330 U.S. 386 (1947). It also may require state governors to enforce the Extradition Clause,

[12] **Question:** Applying Alito's reasoning in *Murphy v. National Collegiate Athletic Ass'n*, if Congress were interested in prohibiting sports gambling despite state laws authorizing it, how might Congress amend the Professional and Amateur Sports Protection Act to be constitutional?

as in *Puerto Rico v. Branstad*, 483 U.S. 219 (1987). Congress also may not tell state executive officials what to do, as in *Printz*—unless the order is part of a generally applicable regulatory scheme, as in *Garcia v. San Antonio Metropolitan Transit Authority*, 469 U.S. 528 (1985) (affirming Congress's authority to regulate public and private mass-transit systems), or *Reno v. Condon*, 528 U.S. 141 (2000) (same for public and private entities that disperse information regarding motor vehicles). And Congress may not prohibit states from legislating, as in *Murphy*—but it may preempt contrary state legislation, as in *Hines v. Davidowitz*, 312 U.S. 52 (1941) (finding that Pennsylvania's state immigrant registration system was preempted by the federal Alien Registration Act), or *Arizona v. United States*, 567 U.S. 387 (2012) (finding that Arizona's immigration laws were preempted by the Immigration and Naturalization Act).

12.2 ARTICLE 1, SECTION 9

In contrast with the anticommandeering doctrine, which is an implied limit on Congress's power, there are numerous express limits on Congress's power listed in Article I, Section 9. Previous sections discussed several of Section 9's limits that relate to taxing and spending, including the prohibition on regulating the slave trade before 1808 (section 5.2), the requirement that "direct taxes" be apportioned on the basis of each state's population (section 4.1), and the prohibition on withdrawing money from the Treasury without a congressional appropriation (section 6.3). Most of the other limits apply to Congress's regulatory or criminal powers.

Clause 3

The most commonly litigated clause in Section 9 is likely Clause 3, the prohibition on any "Bill of Attainder or ex post facto Law." This prohibition protects "one of the most 'widely held value-judgment[s] in the entire history of human thought' ": the principle that no one should be punished for doing something that was not prohibited by law when it was done. *Rogers v. Tennessee*, 532 U.S. 451, 468 (2001) (Scalia, J., dissenting) (quoting J. Hall, *General Principles of Criminal Law* 59 (2d ed. 1960)).

The prohibition has roots in perceived abuses by Parliament against its political enemies. Before the eighteenth century, when members of Parliament wished to see someone punished, they could call for a costly and time-consuming indictment—or, alternatively, they could pass a statute simply declaring the person guilty of an offense. *See* 3 James Wilson, *Of Crimes, Immediately Against the Community, in The Works of the Honourable James Wilson* 95, 96 (Bird Wilson ed., 1804). During the reign of Henry VIII, for example, Parliament enacted a law declaring that a group of named Irish leaders were "attainted, adjudged, and convicted of high treason," which meant that their property should be confiscated and they should be executed as if they had been found guilty of treason by a jury. *See* 4 William Blackstone, *Commentaries* *44. These sorts of laws became known as *bills of attainder* because their effect was to "attaint," or extinguish, the civil and legal rights of a person, including the person's right to live or devise property. When a bill of attainder retroactively declared it a crime to do whatever the named person had done, the bill was also an *ex post facto law*, meaning that it punished conduct "after the fact."

Bills of attainder and ex post facto laws were heavily criticized by American lawyers after the revolution, and the Constitutional Convention's decision to prohibit both Congress and states from passing them was relatively uncontroversial. *Letter from James Madison to Thomas Jefferson* (Apr. 16, 1781), *reprinted in* 1 The Writings of James Madison 276 (Gaillard Hunt ed., 1900).

The meaning of the term *ex post facto* proved to be ambiguous, however, as litigants argued that all laws that applied retroactively were unconstitutional. In *Calder v. Bull*, 3 U.S. (3 Dall.) 386 (1798), one of the first landmark Supreme Court decisions, the Court disagreed. The justices concluded that the prohibition on ex post facto laws referred only to *criminal* or *punitive* laws that retroactively (1) punished someone for doing something that was not a crime when it was done or (2) inflicted a greater punishment for a crime than the law at the time would have permitted. *Id.* at 389 (opinion of Chase, J.).

Oaths of nonparticipation in Confederate rebellion. The first time the Supreme Court struck down a law as a bill of attainder or ex post facto law was in the aftermath of the Civil War.

After the assassination of President Abraham Lincoln, his successor, Andrew Johnson, announced an extremely lenient amnesty program that pardoned most southerners who took an oath declaring their allegiance to the Union and the Thirteenth Amendment. *See* Eric Foner, *Reconstruction* 182–83 (2014). The pardons infuriated members of Congress as well as legislators in border states like Missouri, who demanded laws to prevent former Confederates from regaining their power and influence. *Id.* To counter the pardons, Congress, in an act of retribution against the Confederacy, passed a statute prohibiting attorneys from practicing in any federal court unless they took an oath that they had taken no part in the Confederate rebellion. Missouri, for its part, extended a similar prohibition and oath to anyone who wanted to practice as a professor, teacher, corporate official, priest, or officer of the state.

In the companion cases of *Ex parte Garland*, 71 U.S. (4 Wall.) 333 (1867), and *Cummings v. Missouri*, 71 U.S. (4 Wall.) 277 (1867), the Supreme Court struck down both laws for violating the prohibition on bills of attainder and ex post facto laws. The intention of the constitutional prohibition, the Court explained in *Cummings*, was "that the rights of the citizen should be secure against deprivation for past conduct by legislative enactment, under any form, however disguised."

Cummings, 71 U.S. (4 Wall.) at 325. Even though the federal and Missouri laws didn't expressly declare that former Confederates were guilty of treason and barred from practicing law or religion, the requirement that lawyers and clergy take an oath declaring that they had never been part of the Confederate rebellion was functionally identical. "The disabilities . . . must be regarded as penalties—they constitute punishment," the Court wrote. *Id.* at 320. The laws deprived people of their rights to practice certain professions or inhabit certain offices, which the Court regarded as a deprivation equivalent to what one would expect after a criminal conviction. *Id.* at 327–31. Furthermore, neither Congress nor Missouri had, before the Civil War, enacted laws declaring that participation in a rebellion could result in the inability to practice law or religion, meaning that the punishments had been imposed retroactively. *Id.* By naming a group of people and punishing them without a trial, the laws violated the Constitution's prohibition on bills of attainder. And by inflicting greater punishment on this group of people beyond whatever statutory punishments existed at the time of the rebellion, the laws violated the prohibition on ex post facto laws. *Id.* at 331–32.

Punishment versus regulation. In the 150 years since *Garland* and *Cummings*, litigation around the prohibition on bills of attainder and ex post facto laws has tended to focus on whether a law is an invalid *punishment* for past conduct or, instead, a valid *regulation* of future conduct.

For example, in *Murphy v. Ramsey*, 114 U.S. 15 (1885), the Court upheld a law that denied polygamists the right to vote. The Court explained that the law was a valid regulation of future voting standards, not a punishment for past acts of polygamy. 114 U.S. at 43. But in *United States v. Brown*, 381 U.S. 437 (1965), the Court struck down a law that made it a crime for a Communist to serve as an employee of a labor union. The *Brown* Court explained that the law was designed to punish Communists for their previous actions rather than to regulate who should be allowed to serve in a labor union. 381 U.S. at 450. The difference between an invalid punishment and a valid regulation, the Court emphasized, was that a punishment applied to certain people exclusively because of their past conduct, whereas a regulation created an objective standard of conduct that generally applied to all people who possess certain characteristics or who are likely to commit certain acts in the future. *Id.* at 453–60.

In later cases, the Court added that whether a law is a punishment depends on a multifactor test that includes an examination of the legislature's expressed intent, the unstated purpose of the law, and the law's effects. *Seling v. Young*, 531 U.S. 250 (2001); *see, e.g., Flemming v. Nestor,* 363 U.S. 603 (1960) (upholding a law denying pensions to deported immigrants, including an alleged Communist, because the law was a regulation of pensions to keep them administrable, not a punishment of a belief in Communism); *United States v. Lovett*, 328 U.S. 303 (1946) (striking down a law forbidding the executive branch from paying the salaries of three named alleged Communists).

Clause 6

Far less commonly litigated is Section 9, Clause 6, which declares that "[n]o Preference shall be given by any Regulation of Commerce or Revenue to the Ports of one State over those of another."

In the few cases to interpret this clause, the Court has explained that the clause's purpose was to prevent Congress from preferring certain ports because of their location in a particular state—for example, by directing foreign commerce to go through Connecticut's ports rather than through New York's ports. The clause does not, by contrast, prevent Congress from allowing states to supervise and regulate the entry into their ports. *Thompson v. Darden*, 198 U.S. 310 (1905). The clause also doesn't prohibit Congress from discriminating among individual ports because of their geographic uniqueness. "Congress, acting under the commerce clause, causes many things to be done that greatly benefit particular ports and which incidentally result to the disadvantage of other ports in the same or neighboring States," the Court explained in *Louisiana Public Service Commission v. Texas & New Orleans Railroad*. 284 U.S. 125, 131 (1931). "The establishing of ports of entry, erection and operation of lighthouses, improvement of rivers and harbors, and the providing of structures for the convenient and economical handling of traffic, are examples. . . . It is clear that the Constitution does not forbid [these things]." *Id.* at 131–32.

Clause 8

Another clause of Section 9 that has not been the subject of much litigation—but that may prove to be important in the future—is Clause 8, which declares, "No Title of Nobility shall be granted by the United States: And no Person holding any Office of Profit or Trust under them, shall, without the Consent of the Congress, accept of any present, Emolument, Office, or Title, of any kind whatever, from any King, Prince, or foreign State."

Until recently, the most important aspect of this clause was its prohibition on titles of nobility. *See, e.g.*, 13 Op. Att'y Gen. 538 (1871) (opinion of Attorney General Amos T. Akerman explaining that the clause allows foreign ministers to work for foreign nations up to the point of creating an official relationship between the minister and the foreign government).

However, since the election of President Donald Trump, several litigants have invoked the clause's prohibition on the acceptance of "[e]molument[s]" to challenge the president's decision to knowingly profit from his hotels and other businesses that catered to foreign diplomats and state-owned businesses. Litigants challenging Trump's alleged violation of the Emoluments Clause argued that *emolument* refers broadly to a salary, profit, or other monetary interest. Under this interpretation, the clause prohibits anyone in the executive or judicial branches from receiving any money from anyone affiliated with a foreign government—even if that money comes indirectly in the form of owning shares in a company that does business with foreign countries.

During Trump's presidency, however, no federal appeals court considered the question on the merits. *See, e.g., Citizens for Resp. & Ethics in Wash. v. Trump*, 939 F.3d 131 (2d Cir. 2019) (holding that the plaintiffs had standing to sue and remanding for determination on the merits); *In re Trump*, 928 F.3d 360 (4th Cir. 2019) (dismissing for lack of standing); *Blumenthal v. Trump*, 949 F.3d 14 (D.C. Cir. 2020) (dismissing for lack of standing). In January 2021, after Trump's term in office expired, the Supreme Court dismissed the still-pending litigation as moot.

12.3 THE BILL OF RIGHTS

Most members of the Constitutional Convention, including James Madison, believed that the enumerated powers of Article I, Section 8, and the enumerated limits of Article I, Section 9, were sufficient to ensure that Congress would not become an abusive central government. But several delegates complained that Section 9 was too short: it omitted a lengthy declaration of rights protecting the freedom of conscience, the freedom of the press, and the protection against deprivations without due process of law. 2 *The Records of the Federal Convention of 1787*, at 587–88, 617–18 (Max Farrand ed., 1911). Although these delegates were outvoted during the convention, the omission of a bill of rights proved to be a major sticking point during the debates over ratification. Several state conventions, from Massachusetts to Virginia, demanded that the first Congress add a bill of rights to the Constitution as amendments.

The ratification debates convinced Madison and other members of the first Congress in 1789 to draft a bill of rights. Nevertheless, Madison may never have been entirely convinced that a federal bill of rights was truly necessary. In contrast with state constitutions, which typically gave state legislatures plenary powers subject to the enumerated limits of a state's own bill of rights, the U.S. Constitution gave Congress only a handful of enumerated powers that each had their own implied limits. Moreover, in contrast with state legislation, which typically applied domestically and could regulate any aspect of a person's life, Congress was expected to spend most of its time regulating foreign commerce, imposts, and other things that only indirectly affected Americans' daily lives. Accordingly, Madison expected that a federal bill of rights would rarely be invoked as a limit on Congress's power. *See* Michael J. Klarman, *The Framers' Coup: The Making of the United States Constitution* 547 (2016).

Madison's prediction proved to be correct—at least for the country's first seventy-five years. Before the Civil War, the Supreme Court only once struck down a major law for violating one of the amendments to the Constitution. That case was *Dred Scott v. Sandford*, 60 U.S. (19 How.) 393 (1857). The Court in *Dred Scott* went out of its way to declare that Congress had no power to abolish slavery in northern territories because of the Fifth Amendment's declaration that "No person shall . . . be deprived of . . . property, without due process of law." *Dred Scott*, 60 U.S. (19 How.) at 450. The Court's protection of the property interests of enslavers was an inauspicious start to its use of the Bill of Rights to strike down legislation.

For years after *Dred Scott*, the Court rarely invoked the federal Bill of Rights as a limit on Congress's power. Far more often, as Madison predicted, the Court instead evaluated whether Congress had exceeded one of its enumerated powers, such as its taxing power or its power to regulate commerce. Although the Court often invoked the Tenth Amendment to explain the limits on Congress's enumerated powers, it generally invoked the Tenth Amendment not as a freestanding limit but as an illustration of the Constitution's structure.

Even today, the Bill of Rights is infrequently invoked against Congress relative to the other limits on its power. Yet the Bill of Rights has always been an important *conceptual* limit on Congress's power. For example, no exercise of Congress's spending power is valid if it deprives someone of a jury trial in violation of the Seventh Amendment, and no regulation of interstate commerce is valid if it constitutes cruel and unusual punishment in violation of the Eighth Amendment.

12.3.1

District of Columbia v. Heller

554 U.S. 570 (2008)

An important illustration of the historical and practical role of the Bill of Rights as a limit on Congress's power is the Supreme Court's interpretation of the Second Amendment. The Second Amendment declares, in full, "A well regulated Militia, being necessary to the security of a free State, the right of the people to keep and bear Arms, shall not be infringed."

Over the years, this oddly structured sentence has lent itself to two interpretations. One, a "states' rights" reading, interprets the sentence as a protection of state militias. Adherents of this reading emphasize that the states that fought the Revolutionary War did so by raising and maintaining militias of local volunteers. Under this reading, the Second Amendment therefore prohibits Congress from interfering with states' regulations of their militias or their armaments. The alternative interpretation, an "individual's right" reading, views the sentence as a protection of an individual's right of self-defense. Adherents of this reading stress that before the Constitution was ratified, individuals had "the right . . . to keep and bear Arms" in order to defend themselves and their communities. Under this reading, the Second Amendment prohibits Congress from interfering with that preexisting right.

For two hundred years or so, the "states' rights" interpretation of the Second Amendment was the dominant one among Supreme Court justices. This interpretation was most prominently illustrated after Congress passed the National Firearms Act of 1934, Pub. L. No. 474, 48 Stat. 1236, which required owners of sawed-off shotguns and other specified firearms to register their firearms with the government. When a resident of Arkansas, Jack Miller, was indicted for violating the law, he complained that the Second Amendment prohibited Congress from regulating the personal ownership of firearms. But in *United States v. Miller*, 307 U.S. 174 (1939), the Court invoked the states' rights interpretation of the Second Amendment to sustain the law and the indictment. The Court explained that the Constitution recognized the existence of state militias and their role in winning the Revolutionary War. "With obvious purpose to assure the continuation and render possible the effectiveness of such forces," the Court wrote, "the declaration and guarantee of the Second Amendment were made. It must be interpreted and applied with that end in view." *Miller*, 307 U.S. at 178. Interpreting the Second Amendment to preserve state militias, the Court concluded that

> [i]n the absence of any evidence tending to show that possession or use of a "shotgun having a barrel of less than eighteen inches in length" at this time has some reasonable relationship to the preservation or efficiency of a well regulated militia, we cannot say that the Second Amendment guarantees the right to keep and bear such an instrument.

Id.

On the basis of *Miller*, Congress considered several proposals for the national registration or prohibition of firearms. *See, e.g.*, Gun Control Act of 1968, Pub. L. No. 90–351, 82 Stat. 226; Nat'l Comm'n on Reform of Fed. Crim. L., *Final Report* (1971).

Beginning in the 1980s, however, legal scholars began to defend the "individual's right" interpretation of the Second Amendment as being more consistent with how the Second Amendment would have been understood when it was ratified in the 1790s. *See, e.g.*, Stephen P. Halbrook, *That Every Man Be Armed* (1984); Don B. Kates Jr., *Handgun Prohibition and the Original Meaning of the Second Amendment*, 82 Mich. L. Rev. 204 (1984). By the 2000s, prominent conservative and libertarian scholars had reached a consensus that *Miller* was wrongly decided. They argued that the Second Amendment protects an individual's right to own a firearm regardless of whether the firearm is reasonably related to a militia. *See, e.g.*, Randy E. Barnett, *Was the Right to Keep and Bear Arms Conditioned on Service in an Organized Militia?*,

83 Tex. L. Rev. 237 (2004) (book review); Eugene Volokh, *Necessary to the Security of a Free State*, 83 Notre Dame L. Rev. 1 (2007).

In 2004, a federal police officer named Dick Heller invoked the "individual's right" interpretation of the Second Amendment to challenge a code of federal laws that, in effect, prohibited the ownership of handguns within the District of Columbia. Overlapping provisions of the Code made it a crime for anyone to carry an unregistered firearm. They also prohibited anyone from registering a handgun. Although the Code allowed some exceptions to these prohibitions, it required all lawfully owned firearms to be kept "unloaded and dissembled or bound by a trigger lock or similar device," even when in a home. *Dist. of Columbia v. Heller*, 554 U.S. 570, 575 (2008). The net effect of these laws meant that Heller was allowed to carry a handgun while he was on duty protecting federal property, but he was not allowed to keep any handguns in his home, nor could he keep a long gun in his home without a trigger lock.

In *District of Columbia v. Heller*, 554 U.S. 570 (2008), the Court ruled in favor of Heller.

■ JUSTICE SCALIA delivered the opinion of the Court.[13]

We consider whether a District of Columbia prohibition on the possession of usable handguns in the home violates the Second Amendment to the Constitution. . . . We turn first to the meaning of the Second Amendment.

A

The Second Amendment provides: "A well regulated Militia, being necessary to the security of a free State, the right of the people to keep and bear Arms, shall not be infringed." In interpreting this text, we are guided by the principle that "[t]he Constitution was written to be understood by the voters; its words and phrases were used in their normal and ordinary as distinguished from technical meaning." Normal meaning may of course include an idiomatic meaning, but it excludes secret or technical meanings that would not have been known to ordinary citizens in the founding generation.

The two sides in this case have set out very different interpretations of the Amendment. Petitioners and today's dissenting Justices believe that it protects only the right to possess and carry a firearm in connection with militia service. Respondent argues that it protects an individual right to possess a firearm unconnected with service in a militia, and to use that arm for traditionally lawful purposes, such as self-defense within the home.

The Second Amendment is naturally divided into two parts: its prefatory clause and its operative clause. The former does not limit the latter grammatically, but rather announces a purpose. The Amendment could be rephrased, "Because a well regulated Militia is necessary to the security of a free State, the right of the people to keep and bear Arms shall not be infringed." See J. Tiffany, A Treatise on Government and Constitutional Law § 585, p. 394 (1867); Brief for Professors of Linguistics and English as *Amici Curiae* 3 (hereinafter Linguists' Brief). Although this structure of the Second Amendment is unique in our Constitution, other legal documents of the founding era, particularly individual-rights provisions of state constitutions, commonly

[13] **As You Read, Consider:** What principles does Justice Antonin Scalia consider to make sense of the Second Amendment's ambiguous language? Are they the same principles that Justice John Paul Stevens invokes in dissent, or do the two justices emphasize different values?

included a prefatory statement of purpose. See generally Volokh, The Commonplace Second Amendment, 73 N.Y.U. L. Rev. 793, 814–821 (1998).

Logic demands that there be a link between the stated purpose and the command. The Second Amendment would be nonsensical if it read, "A well regulated Militia, being necessary to the security of a free State, the right of the people to petition for redress of grievances shall not be infringed." That requirement of logical connection may cause a prefatory clause to resolve an ambiguity in the operative clause. ("The separation of church and state being an important objective, the teachings of canons shall have no place in our jurisprudence." The preface makes clear that the operative clause refers not to canons of interpretation but to clergymen.) But apart from that clarifying function, a prefatory clause does not limit or expand the scope of the operative clause. . . . Therefore, while we will begin our textual analysis with the operative clause, we will return to the prefatory clause to ensure that our reading of the operative clause is consistent with the announced purpose.

1. Operative Clause.

a. "Right of the People." The first salient feature of the operative clause is that it codifies a "right of the people." The unamended Constitution and the Bill of Rights use the phrase "right of the people" two other times, in the First Amendment's Assembly-and-Petition Clause and in the Fourth Amendment's Search-and-Seizure Clause. The Ninth Amendment uses very similar terminology ("The enumeration in the Constitution, of certain rights, shall not be construed to deny or disparage others retained by the people"). All three of these instances unambiguously refer to individual rights, not "collective" rights, or rights that may be exercised only through participation in some corporate body.[14]

Three provisions of the Constitution refer to "the people" in a context other than "rights"—the famous preamble ("We the people"), § 2 of Article I (providing that "the people" will choose members of the House), and the Tenth Amendment (providing that those powers not given the Federal Government remain with "the States" or "the people"). Those provisions arguably refer to "the people" acting collectively—but they deal with the exercise or reservation of powers, not rights. Nowhere else in the Constitution does a "right" attributed to "the people" refer to anything other than an individual right.

What is more, in all six other provisions of the Constitution that mention "the people," the term unambiguously refers to all members of the political community, not an unspecified subset. . . .

This contrasts markedly with the phrase "the militia" in the prefatory clause. As we will describe below, the "militia" in colonial America consisted of a subset of "the people"—those who were male, able bodied, and within a certain age range. Reading the Second Amendment as protecting only the right to "keep and bear Arms" in an organized militia therefore fits poorly with the operative clause's description of the holder of that right as "the people."

We start therefore with a strong presumption that the Second Amendment right is exercised individually and belongs to all Americans.

b. "Keep and Bear Arms." We move now from the holder of the right—"the people"—to the substance of the right: "to keep and bear Arms."

Before addressing the verbs "keep" and "bear," we interpret their object: "Arms." The 18th-century meaning is no different from the meaning today. The 1773 edition

[14] **Question:** Do you agree that the First Amendment's protection of the "right of the people peaceably to assemble" unambiguously refers to an individual right, not a collective right?

of Samuel Johnson's dictionary defined "arms" as "[w]eapons of offence, or armour of defence." 1 Dictionary of the English Language 106 (4th ed.) (reprinted 1978) (hereinafter Johnson). . . . The term was applied, then as now, to weapons that were not specifically designed for military use and were not employed in a military capacity. . . .

Some have made the argument, bordering on the frivolous, that only those arms in existence in the 18th century are protected by the Second Amendment. We do not interpret constitutional rights that way. Just as the First Amendment protects modern forms of communications, and the Fourth Amendment applies to modern forms of search, the Second Amendment extends, prima facie, to all instruments that constitute bearable arms, even those that were not in existence at the time of the founding.

We turn to the phrases "keep arms" and "bear arms." Johnson defined "keep" as, most relevantly, "[t]o retain; not to lose," and "[t]o have in custody." Johnson 1095. Webster defined it as "[t]o hold; to retain in one's power or possession." No party has apprised us of an idiomatic meaning of "keep Arms." Thus, the most natural reading of "keep Arms" in the Second Amendment is to "have weapons."

The phrase "keep arms" was not prevalent in the written documents of the founding period that we have found, but there are a few examples, all of which favor viewing the right to "keep Arms" as an individual right unconnected with militia service. William Blackstone, for example, wrote that Catholics convicted of not attending service in the Church of England suffered certain penalties, one of which was that they were not permitted to "keep arms in their houses." 4 Commentaries on the Laws of England 55 (1769) (hereinafter Blackstone). . . .

At the time of the founding, as now, to "bear" meant to "carry." See Johnson 161; Webster; T. Sheridan, A Complete Dictionary of the English Language (1796); 2 Oxford English Dictionary 20 (2d ed.1989) (hereinafter Oxford). When used with "arms," however, the term has a meaning that refers to carrying for a particular purpose—confrontation. . . . Although the phrase implies that the carrying of the weapon is for the purpose of "offensive or defensive action," it in no way connotes participation in a structured military organization.

From our review of founding-era sources, we conclude that this natural meaning was also the meaning that "bear arms" had in the 18th century. In numerous instances, "bear arms" was unambiguously used to refer to the carrying of weapons outside of an organized militia. The most prominent examples are those most relevant to the Second Amendment: nine state constitutional provisions written in the 18th century or the first two decades of the 19th, which enshrined a right of citizens to "bear arms in defense of themselves and the state" or "bear arms in defense of himself and the state." It is clear from those formulations that "bear arms" did not refer only to carrying a weapon in an organized military unit. Justice James Wilson interpreted the Pennsylvania Constitution's arms-bearing right, for example, as a recognition of the natural right of defense "of one's person or house"—what he called the law of "self preservation." 2 Collected Works of James Wilson 1142, and n. x (K. Hall & M. Hall eds.2007) (citing Pa. Const., Art. IX, § 21 (1790)). That was also the interpretation of those state constitutional provisions adopted by pre-Civil War state courts. These provisions demonstrate—again, in the most analogous linguistic context—that "bear arms" was not limited to the carrying of arms in a militia. . . .

c. Meaning of the Operative Clause. Putting all of these textual elements together, we find that they guarantee the individual right to possess and carry weapons in case of confrontation. This meaning is strongly confirmed by the historical background of the Second Amendment. We look to this because it has always been widely understood that the Second Amendment, like the First and Fourth

Amendments, codified a *pre-existing* right. The very text of the Second Amendment implicitly recognizes the pre-existence of the right and declares only that it "shall not be infringed." . . .

Between the Restoration and the Glorious Revolution, the Stuart Kings Charles II and James II succeeded in using select militias loyal to them to suppress political dissidents, in part by disarming their opponents. See J. Malcolm, To Keep and Bear Arms 31–53 (1994) (hereinafter Malcolm); L. Schwoerer, The Declaration of Rights, 1689, p. 76 (1981). Under the auspices of the 1671 Game Act, for example, the Catholic Charles II had ordered general disarmaments of regions home to his Protestant enemies. See Malcolm 103–106. These experiences caused Englishmen to be extremely wary of concentrated military forces run by the state and to be jealous of their arms. They accordingly obtained an assurance from William and Mary, in the Declaration of Rights (which was codified as the English Bill of Rights), that Protestants would never be disarmed: "That the Subjects which are Protestants, may have Arms for their Defence suitable to their Conditions, and as allowed by Law." 1 W. & M., ch. 2, § 7, in 3 Eng. Stat. at Large 441. This right has long been understood to be the predecessor to our Second Amendment. . . . It was clearly an individual right, having nothing whatever to do with service in a militia. To be sure, it was an individual right not available to the whole population, given that it was restricted to Protestants, and like all written English rights it was held only against the Crown, not Parliament. . . . But it was secured to them as individuals, according to "libertarian political principles," not as members of a fighting force. . . .

There seems to us no doubt, on the basis of both text and history, that the Second Amendment conferred an individual right to keep and bear arms. Of course the right was not unlimited, just as the First Amendment's right of free speech was not. Thus, we do not read the Second Amendment to protect the right of citizens to carry arms for *any sort* of confrontation, just as we do not read the First Amendment to protect the right of citizens to speak for *any purpose*. Before turning to limitations upon the individual right, however, we must determine whether the prefatory clause of the Second Amendment comports with our interpretation of the operative clause.

2. Prefatory Clause.

The prefatory clause reads: "A well regulated Militia, being necessary to the security of a free State. . . ."

a. "Well-Regulated Militia." In *United States v. Miller,* 307 U.S. 174, 179 (1939), we explained that "the Militia comprised all males physically capable of acting in concert for the common defense." That definition comports with founding-era sources. . . .

[T]he adjective "well-regulated" implies nothing more than the imposition of proper discipline and training. See Johnson 1619 ("Regulate": "To adjust by rule or method"); Rawle 121–122; cf. Va. Declaration of Rights § 13 (1776), in 7 Thorpe 3812, 3814 (referring to "a well-regulated militia, composed of the body of the people, trained to arms").

b. "Security of a Free State." The phrase "security of a free State" meant "security of a free polity," not security of each of the several States as the dissent below argued, see 478 F.3d, at 405, and n. 10. Joseph Story wrote in his treatise on the Constitution that "the word 'state' is used in various senses [and in] its most enlarged sense it means the people composing a particular nation or community." 1 Story § 208; see also 3 *id.,* § 1890 (in reference to the Second Amendment's prefatory clause: "The militia is the natural defence of a free country"). It is true that the term "State" elsewhere in the Constitution refers to individual States, but the phrase "security of a free State" and close variations seem to have been terms of art in 18th-century political discourse, meaning a " 'free country' " or free polity. See Volokh, "Necessary to the Security of a Free State," 83 Notre Dame L. Rev. 1, 5 (2007). . . .

3. Relationship Between Prefatory Clause and Operative Clause.

We reach the question, then: Does the preface fit with an operative clause that creates an individual right to keep and bear arms? It fits perfectly, once one knows the history that the founding generation knew and that we have described above. That history showed that the way tyrants had eliminated a militia consisting of all the able-bodied men was not by banning the militia but simply by taking away the people's arms, enabling a select militia or standing army to suppress political opponents. This is what had occurred in England that prompted codification of the right to have arms in the English Bill of Rights.

The debate with respect to the right to keep and bear arms, as with other guarantees in the Bill of Rights, was not over whether it was desirable (all agreed that it was) but over whether it needed to be codified in the Constitution. During the 1788 ratification debates, the fear that the Federal Government would disarm the people in order to impose rule through a standing army or select militia was pervasive in Antifederalist rhetoric. . . . Federalists responded that because Congress was given no power to abridge the ancient right of individuals to keep and bear arms, such a force could never oppress the people. . . . It was understood across the political spectrum that the right helped to secure the ideal of a citizen militia, which might be necessary to oppose an oppressive military force if the constitutional order broke down.

It is therefore entirely sensible that the Second Amendment's prefatory clause announces the purpose for which the right was codified: to prevent elimination of the militia. The prefatory clause does not suggest that preserving the militia was the only reason Americans valued the ancient right; most undoubtedly thought it even more important for self-defense and hunting. But the threat that the new Federal Government would destroy the citizens' militia by taking away their arms was the reason that right—unlike some other English rights—was codified in a written Constitution.[15]

B

Our interpretation is confirmed by analogous arms-bearing rights in state constitutions that preceded and immediately followed adoption of the Second Amendment. . . . Pennsylvania's Declaration of Rights of 1776 said: "That the people have a right to bear arms *for the defence of themselves* and the state . . . ." § XIII, in 5 Thorpe 3082, 3083 (emphasis added). In 1777, Vermont adopted the identical provision, except for inconsequential differences in punctuation and capitalization. See Vt. Const., ch. 1, § XV, in 6 *id.,* at 3741. . . .

D

We now address how the Second Amendment was interpreted from immediately after its ratification through the end of the 19th century. . . .

---

[15] **Questions:** Are you persuaded by Scalia's interpretation of the prefatory clause's relationship to the operative clause? Consider the following clause from the Texas Constitution: "A general diffusion of knowledge being essential to the preservation of the liberties and rights of the people, it shall be the duty of the Legislature of the State to establish . . . an efficient system of public free schools." Tex. Const. art. VII, § 1. Might such a clause reasonably be interpreted to protect an individual right to a free public education, despite the preface's emphasis on a "diffusion of knowledge" within a wider community?

E

We now ask whether any of our precedents forecloses the conclusions we have reached about the meaning of the Second Amendment. . . .

Justice STEVENS places overwhelming reliance upon this Court's decision in *Miller,* 307 U.S. 174. . . . And what is, according to Justice STEVENS, the holding of *Miller* that demands such obeisance? That the Second Amendment "protects the right to keep and bear arms for certain military purposes, but that it does not curtail the Legislature's power to regulate the nonmilitary use and ownership of weapons." *Post,* at 2823.

Nothing so clearly demonstrates the weakness of Justice STEVENS' case. *Miller* did not hold that and cannot possibly be read to have held that. The judgment in the case upheld against a Second Amendment challenge two men's federal indictment for transporting an unregistered short-barreled shotgun in interstate commerce, in violation of the National Firearms Act, 48 Stat. 1236. It is entirely clear that the Court's basis for saying that the Second Amendment did not apply was *not* that the defendants were "bear[ing] arms" not "for . . . military purposes" but for "nonmilitary use," *post,* at 2823. Rather, it was that the *type of weapon at issue* was not eligible for Second Amendment protection: "In the absence of any evidence tending to show that the possession or use of a [short-barreled shotgun] at this time has some reasonable relationship to the preservation or efficiency of a well regulated militia, we cannot say that the Second Amendment guarantees the right to keep and bear *such an instrument.*" 307 U.S., at 178 (emphasis added). "Certainly," the Court continued, "it is not within judicial notice that this weapon is any part of the ordinary military equipment or that its use could contribute to the common defense." *Ibid.* Beyond that, the opinion provided no explanation of the content of the right.

This holding is not only consistent with, but positively suggests, that the Second Amendment confers an individual right to keep and bear arms (though only arms that "have some reasonable relationship to the preservation or efficiency of a well regulated militia"). Had the Court believed that the Second Amendment protects only those serving in the militia, it would have been odd to examine the character of the weapon rather than simply note that the two crooks were not militiamen. . . . *Miller* stands only for the proposition that the Second Amendment right, whatever its nature, extends only to certain types of weapons. . . .

We conclude that nothing in our precedents forecloses our adoption of the original understanding of the Second Amendment. It should be unsurprising that such a significant matter has been for so long judicially unresolved. For most of our history, the Bill of Rights was not thought applicable to the States, and the Federal Government did not significantly regulate the possession of firearms by law-abiding citizens. Other provisions of the Bill of Rights have similarly remained unilluminated for lengthy periods. This Court first held a law to violate the First Amendment's guarantee of freedom of speech in 1931, almost 150 years after the Amendment was ratified, see *Near v. Minnesota ex rel. Olson,* 283 U.S. 697 (1931), and it was not until after World War II that we held a law invalid under the Establishment Clause, see *Illinois ex rel. McCollum v. Board of Ed. of School Dist. No. 71, Champaign Cty.*, 333 U.S. 203 (1948). Even a question as basic as the scope of proscribable libel was not addressed by this Court until 1964, nearly two centuries after the founding. See *New York Times Co. v. Sullivan,* 376 U.S. 254 (1964). It is demonstrably not true that, as Justice STEVENS claims, *post,* at 2844–2845, "for most of our history, the invalidity of Second-Amendment-based objections to firearms regulations has been well settled and uncontroversial." For most of our history the question did not present itself.

III

Like most rights, the right secured by the Second Amendment is not unlimited.[16] From Blackstone through the 19th-century cases, commentators and courts routinely explained that the right was not a right to keep and carry any weapon whatsoever in any manner whatsoever and for whatever purpose. For example, the majority of the 19th-century courts to consider the question held that prohibitions on carrying concealed weapons were lawful under the Second Amendment or state analogues. Although we do not undertake an exhaustive historical analysis today of the full scope of the Second Amendment, nothing in our opinion should be taken to cast doubt on longstanding prohibitions on the possession of firearms by felons and the mentally ill, or laws forbidding the carrying of firearms in sensitive places such as schools and government buildings, or laws imposing conditions and qualifications on the commercial sale of arms.

We also recognize another important limitation on the right to keep and carry arms. *Miller* said, as we have explained, that the sorts of weapons protected were those "in common use at the time." 307 U.S., at 179. We think that limitation is fairly supported by the historical tradition of prohibiting the carrying of "dangerous and unusual weapons." . . .

It may be objected that if weapons that are most useful in military service—M-16 rifles and the like—may be banned, then the Second Amendment right is completely detached from the prefatory clause. But as we have said, the conception of the militia at the time of the Second Amendment's ratification was the body of all citizens capable of military service, who would bring the sorts of lawful weapons that they possessed at home to militia duty. It may well be true today that a militia, to be as effective as militias in the 18th century, would require sophisticated arms that are highly unusual in society at large. Indeed, it may be true that no amount of small arms could be useful against modern-day bombers and tanks. But the fact that modern developments have limited the degree of fit between the prefatory clause and the protected right cannot change our interpretation of the right.

IV

We turn finally to the law at issue here. As we have said, the law totally bans handgun possession in the home. It also requires that any lawful firearm in the home be disassembled or bound by a trigger lock at all times, rendering it inoperable.

As the quotations earlier in this opinion demonstrate, the inherent right of self-defense has been central to the Second Amendment right. The handgun ban amounts to a prohibition of an entire class of "arms" that is overwhelmingly chosen by American society for that lawful purpose. The prohibition extends, moreover, to the home, where the need for defense of self, family, and property is most acute. Under any of the standards of scrutiny that we have applied to enumerated constitutional rights, banning from the home "the most preferred firearm in the nation to 'keep' and use for protection of one's home and family," would fail constitutional muster.

Few laws in the history of our Nation have come close to the severe restriction of the District's handgun ban. And some of those few have been struck down. In *Nunn v. State*, the Georgia Supreme Court struck down a prohibition on carrying pistols openly (even though it upheld a prohibition on carrying concealed weapons). See 1 Ga., at 251. In *Andrews v. State*, the Tennessee Supreme Court likewise held that a statute that forbade openly carrying a pistol "publicly or privately, without regard

[16] **Question:** Imagine that Congress decided to prohibit everyone from possessing AR-15-style semiautomatic rifles, which have often been used in a recent epidemic of school shootings. In light of Scalia's discussion of the Second Amendment's limits, could Congress constitutionally pass such a law?

to time or place, or circumstances," 50 Tenn., at 187, violated the state constitutional provision (which the court equated with the Second Amendment). That was so even though the statute did not restrict the carrying of long guns. *Ibid.* See also *State v. Reid,* 1 Ala. 612, 616–617 (1840) ("A statute which, under the pretence of regulating, amounts to a destruction of the right, or which requires arms to be so borne as to render them wholly useless for the purpose of defence, would be clearly unconstitutional").

It is no answer to say, as petitioners do, that it is permissible to ban the possession of handguns so long as the possession of other firearms (*i.e.,* long guns) is allowed. It is enough to note, as we have observed, that the American people have considered the handgun to be the quintessential self-defense weapon. There are many reasons that a citizen may prefer a handgun for home defense: It is easier to store in a location that is readily accessible in an emergency; it cannot easily be redirected or wrestled away by an attacker; it is easier to use for those without the upper-body strength to lift and aim a long gun; it can be pointed at a burglar with one hand while the other hand dials the police. Whatever the reason, handguns are the most popular weapon chosen by Americans for self-defense in the home, and a complete prohibition of their use is invalid.

We must also address the District's requirement (as applied to respondent's handgun) that firearms in the home be rendered and kept inoperable at all times. This makes it impossible for citizens to use them for the core lawful purpose of self-defense and is hence unconstitutional. . . .

In sum, we hold that the District's ban on handgun possession in the home violates the Second Amendment, as does its prohibition against rendering any lawful firearm in the home operable for the purpose of immediate self-defense. Assuming that Heller is not disqualified from the exercise of Second Amendment rights, the District must permit him to register his handgun and must issue him a license to carry it in the home. . . .

■ JUSTICE STEVENS, with whom JUSTICE SOUTER, JUSTICE GINSBURG, and JUSTICE BREYER join, dissenting.

The question presented by this case is not whether the Second Amendment protects a "collective right" or an "individual right." Surely it protects a right that can be enforced by individuals. But a conclusion that the Second Amendment protects an individual right does not tell us anything about the scope of that right.

Guns are used to hunt, for self-defense, to commit crimes, for sporting activities, and to perform military duties. The Second Amendment plainly does not protect the right to use a gun to rob a bank; it is equally clear that it *does* encompass the right to use weapons for certain military purposes. Whether it also protects the right to possess and use guns for nonmilitary purposes like hunting and personal self-defense is the question presented by this case. The text of the Amendment, its history, and our decision in *United States v. Miller,* 307 U.S. 174 (1939), provide a clear answer to that question.

The Second Amendment was adopted to protect the right of the people of each of the several States to maintain a well-regulated militia. It was a response to concerns raised during the ratification of the Constitution that the power of Congress to disarm the state militias and create a national standing army posed an intolerable threat to the sovereignty of the several States. Neither the text of the Amendment nor the arguments advanced by its proponents evidenced the slightest interest in limiting any legislature's authority to regulate private civilian uses of firearms. Specifically, there is no indication that the Framers of the Amendment intended to enshrine the common-law right of self-defense in the Constitution.

In 1934, Congress enacted the National Firearms Act, the first major federal firearms law. Sustaining an indictment the Act, this Court held that, "[i]n the absence of any evidence tending to show that possession or use of a 'shotgun having a barrel of less than eighteen inches in length' at this time has some reasonable relationship to the preservation or efficiency of a well regulated militia, we cannot say that the Second Amendment guarantees the right to keep and bear such an instrument." *Miller*, 307 U.S., at 178. The view of the Amendment we took in *Miller*—that it protects the right to keep and bear arms for certain military purposes, but that it does not curtail the Legislature's power to regulate the nonmilitary use and ownership of weapons—is both the most natural reading of the Amendment's text and the interpretation most faithful to the history of its adoption.

Since our decision in *Miller,* hundreds of judges have relied on the view of the Amendment we endorsed there. . . . No new evidence has surfaced since [then] supporting the view that the Amendment was intended to curtail the power of Congress to regulate civilian use or misuse of weapons. Indeed, a review of the drafting history of the Amendment demonstrates that its Framers *rejected* proposals that would have broadened its coverage to include such uses.

The opinion the Court announces today fails to identify any new evidence supporting the view that the Amendment was intended to limit the power of Congress to regulate civilian uses of weapons. Unable to point to any such evidence, the Court stakes its holding on a strained and unpersuasive reading of the Amendment's text; significantly different provisions in the 1689 English Bill of Rights, and in various 19th-century State Constitutions; postenactment commentary that was available to the Court when it decided *Miller;* and, ultimately, a feeble attempt to distinguish *Miller* that places more emphasis on the Court's decisional process than on the reasoning in the opinion itself.

Even if the textual and historical arguments on both sides of the issue were evenly balanced, respect for the well-settled views of all of our predecessors on this Court, and for the rule of law itself, would prevent most jurists from endorsing such a dramatic upheaval in the law. As Justice Cardozo observed years ago, the "labor of judges would be increased almost to the breaking point if every past decision could be reopened in every case, and one could not lay one's own course of bricks on the secure foundation of the courses laid by others who had gone before him." The Nature of the Judicial Process 149 (1921). . . .[17]

NOTE: INCORPORATION AND POST-BILL OF RIGHTS AMENDMENTS

Two additional subjects are worth mentioning with regard to the Bill of Rights and limits on Congress's power: incorporation and post-Bill of Rights amendments.

Incorporation. The Bill of Rights has always been interpreted to apply only to the federal government, not to the states. But, as discussed in a later section (40.5), the Fourteenth Amendment has been interpreted to apply most of the rights protected by the Bill of Rights to the states via a doctrine known as "incorporation." Thus, in *McDonald v. Chicago*, 561 U.S. 742

[17] **Question:** In writing on *District of Columbia v. Heller* and originalism, Professor Lawrence B. Solum argues that the majority grounded its analysis in the idea that the "linguistic meaning of the Second Amendment was fixed by linguistic facts . . . at the time of utterance, not before and not after." District of Columbia v. Heller *and Originalism*, 103 Nw. U. L. Rev. 923, 946–47 (2009). In your opinion, should this type of analysis—which Solum refers to as the fixation thesis—be considered decisive in light of countervailing principles?

(2010), a majority of the Court held that the Fourteenth Amendment effectively applies *Heller* to state and local gun-control laws.

Post-Bill of Rights amendments. In addition to the Bill of Rights, there are a number of other amendments that limit Congress's power. As will be discussed later in the casebook, the Eleventh Amendment generally prohibits Congress from authorizing an individual to sue a state in federal court. The Reconstruction amendments (Thirteenth–Fifteenth) and voting-rights amendments (Fifteenth, Nineteenth, Twenty-Fourth, and Twenty-Sixth) also impose generally applicable limits on Congress's powers. Finally, the Twenty-Seventh Amendment prohibits Congress from raising the salary of members of Congress until after an intervening election.

This Twenty-Seventh Amendment, ratified in 1992, was one of the original twelve submitted to the states by Congress in 1789. Not enough states ratified it in 1791 to make it part of the Bill of Rights, however. Nevertheless, an intrepid student researcher rediscovered the amendment two hundred years later and successfully argued that it was not too late for remaining states to ratify it. *See generally* Richard B. Bernstein, *The Sleeper Wakes: The History and Legacy of the Twenty-Seventh Amendment*, 61 Fordham L. Rev. 497 (1992).

CHAPTER 13

What Is the Scope of Congress's War Powers?

PREAMBLE: We the People of the United States, in Order to form a more perfect Union, establish Justice, insure domestic Tranquility, provide for the common defence, promote the general Welfare, and secure the Blessings of Liberty to ourselves and our Posterity, do ordain and establish this Constitution for the United States of America.

ARTICLE I, SECTION 8, CLAUSE 11: The Congress shall have Power . . . To declare War, grant Letters of Marque and Reprisal, and make Rules concerning Captures on Land and Water;

CLAUSE 12: To raise and support Armies, but no Appropriation of Money to that Use shall be for a longer Term than two Years;

CLAUSE 13: To provide and maintain a Navy;

CLAUSE 14: To make Rules for the Government and Regulation of the land and naval Forces;

CLAUSE 15: To provide for calling forth the Militia to execute the Laws of the Union, suppress Insurrections and repel Invasions;

CLAUSE 16: To provide for organizing, arming, and disciplining, the Militia, and for governing such Part of them as may be employed in the Service of the United States, reserving to the States respectively, the Appointment of the Officers, and the Authority of training the Militia according to the discipline prescribed by Congress; . . .—And

CLAUSE 18: To make all Laws which shall be necessary and proper for carrying into Execution the foregoing Powers, and all other Powers vested by this Constitution in the Government of the United States, or in any Department or Officer thereof.

ARTICLE I, SECTION 9, CLAUSE 2: The Privilege of the Writ of Habeas Corpus shall not be suspended, unless when in Cases of Rebellion or Invasion the public Safety may require it.

ARTICLE II, SECTION 2, CLAUSE 1: The President shall be Commander in Chief of the Army and Navy of the United States, and of the Militia of the several States, when called into the actual Service of the United States. . . .

ARTICLE III, SECTION 3, CLAUSE 1: Treason against the United States, shall consist only in levying War against them, or in adhering to their Enemies, giving them Aid and Comfort. No Person shall be convicted of Treason unless on the Testimony of two Witnesses to the same overt Act, or on Confession in open Court.

CLAUSE 2: The Congress shall have Power to declare the Punishment of Treason, but no Attainder of Treason shall work Corruption of Blood, or Forfeiture except during the Life of the Person attainted.

ARTICLE IV, SECTION 4: The United States shall guarantee to every State in this Union a Republican Form of Government, and shall protect each of them against Invasion; and on Application of the Legislature, or of the Executive (when the Legislature cannot be convened), against domestic Violence.

13.1 THE SOURCE OF THE WAR POWERS

The text of Article I, Section 8, Clause 11, of the Constitution gives Congress the power to "declare War" but not a broader power to *conduct* war. In fact, the Constitutional Convention voted 7–2 to amend an earlier draft of the Constitution that would have given Congress the power to "make war." 2 *The Records of the Federal Convention of 1787*, at 318–19 (Max Farrand ed., 1911). The delegates who supported the amendment overcame the objections of two sets of opponents. The first opponents wanted the president alone to have the power to commence and conduct war, on the theory that Congress would be too slow and deliberative to repel invasions or command soldiers. The other opponents accepted that the president should oversee a war but wanted Congress alone to have the power to commence war, on the theory that the president would be as rash as English monarchs had long been. James Madison proposed the term *declare* as a compromise position: Congress could decide whether to enter into an armed conflict, "leaving to the Executive the power to repel sudden attacks." *Id.* at 318; *see* 3 Joseph Story, *Commentaries on the Constitution of the United States* 1187 (1833). The final version of Article IV also required the United States to "protect [the states] from Invasion."

Although the power to declare war could have been interpreted as a modest power to decide whether to formally enter into an armed conflict, it has instead been interpreted quite broadly. Madison, for example, didn't believe that Congress had the power to regulate immigration in peacetime, but he did think that Congress's power to declare war also gave it the power to deport residents of countries with which the United States had a hostile relationship. Report of 1800 (Jan. 7, 1800), *in* 17 *The Papers of James Madison* 303–51 (William T. Hutchinson et al. eds., 1991); *see also Ludecke v. Watkins*, 335 U.S. 160 (1948) (upholding the president's power to deport a German national during and immediately after World War II). Chief Justice John Marshall soon wrote that this enumerated power also gave Congress the implied power to "carry on war, by armies and navies, and other suitable means and methods of warfare." *McCulloch v. Maryland*, 17 U.S. (4 Wheat.) 316, 324 (1819). Later justices expanded this interpretation still further, writing after the Civil War that "the power to declare war involves the power to prosecute it by all means and in any manner in which war may be legitimately prosecuted." *Miller v. United States*, 78 U.S. 268, 305 (1870).

Of course, the power to "declare War" is not the only war-related power that Article I confers. It is supplemented by several other powers, including the power to raise, support, maintain, and regulate armies, a navy, and a militia. In the aggregate, these are often collectively referred to as the "war powers." *See, e.g., Lichter v. United States*, 334 U.S. 742, 754–55 (1948). Alexander Hamilton argued that these aggregate powers ought to be interpreted without limit to include any power that may be necessary to meet whatever national emergencies the country might face in the unforeseeable future. *The Federalist No. 23*, at 146 (Alexander Hamilton) (Jacob E. Cooke ed., 1961).

Indeed, the perceived need to give Congress discretion over war has proved so great that the Supreme Court has occasionally suggested that Congress would have plenary power to conduct a war even if the Constitution had been silent on the subject. Like the power to exclude immigrants at the border, the Court has described Congress's power over war as an inherent attribute of sovereignty. "The powers to declare and wage war, to conclude peace, to make treaties, to maintain diplomatic relations with other sovereignties," the Court wrote shortly before World War II, "if they had never been mentioned in the Constitution, would have vested in the Federal Government as necessary concomitants of nationality." *United States v. Curtiss-Wright Exp. Corp.*, 299 U.S. 304, 318 (1936).

13.2 THE POWER TO PREPARE FOR WAR

Whether the source of Congress's war powers is (1) the power to declare war, (2) the aggregate of the war-related powers in Article I, or (3) an inherent feature of sovereignty, the war powers themselves have been interpreted to give Congress vast authority to prepare for war.

Federalization of the militia

Traditionally, Congress relied on states to prepare for war. During the American Revolution, states established their own "militias," or informal armed services, which were typically organized at the town or county level. The Confederation Congress raised the Continental Army by asking each state to send a quota of these militia members for service. After victory in the Revolutionary War and the ratification of the Constitutional Convention, Congress passed an act delegating to the president the power to "call forth" the state militias to repel invasions, to suppress insurrections, or to enforce federal law—the three actions for which Article I, Section 8, allows Congress to call forth the militia. Militia Act of 1795, ch. 36, § 2, 1 Stat. 424 (1795). Early opinions interpreting this statute explained that Congress has nearly unlimited power to train, regulate, and punish members of the militia. *Martin v. Mott*, 25 U.S. (12 Wheat.) 19 (1827); *Houston v. Moore*, 18 U.S. (5 Wheat.) 1 (1820).

Congress heavily relied on state militias through the War of 1812 (to repel an "invasion") and the Civil War (to suppress an "insurrection"). *See Tyler v. Defrees*, 78 U.S. (11 Wall.) 331 (1871); *Texas v. White*, 74 U.S. (7 Wall.) 700 (1869). But Congress began to permanently "federalize" the state militias shortly before World War I with the National Defense Act of 1916, Pub. L. No. 64–85, 39 Stat. 166. This statute provided that state militias would be permanently controlled and regulated by the federal government, under the new name *National Guard*. In 1933, Congress added that anyone who enrolled in their state National Guard would also be simultaneously enrolled in the "National Guard of the United States," which Congress designated as part of the U.S. Army. *See* Act of June 13, 1933, Pub. L. No. 73–64, 48 Stat. 153.

In the 1980s, Congress passed a series of laws that allowed the president to send National Guard members abroad even absent an invasion, an insurrection, or an obstruction of federal law. When governors challenged these laws as violations of limits within Article I's Militia Clauses, the Supreme Court upheld these laws in *Perpich v. Department of Justice*, 496 U.S. 334 (1990). It explained that Congress's war powers gave it wide authority to "raise . . . Armies"; that National Guard members were now part of the U.S. Army; and that therefore when Congress sends a National Guard unit overseas, it is doing so as part of its power over the army, not over the more limited constitutional militia. *Perpich*, 496 U.S. at 349–50. But the Court also wrote that when the federal government has not called the National Guard into active federal service, states retain their long-standing authority to train their own guard under federal standards and to rely on their guard to address state emergencies. *Id.* at 351.

Drafting or conscription of soldiers

In addition to federalizing the militia, Congress has also prepared for war by drafting or conscripting soldiers. During the Revolutionary War, the power to conscript soldiers was wielded by the states and was included in most early state constitutions. *See, e.g.*, Pa. Const. of 1776, dec. of rights, art. I. Although the Confederation Congress did not draft soldiers directly, it set quotas and resolved that states should use their compulsory powers to fulfill them. The first U.S. Congresses maintained this quota system: by the War of 1812, the U.S. Army consisted both of enlisted soldiers and of state-supplied militias of conscripts and volunteers.

But during the Civil War, Congress enacted the Enrollment Act of 1863, ch. 75, 12 Stat. 731, which, for the first time, made every male citizen between the ages of twenty and forty-five subject to be drafted into service in the national army. The law provided that a person so drafted would have the choice of enlisting in the army, furnishing "an acceptable substitute to take his place," or paying the federal government $300 to hire another substitute. Enrollment Act, 12 Stat. at 733.

The Enrollment Act precipitated riots in many northern cities, notably New York City. There, armed mobs of white, working-class residents protested the draft by terrorizing the local black population, whom the mobs blamed for the Civil War. Over four days, the mobs lynched eleven black men, beat over two thousand more, and destroyed countless homes and churches. It took five regiments of U.S. soldiers ordered back from Gettysburg to finally suppress the disorder. *See* Iver Bernstein, *The New York City Draft Riots* 3–8 (1991).

Despite this violence, Congress's power to conduct a draft did not reach the Supreme Court until World War I, in a series of cases known as the *Selective Draft Law Cases*, 245 U.S. 366 (1918). The cases challenged a 1916 law that, among other things, authorized the president to subject all male citizens between the ages of twenty-one and thirty to duty in the national army. *See* Act of June 3, 1916, Pub. L. No. 64–85, 39 Stat. 166, 211. The challengers, a group of adult male citizens, argued that the Constitution gave Congress the power to "raise . . . Armies," but it did not give Congress the power to do so by force. The Supreme Court disagreed, remarking that the draftees' claim "challenges the existence of all power, for a governmental power which has no sanction to it and which therefore can only be exercised provided the citizen consents to its exertion is in no substantial sense a power." *Selective Draft Law Cases*, 245 U.S. at 378. The Court also wrote at length about the history of conscription afterward to support its conclusion that conscription was a necessary and proper means of raising an army. *Id.* at 378–88; *see also Cox v. Wood*, 247 U.S. 3 (1918).

Since the *Selective Draft Law Cases*, Congress has adopted a permanent selective-service program, 50 U.S.C. §§ 451–73 (1948), under which all adult men, with some exceptions, are required to register for a possible draft. In *United States v. O'Brien*, 391 U.S. 367 (1968), the Court upheld a statute that prohibited the knowing destruction of draft cards. And in *Rostker v. Goldberg*, 453 U.S. 57 (1981), the Court upheld the selective-service system—which, again, applied only to men—against a sex-discrimination challenge. The Court explained that "in no other area has the Court accorded Congress greater deference" than "in the context of Congress' authority over national defense and military matters." *Goldberg*, 453 U.S. at 64–65. Applying that deference, the Court allowed Congress to determine whether military necessity compelled a male-only draft.

Enactment of peacetime statutes

Congress's war powers have also served as the basis for many peacetime statutes that could arguably prepare the United States for war if it later arose. For example, shortly after World War I ended, the Supreme Court upheld the Wartime Prohibition Act of 1918, Pub. L. No. 65–243, 40 Stat. 1045, which saved grain by prohibiting the sale of beverages with an alcohol content of greater than 1.28 percent. *Hamilton v. Ky. Distilleries Co.*, 251 U.S. 146 (1919). The Court explained that even though it was no longer "wartime," Congress had to have the power to prepare for the renewal of hostilities, including by conserving a needed supply. *Id.* at 160–61. More consequentially, in *Ashwander v. Tennessee Valley Authority*, the Court upheld the power of the federal government to construct a hydroelectric dam in 1926 to provide "an abundant supply of electric energy in the event of war." 297 U.S. 288, 328 (1936). Even without any war in sight, the Court maintained that Congress's war powers included the power to operate the dam and to sell excess energy. The Court later repeatedly upheld price and wage controls when there was a reasonable connection to preparing for war—even if a war had recently ended. *See, e.g.*, *Woods v. Cloyd W. Miller Co.*, 333 U.S. 138 (1948); *Yakus v. United States*, 321 U.S. 414 (1944); *Block v. Hirsh*, 256 U.S. 153 (1921).

In light of these precedents, Congress has styled much of its peacetime legislation as an exercise of its war powers. For example, Congress invoked its war powers to create the interstate highway system, formally known as the "National System of Interstate and Defense Highways." *See* Federal Aid Highway Act of 1956, Pub. L. No. 84–627, 70 Stat. 374, 378. Similarly, after the Soviet Union launched Sputnik into orbit the following year, Congress invoked its war powers to create the National Aeronautics and Space Administration. National Aeronautics and Space Act of 1958, Pub. L. No. 85–568, 72 Stat. 426; *see* Margaret O'Mara, *The Code* 44–45 (2019). For the first time, Congress also extended federal financial assistance to local schools. It explained that its purpose was "[t]o strengthen the national defense and assist in the expansion and improvement of educational programs to meet critical national needs." *See* National Defense Education Act of 1958, Pub. L. No. 85–864, 72 Stat. 1580, 1580.

13.3 THE POWER TO INITIATE WAR

Although Congress has the power to declare war, it has only exercised this power on five occasions: the War of 1812, the Mexican-American War in 1846, the Spanish-American War in 1898, World War I in 1917, and World War II in 1941. In dozens of other armed conflicts, Congress has initiated war by authorizing the use of military force against an enemy without formally declaring war.

In *Bas v. Tingy*, 4 U.S. (4 Dall.) 37 (1800), the Supreme Court upheld a statute that authorized the president to protect American shipping from French attacks. *See* Act of July 9, 1798, ch. 68, 1 Stat. 578. The Court held that Congress's enumerated power to declare a formal, or "perfect," war also included the implied power to authorize an informal, or "imperfect," war. *Bas*, 4 U.S. at 46.

After *Bas*, there remained an open question regarding whether any formal or informal declaration by Congress was necessary before the president could initiate hostilities with an enemy. Characteristically, Alexander Hamilton argued that no such declaration was needed when another nation declared war on the United States. 7 *Works of Alexander Hamilton* 746–47 (John C. Hamilton ed., 1851). By contrast, Thomas Jefferson doubted the president's power to initiate hostilities absent a declaration by Congress or an actual invasion. *Messages and Papers of the Presidents* 326, 327 (James D. Richardson ed., 1896). This debate remained somewhat hypothetical, however, until the Civil War.

13.3.1

The Brig Amy Warwick (The Prize Cases)

67 U.S. (2 Black) 635 (1862)

On April 12, 1861, South Carolina soldiers fired the first shots of the Civil War on Fort Sumter in Charleston Harbor. At the time, Congress was not in session and would not reconvene until July 4. In the meantime, the recently inaugurated President Abraham Lincoln initiated a blockade of southern ports, suspended habeas corpus, and called forth 75,000 militia members. The federal blockade soon seized four ships and condemned them as "prizes" of war. *The Prize Cases*, 67 U.S. (2 Black) 635, 636 (1862).

In *The Brig Amy Warwick* (*The Prize Cases*), 67 U.S. (2 Black) 635 (1862), the owners of these four ships appealed to the Supreme Court with two arguments. First, they contended that only Congress had the power to authorize the seizure of enemies' ships during wartime, yet Congress never formally declared war against the rebelling states. Second, they argued that even if Congress had authorized the seizure, principles of international law prohibited warring nations from seizing the ships of *neutrals*, or people who were not technically *enemies*. *See* Oona A. Hathaway & Scott Shapiro, *The Internationalists* 90–91 (2017).

While their case progressed, Congress reconvened and passed several laws that ratified the president's actions. *See, e.g.*, Act of Aug. 6, 1861, ch. 40, 12 Stat. 319. Yet even as observers called the conflict a *civil war*, Congress refused to declare war because it regarded the Confederacy as an illegal rebellion. This lack of an official declaration of war did not sway the Court, which ruled in favor of the blockade and prizes of war.

■ MR. JUSTICE GRIER delivered the opinion of the Court.[1]

There are certain propositions of law which must necessarily affect the ultimate decision of these cases. . . .

They are, 1st. Had the President a right to institute a blockade of ports in possession of persons in armed rebellion against the Government, on the principles of international law, as known and acknowledged among civilized States?

2d. Was the property of persons domiciled or residing within those States a proper subject of capture on the sea as "enemies' property?"

[I.] [T]he right of prize and capture has its origin in the '*jus belli*,' and is governed and adjudged under the law of nations. To legitimate the capture of a neutral vessel or property on the high seas, a war must exist *de facto*, and the neutral must have a knowledge or notice of the intention of one of the parties belligerent to use this mode of coercion against a port, city, or territory, in possession of the other.

---

[1] **As You Read, Consider:** The Civil War was not a formally declared war between the United States and an independent state. How does this technicality influence Justice Robert Grier's perspective regarding Congress's powers to "declare War" or "call[ ] forth the Militia to execute the Laws of the Union, suppress Insurrections and repel Invasions"?

Let us enquire whether, at the time this blockade was instituted, a state of war existed which would justify a resort to these means of subduing the hostile force.

War has been well defined to be, 'That state in which a nation prosecutes its right by force.'

The parties belligerent in a public war are independent nations. But it is not necessary to constitute war, that both parties should be acknowledged as independent nations or sovereign States. A war may exist where one of the belligerents, claims sovereign rights as against the other.

Insurrection against a government may or may not culminate in an organized rebellion, but a civil war always begins by insurrection against the lawful authority of the Government. A civil war is never solemnly declared; it becomes such by its accidents—the number, power, and organization of the persons who originate and carry it on. When the party in rebellion occupy and hold in a hostile manner a certain portion of territory; have declared their independence; have cast off their allegiance; have organized armies; have commenced hostilities against their former sovereign, the world acknowledges them as belligerents, and the contest a *war. They* claim to be in arms to establish their liberty and independence, in order to become a sovereign State, while the sovereign party treats them as insurgents and rebels who owe allegiance, and who should be punished with death for their treason.

The laws of war, as established among nations, have their foundation in reason, and all tend to mitigate the cruelties and misery produced by the scourge of war. Hence the parties to a civil war usually concede to each other belligerent rights. They exchange prisoners, and adopt the other courtesies and rules common to public or national wars. . . .

As a civil war is never publicly proclaimed, *eo nomine*, against insurgents, its actual existence is a fact in our domestic history which the Court is bound to notice and to know.

The true test of its existence, as found in the writings of the sages of the common law, may be thus summarily stated: 'When the regular course of justice is interrupted by revolt, rebellion, or insurrection, so that the Courts of Justice cannot be kept open, *civil war exists* and hostilities may be prosecuted on the same footing as if those opposing the Government were foreign enemies invading the land.'

By the Constitution, Congress alone has the power to declare a national or foreign war. It cannot declare war against a State, or any number of States, by virtue of any clause in the Constitution. The Constitution confers on the President the whole Executive power. He is bound to take care that the laws be faithfully executed. He is Commander-in-chief of the Army and Navy of the United States, and of the militia of the several States when called into the actual service of the United States. He has no power to initiate or declare a war either against a foreign nation or a domestic State. But by the Acts of Congress of February 28th, 1795, and 3d of March, 1807, he is authorized to called out the militia and use the military and naval forces of the United States in case of invasion by foreign nations, and to suppress insurrection against the government of a State or of the United States.

If a war be made by invasion of a foreign nation, the President is not only authorized but bound to resist force by force.[2] He does not initiate the war, but is bound to accept the challenge without waiting for any special legislative authority.

---

[2] **Questions:** From where does Grier derive the idea that the president may "resist force by force"? From the president's duty as "Commander-in-chief"? From the United States' responsibility to "protect [the states] against Invasion"? Or from nontextual principles? How does the answer to this question affect Congress's Article I power to retroactively authorize a blockade?

And whether the hostile party be a foreign invader, or States organized in rebellion, it is none the less a war, although the declaration of it be '*unilateral*.' Lord Stowell (1 Dodson, 247) observes, 'It is not the less a war on *that account*, for war may exist without a declaration on either side. It is so laid down by the best writers on the law of nations. A declaration of war by one country only, is not a mere challenge to be accepted or refused at pleasure by the other.

The battles of Palo Alto and Resaca de la Palma had been fought before the passage of the Act of Congress of May 13th, 1846, which recognized '*a state of war as existing by the act of the Republic of Mexico*.' This act not only provided for the future prosecution of the war, but was itself a vindication and ratification of the Act of the President in accepting the challenge without a previous formal declaration of war by Congress.

This greatest of civil wars was not gradually developed by popular commotion, tumultuous assemblies, or local unorganized insurrections. However long may have been its previous conception, it nevertheless sprung forth suddenly from the parent brain, a Minerva in the full panoply of *war*. The President was bound to meet it in the shape it presented itself, without waiting for Congress to baptize it with a name; and no name given to it by him or them could change the fact.

It is not the less a civil war, with belligerent parties in hostile array, because it may be called an 'insurrection' by one side, and the insurgents be considered as rebels or traitors. It is not necessary that the independence of the revolted province or State be acknowledged in order to constitute it a party belligerent in a war according to the law of nations. Foreign nations acknowledge it as war by a declaration of neutrality. . . .

As soon as the news of the attack on Fort Sumter, and the organization of a government by the seceding States, assuming to act as belligerents, could become known in Europe, to wit, on the 13th of May, 1861, the Queen of England issued her proclamation of neutrality, 'recognizing hostilities as existing between the Government of the United States of American and *certain States* styling themselves the Confederate States of America.' This was immediately followed by similar declarations or silent acquiescence by other nations.

After such an official recognition by the sovereign, a citizen of a foreign State is estopped to deny the existence of a war with all its consequences as regards neutrals. They cannot ask a Court to affect a technical ignorance of the existence of a war, which all the world acknowledges to be the greatest civil war known in the history of the human race, and thus cripple the arm of the Government and paralyze its power by subtle definitions and ingenious sophisms.

The law of nations is also called the law of nature; it is founded on the common consent as well as the common sense of the world. It contains no such anomalous doctrine as that which this Court are now for the first time desired to pronounce, to wit: That insurgents who have risen in rebellion against their sovereign, expelled her Courts, established a revolutionary government, organized armies, and commenced hostilities, are not *enemies* because they are *traitors;* and a war levied on the Government by traitors, in order to dismember and destroy it, is not a *war* because it is an 'insurrection.'

Whether the President in fulfilling his duties, as Commander-in-chief, in suppressing an insurrection, has met with such armed hostile resistance, and a civil war of such alarming proportions as will compel him to accord to them the character of belligerents, is a question to be decided *by him*, and this Court must be governed by the decisions and acts of the political department of the Government to which this power was entrusted. 'He must determine what degree of force the crisis demands.'

The proclamation of blockade is itself official and conclusive evidence to the Court that a state of war existed which demanded and authorized a recourse to such a measure, under the circumstances peculiar to the case. . . .[3]

If it were necessary to the technical existence of a war, that it should have a legislative sanction, we find it in almost every act passed at the extraordinary session of the Legislature of 1861, which was wholly employed in enacting laws to enable the Government to prosecute the war with vigor and efficiency. And finally, in 1861, we find Congress '*ex majore cautela*' and in anticipation of such astute objections, passing an act 'approving, legalizing, and making valid all the acts, proclamations, and orders of the President, &c., as if they had been *issued and done under the previous express authority* and direction of the Congress of the United States.' . . .

The objection made to this act of ratification, that it is *ex post facto*, and therefore unconstitutional and void, might possibly have some weight on the trial of an indictment in a criminal Court. But precedents from that source cannot be received as authoritative in a tribunal administering public and international law.

[T]herefore we are of the opinion that the President had a right, *jure belli*, to institute a blockade of ports in possession of the States in rebellion, which neutrals are bound to regard. . . .

II. We come now to the consideration of the second question. What is included in the term '*enemies' property?*

Is the property of all persons residing within the territory of the States now in rebellion, captured on the high seas, to be treated as 'enemies' property' whether the owner be in arms against the Government or not?

The right of one belligerent not only to coerce the other by direct force, but also to cripple his resources by the seizure or destruction of his property, is a necessary result of a state of war. Money and wealth, the products of agriculture and commerce, are said to be the sinews of war, and as necessary in its conduct as numbers and physical force. Hence it is, that the laws of war recognize the right of a belligerent to cut these sinews of the power of the enemy, by capturing his property on the high seas.[4]

The appellants contend that the term 'enemy' is properly applicable to those only who are subjects or citizens of a foreign State at war with our own. . . . They insist, moreover, that the President himself, in his proclamation, admits that great numbers of the persons residing within the territories in possession of the insurgent government, are loyal in their feelings, and forced by compulsion and the violence of the rebellious and revolutionary party and its '*de facto* government' to submit to their laws and assist in their scheme of revolution; that the acts of the usurping government cannot legally sever the bond of their allegiance; they have, therefore, a co-relative right to claim the protection of the government for their persons and property, and to be treated as loyal citizens, till legally convicted of having renounced their allegiance and made war against the Government by treasonably resisting its laws.

---

3 **Questions:** Grier's point may seem obvious—*of course* the federal government can prosecute the Civil War even if it is not technically a war. But does his analysis offer any guidance for determining when a more ambiguous war is occurring? If Congress declared a "War on Drugs," a "War on Poverty," or an unofficial war in Vietnam, could it then invoke its war powers to forcibly seize and destroy property?

4 **Question:** The Constitution authorizes Congress to declare war as well as suppress insurrections and repel invasions. If these powers imply that Congress can seize and destroy property, is there anything Congress cannot do in prosecuting a war or suppressing an insurrection?

They contend, also, that insurrection is the act of individuals and not of a government or sovereignty; that the individuals engaged are subjects of law. That confiscation of their property can be effected only under a municipal law. That by the law of the land such confiscation cannot take place without the conviction of the owner of some offence, and finally that the secession ordinances are nullities and ineffectual to release any citizen from his allegiance to the national Government, and consequently that the Constitution and Laws of the United States are still operative over persons in all the States for punishment as well as protection.

This argument rests on the assumption of two propositions, each of which is without foundation on the established law of nations. It assumes that where a civil war exists, the party belligerent claiming to be sovereign, cannot, for some unknown reason, exercise the rights of belligerents, although the revolutionary party may. Being sovereign, he can exercise only sovereign rights over the other party. The insurgent may be killed on the battle-field or by the executioner; his property on land may be confiscated under the municipal law; but the commerce on the ocean, which supplies the rebels with means to support the war, cannot be made the subject of capture under the laws of war, because it is '*unconstitutional!!!*' . . .[5]

Under the very peculiar Constitution of this Government, although the citizens owe supreme allegiance to the Federal Government, they owe also a qualified allegiance to the State in which they are domiciled. Their persons and property are subject to its laws.

Hence, in organizing this rebellion, they have *acted as States* claiming to be sovereign over all persons and property within their respective limits, and asserting a right to absolve their citizens from their allegiance to the Federal Government. Several of these States have combined to form a new confederacy, claiming to be acknowledged by the world as a sovereign State. Their right to do so is now being decided by wager of battle. The ports and territory of each of these States are held in hostility to the General Government. It is no loose, unorganized insurrection, having no defined boundary or possession. It has a boundary marked by lines of bayonets, and which can be crossed only by force—south of this line is enemies' territory, because it is claimed and held in possession by an organized, hostile and belligerent power.

All persons residing within this territory whose property may be used to increase the revenues of the hostile power are, in this contest, liable to be treated as enemies, though not foreigners. They have cast off their allegiance and made war on their Government, and are none the less enemies because they are traitors. . . .

■ MR. JUSTICE NELSON dissented, joined by MR. CHIEF JUSTICE TANEY, MR. JUSTICE CATRON, and MR. JUSTICE CLIFFORD.

13.4 THE POWER TO WAGE WAR SUCCESSFULLY

The *Prize Cases*, 67 U.S. (2 Black) 635 (1862), addressed the federal government's power not only to initiate war but also to prosecute a war by blockading enemy ports and seizing and condemning ships. In this respect, the case was one of many that have assessed the scope of Congress's power to wage war *successfully*. This power has been relatively unchallenged on the battlefield: Congress's power to declare

5 **Question:** In 2011, the federal government used a drone to target and kill a U.S. citizen, Anwar al-Awlaki, who the government suspected was planning to attack the United States on behalf of Al-Qaeda. Does this passage authorize similar uses of force against U.S. citizens?

war and the president's power to oversee a war have long been presumed to include the power to destroy or confiscate lives and property that are caught up in the armed conflict. *See, e.g.*, *Dow v. Johnson*, 100 U.S. 158 (1880) (prohibiting a soldier from recovering damages against a U.S. military officer for injuries sustained in battle); *Brown v. United States*, 12 U.S. (8 Cranch) 110 (1814) (upholding the confiscation of enemy property). As in the *Prize Cases*, the Supreme Court has also repeatedly authorized the federal government to seize or destroy property owned by U.S. citizens, without compensation, if necessary to prevent the property from falling into enemy hands. *See, e.g.*, *United States v. Pacific Railroad*, 120 U.S. 227 (1887). Indeed, as we will see, President Abraham Lincoln described the Emancipation Proclamation of 1863 as "a fit and necessary war measure for suppressing [the southern] rebellion." 2 *Abraham Lincoln: Complete Works* 287 (John G. Nicolay & John Hay eds., New York, Century Co. 1894).

Far more legally controversial have been Congress's *domestic* powers to wage war successfully. The Supreme Court has evaluated three types of extraordinary power that can be invoked in the name of winning an ongoing war: (1) the federal government's power to impose martial law and replace civilian courts with military tribunals, (2) the federal government's power to relocate entire races or nationalities suspected of being disloyal, and (3) the federal government's power to detain people indefinitely after they have been captured abroad. The next case discusses the first of these powers.

13.4.1

Ex parte Milligan

71 U.S. (4 Wall.) 2 (1866)

Shortly before the Civil War, the Supreme Court upheld Congress's power to create military courts (*courts-martial*) with the unreviewable power to enforce certain rules and regulations that applied only to members of the military. *Dynes v. Hoover*, 61 U.S. (20 How.) 65 (1858). After South Carolina fired on Fort Sumter, Lincoln extended the jurisdiction of these courts-martial to anyone suspected of interfering with the railroad lines connecting Washington, D.C., with the northern states. Lincoln did this by suspending the writ of habeas corpus, which allows prisoners to contest the legality of their detention in a civilian court. *See* Order to Suspend Habeas Corpus, Apr. 27, 1861, *in* 2 *Abraham Lincoln: Complete Works*, *supra*, at 39.

Applying the president's instructions, an army officer arrested John Merryman, a Confederate sympathizer suspected of burning railroad bridges in Maryland. When Merryman applied for a writ of habeas corpus from the local federal circuit court, the arresting officer treated the application as illegal because the president had suspended the writ. But the presiding officer of the circuit court happened to be the chief justice of the United States, Roger Taney.

In *Ex parte Merryman*, 17 F. Cas. 144 (C.C.D. Md. 1861) (No. 9487), Taney ruled that Congress, not the president, had the exclusive power to suspend the writ of habeas corpus. Taney conceded that a clause of the Constitution permitted the suspension of habeas corpus "when in Cases of Rebellion or Invasion the public Safety may require it." U.S. Const. art. I, § 9, cl. 2. But he observed that this Suspension Clause appears in Article I, which "is devoted to the legislative department of the United States, and has not the slightest reference to the executive department." *Merryman*, 17 F. Cas. at 148. Taney added that

> [e]ven if the privilege of the writ of habeas corpus were suspended by act of congress, [if] a party not subject to the rules and articles of war were afterwards arrested and imprisoned by regular judicial process, he could not be detained in prison, or brought to trial before a military tribunal.

Id. at 149. He held that the Sixth Amendment guarantees a speedy jury trial to all noncombatants accused of a crime. *Id.*

Ex parte Merryman was published in May 1861, but Lincoln refused to recognize its legitimacy. He asked rhetorically, "Are all the laws, *but one* [the right of habeas corpus], to go unexecuted, and the government itself to go to pieces, lest that one be violated?" *See* James McPherson, *Battle Cry of Freedom* 287–89 (1988). Instead, while Taney watched without any soldiers of his own to enforce his opinion, the president suspended habeas corpus across the country and extended the powers of courts-martial to anyone "affording aid and comfort to rebels against the authority of the United States." Proclamation Suspending the Writ of Habeas Corpus (Sept. 24, 1862), *in* 2 *Abraham Lincoln: Complete Works*, *supra*, at 239. In 1863, Congress ratified the president's actions and authorized the continued suspension of habeas corpus for as long as "said rebellion continue." Act of Mar. 3, 1863, ch. 81, 12 Stat. 755.

For the remainder of the Civil War, several northern states, including Indiana, were organized into military districts and overseen by military officers. Many of these commanding officers tried U.S. citizens suspected of aiding the Confederacy in courts-martial rather than in civilian courts. In 1864, a military tribunal in Indianapolis convicted Lambdin Milligan and three other men of aiding the Confederacy. Milligan was sentenced to death.

Before this death sentence could be carried out, however, the Civil War effectively ended in April 1865. Milligan therefore petitioned for a writ of habeas corpus under Congress's 1863 law, challenging his conviction on the ground that his military trial violated his Sixth Amendment-protected right to a jury trial in a civilian court.

The Supreme Court considered the question in *Ex parte Milligan*, 71 U.S. (4 Wall.) 2 (1866), a year after the Civil War concluded—and concluded that the United States overstepped its bounds with regard to Milligan.

■ MR. JUSTICE DAVIS delivered the opinion of the Court.[6]

During the late wicked Rebellion, the temper of the times did not allow that calmness in deliberation and discussion so necessary to a correct conclusion of a purely judicial question. Then, considerations of safety were mingled with the exercise of power; and feelings and interests prevailed which are happily terminated. Now that the public safety is assured, this question, as well as all others, can be discussed and decided without passion or the admixture of any element not required to form a legal judgment. We approach the investigation of this case, fully sensible of the magnitude of the inquiry and the necessity of full and cautious deliberation. . . .

The controlling question in the case is this: Upon the facts stated in Milligan's petition, and the exhibits filed, had the military commission mentioned in it jurisdiction, legally, to try and sentence him? Milligan, not a resident of one of the rebellious states, or a prisoner of war, but a citizen of Indiana for twenty years past, and never in the military or naval service, is, while at his home, arrested by the military power of the United States, imprisoned, and, on certain criminal charges preferred against him, tried, convicted, and sentenced to be hanged by a military commission, organized under the direction of the military commander of the military district of Indiana. Had this tribunal the legal power and authority to try and punish this man?

No graver question was ever considered by this court, nor one which more nearly concerns the rights of the whole people; for it is the birthright of every American citizen when charged with crime, to be tried and punished according to law. The power of punishment is, alone through the means which the laws have provided for that purpose, and if they are ineffectual, there is an immunity from punishment, no matter how great an offender the individual may be, or how much his crimes may have shocked the sense of justice of the country, or endangered its safety. By the protection of the law human rights are secured; withdraw that protection, and they are at the mercy of wicked rulers, or the clamor of an excited people. If there was law to justify this military trial, it is not our province to interfere; if there was not, it is our duty to declare the nullity of the whole proceedings. The decision of this question does not depend on argument or judicial precedents, numerous and highly illustrative as they are. These precedents inform us of the extent of the struggle to preserve liberty and to relieve those in civil life from military trials. The founders of our government were familiar with the history of that struggle; and secured in a written constitution every right which the people had wrested from power during a contest of ages. By that Constitution and the laws authorized by it this question must be determined. The provisions of that instrument on the administration of criminal justice are too plain and direct, to leave room for misconstruction or doubt of their true meaning. Those applicable to this case are found in that clause of the original Constitution which says, "That the trial of all crimes, except in case of impeachment, shall be by jury;" and in the fourth, fifth, and sixth articles of the amendments. The fourth proclaims the right to be secure in person and effects against unreasonable search and seizure; and directs that a judicial warrant shall not issue "without proof of probable cause supported by oath or affirmation." The fifth declares "that no person shall be held to answer for a capital or otherwise infamous crime unless on presentment by a grand jury, except in cases arising in the land or naval forces, or

---

[6] **As You Read, Consider:** Justice David Davis identifies the question raised by Lambdin Milligan's case as the "grave[st] question . . . ever considered by this court." What does he think is the role of a civilian court during wartime, and under what circumstances does he think a military tribunal is acceptable?

in the militia, when in actual service in time of war or public danger, nor be deprived of life, liberty, or property, without due process of law." And the sixth guarantees the right of trial by jury, in such manner and with such regulations that with upright judges, impartial juries, and an able bar, the innocent will be saved and the guilty punished. . . . These securities for personal liberty thus embodied, were such as wisdom and experience had demonstrated to be necessary for the protection of those accused of crime. And so strong was the sense of the country of their importance, and so jealous were the people that these rights, highly prized, might be denied them by implication, that when the original Constitution was proposed for adoption it encountered severe opposition; and, but for the belief that it would be so amended as to embrace them, it would never have been ratified.

Time has proven the discernment of our ancestors; for even these provisions, expressed in such plain English words, that it would seem the ingenuity of man could not evade them, are now, after the lapse of more than seventy years, sought to be avoided. Those great and good men foresaw that troublous times would arise, when rulers and people would become restive under restraint, and seek by sharp and decisive measures to accomplish ends deemed just and proper; and that the principles of constitutional liberty would be in peril, unless established by irrepealable law. The history of the world had taught them that what was done in the past might be attempted in the future. The Constitution of the United States is a law for rulers and people, equally in war and in peace, and covers with the shield of its protection all classes of men, at all times, and under all circumstances. No doctrine, involving more pernicious consequences, was ever invented by the wit of man than that any of its provisions can be suspended during any of the great exigencies of government. Such a doctrine leads directly to anarchy or despotism, but the theory of necessity on which it is based is false; for the government, within the Constitution, has all the powers granted to it, which are necessary to preserve its existence; as has been happily proved by the result of the great effort to throw off its just authority.

Have any of the rights guaranteed by the Constitution been violated in the case of Milligan? and if so, what are they?

Every trial involves the exercise of judicial power; and from what source did the military commission that tried him derive their authority? Certainly no part of the judicial power of the country was conferred on them; because the Constitution expressly vests it "in one supreme court and such inferior courts as the Congress may from time to time ordain and establish," and it is not pretended that the commission was a court ordained and established by Congress. They cannot justify on the mandate of the President; because he is controlled by law, and has his appropriate sphere of duty, which is to execute, not to make, the laws; and there is "no unwritten criminal code to which resort can be had as a source of jurisdiction."

But it is said that the jurisdiction is complete under the "laws and usages of war."

It can serve no useful purpose to inquire what those laws and usages are, whence they originated, where found, and on whom they operate; they can never be applied to citizens in states which have upheld the authority of the government, and where the courts are open and their process unobstructed. This court has judicial knowledge that in Indiana the Federal authority was always unopposed, and its courts always open to hear criminal accusations and redress grievances; and no usage of war could sanction a military trial there for any offence whatever of a citizen in civil life, in nowise connected with the military service. Congress could grant no such power; and to the honor of our national legislature be it said, it has never been provoked by the state of the country even to attempt its exercise. One of the plainest constitutional provisions was, therefore, infringed when Milligan was tried by a court not ordained and established by Congress, and not composed of judges appointed during good behavior.[7]

Why was he not delivered to the Circuit Court of Indiana to be proceeded against according to law? No reason of necessity could be urged against it; because Congress had declared penalties against the offences charged, provided for their punishment, and directed that court to hear and determine them. And soon after this military tribunal was ended, the Circuit Court met, peacefully transacted its business, and adjourned. It needed no bayonets to protect it, and required no military aid to execute its judgments. It was held in a state, eminently distinguished for patriotism, by judges commissioned during the Rebellion, who were provided with juries, upright, intelligent, and selected by a marshal appointed by the President. The government had no right to conclude that Milligan, if guilty, would not receive in that court merited punishment; for its records disclose that it was constantly engaged in the trial of similar offences, and was never interrupted in its administration of criminal justice. If it was dangerous, in the distracted condition of affairs, to leave Milligan unrestrained of his liberty, because he "conspired against the government, afforded aid and comfort to rebels, and incited the people to insurrection," the *law* said arrest him, confine him closely, render him powerless to do further mischief; and then present his case to the grand jury of the district, with proofs of his guilt, and, if indicted, try him according to the course of the common law. If this had been done, the Constitution would have been vindicated, the law of 1863 enforced, and the securities for personal liberty preserved and defended.[8]

Another guarantee of freedom was broken when Milligan was denied a trial by jury. The great minds of the country have differed on the correct interpretation to be given to various provisions of the Federal Constitution; and judicial decision has been often invoked to settle their true meaning; but until recently no one ever doubted that the right of trial by jury was fortified in the organic law against the power of attack. It is now assailed; but if ideas can be expressed in words, and language has any meaning, this right—one of the most valuable in a free country—is preserved to every one accused of crime who is not attached to the army, or navy, or militia in actual service. The sixth amendment affirms that "in all criminal prosecutions the accused shall enjoy the right to a speedy and public trial by an impartial jury," language broad enough to embrace all persons and cases; but the fifth, recognizing the necessity of an indictment, or presentment, before any one can be held to answer for high crimes, "excepts cases arising in the land or naval forces, or in the militia, when in actual service, in time of war or public danger;" and the framers of the Constitution, doubtless, meant to limit the right of trial by jury, in the sixth amendment, to those persons who were subject to indictment or presentment in the fifth.

The discipline necessary to the efficiency of the army and navy, required other and swifter modes of trial than are furnished by the common law courts; and, in pursuance of the power conferred by the Constitution, Congress has declared the kinds of trial, and the manner in which they shall be conducted, for offences committed while the party is in the military or naval service. Every one connected with these branches of the public service is amenable to the jurisdiction which Congress has created for their government, and, while thus serving, surrenders his

---

7 **Question:** Davis here emphasizes that Milligan was captured in Indiana, a northern state whose loyalty to the Union was unquestioned. Might his analysis have been different if Milligan had been captured in the neighboring state of Kentucky, the site of several pitched battles?

8 **Questions:** Does this passage suggest that there is never an excuse to try a civilian in a military tribunal as opposed to a civilian court? What if there is a serious allegation that the defendant's allies might attack the courthouse in retaliation? *Cf.* Scott Shane & Benjamin Weiser, *U.S. Drops Plan for a 9/11 Trial in New York City*, N.Y. Times, Jan. 29, 2010, at A1.

right to be tried by the civil courts.[9] All other persons, citizens of states where the courts are open, if charged with crime, are guaranteed the inestimable privilege of trial by jury. This privilege is a vital principle, underlying the whole administration of criminal justice; it is not held by sufferance, and cannot be frittered away on any plea of state or political necessity. When peace prevails, and the authority of the government is undisputed, there is no difficulty of preserving the safeguards of liberty; for the ordinary modes of trial are never neglected, and no one wishes it otherwise; but if society is disturbed by civil commotion—if the passions of men are aroused and the restraints of law weakened, if not disregarded—these safeguards need, and should receive, the watchful care of those intrusted with the guardianship of the Constitution and laws. In no other way can we transmit to posterity unimpaired the blessings of liberty, consecrated by the sacrifices of the Revolution.

It is claimed that martial law covers with its broad mantle the proceedings of this military commission. The proposition is this: that in a time of war the commander of an armed force (if in his opinion the exigencies of the country demand it, and of which he is to judge), has the power, within the lines of his military district, to suspend all civil rights and their remedies, and subject citizens as well as soldiers to the rule of his will; and in the exercise of his lawful authority cannot be restrained, except by his superior officer or the President of the United States.

If this position is sound to the extent claimed, then when war exists, foreign or domestic, and the country is subdivided into military departments for mere convenience, the commander of one of them can, if he chooses, within his limits, on the plea of necessity, with the approval of the Executive, substitute military force for and to the exclusion of the laws, and punish all persons, as he thinks right and proper, without fixed or certain rules.

The statement of this proposition shows its importance; for, if true, republican government is a failure, and there is an end of liberty regulated by law. Martial law, established on such a basis, destroys every guarantee of the Constitution, and effectually renders the "military independent of and superior to the civil power"—the attempt to do which by the King of Great Britain was deemed by our fathers such an offence, that they assigned it to the world as one of the causes which impelled them to declare their independence. Civil liberty and this kind of martial law cannot endure together; the antagonism is irreconcilable; and, in the conflict, one or the other must perish.[10]

This nation, as experience has proved, cannot always remain at peace, and has no right to expect that it will always have wise and humane rulers, sincerely attached to the principles of the Constitution. Wicked men, ambitious of power, with hatred of liberty and contempt of law, may fill the place once occupied by Washington and Lincoln; and if this right is conceded, and the calamities of war again befall us, the dangers to human liberty are frightful to contemplate. If our fathers had failed to provide for just such a contingency, they would have been false to the trust reposed in them. They knew—the history of the world told them—the nation they were founding, be its existence short or long, would be involved in war; how often or how

[9] **Question:** Davis here explains one circumstance in which it is appropriate to try people in a military tribunal without a jury: when they are members of the military. What distinguishes members of the military from Milligan in this case?

[10] **Question:** Davis emphatically rejects the idea that a military commander can ignore constitutional limits like the Sixth Amendment's guarantee of a jury trial. Yet in the *Prize Cases*, the Court authorized the federal government to seize the private property of rebel allies, even though the Fifth Amendment ordinarily requires the federal government to pay just compensation when it takes property. Why might Congress's war powers authorize takings without just compensation but not the suspension of other civil rights?

long continued, human foresight could not tell; and that unlimited power, wherever lodged at such a time, was especially hazardous to freemen. For this, and other equally weighty reasons, they secured the inheritance they had fought to maintain, by incorporating in a written constitution the safeguards which time had proved were essential to its preservation. Not one of these safeguards can the President, or Congress, or the Judiciary disturb, except the one concerning the writ of habeas corpus.

It is essential to the safety of every government that, in a great crisis, like the one we have just passed through, there should be a power somewhere of suspending the writ of habeas corpus. In every war, there are men of previously good character, wicked enough to counsel their fellow-citizens to resist the measures deemed necessary by a good government to sustain its just authority and overthrow its enemies; and their influence may lead to dangerous combinations. In the emergency of the times, an immediate public investigation according to law may not be possible; and yet, the peril to the country may be too imminent to suffer such persons to go at large. Unquestionably, there is then an exigency which demands that the government, if it should see fit in the exercise of a proper discretion to make arrests, should not be required to produce the persons arrested in answer to a writ of habeas corpus. The Constitution goes no further. It does not say after a writ of habeas corpus is denied a citizen, that he shall be tried otherwise than by the course of the common law; if it had intended this result, it was easy by the use of direct words to have accomplished it. The illustrious men who framed that instrument were guarding the foundations of civil liberty against the abuses of unlimited power; they were full of wisdom, and the lessons of history informed them that a trial by an established court, assisted by an impartial jury, was the only sure way of protecting the citizen against oppression and wrong. Knowing this, they limited the suspension to one great right, and left the rest to remain forever inviolable. But, it is insisted that the safety of the country in time of war demands that this broad claim for martial law shall be sustained. If this were true, it could be well said that a country, preserved at the sacrifice of all the cardinal principles of liberty, is not worth the cost of preservation. Happily, it is not so.

It will be borne in mind that this is not a question of the power to proclaim martial law, when war exists in a community and the courts and civil authorities are overthrown. Nor is it a question what rule a military commander, at the head of his army, can impose on states in rebellion to cripple their resources and quell the insurrection. The jurisdiction claimed is much more extensive. The necessities of the service, during the late Rebellion, required that the loyal states should be placed within the limits of certain military districts and commanders appointed in them; and, it is urged, that this, in a military sense, constituted them the theatre of military operations; and, as in this case, Indiana had been and was again threatened with invasion by the enemy, the occasion was furnished to establish martial law. The conclusion does not follow from the premises. If armies were collected in Indiana, they were to be employed in another locality, where the laws were obstructed and the national authority disputed. On her soil there was no hostile foot; if once invaded, that invasion was at an end, and with it all pretext for martial law. Martial law cannot arise from a threatened invasion. The necessity must be actual and present; the invasion real, such as effectually closes the courts and deposes the civil administration.[11]

---

[11] **Question:** Davis concedes in this paragraph that there are some circumstances when martial law and military tribunals may be justified. How does he expect a court to be able to identify when "[t]he necessity [is] actual and present"?

It is difficult to see how the safety of the country required martial law in Indiana. If any of her citizens were plotting treason, the power of arrest could secure them, until the government was prepared for their trial, when the courts were open and ready to try them. It was as easy to protect witnesses before a civil as a military tribunal; and as there could be no wish to convict, except on sufficient legal evidence, surely an ordained and established court was better able to judge of this than a military tribunal composed of gentlemen not trained to the profession of the law.

It follows, from what has been said on this subject, that there are occasions when martial rule can be properly applied. If, in foreign invasion or civil war, the courts are actually closed, and it is impossible to administer criminal justice according to law, then, on the theatre of active military operations, where war really prevails, there is a necessity to furnish a substitute for the civil authority, thus overthrown, to preserve the safety of the army and society; and as no power is left but the military, it is allowed to govern by martial rule until the laws can have their free course. As necessity creates the rule, so it limits its duration; for, if this government is continued after the courts are reinstated, it is a gross usurpation of power. Martial rule can never exist where the courts are open, and in the proper and unobstructed exercise of their jurisdiction. It is also confined to the locality of actual war. Because, during the late Rebellion it could have been enforced in Virginia, where the national authority was overturned and the courts driven out, it does not follow that it should obtain in Indiana, where that authority was never disputed, and justice was always administered. And so in the case of a foreign invasion, martial rule may become a necessity in one state, when, in another, it would be "mere lawless violence." . . .[12]

NOTE: MARTIAL LAW AND THE SUSPENSION OF HABEAS CORPUS

Although the Supreme Court overturned Milligan's conviction in Indiana, it recognized that martial law could validly be imposed in Virginia and other states that had actually rebelled against the Union. A year after *Milligan*, Congress passed the first of four Military Reconstruction Acts, ch. 153, 14 Stat. 428 (1867), which created five military districts in the South to be administered by military generals. These laws exercised enormous power to reshape southern government: they required southern states to adopt new constitutions allowing black men to vote, they determined who was eligible to participate in constitutional conventions, and they gave military governors the power to oversee military tribunals and local governments in their districts' states until the states established satisfactory constitutions. *See* Eric Foner, *Reconstruction* 273–80 (2014). In fact, Congress was so worried about the constitutionality of these laws that it temporarily stripped the Supreme Court of jurisdiction to hear appeals challenging their legality. *See* Act of Feb. 5, 1867, ch. 28, 14 Stat. 385; *Ex parte McCardle*, 74 U.S. (7 Wall.) 506 (1869) (upholding the jurisdiction-stripping laws). Congress had no need to worry, though. In *Texas v. White*, the Court upheld the Military Reconstruction Acts as an exercise of Congress's "power to suppress insurrection and carry on war" as well as its duty "to guarantee to every

[12] **Question:** *Milligan* is a bold opinion that repudiated the federal government's claim of special powers during wartime. The opinion was also issued in 1866, after the Civil War was over. Do you think that the Court would have written the same opinion at the height of the war three years earlier—even after President Abraham Lincoln announced that he would ignore the federal court's decision in *Ex parte Merryman*?

State in the Union a republican form of government." 74 U.S. (7 Wall.) 700, 727 (1869).

In the years following Reconstruction, Congress occasionally suspended the writ of habeas corpus to combat the Ku Klux Klan and other insurrections. *See, e.g.*, Act of July 1, 1902, Pub. L. No. 57–235, 32 Stat. 691, 692; Act of Apr. 20, 1871, ch. 22, 17 Stat. 13, 14. When Congress organized a territorial government for Hawaii in 1900, it also authorized the governor to suspend habeas corpus and declare "martial law" during an emergency. *See* Act of Apr. 30, 1900, ch. 339, 31 Stat. 141, 153. The governor invoked this provision eight hours after the Japanese bombing of Pearl Harbor in 1941, putting the island's government in the hands of a military officer. For three years during World War II, the military restricted travel, censored the press, froze wages, required people to work, and even set hours kept by bowling alleys. *See* Daniel Immerwahr, *How to Hide an Empire* 174–77 (2019). Anyone who broke the law could be punished by juryless military tribunals. *Id.*

As in *Milligan*, the Supreme Court weighed in on the legality of Hawaii's martial rule only after World War II ended. In *Duncan v. Kahanamoku*, 327 U.S. 304 (1946), the Court reversed the convictions of two civilian petitioners on the ground that martial law had been extended far beyond the time when Hawaii was under an actual threat of invasion. The Court held that the relevant statute was "intended to authorize the military to act vigorously for the maintenance of an orderly civil government and for the defense of the island against actual or threatened rebellion or invasion, [but] was not intended to authorize the supplanting of courts by military tribunals." *Duncan*, 327 U.S. at 324.

Since *Duncan*, the Court has emphasized that the suspension of the writ of habeas corpus will not be implied and can only take place after Congress's clear intent to do so. *INS v. St. Cyr*, 533 U.S. 289 (2001). At the same time, the Court has also upheld laws denying certain immigrants and prisoners the opportunity to bring habeas claims. *See, e.g., Dep't of Homeland Sec. v. Thuraissigiam*, 140 S. Ct. 1959 (2020) (upholding a law that authorized the summary deportation of immigrants apprehended near the border because habeas is a remedy for unlawful confinement, not unlawful deportation); *Felker v. Turpin*, 518 U.S. 651, 664 (1996) (upholding a law that made it more difficult to file second or successive habeas petitions).

13.4.2

Hirabayashi v. United States

320 U.S. 81 (1943)

The imposition of martial law in *Merryman*, *Milligan*, and *Duncan* involved the replacement of civilian courts with military tribunals for *all* U.S. citizens in particular regions. But in the name of waging war successfully, Congress has also asserted the power to relocate and detain *entire classes* of civilians suspected of being enemies. Indeed, an early Congress passed the Alien Enemy Act of 1798, which authorized the president to arrest, detain, and deport "all natives, citizens, denizens, or subjects" of any nation at war with the United States. Alien Enemy Act, ch. 66, 1 Stat. 577. Even James Madison, who argued that Congress had no such power over "alien friends," conceded that Congress had this power over "alien enemies." Report of 1800 (Jan. 7, 1800), *in* 17 *The Papers of James Madison* 303–51 (William T. Hutchinson et al. eds., 1991).

The federal government most infamously exercised this power during World War II against U.S. citizens of Japanese ancestry. On February 19, 1942, two months after Congress declared war against Japan, President Franklin D. Roosevelt issued Executive Order No. 9066. The order authorized the secretary of war "to prescribe military areas in such places and of such extent as he or the appropriate Military Commander may determine, from which any or all persons may be excluded." Exec. Order No. 9066, 7 Fed. Reg. 1407 (Feb. 19, 1942). Applying this order, the relevant military commander declared that the Pacific Coast was "particularly subject to attack . . . and acts of sabotage, thereby requiring the adoption of military measures necessary to establish safeguards against such enemy operations." 7 Fed. Reg. 2320 (Mar. 2, 1942). The commander added that "such persons or classes of persons as the situation may require" would be excluded from sensitive areas. *Id.* On March 21, 1942, Congress passed a law making it a crime to remain in an area contrary to the restrictions prescribed by a military commander. Pub. L. No. 77–503, 56 Stat. 173.

Three days later, a military commander imposed an 8:00 p.m. curfew on "all alien Germans, all alien Italians, and all persons of Japanese ancestry" within "Military Area No. 1" in the state of Washington. 7 Fed. Reg. 2543 (Mar. 24, 1942). Although this order nominally applied to German and Italian immigrants, its obvious targets were Americans of Japanese ancestry—the majority of whom lived on the Pacific Coast. The same commander even ordered "all persons of Japanese ancestry, both alien and non-alien," to report to a "Civil Control Station" in Seattle, where they would eventually be resettled in concentration camps. *Id.* at 2601.

Gordon Kiyoshi Hirabayashi was a 23-year-old U.S. citizen of Japanese ancestry. A recent graduate of the University of Washington, he elected to defy the 8:00 p.m. curfew with the support of the American Friends Service Committee and the American Civil Liberties Union. After turning himself in to the Federal Bureau of Investigation (FBI), he was convicted of violating the restrictions of a military commander. On appeal, he challenged Congress's power to enforce a curfew against U.S. citizens of Japanese ancestry.

By the time the Supreme Court rejected Hirabayashi's argument in *Hirabayashi v. United States*, 320 U.S. 81 (1943), the FBI had, in fact, discovered one operation to commit acts of sabotage in the United States—but the saboteurs were all of *German* descent and lived in areas far removed from the Pacific curfew. *See Ex parte Quirin*, 317 U.S. 1 (1942).

■ MR. CHIEF JUSTICE STONE delivered the opinion of the Court.[13]

[A]ppellant does not deny that he knowingly failed to obey the curfew order as charged in the second count of the indictment, or that the order was authorized by the terms of Executive Order No. 9066, or that the challenged Act of Congress purports to punish with criminal penalties disobedience of such an order. His contentions are only that Congress unconstitutionally delegated its legislative power to the military commander by authorizing him to impose the challenged regulation, and that, even if the regulation were in other respects lawfully authorized, the Fifth Amendment prohibits the discrimination made between citizens of Japanese descent and those of other ancestry. . . .

It will be evident from the legislative history that the Act of March 21, 1942, contemplated and authorized the curfew order which we have before us. . . . [In fact, the] conclusion is inescapable that Congress, by the Act of March 21, 1942, ratified and confirmed Executive Order No. 9066. *Prize Cases* (*The Amy Warwick*), 2 Black 635, 671. And so far as it lawfully could, Congress authorized and implemented such curfew orders as the commanding officer should promulgate pursuant to the Executive Order of the President. The question then is not one of Congressional power to delegate to the President the promulgation of the Executive Order, but whether, acting in cooperation, Congress and the Executive have constitutional authority to impose the curfew restriction here complained of. We must consider also whether, acting together, Congress and the Executive could leave it to the designated military commander to appraise the relevant conditions and on the basis of that appraisal to say whether, under the circumstances, the time and place were appropriate for the promulgation of the curfew order and whether the order itself was an appropriate means of carrying out the Executive Order for the 'protection against espionage and against sabotage' to national defense materials, premises and utilities. For reasons presently to be stated, we conclude that it was within the constitutional power of Congress and the executive arm of the Government to prescribe this curfew order for the period under consideration and that its promulgation by the military commander involved no unlawful delegation of legislative power.

Executive Order No. 9066, promulgated in time of war for the declared purpose of prosecuting the war by protecting national defense resources from sabotage and espionage, and the Act of March 21, 1942, ratifying and confirming the Executive Order, were each an exercise of the power to wage war conferred on the Congress and on the President, as Commander in Chief of the armed forces, by Articles I and II of the Constitution. See *Ex parte Quirin*, 317 U.S. 1, 25, 26. We have no occasion to consider whether the President, acting alone, could lawfully have made the curfew order in question, or have authorized others to make it. For the President's action has the support of the Act of Congress, and we are immediately concerned with the question whether it is within the constitutional power of the national government, through the joint action of Congress and the Executive, to impose this restriction as an emergency war measure. The exercise of that power here involves no question of martial law or trial by military tribunal. Cf. *Ex parte Milligan*, 4 Wall. 2. Appellant has

---

13 **As You Read, Consider:** The enumerated basis of Congress's war powers are the powers to "declare War" and to call forth the militia to "suppress Insurrections and repel Invasions." The Constitution also makes the president "Commander in Chief." Chief Justice Harlan Stone generalizes these discrete clauses into a broad power to "wage war successfully." Is his interpretation fair?

been tried and convicted in the civil courts and has been subjected to penalties prescribed by Congress for the acts committed.

The war power of the national government is 'the power to wage war successfully'. See Charles Evans Hughes, War Powers Under the Constitution, 42 A.B.A.Rep. 232, 238.[14] It extends to every matter and activity so related to war as substantially to affect its conduct and progress. The power is not restricted to the winning of victories in the field and the repulse of enemy forces. It embraces every phase of the national defense, including the protection of war materials and the members of the armed forces from injury and from the dangers which attend the rise, prosecution and progress of war. *Prize Cases, supra*; *Miller v. United States*, 11 Wall. 268, 303, 314; *Selective Draft Law Cases* (*Arver v. United States*), 245 U.S. 366. Since the Constitution commits to the Executive and to Congress the exercise of the war power in all the vicissitudes and conditions of warfare, it has necessarily given them wide scope for the exercise of judgment and discretion in determining the nature and extent of the threatened injury or danger and in the selection of the means for resisting it. *Ex parte Quirin, supra*, 317 U.S. 28, 29; *cf. Prize Cases, supra*, 2 Black 670. Where, as they did here, the conditions call for the exercise of judgment and discretion and for the choice of means by those branches of the Government on which the Constitution has placed the responsibility of warmaking, it is not for any court to sit in review of the wisdom of their action or substitute its judgment for theirs.

The actions taken must be appraised in the light of the conditions with which the President and Congress were confronted in the early months of 1942, many of which since disclosed, were then peculiarly within the knowledge of the military authorities. On December 7, 1941, the Japanese air forces had attacked the United States Naval Base at Pearl Harbor without warning, at the very hour when Japanese diplomatic representatives were conducting negotiations with our State Department ostensibly for the peaceful settlement of differences between the two countries. Simultaneously or nearly so, the Japanese attacked Malaysia, Hong Kong, the Philippines, and Wake and Midway Islands. On the following day their army invaded Thailand. Shortly afterwards they sank two British battleships. On December 13th, Guam was taken. On December 24th and 25th they captured Wake Island and occupied Hong Kong. On January 2, 1942, Manila fell, and on February 10th Singapore, Britain's great naval base in the East, was taken. On February 27th the battle of the Java Sea resulted in a disastrous naval defeat to the United Nations. By the 9th of March Japanese forces had established control over the Netherlands East Indies; Rangoon and Burma were occupied; Bataan and Corregidor were under attack.

Although the results of the attack on Pearl Harbor were not fully disclosed until much later, it was known that the damage was extensive, and that the Japanese by their successes had gained a naval superiority over our forces in the Pacific which might enable them to seize Pearl Harbor, our largest naval base and the last stronghold of defense lying between Japan and the west coast. That reasonably prudent men charged with the responsibility of our national defense had ample ground for concluding that they must face the danger of invasion, take measures against it,

---

[14] **Questions:** Charles Evans Hughes had recently resigned as chief justice of the United States. Thirty years earlier, during World War I, he delivered a famous lecture to the American Bar Association that Stone quotes in this paragraph. Hughes argued that the U.S. Constitution was "a *fighting* constitution" whose enumerated powers permitted Congress to impose a national draft, to expansively regulate the domestic economy, and "to enact whatever legislation is necessary to prosecute [a] war with vigor and success." Charles Evans Hughes, *War Powers Under the Constitution*, 42 A.B.A. Rep. 232, 238–39 (1917); *see* Matthew C. Waxman, *The Power to Wage War Successfully*, 117 Colum. L. Rev. 613, 614 (2017). Do you agree? How does Gordon Hirabayashi's case affect your perspective?

and in making the choice of measures consider our internal situation, cannot be doubted.

The challenged orders were defense measures for the avowed purpose of safeguarding the military area in question, at a time of threatened air raids and invasion by the Japanese forces, from the danger of sabotage and espionage. As the curfew was made applicable to citizens residing in the area only if they were of Japanese ancestry, our inquiry must be whether in the light of all the facts and circumstances there was any substantial basis for the conclusion, in which Congress and the military commander united, that the curfew as applied was a protective measure necessary to meet the threat of sabotage and espionage which would substantially affect the war effort and which might reasonably be expected to aid a threatened enemy invasion. The alternative which appellant insists must be accepted is for the military authorities to impose the curfew on all citizens within the military area, or on none. In a case of threatened danger requiring prompt action, it is a choice between inflicting obviously needless hardship on the many, or sitting passive and unresisting in the presence of the threat. We think that constitutional government, in time of war, is not so powerless and does not compel so hard a choice if those charged with the responsibility of our national defense have reasonable ground for believing that the threat is real.

When the orders were promulgated there was a vast concentration, within Military Areas No. 1 and 2, of installations and facilities for the production of military equipment, especially ships and airplanes. Important Army and Navy bases were located in California and Washington. Approximately one-fourth of the total value of the major aircraft contracts then let by Government procurement officers were to be performed in the State of California. California ranked second, and Washington fifth, of all the states of the Union with respect to the value of shipbuilding contracts to be performed.

In the critical days of March, 1942, the danger to our war production by sabotage and espionage in this area seems obvious. The German invasion of the Western European countries had given ample warning to the world of the menace of the 'fifth column.' Espionage by persons in sympathy with the Japanese Government had been found to have been particularly effective in the surprise attack on Pearl Harbor. At a time of threatened Japanese attack upon this country, the nature of our inhabitants' attachments to the Japanese enemy was consequently a matter of grave concern. Of the 126,000 persons of Japanese descent in the United States, citizens and non-citizens, approximately 112,000 resided in California, Oregon and Washington at the time of the adoption of the military regulations. Of these approximately two-thirds are citizens because born in the United States. Not only did the great majority of such persons reside within the Pacific Coast states but they were concentrated in or near three of the large cities, Seattle, Portland and Los Angeles, all in Military Area No. 1.

There is support for the view that social, economic and political conditions which have prevailed since the close of the last century, when the Japanese began to come to this country in substantial numbers, have intensified their solidarity and have in large measure prevented their assimilation as an integral part of the white population. In addition, large numbers of children of Japanese parentage are sent to Japanese language schools outside the regular hours of public schools in the locality. Some of these schools are generally believed to be sources of Japanese nationalistic propaganda, cultivating allegiance to Japan. Considerable numbers, estimated to be approximately 10,000, of American-born children of Japanese parentage have been sent to Japan for all or a part of their education.

Congress and the Executive, including the military commander, could have attributed special significance, in its bearing on the loyalties of persons of Japanese descent, to the maintenance by Japan of its system of dual citizenship. Children born in the United States of Japanese alien parents, and especially those children born before December 1, 1924, are under many circumstances deemed, by Japanese law, to be citizens of Japan. No official census of those whom Japan regards as having thus retained Japanese citizenship is available, but there is ground for the belief that the number is large.

The large number of resident alien Japanese, approximately one-third of all Japanese inhabitants of the country, are of mature years and occupy positions of influence in Japanese communities. The association of influential Japanese residents with Japanese Consulates has been deemed a ready means for the dissemination of propaganda and for the maintenance of the influence of the Japanese Government with the Japanese population in this country.

As a result of all these conditions affecting the life of the Japanese, both aliens and citizens, in the Pacific Coast area, there has been relatively little social intercourse between them and the white population. The restrictions, both practical and legal, affecting the privileges and opportunities afforded to persons of Japanese extraction residing in the United States, have been sources of irritation and may well have tended to increase their isolation, and in many instances their attachments to Japan and its institutions.[15]

Viewing these data in all their aspects, Congress and the Executive could reasonably have concluded that these conditions have encouraged the continued attachment of members of this group to Japan and Japanese institutions. These are only some of the many considerations which those charged with the responsibility for the national defense could take into account in determining the nature and extent of the danger of espionage and sabotage, in the event of invasion or air raid attack. The extent of that danger could be definitely known only after the event and after it was too late to meet it. Whatever views we may entertain regarding the loyalty to this country of the citizens of Japanese ancestry, we cannot reject as unfounded the judgment of the military authorities and of Congress that there were disloyal members of that population, whose number and strength could not be precisely and quickly ascertained. We cannot say that the war-making branches of the Government did not have ground for believing that in a critical hour such persons could not readily be isolated and separately dealt with, and constituted a menace to the national defense and safety, which demanded that prompt and adequate measures be taken to guard against it.

Appellant does not deny that, given the danger, a curfew was an appropriate measure against sabotage. It is an obvious protection against the perpetration of sabotage most readily committed during the hours of darkness. If it was an appropriate exercise of the war power its validity is not impaired because it has restricted the citizen's liberty. Like every military control of the population of a dangerous zone in war time, it necessarily involves some infringement of individual liberty, just as does the police establishment of fire lines during a fire, or the

---

[15] **Questions:** Stone here is alluding to racist state and federal laws that prohibited residents of Japanese origin from becoming citizens, owning land, or living in certain neighborhoods. He is suggesting that Congress acted rationally when it presumed that Japanese Americans might be resentful of these restrictions and therefore disloyal to the United States. Do you agree with Stone that, as unjust as these discriminatory laws were, they support deferring to the government's judgment about which actions are necessary to "wage war successfully"? Or do you agree with the Yale law professor Eugene V. Rostow, who criticized the Court's failure to evaluate for itself the factual basis for the government's action—as the Court did in *Ex parte Milligan*? *See* Eugene V. Rostow, *The Japanese American Cases—A Disaster*, 54 Yale L.J. 489, 530 (1945). What is the proper role of the judiciary in determining which actions are appropriate exercises of Congress's war powers?

confinement of people to their houses during an air raid alarm—neither of which could be thought to be an infringement of constitutional right. Like them, the validity of the restraints of the curfew order depends on all the conditions which obtain at the time the curfew is imposed and which support the order imposing it.

But appellant insists that the exercise of the power is inappropriate and unconstitutional because it discriminates against citizens of Japanese ancestry, in violation of the Fifth Amendment. The Fifth Amendment contains no equal protection clause and it restrains only such discriminatory legislation by Congress as amounts to a denial of due process. Congress may hit at a particular danger where it is seen, without providing for others which are not so evident or so urgent.[16]

Distinctions between citizens solely because of their ancestry are by their very nature odious to a free people whose institutions are founded upon the doctrine of equality. For that reason, legislative classification or discrimination based on race alone has often been held to be a denial of equal protection. *Yick Wo v. Hopkins*, 118 U.S. 356. We may assume that these considerations would be controlling here were it not for the fact that the danger of espionage and sabotage, in time of war and of threatened invasion, calls upon the military authorities to scrutinize every relevant fact bearing on the loyalty of populations in the danger areas. Because racial discriminations are in most circumstances irrelevant and therefore prohibited, it by no means follows that, in dealing with the perils of war, Congress and the Executive are wholly precluded from taking into account those facts and circumstances which are relevant to measures for our national defense and for the successful prosecution of the war, and which may in fact place citizens of one ancestry in a different category from others. 'We must never forget, that it is a constitution we are expounding', 'a constitution intended to endure for ages to come, and, consequently, to be adapted to the various crises of human affairs'. *McCulloch v. Maryland*, 4 Wheat. 316, 407, 415. The adoption by Government, in the crisis of war and of threatened invasion, of measures for the public safety, based upon the recognition of facts and circumstances which indicate that a group of one national extraction may menace that safety more than others, is not wholly beyond the limits of the Constitution and is not to be condemned merely because in other and in most circumstances racial distinctions are irrelevant. . . .

We need not now attempt to define the ultimate boundaries of the war power. We decide only the issue as we have defined it—we decide only that the curfew order as applied, and at the time it was applied, was within the boundaries of the war power. In this case it is enough that circumstances within the knowledge of those charged with the responsibility for maintaining the national defense afforded a rational basis for the decision which they made. Whether we would have made it is irrelevant. . . .[17]

---

[16] **Note:** In addition to challenging the Article I source of the curfew law, Gordon Hirabayashi challenged the law as unconstitutionally discriminatory in violation of the Fifth Amendment. We will discuss this second argument, which Stone quickly rejects, in a later section on racial discrimination (section 45.2).

[17] **Questions:** In *Milligan*, the Supreme Court emphatically rejected the federal government's claim that martial law was necessary to repel a threatened, but not yet actual, invasion. Does *Hirabayashi* modify *Milligan*'s analysis? Stone concedes in this final paragraph that there might be some "ultimate boundaries of the war power." What rule would you adopt to determine which actions are necessary to "wage war successfully" and which exceed the government's power?

NOTE: CONSTITUTIONALITY OF INTERNMENT

None of the justices dissented from *Hirabayashi*, which remains good law. The case challenged only the curfew, however, not the exclusion or relocation of U.S. citizens of Japanese ancestry. By 1944, over 100,000 of the 127,000 Japanese Americans living in the United States had been forcibly relocated into concentration camps away from the Pacific Coast, where they were crammed into military barracks unsuitable for family life. Many of the internees were allowed to leave only if they renounced their U.S. citizenship and departed for Japan. *See* Mae Ngai, *Impossible Subjects* 188–92 (2014).

In *Korematsu v. United States*, 323 U.S. 214 (1944), the Supreme Court upheld the exclusion of Japanese American residents from the West Coast, relying heavily on *Hirabayashi*. (We will read *Korematsu* later (section 45.2) because of its relevance to the development of equal-protection jurisprudence.)

The same day as *Korematsu*, however, the Court also announced *Ex parte Endo*, in which the Court held that the federal government could not relocate or indefinitely detain "citizens who are concededly loyal." 323 U.S. 283, 297 (1944). The Court explained that "[a] citizen who is concededly loyal presents no problem of espionage or sabotage. Loyalty is a matter of the heart and mind not of race, creed, or color. He who is loyal is by definition not a spy or a saboteur." *Id.* at 302. Because the power to detain was "derived from the power to protect the war effort against espionage and sabotage, detention which has no relationship to that objective is unauthorized." *Id.*

The federal government was nevertheless slow to react to *Endo*, and the internment of Japanese Americans continued until 1946. In 1988, Congress formally apologized for the federal government's treatment of Japanese Americans, granting $20,000 in reparations to each surviving internee. Civil Liberties Act of 1988, Pub. L. No. 100–383, 102 Stat. 904.

NOTE: PUNISHMENT OF TRAITORS

Although U.S. citizens such as Hirabayashi were concededly loyal, Congress has, at times, targeted and punished people suspected of being traitors or subversives. Through the 1960s, for example, the Supreme Court repeatedly affirmed Congress's power to punish people who actively sought to disrupt the federal war effort or to give aid to the Soviet Union, with whom the United States had not declared war. *See, e.g., Schenck v. United States*, 249 U.S. 47 (1919); *Debs v. United States*, 249 U.S. 211 (1919); *Abrams v. United States*, 250 U.S. 616 (1919). The Court also upheld Congress's power to regulate and punish members of the Communist Party who allegedly sought to forcibly overthrow the U.S. government. *See, e.g., Dennis v. United States*, 341 U.S. 494 (1951).

Absent the First Amendment's protection of free speech and association, Congress's war powers would likely continue to support such regulation. But the Supreme Court has since enforced the First Amendment as an external limit on Congress's war powers. *See, e.g., United States v. Robel*, 389 U.S. 258 (1967); *United States v. Brown*, 381 U.S. 437 (1965).

Related to Congress's war powers is its power "to declare the Punishment of Treason." U.S. Const. art. III, § 3, cl. 2. The Constitution sets several limits on this power: "Treason against the United States, shall consist only in levying War against them, or in adhering to their Enemies, giving them Aid and Comfort. No Person shall be convicted of Treason unless on the Testimony of two Witnesses to the same overt Act, or on Confession in open Court." *Id.* cl. 1. In practice, these limits have been interpreted literally. Evidence that former vice president Aaron Burr had plotted to commit treason was dismissed for failing to include "two Witnesses to the same overt Act." *United States v. Burr*, 8 U.S. (4 Cranch) 469, app. (1807); *see also Cramer v. United States*, 325 U.S. 1 (1945). Treason charges against Burr's confederates were also dismissed because they were charged with conspiring to subvert the federal government by force, not levying war as the Constitution requires. *Ex parte Bollman*, 8 U.S. (4 Cranch) 75, 126 (1807). Similarly, treason charges against abolitionists who forcibly resisted the Fugitive Slave Act of 1850 were also dismissed because such resistance also did not constitute levying war. *United States v. Hanway*, 26 F. Cas. 105 (C.C.E.D. Pa. 1851) (No. 15299).

These limits on the power to punish traitors mean that only a handful of people have ever been convicted of treason over the course of more than two centuries. This handful includes several participants in the Whiskey Rebellion of 1794. *See United States v. Vigol*, 29 F. Cas. 376 (C.C.D. Pa. 1795) (No. 16621); *United States v. Mitchell*, 26 F. Cas. 1277 (C.C.D. Pa. 1795) (No. 15788). It also includes the family members of Herbert Hans Haupt, a German saboteur during World War II. *Haupt v. United States*, 330 U.S. 631 (1947). The most recent person to be convicted of treason is Tomoya Kawakita, a dual U.S.-Japanese citizen who worked in a Japanese prisoner of war (POW) camp during World War II and was charged with mistreating American POWs. *See Kawakita v. United States*, 343 U.S. 717 (1952). Far more common have been convictions under federal statutes that prohibit conspiring to commit espionage or to give aid to an enemy. *See, e.g., United States v. Rosenberg*, 195 F.2d 583 (2d Cir. 1952), *cert denied*, 344 U.S. 889 (1952) (upholding the convictions of Ethel and Julius Rosenberg).

Surprisingly, few if any of the thousands of people who joined the Confederacy during the Civil War were convicted of treason by a federal court. *See* William A. Blair, *With Malice Toward Some* 52–53 (2014). A disappointed Congress eager to punish southerners instead adopted the Fourteenth Amendment, Section 3 of which disqualified from holding office any official who "engaged in insurrection or rebellion against the [Constitution]" or who gave "aid or comfort to the enemies thereof." *Id.* at 292–93.

During the war, Congress also attempted to "punish Treason and Rebellion" by seizing and confiscating the property of anyone convicted of giving aid and comfort to the Confederacy. Act of July 17, 1862, ch. 195, 12 Stat. 589. The law did not actually define such aid as *treason*, however, and the Supreme Court upheld it "as an exercise of the war powers of the government." *Miller v. United States*, 78 U.S. (11 Wall.) 268, 304–05 (1871).

13.4.3

Boumediene v. Bush

553 U.S. 723 (2008)

In addition to authorizing martial law and relocating U.S. citizens to win a war, Congress has also detained and summarily punished enemy combatants after they have been captured.

On the battlefield, the federal government traditionally exercised near plenary constitutional power—subject only to the limits of international law—to execute enemy combatants, detain them, or otherwise prevent them from rejoining the fight. *See* John Fabian Witt, *Lincoln's Code: The Laws of War in American History* 94–99 (2005).

This power traditionally extended off the battlefield as well. For example, during World War II, a group of German saboteurs arrived by submarine in Long Island. The saboteurs were spotted by a member of the U.S. Coast Guard, whom they unsuccessfully attempted to bribe. *See* Noah Feldman, *Scorpions* 216–25 (2010). Instead of trying the captured Germans in federal court, President Franklin D. Roosevelt appointed a military commission to try them without a jury. In *Ex parte Quirin*, 317 U.S. 1 (1942), the Supreme Court unanimously upheld the constitutionality of this military proceeding. The Court explained that Congress had constitutionally authorized such a commission in its declaration of war on Germany. "An important incident to the conduct of war is the adoption of measures by the military command not only to repel and defeat the enemy," the Court explained, "but to seize and subject to disciplinary measures those enemies who in their attempt to thwart or impede our military effort have violated the law of war." *Ex parte Quirin*, 317 U.S. at 28–29. The Court reaffirmed this holding after World War II ended. In *In re Yamashita*, 327 U.S. 1 (1946), the Court authorized the use of a military commission to try a Japanese general for conduct committed by his soldiers during Japan's wartime occupation of the U.S. territory of the Philippines.

The Court only began to reconsider this use of military commissions during the so-called War on Terror following the September 11 attacks. On September 14, 2001, Congress passed the Authorization for the Use of Military Force (AUMF), Pub. L. No. 107–40, 115 Stat. 224. The AUMF authorized the president "to use all necessary and appropriate force against those nations, organizations, or persons he determines . . . aided the terrorist attacks that occurred on September 11, 2001, or harbored such organizations or persons, in order to prevent any future acts of international terrorism against the United States." AUMF, 115 Stat. 224. President George W. Bush subsequently ordered U.S. armed forces to Afghanistan to subdue the Al-Qaeda terrorist network and the Taliban regime that was thought to support it. As part of this military campaign, U.S. soldiers captured thousands of people, including several U.S. citizens. Many of these prisoners were indefinitely detained without access to civil courts, with some sent to a U.S. military base on Guantánamo Bay in Cuba.

Between 2004 and 2008, the Supreme Court heard six cases challenging the legality of these detentions. The first, *Hamdi v. Rumsfeld*, 542 U.S. 507 (2004), questioned whether it was constitutional for the federal government to indefinitely detain Yaser Hamdi, a U.S. citizen captured in a combat zone. The Bush administration claimed that Congress constitutionally authorized such a detention in the AUMF when it authorized the president "to use all necessary and appropriate force." A fractured plurality of the Supreme Court agreed. Citing *Ex parte Quirin*, the Court first held that Congress had the constitutional power to detain suspected enemy "combatants," including U.S. citizens. *Hamdi*, 542 U.S. at 518. The Court explained that the federal government often needed "to prevent captured individuals from returning to the field of battle and taking up arms once again." *Id.* But the Court also held that "detention may last no longer than active hostilities," and "indefinite detention for the purpose of interrogation is not authorized." *Id.* at 521. The Court further limited its holding by clarifying that Congress had not suspended the writ of habeas corpus with the AUMF, and therefore "our opinion only finds legislative authority to detain under the AUMF once it is sufficiently clear that the individual is, in fact, an enemy combatant." *Id.* at 523. So, even though Hamdi's seizure took place in a combat zone, he was entitled to provide evidence to refute his enemy-combatant status before an impartial tribunal—including by filing a habeas petition in federal district court if the military's fact-finding procedure proved inadequate.

Although *Hamdi* addressed the detention of U.S. citizens, *Rasul v. Bush*, 542 U.S. 466 (2004), held that noncitizen combatants captured abroad and detained in Guantánamo Bay could also bring habeas petitions in federal district court. *Rasul* distinguished an earlier case, *Johnson v. Eisentrager*, 339 U.S. 763 (1950), in which the Supreme Court held that noncitizen combatants detained abroad could not contest their detentions in federal court. The Supreme Court explained that the writ of habeas corpus is intended to allow prisoners to contest their unlawful detention, so a federal district court can grant the writ whenever it has jurisdiction over a prisoner's custodian. Federal courts do not typically exercise jurisdiction over custodians abroad or in war zones. But the Supreme Court found that the federal habeas statute permitted the U.S. District Court for the District of Columbia to exercise jurisdiction over the naval officers supervising Guantánamo Bay, over which the United States exercised exclusive control. *Rasul*, 542 U.S. at 476. *But see Rumsfeld v. Padilla*, 542 U.S. 426 (2004) (holding that the D.C. court did not have jurisdiction over a detainee's suit against the secretary of defense, Donald Rumsfeld).

In response to *Hamdi* and *Rasul*, Congress passed the Detainee Treatment Act of 2005 (DTA), Pub. L. No. 109–148, 119 Stat. 2680. The

DTA amended the federal habeas statute to eliminate all federal habeas jurisdiction over Guantánamo detainees. But in a case involving Osama bin Laden's driver and bodyguard, Salim Hamdan, the Supreme Court held that this statute did not apply to detainees whose cases were already pending at the time of enactment. *Hamdan v. Rumsfeld*, 548 U.S. 557 (2006). Congress responded by passing the Military Commissions Act of 2006 (MCA), Pub. L. No. 109–366, 120 Stat. 2600. The MCA amended the DTA to apply to pending cases of enemy combatants.

Together, the DTA and MCA authorized the Guantánamo prison guards to indefinitely hold noncitizens captured abroad without providing them with an opportunity to contest their status in federal court as enemy combatants. (Citizen detainees, even those captured abroad, could continue to file habeas petitions on the basis of *Hamdi. See Munaf v. Geren*, 553 U.S. 674 (2008).)

In *Boumediene v. Bush*, 553 U.S. 723 (2008), a group of Guantánamo detainees, led by a Bosnian man named Lakhdar Boumediene, challenged this arrangement as a violation of the Suspension Clause, which prohibits the suspension of the writ of habeas corpus "unless when in Cases of Rebellion or Invasion the public safety may require it." U.S. Const. art. I, § 9, cl. 2.

The Court's holding reinforced the importance of the writ.

■ JUSTICE KENNEDY delivered the opinion of the Court.[18]

Petitioners are aliens designated as enemy combatants and detained at the United States Naval Station at Guantanamo Bay, Cuba. There are others detained there, also aliens, who are not parties to this suit.

Petitioners present a question not resolved by our earlier cases relating to the detention of aliens at Guantanamo: whether they have the constitutional privilege of habeas corpus, a privilege not to be withdrawn except in conformance with the Suspension Clause, Art. I, § 9, cl. 2. We hold these petitioners do have the habeas corpus privilege. . . . Therefore § 7 of the Military Commissions Act of 2006 (MCA), 28 U.S.C. § 2241(e), operates as an unconstitutional suspension of the writ. . . .

I

Under the Authorization for Use of Military Force (AUMF), § 2(a), 115 Stat. 224, note following 50 U.S.C. § 1541, the President is authorized "to use all necessary and appropriate force against those nations, organizations, or persons he determines planned, authorized, committed, or aided the terrorist attacks that occurred on September 11, 2001, or harbored such organizations or persons, in order to prevent any future acts of international terrorism against the United States by such nations, organizations or persons."

In *Hamdi v. Rumsfeld,* 542 U.S. 507 (2004), five Members of the Court recognized that detention of individuals who fought against the United States in Afghanistan "for the duration of the particular conflict in which they were captured, is

[18] **As You Read, Consider:** Where the *Prize Cases* and *Hirabayashi v. United States* gave Congress enormous discretion to "wage war successfully," *Ex parte Milligan* and *Boumediene v. Bush* attempt to cabin that discretion. Does a rule emerge from these four cases about what is acceptable for Congress to do to win a war—particularly an undeclared war like the Civil War or the War on Terror, where affected people deny that they are participants in the war?

so fundamental and accepted an incident to war as to be an exercise of the 'necessary and appropriate force' Congress has authorized the President to use." *Id.,* at 518 (plurality opinion of O'Connor, J.). After *Hamdi,* the Deputy Secretary of Defense established Combatant Status Review Tribunals (CSRTs) to determine whether individuals detained at Guantanamo were "enemy combatants," as the Department defines that term. . . .

Interpreting the AUMF, the Department of Defense ordered the detention of these petitioners, and they were transferred to Guantanamo. Some of these individuals were apprehended on the battlefield in Afghanistan, others in places as far away from there as Bosnia and Gambia. All are foreign nationals, but none is a citizen of a nation now at war with the United States. Each denies he is a member of the al Qaeda terrorist network that carried out the September 11 attacks or of the Taliban regime that provided sanctuary for al Qaeda. Each petitioner appeared before a separate CSRT; was determined to be an enemy combatant; and has sought a writ of habeas corpus in the United States District Court for the District of Columbia. . . .[19]

II

As a threshold matter, we must decide whether MCA § 7 denies the federal courts jurisdiction to hear habeas corpus actions pending at the time of its enactment. We hold the statute does deny that jurisdiction, so that, if the statute is valid, petitioners' cases must be dismissed. . . .

III

In deciding the constitutional questions now presented we must determine whether petitioners are barred from seeking the writ or invoking the protections of the Suspension Clause either because of their status, *i.e.,* petitioners' designation by the Executive Branch as enemy combatants, or their physical location, *i.e.,* their presence at Guantanamo Bay. The Government contends that noncitizens designated as enemy combatants and detained in territory located outside our Nation's borders have no constitutional rights and no privilege of habeas corpus. Petitioners contend they do have cognizable constitutional rights and that Congress, in seeking to eliminate recourse to habeas corpus as a means to assert those rights, acted in violation of the Suspension Clause. . . .

The Framers viewed freedom from unlawful restraint as a fundamental precept of liberty, and they understood the writ of habeas corpus as a vital instrument to secure that freedom. . . . [This] is evident from the care taken to specify the limited grounds for its suspension: "The Privilege of the Writ of Habeas Corpus shall not be suspended, unless when in Cases of Rebellion or Invasion the public Safety may require it." Art. I, § 9, cl. 2. . . .

The Clause protects the rights of the detained by a means consistent with the essential design of the Constitution. It ensures that, except during periods of formal suspension, the Judiciary will have a time-tested device, the writ, to maintain the "delicate balance of governance" that is itself the surest safeguard of liberty. See *Hamdi,* 542 U.S., at 536 (plurality opinion). The Clause protects the rights of the detained by affirming the duty and authority of the Judiciary to call the jailer to account. . . .

---

[19] **Question:** One of the difficulties that connects the Guantánamo cases is that many of the people detained there, like Lakhdar Boumediene, denied that they were enemies. This would not have been a problem in the 1780s, when British soldiers wore their characteristic red uniforms. An underlying question of this case, therefore, is this: How much discretion should the federal government have to unilaterally assert that a person is an enemy, particularly when the person was captured abroad and is being detained in an overseas military base?

We know that at common law a petitioner's status as an alien was not a categorical bar to habeas corpus relief. See, *e.g.*, *Sommersett's Case*, 20 How. St. Tr. 1, 80–82 (1772) (ordering an African slave freed upon finding the custodian's return insufficient). . . .

[But, d]rawing from its position that at common law the writ ran only to territories over which the Crown was sovereign, the Government says the Suspension Clause affords petitioners no rights because the United States does not claim sovereignty over the place of detention.

Guantanamo Bay is not formally part of the United States. See DTA § 1005(g), 119 Stat. 2743. And under the terms of the lease between the United States and Cuba, Cuba retains "ultimate sovereignty" over the territory while the United States exercises "complete jurisdiction and control." See Lease of Lands for Coaling and Naval Stations, Feb. 23, 1903, U.S.-Cuba, Art. III, T.S. No. 418 (hereinafter 1903 Lease Agreement); *Rasul*, 542 U.S., at 471. . . . We therefore do not question the Government's position that Cuba, not the United States, maintains sovereignty, in the legal and technical sense of the term, over Guantanamo Bay. But this does not end the analysis. Our cases do not hold it is improper for us to inquire into the objective degree of control the Nation asserts over foreign territory. . . . As we did in *Rasul*, . . . we take notice of the obvious and uncontested fact that the United States, by virtue of its complete jurisdiction and control over the base, maintains *de facto* sovereignty. . . .

The United States has maintained complete and uninterrupted control of the bay for over 100 years. At the close of the Spanish-American War, Spain ceded control over the entire island of Cuba to the United States and specifically "relinquishe[d] all claim[s] of sovereignty . . . and title." See Treaty of Paris, Dec. 10, 1898, U.S.-Spain, Art. I, 30 Stat. 1755, T.S. No. 343. From the date the treaty with Spain was signed until the Cuban Republic was established on May 20, 1902, the United States governed the territory "in trust" for the benefit of the Cuban people. *Neely v. Henkel*, 180 U.S. 109, 120 (1901); H. Thomas, Cuba or The Pursuit of Freedom 436, 460 (1998). And although it recognized, by entering into the 1903 Lease Agreement, that Cuba retained "ultimate sovereignty" over Guantanamo, the United States continued to maintain the same plenary control it had enjoyed since 1898. Yet the Government's view is that the Constitution had no effect there, at least as to noncitizens, because the United States disclaimed sovereignty in the formal sense of the term. . . .

Our basic charter cannot be contracted away like this. The Constitution grants Congress and the President the power to acquire, dispose of, and govern territory, not the power to decide when and where its terms apply. Even when the United States acts outside its borders, its powers are not "absolute and unlimited" but are subject "to such restrictions as are expressed in the Constitution." *Murphy v. Ramsey*, 114 U.S. 15, 44 (1885). To hold the political branches have the power to switch the Constitution on or off at will . . . would permit a striking anomaly in our tripartite system of government, leading to a regime in which Congress and the President, not this Court, say "what the law is." *Marbury v. Madison*, 1 Cranch 137, 177 (1803). . . .[20]

As we recognized in *Rasul*, the outlines of a framework for determining the reach of the Suspension Clause are suggested by the factors the Court relied upon in

[20] **Question:** The Supreme Court has gone back and forth on the question of whether the Constitution restricts Congress's power outside the United States to the same degree that it restricts Congress's power within the United States. What principles, if any, would support interpreting the Constitution to give Congress more discretion outside the United States' formal borders?

[*Johnson v. Eisentrager*, 339 U.S. 763 (1950)]. . . .[21] [W]e conclude that at least three factors are relevant in determining the reach of the Suspension Clause: (1) the citizenship and status of the detainee and the adequacy of the process through which that status determination was made; (2) the nature of the sites where apprehension and then detention took place; and (3) the practical obstacles inherent in resolving the prisoner's entitlement to the writ.

Applying this framework, we note at the onset that the status of these detainees is a matter of dispute. Petitioners, like those in *Eisentrager*, are not American citizens. But the petitioners in *Eisentrager* did not contest, it seems, the Court's assertion that they were "enemy alien[s]." *Ibid.* In the instant cases, by contrast, the detainees deny they are enemy combatants. They have been afforded some process in CSRT proceedings to determine their status; but, unlike in *Eisentrager*, there has been no trial by military commission for violations of the laws of war. The difference is not trivial. The records from the *Eisentrager* trials suggest that, well before the petitioners brought their case to this Court, there had been a rigorous adversarial process to test the legality of their detention. . . .

As to the second factor relevant to this analysis, the detainees here are similarly situated to the *Eisentrager* petitioners in that the sites of their apprehension and detention are technically outside the sovereign territory of the United States. As noted earlier, this is a factor that weighs against finding they have rights under the Suspension Clause. [But in] every practical sense Guantanamo is not abroad; it is within the constant jurisdiction of the United States. See *Rasul*, 542 U.S., at 480.

As to the third factor, we recognize, as the Court did in *Eisentrager*, that there are costs to holding the Suspension Clause applicable in a case of military detention abroad. Habeas corpus proceedings may require expenditure of funds by the Government and may divert the attention of military personnel from other pressing tasks. While we are sensitive to these concerns, we do not find them dispositive. Compliance with any judicial process requires some incremental expenditure of resources. Yet civilian courts and the Armed Forces have functioned alongside each other at various points in our history. See, *e.g.*, *Duncan v. Kahanamoku*, 327 U.S. 304 (1946); *Ex parte Milligan*, 4 Wall. 2 (1866). The Government presents no credible arguments that the military mission at Guantanamo would be compromised if habeas corpus courts had jurisdiction to hear the detainees' claims. And in light of the plenary control the United States asserts over the base, none are apparent to us. . . .

It is true that before today the Court has never held that noncitizens detained by our Government in territory over which another country maintains *de jure* sovereignty have any rights under our Constitution. But the cases before us lack any precise historical parallel. They involve individuals detained by executive order for the duration of a conflict that, if measured from September 11, 2001, to the present, is already among the longest wars in American history. See Oxford Companion to American Military History 849 (1999). The detainees, moreover, are held in a territory that, while technically not part of the United States, is under the complete and total

---

21 **Note:** In *Johnson v. Eisentrager*, 339 U.S. 763 (1950), the Court considered the case of twenty-one German nationals convicted by a military commission in China of illegally fighting against the United States after World War II ended. The Germans wanted to petition a federal district court for a writ of habeas corpus, but the Supreme Court observed that "[w]e are cited to no instance where a court, in this or any other country where the writ is known, has issued it on behalf of an alien enemy who, at no relevant time and in no stage of his captivity, has been within its territorial jurisdiction." *Eisentrager*, 339 U.S. at 768. In these paragraphs, Justice Anthony Kennedy distinguishes the situation of the Guantánamo detainees from that of the Germans.

control of our Government. Under these circumstances the lack of a precedent on point is no barrier to our holding.

We hold that Art. I, § 9, cl. 2, of the Constitution has full effect at Guantanamo Bay. If the privilege of habeas corpus is to be denied to the detainees now before us, Congress must act in accordance with the requirements of the Suspension Clause. This Court may not impose a *de facto* suspension by abstaining from these controversies. The MCA does not purport to be a formal suspension of the writ; and the Government, in its submissions to us, has not argued that it is. Petitioners, therefore, are entitled to the privilege of habeas corpus to challenge the legality of their detention. . . .[22]

■ JUSTICE SCALIA, with whom THE CHIEF JUSTICE, JUSTICE THOMAS, and JUSTICE ALITO join, dissenting. . . .

Today, for the first time in our Nation's history, the Court confers a constitutional right to habeas corpus on alien enemies detained abroad by our military forces in the course of an ongoing war. . . .

The category of prisoner comparable to these detainees are not the *Eisentrager* criminal defendants, but the more than 400,000 prisoners of war detained in the United States alone during World War II. Not a single one was accorded the right to have his detention validated by a habeas corpus action in federal court—and that despite the fact that they were present on U.S. soil. . . . The Court's analysis produces a crazy result: Whereas those convicted and sentenced to death for war crimes are without judicial remedy, all enemy combatants detained during a war, at least insofar as they are confined in an area . . . over which the United States exercises "absolute and indefinite" control, may seek a writ of habeas corpus in federal court. And, as an even more bizarre implication from the Court's reasoning, those prisoners whom the military plans to try by full-dress Commission at a future date may file habeas petitions and secure release before their trials take place.

There is simply no support for the Court's assertion that constitutional rights extend to aliens held outside U.S. sovereign territory. . . .[23]

NOTE: AFTERMATH OF *BOUMEDIENE*

Boumediene held that Guantánamo Bay detainees should have an opportunity to contest the legality of their detention in federal court. Later that year, after the election of a Democratic president, Barack Obama, it appeared that the Guantánamo detention camp would be permanently closed even before the detained prisoners had their day in court. But even a Democratic-controlled Congress continued to believe that the Guantánamo detainees were the equivalent of POWs—not criminals who deserved judicial trials. After Obama signed an executive order promising to close Guantánamo and transfer or release its remaining three hundred detainees

---

[22] **Note:** To recap the Court's holding: Boumediene, a Bosnian citizen held in Guantánamo Bay, wants to petition for a writ of habeas corpus. Congress has said he cannot. But where the Suspension Clause applies, it prohibits Congress from suspending the writ "unless when in Cases of Rebellion or Invasion the public safety may require it." Neither circumstance applies here, and Congress has not attempted to formally suspend the writ. Congress has therefore violated the Suspension Clause if the clause's protection applies to noncitizens in Guantánamo Bay. The Court applies a three-factor test to conclude that its protection does apply.

[23] **Questions:** Do you agree with Justice Antonin Scalia that *Boumediene*'s result is "crazy" and that noncitizens held abroad should have no constitutional protection? Does extending constitutional protection in this manner undermine the federal government's ability to conduct a war?

by 2010, *see* 74 Fed. Reg. 4897 (2009), Congress overwhelmingly passed a law prohibiting the expenditure of funds to accomplish these goals, Act of June 24, 2009, Pub. L. No. 111–32, 123 Stat. 1859. Two years later, Congress passed an even more restrictive law that prohibited the president from transferring Guantánamo prisoners to mainland prisons. *See* Act of Jan. 7, 2011, Pub. L. No. 111–383, 124 Stat. 4137. Ten years later, in 2021, there were still forty detainees in Guantánamo Bay.

Thanks to *Boumediene*, the Guantánamo detainees did have an opportunity to petition for habeas relief in federal court by challenging their status as "enemy combatants." But when the U.S. Court of Appeals for the District of Columbia Circuit began hearing detainee appeals, it revealed that it was not sympathetic to their situation. In one case, lawyers from the Department of Justice argued that the government should have to prove by the *preponderance of the evidence* that the detainee met the definition of a detainable enemy—meaning that it was more than 50 percent likely that the detainee was a member of Al-Qaeda. But Judge Janice Rogers Brown responded that this standard was too high: *some evidence* was enough, even if seemingly outweighed by countervailing evidence. *Al-Bihani v. Obama*, 590 F.3d 866 (D.C. Cir. 2010); *see* Charlie Savage, *Power Wars* 300–01 (2017). The Supreme Court declined to hear further appeals by the detainees, leaving similar rulings in place. Within a few years of *Boumediene*, therefore, the opinion had been rendered toothless. Savage, *supra*, at 300.

13.5 THE POWER TO CARE FOR THE ARMED FORCES

Beyond Congress's powers to prepare for war, declare war, and prosecute a war, Congress also has the power to care for the armed forces by making rules for the government and regulation of the army, navy, and militia. From the beginning of the federal armed forces, Congress has enacted such rules, which are today codified as the Uniform Code of Military Justice of 1950, Pub. L. No. 506, 64 Stat. 107, *amended by* the Military Justice Act of 1968, Pub. L. No. 90–632, 82 Stat. 1335. As far as U.S. soldiers are concerned, the Supreme Court gives Congress wide deference to issue and enforce these rules. *United States v. Williams*, 302 U.S. 46 (1937). Congress may punish conduct that would be vague or impermissible for civilians, such as the standard requiring officers to engage in conduct becoming "an officer and a gentleman." *Parker v. Levy*, 417 U.S. 733 (1974).

Although courts-martial are the exclusive courts used to try active-duty service members, the Supreme Court has allowed service members to file habeas petitions with federal courts to review denials of due process. *Burns v. Wilson*, 346 U.S. 137 (1953). The Military Justice Act of 1968 also created a civilian appellate court, the Court of Military Appeals, to review the courts-martial decisions of the various services. This court, today known as the Court of Appeals for the Armed Forces, has held that service members are entitled to all constitutional rights except those expressly or by implication inapplicable to the military. *See, e.g.*, *United States v. Tempia*, 16 U.S.C.M.A. 629, 37 C.M.R. 249 (1967).

In *Ortiz v. United States*, 138 S. Ct. 2165 (2018), the Supreme Court held that it has appellate jurisdiction to review decisions of the Court of Appeals for the Armed Forces even though it is not an Article III court.

Consistent with its holdings in *Ex parte Milligan*, 71 U.S. (4 Wall.) 2 (1866), and *Duncan v. Kahanamoku*, 327 U.S. 304 (1946), the Supreme Court has also limited the reach of courts-martial beyond active-duty service members. In *United States ex rel. Toth v. Quarles*, 350 U.S. 11 (1955), the Court prohibited the federal government from trying an honorably discharged soldier by court-martial for earlier conduct performed while in service. And in *Reid v. Covert*, 354 U.S. 1 (1957), the Court voided the capital court-martial convictions of two civilians accused of murdering their soldier husbands while they were stationed in Japan. *Reid*'s prohibition against using court-martials to try civilians during peacetime has since been extended to noncapital crimes and to civilian employees of the military. *See Grisham v. Hagan*, 361 U.S. 278 (1960); *Kinsella v. United States*, 361 U.S. 234 (1960).

CHAPTER 14

WHAT IS THE SCOPE OF CONGRESS'S POWER TO MAKE AND ENFORCE TREATIES?

ARTICLE I, SECTION 8, CLAUSE 18: The Congress shall have Power . . . To make all Laws which shall be necessary and proper for carrying into Execution the foregoing Powers, and all other Powers vested by this Constitution in the Government of the United States, or in any Department or Officer thereof.

ARTICLE II, SECTION 2, CLAUSE 2: The President . . . shall have Power, by and with the Advice and Consent of the Senate, to make Treaties, provided two thirds of the Senators present concur. . . .

ARTICLE VI, PARAGRAPH 2: This Constitution, and the Laws of the United States which shall be made in Pursuance thereof; and all Treaties made, or which shall be made, under the Authority of the United States, shall be the supreme Law of the Land; and the Judges in every State shall be bound thereby, any Thing in the Constitution or Laws of any State to the Contrary notwithstanding.

TENTH AMENDMENT (1791): The powers not delegated to the United States by the Constitution, nor prohibited by it to the States, are reserved to the States respectively, or to the people.

14.1 THE POWER TO CONSENT TO AND TERMINATE TREATIES

For most of the Constitutional Convention, the draft Constitution gave the Senate all power over "treaties," that is, international agreements between the United States and foreign nations. *See* 2 *The Records of the Federal Convention of 1787*, at 183 (Max Farrand ed., 1911). Giving this power to the Senate continued the foreign affairs responsibilities of the Confederation Congress, which lacked a separate executive and therefore was collectively responsible for appointing ambassadors and conducting the United States' diplomacy.

But the convention ultimately concluded that a single person needed to be able to seize the initiative in negotiating treaties. *See The Federalist No. 64*, at 435–46 (John Jay) (Jacob E. Cooke ed., 1961). The final document empowered the president alone to negotiate any treaty, leaving the Senate responsible for accepting the treaty as is, accepting it with new conditions, or rejecting it. *See United States v. Curtiss-Wright Corp.*, 299 U.S. 304, 319 (1936).

The procedure for creating a treaty is not complicated: the president submits a treaty to the Senate, two-thirds of the Senate consents (with or without conditions), and the president then ratifies the Senate's decision.

The procedure for terminating a treaty, by contrast, is not described by the Constitution. The Senate has occasionally contended that terminating a treaty should require the same procedure as creating the treaty: the consent of the president and two-thirds of the Senate. *See* S. Rep. No. 34–97, at 6–7 (1856). Some presidents have disagreed, claiming that they have the power to unilaterally abrogate treaties by executive action. During the Civil War, for example, President Abraham Lincoln terminated a treaty with Great Britain regulating the size of the naval force on the Great Lakes. Like many of the president's actions, this one was later ratified by Congress. Act of Feb. 9, 1865, Res. No. 13, 13 Stat. 568 (1865). But the legitimacy of the president's unilateral power remains unresolved. *See Goldwater v. Carter*, 617 F.2d 697 (D.C. Cir. 1979) (en banc), *vacated & remanded*, 444 U.S. 996 (1979) (divided on the merits on President Jimmy Carter's power to terminate a treaty with Taiwan).

Treaties are more commonly terminated by Congress *and* the president enacting an ordinary statute that contradicts an earlier treaty's terms. As early as the "imperfect" war with France in 1798, Congress and the president dissolved a preexisting treaty by passing a statute. *See Bas v. Tingy*, 4 U.S. (4 Dall.) 37, 40 (1800). Congress and the president have also enacted statutes to abrogate treaties with Indian nations. *See Lone Wolf v. Hitchcock*, 187 U.S. 553 (1903). Even when a treaty's terms forbid the United States from abrogating it as a matter of international law, the Supreme Court has recognized the power of Congress and the president to do so as a matter of domestic constitutional law. *See The Chinese Exclusion Case*, 130 U.S. 581, 600 (1889) (quoting *Head Money Cases*, 112 U.S. 580, 599 (1884)). But the president is a necessary actor in this respect. Even when both houses of Congress have passed resolutions denouncing certain treaties and directing the president to cancel them—*see, e.g.*, Act of June 5, 1920, Pub. L. No. 66–261, 41 Stat. 1007—the president has sometimes declined to do so. *See Van der Weyde v. Ocean Transp. Co.*, 297 U.S. 114 (1936).

The Supreme Court has declined to recognize the termination of a treaty by any means other than presidential or congressional action. For example, when a foreign state has allegedly breached a treaty, the Supreme Court has declared that the existence of a breach or the effect of the breach is a political question that must be decided by the president or Congress. *See, e.g.*, *Clark v. Allen*, 331 U.S. 503, 511 (1947); *Ware v. Hylton*, 3 U.S. (3 Dall.) 199, 260 (1796).

14.2 THE POWER TO ENFORCE TREATIES

When the Senate ratifies a treaty, the United States becomes committed to following the treaty's terms as a matter of *international* law. That is, foreign states will expect the United States to comply with the treaty's terms. But the treaty does not necessarily have any effect as a matter of *domestic* law. Whether it has any effect depends on whether the treaty is "self-executing" or "non-self-executing."

The Supreme Court first discussed this distinction in *Foster v. Neilson*, 27 U.S. (2 Pet.) 253 (1829). The case concerned a treaty between the United States and Spain that ceded part of Florida to the United States. The treaty specified that certain private grants of lands "shall be ratified and confirmed"—in the future, that is. *Foster*, 27 U.S. (2 Pet.) at 310. But the treaty did not directly ratify or confirm the grants. The Court therefore interpreted the language to mean that the United States had promised Spain that Congress would pass a law ratifying and confirming the grants but that the treaty otherwise had no domestic effect.

The Court explained thus:

> A treaty is in its nature a contract between two nations, not a legislative act. It does not generally effect, of itself, the object to be accomplished, especially so far as its operation is infra-territorial; but is carried into execution by the sovereign power of the respective parties to the instrument.
>
> In the United States a different principle is established. Our constitution declares a treaty to be the law of the land. It is, consequently, to be regarded in courts of justice as equivalent to an act of the legislature, whenever it operates of itself without the aid of any legislative provision. But when the terms of the stipulation import a contract, when either of the parties engages to perform a particular act, the treaty addresses itself to the political, not the judicial department; and the legislature must execute the contract before it can become a rule for the Court.

Id. at 314. In other words, when a treaty's wording indicates that it operates immediately, it is self-executing and has a domestic effect. Otherwise, the treaty is non-self-executing, and Congress must pass a law putting the treaty into domestic effect.

The difference between a self-executing treaty and a non-self-executing treaty is significant. The Supremacy Clause declares that treaties are part of the "supreme Law of the Land" and the equivalent of federal statutes. U.S. Const. art. VI, para. 2. So if a treaty is self-executing, it is as if the president and Senate passed a law without the House's involvement. For this reason, the House has long objected to self-executing treaties that appropriate funds from the Treasury without the House's consent. *See, e.g.*, Act of Mar. 1, 1816, ch. 22, 3 Stat. 255 (1816). States have also expressed concern about self-executing treaties that preempt state laws or confer new legal rights on their residents. *See, e.g.*, *Sanchez-Llamas v. Oregon*, 548 U.S. 331, 370 (2006).

Although non-self-executing treaties do not have any domestic effect on their own, they do invite Congress to pass a statute putting their terms into effect. This invitation raises an important question: When

Congress wants to execute a treaty, is it limited to exercising its enumerated powers under the Constitution, or—per Article I, Section 8, Clause 18—may it pass any law "necessary and proper for carrying into Execution" the treaty's terms? Early on, Thomas Jefferson objected that no treaty should be interpreted as giving Congress new powers, "for surely the President and Senate cannot do by treaty what the whole Government is interdicted from doing in any way." *Jefferson's Manual of Parliamentary Practice* § 594. The Supreme Court has occasionally agreed: "It need hardly be said that a treaty cannot change the Constitution or be held valid if it be in violation of that instrument." *The Cherokee Tobacco*, 78 U.S. (11 Wall.) 616, 620 (1871). But since the late nineteenth century, the Court has declared that the Necessary and Proper Clause confers upon Congress "the power to enact such legislation as is appropriate to give efficacy to any stipulations which it is competent for the President by and with the advice and consent of the Senate to insert in a treaty with a foreign power." *Neely v. Henkel*, 180 U.S. 109, 121 (1901); *see, e.g., Baldwin v. Franks*, 120 U.S. 678, 683 (1887).

14.2.1

Missouri v. Holland

252 U.S. 416 (1920)

The scope of Congress's power to enforce a non-self-executing treaty was the subject of *Missouri v. Holland*, 252 U.S. 416 (1920).

In 1913, during an era when the Supreme Court narrowly interpreted Congress's powers under the Commerce Clause, Congress attempted to protect certain birds that migrated across the United States. *See* Act of Mar. 4, 1913, Pub. L. No. 62–430, 37 Stat. 828. Federal district courts quickly invalidated this legislation. *See, e.g., United States v. Shauver*, 214 F. 154 (E.D. Ark. 1914). So, in 1916, President Woodrow Wilson and the Senate ratified a treaty in which the United States and Canada both promised to protect migratory birds. Congress then passed the Migratory Bird Treaty Act of 1918, Pub. L. No. 65–186, to "give effect" to the treaty—even though federal courts had just said Congress ordinarily lacks the power to protect migratory birds. *Holland*, 252 U.S. at 431.

In *Holland*, the Court's ruling was a win for migratory birds.

■ MR. JUSTICE HOLMES delivered the opinion of the Court.[1]

This is a bill in equity brought by the State of Missouri to prevent a game warden of the United States from attempting to enforce the Migratory Bird Treaty Act of July 3, 1918, c. 128, 40 Stat. 755, and the regulations made by the Secretary of Agriculture in pursuance of the same. The ground of the bill is that the statute is an

[1] **As You Read, Consider:** The Necessary and Proper Clause empowers Congress to "carry[ ] into Execution . . . [all] Powers vested by this Constitution in the Government of the United States." Does Justice Oliver Wendell Holmes interpret this clause to allow Congress to carry into execution the president and Senate's power to *make* treaties, or does he think it allows Congress to carry into execution the content of the treaties?

unconstitutional interference with the rights reserved to the States by the Tenth Amendment, and that the acts of the defendant done and threatened under that authority invade the sovereign right of the State and contravene its will manifested in statutes. . . .

To answer this question it is not enough to refer to the Tenth Amendment, reserving the powers not delegated to the United States, because by Article II, § 2, the power to make treaties is delegated expressly, and by Article VI treaties made under the authority of the United States, along with the Constitution and laws of the United States made in pursuance thereof, are declared the supreme law of the land. If the treaty is valid there can be no dispute about the validity of the statute under Article I, § 8, as a necessary and proper means to execute the powers of the Government. The language of the Constitution as to the supremacy of treaties being general, the question before us is narrowed to an inquiry into the ground upon which the present supposed exception is placed.

It is said that a treaty cannot be valid if it infringes the Constitution, that there are limits, therefore, to the treaty-making power, and that one such limit is that what an act of Congress could not do unaided, in derogation of the powers reserved to the States, a treaty cannot do. An earlier act of Congress that attempted by itself and not in pursuance of a treaty to regulate the killing of migratory birds within the States had been held bad in the District Court. *United States v. Shauver*, 214 Fed. Rep. 154. *United States v. McCullagh*, 221 Fed. Rep. 288. Those decisions were supported by arguments that migratory birds were owned by the States in their sovereign capacity for the benefit of their people, and that . . . this control was one that Congress had no power to displace. The same argument is supposed to apply now with equal force.

Whether the two cases cited were decided rightly or not they cannot be accepted as a test of the treaty power. Acts of Congress are the supreme law of the land only when made in pursuance of the Constitution, while treaties are declared to be so when made under the authority of the United States. It is open to question whether the authority of the United States means more than the formal acts prescribed to make the convention. We do not mean to imply that there are no qualifications to the treaty-making power; but they must be ascertained in a different way. It is obvious that there may be matters of the sharpest exigency for the national well being that an act of Congress could not deal with but that a treaty followed by such an act could, and it is not lightly to be assumed that, in matters requiring national action, "a power which must belong to and somewhere reside in every civilized government" is not to be found. *Andrews v. Andrews*, 188 U.S. 14, 33. What was said in that case with regard to the powers of the States applies with equal force to the powers of the nation in cases where the States individually are incompetent to act. . . . With regard to that we may add that when we are dealing with words that also are a constituent act, like the Constitution of the United States, we must realize that they have called into life a being the development of which could not have been foreseen completely by the most gifted of its begetters. It was enough for them to realize or to hope that they had created an organism; it has taken a century and has cost their successors much sweat and blood to prove that they created a nation. The case before us must be considered in the light of our whole experience and not merely in that of what was said a hundred years ago. The treaty in question does not contravene any prohibitory words to be found in the Constitution. The only question is whether it is forbidden by some invisible radiation from the general terms of the Tenth Amendment. We must consider what this country has become in deciding what that Amendment has reserved.[2]

---

[2] **Question:** In this paragraph, Holmes is articulating the principle of *living constitutionalism*: the text of the Constitution should be interpreted with respect to modern

The State as we have intimated founds its claim of exclusive authority upon an assertion of title to migratory birds, an assertion that is embodied in statute. No doubt it is true that as between a State and its inhabitants the State may regulate the killing and sale of such birds, but it does not follow that its authority is exclusive of paramount powers. . . .

As most of the laws of the United States are carried out within the States and as many of them deal with matters which in the silence of such laws the State might regulate, such general grounds are not enough to support Missouri's claim. Valid treaties of course "are as binding within the territorial limits of the States as they are elsewhere throughout the dominion of the United States." *Baldwin v. Franks*, 120 U.S. 678, 683. No doubt the great body of private relations usually fall within the control of the State, but a treaty may override its power. . . .

Here a national interest of very nearly the first magnitude is involved. It can be protected only by national action in concert with that of another power. The subject-matter is only transitorily within the State and has no permanent habitat therein. But for the treaty and the statute there soon might be no birds for any powers to deal with. We see nothing in the Constitution that compels the Government to sit by while a food supply is cut off and the protectors of our forests and our crops are destroyed. It is not sufficient to rely upon the States. The reliance is vain, and were it otherwise, the question is whether the United States is forbidden to act. We are of opinion that the treaty and statute must be upheld.[3]

NOTE: SCOPE OF *HOLLAND*

The treaty at issue in *Holland* was uncontroversial. But the principle announced in *Holland* was momentous, particularly when the United States entered into a series of expansive multilateral treaties after World War II. If the Constitution gave Congress the power to execute these treaties, then each treaty had the power to dramatically increase Congress's powers relative to the states.

For example, the United Nations Charter of 1945 and the Universal Declaration of Human Rights of 1948 prohibited racial discrimination with respect to economic, social, political, cultural, and civic rights. The National Association for the Advancement of Colored People (NAACP), among other organizations, argued that these treaties gave Congress all the power it needed to eliminate racial segregation in the South. *See* NAACP, *An Appeal to the World!* (W. E. B. Du Bois ed., 1947). Similarly, the North Atlantic Treaty of 1949 created the North Atlantic Treaty Organization (NATO) and pledged the United States to defend allied states in North America and Western Europe. President Harry Truman argued that this treaty empowered him to unilaterally send soldiers overseas. *See Assignment of Ground Forces of the United States to Duty in the European Area: Hearings*

---

developments that may have been unforeseen by the Constitution's authors. How do such developments influence his interpretation?

[3] **Questions:** Under Holmes's interpretation of the Necessary and Proper Clause as applied to treaties, are there any limits on what laws Congress can enact to enforce a treaty? If the United States entered into a treaty in which it promised to ban the publication of newspapers criticizing the treaty partner, would the First Amendment's protection of a free press restrict Congress's power to execute the treaty?

Before the S. Comms. on Foreign Relations and Armed Services, 82d Cong. 92 (1951).

Bricker Amendment. These sorts of arguments prompted Senate Republicans, led by John W. Bricker, to propose a constitutional amendment overruling *Holland*: "A treaty shall become effective as internal law in the United States only through legislation which would be valid in the absence of treaty." S.J. Res. 43, 82d Cong., 1st Sess., § 2 (1953). This so-called Bricker Amendment also would have prohibited the president from entering into international agreements without Senate ratification—a topic that we will discuss later in the context of the president's power to conduct foreign affairs (section 32.1).

The Bricker Amendment ignited fierce opposition from Senate Democrats, led by Lyndon B. Johnson. It was also opposed by the Republican administration of President Dwight D. Eisenhower, who called it "a blind violation of the Constitution by stupid, blind isolationists." Robert A. Caro, *Master of the Senate* 528 (2003). After a year of debate that played out in Senate cloakrooms and on the front pages of national newspapers, the Senate voted down the final version of the Bricker Amendment by a single vote. *Id.* at 527–40.

Narrow interpretation of *Holland* in *Covert*. Although the Bricker Amendment was extinguished, a plurality of the Supreme Court has carried its torch. In *Reid v. Covert*, 354 U.S. 1 (1957), the Court considered the case of a civilian who had been tried by a court-martial. The United States was party to an international agreement that permitted the court-martial in this setting, even though the juryless proceeding violated the Bill of Rights. Writing for four justices, Justice Hugo Black rejected the federal government's argument that it could "exercise power under an international agreement without observing constitutional prohibitions." *Covert*, 345 U.S. at 17. Such a construction of the Constitution, Black wrote, "would permit amendment of that document in a manner not sanctioned by Article V." *Id.* Black interpreted *Holland* narrowly to stand only for the proposition that when Congress legislates to enforce a treaty, "the Tenth Amendment is no barrier." *Id.* at 17–18. He emphasized that *Holland* had "carefully noted that the treaty involved was not inconsistent with any specific provision of the Constitution," such as the Bill of Rights. *Id.*

Narrow interpretation of *Holland* in *Bond*. The Court recently declined another opportunity to overrule *Holland* in a case involving the Chemical Weapons Convention Implementation Act of 1998, Pub. L. No. 105–277, 112 Stat. 2681. The act enforced a treaty prohibiting the use of chemicals in warfare. The act's language was broad, however, and the federal government invoked it to prosecute Carol Anne Bond, a civilian who purchased chemicals from Amazon and used them to attack a woman with whom her husband was having an affair. *Bond v. United States*, 572 U.S. 844 (2014). Bond argued that the statute was unconstitutional: Congress has no internal police power, and the Necessary and Proper Clause empowers Congress to help the president make treaties, not to *implement* treaties already made. *Id.* at 875 (Scalia, J., concurring in the judgment). But while three justices agreed with Bond, a majority dodged the question by interpreting the statute not to apply to basic assault. Applying the clear-statement rule of *Gregory v. Ashcroft*, 501 U.S. 452 (1991), the Court considered the statute's scope ambiguous. The majority wrote that it would not interpret such a statute to override the "usual constitutional balance of federal and state powers." *Bond*, 572 U.S. at 858. It concluded, "[I]n this curious case, we can insist on a clear indication that Congress meant to reach purely local crimes, before interpreting the statute's expansive language in a way that intrudes on the police power of the States." *Id.* at 860.

CHAPTER 15

WHAT IS THE SCOPE OF CONGRESS'S POWER TO CONSTITUTE TRIBUNALS?

ARTICLE I, SECTION 8, CLAUSE 9: The Congress shall have Power . . . To constitute Tribunals inferior to the supreme Court; . . .—And

> **CLAUSE 18:** To make all Laws which shall be necessary and proper for carrying into Execution the foregoing Powers, and all other Powers vested by this Constitution in the Government of the United States, or in any Department or Officer thereof.

ARTICLE III, SECTION 1: The judicial Power of the United States, shall be vested in one supreme Court, and in such inferior Courts as the Congress may from time to time ordain and establish. The Judges, both of the supreme and inferior Courts, shall hold their Offices during good Behaviour, and shall, at stated Times, receive for their Services, a Compensation, which shall not be diminished during their Continuance in Office.

ARTICLE III, SECTION 2, CLAUSE 2: In all Cases affecting Ambassadors, other public Ministers and Consuls, and those in which a State shall be Party, the supreme Court shall have original Jurisdiction. In all the other Cases before mentioned, the supreme Court shall have appellate Jurisdiction, both as to Law and Fact, with such Exceptions, and under such Regulations as the Congress shall make.

15.1 THE POWER TO CREATE COURTS

During the 1787 Constitutional Convention, most delegates agreed that the Constitution needed to create a Supreme Court with the power to compel states to enforce treaties and to recognize national obligations. But the delegates were conflicted about whether the Supreme Court would be the full extent of the federal judiciary. One group of delegates wanted to supplement the Supreme Court with an entirely new system of federal trial courts to ensure that litigants bringing federal claims or suing out of state could bring their claims before a relatively nonpartisan tribunal. Another group thought that a Supreme Court was enough: as long as the Court had the power to review state-court cases, then state trial and appellate courts already provided an effective, nonpartisan judiciary for hearing all claims.

Eventually, both groups decided to punt the question. The resulting Constitution left it to Congress "to constitute Tribunals inferior to the supreme Court." *See* 2 *The Records of the Federal Convention of 1787*, at 79 (Max Farrand ed., 1911). Indeed, the Constitution didn't even specify the Supreme Court's membership or responsibilities, other than that it would have a "Chief Justice," Article I, Section 3, and that it would exercise the "judicial Power" in certain cases and controversies, Article III, Section 2.

Judiciary Act of 1789

The first Congress got to work with the Judiciary Act of 1789, ch. 20, 1 Stat. 73, creating a three-tiered system of federal courts.

At the top was a Supreme Court with "a chief justice and five associate justices," *id.*, although the Constitution said nothing about associate justices. Congress slowly expanded the Court's membership over the decades to an all-time high of ten members in 1863. Act of Mar. 3, 1863, ch. 100, 12 Stat. 794. But in 1866, during the acrimonious presidency of Andrew Johnson, Congress prohibited the president from appointing new justices as old ones died or retired, bringing the number down to eight. A month after Johnson left office in 1869, Congress set the number of Supreme Court justices at nine. Act of Apr. 10, 1869, ch. 22, 16 Stat. 44. That number has remained ever since. In 1937, President Franklin D. Roosevelt famously asked Congress to pass legislation empowering him to "pack" the Supreme Court by supplementing the six justices over the age of seventy with his own appointments. Congress rejected the proposal, but the Supreme Court soon began upholding Roosevelt's New Deal programs, making the issue moot. *See generally* Jeff Shesol, *Supreme Power* 429 (2011).

Below the Supreme Court, the first Congress also created a system of thirteen district courts and three intermediate courts, called "circuit courts." The district courts looked a lot like they do today: they were the trial courts of the federal system. But the intermediate circuit courts were very different from today's courts of appeal. They each consisted of two Supreme Court justices and one district judge who met twice annually to literally "ride circuit," that is, to go from place to place hearing both trials and appeals. Judiciary Act, 1 Stat. at 74–75. Riding circuit along eighteenth-century roads was uncomfortable enough that many Supreme Court justices simply resigned: four chief justices served in the Court's first twelve years.

Judiciary Act of 1801

The justices who remained on the Court complained so loudly about riding circuit that Congress abolished the practice in February 1801. Judiciary Act of 1801, ch. 4, 2 Stat. 89. The 1801 law replaced the previous system with six new circuits, each with three dedicated "circuit judges." This reform placated the Supreme Court justices by allowing them to stay in Washington. It also served President John Adams, allowing him to confirm eighteen new circuit judges before his rival, Thomas Jefferson, could take the presidential oath of office in March 1801. For this second reason, the law became known by Jefferson's partisan allies as the Midnight Judges Act. *See generally* Kathryn Turner, *The Midnight Judges*, 109 U. Pa. L. Rev. 494 (1961).

In addition to creating the new position of circuit judge, the Midnight Judges Act also created several dozen new trial positions, including justices of the peace for the District of Columbia. So many positions were created, in fact, that the Adams administration was unable to deliver all of the commissions entitling the commission recipients to be judges.

When Jefferson became president, his administration resisted the Midnight Judges Act by withholding the commissions for these new judges—giving rise to the controversy at issue in *Marbury v. Madison*, 5 U.S. (1 Cranch) 137 (1803) (see section 3.1). In 1802, Jefferson and his allies in Congress went even further and attempted to kick all of the newly commissioned Federalist judges out of office.

Judiciary Act of 1802

With the Judiciary Act of 1802, ch. 8, 2 Stat. 132, Congress repealed the Midnight Judges Act and prohibited the Federalist-dominated circuit courts from hearing any cases. The repeal law, in other words, effectively abolished the new judicial offices created by the federalists. Yet the law said nothing about Adams's appointees, who still held paper commissions that authorized them to serve on these now-powerless courts. Federalist opponents of the repeal law therefore challenged its constitutionality in federal court. They claimed that effectively abolishing a judge's position violated Article III of the Constitution, which states that all federal judges "shall hold their Offices during good Behaviour."

In *Stuart v. Laird*, 5 U.S. (1 Cranch) 299 (1803), the Supreme Court upheld the repeal law. The decision came one week after *Marbury v. Madison*, in which the Court declined to order the secretary of state, James Madison, to deliver William Marbury's commission as justice of the peace. The *Stuart* Court was equally conciliatory, sustaining the 1802 repeal law without giving any express opinion about its constitutionality.

The Court did, however, explicitly state that Congress could compel Supreme Court justices to once again ride circuit. *Id.* at 309. For the next century, Supreme Court justices therefore continued to ride circuit. Only in 1891 did Congress create the modern judicial system, in which dedicated circuit judges sit on intermediate "courts of appeals" between the district courts and the Supreme Court. Judiciary Act of 1891, ch. 517, 26 Stat. 826.

Jurisdiction of courts

As part of its power to create and abolish federal courts, Congress has also defined the jurisdiction of particular federal courts—a practice that the Supreme Court has repeatedly upheld under the Necessary and Proper Clause. *See Sheldon v. Sill*, 49 U.S. (8 How.) 441, 448–49 (1850); *Bank of the United States v. Halstead*, 23 U.S. (10 Wheat.) 51, 53–55 (1825); *United States v. Hudson & Goodwin*, 11 U.S. (7 Cranch) 32, 33

(1812); *Ex parte Bollman*, 8 U.S. (4 Cranch) 75, 103 (1807); *Turner v. Bank of N. Am.*, 4 U.S. (4 Dall.) 8, 11 (1799).

For example, in the years after the first Judiciary Act, Congress gave federal district courts the power to hear only cases between citizens of different states—a type of jurisdiction known as *diversity jurisdiction*. But Congress withheld from these courts the power to hear nondiverse cases arising under the Constitution or federal law. Litigants who wanted to present a "federal question" therefore had to bring their claim in state court unless they could find an out-of-state party to sue in federal court. Congress permanently gave federal district courts original jurisdiction to hear all federal claims only in 1875. Act of Mar. 3, 1875, ch. 137, 18 Stat. 470.

In the meantime, Congress steadily added provisions allowing defendants to "remove" certain cases from state courts to federal courts—another type of jurisdiction that district courts continue to exercise. *See, e.g.*, *Tennessee v. Davis*, 100 U.S. 257, 261–63 (1880); *Ry. Co. v. Whitton*, 80 U.S. (13 Wall.) 270, 289–90 (1872).

Specialized courts

Congress has also created specialized federal courts with even more limited powers than the nineteenth-century district courts. As part of its war powers, for instance, Congress created courts-martial to enforce military discipline. *See, e.g.*, *Dynes v. Hoover*, 61 U.S. (20 How.) 65, 79 (1858). As discussed earlier (section 13.4), Congress has also authorized military tribunals to hear claims involving certain civilians and enemy combatants. Relatedly, when Congress first organized federal territories, it empowered territorial legislatures to create territorial courts with the power to hear claims arising in their territory. *See, e.g.*, *Am. Ins. Co. v. Canter*, 26 U.S. (1 Pet.) 511 (1828). And when Congress began building the modern administrative state in the early twentieth century, it often created courts like the Commerce Court, which temporarily enforced orders of the Interstate Commerce Commission, a federal agency. Act of June 18, 1910, Pub. L. No. 61–218, 36 Stat. 539; *see also* Act of Oct. 22, 1913, Pub. L. No. 63–32, 38 Stat. 208, 219 (abolishing the Commerce Court).

Similar specialized courts have included the Emergency Price Court of Appeals, which heard cases during World War II involving federal price controls, *see* Act of Jan. 30, 1942, Pub. L. No. 77–421, 56 Stat. 23; the Judicial Panel on Multidistrict Litigation, which has the power to transfer actions pending in multiple districts to a single district for trial, *see* Act of Apr. 29, 1968, Pub. L. No. 90–296, 82 Stat. 109; the FISA Court, which hears applications for warrants regarding intelligence activities, *see* Foreign Intelligence Surveillance Act of 1978, Pub. L. No. 95–511, 92 Stat. 1783, 1788; the U.S. Court of International Trade, which hears cases involving international trade and customs issues, *see* Customs Courts Act of 1980, Pub. L. No. 96–417, 94 Stat. 1727; and the U.S. Court of Appeals for the Federal Circuit, which exercises exclusive jurisdiction over appeals regarding patents and trademarks, monetary claims against the United States, civil service disputes, and trade and customs issues, *see* Federal Courts Improvement Act of 1982, Pub. L. No. 97–164, 96 Stat. 25, 37.

Specialized federal courts have occasionally raised significant constitutional issues involving the separation of powers. After Watergate, for instance, Congress passed the Ethics in Government Act of 1978, Pub. L. No. 95–521, 92 Stat. 1824, which created the Special Division of the U.S. Court of Appeals for the D.C. Circuit. Congress gave this division the responsibility of appointing and supervising an independent counsel to prosecute charges of illegality within the executive branch. In 1988, Ted Olson, a lawyer in the administration of President Ronald Reagan, challenged the statute's constitutionality after an independent counsel was appointed to investigate whether Olson had illegally withheld information from Congress. In *Morrison v. Olson*, 487 U.S. 654 (1988), the Supreme Court upheld the statute over a vigorous dissent from Justice Antonin Scalia. Although Scalia argued that the statute unconstitutionally encroached on the president's exclusive responsibility to ensure that the laws be faithfully executed, a majority of the Court thought that appointing an independent counsel was an acceptable responsibility for courts, which often appoint special masters and other investigatory bodies to assist them with fact-finding. *See also Mistretta v. United States*, 488 U.S. 361 (1989) (upholding the placement of the U.S. Sentencing Commission in the judicial branch instead of the executive branch).

15.1.1

Northern Pipeline Construction Co. v. Marathon Pipe Line Co.

458 U.S. 50 (1982)

Perhaps the most important constitutional issue raised when Congress exercises its power to constitute tribunals is whether Congress needs to comply with the two protections of federal judges listed in Article III: tenure protection and salary protection. Article III states that "Judges, both of the supreme and inferior Courts, shall hold their Offices during *good Behaviour* and shall, at stated Times, receive for their Services, a Compensation, which shall not be diminished during their Continuance in Office" (emphasis added). During the ratification debates, Alexander Hamilton stressed the importance of these provisions, explaining that they guaranteed judicial independence by protecting federal judges from the other two branches. *See The Federalist No. 79*, at 531 (Alexander Hamilton) (Jacob Cooke ed., 1961). Absent the tenure protection of being allowed to hold office "during good Behaviour," judges might be removed if they failed to issue decisions in line with the political branches' views. And absent the salary protection of "a Compensation, which shall not be diminished," judges might be punished by Congress for disfavored decisions.

In the abstract, Article III's protections are relatively straightforward: judges on the federal district courts, the courts of appeal, and the Supreme Court cannot have their salaries reduced or tenures eliminated. *See United States v. Will*, 449 U.S. 200, 224–30 (1980). But it has long been a challenge to determine which other courts must be eligible for these protections. For example, imagine that Congress created a fourth court that looked exactly like a federal district court but was called a *magistrate court* and staffed with "magistrates" instead of district judges. If Congress could give these magistrates the same powers as district judges but only for five-year terms instead of lifetime appointments, then these alternatives to district courts might entirely replace tenure- and salary-protected courts, which would be unconstitutional.

On the flip side, it cannot be that everyone who acts in a judicial capacity deserves Article III protections. To take a different example, imagine Congress empowered the secretary of defense to determine whether elderly men were veterans who deserved a pension reserved for injured soldiers. *Cf.* Act of Mar. 23, 1792, ch. 11, 1 Stat. 243. This sort of fact-finding is something that a federal judge theoretically could decide. But if deciding facts alone meant that the secretary of defense deserved the protections of Article III, then any executive officer given responsibility for making a fact-finding decision would get a lifetime appointment and a permanent salary.

The Court has therefore had to come up with a test to distinguish fact finders that deserve Article III's tenure and salary protections from fact finders whose salary and tenure may be eliminated. *See, e.g.*, *Williams v. United States*, 289 U.S. 553 (1933); *Cary v. Curtis*, 44 U.S. (3 How.) 236 (1845). The main test that the Court has used distinguishes "private rights" from "public rights."

So-called *private-rights claims* are claims that historically have been vindicated by one private party going to court to seek redress from another private party. These sorts of claims include contracts, torts, and property claims. The Supreme Court has emphasized that, in general, private-rights claims must be heard by a court protected by Article III, called an *Article III court*.

The Court has distinguished these private-rights claims from claims involving *public rights*, or rights created and maintained solely by the government. A federal pension is a good example of a public right: because Congress has created the right to a pension, it can determine for itself whether a particular individual deserves that pension—or, alternatively, it can ask an untenured executive official or a tenured Article III court to make the same determination. Recognizing Congress's discretion to determine how to administer federally created rights, the

Supreme Court has held that public-rights claims may be heard by what it calls *Article I courts*, or fact finders subject to Congress's control. *See, e.g.*, *McAllister v. United States*, 141 U.S. 174 (1891) (judges in Article I courts may be removable by the president); *United States v. Fisher*, 109 U.S. 143 (1883) (judges in Article I courts may have their salaries reduced by the president).

The Supreme Court first developed this distinction in a case called *Murray's Lessee v. Hoboken Land & Improvement Co.*, 59 U.S. (18 How.) 272 (1856). The Court explained that Congress generally has complete control over whether to award public rights, such as who should receive a pension, whether an immigrant deserves asylum, or whether a soldier should be expelled from the military. The Court has therefore considered it reasonable for Congress to determine whether claims involving public rights should be adjudicated by Article III courts or by executive-branch officials. By contrast, when it comes to private rights, like contract disputes, the Court has held that Congress doesn't have the same discretion to withhold the right to a remedy in an Article III court. On the basis of this distinction, the Court has allowed Article I courts to administer monetary claims against the United States, *McElrath v. United States*, 102 U.S. 426 (1880); disputes involving customs and internal revenue issues, *Ex parte Bakelite Corp.*, 279 U.S. 438 (1929); questions involving the disposal of public lands, *United States v. Coe*, 155 U.S. 76 (1894); questions concerning membership in tribes, *Wallace v. Adams*, 204 U.S. 415 (1907); diplomatic and consular issues, *In re Ross*, 140 U.S. 453 (1891); military justice issues, *Dynes v. Hoover*, 61 U.S. (20 How.) 65, 79 (1858); and territorial issues, *Am. Ins. Co. v. Canter*, 26 U.S. 511 (1828).

The public-rights/private-rights distinction presented a major problem for early administrative agencies. In *Crowell v. Benson*, 285 U.S. 22 (1932), the Supreme Court heard a challenge to a federal administrative scheme in which an executive-branch official determined whether a maritime employer owed compensation to an employee. The Court considered this sort of fact-finding a classic example "of private right, that is, of the liability of one individual to another." *Id.* at 51. But the Court did not consider the involvement of a private right the end of the matter. The administrative scheme allowed either of the parties to appeal the executive official's findings to an Article III district court, which had final say on whether to accept or reject the official's facts. Moreover, the official's role was limited to finding particular facts; it could not issue orders without the district court's approval. Despite the existence of a private-rights claim, the Supreme Court upheld the administrative scheme on the ground that the executive official was an adjunct who provided mere "assistance" to the district court, similar to a court-appointed investigator like a special master. *Id.* at 51–52.

Over the next forty years, *Crowell*'s adjunct or assistance principle formed the basis for the creation of the modern administrative state.

Crowell adjunct/assistant

Congress created numerous agencies, including the National Labor Relations Board and the Occupational Safety and Health Administration; empowered them to find facts and even issue orders regarding congressionally created private rights; and complied with *Crowell* by making these orders appealable to an Article III court. *See, e.g., Atlas Roofing Co. v. OSHRC*, 430 U.S. 442 (1977); *NLRB v. Jones & Laughlin Steel Corp.*, 301 U.S. 1 (1937).

On the basis of *Crowell* and its adjunct principle, Congress enacted the Bankruptcy Act of 1978, Pub. L. No. 95–598, 92 Stat. 2549. The act was a major overhaul of the bankruptcy court system. Before 1978, federal bankruptcy proceedings were resolved in federal district courts, which typically appointed "referees" to present findings and recommendations for a federal district judge to approve or amend. After 1978, Congress replaced these referees with adjuncts to district courts called *bankruptcy courts* and gave these bankruptcy courts the same power as district courts to issue final judgments in any case involving bankruptcy—even if the case involved other federal or state claims. Congress did not, however, give bankruptcy judges the tenure or salary protections of Article III. Instead, it allowed bankruptcy judges to serve only for fourteen-year terms.

To comply with *Crowell*, Congress gave litigants the right to appeal decisions of a bankruptcy court to a district court, which could reverse any decisions that were "clearly erroneous"—a highly deferential standard of review. *Crowell*, 285 U.S. at n.13. The law thus presented a stark version of the hypothetical above: Can Congress create a system of federal courts that look like district courts but lack Article III's protections, as long as an Article III court has some power to review their decisions on appeal?

A fractured Supreme Court provided an answer—in the negative!—in a bankruptcy case, *Northern Pipeline Construction Co. v. Marathon Pipe Line Co.*, 458 U.S. 50 (1982). As part of its bankruptcy proceedings, Northern Pipeline Construction Co. sued Marathon Pipe Line Co. in bankruptcy court for an alleged breach of contract, which is a state-law claim. Marathon sought dismissal of the suit on the ground that the Bankruptcy Act unconstitutionally conferred judicial power upon judges who lacked Article III's tenure and salary protections.

■ JUSTICE BRENNAN announced the judgment of the Court and delivered an opinion, in which JUSTICE MARSHALL, JUSTICE BLACKMUN, and JUSTICE STEVENS joined.[1]

[W]e turn to the question presented for decision: whether the Bankruptcy Act of 1978 violates the command of Art. III that the judicial power of the United States must be vested in courts whose judges enjoy the protections and safeguards specified in that Article.

---

[1] **As You Read, Consider:** Article III expressly restricts Congress's power to diminish the tenure and salary protections of "Judges." What is the justification for allowing Congress, in some instances, to create "legislative" or "Art. I" courts whose judges lack these protections?

It is undisputed that the bankruptcy judges whose offices were created by the Bankruptcy Act of 1978 do not enjoy the protections constitutionally afforded to Art. III judges. . . . [But] Appellants suggest two grounds for upholding the Act's conferral of broad adjudicative powers upon judges unprotected by Art. III. First, it is urged that "pursuant to its enumerated Article I powers, Congress may establish legislative courts that have jurisdiction to decide cases to which the Article III judicial power of the United States extends." Brief for United States 9. Referring to our precedents upholding the validity of "legislative courts," appellants suggest that "the plenary grants of power in Article I permit Congress to establish non-Article III tribunals in 'specialized areas having particularized needs and warranting distinctive treatment,' " such as the area of bankruptcy law. *Ibid.* Second, appellants contend that even if the Constitution does require that this bankruptcy-related action be adjudicated in an Art. III court, the Act in fact satisfies that requirement. "Bankruptcy jurisdiction was vested in the district court" of the judicial district in which the bankruptcy court is located, "and the exercise of that jurisdiction by the adjunct bankruptcy court was made subject to appeal as of right to an Article III court." Brief for United States 12. Analogizing the role of the bankruptcy court to that of a special master, appellants urge us to conclude that this "adjunct" system established by Congress satisfies the requirements of Art. III. We consider these arguments in turn.[2]

Gov arg

Appellants contend [that the bankruptcy courts are "legislative" or "Art. I" courts]. In advancing this argument, appellants rely upon cases in which we have identified certain matters that "congress may or may not bring within the cognizance of [Art. III courts], as it may deem proper." *Murray's Lessee v. Hoboken Land & Improvement Co.*, 18 How. 272, 284 (1856). But when properly understood, these precedents represent no broad departure from the constitutional command that the judicial power of the United States must be vested in Art. III courts. Rather, they reduce to three narrow situations not subject to that command, each recognizing a circumstance in which the grant of power to the Legislative and Executive Branches was historically and constitutionally so exceptional that the congressional assertion of a power to create legislative courts was consistent with, rather than threatening to, the constitutional mandate of separation of powers. These precedents simply acknowledge that the literal command of Art. III, assigning the judicial power of the United States to courts insulated from Legislative or Executive interference, must be interpreted in light of the historical context in which the Constitution was written, and of the structural imperatives of the Constitution as a whole.[3]

Appellants first rely upon a series of cases in which this Court has upheld the creation by Congress of non-Art. III "territorial courts." This exception from the general prescription of Art. III dates from the earliest days of the Republic, when it was perceived that the Framers intended that as to certain geographical areas, in which no State operated as sovereign, Congress was to exercise the general powers of

---

[2] **Question:** The Court here is quoting excerpts from a brief by the U.S. solicitor general, who is joining Northern Pipeline in defending the constitutionality of the Bankruptcy Act. The solicitor general's position is, roughly, that (1) bankruptcy judges who lack tenure and salary protections can hear all claims arising out of bankruptcy, including state-law contract claims; and (2) any constitutional difficulty is rendered harmless by the fact that litigants can appeal the bankruptcy judge's decision to a district court that *does* have tenure and salary protections. Does either of these points resolve the concern that if Congress can create these sorts of Article I courts, they might one day displace all Article III courts that have tenure and salary protections?

[3] **Question:** In the next few paragraphs, Justice William Brennan identifies three circumstances in which the Supreme Court has allowed Congress to create courts whose judges do not have tenure and salary protections: (1) courts for territories and the District of Columbia, (2) military tribunals, and (3) cases involving "public rights." What do these three examples all have in common?

government. For example, in *American Ins. Co. v. Canter*, 1 Pet. 511 (1828), the Court observed that Art. IV bestowed upon Congress alone a complete power of government over territories not within the States that constituted the United States. The Court then acknowledged Congress' authority to create courts for those territories that were not in conformity with Art. III. Such courts were

> "[C]reated in virtue of the general right of sovereignty which exists in the government, or in virtue of that clause which enables Congress to make all needful rules and regulations, respecting the territory belonging to the United States. The jurisdiction with which they are invested . . . is conferred by Congress, in the execution of those general powers which that body possesses over the territories of the United States. Although admiralty jurisdiction can be exercised in the states in those Courts, only, which are established in pursuance of the third article of the Constitution; the same limitation does not extend to the territories. In legislating for them, Congress exercises the combined powers of the general, and of a state government." 1 Pet., at 546.

The Court followed the same reasoning when it reviewed Congress' creation of non-Art. III courts in the District of Columbia. It noted that there was in the District

> "[N]o division of powers between the general and state governments. Congress has the entire control over the district for every purpose of government; and it is reasonable to suppose, that in organizing a judicial department here, all judicial power necessary for the purposes of government would be vested in the courts of justice." *Kendall v. United States*, 12 Pet. 524, 619 (1838).

Appellants next advert to a second class of cases—those in which this Court has sustained the exercise by Congress and the Executive of the power to establish and administer courts-martial. The situation in these cases strongly resembles the situation with respect to territorial courts: It too involves a constitutional grant of power that has been historically understood as giving the political Branches of Government extraordinary control over the precise subject matter at issue. Article I, § 8, cls. 13, 14, confer upon Congress the power "[t]o provide and maintain a Navy," and "[t]o make Rules for the Government and Regulation of the land and naval Forces." The Fifth Amendment, which requires a presentment or indictment of a grand jury before a person may be held to answer for a capital or otherwise infamous crime, contains an express exception for "cases arising in the land or naval forces." And Art. II, § 2, cl. 1, provides that "The President shall be Commander in Chief of the Army and Navy of the United States, and of the Militia of the several States, when called into the actual Service of the United States." Noting these constitutional directives, the Court in *Dynes v. Hoover*, 20 How. 65 (1857), explained:

> "These provisions show that Congress has the power to provide for the trial and punishment of military and naval offences in the manner then and now practiced by civilized nations; and that the power to do so is given without any connection between it and the 3d article of the Constitution defining the judicial power of the United States; indeed, that the two powers are entirely independent of each other." *Id.*, at 79.

Finally, appellants rely on a third group of cases, in which this Court has upheld the constitutionality of legislative courts and administrative agencies created by Congress to adjudicate cases involving "public rights." The "public rights" doctrine was first set forth in *Murray's Lessee v. Hoboken Land & Improvement Co.*, 18 How. 272 (1856):

> "[W]e do not consider congress can either withdraw from judicial cognizance any matter which, from its nature, is the subject of a suit at the common law, or in equity, or admiralty; nor, on the other hand, can it bring under the judicial power a matter which, from its nature, is not a subject for judicial determination. At the same time there are matters, *involving public rights*, which may be presented in such form that the judicial power is capable of acting on them, and which are susceptible of judicial determination, but which congress may or may not bring within the cognizance of the courts of the United States, as it may deem proper." *Id.*, at 284 (emphasis added).

This doctrine may be explained in part by . . . the principle of separation of powers, and a historical understanding that certain prerogatives were reserved to the political Branches of Government. The doctrine extends only to matters arising "between the Government and persons subject to its authority in connection with the performance of the constitutional functions of the executive or legislative departments," *Crowell v. Benson*, 285 U. S. 22, 50 (1932), and only to matters that historically could have been determined exclusively by those departments, see *Ex parte Bakelite Corp.*, *supra*, at 458. The understanding of these cases is that the Framers expected that Congress would be free to commit such matters completely to nonjudicial executive determination, and that as a result there can be no constitutional objection to Congress' employing the less drastic expedient of committing their determination to a legislative court or an administrative agency. *Crowell v. Benson*, *supra*, at 50.

The public-rights doctrine is grounded in a historically recognized distinction between matters that could be conclusively determined by the Executive and Legislative Branches and matters that are "inherently . . . judicial." *Ex parte Bakelite Corp.*, *supra*, at 458. See *Murray's Lessee v. Hoboken Land & Improvement Co.*, 18 How., at 280–282. For example, the Court in *Murray's Lessee* looked to the law of England and the States at the time the Constitution was adopted, in order to determine whether the issue presented was customarily cognizable in the courts. *Ibid.* Concluding that the matter had not traditionally been one for judicial determination, the Court perceived no bar to Congress' establishment of summary procedures, outside of Art. III courts, to collect a debt due to the Government from one of its customs agents. . . .

The distinction between public rights and private rights has not been definitively explained in our precedents. Nor is it necessary to do so in the present cases, for it suffices to observe that a matter of public rights must at a minimum arise "between the government and others." *Ex parte Bakelite Corp.*, *supra*, at 451. In contrast, "the liability of one individual to another under the law as defined," *Crowell v. Benson*, *supra*, at 51, is a matter of private rights. Our precedents clearly establish that *only* controversies in the former category may be removed from Art. III courts and delegated to legislative courts or administrative agencies for their determination. Private-rights disputes, on the other hand, lie at the core of the historically recognized judicial power.

In sum, this Court has identified three situations in which Art. III does not bar the creation of legislative courts. In each of these situations, the Court has recognized certain exceptional powers bestowed upon Congress by the Constitution or by historical consensus. Only in the face of such an exceptional grant of power has the Court declined to hold the authority of Congress subject to the general prescriptions of Art. III.

We discern no such exceptional grant of power applicable in the cases before us. The courts created by the Bankruptcy Act of 1978 do not lie exclusively outside the States of the Federal Union, like those in the District of Columbia and the Territories. Nor do the bankruptcy courts bear any resemblance to courts-martial, which are founded upon the Constitution's grant of plenary authority over the Nation's military forces to the Legislative and Executive Branches. Finally, the substantive legal rights at issue in the present action cannot be deemed "public rights." Appellants argue that a discharge in bankruptcy is indeed a "public right," similar to such congressionally created benefits as "radio station licenses, pilot licenses, or certificates for common carriers" granted by administrative agencies. See Brief for United States 34. But the restructuring of debtor-creditor relations, which is at the core of the federal bankruptcy power, must be distinguished from the adjudication of state-created private rights, such as the right to recover contract damages that is at issue in this case. The former may well be a "public right," but the latter obviously is not. Appellant Northern's right to recover contract damages to augment its estate is "one of private right, that is, of the liability of one individual to another under the law as defined." *Crowell v. Benson*, 285 U. S., at 51. . . .[4]

Appellants advance a second argument for upholding the constitutionality of the Act: that "viewed within the entire judicial framework set up by Congress," the bankruptcy court is merely an "adjunct" to the district court, and that the delegation of certain adjudicative functions to the bankruptcy court is accordingly consistent with the principle that the judicial power of the United States must be vested in Art. III courts. See Brief for United States 11–13, 37–45. As support for their argument, appellants rely principally upon *Crowell v. Benson*, 285 U. S. 22 (1932), . . . in which we approved the use of administrative agencies and magistrates as adjuncts to Art. III courts. Brief for United States 40–42. The question to which we turn, therefore, is whether the Act has retained "the essential attributes of the judicial power," *Crowell v. Benson, supra*, at 51, in Art. III tribunals.

The essential premise underlying appellants' argument is that even where the Constitution denies Congress the power to establish legislative courts, Congress possesses the authority to assign certain factfinding functions to adjunct tribunals. It is, of course, true that while the power to adjudicate "private rights" must be vested in an Art. III court, see Part III, *supra*,

> "this Court has accepted factfinding by an administrative agency, . . . as an adjunct to the Art. III court, analogizing the agency to a jury or a special master and permitting it in admiralty cases to perform the function of the special master. *Crowell v. Benson*, 285 U. S. 22, 51–65 (1932)." *Atlas Roofing Co. v. Occupational Safety and Health Review Comm'n*, 430 U. S., at 450, n. 7.

The use of administrative agencies as adjuncts was first upheld in *Crowell* v. *Benson*, *supra*. The congressional scheme challenged in *Crowell* empowered an administrative agency, the United States Employees' Compensation Commission, to make initial factual determinations pursuant to a federal statute requiring employers to compensate their employees for work-related injuries occurring upon the navigable waters of the United States. The Court began its analysis by noting that the federal statute administered by the Compensation Commission provided for compensation of injured employees "irrespective of fault," and that the statute also prescribed a fixed

---

[4] **Question:** Brennan concluded in the previous paragraph that Congress cannot allow Article I courts to hear claims involving private rights, as this bankruptcy court did. But if a litigant can always appeal a private-right claim to an Article III district court, doesn't that appellate relationship protect the continued existence of Article III's tenure and salary protections? The Court's answer to this question could affect the constitutionality of the administrative state, which often relies on administrative agencies to resolve factual disputes before the dispute is appealed to an Article III court.

and mandatory schedule of compensation. *Id.*, at 38. The agency was thus left with the limited role of determining "questions of fact as to the circumstances, nature, extent and consequences of the injuries sustained by the employee for which compensation is to be made." *Id.*, at 54. The agency did not possess the power to enforce any of its compensation orders: On the contrary, every compensation order was appealable to the appropriate federal district court, which had the sole power to enforce it or set it aside, depending upon whether the court determined it to be "in accordance with law" and supported by evidence in the record. *Id.*, at 44–45, 48. The Court found that in view of these limitations upon the Compensation Commission's functions and powers, its determinations were "closely analogous to findings of the amount of damages that are made, according to familiar practice, by commissioners or assessors." *Id.*, at 54. Observing that "there is no requirement that, in order to maintain the essential attributes of the judicial power, all determinations of fact in constitutional courts shall be made by judges," *id.*, at 51, the Court held that Art. III imposed no bar to the scheme enacted by Congress, *id.*, at 54.

Crowell involved the adjudication of congressionally created rights. But this Court has sustained the use of adjunct factfinders even in the adjudication of constitutional rights—so long as those adjuncts were subject to sufficient control by an Art. III district court. . . .

Yet it is equally plain that Congress has vested the "adjunct" bankruptcy judges with powers over Northern's state-created right that far exceed the powers that it has vested in administrative agencies that adjudicate only rights of Congress' own creation.

Unlike the administrative scheme that we reviewed in *Crowell*, the Act vests all "essential attributes" of the judicial power of the United States in the "adjunct" bankruptcy court. First, the agency in *Crowell* made only specialized, narrowly confined factual determinations regarding a particularized area of law. In contrast, the subject-matter jurisdiction of the bankruptcy courts encompasses not only traditional matters of bankruptcy, but also "all civil proceedings arising under title 11 or arising in or *related to* cases under title 11." Second, while the agency in *Crowell* engaged in statutorily channeled factfinding functions, the bankruptcy courts exercise "*all* of the jurisdiction" conferred by the Act on the district courts. Third, the agency in *Crowell* possessed only a limited power to issue compensation orders pursuant to specialized procedures, and its orders could be enforced only by order of the district court. By contrast, the bankruptcy courts exercise all ordinary powers of district courts, including the power to preside over jury trials, the power to issue declaratory judgments, the power to issue writs of habeas corpus, and the power to issue any order, process, or judgment appropriate for the enforcement of the provisions of Title 11. Fourth, while orders issued by the agency in *Crowell* were to be set aside if "not supported by the evidence," the judgments of the bankruptcy courts are apparently subject to review only under the more deferential "clearly erroneous" standard. Finally, the agency in *Crowell* was required by law to seek enforcement of its compensation orders in the district court. In contrast, the bankruptcy courts issue final judgments, which are binding and enforceable even in the absence of an appeal. In short, the "adjunct" bankruptcy courts created by the Act exercise jurisdiction behind the facade of a grant to the district courts, and are exercising powers far greater than those lodged in the adjuncts approved in [*Crowell*].[5]

[5] **Question:** Here, Brennan rejects the argument that Congress can create bankruptcy courts with the same powers as Article III courts but without Article III's protections—even when Article III courts are available to review the bankruptcy courts' decisions on appeal. But as he notes in this paragraph, the judgments of bankruptcy courts are "subject to review only

We conclude that . . . the Bankruptcy Act of 1978[ ] has impermissibly removed most, if not all, of "the essential attributes of the judicial power" from the Art. III district court, and has vested those attributes in a non-Art. III adjunct. Such a grant of jurisdiction cannot be sustained as an exercise of Congress' power to create adjuncts to Art. III courts.

■ JUSTICE REHNQUIST, with whom JUSTICE O'CONNOR joins, concurring in the judgment.

NOTE: ARTICLE I COURTS

Congress responded to *Northern Pipeline* with the Bankruptcy Amendments and Federal Judgeship Act of 1984, which allowed any party to seek de novo review of certain non-"core" bankruptcy court findings by an Article III court. Pub. L. No. 98–353, 98 Stat. 333, 341. This amendment responded to one of the problems raised by *Northern Pipeline*: before the amendment, district courts could reverse bankruptcy court findings only if the findings were clearly erroneous.

But in a bankruptcy case involving the estate of model and actress Anna Nicole Smith (married name: Marshall), the Supreme Court held that Congress's amendments didn't resolve the rest of the problems raised by *Northern Pipeline*. Specifically, the Court held in *Stern v. Marshall*, 564 U.S. 462 (2011), that Article III prohibits a bankruptcy court from exercising jurisdiction over any private-rights claims, even if they are reviewable de novo on appeal. Chief Justice John Roberts wrote for the majority that given the enormous powers Congress had vested in bankruptcy courts, "a bankruptcy court can no more be deemed a mere 'adjunct' of the district court than a district court can be deemed such an 'adjunct' of the court of appeals." *Stern*, 564 U.S. at 500. Regardless of whether appeal to an Article III court was available, the Supreme Court limited bankruptcy courts' jurisdiction to public-rights claims, which it defined as (1) claims deriving from a "federal regulatory scheme" or (2) claims in which "an expert Government agency is deemed essential to a limited regulatory objective." *Id.* at 490; *Granfinanciera, S.A. v. Nordberg*, 492 U.S. 33, 51–55 (1989) (providing a similar definition for when an Article I court may decide a case without the jury required by the Seventh Amendment); *see also Oil States Energy Servs., LLC v. Greene's Energy Grp., LLC*, 138 S. Ct. 1365, 1373 (2018) (finding that the administration of patents is "squarely within the public-rights doctrine").

After *Stern*, the only contexts in which an Article I court or agency may resolve private-rights claims are those in which the fact finder has such limited powers that it doesn't threaten the integrity of Article III courts or interfere with separation-of-powers principles. *See CFTC v. Schor*, 478 U.S. 833 (1986); *Thomas v. Union Carbide Agric. Prods. Co.*, 473 U.S. 568 (1985). In addition, an Article I court may resolve a private-rights claim if all parties to the claim voluntarily consent to the court's exercise of jurisdiction—as if

---

under the more deferential 'clearly erroneous' standard." Would this appellate relationship be constitutional if Article III courts could review bankruptcy courts de novo?

For the Court's answer, see *Stern v. Marshall*, discussed in the note following this case.

the Article I court were a private arbitrator. *See Wellness Int'l Network, Ltd. v. Sharif*, 575 U.S. 665 (2015).

15.2 THE POWER TO REGULATE THE JUDICIARY

As a necessary and proper exercise of its power to *create* federal courts, Congress has also *regulated* federal courts. The Judiciary Act of 1789, for example, created federal district courts but withheld from them any power to hear certain cases, including federal-question cases, involving parties from the same state. Even though Article III confers broad federal-question jurisdiction on federal courts, the Supreme Court has explained that Congress may define and withhold Article III jurisdiction as part of its power to create inferior courts. *See Sheldon v. Sill*, 49 U.S. (8 How.) 441 (1850).

Congress's power to regulate the jurisdiction of federal courts also applies to the Supreme Court. Article III specifically states that "the supreme Court shall have appellate Jurisdiction, both as to Law and Fact, with such Exceptions, and under such Regulations as the Congress shall make." Applying this language, Congress has prohibited the Supreme Court from hearing certain types of cases, including cases with less than a minimum amount in controversy. *See Barry v. Mercein*, 46 U.S. (5 How.) 103, 119 (1847). Approvingly, the Supreme Court has held that although Article III allows the Court to hear many different types of cases, the Court's exercise of appellate jurisdiction depends on whatever Congress decides by statute. *Daniels v. R.R. Co.*, 70 U.S. (3 Wall.) 250, 254 (1865). The only power that Congress definitively lacks, in this respect, is the power to vest the Supreme Court with jurisdiction not also authorized by Article III itself. *See Marbury v. Madison*, 5 U.S. (1 Cranch) 137 (1803).

Congress's power to withhold jurisdiction from federal courts has other applications, some more controversial than others. On the less controversial end of the spectrum, Congress has required challengers of certain federal laws, such as the Voting Rights Act of 1965, to litigate their claims in specific federal courts, such as the U.S. District Court for the District of Columbia. *See* Pub. L. No. 89–110, 79 Stat. 437; *South Carolina v. Katzenbach*, 383 U.S. 301, 331 (1966) (upholding the law); *see also Lockerty v. Phillips*, 319 U.S. 182 (1943) (upholding a provision of the Emergency Price Control Act of 1942, Pub. L. No. 77–421, 56 Stat. 23, 31–33, that required anyone challenging the act's constitutionality to bring the claim in a newly created Emergency Court of Appeals). On the more controversial end of the spectrum, Congress has occasionally attempted to insulate certain controversial statutes from judicial review entirely.

15.2.1

Ex parte McCardle

74 U.S. (7 Wall.) 506 (1869)

As discussed in the section on Congress's powers to wage war successfully (section 13.4), after the Civil War, Congress passed several Military Reconstruction Acts to govern the defeated South. *See, e.g.*, Act of Mar. 2, 1867, ch. 153, 14 Stat. 428. The acts created five military districts in the South and authorized a general appointed by the president to administer the government for each district. These acts extended federal power further than ever before: regulating state constitutions, determining who could vote, and empowering governors to oversee the trials of civilians in military tribunals. *See* Eric Foner, *Reconstruction* 273–80 (2014). But when the Supreme Court overturned a conviction obtained by a military tribunal in *Ex parte Milligan*, 71 U.S. (4 Wall.) 2 (1866), Congress became fearful that the Supreme Court would also strike down the Reconstruction Acts.

One of the people arrested under the Reconstruction Acts was a Mississippi newspaper editor named William H. McCardle. A military tribunal tried and convicted McCardle on libel charges for printing several articles in his newspaper opposing Congress's Reconstruction policies. McCardle petitioned the local circuit court for a writ of habeas corpus, which it denied. He then appealed directly to the Supreme Court under an 1867 statute that authorized the Court to hear habeas claims on appeal. Act of Feb. 5, 1867, ch. 28, 14 Stat. 385.

When the case reached the Supreme Court, the administration of President Andrew Johnson was so hostile to Reconstruction that it refused to defend the constitutionality of the Reconstruction Acts. 6 Charles Fairman, *History of the Supreme Court of the United States: Reconstruction and Reunion, 1868–88*, at 436 (1971). Ultimately, Senator Lyman Trumbull was brought on to defend his own statute before the Court. *Id.* After the Supreme Court heard oral argument in McCardle's case, however, the senator returned to Congress fearful about the future of the Reconstruction Acts. *Id.* at 459–69.

To prevent the Court from issuing a decision, Congress repealed the 1867 law that allowed McCardle to appeal from the military tribunal to the Supreme Court. *Id.* The main question before the Court in *Ex parte McCardle*, 74 U.S. (7 Wall.) 506 (1869), therefore, was not whether the Reconstruction Acts validly authorized McCardle's conviction but whether the Supreme Court had jurisdiction to hear McCardle's habeas petition.

The Court's dismissal for lack of jurisdiction was its answer.

■ THE CHIEF JUSTICE delivered the opinion of the Court.[6]

The first question necessarily is that of jurisdiction; for, if the act of March, 1868, takes away the jurisdiction defined by the act of February, 1867, it is useless, if not improper, to enter into any discussion of other questions.

It is quite true, as was argued by the counsel for the petitioner, that the appellate jurisdiction of this court is not derived from acts of Congress. It is, strictly speaking, conferred by the Constitution. But it is conferred "with such exceptions and under such regulations as Congress shall make." . . .

In the case of *Durousseau v. The United States*, particularly, the whole matter was carefully examined, and the court held, that while "the appellate powers of this court are not given by the judicial act, but are given by the Constitution," they are, nevertheless, "limited and regulated by that act, and by such other acts as have been passed on the subject." The court said, further, that the judicial act was an exercise of the power given by the Constitution to Congress "of making exceptions to the appellate jurisdiction of the Supreme Court." "They have described affirmatively," said the court, "its jurisdiction, and this affirmative description has been understood to imply a negation of the exercise of such appellate power as is not comprehended within it."

The principle that the affirmation of appellate jurisdiction implies the negation of all such jurisdiction not affirmed having been thus established, it was an almost necessary consequence that acts of Congress, providing for the exercise of jurisdiction, should come to be spoken of as acts granting jurisdiction, and not as acts making exceptions to the constitutional grant of it.

The exception to appellate jurisdiction in the case before us, however, is not an inference from the affirmation of other appellate jurisdiction. It is made in terms. The provision of the act of 1867, affirming the appellate jurisdiction of this court in cases of habeas corpus is expressly repealed. It is hardly possible to imagine a plainer instance of positive exception.

We are not at liberty to inquire into the motives of the legislature. We can only examine into its power under the Constitution; and the power to make exceptions to the appellate jurisdiction of this court is given by express words.

What, then, is the effect of the repealing act upon the case before us? We cannot doubt as to this. Without jurisdiction the court cannot proceed at all in any cause. Jurisdiction is power to declare the law, and when it ceases to exist, the only function remaining to the court is that of announcing the fact and dismissing the cause. And this is not less clear upon authority than upon principle.

Several cases were cited by the counsel for the petitioner in support of the position that jurisdiction of this case is not affected by the repealing act. But none of them, in our judgment, afford any support to it. They are all cases of the exercise of judicial power by the legislature, or of legislative interference with courts in the exercising of continuing jurisdiction.

On the other hand, the general rule, supported by the best elementary writers, is, that "when an act of the legislature is repealed, it must be considered, except as to transactions past and closed, as if it never existed." . . . It is quite clear, therefore, that this court cannot proceed to pronounce judgment in this case, for it has no longer jurisdiction of the appeal; and judicial duty is not less fitly performed by declining

[6] **As You Read, Consider:** Keep in mind the facts of this case: the Supreme Court *heard oral argument* in a case evaluating the Reconstruction Acts' constitutionality, so Congress repealed the statute that allowed the petitioner to bring his claim before the Supreme Court. How does the Court evaluate this highly controversial exercise of jurisdiction stripping?

ungranted jurisdiction than in exercising firmly that which the Constitution and the laws confer.

Counsel seem to have supposed, if effect be given to the repealing act in question, that the whole appellate power of the court, in cases of habeas corpus, is denied. But this is an error. The act of 1868 does not except from that jurisdiction any cases but appeals from Circuit Courts under the act of 1867. It does not affect the jurisdiction which was previously exercised.[7]

The appeal of the petitioner in this case must be

DISMISSED FOR WANT OF JURISDICTION.

NOTE: CONGRESS'S POWER TO CURB JURISDICTION

McCardle represents a high-water mark of Congress's successful efforts to insulate a particular case from judicial review. But the significance of the case remains unclear. As the decision itself noted, the 1868 law didn't eliminate *all* paths by which someone could seek judicial review of the Reconstruction Acts; rather, it eliminated only the path opened by the 1867 law. Indeed, later that same year, the Supreme Court held that it continued to have authority under the Judiciary Act of 1789 to review a certiorari petition from a lower court's denial of a military prisoner's habeas petition. *Ex parte Yerger*, 75 U.S. (8 Wall.) 85 (1869). This second case has long led observers to question how the Court would respond if Congress passed a statute permanently insulating another law from judicial review. *See* Henry P. Monaghan, *Jurisdiction Stripping Circa 2020: What* the Dialogue *(Still) Has to Teach Us*, 69 Duke L.J. 1 (2019); Henry M. Hart Jr., *The Power of Congress to Limit the Jurisdiction of Federal Courts: An Exercise in Dialectic*, 66 Harv. L. Rev. 1362 (1953). This question is more real than speculative as both Democrats and Republicans have recently attempted to protect favored legislation from hostile federal courts. *See, e.g.*, H.R. 1, § 4, 117th Cong. (2021) (requiring constitutional challenges to a major voting-rights bill to be brought in the U.S. District Court for the District of Columbia); H.R. 3313, 108th Cong. (2004) (prohibiting federal courts from reviewing same-sex marriage cases).

***Patchak* and expansive judiciary power.** In *Patchak v. Zinke*, the Court offered one answer: "When Congress strips federal courts of jurisdiction, it exercises a valid legislative power no less than when it lays taxes, coins money, declares war, or invokes any other power that the Constitution grants it." 138 S. Ct. 897, 906 (2018). The Court continued: "So long as Congress does not violate other constitutional provisions, its 'control over the jurisdiction of the federal courts' is 'plenary.' " *Id.* This answer built on four lines of cases, each of which illustrated marginal limits on a quite-expansive power.

---

[7] **Questions:** Chief Justice Salmon Chase ends his opinion with a reminder that Congress's 1868 repeal statute "does not affect the jurisdiction which was previously exercised." In other words, someone like William H. McCardle can try again to bring his claim to the Supreme Court through the procedures that existed before 1867. How significant do you think this fact is for the Court's decision? If McCardle had no way of returning to the Supreme Court, might the case have come out differently?

One line has upheld various attempts by Congress to forestall an expected decision, including by raising the amount-in-controversy requirement for jurisdiction, *R.R. Co. v. Grant*, 98 U.S. 398 (1878), or by confining the Supreme Court's review to questions of law as opposed to questions of fact, *The Francis Wright*, 105 U.S. 381 (1882). More recently, in *Felker v. Turpin*, 518 U.S. 651 (1996), the Court upheld the Antiterrorism and Effective Death Penalty Act (AEDPA) of 1996, which prohibited federal appellate courts from hearing a prisoner's "second or successive" habeas petition unless a judge issued a "certificate of appealability" determining that the petition had arguable merit. Pub. L. No. 104–132, 110 Stat. 1214, 1217. Although AEDPA has made it very difficult for prisoners to challenge their detention more than once, the *Felker* Court held that Congress has discretion to regulate courts' jurisdiction in this manner.

A second line of cases has recognized that Congress's power to regulate federal courts' jurisdiction over habeas petitions may sometimes be limited by the Constitution's Suspension Clause, which states that "[t]he Privilege of the Writ of Habeas Corpus shall not be suspended, unless when in Cases of Rebellion or Invasion the public Safety may require it." U.S. Const. art. I, § 9, cl. 2. In *INS v. St. Cyr*, 533 U.S. 289 (2001), the Court undermined a restrictive obstacle for immigration-related challenges, holding that the Court would require a clear statement from Congress before it interpreted a statute to deny people the ability to contest their detention in federal court. And in *Boumediene v. Bush*, 553 U.S. 723 (2008), the Court held that the Suspension Clause prohibited Congress from permanently denying detained people a fair procedure for contesting their detention unless Congress expressly invoked the Suspension Clause. Yet in *Department of Homeland Security v. Thuraissigiam*, 140 S. Ct. 1959 (2020), the Court upheld the constitutionality of a statute that prohibited certain immigrants from challenging their *deportation* in federal court, concluding that deportation was distinct from indefinite detention.

A third line of cases recognizes another potential limit: Congress may not allow any court but an Article III court to overturn another Article III court's final judgment. This limit first arose in 1792 when Congress passed a statute that required Article III judges to administer pension claims arising from the Revolutionary War. Act of Mar. 23, 1792, ch. 11, 1 Stat. 243, 244. The Supreme Court objected that this act also allowed the secretary of war to review—and reject—the Article III court's judgment. *See Hayburn's Case*, 2 U.S. (2 Dall.) 409 (1792). In later cases, the Court emphasized that no statutory scheme can permit Congress or an executive officer to review and reject the decision of an Article III fact finder. *See Chi. & S. Air Lines* v. *Waterman S.S. Corp.*, 333 U.S. 103 (1948); *Gordon v. United States*, 69 U.S. (2 Wall.) 561 (1864). By contrast, the Court has upheld statutory schemes that allow the Supreme Court or any other Article III court to review and reject an Article I court's judgment—even though the text of Article III itself appears to limit the Supreme Court's appellate jurisdiction to Article III cases. *See Ortiz v. United States*, 138 S. Ct. 2165 (2018); *D.C. Ct. of Appeals v. Feldman*, 460 U.S. 462 (1983); *Pope v. United States*, 323 U.S. 1 (1944); *De Groot v. United States*, 72 U.S. (5 Wall.) 419 (1867).

A fourth line of cases recognizes a final limit: Congress may not usurp a court's power to interpret and apply the law to the circumstances before it. The landmark case in this line also arose out of the Reconstruction era. During the Civil War, Congress passed the Confiscation Act of 1862, ch. 145, 12 Stat. 589, which authorized the president to seize the property of anyone who participated in the Confederate rebellion. President Abraham Lincoln invoked this act as a legal basis for the Emancipation Proclamation. Yet he and his successor, Andrew Johnson, also issued proclamations that undermined the act by pardoning many ex-Confederates if they took an oath of loyalty. In 1870, the Supreme Court held that the receipt of a pardon entitled an ex-Confederate to regain his (non-enslaved) property by going to the U.S. Court of Claims, an Article I court. *United States v. Padelford*, 76 U.S. (9 Wall.) 531 (1870). Immediately afterward, Congress passed a law that attempted to reverse this decision. *See* Act of July 12, 1870, 16 Stat. 230, 235. In effect, the law declared that receipt of a pardon was evidence of a person's *dis*loyalty. And if anyone with a pardon had already gone to the U.S. Court of Claims to recover property, the law instructed the Supreme Court, on appeal, to dismiss the case for lack of jurisdiction.

***Klein* and limits on congressional power.** In *United States v. Klein*, 80 U.S. (13 Wall.) 128 (1872), the Court invalidated this last provision. "It seems to us that this is not an exercise of the acknowledged power of Congress to make exceptions and prescribe regulations to the appellate power," the Court wrote. *Klein*, 80 U.S. (13 Wall.) at 146. Instead, the Court considered the law to be "the application of a rule of decision, in causes pending, prescribed by Congress." *Id.* The Court offered two reasons why it was unconstitutional for Congress "to prescribe a rule for the decision of a cause in a particular way." *Id.* First, Congress had no power to invalidate the effect of a presidential pardon without interfering with the president's Article II powers. Second, if Congress had the power to "prescribe rules of decision to the Judicial Department of the government in cases pending before it," the Court suggested that Congress would also have the power to ignore or eliminate the Court's ability to serve as an independent branch of government. *Id.* In enacting this law, "Congress has inadvertently passed the limit which separates the legislative from the judicial power," the Court concluded. *Id.* at 147.

Klein thus held that Congress possesses the power to regulate the Supreme Court's appellate jurisdiction, but not the power to "prescribe a rule for the decision of a cause in a particular way." *Id.* at 146. Taken at face value, this language suggests that Congress lacks the power to amend a statute retroactively so that a case decided one way in a trial court must be decided differently on appeal.

***Peterson* and retroactive regulations.** But when the Court has recently considered statutes that do just this, the Court has narrowly limited *Klein* to its facts. *See, e.g.*, *Plaut v. Spendthrift Farms, Inc.*, 514 U.S. 211 (1995) (writing that Congress could retroactively apply a new law to pending cases but could not require federal courts to reopen final judgments). Indeed, the Court effectively overruled *Klein* in a 2016 case involving the state bank of Iran, *Bank Markazi v. Peterson*, 578 U.S. 212 (2016).

Since the 1980s, thousands of victims of bombings in the Middle East, including the 1983 truck bombings of a barracks in Beirut, have obtained judgments against Iran for its role in supporting state-sponsored terrorism. To satisfy these judgments, a group of plaintiffs obtained court orders preventing the central bank of Iran, Bank Markazi, from shifting approximately $1.75 billion out of a particular New York bank account. In one of these court proceedings in the U.S. District Court for the Southern District of New York, Bank Markazi objected that existing federal law didn't authorize federal courts to seize this particular bank account. Before the district court resolved the dispute, however, Congress passed the Iran Threat Reduction and Syria Human Rights Act of 2012, Pub. L. No. 112–158, 126 Stat. 1214. One of the provisions of the law authorized federal district courts to seize

> the financial assets that are identified in and the subject of proceedings in the United States District Court for the Southern District of New York in Peterson et al. v. Islamic Republic of Iran et al., Case No. 10 Civ. 4518 (BSJ)(GWG), that were restrained by restraining notices and levies secured by the plaintiffs in those proceedings.

Id. at 1259. Bank Markazi objected that this provision effectively dictated the result of a pending case, violating the separation-of-powers principle of *Klein*.

The Supreme Court disagreed. Writing for a 6–2 majority, Justice Ruth Bader Ginsburg interpreted *Klein* to the point of insignificance as a case about Congress's power to interfere with the president's pardon power. At most, Ginsburg wrote, the decision stood for the proposition that Congress may not "compel[ ] . . . findings or results under old law" by failing to supply "any new legal standard effectuating the lawmakers' reasonable policy judgment." *Bank Markazi*, 136 S. Ct. at 1326. By contrast, Ginsburg cited dozens of cases in which the Supreme Court had already upheld (1) laws that retroactively "direct[ed] courts to apply newly enacted, outcome-altering legislation in pending civil cases," *see, e.g.*, *Plaut*, 514 U.S. 211; (2) "laws that governed one or a very small number of specific subjects," *see, e.g.*, *Pennsylvania v. Wheeling & Belmont Bridge Co.*, 18 How. 421 (1856); and (3) laws that "exercised control over claims against foreign states and the disposition of foreign-state property in the United States," *see, e.g.*, *Dames & Moore v. Regan*, 453 U.S. 654 (1981). *Bank Markazi*, 136 S. Ct. at 1325, 1328. Justice Ginsburg therefore concluded that Congress had the power to apply new governing standards to Bank Markazi's specific, pending case.

NOTE: CONGRESS'S OTHER POWERS TO REGULATE THE JUDICIARY

In addition to regulating the federal judiciary's jurisdiction, Congress also has significant power to regulate virtually every other aspect of the judiciary's business.

Writs. Perhaps the most important power possessed by a judge is the power to issue binding orders, or *writs,* commanding someone else to comply with a decision.

As just mentioned, Congress has routinely regulated judges' power to issue writs of habeas corpus that command a custodian to release someone from detention. *See, e.g.*, Antiterrorism and Effective Death Penalty Act of 1996, Pub. L. No. 104–132, 110 Stat. 1214, 1217 (setting very restrictive standards for state and "second or successive" habeas petitions); Act of Nov. 2, 1996, Pub. L. 89–711, § 2, 80 Stat. 1105, 1105–06 (setting moderately restrictive standards for when a federal court could issue habeas relief to a state prisoner); Habeas Corpus Act of 1867, Pub. L. 39–28, 14 Stat. 385, 385–87 (authorizing federal courts to consider habeas petitions from convicted prisoners).

Congress has also regulated more mundane writs, including federal courts' power to issue writs of mandamus that order federal or state officers to execute a law, raise state taxes, or otherwise remedy a petitioner's grievance. *See, e.g.*, Act of Oct. 5, 1962, Pub. L. 87–748, 76 Stat. 744, 744 (enhancing federal courts' power to command state and federal executive officers); Judiciary Act of 1789, ch. 20, 1 Stat. 73 (authorizing federal courts to issue various writs); *see also, e.g.*, *Missouri v. Jenkins*, 495 U.S. 33, 57–58 (upholding a federal court's power under these statutes to order local authorities to increase taxes to pay for desegregation remedies).

Injunctions. Congress has also regulated federal courts' power to issue *injunctions*: equitable orders commanding someone to cease their conduct. *See, e.g.*, Judiciary Act of 1793, ch. 22, 1 Stat. 333 (prohibiting federal courts from issuing injunctions to stay state-court proceedings unless necessary to aid their jurisdiction, effectuate their judgments, or enforce bankruptcy proceedings); Judiciary Act of 1789, ch. 20, 1 Stat. 73 (providing that no equity suit should be maintained where there was a full and adequate remedy at law).

Occasionally, Congress has used this power to stop federal courts from interfering in particular issues. *See, e.g.*, Tax Injunction Act, Pub. L. No. 75–332, ch. 726, 50 Stat. 738 (1937) (codified as amended at 28 U.S.C. § 1341) (prohibiting federal courts from issuing injunctions to restrain the collection of state taxes); Tax Anti-Injunction Act, ch. 169, § 10, 14 Stat. 475 (1867) (same with federal taxes). For example, after the Supreme Court upheld the power of federal courts to enjoin state officers from enforcing unconstitutional laws, Congress provided that such injunctions could be issued only by panels of three federal judges. Three-Judge Court Act, Act of June 18, 1910, ch. 309, § 17, 36 Stat. 557; *see* Act of Aug. 12, 1976, Pub. L. No. 94–381, 90 Stat. 1119 (repealing the 1910 law for most cases with some exceptions, including voting-rights and districting cases). Furthermore, after decades in which federal courts enjoined unions from striking, Congress passed the Norris-La Guardia Act of 1932, Pub. L. No. 72–65, 47 Stat. 70, which forbade the use of injunctions in labor disputes unless certain conditions were satisfied. And with the Emergency Price Control Act of 1942, Pub. L. No. 77–421, 56 Stat. 23, Congress prohibited federal courts from enjoining wartime price controls by giving exclusive jurisdiction over the issue to a specialized court, the Emergency Court of Appeals. *See Lockerty v. Phillips*, 319 U.S. 182, 186–87 (1943). Controversially, the Supreme Court upheld this law even though it prohibited criminal defendants charged with violating the price controls from challenging the law's legality in their trials. *See Yakus v. United States*, 321 U.S. 414, 426, 446–48 (1944).

Rules. Congress has also regulated the *rules* that govern courts' procedure, including when courts may meet, how they may appoint officers, how writs may be issued, and more. *See, e.g.*, Judiciary Act of 1789, ch. 20, 1 Stat. 73 (issuing rules for the Supreme Court and inferior courts); 48 Stat. 1064 (1934) (authorizing the Supreme Court to prescribe the Federal Rules of Civil Procedure and other rules of practice for lower federal courts).

These statutes have been upheld even when they have had the effect of delaying for years when a court, including the Supreme Court, could hear a particular case. *See, e.g.*, *Sibbach v. Wilson*, 312 U.S. 1 (1941). For example, a month after President Thomas Jefferson signed into law the controversial 1802 statute abolishing the judicial positions created by John Adams, Congress also canceled the Supreme Court's next sitting. Judiciary Act of 1802, ch. 31, 2 Stat. 156. This meant that the Supreme Court didn't consider the 1802 law's constitutionality for over a year—and in the meantime, it had to comply with its requirements by once again riding circuit.

Punishment of contempt/disobedience. Finally, Congress has also regulated federal courts' power to punish *contempt*, or disobedience, with its orders. *See, e.g.*, Act of Mar. 2, 1831, ch. 99, 4 Stat. 487, 488 (imposing limits on courts' power to punish contempt outside the presence of the court); Judiciary Act of 1789, 1 Stat. 73, 83 (conferring the power to punish "contempts of authority"). The Supreme Court has suggested that this power of Congress is not unlimited, however, because "[t]he power to punish for contempts is inherent in all courts." *Ex parte Robinson*, 86 U.S. (19 Wall.) 505 (1874).

Power of federal courts. Absent action by Congress, the Supreme Court has suggested that federal courts possess the inherent power to respond to any problem "confronting the court's fair administration of justice," as long as the power is "a reasonable response to a specific problem" and doesn't "contradict any express rule or statute." *Dietz v. Bouldin*, 579 U.S. 40, 46 (2016). Such inherent powers include the power to issue rules, hear motions, and stay or dismiss proceedings. *Id.*

CHAPTER 16

WHAT IS THE SCOPE OF CONGRESS'S POWER WITH RESPECT TO THE FEDERAL DISTRICT AND FEDERAL ENCLAVES?

ARTICLE I, SECTION 8, CLAUSE 17: The Congress shall have Power . . . To exercise exclusive Legislation in all Cases whatsoever, over such District (not exceeding ten Miles square) as may, by Cession of particular States, and the Acceptance of Congress, become the Seat of the Government of the United States, and to exercise like Authority over all Places purchased by the Consent of the Legislature of the State in which the Same shall be, for the Erection of Forts, Magazines, Arsenals, dock-Yards, and other needful Buildings;—And

> **CLAUSE 18:** To make all Laws which shall be necessary and proper for carrying into Execution the foregoing Powers, and all other Powers vested by this Constitution in the Government of the United States, or in any Department or Officer thereof.

TWENTY-THIRD AMENDMENT, SECTION 1 (1961): The District constituting the seat of Government of the United States shall appoint in such manner as the Congress may direct: A number of electors of President and Vice President equal to the whole number of Senators and Representatives in Congress to which the District would be entitled if it were a State, but in no event more than the least populous State; they shall be in addition to those appointed by the States, but they shall be considered, for the purposes of the election of President and Vice President, to be electors appointed by a State; and they shall meet in the District and perform such duties as provided by the twelfth article of amendment.

The District and Enclave Clause

In June 1783, while the Congress of the Confederation was meeting at the Pennsylvania statehouse in Philadelphia, an armed group of soldiers descended on the building demanding payment for their service during the Revolutionary War. Stephen J. Markman, *Statehood for the District of Columbia*, 46–47 (1988). Congress urgently asked the Pennsylvania militia for protection, but the state's leaders sided with the soldiers. Unable to respond to the mutiny on its own, Congress fled to nearby Princeton, New Jersey. It eventually relocated the federal capital to New York City. *See* Jeffery M. Dorwart, *Invasion and Insurrection* 161–67, 179 (2008).

The Confederation Congress's early experience with armed insurrection is likely why the Constitution gives Congress the power

> [t]o exercise exclusive Legislation in all Cases whatsoever, over such District (not exceeding ten Miles square) as may, by Cession of particular States, and the Acceptance of Congress, become the Seat of the Government of the United States, and to exercise like Authority over all Places purchased by the Consent of the Legislature of the State in which the Same shall be, for the Erection of Forts, Magazines, Arsenals, dock-Yards, and other needful buildings.

U.S. Const. art. I, § 8, cl. 17. Today, more than seven hundred thousand people live in places governed by this clause—Article I, Section 8, Clause 17—which in its entirety is called the District and Enclave Clause.

16.1 THE FEDERAL DISTRICT

The first half of this clause, sometimes called the District Clause, envisioned that Congress would accept a cession of land from a state and govern it as a federal capital. The first Congress did just that, passing the Residence Act of 1790, which placed the capital by "the river Potomac." Residence Act, ch. 28, 1 Stat. 130, 130. The location of the new district was part of a compromise. In exchange for allowing the federal government to assume the war debts of all the states—something the southern states opposed—the capital would be located in the South. *See* Ron Chernow, *Alexander Hamilton* 330 (2005). President George Washington selected the final site of the district to include the existing cities of Alexandria, Virginia, and Georgetown, Maryland.

Categorization of the district

In 1801, Congress organized the newly named "District of Columbia" and divided it into two counties: Washington County on the north side of the Potomac and Alexandria County on the south side. Act of Feb. 27, 1801, ch. 15, 2 Stat. 103. Congress soon chartered the "city of Washington" within Washington County. Act of May 3, 1802, ch. 53, 2 Stat. 195. The charter provided for a twelve-member city council and a mayor who would be appointed by the president. It also gave the city the power to enact and enforce ordinances, taxes, and penalties. Thus, at the time of its creation, the District of Columbia resembled a state. It had two counties—Washington and Alexandria—in which there were three cities: Washington, D.C.; Alexandria, D.C.; and Georgetown, D.C.

Because of this resemblance to a state, early courts had a difficult time determining where it fit in the constitutional order. For example, both the Judiciary Act of 1789 and Article III of the Constitution gave federal courts the power to hear "Controversies . . . between Citizens of different States." Invoking this jurisdiction, early residents of the District of Columbia sued a Virginian in federal court. But in *Hepburn v. Ellzey*, the Supreme Court dismissed the case for lack of jurisdiction, writing that "the word state is used in the constitution as designating a member of the union," not the federal district. 6 U.S. (2 Cranch) 445, 452 (1805). Accordingly, residents of the District of Columbia were constitutionally unable to sue residents of other states in federal court.

In writing about this outcome, the Court noted that "it is extraordinary that the courts of the United States, which are open to aliens, and to the citizens of every state in the union, should be closed upon them." *Id.* at 453. But, the Court wrote, the district was simply not a "state." *Id.* Otherwise, it would be entitled to a representative, two senators, three presidential electors, and other attributes of a state—which the litigants before it were not arguing for. *See id.* at 452–53.

Taxation in the district

This conclusion of *Hepburn*—that residents of the District of Columbia did not have the same constitutional rights as residents of Virginia or Maryland—was in tension with the maxim that launched the American Revolution: "No taxation without representation." Thus, fifteen years after *Hepburn*, the Court considered whether Congress had the authority to impose a direct tax on the people of the District of Columbia without also giving its residents elected representatives in Congress. In *Loughborough v. Blake*, Chief Justice John Marshall concluded that the needs of the "American empire" meant that Congress could not afford to give political representation to every constituency it taxed. 18 U.S. (5 Wheat.) 317, 324 (1820).

Thinking ahead to how Congress might govern "the territory west of the Missouri," Marshall thought it absurd that the Constitution could prohibit Congress from taxing residents of the District of Columbia and the territories simply because they had no voting representatives in Congress. *Id.* at 318–19. The people who chose to live in these places had "voluntarily relinquished the right of representation, and ha[d] adopted the whole body of Congress for its legitimate government," he wrote. *Id.* at 324.

> Although in theory it might be more congenial to the spirit of our institutions to admit a representative from the district, it may be doubted, whether, in fact, its interests would be rendered thereby the more secure; and certainly the constitution does not consider their want of a representative in Congress as exempting it from equal taxation.

Id. at 324–25.

As *Loughborough* indicated, the Court has historically treated "the whole body of Congress" as the government for the District of Columbia—even when Congress has allowed the cities within the District of Columbia to elect their own mayors. *See* Act of May 15, 1820, ch. 104, 3 Stat. 583. In *Cohens v. Virginia*, 19 U.S. (6 Wheat.) 264 (1821), the Court explained that when Congress legislates for the District of Columbia, it assumes the role of both the national legislature and a state legislature, with as much power over the district as a state has over its cities.

Court system in the district

The District of Columbia's courts illustrate Congress's state-like powers over the district. As discussed previously (section 15.1), when Congress creates a federal court, it is ordinarily bound by the provisions of Article III that protect the tenure and salaries of federal judges. States, by contrast, are not bound by these limits and may create state courts on which justices serve without tenure or salary protections. When the Supreme Court has considered Congress's powers to create courts in the District of Columbia, it has relied heavily on this state analogy to conclude that Congress "possesses a dual authority over the District and may clothe the courts of the District not only with the jurisdiction and powers of federal courts in the several States but with such authority as a State may confer on her courts." *Keller v. Potomac Elec. Power Co.*, 261 U.S. 428, 443 (1923).

Accordingly, the Court has allowed Congress to create Article I courts in the District of Columbia without tenure or salary protections, *Kendall v. United States ex rel. Stokes,* 37 U.S. (12 Pet.) 524, 619 (1838); it has allowed these Article I courts to enforce federal law and claims of private right, *Palmore v. United States*, 411 U.S. 389 (1973); and it has even allowed *Article III* courts in the district to exercise powers that federal courts lack elsewhere, including the power to act like an administrative agency within the executive branch, *see, e.g., O'Donoghue v. United States,* 289 U.S. 516 (1933). Notably, in *National Mutual Insurance Co. v. Tidewater Transfer Co.*, the Court even held that Congress had the power to effectively overrule *Hepburn*: the Court allowed Congress to give residents of the District of Columbia the right to claim diversity jurisdiction in federal court—even though Article III reserves such jurisdiction to "Citizens of different *States.*" *Tidewater Transfer Co.*, 337 U.S. 582, 588–91 (1949).

Federal plenary power

The history of Congress's relationship with the District of Columbia is a history of plenary power. Where Congress ordinarily must justify its legislation by pointing to a specific enumerated power, the Supreme Court has interpreted Article I's grant of power to "exercise exclusive Legislation in all Cases whatsoever, over [the] District," as authorizing Congress (1) to tax the people of the District of Columbia without providing them with representation, *see Loughborough*; (2) to create Article I courts that ignore the tenure and salary protections of Article III, *see Kendall*; (3) to empower Article III courts to perform administrative functions overseen by an executive officer, *see O'Donoghue*; (4) to delegate its lawmaking power to a local government, *see District of Columbia v. John R. Thompson Co.*, 346 U.S. 100 (1953);

and (5) to empower that local government to enact legislation that Congress lacks the power to enact outside the District of Columbia, *see id.*

In the tribal context, where Congress has similar plenary powers, the Supreme Court has interpreted Congress's power so broadly that the Court has refused to consider claims that Congress has violated the limits of the Bill of Rights. *See Lone Wolf v. Hitchcock*, 187 U.S. 553 (1903). It therefore might seem reasonable to argue that the Bill of Rights also doesn't limit Congress when it legislates for the District of Columbia. However, the Court has determined otherwise.

The right to a jury trial is one example. Although both Article III and the Sixth Amendment protect the right to a jury trial, both contain language that suggests that this protection applies only to states. The Sixth Amendment references a "State," and Article III says that criminal trials "shall be by Jury . . . in the State where the said Crimes shall have been committed." In *Hepburn*, the Supreme Court expressly held that the District of Columbia is not a "State" for purposes of Article III's grant of diversity jurisdiction. So, when the federal government prosecuted people in the District of Columbia, it occasionally argued that a jury trial was not required. But in *Callan v. Wilson*, the Supreme Court emphatically held that the right to a jury trial—along with the rest of the Bill of Rights—applies to the District of Columbia just as it applies in the states:

> There is nothing in the history of the Constitution or of the original amendments to justify the assertion that the people of this District may be lawfully deprived of the benefit of any of the constitutional guaranties of life, liberty, and property—especially of the privilege of trial by jury in criminal cases.

127 U.S. 540, 550 (1888). Examining that history, the Court concluded that "it was taken for granted" by the Constitution's framers that the right to a jury trial would apply in the District of Columbia. *Id.*

Accordingly, the Supreme Court has often applied the Bill of Rights to laws passed by Congress with respect to the District of Columbia or to laws passed by the District of Columbia itself—despite Congress's plenary powers. Famous examples include a case striking down a minimum wage law under the Due Process Clause of the Fifth Amendment, *Adkins v. Children's Hosp.*, 261 U.S. 525 (1923); a case striking down a school segregation policy under the equal-protection principle embodied in the Due Process Clause, *Bolling v. Sharpe*, 347 U.S. 497 (1954); and a case striking down a gun-control ordinance under the Second Amendment, *District of Columbia v. Heller*, 554 U.S. 570 (2008).

16.1.1
District of Columbia v. John R. Thompson Co.

346 U.S. 100 (1953)

The best illustration of Congress's power "[t]o exercise exclusive Legislation in all Cases whatsoever, over [the] District [of Columbia]," concerns slavery and race.

Before the Civil War, few white Americans believed that Congress had the power to abolish slavery or the slave trade within the southern states. But most believed that Congress *did* have such power in the District of Columbia. One group that certainly thought so comprised the people of Alexandria, D.C.—a slave port located south of the Potomac River. In the 1840s, fearing that Congress might soon abolish slavery in the district, the white residents of Alexandria petitioned Congress to "retrocede" the land back to Virginia. There were two problems with this petition. One, when Virginia first ceded Alexandria to the federal government in 1789, the Virginia legislature declared that the cession would last "forever." 1789 Va. Acts 19. Two, while Article I gives Congress the power to *acquire* territory for the federal district, it does not give Congress explicit authority to *dispose of* any part of the federal district. Nevertheless, Congress agreed to return Alexandria to Virginia after a referendum. Act of July 9, 1846, ch. 35, 9 Stat. 35. Four years later, Congress abolished the slave trade in the District of Columbia. Act of Sept. 20, 1850, ch. 63, 9 Stat. 467. Congress went even further during the Civil War, abolishing slavery in the district, as the Alexandrians predicated (but compensating former owners of enslaved people). *See* Act of Apr. 16, 1862, ch. 54, 12 Stat. 376.

During the Reconstruction era that followed the Civil War, as Congress protected the right of black people to vote throughout the South, Congress transformed the government of the District of Columbia to reflect the prevailing democratic ethos. The D.C. Organic Act of 1871 combined Washington, Georgetown, and the county surrounding them into a single "territorial government"—the District of Columbia—with an elected legislature for the first time. Act of Feb. 21, 1871, ch. 112, 16 Stat. 419. The D.C. legislature immediately went to work passing antidiscrimination laws. One made it a crime for the owner of any "restaurant, hotel, ice-cream saloon, or soda-fountain" to engage in racial discrimination. *Statutes in Force in the District of Columbia*, Misc. Doc. No. 42-25, at 219 (1872).

This elected legislature lasted only three years, however, as the economy sputtered and white opposition to Reconstruction grew more intense. In 1874, Congress abolished the District of Columbia's multiracial democracy and opted to resume directly legislating for the district once again. Act of June 20, 1874, ch. 337, 18 Stat. 116; *see* David W. Blight, *Frederick Douglass* 549–50 (2019). Yet Congress never repealed the antidiscrimination laws that the D.C. legislature passed between 1871 and 1874; it simply created a presidentially appointed board of commissioners for the district that declined to enforce old laws.

Mary Church Terrell, one of the first black women to receive a college degree in the United States, moved to the District of Columbia shortly after Congress resumed legislating for it. While there, she witnessed the effect of decisions like the *Civil Rights Cases*, 109 U.S. 3 (1883), in which the Supreme Court held that Congress had no power to prohibit racial discrimination within the states. Throughout the South, states and local governments responded by adopting segregation laws that subordinated the status of black residents. The District of Columbia followed this trend. Restaurants and streetcars that once catered to Terrell began enforcing their own Jim Crow policies. During the administration of President Woodrow Wilson—the first southerner to occupy the White House since the Civil War—even the federal workforce became racially segregated. *See* Joan Quigley, *Just Another Southern Town* 78 (2016).

These developments radicalized Terrell. She became one of the founding members of the National Association for the Advancement of Colored People (NAACP) in 1909, she organized a national network of black women to combat lynching and work toward granting women the right to vote, and she became a nationally recognized speaker and civil rights activist. *See* Martha S. Jones, *Vanguard* 153–66 (2020). In the 1940s, when she was over 80 years old, she was still leading sit-ins and protests to force D.C. businesses to desegregate their facilities.

During one of these campaigns, a national report on segregation in the District of Columbia uncovered the existence of one of the Reconstruction-era antidiscrimination laws. The report observed that the law had "mysteriously disappeared from the compiled statutes of the District, and it cannot be found in present codes. Since there is no record of its repeal, some lawyers speculate that it may still be technically in full force and effect." Kenesaw M. Landis, *Segregation in Washington* 18 (1948).

Terrell immediately grasped the significance of this report. Quigley, *supra*, at 296. She soon led a group of civil rights activists into Thompson's Restaurant, a segregated lunch counter near the White House. When the restaurant refused to serve her, she brought a claim with the District of Columbia's board of commissioners, asking the board to enforce the district's old antidiscrimination laws. The John R. Thompson Company defended itself from this prosecution by arguing that Congress had no power to prohibit segregation in restaurants.

A decade before *Heart of Atlanta Motel, Inc. v. United States*, 379 U.S. 241 (1964)—during the same term when it heard oral arguments in *Brown v. Board of Education* (*Brown I*), 347 U.S. 483 (1954)—the Supreme Court in *District of Columbia v. John R. Thompson Co.*, 346 U.S. 100 (1953), considered whether Congress could delegate to the District of Columbia the power to enact an antidiscrimination ordinance.

Terrell lived long enough to enjoy a successful conclusion to the case that she initiated.

■ MR. JUSTICE DOUGLAS delivered the opinion of the Court.[1]

This is a criminal proceeding prosecuted by information against respondent for refusal to serve certain members of the Negro race at one of its restaurants in the District of Columbia solely on account of the race and color of those persons. The information is in four counts, the first charging a violation of the Act of the Legislative Assembly of the District of Columbia, June 20, 1872, and the others charging violations of the Act of the Legislative Assembly of the District of Columbia, June 26, 1873, Dist. Col. Laws 1871–1873, pp. 65, 116. Each Act makes it a crime to discriminate against a person on account of race or color or to refuse service to him on that ground. . . . [T]he Court of Appeals held that the 1872 and 1873 Acts were unenforceable and that the entire information should be dismissed. 92 U. S. App. D. C. 34, 203 F. 2d 579. . . .

I.

The history of congressional legislation dealing with the District of Columbia begins with the Act of July 16, 1790, 1 Stat. 130, by which the District was established as the permanent seat of the Government of the United States. We need not review for the purposes of this case the variety of congressional enactments pertaining to the management of the affairs of the District between that date and 1871. It is with the Organic Act of February 21, 1871, 16 Stat. 419, that we are particularly concerned.

That Act created a government by the name of the District of Columbia, constituted it "a body corporate for municipal purposes" with all of the powers of a municipal corporation "not inconsistent with the Constitution and laws of the United States and the provisions of this act," and gave it jurisdiction over all the territory within the limits of the District. § 1. The Act vested "legislative power and authority" in a Legislative Assembly consisting of a Council and a House of Delegates, members of the Council to be appointed by the President with the advice and consent of the Senate and members of the House of Delegates to be elected by male citizens residing in the District. §§ 5, 7. The Act provided, with exceptions not material here, that "the legislative power of the District shall extend to all rightful subjects of legislation within said District, consistent with the Constitution of the United States and the provisions of this act." § 18. All acts of the Legislative Assembly were made subject at all times "to repeal or modification" by Congress. § 18. And it was provided that nothing in the Act should be construed to deprive Congress of "the power of legislation" over the District "in as ample manner as if this law had not been enacted." § 18. Executive power was vested in a governor appointed by the President by and with the advice of the Senate. § 2. And it was provided that the District should have in the House of Representatives an elected delegate having the same rights and privileges as those of delegates from federal territories. § 34.

This government (which was short-lived) was characterized by the Court as a "territorial government." *Eckloff* v. *District of Columbia,* 135 U.S. 240, 241. The analogy is an apt one. The grant to the Legislative Assembly by § 18 of legislative power which extends "to all rightful subjects of legislation" is substantially identical with the grant of legislative power to territorial governments which reads: "The legislative power of every Territory shall extend to all rightful subjects of legislation not inconsistent with the Constitution and laws of the United States." R. S. § 1851.

---

1 **As You Read, Consider:** The Constitution gives Congress the power to exercise "exclusive Legislation in all Cases whatsoever" over the District of Columbia. Does the Court consider this an unlimited grant of power?

The power of Congress over the District and its power over the Territories are phrased in very similar language in the Constitution. Article I, § 8, cl. 17 of the Constitution provides that "The Congress shall have Power . . . To exercise exclusive Legislation in all Cases whatsoever, over such District (not exceeding ten Miles square) as may, by Cession of particular States, and the Acceptance of Congress, become the Seat of the Government of the United States." Article IV, § 3, cl. 2 of the Constitution grants Congress authority over territories in the following words: "The Congress shall have Power to dispose of and make all needful Rules and Regulations respecting the Territory or other Property belonging to the United States. . . ."

The power of Congress to delegate legislative power to a territory is well settled. The power which Congress constitutionally may delegate to a territory (subject of course to "the right of Congress to revise, alter, and revoke,") covers all matters "which, within the limits of a State, are regulated by the laws of the State only."[2]

The power of Congress to grant self-government to the District of Columbia under Art. I, § 8, cl. 17 of the Constitution would seem to be as great as its authority to do so in the case of territories. But a majority of the judges of the Court of Appeals held that Congress had the constitutional authority to delegate "municipal" but not "general" legislative powers and that the Acts of 1872 and 1873, being in the nature of civil rights legislation, fell in the latter group and were for Congress alone to enact. In reaching that conclusion the Court of Appeals relied upon . . . *Metropolitan R. Co.* v. *District of Columbia,* 132 U. S. 1. . . .

[*Metropolitan*] presented the question of the capacity of the District of Columbia to sue. The Court held that it might do so, noting that while the District was "a separate political community," its sovereign power was lodged in the Congress. "The subordinate legislative powers of a municipal character which have been or may be lodged in the city corporations, or in the District corporation, do not make those bodies sovereign. Crimes committed in the District are not crimes against the District, but against the United States. Therefore, whilst the District may, in a sense, be called a State, it is such in a very qualified sense." P. 9. But there is no suggestion in that case that Congress lacks the authority under the Constitution to delegate the powers of home rule to the District.

The power of Congress over the District of Columbia relates not only to "national power" but to "all the powers of legislation which may be exercised by a state in dealing with its affairs." There is no reason why a state, if it so chooses, may not fashion its basic law so as to grant home rule or self-government to its municipal corporations. The Court in *Barnes* v. *District of Columbia,* 91 U. S. 540, 544, in construing the Organic Act of February 21, 1871, the one with which we are presently concerned, stated: "A municipal corporation, in the exercise of all of its duties, including those most strictly local or internal, is but a department of the State. The legislature may give it all the powers such a being is capable of receiving, making it a miniature State within its locality."

This is the theory which underlies the constitutional provisions of some states allowing cities to have home rule. So it is that decision after decision has held that the delegated power of municipalities is as broad as the police power of the state, except as that power may be restricted by terms of the grant or by the state

---

[2] **Questions:** Note how Justice William O. Douglas arrives at the conclusion of this paragraph: when Congress legislates for the District of Columbia, its power is equivalent to that of a state legislating for a city (or Congress legislating for a territory, like Puerto Rico). Does this imply that Congress could create a court system for the District of Columbia, whose judges lack Article III tenure and salary protections, as many states do? Could Congress make the mayor of the district an elected official even though the Constitution requires that all other federal officers must be appointed?

constitution. See McQuillin, The Law of Municipal Corporations (3d ed. 1949), § 16.02 *et seq.* And certainly so far as the Federal Constitution is concerned there is no doubt that legislation which prohibits discrimination on the basis of race in the use of facilities serving a public functions is within the police power of the states. It would seem then that on the analogy of the delegation of powers of self-government and home rule both to municipalities and to territories there is no constitutional barrier to the delegation by Congress to the District of Columbia of full legislative power, subject of course to constitutional limitations to which all lawmaking is subservient and subject also to the power of Congress at any time to revise, alter, or revoke the authority granted.

There is, however, a suggestion that the power of Congress "To exercise exclusive Legislation" granted by Art. I, § 8, cl. 17 of the Constitution is nondelegable because it is "exclusive." But it is clear from the history of the provision that the word "exclusive" was employed to eliminate any possibility that the legislative power of Congress over the District was to be concurrent with that of the ceding states. See The Federalist, No. 43; 3 Elliot's Debates (2d ed. 1876), pp. 432–433; 2 Story, Commentaries on the Constitution of the United States (4th ed. 1873), § 1218. Madison summed up the need for an "exclusive" power in the Congress as follows:

"Let me remark, if not already remarked, that there must be a cession, by particular states, of the district to Congress, and that the states may settle the terms of the cession. The states may make what stipulation they please in it, and, if they apprehend any danger, they may refuse it altogether. How could the general government be guarded from the undue influence of particular states, or from insults, without such exclusive power?" Elliot's *op. cit., supra,* p. 433.

We conclude that the Congress had the authority under Art. I, § 8, cl. 17 of the Constitution to delegate its lawmaking authority to the Legislative Assembly of the municipal corporation which was created by the Organic Act of 1871 and that the "rightful subjects of legislation" within the meaning of § 18 of that Act was as broad as the police power of a state so as to include a law prohibiting discriminations against Negroes by the owners and managers of restaurants in the District of Columbia. . . .

II.

There remains for consideration only whether the Acts of 1872 and 1873 were abandoned or repealed as a result of non-use and administrative practice. There was one view in the Court of Appeals that these laws are presently unenforceable for that reason. We do not agree. The failure of the executive branch to enforce a law does not result in its modification or repeal. The repeal of laws is as much a legislative function as their enactment.

Congress has had the power to repeal the 1872 and 1873 Acts from the dates of their passage by the Legislative Assembly. But as we have seen, it has not done so.

Congress also has had the authority to delegate to a municipal government for the District the power to pass laws which would alter or repeal the Acts of the Legislative Assembly. As we have seen, the Organic Act of the District of Columbia approved June 11, 1878, withdrew legislative powers from the municipal government. In 1892 the Commissioners were given legislative power as respects "reasonable and usual police regulations." That legislative authority could have been employed to repeal the Acts of 1872 and 1873. For as we have noted, regulation of restaurants is a matter plainly within the scope of police regulations. But the Commissioners passed no ordinances dealing with the rights of Negroes in the restaurants of the District. . . .

NOTE: HOME RULE IN THE DISTRICT OF COLUMBIA

John R. Thompson Co. did not merely affirm Congress's plenary power to prohibit racial discrimination in the District of Columbia. It also affirmed Congress's power to delegate lawmaking authority to the District of Columbia's voters. In the wake of this decision, the federal government delegated such authority to the district for the first time since 1871.

The formal process of "home rule" began in 1960, when Congress proposed the Twenty-Third Amendment. Ratified in 1961, the Amendment empowered the people of the District of Columbia to participate in presidential elections as if the district were the least-populated state.

Congress later proposed another constitutional amendment that would have empowered the people of the District of Columbia to elect congressional representatives and senators. *See* H.R.J. Res. 554, 95th Cong. (1978). However, only sixteen states ratified the amendment before it expired under its own terms.

Home rule has instead proceeded by statute and regulation. In 1967, President Lyndon Johnson replaced the presidentially appointed commission that had administered the District of Columbia since 1874 with a city council led by an appointed mayor/commissioner. *See* Reorganization Plan No. 3 of 1967, 32 Fed. Reg. 11,669 (June 1, 1967). The first mayor he appointed was the appropriately named Walter Washington—one of the first black mayors of a major city in American history. Around the same time, Congress empowered the people of the district to elect a nonvoting "delegate" to Congress. *See* Act of Sept. 22, 1970, Pub. L. No. 91–405, 84 Stat. 845.

The government of the District of Columbia assumed its current form in 1973, when Congress passed the District of Columbia Self-Government and Governmental Reorganization Act, Pub. L. No. 93–198, 87 Stat. 774 (1973), commonly known as the D.C. Home Rule Act. The District of Columbia today blends attributes of a state government and a city government. Like a city, the district has an elected mayor and an elected "District of Columbia Council" with the power to pass laws subject to preemption by Congress. District of Columbia Self-Government and Governmental Reorganization Act, 87 Stat. at 777. Like a state, the district has an elected attorney general and a dual system of local courts and federal courts. *See* D.C. Code § 1–204.35 (2021). The D.C. Court of Appeals, an Article I court, hears cases involving local law and is analogous to a state court. *See* District of Columbia Court Reorganization Act of 1970, Pub. L. No. 91–358, 84 Stat. 473, 475. The U.S. Court of Appeals for the D.C. Circuit, an Article III court, hears cases involving federal law. *Id.* In contrast with the District of Columbia's elected legislature and chief executive, the judges on both of these courts are appointed by the president and confirmed by the Senate, as is the U.S. attorney who acts as a local and federal prosecutor.

16.2 FEDERAL ENCLAVES

The same clause of Article I that gives Congress plenary authority over the District of Columbia also empowers Congress "to exercise like

Authority over all Places purchased by the Consent of the Legislature of the State in which the Same shall be, for the Erection of Forts, Magazines, Arsenals, dock-Yards, and other needful Buildings." This provision is sometimes called the Enclave Clause, and it currently applies to thousands of military bases, office buildings, and other federally owned property throughout the United States.

Just as Congress acquired land from Maryland and Virginia for use as the District of Columbia, the federal government has long "purchased" and exercised exclusive jurisdiction over land for federal purposes. *See, e.g.*, Act of Apr. 30, 1790, ch. 9, 1 Stat. 112, 113 (punishing crimes committed in places under federal jurisdiction). Although the language of the Enclave Clause suggests that it applies only when places are purchased for specifically enumerated purposes, the Supreme Court has interpreted the clause capaciously to allow Congress to purchase and exercise exclusive jurisdiction over property for any purpose as long as the state conveying the property consents. *See Collins v. Yosemite Park Co.*, 304 U.S. 518 (1938).

Before the 1930s, the Supreme Court interpreted the Enclave Clause with what has been called the *extraterritoriality doctrine*. Under this doctrine, once a state consented to the federal acquisition of property, the state's jurisdiction over the property ceased to exist. *See, e.g.*, *Battle v. United States*, 209 U.S. 36 (1908). This meant that a state could not punish crimes, tax residents, or otherwise regulate people on the conveyed property. *See, e.g.*, *Surplus Trading Co. v. Cook*, 281 U.S. 647 (1930); *W. Union Tel. Co. v. Chiles*, 214 U.S. 274 (1909).

Congress, however, generally failed to pass sufficient laws to govern and regulate the millions of people living in federal enclaves. So in *Chicago, Rock Island & Pacific Railway Co. v. McGlinn*, 114 U.S. 542 (1885), the Court held that any state laws that were in force *before* the enclave was conveyed generally continued to apply until abrogated by Congress—a doctrine developed by analogy to what happens under international law after territory is conquered. Similarly, in *James v. Dravo Contracting Co.*, the Court held that states could specifically "reserve[ ]" some aspects of their jurisdiction over the conveyed enclave. 302 U.S. 134, 145 (1937); *see also Palmer v. Barrett*, 162 U.S. 399 (1896) (upholding a state's conditional conveyance of property to the federal government).

Soon, Congress began passing legislation that permitted certain state laws or taxes to apply to federal enclaves. *See, e.g.*, Act of Feb. 3, 1928, Pub. L. No. 70–12, 45 Stat. 54. For example, in 1940, Congress passed the Buck Act, which empowered states and local governments to levy taxes on people who work within their territorial boundaries in federal enclaves. Act of Oct. 9, 1940, Pub. L. No. 76–819, 54 Stat. 1059. The Supreme Court interpreted this act in its most important decision affecting enclaves, *Howard v. Commissioners of Sinking Fund*, 344 U.S. 624 (1953). The case involved the City of Louisville, Kentucky, which annexed the land around a naval ordnance plant and invoked the Buck Act to tax the plant's employees. Some of the employees objected to the legal "fiction" that a Kentucky city could claim jurisdiction over land that Kentucky had ceded to the federal government. *Howard*, 344 U.S. at 627, It seemed as odd to them as if Maryland levied a tax on the people of the District of Columbia. But in *Howard*, the Court upheld the annexation. Although the Court recognized the conceptual difficulty posed by the extraterritoriality doctrine, which it called the "fiction of a state within a state," the Court also observed that the city's change of municipal boundaries "did not interfere in the least with the jurisdiction of the United States within the area or with its use or disposition of the property." *Id.* at 626–27. The Court concluded, "The sovereign rights in this dual relationship are not antagonistic. . . . It is friction, not fiction, to which we must give heed." *Id.* at 627.

Although the District and Enclave Clause states that Congress's jurisdiction over a federal enclave is "exclusive," in *Offutt Housing Co. v. Sarpy County*, 351 U.S. 253 (1956), the Court explained that *Howard*'s "friction, not fiction" doctrine meant that Congress validly exercised its exclusive jurisdiction when it passed laws like the Buck Act that permitted a state to regulate federal enclaves—just as Congress could permit states to regulate federally recognized tribes.

In *Evans v. Cornman*, 398 U.S. 419 (1970), the Supreme Court went even further. *Evans* declared that as long as there was no "friction," states could exercise jurisdiction over federal enclaves even when Congress had not yet acted. That case held that Maryland violated the Fourteenth Amendment's Equal Protection Clause when it prohibited residents of federal enclaves or reservations, like the National Institutes of Health (NIH), from voting in Maryland elections. Maryland argued that these residents were not residents of Maryland but more like residents of the nearby District of Columbia. But the Court observed that in the years after *Howard*, Maryland had already begun to regulate these residents by requiring them to obtain Maryland driver's licenses, go to Maryland public schools, and otherwise act as though they lived in Maryland. Such laws were valid under *Howard*, the Court explained, as long as they didn't interfere with the United States' jurisdiction over the federal reservation of the NIH. It was therefore arbitrary for Maryland to exclude these same residents from voting.

CHAPTER 17

WHAT IS THE SCOPE OF CONGRESS'S POWER WITH RESPECT TO TRIBES?

ARTICLE I, SECTION 8, CLAUSE 3: The Congress shall have Power . . . To regulate Commerce with foreign Nations, and among the several States, and with the Indian Tribes; . . .—And

CLAUSE 18: To make all Laws which shall be necessary and proper for carrying into Execution the foregoing Powers, and all other Powers vested by this Constitution in the Government of the United States, or in any Department or Officer thereof.

ARTICLE II, SECTION 2, CLAUSE 2: The President . . . shall have Power, by and with the Advice and Consent of the Senate, to make Treaties, provided two thirds of the Senators present concur. . . .

Four Eras of Federal Policy Regarding Tribes

Centuries before the ratification of the U.S. Constitution in 1788, tens of millions of American Indians, Pacific Islanders, and Alaska Natives lived in North America and the Pacific. But after 1492, European diseases, war, and near-genocidal practices decimated the Native population. By 1800, only approximately 600,000 Native people lived within the present territorial boundaries of the United States. *See* Russell Thornton, *American Indian Holocaust and Survival: A Population History since 1492*, at 133 (1990). By 1900, the number was a mere 250,000. *Id.* Although the Native population has since recovered to seventeenth-century levels, with over five million American Indians and Alaska Natives living in the United States as of the 2020 census, this recovery has occurred in spite of decades of hostile policies by the federal government to take Native land, remove tribes to federally created reservations, assimilate tribal culture into white American culture, and terminate tribal self-government. *See id.* at 44.

Federal policy toward American Indians can be divided into four eras: the treaty era (1788–1870), the assimilation era (1871–1933), the self-determination era (1934–1939 and 1968–present), and the termination era (1940–1967).

17.1 THE SOURCE OF FEDERAL AND STATE POWER (THE TREATY ERA)

The treaty era began with the ratification of the U.S. Constitution, which empowered the federal government to "make Treaties," U.S.

Const. art. II, § 2, cl. 2, and "regulate Commerce . . . with the Indian Tribes," *id.* art. I, § 8, cl. 3. This era coincided with the initial expansion of the United States' territorial boundaries. At the time of ratification, the various peace treaties that ended the Revolutionary War set the United States' western boundary at the Mississippi River; northern boundary at the Great Lakes; eastern boundary at the Atlantic Ocean; and southern boundary at East and West Florida, both claimed by Spain. Within these expansive boundaries, three groups claimed the power to govern the land.

One group of claimants comprised the individual states whose western borders had never been clearly defined. Most of the first thirteen states had been created by grants from the British Crown that defined their boundaries as extending from "sea to sea," or from the Atlantic Ocean to the Pacific Ocean. *See, e.g.*, 7 *Abridgment of the Debates of Congress, From 1789 to 1856*, at 75 (John C. Rives ed., 1858). Much of the current state of Ohio, for example, was claimed by Connecticut as part of its western reserve. Connecticut's claim lives on in the name of the Case Western Reserve University in Cleveland.

A second claimant was the federal government. Beginning in the 1780s, the Confederation Congress began asking the various states to cede their western reserves to the United States as a fundraising measure. The federal government planned to organize this western land into a territory, establish a government for this territory, sell individual parcels of the territory's land to white settlers, and eventually admit sections of the territory into the Union as new states. The federal government could then use the revenue from the sales toward paying off its war debt. The Confederation Congress took its first step toward implementing this plan in 1787, when it created a government for the "Territory of the United States, North-West of the River Ohio." 32 *Journals of the Continental Congress* 334 (Roscoe R. Hill ed., 1936). This decree, the Northwest Ordinance, was passed while the Constitutional Convention was meeting in Philadelphia. Aware of the ordinance, the convention codified the plan in Article IV, Section 3, of the Constitution, which empowered Congress "to dispose of and make all needful Rules and Regulations respecting the Territory or other Property belonging to the United States" and to admit "New States . . . into this Union."

The third claimants, of course, were Native tribes. In the Northeast lived two broad groupings of tribes. Along the Atlantic Coast was a polymorphous collection of Algonquian-speaking tribes, including the Powhatan, Massachusett, Mohegan, Delaware, Pequot, Wampanoag, and others. *See* David Treuer, *The Heartbeat of Wounded Knee* 39 (2019). Farther inland was a more centralized alliance of five tribes known as the Iroquois Confederacy, comprising the Cayuga, Oneida, Seneca, Onondaga, and Mohawk. *Id.* Between 1600 and 1788, however, European settlers decimated the coastal Algonquians, who bore the brunt of war, disease, and forcible removal. But the inland Iroquois thrived by engaging in profitable trading alliances with European settlers. White settlement nevertheless pushed the Iroquois westward so that by 1788 many Iroquois were living amid other powerful tribes along the Great Lakes. *Id.* at 46.

The Great Lakes tribes included, among others, the Huron, Shawnee, Odawa, Potawatomi, Sac, Fox, Menominee, Ho-Chunk, Mandan, Arikara, Hidatsa, Ojibwe, Miami, Cree, Osage, and "Sioux" (the French name for the Oceti Sakowin, a confederacy of seven "council fires" that included the Lakota). *Id.* With the exception of the Huron, which concentrated on agriculture, most of these tribes were dispersed in small, mobile villages. Many of these tribes had long participated in the fur trade, using diplomacy to balance the interests of the French, British Canadians, and British Americans against one another. *See* Richard White, *The Middle Ground* 142–85 (1991). The Seven Years' War and the American Revolution marked a devastating turning point for many of these Great Lakes tribes because they disrupted colonial alliances and left the United States as the sole colonial force in the region. *Id.* at 413–68; Treuer, *supra*, at 50–51. Several tribes, notably the Lakota, took advantage of the situation. In the wake of the American Revolution, the Lakota used European horses and guns to conquer vast territories along the Mississippi and Missouri Rivers. *See* Pekka Hämäläinen, *Lakota America* 90–117 (2019). But most tribes suffered, particularly as the fur trade rendered beavers extinct east of the Mississippi River. By the 1790s, the United States had enormous leverage to demand land concessions from the Great Lakes tribes—concessions that were codified in treaties. Treuer, *supra*, at 51.

Meanwhile, centuries of experience with intermittent Spanish settlers prompted the tribes in the Southeast to consolidate into a dozen "supertribes," including the Chickasaw, Choctaw, Muscogee, Creek, Cherokee, Yamasee, Catawba, Miccosukee, and Seminole. *Id.* at 32. Even after the American Revolution, these tribes remained powerful enough to govern themselves within enormous sections of land claimed by Georgia, the Carolinas, and Virginia.

One of these southeastern tribes, the Cherokee Nation, attempted to protect its land from white intrusion by turning to the Supreme Court.

17.1.1

Worcester v. Georgia

31 U.S. 515 (1832)

After decades of watching American settlers attempt to eliminate their Native neighbors, the Cherokee Nation began the nineteenth century by emphasizing how much it had in common with the United States. *See* Claudio Saunt, *Unworthy Republic: The Dispossession of Native Americans and the Road to Indian Territory* 11–14 (2020). The Cherokee had a capital called New Echota, from which a centralized government and judiciary administered a nation of yeoman farmers. Treuer, *supra*, at 32–33. They drafted a constitution modeled on the U.S. Constitution, published a bilingual newspaper, and sent diplomats to Congress. *Id.* They even elected a chief executive, John Ross, who grew up speaking English and dressing in western suits. *Id.* at 32. For his part, Ross explained to the U.S. Senate that the Cherokee had become "like the white-man in manners, morals and religion." Daniel Immerwahr, *How to Hide an Empire* 36–37 (2019).

Despite the Cherokee Nation's similarities with the United States, the state government of Georgia regarded the Cherokee as inferior—and in the way. The Cherokee Nation's territory included highly fertile land within the current borders of Georgia. White politicians hoped to take possession of this land for the future of slave-based capitalism. *See* Hämäläinen, *supra*, at 209–10. In 1802, Georgia even ceded its western reserves in Alabama and Mississippi to the federal government on the condition that Congress remove the Cherokee Nation from Georgia's jurisdiction. *See* Treuer, *supra*, at 34. President Thomas Jefferson obliged, writing that the federal government would require tribes to "either incorporate with us as citizens of the United States, or remove beyond the Mississippi." Letter from President Jefferson to William Henry Harrison (Feb. 27, 1803), *in Documents of United States Indian Policy* 22–23 (Francis Paul Prucha ed., 2000). Jefferson added, "Should any tribe be foolhardy enough to take up the hatchet at any time, the seizing of the whole country of that tribe, and driving them across the Mississippi as the only condition of peace, would be an example to others, and a furtherance of our final consolidation." *Id.*

At first, the federal government conducted Jefferson's policy of removal and assimilation by negotiating a series of treaties that guaranteed the federal government's protection in exchange for cessions of land and sovereignty. For instance, in the Treaty of Hopewell of 1785, the Cherokee agreed that in exchange for peace and the United States' recognition of the Cherokee Nation's boundaries, the Cherokee would acknowledge "all the Cherokees to be under the protection of the United States of America, and of no other sovereign whosoever." 2 *Indian Affairs: Laws and Treaties* 6 (Charles J. Kappler ed., 1903). The treaty added that

> [f]or the benefit and comfort of the Indians, and for the prevention of injuries or oppressions on the part of the citizens or Indians; the United States in Congress assembled shall have the sole and exclusive right of regulating the trade with the Indians, and managing all their affairs, as they think proper.

Id. at 7. Six years later, in the Treaty of Holston of 1791, the Cherokee ceded eastern sections of their land to the United States in exchange for "valuable goods" and an annual payment of $1,000. *Id.* at 23–24. Similar treaties ceding more land were signed through the 1820s.

These treaties were not signed fast enough for Georgia, however, particularly after gold was discovered on Cherokee land in 1829. In 1830,

Georgia passed a law declaring the Cherokee Constitution invalid and prohibiting the assemblage of any court or legislature "under pretext of authority from the Cherokee tribe." *Laws of the Colonial and State Governments Relating to Indians and Indian Affairs* 220–22 (Washington, Thompson & Romans 1832). Georgia also made it a crime for any white person to reside within the Cherokee Nation without a written license from the governor of Georgia. *Id.* Subsequent laws boldly allotted Cherokee land to white people and authorized Georgia's governor to seize Cherokee gold. *Id.* at 223–29. Georgia enacted these laws with the support of President Andrew Jackson, who himself signed into law the federal Indian Removal Act of 1830, ch. 148, 4 Stat. 411. This federal law authorized the president to grant tribes unsettled lands west of the Mississippi in exchange for tribal land "within the limits of any of the states." Indian Removal Act, 4 Stat. at 412.

In the face of this hostility, the Cherokee's chief, John Ross, filed an original action in the Supreme Court on behalf of the Cherokee Nation. He had reason to believe that the Court would be receptive to his grievances, thanks to a case from several years earlier, *Johnson v. M'Intosh*, 21 U.S. (8 Wheat.) 543 (1823). In *Johnson*, Chief Justice John Marshall wrote a lengthy opinion cataloging and rationalizing the history of European conquest of North America—yet he also recognized some limited rights that tribes could claim from the United States. In short, the chief justice concluded that under European practice, the first European nation to "discover" non-European land gained the exclusive right to sell or dispose of the land as it wished. 21 U.S. (8 Wheat.) at 576–77. Any native people living on that land were considered "conquered" subjects who could be dealt with by the conqueror however it wished. *Id.* at 589. But the chief justice also recognized a "general rule, that the conquered shall not be wantonly oppressed" and that all conquerors had the duty to preserve, within reason, the right of conquered people to continue to peacefully occupy their lands. *Id.* In the context of the United States—which inherited its territory from earlier British and other European conquests—Marshall wrote that the federal government therefore had the exclusive right to dispose of tribal lands; but until it did so, it had a duty to protect any peaceful tribes living within the United States' boundaries. *Id.* at 591.

Ross may have hoped for the Supreme Court to reaffirm this duty of protection in the case he brought before the Supreme Court, *Cherokee Nation v. Georgia*, 30 U.S. (5 Pet.) 1 (1831). But Marshall, still on the Court, dismissed the case for lack of jurisdiction. Article III of the U.S. Constitution gives the Supreme Court original jurisdiction over controversies "between a State . . . and foreign States." Most other sorts of controversies must be heard in a trial court before they can be appealed to the Supreme Court. *See Marbury v. Madison*, 5 U.S. (1 Cranch) 137, 176 (1803). While the Cherokee Nation considered itself a "foreign State[ ]" that could sue Georgia in the Supreme Court without first going to a trial court, Marshall disagreed. He wrote that tribes were unlike all other foreign states for four reasons: (1) tribes were thought to be within the jurisdictional limits of the United States; (2) they were mentioned separately from "foreign Nations" in the Commerce Clause; (3) they had acknowledged themselves by treaties to be under the protection of the United States; and (4) they had also, by treaties, given the United States power to regulate their trade and manage their affairs. *Cherokee Nation*, 30 U.S. (5 Pet.) at 17–20. Rather than call tribes *foreign states*, Marshall explained, "[t]hey may, more correctly, perhaps, be denominated domestic dependent nations." *Id.* at 17. Marshall noted that tribes were "so completely under the sovereignty and dominion of the United States" that any attempt by a European power to form a political connection with a tribe would be considered an invasion of the United States. *Id.* In an analogy that would haunt federal Indian policy for generations, Marshall concluded that tribes' relationship to the United States was less like that of two sovereign nations and more like "that of a ward to his guardian." *Id.*

Undeterred by this jurisdictional setback, Ross's legal team found a new plaintiff. While *Cherokee Nation* was being argued, a missionary from Vermont named Samuel Worcester was arrested, convicted, and imprisoned for violating Georgia's 1830 law that prohibited any white person from living within the Cherokee Nation without a license from the governor. Worcester defended himself in court, arguing that Georgia had no authority over the Cherokee Nation. He observed that the United States had signed treaties in 1785, 1791, and onward that had consistently given the United States the *exclusive* right to regulate trade with the tribe. As Worcester appealed his way to the Supreme Court, he was represented by the same lawyers who had argued *Cherokee Nation*.

This time, to the benefit of the Cherokee, the Supreme Court, in *Worcester v. Georgia*, 31 U.S. 515 (1832), considered the merits of whether Georgia could assert power over the Cherokee Nation despite federal treaties giving Congress the exclusive right to do so.

■ MR. CHIEF JUSTICE MARSHALL delivered the opinion of the Court.[1]

[W]e must inquire and decide whether the act of the legislature of Georgia, under which the plaintiff in error has been prosecuted and condemned, be consistent with, or repugnant to, the constitution, laws and treaties of the United States. . . . The extra-territorial power of every legislature being limited in its action, to its own citizens or subjects, the very passage of this act is an assertion of jurisdiction over the Cherokee nation, and of the rights and powers consequent on jurisdiction.

The first step, then, in the inquiry, which the constitution and laws impose on this court, is an examination of the rightfulness of this claim.

America, separated from Europe by a wide ocean, was inhabited by a distinct people, divided into separate nations, independent of each other and of the rest of

---

[1] **As You Read, Consider:** Georgia's main argument in this case is that if you look at a map of "Georgia"—as defined by the 1732 charter bringing the Georgia colony into existence—the Cherokee Nation is located within Georgia's borders. Why doesn't Chief Justice John Marshall think Georgia has jurisdiction over white people within the Cherokee Nation?

the world, having institutions of their own, and governing themselves by their own laws. . . . But power, war, conquest, give rights, which, after possession, are conceded by the world; and which can never be controverted by those on whom they descend. . . .

The great maritime powers of Europe discovered and visited different parts of this continent at nearly the same time. The object was too immense for any one of them to grasp the whole; and the claimants were too powerful to submit to the exclusive or unreasonable pretensions of any single potentate. To avoid bloody conflicts, which might terminate disastrously to all, it was necessary for the nations of Europe to establish some principle which all would acknowledge, and which should decide their respective rights as between themselves. This principle, suggested by the actual state of things, was, "that discovery gave title to the government by whose subjects or by whose authority it was made, against all other European governments, which title might be consummated by possession." [*Johnson v. M'Intosh,*] 8 Wheat. 573 [(1823)].

This principle, acknowledged by all Europeans, because it was the interest of all to acknowledge it, gave to the nation making the discovery, as its inevitable consequence, the sole right of acquiring the soil and of making settlements on it. It was an exclusive principle which shut out the right of competition among those who had agreed to it; not one which could annul the previous rights of those who had not agreed to it. . . .

Soon after Great Britain determined on planting colonies in America, the king granted charters to companies of his subjects who associated for the purpose of carrying the views of the crown into effect, and of enriching themselves. The first of these charters was made before possession was taken of any part of the country. They purport, generally, to convey the soil, from the Atlantic to the South Sea. This soil was occupied by numerous and warlike nations, equally willing and able to defend their possessions. The extravagant and absurd idea, that the feeble settlements made on the sea coast, or the companies under whom they were made, acquired legitimate power by them to govern the people, or occupy the lands from sea to sea, did not enter the mind of any man. They were well understood to convey the title which, according to the common law of European sovereigns respecting America, they might rightfully convey, and no more. This was the exclusive right of purchasing such lands as the natives were willing to sell. The crown could not be understood to grant what the crown did not affect to claim; nor was it so understood. . . .

The charter to Georgia professes to be granted for the charitable purpose of enabling poor subjects to gain a comfortable subsistence by cultivating lands in the American provinces, "at present waste and desolate." . . . These motives for planting the new colony are incompatible with the lofty ideas of granting the soil, and all its inhabitants from sea to sea. They demonstrate the truth, that these grants asserted a title against Europeans only, and were considered as blank paper so far as the rights of the natives were concerned. The power of war is given only for defence, not for conquest.[2]

The charters contain passages showing one of their objects to be the civilization of the Indians, and their conversion to Christianity—objects to be accomplished by conciliatory conduct and good example; not by extermination. . . .

---

[2] **Note:** Marshall here is explaining that Georgia's colonial charter gave its government the power to *purchase* land from Indians, not to *exterminate* them. This alone doesn't resolve, however, whether the State of Georgia can now regulate white people within the territory granted in the charter.

This was the settled state of things when the war of our revolution commenced. The influence of our enemy was established; her resources enabled her to keep up that influence; and the colonists had much cause for the apprehension that the Indian nations would, as the allies of Great Britain, add their arms to hers. This, as was to be expected, became an object of great solicitude to congress. Far from advancing a claim to their lands, or asserting any right of dominion over them, congress resolved "that the securing and preserving the friendship of the Indian nations appears to be a subject of the utmost moment to these colonies." . . .

During the war of the revolution, the Cherokees took part with the British. After its termination, the United States, though desirous of peace, did not feel its necessity so strongly as while the war continued. Their political situation being changed, they might very well think it advisable to assume a higher tone, and to impress on the Cherokees the same respect for congress which was before felt for the king of Great Britain. This may account for the language of the treaty of Hopewell. . . .

The treaty of Hopewell seems not to have established a solid peace. To accommodate the differences still existing between the state of Georgia and the Cherokee nation, the treaty of Holston was negotiated in July 1791. . . . The mutual desire of establishing permanent peace and friendship, and of removing all causes of war, is honestly avowed, and, in pursuance of this desire, the first article declares, that there shall be perpetual peace and friendship between all the citizens of the United States of America and all the individuals composing the Cherokee nation.

The second article repeats the important acknowledgement, that the Cherokee nation is under the protection of the United States of America, and of no other sovereign whosoever. . . . This relation was that of a nation claiming and receiving the protection of one more powerful: not that of individuals abandoning their national character, and submitting as subjects to the laws of a master. . . .

The fourth article declares, that "the boundary between the United States and the Cherokee nation shall be as follows: beginning," & c. . . . A boundary is described, between nation and nation, by mutual consent. . . .

By the sixth article, it is agreed, on the part of the Cherokees, that the United States shall have the sole and exclusive right of regulating their trade. . . .

This treaty, thus explicitly recognizing the national character of the Cherokees, and their right of self government; thus guarantying their lands; assuming the duty of protection, and of course pledging the faith of the United States for that protection; has been frequently renewed, and is now in full force. . . .[3]

From the commencement of our government, congress has passed acts to regulate trade and intercourse with the Indians; which treat them as nations, respect their rights, and manifest a firm purpose to afford that protection which treaties stipulate. . . . In 1819, congress passed an act for promoting those humane designs of civilizing the neighbouring Indians, which had long been cherished by the executive. . . .[4] This act avowedly contemplates the preservation of the Indian nations as an object sought by the United States, and proposes to effect this object by civilizing and converting them from hunters into agriculturists. . . . This act furnishes

---

3 **Question:** Marshall is summarizing the 1791 Treaty of Holston, in which the United States promised to protect the Cherokee Nation and claimed the exclusive right to regulate trade with it. If this federal treaty conflicts with Georgia's claim of jurisdiction, how does the Constitution resolve the conflict?

4 **Note:** Marshall is alluding to the Civilization Fund Act of 1819, in which Congress attempted to encourage agriculture among Native tribes "for the purpose of providing against the further decline and final extinction of the Indian tribes." Civilization Fund Act, ch. 85, 3 Stat. 516.

strong additional evidence of a settled purpose to fix the Indians in their country by giving them security at home.

The treaties and laws of the United States contemplate the Indian territory as completely separated from that of the states; and provide that all intercourse with them shall be carried on exclusively by the government of the union.

Is this the rightful exercise of power, or is it usurpation?[5]

While these states were colonies, this power, in its utmost extent, was admitted to reside in the crown. When our revolutionary struggle commenced, congress was composed of an assemblage of deputies acting under specific powers granted by the legislatures, or conventions of the several colonies. . . . Without any written definition of powers, they employed diplomatic agents to represent the United States at the several courts of Europe; offered to negotiate treaties with them, and did actually negotiate treaties with France. From the same necessity, and on the same principles, congress assumed the management of Indian affairs; first in the name of these United Colonies; and, afterwards, in the name of the United States. . . .

[After 1787, the Constitution conferred] on congress the powers of war and peace; of making treaties, and of regulating commerce with foreign nations, and among the several states, and with the Indian tribes. These powers comprehend all that is required for the regulation of our intercourse with the Indians. . . .

The Indian nations had always been considered as distinct, independent political communities, retaining their original natural rights, as the undisputed possessors of the soil, from time immemorial, with the single exception of that imposed by irresistible power, which excluded them from intercourse with any other European potentate than the first discoverer of the coast of the particular region claimed: and this was a restriction which those European potentates imposed on themselves, as well as on the Indians. The very term "nation," so generally applied to them, means "a people distinct from others." The constitution, by declaring treaties already made, as well as those to be made, to be the supreme law of the land, has adopted and sanctioned the previous treaties with the Indian nations, and consequently admits their rank among those powers who are capable of making treaties. The words "treaty" and "nation" are words of our own language, selected in our diplomatic and legislative proceedings, by ourselves, having each a definite and well understood meaning. We have applied them to Indians, as we have applied them to the other nations of the earth. They are applied to all in the same sense.

Georgia, herself, has furnished conclusive evidence that her former opinions on this subject concurred with those entertained by her sister states, and by the government of the United States. Various acts of her legislature have been cited in the argument, including the contract of cession made in the year 1802, all tending to prove her acquiescence in the universal conviction that the Indian nations possessed a full right to the lands they occupied, until that right should be extinguished by the United States, with their consent: that their territory was separated from that of any state within whose chartered limits they might reside, by a boundary line, established by treaties: that, within their boundary, they possessed rights with which no state could interfere: and that the whole power of regulating the intercourse with them, was vested in the United States. . . . Her new series of laws, manifesting her abandonment of these opinions, appears to have commenced in December 1828. . . .

---

[5] **Note:** Recall that in *McCulloch v. Maryland*, Marshall structured his opinion by asking (1) whether the federal law establishing a bank was constitutional and (2) whether the state law was an obstacle to the federal government's purposes. This opinion is structured in the same way.

The Cherokee nation, then, is a distinct community occupying its own territory, with boundaries accurately described, in which the laws of Georgia can have no force, and which the citizens of Georgia have no right to enter, but with the assent of the Cherokees themselves, or in conformity with treaties, and with the acts of congress. The whole intercourse between the United States and this nation, is, by our constitution and laws, vested in the government of the United States.

The act of the state of Georgia, under which the plaintiff in error was prosecuted, is consequently void, and the judgment a nullity. . . .[6]

NOTE: AFTERMATH OF *WORCESTER*

Johnson, *Cherokee Nation*, and *Worcester* are today known as the *Marshall Trilogy*. The chief justice interpreted the Constitution and federal treaties as conferring upon the United States broad and exclusive powers over land occupied by tribes, which he referred to as "domestic dependent nations." *Cherokee Nation*, 30 U.S. at 17. This federal exclusivity meant that states like Georgia had no similar power to enact extraterritorial laws over tribal land, including over white people living there.

Fate of Worcester. Nevertheless, even though the Supreme Court voided Worcester's conviction, Georgia's governor, Wilson Lumpkin, refused to free Worcester from state prison for years. (In a famous but apocryphal statement, President Andrew Jackson supposedly said, "Well, John Marshall has made his decision, now let him enforce it." 1 Horace Greeley, *The American Conflict* 106 (1864).) After waiting unsuccessfully for the president to free him from Georgia's prison, Worcester eventually capitulated to Georgia's claim of authority and accepted a pardon from Governor Lumpkin. *See* Saunt, *supra*, at 168.

Fate of Native Americans. *Worcester* was soon followed by the Trail of Tears, the name given to the forced relocation of the Cherokee, Muscogee, Seminole, Chickasaw, and Choctaw Nations from the southeastern United States to a new "Indian Territory" west of the Mississippi River. *Id.* at 173–200. The federal government conducted these relocations at gunpoint after coercing the various tribes to sign agreements pursuant to the Indian Removal Act of 1830. Although John Ross resisted selling the Cherokee's land for five years, a dissident minority of tribal leaders signed the Treaty of New Echota in 1835. *Id.* at 238–29. This treaty became the legal basis for compelling sixteen thousand Cherokees to march to present-day Oklahoma. At least four thousand of these refugees died of famine or disease along the way. Brian Hicks, *Toward the Setting Sun* 312 (2012).

> Although removal failed to deport all Native Americans east of the Mississippi, its successes—roughly one hundred thousand Indians cleared out, a hundred million acres of fecund black soil opened for cotton, the future of slave capitalism secured—conditioned the Americans to see themselves and the world in a new light.

---

[6] **Questions:** Marshall concludes that Georgia's laws cannot be enforced in the Cherokee Nation's territory because the laws are preempted. But are they preempted by the specific laws and treaties he quoted at the beginning of this opinion, by the Constitution itself, or by both?

In other words, after this opinion, can other states regulate people in the territory of tribes not covered by the treaties with the Cherokee Nation?

Hämäläinen, *supra*, at 210.

17.2 FEDERAL PLENARY POWER (THE ASSIMILATION ERA)

Through the 1860s, the federal government negotiated and enforced treaties similar to the Treaty of New Echota with other tribes. Most of these treaties compelled the tribes to exchange their traditional lands for federally administered reservations in the "Indian Territory," which at first stretched from Oregon to Arkansas. *See* Daniel Immerwahr, *How to Hide an Empire* 42–45 (2019). To compensate for poor soil and hunting prospects, the federal government agreed to provide reservation Indians with food and other resources—creating a relationship of dependence that the federal government exploited. By withholding food, the federal government could force tribes to renegotiate these treaties and cede land for white settlement. By 1889, all that was left of the Indian Territory was its southern tip: present-day Oklahoma. *Id.* Even this much-diminished Indian Territory was soon opened to white settlers in a land rush memorialized in the name of the University of Oklahoma's mascot, the Sooners—some white people claimed the land "sooner" than was legally permitted. *See* Simon Winchester, *Land* 123–25, 151–58 (2021).

At first, the federal government regulated reservations in the Indian Territory with the treaties that created the reservations. Broad clauses in these treaties gave Congress extensive jurisdiction over tribes, including the power to do things like prohibit the sale of liquor on tribal land. *See United States v. Forty-Three Gallons of Whiskey*, 93 U.S. 188, 197 (1876). As Congress admitted new states around these reservations, the Supreme Court reaffirmed the holding of *Worcester v. Georgia*, 31 U.S. 515 (1832), that federal Indian treaties preempted contrary state legislation, including laws that attempted to tax or regulate tribal members. *See, e.g., The Kansas Indians*, 72 U.S. (5 Wall.) 737, 757, 759, 761 (1867). These treaties continue to prohibit states from taxing or regulating most on-reservation activities, such as gambling or fishing. *Washington v. Wash. State Com. Passenger Fishing Vessel Ass'n*, 443 U.S. 658, 695 (1979); *Puyallup Tribe v. Dep't of Game*, 433 U.S. 165, 175–77 (1977).

In 1871, however, the federal government announced an abrupt change of policy. Members of the House of Representatives, long jealous of how senators alone could use Indian treaties to give patronage to railroad companies and other allies, demanded an end to the treaty system. *See* Richard White, *Railroaded* 76–77 (2012). The Indian Appropriations Act of 1871 declared that "hereafter no Indian nation or tribe within the territory of the United States shall be acknowledged or recognized as an independent nation, tribe, or power with whom the United States may contract by treaty." Indian Appropriations Act, ch. 120, 16 Stat. 544, 566.

Rather than negotiate new treaties with tribes, Congress began passing statutes that regulated tribes in a manner inconsistent with prior treaty provisions. *See, e.g.*, *Ward v. Race Horse*, 163 U.S. 504 (1896); *Cherokee Nation v. S. Kan. Ry.*, 135 U.S. 641 (1890); *The Cherokee Tobacco Case*, 78 U.S. (11 Wall.) 616 (1871). For example, to "assimilate" Indian children into white culture, Congress passed a law that required the secretary of the interior to "secure the attendance of Indian children of suitable age and health at schools established and maintained for their benefit." Indian Appropriations Act of 1891, ch. 543, 26 Stat. 989, 1014. The headmaster of the most famous of these schools was Richard Pratt of the Carlisle Indian Industrial School of Pennsylvania. In a speech to a group of charities, Pratt explained that forcing tens of thousands of children to attend boarding schools far away from their families and culture was a more humane policy than massacring them. "A great general has said that the only good Indian is a dead one," Pratt said, repeating a statement attributed to the Civil War general Philip Sheridan. "In a sense, I agree with the sentiment, but only in this: that all the Indian there is in the race should be dead. Kill the Indian in him, and save the man." *Official Report of the Nineteenth Annual Conference of Charities and Correction* 46–59 (1892); *see* David Treuer, *The Heartbeat of Wounded Knee* 132–43 (2019).

17.2.1

Lone Wolf v. Hitchcock

187 U.S. 553 (1903)

Where *Cherokee Nation v. Georgia*, 30 U.S. (5 Pet.) 1 (1831), resolved Congress's exclusive power to regulate tribes by treaty, cases after 1871 resolved the constitutionality of Congress's power to regulate tribes by statute.

The first major test reached the Supreme Court after Congress passed the Major Crimes Act of 1885, ch. 342, 23 Stat. 385. The act gave federal courts exclusive jurisdiction over a list of offenses when committed by a Native person on a reservation, including murder. Soon after the act's passage, a member of the Hoopa Valley Tribe named Kagama killed another tribal member on the Hoopa Valley Reservation, within California's boundaries. Federal prosecutors indicted Kagama for violating the Major Crimes Act. But Kagama responded that only California could prosecute murder; Congress's power to regulate "Commerce . . . with the Indian tribes," U.S. Const. art I, § 8, cl. 3, did not include the power to prohibit state-law crimes. In *United States v. Kagama*, adopting a narrow interpretation of the Commerce Clause, the Supreme Court agreed that the term *commerce* did not permit Congress to authorize "a system of criminal laws for Indians living peaceably in their reservations." 118 U.S. 375, 378 (1886). But the Court nevertheless upheld the Major Crimes Act on different grounds. Applying the metaphor from the Marshall Trilogy that tribes are "wards of the nation," the Court explained that Congress *had* to have the power to protect them:

> It seems to us that this is within the competency of Congress. These Indian tribes *are* the wards of the nation. They are communities *dependent* on the United States. Dependent largely for their daily food. Dependent for their political rights. . . . The power of the General Government over these remnants of a race once powerful, now weak and diminished in numbers, is necessary to their protection, as well as to the safety of those among whom they dwell. It must exist in that government, because it never has existed anywhere else, because the theatre of its exercise is within the geographical limits of the United States, because it has never been denied, and because it alone can enforce its laws on all the tribes.

Id. at 383–84. *Kagama* represented a major expansion of Congress's power to legislate directly for tribes.

The following year, Congress continued its assimilation policy by enacting the General Allotment Act of 1887, ch. 119, 24 Stat. 388, commonly called the *Dawes Act* after its sponsor, Senator Henry L. Dawes of Massachusetts. The purpose of this law was to abolish communal land, powwows, and other practices that distinguished tribes from the supposedly "civilized life" surrounding them. 24 Stat. at 390. The law worked by authorizing the president to survey communal land on reservations and divide the land into "allotments" for individual tribal members. *Id.* Tribal members could dispose of their allotments as they pleased. In exchange for agreeing to divide their land in this way, a tribe's members would gain U.S. citizenship. *Id.* To determine who was a tribal member eligible to receive an allotment, the United States also began the controversial practice of "enrollment," in which federal agents measured Natives' "blood quantum," or how much "Indian blood" (full blood, half, quarter, eighth) they allegedly had. Treuer, *supra*, at 143–47.

Allotment and enrollment gave federal agents far-reaching discretion to determine who was a tribal member and which members would receive which land. Federal agents typically reserved each reservation's richest farmland and lakeshores for sale to white settlers, who could purchase the land in "fee simple," meaning that they could live on it and sell it without the tribe's permission, along with its vested immunity from state regulation. *See Choate v. Trapp*, 224 U.S. 665 (1912); *Jones v. Meehan*, 175 U.S. 1 (1899). The Dawes Act was incredibly destructive. By the time Congress repealed it in 1934, Indian landholdings had dropped from 138 million acres to 48 million acres. Treuer, *supra*, at 147–51.

The Dawes Act and its successor statutes violated many preexisting treaties that recognized the indivisibility of tribal land. In 1892, after the federal government allegedly persuaded a majority of the Kiowa to allot their reservation in present-day Oklahoma, the Kiowa chief, Lone Wolf, protested that an 1867 treaty prohibited any agreement to divide the reservation "unless executed and signed by at least three-fourths of all the adult male Indians occupying the same." *Lone Wolf v. Hitchcock*, 187 U.S. 553, 564 (1903) (citing the treaty). Lone Wolf sued to contest the legality of the federal allotment statutes in light of this treaty. The question before the Supreme Court in *Lone Wolf v. Hitchcock*, 187 U.S. 553 (1903), was whether Congress's unenumerated power over tribes could abrogate an existing treaty.

In answering this question, the Court declined to place any limits on Congress's unenumerated power.

■ JUSTICE WHITE delivered the opinion of the Court.[7]

[T]he twelfth article [of the 1867 treaty between the United States and the Kiowa tribe] reads as follows:

"Article 12. No treaty for the cession of any portion or part of the reservation herein described, which may be held in common, shall be of any validity or force as against the said Indians, unless executed and signed by at least three fourths of all the adult male Indians occupying the same, and no cession by the tribe shall be understood or construed in such manner as to deprive, without his consent, any individual member of the tribe of his rights to any tract of land selected by him as provided in article III (VI) of this treaty."

The appellants base their right to relief on the proposition that by the effect of the article just quoted the confederated tribes of Kiowas, Comanches and Apaches were vested with an interest in the lands held in common within the reservation, which interest could not be divested by Congress in any other mode than that specified in the said twelfth article, and that as a result of the said stipulation the interest of the Indians in the common lands fell within the protection of the Fifth Amendment to the Constitution of the United States, and such interest—indirectly at least—came under the control of the judicial branch of the government. We are unable to yield our assent to this view.

The contention in effect ignores the status of the contracting Indians and the relation of dependency they bore and continue to bear towards the government of the United States. To uphold the claim would be to adjudge that the indirect operation of the treaty was to materially limit and qualify the controlling authority of Congress in respect to the care and protection of the Indians, and to deprive Congress, in a possible emergency, when the necessity might be urgent for a partition and disposal of the tribal lands, of all power to act, if the assent of the Indians could not be obtained.

Now, it is true that in decisions of this court, the Indian right of occupancy of tribal lands, whether declared in a treaty or otherwise created, has been stated to be sacred, or, as sometimes expressed, as sacred as the fee of the United States in the same lands. *Johnson v. M'Intosh*, (1823) 8 Wheat. 543, 574; *Cherokee Nation v. Georgia*, (1831) 5 Pet. 1, 48; *Worcester v. Georgia*, (1832) 6 Pet. 515, 581. But in none of these cases was there involved a controversy between Indians and the

[7] **As You Read, Consider:** In the *Chinese Exclusion Case* (see section 10.3), the Supreme Court upheld Congress's power to pass a statute abrogating a treaty with a foreign state. But the Court was, at best, ambiguous about the source of Congress's power to pass a statute excluding immigrants. How does Justice Edward White describe the source and scope of Congress's power with respect to tribes—particularly a tribe claiming that the abrogation of this particular treaty violates the Fifth Amendment's prohibition against taking land without just compensation?

government respecting the power of Congress to administer the property of the Indians. The questions considered in the cases referred to, which either directly or indirectly had relation to the nature of the property rights of the Indians, concerned the character and extent of such rights as respected States or individuals. In one of the cited cases it was clearly pointed out that Congress possessed a paramount power over the property of the Indians, by reason of its exercise of guardianship over their interests, and that such authority might be implied, even though opposed to the strict letter of a treaty with the Indians. . . .

Plenary authority over the tribal relations of the Indians has been exercised by Congress from the beginning, and the power has always been deemed a political one, not subject to be controlled by the judicial department of the government.[8] Until the year 1871 the policy was pursued of dealing with the Indian tribes by means of treaties, and, of course, a moral obligation rested upon Congress to act in good faith in performing the stipulations entered into on its behalf. But, as with treaties made with foreign nations, *Chinese Exclusion Case*, 130 U.S. 581, 600, the legislative power might pass laws in conflict with treaties made with the Indians. *The Cherokee Tobacco*, 11 Wall. 616.

The power exists to abrogate the provisions of an Indian treaty, though presumably such power will be exercised only when circumstances arise which will not only justify the government in disregarding the stipulations of the treaty, but may demand, in the interest of the country and the Indians themselves, that it should do so. When, therefore, treaties were entered into between the United States and a tribe of Indians it was never doubted that the power to abrogate existed in Congress, and that in a contingency such power might be availed of from considerations of governmental policy, particularly if consistent with perfect good faith towards the Indians[.] *United States v. Kagama* (1885), 118 U.S. 375. . . .

In view of the legislative power possessed by Congress over treaties with the Indians and Indian tribal property, we may not specially consider the contentions pressed upon our notice that the signing by the Indians of the agreement of October 6, 1892, was obtained by fraudulent misrepresentations and concealment, that the requisite three fourths of adult male Indians had not signed, as required by the twelfth article of the treaty of 1867, and that the treaty as signed had been amended by Congress without submitting such amendments to the action of the Indians, since all these matters, in any event, were solely within the domain of the legislative authority and its action is conclusive upon the courts. . . .

Indeed, the controversy which this case presents is concluded by the decision in *Cherokee Nation v. Hitchcock*, 187 U.S. 294, decided this term, where it was held that full administrative power was possessed by Congress over Indian tribal property. In effect, the action of Congress now complained of was but an exercise of such power, a mere change in the form of investment of Indian tribal property, the property of those who, as we have held, were in substantial effect the wards of the government. We must presume that Congress acted in perfect good faith in the dealings with the Indians of which complaint is made, and that the legislative branch of the government exercised its best judgment in the premises. In any event, as Congress possessed full power in the matter, the judiciary cannot question or inquire into the motives which prompted the enactment of this legislation. If injury was occasioned, which we do not

---

8 **Questions:** What, precisely, does White mean by *plenary authority*? Does he mean the same thing as in *Gibbons v. Ogden* when Chief Justice John Marshall described the Commerce Clause as "plenary" and subject to the restraints of "elections" and not courts? 22 U.S. (9 Wheat.) 1, 197 (1824). Or does he mean that the power comes from a source outside of the Constitution's enumerated powers? Either way, how does this description of Congress's power excuse the alleged violation of the Fifth Amendment?

wish to be understood as implying, by the use made by Congress of its power, relief must be sought by an appeal to that body for redress and not to the courts. The legislation in question was constitutional . . . .[9]

NOTE: PLENARY POWER DOCTRINE

Lone Wolf represents the high-water mark of the "plenary power" doctrine, in which Congress's power with respect to tribes was deemed effectively unreviewable. Congress took advantage of this power repeatedly over the next thirty years to continue its paternalistic policy of assimilation. For example, in *United States v. Sandoval*, the Court upheld a statute prohibiting the sale of liquor on a reservation, holding that Congress's power is plenary as long as it respects "distinctly Indian communities." 231 U.S. 28, 46 (1913). And in *United States v. Nice*, 241 U.S. 591 (1916), the Court declared that Congress's power extended even to Native people who had become U.S. citizens under the terms of the Dawes Act. The Court therefore upheld a statute that prohibited the off-reservation sales of liquor to members of any Indian tribe: "Commerce with the Indian tribes, means commerce with the individuals composing those tribes." *Nice*, 241 U.S. at 597.

Thanks to *Kagama*, the federal government was also free to adopt and enforce a Code of Indian Offenses, which prohibited a lengthy list of practices that the federal government regarded as "a great hindrance to the civilization of the Indians." Treuer, *supra*, at 153–55. Most destructively, the code outlawed various religious observances among tribes, including "heathenish dances, such as the sun-dance," and other "evil practices." *Id.* Even though the First Amendment generally forbids the federal government from "prohibiting the free exercise [of religion]," the Court in *Lone Wolf* indicated that it would not entertain a challenge under the Bill of Rights to Congress's plenary power over Indians. As a consequence, Native religious practices were criminalized for decades.

American Indians responded with a century of resistance and activism led by the National Indian Defense Association, founded in 1885; the American Indian Defense Association, founded in 1923; and, most radically, the American Indian Movement (AIM), founded in 1968. AIM organized a series of national events in the 1970s, including the occupation of Alcatraz Island; the takeover of Wounded Knee, South Dakota; and a national caravan called the Trail of Broken Treaties. Collectively, these AIM events called for the restoration of treaty relations between the United States and Indian tribes, the return of 110 million acres of land, and a recognition of tribal sovereignty. *See* Pekka Hämäläinen, *Lakota America* 386–90 (2019).

The international attention generated by AIM prompted Congress to enact the modest American Indian Religious Freedom Act of 1978, which declared that "[o]n and after August 11, 1978, it shall be the policy of the

[9] **Question:** In *Cherokee Nation v. Hitchcock,* White wrote another opinion in which he concluded that Congress's regulation of tribal land was a "political" question. 187 U.S. 294, 308 (1902). In this case, he therefore quickly dismisses the Fifth Amendment argument on the same grounds. Does this opinion imply that Congress could abridge other protections of the Bill of Rights without judicial oversight? Could Congress prohibit the free exercise of Native religions?

United States to protect and preserve for American Indians their inherent right of freedom to believe, express, and exercise the traditional religions of the American Indian, Eskimo, Aleut, and Native Hawaiians." Pub. L. No. 95–341, 92 Stat. 469. This statute, not the First Amendment, remains the federal source of protection for Native religious practices.

17.3 TRIBAL POWER (THE SELF-DETERMINATION ERA)

The assimilation era lasted through the 1920s, as Congress displaced tribal land and extinguished tribal religious and cultural practices. *See generally* David Treuer, *The Heartbeat of Wounded Knee* 151–75 (2019). The era only ended with World War I, after more than seventeen thousand Indian men—most of whom were not U.S. citizens—fought for the United States. *Id.* at 177–99. After the war, Congress enacted the Indian Citizenship Act of 1924, which extended U.S. citizenship to "all non-citizen Indians born within the territorial limits of the United States." Pub. L. No. 68–175, 43 Stat. 253. Four years later, Lewis Meriam, a federal investigator, published a massive report excoriating the effects of the federal government's prior Indian policy. Treuer, *supra*, at 201–02.

Indian Reorganization Act of 1934. The administration of President Franklin D. Roosevelt responded to the Meriam report by signing into law the Indian Reorganization Act of 1934, Pub. L. No. 73–383, 48 Stat. 984. This revolutionary law effectively repealed the Dawes Act, ended the practice of allotment, and created processes by which some of the land already lost could be "restore[d] to tribal ownership." Indian Reorganization Act, 48 Stat. at 984. These processes generally authorized the United States to reacquire allotted land and hold the land "in trust" for each tribe's common use. *Id.* at 985.

Section 16 of the law also authorized any tribe to "adopt an appropriate constitution and bylaws," which, when "ratified by a majority vote of the adult Indians living on the reservation," would become the basic law of the tribe. Many tribes were understandably suspicious of the federal government's proposals for reorganization. *Id.* at 987. Yet, by 1938, 172 out of 245 federally recognized tribes voted to ratify their own constitutions. Treuer, *supra*, at 207. Today, the majority of federally recognized tribes continue to have their own constitutions, governments, laws, judicial procedures, and methods for determining who can be enrolled as a tribal member.

Talton. Although 1934 marked a turning point in the federal government's recognition of tribal self-government, tribes had, of course, governed themselves effectively for millennia. For this reason, when the Supreme Court has considered whether the U.S. Constitution applies to a tribe's own laws, the Court has answered no.

It first reached this conclusion in 1896, when Bob Talton, a member of the Cherokee Nation, was indicted by a tribal grand jury for murdering another tribal member. Talton protested that this indictment was unconstitutional because the grand jury that indicted him consisted of only five people. The Fifth Amendment to the U.S. Constitution, by contrast, has been interpreted to require that federal grand juries consist of at least sixteen people. So Talton took his claim to the U.S. Supreme Court, asking the Court to vacate his indictment.

In *Talton v. Mayes*, 163 U.S. 376 (1896), the Court declined to apply the U.S. Constitution to the Cherokee Nation's judicial procedure. It explained that the Fifth Amendment is a limitation only upon the powers of the federal government, whereas "the powers of local self government enjoyed by the Cherokee nation existed prior to the Constitution." *Talton*, 163 U.S. at 384. The Court therefore concluded that the Cherokee Nation's powers are "not operated upon by the Fifth Amendment." *Id.* This holding was not a limitation on the plenary power doctrine—to the contrary, the Court emphasized that the Cherokee Nation's "attributes of local self government . . . are subject to the supreme legislative authority of the United States." *Id.* But the Court insisted that "the existence of the right in Congress to regulate the manner in which the local powers of the Cherokee nation shall be exercised does not render such local powers Federal powers arising from and created by the Constitution of the United States." *Id.*

Indian Civil Rights Act of 1968. Congress amended this situation with the Indian Civil Rights Act of 1968, which created a statutory Bill of Rights to limit any "Indian tribe in exercising powers of self-government." Pub. L. No. 90–284, 82 Stat. 77. The law effectively applied most of the First, Fourth, Fifth, Sixth, Eighth, and Fourteenth Amendments to tribes, while omitting certain clauses such as the grand jury requirement at issue in *Talton*.

The Supreme Court interpreted the Indian Civil Rights Act in one of three seminal 1978 cases regarding tribal sovereignty.

In the first, *Santa Clara Pueblo v. Martinez*, 436 U.S. 49 (1978), the Court evaluated a claim by a woman who challenged a tribal membership law that explicitly discriminated on the basis of sex. The Court reiterated *Talton*'s holding that the U.S. Constitution's Equal Protection Clause did not apply to the tribe. And even though the Indian Civil Rights Act included an equal-protection clause, the Supreme Court held that two considerations prohibited federal courts from hearing challenges to enforce the act. First, unlike most federal civil rights statutes, the act itself contained no provision authorizing anyone to sue to enforce its terms. Second, the Court recognized that tribes possess a "common-law immunity from suit traditionally enjoyed by sovereign powers." *Martinez*, 436 U.S. at 58 (citing *Turner v. United States*, 248 U.S. 354, 358 (1919)). As in *Talton*, the Court emphasized that Congress had the power to amend both of these considerations—it could authorize civil actions or waive the tribe's sovereign immunity from suit. But the Court concluded that "without congressional authorization, the Indian Nations are exempt from suit." *Id.* at 59; *see also Michigan v. Bay Mills Indian Cmty.*, 572 U.S. 782 (2014) (tribal sovereign immunity prohibits states from suing any tribe—including in state court—absent a waiver by the tribe or by Congress).

In the second case, *United States v. Wheeler*, 435 U.S. 313 (1978), the Court held that tribes' inherent sovereignty also gave them the power to criminally prosecute tribal members. Citing *Cherokee Nation v. Georgia*, 30 U.S. (5 Pet.) 1 (1831), and *Worcester v. Georgia*, 31 U.S. 515 (1832), the Court explained that tribal sovereignty predated the United States. Therefore "Indian tribes still possess those aspects of sovereignty not withdrawn by treaty or statute, or by implication as a necessary result of their dependent status." *Wheeler*, 435 U.S. at 323. Emphasizing again that Congress could limit or extinguish this sovereignty, the Court reiterated that "until Congress acts, the tribes retain their existing sovereign powers." *Id.* These sovereign powers included the power to punish tribal offenders, which had never been given up to Congress.

In the third case, *Oliphant v. Suquamish Indian Tribe*, 435 U.S. 191 (1978), the Court limited this tribal sovereignty with respect to *nonmembers*—even those who live on reservations. Citing *Johnson v. M'Intosh*, 21 U.S. (8 Wheat.) 543 (1823), the Court wrote that virtually every federally recognized tribe had submitted to "the overriding sovereignty of the United States" by the nineteenth century. By submitting to this overriding sovereignty, the Court held, "Indian tribes therefore necessarily give up their power to try non-Indian citizens of the United States except in a manner acceptable to Congress." *Oliphant*, 435 U.S. at 210. Although the Court recognized that many non-Indians commit crimes on reservations, the Court held that "these are considerations for Congress to weigh in deciding whether Indian tribes should finally be authorized to try non-Indians." *Id.* at 212; *see Duro v. Reina*, 495 U.S. 676 (1990) (clarifying *Oliphant* to hold that tribes lack the inherent power to prosecute *nonmembers*, not just *non-Indians*).

These three cases, in short, held that tribal governments (1) are not subject to the limits of the U.S. Constitution, (2) possess sovereign immunity from civil claims in federal court, (3) have inherent sovereign powers to criminally prosecute tribal members, and (4) have no similar sovereign powers to criminally prosecute nonmembers. They also held that all four attributes are subject to change by Congress. *See South Dakota v. Bourland*, 508 U.S. 679 (1993) (discussing an example of Congress's reduction of sovereign rights). In fact, since 1978, Congress has given tribes the authority to criminally prosecute nonmember Indians of a different tribe—although it has never given tribes the power to prosecute non-Indians. *See United States v. Lara*, 541 U.S. 193 (2004).

17.3.1
Montana v. United States

450 U.S. 544 (1981)

In the years since 1978, when the Supreme Court held that tribes' *criminal* jurisdiction over nonmembers is limited to whatever Congress allows, the most contested attribute of tribes' inherent sovereign power has been their *civil* jurisdiction over nonmembers. This issue arises frequently. One of the long-term consequences of the Dawes Act has been that the land within many reservation boundaries is owned by white people and other nonmembers in "fee simple," which, as noted earlier, means that they can live on it and sell it without the tribe's permission. Some reservations are also very large and contain highways on which nonmembers regularly pass through. This has given rise to many disputes over the power of tribal governments to regulate the enormous number of nonmembers who live, work, and travel on reservations. *See United States v. Cooley*, 141 S. Ct. 1638, 1645 (2021) ("3.5 million of the 4.6 million people living in American Indian areas in the 2010 census were non-Indians.").

At issue in the following case, *Montana v. United States*, 450 U.S. 544 (1981), was whether the Crow Tribe could prohibit hunting and fishing on land within the reservation owned by non-Indians. As you will see, the Court's answer is no: "the inherent sovereign powers of an Indian tribe do not extend to the activities of nonmembers of the tribe." *Montana*, 450 U.S. at 565. But the second-to-last paragraph excerpted here contains two exceptions to this "general proposition" that today serve as the basis for the inherent power of tribes over nonmembers.

■ JUSTICE STEWART delivered the opinion of the Court.[10]

This case concerns the sources and scope of the power of an Indian tribe to regulate hunting and fishing by non-Indians on lands within its reservation owned in fee simple by non-Indians. Relying on its purported ownership of the bed of the Big Horn River, on the treaties which created its reservation, and on its inherent power as a sovereign, the Crow Tribe of Montana claims the authority to prohibit all hunting and fishing by nonmembers of the Tribe on non-Indian property within reservation boundaries. . . .

I

The Crow Indians originated in Canada, but some three centuries ago they migrated to what is now southern Montana. In the 19th century, warfare between the Crows and several other tribes led the tribes and the United States to sign the First Treaty of Fort Laramie of 1851, in which the signatory tribes acknowledged various designated lands as their respective territories. The treaty identified approximately 38.5 million acres as Crow territory and, in Article 5, specified that, by making the treaty, the tribes did not "surrender the privilege of hunting, fishing, or passing over"

---

[10] **As You Read, Consider:** When someone from Montana visits land they own in Idaho or Canada, they are subject to Idaho or Canadian law—even if they are ineligible to vote in those places. Why does Justice Potter Stewart think the rule should be different when a white person from Montana visits land owned by other white people on the Crow Reservation?

any of the lands in dispute. In 1868, the Second Treaty of Fort Laramie established a Crow Reservation of roughly 8 million acres, including land through which the Big Horn River flows. By Article II of the treaty, the United States agreed that the reservation "shall be . . . set apart for the absolute and undisturbed use and occupation" of the Crow Tribe, and that no non-Indians except agents of the Government "shall ever be permitted to pass over, settle upon, or reside in" the reservation.

Several subsequent Acts of Congress reduced the reservation to slightly fewer than 2.3 million acres. In addition, the General Allotment Act of 1887, ch. 119, 24 Stat. 388, and the Crow Allotment Act of 1920, 41 Stat. 751, authorized the issuance of patents in fee to individual Indian allottees within the reservation. Under these Acts, an allottee could alienate his land to a non-Indian after holding it for 25 years. Today, roughly 52 percent of the reservation is allotted to members of the Tribe and held by the United States in trust for them, 17 percent is held in trust for the Tribe itself, and approximately 28 percent is held in fee by non-Indians. The State of Montana owns in fee simple 2 percent of the reservation, the United States less than 1 percent.

Since the 1920's, the State of Montana has stocked the waters of the reservation with fish, and the construction of a dam by the United States made trout fishing in the Big Horn River possible. The reservation also contains game, some of it stocked by the State. Since the 1950's, the Crow Tribal Council has passed several resolutions respecting hunting and fishing on the reservation, including Resolution No. 74–05, the occasion for this lawsuit. That resolution prohibits hunting and fishing within the reservation by anyone who is not a member of the Tribe. The State of Montana, however, has continued to assert its authority to regulate hunting and fishing by non-Indians within the reservation. . . .

III

Though the parties in this case have raised broad questions about the power of the Tribe to regulate hunting and fishing by non-Indians on the reservation, the regulatory issue before us is a narrow one. The Court of Appeals held that the Tribe may prohibit nonmembers from hunting or fishing on land belonging to the Tribe or held by the United States in trust for the Tribe, and with this holding we can readily agree. We also agree with the Court of Appeals that if the Tribe permits nonmembers to fish or hunt on such lands, it may condition their entry by charging a fee or establishing bag and creel limits. What remains is the question of the power of the Tribe to regulate non-Indian fishing and hunting on reservation land owned in fee by nonmembers of the Tribe. The Court of Appeals held that, with respect to fee-patented lands, the Tribe may regulate, but may not prohibit, hunting and fishing by non-members resident owners or by those, such as tenants or employees, whose occupancy is authorized by the owners. The court further held that the Tribe may totally prohibit hunting and fishing on lands within the reservation owned by non-Indians who do not occupy that land.

The Court of Appeals . . . identified that power as an incident of the inherent sovereignty of the Tribe over the entire Crow Reservation. But "inherent sovereignty" is not so broad as to support the application of Resolution No. 74–05 to non-Indian lands.

This Court most recently reviewed the principles of inherent sovereignty in *United States v. Wheeler*, 435 U.S. 313 (1978). In that case, noting that Indian tribes are "unique aggregations possessing attributes of sovereignty over both their members and their territory," the Court upheld the power of a tribe to punish tribal members who violate tribal criminal laws. But the Court was careful to note that, through their original incorporation into the United States as well as through specific treaties and statutes, the Indian tribes have lost many of the attributes of sovereignty. The Court distinguished between those inherent powers retained by the tribes and those divested:

> "The areas in which such implicit divestiture of sovereignty has been held to have occurred are those involving *the relations between an Indian tribe and nonmembers of the tribe*. . . .
>
> These limitations rest on the fact that the dependent status of Indian tribes within our territorial jurisdiction is necessarily inconsistent with their freedom independently *to determine their external relations*. But the powers of self-government, including the power to prescribe and enforce internal criminal laws, are of a different type. They involve *only the relations among members of a tribe*. Thus, they are not such powers as would necessarily be lost by virtue of a tribe's dependent status." *Ibid.* (Emphasis added.)

Thus, in addition to the power to punish tribal offenders, the Indian tribes retain their inherent power to determine tribal membership, to regulate domestic relations among members, and to prescribe rules of inheritance for members. *Id.*, at 322, n. 18. But exercise of tribal power beyond what is necessary to protect tribal self-government or to control internal relations is inconsistent with the dependent status of the tribes, and so cannot survive without express congressional delegation. *United States v. Kagama*, 118 U.S. 375, 381–382. Since regulation of hunting and fishing by nonmembers of a tribe on lands no longer owned by the tribe bears no clear relationship to tribal self-government or internal relations, the general principles of retained inherent sovereignty did not authorize the Crow Tribe to adopt Resolution No. 74–05.[11]

The Court recently applied these general principles in *Oliphant v. Suquamish Indian Tribe*, 435 U.S. 191, rejecting a tribal claim of inherent sovereign authority to exercise criminal jurisdiction over non-Indians. Stressing that Indian tribes cannot exercise power inconsistent with their diminished status as sovereigns, the Court quoted Justice Johnson's words in his concurrence in *Fletcher v. Peck*, 6 Cranch 87, 147—the first Indian case to reach this Court—that the Indian tribes have lost any "right of governing every person within their limits except themselves." 435 U. S., at 209. Though *Oliphant* only determined inherent tribal authority in criminal matters, the principles on which it relied support the general proposition that the inherent sovereign powers of an Indian tribe do not extend to the activities of nonmembers of the tribe.[12] To be sure, Indian tribes retain inherent sovereign power to exercise some forms of civil jurisdiction over non-Indians on their reservations, even on non-Indian fee lands. A tribe may regulate, through taxation, licensing, or other means, the activities of nonmembers who enter consensual relationships with the tribe or its members, through commercial dealing, contracts, leases, or other arrangements. A tribe may also retain inherent power to exercise civil authority over the conduct of non-Indians on fee lands within its reservation when that conduct threatens or has

---

[11] **Question:** Here, Stewart recognizes several inherent powers of tribes, including the power to regulate their own members. Beyond Supreme Court precedent and its claims about tribes' "diminished status as sovereigns," is there any persuasive explanation for why tribes should lack the power to regulate nonmembers within their borders?

[12] **Questions:** After announcing a "general proposition" that tribes cannot regulate nonmembers, Stewart concedes that there are two circumstances when it is appropriate for tribes to regulate "non-Indians on their reservations." Today, these circumstances are known as the *Montana* exceptions. What principles do these exceptions balance or vindicate?

Note also that this paragraph discusses tribes' power over "non-Indians," not just nonmembers. Is there any justification for a rule that would give the Crow Tribe more power to regulate a member of the Cherokee Nation on its reservation than it would have over a white person on its reservation?

some direct effect on the political integrity, the economic security, or the health or welfare of the tribe.

No such circumstances, however, are involved in this case. Non-Indian hunters and fishermen on non-Indian fee land do not enter any agreements or dealings with the Crow Tribe so as to subject themselves to tribal civil jurisdiction. And nothing in this case suggests that such non-Indian hunting and fishing so threaten the Tribe's political or economic security as to justify tribal regulation. . . .

NOTE: *MONTANA* EXCEPTIONS

Although *Montana* recognized that tribes have the inherent power to regulate the activities of their own members, the Court held that as a "general proposition," tribes have no similar power to regulate non-Indians on non-Indian fee lands—that is, white people within a reservation's boundaries on land that is not owned by the tribe, its members, or the federal government. *Montana,* 450 U.S. at 565. But the second-to-last paragraph of the opinion describes two exceptions to this rule that today are frequently litigated.

Consensual regulations. Under the first *Montana* exception, tribes have the inherent power to regulate "the activities of nonmembers who enter consensual relationships with the tribe or its members." *Id.* In theory, this means that when a nonmember wants to live or do business on a reservation, the tribe can require the nonmember to consent to tribal law—just like a state like Montana can require any visitor to the state to consent to Montana law. But in *Plains Commerce Bank v. Long Family Land & Cattle Co.*, 554 U.S. 316 (2008), a 5–4 Court interpreted the first *Montana* exception narrowly to prohibit a tribe from preventing a bank from foreclosing on reservation land owned by a nonmember. The majority opinion, written by Chief Justice John Roberts, emphasized that the bank's issuance of a mortgage within a reservation was not the same thing as consenting to tribal authority. *Plains Commerce Bank*, 554 U.S. at 337. In a telling paragraph, he explained his concern about "subjecting nonmembers to tribal regulatory authority without commensurate consent":

> Tribal sovereignty, it should be remembered, is a sovereignty outside the basic structure of the Constitution. The Bill of Rights does not apply to Indian tribes. Indian courts differ from traditional American courts in a number of significant respects. And nonmembers have no part in tribal government—they have no say in the laws and regulations that govern tribal territory. Consequently, those laws and regulations may be fairly imposed on nonmembers only if the nonmember has consented, either expressly or by his actions. Even then, the regulation must stem from the tribe's inherent sovereign authority to set conditions on entry, preserve tribal self-government, or control internal relations. See *Montana,* 450 U.S., at 564.

Plains Commerce Bank, 554 U.S. at 337.

Threats to tribal security. If the existence of "commensurate consent" defines the first *Montana* exception, the existence of a threat to tribal security defines the second. The second *Montana* exception allows tribes to enact whatever regulations are necessary to protect the "political integrity, the economic security, or the health or welfare of the tribe." *Montana*, 450 U.S. at 566. The Court most recently applied this exception to uphold the exercise of tribal power in *United States v. Cooley*, 141 S. Ct. 1638 (2021). At issue was whether a member of the Crow Police Department could stop and search the car of a white driver who was acting suspiciously on a U.S. Highway within the Crow reservation in Montana. The Court unanimously agreed that such a stop was permissible. "The second [*Montana* exception] fits the present case, almost like a glove," the Court wrote. *Id.* at 1643. "The phrase speaks of the protection of the 'health or welfare of the tribe.' To deny a tribal police officer authority to search and detain for a reasonable time any person he or she believes may commit or has committed a crime would make it difficult for tribes to protect themselves against ongoing threats." *Id.* Nevertheless, the Court cautioned that it was not authorizing tribes to criminally prosecute nonmembers or even to adjudicate civil suits arising out of car accidents that took place on public highways. *Id.* at 1644 (citing *Strate v. A-1 Contractors*, 520 U.S. 438, 456–59 (1997)).

17.4 MODERN FEDERAL AND STATE POWER (THE TERMINATION ERA)

The federal government's policy of tribal self-determination has not caused Congress to cease passing laws to regulate tribes. Throughout the twentieth and twenty-first centuries, Congress has continued to exercise its plenary power over tribes to take land into trust, approve tribal constitutions, and attempt to assist tribal self-government. The Court has, however, abandoned the rationale of *Lone Wolf v. Hitchcock*, 187 U.S. 553 (1903), for this plenary power. "The source of federal authority over Indian matters has been the subject of some confusion," the Court wrote in 1973, "but it is now generally recognized that the power derives from federal responsibility for regulating commerce with Indian tribes and for treaty making." *McClanahan v. Ariz. Tax Comm'n*, 411 U.S. 164, 172 n.7 (1973).

Pro-Indian standard of statute/treaty interpretation

Generally speaking, the Supreme Court has adjusted its interpretation of federal law by applying a canon that statutes should be "liberally construed" in favor of Indians. *Carpenter v. Shaw*, 280 U.S. 363, 367 (1930). For example, the Court requires a clear statement of Congress's intent before it will interpret a federal statute to divest a tribe of land, diminish the tribe's boundaries, or narrow the tribe's sovereign powers. *See, e.g.*, *Nebraska v. Parker*, 577 U.S. 481, 489–93 (2016).

This canon of interpretation proved significant in *McGirt v. Oklahoma*, 140 S. Ct. 2452 (2020), in which the Court concluded that nineteenth century treaties created an expansive reservation for the Creek Nation in Oklahoma that Congress never withdrew with subsequent legislation. *McGirt*, 140 S. Ct. at 2482. Applying *Worcester v. Georgia*, 31 U.S. 515 (1832), the Court also rejected the suggestion that states have the authority to unilaterally reduce the size of reservations within their borders. *Id.* at 2477. Nevertheless, in an effort to reduce the practical impact of its decision, the Court declared that "[s]tates are otherwise free to apply their criminal laws in cases of non-Indian victims and defendants, including within Indian country." *Id.* at 2479 (citing *United States v. McBratney*, 104 U.S. 621, 624 (1882), which prohibited the federal government from prosecuting white people on tribal land in Colorado). This declaration is in serious tension with the holding of *Worcester*, suggesting that the Court will soon have to resolve uncertainty about the scope of state jurisdiction over non-Indians on tribal land.

In addition to applying a pro-Indian standard for interpreting statutes and treaties, the modern Court also applies a deferential standard of scrutiny when evaluating laws that allegedly violate equal-protection principles by benefiting Indians over non-Indians. In the landmark case of *Morton v. Mancari*, 417 U.S. 535, 554–55 (1974), the Court upheld a hiring preference given to Indians within the Bureau of Indian Affairs after the preference was challenged as racially discriminatory. The Court held that the strict scrutiny the Court usually applied to racial classifications was not warranted because "the preference is political, rather than racial in nature." *Mancari*, 417 U.S. at 553 n.24. The Court explained that Congress had long distinguished between Indians and non-Indians; that the preference was enacted to give Indians "a greater degree of self-government, both politically and economically"; and that the preference was "not directed towards a 'racial' group consisting of 'Indians'; instead it applies only to members of 'federally recognized tribes.'" *Id.* at 553–54. Analogizing the preference to a law that required a member of a city council to reside within the city governed by the council, the Court deferred to Congress's judgment about how best to "further the cause of Indian self-government." *Id.*; *see also Del. Tribal Bus. Comm. v. Weeks*, 430 U.S. 73 (1977) (applying the *Mancari* standard to sustain a classification that inadvertently disfavored one group of Indians as compared to another group).

Public Law 280

Nevertheless, Congress has not, in fact, always acted to further the cause of Indian self-government. In 1953, Congress passed a statute that conferred "jurisdiction on the States of California, Minnesota, Nebraska, Oregon, and Wisconsin, with respect to criminal offenses and civil causes of action committed or arising on Indian reservations within such States." Pub. L. 83–280, 67 Stat. 588, 588. The law, known as "Public Law 280," was one of several laws passed between 1940 and 1960 that resisted the general trend toward tribal self-government, and it quickly became infamous among Indian communities because it took effect without tribal consent and threatened to "terminate" the ability of tribes to enforce their own laws. David Treuer, *The Heartbeat of Wounded Knee* 255–56 (2019). By 1968, almost a dozen additional states had invoked Public Law 280 to exercise jurisdiction over tribes without their consent. *Id.* at 256.

But Public Law 280 had a few terms that were favorable to tribes. In *Three Affiliated Tribes v. Wold Engineering*, 476 U.S. 877 (1986), the Court held that the states that invoked Public Law 280 waived their own sovereign immunity, and that they therefore had a duty to open up their state courts to lawsuits brought by Indians against non-Indians for activities on reservations. Even more significantly, in *Bryan v. Itasca County*, 426 U.S. 373 (1976), the Supreme Court interpreted Public Law 280 to give states power to enforce *criminal* laws on reservations but not *civil* laws. *See, e.g.*, *New Mexico v. Mescalero Apache Tribe*, 462 U.S. 324, 343–44 (1983) (interpreting Public Law 280 as preempting New Mexico's civil laws governing on-reservation hunting and fishing by nonmembers).

The criminal-versus-civil distinction of *Bryan* proved to be particularly important after *California v. Cabazon Band of Mission Indians*, 480 U.S. 202, 220–22 (1987), in which the Supreme Court held that state regulation of gambling was a civil, not criminal, matter. The *Cabazon Band* decision paved the way for tribes to open casinos and other businesses on their reservations despite state laws to the contrary. To regulate these new casinos, Congress quickly enacted the Indian Gaming Regulatory Act of 1988, Pub. L. No. 100–497, 102 Stat. 2467. Since the act was passed, the Indian gaming industry has grown into a $34 billion-per-year industry—exceeding the value of the United States' non-Indian gaming industry by almost a billion dollars. *See* Press Release, Nat'l Indian Gaming Comm., 2018 Indian Gaming Revenues (Sept. 12, 2019).

State taxation of tribal land

Congress's approval of specified state *regulation* of tribal land has also accompanied the Supreme Court's approval of state *taxation* of tribal land—at least as long as Congress hasn't preempted such taxation. The Court announced this new rule in *Oklahoma Tax Commission v. Texas Co.*, 336 U.S. 342 (1949), which overruled several prior decisions to hold that states could collect nondiscriminatory state production and excise taxes from non-Indians who leased restricted Indian lands. In a pair of cases in 1973, the Court expanded this doctrine to hold that states could also tax Indians for off-reservation activities, *Mescalero Apache Tribe v. Jones*, 411 U.S. 145 (1973), but not on-reservation activities, *McClanahan v. Ariz. Tax Comm'n*, 411 U.S. 164 (1973). The Court explained that this new doctrine was consistent with *Worcester* because Congress always had the power to stop states from collecting taxes.

In *White Mountain Apache Tribe v. Bracker*, 448 U.S. 136 (1980), the Court adopted a balancing test for these sorts of state taxes in which it weighed state, tribal, and federal interests against one another. But after a brief period in which it struck down state laws under the *Bracker* test, the Court has indicated that it will only strike down a tax where the state has "asserted no legitimate regulatory interest that might justify the tax." *Cotton Petroleum Corp. v. New Mexico*, 490 U.S. 163 (1989) (upholding state tax on oil extracted from Indian territory); *see Ramah Navajo Sch. Bd. v. Bureau of Revenue*, 458 U.S. 832 (1982) (striking tax of construction company on reservation as preempted). In *County of Yakima v. Confederated Tribes & Bands of the Yakima Indian Nation*, the Court interpreted the Dawes Act itself as authorizing certain types of property taxation and determined that any inconsistency with tribal self-determination was a "policy" argument properly presented to Congress, not to the justices. 502 U.S. 251, 265 (1992).

CHAPTER 18

WHAT IS THE SCOPE OF CONGRESS'S POWER WITH RESPECT TO ARTICLE IV?

ARTICLE I, SECTION 8, CLAUSE 18: The Congress shall have Power . . . To make all Laws which shall be necessary and proper for carrying into Execution the foregoing Powers, and all other Powers vested by this Constitution in the Government of the United States, or in any Department or Officer thereof.

ARTICLE IV, SECTION 1: Full Faith and Credit shall be given in each State to the public Acts, Records, and judicial Proceedings of every other State. And the Congress may by general Laws prescribe the Manner in which such Acts, Records and Proceedings shall be proved, and the Effect thereof.

ARTICLE IV, SECTION 2, CLAUSE 1: The Citizens of each State shall be entitled to all Privileges and Immunities of Citizens in the several States.

CLAUSE 2: A Person charged in any State with Treason, Felony, or other Crime, who shall flee from Justice, and be found in another State, shall on Demand of the executive Authority of the State from which he fled, be delivered up, to be removed to the State having Jurisdiction of the Crime.

CLAUSE 3: No Person held to Service or Labour in one State, under the Laws thereof, escaping into another, shall, in Consequence of any Law or Regulation therein, be discharged from such Service or Labour, but shall be delivered up on Claim of the Party to whom such Service or Labour may be due.

ARTICLE IV, SECTION 3, CLAUSE 1: New States may be admitted by the Congress into this Union; but no new State shall be formed or erected within the Jurisdiction of any other State; nor any State be formed by the Junction of two or more States, or Parts of States, without the Consent of the Legislatures of the States concerned as well as of the Congress.

CLAUSE 2: The Congress shall have Power to dispose of and make all needful Rules and Regulations respecting the Territory or other Property belonging to the United States; and nothing in this Constitution shall be so construed as to Prejudice any Claims of the United States, or of any particular State.

ARTICLE IV, SECTION 4: The United States shall guarantee to every State in this Union a Republican Form of Government, and shall protect each of them against Invasion; and on Application of the Legislature, or of the Executive (when the Legislature cannot be convened), against domestic Violence.

TENTH AMENDMENT (1791): The powers not delegated to the United States by the Constitution, nor prohibited by it to the States, are reserved to the States respectively, or to the people.

Article IV Clauses

In contrast with Article I, which comprehensively describes the legislative powers given to Congress, Article IV reads like a multilateral treaty. Instead of detailing powers and limits, Article IV contains a list of obligations that each state owes to the others. This structure reflects, in part, the fact that many of Article IV's terms were copied straight out of Article IV of the Articles of Confederation.

The scope of Congress's power with respect to Article IV varies with the various clauses in Article IV: Full Faith and Credit Clause, Privileges and Immunities Clause, Fugitive Slave and Extradition Clauses, Territory Clause, Admissions Clause, Property Clause, and Guarantee Clause.

18.1 THE FULL FAITH AND CREDIT CLAUSE

The first section in Article IV, the Full Faith and Credit Clause, generally requires each state to respect the contracts, marriages, property rights, and judgments of other states. Absent the clause, a marriage or divorce performed in Massachusetts might not be recognized by the courts of Connecticut and vice versa.

Unlike the Confederation's version of the clause, which was self-executing, the Constitution's version expressly empowers Congress to "prescribe the Manner" by which a person from one state might prove the existence of their legal rights in other states. The first Congress enforced this provision early on, declaring that legal records and judicial proceedings "shall have such faith and credit given to them in every court within the United States, as they have by law or usage in the courts of the state from whence the said records are or shall be taken." Act of May 26, 1790, ch. 11, 1 Stat. 122; *see, e.g.*, *Cooper v. Newell*, 173 U.S. 555, 566–67 (1899) (holding that each court must treat legal records as the jurisdiction that created them would treat them).

Scholars have long argued that Congress could go further than this 1790 law. Edward S. Corwin wrote in a famous 1933 article:

> Congress has the power under the clause to decree the effect that the statutes of one state shall have in other states. This being so, it does not seem extravagant to argue that Congress may under the clause describe a certain type of divorce and say that it shall be granted recognition throughout the Union and that no other kind shall. Or to speak in more general terms, Congress has under the clause power to enact standards whereby uniformity of state legislation may be secured as to almost any matter in connection with which interstate recognition of private rights would be useful and valuable.

The "Full Faith and Credit" Clause, 81 U. Pa. L. Rev. 371, 388 (1933). Other scholars have agreed that, in theory, Congress "remains entirely free to determine the effect of state records in other states." Stephen E. Sachs, *Full Faith and Credit in the Early Congress*, 95 Va. L. Rev. 1201, 1207 (2009).

But, in practice, Congress hasn't attempted to test the limits of its powers under the clause. Instead, the meaning of the clause itself has been disputed over the decades as states have rejected controversial legislation and judicial rulings from other states.

Slavery laws dispute

The first major dispute over the Full Faith and Credit Clause concerned slavery. In the nineteenth century, northerners and southerners both argued that the Full Faith and Credit Clause applied less strictly to statutes than to judgments, and therefore states didn't have to recognize other states' laws creating or abolishing property rights in enslaved people. *See Dred Scott v. Sandford*, 60 U.S. (19 How.) 393, 460 (1857) (Nelson, J., concurring).

A form of this argument has developed into the modern rule: states may decline to enforce other states' laws if they conflict with their own public policy—at least as long as that policy is not one of general "hostility" toward enforcing other states' laws. *Franchise Tax Bd. of Cal. v. Hyatt*, 578 U.S. 171, 178 (2016).

Financial markets dispute

A second dispute concerned financial markets. In the early twentieth century, some states objected to recognizing speculative contracts. Mississippi, for example, treated contracts that bet on the future price of cotton as a form of gambling—prompting its residents to enforce cotton futures contracts in neighboring states.

In one case, a Mississippi resident tried to enforce a futures contract in Missouri, whose courts sided with the resident only after misinterpreting Mississippi's law on the subject. The resident went back to Mississippi to get its courts to enforce the Missouri judgment. But the Mississippi courts refused to do so on the ground that the Missouri court incorrectly applied Mississippi law—which, again, banned speculative contracts. The Supréme Court reversed, holding that as long as an out-of-state court has *jurisdiction* to hear a dispute, then its judgments on the *merits* must be enforced under the Full Faith and Credit Clause. *Fauntleroy v. Lum*, 210 U.S. 230 (1908).

Divorce laws dispute

This distinction between merits and jurisdiction became important for a third major dispute: divorce laws. Before the advent of no-fault divorce laws in 1969, it was difficult for couples to obtain a divorce absent proof of infidelity or other misconduct. Nevada had unusually lax divorce rules, however. Thus, married individuals from across the country temporarily moved there, obtained a unilateral divorce decree from a Nevada court, and moved back to their home states to enforce their Nevada judgments.

In two cases in the 1940s, the Supreme Court held that for purposes of the Full Faith and Credit Clause, a court had to enforce a Nevada divorce decree absent evidence that the person who obtained it was never domiciled in Nevada, even temporarily. *See Williams v. North Carolina*, 325 U.S. 226, 239 (1945); *Williams v. North Carolina*, 317 U.S. 287, 302–04 (1942).

Since then, the Court has held that divorces are "divisible," so a Nevada court can end a marriage without affecting how other states determine property, alimony, and custody rights. *Armstrong v. Armstrong*, 350 U.S. 568, 571 (1956).

Marriage laws dispute

Finally, a more recent dispute has concerned marriages, particularly in the decade between 2004, when Massachusetts became the first state to recognize same-sex marriages, and 2015, when the Supreme Court recognized them nationwide in *Obergefell v. Hodges*, 57 U.S. 644 (2015).

For example, in 2007, a Georgia court allowed V.L., the same-sex partner of E.L., to adopt E.L.'s biological children. The couple moved to Alabama and eventually split up, leading V.L. to seek visitation rights in an Alabama court. In 2015, despite *Obergefell*, the Alabama Supreme Court denied V.L.'s request after it refused to recognize the Georgia court's adoption decree. The U.S. Supreme Court reversed, holding that the Alabama court was required to grant the decree full faith and credit because the decree appeared on its face to have been issued by a court with competent jurisdiction, and there was no established Georgia law to the contrary. *V.L. v. E.L.*, 577 U.S. 404, 408–10 (2016).

18.2 THE PRIVILEGES AND IMMUNITIES CLAUSE

The Privileges and Immunities Clause—Article IV, Section 2, Clause 1—has its origin in the charters of English colonial corporations, which often included a provision guaranteeing that anyone who traveled or was born overseas would have the same "liberties, franchises, and immunities" as if they had never left England. *See* Mary Sarah Bilder, *Charter Constitutionalism*, 94 N.C. L. Rev. 1545, 1577–84 (2016). The Articles of Confederation expanded this protection to guarantee that "the free inhabitants" of each state would have the same privileges and immunities "of free citizens" in other states, including the right to travel and do business. But this language was confusing: Did it mean that a *noncitizen* of one state had all the rights of *citizenship* in another? The Constitution's version was intended to clarify the text and make it into "the basis of the Union": citizens of every state deserve to be treated equally no matter where in the nation they go. *The Federalist No. 80*, at 537–38 (Alexander Hamilton) (Jacob E. Cooke ed., 1961).

The Constitution's version of the Privileges and Immunities Clause was not, however, as clear as its authors intended: slavery complicated the clause's interpretation in the early nineteenth century. In northern states such as Massachusetts, black people could become citizens of the state and vote. But in southern states such as South Carolina, black people were presumptively enslaved unless they could provide documentation proving their freedom. *See* Paul Finkelman, *States' Rights, Southern Hypocrisy, and the Crisis of the Union*, 45 Akron L. Rev. 449, 464 (2012). If the Privileges and Immunities Clause were interpreted literally, laws discriminating against black people might be unconstitutional as applied to black citizens of northern states.

The most famous antebellum interpretation of the clause failed to resolve this question of whether the clause applied to free black people. In *Corfield v. Coryell*, a case decided by a Supreme Court justice riding circuit, Justice Bushrod Washington interpreted the clause as a guarantee to the citizens of each state

> those privileges and immunities which are, in their nature, fundamental; which belong, of right, to the citizens of all free governments; and which have, at all times, been enjoyed by the citizens of the several states which compose this Union, from the time of their becoming free, independent, and sovereign.

6 F. Cas. 546, 551 (C.C.E.D. Pa. 1823) (No. 3230).

The *Corfield* case involved a New Jersey law that allowed only inhabitants of New Jersey to gather oysters in the state. Washington rejected the argument that harvesting a state's limited natural resources was a privilege or immunity protected by Article IV. Rather, he proposed the following influential list of privileges and immunities:

> Protection by the government; the enjoyment of life and liberty, with the right to acquire and possess property of every kind, and to pursue and obtain happiness and safety; subject nevertheless to such restraints as the government may justly prescribe for the general good of the whole. The right of a citizen of one state to pass through, or to reside in any other state, for purposes of trade, agriculture, professional pursuits, or otherwise; to claim the benefit of the writ of habeas corpus; to institute and maintain actions of any kind in the courts of the state; to take, hold and dispose of property, either real or personal; and an exemption from higher taxes or impositions than are paid by the other citizens of the state; may be mentioned as some of the particular privileges and immunities of citizens, which are clearly embraced by the general description of privileges deemed to be fundamental: to which may be added, the elective franchise, as regulated and established by the laws or constitution of the state in which it is to be exercised. These, and many others which might be mentioned, are, strictly speaking, privileges and immunities. . . .

Corfield, 6 F. Cas. at 551–52.

The Supreme Court relied on Washington's theory in *Dred Scott v. Sandford*, 60 U.S. (19 How.) 393 (1857), in which it held that black people could never become citizens of the United States. As will be discussed in a later section (18.4), Chief Justice Roger Taney feared that if black people were entitled to Washington's list of rights, then black people from Massachusetts would have the same right as white citizens to travel to southern states and carry firearms among southern black people, "inevitably producing discontent and insubordination among them, and endangering the peace and safety of the State." *Dred Scott*, 60 U.S. (19 How.) at 417.

Congress later repudiated *Dred Scott* after the Civil War. Yet it too relied on Washington's theory when it passed the Civil Rights Act of 1866, ch. 31, 14 Stat. 27. The act declared that all U.S. citizens of every race had the right "to make and enforce contracts, to sue, be parties, and give evidence, to inherit, purchase, lease, sell, hold, and convey real and personal property, and to full and equal benefit of all laws and proceedings for the security of person and property, as is enjoyed by white citizens." Civil Rights Act, 14 Stat. at 27. But conservatives in Congress stridently contended that unlike with the Full Faith and Credit Clause, nothing in the Privileges and Immunities Clause empowered Congress to define its terms. *See* Note, *Congress's Power to Define the Privileges and Immunities of Citizenship*, 128 Harv. L. Rev. 1206, 1218 (2015). The constitutionality of the Civil Rights Act thus seemed vulnerable until Congress proposed the Fourteenth Amendment, Section 1 of which explicitly gave Congress the power to enforce a new clause protecting "the privileges or immunities of citizens of the United States" from state interference.

Despite this legislative history, in the *Slaughter-House Cases*, 83 U.S. (16 Wall.) 36 (1873), the Supreme Court rejected the idea that Congress had any role to play in the enforcement of Article IV's Privileges and Immunities Clause. The Court wrote instead that Article IV protected a "class of rights which the *State governments* were created to establish and secure." *Slaughter-House Cases*, 83 U.S. (16 Wall.) at 76 (emphasis added); *see also Baldwin v. Franks*, 120 U.S. 678, 661–62 (1887); *United States v. Harris*, 106 U.S. 629, 643 (1883). Two decades later, the Court also firmly rejected the theory that the Privileges and Immunities Clause protects a freestanding class of fundamental or natural rights beyond whatever rights states choose to grant their own citizens. *McKane v. Durston*, 153 U.S. 684, 687–88 (1894).

Today, the *Slaughter-House Cases* continues to provide the primary, if narrow, interpretation of the Privileges and Immunities Clause:

> Its sole purpose was to declare to the several States, that whatever those rights, as you grant or establish them to your own citizens, or as you limit or qualify, or impose restrictions on their exercise, the same, neither more nor less, shall be the measure of the rights of citizens of other States within your jurisdiction.

Slaughter-House Cases, 83 U.S. (16 Wall.) at 77. In other words, the clause is an antidiscrimination provision: states may not discriminate against out-of-state citizens "with respect to those 'privileges' and 'immunities' bearing upon the vitality of the Nation as a single entity." *Baldwin v. Mont. Fish & Game Comm'n*, 436 U.S. 371, 383 (1978).

Applying this standard, the Court has struck down laws that allow only state residents to access courts, own property, or receive free medical care. *See Doe v. Bolton*, 410 U.S. 179, 200 (1973); *Canadian N. Ry. Co. v. Eggen*, 252 U.S. 553, 562–63 (1920); *Blake v. McClung*, 172 U.S. 239, 246 (1898).

By contrast, the Court has upheld state laws that allow only that state's citizens to vote; hold office; or access scarce resources, like fish or game. *See, e.g., Baldwin*, 436 U.S. at 383. The Court has also upheld laws that discriminate against a state's *own* citizens unless the law discriminates against out-of-state citizens too. *See United Bldg. & Constr. Trades Council v. Mayor of Camden*, 465 U.S. 208, 220–22 (1984); *Bradwell v. Illinois*, 83 U.S. (16 Wall.) 130, 138 (1873).

18.3 THE FUGITIVE SLAVE AND EXTRADITION CLAUSES

Among the fifty-five delegates who arrived at the Constitutional Convention in 1787, almost half, twenty-five, owned enslaved people. *See* Andrew Delblanco, *The War Before the War: Fugitive Slaves and the Struggle for America's Soul from the Revolution to the Civil War* 66 (2018). George Washington brought three of his over two hundred enslaved people to Philadelphia, and other delegates arrived with black valets, cooks, and housemaids. Only three delegates—Alexander Hamilton, Benjamin Franklin, and William Livingston—belonged to abolition societies. Even among them, Hamilton married into a slave-owning family, and Franklin owned enslaved people until his death. *Id.*

In this context, one pressing issue for many of the delegates was what should happen when an enslaved person escaped from one state into another. At the outbreak of the American Revolution, the Crown governor of Virginia, the Earl of Dunmore, issued a proclamation promising to free any enslaved person who escaped to fight for the British. Dunmore's proclamation prompted as many as one hundred thousand enslaved people to flee to British lines and fight for the British. This mass exodus caused a sensation among America's white elite; even Benjamin Franklin called Dunmore's proclamation barbaric. *Id.* at 73. When the war ended, American negotiators demanded that the Treaty of Paris prohibit British forces from "carrying away any negroes or other property of American inhabitants" as they withdrew from American territory. *Id.* at 75.

Although the "carrying away" clause of the Treaty of Paris was poorly enforced, the end of the Revolutionary War left tens of thousands of formerly enslaved people in places like New York. As the New York government negotiated with other states over the future status of these refugees, Hamilton called it an "act of perfidy" to send people back into slavery after they had been "induced to quit their masters on the faith of official proclamations, promising them liberty." *Id.* at 76. John Jay, the president of the New York Manumission Society, agreed with Hamilton, but he also thought it unjust not to compensate the enslavers who had lost their property. *Id.* at 77.

As this dilemma played out in state politics, the Confederation Congress, meeting in New York City, passed an act to organize the territory northwest of the Ohio River. The Northwest Ordinance banned slavery in the territory but also sought to prevent a situation like that of the New York refugees from arising again. It declared:

> There shall be neither slavery nor involuntary servitude in the said territory, otherwise than in the punishment of crimes whereof the party shall have been duly convicted: Provided, always, That any person escaping into the same, from whom labor or service is lawfully claimed in any one of the original States, such fugitive may be lawfully reclaimed and conveyed to the person claiming his or her labor or service.

32 *Journals of the Continental Congress* 343 (Roscoe R. Hill ed., 1936).

In August 1787, a month after the Confederation Congress enacted the Northwest Ordinance, two delegates from South Carolina requested that "some provision should be included in favor of property in slaves." 2 *Records of the Federal Convention of 1787*, at 443 (Max Farrand ed., 1911). They proposed to add a phrase requiring "fugitive slaves and servants to be delivered up like criminals." *Id.* Several delegates objected to this proposal, complaining that states should not be obligated to return fugitives from slavery at taxpayer expense, so the South Carolinians withdrew their proposal and replaced it with what became the Fugitive Slave Clause.

The final version of the Fugitive Slave Clause—Article IV, Section 2, Clause 3—prohibited states from freeing fugitives from slavery, declaring that "No Person held to Service or Labour in one State, under the Laws thereof, escaping into another, shall, in Consequence of any Law or Regulation therein, be discharged from such Service or Labour." The final version also required that any fugitives from slavery "shall be delivered up on Claim of the Party to whom such Service or Labour may be due"—a parallel to the Extradition Clause, Article IV, Section 2, Clause 2—although it didn't specify who was responsible for doing so. Delblanco, *supra*, at 79. The clause was then added to the draft constitution without debate. *Id.* at 80.

18.3.1

Prigg v. Pennsylvania

41 U.S. (16 Pet.) 539 (1842)

Although neither part of the Fugitive Slave Clause provoked much debate in the Constitutional Convention, the clause left ambiguous a crucial question: Who was responsible for ensuring that fugitives from slavery be "delivered up": private parties, states, or Congress?

Congress sought to resolve this question with the Fugitive Slave Act of 1793, ch. 2, 1 Stat. 302. The act empowered private captors, acting on behalf of slave owners, to arrest anyone they suspected was a fugitive from slavery. Fugitive Slave Act, 1 Stat. at 302–05. If a captor took a black person before a state or federal judge and offered "oral testimony or affidavit" that the person was a fugitive from slavery, the law then required the judge to issue a certificate empowering the captor to take the black person out of the state. *Id.*

Like the Fugitive Slave Clause, the Fugitive Slave Act of 1793 passed with relatively little fanfare. But over the next half century, the clause and act became the most controversial features of the federal government. This controversy was partially a consequence of massive changes in state law and partially a consequence of the act's minimal protections for black people. By the early nineteenth century, every northern state had begun to abolish slavery. Yet the clause and act ensured that none of these states could provide their black residents with sanctuary from the horrors of enslavement. White captors could, with impunity, storm a black person's home; drag the black person and his or her family to a local judge; and, within days, carry them to a southern plantation or auction block. As a consequence, white captors found it profitable to kidnap any northern black person they encountered. *See, e.g.*, Solomon Northup, *Twelve Years a Slave* (Auburn, N.Y., Derby & Miller 1853).

In this climate, northern jurists began to argue that the Fugitive Slave Act was unconstitutional. *See* Delblanco, *supra*, at 177–78. Some argued that Article IV gave Congress no role to play in the enforcement of the Fugitive Slave Clause. *See* Robert Cover, *Justice Accused: Antislavery and the Judicial Process* 149–58, 233 (1975). Others added that Congress could not commandeer state judges by requiring them to participate in the enforcement of federal law. *See, e.g.*, 1 James Kent, *Commentaries on American Law* 396–404 (1826). Eventually, Pennsylvania and other northern states began passing laws "for the protection of free people of color, and to prevent kidnapping." 1825 Pa. Laws 150 (1826). Pennsylvania's antikidnapping law required a captor to first obtain a warrant from a Pennsylvania judge before arresting someone—giving black people time to flee. *Id.* at 151. The law also required the captor to obtain a certificate from a state judge before removing the black person to the South. *Id.* If the captor failed to comply with either of these provisions, the law made it a felony to "take, carry away, or seduce, any negro or mulatto from any part of [the state] . . ., with a design and intention of selling and disposing of, or causing to be sold, . . . such negro or mulatto, as a slave or servant." *Id.* at 150.

In 1832, an enslaved woman named Margaret Morgan fled from Maryland to Pennsylvania, where she joined her free black husband. Over the next five years, Morgan started a new life and gave birth to a child. But in 1837, a white woman in Maryland hired a lawyer named Edward Prigg "to seize and arrest the said negro woman." *Prigg v. Pennsylvania*, 41 U.S. (16 Pet.) 539, 556 (1842). Prigg went to Pennsylvania, obtained a warrant for Morgan's arrest, and brought her and her child before a local magistrate. But the magistrate refused to grant Prigg a certificate allowing him to take Morgan's family south. So Prigg simply dragged Morgan and her child to Maryland by force. An outraged Pennsylvania court convicted an absent Prigg of kidnapping. The state then negotiated with Maryland to bring Prigg's appeal to the Supreme Court.

The Massachusetts-born justice and Harvard Law School professor Joseph Story wrote the majority opinion in *Prigg v. Pennsylvania*, 41 U.S. (16 Pet.) 539 (1842). He considered two questions:

(1) Was the Fugitive Slave Act constitutional?

(2) If so, did the act or the Fugitive Slave Clause itself preempt Pennsylvania's antikidnapping law?

Story's opinion sided with Prigg.

■ MR. JUSTICE STORY delivered the opinion of the Court.[1]

1. The question arising in the case, as to the constitutionality of the statute of Pennsylvania, has been most elaborately argued at the bar. The counsel for the plaintiff in error have contended that the statute of Pennsylvania is unconstitutional; first, because Congress has the exclusive power of legislation upon the subject-matter under the Constitution of the United States, and under the act of the 12th of February, 1793, ch. 51, (7), which was passed in pursuance thereof; secondly, that if this power is not exclusive in Congress, still the concurrent power of the state legislatures is suspended by the actual exercise of the power by Congress; and thirdly, that if not suspended, still the statute of Pennsylvania, in all its provisions applicable to this case, is in direct collision with the act of Congress, and therefore is unconstitutional and void. The counsel for Pennsylvania maintain the negative of all these points.

Few questions which have ever come before this Court involve more delicate and important considerations; and few upon which the public at large may be presumed to feel a more profound and pervading interest. We have accordingly given them our most deliberate examination. . . .

---

1 **As You Read, Consider:** A federal law like the Fugitive Slave Act can preempt a state law only if Congress had the power to enact the federal law. But unlike several other clauses in Article IV, the Fugitive Slave Clause contains no grant of power to Congress. The clause merely declares that fugitives from slavery "shall be delivered up." What, then, gives Congress the power to enforce the clause's terms? How does Justice Joseph Story's answer to this question compare to the structurally similar opinion of *McCulloch v. Maryland*?

There are two clauses in the Constitution upon the subject of fugitives, which stand in juxtaposition with each other, and have been thought mutually to illustrate each other. They are both contained in the second section of the fourth article, and are in the following words:

> A person charged in any state with treason, felony, or other crime, who shall flee from justice, and be found in another state, shall, on demand of the executive authority of the state from which he fled, be delivered up, to be removed to the state having jurisdiction of the crime.[2]
>
> No person held to service or labour in one state under the laws thereof, escaping into another, shall in consequence of any law or regulation therein, be discharged from such service or labour; but shall be delivered up, on claim of the party to whom such service or labour may be due.

The last clause is that, the true interpretation whereof is directly in judgment before us. Historically, it is well known, that the object of this clause was to secure to the citizens of the slaveholding states the complete right and title of ownership in their slaves, as property, in every state in the Union into which they might escape from the state where they were held in servitude. The full recognition of this right and title was indispensable to the security of this species of property in all the slaveholding states; and, indeed, was so vital to the preservation of their domestic interests and institutions, that it cannot be doubted that it constituted a fundamental article, without the adoption of which the Union could not have been formed.[3] Its true design was to guard against the doctrines and principles prevalent in the non-slaveholding states, by preventing them from intermeddling with, or obstructing, or abolishing the rights of the owners of slaves.

By the general law of nations, no nation is bound to recognise the state of slavery, as to foreign slaves found within its territorial dominions, when it is in opposition to its own policy and institutions, in favour of the subjects of other nations where slavery is recognised. If it does it, it is as a matter of comity, and not as a matter of international right. The state of slavery is deemed to be a mere municipal regulation, founded upon and limited to the range of the territorial laws. This was fully recognised in *Somerset's Case*, which was decided before the American revolution.[4] It is manifest from this consideration, that if the Constitution had not contained this clause, every non-slaveholding state in the Union would have been at liberty to have declared free all runaway slaves coming within its limits, and to have given them entire immunity and protection against the claims of their masters; a course which would have created the most bitter animosities, and engendered perpetual strife between the different states. The clause was, therefore, of the last importance to the safety and security of the southern states; and could not have been surrendered by them without endangering their whole property in slaves. The clause was accordingly adopted into the Constitution by the unanimous consent of the framers of it; a proof at once of its intrinsic and practical necessity.

---

2 **Note:** The first clause is the Extradition Clause, which applies to all fugitives. The second clause is the Fugitive Slave Clause.

3 **Question:** Story here writes that "it cannot be doubted" that "the Union could not have been formed" absent the Fugitive Slave Clause. But the clause was introduced toward the end of the Constitutional Convention and prompted little debate. Story later credits this lack of debate as "proof at once of its intrinsic and practical necessity." Why is this mythologizing of the clause's importance necessary to Story's interpretation?

4 **Note:** *Somerset v. Stewart*, [1772] Eng. Rep. 499 (KB), was a landmark British decision holding that slavery could not exist in the United Kingdom unless Parliament passed a statute legalizing it there. The court declared that slavery was "so odious, that nothing can be suffered to support it, but positive law." *Somerset*, [1772] Eng. Rep. at 510.

How, then, are we to interpret the language of the clause? The true answer is, in such a manner, as, consistently with the words, shall fully and completely effectuate the whole objects of it. If by one mode of interpretation the right must become shadowy and unsubstantial, and without any remedial power adequate to the end; and by another mode it will attain its just end and secure its manifest purpose; it would seem, upon principles of reasoning, absolutely irresistible, that the latter ought to prevail: No Court of justice can be authorized so to construe any clause of the Constitution as to defeat its obvious ends, when another construction, equally accordant with the words and sense thereof, will enforce and protect them.

The clause manifestly contemplates the existence of a positive, unqualified right on the part of the owner of the slave, which no state law or regulation can in any way qualify, regulate, control, or restrain. The slave is not to be discharged from service or labour, in consequence of any state law or regulation. . . .

[T]he owner must, therefore, have the right to seize and repossess the slave, which the local laws of his own state confer upon him as property; and we all know that this right of seizure and recaption is universally acknowledged in all the slaveholding states. . . . Upon this ground we have not the slightest hesitation in holding, that, under and in virtue of the Constitution, the owner of a slave is clothed with entire authority, in every state in the Union, to seize and recapture his slave, whenever he can do it without any breach of the peace, or any illegal violence. In this sense, and to this extent this clause of the Constitution may properly be said to execute itself; and to require no aid from legislation, state or national.

But the clause of the Constitution does not stop here; nor indeed, consistently with its professed objects, could it do so.[5] Many cases must arise in which, if the remedy of the owner were confined to the mere right of seizure and recaption, he would be utterly without any adequate redress. He may not be able to lay his hands upon the slave. He may not be able to enforce his rights against persons who either secrete or conceal, or withhold the slave. He may be restricted by local legislation as to the mode of proofs of his ownership; as to the Courts in which he shall sue, and as to the actions which he may bring; or the process he may use to compel the delivery of the slave. Nay, the local legislation may be utterly inadequate to furnish the appropriate redress, by authorizing no process in rem, or no specific mode of repossessing the slave, leaving the owner, at best, not that right which the Constitution designed to secure—a specific delivery and repossession of the slave, but a mere remedy in damages; and that perhaps against persons utterly insolvent or worthless. . . .

If, therefore, the clause of the Constitution had stopped at the mere recognition of the right, without providing or contemplating any means by which it might be established and enforced in cases where it did not execute itself, it is plain that it would have, in a great variety of cases, a delusive and empty annunciation. If it did not contemplate any action either through state or national legislation, as auxiliaries to its more perfect enforcement in the form of remedy, or of protection, then, as there would be no duty on either to aid the right, it would be left to the mere comity of the states to act as they should please; and would depend for its security upon the changing course of public opinion, the mutations of public policy, and the general adaptations of remedies for purposes strictly according to the lex fori.

---

[5] **Questions:** Over the next few paragraphs, Story is making the argument that the Fugitive Slave Clause would be "utterly inadequate" if it didn't authorize Congress to supplement its terms by appropriate legislation. Do you find his argument persuasive? Why doesn't this clause appear in Article I then?

And this leads us to the consideration of the other part of the clause, which implies at once a guaranty and duty. It says, "But he (the slave) shall be delivered up on claim of the party to whom such service or labour may be due." Now, we think it exceedingly difficult, if not impracticable, to read this language and not to feel that it contemplated some farther remedial redress than that which might be administered at the hands of the owner himself. A claim is to be made. What is a claim? It is, in a just juridical sense, a demand of some matter as of right made by one person upon another, to do or to forbear to do some act or thing as a matter of duty. . . . The slave is to be delivered up on the claim. By whom to be delivered up? In what mode to be delivered up? How, if a refusal takes place, is the right of delivery to be enforced? Upon what proofs? What shall be the evidence of a rightful recaption or delivery? When and under what circumstances shall the possession of the owner, after it is obtained, be conclusive of his right, so as to preclude any further inquiry or examination into it by local tribunals or otherwise, while the slave, in possession of the owner, is in transitu to the state from which he fled?

These, and many other questions, will readily occur upon the slightest attention to the clause; and it is obvious that they can receive but one satisfactory answer. They require the aid of legislation to protect the right, to enforce the delivery, and to secure the subsequent possession of the slave. If, indeed, the Constitution guarantees the right, and if it requires the delivery upon the claim of the owner, (as cannot well be doubted,) the natural inference certainly is, that the national government is clothed with the appropriate authority and functions to enforce it. The fundamental principle applicable to all cases of this sort, would seem to be, that where the end is required, the means are given; and where the duty is enjoined, the ability to perform it is contemplated to exist on the part of the functionaries to whom it is entrusted.[6] The clause is found in the national Constitution, and not in that of any state. It does not point out any state functionaries, or any state action to carry its provisions into effect. The states cannot, therefore, be compelled to enforce them; and it might well be deemed an unconstitutional exercise of the power of interpretation, to insist that the states are bound to provide means to carry into effect the duties of the national government, nowhere delegated or intrusted to them by the Constitution. On the contrary, the natural, if not the necessary conclusion is, that the national government, in the absence of all positive provisions to the contrary, is bound, through its own proper departments, legislative, judicial, or executive, as the case may require, to carry into effect all the rights and duties imposed upon it by the Constitution. The remark of Mr. Madison, in the Federalist, (No. 43,) would seem in such cases to apply with peculiar force. "A right (says he) implies a remedy; and where else would the remedy be deposited, than where it is deposited by the Constitution?" meaning, as the context shows, in the government of the United States. . . .

Congress has taken this very view of the power and duty of the national government. As early as the year 1791, the attention of Congress was drawn to it, . . . in consequence of some practical difficulties arising under the other clause, respecting fugitives from justice escaping into other states. The result of their deliberations, was the passage of the act of the 12th of February, 1793, ch. 51. . . .

In a general sense, this act may be truly said to cover the whole ground of the Constitution, both as to fugitives from justice, and fugitive slaves; that is, it covers both the subjects, in its enactments. . . . If this be so, then it would seem, upon just principles of construction, that the legislation of Congress, if constitutional, must supersede all state legislation upon the same subject; and by necessary implication

---

6 **Question:** "[W]here the end is required, the means are given." Where does this language come from?

prohibit it. For if Congress have a constitutional power to regulate a particular subject, and they do actually regulate it in a given manner, and in a certain form, it cannot be that the state legislatures have a right to interfere; and, as it were, by way of complement to the legislation of Congress, to prescribe additional regulations, and what they may deem auxiliary provisions for the same purpose. In such a case, the legislation of Congress, in what it does prescribe, manifestly indicates that it does not intend that there shall be any farther legislation to act upon the subject-matter. Its silence as to what it does not do, is as expressive of what its intention is as the direct provisions made by it. . . .

But it has been argued, that the act of Congress is unconstitutional, because it does not fall within the scope of any of the enumerated powers of legislation confided to that body; and therefore it is void. Stripped of its artificial and technical structure, the argument comes to this, that although rights are exclusively secured by, or duties are exclusively imposed upon the national government, yet, unless the power to enforce these rights, or to execute these duties can be found among the express powers of legislation enumerated in the Constitution, they remain without any means of giving them effect by any act of Congress; and they must operate solely *proprio vigore*, however defective may be their operation; nay, even although, in a practical sense, they may become a nullity from the want of a proper remedy to enforce them, or to provide against their violation. If this be the true interpretation of the Constitution, it must, in a great measure, fail to attain many of its avowed and positive objects as a security of rights, and a recognition of duties. Such a limited construction of the Constitution has never yet been adopted as correct, either in theory or practice. No one has ever supposed that Congress could, constitutionally, by its legislation, exercise powers, or enact laws beyond the powers delegated to it by the Constitution; but it has, on various occasions, exercised powers which were necessary and proper as means to carry into effect rights expressly given, and duties expressly enjoined thereby. The end being required, it has been deemed a just and necessary implication, that the means to accomplish it are given also; or, in other words, that the power flows as a necessary means to accomplish the end.[7]

Thus, for example, although the Constitution has declared that representatives shall be apportioned among the states according to their respective federal numbers; and, for this purpose, it has expressly authorized Congress, by law, to provide for an enumeration of the population every ten years; yet the power to apportion representatives after this enumeration is made, is nowhere found among the express powers given to Congress, but it has always been acted upon as irresistibly flowing from the duty positively enjoined by the Constitution. Treaties made between the United States and foreign powers, often contain special provisions, which do not execute themselves, but require the interposition of Congress to carry them into effect, and Congress has constantly, in such cases, legislated on the subject; yet, although the power is given to the executive, with the consent of the senate, to make treaties, the power is nowhere in positive terms conferred upon Congress to make laws to carry the stipulations of treaties into effect. It has been supposed to result from the duty of the national government to fulfil all the obligations of treaties. . . .

These cases are put merely by way of illustration, to show that the rule of interpretation, insisted upon at the argument, is quite too narrow to provide for the ordinary exigencies of the national government, in cases where rights are intended to be absolutely secured, and duties are positively enjoined by the Constitution.

---

7 **Question:** The Necessary and Proper Clause empowers Congress to "make all Laws which shall be necessary and proper for carrying into Execution . . . [all] Powers vested by this Constitution *in the Government of the United States*." U.S. Const. art. I, § 8, cl. 18 (emphasis added). Does the Fugitive Slave Clause vest powers in the federal government?

The very act of 1793, now under consideration, affords the most conclusive proof that Congress has acted upon a very different rule of interpretation, and has supposed that the right as well as the duty of legislation on the subject of fugitives from justice, and fugitive slaves was within the scope of the constitutional authority conferred on the national legislature. . . .

We hold the act to be clearly constitutional in all its leading provisions, and, indeed, with the exception of that part which confers authority upon state magistrates, to be free from reasonable doubt and difficulty upon the grounds already stated.[8] As to the authority so conferred upon state magistrates, while a difference of opinion has existed, and may exist still on the point, in different states, whether state magistrates are bound to act under it; none is entertained by this Court that state magistrates may, if they choose, exercise that authority, unless prohibited by state legislation. . . .

anticommandeering

We entertain no doubt whatsoever, that the states, in virtue of their general police power, possess full jurisdiction to arrest and restrain runaway slaves, and remove them from their borders, and otherwise to secure themselves against their depredations and evil example, as they certainly may do in cases of idlers, vagabonds, and paupers. The rights of the owners of fugitive slaves are in no just sense interfered with, or regulated by such a course; and in many cases, the operations of this police power, although designed essentially for other purposes, for the protection, safety, and peace of the state, may essentially promote and aid the interests of the owners. But such regulations can never be permitted to interfere with or to obstruct the just rights of the owner to reclaim his slave, derived from the Constitution of the United States; or with the remedies prescribed by Congress to aid and enforce the same.

states can supplement so not field preempted? conflict preemption?

Upon these grounds, we are of opinion that the act of Pennsylvania upon which this indictment is founded, is unconstitutional and void. . . .

NOTE: AFTERMATH OF *PRIGG*

Prigg was a disappointing decision for northern antislavery advocates. But these advocates quickly grasped the significance of its caveat that Congress likely did not have the authority to *require* state officials to enforce the Fugitive Slave Act—particularly when such officials were "prohibited by state legislation" from cooperating. *Prigg*, 41 U.S. (16 Pet.) at 622. Applying this caveat, Massachusetts led several states in passing a type of "personal liberty law" that prohibited state officials from making state facilities available for the enforcement of the Fugitive Slave Act. *See* 1843 Mass. Acts 33. Because there were so few federal judges in the 1840s, these laws effectively suspended the operation of the Fugitive Slave Act.

Congress responded to this northern resistance by passing the Fugitive Slave Act of 1850, ch. 60, 9 Stat. 462. This new act authorized the appointment of a "commissioner" for each Article I court in each state—an official empowered to issue arrest warrants, to order private citizens to execute the warrants, and to sit as a court for determining whether an arrested person was free or a fugitive from slavery. The act provided that

---

8 **Question:** In this paragraph, Story refers to a section of the Fugitive Slave Act that requires state magistrates to enforce its terms. He suggests that the compulsion of state officers may be unconstitutional—the first illustration of the anticommandeering doctrine.

Given the tenor of the rest of this opinion, however, why wouldn't Congress have the implied power to compel state officers to enforce the Fugitive Slave Clause?

each commissioner would be paid $10 for each person he determined was a fugitive and $5 for each person he determined was free. *Id.* at 463–64. All in all, the act dramatically expanded the federal government's role in enforcing the Fugitive Slave Clause. At one point in 1854, President Franklin Pierce even dispatched 1,500 soldiers to Boston to escort a single fugitive, Anthony Burns, to a ship that would return Burns to slavery. *See* Delblanco, *supra*, at 308–09.

Cases in the years following were a dizzying flip-flop between embracing and discarding the anticommandeering doctrine, which holds that Article I, Section 8, does not permit Congress to direct state legislatures or state officers to enforce federal law (see section 12.1).

Discarding the doctrine. When cases involving the 1793 and 1850 versions of the Fugitive Slave Act reached the Supreme Court, the Court continued to uphold the laws as necessary and proper methods of enforcing the Fugitive Slave Clause. *See Moore v. Illinois*, 55 U.S. (14 How.) 13 (1853) (upholding the 1850 law as well as a state law that increased the penalty for harboring a fugitive from slavery); *Jones v. Van Zandt*, 46 U.S. (5 How.) 215 (1847) (upholding the conviction of an abolitionist who aided the escape of enslaved people from Kentucky to Ohio).

However, in 1854, the Supreme Court of Wisconsin ignored these holdings when it ordered federal officers to release a white man, Sherman Booth, whom they had arrested under the Fugitive Slave Act of 1850 for helping a black fugitive escape from their custody. *In re Booth*, 3 Wis. 1 (1854). The Wisconsin court decided for itself that the federal arrest was unconstitutional because the law exceeded Congress's power, violated the tenure and salary protections of Article III, and also violated the Due Process Clause of the Fifth Amendment (because of the conflict of interest posed by the fee system).

When the Supreme Court of the United States granted a writ of certiorari to review the Wisconsin decision, the Wisconsin court refused to cooperate. Nevertheless, in *Ableman v. Booth*, 62 U.S. 506, 526 (1859), the Supreme Court reversed the Wisconsin court's decision, holding that state courts have no power to disagree with federal courts about the constitutionality of federal law. The Court also applied the principle of *McCulloch v. Maryland*, 17 U.S. (4 Wheat.) 316 (1819), to hold that state courts lack the power to interfere with federal officers' enforcement of a valid federal law.

Embracing the doctrine. Despite *Ableman*, the Supreme Court continued to maintain its position from *Prigg* that northern states weren't *required* to enforce the Fugitive Slave Act.

In *Kentucky v. Dennison*, 65 U.S. (24 How.) 66 (1861), a few months before the Civil War began, the Court considered for the first time the constitutionality of the extradition provisions of the Fugitive Slave Act of 1793. The first two provisions of the act enforced the Extradition Clause by requiring state governors to "deliver up" any fugitives from justice on the request of another state. But William Dennison, the governor of Ohio, ignored a request by Kentucky's governor to extradite a free black person who had been indicted for "the crime of assisting a slave to escape." *Dennison*, 65 U.S. (24 How.) at 68.

The Supreme Court held that Congress could not "command and coerce obedience" by Ohio's governor because "the Federal Government, under the Constitution, has no power to impose on a State officer, as such, any duty whatever, and compel him to perform it." *Id.* at 107. The Court explained that even though the Extradition Clause imposed a duty on all governors to comply with other states' extradition requests, "if the Governor of Ohio refuses to discharge this duty, there is no power delegated to the General Government, either through the Judicial Department or any other department, to use any coercive means to compel him." *Id.* at 109–110.

Discarding the doctrine again. Over a century later, the Supreme Court reconsidered this language and overruled *Dennison*, holding that Congress *did* have the power to compel a state officer to enforce the Extradition Clause. *See Puerto Rico v. Branstad*, 483 U.S. 219 (1987). Citing the "mandatory language" of the Extradition Clause and the fraught circumstances in which *Dennison* was decided, the Court dismissed *Dennison* "as the product of another time." *Branstad*, 483 U.S. at 230.

Embracing the doctrine again. But only a few years later, the Supreme Court decided *New York v. United States*, 505 U.S. 144 (1992), and *Printz v. United States*, 521 U.S. 898 (1997), which resurrected the anticommandeering principle underlying *Prigg* and *Dennison*. Neither case overruled *Branstad*, however. Instead, the Court sought to distinguish *Branstad*—first as a case holding that federal *courts* have the power to compel state officers to enforce the Constitution or federal law, *New York*, 505 U.S. at 179, and then as a case merely allowing the "direct implementation . . . of the Extradition Clause of the Constitution itself," *Printz*, 521 U.S. at 909.

18.4 THE TERRITORY CLAUSE

The Fugitive Slave Clause was only one of the clauses at the center of the antebellum dispute that precipitated the Civil War. Another was the Territory Clause—Article IV, Section 3, Clause 2—which gives Congress the "[p]ower to dispose of and make all needful Rules and Regulations respecting the Territory or other Property belonging to the United States." Because Article IV also provides that "[n]ew States may be admitted by the Congress into this Union"—and because each state receives two senators—every decision regarding whether to allow or prohibit slavery in a territory affected the political power of slavery's advocates in the Senate. As a consequence, many of the most bitter congressional debates in the country's first century concerned the organization of new territories.

Northwest Ordinance and abolition of slavery in territories

The United States first acquired federal territory in the 1780s when the Confederation Congress asked states to cede their claims to land west of the Appalachian Mountains. Several states accompanied these cessions with a condition that Congress had to administer the land for the eventual admission of new states. Thus, in 1787, the Confederation Congress passed the Northwest Ordinance, which established a "temporary government" for this ceded territory north of the Ohio River. 32 *Journals of the Continental Congress* 334–43 (Roscoe R. Hill ed., 1936). This ordinance set three important precedents for how territorial governments would be organized in the future. First, it authorized the appointment of a territorial governor and the establishment of an elected territorial legislature. *Id.* at 335–38. Second, it outlined the process by which sections of the territory could be admitted into the Union as new states "on an equal footing with the original States." *Id.* at 339. Third, and most importantly, it permanently abolished slavery in the territory, declaring that "[t]here shall be neither Slavery nor involuntary Servitude in the said territory otherwise than in punishment of crimes." *Id.* at 343.

When the Confederation Congress passed the Northwest Ordinance in 1787, the Constitutional Convention was meeting in Philadelphia. The convention likely adopted the Territory Clause to permit the new Congress to enact laws similar to the Northwest Ordinance—and the first Congress did just that in 1789, reenacting the Northwest Ordinance. *See* Act of Aug. 7, 1789, ch. 8, 1 Stat. 50. This reenactment established a lasting interpretation that the Territory Clause permitted Congress to abolish slavery in U.S. territory—even if Congress lacked the power to abolish slavery in the states.

Confirming this interpretation of the Territory Clause, when North Carolina and Georgia later ceded their own western territories to Congress, they did so on the condition that "no regulation made or to be made, by Congress, shall tend to emancipate slaves." 4 *Territorial Papers of the United States* 3, 7 (Clarence Carter ed., 1936). Congress complied with this condition when it organized the Southwest Territory south of the Ohio River. *See* Act of May 26, 1790, ch. 14, 1 Stat. 123. As a result, the Ohio River became the de facto dividing line that separated free territory from slave territory.

Louisiana Territory and slavery

The admission of states from northern and southern territories was relatively uncontroversial through 1803, when France offered to sell to the United States its massive Louisiana Territory west of the Mississippi River. At first, President Thomas Jefferson balked on the ground that the Territory Clause empowered Congress to *dispose* of territory, but nothing authorized Congress to *acquire* territory from a foreign power. *See* Letter from Thomas Jefferson to John Dickinson (Aug. 9, 1803), *in* 41 *The Papers of Thomas Jefferson* 169 (Barbara B. Oberg ed., 2014). But when Congress failed to act on a proposed constitutional amendment to expressly give it this power, Jefferson agreed to purchase the territory as an exercise of the treaty power. The purchase doubled the United States' land area—and also forced Congress to consider whether to extend slavery further west.

The question of slavery's expansion reached a crisis point in 1819 when the Senate was divided between eleven free states and eleven slave states. At the time, the Louisiana Territory had been subdivided into several smaller territories, including the Missouri Territory northwest of the Ohio River. When the House of Representatives voted to admit the Missouri Territory as a state, a representative from New York, James Tallmadge Jr., proposed an amendment to permanently prohibit the introduction of slavery into the new state. *See* Don E. Fehrenbacher, *Slavery, Law, and Politics* 49 (1981). The House also debated a bill to organize a new territory southwest of the Ohio River—the Arkansas Territory—in which slavery would also be abolished. *Id.* at 49–50. Southern members of Congress passionately opposed both bills. Most argued that the Territory Clause gave Congress no power to permanently abolish slavery in a new state, while some made the more radical argument that Congress also had no power to abolish slavery in the territories. *See id.* at 50–53.

Missouri Compromise of 1820

Congress resolved the standoff over the admission of Missouri by adopting what became known as the Missouri Compromise of 1820. The compromise had three parts. First, Congress enabled the new state of Maine to be admitted from territory ceded by Massachusetts. Act of Mar. 3, 1820, ch. 19, 3 Stat. 544. Second, Congress enabled the new state of Missouri to be admitted without any restriction on whether the state could permit slavery. Act of Mar. 6, 1820, ch. 22, 3 Stat. 545. Third, the act admitting Missouri declared that "slavery and involuntary servitude, otherwise than in the punishment of crimes," would be "forever prohibited" in territories north of 36°, 30′—or the line of latitude extending from Missouri's southern border—except for Missouri. *Id.* at 548.

During the lengthy debate over the Missouri Compromise, several high-profile southerners, including James Madison and John C. Calhoun, contested the constitutionality of Congress's power to forever prohibit slavery in territories north of the Missouri Compromise line. Fehrenbacher, *supra*, at 52–54. Although the Supreme Court did not immediately weigh in, Chief Justice John Marshall delivered an opinion in an unrelated case that strongly suggested that the Missouri Compromise was constitutional. The case, *American Insurance Co. v. Canter*, 26 U.S. 511 (1828), involved Congress's power to create Article I courts in the Florida Territory. Writing for the Court, Marshall emphatically declared that Congress had the "unquestioned" power to govern the territories as it saw fit. *Canter*, 26 U.S. at 542–43. He wrote:

> Perhaps the power of governing a territory belonging to the United States, which has not, by becoming a state, acquired the

> means of self-government, may result necessarily from the facts, that it is not within the jurisdiction of any particular state, and is within the power and jurisdiction of the United States.

Id. at 542. Alternatively, "[t]he right to govern may be the inevitable consequence of the right to acquire territory." *Id.* at 543. Either way, when Congress legislated for a territory, it wasn't subject to ordinary constitutional restrictions. Instead, Marshall wrote, "Congress exercises the combined powers of the general, and of a state government." *Id.* at 546.

The Missouri Compromise lasted for nearly thirty years. Territories north of the line, including Iowa, were admitted as free states. Territories south of the line, including Arkansas, were admitted as slave states. *See* Fehrenbacher, *supra*, at 55. And in 1845, when Congress annexed the slaveholding Republic of Texas—a renegade province of Mexico that declared independence after Mexico abolished slavery—Congress reaffirmed that slavery would be "prohibited" in any states carved out of Texas north of the Missouri Compromise line. Act of Mar. 1, 1845, no. 8, 5 Stat. 797, 798. Nevertheless, proponents of slavery like John C. Calhoun continued to protest Congress's power to abolish slavery anywhere. Invoking the Fifth Amendment's protection of life, liberty, and property, Calhoun asked, "Are not slaves property and if so, how can Congress any more take away property of a master in his slave . . . than it could his life and liberty? They stand on the same ground." Robert Elder, *Calhoun* 238 (2021).

Compromise of 1850

Congress's annexation of Texas marked the beginning of the end of the Missouri Compromise. The annexation precipitated the Mexican-American War, in which the United States seized vast new territories from present-day Colorado to the Pacific Ocean. *See* Fehrenbacher, *supra*, at 59–61. In 1846, David Wilmot of Pennsylvania introduced a proviso to an appropriation bill that would prohibit the introduction of slavery into all of this new territory. *Id.* at 62–63. Southerners, led by Calhoun, responded that Congress had no power to prevent the citizens of any states from "emigrating with their property" into the territories. *Id.* The Wilmot proviso, which was universally supported by a bipartisan bloc of northern politicians and universally condemned by a bipartisan bloc of southern politicians, was defeated. *Id.* at 63–64. This sectional conflict transformed the party system and signaled that the expansion of slavery into the territories had become the defining issue of American politics. *See* David M. Potter, *The Impending Crisis* 18–23 (2011).

Congress temporarily resolved the sectional crisis with the Compromise of 1850. To appease southerners, Congress enacted the second Fugitive Slave Act of 1850, ch. 60, 9 Stat. 462. To appease northerners, Congress admitted California as a free state, giving the

North a one-state majority in the Senate. *See* Act of Sept. 9, 1850, ch. 50, 9 Stat. 452.

Kansas-Nebraska Act of 1854

Southern senators nevertheless feared that if the Missouri Compromise line remained static, free states would soon overwhelm slave states. When an Illinois senator, Stephen A. Douglas, proposed a bill to facilitate a transcontinental railroad through northern territory, southerners supported his proposal on the condition that the Missouri Compromise be repealed. *See* Potter, *supra*, at 167–71.

Debate over the measure culminated in the Kansas-Nebraska Act of 1854, ch. 59, 10 Stat. 277, which organized the Kansas Territory and Nebraska Territory out of parts of the former Louisiana Territory. Although these territories were north of the Missouri Compromise line, the new law allowed the white residents of these territories to decide for themselves whether or not to legalize slavery. Kansas-Nebraska Act, 10 Stat. at 277. Americans from the North and South soon swarmed into the Kansas Territory with the goal of being the first group to send a proposed free or slave constitution to Congress. As John Brown and other New Englanders literally battled southerners from neighboring Missouri, journalists described the territory as "Bleeding Kansas." Potter, *supra*, at 212–24.

18.4.1

Dred Scott v. Sandford

60 U.S. 393 (1857)

As the United States steadily progressed toward civil war, President James Buchanan declared in 1857 that the issue of slavery in the territories was "a judicial question which legitimately belongs to the Supreme Court of the United States, before whom it is now pending, and will, it is understood, be speedily and finally settled." Potter, *supra*, at 287. Buchanan was alluding to the case of Dred and Harriet Scott—a black married couple who had sued for their family's freedom. *See* Amanda Frost, *You Are Not American* 14–16 (2021).

During the 1830s, Dred Scott was enslaved by an army surgeon from Missouri who took him to Illinois and the Wisconsin Territory, in present-day Minnesota. While living in the Wisconsin Territory, Scott met and married another enslaved person named Harriet Robinson. After the wedding, the couple continued to be enslaved by Dred Scott's owner despite Congress's declaration in the Missouri Compromise that slavery would be "forever prohibited" in northern territories. When the Scotts and their children returned to Missouri, they sued for their family's freedom, arguing that they had been freed by living in free territory.

Missouri state courts permitted similar suits for freedom, which were victorious often enough that the Scotts had reason to be optimistic about their chance of success. *See* Fehrenbacher, *supra*, at 129–30. But after a trial court freed the Scotts, the Missouri Supreme Court reversed. The court announced that northern states had become so opposed to slavery that Missouri had no choice but to retaliate by refusing to respect the emancipatory effect of northern laws. *Id.* at 137–38.

Rather than appeal this decision to the Supreme Court, the Scotts' lawyers began a new suit on their behalf in federal court. *Id.* at 140. At the time, Congress limited the jurisdiction of federal courts only to controversies "between Citizens of different States," as Article III of the Constitution allowed. But shortly before the Missouri-bound Scotts initiated their suit, their ownership was transferred to a citizen of New York. *Id.* at 140–43. The trial court therefore accepted jurisdiction as a case involving citizens of Missouri and a citizen of New York. But the court rejected the Scotts' argument that Congress had permanently freed them with the Missouri Compromise; it concluded instead that Missouri had reenslaved the Scotts when they returned to the state. *Id.* at 143–47.

The Scotts then appealed to the Supreme Court, led at the time by Chief Justice Roger Taney of Maryland. Of the Court's nine justices, seven had been appointed by slave-owning presidents, and five belonged to slave-owning families. Frost, *supra*, at 20.

Taney and a majority of the Court hoped (in vain, as it turned out) to use the Scotts' case to permanently resolve the sectional conflict that had gripped the United States since 1820. Fehrenbacher, *supra*, at 165–68. Taney's opinion in *Dred Scott v. Sandford*, 60 U.S. 393 (1857), considered two questions:

(1) Can allegedly free black people be "Citizens" whom Article III permitted to sue in federal court?

(2) In the alternative, assuming that only free people can be "Citizens," did the Missouri Compromise free the Scotts?

The Court answered no to both questions.

■ MR. CHIEF JUSTICE TANEY delivered the opinion of the Court.[9]

[I. Are the Scotts "Citizens" for purposes of Article III?]

The question is simply this: Can a negro, whose ancestors were imported into this country, and sold as slaves, become a member of the political community formed and brought into existence by the Constitution of the United States, and as such become entitled to all the rights, and privileges, and immunities, guarantied by that instrument to the citizen? One of which rights is the privilege of suing in a court of the United States in the cases specified in the Constitution. . . .

We think they [can] not, and that they are not included, and were not intended to be included, under the word "citizens" in the Constitution, and can therefore claim none of the rights and privileges which that instrument provides for and secures to citizens of the United States. On the contrary, they were at that time considered as a

[9] **As You Read, Consider:** Chief Justice Roger Taney answers both the citizenship question and the territorial question with reference to what it would mean if the Scotts were citizens who could be freed in the territories by Congress. What, precisely, is Taney worried about?

subordinate and inferior class of beings, who had been subjugated by the dominant race, and, whether emancipated or not, yet remained subject to their authority, and had no rights or privileges but such as those who held the power and the Government might choose to grant them.

It is not the province of the court to decide upon the justice or injustice, the policy or impolicy, of these laws. The decision of that question belonged to the political or law-making power; to those who formed the sovereignty and framed the Constitution. The duty of the court is, to interpret the instrument they have framed, with the best lights we can obtain on the subject, and to administer it as we find it, according to its true intent and meaning when it was adopted.

It becomes necessary, therefore, to determine who were citizens of the several States when the Constitution was adopted.[10] And in order to do this, we must recur to the Governments and institutions of the thirteen colonies, when they separated from Great Britain and formed new sovereignties, and took their places in the family of independent nations. We must inquire who, at that time, were recognised as the people or citizens of a State, whose rights and liberties had been outraged by the English Government. . . .

It is difficult at this day to realize the state of public opinion in relation to that unfortunate race, which prevailed in the civilized and enlightened portions of the world at the time of the Declaration of Independence, and when the Constitution of the United States was framed and adopted. But the public history of every European nation displays it in a manner too plain to be mistaken.

They had for more than a century before been regarded as beings of an inferior order, and altogether unfit to associate with the white race, either in social or political relations; and so far inferior, that they had no rights which the white man was bound to respect; and that the negro might justly and lawfully be reduced to slavery for his benefit.[11] He was bought and sold, and treated as an ordinary article of merchandise and traffic, whenever a profit could be made by it. This opinion was at that time fixed and universal in the civilized portion of the white race. It was regarded as an axiom in morals as well as in politics, which no one thought of disputing, or supposed to be open to dispute; and men in every grade and position in society daily and habitually acted upon it in their private pursuits, as well as in matters of public concern, without doubting for a moment the correctness of this opinion.

And in no nation was this opinion more firmly fixed or more uniformly acted upon than by the English Government and English people. They not only seized them on the coast of Africa, and sold them or held them in slavery for their own use; but they took them as ordinary articles of merchandise to every country where they could make a profit on them, and were far more extensively engaged in this commerce than any other nation in the world.

The opinion thus entertained and acted upon in England was naturally impressed upon the colonies they founded on this side of the Atlantic. And, accordingly, a negro of the African race was regarded by them as an article of property, and held, and bought and sold as such, in every one of the thirteen colonies which united in the Declaration of Independence, and afterwards formed the

---

10 **Question:** Taney analyzes the citizenship question by exclusively asking whether black people would have been considered citizens "when the Constitution was adopted." Should the answer to this empirical question predominate over other interpretive principles?

11 **Questions:** This paragraph contains the most notorious line of Taney's opinion: black people in the 1700s were considered "so far inferior, that they had no rights which the white man was bound to respect." What evidence does Taney rely on to support this historical claim? Is he wrong?

Constitution of the United States. The slaves were more or less numerous in the different colonies, as slave labor was found more or less profitable. But no one seems to have doubted the correctness of the prevailing opinion of the time.

The legislation of the different colonies furnishes positive and indisputable proof of this fact.

It would be tedious, in this opinion, to enumerate the various laws they passed upon this subject. It will be sufficient, as a sample of the legislation which then generally prevailed throughout the British colonies, to give the laws of two of them; one being still a large slaveholding State, and the other the first State in which slavery ceased to exist.

The province of Maryland, in 1717, (ch. 13, s. 5,) passed a law [prohibiting] "any free negro or mulatto [from intermarrying] with any white [person]. . . ."

The other colonial law to which we refer was passed by Massachusetts in 1705, (chap. 6.) It . . . provides, . . . "that none of her Majesty's English or Scottish subjects, nor of any other Christian nation, within this province, shall contract matrimony with any negro or mulatto; nor shall any person, duly authorized to solemnize marriage, presume to join any such in marriage, on pain of forfeiting the sum of fifty pounds. . . ."

We give both of these laws in the words used by the respective legislative bodies, because the language in which they are framed, as well as the provisions contained in them, show, too plainly to be misunderstood, the degraded condition of this unhappy race. They were still in force when the Revolution began, and are a faithful index to the state of feeling towards the class of persons of whom they speak, and of the position they occupied throughout the thirteen colonies, in the eyes and thoughts of the men who framed the Declaration of Independence and established the State Constitutions and Governments. They show that a perpetual and impassable barrier was intended to be erected between the white race and the one which they had reduced to slavery, and governed as subjects with absolute and despotic power, and which they then looked upon as so far below them in the scale of created beings, that intermarriages between white persons and negroes or mulattoes were regarded as unnatural and immoral, and punished as crimes, not only in the parties, but in the person who joined them in marriage. And no distinction in this respect was made between the free negro or mulatto and the slave, but this stigma, of the deepest degradation, was fixed upon the whole race. . . .

The language of the Declaration of Independence is equally conclusive: . . . [It says]: "We hold these truths to be self-evident: that all men are created equal; that they are endowed by their Creator with certain unalienable rights; that among them is life, liberty, and the pursuit of happiness; that to secure these rights, Governments are instituted, deriving their just powers from the consent of the governed."

The general words above quoted would seem to embrace the whole human family, and if they were used in a similar instrument at this day would be so understood. But it is too clear for dispute, that the enslaved African race were not intended to be included, and formed no part of the people who framed and adopted this declaration; for if the language, as understood in that day, would embrace them, the conduct of the distinguished men who framed the Declaration of Independence would have been utterly and flagrantly inconsistent with the principles they asserted; and instead of the sympathy of mankind, to which they so confidently appealed, they would have deserved and received universal rebuke and reprobation.[12]

---

12 **Question:** Taney here observes that if the authors of the Declaration of Independence had black people in mind when they wrote "all men are created equal," they would have been

Yet the men who framed this declaration were great men—high in literary acquirements—high in their sense of honor, and incapable of asserting principles inconsistent with those on which they were acting. They perfectly understood the meaning of the language they used, and how it would be understood by others; and they knew that it would not in any part of the civilized world be supposed to embrace the negro race, which, by common consent, had been excluded from civilized Governments and the family of nations, and doomed to slavery. They spoke and acted according to the then established doctrines and principles, and in the ordinary language of the day, and no one misunderstood them. The unhappy black race were separated from the white by indelible marks, and laws long before established, and were never thought of or spoken of except as property, and when the claims of the owner or the profit of the trader were supposed to need protection.

This state of public opinion had undergone no change when the Constitution was adopted, as is equally evident from its provisions and language. . . . [T]here are two clauses in the Constitution which point directly and specifically to the negro race as a separate class of persons, and show clearly that they were not regarded as a portion of the people or citizens of the Government then formed.

One of these clauses reserves to each of the thirteen States the right to import slaves until the year 1808. . . . And by the other provision the States pledge themselves to each other to maintain the right of property of the master, by delivering up to him any slave who may have escaped from his service. . . .[13]

[T]hese two provisions show, conclusively, that neither the description of persons therein referred to, nor their descendants, were embraced in any of the other provisions of the Constitution; for certainly these two clauses were not intended to confer on them or their posterity the blessings of liberty, or any of the personal rights so carefully provided for the citizen. . . .

It is [also] obvious that [members of the negro race] were not even in the minds of the framers of the Constitution when they were conferring special rights and privileges upon the citizens of a State in every other part of the Union. . . .[14] Indeed, when we look to the condition of this race in the several States at the time, it is impossible to believe that these rights and privileges were intended to be extended to them. . . . In addition to those [laws] already referred to, it is sufficient to say, . . . that in no part of the country except Maine, did the African race, in point of fact, participate equally with the whites in the exercise of civil and political rights. . . .

The legislation of the States therefore shows, in a manner not to be mistaken, the inferior and subject condition of that race at the time the Constitution was adopted, and long afterwards, throughout the thirteen States by which that instrument was framed; and it is hardly consistent with the respect due to these States, to suppose that they regarded at that time, as fellow-citizens and members of the sovereignty, a class of beings whom they had thus stigmatized. . . .

More especially, it cannot be believed that the large slaveholding States regarded them as included in the word citizens, or would have consented to a Constitution which might compel them to receive them in that character from another

---

flagrant hypocrites. He resolves this hypocrisy by concluding that they must not have intended to include black people among "We the People." Is he wrong?

[13] **Note:** Taney is describing the Slave Trade Clause of Article I and the Fugitive Slave Clause of Article IV.

[14] **Question:** Taney here is alluding to the Privileges and Immunities Clause of Article IV, which declares, "The Citizens of each State shall be entitled to all Privileges and Immunities of Citizens in the several States." Why does he think that this clause provides convincing evidence that the framers of the Constitution could not have intended for black people to be citizens? cause then they'd be free

State. For if they were so received, and entitled to the privileges and immunities of citizens, it would exempt them from the operation of the special laws and from the police regulations which they considered to be necessary for their own safety. It would give to persons of the negro race, who were recognised as citizens in any one State of the Union, the right to enter every other State whenever they pleased, singly or in companies, without pass or passport, and without obstruction, to sojourn there as long as they pleased, to go where they pleased at every hour of the day or night without molestation . . .; and it would give them the full liberty of speech in public and in private upon all subjects upon which its own citizens might speak; to hold public meetings upon political affairs, and to keep and carry arms wherever they went. And all of this would be done in the face of the subject race of the same color, both free and slaves, and inevitably producing discontent and insubordination among them, and endangering the peace and safety of the State. . . .

[The Privileges and Immunities Clause declares that if a person] ranks as a citizen in the State to which he belongs, within the meaning of the Constitution of the United States, then, whenever he goes into another State, the Constitution clothes him, as to the rights of person, with all the privileges and immunities which belong to citizens of the State. . . . [T]hese rights are of a character and would lead to consequences which make it absolutely certain that the African race were not included under the name of citizens of a State, and were not in the contemplation of the framers of the Constitution when these privileges and immunities were provided for the protection of the citizen in other States. . . .

We have the language of the Declaration of Independence and of the Articles of Confederation, in addition to the plain words of the Constitution itself; we have the legislation of the different States, before, about the time, and since, the Constitution was adopted; we have the legislation of Congress, from the time of its adoption to a recent period . . ., all concurring together, and leading to the same result. And if anything in relation to the construction of the Constitution can be regarded as settled, it is that which we now give to the word "citizen" and the word "people."

[U]pon a full and careful consideration of the subject, the court is of opinion, that . . . Dred Scott was not a citizen of Missouri within the meaning of the Constitution of the United States, and not entitled as such to sue in its courts; and, consequently, that the Circuit Court had no jurisdiction of the case, and that the judgment on the plea in abatement is erroneous. . . .[15]

[II. Were the Scotts freed by the Missouri Compromise?]

We are aware that doubts are entertained by some of the members of the court, whether the plea in abatement is legally before the court upon this writ of error. . . . [Y]et the question as to the jurisdiction of the Circuit Court is [also] presented on the [merits]; for [Scott] admits that he and his wife were born slaves, but endeavors to make out his title to freedom and citizenship by showing that they were taken by their owner to certain places, hereinafter mentioned, where slavery could not by law

[15] **Note:** Taney completes the first half of *Dred Scott v. Sandford* by concluding that no black person, enslaved or free, can be a citizen under the U.S. Constitution. The case is therefore over: the Court lacks jurisdiction under Article III.

Yet in the next half, Taney finds an excuse to consider the question of whether Congress has the power to abolish slavery in the territories. Critics would later malign his reasoning and treat the second half of the opinion as dicta, but his argument is straightforward: No one supposed that enslaved people were citizens. If Congress lacked the power to free the Scotts, then the Scotts were still enslaved. Taney writes that resolving the question of Congress's power is therefore a second and potentially more persuasive explanation for why the Court lacks jurisdiction.

exist, and that they thereby became free, and upon their return to Missouri became citizens of that State.

Now, if the removal of which he speaks did not give them their freedom, then by his own admission he is still a slave; and whatever opinions may be entertained in favor of the citizenship of a free person of the African race, no one supposes that a slave is a citizen of the State or of the United States. If, therefore, the acts done by his owner did not make them free persons, he is still a slave, and certainly incapable of suing in the character of a citizen. . . .

We proceed, therefore, to inquire whether the facts relied on by the plaintiff entitled him to his freedom. . . .

[T]he act of Congress, upon which the plaintiff relies, declares that slavery and involuntary servitude, except as a punishment for crime, shall be forever prohibited in all that part of the territory ceded by France, under the name of Louisiana, which lies north of thirty-six degrees thirty minutes north latitude, and not included within the limits of Missouri. And the difficulty which meets us at the threshold of this part of the inquiry is, whether Congress was authorized to pass this law under any of the powers granted to it by the Constitution; for if the authority is not given by that instrument, it is the duty of this court to declare it void and inoperative, and incapable of conferring freedom upon any one who is held as a slave under the laws of any one of the States.

The counsel for the plaintiff has laid much stress upon that article in the Constitution which confers on Congress the power "to dispose of and make all needful rules and regulations respecting the territory or other property belonging to the United States;" but, in the judgment of the court, that provision has no bearing on the present controversy, and the power there given, whatever it may be, is confined, and was intended to be confined, to the territory which at that time belonged to, or was claimed by, the United States, and was within their boundaries as settled by the treaty with Great Britain, and can have no influence upon a territory afterwards acquired from a foreign Government. It was a special provision for a known and particular territory, and to meet a present emergency, and nothing more.[16]

A brief summary of the history of the times . . . will show the correctness of this proposition.

[Various states ceded their western lands to help pay off the United States' war debt. By 1787, when both the Northwest Ordinance and Constitution were drafted, all states but North Carolina and Georgia had done this. The Territory Clause, therefore, had only the sale of this territory in mind.]

The language used in the clause, the arrangement and combination of the powers, and the somewhat unusual phraseology it uses, when it speaks of the political power to be exercised in the government of the territory, all indicate the design and meaning of the clause to be such as we have mentioned. It does not speak of any territory, nor of Territories, but . . . only to the territory of the United States—that is, to a territory then in existence, and then known or claimed as the territory of the United States. It begins its enumeration of powers by that of disposing, in other words, making sale of the lands, or raising money from them. . . . It then gives the power which was necessarily associated with the disposition and sale of the lands—that is, the power of making needful rules and regulations respecting the territory. And whatever construction may now be given to these words, every one, we think, must admit that they are not the words usually employed by statesmen in giving supreme

---

16 **Question:** Taney here concludes that the Territory Clause cannot be interpreted to give Congress the power to regulate the Louisiana Territory. What powers does he think the clause gives Congress?

power of legislation. They are certainly very unlike the words used in the power granted to legislate over territory which the new Government might afterwards itself obtain by cession from a State, either for its seat of Government, or for forts, magazines, arsenals, dock yards, and other needful buildings. . . .[17]

The concluding words of the clause appear to render this construction irresistible; for, after the provisions we have mentioned, it proceeds to say, "that nothing in the Constitution shall be so construed as to prejudice any claims of the United States, or of any particular State." . . . [W]hen [this] latter provision relates so obviously to the unappropriated lands not yet ceded by [North Carolina and Georgia], and the first clause makes provision for those then actually ceded, it is impossible, by any just rule of construction, to make the first provision general, and extend to all territories, which the Federal Government might in any way afterwards acquire, when the latter is plainly and unequivocally confined to a particular territory; which was a part of the same controversy, and involved in the same dispute, and depended upon the same principles. The union of the two provisions in the same clause shows that they were kindred subjects; and that the whole clause is local, and relates only to lands, within the limits of the United States, which had been or then were claimed by a State; and that no other territory was in the mind of the framers of the Constitution, or intended to be embraced in it. . . .[18]

This brings us to examine by what provision of the Constitution the present Federal Government, under its delegated and restricted powers, is authorized to acquire territory outside of the original limits of the United States, and what powers it may exercise therein over the person or property of a citizen of the United States, while it remains a Territory, and until it shall be admitted as one of the States of the Union.

There is certainly no power given by the Constitution to the Federal Government to establish or maintain colonies bordering on the United States or at a distance, to be ruled and governed at its own pleasure; nor to enlarge its territorial limits in any way, except by the admission of new States. . . . [N]o power is given to acquire a Territory to be held and governed permanently in that character. . . .

[That said, t]he power to expand the territory of the United States by the admission of new States is plainly given; and in the construction of this power by all the departments of the Government, it has been held to authorize the acquisition of territory, not fit for admission at the time, but to be admitted as soon as its population and situation would entitle it to admission. It is acquired to become a State, and not to be held as a colony and governed by Congress with absolute authority; and as the propriety of admitting a new State is committed to the sound discretion of Congress, the power to acquire territory for that purpose, to be held by the United States until it is in a suitable condition to become a State upon an equal footing with the other States, must rest upon the same discretion. It is a question for the political department of the Government, and not the judicial; and whatever the political department of the Government shall recognise as within the limits of the United States, the judicial

---

17 **Question:** Do you agree with Taney that the Territory Clause's choice of words does not give Congress plenary power over the territories? He contrasts it with the District Clause, which empowers Congress to "exercise exclusive Legislation in all Cases whatsoever" over the District and places purchased for forts, magazines, and the like.

18 **Questions:** Taney here is making an even more provocative interpretation of the Territory Clause: it applies only to the territory that the United States possessed in 1787; it does not apply to "all territories, which the Federal Government might in any way afterwards acquire." Do you find his reasoning persuasive? If the Territory Clause doesn't give Congress power to legislate for territories like the Louisiana or Wisconsin Territory, does Taney think that any other clause does?

department is also bound to recognise, and to administer in it the laws of the United States, so far as they apply. . . .[19]

Taking this rule to guide us, it may be safely assumed that citizens of the United States who migrate to a Territory belonging to the people of the United States, cannot be ruled as mere colonists, dependent upon the will of the General Government, and to be governed by any laws it may think proper to impose. The principle upon which our Governments rest, and upon which alone they continue to exist, is the union of States, sovereign and independent within their own limits in their internal and domestic concerns, and bound together as one people by a General Government, possessing certain enumerated and restricted powers, delegated to it by the people of the several States, and exercising supreme authority within the scope of the powers granted to it, throughout the dominion of the United States. A power, therefore, in the General Government to obtain and hold colonies and dependent territories, over which they might legislate without restriction, would be inconsistent with its own existence in its present form. . . .

The power to acquire necessarily carries with it the power to preserve and apply to the purposes for which it was acquired. [When the United States acquired the Louisiana Territory, the] form of government to be established necessarily rested in the discretion of Congress. . . . [S]ome form of civil authority would be absolutely necessary to organize and preserve civilized society, and prepare it to become a State; and what is the best form must always depend on the condition of the Territory at the time, and the choice of the mode must depend upon the exercise of a discretionary power by Congress, acting within the scope of its constitutional authority, and not infringing upon the rights . . . of the citizen who might go there. . . .

The powers of the Government and the rights and privileges of the citizen are regulated and plainly defined by the Constitution itself. . . . It has no power of any kind beyond it; and it cannot, when it enters a Territory of the United States, put off its character, and assume discretionary or despotic powers which the Constitution has denied to it. It cannot create for itself a new character separated from the citizens of the United States, and the duties it owes them under the provisions of the Constitution. The Territory being a part of the United States, the Government and the citizen both enter it under the authority of the Constitution, with their respective rights defined and marked out; and the Federal Government can exercise no power over his person or property, beyond what that instrument confers, nor lawfully deny any right which it has reserved. . . .[20]

For example, no one, we presume, will contend that Congress can make any law in a Territory respecting the establishment of religion, or the free exercise thereof, or abridging the freedom of speech or of the press, or the right of the people of the Territory peaceably to assemble, and to petition the Government for the redress of grievances.

---

[19] **Questions:** Taney here interprets the clause of Article IV that permits Congress to admit new states into the Union. Does he think that *this* clause gives Congress plenary power to legislate for the territories? If not, what implied limits does he think the clause imposes?

Note also what Taney worries would result if Congress possessed unlimited power over the territories: Congress might maintain them as "colonies" to be "ruled and governed at its own pleasure." Do you agree that opposition to imperialism is a persuasive interpretive principle for setting limits on Congress's power over territories?

[20] **Questions:** Taney in these paragraphs is arguing that when Congress legislates for the territories, it is as bound by the Bill of Rights as when Congress legislates within the states. Do you agree that this is a just principle?

Which limitation of the Bill of Rights does Taney think prevents Congress from prohibiting the introduction of slavery?

Nor can Congress deny to the people the right to keep and bear arms, nor the right to trial by jury, nor compel any one to be a witness against himself in a criminal proceeding.

These powers, and others, in relation to rights of person, which it is not necessary here to enumerate, are, in express and positive terms, denied to the General Government; and the rights of private property have been guarded with equal care. . . . [T]he fifth amendment to the Constitution . . . provides that no person shall be deprived of life, liberty, and property, without due process of law. And an act of Congress which deprives a citizen of the United States of his liberty or property, merely because he came himself or brought his property into a particular Territory of the United States, and who had committed no offence against the laws, could hardly be dignified with the name of due process of law. . . .

It seems, however, to be supposed, that there is a difference between property in a slave and other property, and that different rules may be applied to it in expounding the Constitution of the United States. And the laws and usages of nations, and the writings of eminent jurists upon the relation of master and slave and their mutual rights and duties, and the powers which Governments may exercise over it, have been dwelt upon in the argument.

But . . . [t]he powers of the Government, and the rights of the citizen under it, are positive and practical regulations plainly written down. The people of the United States have delegated to it certain enumerated powers, and forbidden it to exercise others. It has no power over the person or property of a citizen but what the citizens of the United States have granted. . . . And if the Constitution recognises the right of property of the master in a slave, and makes no distinction between that description of property and other property owned by a citizen, no tribunal, acting under the authority of the United States, . . . has a right to draw such a distinction, or deny to it the benefit of the provisions and guarantees which have been provided for the protection of private property against the encroachments of the Government. . . .

Upon these considerations, . . . the act of Congress which prohibited a citizen from holding and owning property of this kind in the territory of the United States north of the line therein mentioned, is not warranted by the Constitution, and is therefore void; and . . . neither Dred Scott himself, nor any of his family, were made free by being carried into this territory. . . . Upon the whole, therefore, it is the judgment of this court, . . . that the plaintiff in error is not a citizen of Missouri, in the sense which that word is used in the Constitution. . . .[21]

■ MR. JUSTICE CURTIS dissenting.[22]

[T]here is not, in my judgment, anything in the language, the history, or the subject-matter of [the Territory Clause], which restricts its operation to territory owned by the United States when the Constitution was adopted. . . . Nor do the particular terms employed, in my judgment, tend in any degree to restrict [its grant of] legislative power. Power granted to a Legislature to make all needful rules and

---

21 **Questions:** What is the bottom-line holding of this second half of the opinion? What, precisely, prevents Congress from freeing enslaved people in the territories?

22 **Questions:** Justice Benjamin Curtis of Massachusetts sharply dissented from Taney's first conclusion, i.e., that black people could never become citizens. Curtis's position would be vindicated in 1868, when the Fourteenth Amendment declared that all people born in the United States—with some exceptions—were citizens.

This excerpt picks up where Curtis addresses Taney's second conclusion, which evaluated Congress's power to abolish slavery in the territories. Where in the Constitution does Curtis locate Congress's power to legislate for the territories? Why, precisely, does he disagree with Taney about whether the Constitution prohibits Congress from freeing enslaved people in the territories?

regulations respecting the territory, is a power to pass all needful laws respecting it. . . .

If, then, this clause does contain a power to legislate respecting the territory, what are the limits of that power? To this I answer, that, in common with all the other legislative powers of Congress, it finds limits in the express prohibitions on Congress not to do certain things; that, in the exercise of the legislative power, Congress cannot pass an *ex post facto* law or bill of attainder; and so in respect to each of the other prohibitions contained in the Constitution.

Besides this, the rules and regulations must be needful. But undoubtedly the question whether a particular rule or regulation be needful, must be finally determined by Congress itself. Whether a law be needful, is a legislative or political, not a judicial, question. Whatever Congress deems needful is so, under the grant of power. Nor am I aware that it has ever been questioned that laws providing for the temporary government of the settlers on the public lands are needful, not only to prepare them for admission to the Union as States, but even to enable the United States to dispose of the lands. . . .

[It] is insisted, that whatever other powers Congress may have respecting the territory of the United States, the subject of negro slavery forms an exception. . . . [But] what positive prohibition exists in the Constitution, which restrained Congress from enacting a law in 1820 to prohibit slavery north of thirty-six degrees thirty minutes north latitude?

The only one suggested is that clause in the [Fifth Amendment,] which declares that no person shall be deprived of his life, liberty, or property, without due process of law. . . .

[But in] the great and leading case of *Prigg v. The State of Pennsylvania*, 16 Peters 594, this court [said:] The state of slavery is deemed to be a mere municipal regulation, founded on and limited to the range of territorial laws. . . . [S]lavery is limited to the range of the laws under which it is sanctioned. . . . And not only must the status of slavery be created and measured by municipal law, but the rights, powers, and obligations, which grow out of that status, must be defined, protected, and enforced, by such laws. . . .

[I think it is] rational to conclude that they who framed and adopted the Constitution were aware that persons held to service under the laws of a State are property only to the extent and under the conditions fixed by those laws; that they must cease to be available as property, when their owners voluntarily place them permanently within another jurisdiction, where no municipal laws on the subject of slavery exist; and that, being aware of these principles, and having said nothing to interfere with or displace them, or to compel Congress to legislate in any particular manner on the subject, and having empowered Congress to make all needful rules and regulations respecting the territory of the United States, it was their intention to leave to the discretion of Congress what regulations, if any, should be made concerning slavery therein. . . .

It must be remembered that [the Fifth Amendment's Due Process Clause] is not peculiar to the Constitution of the United States; it was borrowed from Magna Charta . . . and has existed in all the States. . . . [I]f a prohibition of slavery in a territory in 1820 violated this principle of Magna Charta, the ordinance of 1787 also violated it. . . . [So, too, did Congress's prohibition of the slave trade in 1808.] A citizen of the United States owns slaves in Cuba, and brings them to the United

States, where they are set free by the legislation of Congress. Does this legislation deprive him of his property without due process of law?[23]

NOTE: AFTERMATH OF *DRED SCOTT*

Dred Scott was immediately condemned by many northerners as the worst opinion in Supreme Court history. *See* Potter, *supra*, at 279–90. A majority of the Court—consisting of the five southern justices and one northerner—had emphatically concluded that no black person, enslaved or free, could become a citizen under the Constitution. Nor could Congress do anything to prevent the westward expansion of slavery. Applying these conclusions, the majority had also invalidated a major act of Congress for the first time since *Marbury v. Madison*, 5 U.S. (1 Cranch) 137 (1803). All of this was anathema in the North. As discussed previously (sections 3.2, 18.3), northern states responded by directly resisting the Supreme Court's authority—as when the Wisconsin Supreme Court attempted to obstruct the enforcement of the Fugitive Slave Act of 1850. *See Ableman v. Booth*, 62 U.S. 506 (1859).

South Carolina, in turn, cited this northern resistance among its reasons for seceding from the United States in 1860. *See Journal of the Convention of the People of South Carolina* 461 (R. W. Gibbes, Columbia, S.C. 1862). The South Carolina convention argued that Wisconsin and thirteen other northern states had "enacted laws which either nullify the [Fugitive Slave Acts of 1793 and 1850] or render useless any attempt to execute them." *Id.* at 464. South Carolina also accused the "non-slaveholding States" of "elevating to citizenship, persons, who, by the supreme law of the land, are incapable of becoming citizens." *Id.* at 465. Finally, the northern states had "denied the rights of property established in fifteen of the States and recognized by the Constitution." *Id.* "Thus," South Carolina concluded, "the constituted compact has been deliberately broken and disregarded by the non-slaveholding States, and the consequence follows that South Carolina is released from her obligation." *Id.*

As mentioned earlier (section 3.2), President Abraham Lincoln challenged the Supreme Court's interpretive supremacy in his inaugural address, declaring in 1861 that the Court was entitled to respect but not unquestioned deference. 7 *A Compilation of the Messages and Papers of the Presidents* 3210–11 (James D. Richardson ed., 1897). He also condemned South Carolina's conclusion that a state could remedy any alleged constitutional violations by unilaterally seceding. The Fugitive Slave Clause was "as well enforced, perhaps, as any law can ever be in a community where the moral sense of the people imperfectly supports the law itself," he observed. *Id.* at 3211. He also argued that the Constitution did not establish a mere "compact," but "a more perfect Union": one whose "perpetual" bonds could not "be peaceably unmade by less than all the parties who made it." *Id.* at 3208.

[23] **Question:** Curtis suggests that the majority opinion threatens not only the abolition of slavery in the territories but also in northern states. Why?

This dispute over the nature of the Constitution—Union versus compact, judicial supremacy versus popular constitutionalism, proslavery versus antislavery—was resolved not in the Supreme Court but in the Civil War. In 1861, after South Carolina troops fired on a federal fort in Charleston Harbor, Lincoln and Congress dispatched soldiers to defend the Union. Potter, *supra*, at 582. Despite *Dred Scott*'s holding that Congress lacked the power to abolish slavery in the territories, Congress and the president soon enacted An Act to Secure Freedom to All Persons within the Territories, ch. 111, 12 Stat. 432 (1862), which did what its title suggested.

Congress completed its repudiation of *Dred Scott* after the Union won the Civil War, when it proposed the Fourteenth Amendment. The opening sentence of the new amendment, ratified in 1868, declared that "[a]ll persons born or naturalized in the United States, and subject to the jurisdiction thereof, are citizens of the United States and of the state wherein they reside."

18.4.2

Downes v. Bidwell

182 U.S. 244 (1901)

If there was one thing that the *Dred Scott* majority and dissenters all agreed upon, it was that the Constitution doesn't permit Congress to "legislate without restriction" in the territories; Congress is always limited by the Bill of Rights. *Dred Scott*, 60 U.S. (19 How.) at 448. Congress itself accepted this limitation in 1874, declaring that "[t]he Constitution and all laws of the United States which are not locally inapplicable shall have the same force and effect within all the organized Territories, and in every Territory hereafter organized, as elsewhere within the United States." Rev. Stat. § 1891 (1874).

But this widely shared belief that "the Constitution followed the flag" was upended in 1898 when the United States went to war with Spain. In the war's aftermath, Secretary of War Elihu Root revised the principle to reflect a new reality: "the Constitution follows the flag—but doesn't quite catch up with it." 1 Arthur Wallace Dunn, *From Harrison to Harding* 257 (1922).

The Spanish-American War lasted only three months but wrought profound changes in the map of the United States. In the Treaty of Paris that ended the war, Spain ceded to the United States sovereignty over three populous island groups: Puerto Rico, the Philippines, and Guam. *See* 11 U.S.T. 615 (1898). The treaty also gave the United States jurisdiction over Cuba, including Guantánamo Bay. That same year, the United States also annexed the Republic of Hawaii, an independent nation founded after U.S. citizens overthrew the archipelago's constitutional monarchy in a coup backed by U.S. Marines. *See* Julia Flynn Siler, *Lost Kingdom* 212–19 (2012).

As Taney observed in *Dred Scott*, the United States generally acquired territory with the assumption that Congress would allow white settlers to govern themselves with a territorial government and then petition for admission as a state. Taney thought it inconceivable that the federal government might "establish or maintain colonies . . . at a distance, to be ruled and governed at its own pleasure." *Dred Scott*, 60 U.S. at 446.

But after 1898, as members of Congress and the executive branch debated how to govern the United States' new islands, most were unwilling to extend U.S. citizenship to the islands' residents, much less put the islands on a path toward statehood or independence. *See* Sam Erman, *Almost Citizens* 40–41 (2019). The Philippines alone had eleven million people—almost twice the size of New York, the most populous state. If brown-skinned Filipinos were allowed to elect members of Congress, they would profoundly influence national policy. Yet in the jingoistic atmosphere of a budding "American Empire," members of Congress were equally loath not to "[t]ake up the White Man's burden" and civilize their "new-caught sullen peoples." 32 Cong. Rec. 1532 (Feb. 7, 1899) (statement of Sen. Benjamin Tillman) (quoting Rudyard Kipling, *The White Man's Burden*, McClure's Mag., Feb. 1899, at 290). As one historian has written, "it was an argument about a trilemma. Republicanism, white supremacy, and overseas expansion—the country could have at most two." Daniel Immerwahr, *How to Hide an Empire* 80 (2019).

The Supreme Court considered the trilemma in a series of cases known as the *Insular Cases*. The first and most important of these cases, *Downes v. Bidwell*, 182 U.S. 244 (1901), involved what was superficially a minor issue: the applicability of a tariff on oranges from Puerto Rico. In 1900, Congress passed the Foraker Act, ch. 191, 31 Stat. 77, which replaced Puerto Rico's military governor with a civilian government. To fund the new government until it could enact its own local taxes, the act imposed a temporary tariff on "all merchandise coming into the United States from Porto Rico." Foraker Act, 31 Stat. at 77. Rather than pay this tariff, Samuel Downes, an orange importer, sued George Bidwell, the U.S. customs inspector for the Port of New York, arguing that the tariff violated the Taxing Clause of Article I, Section 8, which declares that "Duties, Imposts and Excises shall be uniform throughout the United States." He argued that the tariff wasn't "uniform" because it treated Puerto Rico differently than it treated the states.

When the case reached the Supreme Court, all of the justices agreed that the tariff would be unconstitutional if the phrase *throughout the United States* included Puerto Rico. However, a fractured majority held that Puerto Rico was *subordinate* to the United States but not *part of it*. Justice Henry Brown was the only justice to join his plurality opinion. Justice Edward White—a former Confederate officer who would soon invent the "plenary power" doctrine in the context of Native tribes—

wrote an influential concurrence that established a lasting distinction between "incorporated" and "unincorporated" territories.

■ MR. JUSTICE BROWN . . . announced the conclusion and judgment of the Court.[24]

In the case of *De Lima* v. *Bidwell,* just decided, we held that upon the ratification of the treaty of peace with Spain, Porto Rico ceased to be a foreign country, and became a territory of the United States. . . . We are now asked to hold that it became a part of the *United States* within that portion of the Constitution which declares that "all duties, imposts and excises shall be uniform throughout the United States." Art. I, sec. 8. If Porto Rico be a part of the United States, the Foraker act imposing duties upon its products is unconstitutional. . . .

The question of the legal relations between the States and the newly acquired territories first became the subject of public discussion in connection with the purchase of Louisiana in 1803. . . . It is unnecessary to enter into the details of this debate. . . . Suffice it to say that the [prevailing side] took the ground that, under the constitutional power to make treaties, there was ample power to acquire territory, and to hold and govern it under laws to be passed by Congress; and that as Louisiana was incorporated into the Union as a territory, and not as a State, a stipulation for citizenship became necessary. . . . Congress, not only in organizing the territory of Louisiana by act of March 26, 1804, but all other territories carved out of this vast inheritance, has assumed that the Constitution did not extend to them of its own force, and has in each case made special provision, either that their legislatures shall pass no law inconsistent with the Constitution of the United States, or that the Constitution or laws of the United States shall be the supreme laws of such territories. . . .

Indeed, the practical interpretation put by Congress upon the Constitution has been long continued and uniform to the effect that the Constitution is applicable to territories acquired by purchase or conquest only when and so far as Congress shall so direct.[25] Notwithstanding its duty to "guarantee to every State in this Union a republican form of government," Art. IV, sec. 4, . . . Congress did not hesitate, in the original organization of the territories of Louisiana, Florida, the Northwest Territory, and its subdivisions of Ohio, Indiana, Michigan, Illinois and Wisconsin, and still more recently in the case of Alaska, to establish a form of government bearing a much greater analogy to a British crown colony than a republican State of America, and to vest the legislative power either in a governor and council, or a governor and judges, to be appointed by the President. It was not until they had attained a certain population that power was given them to organize a legislature by vote of the people. In all these cases, as well as in Territories subsequently organized west of the Mississippi, Congress thought it necessary either to extend the Constitution and laws of the United States over them, or to declare that the inhabitants should be entitled to enjoy the right of trial by jury, of bail, and of the privilege of the writ of *habeas corpus*, as well as other privileges of the bill of rights.

We are also of opinion that the power to acquire territory by treaty implies not only the power to govern such territory, but to prescribe upon what terms the United

---

24 **As You Read, Consider:** For all of *Dred Scott v. Sandford*'s faults, Chief Justice Roger Taney was strongly opposed to the idea that the Constitution meant one thing in the states and a different thing in the territories. Do the opinions of Justices Henry Brown and Edward White agree? What do they think gives Congress the power to legislate for the territories, and what limits do they think the Constitution imposes?

25 **Note:** In these opening paragraphs, Brown is describing how, as a matter of historical practice, Congress has felt the need to expressly "incorporate" new possessions into the Union as territories and then determine by statute which provisions of the Constitution are "applicable." This idea of incorporation and applicability is central to White's more influential concurring opinion.

States will receive its inhabitants, and what their *status* shall be in what Chief Justice Marshall termed the "American Empire." There seems to be no middle ground between this position and the doctrine that if their inhabitants do not become, immediately upon annexation, citizens of the United States, their children thereafter born, whether savages or civilized, are such, and entitled to all the rights, privileges and immunities of citizens.[26] If such be their *status,* the consequences will be extremely serious. Indeed, it is doubtful if Congress would ever assent to the annexation of territory upon the condition that its inhabitants, however foreign they may be to our habits, traditions and modes of life, shall become at once citizens of the United States. . . .

Grave apprehensions of danger are felt by many eminent men—a fear lest an unrestrained possession of power on the part of Congress may lead to unjust and oppressive legislation, in which the natural rights of territories, or their inhabitants, may be engulfed in a centralized despotism. These fears, however, find no justification in the action of Congress in the past century, nor in the conduct of the British Parliament towards its outlying possessions since the American Revolution. Indeed, in the only instance in which this court has declared an act of Congress unconstitutional as trespassing upon the rights of territories, (the Missouri Compromise,) such action was dictated by motives of humanity and justice, and so far commanded popular approval as to be embodied in the Thirteenth Amendment to the Constitution. There are certain principles of natural justice inherent in the Anglo-Saxon character which need no expression in constitutions or statutes to give them effect or to secure dependencies against legislation manifestly hostile to their real interests. Even in the Foraker act itself, the constitutionality of which is so vigorously assailed, power was given to the legislative assembly of Porto Rico to repeal the very tariff in question in this case, a power it has not seen fit to exercise. The words of Chief Justice Marshall in *Gibbons* v. *Ogden,* 9 Wheat. 1, with respect to the power of Congress to regulate commerce, are pertinent in this connection: . . . ["]The wisdom and discretion of Congress, their identity with the people, and the influence which their constituents possess at elections, are, in this, as in many other instances, . . . the sole restraints on which they have relied to secure them from its abuse. They are the restraints on which the people must often rely on solely, in all representative governments." . . .

We suggest, without intending to decide, that there may be a distinction between certain natural rights, enforced in the Constitution by prohibitions against interference with them, and what may be termed artificial or remedial rights, which are peculiar to our own system of jurisprudence.[27] Of the former class are the rights to one's own religious opinion and to a public expression of them, or, as sometimes said, to worship God according to the dictates of one's own conscience; the right to personal liberty and individual property; to freedom of speech and of the press; to free access to courts of justice, to due process of law and to an equal protection of the laws; to immunities from unreasonable searches and seizures, as well as cruel and unusual punishments; and to such other immunities as are indispensable to a free government. Of the latter class are the rights to citizenship, to suffrage, *Minor* v.

[26] **Note:** Brown is alluding in this paragraph to the Fourteenth Amendment, which provides that all people born in the United States "and subject to the jurisdiction thereof" automatically become citizens of the United States. He is suggesting how horrible it would be if all people in a newly acquired territory automatically became U.S. citizens within a generation.

[27] **Question:** Despite his deferential attitude toward Congress in the previous paragraph, Brown proposes that Congress might be limited by certain "natural rights" when it legislates for the territories. For Brown, what distinguishes these rights from what he calls artificial rights? Note that in *Minor v. Happersett*, 88 U.S. (21 Wall.) 162 (1875), the Court held that the Constitution did not prohibit states from denying the right to vote to female U.S. citizens.

Happersett, 21 Wall. 162, and to the particular methods of procedure pointed out in the Constitution, which are peculiar to Anglo-Saxon jurisprudence, and some of which have already been held by the States to be unnecessary to the proper protection of individuals. . . . We do not desire, however, to anticipate the difficulties which would naturally arise in this connection, but merely to disclaim any intention to hold that the inhabitants of these territories are subject to an unrestrained power on the part of Congress to deal with them upon the theory that they have no rights which it is bound to respect. . . .

The liberality of Congress in legislating the Constitution into all our contiguous territories has undoubtedly fostered the impression that it went there by its own force, but there is nothing in the Constitution itself, and little in the interpretation put upon it, to confirm that impression. . . . In short, there is absolute silence upon the subject. The executive and legislative departments of the government have for more than a century interpreted this silence as precluding the idea that the Constitution attached to these territories as soon as acquired, and unless such interpretation be manifestly contrary to the letter or spirit of the Constitution, it should be followed by the judicial department. . . . A false step at this time might be fatal to the development of what Chief Justice Marshall called the American Empire. . . .

We are therefore of opinion that the Island of Porto Rico is a territory appurtenant and belonging to the United States, but not a part of the United States within the revenue clauses of the Constitution; that the Foraker act is constitutional, so far as it imposes duties upon imports from such island, and that the plaintiff cannot recover back the duties exacted in this case.

■ MR. JUSTICE WHITE, . . . uniting in the judgment. . . .[28]

[I concur in the result reached by Mr. Justice Brown, but] the reasons which cause me to do so are different from, if not in conflict with, that opinion. . . . [L]et me state and concede the soundness of some principles . . . .

First. The government of the United States was born of the Constitution, and all powers which it enjoys or may exercise must be either derived expressly or by implication from that instrument. . . .

Second. Every function of the government being thus derived from the Constitution, it follows that that instrument is everywhere and at all times potential in so far as its provisions are applicable.

Third. Hence it is that wherever a power is given by the Constitution and there is a limitation imposed on the authority, such restriction operates upon and confines every action on the subject within its constitutional limits.

Fourth. Consequently it is impossible to conceive that where conditions are brought about to which any particular provision of the Constitution applies, its controlling influence may be frustrated by the action of any or all of the departments of the government. Those departments, when discharging, within the limits of their constitutional power, the duties which rest on them, may of course deal with the subjects committed to them in such a way as to cause the matter dealt with to come under the control of provisions of the Constitution which may not have been previously

---

28 **Questions:** White begins his opinion by emphasizing that Congress has no power except for the powers granted to it by the Constitution and that Congress's power is always limited by the Constitution. Yet he makes an important move in his fourth principle when he suggests that some provisions of the Constitution may not be "applicable" until the political branches "cause the matter dealt with to come under [the provisions'] control." What do you think he means by this? Is it the same as Brown's declaration above that when the United States acquires territory, Congress may "prescribe upon what terms the United States will receive its inhabitants, and what their *status* shall be in what Chief Justice Marshall termed the 'American Empire' "?

applicable. But this does not conflict with the doctrine just stated, or presuppose that the Constitution may or may not be applicable at the election of any agency of the government.

Fifth. The Constitution has undoubtedly conferred on Congress the right to create such municipal organizations as it may deem best for all the territories of the United States whether they have been incorporated or not, to give to the inhabitants as respects the local governments such degree of representation as may be conducive to the public well-being, to deprive such territory of representative government if it is considered just to do so, and to change such local governments at discretion. . . . [T]here is an instance which exemplifies the exercise of the power substantially in all its forms, in such an apt way that reference is made to it. The instance referred to is the District of Columbia, which has had from the beginning different forms of government conferred upon it by Congress, some largely representative, others only partially so, until, at the present time, the people of the District live under a local government totally devoid of local representation, in the elective sense, administered solely by officers appointed by the President, Congress, in which the District has no representative in effect, acting as the local legislature.

In some adjudged cases the power to locally govern at discretion has been declared to arise as an incident to the right to acquire territory. In others it has been rested upon the clause of section 3, Article IV, of the Constitution, which vests Congress with the power to dispose of and make all needful rules and regulations respecting the territory or other property of the United States. [*See American Insurance Co. v. Canter*, 1 Pet. 511.] But this divergence, if not conflict of opinion, does not imply that the authority of Congress to govern the territories is outside of the Constitution, since in either case the right is founded on the Constitution, although referred to different provisions of that instrument.

Whilst, therefore, there is no express or implied limitation on Congress in exercising its power to create local governments for any and all of the territories, by which that body is restrained from the widest latitude of discretion, it does not follow that there may not be inherent, although unexpressed, principles which are the basis of all free government which cannot be with impunity transcended. But this does not suggest that every express limitation of the Constitution which is applicable has not force, but only signifies that even in cases where there is no direct command of the Constitution which applies, there may nevertheless be restrictions of so fundamental a nature that they cannot be transgressed. . . .[29]

Sixth. As Congress in governing the territories is subject to the Constitution, it results that all the limitations of the Constitution which are applicable to Congress in exercising this authority necessarily limit its power on this subject. It follows also that every provision of the Constitution which is applicable to the territories is also controlling therein. To justify a departure from this elementary principle by a criticism of the opinion of Mr. Chief Justice Taney in *Scott v. Sandford* 19 How. 393, appears to me to be unwarranted. Whatever may be the view entertained of the correctness of the opinion of the court in that case, in so far as it interpreted a particular provision of the Constitution concerning slavery and decided that as so construed it was in force in the territories, this in no way affects the principle which that decision

[29] **Question:** In this paragraph, White suggests that Congress has the same latitude to operate in the territories as it has in the District of Columbia, yet in both cases it may be limited by certain "fundamental" restrictions. He doesn't yet say what these restrictions are. What do you think he is referring to?

announced, that the applicable provisions of the Constitution were operative. That doctrine was concurred in by the dissenting judges. . . .[30]

Seventh. In the case of the territories, as in every other instance, when a provision of the Constitution is invoked, the question which arises is, not whether the Constitution is operative, for that is self-evident, but whether the provision relied on is applicable.

Eighth. As Congress derives its authority to levy local taxes for local purposes within the territories, not from the general grant of power to tax as expressed in the Constitution, it follows that its right to locally tax is not to be measured by the provision empowering Congress "To lay and collect Taxes, Duties, Imposts and Excises," and is not restrained by the requirement of uniformity throughout the United States. But the power just referred to, as well as the qualification of uniformity, restrains Congress from imposing an impost duty on goods coming into the United States from a territory which has been incorporated into and forms a part of the United States. . . .

From these conceded propositions it follows that Congress in legislating for Porto Rico was only empowered to act within the Constitution and subject to its applicable limitations, and that every provision of the Constitution which applied to a country situated as was that island, was potential in Porto Rico.

And the determination of what particular provision of the Constitution is applicable, generally speaking, in all cases, involves an inquiry into the situation of the territory and its relations to the United States. This is well illustrated by some of the decisions of this court which are cited in the margin. [*E.g., American Insurance Co. v. Canter*, 1 Pet. 511.] Some of these decisions hold on the one hand that, growing out of the presumably ephemeral nature of a territorial government, the provisions of the Constitution relating to the life tenure of judges is inapplicable to courts created by Congress, even in territories which are incorporated into the United States, and some on the other hand decide that the provisions as to common-law juries found in the Constitution are applicable under like conditions; that is to say, although the judge presiding over a jury need not have the constitutional tenure, yet the jury must be in accordance with the Constitution. . . .

Albeit, as a general rule, the *status* of a particular territory has to be taken in view when the applicability of any provisions of the Constitution is questioned, it does not follow when the Constitution has absolutely withheld from the government all power on a given subject, that such an inquiry is necessary.[31] Undoubtedly, there are

---

[30] **Questions:** White is not being very clear with these various propositions. But he is reaching the conclusion that Congress's power to acquire territory includes the power to determine whether the territory should be "incorporated" into the Union, thus making otherwise inapplicable constitutional provisions "applicable."

This leaves two open questions: First, how does the Court know when a territory has been "incorporated into and forms a part of the United States"? Second, when dealing with territories like Puerto Rico—which White evidently thinks has not yet been incorporated—which of the Constitution's limitations on Congress are always applicable, and which are within the authority of Congress to decide?

In the remainder of this opinion, how does White answer these two questions?

Don't worry if you're finding White's analysis hard to follow. In his dissenting opinion, Justice John Marshall Harlan complained, "I am constrained to say that this idea of 'incorporation' has some occult meaning which my mind does not apprehend. It is enveloped in some mystery which I am unable to unravel."

[31] **Questions:** In this paragraph, White distinguishes two types of constitutional limits: (1) "mere regulations as to the form and manner in which a conceded power may be exercised" (which may or may not be applicable depending on the status of a particular territory) and (2) "general prohibitions in the Constitution in favor of the liberty and property of the citizen" (which are always applicable). In which category does he place the Sixth Amendment right to a trial by jury? In light of your answer, what do you think he means by "general prohibitions" that

general prohibitions in the Constitution in favor of the liberty and property of the citizen which are not mere regulations as to the form and manner in which a conceded power may be exercised, but which are an absolute denial of all authority under any circumstances or conditions to do particular acts. In the nature of things, limitations of this character cannot be under any circumstances transcended, because of the complete absence of power. . . .

There is in reason then no room in this case to contend that Congress can destroy the liberties of the people of Porto Rico by exercising in their regard powers against freedom and justice which the Constitution has absolutely denied. There can also be no controversy as to the right of Congress to locally govern the island of Porto Rico as its wisdom may decide and in so doing to accord only such degree of representative government as may be determined on by that body. . . .

It is insisted, however, that, conceding the right of the government of the United States to acquire territory, . . . [all] territory when acquired becomes absolutely incorporated into the United States, [and] every provision of the Constitution which would apply under that situation is controlling in such acquired territory. This, however, is but to admit the power to acquire and immediately to deny its beneficial existence.

The general principle of the law of nations, . . . is that acquired territory, in the absence of agreement to the contrary, will bear such relation to the acquiring government as may be by it determined. . . . Suppose at the termination of a war the hostile government had been overthrown and the entire territory or a portion thereof was occupied by the United States, and . . . it became necessary for the United States to hold the conquered country for an indefinite period, or at least until such time as Congress deemed that it should be either released or retained because it was apt for incorporation into the United States. If holding was to have the effect which is now claimed for it, would not the exercise of judgment respecting the retention be so fraught with danger to the American people that it could not be safely exercised? . . .[32]

But, it is argued, all the instances previously referred to may be conceded, for they but illustrate the rule *inter arma silent leges* [i.e., in times of war, the law falls silent]. Hence, they do not apply to acts done after the cessation of hostilities when a treaty of peace has been concluded. This not only begs the question, but also embodies a fallacy. . . . The fallacy lies in admitting the right to exercise the power, if only it is exerted by the military arm of the government, but denying it wherever the civil power comes in to regulate and make the conditions more in accord with the spirit of our free institutions. Why it can be thought, although under the Constitution the military arm of the government is in effect the creature of Congress, that such arm may exercise a power without violating the Constitution, and yet Congress—the creator—may not regulate, I fail to comprehend. . . .

If the proposition [that the entire Constitution follows the flag] be true, then millions of inhabitants of alien territory, if acquired by treaty, can, without the desire

---

Congress may *never* transcend? Are these the same as the "fundamental" restrictions that he referenced in the fifth proposition above?

[32] **Questions:** Just as Brown did, White here is suggesting why it would be horrible if the United States were required to extend the Constitution and all of its limitations to every territory it controlled, no matter its situation. In light of the United States' more recent wars and humanitarian actions overseas, do you agree that American foreign policy requires that Congress and the president have more constitutional flexibility abroad than they do within the United States? For example, when the U.S. military occupies an overseas area like Iraq or Afghanistan, should the residents of those places be protected by the Second Amendment's right to bear arms?

or consent of the people of the United States speaking through Congress, be immediately and irrevocably incorporated into the United States, and the whole structure of the government be overthrown. . . . Conceding that the conception upon which the Constitution proceeds is that no territory as a general rule should be acquired unless the territory may reasonably be expected to be worthy of statehood, the determination of when such blessing is to be bestowed is wholly a political question, and the aid of the judiciary cannot be invoked to usurp political discretion in order to save the Constitution from imaginary or even real dangers. . . .

The result of what has been said is that whilst in an international sense Porto Rico was not a foreign country, since it was subject to the sovereignty of and was owned by the United States, it was foreign to the United States in a domestic sense, because the island had not been incorporated into the United States, but was merely appurtenant thereto as a possession. As a necessary consequence, the . . . [uniformity requirement of Article I] was not applicable to Congress in legislating for Porto Rico. . .

■ MR. JUSTICE HARLAN, dissenting. . . .

[I]n my opinion Porto Rico became, at least after the ratification of the treaty with Spain, a part of and subject to the jurisdiction of the United States in respect of all its territory and people, and Congress could not thereafter impose any duty, impost or excise with respect to that island and its inhabitants, which departed from the rule of uniformity established by the Constitution.

NOTE: INCORPORATED VERSUS UNINCORPORATED TERRITORIES

The plurality and concurrence in *Downes* reached the same conclusion—the "uniformity" limit on federal taxes didn't apply to Puerto Rico—but with different rationales. Brown's plurality opinion held that Puerto Rico wasn't part of the "United States" for purposes of the Constitution's text. White's concurrence held that the Constitution applies differently to different territories, and "the determination of what particular provision of the Constitution is applicable, generally speaking, in all cases, involves an inquiry into the situation of the territory and its relations to the United States." *Downes*, 182 U.S. at 293. When a territory is "incorporated into the United States," White wrote, then most provisions apply, except for those that are functionally inapplicable, such as the tenure and salary protections of Article III at issue in *American Insurance Co. v. Canter*. 26 U.S. (1 Pet.) 511 (1828). *Downes*, 182 U.S. at 293. But when Congress has not chosen to incorporate a territory into the United States, then the only provisions that apply are those "restrictions of so fundamental a nature that they cannot be transgressed." *Id.* at 291.

Incorporated/unincorporated distinction. In subsequent cases, the Supreme Court adopted White's distinction between incorporated and unincorporated territories, giving Congress enormous latitude to govern the newly acquired islands at issue in the cases. In *Hawaii v. Mankichi*, 190 U.S. 197 (1903), and *Dorr v. United States*, 195 U.S. 138 (1904), the Court held that the Fifth Amendment right to a grand jury indictment didn't apply to Hawaii, and the Sixth Amendment right to a jury trial didn't apply to the Philippines, because neither right was "fundamental" and because Congress hadn't incorporated either territory. The *Dorr* Court explained that a contrary rule—one requiring Congress to respect the Fifth and Sixth

Amendments in the territories—would mean that "[i]f the United States, impelled by its duty or advantage, shall acquire territory peopled by savages, . . . it must establish there the trial by jury. To state such a proposition demonstrates the impossibility of carrying it into practice." 195 U.S. at 148; *see also Ocampo v. United States*, 234 U.S. 91 (1914) (authorizing indictments without grand juries in the Philippines). And in *Balzac v. Puerto Rico*, 258 U.S. 298 (1922), a case decided after Congress granted U.S. citizenship to the people of Puerto Rico, 39 Stat. 951 (1917), the Court continued to hold that the territory would not be incorporated until Congress expressly said as much. "Incorporation has always been a step, and an important one, leading to statehood," the Court wrote. *Balzac*, 258 U.S. at 311. The importance of incorporation "requires us not lightly to infer . . . an intention to incorporate in the Union these distant ocean communities of a different origin and language from those of our continental people." *Id.*

As in the tribal context, the Court eventually retreated from the racist overtones of the *Insular Cases* without abandoning the cases' foundational principles. In *Cincinnati Soap Co. v. United States*, 301 U.S. 308 (1937), the Court upheld Congress's power to delegate its lawmaking authority to a territorial legislature in a decision analogous to *District of Columbia v. John R. Thompson Co.*, 346 U.S. 100 (1953) (see section 16.1). Within a decade, the federal government told the United Nations that it would "develop self-government" in its territories. T.S. No. 993. In 1946, it granted the Philippines independence. Act of Mar. 24, 1934, Pub. L. No. 73–127, 48 Stat. 456. In 1947, it made the governor of Puerto Rico elected, not appointed. Act of Aug. 5, 1947, Pub. L. No. 80–361, 61 Stat. 770. And in 1950, Congress authorized Puerto Rico to form its own constitution. The constitution became law in 1952, after Congress approved it with several conditions, including a condition that Puerto Rico would be subject to certain federal laws and "the applicable provisions of the Constitution of the United States." Act of Jul. 3, 1952, Pub. L. No. 82–447, 66 Stat. 327.

Skepticism regarding *Insular Cases*. In this context, some members of the Court even expressed doubt about the continued vitality of the *Insular Cases*, writing

> that neither the cases nor their reasoning should be given any further expansion. The concept that the Bill of Rights and other constitutional protections against arbitrary government are inoperative when they become inconvenient or when expediency dictates otherwise is a very dangerous doctrine and if allowed to flourish would destroy the benefit of a written Constitution and undermine the basis of our Government.

Reid v. Covert, 354 U.S. 1, 14 (1957) (plurality opinion); *see also Calero-Toledo v. Pearson Yacht Leasing Co.,* 416 U.S. 663 (1974) (interpreting the statute approving the Puerto Rico Constitution as extending principles of the U.S. Constitution to Puerto Rico); *Examining Bd. v. Flores de Otero*, 426 U.S. 572 (1976) (same with respect to equal-protection principles of the U.S. Constitution); *Califano v. Torres*, 435 U.S. 1 (1978) (same with due process principles).

Puerto Rico and plenary power of Congress. But the Court has at the same time indicated—without citing the *Insular Cases*—that unincorporated territories such as Puerto Rico remain subject to Congress's plenary power. In *Califano v. Torres*, 435 U.S. 1 (1978), and *Harris v. Rosario*, 446 U.S. 651 (1980), the Court held that Congress could withhold federal aid programs from Puerto Rico and reserve it for residents of states and the District of Columbia. The *Califano* Court explained that "Congress has the power to treat Puerto Rico differently, and that every federal program does not have to be extended to it. Puerto Rico has a relationship to the United States 'that has no parallel in our history.'" 435 U.S. at 3 n.4.

The Court emphasized the significance of these decisions in *Puerto Rico v. Franklin California Tax-Free Trust*, 579 U.S. 115 (2016), a case in which the Court determined that Congress had excluded Puerto Rico from taking advantage of federal bankruptcy law. Nevertheless, the same decision also held that Congress had preempted a 2014 Puerto Rico law that sought to reorganize billions of dollars in debt it accumulated thanks in part to federal tax policy. *See, e.g.*, Small Business Job Protection Act of 1996, Pub. L. No. 104–188, 110 Stat. 1755. With Puerto Rico preempted from enacting its own solution to a major fiscal crisis, Congress enacted the Puerto Rico Oversight, Management, and Economic Stability Act (PROMESA), which created an unelected financial oversight board to administer Puerto Rico's finances and rewrite certain territorial laws. Pub. L. No. 114–187, 130 Stat. 549. Although Puerto Rico continues to have its own constitution, the Supreme Court has reiterated that the constitution is a product of federal law and that Congress retains the ultimate sovereignty over the island. *See Puerto Rico v. Sanchez Valle*, 579 U.S. 59, 74–77 (2016).

18.5 THE ADMISSIONS CLAUSE

The admission of new states has long been a contentious subject in U.S. history. Article XI of the Articles of Confederation authorized Canada to be admitted into the Union but warned that "no other colony shall be admitted into the same, unless such admission be agreed to by nine states"—a supermajority.

The U.S. Constitution made things easier. The Admissions Clause—Article IV, Section 3, Clause 1—declares:

> New States may be admitted by the Congress into this Union; but no new State shall be formed or erected within the Jurisdiction of any other State; nor any State be formed by the Junction of two or more States, or Parts of States, without the Consent of the Legislatures of the States concerned as well as of the Congress.

This oddly structured sentence has been interpreted to authorize a simple majority of Congress to admit new states—something Congress has done thirty-seven times. Some states, like Kentucky, Tennessee, and Maine, were admitted from territory voluntarily ceded by other states. Other states, like Vermont, Texas, West Virginia, and Hawaii, were admitted from places that had contentiously declared their independence. The rest were admitted from "incorporated" federal territories.

Controversial admissions

Nevertheless, as discussed in the previous section on territories, the admission of new states has been controversial because it carries the potential to change the balance of power in the Senate. For decades, the early Congresses admitted new states by attempting to pair new slave states with new free states (like Missouri and Maine in 1820, and Florida and Iowa in 1846). Since the end of the Civil War, the admission of new states has been seen as a partisan issue: Hawaii and Alaska were paired in 1959 on the assumption that Hawaii would be reliably Republican and Alaska would be reliably Democrat. (The opposite turned out to be true.) Today, the admission of Puerto Rico and the District of Columbia as new states has been debated as a policy that would likely benefit Democrats.

Equal-footing doctrine

Despite Congress's expectations about what a potential state will look like, Congress doesn't have much control over states once they are admitted into the Union, thanks to a legal rule known as the *equal-footing doctrine*.

The doctrine has its origin in the early cessions of land from states to the federal government. In 1784, three years after Virginia ceded land that became part of the Northwest Territory, Virginia added a condition that Congress eventually had to admit the land as "distinct Republican States ... having the same rights of Sovereignty, Freedom and Independence as the other States." 2 *The Territorial Papers of the United States* 7 (Clarence Edwin Carter ed., 1934). Other states included similar conditions, and the Confederation Congress accepted and codified them in the Northwest Ordinance of 1787. *See, e.g.*, 32 *Journals of the Continental Congress* 343 (1936). At the same time, delegates attending the Constitutional Convention rejected a proposal that would have constitutionally required that "new States shall be admitted on the same terms with the original States." 2 *The Records of the Federal Convention of 1787*, at 454 (Max Farrand ed., 1911). But in the 1790s, when Congress actually began admitting new states, its acts of admission generally admitted each new state "on an equal footing with the original states, in all respects whatever." Act of Jun. 1, 1796, ch. 47, 1 Stat. 491, 491–92.

These early acts of admission set a precedent that Congress continued to follow, even with respect to territory beyond the thirteen states' original cessions. For example, Congress admitted the state of Louisiana "on an equal footing," even though Napoleon didn't include a condition requiring as much when France ceded the Louisiana Territory to the United States. Act of Apr. 8, 1812, ch. 50, 2 Stat. 701. Congress did the same with its act admitting Texas, which considered itself an independent nation. Joint Resolution of Dec. 29, 1845, No. 1, 9 Stat. 108.

Court rulings on legal effect of equal footing *language*

In 1845, the same year that Congress admitted Texas, the Supreme Court considered the legal effect of this *equal footing* language for the first time.

The principal case involved conflicting claims over swampland near present-day Mobile, Alabama, which had been ceded to the United States by Georgia in 1802. After 1819, when the United States admitted Alabama as a state on an "equal footing" with the other states, the United States continued to claim ownership over the swamp. But when the thirteen original states ratified the Constitution, they retained sovereignty over all navigable waters and the soil beneath them, including swampland. *See Martin v. Waddell*, 41 U.S. (16 Pet.) 367 (1842). So, in *Pollard's Lessee v. Hagan*, the Court held that Congress's act admitting Alabama must have ceded the swampland to Alabama, or else Alabama would not have been admitted on an "equal footing" with the other states. 44 U.S. (3 How.) 212, 229 (1845).

The equal-footing doctrine and slavery

Pollard's Lessee was an interpretation of a federal act of admission, not the Constitution. But its "equal footing" language reappeared in a contemporary debate over the constitutionality of Congress's power to permanently abolish slavery in new states admitted from western territories. After the Mexican-American War began in 1846, Representative David Wilmot of Pennsylvania proposed "that neither slavery nor involuntary servitude shall ever exist" in any territories acquired from Mexico. *See* Robert Elder, *Calhoun* 455 (2021). His proposed legislation would also prohibit the admission of any state whose constitution permitted slavery. *See* Cong. Globe, 29th Cong., 2d Sess. 454 (1847). The Senate's most ardent defender of slavery, John C. Calhoun, responded that Wilmot's proviso would unconstitutionally violate the "perfect equality between the members of this republic." *Id.* Calhoun offered two objections. First, he argued that the ban on slavery in the territories would discriminate against the rights of southern states to send their residents and property into federal territory on the same terms as northern states. The proviso therefore derogated "that perfect equality which belongs to [states] as members of this Union." *Id.* at 455. Second, he considered it "a fundamental principle of our political system" that "every State about to become a member of this Union has a right to form its own Government as it pleases; and that, in order to be admitted, there is but one qualification, and that is, that the government shall be republican." *Id.* at 454. Although Calhoun conceded that "no express provision" of the Constitution protected this equality of the states, he thought that such equality was essential "to maintain the absolute right of individuals in every possible condition to govern themselves!" *Id.* The so-called Wilmot Proviso never passed.

Perpetual theory of the Constitution

Closely related to Calhoun's theory of state equality was his understanding that the U.S. Constitution was a "compact" among equal sovereigns. *See* Elder, *supra*, at 271–77. Just as nation-states could unilaterally nullify treaty obligations if another nation-state violated the treaty's terms, the compact theory of the Constitution held that disgruntled states could unilaterally nullify federal laws or secede if the federal government violated the Constitution. *Id.* Opponents of the compact theory, like President Abraham Lincoln, rejected the constitutionality of secession. From Lincoln's perspective, the Articles of Confederation had created a "perpetual Union" that the U.S. Constitution made "more perfect." A Union would not be more perfect if states could unilaterally leave. *See* Noah Feldman, *The Broken Constitution* 138–40 (2021).

As discussed earlier (section 18.4), when South Carolina seceded in 1860, it embraced Calhoun's compact theory; the army of the "Union" embraced Lincoln's perpetual-union theory. The Supreme Court weighed in only after the Union victory in the Civil War, in a decision that embraced Lincoln's view of perpetual union along with a limited version of Calhoun's argument for state sovereignty.

The decision, *Texas v. White*, 74 U.S. (7 Wall.) 700 (1869), asked whether the state of Texas had, legally, left the Union when it joined the Confederacy in 1861. The Court explained that a "state" for purposes of the Constitution was "a political community of free citizens, occupying a territory of defined boundaries, and organized under a government sanctioned and limited by a written constitution, and established by the consent of the governed." *Id.* at 721. The Court distinguished this political community from the *government* of the state, which, in Texas's case, had voted to secede. But even though Texas had once been an independent nation, the Court emphasized that its admission into the Union inalterably changed its status and deprived its government of the unilateral power to make all decisions for the state:

> When, therefore, Texas became one of the United States, she entered into an indissoluble relation. All the obligations of perpetual union, and all the guaranties of republican government in the Union, attached at once to the State. The act which consummated her admission into the Union was something more than a compact; it was the incorporation of a new member into the political body. And it was final. The union between Texas and the other States was as complete, as perpetual, and as indissoluble as the union between the original States. There was no place for reconsideration, or revocation, except through revolution, or through consent of the States.

Id. at 725–26.

This language repudiated the Confederacy's view that states were so sovereign they could reclaim their independence. But the Court added that states retained a limited sovereignty, recognized by the Tenth Amendment, that the federal government could not abolish. "[T]he preservation of the States, and the maintenance of their governments, are as much within the design and care of the Constitution as the preservation of the Union and the maintenance of the National government," the Court wrote. *Id.* at 725. In the context of Reconstruction, the decision warned Congress that the Court would not likely tolerate the treatment of Southern states as if they were conquered territory.

18.5.1

Coyle v. Smith

221 U.S. 559 (1911)

The Civil War temporarily resolved many antebellum debates over the sovereign status of states after their admission. In particular, the Union's victory repudiated John C. Calhoun's argument that the Constitution implicitly protected the "perfect equality" of the states in a manner that prohibited Congress from discriminating against Southern states or requiring territories to satisfy certain antislavery conditions before their admission as new states. *See* Cong. Globe, 29th Cong., 2d Sess. 454 (1847). But one question that remained unresolved was whether the Admissions Clause gave Congress power with respect to new states *after* their admission that Congress lacked with respect to existing states. For example, the Missouri Compromise of 1820 not only "forever prohibited" slavery from certain federal territory, but also implicitly prohibited the future introduction of slavery in states formed from that territory. *See* 3 Stat. 545.

The question of Congress's power to use the Admissions Clause to impose permanent conditions on the admission of new states arose in 1867, when Congress passed laws to admit Colorado and Nebraska into the Union. Like all previous enabling acts, the Nebraska law admitted the state "upon an equal footing with the original States in all respects whatsoever." Act of Feb. 9, 1867, ch. 36, 14 Stat. 391, 391–92. Yet the law also required the state to include in its constitution a "fundamental condition that within the State of Nebraska there shall be no denial of the elective franchise, or of any other right, to any person, by reason of race or color . . . ." *Id.* In a veto message, President Andrew Johnson objected to the "incongruity" between Congress's admission of Nebraska on an "equal footing" and its attempt to "regulate the elective franchise of [the] State." 8 *The Compilation of the Messages and Papers of the Presidents* 3688–89 (James D. Richardson ed., 1897). He argued that nothing in the Constitution permitted Congress to determine who could vote in existing states, so Nebraska would be treated unequally. (The Fifteenth Amendment, which bans racial discrimination in voting, had not yet been proposed or ratified.) But Congress overrode the veto, enabling Nebraska to enter the Union so long as its constitution allowed black people to vote.

Nebraska never attempted to challenge this permanent condition on its admission. The Supreme Court therefore never reviewed it. But the Court considered the same issue for the first time in the following case, *Coyle v. Smith*, 221 U.S. 559 (1911).

In 1906, when Congress passed an enabling act to permit Oklahoma to enter the Union, it declared that "[t]he capital of said State shall temporarily be at the city of Guthrie, in the present Territory of Oklahoma and shall not be changed therefrom previous to [1913]." Act of June 16, 1906, Pub. L. 59–234, 34 Stat. 267, 269. The act provided that the Oklahoma legislature could move the capital after 1913. However, the new state of Oklahoma couldn't wait, and its legislature moved the capital to Oklahoma City in 1910. This move outraged a group of Guthrie residents who owned large property interests in the temporary capital. They challenged Oklahoma's decision to move the capital as a violation of the federal enabling act. The state responded that the federal enabling act was unconstitutional.

In reviewing the constitutionality of Congress's restriction, the Court constitutionalized the equal-footing doctrine.

■ MR. JUSTICE LURTON delivered the opinion of the Court.[33]

This is a writ of error to the Supreme Court of Oklahoma to review the judgment of that court upholding a legislative act of the State providing for the removal of its capital from Guthrie to Oklahoma City . . . . The only question for review by us is whether the provision of the [federal] enabling act was a valid limitation upon the power of the State after its admission, which overrides any subsequent state legislation repugnant thereto.

The power to locate its own seat of government and to determine when and how it shall be changed from one place to another, and to appropriate its own public funds for that purpose, are essentially and peculiarly state powers. That one of the original thirteen States could now be shorn of such powers by an act of Congress would not be for a moment entertained. The question then comes to this: Can a State be placed upon a plane of inequality with its sister States in the Union if the Congress chooses to impose conditions which so operate, at the time of its admission? The argument is, that while Congress may not deprive a State of any power which it *possesses*, it may, as a condition to the admission of a new State, constitutionally restrict its authority, to the extent at least, of suspending its powers for a definite time in respect to the location of its seat of government. . . .

---

[33] **As You Read, Consider:** In the century before this decision, when Congress admitted new states into the Union, it usually included statutory language declaring that the new states would be admitted on an "equal footing" with existing states. In earlier cases such as *Pollard's Lessee v. Hagan*, 44 U.S. (3 How.) 212 (1845), the Supreme Court interpreted the meaning of this statutory language. In this decision, when Justice Horace Lurton discusses the equality of the states, is he interpreting a federal statute or the Constitution itself?

The position of counsel for the appellants is substantially this: That the power of Congress to admit new States and to determine whether or not its fundamental law is republican in form, are political powers, and as such, uncontrollable by the courts. That Congress may in the exercise of such power impose terms and conditions upon the admission of the proposed new State, which, if accepted, will be obligatory, although they operate to deprive the State of powers which it would otherwise possess, and, therefore, not admitted upon "an equal footing with the original States."

The power of Congress in respect to the admission of new States is found in the third section of the fourth Article of the Constitution. . . . But what is this power? It is not to admit political organizations which are less or greater, or different in dignity or power, from those political entities which constitute the Union. It is, as strongly put by counsel, a "power to admit States."

The definition of "a State" is found in the powers possessed by the original States which adopted the Constitution, a definition emphasized by the terms employed in all subsequent acts of Congress admitting new States into the Union. The first two States admitted into the Union were the States of Vermont and Kentucky, one as of March 4, 1791, and the other as of June 1, 1792. No terms or conditions were exacted from either. Each act declares that the State is admitted "as a new and *entire member* of the United States of America." 1 Stat. 189, 191. Emphatic and significant as is the phrase admitted as "an entire member," even stronger was the declaration upon the admission in 1796 of Tennessee, as the third new State, it being declared to be "one of the United States of America," "on an equal footing with the original States in all respects whatsoever," phraseology which has ever since been substantially followed in admission acts, concluding with the Oklahoma act, which declares that Oklahoma shall be admitted "on an equal footing with the original States."

The power is to admit "new States into *this* Union."

"This Union" was and is a union of States, equal in power, dignity and authority, each competent to exert that residuum of sovereignty not delegated to the United States by the Constitution itself. To maintain otherwise would be to say that the Union, through the power of Congress to admit new States, might come to be a union of States unequal in power, as including States whose powers were restricted only by the Constitution, with others whose powers had been further restricted by an act of Congress accepted as a condition of admission. Thus it would result, first, that the powers of Congress would not be defined by the Constitution alone, but in respect to new States, enlarged or restricted by the conditions imposed upon new States by its own legislation admitting them into the Union; and, second, that such new States might not exercise all of the powers which had not been delegated by the Constitution, but only such as had not been further bargained away as conditions of admission.[34]

The argument that Congress derives from the duty of "guaranteeing to each State in this Union a republican form of government," power to impose restrictions upon a new State which deprives it of equality with other members of the Union, has no merit. It may imply the duty of such new State to provide itself with such state government, and impose upon Congress the duty of seeing that such form is not

---

[34] **Question:** Lurton holds that the Admissions Clause does not give Congress the power to create two classes of states: some with all their powers and others with whatever powers were not "bargained away as conditions of admission." Why not?

changed to one anti-republican, but it obviously does not confer power to admit a new State which shall be any less a State than those which compose the Union.[35]

Has Oklahoma been admitted upon an equal footing with the original States? If she has, she by virtue of her jurisdictional sovereignty as such a State may determine for her own people the proper location of the local seat of government. She is not equal in power to them if she cannot.

In *Texas* v. *White,* 7 Wall. 700, 725, Chief Justice Chase said in strong and memorable language that, "the Constitution, in all of its provisions looks to an indestructible Union, composed of indestructible States." . . .

To this we may add that the constitutional equality of the States is essential to the harmonious operation of the scheme upon which the Republic was organized. When that equality disappears we may remain a free people, but the Union will not be the Union of the Constitution.

NOTE: THE EQUAL-FOOTING DOCTRINE AFTER *COYLE*

As we will see in a section on Congress's power to enforce the Reconstruction amendments (section 21.2), the Supreme Court has limited the equal-footing doctrine to the admission of new states. *See South Carolina v. Katzenbach*, 383 U.S. 301, 328–29 (1966) ("The doctrine of the equality of States . . . applies only to the terms upon which States are admitted to the Union, and not to the remedies for local evils which have subsequently appeared."). But the Court has recently revived *Coyle* to limit Congress's power to preempt the voting laws of some states but not others. *See Shelby Cnty. v. Holder*, 570 U.S. 529, 544 (2013) ("*Coyle* concerned the admission of new States, and *Katzenbach* rejected the notion that the principle operated as a *bar* on differential treatment outside that context. At the same time, . . . the fundamental principle of equal sovereignty remains highly pertinent in assessing subsequent disparate treatment of States.").

18.6 THE PROPERTY CLAUSE

One condition that Congress has often included in acts admitting new states is a reservation of federal possession of specified land, highways, and structures. *See, e.g., Stearns v. Minnesota*, 179 U.S. 223 (1900). Congress's power to enforce this sort of condition after statehood comes from Section 3, Clause 2, in Article IV, which gives Congress the "Power to dispose of and make all needful Rules and Regulations respecting the Territory or other Property belonging to the United

---

[35] **Questions:** In addition to rejecting the applicability of the Admissions Clause, Lurton also rejects the applicability of the Guarantee Clause, which provides that "the United States shall guarantee to every State in this Union a Republican Form of Government."

Do these holdings have any relevance for Congress's power to exercise other clauses of the Constitution in a manner that treats some states differently from others? In other words, do they vindicate an argument once made by Senator John C. Calhoun, that the "perfect equality" of the states prohibited Congress from enacting tariffs and antislavery laws that allegedly treated Southern states differently from Northern states? *See* Cong. Globe, 29th Cong., 2d Sess. 454 (1847).

For example, could Congress exercise the Commerce Clause to preempt the laws of some states but not other states? What about exercising the General Welfare Clause to grant money to states recently hit by a hurricane?

States." Applying this clause, Congress has retained ownership over massive amounts of land, all navigable waters, and other "Property." *See, e.g., PPL Montana, LLC v. Montana*, 565 U.S. 576 (2012) (by default, when a new state is admitted on an equal footing, the United States retains ownership over navigable rivers and coastal waters, while states are given title to riverbeds, tidal lands, and shorelines). Today, the federal government owns approximately 28 percent of the United States' total land area, the vast majority of which is located in eleven western states and Alaska. Carol Hardy Vincent et al., Cong. Rsch. Serv., R42346, *Federal Land Ownership* 1 (2020).

Camfield *and government power over its own property*

The Supreme Court considered the relationship between federal lands and newly admitted states at length in *Camfield v. United States*, 167 U.S. 518 (1897). The case involved federal lands in Colorado over which the United States retained ownership after Congress admitted Colorado as a state. To stimulate economic development, Congress sold some of its land to railroad companies in a checkerboard pattern along rail lines—[$$][U.S.][$$][U.S.][$$]—allowing the railroad to resell its squares to private purchasers while preserving ownership over the remaining squares for the United States. In 1885, Congress passed an act prohibiting anyone from erecting fences or other enclosures in a manner that would interfere with the United States' right to use and occupy its own land. Act of Feb. 25, 1885, ch. 149, 23 Stat. 321. This law had the practical effect of preventing ranchers on "private" squares from building fences on their own property.

The *Camfield* Court upheld the act and, in the process, described the federal government's power over its "Property." "While the lands in question are all within the State of Colorado," the Court began, "the Government has, with respect to its own lands, the rights of an ordinary proprietor, to maintain its possession and to prosecute trespassers. It may deal with such lands precisely as a private individual may deal with his farming property." *Camfield*, 167 U.S. at 524. At the same time, the *Camfield* Court wrote, the federal government was a *government* that "doubtless has a power over its own property analogous to the police power of the several States." *Id.* at 525. The Court interpreted this to mean that Congress not only had the power to enact a law forbidding fences on *federal* property, but also, if "necessary for the protection of the public," had the power to enact a law forbidding fences on nearby *private* property. *Id.* The Court concluded:

> While we do not undertake to say that Congress has the unlimited power to legislate against nuisances within a State, which it would have within a Territory, we do not think the admission of a Territory as a State deprives it of the power of legislating for the protection of the public lands . . . so long as such power is directed solely to its own protection.

Id. at 525–26. "A different rule would place the public domain of the United States completely at the mercy of state legislation." *Id.* at 526.

*Post-*Camfield *plenary power over property*

Since *Camfield*, the Supreme Court has generally treated federal property the same way that it treats federal enclaves. Congress's power over its property is plenary, and it may enact all "needful Rules" that, in its discretion, it determines are necessary. *See Light v. United States*, 220 U.S. 523 (1911). Even though federal property may be within the boundaries of a state, Congress's laws with respect to its property preempt any contrary state laws. *See Kleppe v. New Mexico*, 426 U.S. 529 (1976). Moreover, until the federal government sells or otherwise disposes of its property, states may not tax the property, nor may they otherwise interfere with the federal government's jurisdiction over it. *See Van Brocklin v. Tennessee*, 117 U.S. 151 (1886). But applying the "friction, not fiction" approach (see section 16.2), absent action by Congress, states may, in some instances, exercise some jurisdiction over activities on federal land as long as the laws don't interfere with the federal government's purposes. *Cal. Coastal Comm'n v. Granite Rock Co.*, 480 U.S. 572 (1987).

One complication with federal lands that doesn't apply to federal enclaves is the fact that Congress often sells or leases its lands to states or private individuals. Even though the Court has interpreted the Admissions Clause to prohibit Congress from enacting permanent conditions on the admission of new states, Congress's separate power "to dispose of . . . Property belonging to the United States" *does* give it plenary authority to prescribe the manner and conditions by which title over federal property may be transferred to other people. *Gibson v. Chouteau*, 80 U.S. (13 Wall.) 92 (1872). The Court has interpreted this principle capaciously. For example, the Court has upheld Congress's power to include a permanent covenant in its grant of land to a city, prohibiting the land from ever being sold or leased to a private corporation. *United States v. City of San Francisco*, 310 U.S. 16 (1940).

18.7 THE GUARANTEE CLAUSE

The final section of Article IV provides that "[t]he United States shall guarantee to every State in this Union a Republican Form of Government, and shall protect each of them against Invasion; and on Application of the Legislature, or of the Executive (when the Legislature cannot be convened), against domestic Violence." This clause was likely influenced by Shays' Rebellion in 1786 Massachusetts, an episode of domestic violence to which the Confederation Congress was unable to respond effectively. *See* Michael J. Klarman, *The Framers' Coup* 673 n.117 (2016). Early drafts of the Guarantee Clause imposed on the federal government a duty to protect states against foreign invasion or internal insurrection—a power conferred by Article I, Section 8, Clause

15. *See* 1 *The Records of the Federal Convention of 1787*, at 22, 193–94, 206 (Max Farrand ed., 1911). But the final version of the clause reflects the idea "that no State be at liberty to form any other than a Republican Govt." 2 *id.* at 47–49.

As discussed earlier in the context of political questions (section 3.4), the Supreme Court has long rejected calls for it to enforce the Guarantee Clause. *See Luther v. Borden*, 48 U.S. 1 (1849). Instead, the Court has repeatedly emphasized that "it rests with Congress to decide what government is the established one in a State . . . as well as its republican character." *Id.* at 42; *see also Baker v. Carr*, 369 U.S. 186 (1962); *Pac. States Tel. & Tel. Co. v. Oregon*, 223 U.S. 118 (1912).

Accepting its responsibility to enforce the Guarantee Clause, Congress has, at times, extensively relied on this "sleeping giant of the Constitution." Cong. Globe, 40th Cong., 1st Sess. 614 (1867). It proved particularly important after the Civil War, when Congress attempted to reconstruct southern states as multiracial democracies. *See* Eric Foner, *Reconstruction* 239–51 (2014). For example, Congress invoked the clause to support the Civil Rights Act of 1866, ch. 31, 14 Stat. 27, which gave black people many of the same legal rights as white people. It also invoked the clause to support the Reconstruction Acts of 1867, ch.153, 14 Stat. 428, which put several former Confederate states under the oversight of military governors until they adopted racially egalitarian constitutions. In *Texas v. White*, the Supreme Court wrote approvingly that "the power to carry into effect the clause of guaranty is primarily a legislative power that resides in Congress." 74 U.S. (7 Wall.) 700, 729–30 (1869). Given the circumstances, the Court held that Congress had extensive powers to regulate a state "with a view to the re-establishment of a republican government, under an amended constitution, and to the restoration of the State to her former constitutional relations." *Id.*

Even though Congress's actions during Reconstruction continue to offer an important precedent for interpreting the Guarantee Clause broadly, the scholarly consensus among white historians in the early twentieth century was that Reconstruction was a "tragic era" in which Congress overstepped constitutional limits to mistakenly enfranchise black people. *See, e.g.*, Claude G. Bowers, *The Tragic Era: The Revolution After Lincoln*, at v (1929) ("The Constitution was treated as a doormat on which politicians and army officers wiped their feet after wading in the muck."); William A. Dunning, *Essays in the Civil War and Reconstruction and Related Topics* 366–68 (1898) (praising anti-Reconstruction Supreme Court cases that allowed "Southern whites [to make] enormous positive advances in the suppression of the other race"); *see also* W.E.B. Du Bois, *Black Reconstruction in America* 719 (1935) (criticizing "a nation-wide university attitude . . . by which propaganda against the Negro has been carried on unquestioned"). Perhaps reflecting this consensus, the Supreme Court narrowly interpreted the clause in *Coyle v. Smith* as irrelevant to whether Congress could determine a state's capital or set permanent conditions on a state's admission into the Union. *See* 221 U.S. 559, 567–68 (1911).

Today, even after more recent historians have redeemed the value and reputation of Reconstruction as the basis for modern federal civil-rights law in the United States, the Guarantee Clause remains "an infrequent basis for litigation." *New York v. United States*, 505 U.S. 144, 185–86 (1992). The clause also remains a relatively untested source of congressional power. But its significance to Reconstruction has led scholars and members of Congress to describe the clause as "an independent source of legislative power to restructure state governments in conformity with republican principles." Francesca L. Procaccini, *Reconstructing State Republics*, 89 Fordham L. Rev. 2157, 2198 (2021); *see also* H.R. 1, 117th Cong. § 3(2) (2021) ("Congress finds that its authority and responsibility to enforce the Guarantee Clause is particularly strong given that Federal courts have not enforced this clause because they understood that its enforcement is committed to Congress by the Constitution.").

CHAPTER 19

HOW ARE AMENDMENTS PROPOSED AND RATIFIED?

ARTICLE V: The Congress, whenever two thirds of both Houses shall deem it necessary, shall propose Amendments to this Constitution, or, on the Application of the Legislatures of two thirds of the several States, shall call a Convention for proposing Amendments, which, in either Case, shall be valid to all Intents and Purposes, as Part of this Constitution, when ratified by the Legislatures of three fourths of the several States, or by Conventions in three fourths thereof, as the one or the other Mode of Ratification may be proposed by the Congress; Provided that no Amendment which may be made prior to the Year One thousand eight hundred and eight shall in any Manner affect the first and fourth Clauses in the Ninth Section of the first Article [*i.e.*, the ban on prohibiting the importation of enslaved people and the enumeration requirement for direct taxes]; and that no State, without its Consent, shall be deprived of its equal Suffrage in the Senate.

19.1 PROPOSING A CONSTITUTIONAL AMENDMENT

One of the major defects of the Articles of Confederation was that the standard for amending its terms was impossibly high. The final provision, Article XII, stated that

> the Articles of this Confederation shall be inviolably observed by every State, and the Union shall be perpetual; nor shall any alteration at any time hereafter be made in any of them; unless such alteration be agreed to in a Congress of the United States, and be afterwards confirmed by the legislatures of every State.

Although the Confederation Congress proposed several amendments that would have empowered Congress to levy certain taxes and regulate foreign commerce, individual states, such as Rhode Island or New York, successfully vetoed each amendment. The impracticability of amending the Articles was perhaps the main reason why members of the 1787 Philadelphia Convention proposed an entirely new government rather than modest fixes to the existing structure.

Article V

In theory, Article V of the Constitution made amendment significantly easier. It offered two methods for proposing amendments instead of one. First, a two-thirds vote of Congress. Second, a "Convention" initiated by the application of the legislatures from two-thirds of the states. Article V also offered a lower threshold for how many state approvals were needed to ratify an amendment: only three-quarters instead of all of them. Finally, Article V theoretically allowed the amendment of any part of the Constitution, excepting an amendment that (1) deprived a state of its equal suffrage in the Senate, (2) abolished the slave trade before 1808, or (3) repealed the limitation on direct taxes before 1808.

For many observers, including Thomas Jefferson, Article V didn't make amendments easy enough. Jefferson, in a letter to James Madison in 1789, famously said that "[n]o society can make a perpetual constitution, or even a perpetual law. The earth belongs always to the living generation." Letter from Thomas Jefferson to James Madison (Sept. 6, 1789), *reprinted in* 15 *The Papers of Thomas Jefferson* 392, 392–98 (Julian P. Boyd ed., 1958). From this premise, Jefferson argued that constitutions ought to expire every nineteen years so that new generations could receive the same ability as older generations to determine for themselves which fundamental laws should bind them. Reflecting a similar sentiment, some early state constitutions, such as the 1780 Massachusetts Constitution, called for a new constitutional convention to meet automatically after fifteen years. But the delegates to the Philadelphia Convention were far more skeptical of what new conventions might do. *See* 2 *The Records of the Federal Convention of 1787*, at 557–59, 629–30 (Max Farrand ed., 1911).

Proposal by convention

In practice, Article V's provisions have made it very difficult to propose and ratify constitutional amendments. Since 1789, no "Convention for proposing Amendments" has ever been called, although almost every state has applied for such a convention at one time or another. *See* Lawrence Lessig, *Republic, Lost* 291–94 (2015). States have typically called for a convention on a specific issue, even though nothing in the text of Article V contains an enforcement mechanism to ensure that the subsequent convention would be limited to that issue. Only one state was lacking in 1912 amid calls for a convention to propose the popular election of the Senate; only one state was lacking in the 1960s amid calls to repeal the Supreme Court's one-person, one-vote cases; and between 1970 and 2017, at least twenty-eight out of the necessary thirty-four states called for a convention to propose an amendment requiring the federal government to balance its budget. *See* Michael Leachman & David A. Super, Cent. on Budget & Pol'y Priorities, *States Likely Could Not Control Constitutional Convention on Balanced Budget Amendment or Other Issues* (2017).

Because the convention process has not been tested, many questions remain unanswered. It is not clear when and how a convention should be convened. It is not clear whether applications must be contemporaneous with each other or whether they may be separated by years or decades. It is not clear whether a convention could be limited to consideration of a single subject. And it is not clear whether a court could compel Congress to call a convention after the necessary number of applications have arrived. *See generally* Russell L. Caplan, *Constitutional Brinksmanship: Amending the Constitution by National Convention* (1988).

Congressional proposal

In contrast with the process of proposing amendments by convention, Congress has proposed thirty-three amendments by itself over the past 250 years. Twenty-seven have been ratified. This number still is not a lot—Massachusetts, over a similar period, has proposed 127 amendments and ratified 117. But familiarity with congressionally proposed amendments has led to more clarity about the procedure.

The first question Congress faced about the procedure for proposing amendments related to Article V's requirement that "Congress, whenever two thirds of both Houses *shall deem it necessary*, shall propose Amendments to this Constitution" (emphasis added). This sentence left it ambiguous whether Congress must first vote to "deem it necessary" to amend the Constitution before actually proposing an amendment. In debating the amendments that became the Bill of Rights, the first Congress decided that the two-thirds vote applied only to the act of proposing amendments, which, by implication, satisfied the "deem it necessary" standard. 1 Annals of Cong. 430 (1789).

The next question was whether proposed amendments should be added into the text of the Constitution or whether they should be appended to the end of the Constitution. James Madison wanted amendments to be inserted into the text: he embedded the opening words of one of his amendments—*Congress shall make no law respecting an establishment of religion, or prohibiting the free exercise thereof*—into other limits on Congress's power in Article I, Section 9. *See* Jonathan Gienapp, *The Second Creation: Fixing the American Constitution at the Founding Era* 179 (2018). But Madison's proposal was defeated by Roger Sherman, who argued that the Constitution's original parchment was sanctified and should be undisturbed. *See id*. As a result, the first ten amendments were added as new "Articles" at the end of the document.

Another question arose in 1795, after Congress proposed and the states ratified the Eleventh Amendment (which prohibited federal courts from entertaining certain suits brought against states). Unlike with ordinary legislation, President George Washington did not sign the amendment before it was proposed. A Pennsylvania merchant named Levi Hollingsworth argued that the amendment was therefore invalid. But during oral argument, Justice Samuel Chase in *Hollingsworth v. Virginia*, 3 U.S. (3 Dall.) 378 (1798), expressed skepticism that the president had any role to play in the amendment process. "The negative of the President applies only to the ordinary cases of legislation: He has nothing to do with the proposition, or adoption, of amendments to the Constitution," Chase said. *Hollingsworth*, 3 U.S. (3 Dall.) at 382 n.*. The rest of the Court in *Hollingsworth* said only that the Eleventh Amendment had been properly ratified. But *Hollingsworth* has been subsequently interpreted as holding that "Presidential approval was unnecessary for a proposed constitutional amendment." *INS v. Chadha*,

462 U.S. 919, 955 n.21 (1983); *see also Hawke v. Smith*, 253 U.S. 221, 228–30 (1920).

Challenges to amendments

A comprehensive challenge was brought in 1920 against the Eighteenth Amendment, which authorized Congress to prohibit the sale of intoxicating liquors in the United States. In *Rhode Island v. Palmer* (*National Prohibition Cases*), 253 U.S. 350 (1920), the Court's opinion comprised a half-dozen bullet points that each summarily disposed of an objection to the amendment. One affirmed Congress's 1789 conclusion that both Houses could propose an amendment by a two-thirds vote of those members present: "An express declaration that they regarded it as necessary is not essential." *Nat'l Prohibition Cases*, 253 U.S. at 386. Another rejected the argument that the purpose of Article V was merely to correct errors in the framing of the Constitution—not to give Congress access to police powers that previously belonged to states. The Court therefore upheld the amendment. *Id.*

The Court also rejected a challenge to the Nineteenth Amendment, which prohibited states from denying the right to vote on the basis of sex. Maryland had voted against the amendment, and opponents from Maryland creatively claimed that the amendment deprived their state of its equal suffrage in the Senate. *See Leser v. Garnett*, 258 U.S. 130, 137 (1922). Their argument was that Maryland's senators would now be chosen by voters whom the state itself had never authorized to vote. But the Court dismissed this argument because the Nineteenth Amendment was materially identical to the unchallenged Fifteenth Amendment, which prohibited denying the right to vote on the basis of race. *See id.* at 136–37.

19.2 RATIFYING A CONSTITUTIONAL AMENDMENT

Article V states that an amendment becomes "Part of this Constitution, when ratified by the Legislatures of three fourths of the several States, or by Conventions in three fourths thereof, as the one or the other Mode of Ratification may be proposed by the Congress."

Ratification by legislatures versus conventions

This gives Congress two options for ratifying an amendment: "Legislatures" or "Conventions." Although the Constitution itself was ratified by state conventions, Congress has accompanied almost every proposal for a constitutional amendment with a resolution calling for ratification by "the Legislatures of the several States." *See* Resolution No. 3 of Sep. 23, 1789, 1 Stat. 97. The one exception was the Twenty-First Amendment, which, when ratified by state conventions in 1933, repealed the Eighteenth Amendment's establishment of national prohibition.

One reason for Congress's choice of ratification by convention may have been a Supreme Court case two years earlier, *United States v. Sprague*, in which the Court considered a challenge to the Eighteenth Amendment on the ground that it should have been ratified by conventions. 282 U.S. 716, 729–30 (1931). The argument was that state legislatures could ratify amendments that affected the powers "reserved to the States" by the Tenth Amendment, but only conventions of the people could ratify amendments that affected the powers "reserved . . . to the people." *Id.* at 733. The Court summarily rejected that challenge—which would have invalidated the Thirteenth Amendment's abolition of slavery—but the challenge may have influenced Congress's choice of a convention when it proposed the repeal of the Eighteenth Amendment shortly afterward.

The Court has interpreted the term *legislatures* literally to refer only to actual legislatures: the lawmaking body of the type that existed in 1789. As a consequence, the Court held in *Hawke v. Smith*, 253 U.S. 221 (1920), that a state may not validly condition ratification of a proposed constitutional amendment on its approval by a referendum. *Hawke* created some tension when the Court later held that the term *legislature* could refer to a popular initiative or referendum for purposes of Article I, Section 4: "The Times, Places and Manner of holding Elections for Senators and Representatives, shall be prescribed in each State by the Legislature thereof." In upholding Arizona's independent redistricting commission, which had been created by a popular initiative, the Court in *Arizona State Legislature v. Arizona Independent Redistricting Commission*, 576 U.S. 787 (2015), explained that Article V and Article I, Section 4, impose different functions on states and therefore can tolerate different interpretations of the same term. The Article V clause imposes a "federal" function on states and does not call for "an act of legislation within the proper sense of the word," the Court wrote. *Ariz. Indep. Redistricting Comm'n*, 576 U.S. at 806. But Article I, Section 4, concerns the power to legislate, which "is derived from the people of the State" and is subject to a state's own procedure for making laws. *Id.* at 807.

Certification of ratification

Once three-quarters of the states ratify an amendment, the amendment becomes "Part of this Constitution." As simple as this procedure sounds, however, Article V contains no language regarding who is responsible for determining whether a sufficient number of states have ratified the amendment. Is it the final state? Congress? The Supreme Court?

Since 1818, Congress has taken the lead and provided by law that each state legislature should send notice of its ratification to a specified official in the executive branch. The official must then "certif[y]" when the amendment has received a sufficient number of votes to become part of the Constitution. Act of Apr. 20, 1818, ch. 80, 3 Stat. 439. From 1818 to 1951, this official was the secretary of state; from 1951 to 1984, it was the administrator of general services; and since 1984, it has been the archivist of the United States. *See* National Archives and Records Administration Act of 1984, Pub. L. No. 98–497, 98 Stat. 2280, 2291; Act of Oct. 31, 1951, Pub. L. No. 82–248, 65 Stat. 710.

But even though the archivist now certifies how many states have ratified an amendment, both houses of Congress have traditionally also adopted resolutions declaring that an amendment is now part of the Constitution. *See, e.g.*, 15 Stat. 709–10 (1868); H.R. Con. Res. 320, 102d Cong. (1992); S. Con. Res. 120, 102d Cong. (1992). Nevertheless, the executive branch has currently taken the position that Article V gives Congress no role after submitting proposed amendments for ratification. 16 Op. O.L.C. 102, 125 (1992); *see also* Ratification of the Equal Rights Amendment, 44 Op. O.L.C. ___, slip op. at 3–4 (Jan. 6, 2020).

This procedure has raised two complications:

(1) What happens when a state "rescinds" an earlier vote to ratify an amendment?

(2) How much time may pass between an amendment's proposal and its ratification?

Rescissions and ratification

The first complication, regarding rescissions, most famously arose when Congress proposed the Fourteenth Amendment in 1866. During the ratification process, the United States included thirty-seven states, of which eleven had seceded during the Civil War. This meant that ratification depended on twenty-eight states. But with one exception, every state legislature in the former Confederacy rejected the amendment, dooming it to fail. Congress responded in March 1867 by passing the Reconstruction Acts—discussed earlier in the sections on the war powers (section 13.4) and the Guarantee Clause (section 18.7)—which required each of the remaining "rebel States" to ratify the Fourteenth Amendment before "said State shall be declared entitled to representation in Congress." Act of Mar. 2, 1867, ch. 153, 14 Stat. 428, 429. But before any of these states ratified the amendment in 1868, two northern states, New Jersey and Ohio, "withdrew" their ratifications.

On July 20, 1868, the secretary of state, William H. Seward, announced that the Fourteenth Amendment had been ratified by the necessary twenty-eight states if Ohio's and New Jersey's rescissions had been "ineffectual." 15 Stat. 707. His tally also included seven southern states that had initially voted to reject the amendment but that approved it after adopting new state constitutions that allowed black men to vote. *See* Eric Foner, *The Second Founding* 91 (2019). The next day, July 21, both houses of Congress concurrently resolved that the Fourteenth Amendment had been ratified by the requisite number of states, including Ohio and New Jersey. 15 Stat. at 709–10. On July 28, Secretary

Seward "further certif[ied]" that the amendment had also been ratified by Alabama and Georgia in the days since his initial announcement. *Id.* at 711.

Because Georgia's ratification brought the total number of ratifying states to twenty-eight without counting Ohio and New Jersey, no court has ever considered whether Ohio's and New Jersey's withdrawals of their ratification votes were effective. *But see* Brief for United States at 46, *United States v. Wong Kim Ark*, 169 U.S. 649 (1898) (No. 449) (suggesting that the Fourteenth Amendment, "so far as the ten Southern States were concerned, was of something more than doubtful validity"). But both Congress and the executive branch have, historically, agreed that once a state acts favorably on a resolution of ratification, it has exhausted its jurisdiction over the subject and cannot rescind its vote. *See* 89 Cong. Globe, 41st Cong., 2d Sess. 1477–81 (1870) (statement of Sen. Roscoe Conkling).

Timing and ratification

The second complication, regarding timing, has been an issue since 1917, when Congress included language in the Eighteenth Amendment that declared that the amendment "shall be inoperative unless it shall have been ratified . . . within seven years from the date of the submission hereof." Congress proceeded to use similar language in most new amendments it proposed. Beginning with the Twenty-Third Amendment in 1960, however, Congress has generally included the time limit in a joint resolution accompanying the amendment as opposed to in the amendment itself. *See, e.g.*, S.J. Res. 39, 86th Cong., 74 Stat. 1057 (1960).

Challenge to Eighteenth Amendment. In *Dillon v. Gloss*—yet another challenge to the Eighteenth Amendment—the Supreme Court upheld Congress's power to prescribe "reasonable" time limitations for ratification. 256 U.S. 368, 376 (1921). The Court also implied that it would be "quite untenable" if

> four amendments proposed long ago—two in 1789, one in 1810 and one in 1861—are still pending and in a situation where their ratification in some of the States many years since by representatives of generations now largely forgotten may be effectively supplemented in enough more States to make three-fourths by representatives of the present or some future generation.

Id. at 375. The Court explained that contemporaneous ratification was necessary for "a decisive expression of the people's will." *Id.* at 374.

Proposed Child Labor Amendment. The Court walked back this opinion a few years later in a case that considered whether an amendment empowering Congress to prohibit child labor (see section 19.3) could be ratified thirteen years after the amendment was submitted to the states in 1924. The case arose out of Kansas, which in 1925 voted to reject the amendment. In 1933, however, there was an aggressive campaign in favor of the amendment, and the Kansas House voted to approve it. The vote was close in Kansas's forty-member Senate: twenty senators voted in favor of the amendment and twenty against, leaving the lieutenant governor to cast the tie-breaking vote in favor of the amendment. This infuriated the twenty losing senators, including Rolla Coleman, who sued to enjoin Kansas's secretary of state, Clarence Miller, from delivering the ratification vote to Congress.

In *Coleman v. Miller*, 307 U.S. 433 (1939), the Court decided several questions in favor of the amendment's proponents. First, Chief Justice Charles Evans Hughes wrote that the Court would express no opinion about whether the lieutenant governor was part of Kansas's legislature for purposes of Article V; the Court was evenly divided about whether this was a political question. *Coleman*, 307 U.S. at 447. Second, Hughes wrote that Kansas's earlier rejection of the child labor amendment didn't prevent the legislature from later approving the amendment. Citing the history of the Fourteenth Amendment's ratification, the chief justice wrote that

> the question of the efficacy of ratifications by state legislatures, in the light of previous rejection or attempted withdrawal, should be regarded as a political question pertaining to the political departments, with the ultimate authority in the Congress in the exercise of its control over the promulgation of the adoption of the amendment.

Id. at 450. Third, the Court held that it was also up to the political branches to decide "what is a reasonable period within which ratification may be had . . . and determine accordingly the validity of ratifications." *Id.* at 452–53. The chief justice concluded:

> Our decision that the Congress has the power under Article V to fix a reasonable limit of time for ratification in proposing an amendment proceeds upon the assumption that the question, what is a reasonable time, lies within the congressional province. If it be deemed that such a question is an open one when the limit has not been fixed in advance, we think that it should also be regarded as an open one for the consideration of the Congress when, in the presence of certified ratifications by three-fourths of the States, the time arrives for the promulgation of the adoption of the amendment. The decision by the Congress, in its control of the action of the Secretary of State, of the question whether the amendment had been adopted within a reasonable time would not be subject to review by the courts.

Id. at 454.

The precedential value of *Coleman* is questionable: four of the six justices in the majority held that the entire issue was a political question not subject to judicial guidance as "Congress has sole and complete control over the amending process, subject to no judicial review." *Id.* at 459 (Black, J., concurring).

Twenty-Seventh Amendment. Some of the questions underlying *Coleman* continue to be unresolved. One of these questions became apparent in the process of ratifying the Twenty-Seventh Amendment.

In 1982, a sophomore at the University of Texas named Gregory Watson wrote a research paper about the twelve amendments originally proposed by Congress in 1789, only ten of which were ratified as part of the Bill of Rights. Arguing that the ratification process for the other two amendments was still pending, Watson became a "one-man band," urging states to pass one of the amendments to limit Congress's ability to raise the salary of its members. Richard L. Berke, *1789 Amendment Is Ratified but Now the Debate Begins*, N.Y. Times, May 8, 1992, at A1.

In 1992, Michigan became the thirty-eighth state to ratify what became the Twenty-Seventh Amendment—almost 203 years after Congress first proposed it. The archivist of the United States and Congress soon each declared that the amendment was now part of the Constitution despite the incredibly long ratification process. They disagreed, however, about which branch was responsible for determining whether the amendment had been validly ratified. *Id.*

Proposed Equal Rights Amendment. The other context in which the *Coleman* questions remain relevant is with the proposed Equal Rights Amendment (see section 19.3), which declares that "Equality of rights under the law shall not be denied or abridged by the United States or by any state on account of sex."

When Congress first proposed this amendment in 1972, it included a seven-year ratification deadline in its resolution sending the amendment to the states. *See* H.J. Res. 208, 92d Cong., 86 Stat. 1523 (1972). Soon, thirty-five of the necessary thirty-eight states voted to approve the amendment. But Phyllis Schlafly, a conservative activist, mobilized opposition that stalled the momentum in favor of the amendment. *See* Marjorie J. Spruill, *Divided We Stand* 2–10 (2017). She eventually persuaded five of the approving states to withdraw their approvals—although in one of these states, Kentucky, the governor vetoed the withdrawal vote.

In 1978, Congress responded by passing a joint resolution to extend the ratification deadline through 1982. H.J. Res. 638, 95th Cong., 92 Stat. 3799 (1978). Although some members of Congress were conflicted about its power to extend a deadline for ratification, most members considered it significant that the deadline had been set by a congressional resolution, not in the text of the amendment itself. *See Equal Rights Amendment Extension: Hearings Before the S. Judiciary Subcomm. on the Constitution*, 95th Cong., 2d Sess. (1978).

However, in *Idaho v. Freeman*, 529 F. Supp. 1107 (D. Idaho 1981), a federal district court held that Congress had no power to extend any deadlines, including one established by a resolution. The Supreme Court took up an appeal from this decision, but it vacated the district court judgment as moot after the 1982 deadline passed without any additional states voting to approve the amendment. *Nat'l Org. for Women v. Idaho*, 459 U.S. 809 (1982).

Decades after the second deadline expired in 1982, Nevada, Illinois, and Virginia all ratified the amendment, bringing the total number of states that have ever approved the amendment to thirty-eight. In January 2020, these three states sued to require the archivist of the United States to certify that the amendment has been ratified. A federal district court rejected the argument, holding that the states lacked standing to contest the matter in court. *Virginia v. Ferriero*, 525 F. Supp. 3d 35, 47 (2021). The court nevertheless opined that the congressionally imposed deadlines were valid. *Id.* at 61. Like previous district court opinions to consider the issue, the court left unresolved (1) whether Congress can rescind the existing deadline and confirm that the amendment has been ratified and (2) whether federal courts will defer to Congress's judgment or resolve the issue on their own. *Compare* Walter E. Dellinger III, *The Legitimacy of Constitutional Change: Rethinking the Amendment Process*, 97 Harv. L. Rev. 386, 387 (1983) (calling for vigorous judicial review of the amendment process), *with* Laurence H. Tribe, *A Constitution We Are Amending: In Defense of a Restrained Judicial Role*, 97 Harv. L. Rev. 433 (1983) (calling for the opposite).

19.3 AMENDMENTS PROPOSED BY CONGRESS BUT NEVER RATIFIED

Amendments proposed by Congress but never ratified by enough states to take effect are included below.

Congressional Apportionment Amendment (1789, ratified by 11 states): After the first enumeration required by the first article of the Constitution, there shall be one Representative for every thirty thousand, until the number shall amount to one hundred, after which the proportion shall be so regulated by Congress, that there shall be not less than one hundred Representatives, nor less than one Representative for every forty thousand persons, until the number of Representatives shall amount to two hundred; after which the proportion shall be so regulated by Congress, that there shall not be less than two hundred Representatives, nor more than one Representative for every fifty thousand persons.

Titles of Nobility Amendment (1810, ratified by 12 states): If any citizen of the United States shall accept, claim, receive or retain any title of nobility or honour, or shall, without the consent of Congress, accept and retain any present, pension, office or emolument of any kind whatever, from any emperor, king, prince or foreign power, such person shall cease to be a citizen of the United States, and shall be incapable of holding any office of trust or profit under them, or either of them.

Corwin Amendment (1861, ratified by 5 states): No amendment shall be made to the Constitution which will authorize or give to Congress the power to abolish or interfere, within any State, with the domestic institutions thereof, including that of persons held to labor or service by the laws of said State.

Child Labor Amendment (1924, ratified by 28 states), section 1: The Congress shall have power to limit, regulate, and prohibit the labor of persons under 18 years of age.

> **section 2:** The power of the several States is unimpaired by this article except that the operation of State laws shall be suspended to the extent necessary to give effect to legislation enacted by the Congress.

Equal Rights Amendment (1972, ratified by 38 states), section 1: Equality of rights under the law shall not be denied or abridged by the United States or by any State on account of sex.

> **section 2:** The Congress shall have the power to enforce, by appropriate legislation, the provisions of this article.
>
> **section 3:** This amendment shall take effect two years after the date of ratification.

D.C. Voting Rights Amendment (1978, ratified by 16 states), section 1: For purposes of representation in the Congress, election of the President and Vice President, and article V of this Constitution, the District constituting the seat of government of the United States shall be treated as though it were a State.

> **section 2:** The exercise of the rights and powers conferred under this article shall be by the people of the District constituting the seat of government, and as shall be provided by the Congress.
>
> **section 3:** The twenty-third article of amendment to the Constitution of the United States is hereby repealed [i.e., the amendment giving the District three electoral votes for president].
>
> **section 4:** This article shall be inoperative, unless it shall have been ratified as an amendment to the Constitution by the legislatures of three-fourths of the several States within seven years from the date of its submission.

CHAPTER 20

What Is the Scope of Congress's Power to Enforce the Reconstruction and Voting-Rights Amendments Against Personal Violations?

THIRTEENTH AMENDMENT (1865), SECTION 1: Neither slavery nor involuntary servitude, except as a punishment for crime whereof the party shall have been duly convicted, shall exist within the United States, or any place subject to their jurisdiction.

SECTION 2: Congress shall have power to enforce this article by appropriate legislation.

FOURTEENTH AMENDMENT (1868), SECTION 1: All persons born or naturalized in the United States, and subject to the jurisdiction thereof, are citizens of the United States and of the State wherein they reside. No State shall make or enforce any law which shall abridge the privileges or immunities of citizens of the United States; nor shall any State deprive any person of life, liberty, or property, without due process of law; nor deny to any person within its jurisdiction the equal protection of the laws.

SECTION 2: Representatives shall be apportioned among the several States according to their respective numbers, counting the whole number of persons in each State, excluding Indians not taxed. But when the right to vote at any election for the choice of electors for President and Vice-President of the United States, Representatives in Congress, the Executive and Judicial officers of a State, or the members of the Legislature thereof, is denied to any of the male inhabitants of such State, being twenty-one years of age, and citizens of the United States, or in any way abridged, except for participation in rebellion, or other crime, the basis of representation therein shall be reduced in the proportion which the number of such male citizens shall bear to the whole number of male citizens twenty-one years of age in such State.

SECTION 3: No person shall be a Senator or Representative in Congress, or elector of President and Vice-President, or hold any office, civil or military, under the United States, or under any State, who, having previously taken an oath, as a member of Congress, or as an officer of the United States, or as a member of any State legislature, or as an executive or judicial officer of any State, to support the Constitution of the United States, shall have engaged in insurrection or rebellion against the same, or given aid or comfort to the enemies thereof. But Congress may by a vote of two-thirds of each House, remove such disability.

SECTION 4: The validity of the public debt of the United States, authorized by law, including debts incurred for payment of pensions and bounties for services in suppressing insurrection or rebellion, shall not be questioned. But neither the United States nor any State shall assume or pay any debt or obligation incurred in aid of insurrection or rebellion against the United States, or any claim for the loss or emancipation of any slave; but all such debts, obligations and claims shall be held illegal and void.

SECTION 5: The Congress shall have the power to enforce, by appropriate legislation, the provisions of this article.

FIFTEENTH AMENDMENT (1870), SECTION 1: The right of citizens of the United States to vote shall not be denied or abridged by the United States or by any State on account of race, color, or previous condition of servitude—

SECTION 2: The Congress shall have the power to enforce this article by appropriate legislation.

NINETEENTH AMENDMENT (1920), SECTION 1: The right of citizens of the United States to vote shall not be denied or abridged by the United States or by any State on account of sex.

SECTION 2: Congress shall have power to enforce this article by appropriate legislation.

TWENTY-FOURTH AMENDMENT (1964), SECTION 1: The right of citizens of the United States to vote in any primary or other election for President or Vice President, for electors for President or Vice President, or for Senator or Representative in Congress, shall not be denied or abridged by the United States or any State by reason of failure to pay any poll tax or other tax.

SECTION 2: The Congress shall have power to enforce this article by appropriate legislation.

TWENTY-SIXTH AMENDMENT (1971), SECTION 1: The right of citizens of the United States, who are eighteen years of age or older, to vote shall not be denied or abridged by the United States or by any State on account of age.

SECTION 2: The Congress shall have power to enforce this article by appropriate legislation.

20.1 RECONSTRUCTION AND REDEMPTION

The Civil War fundamentally changed the relationship between the federal government and the states. It inspired the Reconstruction era, in which the federal government tried to take a more active role in individual rights. It also inspired a backlash against Reconstruction, in which white people tried to "redeem" white supremacy in the South.

Pre-Civil War federal-state relationship

Before December 1860, when South Carolina voted to secede, the entire federal government consisted of about thirty thousand postal workers; sixteen thousand soldiers; and 5,837 civil officers, employees, judges, and members of Congress. *See* Daniel A. Farber, *Lincoln, Presidential Power, and the Rule of Law*, 113 Nw. U. L. Rev. 667, 679–80 (2018). The federal government passed little legislation relative to the typical state government. And under the dominant ideology of dual federalism, the federal government's jurisdictional "sphere" was far narrower than the sphere of the states. As French journalist Alexis de

Tocqueville wrote after touring the United States in the 1830s, the Constitution gave the federal government supreme authority over war, foreign affairs, and other "cases in which the nation has to appear as a single and undivided power," but these issues didn't "immediately affect private citizens" and were "very far removed from its subjects." *Democracy in America* 364 (Henry Reeve trans., New York, George Adlard 1838). By contrast, the several states had their own exclusive authority to "maintain the liberty, regulate the rights, protect the fortune, and secure the life and the whole future prosperity of every citizen." *Id.* at 364–65. "In this division of the rights of sovereignty," de Tocqueville continued, "the share of the Union seems at first sight to be more considerable than that of the States; but a more attentive investigation shows it to be less so. The undertakings of the Government of the Union are more vast, but their influence is more rarely felt." *Id.* at 365.

The political and economic force that maintained this federal distance from ordinary people was slavery. In 1860, there were four million enslaved people in the United States, each of whom, on average, could be valued at approximately $150,000 in 2016 dollars. *See* Samuel H. Williamson & Louis P. Cain, *Measuring Slavery in 2016 Dollars* (2017). Total investment in enslaved people represented about half of the South's regional wealth, and the cotton and other agricultural goods produced by enslaved people were vital to the North's manufacturers, merchants, and bankers. *See* Eric Foner, *The Second Founding* 1–6 (2019). Ten of the first twelve presidents—all but John Adams and his son—enslaved people while in office. In this environment, debates about the federal government's power nearly always acknowledged a "federal consensus": the national government had no power to take direct action against slavery. *Id.* at 2. Even more, many felt that because the federal government couldn't regulate slavery within the states, the federal government couldn't regulate other domestic affairs within the states either.

Civil War and evolving northern outlook on slavery

At the outset of the Civil War, northern members of Congress attempted to pacify the seceding southern states by pledging that Congress would never interfere with slavery within the states. *See* David M. Potter, *The Impending Crisis* 550–51 (2011). In March 1861, the outgoing Congress approved a constitutional amendment proposed by Ohio representative Thomas Corwin that declared that "[n]o amendment shall be made to the Constitution which will authorize or give to Congress the power to abolish or interfere, within any State, with the domestic institutions thereof, including that of persons held to labor or service by the laws of said State." Joint Resolution of Mar. 2, 1861, 12 Stat. 251. President Abraham Lincoln endorsed this amendment in his first inaugural address, declaring that it was already "implied constitutional law." 6 *The Life and Works of Abraham Lincoln* 133 (Marion Mills Miller ed., 1907). For Lincoln and many white northerners, the immediate controversy that precipitated the Civil War was whether slavery would be extended into the territories, not whether Congress would abolish it within the South.

This northern sentiment changed rapidly as the Civil War progressed and hundreds of thousands of black people escaped and fought their way to Union lines. These fugitives from slavery created enormous pressure for the Union army, prompting Lincoln to propose that Congress free the fugitives; compensate their owners; and deport the fugitives to another country, such as Liberia or Panama. Foner, *supra*, at 25. But the military simply began treating the fugitives as "contraband," putting them to work toward the Union war effort just as they would other weapons or supplies captured from the enemy. *Id.*

By the summer of 1862, Congress responded to these developments with a series of laws. The first invoked the District Clause to abolish slavery (with compensation) within the District of Columbia. Act of Apr. 16, 1862, ch. 54, 12 Stat. 376. The second invoked the Territory Clause to abolish slavery (without compensation) in the territories. Act of June 19, 1862, ch. 111, 12 Stat. 432. The third invoked Congress's war powers to declare that

> all slaves of persons who shall hereafter be engaged in rebellion against the government of the United States, . . . escaping from such persons and taking refuge within the lines of the army, . . . or being within any place occupied by rebel forces and afterwards occupied by the forces of the United States, shall be deemed captives of war, and shall be forever free of their servitude.

Act of July 16, 1862, ch. 190, 12 Stat. 589, 591. This final act also authorized the president to employ black people toward the war effort; to colonize them in "some tropical country beyond the limits of the United States"; or, "by proclamation, to extend to persons who may have participated in the existing rebellion, in any State or part thereof, pardon and amnesty, with such exceptions and at such time and on such conditions as he may deem expedient for the public welfare." *Id.* at 592.

Lincoln expanded on this statutory authority in September 1862. He issued a proclamation formally notifying the Confederate rebels that unless they surrendered within one hundred days, he would declare that "all persons held as slaves" within any area held by the rebels would be "forever free." 12 Stat. 1267 (1862). On January 1, 1863, President Lincoln followed through with the Emancipation Proclamation, declaring, "by virtue of the power in me vested as Commander-in-Chief, . . . and as a fit and necessary war measure, . . . that all persons held as slaves within [rebel-occupied] parts of States, are, and henceforward shall be free." 12 Stat. 1268, 1269 (1863). The 1863 proclamation also empowered black people to become soldiers. The destruction of slavery—

and racial discrimination—became an objective of the Union army for the first time. *See* Foner, *supra*, at 27.

Thirteenth Amendment, enforcement powers, and Civil Rights Act

Two years later, in 1865 when the Reconstruction era began, Congress proposed the Thirteenth Amendment to constitutionalize the Emancipation Proclamation. 13 Stat. 567 (1865). The amendment also freed enslaved people in northern and border states whose status had been unaffected by the proclamation. Its first section borrowed language from the Northwest Ordinance of 1787 to declare that "[n]either slavery nor involuntary servitude, except as a punishment for crime whereof the party shall have been duly convicted, shall exist within the United States." Its second section empowered Congress "to enforce this article by appropriate legislation." In contrast with all prior amendments—which limited Congress's power—the new amendment gave Congress new power and also imposed limits on states and individuals.

Congress's new power proved important after Lincoln was assassinated in April 1865. Lincoln's successor, Andrew Johnson, was a white supremacist who eventually became a close ally of the defeated southern states. Although he demanded that each southern state ratify the Thirteenth Amendment as a condition of resuming its place in the Union, he looked the other way as states like Mississippi attempted to preserve slavery in everything but name. Foner, *supra*, at 38. Mississippi passed so-called black codes that made it an offense for any "freedman, free Negro, or mulatto" to do a number of ordinary things. 1866 Miss. Laws 82. Punishable offenses included not having a job, not being able to pay a special tax imposed only on black people, and not treating a white person with respect. *Id.* Taking advantage of the Thirteenth Amendment's allowance for slavery as punishment for a crime, Mississippi punished these offenses by fining the black people and auctioning them "to any white person who will pay said fine." *Id.* Congress responded to these black codes by passing an act to prohibit the kidnapping of black people, Act of May 21, 1866, ch. 86, 14 Stat. 50; an act to abolish "peonage," or debt slavery, Act of Mar. 2, 1867, ch. 187, 14 Stat. 546; and the Civil Rights Act of 1866, ch. 31, 14 Stat. 27, one of the most important federal laws in American history.

The Civil Rights Act repudiated the holding of *Dred Scott v. Sandford*, 60 U.S. 393 (1857), by providing that "all persons born in the United States . . ., excluding Indians not taxed, are hereby declared to be citizens of the United States." 14 Stat. at 27. It also was the first federal statute to define the meaning of U.S. citizenship. Section 1 of the act declared that U.S. citizens had the same right "as is enjoyed by white citizens" to contract, to own property, to access courts, and to enjoy "the full and equal benefit of all laws." *Id.* It also provided that all citizens would be subject to the same "punishment, pains, and penalties" as white citizens, notwithstanding "any law, statute, ordinance, regulation, or custom, to the contrary." *Id.* Section 2 made it a federal crime for any person, "under color of law," to deprive someone of a right protected by the act. *Id.*

Most of the rights protected by the Civil Rights Act related to issues that Alexis de Tocqueville would have regarded as within the exclusive jurisdiction of states, not the national jurisdiction of Congress. This troubled Johnson, who vetoed the law after strongly objecting to its constitutionality. "[I]f Congress can abrogate all State laws of discrimination between the two races in the matter of real estate, of suits, and of contracts," Johnson warned, then Congress would also have the power to "repeal the State laws as to the contract of marriage between the two races" or to "repeal in the same way all State laws discriminating between the two races on the subjects of suffrage and office." 6 *The Compilation of the Messages and Papers of the Presidents* 405 (James D. Richardson ed., 1911). Any exercise of federal power that set a precedent for interracial marriages or black voters represented to Johnson a radical departure from the "federal consensus" existing before the war. President Johnson concluded:

> In all our history, in all our experience as people living under Federal and State law, no such system as that contemplated by the details of this bill has ever before been proposed or adopted. They establish for the security of the colored race safeguards which go infinitely beyond any that the General Government has ever provided for the white race. In fact, the distinction of race and color is by the bill made to operate in favor of the colored and against the white race. They interfere with the municipal legislation of the States, with the relations existing exclusively between a State and its citizens, or between inhabitants of the same State—an absorption and assumption of power by the General Government which, if acquiesced in, must sap and destroy our federative system of limited powers and break down the barriers which preserve the rights of the States. It is another step, or rather stride, toward centralization and the concentration of all legislative powers in the National Government. The tendency of the bill must be to resuscitate the spirit of rebellion and to arrest the progress of those influences which are more closely drawing around the States the bonds of union and peace.

Id.

Despite this vocal protest and Johnson's veto, Congress passed the Civil Rights Act.

Fourteenth Amendment, expanded powers, and Reconstruction Acts

Some members of Congress, particularly John Bingham of Ohio, continued to complain that nothing in the Constitution empowered Congress to enact such a sweeping law—not the Privileges and

Immunities Clause, not the Guarantee Clause, and not Section 2 of the Thirteenth Amendment. Bingham therefore argued that Congress should propose a new constitutional amendment, one declaring, in full, that

> Congress shall have power to make all laws which shall be necessary and proper to secure to the citizens of each State all privileges and immunities of citizens in the several States, and to all persons in the several States equal protection in the rights of life, liberty, and property.

Cong. Globe, 39th Cong., 1st Sess. 1088 (1866).

After months of rewording, Bingham's proposal became the core of Sections 1 and 5 of the Fourteenth Amendment. The Fourteenth Amendment was a sweeping, omnibus package. In addition to definitively empowering Congress to pass the Civil Rights Act of 1866, the final version also included several self-executing limits on the powers of the states. Section 1 constitutionalized the principle of birthright citizenship and prohibited states from abridging "the privileges or immunities of citizens"; depriving "any person of life, liberty, or property without due process of law"; and denying to any person "the equal protection of the laws." Section 5 empowered Congress to enforce these prohibitions by "appropriate legislation." These sections marked a major change in American federalism by empowering the national state to protect the rights of individuals. Foner, *supra*, at 83. No longer would the federal government be prohibited from defining and defending people's domestic civil rights.

The rest of the amendment, meanwhile, responded to a political threat posed by the readmission of southern representatives to Congress. Before the Civil War, the Three-Fifths Clause of Article I entitled southern states to count three-fifths of their enslaved population for purposes of congressional representation. Now that no one would be enslaved, southern states would be able to count five-fifths of their free black population—even if the states continued to disenfranchise them. Few northerners relished the prospect of all-white constituencies in the South sending large delegations of ex-Confederates to future Congresses. But most also didn't want to require all states to enfranchise black citizens; after all, the vast majority of Union states continued to prohibit black people from voting. *See* Foner, *supra*, at 81–83.

Section 2 tried to resolve this puzzle by adopting a convoluted penalty scheme that reduced a state's representation in Congress if it disenfranchised male citizens for any reason other than as a penalty for a crime. In contrast with Sections 1 and 5, which empowered the federal government to protect the rights of individuals, Section 2 preserved the traditions of federalism that envisioned state control over voting requirements. *Id*. It also, for the first time, added the word *male* to the Constitution, drawing the enmity of feminists like Susan B. Anthony and

Elizabeth Cady Stanton. "If that word 'male' be inserted,'" Stanton warned, "it will take us a century at least to get it out." *Id.*

Section 3, meanwhile, sought to ensure that, even without black suffrage, state governments in the South would be so constituted as to make federal intervention unnecessary. *Id.* at 83–84. Where an early draft would have prohibited all people who had "engaged in insurrection or rebellion" from voting, the final draft prohibited them from holding state or federal office. *Id.*

Section 4, in turn, prohibited future Congresses from assuming the Confederacy's war debt or compensating former enslavers for abolition. Along with the remainder of the Fourteenth Amendment, it tried to create a multiracial national democracy out of a confederation built on racial subordination. *Id.*

Southern state legislatures—largely elected by white ex-Confederates—initially rejected the Fourteenth Amendment. Congress responded by passing the first of four Reconstruction Acts, the Reconstruction Act of 1867, which required the "rebel States" to ratify the amendment before they would be "entitled to representation in Congress." Reconstruction Act, ch. 153, 14 Stat. 428, 429. This condition—along with the rest of Congress's Reconstruction program—led to the establishment of multiracial governments in the South for the first time in its history. Under the terms of the Reconstruction Acts, southern states enfranchised black voters; ratified progressive state constitutions; elected the first black officeholders; and, ultimately, ratified the Fourteenth Amendment.

Fifteenth Amendment, expanded powers, and enforcement acts

By 1868, black supporters had made themselves into a critical constituency of the Republican Party. Republicans in Congress soon began to debate a Fifteenth Amendment to require that all states, including in the North, enfranchise black voters. *See* Foner, *supra*, at 98–100.

The Fifteenth Amendment proved complicated to actually draft, however, because the Republican Party was internally conflicted about who else, besides black men, should be allowed to vote. Radicals in Congress, along with Senator John Sherman of Ohio, favored a broad amendment to guarantee the right of all male citizens to vote. *Id.* at 101–03. But this proposal alienated senators from the East Coast, who worried about its application to Irish immigrants. *Id.* It also scared senators from the West Coast, who worried about its application to Chinese immigrants. *Id.* Senators on both coasts also defended their states' property qualifications, literacy tests, and bans on voting by formerly incarcerated people or by ex-Confederates. After a contentious debate, the Senate whittled down the proposed amendment to the weakest language possible: it prohibited states from denying citizens the right to vote "on account of race, color, or previous condition of servitude."

Like the Thirteenth and Fourteenth Amendments, the Fifteenth Amendment also empowered Congress to enforce its terms.

Many members of Congress, notably Bingham, fiercely criticized an amendment that they thought would be too easy for states to evade. Senator Henry Wilson of Massachusetts warned that unless the amendment also barred discrimination on the basis of birthplace, property, education, and religious creed, then southern states would simply adopt measures like literacy tests for potential black voters, accomplishing nothing. *Id.* at 104–08. Susan B. Anthony considered the amendment a "humiliation" that left women "the only human beings outside of state prisons and lunatic asylums adjudged incompetent" to cast a ballot. *Id.* at 113–15. Her longtime collaborator, Elizabeth Cady Stanton, used more effusive language, charging the amendment with placing "the ignorant Chinaman, the Germans . . . who harness their wives to the plow with cows and horses, and the Southern Negroes, as rulers over our educated women." *Id.*

Despite these protests, the Fifteenth Amendment was ratified in 1870, joining the Thirteenth and Fourteenth Amendments in significantly enlarging Congress's powers beyond Articles I and IV. Congress began to wield these powers almost immediately as Confederate sympathizers throughout the South used violence, intimidation, and lynchings to terrorize potential black voters into staying away from the polls. Many of these sympathizers joined a loosely knit paramilitary organization called the Ku Klux Klan, which emerged during the 1860s with the goal of "redeeming" southern states and returning them to rule by white Democrats instead of multiracial coalitions of Republicans. *See* Foner, *supra*, at 116–22.

In 1870, Congress received hundreds of pages of reports about the inability or unwillingness of southern states to cope with the surge of Klan terrorism and activity. *See* Eric Foner, *Reconstruction* 454 (2014). A particularly egregious problem was that in many southern states, state officers simply refused to enforce criminal laws against Klan members—in violation of the recently ratified Fourteenth Amendment. "[C]ertain States have denied to persons within their jurisdiction the equal protection of the laws. The proof on this point is voluminous and unquestionable," one member of Congress complained. Cong. Globe, 42d Cong., 1st Sess., app. 166 (1871). He continued, "[M]en were murdered, houses were burned, women were outraged, men were scourged, and officers of the law shot down; and the State made no successful effort to bring the guilty to punishment or afford protection or redress to the outraged and innocent." *Id.* These reports persuaded Congress and the new president, Ulysses S. Grant, to enact several "enforcement acts" to enforce the Reconstruction amendments, suppress the Klan, and entrench the multiracial democracies then under attack.

The first of these acts, the Enforcement Act of 1870, ch. 114, 16 Stat. 140, expanded the scope of the Civil Rights Act of 1866 and prohibited states from preventing people from voting in an election on account of their race. The act also created a code of new criminal offenses relating to voting rights. One of these made it a crime for "any person" to conspire with others to "injure, oppress, threaten, or intimidate any citizen with intent to hinder his free exercise and enjoyment of any right or privilege granted or secured to him by the Constitution or laws of the United States," including the right to vote. Enforcement Act, 16 Stat. at 141.

As federal prosecutors from the newly created Department of Justice traveled to the South to enforce this act's terms, Congress passed two more enforcement acts. The Second Enforcement Act of 1871, ch. 99, 16 Stat. 433, empowered federal judges and U.S. marshals to supervise local polling places and protect black voters. The Third Enforcement Act of 1871, also known as the Ku Klux Klan Act of 1871, ch. 22, 17 Stat. 13, made it a crime for two or more people to conspire to deprive someone of the equal protection of the laws. In a section that would become profoundly important decades after it was codified as 42 U.S.C. § 1983, the Ku Klux Klan Act also authorized people whose constitutional or statutory rights were violated to sue the perpetrator in federal court.

End of the Reconstruction era

Newly empowered federal prosecutors, federal courts, and, in some areas, federal soldiers became a critical source of protection for the civil rights of black people within southern states. But in each election after 1870, white vigilantes assassinated thousands of black voters and suppressed Republican turnout in massacres from Colfax, Louisiana, to Hamburg, South Carolina. *See* Foner, *supra*, at 143–46. Principally because of this violence, in 1874, Democrats retook control of both houses of Congress for the first time since the Civil War.

Reconstruction drew to an abrupt close after the presidential election of 1876, when enough electoral votes were contested that neither Rutherford B. Hayes, a Republican, nor Samuel J. Tilden, a Democrat, could claim a decisive victory. In early 1877, their two parties agreed to a compromise by which the Democrats would accept Hayes in the White House in exchange for Hayes's abandonment of federal intervention on behalf of the fundamental rights of black citizens. Although Hayes did not, as legend has it, remove any federal troops from the South, he did order federal soldiers to stop protecting black voters and officeholders. Eric Foner, *Reconstruction* 582–83 (2014).

20.1.1

United States v. Stanley (The Civil Rights Cases)

109 U.S. 3 (1883)

Reconstruction lasted only a decade before it ended in 1876, but it wrought dramatic changes. In 1865, before it began, the U.S. Constitution divided power between the federal and state governments in such a way that states possessed the exclusive authority to protect—and decline to protect—the liberty and equality of their residents. Even as states across the country used this authority to entrench political economies built on slavery and other forms of racial subordination, the federal government could only intervene by exercising its war powers. But the Thirteenth, Fourteenth, and Fifteenth Amendments empowered Congress to abolish slavery and prohibit states from unfairly depriving any person of liberty; equality under the law; and, in the case of men, the right to vote. Congress then exercised its new powers to rewrite state constitutions, prosecute white vigilantes, redistribute resources, and otherwise allow black residents to participate in democratic self-governance for the first time.

These profound changes generated such a vicious backlash among white supremacists that the "counter-revolution of 1876" did not exhaust itself with the formal end of Reconstruction. *See* W. E. B. Du Bois, *Black Reconstruction in America* 667, 690 (1935). As white resistance in the South persuaded northern supporters of Reconstruction to abandon the project, the Supreme Court embarked on a campaign to repudiate the idea that Reconstruction made any permanent changes in the antebellum constitutional order. Narrowly interpreting the Thirteenth, Fourteenth, and Fifteenth Amendments, the Court announced that "we do not see in those amendments any purpose to destroy the main features of the general system." *Slaughter-House Cases*, 83 U.S. (16 Wall.) 36, 82 (1873). Instead, the Court treated federalism as an implied limit on Congress's capacity to protect civil rights domestically—even when Congress was exercising one of its new powers.

The first major case interpreting Congress's new powers arose out of an 1873 massacre of black officeholders in Colfax, Louisiana. There, a paramilitary group of hundreds of armed white Democrats assaulted a state courthouse occupied by black Republicans. *See* Foner, *Reconstruction*, *supra*, at 437. The courthouse was the seat of local government. The Republicans inside were attempting to protect recently elected Republican officeholders as well as black families in the area. But the white Democrats murdered dozens of the people inside after announcing, "Boys, this is a struggle for white supremacy." Charles Lane, *The Day Freedom Died* 91 (2008).

A federal prosecutor indicted William Cruikshank and nearly one hundred other white people for violating the Enforcement Act of 1870, which prohibited the intimidation of any citizen "with intent to prevent or hinder his free exercise and enjoyment of any right or privilege granted or secured to him by the Constitution or laws of the United States." Enforcement Act, ch. 114, 16 Stat. 140, 141. The indictment alleged that the murderers had hindered the victims' Fourteenth Amendment rights. But in *United States v. Cruikshank*, 92 U.S. 542 (1876), the Supreme Court dismissed these charges on the ground that Congress's power to enforce the Fourteenth Amendment extended only to action by a *state*, not individual murderers. Writing for a near-unanimous Court, Chief Justice Morrison Waite of Ohio centered his analysis on the Fourteenth Amendment's text, which declares that "[n]o State shall" violate its terms:

> The fourteenth amendment prohibits a State from depriving any person of life, liberty, or property, without due process of law; but this adds nothing to the rights of one citizen as against another. It simply furnishes an additional guaranty against any encroachment by the States upon the fundamental rights which belong to every citizen as a member of society. . . . [The Equal Protection Clause, similarly, does not] add any thing to the rights which one citizen has under the Constitution against another. The equality of the rights of citizens is a principle of republicanism. Every republican government is in duty bound to protect all its citizens in the enjoyment of this principle, if within its power. That duty was originally assumed by the States; and it still remains there. The only obligation resting upon the United States is to see that the States do not deny the right. This the amendment guarantees, but no more. The power of the national government is limited to the enforcement of this guaranty.

Cruikshank, 92 U.S. at 554–55.

Federal prosecutors fared no better in *United States v. Harris*, 106 U.S. 629 (1883). That case arose after a lynch mob of twenty white people hauled four black people out of a county jail and beat one of them to death. Federal prosecutors charged members of the mob with violating the Ku Klux Klan Act of 1871, which prohibited "two or more persons within any State . . . of depriving any person or any class of persons of the equal protection of the laws." Ku Klux Klan Act, ch. 22, 17 Stat. 13, 13.

As in *Cruikshank*, the Court dismissed the prosecution because the offense was unconstitutionally overbroad. "It is perfectly clear from the language of the first section [of the Fourteenth Amendment], that its purpose . . . was to place a restraint upon the action of the States," the Court wrote. *Harris*, 106 U.S. at 638. But "the section of the law under consideration is directed exclusively against the action of private persons, without reference to the laws of the States or their administration by her officers." *Id.* at 640. The Court added that the offense couldn't be justified under the Thirteenth or Fifteenth Amendment either because if "one private person can deprive another of the equal protection of the laws [merely] by the commission of some offen[s]e against the laws which protect the rights of persons, as by theft, burglary, arson, libel, assault, or murder," then Congress would have "the power to punish every crime by which the right of any person to life, property, or reputation is invaded." *Id.* at 643. The Court thought it was "clearly unsound" to interpret the Reconstruction amendments as "invest[ing] congress with power over the whole catalogue of crimes." *Id.*

The final blow against congressional power to enforce the Reconstruction amendments was the inappropriately named *Civil Rights Cases*, 109 U.S. 3 (1883), which interpreted the final civil rights act passed by the Reconstruction Congress, the Civil Rights Act of 1875, ch. 114, 18 Stat. 335.

Congress first debated a federal public accommodations law in 1870, when multiracial Republican governments still predominated in the South. One of these governments' main priorities was to dismantle the black codes and other forms of white supremacy that had existed for centuries. Louisiana's constitution of 1868, for example, declared that "[a]ll persons shall enjoy equal rights and privileges upon any conveyance of a public character; and all places of business, or of public resort." La. Const. of 1868, art. 13. The proposed federal civil rights act promised to extend these protections nationwide.

The need for a federal antidiscrimination law grew as white Democrats in southern states targeted local antidiscrimination laws as part of their efforts to "redeem" their state governments. Between 1870 and 1874, as the Ku Klux Klan and other paramilitary organizations violently suppressed Republican voters, "redeemed" southern governments drafted new constitutions and laws that required racial separation in public schools, on railroads, in hotels, and in other public places. Foner, *Reconstruction*, *supra*, at 420–23.

Shortly after the 1874 election—when resurgent Democrats won control of the House of Representatives for the first time since the Civil War—the lame-duck, Republican-controlled Congress finally passed a federal civil rights act. Seven black senators and representatives, all of whom had been elected from reconstructed southern states, joined the rest of Congress in enacting the Civil Rights Act of 1875, a sweeping final statute of the Reconstruction era. It declared:

> That all persons within the jurisdiction of the United States shall be entitled to the full and equal enjoyment of the accommodations, advantages, facilities, and privileges of inns, public conveyances on land or water, theaters, and other places of public amusement; subject only to the conditions and limitations established by law, and applicable alike to citizens of every race and color, regardless of any previous condition of servitude.

Civil Rights Act, 18 Stat. at 336.

Democrats and some white Republicans in Congress condemned the Civil Rights Act of 1875 as an unwarranted exercise of federal power. They argued that nothing in the Reconstruction amendments permitted Congress to promote "social equality" or to prohibit "private" discrimination. Foner, *The Second Founding*, *supra*, at 141–43. But black

Republicans in Congress, including Robert B. Elliott of South Carolina, answered that Congress undoubtedly had the power to "legislate against a plain discrimination made by state laws or state customs against that very race for whose complete freedom and protection these great amendments [had been adopted]." *Id.* Elliott explained that even if the Fourteenth Amendment applies only to "States," states deny people the "equal protection of the laws" both when they enact discriminatory laws as well as when they fail to address inequality perpetuated by private discrimination. *Id.* at 143. He and his allies also argued that the act was justified by the Thirteenth Amendment, which permitted Congress to abolish the lasting effects of slavery.

The *Civil Rights Cases* reached the Supreme Court as a consolidated appeal of five separate indictments: two against hotel owners in Kansas and Missouri who refused to admit black visitors, two against theater owners in San Francisco and New York City who refused to seat black patrons, and one against the operator of a Tennessee railroad who refused to allow a black woman to ride in a "ladies' car." 109 U.S. 3, 4 (1883).

The Court's ruling severely constrained Congress's power to protect civil rights.

■ BRADLEY, J.[1]

[I]t is obvious that the primary and important question in all the cases is the constitutionality of the law; for if the law is unconstitutional none of the prosecutions can stand. . . .

[I. Is the law an exercise of the Fourteenth Amendment?]

The essence of the law is . . . to declare that, in the enjoyment of the accommodations and privileges of inns, public conveyances, theaters, and other places of public amusement, no distinction shall be made between citizens of different race or color, or between those who have, and those who have not, been slaves. . . . The second section makes it a penal offense in any person to deny to any citizen of any race or color, regardless of previous servitude, any of the accommodations or privileges mentioned in the first section.

Has Congress constitutional power to make such a law? Of course, no one will contend that the power to pass it was contained in the Constitution before the adoption of the last three amendments. The power is sought, first, in the Fourteenth Amendment, and the views and arguments of distinguished Senators, advanced while

---

1 **As You Read, Consider:** In his opinion, Justice Joseph Bradley emphasizes the text of Section 1 of the Fourteenth Amendment. Yet Section 5 of the Fourteenth Amendment empowers Congress "to enforce, by appropriate legislation, the provisions of this article." The term *appropriate* is an allusion to Chief Justice John Marshall's definition of the Necessary and Proper Clause in *McCulloch v. Maryland*, 17 U.S. (4 Wheat.) 316, 421 (1819) ("Let the end be legitimate . . . and all means which are *appropriate*, which . . . consist with the letter and spirit of the Constitution, are Constitutional." (emphasis added)).

In light of the breadth of the term *appropriate*, supporters offered three arguments to justify the Civil Rights Act of 1875: First, Section 5 of the Fourteenth Amendment gives Congress the same authority as the Supreme Court to determine what violates Section 1. Second, it is "appropriate" for Congress to enforce the spirit of the Fourteenth Amendment by prohibiting discrimination that might not violate the letter of Section 1. Third, a "State" violates Section 1 when it fails to pass its own antidiscrimination legislation, and it is therefore "appropriate" for Congress to remedy the violation. Does Bradley address any of these arguments?

the law was under consideration, claiming authority to pass it by virtue of that amendment, are the principal arguments adduced in favor of the power. . . .

The first section of the Fourteenth Amendment,—which is the one relied on,—after declaring who shall be citizens of the United States, and of the several States, is prohibitory in its character, and prohibitory upon the States. It declares that: 'No State shall make or enforce any law which shall abridge the privileges or immunities of citizens of the United States; nor shall any State deprive any person of life, liberty, or property without due process of law; nor deny to any person within its jurisdiction the equal protection of the laws.'

It is State action of a particular character that is prohibited.[2] Individual invasion of individual rights is not the subject-matter of the amendment. It has a deeper and broader scope. It nullifies and makes void all State legislation, and State action of every kind, which impairs the privileges and immunities of citizens of the United States, or which injures them in life, liberty, or property without due process of law, or which denies to any of them the equal protection of the laws. It not only does this, but, in order that the national will, thus declared, may not be a mere brutum fulmen [i.e., *an empty threat*], the last section of the amendment invests Congress with power to enforce it by appropriate legislation. To enforce what? To enforce the prohibition. To adopt appropriate legislation for correcting the effects of such prohibited State law and State acts, and thus to render them effectually null, void, and innocuous. This is the legislative power conferred upon Congress, and this is the whole of it. It does not invest Congress with power to legislate upon subjects which are within the domain of State legislation; but to provide modes of relief against State legislation, or State action, of the kind referred to. It does not authorize Congress to create a code of municipal law for the regulation of private rights; but to provide modes of redress against the operation of State laws, and the action of State officers, executive or judicial, when these are subversive of the fundamental rights specified in the amendment.[3] Positive rights and privileges are undoubtedly secured by the Fourteenth Amendment; but they are secured by way of prohibition against State laws and State proceedings affecting those rights and privileges, and by power given to Congress to legislate for the purpose of carrying such prohibition into effect; and such legislation must necessarily be predicated upon such supposed State laws or State proceedings, and be directed to the correction of their operation and effect. . . .

An apt illustration of this distinction may be found in some of the provisions of the original Constitution. Take the subject of contracts, for example. The Constitution prohibited the States from passing any law impairing the obligation of contracts. This did not give to Congress power to provide laws for the general enforcement of contracts; nor power to invest the courts of the United States with jurisdiction over contracts, so as to enable parties to sue upon them in those courts. It did, however, give the power to provide remedies by which the impairment of contracts by State legislation might be counteracted and corrected; and this power was exercised. The remedy which Congress actually provided was that contained in the twenty-fifth section of the Judiciary Act of 1789, giving to the Supreme Court of the United States

---

[2] **Note:** This paragraph is the origin of the "state action" doctrine, which provides that Section 1 of the Fourteenth Amendment applies only to states, not to individuals.

[3] **Questions:** Here, Bradley is explaining that Congress's power is *remedial*, not *definitional*. Referencing another clause in the Constitution that prohibits states from "impairing the Obligation of Contracts," he notes that this clause did not empower Congress to define what counts as a contract or to federalize all contract law. Rather, all Congress could do was allow federal courts to remedy unconstitutional state laws.

Do you find the analogy persuasive? What about the Fugitive Slave Clause? Recall that in *Prigg v. Pennsylvania*, the Court allowed Congress to enact the Fugitive Slave Act of 1793 in order to enforce the spirit of that clause and protect the rights of enslavers.

jurisdiction by writ of error to review the final decisions of State courts whenever they should sustain the validity of a State statute or authority, alleged to be repugnant to the Constitution or laws of the United States. By this means, if a State law was passed impairing the obligation of a contract, and the State tribunals sustained the validity of the law, the mischief could be corrected in this court. The legislation of Congress, and the proceedings provided for under it, were corrective in their character. No attempt was made to draw into the United States courts the litigation of contracts generally, and no such attempt would have been sustained. We do not say that the remedy provided was the only one that might have been provided in that case. Probably Congress had power to pass a law giving to the courts of the United States direct jurisdiction over contracts alleged to be impaired by a State law; and, under the broad provisions of the act of March 3, 1875, giving to the circuit courts jurisdiction of all cases arising under the Constitution and laws of the United States, it is possible that such jurisdiction now exists. But under that or any other law, it must appear, as well by allegation as proof at the trial, that the Constitution had been violated by the action of the State legislature. Some obnoxious State law passed, or that might be passed, is necessary to be assumed in order to lay the foundation of any federal remedy in the case, and for the very sufficient reason that the constitutional prohibition is against *State laws* impairing the obligation of contracts.

And so in the present case, until some State law has been passed, or some State action through its officers or agents has been taken, adverse to the rights of citizens sought to be protected by the Fourteenth Amendment, no legislation of the United States under said amendment, nor any proceeding under such legislation, can be called into activity, for the prohibitions of the amendment are against State laws and acts done under State authority. Of course, legislation may and should be provided in advance to meet the exigency when it arises, but it should be adapted to the mischief and wrong which the amendment was intended to provide against; and that is, State laws or State action of some kind adverse to the rights of the citizen secured by the amendment. Such legislation cannot properly cover the whole domain of rights appertaining to life, liberty, and property, defining them and providing for their vindication.[4] That would be to establish a code of municipal law regulative of all private rights between man and man in society. It would be to make Congress take the place of the State legislatures and to supersede them. It is absurd to affirm that, because the rights of life, liberty, and property (which include all civil rights that men have) are by the amendment sought to be protected against invasion on the part of the state without due process of law, Congress may, therefore, provide due process of law for their vindication in every case; and that, because the denial by a State to any persons of the equal protection of the laws is prohibited by the amendment, therefore Congress may establish laws for their equal protection. In fine, the legislation which Congress is authorized to adopt in this behalf is not general legislation upon the rights of the citizen, but corrective legislation; that is, such as may be necessary and proper for counteracting such laws as the States may adopt or enforce, and which by the amendment they are prohibited from making or enforcing, or such acts and proceedings as the States may commit or take, and which by the amendment they are prohibited from committing or taking. It is not necessary

---

[4] **Questions:** Bradley expresses concern in the next few paragraphs that if Congress has the power to enact an antidiscrimination law, then it is difficult to imagine a limiting principle on what other kinds of domestic legislation it can pass.

But his interpretation of Section 5 raises the opposite problem: if Congress *cannot* enact this antidiscrimination law, what kinds of laws is it empowered to pass? Judging by Bradley's analysis, must Congress wait for a state to violate Section 1 before it can remedy the violation, or can it also pass prophylactic legislation?

for us to state, if we could, what legislation would be proper for Congress to adopt. It is sufficient for us to examine whether the law in question is of that character.

An inspection of the law shows that it makes no reference whatever to any supposed or apprehended violation of the Fourteenth Amendment on the part of the states. It is not predicated on any such view. It proceeds *ex directo* to declare that certain acts committed by individuals shall be deemed offenses, and shall be prosecuted and punished by proceedings in the courts of the United States. It does not profess to be corrective of any constitutional wrong committed by the States; it does not make its operation to depend upon any such wrong committed. It applies equally to cases arising in states which have the justest laws respecting the personal rights of citizens, and whose authorities are ever ready to enforce such laws as to those which arise in States that may have violated the prohibition of the amendment. In other words, it steps into the domain of local jurisprudence, and lays down rules for the conduct of individuals in society towards each other, and imposes sanctions for the enforcement of those rules, without referring in any manner to any supposed action of the state or its authorities.

If this legislation is appropriate for enforcing the prohibitions of the amendment, it is difficult to see where it is to stop. Why may not Congress, with equal show of authority, enact a code of laws for the enforcement and vindication of all rights of life, liberty, and property? If it is supposable that the States may deprive persons of life, liberty, and property without due process of law, (and the amendment itself does suppose this,) why should not Congress proceed at once to prescribe due process of law for the protection of every one of these fundamental rights, in every possible case, as well as to prescribe equal privileges in inns, public conveyances, and theaters. The truth is that the implication of a power to legislate in this manner is based upon the assumption that if the States are forbidden to legislate or act in a particular way on a particular subject, and power is conferred upon Congress to enforce the prohibition, this gives Congress power to legislate generally upon that subject, and not merely power to provide modes of redress against such State legislation or action. The assumption is certainly unsound. It is repugnant to the Tenth Amendment of the Constitution, which declares that powers not delegated to the United States by the Constitution, nor prohibited by it to the States, are reserved to the States respectively or to the people. . . .

In this connection it is proper to state that civil rights, such as are guarantied by the Constitution against State aggression, cannot be impaired by the wrongful acts of individuals, unsupported by State authority in the shape of laws, customs, or judicial or executive proceedings.[5] The wrongful act of an individual, unsupported by any such authority, is simply a private wrong, or a crime of that individual; an invasion of the rights of the injured party, it is true, whether they affect his person, his property, or his reputation; but if not sanctioned in some way by the State, or not done under State authority, his rights remain in full force, and may presumably be vindicated by resort to the laws of the State for redress. An individual cannot deprive a man of his right to vote, to hold property, to buy and to sell, to sue in the courts, or to be a witness or a juror; he may, by force or fraud, interfere with the enjoyment of the right in a particular case; he may commit an assault against the person, or commit murder, or use ruffian violence at the polls, or slander the good name of a fellow-citizen; but unless protected in these wrongful acts by some shield of State law or State authority,

---

[5] **Questions:** Here, Bradley is offering a second objection to the Civil Rights Act. Not only is the act not *remedial*, he writes, but it also applies to *individuals* rather than states. Why can't an individual participate in denying someone the equal protection of the laws? Why doesn't a state deny someone the equal protection of the laws when it fails to protect that person from hostile individuals?

he cannot destroy or injure the right; he will only render himself amenable to satisfaction or punishment; and amenable therefor to the laws of the State where the wrongful acts are committed. Hence, in all those cases where the Constitution seeks to protect the rights of the citizen against discriminative and unjust laws of the State by prohibiting such laws, it is not individual offenses, but abrogation and denial of rights, which it denounces, and for which it clothes the Congress with power to provide a remedy. This abrogation and denial of rights, for which the States alone were or could be responsible, was the great seminal and fundamental wrong which was intended to be remedied. And the remedy to be provided must necessarily be predicated upon that wrong. It must assume that in the cases provided for, the evil or wrong actually committed rests upon some State law or State authority for its excuse and perpetration.

Of course, these remarks do not apply to those cases in which Congress is clothed with direct and plenary powers of legislation over the whole subject, accompanied with an express or implied denial of such power to the States, as in the regulation of commerce with foreign nations, among the several States, and with the Indian tribes, the coining of money, the establishment of post-offices and post-roads, the declaring of war, etc. In these cases Congress has power to pass laws for regulating the subjects specified, in every detail, and the conduct and transactions of individuals respect thereof. But where a subject is not submitted to the general legislative power of Congress, but is only submitted thereto for the purpose of rendering effective some prohibition against particular State legislation or state action in reference to that subject, the power given is limited by its object, and any legislation by Congress in the matter must necessarily be corrective in its character, adapted to counteract and redress the operation of such prohibited State laws or proceedings of State officers.[6]

If the principles of interpretation which we have laid down are correct, as we deem them to be,—and they are in accord with the principles laid down in the cases before referred to, as well as in the recent case of *United States v. Harris*, 106 U.S. 629, it is clear that the law in question cannot be sustained by any grant of legislative power made to Congress by the Fourteenth Amendment. That amendment prohibits the States from denying to any person the equal protection of the laws, and declares that Congress shall have power to enforce, by appropriate legislation, the provisions of the amendment. The law in question, without any reference to adverse State legislation on the subject, declares that all persons shall be entitled to equal accommodation and privileges of inns, public conveyances, and places of public amusement, and imposes a penalty upon any individual who shall deny to any citizen such equal accommodations and privileges. This is not corrective legislation; it is primary and direct; it takes immediate and absolute possession of the subject of the right of admission to inns, public conveyances, and places of amusement. It supersedes and displaces State legislation on the same subject, or only allows it permissive force. It ignores such legislation, and assumes that the matter is one that belongs to the domain of national regulation. Whether it would not have been a more effective protection of the rights of citizens to have clothed Congress with plenary power over the whole subject, is not now the question. What we have to decide is, whether such plenary power has been conferred upon Congress by the Fourteenth Amendment, and, in our judgment, it has not. . . .

---

[6] **Question:** Bradley distinguishes Congress's remedial power under Section 5 of the Fourteenth Amendment from its "direct and plenary powers" under Article I. Why is it appropriate for Congress to directly regulate individuals under, say, the Commerce Clause, but not in this case?

We have . . . discussed the validity of the law in reference to cases arising in the States only; and not in reference to cases arising in the Territories or the District of Columbia, which are subject to the plenary legislation of Congress in every branch of municipal regulation. Whether the law would be a valid one as applied to the Territories and the District is not a question for consideration in the cases before us; they all being cases arising within the limits of States. And whether Congress, in the exercise of its power to regulate commerce among the several States, might or might not pass a law regulating rights in public conveyances passing from one State to another, is also a question which is not now before us, as the sections in question are not conceived in any such view.[7]

[II. Is the law an exercise of the Thirteenth Amendment?]

But the power of Congress to adopt direct and primary, as distinguished from corrective, legislation on the subject in hand, is sought, in the second place, from the Thirteenth Amendment, which abolishes slavery. This amendment declares 'that neither slavery, nor involuntary servitude, except as a punishment for crime, whereof the party shall have been duly convicted, shall exist within the United States, or any place subject to their jurisdiction;' and it gives Congress power to enforce the amendment by appropriate legislation.[8]

This amendment, as well as the Fourteenth, is undoubtedly self-executing without any ancillary legislation, so far as its terms are applicable to any existing state of circumstances. By its own unaided force it abolished slavery, and established universal freedom. Still, legislation may be necessary and proper to meet all the various cases and circumstances to be affected by it, and to prescribe proper modes of redress for its violation in letter or spirit. And such legislation may be primary and direct in its character; for the amendment is not a mere prohibition of State laws establishing or upholding slavery, but an absolute declaration that slavery or involuntary servitude shall not exist in any part of the United States.

It is true that slavery cannot exist without law any more than property in lands and goods can exist without law, and therefore the Thirteenth Amendment may be regarded as nullifying all State laws which establish or uphold slavery. But it has a reflex character also, establishing and decreeing universal civil and political freedom throughout the United States; and it is assumed that the power vested in Congress to enforce the article by appropriate legislation, clothes Congress with power to pass all laws necessary and proper for abolishing all badges and incidents of slavery in the United States; and upon this assumption it is claimed that this is sufficient authority for declaring by law that all persons shall have equal accommodations and privileges in all inns, public conveyances, and places of public amusement; the argument being that the denial of such equal accommodations and privileges is in itself a subjection to a species of servitude within the meaning of the amendment. Conceding the major proposition to be true, that Congress has a right to enact all necessary and proper laws for the obliteration and prevention of slavery, with all its badges and incidents, is the minor proposition also true, that the denial to any person of admission to the accommodations and privileges of an inn, a public conveyance, or a theater, does subject that person to any form of servitude, or tend to fasten upon

---

7 **Note:** Note Bradley's caveats here. The Supreme Court would later uphold antidiscrimination laws passed under these exceptions in *District of Columbia v. John R. Thompson Co.*, 346 U.S. 100 (1953) (District Clause), and *Heart of Atlanta Motel, Inc. v. United States*, 379 U.S. 241 (1964) (Commerce Clause).

8 **Question:** In the first half of his opinion, Bradley distinguished Congress's remedial powers under the Fourteenth Amendment from its direct and plenary powers under the Commerce Clause. Does he think the Thirteenth Amendment is "remedial" or "plenary"?

him any badge of slavery? If it does not, then power to pass the law is not found in the Thirteenth Amendment.[9]

In a very able and learned presentation of the cognate question as to the extent of the rights, privileges, and immunities of citizens which cannot rightfully be abridged by state laws under the Fourteenth Amendment, made in a former case, a long list of burdens and disabilities of a servile character, incident to feudal vasslage in France, and which were abolished by the decrees of the National Assembly, was presented for the purpose of showing that all inequalities and observances exacted by one man from another, were servitudes or badges of slavery, which a great nation, in its effort to establish universal liberty, made haste to wipe out and destroy. . . .

But is there any similarity between such servitudes and a denial by the owner of an inn, a public conveyance, or a theater, of its accommodations and privileges to an individual, even though the denial be founded on the race or color of that individual? Where does any slavery or servitude, or badge of either, arise from such an act of denial? . . . It may be that by the Black Code, (as it was called,) in the times when slavery prevailed, the proprietors of inns and public conveyances were forbidden to receive persons of the African race, because it might assist slaves to escape from the control of their masters. This was merely a means of preventing such escapes, and was no part of the servitude itself. A law of that kind could not have any such object now, however justly it might be deemed an invasion of the party's legal right as a citizen. . . .

The long existence of African slavery in this country gave us very distinct notions of what it was, and what were its necessary incidents. Compulsory service of the slave for the benefit of the master, restraint of his movements except by the master's will, disability to hold property, to make contracts, to have a standing in court, to be a witness against a white person, and such like burdens and incapacities were the inseparable incidents of the institution. Severer punishments for crimes were imposed on the slave than on free persons guilty of the same offenses. Congress, as we have seen, by the Civil Rights Bill of 1866, passed in view of the Thirteenth Amendment, before the Fourteenth was adopted, undertook to wipe out these burdens and disabilities, the necessary incidents of slavery, constituting its substance and visible from; and to secure to all citizens of every race and color, and without regard to previous servitude, those fundamental rights which are the essence of civil freedom, namely, the same right to make and enforce contracts, to sue, be parties, give evidence, and to inherit, purchase, lease, sell, and convey property, as is enjoyed by white citizens.[10] Whether this legislation was fully authorized by the Thirteenth Amendment alone, without the support which it afterwards received from the Fourteenth Amendment, after the adoption of which it was re-enacted with some additions, it is not necessary to inquire. It is referred to for the purpose of showing that at that time (in 1866) Congress did not assume, under the authority given by the Thirteenth Amendment, to adjust what may be called the social rights of men and races in the community; but only to declare and vindicate those fundamental rights

---

[9] **Question:** Bradley here suggests that the Thirteenth Amendment gives Congress the power not only to remedy violations of the letter of the Thirteenth Amendment but also to enact laws to enforce the spirit of the Thirteenth Amendment by abolishing all "badges and incidents" of slavery. Why doesn't Congress have the same power under the Fourteenth Amendment?

[10] **Question:** Bradley is writing approvingly of the Civil Rights Act of 1866, which, among other things, declared that black citizens had the same right as white citizens to enter into contracts. If Congress had the power to enact that law, is there any reason why Congress does not have the power to prohibit white proprietors from denying hotel rooms or theater tickets to black customers?

which appertain to the essence of citizenship, and the enjoyment or deprivation of which constitutes the essential distinction between freedom and slavery.

We must not forget that the province and scope of the Thirteenth and Fourteenth Amendments are different: the former simply abolished slavery: the latter prohibited the States from abridging the privileges or immunities of citizens of the United States, from depriving them of life, liberty, or property without due process of law, and from denying to any the equal protection of the laws. The amendments are different, and the powers of Congress under them are different. What Congress has power to do under one, it may not have power to do under the other. Under the Thirteenth Amendment, it has only to do with slavery and its incidents. Under the Fourteenth Amendment, it has power to counteract and render nugatory all state laws and proceedings which have the effect to abridge any of the privileges or immunities which have the effect to abridge any deprive them of life, liberty, or property without due process of law, or to deny to any of them the equal protection of the laws. Under the Thirteenth Amendment the legislation, so far as necessary or proper to eradicate all forms and incidents of slavery and involuntary servitude, may be direct and primary, operating upon the acts of individuals, whether sanctioned by State legislation or not; under the Fourteenth, as we have already shown, it must necessarily be, and can only be, corrective in its character, addressed to counteract and afford relief against State regulations or proceedings.

The only question under the present head, therefore, is, whether the refusal to any persons of the accommodations of an inn, or a public conveyance, or a place of public amusement, by an individual, and without any sanction or support from any State law or regulation, does inflict upon such persons any manner of servitude, or form of slavery, as those terms are understood in this country? Many wrongs may be obnoxious to the prohibitions of the Fourteenth Amendment which are not, in any just sense, incidents or elements of slavery. Such, for example, would be the taking of private property without due process of law; or allowing persons who have committed certain crimes (horse stealing, for example) to be seized and hung by the *posse comitatus* without regular trial; or denying to any person, or class of persons, the right to pursue any peaceful avocations allowed to others. What is called class legislation would belong to this category, and would be obnoxious to the prohibitions of the Fourteenth Amendment, but would not to the prohibitions of the Fourteenth Amendment but would not necessarily be so to the Thirteenth, when not involving the idea of any subjection of one man to another. . . .

Now, conceding, for the sake of the argument, that the admission to an inn, a public conveyance, or a place of public amusement, on equal terms with all other citizens, is the right of every man and all classes of men, is it any more than one of those rights which the states by the Fourteenth Amendment are forbidden to deny to any person? And is the Constitution violated until the denial of the right has some state sanction or authority? Can the act of a mere individual, the owner of the inn, the public conveyance, or place of amusement, refusing the accommodation, be justly regarded as imposing any badge of slavery or servitude upon the applicant, or only as inflicting an ordinary civil injury, properly cognizable by the laws of the state, and presumably subject to redress by those laws until the contrary appears?

After giving to these questions all the consideration which their importance demands, we are forced to the conclusion that such an act of refusal has nothing to do with slavery or involuntary servitude, and that if it is violative of any right of the party, his redress is to be sought under the laws of the State; or, if those laws are adverse to his rights and do not protect him, his remedy will be found in the corrective legislation which Congress has adopted, or may adopt, for counteracting the effect of State laws, or State action, prohibited by the Fourteenth Amendment. It would be running the slavery argument into the ground to make it apply to every act of discrimination which a person may see fit to make as to the guests he will entertain, or as to the people he will take into his coach or cab or car, or admit to his concert or theater, or deal with in other matters of intercourse or business. Innkeepers and public carriers, by the laws of all the States, so far as we are aware, are bound, to the extent of their facilities, to furnish proper accommodation to all unobjectionable persons who in good faith apply for them. If the laws themselves make any unjust discrimination, amenable to the prohibitions of the Fourteenth Amendment, Congress has full power to afford a remedy under that amendment and in accordance with it.

When a man has emerged from slavery, and by the aid of beneficent legislation has shaken off the inseparable concomitants of that state, there must be some stage in the progress of his elevation when he takes the rank of a mere citizen, and ceases to be the special favorite of the laws, and when his rights as a citizen, or a man, are to be protected in the ordinary modes by which other men's rights are protected.[11] There were thousands of free colored people in this country before the abolition of slavery, enjoying all the essential rights of life, liberty, and property the same as white citizens; yet no one, at that time, thought that it was any invasion of their personal *status* as freemen because they were not admitted to all the privileges enjoyed by white citizens, or because they were subjected to discriminations in the enjoyment of accommodations in inns, public conveyances, and places of amusement. Mere discriminations on account of race or color were not regarded as badges of slavery. If, since that time, the enjoyment of equal rights in all these respects has become established by constitutional enactment, it is not by force of the Thirteenth Amendment, (which merely abolishes slavery,) but by force of the [Fourteenth] and Fifteenth Amendments.

On the whole, we are of opinion that no countenance of authority for the passage of the law in question can be found in either the Thirteenth or Fourteenth Amendment of the Constitution; and no other ground of authority for its passage being suggested, it must necessarily be declared void, at least so far as its operation in the several States is concerned. . . .

■ HARLAN, J., dissenting.[12]

The opinion in these cases proceeds, as it seems to me, upon grounds entirely too narrow and artificial. The substance and spirit of the recent amendments of the Constitution have been sacrificed by a subtle and ingenious verbal criticism. 'It is not the words of the law but the internal sense of it that makes the law. The letter of the law is the body; the sense and reason of the law is the soul.' Constitutional provisions, adopted in the interest of liberty, and for the purpose of securing, through national legislation, if need be, rights inhering in a state of freedom, and belonging to American citizenship, have been so construed as to defeat the ends the people desired to accomplish, which they attempted to accomplish, and which they supposed they had accomplished by changes in their fundamental law. By this I do not mean that the

---

[11] **Questions:** Earlier, Bradley wrote that the Thirteenth Amendment empowered Congress to "pass all laws necessary and proper for abolishing all badges and incidents of slavery in the United States." But in these two paragraphs, Bradley suggests (1) that racial discrimination has nothing to do with slavery, and (2) too much time has elapsed since the abolition of slavery—eighteen years—for Congress to continue exercising this power.

Whether or not you agree with Bradley's conclusion, do you agree that there must be *some* time and subject limits after the abolition of slavery when Congress's power to enforce that abolition comes to an end? Or should the Thirteenth Amendment be interpreted to give Congress permanent authority to combat all legacies of slavery even decades later?

[12] **Question:** Justice John Marshall Harlan, a former slave owner from Kentucky, was a frequent lone dissenter in the Supreme Court's early decisions interpreting the Thirteenth and Fourteenth Amendments. Why, precisely, does he disagree with the majority opinion here?

determination of these cases should have been materially controlled by considerations of mere expediency or policy. I mean only, in this form, to express an earnest conviction that the court has departed from the familiar rule requiring, in the interpretation of constitutional provisions, that full effect be given to the intent with which they were adopted.

The purpose of the first section of the act of Congress of March 1, 1875, was to prevent race discrimination. . . . The court adjudges that Congress is without power, under either the Thirteenth or Fourteenth Amendment, to establish such [legislation]. . . . Before considering the particular language and scope of these amendments it will be proper to recall the relations which, prior to their adoption, subsisted between the national government and the institution of slavery, as indicated by the provisions of the Constitution, the legislation of Congress, and the decisions of this court. In this mode we may obtain keys with which to open the mind of the people, and discover the thought intended to be expressed.

In section 2 of article 4 of the Constitution it was provided that 'no person held to service or labor in one State, under the laws thereof, escaping into another, shall, in consequence of any law or regulation therein, be discharged from such service or labor, but shall be delivered up on claim of the party to whom such service or labor may be due.' Under the authority of this clause Congress passed the Fugitive Slave Law of 1793, establishing the mode for the recovery of a fugitive slave, and prescribing a penalty against any person knowingly and willingly obstructing or hindering the master, his agent or attorney, in seizing, arresting, and recovering the fugitive, or who should rescue the fugitive from him, or who should harbor or conceal the slave after notice that he was a fugitive.

In *Prigg v. Commonwealth of Pennsylvania* 16 Pet. 539, this court had occasion to define the powers and duties of Congress in reference to fugitives from labor. Speaking by Mr. Justice STORY, the court [declared] . . . That Congress is not restricted to legislation for the execution of its powers expressly granted; but, for the protection of rights guarantied by the Constitution, it may employ, through legislation, such means, not prohibited, as are necessary and proper, or such as are appropriate, to attain the ends proposed; . . . and That the right of the master to have his slave, thus escaping, delivered up on claim, being guaranteed by the Constitution, the fair implication was that the national government was clothed with appropriate authority and functions to enforce it. . . .

We have seen that the power of Congress, by legislation, to enforce the master's right to have his slave delivered up on claim was *implied* from the recognition of that right in the national Constitution. . . . This court has uniformly held that the national government has the power, whether expressly given or not, to secure and protect rights conferred or guarantied by the constitution. That doctrine ought not now to be abandoned, when the inquiry is not as to an implied power to protect the master's rights, but what may congress do, under powers expressly granted, for the protection of freedom, and the rights necessarily inhering in a state of freedom.

I do not contend that the Thirteenth [or Fourteenth] Amendment invests congress with authority, by legislation, to regulate the entire body of the civil rights which citizens enjoy, or may enjoy, in the several states. But I hold that since slavery . . . was the moving or principal cause of the adoption of [those amendments], and since that institution rested wholly upon the inferiority, as a race, of those held in bondage, their freedom necessarily involved immunity from, and protection against, all discrimination against them, because of their race, in respect of such civil rights as belong to freemen of other races. Congress, therefore, under its express power to enforce [those amendments], by appropriate legislation, may enact laws to protect that people against the deprivation, *on account of their race*, of any civil rights enjoyed by other freemen in the same State; and such legislation may . . . operat[e] upon States, their officers and agents, and also upon, at least, such individuals and corporations as exercise public functions and wield power and authority under the State. . . .

NOTE: AFTERMATH OF THE *CIVIL RIGHTS CASES*

The *Civil Rights Cases* severely limited Congress's power to enforce the Reconstruction amendments.

Regarding the Thirteenth Amendment, the majority conceded that Congress could enact "all necessary and proper laws for the obliteration and prevention of slavery with all its badges and incidents." *Civil Rights Cases*, 109 U.S. at 21. Such laws could also apply to private individuals—a point that the Court later reemphasized in upholding an 1867 statute, 14 Stat. 546, which outlawed peonage, or debt slavery. *See United States v. Gaskin*, 320 U.S. 527 (1944); *Clyatt v. United States*, 197 U.S. 207 (1905); Douglas A. Blackmon, *Slavery by Another Name: The Re-enslavement of Black Americans from the Civil War to World War II* 174–75, 264 (2008).

But the Court narrowly interpreted the other "badges and incidents" of slavery to include only the disabilities remedied by the Civil Rights Act of 1866. *Civil Rights Cases*, 109 U.S. at 35. Interpreting the Thirteenth Amendment to apply to all racial discrimination, the Court wrote, "would be running the slavery argument into the ground." *Id.* at 24. On this basis, the Court later overturned the convictions of three white men who conspired to violently drive black workers from their employment in a lumber mill. The Court explained that such private intimidation wasn't sufficiently analogous to the disabilities of slavery to fall under the Thirteenth Amendment. *See Hodges v. United States*, 203 U.S. 1 (1906); *see also United States v. Kozminski*, 487 U.S. 931 (1988) (compulsion of servitude through "psychological coercion" is also not prohibited).

As for the Fourteenth Amendment, the Court conceded that the amendment broadly protected the equality of black people and their fundamental rights of citizenship. But the Court narrowly interpreted Section 5 of the amendment as empowering Congress only to enact remedial legislation, and only in response to "State laws or State action" of some kind. *Civil Rights Cases*, 109 U.S. at 52. If Congress had the plenary power to prohibit private discrimination, the Court wrote, then Congress could "establish a code of municipal law regulative of all private rights" and "take the place of the State legislatures." *Id.* at 13. This conclusion, ironically, echoed Andrew Johnson's veto of the Civil Rights Act of 1866—the same veto that prompted Congress to propose the Fourteenth Amendment in the first place. *See* Foner, *The Second Founding*, *supra*, at 152.

The *Civil Rights Cases* didn't address the Fifteenth Amendment. The following year, however, in *Ex parte Yarbrough*, 110 U.S. 651 (1884)—which is excerpted later (section 22.3)—the Court held that Article I, Section 4, gave Congress the power to prohibit private individuals from interfering with the right to vote in federal elections. Otherwise, the Court warned, the federal government would be helpless if people committed voter fraud, bribery, or other corrupt schemes to influence elections. *Id.* at 661. But in *James v. Bowman*, 190 U.S. 127 (1903), the Court struck down a provision of the Enforcement Act of 1870, ch. 114, 16 Stat. 140, which enforced the Fifteenth Amendment to prohibit private individuals from preventing others from exercising their right to vote on account of their race. Citing the *Civil Rights Cases* and *Harris*, the Court held that the Fifteenth Amendment "relates solely to action 'by the United States or by any state,' and does not contemplate wrongful individual acts. It is in this respect similar to . . . the Fourteenth Amendment." *James*, 190 U.S. at 136.

20.2 THE SECOND RECONSTRUCTION

In 1894, with Democrats in control of both houses of Congress and the White House for the first time since before the Civil War, Congress repealed most of the Enforcement Acts. *See* Act of Feb. 8, 1894, ch. 25, 28 Stat. 36. By the time Congress established the U.S. Code in 1926, only a handful of scattered provisions from Congress's once-lengthy Reconstruction laws survived, and their constitutionality remained suspect. *See* Act of June 30, 1926, ch. 712, 44 Stat. 777.

One provision, 42 U.S.C. § 1971 (now 52 U.S.C. § 10101), codified the Enforcement Act of 1870's prohibition on racial discrimination in voting. But *James v. Bowman*, 190 U.S. 127 (1903), denied the constitutionality of this provision as applied to private individuals.

A second set of provisions, 42 U.S.C. §§ 1981–82, codified the first section of the Civil Rights Act of 1866. As amended, these statutes declared that all people in the United States had the same right to contract, sue, and own property as white citizens.

Two more provisions, 18 U.S.C. § 241 and 42 U.S.C. § 1985(3), codified the provisions of the Ku Klux Klan Act of 1871 that were at issue in *United States v. Harris*, 106 U.S. 629 (1883). As amended, § 241 made it a crime for two or more people to conspire to deprive someone of a right secured by the Constitution or federal law, while § 1985(3) authorized the victim to bring a civil action.

A final set of provisions, 18 U.S.C. § 242 and 42 U.S.C. § 1983, codified, respectively, the second section of the Civil Rights Act of 1866 and the first section of the Ku Klux Klan Act of 1871. Section 242 made it a crime for any person, acting "under color of any law," to deprive someone of any "rights, privileges, or immunities secured or protected by the Constitution or laws of the United States." Section 1983 used similar language to authorize the victim to bring a civil action.

All of these statutes lay dormant until the 1940s. Southern states, meanwhile, took advantage of federal deference by enacting comprehensive segregation codes, also known as Jim Crow laws, that subordinated and disenfranchised black people. In Louisiana, for example, where black people represented half the population, there were over 130,000 eligible black voters in 1896. By 1910, after Louisiana adopted a new constitution and a series of new laws, the number of eligible black voters dropped to 730. *See* Richard H. Pildes, *Democracy, Anti-Democracy, and the Canon*, 17 Const. Comment. 303 (2000).

One type of disenfranchisement law on which Louisiana and other southern states heavily relied was a "white primary." Rather than prohibit black people from voting in elections, these laws authorized political parties to conduct earlier "primary" elections. The Democratic Party, in turn, prohibited black people from voting in its primary elections as a matter of its own internal rules. This whole scheme took advantage of the state action doctrine announced in the *Civil Rights Cases*, 109 U.S. 3 (1883), as well as the fact that by 1900 the Democratic Party was so dominant in the South that general elections were often uncontested. Because the Democratic Party appeared to be more analogous to a private individual than to a state official, neither the Fifteenth Amendment nor the enforcement acts seemed to apply to its rules. *See* Michael J. Klarman, *From Jim Crow to Civil Rights* 135 (2006).

These white primaries were ubiquitous in 1940 when the Department of Justice under President Franklin D. Roosevelt charged a Louisiana voting commissioner, Patrick Classic, with violating the Civil Rights Act of 1866, now 18 U.S.C. § 242. In *United States v. Classic*, the federal prosecutors alleged that Classic acted "under color of law" to deprive black voters of their constitutional rights when he counted the ballots cast in a whites-only primary election for a congressional representative. 313 U.S. 299, 308 (1941). In *Classic*, the Supreme Court held that "where the primary is by law made an integral part of the election machinery," Congress had the constitutional power to regulate it. *Id.* at 318.

Three years later, in a case brought under the civil equivalent of § 242, now 42 U.S.C. § 1983, the Court held that Congress had the power to prohibit racial discrimination in Texas's white primary even though Texas repealed all of its laws authorizing the primary. The Fifteenth Amendment, the Court wrote,

> grants to all citizens a right to participate in the choice of elected officials without restriction by any state because of race. This grant to the people of the opportunity for choice is not to be nullified by a State through casting its electoral process in a form which permits a private organization to practice racial discrimination in the election. Constitutional rights would be of little value if they could be thus indirectly denied.

Smith v. Allwright, 321 U.S. 649, 664 (1944).

Classic and *Allwright* appeared to reconsider the *Civil Rights Cases*' distinction between Congress's power to remedy state action and its lack of power to remedy private constitutional violations that resulted from state inaction. Later cases maintained a distinction between "rights that flow from the substantive powers of the Federal Government and may clearly be protected from private interference," such as the right to vote in a federal election, "and interests which the Constitution only guarantees from interference by States." *United States v. Williams*, 341 U.S. 70, 78 (1951) (plurality opinion). In 1957, when Congress passed the first federal civil rights act since 1875, it abided by this distinction by prohibiting "any person, whether acting under color of law or otherwise," from intimidating or preventing someone from voting in a federal election. Civil Rights Act of 1957, Pub. L. No. 85–315, 71 Stat. 634, 637. In *United States v. Raines*, the Supreme Court upheld this statute as applied to a state official, leaving to another day "whatever precisely may be the reach of the Fifteenth Amendment" to private individuals. 362 U.S. 17, 25 (1960).

Five years after *Raines*, Congress boldly added a provision to the landmark Voting Rights Act of 1965 that prohibited any person, whether acting under color of law or otherwise, from intimidating voters in a state or local election. Pub. L. No. 89–110, 79 Stat. 437, 443. As *Ex parte Yarbrough*, 110 U.S. 651 (1884), authorized Congress to prohibit private interference only in a *federal* election, this provision would be constitutional as applied to private individuals only if the Fifteenth Amendment's reach extends that far. The Supreme Court has yet to evaluate such a case.

20.2.1

United States v. Guest

383 U.S. 745 (1966)

As discussed earlier with regard to Congress's power to regulate interstate commerce in the realm of civil rights law (section 9.1), when Congress enacted the Civil Rights Act of 1964, it relied on the Commerce Clause, not Section 5 of the Fourteenth Amendment. Its choice was principally determined by the *Civil Rights Cases*, which struck down the Civil Rights Act of 1875 on the ground that Section 5 of the Fourteenth Amendment didn't permit Congress to prohibit racial discrimination by private individuals. But the *Civil Rights Cases* also included the caveat that "whether Congress, in the exercise of its power to regulate commerce among the several States, might or might not pass a law regulating rights in public conveyances passing from one State to another, is . . . a question which is not now before us." *The Civil Rights Cases*, 109 U.S. at 19. The 1964 Congress took advantage of that caveat to enact an antidiscrimination law that was materially identical to the Civil Rights Act of 1875—except that it applied only to businesses that substantially affected interstate commerce.

A week after the passage of the Civil Rights Act of 1964, a black military reserve officer named Lemuel Penn was murdered by members of the Ku Klux Klan. They stopped him while he was driving from Fort Benning, in Georgia, to his home in Washington, D.C. When the suspects were tried in Georgia state court, they were acquitted by an all-white jury. Federal prosecutors eventually charged two of the suspects, including Herbert Guest, with violating a surviving section of the Ku Klux Klan Act of 1871, now 18 U.S.C. § 241, that made it a crime for "two or more persons [to] conspire to injure, oppress, threaten, or intimidate any citizen in the free exercise or enjoyment of any right or privilege secured to him by the Constitution or laws of the United States." The indictment charged Guest with conspiring to deprive Penn of his right to use state facilities (i.e., state highways and state-owned rest stops) without racial discrimination.

In *United States v. Guest*, 383 U.S. 745 (1966), the Court took an opportunity to revisit—and revise—the state action doctrine of the *Civil Rights Cases*.

■ MR. JUSTICE STEWART delivered the opinion of the Court.[13]

The six defendants in this case were indicted by a United States grand jury in the Middle District of Georgia for criminal conspiracy in violation of 18 U.S.C. § 241. . . . [T]he indictment alleged a single conspiracy by the defendants to deprive Negro citizens of the free exercise and enjoyment of several specified rights secured by the Constitution and laws of the United States . . . [including] rights protected by the Equal Protection Clause of the Fourteenth Amendment. . . . [But] the indictment in the present case names no person alleged to have acted in any way under the color of state law. The argument is therefore made that, since there exist no Equal Protection Clause rights against wholly private action, the judgment of the District Court on this branch of the case must be affirmed. On its face, the argument is unexceptionable. The Equal Protection Clause speaks to the State or to those acting under the color of its authority.

In this connection, we emphasize that § 241 by its clear language incorporates no more than the Equal Protection Clause itself; the statute does not purport to give substantive, as opposed to remedial, implementation to any rights secured by that Clause. Since we therefore deal here only with the bare terms of the Equal Protection Clause itself, nothing said in this opinion goes to the question of what kinds of other and broader legislation Congress might constitutionally enact under § 5 of the Fourteenth Amendment to implement that Clause or any other provision of the Amendment.

It is a commonplace that rights under the Equal Protection Clause itself arise only where there has been involvement of the State or of one acting under the color of its authority. The Equal Protection Clause 'does not * * * add any thing to the rights which one citizen has under the Constitution against another.' *United States v. Cruikshank*, 92 U.S. 542, 554—555. As Mr. Justice Douglas more recently put it, 'The Fourteenth Amendment protects the individual against state action, not against wrongs done by individuals.' *United States v. Williams*, 341 U.S. 70, 92 (dissenting opinion). This has been the view of the Court from the beginning. *United States v. Cruikshank, supra*; *United States v. Harris*, 106 U.S. 629; *Civil Rights Cases*, 109 U.S. 3. It remains the Court's view today.

---

[13] **As You Read, Consider:** The *Civil Rights Cases* held that Congress's power to enforce the Fourteenth Amendment—including in statutes like 18 U.S.C. § 241—was limited to remedying "State action." 109 U.S. 3, 6 (1883). Does Justice Potter Stewart apply that doctrine, modify it, or overrule it?

This is not to say, however, that the involvement of the State need be either exclusive or direct. In a variety of situations the Court has found state action of a nature sufficient to create rights under the Equal Protection Clause even though the participation of the State was peripheral, or its action was only one of several co-operative forces leading to the constitutional violation.[14]

This case, however, requires no determination of the threshold level that state action must attain in order to create rights under the Equal Protection Clause. This is so because, contrary to the argument of the litigants, the indictment in fact contains an express allegation of state involvement sufficient at least to require the denial of a motion to dismiss. One of the means of accomplishing the object of the conspiracy, according to the indictment, was 'By causing the arrest of Negroes by means of false reports that such Negroes had committed criminal acts.' . . . [T]he allegation is broad enough to cover a charge of active connivance by agents of the State in the making of the 'false reports,' or other conduct amounting to official discrimination clearly sufficient to constitute denial of rights protected by the Equal Protection Clause. Although it is possible that a bill of particulars, or the proof if the case goes to trial, would disclose no co-operative action of that kind by officials of the State, the allegation in enough to prevent dismissal of this branch of the indictment.

■ MR. JUSTICE CLARK, with whom MR. JUSTICE BLACK and MR. JUSTICE FORTAS join, concurring.

I join the opinion of the Court in this case but believe it worthwhile to comment on its [discussion of the Fourteenth Amendment.] . . .

The Court carves out of its opinion the question of the power of Congress, under § 5 of the Fourteenth Amendment, to enact legislation implementing the Equal Protection Clause or any other provision of the Fourteenth Amendment. The Court's interpretation of the indictment clearly avoids the question whether Congress, by appropriate legislation, has the power to punish private conspiracies that interfere with Fourteenth Amendment rights, such as the right to utilize public facilities. My Brother BRENNAN, however, says that the Court's disposition constitutes an acceptance of appellees' aforesaid contention as to § 241. Some of his language further suggests that the Court indicates *sub silentio* that Congress does not have the power to outlaw such conspiracies. Although the Court specifically rejects any such connotation, it is, I believe, both appropriate and necessary under the circumstances here to say that there now can be no doubt that the specific language of § 5 empowers the Congress to enact laws punishing all conspiracies—with or without state action—that interfere with Fourteenth Amendment rights.

■ MR. JUSTICE BRENNAN, with whom THE CHIEF JUSTICE and MR. JUSTICE DOUGLAS join, concurring in part and dissenting in part.[15]

I agree with so much of [the majority] as construes 18 U.S.C. § 241 to encompass conspiracies to injure, oppress, threaten or intimidate citizens in the free exercise or enjoyment of Fourteenth Amendment rights. . . . I do not agree, however, with the remainder . . . which holds, as I read the opinion, that a conspiracy to interfere with the exercise of the right to equal utilization of state facilities is not, within the meaning of § 241, a conspiracy to interfere with the exercise of a 'right * * *

[14] **Questions:** Is this the same standard that the Court applied in the *Civil Rights Cases*? Would that case have come out the same way under this "peripheral" action test?

[15] **Questions:** In the previous concurring opinion, three justices indicated that they would overrule the state action doctrine. Would the three justices in this concurring opinion—the most liberal justices on the Warren Court—also overrule the state action doctrine? About what do the three opinions in this case disagree?

secured * * * by the Constitution' unless discriminatory conduct by state officers is involved in the alleged conspiracy. . . .

For me, the right to use state facilities without discrimination on the basis of race is, within the meaning of § 241, a right created by, arising under and dependent upon the Fourteenth Amendment and hence is a right 'secured' by that Amendment. . . . The Fourteenth Amendment commands the State to provide the members of all races with equal access to the public facilities it owns or manages, and the right of a citizen to use those facilities without discrimination on the basis of race is a basic corollary of this command. Whatever may be the status of the right to equal utilization of privately owned facilities, it must be emphasized that we are here concerned with the right to equal utilization of public facilities owned or operated by or on behalf of the State. To deny the existence of this right or its constitutional stature is to deny the history of the last decade, or to ignore the role of federal power, predicated on the Fourteenth Amendment, in obtaining nondiscriminatory access to such facilities. . . .

My view as to the scope of § 241 requires that I reach the question of constitutional power—whether § 241 or legislation indubitably designed to punish entirely private conspiracies to interfere with the exercise of Fourteenth Amendment rights constitutes a permissible exercise of the power granted to Congress by § 5 of the Fourteenth Amendment 'to enforce, by appropriate legislation, the provisions of' the Amendment.

A majority of the members of the Court expresses the view today that § 5 empowers Congress to enact laws punishing all conspiracies to interfere with the exercise of Fourteenth Amendment rights, whether or not state officers or others acting under the color of state law are implicated in the conspiracy. Although the Fourteenth Amendment itself, according to established doctrine, 'speaks to the State or to those acting under the color of its authority,' legislation protecting rights created by that Amendment, such as the right to equal utilization of state facilities, need not be confined to punishing conspiracies in which state officers participate. Rather, § 5 authorizes Congress to make laws that it concludes are reasonably necessary to protect a right created by and arising under that Amendment; and Congress is thus fully empowered to determine that punishment of private conspiracies interfering with the exercise of such a right is necessary to its full protection. It made that determination in enacting § 241, and, therefore § 241 is constitutional legislation as applied to reach the private conspiracy alleged in the second numbered paragraph of the indictment.

I acknowledge that some of the decisions of this Court, most notably an aspect of the *Civil Rights Cases*, 109 U.S. 3, 11, have declared that Congress' power under § 5 is confined to the adoption of 'appropriate legislation for correcting the effects of * * * prohibited state law and state acts, and thus to render them effectually null, void, and innocuous.' I do not accept—and a majority of the Court today rejects—this interpretation of § 5. It reduces the legislative power to enforce the provisions of the Amendment to that of the judiciary; and it attributes a far too limited objective to the Amendment's sponsors. . . .[16]

Viewed in its proper perspective, § 5 of the Fourteenth Amendment appears as a positive grant of legislative power, authorizing Congress to exercise its discretion in fashioning remedies to achieve civil and political equality for all citizens. No one would deny that Congress could enact legislation directing state officials to provide

---

[16] **Questions:** Justice William Brennan observes here that a majority of the Court rejects the *Civil Rights Cases*' interpretation of Section 5. Does this decision therefore overrule the *Civil Rights Cases*? Applying Brennan's opinion, are there any limits on Congress's power to enforce the Fourteenth Amendment?

Negroes with equal access to state schools, parks and other facilities owned or operated by the State. Nor could it be denied that Congress has the power to punish state officers who, in excess of their authority and in violation of state law, conspire to threaten, harass and murder Negroes for attempting to use these facilities. And I can find no principle of federalism nor word of the Constitution that denies Congress power to determine that in order adequately to protect the right to equal utilization of state facilities, it is also appropriate to punish other individuals—not state officers themselves and not acting in concert with state officers—who engage in the same brutal conduct for the same misguided purpose. . . .

20.2.2

Jones v. Alfred H. Mayer Co.

392 U.S. 409 (1968)

The Supreme Court's opinions in *Guest* were fractured, but they nevertheless clearly indicated that a majority of the Court—the three justices who joined Justice Tom Clark's opinion and the three justices who joined Justice William Brennan's opinion—believed that Congress had the power to enforce the Fourteenth Amendment against private individuals. In *Griffin v. Breckenridge*, 403 U.S. 88 (1971), the Court explicitly held as much, upholding 42 U.S.C. § 1985(3), which authorizes a person to seek damages against two or more people who conspire to deprive the person of the equal protection of the laws. Even though the criminal counterpart to this statute was struck down in *Harris*, the Court upheld a civil suit against a group of white people who conspired to assault black victims on the mistaken belief that they were civil rights workers. Although a "century of Fourteenth Amendment adjudication has . . . made it understandably difficult to conceive of what might constitute a deprivation of the equal protection of the laws by private persons," the Court wrote, "there is nothing inherent in the phrase that requires the action working the deprivation to come from the State." *Griffin*, 403 U.S. at 97.

The Court took a similarly broad view of the Thirteenth Amendment. Although the *Civil Rights Cases* struck down the Civil Rights Act of 1875, the Court favorably described the earlier Civil Rights Act of 1866 as a constitutional exercise of the Thirteenth and Fourteenth Amendments. The 1866 act nevertheless lay dormant for decades as 42 U.S.C. §§ 1981–82, which, as amended, declared that "[a]ll citizens of the United States shall have the same right, in every State and Territory, as is enjoyed by white citizens thereof to inherit, purchase, lease, sell, hold, and convey real and personal property." 42 U.S.C. § 1982.

In the early 1960s, the 1866 act caught the attention of the Freedom of Residence Committee of St. Louis, Missouri. The committee was a group of black and white activists who provided legal and limited financial support to black home buyers seeking to purchase homes in "white" areas of the city. Walter Johnson, *The Broken Heart of America* 320–21 (2020). Their opponents included the St. Louis Real Estate

Exchange, which assured clients that realtors in St. Louis had ways to "weed out the n—s" without involving the state or local government. *Id.*

The Freedom of Residence Committee soon helped Joseph Lee and Barbara Jo Jones—an interracial couple—sue the Alfred H. Mayer Company for violating the 1866 act. *Id.* The company was a housing developer in nearby Florissant, Missouri, that refused to sell homes to black people.

In *Jones v. Alfred H. Mayer Co.*, 392 U.S. 409 (1968), the Court upheld the application of the Civil Rights Act of 1866.

Related note: As the case made its way to the Supreme Court, Congress passed the Fair Housing Act of 1968, Pub. L. No. 90–284, 82 Stat. 73, 81, which broadly prohibited private individuals from refusing to sell or rent a home to any person because of race, color, religion, sex, familial status, or national origin. Although the 1968 act was passed too late to make it into the following case, its constitutionality turned on the same question of whether Congress could prohibit private housing discrimination where interstate commerce was unaffected.

■ MR. JUSTICE STEWART delivered the opinion of the Court.[17]

In this case we are called upon to determine the scope and constitutionality of an Act of Congress, 42 U.S.C. s 1982. . . . We hold that § 1982 bars all racial discrimination, private as well as public, in the sale or rental of property, and that the statute, thus construed, is a valid exercise of the power of Congress to enforce the Thirteenth Amendment. . . .

We begin with the language of the statute itself. In plain and unambiguous terms, § 1982 grants to all citizens, without regard to race or color, "the same right" to purchase and lease property "as is enjoyed by white citizens." As the Court of Appeals in this case evidently recognized, that right can be impaired as effectively by "those who place property on the market" as by the State itself. For, even if the State and its agents lend no support to those who wish to exclude persons from their communities on racial grounds, the fact remains that, whenever property "is placed on the market for whites only, whites have a right denied to Negroes." So long as a Negro citizen who wants to buy or rent a home can be turned away simply because he is not white, he cannot be said to enjoy "the *same* right * * * as is enjoyed by white citizens * * * to * * * purchase (and) lease * * * real and personal property." 42 U.S.C. s 1982. (Emphasis added.)

On its face, therefore, § 1982 appears to prohibit all discrimination against Negroes in the sale or rental of property—discrimination by private owners as well as discrimination by public authorities. Indeed, even the respondents seem to concede that, if § 1982 "means what it says"—to use the words of the respondents' brief—then it must encompass every racially motivated refusal to sell or rent and cannot be confined to officially sanctioned segregation in housing. Stressing what they consider to be the revolutionary implications of so literal a reading of § 1982, the respondents argue that Congress cannot possibly have intended any such result. Our examination

---

17 **As You Read, Consider:** Section 2 of the Thirteenth Amendment, like Section 5 of the Fourteenth Amendment, empowers Congress to enforce the amendment's terms by "appropriate" legislation. Who does Justice Potter Stewart (author of the majority opinion in *United States v. Guest*) think should be the primary interpreter of which laws are appropriate: Congress or the Court?

of the relevant history, however, persuades us that Congress meant exactly what it said. . . .

In its original form, 42 U.S.C. § 1982 was part of § 1 of the Civil Rights Act of 1866. That section was cast in sweeping terms. . . . The crucial language for our purposes was that which guaranteed all citizens "the same right, in every State and Territory in the United States, * * * to inherit, purchase, lease, sell, hold, and convey real and personal property * * * as is enjoyed by white citizens * * *." To the Congress that passed the Civil Rights Act of 1866, it was clear that the right to do these things might be infringed not only by "State or local law" but also by "custom, or prejudice." Thus, when Congress provided in § 1 of the Civil Rights Act that the right to purchase and lease property was to be enjoyed equally throughout the United States by Negro and white citizens alike, it plainly meant to secure that right against interference from any source whatever, whether governmental or private. . . .

In attempting to demonstrate the contrary, the respondents rely heavily upon the fact that the Congress which approved the 1866 statute wished to eradicate the recently enacted Black Codes—laws which had saddled Negroes with "onerous disabilities and burdens, and curtailed their rights * * * to such an extent that their freedom was of little value * * *." *Slaughter-House Cases*, 16 Wall. 36, 70. The respondents suggest that the only evil Congress sought to eliminate was that of racially discriminatory laws in the former Confederate States. But the Civil Rights Act was drafted to apply throughout the country, and its language was far broader than would have been necessary to strike down discriminatory statutes. . . .

On January 5, 1866, Senator [Lyman] Trumbull introduced . . . the bill which later became the Civil Rights Act of 1866. He described its objectives in terms that belie any attempt to read it narrowly:

"Mr. President, I regard the bill to which the attention of the Senate is now called as the most important measure that has been under its consideration since the adoption of the constitutional amendment abolishing slavery. That amendment declared that all persons in the United States should be free. This measure is intended to give effect to that declaration and secure to all persons within the United States practical freedom. There is very little importance in the general declaration of abstract truths and principles unless they can be carried into effect, unless the persons who are to be affected by them have some means of availing themselves of their benefits."

Of course, Senator Trumbull's bill would, as he pointed out, "destroy all (the) discriminations" embodied in the Black Codes, but it would do more: It would affirmatively secure for all men, whatever their race or color, what the Senator called the "great fundamental rights": "the right to acquire property, the right to go and come at pleasure, the right to enforce rights in the courts, to make contracts, and to inherit and dispose of property." As to those basic civil rights, the Senator said, the bill would "break down *all* discrimination between black men and white men." . . .

President Andrew Johnson vetoed the Act on March 27, and in the brief congressional debate that followed, his supporters characterized its reach in all embracing terms. . . . Those observations elicited no reply. On April 6 the Senate, and on April 9 the House, overrode the President's veto by the requisite majorities, and the Civil Rights Act of 1866 became law.

In light of the concerns that led Congress to adopt it and the contents of the debates that preceded its passage, it is clear that the Act was designed to do just what its terms suggest: to prohibit all racial discrimination, whether or not under color of law, with respect to the rights enumerated therein—including the right to purchase or lease property.

originalism/purposivism
textualism also

Nor was the scope of the 1866 Act altered when it was re-enacted in 1870, some two years after the ratification of the Fourteenth Amendment. It is quite true that some members of Congress supported the Fourteenth Amendment "in order to eliminate doubt as to the constitutional validity of the Civil Rights Act as applied to the States." *Hurd v. Hodge*, 334 U.S. 24, 32–33. But it certainly does not follow that the adoption of the Fourteenth Amendment or the subsequent readoption of the Civil Rights Act were meant somehow to *limit* its application to state action. The legislative history furnishes not the slightest factual basis for any such speculation, and the conditions prevailing in 1870 make it highly implausible. For by that time most, if not all, of the former Confederate States, then under the control of "reconstructed" legislatures, had formally repudiated racial discrimination, and the focus of congressional concern had clearly shifted from hostile statutes to the activities of groups like the Ku Klux Klan, operating wholly outside the law.

Against this background, it would obviously make no sense to assume, without any historical support whatever, that Congress made a silent decision in 1870 to exempt private discrimination from the operation of the Civil Rights Act of 1866. . . .

The remaining question is whether Congress has power under the Constitution to do what § 1982 purports to do: to prohibit all racial discrimination, private and public, in the sale and rental of property. Our starting point is the Thirteenth Amendment, for it was pursuant to that constitutional provision that Congress originally enacted what is now § 1982. . . .

As its text reveals, the Thirteenth Amendment "is not a mere prohibition of state laws establishing or upholding slavery, but an absolute declaration that slavery or involuntary servitude shall not exist in any part of the United States." *Civil Rights Cases*, 109 U.S. 3, 20. It has never been doubted, therefore, "that the power vested in Congress to enforce the article by appropriate legislation," *ibid.*, includes the power to enact laws "direct and primary, operating upon the acts of individuals, whether sanctioned by state legislation or not." *Id.*, at 23.

Thus, the fact that § 1982 operates upon the unofficial acts of private individuals, whether or not sanctioned by state law, presents no constitutional problem. If Congress has power under the Thirteenth Amendment to eradicate conditions that prevent Negroes from buying and renting property because of their race or color, then no federal statute calculated to achieve that objective can be thought to exceed the constitutional power of Congress simply because it reaches beyond state action to regulate the conduct of private individuals. The constitutional question in this case, therefore, comes to this: Does the authority of Congress to enforce the Thirteenth Amendment "by appropriate legislation" include the power to eliminate all racial barriers to the acquisition of real and personal property? We think the answer to that question is plainly yes.

"By its own unaided force and effect," the Thirteenth Amendment "abolished slavery, and established universal freedom." *Civil Rights Cases*, 109 U.S. 3, 20. Whether or not the Amendment *itself* did any more than that—a question not involved in this case—it is at least clear that the Enabling Clause of that Amendment empowered Congress to do much more. For that clause clothed "Congress with power to pass *all laws necessary and proper for abolishing all badges and incidents of slavery in the United States.*" *Ibid.* (Emphasis added.)[18]

[18] **Question:** Section 2 of the Thirteenth Amendment empowers Congress to enforce Section 1 of the Thirteenth Amendment by "appropriate" legislation. Yet Stewart here is suggesting that even if a practice like housing discrimination doesn't violate the letter of Section 1, Congress has the power "to do much more." Is this interpretation of the Thirteenth Amendment compatible with the *Civil Rights Cases*' interpretation of the neighboring Fourteenth Amendment? Recall that in the *Civil Rights Cases*, the Court held that Congress's

Those who opposed passage of the Civil Rights Act of 1866 argued in effect that the Thirteenth Amendment merely authorized Congress to dissolve the legal bond by which the Negro slave was held to his master. Yet many had earlier opposed the Thirteenth Amendment on the very ground that it would give Congress virtually unlimited power to enact laws for the protection of Negroes in every State. And the majority leaders in Congress—who were, after all, the authors of the Thirteenth Amendment—had no doubt that its Enabling Clause contemplated the sort of positive legislation that was embodied in the 1866 Civil Rights Act. Their chief spokesman, Senator Trumbull of Illinois, the Chairman of the Judiciary Committee, had brought the Thirteenth Amendment to the floor of the Senate in 1864. In defending the constitutionality of the 1866 Act, he argued that, if the narrower construction of the Enabling Clause were correct, then

> the trumpet of freedom that we have been blowing throughout the land has given an 'uncertain sound,' and the promised freedom is a delusion. Such was not the intention of Congress, which proposed the constitutional amendment, nor is such the fair meaning of the amendment itself. * * * I have no doubt that under this provision * * * we may destroy all these discriminations in civil rights against the black man; and if we cannot, our constitutional amendment amounts to nothing. It was for that purpose that the second clause of that amendment was adopted, which says that Congress shall have authority, by appropriate legislation, to carry into effect the article prohibiting slavery. Who is to decide what that appropriate legislation is to be? The Congress of the United States; and it is for Congress to adopt such appropriate legislation as it may think proper, so that it be a means to accomplish the end.

Surely Senator Trumbull was right. Surely Congress has the power under the Thirteenth Amendment rationally to determine what are the badges and the incidents of slavery, and the authority to translate that determination into effective legislation. Nor can we say that the determination Congress has made is an irrational one. For this Court recognized long ago that, whatever else they may have encompassed, the badges and incidents of slavery—its "burdens and disabilities"—included restraints upon "those fundamental rights which are the essence of civil freedom, namely, the same right * * * to inherit, purchase, lease, sell and convey property, as is enjoyed by white citizens." *Civil Rights Cases*, 109 U.S. 3, 22. Just as the Black Codes, enacted after the Civil War to restrict the free exercise of those rights, were substitutes for the slave system, so the exclusion of Negroes from white communities became a substitute for the Black Codes. And when racial discrimination herds men into ghettos and makes their ability to buy property turn on the color of their skin, then it too is a relic of slavery.[19]

Negro citizens, North and South, who saw in the Thirteenth Amendment a promise of freedom—freedom to "go and come at pleasure" and to "buy and sell when they please"—would be left with "a mere paper guarantee" if Congress were powerless to assure that a dollar in the hands of a Negro will purchase the same thing as a dollar in the hands of a white man. At the very least, the freedom that Congress is empowered to secure under the Thirteenth Amendment includes the

---

power under Section 5 of the Fourteenth Amendment was limited to remedying violations of Section 1 of the Fourteenth Amendment—which only states could violate.

[19] **Questions:** Applying this test of Congress's power under Section 2 of the Thirteenth Amendment, is there anything that Congress cannot do in the name of eliminating racial subordination? For example, could Congress decide that racial disparities in mass incarceration are a "relic of slavery," and therefore it is appropriate for Congress to pass legislation reducing the sentences of people confined in state and local prisons?

freedom to buy whatever a white man can buy, the right to live wherever a white man can live. If Congress cannot say that being a free man means at least this much, then the Thirteenth Amendment made a promise the Nation cannot keep.

Representative Wilson of Iowa was the floor manager in the House for the Civil Rights Act of 1866. In urging that Congress had ample authority to pass the pending bill, he recalled the celebrated words of Chief Justice Marshall in *McCulloch v. State of Maryland*, 4 Wheat. 316, 421:

> Let the end by legitimate, let it be within the scope of the constitution, and all means which are appropriate, which are plainly adapted to that end, which are not prohibited, but consist with the letter and spirit of the constitution, are constitutional.

"The end is legitimate," the Congressman said, "because it is defined by the Constitution itself. The end is the maintenance of freedom * * *. A man who enjoys the civil rights mentioned in this bill cannot be reduced to slavery. * * * This settles the appropriateness of this measure, and that settles its constitutionality."

We agree. The judgment is reversed.

NOTE: CONTINUED VITALITY OF THE CIVIL RIGHTS ACT OF 1866

The Supreme Court has continued to apply the Civil Rights Act of 1866—as reenacted in 1870—to "break down *all* discrimination" with respect to contracts, torts, and property ownership. *Alfred H. Mayer Co.*, 392 U.S. at 432. In *Sullivan v. Little Hunting Park*, 396 U.S. 229, 236–38 (1969), the Court applied the law to prohibit a neighborhood recreational club from turning away black homeowners when membership ordinarily went with the lease or ownership of houses in the area. In *Runyon v. McCrary*, 427 U.S. 160, 179 (1976), the Court applied the law to prohibit a private school from discriminating against black parents of prospective students, holding that such parents had the same right as white parents to make and enforce contracts with the school. And in *Johnson v. Railway Express Agency, Inc.*, 421 U.S. 454, 459–60 (1975), and *McDonald v. Santa Fe Trail Transportation Co.*, 427 U.S. 273, 286–87 (1976), the Court applied the law to prohibit racial discrimination in private employment—including when the victim was white.

20.3 THE MODERN POWER TO ENFORCE THE FOURTEENTH AND FIFTEENTH AMENDMENTS AGAINST PERSONAL VIOLATIONS

After *United States v. Guest*, 383 U.S. 745 (1966), and *Jones v. Alfred H. Mayer Co.*, 392 U.S. 409 (1968), it appeared that the *Civil Rights Cases*, 109 U.S. 3 (1883), and the Supreme Court's other Redemption-era cases were no longer good law. But the Court returned to *Guest*—and the *Civil Rights Cases*—in a 2000 case that reinterpreted Congress's power to enforce the Fourteenth Amendment against a private individual.

20.3.1

United States v. Morrison

529 U.S. 598 (2000)

The Violence Against Women Act of 1994 authorized "victims of crimes of violence motivated by gender" to sue and collect damages from the people who injured them. Pub. L. No. 103–322, 108 Stat. 1796, 1941. Congress justified the law as an execution of two provisions: the Commerce Clause of Article I and Section 5 of the Fourteenth Amendment.

Applying the law, a Virginia Tech student named Christy Brzonkala filed suit in federal court against a classmate, Antonio Morrison. She accused Morrison of sexually assaulting her, raping her, and bragging about it to other students. Morrison responded by attacking the constitutionality of the Violence Against Women Act, arguing that it was beyond Congress's power to enact.

The Court in *United States v. Morrison*, 529 U.S. 598 (2000), agreed with Morrison that the law wasn't justified by the Commerce Clause because "[g]ender-motivated crimes of violence are not, in any sense of the phrase, economic activity." 529 U.S. 598, 613 (2000). But it still had to consider the argument that the law was appropriate to remedy systematic violations of the Equal Protection Clause. Defending the law, the U.S. solicitor general explained that twentieth-century state courts had failed in their duty to equally protect women from gender-motivated violence, just as nineteenth-century state courts had failed in their duty to equally protect black people from racially motivated violence. The solicitor general sought to distinguish the *Civil Rights Cases* by observing that the 1883 Court never considered the argument that a state can violate the Fourteenth Amendment by neglecting to provide sufficient remedies for civil rights violations by individuals.

The Court's decision established that the *Civil Rights Cases* still had teeth.

■ CHIEF JUSTICE REHNQUIST delivered the opinion of the Court.[20]

[B]ecause we conclude that the Commerce Clause does not provide Congress with authority to enact § 13981, we address petitioners' alternative argument that the section's civil remedy should be upheld as an exercise of Congress' remedial power under § 5 of the Fourteenth Amendment. As noted above, Congress expressly invoked the Fourteenth Amendment as a source of authority to enact § 13981. . . .

Petitioners' § 5 argument is founded on an assertion that there is pervasive bias in various state justice systems against victims of gender-motivated violence. This assertion is supported by a voluminous congressional record. Specifically, Congress

---

[20] **As You Read, Consider:** In *United States v. Guest*, a majority of the Court repudiated the holding of the *Civil Rights Cases* and announced that Congress could enforce the Fourteenth Amendment by passing laws that directly regulated individuals. How does Chief Justice William Rehnquist balance the precedential value of *Guest* against that of the *Civil Rights Cases*?

received evidence that many participants in state justice systems are perpetuating an array of erroneous stereotypes and assumptions. Congress concluded that these discriminatory stereotypes often result in insufficient investigation and prosecution of gender-motivated crime, inappropriate focus on the behavior and credibility of the victims of that crime, and unacceptably lenient punishments for those who are actually convicted of gender-motivated violence. Petitioners contend that this bias denies victims of gender-motivated violence the equal protection of the laws and that Congress therefore acted appropriately in enacting a private civil remedy against the perpetrators of gender-motivated violence to both remedy the States' bias and deter future instances of discrimination in the state courts. . . .

However, the language and purpose of the Fourteenth Amendment place certain limitations on the manner in which Congress may attack discriminatory conduct. These limitations are necessary to prevent the Fourteenth Amendment from obliterating the Framers' carefully crafted balance of power between the States and the National Government. Foremost among these limitations is the time-honored principle that the Fourteenth Amendment, by its very terms, prohibits only state action. "[T]he principle has become firmly embedded in our constitutional law that the action inhibited by the first section of the Fourteenth Amendment is only such action as may fairly be said to be that of the States. That Amendment erects no shield against merely private conduct, however discriminatory or wrongful." *Shelley v. Kraemer*, 334 U.S. 1, 13, and n. 12 (1948).[21]

Shortly after the Fourteenth Amendment was adopted, we decided two cases interpreting the Amendment's provisions, *United States v. Harris*, 106 U.S. 629 (1883), and the *Civil Rights Cases*, 109 U.S. 3 (1883). In *Harris*, the Court considered a challenge to § 2 of the Civil Rights Act of 1871. That section sought to punish "private persons" for "conspiring to deprive any one of the equal protection of the laws enacted by the State." 106 U.S., at 639. We concluded that this law exceeded Congress' § 5 power because the law was "directed exclusively against the action of private persons, without reference to the laws of the State, or their administration by her officers." *Id.*, at 640. . . .

We reached a similar conclusion in the *Civil Rights Cases*. In those consolidated cases, we held that the public accommodation provisions of the Civil Rights Act of 1875, which applied to purely private conduct, were beyond the scope of the § 5 enforcement power. 109 U.S., at 11. See also, *e.g.*, *United States v. Cruikshank*, 92 U.S. 542, 554 (1875) ("The fourteenth amendment prohibits a state from depriving any person of life, liberty, or property, without due process of law; but this adds nothing to the rights of one citizen as against another. It simply furnishes an additional guaranty against any encroachment by the States upon the fundamental rights which belong to every citizen as a member of society").

The force of the doctrine of *stare decisis* behind these decisions stems not only from the length of time they have been on the books, but also from the insight attributable to the Members of the Court at that time. Every Member had been appointed by President Lincoln, Grant, Hayes, Garfield, or Arthur—and each of their

---

21 **Questions:** Here, Rehnquist reaffirms the state action doctrine as a limiting principle on the Fourteenth Amendment to prevent it from obliterating the "Framers'" balance of power. Which Framers is he talking about—those who framed the original Constitution in 1789 or those who framed the amended Constitution in 1868? If he is referring to 1789, is it a fair assumption that the authors of the Fourteenth Amendment did not intend to change the relationship between Congress and the states?

judicial appointees obviously had intimate knowledge and familiarity with the events surrounding the adoption of the Fourteenth Amendment.[22]

Petitioners contend that . . . more recent decisions have in effect overruled this longstanding limitation on Congress' § 5 authority. They rely on *United States v. Guest*, 383 U.S. 745 (1966), for the proposition that the rule laid down in the *Civil Rights Cases* is no longer good law. In *Guest*, the Court reversed the construction of an indictment under 18 U.S.C. § 241, saying in the course of its opinion that "we deal here with issues of statutory construction, not with issues of constitutional power." 383 U.S., at 749. Three Members of the Court, in a separate opinion by Justice Brennan, expressed the view that the *Civil Rights Cases* were wrongly decided, and that Congress could under § 5 prohibit actions by private individuals. 383 U.S., at 774 (opinion concurring in part and dissenting in part). Three other Members of the Court, who joined the opinion of the Court, joined a separate opinion by Justice Clark which in two or three sentences stated the conclusion that Congress could "punis[h] all conspiracies—with or without state action—that interfere with Fourteenth Amendment rights." *Id.*, at 762 (concurring opinion). . . .

Though these three Justices saw fit to opine on matters not before the Court in *Guest*, the Court had no occasion to revisit the *Civil Rights Cases* and *Harris*, having determined "the indictment [charging private individuals with conspiring to deprive blacks of equal access to state facilities] in fact contain[ed] an express allegation of state involvement." 383 U.S., at 756. The Court concluded that the implicit allegation of "active connivance by agents of the State" eliminated any need to decide "the threshold level that state action must attain in order to create rights under the Equal Protection Clause." *Ibid.* All of this Justice Clark explicitly acknowledged. See *id.*, at 762 (concurring opinion) ("The Court's interpretation of the indictment clearly avoids the question whether Congress, by appropriate legislation, has the power to punish private conspiracies that interfere with Fourteenth Amendment rights, such as the right to utilize public facilities").

To accept petitioners' argument, moreover, one must add to the three Justices joining Justice Brennan's reasoned explanation for his belief that the *Civil Rights Cases* were wrongly decided, the three Justices joining Justice Clark's opinion who gave no explanation whatever for their similar view. This is simply not the way that reasoned constitutional adjudication proceeds. We accordingly have no hesitation in saying that it would take more than the naked dicta contained in Justice Clark's opinion, when added to Justice Brennan's opinion, to cast any doubt upon the enduring vitality of the *Civil Rights Cases* and *Harris*. . . .

We believe that the description of the § 5 power contained in the *Civil Rights Cases* is correct:

"But where a subject is not submitted to the general legislative power of Congress, but is only submitted thereto for the purpose of rendering effective some prohibition against particular [s]tate legislation or [s]tate action in reference to that subject, the power given is limited by its object, and any legislation by Congress in the matter must necessarily be corrective in its character, adapted to counteract and redress the operation of such prohibited state laws or proceedings of [s]tate officers." 109 U.S., at 18.

Petitioners alternatively argue that, unlike the situation in the *Civil Rights Cases*, here there has been gender-based disparate treatment by state authorities, whereas

[22] **Question:** Here, Rehnquist is observing that the authors of the *Civil Rights Cases* were all Republicans. Yet when the *Civil Rights Cases* were decided in 1883, Reconstruction was over and the backlash was in its heyday. Do you agree with Rehnquist regarding how much weight stare decisis deserves in this context?

in those cases there was no indication of such state action. There is abundant evidence, however, to show that the Congresses that enacted the Civil Rights Acts of 1871 and 1875 had a purpose similar to that of Congress in enacting § 13981: There were state laws on the books bespeaking equality of treatment, but in the administration of these laws there was discrimination against newly freed slaves. The statement of Representative Garfield in the House and that of Senator Sumner in the Senate are representative:

"[T]he chief complaint is not that the laws of the State are unequal, but that even where the laws are just and equal on their face, yet, by a systematic maladministration of them, or a neglect or refusal to enforce their provisions, a portion of the people are denied equal protection under them." Cong. Globe, 42d Cong., 1st Sess., App. 153 (1871) (statement of Rep. Garfield).

"The Legislature of South Carolina has passed a law giving precisely the rights contained in your 'supplementary civil rights bill.' But such a law remains a dead letter on her statute-books, because the State courts, comprised largely of those whom the Senator wishes to obtain amnesty for, refuse to enforce it." Cong. Globe, 42d Cong., 2d Sess., 430 (1872) (statement of Sen. Sumner).

But even if that distinction were valid, we do not believe it would save § 13981's civil remedy. For the remedy is simply not "corrective in its character, adapted to counteract and redress the operation of such prohibited [s]tate laws or proceedings of [s]tate officers." *Civil Rights Cases, supra*, at 18. Or, as we have phrased it in more recent cases, prophylactic legislation under § 5 must have a "congruence and proportionality between the injury to be prevented or remedied and the means adopted to that end." *Florida Prepaid Postsecondary Ed. Expense Bd. v. College Savings Bank*, 527 U.S. 627, 639 (1999). Section 13981 is not aimed at proscribing discrimination by officials which the Fourteenth Amendment might not itself proscribe; it is directed not at any State or state actor, but at individuals who have committed criminal acts motivated by gender bias.[23]

In the present cases, for example, § 13981 visits no consequence whatever on any Virginia public official involved in investigating or prosecuting Brzonkala's assault. The section is, therefore, unlike any of the § 5 remedies that we have previously upheld. . . .

For these reasons, we conclude that Congress' power under § 5 does not extend to the enactment of § 13981.

---

[23] **Questions:** Has Rehnquist overruled *Guest*? Applying the standard that he outlines in this paragraph, how could Congress reenact the Violence Against Women Act to permit lawsuits against people who commit "crimes of violence motivated by gender"?

CHAPTER 21

What Is the Scope of Congress's Power to Enforce the Reconstruction and Voting Rights Amendments Against State Violations?

THIRTEENTH AMENDMENT (1865), SECTION 1: Neither slavery nor involuntary servitude, except as a punishment for crime whereof the party shall have been duly convicted, shall exist within the United States, or any place subject to their jurisdiction.

SECTION 2: Congress shall have power to enforce this article by appropriate legislation.

FOURTEENTH AMENDMENT (1868), SECTION 1: All persons born or naturalized in the United States, and subject to the jurisdiction thereof, are citizens of the United States and of the State wherein they reside. No State shall make or enforce any law which shall abridge the privileges or immunities of citizens of the United States; nor shall any State deprive any person of life, liberty, or property, without due process of law; nor deny to any person within its jurisdiction the equal protection of the laws.

SECTION 5: The Congress shall have the power to enforce, by appropriate legislation, the provisions of this article.

FIFTEENTH AMENDMENT (1870), SECTION 1: The right of citizens of the United States to vote shall not be denied or abridged by the United States or by any State on account of race, color, or previous condition of servitude—

SECTION 2: The Congress shall have the power to enforce this article by appropriate legislation.

NINETEENTH AMENDMENT (1920), SECTION 1: The right of citizens of the United States to vote shall not be denied or abridged by the United States or by any State on account of sex.

SECTION 2: Congress shall have power to enforce this article by appropriate legislation.

TWENTY-FOURTH AMENDMENT (1964), SECTION 1: The right of citizens of the United States to vote in any primary or other election for President or Vice President, for electors for President or Vice President, or for Senator or Representative in Congress, shall not be denied or abridged by the United States or any State by reason of failure to pay any poll tax or other tax.

SECTION 2: The Congress shall have power to enforce this article by appropriate legislation.

TWENTY-SIXTH AMENDMENT (1971), SECTION 1: The right of citizens of the United States, who are eighteen years of age or older, to vote shall not be denied or abridged by the United States or by any State on account of age.

SECTION 2: The Congress shall have power to enforce this article by appropriate legislation.

21.1 RECONSTRUCTION AND REDEMPTION

In contrast with its parsimonious interpretation of Congress's powers to enforce the Reconstruction amendments against violations by *private* individuals, the Supreme Court of the nineteenth century was relatively generous when interpreting Congress's powers against *state* officials. As the Court wrote of the Fourteenth Amendment in the *Civil Rights Cases*, "it is State action of a particular character that is prohibited." 109 U.S. 3, 11 (1883). Accordingly, when the Court first considered a series of actions brought against state officers, the Court held that Congress had the power to regulate their conduct. "Congress, by virtue of the fifth section of the Fourteenth Amendment, may enforce the prohibitions whenever they are disregarded by either the Legislative, the Executive, or the Judicial Department of the State," the Court wrote. *Virginia v. Rives*, 100 U.S. 313, 318 (1880). "The mode of enforcement is left to its discretion." *Id.*

Denial of rights and removal to federal court

For example, in *Strauder v. West Virginia*, 100 U.S. 303 (1880), the Supreme Court upheld a provision of the Civil Rights Act of 1866, ch. 31, 14 Stat. 27, that authorized any criminal defendants whose constitutional rights were being denied in state court to remove their trial to federal court. The case involved Taylor Strauder, a formerly enslaved person who was indicted for murder by an all-white West Virginia jury. Invoking the Civil Rights Act, Strauder complained that a fair trial in state court was impossible because West Virginia law prohibited black people from serving on juries.

The Court agreed that such a state law violated the Equal Protection Clause:

> It is not easy to comprehend how it can be said that while every white man is entitled to a trial by a jury selected from persons of his own race or color, or, rather, selected without discrimination against his color, and a negro is not, the latter is equally protected by the law with the former.

Strauder, 100 U.S. at 309. The Court also held that Congress had the power to remedy this constitutional violation by empowering Strauder to remove his trial to a federal court. Citing *Prigg v. Pennsylvania*, 41 U.S. (16 Pet.) 539 (1842), the *Strauder* Court explained that "[a] right or an immunity, whether created by the Constitution or only guaranteed by it, even without any express delegation of power, may be protected by

Congress . . . in the legitimate exercise of its legislative discretion." *Strauder*, 100 U.S. at 310–11.

Juror discrimination and state judges as defendants

The Court went even further in *Ex parte Virginia*, 100 U.S. 339 (1880), upholding a prosecution against a Virginia judge for violating a section of the Civil Rights Act of 1875, ch. 114, 18 Stat. 335, which made it a criminal offense for a state official to disqualify any citizen from a jury "on account of race, color, or previous condition of servitude." *Ex parte Virginia*, 100 U.S. at 336.

When Congress enacted this legislation in 1875, no federal court had yet considered whether the Fourteenth Amendment prohibited racial discrimination against potential jurors. Yet the Court emphasized that Section 5 of the amendment left the interpretation of the Fourteenth Amendment to Congress. "It is not said the *judicial power* of the general government shall extend to enforcing [its] prohibitions," the Court wrote. *Id.* at 345 (emphasis added). "It is the power of Congress which has been enlarged: Congress is authorized to *enforce* the prohibitions by appropriate legislation." *Id.* (emphasis added). The Court continued,

> Whatever legislation is appropriate, that is, adapted to carry out the objects the amendments have in view, whatever tends to enforce submission to the prohibitions they contain, and to secure to all persons the enjoyment of perfect equality of civil rights and the equal protection of the laws against State denial or invasion, if not prohibited, is brought within the domain of congressional power.

Id. at 345–46.

Another complication that the Court considered in *Ex parte Virginia* was the unusual identity of the criminal defendants: state judges. Under the law of every state, judges traditionally were immune from civil or criminal liability. Virginia complained on behalf of its judges that Congress had no authority to interfere with the state's sovereignty like this. But the Court emphasized that in expanding Congress's power, the Fourteenth Amendment had imposed radical "restrictions of State power. . . . Indeed, every addition of power to the general government involves a corresponding diminution of the governmental powers of the States." *Id.* at 346. When the Fourteenth Amendment gave Congress power to enforce its terms, therefore, it empowered Congress to restrict the conduct of state officers. "Such legislation must act upon persons, not upon the abstract thing denominated a State, but upon the persons who are the agents of the State in the denial of the rights which were intended to be secured," the Court wrote. *Id.* at 347. "This must be so, or the constitutional prohibition has no meaning. Then the State has clothed one of its agents with power to annul or to evade it." *Id.*

Over the next century, the Court continued to uphold federal prosecutions brought under the Reconstruction-era enforcement acts against state officers. *See, e.g.*, *United States v. Johnson*, 390 U.S. 563 (1968); *United States v. Price*, 383 U.S. 787 (1966).

Voting rights and narrow interpretation of enforcement acts

However, in the context of voting rights, the Court narrowly interpreted some of the acts to the point of insignificance.

For example, in *United States v. Reese*, 92 U.S. 214 (1876), the Court dismissed an indictment that charged two Kentucky election officials with violating the Enforcement Act of 1870, ch. 114, 16 Stat. 140, by refusing to count the ballot of a qualified black voter. The Court held that the act was unconstitutionally overbroad: the Fifteenth Amendment prohibits state officials from excluding voters "on account of race," but the enforcement act failed to mention race in the specific section that made it a crime for state officials to wrongfully fail to count a ballot. *Reese*, 92 U.S. at 218–19.

In *Screws v. United States*, 325 U.S. 91 (1945), the Court similarly held that where a sheriff was federally prosecuted under the Civil Rights Act of 1866 for arresting and beating a black man to death, the prosecutors had to prove that the sheriff acted with the specific intent of depriving the black man of his constitutional rights. This meant that federal prosecutors who wanted to vindicate the murders of civil rights activists had to prove that the activists were murdered because of their intention to vote, not because they were black. "Within the tiny fraternity of civil rights prosecutors, the decision was an unpleasant echo of *Dred Scott*." Taylor Branch, *Parting the Waters: America in the King Years* 408–09 (1989).

21.1.1

Giles v. Harris

189 U.S. 475 (1903)

Perhaps the most infamous example of the Supreme Court's attitude toward Congress's ability to protect the right to vote was the following, brief decision.

Jackson Giles was a literate black janitor and a Republican Party activist in Montgomery, Alabama, where black people had been eligible to vote since 1868. But after the Alabama government was "redeemed" by white Democrats in 1874, the state steadily began to contract the list of eligible black voters. In 1900, the year before Alabama adopted a new state constitution, there were 181,471 eligible black voters; by 1901, there were only 3,000. *See* Richard H. Pildes, *Democracy, Anti-Democracy, and the Canon*, 17 Const. Comment. 303 (2000). Even though black residents represented majorities or nearly half of the population in Alabama, Florida, Georgia, Louisiana, Mississippi, and South Carolina, these and other states used discretionary tests, poll taxes, and other arbitrary practices to deny Giles and other black residents the franchise.

Giles filed suit under the Ku Klux Klan Act of 1871, ch. 22, 17 Stat. 13—now 42 U.S.C. § 1983—alleging that state officials had violated his rights under the Fourteenth and Fifteenth Amendments by enforcing the 1901 Alabama Constitution. Section 1983 authorized courts to provide a remedy "in an action at law, suit in equity, or other proper proceeding for redress"—and Giles wanted a federal court to order Alabama officials to readmit him and five thousand other black people to the voter rolls. At issue was whether the Supreme Court would allow black litigants to use the surviving Reconstruction-era statutes to stem the legal establishment of white supremacy throughout the South, or whether the Court would stand by as the white counterrevolution entrenched itself in society.

The Court opted to stand by.

■ MR. JUSTICE HOLMES delivered the opinion of the Court.[1]

This is a bill in equity brought by a colored man, on behalf of himself "and on behalf of more than five thousand negroes, citizens of the county of Montgomery, Alabama, similarly situated and circumstanced as himself," against the board of registrars of that county. The prayer of the bill is in substance that the defendants may be required to enroll upon the voting lists the name of the plaintiff and of all other qualified members of his race who applied for registration before August 1, 1902, and were refused, and that certain sections of the Constitution of Alabama, viz., §§ 180, 181, 183, 184, 185, 186, 187, and 188 of article 8, may be declared contrary to the 14th and 15th Amendments of the Constitution of the United States, and void.

The allegations of the bill may be summed up as follows: The plaintiff is subject to none of the disqualifications set forth in the Constitution of Alabama and is entitled to vote,—entitled, as the bill plainly means, under the Constitution as it is. He applied in March, 1902, for registration as a voter, and was refused arbitrarily on the ground of his color, together with large numbers of other duly qualified negroes, while all white men were registered. The same thing was done all over the state. Under § 187 of article 8 of the Alabama Constitution, persons registered before January 1, 1903, remain [voters] for life unless they become disqualified by certain crimes, etc., while after that date severer tests come into play which would exclude, perhaps, a large part of the black race. Therefore by the refusal the plaintiff and the other negroes excluded were deprived, not only of their vote at an election which has taken place since the bill was filed, but of the permanent advantage incident to registration before 1903. The white men generally are registered for good under the easy test, and the black men are likely to be kept out in the future as in the past. This refusal to register the blacks was part of a general scheme to disfranchise them, to which the defendants and the state itself, according to the bill, were parties. The defendants accepted their office for the purpose of carrying out the scheme. The part taken by the state, that is, by the white population which framed the Constitution, consisted in shaping that instrument so as to give opportunity and effect to the wholesale fraud which has been practised. . . .

---

1 **As You Read, Consider:** Does Justice Oliver Wendell Holmes agree with Jackson Giles that Alabama's new constitution violates the Fourteenth and Fifteenth Amendments? What does his answer reveal about the power of the Supreme Court to enforce constitutional limits in the face of hostile public opinion?

The certificate of the circuit judge raises the single question of the jurisdiction of the court. The plaintiff contends that this jurisdiction is given expressly by Rev. Stat. § 629, coupled with [42 U.S.C. § 1983], which provides that every person who, under color of a state 'statute, ordinance, regulation, custom, or usage,' 'subjects, or causes to be subjected, any citizen of the United States or other person within the jurisdiction thereof to the deprivation of any rights, privileges, or immunities secured by the Constitution and laws, shall be liable to the party injured in an action at law, suit in equity, or other proper proceeding for redress.' . . .

It seems to us impossible to grant the equitable relief which is asked.[2] It will be observed, in the first place, that the language of § [1983] does not extend the sphere of equitable jurisdiction in respect of what shall be held an appropriate subject-matter for that kind of relief. The words are, 'shall be liable to the party injured in an action at law, suit in equity, or other proper proceeding for redress.' They allow a suit in equity only when that is the proper proceeding for redress, and they refer to existing standards to determine what is a proper proceeding. The traditional limits of proceedings in equity have not embraced a remedy for political wrongs. But we cannot forget that we are dealing with a new and extraordinary situation, and we are unwilling to stop short of the final considerations which seem to us to dispose of the case.

The difficulties which we cannot overcome are two, and the first is this: The plaintiff alleges that the whole registration scheme of the Alabama Constitution is a fraud upon the Constitution of the United States, and asks us to declare it void. . . .[3] [He then] asks to be registered as a party qualified under the void instrument. If, then, we accept the conclusion which it is the chief purpose of the bill to maintain, how can we make the court a party to the unlawful scheme by accepting it and adding another voter to its fraudulent lists? If a white man came here on the same general allegations, admitting his sympathy with the plan, but alleging some special prejudice that had kept him off the list, we hardly should think it necessary to meet him with a reasoned answer. But the relief cannot be varied because we think that in the future the particular plaintiff is likely to try to overthrow the scheme. If we accept the plaintiff's allegations for the purposes of his case, he cannot complain. We must accept or reject them. It is impossible simply to shut our eyes, put the plaintiff on the lists, be they honest or fraudulent, and leave the determination of the fundamental question

---

[2] **Question:** The term *equity* refers to the power of a court to provide novel and flexible remedies for injustice when damages or other after-the-fact legal remedies are insufficient. Injunctions are common forms of equitable relief. To determine whether it is appropriate to issue an injunction or other forms of equitable relief, courts typically balance how the relief would serve the personal interest of the petitioner against how the relief might harm the public interest.

Why does Holmes think it inappropriate for the Court to issue an injunction compelling the Alabama defendants to register Giles and other black voters?

[3] **Questions:** Holmes's language in these two paragraphs is a little difficult to penetrate. He is offering two reasons why it would be inappropriate for the Court to issue an injunction requiring Alabama officers to register Giles. First, if Giles is correct that Alabama's 1901 constitution violates the Fourteenth and Fifteenth Amendments, then it would be inappropriate for the Court to register Giles without also invalidating the entire 1901 constitution. Second, it is not clear how the Court would enforce such an injunction when "the great mass of the white population intends to keep the blacks from voting." (To support this second point, he cites a case, *Hans v. Louisiana*, 134 U.S. 1 (1890), in which the Court held that federal courts cannot issue injunctions against state *governments* (in contrast with state *officers*). We will look at this case in detail in a later section of this casebook on sovereign immunity (section 35.1).)

Do these two reasons persuade you that it would be inappropriate for the Court to remedy Alabama's disenfranchisement of Giles? Or do you agree with Professor Richard H. Pildes, who wrote that *Giles v. Harris* failed a "fundamental constitutional test of whether massive disfranchisement would be permitted under the shadow of the Fifteenth Amendment"? Richard H. Pildes, *Keeping Legal History Meaningful*, 19 Const. Comment. 645, 648 (2002).

for the future. If we have an opinion that the bill is right on its face, or if we are undecided, we are not at liberty to assume it to be wrong for the purposes of decision. It seems to us that unless we are prepared to say that it is wrong, that all its principal allegations are immaterial, and that the registration plan of the Alabama Constitution is valid, we cannot order the plaintiff's name to be registered. It is not an answer to say that if all the blacks who are qualified according to the letter of the instrument were registered, the fraud would be cured. In the first place, there is no probability that any way now is open by which more than a few could be registered; but, if all could be, the difficulty would not be overcome. If the sections of the Constitution concerning registration were illegal in their inception, it would be a new doctrine in constitutional law that the original invalidity could be cured by an administration which defeated their intent. We express no opinion as to the alleged fact of their unconstitutionality beyond saying that we are not willing to assume that they are valid, in the face of the allegations and main object of the bill, for the purpose of granting the relief which it was necessary to pray in order that that object should be secured.

The other difficulty is of a different sort, and strikingly reinforces the argument that equity cannot undertake now, any more than it has in the past, to enforce political rights. . . . In determining whether a court of equity can take jurisdiction, one of the first questions is what it can do to enforce any order that it may make. This is alleged to be the conspiracy of a state, although the state is not and could not be made a party to the bill. *Hans v. Louisiana*, 134 U.S. 1. The circuit court has no constitutional power to control its action by any direct means. And if we leave the state out of consideration, the court has as little practical power to deal with the people of the state in a body. The bill imports that the great mass of the white population intends to keep the blacks from voting. To meet such an intent something more than ordering the plaintiff's name to be inscribed upon the lists of 1902 will be needed. If the conspiracy and the intent exist, a name on a piece of paper will not defeat them. Unless we are prepared to supervise the voting in that state by officers of the court, it seems to us that all that the plaintiff could get from equity would be an empty form. Apart from damages to the individual, relief from a great political wrong, if done, as alleged, by the people of a state and the state itself, must be given by them or by the legislative and political department of the government of the United States.

■ MR. JUSTICE BREWER dissenting:

I am unable to concur in either the opinion or judgment in this case. The single question is whether the circuit court of the United States had jurisdiction. Accepting the statement of facts in the opinion of the majority as sufficiently full, it appears that the plaintiff was entitled to a place on the permanent registry and was denied it by the defendants, the board of registrars in the county in which he lived. No one was allowed to vote who was not registered. He desired to vote at the coming election for representative in Congress. He was deprived of that right by the action of the defendants. . . .

21.2 THE SECOND RECONSTRUCTION

The Ku Klux Klan Act of 1871, ch. 22, 17 Stat. 13, now 42 U.S.C. § 1983, lay dormant for a generation after the Supreme Court dismissed its effectiveness in *Giles v. Harris*, 189 U.S. 475 (1903). With the Court announcing that the statute gave courts too little power to stop "the great mass of the white population [that] intends to keep the blacks from voting," southern governments continued to systematically exclude black voters from the rolls. Writing his classic account of Reconstruction in

1935, W. E. B. Du Bois wrote in amazement that "[i]n no other civilized and modern land has so great a group of people, most of whom were able to read and write, been allowed so small a voice in their own government." W. E. B. Du Bois, *Black Reconstruction in America* 694 (1935). By the time the Supreme Court finally weighed in against the "white primary" in *United States v. Classic*, 313 U.S. 299 (1941), fewer than one out of five black people in the South were registered to vote, and most of them didn't dare cast ballots because of fear of violence or retaliation. *See* Robert A. Caro, *Master of the Senate*, at xii (2003).

Beginning in the 1940s, however, lawyers in the National Association for the Advancement of Colored People's Legal Defense Fund (NAACP LDF) began invoking § 1983 as part of their decades-long challenge to laws that maintained racial segregation. *See* Michael Klarman, *From Jim Crow to Civil Rights: The Supreme Court and the Struggle for Racial Equality* 143–62 (2004). In fact, § 1983 provided the cause of action by which challengers to racial segregation in public schools reached the Supreme Court in *Brown v. Board of Education* (*Brown I*), 347 U.S. 483 (1954), culminating in a sweeping opinion that invalidated all state laws that maintained racially separate school systems. In contrast with Justice Oliver Wendell Holmes's skepticism in *Giles* about the Supreme Court's preparedness "to supervise the voting in [a] state by officers of the court," 189 U.S. at 488, the Court after *Brown* authorized federal judges to supervise the desegregation of schools in the face of massive resistance by state officers. *See, e.g.*, *Griffin v. Cnty. Sch. Bd.*, 377 U.S. 218 (1964); *Cooper v. Aaron*, 358 U.S. 1 (1958). Eventually, as Holmes predicted, federal courts' desegregation orders often required federal soldiers, new laws, and decades of judicial supervision to actually enforce their terms.

Brown *and enforcement of Reconstruction amendments*

We will revisit *Brown* and its aftermath in a later discussion about how the Fourteenth Amendment limits states by its own terms (section 45.2). For now, we'll consider *Brown*'s under-the-surface implications for Congress's authority to enforce the Reconstruction amendments. Two stand out.

First, *Brown* demonstrated the potential effectiveness of § 1983 as a modern tool for remedying constitutional violations. This potential grew exponentially after *Monroe v. Pape*, 365 U.S. 167 (1961), which closely interpreted § 1983's text. Section 1983 makes a person liable for a constitutional violation only when that person acts "under color of [law]." *Monroe*, 365 U.S. at 168. Until *Monroe*, most litigants had interpreted this phrase narrowly to mean that the state law itself had to allegedly violate the Constitution, as in *Brown*. But the *Monroe* Court interpreted the phrase broadly to mean that anyone "clothed with the authority of state law" could be held liable for violating the Constitution. *Id.* at 184 (quoting *United States v. Classic*, 313 U.S. 299, 326 (1941)). This meant that litigants could use § 1983 to challenge the unconstitutional conduct of a state official even when the official's conduct also violated state law. Soon, litigants began bringing § 1983 claims against state officials all over the country for all kinds of constitutional violations. Today, § 1983 claims represent an enormous percentage of the cases that federal district courts hear every year. They are the main vehicle by which litigants challenge unconstitutional state laws, police misconduct, prison abuse, and other violations by state officers. *See, e.g.*, *Obergefell v. Hodges*, 576 U.S. 644 (2015); *Roe v. Wade*, 410 U.S. 113 (1973); *Pierson v. Ray*, 386 U.S. 547 (1967).

The second, and most important, implication of *Brown* for Congress's power to enforce the Reconstruction amendments was that for the first time in its history, the Supreme Court demonstrated a willingness to supervise the enforcement of the Reconstruction amendments against the collective hostility of southern states. Congress responded by passing the first civil rights statute since Reconstruction, the Civil Rights Act of 1957, Pub. L. No. 85–315, 71 Stat. 634. Although this law's effects were modest—authorizing the attorney general to seek injunctive relief in federal courts to prevent interference with the voting rights of citizens—it represented the first time since 1875 that all three branches of the federal government aligned themselves to protect the civil rights of black people. *See* Caro, *supra*, at 996–1004. Congress soon followed with two more civil rights acts that expanded the federal government's role in supervising southern elections.

Civil Rights Act of 1960 and its shortcomings

The first of these laws, the Civil Rights Act of 1960, authorized federal courts to register all qualified voters in a city or county on proof that the jurisdiction had a "pattern or practice" of discrimination. Pub. L. No. 86–449, 74 Stat. 86, 90. The law was a response to the persistent evasion of the 1957 act by southern jurisdictions, which typically registered individual black plaintiffs while keeping the polls closed to the vast majority of black voters in an area. *See* Taylor Branch, *Parting the Waters* 303–04, 331–32 (1989).

But even this law only permitted courts to desegregate one county at a time. More importantly, it didn't stop southern jurisdictions from adopting new techniques to bar eligible voters from participating in future elections. For example, Louisiana and other states adopted literacy tests that asked questions so absurd that the county registrar had complete discretion over whether an applicant passed. One of the more famous questions asked, "How many bubbles are in a bar of soap?" John Lewis, *Now We Know That Not All Votes Count*, N.Y. Times, Dec. 2, 2000, at A19.

Under the nominal protection of the 1957 and 1960 Civil Rights Acts, activists throughout the South attempted to register black voters despite intimidation, assassinations, economic reprisals, and other efforts to keep them away from the polls. In early 1965, an Alabama state trooper even shot a black activist named Jimmie Lee Jackson. In response, the Southern Christian Leadership Conference—a network of preachers led by Martin Luther King Jr.—organized a march from Selma, Alabama, to the state capital of Montgomery. The marchers demanded a comprehensive voting rights act that could meaningfully respond to southern intransigence. But when they attempted to leave Selma via the Edmund Pettus Bridge, they were tear-gassed and beaten on live television by state troopers. *See* Taylor Branch, *At Canaan's Edge* 49–73 (2006).

21.2.1

South Carolina v. Katzenbach

383 U.S. 301 (1966)

International outrage over this "Bloody Sunday" helped activists build a nationwide coalition around a sweeping new law, the Voting Rights Act of 1965, Pub. L. No. 89–110, 79 Stat. 437.

The Voting Rights Act was a revolutionary piece of legislation. Like previous voting-rights laws, Section 2 prohibited any state or local government from maintaining a "voting qualification or prerequisite to voting, or standard, practice, or procedure" that abridged the right of any citizen to vote on account of race or color. Voting Rights Act, 79 Stat. at 437. But rather than rely on case-by-case litigation to challenge abridgments one at a time, Sections 4 and 5 established a new procedure known as *preclearance review*. Section 4(b) announced that certain states and local governments would be subject to federal oversight because of their low voter turnout and their use of discriminatory tests in the 1964 federal elections. *Id.* at 438. Section 4(a) and Section 5 provided that these so-called covered jurisdictions would be prohibited from enforcing or changing their voting laws without permission from the U.S. attorney general or a three-judge panel of the U.S. District Court for the District of Columbia. *Id.* at 438–39. Section 3 authorized the U.S. attorney general to "bail in" and cover additional jurisdictions that used discriminatory tests or devices. *Id.* at 437. If a covered jurisdiction wanted to "bail out" and regain full autonomy to change its election laws, Section 4(a) provided that the jurisdiction had to prove to the attorney general or district court that it had refrained from using any discriminatory test or device for five years. *Id.* at 438. Other sections of the act imposed additional restrictions on covered jurisdictions, including the possibility that federal courts would appoint examiners to register voters. *Id.* at 439.

When the Voting Rights Act took effect, its formula immediately treated Alabama, Alaska, Georgia, Louisiana, Mississippi, South Carolina, Virginia, twenty-six counties in North Carolina, and one county in Arizona as covered jurisdictions subject to preclearance review. If any of these states or counties wanted to change their election laws, they first needed to obtain the approval of federal officials or judges in the District of Columbia.

South Carolina, one of the covered jurisdictions, immediately challenged the constitutionality of the Voting Rights Act in the Supreme Court. It offered three reasons why the act was not authorized by Congress's enforcement power under the Fifteenth Amendment. First, South Carolina contended that Congress had no power to enforce an amendment by outlawing conduct that didn't violate the amendment. It observed that the Voting Rights Act banned all literacy tests even though the Supreme Court had recently held that most literacy tests were constitutional under the Fourteenth and Fifteenth Amendments. *See Lassiter v. Northampton Cnty. Bd. of Elections*, 360 U.S. 45, 50–54 (1959). Second, South Carolina contended that Congress had no power to discriminate against certain states, which it contended deprived the states of their "equal footing" with other states. For support, South Carolina alluded to *Coyle v. Smith*, 221 U.S. 559 (1911), a case excerpted above (section 18.5). There, the Supreme Court held that Congress's power to admit new states did not permit Congress to condition Oklahoma's admission on its acceptance of lasting restrictions that Congress could not impose on existing states—such as where Oklahoma could locate its state capital. *Coyle*, 221 U.S. at 579. Finally, South Carolina also contended that Congress had no power to impose rigorous preclearance review on any state. It observed that a state's ability to regulate its own elections was a fundamental feature of its sovereignty, and it argued that it was an inappropriate use of federal power to prohibit a state from changing its own laws.

In *South Carolina v. Katzenbach*, 383 U.S. 301 (1966), the attorney general, Nicholas Katzenbach, successfully defended the act.

■ MR. CHIEF JUSTICE WARREN delivered the opinion of the Court.[4]

[T]he Voting Rights Act was designed by Congress to banish the blight of racial discrimination in voting, which has infected the electoral process in parts of our country for nearly a century. The Act creates stringent new remedies for voting discrimination where it persists on a pervasive scale, and in addition the statute strengthens existing remedies for pockets of voting discrimination elsewhere in the country. Congress assumed the power to prescribe these remedies from § 2 of the Fifteenth Amendment, which authorizes the National Legislature to effectuate by "appropriate" measures the constitutional prohibition against racial discrimination in voting. We hold that the [Act is] . . . an appropriate means for carrying out Congress' constitutional responsibilities and [is] consonant with all other provisions of the Constitution.

I.

The constitutional propriety of the Voting Rights Act of 1965 must be judged with reference to the historical experience which it reflects. Before enacting the

[4] **As You Read, Consider:** How does Chief Justice Earl Warren address each of South Carolina's three main arguments? What standard does he offer to evaluate whether a federal law is "appropriate" for enforcing the Reconstruction amendments?

measure, Congress explored with great care the problem of racial discrimination in voting. . . . Two points emerge vividly from the voluminous legislative history of the Act contained in the committee hearings and floor debates. First: Congress felt itself confronted by an insidious and pervasive evil which had been perpetuated in certain parts of our country through unremitting and ingenious defiance of the Constitution. Second: Congress concluded that the unsuccessful remedies which it had prescribed in the past would have to be replaced by sterner and more elaborate measures in order to satisfy the clear commands of the Fifteenth Amendment. We pause here to summarize the majority reports of the House and Senate Committees, which document in considerable detail the factual basis for these reactions by Congress. . . .

The Fifteenth Amendment to the Constitution was ratified in 1870. Promptly thereafter Congress passed the Enforcement Act of 1870, which made it a crime for public officers and private persons to obstruct exercise of the right to vote. The statute was amended in the following year to provide for detailed federal supervision of the electoral process, from registration to the certification of returns. As the years passed and fervor for racial equality waned, enforcement of the laws became spotty and ineffective, and most of their provisions were repealed in 1894. The remnants have had little significance in the recently renewed battle against voting discrimination.

Meanwhile, beginning in 1890, the States of Alabama, Georgia, Louisiana, Mississippi, North Carolina, South Carolina, and Virginia enacted tests still in use which were specifically designed to prevent Negroes from voting. Typically, they made the ability to read and write a registration qualification and also required completion of a registration form. These laws were based on the fact that as of 1890 in each of the named States, more than two-thirds of the adult Negroes were illiterate while less than one-quarter of the adult whites were unable to read or write. At the same time, alternate tests were prescribed in all of the named States to assure that white illiterates would not be deprived of the franchise. These included grandfather clauses, property qualifications, "good character" tests, and the requirement that registrants "understand" or "interpret" certain matter. . . .

According to the evidence in recent Justice Department voting suits, [discriminatory application of voting tests] is now the principal method used to bar Negroes from the polls. . . . White applicants for registration have often been excused altogether from . . . literacy and understanding tests or have been given easy versions, have received extensive help from voting officials, and have been registered despite serious errors in their answers. Negroes, on the other hand, have typically been required to pass difficult versions of all the tests, without any outside assistance and without the slightest error. . . .

In recent years, Congress has repeatedly tried to cope with the problem by facilitating case-by-case litigation against voting discrimination. . . . Despite the earnest efforts of the Justice Department and of many federal judges, these new laws have done little to cure the problem of voting discrimination. According to estimates by the Attorney General during hearings on the Act, registration of voting-age Negroes in Alabama rose only from 14.2% to 19.4% between 1958 and 1964; in Louisiana it barely inched ahead from 31.7% to 31.8% between 1956 and 1965; and in Mississippi it increased only from 4.4% to 6.4% between 1954 and 1964. In each instance, registration of voting-age whites ran roughly 50 percentage points or more ahead of Negro registration.

The previous legislation has proved ineffective for a number of reasons. Voting suits are unusually onerous to prepare, sometimes requiring as many as 6,000 man-hours spent combing through registration records in preparation for trial. Litigation has been exceedingly slow, in part because of the ample opportunities for delay afforded voting officials and others involved in the proceedings. Even when favorable decisions have finally been obtained, some of the States affected have merely switched to discriminatory devices not covered by the federal decrees or have enacted difficult new tests designed to prolong the existing disparity between white and Negro registration. Alternatively, certain local officials have defied and evaded court orders or have simply closed their registration offices to freeze the voting rolls.

During the hearings and debates on the Act, Selma, Alabama, was repeatedly referred to as the pre-eminent example of the ineffectiveness of existing legislation. In Dallas County, of which Selma is the seat, there were four years of litigation by the Justice Department and two findings by the federal courts of widespread voting discrimination. Yet in those four years, Negro registration rose only from 156 to 383, although there are approximately 15,000 Negroes of voting age in the county. Any possibility that these figures were attributable to political apathy was dispelled by the protest demonstrations in Selma in the early months of 1965. . . . The House Committee on the Judiciary summed up the reaction of Congress to these developments in the following words: "Four years is too long. The burden is too heavy—the wrong to our citizens is too serious—the damage to our national conscience is too great not to adopt more effective measures than exist today. Such is the essential justification for the pending bill." House Report 11.

II.

The Voting Rights Act of 1965 reflects Congress' firm intention to rid the country of racial discrimination in voting. The heart of the Act is a complex scheme of stringent remedies aimed at areas where voting discrimination has been most flagrant. . . .

We now turn to a detailed description of [the sections of the Act being challenged] and their present status.

[The "coverage formula" of § 4(b) of the Voting Rights Act covers South Carolina and other states that used a "test or device" and had a voter turnout of less than 50 percent in the 1964 presidential election. As a "covered jurisdiction," South Carolina is prohibited by § 4(a) from maintaining its literacy test and poll tax. It is also prohibited by § 5 from extending the closing hour at polling places from 6 p.m. to 7 p.m. because the state may not enforce changes in its voting laws without the permission of the attorney general or a three-judge district court.][5]

III.

These provisions of the Voting Rights Act of 1965 are challenged on the fundamental ground that they exceed the powers of Congress and encroach on an area reserved to the States by the Constitution. South Carolina and certain of the *amici curiae* also . . . argue that the coverage formula prescribed in § 4(a)–(d) violates the principle of the equality of States . . . . [T]he basic question presented by the case [is]: Has Congress exercised its powers under the Fifteenth Amendment in an appropriate manner with relation to the States?

The ground rules for resolving this question are clear. The language and purpose of the Fifteenth Amendment, the prior decisions construing its several provisions, and the general doctrines of constitutional interpretation, all point to one fundamental principle. As against the reserved powers of the States, Congress may use any rational means to effectuate the constitutional prohibition of racial discrimination in voting. . . .

---

[5] **Question:** In preparation for this litigation, South Carolina attempted to *extend* the time to vote on Election Day by an hour. Why might it be appropriate for Congress to require a state to seek the permission of federal officials before enacting a change that makes it easier for people to vote?

Section 1 of the Fifteenth Amendment declares that "[t]he right of citizens of the United States to vote shall not be denied or abridged by the United States or by any State on account of race, color, or previous condition of servitude." This declaration has always been treated as self-executing and has repeatedly been construed, without further legislative specification, to invalidate state voting qualifications or procedures which are discriminatory on their face or in practice. See *Neal v. Delaware*, 103 U. S. 370; *Guinn v. United States*, 238 U. S. 347; *Myers v. Anderson*, 238 U. S. 368; *Lane v. Wilson*, 307 U. S. 268; *Smith v. Allwright*, 321 U. S. 649; *Schnell v. Davis*, 336 U. S. 933; *Terry v. Adams*, 345 U. S. 461; *United States v. Thomas*, 362 U. S. 58; *Gomillion v. Lightfoot*, 364 U. S. 339; *Alabama v. United States*, 371 U. S. 37; *Louisiana v. United States*, 380 U. S. 145. . . . The gist of the matter is that the Fifteenth Amendment supersedes contrary exertions of state power. . . .

South Carolina contends that the cases cited above are precedents only for the authority of the judiciary to strike down state statutes and procedures—that to allow an exercise of this authority by Congress would be to rob the courts of their rightful constitutional role.[6] On the contrary, § 2 of the Fifteenth Amendment expressly declares that "Congress shall have power to enforce this article by appropriate legislation." By adding this authorization, the Framers indicated that Congress was to be chiefly responsible for implementing the rights created in § 1. "It is the power of Congress which has been enlarged. Congress is authorized to *enforce* the prohibitions by appropriate legislation. Some legislation is contemplated to make the [Civil War] amendments fully effective." *Ex parte Virginia*, 100 U. S. 339, 345. Accordingly, in addition to the courts, Congress has full remedial powers to effectuate the constitutional prohibition against racial discrimination in voting.

Congress has repeatedly exercised these powers in the past, and its enactments have repeatedly been upheld. For recent examples, see the Civil Rights Act of 1957, which was sustained in *United States v. Raines*, 362 U. S. 17 . . . . On the rare occasions when the Court has found an unconstitutional exercise of these powers, in its opinion Congress had attacked evils not comprehended by the Fifteenth Amendment. See *United States v. Reese*, 92 U. S. 214; *James v. Bowman*, 190 U. S. 127.

The basic test to be applied in a case involving § 2 of the Fifteenth Amendment is the same as in all cases concerning the express powers of Congress with relation to the reserved powers of the States. Chief Justice Marshall laid down the classic formulation, 50 years before the Fifteenth Amendment was ratified:

"Let the end be legitimate, let it be within the scope of the constitution, and all means which are appropriate, which are plainly adapted to that end, which are not prohibited, but consist with the letter and spirit of the constitution, are constitutional." *McCulloch v. Maryland*, 4 Wheat. 316, 421.

The Court has subsequently echoed his language in describing each of the Civil War Amendments[. *Ex parte Virginia*, 100 U. S., at 345–346.] . . .[7]

---

6 **Questions:** What is Warren saying here about the proper roles of Congress and the Supreme Court in interpreting the Fifteenth Amendment? If the Supreme Court says that something doesn't violate Section 1 of the amendment, can Congress nevertheless exercise its Section 2 powers to prohibit it?

7 **Questions:** In these paragraphs, Warren concludes that Congress's power to enforce the Fifteenth Amendment under Section 2 is as broad as the Necessary and Proper Clause, and certainly more extensive than the Fifteenth Amendment's narrow prohibitions in Section 1. But does he offer any guidance about how to resolve a conflict between Congress's and the Court's interpretation of Section 1? For example, suppose the Court declares that a particular test

We therefore reject South Carolina's argument that Congress may appropriately do no more than to forbid violations of the Fifteenth Amendment in general terms—that the task of fashioning specific remedies or of applying them to particular localities must necessarily be left entirely to the courts. Congress is not circumscribed by any such artificial rules under § 2 of the Fifteenth Amendment. In the oft-repeated words of Chief Justice Marshall, referring to another specific legislative authorization in the Constitution, "This power, like all others vested in Congress, is complete in itself, may be exercised to its utmost extent, and acknowledges no limitations, other than are prescribed in the constitution." *Gibbons v. Ogden*, 9 Wheat. 1, 196.

IV.

Congress exercised its authority under the Fifteenth Amendment in an inventive manner when it enacted the Voting Rights Act of 1965. First: The measure prescribes remedies for voting discrimination which go into effect without any need for prior adjudication. This was clearly a legitimate response to the problem, for which there is ample precedent under other constitutional provisions. See *Katzenbach v. McClung*, 379 U. S. 294; *United States v. Darby*, 312 U. S. 100. Congress had found that case-by-case litigation was inadequate to combat widespread and persistent discrimination in voting, because of the inordinate amount of time and energy required to overcome the obstructionist tactics invariably encountered in these lawsuits. After enduring nearly a century of systematic resistance to the Fifteenth Amendment, Congress might well decide to shift the advantage of time and inertia from the perpetrators of the evil to its victims. . . .

Second: The Act intentionally confines these remedies to a small number of States and political subdivisions which in most instances were familiar to Congress by name. This, too, was a permissible method of dealing with the problem. Congress had learned that substantial voting discrimination presently occurs in certain sections of the country, and it knew no way of accurately forecasting whether the evil might spread elsewhere in the future. In acceptable legislative fashion, Congress chose to limit its attention to the geographic areas where immediate action seemed necessary. The doctrine of the equality of States, invoked by South Carolina, does not bar this approach, for that doctrine applies only to the terms upon which States are admitted to the Union, and not to the remedies for local evils which have subsequently appeared. See *Coyle v. Smith*, 221 U. S. 559, and cases cited therein. . . .[8]

Coverage formula.

We now consider the related question of whether the specific States and political subdivisions within § 4 (b) of the Act were an appropriate target for the new remedies. South Carolina contends that the coverage formula is awkwardly designed in a number of respects and that it disregards various local conditions which have nothing to do with racial discrimination.[9] These arguments, however, are largely beside the point. Congress began work with reliable evidence of actual voting discrimination in a great majority of the States and political subdivisions affected by the new remedies

---

violates Section 1 of the Fifteenth Amendment. Could Congress declare that the test is, in fact, constitutional?

[8] **Question:** This last sentence will prove significant when the Court returns to "[t]he doctrine of the equality of States" in *Shelby County v. Holder*. In *Coyle v. Smith*, the Court held that Congress could not enforce a law that admitted Oklahoma into the Union but restricted where it could locate its state capital. South Carolina cited the case for the proposition that each state is admitted into the Union on an equal footing with all other states, and Congress therefore cannot discriminate against particular states. How does Warren interpret *Coyle*?

[9] **Question:** This paragraph will also prove significant in *Shelby County*. What kind of test does Warren employ to determine whether the coverage formula is an appropriate exercise of congressional power under Section 2 of the Fifteenth Amendment?

of the Act. The formula eventually evolved to describe these areas was relevant to the problem of voting discrimination, and Congress was therefore entitled to infer a significant danger of the evil in the few remaining States and political subdivisions covered by § 4(b) of the Act. No more was required to justify the application to these areas of Congress' express powers under the Fifteenth Amendment. . . .

To be specific, the new remedies of the Act are imposed on [seven] States . . . in which federal courts have repeatedly found substantial voting discrimination. . . . [These states] share two characteristics incorporated by Congress into the coverage formula: the use of tests and devices for voter registration, and a voting rate in the 1964 presidential election at least 12 points below the national average. Tests and devices are relevant to voting discrimination because of their long history as a tool for perpetrating the evil; a low voting rate is pertinent for the obvious reason that widespread disenfranchisement must inevitably affect the number of actual voters. Accordingly, the coverage formula is rational in both practice and theory. It was therefore permissible to impose the new remedies on the few remaining States and political subdivisions covered by the formula, at least in the absence of proof that they have been free of substantial voting discrimination in recent years. . . .

Acknowledging the possibility of overbreadth, the Act provides for termination of special statutory coverage at the behest of States and political subdivisions in which the danger of substantial voting discrimination has not materialized during the preceding five years. Despite South Carolina's argument to the contrary, Congress might appropriately limit litigation under this provision to a single court in the District of Columbia, pursuant to its constitutional power under Art. III, § 1, to "ordain and establish" inferior federal tribunals. See *Yakus v. United States*, 321 U. S. 414, 427–431; *Lockerty v. Phillips*, 319 U. S. 182. At the present time, contractual claims against the United States for more than $10,000 must be brought in the Court of Claims, and, until 1962, the District of Columbia was the sole venue of suits against federal officers officially residing in the Nation's Capital. We have discovered no suggestion that Congress exceeded constitutional bounds in imposing these limitations on litigation against the Federal Government, and the Act is no less reasonable in this respect. . . .

Suspension of tests.

We now arrive at consideration of the specific remedies prescribed by the Act for areas included within the coverage formula. South Carolina assails the temporary suspension of existing voting qualifications, reciting the rule laid down by *Lassiter v. Northampton County Bd. of Elections*, 360 U. S. 45, that literacy tests and related devices are not in themselves contrary to the Fifteenth Amendment.[10] In that very case, however, the Court went on to say, "Of course a literacy test, fair on its face, may be employed to perpetuate that discrimination which the Fifteenth Amendment was designed to uproot." *Id.*, at 53. The record shows that in most of the States covered by the Act, including South Carolina, various tests and devices have been instituted with the purpose of disenfranchising Negroes, have been framed in such a way as to facilitate this aim, and have been administered in a discriminatory fashion for many years. Under these circumstances, the Fifteenth Amendment has clearly been violated. . . .

The Act suspends literacy tests and similar devices for a period of five years from the last occurrence of substantial voting discrimination. This was a legitimate

---

10 **Question:** Warren here addresses the apparent conflict between Congress's exercise of Section 2 of the Fifteenth Amendment to ban literacy tests and *Lassiter v. Northampton County Board of Elections*, in which the Supreme Court upheld the use of literacy tests under Section 1 of the Fifteenth Amendment. How does Warren resolve the inconsistency?

response to the problem, for which there is ample precedent in Fifteenth Amendment cases. . . . Congress knew that continuance of the tests and devices in use at the present time, no matter how fairly administered in the future, would freeze the effect of past discrimination . . . .

Review of new rules.

The Act suspends new voting regulations pending scrutiny by federal authorities to determine whether their use would violate the Fifteenth Amendment. This may have been an uncommon exercise of congressional power, as South Carolina contends, but the Court has recognized that exceptional conditions can justify legislative measures not otherwise appropriate.[11] Congress knew that some of the States covered by § 4(b) of the Act had resorted to the extraordinary stratagem of contriving new rules of various kinds for the sole purpose of perpetuating voting discrimination in the face of adverse federal court decrees. Congress had reason to suppose that these States might try similar maneuvers in the future in order to evade the remedies for voting discrimination contained in the Act itself. Under the compulsion of these unique circumstances, Congress responded in a permissibly decisive manner. . . .

* * *

After enduring nearly a century of widespread resistance to the Fifteenth Amendment, Congress has marshalled an array of potent weapons against the evil, with authority in the Attorney General to employ them effectively. . . . We here hold that the portions of the Voting Rights Act properly before us are a valid means for carrying out the commands of the Fifteenth Amendment. Hopefully, millions of non-white Americans will now be able to participate for the first time on an equal basis in the government under which they live. We may finally look forward to the day when truly "[t]he right of citizens of the United States to vote shall not be denied or abridged by the United States or by any State on account of race, color, or previous condition of servitude."[12]

21.3 THE MODERN POWER TO DEFINE THE SCOPE OF THE RECONSTRUCTION AMENDMENTS

One of South Carolina's arguments that is a little hard to decipher from the Court's opinion in *South Carolina v. Katzenbach* is its contention that only federal courts, not Congress, could determine what was a violation of the Fifteenth Amendment—"that to allow an exercise of this authority by Congress would be to rob the courts of their rightful constitutional role." 383 U.S. 301, 325 (1966). South Carolina was referring to *Lassiter v. Northampton County Board of Elections*, 360 U.S. 45 (1959), and *Guinn v. United States*, 238 U.S. 347 (1915)—two cases in which the Supreme Court had earlier upheld a state's and county's use of literacy tests as voting qualifications despite the Fourteenth,

[11] **Question:** Warren writes that "exceptional conditions can justify legislative measures not otherwise appropriate." Does this imply that preclearance would no longer be appropriate if exceptional conditions no longer existed?

[12] **Questions:** The Warren Court was quite deferential toward Congress's exercise of its power to enforce the Reconstruction amendments. Does *South Carolina v. Katzenbach* impose any limits on that power? If Congress determined that voter ID and in-person voting requirements disproportionately harmed black voters, could it require states to allow all voters to vote by mail without identification in presidential, congressional, and state elections?

Fifteenth, Seventeenth, and Nineteenth Amendments. South Carolina's argument was, essentially, this: If the Supreme Court allowed states to use literacy tests under the Fifteenth Amendment, then how could Congress enforce the Fifteenth Amendment by saying that literacy tests are no longer valid? The *Katzenbach* Court's curt response was that "the Framers indicated that Congress was to be chiefly responsible for implementing the rights" created by the Reconstruction amendments and that the Voting Rights Act was, in any event, consistent with *Lassiter*'s interpretation of the Reconstruction amendments. *Id.* at 326.

Legislative power of enforcement of Reconstruction amendments

The Court had a more difficult time dodging this question in another Voting Rights Act case later the same year, *Katzenbach v. Morgan*, 384 U.S. 641 (1966). One of the provisions of the Voting Rights Act, Section 4(e), specifically prohibited the use of English-language literacy tests for any voter who successfully completed sixth grade in Puerto Rico. Congress justified this provision under Section 5 of the Fourteenth Amendment, concluding that it was necessary to enforce the Equal Protection Clause. This provision had the effect of invalidating the election laws of New York, a state that was home to hundreds of thousands of U.S. citizens who had been educated in Puerto Rico. But New York's attorney general challenged Section 4(e) in light of *Lassiter*'s embrace of a near-identical literacy test, arguing that "an exercise of congressional power under § 5 of the Fourteenth Amendment that prohibits the enforcement of state law can only be sustained if the judicial branch determines that the state law is prohibited by the provisions of the Amendment that Congress sought to enforce." *Morgan*, 384 U.S. at 648.

In an opinion announcing a bold new test, Justice William Brennan disagreed with New York. He declared that Section 5 empowered Congress to decide for itself how best to "*enforce* the prohibitions" of the Reconstruction Amendments:

> A construction of § 5 that would require a judicial determination that the enforcement of the state law precluded by Congress violated the Amendment, as a condition of sustaining the congressional enactment, would depreciate both congressional resourcefulness and congressional responsibility for implementing the Amendment. It would confine the legislative power in this context to the insignificant role of abrogating only those state laws that the judicial branch was prepared to adjudge unconstitutional, or of merely informing the judgment of the judiciary by particularizing the "majestic generalities" of § 1 of the Amendment.
>
> Thus our task in this case is not to determine whether the New York English literacy requirement as applied to deny the right to vote to a person who successfully completed the sixth grade

> in a Puerto Rican school violates the Equal Protection Clause. Accordingly, our decision in *Lassiter v. Northampton Election Bd.*, 360 U. S. 45, sustaining the North Carolina English literacy requirement as not in all circumstances prohibited by the first sections of the Fourteenth and Fifteenth Amendments, is inapposite. *Lassiter* did not present the question before us here: Without regard to whether the judiciary would find that the Equal Protection Clause itself nullifies New York's English literacy requirement as so applied, could Congress prohibit the enforcement of the state law by legislating under § 5 of the Fourteenth Amendment? In answering this question, our task is limited to determining whether such legislation is, as required by § 5, appropriate legislation to enforce the Equal Protection Clause. . . . By including § 5 the draftsmen sought to grant to Congress, by a specific provision applicable to the Fourteenth Amendment, the same broad powers expressed in the Necessary and Proper Clause, Art. I, § 8, cl. 18.

Id. at 648–50 (quoting *Ex parte Virginia*, 100 U.S. 339, 345 (1879) (emphasis in original), for quoted phrase before the colon).

Applying this test, Brennan concluded that a law banning the use of English-literacy tests was necessary and proper for one of two alternative reasons.

First, given how deferential the necessary-and-proper test is in most circumstances, the Court would sustain Congress's exercise of power as long as it could "perceive a basis upon which Congress might predicate a judgment" that New York's English literacy test violated the Fourteenth Amendment. *Id.* at 656. This deference was justified, Brennan explained, because Congress "brought a specially informed legislative competence" to bear on the question, and "it was Congress' prerogative to weigh" the state's justifications for the tests against the burdens they imposed on Puerto Rican voters. *Id.* at 655–66. In this respect, Congress was entitled to arrive at a different conclusion about the tests' constitutionality than the Court alone might have reached.

Second, and alternatively, Brennan wrote that Congress might have agreed with the *Lassiter* Court that the literacy test itself complied with the Fourteenth Amendment, while deciding that eliminating the test was an appropriate means of remedying a separate constitutional violation. *Id.* at 652–53. The effect of the test had been to disenfranchise hundreds of thousands of Puerto Rican voters, who were then subject to unconstitutionally discriminatory state and local treatment. By giving Puerto Rican voters the franchise, Congress might have intended to "enable[ ] the Puerto Rican minority better to obtain 'perfect equality of civil rights and the equal protection of the laws.' " *Id.* at 653. Either way, the case illustrated that Congress could appropriately consider many factors beyond those that guided the Supreme Court. Therefore,

Congress's power to enforce the Reconstruction amendments could not be limited by how a court would enforce them.

Beyond Supreme Court interpretations

Morgan's announcement that Congress could, in effect, define the substantive scope of the Reconstruction amendments quickly led members of Congress to propose new laws that would enforce the Reconstruction amendments by overruling controversial Supreme Court interpretations of them. For example, as will be discussed later (sections 40.5, 43.1), the Supreme Court has interpreted the Due Process Clause of the Fourteenth Amendment to prohibit states from, among other things, convicting someone of a crime after an involuntary confession, *see Miranda v. Arizona*, 384 U.S. 436 (1966); and criminalizing a woman's liberty to have an abortion, *see Roe v. Wade*, 410 U.S. 113 (1973). Invoking *Morgan*, conservative members of Congress argued that Congress had the power to enforce the Fourteenth Amendment by reversing these precedents. *See, e.g.*, Omnibus Crime Control and Safe Streets Act of 1968, Pub. L. No. 90–351, 82 Stat. 197, 210 (attempting to reverse *Miranda*); *The Human Life Bill: Hearings Before the S. Judiciary Subcomm. on Separation of Powers*, 97th Cong., 1st Sess. (1981) (discussing an attempt to reverse *Roe*).

Progressive members of Congress, meanwhile, proposed sweeping new voting-rights laws that went well beyond how the Supreme Court had previously interpreted the Reconstruction amendments. In 1970, for instance, student activists protested the fact that eighteen-year-olds weren't old enough to vote in many states even though they were old enough to be drafted into the Vietnam War. Congress responded by enforcing the Reconstruction amendments to lower the voting age to eighteen in all elections—federal, state, and local. *See* Voting Rights Act Amendments of 1970, Pub. L. No. 91–285, 84 Stat. 314, 316. The Supreme Court had never even hinted that a voting age of twenty-one violated the Reconstruction amendments, raising the question of whether Congress could decide for itself how to interpret the amendments in this context.

In *Oregon v. Mitchell*, 400 U.S. 112 (1970), a fractured Supreme Court divided on the question. Four justices, led by Brennan, interpreted *Morgan* expansively to hold that Congress could rationally decide for itself whether discrimination on the basis of age violated the Fourteenth Amendment. *Mitchell*, 400 U.S. at 248–50. Three justices, led by Potter Stewart, interpreted *Morgan* in light of its alternative rationale: Congress "may paint with a much broader brush" than the Supreme Court in making decisions about how to remedy discriminatory state action, but this limited discretion didn't permit Congress to determine the substantive scope of the Fourteenth Amendment by lowering the voting age. *Id.* at 284. One justice, John Marshall Harlan II, would have rejected *Morgan* entirely. *Id.* at 209. The final justice, Hugo Black, wrote a controlling opinion that applied *Morgan*'s deference to Congress's enforcement power only in cases of "racial discrimination," not in cases of age discrimination. *Id.* at 129. But, citing an earlier decision, Black thought that Congress independently had the power under Article I, Section 4, to regulate federal elections. *Id.* at 124 (citing *Ex parte Yarbrough*, 110 U.S. 651 (1884)). This breakdown meant there were five votes in favor of Congress's power to lower the voting age in *federal* elections but only four votes in favor of Congress's power to lower the voting age in *state* elections.

Despite this fractured opinion on the question of age discrimination, a much larger majority of the *Mitchell* Court agreed that Congress appropriately enforced the Fourteenth Amendment with other provisions of the Voting Rights Act Amendments of 1970. In particular, the Court upheld Congress's power to impose a nationwide ban on literacy tests and to establish a nationwide standard for residency requirements. *Mitchell*, 400 U.S. at 118.

Moreover, *Mitchell* itself did not permanently resolve the question of age discrimination in voting. In 1971, Congress proposed the Twenty-Sixth Amendment. When it was ratified a few months later, its terms prohibited states from denying the franchise to anyone eighteen or older on the basis of age. It also gave Congress new power to enforce its prohibition by appropriate legislation.

Discriminatory effect versus discriminatory purpose

The next time the Court had cause to review Congress's power to enforce the Reconstruction amendments, it sided with Congress. The case arose out of the actions of two southern cities—Mobile, Alabama, and Rome, Georgia—each of which had made it more difficult for black residents to elect candidates of their choice. But the challengers in both cases could only show that the cities' actions had had a discriminatory *effect*; they could not show that the actions had been made with a discriminatory *purpose*. The Mobile challengers argued that evidence of a discriminatory effect was enough to prove that Mobile's actions violated the nationwide prohibitions of the Voting Rights Act—which the Supreme Court interpreted to embody the same standards as Section 1 of the Fifteenth Amendment. The Rome challengers argued that regardless of the proof needed to show a violation of Section 1 of the Fifteenth Amendment, Congress had permissibly enforced Section 2 of the Fifteenth Amendment by passing the preclearance provisions of the Voting Rights Act, which required proof only of a discriminatory effect.

In *City of Mobile v. Bolden*, 446 U.S. 55 (1980), the Court upheld Mobile's actions under the standard it used to evaluate Section 1 of the Fifteenth Amendment, concluding that a challenger had to prove that the actions were made with a discriminatory *purpose*—a more restrictive standard than a discriminatory *effect* test. *Bolden*, 446 U.S. at 60–61.

But in *City of Rome v. United States*, 446 U.S. 156 (1980), the Court held that Congress could permissibly enforce Section 2 of the Fifteenth Amendment by requiring the less deferential discriminatory effect test. Writing for the *Rome* majority, Justice Thurgood Marshall—who had formerly served as the lead attorney for the National Association for the Advancement of Colored People's Legal Defense Fund (NAACP LDF)—wrote that "under § 2 of the Fifteenth Amendment, Congress may prohibit practices that in and of themselves do not violate § 1 of the Amendment, so long as the prohibitions attacking racial discrimination in voting are 'appropriate,' as that term is defined in *McCulloch v. Maryland* and *Ex parte Virginia*." *Rome*, 446 U.S. at 177. The Court indicated that it would uphold any enforcement of the Reconstruction amendments consistent with the spirit of the amendments. *Id.* at 176–77.

Rome again raised the possibility that Congress might attempt to *overrule* a Supreme Court precedent. Two years later, however, the Court emphasized limits on Congress's power. "Congress's power [to enforce the Reconstruction amendments] is limited to adopting measures to enforce the guarantees of the Amendment[s]," the Court wrote. Each enforcement section "grants Congress no power to restrict, abrogate, or dilute these guarantees." *Miss. Univ. for Women v. Hogan*, 458 U.S. 718, 731–33 (1982).

21.3.1

City of Boerne v. Flores

521 U.S. 507 (1997)

Congress finally did attempt to explicitly overrule a Supreme Court precedent when it passed the Religious Freedom Restoration Act of 1993, Pub. L. No. 103–141, 107 Stat. 1488, commonly known as RFRA (pronounced "RIFF-rah"). Congress enacted RFRA in direct response to a 1990 Supreme Court decision that interpreted the Due Process Clause of the Fourteenth Amendment.

To preview a topic that will be covered in far more detail later (section 39.1 ff.), the First Amendment and other provisions of the Bill of Rights apply only to the federal government—none of them limit the powers of states. *See Barron ex rel. Tiernan v. Mayor of Balt.*, 32 U.S. (7 Pet.) 243 (1833). A central goal of the drafters of the Fourteenth Amendment was to "incorporate" the Bill of Rights so that it limited states and local governments. By the mid-twentieth century, the Supreme Court accomplished this goal through its interpretation of the Due Process Clause of the Fourteenth Amendment, which prohibits states from depriving "any person of life, liberty, or property without due process of law." The Court held, essentially, that *liberty* for purposes of the Due Process Clause includes the liberties of the Bill of Rights, and states cannot deprive a person of these liberties without a sufficient reason. *Cantwell v. Connecticut*, 310 U. S. 296, 303 (1940).

In a famous mid-twentieth-century case, *Sherbert v. Verner*, 374 U.S. 398 (1963), the Court adopted a test for how it would apply the First Amendment to the states via the Due Process Clause. The Court held that when a state law interfered with the "free exercise" of a person's religion, the law could stand only if it was *narrowly tailored* to serve a *compelling* purpose. *Sherbert*, 374 U.S. at 403. This *Sherbert* rule lasted for nearly thirty years, but it led to several results that the Court found absurd. In particular, it suggested that if a person had a religious objection to generally applicable requirements like paying taxes or complying with antidiscrimination laws, then the laws had to satisfy a really demanding standard.

Eventually, in *Employment Division v. Smith*, 494 U.S. 872 (1990), a 5–4 majority of the Court proposed a less demanding test for generally applicable laws that don't target religious exercise: they merely had to be *rationally related* to a *legitimate* state interest. *Smith*, 494 U.S. at 890. This new *Smith* test drew the bipartisan ire of members of Congress.

With RFRA, Congress declared that it was exercising its powers under Section 5 of the Fourteenth Amendment to overrule *Smith* and bring back *Sherbert*. RFRA required state and federal courts to apply the *Sherbert* test whenever a person claimed that a law was imposing a substantial burden on religious exercise.

In the following case, *City of Boerne v. Flores*, 521 U.S. 507 (1997), a Texas city named Boerne (pronounced "Bur-nee") passed a historic preservation ordinance that restricted construction in a particular district. When a Catholic church in the district applied for a building permit, local zoning authorities enforced the ordinance and denied the permit. The Archbishop of San Antonio, Patrick Fernández Flores, argued that the ordinance violated RFRA. The city, in turn, argued that RFRA unconstitutionally exceeded Congress's powers to enforce the Reconstruction amendments—an argument that reached the Supreme Court.

Congress's powers took a hit under the Court's ruling in *City of Boerne*.

■ JUSTICE KENNEDY delivered the opinion of the Court.[13]

[T]he parties disagree over whether RFRA is a proper exercise of Congress' § 5 power "to enforce" by "appropriate legislation" the constitutional guarantee that no State shall deprive any person of "life, liberty, or property, without due process of law," nor deny any person "equal protection of the laws."

In defense of the Act, respondent the Archbishop contends, with support from the United States, that RFRA is permissible enforcement legislation. Congress, it is

---

[13] **As You Read, Consider:** Justice Anthony Kennedy announces a very different test to evaluate Congress's power to enforce the Reconstruction amendments than did Chief Justice Earl Warren in *South Carolina v. Katzenbach*. What principles does he invoke to justify the limits that he imposes on Congress?

said, is only protecting by legislation one of the liberties guaranteed by the Fourteenth Amendment's Due Process Clause, the free exercise of religion, beyond what is necessary under [*Employment Division v. Smith* 494 U. S. 872 (1990)]. It is said the congressional decision . . . accords with the settled understanding that § 5 includes the power to enact legislation designed to prevent, as well as remedy, constitutional violations. It is further contended that Congress' § 5 power is not limited to remedial or preventive legislation.

[A]

All must acknowledge that § 5 is "a positive grant of legislative power" to Congress, *Katzenbach v. Morgan*, 384 U. S. 641, 651 (1966); *Ex parte Virginia*, 100 U. S. 339, 345–346 (1880). . . .

Legislation which deters or remedies constitutional violations can fall within the sweep of Congress' enforcement power even if in the process it prohibits conduct which is not itself unconstitutional and intrudes into "legislative spheres of autonomy previously reserved to the States." For example, the Court upheld a suspension of literacy tests and similar voting requirements under Congress' parallel power to enforce the provisions of the Fifteenth Amendment, see U. S. Const., Amdt. 15, § 2, as a measure to combat racial discrimination in voting, *South Carolina v. Katzenbach*, 383 U. S. 301, 308 (1966), despite the facial constitutionality of the tests under *Lassiter v. Northampton County Bd. of Elections*, 360 U. S. 45 (1959). We have also concluded that other measures protecting voting rights are within Congress' power to enforce the Fourteenth and Fifteenth Amendments, despite the burdens those measures placed on the States. *South Carolina v. Katzenbach*, *supra* (upholding several provisions of the Voting Rights Act of 1965); *Katzenbach v. Morgan*, *supra* (upholding ban on literacy tests that prohibited certain people schooled in Puerto Rico from voting); *Oregon v. Mitchell*, 400 U. S. 112 (1970) (upholding 5-year nationwide ban on literacy tests and similar voting requirements for registering to vote); *City of Rome v. United States*, 446 U. S. 156, 161 (1980) (upholding 7-year extension of the Voting Rights Act's requirement that certain jurisdictions preclear any change to a " 'standard, practice, or procedure with respect to voting' "). . . .

It is also true, however, that "[a]s broad as the congressional enforcement power is, it is not unlimited." *Oregon v. Mitchell*, *supra*, at 128 (opinion of Black, J.). In assessing the breadth of § 5's enforcement power, we begin with its text. Congress has been given the power "to enforce" the "provisions of this article." We agree with respondent, of course, that Congress can enact legislation under § 5 enforcing the constitutional right to the free exercise of religion. The "provisions of this article," to which § 5 refers, include the Due Process Clause of the Fourteenth Amendment. Congress' power to enforce the Free Exercise Clause follows from our holding in *Cantwell v. Connecticut*, 310 U. S. 296, 303 (1940), that the "fundamental concept of liberty embodied in [the Fourteenth Amendment's Due Process Clause] embraces the liberties guaranteed by the First Amendment." . . .

Congress' power under § 5, however, extends only to "enforc[ing]" the provisions of the Fourteenth Amendment. The Court has described this power as "remedial," *South Carolina v. Katzenbach*, *supra*, at 326. The design of the Amendment and the text of § 5 are inconsistent with the suggestion that Congress has the power to decree the substance of the Fourteenth Amendment's restrictions on the States.[14] Legislation which alters the meaning of the Free Exercise Clause

---

[14] **Questions:** Kennedy here distinguishes Congress's power to "enforce" the Fourteenth Amendment from a power "to determine what constitutes a constitutional violation." Is this distinction compatible with the Court's decisions from the 1960s, like *South Carolina v. Katzenbach* and *Jones v. Alfred H. Mayer Co.*? What about the *Civil Rights Cases*?

cannot be said to be enforcing the Clause. Congress does not enforce a constitutional right by changing what the right is. It has been given the power "to enforce," not the power to determine what constitutes a constitutional violation. Were it not so, what Congress would be enforcing would no longer be, in any meaningful sense, the "provisions of [the Fourteenth Amendment]."

While the line between measures that remedy or prevent unconstitutional actions and measures that make a substantive change in the governing law is not easy to discern, and Congress must have wide latitude in determining where it lies, the distinction exists and must be observed. There must be a congruence and proportionality between the injury to be prevented or remedied and the means adopted to that end. Lacking such a connection, legislation may become substantive in operation and effect. . . .[15]

As enacted, the Fourteenth Amendment confers substantive rights against the States which, like the provisions of the Bill of Rights, are self-executing. Cf. *South Carolina v. Katzenbach*, 383 U. S., at 325 (discussing Fifteenth Amendment). The power to interpret the Constitution in a case or controversy remains in the Judiciary. . . .

The remedial and preventive nature of Congress' enforcement power, and the limitation inherent in the power, were confirmed in our earliest cases on the Fourteenth Amendment. In the *Civil Rights Cases*, 109 U. S. 3 (1883), the Court invalidated sections of the Civil Rights Act of 1875 which prescribed criminal penalties for denying to any person "the full enjoyment of" public accommodations and conveyances, on the grounds that it exceeded Congress' power by seeking to regulate private conduct. The Enforcement Clause, the Court said, did not authorize Congress to pass "general legislation upon the rights of the citizen, but corrective legislation, that is, such as may be necessary and proper for counteracting such laws as the States may adopt or enforce, and which, by the amendment, they are prohibited from making or enforcing. . . ." *Id.*, at 13–14. The power to "legislate generally upon" life, liberty, and property, as opposed to the "power to provide modes of redress" against offensive state action, was "repugnant" to the Constitution. *Id.*, at 15. See also *United States v. Reese*, 92 U. S. 214, 218 (1876); *United States v. Harris*, 106 U. S. 629, 639 (1883); *James v. Bowman*, 190 U. S. 127, 139 (1903). Although the specific holdings of these early cases might have been superseded or modified, see, *e.g.*, *Heart of Atlanta Motel, Inc. v. United States*, 379 U. S. 241 (1964); *United States v. Guest*, 383 U. S. 745 (1966), their treatment of Congress' § 5 power as corrective or preventive, not definitional, has not been questioned. . . .

Recent cases have continued to revolve around the question whether § 5 legislation can be considered remedial. In *South Carolina v. Katzenbach*, *supra*, we emphasized that "[t]he constitutional propriety of [legislation adopted under the Enforcement Clause] must be judged with reference to the historical experience . . . it reflects." 383 U. S., at 308. There we upheld various provisions of the Voting Rights Act of 1965, finding them to be "remedies aimed at areas where voting discrimination has been most flagrant," *id.*, at 315, and necessary to "banish the blight of racial discrimination in voting, which has infected the electoral process in parts of our country for nearly a century," *id.*, at 308. . . .

After *South Carolina v. Katzenbach*, the Court continued to acknowledge the necessity of using strong remedial and preventive measures to respond to the

---

[15] **Question:** Kennedy calls for a "congruence" and "proportionality" between a valid exercise of the Fourteenth Amendment and the injury to be prevented or remedied. Although he doesn't define these terms, later cases interpret *congruent* to mean similar in nature or kind, while *proportional* means similar in intensity or degree. How might these two considerations distinguish a "substantive" law from a "remedial" law?

widespread and persisting deprivation of constitutional rights resulting from this country's history of racial discrimination. See *Oregon v. Mitchell*, 400 U. S., at 132; *City of Rome*, 446 U. S., at 182; *Morgan*, 384 U. S., at 656. . . .

Any suggestion that Congress has a substantive, nonremedial power under the Fourteenth Amendment is not supported by our case law. In *Oregon v. Mitchell*, *supra*, at 112, a majority of the Court concluded Congress had exceeded its enforcement powers by enacting legislation lowering the minimum age of voters from 21 to 18 in state and local elections. The five Members of the Court who reached this conclusion explained that the legislation intruded into an area reserved by the Constitution to the States. See 400 U. S., at 125 (opinion of Black, J.); *id.*, at 154 (opinion of Harlan, J.); *id.*, at 294 (opinion of Stewart, J., joined by Burger, C. J., and Blackmun, J.). Four of these five were explicit in rejecting the position that § 5 endowed Congress with the power to establish the meaning of constitutional provisions. See *id.*, at 209 (opinion of Harlan, J.); *id.*, at 296 (opinion of Stewart, J.). Justice Black's rejection of this position might be inferred from his disagreement with Congress' interpretation of the Equal Protection Clause. See *id.*, at 125.

There is language in our opinion in *Katzenbach v. Morgan*, 384 U. S. 641 (1966), which could be interpreted as acknowledging a power in Congress to enact legislation that expands the rights contained in § 1 of the Fourteenth Amendment. This is not a necessary interpretation, however, or even the best one. . . . [All the *Morgan* Court did was perceive] a factual basis on which Congress could have concluded that New York's literacy requirement "constituted an invidious discrimination in violation of the Equal Protection Clause." *Id.*, at 656. . . . As Justice Stewart explained in *Oregon v. Mitchell*, *supra*, at 296, interpreting *Morgan* to give Congress the power to interpret the Constitution "would require an enormous extension of that decision's rationale."[16]

If Congress could define its own powers by altering the Fourteenth Amendment's meaning, no longer would the Constitution be "superior paramount law, unchangeable by ordinary means." It would be "on a level with ordinary legislative acts, and, like other acts, . . . alterable when the legislature shall please to alter it." *Marbury v. Madison*, 1 Cranch, at 177. Under this approach, it is difficult to conceive of a principle that would limit congressional power. Shifting legislative majorities could change the Constitution and effectively circumvent the difficult and detailed amendment process contained in Article V.

We now turn to consider whether RFRA can be considered enforcement legislation under § 5 of the Fourteenth Amendment.

B

Respondent contends that RFRA is a proper exercise of Congress' remedial or preventive power.[17] The Act, it is said, is a reasonable means of protecting the free exercise of religion as defined by *Smith*. It prevents and remedies laws which are enacted with the unconstitutional object of targeting religious beliefs and practices.

---

[16] **Question:** The General Welfare Clause of Article I empowers Congress to "provide for the . . . general Welfare of the United States." The Court has never suggested that Congress cannot define for itself what general welfare means. Do you agree with Kennedy that it would be incompatible with written constitutionalism for Congress to be able to define the scope of what is "appropriate" to enforce the Fourteenth Amendment?

[17] **Questions:** In the next few paragraphs, Kennedy distinguishes RFRA's relationship to *Employment Division v. Smith* from the Voting Rights Act's relationship to *Lassiter v. Northampton County Board of Elections*. In both cases, Congress effectively overruled an earlier Supreme Court case. Does Kennedy persuade you that the Voting Rights Act was "remedial" and RFRA was not? Even if he is correct, do you agree that the Reconstruction amendments should not permit Congress to enact "substantive" legislation?

See *Church of Lukumi Babalu Aye, Inc. v. Hialeah*, 508 U. S. 520, 533 (1993). To avoid the difficulty of proving such violations, it is said, Congress can simply invalidate any law which imposes a substantial burden on a religious practice unless it is justified by a compelling interest and is the least restrictive means of accomplishing that interest. If Congress can prohibit laws with discriminatory effects in order to prevent racial discrimination in violation of the Equal Protection Clause, see *City of Rome*, 446 U. S., at 177, then it can do the same, respondent argues, to promote religious liberty.

While preventive rules are sometimes appropriate remedial measures, there must be a congruence between the means used and the ends to be achieved. The appropriateness of remedial measures must be considered in light of the evil presented. See *South Carolina v. Katzenbach*, 383 U. S., at 308. Strong measures appropriate to address one harm may be an unwarranted response to another, lesser one. *Id.*, at 334.

A comparison between RFRA and the Voting Rights Act is instructive. In contrast to the record which confronted Congress and the Judiciary in the voting rights cases, RFRA's legislative record lacks examples of modern instances of generally applicable laws passed because of religious bigotry. The history of persecution in this country detailed in the hearings mentions no episodes occurring in the past 40 years. . . . This lack of support in the legislative record, however, is not RFRA's most serious shortcoming. Judicial deference, in most cases, is based not on the state of the legislative record Congress compiles but "on due regard for the decision of the body constitutionally appointed to decide." *Oregon v. Mitchell*, 400 U. S., at 207 (opinion of Harlan, J.). As a general matter, it is for Congress to determine the method by which it will reach a decision.

Regardless of the state of the legislative record, RFRA cannot be considered remedial, preventive legislation, if those terms are to have any meaning. RFRA is so out of proportion to a supposed remedial or preventive object that it cannot be understood as responsive to, or designed to prevent, unconstitutional behavior. It appears, instead, to attempt a substantive change in constitutional protections. Preventive measures prohibiting certain types of laws may be appropriate when there is reason to believe that many of the laws affected by the congressional enactment have a significant likelihood of being unconstitutional. See *City of Rome*, 446 U. S., at 177. Remedial legislation under § 5 "should be adapted to the mischief and wrong which the [Fourteenth] [A]mendment was intended to provide against." *Civil Rights Cases*, 109 U. S., at 13.

RFRA is not so confined. Sweeping coverage ensures its intrusion at every level of government, displacing laws and prohibiting official actions of almost every description and regardless of subject matter. RFRA's restrictions apply to every agency and official of the Federal, State, and local Governments. RFRA applies to all federal and state law, statutory or otherwise, whether adopted before or after its enactment. RFRA has no termination date or termination mechanism. Any law is subject to challenge at any time by any individual who alleges a substantial burden on his or her free exercise of religion.

The reach and scope of RFRA distinguish it from other measures passed under Congress' enforcement power, even in the area of voting rights. In *South Carolina v. Katzenbach*, the challenged provisions were confined to those regions of the country where voting discrimination had been most flagrant, see 383 U. S., at 315, and affected a discrete class of state laws, *i.e.*, state voting laws. Furthermore, to ensure that the reach of the Voting Rights Act was limited to those cases in which constitutional violations were most likely (in order to reduce the possibility of overbreadth), the coverage under the Act would terminate "at the behest of States and political subdivisions in which the danger of substantial voting discrimination has not materialized during the preceding five years." *Id.*, at 331. . . . This is not to say, of course, that § 5 legislation requires termination dates, geographic restrictions, or egregious predicates. Where, however, a congressional enactment pervasively prohibits constitutional state action in an effort to remedy or to prevent unconstitutional state action, limitations of this kind tend to ensure Congress' means are proportionate to ends legitimate under § 5.

The stringent test RFRA demands of state laws reflects a lack of proportionality or congruence between the means adopted and the legitimate end to be achieved. If an objector can show a substantial burden on his free exercise, the State must demonstrate a compelling governmental interest and show that the law is the least restrictive means of furthering its interest. Claims that a law substantially burdens someone's exercise of religion will often be difficult to contest. . . . Requiring a State to demonstrate a compelling interest and show that it has adopted the least restrictive means of achieving that interest is the most demanding test known to constitutional law. . . . This is a considerable congressional intrusion into the States' traditional prerogatives and general authority to regulate for the health and welfare of their citizens.

The substantial costs RFRA exacts, both in practical terms of imposing a heavy litigation burden on the States and in terms of curtailing their traditional general regulatory power, far exceed any pattern or practice of unconstitutional conduct under the Free Exercise Clause as interpreted in *Smith*. Simply put, RFRA is not designed to identify and counteract state laws likely to be unconstitutional because of their treatment of religion. . . .

Our national experience teaches that the Constitution is preserved best when each part of the Government respects both the Constitution and the proper actions and determinations of the other branches. When the Court has interpreted the Constitution, it has acted within the province of the Judicial Branch, which embraces the duty to say what the law is. *Marbury v. Madison*, 1 Cranch, at 177. When the political branches of the Government act against the background of a judicial interpretation of the Constitution already issued, it must be understood that in later cases and controversies the Court will treat its precedents with the respect due them under settled principles, including *stare decisis*, and contrary expectations must be disappointed. RFRA was designed to control cases and controversies, such as the one before us; but as the provisions of the federal statute here invoked are beyond congressional authority, it is this Court's precedent, not RFRA, which must control. . . .[18]

NOTE: "CONGRUENCE AND PROPORTIONALITY" REVIEW

In contrast with the *Katzenbach* decisions, which interpreted the Reconstruction amendments to give Congress "the same broad powers expressed in the Necessary and Proper Clause," 384 U.S. at 650, the *City of Boerne* test imposed two new limits on Congress's enforcement power drawn

[18] **Question:** In contrast with other federalism decisions of the 1990s, it is difficult to imagine how Congress could have responded to the Supreme Court's decision in *City of Boerne v. Flores* by reenacting RFRA's application to state and local laws. If Congress remained eager to protect religious liberty at the state and local level, how might it have done so?

Note, also, that *City of Boerne*'s holding applied only to Congress's power to regulate state laws. It did not restrict Congress's power to regulate federal laws. RFRA remains in the U.S. Code, and religious petitioners continue to challenge federal regulations for imposing substantial burdens on their religious exercise. *See, e.g., Burwell v. Hobby Lobby Stores, Inc.*, 573 U.S. 682 (2014).

from the *Civil Rights Cases*, 109 U.S. 3 (1883): "There must be a congruence and proportionality between the injury to be prevented or remedied and the means adopted to that end." *City of Boerne*, 521 U.S. at 520. Although the Court didn't explain the difference between these two terms, later cases suggest that *congruence* refers to a reasonable relationship between the nature of the injury and Congress's remedy (i.e., unconstitutional restrictions on voting may be remedied by making it easier to vote), while *proportionality* refers to a reasonable relationship between the intensity of the injury and Congress's remedy (i.e., pervasive restrictions on voting may be remedied by dramatic limits on states' ability to change their laws).

Sovereign immunity. For the next decade after *City of Boerne*, Congress's enforcement powers were most contested in the context of sovereign immunity. As will be discussed later in an examination of the Eleventh Amendment (section 35.1), the Supreme Court has held that when the thirteen original states declared independence, they inherited the British Crown's immunity from being sued without its consent. This immunity became particularly important toward the end of the twentieth century, as Congress passed antidiscrimination laws that applied to all employers, including states, such as the Age Discrimination in Employment Act of 1967, Pub. L. No. 90–202, 81 Stat. 602; the Americans with Disabilities Act of 1990, Pub. L. No. 101–336, 104 Stat. 327; and the Family and Medical Leave Act of 1993, Pub. L. No. 103–3, 107 Stat. 6. As individuals attempted to sue state employers for violating these statutes, the Court held that Congress may not exercise its Article I powers to authorize individuals to sue a state without its consent. *See Seminole Tribe of Fla. v. Florida*, 517 U.S. 44 (1996).

Sovereign immunity and the Reconstruction amendments. But in *Fitzpatrick v. Bitzer*, 427 U.S. 445 (1976), the Court held that this limit on Congress's ability to exercise powers under *Article I* didn't apply to Congress's ability to exercise powers under the *Reconstruction amendments*. Citing the *Katzenbach* cases and *Ex parte Virginia*, 100 U.S. 339 (1880), the Court explained that the Reconstruction amendments were enacted after the Eleventh Amendment and that they were intended to "sanction[ ] intrusions by Congress . . . into the judicial, executive, and legislative spheres of autonomy previously reserved to the States." *Fitzpatrick*, 427 U.S. at 455. Federalism limits like sovereign immunity therefore don't necessarily apply with the same force when Congress legislates pursuant to the Reconstruction amendments. *Id.* at 455–56. This decision led Congress to cast many of its antidiscrimination statutes as methods of enforcing the Reconstruction and voting-rights amendments—leading to a showdown regarding whether those statutes were congruent and proportional to the problems that they allegedly remedied.

The first two cases in this post-*City of Boerne* contest were the companion cases of *Florida Prepaid Postsecondary Education Expense Board v. College Savings Bank*, 527 U.S. 627 (1999), and *College Savings Bank v. Florida Prepaid Postsecondary Education Expense Board*, 527 U.S. 666 (1999). In each case, a bank sued a Florida agency for intellectual property violations: the first under a 1992 amendment to the federal patent law, 106 Stat. 4230, and the second under a 1992 amendment to the federal trademark law, 106 Stat. 3567, which the banks cast as a method of enforcing the Fourteenth Amendment.

The Court disagreed, emphasizing the absence of any legislative or statutory history in which Congress identified a pattern of unconstitutional intellectual property infringement by the states or the unconstitutional denial of a state remedy for such violations. In both cases, the Court suggested that Congress had to have *constitutional* injuries in mind when it enforced the Fourteenth Amendment—that is, there had to be evidence that the law was a congruent and proportionate response to state violations of the Fourteenth Amendment.

The Court also made this point part of its holding in *Kimel v. Florida Board of Regents*, 528 U.S. 62 (2000), in which it held that the Age Discrimination in Employment Act could not abrogate a state's sovereign immunity because Congress had identified no pattern of states engaging in *unconstitutional* age discrimination that independently violated the Equal Protection Clause.

A particularly controversial application of the congruence and proportionality test was *Board of Trustees v. Garrett*, 531 U.S. 356 (2001), in which Patricia Garrett, a nurse at the University of Alabama who had been diagnosed with cancer, alleged that the university violated the Americans with Disabilities Act. She argued that the university had failed to provide her with "reasonable accommodations," such as time off to receive treatment. Unlike with previous statutes, Garrett could point to an extensive legislative record documenting discrimination by states on the basis of disability, and also recent Supreme Court precedent showing that discrimination on the basis of disability could, in some instances, violate the Equal Protection Clause. But the Court interpreted its equal-protection precedent narrowly as holding "that States are not required by the Fourteenth Amendment to make special accommodations for the disabled, so long as their actions toward such individuals are rational." *Garrett*, 531 U.S. at 367 (citing *Cleburne v. Cleburne Living Ctr., Inc.*, 473 U.S. 432 (1985)). Because the legislative record behind the Americans with Disabilities Act showed a pattern of state discrimination but not a pattern of *irrational* state discrimination, the Court held that Congress had not "identified a history and pattern of unconstitutional employment discrimination by the States against the disabled. . . . Congress' § 5 authority is appropriately exercised only in response to state transgressions." *Id.* at 368.

Presumptively unconstitutional discrimination. In more recent cases, the Court has departed in some contexts from *Kimel*'s and *Garrett*'s demanding versions of the congruence and proportionality test.

In *Nevada Department of Human Resources v. Hibbs*, 538 U.S. 721 (2003), the Court held that the Family and Medical Leave Act satisfied the congruence and proportionality test because it attempted to remedy a type of discrimination—discriminatory sex-based stereotypes about family care—that the Court had previously recognized as presumptively unconstitutional. Even though Congress had not developed as extensive a legislative record of discrimination as in *Garrett*, the Court suggested that such a record was unnecessary when Congress was acting to remedy race- or sex-based discrimination, which is usually unconstitutional. By contrast, the Court wrote, discrimination on the basis of age and disability is presumptively constitutional, and therefore Congress needs more evidence when it seeks to remedy such discrimination. *Hibbs*, 538 U.S. at 736.

Hibbs suggests that Congress's substantive power to enforce the Reconstruction amendments depends, in large part, on the standard that the Court has used to determine whether the injury at issue independently violates the Constitution. As we will read in detail in later sections, when the Court today interprets the Fourteenth Amendment, it applies a deferential test to most legislation that allegedly treats people differently or that deprives someone of an important right, but it applies stricter scrutiny to legislation that creates a "suspect" classification (i.e., a classification on the basis of race or sex) or that deprives someone of a "fundamental" right (i.e., a constitutionally protected right such as the right to vote). So, although in *Garrett* the Court held that the Americans with Disabilities Act couldn't ordinarily satisfy the congruence and proportionality test, in *Tennessee v. Lane*, 541 U.S. 509 (2004), the Court held that the same statute could satisfy the test when applied to prevent the denial of a fundamental right, such as the right to access a court. And although in *Hibbs* the Court held that the Family and Medical Leave Act satisfied the test, in *Coleman v. Court of Appeals*, 566 U.S. 30 (2012), the Court held that the sick-leave provisions of the same statute didn't satisfy the test because those provisions were intended to ameliorate discrimination on the basis of illness—which is not a suspect classification—as opposed to discrimination on the basis of sex.

21.4 THE MODERN POWER TO TREAT STATES DIFFERENTLY

In *South Carolina v. Katzenbach*, 383 U.S. 301 (1966), South Carolina didn't argue only that Congress had no power to define the substantive scope of the Reconstruction amendments. It also argued that the Voting Rights Act violated "[t]he doctrine of the equality of States" because Section 4's coverage formula targeted "a small number of States and political subdivisions which in most instances were familiar to Congress by name." *Katzenbach*, 383 U.S. at 328.

South Carolina was referring to *Coyle v. Smith*, 221 U.S. 559 (1911), a case discussed earlier with regard to the Admissions Clause (section 18.5). *Coyle* arose out of Congress's admission of Oklahoma into the Union. When Oklahoma was a territory, Congress exercised its power under the Territory Clause to locate Oklahoma's capital in the city of Guthrie. In 1906, after white residents of Oklahoma applied for statehood, Congress passed an enabling act that permitted Oklahoma to enter the Union on the condition that the new state keep its capital in Guthrie until 1913. Act of June 16, 1906, Pub. L. No. 59–234, 34 Stat. 267. The new state of Oklahoma nevertheless moved its capital to Oklahoma City in 1910—triggering litigation. In *Coyle*, the Supreme Court held that Congress's condition was unenforceable. The Court explained that once a state is admitted on an "equal footing" with the other states, Congress may not reserve for itself more power over one state than it could constitutionally exercise over other states. *Coyle*, 221 U.S. at 580.

When South Carolina invoked this principle in opposition to Section 4(b) of the Voting Rights Act, the *Katzenbach* Court cited *Coyle* to reject South Carolina's argument. It wrote that *Coyle*'s doctrine "applies only to the terms upon which States are admitted to the Union, and not to the remedies for local evils which have subsequently appeared." *Katzenbach*, 383 U.S. at 329.

Voting Rights Act Amendments of 1970 and 1975

Section 4(b)'s coverage formula determined whether a state was subject to Section 5's preclearance review procedure. Although this procedure was initially scheduled to expire after five years, Congress reauthorized it in 1970 for five additional years. *See* Voting Rights Act Amendments of 1970, Pub. L. No. 91–284, 84 Stat. 314, 315. Congress also updated Section 4(b)'s coverage formula with data from 1968. *Id.* This swept in several counties in California, New Hampshire, and New York.

In 1975, Congress reauthorized the Voting Rights Act's preclearance procedure for seven more years, and extended its coverage with data from 1972. *See* Voting Rights Act Amendments of 1975, Pub. L. No. 94–73, 89 Stat. 400, 401. Congress also amended the definition of a discriminatory *test* to include the practice of providing English-only voting materials in places where over 5 percent of voting-age citizens spoke a language other than English. *Id.*; *see Gaston Cnty. v. United States*, 395 U.S. 285 (1969) (holding that evidence of past educational discrimination could justify preventing a county from instituting a literacy test). After these amendments, Arizona and Texas became covered jurisdictions, as did several counties in California, Florida, Michigan, New York, North Carolina, and South Dakota.

As Congress expanded the reach of Section 4(b)'s coverage formula, the Supreme Court expanded the strength of Section 5's preclearance review. Covered jurisdictions subject to preclearance needed the permission of the U.S. attorney general or a three-judge district court before making any changes to their electoral practices, including apportionment and districting, adoption of at-large instead of district elections, candidate qualification regulations, provisions for the assistance of illiterate voters, movement of polling places, adoption of appointive instead of elective positions, annexations, and public-employer restrictions on employees running for public office. *See Allen v. State Bd. of Elections*, 393 U.S. 544 (1969); *Perkins v. Matthews*, 400 U.S. 379 (1971); *Georgia v. United States*, 411 U.S. 526 (1973); *Dougherty Cnty. Bd. of Educ. v. White*, 439 U.S. 32 (1978).

Voting Rights Act Amendments of 1982 and 2006

By the time Congress once again considered whether to reauthorize Section 5's preclearance procedure in 1982, limiting the Voting Rights Act's scope had become a major priority among conservative lawyers in the Department of Justice under President Ronald Reagan. One of these lawyers was a rising star named John Roberts. *See* Joan Biskupic, *The Chief: The Life and Turbulent Times of Chief Justice John Roberts* 70–76 (2019). Roberts wrote dozens of memos urging senators to dilute the Voting Rights Act's protections, calling them "the most intrusive interference imaginable by federal courts into state and local processes." Ari Berman, *Give Us the Ballot: The Modern Struggle for Voting Rights in America* 150 (2015).

In the face of Roberts's memos, Congress expanded the scope of the Voting Rights Act and extended Section 5's preclearance provisions for twenty-five years. *See* Voting Rights Act Amendments of 1982, Pub. L. No. 97–205, 96 Stat. 131. Congress did not, however, update Section 4(b)'s coverage formula to determine which jurisdictions would be subject to preclearance. Nevertheless, when the Supreme Court interpreted the amendments, it reaffirmed Congress's power to exercise wide discretion in enforcing the Fifteenth Amendment beyond how the Court would have interpreted it alone. *See, e.g.*, *Lopez v. Monterey Cnty.*, 525 U.S. 266 (1999); *Thornburg v. Gingles*, 478 U.S. 30 (1986).

In 2006, Congress again reauthorized the preclearance provisions of the Voting Rights Act for another twenty-five years without changing the coverage formula under Section 4(b). *See* Fannie Lou Hamer, Rosa Parks, and Coretta Scott King Voting Rights Act Reauthorization and Amendments Act of 2006, Pub. L. No. 190–246, 120 Stat. 577. Instead, Congress continued to define covered jurisdictions with data from 1972.

21.4.1

Shelby County v. Holder

570 U.S. 529 (2013)

A year before Congress reauthorized the Voting Rights Act's preclearance provisions in 2006, John Roberts joined the Supreme Court as chief justice. The new Roberts Court was far less deferential to Congress's power than the previous Supreme Court had been.

Shortly after Congress reauthorized the Voting Rights Act, a Texas utility district brought a suit challenging the act's constitutionality using the same "equality of States" argument that South Carolina had made in 1966. In *Northwest Austin Municipal Utility District No. 1 v. Holder*, the Supreme Court resolved the case on statutory grounds, but it also expressed serious doubts about the constitutionality of Section 5's preclearance procedures. 557 U.S. 193, 202–03 (2009). An 8–1 majority explained that Section 5 "imposes substantial 'federalism costs'" and "differentiates between the States, despite our historic tradition that all the States enjoy 'equal sovereignty.'" *Id.* at 202–03.

Four years later, another covered jurisdiction—Shelby County, Alabama—brought another challenge to Section 4(b)'s coverage formula and Section 5's preclearance provisions. The Court's decision in *Shelby County v. Holder*, 570 U.S. 529 (2013), imposed a new, restrictive limit on Congress's power to enforce the Fifteenth Amendment.

■ CHIEF JUSTICE ROBERTS delivered the opinion of the Court.[19]

The Voting Rights Act of 1965 employed extraordinary measures to address an extraordinary problem. Section 5 of the Act required States to obtain federal permission before enacting any law related to voting—a drastic departure from basic principles of federalism. And § 4 of the Act applied that requirement only to some States—an equally dramatic departure from the principle that all States enjoy equal sovereignty. This was strong medicine, but Congress determined it was needed to address entrenched racial discrimination in voting, "an insidious and pervasive evil which had been perpetuated in certain parts of our country through unremitting and ingenious defiance of the Constitution." *South Carolina v. Katzenbach*, 383 U.S. 301, 309 (1966). As we explained in upholding the law, "exceptional conditions can justify legislative measures not otherwise appropriate." *Id.*, at 334. Reflecting the unprecedented nature of these measures, they were scheduled to expire after five years. See Voting Rights Act of 1965, § 4(a), 79 Stat. 438.

Nearly 50 years later, they are still in effect; indeed, they have been made more stringent, and are now scheduled to last until 2031. There is no denying, however, that the conditions that originally justified these measures no longer characterize voting in the covered jurisdictions. By 2009, "the racial gap in voter registration and turnout [was] lower in the States originally covered by § 5 than it [was] nationwide." *Northwest Austin Municipal Util. Dist. No. One v. Holder*, 557 U.S. 193, 203–204 (2009). Since that time, Census Bureau data indicate that African-American voter turnout has come to exceed white voter turnout in five of the six States originally covered by § 5, with a gap in the sixth State of less than one half of one percent.

At the same time, voting discrimination still exists; no one doubts that. The question is whether the Act's extraordinary measures, including its disparate treatment of the States, continue to satisfy constitutional requirements. As we put it a short time ago, "the Act imposes current burdens and must be justified by current needs." *Northwest Austin*, 557 U.S., at 203. . . .

II

[T]he Constitution and laws of the United States are "the supreme Law of the Land." U.S. Const., Art. VI, cl. 2. State legislation may not contravene federal law. The Federal Government does not, however, have a general right to review and veto state enactments before they go into effect. A proposal to grant such authority to "negative" state laws was considered at the Constitutional Convention, but rejected in favor of allowing state laws to take effect, subject to later challenge under the

---

[19] **As You Read, Consider:** In this opinion, Chief Justice John Roberts introduces a novel limitation on Congress's power to enforce the Reconstruction amendments: the "equal sovereignty" principle. How does his application of this principle compare with Justice Anthony Kennedy's application of the "congruence and proportionality" standard in *City of Boerne v. Flores*, or Chief Justice Earl Warren's application of the *McCulloch v. Maryland* standard in *South Carolina v. Katzenbach*? Would all three tests yield different results in this case?

Supremacy Clause. See 1 Records of the Federal Convention of 1787, pp. 21, 164–168 (M. Farrand ed. 1911); 2 *id.*, at 27–29, 390–392.[20]

Outside the strictures of the Supremacy Clause, States retain broad autonomy in structuring their governments and pursuing legislative objectives. Indeed, the Constitution provides that all powers not specifically granted to the Federal Government are reserved to the States or citizens. Amdt. 10. This "allocation of powers in our federal system preserves the integrity, dignity, and residual sovereignty of the States." *Bond v. United States*, 564 U.S. ___, ___ (2011). But the federal balance "is not just an end in itself: Rather, federalism secures to citizens the liberties that derive from the diffusion of sovereign power." *Ibid.* (internal quotation marks omitted).

More specifically, " 'the Framers of the Constitution intended the States to keep for themselves, as provided in the Tenth Amendment, the power to regulate elections.' " *Gregory v. Ashcroft*, 501 U.S. 452, 461–462. Of course, the Federal Government retains significant control over federal elections. For instance, the Constitution authorizes Congress to establish the time and manner for electing Senators and Representatives. Art. I, § 4, cl. 1. But States have "broad powers to determine the conditions under which the right of suffrage may be exercised." And "[e]ach State has the power to prescribe the qualifications of its officers and the manner in which they shall be chosen." *Boyd v. Nebraska ex rel. Thayer*, 143 U.S. 135 (1892). Drawing lines for congressional districts is likewise "primarily the duty and responsibility of the State." *Perry v. Perez*, 565 U.S. ___, ___, 132 S.Ct. 934, 940 (2012) (*per curiam*).

Not only do States retain sovereignty under the Constitution, there is also a "fundamental principle of *equal* sovereignty" among the States.[21] *Northwest Austin*, *supra*, at 203 (citing *Lessee of Pollard v. Hagan*, 3 How. 212, 223 (1845); and *Texas v. White*, 7 Wall. 700, 725–726 (1869); emphasis added). Over a hundred years ago, this Court explained that our Nation "was and is a union of States, equal in power, dignity and authority." *Coyle v. Smith*, 221 U.S. 559, 567 (1911). Indeed, "the constitutional equality of the States is essential to the harmonious operation of the scheme upon which the Republic was organized." *Id.*, at 580. *Coyle* concerned the admission of new States, and *Katzenbach* rejected the notion that the principle operated as a *bar* on differential treatment outside that context. 383 U.S., at 328–329. At the same time, as we made clear in *Northwest Austin*, the fundamental principle of equal sovereignty remains highly pertinent in assessing subsequent disparate treatment of States. 557 U.S., at 203.

The Voting Rights Act sharply departs from these basic principles. It suspends "*all* changes to state election law—however innocuous—until they have been

[20] **Question:** Roberts's opening observations raise a question: Why doesn't the Voting Rights Act violate the anticommandeering doctrine? For one answer, see *New York v. United States*, 505 U.S. 144, 207 n.3 (1992) (White, J., concurring in part and dissenting in part) ("[In contexts outside of Article I], principles of federalism have not insulated States from mandates by the National Government. The Court has upheld congressional statutes that impose clear directives on state officials, including those enacted pursuant to the Extradition Clause, *see, e.g., Puerto Rico v. Branstad*, 483 U.S. 291, 227–228 (1987), the post-Civil War Amendments, *see, e.g., South Carolina v. Katzenbach*, 383 U.S. 301, 319–320, 334–335 (1966), as well as congressional statutes that require state courts to hear certain actions, *see, e.g., Testa v. Katt*, 330 U.S. 386, 392–94 (1947).").

[21] **Question:** In this paragraph, Roberts invokes the same sort of "equal sovereignty" argument that South Carolina invoked in its suit against the Voting Rights Act in 1966. The *South Carolina v. Katzenbach* Court rejected the argument that Congress is *barred* from treating existing states differently from one another, and Roberts appears to accept that conclusion. Precisely what role, then, does Congress's differential treatment of states play in Roberts's analysis of the Voting Rights Act?

precleared by federal authorities in Washington, D.C." *Id.*, at 202. States must beseech the Federal Government for permission to implement laws that they would otherwise have the right to enact and execute on their own, subject of course to any injunction in a § 2 action. The Attorney General has 60 days to object to a preclearance request, longer if he requests more information. If a State seeks preclearance from a three-judge court, the process can take years.

And despite the tradition of equal sovereignty, the Act applies to only nine States (and several additional counties). While one State waits months or years and expends funds to implement a validly enacted law, its neighbor can typically put the same law into effect immediately, through the normal legislative process. Even if a noncovered jurisdiction is sued, there are important differences between those proceedings and preclearance proceedings; the preclearance proceeding "not only switches the burden of proof to the supplicant jurisdiction, but also applies substantive standards quite different from those governing the rest of the nation." 679 F.3d, at 884 (Williams, J., dissenting) (case below).

All this explains why, when we first upheld the Act in 1966, we described it as "stringent" and "potent." *Katzenbach*, 383 U.S., at 308, 315, 337. We recognized that it "may have been an uncommon exercise of congressional power," but concluded that "legislative measures not otherwise appropriate" could be justified by "exceptional conditions." *Id.*, at 334. We have since noted that the Act authorizes federal intrusion into sensitive areas of state and local policymaking, and represents an extraordinary departure from the traditional course of relations between the States and the Federal Government. . . .[22]

In 1966, we found these departures from the basic features of our system of government justified. The "blight of racial discrimination in voting" had "infected the electoral process in parts of our country for nearly a century." *Katzenbach*, 383 U.S., at 308. Several States had enacted a variety of requirements and tests "specifically designed to prevent" African-Americans from voting. *Id.*, at 310. Case-by-case litigation had proved inadequate to prevent such racial discrimination in voting, in part because States "merely switched to discriminatory devices not covered by the federal decrees," "enacted difficult new tests," or simply "defied and evaded court orders." *Id.*, at 314. Shortly before enactment of the Voting Rights Act, only 19.4 percent of African-Americans of voting age were registered to vote in Alabama, only 31.8 percent in Louisiana, and only 6.4 percent in Mississippi. *Id.*, at 313, 86 S.Ct. 803. Those figures were roughly 50 percentage points or more below the figures for whites. *Ibid.* . . .

At the time, the coverage formula—the means of linking the exercise of the unprecedented authority with the problem that warranted it—made sense. We found that "Congress chose to limit its attention to the geographic areas where immediate action seemed necessary." *Katzenbach*, 383 U.S., at 328. . . .

Nearly 50 years later, things have changed dramatically. Shelby County contends that the preclearance requirement, even without regard to its disparate coverage, is now unconstitutional. Its arguments have a good deal of force. In the covered jurisdictions, "[v]oter turnout and registration rates now approach parity. Blatantly discriminatory evasions of federal decrees are rare. And minority candidates hold office at unprecedented levels." *Northwest Austin*, 557 U.S., at 202. The tests

[22] **Questions:** In these paragraphs, is Roberts suggesting that Congress must demonstrate that "exceptional conditions" exist before it can *ever* treat two states differently? Or is he saying that only "exceptional conditions" can justify differential treatment when Congress engages in an "extraordinary departure from the traditional course of relations between the States and the Federal Government"?

and devices that blocked access to the ballot have been forbidden nationwide for over 40 years. See § 6, 84 Stat. 315; § 102, 89 Stat. 400.

Those conclusions are not ours alone. Congress said the same when it reauthorized the Act in 2006, writing that "[s]ignificant progress has been made in eliminating first generation barriers experienced by minority voters, including increased numbers of registered minority voters, minority voter turnout, and minority representation in Congress, State legislatures, and local elected offices." § 2(b)(1), 120 Stat. 577. . . . That Report also explained that there have been "significant increases in the number of African-Americans serving in elected offices"; more specifically, there has been approximately a 1,000 percent increase since 1965 in the number of African-American elected officials in the six States originally covered by the Voting Rights Act. *Id.*, at 18. . . .

There is no doubt that these improvements are in large part *because of* the Voting Rights Act. The Act has proved immensely successful at redressing racial discrimination and integrating the voting process. See § 2(b)(1), 120 Stat. 577. During the "Freedom Summer" of 1964, in Philadelphia, Mississippi, three men were murdered while working in the area to register African-American voters. See *United States v. Price,* 383 U.S. 787 (1966). On "Bloody Sunday" in 1965, in Selma, Alabama, police beat and used tear gas against hundreds marching in support of African-American enfranchisement. Today both of those towns are governed by African-American mayors. Problems remain in these States and others, but there is no denying that, due to the Voting Rights Act, our Nation has made great strides.

Yet the Act has not eased the restrictions in § 5 or narrowed the scope of the coverage formula in § 4(b) along the way. Those extraordinary and unprecedented features were reauthorized—as if nothing had changed. In fact, the Act's unusual remedies have grown even stronger. When Congress reauthorized the Act in 2006, it did so for another 25 years on top of the previous 40—a far cry from the initial five-year period. See 42 U.S.C. § 1973b(a)(8). Congress also expanded the prohibitions in § 5. [See 42 U.S.C. §§ 1973c(b)–(c).] [T]he bar that covered jurisdictions must clear has been raised even as the conditions justifying that requirement have dramatically improved. . . .

Respondents do not deny that there have been improvements on the ground, but argue that much of this can be attributed to the deterrent effect of § 5, which dissuades covered jurisdictions from engaging in discrimination that they would resume should § 5 be struck down. Under this theory, however, § 5 would be effectively immune from scrutiny; no matter how "clean" the record of covered jurisdictions, the argument could always be made that it was deterrence that accounted for the good behavior.

The provisions of § 5 apply only to those jurisdictions singled out by § 4. We now consider whether that coverage formula is constitutional in light of current conditions.

III

When upholding the constitutionality of the coverage formula in 1966, we concluded that it was "rational in both practice and theory." *Katzenbach*, 383 U.S., at 330. The formula looked to cause (discriminatory tests) and effect (low voter registration and turnout), and tailored the remedy (preclearance) to those jurisdictions exhibiting both.

By 2009, however, we concluded that the "coverage formula raise[d] serious constitutional questions." *Northwest Austin*, 557 U.S., at 204. As we explained, a statute's "current burdens" must be justified by "current needs," and any "disparate geographic coverage" must be "sufficiently related to the problem that it targets." *Id.*, at 203.[23] The coverage formula met that test in 1965, but no longer does so.

Coverage today is based on decades-old data and eradicated practices. The formula captures States by reference to literacy tests and low voter registration and turnout in the 1960s and early 1970s. But such tests have been banned nationwide for over 40 years. And voter registration and turnout numbers in the covered States have risen dramatically in the years since. Racial disparity in those numbers was compelling evidence justifying the preclearance remedy and the coverage formula. See, *e.g.*, *Katzenbach*, *supra*, at 313, 329–330. There is no longer such a disparity.

In 1965, the States could be divided into two groups: those with a recent history of voting tests and low voter registration and turnout, and those without those characteristics. Congress based its coverage formula on that distinction. Today the Nation is no longer divided along those lines, yet the Voting Rights Act continues to treat it as if it were. . . .

The Government [argues] that because the formula was relevant in 1965, its continued use is permissible so long as any discrimination remains in the States Congress identified back then—regardless of how that discrimination compares to discrimination in States unburdened by coverage. This argument does not look to "current political conditions," *Northwest Austin*, *supra*, at 203, but instead relies on a comparison between the States in 1965. That comparison reflected the different histories of the North and South. It was in the South that slavery was upheld by law until uprooted by the Civil War, that the reign of Jim Crow denied African-Americans the most basic freedoms, and that state and local governments worked tirelessly to disenfranchise citizens on the basis of race. The Court invoked that history—rightly so—in sustaining the disparate coverage of the Voting Rights Act in 1966. See *Katzenbach*, *supra*, at 308 ("The constitutional propriety of the Voting Rights Act of 1965 must be judged with reference to the historical experience which it reflects.").

But history did not end in 1965. By the time the Act was reauthorized in 2006, there had been 40 more years of it. In assessing the "current need[ ]" for a preclearance system that treats States differently from one another today, that history cannot be ignored. During that time, largely because of the Voting Rights Act, voting tests were abolished, disparities in voter registration and turnout due to race were erased, and African-Americans attained political office in record numbers. And yet the coverage formula that Congress reauthorized in 2006 ignores these developments, keeping the focus on decades-old data relevant to decades-old problems, rather than current data reflecting current needs.

The Fifteenth Amendment commands that the right to vote shall not be denied or abridged on account of race or color, and it gives Congress the power to enforce that command. The Amendment is not designed to punish for the past; its purpose is to ensure a better future. To serve that purpose, Congress—if it is to divide the States—must identify those jurisdictions to be singled out on a basis that makes sense in light of current conditions. . . .

---

[23] **Question:** Roberts here is announcing a test for how to evaluate the constitutionality of the coverage formula. Is it any different from the congruence and proportionality test of *City of Boerne*? *See* Ellen D. Katz, *Dismissing Deterrence*, 127 Harv. L. Rev. F. 248, 249 (2014) ("Immobilized by *Shelby County*, preclearance had been vulnerable to attack since 1997 when the Supreme Court decided *City of Boerne v. Flores*. That decision and its progeny demanded a far tighter connection between constitutional violations and congressionally crafted remedies than prior precedent had required.")

* * *

[C]ongress could have updated the coverage formula at [any] time, but did not do so. Its failure to act leaves us today with no choice but to declare § 4(b) unconstitutional. The formula in that section can no longer be used as a basis for subjecting jurisdictions to preclearance.

Our decision in no way affects the permanent, nationwide ban on racial discrimination in voting found in § 2. We issue no holding on § 5 itself, only on the coverage formula. Congress may draft another formula based on current conditions. Such a formula is an initial prerequisite to a determination that exceptional conditions still exist justifying such an "extraordinary departure from the traditional course of relations between the States and the Federal Government." . . .[24]

■ JUSTICE GINSBURG, with whom JUSTICE BREYER, JUSTICE SOTOMAYOR, and JUSTICE KAGAN join, dissenting.

In the Court's view, the very success of § 5 of the Voting Rights Act demands its dormancy. Congress was of another mind. Recognizing that large progress has been made, Congress determined, based on a voluminous record, that the scourge of discrimination was not yet extirpated. The question this case presents is who decides whether, as currently operative, § 5 remains justifiable, this Court, or a Congress charged with the obligation to enforce the post-Civil War Amendments "by appropriate legislation." With overwhelming support in both Houses, Congress concluded that, for two prime reasons, § 5 should continue in force, unabated. First, continuance would facilitate completion of the impressive gains thus far made; and second, continuance would guard against backsliding. Those assessments were well within Congress' province to make and should elicit this Court's unstinting approbation. . . .

It is well established that Congress' judgment regarding exercise of its power to enforce the Fourteenth and Fifteenth Amendments warrants substantial deference. . . . The basis for this deference is firmly rooted in both constitutional text and precedent. The Fifteenth Amendment, which targets precisely and only racial discrimination in voting rights, states that, in this domain, "Congress shall have power to enforce this article by appropriate legislation." In choosing this language, the Amendment's framers invoked Chief Justice Marshall's formulation of the scope of Congress' powers under the Necessary and Proper Clause. . . .

It cannot tenably be maintained that the VRA, an Act of Congress adopted to shield the right to vote from racial discrimination, is inconsistent with the letter or spirit of the Fifteenth Amendment, or any provision of the Constitution read in light of the Civil War Amendments. . . . The stated purpose of the Civil War Amendments was to arm Congress with the power and authority to protect all persons within the Nation from violations of their rights by the States. In exercising that power, then, Congress may use "all means which are appropriate, which are plainly adapted" to the constitutional ends declared by these Amendments. *McCulloch*, 4 Wheat., at 421. So when Congress acts to enforce the right to vote free from racial discrimination, we

---

[24] **Question:** President Donald Trump's main legislative achievement was the Tax Cuts and Jobs Act of 2017, Pub. L. No. 115–97, 131 Stat. 2054. Before the act, taxpayers could deduct from their federal tax bill money that they spent on state and local taxes. But the act capped this deduction. This cap disproportionately affected people in states with the highest tax rates, which tend to be coastal, Democratic-voting states like New York. After *Shelby County*, must Congress demonstrate that "exceptional conditions" justify its differential treatment of these states? *See New York v. Mnuchin*, 408 F. Supp. 3d 399, 420–21 (S.D.N.Y. 2019) (discussing Shelby County's application to the act).

ask not whether Congress has chosen the means most wise, but whether Congress has rationally selected means appropriate to a legitimate end. . . .

[But the Court holds] that § 4(b)'s coverage formula is unconstitutional. It pins this result, in large measure, to "the fundamental principle of equal sovereignty." In *Katzenbach*, however, the Court held, in no uncertain terms, that the principle "*applies only to the terms upon which States are admitted to the Union*, and not to the remedies for local evils which have subsequently appeared." 383 U.S., at 328–329 (emphasis added). . . . [T]he Court clouds that once clear understanding . . . to convey that the principle of equal sovereignty "remains highly pertinent in assessing subsequent disparate treatment of States." . . .

Today's unprecedented extension of the equal sovereignty principle outside its proper domain—the admission of new States—is capable of much mischief. Federal statutes that treat States disparately are hardly novelties. See, *e.g.*, 42 U.S.C. § 10136 (specifying rules applicable to Nevada's Yucca Mountain nuclear waste site, and providing that "[n]o State, other than the State of Nevada, may receive financial assistance under this subsection. . . ."). . . .

[The Court also] strikes § 4(b)'s coverage provision because, in its view, the provision is not based on "current conditions." *Ante*, at 2627. It discounts, however, that one such condition was the preclearance remedy in place in the covered jurisdictions, a remedy Congress designed both to catch discrimination before it causes harm, and to guard against return to old ways. Volumes of evidence supported Congress' determination that the prospect of retrogression was real. Throwing out preclearance when it has worked and is continuing to work to stop discriminatory changes is like throwing away your umbrella in a rainstorm because you are not getting wet. . . .

The sad irony of today's decision lies in its utter failure to grasp why the VRA has proven effective. The Court appears to believe that the VRA's success in eliminating the specific devices extant in 1965 means that preclearance is no longer needed. With that belief, and the argument derived from it, history repeats itself. The same assumption—that the problem could be solved when particular methods of voting discrimination are identified and eliminated—was indulged and proved wrong repeatedly prior to the VRA's enactment. Unlike prior statutes, which singled out particular tests or devices, the VRA is grounded in Congress' recognition of the "variety and persistence" of measures designed to impair minority voting rights. *Katzenbach*, 383 U.S., at 311. In truth, the evolution of voting discrimination into more subtle second-generation barriers is powerful evidence that a remedy as effective as preclearance remains vital to protect minority voting rights and prevent backsliding. . . .

Aftermath of Shelby County

Shelby County was an extraordinary decision. Rep. John Lewis of Georgia, who was beaten on the Edmund Pettus Bridge in 1965, lamented that it "stuck a dagger into the heart of the Voting Rights Act." *John Lewis and Others React to the Supreme Court's Voting Rights Act Ruling*, Wash. Post., June 25, 2013. Lewis explained that while the court did not deny that voter discrimination still exists, "it gutted the most powerful tool this nation has ever had to stop discriminatory voting practices from becoming law. Those justices were never beaten or jailed for trying to register to vote. They have no friends who gave their lives for the right to vote. I want to say to them, Come and walk in my shoes." *Id.*

In response to the decision, formerly covered jurisdictions, including Alabama, immediately enacted dozens of laws that made it more difficult for voters of color to vote. Reading *Shelby County* from the perspective of 2020, Professor Michael Klarman argued that the "post-*Shelby County* behavior of southern states [in adopting more restrictive voter registration laws] suggests that the deterrence argument was entitled to greater credence." Michael J. Klarman, *The Supreme Court, 2020 Term—Foreword: The Degradation of American Democracy*, 134 Harv. L. Rev. 1, 183–84 (2020). Nevertheless, in 2021, the Court further limited the scope of the Voting Rights Act. In *Brnovich v. Democratic National Committee*, 141 S. Ct. 2321, 2339–40 (2021), the Court narrowly interpreted a provision of the act that prohibits any state voting rule "which results in a denial or abridgement of the right of any citizen of the United States to vote on account of race or color." 52 U.S.C. § 10301. Although members of Congress attempted to amend this provision in 1982 to apply whenever a voting rule disparately impacts voters of color, the Court rejected this interpretation of the final amendment as "a radical project" that "would have the potential to invalidate just about any voting rule a State adopts." *Id.* at 2341, 2343. Instead, the Court adopted a restrictive five-factor test for determining when the provision applied. *Id.* at 2339–40. The *Brnovich* Court did not invoke any constitutional principles in its interpretation of the provision. But its conclusion that the act should prohibit only the most egregious examples of voter suppression is consistent with *Shelby County*'s treatment of the Voting Rights Act's broad scope as an "extraordinary departure from the traditional course of relations between the States and the Federal Government." *Shelby County v. Holder*, 570 U.S. 529, 557 (2013).

Equal sovereignty

Shelby County was also the first time the Supreme Court applied the idea of "the constitutional equality of the States" to limit Congress's power to regulate existing states. *See* Leah M. Litman, *Inventing Equal Sovereignty*, 114 Mich. L. Rev. 1207, 1211 (2016) (calling equal sovereignty "a kind of invented tradition—a social practice whose authority allegedly stems from longstanding observance, but which turns out to be somewhat recent in origin"). As the majority opinion recognized, prior cases like *South Carolina v. Katzenbach*, 383 U.S. 301 (1966), had "rejected the notion that the principle operated as a *bar* on differential treatment." *Holder*, 570 U.S. at 544. Nevertheless, the Court treated equal sovereignty as a relevant factor in applying a new balancing test that looks nearly identical to the congruence and proportionality test from *City of Boerne v. Flores*, 521 U.S. 507 (1997). Where *Flores* determined whether an exercise of the Fourteenth Amendment was "appropriate" by asking whether it was congruent and proportional to remedying a constitutional violation, *Shelby County* determined whether an exercise of the Fifteenth Amendment was "appropriate" by asking whether its "current burdens" were justified by "current needs," and whether its "disparate geographic coverage" was "sufficiently related to the problem that it targets." 570 U.S. at 542. The Court concluded that the Voting Rights Act's coverage formula was no longer appropriate because its "extraordinary departure from the traditional course of relations between the States and the Federal Government"—including its disparate coverage, but also including its regulation of state voting laws—were no longer justified. *Id.* at 545.

In the years since *Shelby County*, the Court has occasionally invoked the equal sovereignty principle without much elaboration, leaving its range of applications open to question. *See, e.g.*, *Franchise Tax Bd. v. Hyatt*, 578 U.S. 171, 179 (2016) (invoking "the 'constitutional equality' among the states" to invalidate a *state* law).

CHAPTER 22

HOW ARE THE MEMBERS OF CONGRESS CHOSEN?

ARTICLE I, SECTION 2, CLAUSE 1: The House of Representatives shall be composed of Members chosen every second Year by the People of the several States, and the Electors in each State shall have the Qualifications requisite for Electors of the most numerous Branch of the State Legislature.

CLAUSE 3: Representatives and direct Taxes shall be apportioned among the several States which may be included within this Union, according to their respective Numbers, which shall be determined by adding to the whole Number of free Persons, including those bound to Service for a Term of Years, and excluding Indians not taxed, three fifths of all other Persons. The actual Enumeration shall be made within three Years after the first Meeting of the Congress of the United States, and within every subsequent Term of ten Years, in such Manner as they shall by Law direct. The Number of Representatives shall not exceed one for every thirty Thousand, but each State shall have at Least one Representative; and until such enumeration shall be made, the State of New Hampshire shall be entitled to chuse three, Massachusetts eight, Rhode-Island and Providence Plantations one, Connecticut five, New-York six, New Jersey four, Pennsylvania eight, Delaware one, Maryland six, Virginia ten, North Carolina five, South Carolina five, and Georgia three.

CLAUSE 4: When vacancies happen in the Representation from any State, the Executive Authority thereof shall issue Writs of Election to fill such Vacancies.

CLAUSE 5: The House of Representatives shall chuse their Speaker and other Officers. . . .

ARTICLE I, SECTION 3, CLAUSE 1: The Senate of the United States shall be composed of two Senators from each State, chosen by the Legislature thereof, for six Years; and each Senator shall have one Vote.

CLAUSE 2: Immediately after they shall be assembled in Consequence of the first Election, they shall be divided as equally as may be into three Classes. The Seats of the Senators of the first Class shall be vacated at the Expiration of the second Year, of the second Class at the Expiration of the fourth Year, and of the third Class at the Expiration of the sixth Year, so that one third may be chosen every second Year; and if Vacancies happen by Resignation, or otherwise, during the Recess of the Legislature of any State, the Executive thereof may make temporary Appointments until the next Meeting of the Legislature, which shall then fill such Vacancies.

CLAUSE 4: The Vice President of the United States shall be President of the Senate, but shall have no Vote, unless they be equally divided.

CLAUSE 5: The Senate shall chuse their other Officers, and also a President pro tempore, in the Absence of the Vice President, or when he shall exercise the Office of President of the United States.

ARTICLE I, SECTION 4, CLAUSE 1: The Times, Places and Manner of holding Elections for Senators and Representatives, shall be prescribed in each State by the

Legislature thereof; but the Congress may at any time by Law make or alter such Regulations, except as to the Places of chusing Senators.

CLAUSE 2: The Congress shall assemble at least once in every Year, and such Meeting shall be on the first Monday in December, unless they shall by Law appoint a different Day.

SEVENTEENTH AMENDMENT (1913), CLAUSE 1: The Senate of the United States shall be composed of two Senators from each State, elected by the people thereof, for six years; and each Senator shall have one vote. The electors in each State shall have the qualifications requisite for electors of the most numerous branch of the State legislatures.

CLAUSE 2: When vacancies happen in the representation of any State in the Senate, the executive authority of such State shall issue writs of election to fill such vacancies: Provided, That the legislature of any State may empower the executive thereof to make temporary appointments until the people fill the vacancies by election as the legislature may direct.

TWENTIETH AMENDMENT (1933), SECTION 1: The terms of the President and the Vice President shall end at noon on the 20th day of January, and the terms of Senators and Representatives at noon on the 3d day of January, of the years in which such terms would have ended if this article had not been ratified; and the terms of their successors shall then begin.

SECTION 2: The Congress shall assemble at least once in every year, and such meeting shall begin at noon on the 3d day of January, unless they shall by law appoint a different day.

22.1 THE THREE-FIFTHS CLAUSE AND THE ENUMERATION CLAUSE

So far, this casebook has emphasized the *powers* of Congress, including its powers to tax, to provide for the general welfare, to regulate individuals, to conduct war, and to protect the basic civil rights of everyone who lives in the United States. When these powers are viewed in the aggregate, it is evident that Congress is an incredibly powerful institution, capable of legislating on a vast array of topics while also preempting any contrary state actions. Perhaps the most persuasive justification for awarding all of these powers to Congress is that, as the national legislature, it is representative of "We the People of the United States." *See McCulloch v. Maryland*, 17 U.S. (4 Wheat.) 316, 402–05 (1819). But determining who, exactly, are members of "We the People" has been a divisive question since the Constitution was drafted.

Three methods of counting "We the People"

When the Constitutional Convention met in 1787 and attempted to construct a new national legislature, the delegates had three broad answers to the question of who should count toward "We the People" for purposes of congressional representation.

First, the "People" could include *all* people—regardless of where they lived or whether they were eligible to vote—because Congress should be a legislature for the entire nation. Advocates of this view included representatives from large southern states, who proposed that each state should send representatives to Congress in proportion to their total population. As James Madison and his allies from Virginia complained about the Articles of Confederation—in which each state had only one vote in Congress—it was inequitable for the 140,000 people who lived in Delaware and Rhode Island to have more votes in Congress than the 800,000 people who lived in Virginia. Michael J. Klarman, *The Framers' Coup* 130–31 (2016).

Second, "We the People" could include *citizens* or *eligible voters* because only these people would be members of the community that elected members of Congress. Advocates of this view included representatives from large northern states, who opposed allowing southern states to count disenfranchised and enslaved people toward their representation in Congress. As Elbridge Gerry of Massachusetts argued, it didn't make sense to give southern slave owners extra votes for each of the people they owned when the owners of other property received no such extra votes. If "blacks, who were property in the South," counted, then so should "the cattle and horses of the North," he argued. 1 *The Records of the Federal Convention of 1787*, at 201 (Max Farrand ed., 1911); *see* Michael J. Klarman, *The Framers' Coup: The Making of the United States Constitution* 268 (2016).

Finally, "We the People" could refer not to individuals but to *states* because states were the formal constituents under the Articles of Confederation and state legislatures continued to represent voters more immediately than a federal legislature could. Advocates of this view included delegates from small states like New Jersey, which wanted to continue giving each state delegation an equal vote in Congress. Klarman, *supra,* at 268–71. These delegates argued that population was not the only relevant consideration for a representative legislature. To avoid a situation in which dense concentrations of people could overwhelm political minorities scattered elsewhere, they proposed a Congress that would be proportionally representative not only by population but also by geography, property, ideology, and other communities of interest.

Constitutional Convention compromise

After spending an entire month of its four-month convention resolving these disagreements, the delegates in Philadelphia reached a compromise that incorporated proposals from all three groups. To appease small states, Article I of the Constitution divided Congress into two houses—a House of Representatives and a Senate—and Section 3, Clause 1, allowed each state legislature to elect equal numbers of senators to the Senate, regardless of population. To appease large states, Article I, Section 2, Clause 3, allowed each state to send representatives to the House "according to their respective numbers." And as a compromise between large northern states and large southern states,

Article I, Section 2, Clause 3, set out a formula for determining which disenfranchised people should count for purposes of a state's "numbers": "their respective numbers . . . shall be determined by adding to the whole Number of free Persons, including those bound to Service for a Term of Years, and excluding Indians not taxed, three fifths of all other Persons."

Three-Fifths Clause

The Three-Fifths Clause—Article I, Section 2, Clause 3—is often seen today as an indication that the delegates at the Constitutional Convention viewed each enslaved person as three-fifths of a free person. To some extent, this perspective is accurate: the delegates accepted the three-fifths ratio as an approximation of how much less they assumed enslaved workers contributed to a state's tax base than free workers—as they believed that enslaved workers had "no interest in their labor" and an incentive to do "as little as possible." *See* Klarman, *supra*, at 270–71. But what this modern view often misses is that the advocates for counting enslaved people *at all* were the slaveholders who actively disenfranchised and subordinated them. It was northern opponents of this disenfranchisement who insisted that only three-fifths of enslaved people be counted.

Enumeration Clause

Even after the Three-Fifths Clause was repealed by the Thirteenth and Fourteenth Amendments, the divide over whether Congress should represent *all people* or only *eligible voters* continues to animate political debates. In fact, this debate surfaces every decade. After tying a state's representation in the House to its population—and counting, for population purposes, not just white male voters but all people excluding "Indians not taxed"—the Constitutional Convention added the Enumeration Clause in Article 1, Section 2, Clause 3: a requirement that Congress regularly conduct an "actual Enumeration" every ten years. Congress has conducted this enumeration, popularly known as the census, every decade since 1790.

The primary purpose of the census is to ascertain the number of people in every state so that Congress can adjust the number of representatives each state can send to the House. Initially, because Article I determined how many representatives each state could send to the first Congress, there were sixty-five representatives for approximately 4,000,000 people, or one representative for every 60,000 people. The tiny number of representatives was a major point of disagreement in the debates over ratification. After the first census in 1790, the number of representatives was increased to one hundred and five, or one representative for every 40,000 people. The House kept growing until 1911, when Congress effectively capped the number of representatives at 435. *See* Act of Aug. 3, 1911, Pub. L. No. 62–5, 37 Stat. 13; *see also* Hawaii Enabling Act of 1959, Pub. L. No. 86–3, 73 Stat. 8.

Since then, Congress has followed each census by reallocating representatives from states whose populations have declined relative to other states—provided that "each State shall have at Least one Representative." U.S. Const. art. I, § 2, cl. 3.

The census has become far more than an opportunity to count how many people live in each state for purposes of representation. Administrators of the census have also used it to assess basic demographic information about the country, such as age, sex, race, and occupation. *See The Legal Tender Cases*, 79 U.S. (12 Wall.) 457 (1871). Yet the census remains critical for determining each state's political power, and states frequently challenge census-related decisions in court. After the 1990 census, for example, Montana challenged the method by which Congress decided to reallocate one of Montana's representatives to a faster-growing state. The Supreme Court rejected this challenge in *U.S. Department of Commerce v. Montana*, 503 U.S. 442 (1992), holding that the Enumeration Clause gives Congress discretion in how to apportion representatives as equally as possible. Similarly, after the 2000 census, Utah (which lost a representative) challenged the method by which the census used statistics to impute the number of people in an area that enumerators were unable to count. In *Utah v. Evans*, 536 U.S. 452 (2002), the Court agreed that the Constitution requires Congress to conduct an "actual Enumeration" but held that this requirement was compatible with using statistics to fill in missing data.

22.1.1

Department of Commerce v. New York

139 S. Ct. 2551 (2019)

More recently, the census has come under scrutiny for reasons analogous to the initial controversy surrounding the Three-Fifths Clause. Like northern delegates who once opposed counting disenfranchised people in the South, some officials in states with relatively few immigrants have complained that counting all people and not just eligible voters increases the political power of voters in states with large immigrant populations.

Agreeing with these officials in 2017, President Donald Trump's administration proposed asking respondents about their citizenship status in the 2020 census. Although this question had been asked in most previous censuses before 2000, the Census Bureau itself predicted that adding such a question in 2020 would discourage noncitizens from responding. Thus, in light of the Constitution's requirement that Congress conduct an actual enumeration, a group of states led by Democratic attorneys general challenged the inclusion of this question in *Department of Commerce v. New York*, 139 S. Ct. 2551 (2019).

Based on the history of the census, the Court ruled the question constitutional—yet still disallowed it.

■ CHIEF JUSTICE ROBERTS delivered the opinion of the Court.[1]

The Secretary of Commerce decided to reinstate a question about citizenship on the 2020 census questionnaire. A group of plaintiffs challenged that decision on constitutional and statutory grounds. We now decide whether the Secretary violated the Enumeration Clause of the Constitution, the Census Act, or otherwise abused his discretion.

I

In order to apportion Members of the House of Representatives among the States, the Constitution requires an "Enumeration" of the population every 10 years, to be made "in such Manner" as Congress "shall by Law direct." Art. I, § 2, cl. 3; Amdt. 14, § 2. In the Census Act, Congress delegated to the Secretary of Commerce the task of conducting the decennial census "in such form and content as he may determine." 13 U. S. C. § 141(a). The Secretary is aided in that task by the Census Bureau, a statistical agency housed within the Department of Commerce. See §§ 2, 21.

The population count derived from the census is used not only to apportion representatives but also to allocate federal funds to the States and to draw electoral districts. *Wisconsin v. City of New York*, 517 U.S. 1, 5–6 (1996). The census additionally serves as a means of collecting demographic information, which "is used for such varied purposes as computing federal grant-in-aid benefits, drafting of legislation, urban and regional planning, business planning, and academic and social studies." *Baldrige v. Shapiro*, 455 U.S. 345, 353–54 (1982). Over the years, the census has asked questions about (for example) race, sex, age, health, education, occupation, housing, and military service. It has also asked about radio ownership, age at first marriage, and native tongue. The Census Act obliges everyone to answer census questions truthfully and requires the Secretary to keep individual answers confidential, including from other Government agencies. §§ 221, 8(b), 9(a).

There have been 23 decennial censuses from the first census in 1790 to the most recent in 2010. Every census between 1820 and 2000 (with the exception of 1840) asked at least some of the population about their citizenship or place of birth. . . .

The Census Bureau and former Bureau officials have resisted occasional proposals to resume asking a citizenship question of everyone, on the ground that doing so would discourage noncitizens from responding to the census and lead to a less accurate count of the total population. . . .

In March 2018, Secretary of Commerce Wilbur Ross announced in a memo that he had decided to reinstate a question about citizenship on the 2020 decennial census questionnaire. The Secretary stated that he was acting at the request of the Department of Justice (DOJ), which sought improved data about citizen voting-age population for purposes of enforcing the Voting Rights Act (or VRA)—specifically the Act's ban on diluting the influence of minority voters by depriving them of single-member districts in which they can elect their preferred candidates. DOJ explained that federal courts determine whether a minority group could constitute a majority in a particular district by looking to the citizen voting-age population of the group. . . .

The Secretary "carefully considered" the possibility that reinstating a citizenship question would depress the response rate. But . . . the Secretary determined that "the

[1] **As You Read, Consider:** Chief Justice John Roberts frames his opinion as a question of whether courts should police the political branches' discretion in administering the census. If Congress and the president agree that the census should include a particular question, do you think that the Enumeration Clause provides any clear legal standards by which the Supreme Court could intervene?

need for accurate citizenship data and the limited burden that the reinstatement of the citizenship question would impose outweigh fears about a potentially lower response rate." . . .

Shortly after the Secretary announced his decision, two groups of plaintiffs filed suit in Federal District Court in New York, challenging the decision on several grounds[, including] that the Secretary's decision violated the Enumeration Clause of the Constitution. . . .

III

The Enumeration Clause of the Constitution does not provide a basis to set aside the Secretary's decision. The text of that clause "vests Congress with virtually unlimited discretion in conducting the decennial 'actual Enumeration,' " and Congress "has delegated its broad authority over the census to the Secretary." *Wisconsin*, 517 U.S. at 19. Given that expansive grant of authority, we have rejected challenges to the conduct of the census where the Secretary's decisions bore a "reasonable relationship to the accomplishment of an actual enumeration." *Id.*

Respondents ask us to evaluate the Secretary's decision to reinstate a citizenship question under that "reasonable relationship" standard, but . . . a different analysis is needed here. Our cases applying that standard concerned decisions about the population count itself—such as a postcensus decision not to use a particular method to adjust an undercount, *id.*, and a decision to allocate overseas military personnel to their home States, *Franklin v. Massachusetts*, 505 U.S. 788, 790–91 (1992). We have never applied the standard to decisions about what kinds of demographic information to collect in the course of taking the census. Indeed, as the District Court recognized, applying the "reasonable relationship" standard to *every* census-related decision "would lead to the conclusion that it is unconstitutional to ask *any* demographic question on the census" because "asking such questions bears no relationship whatsoever to the goal of an accurate headcount." Yet demographic questions have been asked in *every* census since 1790, and questions about citizenship in particular have been asked for nearly as long. Like the District Court, we decline respondents' invitation to measure the constitutionality of the citizenship question by a standard that would seem to render every census since 1790 unconstitutional.[2]

We look instead to Congress's broad authority over the census, as informed by long and consistent historical practice. All three branches of Government have understood the Constitution to allow Congress, and by extension the Secretary, to use the census for more than simply counting the population. Since 1790, Congress has sought, or permitted the Secretary to seek, information about matters as varied as age, sex, marital status, health, trade, profession, literacy, and value of real estate owned. Since 1820, it has sought, or permitted the Secretary to seek, information about citizenship in particular. . . . While we have never faced the question directly, we have assumed that Congress has the power to use the census for information-gathering purposes, see *Legal Tender Cases*, 12 Wall. 457, 536 (1871), and we have recognized the role of the census as a "linchpin of the federal statistical system by collecting data on the characteristics of individuals, households, and housing units throughout the country," *Department of Commerce v. United States House of Representatives*, 525 U.S. 316, 341 (1999).

---

2 **Question:** Do you agree with Roberts that it would be inappropriate for the Supreme Court to evaluate the relevance of each census question to the goal of an accurate headcount? To the extent that demographic questions do, in fact, compromise the accuracy of the count, why shouldn't the Court intervene?

That history matters.[3] Here, as in other areas, our interpretation of the Constitution is guided by a Government practice that "has been open, widespread, and unchallenged since the early days of the Republic." *NLRB v. Noel Canning*, 573 U.S. 513, 572 (2014) (Scalia, J., concurring in judgment). In light of the early understanding of and long practice under the Enumeration Clause, we conclude that it permits Congress, and by extension the Secretary, to inquire about citizenship on the census questionnaire. We need not, and do not, decide the constitutionality of any other question that Congress or the Secretary might decide to include in the census. . . .

NOTE: AFTERMATH OF *DEPARTMENT OF COMMERCE*

After deciding the above constitutional question, the Supreme Court in *Department of Commerce* went on to invalidate the Trump administration's inclusion of a citizenship question on statutory grounds. The Administrative Procedure Act requires agencies to offer a "reasoned explanation" for their decisions. 5 U.S.C. § 706. The Court concluded that the explanation offered by the secretary of commerce—helping to enforce the Voting Rights Act—was, in fact, "contrived" and "incongruent with what the record reveals about the agency's priorities and decisionmaking process." *Dep't of Com.*, 139 S. Ct. at 2575. The Court gave the administration the opportunity to try again with "something better than the explanation offered for the action taken in this case," *id.* at 2576, but, in July 2019, the administration declined to do so.

22.2 VOTER QUALIFICATIONS FOR HOUSE AND SENATE ELECTIONS

After the Constitutional Convention agreed to make the Senate representative by state and the House representative by population, the delegates still had to decide how members of the Senate and House would be elected.

Senate

The Senate turned out to be an easier decision. Under the Articles of Confederation, delegates to the Confederation Congress were elected by state legislatures. As the Senate's existence was largely justified as a continuation of the Confederation Congress, the convention continued this practice of allowing state legislatures to elect senators. James Madison defended this choice as "giving to the state governments such an agency in the formation of the federal government." *Federalist No. 62*, at 416 (James Madison) (Jacob E. Cooke ed., 1961). He argued that voters in the ratification debates shouldn't fear a too-powerful federal government because "[n]o law or resolution can now be passed without

---

[3] **Questions:** Precisely why should the history of the census matter in this case? Is it because the federal government has a reliance interest on asking demographic questions during the census? Is it because a long history of asking demographic questions suggests that Congress and the president have considered the constitutional issue in depth?

In other words, if 2020 were the first time the census asked about citizenship, should the result be any different?

the concurrence, first, of a majority of the people, and then, of a majority of the states." *Id.* at 417.

House

More difficult was who should be allowed to elect House members. Although many of the state constitutions adopted in the 1770s and 1780s dramatically expanded who could vote for state legislators, most still limited the franchise to white men with property. Even in New Jersey—whose 1776 constitution gave voting rights to "all inhabitants of this colony," including black men, women, and noncitizens—the franchise was still limited to people "who are worth fifty pounds," or about the average yearly wage of a skilled tradesperson. *See* N.J. Const. of 1776, art. IV. While some of the delegates in Philadelphia, notably Benjamin Franklin, opposed all property qualifications on the merits, most favored at least some property qualifications as a "necessary defense against the dangerous influence of those multitudes without property and without principle." Michael J. Klarman, *The Framers' Coup* 179 (2016).

Even delegates who were adamantly in favor of property qualifications found it difficult, however, to agree on which qualifications to embrace. Many delegates also worried that including qualifications in the Constitution would make ratification more difficult because "[t]he people will not readily subscribe to the national Constitution if it should subject them to be disfranchised." *Id.* For these practical reasons, the delegates settled on the current language of Article I, Section 2, writing that "the Electors in each State shall have the Qualifications requisite for Electors of the most numerous Branch of the State Legislature." This permitted states to set their own qualifications—property and otherwise—for the "Electors," or voters, of federal House representatives. However, the language prohibited states from applying different voter qualifications for House elections than for their own state assemblies.

Seventeenth Amendment

Congress in the nineteenth century exercised its Section 4 power not only to regulate House elections but also to regulate how state legislatures elected members of the U.S. Senate. *See Ex parte Yarbrough*, 110 U.S. 651 (1884). In particular, by the 1860s, the election of U.S. senators had become one of the most important functions of state legislatures. This meant that elections for state senators and representatives had become, in effect, proxy elections for the U.S. Senate—much in the same way that, for some voters today, the election of presidents is important mainly because of judicial nominations. It became typical in the nineteenth century for a state legislature to deadlock when its house was controlled by one party and its senate controlled by another.

Congress sought to break these deadlocks in 1866 with a law requiring every state legislature to meet every day during a vacancy until a U.S. senator was elected. *See* Act of July 25, 1866, ch. 245, 14 Stat. 243. This law didn't have the desired effect: vacancies remained unfilled for long periods. Meanwhile, businesses and political organizations strongly influenced the selection of U.S. senators through their disproportionate power in local house and senate races, and in local elections it became more important who a candidate would vote for as opposed to how the candidate planned to legislate for the state. *See* David Schleicher, *The Seventeenth Amendment and Federalism in the Age of National Political Parties*, 65 Hast. L.J. 1043, 1073–75 (2014).

By statute or common understanding, at least twenty-nine states by 1912 began holding popular referenda to nominate their senators, allowing the legislature to pick the winner and get on with its business. 1 George Haynes, *The Senate of the United States* 79–117 (1938). That same year, Congress proposed the Seventeenth Amendment, which stated that U.S. senators would be "elected by the people" who had "the qualifications requisite for electors of the most numerous branch of the State legislatures." Once ratified by thirty-six states in April 1913, the amendment effectively made elections for senators constitutionally equivalent to elections for House members.

A final constitutional change to the Senate (and the House) was made with the Twentieth Amendment in 1933. Until that year, the president and members of Congress were elected in November and inaugurated on March 4 of the following year. As the "midnight judges" of *Marbury v. Madison* illustrated, this was a very long gap for a lame-duck Congress to remain in power. In addition, in crises such as the Civil War and the Great Depression, it meant that incoming Congresses and presidential administrations had to sit on their hands while people elsewhere reacted to their elections. Yet Congress lacked the power to move the March 4 date on its own without interfering with the "six Years" and "four Years" that senators and presidents were guaranteed in office. So, in 1932, Congress proposed an amendment to move the inauguration of the president to January 20 and the inauguration of Congress to January 3. On January 23, 1933, enough states ratified the Twentieth Amendment to make it law—not in time for President-elect Franklin D. Roosevelt, however, who became the last president to hold his inauguration ceremony in March.

22.3 THE TIMES, PLACES, AND MANNER OF HOLDING CONGRESSIONAL ELECTIONS

In addition to allowing state legislatures to set voter qualifications for House and, indirectly, Senate elections, Article I also allowed state legislatures in Section 4, Clause 1, to prescribe the "Times, Places and Manner of holding Elections for Senators and Representatives." But unlike with voter qualifications, Article I, Section 4, gave Congress the power to "make or alter such Regulations, except as to the Places of chusing Senators."

This clause terrified many opponents of the Constitution during the ratification debates. Some critics worried that Congress might regulate the times of elections to "never" or, alternatively, regulate the places of elections to cities where supporters were concentrated. *See* Michael J. Klarman, *The Framers' Coup: The Making of the United States Constitution* 342 (2016).

But supporters of the Constitution argued that Congress had to possess this revisionary power to ensure that representatives were always chosen "*by the people*" and not by a particular state's "unequal mode of representation." 5 *Documentary History of the Ratification of the Constitution* 1279 (John P. Kaminski et al. eds., 2000). In the Massachusetts ratifying convention, for example, Rufus King pointed to Rhode Island, South Carolina, and Virginia as states whose legislatures already used malapportioned electoral districts, voice votes as opposed to ballots, and other tactics to entrench their own power. *Id.*

Today, American elections contain many features that most voters take for granted but that were first introduced as exercises of Congress's Section 4 power. For example, before 1842, many states elected their representatives through statewide, at-large elections that allowed 51 percent of a state's voters to elect 100 percent of the state's representatives. Exercising its power to "alter" these regulations in 1842, Congress required every state to use single-member districts to elect representatives—a practice that continues today. *See* Act of June 25, 1842, ch. 47, 5 Stat. 491. Equally influential, in 1872, Congress required states with multiple House districts to draw "districts composed of contiguous territory, and containing as nearly as practicable an equal number of inhabitants." Act of Feb. 2, 1872, ch.11, 17 Stat. 28. That same law also, for the first time, specified a common day for the election of representatives: "[t]he Tuesday next after the first Monday in November, in every second year." *Id.*; *see* 2 U.S.C. § 7.

22.3.1

Ex parte Yarbrough

110 U.S. 651 (1884)

One of Congress's most significant exercises of its Section 4 power was during Reconstruction.

As discussed earlier in analysis of the Reconstruction amendments (sections 20.1, 21.1), Congress passed several laws to enforce the Thirteenth, Fourteenth, and Fifteenth Amendments. For example, the Ku Klux Klan Act of 1871 made it a crime

> to prevent, by force, intimidation, or threat, any citizen who is lawfully entitled to vote from giving his support or advocacy, in a legal manner, towards or in favor of the election of any lawfully qualified person as an elector for President or Vice-President, or as a member of the Congress of the United States.

Ku Klux Klan Act, ch. 22, 17 Stat. 13, 13–14. Meanwhile, the Enforcement Act of 1870 made it a crime to intimidate a citizen "in the free exercise or enjoyment of any right or privilege secured to him by the Constitution." Enforcement Act, ch. 114, 16 Stat. 140, 141.

Yet when these laws reached the Supreme Court, the Court invalidated or declined to enforce nearly every law on technical grounds. In *United States v. Reese*, 92 U.S. 214 (1876), the Court dismissed an indictment against two Kentucky election officials who refused to count the ballot of a black voter. The Court explained that the relevant acts failed to mention race and therefore could not have been intended to enforce the Fifteenth Amendment's prohibition on racial discrimination in voting. *Reese*, 92 U.S. at 218–20. Then, in *United States v. Harris*, the Court suggested that neither the Fourteenth nor the Fifteenth Amendment permitted Congress to regulate the conduct of private individuals as opposed to state officers. 106 U.S. 629, 636–39 (1883).

Nevertheless, federal prosecutors persisted in prosecuting members of the Ku Klux Klan for violating the various enforcement acts. Rather than justify the prosecutions under the Fifteenth Amendment, however, they turned to Article I, Section 4. The Supreme Court first evaluated this argument in *Ex parte Yarbrough*, 110 U.S. 651 (1884), a case involving a group of Ku Klux Klansmen accused of violating the Enforcement Act of 1870 and the Ku Klux Klan Act of 1871.

The decision was a win for Congress's power to protect voting rights.

■ MR. JUSTICE MILLER delivered the opinion of the Court.[4]

This case originates in this court by an application for a writ of habeas corpus on the part of Jasper Yarbrough and seven other persons, who allege that they are confined by the jailer of Fulton County in the custody of the United States Marshal for the Northern District of Georgia, and that the trial, conviction, and sentence in the Circuit Court of the United States for that District, under which they are held, were illegal, null, and void. . . .

Stripped of its technical verbiage, the offense charged in this indictment is that the defendants conspired to intimidate Berry Saunders, a citizen of African descent, in the exercise of his right to vote for a member of the Congress of the United States, and, in the execution of that conspiracy, they beat, bruised, wounded, and otherwise maltreated him. . . .

That a government whose essential character is republican, whose executive head and legislative body are both elective, whose numerous and powerful branch of the legislature is elected by the people directly, has no power by appropriate laws to secure this election from the influence of violence, of corruption, and of fraud, is a proposition so startling as to arrest attention and demand the gravest consideration. If this government is anything more than a mere aggregation of delegated agents of other States and governments, each of which is superior to the general government,

---

[4] **As You Read, Consider:** Justice Samuel Miller's opinion in *Ex parte Yarbrough* was one of the only examples in the nineteenth century in which the Supreme Court upheld the application of one of the Reconstruction enforcement acts to private individuals. Why does Miller interpret Congress's powers under Section 4 more capaciously than Congress's powers to enforce the Fourteenth and Fifteenth Amendments?

it must have the power to protect the elections on which its existence depends from violence and corruption.

If it has not this power, it is left helpless before the two great natural and historical enemies of all republics, open violence and insidious corruption.

The proposition that it has no such power is supported by the old argument often heard, often repeated, and in this Court never assented to, that, when a question of the power of Congress arises, the advocate of the power must be able to place his finger on words which expressly grant it. The brief of counsel before us, though directed to the authority of that body to pass criminal laws, uses the same language. Because there is no express power to provide for preventing violence exercised on the voter as a means of controlling his vote, no such law can be enacted. It destroys at one blow, in construing the Constitution of the United States, the doctrine universally applied to all instruments of writing, that what is implied is as much a part of the instrument as what is expressed. This principle, in its application to the Constitution of the United States, more than to almost any other writing, is a necessity by reason of the inherent inability to put into words all derivative powers—a difficulty which the instrument itself recognizes by conferring on Congress the authority to pass all laws necessary and proper to carry into execution the powers expressly granted, and all other powers vested in the government or any branch of it by the Constitution. Article I, sec. 8, clause 18.[5]

We know of no express authority to pass laws to punish theft or burglary of the treasury of the United States. Is there therefore no power in Congress to protect the treasury by punishing such theft and burglary?

Are the mails of the United States, and the money carried in them, to be left at the mercy of robbers and of thieves who may handle the mail because the Constitution contains no express words of power in Congress to enact laws for the punishment of those offenses? The principle, if sound, would abolish the entire criminal jurisdiction of the courts of the United States, and the laws which confer that jurisdiction. . . .

[Article 1, section 4] declares that "[t]he times, places, and manner of holding elections for senators and representatives shall be prescribed in each State by the legislature thereof; but the Congress may at any time make or alter such regulations, except as to the place of choosing senators."

It was not until 1842 that Congress took any action under the power here conferred, when, conceiving that the system of electing all the members of the house of representatives from a State by general ticket, as it was called—that is, every elector voting for as many names as the State was entitled to representatives in that house—worked injustice to other States which did not adopt that system, and gave an undue preponderance of power to the political party which had a majority of votes in the State, however small, enacted that each member should be elected by a separate district, composed of contiguous territory. 5 Stat. 491.

And to remedy more than one evil arising from the election of members of Congress occurring at different times in the different States, Congress, by the act of February 2, 1872, 30 years later, required all the elections for such members to be held on the Tuesday after the first Monday in November in 1876, and on the same day of every second year thereafter.

---

[5] **Question:** The Court here is invoking the Necessary and Proper Clause to explain why Congress has the implied power "to secure [federal elections] from the influence of violence, of corruption, and of fraud." Why does the Court think it is proper to impose criminal penalties on private individuals as an exercise of Congress's power to regulate federal elections?

The frequent failures of the legislatures of the States to elect senators at the proper time, by one branch of the legislature voting for one person and the other branch for another person, and refusing in any manner to reconcile their differences, led Congress to pass an act which compelled the two bodies to meet in joint convention, and fixing the day when this should be done, and requiring them so to meet on every day thereafter and vote for a senator until one was elected.

In like manner, Congress has fixed a day, which is to be the same in all the States, when the electors for president and vice-president shall be appointed.

Now the day fixed for electing members of Congress has been established by Congress without regard to the time set for election of state officers in each State, and, but for the fact that the state legislatures have, for their own accommodation, required state elections to be held at the same time, these elections would be held for Congressmen alone at the same time fixed by the act of Congress.[6]

Will it be denied that it is in the power of that body to provide laws for the proper conduct of those elections? To provide, if necessary, the officers who shall conduct them and make return of the result? And especially to provide, in an election held under its own authority, for security of life and limb to the voter while in the exercise of this function? Can it be doubted that Congress can, by law, protect the act of voting, the place where it is done, and the man who votes from personal violence or intimidation, and the election itself from corruption or fraud?

If this be so, and it is not doubted, are such powers annulled because an election for state officers is held at the same time and place? Is it any less important that the election of members of Congress should be the free choice of all the electors, because state officers are to be elected at the same time? *Ex parte Siebold*, 100 U. S. 371.

These questions answer themselves, and it is only because the Congress of the United States, through long habit and long years of forbearance, has, in deference and respect to the States, refrained from the exercise of these powers that they are now doubted.

But when, in the pursuance of a new demand for action, that body, as it did in the cases just enumerated, finds it necessary to make additional laws for the free, the pure, and the safe exercise of this right of voting, they stand upon the same ground, and are to be upheld for the same reasons.

It is said that the parties assaulted in these cases are not officers of the United States, and their protection in exercising the right to vote by Congress does not stand on the same ground.

But the distinction is not well taken. The power in either case arises out of the circumstance that the function in which the party is engaged or the right which he is about to exercise is dependent on the laws of the United States.

In both cases, it is the duty of that government to see that he may exercise this right freely, and to protect him from violence while so doing, or on account of so doing. This duty does not arise solely from the interest of the party concerned, but from the necessity of the government itself that its service shall be free from the adverse influence of force and fraud practiced on its agents, and that the votes by

---

[6] **Questions:** Article I, Section 4, permits Congress to regulate the "Times, Places and Manner" of *congressional* elections but says nothing about presidential or state elections. If Jasper Yarbrough could conclusively prove that he attacked black voters because of how they might vote in a state election, do you agree with Miller that Congress should nevertheless be able to intervene? Is such an intervention necessary and proper to regulate the "Manner" of holding congressional elections?

which its members of Congress and its President are elected shall be the free votes of the electors, and the officers thus chosen the free and uncorrupted choice of those who have the right to take part in that choice.

This proposition answers also another objection to the constitutionality of the laws under consideration, namely, that the right to vote for a member of Congress is not dependent upon the Constitution or laws of the United States, but is governed by the law of each State respectively.

If this were conceded, the importance to the general government of having the actual election—the voting for those members, free from force and fraud—is not diminished by the circumstance that the qualification of the voter is determined by the law of the State where he votes. It equally affects the government; it is as indispensable to the proper discharge of the great function of legislating for that government that those who are to control this legislation shall not owe their election to bribery or violence, whether the class of persons who shall vote is determined by the law of the State, or by the laws of the United States, or by their united result.

But it is not correct to say that the right to vote for a member of Congress does not depend on the Constitution of the United States.[7]

The office, if it be properly called an office, is created by that Constitution, and by that alone. It also declares how it shall be filled—namely, by election. Its language is: "The house of representatives shall be composed of members chosen every second year by the people of the several States; and the electors in each State shall have the same qualifications requisite for electors of the most numerous branch of the state legislature." Article I, section 2.

The States, in prescribing the qualifications of voters for the most numerous branch of their own legislatures, do not do this with reference to the election for members of Congress. Nor can they prescribe the qualification for voters for those *eo nominee*[, or, "by that name"]. They define who are to vote for the popular branch of their own legislature, and the Constitution of the United States says the same persons shall vote for members of Congress in that State. It adopts the qualification thus furnished as the qualification of its own electors for members of Congress.

It is not true, therefore, that electors for members of Congress owe their right to vote to the state law, in any sense which makes the exercise of the right to depend exclusively on the law of the State.

Counsel for petitioners, seizing upon the expression found in the opinion of the court in the case of *Minor v. Happersett*, 21 Wall. 178, that "the Constitution of the United States does not confer the right of suffrage upon anyone," without reference to the connection in which it is used, insists that the voters in this case do not owe their right to vote in any sense to that instrument.

But the court was combating the argument that this right was conferred on all citizens, and therefore upon women as well as men.

In opposition to that idea, it was said the Constitution adopts as the qualification for voters of members of Congress that which prevails in the State where the voting

---

7 **Questions:** Nothing in the Constitution affirmatively guarantees the right to vote. Instead, it restricts the reasons that governments can offer for *denying* the right to vote. The Fifteenth Amendment, for example, states only that "[t]he right of citizens of the United States to vote shall not be denied or abridged . . . on account of race."

In this case, the Ku Klux Klan Act of 1871 made it a crime to intimidate a citizen "in the free exercise or enjoyment of any right or privilege secured to him by the Constitution." Do you agree with Miller that the right to vote for members of Congress should be considered a "right . . . secured . . . by the Constitution"? Which clause of the Constitution does he think secures this right?

is to be done; therefore, said the opinion, the right is not definitely conferred on any person or class of persons by the Constitution alone, because you have to look to the law of the State for the description of the class. But the court did not intend to say that, when the class or the person is thus ascertained, his right to vote for a member of Congress was not fundamentally based upon the Constitution, which created the office of member of Congress, and declared it should be elective, and pointed to the means of ascertaining who should be electors. . . .

It is as essential to the successful working of this government that the great organisms of its executive and legislative branches should be the free choice of the people as that the original form of it should be so. . . .

If the recurrence of such acts as these prisoners stand convicted of are too common in one quarter of the country, and give omen of danger from lawless violence, the free use of money in elections, arising from the vast growth of recent wealth in other quarters, presents equal cause for anxiety.

If the government of the United States has within its constitutional domain no authority to provide against these evils—if the very sources of power may be poisoned by corruption or controlled by violence and outrage, without legal restraint—then indeed is the country in danger, and its best powers, its highest purposes, the hopes which it inspires, and the love which enshrines it are at the mercy of the combinations of those who respect no right but brute force on the one hand, and unprincipled corruptionists on the other.[8]

NOTE: CONGRESS'S POWER TO REGULATE ELECTIONS

One passage of *Ex parte Yarbrough* called upon Congress to control "the free use of money in elections." 110 U.S. at 667. Two decades later, Congress enacted the Tillman Act of 1907, Pub. L. No. 59–36, 34 Stat. 864. The Tillman Act was the first federal law that prohibited banks and corporations from making contributions in federal elections. As revised and amended by the Federal Corrupt Practices Act of 1925, Pub. L. No. 68–506, 43 Stat. 1053, 1070, and the Federal Election Campaign Act Amendments of 1974, Pub. L. No. 93–443, 88 Stat. 1263, the Tillman Act forms the bedrock of modern federal election law.

Interpreting these and similar laws, the Supreme Court has upheld Congress's power to punish state officials for failing to comply with federal election regulations. *See, e.g.*, *Ex parte Siebold*, 100 U.S. 371 (1880) (upholding the indictment of state election officials for violating a federal bribery statute); *United States v. Mosley*, 238 U.S. 383 (1915) (upholding the indictment of state election officials for making false election returns). The Court has also upheld Congress's power to punish private citizens for doing the same—even in primary elections established by a political party. *See, e.g.*, *United States v. Classic*, 313 U.S. 299 (1941) (upholding an indictment for falsely counting the ballots of voters in Louisiana's Democratic primary).

However, in *Citizens United v. Federal Election Commission*, 558 U.S. 310 (2010), the Supreme Court struck down a federal prohibition on corporate political expenditures—a ban whose legacy dated back to the

---

8 **Question:** Consider cases like the *Civil Rights Cases*, *United States v. Guest*, and *United States v. Morrison*. How does Miller's opinion in *Ex parte Yarbrough* compare to the holdings of those cases, which considered the scope of Congress's power to enforce Fourteenth Amendment rights against personal violations?

Tillman Act—as a violation of the Free Speech Clause of the First Amendment. While *Citizens United* is primarily a First Amendment case, it is notable that the Court did not question Congress's Section 4 power to regulate elections.

22.3.2

Wesberry v. Sanders

376 U.S. 1 (1964)

Congress followed *Ex parte Yarbrough* by continuing to regulate electoral districts as it had before the case. While preserving its 1872 requirement that all congressional districts contain equal numbers of inhabitants, in 1901 Congress added a requirement that all districts must be composed of "compact territory." Act of Jan. 16, 1901, ch. 93, 31 Stat. 733.

In 1929, however, following Congress's failure to reapportion districts after the 1920 census, Congress no longer required states to adhere to any compactness and equal population requirements. *See* Act of June 18, 1929, Pub. L. No. 71–13, 46 Stat. 21; *Wood v. Broom*, 287 U.S. 1, 6 (1932). As a result of population changes, by the 1940s, congressional districts in several states were severely malapportioned, with some districts containing a fraction of the population of neighboring districts.

In the wake of Illinois's failure to reapportion its electoral districts after the 1930 and 1940 censuses, Kenneth Colegrove, a political scientist at Northwestern University, sued Illinois's governor, Dwight Green, in federal court. Chicago had been a major hub for migrants from the South during World War II, and its congressional districts swelled compared to the congressional districts in Illinois's rural counties. Colegrove argued that this districting scheme violated Chicagoans' right to vote—recognized by *Ex parte Yarbrough* as protected by Article I, Section 2—because their votes effectively counted for less than those of their rural neighbors.

In *Colegrove v. Green*, however, a 4–3 plurality of the Supreme Court dismissed Colegrove's challenge as a political question "beyond its competence." 328 U.S. 549, 551 (1946). Justice Felix Frankfurter wrote that even if Colegrove were correct about what the Constitution required, "[of] course no court can affirmatively re-map the Illinois districts so as to bring them more in conformity with the standards of fairness for a representative system." *Id.* at 549. "At best," he continued, "we could only declare the existing electoral system invalid," *id.*, potentially leaving the state in a new position "worse than the first," *id.* at 553. More importantly, he concluded, "[a]uthority for dealing with such problems resides elsewhere." *Id.* at 554. Quoting Section 4's grant of power to Congress, the Court concluded:

> The short of it is that the Constitution has conferred upon Congress exclusive authority to secure fair representation by

> the States in the popular House, and left to that House determination whether States have fulfilled their responsibility. If Congress failed in exercising its powers, whereby standards of fairness are offended, the remedy ultimately lies with the people. Whether Congress faithfully discharges its duty or not, the subject has been committed to the exclusive control of Congress. An aspect of government from which the judiciary, in view of what is involved, has been excluded by the clear intention of the Constitution cannot be entered by the federal courts because Congress may have been in default in exacting from States obedience to its mandate.

Id.

Colegrove was decided by only seven justices because one justice had recently died and another didn't participate. Voters therefore continued pressing the issue. In 1961, the Supreme Court heard another malapportionment challenge brought against Tennessee's secretary of state, Joseph Cordell Carr. This challenge was not to Tennessee's *congressional* districts but to its *state legislative* districts—a significant difference that that will be discussed later (section 50.3). But because of *Colegrove*'s political-question holding, the main issue was whether the Court had the power to consider any malapportionment challenges.

After hearing six hours of oral arguments over two sessions, the Court issued five opinions taking up 163 pages. The majority opinion in *Baker v. Carr*, 369 U.S. 186 (1962), written by Justice William Brennan, spent most of its analysis summarizing the Supreme Court's history of political-question cases, including *Marbury v. Madison*, 5 U.S. (1 Cranch) 137 (1903). The opinion concluded with the following summary of its political-question cases:

> It is apparent that several formulations which vary slightly according to the settings in which the questions arise may describe a political question, although each has one or more elements which identify it as essentially a function of the separation of powers. Prominent on the surface of any case held to involve a political question is found [1] a textually demonstrable constitutional commitment of the issue to a coordinate political department; or [2] a lack of judicially discoverable and manageable standards for resolving it; or [3] the impossibility of deciding without an initial policy determination of a kind clearly for nonjudicial discretion; or [4] the impossibility of a court's undertaking independent resolution without expressing lack of the respect due coordinate branches of government; or [5] an unusual need for unquestioning adherence to a political decision already made; or [6] the potentiality of embarrassment from multifarious pronouncements by various departments on one question.

Unless one of these formulations is inextricable from the case at bar, there should be no dismissal for nonjusticiability on the ground of a political question's presence. The doctrine of which we treat is one of "political questions," not one of "political cases." . . . The cases we have reviewed show the necessity for discriminating inquiry into the precise facts and posture of the particular case, and the impossibility of resolution by any semantic cataloguing.

Baker, 369 U.S. at 217–18. The *Baker* Court concluded by sharply criticizing *Colegrove* and holding that the Tennessee plaintiffs' challenge to the state's legislative districts was not a political question.

The following year, the Court heard arguments in another *Colegrove*-like case, *Wesberry v. Sanders*, 376 U.S. 1 (1964), in which James Wesberry, a Georgia resident, successfully challenged his state's failure to reapportion its congressional districts since 1931.

■ MR. JUSTICE BLACK delivered the opinion of the Court.[9]

Appellants are citizens and qualified voters of Fulton County, Georgia, and as such are entitled to vote in congressional elections in Georgia's Fifth Congressional District. That district, one of ten created by a 1931 Georgia statute, includes Fulton, DeKalb, and Rockdale Counties, and has a population, according to the 1960 census, of 823,680. The average population of the ten districts is 394,312, less than half that of the Fifth. One district, the Ninth, has only 272,154 people, less than one-third as many as the Fifth. Since there is only one Congressman for each district, this inequality of population means that the Fifth District's Congressman has to represent from two to three times as many people as do Congressmen from some of the other Georgia districts.

Claiming that these population disparities deprived them and voters similarly situated of a right under the Federal Constitution to have their votes for Congressmen given the same weight as the votes of other Georgians, the appellants brought this action. . . . [But] a majority of the court [below] dismissed the complaint, citing as their guide Mr. Justice Frankfurter's minority opinion in *Colegrove v. Green*, 328 U. S. 549, an opinion stating that challenges to apportionment of congressional districts raised only "political" questions, which were not justiciable. . . .

[I]

The Court in *Baker* [*v. Carr*, 369 U.S. 186 (1962)] pointed out that the opinion of Mr. Justice Frankfurter in *Colegrove*, upon the reasoning of which the majority below leaned heavily . . ., was approved by only three of the seven Justices sitting. After full consideration of *Colegrove*, the Court in *Baker* held (1) that the District Court had jurisdiction of the subject matter; (2) that the qualified Tennessee voters there had standing to sue; and (3) that the plaintiffs had stated a justiciable cause of action on which relief could be granted.

---

[9] **As You Read, Consider:** At issue in James Wesberry's case is whether Georgia has done anything wrong by drawing congressional districts of unequal populations. Although Congress once exercised its Article I, Section 4, power to require equal populations, it had not reaffirmed this requirement for decades. Why does Justice Hugo Black think that the Supreme Court can resolve this issue on its own rather than waiting for Congress to enact a new equal-population law?

The reasons which led to these conclusions in *Baker* are equally persuasive here. . . .

Mr. Justice Frankfurter's *Colegrove* opinion contended that Art. I, § 4, of the Constitution had given Congress "exclusive authority" to protect the right of citizens to vote for Congressmen, but . . . nothing in the language of that article gives support to a construction that would immunize state congressional apportionment laws which debase a citizen's right to vote from the power of courts to protect the constitutional rights of individuals from legislative destruction, a power recognized at least since our decision in *Marbury v. Madison*, 1 Cranch 137, in 1803. The right to vote is too important in our free society to be stripped of judicial protection by such an interpretation of Article I. . . . We therefore hold that the District Court erred in dismissing the complaint.

[II]

This brings us to the merits. We agree with the District Court that the 1931 Georgia apportionment grossly discriminates against voters in the Fifth Congressional District. A single Congressman represents from two to three times as many Fifth District voters as are represented by each of the Congressmen from the other Georgia congressional districts. The apportionment statute thus contracts the value of some votes and expands that of others. If the Federal Constitution intends that, when qualified voters elect members of Congress, each vote be given as much weight as any other vote, then this statute cannot stand.

We hold that, construed in its historical context, the command of Art. I, § 2 that Representatives be chosen "by the People of the several States" means that, as nearly as is practicable, one man's vote in a congressional election is to be worth as much as another's. This rule is followed automatically, of course, when Representatives are chosen as a group on a statewide basis, as was a widespread practice in the first 50 years of our Nation's history. It would be extraordinary to suggest that, in such statewide elections, the votes of inhabitants of some parts of a State, for example, Georgia's thinly populated Ninth District, could be weighted at two or three times the value of the votes of people living in more populous parts of the State, for example, the Fifth District around Atlanta. We do not believe that the Framers of the Constitution intended to permit the same vote-diluting discrimination to be accomplished through the device of districts containing widely varied numbers of inhabitants. To say that a vote is worth more in one district than in another would not only run counter to our fundamental ideas of democratic government, it would cast aside the principle of a House of Representatives elected "by the People," a principle tenaciously fought for and established at the Constitutional Convention. The history of the Constitution, particularly that part of it relating to the adoption of Art. I, § 2, reveals that those who framed the Constitution meant that, no matter what the mechanics of an election, whether statewide or by districts, it was population which was to be the basis of the House of Representatives. . . .

The debates at the Convention make at least one fact abundantly clear: that, when the delegates agreed that the House should represent "people," they intended that, in allocating Congressmen, the number assigned to each State should be determined solely by the number of the State's inhabitants. The Constitution embodied Edmund Randolph's proposal for a periodic census to ensure "fair representation of the people," an idea endorsed by Mason as assuring that "numbers of inhabitants" should always be the measure of representation in the House of Representatives. The Convention also overwhelmingly agreed to a resolution offered by Randolph to base future apportionment squarely on numbers and to delete any reference to wealth. And the delegates defeated a motion made by Elbridge Gerry to limit the number of Representatives from newer Western States so that it would never exceed the number from the original States. . . .

It would defeat the principle solemnly embodied in the Great Compromise—equal representation in the House for equal numbers of people—for us to hold that, within the States, legislatures may draw the lines of congressional districts in such a way as to give some voters a greater voice in choosing a Congressman than others. The House of Representatives, the Convention agreed, was to represent the people as individuals, and on a basis of complete equality for each voter. The delegates were quite aware of what Madison called the "vicious representation" in Great Britain whereby "rotten boroughs" with few inhabitants were represented in Parliament on or almost on a par with cities of greater population. Wilson urged that people must be represented as individuals, so that America would escape the evils of the English system, under which one man could send two members to Parliament to represent the borough of Old Sarum, while London's million people sent but four. . . .

Madison, in *The Federalist*, described the system of division of States into congressional districts, the method which he and others assumed States probably would adopt: "The city of Philadelphia is supposed to contain between fifty and sixty thousand souls. It will therefore form nearly two districts for the choice of Federal Representatives."

"[N]umbers," he said, not only are a suitable way to represent wealth, but, in any event, "are the only proper scale of representation." In the state conventions, speakers urging ratification of the Constitution emphasized the theme of equal representation in the House which had permeated the debates in Philadelphia. . . .

It is in the light of such history that we must construe Art. I, § 2, of the Constitution, which, carrying out the ideas of Madison and those of like views, provides that Representatives shall be chosen "by the People of the several States," and shall be "apportioned among the several States . . . according to their respective Numbers." It is not surprising that our Court has held that this Article gives persons qualified to vote a constitutional right to vote and to have their votes counted. *Ex Parte Yarbrough*, 110 U. S. 651. Not only can this right to vote not be denied outright, it cannot, consistently with Article I, be destroyed by alteration of ballots, see *United States v. Classic*, 313 U. S. 299, or diluted by stuffing of the ballot box, see *United States v. Saylor*, 322 U. S. 385. No right is more precious in a free country than that of having a voice in the election of those who make the laws under which, as good citizens, we must live. Other rights, even the most basic, are illusory if the right to vote is undermined. Our Constitution leaves no room for classification of people in a way that unnecessarily abridges this right.[10]

In urging the people to adopt the Constitution, Madison said in No. 57 of The Federalist: "Who are to be the electors of the Federal Representatives? Not the rich more than the poor; not the learned more than the ignorant; not the haughty heirs of distinguished names more than the humble sons of obscure and unpropitious fortune. The electors are to be the great body of the people of the United States."

Readers surely could have fairly taken this to mean, "one person, one vote."

---

[10] **Question:** Here, Black establishes the principle that Article I, Section 2, of the Constitution *requires* that congressional districts contain equal populations—even though Congress itself didn't require districts until 1842 and equally populated districts until 1872. Suppose Congress exercised its power under Article I, Section 4, and required states to adopt a system of proportional representation for House elections. Under this system, each state holds statewide elections and sends to Congress representatives belonging to particular parties in proportion to each party's share of the statewide vote. Would such a law be compatible with Black's analysis?

While it may not be possible to draw congressional districts with mathematical precision, that is no excuse for ignoring our Constitution's plain objective of making equal representation for equal numbers of people the fundamental goal for the House of Representatives. That is the high standard of justice and common sense which the Founders set for us.

NOTE: ONE PERSON, ONE VOTE

In the years since *Wesberry* and its companion case, *Reynolds v. Sims*, 377 U.S. 533 (1964), the Supreme Court has continued to require states to reapportion congressional and state legislative districts after every census. The decisions have had an enormous effect on American democracy by preventing state legislatures from crafting districts favoring rural areas over cities and suburbs. *See* Daryl J. Levinson, *The Supreme Court, 2015 Term—Foreword: Looking for Power in Public Law*, 130 Harv. L. Rev. 4, 123 (2016). The decisions also heavily involved federal courts in an area of politics once occupied exclusively by Congress and state legislatures. Redistricting and apportionment questions are, today, routinely litigated.

With regard to congressional districts, the Court has interpreted Article I, Section 2, to require that states "make a good-faith effort to achieve precise mathematical equality." *Kirkpatrick v. Preisler*, 394 U.S. 526, 530 (1969). Even average population deviations of 0.745 percent are "not legally acceptable" if they are avoidable. *White v. Weiser*, 412 U.S. 783 (1973). Since the 1980s, the Court has encouraged states to use computers to reach this mathematical equality. *Karcher v. Daggett*, 462 U.S. 725, 733 (1983). Today, virtually all legislative maps are drawn with computers to create congressional districts of equal population within each state.

22.3.3

Rucho v. Common Cause

139 S. Ct. 2484 (2019)

Population imbalances are not the only problem that can harm voters in particular congressional districts. In *Davis v. Bandemer*, 478 U.S. 109 (1986), the Supreme Court held that voters could also challenge partisan gerrymanders: legislative districts mapped with the goal of increasing the representation of one political party at the expense of another. Unlike with its "one person, one vote" cases, however, members of the Court failed to agree on a standard for evaluating partisan gerrymandering claims, mainly because they failed to agree on whether the Constitution required proportional representation by party. That is, a majority of the Court did not agree that the Constitution required that if 75 percent of a state's voters supported Republican representatives, 75 percent of the state's congressional delegation should actually be Republicans.

In *Vieth v. Jubelirer*, Justice Antonin Scalia and three other justices rejected one partisan gerrymandering claim for this reason:

> Assuming . . . that the effects of partisan gerrymandering can be determined, . . . [any] standard rests upon the principle that groups (or at least political-action groups) have a right to proportional representation. But the Constitution contains no such principle. . . . It nowhere says that farmers or urban dwellers, Christian fundamentalists or Jews, Republicans or Democrats, must be accorded political strength proportionate to their numbers.

541 U.S. 267, 287–88 (2004).

Voters in many states responded to inaction by the Supreme Court and Congress by proposing the creation of "independent redistricting commissions": nonpartisan agencies with the authority to redraw congressional and state legislative districts after each census. Because state legislators often have an interest in maintaining the electoral districts that got them elected, these commissions have typically been created in states that allow voters to propose constitutional amendments or laws as ballot questions.

In 2012, however, after Arizona voters adopted an initiative that created a redistricting commission for that state, the state legislature challenged the law on the ground that Article I, Section 4, permitted only "the Legislature" to prescribe the "Times, Places and Manner of holding Elections." In *Arizona State Legislature v. Arizona Independent Redistricting Commission*, 576 U.S. 787 (2015), the Supreme Court narrowly upheld the voter-created commission. Justice Ruth Bader Ginsburg, writing for a 5–4 majority, agreed with the district court that "the word 'Legislature' in the Elections Clause refers to the legislative process used in [a] state, determined by that state's own constitution and laws." *Ariz. State Legislature*, 576 U.S. at 799. Drawing on the Arizona Constitution and the history of state referenda and initiatives, the Court concluded that in Arizona, the "Legislature" included the governor (when the governor issues a veto) and the electorate (when voters create laws through initiatives). *Id.* at 807–09.

Chief Justice John Roberts issued a sharply worded dissent that began:

> Just over a century ago, Arizona became the second State in the Union to ratify the Seventeenth Amendment. That Amendment transferred power to choose United States Senators from "the Legislature" of each State, Art. I, § 3, to "the people thereof." The Amendment resulted from an arduous, decades-long campaign in which reformers across the country worked hard to garner approval from Congress and three-quarters of the States.
>
> What chumps! Didn't they realize that all they had to do was interpret the constitutional term "the Legislature" to mean "the people"? The Court today performs just such a magic trick with the Elections Clause. Art. I, § 4.

Id. at 825–26.

Three years after *Arizona State Legislature*, Justice Anthony Kennedy retired. Not only had he been in *Arizona State Legislature*'s 5–4 majority, but he had also voted with four other justices in *Vieth* to continue holding that gerrymandering claims were justiciable. The following case, *Rucho v. Common Cause*, 139 S. Ct. 2484 (2019), was the first partisan gerrymandering case that the Court heard after Kennedy's retirement.

His replacement, Justice Brett Kavanaugh, joined the 5–4 majority that declined to find the claims justiciable.

■ CHIEF JUSTICE ROBERTS delivered the opinion of the Court.[11]

Voters and other plaintiffs in North Carolina and Maryland challenged their States' congressional districting maps as unconstitutional partisan gerrymanders. . . . These cases require us to consider once again whether claims of excessive partisanship in districting are "justiciable"—that is, properly suited for resolution by the federal courts. This Court has not previously struck down a districting plan as an unconstitutional partisan gerrymander, and has struggled without success over the past several decades to discern judicially manageable standards for deciding such claims. The districting plans at issue here are highly partisan, by any measure. The question is whether the courts below appropriately exercised judicial power when they found them unconstitutional as well.

I

The first case involves a challenge to the congressional redistricting plan enacted by the Republican-controlled North Carolina General Assembly in 2016. The Republican legislators leading the redistricting effort instructed their mapmaker to use political data to draw a map that would produce a congressional delegation of ten Republicans and three Democrats. As one of the two Republicans chairing the redistricting committee stated, "I think electing Republicans is better than electing Democrats. So I drew this map to help foster what I think is better for the country." He further explained that the map was drawn with the aim of electing ten Republicans and three Democrats because he did "not believe it [would be] possible to draw a map with 11 Republicans and 2 Democrats." . . .

The second case before us is [from Maryland]. In 2011, the Maryland Legislature—dominated by Democrats—undertook to redraw the lines of that State's eight congressional districts. The Governor at the time, Democrat Martin O'Malley, led the process. He appointed a redistricting committee to help redraw the map, and asked Congressman Steny Hoyer, who has described himself as a "serial gerrymanderer," to advise the committee. The Governor later testified that his aim was to "use the redistricting process to change the overall composition of Maryland's congressional delegation to 7 Democrats and 1 Republican by flipping" one district. "[A] decision was made to go for the Sixth," which had been held by a Republican for nearly two decades. To achieve the required equal population among districts,

---

11 **As You Read, Consider:** Like Justice Hugo Black in *Wesberry v. Sanders*, Chief Justice John Roberts begins this opinion by addressing whether the question before the Court is a *legal* question that the federal judiciary can resolve, or whether it is a *political* question that would be best left to Congress. Both cases interpreted the six factors described in *Baker v. Carr*, 369 U.S. 186 (1962), excerpted in the textual discussion preceding *Wesberry*. Why does Roberts reach a different conclusion than Black? If the *Wesberry* Court had applied Roberts's analysis, would the Court have dismissed the case as a political question instead of announcing its famous "one person, one vote" principle?

only about 10,000 residents needed to be removed from that district. The 2011 Plan accomplished that by moving roughly 360,000 voters out of the Sixth District and moving 350,000 new voters in. . . .

[II]

Chief Justice Marshall famously wrote that it is "the province and duty of the judicial department to say what the law is." *Marbury v. Madison*, 1 Cranch 137, 177 (1803). Sometimes, however, "the law is that the judicial department has no business entertaining the claim of unlawfulness—because the question is entrusted to one of the political branches or involves no judicially enforceable rights." *Vieth v. Jubelirer*, 541 U. S. 267, 277 (2004). In such a case the claim is said to present a "political question" and to be nonjusticiable—outside the courts' competence and therefore beyond the courts' jurisdiction. *Baker v. Carr*, 369 U. S. 186, 217 (1962). Among the political question cases the Court has identified are those that lack "judicially discoverable and manageable standards for resolving [them]." . . .

Partisan gerrymandering is nothing new. Nor is frustration with it. The practice was known in the Colonies prior to Independence, and the Framers were familiar with it at the time of the drafting and ratification of the Constitution. See *Vieth*, 541 U.S. at 274. During the very first congressional elections, George Washington and his Federalist allies accused Patrick Henry of trying to gerrymander Virginia's districts against their candidates—in particular James Madison, who ultimately prevailed over fellow future President James Monroe.

In 1812, Governor of Massachusetts and future Vice President Elbridge Gerry notoriously approved congressional districts that the legislature had drawn to aid the Democratic-Republican Party. The moniker "gerrymander" was born when an outraged Federalist newspaper observed that one of the misshapen districts resembled a salamander. See *Vieth*, 541 U.S. at 274. By 1840, the gerrymander was a recognized force in party politics and was generally attempted in all legislation enacted for the formation of election districts. It was generally conceded that each party would attempt to gain power which was not proportionate to its numerical strength.

The Framers addressed the election of Representatives to Congress in the Elections Clause. Art. I, § 4, cl. 1. That provision assigns to state legislatures the power to prescribe the "Times, Places and Manner of holding Elections" for Members of Congress, while giving Congress the power to "make or alter" any such regulations. Whether to give that supervisory authority to the National Government was debated at the Constitutional Convention. When those opposed to such congressional oversight moved to strike the relevant language, Madison came to its defense:

"[T]he State Legislatures will sometimes fail or refuse to consult the common interest at the expense of their local coveniency or prejudices. . . . Whenever the State Legislatures had a favorite measure to carry, they would take care so to mould their regulations as to favor the candidates they wished to succeed." 2 Records of the Federal Convention of 1787, at 240–241.

During the subsequent fight for ratification, the provision remained a subject of debate. Antifederalists predicted that Congress's power under the Elections Clause would allow Congress to make itself "omnipotent," setting the "time" of elections as never or the "place" in difficult to reach corners of the State. Federalists responded that, among other justifications, the revisionary power was necessary to counter state legislatures set on undermining fair representation, including through malapportionment. M. Klarman, The Framers' Coup: The Making of the United States Constitution 340–342 (2016). The Federalists were, for example, concerned that newly developing population centers would be deprived of their proper electoral weight, as some cities had been in Great Britain.

Congress has regularly exercised its Elections Clause power, including to address partisan gerrymandering. The Apportionment Act of 1842, which required single-member districts for the first time, specified that those districts be "composed of contiguous territory," 5 Stat. 491, in "an attempt to forbid the practice of the gerrymander." Later statutes added requirements of compactness and equality of population. 31 Stat. 733; 17 Stat. 28. (Only the single member district requirement remains in place today. 2 U. S. C. § 2c.) Congress also used its Elections Clause power in 1870, enacting the first comprehensive federal statute dealing with elections as a way to enforce the Fifteenth Amendment. 16 Stat. 140. Starting in the 1950s, Congress enacted a series of laws to protect the right to vote through measures such as the suspension of literacy tests and the prohibition of English-only elections.

Appellants suggest that, through the Elections Clause, the Framers set aside electoral issues such as the one before us as questions that only Congress can resolve. See *Baker*, 369 U.S. at 217. We do not agree. In two areas—one-person, one-vote and racial gerrymandering—our cases have held that there is a role for the courts with respect to at least some issues that could arise from a State's drawing of congressional districts. See *Wesberry v. Sanders*, 376 U. S. 1 (1964); *Shaw v. Reno*, 509 U. S. 630 (1993) (*Shaw I*).

But the history is not irrelevant. The Framers were aware of electoral districting problems and considered what to do about them. They settled on a characteristic approach, assigning the issue to the state legislatures, expressly checked and balanced by the Federal Congress. As Alexander Hamilton explained, "it will . . . not be denied that a discretionary power over elections ought to exist somewhere. It will, I presume, be as readily conceded that there were only three ways in which this power could have been reasonably modified and disposed: that it must either have been lodged wholly in the national legislature, or wholly in the State legislatures, or primarily in the latter, and ultimately in the former." The Federalist No. 59, p. 362 (C. Rossiter ed. 1961). At no point was there a suggestion that the federal courts had a role to play. Nor was there any indication that the Framers had ever heard of courts doing such a thing.

Courts have nevertheless been called upon to resolve a variety of questions surrounding districting. Early on, doubts were raised about the competence of the federal courts to resolve those questions. See *Colegrove v. Green*, 328 U.S. 549 (1946).

In the leading case of *Baker v. Carr*, voters in Tennessee complained that the State's districting plan for state representatives "debase[d]" their votes, because the plan was predicated on a 60-year-old census that no longer reflected the distribution of population in the State. The plaintiffs argued that votes of people in overpopulated districts held less value than those of people in less-populated districts, and that this inequality violated the Equal Protection Clause of the Fourteenth Amendment. The District Court dismissed the action on the ground that the claim was not justiciable, relying on this Court's precedents, including *Colegrove*. *Baker v. Carr*, 179 F. Supp. 824, 825, 826 (MD Tenn. 1959). This Court reversed. It identified various considerations relevant to determining whether a claim is a nonjusticiable political question, including whether there is "a lack of judicially discoverable and manageable standards for resolving it." 369 U. S., at 217. The Court concluded that the claim of population inequality among districts did not fall into that category, because such a claim could be decided under basic equal protection principles. Id., at 226. In *Wesberry v. Sanders*, the Court extended its ruling to malapportionment of congressional districts, holding that Article I, § 2, required that "one man's vote in a congressional election is to be worth as much as another's." 376 U. S., at 8. . . .

Another line of challenges to districting plans has focused on race. Laws that explicitly discriminate on the basis of race, as well as those that are race neutral on their face but are unexplainable on grounds other than race, are of course presumptively invalid. The Court applied those principles to electoral boundaries in *Gomillion v. Lightfoot*, concluding that a challenge to an "uncouth twenty-eight sided" municipal boundary line that excluded black voters from city elections stated a constitutional claim. 364 U. S. 339, 340 (1960). In *Wright v. Rockefeller*, 376 U. S. 52 (1964), the Court extended the reasoning of *Gomillion* to congressional districting.

Partisan gerrymandering claims have proved far more difficult to adjudicate. The basic reason is that, while it is illegal for a jurisdiction to depart from the one-person, one-vote rule, or to engage in racial discrimination in districting, a jurisdiction may engage in constitutional political gerrymandering.

To hold that legislators cannot take partisan interests into account when drawing district lines would essentially countermand the Framers' decision to entrust districting to political entities. The "central problem" is not determining whether a jurisdiction has engaged in partisan gerrymandering. It is "determining when political gerrymandering has gone too far." *Vieth*, 541 U. S., at 296 (plurality opinion). . . .

We first considered a partisan gerrymandering claim in *Gaffney v. Cummings* in 1973. There we rejected an equal protection challenge to Connecticut's redistricting plan, which "aimed at a rough scheme of proportional representation of the two major political parties" by "wiggl[ing] and joggl[ing] boundary lines" to create the appropriate number of safe seats for each party. 412 U.S. at 738, 752 n.18. In upholding the State's plan, we reasoned that districting "inevitably has and is intended to have substantial political consequences." *Id.*, at 753.

Thirteen years later, in *Davis v. Bandemer*, we addressed a claim that Indiana Republicans had cracked and packed Democrats in violation of the Equal Protection Clause. 478 U.S. 109, 116–117 (1986). A majority of the Court agreed that the case was justiciable, but the Court splintered over the proper standard to apply. . . .

Eighteen years later, in *Vieth*, the plaintiffs complained that Pennsylvania's legislature "ignored all traditional redistricting criteria, including the preservation of local government boundaries," in order to benefit Republican congressional candidates. 541 U.S. at 272–273. Justice Scalia wrote for a four-Justice plurality. He would have held that the plaintiffs' claims were nonjusticiable because there was no "judicially discernible and manageable standard" for deciding them. Justice Kennedy, concurring in the judgment, noted "the lack of comprehensive and neutral principles for drawing electoral boundaries [and] the absence of rules to limit and confine judicial intervention." *Id.*, at 306–307. He nonetheless left open the possibility that "in another case a standard might emerge." *Id.*, at 312. Four Justices dissented. . . .

[III]

Partisan gerrymandering claims rest on an instinct that groups with a certain level of political support should enjoy a commensurate level of political power and influence. Explicitly or implicitly, a districting map is alleged to be unconstitutional because it makes it too difficult for one party to translate statewide support into seats in the legislature. But such a claim is based on a "norm that does not exist" in our electoral system—"statewide elections for representatives along party lines."

Partisan gerrymandering claims invariably sound in a desire for proportional representation.[12] As Justice O'Connor put it, such claims are based on "a conviction that the greater the departure from proportionality, the more suspect an apportionment plan becomes." *Ibid.* "Our cases, however, clearly foreclose any claim that the Constitution requires proportional representation or that legislatures in reapportioning must draw district lines to come as near as possible to allocating seats to the contending parties in proportion to what their anticipated statewide vote will be."

The Founders certainly did not think proportional representation was required. For more than 50 years after ratification of the Constitution, many States elected their congressional representatives through at-large or "general ticket" elections. Such States typically sent single-party delegations to Congress.

That meant that a party could garner nearly half of the vote statewide and wind up without any seats in the congressional delegation. The Whigs in Alabama suffered that fate in 1840: "their party garnered 43 percent of the statewide vote, yet did not receive a single seat." When Congress required single-member districts in the Apportionment Act of 1842, it was not out of a general sense of fairness, but instead a (mis)calculation by the Whigs that such a change would improve their electoral prospects.

Unable to claim that the Constitution requires proportional representation outright, plaintiffs inevitably ask the courts to make their own political judgment about how much representation particular political parties *deserve*—based on the votes of their supporters—and to rearrange the challenged districts to achieve that end. But federal courts are not equipped to apportion political power as a matter of fairness, nor is there any basis for concluding that they were authorized to do so. . . .

The initial difficulty in settling on a "clear, manageable and politically neutral" test for fairness is that it is not even clear what fairness looks like in this context. There is a large measure of "unfairness" in any winner-take-all system. Fairness may mean a greater number of competitive districts. Such a claim seeks to undo packing and cracking so that supporters of the disadvantaged party have a better shot at electing their preferred candidates. But making as many districts as possible more competitive could be a recipe for disaster for the disadvantaged party. As Justice White has pointed out, "[i]f all or most of the districts are competitive . . . even a narrow statewide preference for either party would produce an overwhelming majority for the winning party in the state legislature." *Bandemer*, 478 U.S. at 130.

On the other hand, perhaps the ultimate objective of a "fairer" share of seats in the congressional delegation is most readily achieved by yielding to the gravitational pull of proportionality and engaging in cracking and packing, to ensure each party its "appropriate" share of "safe" seats. Such an approach, however, comes at the expense of competitive districts and of individuals in districts allocated to the opposing party.

Or perhaps fairness should be measured by adherence to "traditional" districting criteria, such as maintaining political subdivisions, keeping communities of interest

---

[12] **Questions:** In these paragraphs, Roberts rejects the idea that the Constitution supplies a legal standard—proportional representation by party—for evaluating whether a partisan gerrymander goes too far. In other words, he does not think that Article I, Section 2, requires that a quarter of a state's congressional delegation be Republicans if a quarter of the state's voters supported Republicans.

There is some controversy about whether Roberts is correct about what the Founders expected. But assuming that he is correct, would it be constitutional for Congress after this opinion to require proportional representation by party in congressional elections? If your answer is yes, then is Roberts correct that partisan gerrymandering really is a political question that should be left to Congress?

together, and protecting incumbents. But protecting incumbents, for example, enshrines a particular partisan distribution. And the "natural political geography" of a State—such as the fact that urban electoral districts are often dominated by one political party—can itself lead to inherently packed districts. . . .

Deciding among just these different visions of fairness (you can imagine many others) poses basic questions that are political, not legal. There are no legal standards discernible in the Constitution for making such judgments, let alone limited and precise standards that are clear, manageable, and politically neutral. Any judicial decision on what is "fair" in this context would be an "unmoored determination" of the sort characteristic of a political question beyond the competence of the federal courts.

And it is only after determining how to define fairness that you can even begin to answer the determinative question: "How much is too much?" At what point does permissible partisanship become unconstitutional? . . .

Appellees contend that if we can adjudicate one-person, one-vote claims, we can also assess partisan gerrymandering claims. But the one-person, one-vote rule is relatively easy to administer as a matter of math. The same cannot be said of partisan gerrymandering claims, because the Constitution supplies no objective measure for assessing whether a districting map treats a political party fairly. It hardly follows from the principle that each person must have an equal say in the election of representatives that a person is entitled to have his political party achieve representation in some way commensurate to its share of statewide support.

More fundamentally, "vote dilution" in the one-person, one-vote cases refers to the idea that each vote must carry equal weight. In other words, each representative must be accountable to (approximately) the same number of constituents. That requirement does not extend to political parties. It does not mean that each party must be influential in proportion to its number of supporters. . . .

Nor do our racial gerrymandering cases provide an appropriate standard for assessing partisan gerrymandering.[13] "[N]othing in our case law compels the conclusion that racial and political gerrymanders are subject to precisely the same constitutional scrutiny. . . .["] Unlike partisan gerrymandering claims, a racial gerrymandering claim does not ask for a fair share of political power and influence, with all the justiciability conundrums that entails. It asks instead for the elimination of a racial classification. A partisan gerrymandering claim cannot ask for the elimination of partisanship. . . .

V

Excessive partisanship in districting leads to results that reasonably seem unjust. But the fact that such gerrymandering is "incompatible with democratic principles," *Arizona State Legislature*, 576 U. S., at ___ (slip op., at 1), does not mean that the solution lies with the federal judiciary. We conclude that partisan gerrymandering claims present political questions beyond the reach of the federal courts. Federal judges have no license to reallocate political power between the two

---

[13] **Questions:** The racial gerrymandering cases to which Roberts is referring held that the Fourteenth Amendment prohibits states from using race as the "predominant" reason for deciding how to draw congressional or state legislative districts. These cases will be discussed later (section 50.2). But judging by Roberts's description of them, do you accept his explanation for why racial gerrymandering is a justiciable issue while partisan gerrymandering is not? Does this opinion raise the risk that states interested in conducting *racial* gerrymandering will announce that what they're doing is engaging in *partisan* gerrymandering in order to avoid litigation? *See* Richard L. Hasen, *Race or Party?: How Courts Should Think About Republican Efforts to Make It Harder to Vote in North Carolina and Elsewhere*, 127 Harv. L. Rev. F. 58, 61 (2014) ("When party and race coincide, . . . it is much harder to separate racial and partisan intent and effect.").

major political parties, with no plausible grant of authority in the Constitution, and no legal standards to limit and direct their decisions. "[J]udicial action must be governed by *standard*, by *rule*," and must be "principled, rational, and based upon reasoned distinctions" found in the Constitution or laws. *Vieth*, 541 U.S. at 278. Judicial review of partisan gerrymandering does not meet those basic requirements. . . .

What the appellees and dissent seek is an unprecedented expansion of judicial power. We have never struck down a partisan gerrymander as unconstitutional—despite various requests over the past 45 years. The expansion of judicial authority would not be into just any area of controversy, but into one of the most intensely partisan aspects of American political life. That intervention would be unlimited in scope and duration—it would recur over and over again around the country with each new round of districting, for state as well as federal representatives. Consideration of the impact of today's ruling on democratic principles cannot ignore the effect of the unelected and politically unaccountable branch of the Federal Government assuming such an extraordinary and unprecedented role.

Our conclusion does not condone excessive partisan gerrymandering. Nor does our conclusion condemn complaints about districting to echo into a void. The States, for example, are actively addressing the issue on a number of fronts. In 2015, the Supreme Court of Florida struck down that State's congressional districting plan as a violation of the Fair Districts Amendment to the Florida Constitution. *League of Women Voters of Florida v. Detzner*, 172 So. 3d 363 (2015). The dissent wonders why we can't do the same. The answer is that there is no "Fair Districts Amendment" to the Federal Constitution. Provisions in state statutes and state constitutions can provide standards and guidance for state courts to apply. . . . Indeed, numerous other States are restricting partisan considerations in districting through legislation. One way they are doing so is by placing power to draw electoral districts in the hands of independent commissions. For example, in November 2018, voters in Colorado and Michigan approved constitutional amendments creating multimember commissions that will be responsible in whole or in part for creating and approving district maps for congressional and state legislative districts. See Colo. Const., Art. V, §§ 44, 46; Mich. Const., Art. IV, § 6. Missouri is trying a different tack. Voters there overwhelmingly approved the creation of a new position—state demographer—to draw state legislative district lines. Mo. Const., Art. III, § 3. . . .

As noted, the Framers gave Congress the power to do something about partisan gerrymandering in the Elections Clause. The first bill introduced in the 116th Congress would require States to create 15-member independent commissions to draw congressional districts and would establish certain redistricting criteria, including protection for communities of interest, and ban partisan gerrymandering. H. R. 1, 116th Cong., 1st Sess., §§ 2401, 2411 (2019). . . .[14]

We express no view on any of these pending proposals. We simply note that the avenue for reform established by the Framers, and used by Congress in the past, remains open.

* * *

No one can accuse this Court of having a crabbed view of the reach of its competence. But we have no commission to allocate political power and influence in

[14] **Question:** The bill that Roberts is referring to, H.R. 1, has long been a major priority of most congressional Democrats. In addition to requiring states to (1) adopt independent redistricting commissions, the bill would also require states to (2) establish systems of automatic, same-day registration and (3) allow formerly incarcerated people to vote if they are otherwise eligible under state law. In light of *Ex parte Yarbrough*, *Wesberry*, and *Rucho v. Common Cause*, do you think that all three of these provisions are constitutional exercises of Congress's power under Article I, Section 4?

the absence of a constitutional directive or legal standards to guide us in the exercise of such authority. "It is emphatically the province and duty of the judicial department to say what the law is." *Marbury v. Madison*, 1 Cranch, at 177. In this rare circumstance, that means our duty is to say "this is not law."

■ JUSTICE KAGAN, with whom JUSTICE GINSBURG, JUSTICE BREYER, and JUSTICE SOTOMAYOR join, dissenting.

For the first time ever, this Court refuses to remedy a constitutional violation because it thinks the task beyond judicial capabilities.

And not just any constitutional violation. The partisan gerrymanders in these cases deprived citizens of the most fundamental of their constitutional rights: the rights to participate equally in the political process, to join with others to advance political beliefs, and to choose their political representatives. In so doing, the partisan gerrymanders here debased and dishonored our democracy, turning upside-down the core American idea that all governmental power derives from the people. These gerrymanders enabled politicians to entrench themselves in office as against voters' preferences. They promoted partisanship above respect for the popular will. They encouraged a politics of polarization and dysfunction. If left unchecked, gerrymanders like the ones here may irreparably damage our system of government.

And checking them is *not* beyond the courts. The majority's abdication comes just when courts across the country, including those below, have coalesced around manageable judicial standards to resolve partisan gerrymandering claims. Those standards satisfy the majority's own benchmarks. They do not require—indeed, they do not permit—courts to rely on their own ideas of electoral fairness, whether proportional representation or any other. And they limit courts to correcting only egregious gerrymanders, so judges do not become omnipresent players in the political process. But yes, the standards used here do allow—as well they should—judicial intervention in the worst-of-the-worst cases of democratic subversion, causing blatant constitutional harms. In other words, they allow courts to undo partisan gerrymanders of the kind we face today from North Carolina and Maryland. In giving such gerrymanders a pass from judicial review, the majority goes tragically wrong.

CHAPTER 23

WHAT ARE CONGRESS'S NONLEGISLATIVE POWERS?

ARTICLE I, SECTION 2, CLAUSE 2: No Person shall be a Representative who shall not have attained to the Age of twenty five Years, and been seven Years a Citizen of the United States, and who shall not, when elected, be an Inhabitant of that State in which he shall be chosen.

CLAUSE 5: The House of Representatives shall chuse their Speaker and other Officers . . . .

ARTICLE I, SECTION 3, CLAUSE 3: No Person shall be a Senator who shall not have attained to the Age of thirty Years, and been nine Years a Citizen of the United States, and who shall not, when elected, be an Inhabitant of that State for which he shall be chosen.

CLAUSE 4: The Vice President of the United States shall be President of the Senate but shall have no Vote, unless they be equally divided.

ARTICLE I, SECTION 5, CLAUSE 1: Each House shall be the Judge of the Elections, Returns and Qualifications of its own Members, and a Majority of each shall constitute a Quorum to do Business; but a smaller Number may adjourn from day to day, and may be authorized to compel the Attendance of absent Members, in such Manner, and under such Penalties as each House may provide.

CLAUSE 2: Each House may determine the Rules of its Proceedings, punish its Members for disorderly Behaviour, and, with the Concurrence of two thirds, expel a Member.

CLAUSE 3: Each House shall keep a Journal of its Proceedings, and from time to time publish the same, excepting such Parts as may in their Judgment require Secrecy; and the Yeas and Nays of the Members of either House on any question shall, at the Desire of one fifth of those Present, be entered on the Journal.

CLAUSE 4: Neither House, during the Session of Congress, shall, without the Consent of the other, adjourn for more than three days, nor to any other Place than that in which the two Houses shall be sitting.

ARTICLE I, SECTION 6, CLAUSE 1: The Senators and Representatives shall receive a Compensation for their Services, to be ascertained by Law, and paid out of the Treasury of the United States. They shall in all Cases, except Treason, Felony and Breach of the Peace, be privileged from Arrest during their Attendance at the Session of their respective Houses, and in going to and returning from the same; and for any Speech or Debate in either House, they shall not be questioned in any other Place.

CLAUSE 2: No Senator or Representative shall, during the Time for which he was elected, be appointed to any civil Office under the Authority of the United States, which shall have been created, or the Emoluments whereof shall have been encreased during such time; and no Person holding any Office under the United States, shall be a Member of either House during his Continuance in Office.

Importance of Nonlegislative Powers

Most of the debate during the Constitutional Convention was over the composition of Congress and the legislative powers granted to it. But the Constitution also granted Congress many parliamentary, or nonlegislative, powers, including the power to investigate, to determine its own rules, to speak and debate freely, and to exclude and expel members. Although these powers are less controversial than, say, Congress's power to tax, they are vital for Congress to legislate effectively and to push back against the other branches.

23.1 THE POWER TO INVESTIGATE, SUBPOENA, AND HOLD IN CONTEMPT

Nothing in the Constitution expressly gives Congress the power to hire researchers, hold hearings, subpoena witnesses and documents, and otherwise investigate the world around it. The closest it comes is in Article II, Section 3, which requires the president to "give to the Congress Information of the State of the Union, and recommend to their Consideration such Measures as he shall judge necessary and expedient."

In apparent compliance with this clause, Secretary of the Treasury Alexander Hamilton wielded enormous power with the first Congress, submitting his First Report on the Public Credit (1790), Report on a National Bank (1790), and Report on the Subject of Manufactures (1791) as the main sources of economic information for Congress. Congress largely adopted these reports as the basis of its early economic legislation, and its first appropriations acts essentially tracked budget estimates submitted by Hamilton. *See* Josh Chafetz, *Congress's Constitution: Legislative Authority and the Separation of Powers* 58 (2017).

As reliant as Congress was on Hamilton, however, the House maintained its independence in conducting investigations into other matters. Earlier legislatures, including Parliament, the Confederation Congress, and state and colonial legislatures, had all conducted investigations regarding proposed legislation and impeachments. The first House was no different. In 1792, for example, following news that a coalition of Miami, Shawnee, and Delaware had defeated hundreds of U.S. soldiers serving in the Northwest Territory under Major General Arthur St. Clair, the House resolved, 44–10, "[t]hat a committee be appointed to inquire into the causes of the failure of the late expedition under Major General St. Clair; and that the said committee be empowered to call for such persons, papers, and records, as may be necessary to assist their inquiries." 3 Annals of Cong. 493 (1792). Although opponents of the resolution warned that Congress might not have the power to investigate the executive branch, supporters, including James Madison, maintained that "an inquiry into the expenditure of all public money was the indispensable duty of this House" and that a committee investigation "would be able to throw more light on the subject, and then the House would be able to determine how to proceed." *Id.* at 492. Later Houses continued to compel witnesses to testify about information needed to legislate properly, including on tariff rates, 4 Reg. Deb. 862–89 (1827); "the condition of the various executive departments [and] the ability and integrity with which they have been conducted," 13 Reg. Deb. 1057–67 (1836); and John Brown's raid of Harper's Ferry in 1859, Cong. Globe, 36th Cong., 1st Sess. 1100–09 (1860).

To enforce their orders compelling people to testify under oath, both houses of Congress determined that they also had the power to hold witnesses in "contempt of Congress"—that is, to order the House's or Senate's sergeant at arms to arrest a witness and, if necessary, imprison the witness in the Capitol. As with the general power to investigate, the power to hold in contempt had long been wielded by Parliament, the Confederation Congress, and colonial legislatures, usually against people who allegedly breached a legislative privilege. *See* Chafetz, *supra*, at 153–73.

In 1821, for example, when a man named John Anderson allegedly bribed a House member, the House found him guilty of contempt and ordered him imprisoned. Anderson sued the sergeant at arms for false imprisonment on the ground that no constitutional provision authorized this proceeding. The Supreme Court unanimously rejected this argument, declaring the House's contempt power analogous to the contempt power of federal courts. If Congress lacked the power to punish people like Anderson, the Court declared, it would "obviously lead[ ] to the total annihilation of the power of the House of Representatives to guard itself from contempts, and leaves it exposed to every indignity and interruption that rudeness, caprice, or even conspiracy, may meditate against it." *Anderson v. Dunn*, 19 U.S. 204, 228 (1821).

But holding someone in contempt for bribery is a bit different than holding someone in contempt for failing to testify. When the Supreme Court first confronted the latter issue in *Kilbourn v. Thompson*, the Court expressed skepticism that either house of Congress had the "general power of making inquiry into the private affairs of the citizen." 103 U.S. 168, 190 (1880). Leaving open the question of whether the House or Senate could punish someone for failing to testify about an issue over which Congress had power to legislate, the Court held that where the House lacked such a power, it definitely lacked the power to hold someone in contempt. It reaffirmed this limitation in *Marshall v. Gordon*, 243 U.S. 521 (1917), where it ordered the release of someone held in contempt for publishing allegedly defamatory material about a House member.

In the case *In re Chapman*, 166 U.S. 661 (1897), however, the Court affirmed, for the first time, that the Senate could investigate and punish a witness for failing to answer questions regarding the misconduct of a senator—something the Senate had the power to punish under the Expulsion Clause of Article I, Section 5. That case set the stage for the following case, in which the Court attempted to definitively settle Congress's investigation and contempt power.

23.1.1

McGrain v. Daugherty

273 U.S. 135 (1927)

On April 14, 1922, the *Wall Street Journal* published a front-page story reporting that the U.S. government had secretly signed a deal to allow Harry F. Sinclair, an oil tycoon, to develop an oil field that the government was reserving for the U.S. Navy in Wyoming. *See Sinclair Consolidated in Big Oil Deal with U.S.*, Wall St. J., Apr. 14, 1922, at 1. The oil field, named for the nearby Teapot Dome rock formation, soon lent its name to a brewing scandal over why the government had signed this deal in secret and without competitive bidding. At the time, the U.S. Navy was the country's largest oil consumer, and the contracts to develop its oil reserves were highly coveted. Yet, for some reason, one year earlier, President Warren G. Harding had signed an executive order transferring authority over the navy's oil reserves from the secretary of the navy to the secretary of the interior, Albert B. Fall. *See* Exec. Order No. 3474 (May 31, 1921).

A day after the *Wall Street Journal* story broke, one of Wyoming's senators called for a Senate investigation of the deal. Over the next five years, Senator Thomas Walsh of Montana led a committee investigation that uncovered evidence that Secretary Fall had received the modern equivalent of $7 million in gifts and no-interest loans in exchange for issuing the development contracts for Teapot Dome and another oil field in California. *See* Laton McCartney, *The Teapot Dome Scandal* 108–09 (2008). The massive bribery scandal—the biggest federal scandal until Watergate—also implicated other members of the Harding administration, including Harding's attorney general and political fixer, Harry M. Daugherty. *Id.* at 9.

In 1924, Daugherty resigned in disgrace, leading Senate investigators to issue a subpoena to his older brother, Mally Daugherty, compelling him to testify. Mally ignored the subpoena on the ground that the Senate had no power to compel testimony of a private citizen. The Senate responded by ordering its deputy sergeant at arms, John McGrain, to arrest Mally and bring him before the Walsh committee. But when McGrain arrested Mally in Cincinnati, Mally petitioned the local federal district court for a writ of habeas corpus. The court granted Mally's petition, evaluated the legality of McGrain's arrest, and ordered Mally freed because, it ruled, the Senate had no power to compel Mally to answer its questions.

On behalf of the Senate, the sergeant at arms appealed the district court's order to the Supreme Court, which heard arguments in 1924 and issued its opinion in 1927, after the full scope of the Teapot Dome scandal had been revealed. The Court in *McGrain v. Daugherty*, 273 U.S. 135 (1927), examined—and decided in favor of the Senate—two questions: First, does the Senate have the power to compel testimony from a private individual for a constitutional legislative function? Second, was the Senate in this case seeking testimony for a constitutional legislative function?

■ MR. JUSTICE VAN DEVANTER delivered the opinion of the Court.[1]

This is an appeal from the final order in a proceeding in *habeas corpus* discharging a recusant witness held in custody under process of attachment issued from the United States Senate in the course of an investigation which it was making of the administration of the Department of Justice. . . . .

We have given the case earnest and prolonged consideration because the principal questions involved are of unusual importance and delicacy. They are (a) whether the Senate—or the House of Representatives, both being on the same plane in this regard—has power, through its own process, to compel a private individual to appear before it or one of its committees and give testimony needed to enable it efficiently to exercise a legislative function belonging to it under the Constitution, and (b) whether it sufficiently appears that the process was being employed in this instance to obtain testimony for that purpose. . . .

[Question 1: The Senate's power to compel testimony]

The Constitution provides for a Congress consisting of a Senate and House of Representatives and invests it with "all legislative powers" granted to the United States, and with power "to make all laws which shall be necessary and proper" for carrying into execution these powers and "all other powers" vested by the Constitution in the United States or in any department or officer thereof. Art. I, secs 1, 8. Other provisions show that, while bills can become laws only after being considered and passed by both houses of Congress, each house is to be distinct from the other, to have its own officers and rules, and to exercise its legislative function independently. Art. I, secs. 2, 3, 5, 7. But there is no provision expressly investing either house with power to make investigations and exact testimony to the end that it may exercise its legislative function advisedly and effectively. So the question arises whether this power is so far incidental to the legislative function as to be implied.

In actual legislative practice power to secure needed information by such means has long been treated as an attribute of the power to legislate. It was so regarded in the British Parliament and in the Colonial legislatures before the American Revolution; and a like view has prevailed and been carried into effect in both houses of Congress and in most of the state legislatures.

This power was both asserted and exerted by the House of Representatives in 1792, when it appointed a select committee to inquire into the St. Clair expedition and authorized the committee to send for necessary persons, papers and records. Mr. Madison, who had taken an important part in framing the Constitution only five years before, and four of his associates in that work, were members of the House of Representatives at the time, and all voted for the inquiry. 3 Cong. Ann. 494. Other exertions of the power by the House of Representatives, as also by the Senate, are shown in the citations already made. Among those by the Senate, the inquiry ordered in 1859 respecting the raid by John Brown and his adherents on the armory and arsenal of the United States at Harper's Ferry is of special significance. The resolution

[1] **As You Read, Consider:** From where in the Constitution does Congress derive its power to compel testimony? How does Justice Willis Van Devanter respond to claims that Congress could abuse its power to investigate and compel testimony?

precedent

nec & prop

implied pow

directing the inquiry authorized the committee to send for persons and papers, to inquire into the facts pertaining to the raid and the means by which it was organized and supported, and to report what legislation, if any, was necessary to preserve the peace of the country and protect the public property. The resolution was briefly discussed and adopted without opposition. Cong. Globe, 36th Cong., 1st Sess., pp. 141, 152. Later on the committee reported that Thaddeus Hyatt, although subpoenaed to appear as a witness, had refused to do so; whereupon the Senate ordered that he be attached and brought before it to answer for his refusal. When he was brought in he answered by challenging the power of the Senate to direct the inquiry and exact testimony to aid it in exercising its legislative function. The question of power thus presented was thoroughly discussed by several senators—Mr. Sumner of Massachusetts taking the lead in denying the power and Mr. Fessenden of Maine in supporting it. Sectional and party lines were put aside and the question was debated and determined with special regard to principle and precedent. The vote was taken on a resolution pronouncing the witness's answer insufficient and directing that he be committed until he should signify that he was ready and willing to testify. The resolution was adopted—44 senators voting for it and 10 against. Cong. Globe, 36th Cong., 1st Sess., pp. 1100–1109, 3006–3007. . . .

precedent

The deliberate solution of the question on that occasion has been accepted and followed on other occasions by both houses of Congress, and never has been rejected or questioned by either.

The state courts quite generally have held that the power to legislate carries with it by necessary implication ample authority to obtain information needed in the rightful exercise of that power, and to employ compulsory process for the purpose. . . . An instructive decision on the question is also found in *Ex parte Dansereau* (1875), 19 L.C. Jur. 210, where the legislative assembly of the Province of Quebec was held to possess this power as a necessary incident of its power to legislate.

We have referred to the practice of the two houses of Congress; and we now shall notice some significant congressional enactments. May 3, 1798, c. 36, 1 Stat. 554, Congress provided that oaths or affirmations might be administered to witnesses by the President of the Senate, the Speaker of the House of Representatives, the chairman of a committee of the whole, or the chairman of a select committee, "in any case under their examination." . . . January 24, 1857, c. 19, 11 Stat. 155, it passed "An Act more effectually to enforce the attendance of witnesses on the summons of either house of Congress, and to compel them to discover testimony." This act provided, first, that any person summoned as a witness to give testimony or produce papers in any matter under inquiry before either house of Congress, or any committee of either house, who should wilfully make default, or, if appearing, should refuse to answer any question pertinent to the inquiry, should . . . be deemed guilty of a misdemeanor and be subject to indictment and punishment as there prescribed. . . .

[These statutes] show very plainly that Congress intended thereby (a) to recognize the power of either house to institute inquiries and exact evidence touching subjects within its jurisdiction and on which it was disposed to act; (b) to recognize that such inquiries may be conducted through committees; (c) to subject defaulting and contumacious witnesses to indictment and punishment in the courts, and thereby to enable either house to exert the power of inquiry "more effectually"; and (d) to open the way for obtaining evidence in such an inquiry, which otherwise could not be obtained, by exempting witnesses required to give evidence therein from criminal and penal prosecutions in respect of matters disclosed by their evidence. . . .

While [our own] cases are not decisive of the question we are considering, they definitely settle two propositions which we recognize as entirely sound and having a bearing on its solution: One, that the two houses of Congress, in their separate relations, possess not only such powers as are expressly granted to them by the Constitution, but such auxiliary powers as are necessary and appropriate to make the express powers effective; and, the other, that neither house is invested with "general" power to inquire into private affairs and compel disclosures but only with such limited power of inquiry as is shown to exist when the rule of constitutional interpretation just stated is rightly applied. . . .

With this review of the legislative practice, congressional enactments and court decisions, we proceed to a statement of our conclusions on the question.

We are of opinion that the power of inquiry—with process to enforce it—is an essential and appropriate auxiliary to the legislative function. It was so regarded and employed in American legislatures before the Constitution was framed and ratified. Both houses of Congress took this view of it early in their history . . . and both houses have employed the power accordingly up to the present time. . . . So, when their practice in the matter is appraised according to the circumstances in which it was begun and to those in which it has been continued, it falls nothing short of a practical construction, long continued, of the constitutional provisions respecting their powers, and therefore should be taken as fixing the meaning of those provisions, if otherwise doubtful.[2]

We are further of opinion that the provisions are not of doubtful meaning, but, as was held by this Court in the cases we have reviewed, are intended to be effectively exercised, and therefore to carry with them such auxiliary powers as are necessary and appropriate to that end.[3] While the power to exact information in aid of the legislative function was not involved in those cases, the rule of interpretation applied there is applicable here. A legislative body cannot legislate wisely or effectively in the absence of information respecting the conditions which the legislation is intended to affect or change; and where the legislative body does not itself possess the requisite information—which not infrequently is true—recourse must be had to others who do possess it. Experience has taught that mere requests for such information often are unavailing, and also that information which is volunteered is not always accurate or complete; so some means of compulsion are essential to obtain what is needed. All this was true before and when the Constitution was framed and adopted. In that period the power of inquiry—with enforcing process—was regarded and employed as a necessary and appropriate attribute of the power to legislate—indeed, was treated as inhering in it. Thus there is ample warrant for thinking, as we do, that the constitutional provisions which commit the legislative function to the two houses are intended to include this attribute to the end that the function may be effectively exercised.

The contention is earnestly made on behalf of the witness that this power of inquiry, if sustained, may be abusively and oppressively exerted. If this be so, it affords no ground for denying the power. The same contention might be directed against the power to legislate, and of course would be unavailing. We must assume, for present purposes, that neither house will be disposed to exert the power beyond

---

2 **Questions:** Van Devanter here says that Congress's historical practice can have the practical effect of "fixing the meaning" of the Constitution. Why? Is the opposite true? For example, if today's Congress tries something new for the first time, does its failure to adopt the practice earlier "fix" the Constitution to mean that Congress lacks such a novel power?

3 **Question:** Van Devanter holds that each house of Congress has the implied power to take actions that are "necessary and appropriate" for enforcing its enumerated powers to legislate, expel, make rules, etc. Yet the Necessary and Proper Clause does not literally apply; it defines only what kind of laws Congress may pass. Do you agree that Congress should nevertheless have implied powers *before* it legislates?

its proper bounds, or without due regard to the rights of witnesses. But if, contrary to this assumption, controlling limitations or restrictions are disregarded, the decisions in *Kilbourn v. Thompson* and *Marshall v. Gordon* point to admissible measures of relief. And it is a necessary deduction from the decisions in *Kilbourn v. Thompson* and *In re Chapman* that a witness rightfully may refuse to answer where the bounds of the power are exceeded or the questions are not pertinent to the matter under inquiry.[4]

[Question 2: The application of this power here]

We come now to the question whether it sufficiently appears that the purpose for which the witness's testimony was sought was to obtain information in aid of the legislative function. The court below answered the question in the negative and put its decision largely on this ground, . . . ["T]hat in the second resolution the Senate has expressly avowed that the investigation is in aid of other action than legislation. Its purpose is to 'obtain information necessary as a basis for such legislative and other action as the Senate may deem necessary and proper.' This indicates that the Senate is contemplating the taking of action other than legislative, as the outcome of the investigation, at least the possibility of so doing. The extreme personal cast of the original resolutions; the spirit of hostility towards the then Attorney General which they breathe; that it was not avowed that legislative action was had in view until after the action of the Senate had been challenged; and that the avowal then was coupled with an avowal that other action was had in view—are calculated to create the impression that the idea of legislative action being in contemplation was an afterthought. . . . That the Senate has in contemplation the possibility of taking action other than legislation as an outcome of the investigation, as thus expressly avowed, would seem of itself to invalidate the entire proceeding. . . ."

We are of opinion that the court's ruling on this question was wrong, and that it sufficiently appears, when the proceedings are rightly interpreted, that the object of the investigation and of the effort to secure the witness's testimony was to obtain information for legislative purposes.

It is quite true that the resolution directing the investigation does not in terms avow that it is intended to be in aid of legislation; but it does show that the subject to be investigated was the administration of the Department of Justice—whether its functions were being properly discharged or were being neglected or misdirected, and particularly whether the Attorney General and his assistants were performing or neglecting their duties in respect of the institution and prosecution of proceedings to punish crimes and enforce appropriate remedies against the wrongdoers—specific instances of alleged neglect being recited. Plainly the subject was one on which legislation could be had and would be materially aided by the information which the investigation was calculated to elicit. This becomes manifest when it is reflected that the functions of the Department of Justice, the powers and duties of the Attorney General and the duties of his assistants, are all subject to regulation by congressional legislation, and that the department is maintained and its activities are carried on

---

4 **Questions:** The decisions that Van Devanter is referring to in this paragraph held that neither house of Congress could require a witness to answer questions that are not necessary and proper for exercising its powers to legislate, make rules, expel members, etc. Do you agree that this is sufficient protection?

Consider what happened after the Court issued this opinion. A decade later, the House of Representatives established the House Un-American Activities Committee, which subpoenaed alleged subversives in the federal government. In 1950, Senator Joseph McCarthy initiated his own investigation of alleged Communists. These investigations ruined many people's lives while revealing little evidence of espionage.

If you were on the *McGrain v. Daugherty* Court and knew that these sorts of investigations were on the horizon, would you have modified Van Devanter's opinion?

under such appropriations as in the judgment of Congress are needed from year to year.

The only legitimate object the Senate could have in ordering the investigation was to aid it in legislating; and we think the subject-matter was such that the presumption should be indulged that this was the real object. An express avowal of the object would have been better; but in view of the particular subject-matter was not indispensable. . . .

We conclude that the investigation was ordered for a legitimate object; that the witness wrongfully refused to appear and testify before the committee and was lawfully attached; that the Senate is entitled to have him give testimony pertinent to the inquiry, either at its bar or before the committee; and that the district court erred in discharging him from custody under the attachment. . . .

NOTE: LIMITS ON CONGRESS'S POWER TO INVESTIGATE

Although *McGrain* remains the leading precedent for Congress's power to investigate and hold someone in contempt, later cases have refined and limited its powers, particularly after high-profile abuses of the investigation and contempt powers in the early years of the Cold War by the Senate Permanent Subcommittee on Investigations, chaired by Joseph McCarthy of Wisconsin, and the House Committee on Un-American Activities, whose contempt convictions led to the blacklisting of dozens of left-wing intellectuals and entertainment figures.

One of the more important limits was imposed by *Watkins v. United States*, 354 U.S. 178 (1957), a case involving an alleged Communist, in which the Court held that witnesses before Congress were protected by the Bill of Rights, including the Fifth Amendment's protection against self-incrimination and deprivations of liberty without due process. This limit allows witnesses to refuse to answer questions that are not "pertinent to the question under inquiry"—or that might lead to their later prosecution. *Watkins*, 354 U.S. at 207–08.

Recently, in *Trump v. Mazars USA, LLP*, 140 S. Ct. 2019 (2020), the Court introduced another limit on Congress's subpoena power. In April 2019, three House committees issued four subpoenas to banks and other companies seeking the financial records of President Donald Trump and his affiliated businesses. *See Mazars*, 140 S. Ct. at 2026. Trump sued the banks in his personal capacity to quash the subpoenas. When the case reached the Supreme Court, Chief Justice John Roberts reaffirmed *McGrain*'s holding that "each House has power 'to secure needed information' in order to legislate." *Id.* at 2031–32. But he added that "the usual rules for congressional subpoenas" change when the president's personal documents are at stake. *Id.* at 2032 (quoting *United States v. Nixon*, 418 U.S. 683, 713 (1974)). Invoking the separation of powers, Roberts explained that "without limits on its subpoena powers, Congress could . . . aggrandize itself at the President's expense." *Id.* at 2034. The Court therefore held that when a subpoena seeks the president's personal information, courts must ensure that the subpoena is narrowly tailored to advance a legislative purpose significant enough to justify any burdens that it imposes on the president. *Id.* at 2036.

23.2 THE FREEDOM FROM ARREST AND OF SPEECH AND DEBATE

Congress develops laws not only by collecting information; its members also speak and debate with one another about the wisdom and constitutionality of a proposed course of action. Congress's ability to legislate would therefore be seriously curtailed if members could be punished by the executive branch or courts for what members introduced or said to one another.

These sorts of punishments happened often in English history. In 1512, for example, a local court in England's largest tin-mining region fined and imprisoned Richard Strode, a member of Parliament, because he had introduced bills to regulate the tin industry. *See* Josh Chafetz, *Congress's Constitution: Legislative Authority and the Separation of Powers* 201–11 (2017). Parliament's experience with attempts to silence its members led to its enforcement of a strong norm, codified in the 1688 Bill of Rights, "that the Freedome of Speech and Debates or Proceedings in Parlyament ought not to be impeached or questioned in any Court or Place out of Parlyament."

The Constitutional Convention adopted similar language in Article I, Section 6:

> They shall in all Cases, except Treason, Felony and Breach of the Peace, be privileged from Arrest during their Attendance at the Session of their respective Houses, and in going to and returning from the same; and for any Speech or Debate in either House, they shall not be questioned in any other Place.

Justice Joseph Story, in his influential book, called both privileges "great and vital." *Commentaries on the Constitution* § 866 (1833). Without these, he wrote, "all other privileges would be comparatively unimportant or ineffectual." *Id.*

Despite Story's words, the protection from arrest has proved to be next to useless. In the 1930s, Huey Long was one of the country's most powerful and outspoken proponents of left-wing populism, first as the governor of Louisiana and later as a U.S. senator. His speeches and policies made him many enemies. In 1933, while he was serving in the Senate, one of the targets of his speeches sued him for defamation. He challenged this suit under the Privilege from Arrest Clause, but the Supreme Court rejected his claim in a brief opinion. *Long v. Ansell*, 293 U.S. 76, 82 (1934). Interpreting historical precedents from Parliament and state legislatures, the Court concluded "that the immunity is limited to arrest . . . in civil suits"—that is, attempts to confine a person until that person pays a judgment or complies with a civil order, in contrast with a criminal arrest or, in Long's case, a service of process. *Id.* at 82–83. "When the Constitution was adopted, arrests in civil suits were still common in America," the Court wrote. *Id.* at 83. "It is only to such arrests that the provision applies." *Id.*

The clause's protection of the freedom of speech or debate has had longer legs. In *Kilbourn v. Thompson*, 103 U.S. 168 (1880), one of the cases about Congress's contempt power, Hallet Kilbourn sued not only the sergeant at arms who arrested him—John G. Thompson—but also the members of the House who had voted to hold him in contempt. Although the Court agreed with Kilbourn that contempt was unwarranted in his case, it disagreed that he could sue members of the House for their votes. Tracing the history of the Speech or Debate Clause through Parliament and colonial legislatures, the Court wrote that "[i]t would be a narrow view of the constitutional provision to limit it to words spoken in debate." *Kilbourn*, 103 U.S. at 204. For "if a report, or a resolution, or a vote is not a speech or debate, of what value is the constitutional protection?" *Id.* at 201. A better reading, the Court concluded, is to interpret the rule in light of its historical purpose in protecting legislators as they develop legislation and policy:

> The reason of the rule is as forcible in its application to written reports presented in that body by its committees, to resolutions offered, which, though in writing, must be reproduced in speech, and to the act of voting, whether it is done vocally or by passing between the tellers. In short, to things generally done in a session of the House by one of its members in relation to the business before it.

Id. at 204.

The *Kilbourn* Court reserved the question of whether the clause protected members of Congress from being prosecuted for crimes, writing that "we are not prepared to say that such an utter perversion of their powers to a criminal purpose would be screened from punishment by the constitutional provision for freedom of debate." *Id.* at 205. Although the Court held in *United States v. Johnson*, 383 U.S. 169 (1966), that a criminal trial could not examine the context behind a speech to determine whether a member accepted a bribe in order to make it, in *United States v. Brewster*, 408 U.S. 501 (1972), the Court reversed course and held that a member could be charged with accepting a bribe as long as the charge didn't call into question a legislative act or the motivation behind it.

Other disputes over the Speech or Debate Clause have turned over (1) whether its protection is limited to congressional members as opposed to their aides and (2) whether it applies to unofficial speeches and debates, such as press conferences. Both questions arose in the following case.

23.2.1

Gravel v. United States

408 U.S. 606 (1972)

In the late spring of 1971, the *New York Times* published a front-page story about a leaked three-thousand-page research study conducted by the Pentagon in secret. *See* Neil Sheehan, *Vietnam Archive: Pentagon Study Traces 3 Decades of Growing U.S. Involvement*, Jun. 13, 1971, at 1. The so-called Pentagon Papers detailed how, from 1945 to 1967, the U.S. government had systematically lied to the public about its role and intentions in escalating American military involvement in Vietnam. The story was sensational. On the request of the Nixon administration, a federal court ordered the *New York Times* to cease publication after three articles.

To evade this court order, a reporter at the *Washington Post* sent another leaked copy of the Pentagon Papers to Senator Mike Gravel of Alaska. *See* Chafetz, *supra*, at 215–16. Taking advantage of the Speech or Debate Clause, Gravel convened a nighttime meeting of the Senate Subcommittee on Public Buildings and Grounds and spent an hour reading excerpts of the Pentagon Papers aloud. *Id.* With the help of an aide, Leonard Rodberg, he then entered the remainder of the forty-seven volumes into the public record. *Id.* Afterward, he and the aide sought to arrange the private publication of the Pentagon Papers by a Boston-based publisher.

The Department of Justice, investigating whether any of this violated federal antileaking laws, asked a federal court to subpoena Gravel and Rodberg to testify before a grand jury. *Id.* Gravel and Rodberg moved to quash, or cancel, the subpoenas on the ground that they violated the Speech or Debate Clause. The district court and court of appeals agreed with respect to the senator's conduct before the subcommittee. Both courts, however, would have allowed the senator and his aide to be questioned regarding the private publication of the Pentagon Papers.

Gravel petitioned the Supreme Court for a writ of certiorari. In *Gravel v. United States*, 408 U.S. 606 (1972), the Court heard arguments about (1) whether Rodberg, an aide, was protected by the clause and (2) whether the clause applied to how Gravel originally received the Pentagon Papers and how he planned to publish them.

The Court construed the Speech or Debate Clause narrowly.

■ Opinion of the Court by MR. JUSTICE WHITE.[5]

I

[B]ecause the claim is that a Member's aide shares the Member's constitutional privilege, we consider first whether and to what extent Senator Gravel himself is exempt from process or inquiry by a grand jury investigating the commission of a crime. Our frame of reference is Art. I, § 6, cl. 1, of the Constitution:

"The Senators and Representatives shall . . . in all Cases, except Treason, Felony and Breach of the Peace, be privileged from Arrest during their Attendance at the Session of their respective Houses, and in going to and returning from the same;

[5] **As You Read, Consider:** What does Justice Byron White think is the purpose of the Speech or Debate Clause? Does he interpret the clause narrowly or broadly?

and for any Speech or Debate in either House, they shall not be questioned in any other Place."

The last sentence of the Clause provides Members of Congress with two distinct privileges. Except in cases of "Treason, Felony and Breach of the Peace," the Clause shields Members from arrest while attending or traveling to and from a session of their House. History reveals, and prior cases so hold, that this part of the Clause exempts Members from arrest in civil cases only. [*Long v. Ansell*, 293 U. S. 76, 83 (1934)]. Nor does freedom from arrest confer immunity on a Member from service of process as a defendant in civil matters or as a witness in a criminal case. . . . It is, therefore, sufficiently plain that the constitutional freedom from arrest does not exempt Members of Congress from the operation of the ordinary criminal laws, even though imprisonment may prevent or interfere with the performance of their duties as Members. . . . Indeed, implicit in the narrow scope of the privilege of freedom from arrest is, as Jefferson noted, the judgment that legislators ought not to stand above the law they create but ought generally to be bound by it as are ordinary persons. T. Jefferson, Manual of Parliamentary Practice, S. Doc. No. 92-1, p. 437 (1971).

In recognition, no doubt, of the force of this part of § 6, Senator Gravel disavows any assertion of general immunity from the criminal law. But he points out that the last portion of § 6 affords Members of Congress another vital privilege—they may not be questioned in any other place for any speech or debate in either House. The claim is not that while one part of § 6 generally permits prosecutions for treason, felony, and breach of the peace, another part nevertheless broadly forbids them. Rather, his insistence is that the Speech or Debate Clause at the very least protects him from criminal or civil liability and from questioning elsewhere than in the Senate, with respect to the events occurring at the subcommittee hearing at which the Pentagon Papers were introduced into the public record. To us this claim is incontrovertible. The Speech or Debate Clause was designed to assure a co-equal branch of the government wide freedom of speech, debate, and deliberation without intimidation or threats from the Executive Branch. It thus protects Members against prosecutions that directly impinge upon or threaten the legislative process. We have no doubt that Senator Gravel may not be made to answer—either in terms of questions or in terms of defending himself from prosecution—for the events that occurred at the subcommittee meeting. . . .

Even so, the United States strongly urges that because the Speech or Debate Clause confers a privilege only upon "Senators and Representatives," Rodberg himself has no valid claim to constitutional immunity from grand jury inquiry. In our view, both courts below correctly rejected this position. . . . Both courts recognized what the Senate of the United States urgently presses here: that it is literally impossible, in view of the complexities of the modern legislative process, with Congress almost constantly in session and matters of legislative concern constantly proliferating, for Members of Congress to perform their legislative tasks without the help of aides and assistants; that the day-to-day work of such aides is so critical to the Members' performance that they must be treated as the latter's alter egos; and that if they are not so recognized, the central role of the Speech or Debate Clause—to prevent intimidation of legislators by the Executive and accountability before a possibly hostile judiciary, *United States v. Johnson*, 383 U. S. 169, 181 (1966), will inevitably be diminished and frustrated. . . .

II

We are convinced also that the Court of Appeals correctly determined that Senator Gravel's alleged arrangement with Beacon Press to publish the Pentagon Papers was not protected speech or debate within the meaning of Art. I, § 6, cl. 1, of the Constitution.

Prior cases have read the Speech or Debate Clause "broadly to effectuate its purposes," *United States v. Johnson*, 383 U. S., at 180, and have included within its reach anything "generally done in a session of the House by one of its members in relation to the business before it." *Kilbourn v. Thompson*, 103 U. S., at 204. . . . But the Clause has not been extended beyond the legislative sphere. That Senators generally perform certain acts in their official capacity as Senators does not necessarily make all such acts legislative in nature. Members of Congress are constantly in touch with the Executive Branch of the Government and with administrative agencies—they may cajole, and exhort with respect to the administration of a federal statute—but such conduct, though generally done, is not protected legislative activity. . . .

Legislative acts are not all-encompassing. The heart of the Clause is speech or debate in either House. Insofar as the Clause is construed to reach other matters, they must be an integral part of the deliberative and communicative processes by which Members participate in committee and House proceedings with respect to the consideration and passage or rejection of proposed legislation or with respect to other matters which the Constitution places within the jurisdiction of either House. . . . Here, private publication by Senator Gravel through the cooperation of Beacon Press was in no way essential to the deliberations of the Senate; nor does questioning as to private publication threaten the integrity or independence of the Senate by impermissibly exposing its deliberations to executive influence. The Senator had conducted his hearings; the record and any report that was forthcoming were available both to his committee and the Senate. Insofar as we are advised, neither Congress nor the full committee ordered or authorized the publication. We cannot but conclude that the Senator's arrangements with Beacon Press were not part and parcel of the legislative process. . . .[6]

NOTE: PUBLIC DISSEMINATION

Gravel's obvious goal in entering the Pentagon Papers into the record was to publicly disseminate their contents. But the *Gravel* Court held that the private publication of the Pentagon Papers was unprotected by the Speech or Debate Clause, and subsequent cases have further limited the clause's protection for this sort of publication. In *Doe v. McMillan*, the Court held that the clause protects the publication of reports "for the information and use of Members in the performance of their legislative duties" but does *not* protect publication to "inform[ ] the public concerning matters pending before Congress." 412 U.S. 306, 314 (1973). It regarded this latter purpose as not "an integral part" of the legislative process. *Id.* In *Hutchinson v.*

---

[6] **Questions:** Consider what members of Congress spend much of their time doing: holding press conferences, tweeting, fundraising, and otherwise rallying public awareness around their legislative agenda. Do you agree with White that, even in a world in which public opinion determines what sort of legislation will pass or fail, any attempt to shape this opinion outside of Congress is not "legislative activity"?

By contrast, consider the actions of several members of Congress in the wake of the 2020 election. As President Donald Trump complained that the election was fraudulent, two senators announced on the Senate floor that they would object to the certification of electoral votes when Congress assembled for that purpose on January 6, 2021. Other members allegedly sent emails and text messages to help plan an outdoor rally, scheduled the same day, with the goal of pressuring additional lawmakers to object. Some of these members spoke at the rally, urging participants to "fight for America"; rally participants ultimately stormed the Capitol by force, leading to several deaths. *See* Catie Edmonson & Luke Broadwater, *Before Capitol Riot, Republican Lawmakers Fanned the Flames*, N.Y. Times, Jan. 29, 2021. Would all of the members' actions be protected by the Speech or Debate Clause?

Proxmire, 443 U.S. 111 (1979), the Court added that press releases and communications with constituents are similarly unprotected because they are not integral to legislative matters.

23.3 THE POWER TO EXCLUDE, PUNISH, AND EXPEL

Although the Constitutional Convention was never able to reach anything more than a wishy-washy consensus on the appropriate qualifications for voters, at least with regard to House members, it was able to decide on some specific qualifications for members of Congress. For both representatives and senators, Sections 2 and 3 of Article I prescribed age, citizenship, and residency requirements. Section 5 also gave each house the power to judge "the Elections, Returns and Qualifications of its own Members," as well as the power to "punish its Members for disorderly Behaviour, and, with the Concurrence of two thirds, expel a Member." Like the power to investigate and the freedom of speech, these powers were familiar to the British Parliament and state legislatures. As one Federalist argued during the ratification debate in Massachusetts, "[n]o one, who professes to be governed by reason, will dispute the propriety of any assembly's being the judge of the qualifications requisite to constitute a member of their own body." 5 *Documentary History of the Ratification of the Constitution* 479 (John P. Kaminski et al. eds., 1998).

As soon became apparent, however, it was not obvious whether Congress's power to judge the "Qualifications" of its members was limited to the power to check a member-elect's age, citizenship, and residency, or whether it also included the additional power to create *new* qualifications such as good moral character. In *Luther v. Borden*, when the Supreme Court held that the legitimacy of Rhode Island's government was a political question, it suggested that Congress could exclude any senators and representatives from a state that failed to be adequately "republican" in violation of the Guarantee Clause of Article IV. 48 U.S. (7 How.) 1, 42 (1849). Congress did just that after the Civil War. As states of the former Confederacy held elections and sent representatives and senators to Congress, both houses informally excluded the members-elect from sitting until satisfied with their loyalty. *See, e.g.*, 1 *Hinds' Precedents of the House of Representatives of the United States* §§ 445, 449–51 (Asher C. Hinds ed., 1907). Congress codified this practice with the first Reconstruction Act of 1867, ch. 153, 14 Stat. 428. That statute excluded representatives of former Confederate states from Congress absent evidence that their state's government allowed black men to vote and had ratified the then-pending Fourteenth Amendment.

The Supreme Court never evaluated the legality of this exclusion, but in the years after Reconstruction, it approached Congress's powers to judge elections and punish and expel members with deference. In a case upholding the Senate's power to compel a witness to testify about the misconduct of a member, *In re Chapman*, the Court explained that the investigatory power was implied by the Senate's power to punish and expel members, which "extends to all cases where the offense is such as in the judgment of the Senate is inconsistent with the trust and duty of a member." 166 U.S. 661, 669 (1897). In *Barry v. United States ex rel. Cunningham*, 279 U.S. 597 (1929), the Court added that the Senate had similarly broad powers to investigate the election of a senator-elect who had allegedly received bribes. Article I, Section 5, the Court explained, "carries with it authority to take such steps as may be appropriate and necessary to secure information upon which to decide concerning elections." *Barry*, 279 U.S. at 613. This gave the Senate the power not only "to compel [witnesses] to answer pertinent questions, to determine the facts and apply the appropriate rules of law, and, finally, to render a judgment" but also to exclude senators-elect if it determined that they had not been properly elected. *Id.*

Chapman and *Barry* appeared to give both houses of Congress broad authority to exclude members for whatever reasons they wished. But it was not until 1969 that the Court directly reviewed Congress's power to exclude a member on the basis of qualifications not expressed in the text of Article I, Section 2.

23.3.1

Powell v. McCormack

395 U.S. 486 (1969)

Adam Clayton Powell Jr., a gregarious representative from Harlem, was the most powerful black member of Congress in the 1960s. As chair of the House Committee on Education and Labor, he was outspoken on civil rights issues and an important shepherd of the decade's progressive legislation. He was also, in the eyes of many of his colleagues, corrupt. In 1966, an investigation by a House subcommittee reported that Powell had taken private trips at public expense and had directed illegal payments to his wife.

When the ninetieth Congress met to take the oath of office in January 1967, Powell was deposed of his chairmanship and asked to step aside while the oath was administered to other members-elect. Joseph A. Loftus, *Democrats Vote to Oust Powell as House Committee's Chairman; He May Be Kept from Seat Today*, N.Y. Times, Jan. 10, 1967, at 1. Powell called the proceedings "a lynching—Northern style." *Id.* He argued that he was being singled out for conduct that every other member had exhibited. *See* Wil Haygood, *The King of Cats: The Life and Times of Adam Clayton Powell Jr.* 351–52 (1994). His claim that the proceedings were racially motivated was supported by the fact that Julian Bond, a prominent civil rights leader, had been similarly excluded from sitting on the Georgia legislature because of his antiwar views—an exclusion that the Supreme Court rejected on First Amendment grounds in *Bond v. Floyd*, 385 U.S. 116 (1966).

Nevertheless, by a vote of 363 to 65, the House adopted a resolution providing for a select committee to determine whether Powell was qualified to become a member of the ninetieth Congress. Powell refused to testify before the House committee on anything "other than his eligibility under the standing qualifications of Art. I, § 2," which he called the exclusive requirements for membership. *See Powell v. McCormack*, 395 U.S. 486, 492 (1969). That section states: "No Person shall be a Representative who shall not have attained to the Age of twenty five Years, and been seven Years a Citizen of the United States, and who shall not, when elected, be an Inhabitant of that State in which he shall be chosen."

The committee found that Powell met the qualifications of Article I, Section 2, and therefore must be seated—after which he could be censured and fined. But the House rejected this recommendation 222–202. *See Powell*, 395 U.S. at 492. Afterward, Speaker of the House John W. McCormack called for a majority vote on a resolution, H.R. Res. 278, 90th Cong. (1967), to exclude Powell from his seat. This was adopted 307–116—more than the two-thirds necessary to expel a member. *See Powell*, 395 U.S. at 493.

Powell subsequently sued the speaker and several members of the House staff, including the sergeant at arms, for their roles in excluding him from office. As his case wound its way to the Supreme Court, he also ran again for office, successfully winning back his seat in the 1968 election. *Id.* at 495.

By the time the Supreme Court heard Powell's case in 1969, Powell had been seated as a member of the ninety-first Congress. But the question remained whether the House had acted constitutionally in excluding him from the ninetieth Congress. The below excerpt picks up after the Court determined that the case was not moot because Powell had never been paid his salary as a member of the ninetieth Congress. The three remaining questions in *Powell v. McCormack* were (1) whether Powell's lawsuit was barred by the Speech or Debate Clause, (2) whether H.R. Res. 278 could be understood as a vote to expel rather than to exclude Powell, and (3) whether Congress's power to exclude members for reasons other than those listed in Article I, Section 2, was a political question.

In answering these questions, the Court determined that Powell had the right to serve in the ninetieth Congress and should not have been excluded.

■ MR. CHIEF JUSTICE WARREN delivered the opinion of the Court.[7]

In November 1966, petitioner Adam Clayton Powell, Jr., was duly elected from the 18th Congressional District of New York to serve in the United States House of

[7] **As You Read, Consider:** Article I, Section 2, includes an age, citizenship, and residence requirement but does not state whether Congress can introduce additional qualifications. Section 5, meanwhile, states that "[e]ach House shall be the Judge of the Elections, Returns and Qualifications of its own Members." How does Chief Justice Earl Warren conclude whether this

Representatives for the 90th Congress. However, pursuant to a House resolution, he was not permitted to take his seat. Powell (and some of the voters of his district) then filed suit in Federal District Court, claiming that the House could exclude him only if it found he failed to meet the standing requirements of age, citizenship, and residence contained in Art. I, § 2, of the Constitution—requirements the House specifically found Powell met—and thus had excluded him unconstitutionally. . . . [We have determined] that petitioner Powell is entitled to a declaratory judgment that he was unlawfully excluded from the 90th Congress. . . .

III.

SPEECH OR DEBATE CLAUSE.

Respondents assert that the Speech or Debate Clause of the Constitution, Art. I, § 6, is an absolute bar to petitioners' action. . . . Our cases make it clear that the legislative immunity created by the Speech or Debate Clause performs an important function in representative government. . . . [But] [l]egislative immunity does not, of course, bar all judicial review of legislative acts. That issue was settled by implication as early as 1803, see *Marbury v. Madison*, 1 Cranch 137, and expressly in *Kilbourn v. Thompson*, the first of this Court's cases interpreting the reach of the Speech or Debate Clause. . . .[8]

[P]etitioners brought this suit against several House employees—the Sergeant at Arms, the Doorkeeper and the Clerk—as well as several Congressmen. . . . That House employees are acting pursuant to express orders of the House does not bar judicial review of the constitutionality of the underlying legislative decision. *Kilbourn* decisively settles this question, since [in that case] the Sergeant at Arms was held liable for false imprisonment even though he did nothing more than execute the House Resolution that Kilbourn be arrested and imprisoned.

In *Kilbourn* . . . we thus dismissed the action against members of Congress but did not regard the Speech or Debate Clause as a bar to reviewing the merits of the challenged congressional action since congressional employees were also sued. Similarly, though this action may be dismissed against the Congressmen[,] petitioners are entitled to maintain their action against House employees and to judicial review of the propriety of the decision to exclude petitioner Powell. . . .

IV.

EXCLUSION OR EXPULSION.

The resolution excluding petitioner Powell was adopted by a vote in excess of two-thirds of the 434 Members of Congress—307 to 116. 113 Cong. Rec. 5037–5038. Article I, § 5, grants the House authority to expel a member "with the Concurrence of two thirds." Respondents assert that the House may expel a member for any reason whatsoever and that, since a two-thirds vote was obtained, the procedure by which Powell was denied his seat in the 90th Congress should be regarded as an expulsion, not an exclusion. . . .

Although respondents repeatedly urge this Court not to speculate as to the reasons for Powell's exclusion, their attempt to equate exclusion with expulsion would require a similar speculation that the House would have voted to expel Powell had it been faced with that question. Powell had not been seated at the time House

---

textual commitment makes the question of qualifications a political question for the House to decide?

8 **Question:** Prior cases establishing the scope of the Speech or Debate Clause make clear that Adam Clayton Powell Jr. could not have sued the members of Congress who voted to exclude him. Do you agree with Warren that Powell can nevertheless challenge the constitutionality of the House's exclusion by suing the *sergeant at arms*?

Resolution No. 278 was debated and passed. . . . The Speaker [explained] that "action by a majority vote would be in accordance with the rules." *Ibid.* Had [Resolution No. 278] been regarded as an attempt to expel Powell, a two-thirds vote would have been constitutionally required. The Speaker ruled that the House was voting to exclude Powell, and we will not speculate what the result might have been if Powell had been seated and expulsion proceedings subsequently instituted. . . .[9]

VI.

JUSTICIABILITY.

[R]espondents maintain that [this case] presents only a political question. . . . In *Baker v. Carr, supra,* . . . [a]fter reviewing our decisions in this area, we concluded that on the surface of any case held to involve a political question was at least one of the following formulations:

> "[1] a textually demonstrable constitutional commitment of the issue to a coordinate political department; or [2] a lack of judicially discoverable and manageable standards for resolving it; or [3] the impossibility of deciding without an initial policy determination of a kind clearly for nonjudicial discretion; or [4] the impossibility of a court's undertaking independent resolution without expressing lack of the respect due coordinate branches of government; or [5] an unusual need for unquestioning adherence to a political decision already made; or [6] the potentiality of embarrassment from multifarious pronouncements by various departments on one question."

Respondents' [principal] contention is that this case presents a political question because under Art. I, § 5, there has been a "textually demonstrable constitutional commitment" to the House of the "adjudicatory power" to determine Powell's qualifications. Thus it is argued that the House, and the House alone, has power to determine who is qualified to be a member. . . .

In order to determine the scope of any "textual commitment" under Art. I, § 5, we necessarily must determine the meaning of the phrase to "be the Judge of the Qualifications of its own Members." Petitioners argue that the records of the debates during the Constitutional Convention; available commentary from the post-Convention, pre-ratification period; and early congressional applications of Art. I, § 5, support their construction of the section. Respondents insist, however, that a careful examination of the pre-Convention practices of the English Parliament and American colonial assemblies demonstrates that by 1787, a legislature's power to judge the qualifications of its members was generally understood to encompass exclusion or expulsion on the ground that an individual's character or past conduct rendered him unfit to serve. . . .

Our examination of the relevant historical materials leads us to the conclusion that petitioners are correct and that the Constitution leaves the House without authority to *exclude* any person, duly elected by his constituents, who meets all the requirements for membership expressly prescribed in the Constitution.

a. The Pre-Convention Precedents.

[There are a number of precedents from sixteenth- and seventeenth-century England and America in which legislatures excluded elected members, including the

---

[9] **Questions:** Here, Warren is observing that members who voted to *exclude* Powell might have voted differently if they knew that a two-thirds vote for *expulsion* was required. Do you agree? Or does the lopsided vote suggest that this suit need not be decided because there was no way that Powell could have sat in the ninetieth Congress?

controversial exclusion of John Wilkes for seditious libel in 1764. The House of Commons repudiated his exclusion in 1782.]

With the successful resolution of Wilkes' long and bitter struggle for the right of the British electorate to be represented by men of their own choice, it is evident that, on the eve of the Constitutional Convention, English precedent stood for the proposition that "the law of the land had regulated the qualifications of members to serve in parliament" and those qualifications were "not occasional but fixed." 16 Parl. Hist. Eng. 589, 590 (1769). Certainly English practice did not support, nor had it ever supported, respondents' assertion that the power to judge qualifications was generally understood to encompass the right to exclude members-elect for general misconduct not within standing qualifications. . . .

b. Convention Debates.

Relying heavily on Charles Warren's analysis of the Convention debates, petitioners argue that the proceedings manifest the Framers' unequivocal intention to deny either branch of Congress the authority to add to or otherwise vary the membership qualifications expressly set forth in the Constitution. We do not completely agree, for the debates are subject to other interpretations. However, we have concluded that the records of the debates, viewed in the context of the bitter struggle for the right to freely choose representatives which had recently concluded in England and in light of the distinction the Framers made between the power to expel and the power to exclude, indicate that petitioners' ultimate conclusion is correct.[10]

The Convention opened in late May 1787. By the end of July, the delegates adopted, with a minimum of debate, age requirements for membership in both the Senate and the House. . . . [After tabling a vigorous debate over whether to introduce property qualifications, the delegates unanimously adopted the citizenship and residency requirements embodied in Article I, Section 2.]

On August 10, the Convention considered the Committee of Detail's proposal that the "Legislature of the United States shall have authority to establish such uniform qualifications of the members of each House, with regard to property, as to the said Legislature shall seem expedient." *Id.*, at 179. The debate on this proposal discloses much about the views of the Framers on the issue of qualifications. For example, James Madison urged its rejection, stating that the proposal would vest "an improper & dangerous power in the Legislature. The qualifications of electors and elected were fundamental articles in a Republican Govt. and ought to be fixed by the Constitution. If the Legislature could regulate those of either, it can by degrees subvert the Constitution. A Republic may be converted into an aristocracy or oligarchy as well by limiting the number capable of being elected, as the number authorised to elect. . . ." *Id.*, at 249–250.

Significantly, Madison's argument was not aimed at the imposition of a property qualification as such, but rather at the delegation to the Congress of the discretionary power to establish any qualifications. . . . Shortly thereafter, the Convention rejected . . . the Committee's proposal. Later the same day, the Convention adopted without

[10] **Question:** Warren is relying heavily on a 1911 transcription of the Constitutional Convention's debates by Max Farrand, a Yale historian. Yet Farrand himself relied heavily on notes completed by James Madison after the convention concluded. In fact, Madison continued to revise his notes well into the nineteenth century, sometimes to make his own positions seem more reasonable in light of subsequent events. *See* Mary Sarah Bilder, *Madison's Hand: Revising the Constitutional Convention* 9–13 (2015). Does it nevertheless make sense for the Supreme Court to rely on these edited notes to determine the intent of the Constitution's authors?

debate the provision authorizing each House to be "the judge of the . . . qualifications of its own members." *Id.*, at 254.

One other decision made the same day is very important to determining the meaning of Art. I, § 5. When the delegates reached the Committee of Detail's proposal to empower each House to expel its members, Madison "observed that the right of expulsion . . . was too important to be exercised by a bare majority of a quorum: and in emergencies [one] faction might be dangerously abused." *Id.*, at 254. He therefore moved that "with the concurrence of two-thirds" be inserted. With the exception of one State, whose delegation was divided, the motion was unanimously approved without debate. . . . The importance of this decision cannot be over-emphasized. None of the parties to this suit disputes that prior to 1787 the legislative powers to judge qualifications and to expel were exercised by a majority vote. Indeed, without exception, the English and colonial antecedents to Art. I, § 5, cls. 1 and 2, support this conclusion. Thus, the Convention's decision to increase the vote required to expel, because that power was "too important to be exercised by a bare majority," while at the same time not similarly restricting the power to judge qualifications, is compelling evidence that they considered the latter already limited by the standing qualifications previously adopted. . . .

Petitioners also argue that the post-Convention debates over the Constitution's ratification support their interpretation of § 5. For example, they emphasize Hamilton's reply to the antifederalist charge that the new Constitution favored the wealthy and well-born:

> "The truth is that there is no method of securing to the rich the preference apprehended but by prescribing qualifications of property either for those who may elect or be elected. But this forms no part of the power to be conferred upon the national government. Its authority would be expressly restricted to the regulation of the *times*, the *places*, the *manner* of elections. *The qualifications of the persons who may choose or be chosen, as has been remarked upon other occasions, are defined and fixed in the Constitution, and are unalterable by the legislature.*" The Federalist Papers 371 (Mentor ed. 1961). (Emphasis in last sentence added.) . . .

c. Post-Ratification.

As clear as these statements appear, respondents dismiss them as "general statements . . . directed to other issues." They suggest that far more relevant is Congress' own understanding of its power to judge qualifications as manifested in post-ratification exclusion cases. Unquestionably, both the House and the Senate have excluded members-elect for reasons other than their failure to meet the Constitution's standing qualifications. For almost the first 100 years of its existence, however, Congress strictly limited its power to judge the qualifications of its members to those enumerated in the Constitution.

Congress was first confronted with the issue in 1807, when the eligibility of William McCreery was challenged because he did not meet additional residency requirements imposed by the State of Maryland. In recommending that he be seated, the House Committee of Elections reasoned:

> "The committee proceeded to examine the Constitution, with relation to the case submitted to them, and find that qualifications of members are therein determined, without reserving any authority to the State Legislatures to change, add to, or diminish those qualifications; and that, by that instrument, Congress is constituted the sole judge of the qualifications prescribed by it, and are obliged to decide agreeably to the Constitutional rules . . . ." 17 Annals of Cong. 871 (1807). . . .

The chairman emphasized that the committee's narrow construction of the power of the House to judge qualifications was compelled by the "fundamental principle in a free government," *id.*, at 873, that restrictions upon the people to choose their own representatives must be limited to those "absolutely necessary for the safety of the society." *Id.*, at 874. At the conclusion of a lengthy debate, which tended to center on the more narrow issue of the power of the States to add to the standing qualifications set forth in the Constitution, the House agreed by a vote of 89 to 18 to seat Congressman McCreery. *Id.*, at 1237. See 1 A. Hinds, Precedents of the House of Representatives of the United States § 414 (1907) (hereinafter cited as Hinds).

There was no significant challenge to these principles for the next several decades. They came under heavy attack, however, "during the stress of civil war [but initially] the House of Representatives declined to exercise the power [to exclude], even under circumstances of great provocation." Rules of the House of Representatives, H. R. Doc. No. 529, 89th Cong., 2d Sess., § 12, p. 7 (1967). The abandonment of such restraint, however, was among the casualties of the general upheaval produced in war's wake. In 1868, the House voted for the first time in its history to exclude a member-elect. It refused to seat two duly elected representatives for giving aid and comfort to the Confederacy. See 1 Hinds §§ 449–451. "This change was produced by the North's bitter enmity toward those who failed to support the Union cause during the war, and was effected by the Radical Republican domination of Congress. It was a shift brought about by the naked urgency of power and was given little doctrinal support." Comment, Legislative Exclusion: Julian Bond and Adam Clayton Powell, 35 U. Chi. L. Rev. 151, 157 (1967). From that time until the present, congressional practice has been erratic; and on the few occasions when a member-elect was excluded although he met all the qualifications set forth in the Constitution, there were frequently vigorous dissents. Even the annotations to the official manual of procedure for the 90th Congress manifest doubt as to the House's power to exclude a member-elect who has met the constitutionally prescribed qualifications. See Rules of the House of Representatives, H. R. Doc. No. 529, 89th Cong., 2d Sess., § 12, pp. 7–8 (1967).[11]

Had these congressional exclusion precedents been more consistent, their precedential value still would be quite limited. See Note, The Power of a House of Congress to Judge the Qualifications of its Members, 81 Harv. L. Rev. 673, 679 (1968). That an unconstitutional action has been taken before surely does not render that same action any less unconstitutional at a later date. Particularly in view of the Congress' own doubts in those few cases where it did exclude members-elect, we are not inclined to give its precedents controlling weight. The relevancy of prior exclusion cases is limited largely to the insight they afford in correctly ascertaining the draftsmen's intent. Obviously, therefore, the precedential value of these cases tends to increase in proportion to their proximity to the Convention in 1787. See *Myers v. United States*, 272 U.S. 52, 175 (1926). And, what evidence we have of Congress' early understanding confirms our conclusion that the House is without power to exclude any member-elect who meets the Constitution's requirements for membership.

d. Conclusion.

Had the intent of the Framers emerged from these materials with less clarity, we would nevertheless have been compelled to resolve any ambiguity in favor of a

---

[11] **Question:** Note the way that Warren dismisses the significance of precedents set during the Reconstruction era. This has been a common pattern since the Court condemned the impeachment of President Andrew Johnson in *Myers v. United States*, 272 U.S. 51 (1926) (see section 27.3). Do you agree that congressional exclusion of former Confederates should have little bearing in an opinion whose analysis is dominated by the principle of settled practice?

narrow construction of the scope of Congress' power to exclude members-elect. A fundamental principle of our representative democracy is, in Hamilton's words, "that the people should choose whom they please to govern them." 2 Elliot's Debates 257. As Madison pointed out at the Convention, this principle is undermined as much by limiting whom the people can select as by limiting the franchise itself. In apparent agreement with this basic philosophy, the Convention adopted his suggestion limiting the power to expel. To allow essentially that same power to be exercised under the guise of judging qualifications, would be to ignore Madison's warning, borne out in the Wilkes case and some of Congress' own post-Civil War exclusion cases, against "vesting an improper & dangerous power in the Legislature." 2 Farrand 249. Moreover, it would effectively nullify the Convention's decision to require a two-thirds vote for expulsion. Unquestionably, Congress has an interest in preserving its institutional integrity, but in most cases that interest can be sufficiently safeguarded by the exercise of its power to punish its members for disorderly behavior and, in extreme cases, to expel a member with the concurrence of two-thirds. In short, both the intention of the Framers, to the extent it can be determined, and an examination of the basic principles of our democratic system persuade us that the Constitution does not vest in the Congress a discretionary power to deny membership by a majority vote.

For these reasons, we have concluded that Art. I, § 5, is at most a "textually demonstrable commitment" to Congress to judge only the qualifications expressly set forth in the Constitution. Therefore, the "textual commitment" formulation of the political question doctrine does not bar federal courts from adjudicating petitioners' claims. . . . Nor are any of the other formulations of a political question "inextricable from the case at bar." *Baker* v. *Carr, supra,* at 217. Petitioners seek a determination that the House was without power to exclude Powell from the 90th Congress, which, we have seen, requires an interpretation of the Constitution—a determination for which clearly there are "judicially . . . manageable standards." Finally, a judicial resolution of petitioners' claim will not result in "multifarious pronouncements by various departments on one question." For, as we noted in *Baker* v. *Carr, supra,* at 211, it is the responsibility of this Court to act as the ultimate interpreter of the Constitution. *Marbury* v. *Madison,* 1 Cranch 137 (1803). Thus, we conclude that petitioners' claim is not barred by the political question doctrine, and, having determined that the claim is otherwise generally justiciable, we hold that the case is justiciable. . . .

Further, analysis of the "textual commitment" under Art. I, § 5, has demonstrated that in judging the qualifications of its members Congress is limited to the standing qualifications prescribed in the Constitution. Respondents concede that Powell met these. Thus, there is no need to remand this case to determine whether he was entitled to be seated in the 90th Congress. Therefore, we hold that, since Adam Clayton Powell, Jr., was duly elected by the voters of the 18th Congressional District of New York and was not ineligible to serve under any provision of the Constitution, the House was without power to exclude him from its membership. . . .[12]

---

[12] **Questions:** *McGrain v. Daugherty*, *Gravel v. United States*, and *Powell v. McCormack* are all examples of the Supreme Court policing Congress's nonlegislative powers and immunities. One implication is that when Congress seeks to exercise its subpoena or exclusion powers, it must consider how a federal court would evaluate its actions. Consider an alternative universe in which the Court instead announced that all three cases were political questions about which courts must defer to Congress. How would that universe be different? What are the trade-offs involved in declaring these issues to be justiciable?

NOTE: STATES' POWERS TO ADD QUALIFICATIONS

The Court in *McCormack* discussed an example from 1807 in which Congress admitted a representative-elect from Maryland despite that state's stricter residency qualifications. A similar issue faced the Court in the 1990s. During the 1994 midterm elections, the House minority leader, Newt Gingrich, proposed a "Contract with America," in which he promised that a Republican majority would enact term limits on members of Congress. Even before he led the Republicans to a sweeping victory, many states, including Arkansas, adopted term limits for members of Congress as part of their own constitutions. After the 1994 midterm elections, Ray Thornton, a Democratic representative from Arkansas, challenged his state's prohibition on running for Congress if he had already served three terms in the House. In *U.S. Term Limits v. Thornton*, 514 U.S. 779 (1995), a 5–4 majority agreed with Thornton that a term limit was functionally a qualification on who could be admitted to Congress and that its holding in *McCormack* prohibited not only the House but also states from adding to the qualifications in Article I, Section 2.

Missouri voters followed this decision by adopting a state constitutional amendment in 1996 that instructed Missouri candidates for Congress to support a "Congressional Term Limits Amendment" to the U.S. Constitution. The state provision stated that if a candidate refused to pledge support for the federal amendment, "DECLINED TO PLEDGE TO SUPPORT TERM LIMITS" would be printed on all primary and general election ballots next to that candidate's name. In *Cook v. Gralike*, the Court unanimously held that the amendment attempted to add the same qualification that the Court had rejected in *U.S. Term Limits* and was not authorized by the Elections Clause's grant of power for states to "regulate" federal elections. 531 U.S. 510, 530 (2001).

23.4 THE POWER TO DETERMINE RULES, CHOOSE A SPEAKER, AND FILIBUSTER LEGISLATION AND NOMINATIONS

Congress's final major nonlegislative power is the power to "determine the Rules of its Proceedings" and, in the case of the House, to choose a "Speaker." As with Congress's other nonlegislative powers, these powers originate from the practices of Parliament and state and colonial legislatures. The House of Commons, for example, frequently battled with the British Crown over the power to choose its own speaker—a power that the Crown often did not recognize. Similarly, in the lead-up to the American Revolution, several colonial assemblies feuded with Crown-appointed governors over the power to choose their own leaders. In these disputes and others, Parliament and the colonial assemblies relied heavily on "Journals" of their proceedings in which they could list notable precedents where the Crown had given in to their demands. *See* Nicholas Handler, *Rediscovering the Journal Clause: The Lost History of Legislative Constitutional Interpretation*, 21 J. Const. L. 1219, 1221

(2019) ("[T]he Journals are law-producing documents, and a critical medium through which Parliament and later Congress historically engaged in constitutional interpretation."). By allowing each house to make its own rules, keep its own journals, and choose its own officers—except in the case of the Senate, whose presiding officer was the vice president—the Constitutional Convention assisted Congress in maintaining its independence from the other branches. *See* Josh Chafetz, *Congress's Constitution: Legislative Authority and the Separation of Powers* 274–80 (2017).

The rulemaking power developed differently in the House than in the Senate.

The House of Representatives

In the House's first two decades, the most important rules of procedure were the ones that created "standing committees," such as the House Ways and Means Committee, through which longtime members could develop expertise in various issues without having to rely on reports from Alexander Hamilton or other executive branch officers. In 1810, Speaker Henry Clay steadily increased the number of these committees, also establishing the precedent that the speaker could appoint every committee's chair and membership by a majority vote. This gave the speaker an enormous amount of power—which only increased over the next century thanks to one of these committees, the Committee on Rules. *See id.*

The purpose of the Rules Committee, established in 1789, was, at first, limited to proposing general rules for debates within the House. But the committee's members were soon given the privilege of calling its reports, or "special rules," to the floor of the House at any time, no matter what else was on the legislative calendar. In 1880, a powerful member of the Rules Committee, Thomas Reed, successfully introduced a special rule to the House floor that had the effect of bringing a specific piece of legislative business to the front of the House's lengthy queue. Overnight, Reed's action converted the House's reputation from a "large and unwieldy" body whose legislation was constantly being obstructed into an efficient institution led by a powerful speaker in complete control of its agenda. Soon after this parliamentary maneuver, Reed was elected speaker and earned the nickname "Czar Reed" for the influence that he wielded. *See id.* at 282–87.

Since Reed's day, the responsibilities of the Rules Committee have included not only introducing bills and resolutions to the House floor but also establishing the procedures by which business can be debated by members. This has occasionally engendered controversy. In 1890, for example, the Democratic minority in the House reacted to Czar Reed's power by taking advantage of Clause 1 of Article I, Section 5, which reads, "[A] Majority of each [House] shall constitute a Quorum to do Business." Under long-standing House precedent, members counted for quorum purposes only if they voted. So Democratic members began refusing to vote on bills—denying the House a quorum to do business unless nearly all of the Republicans were physically present. Reed responded by ordering the clerk of the House to count all members physically present for quorum purposes, enraging the Democratic members, who complained that Reed's rule change was unconstitutional. *See* 4 *Hinds' Precedents of the House of Representatives of the United States* §§ 2895–2905 (Asher C. Hinds ed., 1907).

Two years after Reed codified this new quorum rule as House Rule XV, a cloth importer who objected to a newly enacted customs duty challenged the statute that created the duty on the ground that the House had passed it in violation of the Quorum Clause. But in *United States v. Ballin*, the Supreme Court sustained the statute, holding that Reed's rule change was one of many ways that the House could comply with the Quorum Clause's requirement of a "Majority":

> The Constitution empowers each house to determine its rules of proceedings. It may not by its rules ignore constitutional restraints or violate fundamental rights, and there should be a reasonable relation between the mode or method of proceeding established by the rule and the result which is sought to be attained. But within these limitations, all matters of method are open to the determination of the house, and it is no impeachment of the rule to say that some other way would be better, more accurate, or even more just.

144 U.S. 1, 5 (1892).

Despite *Ballin*'s deference to the House's rules, the Court was careful to explain that the House's rulemaking power was not unreviewable. It would be impermissible, the Court suggested, for the House to create a rule saying that two or three members could constitute a quorum. And in *Christoffel v. United States*, 338 U.S. 84 (1949), one of the cases in which the Court reviewed a House committee's interrogation of an alleged Communist, the Court evaluated for itself whether the committee had acted with a quorum despite Rule XV's presumption that a quorum is present absent a roll call. *See also Yellin v. United States*, 374 U.S. 109 (1963) (guaranteeing the procedural rights of witnesses before congressional committees). In *United States v. Smith*, the Court similarly disagreed with the Senate about how to interpret one of its own rules, justifying its judicial review of Senate rules by writing that where "the construction to be given to the rules affects persons other than members of the Senate, the question presented is of necessity a judicial one." 286 U.S. 6, 33 (1932).

Applying these precedents, courts have recently evaluated the House's power to use its rules to affect people outside of the chamber. For example, one House rule permits individual committees to issue subpoenas—something that the House Oversight and Reform Committee did to request financial records from President Donald Trump's accounting firm. *See* Ben Miller-Gootnick, *How the House Sues*, 2021 U. Ill. L. Rev. 607, 633. In *Trump v. Mazars*, the U.S. Court of Appeals for the D.C. Circuit upheld this rule, holding that "unless and until Congress adopts a rule that offends the Constitution, the courts get no vote in how each chamber chooses to run its internal affairs." 940 F.3d 710, 743–44 (D.C. Cir. 2019). The House has similarly adopted a rule that creates a five-member group of legislators—the Bipartisan Legal Advisory Group (BLAG)—that "speaks for, and articulates the institutional position of, the House in all litigation matters." H.R. Res. 5, 114th Cong. (2015). Today, BLAG routinely initiates or intervenes in litigation on behalf of the House as if the entire House voted to authorize each of its decisions. *See* Miller-Gootnick, *supra*, at 609.

The Senate

The Senate's rules, in contrast with those of the House, have, historically, diffused power away from a single leader and given individual senators significant leverage over its business. This trajectory perhaps reflects the fact that where the House can choose its own speaker, Article I makes the vice president the leader of the Senate.

The Senate's disaggregation of power began with its first standing rules, compiled and published by Vice President Thomas Jefferson in his 1801 *A Manual of Parliamentary Practice for the Use of the Senate of the United States*, which gave each member broad power to debate motions and propose amendments in order to build consensus. These powers were limited by a "previous question" rule, which authorized senators to close debate and vote immediately on the pending motion. But in 1806, in "one of the most significant copy edits in American history," the Senate eliminated the previous-question rule, which it considered unnecessary in light of prevailing norms against superfluous debate. Adam Jentleson, *Kill Switch: The Rise of the Modern Senate* 46–47 (2021). The Senate eliminated another important limit on debate in 1828 after Vice President John C. Calhoun used his power as presiding officer to cut off political opponents. *Id.* at 48–49. Instead of giving the chair discretion to enforce the norm against superfluous debate, the Senate voted to formally codify the presiding officer's power to recognize senators who wished to speak. *Id.* This rule change eventually evolved into a tradition of unlimited debate checked only by the unanimous consent of the entire Senate. By the twentieth century, when the House had a speaker who could assign committee chairs and bring bills to the floor for a scheduled vote, the Senate collectively assigned committee chairs on the basis of seniority, and individual senators could debate and amend bills forever. *See* Chafetz, *supra*, at 284–89.

Unlimited debate in the Senate became an important tool for members of the minority party to delay or obstruct disfavored legislation—a practice known as the *filibuster*. The practice began in the 1840s after Calhoun resigned from the vice presidency and was elected to the Senate from South Carolina. In 1841, as one of the most dominant proslavery figures in Senate history, Calhoun organized other southern senators to delay unfavorable legislation by debating it as long as they could. Jentleson, *supra*, at 50–51. He defended these tactics by arguing that each section of the country—particularly sections in the political minority—should have "a negative on the others." *Id.* at 53–57. By tying the right of unlimited debate to "minority rights," he established a precedent that southern senators wielded to delay civil rights legislation for the remainder of the nineteenth century. *Id.* at 59–61. In 1891, southern senators even defeated a bill to restore the previous-question rule. *Id.* at 62–63.

Although civil rights bills were, by far, the most frequent targets of the filibuster, the most consequential filibuster concerned a 1917 bill that would have armed merchant ships against German U-boat attacks. In light of the exigencies of World War I, the Senate responded to this filibuster by adopting the French National Assembly's practice of "cloture," by which debate could be cut off with a two-thirds vote. Chafetz, *supra*, at 290. Supporters hoped that this new rule—codified in paragraph 2 of Senate Rule XXII—would restore the previous-question rule and formalize senators' power to quickly move past filibusters. But ironically, this new rule had the exact opposite effect. By codifying a supermajority requirement into the Senate rules, Rule XXII enhanced a delaying tactic into a veto. Jentleson, *supra*, at 66–67. Before the rule, a majority could simply wait out a filibustering minority. But after Rule XII, the Senate's twenty southern senators could demand that the majority prove it had the votes to end debate. *Id.* at 67–68. These senators took advantage of Rule XXII by indefinitely filibustering bills supported by a majority of voters, House members, and senators—such as bills to end lynching or eliminate poll taxes. *Id.* In 1948, Senator Richard Russell Jr. of Georgia, the leader of the southern bloc, successfully expanded Rule XXII's reach to include everything that the Senate did, from procedural motions to judicial and executive nominations. *Id.* at 83.

The Civil Rights Act of 1964 represented the first time that the Senate overcame a southern filibuster—after eleven unsuccessful attempts dating to the advent of cloture in 1917. *Id.* at 107. Yet rather than respond to this victory by eliminating the filibuster, the Senate expanded its application. From the end of Reconstruction until 1964, the only bills that had ever been stopped by filibusters were civil rights bills. *Id.* at 108. After 1964, by contrast, filibusters steadily became a routine part of the legislative process. Moreover, as with the advent of cloture in Rule XXII, attempts to reduce abuse backfired. For example, in 1975, a series of filibusters by the segregationist Senator James Allen of Alabama pushed the Senate to reform the cloture rule. The Senate reduced the supermajority threshold from two-thirds to three-fifths and also adopted new procedures that permitted the Senate to move on to other business in response to a threatened filibuster. *Id.* at 210. Yet the advent of the "silent" filibuster only made it easier to wield. Now, senators could merely signal their intent to filibuster and place a "hold" on nominations, legislation, and everything else that the Senate did. *Id.* at 211.

As filibusters became pervasive in the 1990s and 2000s, some outside litigants challenged their constitutionality. *See, e.g.*, *Page v. Shelby*, 995 F. Supp. 23 (D.D.C. 1998); *Jud. Watch, Inc. v. U.S. Senate*, 432 F.3d 359 (D.C. Cir. 2005). Litigants complained that Rule XXII effectively imposed a supermajority requirement on everything that the Senate did, even though the Constitution required supermajorities only for specific actions like ratifying treaties or overcoming presidential vetoes. But none of these challenges have reached the merits. For example, in *Common Cause v. Biden*, 748 F.3d 1280 (D.C. Cir. 2014), the U.S. Court of Appeals for the D.C. Circuit held that the Rules Clause gave senators exclusive responsibility for modifying and enforcing Rule XXII and that the Speech or Debate Clause prohibited plaintiffs from suing the senators who voted against cloture on a particular bill.

Although the supermajority threshold for cloture has applied to legislation *and* nominations since 1948, recent Senates have lowered the threshold for nominations to a majority vote. In 2013, after a Republican minority filibustered fifty-nine nominees to positions in the Obama administration and seventeen nominees to the federal judiciary, the Senate voted 52–48 "that the vote on cloture under rule XXII for all nominations other than for the Supreme Court of the United States is by majority vote." 159 Cong. Rec. S8417–18 (daily ed. Nov. 21, 2013). In 2017, after a Democratic minority filibustered the nomination of Neil Gorsuch to the Supreme Court, the Senate voted 52–48 "that the vote on cloture, under the precedent set on November 21, 2013, is a majority vote for all nominations." 163 Cong. Rec. S2389–90 (Apr. 6, 2017). Neither of these procedural rulings changed the text of Rule XXII, however, which continues to apply to "any measure, motion, other matter pending before the Senate."

CHAPTER 24

WHAT ARE THE LIMITS ON HOW CONGRESS ENACTS LEGISLATION?

ARTICLE I, SECTION 5, CLAUSE 3: Each House shall keep a Journal of its Proceedings, and from time to time publish the same, excepting such Parts as may in their Judgment require Secrecy; and the Yeas and Nays of the Members of either House on any question shall, at the Desire of one fifth of those Present, be entered on the Journal.

ARTICLE I, SECTION 6, CLAUSE 2: No Senator or Representative shall, during the Time for which he was elected, be appointed to any civil Office under the Authority of the United States, which shall have been created, or the Emoluments whereof shall have been encreased during such time; and no Person holding any Office under the United States, shall be a Member of either House during his Continuance in Office.

ARTICLE I, SECTION 7, CLAUSE 1: All Bills for raising Revenue shall originate in the House of Representatives; but the Senate may propose or concur with Amendments as on other Bills.

CLAUSE 2: Every Bill which shall have passed the House of Representatives and the Senate, shall, before it become a Law, be presented to the President of the United States; If he approve he shall sign it, but if not he shall return it, with his Objections to that House in which it shall have originated, who shall enter the Objections at large on their Journal, and proceed to reconsider it. If after such Reconsideration two thirds of that House shall agree to pass the Bill, it shall be sent, together with the Objections, to the other House, by which it shall likewise be reconsidered, and if approved by two thirds of that House, it shall become a Law. But in all such Cases the Votes of both Houses shall be determined by yeas and Nays, and the Names of the Persons voting for and against the Bill shall be entered on the Journal of each House respectively. If any Bill shall not be returned by the President within ten Days (Sundays excepted) after it shall have been presented to him, the Same shall be a Law, in like Manner as if he had signed it, unless the Congress by their Adjournment prevent its Return, in which Case it shall not be a Law.

CLAUSE 3: Every Order, Resolution, or Vote to which the Concurrence of the Senate and House of Representatives may be necessary (except on a question of Adjournment) shall be presented to the President of the United States; and before the Same shall take Effect, shall be approved by him, or being disapproved by him, shall be repassed by two thirds of the Senate and House of Representatives, according to the Rules and Limitations prescribed in the Case of a Bill.

24.1 BICAMERALISM, PRESENTMENT, AND THE VETO

Anyone who has heard the *Schoolhouse Rock!* segment "I'm Just a Bill" is already familiar with the basics of Article I, Section 7, Clause 2. Before becoming a law, a bill must pass both houses of Congress, a requirement known as *bicameralism*. Then it must be "presented" to the president. The president can then (1) sign the bill, making it a law immediately; (2) "return it"—that is, veto it—giving both houses the opportunity to override the veto with a two-thirds vote; or (3) do nothing, making it a law "ten Days (Sundays excepted) after it shall have been presented to him, . . . unless the Congress by their Adjournment prevent its Return, in which Case it shall not be a Law." Clause 3 appears to apply this same procedure to every "Order, Resolution, or Vote to which the Concurrence of the Senate and House of Representatives may be necessary."

In most cases, these requirements are straightforward. But, historically, they have presented three interpretive problems.

Line-item veto

First, imagine a scenario in which the president asks Congress in the State of the Union Address to pass a bill containing X—with X being, say, a requirement that school buses stop at railroad crossings. Both houses of Congress comply, but they present the president an omnibus bill that also contains their own priorities: Y and Z. Can the president sign only the part of the bill with X while vetoing parts Y and Z? This sort of action is called a *line-item veto*.

In 1996, Congress passed and the president signed the Line Item Veto Act of 1996, Pub. L. 104–130, 110 Stat. 1200, which permitted the president to sign a bill and immediately afterward issue a signing statement canceling or reducing the dollar amounts of some of the bill's provisions. This statute copied the practice of several states, including Massachusetts, which have long permitted governors to exercise similar line-item vetoes.

But in *Clinton v. City of New York*, 524 U.S. 417 (1998), the Supreme Court held that the 1996 act violated the Constitution's bicameralism and presentment requirements. The Court explained that once the president signs a bill, it becomes a law. In permitting the president to amend a signed bill, the act had the effect of permitting the president to amend an existing law. But, the Court declared, "[t]here is no provision in the Constitution that authorizes the President to enact, to amend, or to repeal statutes." *Clinton*, 524 U.S. at 438. Rather, quoting George Washington, the Court held that the Presentment Clause requires the president to "either 'approve all the parts of a Bill, or reject it in toto.'" *Id*. at 440.

Pocket veto

Second, imagine a scenario in which both houses of Congress pass a bill and present it to the president. After waiting for the president to act for nine days, Congress temporarily recesses for the weekend, leaving behind a staff member in case the president vetoes and "returns" the bill.

On the tenth day, while Congress is in its weekend recess, the president does nothing. Has the bill become a law because the president has failed to act on it, or has the bill not become a law because "the Congress by their Adjournment [has] prevent[ed] its Return"? This sort of situation is called a *pocket veto*.

Nearly every president since James Madison has attempted such a veto, either because writing up a veto statement is politically unpalatable or because, unlike with normal vetoes, Section 7 doesn't permit both houses of Congress to override a pocket veto. But unlike a normal bill in which there is clearly either a signature or a veto statement, the legal status of a pocket-vetoed bill depends on the status of Congress.

At first, in the appropriately named *Pocket Veto Case*, 279 U.S. 655 (1929), the Court held that the bill in the above scenario has *not* become a law because the House was not in session on the tenth day. "We find no substantial basis for the suggestion that, although the House in which the bill originated is not in session, the bill may nevertheless be returned," the Court wrote. *Pocket Veto Case*, 279 U.S. at 683. It added that the term *House* in Section 7 refers not to an empty chamber but rather to a chamber with a quorum "to do all the business that comes before [it, including] . . . the reconsideration of a bill which has been vetoed by the President." *Id.* at 682.

But in *Wright v. United States*, the Court reversed itself, finding that its earlier decision "would frustrate the fundamental purposes of the constitutional provision as to action upon bills." 302 U.S. 583, 594 (1938). These purposes, the Court wrote, are "(1) [t]hat the President shall have suitable opportunity to consider the bills presented to him, and (2) that the Congress shall have suitable opportunity to consider his objections to bills and, on such consideration, to pass them over his veto provided there are requisite votes." *Id.* at 596. In light of these two purposes, the Court held that it would be "extremely technical" to hold that a House in recess doesn't have a suitable opportunity to consider the president's objections to bills. *Id.* at 597. Instead, it held that "where the Congress has not adjourned and the House in which the bill originated is in recess for not more than three days," then the president can either return the bill to an appropriate officer in the House or the president can wait ten days and the bill will become a law. *Id.* at 598,

Legislative veto

Third, imagine a scenario in which Congress passes and the president signs a law that gives an executive officer the power to do X. But, out of legislators' fear that the officer might do X poorly, the law states that a majority vote of either house has the power to veto the officer's action within thirty days. So, the officer goes, does X poorly, and the Senate passes a resolution vetoing the officer's decision. Has the Senate violated the bicameralism and presentment requirements because it effectively changed the law regarding X without the House and president's approval, or was the Senate's resolution an "Order, Resolution, or Vote to which the Concurrence of the Senate and House [wasn't] necessary"? This situation is called a *legislative veto*.

Beginning in 1932, the legislative veto became an incredibly popular type of legislation. *See* Act of June 30, 1932, Pub. L. No. 72–212, 47 Stat. 382, 414. By 1983, legislative vetoes had been enacted in almost three hundred provisions.

They were justified on several grounds. For one thing, the period between the 1930s and 1980s saw the growth of dozens of administrative agencies and the creation of a tremendously powerful administrative state; as Congress delegated to the executive branch what Congress had once done itself, it made sense to many legislators that Congress should be able to review and veto what the executive branch was doing. *See* Daphna Renan, *Pooling Powers*, 115 Colum. L. Rev. 211, 236–38 (2015). For another thing, the legislative veto appeared to be justified by the existence of two separate bicameralism and presentment clauses in Section 7: Clause 2, which applied to "Bill[s]"; and Clause 3, which applied to orders, resolutions, or votes "to which the Concurrence of the Senate and House *may be* necessary" (emphasis added). Not all resolutions require the concurrence of both houses; a resolution to change a Senate rule, for example, can be passed by the Senate alone. Thus, many legislators argued that legislative vetoes are analogous to one-house resolutions and, therefore, don't require bicameralism and presentment.

24.1.1.

Immigration & Naturalization Service v. Chadha

462 U.S. 919 (1983)

The following case, *Immigration & Naturalization Service v. Chadha*, 462 U.S. 919 (1983), involves the third scenario above: the legislative veto. In 1975, a section of the Immigration and Nationality Act authorized the U.S. attorney general to suspend the deportation of a noncitizen if the attorney general found that certain criteria were met. A different section of the statute, § 244(c)(2), authorized the House or Senate to pass a resolution vetoing the attorney general's decision. Both things happened to Jagdish Rai Chadha, a man born to Indian parents in the British colony of Kenya. Chadha had been living in the United States on a student visa when Kenya declared its independence. Due to bad luck, he lost his right to live in Kenya, the United Kingdom, and India. Taking account of Chadha's situation, the attorney general suspended his deportation. But a member of the House who apparently wanted Chadha out of this country urged his colleagues to pass a disapproval resolution. Chadha was then ordered deported.

Chadha challenged the deportation order on the ground that legislative vetoes violate Article I, Section 7. The Court agreed that a one-house legislative veto does not pass constitutional muster.

The following excerpt picks up after the Supreme Court determined that his challenge wasn't a political question.

■ CHIEF JUSTICE BURGER delivered the opinion of the Court.[1]

[This case] presents a challenge to the constitutionality of the provision in § 244(c)(2) of the Immigration and Nationality Act, 66 Stat. 216, as amended, 8 U. S. C. § 1254(c)(2), authorizing one House of Congress, by resolution, to invalidate the decision of the Executive Branch, pursuant to authority delegated by Congress to the Attorney General of the United States, to allow a particular deportable alien to remain in the United States. . . .

III

Since 1932, when the first veto provision was enacted into law, 295 congressional veto-type procedures have been inserted in 196 different statutes. . . . [The government] undertakes to make a case for the proposition that the one-House veto is a useful "political invention," and we need not challenge that assertion. . . . But policy arguments supporting even useful "political inventions" are subject to the demands of the Constitution which defines powers and, with respect to this subject, sets out just how those powers are to be exercised.

The Presentment Clauses

The records of the Constitutional Convention reveal that the requirement that all legislation be presented to the President before becoming law was uniformly accepted by the Framers. Presentment to the President and the Presidential veto were considered so imperative that the draftsmen took special pains to assure that these requirements could not be circumvented. During the final debate on Art. I, § 7, cl. 2, James Madison expressed concern that it might easily be evaded by the simple expedient of calling a proposed law a "resolution" or "vote" rather than a "bill." 2 Farrand 301–302. As a consequence, Art. I, § 7, cl. 3, was added. 2 Farrand 304–305.

The decision to provide the President with a limited and qualified power to nullify proposed legislation by veto was based on the profound conviction of the Framers that the powers conferred on Congress were the powers to be most carefully circumscribed. It is beyond doubt that lawmaking was a power to be shared by both Houses and the President. . . .

The President's role in the lawmaking process also reflects the Framers' careful efforts to check whatever propensity a particular Congress might have to enact oppressive, improvident, or ill-considered measures. The President's veto role in the legislative process was described later during public debate on ratification: "It establishes a salutary check upon the legislative body, calculated to guard the community against the effects of faction, precipitancy, or of any impulse unfriendly to the public good, which may happen to influence a majority of that body. . . ." The Federalist No. 73, *supra,* at 458 (A. Hamilton).

---

[1] **As You Read, Consider:** The statute under review in this decision, the Immigration and Nationality Act of 1952, was enacted by the procedure mandated by Article I, Section 7: it passed both houses of Congress, was presented to the president, and was ultimately enacted over his veto. Why, then, does Chief Justice Warren Burger think that the law violates Article I, Section 7? How does he distinguish agency regulations, which change the law yet do not go through the bicameralism and presentment requirements of Article I, Section 7?

Bicameralism

The bicameral requirement of Art. I, §§ 1, 7, was of scarcely less concern to the Framers than was the Presidential veto and indeed the two concepts are interdependent. By providing that no law could take effect without the concurrence of the prescribed majority of the Members of both Houses, the Framers reemphasized their belief, already remarked upon in connection with the Presentment Clauses, that legislation should not be enacted unless it has been carefully and fully considered by the Nation's elected officials. In the Constitutional Convention debates on the need for a bicameral legislature, James Wilson, later to become a Justice of this Court, commented:

> "Despotism comes on mankind in different shapes. sometimes in an Executive, sometimes in a military, one. Is there danger of a Legislative despotism? Theory & practice both proclaim it. If the Legislative authority be not restrained, there can be neither liberty nor stability; and it can only be restrained by dividing it within itself, into distinct and independent branches. In a single house there is no check, but the inadequate one, of the virtue & good sense of those who compose it." 1 Farrand 254. . . .

However familiar, it is useful to recall that apart from their fear that special interests could be favored at the expense of public needs, the Framers were also concerned, although not of one mind, over the apprehensions of the smaller states. Those states feared a commonality of interest among the larger states would work to their disadvantage; representatives of the larger states, on the other hand, were skeptical of a legislature that could pass laws favoring a minority of the people. See 1 Farrand 176–177, 484–491. It need hardly be repeated here that the Great Compromise, under which one House was viewed as representing the people and the other the states, allayed the fears of both the large and small states.

We see therefore that the Framers were acutely conscious that the bicameral requirement and the Presentment Clauses would serve essential constitutional functions. The President's participation in the legislative process was to protect the Executive Branch from Congress and to protect the whole people from improvident laws. The division of the Congress into two distinctive bodies assures that the legislative power would be exercised only after opportunity for full study and debate in separate settings. The President's unilateral veto power, in turn, was limited by the power of two-thirds of both Houses of Congress to overrule a veto thereby precluding final arbitrary action of one person. See *id.*, at 99–104. It emerges clearly that the prescription for legislative action in Art. I, §§ 1, 7, represents the Framers' decision that the legislative power of the Federal Government be exercised in accord with a single, finely wrought and exhaustively considered, procedure.

IV

The Constitution sought to divide the delegated powers of the new Federal Government into three defined categories, Legislative, Executive, and Judicial, to assure, as nearly as possible, that each branch of government would confine itself to its assigned responsibility. The hydraulic pressure inherent within each of the separate Branches to exceed the outer limits of its power, even to accomplish desirable objectives, must be resisted. . . .

[T]he challenged action under § 244(c)(2) is of the kind to which the procedural requirements of Art. I, § 7, apply. Not every action taken by either House is subject to the bicameralism and presentment requirements of Art. I. Whether actions taken by either House are, in law and fact, an exercise of legislative power depends not on their form but upon "whether they contain matter which is properly to be regarded as legislative in its character and effect." S. Rep. No. 1335, 54th Cong., 2d Sess., 8 (1897).

Examination of the action taken here by one House pursuant to § 244(c)(2) reveals that it was essentially legislative in purpose and effect. In purporting to exercise power defined in Art. I, § 8, cl. 4, to "establish an uniform Rule of Naturalization," the House took action that had the purpose and effect of altering the legal rights, duties, and relations of persons, including the Attorney General, Executive Branch officials and Chadha, all outside the Legislative Branch. Section 244(c)(2) purports to authorize one House of Congress to require the Attorney General to deport an individual alien whose deportation otherwise would be canceled under § 244. The one-House veto operated in these cases to overrule the Attorney General and mandate Chadha's deportation; absent the House action, Chadha would remain in the United States. Congress has *acted* and its action has altered Chadha's status.[2]

The legislative character of the one-House veto in these cases is confirmed by the character of the congressional action it supplants. Neither the House of Representatives nor the Senate contends that, absent the veto provision in § 244(c)(2), either of them, or both of them acting together, could effectively require the Attorney General to deport an alien once the Attorney General, in the exercise of legislatively delegated authority, had determined the alien should remain in the United States. Without the challenged provision in § 244(c)(2), this could have been achieved, if at all, only by legislation requiring deportation. Similarly, a veto by one House of Congress under § 244(c)(2) cannot be justified . . . as a repeal of § 244 as applied to Chadha. Amendment and repeal of statutes, no less than enactment, must conform with Art. I.

The nature of the decision implemented by the one-House veto in these cases further manifests its legislative character. After long experience with the clumsy, time-consuming private bill procedure, Congress made a deliberate choice to delegate to the Executive Branch, and specifically to the Attorney General, the authority to allow deportable aliens to remain in this country in certain specified circumstances. It is not disputed that this choice to delegate authority is precisely the kind of decision that can be implemented only in accordance with the procedures set out in Art. I. Disagreement with the Attorney General's decision on Chadha's deportation—that is, Congress' decision to deport Chadha—no less than Congress' original choice to delegate to the Attorney General the authority to make that decision, involves determinations of policy that Congress can implement in only one way; bicameral passage followed by presentment to the President. Congress must abide by its delegation of authority until that delegation is legislatively altered or revoked.

Finally, we see that when the Framers intended to authorize either House of Congress to act alone and outside of its prescribed bicameral legislative role, they narrowly and precisely defined the procedure for such action. There are four provisions in the Constitution, explicit and unambiguous, by which one House may act alone with the unreviewable force of law, not subject to the President's veto:

(a) The House of Representatives alone was given the power to initiate impeachments. Art. I, § 2, cl. 5;

exceptions

Exceptions

---

[2] **Questions:** Burger here notes that the House has, effectively, changed the law for Chadha by reversing the attorney general's decision to suspend his deportation. He concludes that the House violated Article I, Section 7. But why isn't the attorney general's suspension decision also subject to Article I, Section 7? After all, had the attorney general not acted, Chadha would have been deportable. The attorney general therefore "altered Chadha's status" as much as the House did—right?

(b) The Senate alone was given the power to conduct trials following impeachment on charges initiated by the House and to convict following trial. Art. I, § 3, cl. 6;

exceptions

(c) The Senate alone was given final unreviewable power to approve or to disapprove Presidential appointments. Art. II, § 2, cl. 2;

(d) The Senate alone was given unreviewable power to ratify treaties negotiated by the President. Art. II, § 2, cl. 2.

Clearly, when the Draftsmen sought to confer special powers on one House, independent of the other House, or of the President, they did so in explicit, unambiguous terms.[3] These carefully defined exceptions from presentment and bicameralism underscore the difference between the legislative functions of Congress and other unilateral but important and binding one-House acts provided for in the Constitution. These exceptions are narrow, explicit, and separately justified; none of them authorize the action challenged here. On the contrary, they provide further support for the conclusion that congressional authority is not to be implied and for the conclusion that the veto provided for in § 244(c)(2) is not authorized by the constitutional design of the powers of the Legislative Branch. . . .

The veto authorized by § 244(c)(2) doubtless has been in many respects a convenient shortcut; the "sharing" with the Executive by Congress of its authority over aliens in this manner is, on its face, an appealing compromise. In purely practical terms, it is obviously easier for action to be taken by one House without submission to the President; but it is crystal clear from the records of the Convention, contemporaneous writings and debates, that the Framers ranked other values higher than efficiency. . . .

The choices we discern as having been made in the Constitutional Convention impose burdens on governmental processes that often seem clumsy, inefficient, even unworkable, but those hard choices were consciously made by men who had lived under a form of government that permitted arbitrary governmental acts to go unchecked. There is no support in the Constitution or decisions of this Court for the proposition that the cumbersomeness and delays often encountered in complying with explicit constitutional standards may be avoided, either by the Congress or by the President. With all the obvious flaws of delay, untidiness, and potential for abuse, we have not yet found a better way to preserve freedom than by making the exercise of power subject to the carefully crafted restraints spelled out in the Constitution. . . .[4]

■ JUSTICE WHITE, dissenting.

Today the Court not only invalidates § 244(c)(2) of the Immigration and Nationality Act, but also sounds the death knell for nearly 200 other statutory provisions in which Congress has reserved a "legislative veto.' For this reason, the Court's decision is of surpassing importance. And it is for this reason that the Court would have been well advised to decide the cases, if possible, on the narrower grounds of separation of powers, leaving for full consideration the constitutionality of

---

3 **Question:** This section of Burger's opinion emphasizes his objections to the *one-house* legislative veto. But does the rest of his opinion suggest that it would have been constitutional for Congress to engage in a *two-house* veto of the attorney general's decision without presenting that veto for the president's signature?

4 **Questions:** Does Congress need to pass a new law each time it wishes to "veto" an agency decision? What effect might *Immigration & Naturalization Service v. Chadha* have had on how Congress drafts and passes new laws? *See* James Q. Wilson, *Bureaucracy* 268 (1989) (emphasizing Congress's unwillingness to delegate as much power to the executive branch after *Chadha*).

other congressional review statutes operating on such varied matters as war powers and agency rulemaking, some of which concern the independent regulatory agencies.

The prominence of the legislative veto mechanism in our contemporary political system and its importance to Congress can hardly be overstated. It has become a central means by which Congress secures the accountability of executive and independent agencies. Without the legislative veto, Congress is faced with a Hobson's choice: either to refrain from delegating the necessary authority, leaving itself with a hopeless task of writing laws with the requisite specificity to cover endless special circumstances across the entire policy landscape, or in the alternative, to abdicate its law-making function to the Executive Branch and independent agencies. To choose the former leaves major national problems unresolved; to opt for the latter risks unaccountable policymaking by those not elected to fill that role. Accordingly, over the past five decades, the legislative veto has been placed in nearly 200 statutes. The device is known in every field of governmental concern: reorganization, budgets, foreign affairs, war powers, and regulation of trade, safety, energy, the environment, and the economy. . . .

The Court's holding today that all legislative-type action must be enacted through the lawmaking process ignores that legislative authority is routinely delegated to the Executive Branch, to the independent regulatory agencies, and to private individuals and groups.[5]

> "The rise of administrative bodies probably has been the most significant legal trend of the last century. . . . They have become a veritable fourth branch of the Government, which has deranged our three-branch legal theories. . . ." *FTC* v. *Ruberoid Co.,* 343 U. S. 470, 487 (1952) (Jackson, J. dissenting).

This Court's decisions sanctioning such delegations make clear that Art. I does not require all action with the effect of legislation to be passed as a law. . . . [Our] cases establish that by virtue of congressional delegation, legislative power can be exercised by independent agencies and Executive departments without the passage of new legislation. For some time, the sheer amount of law—the substantive rules that regulate private conduct and direct the operation of government—made by the agencies has far outnumbered the lawmaking engaged in by Congress through the traditional process. There is no question but that agency rulemaking is lawmaking in any functional or realistic sense of the term. . . . These regulations bind courts and officers of the Federal Government, may pre-empt state law, and grant rights to and impose obligations on the public. In sum, they have the force of law.

If Congress may delegate lawmaking power to independent and Executive agencies, it is most difficult to understand Art. I as prohibiting Congress from also reserving a check on legislative power for itself. Absent the veto, the agencies receiving delegations of legislative or quasi-legislative power may issue regulations having the force of law without bicameral approval and without the President's signature. It is thus not apparent why the reservation of a veto over the exercise of that legislative power must be subject to a more exacting test. In both cases, it is enough that the initial statutory authorizations comply with the Art. I requirements.

---

5 **Questions:** Despite Justice Byron White's warning, the Supreme Court has not followed *Chadha* by invalidating every regulation issued by every administrative agency. Do you think this is because White was wrong and there really is a principled distinction between legislative vetoes and executive regulations? Or might there be some other reason?

NOTE: AFTERMATH OF *CHADHA*

Thanks to the Supreme Court's decision, Chadha was allowed to remain in the United States. By 1985, he had become a U.S. citizen.

In contrast, the 295 legislative vetoes identified by the Court were less lucky. Within one year, the Supreme Court confirmed that *Chadha*'s holding applied to all legislative vetoes, not just one-house vetoes. *Consumers Union v. FTC*, 691 F.2d 575 (D.C. Cir. 1982), *aff'd sub nom. Process Gas Consumers Grp. v. Consumer Energy Council*, 463 U.S. 1216 (1983). Congress then spent several years afterward replacing existing legislative vetoes with review provisions that take effect only after both houses and the president agree.

Nevertheless, many statutes remain that function like legislative vetoes even if they are not literally the same mechanism as in *Chadha. See generally* Louis Fisher, Cong. Rsch. Serv., *Legislative Vetoes After* Chadha (2005). Indeed, Congress has even preserved the nonenforceable legislative veto in several statutory schemes to preserve the "practical accommodation between executive agencies and congressional committees." Louis Fisher, *The Legislative Veto: Invalidated, It Survives*, Law & Contemp. Probs., Autumn 1993, at 273, 273–75; *see also* Renan, *supra*, at 237–38. Congress has also turned to alternative methods of overseeing the executive branch, including by withholding appropriations from agencies that fail to comply with congressional requests. As then-Senator Joe Biden wrote in an article shortly after *Chadha* was decided, the decision was "much more of an inconvenience than a disaster." Senator Joseph R. Biden Jr., *Who Needs the Legislative Veto?*, 35 Syracuse L. Rev. 685, 688 (1984).

24.2 THE JOURNAL CLAUSE, THE INELIGIBILITY CLAUSE, AND THE ORIGINATION CLAUSE

The bicameralism and presentment requirements are the most important procedural requirements for how Congress may exercise its legislative powers, but they are not the only ones. Nevertheless, the Supreme Court has never held that Congress has violated any of the other requirements, so this section will run through them only briefly.

Journal Clause

Section 5 requires each house "to keep a Journal of its Proceedings." As discussed earlier, one benefit of keeping a journal is to establish precedents that either house can return to in disputes with other branches. But an obvious purpose of *requiring* a journal is publicity: ensuring that voters at home and state legislatures could evaluate their representatives' conduct. 2 Joseph Story, *Commentaries on the Constitution of the United States* § 840 (1833).

Very early in Congress's history, however, both houses agreed that the Journal Clause demanded only a bare-bones recitation of what each house did. In fact, the Senate kept its debates entirely secret for its first five years.

Even after the Senate allowed visitors, for Congress's first century, congressional debates were made public primarily through newspaper accounts. After 1834, private publishers began compiling newspaper accounts and other summaries of the debates as the *Annals of Congress* (1789–1824), the *Register of Debates* (1824–1837), and the *Congressional Globe* (1837–1873). Finally, in 1873, Congress began printing its own debates as the *Congressional Record. See* Josh Chafetz, *Congress's Constitution: Legislative Authority and the Separation of Powers* 281–82 (2017). In 1979, the House began broadcasting debates on C-SPAN, and in 1986 the Senate followed.

Ineligibility Clause

Section 6 prohibits members of Congress from becoming "Officers" of the United States (1) while serving as a member of Congress, or (2) if they participated in increasing the salary of the office. The purpose of the Ineligibility Clause was to remove improper bias, helping to ensure (in small part) that the people who passed laws would not be the officers who immediately benefited from them.

But the clause's prohibition has long been interpreted to apply only to one session of Congress—meaning that if the fifty-third Congress votes to increase an office's salary, any of its members may become eligible for that office in the fifty-fourth Congress. 2 Story, *supra,* § 864. In practice, this interpretation means that the clause applies only where the president nominates a member of Congress to become an officer immediately after Congress has just voted to increase that officer's salary.

In that situation, Congress typically follows a precedent it established with a 1909 law, ch. 137, 35 Stat. 626, in which it reduces the salary of the office to previous levels so that the member is eligible to be confirmed. Since the 1973 nomination of Senator William Saxbe to become attorney general, this procedure has become known as the *Saxbe fix. See* Mark Tushnet, *Constitutional Workarounds*, 87 Tex. L. Rev. 1499, 1501 (2009).

Occasionally, members of Congress have failed to comply with the Saxbe fix. For example, Hugo Black, a senator from Alabama, was nominated to become a Supreme Court justice almost immediately after Congress had voted to raise the justices' salaries. Nevertheless, a challenge to Black's appointment was dismissed by the Supreme Court for lack of standing. *Ex parte Levitt*, 302 U.S. 633 (1937).

Origination Clause

Finally, the Origination Clause of Section 7 requires "Bills for raising Revenue" to originate in the House of Representatives. This requirement, part of the Constitutional Convention's Connecticut Compromise that resulted in the House and Senate, was modeled on the practice of the British Parliament in which the House of Commons could propose new taxes and the House of Lords had no power to amend its tax bills.

The proponents of the Origination Clause explained that because members of the House of Representatives were elected by the people, the principle of "no taxation without representation" meant that only the House should have any authority over revenue bills. But later in the Constitutional Convention, delegates severely weakened this clause by adding the proviso that "the Senate may propose or concur with Amendments as on other Bills." The Origination Clause's supporters, such as Elbridge Gerry, complained that this change turned the clause into a farce because the House could propose a revenue bill about one thing, which the Senate could replace with its own revenue bill about a completely different matter.

In practice, this is exactly what has happened. Although the Supreme Court has been invited to strike down laws a dozen times for violating the Origination Clause, each time it has upheld the law because (1) the law originated in the Senate but was not passed for the purpose of "raising Revenue," or (2) the law originated in the House and was properly amended by the Senate.

An example of the first scenario is *United States v. Munoz-Flores*, 495 U.S. 385 (1990), in which the Court upheld a Senate-originated law that imposed mandatory monetary penalties on people convicted of certain crimes. The Court explained that the Origination Clause applied only to bills whose primary purpose was to raise general revenue—not to a statute that happened to raise revenue in order to support a larger program or regulation. *See also Field v. Clark*, 143 U.S. 649, 696 (1892) (a tariff is not a revenue bill because its purpose is also to encourage domestic industry); *Twin City Nat'l Bank v. Nebeker*, 167 U.S. 196, 202 (1897) (a tax on circulating notes is not a revenue bill because its purpose is to support a national currency).

For an example of the second scenario, consider the legislative history of the bill that became the Affordable Care Act of 2010: it originated in the House as a tax to aid service members, was passed by the House, and then was erased by a Senate amendment that substituted its text with that of the major health-care regulation. In *Sissel v. United States Department of Health & Human Services*, some members of the court of appeals wrote that the act wasn't a revenue bill because its purpose was to regulate health care. 760 F.3d 1 (D.C. Cir. 2014), *reh'g en banc denied*, 799 F.3d 1035, 1041 (D.C. Cir. 2015) (Rogers, Pillard, and Wilkins, JJ., concurring in denial of rehearing en banc). Meanwhile, Brett Kavanaugh, a circuit court judge at the time, argued that it was a revenue bill, but it properly originated in the House. *Id.* at 1049 (Kavanaugh, J., dissenting from denial of rehearing en banc). *See also Flint v. Stone Tracy Co.*, 220 U.S. 107, 143 (1911) (upholding a similar Senate substitution).

PART TWO

The Executive Branch

CHAPTER 25

WHAT IS THE "EXECUTIVE POWER," AND HOW DOES IT DIFFER FROM THE "LEGISLATIVE POWERS"?

ARTICLE I, SECTION 1: All legislative Powers herein granted shall be vested in a Congress of the United States, which shall consist of a Senate and House of Representatives.

ARTICLE I, SECTION 3, CLAUSE 4: The Vice President of the United States shall be President of the Senate, but shall have no Vote, unless they be equally divided.

> **CLAUSE 5:** The Senate shall chuse their other Officers, and also a President pro tempore, in the Absence of the Vice President, or when he shall exercise the Office of President of the United States.

ARTICLE I, SECTION 7, CLAUSE 2: Every Bill which shall have passed the House of Representatives and the Senate, shall, before it become a Law, be presented to the President of the United States; If he approve he shall sign it, but if not he shall return it, with his Objections to that House in which it shall have originated, who shall enter the Objections at large on their Journal, and proceed to reconsider it. . . .

> **CLAUSE 3:** [Same as above for] Every Order, Resolution, or Vote to which the Concurrence of the Senate and House of Representatives may be necessary. . . .

ARTICLE II, SECTION 1, CLAUSE 1: The executive Power shall be vested in a President of the United States of America. . . .

> **CLAUSE 8:** Before he enter on the Execution of his Office, he shall take the following Oath or Affirmation:—"I do solemnly swear (or affirm) that I will faithfully execute the Office of President of the United States, and will to the best of my Ability, preserve, protect and defend the Constitution of the United States."

ARTICLE II, SECTION 2, CLAUSE 1: The President shall be Commander in Chief of the Army and Navy of the United States, and of the Militia of the several States, when called into the actual Service of the United States; he may require the Opinion, in writing, of the principal Officer in each of the executive Departments, upon any Subject relating to the Duties of their respective Offices, and he shall have Power to grant Reprieves and Pardons for Offences against the United States, except in Cases of Impeachment.

> **CLAUSE 2:** He shall have Power, by and with the Advice and Consent of the Senate, to make Treaties, provided two thirds of the Senators present concur; and he shall nominate, and by and with the Advice and Consent of the Senate, shall appoint Ambassadors, other public Ministers and Consuls, Judges of the supreme Court, and all other Officers of the United States, whose Appointments are not herein otherwise provided for, and which shall be established by Law: but the Congress may by Law vest the Appointment of such inferior Officers, as

they think proper, in the President alone, in the Courts of Law, or in the Heads of Departments.

CLAUSE 3: The President shall have Power to fill up all Vacancies that may happen during the Recess of the Senate, by granting Commissions which shall expire at the End of their next Session.

ARTICLE II, SECTION 3: He shall from time to time give to the Congress Information of the State of the Union, and recommend to their Consideration such Measures as he shall judge necessary and expedient; he may, on extraordinary Occasions, convene both Houses, or either of them, and in Case of Disagreement between them, with Respect to the Time of Adjournment, he may adjourn them to such Time as he shall think proper; he shall receive Ambassadors and other public Ministers; he shall take Care that the Laws be faithfully executed, and shall Commission all the Officers of the United States.

25.1 THE VESTING CLAUSES OF ARTICLE I AND ARTICLE II

The opening clause of Article I vests Congress with "All legislative Powers *herein granted*." The use of the phrase *herein granted* has long been commonly interpreted to refer to the list of powers enumerated in Article I and, to a lesser extent, Article II (e.g., the power to make treaties), Article III (e.g., the power to establish tribunals), Article IV (e.g., the power to regulate territories, admit new states, and enforce the various other clauses), and the Reconstruction and voting-rights amendments. This isn't the only way to interpret the opening phrase. *See generally* Richard Primus, *Herein of "Herein Granted": Why Article I's Vesting Clause Does Not Support the Doctrine of Enumerated Powers*, 36 Const. Comment. 301, 331 (2020) (interpreting the phrase as a meaningless artifact of the Constitution's drafting process). However, this interpretation is consistent with a widely shared assumption that when Congress does something, it generally needs to point to one of the "Powers herein granted" that authorizes it to act, such as the Necessary and Proper Clause. The exceptions to this rule—Congress's "inherent" power to regulate tribes or to acquire territory, for example—are notable for their controversy, rarity, and historical justifications, such as white supremacy or a demand for empire.

Article II is different. It begins, "The executive Power shall be vested in a President of the United States of America." And unlike Article I, there is no comprehensive list, analogous to Article I, Section 8, of everything that might compose the "executive Power." Instead, Article II reads as if the term *executive power* should have a familiar scope. And perhaps it did at one point. When the Constitutional Convention opened in 1787, the Virginia delegation began the debate by proposing the creation of "a National Executive . . . to be chosen by the National Legislature, . . . and that besides a general authority to execute the National laws, it ought to enjoy the Executive rights vested in Congress by the Confederation." 1 *The Records of the Federal Convention of 1787*, at 21 (Max Farrand ed., 1911). However, the delegation didn't specify what this meant.

Unfortunately, the "Executive rights" of the Confederation Congress weren't specified anywhere else either. At the time, *President of the United States in Congress Assembled* referred to the presiding officer of the Confederation Congress. This unremarkable officer chaired meetings but exercised no powers independent of Congress as a whole. Congress, not any particular individual, was responsible for overseeing the Revolutionary War, appointing ambassadors, executing federal policies, and performing all of the other tasks of the federal government. The closest Congress came to creating an independent executive branch was a "committee of the states," consisting of one delegate per state, to manage the government while Congress was in recess. *See* Michael Klarman, *The Framers' Coup: The Making of the United States Constitution* 213 (2016).

The states, by contrast, did have a history of independent "executive" officers. During the colonial era, most of the thirteen colonies were governed by royal governors appointed by the British Crown. Acting as agents of the Crown, these governors typically had responsibilities such as signing or vetoing legislation passed by the colonial assemblies, dissolving and convening the assemblies at their discretion, appointing judges and officers to enforce colonial law, and commanding colonial armed forces. *See* Robert Middlekauff, *The Glorious Cause* 135 (2005). For its part, the Crown exercised similar functions with respect to the British Parliament—while also issuing pardons, making treaties, receiving and appointing ambassadors from foreign states, and deciding when to make war or peace. The first twelve grievances listed in the Declaration of Independence all relate to unilateral actions of the Crown and governors that the colonists found abusive, such as vetoing "wholesome" laws, maintaining standing armies, and dissolving colonial assemblies.

In part because of how these various powers had been abused, the state constitutions of the 1770s and 1780s all created weak executive officers dependent on state legislatures—if they created executives at all. On one extreme was New Hampshire, which followed Congress in vesting all power in the legislature. Although New Hampshire designated the leader of the legislature's upper house the "President," it gave this person no additional powers. N.H. Const. of 1776, ¶ 3. Pennsylvania didn't retreat quite as far from an independent executive: it lodged the power to appoint judges and the power to execute laws in the "president" of an elected "supreme executive council"—but it, too, cabined the president's independence by giving the legislature a role in appointing the position. Pa. Const. of 1776, §§ 19–20. The most powerful chief executive belonged to Massachusetts, whose constitution gave a popularly elected "supreme executive magistrate"—the governor—the power to veto laws, appoint officers, execute the law, and command the armed forces. Mass. Const. of

1780, pt. 2, ch. 2, arts. I–VIII. But even Massachusetts's governor could exercise some of these functions, such as the power to appoint officers, only with the advice of a "council" chosen from the state senate. *See, e.g.*, *id.* art. IX.

So, at the very least, when the Constitution was written, there were some inconsistencies about how to define executive powers. There wasn't even a consensus about whether a chief executive had to be a single person, as in Massachusetts, or a council, as in Pennsylvania. Nor was there consensus about how executives were generally appointed: they could be elected in part by the legislature, as in Pennsylvania, or by the people, as in Massachusetts.

With this context in mind, let's return to the opening sentence—"The executive Power shall be vested in a President of the United States of America"—and ask again what the Constitution means by the term *executive power*.

25.1.1
Opinions on the Proclamation of Neutrality

15 The Papers of Alexander Hamilton 33 (Harold C. Syrett ed., 1969) (1793)
15 The Papers of James Madison 66 (Thomas A. Mason ed., 1985) (1793)

There are two basic interpretations of the opening sentence of Article II, often called the Vesting Clause.

One is that the clause functions like the opening sentence of Article I: it explains who can wield the executive power (a "President of the United States," as opposed to the "Congress of the United States"), but it doesn't grant any powers on its own. Rather, the executive powers granted by the Constitution are located elsewhere: in the clauses that give the president (1) the powers to recommend laws, to veto laws, and to convene or adjourn Congress; (2) the power to appoint judges, ambassadors, and federal officers; (3) the duty to take care that the laws be faithfully executed; (4) the power to grant pardons for federal offenses; (5) the power to command the armed forces; and (6) the powers to make treaties and to receive ambassadors. Following this interpretation's intuitive logic, we'll turn to each of these clauses in detail in the next few sections.

A second interpretation extracts meaning out of the textual differences between the opening sentences of Article I and Article II. It contends that the Vesting Clause *alone* is the principal source of presidential power. From this perspective, it matters enormously that the legislative powers vested by Article I are those "herein granted" by the rest of the document, whereas the executive power vested by Article II doesn't have such a qualification. Adherents of this theory argue that if Article II began and ended with the Vesting Clause, then the president could constitutionally veto laws, appoint officers, grant pardons, and do all sorts of things that prior executives could do.

These two competing interpretations first clashed in a 1793 debate that paralleled the 1791 debate over Congress's implied powers to charter a bank. The characters in this second debate were the same: on one side was the secretary of state, Thomas Jefferson; and on the other was the secretary of the Treasury, Alexander Hamilton.

The controversy erupted when revolutionary France declared war on Great Britain in early 1793. This war implicated the United States; during the Revolutionary War, the United States had signed an indispensable treaty with France that established a "defensive alliance" between the two countries. But President George Washington didn't want to enter another war, so he asked his cabinet whether he had the constitutional authority to issue a proclamation stating that the United States wasn't bound by its treaty obligations to declare war on Great Britain. Jefferson said no; Hamilton said yes.

Jefferson argued that Article II gave the president no explicit power to issue a proclamation of neutrality, just as he had once argued that Article I gave Congress no explicit power to charter a bank. Jefferson instead emphasized that Article I empowers *Congress* to decide whether or not to declare war. Moreover, while Article II authorizes the president to "make Treaties," the president can do so only with the consent of two-thirds of the Senate. He therefore contended that only Congress could decide whether to adhere to treaties.

Hamilton, by contrast, argued that the Vesting Clause gave the president all powers implied by the term *executive*—including the power to interpret the meaning of the existing treaty with France. This implied-powers argument was analogous to his earlier argument that Congress had the power to charter a bank. It was similarly persuasive. Washington agreed with Hamilton, leading Jefferson to resign from the cabinet in disgust.

A few months later, Hamilton published in a newspaper the following defense of the proclamation of neutrality. After reading it, Jefferson wrote to his ally, James Madison, "For god's sake, my dear Sir, take up your pen, select the most striking heresies, and cut him to pieces in the face of the public." 26 *The Papers of Thomas Jefferson* 443 (John Catanzariti ed., 1995). Madison reluctantly obliged.

■ [Alexander Hamilton,] Pacificus No. 1, [June 29, 1793][1]

[T]he objections which have been raised against the Proclamation of Neutrality lately issued by the President have been urged in a spirit of acrimony and invective, which demonstrates, that more was in view than merely a free discussion of an important public measure; that the discussion covers a design of weakening the confidence of the People in the author of the measure; in order to remove or lessen a powerful obstacle to the success of an opposition to the Government, which

---

1 **As You Read, Consider:** No statute authorized President George Washington to issue a proclamation of neutrality. Precisely where, then, does Alexander Hamilton locate the source of the president's power to do this? How does James Madison respond?

however it may change its form, according to circumstances, seems still to be adhered to and pursued with persevering Industry. . . .

In order to judge of the solidity of . . . [the constitutional] objection, it is necessary to examine what is the nature and design of a proclamation of neutrality.

The true nature & design of such an act is—to *make known* to the powers at War and to the Citizens of the Country, whose Government does the Act that such country is in the condition of a Nation at Peace with the belligerent parties, and under no obligations of Treaty, to become an *associate in the war* with either of them; that this being its situation its intention is to observe a conduct conformable with it and to perform towards each the duties of neutrality; and as a consequence of this state of things, to give warning to all within its jurisdiction to abstain from acts that shall contravene those duties, under the penalties which the laws of the land (of which the law of Nations is a part) annexes to acts of contravention. . . .

If this be a just view of the true force and import of the Proclamation, it will remain to see whether the President in issuing it acted within his proper sphere, or stepped beyond the bounds of his constitutional authority and duty.

It will not be disputed that the management of the affairs of this country with foreign nations is confided to the Government of the UStates.

It can as little be disputed, that a Proclamation of Neutrality, where a Nation is at liberty to keep out of a War in which other Nations are engaged and means so to do, is a *usual* and a *proper* measure. *Its main object and effect are to prevent the Nation being immediately responsible for acts done by its citizens, without the privity or connivance of the Government, in contravention of the principles of neutrality*; an object of the greatest moment to a Country whose true interest lies in the preservation of peace.

The inquiry then is—what department of the Government of the UStates is the proper one to make a declaration of Neutrality in the cases in which the engagements of the Nation permit and its interests require such a declaration.

A correct and well informed mind will discern at once that it can belong neither to the Legislative nor Judicial Department and of course must belong to the Executive.

The Legislative Department is not the *organ* of intercourse between the UStates and foreign Nations. It is charged neither with *making* nor *interpreting* Treaties. It is therefore not naturally that Organ of the Government which is to pronounce the existing condition of the Nation, with regard to foreign Powers, or to admonish the Citizens of their obligations and duties as founded upon that condition of things. Still less is it charged with enforcing the execution and observance of these obligations and those duties.[2]

It is equally obvious that the act in question is foreign to the Judiciary Department of the Government. The province of that Department is to decide litigations in particular cases. It is indeed charged with the interpretation of treaties; but it exercises this function only in the litigated cases; that is where contending parties bring before it a specific controversy. It has no concern with pronouncing upon the external political relations of Treaties between Government and Government. This position is too plain to need being insisted upon.[3]

---

[2] **Question:** Article I makes Congress responsible for "declaring War." Do you agree with Hamilton that it is nevertheless not Congress's role to "pronounce the existing condition of the Nation," i.e., to declare *peace* or *neutrality*?

[3] **Question:** Here, Hamilton argues that the United States' relationship with France and Great Britain is a *political* question, not a legal question. Is this view consistent with later articulations of the political question doctrine?

It must then of necessity belong to the Executive Department to exercise the function in Question—when a proper case for the exercise of it occurs.

It appears to be connected with that department in various capacities, as the *organ* of intercourse between the Nation and foreign Nations—as the interpreter of the National Treaties in those cases in which the Judiciary is not competent, that is in the cases between Government and Government—as that Power, which is charged with the Execution of the Laws, of which Treaties form a part—as that Power which is charged with the command and application of the Public Force.

This view of the subject is so natural and obvious—so analogous to general theory and practice—that no doubt can be entertained of its justness, unless such doubt can be deduced from particular provisions of the Constitution of the UStates.

Let us see then if cause for such doubt is to be found in that constitution.

The second Article of the Constitution of the UStates, section 1st, establishes this general Proposition, That "The Executive Power shall be vested in a President of the United States of America."

The same article[, section 2d,] proceeds to designate particular cases of Executive Power. It declares among other things that the President shall be Commander in Chief of the army and navy of the UStates and of the Militia of the several states when called into the actual service of the UStates, that he shall have power by and with the advice of the senate to make treaties; that it shall be his duty to receive ambassadors and other public Ministers and to take care that the laws be faithfully executed.

It would not consist with the rules of sound construction to consider this enumeration of particular authorities as derogating from the more comprehensive grant contained in the general clause, further than as it may be coupled with express restrictions or qualifications; as in regard to the cooperation of the Senate in the appointment of Officers and the making of treaties; which are qualifications of the general executive powers of appointing officers and making treaties: Because the difficulty of a complete and perfect specification of all the cases of Executive authority would naturally dictate the use of general terms—and would render it improbable that a specification of certain particulars was designd as a substitute for those terms, when antecedently used. The different mode of expression employed in the constitution in regard to the two powers the Legislative and the Executive serves to confirm this inference. In the article which grants the legislative powers of the Govertnt. the expressions are—"*All Legislative powers herein granted shall be vested in a Congress of the UStates*"; in that which grants the Executive Power the expressions are, as already quoted "The Executive Power shall be vested in a President of the UStates of America."[4]

The enumeration ought rather therefore to be considered as intended by way of greater caution, to specify and regulate the principal articles implied in the definition of Executive Power; leaving the rest to flow from the general grant of that power,

---

[4] **Questions:** Hamilton is arguing that there is a meaningful distinction between the opening sentences of Article I and Article II. The opening sentence of Article I vests in Congress only those legislative powers "herein granted." The rest of Article I then provides what those enumerated powers are. But Hamilton writes here that the opening sentence of Article II gives the president *all* "Executive Power." The rest of Article II is merely a list of "exceptions and qualifications" for that initial grant of power. Is this a coherent interpretation of Article II, or a lawyer's creative argument to save a client in a difficult situation? Isn't it a far more intuitive interpretation that Article II gives the president the specific executive powers listed in Article II?

interpreted in conformity to other parts of the constitution and to the principles of free government.

The general doctrine then of our constitution is, that the Executive Power of the Nation is vested in the President; subject only to the *exceptions* and *qu[a]lifications* which are expressed in the instrument.

Two of these have been already noticed—the participation of the Senate in the appointment of Officers and the making of Treaties. A third remains to be mentioned the right of the Legislature "to declare war and grant letters of marque and reprisal."

With these exceptions the Executive Power of the Union is completely lodged in the President. This mode of construing the Constitution has indeed been recognized by Congress in formal acts, upon full consideration and debate. The power of removal from office is an important instance.[5]

And since upon general principles for reasons already given, the issuing of a proclamation of neutrality is merely an Executive Act; since also the general Executive Power of the Union is vested in the President, the conclusion is, that the step, which has been taken by him, is liable to no just exception. . . .

It may be observed that this Inference would be just if the power of declaring war had not been vested in the Legislature, but that this power naturally includes the right of judging whether the Nation is under obligations to make war or not.

The answer to this is, that however true it may be, that the right of the Legislature to declare war includes the right of judging whether the Nation be under obligations to make War or not—it will not follow that the Executive is in any case excluded from a similar right of Judgment, in the execution of its own functions.

If the Legislature have a right to make war on the one hand—it is on the other the duty of the Executive to preserve Peace till war is declared; and in fulfilling that duty, it must necessarily possess a right of judging what is the nature of the obligations which the treaties of the Country impose on the Government; and when in pursuance of this right it has concluded that there is nothing in them inconsistent with a *state* of neutrality, it becomes both its province and its duty to enforce the laws incident to that state of the Nation. The Executive is charged with the execution of all laws, the laws of Nations as well as the Municipal law, which recognises and adopts those laws. It is consequently bound, by faithfully executing the laws of neutrality, when that is the state of the Nation, to avoid giving a cause of war to foreign Powers.[6]

This is the direct and proper end of the proclamation of neutrality. It declares to the UStates their situation with regard to the Powers at war and makes known to the Community that the laws incident to that situation will be enforced. In doing this, it conforms to an established usage of Nations, the operation of which as before remarked is to obviate a responsibility on the part of the whole Society, for secret and unknown violations of the rights of any of the warring parties by its citizens.

Those who object to the proclamation will readily admit that it is the right and duty of the Executive to judge of, or to interpret, those articles of our treaties which

---

[5] **Note:** "The power of removal from office" refers to a high-profile debate in 1789 over whether a president could remove an executive officer without statutory authorization. Madison, then a member of Congress, argued that such a power could be inferred from the text of Article II. This debate will later be the subject of *Myers v. United States* (see section 27.3).

[6] **Question:** The reason that the proclamation of neutrality was so controversial was because the United States had earlier ratified a treaty with the prerevolutionary Kingdom of France. The proclamation of neutrality declared that the United States would not consider itself bound by those treaty obligations because the French Republic deposed the monarch. In this context, is issuing a declaration of neutrality really the same thing as executing the president's constitutionally imposed duty to "take Care that the Laws be faithfully executed"?

give to France particular privileges, in order to the enforcement of those privileges: But the necessary consequence of this is, that the Executive must judge what are the proper bounds of those privileges—what rights are given to other nations by our treaties with them—what rights the law of Nature and Nations gives and our treaties permit, in respect to those Nations with whom we have no treaties; in fine what are the reciprocal rights and obligations of the United States & of all & each of the powers at War.

The right of the Executive to receive ambassadors and other public Ministers may serve to illustrate the relative duties of the Executive and Legislative Departments. This right includes that of judging, in the case of a Revolution of Government in a foreign Country, whether the new rulers are competent organs of the National Will and ought to be recognised or not: And where a treaty antecedently exists between the UStates and such nation that right involves the power of giving operation or not to such treaty. For until the new Government is *acknowledged,* the treaties between the nations, as far at least as regards *public* rights, are of course suspended.

This power of determ[in]ing virtually in the case supposed upon the operation of national Treaties as a consequence, of the power to receive ambassadors and other public Ministers, is an important instance of the right of the Executive to decide the obligations of the Nation with regard to foreign Nations.[7] To apply it to the case of France, if there had been a Treaty of alliance *offensive* and defensive between the UStates and that Country, the unqualified acknowledgement of the new Government would have put the UStates in a condition to become an associate in the War in which France was engaged—and would have laid the Legislature under an obligation, if required, and there was otherwise no valid excuse, of exercising its power of declaring war.[8]

This serves as an example of the right of the Executive, in certain cases, to determine the condition of the Nation, though it may consequentially affect the proper or improper exercise of the Power of the Legislature to declare war. The Executive indeed cannot control the exercise of that power—further than by the exer[c]ise of its general right of objecting to all acts of the Legislature; liable to being overruled by two thirds of both houses of Congress. The Legislature is free to perform its own duties according to its own sense of them—though the Executive in the exercise of its constitutional powers, may establish an antecedent state of things which ought to weigh in the legislative decisions. From the division of the Executive Power there results, in reference to it, a *concurrent* authority, in the distributed cases.

Hence in the case stated, though treaties can only be made by the President and Senate, their activity may be continued or suspended by the President alone.

---

7 **Question:** Hamilton is now quoting the clause of Article II that imposes on the president the duty to "receive Ambassadors." Do you agree with Hamilton that this phrase is evidence that the executive power includes the power to determine which foreign governments to recognize? This interpretation will later be the subject of *Zivotofsky ex rel. Zivotofsky v. Kerry* (see section 32.4).

8 **Questions:** Perhaps the strongest argument against Hamilton's position is that the Constitution vests Congress with the power to declare war; therefore, Congress alone should have the power to declare neutrality or revise treaties. Hamilton is responding that war and treaties are inherently *executive* actions, not legislative actions. Therefore, the Constitution's grant to Congress of the power to declare war and ratify treaties should be treated as narrow exceptions to the president's executive power.

Does Hamilton's interpretation of executive power raise the possibility of an unlimited chief executive, or does he offer guidance about potential limits? Under Hamilton's interpretation, how could Congress overcome a president's veto if Congress disagrees with the president about his proclamation of neutrality?

No objection has been made to the Presidents having acknowleged the Republic of France, by the Reception of its Minister, without having consulted the Senate; though that body is connected with him in the making of Treaties, and though the consequence of his act of reception is to give operation to the Treaties heretofore made with that Country: But he is censured for having declared the UStates to be in a state of peace & neutrality, with regard to the Powers at War; because the right of *changing* that state & *declaring war* belongs to the Legislature.

It deserves to be remarked, that as the participation of the senate in the making of Treaties and the power of the Legislature to declare war are exceptions out of the general "Executive Power" vested in the President, they are to be construed strictly—and ought to be extended no further than is essential to their execution.

While therefore the Legislature can alone declare war, can alone actually transfer the nation from a state of Peace to a state of War—it belongs to the "Executive Power," to do whatever else the laws of Nations cooperating with the Treaties of the Country enjoin. . . .

But though it has been thought adviseable to vindicate the authority of the Executive on this broad and comprehensive ground—it was not absolutely necessary to do so. That clause of the constitution which makes it his duty to "take care that the laws be faithfully executed" might alone have been relied upon, and this simple process of argument pursued.[9]

The President is the constitutional Executor of the laws. Our Treaties and the laws of Nations form a part of the law of the land. He who is to execute the laws must first judge for himself of their meaning. In order to the observance of that conduct, which the laws of nations combined with our treaties prescribed to this country, in reference to the present War in Europe, it was necessary for the President to judge for himself whether there was any thing in our treaties incompatible with an adherence to neutrality. Having judged that there was not, he had a right, and if in his opinion the interests of the Nation required it, it was his duty, as Executor of the laws, to proclaim the neutrality of the Nation, to exhort all persons to observe it, and to warn them of the penalties which would attend its non observance.

The Proclamation has been represented as enacting some new law. This is a view of it entirely erroneous. It only proclaims a *fact* with regard to the *existing state* of the Nation, informs the citizens of what the laws previously established require of them in that state, & warns them that these laws will be put in execution against the Infractors of them. . . .

■ [James Madison,] Helvidius No. 1, [Aug. 24, 1793]

Several pieces with the signature of Pacificus were lately published, which have been read with singular pleasure and applause, by the foreigners and degenerate citizens among us, who hate our republican government, and the French revolution. . . .

The substance of the first piece, sifted from its inconsistencies and its vague expressions, may be thrown into the following propositions: That the powers of declaring war and making treaties are, in their nature, executive powers:

---

[9] **Question:** Hamilton appears to hedge in these final paragraphs. Rather than locate the president's power in the Vesting Clause, he suggests that the proclamation of neutrality represents the fulfillment of the president's enumerated duty to "take Care that the Laws be faithfully executed." Either way, he argues that the president possesses implied powers to proclaim neutrality. Is either interpretation of Article II as persuasive as his earlier argument with Thomas Jefferson, in which he argued that the Necessary and Proper Clause vests Congress with the implied power to charter a bank?

That being particularly vested by the constitution in other departments, they are to be considered as exceptions out of the general grant to the executive department:

That being, as exceptions, to be construed strictly, the powers not strictly within them, remain with the executive:

That the executive consequently, as the organ of intercourse with foreign nations, and the interpreter and executor of treaties, and the law of nations, is authorised, to expound all articles of treaties, those involving questions of war and peace, as well as others; to judge of the obligations of the United States to make war or not . . .; and, to pronounce the state of things resulting from the obligations of the United States, as understood by the executive: . . . .[10]

If there be any countenance to these positions, it must be found either 1st, in the writers, of authority, on public law; or 2d, in the quality and operation of the powers to make war and treaties; or 3d, in the constitution of the United States.

[1.] It would be of little use to enter far into the first source of information, not only because our own reason and our own constitution, are the best guides; but because a just analysis and discrimination of the powers of government, according to their executive, legislative and judiciary qualities are not to be expected in the works of the most received jurists, who wrote before a critical attention was paid to those objects, and with their eyes too much on monarchical governments, where all powers are confounded in the sovereignty of the prince. . . .

2. If we consult for a moment, the nature and operation of the two powers to declare war and make treaties, it will be impossible not to see that they can never fall within a proper definition of executive powers. The natural province of the executive magistrate is to execute laws, as that of the legislature is to make laws. All his acts therefore, properly executive, must pre-suppose the existence of the laws to be executed. A treaty is not an execution of laws: it does not pre-suppose the existence of laws. It is, on the contrary, to have itself the force of a *law*, and to be carried into *execution*, like all *other laws*, by the *executive magistrate*. To say then that the power of making treaties which are confessedly laws, belongs naturally to the department which is to execute laws, is to say, that the executive department naturally includes a legislative power. In theory, this is an absurdity—in practice a tyranny.

The power to declare war is subject to similar reasoning. A declaration that there shall be war, is not an execution of laws: it does not suppose pre-existing laws to be executed: it is not in any respect, an act merely executive. It is, on the contrary, one of the most deliberative acts that can be performed; and when performed, has the effect of *repealing* all the *laws* operating in a state of peace, so far as they are inconsistent with a state of war: and of *enacting* as *a rule for the executive*, a *new code* adapted to the relation between the society and its foreign enemy. In like manner a conclusion of peace *annuls* all the *laws* peculiar to a state of war, and *revives* the general *laws* incident to a state of peace. . . .

From this view of the subject it must be evident, that although the executive may be a convenient organ of preliminary communications with foreign governments, on the subjects of treaty or war; and the proper agent for carrying into execution the final determinations of the competent authority; yet it can have no pretensions from the

---

[10] **Question:** Here, Madison is focusing his attention on Hamilton's argument that the first sentence of Article II vests the president with all "executive Power"—including the powers over war, treaties, and peace—subject to the qualifications of Article I and II. In the next few paragraphs, Madison calls this interpretation "monarchical." How does Madison distinguish between which powers the president can exercise on his own and which must first be delegated by Congress?

nature of the powers in question compared with the nature of the executive trust, to that essential agency which gives validity to such determinations. . . .

3. It remains to be enquired whether there be any thing in the constitution itself which shews that the powers of making war and peace are considered as of an executive nature, and as comprehended within a general grant of executive power. . . .

In the general distribution of powers, we find that of declaring war expressly vested in the Congress, where every other legislative power is declared to be vested, and without any other qualification than what is common to every other legislative act. The constitutional idea of this power would seem then clearly to be, that it is of a legislative and not an executive nature.

This conclusion becomes irresistible, when it is recollected, that the constitution cannot be supposed to have placed either any power legislative in its nature, entirely among executive powers, or any power executive in its nature, entirely among legislative powers, without charging the constitution, with that kind of intermixture and consolidation of different powers, which would violate a fundamental principle in the organization of free governments. If it were not unnecessary to enlarge on this topic here, it could be shewn, that the constitution was originally vindicated, and has been constantly expounded, with a disavowal of any such intermixture.

The power of treaties is vested jointly in the President and in the Senate, which is a branch of the legislature. From this arrangement merely, there can be no inference that would necessarily exclude the power from the executive class: since the senate is joined with the President in another power, that of appointing to offices, which as far as relate to executive offices at least, is considered as of an executive nature. Yet on the other hand, there are sufficient indications that the power of treaties is regarded by the constitution as materially different from mere executive power, and as having more affinity to the legislative than to the executive character.

One circumstance indicating this, is the constitutional regulation under which the senate give their consent in the case of treaties. In all other cases the consent of the body is expressed by a majority of voices. In this particular case, a concurrence of two thirds at least is made necessary, as a substitute or compensation for the other branch of the legislature, which on certain occasions, could not be conveniently a party to the transaction.

But the conclusive circumstance is, that treaties when formed according to the constitutional mode, are confessedly to have the force and operation of *laws*, and are to be a rule for the courts in controversies between man and man, as much as any *other laws*. They are even emphatically declared by the constitution to be "the supreme law of the land."

So far the argument from the constitution is precisely in opposition to the doctrine. As little will be gained in its favour from a comparison of the two powers, with those particularly vested in the President alone.[11]

As there are but few it will be most satisfactory to review them one by one.

"The President shall be commander in chief of the army and navy of the United States, and of the militia when called into the actual service of the United States."

---

[11] **Question:** Madison has rejected Hamilton's position that treaties are inherently executive and now turns to an examination of each clause in Article II to see whether they authorize a proclamation of neutrality. How does this analysis compare to Thomas Jefferson's line-by-line rejection of Hamilton's argument that Congress had the implied power to charter a bank?

There can be no relation worth examining between this power and the general power of making treaties. And instead of being analogous to the power of declaring war, it affords a striking illustration of the incompatibility of the two powers in the same hands. Those who are to *conduct a war* cannot in the nature of things, be proper or safe judges, whether *a war ought* to be *commenced, continued*, or *concluded*. They are barred from the latter functions by a great principle in free government, analogous to that which separates the sword from the purse, or the power of executing from the power of enacting laws.

"He may require the opinion in writing of the principal officers in each of the executive departments upon any subject relating to the duties of their respective offices; and he shall have power to grant reprieves and pardons for offences against the United States, except in case of impeachment." These powers can have nothing to do with the subject.

"The President shall have power to fill up vacancies that may happen during the recess of the senate, by granting commissions which shall expire at the end of the next session." The same remark is applicable to this power, as also to that of "receiving ambassadors, other public ministers and consuls." The particular use attempted to be made of this last power will be considered in another place.

"He shall take care that the laws shall be faithfully executed and shall commission all officers of the United States." To see the laws faithfully executed constitutes the essence of the executive authority. But what relation has it to the power of making treaties and war, that is, of determining what the *laws shall be* with regard to other nations? No other certainly than what subsists between the powers of executing and enacting laws; no other consequently, than what forbids a coalition of the powers in the same department.

I pass over the few other specified functions assigned to the President, such as that of convening of the legislature, &c. &c. which cannot be drawn into the present question. . . .

Thus it appears that by whatever standard we try this doctrine, it must be condemned as no less vicious in theory than it would be dangerous in practice. . . .

Whence then can the writer have borrowed it?

There is but one answer to this question.[12]

The power of making treaties and the power of declaring war, are *royal prerogatives* in the *British government*, and are accordingly treated as Executive prerogatives by *British commentators*. . . .

We shall be the more confirmed in the necessity of this solution of the problem, by looking back to the era of the Constitution, and satisfying ourselves that the writer could not have been misled by the doctrines maintained by our own commentators on our own government. That I may not ramble beyond prescribed limits, I shall content myself with an extract from a work which entered into a systematic explanation and defence of the Constitution, and to which there has frequently been ascribed some influence in conciliating the public assent to the government in the form proposed. . . .

---

[12] **Question:** In the next few paragraphs, Madison accuses Hamilton of being not only a monarchist but also a hypocrite. Even though both of these essays were published under pseudonyms, Madison makes fun of Hamilton by quoting Hamilton's words from *The Federalist*, in which Hamilton rejected the argument that treaties were executive and not legislative. What does this disagreement suggest about the present-day reliance on *The Federalist* as an objective explanation of the Constitution's true meaning?

> "Tho' several writers on the subject of government place that power (of *making treaties*) in the class of *Executive authorities*, yet this is *evidently* an *arbitrary disposition*. For if we attend *carefully*, to its operation, it will be found to partake more of the legislative than of the executive character, though it does not seem strictly to fall within the definition of either of them. The essence of the legislative authority, is to enact laws; or in other words, to prescribe rules for the regulation of the society. While the execution of the laws and the employment of the common strength, either for this purpose, or for the common defense, seem to comprise *all* functions of the Executive magistrate. The power of making treaties is *plainly* neither the one nor the other. . . ."[13]
>
> It will not fail to be remarked on this commentary, that whatever doubts may be started as to the correctness of its reasoning against the legislative nature of the power to make treaties: it is clear, *consistent* and *confident*, in deciding that the power is *plainly* and *evidently* not an executive power.

NOTE: PRESIDENT'S LEGISLATIVE POWERS

As we will see, Hamilton's interpretation of the Vesting Clause carried the day in 1793 and remains the dominant view among executive branch officers. Indeed, when Thomas Jefferson became president, he took a similarly broad view of Article II to justify the Louisiana Purchase. Today, Hamilton's view animates the president's implied powers to remove executive officers, *see Myers v. United States*, 272 U.S. 52 (1926); *Seila Law LLC v. Consumer Fin. Prot. Bureau*, 140 S. Ct. 2183 (2020); and to conduct foreign affairs, *see United States v. Curtiss-Wright Exp. Corp.*, 299 U.S. 304 (1936); *Zivotofsky ex rel. Zivotofsky v. Kerry*, 576 U.S. 1059 (2015).

25.2 CONGRESS'S INABILITY TO DELEGATE LEGISLATIVE POWER

Many debates over the president's powers—from old debates over proclamations of neutrality to recent debates over the power to order air strikes abroad—concern whether a particular power is "legislative" or "executive." Alexander Hamilton and James Madison each provide various ways of answering this question: appealing to historical practice, considering functionally whether a power looks more like making new law or executing existing law, and considering whether a power is placed in Article I or Article II.

Complicating this debate are the many so-called executive powers that undoubtedly relate to making new laws and that are occasionally found in Article I. Article II of the Constitution also gives the president power that can functionally be described as making laws rather than executing laws. Although the line between legislative powers and executive power is sometimes hazy, the Supreme Court has tried to clarify it with the "nondelegation" doctrine.

---

[13] **Note:** This block quote is from *Federalist No. 75*, written by Hamilton a few years earlier. While pretending not to know who the author is, Madison is making fun of Hamilton for departing from his previous "*confident*" position.

Articles I and II presidential legislative powers

Veto power. One of the Article I presidential powers that relates to making new laws is the president's power to veto legislation, discussed in the section on how Congress enacts legislation (section 24.1). Such a power has historically been wielded by the British Crown, which alone (still) has the power to determine whether to assent to an act of Parliament. Royal governors generally also exercised a veto power (and still do in former British colonies like Canada and Australia), as did the governor of Massachusetts after the American Revolution. During the Constitutional Convention, James Madison proposed that the executive have the power to veto federal and state legislation while sitting alongside Supreme Court justices as one member of a "council of revision." *See* Michael Klarman, *The Framers' Coup: The Making of the United States Constitution* 222 (2016). The convention slowly chipped away at this proposal, instead giving the executive alone a veto only over federal legislation—a veto that could be overridden by a supermajority of Congress.

The first six presidential administrations exercised the veto power sparingly—eleven times through 1829. All of these vetoes were delivered on the ground that the president believed that the bill before him was unconstitutional. One such example was when President James Madison vetoed the "bonus bill" that would have used revenue from the Second Bank of the United States to pay for infrastructure projects (see section 6.1).

President Andrew Jackson fundamentally changed the nature of the veto power when he vetoed the rechartering of the Second Bank in 1832. As discussed earlier (section 3.2), Jackson explained that Article II required the president to take an oath to "preserve, protect and defend the Constitution." 8 Reg. Deb. app. 73–76 (1832). Although the Supreme Court had recently upheld the bank in *McCulloch v. Maryland*, 17 U.S. (4 Wheat.) 316 (1819), Jackson argued that this oath required him to decide for himself whether the bank was constitutional, and "the authority of the Supreme Court must not . . . be permitted to control the Congress or the Executive when acting in their legislative capacities." 8 Reg. Deb. app. at 76. Jackson could have ended his veto message there with that blunt rebuke of the Supreme Court's interpretive supremacy. But he continued by arguing that even if the bank were *constitutionally* necessary and proper, he disagreed that the bank was *politically* necessary or proper. That is, Jackson announced that he disagreed with Congress about the political merits of the bank. He used his veto, therefore, as if he were a third house of the legislature, writing, "The opinion of the judges has no more authority over Congress than the opinion of Congress over the judges, and on that point the President is independent of both." *Id.*

Jackson's political veto outraged his opponents, who called the president "King Andrew" and began to call themselves "Whigs" after the

British political party that had historically opposed absolute monarchy. *See* Jon Meacham, *American Lion: Andrew Jackson in the White House* 209–12, 230–38 (2009). But over time, Jackson's interpretation of the veto power became widely shared among future presidential administrations. Where Jackson's twelve vetoes eclipsed the total number of vetoes issued before his time, some presidents after him have issued hundreds of vetoes. Today, the president is a central figure in the legislative process.

Power to propose laws. Article II, Section 3, declares that the president "shall from time to time give to the Congress Information of the State of the Union, and recommend to their Consideration such Measures as he shall judge necessary and expedient." As noted in the discussion of Congress's power to investigate (section 23.1), this is the only clause of the Constitution that expressly mentions how Congress can acquire information. Taking this duty literally, the first secretary of the Treasury, Alexander Hamilton, not only provided Congress with data about the state of the economy but also provided draft bills and budgets for Congress to adopt. *See* Josh Chafetz, *Congress's Constitution: Legislative Authority and the Separation of Powers* 58 (2016).

After Congress adopted its modern system of legislative hearings in the nineteenth century, a long series of presidents declined to "usurp" legislative powers by proposing legislation. *See, e.g.*, 6 *Messages and Papers of the Presidents* 2513–19, 2561–62, 2608–15 (James D. Richardson ed., 1902). Instead, the president delivered an annual message by letter for a member or clerk of Congress to read aloud.

But in 1913, President Woodrow Wilson became the first president in over a century to deliver his State of the Union address in person to Congress, inaugurating a tradition of using the speech to advance the president's legislative agenda. A. Scott Berg, *Wilson* 292–94 (2014). Like Hamilton, executive officials today also routinely send draft bills and budgets to Congress for its approval.

Power to convene and dissolve the legislature. Article II, Section 3, also empowers the president to, "on extraordinary Occasions, convene both Houses, or either of them, and in Case of Disagreement between them, with Respect to the Time of Adjournment, he may adjourn them to such Time as he shall think proper." This power to convene and dissolve the legislature has been exercised by the British Crown for almost as long as Parliament has been in existence. The president has also frequently summoned both houses of Congress into "special sessions" for legislative purposes and the Senate alone for "executive sessions" to consider nominations or treaties.

A famous example occurred in 1861. At the time, Congress typically held a special session for a week or two after the president's inauguration in March but didn't meet again until the following December. Shortly after President Abraham Lincoln was inaugurated, however, rebels in South Carolina fired the opening shots of the Civil War on Fort Sumter.

Lincoln summoned Congress to reconvene months early, on July 4. In the meantime, he had to act alone—ordering the blockade of southern ports and the suspension of habeas corpus that were at issue in the *Prize Cases*, 67 U.S. (2 Black) 635 (1863), and *Ex parte Merryman*, 17 F. Cas. 144 (C.C.D. Md. 1861) (No. 9487). Like Jackson in his veto message, Lincoln defended his unilateral actions by invoking the clause of Article II that requires him to swear to "preserve, protect and defend the Constitution." 6 *Messages and Papers of the Presidents*, *supra*, at 25. But the July 4 session of Congress ratified most of his actions anyway.

Vice presidential power as Senate's presiding officer. One final legislative power worth mentioning is the vice president's role as the "President"—the presiding officer—of the Senate. This has a parallel in some bicameral colonial legislatures, in which the governor sat in the upper house of the legislature. New York's constitution of 1777 made the "lieutenant-governor" the president of the state senate, and it appears that the U.S. Constitution cut and pasted New York's provision. *See* N.Y. Const. of 1777, art. XX. Vice President John C. Calhoun established the precedent that a vice president can cut off and direct debates on the Senate floor—a practice that has since been abandoned. *See* Adam Jentleson, *Kill Switch: The Rise of the Modern Senate* 48–49 (2021). Vice presidents since Calhoun have characterized their duties in the Senate as "not worth a bucket of warm piss." Robert Caro, *The Passage of Power* 110 (2013). But Vice President Dick Cheney famously argued that by virtue of his role in the Senate, the vice president was not within the executive branch and therefore immune from an executive order requiring executive-branch entities to disclose classified documents. *See* Charlie Savage, *Takeover* 163–64 (2008).

Nondelegation doctrine

The president's powers to veto legislation, propose laws, and convene and dissolve the legislature suggest that there isn't an obvious distinction between executive and legislative powers. And just as President George Washington's proclamation of neutrality could be understood by Hamilton as an executive interpretation of an existing treaty and by Madison as a legislative change in the law, other actions can often be characterized by different people as falling on either side of the legislative/executive line. Nevertheless, the Supreme Court has, historically, attempted to maintain this line and prevent one branch from crossing to the other side. The term that the Court has used to describe its ban on lawmaking by an executive official is *nondelegation doctrine*.

For its first century of existence, the nondelegation doctrine stalked the halls of Congress without ever laying hands on a statutory victim. As the president of the American Bar Association wrote in 1916, "the old doctrine prohibiting the delegation of legislative power has virtually retired from the field and given up the fight." *Addresses on Government and Citizenship by Elihu Root* 535 (Robert Bacon & James Brown Scott eds., 1916).

The doctrine first arose in the early nineteenth century while the federal government was attempting to chart a neutral course through Napoleonic France's various wars with Great Britain. After France and Great Britain began seizing U.S. ships instead of letting them dock in the other country's ports, Congress retaliated by passing the Non-Intercourse Act of 1809, ch. 24, 2 Stat. 528. This law prohibited the importation of goods into the United States from either country for one year—but it expired in 1810 without having much of an effect. The ineffectiveness of this first law inspired Congress to pass a second law, often called "Macon's Bill Number 2." *See* Act of May 1, 1810, ch. 39, 2 Stat. 605. Macon's Bill Number 2 provided that if the president proclaimed that one of the two countries agreed to stop seizing U.S. ships, then the Non-Intercourse Act would be "revived and have full force and effect" with respect only to the other country—unless that country also agreed to respect U.S. neutrality. Act of May 1, 2 Stat. at 606. Later that year, Napoleon Bonaparte of France took advantage of the situation by sending President James Madison a message that France would stop interfering with U.S. commerce. Madison issued the statutory proclamation, and the British didn't respond. *See* Michael Beschloss, *Presidents of War* 45–48 (2018). The United States therefore began seizing goods imported from Great Britain, including goods carried on a brig called the *Aurora*. Similar seizures contributed to the War of 1812 with Great Britain.

The owner of the goods seized from the *Aurora* complained that Macon's Bill Number 2 had unconstitutionally given the president legislative power by authorizing him to "revive[ ]" an otherwise expired law. Pointing to the opening sentence of Article I—"All legislative Powers herein granted shall be vested in a Congress"—the owner argued that only Congress can exercise legislative powers, and therefore Congress cannot delegate those legislative powers to anyone else. The Supreme Court interpreted Macon's Bill Number 2 differently: not as a delegation of lawmaking power but as an ordinary statute whose terms took effect after certain conditions were met. "[W]e can see no sufficient reason why the legislature should not exercise its discretion in reviving the Act of March 1, 1809, either expressly or conditionally, as its judgment should direct," the Court wrote. *The Brig Aurora*, 11 U.S. (7 Cranch) 382, 387 (1813). *The Brig Aurora* essentially announced that no constitutional obstacle prevented Congress from conditioning a law's effect on whether a certain fact existed, while leaving it to others to determine those facts.

A few years later, the Court added to this holding in a challenge to the Judiciary Act of 1789, which empowered courts "to make and establish all necessary rules for the orderly conducting of business in the said courts." Judiciary Act of 1789, ch. 20, 1 Stat. 73, 83. The challenger argued that this law was different from Macon's Bill Number 2: rather than condition a law's effect on the existence of certain facts, Congress had simply allowed another branch of government to determine policies. But the Supreme Court didn't think this alone was a problem: "Congress may certainly delegate to others powers which the legislature may rightfully exercise itself," Chief Justice John Marshall wrote. *Wayman v. Southard*, 23 U.S. (10 Wheat.) 1, 42 (1825).

Marshall accepted, in principle, the challenger's argument that Congress could not "delegate to the courts or to any other tribunals powers which are strictly and exclusively legislative." *Id.* at 43. But, the chief justice added, it was unreasonable to expect that every law would provide for every contingency. Any law authorizing a person to do something necessarily entails giving that person discretion about how to respond to minutiae or unforeseen events. The chief justice suggested that the line distinguishing a law that improperly delegates legislative power from a law that properly "commit[s] something to the discretion of the other departments" was determined by the delegation's importance: really important things "must be entirely regulated by the legislature itself," while "those of less interest" could be delegated to other people by "a general provision" authorizing them to "to fill up the details." *Id.* at 43, 46. The chief justice didn't elaborate on this point, however, nor did he think that it was appropriate for a court to precisely draw the line. Instead, he called the boundary between a proper and improper delegation "a subject of delicate and difficult inquiry, into which a court will not enter unnecessarily." *Id.* at 46.

It is not obvious where Marshall came up with the idea that some delegations of congressional power might cross a "line" and be unconstitutional. As early as 1789, the first Congresses delegated enormous and open-ended rulemaking authority to a vast array of agencies. *See* Julian Davis Mortenson & Nicholas Bagley, *Delegation at the Founding*, 121 Colum. L. Rev. 1, 43 (2021). For example, the Northwest Ordinance conveyed standardless discretion to the governor and judges of the Northwest Territory to craft the entire body of laws for the territory. *Id.* at 79. Few, if any, of these delegations appear to have been controversial. At most, the only contemporary protest was levied against the idea that Congress might irrevocably alienate its power to make laws. *Id.* at 6.

Even after *Wayman*, Congress continued to delegate lawmaking authority to Article I courts like the Court of Claims, agencies like the Interstate Commerce Commission, and territorial councils like the Arizona Territorial Legislature. As discussed in the section on Article I courts and territories (section 15.1), Marshall was quite tolerant of these delegations to what he called "legislative" or territorial courts. *See, e.g.*, *Am. Ins. Co. v. Canter*, 26 U.S. 511 (1828). By the twentieth century, Congress consistently focused its own attention on setting general policies while authorizing what became known as the "administrative state" to fill up the details. *See* Dwight Waldo, *The Administrative State* 124–25 (1948).

As Congress committed more of its important functions to administrative agencies, it increasingly tested even the deferential boundaries established by Marshall. For example, in the mid-nineteenth century, tariff rates were one of the most contested issues on Congress's legislative calendar. But by the end of the century, Congress was delegating some tariff-related responsibilities to the president, authorizing him to suspend importations from countries that had "unequal and unreasonable" trade restrictions on the United States. *See* Tariff Act of 1890, ch. 1244, 26 Stat. 567, 612. Evaluating this delegation, the Court repeated its mantra that "Congress cannot delegate legislative power to the president," calling this "a principle universally recognized as vital to the integrity and maintenance of the system of government ordained by the constitution." *Field v. Clark*, 143 U.S. 649, 692 (1892). But the Court held that these tariff laws were functionally identical to the statutes in *The Brig Aurora*. Both sets of laws established general policies—don't freely trade with governments that don't reciprocate—and gave the president discretion to determine when a fact existed to set those policies in motion. *Id.* Plus, the president wasn't actually setting tariff rates.

Even that last fact changed in 1922, when Congress authorized the president to set individual tariff rates for each country with the goal of helping domestic producers compete with foreign producers. To assist the president, Congress authorized an administrative agency, the United States Tariff Commission, to consider various factors such as the price of a particular article and the competitive advantages other countries possessed in manufacturing it. *See* Fordney-McCumber Tariff Act of 1922, ch. 356, 42 Stat. 858.

An importer who paid higher rates under this law complained that Congress had never delegated its taxing power before; such a power surely ranked among Congress's most important functions. But the Court upheld the delegation, this time explaining that the importance of the power didn't matter. All that mattered was whether Congress had offered the president sufficient guidance so that he was *executing* a policy rather than *creating* a new one. "It is conceded by counsel that Congress may use executive officers in the application and enforcement of a policy declared in law by Congress, and authorize such officers, in the application of the congressional declaration, to enforce it by regulation equivalent to law," the Court wrote in *J.W. Hampton, Jr. & Co. v. United States,* 276 U.S. 394, 409 (1928). "If Congress shall lay down by legislative act an *intelligible principle* to which the person or body authorized to fix such rates is directed to conform, such legislative action is not a forbidden delegation of legislative power." *Id.* (emphasis added).

25.2.1

Panama Refining Co. v. Ryan

293 U.S. 388 (1935)

Despite the lackluster impression of the nondelegation doctrine in the first half of its life, the doctrine finally came out swinging—briefly but vigorously—against President Franklin D. Roosevelt's New Deal during the Great Depression.

When the Depression hit in 1929, the petroleum industry was one of the first affected. Hundreds of new oil wells had been constructed in the 1920s, producing such an oversupply of oil that the price collapsed with the economy. Several of the largest oil-producing states immediately adopted quotas to prevent overproduction. But many oil producers in these states simply ignored the quotas, packed their oil into tankers, and sold it elsewhere. This "hot oil," as it became known, was such a problem that the governors of Texas and Oklahoma even sent members of the National Guard to close down oil wells by force.

Congress responded with the National Industrial Recovery Act of 1933, Pub. L. No. 73–67, 48 Stat. 195, Roosevelt's landmark proposal to revive the economy. Section 1 of the act declared the existence of a "national emergency" that was due, in part, to "obstructions to the free flow of interstate and foreign commerce which tend to diminish the amount thereof," as well as "unfair competitive practices." *Id.* Section 9(c) addressed hot oil, declaring, "The President is authorized to prohibit the transportation in interstate and foreign commerce of petroleum and the products thereof produced or withdrawn from storage in excess of the amount permitted to be produced or withdrawn from storage by any state law." *Id.* at 200. The section also made it a crime to violate any of the president's orders.

A hallmark of the early New Deal was Roosevelt's willingness to experiment to fix the economy, sometimes without much forethought. Over the summer of 1933, the president rushed to sign dozens of executive orders to enforce the act's provisions, including an order that simply quoted Section 9(c) and made it a crime to transport hot oil across state lines. His process was so rushed, in fact, that when the Panama Refining Company sued to challenge the act's criminal penalties, including those authorized by Section 9(c), the administration couldn't find original copies of the orders creating them. Only after the case reached the Supreme Court did a government lawyer realize, to his embarrassment, that some of the penalties authorized by the president's first round of orders had been accidentally amended out of existence by a second round of orders. *See* Robert L. Stern, *The Commerce Clause and the National Economy*, 59 Harv. L. Rev. 645, 656–57 (1946).

Although the government quickly fixed this problem, it galled the justices in *Panama Refining Co. v. Ryan*, 293 U.S. 388 (1935), to learn that Congress had authorized the president to create new crimes in such a slipshod manner. Justice Louis Brandeis, an ideological ally of Roosevelt, lamented at oral argument that nothing in the statute required the president to justify his actions or make any findings of fact. Jeff Shesol, *Supreme Power* 90 (2010).

Nevertheless, it seemed that the government had little reason to fear that Section 9(c) was in danger under the nondelegation doctrine. Of its 195-page brief, the government dedicated a scant three pages to answer the oil company's argument that Section 9(c) was an unconstitutional delegation of legislative power. Stern, *supra*, at 657. This would prove to be a mistake.

■ MR. CHIEF JUSTICE HUGHES delivered the opinion of the Court.[14]

[S]ection 9(c) is assailed upon the ground that it is an unconstitutional delegation of legislative power. The section purports to authorize the President to pass a prohibitory law. The subject to which this authority relates is defined. It is the transportation in interstate and foreign commerce of petroleum and petroleum products which are produced or withdrawn from storage in excess of the amount permitted by state authority. Assuming for the present purpose, without deciding, that the Congress has power to interdict the transportation of that excess in interstate and foreign commerce, the question whether that transportation shall be prohibited by law is obviously one of legislative policy. Accordingly, we look to the statute to see whether the Congress has declared a policy with respect to that subject; whether the Congress has set up a standard for the President's action; whether the Congress has required any finding by the President in the exercise of the authority to enact the prohibition.

Section 9(c) is brief and unambiguous. It does not attempt to control the production of petroleum and petroleum products within a State. It does not seek to lay down rules for the guidance of state legislatures or state officers. It leaves to the States and to their constituted authorities the determination of what production shall be permitted. It does not qualify the President's authority by reference to the basis, or extent, of the State's limitation of production. Section 9(c) does not state whether, or in what circumstances or under what conditions, the President is to prohibit the transportation of the amount of petroleum or petroleum products produced in excess of the State's permission. It establishes no criterion to govern the President's course. It does not require any finding by the President as a condition of his action. The Congress in § 9(c) thus declares no policy as to the transportation of the excess production. So far as this section is concerned, it gives to the President an unlimited authority to determine the policy and to lay down the prohibition, or not to lay it down, as he may see fit. And disobedience to his order is made a crime punishable by fine and imprisonment.

---

[14] **As You Read, Consider:** In the decades before this decision, the Supreme Court offered three rules for distinguishing a valid delegation of legislative power from an invalid delegation. One rule would require Congress to set important policies and allow agents only to "fill up the details." *Wayman v. Southard*, 23 U.S. (10 Wheat.) 1, 42 (1825). A second rule would require Congress to make all rules and allow agents only to determine when certain rules should take effect. *The Brig Aurora*, 11 U.S. (7 Cranch) 382, 387 (1813). And a third rule would allow Congress to delegate any authority to agents as long as it supplies an "intelligible principle" for how the agents must exercise that authority. *J.W. Hampton, Jr. & Co. v. United States*, 276 U.S. 394, 411 (1928). Does Chief Justice Charles Evans Hughes think that the hot oil law survives under any of these rules?

We examine the context to ascertain if it furnishes a declaration of policy or a standard of action, which can be deemed to relate to the subject of § 9(c) and thus to imply what is not there expressed. It is important to note that § 9 is headed "Oil Regulation,"—that is, § 9 is the part of the National Industrial Recovery Act which particularly deals with that subject matter. But the other provisions of § 9 afford no ground for implying a limitation of the broad grant of authority in § 9(c). . . .

We turn to the other provisions of Title I of the Act.

The first section is a "declaration of policy." It declares that a national emergency exists "which is productive of widespread unemployment and disorganization of industry, which burdens interstate and foreign commerce, affects public welfare, and undermines the standards of living of the American people." It is declared to be the policy of Congress "to remove obstructions to the free flow of interstate and foreign commerce which tend to diminish the amount thereof." . . .

This general outline of policy contains nothing as to the circumstances or conditions in which transportation of petroleum or petroleum products should be prohibited,—nothing as to the policy of prohibiting, or not prohibiting, the transportation of production exceeding what the States allow. The general policy declared is "to remove obstructions to the free flow of interstate and foreign commerce." . . . It is manifest that this broad outline is simply an introduction of the Act, leaving the legislative policy as to particular subjects to be declared and defined, if at all, by the subsequent sections.

It is no answer to insist that deleterious consequences follow the transportation of "hot oil,"—oil exceeding state allowances. The Congress did not prohibit that transportation. The Congress did not undertake to say that the transportation of "hot oil" was injurious. The Congress did not say that transportation of that oil was "unfair competition." The Congress did not declare in what circumstances that transportation should be forbidden, or require the President to make any determination as to any facts or circumstances. Among the numerous and diverse objectives broadly stated, the President was not required to choose. The President was not required to ascertain and proclaim the conditions prevailing in the industry which made the prohibition necessary. The Congress left the matter to the President without standard or rule, to be dealt with as he pleased. The effort by ingenious and diligent construction to supply a criterion still permits such a breadth of authorized action as essentially to commit to the President the functions of a legislature rather than those of an executive or administrative officer executing a declared legislative policy. We find nothing in § 1 which limits or controls the authority conferred by § 9(c). . . .

Fifth. The question whether such a delegation of legislative power is permitted by the Constitution is not answered by the argument that it should be assumed that the President has acted, and will act, for what he believes to be the public good. The point is not one of motives but of constitutional authority, for which the best of motives is not a substitute. While the present controversy relates to a delegation to the President, the basic question has a much wider application. If the Congress can make a grant of legislative authority of the sort attempted by § 9(c), we find nothing in the Constitution which restricts the Congress to the selection of the President as grantee. The Congress may vest the power in the officer of its choice or in a board or commission such as it may select or create for the purpose. Nor, with respect to such a delegation, is the question concerned merely with the transportation of oil, or of oil produced in excess of what the State may allow. If legislative power may thus be vested in the President, or other grantee, as to that excess of production, we see no reason to doubt that it may similarly be vested with respect to the transportation of oil without reference to the State's requirements. . . .

The Constitution provides that "All legislative powers herein granted shall be vested in a Congress of the United States, which shall consist of a Senate and House of Representatives." Art. I, § 1. And the Congress is empowered "To make all laws which shall be necessary and proper for carrying into execution" its general powers. Art. I, § 8, par. 18. The Congress manifestly is not permitted to abdicate, or to transfer to others, the essential legislative functions with which it is thus vested. Undoubtedly legislation must often be adapted to complex conditions involving a host of details with which the national legislature cannot deal directly. The Constitution has never been regarded as denying to the Congress the necessary resources of flexibility and practicality, which will enable it to perform its function in laying down policies and establishing standards, while leaving to selected instrumentalities the making of subordinate rules within prescribed limits and the determination of facts to which the policy as declared by the legislature is to apply. Without capacity to give authorizations of that sort we should have the anomaly of a legislative power which in many circumstances calling for its exertion would be but a futility. But the constant recognition of the necessity and validity of such provisions, and the wide range of administrative authority which has been developed by means of them, cannot be allowed to obscure the limitations of the authority to delegate, if our constitutional system is to be maintained. . . .

[In *The Brig Aurora*, 7 Cranch 382, the Court announced a principle distinguishing an improper delegation of power to make the law, which necessarily involves a discretion as to what it shall be, and a proper delegation of authority or discretion as to how a law should be executed.] Applying that principle, authorizations given by Congress to selected instrumentalities for the purpose of ascertaining the existence of facts to which legislation is directed, have constantly been sustained. Moreover, the Congress may not only give such authorizations to determine specific facts but may establish primary standards, devolving upon others the duty to carry out the declared legislative policy, that is, as Chief Justice Marshall expressed it, "to fill up the details" under the general provisions made by the legislature. *Wayman v. Southard,* 10 Wheat. 1, 43. . . .

The applicable considerations were reviewed in *Hampton & Co. v. United States,* 276 U.S. 394, where the Court dealt with the so-called "flexible tariff provision" of the Act of September 21, 1922 (42 Stat. 858, 941, 942), and with the authority which it conferred upon the President. [T]he Court said, "If Congress shall lay down by legislative act an intelligible principle to which the person or body authorized to fix such rates is directed to conform, such legislative action is not a forbidden delegation of legislative power. . . .["][15]

Thus, in every case in which the question has been raised, the Court has recognized that there are limits of delegation which there is no constitutional authority to transcend. We think that § 9(c) goes beyond those limits. As to the transportation of oil production in excess of state permission, the Congress has declared no policy, has established no standard, has laid down no rule. There is no requirement, no

[15] **Question:** The National Emergencies Act of 1976 provides that "the President is authorized to declare [a] national emergency." Pub. L. No. 90–412, 90 Stat. 1255. Such a declaration activates over one hundred "special or extraordinary power[s]" that the president may use to respond to a crisis. *Id.* In 2019, President Donald Trump invoked this provision to declare a national emergency on the southern border caused by the illegal entry of "criminals, gang members, and illicit narcotics." Proc. No. 9844, 84 Fed. Reg. 4949 (Feb. 15, 2019). Invoking an "extraordinary power" made available by the act, he directed the reappropriation of funds from the military's budget to construct a border wall.

Would the National Emergencies Act's delegation of authority to the president survive Hughes's analysis in these paragraphs?

definition of circumstances and conditions in which the transportation is to be allowed or prohibited.

If § 9(c) were held valid, it would be idle to pretend that anything would be left of limitations upon the power of the Congress to delegate its law-making function. The reasoning of the many decisions we have reviewed would be made vacuous and their distinctions nugatory. Instead of performing its law-making function, the Congress could at will and as to such subjects as it chose transfer that function to the President or other officer or to an administrative body. The question is not of the intrinsic importance of the particular statute before us, but of the constitutional processes of legislation which are an essential part of our system of government. . . .

NOTE: AFTERMATH OF *PANAMA REFINING*

Chief Justice Charles Evans Hughes waited until the stock market closed before announcing the Court's decision in *Panama Refining* because he knew that it would have an enormous effect on the economy. In fact, *Panama Refining* has continued to have an effect on the economy and other aspects of society.

Application of the nondelegation doctrine. By 1935, Congress had enacted several New Deal statutes whose "intelligible principle" was no more apparent than that of Section 9(c). *See* Shesol, *supra*, at 90. Over the next two years, the Court wielded the nondelegation doctrine as an ax to chop down these statutes and the regulations built on top of them. In *A.L.A. Schechter Poultry Corp. v. United States*, which we read in one of the sections on Congress's historical power to regulate interstate commerce (section 8.2), the Court struck down part of the National Industrial Relations Act both because it regulated "indirect" effects on commerce and because it delegated to the president "unfettered discretion to make whatever laws he thinks may be needed or advisable for the rehabilitation and expansion of trade or industry." 295 U.S. 495, 538 (1935). The section at issue permitted the president to approve codes of "fair competition" drafted by members of the poultry industry, including an agreed-upon minimum wage that the Schechter brothers had violated; however, the Court complained that the section permitted the president to approve virtually any regulation without meaningful standards to guide or constrain the president's judgment. *Id.* at 540.

Relatedly, in *Carter v. Carter Coal Co.*, 298 U.S. 238 (1936), the Court struck down a 1935 act that permitted coal companies themselves to get together and vote on binding codes to fix the maximum hours and minimum wages for the industry. This time, the Court held that the delegation to private entities itself was unlawful. "The power conferred upon the majority [of coal companies] is, in effect, the power to regulate the affairs of an unwilling minority," the Court wrote. *Carter Coal*, 298 U.S. at 311. "This is legislative delegation in its most obnoxious form; for it is not even delegation to an official or an official body, presumptively disinterested, but to private persons whose interests may be and often are adverse to the interests of others in the same business." *Id.*

Disregard of the nondelegation doctrine. But even as the Court attacked early New Deal legislation, it blunted the nondelegation doctrine's impact in areas where the Court had already been deferential. For example, Congress had, since the Northwest Ordinance, authorized territorial legislatures to literally make new laws. Even though Congress never provided intelligible principles to accompany these delegations of power, the Court wrote in 1937 that the nondelegation doctrine simply didn't apply in this context: "In dealing with the territories . . ., this nation has all the powers of other sovereign nations, and Congress in legislating is not subject to the same restrictions which are imposed in respect of laws for the United States considered as a political body of states in union." *Cincinnati Soap Co. v. United States*, 301 U.S. 308, 232 (1937); *see also District of Columbia v. John R. Thompson Co.*, 346 U.S. 100 (1953) (same for the District of Columbia).

Even a case like *Carter Coal* was quickly cabined; only a few years later, the Court emphasized that Congress could continue to condition the effect of legislation on a vote by private entities. *See Currin v. Wallace*, 306 U.S. 1 (1939). The problem with *Carter Coal*, the Court explained, was that Congress had allowed a group of producers to "make the law." *Id.* at 15.

These and the many earlier exceptions to the nondelegation doctrine soon overwhelmed the few instances in which the Court held that the doctrine applied. In all the years since *Carter Coal* in 1936, the Court has never struck down a statute as an unconstitutional delegation of legislative power. Instead, applying the standard established in *J.W. Hampton, Jr. & Co. v. United States*, 276 U.S. 394 (1928), it has held that a delegation of power isn't "legislative" as long as there is an "intelligible principle" to guide an entity's execution of congressional policy. *See, e.g., Mistretta v. United States*, 488 U.S. 361, 372 (1989) (upholding a law authorizing the U.S. Sentencing Commission to promulgate federal criminal sentencing guidelines after considering seven factors); *Am. Power & Light Co. v. SEC*, 329 U.S. 90, 96 (1940) (upholding a law authorizing the Securities and Exchange Commission to regulate holding companies to prevent "unfairly or inequitably distribut[ing] voting power").

As Justice Elena Kagan summarized in *Gundy v. United States*:

> [T]his Court has held that a delegation is constitutional so long as Congress has set out an "intelligible principle" to guide the delegee's exercise of authority. *J. W. Hampton, Jr., & Co.*, 276 U.S. at 409. Or in a related formulation, the Court has stated that a delegation is permissible if Congress has made clear to the delegee "the general policy" he must pursue and the "boundaries of [his] authority." *American Power & Light*, 329 U.S. at 105. Those standards, the Court has made clear, are not demanding. "[W]e have 'almost never felt qualified to second-guess Congress regarding the permissible degree of policy judgment that can be left to those executing or applying the law.'" *Whitman*, 531 U.S. at 474–475, 121 S.Ct. 903 (quoting *Mistretta*, 488 U.S. at 416 (Scalia, J., dissenting)). Only twice in this country's history (and that in a single year) have we found a delegation excessive—in each case because "Congress had failed to articulate *any* policy or standard" to confine discretion. *Mistretta*, 488 U.S. at 373, n. 7 (emphasis

> added); see *A.L.A. Schechter Poultry Corp. v. United States*, 295 U.S. 495 (1935); *Panama Refin. Co. v. Ryan*, 293 U.S. 388 (1935). By contrast, we have over and over upheld even very broad delegations. Here is a sample: We have approved delegations to various agencies to regulate in the "public interest." See, e.g., *National Broadcasting Co.*, 319 U.S. at 216; *New York Central Securities Corp. v. United States*, 287 U.S. 12, 24 (1932). We have sustained authorizations for agencies to set "fair and equitable" prices and "just and reasonable" rates. *Yakus*, 321 U.S. at 422; *FPC v. Hope Natural Gas Co.*, 320 U.S. 591 (1944). We more recently affirmed a delegation to an agency to issue whatever air quality standards are "requisite to protect the public health." *Whitman*, 531 U.S. at 472. And so forth.

139 S. Ct. 2116, 2129 (2019).

In fact, in a pattern similar to the century before 1935, the Court has continued to invoke the nondelegation doctrine as a bogeyman. *See, e.g., Nat'l Cable Television Ass'n, Inc. v. United States*, 415 U.S. 336, 342 (1974). In some cases, it has even emphasized implied limits in statutory language to avoid triggering the nondelegation doctrine. *See, e.g., Whitman v. Am. Trucking Ass'n*, 531 U.S. 457 (2001) (interpreting a statute that authorizes the Environmental Protection Agency to set air quality standards at the level that is "requisite to protect the public health" as *not* permitting standards at a level that is "lower or higher than is necessary").

The Court recently emphasized these sorts of implied limits in *Gundy*, a 2019 case interpreting the Sex Offender Registration and Notification Act of 2006 (SORNA), Pub. L. No. 109–248, 120 Stat. 587. SORNA generally required new "sex offenders" to register with the federal government before being sentenced. For sex offenders who had already been sentenced before 2006, it permitted the attorney general to "specify the applicability" of SORNA's registration requirements to them. SORNA, 120 Stat. at #. Considering whether this statute violated the nondelegation doctrine, Kagan wrote for a plurality that "[t]he constitutional question is whether Congress has supplied an intelligible principle to guide the delegee's use of discretion." *Gundy,* 139 S. Ct. at 2123. Answering this question, she continued, required looking at the statute's "text, considered alongside its context, purpose, and history," to see whether it provided sufficiently "definite" standards. *Id.* Conducting this inquiry, Kagan thought that the statute supplied an intelligible principle: the attorney general must "apply SORNA to all pre-Act offenders as feasible." *Id.* If this principle were insufficiently intelligible, she concluded, "then most of Government is unconstitutional—dependent as Congress is on the need to give discretion to executive officials to implement its programs." *Id.* at 2130.

But another four justices indicated in separate opinions in *Gundy* that they thought Kagan was overstating the importance of the "intelligible principle" test and would return to the tests laid out in *The Brig Aurora*; *Wayman v. Southard*, 23 U.S. (10 Wheat.) 1 (1825); *Field v. Clark*, 143 U.S. 649 (1892); and *Panama Refining. See Gundy*, 139 S. Ct. at 2131 (Alito, J., concurring in the judgment); *id.* at 2138–39 (Gorsuch, J., dissenting). Later that year, a fifth justice, who hadn't participated in *Gundy*, Brett Kavanaugh, expressed his agreement with the *Gundy* dissenters that the Court should, in effect, return to Chief Justice Marshall's test in *Wayman* and distinguish "those important subjects which must be entirely regulated by the legislature itself from those of less interest in which a general provision may be made and power given to those who are to act under such general provisions to fill up the details." *Wayman*, 23 U.S. (10 Wheat.) at 43; *see Paul v. United States*, 140 S. Ct. 342 (2019) (Kavanaugh, J., respecting the denial of certiorari).

Preemptive effect of executive regulations. In Article VI, Paragraph 2, the Supremacy Clause provides that the Constitution and "the Laws of the United States" are the "supreme Law of the land . . ., any Thing in the Constitution or Laws of any State to the Contrary notwithstanding." As we read earlier (section 11.2), when a state takes an action that is inconsistent with a congressional statute, the state's action is "preempted" under the Supremacy Clause and cannot be enforced. *See, e.g.*, *Arizona v. United States*, 567 U.S. 387 (2012).

Federal regulations are similarly preemptive. When Congress validly delegates authority to the president or another executive official, it often also authorizes that official to issue rules, orders, or other regulations to execute its statutory authority. *See, e.g.*, Interstate Commerce Act of 1887, ch. 104, 24 Stat. 379, 386. These regulations, if they are valid exercises of statutory authority, also are "Laws of the United States" and generally carry the same force as the statute that authorized them. *See United States v. Shimer*, 367 U.S. 374, 383 (1961). Moreover, the Supreme Court has held that their preemptive force doesn't depend on whether Congress expressly authorized the regulation to displace state law. "The statutorily authorized regulations of an agency will pre-empt any state or local law that conflicts with such regulations or frustrates the purposes thereof," the Court wrote in *City of New York v. FCC*, and "in proper circumstances the agency may determine that its authority is exclusive and pre-empts any state efforts to regulate in the forbidden area." 486 U.S. 57, 64 (1988).

In practice, questions about regulatory preemption follow a different pattern than questions about statutory preemption. With federal statutes, courts generally ask (1) whether the statute was a valid exercise of constitutional authority and, if so, (2) whether Congress intended to displace state laws that conflict with its policies. *See, e.g.*, *Hines v. Davidowitz*, 312 U.S. 52, 70 (1941). With federal regulations, courts ask the same two questions about the authorizing statute—*and* if the statute is constitutional but not preemptive on its own, they also ask (3) whether the regulation was a valid exercise of statutory authority and, if so, (4) whether the regulator intended to displace state laws that conflict with its policies. *See, e.g.*, *City of New York*, 486 U.S. at 64.

As we will see later, this question becomes slightly more complicated in the limited contexts where the president or another executive official can issue an order without statutory authority. *See Dalton v. Specter*, 511 U.S. 462, 472 (1992).

25.3 CONGRESS'S INABILITY TO EXERCISE EXECUTIVE POWER

The nondelegation doctrine is the principle that the Supreme Court uses to prohibit Congress from allowing other governmental entities to exercise Congress's *legislative* power. But sometimes the Court has also intervened to prohibit Congress from exercising federal *executive* power. We saw one example of this earlier in the context of the legislative veto (section 24.1): Congress may not reserve for itself the power to veto the actions of executive-branch officials except by laws that satisfy the rules of Article I, Section 7, on bicameralism and presentment. *See INS v. Chadha*, 462 U.S. 919 (1983); *Consumers Union v. FTC*, 691 F.2d 575 (D.C. Cir. 1982), *aff'd sub nom. Process Gas Consumers Grp. v. Consumer Energy Council*, 463 U.S. 1216 (1983).

25.3.1

Bowsher v. Synar

478 U.S. 714 (1986)

The following case, *Bowsher v. Synar*, 478 U.S. 714 (1986), illustrates what it looks like to the Court when Congress exercises executive power.

The case considered the Balanced Budget and Emergency Deficit Control Act of 1985, a complicated law that attempted to eliminate the federal budget deficit. Pub. L. No. 99–177, §§ 200–275, 99 Stat. 1037, 1038. The law provided that if federal spending in an upcoming year was projected to exceed a "maximum deficit amount," then spending on defense and nondefense programs had to be cut in equal amounts to reach the targeted deficit level. *Id.* at 1063. To calculate these spending cuts, the law required the "comptroller general"—a legislative official appointed by the president but removable only by Congress—to "review and consider" budget estimates generated by the Congressional Budget Office and the White House. *Id.* at 1068. The comptroller general then had to "issue a report to the President" specifying which programs should be cut to eliminate the deficit. *Id.* The law provided that the president then had to accept these recommendations.

Mike Synar, a member of Congress who voted against the law, sued to enjoin the comptroller general, Charles Bowsher, from enforcing it. Synar argued that the law unconstitutionally gave executive responsibilities to an officer subject to control only by the legislature, not the president. But Bowsher responded that Congress employed hundreds of employees who performed similar tasks—from the sergeant at arms to the staff of the Congressional Budget Office—none of whom was constitutionally suspect. Therefore, Bowsher argued, there was nothing unusual about assigning him to prepare the act's report.

The issue ultimately boiled down to whether the act gave the comptroller general, a member of the legislative branch, executive power to exercise. The Court determined that it did—and that it shouldn't.

■ CHIEF JUSTICE BURGER delivered the opinion of the Court.[16]

[W]e noted recently that "[t]he Constitution sought to divide the delegated powers of the new Federal Government into three defined categories, Legislative, Executive, and Judicial." *INS v. Chadha,* 462 U. S. 919, 951 (1983). The declared purpose of separating and dividing the powers of government, of course, was to "diffus[e] power the better to secure liberty." *Youngstown Sheet & Tube Co. v. Sawyer,* 343 U. S. 579, 635 (1952) (Jackson, J., concurring). Justice Jackson's words echo the famous warning of Montesquieu, quoted by James Madison in The Federalist No. 47, that " 'there can be no liberty where the legislative and executive powers are united in the same person, or body of magistrates'. . . ." . . .

Even a cursory examination of the Constitution reveals the influence of Montesquieu's thesis that checks and balances were the foundation of a structure of government that would protect liberty. The Framers provided a vigorous Legislative Branch and a separate and wholly independent Executive Branch, with each branch responsible ultimately to the people. The Framers also provided for a Judicial Branch equally independent with "[t]he judicial Power . . . extend[ing] to all Cases, in Law and Equity, arising under this Constitution, and the Laws of the United States." Art. III, § 2.

Other, more subtle, examples of separated powers are evident as well. Unlike parliamentary systems such as that of Great Britain, no person who is an officer of the United States may serve as a Member of the Congress. Art. I, § 6. Moreover, unlike parliamentary systems, the President, under Article II, is responsible not to the Congress but to the people, subject only to impeachment proceedings which are exercised by the two Houses as representatives of the people. Art. II, § 4. And even in the impeachment of a President the presiding officer of the ultimate tribunal is not a member of the Legislative Branch, but the Chief Justice of the United States. Art. I, § 3.

That this system of division and separation of powers produces conflicts, confusion, and discordance at times is inherent, but it was deliberately so structured to assure full, vigorous, and open debate on the great issues affecting the people and to provide avenues for the operation of checks on the exercise of governmental power. . . .

IV

Appellants urge that the Comptroller General performs his duties independently and is not subservient to Congress. . . . [T]his contention does not bear close scrutiny.

INS v. Chadha

The critical factor lies in the provisions of the statute defining the Comptroller General's office relating to removability.[17] Although the Comptroller General is nominated by the President from a list of three individuals recommended by the Speaker of the House of Representatives and the President *pro tempore* of the

---

16 **As You Read, Consider:** What test does Chief Justice Warren Burger use to determine whether the comptroller general is an "executive" or a "legislative" officer? Does he think that legislative officers are inherently unconstitutional, or only that they are constitutionally disabled from performing certain "executive" functions?

17 **Questions:** Why do you think Burger stresses who can remove the comptroller general in determining whether the comptroller general is a legislative officer? The president can be removed by Congress via impeachment; the attorney general occupies an office that Congress could, theoretically, abolish. Are the president and attorney general legislative officers too?

Senate, see 31 U. S. C. § 703(a)(2), and confirmed by the Senate, he is removable only at the initiative of Congress. He may be removed not only by impeachment but also by joint resolution of Congress "at any time" resting on any one of the following bases: "(i) permanent disability; (ii) inefficiency; (iii) neglect of duty; (iv) malfeasance; or (v) a felony or conduct involving moral turpitude." 31 U. S. C. § 703(e)(1)B.

This provision was included, as one Congressman explained in urging passage of the Act, because Congress "felt that [the Comptroller General] should be brought under the sole control of Congress, so that Congress at any moment when it found he was inefficient and was not carrying on the duties of his office as he should and as the Congress expected, could remove him without the long, tedious process of a trial by impeachment." 61 Cong. Rec. 1081 (1921). . . .

The Comptroller General heads the General Accounting Office (GAO), "an instrumentality of the United States Government independent of the executive departments," 31 U. S. C. § 702(a), which was created by Congress in 1921 as part of the Budget and Accounting Act of 1921, 42 Stat. 23. Congress created the office because it believed that it "needed an officer, responsible to it alone, to check upon the application of public funds in accordance with appropriations." H. Mansfield, The Comptroller General: A Study in the Law and Practice of Financial Administration 65 (1939).

It is clear that Congress has consistently viewed the Comptroller General as an officer of the Legislative Branch. The Reorganization Acts of 1945 and 1949, for example, both stated that the Comptroller General and the GAO are "a part of the legislative branch of the Government." 59 Stat. 616; 63 Stat. 205. Similarly, in the Accounting and Auditing Act of 1950, Congress required the Comptroller General to conduct audits "as an agent of the Congress." 64 Stat. 835.

Over the years, the Comptrollers General have also viewed themselves as part of the Legislative Branch. In one of the early Annual Reports of Comptroller General, the official seal of his office was described as reflecting

> "the independence of judgment to be exercised by the General Accounting Office, subject to the control of the legislative branch. . . . The combination represents an agency of the Congress independent of other authority auditing and checking the expenditures of the Government as required by law and subjecting any questions arising in that connection to quasi-judicial determination." GAO Ann. Rep. 5–6 (1924).

[In 1945], Comptroller General Warren, who had been a Member of Congress for 15 years before being appointed Comptroller General, testified: "During most of my public life, . . . I have been a member of the legislative branch. Even now, although heading a great agency, it is an agency of the Congress, and *I am an agent of the Congress.*" . . . .

Against this background, we see no escape from the conclusion that, because Congress has retained removal authority over the Comptroller General, he may not be entrusted with executive powers. The remaining question is whether the Comptroller General has been assigned such powers in the Balanced Budget and Emergency Deficit Control Act of 1985.

V

The primary responsibility of the Comptroller General under the instant Act is the preparation of a "report." This report must contain detailed estimates of projected federal revenues and expenditures. The report must also specify the reductions, if any, necessary to reduce the deficit to the target for the appropriate fiscal year. The reductions must be set forth on a program-by-program basis.

In preparing the report, the Comptroller General is to have "due regard" for the estimates and reductions set forth in a joint report submitted to him by the Director of [the Congressional Budget Office] and the Director of OMB, the President's fiscal and budgetary adviser. However, the Act plainly contemplates that the Comptroller General will exercise his independent judgment and evaluation with respect to those estimates. The Act also provides that the Comptroller General's report "shall explain fully any differences between the contents of such report and the report of the Directors." § 251(b)(2).

Appellants suggest that the duties assigned to the Comptroller General in the Act are essentially ministerial and mechanical so that their performance does not constitute "execution of the law" in a meaningful sense. On the contrary, we view these functions as plainly entailing execution of the law in constitutional terms. Interpreting a law enacted by Congress to implement the legislative mandate is the very essence of "execution" of the law. Under § 251, the Comptroller General must exercise judgment concerning facts that affect the application of the Act. He must also interpret the provisions of the Act to determine precisely what budgetary calculations are required. Decisions of that kind are typically made by officers charged with executing a statute.

The executive nature of the Comptroller General's functions under the Act is revealed in § 252(a)(3) which gives the Comptroller General the ultimate authority to determine the budget cuts to be made. Indeed, the Comptroller General commands the President himself to carry out, without the slightest variation (with exceptions not relevant to the constitutional issues presented), the directive of the Comptroller General as to the budget reductions:

"The [Presidential] order *must provide* for reductions in the manner specified in section 251(a)(3), *must incorporate* the provisions of the [Comptroller General's] report submitted under section 251(b), and *must be consistent with such report in all respects*. . . ." § 252(a)(3) (emphasis added). . . .

Congress of course initially determined the content of the Balanced Budget and Emergency Deficit Control Act; and undoubtedly the content of the Act determines the nature of the executive duty. However, as *Chadha* makes clear, once Congress makes its choice in enacting legislation, its participation ends. Congress can thereafter control the execution of its enactment only indirectly—by passing new legislation. *Chadha,* 462 U. S., at 958. By placing the responsibility for execution of the Balanced Budget and Emergency Deficit Control Act in the hands of an officer who is subject to removal only by itself, Congress in effect has retained control over the execution of the Act and has intruded into the executive function. The Constitution does not permit such intrusion. . . .[18]

NOTE: WHAT COUNTS AS AN "EXECUTIVE" FUNCTION

Although the *Bowsher* Court invalidated one of the powers delegated by statute to the comptroller general, legislative officers continue to exercise dozens of distinct powers, including powers that exert control over the executive branch. *See* Benjamin Miller-Gootnick, *How the House Sues*, 2021 U. Ill. L. Rev. 607, 646 (2021). The hundreds of employees in the

---

[18] **Question:** In light of this decision, how could Congress amend the Balanced Budget and Emergency Deficit Control Act to either render the comptroller general an executive officer or ensure that the powers exercised by the comptroller general are legislative, not executive?

Congressional Research Service operate a multimillion-dollar budget and provide "comprehensive and reliable legislative research analysis" to Congress. *Id.* The Congressional Budget Office produces reports and cost estimates on proposed legislation that can have the practical effect of vetoing legislation that would add to the federal deficit. *Id.* And the Government Accountability Office (GAO)—the home of the comptroller general—monitors spending by the executive branch and has the statutory authority to issue legally binding judgments that an executive agency is failing to comply with appropriation laws. *Id.* at 647–48. In one recent instance, the GAO determined that the Trump administration had improperly failed to spend $91 million appropriated to research programs at the Department of Energy. *Id.* at 648. As a result, the Department of Energy began funding the programs. *Id.*

Another executive-like function that Congress has increasingly exercised over the past decade is litigation. In 2019, for example, the House of Representatives sued the secretary of the Treasury, Steven Mnuchin, to prevent the Trump administration from spending money to build a border wall. *Id.* at 617. Litigation, of course, is a function usually performed by the Department of Justice, an executive agency. Yet even the *Bowsher* Court noted without comment in a footnote that the comptroller general, a legislative officer, has been assigned the "duty to bring suit" since 1921. *Bowsher*, 478 U.S. at 734 n.9. And in 2013 when the Bipartisan Legal Advisory Group of the House of Representatives intervened in a case that reached the Supreme Court, the Court accepted that the House could provide a "capable defense" of a federal statute that the Department of Justice refused to defend. *See United States v. Windsor*, 570 U.S. 744, 754, 762–63 (2013).

CHAPTER 26

HOW IS THE PRESIDENT CHOSEN?

ARTICLE II, SECTION 1, CLAUSE 1: The executive Power shall be vested in a President of the United States of America. He shall hold his Office during the Term of four Years, and, together with the Vice President, chosen for the same Term, be elected, as follows:

CLAUSE 2: Each State shall appoint, in such Manner as the Legislature thereof may direct, a Number of Electors, equal to the whole Number of Senators and Representatives to which the State may be entitled in the Congress: but no Senator or Representative, or Person holding an Office of Trust or Profit under the United States, shall be appointed an Elector.

CLAUSE 3: The Electors shall meet in their respective States, and vote by Ballot for two Persons, of whom one at least shall not be an Inhabitant of the same State with themselves. And they shall make a List of all the Persons voted for, and of the Number of Votes for each; which List they shall sign and certify, and transmit sealed to the Seat of the Government of the United States, directed to the President of the Senate. The President of the Senate shall, in the Presence of the Senate and House of Representatives, open all the Certificates, and the Votes shall then be counted. The Person having the greatest Number of Votes shall be the President, if such Number be a Majority of the whole Number of Electors appointed; and if there be more than one who have such Majority, and have an equal Number of Votes, then the House of Representatives shall immediately chuse by Ballot one of them for President; and if no Person have a Majority, then from the five highest on the List the said House shall in like Manner chuse the President. But in chusing the President, the Votes shall be taken by States, the Representation from each State having one Vote; A quorum for this Purpose shall consist of a Member or Members from two thirds of the States, and a Majority of all the States shall be necessary to a Choice. In every Case, after the Choice of the President, the Person having the greatest Number of Votes of the Electors shall be the Vice President. But if there should remain two or more who have equal Votes, the Senate shall chuse from them by Ballot the Vice President.

CLAUSE 4: The Congress may determine the Time of chusing the Electors, and the Day on which they shall give their Votes; which Day shall be the same throughout the United States.

CLAUSE 5: No Person except a natural born Citizen, or a Citizen of the United States, at the time of the Adoption of this Constitution, shall be eligible to the Office of President; neither shall any Person be eligible to that Office who shall not have attained to the Age of thirty five Years, and been fourteen Years a Resident within the United States.

CLAUSE 6: In Case of the Removal of the President from Office, or of his Death, Resignation, or Inability to discharge the Powers and Duties of the said Office, the Same shall devolve on the Vice President, and the Congress may by Law provide for the Case of Removal, Death, Resignation or Inability, both of the President and Vice President, declaring what Officer shall then act as President, and such Officer shall act accordingly, until the Disability be removed, or a President shall be elected.

CLAUSE 7: The President shall, at stated Times, receive for his Services, a Compensation, which shall neither be encreased nor diminished during the Period for which he shall have been elected, and he shall not receive within that Period any other Emolument from the United States, or any of them.

TWELFTH AMENDMENT (1804): The Electors shall meet in their respective states and vote by ballot for President and Vice-President, one of whom, at least, shall not be an inhabitant of the same state with themselves; they shall name in their ballots the person voted for as President, and in distinct ballots the person voted for as Vice-President, and they shall make distinct lists of all persons voted for as President, and of all persons voted for as Vice-President, and of the number of votes for each, which lists they shall sign and certify, and transmit sealed to the seat of the government of the United States, directed to the President of the Senate;—the President of the Senate shall, in the presence of the Senate and House of Representatives, open all the certificates and the votes shall then be counted;—The person having the greatest number of votes for President, shall be the President, if such number be a majority of the whole number of Electors appointed; and if no person have such majority, then from the persons having the highest numbers not exceeding three on the list of those voted for as President, the House of Representatives shall choose immediately, by ballot, the President. But in choosing the President, the votes shall be taken by states, the representation from each state having one vote; a quorum for this purpose shall consist of a member or members from two-thirds of the states, and a majority of all the states shall be necessary to a choice. And if the House of Representatives shall not choose a President whenever the right of choice shall devolve upon them, before the fourth day of March next following, then the Vice-President shall act as President, as in case of the death or other constitutional disability of the President.—The person having the greatest number of votes as Vice-President, shall be the Vice-President, if such number be a majority of the whole number of Electors appointed, and if no person have a majority, then from the two highest numbers on the list, the Senate shall choose the Vice-President; a quorum for the purpose shall consist of two-thirds of the whole number of Senators, and a majority of the whole number shall be necessary to a choice. But no person constitutionally ineligible to the office of President shall be eligible to that of Vice-President of the United States.

TWENTIETH AMENDMENT (1933), SECTION 1: The terms of the President and the Vice President shall end at noon on the 20th day of January, and the terms of Senators and Representatives at noon on the 3d day of January, of the years in which such terms would have ended if this article had not been ratified; and the terms of their successors shall then begin. . . .

SECTION 3: If, at the time fixed for the beginning of the term of the President, the President elect shall have died, the Vice President elect shall become President. If a President shall not have been chosen before the time fixed for the beginning of his term, or if the President elect shall have failed to qualify, then the Vice President elect shall act as President until a President shall have qualified; and the Congress may by law provide for the case wherein neither a President elect nor a Vice President elect shall have qualified, declaring who shall then act as President, or the manner in which one who is to act shall be selected, and such person shall act accordingly until a President or Vice President shall have qualified.

SECTION 4: The Congress may by law provide for the case of the death of any of the persons from whom the House of Representatives may choose a President whenever the right of choice shall have devolved upon them, and for the case of the death of any of the persons from whom the Senate may choose a Vice President whenever the right of choice shall have devolved upon them.

TWENTY-SECOND AMENDMENT (1951), SECTION 1: No person shall be elected to the office of the President more than twice, and no person who has held the office of President, or acted as President, for more than two years of a term to which some other person was elected President shall be elected to the office of the President more than once. But this Article shall not apply to any person holding the office of President when this Article was proposed by the Congress, and shall not prevent any person who may be holding the office of President, or acting as President, during the term within which this Article becomes operative from holding the office of President or acting as President during the remainder of such term.

TWENTY-THIRD AMENDMENT (1961), SECTION 1: The District constituting the seat of Government of the United States shall appoint in such manner as the Congress may direct: A number of electors of President and Vice President equal to the whole number of Senators and Representatives in Congress to which the District would be entitled if it were a State, but in no event more than the least populous State; they shall be in addition to those appointed by the States, but they shall be considered, for the purposes of the election of President and Vice President, to be electors appointed by a State; and they shall meet in the District and perform such duties as provided by the twelfth article of amendment.

TWENTY-FIFTH AMENDMENT (1967), SECTION 1: In case of the removal of the President from office or of his death or resignation, the Vice President shall become President.

SECTION 2: Whenever there is a vacancy in the office of the Vice President, the President shall nominate a Vice President who shall take office upon confirmation by a majority vote of both Houses of Congress.

SECTION 3: Whenever the President transmits to the President pro tempore of the Senate and the Speaker of the House of Representatives his written declaration that he is unable to discharge the powers and duties of his office, and until he transmits to them a written declaration to the contrary, such powers and duties shall be discharged by the Vice President as Acting President.

SECTION 4: Whenever the Vice President and a majority of either the principal officers of the executive departments or of such other body as Congress may by law provide, transmit to the President pro tempore of the Senate and the Speaker of the House of Representatives their written declaration that the President is unable to discharge the powers and duties of his office, the Vice President shall immediately assume the powers and duties of the office as Acting President. Thereafter, when the President transmits to the President pro tempore of the Senate and the Speaker of the House of Representatives his written declaration that no inability exists, he shall resume the powers and duties of his office unless the Vice President and a majority of either the principal officers of the executive department or of such other body as Congress may by law provide, transmit within four days to the President pro tempore of the Senate and the Speaker of the House of Representatives their written declaration that the President is unable to discharge the powers and duties of his office. Thereupon Congress shall decide the issue, assembling within forty-eight hours for that purpose if not in session. If the Congress, within twenty-one days after receipt of the latter written declaration, or, if Congress is not in session, within twenty-one days after Congress is required to assemble, determines by two-thirds vote of both Houses that the President is unable to discharge the powers and duties of his office, the Vice President shall continue to discharge the same as Acting President; otherwise, the President shall resume the powers and duties of his office.

26.1 THE ELECTORAL COLLEGE

The opening sentence of Article II not only distinguishes the "executive Power" from the "legislative Powers" that open Article I. It also declares that the executive power shall be vested in "a President of the United States of America." At the very least, this sentence identifies that the chief executive is a single person, the president, and not a committee of the states (as in the Confederation Congress) or a supreme executive council (as in Pennsylvania).

This point—that the chief executive would be a *unitary* individual, as opposed to a *plural* committee—was debated at length in the opening weeks of the Constitutional Convention. *See* Michael Klarman, *The Framers' Coup: The Making of the United States Constitution* 213 (2016). James Madison, Alexander Hamilton, and other proponents of strong executive power opened the debate by arguing that the absence of a single chief executive was a major flaw of the Confederation Congress. The Congress had a reputation for indecisively responding to imminent threats such as Shays' Rebellion, when wealthy property owners had to rely on a private militia instead of federal troops to open courthouses in western Massachusetts. Opposing Madison and Hamilton were George Mason of Virginia and William Paterson of New Jersey, who contended that a single chief executive would lead to a return of monarchy. Mason and Paterson added that an executive committee could have members appointed from various sections of the country as opposed to from a single place. A single chief executive from Virginia, by contrast, might favor southern states over northern states, and the opposite might be true for a single chief executive from Massachusetts. *Id.* at 216–17.

The convention ultimately voted 7–3 in favor of a single chief executive—given the title of *president* by the end of the summer. The convention also rejected a plan to require the president to consult some sort of executive council before making major decisions. Instead, the convention voted to require the president to consult with the Senate before making appointments or treaties. *Id.* at 223–24. But as a vestige of this debate, the final Article II, Section 2, authorized the president to "require the Opinion in writing, of the principal Officer in each of the executive Departments, upon any Subject relating to the Duties of their respective Offices."

This left a final question, one debated incessantly during the convention, of who would elect this unitary chief executive.

Discarded ideas for electing the president

Although there was no consensus on this question until the end of the convention, there was virtually uniform agreement throughout the summer that the people should *not* be allowed to elect the president. The delegates raised three major problems with direct elections. First, most delegates assumed that the vast majority of people would be ignorant of national politics and have no capacity to accurately evaluate the merits of candidates from across an enormous country in which communication and transportation networks were slow and cumbersome. Second, the delegates also assumed that, due to their ignorance about people from other places, most people would vote for candidates from their home states, thus disadvantaging small states. Third, several southern delegates vigorously objected that enslaved people would count for nothing in popular elections, thus diminishing the influence of southern states. Combined, these three arguments led the convention to defeat all proposals for direct elections, including once by a 9–1 vote. *Id.* at 228.

With direct elections off the table, the delegates instead debated whether Congress or state legislatures would elect the chief executive. Each of these proposals raised logistical and ideological problems.

With Congress, the delegates couldn't decide on whether both houses of Congress should elect the president separately or as a single body. They also couldn't decide on how to ensure that congressional election wouldn't make the president too dependent on Congress. Proponents of congressional elections offered various solutions to this second problem, such as giving the executive a long, fixed term; tenure to serve that term during good behavior; and ineligibility for reelection. *Id.* at 226–29.

Election by state legislatures seemed like it would better ensure the chief executive's independence from Congress. But logistically the plan seemed too complicated. State legislatures, presumably, would also have little knowledge of candidates from other states. Moreover, election by state legislatures also carried the risk of creating an executive too aligned with state interests to lead a strong federal government. *Id.*

"Electors" compromise

After debates over these proposals reached an impasse, James Wilson of Pennsylvania improvised with a variety of ideas, including the creation of a national grand jury, chosen by lot among a small number of national legislators, that would presumably be able to evaluate the evidence and decide who was best suited to be president. Eventually, a mediation committee forged this idea into what appeared to be an elegant compromise: authorize state legislatures to appoint independent "electors," who would then meet with the electors from other states and decide as a body whom to support for president. The delegates presumed that states would appoint only their most prominent and knowledgeable citizens as electors. Moreover, they believed that because all of the states' electors would meet simultaneously in their own states, the process would be "impossible to corrupt." *Id.* at 231. This electoral system also placated southern delegates who opposed the direct election of the president, as it provided that each state would have as many electors as they had senators and representatives, allowing states to count three-fifths of enslaved people toward their electors. *Id.* at 231–32.

One final compromise reached by the convention was that no candidate for president would be elected without securing a "[m]ajority of the whole Number of Electors appointed." Because of the logistical challenges of national elections, George Mason predicted that "nineteen times in twenty" the electors would fail to reach a majority. *Id.* at 232. In this event, the convention provided, the House of Representatives would choose the president from among the five highest vote-getters. *Id.* at 233. To preserve the influence of small states within this process, Article II, Section 1, declared that all of the delegates in the House would vote as state delegations, with "the Representation from each State having one Vote."

Although neither the convention nor the Constitution used the term *Electoral College*, this became the name for the system they proposed. To reiterate the delegates' principal assumptions, they assumed that (1) state legislatures would appoint juries of (2) prominent people who would meet, consider the merits of the candidates, and decide as a body whom to support for president—after which (3) most elections would be decided by the House among the five highest vote-getters because no candidate would receive a majority of electoral votes. All three of these assumptions would, eventually, prove to be mistaken.

First, from the get-go, many state legislatures used methods other than direct appointment to "appoint" their electors. In the first presidential election of 1788–1789, six state legislatures directly appointed their electors (Connecticut, Georgia, Massachusetts, New Hampshire, New Jersey, and South Carolina), but four state legislatures (Delaware, Maryland, Pennsylvania, and Virginia) authorized the appointment of electors by popular vote. (All of the states' electors unanimously voted for George Washington.) By the fifth presidential election, in 1804, a majority of states appointed their electors by popular vote. By 1832, only the legislature of South Carolina continued to appoint its state's electors. *See Congressional Quarterly's Guide to U.S. Elections* 255 (John L. Moore ed., 1985). Although the vast majority of the delegates opposed electing the president by popular vote, the popular vote for electors has become the universal method of election.

Second, with the development of political parties in the 1790s, the appointment of electors soon became a partisan affair, in which electors were evaluated more for which party's candidate they would support than for their individual prominence in the community. *See* John H. Aldrich, *Why Parties? The Origin and Transformation of Political Parties in America* 65–68 (1995). Voting for electors quickly became a proxy contest for presidential candidates. Today, it has become so ingrained that electors will vote for their party's candidates that ballots in the vast majority of states simply list the names of presidential candidates without naming the electors who are literally chosen by the voters. *See*

Ray v. Blair, 343 U.S. 214, 228–29 (1952) (noticing this pattern). This distinction—that voters in presidential elections elect *electors*, not *presidential candidates*—only becomes apparent when "faithless" electors cast votes for their own choice of candidate, as in 2016, when three electors voted for former secretary of state Colin Powell and one each voted for Senator Bernie Sanders; Governor John Kasich; Senator Ron Paul; and Faith Spotted Eagle, a Yankton Sioux activist from South Dakota. *See* Jonathan Martin & Michael Wines, *Electoral College Settles Donald Trump's Victory, but Little Else*, N.Y. Times, Dec. 19, 2016, at A1.

Third, in part because of party politics, George Mason's prediction that nineteen out of twenty elections would be decided by the House proved entirely backward: the House has decided only two out of almost sixty presidential elections, in 1800 and 1824.

26.1.1

McPherson v. Blacker

146 U.S. 1 (1892)

Although the Electoral College today looks nothing like what some members of the Constitutional Convention expected, it still bears vestiges of the original scheme. One of those vestiges is the discretion that Article II, Section 1, gives to state legislatures. Even though almost all states today appoint electors based on the winner of the popular vote within each state, Article II, Section 1, declares that "[e]ach State shall appoint" these electors "in such Manner as the Legislature thereof may direct." Presumably, this means that a state could appoint its electors in some manner other than the winner of the in-state popular vote.

Before the 1892 presidential election, Michigan appointed all thirteen of its electors based on the winner of the popular vote within the state. But in 1891, the Democratic-controlled state legislature passed a law that authorized each congressional district to vote for different sets of electors. This law had the practical effect of assisting Democrats: Michigan as a whole was reliably Republican in presidential elections, but now the state would elect several Democratic electors.

In *McPherson v. Blacker*, 146 U.S. 1 (1892), William McPherson, a Republican nominee for presidential elector, sued the Democratic secretary of state, Robert Blacker, to have the law declared void. The Court's ruling, however, was a disappointment for Republicans.

■ MR. CHIEF JUSTICE FULLER . . . delivered the opinion of the Court.[1]

On behalf of plaintiffs in error it is contended that the act is void because in conflict with . . . clause two of section one of Article II of the Constitution of the United States . . . : "Each State shall appoint, in such Manner as the Legislature thereof may

[1] **As You Read, Consider:** Article II, Section 1, declares that "[e]ach State shall appoint" electors "in such Manner as the Legislature thereof may direct." Does Chief Justice Melville Fuller impose any limits on this power?

direct, a Number of Electors, equal to the whole Number of Senators and Representatives to which the State may be entitled in the Congress. . . ."

The manner of the appointment of electors directed by the act of Michigan is the election of an elector and an alternate elector in each of the twelve Congressional districts into which the State of Michigan is divided, and of an elector and an alternate elector at large in each of two districts defined by the act. It is insisted that it was not competent for the legislature to direct this manner of appointment because the State is to appoint as a body politic and corporate, and so must act as a unit and cannot delegate the authority to subdivisions created for the purpose; and it is argued that the appointment of electors by districts is not an appointment by the State, because all its citizens otherwise qualified are not permitted to vote for all the presidential electors.

def. of State

"A State in the ordinary sense of the Constitution," said Chief Justice Chase, *Texas v. White*, 7 Wall. 700, 721, "is a political community of free citizens, occupying a territory of defined boundaries, and organized under a government sanctioned and limited by a written constitution, and established by the consent of the governed." The State does not act by its people in their collective capacity, but through such political agencies as are duly constituted and established. The legislative power is the supreme authority except as limited by the constitution of the State, and the sovereignty of the people is exercised through their representatives in the legislature unless by the fundamental law power is elsewhere reposed. The Constitution of the United States frequently refers to the State as a political community, and also in terms to the people of the several States and the citizens of each State. What is forbidden or required to be done by a State is forbidden or required of the legislative power under state constitutions as they exist. The clause under consideration does not read that the people or the citizens shall appoint, but that "each State shall"; and if the words "in such manner as the legislature thereof may direct," had been omitted, it would seem that the legislative power of appointment could not have been successfully questioned in the absence of any provision in the state constitution in that regard. Hence the insertion of those words, while operating as a limitation upon the State in respect of any attempt to circumscribe the legislative power, cannot be held to operate as a limitation on that power itself.

If the legislature possesses plenary authority to direct the manner of appointment, and might itself exercise the appointing power by joint ballot or concurrence of the two houses, or according to such mode as designated, it is difficult to perceive why, if the legislature prescribes as a method of appointment choice by vote, it must necessarily be by general ticket and not by districts. In other words, the act of appointment is none the less the act of the State in its entirety because arrived at by districts, for the act is the act of political agencies duly authorized to speak for the State, and the combined result is the expression of the voice of the State, a result reached by direction of the legislature, to whom the whole subject is committed. . . .

By original clause three of section one of Article II, and by the Twelfth Amendment which superseded that clause, in case of a failure in the election of President by the people, the House of Representatives is to choose the President; and "the vote shall be taken by States, the representation from each State having one vote." The State acts as a unit and its vote is given as a unit, but that vote is arrived at through the votes of its representatives in Congress elected by districts.

The State also acts individually through its electoral college, although, by reason of the power of its legislature over the manner of appointment, the vote of its electors may be divided.

The Constitution does not provide that the appointment of electors shall be by popular vote, nor that the electors shall be voted for upon a general ticket, nor that the majority of those who exercise the elective franchise can alone choose the electors. It recognizes that the people act through their representatives in the legislature, and leaves it to the legislature exclusively to define the method of effecting the object. . . .

It has been said that the word "appoint" is not the most appropriate word to describe the result of a popular election. Perhaps not; but it is sufficiently comprehensive to cover that mode, and was manifestly used as conveying the broadest power of determination. It was used in Article V of the Articles of Confederation, which provided that "delegates shall be annually appointed in such manner as the legislature of each State shall direct;" and in the resolution of Congress of February 21, 1787, which declared it expedient that "a convention of delegates who shall have been appointed by the several States," should be held. The appointment of delegates was, in fact, made by the legislatures directly, but that involved no denial of authority to direct some other mode. The Constitutional Convention, by resolution of September 17, 1787, expressed the opinion that the Congress should fix a day "on which electors should be appointed by the States which shall have ratified the same," etc., and that "after such publication, the electors should be appointed, and the Senators and Representatives elected."

The Journal of the Convention discloses that propositions that the President should be elected by "the citizens of the United States," or by the "people," or "by electors to be chosen by the people of the several States," instead of by the Congress, were voted down, (Jour. Con. 286, 288; 1 Elliot's Deb. 208, 262,) as was the proposition that the President should be "chosen by electors appointed for that purpose by the legislatures of the States," though at one time adopted. Jour. Con. 190; 1 Elliot's Deb. 208, 211, 217. And a motion to postpone the consideration of the choice "by the national legislature," in order to take up a resolution providing for electors to be elected by the qualified voters in districts, was negatived in Committee of the Whole. Jour. Con. 92; 1 Elliot's Deb. 156. Gerry proposed that the choice should be made by the State executives; Hamilton, that the election be by electors chosen by the people; James Wilson and Gouverneur Morris were strongly in favor of popular vote; Ellsworth and Luther Martin preferred the choice by electors elected by the legislatures; and Roger Sherman, appointment by Congress. The final result seems to have reconciled contrariety of views by leaving it to the state legislatures to appoint directly by joint ballot or concurrent separate action, or through popular election by districts or by general ticket, or as otherwise might be directed.

Therefore, on reference to contemporaneous and subsequent action under the clause, we should expect to find, as we do, that various modes of choosing the electors were pursued, as, by the legislature itself on joint ballot; by the legislature through a concurrent vote of the two houses; by vote of the people for a general ticket; by vote of the people in districts; by choice partly by the people voting in districts and partly by the legislature; by choice by the legislature from candidates voted for by the people in districts; and in other ways, as, notably, by North Carolina in 1792, and Tennessee in 1796 and 1800. No question was raised as to the power of the State to appoint, in any mode its legislature saw fit to adopt, and none that a single method, applicable without exception, must be pursued in the absence of an amendment to the Constitution. The district system was largely considered the most equitable, and Madison wrote that it was that system which was contemplated by the framers of the Constitution, although it was soon seen that its adoption by some

States might place them at a disadvantage by a division of their strength, and that a uniform rule was preferable.[2]

At the first presidential election the appointment of electors was made by the legislatures of Connecticut, Delaware, Georgia, New Jersey and South Carolina. Pennsylvania, by act of October 4, 1788, Acts Penn. 1787–1788, p. 513, provided for the election of electors on a general ticket. Virginia, by act of November 17, 1788, was divided into twelve separate districts and an elector elected in each district, while for the election of Congressmen the State was divided into ten other districts. Laws Va. Oct. Sess. 1788, pp. 1, 2; 12 Henning's Stat. 648. In Massachusetts the general court, by resolve of November 17, 1788, divided the State into districts for the election of Representatives in Congress, and provided for their election December 18, 1788, and that at the same time the qualified inhabitants of each district should give their votes for two persons as candidates for an elector of President and Vice President of the United States, and, from the two persons in each district having the greatest number of votes, the two houses of the general court by joint ballot should elect one as elector, and in the same way should elect two electors at large. Mass. Resolves, 1788, p. 53. In Maryland, under act of December 22, 1788, electors were elected on general ticket, five being residents of the Western Shore and three of the Eastern Shore. Laws Md. 1788, Nov. Sess. c. 10. In New Hampshire an act was passed November 12, 1788, Laws N.H. 1789, p. 167, providing for the election of five electors by majority popular vote, and in case of no choice that the legislature should appoint out of so many of the candidates as equalled double the number of electors elected. There being no choice the appointment was made by the legislature. The senate would not agree to a joint ballot, and the house was compelled, that the vote of the State might not be lost, to concur in the electors chosen by the senate. The State of New York lost its vote through a similar contest. The assembly was willing to elect by joint ballot of the two branches or to divide the electors with the senate, but the senate would assent to nothing short of a complete negative upon the action of the assembly, and the time for election passed without an appointment. North Carolina and Rhode Island had not then ratified the Constitution.

[In the next three presidential elections,] while most of the States adopted the general ticket system, the district method obtained in Kentucky until 1824; in Tennessee and Maryland until 1832; in Indiana in 1824 and 1828; in Illinois in 1820 and 1824; and in Maine in 1820, 1824 and 1828. Massachusetts used the general ticket system, in 1804, chose electors by joint ballot of the legislature in 1808 and in 1816, used the district system again in 1812 and in 1820, and returned to the general ticket system in 1824. In New York the electors were elected in 1828 by districts, the district electors choosing the electors at large. The appointment of electors by the legislature, instead of by popular vote, was made use of by North Carolina, Vermont and New Jersey in 1812.

In 1824 the electors were chosen by popular vote[—]by districts, and by general ticket[—]in all the States excepting Delaware, Georgia, Louisiana, New York, South Carolina, and Vermont, where they were still chosen by the legislature. After 1832 electors were chosen by general ticket in all the States excepting South Carolina, where the legislature chose them up to and including 1860. . . .

---

[2] **Question:** Fuller is referencing a constitutional amendment favored by James Madison that would require each state to hold elections for electors in each congressional district, thus ensuring that a closely divided state would not award all of its electoral votes to the winner of a statewide election. As Fuller observes, most states thought that the "district system" was fairer than a winner-take-all "general ticket" system. But unless every state adopted the district system, district states typically attracted less attention from presidential campaigns than general-ticket states. Why, then, did Michigan adopt a district system?

Mr. Justice Story, in considering the subject in his Commentaries on the Constitution, and writing nearly fifty years after the adoption of that instrument, after stating that "in some States the legislatures have directly chosen the electors by themselves; in others, they have been chosen by the people by a general ticket throughout the whole State; and in others, by the people by electoral districts, fixed by the legislature, a certain number of electors being apportioned to each district," adds: "No question has ever arisen as to the constitutionality of either mode, except that by a direct choice by the legislature. But this, though often doubted by able and ingenious minds, (3 Elliot's Deb. 100, 101,) has been firmly established in practice ever since the adoption of the Constitution, and does not now seem to admit of controversy, even if a suitable tribunal existed to adjudicate upon it." And he remarks that "it has been thought desirable by many statesmen to have the Constitution amended so as to provide for a uniform mode of choice by the people." Story Const. 1st Ed. § 1466. . . .

From this review, in which we have been assisted by the laborious research of counsel, and which might have been greatly expanded, it is seen that from the formation of the government until now the practical construction of the clause has conceded plenary power to the state legislatures in the matter of the appointment of electors. . . .[3]

In short, the appointment and mode of appointment of electors belong exclusively to the States under the Constitution of the United States. They are, as remarked by Mr. Justice Gray in *In re Green,* 134 U.S. 377, 379, "no more officers or agents of the United States than are the members of the state legislatures when acting as electors of Federal senators, or the people of the States when acting as the electors of representatives in Congress." Congress is empowered to determine the time of choosing the electors and the day on which they are to give their votes, which is required to be the same day throughout the United States, but otherwise the power and jurisdiction of the State is exclusive, with the exception of the provisions as to the number of electors and the ineligibility of certain persons, so framed that Congressional and Federal influence might be excluded.

The question before us is not one of policy but of power, and while public opinion had gradually brought all the States as matter of fact to the pursuit of a uniform system of popular election by general ticket, that fact does not tend to weaken the force of contemporaneous and long continued previous practice when and as different views of expediency prevailed. The prescription of the written law cannot be overthrown because the States have latterly exercised in a particular way a power which they might have exercised in some other way. The construction to which we have referred has prevailed too long and been too uniform to justify us in interpreting the language of the Constitution as conveying any other meaning than that heretofore ascribed, and it must be treated as decisive.

It is argued that the district mode of choosing electors, while not obnoxious to constitutional objection, if the operation of the electoral system had conformed to its original object and purpose, had become so in view of the practical working of that system. Doubtless it was supposed that the electors would exercise a reasonable independence and fair judgment in the selection of the Chief Executive, but experience soon demonstrated that, whether chosen by the legislatures or by popular suffrage on general ticket or in districts, they were so chosen simply to register the will of the appointing power in respect of a particular candidate. In relation, then, to the independence of the electors the original expectation may be said to have been

[3] **Question:** Suppose that before the 2024 presidential election, the state legislatures of Michigan, Pennsylvania, and Wisconsin declared that they would award the state's electoral votes to the Republican candidate. Does Article II provide objecting voters with any recourse?

frustrated. But we can perceive no reason for holding that the power confided to the States by the Constitution has ceased to exist because the operation of the system has not fully realized the hopes of those by whom it was created. Still less can we recognize the doctrine, that because the Constitution has been found in the march of time sufficiently comprehensive to be applicable to conditions not within the minds of its framers, and not arising in their time, it may, therefore, be wrenched from the subjects expressly embraced within it, and amended by judicial decision without action by the designated organs in the mode by which alone amendments can be made. . . .[4]

NOTE: STATES' PLENARY POWER TO REGULATE PRESIDENTIAL ELECTIONS

The Court in *McPherson* declared that Article II, Section 1, gives states "plenary power" to determine how to appoint their electors. *McPherson*, 146 U.S. at 35. In the context of 1892 Michigan, this meant that the state could allocate its electors by the popular votes of districts as opposed to by the state as a whole.

In a later case, the Court held that state legislatures also have power to require potential electors to pledge themselves to support a particular party's candidate for president. In *Ray v. Blair*, 343 U.S. 214 (1952), the Court upheld an Alabama law that required potential presidential electors to pledge themselves to support a particular party's presidential candidate. The Court held that "[n]either the language of Art. II, § 1, nor that of the Twelfth Amendment forbids a party to require from candidates [for elector] in its primary a pledge of political conformity with the aims of the party." *Ray*, 343 U.S. at 225. Indeed, thirty-two states today have pledge laws that require electors' ballots to reflect the state vote. Fifteen states go further, either fining or replacing electors if they vote for someone other than the candidates of the political party that nominated them. *Chiafolo v. Washington*, 140 S. Ct. 2316, 2321–22 (2020); *see, e.g.*, Mich. Comp. Laws § 168.47 (2019).

The Court recently affirmed state legislatures' plenary power under Article II to appoint electors and determine the manner in which their appointment is made. In *Chiafolo v. Washington*, 140 S. Ct. 2316 (2020), three Washington electors who pledged to support Hillary Clinton in the 2016 presidential election violated their oaths. Although Clinton carried the state vote, the electors voted for Colin Powell, hoping to encourage other electors to vote for an alternative candidate and punt the election to the House of Representatives. *See* Jesse Wegman, *Let the People Pick the President* 1–10 (2020). Under Washington law at the time, an elector who did not vote for his party's candidate was subject to a $1,000 fine. The Court affirmed the state's ability to prevent this "faithless" voting. Writing for the majority, Justice Elena Kagan noted that Article II gives states the power to

---

[4] **Questions:** Recall that in cases like *McGrain v. Daughtery* and *Powell v. McCormack*, the Supreme Court emphasized that long-standing historical practice could "fix" the meaning of the Constitution. Why doesn't a widespread public expectation fix Article II to mean that the appointment of presidential electors requires popular, winner-take-all elections? After the 2020 presidential election, President Donald Trump urged state legislatures to appoint Republican slates of electors—even in states where he lost the popular vote. Would such an appointment be unconstitutional under Article II?

appoint electors "in such Manner as the Legislature thereof may direct," a power that included setting conditions on the electors' appointment. The Court held that states may enforce a presidential elector's pledge to support its party's nominee. *Chiafolo*, 140 S. Ct. at 2320, 2322.

Limits on state plenary power. The Court in *McPherson*, however, noted an important exception to state plenary power: "Congress is empowered to determine the time of choosing the electors and the day on which they are to give their votes." In *Ex parte Yarbrough*, a case discussed in the context of Congress's power to regulate congressional elections (section 22.3), the Court held that Congress had the power to prevent fraud or intimidation in all federal elections, congressional and presidential, because "the importance to the general government of having the actual election—the voting for [presidential electors]—free from force and fraud is not diminished by the circumstance that the qualification of the voter is determined by the law of the State where he votes." 110 U.S. 651, 663 (1884).

The Court expanded on this point in *Burroughs & Cannon v. United States*, explaining that it was necessary and proper for Congress to regulate political expenditures in presidential elections as long as the regulation doesn't "interfere with the power of a state to appoint electors or the manner in which their appointment shall be made." 290 U.S. 534, 544 (1934).

And in *Oregon v. Mitchell*, a case upholding Congress's power to reduce the voting age in presidential elections to eighteen, Justice Hugo Black cited these earlier cases to hold that "[i]t cannot be seriously contended that Congress has less power over the conduct of presidential elections than it has over congressional elections." 400 U.S. 112, 124, n.7 (1970). A plurality contended that Section 5 of the Fourteenth Amendment empowered Congress to reach the same result. *Id.* at 278–81 (opinion of Brennan, J.).

Finally, there are also constitutional limits on state plenary power. For example, state laws enacted pursuant to Article II, Section 1, must meet the requirements of the Equal Protection Clause of the Fourteenth Amendment. *See Bush v. Gore*, 531 U.S. 98, 104–05 (2000) (declaring that a state could not apply arbitrarily different standards when counting votes for presidential electors); *Williams v. Rhodes*, 393 U.S. 23, 31 (1968) (preventing a state from limiting ballot access to the electors of two major parties). In addition, in *Bush v. Gore*, Chief Justice William Rehnquist controversially reasoned that the Supreme Court wasn't obligated to defer to the judgments of Florida state courts regarding how the state counted votes for presidential electors because Article II, Section 1, applies only to the *legislature* and not to a state's courts. 531 U.S. at 112–13 (Rehnquist, C.J., concurring).

Unresolved issue of adding to qualifications of president. One unresolved issue that has recently become important is whether state legislatures, by virtue of their plenary power to appoint electors, may, in effect, add to the qualifications of the president. You may recall from the discussion of Congress's power to exclude members (section 23.3) that the Court has repeatedly held that neither Congress nor states may add to the Constitution's three qualifications for members of Congress: age, citizenship, and residency. *See, e.g.*, *Cook v. Gralike*, 531 U.S. 510, 523 (2001) (striking down a law penalizing candidates who didn't favor term limits); *U.S. Term Limits, Inc. v. Thornton*, 514 U.S. 779, 798 (1995) (striking down a law imposing term limits on candidates); *Powell v. McCormack*, 395 U.S. 486, 522 (1969) (invalidating a vote to exclude a member of Congress due to allegations of corruption). The Constitution includes similar qualifications for the president: the president must be a "natural born Citizen," at least thirty-five years old, and a resident of the United States for at least fourteen years.

In 2019, California passed a law, S.B. 27, that would require candidates for president to publish their income tax returns in order to have their name placed upon a primary election ballot. 2019 Cal. Stat. ch. 121. But later that year, a federal district court struck down the law under *U.S. Term Limits v. Thornton*, 514 U.S. 779 (1995)—even though that case interpreted state power under the Congressional Elections Clause of Article I, Section 4, and not the Presidential Elections Clause of Article II, Section 1. *See Griffin v. Padilla*, 408 F. Supp. 3d 1169, 1180–81 (E.D. Cal. 2019).

As an aside, it is not clear what the term *natural born citizen* means. It could mean someone born in the United States. But before the Fourteenth Amendment, not all people born in the United States were considered citizens. Moreover, Congress provided in the Naturalization Act of 1790 that children born abroad of U.S. citizens "shall be considered as natural born citizens." Naturalization Act, ch. 3, 1 Stat. 103, 104. This statute followed earlier statutes from eighteenth-century Great Britain that declared that certain people born abroad would be "natural-born subjects" of the British Crown. *See, e.g.*, British Nationality Act 1730, 4 Geo. 2 c. 21 (Gr. Brit.). Although this issue was almost tested when John McCain ran for president—he was born in the Panama Canal Zone, an unincorporated territory—it has yet to be adjudicated.

NOTE: ATTEMPTS TO REFORM THE ELECTORAL COLLEGE

Nearly one-tenth of all constitutional amendments proposed in Congress have sought to reform or abolish the Electoral College. *See* Wegman, *supra*, at 126–28. Such calls have intensified since the 2016 election, when a presidential candidate was elected without winning a majority of votes for the second time in sixteen years. Professor Lawrence Lessig, for example, has proposed a constitutional amendment that would award the support of each state's electors to the top two candidates on a "fractional proportional" basis: the candidates would receive votes equal to their percentage of the overall state results. *See id.* at 182–89. This proposal, among others, has highlighted questions around what values the Electoral College serves today and whether it is a system worth keeping. *See, e.g.*, Akhil Reed Amar, *The Troubling Reason the Electoral College Exists*, Time, Nov. 26, 2018 (arguing that the Electoral College was invented to protect slavery); Lawrence Lessig, *The Constitution Lets the Electoral College Choose the Winner. They Should Choose Clinton*, Wash. Post, Nov. 24, 2016 (criticizing the Electoral College but not proposing its abolition); Allen Guelzo & James Hulme, Opinion, *In Defense of the Electoral College*, Wash. Post, Nov. 15, 2016 (defending the Electoral College).

Some reform proposals do not require a constitutional amendment. The most prominent "subconstitutional" proposal, the National Popular Vote Interstate Compact, represents an agreement among sixteen states, together holding a total of 196 electoral votes, to appoint their states' electors based on the outcome of the national popular vote in the presidential election. Wegman, *supra*, at 21–24. The compact would not take effect until states collectively holding 270 electoral votes have adopted it. The compact has received limited, but increasing, attention in legal scholarship. John Koza staked out many of the key terms of the debate, advancing a comprehensive case in favor of the compact. *See* John Koza et al., *Every Vote Equal: A State-Based Plan for Electing the President by National Popular Vote* (2006). The strongest legal objection to such a proposal is that many interstate compacts require the approval of Congress to take effect—raising the prospect of litigation if Congress fails to approve the compact. *See* Wegman, *supra*, at 196–203. (Interstate compacts are discussed in section 38.2.)

26.2 THE PRESIDENTIAL AMENDMENTS

The constitutional method by which the president is chosen has been amended five times.

Twelfth Amendment

The Twelfth Amendment, ratified in 1804, was a response to the embarrassing election of 1800, which revealed a major flaw in the original version of Article II.

As originally written, Article II, Section 1, didn't distinguish between electoral votes for president and those for vice president. Each elector would vote for "two Persons": the person who received the most electoral votes would be president, and the runner-up would be vice president. Article II also provided that the outgoing House would break a tie if two candidates received the same number of electoral votes.

Such a tie inadvertently resulted from the election of 1800, when Thomas Jefferson and his running mate, Aaron Burr, each received seventy-three electoral votes—sending the election to the House. Unfortunately for Jefferson, a majority of state delegations in the House were controlled by members of the Federalist Party, which opposed him. For thirty-five ballots, enough of these Federalist-controlled state delegations tried to stick it to Jefferson by supporting Burr for president that neither Jefferson nor Burr received the necessary majority of votes. The deadlock was finally broken thanks in part to the vigorous campaigning of Alexander Hamilton, who urged Federalists in the House to support Jefferson. *See* Ron Chernow, *Alexander Hamilton* 644–45, 677–78 (2004).

After the House elected Jefferson to become the third president, Congress proposed the Twelfth Amendment, which (1) required presidential electors to cast one vote for "President" and one for "Vice-President" and (2) made the vice president the person who received the most votes for that office, as opposed to the person who received the second-most votes for president.

Twentieth Amendment

The Twentieth Amendment, ratified in 1933, shortened the time between Election Day and Inauguration Day.

Before then, historical practice and congressional statutes had set Election Day as the first Tuesday after the first Monday in November, and Inauguration Day as March 4. But such a long gap between the two days created three major problems. First, the gap became dangerous as travel and communication networks improved—Abraham Lincoln and Franklin D. Roosevelt each had to wait almost five months before they could respond to crises unfolding around them. Second, it created a long lame-duck session of Congress in which the legislature couldn't get much done. And third, it contributed to a situation like that in 1801, in which a House that had just been kicked out of office could decide the future president. *See* S. Rep. No. 72–26, at 2–6 (1932).

Yet Congress could not change Inauguration Day by statute without shortening the constitutionally mandated four-year term for the president and six-year term for senators. The Twentieth Amendment fixed this problem. Franklin D. Roosevelt was the last president inaugurated on March 4. And pursuant to Section 3 of the Twentieth Amendment, Congress passed the Presidential Succession Act of 1948, Pub. L. No. 80–771, § 19, which addressed the situation of a president-elect failing to qualify before Inauguration Day.

Twenty-Second Amendment

The Twenty-Second Amendment, ratified in 1951, was proposed after Roosevelt controversially but successfully pursued a third and fourth term as president. Congress intended the amendment to serve as a referendum on whether someone in the future should be able to follow in Roosevelt's footsteps.

Interestingly, the language of the amendment creates a puzzle about whether a two-term president could serve as vice president. *See* Bruce G. Peabody & Scott E. Gant, *The Twice and Future President: Constitutional Interstices and the Twenty-Second Amendment*, 83 Minn. L. Rev. 565, 612–26 (1999). The amendment prohibits a two-term president from being "elected" again, but it doesn't say anything about that person *succeeding* to the presidency from the vice presidency if the president dies or resigns. At the same time, the last sentence of the Twelfth Amendment states that "no person constitutionally ineligible to the office of President shall be eligible to that of Vice-President of the United States." This puzzle briefly became a live issue when Hillary Clinton speculated in 2015 about picking former president Bill Clinton as vice president. Tom

LoBianco, *Hillary Clinton: Bill as VP Has "Crossed Her Mind,"* CNN, Sept. 15, 2015.

Twenty-Third Amendment

The Twenty-Third Amendment, ratified in 1961, authorized the District of Columbia to appoint three presidential electors. The Congress that proposed this amendment noted that the District of Columbia's population paid taxes, served in the armed forces, and outnumbered the populations of thirteen states, yet couldn't vote for president. H.R. Rep. No. 86–1698, at 2 (1960).

Twenty-Fifth Amendment

Finally, the Twenty-Fifth Amendment, proposed after the assassination of John F. Kennedy and ratified in 1967, resolved several questions about presidential succession that had been serious problems for decades. The oldest of these problems stretched back to 1841, when President William Henry Harrison became the first president to die in office. At the time, it was unclear whether his vice president, John Tyler, became the nation's tenth president or whether Tyler remained the vice president but could now exercise the duties of the president. Tyler insisted that he was now the president, and the seven vice presidents turned presidents afterward followed suit. But until the Twenty-Fifth Amendment, there was no mechanism by which any president could appoint a new vice president when that office was vacant.

Section 1 of the Twenty-Fifth Amendment codified Tyler's practice, and Section 2 authorized a president to fill a vacant vice presidency with the consent of both the House and the Senate. This second section proved critical during the administration of President Richard Nixon. In 1973, Vice President Spiro Agnew resigned after being indicted for bribery, and Section 2 authorized President Nixon to nominate a new vice president, Gerald Ford. A year later, in 1974, Nixon resigned, allowing Gerald Ford to succeed him without ever having been elected to an executive office. President Ford then nominated a new vice president, Nelson Rockefeller, who was confirmed later that year.

Sections 3 and 4 of the Twenty-Fifth Amendment also resolved what should happen when a president remained alive but was no longer able to function in the office. This situation occurred in 1881, when President James Garfield lay in a coma for ninety days after being shot by an assassin; and in 1919, when President Woodrow Wilson suffered a severe stroke. For the last eighteen months of Wilson's presidency, his wife, Edith, became the de facto president by conducting presidential business on his behalf. The Twenty-Fifth Amendment provided that if a similar situation occurred in the future, a president or the president's cabinet could transfer the president's powers and duties to the vice president, who would serve as "Acting President" for as long as the president remained incapacitated. This situation has occurred twice since the amendment's ratification: Vice President George H. W. Bush became acting president in 1985 while President Ronald Reagan underwent a colonoscopy procedure, and Vice President Dick Cheney became acting president in 2002 and 2007 while President George W. Bush underwent the same procedure. *See* Peter Baker, *Days of Fire* 206 (2014).

Section 4 of the Twenty-Fifth Amendment—which allows the vice president to assume the title of "Acting President" if the cabinet determines that the president is "unable to discharge the powers and duties of his office"—grew in prominence during Donald Trump's presidency. Critics inside and outside the White House complained that the president was too erratic to be given responsibility for the United States' nuclear arsenal. *See* Anonymous, *I Am Part of the Resistance Inside the Trump Administration*, N.Y. Times, Sept. 5, 2018, at A23; Louis Cholden-Brown, Daisy de Wolff, Marcello Figueroa & Kathleen McCullough, *Protecting Against an Unable President: Reforms for Invoking the 25th Amendment and Overseeing Presidential Nuclear Launch Authority* (Jan. 2020). These complaints grew louder after President Trump was diagnosed with COVID-19 and treated with steroids that could affect his judgment. *See, e.g.*, Rose McDermott, *Trump's COVID-19 Diagnosis and Presidential Illness*, Pol. & Life Scis., Nov. 6, 2020. In January 2021, after the president "encouraged" a "massive violent invasion of the United States Capitol" to disrupt Congress's certification of the 2020 electoral votes, the House of Representatives formally called upon Vice President Mike Pence to invoke Section 4. H.R. Res. 21, 117th Cong. (2021). The vice president declined, leaving open the question of whether the Twenty-Fifth Amendment authorizes the removal of a president for reasons other than medical incapacity.

CHAPTER 27

What Is the Scope of the President's Power to Manage the Executive Branch?

ARTICLE I, SECTION 3, CLAUSE 4: Neither House, during the Session of Congress, shall, without the Consent of the other, adjourn for more than three days, nor to any other Place than that in which the two Houses shall be sitting.

ARTICLE II, SECTION 1, CLAUSE 1: The executive Power shall be vested in a President of the United States of America. . . .

ARTICLE II, SECTION 2, CLAUSE 1: The President . . . may require the Opinion, in writing, of the principal Officer in each of the executive Departments, upon any Subject relating to the Duties of their respective Offices. . . .

> **CLAUSE 2:** He shall have Power, by and with the Advice and Consent of the Senate, to make Treaties, provided two thirds of the Senators present concur; and he shall nominate, and by and with the Advice and Consent of the Senate, shall appoint Ambassadors, other public Ministers and Consuls, Judges of the supreme Court, and all other Officers of the United States, whose Appointments are not herein otherwise provided for, and which shall be established by Law: but the Congress may by Law vest the Appointment of such inferior Officers, as they think proper, in the President alone, in the Courts of Law, or in the Heads of Departments.
>
> **CLAUSE 3:** The President shall have Power to fill up all Vacancies that may happen during the Recess of the Senate, by granting Commissions which shall expire at the End of their next Session.

ARTICLE II, SECTION 3, CLAUSE 1: [H]e shall receive Ambassadors and other public Ministers; he shall take Care that the Laws be faithfully executed, and shall Commission all the Officers of the United States.

27.1 The Power to Make Appointments

The Confederation Congress was responsible for appointing executive officers in the 1780s, and for the first two months of the Constitutional Convention, many delegates agreed that the Senate would be responsible for appointments going forward. This agreement was based on the assumption that no individual person could possibly have firsthand knowledge of as many qualified candidates for office as might need to be appointed under the new federal government. *See* Michael Klarman, *The Framers' Coup: The Making of the United States Constitution* 222–23 (2016). But after the Connecticut Compromise converted the Senate into a chamber in which small states had the same representation as large states, delegates from large states, including

James Madison, lobbied to move the appointment power to the executive. *Id.* at 223. To placate opponents who remained concerned about the president's limited knowledge, Madison successfully argued for a mechanism like that of Massachusetts's government, in which the president could seek the advice of the Senate and confirm nominees with the Senate's approval. *Id.* To guard against corrupt appointments, the convention also added the Ineligibility Clause to prohibit members of Congress from simultaneously serving as executive officers (see section 24.2). *Id.* at 224–26.

Steps in appointment process

The Constitution describes three steps in the process for the appointment of most officers, not all of which must be satisfied for every officer: (1) nomination, (2) advice and consent, and (3) appointment and commission.

The first two steps, nomination and advice and consent, are described by the Appointments Clause of Article II, Section 2, which states that the president "shall nominate, and by and with the Advice and Consent of the Senate, shall appoint Ambassadors, other public Ministers and Consuls, Judges of the supreme Court, and all other Officers of the United States, whose Appointments are not herein otherwise provided for, and which shall be established by Law." Although this language suggests that the Senate may give advice on a nominee before offering its consent, the sentence as a whole has long been interpreted to mean that only the president can nominate an officer who is subject to the Appointments Clause. *See* 3 Op. Att'y Gen. 188–89 (1837). In practice, the Senate's only responsibility is to decide whether to offer its consent to the appointment of the president's nominee; unlike with treaties, the Senate does not offer revisions or conditions on its confirmation of a nominee.

The Appointments Clause doesn't require the first two steps for all officers; it requires them only for those "whose Appointments are not herein otherwise provided for." This language alludes to three exceptions by which officers may be appointed using alternative procedures. One exception is for *constitutional officers* whose appointments are described by other sections of the Constitution. Presidential electors, for example, are appointed by the states, while the vice president is appointed either by presidential electors or by the procedure of the Twenty-Fifth Amendment. A second exception is for *inferior officers*, which are described in the next section of the Appointments Clause: "Congress may by Law vest the Appointment of such inferior Officers, as they think proper, in the President alone, in the Courts of Law, or in the Heads of Departments." Although this language suggests that many officers may be appointed by people other than the president with or without the consent of the Senate, it doesn't define who counts as an "inferior Officer"—a point we will return to shortly. The third exception is for *recess appointments*, which are described in the Recess Appointments Clause of Article II, Section 2: "The President shall have Power to fill up all Vacancies that may happen during the Recess of the Senate, by granting Commissions which shall expire at the End of their next Session." We will return to this clause shortly as well.

Once the Senate advises about and consents to the appointment of a nominee—or once the office seeker is appointed by other means—that person still can't take office until receiving a "Commission." The Commissions Clause of Article II, Section 3, provides that the president has the duty to "Commission all the Officers of the United States." This generally entails (1) signing a document stating that a person is entitled to hold a particular office, (2) affixing the seal of the United States to that document, and (3) delivering the document to the office seeker. As you may recall from *Marbury v. Madison*, the Supreme Court interpreted the Commissions Clause to conclude that although office seekers cannot start exercising the duties of their office until they've received a commission, they are entitled to the commission as soon as it is signed, and they may therefore go to (a district) court to compel its delivery. 5 U.S. (1 Cranch) 137, 157–58 (1803). But before and after *Marbury*, the executive branch has interpreted this clause to conclude that the president is free to withhold even a signed commission. *See* 12 Op. Att'y Gen. 306 (1867).

Once an office seeker receives a commission, that person is in office. Any power that the Senate may have once possessed over the nomination is over. In *United States v. Smith*, the Supreme Court explained that the Senate's power is merely to advise about and consent to the appointment of a nominee; it may not remove a commissioned officer from office by retroactively withdrawing its consent. 286 U.S. 6, 47–48 (1932).

Definition of officer

This three-step appointment procedure has led to several long-standing questions, the most important of which are the following:

(1) Who are "Officers of the United States" subject to the Appointments Clause?

(2) Who among those officers is an "inferior Officer" whose appointment may be provided for without the advice and consent of the Senate?

Regarding the first question, there is evidence that at least some of the delegates at the Constitutional Convention might have used the term *officer* to describe "any individual who had ongoing responsibility for a governmental duty." Jennifer L. Mascott, *Who Are "Officers of the United States"?*, 70 Stan. L. Rev. 443, 450 (2018). These delegates would have considered nearly all federal employees—from the secretary of state to a postal clerk—to be officers subject to the Appointments Clause. But the federal government was relatively small through the early nineteenth century, obviating any practical difficulty in complying with one of the

Appointments Clause's procedures. This changed over the course of the nineteenth century in two ways.

First, until 1855, no federal statute governed the appointment of ambassadors and other formal and informal diplomats. *See* Act of Mar. 1, 1855, ch. 133, 10 Stat. 619. Instead, the president typically nominated diplomats on the fly, creating new offices by asking the Senate to confirm them. *See, e.g.*, 26 Annals of Cong. 694–722 (1814). Eventually, the president began appointing some diplomats without Senate confirmation, as when President Millard Filmore secretly appointed Commodore Matthew C. Perry to open trade with Japan in 1852. *See* 7 Op. Att'y Gen. 205 (1855). Today, it remains common for presidents to unilaterally appoint special envoys without Senate confirmation, as when President Harry Truman appointed Justice Robert Jackson to serve as chief prosecutor at the Nuremberg trials after World War II, when President Richard Nixon appointed Henry Kissinger to negotiate a cease-fire in the Vietnam War, and when President Donald Trump appointed Kurt Volker as special envoy to Ukraine.

An even bigger change over the course of the nineteenth century was the federal government's increase in size, particularly after the Civil War. The federal government employed fewer than four thousand people in 1800 but more than fifty thousand by 1870. 2 Cong. Rec. 2053 (1874). These new federal officials included thousands of tax collectors, clerks, doctors, teamsters, and other functionaries. Many departments grew because of wartime needs, but many also grew because federal offices were patronage positions: political parties financed themselves by filling federal offices in exchange for the office seekers' payment of an "assessment" to the person who appointed them. "They see nothing wrong in the rule, that to the victor belong the spoils of the enemy," one senator said after Andrew Jackson's election in 1829. Jon Meacham, *American Lion* 83 (2009).

The Supreme Court first addressed the appointment of federal officials in *United States v. Hartwell*, 73 U.S. (6 Wall.) 385 (1868), a case that incidentally evaluated whether a clerk who worked for the Treasury Department was constitutionally appointed. The Court defined *officer* as someone who fills an office. It defined *office* as "a public station, or employment, conferred by the appointment of government. The term embraces the ideas of tenure, duration, emolument, and duties." *Hartwell*, 73 U.S. (6 Wall.) at 393. Applying these definitions, the Court considered the clerk an officer whose appointment was valid because a "Head of Department[ ]"—the secretary of the Treasury—indirectly approved his hiring by the assistant treasurer.

But a decade later, in *United States v. Germaine*, 99 U.S. 508 (1879), the Court held that *Hartwell*'s definition of *officer* did *not* apply to a civil surgeon hired by the commissioner of pensions to examine pension claimants. Instead, the Court created a new hierarchy that included three types of federal appointees. At the top were "principal Officers"—

the heads of departments—whom the Appointments Clause required to be appointed by the president with the consent of the Senate. (The Court adopted the term *principal* from the clause in Article II, Section 2, that authorizes the president to "require the Opinion, in writing, of the principal Officer in each of the executive Departments.") *Germaine*, 99 U.S. at 511. Underneath these were "inferior Officers," whom the Appointments Clause required to be appointed by the president, a court, or a principal officer. Inferior officers included everyone who worked in a "continuing and permanent" office as defined by *Hartwell*. *Id.* at 511–12. But anyone who had merely "occasional or temporary" duties, like a civil surgeon hired to examine particular pensioners, was merely an "employé." *Id.* at 509, 512. The Court held that the thousands of employees who worked for the federal government in an informal capacity could be hired without resorting to the procedures of the Appointments Clause. *Id.* at 512.

Civil service reform

Around the same time as *Germaine*, Congress began to tackle corruption in federal office-seeking by embarking on civil service reform. The first of these laws attempted to eliminate the practice of assessments by prohibiting most officers from "requesting, giving to, or receiving from any other officer or employee of the Government, any money or property or other thing of value for political purposes." Act of Aug. 15, 1876, ch. 287, § 6, 19 Stat. 143, 169. In *Ex parte Curtis*, the Supreme Court upheld this statute as part of a long line of statutes that "regulat[es] in some particulars the conduct of certain officers and employees of the United States." 106 U.S. 371, 372 (1882). Drawing on dozens of similar laws—including a 1789 law that made it unlawful for certain officers of the Treasury Department to engage in the business of trade, and an 1853 law that prohibited federal officers from pursuing financial claims in court against the United States—the Court held that Congress had discretion to regulate the appointment, conduct, and removal of executive officials. *Id.* at 373.

The Court announced *Ex parte Curtis* shortly after President James Garfield had been assassinated by a disgruntled office seeker. The assassination increased calls for civil service reform. The year after *Ex parte Curtis*, Congress enacted the Pendleton Civil Service Reform Act of 1883, ch. 27, 22 Stat. 403. The Pendleton Act replaced much of the spoils system with "civil service" examinations, providing that certain federal officers or employees could be hired only for how well they did on the examinations. It also imposed criminal penalties for firing existing officers or employees for political reasons. *Id.* at 407. Although the law didn't apply to all federal officers or employees, it had the practical effect of protecting a significant number of Republicans in the executive branch. When Democrats next controlled Congress and the White House, they expanded the act's protections to gain the same benefit. This pattern continued until the late twentieth century, when most federal officers and employees were subject to civil service examinations, were protected from removal except for "just cause," and were prohibited from taking part in political campaigns. *See, e.g.*, Ethics in Government Act of 1978, Pub. L. No. 95–521, 92 Stat. 1824; Civil Service Reform Act of 1978, Pub. L. No. 95–454, 92 Stat. 1111; Act of Aug. 2, 1939, Pub. L. No. 76–252, 53 Stat. 1147; Act of Aug. 24, 1912, Pub. L. No. 62–336, 37 Stat. 539; *see also United Public Workers v. Mitchell*, 330 U.S. 75 (1947) (sustaining the statutory prohibition on political campaigning).

27.1.1

Buckley v. Valeo

424 U.S. 1 (1976)

In the following case, *Buckley v. Valeo*, 424 U.S. 1 (1976), the Supreme Court addressed the extent of Congress's power to regulate the appointment of federal officers. It also adopted the modern definition of an "Officer" subject to the Appointments Clause.

The case evaluated the constitutionality of the Federal Election Commission (FEC). Created in 1974 after the Watergate scandal, the commission was charged with regulating federal elections and enforcing federal campaign finance laws. To ensure that the commission's six voting members would be relatively nonpartisan, Congress authorized the president to appoint only two members subject to confirmation by the Senate *and* the House. It also provided that two members would be appointed by the president pro tempore of the Senate on the recommendations of the majority and minority leaders, while two would be appointed by the Speaker of the House on the recommendations of the majority and minority leaders. *See* Federal Election Campaign Act Amendments of 1974, Pub. L. No. 93–443, 88 Stat. 1263. This appointment scheme raised two questions:

(1) Were the commission's members "Officers" subject to the Appointments Clause?

(2) If so, did the clause permit members of Congress to make the appointments?

The federal government defended the scheme on the ground that the commissioners were legislative officers, not executive officers, and, moreover, that Congress had the authority to regulate the appointment of officers however it chose.

The Court was unconvinced by the government's arguments.

■ PER CURIAM.[1]

These appeals present constitutional challenges to the key provisions of the Federal Election Campaign Act of 1971 (Act), and related provisions of the Internal Revenue Code of 1954, all as amended in 1974. . . .

Appellants urge that since Congress has given the [Federal Election] Commission wide-ranging rulemaking and enforcement powers with respect to the substantive provisions of the Act, Congress is precluded under the principle of separation of powers from vesting in itself the authority to appoint those who will exercise such authority. Their argument is based on the language of [the Appointments Clause] of Art. II, § 2, cl. 2, of the Constitution. . . .

1. Separation of Powers

[O]ur inquiry of necessity touches upon the fundamental principles of the Government established by the Framers of the Constitution, and all litigants and all of the courts which have addressed themselves to the matter start on common ground in the recognition of the intent of the Framers that the powers of the three great branches of the National Government be largely separate from one another.

James Madison, writing in the Federalist No. 47, defended the work of the Framers against the charge that these three governmental powers were not *entirely* separate from one another in the proposed Constitution. He asserted that while there was some admixture, the Constitution was nonetheless true to Montesquieu's well-known maxim that the legislative, executive, and judicial departments ought to be separate and distinct. . . .

Yet it is also clear from the provisions of the Constitution itself, and from the Federalist Papers, that the Constitution by no means contemplates total separation of each of these three essential branches of Government. The President is a participant in the lawmaking process by virtue of his authority to veto bills enacted by Congress. The Senate is a participant in the appointive process by virtue of its authority to refuse to confirm persons nominated to office by the President. The men who met in Philadelphia in the summer of 1787 were practical statesmen, experienced in politics, who viewed the principle of separation of powers as a vital check against tyranny. But they likewise saw that a hermetic sealing off of the three branches of Government from one another would preclude the establishment of a Nation capable of governing itself effectively. . . .

The Framers regarded the checks and balances that they had built into the tripartite Federal Government as a self-executing safeguard against the encroachment or aggrandizement of one branch at the expense of the other. As Madison put it in Federalist No. 51: "This [is a] policy of supplying, by opposite and rival interests, the defect of better motives. . . . ["] . . .

2. The Appointments Clause

The principle of separation of powers was not simply an abstract generalization in the minds of the Framers: it was woven into the document that they drafted in Philadelphia in the summer of 1787. Article I, § 1, declares: "All legislative Powers herein granted shall be vested in a Congress of the United States." Article II, § 1, vests the executive power "in a President of the United States of America," and Art. III, § 1, declares that "The judicial Power of the United States, shall be vested in one supreme Court, and in such inferior Courts as the Congress may from time to time

[1] **As You Read, Consider:** How does the Court define who is an "Officer" under the Appointments Clause and who is an "inferior" officer that can be appointed without the advice and consent of the Senate? If a federal official is appointed outside the scope of the Appointments Clause, what limits does the Court impose on that official?

ordain and establish." The further concern of the Framers of the Constitution with maintenance of the separation of powers is found in the so-called "Ineligibility" and "Incompatibility" Clauses contained in Art. I, § 6. . . .

It is in the context of these cognate provisions of the document that we must examine the language of Art. II. § 2, cl. 2, which appellants contend provides the only authorization for appointment of those to whom substantial executive or administrative authority is given by statute. Because of the importance of its language, we again set out the provision:

> "[The President] shall nominate, and by and with the Advice and Consent of the Senate, shall appoint Ambassadors, other public Ministers and Consuls, Judges of the supreme Court, and all other Officers of the United States, whose Appointments are not herein otherwise provided for, and which shall be established by Law: but the Congress may by Law vest the Appointment of such inferior Officers, as they think proper, in the President alone, in the Courts of Law, or in the Heads of Departments."

The Appointments Clause could, of course, be read as merely dealing with etiquette or protocol in describing "Officers of the United States," but the drafters had a less frivolous purpose in mind. This conclusion is supported by language from *United States v. Germaine,* 99 U. S. 508, 509–510 (1879):

> "The Constitution for purposes of appointment very clearly divides all its officers into two classes. The primary class requires a nomination by the President and confirmation by the Senate. But foreseeing that when offices became numerous, and sudden removals necessary, this mode might be inconvenient, it was provided that, in regard to officers inferior to those specially mentioned, Congress might by law vest their appointment in the President alone, in the courts of law, or in the heads of departments. *That all persons who can be said to hold an office under the government about to be established under the Constitution were intended to be included within one or the other of these modes of appointment there can be but little doubt.*" (Emphasis supplied.)

We think that the term "Officers of the United States" as used in Art. II, defined to include "all persons who can be said to hold an office under the government" in *United States v. Germaine, supra,* is a term intended to have substantive meaning. We think its fair import is that any appointee exercising significant authority pursuant to the laws of the United States is an "Officer of the United States," and must, therefore, be appointed in the manner prescribed by § 2, cl. 2, of that Article.[2]

If "all persons who can be said to hold an office under the government about to be established under the Constitution were intended to be included within one or the other of these modes of appointment," *United States v. Germaine, supra,* it is difficult to see how the members of the Commission may escape inclusion. . . .[162][3]

---

[2] **Questions:** The Court here defines the term *officer* to mean someone "exercising significant authority pursuant to the laws of the United States." By this definition, is an Article I immigration judge an officer who must be appointed under Article II's procedure? What about the governor of Puerto Rico or the mayor of the District of Columbia—must they be appointed, not elected?

[162] "*Officers of the United States*" does not include all employees of the United States, but there is no claim made that the Commissioners are employees of the United States, rather than officers. Employees are lesser functionaries subordinate to officers of the United States, see *United States* v. *Germaine*, 99 U. S. 508 (1879), whereas the Commissioners, appointed for a statutory term, are not subject to the control or direction of any other executive, judicial, or legislative authority.

[3] **Questions:** The Court describes an important exception to its definition of *officer* in footnote 162: "employees," or "lesser functionaries," are *not* officers who must be appointed

Although two members of the Commission are initially selected by the President, his nominations are subject to confirmation not merely by the Senate, but by the House of Representatives as well. The remaining four voting members of the Commission are appointed by the President *pro tempore* of the Senate and by the Speaker of the House. While the second part of the Clause authorizes Congress to vest the appointment of the officers described in that part in "the Courts of Law, or in the Heads of Departments," neither the Speaker of the House nor the President *pro tempore* of the Senate comes within this language. . . .

Thus with respect to four of the six voting members of the Commission, neither the President, the head of any department, nor the Judiciary has any voice in their selection.

The Appointments Clause specifies the method of appointment only for "Officers of the United States" whose appointment is not "otherwise provided for" in the Constitution. But there is no provision of the Constitution remotely providing any alternative means for the selection of the members of the Commission or for anybody like them. Appellee Commission has argued, and the Court of Appeals agreed, that the Appointments Clause of Art. II should not be read to exclude the "inherent power of Congress" to appoint its own officers to perform functions necessary to that body as an institution. But there is no need to read the Appointments Clause contrary to its plain language in order to reach the result sought by the Court of Appeals. Article I, § 3, cl. 5, expressly authorizes the selection of the President *pro tempore* of the Senate, and § 2, cl. 5, of that Article provides for the selection of the Speaker of the House. Ranking nonmembers, such as the Clerk of the House of Representatives, are elected under the internal rules of each House and are designated by statute as "officers of the Congress." . . . Contrary to the fears expressed by the majority of the Court of Appeals, nothing in our holding with respect to Art. II, § 2, cl. 2, will deny to Congress "all power to appoint its own inferior officers to carry out appropriate legislative functions." . . .

Appellee Commission and *amici* [emphasize] . . . the extraordinary authority reposed in Congress to regulate elections . . ., by virtue of the power conferred in Art. I, § 4. [They point to this Court's holdings that Congress] has very broad authority to prevent corruption in national Presidential elections. *Burroughs v. United States,* 290 U.S. 534 (1934). . . . [And] whatever shortcomings the provisions for the appointment of members of the Commission might have under Art. II, Congress had ample authority under the Necessary and Proper Clause of Art. I to effectuate this result. . . .

We do not agree. The proper inquiry when considering the Necessary and Proper Clause is not the authority of Congress to create an office or a commission, which is broad indeed, but rather its authority to provide that its own officers may make appointments to such office or commission. . . . Congress could not, merely because it concluded that such a measure was "necessary and proper" to the discharge of its substantive legislative authority, pass a bill of attainder or *ex post facto* law contrary to the prohibitions contained in § 9 of Art. I. No more may it vest in itself, or in its officers, the authority to appoint officers of the United States when the Appointments Clause by clear implication prohibits it from doing so. . . .[4]

---

under the procedure of Article II. What justifies the recognition of this exception? What distinguishes an officer from an employee? Is the president's chief of staff an officer or an employee?

[4] **Question:** Previous sections describe Congress's enormous power to create Article I courts outside the confines of Article III. Why, then, would the Necessary and Proper Clause not permit Congress to create new "Article I officers" outside the confines of Article II?

3. The Commission's Powers

Thus, on the assumption that all of the powers granted in the statute may be exercised by an agency whose members *have been* appointed in accordance with the Appointments Clause, the ultimate question is which, if any, of those powers may be exercised by the present voting Commissioners, none of whom *was* appointed as provided by that Clause. . . .

Insofar as the powers confided in the Commission are essentially of an investigative and informative nature, falling in the same general category as those powers which Congress might delegate to one of its own committees, there can be no question that the Commission as presently constituted may exercise them. *McGrain v. Daugherty,* 273 U. S. 135 (1927). . . .

But when we go beyond this type of authority to the more substantial powers exercised by the Commission, we reach a different result. The Commission's enforcement power, exemplified by its discretionary power to seek judicial relief, is authority that cannot possibly be regarded as merely in aid of the legislative function of Congress. A lawsuit is the ultimate remedy for a breach of the law, and it is to the President, and not to the Congress, that the Constitution entrusts the responsibility to "take Care that the Laws be faithfully executed."

Congress may undoubtedly under the Necessary and Proper Clause create "offices" . . . and provide such method of appointment to those "offices" as it chooses. But Congress' power under that Clause is inevitably bounded by the express language of Art. II, § 2, cl. 2, and unless the method it provides comports with the latter, the holders of those offices will not be "Officers of the United States." They may, therefore, properly perform duties only in aid of those functions that Congress may carry out by itself, or in an area sufficiently removed from the administration and enforcement of the public law as to permit their being performed by persons not "Officers of the United States." . . .[5]

NOTE: DEFINITION OF *OFFICER*

Buckley established a new definition of *officer* for purposes of the Appointments Clause: "any appointee exercising significant authority pursuant to the laws of the United States is an 'Officer of the United States,' and must, therefore, be appointed in the manner prescribed by § 2, cl. 2, of [Article II]." 424 U.S. at 126. This broad definition joined *United States v. Germaine*'s earlier definition that an officer is someone who exercises "continuing and permanent" authority. 99 U.S. 508, 511–12 (1879). Like *Germaine*, the *Buckley* Court also added in footnote 162 that the thousands of "lesser functionaries" who failed to meet these definitions were mere "employees" who could be hired by methods other than those listed in the Appointments Clause. *Buckley*, 424 U.S. at 126 n.162. In *Freytag v. Commissioner*, 501 U.S. 868 (1991), and *Lucia v. SEC*, 138 S. Ct. 2044 (2019), the Court used these tests to conclude that judges of Article I courts—trial judges of the U.S. Tax Court and administrative law judges of the Securities

---

[5] **Question:** Note that the Court does not declare that the Federal Election Commission is unconstitutional merely because its officers were appointed outside the procedures of Article II. Instead, as in *Bowsher v. Synar*, it considers the commissioners to be "legislative officers" and asks whether such legislative officers are unconstitutionally exercising executive power that only Article II appointees may exercise. How does the Court distinguish between "legislative" power that the commissioners may exercise and "executive" power that they may not?

and Exchange Commission—were officers subject to the Appointments Clause, not employees.

Principal versus inferior officers. Although the *Buckley* Court didn't distinguish "principal" officers (who must be appointed by the president with Senate consent) from "inferior" officers (who could be appointed by the president, a court of law, or the head of a department), the Court adopted a functional distinction in *Edmond v. United States*, 520 U.S. 651 (1997). "Whether one is an 'inferior' officer depends on whether he has a superior," the Court wrote. *Edmond*, 520 U.S. at 662. " '[I]nferior officers' are officers whose work is directed and supervised at some level by others who were appointed by Presidential nomination with the advice and consent of the Senate." *Id.* at 663. Invoking this standard, in 2021 the Court invalidated a statute regulating the appointment of administrative patent judges by a principal officer, the Secretary of Commerce. Because these so-called APJs were authorized to issue binding decisions on behalf of the Executive Branch without review by any other executive officer, the Court held "that the unreviewable authority wielded by APJs . . . is incompatible with their appointment by the Secretary to an inferior office." *United States v. Arthrex, Inc.*, 141 S. Ct. 1970, 1985 (2021).

Heads of departments. As the *Buckley* Court emphasized, not all important officials are heads of departments. *Buckley* held that the speaker of the House and the president pro tempore of the Senate are not heads of departments. In *Freytag*, the Court held that the chief judge of the U.S. Tax Court, an Article I court, also wasn't the head of a department, but the court *was* a "Cour[t] of Law." 501 U.S. at 889–90.

Officers and temporary vacancies. Once a person is nominated by the president and confirmed by the Senate, that person is an officer who may validly exercise executive power as defined by the *Buckley* Court. The Court has also held that "Congress may increase the power and duties of an existing office without thereby rendering it necessary that the incumbent should be again nominated and appointed." *Shoemaker v. United States*, 147 U.S. 282, 301 (1893). Applying this precedent to reform the procedure by which the president can fill temporary vacancies, Congress enacted the Federal Vacancies Reform Act of 1998, Pub. L. No. 105–277, 112 Stat. 2681–611. The act allows any Senate-confirmed officer to "perform the functions and duties of [a] vacant office temporarily in an acting capacity." *Id.* at 2681–611. President Donald Trump notably applied this act to an unprecedented degree to avoid nominating cabinet officers. Anne Joseph O'Connell, *Actings*, 120 Colum. L. Rev. 613, 617 (2020).

Territorial and District of Columbia officers. *Buckley*'s definition of *Officer of the United States*—a person who exercises "significant authority pursuant to the laws of the United States," 424 U.S. at 126—was broad enough to sweep in many elected officials, particularly in the territories and the District of Columbia. This would not have been a problem in the nineteenth century, when territorial governors and district commissioners were appointed by the president with Senate consent. But since the mid-twentieth century, territorial governors and the District of Columbia mayor have all been *elected*—raising the question of whether they are officers who must be appointed. *See* Nikolas Bowie, *Will Puerto Rico Still Be Allowed to Govern Itself?*, N.Y. Times, Oct. 9, 2019.

The Supreme Court recently answered this question in *Financial Oversight and Management Board for Puerto Rico v. Aurelius Investment, LLC*, 140 S. Ct. 1649 (2020). In a unanimous opinion by Justice Stephen Breyer, the Court held that the Appointments Clause

> *does* restrict the appointment of 'Officers of the United States' with duties in or related to the District of Columbia or an Article IV entity, [but] it *does not* restrict the appointment of local officers that Congress vests with primarily local duties under Article IV, § 3, or Article I, § 8, cl. 17.

Id. at 1661 (emphasis added). The Court offered two explanations for why it needed to distinguish between "local" and "national" officers: First, the history of territories and the District of Columbia reflects "long-standing use of various methods for selecting officials with primarily local responsibilities." *Id.* at 1660. Second, Article II applies to "Officers *of the United States*," not officers of the *territories* or the *District of Columbia*. *Id.* at 1657–58 (emphasis added).

Applying this new distinction, the Court held that the Appointments Clause does not restrict the selection of members of the Financial Oversight and Management Board, a powerful board created by Congress to govern many of Puerto Rico's financial decisions. Although the oversight board could administer oaths, issue subpoenas, demand data, and oversee Puerto Rico's fiscal and budgetary plans, the Court concluded that all of these powers were "primarily local powers and duties" because they were all conducted in or on behalf of the Puerto Rican government. *Id.* at 1661–62. Justice Sonia Sotomayor, whose parents were born in Puerto Rico, "reluctantly" agreed with the court's judgment but wrote separately to emphasize Puerto Rico's status as "autonomous political entity." *Id.* at 1673, 1683. Given that autonomous status, she wrote, the Court's ruling "seems anomalous," placing the board "in a twilight zone of accountability, neither selected by Puerto Rico itself nor subject to the strictures of the Appointments Clause." *Id.* at 1683.

27.2 THE POWER TO MAKE RECESS APPOINTMENTS

In addition to authorizing the president to appoint all principal officers and some inferior officers, Article II also gives the president "[p]ower to fill up all Vacancies that may happen during the Recess of the Senate, by granting Commissions which shall expire at the End of their next Session." During the ratification debates, Alexander Hamilton wrote that the purpose of this clause was to establish "an auxiliary method of appointment, in cases to which the general method was inadequate." *Federalist No. 67*, at 455 (Alexander Hamilton) (Jacob Cooke ed., 1961).

The president, historically, has invoked this clause often. For most of U.S. history, Congress took an extensive recess between a special session in March and its first substantive session in December, giving the president plenty of opportunities to appoint officers, cabinet secretaries, and even Supreme Court justices like William Brennan. Although such appointments expire at the end of the next congressional session, the president can, before or after the appointment expires, nominate the appointee to the Senate for its advice and consent.

27.2.1

NLRB v. Noel Canning

573 U.S. 513 (2014)

Today, recess appointments are more challenging because Congress meets as an almost-continuing body—particularly when one house of Congress is controlled by a different party than the president's party.

This was the case for the one hundred twelfth Congress. After the 2010 election during the Democratic administration of President Barack Obama, Republicans controlled the House and had enough members in the Senate to filibuster presidential nominations. As Obama's nominations stalled, he looked more favorably toward recess appointments—which the House attempted to stop. Article I, Section 5, provides that "[n]either House, during the Session of Congress, shall, without the Consent of the other, adjourn for more than three days." To deny Obama the opportunity to make recess appointments, the Republican-controlled House refused to consent to adjournments of more than three days. In part because of this refusal, on December 17, 2011, the Senate went into a recess until January 20, 2012, but provided that every three days it would convene in a pro forma session in which an individual senator would arrive, bang a gavel, and immediately adjourn. The resolution convening the pro forma session provided that the Senate would conduct "no business" during the monthlong break. S. Journal, 112th Cong., 1st Sess. 923 (2011).

On January 4, 2012, shortly after one of these pro forma sessions, Obama appointed three members of the National Labor Relations Board (NLRB) without Senate approval. The president insisted that the Senate was in the middle of a monthlong recess because the Senate wasn't available to transact business until January 20. The president also explained that there were three vacancies in the NLRB that he had the power to fill.

But when the NLRB issued a ruling against Noel Canning, a Pepsi distribution company, the company challenged the constitutionality of the board members' appointments. It countered that the Recess Appointments Clause didn't refer to *any* recess but "*the* Recess of the Senate" (emphasis added)—that is, the annual recess that separates the first session of a particular Congress from the second session. Noel Canning also argued that the Recess Appointments Clause applied only to "*Vacancies that may happen* during the Recess" (emphasis added)—

that is, to offices that were occupied when the single recess began but that became vacant while the recess was ongoing. Finally, Noel Canning argued that even if it were wrong about these two arguments, a three-day recess was simply too short to allow the president to finesse his way around the normal Appointments Clause practice.

When *NLRB v. Noel Canning*, 573 U.S. 513 (2014), reached the Supreme Court, the Court considered all three questions:

(1) What is meant by the phrase *the Recess of the Senate*?

(2) What is meant by the phrase *Vacancies that may happen during the Recess*?

(3) Was the January 2012 recess three days or thirty-four days, and was either too brief for a recess appointment?

The Court's answers invalidated Obama's appointments.

■ JUSTICE BREYER delivered the opinion of the Court.[6]

Ordinarily the President must obtain "the Advice and Consent of the Senate" before appointing an "Office[r] of the United States." U.S. Const., Art. II, § 2, cl. 2. But the Recess Appointments Clause creates an exception. It gives the President alone the power "to fill up all Vacancies that may happen during the Recess of the Senate, by granting Commissions which shall expire at the End of their next Session." Art. II, § 2, cl. 3. We here consider three questions about the application of this Clause. . . .

[II]

Before turning to the specific questions presented, we shall mention two background considerations that we find relevant to all three. First, *the Recess Appointments Clause sets forth a subsidiary, not a primary, method for appointing officers of the United States*. The immediately preceding Clause—Article II, Section 2, Clause 2—provides the primary method of appointment. It says that the President "shall nominate, *and by and with the Advice and Consent of the Senate,* shall appoint . . . [all] Officers of the United States" (emphasis added). . . . We seek to interpret the [Recess Appointments] Clause as granting the President the power to make appointments during a recess but not offering the President the authority routinely to avoid the need for Senate confirmation.

Second, *in interpreting the Clause, we put significant weight upon historical practice*. For one thing, the interpretive questions before us concern the allocation of power between two elected branches of Government. . . . "[L]ong settled and established practice is a consideration of great weight in a proper interpretation of constitutional provisions" regulating the relationship between Congress and the President. *The Pocket Veto Case,* 279 U.S. 655, 689 (1929). . . . [There] is a great deal of history to consider here. Presidents have made recess appointments since the beginning of the Republic. . . . We have not previously interpreted the Clause, and, when doing so for the first time in more than 200 years, we must hesitate to upset the compromises and working arrangements that the elected branches of Government themselves have reached.

---

6 **As You Read, Consider:** Which interpretive principles does Justice Stephen Breyer rely upon to answer Noel Canning's three questions? Do you agree that the text alone cannot answer any of the questions?

III

The first question concerns the scope of the phrase *"the recess* of the Senate." Art. II, § 2, cl. 3 (emphasis added). The Constitution provides for congressional elections every two years. And the 2-year life of each elected Congress typically consists of two formal 1-year sessions, each separated from the next by an "inter-session recess." The Senate or the House of Representatives announces an inter-session recess by approving a resolution stating that it will "adjourn *sine die," i.e.,* without specifying a date to return (in which case Congress will reconvene when the next formal session is scheduled to begin).

The Senate and the House also take breaks in the midst of a session. The Senate or the House announces any such "intra-session recess" by adopting a resolution stating that it will "adjourn" to a fixed date, a few days or weeks or even months later. All agree that the phrase "the recess of the Senate" covers inter-session recesses. The question is whether it includes intra-session recesses as well.

In our view, the phrase "the recess" includes an intra-session recess of substantial length. Its words taken literally can refer to both types of recess. Founding-era dictionaries define the word "recess," much as we do today, simply as "a period of cessation from usual work." 13 The Oxford English Dictionary 322–323 (2d ed. 1989) (hereinafter OED) (citing 18th- and 19th-century sources for that definition of "recess"). . . . The Founders themselves used the word to refer to intra-session, as well as to inter-session, breaks. . . .

We recognize that the word "the" in "*the* recess" might suggest that the phrase refers to the single break separating formal sessions of Congress. That is because the word "the" frequently (but not always) indicates "a particular thing." 2 Johnson 2003. But the word can also refer "to a term used generically or universally." 17 OED 879. The Constitution, for example, directs the Senate to choose a President *pro tempore* "in *the* Absence of the Vice-President." Art. I, § 3, cl. 5 (emphasis added). . . .

The constitutional text is thus ambiguous. And we believe the Clause's purpose demands the broader interpretation. The Clause gives the President authority to make appointments during "the recess of the Senate" so that the President can ensure the continued functioning of the Federal Government when the Senate is away. The Senate is equally away during both an inter-session and an intra-session recess. . . .

History also offers strong support for the broad interpretation. . . . Since 1929, . . . Congress has shortened its inter-session breaks as it has taken longer and more frequent intra-session breaks; Presidents have correspondingly made more intra-session recess appointments. Indeed, if we include military appointments, Presidents have made thousands of intra-session recess appointments. President Franklin Roosevelt, for example, commissioned Dwight Eisenhower as a permanent Major General during an intra-session recess; President Truman made Dean Acheson Under Secretary of State; and President George H.W. Bush reappointed Alan Greenspan as Chairman of the Federal Reserve Board.

Not surprisingly, the publicly available opinions of Presidential legal advisers that we have found are nearly unanimous in determining that the Clause authorizes these appointments. . . .

What about the Senate? Since Presidents began making intra-session recess appointments, individual Senators have taken differing views about the proper definition of "the recess." . . . But neither the Senate considered as a body nor its committees, despite opportunities to express opposition to the practice of intra-session recess appointments, has done so.[7] Rather, to the extent that the Senate or a Senate committee has expressed a view, that view has favored a functional definition of "recess," and a functional definition encompasses intra-session recesses. . . .

The greater interpretive problem is determining how long a recess must be in order to fall within the Clause. Is a break of a week, or a day, or an hour too short to count as a "recess"? The Clause itself does not say. . . .

The Recess Appointments Clause seeks to permit the Executive Branch to function smoothly when Congress is unavailable. And though Congress has taken short breaks for almost 200 years, and there have been many thousands of recess appointments in that time, we have not found a single example of a recess appointment made during an intra-session recess that was shorter than 10 days. . . . The lack of examples suggests that the recess-appointment power is not needed in that context. . . .[8]

In sum, we conclude that the phrase "the recess" applies to both intra-session and inter-session recesses. . . . [But] a recess lasting less than 10 days is presumptively too short. . . .

IV

The second question concerns the scope of the phrase "vacancies *that may happen* during the recess of the Senate." Art. II, § 2, cl. 3 (emphasis added). All agree that the phrase applies to vacancies that initially occur during a recess. But does it also apply to vacancies that initially occur before a recess and continue to exist during the recess? In our view the phrase applies to both kinds of vacancy. . . .

Thomas Jefferson wrote that the Clause is "certainly susceptible of [two] constructions." Letter to Wilson Cary Nicholas (Jan. 26, 1802), in 36 Papers of Thomas Jefferson 433 (B. Oberg ed., 2009). It "may mean 'vacancies that may happen to be' or 'may happen to fall' " during a recess. *Ibid.* . . . [T]he Clause is ambiguous. *The Pocket Veto Case,* 279 U.S., at 690. And the broader reading, we believe, is at least a permissible reading of a " 'doubtful' " phrase. *Ibid.* We consequently go on to consider the Clause's purpose and historical practice.

The Clause's purpose strongly supports the broader interpretation. That purpose is to permit the President to obtain the assistance of subordinate officers when the Senate, due to its recess, cannot confirm them. . . .

[Moreover, every] Attorney General to consider the question throughout the Nation's history has [adopted the broader interpretation]. . . .

Did the Senate object? [In] 1862 Attorney General Bates [referred] to "the unbroken acquiescence of the Senate" in support of the broad interpretation. 10 Op. Atty. Gen., at 356. . . . Then in 1863 the Senate Judiciary Committee disagreed with the broad interpretation. It issued a report concluding that a vacancy "must have its inceptive point after one session has closed and before another session has begun."

---

[7] **Questions:** Why do you think Breyer considers whether the Senate has ever "express[ed] opposition" to intrasession recess appointments? Suppose that after reading this opinion, the Senate raised an objection. Would that signal that this decision was wrong?

[8] **Questions:** Breyer here suggests that a ten-day intrasession recess is too short to trigger the Recess Appointments Clause because there are no historical examples of such a recess appointment. But the recess appointment at issue in *this* litigation was arguably made during such a recess. Suppose that this particular appointment had gone unchallenged and the Supreme Court instead considered the *second* time a president made a recess appointment during a similarly short recess. Would that have changed the Court's outcome? If not, why not—there is no longer a settled historical practice, right? If so, isn't relying on historical practice pretty arbitrary in that it relies on contingent and possibly random circumstances?

S.Rep. No. 80, 37th Cong., 3d Sess., p. 3. And the Senate then passed the Pay Act, which provided that "no money shall be paid . . . as a salary, to any person appointed during the recess of the Senate, to fill a vacancy . . . which . . . existed while the Senate was in session." Act of Feb. 9, 1863, § 2, 12 Stat. 646. . . . [But] the Senate subsequently abandoned its hostility. . . . [I]n 1940 Congress amended the Pay Act to authorize salary payments . . . that did not initially occur during a recess but happened to exist during that recess. By paying salaries to this kind of recess appointee, the 1940 Senate (and later Senates) in effect supported the President's interpretation of the Clause.

The upshot is that the President has consistently and frequently interpreted the Recess Appointments Clause to apply to vacancies that initially occur before, but continue to exist during, a recess of the Senate. The Senate as a body has not countered this practice for nearly three-quarters of a century, perhaps longer. The tradition is long enough to entitle the practice "to great regard in determining the true construction" of the constitutional provision. *The Pocket Veto Case,* 279 U.S., at 690. And we are reluctant to upset this traditional practice where doing so would seriously shrink the authority that Presidents have believed existed and have exercised for so long. . . .

V

The third question concerns the calculation of the length of the Senate's "recess." On December 17, 2011, the Senate by unanimous consent adopted a resolution to convene "*pro forma* session[s]" only, with "no business . . . transacted," on every Tuesday and Friday from December 20, 2011, through January 20, 2012. 2011 S.J. 923. At the end of each *pro forma* session, the Senate would "adjourn until" the following *pro forma* session. *Ibid.* . . .

The President made the recess appointments before us on January 4, 2012, in between the January 3 and the January 6 *pro forma* sessions. We must determine the significance of these sessions—that is, whether, for purposes of the Clause, we should treat them as periods when the Senate was in session or as periods when it was in recess. If the former, the period between January 3 and January 6 was a 3-day recess, which is too short to trigger the President's recess-appointment power. If the latter, however, then the 3-day period was part of a much longer recess during which the President did have the power to make recess appointments. . . .

We hold that, for purposes of the Recess Appointments Clause, the Senate is in session when it says it is, provided that, under its own rules, it retains the capacity to transact Senate business. The Senate met that standard here.

The standard we apply is consistent with the Constitution's broad delegation of authority to the Senate to determine how and when to conduct its business. The Constitution explicitly empowers the Senate to "determine the Rules of its Proceedings." Art. I, § 5, cl. 2. . . . Furthermore, . . . [w]e generally take at face value the Senate's own report of its actions. When, for example, . . . the Journal of the Senate indicates that a quorum was present, under a valid Senate rule, at the time the Senate passed a bill, we will not consider an argument that a quorum was not, in fact, present. *Ballin, supra,* at 9. The Constitution requires the Senate to keep its Journal, Art. I, § 5, cl. 3, and "if reference may be had to" it, "it must be assumed to speak the truth," *Ballin, supra,* at 4.

For these reasons, we conclude that we must give great weight to the Senate's own determination of when it is and when it is not in session. But our deference to the Senate cannot be absolute. When the Senate is without the *capacity* to act, under its own rules, it is not in session even if it so declares. . . . The purpose of the Clause is to ensure the continued functioning of the Federal Government while the Senate is unavailable. This purpose would count for little were we to treat the Senate as though it were in session even when it lacks the ability to provide its "advice and consent." Art. II, § 2, cl. 2. . . .

Applying this standard, we find that the *pro forma* sessions were sessions for purposes of the Clause. First, the Senate said it was in session. . . .

Second, the Senate's rules make clear that during its *pro forma* sessions, despite its resolution that it would conduct no business, the Senate retained the power to conduct business. . . . Indeed, the Senate passed a bill by unanimous consent during the second *pro forma* session after its December 17 adjournment. 2011 S.J. 924. . . .

Given our answer to the last question before us, we conclude that the Recess Appointments Clause does not give the President the constitutional authority to make the appointments here at issue. . . .

NOTE: ACTING OFFICERS

Recess appointments are not the only method that presidents have used to appoint principal officers without Senate confirmation. For over a century, presidents have also claimed an inherent power to designate "acting" officers to temporarily exercise the powers of a vacant office. *See, e.g.*, 6 Op. Att'y Gen. 358 (1854).

In 1998, after a dispute with President Bill Clinton over these sorts of acting officers, Congress passed the Federal Vacancies Reform Act of 1998, which codified a procedure for when a principal officer "dies, resigns, or is otherwise unable to perform the functions and duties of the office." Pub. L. No. 105–277, 112 Stat. 2681. By default, the act provides that "the first assistant to the office of such officer shall perform the functions and duties of the office temporarily in an acting capacity." *Id.* at 2681–611. But it also allows the president to appoint as an acting officer (1) any other officer who has been confirmed by the Senate or (2) any officer or employee in the vacant office's department. President Donald Trump extensively relied on this statute to fill vacant offices on the theory that "[i]t gives me more flexibility." Anne Joseph O'Connell, *Actings*, 120 Colum. L. Rev. 613, 617 (2020). In the first three years of his administration, he appointed thirty acting cabinet secretaries—more than any of his predecessors had over their entire presidencies. *Id.* at 643.

27.3 THE POWER TO APPOINT AND REMOVE SUBORDINATE OFFICERS

Although the Appointments Clause and the Recess Appointments Clause explicitly give the president power to *appoint* "Officers of the United States," no clause explicitly gives the president power to *remove* such officers. Yet when it comes to ensuring that someone follows orders, the power to fire that person can be more important than the power to hire that person.

Initial debate over removal power

When the first Congress created the first executive department—the Department of Foreign Affairs—it spent considerable energy debating whether to include language declaring that the secretary of foreign affairs was "[t]o be removable from office by the President of the United States." 1 Annals of Cong. 473 (1789). The debate raised four interpretations of the Constitution's removal power. *See* Jonathan Gienapp, *The Second Creation* 125–63 (2018).

The first interpretation focused on the text of the Constitution and concluded that the only clause relating to removal was the clause in Article II, Section 4, on impeachment—"The President, Vice President and all civil Officers of the United States, shall be removed from Office on Impeachment for, and Conviction of, Treason, Bribery, or other high Crimes and Misdemeanors"—thus, the only basis for removal was impeachment. Supporting this interpretation was the theory, later announced in *Marbury v. Madison*, 5 U.S. (1 Cranch) 137 (1803), that officeholders have a vested property interest in their office. Under this interpretation, officeholders could be deprived of their property only after a fair proceeding, like an impeachment trial. 1 Annals of Cong. at 489–90. But most members of Congress thought that "we shall be in a deplorable situation indeed" if impeachment were the only method of removing any officer. Gienapp, *supra*, at 133.

A second interpretation considered "the power of appointing and dismissing to be united in their natures." 1 Annals of Cong. at 473. Under this interpretation, if the president and the Senate had the power to appoint the secretary of foreign affairs, then they should also have the power to remove the secretary and appoint a replacement. But some members of Congress objected that this was not a generalizable principle. For example, presidential electors had the power to appoint the president without the power of removal. It was also not obvious that the president and Senate should be able to remove judges who they thought behaved badly. Complicating this interpretation was disagreement about just who had the power of "appointing" the secretary: the president *and* the Senate, or just the president with the Senate's advice and consent. *Id.* at 483–84.

A third interpretation focused on the Necessary and Proper Clause to argue that if Congress could create the secretary of foreign affairs, it could also decide how the secretary should be removed. The secretary of foreign affairs was a "creature of the law," one member of Congress explained. *Id.* at 496. "[B]ecause the law establishes the office, [it] has the power of creating him in what shape the Legislature pleases." *Id.*

A fourth interpretation, raised by James Madison, argued that the Vesting Clause gave the president the "executive Power," and "inasmuch as the power of removal is of an executive nature, and not affected by any constitutional exception, it is beyond the reach of the legislative body."

Id. at 482. (Ironically, Madison later criticized Alexander Hamilton for making this sort of argument with respect to the proclamation of neutrality.) Other members of Congress supported Madison's argument by alluding to the clause of Article II, Section 3, that gave the president the duty to "take Care that the Laws be faithfully executed." One explained, "I take it that the best principle is, that he who is responsible for the conduct of the officer, ought to have the power of removing him." 1 Annals of Cong. at 483.

A majority of the House ultimately agreed that "all officers concerned in executive business should depend upon the will of the President for their continuance in office." *Id.* at 637. Beyond that point, however, there was little agreement about whether this position was merely the best policy for Congress to adopt—or whether it was constitutionally required. *See* Gienapp, *supra*, at 159–63. The final statute creating the Department of Foreign Affairs failed to resolve this basic ambiguity. Instead, it merely alluded to the president's removal power, declaring what would happen "whenever the principal officer shall be removed from office by the President." Act of July 27, 1789, ch. 4, 1 Stat. 28, 29. The first foreign secretary, Thomas Jefferson, later removed himself by resigning.

The removal debate wasn't over, however. When Congress next created the Department of the Treasury, Madison argued that one of the officers, the comptroller of the Treasury, was more of a "judicial" officer than an "executive" officer because his role was primarily to decide upon the justice of claims against the United States. 1 Annals of Cong. at 635–36. After considering "the nature of this office," Madison argued that he was "very well satisfied" that Congress could make this quasi-judicial officer dependent upon Congress as well as the president. *Id.* at 636–39. The final statute creating the Department of the Treasury implied that the principal officer of the Treasury Department could be removed by the president but made no provision for the removal of the comptroller. Act of Sept. 2, 1789, ch. 12, 1 Stat. 65, 67.

Take Care Clause

The removal debate continued through the entire nineteenth century with major consequences. Executive-branch interpretations typically focused on the Take Care Clause, which required the president to "take Care that the Laws be faithfully executed." At first, attorneys general interpreted this clause narrowly as a duty to hold criminally negligent officials accountable—perhaps through removal, or perhaps instead through impeachment or criminal prosecutions. 1 Op. Att'y Gen. 624 (1823). But President Andrew Jackson and his attorney general, Roger Taney, argued that the clause gave the president the implied power to control any members of the executive branch by removing them if necessary. *See* 2 Op. Att'y Gen. 482 (1831).

The Jackson administration raised this point during a fierce debate with Congress over control of the Second Bank of the United States. The president wanted the secretary of the Treasury to remove all federal deposits from the bank, while Congress wanted the secretary to protect the bank. When the secretary refused to comply with Jackson's order, Jackson fired him with a message to Congress that mirrored Madison's position in the debate over the secretary of foreign affairs:

> By the Constitution "the executive power is vested in a President of the United States." Among the duties imposed upon him and which he is sworn to perform, is that of "taking care that the laws be faithfully executed." . . . The whole executive power being vested in the President, who is responsible for its exercise, it is a necessary consequence that he should have a right to employ agents of his own choice to aid him in the performance of his duties, and to discharge them when he is no longer willing to be responsible for their acts. In strict accordance with this principle, the power of removal, which, like that of appointment, is an original executive power, is left unchecked by the Constitution in relation to all executive officers, for whose conduct the President is responsible, while it is taken from him in relation to judicial officers, for whose acts he is not responsible.

3 *Messages and Papers of the Presidents* 79–80 (James D. Richardson ed., 1896).

The Supreme Court weighed in on this debate a few years later when it mediated another dispute between Congress and President Jackson. The president ordered his postmaster general, Amos Kendall, to refuse to pay money to several postal carriers, including William B. Stokes. Congress responded by passing a special act ordering Kendall to pay the carriers. Act of July 2, 1836, ch. 284, 6 Stat. 665. Kendall argued that this law violated the Take Care Clause because the "the Postmaster General was alone subject to the direction and control of the President," not to Congress. But in *Kendall v. United States ex rel. Stokes*, 37 U.S. (12 Pet.) 524 (1838), the Court sided with Congress. "There are certain political duties imposed upon many officers in the Executive Department the discharge of which is under the direction of the President," the Court wrote. *Stokes*, 37 U.S. (12 Pet.) at 610. "But it would be an alarming doctrine that Congress cannot impose upon any executive officer any duty they may think proper . . . subject to the control of the law, and not to the direction of the President." *Id.* Without drawing a line between duties that could be enforced by statute and duties subject only to presidential control, the Court "emphatically" declared that "where the duty enjoined is of a mere ministerial character," Congress could require executive officers to cooperate. *Id.*

But in later cases, when Congress by statute required the president alone to perform an action, the Court, based on Jackson's theory that the president embodied the entire executive branch, authorized the president to delegate these responsibilities to subordinates. *See, e.g.*, *Williams v. United States*, 42 U.S. (1 How.) 290 (1843); *Wilcox v. Jackson*, 38 U.S. (13 Pet.) 498 (1839). *But see* 7 Op. Att'y Gen. 453 (1855) (arguing that the president could not delegate constitutional duties such as the pardon power or the responsibilities of commander in chief).

Tenure of Office Act

The conflict between Congress and the president over the removal power reached a breaking point during the administration of Andrew Johnson, who succeeded Abraham Lincoln at the end of the Civil War. As discussed earlier (sections 12.2, 20.1), Johnson began his administration by proposing lenient terms for former Confederate states to resume their standing in the Union, and he vetoed the Civil Rights Act of 1866 and other legislation intended to protect the civil rights of black people. Congress took Reconstruction into its own hands with the Reconstruction Acts of 1867, which placed every southern state except for Tennessee under the supervision of military generals. These generals, in turn, were supervised by the secretary of war, Edwin Stanton. To protect the generals from Johnson, Congress passed a law in 1867 that required "any orders or instructions relating to military operations" to be issued through the general of the army, Ulysses S. Grant. Act of Mar. 2, 1867, ch. 170, 14 Stat. 485, 486–87. Congress also passed the Tenure of Office Act of 1867, which made it a "high misdemeanor[ ]" for the president to remove certain civil officers without the Senate's consent. Tenure of Office Act, ch. 154, 14 Stat. 430, 431.

The Tenure of Office Act's applicability to Secretary of War Stanton was ambiguous. But some members of the Johnson administration called the law "*palpably* unconstitutional," persuading the president to spurn the law and fire Stanton. Ron Chernow, *Grant* 595–98 (2017). As the president fired Stanton, he sent a defiant message to Congress accusing it of conspiring to replace white governments with black politicians who had "shown a constant tendency to relapse into barbarism." *Id.* at 598–99.

Shortly afterward, the House sent eleven articles of impeachment to the Senate, most of which turned on the president's alleged violation of the Tenure of Office Act (although the real issue was the president's attempts to disrupt congressional Reconstruction). *Id.* Although Republicans wielded a supermajority in the Senate, Johnson was acquitted by a single vote. He was saved by two authors of the Tenure of Office Act, who insisted that its terms did not apply to Stanton. *See* 3 *Trial of Andrew Johnson* 322–23 (Washington, Gov't Printing Office 1868). Many observers speculated that the president made a deal with some moderate Republicans to cease interfering in Reconstruction. *See* Annette Gordon-Reed, *Andrew Johnson* 140–41 (2011). Regardless of the reason for Johnson's acquittal, the Tenure of Office Act remained on the books for decades.

Yet as Reconstruction ended in the face of a conservative counterrevolution, white historians sympathetic to the Lost Cause began to redeem Johnson's memory. They argued that the Tenure of Office Act was an unconstitutional "assertion of congressional supremacy over the judicial and executive branches of government" in order to effect "congressional supremacy in the conquered South." William A. Dunning, *Reconstruction* 86–89, 93 (1907).

And as Reconstruction grew more unpopular among white historians, the Supreme Court impliedly sided with Johnson, holding that, absent a statute involving the Senate in the removal process, the president could summarily fire an executive officer who had been appointed with the Senate's consent—even if a statute gave the officer a fixed term or made that officer subject to removal only for specified reasons. *See Shurtleff v. United States*, 189 U.S. 311 (1903); *Parsons v. United States*, 167 U.S. 324 (1897). The Court also held that the president always had the power to remove an inferior officer by nominating and confirming a replacement. *See Wallace v. United States*, 257 U.S. 541 (1922); *Quackenbush v. United States*, 117 U.S. 20 (1900); *Blake v. United States*, 103 U.S. 227 (1881).

27.3.1

Myers v. United States

272 U.S. 52 (1926)

It wasn't until the 1920s that the Supreme Court finally reviewed the constitutionality of a statute that, like the Tenure of Office Act, specifically prohibited the president from removing an executive officer without the permission of the Senate. The statute at issue was an 1876 law that reorganized the Department of the Post Office. At the time, the post office was a cabinet-level department whose enormous number of employees made it the most important source of patronage in the federal government. The law gave postmasters four-year terms and made them appointable and removable only "by the President by and with the advice and consent of the Senate." Act of July 12, 1876, ch. 179, 19 Stat. 80.

In 1913, shortly after becoming the second Democrat elected to the presidency since the Civil War, Woodrow Wilson appointed a man named Frank Myers as postmaster of Portland, Oregon. Wilson reappointed Myers in 1917, after which Myers tumbled into a series of factional brawls with a senator, member of Congress, and mayor of Portland. In 1920, after the mayor publicized that Myers was refusing to give returning World War I veterans their old jobs back, even the Wilson administration turned on him. Ultimately, Wilson's postmaster general fired Myers on the president's behalf. Myers responded by pointing to the 1876 statute and suing the government to collect his lost salary. *See*

Jonathan L. Entin, *The Curious Case of the Pompous Postmaster*, 65 Case W. Res. L. Rev. 1059, 1061–65 (2015).

By the time *Myers v. United States*, 272 U.S. 52 (1926), reached the Supreme Court, the chief justice was William Howard Taft, the former president who had lost to Wilson in his bid for a second term. Taft had long been a critic of Reconstruction generally and the Tenure of Office Act specifically, which he called an "undue stretch of legislative power." William Howard Taft, *Four Aspects of Civic Duty* 59 (1906). A firm believer in judicial supremacy, Taft used Myers's case as an opportunity to invalidate the Tenure of Office Act and vindicate Johnson's opposition to the Reconstruction Congress. "As I study the injustice that the radical Republicans did to Andrew Johnson, I am humiliated as a Republican," Taft explained to his colleague, Justice Pierce Butler, while writing the following opinion. *See* Nikolas Bowie & Daphna Renan, *The Separation-of-Powers Counterrevolution*, 131 Yale L.J. 3000, 3052 (2022).

■ MR. CHIEF JUSTICE TAFT delivered the opinion of the Court.[9]

This case presents the question whether under the Constitution the President has the exclusive power of removing executive officers of the United States whom he has appointed by and with the advice and consent of the Senate. . . .

There is no express provision respecting removals in the Constitution, except as Section 4 of Article II, . . . provides for removal from office by impeachment. The subject was not discussed in the Constitutional Convention. Under the Articles of Confederation, Congress was given the power of appointing certain executive officers of the Confederation, and during the Revolution and while the Articles were given effect, Congress exercised the power of removal.

Consideration of the executive power was initiated in the Constitutional Convention by the seventh resolution in the Virginia Plan. . . . It gave to the Executive "all the executive powers of the Congress under the Confederation," which would seem therefore to have intended to include the power of removal which had been exercised by that body as incident to the power of appointment. . . .

In the House of Representatives of the First Congress, on Tuesday, May 18, 1789, Mr. Madison moved in the Committee of the Whole that there should be established . . . a Department of Foreign Affairs, but a discussion ensued as to making the Secretary removable by the President. "The question was now taken and carried, by a considerable majority, in favor of declaring the power of removal to be in the President." 1 *Annals of Congress*, 383. . . .[10]

The discussion was a very full one. . . . Of the members of the House, eight had been in the Constitutional Convention . . . . Ten of the Senators had been in the

[9] **As You Read, Consider:** Congress created the office and responsibilities of local postmasters by virtue of its power under the Necessary and Proper Clause. Article II specifically authorized Congress to decide for itself whether to vest the appointment of the postmaster in the president, the courts, or the head of a department. Nothing in the Constitution specifically prohibited Congress from regulating how the postmaster could be removed. And President Ulysses S. Grant signed the 1876 law at issue in this case, indicating his agreement with its terms. Where in the Constitution, then, does Chief Justice William Howard Taft locate the president's exclusive and invulnerable power to remove executive officers?

[10] **Question:** The debate to which Taft is referring, discussed in the notes before this case, resolved that the president *could* remove executive officers but left open the question of whether Congress could take that power away. Why does Taft interpret the debate as conclusively determining that the president *exclusively* had the power to remove executive officers?

Constitutional Convention, and of them six voted that the power of removal was in the President alone. The bill having passed as it came from the House was signed by President Washington and became a law. 1 Stat. 28, c. 4. . . .

It is convenient in the course of our discussion of this case to review the reasons advanced by Mr. Madison and his associates for their conclusion, supplementing them, so far as may be, by additional considerations which lead this Court to concur therein.

First. Mr. Madison insisted that Article II by vesting the executive power in the President was intended to grant to him the power of appointment and removal of executive officers except as thereafter expressly provided in that Article.[11] He pointed out that one of the chief purposes of the Convention was to separate the legislative from the executive functions. . . . Their union under the Confederation had not worked well, as the members of the convention knew. Montesquieu's view that the maintenance of independence as between the legislative, the executive and the judicial branches was a security for the people had their full approval. Madison in the Convention, 2 Farrand, Records of the Federal Convention, 56. *Kendall v. United States,* 12 Peters 524, 610. Accordingly, the Constitution was so framed as to vest in the Congress all legislative powers therein granted, to vest in the President the executive power, and to vest in one Supreme Court and such inferior courts as Congress might establish, the judicial power. From this division on principle, the reasonable construction of the Constitution must be that the branches should be kept separate in all cases in which they were not expressly blended, and the Constitution should be expounded to blend them no more than it affirmatively requires. . . .

The vesting of the executive power in the President was essentially a grant of the power to execute the laws. But the President alone and unaided could not execute the laws. He must execute them by the assistance of subordinates. . . . As he is charged specifically to take care that they be faithfully executed, the reasonable implication, even in the absence of express words, was that as part of his executive power he should select those who were to act for him under his direction in the execution of the laws. The further implication must be, . . . that as his selection of administrative officers is essential to the execution of the laws by him, so must be his power of removing those for whom he can not continue to be responsible. Fisher Ames, 1 *Annals of Congress*, 474. . . .

Second. The view of Mr. Madison and his associates was that not only did the grant of executive power to the President in the first section of Article II carry with it the power of removal, but the express recognition of the power of appointment in the second section enforced this view on the well approved principle of constitutional and statutory construction that the power of removal of executive officers was incident to the power of appointment.[12] It was agreed by the opponents of the bill, with only one or two exceptions, that as a constitutional principle the power of appointment carried

---

[11] **Question:** This first argument is resonant of Alexander Hamilton's interpretation of the Vesting Clause: it gives the president all "executive Power" that has not been qualified or taken away. Yet the Constitution also gives the president the duty to "take Care that the Laws be faithfully executed." And unlike with Hamilton's defense of the proclamation of neutrality, here Congress has enacted a statute regulating how the president can exercise his power. If Taft is correct that the president's executive power can overcome a statute, is there anything Congress can do to limit a president in any context?

[12] **Questions:** Does the power to appoint someone necessarily convey the power to remove that person? Consider senators: under the original Constitution, state legislatures appointed senators yet could not remove them before the senators' six-year term expired.

Even if Taft is correct on this point, Myers was appointed by the president with the advice and consent of the Senate. Why would it be inappropriate for Congress to require that he be removed with the advice and consent of the Senate?

with it the power of removal. Roger Sherman, 1 *Annals of Congress*, 491. This principle as a rule of constitutional and statutory construction, then generally conceded, has been recognized ever since. *Shurtleff v. United States,* 189 U.S. 311, 315. The reason for the principle is that those in charge of and responsible for administering functions of government who select their executive subordinates need in meeting their responsibility to have the power to remove those whom they appoint. . . .

Under section 2 of Article II, however, the power of appointment by the Executive is restricted in its exercise by the provision that the Senate, a part of the legislative branch of the Government, may check the action of the Executive by rejecting the officers he selects. Does this make the Senate part of the removing power? . . .

[No.] The power to prevent the removal of an officer who has served under the President is different from the authority to consent to or reject his appointment. When a nomination is made, it may be presumed that the Senate is, or may become, as well advised as to the fitness of the nominee as the President, but in the nature of things the defects in ability or intelligence or loyalty in the administration of the laws of one who has served as an officer under the President, are facts as to which the President, or his trusted subordinates, must be better informed than the Senate, and the power to remove him may, therefore, be regarded as confined, for very sound and practical reasons, to the governmental authority which has administrative control. The power of removal is incident to the power of appointment, not to the power of advising and consenting to appointment, and when the grant of the executive power is enforced by the express mandate to take care that the laws be faithfully executed, it emphasizes the necessity for including within the executive power as conferred the exclusive power of removal. . . .

Third. Another argument urged against the constitutional power of the President alone to remove executive officers appointed by him with the consent of the Senate is that, in the absence of an express power of removal granted to the President, power to make provision for removal of all such officers is vested in the Congress by section 8 of Article I. . . .

[But a] reference of the whole power of removal to general legislation by Congress is quite out of keeping with the plan of government devised by the framers of the Constitution. It could never have been intended to leave to Congress unlimited discretion to vary fundamentally the operation of the great independent executive branch of government and thus most seriously to weaken it. It would be a delegation by the Convention to Congress of the function of defining the primary boundaries of another of the three great divisions of government. . . .

It is reasonable to suppose also that, had it been intended to give to Congress power to regulate or control removals in the manner suggested, it would have been included among the specifically enumerated legislative powers in Article I, or in the specified limitations on the executive power in Article II. The difference between the grant of legislative power under Article I to Congress, which is limited to powers therein enumerated, and the more general grant of the executive power to the President under Article II, is significant. The fact that the executive power is given in general terms strengthened by specific terms where emphasis is appropriate, and limited by direct expressions where limitation is needed and that no express limit is placed on the power of removal by the executive, is a convincing indication that none was intended.

It is argued that the denial of the legislative power to regulate removals in some way involves the denial of power to prescribe qualifications for office, or reasonable classification for promotion, and yet that has been often exercised. We see no conflict between the latter power and that of appointment and removal, provided of course that the qualifications do not so limit selection and so trench upon executive choice as to be in effect legislative designation. As Mr. Madison said in the First Congress:[13]

> "The powers relative to offices are partly Legislative and partly Executive. The Legislature creates the office, defines the powers, limits its duration and annexes a compensation. This done, the Legislative power ceases. They ought to have nothing to do with designating the man to fill the office. That I conceive to be of an Executive nature. Although it be qualified in the Constitution, I would not extend or strain that qualification beyond the limits precisely fixed for it. We ought always to consider the Constitution with an eye to the principles upon which it was founded. . . ." 1 *Annals of Congress*, 581, 582. . . .

Fourth. Mr. Madison and his associates pointed out with great force the unreasonable character of the view that the Convention intended, without express provision, to give to Congress or the Senate, in case of political or other differences, the means of thwarting the Executive in the exercise of his great powers and in the bearing of his great responsibility, by fastening upon him, as subordinate executive officers, men who by their inefficient service under him, by their lack of loyalty to the service, or by their different views of policy, might make his taking care that the laws be faithfully executed most difficult or impossible. . . .[14]

Made responsible under the Constitution for the effective enforcement of the law, the President needs as an indispensable aid to meet it the disciplinary influence upon those who act under him of a reserve power of removal. . . . Each head of a department is and must be the President's *alter ego* in the matters of that department where the President is required by law to exercise authority. . . . The moment that he loses confidence in the intelligence, ability, judgment or loyalty of any one of them, he must have the power to remove him without delay. To require him to file charges and submit them to the consideration of the Senate might make impossible that unity and co-ordination in executive administration essential to effective action. . . .

Of course there may be duties so peculiarly and specifically committed to the discretion of a particular officer as to raise a question whether the President may overrule or revise the officer's interpretation of his statutory duty in a particular instance. Then there may be duties of a quasi-judicial character imposed on executive officers and members of executive tribunals whose decisions after hearing affect interests of individuals, the discharge of which the President can not in a particular case properly influence or control. But even in such a case he may consider the decision after its rendition as a reason for removing the officer, on the ground that the discretion regularly entrusted to that officer by statute has not been on the whole

---

[13] **Question:** Is Taft's distinction here persuasive—i.e., that the Necessary and Proper Clause empowers Congress to regulate the *duration* of an office, yet Congress cannot regulate how an officer may be removed?

[14] **Questions:** With these four arguments, Taft is embracing what is sometimes called the "unitary executive" theory: the Constitution vests in the "executive Power" in the president alone and gives the president alone the duty to "take Care that the Laws be faithfully executed." An implication of this theory is that all executive officers are mere alter egos of the president, and the president must therefore be able to remove subordinates whom the president cannot trust to faithfully execute duties for which the president alone will be held responsible.

In this case, however, President Woodrow Wilson *violated* a law that required him to seek Senate approval before removing a postmaster. What explains why a president's duty to faithfully execute the laws might authorize the president to violate a particular law that regulates the president's conduct? Does Taft think that the president could violate all laws that regulate the executive branch or that insulate certain decisions from presidential influence? Could a president overrule a U.S. attorney's decision regarding whether to prosecute someone?

intelligently or wisely exercised. Otherwise he does not discharge his own constitutional duty of seeing that the laws be faithfully executed.

We have devoted much space to this discussion and decision of the question of the Presidential power of removal in the First Congress, not because a Congressional conclusion on a constitutional issue is conclusive, but, first, because of our agreement with the reasons upon which it was avowedly based; second, because this was the decision of the First Congress, on a question of primary importance in the organization of the Government, made within two years after the Constitutional Convention and within a much shorter time after its ratification; and, third, because that Congress numbered among its leaders those who had been members of the Convention. It must necessarily constitute a precedent upon which many future laws supplying the machinery of the new Government would be based, and, if erroneous, it would be likely to evoke dissent and departure in future Congresses. It would come at once before the executive branch of the Government for compliance, and might well be brought before the judicial branch for a test of its validity. As, we shall see, it was soon accepted as a final decision of the question by all branches of the Government. . . .

A typical case of such acquiescence was that of Alexander Hamilton . . ., as is shown by his view of Washington's first proclamation of neutrality in the war between France and Great Britain. That proclamation was at first criticized as an abuse of executive authority. It has now come to be regarded as one of the greatest and most valuable acts of the first President's Administration, and has been often followed by succeeding Presidents. Hamilton's argument was that the Constitution, by vesting the executive power in the President, gave him the right, as the organ of intercourse between the Nation and foreign nations, to interpret national treaties and to declare neutrality. He deduced this from Article II of the Constitution on the executive power, and followed exactly the reasoning of Madison and his associates as to the executive power upon which the legislative decision of the First Congress as to Presidential removals depends, and he cites it as authority. . . .

[Based on earlier opinions of the Supreme Court, attorneys general, and members of Congress from 1789 through the Civil War], then, the facts as to acquiescence by all branches of the Government in the legislative decision of 1789, as to executive officers, whether superior or inferior, we find that from 1789 until 1863, a period of 74 years, there was no act of Congress, no executive act, and no decision of this Court at variance with the declaration of the First Congress, but there was, as we have seen, clear, affirmative recognition of it by each branch of the Government. . . .

We come now to a period in the history of the Government when both Houses of Congress attempted to reverse this constitutional construction and to subject the power of removing executive officers appointed by the President and confirmed by the Senate to the control of the Senate—indeed, finally, to the assumed power in Congress to place the removal of such officers anywhere in the Government.[15]

This reversal grew out of the serious political difference between the two Houses of Congress and President Johnson. There was a two-thirds majority of the Republican party in control of each House of Congress, which resented what it feared would be Mr. Johnson's obstructive course in the enforcement of the reconstruction measures, in respect of the States whose people had lately been at war against the

[15] **Question:** The actions of the Reconstruction Congress represent a powerful counterargument to Taft's claim that all branches acquiesced to the idea that Congress could not regulate the power of the president to remove executive officers. Indeed, the 1876 law is one of many since the Civil War that regulated the removal of executive officers. How does Taft evaluate the precedential value of these counterexamples?

National Government. . . . [T]he chief legislation in support of the reconstruction policy of Congress was the Tenure of Office Act, of March 2, 1867, 14 Stat. 430, c. 154, providing . . . that certain heads of departments, including the Secretary of War, should hold their offices during the term of the President by whom appointed and one month thereafter subject to removal by consent of the Senate. The Tenure of Office Act was vetoed, but it was passed over the veto. The House of Representatives preferred articles of impeachment against President Johnson for refusal to comply with, and for conspiracy to defeat, the legislation above referred to, but he was acquitted for lack of a two-thirds vote for conviction in the Senate. . . .

The extreme provisions of all this legislation were a full justification for the considerations so strongly advanced by Mr. Madison and his associates in the First Congress for insisting that the power of removal of executive officers by the President alone was essential in the division of powers between the executive and the legislative bodies. It exhibited in a clear degree the paralysis to which a partisan Senate and Congress could subject the executive arm and destroy the principle of executive responsibility and separation of the powers, sought for by the framers of our Government, if the President had no power of removal save by consent of the Senate. It was an attempt to re-distribute the powers and minimize those of the President.

After President Johnson's term ended, the injury and invalidity of the Tenure of Office Act in its radical innovation were immediately recognized by the Executive and objected to. General Grant, succeeding Mr. Johnson in the Presidency, earnestly recommended in his first message the total repeal of the act . . . . The feeling growing out of the controversy with President Johnson retained the act on the statute book until 1887, when it was repealed. 24 Stat. 500, c. 353. During this interval, . . . [in] 1876 the act here under discussion was passed, making the consent of the Senate necessary both to the appointment and removal of first, second and third class postmasters. . . .

What, then, are the elements that enter into our decision of this case? We have first a construction of the Constitution made by a Congress which was to provide by legislation for the organization of the Government in accord with the Constitution which had just then been adopted, and in which there were, as representatives and senators, a considerable number of those who had been members of the Convention that framed the Constitution and presented it for ratification. . . . This Court has repeatedly laid down the principle that a contemporaneous legislative exposition of the Constitution when the founders of our Government and framers of our Constitution were actively participating in public affairs, acquiesced in for a long term of years, fixes the construction to be given its provisions. *Prigg v. Pennsylvania*, 16 Pet. 544; *McPherson v. Blacker*, 146 U.S. 1, 28.

We are now asked to set aside this construction, thus buttressed, and adopt an adverse view, because the Congress of the United States did so during a heated political difference of opinion between the then President and the majority leaders of Congress over the reconstruction measures adopted as a means of restoring to their proper status the States which attempted to withdraw from the Union at the time of the Civil War. . . . Without animadverting on the character of the measures taken, we are certainly justified in saying that they should not be given the weight affecting proper constitutional construction to be accorded to that reached by the First Congress of the United States during a political calm and acquiesced in by the whole Government for three-quarters of a century, especially when the new construction contended for has never been acquiesced in by either the executive or the judicial departments. . . . When, on the merits, we find our conclusion strongly favoring the view which prevailed in the First Congress, we have no hesitation in holding that conclusion to be correct; and it therefore follows that the Tenure of Office Act of 1867, in so far as it attempted to prevent the President from removing executive officers who had been appointed by him by and with the advice and consent of the Senate, was invalid, and that subsequent legislation of the same effect was equally so.

For the reasons given, we must therefore hold that the provision of the law of 1876, by which the unrestricted power of removal of first class postmasters is denied to the President, is in violation of the Constitution, and invalid. . . .

NOTE: AFTERMATH OF *MYERS*

Myers was a sweeping, provocative decision that cast into doubt dozens of statutes in which Congress had attempted to protect executive officers from removal. Two kinds of statutes appeared to be in particular trouble: (1) civil service reform laws, in which Congress protected inferior officers from being fired for political reasons; and (2) so-called independent agencies—including the Interstate Commerce Commission and the Federal Trade Commission—in which members could be removed only "for cause," meaning for inefficiency, neglect, or malfeasance in office. The purpose of both protections was to ensure that administrative officers would base their decisions on professional considerations rather than the political wishes of the president's party.

Retreat from *Myers* in *Humphrey's Executor*. A decade after *Myers*, the Court reconsidered the decision's effect on civil service reform and independent agencies in *Humphrey's Executor v. United States*, 295 U.S. 602 (1935).

In 1931, a Republican president, Herbert Hoover, nominated William E. Humphrey to sit for a seven-year term on the Federal Trade Commission, the agency in charge of antitrust activities. The act creating the commission stated that members could be removed by the president only for cause. Two years later, the newly elected Democratic president, Franklin D. Roosevelt, fired Humphrey on the ground "that the aims and purposes of the Administration with respect to the work of the Commission can be carried out most effectively with personnel of my own selection." *Humphrey's Executor*, 295 U.S. at 618. Humphrey died shortly afterward, but, as in *Myers*, the executor of his estate sued the United States to recover his lost salary.

In *Humphrey's Executor*, the Court distinguished *Myers* to hold that Roosevelt lacked the power to override Humphrey's statutory protection from removal. Although the Court again turned to James Madison's arguments in 1789, it focused not on the debate over the secretary of foreign affairs but on the later debate over the comptroller of the Treasury. There, Madison had argued that Congress could ensure the congressional dependence of an officer whose duties were not purely executive but who also had judge-like functions of assessing the legitimacy of claims against the United States. *Id.* at 631. The Court agreed with Madison's position as a reflection of the separation of powers: while the president might have plenary power to remove "purely executive officers," the president had fewer powers to remove "quasi-legislative and quasi-judicial bodies" and no powers at all with respect to "the legislative or judicial departments of the government." *Id.* at 628–29. Treating *Myers* as an application of Madison's thought with respect to purely executive officers alone, the Court held that the president's power to override statutory protections from removal, such as a fixed term or for-cause protections, "will depend upon the character of the office." *Id.* at 631–32. Applying this standard, the Court found that the president could not override these protections for members of the Federal Trade Commission because "[i]n administering the provisions of the statute in respect of 'unfair methods of competition'—that is to say in filling in and administering the details embodied by that general standard—the commission acts in part quasi-legislatively and in part quasi-judicially." *Id.* at 628; *see also Wiener v. United States*, 357 U.S. 349 (1958) (in the face of a silent statute, the president has no power to remove members of the War Claims Commission, an adjudicatory body).

Further retreat from *Myers* in *Nixon*. After *Humphrey's Executor*, the Court steadily retreated from *Myers*, particularly after the Watergate scandal.

In 1973, while Congress was investigating the administration of President Richard Nixon for its role in the 1972 break-in of the Democratic National Committee's headquarters at the Watergate Hotel, the president nominated Elliot Richardson to serve as attorney general. During the nomination hearings, the Senate communicated to Richardson that he would be confirmed only if he agreed to appoint a "special prosecutor" to conduct his own independent investigation. Richardson agreed; appointed a Harvard Law School professor, Archibald Cox; and promulgated regulations that Cox would be removed only for "extraordinary improprieties." 38 Fed. Reg. 14,688 (1973).

But later that year, when Cox refused a direct order from the president not to subpoena tapes that the president had secretly recorded of his Oval Office conversations, the president ordered his attorney general to fire Cox. Richardson resigned rather than cooperate, as did the deputy attorney general, because both had promised Congress that they wouldn't interfere with the special prosecutor. *See* John W. Dean, *Blind Ambition* 382 (2016). Eventually, the solicitor general, Robert Bork, fired Cox—and the whole event became known as the "Saturday Night Massacre."

Cox's original subpoena reached the Supreme Court in *United States v. Nixon*, 418 U.S. 683 (1974), a case that we will consider shortly. Even though a prosecutor is an "executive" official, the Court upheld the special prosecutor's power to seek the subpoena while failing to comment on his protections from presidential removal. Nixon resigned soon afterward.

Affirmation of independence of independent counsel in *Morrison*. In the wake of the Watergate scandal and the Saturday Night Massacre, Congress passed the Ethics in Government Act of 1978, Pub. L. No. 95–521, 92 Stat. 1824, which established the office of "independent counsel" to investigate and prosecute high-ranking members of the executive branch for violating federal criminal law. In granting the counsel "full power and independent authority" to investigate the Department of Justice, the act provided that the independent counsel could be removed only (1) on impeachment and conviction; (2) after completing the investigation; or (3) "by the personal action of the Attorney General and only for good cause, physical disability, mental incapacity, or any other condition that substantially impairs the performance of such independent counsel's duties." Ethics in Government Act, 92 Stat. at 1872.

In 1982, a House committee investigating the federal government's handling of toxic "Superfund" sites issued a subpoena to the head of the Environmental Protection Agency, Anne Gorsuch—the mother of Justice Neil Gorsuch. When President Ronald Reagan consulted with the Department of Justice's Office of Legal Counsel, the head of the office, Ted Olson, recommended that the president order Gorsuch not to comply with the subpoena on the ground that it unduly interfered with the executive branch's internal deliberations. Reagan issued the order, Gorsuch defied the subpoena, and an infuriated House of Representatives held Gorsuch in contempt. *See* Philip Shabecoff, *House Charges Head of E.P.A. with Contempt*, N.Y. Times, Dec. 17, 1982, at A1. The House also called Olson to testify about his recommendation to the president. Concluding that Olson's testimony had been misleading, the House called for the appointment of an independent counsel to investigate. Olson challenged the constitutionality of this appointment, arguing in part that the counsel's removal protections unconstitutionally interfered with the president's power to remove and control executive officers.

In *Morrison v. Olson*, 487 U.S. 654 (1988), the Court held that the independent counsel's appointment, along with its removal limitations, did not impermissibly interfere with the president's Article II power. While *Humphrey's Executor* had relied on formal distinctions between "purely executive" and "quasi-legislative" and "quasi-judicial" officers, the *Morrison* Court took a functional approach, considering whether the counsel's removal protections were "of such a nature that they impede[d] the President's ability to perform his constitutional duty" to faithfully execute federal law. 487 U.S. at 691. The Court concluded that they did not "sufficiently deprive" the president of control over the independent counsel and the executive branch. *Id.* at 693.

Justice Antonin Scalia was the only justice to disagree with the *Morrison* majority, but his dissent became legendary in conservative circles. Critiquing the majority's approach as an "ad hoc, standardless" inquiry, Scalia emphasized a unitary view of the executive: all executive power is vested in the president, who has broad power under *Myers* to remove at will any executive officer, including the independent counsel. *Id.* at 712. The dissent foresaw disaster for the executive branch: unless the Court intervened to protect the president's removal power, Congress would place more restraints on the presidency until it swallowed the executive branch whole:

> Frequently an issue of this sort will come before the Court clad, so to speak, in sheep's clothing: the potential of the asserted principle to effect important change in the equilibrium of power is not immediately evident, and must be discerned by a careful and perceptive analysis. But this wolf comes as a wolf.

Id. at 699.

Limited protections for executive officers in *Free Enterprise Fund*. Since 1988, the Court has limited congressional protections of executive officers.

Most notably, in *Free Enterprise Fund v. Public Co. Accounting Oversight Board*, the Court held that Congress unconstitutionally interfered with the president's ability to "take Care that the Laws be faithfully executed" when it insulated an inferior officer from removal with two levels of protection. 561 U.S. 477, 497 (2010). The statutory protection at issue was part of the Sarbanes-Oxley Act of 2002, Pub. L. No. 107–204, 116 Stat. 745, passed in the wake of the Enron scandal. The act made members of the Public Company Accounting Oversight Board (PCAOB (pronounced "PEEK-a-boo")) removable by officers of the Securities and Exchange Commission (SEC) only "for good cause shown." *Id.* at 752. But the Court described members of the SEC as enjoying similar for-cause protections from removal, making it practically impossible for the president to control members of the PCAOB. Calling this a "novel" and "unusual situation," the Court struck down PCAOB's for-cause protection on the ground that "two layers are not the same as one." *Id.* at 501.

Ironically, the statute creating the SEC—drafted between the years of *Myers* and *Humphrey's Executor*—did *not* expressly include any for-cause protection from removal. *See* Note, *The SEC Is Not an Independent Agency*, 126 Harv. L. Rev. 781 (2013). But after the Court was made aware of this inconvenient fact, it allowed the parties to stipulate that SEC commissioners had removal protection and to "decide the case with that understanding." *Free Enter. Fund*, 561 U.S. at 781–82.

27.3.2

Seila Law LLC v. Consumer Financial Protection Bureau

140 S. Ct. 2183 (2020)

For almost a century, the Court retreated from *Myers*'s sweeping view of the president's removal power, adopting a variety of alternative tests that preserved Congress's power to regulate executive officers and insulate them from removal by a hostile president. But in 2020, the Court reaffirmed *Myers*'s basic premise.

In the wake of the 2008 financial crisis, Congress established the Consumer Financial Protection Bureau, an independent regulatory agency entrusted with protecting consumers in the financial sector. First proposed in 2007 by then-professor Elizabeth Warren, the bureau includes within its jurisdiction banks, credit unions, payday lenders, debt collectors, and other financial companies. But while Warren had envisioned a multimember board to oversee the new agency, Congress provided that the bureau would be led by a single director, who would serve a five-year term and could not be removed by the president except for inefficiency, neglect, or malfeasance.

In 2017, the bureau investigated Seila Law LLC, a California-based law firm that provided debt-relief services. When the bureau directed Seila Law to produce documentation of its business practices, Seila Law declined to comply and challenged the constitutionality of the agency. At the time, the bureau was led by an acting official whom President Donald Trump could remove at will under the terms of the Federal Vacancies Reform Act.

Nevertheless, in *Seila Law LLC v. CFPB*, 140 S. Ct. 2183 (2020), the Court considered whether the bureau's single-director structure impermissibly intruded on the president's powers—and decided that it did.

■ CHIEF JUSTICE ROBERTS delivered the opinion of the Court. . . .[16]

In the wake of the 2008 financial crisis, Congress established the Consumer Financial Protection Bureau (CFPB), an independent regulatory agency tasked with ensuring that consumer debt products are safe and transparent. In organizing the CFPB, Congress deviated from the structure of nearly every other independent administrative agency in our history. Instead of placing the agency under the leadership of a board with multiple members, Congress provided that the CFPB would be led by a single Director, who serves for a longer term than the President and cannot be removed by the President except for inefficiency, neglect, or malfeasance. The CFPB Director has no boss, peers, or voters to report to. Yet the Director wields vast rulemaking, enforcement, and adjudicatory authority over a significant portion of the U. S. economy. The question before us is whether this arrangement violates the Constitution's separation of powers.

Under our Constitution, the "executive Power"—all of it—is "vested in a President," who must "take Care that the Laws be faithfully executed." Art. II, § 1, cl. 1; *id.*, § 3. Because no single person could fulfill that responsibility alone, the Framers expected that the President would rely on subordinate officers for assistance. Ten years ago, in *Free Enterprise Fund v. Public Company Accounting Oversight Bd.*, 561 U.S. 477 (2010), we reiterated that, "as a general matter," the Constitution gives the President "the authority to remove those who assist him in carrying out his duties," *id.*, at 513–514. "Without such power, the President could not be held fully accountable for discharging his own responsibilities; the buck would stop somewhere else." *Id.*, at 514.

The President's power to remove—and thus supervise—those who wield executive power on his behalf follows from the text of Article II, was settled by the First Congress, and was confirmed in the landmark decision *Myers v. United States*, 272 U.S. 52 (1926). Our precedents have recognized only two exceptions to the President's unrestricted removal power. In *Humphrey's Executor* v. *United States*, 295 U.S. 602 (1935), we held that Congress could create expert agencies led by a

---

[16] **As You Read, Consider:** In the years separating *Myers v. United States* from this decision, the Supreme Court authorized Congress to protect multimember agencies and executive officers from removal by the president as long as the protections were not "of such a nature that they impede[d] the President's ability to perform his constitutional duty" to faithfully execute federal law. *Morrison v. Olson*, 487 U.S. 654, 691 (1988). Does Chief Justice John Roberts apply this rule to the Consumer Financial Protection Bureau, or does he overrule it? What is so intrusive about protecting a single agency head compared to a multimember agency head?

group of principal officers removable by the President only for good cause. And in *United States v. Perkins*, 116 U.S. 483 (1886), and *Morrison v. Olson*, 487 U.S. 654 (1988), we held that Congress could provide tenure protections to certain *inferior* officers with narrowly defined duties.

We are now asked to extend these precedents to a new configuration: an independent agency that wields significant executive power and is run by a single individual who cannot be removed by the President unless certain statutory criteria are met. We decline to take that step. While we need not and do not revisit our prior decisions allowing certain limitations on the President's removal power, there are compelling reasons not to extend those precedents to the novel context of an independent agency led by a single Director. Such an agency lacks a foundation in historical practice and clashes with constitutional structure by concentrating power in a unilateral actor insulated from Presidential control. . . .

"Perhaps the most telling indication of [a] severe constitutional problem" with an executive entity "is [a] lack of historical precedent" to support it. An agency with a structure like that of the CFPB is almost wholly unprecedented. . . .[17]

In addition to being a historical anomaly, the CFPB's single-Director configuration is incompatible with our constitutional structure. Aside from the sole exception of the Presidency, that structure scrupulously avoids concentrating power in the hands of any single individual.

"The Framers recognized that, in the long term, structural protections against abuse of power were critical to preserving liberty." *Bowsher*, 478 U.S., at 730. Their solution to governmental power and its perils was simple: divide it. To prevent the "gradual concentration" of power in the same hands, they enabled "[a]mbition . . . to counteract ambition" at every turn. The Federalist No. 51, p. 349 (J. Cooke ed. 1961) (J. Madison). At the highest level, they "split the atom of sovereignty" itself into one Federal Government and the States. They then divided the "powers of the new Federal Government into three defined categories, Legislative, Executive, and Judicial." *Chadha*, 462 U.S., at 951.

They did not stop there. Most prominently, the Framers bifurcated the federal legislative power into two Chambers: the House of Representatives and the Senate, each composed of multiple Members and Senators. Art. I, §§ 2, 3.

The Executive Branch is a stark departure from all this division. The Framers viewed the legislative power as a special threat to individual liberty, so they divided that power to ensure that "differences of opinion" and the "jarrings of parties" would "promote deliberation and circumspection" and "check excesses in the majority." See The Federalist No. 70, at 475 (A. Hamilton). By contrast, the Framers thought it necessary to secure the authority of the Executive so that he could carry out his unique responsibilities. See *id.*, No. 70, at 475–478. As Madison put it, while "the weight of the legislative authority requires that it should be . . . divided, the weakness of the executive may require, on the other hand, that it should be fortified." *Id.*, No. 51, at 350. . . .

To justify and check *that* authority—unique in our constitutional structure—the Framers made the President the most democratic and politically accountable official in Government.[18] Only the President (along with the Vice President) is elected by

---

[17] **Questions:** Why should the "lack of historical precedent" suggest anything about the unconstitutionality of an executive entity? Does it make sense to interpret the Constitution as if all constitutionally permissible arrangements have been tried? For a counterargument, see Leah M. Litman, *Debunking Antinovelty*, 66 Duke L.J. 1407 (2017).

[18] **Questions:** As discussed previously (sections 26.1–26.2), the delegates to the Constitutional Convention notably refused to make the president directly accountable to voters.

the entire Nation. And the President's political accountability is enhanced by the solitary nature of the Executive Branch, which provides "a single object for the jealousy and watchfulness of the people." *Id.,* at 479. The President "cannot delegate ultimate responsibility or the active obligation to supervise that goes with it," because Article II "makes a single President responsible for the actions of the Executive Branch." *Free Enterprise Fund,* 561 U.S., at 496–497.

The resulting constitutional strategy is straightforward: divide power everywhere except for the Presidency, and render the President directly accountable to the people through regular elections. In that scheme, individual executive officials will still wield significant authority, but that authority remains subject to the ongoing supervision and control of the elected President. Through the President's oversight, "the chain of dependence [is] preserved," so that "the lowest officers, the middle grade, and the highest" all "depend, as they ought, on the President, and the President on the community." 1 Annals of Cong. 499 (J. Madison).

The CFPB's single-Director structure contravenes this carefully calibrated system by vesting significant governmental power in the hands of a single individual accountable to no one. The Director is neither elected by the people nor meaningfully controlled (through the threat of removal) by someone who is. . . . Yet the Director may *unilaterally,* without meaningful supervision, issue final regulations, oversee adjudications, set enforcement priorities, initiate prosecutions, and determine what penalties to impose on private parties. With no colleagues to persuade, and no boss or electorate looking over her shoulder, the Director may dictate and enforce policy for a vital segment of the economy affecting millions of Americans.

The CFPB Director's insulation from removal by an accountable President is enough to render the agency's structure unconstitutional. . . .

It is true that "there is no 'removal clause' in the Constitution," *id.,* at 1, but neither is there a "separation of powers clause" or a "federalism clause." These foundational doctrines are instead evident from the Constitution's vesting of certain powers in certain bodies. As we have explained many times before, the President's removal power stems from Article II's vesting of the "executive Power" in the President. *Free Enterprise Fund,* 561 U.S., at 483 (quoting Art. II, § 1, cl. 1). . . . [T]hat power generally includes the ability to supervise and remove the agents who wield executive power in his stead. While we have previously upheld limits on the President's removal authority in certain contexts, we decline to do so when it comes to principal officers who, acting alone, wield significant executive power. The Constitution requires that such officials remain dependent on the President, who in turn is accountable to the people.[19]

■ JUSTICE KAGAN, with whom JUSTICE GINSBURG, JUSTICE BREYER, and JUSTICE SOTOMAYOR join, . . . dissenting in part.

They instead authorized state legislatures to appoint presidential electors, expecting that these electors would divide often enough to throw the election of the president to the House of Representatives. If Roberts is guided by the principle of popular sovereignty, why, then, does he not trust a statutory regulation of the president's removal authority that was enacted by the House of Representatives, the Senate, *and* the president? Couldn't the president veto this sort of democratically enacted law if it was too intrusive?

[19] **Question:** Roberts's opinion did not strike down the Consumer Financial Protection Bureau; it merely invalidated the "insulation from removal" and authorized the president to remove the bureau director at will. But in light of the "limits on the President's removal authority" that Roberts says he is not reevaluating in this opinion, if Congress wanted to preserve the independence of the bureau to the greatest extent possible, how could it do so while complying with this opinion?

Throughout the Nation's history, this Court has left most decisions about how to structure the Executive Branch to Congress and the President, acting through legislation they both agree to. In particular, the Court has commonly allowed those two branches to create zones of administrative independence by limiting the President's power to remove agency heads. The Federal Reserve Board. The Federal Trade Commission (FTC). The National Labor Relations Board. Statute after statute establishing such entities instructs the President that he may not discharge their directors except for cause—most often phrased as inefficiency, neglect of duty, or malfeasance in office. Those statutes, whose language the Court has repeatedly approved, provide the model for the removal restriction before us today. If precedent were any guide, that provision would have survived its encounter with this Court—and so would the intended independence of the Consumer Financial Protection Bureau (CFPB). . . .

I

The text of the Constitution, the history of the country, the precedents of this Court, and the need for sound and adaptable governance—all stand against the majority's opinion. They point not to the majority's "general rule" of "unrestricted removal power" with two grudgingly applied "exceptions." Rather, they bestow discretion on the legislature to structure administrative institutions as the times demand, so long as the President retains the ability to carry out his constitutional duties. And most relevant here, they give Congress wide leeway to limit the President's removal power in the interest of enhancing independence from politics in regulatory bodies like the CFPB.

What does the Constitution say about the separation of powers—and particularly about the President's removal authority? (Spoiler alert: about the latter, nothing at all. . . .)

The majority offers the civics class version of separation of powers—call it the Schoolhouse Rock definition of the phrase. The Constitution's first three articles, the majority recounts, "split the atom of sovereignty" among Congress, the President, and the courts. And by that mechanism, the Framers provided a "simple" fix "to governmental power and its perils."

There is nothing wrong with that as a beginning (except the adjective "simple"). . . . The problem lies in treating the beginning as an ending too—in failing to recognize that the separation of powers is, by design, neither rigid nor complete. Blackstone, whose work influenced the Framers on this subject as on others, observed that "every branch" of government "supports and is supported, regulates and is regulated, by the rest." 1 W. Blackstone, Commentaries on the Laws of England 151 (1765). . . .

One way the Constitution reflects that vision is by giving Congress broad authority to establish and organize the Executive Branch. Article II presumes the existence of "Officer[s]" in "executive Departments." § 2, cl. 1. But it does not, as you might think from reading the majority opinion, give the President authority to decide what kinds of officers—in what departments, with what responsibilities—the Executive Branch requires. Instead, Article I's Necessary and Proper Clause puts those decisions in the legislature's hands. Congress has the power "[t]o make all Laws which shall be necessary and proper for carrying into Execution" not just its own enumerated powers but also "all other Powers vested by this Constitution in the Government of the United States, or in any Department or Officer thereof." § 8, cl. 18. Similarly, the Appointments Clause reflects Congress's central role in structuring the Executive Branch. Yes, the President can appoint principal officers, but only as the legislature "shall . . . establish[ ] by Law" (and of course subject to the Senate's advice and consent). Art. II, § 2, cl. 2. And Congress has plenary power to decide not only what inferior officers will exist but also who (the President or a head of department) will appoint them. So as Madison told the first Congress, the legislature gets to "create[ ] the office, define[ ] the powers, [and] limit[ ] its duration." 1 Annals of Cong. 582 (1789). The President, as to the construction of his own branch of government, can only try to work his will through the legislative process.[20]

The majority relies for its contrary vision on Article II's Vesting Clause, but the provision can't carry all that weight. Or as Chief Justice Rehnquist wrote of a similar claim in *Morrison v. Olson*, 487 U.S. 654 (1988), "extrapolat[ing]" an unrestricted removal power from such "general constitutional language"—which says only that "[t]he executive Power shall be vested in a President"—is "more than the text will bear." *Id.*, at 690, n. 29. Dean John Manning has well explained why, even were it not obvious from the Clause's "open-ended language." *Separation of Powers as Ordinary Interpretation*, 124 Harv. L. Rev. 1939, 1971 (2011). The Necessary and Proper Clause, he writes, makes it impossible to "establish a constitutional violation simply by showing that Congress has constrained the way '[t]he executive Power' is implemented"; that is exactly what the Clause gives Congress the power to do. *Id.*, at 1967. . . .

Nor can the Take Care Clause come to the majority's rescue. That Clause cannot properly serve as a "placeholder for broad judicial judgments" about presidential control. Goldsmith & Manning, *The Protean Take Care Clause*, 164 U. Pa. L. Rev. 1835, 1867 (2016). To begin with, the provision—"he shall take Care that the Laws be faithfully executed"—speaks of duty, not power. Art. II, § 3. To be sure, the imposition of a duty may imply a grant of power sufficient to carry it out. But again, the majority's view of that power ill comports with founding-era practice, in which removal limits were common. . . . And yet more important, the text of the Take Care Clause requires only enough authority to make sure "the laws [are] faithfully executed"—meaning with fidelity to the law itself, not to every presidential policy preference. . . .

Finally, recall the Constitution's telltale silence: Nowhere does the text say anything about the President's power to remove subordinate officials at will. The majority professes unconcern. After all, it says, "neither is there a 'separation of powers clause' or a 'federalism clause.' " But those concepts are carved into the Constitution's text—the former in its first three articles separating powers, the latter in its enumeration of federal powers and its reservation of all else to the States. And anyway, at-will removal is hardly such a "foundational doctrine[ ]," *ibid.*: You won't find it on a civics class syllabus. That's because removal is a tool—one means among many, even if sometimes an important one, for a President to control executive officials. To find that authority hidden in the Constitution as a "general rule" is to discover what is nowhere there. . . .

As Chief Justice Marshall wrote when he upheld the first independent financial agency: "To have prescribed the means by which government should, in all future time, execute its powers, would have been to change, entirely, the character of the

---

[20] **Questions:** Justice Elena Kagan's dissent emphasizes that the Consumer Financial Protection Bureau and other administrative agencies are all created by legislation that Congress and the president negotiate. To the extent that an agency regulation is "necessary and proper for carrying into Execution" the president's powers, she would leave it to Congress and the president to hash out issues using their own expertise, which the judiciary lacks. But what about contexts like the Tenure of Office Act of 1867, which Congress enacted over President Andrew Johnson's veto? Does the existence of veto overrides suggest that there should be *some* role for the judiciary in policing the separation of powers? Or do the principles underlying her argument suggest that the judiciary should be deferential to Congress's discretion even in these circumstances?

instrument." *McCulloch*, 4 Wheat. at 415. . . . And if the Constitution, for those reasons, does not lay out immutable rules, then neither should judges. This Court has usually respected that injunction. It has declined to second-guess the work of the political branches in creating independent agencies like the CFPB. In reversing course today—in spurning a "pragmatic, flexible approach to American governance" in favor of a dogmatic, inflexible one—the majority makes a serious error. . . .[21]

[II]

The question here . . . is whether including [a] for-cause standard [for the CFPB Director] in the statute creating the CFPB violates the Constitution. . . .

The analysis is as simple as simple can be. The CFPB Director exercises the same powers, and receives the same removal protections, as the heads of other, constitutionally permissible independent agencies. How could it be that this opinion is a dissent?

The majority focuses on one (it says sufficient) reason: The CFPB Director is singular, not plural. And a solo CFPB Director does not fit within either of the majority's supposed exceptions. He is not an inferior officer, so (the majority says) *Morrison* does not apply; and he is not a multimember board, so (the majority says) neither does *Humphrey's*. Further, the majority argues, "[a]n agency with a [unitary] structure like that of the CFPB" is "novel"—or, if not quite that, "almost wholly unprecedented." Finally, the CFPB's organizational form violates the "constitutional structure" because it vests power in a "single individual" who is "insulated from Presidential control."

I'm tempted at this point just to say: No. All I've explained about constitutional text, history, and precedent invalidates the majority's thesis. But I'll set out here some more targeted points, taking step by step the majority's reasoning.

First, as I'm afraid you've heard before, the majority's "exceptions" (like its general rule) are made up. To begin with, our precedents reject the very idea of such exceptions. "The analysis contained in our removal cases," *Morrison* stated, shuns any attempt "to define rigid categories" of officials who may (or may not) have job protection. 487 U.S., at 689. . . . Those opinions mention the "groupness" of the agency head only in their background sections. The majority picks out that until-now-irrelevant fact to distinguish the CFPB, and constructs around it an until-now-unheard-of exception. So if the majority really wants to see something "novel," it need only look to its opinion. . . .

[T]o make sense on the majority's own terms, the distinction between singular and plural agency heads must rest on a theory about why the former more easily "slip" from the President's grasp. But the majority has nothing to offer. In fact, the opposite is more likely to be true: To the extent that such matters are measurable, individuals are easier than groups to supervise. . . . Just consider your everyday experience: It's easier to get one person to do what you want than a gaggle. So too, you know exactly whom to blame when an individual—but not when a group—does a job badly. The same is true in bureaucracies. . . .

[Yet] the majority . . . says a single head is the greater threat because he may wield power "*unilaterally*" and "[w]ith no colleagues to persuade." So the CFPB falls

[21] **Questions:** Is Kagan's criticism of judicial review limited to the specific context of the power of Congress and the president to create administrative agencies by statute, or is it generalizable to all federal legislation? For example, Congress presumably has far more expertise than the Supreme Court regarding tax policy, the regulation of commerce, and spending decisions. Is judicial review in defense of "the Constitution's general structure" and "implicit values" any more warranted in those settings than in this one?

victim to what the majority sees as a constitutional anti-power-concentration principle (with an exception for the President). . . .

If you've never heard of a statute being struck down on that ground, you're not alone. It is bad enough to "extrapolat[e]" from the "general constitutional language" of Article II's Vesting Clause an unrestricted removal power constraining Congress's ability to legislate under the Necessary and Proper Clause. It is still worse to extrapolate from the Constitution's general structure (division of powers) and implicit values (liberty) a limit on Congress's express power to create administrative bodies. And more: to extrapolate from such sources a distinction as prosaic as that between the SEC and the CFPB—*i.e.,* between a multi-headed and single-headed agency. That is, to adapt a phrase (or two) from our precedent, "more than" the emanations of "the text will bear." *Morrison,* 487 U.S., at 690, n. 29. By using abstract separation-of-powers arguments for such purposes, the Court "appropriate[s]" the "power delegated to Congress by the Necessary and Proper Clause" to compose the government. Manning, Foreword: The Means of Constitutional Power, 128 Harv. L. Rev. 1, 78 (2014). In deciding for itself what is "proper," the Court goes beyond its own proper bounds.

And in doing so, the majority again reveals its lack of interest in how agencies work. First, the premise of the majority's argument—that the CFPB head is a mini-dictator, not subject to meaningful presidential control[—]is wrong. As this Court has seen in the past, independent agencies are not fully independent. A for-cause removal provision, as noted earlier, leaves "ample" control over agency heads in the hands of the President. *Morrison,* 487 U.S., at 692. He can discharge them for failing to perform their duties competently or in accordance with law, and so ensure that the laws are "faithfully executed." U. S. Const., Art. II, § 3. And he can use the many other tools attached to the Office of the Presidency—including in the CFPB's case, rulemaking review—to exert influence over discretionary policy calls. Second, the majority has nothing but intuition to back up its essentially functionalist claim that the CFPB would be less capable of exercising power if it had more than one Director. Although a multimember format tends to frustrate the President's control over an agency, it may not lessen the agency's own ability to act with decision and dispatch. (Consider, for a recent example, the Federal Reserve Board.) That effect presumably would depend on the agency's internal organization, voting rules, and similar matters. At the least: If the Court is going to invalidate statutes based on empirical assertions like this one, it should offer some empirical support. It should not pretend that its assessment that the CFPB wields more power more dangerously than the SEC comes from someplace in the Constitution. But today the majority fails to accord even that minimal respect to Congress.

III

Recall again how this dispute got started. In the midst of the Great Recession, Congress and the President came together to create an agency with an important mission. It would protect consumers from the reckless financial practices that had caused the then-ongoing economic collapse. Not only Congress but also the President thought that the new agency, to fulfill its mandate, needed a measure of independence. So the two political branches, acting together, gave the CFPB Director the same job protection that innumerable other agency heads possess. All in all, those branches must have thought, they had done a good day's work. Relying on their experience and knowledge of administration, they had built an agency in the way best suited to carry out its functions. . . . They had governed.

And now consider how the dispute ends—with five unelected judges rejecting the result of that democratic process. . . . [The majority] jettisons a measure Congress and the President viewed as integral to the way the agency should operate

. . . even though the Constitution grants to Congress, acting with the President's approval, the authority to create and shape administrative bodies. . . .

NOTE: AFTERMATH OF *SEILA LAW*

Seila Law illustrates the Supreme Court's recent skepticism of Congress's power to regulate the removal of executive officers. Even though Congress and President Barack Obama agreed upon the law that authorized the president to remove the head of the Consumer Financial Protection Bureau for "inefficiency, neglect of duty, or malfeasance in office," and even though there was no indication that this tenure protection had even affected Seila Law's situation, the Court held that any sort of statutory tenure protection was prohibited by Article II's vesting of "executive Power" to the president. *Seila Law LLC v. CFPB*, 140 S. Ct. 2183, 2197 (2020). The Court reaffirmed this holding the following year when it invalidated a statute whose tenure protection the Court conceded was "modest." *Collins v. Yellen*, 141 S. Ct. 1761 (2021). The statute governing the single-member director of the Federal Housing Finance Agency authorized the president to remove the director "for cause," which included disobeying a presidential order. *Id.* at 1786. Nevertheless, the Court held that " 'for cause' . . . does not mean the same thing as 'at will,' and therefore the removal restriction in the [statute] violates the separation of powers." *Id.* at 1787.

Although the Supreme Court's modern removal jurisprudence is associated with the conservative legal movement, the first president to take advantage of the Court's holding in *Seila Law* was a Democrat, Joe Biden. Early in his presidency, Biden fired several officers who had been appointed by his Republican predecessor despite statutory tenure provisions that nominally protected the officers from removal. *See, e.g.*, Jim Tankersley, *Biden Fires Trump Appointee as Head of Social Security Administration*, N.Y. Times, Jul. 9, 2021, at A11. Ironically, Republicans in Congress complained that the president's actions were "unprecedented and unlawful." *See* Press Release, U.S. Sen. Comm. on Finance, Crapo, Scott, Young, Brady and Reed ask GAO to Clarify Authorities and Term of Acting SSA Commissioner, Aug. 24, 2021.

NOTE: CONGRESSIONAL ORDERS AND THE APPROPRIATIONS CLAUSE

Despite the Supreme Court's restrictions on Congress's power to protect executive officials from being removed by the president, there are many instances in which Congress can *order* executive officials to comply with congressional orders. The most important concerns the Appropriations Clause of Article I, Section 9, which states, "No Money shall be drawn from the Treasury, but in Consequence of Appropriations made by Law."

In *Stokes*, the case about Congress's power to compel the postmaster general to pay an individual, the Supreme Court based its decision, in part, on Congress's unique power to compel where money from the Treasury may be spent. Nevertheless, in the face of statutes ordering the expenditure of money on certain projects, Thomas Jefferson and subsequent presidents declined to spend the money on the ground that the expenditure is no longer necessary or the money can be better spent in the future. *See, e.g.*, 1 *Messages and Papers of the Presidents* 348, 360 (James D. Richardson ed., 1909) (Jefferson). The Nixon administration expanded and vocally defended this practice of "impoundment," arguing that the president had to have the discretion to determine how best to satisfy the executive branch's many statutory responsibilities. Members of Congress disagreed, criticizing the president for issuing what was, in effect, a line-item veto of congressional appropriations.

In 1974, Congress ended the controversy by passing the Congressional Budget and Impoundment Control Act, 88 Stat. 332, which authorized court actions by the comptroller general to compel the executive branch to spend funds as directed. Shortly afterward, in *Train v. City of New York*, 420 U.S. 35 (1975), the Court held that Nixon had no discretion to impound money appropriated for the Environmental Protection Agency. This decision—and the impoundment controversy generally—became relevant again in 2019, when officials in the Trump administration ordered the Department of Defense to withhold appropriated funds from Ukraine until its president, Volodymyr Zelensky, announced that he would investigate the son of Trump's political rival, Joe Biden. This "abuse of power" formed the basis of the first article of impeachment brought against Trump in 2019. *See* H.R. Res. 755, 116th Cong. (2019).

CHAPTER 28

WHAT IS THE SCOPE OF THE PRESIDENT'S IMMUNITY FROM INVESTIGATIONS?

ARTICLE I, SECTION 1: All legislative Powers herein granted shall be vested in a Congress of the United States, which shall consist of a Senate and House of Representatives.

ARTICLE II, SECTION 3, CLAUSE 1: The President . . . shall take Care that the Laws be faithfully executed, and shall Commission all the Officers of the United States.

28.1 EXECUTIVE PRIVILEGE

For hundreds of years, lawyers in the United States have consulted with clients with the expectation that neither could be compelled to disclose their communications to courts or other government officials. *See Attorney-Client Privilege in the United States* § 1:1 (Kevin T. Barnett et al. eds., 2019). The American Bar Association calls this "attorney-client privilege" the "crown jewel of the legal profession" as it allows clients to candidly seek legal advice without fear of inadvertently incriminating themselves or others. John M. Barkett, *Attorney-Client Privilege*, 45 Litig. J. 34 (2019). In the twentieth century, the privilege expanded in various ways to also include the work product that lawyers prepare on behalf of their clients—including interviews, statements, memoranda, correspondence, briefs, mental impressions, and personal beliefs. *See Hickman v. Taylor*, 329 U.S. 495, 511 (1947). But as established as these privileges are in the private sector, they are considerably more controversial when the client is the president of the United States and the communications and work product are documents prepared by executive-branch officials.

Role of the Department of Justice

Early in American history, when Congress or federal courts asked presidents for information, presidents often asserted the right to exercise discretion in selecting how they would respond. *See, e.g.*, *United States v. Burr*, 25 F. Cas. 30 (C.C.D. Va. 1807). Yet it took decades for this presidential discretion to evolve into the modern concept of "executive privilege" that protects all executive-branch officials.

For most of the century, when executive-branch officials were taken to court, they hired their own lawyers to defend themselves. This was the case in 1853, when the U.S. marshal for the state of Indiana was sued for falsely arresting a free black man in an attempt to enforce the Fugitive

Slave Act of 1850. A senator from Indiana asked the attorney general, Caleb Cushing, for his opinion on whether the president could constitutionally authorize the federal government to pay for the marshal's counsel. The attorney general answered that as part of the president's duty to "take Care that the Laws be faithfully executed," it would be appropriate for lawyers employed by the United States to defend officials in their faithful execution of acts of Congress. 6 Op. Att'y Gen. 220, 221–22 (1853).

Two decades later, Congress created the Department of Justice to coordinate litigation involving federal officials and to replace the prior system of outside lawyers counseling individual clients. *See* Ron Chernow, *Grant* 700 (2017). Over the next several decades, Justice Department lawyers not only defended executive officials but also began taking the executive branch's side in disputes with Congress—including by attacking the constitutionality of certain laws. *See, e.g.*, *United States v. Lovett,* 328 U.S. 303, 306 (1946); *Developments in the Law—Government Counsel and Their Obligations*, 121 Harv. L. Rev. 1409 (2008). These lawyers also began refusing demands for information from congressional investigators and federal judges on the ground that their client was the executive branch, which was entitled to the same sorts of privileges as any other client.

Eisenhower and the invocation of executive privilege

President Dwight D. Eisenhower established the modern precedent for invoking executive privilege in 1954, during the height of the Red Scare. At the time, Senator Joe McCarthy had spent years announcing without evidence that Communists had infiltrated the highest ranks of the State Department, academia, and Hollywood. Yet when McCarthy turned his attention to the U.S. military, the former general Eisenhower issued an order prohibiting anyone within the executive branch from submitting documents or any other evidence to McCarthy's committee. *See* Jean Edward Smith, *Eisenhower in War and Peace* 592 (2013). The order ground the McCarthy hearings to a halt. *Id.* Yet Arthur Schlesinger Jr., writing decades later, called it "the most absolute assertion of presidential right to withhold information from Congress ever uttered to that day in American history." Arthur Schlesinger Jr., *The Imperial Presidency* 156 (1973).

In 1958, Eisenhower's attorney general, William P. Rogers, defended the president by identifying five categories of what he called *executive privilege*: (1) information relating to the military and "the field of foreign affairs"; (2) information "made confidential by statute"; (3) information "in the area of pending litigation"; (4) information relating to "internal government affairs"; and (5) investigative files, reports, and other records incidental to the making of policy. William P. Rogers, *Constitutional Law: The Papers of the Executive Branch*, 44 A.B.A. J. 941, 941–42 (1958). For support, the attorney general pointed to earlier presidents who refused congressional calls for papers, including George Washington, who maintained that he "ought to communicate such papers as the public good would permit, and ought to refuse those, the disclosure of which would injure the public." *Id.* at 944. In later congressional hearings, the assistant attorney general for President Richard Nixon, William Rehnquist, drew upon similar historical examples to defend the privilege. *Executive Privilege: The Withholding of Information by the Executive: Hearing Before the Subcomm. on the Separation of Powers of the S. Comm. on the Judiciary*, 92d Cong. 420–43 (1971).

Pushback against executive privilege

Nevertheless, the executive branch's claim of privilege was fiercely contested. Legal historians such as Raoul Berger refuted Rehnquist and Rogers's claims of precedent and argued that executive privilege was a "constitutional myth" that shouldn't be recognized by Congress or the courts. *See* Raoul Berger, *Executive Privilege* (1974). Members of Congress argued that Supreme Court decisions such as *McGrain v. Daugherty*, 273 U.S. 135 (1927), had recognized Congress's inherent power under Article I, Section 1, to compel the production of information relevant to its legislative powers, including the power of impeachment.

Congress codified an aspect of this power with the Freedom of Information Act of 1966, which offered members of the public a method to compel the disclosure of governmental documents, with several notable exceptions (including classified matters, certain interagency memoranda, and investigatory matters). Pub. L. No. 89–554, 80 Stat. 378, 383.

Courts, meanwhile, had long asserted the power to require the executive branch to turn over requested documents, even as judges exercised their discretion not to push the issue when the executive branch claimed that compelled disclosure would compromise military secrets or other confidential information. *See, e.g.*, *United States v. Reynolds*, 345 U.S. 1, 10 (1953); *Totten v. United States*, 92 U.S. 105, 107 (1875); *United States v. Burr*, 25 F. Cas. 30, 37–38 (C.C.D. Va. 1807). And in the landmark case of *Brady v. Maryland*, the Supreme Court held that all prosecutors had a constitutional obligation to disclose evidence that might exonerate an accused defendant. 373 U.S. 83, 90 (1963).

28.1.1

United States v. Nixon

418 U.S. 683 (1974)

Executive privilege became a major constitutional issue after news of the Watergate scandal broke in the summer of 1972.

The scandal began when five men were arrested inside the Watergate Hotel in Washington, D.C., while attempting to break into the headquarters of the Democratic National Committee. An investigation by the Federal Bureau of Investigation (FBI) and two journalists for the *Washington Post*, Bob Woodward and Carl Bernstein, uncovered evidence that the burglars had been paid by the Committee for the Re-Election of the President, the organization set up to reelect President Richard Nixon in that fall's elections. The president publicly denied any association with the break-in while privately working to ensure that the burglars pleaded guilty without revealing the campaign's involvement in their plan.

But after the president cruised to a landslide victory in November, one of the burglars, James McCord, wrote a letter to the judge overseeing his case stating that he had perjured himself and pleaded guilty because of "political pressure." *See* Keith W. Olson, *Watergate* 60 (2016). When news of this letter reached the Oval Office, Nixon candidly discussed with his White House counsel, John Dean, the need to distance himself both from the burglary and from the pressure put on the burglars to perjure themselves—effecting what Dean later called "a cover-up of the cover-up." John W. Dean, *The Nixon Defense* 344 (2014). Nixon ultimately fired several of his aides, including Dean, expecting them to take responsibility for the break-in and purge a growing "cancer" on the presidency. *See* Olson, *supra*, at 74.

Around the same time, in early 1973, the Senate appointed a select committee to investigate illegal activities during the 1972 campaign. During highly publicized hearings over the summer of 1973, Dean testified before the committee that he believed his Oval Office conversations had been secretly recorded. Another White House aide later testified that a tape-recording system automatically recorded everything spoken in the Oval Office. *See* Olson, *supra*, at 101.

When the existence of the secret tapes became public, a special prosecutor who had been appointed to investigate the Watergate burglary, Archibald Cox, requested a judicial order for the president to turn over the tapes. Nixon ordered officials in the Department of Justice to fire him—leading the attorney general and some high-ranking officials to resign in the Saturday Night Massacre (see section 27.3). Cox's firing generated so much bad publicity for the president that Congress initiated impeachment proceedings, and the acting attorney general appointed a new special prosecutor, Leon Jaworski.

In early 1974, Jaworski obtained an indictment from a federal grand jury charging seven people with offenses relating to the cover-up of the Watergate burglary; the grand jury also named Nixon as an unindicted coconspirator. To prosecute the indictment, Jaworski also moved for the federal court to issue a subpoena *duces tecum*—an order to produce evidence—directing Nixon to produce tape recordings and documents relating to conversations that the president had with aides at specific dates and times. Although the president publicly released edited transcripts of many of the requested tapes, he moved to quash the indictment on the ground that the tapes themselves were protected by absolute executive privilege.

The Supreme Court heard oral argument in *United States v. Nixon*, 418 U.S. 683 (1974), in early July 1974 and issued the following unanimous opinion by the end of the month. The opinion affirmed the ruling of the district court, which held that although subpoenaed material is "presumptively privileged," a special prosecutor can overcome that privilege with "a sufficient showing to rebut th[at] presumption." *Nixon*, 418 U.S. at 713–14.

■ MR. CHIEF JUSTICE BURGER delivered the opinion of the Court.[1]

[A]

We turn to the claim that the subpoena should be quashed because it demands "confidential conversations between a President and his close advisors that it would be inconsistent with the public interest to produce." App. 48a. The first contention is a broad claim that the separation of powers doctrine precludes judicial review of a President's claim of privilege. The second contention is that if he does not prevail on the claim of absolute privilege, the court should hold as a matter of constitutional law that the privilege prevails over the subpoena *duces tecum*. . . .

B

In support of his claim of absolute privilege, the President's counsel urges two grounds, one of which is common to all governments and one of which is peculiar to our system of separation of powers. The first ground is the valid need for protection of communications between high Government officials and those who advise and assist them in the performance of their manifold duties; the importance of this confidentiality is too plain to require further discussion. Human experience teaches that those who expect public dissemination of their remarks may well temper candor with a concern for appearances and for their own interests to the detriment of the decisionmaking process. Whatever the nature of the privilege of confidentiality of Presidential communications in the exercise of Art. II powers, the privilege can be said to derive from the supremacy of each branch within its own assigned area of constitutional duties. Certain powers and privileges flow from the nature of enumerated powers; the protection of the confidentiality of Presidential communications has similar constitutional underpinnings.

The second ground asserted by the President's counsel in support of the claim of absolute privilege rests on the doctrine of separation of powers. Here it is argued that the independence of the Executive Branch within its own sphere insulates a President from a judicial subpoena in an ongoing criminal prosecution, and thereby protects confidential Presidential communications.

However, neither the doctrine of separation of powers, nor the need for confidentiality of high-level communications, without more, can sustain an absolute, unqualified Presidential privilege of immunity from judicial process under all circumstances. The President's need for complete candor and objectivity from advisers calls for great deference from the courts. However, when the privilege depends solely on the broad, undifferentiated claim of public interest in the confidentiality of such conversations, a confrontation with other values arises. Absent

[1] **As You Read, Consider:** This is the first Supreme Court opinion to consider whether a president could claim an "executive privilege" and decline to comply with a judicial demand for information. What part of the Constitution would justify such a privilege? Does Chief Justice Warren Burger, an appointee of President Richard Nixon, agree that the privilege exists?

a claim of need to protect military, diplomatic, or sensitive national security secrets, we find it difficult to accept the argument that even the very important interest in confidentiality of Presidential communications is significantly diminished by production of such material for *in camera* inspection[2] with all the protection that a district court will be obliged to provide.[3]

The impediment that an absolute, unqualified privilege would place in the way of the primary constitutional duty of the Judicial Branch to do justice in criminal prosecutions would plainly conflict with the function of the courts under Art. III. In designing the structure of our Government and dividing and allocating the sovereign power among three co-equal branches, the Framers of the Constitution sought to provide a comprehensive system, but the separate powers were not intended to operate with absolute independence. . . .

To read the Art. II powers of the President as providing an absolute privilege as against a subpoena essential to enforcement of criminal statutes on no more than a generalized claim of the public interest in confidentiality of nonmilitary and nondiplomatic discussions would upset the constitutional balance of "a workable government" and gravely impair the role of the courts under Art. III.

C

Since we conclude that the legitimate needs of the judicial process may outweigh Presidential privilege, it is necessary to resolve those competing interests in a manner that preserves the essential functions of each branch. The right and indeed the duty to resolve that question does not free the Judiciary from according high respect to the representations made on behalf of the President. *United States v. Burr*, 25 F. Cas. 187, 190, 191–192 (No. 14,694) (CC Va. 1807).[4]

The expectation of a President to the confidentiality of his conversations and correspondence, like the claim of confidentiality of judicial deliberations, for example, has all the values to which we accord deference for the privacy of all citizens and, added to those values, is the necessity for protection of the public interest in candid, objective, and even blunt or harsh opinions in Presidential decision-making. A President and those who assist him must be free to explore alternatives in the process of shaping policies and making decisions and to do so in a way many would be unwilling to express except privately. These are the considerations justifying a presumptive privilege for Presidential communications. The privilege is fundamental to the operation of Government and inextricably rooted in the separation of powers under the Constitution. In *Nixon v. Sirica,* 159 U. S. App. D. C. 58, 487 F. 2d 700 (1973), the Court of Appeals held that such Presidential communications are "presumptively privileged," *id.,* at 75, 487 F. 2d, at 717, and this position is accepted by both parties in the present litigation. We agree with Mr. Chief Justice Marshall's observation, therefore, that "[i]n no case of this kind would a court be required to proceed against the president as against an ordinary individual." *United States v. Burr,* 25 F. Cas., at 192.

But this presumptive privilege must be considered in light of our historic commitment to the rule of law. This is nowhere more profoundly manifest than in our

---

[2] **Note:** The phrase *in camera inspection* refers to a judicial procedure in which a judge privately reviews confidential documents.

[3] **Questions:** Does Burger here recognize the legitimacy of a claim of executive privilege "to protect military, diplomatic, or sensitive national security secrets"? Where does the privilege come from?

[4] **Note:** Burger here cites one of the first cases that considered the question of whether a president must divulge information to a court. In *Trump v. Vance* (see section 28.2), Chief Justice John Roberts summarizes *United States v. Burr* at length.

view that "the twofold aim [of criminal justice] is that guilt shall not escape or innocence suffer." *Berger v. United States,* 295 U. S., at 88. We have elected to employ an adversary system of criminal justice in which the parties contest all issues before a court of law. The need to develop all relevant facts in the adversary system is both fundamental and comprehensive. The ends of criminal justice would be defeated if judgments were to be founded on a partial or speculative presentation of the facts. The very integrity of the judicial system and public confidence in the system depend on full disclosure of all the facts, within the framework of the rules of evidence. To ensure that justice is done, it is imperative to the function of courts that compulsory process be available for the production of evidence needed either by the prosecution or by the defense. . . .[5]

In this case the President challenges a subpoena served on him as a third party requiring the production of materials for use in a criminal prosecution; he does so on the claim that he has a privilege against disclosure of confidential communications. He does not place his claim of privilege on the ground they are military or diplomatic secrets. As to these areas of Art. II duties the courts have traditionally shown the utmost deference to Presidential responsibilities. In *C. & S. Air Lines v. Waterman S. S. Corp.,* 333 U. S. 103, 111 (1948), dealing with Presidential authority involving foreign policy considerations, the Court said:

> "The President, both as Commander-in-Chief and as the Nation's organ for foreign affairs, has available intelligence services whose reports are not and ought not to be published to the world. It would be intolerable that courts, without the relevant information, should review and perhaps nullify actions of the Executive taken on information properly held secret." . . .

No case of the Court, however, has extended this high degree of deference to a President's generalized interest in confidentiality. Nowhere in the Constitution, as we have noted earlier, is there any explicit reference to a privilege of confidentiality, yet to the extent this interest relates to the effective discharge of a President's powers, it is constitutionally based.

The right to the production of all evidence at a criminal trial similarly has constitutional dimensions. The Sixth Amendment explicitly confers upon every defendant in a criminal trial the right "to be confronted with the witnesses against him" and "to have compulsory process for obtaining witnesses in his favor." Moreover, the Fifth Amendment also guarantees that no person shall be deprived of liberty without due process of law. It is the manifest duty of the courts to vindicate those guarantees, and to accomplish that it is essential that all relevant and admissible evidence be produced.

In this case we must weigh the importance of the general privilege of confidentiality of Presidential communications in performance of the President's responsibilities against the inroads of such a privilege on the fair administration of criminal justice. The interest in preserving confidentiality is weighty indeed and entitled to great respect. However, we cannot conclude that advisers will be moved to temper the candor of their remarks by the infrequent occasions of disclosure because of the possibility that such conversations will be called for in the context of a criminal prosecution.

---

5 **Questions:** Burger appears to weigh a president's interest in confidentiality—nebulously supported by Article II—against various judicial interests in obtaining all relevant information. Which provisions of the Constitution support the judiciary's demand for information? How can a court fairly weigh the judiciary's abstract interests against those of the president?

On the other hand, the allowance of the privilege to withhold evidence that is demonstrably relevant in a criminal trial would cut deeply into the guarantee of due process of law and gravely impair the basic function of the courts. A President's acknowledged need for confidentiality in the communications of his office is general in nature, whereas the constitutional need for production of relevant evidence in a criminal proceeding is specific and central to the fair adjudication of a particular criminal case in the administration of justice. Without access to specific facts a criminal prosecution may be totally frustrated. The President's broad interest in confidentiality of communications will not be vitiated by disclosure of a limited number of conversations preliminarily shown to have some bearing on the pending criminal cases.

We conclude that when the ground for asserting privilege as to subpoenaed materials sought for use in a criminal trial is based only on the generalized interest in confidentiality, it cannot prevail over the fundamental demands of due process of law in the fair administration of criminal justice. The generalized assertion of privilege must yield to the demonstrated, specific need for evidence in a pending criminal trial.

D

We have earlier determined that the District Court did not err in authorizing the issuance of the subpoena. If a President concludes that compliance with a subpoena would be injurious to the public interest he may properly, as was done here, invoke a claim of privilege on the return of the subpoena. Upon receiving a claim of privilege from the Chief Executive, it became the further duty of the District Court to treat the subpoenaed material as presumptively privileged and to require the Special Prosecutor to demonstrate that the Presidential material was "essential to the justice of the [pending criminal] case." *United States v. Burr,* 25 F. Cas., at 192.[6] Here the District Court treated the material as presumptively privileged, proceeded to find that the Special Prosecutor had made a sufficient showing to rebut the presumption, and ordered an *in camera* examination of the subpoenaed material. On the basis of our examination of the record we are unable to conclude that the District Court erred in ordering the inspection. Accordingly we affirm the order of the District Court that subpoenaed materials be transmitted to that court. . . .

NOTE: CRIMINAL, CIVIL, AND CONGRESSIONAL SUBPOENAS

Nixon resigned two weeks after the Supreme Court rejected his argument that his interest in confidential conversations outweighed the district court's constitutional obligation to provide a fair process to criminal defendants.

Three years later, the Court rejected a similar argument in *Nixon v. Administrator of General Services*, 433 U.S. 425 (1977), which upheld the Presidential Recordings and Materials Preservation Act of 1974, Pub. L. No. 93–525, 88 Stat. 1695. The act directed the administrator of general services to take custody of Nixon's records so that archivists could preserve selected material for future historians—leading Nixon to claim that such compelled disclosure would again violate the executive branch's interest in confidential conversations. The Court held that this interest in secrecy was outweighed by Congress's broad investigatory power and the need to preserve materials

[6] **Question:** Burger here introduces a final rule: in weighing a president's interest in confidentiality against the judiciary's interest in information, a court must ask whether the information is "essential." What factors might a court consider in determining whether information is essential?

for future academic use or use in civil or criminal litigation. *Adm'r of Gen. Servs.*, 433 U.S. at 453–54. The Court also observed that the archival screening process would protect against the accidental disclosure of confidential information. *Id.* at 455.

Civil versus criminal subpoenas. But in the years after these two Nixon cases, the Court became more deferential to claims of executive privilege. In *Cheney v. United States District Court*, 542 U.S. 367 (2004), the Court considered Vice President Dick Cheney's claim that he should not be forced to comply with a civil discovery request to disclose information about a national energy task force in which he participated. Although the Supreme Court remanded the case to the court of appeals without resolving the question of executive privilege, the majority emphasized that Cheney's claim of privilege was stronger than Nixon's claim because Cheney's case involved a *civil* subpoena and Nixon's case involved a *criminal* subpoena. The Court explained that this difference was "not just a matter of formalism": unlike criminal subpoenas, civil subpoenas (1) were not needed to protect the constitutional rights of criminal defendants, (2) were requested by random civil plaintiffs rather than publicly accountable prosecutors, and (3) asked for "everything under the sky" instead of precisely identifying relevant and admissible information. *Cheney*, 542 U.S. at 383–87. The Court thought that civil subpoenas would therefore more likely be an "unnecessary intrusion into the operation of the Office of the President." *Id.* at 387.

Congressional subpoenas. In *Senate Select Committee on Presidential Campaign Activities v. Nixon*, 498 F.2d 725 (D.C. Cir. 1974), an appellate court denied the Senate committee investigating Watergate access to White House tapes that it had subpoenaed. But the Supreme Court never evaluated a claim of executive privilege against a *congressional* subpoena issued as part of Congress's power to conduct investigations. Rather, Congress enforced its subpoenas against executive officials without seeking help from the federal judiciary. It pursued two methods.

First, Congress began to impeach executive officials who violated its subpoenas. One of the drafted articles of impeachment against Nixon charged him with failure to comply with congressional subpoenas. H.R. Rep. No. 93–1305 (1974). And in December 2019, the House charged President Donald Trump with "obstruction of Congress" for ordering executive officials not to comply with similar subpoenas. H.R. Res. 755, 116th Cong. (2019).

Second, Congress began holding executive officials in contempt. As noted earlier in the discussion about congressional subpoenas (section 23.1), when private individuals have resisted congressional demands for information, Congress has historically held the individuals in contempt and ordered their arrest by a sergeant at arms—a practice that the Supreme Court upheld in *McGrain*. Beginning in 1982, Congress began holding executive officials in contempt as well. *See* Note, *The Conflict Between Executive Privilege and Congressional Oversight: The Gorsuch Controversy*, 1983 Duke L.J. 1333, 1333. Rather than arrest these officials, Congress typically used the threat of arrest, legislation, or judicial enforcement to negotiate with the executive branch. *See* Josh Chafetz, *The House Can Play Hardball, Too. It Can Arrest Giuliani*, N.Y. Times, Oct. 10, 2019. *But see*

Jonathan David Shaub, *The Executive's Privilege*, 70 Duke L.J. 1, 48 (2020) (arguing that Congress lacks mechanisms to unilaterally effectuate arrests of executive officials).

28.1.2

Trump v. Mazars USA, LLP

140 S. Ct. 2019 (2020)

The federal judiciary did intervene when Congress attempted to seek information about Trump's personal finances—but not at the request of Congress itself. Rather, Trump initiated the litigation.

When Trump ran for office in 2016, he refused to make his tax returns public. His action rejected a long-standing norm that allowed voters to evaluate whether presidential candidates had violated the law or would financially benefit from their own policy proposals. After the allegedly self-made billionaire was elected president, a 2018 investigation by the *New York Times* revealed not only that Trump had inherited much of his wealth but also that he had sustained much of that wealth by committing legally suspect tax dodges in the 1990s. *See* David Barstow, Susanne Craig & Russ Buettner, *Trump Took Part in Suspect Schemes to Evade Tax Bills*, N.Y. Times, Oct. 3, 2018, at A1. After the Democratic Party took control of the House of Representatives in 2019, three House committees investigating Trump's tax returns issued subpoenas to several financial institutions, including Trump's personal accounting firm, Mazars USA, LLP.

In his personal capacity, Trump contested the subpoenas by suing in federal court to request a judicial order invalidating the subpoenas. With help from lawyers for the Department of Justice, he argued that no legislative purpose justified the subpoenas, violating the standard established in *McGrain*. He also argued that if the subpoenas were valid, judges should employ the same standard as in *Nixon* to hold that his constitutional interest in confidentiality outweighed Congress's constitutional interest in seeking information.

In *Trump v. Mazars USA, LLP*, 140 S. Ct. 2019 (2020), the Court ruled that the separation of powers must be considered in cases involving congressional subpoenas of the president.

■ CHIEF JUSTICE ROBERTS delivered the opinion of the Court.[7]

Over the course of five days in April 2019, three committees of the U. S. House of Representatives issued four subpoenas seeking information about the finances of President Donald J. Trump, his children, and affiliated businesses. We have held that the House has authority under the Constitution to issue subpoenas to assist it in carrying out its legislative responsibilities. The House asserts that the financial

---

[7] **As You Read, Consider:** This opinion was the first in over two hundred years in which the Supreme Court considered whether Congress could subpoena information from the president. In light of the lengthy history in which Congress and the executive branch negotiated information requests among themselves, why doesn't Chief Justice John Roberts consider the issue a political question that the federal judiciary should not attempt to resolve?

information sought here—encompassing a decade's worth of transactions by the President and his family—will help guide legislative reform in areas ranging from money laundering and terrorism to foreign involvement in U. S. elections. The President contends that the House lacked a valid legislative aim and instead sought these records to harass him, expose personal matters, and conduct law enforcement activities beyond its authority. The question presented is whether the subpoenas exceed the authority of the House under the Constitution. . . .

[A]

Historically, disputes over congressional demands for presidential documents have not ended up in court. Instead, they have been hashed out in the "hurly-burly, the give-and-take of the political process between the legislative and the executive." Hearings on S. 2170 et al. . . ., 94th Cong., 1st Sess., 87 (1975) (A. Scalia, Assistant Attorney General, Office of Legal Counsel).

That practice began with George Washington and the early Congress. In 1792, a House committee requested Executive Branch documents pertaining to General St. Clair's campaign against the Indians in the Northwest Territory, which had concluded in an utter rout of federal forces when they were caught by surprise. . . . Since this was the first such request from Congress, President Washington called a Cabinet meeting, wishing to take care that his response "be rightly conducted" because it could "become a precedent." 1 Writings of Thomas Jefferson 189 (P. Ford ed. 1892).

The meeting . . . ended with the Cabinet of "one mind": The House had authority to "institute inquiries" and "call for papers" but the President could "exercise a discretion" over disclosures, "communicat[ing] such papers as the public good would permit" and "refus[ing]" the rest. *Id.,* at 189–190. President Washington then dispatched [Secretary of State Thomas] Jefferson to speak to individual congressmen and "bring them by persuasion into the right channel." *Id.,* at 190. The discussions were apparently fruitful, as the House later narrowed its request and the documents were supplied without recourse to the courts.

Jefferson, once he became President, followed Washington's precedent. In early 1807, after Jefferson had disclosed that "sundry persons" were conspiring to invade Spanish territory in North America with a private army, 16 Annals of Cong. 686–687, the House requested that the President produce any information in his possession touching on the conspiracy (except for information that would harm the public interest), *id.,* at 336, 345, 359. Jefferson chose not to divulge the entire "voluminous" correspondence on the subject, explaining that . . . "neither safety nor justice" permitted him to "expos[e] names" apart from identifying the conspiracy's "principal actor": Aaron Burr. *Id.,* at 39–40. Instead of the entire correspondence, Jefferson sent Congress particular documents and a special message summarizing the conspiracy. *Id.,* at 39–43. Neither Congress nor the President asked the Judiciary to intervene. Ever since, congressional demands for the President's information have been resolved by the political branches without involving this Court. . . .

During the Reagan administration, [for example,] a House subcommittee subpoenaed all documents related to the Department of the Interior's decision whether to designate Canada a reciprocal country for purposes of the Mineral Lands Leasing Act. President Reagan directed that certain documents be withheld because they implicated his confidential relationship with subordinates. While withholding those documents, the administration made "repeated efforts" at accommodation through limited disclosures and testimony over a period of several months. 6 Op. of Office of Legal Counsel 751, 780 (1982). Unsatisfied, the subcommittee and its parent committee eventually voted to hold the Secretary of the Interior in contempt, and an innovative compromise soon followed: All documents were made available, but only for one day with no photocopying, minimal notetaking, and no participation by non-Members of Congress. *Id.,* at 780–781; see H. R. Rep. No. 97–898, pp. 3–8 (1982). . . .

Congress and the President maintained this tradition of negotiation and compromise—without the involvement of this Court—until the present dispute. Indeed, from President Washington until now, we have never considered a dispute over a congressional subpoena for the President's records. And, according to the parties, the appellate courts have addressed such a subpoena only once, when a Senate committee subpoenaed President Nixon during the Watergate scandal. See *Senate Select Committee on Presidential Campaign Activities v. Nixon,* 498 F.2d 725 (CADC 1974) (en banc)). In that case, the court refused to enforce the subpoena, and the Senate did not seek review by this Court. . . .

Such longstanding practice " 'is a consideration of great weight' " in cases concerning "the allocation of power between [the] two elected branches of Government," and it imposes on us a duty of care to ensure that we not needlessly disturb "the compromises and working arrangements that [those] branches . . . themselves have reached." *NLRB v. Noel Canning,* 573 U.S. 513, 524–526 (2014). With that in mind, we turn to the question presented.

B

Congress has no enumerated constitutional power to conduct investigations or issue subpoenas, but we have held that each House has power "to secure needed information" in order to legislate. *McGrain v. Daugherty,* 273 U.S. 135, 161 (1927). This "power of inquiry—with process to enforce it—is an essential and appropriate auxiliary to the legislative function." *Id.,* at 174. Without information, Congress would be shooting in the dark, unable to legislate "wisely or effectively." *Id.,* at 175. The congressional power to obtain information is "broad" and "indispensable." *Watkins v. United States,* 354 U.S. 178, 187, 215 (1957). It encompasses inquiries into the administration of existing laws, studies of proposed laws, and "surveys of defects in our social, economic or political system for the purpose of enabling the Congress to remedy them." *Id.,* at 187.

Because this power is "justified solely as an adjunct to the legislative process," it is subject to several limitations. *Id.,* at 197. Most importantly, a congressional subpoena is valid only if it is "related to, and in furtherance of, a legitimate task of the Congress." *Id.,* at 187. The subpoena must serve a "valid legislative purpose," *Quinn v. United States,* 349 U.S. 155, 161 (1955); it must "concern[ ] a subject on which legislation 'could be had,' " *Eastland v. United States Servicemen's Fund,* 421 U.S. 491, 506.

Furthermore, Congress may not issue a subpoena for the purpose of "law enforcement," because "those powers are assigned under our Constitution to the Executive and the Judiciary." *Quinn,* 349 U.S. at 161. Thus Congress may not use subpoenas to "try" someone "before [a] committee for any crime or wrongdoing." *McGrain,* 273 U.S. at 179. Congress has no " 'general' power to inquire into private affairs and compel disclosures," *id.,* at 173–174, and "there is no congressional power to expose for the sake of exposure," *Watkins,* 354 U.S. at 200. . . .

Finally, recipients of legislative subpoenas retain their constitutional rights throughout the course of an investigation. See *id.,* at 188, 198. And recipients have long been understood to retain common law and constitutional privileges with respect to certain materials, such as attorney-client communications and governmental communications protected by executive privilege.

C

The President contends, as does the Solicitor General appearing on behalf of the United States, that the usual rules for congressional subpoenas do not govern here because the President's papers are at issue. They argue for a more demanding standard based in large part on cases involving the Nixon tapes—recordings of conversations between President Nixon and close advisers discussing the break-in at the Democratic National Committee's headquarters at the Watergate complex. The tapes were subpoenaed by a Senate committee and the Special Prosecutor investigating the break-in, prompting President Nixon to invoke executive privilege and leading to two cases addressing the showing necessary to require the President to comply with the subpoenas. See *Nixon,* 418 U.S. 683; *Senate Select Committee,* 498 F.2d 725.[8]

Those cases, the President and the Solicitor General now contend, establish the standard that should govern the House subpoenas here. Quoting *Nixon,* the President asserts that the House must establish a "demonstrated, specific need" for the financial information, just as the Watergate special prosecutor was required to do in order to obtain the tapes. 418 U.S. at 713. And drawing on *Senate Select Committee*—the D. C. Circuit case refusing to enforce the Senate subpoena for the tapes—the President and the Solicitor General argue that the House must show that the financial information is "demonstrably critical" to its legislative purpose. 498 F.2d at 731.

We disagree that these demanding standards apply here. Unlike the cases before us, *Nixon* and *Senate Select Committee* involved Oval Office communications over which the President asserted executive privilege. That privilege safeguards the public interest in candid, confidential deliberations within the Executive Branch; it is "fundamental to the operation of Government." *Nixon,* 418 U.S. at 708. As a result, information subject to executive privilege deserves "the greatest protection consistent with the fair administration of justice." *Id.,* at 715. We decline to transplant that protection root and branch to cases involving nonprivileged, private information, which by definition does not implicate sensitive Executive Branch deliberations. . . . Such a categorical approach would represent a significant departure from the longstanding way of doing business between the branches, giving short shrift to Congress's important interests in conducting inquiries to obtain the information it needs to legislate effectively. . . .

D

The House meanwhile would have us ignore that these suits involve the President. Invoking our precedents concerning investigations that did not target the President's papers, the House urges us to uphold its subpoenas because they "relate[ ] to a valid legislative purpose" or "concern[ ] a subject on which legislation could be had." Brief for Respondent 46. . . .

The House's approach fails to take adequate account of the significant separation of powers issues raised by congressional subpoenas for the President's information. Congress and the President have an ongoing institutional relationship as the "opposite and rival" political branches established by the Constitution. The Federalist No. 51, at 349. As a result, congressional subpoenas directed at the President . . . bear little resemblance to criminal subpoenas issued to the President in the course of a specific investigation, *Nixon,* 418 U.S. 683. Unlike those

[8] **Question:** Here, President Donald Trump has not literally asserted executive privilege. But he argues that he should be entitled to an identical protection. Do you agree with him that forcing a president to divulge personal information could harm the workings of the executive branch as much as forcing a president to divulge official information?

subpoenas, congressional subpoenas for the President's information unavoidably pit the political branches against one another.

Far from accounting for separation of powers concerns, the House's approach aggravates them by leaving essentially no limits on the congressional power to subpoena the President's personal records. Any personal paper possessed by a President could potentially "relate to" a conceivable subject of legislation, for Congress has broad legislative powers that touch a vast number of subjects. . . .

Without limits on its subpoena powers, Congress could "exert an imperious controul" over the Executive Branch and aggrandize itself at the President's expense, just as the Framers feared. The Federalist No. 71, at 484 (A. Hamilton). And a limitless subpoena power would transform the "established practice" of the political branches. *Noel Canning,* 573 U.S. at 524. Instead of negotiating over information requests, Congress could simply walk away from the bargaining table and compel compliance in court.

The House and the courts below suggest that these separation of powers concerns are not fully implicated by the particular subpoenas here, but we disagree. We would have to be "blind" not to see what "[a]ll others can see and understand": that the subpoenas do not represent a run-of-the-mill legislative effort but rather a clash between rival branches of government over records of intense political interest for all involved. *Rumely,* 345 U.S. at 44 (quoting *Child Labor Tax Case,* 259 U.S. 20, 37 (1922) (Taft, C. J.)).

The interbranch conflict here does not vanish simply because the subpoenas seek personal papers or because the President sued in his personal capacity. The President is the only person who alone composes a branch of government. As a result, there is not always a clear line between his personal and official affairs. "The interest of the man" is often "connected with the constitutional rights of the place." The Federalist No. 51, at 349. . . . No one can say that the controversy here is less significant to the relationship between the branches simply because it involves personal papers. Quite the opposite. That appears to be what makes the matter of such great consequence to the President and Congress.

In addition, separation of powers concerns are no less palpable here simply because the subpoenas were issued to third parties. Congressional demands for the President's information present an interbranch conflict no matter where the information is held—it is, after all, the President's information. Were it otherwise, Congress could . . . declare open season on the President's information held by schools, archives, internet service providers, e-mail clients, and financial institutions. The Constitution does not tolerate such ready evasion; it "deals with substance, not shadows." *Cummings v. Missouri,* 4 Wall. 277, 325 (1867).[9]

[E]

For more than two centuries, the political branches have resolved information disputes using the wide variety of means that the Constitution puts at their disposal. . . . A balanced approach [by this Court is therefore] necessary, one that takes a "considerable impression" from "the practice of the government," and "resist[s]" the "pressure inherent within each of the separate Branches to exceed the

---

9 **Question:** Roberts has so far offered reasons why the Court will not categorically *invalidate* a congressional subpoena to obtain the president's information, and why it will not categorically *enforce* such a subpoena. That leaves two alternatives: the Court could either (1) adopt a balancing test or (2) hold that the issue is a political question and therefore that the judiciary should not attempt to invalidate *or* enforce such subpoenas. Recall that Congress did not seek judicial review of its subpoenas. Is a balancing test or political-question approach preferable?

outer limits of its power," *INS v. Chadha,* 462 U.S. 919, 951 (1983). We therefore conclude that, in assessing whether a subpoena directed at the President's personal information is "related to, and in furtherance of, a legitimate task of the Congress," courts must perform a careful analysis that takes adequate account of the separation of powers principles at stake, including both the significant legislative interests of Congress and the "unique position" of the President. Several special considerations inform this analysis.[10]

First, courts should carefully assess whether the asserted legislative purpose warrants the significant step of involving the President and his papers. . . . Congress may not rely on the President's information if other sources could reasonably provide Congress the information it needs in light of its particular legislative objective. The President's unique constitutional position means that Congress may not look to him as a "case study" for general legislation.

Unlike in criminal proceedings, where "[t]he very integrity of the judicial system" would be undermined without "full disclosure of all the facts," *Nixon,* 418 U.S. at 709, efforts to craft legislation involve predictive policy judgments that are "not hamper[ed] . . . in quite the same way" when every scrap of potentially relevant evidence is not available, *Cheney,* 542 U.S. at 384; see *Senate Select Committee,* 498 F.2d at 732. While we certainly recognize Congress's important interests in obtaining information through appropriate inquiries, those interests are not sufficiently powerful to justify access to the President's personal papers when other sources could provide Congress the information it needs.

Second, to narrow the scope of possible conflict between the branches, courts should insist on a subpoena no broader than reasonably necessary to support Congress's legislative objective. The specificity of the subpoena's request "serves as an important safeguard against unnecessary intrusion into the operation of the Office of the President." *Cheney,* 542 U.S. at 387.

Third, courts should be attentive to the nature of the evidence offered by Congress to establish that a subpoena advances a valid legislative purpose. The more detailed and substantial the evidence of Congress's legislative purpose, the better. . . .

Fourth, courts should be careful to assess the burdens imposed on the President by a subpoena. We have held that burdens on the President's time and attention stemming from judicial process and litigation, without more, generally do not cross constitutional lines. See *Clinton,* 520 U.S. at 704–705. But burdens imposed by a congressional subpoena should be carefully scrutinized, for they stem from a rival political branch that has an ongoing relationship with the President and incentives to use subpoenas for institutional advantage.

Other considerations may be pertinent as well; one case every two centuries does not afford enough experience for an exhaustive list.

When Congress seeks information "needed for intelligent legislative action," it "unquestionably" remains "the duty of *all* citizens to cooperate." *Watkins,* 354 U.S. at 187. Congressional subpoenas for information from the President, however, implicate

[10] **Questions:** How does the following multifactor test work? First of all, is it exclusive to congressional requests for *personal* information from the president, or does Roberts suggest that this test should apply to congressional requests for *official* information from the executive branch? Second, and with your answer to the previous question in mind, if Congress subpoenas information from the executive branch regarding, say, the Department of Homeland Security's family-separation policy, would this test require the department to comply? Would the "demanding" tests from *United States v. Nixon* and *Senate Select Committee on Presidential Campaign Activities v. Nixon-summarized* by Roberts in Section C-require the department to comply?

special concerns regarding the separation of powers. The courts below did not take adequate account of those concerns. . . .

NOTE: AFTERMATH OF *MAZARS*

Mazars offered lower courts a balancing test for evaluating whether Congress had the power to compel the president (or, by implication, another member of the executive branch) to comply with a subpoena. The Court crafted this test with the ostensible goal of not "needlessly disturb[ing] 'the compromises and working arrangements that [those] branches . . . themselves have reached.'" *Mazars*, 140 S. Ct. at 2031 (quoting *NLRB v. Noel Canning*, 573 U.S. 513, 524–26 (2014) (quoting *The Pocket Veto Case*, 279 U.S. 655, 689 (1929))). But by intervening *at all* instead of dismissing the case as a political question, the Court's test had the practical effect of requiring future subpoenas to be litigated in federal courts. This "judicial self-aggrandizement," wrote Josh Chafetz, law professor, shortly after *Mazars*, "has come at the expense of Congress, which has not only been described in uniformly unflattering terms in the opinions but has also been impeded from carrying out one of its central functions: the use of oversight in ways specifically intended to shape public opinion and inform voters." Josh Chafetz, *Nixon / Trump: Strategies of Judicial Aggrandizement*, 110 Geo. L.J. 125, 128 (2021).

Mazars illustrates how this self-aggrandizement has been costly in terms of justice. The House of Representatives attempted to subpoena financial records from a financial institution but could not do so while Trump litigated the subpoenas all the way to the Supreme Court. The Court's decision—remanding the case back to the lower courts to apply its new balancing test—left the subpoena unresolved before the presidential election in 2020. As a consequence, Congress was unable to enforce its subpoena in time for voters and legislators to consider what it would have found—defeating the likely purpose of the subpoena. *Id.* (manuscript at 20).

Mazars also illustrates how the Court's intervention on behalf of the president has shaped the way in which Congress reacts to noncooperation with a subpoena—and how that has been costly in terms of justice. In addition to seeking Trump's financial records, the House Judiciary Committee also issued a subpoena in early 2019 against former White House Counsel Don McGahn. The committee wanted him to testify regarding its investigation of whether to recommend Trump's impeachment. McGahn and other executive-branch officials refused to testify. Yet the committee also refused to send the sergeant at arms to arrest him. *See* Chafetz, *The House Can Play Hardball, Too*, *supra*. Instead, it sued McGahn in the U.S. District Court for the District of Columbia, seeking a *judicial* injunction to compel McGahn to comply with a *legislative* subpoena. Yet by the time Joe Biden was inaugurated as president in 2021, federal courts still had not concluded whether the House Judiciary Committee even had the power to seek a judicial remedy. *See Comm. on Judiciary of U.S. House of Representatives v. McGahn*, 968 F.3d 755 (D.C. Cir. 2020) (en banc) (holding that the case was justiciable and that the committee had Article III standing to sue McGahn in federal court), *decided on remand by* 973 F.3d 121 (D.C. Cir. 2020) (panel op.) (holding that the committee lacked a cause of action to sue McGahn in federal court), *rehearing en banc granted* Oct. 15, 2020.

The net result is that if Congress issues a subpoena to an executive-branch official, either Congress or the official can invite a federal court to litigate the dispute. What previously required negotiation between Congress and the executive branch is now a question for the federal judiciary to decide.

28.2 EXECUTIVE IMMUNITY

In contrast with executive *privilege*, which refers to an executive official's protection from an order compelling the disclosure of information, executive *immunity* refers to an executive official's protection from being sued. Although both doctrines are intended to protect the executive branch from disruptive intrusion by other branches, they are motivated by slightly different concerns, and they developed from very different backgrounds.

Recognition of executive immunity in Mississippi

The Supreme Court first recognized the concept of executive immunity during Reconstruction, when Mississippi sued President Andrew Johnson to seek the judicial invalidation of the Reconstruction Acts of 1867. Mississippi alleged that the acts were unconstitutional and insisted that the Supreme Court should therefore enjoin the president from enforcing the acts. The attorney general responded that the president was immune from all suits whatsoever except for in cases of impeachment. In *Mississippi v. Johnson*, 71 U.S. (4 Wall.) 475 (1867), the Supreme Court struck a middle ground, siding with the attorney general.

Without deciding whether a president could ever be sued in federal court, the Court offered two reasons why it was inappropriate for a court to attempt to restrain a president from carrying into effect an act of Congress alleged to be unconstitutional. First, the president's enforcement of the Reconstruction Acts involved a significant amount of discretion—not the straightforward "ministerial" action of, say, delivering William Marbury's commission or paying William Stokes's postal carrier salary. The Court thought it "an absurd and excessive extravagance" to suggest that a court might be better able than the president to determine how to take care that even allegedly unconstitutional laws be faithfully executed. *Mississippi*, 71 U.S. (4 Wall.) at 499. Second, if the Court were to intervene, and if the president were to "refuse obedience, it is needless to observe that the court is without the power to enforce its process." *Id.* at 500–01. The Court contrasted its undoubted power to *determine the legal effect* of a congressional or executive action with what Mississippi was asking it to do—that is, to *directly order* Congress or the president to perform or not perform some discretionary action in the abstract. Concluding that neither Congress nor the president "can be restrained in its action by the judicial department," the Court rejected Mississippi's complaint. *Id.*

Mississippi *and effect on subordinate officers*

Although the holding of *Mississippi* was narrow—litigants cannot sue the president to challenge the unconstitutionality of a statute—the opinion has long been interpreted as holding that courts lack the power to review the official action of the president. For example, when federal investigators indicted Vice President Spiro Agnew for bribery in 1973, lawyers in the Department of Justice conceded that the vice president could be criminally indicted but invoked *Mississippi* to argue that the president served a constitutionally unique role that prevented a court from effectively incapacitating him with criminal proceedings. *See* Memorandum from Robert G. Dixon Jr., Assistant Att'y Gen., Office of Legal Couns., Re: Amenability of the President, Vice President and Other Civil Officers to Federal Criminal Prosecution While in Office 23 (Sept. 24, 1973).

In part because of *Mississippi*, litigants seeking to challenge executive actions have typically sought injunctive relief against subordinate executive officials rather than against the president directly. *See, e.g., Youngstown Sheet & Tube Co. v. Sawyer*, 343 U.S. 579 (1952) (considering a case against Charles Sawyer, secretary of commerce, for an allegedly unconstitutional order issued by President Harry Truman). It is not clear whether this legal fiction is still necessary, however. In *Trump v. Hawaii*, 138 S. Ct. 2392 (2018), and *Clinton v. City of New York*, 524 U.S. 417 (1998), the Court considered other governments' challenges to other presidents' allegedly unconstitutional actions without even mentioning *Mississippi*. *See also Trump v. Nat'l Ass'n for the Advancement of Colored People*, 140 S. Ct. 1891 (2020) (similar).

Another effect of the *Mississippi* decision was to encourage litigants injured by an executive action to sue the responsible subordinate officers for damages. At first, the Court generally agreed that executive officers could be held personally liable for their actions. *See, e.g., United States v. Lee*, 106 U.S. 196, 581–82 (1882). But in the landmark case of *Spalding v. Vilas*, the Court indicated that it would be unfair to hold an officer liable for actions taken "within the limits of his authority" because the threat of litigation "would seriously cripple the proper and effective administration of public affairs as entrusted to the executive branch of the government." 161 U.S. 483, 498–99 (1896). Later cases therefore attempted to balance "the view that the threat of liability will make federal officials unduly timid in carrying out their official duties" against the recognition "that official immunity comes at a great cost. An injured party with an otherwise meritorious tort claim is denied compensation simply because he had the misfortune to be injured by a federal official." *Westfall v. Erwin*, 484 U.S. 292, 295 (1988).

Qualified immunity and absolute immunity after Bivens

The first and most famous example of this sort of balancing occurred once again with Richard Nixon. He was sued for actions during his presidency thanks to a case called *Bivens v. Six Unknown Named Agents of the Federal Bureau of Narcotics*, 403 U.S. 388 (1971).

In 1965, federal drug agents raided the Brooklyn home of Webster Bivens, dragging him out of his bed, handcuffing him in front of his wife and children, and threatening to arrest his entire family. Bivens sued the unknown agents for violating his Fourth Amendment right to be free from unreasonable searches and seizures. But the only statute that permits suits for alleged constitutional violations—the Ku Klux Klan Act of 1871, 42 U.S.C. § 1983—applies to officials acting under color of *state* law, not to *federal* officials. Nevertheless, after observing that "[f]or people in Bivens' shoes, it is damages or nothing," the Court held that an implied federal cause of action permitted Bivens to sue for alleged violations of the Constitution. *Bivens*, 403 U.S. at 410 (Harlan, J., concurring). By creating a federal analog to 42 U.S.C. § 1983, *Bivens* raised the possibility that federal officials could be held individually liable for constitutional violations even if they were absolutely immune from ordinary tort claims under *Spalding*.

The Supreme Court considered this possibility in *Butz v. Economou*, 438 U.S. 478 (1978), declining to award absolute immunity to one of Nixon's cabinet secretaries who had been sued for allegedly violating the plaintiff's constitutional rights. Instead, following its prior interpretation of 42 U.S.C. § 1983, the Court held that cabinet officials deserved "qualified" immunity: they would be immune from suit unless they violated a constitutional right so "clearly established" that they should have known about it. *Butz*, 438 U.S. at 498.

And when a whistleblower in the air force named Ernest Fitzgerald brought another *Bivens* claim against Nixon and several of his official aides, the Court awarded this same sort of qualified immunity to the president's aides, writing that there was no principled reason to treat most executive officials, from a federal police officer to a chief of staff, any differently than a cabinet official. *Harlow v. Fitzgerald*, 457 U.S. 800, 809 (1982).

But when it came to Nixon, the Court concluded that absolute immunity was demanded by the president's "unique office, rooted in the constitutional tradition of the separation of powers and supported by our history." *Nixon v. Fitzgerald*, 457 U.S. 731, 749 (1982). The Court began its analysis by interpreting its precedent as establishing "that a court, before exercising jurisdiction, must balance the constitutional weight of the interest to be served against the dangers of intrusion on the authority and functions of the Executive Branch." *Id.* at 754.

On the interest-to-be-served side, the Court wrote that private lawsuits serve weaker interests than "the public interest in an ongoing criminal prosecution," which the Court had recently recognized in the executive-privilege case of *United States v. Nixon*, 418 U.S. 683 (1974). *Id.* Moreover, the Court observed that constitutional violations by the president could be remedied by "formal and informal checks on

Presidential action that do not apply with equal force to other executive officials"—from "the constitutional remedy of impeachment" and "[v]igilant oversight by Congress" to "constant scrutiny by the press" and "a desire to earn reelection." *Id.* at 757.

As for the dangers of intrusion, the Court wrote, "[b]ecause of the singular importance of the President's duties, diversion of his energies by concern with private lawsuits would raise unique risks to the effective functioning of government." *Id.* at 751. The Court explained:

> The President occupies a unique position in the constitutional scheme. Article II, § 1, of the Constitution provides that "[t]he executive Power shall be vested in a President of the United States . . . ." This grant of authority establishes the President as the chief constitutional officer of the Executive Branch, entrusted with supervisory and policy responsibilities of utmost discretion and sensitivity. These include the enforcement of federal law—it is the President who is charged constitutionally to "take Care that the Laws be faithfully executed"; the conduct of foreign affairs—a realm in which the Court has recognized that "[i]t would be intolerable that courts, without the relevant information, should review and perhaps nullify actions of the Executive taken on information properly held secret"; and management of the Executive Branch—a task for which "imperative reasons requir[e] an unrestricted power [in the President] to remove the most important of his subordinates in their most important duties."

Id. at 749–50. In light of all of these responsibilities, the Court concluded that it was "appropriate to recognize absolute Presidential immunity from damages liability for acts within the 'outer perimeter' of his official responsibility." *Id.* at 756.

Official acts versus personal acts

Despite this recognition of the president's broad executive immunity from civil suits for *official* acts, the Court declined to recognize a similar immunity from civil suits for *personal* acts. As the Court's decision in *Trump v. Mazars*, 140 S. Ct. 2019 (2020), illustrates, though, it is not often clear how to distinguish between the official acts and the personal acts of the president. But when the Court has been able to make the distinction, it has held that the president can be sued.

28.2.1

Clinton v. Jones

520 U.S. 681 (1997)

Shortly after Arkansas Governor Bill Clinton announced that he was a candidate in the 1992 presidential election, a woman named Gennifer Flowers publicly accused him of having had an extramarital affair with her for twelve years. Flowers became the first of many women to credibly accuse Clinton of sexual impropriety. *See* Jeffrey Toobin, *A Vast Conspiracy* 228 (2012). Over the next five years, several women would accuse Clinton of committing sexual assault before and after his election to the presidency. One of these women was Paula Jones.

Jones alleged that in 1991, she was staffing a conference in a Little Rock hotel when then-Governor Clinton arrived to give a speech. Later that day, an Arkansas state trooper, Danny Ferguson, allegedly approached Jones and persuaded her to visit the governor in a business suite at the hotel. According to Jones, the governor invited Jones inside, where he sexually assaulted her. *See Jones v. Clinton*, 858 F. Supp. 902 (E.D. Ark. 1994).

Jones kept silent about her story until she read a 1994 article in a conservative magazine, *The American Spectator*, which described how an Arkansas state trooper had secured hotel rooms and other meeting places for the governor's sexual encounters, including an allegedly consensual encounter with a woman named "Paula." Believing that she was being defamed, Jones publicly revealed her story—prompting members of the Clinton administration to brand her as a liar. *See* Toobin, *supra*, at 27.

Jones soon filed suit against the state trooper and Clinton under 42 U.S.C. § 1983 for depriving her of her Fourteenth Amendment right to the equal protection of the laws. Clinton, in response, argued that he was absolutely immune from suit—even though the alleged conduct took place in 1991, a year before he was elected president. Furthermore, he argued that civil trials would be so disruptive to the executive branch and take up so much of the president's time that no president should have to participate in any civil suit until after the president left the White House.

The Court in *Clinton v. Jones*, 520 U.S. 681 (1997), did not find Clinton's arguments persuasive.

■ JUSTICE STEVENS, delivered the opinion of the Court.[11]

This case raises a constitutional and a prudential question concerning the Office of the President of the United States. Respondent, a private citizen, seeks to recover damages from the current occupant of that office based on actions allegedly taken before his term began. The President submits that in all but the most exceptional cases the Constitution requires federal courts to defer such litigation until his term ends and that, in any event, respect for the office warrants such a stay. Despite the force of the arguments supporting the President's submissions, we conclude that they must be rejected. . . .

[11] **As You Read, Consider:** In *Nixon v. Fitzgerald*—a case decided eight years after the Nixon tapes case—the Supreme Court held that a president is absolutely immune from civil suit for *official* acts committed while in office. How does Justice John Paul Stevens apply the principles from that decision to a president's *unofficial* acts committed before becoming president?

IV

Only three sitting Presidents have been defendants in civil litigation involving their actions prior to taking office. Complaints against Theodore Roosevelt and Harry Truman had been dismissed before they took office; the dismissals were affirmed after their respective inaugurations. Two companion cases arising out of an automobile accident were filed against John F. Kennedy in 1960 during the Presidential campaign. After taking office, he unsuccessfully argued that his status as Commander in Chief gave him a right to a stay under the Soldiers' and Sailors' Civil Relief Act of 1940, 50 U. S. C. App. §§ 501–525. The motion for a stay was denied by the District Court, and the matter was settled out of court. Thus, none of those cases sheds any light on the constitutional issue before us.

The principal rationale for affording certain public servants immunity from suits for money damages arising out of their official acts is inapplicable to unofficial conduct. In cases involving prosecutors, legislators, and judges we have repeatedly explained that the immunity serves the public interest in enabling such officials to perform their designated functions effectively without fear that a particular decision may give rise to personal liability. We explained in *Ferri v. Ackerman,* 444 U. S. 193 (1979):

> "As public servants, the prosecutor and the judge represent the interest of society as a whole. The conduct of their official duties may adversely affect a wide variety of different individuals, each of whom may be a potential source of future controversy. The societal interest in providing such public officials with the maximum ability to deal fearlessly and impartially with the public at large has long been recognized as an acceptable justification for official immunity. The point of immunity for such officials is to forestall an atmosphere of intimidation that would conflict with their resolve to perform their designated functions in a principled fashion." *Id.,* at 202–204.

That rationale provided the principal basis for our holding that a former President of the United States was "entitled to absolute immunity from damages liability predicated on his official acts," [*Nixon v.*] *Fitzgerald,* 457 U. S. [731,] 749 [(1982)]. Our central concern was to avoid rendering the President "unduly cautious in the discharge of his official duties." 457 U. S., at 752, n. 32.

This reasoning provides no support for an immunity for *unofficial* conduct. As we explained in *Fitzgerald,* "the sphere of protected action must be related closely to the immunity's justifying purposes." *Id.,* at 755. Because of the President's broad responsibilities, we recognized in that case an immunity from damages claims arising out of official acts extending to the "outer perimeter of his authority." *Id.,* at 757. But we have never suggested that the President, or any other official, has an immunity that extends beyond the scope of any action taken in an official capacity. . . .[12]

Moreover, when defining the scope of an immunity for acts clearly taken *within* an official capacity, we have applied a functional approach. "Frequently our decisions have held that an official's absolute immunity should extend only to acts in performance of particular functions of his office." *Id.,* at 755. Hence, for example, a judge's absolute immunity does not extend to actions performed in a purely administrative capacity. See *Forrester v. White,* 484 U. S. 219, 229–230 (1988).

---

[12] **Question:** Summarizing *Fitzgerald*, the Court notes that a president's claim of executive immunity extends to the "outer perimeter of his authority." Prepresidential conduct is clearly outside this perimeter. But can you also think of an example of a presidential action committed *while in office* that would also be beyond the outer perimeter of the president's authority?

As our opinions have made clear, immunities are grounded in "the nature of the function performed, not the identity of the actor who performed it." *Id.,* at 229.

Petitioner's effort to construct an immunity from suit for unofficial acts grounded purely in the identity of his office is unsupported by precedent. . . .

VI

Petitioner's strongest argument supporting his immunity claim is based on the text and structure of the Constitution. He does not contend that the occupant of the Office of the President is "above the law," in the sense that his conduct is entirely immune from judicial scrutiny. The President argues merely for a postponement of the judicial proceedings that will determine whether he violated any law. His argument is grounded in the character of the office that was created by Article II of the Constitution, and relies on separation-of-powers principles that have structured our constitutional arrangement since the founding.

As a starting premise, petitioner contends that he occupies a unique office with powers and responsibilities so vast and important that the public interest demands that he devote his undivided time and attention to his public duties. He submits that—given the nature of the office—the doctrine of separation of powers places limits on the authority of the Federal Judiciary to interfere with the Executive Branch that would be transgressed by allowing this action to proceed.

We have no dispute with the initial premise of the argument. . . . It does not follow, however, that separation-of-powers principles would be violated by allowing this action to proceed. The doctrine of separation of powers is concerned with the allocation of official power among the three coequal branches of our Government. The Framers "built into the tripartite Federal Government . . . a self-executing safeguard against the encroachment or aggrandizement of one branch at the expense of the other." *Buckley v. Valeo,* 424 U. S., at 122. Thus, for example, the Congress may not exercise the judicial power to revise final judgments, or the executive power to manage an airport. See *J. W. Hampton, Jr., & Co. v. United States,* 276 U. S. 394, 406 (1928). Similarly, the President may not exercise the legislative power to authorize the seizure of private property for public use. *Youngstown,* 343 U. S., at 588. And, the judicial power to decide cases and controversies does not include the provision of purely advisory opinions to the Executive, or permit the federal courts to resolve nonjusticiable questions. . . .

But in this case there is no suggestion that the Federal Judiciary is being asked to perform any function that might in some way be described as "executive." Respondent is merely asking the courts to exercise their core Article III jurisdiction to decide cases and controversies. Whatever the outcome of this case, there is no possibility that the decision will curtail the scope of the official powers of the Executive Branch. The litigation of questions that relate entirely to the unofficial conduct of the individual who happens to be the President poses no perceptible risk of misallocation of either judicial power or executive power.

Rather than arguing that the decision of the case will produce either an aggrandizement of judicial power or a narrowing of executive power, petitioner contends that—as a by product of an otherwise traditional exercise of judicial power—burdens will be placed on the President that will hamper the performance of his official duties. We have recognized that "[e]ven when a branch does not arrogate power to itself . . . the separation-of-powers doctrine requires that a branch not impair another in the performance of its constitutional duties." [See] *Nixon v. Administrator of General Services,* 433 U. S. 425, 443 (1977). As a factual matter, petitioner contends that this particular case—as well as the potential additional litigation that an affirmance of the Court of Appeals judgment might spawn—may impose an unacceptable burden on the President's time and energy, and thereby impair the effective performance of his office.

Petitioner's predictive judgment finds little support in either history or the relatively narrow cómpass of the issues raised in this particular case. As we have already noted, in the more than 200-year history of the Republic, only three sitting Presidents have been subjected to suits for their private actions. If the past is any indicator, it seems unlikely that a deluge of such litigation will ever engulf the Presidency. As for the case at hand, if properly managed by the District Court, it appears to us highly unlikely to occupy any substantial amount of petitioner's time.[13]

Of greater significance, petitioner errs by presuming that interactions between the Judicial Branch and the Executive, even quite burdensome interactions, necessarily rise to the level of constitutionally forbidden impairment of the Executive's ability to perform its constitutionally mandated functions. . . . As Madison explained, separation of powers does not mean that the branches "ought to have no *partial agency* in, or no *control* over the acts of each other." The fact that a federal court's exercise of its traditional Article III jurisdiction may significantly burden the time and attention of the Chief Executive is not sufficient to establish a violation of the Constitution. Two long-settled propositions, first announced by Chief Justice Marshall, support that conclusion.

First, we have long held that when the President takes official action, the Court has the authority to determine whether he has acted within the law. Perhaps the most dramatic example of such a case is our holding that President Truman exceeded his constitutional authority when he issued an order directing the Secretary of Commerce to take possession of and operate most of the Nation's steel mills in order to avert a national catastrophe. *Youngstown Sheet & Tube Co. v. Sawyer,* 343 U. S. 579 (1952). Despite the serious impact of that decision on the ability of the Executive Branch to accomplish its assigned mission, and the substantial time that the President must necessarily have devoted to the matter as a result of judicial involvement, we exercised our Article III jurisdiction to decide whether his official conduct conformed to the law. Our holding was an application of the principle established in *Marbury v. Madison,* 1 Cranch 137 (1803), that "[i]t is emphatically the province and duty of the judicial department to say what the law is." *Id.,* at 177.

Second, it is also settled that the President is subject to judicial process in appropriate circumstances. Although Thomas Jefferson apparently thought otherwise, Chief Justice Marshall, when presiding in the treason trial of Aaron Burr, ruled that a subpoena *duces tecum* could be directed to the President. *United States v. Burr,* 25 F. Cas. 30 (No. 14,692d) (CC Va. 1807). We unequivocally and emphatically endorsed Marshall's position when we held that President Nixon was obligated to comply with a subpoena commanding him to produce certain tape recordings of his conversations with his aides. *United States v. Nixon,* 418 U. S. 683 (1974). As we explained, "neither the doctrine of separation of powers, nor the need for confidentiality of high-level communications, without more, can sustain an absolute, unqualified Presidential privilege of immunity from judicial process under all circumstances." *Id.,* at 706.

Sitting Presidents have responded to court orders to provide testimony and other information with sufficient frequency that such interactions between the Judicial and

[13] **Question:** Stevens appears to concede that distracting litigation could, theoretically, hamper the performance of a president's official duties. Yet he predicts that subjecting a president to civil litigation for unofficial acts would not be distracting. Do you agree with his prediction? Keep in mind that as this case was being decided, President Bill Clinton was being investigated by a special prosecutor, Ken Starr, for conduct relating to Clinton's personal finances.

Executive Branches can scarcely be thought a novelty. . . . President Nixon—as noted above—produced tapes in response to a subpoena *duces tecum,* President Ford complied with an order to give a deposition in a criminal trial, and President Clinton has twice given videotaped testimony in criminal proceedings. Moreover, sitting Presidents have also voluntarily complied with judicial requests for testimony. President Grant gave a lengthy deposition in a criminal case under such circumstances, and President Carter similarly gave videotaped testimony for use at a criminal trial.

In sum, "[i]t is settled law that the separation-of-powers doctrine does not bar every exercise of jurisdiction over the President of the United States." *Fitzgerald,* 457 U. S., at 753–754. If the Judiciary may severely burden the Executive Branch by reviewing the legality of the President's official conduct, and if it may direct appropriate process to the President himself, it must follow that the federal courts have power to determine the legality of his unofficial conduct. The burden on the President's time and energy that is a mere by product of such review surely cannot be considered as onerous as the direct burden imposed by judicial review and the occasional invalidation of his official actions. We therefore hold that the doctrine of separation of powers does not require federal courts to stay all private actions against the President until he leaves office. . . .

VIII

[I]f Congress deems it appropriate to afford the President stronger protection, it may respond with appropriate legislation.[14] As petitioner notes in his brief, Congress has enacted more than one statute providing for the deferral of civil litigation to accommodate important public interests. . . . If the Constitution embodied the rule that the President advocates, Congress, of course, could not repeal it. But our holding today raises no barrier to a statutory response to these concerns. . . .

NOTE: AFTERMATH OF *JONES*

Jones contained two of the most inaccurate predictions in Supreme Court history.

First was Stevens's guess that allowing a president to be sued for unofficial conduct likely would not occupy a substantial amount of the president's time. As soon as Clinton's case returned to the district court in late 1997, Jones's lawyers attempted to bolster Jones's credibility by documenting a pattern of behavior in which Clinton became sexually involved with government employees. One of the women they subpoenaed was a former White House intern named Monica Lewinsky. Although Lewinsky responded in January 1998 with an affidavit denying that she had ever had a physical relationship with the president, she candidly told her friend, Linda Tripp, that she began a sexual relationship with the president during the government shutdown of 1995. *See* Jeffrey Toobin, *A Vast Conspiracy* 177–78 (2012). Tripp secretly recorded her conversations with Lewinsky and sent tapes of what Lewinsky said to Ken Starr, an independent counsel who was investigating real estate transactions in which Clinton had engaged as governor. *Id.* While Starr obtained permission to

---

[14] **Questions:** From the perspective of the present—knowing all that has happened since this 1997 decision—would you advise Congress to draft a statute protecting a president from civil litigation for unofficial acts? Or do you think that the benefits of such litigation have been worth the distractions and burdens that it imposes on a president?

expand his probe into issues of perjury, Clinton gave a deposition in the *Jones* case in which he also denied having had sexual relations with Lewinsky. Days later, news of Tripp's tapes became public and the scandal erupted—occupying a substantial amount of Clinton's time, to say the least.

Clinton later admitted that he had indeed had a sexual relationship with Lewinsky (and Gennifer Flowers), although he continued to deny having sexually harassed Jones or the other women who had accused him of sexual assault. For his misleading January 1998 deposition, Starr accused the president of perjuring himself. *See Referral from Independent Counsel Kenneth W. Starr* 116–28 (1998). The House of Representatives subsequently impeached Clinton on charges of perjury in December 1998. Although Clinton was acquitted by the Senate in 1999, the district court overseeing *Jones* later held the president in contempt.

The second inaccurate prediction by Stevens, which took longer to prove incorrect, was his claim that "it seems unlikely that a deluge of [civil] litigation will ever engulf the Presidency." *Jones*, 520 U.S. at 702. It is difficult to think of a more fitting word than *deluge* to describe the number of civil cases that challenged President Donald Trump's unofficial or prepresidential conduct. *See* Peter Baker, *Trump Is Fighting So Many Legal Battles, It's Hard to Keep Track*, N.Y. Times, Nov. 6, 2019, at A19. As with Clinton, many of these cases involved credible accusations of Trump committing sexual assault before he became president and then defaming his victims afterward. *See, e.g.*, *Carroll v. Trump*, 498 F.Supp.3d 422 (S.D.N.Y. Oct. 27, 2020); Barry Levine & Monique El-Faizy, *All the President's Women* 2–3 (2019). Some of these cases considered the same question of tax evasion that the House of Representatives began investigating in 2019.

28.2.2

Trump v. Vance

140 S. Ct. 2412 (2020)

In 2018, the district attorney of Manhattan, Cy Vance, opened an investigation into "business transactions involving multiple individuals whose conduct may have violated state law." *Trump v. Vance*, 140 S. Ct. 2412, 2419 (2020) (quoting Brief for Respondent Vance at 2). A year later, Vance's office served a subpoena on the same accounting firm at issue in *Mazars*, seeking roughly the same information that Congress sought. Although Trump argued that principles of *executive privilege* protected him from Congress's subpoena, he argued that *executive immunity* made it totally inappropriate for a state prosecutor to investigate his personal information while he was in office.

In *Trump v. Vance*, 140 S. Ct. 2412 (2020), the Supreme Court rejected his argument on the same day that it decided *Mazars*.

■ CHIEF JUSTICE ROBERTS delivered the opinion of the Court.[15]

In our judicial system, "the public has a right to every man's evidence." Since the earliest days of the Republic, "every man" has included the President of the United States. Beginning with Jefferson and carrying on through Clinton, Presidents have uniformly testified or produced documents in criminal proceedings when called upon by federal courts. This case involves—so far as we and the parties can tell—the first *state* criminal subpoena directed to a President. The President contends that the subpoena is unenforceable. We granted certiorari to decide whether Article II and the Supremacy Clause categorically preclude, or require a heightened standard for, the issuance of a state criminal subpoena to a sitting President. . . .

II

In the summer of 1807, all eyes were on Richmond, Virginia. Aaron Burr, the former Vice President, was on trial for treason. Fallen from political grace after his fatal duel with Alexander Hamilton, and with a murder charge pending in New Jersey, Burr followed the path of many down-and-out Americans of his day—he headed West in search of new opportunity. But Burr was a man with outsized ambitions. Together with General James Wilkinson, the Governor of the Louisiana Territory, he hatched a plan to establish a new territory in Mexico, then controlled by Spain. Both men anticipated that war between the United States and Spain was imminent, and when it broke out they intended to invade Spanish territory at the head of a private army.

But while Burr was rallying allies to his cause, tensions with Spain eased and rumors began to swirl that Burr was conspiring to detach States by the Allegheny Mountains from the Union. Wary of being exposed as the principal co-conspirator, Wilkinson took steps to ensure that any blame would fall on Burr. He sent a series of letters to President Jefferson accusing Burr of plotting to attack New Orleans and revolutionize the Louisiana Territory.

Jefferson, who despised his former running mate Burr for trying to steal the 1800 presidential election from him, was predisposed to credit Wilkinson's version of events. The President sent a special message to Congress identifying Burr as the "prime mover" in a plot "against the peace and safety of the Union." 16 Annals of Cong. 39–40 (1807). . . .

The trial that followed was "the greatest spectacle in the short history of the republic," complete with a Founder-studded cast. N. Isenberg, Fallen Founder: The Life of Aaron Burr 351 (2007). People flocked to Richmond to watch, massing in tents and covered wagons along the banks of the James River, nearly doubling the town's population of 5,000. Burr's defense team included Edmund Randolph and Luther Martin, both former delegates at the Constitutional Convention and renowned advocates. Chief Justice John Marshall, who had recently squared off with the Jefferson administration in *Marbury v. Madison,* 1 Cranch 137 (1803), presided as Circuit Justice for Virginia. Meanwhile Jefferson, intent on conviction, orchestrated the prosecution from afar, dedicating Cabinet meetings to the case, peppering the prosecutors with directions, and spending nearly $100,000 from the Treasury on the five-month proceedings.

In the lead-up to trial, Burr, taking aim at his accusers, moved for a subpoena *duces tecum* directed at Jefferson. The draft subpoena required the President to produce an October 21, 1806 letter from Wilkinson and accompanying documents,

---

[15] **As You Read, Consider:** President Donald Trump and the Department of Justice argue that Trump's interest in confidentiality from a state prosecutor is supported not only by Article II but also by the Supremacy Clause. After Chief Justice John Roberts's opinion, when is it appropriate for a *state* court to (1) hold a president liable for suit or (2) demand information from the president? When is it appropriate for a *federal* court to do these two things?

which Jefferson had referenced in his message to Congress. The prosecution opposed the request, arguing that a President could not be subjected to such a subpoena and that the letter might contain state secrets. Following four days of argument, Marshall announced his ruling to a packed chamber.

The President, Marshall declared, does not "stand exempt from the general provisions of the constitution" or, in particular, the Sixth Amendment's guarantee that those accused have compulsory process for obtaining witnesses for their defense. *United States v. Burr,* 25 F.Cas. 30, 33–34 (No. 14,692d) (CC Va. 1807). . . . According to Marshall, the sole argument for exempting the President from testimonial obligations was that his "duties as chief magistrate demand his whole time for national objects." *Ibid.* But, in Marshall's assessment, those demands were "not unremitting." *Ibid.* And should the President's duties preclude his attendance at a particular time and place, a court could work that out upon return of the subpoena. *Ibid.*

Marshall also rejected the prosecution's argument that the President was immune from a subpoena *duces tecum* because executive papers might contain state secrets. "A subpoena duces tecum," he said, "may issue to any person to whom an ordinary subpoena may issue." *Ibid.* . . . As for "the propriety of introducing any papers," that would "depend on the character of the paper, not on the character of the person who holds it." *Id.,* at 34. Marshall acknowledged that the papers sought by Burr could contain information "the disclosure of which would endanger the public safety," but stated that, again, such concerns would have "due consideration" upon the return of the subpoena. *Id.,* at 37.

While the arguments unfolded, Jefferson, who had received word of the motion, wrote to the prosecutor indicating that he would—subject to the prerogative to decide which executive communications should be withheld—"furnish on all occasions, whatever the purposes of justice may require." Letter from T. Jefferson to G. Hay (June 12, 1807), in 10 Works of Thomas Jefferson 398, n. (P. Ford ed. 1905). His "personal attendance," however, was out of the question, for it "would leave the nation without" the "sole branch which the constitution requires to be always in function." Letter from T. Jefferson to G. Hay (June 17, 1807), in *id.,* at 400–401, n.

Before Burr received the subpoenaed documents, Marshall rejected the prosecution's core legal theory for treason and Burr was accordingly acquitted. Jefferson, however, was not done. Committed to salvaging a conviction, he directed the prosecutors to proceed with a misdemeanor (yes, misdemeanor) charge for inciting war against Spain. Burr then renewed his request for Wilkinson's October 21 letter, which he later received a copy of, and subpoenaed a second letter, dated November 12, 1806, which the prosecutor claimed was privileged. Acknowledging that the President may withhold information to protect public safety, Marshall instructed that Jefferson should "state the particular reasons" for withholding the letter. *United States v. Burr,* 25 F.Cas. 187, 192 (No. 14694) (CC Va. 1807). The court, paying "all proper respect" to those reasons, would then decide whether to compel disclosure. *Ibid.* But that decision was averted when the misdemeanor trial was cut short after it became clear that the prosecution lacked the evidence to convict.

In the two centuries since the Burr trial, successive Presidents have accepted Marshall's ruling that the Chief Executive is subject to subpoena. . . . [They have also] uniformly agreed to testify when called in criminal proceedings, provided they could do so at a time and place of their choosing. In 1875, President Grant submitted to a three-hour deposition in the criminal prosecution of a political appointee embroiled in a network of tax-evading whiskey distillers. A century later, President Ford's attempted assassin subpoenaed him to testify in her defense. See *United States v. Fromme,* 405 F.Supp. 578 (ED Cal. 1975). Ford obliged—from a safe distance—in the first videotaped deposition of a President. . . . President Clinton testified three times, twice via deposition pursuant to subpoenas in federal criminal trials of associates implicated during the Whitewater investigation, and once by video for a grand jury investigating possible perjury.

The bookend to Marshall's ruling came in 1974 when the question he never had to decide—whether to compel the disclosure of official communications over the objection of the President—came to a head. That spring, the Special Prosecutor appointed to investigate the break-in of the Democratic National Committee Headquarters at the Watergate complex filed an indictment charging seven defendants associated with President Nixon and naming Nixon as an unindicted co-conspirator. As the case moved toward trial, the Special Prosecutor secured a subpoena *duces tecum* directing Nixon to produce, among other things, tape recordings of Oval Office meetings. Nixon moved to quash the subpoena, claiming that the Constitution provides an absolute privilege of confidentiality to all presidential communications. This Court rejected that argument in *United States v. Nixon,* 418 U.S. 683 (1974), a decision we later described as "unequivocally and emphatically endors[ing] Marshall's" holding that Presidents are subject to subpoena. *Clinton v. Jones,* 520 U.S. 681, 704 (1997).

The *Nixon* Court readily acknowledged the importance of preserving the confidentiality of communications "between high Government officials and those who advise and assist them." 418 U.S. at 705. . . . But, like Marshall two centuries prior, the Court recognized the countervailing interests at stake. Invoking the common law maxim that "the public has a right to every man's evidence," the Court observed that the public interest in fair and accurate judicial proceedings is at its height in the criminal setting, where our common commitment to justice demands that "guilt shall not escape" nor "innocence suffer." *Id.,* at 709. Because these dual aims would be "defeated if judgments" were "founded on a partial or speculative presentation of the facts," the *Nixon* Court recognized that it was "imperative" that "compulsory process be available for the production of evidence needed either by the prosecution or the defense." *Ibid.*

The Court thus concluded that the President's "generalized assertion of privilege must yield to the demonstrated, specific need for evidence in a pending criminal trial." *Id.,* at 713. Two weeks later, President Nixon dutifully released the tapes.

III

The history surveyed above all involved *federal* criminal proceedings. Here we are confronted for the first time with a subpoena issued to the President by a local grand jury operating under the supervision of a *state* court.

In the President's view, that distinction makes all the difference. He argues that the Supremacy Clause gives a sitting President absolute immunity from state criminal subpoenas because compliance with those subpoenas would categorically impair a President's performance of his Article II functions. The Solicitor General, arguing on behalf of the United States, agrees with much of the President's reasoning but does not commit to his bottom line. Instead, the Solicitor General urges us to resolve this case by holding that a state grand jury subpoena for a sitting President's personal records must, at the very least, "satisfy a heightened standard of need," which the Solicitor General contends was not met here. Brief for United States as *Amicus Curiae* 26, 29.

A

We begin with the question of absolute immunity. No one doubts that Article II guarantees the independence of the Executive Branch. As the head of that branch, the President "occupies a unique position in the constitutional scheme." *Nixon v. Fitzgerald,* 457 U.S. 731, 749 (1982). His duties, which range from faithfully executing the laws to commanding the Armed Forces, are of unrivaled gravity and breadth. Quite appropriately, those duties come with protections that safeguard the President's ability to perform his vital functions. See, *e.g., ibid.* (concluding that the President enjoys "absolute immunity from damages liability predicated on his official acts"); *Nixon,* 418 U.S. at 708 (recognizing that presidential communications are presumptively privileged).

In addition, the Constitution guarantees "the entire independence of the General Government from any control by the respective States." As we have often repeated, "States have no power . . . to retard, impede, burden, or in any manner control the operations of the constitutional laws enacted by Congress." *McCulloch v. Maryland,* 4 Wheat. 316, 436 (1819). It follows that States also lack the power to impede the President's execution of those laws.

Marshall's ruling in *Burr,* entrenched by 200 years of practice and our decision in *Nixon,* confirms that *federal* criminal subpoenas do not "rise to the level of constitutionally forbidden impairment of the Executive's ability to perform its constitutionally mandated functions." *Clinton,* 520 U.S. at 702–703. But the President, joined in part by the Solicitor General, argues that *state* criminal subpoenas pose a unique threat of impairment and thus demand greater protection. . . .

1

The President's primary contention, which the Solicitor General supports, is that complying with state criminal subpoenas would necessarily divert the Chief Executive from his duties. He grounds that concern in *Nixon v. Fitzgerald,* which recognized a President's "absolute immunity from damages liability predicated on his official acts." 457 U.S. at 749. In explaining the basis for that immunity, this Court observed that the prospect of such liability could "distract a President from his public duties, to the detriment of not only the President and his office but also the Nation that the Presidency was designed to serve." *Id.,* at 753. The President contends that the diversion occasioned by a state criminal subpoena imposes an equally intolerable burden on a President's ability to perform his Article II functions.

But *Fitzgerald* did not hold that distraction was sufficient to confer absolute immunity. We instead drew a careful analogy to the common law absolute immunity of judges and prosecutors, concluding that a President, like those officials, must "deal fearlessly and impartially with the duties of his office"—not be made "unduly cautious in the discharge of [those] duties" by the prospect of civil liability for official acts. *Id.,* at 751–752. Indeed, we expressly rejected immunity based on distraction alone 15 years later in *Clinton v. Jones.* There, President Clinton argued that the risk of being "distracted by the need to participate in litigation" entitled a sitting President to absolute immunity from civil liability, not just for official acts, as in *Fitzgerald,* but for private conduct as well. 520 U.S. at 694, n. 19. . . . The Court recognized that Presidents constantly face myriad demands on their attention, "some private, some political, and some as a result of official duty." *Id.,* at 705, n. 4. But, the Court concluded, "[w]hile such distractions may be vexing to those subjected to them, they do not ordinarily implicate constitutional . . . concerns." *Ibid.*

The same is true of criminal subpoenas. Just as a "properly managed" civil suit is generally "unlikely to occupy any substantial amount of" a President's time or attention, *id.,* at 702, two centuries of experience confirm that a properly tailored criminal subpoena will not normally hamper the performance of the President's constitutional duties. . . .[16]

[16] **Questions:** Do you agree with Roberts here that a president's time will not be occupied by state criminal subpoenas? Are you persuaded by his observation that states *already* have the power to investigate presidents and prosecute them after they leave office?

The President, however, believes the district attorney is investigating him and his businesses. In such a situation, he contends, the "toll that criminal process . . . exacts from the President is even heavier" than the distraction at issue in *Fitzgerald* and *Clinton,* because "criminal litigation" poses unique burdens on the President's time and will generate a "considerable if not overwhelming degree of mental preoccupation." Brief for Petitioner 16–18, 30.

But the President is not seeking immunity from the diversion occasioned by the prospect of future criminal *liability.* Instead he concedes—consistent with the position of the Department of Justice—that state grand juries are free to investigate a sitting President with an eye toward charging him after the completion of his term. The President's objection therefore must be limited to the *additional* distraction caused by the subpoena itself. But that argument runs up against the 200 years of precedent establishing that Presidents, and their official communications, are subject to judicial process, see *Burr,* 25 F.Cas. at 34, even when the President is under investigation, see *Nixon,* 418 U.S. at 706. . . .

[2]

The President and the Solicitor General nevertheless . . . caution that, while federal prosecutors are accountable to and removable by the President, the 2,300 district attorneys in this country are responsive to local constituencies, local interests, and local prejudices, and might "use criminal process to register their dissatisfaction with" the President. . . . We recognize, as does the district attorney, that harassing subpoenas could, under certain circumstances, threaten the independence or effectiveness of the Executive. Even so, . . . while we cannot ignore the possibility that state prosecutors may have political motivations, here again the law already seeks to protect against the predicted abuse.

First, grand juries are prohibited from engaging in "arbitrary fishing expeditions" and initiating investigations "out of malice or an intent to harass." *United States v. R. Enterprises, Inc.,* 498 U.S. 292, 299 (1991). . . . And, in the event of such harassment, a President would be entitled to the protection of federal courts. The policy against federal interference in state criminal proceedings, while strong, allows "intervention in those cases where the District Court properly finds that the state proceeding is motivated by a desire to harass or is conducted in bad faith." *Huffman v. Pursue, Ltd.,* 420 U.S. 592, 611 (1975).

Second, . . . our holding does not allow States to "run roughshod over the functioning of [the Executive B]ranch." The Supremacy Clause prohibits state judges and prosecutors from interfering with a President's official duties. See, *e.g., Tennessee v. Davis,* 100 U.S. 257, 263 (1880) ("No State government can . . . obstruct [the] authorized officers" of the Federal Government.). Any effort to manipulate a President's policy decisions or to "retaliat[e]" against a President for official acts through issuance of a subpoena would thus be an unconstitutional attempt to "influence" a superior sovereign "exempt" from such obstacles, see *McCulloch,* 4 Wheat. at 427. . . .[17]

Given these safeguards and the Court's precedents, we cannot conclude that absolute immunity is necessary or appropriate under Article II or the Supremacy Clause. . . .

---

[17] **Questions:** How is anyone supposed to determine when a state prosecutor is demanding information for a neutral purpose as opposed to a purpose of harassing a president? Surely Cy Vance, an elected prosecutor, is at least partially motivated by partisan politics, right?

B

We next consider whether a state grand jury subpoena seeking a President's private papers must satisfy a heightened need standard. The Solicitor General would require a threshold showing that . . . the subpoena is a "last resort," meaning the evidence is "not available from any other source" and is needed "now, rather than at the end of the President's term." Brief for United States as *Amicus Curiae* 29. . . .

We disagree . . . .[18] First, such a heightened standard would extend protection designed for official documents to the President's private papers. As the Solicitor General . . . acknowledge[s, this] proposed test is derived from executive privilege cases that trace back to *Burr*. There, Marshall explained that if Jefferson invoked presidential privilege over executive communications, the court would not "proceed against the president as against an ordinary individual" but would instead require an affidavit from the defense that "would clearly show the paper to be essential to the justice of the case." *Burr,* 25 F.Cas. at 192. The Solicitor General . . . would have us apply a similar standard to a President's personal papers. But this argument does not account for the relevant passage from *Burr*: "If there be a paper in the possession of the executive, which is *not of an official nature,* he must stand, as respects that paper, in nearly the same situation with any other individual." *Id.,* at 191 (emphasis added). And it is only "nearly"—and not "entirely"—because the President retains the right to assert privilege over documents that, while ostensibly private, "partake of the character of an official paper." *Id.,* at 191–192. . . .

[Second], the public interest in fair and effective law enforcement cuts in favor of comprehensive access to evidence. Requiring a state grand jury to meet a heightened standard of need would hobble the grand jury's ability to acquire "all information that might possibly bear on its investigation." *R. Enterprises, Inc.,* 498 U.S. at 297. And, even assuming the evidence withheld under that standard were preserved until the conclusion of a President's term, in the interim the State would be deprived of investigative leads that the evidence might yield, allowing memories to fade and documents to disappear. This could frustrate the identification, investigation, and indictment of third parties (for whom applicable statutes of limitations might lapse). More troubling, it could prejudice the innocent by depriving the grand jury of *exculpatory* evidence. . . .

* * *

Two hundred years ago, a great jurist of our Court established that no citizen, not even the President, is categorically above the common duty to produce evidence when called upon in a criminal proceeding. We reaffirm that principle today and hold that the President is neither absolutely immune from state criminal subpoenas seeking his private papers nor entitled to a heightened standard of need. The "guard[ ] furnished to this high officer" lies where it always has—in "the conduct of a court" applying established legal and constitutional principles to individual subpoenas in a manner that preserves both the independence of the Executive and the integrity of the criminal justice system. *Burr,* 25 F.Cas. at 34. . . .

---

[18] **Question:** Roberts here declines to apply the executive-privilege balancing test from *Nixon* to state requests for *personal* documents of the president. Why, then, did he apply a balancing test to *congressional* requests for personal documents of the president?

CHAPTER 29

WHAT IS THE SCOPE OF CONGRESS'S IMPEACHMENT POWER?

ARTICLE I, SECTION 2, CLAUSE 5: The House of Representatives . . . shall have the sole Power of Impeachment.

ARTICLE I, SECTION 3, CLAUSE 6: The Senate shall have the sole Power to try all Impeachments. When sitting for that Purpose, they shall be on Oath or Affirmation. When the President of the United States is tried, the Chief Justice shall preside: And no Person shall be convicted without the Concurrence of two thirds of the Members present.

CLAUSE 7: Judgment in Cases of Impeachment shall not extend further than to removal from Office, and disqualification to hold and enjoy any Office of honor, Trust or Profit under the United States: but the Party convicted shall nevertheless be liable and subject to Indictment, Trial, Judgment and Punishment, according to Law.

ARTICLE II, SECTION 2, CLAUSE 1: The President . . . shall have Power to grant Reprieves and Pardons for Offences against the United States, except in Cases of Impeachment.

ARTICLE II, SECTION 3, CLAUSE 1: [H]e shall take Care that the Laws be faithfully executed, and shall Commission all the Officers of the United States.

ARTICLE II, SECTION 4, CLAUSE 1: The President, Vice President and all civil Officers of the United States, shall be removed from Office on Impeachment for, and Conviction of, Treason, Bribery, or other high Crimes and Misdemeanors.

ARTICLE III, SECTION 2, CLAUSE 3: The Trial of all Crimes, except in Cases of Impeachment, shall be by Jury. . . .

29.1 THE PROCEDURE OF IMPEACHMENT

Several clauses of Articles I, II, and III discuss impeachment without defining the term.

Impeachment and English law

The lack of a constitutional definition likely stems from the fact that by the eighteenth century, impeachment was a well-developed practice in English law. It began hundreds of years earlier as a method by which Parliament could hold royal officials accountable to itself, as opposed to being accountable to just the Crown.

In early modern England, Parliament functioned not only as the supreme legislature in England but also as the supreme judicial court, with the power to hear its own trials and appeals from other courts. Yet through the 1300s, Parliament had little formal control over ministers and other executive officials, who were typically appointed and removed only by the Crown. This lack of control meant that when Parliament enacted a law, it was difficult to compel executive officers to faithfully execute the law as Parliament intended. The only blunt tool at Parliament's disposal was its power to cease funding the government. *See* Josh Chafetz, *Congress's Constitution* 78–79, 81 (2017).

Parliament developed impeachment in the fourteenth century as another tool for forcing executive compliance. Taking advantage of its judicial responsibilities, the House of Commons began indicting ministers who violated Parliament's laws—prosecuting the ministers for treason before the House of Lords. If convicted, the ministers could face the punishment of imprisonment or even death. *Id.* at 79. By the seventeenth century, the House of Commons broadened the definition of *treason* to include not only violations of the law but also the promotion of bad policies with which Parliament disagreed. *Id.* at 84–85. In this manner, Parliament could control executive policy by threatening to impeach and convict ministers who disobeyed its orders. "The consequence, by the end of the reign of Charles II [in 1689], was a Whig constitutional theory that made the king's ministers responsible to Parliament, not simply for the legality, but also for the wisdom of all actions taken by the Crown," legal scholar Josh Chafetz wrote. *Id.* at 88. "On this theory, ministers had a duty to resign from Crown service before carrying out actions odious to the people as represented in Parliament, and the king had a duty to dismiss ministers who had lost the confidence of Parliament." *Id.*

In the 1760s, British jurist William Blackstone summarized the procedure of parliamentary impeachment in his famous work, *Commentaries on the Laws of England*. Blackstone described Parliament as "the supreme court in the kingdom, not only for the making but also for the execution of laws, by the trial of great and enormous offenders . . . in the method of parliamentary impeachment." 4 William Blackstone, *Commentaries* *256. He continued, "The articles of impeachment are a kind of bills of indictment, found by the house of commons, and afterwards tried by the lords, who are, in cases of misdemeanors, considered not only as their own peers, but as the peers of the whole nation." *Id.* at *257. Blackstone wrote that when Parliament sat as a court of impeachment, it sat as "the most high and supreme court of criminal jurisdiction" to try "a prosecution of the already known and established law . . . by the most solemn grand inquest of the whole kingdom." *Id.* at *256. The only difference between impeachment proceedings and other "courts of criminal jurisdiction" was the venue. Because nobles, Crown ministers, and the worst offenders might overawe ordinary criminal tribunals with their influence, Parliament was the only place where they all could be tried by genuinely impartial peers. *Id.* at *258; *see* Nikolas Bowie, *High Crimes Without Law*, 132 Harv. L. Rev. F. 59, 68 (2018).

Impeachment and the Constitutional Convention

The Constitutional Convention adopted a version of this system early in its debates, considering "some mode of displacing an unfit magistrate . . . indispensable." Michael Klarman, *The Framers' Coup: The Making of the United States Constitution* 235 (2016). Article I gives the House of Representatives "the sole Power of Impeachment," which the House can exercise by majority vote. Once the House drafts and votes on articles of impeachment, the House appoints "managers," who prosecute the charges in the Senate. Article I also gives the Senate "the sole Power to try all impeachments." Because the Senate essentially becomes a jury during an impeachment trial, the same article also requires senators to take an "Oath or Affirmation" and stipulates that the chief justice of the United States is to preside when the president is tried. It finally provides that no one may be "convicted" without the vote of two-thirds of the senators present.

The convention also added several changes to parliamentary impeachments. In contrast with Great Britain, in which a conviction for treason could result in the execution of the accused minister, Article I lowers the stakes, declaring that "Judgment in Cases of Impeachment shall not extend further than to removal from Office, and disqualification to hold and enjoy any Office of honor, Trust or Profit under the United States." The article leaves further punishment to a subsequent "Indictment, Trial, Judgment and Punishment, according to Law." Also in contrast with parliamentary impeachments, which defined *treason* capaciously to include abusing an office or issuing a bad policy, Article III limits the definition of *treason* to "consist only in levying War against [the United States], or in adhering to [its] Enemies, giving them Aid and Comfort."

In addition to making these changes, the convention debated two questions: First, who would be subject to impeachment? Second, for what offenses, beyond treason, could a person be impeached?

In Great Britain, although most royal officials could be impeached and removed from office, the Crown itself could not be—for practical and for ideological reasons. On similar grounds, although the vast majority of delegates at the Constitutional Convention agreed that judges and executive officials should be impeachable, many of the delegates argued that the president should not be. Some argued that limiting the president to a single, short term would be sufficient protection from abusive leadership. Others contended that giving Congress the power to impeach the president would make the president too dependent on Congress's wishes to be an effective check on unconstitutional legislation. But most delegates followed Benjamin Franklin's warning that if the president couldn't be removed before the president's term expired, then there would be "recourse . . . to assassination." *Id.* at 235–36. Although some of the pro-removal delegates, including John Dickinson, argued that the president should be removable by a vote of no confidence by a majority of state legislatures, the delegates voted eight states to two to make the president subject to impeachment before the U.S. Supreme Court. *Id.* In the final weeks of the convention, the delegates voted to change the court of impeachment for the president to the Senate, with the chief justice presiding. *Id.* at 237.

The second debate concerned the substantive standard for impeachment. Early on, the convention agreed that an officer could be impeached for "malpractice or neglect of duty"—a low threshold. *Id.* A committee later replaced this standard with "treason, bribery, or corruption," with *corruption* removed in the final weeks. *Id.* In its place, George Mason of Virginia proposed adding *maladministration* to the list of impeachable offenses on the ground that a president could commit many "great and dangerous offenses" without being impeachable for treason or bribery. *Id.* When Madison objected, stating that "[s]o vague a term will be equivalent to a tenure during pleasure of the Senate," the convention substituted for Mason's proposal *other high crimes and misdemeanors. Id.*

Impeachment proceedings and debatable issues

Both of these questions—who can be impeached and for what?—have continued to plague impeachment proceedings.

For example, in July 1797, the Senate discovered that one of Tennessee's first senators, William Blount, was secretly conspiring to seize the Spanish territories of Florida and Louisiana on behalf of Great Britain. Considering this traitorous, the Senate voted to expel Blount from the Senate five days later, prompting the House to impeach him shortly afterward. This raised the puzzle of whether (1) a senator counted as a "civil Officer[ ] of the United States," and (2) if so, whether such an officer could be impeached after already leaving office. The Senate dropped the charges on the first ground, setting a precedent that members of Congress are not themselves "civil Officers" subject to impeachment. *See* 3 *Hinds' Precedents of the House of Representatives of the United States* §§ 2294–318 (1907).

In the decades that followed, the vast majority of impeachments to reach trial—eleven of seventeen—have concerned judges and justices; the other six have been divided between two executive officials and three presidents: Andrew Johnson, Bill Clinton, and Donald Trump. The impeachment of judges has raised its own difficulty because Article III adds that judges "shall hold their Offices during good Behaviour"—a seemingly lesser standard than "high Crimes or Misdemeanors." These competing standards have led some scholars and judges to argue over whether impeachment is the exclusive method of removing judges or whether judges may also be removed by the president or another official on a finding of bad behavior. *See, e.g., Chandler v. Jud. Council,* 398 U.S. 74, 136 (1970) (Douglas, J., dissenting); Raoul Berger, *Impeachment of Judges and "Good Behavior" Tenure,* 79 Yale L.J. 1475 (1970).

Nevertheless, of the seven people who have been removed from office after an impeachment, all seven have been judges charged with high crimes or misdemeanors.

It also remains a fierce debate what the term *high crimes and misdemeanors* even means. Ever since the impeachment of Supreme Court Justice Samuel Chase in 1805—mentioned in the discussion about *Marbury v. Madison* (section 3.1)—impeachment has been a highly partisan affair, with one party arguing that the term includes virtually any abusive conduct and the other party arguing that it refers only to conduct that was criminal at the time it was committed. The Federalist Chase, for instance, was impeached by a House controlled by Thomas Jefferson's Democratic-Republican Party for "highly arbitrary, oppressive and unjust" conduct on the bench. William H. Rehnquist, *Grand Inquests: The Historic Impeachments of Justice Samuel Chase and President Andrew Johnson* 59 (1992). Chase's lawyers defended him in his Senate trial by arguing that issuing unpopular opinions wasn't an indictable offense, and he should therefore be acquitted. "Justice, 'tho it may be an inconvenient restraint on our power, while we are strong, is the only rampart behind which we can find protection when we become weak," the lawyer argued. *See* Robert A. Caro, *Master of the Senate* 13 (2003). Even Democratic-Republicans in the Senate voted to acquit Chase, establishing a precedent that impeachment should not be employed against officials just because their opinions are contrary to those of the party in power. *See id.*

But perhaps the most famous definition of the phrase *high crimes and misdemeanors* comes from Gerald Ford, who, as a leader of House Republicans in 1970, argued that an impeachable offense is "whatever a majority of the House of Representatives considers it to be at a given moment in history." 116 Cong. Rec. 11,913 (1970). Since then, a parade of law professors has joined Ford in rejecting Chase's argument that the phrase *high crimes and misdemeanors* refers to literal crimes or misdemeanors, including Irving Brant's *Impeachment: Trials and Errors* (1972), Raoul Berger's *Impeachment: The Constitutional Problems* (1973), and Charles L. Black Jr.'s *Impeachment: A Handbook* (1974). Today, Charles Black's definition of the term has become something of a consensus: "offenses (1) which are extremely serious, (2) which in some way corrupt or subvert the political and governmental process, and (3) which are plainly wrong in themselves to a person of honor, or to a good citizen, regardless of words on the statute books." Charles L. Black Jr., *Impeachment: A Handbook* 37 (1974); *see, e.g.*, Laurence Tribe & Joshua Matz, *To End a Presidency* 44 (2018); Michael Stokes Paulsen, *To End a (Republican) Presidency*, 132 Harv. L. Rev. 689, 691 (2018). Only a tiny minority of scholars have argued that impeachment should require an indictable offense. *See, e.g.*, Bowie, *supra*.

29.1.1
Benjamin Curtis's Defense of President Johnson

Cong. Globe, 40th Cong., 2d Sess. Supp. 123–34 (1868)

The strongest defense of the impeachment-requires-a-crime definition of *high crimes and misdemeanors* was delivered during the impeachment trial of President Andrew Johnson in 1868.

The principal reason why the House of Representatives impeached Johnson in 1868 was because of his opposition to Congress's Reconstruction policies. Accordingly, most of the eleven articles of impeachment charged the president with having violated the Tenure of Office Act, which prohibited him from removing certain cabinet officials without the Senate's consent. But two of the articles charged Johnson with no crime at all. Instead, in response to a series of speeches in which the president excoriated Congress for its radical commitment to racial equality, the House charged the president with delivering such "intemperate, inflammatory, and scandalous harangues" that he had brought both Congress and "the high office of the President of the United States into contempt." Cong. Globe, 40th Cong., 2d Sess. Supp. 4–5 (1868).

At the time of the president's trial, Republicans controlled the Senate 42–12. Few observers believed that the president had a chance at acquittal in such a hostile environment. Yet when the Senate reached its first vote on one of the speech-related charges, seven Republican senators voted for acquittal, sparing Johnson from removal by a single vote. Some of these senators wrote that they were persuaded by the following argument of Benjamin Curtis, one of the president's attorneys. When he delivered the argument, the Massachusetts-born Curtis was best known for having resigned from the Supreme Court after dissenting in *Dred Scott v. Sandford*, 60 U.S. (19 How.) 393 (1857).

■ MR. CURTIS.[1]

Mr. Chief Justice, I am here to speak to the Senate of the United States sitting in its judicial capacity as a court of impeachment, presided over by the Chief Justice of the United States, for the trial of the President of the United States. This statement sufficiently characterizes what I have to say. . . .

In the front of this inquiry the question presents itself: What are impeachable offences under the Constitution of the United States? Upon this question learned dissertations have been written and printed. One of them is annexed to the argument of the honorable manager who opened the cause for the prosecution. Another one on the other side of the question, written by one of the honorable managers themselves, may be found annexed to the proceedings in the House of Representatives upon the occasion of the first attempt to impeach the President. And there have been others written and published by learned jurists touching this subject.

---

[1] **As You Read, Consider:** All prosecutions are political, yet all also have legal limits. Do you agree with Benjamin Curtis that when the House indicts a president and a Senate sits as a "court of impeachment," they are as bound by the Constitution as if they were a federal prosecutor and a federal district court?

I do not propose to vex the ear of the Senate with any of the precedents drawn from the middle ages. The framers of our Constitution were quite as familiar with them as the learned authors of these treatises, and the framers of our Constitution, as I conceive, have drawn from them the lesson which I desire the Senate to receive, that these precedents are not fit to govern their conduct on this trial.

In my apprehension, the teachings, the requirements, the prohibitions of the Constitution of the United States prove all that is necessary to be attended to for the purposes of this trial. I propose, therefore, instead of a search through the precedents which were made in the times of the Plantagenets, the Tudors, and the Stuarts, and which have been repeated since, to come nearer home and see what provisions of the Constitution of the United States bear on this question, and whether they are not sufficient to settle it. If they are, it is quite immaterial what exists elsewhere.

My first position is, that when the Constitution speaks of "treason, bribery, and other high crimes and misdemeanors," it refers to, and includes only, high criminal offenses against the United States, made so by some law of the United States existing when the acts complained of were done, and I say that this is plainly to be inferred from each and every provision of the Constitution on the subject of impeachment.

"Treason" and "bribery." Nobody will doubt that these are here designated high crimes and misdemeanors against the United States, made such by the laws of the United States, which the framers of the Constitution knew must be passed in the nature of the government they were about to create, because these are offences which strike at the existence of that government. "Other high crimes and misdemeanors." *Noscitur a sociis*. High crimes and misdemeanors; so high that they belong in this company with treason and bribery. That is plain on the face of the Constitution—in the very first step it takes on the subject of impeachment. "High crimes and misdemeanors" against what law? There can be no crime, there can be no misdemeanor without a law, written or unwritten, express or implied. There must be some law, otherwise there is no crime. My interpretation of it is that the language "high crimes and misdemeanors" means "offences against the laws of the United States." Let us see if the Constitution has not said so.[2]

The first clause of the second section of the second article of the Constitution reads thus:

The President of the United States shall have the power to grant reprieves and pardons for offences against the United States, except in cases of impeachment.

"Offences against the United States" would include "cases of impeachment," and they might be pardoned by the President if they were not excepted. Then cases of impeachment are, according to the express declaration of the Constitution itself, cases of offences against the United States.

Still, the learned manager says that this is not a court, and that, whatever may be the character of this body, it is bound by no law. Very different was the understanding of the fathers of the Constitution on this subject. . . .

The next position to which I desire the attention of the Senate is, that there is enough written in the Constitution to prove that this is a court in which a judicial trial is now being carried on. "The Senate of the United States shall have the sole power to try all impeachments." "When the President is tried the Chief Justice shall preside." "The trial of all crimes, except in case of impeachment, shall be by jury." This, then,

---

[2] **Questions:** Curtis's position is not that the phrase *high crimes and misdemeanors* is limited to particular crimes and misdemeanors. Rather, his argument is that if Congress wishes to make something a high crime and misdemeanor, it should do so *before* impeaching an officer for violating the law. Do you think this rule is too formalistic? Do you think that Congress should be able to impeach and convict someone of conduct that was not illegal when it was done?

is the trial of a crime. You are triers, presided over by the Chief Justice of the United States in this particular case, and that on the express words of the Constitution. There is also, according to its express words, to be an acquital or a conviction on this trial for a crime. "No person shall be convicted without the concurrence of two-thirds of the members present." There is also to be a judgment in case there shall be a conviction.

Judgment in cases of impeachment shall not extend further than removal from office and disqualification to hold any office of honor, trust, or profit under the United States.

Here, then, there is the trial of a crime, a trial by a tribunal designated by the Constitution in place of court and jury; a conviction, if guilt is proved; a 'judgment on that conviction; a punishment inflicted by the judgment for a crime; and this on the express terms of the Constitution itself. . . .

I say, then, that it is impossible not to come to the conclusion that the Constitution of the United States has designated impeachable offences as offences against the United States; that it has provided for the trial of those offences; that it has established a tribunal for the purpose of trying them; that it has directed the tribunal, in case of conviction, to pronounce a judgment upon the conviction and inflict a punishment. All this being provided for, can it be maintained that this is not a court, or that it is bound by no law?

But the argument does not rest mainly, I think, upon the provisions of the Constitution concerning impeachment. It is, at any rate, vastly strengthened by the direct prohibitions of the Constitution. "Congress shall pass no bill of attainder or ex post facto law." According to that prohibition of the Constitution, if every member of this body, sitting in its legislative capacity, and every member of the other body, sitting in its legislative capacity, should unite in passing a law to punish an act after the act was done, that law would be a mere nullity. Yet what is claimed by the honorable managers in behalf of members of this body? As a Congress you cannot create a law to punish these acts if no law existed at the time they were done; but sitting here as judges, not only after the fact, but while the case is on trial, you may individually, each one of you, create a law by himself to govern the case.[3]

According to this assumption the same Constitution which has made it a bill of rights of the American citizen, not only as against Congress but as against the legislature of every State in the Union, that no ex post facto law shall be passed—this same Constitution has erected you into a body and empowered every one of you to say *aut inveniam aut faciam*: if I cannot find a law I will make one. Nay, it has clothed every one of you with imperial power; it has enabled you to say, *sic volo, sic jubeo, stat pro ratione voluntas*: I am a law unto myself, by which law I shall govern this case. And, more than that, when each one of you before he took his place here called God to witness that he would administer impartial justice in this case according to the Constitution and the laws, he meant such laws as he might make as he went along. The Constitution, which had prohibited anybody from making such laws, he swore to observe; but he also swore to be governed by his own will; his own individual will was the law which he thus swore to observe; and this special provision of the Constitution, that when the Senate sits in this capacity to try an impeachment the senators shall be on oath, means merely that they shall swear to follow their own individual wills! I respectfully submit, this view cannot consistently and properly be

---

[3] **Question:** Because of the bans on ex post facto laws and bills of attainder, Congress ordinarily lacks the power to punish a person for conduct that was legal when it was done. Do you agree with Curtis that these same bans should apply when Congress impeaches and convicts a person for conduct that was legal when the person engaged in it?

taken of the character of this body, or of the duties and powers incumbent upon it. Look for a moment, if you please, to the other provision. The same search into the English precedents, so far from having made our ancestors who framed and adopted the Constitution in love with them, led them to put into the Constitution a positive and absolute prohibition against any bill of attainder. What is a bill of attainder? It is a case before the Parliament where the Parliament make the law for the facts they find. Each legislator—for it is in their legislative capacity they act, not in a judicial one—is, to use the phrase of the honorable managers, "a law unto himself," and according to his discretion, his views of what is politic or proper under the circumstances, he frames a law to meet the case, and enacts it or votes in its enactment. According to the doctrine now advanced bills of attainder are not prohibited by this Constitution; they are only slightly modified. It is only necessary for the House of Representatives by a majority to vote an impeachment and send up certain articles and have two-thirds of this body vote in favor of conviction, and there is an attainder; and it is done by the same process and depends on identically the same principles as a bill of attainder in the English Parliament. The individual wills of the legislators, instead of the conscientious discharge of the duty of the judges, settle the result.

I submit, then, senators, that this view of the honorable managers of the duties and powers of this body cannot be maintained. But the attempt made by the honorable managers to obtain a conviction upon this tenth article is attended with some peculiarities which I think it is the duty of the counsel to the President to advert to. So far as regards the preceding articles, the first eight articles are framed upon allegations that the President broke a law. I suppose the honorable managers do not intend to carry their doctrine so far as to say that unless you find the President did intentionally break a law those articles are supported. As to those articles there is some law unquestionably, the very gist of the charge being that he broke a law. You must find that the law existed; you must construe it and apply it to the case; you must find his criminal intent wilfully to break the law, before the articles can be supported. But we come now to this tenth article, which depends upon no law at all, but, as I have said, is attended with some extraordinary peculiarities. . . .[4]

29.2 JUDICIAL REVIEW

One reason why so many basic features of impeachment remain contested, including the meaning of the phrase *high crimes and misdemeanors*, is because impeachment remains a rare example of constitutional law regarding which the Supreme Court has, historically, declined to weigh in. Debates over impeachment are thus an example of what debates over the rest of constitutional law might look like absent judicial review, with individual institutions such as the House and Senate defending their own prerogatives and interpretations of the Constitution.

---

[4] **Questions:** Suppose the House impeaches a president for doing something illegal, but the Senate concludes that the president did not, in fact, do what the House accused the president of doing. Should the Senate nevertheless be able to convict a president of committing wrongdoing that was not charged by the House? If not, why not?

29.2.1

Nixon v. United States

506 U.S. 224 (1993)

Even though Benjamin Curtis accused the House managers of contending that the Senate was "bound by no law," Cong. Globe, 40th Cong., 2d Sess. Supp. 134 (1868), the Senate has, in fact, bound itself by rules and precedents. For example, in the Senate's manual, the Senate has codified rules governing how it collects evidence in impeachment proceedings. And through the practice of trying impeachments, the Senate has established several precedents. For example, while a vote to *convict and remove* a civil officer requires a two-thirds vote, Senate precedent dictates that a subsequent vote to *disqualify* that person from ever again holding office is distinct and requires only a majority vote. 3 *Hinds' Precedents of the House of Representatives of the United States* § 2397 (1907). Similarly, during the second impeachment of President Donald Trump, senators cited past precedent to conclude that it had the constitutional power to try the president even after his term in office expired. *See* Nicholas Fandos, *Senate Agrees Trial Is Constitutional, as Trump Consolidates Votes for an Acquittal*, N.Y. Times, Feb. 9, 2021, at A1.

In the following case, *Nixon v. United States*, 506 U.S. 224 (1993), the Supreme Court considered whether it had the power to review these Senate rules and precedents for allegedly violating the Constitution. Ultimately, the Court decided that the issue was a political question, outside of its realm.

■ CHIEF JUSTICE REHNQUIST delivered the opinion of the Court.[5]

Petitioner Walter L. Nixon, Jr., asks this Court to decide whether Senate Rule XI, which allows a committee of Senators to hear evidence against an individual who has been impeached and to report that evidence to the full Senate, violates the Impeachment Trial Clause, Art. I, § 3, cl. 6. That Clause provides that the "Senate shall have the sole Power to try all Impeachments." But before we reach the merits of such a claim, we must decide whether it is "justiciable," that is, whether it is a claim that may be resolved by the courts. We conclude that it is not.

Nixon, a former Chief Judge of the United States District Court for the Southern District of Mississippi, was convicted by a jury of two counts of making false statements before a federal grand jury and sentenced to prison. The grand jury investigation stemmed from reports that Nixon had accepted a gratuity from a Mississippi businessman in exchange for asking a local district attorney to halt the prosecution of the businessman's son. Because Nixon refused to resign from his office as a United States District Judge, he continued to collect his judicial salary while serving out his prison sentence.

On May 10, 1989, the House of Representatives adopted three articles of impeachment for high crimes and misdemeanors. The first two articles charged Nixon

---

[5] **As You Read, Consider:** Chief Justice William Rehnquist offers several reasons why he thinks impeachment is a political question—at least as far as the Supreme Court is concerned. Do you find his reasons persuasive?

with giving false testimony before the grand jury and the third article charged him with bringing disrepute on the Federal Judiciary.

After the House presented the articles to the Senate, the Senate voted to invoke its own Impeachment Rule XI, under which the presiding officer appoints a committee of Senators to "receive evidence and take testimony." Senate Impeachment Rule XI, reprinted in Senate Manual, S. Doc. No. 101-1, p. 186 (1989). The Senate committee held four days of hearings, during which 10 witnesses, including Nixon, testified. Pursuant to Rule XI, the committee presented the full Senate with a complete transcript of the proceeding and a Report stating the uncontested facts and summarizing the evidence on the contested facts. Nixon and the House impeachment managers submitted extensive final briefs to the full Senate and delivered arguments from the Senate floor during the three hours set aside for oral argument in front of that body. Nixon himself gave a personal appeal, and several Senators posed questions directly to both parties. 135 Cong. Rec. S14493–14517 (Nov. 1, 1989). The Senate voted by more than the constitutionally required two-thirds majority to convict Nixon on the first two articles. *Id.,* at S14635 (Nov. 3, 1989). The presiding officer then entered judgment removing Nixon from his office as United States District Judge.

Nixon thereafter commenced the present suit, arguing that Senate Rule XI violates the constitutional grant of authority to the Senate to "try" all impeachments because it prohibits the whole Senate from taking part in the evidentiary hearings. See Art. I, § 3, cl. 6. . . .

A controversy is nonjusticiable—*i. e.,* involves a political question—where there is "a textually demonstrable constitutional commitment of the issue to a coordinate political department; or a lack of judicially discoverable and manageable standards for resolving it . . . ." *Baker v. Carr,* 369 U. S. 186, 217 (1962). But the courts must, in the first instance, interpret the text in question and determine whether and to what extent the issue is textually committed. See *ibid.; Powell v. McCormack,* 395 U. S. 486, 519 (1969). . . .

In this case, we must examine Art. I, § 3, cl. 6, to determine the scope of authority conferred upon the Senate by the Framers regarding impeachment. It provides:

"The Senate shall have the sole Power to try all Impeachments. When sitting for that Purpose, they shall be on Oath or Affirmation. When the President of the United States is tried, the Chief Justice shall preside: And no Person shall be convicted without the Concurrence of two thirds of the Members present."

The language and structure of this Clause are revealing. The first sentence is a grant of authority to the Senate, and the word "sole" indicates that this authority is reposed in the Senate and nowhere else. The next two sentences specify requirements to which the Senate proceedings shall conform: The Senate shall be on oath or affirmation, a two-thirds vote is required to convict, and when the President is tried the Chief Justice shall preside.

Petitioner argues that the word "try" in the first sentence imposes by implication an additional requirement on the Senate in that the proceedings must be in the nature of a judicial trial. From there petitioner goes on to argue that this limitation precludes the Senate from delegating to a select committee the task of hearing the testimony of witnesses, as was done pursuant to Senate Rule XI. " '[T]ry' means more than simply 'vote on' or 'review' or 'judge.' In 1787 and today, trying a case means hearing the evidence, not scanning a cold record." Brief for Petitioner 25. Petitioner concludes from this that courts may review whether or not the Senate "tried" him before convicting him.

There are several difficulties with this position which lead us ultimately to reject it. The word "try," both in 1787 and later, has considerably broader meanings than those to which petitioner would limit it. Older dictionaries define try as "[t]o examine" or "[t]o examine as a judge." See 2 S. Johnson, A Dictionary of the English Language (1785). In more modern usage the term has various meanings. For example, try can mean "to examine or investigate judicially," "to conduct the trial of," or "to put to the test by experiment, investigation, or trial." Webster's Third New International Dictionary 2457 (1971). . . . Based on the variety of definitions, . . . we cannot say that the Framers used the word "try" as an implied limitation on the method by which the Senate might proceed in trying impeachments. . . .

The conclusion that the use of the word "try" in the first sentence of the Impeachment Trial Clause lacks sufficient precision to afford any judicially manageable standard of review of the Senate's actions is fortified by the existence of the three very specific requirements that the Constitution does impose on the Senate when trying impeachments: The Members must be under oath, a two-thirds vote is required to convict, and the Chief Justice presides when the President is tried. These limitations are quite precise, and their nature suggests that the Framers did not intend to impose additional limitations on the form of the Senate proceedings by the use of the word "try" in the first sentence.

Petitioner devotes only two pages in his brief to negating the significance of the word "sole" in the first sentence of Clause 6. As noted above, that sentence provides that "[t]he Senate shall have the sole Power to try all Impeachments." We think that the word "sole" is of considerable significance. Indeed, the word "sole" appears only one other time in the Constitution—with respect to the House of Representatives' "*sole* Power of Impeachment." Art. I, § 2, cl. 5 (emphasis added). The commonsense meaning of the word "sole" is that the Senate alone shall have authority to determine whether an individual should be acquitted or convicted. The dictionary definition bears this out. "Sole" is defined as "having no companion," "solitary," "being the only one," and "functioning . . . independently and without assistance or interference." Webster's Third New International Dictionary 2168 (1971). If the courts may review the actions of the Senate in order to determine whether that body "tried" an impeached official, it is difficult to see how the Senate would be "functioning . . . independently and without assistance or interference."

Nixon asserts that the word "sole" . . . should not bear on the question of justiciability because Art. II, § 2, cl. 1, of the Constitution grants the President pardon authority "except in Cases of Impeachment." He argues that such a limitation on the President's pardon power would not have been necessary if the Framers thought that the Senate alone had authority to deal with such questions. But the granting of a pardon is in no sense an overturning of a judgment of conviction by some other tribunal; it is "[a]n executive action that mitigates or sets aside *punishment* for a crime." Black's Law Dictionary 1113 (6th ed. 1990) (emphasis added). Authority in the Senate to determine procedures for trying an impeached official, unreviewable by the courts, is therefore not at all inconsistent with authority in the President to grant a pardon to the convicted official. The exception from the President's pardon authority of cases of impeachment was a separate determination by the Framers that executive clemency should not be available in such cases. . . .

The history and contemporary understanding of the impeachment provisions support our reading of the constitutional language. The parties do not offer evidence of a single word in the history of the Constitutional Convention or in contemporary commentary that even alludes to the possibility of judicial review in the context of the impeachment powers. This silence is quite meaningful in light of the several explicit references to the availability of judicial review as a check on the Legislature's power with respect to bills of attainder, *ex post facto* laws, and statutes. See The Federalist No. 78, p. 524 (J. Cooke ed. 1961) ("Limitations . . . can be preserved in practice no other way than through the medium of the courts of justice").

The Framers labored over the question of where the impeachment power should lie. Significantly, in at least two considered scenarios the power was placed with the Federal Judiciary. Indeed, James Madison and the Committee of Detail proposed that the Supreme Court should have the power to determine impeachments. Despite these proposals, the Convention ultimately decided that the Senate would have "the sole Power to try all Impeachments." Art. I, § 3, cl. 6. According to Alexander Hamilton, the Senate was the "most fit depositary of this important trust" because its Members are representatives of the people. See The Federalist No. 65, p. 440 (J. Cooke ed. 1961). The Supreme Court was not the proper body because the Framers "doubted whether the members of that tribunal would, at all times, be endowed with so eminent a portion of fortitude as would be called for in the execution of so difficult a task" or whether the Court "would possess the degree of credit and authority" to carry out its judgment if it conflicted with the accusation brought by the Legislature—the people's representative. See *id.,* at 441. In addition, the Framers believed the Court was too small in number: "The awful discretion, which a court of impeachments must necessarily have, to doom to honor or to infamy the most confidential and the most distinguished characters of the community, forbids the commitment of the trust to a small number of persons." *Id.,* at 441–442.[6]

There are two additional reasons why the Judiciary, and the Supreme Court in particular, were not chosen to have any role in impeachments. First, the Framers recognized that most likely there would be two sets of proceedings for individuals who commit impeachable offenses—the impeachment trial and a separate criminal trial. In fact, the Constitution explicitly provides for two separate proceedings. See Art. I, § 3, cl. 7. The Framers deliberately separated the two forums to avoid raising the specter of bias and to ensure independent judgments. . . .

Second, judicial review would be inconsistent with the Framers' insistence that our system be one of checks and balances. In our constitutional system, impeachment was designed to be the *only* check on the Judicial Branch by the Legislature. . . . Judicial involvement in impeachment proceedings, even if only for purposes of judicial review, is counterintuitive because it would eviscerate the "important constitutional check" placed on the Judiciary by the Framers. See *id.,* No. 81, at 545. Nixon's argument would place final reviewing authority with respect to impeachments in the hands of the same body that the impeachment process is meant to regulate.

Nevertheless, Nixon argues that judicial review is necessary in order to place a check on the Legislature. Nixon fears that if the Senate is given unreviewable authority to interpret the Impeachment Trial Clause, there is a grave risk that the Senate will usurp judicial power. The Framers anticipated this objection and created two constitutional safeguards to keep the Senate in check. The first safeguard is that the whole of the impeachment power is divided between the two legislative bodies, with the House given the right to accuse and the Senate given the right to judge. This split of authority "avoids the inconvenience of making the same persons both accusers and judges; and guards against the danger of persecution from the prevalency of a factious spirit in either of those branches." The second safeguard is the two-thirds supermajority vote requirement. Hamilton explained that "[a]s the concurrence of

---

6 **Questions:** Most of this opinion, so far, has explained why the Constitution did not give the impeachment power to the judiciary. What might happen if the Senate convicted a judge (or president) and the Supreme Court reversed the Senate's decision? How would the public evaluate such a result?

two-thirds of the senate will be requisite to a condemnation, the security to innocence, from this additional circumstance, will be as complete as itself can desire." *Ibid.*

In addition to the textual commitment argument, we are persuaded that the lack of finality and the difficulty of fashioning relief counsel against justiciability. See *Baker v. Carr,* 369 U. S., at 210. We agree with the Court of Appeals that opening the door of judicial review to the procedures used by the Senate in trying impeachments would "expose the political life of the country to months, or perhaps years, of chaos." This lack of finality would manifest itself most dramatically if the President were impeached. The legitimacy of any successor, and hence his effectiveness, would be impaired severely, not merely while the judicial process was running its course, but during any retrial that a differently constituted Senate might conduct if its first judgment of conviction were invalidated. Equally uncertain is the question of what relief a court may give other than simply setting aside the judgment of conviction. Could it order the reinstatement of a convicted federal judge, or order Congress to create an additional judgeship if the seat had been filled in the interim?

Petitioner finally contends that a holding of nonjusticiability cannot be reconciled with our opinion in *Powell v. McCormack,* 395 U. S. 486 (1969). The relevant issue in *Powell* was whether courts could review the House of Representatives' conclusion that Powell was "unqualified" to sit as a Member because he had been accused of misappropriating public funds and abusing the process of the New York courts. We stated that the question of justiciability turned on whether the Constitution committed authority to the House to judge its Members' qualifications, and if so, the extent of that commitment. *Id.,* at 519, 521. Article I,§ 5, provides that "Each House shall be the Judge of the Elections, Returns and Qualifications of its own Members." In turn, Art. I, § 2, specifies three requirements for membership in the House: The candidate must be at least 25 years of age, a citizen of the United States for no less than seven years, and an inhabitant of the State he is chosen to represent. We held that, in light of the three requirements specified in the Constitution, the word "qualifications"—of which the House was to be the Judge—was of a precise, limited nature. *Id.,* at 522. . . .

Our conclusion in *Powell* was based on the fixed meaning of "[q]ualifications" set forth in Art. I, § 2. The claim by the House that its power to "be the Judge of the Elections, Returns and Qualifications of its own Members" was a textual commitment of unreviewable authority was defeated by the existence of this separate provision specifying the only qualifications which might be imposed for House membership. The decision as to whether a Member satisfied these qualifications *was* placed with the House, but the decision as to what these qualifications consisted of was not.[7]

In the case before us, there is no separate provision of the Constitution that could be defeated by allowing the Senate final authority to determine the meaning of the word "try" in the Impeachment Trial Clause. We agree with Nixon that courts possess power to review either legislative or executive action that transgresses identifiable textual limits. As we have made clear, "whether the action of [either the Legislative or Executive Branch] exceeds whatever authority has been committed, is itself a delicate exercise in constitutional interpretation, and is a responsibility of this Court as ultimate interpreter of the Constitution." *Baker v. Carr, supra,* at 211; accord, *Powell, supra,* at 521. But we conclude, after exercising that delicate responsibility, that the word "try" in the Impeachment Trial Clause does not provide an identifiable textual limit on the authority which is committed to the Senate.

---

[7] **Questions:** Do you find this distinction between impeachment and exclusion persuasive? If not, does that suggest to you that exclusion should be a political question or, alternatively, that impeachment should be justiciable?

CHAPTER 30

What Is the Scope of the President's Power to Grant Reprieves and Pardons?

ARTICLE II, SECTION 2, CLAUSE 1: The President . . . shall have Power to grant Reprieves and Pardons for Offences against the United States, except in Cases of Impeachment.

ARTICLE II, SECTION 3, CLAUSE 1: He shall . . . take Care that the Laws be faithfully executed, and shall Commission all the Officers of the United States.

30.1 The Power to Grant Reprieves and Pardons

Like *impeachment*, *reprieves* and *pardons* were terms borrowed from British practice. As the ultimate source of law in Great Britain, the Crown exercised the prerogative to forgive a person accused or convicted of a criminal offense, and to determine the legal effect of this forgiveness.

This power could be very controversial. For example, in 1678, after the House of Commons impeached one of King Charles II's highest officials, the king pardoned the official before the House of Lords could vote on whether to convict him. Members of Parliament complained that if such a pardon were legally effective against impeachments, then the Crown could effectively nullify Parliament's power to hold royal officials accountable. *See* Josh Chafetz, *Congress's Constitution: Legislative Authority and the Separation of Powers* 49–50 (2017).

With this episode in mind, the Constitutional Convention gave the president the Crown's pardon power "except in Cases of Impeachment." U.S. Const. art. II, § 2, cl. 1. Beyond that one caveat, however, the delegates generally expected that the president would have the same pardon power as the Crown. As the Supreme Court observed in *The Laura*, "the test of what may be done under the power of pardon granted by our Constitution is, what the King of England could do, by virtue of his pardoning power, at the time of the separation from that country." 114 U.S. 411, 416 (1885). For this reason, early attorneys general and the Supreme Court generally resolved first-impression questions about the scope of the pardon power by borrowing from English precedent.

When, for instance, the Supreme Court considered what, exactly, a pardon was, Chief Justice John Marshall turned to English precedent to conclude that a pardon is a "deed," similar to a deed to transfer property. *United States v. Wilson*, 32 U.S. (7 Pet.) 150, 161 (1833). Once the deed was delivered by the president and accepted by the recipient, the recipient could exhibit the deed in future legal proceedings as evidence that any alleged offense had been forgiven. *Id.* This conception of a pardon mandated that the recipient had to agree to accept the pardon in order for it to be effective—which many recipients chose not to do on the ground that the acceptance of a pardon might be interpreted as an admission of guilt. *See Burdick v. United States*, 236 U.S. 79, 94 (1915).

However, in later cases, the Court modified its conception of a pardon from a *deed* that could be accepted or rejected to a *commutation* that the president could make effective at will. "A pardon in our days is not a private act of grace from an individual happening to possess power. It is a part of the Constitutional scheme," Justice Oliver Wendell Holmes wrote in 1927. "When granted it is the determination of the ultimate authority that the public welfare will be better served by inflicting less than what the judgment fixed. . . . [T]he public welfare, not [the recipient's] consent, determines what shall be done." *Biddle v. Perovich*, 274 U.S. 480, 486 (1927).

Other questions raised by the pardon power included whether the president (1) could condition pardons on the recipient's completion of certain events or (2) issue pardons prospectively before conviction. President James Monroe asked these two questions of his attorney general, William Wirt, as he considered whether to issue prospective pardons provided that the recipients joined the U.S. Navy. To answer the first question about conditions, the attorney general considered English precedent and concluded that "the power of pardoning absolutely includes the power of pardoning conditionally." 1 Op. Att'y Gen. 342 (1820). The attorney general also concluded that Monroe could issue preemptive pardons before indictment or conviction: "There is nothing in the force of the term *pardon* which implies a previous condemnation." *Id.* at 343. But the attorney general did think that the term *pardon* "presupposes an offence." *Id.* It therefore seemed unlikely that a president could issue a pardon in anticipation of an offense, which would authorize the president to dispense with the laws—something Parliament had repudiated Charles II for doing. *See* F. W. Maitland, *Constitutional History of England* 302–06 (2006).

30.1.1

Ex parte Garland

71 U.S. (4 Wall.) 333 (1867)

Presidents Abraham Lincoln and Andrew Johnson later issued blanket, conditional pardons to former Confederates provided that they took an oath of allegiance to support both the Union and the emancipation of formerly enslaved people. However, as discussed earlier with regard to Congress's power to regulate the judiciary (section 15.2), Congress later grew frustrated with these pardons and attempted to nullify their effect. One act that Congress passed in early 1865 was a statute that prohibited people from being admitted to the bar of any federal court unless they could honestly take an oath declaring that they had never participated in the Confederate government. *See* Act of Jan. 24, 1865, ch. 20, 13 Stat. 424. In other words, former Confederate officers could no longer practice law in federal courts.

Augustus Hill Garland, an attorney and a former senator in the Confederate Congress, was a member of the Supreme Court bar when Congress passed its 1865 law. Months after the law excluded him from appearing before the Court, Johnson granted him "a full pardon for all offences committed by his participation, direct or implied, in the Rebellion." *Ex parte Garland*, 71 U.S. (4 Wall.) 333, 375 (1867).

With this pardon in hand, Garland challenged the constitutionality of the 1865 law, complaining that it was a bill of attainder (because it punished a select group of people without a trial), an ex post facto law (because it enhanced the punishment for conduct after the fact), and a violation of the president's pardon power. The government responded that Congress's Article I power to "constitute Tribunals" also gave it the uncontested power to establish qualifications for who could practice before the federal courts.

In *Ex parte Garland*, 71 U.S. (4 Wall.) 333 (1867), the Court found Garland's argument more compelling.

■ MR. JUSTICE FIELD delivered the opinion of the Court.[1]

[The object of the statute passed by Congress] is to exclude [former officers of the Confederacy] from the profession of the law, or at least from its practice in the courts of the United States. As the oath prescribed cannot be taken by these parties, the act, as against them, operates as a legislative decree of perpetual exclusion. And exclusion from any of the professions or any of the ordinary avocations of life for past conduct can be regarded in no other light than as punishment for such conduct. The exaction of the oath is the mode provided for ascertaining the parties upon whom the act is intended to operate, and instead of lessening, increases its objectionable character. All enactments of this kind partake of the nature of bills of pains and penalties, and are subject to the constitutional inhibition against the passage of bills of attainder, under which general designation they are included.

In the exclusion which the statute adjudges it imposes a punishment for some of the acts specified which were not punishable at the time they were committed; and for other of the acts it adds a new punishment to that before prescribed, and it is thus brought within the further inhibition of the Constitution against the passage of an *ex post facto* law. . . .

The profession of an attorney and counsellor is not like an office created by an act of Congress, which depends for its continuance, its powers, and its emoluments upon the will of its creator, and the possession of which may be burdened with any

---

1 **As You Read, Consider:** Congress's argument here is that it doesn't want people to practice law in federal courts if they already violated an oath to protect and defend the Constitution. But Augustus Garland characterizes Congress's law as a "punishment" without a trial for conduct that was not criminal when it was done and for which he had been pardoned by the president. Does Justice Stephen Field agree that Garland is being criminally punished by Congress? What role does Garland's pardon play in the analysis?

conditions not prohibited by the Constitution. Attorneys and counsellors are not officers of the United States; they are not elected or appointed in the manner prescribed by the Constitution for the election and appointment of such officers. They are officers of the court, admitted as such by its order, upon evidence of their possessing sufficient legal learning and fair private character. It has been the general practice in this country to obtain this evidence by an examination of the parties. In this court the fact of the admission of such officers in the highest court of the States to which they respectively belong, for three years preceding their application, is regarded as sufficient evidence of the possession of the requisite legal learning, and the statement of counsel moving their admission sufficient evidence that their private and professional character is fair. The order of admission is the judgment of the court that the parties possess the requisite qualifications as attorneys and counsellors, and are entitled to appear as such and conduct causes therein. From its entry the parties become officers of the court, and are responsible to it for professional misconduct. They hold their office during good behavior, and can only be deprived of it for misconduct ascertained and declared by the judgment of the court after opportunity to be heard has been afforded. Their admission or their exclusion is not the exercise of a mere ministerial power. It is the exercise of judicial power, and has been so held in numerous cases. . . .

The legislature may undoubtedly prescribe qualifications for the office, to which he must conform, as it may, where it has exclusive jurisdiction, prescribe qualifications for the pursuit of any of the ordinary avocations of life. The question, in this case, is not as to the power of Congress to prescribe qualifications, but whether that power has been exercised as a means for the infliction of punishment, against the prohibition of the Constitution. [It has been.] . . .[2]

This view is strengthened by a consideration of the effect of the pardon produced by the petitioner, and the nature of the pardoning power of the President.

The Constitution provides that the President "shall have power to grant reprieves and pardons for offences against the United States, except in cases of impeachment."

The power thus conferred is unlimited, with the exception stated. It extends to every offence known to the law, and may be exercised at any time after its commission, either before legal proceedings are taken, or during their pendency, or after conviction and judgment. This power of the President is not subject to legislative control. Congress can neither limit the effect of his pardon, nor exclude from its exercise any class of offenders. The benign prerogative of mercy reposed in him cannot be fettered by any legislative restrictions.[3]

Such being the case, the inquiry arises as to the effect and operation of a pardon, and on this point all the authorities concur. A pardon reaches both the punishment prescribed for the offence and the guilt of the offender; and when the pardon is full, it releases the punishment and blots out of existence the guilt, so that in the eye of the law the offender is as innocent as if he had never committed the offence. If granted before conviction, it prevents any of the penalties and disabilities

---

[2] **Question:** In concluding that Congress has enacted a bill of attainder and ex post facto law, the Court distinguishes Congress's power to "prescribe qualifications" from its power to inflict "punishment." How might Congress revise its statute to prescribe qualifications without punishing ex-Confederates?

[3] **Questions:** Is this description of the pardon power part of Field's holding, or is it dicta? Suppose Congress enacted a statute that regulated the president's pardon power to make it easier for ordinary people without political connections to obtain executive clemency—for example, a statute that required a president to consider applications for pardons only from those vetted by a Bureau of Pardons. Would this sort of regulation transgress the holding of this opinion?

consequent upon conviction from attaching; if granted after conviction, it removes the penalties and disabilities, and restores him to all his civil rights; it makes him, as it were, a new man, and gives him a new credit and capacity.

There is only this limitation to its operation: it does not restore offices forfeited, or property or interests vested in others in consequence of the conviction and judgment.

The pardon produced by the petitioner is a full pardon "for all offences by him committed, arising from participation, direct or implied, in the Rebellion," and is subject to certain conditions which have been complied with. The effect of this pardon is to relieve the petitioner from all penalties and disabilities attached to the offence of treason, committed by his participation in the Rebellion. So far as that offence is concerned, he is thus placed beyond the reach of punishment of any kind. But to exclude him, by reason of that offence, from continuing in the enjoyment of a previously acquired right, is to enforce a punishment for that offence notwithstanding the pardon. If such exclusion can be effected by the exaction of an expurgatory oath covering the offence, the pardon may be avoided, and that accomplished indirectly which cannot be reached by direct legislation. It is not within the constitutional power of Congress thus to inflict punishment beyond the reach of executive clemency. From the petitioner, therefore, the oath required by the act of January 24th, 1865, could not be exacted, even if that act were not subject to any other objection than the one thus stated. . . .

NOTE: CONGRESS'S POWER TO REGULATE PARDONS

Like the discussion of the removal power in *Myers v. United States*, 272 U.S. 52 (1926) (section 27.3), the Court's opinion in *Garland* is today often interpreted as recognizing a sphere of activity in which the president's action could overrule any congressional statutes to the contrary.

Garland was not the last case to consider the scope of this sphere. Shortly afterward, in *United States v. Klein*, 80 U.S. (13 Wall.) 128 (1872), the Court upheld President Johnson's general amnesty of ex-Confederate soldiers while also invalidating a statute that prohibited ex-Confederates from invoking this pardon in proceedings to recover confiscated property. You may recall this case from an earlier section (section 15.2): one of the Court's conclusions was that Congress lacked the power to "prescribe rules of decision" in cases pending before a court. But the central holding of *Klein* has recently been interpreted to mean that Congress had no power to punish a person for a pardoned offense. *See Bank Markazi v. Peterson*, 578 U.S. 212, 226–28 (2016).

Despite *Garland* and *Klein*, Congress does have some powers to regulate the effect of pardons. As the *Garland* Court observed, one "limitation" on the operation of a presidential pardon is that "it does not restore offices forfeited, or property or interests vested in others in consequence of the conviction and judgment." *Garland*, 71 U.S. (4 Wall.) at 381. What the Court meant by this sentence was that if a convicted person is compelled to pay a fine to the government or restitution to a victim, then a pardon cannot force the government or the third party to return the fine. In *Knote v. United States*, 95 U.S. 149 (1877), the Court explained that under the Appropriations Clause, only Congress—not the president—may force the government to return money to someone convicted of a crime.

The Court has been less clear about whether Article II's grant of the pardon power to the president means that neither Congress nor federal courts can exercise powers that look like pardons. In *The Laura*, the Court upheld a federal amnesty statute that permitted people penalized under certain federal statutes to apply to the secretary of the Treasury for a refund. Although amnesty was something that the president could do with a pardon, the Court held that the pardon power was not "exclusive, in the sense that no other officer can remit forfeitures or penalties incurred for the violation of the laws of the United States." *The Laura*, 114 U.S. at 414. Yet in *Ex parte United States*, 242 U.S. 27 (1916), the Court held that federal courts lack the power to indefinitely suspend a convicted defendant's sentence, allowing the defendant to walk free despite a fact finder's determination of guilt. The Court called this a "quasi pardon" and held that such a remedy "may be afforded by the exertion of the pardoning power." *Id.* at 52.

NOTE: THE PARDON POWER AND "OFFENCES AGAINST THE UNITED STATES"

The president's pardon power extends to Article II's "Offences against the United States," a phrase that has long been interpreted to embrace all federal criminal offenses except in cases of impeachment. *See, e.g.*, 23 Op. Att'y Gen. 360, 363 (1901).

Group pardons. This alone is a broad power that presidents have used not only in individual cases but also in group cases. President Johnson, for example, pardoned all ex-Confederates who violated federal laws prohibiting treason and insurrection. President Jimmy Carter pardoned all Vietnam "draft dodgers": individuals "who may have committed any offense between August 4, 1964 and March 28, 1973 in violation of the Military Selective Service Act." Proclamation No. 4483, 42 Fed. Reg. 4391 (Jan. 21, 1977). Some legal scholars have urged modern presidents to pardon everyone convicted of nonviolent, federal crimes. *See, e.g.*, Jonathan Simon, Article, *Amnesty Now: Ending Prison Overcrowding Through a Categorical Use of the Pardon Power*, 70 U. Miami L. Rev. (2016).

Pardons of presidents and self-pardons. Pardons have long been controversial, particularly when a president is the person pardoned.

Perhaps the most politically damaging pardon in U.S. history was issued by President Gerald Ford a month after succeeding Richard Nixon to the presidency. He granted Nixon a full and unconditional pardon "for all offenses against the United States which he, Richard Nixon, has committed or may have committed or taken part in during the period from January 20, 1969 through August 9, 1974." Proclamation No. 4311, 39 Fed. Reg. 32,601 (Sep. 10, 1974). As Nixon had not yet been impeached when he resigned, he was cleared of all federal wrongdoing.

Since Ford's pardon of Nixon, legal scholars have long debated whether a president could issue a "self-pardon." *See, e.g.*, Brian C. Kalt, Note, *Pardon Me?: The Constitutional Case Against Presidential Self-Pardons*, 106 Yale L.J. 779 (1996). This issue drew more attention during the administration of President Donald Trump, but was not conclusively resolved.

Criminal versus civil offenses. At times, however, the Supreme Court has suggested that the pardon power might extend to more than just the offenses listed in the U.S. criminal code.

It did so most explicitly in a case from the opening years of Prohibition, when a federal court issued a restraining order against Philip Grossman, a Chicago saloon owner, ordering him to stop selling liquor. One year later, Grossman was caught doing just that. Exercising its inherent power to punish contempts of court, the federal court convicted Grossman of criminal contempt and sentenced him to a year of incarceration. When President Calvin Coolidge pardoned Grossman, commuting his sentence to a fine, the district court defied the pardon on the ground that the judiciary's power to punish contempts is not one of the "Offences against the United States" that the president has the power to pardon.

In *Ex parte Grossman*, the Supreme Court upheld the pardon. Interpreting the phrase *offences against the United States* with reference to "British institutions as they were when the [Constitution] was framed and adopted," the Court held that the Pardon Clause was intended to give the president the same pardon power as the King of England, with the one exception for cases of impeachment. 267 U.S. 87, 108–09 (1925). The Court noted that "the term 'offences' is used in the Constitution in a more comprehensive sense than are the terms 'crimes' and 'criminal prosecutions,'" and the phrase *offences against the United States* was inserted into the Constitution "by a Committee on Style, presumably to make clear that the pardon of the President was to operate upon offenses against the United States, as distinguished from offenses against the States." *Id.* at 113, 115. With this background in mind, the Court considered English precedent and found that the King of England "had always exercised the power to pardon contempts of court." *Id.* at 108–09. But, the Court noted, the Crown's pardon power extended only to *criminal* contempts and not to *civil* contempts. With this distinction in mind, the Court categorized Grossman's contempt conviction as criminal, not civil, because it was intended to punish him for violating a court order, not to compel him to comply with an order. The president therefore had the power to pardon him.

Since *Grossman*, some legal scholars have suggested that the president's power to pardon offenses against the United States might extend to civil offenses, such as violations of federal immigration laws. As one law professor wrote in a 2016 opinion piece urging President Barack Obama to pardon the millions of immigrants who are unlawfully present in the United States,

> [i]t's a common assumption that pardons can be used only for criminal offenses, and it's true that they have not been used before for civil immigration violations. However, the Constitution extends the power to all "offenses against the United States," which can be interpreted more broadly than just criminal offenses.

Peter L. Markowitz, *Can Obama Pardon Millions of Immigrants?*, N.Y. Times, July 6, 2016, at A21.

CHAPTER 31

WHAT IS THE SCOPE OF THE PRESIDENT'S ROLE AS "COMMANDER IN CHIEF"?

ARTICLE II, SECTION 2, CLAUSE 1: The President shall be Commander in Chief of the Army and Navy of the United States, and of the Militia of the several States, when called into the actual Service of the United States. . . .

ARTICLE II, SECTION 3, CLAUSE 1: He shall . . . take Care that the Laws be faithfully executed. . . .

31.1 THE POWER TO COMMAND THE ARMED FORCES

Many of the delegates to the Constitutional Convention crafted the position of president with George Washington in mind. He had several qualifications: he was broadly popular in every state; he was the president of the convention itself; and, most importantly, he had successfully served as "commander in chief" of the Continental Army, leading the United States to victory in the Revolutionary War. *See* 2 *Journals of the Continental Congress* 97 (Worthington Chauncey Ford ed., 1905). So, even though the delegates gave *Congress* the powers to "declare War" and to "provide for calling forth the Militia to execute the Laws of the Union, suppress Insurrections and repel Invasions," they did not empower Congress to actually lead these efforts. U.S. Const. art. I, § 8, cls. 11, 15. Instead, they made the president the "Commander in Chief of the Army and Navy of the United States, and of the Militia of the several States, when called into the actual Service of the United States." U.S. Const. art. II, § 2, cl. 1.

The exact powers and duties conferred by the role of commander in chief have never been entirely clear. However, one power that seems relatively intuitive is the power to literally command the armed forces. As Alexander Hamilton predicted after the Constitutional Convention, the commander in chief's authority

> would be nominally the same with that of the king of Great Britain, but in substance much inferior to it. It would amount to nothing more than the supreme command and direction of the military and naval forces, as first General and admiral of the Confederacy; while that of the British king extends to the DECLARING of war and to the RAISING and REGULATING of fleets and armies.

The Federalist No. 69, at 465 (Alexander Hamilton) (Jacob E. Cooke ed., 1961).

In the years since Hamilton's remarks, directing the military has remained the core of the president's commander-in-chief responsibilities. As the Supreme Court observed after the Mexican-American War, the president's

> duty and his power are purely military. As commander in chief, he is authorized to direct the movements of the naval and military forces placed by law at his command, and to employ them in the manner he may deem most effectual to harass and conquer and subdue the enemy.

Fleming v. Page, 50 U.S. (9 How.) 603, 615 (1850). In an early expansion of this power, the Court even added that after hostilities began, a president "may invade the hostile country, and subject it to the sovereignty and authority of the United States." *Id.*; *see also United States v. Burns*, 79 U.S. (12 Wall.) 246 (1871) (considering the secretary of war—and, by implication, the president—a civilian commander of the armed forces).

Presidents have long exercised these "core" commander-in-chief powers. *See* David J. Barron & Martin S. Lederman, *The Commander in Chief at the Lowest Ebb—A Constitutional History*, 121 Harv. L. Rev. 941, 1057 (2008). During the Civil War, President Abraham Lincoln ordered troops to advance on certain targets; during World War I, President Woodrow Wilson settled the question of whether U.S. soldiers would be placed under the independent command of General John J. Pershing as opposed to the multilateral command of British and French leadership; and during World War II, President Harry Truman ordered the deployment of atomic bombs against Japan. Presidents have also stipulated the terms for ending their respective wars even though only Congress has the power to declare war. Wilson, for example, announced his Fourteen Points as principles for achieving peace and ending World War I. *See* A. Scott Berg, *Wilson* 469–503 (2014). By contrast, Truman fired General Douglas MacArthur for insubordinately attempting to expand the Korean War into a war with China and the Soviet Union. *See* David McCullough, *Truman* 999–1018 (1992).

Other recognized commander-in-chief powers include the power to establish the jurisdiction of military commissions, *Madsen v. Kinsella*, 343 U.S. 341, 348 (1952); the power to adopt a code of rules to govern the conduct of armed forces in the field, *see, e.g.*, U.S. War Dep't, *General Orders No. 100* (1863); and the power to employ or remove military officers for strategic or disciplinary reasons, *United States v. Corson*, 114 U.S. 619, 621–22 (1885). Presidents have also employed secret agents to gather information without Senate confirmation or judicial oversight. *See Totten v. United States*, 92 U.S. 105, 106 (1876).

Finally, with the Supreme Court's blessing, the president has also exercised the ultimate power to enforce the rules and regulations that Congress adopts for the military via court-martial. *See Swaim v. United States*, 165 U.S. 553, 564–65 (1897). In 2019, President Donald Trump controversially exercised this power to reverse the punishment of a Navy SEAL who had been charged with war crimes by a court-martial. *See* Press Release, White House, Statement from the Press Secretary (Nov. 15, 2019). He explained, "The President, as Commander-in-Chief, is ultimately responsible for ensuring that the law is enforced and when appropriate, that mercy is granted." *Id.*

31.2 THE POWER TO RESPOND TO EMERGENCIES

If the core of the president's commander-in-chief power is the power to direct the armed forces, at one higher level of generality is the power to use the military to execute federal law and respond to emergencies. This second power has proved far more important over the course of U.S. history—and far more controversial.

Use of the Militia Acts to enforce laws

During President George Washington's first term, Congress passed the Militia Acts of 1792, two laws that, as amended, continue to authorize the president to call forth the militia when needed to execute federal laws, to suppress insurrections, or to repel invasions. *See* Act of May 2, 1792, ch. 28, 1 Stat. 264; Act of May 8, 1792, ch. 33, 1 Stat. 271; *see also* Act of Feb. 28, 1795, ch. 36, 1 Stat. 424; 10 U.S.C. §§ 252–53.

During his second term, Washington invoked the Militia Acts to suppress an "insurrection" in western Pennsylvania commonly known as the "Whiskey Rebellion." *See* Alexis Coe, *You Never Forget Your First: A Biography of George Washington* 157–61 (2020). At one point, he personally took up arms with the federalized militia in the field—although he did so mainly from a carriage. *Id.* at 159.

Although none of Washington's immediate successors attempted to lead troops in the field, many of them followed his example of invoking the Militia Acts and using their role as commander in chief to fulfill their other constitutional responsibility: to "take Care that the Laws be faithfully executed." For example, after Congress passed the Fugitive Slave Act of 1850, President Franklin Pierce authorized U.S. marshals to ensure that the law would be enforced in recalcitrant northern states. *See* 6 Op. Att'y Gen. 446 (1854). In 1854, when crowds in Boston threatened to free a captured fugitive from slavery named Anthony Burns, Pierce ordered the local U.S. attorney to "[i]ncur any expense deemed necessary by the Marshal and yourself for city military, or otherwise, to insure the execution of the law." H.R. Rep. No. 34–182, at 113 (1856) (May 31, 1854). As many as two thousand federal troops were dispatched to Boston, and they guarded the courthouse as Burns was tried and deported to Virginia.

Use of commander-in-chief role to extend laws and fill in gaps

As controversial as Pierce's action was, he was still enforcing laws passed by Congress. In other contexts, presidents occasionally invoked their commander-in-chief responsibilities to *extend* laws passed by Congress or to fill in gaps where Congress had said nothing. Two of these contexts occurred during the administration of President John Adams, when the United States was in an undeclared war with France.

At one point, the United States' cobelligerent, Great Britain, demanded the extradition of a mutinous sailor named Jonathan Robbins under the provisions of the Jay Treaty of 1794. Even though neither the treaty nor any statute authorized anyone to arrest Robbins, Adams issued an arrest warrant anyway. The president's supporters, including the future chief justice John Marshall, argued that the president had to have the power to enforce the Jay Treaty. "[A]lthough the Executive cannot supply a total Legislative omission," Marshall explained, the treaty's terms on extradition were specific enough to authorize the president to deliver up the accused. 10 Annals of Cong. 613–14 (1800).

Shortly after Marshall joined the Supreme Court a year later, he had an opportunity to apply his nuanced rule. Under a 1799 statute, Congress authorized the president to seize U.S. merchant ships going *to* French ports, but not U.S. merchant ships coming *from* French ports. Nevertheless, Adams issued instructions to U.S. frigates ordering them to seize *all* U.S. merchant ships traveling between the ports of the United States and France. When a merchant ship belonging to George Little was seized after leaving a French Caribbean port, Little complained that the president had no authority to order the seizure.

In *Little v. Barreme*, 6 U.S. (2 Cranch) 170 (1804), Chief Justice Marshall agreed that the president had exceeded his power. In contrast with his earlier interpretation of the Jay Treaty, Marshall thought that the statute in Little's case cut against the president's authority:

> It is by no means clear that the president of the United States whose high duty it is to "take care that the laws be faithfully executed," and who is commander in chief of the armies and navies of the United States, might not, without any special authority for that purpose, in the then existing state of things, have empowered the officers commanding the armed vessels of the United States, to seize and send into port for adjudication, American vessels which were forfeited by being engaged in this illicit commerce. But when it is observed that [an act of Congress] gives a special authority to seize on the high seas, and limits that authority to the seizure of vessels bound or sailing *to* a French port, the legislature seem to have prescribed that the manner in which this law shall be carried into execution, was to exclude a seizure of any vessel not bound *to* a French port.

Little, 6 U.S. (2 Cranch) at 177. Accordingly, the Court held that the president's instructions had been issued without authority. *Id.* at 179.

Just as Marshall indicated that he thought the president could act on his own in some but not all contexts, later courts also crafted tests to distinguish between when the commander in chief could act alone and when Congress's approval was required. For example, during the Mexican-American War, an army officer named David Mitchell seized the merchandise of a U.S. citizen, Manuel Harmony, who had followed U.S. soldiers into Mexico in order to trade with both sides. When the case reached the Supreme Court, the Court invalidated this seizure. *See Mitchell v. Harmony*, 54 U.S. (13 How.) 115 (1852). Yet the Court also offered an explanation of when the commander in chief could lawfully seize property without congressional approval:

> There are, without doubt, occasions in which private property may lawfully be taken possession of or destroyed to prevent it from falling into the hands of the public enemy, and also where a military officer . . . may impress private property into the public service or take it for public use. . . .
>
> But we are clearly of opinion, that in all of these cases the danger must be immediate and impending; or the necessity urgent . . . such as will not admit of delay, and where the action of the civil authority would be too late in providing the means which the occasion calls for.

Id. at 134.

31.2.1
The Emancipation Proclamation

12 Stat. 1267 (1863)

The most famous example of a president exercising commander-in-chief responsibilities to extend statutes and fill in statutory omissions occurred during the Civil War. As noted earlier in the discussion of Congress's war powers (section 13.3), Congress was in recess when rebels in South Carolina fired the first shots of the Civil War in April 1861. The newly inaugurated president, Abraham Lincoln, called for Congress to reconvene in a special July 4 session. In the meantime, Lincoln unilaterally suspended habeas corpus, ordered a blockade of southern ports, and called forth seventy-five thousand militia. When Congress reconvened, the president explained that he believed it to be

> an imperative duty upon the incoming Executive to prevent, if possible, the consummation of [any] attempt to destroy the Federal Union. . . . These measures, whether strictly legal or not, were ventured upon under what appeared to be a popular demand and a public necessity, trusting then, as now that Congress would readily ratify them.

7 *Messages and Papers of the Presidents* 3221, 3225 (James D. Richardson ed., 1909).

The Supreme Court upheld Lincoln's actions in the *Prize Cases*, 67 U.S. (2 Black) 635 (1863), a decision that announced a broad interpretation of the president's commander-in-chief power. Even though "Congress alone has the power to declare national or foreign war," the Court wrote, the president has the power to *respond* to hostilities. *The Prize Cases*, 67 U.S. (2 Black) at 668. "If a war be made by invasion of a foreign nation," the Court continued, "the President is not only authorized but bound to resist force by force. He does not initiate the war, but is bound to accept the challenge without waiting for any special legislative authority." *Id.* The Court later observed that the president's duties "as Commander-in-chief" meant that the question of whether he "has met with such armed hostile resistance . . . is a question to be decided by *him*. . . . He must determine what degree of force the crisis demands." *Id.* at 670. These declarations were remarkable, in part, because they were entirely unnecessary to the Court's opinion. As the Court observed in the same passage, Lincoln's conduct had been justified by the earlier Militia Acts, which authorized the president to call forth the militia and to use armed force to suppress insurrections. *Id.* at 668. Moreover, Congress ratified the president's actions in the summer of 1861, eliminating any controversy over the president's unilateral power to act. *Id.* at 670.

One possible explanation for the *Prize Cases*' broad language is the immediate context in which the case was decided. Only two months before the decision, on January 1, 1863, Lincoln issued a wartime proclamation whose legal effect was broader than any statute then allowed. The Emancipation Proclamation, issued as an exercise of the president's commander-in-chief powers, legally freed more than 3.5 million enslaved people living in Confederate states. It also announced that the United States would recruit black soldiers.

At the time Lincoln issued the proclamation, its legality was fiercely contested. *See* Noah Feldman, *The Broken Constitution: Lincoln, Slavery, and the Refounding of America* 283–88 (2021); John Fabian Witt, *Lincoln's Code: The Laws of War in American History* 214–19 (2013). The statute that most closely anticipated it was the Second Confiscation Act of 1862, ch. 190, 12 Stat. 589. That act authorized the president to "cause the seizure of all the estate and property" of anyone "engaged in armed rebellion against the government of the United States, or aiding or abetting such rebellion." Second Confiscation Act, 12 Stat. at 590. It also declared that any enslaved people who escaped from someone "engaged in rebellion" would be "deemed captives of war, and shall be forever free of their servitude." *Id.* at 591. But the act specifically stated that any seizure of property could take place only after a hearing in which the putative owners could argue that they had "not borne arms against the United States in the present rebellion, nor in any way given aid and comfort thereto." *Id.* at 590–91. In other words, the act required the president to give all southerners an opportunity to prove their loyalty before permanently seizing their property or freeing their slaves.

These due process protections of the Second Confiscation Act made the statute practically ineffective in the middle of an armed conflict. *See* Burrus M. Carnahan, *Act of Justice: Lincoln's Emancipation Proclamation and the Law of War* 121 (2007). Yet they may have been constitutionally required. In *Dred Scott v. Sandford*, the Supreme Court held that the Fifth Amendment prohibited the federal government from depriving white people of their property rights in enslaved black people without "due process of law." 60 U.S. (19 How.) 393, 450 (1857). And the Fugitive Slave Act of 1850 continued to make it a crime to "rescue" any fugitive from slavery or to "willingly obstruct, hinder, or prevent" any person from arresting the fugitive. Fugitive Slave Act, ch. 60, 9 Stat. 462, 464. Although the Second Confiscation Act and other laws authorized Union soldiers to treat enslaved people as "contraband" who could be employed on the front lines, the Fugitive Slave Act remained a source of legal protection for white enslavers loyal to the Union. *See* Carnahan, *supra*, at 121–22.

The Emancipation Proclamation arguably failed to abide by the Second Confiscation Act's due process proceedings, and it also arguably contradicted the Fugitive Slave Act of 1850. *See* Feldman, *supra*, at 279–82. Yet Lincoln and his supporters offered several reasons why the proclamation was a legitimate exercise of his powers as commander in chief. First, Lincoln considered the emancipation of millions of people to be an "act of justice" that would motivate northerners to support the war as a moral crusade instead of a legalistic fight over secession. *See* 12 Stat. 1267. Second, he considered the proclamation to be an act of economic and psychological warfare that would deprive the Confederacy of an essential source of labor while recruiting black people to join the Union war effort. *See* Carnahan, *supra*, at 121–22. Third, it was also an act of international diplomacy because it would discourage European nations from joining the Civil War on the side of the Confederacy. *See* Doris Kearns Goodwin, *Team of Rivals* 467–68 (2005). Finally, Lincoln argued that even if enslaved people were legally considered "property," the law of war held that "property, both of enemies and friends, may be taken when needed." Carnahan, *supra*, at 1. As commander in chief, he therefore considered the proclamation to be within the discretion granted to him by the Second Confiscation Act, the Constitution, and the law of war.

■ EMANCIPATION PROCLAMATION (Jan. 1, 1863)[1]

Whereas, on the twenty-second day of September, in the year of our Lord one thousand eight hundred and sixty-two, a proclamation was issued by the President of the United States, containing, among other things, the following, to wit:

---

[1] **As You Read, Consider:** What techniques and subtle arguments does President Abraham Lincoln employ to demonstrate the constitutionality of the Emancipation

That on the first day of January, in the year of our Lord one thousand eight hundred and sixty-three, all persons held as slaves within any State or designated part of a State, the people whereof shall then be in rebellion against the United States, shall be then, thenceforward, and forever free; and the Executive Government of the United States, including the military and naval authority thereof, will recognize and maintain the freedom of such persons, and will do no act or acts to repress such persons, or any of them, in any efforts they may make for their actual freedom.

That the Executive will, on the first day of January aforesaid, by proclamation, designate the States and parts of States, if any, in which the people thereof, respectively, shall then be in rebellion against the United States; and the fact that any State, or the people thereof, shall on that day be, in good faith, represented in the Congress of the United States by members chosen thereto at elections wherein a majority of the qualified voters of such State shall have participated, shall, in the absence of strong countervailing testimony, be deemed conclusive evidence that such State, and the people thereof, are not then in rebellion against the United States.

Now, therefore I, Abraham Lincoln, President of the United States, by virtue of the power in me vested as Commander-in-Chief, of the Army and Navy of the United States in time of actual armed rebellion against the authority and government of the United States, and as a fit and necessary war measure for suppressing said rebellion, do, on this first day of January, in the year of our Lord one thousand eight hundred and sixty-three, and in accordance with my purpose so to do publicly proclaimed for the full period of one hundred days, from the day first above mentioned, order and designate as the States and parts of States wherein the people thereof respectively, are this day in rebellion against the United States, the following, to wit:

Arkansas, Texas, Louisiana, (except the Parishes of St. Bernard, Plaquemines, Jefferson, St. John, St. Charles, St. James Ascension, Assumption, Terrebonne, Lafourche, St. Mary, St. Martin, and Orleans, including the City of New Orleans) Mississippi, Alabama, Florida, Georgia, South Carolina, North Carolina, and Virginia, (except the forty-eight counties designated as West Virginia, and also the counties of Berkley, Accomac, Northampton, Elizabeth City, York, Princess Ann, and Norfolk, including the cities of Norfolk and Portsmouth[)],[2]

and which excepted parts, are for the present, left precisely as if this proclamation were not issued.

And by virtue of the power, and for the purpose aforesaid, I do order and declare that all persons held as slaves within said designated States, and parts of States, are, and henceforward shall be free; and that the Executive government of the United States, including the military and naval authorities thereof, will recognize and maintain the freedom of said persons.

And I hereby enjoin upon the people so declared to be free to abstain from all violence, unless in necessary self-defence; and I recommend to them that, in all cases when allowed, they labor faithfully for reasonable wages.

Proclamation? Do you agree with him that he had the constitutional power to issue the proclamation?

2 **Question:** Lincoln's list of states where the Emancipation Proclamation would take effect excludes places that were, at the time, under Union control. Are these exceptions constitutionally required, or do you think they were listed merely for political reasons?

And I further declare and make known, that such persons of suitable condition, will be received into the armed service of the United States to garrison forts, positions, stations, and other places, and to man vessels of all sorts in said service.

And upon this act, sincerely believed to be an act of justice, warranted by the Constitution, upon military necessity, I invoke the considerate judgment of mankind, and the gracious favor of Almighty God. . . .

NOTE: POWER TO EXPAND STATUTES AND SEIZE PROPERTY

The constitutionality of the Emancipation Proclamation was never tested in the Supreme Court. But it has, of course, been embraced by the court of history. Within two years, Congress proposed the Thirteenth Amendment to abolish slavery throughout the United States, including in the places omitted from the Emancipation Proclamation. Section 4 of the Fourteenth Amendment, ratified in 1868, also prohibited the United States from paying "any claim for the loss or emancipation of any slave." So, the Emancipation Proclamation not only precipitated the freedom of four million black people throughout the United States but also effected the largest seizure in American history of what the law had previously considered property. In 1860, the value of enslaved people in the South represented approximately $3.1 billion, or 48 percent of the region's wealth. *See* Gavin Wright, *Slavery and American Economic Development* 60 (2006). Thanks to the president's action, southern enslavers could no longer claim a property interest in other people.

Seize property. Over the next century, subsequent presidents continued to invoke their role as commander in chief to act beyond what any statute specifically authorized—including, when necessary, to seize property. *See United States v. Russell*, 80 U.S. 623, 628–29 (1871) (authorizing the seizure of property of U.S. citizens where there is an "extreme and imperative" emergency "such as will not admit of delay or resort to any other source of supply" and where "full compensation to the owner" is paid).

Reconstruct governments. As discussed earlier (sections 13.4), in the waning days of the Civil War, Presidents Abraham Lincoln and Andrew Johnson exercised their power as commander in chief to appoint military generals to oversee the conquered southern states—giving the generals broad authority to reconstruct the governments on a republican footing. Two years after the war ended, Congress ratified and enhanced the generals' authority with the Reconstruction Act of 1867, ch. 153, 14 Stat. 428. When the Supreme Court evaluated the situation in *Texas v. White*, the Court wrote that

> [t]he power exercised by the President was supposed, doubtless, to be derived from his constitutional functions, as commander in chief; and, so long as the war continued, it cannot be denied that he might institute temporary government within insurgent districts, occupied by the National forces, or take measures, in any State, for the restoration of the State government faithful to the Union.

74 U.S. 700, 730 (1869). Although the Court thought this action was appropriate, the Court also cautioned that the president must employ "only such means and agents as were authorized by constitutional laws." *Id.* at 730–31.

Suppress insurrections and execute laws. Johnson's successor, Ulysses S. Grant, energetically used the military throughout his administration to suppress lynchings and violent insurrections by the Ku Klux Klan, rifle clubs, the White League, and other white supremacist paramilitary organizations. *See* Ron Chernow, *Grant*, 758, 788–92, 839–43 (2017). Federal soldiers helped to enforce the Ku Klux Klan Act of 1871, for example, by capturing suspects, protecting witnesses, defending courtrooms, and transporting prisoners. *Id.* at 708. Democrats strenuously protested this use of federal troops, which they called "bayonet rule." *Id.* at 601. They also retook control of the House of Representatives and several state legislatures in part by murdering and intimidating Republican voters. *See* Eric Foner, *Reconstruction* 550 (2014).

Congressional Democrats soon led a repudiation of Grant's use of federal soldiers by adding to a federal appropriations bill a rider known as the Posse Comitatus Act of 1878, ch. 263, 20 Stat. 145, 152. The act declared that

> it shall not be lawful to employ any part of the Army of the United States, as a posse comitatus, or otherwise, for the purpose of executing the laws, except in such cases and under such circumstances as such employment of said force may be expressly authorized by the Constitution or by act of Congress.

Posse Comitatus Act, 20 Stat. at 152. The term *posse comitatus* referred to the traditional role of a county sheriff in summoning the armed population of a county to keep the peace. But the obvious purpose of the act was to prohibit future uses of federal soldiers to enforce civil rights laws.

Presidents resisted the Posse Comitatus Act, arguing that it had no legal effect on their powers. For example, when Attorney General Charles Devens considered its effect, he noted that the Militia Acts—first passed in 1792—continued to "expressly authorize[ ]" the president to call forth the militia to suppress insurrections and execute the laws. 16 Op. Att'y Gen. 162, 164 (1878). Future presidents, including Democratic presidents, therefore continued to use the military to enforce federal law.

Perhaps the most notable example of a president using the military to enforce federal law occurred when President Grover Cleveland called forth federal troops to suppress a railroad strike in 1894 that had shut down virtually all major railroads across the country. The Cleveland administration broke the strike when its Department of Justice persuaded a federal court to enjoin the strikers from blocking the flow of U.S. mail—even though no statute specifically authorized such an injunction. "The entire strength of the nation may be used to enforce in any part of the land the full and free exercise of all national powers and the security of all rights entrusted by the Constitution to its care," the Supreme Court wrote approvingly in *In re Debs,* 158 U.S. 564, 582 (1895). The Court continued:

> The strong arm of the national government may be put forth to brush away all obstructions to the freedom of interstate commerce or the transportation of the mails. If the emergency arises, the army of the Nation, and all its militia, are at the service of the Nation to compel obedience to its laws.

Id. at 582.

The 1894 railroad strike marked a new phase in the history of the commander-in-chief power because if the president had the power to stop striking workers during peacetime, then he also had the power during wartime. During World War I and World War II, presidents therefore began invoking their commander-in-chief powers as a legal basis for seizing steel mills, radio stations, aviation plants, coal mines, and other strike-prone industries that they deemed "vital to the defense of the United States." Exec. Order No. 8773, 6 Fed. Reg. 2777 (Jun. 9, 1941); *see, e.g.*, 40 Op. Att'y Gen. 312, 319–20 (1944); Brief for United States at 75–77, *United States v. Midwest Oil Co.*, 236 U.S. 459 (1915); 30 Op. Att'y Gen. 291 (1914). As President Franklin D. Roosevelt explained in a 1942 message to Congress, a "Commander in Chief in wartime . . . has the powers, under the Constitution and under Congressional acts, to take measures necessary to avert a disaster which would interfere with the winning of the war." 88 Cong. Rec. 7044 (1942). The president accompanied this message with a warning: "In the event that the Congress should fail to act, and act adequately, I shall accept the responsibility, and I will act." *Id.*

Congressional expansion of presidential powers. Congress did act. Beginning in World War I with the Trading with the Enemy Act of 1917, Congress codified dozens of expansive powers that the president could exercise whenever "the President shall deem that the public safety demands it." Trading with the Enemy Act, Pub. L. No. 65–91, 40 Stat. 411, 413. During World War II, Congress also ratified several of Roosevelt's executive orders, including his creation of a labor board with the power to adjudicate labor disputes. *See* Exec. Order No. 9017, 7 Fed. Reg. 237 (1942); War Labor Disputes Act of 1943, Pub. L. No. 78–89, 57 Stat. 163; *Emps. Grp. v. Nat'l War Labor Bd.*, 143 F.2d 145 (D.C. Cir. 1944). Most controversially, Congress ratified Roosevelt's 1942 order authorizing military commanders to designate areas from which U.S. citizens of Japanese descent could be excluded or removed. *See* Exec. Order No. 9066, 7 Fed. Reg. 1407 (1942); Act of Mar. 21, 1942, Pub. L. No. 77–503, 56 Stat. 173. As discussed earlier (section 13.4), the order and congressional ratification were first upheld in *Hirabayashi v. United States*, 320 U.S. 81 (1943).

31.2.2

Youngstown Sheet & Tube Co. v. Sawyer

343 U.S. 579 (1952)

Although Congress in the early twentieth century was generally supportive of presidential power in wartime, it also took steps to cabin the president's powers during peacetime—even as the distinction between the two times steadily collapsed. *See* Mary L. Dudziak, *War Time* 33–62 (2012); *Woods v. Cloyd W. Miller Co.*, 333 U.S. 138, 144 (1948) (authorizing Congress to continue exercising war powers after World War II ended). Congress's most notable restrictions affected the president's power to stop strikes—leading to the single most important Supreme Court case on presidential power.

In 1932, in response to a proliferation of antilabor injunctions in the decades after the railroad strike of 1894, Congress enacted the Norris-LaGuardia Act of 1932, Pub. L. No. 72–65, 47 Stat. 70. The law strictly limited the power of federal courts to enjoin private labor disputes. Norris-LaGuardia Act, 47 Stat. at 70–71. The act also increased the bargaining leverage of organized labor, which spent the next two decades organizing most major industries.

In 1947, a Republican-controlled Congress attempted to walk back some of organized labor's advances. Senator Robert A. Taft of Ohio and Representative Fred A. Hartley Jr. of New Jersey each introduced measures to restrict the power of unions. One of these measures proposed to authorize the president not only to break strikes by seizing industries and transferring them into the possession of the federal government but also to legally prohibit strikes among federal workers. Congress had previously given Roosevelt this authority on a temporary basis during World War II, and he had used it to continue wartime production. *See* War Labor Disputes Act of 1943, Pub. L. No. 78–89, 57 Stat. 163, 165. But reauthorizing this power during peacetime proved deeply unpopular. Conservatives in Congress strongly opposed the temporary nationalization of businesses. Progressives feared what President Harry Truman might do with such a power. Although the president ordinarily supported labor unions, he had recently broken a nationwide strike of railroad workers by threatening to "draft them and think about the law later." David McCullough, *Truman* 501–06 (1992). So, the final version of what became known as the Taft-Hartley Act omitted the presidential seizure provision. Instead, it authorized the president to petition a federal court to enjoin a major strike for eighty days pending an impartial study. Labor Management Relations Act of 1947, Pub. L. No. 80–101, 61 Stat. 136, 155. Organized labor called on Truman to veto the law, but Congress enacted the law over his veto. McCullough, *supra*, at 565–66.

Three years later, in 1950, North Korean forces invaded South Korea. Without waiting for congressional approval, Truman announced that he would send U.S. troops to defend South Korea in what he called a "police action for the United Nations." Anthony Leviero, *U.S. "Not at War" President Asserts*, N.Y. Times, June 30, 1950, at 1. He explained that the United Nations Security Council—whose legitimacy the United States recognized by treaty—requested that members of the United Nations "furnish such assistance to the Republic of Korea as may be necessary to repel the armed attack and to restore international peace and security in the area." S.C. Res. 83 (June 27, 1950). The Korean War had begun.

Congress never declared war or explicitly authorized this deployment of U.S. troops. But it did enact the Defense Production Act of 1950, which condoned Truman's foreign policies and gave the president sweeping powers to ensure that domestic industries were producing enough materials "to promote the national defense." Pub. L. 81–774, 64 Stat. 798, 798–99. Exercising this statutory authority, Truman imposed wage and price controls on the entire steel industry. *See* Exec. Order No. 10,161, 15 Fed. Reg. 6105 (1950). But although steel companies profited despite these controls, the companies refused to consent to a single wage increase for two years. When the Truman administration urged the companies to accept a modest wage increase, they wouldn't budge absent an increase in prices. Eventually, the United Steelworkers of America and other labor unions threatened to strike on April 9, 1952. *See* McCullough, *supra*, at 1066–67.

With U.S. soldiers locked in a stalemate in Korea, the Truman administration feared that any stoppage of steel production, even for a short time, would endanger the war effort. Stressing the situation in Korea, the secretary of defense warned him, "[W]e are holding the line with ammunition, and not with the lives of our troops"—meaning a loss of steel would lead to the loss of American lives. *Id.* But the only statute that appeared to give the president any authority to intervene was the Taft-Hartley Act, which he had earlier tried to veto. The president refused to invoke this act: he claimed its injunction procedure would work too slowly to stop a strike, and he saw no sense in seeking only a temporary injunction. He also didn't want to alienate labor in an election year. *Id.* at 1067–68.

Hours before the strike deadline, Truman delivered a prime-time address in which he announced his solution: he would order the secretary of commerce, Charles W. Sawyer, to seize the nation's steel mills. *Public Papers of the Presidents of the United States: Harry S. Truman* 250 (1966) (Apr. 8, 1952); *see* Exec. Order No. 10,340, 17 Fed. Reg. 3139 (1952). "We must have steel," the president declared, explaining that he had a duty as commander in chief to continue supplying soldiers and allies overseas. *Public Papers of the Presidents*, *supra*, at 249–50. The president also explained that he wasn't invoking "the so-called emergency provisions of the Taft-Hartley Act" because they "could not prevent a steel shutdown of at least a week or two." *Id.*

The next day, Truman asked Congress to ratify or countermand his seizure of the steel mills. He added, however, that he didn't believe "that immediate Congressional action is essential." *Id.* at 251. While Congress did nothing, the nation's largest steel companies, including Youngstown Sheet & Tube Company, sued to regain control over the steel mills.

Truman had two reasons to be optimistic about this lawsuit. First, he had appointed four of the Supreme Court's members, including the chief justice, Fred Vinson. The chief justice had even privately assured Truman that his seizure was constitutional. *See* Robert J. Donovan, *Tumultuous Years* 386 (1982). Second, the other five justices had all been appointed by Roosevelt, whose administration had unilaterally seized facilities during World War II. Indeed, when Roosevelt seized an aviation plant in 1941, his attorney general—now Justice Robert Jackson—had explained that the president possessed a "general law-enforcement power conferred by the various acts of Congress," along with "the aggregate of the Presidential powers derived from the Constitution itself." 89 Cong. Rec. 3992 (1943).

Truman's optimism, though, was rash. Jackson's concurring opinion in *Youngstown Sheet & Tube Co. v. Sawyer*, 343 U.S. 579 (1952), contrasts the role he played as a government lawyer with his current position as a justice. It has become the most frequently cited opinion on the president's inherent power to act without statutory authority.

■ MR. JUSTICE BLACK delivered the opinion of the Court.[3]

We are asked to decide whether the President was acting within his constitutional power when he issued an order directing the Secretary of Commerce to take possession of and operate most of the Nation's steel mills. The mill owners argue that the President's order amounts to lawmaking, a legislative function which the Constitution has expressly confided to the Congress and not to the President. The Government's position is that the order was made on findings of the President that his action was necessary to avert a national catastrophe which would inevitably result from a stoppage of steel production, and that in meeting this grave emergency the President was acting within the aggregate of his constitutional powers as the Nation's Chief Executive and the Commander in Chief of the Armed Forces of the United States. . . .

The President's power, if any, to issue the order must stem either from an act of Congress or from the Constitution itself. There is no statute that expressly authorizes the President to take possession of property as he did here. Nor is there any act of Congress to which our attention has been directed from which such a power can fairly be implied. Indeed, we do not understand the Government to rely on statutory authorization for this seizure. There are two statutes which do authorize the President to take both personal and real property under certain conditions. However, the Government admits that these conditions were not met and that the President's order was not rooted in either of the statutes. The Government refers to the seizure provisions of one of these statutes (§ 201(b) of the Defense Production Act) as "much too cumbersome, involved, and time-consuming for the crisis which was at hand."

Moreover, the use of the seizure technique to solve labor disputes in order to prevent work stoppages was not only unauthorized by any congressional enactment; prior to this controversy, Congress had refused to adopt that method of settling labor disputes. When the Taft-Hartley Act was under consideration in 1947, Congress rejected an amendment which would have authorized such governmental seizures in cases of emergency. Apparently it was thought that the technique of seizure, like that

---

3. **As You Read, Consider:** Several of the justices expressly or implicitly compare President Harry Truman's seizure of steel mills with President Abraham Lincoln's Emancipation Proclamation—perhaps because both unilaterally seized "property" in the name of winning a war. Assuming that Lincoln's emancipation of enslaved people was constitutional, what, if anything, would distinguish Truman's seizure of steel mills?

of compulsory arbitration, would interfere with the process of collective bargaining. Consequently, the plan Congress adopted in that Act did not provide for seizure under any circumstances. Instead, the plan sought to bring about settlements by use of the customary devices of mediation, conciliation, investigation by boards of inquiry, and public reports. In some instances temporary injunctions were authorized to provide cooling-off periods. All this failing, unions were left free to strike after a secret vote by employees as to whether they wished to accept their employers' final settlement offer.

It is clear that if the President had authority to issue the order he did, it must be found in some provision of the Constitution. And it is not claimed that express constitutional language grants this power to the President. The contention is that presidential power should be implied from the aggregate of his powers under the Constitution. Particular reliance is placed on provisions in Article II which say that "The executive Power shall be vested in a President . . ."; that "he shall take Care that the Laws be faithfully executed"; and that he "shall be Commander in Chief of the Army and Navy of the United States."

The order cannot properly be sustained as an exercise of the President's military power as Commander in Chief of the Armed Forces. The Government attempts to do so by citing a number of cases upholding broad powers in military commanders engaged in day-to-day fighting in a theater of war. Such cases need not concern us here. Even though "theater of war" be an expanding concept, we cannot with faithfulness to our constitutional system hold that the Commander in Chief of the Armed Forces has the ultimate power as such to take possession of private property in order to keep labor disputes from stopping production. This is a job for the Nation's lawmakers, not for its military authorities.[4]

Nor can the seizure order be sustained because of the several constitutional provisions that grant executive power to the President. In the framework of our Constitution, the President's power to see that the laws are faithfully executed refutes the idea that he is to be a lawmaker. The Constitution limits his functions in the lawmaking process to the recommending of laws he thinks wise and the vetoing of laws he thinks bad. And the Constitution is neither silent nor equivocal about who shall make laws which the President is to execute. The first section of the first article says that "All legislative Powers herein granted shall be vested in a Congress of the United States . . . ." After granting many powers to the Congress, Article I goes on to provide that Congress may "make all Laws which shall be necessary and proper for carrying into Execution the foregoing Powers, and all other Powers vested by this Constitution in the Government of the United States, or in any Department or Officer thereof."

The President's order does not direct that a congressional policy be executed in a manner prescribed by Congress—it directs that a presidential policy be executed in a manner prescribed by the President. The preamble of the order itself, like that of many statutes, sets out reasons why the President believes certain policies should be adopted, proclaims these policies as rules of conduct to be followed, and again, like a statute, authorizes a government official to promulgate additional rules and regulations consistent with the policy proclaimed and needed to carry that policy into execution. The power of Congress to adopt such public policies as those proclaimed by the order is beyond question. It can authorize the taking of private property for

[4] **Question:** After determining that Truman's seizure was not justified by any statute, Justice Hugo Black distinguishes the president's powers in a "theater of war" from the president's domestic powers. Does this distinction make sense in light of the Truman administration's concern that U.S. troops in Korea will run out of ammunition absent the continuous production of steel domestically?

public use. It can make laws regulating the relationships between employers and employees, prescribing rules designed to settle labor disputes, and fixing wages and working conditions in certain fields of our economy. The Constitution does not subject this lawmaking power of Congress to presidential or military supervision or control.[5]

It is said that other Presidents without congressional authority have taken possession of private business enterprises in order to settle labor disputes. But even if this be true, Congress has not thereby lost its exclusive constitutional authority to make laws necessary and proper to carry out the powers vested by the Constitution "in the Government of the United States, or any Department or Officer thereof."

The Founders of this Nation entrusted the lawmaking power to the Congress alone in both good and bad times. It would do no good to recall the historical events, the fears of power and the hopes for freedom that lay behind their choice. Such a review would but confirm our holding that this seizure order cannot stand. . . .

■ MR. JUSTICE FRANKFURTER, concurring.

[T]he question before the Court comes in this setting. Congress has frequently—at least 16 times since 1916—specifically provided for executive seizure of production, transportation, communications, or storage facilities. In every case it has qualified this grant of power with limitations and safeguards. This body of enactments . . . demonstrates that Congress deemed seizure so drastic a power as to require that it be carefully circumscribed whenever the President was vested with this extraordinary authority. The power to seize has uniformly been given only for a limited period or for a defined emergency, or has been repealed after a short period. Its exercise has been restricted to particular circumstances such as "time of war or when was is imminent," the needs of "public safety" or of "national security or defense," or "urgent and impending need." . . .

Congress in 1947 was again called upon to consider whether governmental seizure should be used to avoid serious industrial shutdowns. . . . Under the urgency of telephone and coal strikes in the winter of 1946, Congress addressed itself to the problems raised by "national emergency" strikes and lockouts. The termination of wartime seizure powers on December 31, 1946, brought these matters to the attention of Congress with vivid impact. A proposal that the President be given powers to seize plants to avert a shutdown where the "health or safety" of the Nation was endangered, was thoroughly canvassed by Congress and rejected. No room for doubt remains that the proponents as well as the opponents of the bill which became the Labor Management Relations ["Taft-Hartley"] Act of 1947 clearly understood that as a result of that legislation the only recourse for preventing a shutdown in any basic industry, after failure of mediation, was Congress. Authorization for seizure as an available remedy for potential dangers was unequivocally put aside. . . .

It cannot be contended that the President would have had power to issue this order had Congress explicitly negated such authority in formal legislation. Congress has expressed its will to withhold this power from the President as though it had said so in so many words. The authoritatively expressed purpose of Congress to disallow such power to the President and to require him, when in his mind the occasion arose for such a seizure, to put the matter to Congress and ask for specific authority from

[5] **Questions:** Black's majority opinion holds that the president's only regulatory power—outside the "theater of war"—is to enforce laws passed by Congress. And because Congress has passed no laws authorizing this seizure, the president is powerless to authorize it himself. Do you agree with Black that presidents should be incapable of acting with the force of law absent congressional authorization? How might Black respond to Chief Justice Fred Vinson's dissent, which characterizes the majority opinion as "this messenger-boy concept of the Office, [in which] the President cannot even act to preserve legislative programs from destruction so that Congress will have something left to act upon"?

it, could not be more decisive if it had been written into §§ 206–210 of the Labor Management Relations Act of 1947. . . . By the Labor Management Relations Act of 1947, Congress said to the President, "You may not seize. Please report to us and ask for seizure power if you think it is needed in a specific situation." . . .[6]

It is one thing to draw an intention of Congress from general language and to say that Congress would have explicitly written what is inferred, where Congress has not addressed itself to a specific situation. It is quite impossible, however, when Congress did specifically address itself to a problem, as Congress did to that of seizure, to find secreted in the interstices of legislation the very grant of power which Congress consciously withheld. To find authority so explicitly withheld is not merely to disregard in a particular instance the clear will of Congress. It is to disrespect the whole legislative process and the constitutional division of authority between President and Congress. . . .

■ MR. JUSTICE DOUGLAS, concurring.

There can be no doubt that the emergency which caused the President to seize these steel plants was one that bore heavily on the country. But the emergency did not create power; it merely marked an occasion when power should be exercised. And the fact that it was necessary that measures be taken to keep steel in production does not mean that the President, rather than the Congress, had the constitutional authority to act. The Congress, as well as the President, is trustee of the national welfare. . . .

If we sanctioned the present exercise of power by the President, we would be expanding Article II of the Constitution and rewriting it to suit the political conveniences of the present emergency. Article II which vests the "executive Power" in the President defines that power with particularity. Article II, Section 2 makes the Chief Executive the Commander in Chief of the Army and Navy. But our history and tradition rebel at the thought that the grant of military power carries with it authority over civilian affairs. Article II, Section 3 provides that the President shall "from time to time give to the Congress Information of the State of the Union, and recommend to their Consideration such Measures as he shall judge necessary and expedient." The power to recommend legislation, granted to the President, serves only to emphasize that it is his function to recommend and that it is the function of the Congress to legislate. Article II, Section 3 also provides that the President "shall take Care that the Laws be faithfully executed." But . . . the power to execute the laws starts and ends with the laws Congress has enacted.

The great office of President is not a weak and powerless one. The President represents the people and is their spokesman in domestic and foreign affairs. The office is respected more than any other in the land. It gives a position of leadership that is unique. The power to formulate policies and mould opinion inheres in the Presidency and conditions our national life. The impact of the man and the philosophy he represents may at times be thwarted by the Congress. Stalemates may occur when emergencies mount and the Nation suffers for lack of harmonious, reciprocal action between the White House and Capitol Hill. That is a risk inherent in our system of separation of powers. The tragedy of such stalemates might be avoided by allowing the President the use of some legislative authority. The Framers with memories of the tyrannies produced by a blending of executive and legislative power rejected that

[6] **Question:** Where Black held that Congress merely declined to authorize Truman to seize the steel mill, Justice Felix Frankfurter goes further. He suggests that Congress's failure to enact such authorization in the Taft-Hartley Act was the equivalent of an explicit *rejection* of the president's claimed power "as though it had said so in so many words." But absent a statute that explicitly states "the president cannot do X," how does he know that Congress's failure to pass a provision amounted to a congressional rejection of that provision?

political arrangement. . . . We could not sanction the seizures and condemnations of the steel plants in this case without reading Article II as giving the President not only the power to execute the laws but to make some. . . .[7]

■ MR. JUSTICE JACKSON, concurring in the judgment and opinion of the Court.[8]

That comprehensive and undefined presidential powers hold both practical advantages and grave dangers for the country will impress anyone who has served as legal adviser to a President in time of transition and public anxiety. While an interval of detached reflection may temper teachings of that experience, they probably are a more realistic influence on my views than the conventional materials of judicial decision which seem unduly to accentuate doctrine and legal fiction. But as we approach the question of presidential power, we half overcome mental hazards by recognizing them. The opinions of judges, no less than executives and publicists, often suffer the infirmity of confusing the issue of a power's validity with the cause it is invoked to promote, of confounding the permanent executive office with its temporary occupant. The tendency is strong to emphasize transient results upon policies—such as wages or stabilization—and lose sight of enduring consequences upon the balanced power structure of our Republic.

A judge, like an executive adviser, may be surprised at the poverty of really useful and unambiguous authority applicable to concrete problems of executive power as they actually present themselves. Just what our forefathers did envision, or would have envisioned had they foreseen modern conditions, must be divined from materials almost as enigmatic as the dreams Joseph was called upon to interpret for Pharaoh. A century and a half of partisan debate and scholarly speculation yields no net result but only supplies more or less apt quotations from respected sources on each side of any question. They largely cancel each other. And court decisions are indecisive because of the judicial practice of dealing with the largest questions in the most narrow way.

The actual art of governing under our Constitution does not and cannot conform to judicial definitions of the power of any of its branches based on isolated clauses or even single Articles torn from context. While the Constitution diffuses power the better to secure liberty, it also contemplates that practice will integrate the dispersed powers into a workable government. It enjoins upon its branches separateness but interdependence, autonomy but reciprocity. Presidential powers are not fixed but fluctuate, depending upon their disjunction or conjunction with those of Congress. We may well begin by a somewhat over-simplified grouping of practical situations in which a President may doubt, or others may challenge, his powers, and by distinguishing roughly the legal consequences of this factor of relativity.[9]

---

7 **Question:** Justice William O. Douglas offers a compelling argument for why the president is a powerful figure even absent the unilateral power to act domestically with the force of law. But how would Douglas account for the Emancipation Proclamation? Under his analysis, was the proclamation unconstitutional?

8 **As You Read, Consider:** Justice Robert Jackson's opinion is the most famous and widely cited of all of the *Youngstown Sheet & Tube Co. v. Sawyer* opinions. He begins by alluding to his background as President Franklin D. Roosevelt's attorney general. As attorney general, he issued opinions defending the inherent power of the presidency to seize factories. How does this background shape his opinion?

9 **Questions:** The most widely quoted element of Jackson's opinion is his "somewhat over-simplified grouping" of examples in which a presidential action may be challenged. Everything that any president does can fit within one of these three categories. Indeed, everything that any member of the executive branch does can fit within one of these categories. Can you think of a Supreme Court case that fits within each category? In which category would you find *Myers v. United States* (discussing the removal of executive officers), *Hirabayashi v. United States* (discussing the curfew of Japanese Americans), and the Emancipation Proclamation?

1. When the President acts pursuant to an express or implied authorization of Congress, his authority is at its maximum, for it includes all that he possesses in his own right plus all that Congress can delegate. In these circumstances, and in these only, may he be said (for what it may be worth) to personify the federal sovereignty. If his act is held unconstitutional under these circumstances, it usually means that the Federal Government as an undivided whole lacks power. A seizure executed by the President pursuant to an Act of Congress would be supported by the strongest of presumptions and the widest latitude of judicial interpretation, and the burden of persuasion would rest heavily upon any who might attack it.

2. When the President acts in absence of either a congressional grant or denial of authority, he can only rely upon his own independent powers, but there is a zone of twilight in which he and Congress may have concurrent authority, or in which its distribution is uncertain. Therefore, congressional inertia, indifference or quiescence may sometimes, at least as a practical matter, enable, if not invite, measures on independent presidential responsibility. In this area, any actual test of power is likely to depend on the imperatives of events and contemporary imponderables rather than on abstract theories of law.

3. When the President takes measures incompatible with the expressed or implied will of Congress, his power is at its lowest ebb, for then he can rely only upon his own constitutional powers minus any constitutional powers of Congress over the matter. Courts can sustain exclusive presidential control in such a case only by disabling the Congress from acting upon the subject. Presidential claim to a power at once so conclusive and preclusive must be scrutinized with caution, for what is at stake is the equilibrium established by our constitutional system.[10]

Into which of these classifications does this executive seizure of the steel industry fit? It is eliminated from the first by admission, for it is conceded that no congressional authorization exists for this seizure. That takes away also the support of the many precedents and declarations which were made in relation, and must be confined, to this category.

Can it then be defended under flexible tests available to the second category? It seems clearly eliminated from that class because Congress has not left seizure of private property an open field but has covered it by three statutory policies inconsistent with this seizure. . . . None of these were invoked. In choosing a different and inconsistent way of his own, the President cannot claim that it is necessitated or invited by failure of Congress to legislate upon the occasions, grounds and methods for seizure of industrial properties.[11]

This leaves the current seizure to be justified only by the severe tests under the third grouping, where it can be supported only by any remainder of executive power after subtraction of such powers as Congress may have over the subject. In short, we can sustain the President only by holding that seizure of such strike-bound industries is within his domain and beyond control by Congress. Thus, this Court's first review of such seizures occurs under circumstances which leave presidential

3 categories

---

[10] **Question:** The most controversial of Jackson's three categories is his third: the president's power "at its lowest ebb." His description of this category appears to recognize that there may be examples when a president's action might overcome a statute specifically prohibiting the president from acting. Do the other justices in the majority appear to recognize such a category?

[11] **Questions:** Why doesn't Jackson believe that this case falls within his second category? Truman has acted "in the absence of either a congressional grant or denial of authority," right? Moreover, he invited Congress to condemn or ratify his conduct, yet Congress never acted. Where does Jackson locate a congressional *denial* of authority in this case?

power most vulnerable to attack and in the least favorable of possible constitutional postures.

I did not suppose, and I am not persuaded, that history leaves it open to question, at least in the courts, that the executive branch, like the Federal Government as a whole, possesses only delegated powers. The purpose of the Constitution was not only to grant power, but to keep it from getting out of hand. However, because the President does not enjoy unmentioned powers does not mean that the mentioned ones should be narrowed by a niggardly construction. Some clauses could be made almost unworkable, as well as immutable, by refusal to indulge some latitude of interpretation for changing times. I have heretofore, and do now, give to the enumerated powers the scope and elasticity afforded by what seem to be reasonable, practical implications instead of the rigidity dictated by a doctrinaire textualism.

The Solicitor General seeks the power of seizure in three clauses of the Executive Article, the first reading, "The executive Power shall be vested in a President of the United States of America." Lest I be thought to exaggerate, I quote the interpretation which his brief puts upon it: "In our view, this clause constitutes a grant of all the executive powers of which the Government is capable." If that be true, it is difficult to see why the forefathers bothered to add several specific items, including some trifling ones.[12]

The example of such unlimited executive power that must have most impressed the forefathers was the prerogative exercised by George III, and the description of its evils in the Declaration of Independence leads me to doubt that they were creating their new Executive in his image. Continental European examples were no more appealing. And if we seek instruction from our own times, we can match it only from the executive powers in those governments we disparagingly describe as totalitarian. I cannot accept the view that this clause is a grant in bulk of all conceivable executive power but regard it as an allocation to the presidential office of the generic powers thereafter stated.

The clause on which the Government next relies is that "The President shall be Commander in Chief of the Army and Navy of the United States . . . ." These cryptic words have given rise to some of the most persistent controversies in our constitutional history. Of course, they imply something more than an empty title. But just what authority goes with the name has plagued presidential advisers who would not waive or narrow it by nonassertion yet cannot say where it begins or ends. It undoubtedly puts the Nation's armed forces under presidential command. Hence, this loose appellation is sometimes advanced as support for any presidential action, internal or external, involving use of force, the idea being that it vests power to do anything, anywhere, that can be done with an army or navy.

That seems to be the logic of an argument tendered at our bar—that the President having, on his own responsibility, sent American troops abroad derives from that act "affirmative power" to seize the means of producing a supply of steel for them. To quote, "Perhaps the most forceful illustration of the scope of Presidential power in this connection is the fact that American troops in Korea, whose safety and effectiveness are so directly involved here, were sent to the field by an exercise of

---

[12] **Question:** The solicitor general appears to be referencing Alexander Hamilton's defense of the proclamation of neutrality. This reading of the Vesting Clause was accepted by the Court in *Myers*. Why does Jackson dismiss it? Consider that Jackson took a leave of absence from the Supreme Court in 1946 to serve as the chief prosecutor for the United States in the Nuremberg trials of former leaders of Nazi Germany.

the President's constitutional powers." Thus, it is said, he has invested himself with "war powers."

I cannot foresee all that it might entail if the Court should indorse this argument. Nothing in our Constitution is plainer than that declaration of a war is entrusted only to Congress. Of course, a state of war may in fact exist without a formal declaration. But no doctrine that the Court could promulgate would seem to me more sinister and alarming than that a President whose conduct of foreign affairs is so largely uncontrolled, and often even is unknown, can vastly enlarge his mastery over the internal affairs of the country by his own commitment of the Nation's armed forces to some foreign venture. I do not, however, find it necessary or appropriate to consider the legal status of the Korean enterprise to discountenance argument based on it.[13]

Assuming that we are in a war *de facto,* whether it is or is not a war *de jure,* does that empower the Commander in Chief to seize industries he thinks necessary to supply our army? The Constitution expressly places in Congress power "to raise and *support* Armies" and "to *provide* and *maintain* a Navy." (Emphasis supplied.) This certainly lays upon Congress primary responsibility for supplying the armed forces. Congress alone controls the raising of revenues and their appropriation and may determine in what manner and by what means they shall be spent for military and naval procurement. I suppose no one would doubt that Congress can take over war supply as a Government enterprise. On the other hand, if Congress sees fit to rely on free private enterprise collectively bargaining with free labor for support and maintenance of our armed forces, can the Executive, because of lawful disagreements incidental to that process, seize the facility for operation upon Government-imposed terms?

There are indications that the Constitution did not contemplate that the title Commander in Chief *of the Army and Navy* will constitute him also Commander in Chief of the country, its industries and its inhabitants. He has no monopoly of "war powers," whatever they are. While Congress cannot deprive the President of the command of the army and navy, only Congress can provide him an army or navy to command. It is also empowered to make rules for the "Government and Regulation of land and naval Forces," by which it may to some unknown extent impinge upon even command functions.

That military powers of the Commander in Chief were not to supersede representative government of internal affairs seems obvious from the Constitution and from elementary American history. Time out of mind, and even now in many parts of the world, a military commander can seize private housing to shelter his troops. Not so, however, in the United States, for the Third Amendment says, "No Soldier shall, in time of peace be quartered in any house, without the consent of the Owner, nor in time of war, but in a manner to be prescribed by law." Thus, even in war time, his seizure of needed military housing must be authorized by Congress. It also was expressly left to Congress to "provide for calling forth the Militia to execute the Laws of the Union, suppress Insurrections and repel Invasions . . . ." Such a limitation on the command power, written at a time when the militia rather than a standing army was contemplated as the military weapon of the Republic, underscores the Constitution's policy that Congress, not the Executive, should control utilization of the war power as an instrument of domestic policy. Congress, fulfilling that function, has authorized the President to use the army to enforce certain civil rights. On the other hand. Congress has forbidden him to use the army for the purpose of executing

---

[13] **Questions:** Does this passage—and opinion—suggest that Truman acted unconstitutionally when he unilaterally sent troops overseas to fight in Korea? If not, why not? Why does Jackson even mention the Korean War?

general laws except when *expressly* authorized by the Constitution or by Act of Congress.

While broad claims under this rubric often have been made, advice to the President in specific matters usually has carried overtones that powers, even under this head, are measured by the command functions usual to the topmost officer of the army and navy. Even then, heed has been taken of any efforts of Congress to negative his authority.

We should not use this occasion to circumscribe, much less to contract, the lawful role of the President as Commander in Chief. I should indulge the widest latitude of interpretation to sustain his exclusive function to command the instruments of national force, at least when turned against the outside world for the security of our society. But, when it is turned inward, not because of rebellion but because of a lawful economic struggle between industry and labor, it should have no such indulgence. His command power is not such an absolute as might be implied from that office in a militaristic system but is subject to limitations consistent with a constitutional Republic whose law and policy-making branch is a representative Congress. The purpose of lodging dual titles in one man was to insure that the civilian would control the military, not to enable the military to subordinate the presidential office. No penance would ever expiate the sin against free government of holding that a President can escape control of executive powers by law through assuming his military role. What the power of command may include I do not try to envision, but I think it is not a military prerogative, without support of law, to seize persons or property because they are important or even essential for the military and naval establishment.

The third clause in which the Solicitor General finds seizure powers is that "he shall take Care that the Laws be faithfully executed . . . ." That authority must be matched against words of the Fifth Amendment that "No person shall be . . . deprived of life, liberty or property, without due process of law . . . ." One gives a governmental authority that reaches so far as there is law, the other gives a private right that authority shall go no farther. These signify about all there is of the principle that ours is a government of laws, not of men, and that we submit ourselves to rulers only if under rules.

The Solicitor General lastly grounds support of the seizure upon nebulous, inherent powers never expressly granted but said to have accrued to the office from the customs and claims of preceding administrations. The plea is for a resulting power to deal with a crisis or an emergency according to the necessities of the case, the unarticulated assumption being that necessity knows no law.[14]

Loose and irresponsible use of adjectives colors all nonlegal and much legal discussion of presidential powers. "Inherent" powers, "implied" powers, "incidental" powers, "plenary" powers, "war" powers and "emergency" powers are used, often interchangeably and without fixed or ascertainable meanings.

The vagueness and generality of the clauses that set forth presidential powers afford a plausible basis for pressures within and without an administration for presidential action beyond that supported by those whose responsibility it is to defend his actions in court. The claim of inherent and unrestricted presidential powers has long been a persuasive dialectical weapon in political controversy. While it is not surprising that counsel should grasp support from such unadjudicated claims of power, a judge cannot accept self-serving press statements of the attorney for one

---

14 **Question:** The solicitor general's argument here is similar to statements that Jackson made as attorney general. In light of these statements, what does Jackson think should be the role of an executive-branch lawyer?

of the interested parties as authority in answering a constitutional question, even if the advocate was himself. . . .

The appeal, however, that we declare the existence of inherent powers *ex necessitate* to meet an emergency asks us to do what many think would be wise, although it is something the forefathers omitted. They knew what emergencies were, knew the pressures they engender for authoritative action, knew, too, how they afford a ready pretext for usurpation. We may also suspect that they suspected that emergency powers would tend to kindle emergencies. Aside from suspension of the privilege of the writ of habeas corpus in time of rebellion or invasion, when the public safety may require it, they made no express provision for exercise of extraordinary authority because of a crisis. I do not think we rightfully may so amend their work, and, if we could, I am not convinced it would be wise to do so, although many modern nations have forthrightly recognized that war and economic crises may upset the normal balance between liberty and authority. Their experience with emergency powers may not be irrelevant to the argument here that we should say that the Executive, of his own volition, can invest himself with undefined emergency powers.

Germany, after the First World War, framed the Weimar Constitution, designed to secure her liberties in the Western tradition. However, the President of the Republic, without concurrence of the Reichstag, was empowered temporarily to suspend any or all individual rights if public safety and order were seriously disturbed or endangered. This proved a temptation to every government, whatever its shade of opinion, and in 13 years suspension of rights was invoked on more than 250 occasions. Finally, Hitler persuaded President Von Hindenberg to suspend all such rights, and they were never restored. . . .[15]

Great Britain also has fought both World Wars under a sort of temporary dictatorship created by legislation. As Parliament is not bound by written constitutional limitations, it established a crisis government simply by delegation to its Ministers of a larger measure than usual of its own unlimited power, which is exercised under its supervision by Ministers whom it may dismiss. This has been called the "high-water mark in the voluntary surrender of liberty," but, as Churchill put it, "Parliament stands custodian of these surrendered liberties, and its most sacred duty will be to restore them in their fullness when victory has crowned our exertions and our perseverance." Thus, parliamentary control made emergency powers compatible with freedom.

This contemporary foreign experience may be inconclusive as to the wisdom of lodging emergency powers somewhere in a modern government. But it suggests that emergency powers are consistent with free government only when their control is lodged elsewhere than in the Executive who exercises them. That is the safeguard that would be nullified by our adoption of the "inherent powers" formula. . . .

In the practical working of our Government we already have evolved a technique within the framework of the Constitution by which normal executive powers may be considerably expanded to meet an emergency. Congress may and has granted extraordinary authorities which lie dormant in normal times but may be called into play by the Executive in war or upon proclamation of a national emergency. In 1939, upon congressional request, the Attorney General listed ninety-nine such separate statutory grants by Congress of emergency or wartime executive powers. They were invoked from time to time as need appeared. Under this procedure we retain Government by law—special, temporary law, perhaps, but law nonetheless. The

---

15 **Question:** Once again, Jackson is alluding to expertise he gained as the United States' chief prosecutor at the Nuremberg trials. Is his reference to the history of other countries persuasive for how to interpret the *United States Constitution*?

public may know the extent and limitations of the powers than can be asserted, and persons affected may be informed from the statute of their rights and duties.

In view of the ease, expedition and safety with which Congress can grant and has granted large emergency powers, certainly ample to embrace this crisis, I am quite unimpressed with the argument that we should affirm possession of them without statute. Such power either has no beginning or it has no end. If it exists, it need submit to no legal restraint. I am not alarmed that it would plunge us straightway into dictatorship, but it is at least a step in that wrong direction.[16]

As to whether there is imperative necessity for such powers, it is relevant to note the gap that exists between the President's paper powers and his real powers. The Constitution does not disclose the measure of the actual controls wielded by the modern presidential office. That instrument must be understood as an Eighteenth-Century sketch of a government hoped for, not as a blueprint of the Government that is. Vast accretions of federal power, eroded from that reserved by the States, have magnified the scope of presidential activity. Subtle shifts take place in the centers of real power that do not show on the face of the Constitution.

Executive power has the advantage of concentration in a single head in whose choice the whole Nation has a part, making him the focus of public hopes and expectations. In drama, magnitude and finality his decisions so far overshadow any others that almost alone he fills the public eye and ear. No other personality in public life can begin to compete with him in access to the public mind through modern methods of communications. By his prestige as head of state and his influence upon public opinion he exerts a leverage upon those who are supposed to check and balance his power which often cancels their effectiveness.

Moreover, rise of the party system has made a significant extraconstitutional supplement to real executive power. No appraisal of his necessities is realistic which overlooks that he heads a political system as well as a legal system. Party loyalties and interests, sometimes more binding than law, extend his effective control into branches of government other than his own and he often may win, as a political leader, what he cannot command under the Constitution. . . . I cannot be brought to believe that this country will suffer if the Court refuses further to aggrandize the presidential office, already so potent and so relatively immune from judicial review, at the expense of Congress. . . .

The essence of our free Government is "leave to live by no man's leave, underneath the law"—to be governed by those impersonal forces which we call law. Our Government is fashioned to fulfill this concept so far as humanly possible. The Executive, except for recommendation and veto, has no legislative power. The executive action we have here originates in the individual will of the President and represents an exercise of authority without law. . . . With all its defects, delays and inconveniences, men have discovered no technique for long preserving free government except that the Executive be under the law, and that the law be made by parliamentary deliberations. . . .

---

[16] **Questions:** Jackson indicates here that his opinion rests, in part, on the "ease" with which Congress can grant and contract emergency powers. Does this suggest that he might have arrived at a different conclusion if he could have predicted the far less responsive Congress of the twenty-first century? Does the responsiveness of Congress shape your view about the appropriate use of executive power?

To this end, consider the Deferred Action for Childhood Arrivals (DACA) program, discussed in the note after this case. Should a president have the discretion to act when Congress fails to act for a long time on an important national policy?

■ MR. CHIEF JUSTICE VINSON, with whom MR. JUSTICE REED and MR. JUSTICE MINTON join, dissenting.[17]

[T]hose who suggest that this is a case involving extraordinary powers should be mindful that these are extraordinary times. A world not yet recovered from the devastation of World War II has been forced to face the threat of another and more terrifying global conflict.

Accepting in full measure its responsibility in the world community, the United States was instrumental in securing adoption of the United Nations Charter, approved by the Senate by a vote of 89 to 2. The first purpose of the United Nations is to "maintain international peace and security, and to that end: to take effective collective measures for the prevention and removal of threats to the peace, and for the suppression of acts of aggression or other breaches of the peace, ..." In 1950, when the United Nations called upon member nations "to render every assistance" to repel aggression in Korea, the United States furnished its vigorous support. For almost two full years, our armed forces have been fighting in Korea, suffering casualties of over 108,000 men. Hostilities have not abated. . . . Congressional support of the action in Korea has been manifested by provisions for increased military manpower and equipment and for economic stabilization. . . .

Following the attack in Korea, the President asked for authority to requisition property and to allocate and fix priorities for scarce goods. In the Defense Production Act of 1950, Congress granted the powers requested and, *in addition*, granted power to stabilize prices and wages and to provide for settlement of labor disputes arising in the defense program. The Defense Production Act was extended in 1951, a Senate Committee noting that in the dislocation caused by the programs for purchase of military equipment "lies the seed of an economic disaster that might well destroy the military might we are straining to build." Significantly, the Committee examined the problem "in terms of just one commodity, steel," and found "a graphic picture of the over-all inflationary danger growing out of reduced civilian supplies and rising incomes." Even before Korea, steel production at levels above theoretical 100% capacity was not capable of supplying civilian needs alone. Since Korea, the tremendous military demand for steel has far exceeded the increases in productive capacity. . . .

The President has the duty to execute the foregoing legislative programs. Their successful execution depends upon continued production of steel and stabilized prices for steel. Accordingly, when the collective bargaining agreements between the Nation's steel producers and their employees, represented by the United Steel Workers, were due to expire . . ., and a strike shutting down the entire basic steel industry was threatened, the President acted to avert a complete shutdown of steel production. . . .

Twelve days passed without action by Congress. On April 21, 1952, the President sent a letter to the President of the Senate in which he again described the purpose and need for his action and again stated his position that "The Congress can, if it wishes, reject the course of action I have followed in this matter." Congress has not so acted to this date. . . .

Plaintiffs do not remotely suggest any basis for rejecting the President's finding that *any* stoppage of steel production would immediately place the Nation in peril. . . .

[17] **Question:** Vinson observes that Truman is acting to enforce a ratified treaty—the United Nations Charter. He also reads the Defense Production Act as authorizing the president to act flexibly in the national defense. Yet Frankfurter and Jackson interpreted Congress's actions as if Congress *rejected* the president's conduct. Who do you think offers a more persuasive reading of the situation?

At the time of seizure there was not, and there is not now, the slightest evidence to justify the belief that any strike will be of short duration. . . . [O]ur soldiers and our allies will hardly be cheered with the assurance that the ammunition upon which their lives depend will be forthcoming—"sooner or later," or, in other words, "too little and too late."

Accordingly, if the President has any power under the Constitution to meet a critical situation in the absence of express statutory authorization, there is no basis whatever for criticizing the exercise of such power in this case. . . .

[There are dozens of examples in which presidents earlier exercised power without congressional authorization, including President George Washington's proclamation of neutrality; President John Adams's arrest warrant of Jonathan Robbins; President Thomas Jefferson's initiative in the Louisiana Purchase; and "the Emancipation Proclamation, issued in aid of the successful prosecution of the War Between the States, but wholly without statutory authority"; President Grover Cleveland's use of troops in the railroad strike of 1894; seizures of industrial facilities by Presidents Theodore Roosevelt, William Howard Taft, Woodrow Wilson, and Franklin D. Roosevelt; and President Harry S. Truman's initiation of the Korean War.]

The diversity of views expressed in the six opinions of the majority, the lack of reference to authoritative precedent, . . . the complete disregard of the uncontroverted facts showing the gravity of the emergency and the temporary nature of the taking all serve to demonstrate how far afield one must go to affirm the order of the District Court.[18]

The broad executive power granted by Article II to an officer on duty 365 days a year cannot, it is said, be invoked to avert disaster. Instead, the President must confine himself to sending a message to Congress recommending action. Under this messenger-boy concept of the Office, the President cannot even act to preserve legislative programs from destruction so that Congress will have something left to act upon. . . .

NOTE: AFTERMATH OF *YOUNGSTOWN*

Within hours of the Supreme Court's decision in *Youngstown*, the government gave up possession of the steel mills and the nation's steelworkers went on strike. A month into the strike, "reserves of defense steel melted toward the vanishing point," shutting down production of tanks, weapons, and ammunition. A. H. Raskin, *Steel's 'Big 6' Join in Union Shop Veto*, N.Y. Times, July 3, 1952, at 1. The strike finally ended only after Truman convinced the negotiators to compromise because the United States was going to lose the Korean War without steel. *See* Austin Stevens, *Truman Summons Steel Disputants as Defense Bogs*, N.Y. Times, July 24, 1952, at 1.

In the years since 1952, *Youngstown* has had a profound effect on the constitutional law of presidential power: Justice Robert Jackson's three categories have become the organizing metaphor for understanding Article II.

Category 1. Exercising Jackson's first category—presidential power plus congressional authority—presidents have long continued to invoke the Militia Acts of 1792, as amended, to execute federal law. Only two years after

[18] **Question:** Vinson appears to suggest that the majority opinions would cast doubt on this range of historical actions, including the Emancipation Proclamation. Do you agree?

Youngstown, the Supreme Court declared racial segregation in schools unconstitutional in *Brown v. Board of Education* (*Brown I*), 347 U.S. 493 (1954). Shortly afterward, President Dwight D. Eisenhower invoked the Militia Acts to federalize the Arkansas National Guard and to use federal troops to desegregate the Little Rock Central High School. *See* Exec. Order No. 10,730, 22 Fed. Reg. 7628 (Sep. 24, 1957); 41 Op. Att'y Gen. 313 (1957); *Cooper v. Aaron*, 358 U.S. 1 (1958). President John F. Kennedy did the same thing to suppress rioting by white people against the desegregation of downtown Birmingham and the University of Mississippi. *See* Exec. Order No. 11,053, 27 Fed. Reg. 9681 (Sep. 30, 1962); Exec. Order No. 11,118, 28 Fed. Reg. 9863 (Sep. 10, 1963); *Alabama v. United States*, 373 U.S. 545 (1963); *United States v. Barnett*, 346 F.2d 99 (5th Cir. 1965). President Lyndon Johnson federalized the Alabama National Guard to protect civil rights protestors marching from Selma to Montgomery. *See* Exec. Order No. 11,207, 30 Fed. Reg. 3743 (Mar. 20, 1965); *Williams v. Wallace*, 240 F. Supp. 100 (M.D. Ala. 1965). And so on.

Congress has also continued to grant presidents peacetime and wartime emergency powers. Most of these are codified in two laws: the National Emergencies Act of 1976, Pub. L. No. 94–412, 90 Stat. 1255, and the International Emergency Economic Powers Act of 1977, Pub. L. No. 95–223, 91 Stat. 1626. These acts provide that "the President is authorized to declare [a] national emergency"—after which the president can invoke any number of powers out of a list of hundreds. 90 Stat. 1255. Today, there are dozens of "national emergencies" in effect, including one declared by President Jimmy Carter in 1979 after the Iran hostage crisis.

In February 2019, President Donald Trump controversially declared a national emergency "concerning the southern border of the United States" and invoked various emergency powers to reallocate funding to build a wall along the border. Proclamation No. 9844, 84 Fed. Reg. 4, 949 (Feb. 15, 2019). Several district courts soon declared the reallocation unlawful and issued injunctions prohibiting the president from reapportioning the funds. *See, e.g., Sierra Club v. Trump*, 379 F. Supp. 3d 883 (N.D. Cal. 2019). By the time the Supreme Court granted certiorari to consider the issue, however, President Joe Biden had rescinded his predecessor's declaration of national emergency. *See Biden v. Sierra Club*, 141 S. Ct. 1289 (2021).

Categories 2 and 3. As for Jackson's second and third categories, presidents now routinely argue that unilateral exercises of power either have been silently ratified by Congress or represent illustrations of executive authority with which Congress cannot interfere. Perhaps the most notable recent example is the Deferred Action for Childhood Arrivals (DACA) program.

The administration of President Barack Obama announced the program in a 2012 memorandum whose title implicitly defended the president's unilateral power to create it: "Exercising Prosecutorial Discretion with Respect to Individuals Who Came to the United States as Children." Memorandum from Janet Napolitano, Sec'y of Homeland Sec., Exercising Prosecutorial Discretion with Respect to Individuals Who Came to the United States as Children 1 (June 15, 2012) [hereinafter Napolitano

Memorandum]. This and a follow-on memorandum in 2014 explained that "prosecutorial discretion"—deciding how to allocate limited resources in enforcing federal law—is exclusively "within the authority of the Executive Branch." *Id.*; Memorandum from Jeh Charles Johnson, Sec'y of Homeland Sec., Exercising Prosecutorial Discretion with Respect to Individuals Who Came to the United States as Children and with Respect to Certain Individuals Who Are Parents of U.S. Citizens or Permanent Residents 3 (Nov. 20, 2014) [hereinafter Johnson Memorandum]. Because federal immigration law requires the executive branch to deport millions more people than the government practically can deport at any given time, the memos concluded that, as a matter of discretion, the executive branch shouldn't deport people who came to the United States as children, who went to school, and who haven't been convicted of any serious crimes. *See* Napolitano Memorandum, *supra*, at 1–2; Johnson Memorandum, *supra*, at 4. The memos also concluded that in order to promote the humane enforcement of federal law, the executive branch could authorize these beneficiaries of "deferred action" to work in the United States. *See* Napolitano Memorandum, *supra*, at 1–2; Johnson Memorandum, *supra*, at 4. The 2014 memo also attempted to place DACA within *Youngstown*'s first category: "Although deferred action is not expressly conferred by statute, the practice is referenced and therefore endorsed by implication in several federal statutes." Johnson Memorandum, *supra*, at 2.

Although the Supreme Court has had opportunities to consider the constitutionality of DACA several times since 2012, it has so far declined to do so. *See, e.g.*, *DHS v. Regents of the Univ. of Cal.*, 140 S. Ct. 1891 (2020) (invalidating on procedural grounds the Trump administration's rescission of DACA). Yet in 2016, an evenly divided Supreme Court upheld a lower-court opinion that invalidated a similar program. *See United States v. Texas*, 579 U.S. 547 (2016). The lower court held that the related program, which applied to the *parents* of U.S. citizens or permanent residents, was "not authorized by statute" and was "manifestly contrary" to the Immigration and Nationality Act. *Texas v. United States*, 809 F.3d 134, 181–84 (5th Cir. 2015).

31.3 THE POWER TO DEPLOY FORCE OVERSEAS

As Justice Robert Jackson observed in his concurring opinion in *Youngstown Sheet & Tube Co. v. Sawyer*, one of the contentions made by government lawyers to justify President Harry Truman's seizure of the steel mills was "the fact that American troops in Korea, whose safety and effectiveness are so directly involved here, were sent to the field by an exercise of the President's constitutional powers." 343 U.S. 579, 642 (1952). Although Jackson didn't consider it "necessary or appropriate to consider the legal status of the Korean enterprise," *id.* at 643, Truman's decision to send troops overseas without congressional authorization proved to be as important a legal precedent as *Youngstown* itself. *See* Mary L. Dudziak, Opinion, *The Toxic Legacy of the Korean War*, Wash. Post, Mar. 1, 2019. Never before had a president committed the United States to such a major overseas conflict without a declaration of war, much less without prior approval by Congress. Beyond his powers as commander in chief, the only legal authorities that the president could invoke were the United States' treaty commitments to the United Nations (U.N.) and a U.N. Security Council resolution requesting that the United States defend South Korea. *Authority of the President to Repel the Attack in Korea*, 23 Dep't of State Bull. 173 (1950).

Early examples of overseas deployment of force

Before 1950, presidents had, at times, engaged in armed conflict without the prior consent of Congress. For example, President Abraham Lincoln responded by himself to the outbreak of the Civil War—something the Supreme Court upheld in the *Prize Cases* as the duty "to resist force by force." 67 U.S. (2 Black) 635, 668 (1863). However, the Court characterized Lincoln's actions as a response to an "invasion." *Id.* Sending soldiers overseas was arguably different.

Nevertheless, a few years before the *Prize Cases*, in *Durand v. Hollins*, 8 F. Cas. 111 (C.C.S.D.N.Y. 1860) (No. 4186), Justice Samuel Nelson, riding circuit, upheld President James Buchanan's power to order a U.S. gunship to bombard a town in present-day Nicaragua. The gunboat destroyed the town with the ostensible purpose of protecting U.S. citizens building a canal nearby, and this purpose was good enough for Nelson. "Under our system of government, the citizen abroad is as much entitled to protection as the citizen at home," he wrote, "and the protection, to be effectual or of any avail, may, not unfrequently, require the most prompt and decided action" by the president. *Durand*, 8 F. Cas. at 112.

By the 1950s there had been at least fifty instances, most without congressional authorization, in which presidents had deployed land troops to protect U.S. citizens living in foreign countries. All of these, however, were limited engagements, including the landing of U.S. Marines on "the shores of Tripoli" in 1805 and President William McKinley's deployment of troops to China to suppress the Boxer Rebellion in 1900. *See generally* U.S. Dep't of State, *Right to Protect Citizens in Foreign Countries by Landing Forces* (3d rev. ed. 1934). Later in the twentieth century, President Theodore Roosevelt unilaterally deployed U.S. soldiers to assist a coup in Panama and deployed the U.S. fleet around the world to impress Japan and European powers. *See* Edmund Morris, *Theodore Rex* 282–90, 494–95 (2002). President Franklin D. Roosevelt, meanwhile, unilaterally transferred destroyers to Great Britain before the United States entered World War II. *See* Robert H. Jackson, *Opinion on Exchange of Over-Age Destroyers for Naval and Air Bases*, 34 Am. J. Int'l L. 728 (1940).

Korean War

But the Korean War dwarfed all of these prior examples. Unlike the Civil War, which was characterized as a response to an invasion of the

United States, Truman called his decision to deploy troops a "police action." Anthony Leviero, *U.S. "Not at War" President Asserts*, N.Y. Times, June 30, 1950, at 1. Even as 30,000 U.S. troops landed in South Korea, the president purposefully chose not to seek congressional approval because that would make it more difficult for future presidents to deal with emergencies. *See* David McCullough, *Truman* 789 (1992). (Congress nevertheless continued to fund the military and express its support for U.N. peacekeeping efforts.) And unlike prior deployments of small numbers of troops abroad, Truman deployed over 250,000 U.S. soldiers into a combat zone for a conflict that ultimately lasted for three years, led to tens of thousands of American casualties, and cost the United States billions of dollars. Because neither Congress nor the Supreme Court attempted to stop the Korean War, it marked an important new phase in the president's power to deploy troops overseas.

NATO and the great debate

The Korean War was not the only action of Truman's that enhanced the president's war powers. When the United States helped to establish the North Atlantic Treaty Organization (NATO) a year earlier, the United States agreed by treaty that it would consider an attack on any NATO member an attack on itself. *See* North Atlantic Treaty art. 5, Apr. 4, 1949, 63 Stat. 2241, 34 U.N.T.S. 243. The United States also promised to "assist the Party or Parties so attacked by taking forthwith . . . such action as it deems necessary, including the use of armed force." *Id.* Several critics observed that, as a practical matter, the president alone would be responsible for "taking forthwith . . . such action." *See* Edward S. Corwin, *Who Has the Power to Make War?*, N.Y. Times, July 31, 1949, at 11. And as a legal matter, the treaty appeared to disrupt the distinction between Congress's power to declare war and the president's power to repel an invasion because it made an attack against a NATO ally an attack on the United States. *Id.* at 14.

In January 1951, Senator Kenneth Wherry of Nebraska responded to NATO's disruptive effect by introducing a Senate resolution declaring that "no ground forces of the United States should be assigned to duty in the European area for the purposes of the North Atlantic Treaty"—at least until Congress could adopt a policy regarding their deployment. 97 Cong. Rec. 94 (1951). This led Truman to respond at a press conference that "[u]nder the President's constitutional powers as Commander in Chief of the Armed forces he has the authority to send troops anywhere in the world." *Public Papers of the Presidents of the United States: Harry S. Truman, 1951*, at 19 (1965). The president's supporters explained that as the commander in chief, with the duty to take care that treaties as well as statutes be faithfully executed, the president already had authorization under the North Atlantic Treaty itself to deploy four divisions—tens of thousands of troops—for use by NATO. *See* Henry Steele Commager, *Presidential Power: The Issue Analyzed*, N.Y. Times,

Jan. 14, 1951, at 11. "But, of course," the president said, "the Congress would be consulted before we do it, as we always do." *Public Papers of the Presidents, supra*, at 19.

After what was later called the "great debate" over the president's war powers, Congress decided not to challenge the president's authority to defend NATO allies. *See Assignment of Ground Forces of the United States to Duty in the European Area: Hearings Before the S. Comms. on Foreign Relations and Armed Services*, 82d Cong. 92 (1951). Instead, the Senate passed a "sense of the Senate" resolution in which it approved the president's conduct. S. Res. 99, 82d Cong. § 1 (1951). The Senate also weakly requested that "in the interests of sound constitutional processes, and of national unity and understanding, congressional approval should be obtained of any policy requiring the assignment of American troops abroad." *Id.* § 6.

Vietnam War and the War Powers Resolution

With the Korean War and the "great debate" as two significant precedents for the president's power to deploy troops overseas, Truman's successors unilaterally deployed soldiers to dozens of countries, most notably Vietnam. The legal defense for escalation in Vietnam again relied on the president's powers as commander in chief and his power to enforce a treaty—this time the Southeast Asia Collective Defense Treaty, which established the Southeast Asia Treaty Organization (SEATO), the Pacific counterpart to NATO. *See* Leonard C. Meeker, *The Legality of United States Participation in the Defense of Viet Nam*, 54 Dep't of State Bull. 474, 484–85. In 1964, after a U.S. destroyer was allegedly attacked near Vietnam in the Gulf of Tonkin, Congress authorized the president "to take all necessary measures" to repel any attack against U.S. forces or to assist any SEATO allies, including South Vietnam. Joint Resolution of Aug. 10, 1964, Pub. L. No. 88–408, 78 Stat. 384. Even though it wasn't a formal declaration of war, this authorization led President Lyndon Johnson and his successor to deploy almost three million U.S. soldiers to Vietnam.

By 1973, the widespread feeling that the Vietnam War had been a mistake led Congress to enact—over President Richard Nixon's veto—the War Powers Resolution of 1973. The statute declared:

> The constitutional powers of the President as Commander-in-Chief to introduce United States Armed Forces into hostilities, or into situations where imminent involvement in hostilities is clearly indicated by the circumstances, are exercised only pursuant to (1) a declaration of war, (2) specific statutory authorization, or (3) a national emergency created by attack upon the United States, its territories or possessions, or its armed forces.

Pub. L. No. 93–148, 87 Stat. 555, 555. The statute also required that if armed forces were introduced "into hostilities," then the president had to issue a report explaining the situation to Congress within forty-eight hours. *Id.* at 556. If sixty days passed without a declaration of war or specific statutory authorization, then "the President shall terminate any use of United States Armed Forces." *Id.* The statute also required the president to remove any armed forces from hostilities "if the Congress so directs by concurrent resolution." *Id.* at 557. This last provision—a legislative veto—was made ineffective by *INS v. Chadha*, 462 U.S. 919 (1983).

Unilateral presidential action abroad

Despite the paper limits of the War Powers Resolution, presidents have routinely exercised force abroad without Congress. *See generally* Tess Bridgeman, *War Powers Resolution Reporting: Presidential Practice and the Use of Armed Forces Abroad, 1973–2019* (2020). To enforce U.N. Security Council resolutions, provide humanitarian aid, or serve other national interests, President George H. W. Bush unilaterally introduced twenty-eight thousand troops into Somalia; President Bill Clinton ordered air strikes and troop deployments in Bosnia, Haiti, Kosovo, and Afghanistan; President George W. Bush deployed troops to Haiti; President Barack Obama ordered air strikes in Libya and Yemen; President Donald Trump ordered air strikes throughout the Middle East; and President Joe Biden ordered air strikes in Syria. *See* Samuel Moyn, *Humane* 225–32 (2021).

Unilateral presidential action has usually been defended in one of three ways: (1) self-defense, (2) statutory authorizations for the use of military force, and (3) humanitarian intervention.

Self-defense

In a broad invocation of the president's Article II authority to *defend the United States and its citizens from attack*, presidents have claimed the unilateral power to preemptively deploy military action against other countries.

For example, after the terrorist attacks of September 11, 2001, the Department of Justice's Office of Legal Counsel, which provides legal advice to the president, drafted an opinion concluding that it was "beyond question that the President has the plenary constitutional power to take such military actions as he deems necessary and appropriate . . . both to retaliate for those attacks, and to prevent and deter future assaults on the Nation . . . and the lives of its people, whether at home or overseas." 25 Op. O.L.C. 188, 214 (2001) (John Yoo). The opinion added that Congress had no power to "place any limits on the President's determinations as to any terrorist threat, the amount of military force to be used in response, or the method, timing, and nature of the response." *Id.* A second opinion, issued in the lead-up to the Iraq War in 2002, concluded that the president has the independent constitutional authority to invade a country if the president believes that "a change of regime" would remove threatened weapons that "might endanger our national security because of the risk that such weapons either would be targeted against the United States, or would be used to destabilize the region." 26 Op. O.L.C. 1, 8 (2002) (Jay Bybee). Even though Obama rescinded several related opinions, these two remain authoritative precedents within the executive branch for when the United States may act in self-defense. *See* Jack Goldsmith, *The Soleimani Strike: One Person Decides*, Lawfare (Jan. 3, 2020).

Statutory authorizations for the use of military force

Congress has responded to these broad articulations of presidential power not by imposing more limits, but by giving presidents broad statutory authorization to deploy forces overseas without formally declaring war. These statutes have provided a second defense for what begins as or appears to be unilateral presidential action.

For example, in 1991, when President George H. W. Bush claimed the unilateral authority to enforce a U.N. Security Council resolution to defend Kuwait from an invasion by Iraq, Congress authorized the president to conduct the Persian Gulf War. *See* Authorization for the Use of Military Force Against Iraq Resolution of 1991, Pub. L. No. 102–1, 105 Stat. 3. And after President George W. Bush's administration issued its 2002 opinion describing the president's power to invade Iraq, Congress passed a similar resolution that U.S. forces in the region continue to invoke. *See* Authorization for Use of Military Force Against Iraq Resolution of 2002, Pub. L. No. 107–243, 116 Stat. 1498.

The most commonly invoked of these statutory authorizations is one discussed earlier in the context of Congress's power to detain "enemy combatants" (section 13.4). Three days after September 11, 2001, Congress enacted the Authorization for the Use of Military Force (AUMF) of 2001, Pub. L. No. 107–40, 115 Stat. 224. The AUMF authorized the president "to use all necessary and appropriate force against those nations, organizations, or persons he determines . . . aided the terrorist attacks that occurred on September 11, 2001, or harbored such organizations or persons, in order to prevent any future acts of international terrorism against the United States." *Id.*

Since 2001, presidents have invoked the AUMF to initiate armed conflict in almost a dozen countries, including Afghanistan and Yemen. The AUMF has also been invoked to justify the United States' use of unmanned drones to kill targeted individuals—including U.S. citizens—associated with Al-Qaeda. *See* Memorandum from David Barron, Acting Assistant Att'y Gen., Off. of Legal Couns., Applicability of Federal Criminal Laws and the Constitution to Contemplated Lethal Operations Against Shayk Anwar al-Aulaki (July 16, 2010) [hereinafter Barron Memorandum], *reprinted in N.Y. Times Co. v. U.S. Dep't of Justice*, 756 F.3d 100, 124 (2d Cir. 2014). David Barron, then an acting assistant attorney general in the Obama administration, observed in 2010 that the

Supreme Court had interpreted the AUMF to authorize the detention of U.S. citizens caught on a battlefield. Therefore, Barron argued, "just as the AUMF authorizes the military detention of a U.S. citizen captured abroad who is part of an armed force within the scope of the AUMF, it also authorizes the use of 'necessary and appropriate' lethal force against a U.S. citizen who has joined such an armed force." Barron Memorandum, *reprinted in N.Y. Times Co.*, 756 F.3d at 136 (citing *Hamdi v. Rumsfeld*, 542 U.S. 507, 518 (2004)).

31.3.1

Authority to Use Military Force in Libya

35 Op. O.L.C. 20 (Apr. 1, 2011)

As noted, in addition to defending unilateral executive action on grounds of self-defense and statutory authorizations for the use of military force, the executive branch has also defended the president's unilateral power to use force for humanitarian intervention.

In early 2011, amid the Arab Spring—widespread popular demonstrations seeking governmental reform in Tunisia and Egypt—protests began in Libya against the government of Colonel Muammar Qadhafi. By early March, the Libyan government lost control over the eastern part of the country, including the city of Benghazi. To end the protests, the Libyan government began shooting protestors, bombing cities, and otherwise targeting civilians.

The violence escalated to such an extent that the U.N. Security Council unanimously adopted a resolution "condemning the violence" and urging member states to take "necessary measures" short of military force to "facilitate and support the return of humanitarian agencies and make available humanitarian and related assistance" in Libya. S.C. Res. 1970 (Feb. 26, 2011). The U.S. Senate adopted a similar resolution, as did the League of Arab States and other multinational organizations.

Despite these resolutions, on March 17, 2011, Colonel Qadhafi announced that the Libyan government was going to retake the city of Benghazi by force and show "no mercy and no pity." Dan Bilefsky & Mark Landler, *Military Action Against Qaddafi Is Backed by U.N.*, N.Y. Times, Mar. 18, 2011, at A1. Amid fear that the Libyan government was going to massacre a city nearly the size of Charlotte, North Carolina, the U.N. Security Council adopted a resolution that authorized the use of military force to protect civilians. *See* S.C. Res. 1973 (Mar. 17, 2011). The resolution invited member states "to take all necessary measures . . . to protect civilians and civilian populated areas under threat of attack in the Libyan Arab Jamahiriya, including Benghazi, while excluding a foreign occupation force of any form on any part of Libyan territory." *Id.* ¶ 4.

On March 18, President Obama offered the Libyan government an ultimatum requiring an immediate cease-fire and an end to all civilian attacks if it wished to avoid military intervention. The next day, when it appeared that the Libyan government was continuing its assault on Benghazi, the United States launched air strikes against Libyan targets to enforce the U.N. Security Council resolution.

Consistent with the reporting provisions of the War Powers Resolution, Obama provided a report to Congress less than forty-eight hours later. In the report, Obama explained that "as Commander in Chief and Chief Executive," he had the authority to launch "a limited and well-defined mission in support of international efforts to protect civilians and prevent a humanitarian disaster." Press Release, Text of a Letter from the President to the Speaker of the House of Representatives and the President Pro Tempore of the Senate (Mar. 21, 2011). Emphasizing that "[t]he United States has not deployed ground forces into Libya," the president explained why temporary air strikes were justified:

> Qadhafi's continued attacks and threats against civilians and civilian populated areas are of grave concern to neighboring Arab nations and, as expressly stated in U.N. Security Council Resolution 1973, constitute a threat to the region and to international peace and security. His illegitimate use of force not only is causing the deaths of substantial numbers of civilians among his own people, but also is forcing many others to flee to neighboring countries, thereby destabilizing the peace and security of the region. Left unaddressed, the growing instability in Libya could ignite wider instability in the Middle East, with dangerous consequences to the national security interests of the United States. Qadhafi's defiance of the Arab League, as well as the broader international community . . . represents a lawless challenge to the authority of the Security Council and its efforts to preserve stability in the region. Qadhafi has forfeited his responsibility to protect his own citizens and created a serious need for immediate humanitarian assistance and protection, with any delay only putting more civilians at risk. . . .

Id.

The following memo, Authority to use Military Force in Libya, 35 Op. O.L.C. 20 (Apr. 1, 2011), was written a week later by the Department of Justice's Office of Legal Counsel. It illustrates the third ground for executive unilateralism: humanitarian intervention. It also illustrates the executive branch's position on the legal effect of the War Powers Resolution.

■ MEMORANDUM FOR THE ATTORNEY GENERAL FROM CAROLINE D. KRASS, PRINCIPAL DEPUTY ASST. ATT'Y GEN.[19]

[T]he President explained in his March 21, 2011 report to Congress that the use of military force in Libya serves important U.S. interests in preventing instability in the Middle East and preserving the credibility and effectiveness of the United Nations Security Council. The President also stated that he intended the anticipated United States military operations in Libya to be limited in nature, scope, and duration. . . . In addition, no U.S. ground forces would be deployed, except possibly for any search and rescue missions, and the risk of substantial casualties for U.S. forces would be low. . . . [U]nder these circumstances, the President had constitutional authority, as Commander in Chief and Chief Executive and pursuant to his foreign affairs powers, to direct such limited military operations abroad, even without prior specific congressional approval.

A.

Earlier opinions of this Office and other historical precedents establish the framework for our analysis. As we explained in 1992, Attorneys General and this Office "have concluded that the President has the power to commit United States troops abroad," as well as to "take military action," "for the purpose of protecting important national interests," even without specific prior authorization from Congress. *Authority to Use United States Military Forces in Somalia*, 16 Op. O.L.C. 6, 9 (1992). This independent authority of the President, which exists at least insofar as Congress has not specifically restricted it, derives from the President's "unique responsibility," as Commander in Chief and Chief Executive, for "foreign and military affairs," as well as national security. *Sale v. Haitian Centers Council, Inc.*, 509 U.S. 155, 188 (1993).

The Constitution, to be sure, divides authority over the military between the President and Congress, assigning to Congress the authority to "declare War," "raise and support Armies," and "provide and maintain a Navy," as well as general authority over the appropriations on which any military operation necessarily depends. Yet, under "the historical gloss on the 'executive Power' vested in Article II of the Constitution," the President bears the " 'vast share of responsibility for the conduct of our foreign relations,' " *Am. Ins. Ass'n v. Garamendi*, 539 U.S. 396, 414 (2003) (quoting *Youngstown Sheet & Tube Co. v. Sawyer*, 343 U.S. 579, 610–11 (1952) (Frankfurter, J., concurring)), and accordingly holds "independent authority 'in the areas of foreign policy and national security.' " *Id.* at 429; *Youngstown Sheet & Tube Co.*, 343 U.S. at 635–36 (Jackson, J., concurring). Moreover, the President as Commander in Chief "superintend[s] the military," . . . and "is authorized to direct the movements of the naval and military forces placed by law at his command." *Fleming v. Page*, 50 U.S. (9 How.) 603, 615 (1850). The President also holds "the implicit advantage . . . over the legislature under our constitutional scheme in situations calling for immediate action," given that imminent national security threats and rapidly evolving military and diplomatic circumstances may require a swift response by the United States without the opportunity for congressional deliberation and action. *Presidential Power to Use the Armed Forces Abroad Without Statutory Authorization*, 4A Op. O.L.C. 185, 187 (1980). Accordingly, as Attorney General (later Justice) Robert Jackson observed over half a century ago, "the President's authority has long been recognized as extending to the dispatch of armed forces outside of the United States, either on missions of goodwill or rescue, or for the

[19] **As You Read, Consider:** In light of Justice Robert Jackson's concurring opinion in *Youngstown Sheet & Tube Co. v. Sawyer*, which category—1, 2, or 3—does Caroline Krass, legal counsel, believe describes President Barack Obama's decision to initiate air strikes in Libya? Does her answer confirm Jackson's observation about how executive-branch lawyering is different from judging?

purpose of protecting American lives or property or American interests." *Training of British Flying Students in the United States*, 40 Op. Att'y Gen. 58, 62 (1941).

This understanding of the President's constitutional authority reflects not only the express assignment of powers and responsibilities to the President and Congress in the Constitution, but also, as noted, the "historical gloss" placed on the Constitution by two centuries of practice. *Garamendi*, 539 U.S. at 414. "Our history," this Office observed in 1980, "is replete with instances of presidential uses of military force abroad in the absence of prior congressional approval." *Presidential Power*, 4A Op. O.L.C. at 187; *see generally* Richard F. Grimmett, Cong. Research Serv., R41677, *Instances of Use of United States Armed Forces Abroad, 1798–2010* (2011). Since then, instances of such presidential initiative have only multiplied, with Presidents ordering, to give just a few examples, bombing in Libya (1986), an intervention in Panama (1989), troop deployments to Somalia (1992), Bosnia (1995), and Haiti (twice, 1994 and 2004), air patrols and airstrikes in Bosnia (1993–1995), and a bombing campaign in Yugoslavia (1999), without specific prior authorizing legislation. *See* Grimmett, *supra*, at 13–31. This historical practice is an important indication of constitutional meaning, because it reflects the two political branches' practical understanding, developed since the founding of the Republic, of their respective roles and responsibilities with respect to national defense, and because "[m]atters intimately related to foreign policy and national security are rarely proper subjects for judicial intervention." *Haig*, 453 U.S. at 292. . . .

Indeed, Congress itself has implicitly recognized this presidential authority.[20] The War Powers Resolution ("WPR"), 50 U.S.C. §§ 1541–1548 (2006), a statute Congress described as intended "to fulfill the intent of the framers of the Constitution of the United States," *id.* § 1541(a), provides that, in the absence of a declaration of war, the President must report to Congress within 48 hours of taking certain actions, including introduction of U.S. forces "into hostilities or into situations where imminent involvement in hostilities is clearly indicated by the circumstances." *Id.* § 1543(a). The Resolution further provides that the President generally must terminate such use of force within 60 days (or 90 days for military necessity) unless Congress extends this deadline, declares war, or "enact[s] a specific authorization." *Id.* § 1544(b). As this Office has explained, although the WPR does not itself provide affirmative statutory authority for military operations, *see id.* § 1547(d)(2), the Resolution's "structure . . . recognizes and presupposes the existence of unilateral presidential authority to deploy armed forces" into hostilities or circumstances presenting an imminent risk of hostilities. *Haiti Deployment*, 18 Op. O.L.C. at 175. That structure—requiring a report within 48 hours after the start of hostilities and their termination within 60 days after that—makes sense only if the President may introduce troops into hostilities or potential hostilities without prior authorization by the Congress.[21]

---

[20] **Questions:** Krass does not appear to be arguing that a president could deploy force overseas for humanitarian purposes if Congress explicitly ordered the president not to. Instead, she appears to be arguing that Congress has acquiesced to presidential unilateralism by tolerating examples even as they have "multiplied." Yet, what would it take for Congress to express its dissatisfaction? Consider that in 2019, when Congress passed a joint resolution to "direct the removal of United States Armed Forces from hostilities in the Republic of Yemen," President Donald Trump vetoed the resolution. *See* S.J. Res. 7, 116th Cong. (2019). Would such a vetoed resolution count as a lack of acquiescence?

[21] **Question:** The War Powers Resolution (WPR) explicitly states that a president may deploy U.S. forces into hostilities "*only* pursuant to (1) a declaration of war, (2) specific statutory authorization, or (3) a national emergency." Pub. L. No. 93–148, 87 Stat. at 555 (emphasis added). The WPR follows this statement with the reporting requirements that Krass discusses. Is her interpretation of the WPR—that the WPR itself presupposes the existence of unilateral presidential authority—reasonable?

We have acknowledged one possible constitutionally-based limit on this presidential authority to employ military force in defense of important national interests—a planned military engagement that constitutes a "war" within the meaning of the Declaration of War Clause may require prior congressional authorization.[22] But the historical practice of presidential military action without congressional approval precludes any suggestion that Congress's authority to declare war covers every military engagement, however limited, that the President initiates. In our view, determining whether a particular planned engagement constitutes a "war" for constitutional purposes instead requires a fact-specific assessment of the "anticipated nature, scope, and duration" of the planned military operations. *Haiti Deployment*, 18 Op. O.L.C. at 179. This standard generally will be satisfied only by prolonged and substantial military engagements, typically involving exposure of U.S. military personnel to significant risk over a substantial period. Again, Congress's own key enactment on the subject reflects this understanding. By allowing United States involvement in hostilities to continue for 60 or 90 days, Congress signaled in the WPR that it considers congressional authorization most critical for "major, prolonged conflicts such as the wars in Vietnam and Korea," not more limited engagements. *Id.* at 176. . . .

Applying this fact-specific analysis, we concluded in 1994 that a planned deployment of up to 20,000 United States troops to Haiti to oust military leaders and reinstall Haiti's legitimate government was not a "war" requiring advance congressional approval. *Id.* at 174 n.1, 178–79 & n.10. . . . [We emphasized] ". . . the limited antecedent risk that United States forces would encounter significant armed resistance or suffer or inflict substantial casualties as a result of the deployment." [*Id.*] Similarly, a year later we concluded that a proposed deployment of approximately 20,000 ground troops to enforce a peace agreement in Bosnia and Herzegovina also was not a "war," even though this deployment involved some "risk that the United States [would] incur (and inflict) casualties." *Proposed Bosnia Deployment*, 19 Op. O.L.C. at 333. For more than two years preceding this deployment, the United States had undertaken air operations over Bosnia to enforce a UNSC-declared "no-fly zone," protect United Nations peacekeeping forces, and secure "safe areas" for civilians, including one two-week operation in which NATO attacked hundreds of targets and the United States alone flew over 2300 sorties—all based on the President's "constitutional authority to conduct the foreign relations of the United States and as Commander in Chief and Chief Executive," without a declaration of war or other specific prior approval from Congress. *Letter to Congressional Leaders Reporting on the Deployment of United States Aircraft to Bosnia-Herzegovina*, 1995 Pub. Papers of William J. Clinton 1279, 1280 (Sept. 1, 1995). . . .

B.

Under the framework of these precedents, the President's legal authority to direct military force in Libya turns on two questions: first, whether United States operations in Libya would serve sufficiently important national interests to permit the President's action as Commander in Chief and Chief Executive and pursuant to his authority to conduct U.S. foreign relations; and second, whether the military operations that the President anticipated ordering would be sufficiently extensive in

[22] **Question:** Krass concedes that the president lacks the unilateral power to "declare War." Do you agree with her and the rest of the executive branch that the various examples she cites below do not encroach on Congress's constitutional prerogatives?

"nature, scope, and duration" to constitute a "war" requiring prior specific congressional approval under the Declaration of War Clause.[23]

In prior opinions, this Office has identified a variety of national interests that, alone or in combination, may justify use of military force by the President. In 2004, for example, we found adequate legal authority for the deployment of U.S. forces to Haiti based on national interests in protecting the lives and property of Americans in the country, preserving "regional stability," and maintaining the credibility of United Nations Security Council mandates. Memorandum for Alberto R. Gonzales, Counsel to the President, from Jack L. Goldsmith III, Assistant Attorney General, Office of Legal Counsel, *Re: Deployment of United States Armed Forces to Haiti* at 3–4 (Mar. 17, 2004) ("2004 Haiti Opinion").

In 1995, we similarly concluded that the President's authority to deploy approximately 20,000 ground troops to Bosnia, for purposes of enforcing a peace agreement ending the civil war there, rested on national interests in completing a "pattern of inter-allied cooperation and assistance" established by prior U.S. participation in NATO air and naval support for peacekeeping efforts, "preserving peace in the region and forestalling the threat of a wider conflict," and maintaining the credibility of the UNSC. *Proposed Bosnia Deployment*, 19 Op. O.L.C. at 332–33. And in 1992, we explained the President's authority to deploy troops in Somalia in terms of national interests in providing security for American civilians and military personnel involved in UNSC-supported humanitarian relief efforts and (once again) enforcing UNSC mandates. . . .

In our view, the combination of at least two national interests that the President reasonably determined were at stake here—preserving regional stability and supporting the UNSC's credibility and effectiveness—provided a sufficient basis for the President's exercise of his constitutional authority to order the use of military force. . . .

At the same time, turning to the second element of the analysis, we do not believe that anticipated United States operations in Libya amounted to a "war" in the constitutional sense necessitating congressional approval under the Declaration of War Clause. This inquiry, as noted, is highly fact-specific and turns on no single factor. Here, considering all the relevant circumstances, we believe applicable historical precedents demonstrate that the limited military operations the President anticipated directing were not a "war" for constitutional purposes.

As in the case of the no-fly zone patrols and periodic airstrikes in Bosnia before the deployment of ground troops in 1995 and the NATO bombing campaign in connection with the Kosovo conflict in 1999—two military campaigns initiated without a prior declaration of war or other specific congressional authorization—President Obama determined that the use of force in Libya by the United States would be limited to airstrikes and associated support missions; the President made clear that "[t]he United States is not going to deploy ground troops in Libya." Obama March 18, 2011 Remarks. The planned operations thus avoided the difficulties of withdrawal and risks of escalation that may attend commitment of ground forces . . . to avoid creating a situation in which "Congress may be confronted with circumstances in which the

[23] **Questions:** Consider how this opinion has progressed: Congress has passed a statute, the War Powers Resolution, that appears to expressly prohibit the president from deploying U.S. forces into hostilities without statutory approval. The executive branch has interpreted this statute as *authorizing* the president to deploy U.S. forces into hostilities for 60 days as long as (1) the deployment serves U.S. interests and (2) the deployment doesn't amount to a "war," with *war* being defined extremely narrowly.

Does this opinion provide any meaningful limits on a president's power to deploy U.S. forces overseas? Is there any way for Congress to impose or demand new limits?

exercise of its power to declare war is effectively foreclosed." *Proposed Bosnia Deployment*, 19 Op. O.L.C. at 333. Furthermore, also as in prior operations conducted without a declaration of war or other specific authorizing legislation, the anticipated operations here served a "limited mission" and did not "aim at the conquest or occupation of territory." *Id.* at 332. President Obama directed United States forces to "conduct[ ] a limited and well-defined mission in support of international efforts to protect civilians and prevent a humanitarian disaster"; American airstrikes accordingly were to be "limited in their nature, duration, and scope." Obama March 21, 2011 Report to Congress. . . . Considering the historical practice of even intensive military action—such as the 17-day-long 1995 campaign of NATO airstrikes in Bosnia and some two months of bombing in Yugoslavia in 1999—without specific prior congressional approval, as well as the limited means, objectives, and intended duration of the anticipated operations in Libya, we do not think the "anticipated nature, scope, and duration" of the use of force by the United States in Libya rose to the level of a "war" in the constitutional sense, requiring the President to seek a declaration of war or other prior authorization from Congress.

Accordingly, we conclude that President Obama could rely on his constitutional power to safeguard the national interest by directing the anticipated military operations in Libya—which were limited in their nature, scope, and duration—without prior congressional authorization.

NOTE: AFTERMATH OF THE LIBYAN AIR STRIKES

Libyan air strikes and the sixty-day deadline. As the Office of Legal Counsel (OLC) memo indicates, the Obama administration began its air strikes against the Libyan government while attempting to follow the reporting procedures of the War Powers Resolution. Although the resolution begins by saying that the president lacks the constitutional power to introduce armed forces into overseas "hostilities" absent specific statutory authorization, *see* 87 Stat. 555, the OLC interpreted the statute itself as implicitly sanctioning hostilities short of a war for up to sixty days.

But after the memo was written, as the resolution's sixty-day deadline for ending hostilities drew closer, the prospect that the Obama administration could win specific congressional approval for the air strikes grew more remote. *See* Charlie Savage, *Power Wars* 638–41 (2017). So, a month after the OLC memo argued that the Libyan air strikes were not a "war," the Obama administration began to argue that the air strikes weren't even "hostilities" covered by the War Powers Resolution. Administration lawyers explained that because there were no U.S. ground troops, no serious threat of U.S. casualties, no sustained exchanges of fire with hostile forces, and no significant chance of an escalation, the air strikes didn't rise to the level of "hostilities" that had to be terminated after sixty days. *Id.* at 645. The sixty-day deadline passed with no change in the conduct of the air strikes, indicating that the administration believed that even absent the War Powers Resolution, it had the unilateral power to bomb another country's armed forces for weeks on end in certain circumstances. Obama would later call the worst mistake of his presidency his "fail[ure] to plan for the day after what I think was the right thing to do in intervening in Libya." *See* Allie Malloy & Catherine Treyz, *Obama Admits Worst Mistake of His Presidency*, CNN, Apr. 11, 2016.

Obama, threatened Syrian air strikes, and lack of U.N. Security Council approval. The Obama administration took a less hawkish foreign-policy position in 2013, after the Syrian government of Bashar al-Assad used chemical weapons in violation of both international norms and a rhetorical "red line" drawn by Obama. *See* Peter Baker et al., *Off-the-Cuff Obama Line Put U.S. in Bind on Syria*, N.Y. Times, May 4, 2013, at A1.

At first, the Obama administration threatened to conduct air strikes against Syria similar to those it conducted against Libya. But, unlike with Libya, the U.N. Security Council refused to sanction more air strikes. This refusal carried constitutional implications because of the president's duty to "take Care that the Laws are faithfully executed." As discussed above, Truman invoked this duty to justify his use of force in Korea, which he explained was necessary to faithfully execute the U.N. Charter, a ratified treaty. But the U.N. Charter prohibits member states "from the threat or use of force against the territorial integrity or political independence of any state" when the use of force has not been justified by the Security Council or the "right of self-defense." U.N. Charter art. 2, para. 4. So if the U.N. Charter is one of the "Laws" that the president has a duty to faithfully execute, it arguably prohibited Obama from launching air strikes on Syria.

In response to this sort of legal argument, Obama announced that he would ask Congress for specific authorization to conduct air strikes in Syria. Savage, *supra*, at 650–54. But as the date for a vote drew closer, it appeared that Congress was going to turn down his request.

The situation was defused when Russian president Vladimir Putin proposed that Russia would secure and remove Syria's chemical weapons. This proposal gave Obama a face-saving way to drop his threat. *Id.*

Trump's unilateral actions. Four years later, in the opening months of Trump's administration, the Syrian government again used chemical weapons. This time, rather than seek congressional authorization, Trump unilaterally ordered dozens of cruise missiles to strike a Syrian air base. *See* Michael R. Gordon et al., *Dozens of U.S. Missiles Hit Air Base in Syria*, N.Y. Times, Apr. 6, 2017, at A1. The president justified his conduct on the ground that "[i]t is in [the] vital national security interest of the United States to prevent and deter the spread and use of deadly chemical weapons." *Id.*

In 2018, the president ordered another round of missile strikes against Syria. The OLC concluded "that the President could lawfully direct them because he had reasonably determined that the use of force would be in the national interest and that the anticipated hostilities would not rise to the level of a war in the constitutional sense." *See April 2018 Airstrikes Against Syrian Chemical-Weapons Facilities*, 42 Op. O.L.C. ___ (May 31, 2018) (slip op. at 1).

In 2020, Trump nearly precipitated a war with Iran by ordering the assassination of an Iranian general, Qassim Suleimani, while he was visiting Iraq. *See* Catie Edmonson, *White House Memo Justifying Suleimani Strike Cites No Imminent Threat*, N.Y. Times, Feb. 14, 2020, at A17. In a memorandum to Congress, the Trump administration argued that the strike was justified by the 2002 Iraq Authorization for the Use of Military Force as well as his Article II authority "to protect the Nation from an attack or threat of imminent attack *and to protect important national interests.*" Memorandum, White House Office, Notice on the Legal and Policy Frameworks Guiding the United States' Use of Military Force and Related National Security Operations 1 (Feb. 14, 2020) (emphasis added).

Biden and Syrian air strikes. The executive branch's commitment to unilateral force transcends party lines. Indeed, just as Trump began his administration by unilaterally authorizing air strikes in Syria, Biden began his own administration the same way. *See* Helene Cooper & Eric Schmitt, *Biden Orders Strike in Syria Targeting Iran-Backed Militias*, N.Y. Times, Feb. 25, 2021, at A10. Notably, Biden's press secretary complained in 2017 about the lack of "legal authority" for Trump's air strikes yet defended Biden's similar air strikes in 2021. *Id.* She explained that Biden "took this action pursuant to his Article 2 authority to defend U.S. personnel. The targets were chosen to correspond to the recent attacks on facilities and to deter the risk of additional attacks over the coming weeks." Transcript, Press Gaggle by Press Secretary Jen Psaki (Feb. 26, 2021).

The ineffectiveness of Congress. Professor Jack Goldsmith, a veteran of the OLC, wrote shortly after Trump's first missile strike that "[i]t is a remarkable fact about the U.S. Constitution that 228 years after its creation, we still don't know what limits, if any, it imposes on unilateral presidential uses of military force." *The Constitutionality of the Syria Strike Through the Eyes of the OLC (and the Obama Administration)*, Lawfare (Apr. 7, 2017). Theoretically, Congress could answer Goldsmith's question by introducing new limits on unilateral presidential uses of military force: Congress has the formal power to repeal past authorizations for the use of military force, it could decline to appropriate funds for combat operations, or it could order a president to cease hostilities. Yet Congress has not successfully wielded any of these strategies.

For example, in 2019, bipartisan majorities in Congress voted to direct Trump to remove U.S. troops from Yemen. *See* S.J. Res. 7, 116th Cong. (2019). But the president simply vetoed Congress's joint resolution, and Congress failed to obtain the two-thirds supermajority necessary to override the president's veto. *See* Tess Bridgeman, *Getting Past the Veto on Ending Yemen War: How Congress' Next Moves Can Succeed*, Just Sec. (May 3, 2019) (emphasizing appropriations-based strategies).

The same pattern recurred in 2020 after Trump's unilateral assassination of Iran's general. *See* S.J. Res. 68, 116th Cong. (2020). This second joint resolution warned that Congress's 2001 and 2002 authorizations for the use of military force "do not serve as a specific statutory authorization for the use of force against Iran." *Id.* § 1. It also emphasized that uses of force should follow "a full briefing to Congress and the American public of the issues at stake, a public debate in Congress, and a congressional vote as contemplated by the Constitution." *Id.*

CHAPTER 32

WHAT IS THE SCOPE OF THE PRESIDENT'S POWER TO CONDUCT FOREIGN AFFAIRS?

ARTICLE II, SECTION 2, CLAUSE 1: The President shall be Commander in Chief of the Army and Navy of the United States, and of the Militia of the several States, when called into the actual Service of the United States. . . .

CLAUSE 2: He shall have Power, by and with the Advice and Consent of the Senate, to make Treaties, provided two thirds of the Senators present concur. . . .

ARTICLE II, SECTION 3, CLAUSE 1: He shall . . . receive Ambassadors and other public Ministers; he shall take Care that the Laws be faithfully executed, and shall Commission all the Officers of the United States.

Direct and Indirect Power to Conduct Foreign Affairs

We have so far discussed the meaning of the "executive Power" with respect to several clauses of Article II: (1) the clauses that empower the president to "give to the Congress Information of the State of the Union," to veto legislation, to "convene both Houses, or either of them," and to "adjourn them"; (2) the clauses that empower the president to "nominate," "appoint," "Commission," and remove officers of the United States; (3) the clause requiring the president to "take Care that the Laws be faithfully executed"; and (4) the clause empowering the president "to grant Reprieves and Pardons for Offences against the United States."

Sections 32.2–32.4 consider a final set of Article II clauses that empower the president "make Treaties" and to "receive Ambassadors and other public Ministers." These last two clauses have been interpreted to give the president a vast and, at times, exclusive role in conducting the foreign policy of the United States.

Before we turn to the specific histories of the Treaty Clause and the Reception Clause, however, section 32.1 discusses why the president likely would have had an important foreign policy role even if those clauses didn't exist.

32.1 THE POWER TO REPRESENT THE NATION

Even if there were no constitutional clauses giving specific authority to the president to conduct foreign affairs, the president likely would have had authority to conduct foreign affairs via other constitutional clauses bestowing such authority indirectly. Examples interpreting the

Vesting Clause, the Take Care Clause, and the Appointments Clause established early precedents that the president had substantial powers to conduct foreign affairs. In addition, the State of the Union Clause has given presidents enormous influence in declaring the nation's foreign policy.

Vesting Clause

When Congress passes a law to "regulate Commerce with foreign Nations," per Article I, Section 8, Clause 3, or when the Senate ratifies a treaty, someone has to execute those laws and treaties. As we read earlier with regard to the Vesting Clause (section 25.1), Alexander Hamilton defended President George Washington's power to issue his proclamation of neutrality with just this sort of argument. Hamilton called the president the "*organ* of intercourse between the Nation and Foreign Nations . . . as that Power, which is charged with the Execution of the Laws, of which Treaties form a part—[and] as that Power which is charged with the command and application of the Public Force." 15 *The Papers of Alexander Hamilton* 33 (Harold C. Syrett ed., 1969) (1793).

Take Care Clause

Borrowing language from Hamilton, John Marshall made a similar point in 1800 when he was a member of Congress defending President John Adams's unilateral power to arrest a man named John Robbins. As discussed earlier in the section on the president's power to respond to emergencies (section 31.2), Marshall justified the arrest as an enforcement of a treaty (an extension of the Take Care Clause)—and, Marshall added, only the president had such an enforcement power. "The President is the sole organ of the nation in its external relations, and its sole representative with foreign nations," Marshall declared. 10 Annals of Cong. 613 (1800). "He possesses the whole Executive power. He holds and directs the force of the nation. . . . He must then execute a treaty, where he, and he alone, possesses the means of executing it." *Id.*

Appointments Clause

Even Thomas Jefferson—who disagreed with Hamilton about the legality of Washington's proclamation of neutrality—embraced this theory of the executive power when it came to the appointment of "Ambassadors, other public Ministers and Consuls," i.e., the Appointments Clause. In 1790, when Washington nominated a foreign minister for France, the Senate suggested that the nominee should be appointed to a lower diplomatic position. When the president asked Secretary of State Jefferson for his opinion about this suggestion, Jefferson objected that the Senate was abusing its power. "The transaction of business with foreign nations is Executive altogether. It belongs then to the head of that department," Jefferson wrote. 16 *The Papers of Thomas Jefferson* 378–82 (Julian P. Boyd ed., 1961).

Interpreting the Senate's "advice" and consent role narrowly, Jefferson concluded that only the president had sufficient information and qualifications "to judge of the necessity which calls for a mission to any particular place, or of the particular grade, . . . which special and secret circumstances may call for." *Id.*

State of the Union Clause

In addition to the powers extending from the Vesting Clause, the Take Care Clause, and the Appointments Clause, the State of the Union Clause gives the president a unique platform for "conducting" foreign affairs. The most famous of the early State of the Union addresses occurred in 1823, during a decade when nearly every Latin American colony of Spain and Portugal was fighting for independence. In his message to Congress, President James Monroe focused nearly exclusively on foreign policy—specifically, the United States' approach toward Chile, Mexico, and the other revolutionary governments of the Americas. These republican governments were emerging just as counterrevolutionary monarchies of Europe were fresh from defeating France in the Napoleonic Wars. The Monroe administration feared that the powers of Europe might try to take advantage of the unstable situation in the Americas by surrounding the United States with new, monarchical colonies—thereby threatening the United States' own republican government. Jay Sexton, *The Monroe Doctrine: Empire and Nation in Nineteenth-Century America* 43 (2011). Just as later generations of presidents would fear the establishment of communist governments in the Western Hemisphere, Monroe offered a warning to the monarchies of Europe: the United States would "consider any attempt on their part to extend their system to any portion of this hemisphere as dangerous to our peace and safety." *Id.* at 55–61. He added that he would view any attempt by Europe to threaten the republican governments of the Americas "as the manifestation of an unfriendly disposition toward the United States." *Id.*

The speech announced what later became known as the Monroe Doctrine: the United States wouldn't interfere in the internal affairs of Europe, and, in return, it expected European powers not to interfere in the internal affairs of the Americas. Even though this policy was announced by a president with no input from Congress, successive presidents made the doctrine a defining feature of American foreign policy.

By the turn of the twentieth century, when the U.S. military had become one of the most powerful in the world, President Theodore Roosevelt expanded the doctrine into a justification for the United States' "exercise of an international police power" in the Western Hemisphere. 39 Cong. Rec. 19 (1904). The Roosevelt administration began invoking this "corollary" to the Monroe Doctrine to support a coup in Panama, to break a naval blockade of Venezuela, and to use gunboat diplomacy to resolve conflicts within Latin America. *See* Edmund Morris, *Theodore Rex* 176–94, 282–90 (2002).

32.1.1

United States v. Curtiss-Wright Export Corp.

299 U.S. 304 (1936)

In 1929, President Herbert Hoover's secretary of state applied "the Roosevelt Corollary to the Monroe Doctrine" by mediating a cease-fire between the South American countries of Paraguay and Bolivia. The two countries had long disputed the border area between them, known as the Chaco Basin. Although this cease-fire stopped the fighting, the countries continued to import arms and ammunition from the United States and Europe. War broke out again in 1932, leading the United States to take another proactive role. In 1934, Congress enacted a joint resolution that made it a crime to sell arms or munitions to either country "if the President finds that the prohibition of the sale . . . may contribute to the reestablishment of peace between those countries." Joint Resolution of May 28, 1934, Pub. Res. No. 73–28, 48 Stat. 811. That same day, President Franklin D. Roosevelt issued a proclamation to enforce this prohibition, warning that violations would be "vigorously prosecuted." 48 Stat. at 1744.

Federal prosecutors soon indicted the Curtiss-Wright Export Corporation, a major arms producer, for violating the president's proclamation. But in the wake of the Supreme Court's recent nondelegation decision in *Panama Refining Co. v. Ryan*, 293 U.S. 388 (1935), the corporation's lawyers argued that Congress had unconstitutionally delegated legislative power to the president.

In considering this challenge, the Court declined to consider whether Congress's resolution contained an "intelligible principle" to guide the president's exercise of discretion—as it had done in *Panama Refining*. *Panama Refin.*, 293 U.S. at 430. Instead, the Court in *United States v. Curtiss-Wright Export Corp.*, 299 U.S. 304 (1936), took an entirely different approach—granting the president sweeping power to conduct foreign affairs.

■ MR. JUSTICE SUTHERLAND delivered the opinion of the Court.[1]

On January 27, 1936, an indictment was returned in the court below, the first count of which charges that appellees, beginning with the 29th day of May, 1934, conspired to sell in the United States certain arms of war, namely fifteen machine guns, to Bolivia, a country then engaged in armed conflict in the Chaco, in violation

---

1 **As You Read, Consider:** In *Panama Refining Co. v. Ryan*, the Supreme Court held that Congress violated the nondelegation doctrine when it gave the president unlimited discretion to determine when to criminalize the transportation of "hot oil." The Court complained that "Congress has declared no policy, has established no standard, has laid down no rule. . . . If [this law] were held valid, it would be idle to pretend that anything would be left of limitations upon the power of the Congress to delegate its lawmaking function." 293 U.S. 388, 430 (1935). Why does Justice George Sutherland decline to apply a similar analysis in this case?

of the Joint Resolution of Congress approved May 28, 1934, and the provisions of a proclamation issued on the same day by the President of the United States pursuant to authority conferred by § 1 of the resolution. . . .

It is contended that by the Joint Resolution, the going into effect and continued operation of the resolution was conditioned (a) upon the President's judgment as to its beneficial effect upon the reestablishment of peace between the countries engaged in armed conflict in the Chaco; (b) upon the making of a proclamation, which was left to his unfettered discretion, thus constituting an attempted substitution of the President's will for that of Congress; . . . and ([c]) further, that the extent of its operation in particular cases was subject to limitation and exception by the President, controlled by no standard. In each of these particulars, appellees urge that Congress abdicated its essential functions and delegated them to the Executive.

Whether, if the Joint Resolution had related solely to internal affairs it would be open to the challenge that it constituted an unlawful delegation of legislative power to the Executive, we find it unnecessary to determine. The whole aim of the resolution is to affect a situation entirely external to the United States, and falling within the category of foreign affairs. The determination which we are called to make, therefore, is whether the Joint Resolution, as applied to that situation, is vulnerable to attack under the rule that forbids a delegation of the law-making power. In other words, assuming (but not deciding) that the challenged delegation, if it were confined to internal affairs, would be invalid, may it nevertheless be sustained on the ground that its exclusive aim is to afford a remedy for a hurtful condition within foreign territory?

It will contribute to the elucidation of the question if we first consider the differences between the powers of the federal government in respect of foreign or external affairs and those in respect of domestic or internal affairs. That there are differences between them, and that these differences are fundamental, may not be doubted.[2]

The two classes of powers are different, both in respect of their origin and their nature. The broad statement that the federal government can exercise no powers except those specifically enumerated in the Constitution, and such implied powers as are necessary and proper to carry into effect the enumerated powers, is categorically true only in respect of our internal affairs. In that field, the primary purpose of the Constitution was to carve from the general mass of legislative powers *then possessed by the states* such portions as it was thought desirable to vest in the federal government, leaving those not included in the enumeration still in the states. That this doctrine applies only to powers which the states had, is self evident. And since the states severally never possessed international powers, such powers could not have been carved from the mass of state powers but obviously were transmitted to the United States from some other source. During the colonial period, those powers were possessed exclusively by and were entirely under the control of the Crown. By the Declaration of Independence, "the Representatives of the United States of America" declared the United [not the several] Colonies to be free and independent states, and as such to have "full Power to levy War, conclude Peace, contract Alliances, establish Commerce and to do all other Acts and Things which Independent States may of right do."

---

2 **Question:** Sutherland here distinguishes the federal government's *domestic* powers from its *foreign* powers. He offers a creation myth to demonstrate how these powers came from two different sources. Assuming for the sake of discussion that this myth is true, should constitutional restraints on the federal government's power—in this case, Article I's delegation of legislative power to Congress—cease to apply simply because the federal government is acting abroad?

As a result of the separation from Great Britain by the colonies acting as a unit, the powers of external sovereignty passed from the Crown not to the colonies severally, but to the colonies in their collective and corporate capacity as the United States of America. Even before the Declaration, the colonies were a unit in foreign affairs, acting through a common agency—namely the Continental Congress, composed of delegates from the thirteen colonies. That agency exercised the powers of war and peace, raised an army, created a navy, and finally adopted the Declaration of Independence. Rulers come and go; governments end and forms of government change; but sovereignty survives. A political society cannot endure without a supreme will somewhere. Sovereignty is never held in suspense. When, therefore, the external sovereignty of Great Britain in respect of the colonies ceased, it immediately passed to the Union. That fact was given practical application almost at once. The treaty of peace, made on September 23, 1783, was concluded between his Brittanic Majesty and the "United States of America." 8 Stat.—European Treaties—80.

The Union existed before the Constitution, which was ordained and established among other things to form "a more perfect Union." Prior to that event, it is clear that the Union, declared by the Articles of Confederation to be "perpetual," was the sole possessor of external sovereignty and in the Union it remained without change save in so far as the Constitution in express terms qualified its exercise. The Framers' Convention was called and exerted its powers upon the irrefutable postulate that though the states were several their people in respect of foreign affairs were one. Compare *The Chinese Exclusion Case,* 130 U.S. 581, 604, 606. . . .

It results that the investment of the federal government with the powers of external sovereignty did not depend upon the affirmative grants of the Constitution. The powers to declare and wage war, to conclude peace, to make treaties, to maintain diplomatic relations with other sovereignties, if they had never been mentioned in the Constitution, would have vested in the federal government as necessary concomitants of nationality.[3] Neither the Constitution nor the laws passed in pursuance of it have any force in foreign territory unless in respect of our own citizens; and operations of the nation in such territory must be governed by treaties, international understandings and compacts, and the principles of international law. As a member of the family of nations, the right and power of the United States in that field are equal to the right and power of the other members of the international family. Otherwise, the United States is not completely sovereign. The power to acquire territory by discovery and occupation (*Jones v. United States,* 137 U.S. 202, 212), the power to expel undesirable aliens (*Fong Yue Ting v. United States,* 149 U.S. 698, 705 *et seq.*), . . . none of which is expressly affirmed by the Constitution, nevertheless exist as inherently inseparable from the conception of nationality. This the court recognized, and in each of the cases cited found the warrant for its conclusions not in the provisions of the Constitution, but in the law of nations. . . .

Not only, as we have shown, is the federal power over external affairs in origin and essential character different from that over internal affairs, but participation in the exercise of the power is significantly limited. In this vast external realm, with its important, complicated, delicate and manifold problems, the President alone has the power to speak or listen as a representative of the nation. He *makes* treaties with the advice and consent of the Senate; but he alone negotiates. Into the field of negotiation

---

[3] **Questions:** This passage is, perhaps, the boldest assertion in Supreme Court history—before or since—that the federal government can exercise *sovereign* powers that are neither enumerated nor implied by virtue of the Necessary and Proper Clause. Note that Sutherland has adopted the broad interpretation of the *Chinese Exclusion Case,* in contrast with the enumerated interpretation. As you continue reading, consider: Why does Sutherland feel the need to make such an assertion in the context of this opinion? Does anything turn on the source of the federal government's power?

the Senate cannot intrude; and Congress itself is powerless to invade it. As Marshall said in his great argument of March 7, 1800, in the House of Representatives, "The President is the sole organ of the nation in its external relations, and its sole representative with foreign nations." Annals, 6th Cong., col. 613. The Senate Committee on Foreign Relations at a very early day in our history (February 15, 1816), reported to the Senate, . . . "The President is the constitutional representative of the United States with regard to foreign nations. He manages our concerns with foreign nations and must necessarily be most competent to determine when, how, and upon what subjects negotiation may be urged with the greatest prospect of success. For his conduct he is responsible to the Constitution. . . ." U.S. Senate, Reports, Committee on Foreign Relations, vol. 8, p. 24.[4]

It is important to bear in mind that we are here dealing not alone with an authority vested in the President by an exertion of legislative power, but with such an authority plus the very delicate, plenary and exclusive power of the President as the sole organ of the federal government in the field of international relations—a power which does not require as a basis for its exercise an act of Congress, but which, of course, like every other governmental power, must be exercised in subordination to the applicable provisions of the Constitution. It is quite apparent that if, in the maintenance of our international relations, embarrassment—perhaps serious embarrassment—is to be avoided and success for our aims achieved, congressional legislation which is to be made effective through negotiation and inquiry within the international field must often accord to the President a degree of discretion and freedom from statutory restriction which would not be admissible were domestic affairs alone involved. Moreover, he, not Congress, has the better opportunity of knowing the conditions which prevail in foreign countries, and especially is this true in time of war. He has his confidential sources of information. He has his agents in the form of diplomatic, consular and other officials. Secrecy in respect of information gathered by them may be highly necessary, and the premature disclosure of it productive of harmful results. . . .

The marked difference between foreign affairs and domestic affairs in this respect is recognized by both houses of Congress in the very form of their requisitions for information from the executive departments. In the case of every department except the Department of State, the resolution *directs* the official to furnish the information. In the case of the State Department, dealing with foreign affairs, the President is *requested* to furnish the information "if not incompatible with the public interest." A statement that to furnish the information is not compatible with the public interest rarely, if ever, is questioned.

When the President is to be authorized by legislation to act in respect of a matter intended to affect a situation in foreign territory, the legislator properly bears in mind the important consideration that the form of the President's action—or, indeed, whether he shall act at all—may well depend, among other things, upon the nature of the confidential information which he has or may thereafter receive, or upon the effect which his action may have upon our foreign relations. This consideration, in connection with what we have already said on the subject, discloses the unwisdom of requiring Congress in this field of governmental power to lay down narrowly definite standards by which the President is to be governed. . . .

---

[4] **Questions:** Sutherland complements the above passage about sovereign power by arguing that the president can act in the field of foreign relations even absent statutory authority. Is this passage consistent with the Court's later analysis in cases like *Youngstown Sheet & Tube Co. v. Sawyer*? What if Congress enacted a statute prohibiting the president from regulating some aspect of foreign affairs—would such a statute be enforceable under Sutherland's analysis?

In the light of the foregoing observations, it is evident that this court should not be in haste to apply a general rule which will have the effect of condemning legislation like that under review as constituting an unlawful delegation of legislative power. The principles which justify such legislation find overwhelming support in the unbroken legislative practice which has prevailed almost from the inception of the national government to the present day. . . .

Practically every volume of the United States Statutes contains one or more acts or joint resolutions of Congress authorizing action by the President in respect of subjects affecting foreign relations, which either leave the exercise of the power to his unrestricted judgment, or provide a standard far more general than that which has always been considered requisite with regard to domestic affairs. . . .

We had occasion to review these embargo and kindred acts in connection with an exhaustive discussion of the general subject of delegation of legislative power in a recent case, *Panama Refining Co. v. Ryan,* 293 U.S. 388, 421–422, and in justifying such acts, pointed out that they confided to the President "an authority which was cognate to the conduct by him of the foreign relations of the government."

The result of holding that the joint resolution here under attack is void and unenforceable as constituting an unlawful delegation of legislative power would be to stamp this multitude of comparable acts and resolutions as likewise invalid. And while this court may not, and should not, hesitate to declare acts of Congress, however many times repeated, to be unconstitutional if beyond all rational doubt it finds them to be so, an impressive array of legislation such as we have just set forth, enacted by nearly every Congress from the beginning of our national existence to the present day, must be given unusual weight in the process of reaching a correct determination of the problem. A legislative practice such as we have here, evidenced not by only occasional instances, but marked by the movement of a steady stream for a century and a half of time, goes a long way in the direction of proving the presence of unassailable ground for the constitutionality of the practice, to be found in the origin and history of the power involved, or in its nature, or in both combined. . . .

In *The Laura,* 114 U.S. 411, 416, this court answered a challenge to the constitutionality of a statute authorizing the Secretary of the Treasury to remit or mitigate fines and penalties in certain cases, by repeating the language of a very early case (*Stuart v. Laird,* 1 Cranch 299, 309) that the long practice and acquiescence under the statute was a "practical exposition . . . too strong and obstinate to be shaken or controlled. Of course, the question is at rest, and ought not now to be disturbed." . . . In *Field v. Clark,* 143 U.S. 649, 691, this court declared that ". . . the practical construction of the Constitution, as given by so many acts of Congress, and embracing almost the entire period of our national existence, should not be overruled, unless upon a conviction that such legislation was clearly incompatible with the supreme law of the land." The rule is one which has been stated and applied many times by this court. As examples, see *McCulloch v. Maryland,* 4 Wheat. 316; *Downes v. Bidwell,* 182 U.S. 244.

The uniform, long-continued and undisputed legislative practice just disclosed rests upon an admissible view of the Constitution which, even if the practice found far less support in principle than we think it does, we should not feel at liberty at this late day to disturb. . . .

[B]oth upon principle and in accordance with precedent, we conclude there is sufficient warrant for the broad discretion vested in the President to determine whether the enforcement of the statute will have a beneficial effect upon the reestablishment of peace in the affected countries. . . .[5]

NOTE: NONDELEGATION IN FOREIGN AFFAIRS AND WARTIME

Curtiss-Wright recognized several important principles regarding the federal government's power to conduct foreign affairs, most notably the "plenary and exclusive power of the President as the sole organ of the federal government in the field of international relations." *Curtiss-Wright*, 299 U.S. at 320. Its holding was also important for the development of the nondelegation doctrine and provides one explanation for why the doctrine became dormant after 1936.

In a series of cases during and after World War II, the Court repeatedly upheld broad delegations of authority to the president. The Court explained that the president was the commander in chief and the sole organ of foreign affairs and therefore needed more discretion than when acting domestically during peacetime. These cases included *Hirabayashi v. United States*, 320 U.S. 81 (1943), discussed earlier in the section on Congress's war powers (section 13.4). There, Congress passed an open-ended law ratifying President Franklin D. Roosevelt's executive order that led to the relocation of Japanese Americans living on the West Coast. *See* Act of Mar. 21, 1942, Pub. L. No. 77–503, 56 Stat. 173. The *Hirabayashi* Court saw no need to apply the nondelegation doctrine. As the Court wrote shortly afterward, "while the constitutional structure and controls of our Government are our guides equally in war and in peace, they must be read with the realistic purposes of the entire instrument fully in mind." *Lichter v. United States*, 334 U.S. 742, 782 (1948). The Court has therefore considered it "not necessary that Congress supply administrative officials with a specific formula for their guidance in a field where flexibility and the adaptation of the congressional policy to infinitely variable conditions constitute the essence of the program." *Id.* at 785; *see also Loving v. United States*, 517 U.S. 748, 773–74 (1996) (upholding a delegation with respect to military justice); *Yakus v. United States*, 321 U.S. 414, 424 (1944) (upholding a wartime delegation).

32.2 THE POWER TO MAKE TREATIES AND EXECUTIVE AGREEMENTS

The president has broad power to conduct foreign affairs not only via treaties, a power bestowed by the Constitution, but also via executive agreements, a power bestowed by Congress.

Executive power via treaties

As discussed earlier with regard to Congress's power to ratify and terminate treaties (section 14.1), the Constitutional Convention initially

---

5 **Question:** Sutherland concludes his opinion with a functional and historical argument in favor of interpreting the nondelegation doctrine in a manner that would permit broad delegations in foreign affairs. Are these arguments equally applicable in the domestic context? Consider that in the eight decades after this opinion, the Supreme Court never again invalidated a statute for violating the nondelegation doctrine.

gave the Senate all power over "treaties." *See* 2 *The Records of the Federal Convention of 1787*, at 183 (Max Farrand ed., 1911). But the convention ultimately concluded that it would be better for a single person to be responsible for negotiating the terms of treaties, leaving the Senate responsible only for rejecting or approving the treaty with amendments, reservations, or statements of understanding. Once the Senate approves a treaty, the president has the final say on whether to ratify it, just as the president has the final say on whether to commission an officer confirmed by the Senate. In this respect, the president has the power to "make" treaties.

Historically, presidents have been protective of their exclusive power over treaties. For example, when President George Washington negotiated the Jay Treaty, which established a cordial relationship between the United States and Great Britain, the House of Representatives requested documents relating to the negotiation of the treaty. Washington refused, offering a lengthy defense of his prerogative to withhold the information:

> The nature of foreign negotiations requires caution, and their success must often depend on secrecy; and even when brought to a conclusion a full disclosure of all the measures, demands, or eventual concessions which may have been proposed or contemplated would be extremely impolitic; for this might have a pernicious influence on future negotiations, or produce immediate inconveniences, perhaps danger and mischief, in relation to other powers. The necessity of such caution and secrecy was one cogent reason for vesting the power of making treaties in the President, with the advice and consent of the Senate, the principle on which that body was formed confining it to a small number of members. To admit, then, a right in the House of Representatives to demand and to have as a matter of course all the papers respecting a negotiation with a foreign power would be to establish a dangerous precedent.

1 *Messages and Papers of the Presidents* 194 (James D. Richardson ed., 1896). As the Supreme Court discussed in *United States v. Curtiss-Wright Corp.*, the House accepted the president's refusal. 299 U.S. 304, 319 (1936). Rather than "direct" the president to turn over information about foreign affairs, it began to merely "request" this information. *Id.* at 321.

Executive power via executive agreements

Despite this precedent, the House has always been involved in forming international agreements. In 1792 when Congress established the post office, it authorized the postmaster general to "make arrangements with the postmasters in any foreign country for the reciprocal receipt and delivery of letters." Act of Feb. 20, 1792, ch. 7, 1 Stat. 232, 239. This statute established a precedent by which Congress as a whole could authorize officers in the executive branch to make agreements with foreign nations outside the context of the Treaty Clause. During the nation's first fifty years, the United States was party to sixty treaties, compared with twenty-seven of these "executive agreements." Cong. Rsch. Serv., *Treaties and Other International Agreements: The Role of the United States Senate* 38–40 (2001). But in the two centuries since then, the use of executive agreements authorized by statute has exploded. By World War II, the United States was party to 800 treaties and 1,200 executive agreements. And by 1989, it was party to 890 treaties and over 5,000 executive agreements. *Id.*

However, like the joint resolution at issue in *Curtiss-Wright*, the statutes that authorize executive agreements have typically given the president enormous discretion in a wide range of fields. For example, after the Senate nixed an 1844 treaty to annex the Republic of Texas, Congress voted to give the president authority to negotiate with Texas over the terms of its admission if "in his judgment and discretion [he] deem[s] it most advisable." Joint Resolution of Mar. 1, 1845, No. 8, 5 Stat. 797, 798 (1845). Similarly, with the Lend-Lease Act of 1941, Congress allowed the president to authorize the manufacture and sale of "any defense article for the government of any country whose defense the President deems vital to the defense of the United States." Pub. L. No. 77–11, 55 Stat. 31.

But the most active context in which Congress has authorized executive agreements is international trade. With the Tariff Act of 1890, Congress authorized the president to bargain with foreign nations for reciprocal tariffs with no need for subsequent congressional action. Tariff Act, ch. 1244, 26 Stat. 567, 612. Since then, Congress has expanded the president's authority to negotiate agreements for the reductions of tariffs, and it has given the president authority to put the reductions into effect by proclamation. *See, e.g.*, Trade Act of 1974, Pub. L. No. 93–618, 88 Stat. 1978, 1982; Act of June 12, 1934, Pub. L. No. 73–316, 48 Stat. 943. Indeed, since 1974, Congress has constrained itself with respect to multilateral trade agreements by giving the president fast-track authority. Under this procedure, once the president negotiates and signs certain agreements, Congress must approve or reject implementing legislation under a tight timetable without the possibility of amending or filibustering the agreement before it. *See* Bipartisan Congressional Trade Priorities and Accountability Act of 2015, Pub. L. No. 114–26, 129 Stat. 320; Trade Act of 2002, Pub. L. No. 107–210, 116 Stat. 933.

There have also been contexts in which presidents have signed international agreements without congressional authorization or ratification. Most of these have involved the president's role as commander in chief. During World War II, for example, President Harry S. Truman signed an agreement at Potsdam that directed the end of the war effort and divided the postwar territory of Germany.

Supreme Court acceptance of executive agreements

Although executive agreements have come to displace Article II's procedure for approving treaties, the Supreme Court has generally been tolerant of such agreements. In *Field v. Clark*, discussed earlier in the section on nondelegation (section 25.2), the Court upheld a statute that authorized the president to negotiate reciprocal tariffs. 143 U.S. 649, 692–94 (1892). And in *Tucker v. Alexandroff*, the Court upheld the president's unilateral power to reach certain military agreements with other countries by virtue of the president's power as commander in chief. 183 U.S. 424, 435 (1902). The Court then treated subsequent executive agreements as the legal equivalent of treaties. For example, when President Franklin D. Roosevelt unilaterally agreed to recognize the legitimacy of the Soviet Union in 1933, the Court declared that the recognition was binding domestic law because the president is the "sole organ" of foreign affairs. *United States v. Pink*, 315 U.S. 203, 229–30 (1942); *United States v. Belmont*, 301 U.S. 324, 330 (1937).

Unilateral executive agreements were one of two issues that Senator John W. Bricker hoped to eliminate with the Bricker Amendment in 1953, discussed earlier in the section on Congress's power to enforce treaties (section 14.2). His proposed amendment promised to prohibit Congress from implementing treaties with legislation that Congress ordinarily lacked the power to enact, overruling *Missouri v. Holland*, 252 U.S. 416 (1920). It also declared, "Congress shall have power to regulate all executive and other agreements with any foreign power or international organization. All such agreements shall be subject to the limitations imposed on treaties by this article." S.J. Res. 43, 83d Cong., 1st Sess., § 3 (1953). This provision drew the ire of President Dwight D. Eisenhower, who successfully pushed for its defeat on the ground that it would undermine the president's ability to conduct foreign policy. *See* Robert A. Caro, *Master of the Senate* 528 (2003).

Afterward, in 1957 when the Supreme Court considered two executive agreements that governed the trial of U.S. soldiers on foreign army bases, the Court again upheld the use of such agreements in general, *Wilson v. Girard*, 354 U.S. 524, 530 (1957), while holding that such agreements needed to comply with the Bill of Rights, *Reid v. Covert*, 354 U.S. 1, 5–6 (1957).

32.2.1

Dames & Moore v. Regan

453 U.S. 654 (1981)

In 1953, Eisenhower's administration reached a secret agreement with the United Kingdom to engineer a coup d'état in Iran, whose democratically elected prime minister, Mohammad Mosaddegh, had recently nationalized a British-owned oil company. *See* Tim Weiner, *Legacy of Ashes: The History of the CIA* 92–99 (2008). In Mosaddegh's place, the Eisenhower administration covertly empowered Iran's constitutional monarch, or shah, to rule the country as an authoritarian dictator. *Id.* at 99–103. The shah ruled until 1979, when a coalition of secular and religious demonstrators took to the streets and overthrew the shah's government. *See* Kim Ghattas, *Black Wave: Saudi Arabia, Iran, and the Forty-Year Rivalry That Unraveled Culture, Religion, and Collective Memory in the Middle East* 25–50 (2020). As the revolutionary coalition held a national referendum and established an Islamic republic—a constitutional theocracy—the shah fled to asylum in the United States. *Id.* at 48–49.

In November 1979, a group of radical university students staged a protest against the United States' protection of the shah by breaking into the American embassy in Tehran. *Id.* at 49–50. What began as a brief demonstration spiraled into an occupation when the students held the embassy workers hostage with the support of the Iranian revolution's spiritual and political leader, Ruhollah Khomeini. *Id.*

Ten days into the hostage crisis, President Jimmy Carter declared a national emergency under the International Emergency Economic Powers Act of 1977 (IEEPA), Pub. L. No. 95–223, 91 Stat. 1626, which authorized him to freeze $8 billion in assets that belonged to the Iranian government and were held within the United States. *See* Exec. Order No. 12,170, 44 Fed. Reg. 65,729 (Nov. 14, 1979). The next day, the secretary of the Treasury implemented this freeze with a regulation that, among other things, prohibited any judicial proceeding from executing a judgment against the Iranian government. 31 C.F.R. § 535.203(e) (1979).

This regulation applied to an ongoing lawsuit initiated in December 1979 by an engineering company, Dames & Moore. Dames & Moore was suing the Iranian government in federal district court to collect on a contract that it had performed to study sites for a proposed nuclear power plant in Iran. Despite the regulation, the federal court awarded Dames & Moore a pretrial attachment, or claim of jurisdiction, of over $3 million worth of Iranian assets held in the United States.

Four hundred and forty-four days into the crisis, after a failed attempt by the United States to rescue the hostages by helicopter, the Carter administration reached an agreement with Iran to release the hostages. *See* Ghattas, *supra*, at 50. In exchange for Iran's return of the hostages, the United States promised to unfreeze Iran's assets and "to terminate all litigation as between the Government of each party and the nationals of the other, and to bring about the settlement and termination of all such claims through binding arbitration." *Agreement on the Release of the American Hostages*, 81 Dep't of State Bull. 2 (1981). Carter issued executive orders to implement this agreement the day before his successor, Ronald Reagan, was inaugurated. *See* Exec. Order Nos. 12,276–12,285, 46 Fed. Reg. 7913–32 (Jan. 19, 1981). The new president then "ratified" these orders, adding that any claim that could potentially be presented to the arbitration body established by the agreement "shall have no legal effect in any action now pending in any court of the United States." Exec. Order No. 12,294, 46 Fed. Reg. 14,111 (Feb. 24, 1981).

In light of these executive orders, the district court in the Dames & Moore suit vacated the company's $3 million attachment on Iranian assets and also stayed Dames & Moore's ability to prosecute its suit against the Iranian government. Dames & Moore responded by suing Reagan's secretary of the Treasury, Donald Regan. The company challenged the constitutionality of Reagan's executive orders, which were issued to enforce an executive agreement with Iran that Congress had never authorized. The Reagan administration responded that the orders were authorized by the IEEPA statute that President Carter invoked when he declared a national emergency, as well as by an 1868 statute that authorized the president to obtain the release of hostages.

In *Dames & Moore v. Regan*, 453 U.S. 654 (1981), the Court upheld the power of the executive agreement—thus, although the embassy hostages were released, Dames & Moore's $3 million attachment on Iranian assets was held hostage.

■ JUSTICE REHNQUIST delivered the opinion of the Court.[6]

The questions presented by this case touch fundamentally upon the manner in which our Republic is to be governed. Throughout the nearly two centuries of our Nation's existence under the Constitution, this subject has generated considerable debate. . . . [Yet] as Justice Jackson noted, "[a] judge . . . may be surprised at the poverty of really useful and unambiguous authority applicable to concrete problems of executive power as they actually present themselves." *Youngstown Sheet & Tube Co. v. Sawyer,* 343 U. S. 579, 634 (1952) (concurring opinion).

Our decision today will not dramatically alter this situation, for the Framers "did not make the judiciary the overseer of our government." *Id.,* at 594 (Frankfurter, J., concurring). We are confined to a resolution of the dispute presented to us. That dispute involves various Executive Orders and regulations by which the President nullified attachments and liens on Iranian assets in the United States, directed that these assets be transferred to Iran, and suspended claims against Iran that may be presented to an International Claims Tribunal. This action was taken in an effort to comply with an Executive Agreement between the United States and Iran. . . .

II

The parties and the lower courts . . . have all agreed that much relevant analysis is contained in *Youngstown Sheet & Tube Co. v. Sawyer,* 343 U. S. 579 (1952). Justice Black's opinion for the Court in that case, involving the validity of President Truman's effort to seize the country's steel mills in the wake of a nationwide strike, recognized that "[t]he President's power, if any, to issue the order must stem either from an act of Congress or from the Constitution itself." *Id.,* at 585. Justice Jackson's concurring opinion elaborated in a general way the consequences of different types of interaction between the two democratic branches in assessing Presidential authority to act in any given case. When the President acts pursuant to an express or implied authorization from Congress, he exercises not only his powers but also

---

[6] **As You Read, Consider:** Justice Robert Jackson described his three categories in *Youngstown Sheet & Tube Co. v. Sawyer* as a "somewhat over-simplified grouping" of examples in which presidential actions could be challenged. 343 U.S. 579, 635 (1952). What role do his categories play in Justice William Rehnquist's opinion?

those delegated by Congress. In such a case the executive action "would be supported by the strongest of presumptions and the widest latitude of judicial interpretation, and the burden of persuasion would rest heavily upon any who might attack it." *Id.,* at 637. When the President acts in the absence of congressional authorization he may enter "a zone of twilight in which he and Congress may have concurrent authority, or in which its distribution is uncertain." *Ibid.* In such a case the analysis becomes more complicated, and the validity of the President's action, at least so far as separation-of-powers principles are concerned, hinges on a consideration of all the circumstances which might shed light on the views of the Legislative Branch toward such action, including "congressional inertia, indifference or quiescence." *Ibid.* Finally, when the President acts in contravention of the will of Congress, "his power is at its lowest ebb," and the Court can sustain his actions "only by disabling the Congress from acting upon the subject." *Id.,* at 637–638.

Although we have in the past found and do today find Justice Jackson's classification of executive actions into three general categories analytically useful, . . . Justice Jackson himself recognized that his three categories represented "a somewhat over-simplified grouping," 343 U. S., at 635, and it is doubtless the case that executive action in any particular instance falls, not neatly in one of three pigeonholes, but rather at some point along a spectrum running from explicit congressional authorization to explicit congressional prohibition. This is particularly true as respects cases such as the one before us, involving responses to international crises the nature of which Congress can hardly have been expected to anticipate in any detail.

III

In nullifying post-November 14, 1979, attachments . . ., President Carter . . . relied on § [1702] of the IEEPA, 91 Stat. 1626. . . . [This] provides in part:

> "At the times and to the extent specified in section 1701 of this title, the President may, under such regulations as he may prescribe, by means of instructions, licenses, or otherwise . . . investigate, regulate, direct and compel, nullify, void, prevent or prohibit, any acquisition, holding, withholding, use, transfer, withdrawal, transportation, importation or exportation of, or dealing in, or exercising any right, power, or privilege with respect to, or transactions involving, any property in which any foreign country or a national thereof has any interest . . . by any person, or with respect to any property, subject to the jurisdiction of the United States."

The Government contends that the acts of "nullifying" the attachments and ordering the "transfer" of the frozen assets are specifically authorized by the plain language of the above statute. . . .

[We agree.] . . . This Court has previously recognized that the congressional purpose in authorizing blocking orders is "to put control of foreign assets in the hands of the President . . . ." *Propper v. Clark,* 337 U. S. 472, 493 (1949). Such orders permit the President to maintain the foreign assets at his disposal for use in negotiating the resolution of a declared national emergency. The frozen assets serve as a "bargaining chip" to be used by the President when dealing with a hostile country. [Interpreting blocking orders not to apply to pending claims would] allow individual claimants throughout the country to minimize or wholly eliminate this "bargaining chip" through attachments, garnishments, or similar encumbrances on property. Neither the purpose the statute was enacted to serve nor its plain language supports such a result.

Because the President's action in nullifying the attachments and ordering the transfer of the assets was taken pursuant to specific congressional authorization, it is "supported by the strongest of presumptions and the widest latitude of judicial interpretation, and the burden of persuasion would rest heavily upon any who might attack it." *Youngstown,* 343 U. S., at 637 (Jackson, J., concurring). Under the circumstances of this case, we cannot say that petitioner has sustained that heavy burden. . . .

IV

Although we have concluded that the IEEPA constitutes specific congressional authorization to the President to nullify the attachments and order the transfer of Iranian assets, there remains the question of the President's authority to suspend claims pending in American courts. Such claims have, of course, an existence apart from the attachments which accompanied them. In terminating these claims through Executive Order No. 12294, the President purported to act under authority of both the IEEPA and 22 U. S. C. § 1732, the so-called "Hostage Act."

We conclude that although the IEEPA authorized the nullification of the attachments, it cannot be read to authorize the suspension of the claims. The claims of American citizens against Iran are not in themselves transactions involving Iranian property or efforts to exercise any rights with respect to such property. . . . The terms of the IEEPA therefore do not authorize the President to suspend claims in American courts. . . .

The Hostage Act, passed in 1868, provides:

> "Whenever it is made known to the President that any citizen of the United States has been unjustly deprived of his liberty by or under the authority of any foreign government, . . . [and] it appears to be wrongful and in violation of the rights of American citizenship, the President shall forthwith demand the release of such citizen, and if the release so demanded is unreasonably delayed or refused, the President shall use such means, not amounting to acts of war, as he may think necessary and proper to obtain or effectuate the release. . . ." Rev. Stat. § 2001, 22 U. S. C. § 1732.

We are reluctant to conclude that this provision constitutes specific authorization to the President to suspend claims in American courts. Although the broad language of the Hostage Act suggests it may cover this case, there are several difficulties with such a view. The legislative history indicates that the Act was passed in response to a situation unlike the recent Iranian crisis. Congress in 1868 was concerned with the activity of certain countries refusing to recognize the citizenship of naturalized Americans traveling abroad, and repatriating such citizens against their will. See, *e.g.,* Cong. Globe, 40th Cong., 2d Sess., 4331 (1868). These countries were not interested in returning the citizens in exchange for any sort of ransom. This also explains the reference in the Act to imprisonment "in violation of the rights of American citizenship." Although the Iranian hostage-taking violated international law and common decency, the hostages were not seized out of any refusal to recognize their American citizenship—they were seized precisely *because of their* American citizenship. . . .

Concluding that neither the IEEPA nor the Hostage Act constitutes specific authorization of the President's action suspending claims, however, is not to say that these statutory provisions are entirely irrelevant to the question of the validity of the President's action.[7] We think both statutes highly relevant in the looser sense of

[7] **Questions:** Rehnquist has concluded that (1) a statute authorized Presidents Jimmy Carter and Ronald Reagan to nullify Dames & Moore's *attachment* of Iranian assets, but (2) no statute expressly or implicitly authorized the presidents to suspend Dames & Moore's entire claim against Iran. Why doesn't the absence of statutory authority mean that the president

indicating congressional acceptance of a broad scope for executive action in circumstances such as those presented in this case. . . . [T]he IEEPA delegates broad authority to the President to act in times of national emergency with respect to property of a foreign country. The Hostage Act similarly indicates congressional willingness that the President have broad discretion when responding to the hostile acts of foreign sovereigns. . . .

Although we have declined to conclude that the IEEPA or the Hostage Act directly authorizes the President's suspension of claims for the reasons noted, we cannot ignore the general tenor of Congress' legislation in this area in trying to determine whether the President is acting alone or at least with the acceptance of Congress. As we have noted, Congress cannot anticipate and legislate with regard to every possible action the President may find it necessary to take or every possible situation in which he might act. Such failure of Congress specifically to delegate authority does not, "especially . . . in the areas of foreign policy and national security," imply "congressional disapproval" of action taken by the Executive. *Haig v. Agee, ante,* at 291. On the contrary, the enactment of legislation closely related to the question of the President's authority in a particular case which evinces legislative intent to accord the President broad discretion may be considered to "invite" "measures on independent presidential responsibility," *Youngstown,* 343 U. S., at 637 (Jackson, J., concurring). At least this is so where there is no contrary indication of legislative intent and when, as here, there is a history of congressional acquiescence in conduct of the sort engaged in by the President. It is to that history which we now turn.

Not infrequently in affairs between nations, outstanding claims by nationals of one country against the government of another country are "sources of friction" between the two sovereigns. *United States v. Pink,* 315 U. S. 203, 225 (1942). To resolve these difficulties, nations have often entered into agreements settling the claims of their respective nationals. . . . Consistent with that principle, the United States has repeatedly exercised its sovereign authority to settle the claims of its nationals against foreign countries. Though those settlements have sometimes been made by treaty, there has also been a longstanding practice of settling such claims by executive agreement without the advice and consent of the Senate. Under such agreements, the President has agreed to renounce or extinguish claims of United States nationals against foreign governments in return for lump-sum payments or the establishment of arbitration procedures. . . . It is clear that the practice of settling claims continues today. Since 1952, the President has entered into at least 10 binding settlements with foreign nations, including an $80 million settlement with the People's Republic of China.

Crucial to our decision today is the conclusion that Congress has implicitly approved the practice of claim settlement by executive agreement. This is best demonstrated by Congress' enactment of the International Claims Settlement Act of 1949, 64 Stat. 13, as amended. The Act had two purposes: (1) to allocate to United States nationals funds received in the course of an executive claims settlement with Yugoslavia, and (2) to provide a procedure whereby funds resulting from future settlements could be distributed. To achieve these ends Congress created the International Claims Commission, now the Foreign Claims Settlement Commission, and gave it jurisdiction to make final and binding decisions with respect to claims by United States nationals against settlement funds. By creating a procedure to implement future settlement agreements, Congress placed its stamp of approval on such agreements. Indeed, the legislative history of the Act observed that the United

---

lacks the power to act domestically with the force of law? Wasn't that the holding of the majority opinion in *Youngstown*?

States was seeking settlements with countries other than Yugoslavia and that the bill contemplated settlements of a similar nature in the future. H. R. Rep. No. 770, 81st Cong., 1st Sess. (1949). . . .

Over the years Congress has frequently amended the International Claims Settlement Act to provide for particular problems arising out of settlement agreements, thus demonstrating Congress' continuing acceptance of the President's claim settlement authority. With respect to the Executive Agreement with the People's Republic of China, for example, Congress established an allocation formula for distribution of the funds received pursuant to the Agreement. As with legislation involving other executive agreements, Congress did not question the fact of the settlement or the power of the President to have concluded it. . . .[8]

In addition to congressional acquiescence in the President's power to settle claims, prior cases of this Court have also recognized that the President does have some measure of power to enter into executive agreements without obtaining the advice and consent of the Senate. In *United States v. Pink,* 315 U. S. 203 (1942), for example, the Court upheld the validity of the Litvinov Assignment, which was part of an Executive Agreement whereby the Soviet Union assigned to the United States amounts owed to it by American nationals so that outstanding claims of other American nationals could be paid. The Court explained that the resolution of such claims was integrally connected with normalizing United States' relations with a foreign state: "Power to remove such obstacles to full recognition as settlement of claims of our nationals . . . certainly is a modest implied power of the President. . . ." *Id.,* at 229–230. . . .

In light of all of the foregoing—the inferences to be drawn from the character of the legislation Congress has enacted in the area, such as the IEEPA and the Hostage Act, and from the history of acquiescence in executive claims settlement—we conclude that the President was authorized to suspend pending claims pursuant to Executive Order No. 12294. As Justice Frankfurter pointed out in *Youngstown,* 343 U. S., at 610–611, "a systematic, unbroken, executive practice, long pursued to the knowledge of the Congress and never before questioned . . . may be treated as a gloss on 'Executive Power' vested in the President by § 1 of Art. II." Past practice does not, by itself, create power, but "long-continued practice, known to and acquiesced in by Congress, would raise a presumption that the [action] had been [taken] in pursuance of its consent . . . ." *United States v. Midwest Oil Co.,* 236 U. S. 459, 474 (1915). Such practice is present here and such a presumption is also appropriate. In light of the fact that Congress may be considered to have consented to the President's action in suspending claims, we cannot say that action exceeded the President's powers.

Our conclusion is buttressed by the fact that . . . Congress has not disapproved of the action taken here. Though Congress has held hearings on the Iranian Agreement itself, Congress has not enacted legislation, or even passed a resolution, indicating its displeasure with the Agreement. Quite the contrary, the relevant Senate Committee has stated that the establishment of the Tribunal is "of vital importance to the United States." S. Rep. No. 97–71, p. 5 (1981). We are thus clearly not

---

8 **Questions:** Again, the majority opinion in *Youngstown* concluded that Congress had given President Harry Truman lots of authority over strikes but failed to give Truman the specific seizure authority that he exercised with respect to the steel mills. Several justices interpreted Congress's action as congressional *disapproval* or denial of the authority to seize steel mills. Why, then, does Rehnquist interpret the absence of statutory authority not as "disapproval" but as "acquiescence"? How else could Congress express its disapproval other than by failing to pass a statute expressly or implicitly giving a president power to act?

confronted with a situation in which Congress has in some way resisted the exercise of Presidential authority. . . .[9]

32.3 THE POWER TO ENFORCE TREATIES AND EXECUTIVE AGREEMENTS

Although the executive agreement in *Dames & Moore v. Regan*, 453 U.S. 654 (1981), wasn't expressly authorized by statute, the Supreme Court nevertheless concluded that Congress would have acquiesced to the president's unilateral exercise of power. As a result, just like a valid administrative regulation, the executive agreement carried the force of law and was binding on a federal district court.

In a later case, *American Insurance Ass'n v. Garamendi*, 539 U.S. 396 (2003), the Court elaborated on the preemptive effect of a valid executive order. The decision considered a California law that required insurance companies that did business in Europe from 1920 to 1945 to publicize their records. The law's purpose was to facilitate the ability of Holocaust victims to collect on their insurance plans. But the Court interpreted the state law as inconsistent with executive agreements that presidents had previously entered into with Germany after World War II. *Garamendi*, 539 U.S. at 419–20. The Court held that executive agreements are functionally equivalent to treaties in that they announce "the express foreign policy of the National Government." *Id.* The Court therefore concluded that the state law was preempted under the Supremacy Clause.

Garamendi concluded that the president's power to enact an executive agreement was roughly equivalent to the president's power to make a self-executing treaty. Five years later, the Court considered for the first time whether a president has the same power as Congress to *enforce* a non-self-executing treaty domestically.

32.3.1

Medellín v. Texas

552 U.S. 491 (2008)

At issue was a case in front of the International Court of Justice (ICJ), a tribunal established under the United Nations (U.N.) Charter to adjudicate disputes between member states. In a case known as *Avena* brought by Mexico against the United States, the ICJ held that the United States was violating the Vienna Convention on Consular Relations, a 1969 treaty that governs international agreements. The ICJ

---

[9] **Question:** Rehnquist concludes that the president has an implied power to settle claims—a power that Congress has not "disapproved" but has implicitly accepted. If, after this opinion, Congress were to pass a concurrent or joint resolution condemning the president's exercise of power, would future presidents lose this implied power? Or would future presidents be able to claim *Dames & Moore v. Regan* as a precedent validating their claims of implied power to conduct foreign affairs even in the face of congressional disapproval?

observed that state courts within the United States had failed to inform fifty-one prosecuted Mexican nationals of their right to seek assistance from the Mexican consulate. At the time, the United States had signed a treaty known as the "Optional Protocol" in which it consented to be bound to the decisions of the ICJ on questions of the Vienna Convention.

In 2005, President George W. Bush issued a memorandum in which he declared "that the United States will discharge its international obligations" under the *Avena* decision "by having State courts give effect to the decision . . . in cases filed by the 51 Mexican nationals addressed in that decision." Memorandum from George W. Bush, President of the United States, Compliance with the Decision of the International Court of Justice in Avena (Feb. 28, 2005).

Shortly afterward, one of the Mexican nationals named in the *Avena* decision, José Ernesto Medellín, sought a new trial after the State of Texas convicted him of murder. Medellín's case reached the Supreme Court and presented it with two questions:

(1) Was the *Avena* decision directly enforceable in state court by virtue of the United States' ratification of the U.N. Charter and the Optional Protocol?

(2) If not, did President Bush's memorandum independently make the *Avena* decision enforceable? (In other words, could the *president* enforce the *Avena* decision by issuing a memorandum, or did *Congress alone* have the power to enforce the *Avena* decision under the power to enforce treaties recognized in *Missouri v. Holland*, 252 U.S. 416 (1920)?)

In the following opinion, *Medellín v. Texas*, 552 U.S. 491 (2008), the Court answered no to the first question, holding that the *Avena* decision was the equivalent of a non-self-executing treaty. That left the second question—to which the Court also answered no.

■ CHIEF JUSTICE ROBERTS delivered the opinion of the Court.[10]

[M]edellín . . . argues that the ICJ's judgment in *Avena* is binding on state courts by virtue of the President's February 28, 2005 Memorandum. The United States contends that while the *Avena* judgment does not of its own force require domestic courts to set aside ordinary rules of procedural default, that judgment became the law of the land with precisely that effect pursuant to the President's Memorandum and his power "to establish binding rules of decision that preempt contrary state law." Accordingly, we must decide whether the President's declaration alters our conclusion that the *Avena* judgment is not a rule of domestic law binding in state and federal courts.

---

[10] **As You Read, Consider:** Chief Justice John Roberts has very different views about unilateral presidential power than did his predecessor, William Rehnquist. Yet he also formalistically applies Justice Robert Jackson's three categories from *Youngstown Sheet & Tube Co. v. Sawyer*. How does Roberts interpret the absence of specific congressional authorization allowing the president to enforce a treaty domestically?

A

The United States maintains that the President's constitutional role "uniquely qualifies" him to resolve the sensitive foreign policy decisions that bear on compliance with an ICJ decision and "to do so expeditiously." We do not question these propositions. In this case, the President seeks to vindicate United States interests in ensuring the reciprocal observance of the Vienna Convention, protecting relations with foreign governments, and demonstrating commitment to the role of international law. These interests are plainly compelling.

Such considerations, however, do not allow us to set aside first principles. The President's authority to act, as with the exercise of any governmental power, "must stem either from an act of Congress or from the Constitution itself." *Youngstown, supra,* at 585; *Dames & Moore v. Regan,* 453 U.S. 654, 668 (1981).

Justice Jackson's familiar tripartite scheme provides the accepted framework for evaluating executive action in this area. First, "[w]hen the President acts pursuant to an express or implied authorization of Congress, his authority is at its maximum, for it includes all that he possesses in his own right plus all that Congress can delegate." *Youngstown,* 343 U.S., at 635 (concurring opinion). Second, "[w]hen the President acts in absence of either a congressional grant or denial of authority, he can only rely upon his own independent powers, but there is a zone of twilight in which he and Congress may have concurrent authority, or in which its distribution is uncertain." *Id.,* at 637. In this circumstance, Presidential authority can derive support from "congressional inertia, indifference or quiescence." *Ibid.* Finally, "[w]hen the President takes measures incompatible with the expressed or implied will of Congress, his power is at its lowest ebb," and the Court can sustain his actions "only by disabling the Congress from acting upon the subject." *Id.,* at 637–638.

B

The United States marshals two principal arguments in favor of the President's authority "to establish binding rules of decision that preempt contrary state law." The Solicitor General first argues that the relevant treaties give the President the authority to implement the *Avena* judgment and that Congress has acquiesced in the exercise of such authority. The United States also relies upon an "independent" international dispute-resolution power wholly apart from the asserted authority based on the pertinent treaties. Medellín adds the additional argument that the President's Memorandum is a valid exercise of his power to take care that the laws be faithfully executed.

1

The United States maintains that the President's Memorandum is authorized by the Optional Protocol and the U.N. Charter. That is, because the relevant treaties "create an obligation to comply with *Avena,*" they "*implicitly* give the President authority to implement that treaty-based obligation." As a result, the President's Memorandum is well grounded in the first category of the *Youngstown* framework.

We disagree. The President has an array of political and diplomatic means available to enforce international obligations, but unilaterally converting a non-self-executing treaty into a self-executing one is not among them. The responsibility for transforming an international obligation arising from a non-self-executing treaty into domestic law falls to Congress. *Foster,* 2 Pet., at 315. As this Court has explained, when treaty stipulations are "not self-executing they can only be enforced pursuant to legislation to carry them into effect." *Whitney, supra,* at 194. Moreover, "[u]ntil such act shall be passed, the Court is not at liberty to disregard the existing laws on the subject." *Foster, supra,* at 315.

The requirement that Congress, rather than the President, implement a non-self-executing treaty derives from the text of the Constitution, which divides the treaty-making power between the President and the Senate. The Constitution vests the President with the authority to "make" a treaty. Art. II, § 2. If the Executive determines that a treaty should have domestic effect of its own force, that determination may be implemented in "mak[ing]" the treaty, by ensuring that it contains language plainly providing for domestic enforceability. If the treaty is to be self-executing in this respect, the Senate must consent to the treaty by the requisite two-thirds vote, *ibid.,* consistent with all other constitutional restraints.

Once a treaty is ratified without provisions clearly according it domestic effect, however, whether the treaty will ever have such effect is governed by the fundamental constitutional principle that " '[t]he power to make the necessary laws is in Congress; the power to execute in the President.' " *Hamdan v. Rumsfeld,* 548 U.S. 557, 591 (2006) (quoting *Ex parte Milligan,* 4 Wall. 2, 139 (1866) (opinion of Chase, C. J.)); see U.S. Const., Art. I, § 1 ("All legislative Powers herein granted shall be vested in a Congress of the United States"). As already noted, the terms of a non-self-executing treaty can become domestic law only in the same way as any other law—through passage of legislation by both Houses of Congress, combined with either the President's signature or a congressional override of a Presidential veto. See Art. I, § 7. Indeed, "the President's power to see that the laws are faithfully executed refutes the idea that he is to be a lawmaker." *Youngstown,* 343 U.S., at 587.

A non-self-executing treaty, by definition, is one that was ratified with the understanding that it is not to have domestic effect of its own force. That understanding precludes the assertion that Congress has implicitly authorized the President—acting on his own—to achieve precisely the same result. We therefore conclude, given the absence of congressional legislation, that the non-self-executing treaties at issue here did not "express[ly] or implied[ly]" vest the President with the unilateral authority to make them self-executing. See *id.,* at 635 (Jackson, J., concurring). Accordingly, the President's Memorandum does not fall within the first category of the *Youngstown* framework.[11]

Indeed, the preceding discussion should make clear that the non-self-executing character of the relevant treaties not only refutes the notion that the ratifying parties vested the President with the authority to unilaterally make treaty obligations binding on domestic courts, but also implicitly prohibits him from doing so. When the President asserts the power to "enforce" a non-self-executing treaty by unilaterally creating domestic law, he acts in conflict with the implicit understanding of the ratifying Senate. His assertion of authority, insofar as it is based on the pertinent non-self-executing treaties, is therefore within Justice Jackson's third category, not the first or even the second.

Each of the two means described above for giving domestic effect to an international treaty obligation under the Constitution—for making law—requires joint action by the Executive and Legislative Branches: The Senate can ratify a self-executing treaty "ma[de]" by the Executive, or, if the ratified treaty is not self-executing, Congress can enact implementing legislation approved by the President. It should not be surprising that our Constitution does not contemplate vesting such power in the Executive alone. As Madison explained in The Federalist No. 47, under our constitutional system of checks and balances, "[t]he magistrate in whom the

---

[11] **Question:** As in *Dames & Moore v. Regan*, Roberts concludes that the president has acted without express or implicit congressional authorization. In *Dames & Moore*, the Court nevertheless held that the president had an implied power to settle foreign disputes and that Congress had acquiesced in this power. How does Roberts's analysis depart from that of the *Dames & Moore* Court?

whole executive power resides cannot of himself make a law." J. Cooke ed., p. 326 (1961). That would, however, seem an apt description of the asserted executive authority unilaterally to give the effect of domestic law to obligations under a non-self-executing treaty.

The United States nonetheless maintains that the President's Memorandum should be given effect as domestic law because "this case involves a valid Presidential action in the context of Congressional 'acquiescence.'" Under the *Youngstown* tripartite framework, congressional acquiescence is pertinent when the President's action falls within the second category—that is, when he "acts in absence of either a congressional grant or denial of authority." 343 U.S., at 637 (Jackson, J., concurring). Here, however, as we have explained, the President's effort to accord domestic effect to the *Avena* judgment does not meet that prerequisite.

In any event, even if we were persuaded that congressional acquiescence could support the President's asserted authority to create domestic law pursuant to a non-self-executing treaty, such acquiescence does not exist here. The United States first locates congressional acquiescence in Congress's failure to act following the President's resolution of prior ICJ controversies. A review of the Executive's actions in those prior cases, however, cannot support the claim that Congress acquiesced in this particular exercise of Presidential authority, for none of them remotely involved transforming an international obligation into domestic law and thereby displacing state law.

The United States also directs us to the President's "related" statutory responsibilities and to his "established role" in litigating foreign policy concerns as support for the President's asserted authority to give the ICJ's decision in *Avena* the force of domestic law. Congress has indeed authorized the President to represent the United States before the United Nations, the ICJ, and the Security Council, 22 U.S.C. § 287, but the authority of the President to represent the United States before such bodies speaks to the President's *international* responsibilities, not any unilateral authority to create domestic law. The authority expressly conferred by Congress in the international realm cannot be said to "invite" the Presidential action at issue here. See *Youngstown, supra,* at 637, 72 S.Ct. 863 (Jackson, J., concurring). At bottom, none of the sources of authority identified by the United States supports the President's claim that Congress has acquiesced in his asserted power to establish on his own federal law or to override state law.

None of this is to say, however, that the combination of a non-self-executing treaty and the lack of implementing legislation precludes the President from acting to comply with an international treaty obligation. It is only to say that the Executive cannot unilaterally execute a non-self-executing treaty by giving it domestic effect. That is, the non-self-executing character of a treaty constrains the President's ability to comply with treaty commitments by unilaterally making the treaty binding on domestic courts. The President may comply with the treaty's obligations by some other means, so long as they are consistent with the Constitution. But he may not rely upon a non-self-executing treaty to "establish binding rules of decision that preempt contrary state law."

2

We thus turn to the United States' claim that—independent of the United States' treaty obligations—the Memorandum is a valid exercise of the President's foreign affairs authority to resolve claims disputes with foreign nations. The United States relies on a series of cases in which this Court has upheld the authority of the President to settle foreign claims pursuant to an executive agreement. See *Garamendi,* 539 U.S., at 415; *Dames & Moore,* 453 U.S., at 679–680; *United States v. Pink,* 315

U.S. 203, 229 (1942); *United States v. Belmont,* 301 U.S. 324, 330 (1937). In these cases this Court has explained that, if pervasive enough, a history of congressional acquiescence can be treated as a "gloss on 'Executive Power' vested in the President by § 1 of Art. II." *Dames & Moore, supra,* at 686 (some internal quotation marks omitted).

This argument is of a different nature than the one rejected above. Rather than relying on the United States' treaty obligations, the President relies on an independent source of authority in ordering Texas to put aside its procedural bar to successive habeas petitions. Nevertheless, we find that our claims-settlement cases do not support the authority that the President asserts in this case.

The claims-settlement cases involve a narrow set of circumstances: the making of executive agreements to settle civil claims between American citizens and foreign governments or foreign nationals. See, *e.g., Belmont, supra,* at 327. They are based on the view that "a systematic, unbroken, executive practice, long pursued to the knowledge of the Congress and never before questioned," can "raise a presumption that the [action] had been [taken] in pursuance of its consent." *Dames & Moore, supra,* at 686 . . . . Even still, the limitations on this source of executive power are clearly set forth and the Court has been careful to note that "[p]ast practice does not, by itself, create power." [*Id.*]

The President's Memorandum is not supported by a "particularly longstanding practice" of congressional acquiescence, but rather is what the United States itself has described as "unprecedented action." Indeed, the Government has not identified a single instance in which the President has attempted (or Congress has acquiesced in) a Presidential directive issued to state courts, much less one that reaches deep into the heart of the State's police powers and compels state courts to reopen final criminal judgments and set aside neutrally applicable state laws. The Executive's narrow and strictly limited authority to settle international claims disputes pursuant to an executive agreement cannot stretch so far as to support the current Presidential Memorandum.

3

Medellín argues that the President's Memorandum is a valid exercise of his "take Care" power. The United States, however, does not rely upon the President's responsibility to "take Care that the Laws be faithfully executed." U.S. Const., Art. II, § 3. We think this a wise concession. This authority allows the President to execute the laws, not make them. For the reasons we have stated, the *Avena* judgment is not domestic law; accordingly, the President cannot rely on his Take Care powers here. . . .[12]

32.4 THE POWER TO RECOGNIZE FOREIGN GOVERNMENTS

The clause declaring that the president "shall . . . receive Ambassadors and other public Ministers" might not seem like a source of power. In fact, when Alexander Hamilton discussed the clause in *The Federalist,* he dismissed it as "without consequence," more a "matter of dignity than of authority." *The Federalist No. 69,* at 468 (Alexander

[12] **Question:** Roberts narrowly reads the implied power recognized by *Dames & Moore* and further concludes that the president's duty to "take Care that the Laws be faithfully executed" is inapplicable domestically when there is no domestic law to execute. After this opinion, does the president have any power to issue unilateral regulations domestically absent the express or implied approval of a statute or treaty?

Hamilton) (Jacob E. Cooke ed., 1961). But when he later served in the administration of President George Washington, Hamilton quickly changed his mind. As he wrote in the *Pacificus* essays (see section 25.1), Hamilton regarded the clause as one of the most important textual sources of power for the president to conduct foreign policy.

In 1793 after the French Revolution overthrew the government of Louis XVI, the new French government proposed to send an ambassador, Edmond Charles Genêt, to the United States. In a letter to Washington, Hamilton realized that if the president "receive[d]" Genêt, the United States would implicitly acknowledge the legitimacy of the revolutionary French government. 4 *Works of Alexander Hamilton* 369, 369–96 (Henry Cabot Lodge ed., 1904). Washington agreed—and without consulting Congress, he received Citizen Genêt and thereby recognized the French government. Congress didn't react, setting a precedent that the president had the power to recognize foreign governments.

The following year, when Washington attempted to avoid joining France's war with Great Britain—despite the United States' earlier treaty of alliance with France—Hamilton argued that the president's recognition of France's revolutionary government meant that the United States was no longer bound by a treaty made with France's deposed monarchy. Agreeing, Washington issued his proclamation of neutrality, which Hamilton defended in the *Pacificus* essay, excerpted earlier in the section on the Vesting Clauses (section 25.1). Hamilton wrote in his essay that the Reception Clause gave the president the power "of judging, in the case of a revolution of government in a foreign country, whether the new rulers are competent organs of the national will, and ought to be recognised, or not." 15 *The Papers of Alexander Hamilton* 33 (Harold C. Syrett ed., 1969) (1793).

Over the next century, the president continued to exercise this power to recognize foreign governments. In 1818, when newly independent countries in Latin America were fighting wars of independence against Spain, Congress voted down bills to appropriate money for foreign ministers until the president formally recognized the countries. 32 Annals of Cong. 1570 (1818); Act of May 4, 1882, 3 Stat. 678. When Texas later declared independence from Mexico, Congress similarly appropriated funds for a "diplomatic agent to be sent to the Republic of Texas, whenever the President of the United States . . . shall deem it expedient to appoint such minister." Act of Mar. 3, 1837, 5 Stat. 163, 170. And when President William McKinley and Congress disagreed about whether the United States should recognize Cuba's independence from Spain, Congress capitulated after canvassing historical precedent and concluding that the United States typically recognized foreign countries by receiving their ambassadors. 31 Cong. Rec. 3699–702 (1898); S. Doc. No. 54–56, at 20–22 (1897).

This pattern of presidential and congressional cooperation over recognition continued through the twentieth century, when disputes arose over the recognition of Mexico after 1914, the Soviet Union after 1922, Manchukuo after 1932, and the People's Republic of China after 1949. For three decades after the Chinese civil war, for example, the United States recognized the Republic of China, based in Taiwan, while withholding formal recognition from the People's Republic of China, based on the mainland. But in 1979, President Jimmy Carter unilaterally decided to recognize the People's Republic of China and derecognize the Republic of China. Working with Congress, Carter then signed the Taiwan Relations Act of 1979, Pub. L. No. 96–8, 93 Stat. 14, which treated Taiwan as if it were a legally distinct entity from China. The act nevertheless established close economic and political relationships with Taiwan without formally recognizing it.

The Supreme Court, meanwhile, has treated the question of whether to recognize a foreign country as the archetypal political question. *See, e.g., Kennett v. Chambers*, 55 U.S. (14 How.) 38, 50–51 (1852). In dozens of holdings, the Court has deferred to the other branches to determine a foreign nation's sovereign boundaries, government, ambassadors, and compliance with treaties. *See, e.g., In re Baiz*, 135 U.S. 403 (1890); *Foster v. Neilson*, 27 U.S. (2 Pet.) 253 (1829). Even when the Court issues a decision on the merits in the field of foreign relations, it typically applies considerable deference to the other branches' foreign policy and national security determinations. *See, e.g., Trump v. Hawaii*, 138 S. Ct. 2392 (2018); *Rostker v. Goldberg*, 453 U.S. 57 (1981).

The Court's deference in this area can at times be absolute. Applying a rule known as the "act of state" doctrine, the Court has declared that when the United States recognizes a foreign government, federal courts should not examine the validity of the public acts of those governments within their own territory—such as when a foreign government nationalizes an industry in alleged violation of its own law. *Alfred Dunhill of London, Inc. v. Cuba*, 425 U.S. 682 (1976). In 1976, Congress enacted the Foreign Sovereign Immunities Act of 1976, Pub. L. No. 94–583, 90 Stat. 2891, to guide judges in determining how and whether to award sovereign immunity to a foreign state and its agencies. *See, e.g., Argentine Republic v. Amerada Hess Shipping Corp.*, 488 U.S. 428 (1989).

Despite this general deference, the Court has, occasionally, been asked to weigh in on interbranch disputes with respect to foreign recognition. In 1979, for example, a group of senators led by Barry Goldwater of Arizona sued to enjoin Carter from recognizing the People's Republic of China—a recognition that effectively nullified the Sino-American Mutual Defense Treaty of 1955 with the Republic of China in Taiwan. In *Goldwater v. Carter*, the Court declined to consider the question, with some justices observing that the entire Senate hadn't issued a resolution objecting to Carter's actions. 444 U.S. 996, 998 (1979) (Brennan, J., concurring). Yet in *Zivotofsky ex rel. Zivotofsky v. Clinton*, the Court held that it *could* decide the constitutionality of a statute that effectively ordered the executive branch to recognize Israeli sovereignty over the city of Jerusalem. 566 U.S. 189, 201–02 (2012). That decision cleared the way for the following case three years later.

32.4.1

Zivotofsky ex rel. Zivotofsky v. Kerry

576 U.S. 1059 (2015)

On May 14, 1948, President Harry Truman became the first head of state to recognize the new state of Israel, which declared its independence earlier in the day. *Public Papers of the Presidents of the United States: Harry S. Truman, 1948*, at 258 (1964). This recognition was diplomatically fraught. The United Nations had recently resolved to partition the former British Mandate for Palestine into an independent "Arab State"; an independent "Jewish State"; and the "City of Jerusalem," which would be administered by the United Nations itself. G.A. Res. 181 (II), Future Government of Palestine (Nov. 29, 1947). But many Arab states in the region opposed partition, and the Truman administration believed that its decision to recognize Israel would contribute to an Arab-Israeli war. *See* David McCullough, *Truman* 735–55 (1992).

A war did follow Israel's declaration of independence. Soon, Israel and neighboring Jordan both exercised de facto control over Jerusalem. For six decades afterward, as the status of Jerusalem remained contested, U.S. presidents declined to issue any declaration acknowledging any country's sovereignty over Jerusalem. For American diplomats interested in brokering peace in the region, such as President Bill Clinton's first secretary of state, Warren Christopher, there was "no issue related to the Arab-Israeli negotiations that is more sensitive than Jerusalem." 141 Cong. Rec. 28,967 (1995). Any effort to bring the issue to the forefront was considered "very damaging to the success of the peace process." *Id.*

To avoid compromising the United States' neutrality on the status of Jerusalem, the Department of State adopted a policy of not listing any *country of birth* on the passports of U.S. citizens born in Jerusalem. Instead, the department's policy was simply to record the place of birth as "Jerusalem." This policy bothered members of Congress who wanted the United States to recognize Israeli sovereignty over Jerusalem; thus, Congress responded with the Foreign Relations Authorization Act, Fiscal Year 2003, Pub. L. No. 107–228, 116 Stat. 1350. A section of the act, titled "United States Policy with Respect to Jerusalem as the Capital of Israel," sought to override the policy of the executive branch. It declared, "For purposes of the registration of birth, certification of nationality, or issuance of a passport of a United States citizen born in the city of Jerusalem, the Secretary [of State] shall, upon the request of the citizen or the citizen's legal guardian, record the place of birth as Israel." Foreign Relations Authorization Act, 116 Stat. at 1365–66. Although President

George W. Bush signed the act into law, he issued a signing statement declaring that he would construe the act as advisory, not mandatory. 2 *Public Papers of the Presidents, George W. Bush*, 2002, at 1698 (2005).

In 2002, Menachem Binyamin Zivotofsky was born to U.S. citizens living in Jerusalem. His parents went to the U.S. embassy in Tel Aviv to request that the place of birth on his passport read, "Jerusalem, Israel." The embassy's clerks declined after explaining that under State Department policy, the passport would list only "Jerusalem." Zivotofsky's parents sued on his behalf, seeking to enforce the 2002 statute. In *Zivotofsky ex rel. Zivotofsky v. Clinton*, 566 U.S. 189, 201–02 (2012), the Supreme Court held that the question of this statute's effect was a legal, not a political question.

The merits question returned to the Court shortly afterward in *Zivotofsky ex rel. Zivotofsky v. Kerry*, 576 U.S. 1059 (2015), a case that broadly defined the president's exclusive power to recognize foreign sovereigns.

■ JUSTICE KENNEDY delivered the opinion of the Court.[13]

A delicate subject lies in the background of this case. That subject is Jerusalem. Questions touching upon the history of the ancient city and its present legal and international status are among the most difficult and complex in international affairs. In our constitutional system these matters are committed to the Legislature and the Executive, not the Judiciary. As a result, in this opinion the Court does no more, and must do no more, than note the existence of international debate and tensions respecting Jerusalem. Those matters are for Congress and the President to discuss and consider as they seek to shape the Nation's foreign policies.

2 questions

The Court addresses two questions to resolve the interbranch dispute now before it. First, it must determine whether the President has the exclusive power to grant formal recognition to a foreign sovereign. Second, if he has that power, the Court must determine whether Congress can command the President and his Secretary of State to issue a formal statement that contradicts the earlier recognition. The statement in question here is a congressional mandate that allows a United States citizen born in Jerusalem to direct the President and Secretary of State, when issuing his passport, to state that his place of birth is "Israel." . . .

II

In considering claims of Presidential power this Court refers to Justice Jackson's familiar tripartite framework from *Youngstown Sheet & Tube Co. v. Sawyer,* 343 U.S. 579, 635–638 (1952) (concurring opinion). The framework divides exercises of Presidential power into three categories: First, when "the President acts pursuant to an express or implied authorization of Congress, his authority is at its maximum, for it includes all that he possesses in his own right plus all that Congress can delegate." *Id.,* at 635. Second, "in absence of either a congressional grant or denial of authority" there is a "zone of twilight in which he and Congress may have concurrent authority," and where "congressional inertia, indifference or quiescence may" invite the exercise

[13] **As You Read, Consider:** In contrast with *Youngstown Sheet & Tube Co. v. Sawyer, Dames & Moore v. Regan*, and *Medellín v. Texas*—in which a president claimed the power to act without statutory authorization—here a president has claimed the power to *defy* a statute. Do you agree with Justice Anthony Kennedy that Article II contains implied limits on Congress's power to direct the executive branch? How does this case differ from *Myers v. United States*, in which the Supreme Court restricted Congress's power to regulate the removal of officers?

of executive power. *Id.,* at 637. Finally, when "the President takes measures incompatible with the expressed or implied will of Congress . . . he can rely only upon his own constitutional powers minus any constitutional powers of Congress over the matter." *Ibid.* To succeed in this third category, the President's asserted power must be both "exclusive" and "conclusive" on the issue. *Id.,* at 637–638.

In this case the Secretary contends that § 214(d) infringes on the President's exclusive recognition power by "requiring the President to contradict his recognition position regarding Jerusalem in official communications with foreign sovereigns." In so doing the Secretary acknowledges the President's power is "at its lowest ebb." *Youngstown,* 343 U.S., at 637. Because the President's refusal to implement § 214(d) falls into Justice Jackson's third category, his claim must be "scrutinized with caution," and he may rely solely on powers the Constitution grants to him alone. *Id.,* at 638. . . .

Recognition is a "formal acknowledgement" that a particular "entity possesses the qualifications for statehood" or "that a particular regime is the effective government of a state." Restatement (Third) of Foreign Relations Law of the United States § 203, Comment *a,* p. 84 (1986). It may also involve the determination of a state's territorial bounds. Recognition is often effected by an express "written or oral declaration." 1 J. Moore, Digest of International Law § 27, p. 73 (1906) (Moore). It may also be implied—for example, by concluding a bilateral treaty or by sending or receiving diplomatic agents. *Ibid.*

Legal consequences follow formal recognition. Recognized sovereigns may sue in United States courts, and may benefit from sovereign immunity when they are sued. . . . Recognition at international law, furthermore, is a precondition of regular diplomatic relations. 1 Moore § 27, at 72. Recognition is thus "useful, even necessary," to the existence of a state. *Ibid.*

Despite the importance of the recognition power in foreign relations, the Constitution does not use the term "recognition," either in Article II or elsewhere. The Secretary asserts that the President exercises the recognition power based on the Reception Clause, which directs that the President "shall receive Ambassadors and other public Ministers." Art. II, § 3. As Zivotofsky notes, the Reception Clause received little attention at the Constitutional Convention. In fact, during the ratification debates, Alexander Hamilton claimed that the power to receive ambassadors was "more a matter of dignity than of authority," a ministerial duty largely "without consequence." The Federalist No. 69, p. 420 (C. Rossiter ed. 1961).

At the time of the founding, however, prominent international scholars suggested that receiving an ambassador was tantamount to recognizing the sovereignty of the sending state. See E. de Vattel, The Law of Nations § 78, p. 461 (1758) (J. Chitty ed. 1853) ("[E]very state, truly possessed of sovereignty, has a right to send ambassadors" and "to contest their right in this instance" is equivalent to "contesting their sovereign dignity"). . . . It is a logical and proper inference, then, that a Clause directing the President alone to receive ambassadors would be understood to acknowledge his power to recognize other nations.

This in fact occurred early in the Nation's history when President Washington recognized the French Revolutionary Government by receiving its ambassador. See A. Hamilton, Pacificus No. 1, in The Letters of Pacificus and Helvidius 5, 13–14 (1845). After this incident the import of the Reception Clause became clear—causing Hamilton to change his earlier view. He wrote that the Reception Clause "includes th[e power] of judging, in the case of a revolution of government in a foreign country, whether the new rulers are competent organs of the national will, and ought to be recognised, or not." See *id.,* at 12 . . . . As a result, the Reception Clause provides support, although not the sole authority, for the President's power to recognize other nations.

The inference that the President exercises the recognition power is further supported by his additional Article II powers. It is for the President, "by and with the Advice and Consent of the Senate," to "make Treaties, provided two thirds of the Senators present concur." Art. II, § 2, cl. 2. In addition, "he shall nominate, and by and with the Advice and Consent of the Senate, shall appoint Ambassadors" as well as "other public Ministers and Consuls." *Ibid.*

As a matter of constitutional structure, these additional powers give the President control over recognition decisions. At international law, recognition may be effected by different means, but each means is dependent upon Presidential power. In addition to receiving an ambassador, recognition may occur on "the conclusion of a bilateral treaty," or the "formal initiation of diplomatic relations," including the dispatch of an ambassador. Brownlie 93. The President has the sole power to negotiate treaties, see *United States v. Curtiss-Wright Export Corp.,* 299 U.S. 304, 319 (1936), and the Senate may not conclude or ratify a treaty without Presidential action. The President, too, nominates the Nation's ambassadors and dispatches other diplomatic agents. Congress may not send an ambassador without his involvement. Beyond that, the President himself has the power to open diplomatic channels simply by engaging in direct diplomacy with foreign heads of state and their ministers. The Constitution thus assigns the President means to effect recognition on his own initiative. Congress, by contrast, has no constitutional power that would enable it to initiate diplomatic relations with a foreign nation. Because these specific Clauses confer the recognition power on the President, the Court need not consider whether or to what extent the Vesting Clause, which provides that the "executive Power" shall be vested in the President, provides further support for the President's action here.[14]

The text and structure of the Constitution grant the President the power to recognize foreign nations and governments. The question then becomes whether that power is exclusive. The various ways in which the President may unilaterally effect recognition—and the lack of any similar power vested in Congress—suggest that it is. So, too, do functional considerations. Put simply, the Nation must have a single policy regarding which governments are legitimate in the eyes of the United States and which are not. Foreign countries need to know, before entering into diplomatic relations or commerce with the United States, whether their ambassadors will be received; whether their officials will be immune from suit in federal court; and whether they may initiate lawsuits here to vindicate their rights. These assurances cannot be equivocal.

Recognition is a topic on which the Nation must " 'speak . . . with one voice.' " *American Ins. Assn. v. Garamendi,* 539 U.S. 396, 424 (2003). That voice must be the President's. Between the two political branches, only the Executive has the characteristic of unity at all times. And with unity comes the ability to exercise, to a greater degree, "[d]ecision, activity, secrecy, and dispatch." The Federalist No. 70, p. 424 (A. Hamilton). The President is capable, in ways Congress is not, of engaging in the delicate and often secret diplomatic contacts that may lead to a decision on recognition. See, *e.g., United States v. Pink,* 315 U.S. 203, 229 (1942). He is also better positioned to take the decisive, unequivocal action necessary to recognize

[14] **Question:** Kennedy is observing that the president plays an indispensable role in foreign recognition. But do these observations persuade you that foreign recognition is an *exclusive* power of the president that no statute can regulate? Consider that the statute at issue in this case was signed into law by President George W. Bush, not Congress alone. Consider also that Congress's powers to legislate without the president in *any* context—foreign or domestic—are limited to cases in which Congress can override a presidential veto.

other states at international law. These qualities explain why the Framers listed the traditional avenues of recognition—receiving ambassadors, making treaties, and sending ambassadors—as among the President's Article II powers. . . .

[T]he President since the founding has exercised this unilateral power to recognize new states—and the Court has endorsed the practice. See *Banco Nacional de Cuba v. Sabbatino,* 376 U.S. 398, 410 (1964); *Pink, supra,* at 229; *Williams v. Suffolk Ins. Co.,* 13 Pet. 415, 420 (1839). Texts and treatises on international law treat the President's word as the final word on recognition. See, *e.g.,* Restatement (Third) of Foreign Relations Law § 204, at 89 ("Under the Constitution of the United States the President has exclusive authority to recognize or not to recognize a foreign state or government"). . . .

It remains true, of course, that many decisions affecting foreign relations—including decisions that may determine the course of our relations with recognized countries—require congressional action. Congress may "regulate Commerce with foreign Nations," "establish an uniform Rule of Naturalization," "define and punish Piracies and Felonies committed on the high Seas, and Offences against the Law of Nations," "declare War," "grant Letters of Marque and Reprisal," and "make Rules for the Government and Regulation of the land and naval Forces." U.S. Const., Art. I, § 8. In addition, the President cannot make a treaty or appoint an ambassador without the approval of the Senate. Art. II, § 2, cl. 2. The President, furthermore, could not build an American Embassy abroad without congressional appropriation of the necessary funds. Art. I, § 8, cl. 1. Under basic separation-of-powers principles, it is for the Congress to enact the laws, including "all Laws which shall be necessary and proper for carrying into Execution" the powers of the Federal Government. § 8, cl. 18.

In foreign affairs, as in the domestic realm, the Constitution "enjoins upon its branches separateness but interdependence, autonomy but reciprocity." *Youngstown,* 343 U.S., at 635 (Jackson, J., concurring). Although the President alone effects the formal act of recognition, Congress' powers, and its central role in making laws, give it substantial authority regarding many of the policy determinations that precede and follow the act of recognition itself. If Congress disagrees with the President's recognition policy, there may be consequences. Formal recognition may seem a hollow act if it is not accompanied by the dispatch of an ambassador, the easing of trade restrictions, and the conclusion of treaties. And those decisions require action by the Senate or the whole Congress.

In practice, then, the President's recognition determination is just one part of a political process that may require Congress to make laws. The President's exclusive recognition power encompasses the authority to acknowledge, in a formal sense, the legitimacy of other states and governments, including their territorial bounds. Albeit limited, the exclusive recognition power is essential to the conduct of Presidential duties. The formal act of recognition is an executive power that Congress may not qualify. If the President is to be effective in negotiations over a formal recognition determination, it must be evident to his counterparts abroad that he speaks for the Nation on that precise question. . . .[15]

---

[15] **Questions:** Do you agree with Kennedy that Congress has the exclusive power to "declare War" and "regulate Commerce with foreign Nations" but lacks the power to "qualify" how a president recognizes a foreign nation? Why isn't the president's power to veto legislation sufficient protection of the president's prerogative in this context? How is there any risk that the passage of a statute might compromise the United States' ability to "speak . . . with one voice"?

III

As the power to recognize foreign states resides in the President alone, the question becomes whether § 214(d) infringes on the Executive's consistent decision to withhold recognition with respect to Jerusalem.

Section 214(d) requires that, in a passport or consular report of birth abroad, "the Secretary shall, upon the request of the citizen or the citizen's legal guardian, record the place of birth as Israel" for a "United States citizen born in the city of Jerusalem." 116 Stat. 1366. That is, § 214(d) requires the President, through the Secretary, to identify citizens born in Jerusalem who so request as being born in Israel. But according to the President, those citizens were not born in Israel. As a matter of United States policy, neither Israel nor any other country is acknowledged as having sovereignty over Jerusalem. In this way, § 214(d) "directly contradicts" the "carefully calibrated and longstanding Executive branch policy of neutrality toward Jerusalem." 725 F.3d, at 217, 216.

If the power over recognition is to mean anything, it must mean that the President not only makes the initial, formal recognition determination but also that he may maintain that determination in his and his agent's statements. This conclusion is a matter of both common sense and necessity. If Congress could command the President to state a recognition position inconsistent with his own, . . . Congress in effect would exercise the recognition power.

As Justice Jackson wrote in *Youngstown,* when a Presidential power is "exclusive," it "disabl[es] the Congress from acting upon the subject." 343 U.S., at 637–638 (concurring opinion). Here, the subject is quite narrow: The Executive's exclusive power extends no further than his formal recognition determination. But as to that determination, Congress may not enact a law that directly contradicts it. This is not to say Congress may not express its disagreement with the President in myriad ways. For example, it may enact an embargo, decline to confirm an ambassador, or even declare war. But none of these acts would alter the President's recognition decision. . . .

It is true, as Zivotofsky notes, that Congress has substantial authority over passports. . . . The problem with § 214(d), however, lies in how Congress exercised its authority over passports. It was an improper act for Congress to "aggrandiz[e] its power at the expense of another branch" by requiring the President to contradict an earlier recognition determination in an official document issued by the Executive Branch. *Freytag v. Commissioner,* 501 U.S. 868, 878 (1991). To allow Congress to control the President's communication in the context of a formal recognition determination is to allow Congress to exercise that exclusive power itself. As a result, the statute is unconstitutional. . . .[16]

■ CHIEF JUSTICE ROBERTS, with whom JUSTICE ALITO joins, dissenting.

Today's decision is a first: Never before has this Court accepted a President's direct defiance of an Act of Congress in the field of foreign affairs. We have instead stressed that the President's power reaches "its lowest ebb" when he contravenes the express will of Congress, "for what is at stake is the equilibrium established by our constitutional system." *Youngstown Sheet & Tube Co. v. Sawyer,* 343 U.S. 579, 637–638 (1952) (Jackson, J., concurring). . . .

The first principles in this area are firmly established. The Constitution allocates some foreign policy powers to the Executive, grants some to the Legislature, and

[16] **Questions:** After *Zivotofsky*, could Congress (and the president) enact a law requiring the president to send a message to a foreign country? How far does the "recognition" power extend?

enjoins the President to "take Care that the Laws be faithfully executed." Art. II, § 3. The Executive may disregard "the expressed or implied will of Congress" only if the Constitution grants him a power "at once so conclusive and preclusive" as to "disabl[e] the Congress from acting upon the subject." *Youngstown,* 343 U.S., at 637–638 (1952) (Jackson, J., concurring).

Assertions of exclusive and preclusive power leave the Executive "in the least favorable of possible constitutional postures," and such claims have been "scrutinized with caution" throughout this Court's history. *Id.,* at 640, 638; see *Dames & Moore v. Regan,* 453 U.S. 654, 668–669 (1981). For our first 225 years, no President prevailed when contradicting a statute in the field of foreign affairs. See *Medellín v. Texas,* 552 U.S. 491, 524–532 (2008); *Hamdan v. Rumsfeld,* 548 U.S. 557, 590–595, 613–625 (2006); *Youngstown,* 343 U.S., at 587–589 (majority opinion); *Little v. Barreme,* 2 Cranch 170, 177–179 (1804).[17]

In this case, the President claims the exclusive and preclusive power to recognize foreign sovereigns. The Court devotes much of its analysis to accepting the Executive's contention. I have serious doubts about that position. The majority places great weight on the Reception Clause, which directs that the Executive "shall receive Ambassadors and other public Ministers." Art. II, § 3. But that provision, framed as an obligation rather than an authorization, appears alongside the *duties* imposed on the President by Article II, Section 3, not the *powers* granted to him by Article II, Section 2. Indeed, the People ratified the Constitution with Alexander Hamilton's assurance that executive reception of ambassadors "is more a matter of dignity than of authority" and "will be without consequence in the administration of the government." The Federalist No. 69, p. 420 (C. Rossiter ed. 1961). In short, at the time of the founding, "there was no reason to view the reception clause as a source of discretionary authority for the president." Adler, The President's Recognition Power: Ministerial or Discretionary? 25 Presidential Studies Q. 267, 269 (1995). . . .

[The history also] points in both directions. Some Presidents have claimed an exclusive recognition power, but others have expressed uncertainty about whether such preclusive authority exists. Those in the skeptical camp include Andrew Jackson and Abraham Lincoln, leaders not generally known for their cramped conceptions of Presidential power. Congress has also asserted its authority over recognition determinations at numerous points in history. The majority therefore falls short of demonstrating that "Congress has accepted" the President's exclusive recognition power. In any event, we have held that congressional acquiescence is only "pertinent" when the President acts in the absence of express congressional authorization, not when he asserts power to disregard a statute, as the Executive does here. *Medellín,* 552 U.S., at 528; see *Dames & Moore,*453 U.S., at 678–679.

In sum, although the President has authority over recognition, I am not convinced that the Constitution provides the "conclusive and preclusive" power required to justify defiance of an express legislative mandate. *Youngstown,* 343 U.S., at 638 (Jackson, J., concurring).

NOTE: CURRENT STATUS OF JERUSALEM

Two years after *Zivotofsky*, President Donald Trump dramatically changed the executive branch's policy toward Jerusalem by issuing a proclamation "recognizing Jerusalem as Israel's capital and announcing the

[17] **Question:** Chief Justice John Roberts is an avid proponent of *Myers* and the author of *Seila Law v. Consumer Financial Protection Bureau* (see section 27.3), both of which limited Congress's power to regulate the removal of executive officers. Does he offer a persuasive distinction between that limitation and the one recognized by the majority opinion here?

relocation of our embassy." Proclamation No. 9683, 82 Fed. Reg. 58,331 (Dec. 11, 2017). The president explained that his action was consistent with a 1995 statute, not mentioned by the *Zivotofsky* majority, declaring that it was "the Policy of the United States . . . [that] Jerusalem should be recognized as the capital of the State of Israel." Act of Nov. 8, 1995, Pub. L. No. 104–45, 109 Stat. 398. But the proclamation also noted that "[t]he specific boundaries of Israeli sovereignty in Jerusalem are subject to final status negotiations between the parties. The United States is not taking a position on boundaries or borders." 82 Fed. Reg. at 58,331.

As a result, the effect of Trump's proclamation with respect to U.S. passports remained ambiguous for years. *See* Jennifer K. Elsea, Cong. Rsch. Serv., *So,* Now *Can Menachem Zivotofsky Get His Passport Reissued to Say 'Israel'?* (Mar. 1, 2018). Trump's secretary of state, Michael Pompeo, resolved the ambiguity shortly before the 2020 presidential election when he announced that the U.S. ambassador to Israel would award passports to Jerusalem-born U.S. citizens that listed "Israel" as their place of birth. The first recipient was Menachem Zivotofsky. *See* Press Release, U.S. Embassy Jerusalem, U.S. Embassy Jerusalem Issues First Passport Listing Place of Birth as "Israel" for Applicants Born in Jerusalem (Oct. 30, 2020).

PART THREE

THE JUDICIAL BRANCH

CHAPTER 33

WHAT IS THE "JUDICIAL POWER"?

ARTICLE III, SECTION 1: The judicial Power of the United States, shall be vested in one supreme Court, and in such inferior Courts as the Congress may from time to time ordain and establish. The Judges, both of the supreme and inferior Courts, shall hold their Offices during good Behaviour, and shall, at stated Times, receive for their Services, a Compensation, which shall not be diminished during their Continuance in Office.

ARTICLE III, SECTION 2, CLAUSE 1: The judicial Power shall extend to all Cases, in Law and Equity, arising under this Constitution, the Laws of the United States, and Treaties made, or which shall be made, under their Authority;—to all Cases affecting Ambassadors, other public Ministers and Consuls;—to all Cases of admiralty and maritime Jurisdiction;—to Controversies to which the United States shall be a Party;—to Controversies between two or more States;—between a State and Citizens of another State,—between Citizens of different States,—between Citizens of the same State claiming Lands under Grants of different States, and between a State, or the Citizens thereof, and foreign States, Citizens or Subjects.

ELEVENTH AMENDMENT (1795): The Judicial power of the United States shall not be construed to extend to any suit in law or equity, commenced or prosecuted against one of the United States by Citizens of another State, or by Citizens or Subjects of any Foreign State.

33.1 THE JUDICIAL POWER

Just as the opening sentences of Article I and Article II vest the legislative and executive powers in Congress and the president, the first sentence of Article III vests the "judicial Power" in "one supreme Court" and any "inferior Courts" established by Congress. Beyond this clause, however, Article III does not explicitly define what the term *judicial power* refers to. In addition, unlike Congress and the president, federal courts typically do not invoke their powers on their own initiative. Instead, they generally rely on a *party*, or litigant, to move for the court to exercise the judicial power in a complicated, multistep, and jargon-filled process regulated by Congress.

When reduced to its constitutional minimum, the principal exercise of the judicial power today involves the power *to assume jurisdiction* over a dispute, *to decide the dispute*, and *to compel the disputing parties to comply* with the court's decision.

Power to assume jurisdiction

Jurisdiction refers broadly to the authority of a court to decide a particular dispute and to compel the disputing parties to comply with the court's decision. Jurisdiction can be divided into *personal jurisdiction*, or the power of a court to compel a party to comply with its judgment, and *subject-matter jurisdiction*, or the power of a court to decide a dispute that relates to a particular subject. The personal jurisdiction of federal courts is limited by statute and by constitutional principles of fairness. It will be discussed in a later section on the Due Process Clauses of the Fifth and Fourteenth Amendments (section 40.4). The subject-matter jurisdiction of federal courts is limited by Article III to an enumerated list of "Cases" and "Controversies"—most of which can be further narrowed by acts of Congress. *See Williams v. United States*, 289 U.S. 553, 566–67 (1933).

The terms *cases* and *controversies* do not have objective definitions. Instead, the Supreme Court has interpreted them to describe the sorts of disputes that British and American courts have traditionally decided. One definition of *cases* and *controversies* describes them as raising *legal questions* that judges can resolve by the application of legal rules, versus *political questions* that can be resolved only by the discretion of elected officials. The political question doctrine was first discussed in a section devoted to political questions (section 3.4).

Even when a "Case" or "Controversy" raises a legal question, the Supreme Court has held that the terms describe a particular kind of legal dispute with multiple discrete elements, each of which will be discussed later in terms of standing (section 34.1) and sovereign immunity (section 35.1). Under the doctrine of *standing*, the terms *case* and *controversy* refer to a dispute in which a party alleges a concrete, particularized, and actual or imminent *injury in fact* (section 34.2) that was *caused* by the defendant and can likely be *redressed* by a federal court (section 34.3). In addition, Article III does not permit federal courts to exercise subject-matter jurisdiction over *all* cases and controversies, but only *enumerated* cases that involve particular elements (section 34.5) and controversies that involve particular parties (section 34.6). Finally, the Supreme Court has held that there are certain types of parties who are *immune* from being sued absent their consent or a special action by Congress. Parties that can claim sovereign immunity include states (sections 35.1–35.2), the federal government (section 35.3), and tribes and foreign states (section 35.4).

Power to decide the dispute

When a party presents a justiciable case or controversy before a federal court, the court still will not be able to resolve the dispute absent a *federal cause of action*. A cause of action refers to the elements that a party must prove in order to merit a requested judicial remedy. Some causes of action are *defined by statute* (section 36.1), and some are *implied* (sections 36.2–36.3).

As discussed earlier with regard to Congress's power to regulate federal courts (section 15.2), Congress has passed many statutes to assist courts in reaching their decisions. In addition, the Supreme Court has held that federal courts have the inherent power to respond to any problem "confronting the court's fair administration of justice" so long as the exercise of the power is "reasonable" and does not "contradict any express rule or statute." *Dietz v. Bouldin*, 579 U.S. 40, 46 (2016). Such inherent powers include the power to issue rules, amend records, stay proceedings, hear motions, and refer actions to special fact finders. *Id.* at 1891.

Power to compel compliance with the decision

Finally, Congress has also given federal courts the power to compel disputing parties to comply with the courts' judgments. Even absent statutory authority, the judicial power has been interpreted to include the power to issue *writs*, or orders, *see Ex parte Bollman*, 8 U.S. (4 Cranch) 75, 79 (1807); and the power to punish parties for acting in *contempt*, or disobedience, of the court's authority, *see Michaelson v. United States*, 266 U.S. 42, 65–66 (1924). Both of these exercises of the judicial power can be limited by statute (section 15.2) and by the Due Process Clause (section 40.4).

33.2 THE JUDICIAL POWER AND THE LEGISLATIVE POWER (RETROACTIVITY)

Just as the Supreme Court has attempted to police a boundary between the legislative powers and the executive power, the Court has also at times attempted to prevent federal courts from exercising legislative or executive power.

A long-standing norm holds that courts are distinguished from legislatures by their function, which is not to "pronounce a new law, but to maintain and expound the old one." 1 William Blackstone, *Commentaries* *69. Nevertheless, as we have seen throughout this casebook, federal courts regularly interpret statutes, constitutional provisions, and unwritten legal traditions to reach novel conclusions.

In the civil context, the Supreme Court has resolved this puzzle by formally treating its novel rulings as new interpretations of existing laws. In other words, when the Court announces a novel interpretation of a statute or constitutional provision in a civil case, the Court treats its previous interpretations as if they were incorrect at the time they were decided. For this reason, the Court has declared that all of its decisions in civil cases must be given full retroactive effect and, therefore, must apply to all situations regardless of whether the underlying events predated the Court's announcement of a particular rule. *See Harper v. Virginia Department of Taxation*, 509 U.S. 86, 90 (1993). The Court has explained "that 'the nature of judicial review' strips us of the quintessentially 'legislat[ive]' prerogative to make rules of law retroactive or prospective as we see fit." *Harper*, 509 U.S. at 95.

Yet in the criminal context, the Court has taken a different approach. In *Gideon v. Wainwright*, 372 U.S. 335 (1963), when the Court announced that the Constitution prohibited the government from convicting people in certain circumstances without first providing them with a lawyer, the Court soon confronted the question of whether the countless criminal defendants then in prison would be entitled to new trials if they had already been convicted without a lawyer. *See Linkletter v. Walker*, 381 U.S. 618 (1965). Over the next two decades, the Court expressed concern about the expense of authorizing so many new trials every time it announced a new rule of criminal procedure. Eventually, in *Teague v. Lane*, the Court concluded that most "new rules" should not apply retroactively to defendants who had already exhausted their direct appeals. 489 U.S. 288, 310 (1989). Since *Teague*, the only context in which the Court has applied new criminal rules retroactively is when the rule is "substantive," in that it places "certain kinds of primary, private individual conduct beyond the power of the criminal lawmaking authority to proscribe." *Id.* at 311; *see, e.g.*, *Montgomery v. Louisiana*, 577 U.S. 190, 200 (2016); *see also Edwards v. Vannoy*, 141 S. Ct. 1547, 1555 (2021) (holding explicitly that no procedural rule should apply retroactively in the criminal context).

33.3 THE JUDICIAL POWER AND THE EXECUTIVE POWER (REMEDIES)

In addition to preventing courts from exercising legislative power, the Supreme Court has also, at times, tried to prevent courts from exercising too much executive power. As we'll discuss in a later section on the scope of the federal judiciary's power to remedy equal-protection violations (section 46.1), this issue has most often arisen in the context of decisions ordering states and local governments to desegregate their public schools.

Beginning in the 1950s, white people throughout the United States embarked on a program of "massive resistance," in which they used violent and dilatory strategies to prevent federal decisions from taking effect. *See, e.g.*, *Cooper v. Aaron*, 358 U.S. 1, 4 (1958). These strategies eventually led federal courts to maintain jurisdiction over their cases so that they could oversee the administration of judicial remedies. *See, e.g.*, *Green v. Sch. Bd.*, 391 U.S. 430, 442 (1968). With Supreme Court approval, district courts attempted to remedy violations of the Fourteenth Amendment with a variety of techniques that will be discussed in more detail later (sections 46.1 and 46.2). For example, courts instituted busing programs, redrew school districts' geographic boundaries, and even ordered states to raise taxes to fund remedial education programs. *See, e.g.*, *Milliken v. Bradley* (*Milliken II*), 433 U.S. 267, 291 (1977); *Swann v. Charlotte-Mecklenburg Bd. of Educ.*, 402 U.S. 1, 20–21 (1971).

These executive-like exercises of the judicial power are consistent with equitable powers that courts in the American and British systems have traditionally wielded to ensure that their judgments would take effect. In bankruptcy proceedings, for example, courts often appoint receivers to take control of bankrupt businesses and manage the businesses under the courts' supervision.

Nevertheless, as court-ordered desegregation remedies became politically unpopular, the Supreme Court began cabining courts' remedial powers as a matter of *comity*, or respect for the independent sovereignty of states. *See, e.g.*, *Milliken v. Bradley* (*Milliken I*), 418 U.S. 717, 744 (1974). As a consequence, even where district courts have the power to order tax increases or to fine government officials, the Court has cautioned federal courts not to exercise these powers until less disruptive orders proved insufficient. *See, e.g.*, *Missouri v. Jenkins* (*Jenkins II*), 495 U.S. 33, 50 (1990).

33.4 THE JUDICIAL POWER AND STATES (RULES OF ACCOMMODATION)

Outside the context of desegregation remedies, federal courts often exercise their judicial power in a manner that interferes with the power of states. Such interference takes many forms. Among other things, federal courts (1) enjoin state-court proceedings that are inconsistent with federal proceedings, (2) issue writs of habeas corpus to set aside state-court convictions, (3) adjudicate cases removed from state courts into federal courts, and (4) compel state courts to hear federal cases and compel state officers to comply with federal orders.

The Supreme Court has affirmed federal courts' power to do all of these things while adopting several rules to minimize the disruptive effect of federal power. A course on federal courts will go into all of these rules of accommodation in detail. *See, e.g.*, Richard H. Fallon Jr. et al., *Hart and Wechsler's The Federal Courts and the Federal System* 1061–192 (2015). But, for now, it's worth knowing that four categories of rules exist.

Comity

One category, again, is the rule of *comity*, i.e., the principle that federal courts should generally exercise their powers with restraint to promote cooperation between federal and state governments. *See, e.g.*, *Milliken v. Bradley* (*Milliken I*), 418 U.S. 717, 741 (1974). One application of this principle is the federal court practice of *certification*, in which federal courts are encouraged to ask a state's highest court to answer unsettled questions of state law when the answer might resolve a case before a federal court. *See, e.g.*, *Clay v. Sun Ins. Off. Ltd.*, 363 U.S. 207, 212 (1960).

Exhaustion

The second category of rules of accommodation is *exhaustion*, i.e., the principle that unless Congress says otherwise, litigants ordinarily must exhaust all available state legislative and administrative remedies before seeking relief in federal court. *See, e.g., Prentis v. Atl. Coast Line Co.*, 211 U.S. 210, 230 (1908). This default rule does not require litigants to exhaust state *judicial* remedies, however, because litigants have the choice to pursue state or federal claims. *City Bank Farmers' Tr. Co. v. Schnader*, 291 U.S. 24, 34 (1934).

Statutory accommodation

The third category is a set of rules of accommodation that are required by federal statute.

One rule is *issue and claim preclusion*, required by the federal law that enforces the Full Faith and Credit Clause, 28 U.S.C. § 1738. This law requires federal courts to give preclusive effect to state-court judgments when those judgments would be given preclusive effect by the state's own courts. *See Kramer v. Chem. Constr. Corp.*, 456 U.S. 461, 467 (1982).

A second rule is the *Rooker-Feldman* doctrine, named for two cases that interpreted the federal statute that gives the Supreme Court appellate jurisdiction over state-court proceedings, 28 U.S.C. § 1257. *See D.C. Court of Appeals v. Feldman*, 460 U.S. 462, 487 (1983); *Rooker v. Fid. Tr. Co.*, 263 U.S. 413, 416 (1923). This doctrine holds that § 1257 gives the Supreme Court jurisdiction to review state-court proceedings, but it gives no other federal court the same power of review—meaning that a loser in a state-court proceeding cannot relitigate an identical claim in an inferior federal court. *See Exxon Mobil Corp. v. Saudi Basic Indus. Corp.*, 544 U.S. 280, 284 (2005).

A third rule is the Three-Judge Court Act of 1910, ch. 309, 36 Stat. 539, 557, which, as amended, requires the convening of a three-judge district court to issue any injunction involving the reapportionment of state legislative districts or where otherwise required by an act of Congress. *See* 28 U.S.C. § 2284. The idea behind this law was to make it more difficult for federal courts to strike down state statutes under the doctrine of *Ex parte Young*, 209 U.S. 123 (1908), which we will discuss shortly (section 35.1).

Abstention

The final category of rules of accommodation—and the most complicated—is the rule of *abstention*, i.e., the principle that federal courts should abstain from interfering in state-court proceedings in certain circumstances.

Congress first recognized this principle with the Judiciary Act of 1793, ch. 22, 1 Stat. 333, which, as amended, prohibits any federal court from enjoining any ongoing state-court proceedings unless such an injunction (1) is expressly authorized by an act of Congress, (2) is necessary to aid the federal court's jurisdiction, or (3) is necessary to effectuate its own proceedings. *See* 28 U.S.C. § 2283. Federal courts have taken advantage of these exceptions to enjoin ongoing proceedings that violate federal law or the Constitution. *See, e.g.*, *Mitchum v. Foster*, 407 U.S. 225, 237 (1972) (equitable action under 42 U.S.C. § 1983). But the Supreme Court has warned that even when federal courts have the power to enjoin state-court proceedings, they should abstain from doing so in certain circumstances as a matter of comity.

One circumstance calling for abstention is known as "*Pullman* abstention," named for *Railroad Commission v. Pullman Co.*, 312 U.S. 496, 500–01 (1941), in which the Court instructed lower courts to abstain from exercising jurisdiction over a case if (1) applicable state law would resolve the controversy, (2) the state law is unclear, and (3) a state court's interpretation of its own law would obviate the need for a federal court to decide a federal constitutional issue. "*Burford* abstention," named for *Burford v. Sun Oil Co.*, 319 U.S. 315, 331–32 (1943), instructs lower courts not to exercise jurisdiction when state courts likely have greater expertise in a particularly complex area of state law. "*Thibodaux* abstention" refers to *Louisiana Power & Light Co. v. City of Thibodaux*, 360 U.S. 25, 30 (1959), in which the Court warned lower courts sitting in diversity jurisdiction to allow state courts to decide unsettled issues of state law that are of great public importance to the state. And "*Colorado River* abstention" refers to *Colorado River Water Conservation Dist. v. United States,* 424 U.S. 800, 818 (1976), which instructs courts to abstain from exercising jurisdiction in "exceptional" cases in which the same parties are already prosecuting the identical issues in state court and "piecemeal litigation" might otherwise result.

A special type of abstention, first announced in *Fenner v. Boykin*, 271 U.S. 240, 243 (1926), instructed lower courts not to enjoin state-court criminal proceedings in certain circumstances. The Court reinforced this precedent in 1971 when it announced that federal abstention from state-court criminal proceedings was required by "Our Federalism." *Younger v. Harris*, 401 U.S. 37, 44 (1971). It prohibited federal courts from interfering in ongoing state-court criminal proceedings unless (1) the prosecution was brought in bad faith, (2) the prosecution was one in a series of repeated prosecutions, or (3) the defendant couldn't raise a federal constitutional defense at trial. *Id.* at 45–49. This "*Younger* abstention" has subsequently been expanded to bar the initiation of federal proceedings to interfere with ongoing state administrative proceedings as well as state civil proceedings involving orders uniquely in furtherance of the state courts' ability to perform their judicial functions. *See, e.g.*, *Sprint Commc'ns, Inc. v. Jacobs*, 571 U.S. 69, 73 (2013); *Ohio Civ. Rts. Comm'n v. Dayton Christian Sch., Inc.*, 477 U.S. 619, 628 (1986); *Huffman v. Pursue, Ltd.*, 420 U.S. 592 (1975).

But all kinds of abstention, including *Younger* abstention, apply only to *equitable* exercises of jurisdiction. The Court has held that when a party is seeking damages in federal court, abstention is inappropriate. *Quackenbush v. Allstate Ins. Co.*, 517 U.S. 706, 731 (1996).

CHAPTER 34

TO WHERE DOES THE "JUDICIAL POWER" EXTEND?

ARTICLE III, SECTION 2, CLAUSE 1: The judicial Power shall extend to all Cases, in Law and Equity, arising under this Constitution, the Laws of the United States, and Treaties made, or which shall be made, under their Authority;—to all Cases affecting Ambassadors, other public Ministers and Consuls;—to all Cases of admiralty and maritime Jurisdiction;—to Controversies to which the United States shall be a Party;—to Controversies between two or more States;—between a State and Citizens of another State,—between Citizens of different States,—between Citizens of the same State claiming Lands under Grants of different States, and between a State, or the Citizens thereof, and foreign States, Citizens or Subjects.

34.1 "CASES" AND "CONTROVERSIES"

After vesting the judicial power in federal courts, Article III explains where "[t]he judicial Power shall extend": to specified "Cases" and "Controversies." From the opening years of the country's history, members of the Supreme Court have interpreted this language to prohibit federal courts from exercising the judicial power unless there is an actual *case* or *controversy* before them.

Generally speaking, the Court had held that these terms refer to the sorts of concrete disputes that courts traditionally adjudicate—and not a freestanding power to resolve abstract questions. For example, when President George Washington asked his cabinet whether he had the legal power to issue a proclamation of neutrality in the war between Great Britain and France, he also asked the Supreme Court for its opinion. Chief Justice John Jay responded with "strong arguments against the propriety of our extra-judicially deciding the questions alluded to, especially as the power given by the Constitution to the President, of calling on the heads of departments for opinions, seems to have been purposely as well as expressly united to the executive departments." 3 *Correspondence and Public Papers of John Jay* 487–89 (Henry P. Johnston ed., New York, G.P. Putnam's Sons 1893).

The Court throughout the nineteenth century reiterated that federal courts couldn't issue advisory opinions but rather could only answer questions that "assume such a form that the judicial power is capable of acting on it." *Osborn v. Bank of the United States*, 22 U.S. 738, 819 (1824). The Court considered a question in the "form" of a case or controversy only "when the subject is submitted to it by a party who asserts his rights in the form prescribed by law." *Id.*

In an 1850 opinion, the Court offered an explanation for why it was dangerous to exercise the judicial power in any other form. A man named

John Veazie executed a deed to Nathaniel Lord warranting that he had rights to property claimed by a third person. Without telling the third person, Lord and Veazie initiated a suit to ask a federal court to resolve their "dispute." In *Lord v. Veazie*, the Supreme Court dismissed their collusive suit, calling the men "highly reprehensible" for attempting to resolve a missing person's legal rights without giving the person an opportunity to defend them. 49 U.S. (8 How.) 251, 255 (1850). Before a federal court could exercise the judicial power, the Court wrote, "there must be an actual controversy, and adverse interests." *Id.*

Although the Court has found it impossible to avoid all similarly manufactured suits, the case-or-controversy requirement entered the twentieth century as the Court's attempt to ensure that the parties asking for a federal court's opinion would adequately represent the adverse sides of a dispute. In the following cases, the Court added another consideration.

34.1.1

Massachusetts v. Mellon (Frothingham v. Mellon)

262 U.S. 447 (1923)

In 1921, Congress passed a law known as the Sheppard-Towner Act, Pub. L. No. 67–97, 42 Stat. 224. The act established the United States Children's Bureau to distribute grants to states for the purpose of reducing maternal and infant mortality. At the time, the infant mortality rate in the United States was eighty-six deaths per 1,000 live births—compared to less than six in 1,000 today. *See Birth Statistics and Infant Morality, 1920*, 36 Pub. Health Reps. 2680 (1921). The law was the first peacetime social welfare program in the history of the federal government, passed in part due to the influence of women voters after the ratification of the Nineteenth Amendment in 1920. *See* Edward R. Schlesinger, *The Sheppard-Towner Era*, 6 Am. J. Pub. Health 1034, 1034 (1967). But the law was also controversial. The American Medical Association, among other groups, complained that no emergency in maternal or infant mortality existed. It instead called the act a socialist intrusion into the autonomy of medical professionals. *Id.* at 1036.

Soon after the law took effect, two plaintiffs challenged the law in federal court by suing the secretary of the Treasury, Andrew Mellon. One of the plaintiffs, the Commonwealth of Massachusetts, complained that the federal government was intruding on its sovereign prerogatives by offering states grants that they could not reasonably refuse as a condition for enhancing the federal government's powers. The other, a Massachusetts citizen named Harriet Frothingham, argued that the federal government was spending her tax dollars in an unconstitutional manner. The federal government responded that the plaintiffs were asking for an advisory opinion about the law's constitutionality, not a resolution of their legal rights.

A unanimous Court agreed with the federal government in the combined cases: *Massachusetts v. Mellon* and *Frothingham v. Mellon*, 262 U.S. 447 (1923).

■ MR. JUSTICE SUTHERLAND delivered the opinion of the Court.[1]

These cases were argued and will be considered and disposed of together. . . .

In the *Massachusetts* case it is alleged that the plaintiff's rights and powers as a sovereign State and the rights of its citizens have been invaded and usurped by [the Sheppard-Towner Act's] expenditures and acts; and that, although the State has not accepted the act, its constitutional rights are infringed by the passage thereof and the imposition upon the State of an illegal and unconstitutional option either to yield to the Federal Government a part of its reserved rights or lose the share which it would otherwise be entitled to receive of the moneys appropriated. In the *Frothingham* case plaintiff alleges that the effect of the statute will be to take her property, under the guise of taxation, without due process of law.

We have reached the conclusion that the cases must be disposed of for want of jurisdiction without considering the merits of the constitutional questions.

In the first case, the State of Massachusetts presents no justiciable controversy either in its own behalf or as the representative of its citizens. The appellant in the second suit has no such interest in the subject-matter, nor is any such injury inflicted or threatened, as will enable her to sue.

First. The State of Massachusetts in its own behalf, in effect, complains that the act in question invades the local concerns of the State, and is a usurpation of power, viz: the power of local self government reserved to the States.

Probably, it would be sufficient to point out that the powers of the State are not invaded, since the statute imposes no obligation but simply extends an option which the State is free to accept or reject. But we do not rest here. Under Article III, § 2, of the Constitution, the judicial power of this Court extends "to controversies . . . between a State and citizens of another State" and the Court has original jurisdiction "in all cases . . . in which a State shall be party." The effect of this is not to confer jurisdiction upon the Court merely because a State is a party, but only where it is a party to a proceeding of judicial cognizance. Proceedings not of a justiciable character are outside the contemplation of the constitutional grant. . . .

What, then, is the nature of the right of the State here asserted and how is it affected by this statute? Reduced to its simplest terms, it is alleged that the statute constitutes an attempt to legislate outside the powers granted to Congress by the Constitution and within the field of local powers exclusively reserved to the States. Nothing is added to the force or effect of this assertion by the further incidental allegations that the ulterior purpose of Congress thereby was to induce the States to yield a portion of their sovereign rights; that the burden of the appropriations falls unequally upon the several States; and that there is imposed upon the States an illegal and unconstitutional option either to yield to the Federal Government a part of their reserved rights or lose their share of the moneys appropriated. But what burden is imposed upon the States, unequally or otherwise? Certainly there is none, unless it be the burden of taxation, and that falls upon their inhabitants, who are within the taxing power of Congress as well as that of the States where they reside. Nor does the statute require the States to do or to yield anything. If Congress enacted it with

---

[1] **As You Read, Consider:** Precisely why does Justice George Sutherland think it is inappropriate for a federal court to resolve the claim of Massachusetts or Harriet Frothingham that the Sheppard-Towner Act is unconstitutional? Where, if anywhere, does he think their objections should be resolved?

the ulterior purpose of tempting them to yield, that purpose may be effectively frustrated by the simple expedient of not yielding.

In the last analysis, the complaint of the plaintiff State is brought to the naked contention that Congress has usurped the reserved powers of the several States by the mere enactment of the statute, though nothing has been done and nothing is to be done without their consent; and it is plain that that question, as it is thus presented, is political and not judicial in character, and therefore is not a matter which admits of the exercise of the judicial power. . . .[2]

In *Cherokee Nation v. Georgia,* 5 Pet. 1, . . . Mr. Justice Thompson, with whom Mr. Justice Story concurred, in the course of an opinion, said (p. 75): "It is only where the rights of persons or property are involved, and when such rights can be presented under some judicial form of proceedings, that courts of justice can interpose relief. This court can have no right to pronounce an abstract opinion upon the constitutionality of a state law. Such law must be brought into actual or threatened operation, upon rights properly falling under judicial cognizance, or a remedy is not to be had here." See also *Luther v. Borden,* 7 How. 1; *Mississippi v. Johnson,* 4 Wall. 475, 500. . . .

It follows that in so far as the case depends upon the assertion of a right on the part of the State to sue in its own behalf we are without jurisdiction. In that aspect of the case we are called upon to adjudicate, not rights of person or property, not rights of dominion over physical domain, not quasi-sovereign rights actually invaded or threatened, but abstract questions of political power, of sovereignty, of government. No rights of the State falling within the scope of the judicial power have been brought within the actual or threatened operation of the statute and this Court is as much without authority to pass abstract opinions upon the constitutionality of acts of Congress as it was held to be, in *Cherokee Nation v. Georgia, supra,* of state statutes. . . .[3]

We come next to consider whether the suit may be maintained by the State as the representative of its citizens. To this the answer is not doubtful. We need not go so far as to say that a State may never intervene by suit to protect its citizens against any form of enforcement of unconstitutional acts of Congress; but we are clear that the right to do so does not arise here. Ordinarily, at least, the only way in which a State may afford protection to its citizens in such cases is through the enforcement of its own criminal statutes, where that is appropriate, or by opening its courts to the injured persons for the maintenance of civil suits or actions. But the citizens of Massachusetts are also citizens of the United States. It cannot be conceded that a State, as *parens patriae,* may institute judicial proceedings to protect citizens of the United States from the operation of the statutes thereof. While the State, under some circumstances, may sue in that capacity for the protection of its citizens, it is no part of its duty or power to enforce their rights in respect of their relations with the Federal Government. In that field it is the United States, and not the State, which represents them as *parens patriae,* when such representation becomes appropriate; and to the

---

[2] **Questions:** Sutherland calls Massachusetts's claim a "political" question, not a legal question. Why? In other words, is it because of the nature of the claim or the identity of the claimant?

[3] **Questions:** Sutherland contrasts "abstract questions of political power" with "rights actually invaded or threatened." Why should this distinction matter for whether a question is legal or political? Certainly, the Supreme Court has resolved many cases involving abstract questions of political power: *Hammer v. Dagenhart,* decided a few years earlier, declared a ban on child labor outside the federal government's power. What's the difference between that case and this one?

former, and not to the latter, they must look for such protective measures as flow from that status.[4]

Second. The attack upon the statute in the *Frothingham* case is, generally, the same, but this plaintiff alleges in addition that she is a taxpayer of the United States; and her contention, though not clear, seems to be that the effect of the appropriations complained of will be to increase the burden of future taxation and thereby take her property without due process of law. The right of a taxpayer to enjoin the execution of a federal appropriation act, on the ground that it is invalid and will result in taxation for illegal purposes, has never been passed upon by this Court. In cases where it was presented, the question has either been allowed to pass *sub silentio* or the determination of it expressly withheld. . . .[5]

[It has been a] rule frequently stated by this Court, that resident taxpayers may sue to enjoin an illegal use of the moneys of a municipal corporation. *Roberts v. Bradfield,* 12 App. D.C. 453, 459–460. The interest of a taxpayer of a municipality in the application of its moneys is direct and immediate and the remedy by injunction to prevent their misuse is not inappropriate. . . .

But the relation of a taxpayer of the United States to the Federal Government is very different. His interest in the moneys of the Treasury—partly realized from taxation and partly from other sources—is shared with millions of others; is comparatively minute and indeterminable; and the effect upon future taxation, of any payment out of the funds, so remote, fluctuating and uncertain, that no basis is afforded for an appeal to the preventive powers of a court of equity.

The administration of any statute, likely to produce additional taxation to be imposed upon a vast number of taxpayers, the extent of whose several liability is indefinite and constantly changing, is essentially a matter of public and not of individual concern. If one taxpayer may champion and litigate such a cause, then every other taxpayer may do the same, not only in respect of the statute here under review but also in respect of every other appropriation act and statute whose administration requires the outlay of public money, and whose validity may be questioned. The bare suggestion of such a result, with its attendant inconveniences, goes far to sustain the conclusion which we have reached, that a suit of this character cannot be maintained. It is of much significance that no precedent sustaining the right to maintain suits like this has been called to our attention, although, since the formation of the government, as an examination of the acts of Congress will disclose, a large number of statutes appropriating or involving the expenditure of moneys for non-federal purposes have been enacted and carried into effect.

The functions of government under our system are apportioned. To the legislative department has been committed the duty of making laws; to the executive the duty of executing them; and to the judiciary the duty of interpreting and applying them in cases properly brought before the courts. The general rule is that neither department may invade the province of the other and neither may control, direct or restrain the action of the other. . . . We have no power *per se* to review and annul acts of Congress on the ground that they are unconstitutional. That question may be considered only when the justification for some direct injury suffered or threatened, presenting a justiciable issue, is made to rest upon such an act. Then the power

[4] **Question:** After holding that Massachusetts has not claimed that the federal law has interfered with any of its rights, Sutherland observes that Massachusetts also cannot claim that its citizens are being injured by the federal law. Why not?

[5] **Question:** In contrast with Massachusetts, Frothingham has argued that her legal rights *are* being threatened: she is being forced to pay tax dollars toward a purpose that she believes is unconstitutional. How does Sutherland's dismissal of her case differ from his dismissal of Massachusetts's case?

exercised is that of ascertaining and declaring the law applicable to the controversy. It amounts to little more than the negative power to disregard an unconstitutional enactment, which otherwise would stand in the way of the enforcement of a legal right. The party who invokes the power must be able to show not only that the statute is invalid but that he has sustained or is immediately in danger of sustaining some direct injury as the result of its enforcement, and not merely that he suffers in some indefinite way in common with people generally. If a case for preventive relief be presented the court enjoins, in effect, not the execution of the statute, but the acts of the official, the statute notwithstanding. Here the parties plaintiff have no such case. Looking through forms of words to the substance of their complaint, it is merely that officials of the executive department of the government are executing and will execute an act of Congress asserted to be unconstitutional; and this we are asked to prevent. To do so would be not to decide a judicial controversy, but to assume a position of authority over the governmental acts of another and co-equal department, an authority which plainly we do not possess.[6]

NOTE: STANDING

Although *Mellon* wasn't a radical departure from the case-or-controversy opinions before it, the opinion was an early description of what is now known as *standing*: the doctrine that Article III prohibits federal courts from exercising the judicial power unless a plaintiff can demonstrate a particular relationship to the dispute. As the *Mellon* Court wrote, a plaintiff "must be able to show not only that the statute is invalid but that he has sustained or is immediately in danger of sustaining some direct injury as the result of its enforcement, and not merely that he suffers in some indefinite way in common with people generally." 262 U.S. at 488. The *Mellon* Court offered several justifications for this interpretation of Article III: (1) it's required by the separation of powers, (2) a more lenient rule would lead to people challenging every federal law, and (3) federal courts lack the power to issue advisory opinions.

After *Mellon*, the Court defined *standing* with a variety of imprecise requirements. In addition to *Mellon*'s requirements of (1) a "direct injury" and (2) not a general grievance, the Court held that a case or controversy also (3) "must be definite and concrete," (4) must touch "the legal relations of the parties having adverse legal interests," (5) must be "real and substantial," and (6) must admit "of specific relief through a decree of a conclusive character, as distinguished from an opinion advising what the law would be upon a hypothetical state of facts." *Aetna Life Ins. Co. v. Haworth*, 300 U.S. 229, 240–41 (1937).

During the chief justiceship of Earl Warren, the Court pruned many of these requirements so that the Court could resolve more "political" disputes. In *Baker v. Carr*—a case best known for holding that the apportionment of

---

6 **Questions:** In this final paragraph, Sutherland offers a separation-of-powers explanation of what federal courts do when they engage in judicial review: they do not literally invalidate or strike down unconstitutional legislation but merely "disregard" it or decline to enforce it when resolving a controversy. A freestanding power to invalidate legislation, he argues, would convert the court into a legislature. Do you agree with him that the best way to vindicate this intuition is to require that plaintiffs demonstrate "some direct injury as the result of [a law's] enforcement"? Why would a judicial injunction, in such a case, be less of a threat to the separation of powers?

legislative districts was not a political question—the Court wrote that standing turned on whether the plaintiff "alleged such a personal stake in the outcome of the controversy as to assure that concrete adverseness which sharpens the presentation of issues upon which the court so largely depends for illumination of difficult constitutional questions." 369 U.S. 186, 204 (1962). And in *Flast v. Cohen*, 392 U.S. 83 (1968), the Court appeared to reverse *Mellon*'s holding that individual taxpayers could never have standing. The Court authorized taxpayers to challenge an expenditure of funds in violation of the First Amendment's Establishment Clause, maintaining that the terms *cases* and *controversies* required simply that questions be "presented in an adversary context and in a form historically viewed as capable of resolution through the judicial process." *Flast*, 392 U.S. at 95.

After Earl Warren retired in 1969, the Supreme Court became considerably more circumspect about allowing individuals to challenge the constitutionality of statutes. Abandoning *Flast* and resurrecting *Mellon*, the Court under Chief Justice Warren Burger held that Article III required plaintiffs to prove a "direct injury," not mere adverseness. *United States v. Richardson*, 418 U.S. 166, 172 (1974). The Court also emphasized that there must be a "causal relationship" between the alleged injury and the defendant's practices, *Warth v. Seldin*, 422 U.S. 490, 507 (1975); and that the injury must be "amenable to judicial remedy," *Valley Forge Christian Coll. v. Ams. United*, 454 U.S. 464, 475 (1982). By 1992, the Court distilled these three elements—injury, causation, and redressability—into the "irreducible constitutional minimum of standing." *Lujan v. Defs. of Wildlife*, 504 U.S. 555, 560 (1992).

34.2 THE INJURY-IN-FACT REQUIREMENT

Massachusetts and Harriet Frothingham weren't allowed to challenge the constitutionality of the Sheppard-Towner Act because they hadn't alleged that they were suffering a "direct injury" from the law. *Massachusetts v. Mellon*, 262 U.S. 447, 488 (1923). But the Supreme Court didn't offer much guidance about what would constitute such a direct injury.

The Court provided one answer a decade later.

Alabama Power *era: legal rights*

One of the provisions of the National Industrial Recovery Act of 1933, Pub. L. No. 73–67, 48 Stat. 195, provided federal loans to help rural cities get into the business of distributing electric power. The Alabama Power Company, a private distributor, challenged the constitutionality of four of these loans in federal court. To satisfy *Mellon*'s "direct injury" test, the company argued that it faced the risk of financial loss from the unconstitutional competition.

But in *Alabama Power Co. v. Ickes*, 302 U.S. 464 (1938), the Court was unimpressed. *Mellon*, the Court wrote, established the principle "that the courts have no power to consider in isolation and annul an act of Congress on the ground that it is unconstitutional." *Ala. Power*, 302 U.S. at 479. Courts only have the power to remedy an "injury" as used "in its legal sense, as meaning a wrong which directly results in the violation of a legal right." *Id.* The Court wrote that no one had a legal right to be free from government-supported municipal competition, even if such competition harmed a company's profits. *Id.* In a similar follow-on case, the Court added that a "legal right" referred only to "one of property, one arising out of contract, one protected against tortious invasion, or one founded on a statute which confers a privilege." *Tenn. Elec. Power Co. v. TVA*, 306 U.S. 118, 137 (1939).

The *Alabama Power* test provided a very limited basis for standing: the only people who could challenge the constitutionality of a government action were people who could allege that the action was violating a right protected by the common law or by a statute. But in subsequent cases, the Court expansively heard challenges to statutes by plaintiffs who claimed injuries to their right to collectively bargain, *Joint Anti-Fascist Refugee Comm. v. McGrath*, 341 U.S. 123 (1951); their right to associate, *Nat'l Ass'n for the Advancement of Colored People v. Alabama ex rel. Patterson*, 357 U.S. 449 (1958); their right to vote, *Baker v. Carr*, 369 U.S. 186 (1962); and so on. Within three decades of *Alabama Power*, virtually anyone affected by an allegedly unconstitutional action could claim that the action injured their constitutionally protected legal rights. *See, e.g.*, *Flast v. Cohen*, 392 U.S. 83 (1968).

Camp *era: zones of interest*

The Court finally dispensed with the *Alabama Power* test in *Ass'n of Data Processing Service Organizations v. Camp*, 397 U.S. 150 (1970), another suit involving a company that claimed to be injured by the federal government's unfair assistance of its competitors. Unlike in *Alabama Power*, the Court now authorized the company to sue on the ground that the only test required by *Mellon* was whether "the challenged action has caused [the plaintiff] *injury in fact*, economic or otherwise." *Camp*, 397 U.S. at 152 (emphasis added). Casting aside *Alabama Power*'s "legal right" test as a question that "goes to the merits," the Court explained that standing merely asked "whether the interest sought to be protected by the complainant is arguably within the zone of interests to be protected or regulated by the statute or constitutional guarantee in question." *Id.* at 153. Such an interest could include " 'aesthetic, conservational, and recreational' as well as economic values." *Id.* at 154.

The *Camp* test lasted for a little over two decades, during which the Court generally allowed any plaintiff to challenge any law on the ground that the law would cause an "injury in fact" that was "arguably within the zone of interests to be protected" by a statute or the Constitution. This new test authorized challenges to discriminatory housing practices that harmed plaintiffs' "social benefits of living in an integrated community." *Trafficante v. Metro. Life Ins. Co.*, 409 U.S. 205, 208 (1972). It also authorized challenges to practices that harmed plaintiffs' "[a]esthetic and environmental well-being." *Sierra Club v. Morton*, 405 U.S. 727, 734 (1972).

During the *Camp* era, there were two groups of plaintiffs that the Court occasionally thought lacked an injury in fact. The first included plaintiffs who, like Harriet Frothingham, sought to bring "generalized grievances about the conduct of government" by challenging something that affected the entire nation. *Schlesinger v. Reservists Comm. to Stop the War*, 418 U.S. 208, 225–28 (1974). The Court explained that the purpose of Article III's standing requirement was to maintain the "limited . . . role of the courts in a democratic society" by preventing losers in the political process from using the courts to second-guess Congress or the executive branch. On the ground that certain plaintiffs' injuries were not "concrete," the Court held that it lacked jurisdiction to hear cases concerning the Vietnam War and other controversial expenditures of tax dollars. *See, e.g.*, *United States v. Richardson*, 418 U.S. 166, 175 (1974).

The second group of plaintiffs included those who wanted an injunction to prevent being injured in the future. At first, during the mid-twentieth century, the Court held that any plaintiffs who wanted to challenge the enforcement of an allegedly unconstitutional policy had to subject themselves to enforcement. *See United Pub. Workers v. Mitchell*, 330 U.S. 75, 90 (1947). Absent evidence that a challenged law would *actually* be enforced against the plaintiff, the Court held that the challenge was not "ripe." *Int'l Longshoremen's Union v. Boyd*, 347 U.S. 222, 224 (1954). For example, in *Poe v. Ullman*, the Court refused to hear a challenge to Connecticut's nineteenth-century ban on contraceptives because no one had ever been prosecuted under the statute in its eighty years of existence. 367 U.S. 497, 508 (1961).

After *Camp*, the Court began to relax this ripeness doctrine, holding that "[o]ne does not have to await the consummation of threatened injury to obtain preventive relief. If the injury is certainly impending that is enough." *Reg'l Rail Reorg. Act Cases*, 419 U.S. 102, 143 (1974). Under this new regime, plaintiffs could raise pre-enforcement challenges to government actions as long as there existed a "credible threat" of enforcement. *Babbitt v. United Farm Workers*, 442 U.S. 289, 298 (1979). But the post-*Camp* Court nevertheless maintained that a prospective injury in fact had to be "real and immediate," not "subjective" or "speculative." *Rizzo v. Goode*, 423 U.S. 362, 372 (1976).

The most controversial of these pre-enforcement decisions concerned the Los Angeles Police Department, whose officers in the 1970s routinely stopped black men, frisked them, and put them in illegal chokeholds. One of the department's victims, a black man named Adolph Lyons, sought damages for his chokehold and an injunction against the city to end this practice going forward. But while the Court agreed that Lyons deserved damages, it disagreed that he had standing to request an injunction. It instead called it "no more than speculation" to suggest that absent an injunction, a police officer would subject Lyons to another unconstitutional chokehold "without provocation or legal excuse." *City of Los Angeles v. Lyons*, 461 U.S. 95, 108 (1983).

34.2.1

Lujan v. Defenders of Wildlife

504 U.S. 555 (1992)

The following case, *Lujan v. Defenders of Wildlife*, 504 U.S. 555 (1992), reevaluated what counted as an "injury" under *Mellon* in light of the Court's "concrete" and "immediate" add-ons.

During the administration of President Richard Nixon, Congress passed the Endangered Species Act of 1973, Pub. L. No. 93–205, 87 Stat. 884, which made the secretary of the interior responsible for providing a list of endangered species. While the act was initially interpreted to apply worldwide, the Department of the Interior under President Ronald Reagan issued a regulation that interpreted the statute to apply only domestically. The Defenders of Wildlife and other conservation organizations challenged the new rule as an unreasonable interpretation of the statute. They also alleged that in adopting the new rule, the secretary of the interior had failed to consult with various officials, as the act required.

The government moved for summary judgment, arguing that the conservation organizations wouldn't be injured in fact by the new rule. The challengers answered that they satisfied the *Mellon* test because their members had visited endangered species overseas, planned to return in the future, and would suffer if the species' habitats were destroyed in the meantime. They added that the act itself declared that "any person may commence a civil suit on his own behalf . . . to enjoin any person . . . who is alleged to be in violation of any provision of this Act." *Lujan*, 504 U.S. at 571–72 (quoting Endangered Species Act, 87 Stat. at 900). The two questions before the Court were, therefore, as follows:

(1) Was someone's intent to visit an endangered species overseas an "injury in fact"?

(2) If not, could Congress, in effect, create an injury by giving an otherwise uninjured person a legal right to challenge an unlawful action?

The Court said (1) no and (2) maybe . . . but not in this case.

■ JUSTICE SCALIA delivered the opinion of the Court. . . .[7]

This case involves a challenge to a rule promulgated by the Secretary of the Interior. . . . The preliminary issue, and the only one we reach, is whether respondents here, plaintiffs below, have standing to seek judicial review of the rule. . .

II

While the Constitution of the United States divides all power conferred upon the Federal Government into "legislative Powers," Art. I, § 1, "[t]he executive Power," Art. II, § 1, and "[t]he judicial Power," Art. III, § 1, it does not attempt to define those terms. To be sure, it limits the jurisdiction of federal courts to "Cases" and "Controversies," but an executive inquiry can bear the name "case" (the Hoffa case) and a legislative dispute can bear the name "controversy" (the Smoot-Hawley controversy). Obviously, then, the Constitution's central mechanism of separation of powers depends largely upon common understanding of what activities are appropriate to legislatures, to executives, and to courts. In The Federalist No. 48, Madison expressed the view that "[i]t is not infrequently a question of real nicety in legislative bodies whether the operation of a particular measure will, or will not, extend beyond the legislative sphere," whereas "the executive power [is] restrained within a narrower compass and . . . more simple in its nature," and "the judiciary [is] described by landmarks still less uncertain." The Federalist No. 48. One of those landmarks, setting apart the "Cases" and "Controversies" that are of the justiciable sort referred to in Article III . . . [,] is the doctrine of standing. Though some of its elements express merely prudential considerations that are part of judicial self-government, the core component of standing is an essential and unchanging part of the case-or-controversy requirement of Article III.

Over the years, our cases have established that the irreducible constitutional minimum of standing contains three elements. First, the plaintiff must have suffered an "injury in fact"—an invasion of a legally protected interest which is (a) concrete and particularized, see *Warth v. Seldin,* 422 U. S. 490, 508 (1975); *Sierra Club v. Morton,* 405 U. S. 727, 740–741, n. 16 (1972); and (b) "actual or imminent, not 'conjectural' or 'hypothetical,' " *Whitmore, supra,* at 155 (quoting *Los Angeles v. Lyons,* 461 U. S. 95, 102 (1983)). Second, there must be a causal connection between the injury and the conduct complained of—the injury has to be "fairly. . . trace[able] to the challenged action of the defendant, and not . . . th[e] result [of] the independent action of some third party not before the court." *Simon v. Eastern Ky. Welfare Rights Organization,* 426 U. S. 26, 41–42 (1976). Third, it must be "likely," as opposed to merely "speculative," that the injury will be "redressed by a favorable decision." *Id.,* at 38, 43.[8]

The party invoking federal jurisdiction bears the burden of establishing these elements. Since they are not mere pleading requirements but rather an indispensable part of the plaintiff's case, each element must be supported in the same way as any other matter on which the plaintiff bears the burden of proof, *i.e.,* with the manner and degree of evidence required at the successive stages of the litigation. At the pleading stage, general factual allegations of injury resulting from the defendant's conduct may suffice, for on a motion to dismiss we presume that general allegations embrace those specific facts that are necessary to support the claim. In response to

---

7 **As You Read, Consider:** In *Massachusetts v. Mellon,* the Court framed standing as essential to ensure that the federal judiciary did not engage in legislation. How does Justice Antonin Scalia frame the standing requirement? Why does he think standing is important, and how does his test vindicate its importance?

8 **Questions:** Here, Scalia describes the modern test for standing. What do these elements have to do with the separation of powers? Do they protect only Congress or also the executive branch?

a summary judgment motion, however, the plaintiff can no longer rest on such "mere allegations," but must "set forth" by affidavit or other evidence "specific facts," Fed. Rule Civ. Proc. 56(e), which for purposes of the summary judgment motion will be taken to be true. And at the final stage, those facts (if controverted) must be supported adequately by the evidence adduced at trial. . . .

III

[R]espondents' claim to injury is that the lack of consultation with respect to certain funded activities abroad "increas[es] the rate of extinction of endangered and threatened species." Complaint ¶ 5, App. 13. Of course, the desire to use or observe an animal species, even for purely esthetic purposes, is undeniably a cognizable interest for purpose of standing. See, *e.g., Sierra Club v. Morton,* 405 U. S., at 734. "But the 'injury in fact' test requires more than an injury to a cognizable interest. It requires that the party seeking review be himself among the injured." *Id.,* at 734–735. To survive the Secretary's summary judgment motion, respondents had to submit affidavits or other evidence showing, through specific facts, not only that listed species were in fact being threatened by funded activities abroad, but also that one or more of respondents' members would thereby be "directly" affected apart from their " 'special interest' in th[e] subject." *Id.,* at 735, 739.

With respect to this aspect of the case, the Court of Appeals focused on the affidavits of two Defenders' members—Joyce Kelly and Amy Skilbred. Ms. Kelly stated that she traveled to Egypt in 1986 and "observed the traditional habitat of the endangered Nile crocodile there and intend[s] to do so again, and hope[s] to observe the crocodile directly," and that she "will suffer harm in fact as the result of [the] American . . . role . . . in overseeing the rehabilitation of the Aswan High Dam on the Nile. . . ." App. 101. Ms. Skilbred averred that she traveled to Sri Lanka in 1981 and "observed th[e] habitat" of "endangered species such as the Asian elephant and the leopard" . . .; "[the American-funded] development project," she continued, "will seriously reduce endangered, threatened, and endemic species habitat. . . .["] *Id.,* at 145–146. When Ms. Skilbred was asked at a subsequent deposition if and when she had any plans to return to Sri Lanka, she reiterated that "I intend to go back to Sri Lanka," but confessed that she had no current plans: "I don't know [when]. There is a civil war going on right now. I don't know. Not next year, I will say. In the future." *Id.,* at 318.

[T]hese affidavits . . . plainly contain no facts . . . showing how damage to the species will produce "imminent" injury to Mses. Kelly and Skilbred. That the women "had visited" the areas of the projects before the projects commenced proves nothing. As we have said in a related context, " 'Past exposure to illegal conduct does not in itself show a present case or controversy regarding injunctive relief . . . if unaccompanied by any continuing, present adverse effects.' " *Lyons,* 461 U. S., at 102. And the affiants' profession of an "inten[t]" to return to the places they had visited before—where they will presumably, this time, be deprived of the opportunity to observe animals of the endangered species—is simply not enough. Such "some day" intentions—without any description of concrete plans, or indeed even any specification of *when* the some day will be—do not support a finding of the "actual or imminent" injury that our cases require.

Besides relying upon the Kelly and Skilbred affidavits, respondents propose a series of novel standing theories . . ., [including] the "animal nexus" approach, whereby anyone who has an interest in studying or seeing the endangered animals anywhere on the globe has standing; and the "vocational nexus" approach, under which anyone with a professional interest in such animals can sue. Under these theories, anyone who goes to see Asian elephants in the Bronx Zoo, and anyone who is a keeper of Asian elephants in the Bronx Zoo, has standing to sue because the Director of the Agency for International Development (AID) did not consult with the Secretary [of the Interior] regarding the AID-funded project in Sri Lanka. This is beyond all reason. Standing is not an ingenious academic exercise in the conceivable, but as we have said requires, at the summary judgment stage, a factual showing of perceptible harm. It is clear that the person who observes or works with a particular animal threatened by a federal decision is facing perceptible harm, since the very subject of his interest will no longer exist. . . . It goes beyond the limit, however, and into pure speculation and fantasy, to say that anyone who observes or works with an endangered species, anywhere in the world, is appreciably harmed by a single project affecting some portion of that species with which he has no more specific connection. . . .[9]

IV

The Court of Appeals found that respondents had standing for an additional reason: because they had suffered a "procedural injury." The so-called "citizen-suit" provision of the ESA provides, in pertinent part, that "any person may commence a civil suit on his own behalf (A) to enjoin any person, including the United States and any other governmental instrumentality or agency . . . who is alleged to be in violation of any provision of this chapter." 16 U. S. C. § 1540(g). The court held that, because § 7(a)(2) requires interagency consultation, the citizen-suit provision creates a "procedural righ[t]" to consultation in all "persons"—so that *anyone* can file suit in federal court to challenge the Secretary's (or presumably any other official's) failure to follow the assertedly correct consultative procedure, notwithstanding his or her inability to allege any discrete injury flowing from that failure. To understand the remarkable nature of this holding one must be clear about what it does *not* rest upon: This is not a case where plaintiffs are seeking to enforce a procedural requirement the disregard of which could impair a separate concrete interest of theirs (*e.g.,* the procedural requirement for a hearing prior to denial of their license application, or the procedural requirement for an environmental impact statement before a federal facility is constructed next door to them). Nor is it simply a case where concrete injury has been suffered by many persons, as in mass fraud or mass tort situations. Nor, finally, is it the unusual case in which Congress has created a concrete private interest in the outcome of a suit against a private party for the Government's benefit, by providing a cash bounty for the victorious plaintiff. Rather, the court held that the injury-in-fact requirement had been satisfied by congressional conferral upon *all* persons of an abstract, self-contained, noninstrumental "right" to have the Executive observe the procedures required by law. We reject this view.

We have consistently held that a plaintiff raising only a generally available grievance about government—claiming only harm to his and every citizen's interest in proper application of the Constitution and laws, and seeking relief that no more directly and tangibly benefits him than it does the public at large—does not state an Article III case or controversy. For example, in . . . *Massachusetts v. Mellon,* 262 U. S. 447 (1923), we dismissed for lack of Article III standing a taxpayer suit challenging the propriety of certain federal expenditures. . . . More recent cases are to the same effect. . . .

To be sure, our generalized-grievance cases have typically involved Government violation of procedures assertedly ordained by the Constitution rather than the Congress. But there is absolutely no basis for making the Article III inquiry turn on the source of the asserted right. Whether the courts were to act on their own, or at the invitation of Congress, in ignoring the concrete injury requirement described

---

9 **Questions:** How could the two women in this case have satisfied Scalia's test for an "imminent" injury? If they had purchased plane tickets to visit a particular animal threatened by harm, would that have been enough? If so, what purpose is his test serving?

in our cases, they would be discarding a principle fundamental to the separate and distinct constitutional role of the Third Branch—one of the essential elements that identifies those "Cases" and "Controversies" that are the business of the courts rather than of the political branches. "The province of the court," as Chief Justice Marshall said in *Marbury v. Madison,* 1 Cranch 137, 170 (1803), "is solely, to decide on the rights of individuals." Vindicating the *public* interest (including the public interest in Government observance of the Constitution and laws) is the function of Congress and the Chief Executive. The question presented here is whether the public interest in proper administration of the laws (specifically, in agencies' observance of a particular, statutorily prescribed procedure) can be converted into an individual right by a statute that denominates it as such, and that permits all citizens (or, for that matter, a subclass of citizens who suffer no distinctive concrete harm) to sue. If the concrete injury requirement has the separation-of-powers significance we have always said, the answer must be obvious: To permit Congress to convert the undifferentiated public interest in executive officers' compliance with the law into an "individual right" vindicable in the courts is to permit Congress to transfer from the President to the courts the Chief Executive's most important constitutional duty, to "take Care that the Laws be faithfully executed," Art. II, § 3. It would enable the courts, with the permission of Congress, "to assume a position of authority over the governmental acts of another and co-equal department," *Massachusetts v. Mellon,* 262 U. S., at 489, and to become " 'virtually continuing monitors of the wisdom and soundness of Executive action.' " *Allen, supra,* at 760. We have always rejected that vision of our role . . . .[10]

Nothing in this contradicts the principle that "[t]he . . . injury required by Art. III may exist solely by virtue of 'statutes creating legal rights, the invasion of which creates standing.' " *Warth,* 422 U. S., at 500. . . . [Past illustrations] of that principle [include] Congress' elevating to the status of legally cognizable injuries concrete, *de facto* injuries that were previously inadequate in law (namely, injury to an individual's personal interest in living in a racially integrated community, see *Trafficante v. Metropolitan Life Ins. Co.,* 409 U. S. 205, 208–212 (1972), and injury to a company's interest in marketing its product free from competition, see *Hardin v. Kentucky Utilities Co.,* 390 U. S. 1, 6 (1968)). As we said in *Sierra Club,* "[Statutory] broadening [of] the categories of injury that may be alleged in support of standing is a different matter from abandoning the requirement that the party seeking review must himself have suffered an injury." 405 U. S., at 738. Whether or not the principle . . . can be extended beyond that distinction, it is clear that in suits against the Government, at least, the concrete injury requirement must remain. . . .

■ JUSTICE KENNEDY, with whom JUSTICE SOUTER joins, concurring in part and concurring in the judgment.[11]

[I] join Part IV of the Court's opinion with the following observations. As Government programs and policies become more complex and far reaching, we must be sensitive to the articulation of new rights of action that do not have clear analogs in our common-law tradition. Modern litigation has progressed far from the paradigm of Marbury suing Madison to get his commission, *Marbury v. Madison,* 1 Cranch 137 (1803), or Ogden seeking an injunction to halt Gibbons' steamboat operations,

10 **Question:** Scalia here observes that if Congress had the power to allow *anyone* to file a lawsuit accusing the executive branch of failing to abide by a statute, then it would intrude on the president's duty "to take Care that the Laws be faithfully executed." Yet he also later recognizes that the violation of a statute can injure a person and give that person standing to sue. After this opinion, what options are available if Congress wants to allow individuals to ensure that the executive branch is correctly applying the law?

11 **Question:** Justice Anthony Kennedy's concurring opinion is the controlling opinion in this case. How does he differ from Scalia in his view of Congress's role with respect to standing?

Gibbons v. Ogden, 9 Wheat. 1 (1824). In my view, Congress has the power to define injuries and articulate chains of causation that will give rise to a case or controversy where none existed before, and I do not read the Court's opinion to suggest a contrary view. In exercising this power, however, Congress must at the very least identify the injury it seeks to vindicate and relate the injury to the class of persons entitled to bring suit. The citizen-suit provision of the Endangered Species Act does not meet these minimal requirements, because while the statute purports to confer a right on "any person . . . to enjoin . . . the United States and any other governmental instrumentality or agency . . . who is alleged to be in violation of any provision of this chapter," it does not of its own force establish that there is an injury in "any person" by virtue of any "violation." 16 U. S. C. § 1540(g)(1)(A).

The Court's holding that there is an outer limit to the power of Congress to confer rights of action is a direct and necessary consequence of the case and controversy limitations found in Article III. I agree that it would exceed those limitations if, at the behest of Congress and in the absence of any showing of concrete injury, we were to entertain citizen suits to vindicate the public's nonconcrete interest in the proper administration of the laws. While it does not matter how many persons have been injured by the challenged action, the party bringing suit must show that the action injures him in a concrete and personal way. This requirement is not just an empty formality. It preserves the vitality of the adversarial process by assuring both that the parties before the court have an actual, as opposed to professed, stake in the outcome, and that "the legal questions presented . . . will be resolved, not in the rarified atmosphere of a debating society, but in a concrete factual context conducive to a realistic appreciation of the consequences of judicial action." *Valley Forge Christian College v. Americans United for Separation of Church and State, Inc.,* 454 U. S. 464, 472 (1982). In addition, the requirement of concrete injury confines the Judicial Branch to its proper, limited role in the constitutional framework of Government. . . .

NOTE: AFTERMATH OF *LUJAN*

The *Lujan* Court defined the first requirement of standing as an injury in fact that is "concrete and particularized." *Lujan*, 504 U.S. at 560. These two requirements shortly became a full replacement for the former prohibition on generalized grievances. That prohibition originally emerged in part because the Court feared that generalized grievances would be better remedied through the political process as opposed to through litigation. Since *Lujan*, however, the Court has often upheld a plaintiff's standing to challenge a statutory or constitutional violation even though millions of other people might also have been affected, as long as the violation caused a concrete and particularized injury—for example, where "large numbers of individuals suffer the same common-law injury (say, a widespread mass tort), or where large numbers of voters suffer interference with voting rights conferred by law." *FEC v. Akins*, 524 U.S. 11, 24–25 (1998). Notably, in *Massachusetts v. EPA*, 549 U.S. 497 (2007), a case concerning climate change that could affect the Earth's entire population, the Court allowed Massachusetts to challenge the Environmental Protection Agency's unwillingness to regulate greenhouse gases. The Court explained that "projected rises in sea level would lead to serious loss of coastal property [and] was a 'far cry' from the kind of generalized harm insufficient to ground Article III jurisdiction." *Massachusetts*, 549 U.S. at 515.

The Court elaborated on these two requirements in *Spokeo, Inc. v. Robins*, 578 U.S. 330 (2016). There, a federal statute authorized anyone whose information was inaccurately published by a consumer reporting company to seek damages from the company. Invoking this statute, Thomas Robins sued a "people search engine" called Spokeo for publishing inaccurate information about him on its website. *Id.* at 333. Beyond this legal violation, however, Robins hadn't alleged that the inaccurate information had affected him or harmed his job prospects. *Id.* at 342–43. The Court therefore remanded the case for an analysis of whether his injury was concrete and particularized. *Id.* at 334. For an injury to be "concrete," the Court wrote that the injury "must be '*de facto*'; that is, it must actually exist. . . . [It must be] 'real,' and not 'abstract.' " *Id.* at 340. For an injury to be "particularized," the Court wrote that it "must affect the plaintiff in a personal and individual way." *Id.* at 339. The Court added that while "intangible injuries" could satisfy both requirements, Robins needed to allege more than a "bare procedural violation" of a statute before he could go to court. *Id.* at 342. He also needed evidence that he had been harmed by the violation or that there was a material risk that he would be harmed.

Spokeo also adopted as part of its analysis Kennedy's concurring opinion in *Lujan*. That opinion declared that "Congress has the power to define injuries and articulate chains of causation that will give rise to a case or controversy where none existed before." *Lujan*, 504 U.S. at 580 (Kennedy, J., concurring). Although the *Lujan* Court held that Article III prohibited Congress from authorizing *everyone* to challenge the violation of the Constitution or a statute, subsequent cases, including *Spokeo*, held that Congress has broad powers to accord a plaintiff with "a procedural right to protect *his concrete interests*." *Summers v. Earth Island Inst.*, 555 U.S. 488, 496 (2009); *see also, e.g., Vt. Agency of Nat. Res. v. United States ex rel. Stevens*, 529 U.S. 765, 774 (2000) (finding standing in *qui tam* action where plaintiff sought to vindicate an injury to the United States and the United States assigned a portion of its damages claim to the plaintiff); *Akins*, 524 U.S. 11, 20 (finding standing where plaintiffs claimed that they had been injured in fact by the Federal Election Commission's denial of information to them because Congress had authorized "any person aggrieved" by the denial of information to sue). But as the Court first wrote in *FEC v. Akins* and confirmed in *Spokeo*, the interests involved must be "particular" and "concrete" as opposed to harms of "an abstract and indefinite nature—for example, harm to the 'common concern for obedience to law.' " *Akins*, 524 U.S. at 23.

In the years since *Spokeo*, the Court has repeatedly invoked the "concreteness" requirement as a bar to litigation—even in the face of federal statutes that authorized lawsuits to redress certain types of mismanagement. *See, e.g., TransUnion LLC v. Ramirez*, 141 S. Ct. 2190, 2211–12 (2021) (calling an alleged injury "abstract" instead of "concrete" where plaintiffs complained that a consumer credit company unlawfully included misleading alerts in their credit files but did not also plead that the alerts had been disseminated to third parties); *Thole v. U.S. Bank N.A.*, 140 S. Ct. 1615, 1619 (2020) (same where plaintiffs complained that their pension plan has been unlawfully mismanaged but did not plead that they would have received more benefits as a consequence of good management).

34.2.2

Susan B. Anthony List v. Driehaus

573 U.S. 149 (2014)

The *Lujan* Court held that an injury in fact must be not only "concrete and particularized" but also "actual or imminent, not 'conjectural' or 'hypothetical.'" *Lujan*, 504 U.S. at 560. Just as the first two requirements replaced the prohibition on generalized grievances, the actual or imminent requirements are in the process of replacing the former *ripeness* requirement. In the years since *Lujan*, the Court has continued in a handful of cases to refer to ripeness as if it were distinct from standing. *See, e.g., Trump v. New York*, 141 S. Ct. 530, 535 (2020) (describing ripeness as "related" to standing and "originating in the case-or-controversy requirement of Article III"). But in the following case, *Susan B. Anthony List v. Driehaus*, 573 U.S. 149 (2014), the Court strongly suggested that it would not treat ripeness as an independent consideration distinct from standing.

In 2010, a self-described "pro-life advocacy organization" called Susan B. Anthony List announced that it would publicly oppose the reelection of members of Congress who voted for the Affordable Care Act, which it called a "health care bill that includes taxpayer-funded abortion." *Susan B. Anthony List*, 573 U.S. at 153–54. When the organization attempted to display a billboard denouncing Representative Steve Driehaus of Ohio, he filed a complaint with the Ohio Elections Commission. Under Ohio law, it was illegal to issue "false statement[s]" "during the course of any campaign for nomination or election to public office or office of a political party." *Id.* at 152. Driehaus alleged that this law prohibited the organization from falsely accusing him of voting for "taxpayer-funded abortion." *Id.* at 154.

While the commission proceedings were ongoing, Driehaus lost his election. Although he withdrew his complaint, Susan B. Anthony List and another organization, Coalition Opposed to Additional Spending on Taxes (COAST), immediately sued to enjoin future enforcement of the Ohio false-statement statute. Both groups alleged that their free speech had been unconstitutionally chilled and that they planned to speak on similar issues in the future. They therefore claimed that they were injured by the Ohio law that allowed anyone to hale them into enforcement proceedings. Driehaus and the State of Ohio responded that the case wasn't "ripe" and that the organization's injuries weren't "imminent" because the *earlier* enforcement actions did not mean there would also be *future* enforcement actions. *Id.* at 156.

Although the Court agreed that it was possible that the plaintiffs would not be the subject of future enforcement actions, it nevertheless ruled that they had standing.

■ JUSTICE THOMAS delivered the opinion of the Court.[12]

Petitioners in this case seek to challenge an Ohio statute that prohibits certain "false statements" during the course of a political campaign. The question in this case is whether their preenforcement challenge to that law is justiciable—and in particular, whether they have alleged a sufficiently imminent injury for the purposes of Article III. We conclude that they have. . . .

III

Article III of the Constitution limits the jurisdiction of federal courts to "Cases" and "Controversies." U.S. Const., Art. III, § 2. The doctrine of standing gives meaning to these constitutional limits by "identify[ing] those disputes which are appropriately resolved through the judicial process."[5] *Lujan v. Defenders of Wildlife,* 504 U.S. 555, 560 (1992). The law of Article III standing, which is built on separation-of-powers principles, serves to prevent the judicial process from being used to usurp the powers of the political branches. To establish Article III standing, a plaintiff must show (1) an "injury in fact," (2) a sufficient "causal connection between the injury and the conduct complained of," and (3) a "likel[ihood]" that the injury "will be redressed by a favorable decision." *Lujan, supra,* at 560–561.

This case concerns the injury-in-fact requirement, which helps to ensure that the plaintiff has a "personal stake in the outcome of the controversy." *Warth v. Seldin,* 422 U.S. 490, 498 (1975). An injury sufficient to satisfy Article III must be "concrete and particularized" and "actual or imminent, not 'conjectural' or 'hypothetical.' " *Lujan, supra,* at 560. An allegation of future injury may suffice if the threatened injury is certainly impending, or there is a substantial risk that the harm will occur. . . .

One recurring issue in our cases is determining when the threatened enforcement of a law creates an Article III injury. When an individual is subject to such a threat, an actual arrest, prosecution, or other enforcement action is not a prerequisite to challenging the law. See *Steffel v. Thompson,* 415 U.S. 452, 459 (1974). Instead, we have permitted pre-enforcement review under circumstances that render the threatened enforcement sufficiently imminent. Specifically, we have held that a plaintiff satisfies the injury-in-fact requirement where he alleges "an intention to engage in a course of conduct arguably affected with a constitutional interest, but proscribed by a statute, and there exists a credible threat of prosecution thereunder." *Babbitt v. Farm Workers,* 442 U.S. 289, 298 (1979). . . .[13]

---

[12] **As You Read, Consider:** In cases from the mid-twentieth century, the Supreme Court held that plaintiffs who wanted to challenge the enforcement of an allegedly unconstitutional policy had to subject themselves to enforcement. *See United Public Workers v. Mitchell*, 330 U.S. 75 (1947). Otherwise, their claims were not "ripe" as there was always the possibility that the government would not enforce the policy against them. How does Justice Clarence Thomas describe the "ripeness" or "imminence" requirement? Does he prohibit Susan B. Anthony List from challenging Ohio's law before the law is enforced?

[5] The doctrines of standing and ripeness "originate" from the same Article III limitation. *DaimlerChrysler Corp. v. Cuno*, 547 U.S. 332, 335 (2006). As the parties acknowledge, the Article III standing and ripeness issues in this case "boil down to the same question." *Med-Immune, Inc. v. Genentech, Inc.*, 549 U.S. 118, 128, n. 8 (2007). Consistent with our practice in cases like *Virginia v. American Booksellers Assn., Inc.*, 484 U.S. 383, 392 (1988), and *Babbitt v. Farm Workers*, 442 U.S. 289, 299, n. 11 (1979), we use the term "standing" in this opinion.

[13] **Questions:** What interpretive principles or normative values are vindicated by the Court's interpretation of *cases* and *controversies* to include people who have alleged a "credible

IV

Here, SBA and COAST contend that the threat of enforcement of the false statement statute amounts to an Article III injury in fact. We agree: Petitioners have alleged a credible threat of enforcement. . . .

First, petitioners have alleged "an intention to engage in a course of conduct arguably affected with a constitutional interest." Both petitioners have pleaded specific statements they intend to make in future election cycles. SBA has already stated that representatives who voted for the ACA supported "taxpayer-funded abortion," and it has alleged an "inten[t] to engage in substantially similar activity in the future." COAST has alleged that it previously intended to disseminate materials criticizing a vote for the ACA as a vote "to fund abortions with tax dollars," and that it "desires to make the same or similar statements about other federal candidates who voted for [the ACA]." Because petitioners' intended future conduct concerns political speech, it is certainly "affected with a constitutional interest." *Babbitt, supra,* at 298. . . .

Next, petitioners' intended future conduct is "arguably . . . proscribed by [the] statute" they wish to challenge. *Babbitt, supra,* at 298. The Ohio false statement law sweeps broadly and covers the subject matter of petitioners' intended speech. . . .

Respondents, echoing the Sixth Circuit, contend that SBA's fears of enforcement are misplaced because SBA has not said it " 'plans to lie or recklessly disregard the veracity of its speech.' " The Sixth Circuit reasoned that because SBA "can only be liable for making a statement 'knowing' it is false," SBA's insistence that its speech is factually true "makes the possibility of prosecution for uttering such statements exceedingly slim." *Id.,* at 422.

The Sixth Circuit misses the point. SBA's insistence that the allegations in its press release were true did not prevent the Commission panel from finding probable cause to believe that SBA had violated the law the first time around. And, there is every reason to think that similar speech in the future will result in similar proceedings, notwithstanding SBA's belief in the truth of its allegations. Nothing in this Court's decisions requires a plaintiff who wishes to challenge the constitutionality of a law to confess that he will in fact violate that law. . . .

Finally, the threat of future enforcement of the false statement statute is substantial. Most obviously, there is a history of past enforcement here: SBA was the subject of a complaint in a recent election cycle. We have observed that past enforcement against the same conduct is good evidence that the threat of enforcement is not " 'chimerical.' " . . .

The credibility of that threat is bolstered by the fact that authority to file a complaint with the Commission is not limited to a prosecutor or an agency. Instead, the false statement statute allows "any person" with knowledge of the purported violation to file a complaint. § 3517.153(A). Because the universe of potential complainants is not restricted to state officials who are constrained by explicit guidelines or ethical obligations, there is a real risk of complaints from, for example, political opponents. And petitioners, who intend to criticize candidates for political office, are easy targets.

Finally, Commission proceedings are not a rare occurrence. Petitioners inform us that the Commission " 'handles about 20 to 80 false statement complaints per year,' " Brief for Petitioners 46, and respondents do not deny that the Commission frequently fields complaints alleging violations of the false statement statute. Moreover, respondents have not disavowed enforcement if petitioners make similar

threat" of harm but who have not yet been injured? Why have an injury-in-fact requirement at all if such allegations are sufficient to invoke a federal court's jurisdiction?

statements in the future. In fact, the specter of enforcement is so substantial that the owner of the billboard refused to display SBA's message after receiving a letter threatening Commission proceedings. On these facts, the prospect of future enforcement is far from "imaginary or speculative." . . .

V

In concluding that petitioners' claims were not justiciable, the Sixth Circuit separately considered two other factors: whether the factual record was sufficiently developed, and whether hardship to the parties would result if judicial relief is denied at this stage in the proceedings. Respondents contend that these "prudential ripeness" factors confirm that the claims at issue are nonjusticiable. But we have already concluded that petitioners have alleged a sufficient Article III injury. To the extent respondents would have us deem petitioners' claims nonjusticiable "on grounds that are 'prudential,' rather than constitutional," "[t]hat request is in some tension with our recent reaffirmation of the principle that 'a federal court's obligation to hear and decide' cases within its jurisdiction 'is virtually unflagging.' " *Lexmark Int'l, Inc. v. Static Control Components, Inc.*, 134 S.Ct. 1377, 1386 (2014). . . .

NOTE: PRUDENTIAL STANDING CONSIDERATIONS

Before 2014, when the Supreme Court decided *Susan B. Anthony List*, there existed a half dozen "prudential" considerations that a court could invoke to decline to hear a case or controversy even if the plaintiff satisfied Article III's standing requirements. *See Ashwander v. TVA*, 297 U.S. 288, 346 (1936) (Brandeis, J., concurring). These included the prohibition on "advisory opinions"; the "adverseness" rule; the "zone of interests" test; the "generalized grievance" and "ripeness" doctrines; and other "judicially self-imposed limits on the exercise of federal jurisdiction." *United States v. Windsor*, 570 U.S. 744, 757 (2013).

But as alluded to in Part V of the *Susan B. Anthony List* opinion, these prudential doctrines were in tension with several cases in which the Court held that federal courts have a statutory obligation to hear all disputes over which Congress had validly granted them jurisdiction. *See, e.g., Zwickler v. Koota*, 389 U.S. 241, 248 (1967). And in *Lexmark International, Inc. v. Static Control Components, Inc.*, 572 U.S. 118 (2014), the Court effectively abolished the idea of "prudential standing," reaffirming its conclusion that "a federal court's obligation to hear and decide cases within its jurisdiction is virtually unflagging." *Id.* at 126 (internal quotation marks omitted).

The Court today typically analyzes "prudential standing" issues (1) using an identical analysis as in its jurisdictional standing cases, *see, e.g., Trump v. New York*, 141 S. Ct. 530, 535–36 (2020) (applying "standing" and "ripeness" using an identical analysis), or (2) analyzing whether a plaintiff has a cause of action to sue—a question that will be discussed later (section 36.1), *see, e.g., Bank of Am. Corp. v. City of Miami*, 137 S. Ct. 1296, 1302 (2017) ("Here, we conclude that the City's claims . . . satisfy the 'cause-of-action' (or 'prudential standing') requirement.").

34.3 THE CAUSATION AND REDRESSABILITY REQUIREMENTS

As the Supreme Court announced in *Lujan v. Defenders of Wildlife*, 504 U.S. 555 (1992), and reiterated in *Susan B. Anthony List v. Driehaus*, 573 U.S. 149 (2014), the modern doctrine of standing has three elements: (1) an "injury in fact," (2) a "causal connection between the injury and the conduct complained of," and (3) a "likelihood" that the injury "will be redressed by a favorable decision." *Lujan*, 504 U.S. at 560–61; *Susan B. Anthony List*, 573 U.S. at 166–67. These last two requirements are almost always considered together because they both address the same point: a federal court lacks jurisdiction over a dispute if it has no power to redress the injury in fact.

The Supreme Court developed the modern causation and redressability requirements during the era of *Ass'n of Data Processing Service Organizations v. Camp*, 397 U.S. 150 (1970), in the 1970s. In *Linda R.S. v. Richard D.*, 410 U.S. 614, 615 (1973), an unmarried mother wanted her child's father to provide child support, but the local prosecutor's office had a policy of coercing support only from fathers of children born in wedlock. The mother challenged the constitutionality of this policy, but the Supreme Court appeared concerned about allowing a person to challenge the policies of a prosecutor when the person was "neither prosecuted nor threatened with prosecution." *Linda R.S.*, 410 U.S. at 619. Holding that "a private citizen lacks a judicially cognizable interest in the prosecution or nonprosecution of another," the Court explained that there was no causal connection between the mother's injury in fact (the lack of child support) and the prosecutor's policy. *Id.* Somewhat disingenuously, the Court thought it "only speculative" that prosecuting the father would result in the payment of support as opposed to jail time for the father. *Id.* at 618.

Subsequent cases reaffirmed that a plaintiff seeking to demonstrate standing must prove that it was "likely, as opposed to merely speculative," that a court could remedy the alleged injury by issuing a judgment against the defendant. *Friends of the Earth, Inc. v. Laidlaw Env't Servs. (TOC), Inc.*, 528 U.S. 167, 187 (2000); *see, e.g.*, *Czyzewski v. Jevic Holding Corp.*, 137 S. Ct. 973, 983 (2017) (finding standing despite "the mere *possibility*" that an injury would not be redressable).

Although the causation and redressability requirements can be onerous where they apply, the Court has adopted several exceptions to the requirements. First, in cases challenging affirmative-action programs, the Court has held that white plaintiffs have standing even absent proof that eliminating the affirmative-action program would get them their desired job or position in a school. In *Northeastern Florida Chapter of the Associated General Contractors of America v. City of Jacksonville*, the Court explained that "[t]he 'injury in fact' in an equal protection case in this variety is the denial of equal treatment from the imposition of the barrier, not the ultimate inability to obtain the benefit." 508 U.S. 656, 666 (1993). Second, and for a similar reason, in cases challenging the denial of a procedural right (such as notice and comment before an agency issues a rule), the Court has held that Congress "can loosen the strictures of the redressability prong of our standing inquiry." *Summers v. Earth Island Inst.*, 555 U.S. 488, 497 (2009).

34.3.1
Clapper v. Amnesty International USA

568 U.S. 398 (2013)

In May 2013, a twenty-nine-year-old contractor at the National Security Agency (NSA) named Edward J. Snowden left his job in Hawaii and flew to Hong Kong. There, he invited a select group of journalists to distribute an enormous cache of classified files that he copied from his employer. The files represented the most extraordinary breach of national security secrets in American history. Among other things, they revealed that the Foreign Intelligence Surveillance Act Court (FISA Court) had authorized the federal government to wiretap Americans' international phone calls and to systematically collect Americans' domestic phone and email records without a warrant. *See* Charlie Savage, *Power Wars* 163–68, 399–402 (2017).

Before the Snowden revelations, the only publicly known information about this program came from a 2005 *New York Times* article and a 2006 *USA Today* article. They reported that the NSA had wiretapped or collected phone records from tens of millions of U.S. citizens without a warrant. *Id.* at 399–400; *see* Lesley Cauley, *NSA Has Massive Database of Americans' Phone Calls*, USA Today, May 11, 2006; James Risen & Eric Lichtblau, *Bush Lets U.S. Spy on Callers Without Courts*, N.Y. Times, Dec. 16, 2005, at A1. Those articles prompted the American Civil Liberties Union (ACLU) to seek an injunction blocking the NSA from conducting this warrantless surveillance. To satisfy Article III's injury-in-fact requirement, the ACLU alleged that its lawyers were declining to communicate with their overseas contacts out of fear that the NSA was intercepting their communications without a warrant. But in *ACLU v. NSA*, 493 F.3d 644 (6th Cir. 2007), the U.S. Court of Appeals for the Sixth Circuit held that the ACLU lacked standing. The court explained that it was not only "speculative" that the ACLU's lawyers had even been targeted by the NSA but also equally speculative that a favorable ruling—requiring the NSA to obtain warrants—would allow the ACLU lawyers to "freely engage in conversations and correspond via email without concern." *ACLU*, 493 F.3d at 662, 672–73.

The following year, Congress sought to legalize elements of this surveillance with the FISA Amendments Act of 2008, Pub. L. No. 110–261, 122 Stat. 2436. The newly amended Section 702 of the act permitted the attorney general and director of national intelligence to conduct surveillance of foreign nationals outside the United States—even if they were communicating with a U.S. citizen inside the United States.

Soon, Amnesty International sued James Clapper, the director of national intelligence under President Barack Obama, to challenge the constitutionality of this new law in light of the Fourth Amendment's protection against unreasonable searches. In *Clapper v. Amnesty Int'l USA*, Amnesty International alleged that its lawyers regularly communicated by email and phone with people overseas whom the lawyers believed were likely targets of wiretaps and that their lawyers had "ceased engaging" in these conversations thanks to the act. 568 U.S. 398, 406 (2013).

The Supreme Court issued the following opinion in favor of Clapper in February 2013—only months before the Snowden revelations.

■ JUSTICE ALITO delivered the opinion of the Court.[14]

Section 702 of the Foreign Intelligence Surveillance Act of 1978, 50 U.S.C. § 1881a, allows the Attorney General and the Director of National Intelligence to acquire foreign intelligence information by jointly authorizing the surveillance of individuals who are not "United States persons" and are reasonably believed to be located outside the United States. Before doing so, the Attorney General and the Director of National Intelligence normally must obtain the Foreign Intelligence Surveillance Court's approval. Respondents are United States persons whose work, they allege, requires them to engage in sensitive international communications with individuals who they believe are likely targets of surveillance under § 1881a. Respondents seek a declaration that § 1881a is unconstitutional, as well as an injunction against § 1881a-authorized surveillance. The question before us is whether respondents have Article III standing to seek this prospective relief. . . .

The law of Article III standing, which is built on separation-of-powers principles, serves to prevent the judicial process from being used to usurp the powers of the political branches. In keeping with the purpose of this doctrine, "[o]ur standing inquiry has been especially rigorous when reaching the merits of the dispute would force us to decide whether an action taken by one of the other two branches of the Federal Government was unconstitutional." *Raines, supra,* at 819–820. "Relaxation of standing requirements is directly related to the expansion of judicial power," *United States v. Richardson,* 418 U.S. 166, 188 (1974) (Powell, J., concurring); and we have often found a lack of standing in cases in which the Judiciary has been requested to review actions of the political branches in the fields of intelligence gathering and foreign affairs. . . .

To establish Article III standing, an injury must be "concrete, particularized, and actual or imminent; fairly traceable to the challenged action; and redressable by a favorable ruling." *Monsanto Co. v. Geertson Seed Farms,* 561 U.S. ___, ___ (2010). Although imminence is concededly a somewhat elastic concept, it cannot be stretched beyond its purpose, which is to ensure that the alleged injury is not too speculative for Article III purposes—that the injury is *certainly* impending. Thus, we have repeatedly reiterated that "threatened injury must be *certainly impending* to constitute

---

[14] **As You Read, Consider:** Justice Samuel Alito dismisses Amnesty International's case, in part because he does not believe that the Court could remedy the organization's alleged injury in fact. Why not? Does he think it would be a problem if *no* court could resolve Amnesty International's injury?

injury in fact," and that "[a]llegations of *possible* future injury" are not sufficient. *Whitmore,* 495 U.S., at 158. . . .

Respondents assert that they can establish injury in fact that is fairly traceable to § 1881a because there is an objectively reasonable likelihood that their communications with their foreign contacts will be intercepted under § 1881a at some point in the future. This argument . . . rests on their highly speculative fear that: (1) the Government will decide to target the communications of non-U.S. persons with whom they communicate; (2) in doing so, the Government will choose to invoke its authority under § 1881a rather than utilizing another method of surveillance; (3) the Article III judges who serve on the Foreign Intelligence Surveillance Court will conclude that the Government's proposed surveillance procedures satisfy § 1881a's many safeguards and are consistent with the Fourth Amendment; (4) the Government will succeed in intercepting the communications of respondents' contacts; and (5) respondents will be parties to the particular communications that the Government intercepts. As discussed below, respondents' theory of standing, which relies on a highly attenuated chain of possibilities, does not satisfy the requirement that threatened injury must be certainly impending. Moreover, even if respondents could demonstrate injury in fact, the second link in the above-described chain of contingencies—which amounts to mere speculation about whether surveillance would be under § 1881a or some other authority—shows that respondents cannot satisfy the requirement that any injury in fact must be fairly traceable to § 1881a. . . .[15]

First, it is speculative whether the Government will imminently target communications to which respondents are parties. Section 1881a expressly provides that respondents, who are U.S. persons, cannot be targeted for surveillance under § 1881a. . . . Accordingly, respondents' theory necessarily rests on their assertion that the Government will target *other individuals*—namely, their foreign contacts.

Yet respondents have no actual knowledge of the Government's § 1881a targeting practices. Instead, respondents merely speculate and make assumptions about whether their communications with their foreign contacts will be acquired under § 1881a. For example, journalist Christopher Hedges states: "I have no choice but to *assume* that any of my international communications *may* be subject to government surveillance, and I have to make decisions . . . in light of that *assumption.*" . . . Respondents, however, have set forth no specific facts demonstrating that the communications of their foreign contacts will be targeted. Moreover, because § 1881a at most *authorizes*—but does not *mandate* or *direct*—the surveillance that respondents fear, respondents' allegations are necessarily conjectural. . . . Simply put, respondents can only speculate as to how the Attorney General and the Director of National Intelligence will exercise their discretion in determining which communications to target.

Second, even if respondents could demonstrate that the targeting of their foreign contacts is imminent, respondents can only speculate as to whether the Government will seek to use § 1881a-authorized surveillance (rather than other methods) to do so. The Government has numerous other methods of conducting surveillance, none of which is challenged here. Even after the enactment of the FISA Amendments Act, for example, the Government may still conduct electronic surveillance of persons abroad under the older provisions of FISA so long as it satisfies the applicable

15 **Questions:** Why does Alito think this chain of possibilities is "highly attenuated"? That is, what distinguishes Amnesty International's "speculative" claim of injury from Susan B. Anthony List's "certainly impending" injury? More importantly, how is Amnesty International supposed to prove that this is *not* highly attenuated absent a lawsuit in which it can ask for discovery?

requirements, including a demonstration of probable cause to believe that the person is a foreign power or agent of a foreign power. See § 1805. The Government may also obtain information from the intelligence services of foreign nations. And, although we do not reach the question, the Government contends that it can conduct FISA-exempt human and technical surveillance programs that are governed by Executive Order 12333. See Exec. Order No. 12333, 50 U.S.C. § 401, pp. 543, 547–548. Even if respondents could demonstrate that their foreign contacts will imminently be targeted—indeed, even if they could show that interception of their own communications will imminently occur—they would still need to show that their injury is fairly traceable to § 1881a. But, because respondents can only speculate as to whether any (asserted) interception would be under § 1881a or some other authority, they cannot satisfy the "fairly traceable" requirement.[16]

Third, even if respondents could show that the Government will seek the Foreign Intelligence Surveillance Court's authorization to acquire the communications of respondents' foreign contacts under § 1881a, respondents can only speculate as to whether that court will authorize such surveillance. In the past, we have been reluctant to endorse standing theories that require guesswork as to how independent decisionmakers will exercise their judgment. . . .

Fourth, even if the Government were to obtain the Foreign Intelligence Surveillance Court's approval to target respondents' foreign contacts under § 1881a, it is unclear whether the Government would succeed in acquiring the communications of respondents' foreign contacts. And fifth, even if the Government were to conduct surveillance of respondents' foreign contacts, respondents can only speculate as to whether *their own communications* with their foreign contacts would be incidentally acquired.

In sum, respondents' speculative chain of possibilities does not establish that injury based on potential future surveillance is certainly impending or is fairly traceable to § 1881a. . . .

Respondents' alternative argument—namely, that they can establish standing based on the measures that they have undertaken to avoid § 1881a-authorized surveillance—fares no better. Respondents assert that they are suffering ongoing injuries that are fairly traceable to § 1881a because the risk of surveillance under § 1881a requires them to take costly and burdensome measures to protect the confidentiality of their communications. Respondents claim, for instance, that the threat of surveillance sometimes compels them to avoid certain e-mail and phone conversations, to "tal[k] in generalities rather than specifics," or to travel so that they can have in-person conversations. . . .

Respondents' contention that they have standing because they incurred certain costs as a reasonable reaction to a risk of harm is unavailing—because the harm respondents seek to avoid is not certainly impending. In other words, respondents cannot manufacture standing merely by inflicting harm on themselves based on their fears of hypothetical future harm that is not certainly impending.

---

[16] **Question:** Executive Order No. 12333, 46 Fed. Reg. 59,941 (Dec. 4, 1981), signed by President Ronald Reagan, authorized U.S. intelligence services to collect the content of communications outside the United States. It specifically authorized the collection of "information concerning United States persons . . . in the course of a lawful foreign intelligence . . . investigation." Exec. Order No. 12333, § 2.3(c). Alito is observing that Amnesty International cannot prove that its injury will be caused by § 1881a as opposed to this alternative authority. Does the existence of this alternative persuade you that Amnesty International's challenge is "speculative" and therefore that a federal court should not review the constitutionality of § 1881a?

If the law were otherwise, an enterprising plaintiff would be able to secure a lower standard for Article III standing simply by making an expenditure based on a nonparanoid fear. As Judge Raggi accurately noted, under [this] reasoning, respondents could, "for the price of a plane ticket, . . . transform their standing burden from one requiring a showing of actual or imminent . . . interception to one requiring a showing that their subjective fear of such interception is not fanciful, irrational, or clearly unreasonable." 667 F.3d, at 180. . . .

Another reason that respondents' present injuries are not fairly traceable to § 1881a is that even before § 1881a was enacted, they had a similar incentive to engage in many of the countermeasures that they are now taking. For instance, respondent Scott McKay's declaration describes—and the dissent heavily relies on—Mr. McKay's "knowledge" that thousands of communications involving one of his clients were monitored in the past. But this surveillance was conducted pursuant to FISA authority that predated § 1881a. Thus, because the Government was allegedly conducting surveillance of Mr. McKay's client before Congress enacted § 1881a, it is difficult to see how the safeguards that Mr. McKay now claims to have implemented can be traced to § 1881a.

Because respondents do not face a threat of certainly impending interception under § 1881a, the costs that they have incurred to avoid surveillance are simply the product of their fear of surveillance. . . . Because "[a]llegations of a subjective 'chill' are not an adequate substitute for a claim of specific present objective harm or a threat of specific future harm," [respondents] lack standing. . . .

Respondents [finally] suggest that they should be held to have standing because otherwise the constitutionality of § 1881a could not be challenged. It would be wrong, they maintain, to "insulate the government's surveillance activities from meaningful judicial review." Respondents' suggestion is both legally and factually incorrect. First, " '[t]he assumption that if respondents have no standing to sue, no one would have standing, is not a reason to find standing.' " *Valley Forge Christian College,* 454 U.S., at 489.

Second, our holding today by no means insulates § 1881a from judicial review. As described above, Congress created a comprehensive scheme in which the Foreign Intelligence Surveillance Court evaluates the Government's certifications, targeting procedures, and minimization procedures—including assessing whether the targeting and minimization procedures comport with the Fourth Amendment. § 1881a(a), (c)(1), (i)(2), (i)(3). Any dissatisfaction that respondents may have about the Foreign Intelligence Surveillance Court's rulings—or the congressional delineation of that court's role—is irrelevant to our standing analysis. . . .

NOTE: THE "FAIRLY TRACEABLE" REQUIREMENT

The *Clapper* Court described the causation requirement for standing as a requirement that any alleged injury be "fairly traceable" to the law being challenged. 568 U.S. at 402. The Court in effect wrote that because several sources of law may have authorized the government to conduct surveillance of the plaintiffs, any alleged injury was not "fairly traceable" to the section of the FISA Amendments Act that they were challenging. *Id.*

The Court elaborated on this requirement when it rejected one of the many legal challenges that it heard against the Patient Protection and Affordable Care Act of 2010, Pub. L. No. 111–148, 124 Stat. 119. When Congress first enacted the Affordable Care Act in 2010, it included a provision that penalized certain people who declined to purchase health insurance. This "individual mandate" or "shared responsibility payment" was upheld as an exercise of Congress's taxing power in *NFIB v. Sebelius*, 567 U.S. 519, 567–68 (2012). But in 2017, a Republican-controlled Congress passed the Tax Cuts and Jobs Act of 2017, Pub. L. No. 115–97, 131 Stat. 2054, in which it set the penalty for the individual mandate at zero dollars. A group of twenty states then challenged the Affordable Care Act, arguing that its individual mandate was no longer constitutional because the associated financial penalty no longer produced any revenue for the federal government. The states claimed that the zero-dollar penalty nevertheless unlawfully induced residents to enroll in state-sponsored insurance programs such as Medicaid, which injured the states by requiring them to spend more money on insurance.

In *California v. Texas*, 141 S. Ct. 2104 (2021), the Court dismissed the states' suit for lack of standing. Invoking *Clapper*, Justice Stephen Breyer explained that the states' alleged injury—paying more money on insurance programs—was not " 'fairly traceable' to enforcement of the 'allegedly unlawful' provision of which the plaintiffs complain." *Id.* at 2119. Breyer wrote that the states had failed to provide evidence that any of their residents had actually enrolled in state-sponsored insurance programs because of the zero-dollar penalty. *Id.* at 2117. Rather, most of the people who enrolled in these programs appeared to have done so because the programs "offer their recipients many benefits that have nothing to do with the [zero-dollar penalty]." *Id.* Because only a " 'highly attenuated chain of possibilities' " supported the claim "that an unenforceable mandate will cause [the states'] residents to enroll in valuable benefits programs that they would otherwise forgo," the Court dismissed the suit. *Id.* at 2119 (quoting *Clapper*, 568 U.S. at 410–11).

NOTE: REDRESSABILITY AND MOOTNESS

Even if a plaintiff can satisfy the three requirements of standing *before* the litigation begins, an event during the litigation may deprive the court of its ability to redress the plaintiff's injuries. Such an event renders the litigation *moot*. While mootness sometimes is treated as a separate doctrine from standing, *see, e.g.*, *Friends of the Earth*, 528 U.S. at 190, it is functionally identical to *Lujan*'s redressability requirement. In other words, "[t]o ensure a case remains fit for federal-court adjudication, the parties must have the necessary stake not only at the outset of litigation, but throughout its course." *Camreta v. Greene*, 563 U.S. 692, 701 (2011) (internal quotation marks omitted). If a case becomes moot, there is nothing for a federal court to do but to announce that fact, vacate any judgments, and dismiss the case. *United States v. Munsingwear*, 340 U.S. 36, 39–40 (1950).

Various events can moot a case. If Congress or a legislature changes the challenged law, then there may be no need for a court to remedy the plaintiff's injury. *See, e.g.*, *N.Y. State Rifle & Pistol Ass'n, Inc., v. City of New York*, 140 S. Ct. 1525, 1526 (2020). A change in the status of the parties can also moot a case. In *Arizonans for Official English v. Arizona*, a state employee attacking an English-only work requirement had standing until she resigned from her job following a decision in the trial court—leading the

Supreme Court to vacate the trial-court judgment as moot. 520 U.S. 43, 67 (1997).

The Court has, however, emphasized that a case isn't moot as long as the plaintiff can articulate *some* "concrete interest" in the case that a federal court can remedy. Even if that concrete interest is "small," as long as the issue "is not simply a matter of academic debate, [it] is enough to save [a] case from mootness." *Chafin v. Chafin*, 568 U.S. 165, 176 (2013). The Court reaffirmed this point in *Uzuegbunam v. Preczewski*, a case in which a plaintiff asked only for nominal damages—a single dollar—after he alleged that his public college violated his constitutional right to exercise religion on campus. 141 S. Ct. 792, 801 (2021). "Despite being small, nominal damages are certainly concrete," the Court wrote. *Id.* at 801.

NOTE: "EXCEPTIONS" TO MOOTNESS

The Supreme Court's mootness jurisprudence is full of "exceptions," which can all be understood as situations in which a court can remedy a plaintiff's concrete interest in a case despite an event that would appear to suggest the absence of redressability.

Collateral consequences. First, if the plaintiff's main injury disappears but there remains the possibility of *collateral consequences*, then the plaintiff still has a concrete interest in the litigation. *See, e.g.*, *Super Tire Eng'g Co. v. McCorkle*, 416 U.S. 115, 127 (1974).

Voluntary cessation. Second, "[i]t is well settled that a defendant's voluntary cessation of a challenged practice does not deprive a federal court of its power to determine the legality of the practice." *City of Mesquite v. Aladdin's Castle, Inc.*, 455 U.S. 283, 288–89 (1982). A court can still remedy a plaintiff's harm in this situation because the defendant might repeat the practice after the case is dismissed.

For example, if a government repeals a challenged ordinance but retains the power to reenact precisely the same provision, then the case is moot only where "subsequent events ma[ke] it absolutely clear that the allegedly wrongful behavior could not reasonably be expected to recur." *Trinity Lutheran Church of Columbia, Inc. v. Comer*, 137 S. Ct. 2012, 2019 n.1 (2017).

Similarly, a defendant cannot moot a case by *offering* a plaintiff complete relief—say, by offering the plaintiff a $50 check in a suit for $50 in damages. As long as the settlement offer has not been accepted, both parties retain "the same stake in the litigation that they had at the outset." *Campbell-Ewald Co. v. Gomez*, 577 U.S. 153, 163 (2016).

Capable of repetition yet evading review. The third exception concerns claims that are "capable of repetition yet evading review." *Friends of the Earth*, 528 U.S. at 189–91. These claims arise when a challenged government action concludes before the end of litigation yet there is a reasonable expectation that the government will repeat its action in the future. *Id.* In this situation, the Court has held that it can remedy a plaintiff's *future* injury even after the context for challenging the past injury has concluded.

For example, plaintiffs challenging abortion restrictions can continue their suit even after obtaining an abortion or giving birth. *See Roe v. Wade*, 410 U.S. 113, 124–25 (1973). And in a case challenging short-term contracts, the Court noted that "two years is too short to complete judicial review of the lawfulness of the procurement." *Kingdomware Techs., Inc. v. United States*, 579 U.S. 162, 170 (2016).

Class actions. Finally, when a plaintiff is part of a class action, the case or controversy remains alive as long as (1) the named representative had standing at the initiation of the action and (2) at least one member of the class continues to have a live claim. *United States Parole Comm'n v. Geraghty*, 445 U.S. 388, 396 (1980). For example, in *Sosna v. Iowa*, 419 U.S. 393, 397 (1975), a woman filed a class action against an Iowa divorce statute that imposed a one-year residency requirement on anyone seeking a divorce. The litigation remained pending one year later, after Sosna had lived in Iowa sufficiently long enough to obtain a divorce. *Id.* at 398–99. Sosna's situation didn't fall in the "capable of repetition yet evading review" exception because the Court thought it was unlikely "that she may move from Iowa, only to return and later seek a divorce within one year from her return." *Id.* at 400. But the Court held that while "the controversy is no longer alive as to appellant Sosna, it remains very much alive for the class of persons she has been certified to represent." *Id.* at 401.

NOTE: STANDING ON APPEAL

Standing is usually an obstacle only for a plaintiff. Defendants almost always have a concrete interest in the litigation because an unfavorable judgment will affect their rights or require them to do something. But appeals present two complications.

First, a party that obtains a judgment in its favor arguably lacks any power to maintain the litigation—as there is nothing that the federal court can do further. But the Supreme Court has held that such parties acquire "a judicially cognizable interest in ensuring compliance with that judgment" sufficient to keep the litigation alive. *Salazar v. Buono*, 559 U.S. 700, 712 (2010) (internal quotation marks omitted).

Second, standing is a federal doctrine—an interpretation of Article III. Many states don't have analogous standing rules and therefore allow any interested taxpayers to challenge a government action in state court. *See, e.g.*, *Gregory v. Shurtleff*, 299 P.3d 1098 (Utah 2013). In such circumstances, a *plaintiff* who loses in state court may not appeal to the Supreme Court unless they can prove they had standing under Article III. *See, e.g.*, *Tileston v. Ullman*, 318 U.S. 44, 45–46 (1943). But a *defendant* who loses in state court can often easily prove Article III standing by alleging they have been injured by whatever decree the state court has imposed on them. *See, e.g.*, *ASARCO Inc. v. Kadish*, 490 U.S. 605, 618 (1989).

34.4 THIRD-PARTY STANDING

The three requirements of *Lujan v. Defenders of Wildlife*, 504 U.S. 555 (1992)—injury in fact, causation, and redressability—are at the core of Article III's requirements for a case or controversy. But even when a plaintiff arguably possesses standing to challenge a law's violation of the plaintiff's own rights, the plaintiff may also want to challenge how the law violates other people's rights. This situation arises frequently enough and in different enough settings that the Supreme Court has developed specific rules to analyze each setting.

To the extent that the Court has held that a plaintiff has standing but, as a prudential matter, should not be able to assert the rights of a third party, the present-day validity of such holdings has been called into doubt by the Court's recent abolition of "prudential standing." *See Lexmark Int'l, Inc. v. Static Control Components, Inc.*, 572 U.S. 118, 126 (2014). But most of the Court's third-party standing cases can be understood as specific applications of *Lujan*'s three requirements, particularly its requirement that a plaintiff must have been personally injured in fact. *See, e.g., Hollingsworth v. Perry*, 570 U.S. 693, 707 (2013).

Individuals and third-party standing

The first setting is when a plaintiff injured by a statute challenges the statute because of how it injures a third party. The Supreme Court's usual rule is that a party "generally must assert his own legal rights and interests, and cannot rest his claim to relief on the legal rights or interests of third parties." *Warth v. Seldin*, 422 U.S. 490, 499 (1975). But the Court has upheld what it calls "third-party standing" (1) where "the party asserting the right has a 'close' relationship with the person who possesses the right" and (2) where "there is a 'hindrance' to the possessor's ability to protect his own interests." *Kowalski v. Tesmer*, 543 U.S. 125, 130 (2004).

For example, the Court has frequently heard cases in which doctors or clinics challenge the enforcement of a law against themselves because such enforcement would indirectly infringe on a patient's right to obtain an abortion or contraception. *See, e.g., June Med. Servs. LLC v. Russo*, 140 S. Ct. 2103, 2118–19 (2020); *Griswold v. Connecticut*, 381 U.S. 479, 481 (1965). The Court has also authorized injured parents to assert the rights of their children, *Sessions v. Morales-Santana*, 137 S. Ct. 1678, 1689 (2017); and injured lawyers to assert the rights of their existing clients, *Caplin & Drysdale v. United States*, 491 U.S. 617, 623 n.3 (1989).

But the Court has held that lawyers can't assert the rights of *hypothetical* clients, *Kowalski*, 543 U.S. at 131 (finding no close relationship), or clients who disagree with them, *Whitmore v. Arkansas*, 495 U.S. 149, 165 (1990) (finding no hindrance).

Organizational standing

The second setting is when an organization challenges a statute not just on behalf of itself, but also on behalf of its members.

For example, after the Montgomery bus boycott, Alabama officials attempted to enforce a law requiring the National Association for the Advancement of Colored People (NAACP) to disclose the identity of its members in the state. Such disclosure would open the NAACP's members to intimidation and violence, so the NAACP itself challenged the law in federal court as a violation of its members' rights under the First and Fourteenth Amendments. In *National Ass'n for the Advancement of Colored People v. Alabama ex rel. Patterson*, the Supreme Court agreed that the NAACP was "constitutionally entitled to . . . assert on behalf of its members, a right personal to them to be protected from compelled disclosure by the State of their affiliation with the Association as revealed by the membership lists." 357 U.S. 449, 458–59 (1958).

In later cases, the Court explained that an organization can assert the rights of its members when "(a) its members would otherwise have standing to sue in their own right; (b) the interests it seeks to protect are germane to the organization's purpose; and (c) neither the claim asserted nor the relief requested requires the participation of individual members in the lawsuit." *Hunt v. Wash. State Apple Advert. Comm'n*, 432 U.S. 333, 343 (1977).

State standing

Third, it is common for states to sue to remedy injuries not only to themselves but also to their citizens. *See Louisiana v. Texas*, 176 U.S. 1, 9 (1900).

To remedy injuries to themselves, states have sued to protect their borders, property, air, and other things within their boundaries that they claim "quasi-sovereign" rights over. *See, e.g., Missouri v. Holland*, 252 U.S. 416, 431 (1920); *Pennsylvania v. Wheeling & Belmont Bridge Co.*, 54 U.S. (13 How.) 518, 522 (1852).

To remedy an alleged injury to its citizens, a state may also sue as *parens patriae*, or "parent of the nation," if the injury is of the sort that the state would likely address through its sovereign lawmaking powers if it could. *See Massachusetts v. EPA*, 549 U.S. 497, 520 (2007). For example, the Supreme Court has allowed a state to sue an out-of-state railroad that discriminated against its citizens, *Georgia v. Pa. R.R. Co.*, 324 U.S. 439, 445 (1945).

But the Court has held that a state may not sue merely to protect its citizens from injuries caused by a federal law. As the Court held in *Massachusetts v. Mellon*, 262 U.S. 447, 486 (1923), the United States itself is the *parens patriae* in that situation. So, in cases against a federal agency or officer, the Court has held that a state may only sue when it is seeking to enforce federal law on behalf of its citizens, *Massachusetts v. EPA*, 549 U.S. at 520 n.17, or when it is challenging the federal law for harming its own legal interests, *see, e.g., Dep't of Commerce v. New York*, 139 S. Ct. 2551, 2565 (2019).

Federalism and separation-of-powers standing

Fourth, the Supreme Court has also found standing in the inverse of the above situation, i.e., when individuals sue on behalf of their state's sovereign interests. For example, in *Bond v. United States*, the Court allowed an injured woman, Carol Anne Bond, to challenge a federal law "on grounds that the measure interferes with the powers reserved to States." 564 U.S. 211, 216 (2011). The Court explained that "the individual liberty secured by federalism is not simply derivative of the rights of the States"; rather, federalism's dispersal of power "protects the liberty of the individual from arbitrary power." *Id.* at 222.

Relatedly, injured private parties and local governments have often brought separation-of-powers challenges to remedy alleged injuries against the president—even in cases where the executive branch does not think that the president has been injured. *See, e.g.*, *Seila Law LLC v. Consumer Fin. Prot. Bureau*, 140 S. Ct. 2183, 2195–97 (2020).

Legislator standing

Fifth, legislators often seek to challenge or defend a statute because of how the statute harms them or their "institution." In *Coleman v. Miller*, 307 U.S. 433, 438 (1939), a case in which twenty out of forty members of a state senate sued to challenge an allegedly unconstitutional tiebreaker by the lieutenant governor, the Supreme Court recognized that legislators can, in some instances, suffer an injury in fact due to the loss of the effectiveness of their votes.

But in *Raines v. Byrd*, 521 U.S. 811, 824 (1997), a case in which a member of Congress challenged the constitutionality of the Line Item Veto Act, Pub. L. No. 104–130, 110 Stat. 1200, the Court explained that *Coleman* stood only for the proposition that legislators whose votes would have been sufficient to defeat a specific legislative act have standing to challenge or defend the act. A single legislator's diminished voting power, by contrast, wasn't "particularized." *Raines*, 521 U.S. at 820–21.

However, the Court reaffirmed *Coleman* in *Arizona State Legislature v. Arizona Independent Redistricting Commission*, in which a state legislature authorized some of its members to assert an "institutional injury" to the entire legislative body. 576 U.S. 787, 802 (2015). The Court held that this authorization gave the legislators standing to challenge a state redistricting commission that allegedly "strip[ped] the legislature of its alleged prerogative to initiate redistricting." *Id.* at 2663. In *Committee on Judiciary of the U.S. House of Representatives v. McGahn*, the U.S. Court of Appeals for the D.C. Circuit, sitting en banc, ruled that the House Judiciary Committee had standing to enforce a subpoena on behalf of the entire House against an executive-branch official. 968 F.3d 755, 771–74 (D.C. Cir. 2020).

Agent standing

Sixth, as in *Arizona State Legislature*, the Supreme Court has held that a person or government that is injured by a statute may authorize a trustee, guardian, or other agent to assert its rights on its behalf. *See, e.g., Sprint Comm'ns Co., L.P. v. APCC Servs., Inc.*, 554 U.S. 269, 289 (2008).

But in *Hollingsworth v. Perry*, 570 U.S. 693, 700–01 (2013), the Court dismissed for lack of standing an appeal brought by proponents of Proposition 8, a voter-enacted ballot initiative that eliminated the right of same-sex couples to marry in California. The state's attorney general, Kamala Harris, had refused to defend the proposition in federal court. She instead authorized the proponents to do so. But the Court explained that the California law that authorized the proponents to defend Proposition 8 didn't create the "agency relationship" necessary to give the injured parties the right to control their agent's conduct. *Hollingsworth*, 570 U.S. at 713.

Overbreadth

Finally, the Supreme Court has also allowed plaintiffs to challenge overly broad statutes on the ground that the statutes unconstitutionally regulate constitutionally protected behavior—even if the statutes could constitutionally be applied to the challenger's conduct. *See, e.g., Lewis v. City of New Orleans*, 415 U.S. 130, 134 (1974). This "overbreadth" doctrine typically arises with respect to statutes that regulate speech or the press.

34.5 TYPES OF "CASES"

Even when a case or controversy is before a federal court, Article III doesn't permit federal courts to hear every type of case or controversy. The full scope of cases and controversies is usually covered at length in classes on civil procedure and federal courts. It is nevertheless worth being familiar with the types of cases.

Cases arising under federal law

The first type of case listed in Article III is "all Cases, in Law and Equity, arising under this Constitution, the Laws of the United States, and Treaties made, or which shall be made, under their Authority." This language is usually referred to as *federal-question jurisdiction*. The Supreme Court has read the words "arising under" to refer to "all cases in which a federal question is an ingredient of the action." *Merrill Lynch, Pierce, Fenner & Smith Inc. v. Manning*, 578 U.S. 374, 385 (2016) (internal quotation marks omitted).

But in exercising its power to regulate the jurisdiction of courts, Congress has never authorized federal courts to hear the full extent of their constitutional jurisdiction. For the United States' first eighty years,

Congress didn't authorize federal courts to exercise federal-question jurisdiction at all. *See* Judiciary Act of 1789, ch. 20, 1 Stat. 73. Congress only empowered courts to hear federal questions after the Civil War—and, even then, only when there was a certain amount of money involved. *See* Act of Mar. 3, 1875, ch. 137, 18 Stat. 470; Act of Apr. 9, 1866, ch. 31, 14 Stat. 27.

Only since 1980 has a statute, 28 U.S.C. § 1331(a), empowered courts to hear cases "arising under" federal law without an amount-in-controversy requirement. *See* Act of Dec. 1, 1980, Pub. L. No. 96–486, 94 Stat. 2369; Act of Oct. 21, 1976, Pub. L. No. 94–574, 90 Stat. 2721. Even this general grant of jurisdiction, though, has been interpreted narrowly. Under the "well-pleaded complaint" rule, a civil case "arises under" federal law for purposes of § 1331(a) only when federal law creates the cause of action or the relief sought by the *plaintiff*; a defendant's invocation of a federal defense is usually irrelevant. *See, e.g.*, *Skelly Oil Co. v. Phillips Petroleum Co.*, 339 U.S. 667, 672 (1950).

Other statutes also confer federal-question jurisdiction with respect to specific parties or claims. In 28 U.S.C. § 1343(3), for example, Congress authorized federal courts to exercise federal-question jurisdiction over claims brought to enforce 42 U.S.C. § 1983 and other civil rights statutes. *See Hague v. CIO*, 307 U.S. 496, 513 (1939).

Thanks to various removal statutes, defendants sued in state court can remove their case to federal court as long as (1) the case could have been brought in federal court, (2) the defendant is a federal officer raising a federal-law defense, or (3) the defendant is legally barred from raising a federal civil rights defense in the state proceeding. *See* 28 U.S.C. §§ 1441–43.

Congress has also authorized federal courts to hear suits involving torts, breaches of contract, and other common-law causes of action in contexts where important federal interests, such as labor law, are involved. *See, e.g.*, Labor Management Relations Act of 1947, Pub. L. No. 80–101, 61 Stat. 136, 156.

Finally, when federal courts hear claims involving colorable federal questions, they may also exercise "supplemental" jurisdiction over state-law questions necessary to the disposition of a case. 28 U.S.C. § 1367.

Article III specifically authorizes the Supreme Court to exercise appellate jurisdiction over all "Cases," including federal questions. Congress accordingly has empowered the Court not only to review cases from federal court on appeal or writ of certiorari, 28 U.S.C. §§ 1253–1254, but also to review cases from the "highest court of a state in which a decision could be had" when a federal question was raised in the action or defense, *id.* § 1257(a).

Importantly, this grant of jurisdiction doesn't give the Supreme Court jurisdiction to review state-court cases in which the decision turned solely on an interpretation of state law. It can therefore be ambiguous if a state-court case presents issues involving federal-law *and* state-law claims. To dispel this ambiguity, in *Michigan v. Long*, 463 U.S. 1032 (1983), the Supreme Court announced that whenever a state-court case theoretically could have turned on a federal question, the Supreme Court would presume that it could exercise jurisdiction over the case unless the state court explicitly declared that its decision rested on an "adequate" and "independent" state ground (AISG). *Long*, 463 U.S. at 1041–43. A state ground is adequate when it is broad enough to sustain the judgment and is not an attempt to stifle or evade federal claims. *See, e.g., Nat'l Ass'n for the Advancement of Colored People v. Alabama ex rel. Patterson*, 357 U.S. 449, 457–58 (1958). A state ground is independent when the disposition of a federal question isn't necessary to decide the case. *See, e.g., Raley v. Ohio*, 360 U.S. 423, 435–37 (1959).

Cases affecting ambassadors

The second type of case listed in Article III is "Cases affecting Ambassadors, other public Ministers and Consuls." The Supreme Court has interpreted this clause to involve all cases in which a foreign diplomat is a party (and not merely the subject of the case). *See, e.g., Ex parte Gruber*, 269 U.S. 302, 303 (1925). In contrast with federal-question jurisdiction, Congress authorized federal courts to hear these sorts of cases in the Judiciary Act of 1789. 1 Stat. at 80–81. And even though Article III empowers the Supreme Court to hear cases involving ambassadors as an exercise of its original jurisdiction, Congress has also authorized the Supreme Court to hear such cases on appeal. *See* 28 U.S.C. § 1251(b); *Ames v. Kansas ex rel. Johnston*, 111 U.S. 449, 463–64 (1884).

Cases of admiralty and maritime jurisdiction

The last type of case is "Cases of admiralty and maritime Jurisdiction." When this jurisdiction is properly invoked, the Supreme Court has instructed federal courts to "act as a common-law court, subject to any controlling statutes enacted by Congress." *Air & Liquid Sys. Corp. v. DeVries*, 139 S. Ct. 986, 991 (2019); *see, e.g.*, 28 U.S.C. § 1333.

Although there was once a historical distinction between *admiralty* and *maritime jurisdiction*, today the two terms are used interchangeably. In general, they cover contracts whose "nature and subject matter" concern "maritime commerce," or navigation across rivers, seas, and oceans. *Exxon Corp. v. Cent. Gulf Lines, Inc.*, 500 U.S. 603, 611–12 (1991). They also cover torts, property damage, and seizures that occur on navigable waters or the "high seas" beyond the United States's territorial borders. *See, e.g., Miles v. Apex Marine Corp.*, 498 U.S. 19, 36 (1991); *Prize Cases*, 67 U.S. 635, 672 (1863). Finally, they cover some events that take place on land that are closely connected with maritime commerce. These include a sailor's claim for "maintenance and cure"—day-to-day living expenses and medical bills—for injuries incurred while working. *See, e.g.*, *Atl. Sounding Co. v. Townsend*, 557 U.S. 404, 407 (2009).

34.6 TYPES OF "CONTROVERSIES"

In addition to "Cases," Article III also extends the judicial power to "Controversies" between different types of parties.

Controversies in which the United States is a party

The first type of controversy is one in which "the United States shall be a party."

Although no section of Article I or Article II explicitly gives the United States the power to sue in its own name, the Judiciary Act of 1789, ch. 20, 1 Stat. 73, gave federal courts jurisdiction to hear suits in which the United States was a plaintiff. *See* 28 U.S.C. § 1345. When the issue reached the Supreme Court, it interpreted Article III as implying that the executive branch has the power to sue on behalf of the United States, provided that the United States has an interest in the subject matter and a legal right to the remedy sought. *United States v. San Jacinto Tin Co.*, 125 U.S. 273, 279–80 (1888); *Dugan v. United States*, 16 U.S. (3 Wheat.) 172, 180–81 (1818). The attorney general has exercised this power on behalf of the United States in a number of settings, including to enjoin strikes and enforce federal law. *See, e.g.*, *Arizona v. United States*, 567 U.S. 387 (2012); *In re Debs*, 158 U.S. 564 (1895).

The language of this provision also implies that federal courts have jurisdiction over controversies in which the United States is a defendant. Those controversies present the issue of sovereign immunity, which we will discuss later (section 35.3).

Controversies between two or more states

The second type of controversy involves one state suing another state.

Before 1789, these suits typically involved boundary or territorial disputes and were resolved by the Confederation Congress as a court of last resort. With Article III, the Constitution gave the Supreme Court original jurisdiction over controversies "in which a State shall be Party." The Judiciary Act of 1789 confirmed the Supreme Court's exclusive jurisdiction over cases involving two or more states, but it also gave inferior courts concurrent jurisdiction over cases involving only one state, just as it did with ambassadors. *See* 28 U.S.C. § 1251.

Today, the Supreme Court often hears cases involving multiple states as part of its original jurisdiction. Many of these cases involve boundary disputes and water rights, but some attempt to challenge another state's legislation. *See, e.g.*, *Texas v. Pennsylvania*, 141 S. Ct. 1230 (2020) (dismissing Texas's challenge to Pennsylvania's administration of the 2020 presidential election for lack of standing).

When a state properly invokes the Court's original jurisdiction, the Court sits as a trial court exercising jurisdiction that is "basically equitable in nature." *Kansas v. Nebraska*, 574 U.S. 445, 453 (2015). There are no prescribed rules of decision, so "the court may regulate and mould the process it uses in such a manner as in its judgment will best promote the purposes of justice." *Kentucky v. Dennison*, 65 U.S. (24 How.) 66, 98 (1861). For example, in a case involving an alleged breach of an interstate compact, the Court appointed a special master to investigate and accepted the special master's recommendation that the breaching state disgorge part of its profits. *Kansas*, 574 U.S. at 475. And in a case involving a state that refused to comply with an order, the Court declared that its judgment should be sustained "by every authority of the federal government, judicial, legislative, and executive." *Virginia v. West Virginia*, 246 U.S. 565, 601 (1918). The state soon settled.

The Court does not, however, accept every case that comes before it. Instead, it has treated its exercise of original jurisdiction as discretionary, depending on the seriousness of the claim and the availability of another forum to resolve the dispute. *Texas v. New Mexico*, 462 U.S. 554, 570 (1983). *But see Arizona v. California*, 140 S. Ct. 684, 684–86 (2020) (Thomas, J., dissenting) (arguing that the Court's exercise of original jurisdiction should be mandatory, not discretionary).

Controversies between a state and citizens of another state

The third type of controversy involves "a State and Citizens of another State." As we'll discuss shortly, this provision of Article III was amended by the Eleventh Amendment, which declares, "The judicial power of the United States shall not be construed to extend to any suit in law or equity, commenced or prosecuted against one of the United States by citizens of another state, or by citizens or subjects of any foreign state." As a result, the provision is only invoked today when a state is a plaintiff.

Congress has long given federal courts jurisdiction over "all controversies of a civil nature, where a state is a party." Judiciary Act of 1789, 1 Stat. at 80. Interpreting Article III in light of this language, the Supreme Court held that the term *controversies* refers only to civil cases, meaning that a state could not criminally prosecute a citizen of another state in federal court. *See Wisconsin v. Pelican Ins. Co.*, 127 U.S. 265, 297 (1888).

Once a state is in federal court as a plaintiff, the state must, like any other plaintiff, invoke a cause of action and satisfy the requirements of standing and any other limits on jurisdiction. *See, e.g., Massachusetts v. Mellon*, 262 U.S. 447, 486 (1923).

Controversies between citizens of different states

The next type of controversy involves "Citizens of different States." This is commonly known as "diversity jurisdiction." Along with federal-question jurisdiction, it is the main source of civil cases that reach federal courts.

During the Constitutional Convention, the proponents of diversity jurisdiction wanted federal courts to provide a neutral tribunal for resolving controversies in which local juries might provide a home-state advantage. *See Bank of the United States v. Deveaux*, 9 U.S. (5 Cranch) 61, 87 (1809). This concern is easier to understand today if you analogize the early republic to the modern European Union: just as a German in France might fear that a French court would favor a French defendant, a Virginian in the eighteenth century might fear that a Massachusetts court would favor a Massachusetts defendant. Addressing this fear, Congress authorized federal courts to hear diversity cases in 1789, long before it authorized them to hear federal questions in 1875. *See* Judiciary Act of 1789, 1 Stat. at 78; Judiciary Act of 1875, ch. 137, 18 Stat. 470.

Despite this early action, Congress has never authorized federal courts to exercise the full extent of their jurisdiction under Article III. In *Strawbridge v. Curtiss*, the Court interpreted the Judiciary Act of 1789 to conclude that in diversity cases, there must be "complete" diversity—that is, no party on one side of the controversy can be a citizen of any state of which any party on the other side is a citizen. 7 U.S. (3 Cranch) 267, 267 (1806). The Court later emphasized that *Curtiss* was a statutory interpretation case and that Article III empowers Congress to go further and authorize federal courts to hear controversies in which *at least* one party is from a different state than a party on the other side. *See State Farm Fire & Cas. Co. v. Tashire*, 386 U.S. 523, 530–31 (1967). Congress has taken the Court up on this offer only with respect to corporations—whose shareholders are all deemed to be citizens of a single state. *See* 28 U.S.C. § 1332(c)(1). But the Court has not changed the complete diversity requirement with respect to individuals. In fact, in 1996, Congress added a requirement that diversity cases must have an amount in controversy of at least $75,000. *See* 28 U.S.C. § 1332.

A person's *citizenship* for purposes of Article III is determined by the person's "domicile": the person's permanent home to which they plan to return. *See Knox v. Greenleaf*, 4 U.S. (4 Dall.) 360 (1802). That said, the Supreme Court has, occasionally, struggled to determine who can be a citizen. In *Dred Scott v. Sandford*, 60 U.S. (19 How.) 393 (1857), the Court held that black people could never be citizens—a decision that was overruled by the Civil Rights Act of 1866, ch. 31, 14 Stat. 27, and the Fourteenth Amendment. For a long time, the Court also held that the citizenship of a married woman depended on the citizenship of her husband—even if they lived apart in different states. *See, e.g.*, *Anderson v. Watt*, 138 U.S. 694, 706 (1891). And after going back and forth about whether corporations could be citizens for purposes of Article III, the Court adopted its modern holding that no artificial entity, including a corporation, is a citizen of a state. Instead, entities take on the citizenship of their "members." *Americold Realty Tr. v. ConAgra Foods, Inc.*, 577 U.S.

378, 380–82 (2016). The members of a corporation, however, are subject to a unique rule: by statute, they are deemed to be citizens of the corporation's state of incorporation as well as the state where the corporation has its "principal place of business," or "nerve center." *Hertz Corp. v. Friend*, 559 U.S. 77, 93 (2010); 28 U.S.C. § 1332(c)(1).

Defining the term *states* has proved no less challenging for the Court. As discussed earlier in the context of Congress's power with respect to the District of Columbia (section 16.1), the term *states* has never been interpreted to apply to the federal district or to territories. *See Hepburn v. Ellzey*, 6 U.S. (2 Cranch) 445, 445 (1805). Instead, in *National Mutual Insurance Co. v. Tidewater Transfer Co.*, 337 U.S. 582, 604 (1940), the Court authorized federal courts to hear diversity cases involving citizens of territories and the District of Columbia in a split decision, the reasoning of which remains unclear.

When Congress first authorized federal courts to hear diversity cases, it instructed the courts to apply "the laws of the several states . . . as rules of decision in trials at common law." Judiciary Act of 1789, 1 Stat. at 92. Federal courts generally did that until *Swift v. Tyson*, 41 U.S. (16 Pet.) 1 (1842), a case about whether a preexisting debt was good consideration for an endorsement of a bill of exchange in New York. New York *case law* answered this question, but New York *statutory law* did not—and the Supreme Court held that state-court decisions were not "laws" for purposes of the Judiciary Act. *Swift*, 41 U.S. (16 Pet.) at 18. Instead, the Court held that where a state's "local" or positive law was silent on a question, federal courts must consider "general principles and doctrines of commercial jurisprudence." *Id.* at 19.

Swift invited federal courts sitting in diversity to develop a federal common law to govern torts, contracts, and property disputes—even in contexts where state courts applying state law would reach different conclusions. *See, e.g.*, *Burgess v. Seligman*, 107 U.S. 20, 33 (1883). By the early twentieth century, the divergence between federal common law and state law led some plaintiffs to bring cases in federal court when federal common law was more favorable. In one famous instance, a taxi company even dissolved itself and rechartered in another state to "manufacture" diversity and take advantage of the federal courts' interpretation of contracts. *See Black & White Taxicab & Transfer Co. v. Brown & Yellow Taxicab & Transfer Co.*, 276 U.S. 518, 523, 530 (1928).

The Supreme Court's frustration with the distinction between federal common law and state common law eventually led it to repudiate the *Swift* doctrine. In *Erie Railroad Co. v. Tompkins*, 304 U.S. 64, 69 (1938), a man named Harry J. Tompkins was injured by a train while he was walking along the tracks in Pennsylvania. Had Tompkins sued the railroad in Pennsylvania state court, the state court would have applied Pennsylvania common law and treated him as a trespasser with a high burden of proof. *Id.* at 70. So, he instead sued the railroad in federal court, which would have treated him as a licensee with a low burden of proof. *Id.* When the controversy reached the Supreme Court, neither of the parties asked the Court to reconsider this distinction between state common law and federal common law. But a 5–4 Court nevertheless held that the *Swift* doctrine was unconstitutional—either because it unconstitutionally "introduced grave discrimination by noncitizens against citizens," *id.* at 74, or because "Congress has no power to declare substantive rules of common law applicable in a State," *id.* at 78. Instead of the *Swift* doctrine, the *Erie* Court declared that federal courts sitting in diversity could apply only the federal Constitution, acts of Congress, or "the law of the State [as] declared by its Legislature in a statute or by its highest court in a decision." *Id.* at 78.

Although *Erie* resolved an issue that had vexed the Court for decades, it introduced dozens of puzzles that civil procedure professors love to test. These include identifying "the law of the State," determining whether state procedural rules count as "the law of the State," and assessing whether there is an overriding interest in federal uniformity calling for an exception to *Erie. See, e.g.*, *Hanna v. Plumer*, 380 U.S. 460, 472–74 (1965); *Nolan v. Transocean Air Lines*, 365 U.S. 293, 295–96 (1961).

Controversies between citizens claiming land under grants of different states

During the 1780s, when several states claimed overlapping western reserves of territory, there was a risk that multiple states might grant the same plot of land to multiple people—leading to conflict down the road. The response of the Constitutional Convention was to authorize federal courts to resolve controversies "between Citizens of the same State claiming Lands under Grants of different States." This provision became obsolete with the adoption of the Northwest Ordinance and the Supreme Court's early settlement of boundary disputes. *See, e.g.*, *Pawlet v. Clark*, 13 U.S. (9 Cranch) 292 (1815).

Controversies between a state or its citizens and foreign states

The final set of controversies involves those "between a State, or the Citizens thereof, and foreign States, Citizens or Subjects." As discussed earlier in the context of Congress's power with respect to tribes (section 17.1), the Supreme Court has interpreted the term *foreign states* not to include tribes such as the Cherokee Nation. *See Cherokee Nation v. Georgia*, 30 U.S. (5 Pet.) 1, 17–20 (1831). Instead, the Court has traditionally relied on the State Department or Congress to determine which foreign states have been recognized. *See, e.g.*, *Argentine Republic v. Amerada Hess Shipping Corp.*, 488 U.S. 428, 433–34 (1989); Foreign Sovereign Immunities Act of 1976, Pub. L. No. 94–583, 90 Stat. 2891.

Absent some other form of jurisdiction such as a federal question, this provision doesn't authorize a suit between two foreign nationals or between a foreign national and a foreign state. *See Hodgson & Thompson v. Bowerbank*, 9 U.S. (5 Cranch) 303 (1809). The Court has held that an American must be on one side of the controversy. *Romero v. Int'l Terminal Operating Co.*, 358 U.S. 354, 485–86 (1959).

CHAPTER 35

WHO IS IMMUNE FROM THE JUDICIAL POWER?

ARTICLE III, SECTION 2, CLAUSE 1: The judicial Power shall extend to all Cases, in Law and Equity, arising under this Constitution, the Laws of the United States, and Treaties made, or which shall be made, under their Authority;—to all Cases affecting Ambassadors, other public Ministers and Consuls;—to all Cases of admiralty and maritime Jurisdiction;—to Controversies to which the United States shall be a Party;—to Controversies between two or more States;—between a State and Citizens of another State,—between Citizens of different States,—between Citizens of the same State claiming Lands under Grants of different States, and between a State, or the Citizens thereof, and foreign States, Citizens or Subjects.

ELEVENTH AMENDMENT (1795): The Judicial power of the United States shall not be construed to extend to any suit in law or equity, commenced or prosecuted against one of the United States by Citizens of another State, or by Citizens or Subjects of any Foreign State.

35.1 STATE SOVEREIGN IMMUNITY

During the debate over whether to ratify the Constitution, many Antifederalists objected to the provision of Article III that gave federal courts jurisdiction over controversies between "a State and Citizens of another State." The Antifederalists argued that this language implied that individuals would be able to sue states in federal court, which would be inconsistent with the "sovereignty" of the individual states. *See* Michael Klarman, *The Framers' Coup* 351 (2016). Their complaint became so fervent that Alexander Hamilton, James Madison, and other Federalists tried to assure voters that Article III would have no effect on state sovereign immunity. In one lengthy appeal, Hamilton wrote that it was "inherent in the nature of sovereignty not to be amenable to the suit of an individual *without its consent*," and it would take a "forced and unwarrantable" reading of Article III to authorize such suits. *The Federalist No. 81*, at 487–88 (Alexander Hamilton) (Jacob E. Cooke ed., 1961).

Hamilton's prediction that states would never be sued in federal court was accurate for only about four years. In 1792, a citizen of South Carolina named Alexander Chisholm sued Georgia for failing to repay one of its Revolutionary War debts. Invoking the state's sovereign immunity from suit, Georgia's lawyers refused to appear in court. But in *Chisholm v. Georgia*, 2 U.S. (2 Dall.) 419 (1793), the Supreme Court held that Article III plainly authorized suits between "a State and Citizens of another State." In his opinion, Justice James Wilson directly attacked Hamilton's argument that states were "sovereigns" that could invoke the same immunity that the British Crown had long enjoyed. Wilson observed that the term *sovereign* appeared nowhere in the Constitution; that sovereigns typically had "subjects," not "citizens"; that if anyone could credibly claim to be sovereign, it was not the states themselves but the people of the United States; and that no republican government could claim to be unanswerable to its citizens. *Chisholm*, 2 U.S. (2 Dall.) at 453–64. A majority of the Court therefore concluded that the nation, acting through Congress, could make Georgia or any other state amenable to suit without its consent. *Id.* at 463–66. Only Justice James Iredell dissented. He maintained that no state had ever been sued without its consent and that Article III didn't create a new remedy by implication. *Id.* at 432–33.

Chisholm deeply upset not only many Georgians but also other supporters of state sovereignty, who likely felt betrayed by Hamilton's assurances that the Constitution wouldn't allow this exact result. Within two years of the decision, Congress proposed and the states ratified the Eleventh Amendment, which overturned *Chisholm*'s precise holding. The amendment stated, "The Judicial power of the United States shall not be construed to extend to any suit in law or equity, commenced or prosecuted against one of the United States by Citizens of another State, or by Citizens or Subjects of any foreign State."

This amendment, at first, didn't stop the Supreme Court from authorizing suits against states. When Chief Justice John Marshall joined the Court, he interpreted the text of the amendment literally as doing nothing more than prohibiting a citizen of one state from suing another state in federal court. In one case, the chief justice wrote that Article III continued to give the Supreme Court jurisdiction to review criminal cases brought by a state against one of *its own* citizens. *Cohens v. Virginia*, 19 U.S. (6 Wheat.) 264 (1821). And in another case, he upheld a litigant's suit against a state's treasurer, holding that such a suit was, literally, not a suit "against one of the United States." *Osborn v. Bank of the United States*, 22 U.S. (9 Wheat.) 738, 850 (1824). The *Osborn* Court also embraced the legal fiction that when an officer of a state threatens to enforce an allegedly unconstitutional statute, a suit to enjoin the officer isn't a suit against the state because no state can authorize its agents to violate the federal Constitution. *Id.* at 837–39.

A few years later, a Spanish slave trader named Juan Madrazo sued the governor of Georgia to recover a cargo of enslaved people captured by the state. The suit led Marshall to slightly modify his earlier interpretations of the Eleventh Amendment. He held that the suit against the governor, acting in an official capacity, was indeed a suit against Georgia because Madrazo wanted the governor to divest the state of its claimed property. *See Governor of Ga. v. Madrazo*, 26 U.S. (1 Pet.) 110, 135 (1828). But when Madrazo filed another suit—this time invoking Article III's admiralty jurisdiction—the Court held that the Eleventh Amendment was no obstacle because Article III continued to give federal courts jurisdiction over all admiralty cases regardless of whether a state was a party. *Ex parte Madrazo*, 32 U.S. 627, 632 (1833).

The Supreme Court revisited its sovereign immunity precedents after the Civil War. As discussed throughout these materials, the Reconstruction Congress radically transformed the structure of federalism by enhancing the federal government's power with respect to the states. The Court led the counterrevolution to this development in cases like *Collector v. Day*, 78 U.S. 113 (1871), and the *Civil Rights Cases*, 109 U.S. 3 (1883), both of which limited Congress's power in the name of federalism. The Court applied a similar analysis in its interpretation of the Eleventh Amendment. The Court began to hold that the Eleventh Amendment blocked any suit by a citizen of one state against an official of another state when the other state was the "real party against which . . . the relief is asked and against which the judgment or decree effectively operates." *In re Ayers*, 123 U.S. 443, 506 (1887). In other words, if a suit wanted the state itself to do something—as in Madrazo's first suit against Georgia's governor—the suit was prohibited by the Eleventh Amendment.

This series of decisions culminated in *Hans v. Louisiana*, 134 U.S. 1 (1890).

35.1.1
Hans v. Louisiana
134 U.S. 1 (1890)

Bernard Hans, a citizen of Louisiana, sued the State of Louisiana in federal court to enjoin a provision of the state's post-Reconstruction constitution. He claimed that the state provision violated the Contracts Clause of the federal Constitution—a clause that will be discussed later (section 38.1). The merits of his claim were important only because Hans raised a federal question, and Article III allowed federal courts to hear cases "arising under this Constitution."

Hans took the position that the Eleventh Amendment was irrelevant to his claim. The text of the amendment literally applies only to cases between a state and "Citizens of another State"—and Hans was from Louisiana. He also argued that the amendment did nothing more than repeal the diversity provision of Article III that the *Chisholm* Court had interpreted to authorize a citizen of one state to sue another state in federal court. By contrast, Hans was not invoking Article III's grant of *diversity* jurisdiction, but its separate grant of *federal-question* jurisdiction—just as Madrazo's second suit against Georgia successfully invoked Article III's grant of *admiralty* jurisdiction. Lawyers for the state conceded that Hans's suit wasn't covered by the literal text of the Eleventh Amendment, but they argued that the suit was still barred by the principles underlying the amendment.

The *Hans* Court found the state's argument more compelling.

■ MR. JUSTICE BRADLEY . . . delivered the opinion of the Court.[1]

The question is presented, whether a State can be sued in a Circuit Court of the United States by one of its own citizens upon a suggestion that the case is one that arises under the Constitution or laws of the United States.

The ground taken is, that under the Constitution, as well as under the act of Congress passed to carry it into effect, a case is within the jurisdiction of the federal courts, without regard to the character of the parties, if it arises under the Constitution or laws of the United States, or, which is the same thing, if it necessarily involves a question under said Constitution or laws. The language relied on is that clause of the 3d article of the Constitution, which declares that "the judicial power of the United States shall extend to all cases in law and equity arising under this Constitution, the laws of the United States, and treaties made, or which shall be made, under their authority;" and the corresponding clause of the act conferring jurisdiction upon the Circuit Court, which, as found in the act of March 3, 1875, 18 Stat. 470, c. 137, § 1, is as follows, to wit: "That the Circuit Courts of the United States shall have original cognizance, concurrent with the courts of the several states, of all suits of a civil nature at common law or in equity, . . . arising under the Constitution or laws of the United States, or treaties made, or which shall be made, under their authority." It is said that these jurisdictional clauses make no exception arising from the character of the parties, and, therefore, that a State can claim no exemption from suit, if the case is really one arising under the Constitution, laws or treaties of the United States. It is conceded that where the jurisdiction depends alone upon the character of the parties, a controversy between a State and its own citizens is not embraced within it; but it is contended that though jurisdiction does not exist on that ground, it nevertheless does exist if the case itself is one which necessarily involves a federal question; and with regard to ordinary parties this is undoubtedly true. The question now to be decided is, whether it is true where one of the parties is a State, and is sued as a defendant by one of its own citizens.

That a State cannot be sued by a citizen of another State, or of a foreign state, on the mere ground that the case is one arising under the Constitution or laws of the United States, is clearly established by the decisions of this court in several recent cases. *Louisiana v. Jumel,* 107 U.S. 711; *Hagood v. Southern,* 117 U.S. 52; *In re Ayers,* 123 U.S. 443. Those were cases arising under the Constitution of the United States, upon laws complained of as impairing the obligation of contracts, one of which was the constitutional amendment of Louisiana complained of in the present case. Relief was sought against state officers who professed to act in obedience to those laws. This court held that the suits were virtually against the States themselves and were consequently violative of the Eleventh Amendment of the Constitution, and could not be maintained. It was not denied that they presented cases arising under the Constitution; but, notwithstanding that, they were held to be prohibited by the amendment referred to.

In the present case the plaintiff in error contends that he, being a citizen of Louisiana, is not embarrassed by the obstacle of the Eleventh Amendment, inasmuch as that amendment only prohibits suits against a State which are brought by the citizens of another State, or by citizens or subjects of a foreign State. It is true, the

1 **As You Read, Consider:** Seven years before this decision, in the *Civil Rights Cases*, Justice Joseph Bradley focused on the literal text of the Fourteenth Amendment to conclude that the amendment applied only to "State action" and did not authorize Congress to regulate individuals. 109 U.S. 3, 11 (1883). Here, Bernard Hans has a strong argument that the text of the Eleventh Amendment does not bar his suit against Louisiana. Do textual principles weigh as heavily for Bradley now as they did in 1883? If not, what other principles might be guiding his decision?

amendment does so read: and if there were no other reason or ground for abating his suit, it might be maintainable; and then we should have this anomalous result, that in cases arising under the Constitution or laws of the United States, a State may be sued in the federal courts by its own citizens, though it cannot be sued for a like cause of action by the citizens of other States, or of a foreign state; and may be thus sued in the federal courts, although not allowing itself to be sued in its own courts. If this is the necessary consequence of the language of the Constitution and the law, the result is no less startling and unexpected than was the original decision of this court, that under the language of the Constitution and of the judiciary act of 1789, a State was liable to be sued by a citizen of another State, or of a foreign country. That decision was made in the case of *Chisholm v. Georgia,* 2 Dall. 419, and created such a shock of surprise throughout the country that, at the first meeting of Congress thereafter, the Eleventh Amendment to the Constitution was almost unanimously proposed, and was in due course adopted by the legislatures of the States. This amendment, expressing the will of the ultimate sovereignty of the whole country, superior to all legislatures and all courts, actually reversed the decision of the Supreme Court. It did not in terms prohibit suits by individuals against the States, but declared that the Constitution should not be construed to import any power to authorize the bringing of such suits. The language of the amendment is that "the judicial power of the United States shall *not be construed to extend* to any suit in law or equity, commenced or prosecuted against one of the United States by citizens of another State or by citizens or subjects of any foreign state." The Supreme Court had construed the judicial power as extending to such a suit, and its decision was thus overruled. . . .

This view of the force and meaning of the amendment is important.[2] It shows that, on this question of the suability of the States by individuals, the highest authority of this country was in accord rather with the minority than with the majority of the court in the decision of the case of *Chisholm v. Georgia;* and this fact lends additional interest to the able opinion of Mr. Justice Iredell on that occasion. The other justices were more swayed by a close observance of the letter of the Constitution, without regard to former experience and usage; and because the letter said that the judicial power shall extend to controversies "between a State and citizens of another State;" and "between a State and foreign states, citizens or subjects," they felt constrained to see in this language a power to enable the individual citizens of one State, or of a foreign state, to sue another State of the Union in the federal courts. Justice Iredell, on the contrary, contended that it was not the intention to create new and unheard of remedies, by subjecting sovereign States to actions at the suit of individuals, (which he conclusively showed was never done before,) but only, by proper legislation, to invest the federal courts with jurisdiction to hear and determine controversies and cases, between the parties designated, that were properly susceptible of litigation in courts.

Looking back from our present standpoint at the decision in *Chisholm v. Georgia,* we do not greatly wonder at the effect which it had upon the country. Any such power as that of authorizing the federal judiciary to entertain suits by individuals against the States, had been expressly disclaimed, and even resented, by the great defenders of the Constitution whilst it was on its trial before the American people. As some of

[2] **Question:** Bradley here suggests that the Eleventh Amendment has to be interpreted in light of its purpose and historical context, not just its text. In particular, he argues that the amendment was proposed because the Supreme Court's decision in *Chisholm v. Georgia* created a "shock of surprise throughout the country." Do you agree that this context is persuasive evidence that the Eleventh Amendment should be interpreted far more broadly than its text alone would suggest?

their utterances are directly pertinent to the question now under consideration, we deem it proper to quote them.

The eighty-first number of the Federalist, written by Hamilton, has the following profound remarks: . . .

> "It is inherent in the nature of sovereignty not to be amenable to the suit of an individual *without its consent*. This is the general sense and the general practice of mankind; and the exemption, as one of the attributes of sovereignty, is now enjoyed by the government of every State in the Union. . . . The contracts between a nation and individuals are only binding on the conscience of the sovereign, and have no pretension to a compulsive force. They confer no right of action independent of the sovereign will. To what purpose would it be to authorize suits against States for the debts they owe? How could recoveries be enforced? It is evident that it could not be done without waging war against the contracting State; and to ascribe to the federal courts by mere implication, and in destruction of a pre-existing right of the state governments, a power which would involve such a consequence, would be altogether forced and unwarrantable."

The obnoxious clause to which Hamilton's argument was directed, and which was the ground of the objections which he so forcibly met, was that which declared that "the judicial power shall extend to all . . . controversies between a State and citizens of another State, . . . and between a State and foreign states, citizens or subjects." It was argued by the opponents of the Constitution that this clause would authorize jurisdiction to be given to the federal courts to entertain suits against a State brought by the citizens of another State, or of a foreign state. Adhering to the mere letter, it might be so; and so, in fact, the Supreme Court held in *Chisholm v. Georgia;* but looking at the subject as Hamilton did, and as Mr. Justice Iredell did, in the light of history and experience and the established order of things, the views of the latter were clearly right,—as the people of the United States in their sovereign capacity subsequently decided. . . .

The letter is appealed to now, as it was then, as a ground for sustaining a suit brought by an individual against a State. The reason against it is as strong in this case as it was in that. It is an attempt to strain the Constitution and the law to a construction never imagined or dreamed of. Can we suppose that, when the Eleventh Amendment was adopted, it was understood to be left open for citizens of a State to sue their own state in the federal courts, whilst the idea of suits by citizens of other states, or of foreign states, was indignantly repelled? Suppose that Congress, when proposing the Eleventh Amendment, had appended to it a proviso that nothing therein contained should prevent a State from being sued by its own citizens in cases arising under the Constitution or laws of the United States: can we imagine that it would have been adopted by the States? The supposition that it would is almost an absurdity on its face.

The truth is, that the cognizance of suits and actions unknown to the law, and forbidden by the law, was not contemplated by the Constitution when establishing the judicial power of the United States. Some things, undoubtedly, were made justiciable which were not known as such at the common law; such, for example, as controversies between States as to boundary lines, and other questions admitting of judicial solution. . . . The establishment of this new branch of jurisdiction seemed to be necessary from the extinguishment of diplomatic relations between the States. . . .

The suability of a State without its consent was a thing unknown to the law.[3] This has been so often laid down and acknowledged by courts and jurists that it is hardly necessary to be formally asserted. It was fully shown by an exhaustive examination of the old law by Mr. Justice Iredell in his opinion in *Chisholm v. Georgia;* and it has been conceded in every case since, where the question has, in any way, been presented, even in the cases which have gone farthest in sustaining suits against the officers or agents of States. *Osborn v. Bank of United States,* 9 Wheat. 738; *Davis v. Gray,* 16 Wall. 203. In all these cases the effort was to show, and the court held, that the suits were not against the State or the United States, but against the individuals; conceding that if they had been against either the State or the United States, they could not be maintained. . . .

Some reliance is placed by the plaintiff upon the observations of Chief Justice Marshall, in *Cohens v. Virginia,* 6 Wheat. 264, 410. The Chief Justice was there considering the power of review exercisable by this court over the judgments of a state court, wherein it might be necessary to make the State itself a defendant in error. He showed that this power was absolutely necessary in order to enable the judiciary of the United States to take cognizance of all cases arising under the Constitution and laws of the United States. He also showed that making a State a defendant in error was entirely different from suing a State in an original action in prosecution of a demand against it, and was not within the meaning of the Eleventh Amendment; that the prosecution of a writ of error against a State was not the prosecution of a suit in the sense of that amendment, which had reference to the prosecution, by suit, of claims against a State. . . .

To avoid misapprehension it may be proper to add that, although the obligations of a State rest for their performance upon its honor and good faith, and cannot be made the subjects of judicial cognizance unless the State consents to be sued, or comes itself into court; yet where property or rights are enjoyed under a grant or contract made by a State, they cannot wantonly be invaded. Whilst the State cannot be compelled by suit to perform its contracts, any attempt on its part to violate property or rights acquired under its contracts, may be judicially resisted; and any law impairing the obligation of contracts under which such property or rights are held is void and powerless to affect their enjoyment.[4]

It is not necessary that we should enter upon an examination of the reason or expediency of the rule which exempts a sovereign State from prosecution in a court of justice at the suit of individuals. This is fully discussed by writers on public law. It is enough for us to declare its existence. The legislative department of a State represents its polity and its will; and is called upon by the highest demands of natural and political law to preserve justice and judgment, and to hold inviolate the public obligations. Any departure from this rule, except for reasons most cogent, (of which the legislature, and not the courts, is the judge,) never fails in the end to incur the

---

[3] **Questions:** What exactly is the big deal about allowing a person to sue a state in federal court? Is it merely annoying? A threat to the state's sovereign dignity? Something more fundamental? Consider that thirteen years after this decision, in *Giles v. Harris*, the Supreme Court cited *Hans* as a reason why the Court was powerless to stop Alabama from disenfranchising its black voters. Does *Giles* offer some evidence of what the *Hans* Court might have been worried about?

[4] **Question:** In the previous paragraph, Bradley approvingly cites *Cohens v. Virginia*, in which the Supreme Court held that a state prosecution could be appealed to the U.S. Supreme Court without the state's consent. In these last paragraphs, Bradley adds that if a state "consents to be sued, or comes itself into court" to *enforce* an allegedly unconstitutional law, a defendant can "judicially resist[ ]." Bradley appears to be suggesting that Hans can challenge the constitutionality of Louisiana's law by waiting to be prosecuted in state court, raising a federal defense, and appealing his prosecution to the Supreme Court. What principles does such a requirement vindicate?

odium of the world, and to bring lasting injury upon the State itself. But to deprive the legislature of the power of judging what the honor and safety of the State may require, even at the expense of a temporary failure to discharge the public debts, would be attended with greater evils than such failure can cause. . . .

NOTE: AFTERMATH OF *HANS*

By the time the Supreme Court delivered its opinion in *Hans*, the Eleventh Amendment had become a major obstacle blocking the path of litigants who wanted to stop a state from violating the federal Constitution or a federal statute. Where Marshall's decision in *Osborn* had once authorized a plaintiff to seek an injunction against a state officer enforcing an allegedly unconstitutional law, the Court's opinions in *Louisiana v. Jumel* and *In re Ayers* prohibited any litigant from suing a state officer when the "real party" of the suit was the state itself. *See Ayers*, 123 U.S. 443, 506 (1887); *Jumel*, 107 U.S. 711, 727 (1882). The holding of *Hans* added that no litigant could sue any state without its consent, whether for injunctive relief or for damages. *See Giles v. Harris*, 189 U.S. 475, 488 (1903). So, if a state enacted an unconstitutional law, it appeared that the only avenue for challenging that law was in state court (if the state "consents to be sued") or as a defendant in a civil or criminal prosecution. As *Hans* emphasized, unconstitutional state laws were "void and powerless," 134 U.S. at 21, suggesting that defendants in state court could raise the unconstitutionality of a law as a defense.

One crack in this wall of immunity emerged the same year as *Hans*. In *United States v. North Carolina*, 136 U.S. 211 (1890), the United States sued a state in federal court for the first time, and the Supreme Court decided the controversy without questioning whether such a suit was permissible. Two years later, in *United States v. Texas*, 143 U.S. 621 (1892), the Court held that the United States could sue a state despite the Eleventh Amendment because states impliedly consented to such suits when they joined the Union. The Court reached a similar conclusion in *South Dakota v. North Carolina*, 192 U.S. 286 (1904), in which it announced that states also impliedly consented to being sued under the Supreme Court's original jurisdiction by other states.

A second crack opened with respect to cities, counties, and other local governments. On the principle that a state's sovereign immunity extends only to the state itself and not to its subdivisions, the Court held that the Eleventh Amendment doesn't apply when an individual sues a local government. *See Lincoln Cnty. v. Luning*, 133 U.S. 529, 530 (1890).

A third crack opened with respect to state officers who allegedly committed torts. Concluding that such officers generally act on behalf of themselves and not their governments, the Supreme Court held that plaintiffs could seek damages from officers in their personal capacities, even if the state supported their conduct. *See Tindal v. Wesley*, 167 U.S. 204 (1897).

But the fourth and most consequential crack opened in *Ex parte Young*, 209 U.S. 123 (1908).

35.1.2

Ex parte Young

209 U.S. 123 (1908)

In the early 1900s, populist and progressive activists demanded that governments regulate the unprecedented concentrations of wealth and power that were accumulating in corporations. In response, states like Minnesota began passing a "veritable flood of legislation" that set the maximum rates that railroads and other companies could charge for their services. Richard C. Cortner, *The Iron Horse and the Constitution: The Railroads and the Transformation of the Fourteenth Amendment* 135 (1993). The laws also imposed penalties on anyone who violated their terms—including fines and imprisonment.

As will be discussed in detail later with regard to the Fourteenth Amendment's Due Process Clause (section 41.2), the federal judiciary was initially hostile to these sorts of redistributive measures. In cases like *Lochner v. New York*, 198 U.S. 45 (1905), the Supreme Court invalidated these laws as unconstitutional deprivations of liberty without due process of law.

But the *Hans* and *Ayers* interpretation of the Eleventh Amendment made it difficult for businesses to bring these laws to the attention of a federal court. Those who wanted to contest the constitutionality of Minnesota's maximum-rate law, for example, likely had to violate the law and defend themselves from state prosecution—risking fines and jail if they lost.

The shareholders of the J.P. Morgan-controlled Northern Pacific Railway refused to undergo this risk. *See* Cortner, *supra*, at 141–48. Instead, they asked a federal court to enjoin the state's attorney general, Edward Young, from enforcing Minnesota's maximum-rate law. The shareholders explained that the case presented a federal question, i.e., whether or not the Minnesota law was constitutional. They also argued that their claim was against an officer, not the state, as *Osborn* once allowed. Young responded with what was now a familiar defense: the "real party" from whom relief was demanded was not him but the State of Minnesota, which was protected from suit by the Eleventh Amendment.

The federal court agreed with the shareholders and issued an injunction against Young. When Young enforced the law anyway, the court held Young in contempt. Young sought a writ of habeas corpus from the Supreme Court, asking it to decide whether the lower court had jurisdiction to issue its injunction. The question presented in *Ex parte Young*, 209 U.S. 123 (1908), therefore, was whether the Eleventh Amendment permitted a plaintiff to seek a federal injunction against a state officer in order to prevent the officer from enforcing an allegedly unconstitutional law. A ruling in favor of Young would have required plaintiffs to raise the unconstitutionality of the state law as a defense in a state-court prosecution.

The Court's ruling in *Ex parte Young*, however, was not in favor of Young.

■ MR. JUSTICE PECKHAM . . . delivered the opinion of the Court.[5]

[W]e have . . . upon this record the case of an [allegedly] unconstitutional act of the state legislature and an intention by the Attorney General of the State to endeavor to enforce its provisions, to the injury of the company, in compelling it, at great expense, to defend legal proceedings of a complicated and unusual character, and involving questions of vast importance to all employés and officers of the company, as well as to the company itself. The question that arises is whether there is a remedy that the parties interested may resort to, by going into a Federal court of equity, in a case involving a violation of the Federal Constitution, and obtaining a judicial investigation of the problem, and pending its solution obtain freedom from suits, civil or criminal, by a temporary injunction, and if the question be finally decided favorably to the contention of the company, a permanent injunction restraining all such actions or proceedings.

This inquiry necessitates an examination of the most material and important objection made to the jurisdiction of the Circuit Court, the objection being that the suit is, in effect, one against the State of Minnesota, and that the injunction issued against the Attorney General illegally prohibits state action, either criminal or civil, to enforce obedience to the statutes of the State. . . .

[The Eleventh Amendment] applies to a suit brought against a State by one of its own citizens as well as to a suit brought by a citizen of another State. *Hans v. Louisiana,* 134 U.S. 1. It was adopted after the decision of this court in *Chisholm v. Georgia* (1793), 2 Dall. 419 where it was held that a State might be sued by a citizen of another State. Since that time there have been many cases decided in this court involving the Eleventh Amendment, among them being *Osborn v. United States Bank* (1824), 9 Wheat. 738, 846, 857, which held that the Amendment applied only to those suits in which the State was a party on the record. In the subsequent case of *Governor of Georgia v. Madrazo* (1828), 1 Pet. 110, 122, 123, that holding was somewhat enlarged, and Chief Justice Marshall, delivering the opinion of the court, while citing *Osborn v. United States Bank, supra,* said that where the claim was made, as in the case then before the court, against the Governor of Georgia as governor, and the demand was made upon him, not personally, but officially (for moneys in the treasury of the State and for slaves in possession of the state government), the State might be considered as the party on the record and therefore the suit could not be maintained. . . .

The cases upon the subject were reviewed, and it was held, *In re Ayers,* 123 U.S. 443, that a bill in equity brought against officers of a State, who, as individuals, have no personal interest in the subject-matter of the suit, and defend only as representing the State, where the relief prayed for, if done, would constitute a performance by the State of the alleged contract of the State, was a suit against the State. . . .

---

[5] **As You Read, Consider:** Justice Rufus Peckham was the author of the majority opinion in *Lochner v. United States,* which invalidated a New York labor law designed to assist workers. He also joined the majority in *Giles v. Harris,* which held that the Supreme Court was powerless to enjoin Alabama from disenfranchising black residents. Can this case be explained purely by his pro-business ideology? Or is his interpretation of the Eleventh Amendment consistent with the Court's opinion in *Hans v. Louisiana* two decades earlier?

A suit of such a nature was simply an attempt to make the State itself, through its officers, perform its alleged contract, by directing those officers to do acts which constituted such performance. The State alone had any interest in the question, and a decree in favor of plaintiff would affect the treasury of the State.

On the other hand, *United States v. Lee,* 106 U.S. 196, determined that an individual in possession of real estate under the Government of the United States, which claimed to be its owner, was, nevertheless, properly sued by the plaintiff, as owner, to recover possession, and such suit was not one against the United States, although the individual in possession justified such possession under its authority. . . .

The various authorities we have referred to furnish ample justification for the assertion that individuals, who, as officers of the State, are clothed with some duty in regard to the enforcement of the laws of the State, and who threaten and are about to commence proceedings, either of a civil or criminal nature, to enforce against parties affected an unconstitutional act, violating the Federal Constitution, may be enjoined by a Federal court of equity from such action. . . .[6]

[It is objected that Minnesota authorized the attorney general to enforce its acts. But this is no real objection.] In making an officer of the State a party defendant in a suit to enjoin the enforcement of an act alleged to be unconstitutional it is plain that such officer must have some connection with the enforcement of the act, or else it is merely making him a party as a representative of the State, and thereby attempting to make the State a party. . . .

It is also objected that as the statute does not specifically make it the duty of the Attorney General (assuming he has that general right) to enforce it, he has under such circumstances a full general discretion whether to attempt its enforcement or not, and the court cannot interfere to control him as Attorney General in the exercise of his discretion.

In our view there is no interference with his discretion under the facts herein. There is no doubt that the court cannot control the exercise of the discretion of an officer. It can only direct affirmative action where the officer having some duty to perform not involving discretion, but merely ministerial in its nature, refuses or neglects to take such action. In that case the court can direct the defendant to perform this merely ministerial duty.

The general discretion regarding the enforcement of the laws when and as he deems appropriate is not interfered with by an injunction which restrains the state officer from taking any steps towards the enforcement of an unconstitutional enactment to the injury of complainant. In such case no affirmative action of any nature is directed, and the officer is simply prohibited from doing an act which he had no legal right to do. An injunction to prevent him from doing that which he has no legal right to do is not an interference with the discretion of an officer.

It is also argued that the only proceeding which the Attorney General could take to enforce the statute, so far as his office is concerned, was one by mandamus, which would be commenced by the State in its sovereign and governmental character, and that the right to bring such action is a necessary attribute of a sovereign government. It is contended that the complainants do not complain and they care nothing about any action which Mr. Young might take or bring as an ordinary individual, but that he was complained of as an officer, to whose discretion is confided the use of the name

---

6 **Questions:** The bottom line of Peckham's opinion, announced here, is that the Eleventh Amendment is no bar to a suit seeking to enjoin a state official from violating the Constitution. How is such a suit consistent with *Hans*'s discussion of the Eleventh Amendment's purpose to insulate states from being sued? Is it really credible to say that a state attorney general is distinct from the state itself?

of the State of Minnesota so far as litigation is concerned, and that when or how he shall use it is a matter resting in his discretion and cannot be controlled by any court.

The answer to all this is the same as made in every case where an official claims to be acting under the authority of the State. The act to be enforced is alleged to be unconstitutional, and if it be so, the use of the name of the State to enforce an unconstitutional act to the injury of complainants is a proceeding without the authority of and one which does not affect the State in its sovereign or governmental capacity. It is simply an illegal act upon the part of a state official in attempting by the use of the name of the State to enforce a legislative enactment which is void because unconstitutional.[7] If the act which the state Attorney General seeks to enforce be a violation of the Federal Constitution, the officer in proceeding under such enactment comes into conflict with the superior authority of that Constitution, and he is in that case stripped of his official or representative character and is subjected in his person to the consequences of his individual conduct. The State has no power to impart to him any immunity from responsibility to the supreme authority of the United States. See *In re Ayers, supra,* page 507. It would be an injury to complainant to harass it with a multiplicity of suits or litigation generally in an endeavor to enforce penalties under an unconstitutional enactment, and to prevent it ought to be within the jurisdiction of a court of equity. . . .

It would seem to be clear that the Attorney General, under his power existing at common law and by virtue of . . . various statutes, had a general duty imposed upon him, which includes the right and the power to enforce the statutes of the State, including, of course, the act in question, if it were constitutional. His power by virtue of his office sufficiently connected him with the duty of enforcement to make him a proper party to a suit of the nature of the one now before the United States Circuit Court. . . .

It is proper to add that the right to enjoin an individual, even though a state official, from commencing suits under circumstances already stated does not include the power to restrain a court from acting in any case brought before it, either of a civil or criminal nature, nor does it include power to prevent any investigation or action by a grand jury. The latter body is part of the machinery of a criminal court, and an injunction against a State court would be a violation of the whole scheme of our government. . . .

It has been suggested that the proper way to test the constitutionality of the act is to disobey it, at least once, after which the company might obey the act pending subsequent proceedings to test its validity. But in the event of a single violation the prosecutor might not avail himself of the opportunity to make the test, as obedience to the law was thereafter continued, and he might think it unnecessary to start an inquiry. If, however, he should do so while the company was thereafter obeying the law, several years might elapse before there was a final determination of the question, and if it should be determined that the law was invalid the property of the company would have been taken during that time without due process of law, and there would be no possibility of its recovery.[8]

---

7 **Question:** Peckham is arguing that when a state official attempts to enforce an unconstitutional state law, the official is not *really* acting on behalf of the state because the law is "illegal" and "void because unconstitutional." This is obviously a legal fiction. But is it any less odd than the legal fiction of *Hans*, which held that states are sovereign and incapable of being sued by individuals without their consent?

8 **Question:** Here, Peckham raises several practical problems with a rule that would require a plaintiff to violate a law in order to challenge its constitutionality. These reasons reappear in standing cases like *Susan B. Anthony List v. Driehaus*, which held that an Article III "Case" or "Controversy" exists when a plaintiff challenges a law for which there is a credible threat of enforcement. Yet a contrary rule—one that required violations—would keep more

Another obstacle to making the test on the part of the company might be to find an agent or employé who would disobey the law, with a possible fine and imprisonment staring him in the face if the act should be held valid. Take the passenger rate act, for instance: A sale of a single ticket above the price mentioned in that act might subject the ticket agent to a charge of felony, and upon conviction to a fine of five thousand dollars and imprisonment for five years. It is true the company might pay the fine, but the imprisonment the agent would have to suffer personally. It would not be wonderful if, under such circumstances, there would not be a crowd of agents offering to disobey the law. The wonder would be that a single agent should be found ready to take the risk. . . .

To await proceedings against the company in a state court grounded upon a disobedience of the act, and then, if necessary, obtain a review in this court by writ of error to the highest state court, would place the company in peril of large loss and its agents in great risk of fines and imprisonment if it should be finally determined that the act was valid. This risk the company ought not to be required to take. Over eleven thousand millions of dollars, it is estimated, are invested in railroad property, owned by many thousands of people who are scattered over the whole country from ocean to ocean, and they are entitled to equal protection from the laws and from the courts, with the owners of all other kinds of property, no more, no less. The courts having jurisdiction, Federal or state, should at all times be open to them as well as to others, for the purpose of protecting their property and their legal rights. . . .

Finally it is objected that the necessary result of upholding this suit in the Circuit Court will be to draw to the lower Federal courts a great flood of litigation of this character, where one Federal judge would have it in his power to enjoin proceedings by state officials to enforce the legislative acts of the State, either by criminal or civil actions. To this it may be answered, in the first place, that no injunction ought to be granted unless in a case reasonably free from doubt. We think such rule is, and will be, followed by all the judges of the Federal courts.

And, again, it must be remembered that jurisdiction of this general character has, in fact, been exercised by Federal courts . . . [acting under] the supreme authority of the United States.

This supreme authority, which arises from the specific provisions of the Constitution itself, is nowhere more fully illustrated than in the series of decisions under the Federal *habeas corpus* statute in some of which cases persons in the custody of state officers for alleged crimes against the State have been taken from that custody and discharged by a Federal court or judge, because the imprisonment was adjudged to be in violation of the Federal Constitution. The right to so discharge has not been doubted by this court, and it has never been supposed there was any suit against the State by reason of serving the writ upon one of the officers of the State in whose custody the person was found. . . .

It is somewhat difficult to appreciate the distinction which, while admitting that the taking of such a person from the custody of the State by virtue of service of the writ on the state officer in whose custody he is found, is not a suit against the State, and yet service of a writ on the Attorney General to prevent his enforcing an unconstitutional enactment of a state legislature is a suit against the State. . . .

---

cases out of the federal judiciary. Isn't such a contrary rule therefore more consistent with the Court's own interpretation of the Eleventh Amendment?

NOTE: CONTINUED VITALITY OF *EX PARTE YOUNG*

Ex parte Young established (or, at the very least, reinforced) a major exception to the Eleventh Amendment: a suit for injunctive relief against an officer acting under an allegedly unconstitutional statute isn't a suit against the state itself. Although this doctrine appeared to carve a distinction between a state and its officers who violate the Constitution, the Court was quick to emphasize that a state could still be held responsible for the unconstitutional conduct of its officers. *See Home Tel. & Tel. Co. v. City of Los Angeles*, 227 U.S. 278, 287–89 (1913).

Together, these two points meant that when a state or its officers allegedly violated the federal Constitution, an individual could go to federal court to seek an injunction against an officer's enforcement of the law. Suits against state officers have since become the standard device by which plaintiffs challenge the validity of state legislation in federal courts.

State sovereign immunity faded into obscurity during most of the twentieth century. Although the Supreme Court continued to hold that a state couldn't be sued without its consent, individuals could challenge state laws by seeking injunctions against state officers. On the principle that local governments weren't covered by a state's sovereign immunity, individuals could also pursue claims for damages under 42 U.S.C. § 1983 against local officers. *See Monroe v. Pape*, 365 U.S. 167, 172 (1961). And states and the federal government also continued to sue states directly. *See, e.g., Arizona v. United States*, 567 U.S. 387 (2012).

But the Court's pre-*Young* Eleventh Amendment precedents didn't disappear forever. In *Edelman v. Jordan*, the Court cited *Hans* to hold that "a suit by private parties seeking to impose a liability which must be paid from public funds from the state treasury is barred by the Eleventh Amendment." 415 U.S. 651, 663 (1974). This meant that a suit against an officer of a state could not proceed if the state itself would end up paying money from its treasury. The Court later clarified that the Eleventh Amendment didn't bar suits for monetary relief when the plaintiff was attempting to remedy an ongoing federal constitutional violation, as in the context of *Ex parte Young* or § 1983. *See Quern v. Jordan*, 440 U.S. 332, 337 (1979). But the Court held that the *Ex parte Young* doctrine didn't permit suits alleging that state officers violated *state* law as opposed to federal law. *Pennhurst State Sch. & Hosp. v. Halderman*, 465 U.S. 89, 124–25 (1984).

By the twenty-first century, the Court consolidated its holdings into a single test: "In determining whether the doctrine of *Ex parte Young* avoids an Eleventh Amendment bar to suit, a court need only conduct a straightforward inquiry into whether [the] complaint alleges an ongoing violation of federal law and seeks relief properly characterized as prospective." *Verizon Md. Inc. v. Pub. Serv. Comm'n*, 535 U.S. 635, 645 (2002).

NOTE: AGENCY SOVEREIGN IMMUNITY

Even before *Ex parte Young*, the Supreme Court held that a state's sovereign immunity didn't extend to its cities or counties. *See, e.g., Lincoln*

Cnty. v. Luning, 133 U.S. 529, 530 (1890). Yet even after *Ex parte Young*, the Court continued to hold that a state's sovereign immunity *did* extend to state agencies and officers—as long as the state itself was the "real party in interest" that would be responsible for paying for any judgment out of its treasury. *See Kentucky v. Graham*, 473 U.S. 159, 165–66 (1985) (official-capacity suits "represent only another way of pleading an action against an entity of which an officer is an agent").

But while this distinction between a county/city and an agency/officer is formally straightforward, the Court has found it functionally difficult to determine whether a regional planning agency, school district, or other entity is more like a county or more like an agency. The Court ultimately announced that an entity is more like an agency when the entity acts like an "arm of the state subject to its control." *Lake Cnty. Ests. v. Tahoe Reg'l Plan. Agency*, 440 U.S. 391, 400–02 (1979).

The Court has introduced a number of factors into this arm-of-the-state test, including "the nature of the entity created by state law," the degree of supervision by the state, the level of funding received from the state, and the entity's ability to generate its own revenue. *Mt. Healthy City Bd. of Educ. v. Doyle*, 429 U.S. 274, 280 (1977). If an entity is an "agency" for purposes of this test, the Court has held that it is entitled to the same Eleventh Amendment immunity as the state itself.

This test applies for state officers sued in their official capacities as well. "In an official-capacity claim, the relief sought is only nominally against the official and in fact is against the official's office and thus the sovereign itself. . . . Personal-capacity suits, on the other hand, seek to impose *individual* liability upon a government officer for actions taken under color of state law." *Lewis v. Clarke*, 137 S. Ct. 1285, 1291 (2017).

35.2 CONGRESS'S POWER TO ABROGATE STATE SOVEREIGN IMMUNITY

The Supreme Court has interpreted the Eleventh Amendment as a limit not only on courts but also on Congress. That is, Congress ordinarily may not abrogate state sovereign immunity by passing a statute authorizing individuals to sue states. The Court explained that because "[t]he Eleventh Amendment restricts the judicial power under Article III, . . . Article I cannot be used to circumvent the constitutional limitations placed upon federal jurisdiction." *Seminole Tribe of Florida v. Florida*, 517 U.S. 44, 73 (1996). Nor may Congress circumvent this limit by authorizing individuals to sue states in state court, *Alden v. Maine*, 527 U.S. 706, 711 (1999), or in certain administrative proceedings, *Fed. Maritime Comm'n v. S.C. State Ports Auth.*, 535 U.S. 743, 744 (2002). Congress nevertheless has three options for abrogating a state's sovereign immunity.

First, Congress may use the General Welfare Clause. Because states are always free to waive their sovereign immunity and consent to suit, Congress can solicit a state's consent to be sued as a condition for receiving a federal grant. In such circumstances, though, the Court noted in *Pennhurst State School & Hospital v. Halderman*, "Congress must express clearly its intent to impose conditions on the grant of federal funds so that the States can knowingly decide whether or not to accept those funds." 451 U.S. 1, 24 (1981). In *Pennhurst*, Congress attempted to condition federal grants to state hospitals on the state's willingness to be sued in court if it allegedly engaged in discrimination. But the Supreme Court held that these sorts of conditions must be stated unambiguously. *Id.* at 25.

A second option is the Bankruptcy Clause. Even though this clause appears in Article I, the Supreme Court has interpreted the history and structure of the clause as if it gave Congress power to subordinate state sovereign immunity in the limited context of bankruptcy actions. *See Cent. Va. Cmty. Coll. v. Katz*, 546 U.S. 356, 362–63 (2006).

A third option was discussed earlier with regard to Congress's power to enforce the Reconstruction amendments (section 21.3). The Court has explained that one of the purposes of the Reconstruction amendments was to overturn preexisting arrangements of federalism, including the Eleventh Amendment's prohibition on seeking damages from a state. When seeking to enforce or remedy a violation of those amendments, Congress therefore has the power to abrogate a state's sovereign immunity. *Fitzpatrick v. Bitzer*, 427 U.S. 445, 456 (1976); *see also Monell v. Dep't of Soc. Servs.*, 436 U.S. 658, 701 (1978); *Scheuer v. Rhodes*, 416 U.S. 232, 248 (1974). But the Court has also imposed two limits on this enforcement power. First, the Court has allowed Congress to "abrogate the States' constitutionally secured immunity from suit in federal court only by making its intention unmistakably clear in the language of the statute." *Atascadero State Hosp. v. Scanlon*, 473 U.S. 234, 242 (1985). Applying this clear-statement rule, the Court has held, for example, that the general civil-rights statute first enacted as the Ku Klux Klan Act of 1871, 42 U.S.C. § 1983, "does not explicitly and by clear language indicate on its face an intent to sweep away the immunity of the States; nor does it have a history which focuses directly on the question of state liability and which shows that Congress considered and firmly decided to abrogate the Eleventh Amendment immunity of the States." *Quern v. Jordan*, 440 U.S. 332, 345 (1979). *But see Pulliam v. Allen*, 466 U.S. 522, 540 (1984) (discussing how § 1983 and other federal statutes may permit suits for *injunctive relief* against "all state actors"). Second, there must be "a congruence and proportionality between the injury to be prevented or remedied and the means adopted to that end." *City of Boerne v. Flores*, 521 U.S. 507, 520 (1997). (See section 21.3 for examples of this congruence and proportionality test.)

35.3 FEDERAL SOVEREIGN IMMUNITY

Hans v. Louisiana, 134 U.S. 1 (1890), and *Ex parte Young*, 209 U.S. 123 (1908), were both interpretations of *state* sovereign immunity. By contrast, the sovereign immunity of the United States has developed along a different, but parallel, track.

Chisholm *and need for consent to sue the federal government*

In *Chisholm v. Georgia*, 2 U.S. (2 Dall.) 419 (1793), even as the Supreme Court held that states could be sued without their consent, members of the Court couldn't imagine how a suit against the United States could possibly proceed. Justice William Cushing observed that in a case involving a state defendant or individual citizens, "the national courts are supported in all their legal and constitutional proceedings and judgments by the arm of the executive power of the United States." *Chisholm*, 2 U.S. (2 Dall.) at 478. "[B]ut in cases of actions against the United States, there is no power which the courts can call to their aid." *Id.* From this logic, Cushing reasoned that the United States probably could not be sued without Congress's acknowledgment that the federal government would hold itself liable. Other members of the Court made this need for consent explicit in subsequent cases. *See, e.g., United States v. Clarke*, 33 U.S. (8 Pet.) 436, 444 (1834).

Lee *and suits against officers of the United States*

The first case in which the Supreme Court as a whole conclusively determined the scope of the federal government's sovereign immunity involved the Confederate general Robert E. Lee. During the Civil War, the United States seized Lee's estate in Arlington, Virginia, for his failure to pay property taxes on it. The estate was later put up for auction, and the United States itself purchased it for use as Arlington National Cemetery. After the war, Lee's family attempted to reclaim the estate by suing to eject all federal officers who were allegedly trespassing on their property. Government lawyers responded by seeking to dismiss the suit as a suit against the United States and therefore blocked by sovereign immunity.

In *United States v. Lee*, 106 U.S. 196 (1882), the Court agreed with the federal government that the United States *itself* was immune from suit. The Court wrote that "[e]very government has an inherent right to protect itself against suits, and if, in the liberality of legislation, they are permitted, it is only on such terms and conditions as are prescribed by statute." *Lee*, 106 U.S. at 227 (internal quotation marks omitted). Absent this protection, the Court explained, "the government would be unable to perform the various duties for which it was created." *Id.* The Court therefore held that despite Article III, neither an individual nor a state could sue the United States in any manner other than that authorized by a federal statute. *Id.*

But *United States v. Lee*, like other contemporary decisions, also distinguished suits against the United States from suits against *officers* of the United States. In the Lee family's case, the plaintiffs were not suing the United States itself but were suing to eject the federal officers who had occupied Lee's land after an allegedly illegal auction. The Court therefore concluded that the suit for damages could proceed against these federal officers. The federal government ultimately settled the case for an enormous sum; Lee's house is now known as Arlington House, The Robert E. Lee Memorial, which continues to sit in Arlington National Cemetery. *See* Act of June 30, 1972, Pub. L. No. 92–333, 86 Stat. 401.

The continuing vitality of Lee

Ex parte Young cited *Lee* as an example of an earlier opinion in which the Court distinguished a government from the unconstitutional actions of one of its officers. But *Ex parte Young* didn't address whether a federal officer could be sued for concededly constitutional conduct.

It took the Court decades to answer this question in *See Larson v. Domestic & Foreign Commerce Corp.*, 337 U.S. 682 (1947). There, the Court finally reasoned that it would be inconsistent with the United States's sovereign immunity if the federal government or its officers were sued without their consent for acting pursuant to a constitutionally valid statute. *Larson*, 377 U.S. at 710. Today, the Court holds that plaintiffs can sue federal officers under *Lee* "only where there is a claim that the [officer has violated the Constitution or] . . . was exceeding his delegated powers." *Malone v. Bowdoin*, 369 U.S. 643, 648 (1962) (quoting *Larson*, 337 U.S. at 697).

Sovereign immunity via statute

The Court's holding in *Larson* only reflects a default rule, however. Through the Necessary and Proper Clause, Congress can, by statute, extend immunity to or withhold immunity from itself, its agents, or its instrumentalities. *See, e.g. Yearsley v. W. A. Ross Constr. Co.*, 309 U.S. 18, 20 (1940).

Today, several statutes authorize suits against the United States. These include the Tucker Act of 1887, 28 U.S.C. § 1346(a)(2), which waives immunity for certain contracts and takings claims; the Federal Tort Claims Act of 1946, as amended by the Westfall Act of 1988, 28 U.S.C. §§ 1346(b), 2671, 2679(d), which waives immunity for claims involving certain negligent or official acts of federal officers; and the Administrative Procedure Act of 1946, 5 U.S.C. § 702, as amended in 1976, which waives immunity for claims for injunctive relief against federal agencies. *See also* 28 U.S.C. § 1361 (giving district courts jurisdiction over mandamus actions to compel a federal officer to perform a duty).

35.4 TRIBAL AND FOREIGN SOVEREIGN IMMUNITY

The sovereign immunity of both tribes and foreign states is judicially, not constitutionally created.

Tribal sovereign immunity

As discussed earlier in the context of tribal power (section 17.3), the Supreme Court has long held that "Indian tribes are 'domestic dependent nations' that exercise inherent sovereign authority over their members and territories. Suits against Indian tribes are thus barred by sovereign immunity absent a clear waiver by the tribe or congressional abrogation." *Okla. Tax Comm'n v. Citizen Band Potawatomi Indian Tribe of Okla.*, 498 U.S. 505, 509 (1991) (citing *Santa Clara Pueblo v. Martinez*, 436 U.S. 49, 58 (1978); *Cherokee Nation v. Georgia*, 30 U.S. (5 Pet.) 1, 17 (1831)). The Supreme Court generally interprets the scope of tribal sovereign immunity with reference to its cases interpreting states' Eleventh Amendment immunity. *See, e.g.*, *Lewis v. Clarke*, 137 S. Ct. 1285, 1291 (2017). But tribal sovereign immunity is different from state sovereign immunity in three respects.

First, tribal sovereign immunity is a judicially created doctrine subject to federal law; it is not considered a constitutionally protected feature of tribes. *Kiowa Tribe of Okla. v. Mfg. Techs., Inc.*, 523 U.S. 751, 756 (1998). Immunity therefore functions as a default rule protecting tribes from suits by individuals and states. *Potawatomi*, 498 U.S. at 510. But where the Eleventh Amendment prohibits Congress from interfering with state sovereign immunity in some contexts, the amendment doesn't affect Congress's ability to abrogate a tribe's sovereign immunity. *Id.*

Second, where the Court allows states to sue one another on the presumption that states consented to such suits by joining the Union, *see South Dakota v. North Carolina*, 192 U.S. 286 (1904), the Court hasn't extended the same power to tribes seeking to sue a state. *Blatchford v. Native Vill. of Noatak & Circle Vill.*, 501 U.S. 775, 782 (1991). The Court has explained that "tribes were not at the Constitutional Convention. They were thus not parties to the 'mutuality of . . . concession' that 'makes the States' surrender of immunity from suit by sister States plausible.' " *Kiowa*, 523 U.S. at 756 (quoting *Blatchford*, 501 U.S. at 775 (1991)).

Third, tribal immunity extends not only to activity that takes place within a tribe's jurisdiction but also to a tribe's off-reservation activities, including cigarette sales and ski resorts. *See, e.g.*, *Michigan v. Bay Mills Indian Cmty.*, 572 U.S. 782, 798–800 (2014). Absent congressional modification, states and individuals generally may not tax, regulate, or sue tribes for these activities. *Id.* The Court has explained that "[i]n our interdependent and mobile society . . . tribal immunity extends beyond what is needed to safeguard tribal self-governance." *Kiowa*, 523 U.S. at 758. "[I]t is fundamentally Congress's job, not ours, to determine whether or how to limit tribal immunity. The special brand of sovereignty the tribes retain—both its nature and its extent—rests in the hands of Congress." *Bay Mills*, 572 U.S. at 800.

Foreign sovereign immunity

The immunity of foreign states from suit has also developed as a judicial doctrine, not a constitutional command. *See The Schooner Exch. v. McFaddon*, 11 U.S. (7 Cranch) 116, 147 (1812). As a matter of comity, the Supreme Court refused to allow federal courts to entertain cases involving presidentially recognized friendly foreign sovereigns or their agencies—even when the plaintiff was a state of the Union. *See, e.g.*, *Compania Espanola v. The Navemar*, 303 U.S. 68, 76 (1938).

But in 1952, the State Department announced a new policy asking courts to confine foreign sovereign immunity "to suits involving the foreign sovereign's public acts, and . . . [not] to cases arising out of a foreign state's commercial acts." *Verlinden B.V. v. Cent. Bank of Nigeria*, 461 U.S. 480, 487 (1983). This rule created so many interpretive problems that Congress established its own standards with the Foreign Sovereign Immunities Act of 1976, Pub. L. No. 94–583, 90 Stat. 2891. *See Verlinden*, 461 U.S. at 488. This statute continues to determine the scope of foreign sovereign immunity.

CHAPTER 36

HOW IS THE JUDICIAL POWER INVOKED?

ARTICLE VI, PARAGRAPH 2: This Constitution, and the Laws of the United States which shall be made in Pursuance thereof; and all Treaties made, or which shall be made, under the Authority of the United States, shall be the supreme Law of the Land; and the Judges in every State shall be bound thereby, any Thing in the Constitution or Laws of any State to the Contrary notwithstanding.

THE KU KLUX KLAN ACT OF 1871, CH. 31, 17 STAT. 13 (AS CODIFIED IN 42 U.S.C. § 1983): Every person who, under color of any statute, ordinance, regulation, custom, or usage, of any State or Territory or the District of Columbia, subjects, or causes to be subjected, any citizen of the United States or other person within the jurisdiction thereof to the deprivation of any rights, privileges, or immunities secured by the Constitution and laws, shall be liable to the party injured in an action at law, suit in equity, or other proper proceeding for redress. . . .

THE JUDICIARY ACT OF 1875, CH. 137, 18 STAT. 470 (CURRENT VERSION AT 28 U.S.C. § 1331): [The] courts of the United States shall have original cognizance . . . of all suits of a civil nature at common law or in equity. . . .

THE ADMINISTRATIVE PROCEDURE ACT OF 1946, PUB. L. NO. 79-404, 60 STAT. 237 (AS CODIFIED IN 5 U.S.C. § 702): A person suffering legal wrong because of agency action, or adversely affected or aggrieved by agency action within the meaning of a relevant statute, is entitled to judicial review thereof. . . Nothing herein (1) affects other limitations on judicial review or the power or duty of the court to dismiss any action or deny relief on any other appropriate legal or equitable ground; or (2) confers authority to grant relief if any other statute that grants consent to suit expressly or impliedly forbids the relief which is sought.

36.1 STATUTORY CAUSES OF ACTION (§ 1983 AND THE APA)

The previous several sections have all addressed the question of whether a federal court has jurisdiction to hear a dispute. But even when a court has the *power* to decide a dispute, courts will typically not exercise that power absent instructions about what a party must prove in order to merit a judicial remedy. The name for these instructions is a *cause of action*. A cause of action refers to the legal theory that permits a person to obtain relief from a court.

In state-court proceedings, causes of action often aren't written down but are derived from the common law. These sorts of causes of action are usually covered in classes on state-law torts, contracts, property, and criminal law. *Negligence* is a cause of action, as is *breach of contract*, *nuisance*, and *murder*. If a state-court plaintiff can sufficiently allege that a person has satisfied the elements of one of these causes of action—for example, if a plaintiff alleges that a defendant (1) breached (2) a legal duty owed toward the plaintiff in a manner that (3) actually and (4) proximately caused (5) damage to the plaintiff—then the plaintiff is legally entitled to seek relief in state court.

Federal courts have generally operated on a different theory, particularly since the Supreme Court cases of *United States v. Hudson & Goodwin*, 11 U.S. (7 Cranch) 32 (1812), and *Erie Railroad Co. v. Tompkins*, 304 U.S. 64 (1938). In *Hudson & Goodwin*, the Court held that Congress has permitted federal courts to hear prosecutions involving statutory crimes but not common-law crimes. In *Erie*, the Court announced that "[t]here is no federal general common law," and federal courts must therefore rely on federal statutes or state common law to provide causes of action. *Erie*, 304 U.S. at 78. The *Erie* doctrine is subject to several important exceptions in which federal courts may fashion common-law causes of action. *See, e.g.*, *Clearfield Tr. Co. v. United States*, 318 U.S. 363 (1943). But the general rule is that unlike in state court, a party that wishes to seek the vindication of a federal right in federal court often must point to a statute authorizing the party to seek judicial relief.

Federal cause of action and § 1983

The most important federal cause of action is the Ku Klux Klan Act of 1871, ch. 22, 17 Stat. 13, discussed at length in the section on Congress's power to enforce the Reconstruction amendments (section 20.1). As currently codified in 42 U.S.C. § 1983, the law declares:

> Every person who, under color of any statute, ordinance, regulation, custom, or usage, of any State or Territory or the District of Columbia, subjects, or causes to be subjected, any citizen of the United States or other person within the jurisdiction thereof to the deprivation of any rights, privileges, or immunities secured by the Constitution and laws, shall be liable to the party injured in an action at law, suit in equity, or other proper proceeding for redress.

In other words, anyone whose federal constitutional or statutory rights are violated by a person acting "under color" of state law has a cause of action against that person in federal court. A second statute, 28 U.S.C. § 1343(3), gives federal district courts subject-matter jurisdiction to hear these sorts of claims.

Many of the most important Supreme Court civil cases involving constitutional claims have been brought under § 1983, including *Brown v. Board of Education* (*Brown I*), 347 U.S. 483 (1954), *Roe v. Wade*, 410 U.S. 113 (1973), and *Obergefell v. Hodges*, 576 U.S. 644 (2015). (Criminal cases involving constitutional claims usually arise out of state or federal prosecutions.) As discussed earlier with regard to Congress's power to enforce the Reconstruction amendments (section 21.2), the significance of § 1983 grew exponentially after *Monroe v. Pape*, in which the Court interpreted the phrase *under color of [law]* to mean that anyone "clothed with the authority of state law" could be held liable for violating a person's federal or constitutional rights. 365 U.S. 167, 187 (1961). This meant that litigants could challenge in federal court unconstitutional police misconduct, prison abuse, and other violations by state officers—even when that conduct also violated state law.

Although § 1983 is broad, it doesn't provide a cause of action for every kind of constitutional claim. The Supreme Court has recognized or invented four significant limits: a defendant must be a "person"; absolute and qualified immunity prevent suits against some people; § 1983 doesn't apply to people who act under color of *federal* law; and § 1983 has been interpreted not to abrogate state sovereign immunity.

Qualification of defendant. The text of § 1983 allows a plaintiff to sue only a "person." In *Will v. Michigan Department of State Police*, the Supreme Court held that "a State is [not] a 'person' within the meaning of § 1983." 491 U.S. 58, 62 (1989). This means that when a state passes a law that allegedly violates the Constitution, § 1983 doesn't provide a plaintiff with a cause of action against the state itself. Instead, the cause of action in § 1983 provides a plaintiff with three options for challenging the law. First, it provides a cause of action for *injunctive* relief against *an officer* of the state, including state executives, legislators, and judges. *See id.* at 71 n.10; *Pulliam v. Allen*, 466 U.S. 522, 540 (1984). Second, it also provides a cause of action for *injunctive* and *compensatory* relief against a *local officer or local government*, which are not protected by sovereign immunity. *See Monell v. Dep't of Soc. Servs.*, 436 U.S. 658, 690 (1978); *Scheuer v. Rhodes*, 416 U.S. 232, 237–38 (1974). Third, it provides a cause of action for *compensatory* relief against a state officer only when the officer is sued in their *individual capacity*—that is, when the plaintiff wants damages, the plaintiff can demand that the individual officer pay damages. *See Kentucky v. Graham*, 473 U.S. 159, 165 (1985). The main form of relief barred by the Court's interpretation of § 1983 is *compensatory* relief against officers of the state sued in their *official* capacity—that is, where the plaintiff wants damages but demands that the state pay damages directly or indirectly. *See Will*, 491 U.S. at 62; *see also Quern v. Jordan*, 440 U.S. 332, 345 (1979) (interpreting § 1983 using the Court's clear-statement rule to hold that Congress did not "explicitly and by clear language" abrogate state sovereign immunity).

In light of the options provided by § 1983, most cases seeking to enjoin unconstitutional state laws are suits for injunctive relief against state or local officers. *See, e.g., Roe v. Wade*, 410 U.S. 113 (1973) (using § 1983 to challenge Texas's abortion ban by suing a district attorney).

Unqualified and qualified immunity. A second limit that the Court has read into § 1983 is that when Congress enacted the statute in 1871, Congress didn't abolish traditional forms of immunity that were still in common use at the time. For example, states traditionally extended *unqualified* immunity to judges and legislators—protecting them from being sued for damages caused by their official acts. As the

Supreme Court recently explained in *Trump v. Vance*, this unqualified immunity allowed judges and legislators to issue opinions and pass statutes "fearlessly and impartially" without worrying about owing people damages if one of their opinions or statutes was later found to be unconstitutional. 140 S. Ct. 2412, 2426 (2020). States also extended a form of *qualified* immunity to executive officers. It was qualified in the sense that it wasn't absolute. Instead, qualified immunity applied only as long as an executive officer acted in good faith to execute a law as they reasonably understood it.

In *Pierson v. Ray*, 386 U.S. 547 (1967), the Supreme Court extended both forms of immunity—qualified and unqualified—to a state police officer and judge, respectively, who arrested and convicted a § 1983 plaintiff under a statute that was later found to be unconstitutionally vague. The Court explained that it was unfair to require a judge ever to pay damages for an erroneous interpretation of a law, and it was equally unfair to require a police officer to pay damages "for acting under a statute that he reasonably believed to be valid but that was later held unconstitutional." *Pierson*, 386 U.S. at 555.

As discussed earlier with regard to executive immunity (section 28.2), in *Harlow v. Fitzgerald*, 457 U.S. 800 (1982), the Supreme Court extended qualified immunity to most executive officers sued for violating the Constitution. The Court held that "government officials performing discretionary functions, generally are shielded from liability for civil damages insofar as their conduct does not violate clearly established statutory or constitutional rights of which a reasonable person would have known." *Harlow*, 457 U.S. at 818.

In a subsequent case, the Court explained that a right was "clearly established"—meaning that qualified immunity didn't apply—as long as officers had "fair warning that their conduct violated the Constitution." *Hope v. Pelzer*, 536 U.S. 730, 741 (2002). "Fair warning" was a broad test that made clear "that officials can still be on notice that their conduct violates established law even in novel factual circumstances." *Id.*

But the Court soon abandoned this "fair warning" test and began to interpret the phrase *clearly established* very narrowly. Instead, the Court defined *clearly established right* as one whose "contours were sufficiently definite that any reasonable official in [an officer's] shoes would have understood that he was violating it." *City & Cnty. of San Francisco v. Sheehan*, 575 U.S. 600, 611 (2015). It called this test an "exacting standard" that protects "all but the plainly incompetent or those who knowingly violate the law." *Id.* Under this all-but-the-plainly-incompetent test, qualified immunity quickly became an insurmountable obstacle for many plaintiffs seeking damages under § 1983—particularly in the context of police officers who were sued for using unconstitutionally excessive force. *See, e.g.*, *Kisela v. Hughes*, 138 S. Ct. 1148, 1151 (2018).

Yet in a 2020 decision, *Taylor v. Riojas*, the Court reaffirmed the "fair warning" test and explained that "a general constitutional rule already identified in the decisional law may apply with obvious clarity to the specific conduct in question" even absent a precisely on-point holding. 141 S. Ct. 52, 53–54 (2020) (quoting *Hope*, 536 U.S. at 741).

Actions under federal law. A third limit is that § 1983 only provides a cause of action against a person who acts under color of *state* law, not under federal law. The statute therefore doesn't provide a cause of action against federal officers who violate the Constitution.

State sovereign immunity. In 1979, the Court introduced a fourth and increasingly significant limit on the scope of § 1983 by interpreting it not to abrogate a state's sovereign immunity. This fourth limit provided context for the following case.

36.1.1

Whole Woman's Health v. Jackson

142 S. Ct. 522 (2021)

Even though Congress formally possesses the power to abrogate state sovereign immunity when it enforces the Reconstruction amendments, the Supreme Court has often interpreted federal civil-rights statutes narrowly to insulate states from their operation. As discussed in an earlier section (34.5), the Court has allowed Congress to abrogate a state's sovereign immunity "only by making its intention unmistakably clear in the language of the statute." *Atascadero State Hosp. v. Scanlon*, 473 U.S. 234, 242 (1985).

The Court's most significant and controversial application of this clear-statement rule has been with 42 U.S.C. § 1983. The law clearly provides that any "person" who acts under color of state law to deprive someone "of any rights, privileges, or immunities secured by the Constitution and laws, shall be liable to the party injured in an action at law, suit in equity, or other proper proceeding for redress." The purpose of the law has also long been clear: Congress first passed the statute during Reconstruction in 1871 to give ordinary people the power to sue state and local officials who violated their federally protected rights. *See Mitchum v. Foster*, 407 U.S. 225, 240 (1972). But in 1979, the Court reinterpreted § 1983 to hold that the law "does not explicitly and by clear language indicate on its face an intent to sweep away the immunity of the States; nor does it have a history which focuses directly on the question of state liability and which shows that Congress considered and firmly decided to abrogate the Eleventh Amendment immunity of the States." *Quern v. Jordan*, 440 U.S. 332, 345 (1979).

Applying this revisionist interpretation, the Court held that § 1983 does not provide a cause of action in contexts where state sovereign immunity would protect the defendant. *Id.* At the same time, the Court has conceded that a state's sovereign immunity does not bar § 1983 suits in contexts similar to *Ex parte Young*, where plaintiffs sued state officials to enjoin them from violating the Constitution and federal law. Where the rule from *Ex parte Young* applies, therefore, § 1983 allows plaintiffs to seek injunctions against "all state actors," *Pulliam v. Allen*, 466 U.S. 522, 540 (1984), whether the actors are "executive, legislative, or judicial." *Mitchum*, 407 U.S. at 240.

As a result, § 1983 continues to provide the main cause of action by which plaintiffs sue state and local officials for violating their federally protected rights. In *Obergefell v. Hodges*, 576 U.S. 644 (2015), plaintiffs used § 1983 to challenge Ohio's same-sex marriage ban by suing the director of the Ohio Department of Health. In *Roe v. Wade*, 410 U.S. 113 (1973), plaintiffs used § 1983 to challenge Texas's abortion ban by suing the district attorney for Dallas County. And in *Brown v. Board of Education*, 347 U.S. 483 (1954), plaintiffs used § 1983 to challenge racial segregation at the state and local level by suing a variety of defendants, including the board of education of Topeka, Kansas.

In 2021, however, Texas adopted a novel legislative scheme designed to insulate its laws from § 1983. When the Supreme Court evaluated whether § 1983 permitted it to enjoin the Texas Heartbeat Act, or S.B. 8, the Court expansively interpreted the state's sovereign immunity to dramatically narrow § 1983's cause of action.

Texas legislators passed S.B. 8 to prohibit physicians from "knowingly perfom[ing] or induc[ing] an abortion on a pregnant woman if the physician detected a fetal heartbeat for the unborn child." Tex. Health & Safety Code Ann. § 171.204(a). These state legislators knew that if they authorized state officials to enforce this law, such officials would be liable to suit under § 1983 for violating the clearly established constitutional rights of people seeking abortions. *See Whole Woman's Health v. Hellerstedt*, 579 U.S. 582 (2016) (allowing a § 1983 action for injunctive relief to proceed against Texas state officials responsible for restricting the delivery of abortion services in violation of the Fourteenth Amendment). To evade § 1983, the authors of S.B. 8 therefore prohibited state officials from bringing criminal prosecutions or civil enforcement actions to enforce the law. Instead of relying on these officials, S.B. 8 included a bounty provision that authorized anyone in the country "other than an officer or employee of a state or local governmental entity" to bring a lawsuit in Texas state court against anyone suspected of performing or assisting a prohibited abortion. Tex. Health & Safety Code Ann. § 171.208(a).

To encourage people to file these lawsuits, S.B. 8 provided that any plaintiff who could prove that someone else violated the abortion ban could obtain "statutory damages in an amount of not less than $10,000 for each abortion." *Id.* § 171.208(b). To guarantee the success of these lawsuits, S.B. 8 also introduced abortion-specific procedural rules to make it difficult for abortion providers to defend themselves. Rather than try their luck in unpredictable, rigged, and expensive state-court proceedings, virtually every abortion provider in Texas closed their doors after S.B. 8 took effect.

S.B. 8 was a brazen attempt by state officials to evade existing federal law—precisely the sort of conduct § 1983 was enacted to remedy. *See Mitchum*, 407 U.S. at 240 ("Proponents of the legislation [in 1871] noted that state courts were being used to harass and injure individuals, either because the state courts were powerless to stop deprivations or were in league with those who were bent upon abrogation of federally protected rights."). Despite the efforts of Texas legislators to get around § 1983, S.B. 8 also necessarily required "person[s]" acting under color of state law to enforce its provisions, including the court officials responsible for hearing and enforcing S.B. 8 cases.

Abortion providers therefore invoked § 1983 to obtain a federal injunction against state judges, clerks of court, and other officials responsible for enforcing S.B. 8. But Texas's lawyers responded by invoking the state's sovereign immunity from suit. Because the Court in 1979 interpreted § 1983 not to clearly abrogate state sovereign immunity, the case therefore turned on whether the Eleventh Amendment (and Article III) permitted such a suit to proceed. In *Whole Woman's Health v. Jackson*, 142 S. Ct. 522 (2021), a 5–4 Court held that the most relevant defendants were immune from suit.

■ JUSTICE GORSUCH . . . delivered the opinion of the Court . . . .[1]

The Court granted certiorari before judgment in this case to determine whether, under our precedents, certain abortion providers can pursue a pre-enforcement challenge to a recently enacted Texas statute. . . . In this preliminary posture, the ultimate merits question—whether S. B. 8 is consistent with the Federal Constitution—is not before the Court. Nor is the wisdom of S. B. 8 as a matter of public policy.

A

Turning to the matters that are properly put to us, we begin with the sovereign immunity appeal involving the state-court judge, Austin Jackson, and the state-court clerk, Penny Clarkston. While this lawsuit names only one state-court judge and one state-court clerk as defendants, the petitioners explain that they hope eventually to win certification of a class including all Texas state-court judges and clerks as defendants. In the end, the petitioners say, they intend to seek an order enjoining all state-court clerks from docketing S. B. 8 cases and all state-court judges from hearing them.[2]

---

[1] **As You Read, Consider:** Many of the cases so far in this casebook have addressed *judicial supremacy*, or the question of whether the Supreme Court should have the final word about what the Constitution means when the Court disagrees with Congress and the president. This case and most of the cases that follow in Part IV address *federal supremacy*, or the question of whether federal officials and judges should have the final word about what the Constitution means when they disagree with state officials and judges. Does federal supremacy involve the same balancing of principles as judicial supremacy? For example, when Congress instructs federal courts to stop unconstitutional state action—as it did in 42 U.S.C. § 1983—does a federal court's decision about whether to enjoin a state law involve the same challenge to democratic principles as when a federal court decides on its own whether to enforce a federal law?

[2] **Questions:** Precisely why would a federal injunction against a state court "be a violation of the whole scheme of our Government"? Was this quoted language relevant to the decision in *Ex parte Young*?

Almost immediately, however, the petitioners' theory confronts a difficulty. Generally, States are immune from suit under the terms of the Eleventh Amendment and the doctrine of sovereign immunity. To be sure, in *Ex parte Young,* this Court recognized a narrow exception grounded in traditional equity practice—one that allows certain private parties to seek judicial orders in federal court preventing state executive officials from enforcing state laws that are contrary to federal law. 209 U. S. 123, 159–160 (1908). But as *Ex parte Young* explained, this traditional exception does not normally permit federal courts to issue injunctions against state-court judges or clerks. Usually, those individuals do not enforce state laws as executive officials might; instead, they work to resolve disputes between parties. If a state court errs in its rulings, too, the traditional remedy has been some form of appeal, including to this Court, not the entry of an *ex ante* injunction preventing the state court from hearing cases. As *Ex parte Young* put it, "an injunction against a state court" or its "machinery" "would be a violation of the whole scheme of our Government." *Id.,* at 163.

Nor is that the only problem confronting the petitioners' court-and-clerk theory. Article III of the Constitution affords federal courts the power to resolve only "actual controversies arising between adverse litigants." *Muskrat v. United States,* 219 U. S. 346, 361 (1911). Private parties who seek to bring S. B. 8 suits in state court may be litigants adverse to the petitioners. But the state-court clerks who docket those disputes and the state-court judges who decide them generally are not. Clerks serve to file cases as they arrive, not to participate as adversaries in those disputes. Judges exist to resolve controversies about a law's meaning or its conformance to the Federal and State Constitutions, not to wage battle as contestants in the parties' litigation. As this Court has explained, "no case or controversy" exists "between a judge who adjudicates claims under a statute and a litigant who attacks the constitutionality of the statute." *Pulliam v. Allen,* 466 U. S. 522, 538, n. 18 (1984).[3]

Then there is the question of remedy. Texas Rule of Civil Procedure 24 directs state-court clerks to accept complaints and record case numbers. The petitioners have pointed to nothing in Texas law that permits clerks to pass on the substance of the filings they docket—let alone refuse a party's complaint based on an assessment of its merits. Nor does Article III confer on federal judges some "amorphous" power to supervise "the operations of government" and reimagine from the ground up the job description of Texas state-court clerks. *Raines v. Byrd,* 521 U. S. 811, 829 (1997) (internal quotation marks omitted).

Troubling, too, the petitioners have not offered any meaningful limiting principles for their theory. If it caught on and federal judges could enjoin state courts and clerks from entertaining disputes between private parties under *this* state law, what would stop federal judges from prohibiting state courts and clerks from hearing and docketing disputes between private parties under *other* state laws? And if the state

---

Recall from an earlier section on Congress's power to enforce the Reconstruction Amendments (21.1) that Congress has authorized not only *civil actions* against state judges but also the *criminal prosecution* of state judges who violated the Fourteenth Amendment. *See, e.g., Ex parte Virginia,* 100 U.S. 339, 346 (1880). Even the extremely conservative Court of the 1880s explained that Congress was empowered to enforce the Fourteenth Amendment "against State action, however put forth, whether that action be executive, legislative, or judicial. Such enforcement is no invasion of State sovereignty." *Id.* Otherwise, "the constitutional prohibition has no meaning. Then the State has clothed one of its agents with power to annul or to evade it." *Id.* at 347. Is the outcome in this case nevertheless what the Eleventh Amendment demands?

[3] **Question:** In addition to noting an Eleventh Amendment obstacle, Justice Neil Gorsuch also holds that the plaintiffs in this case have no standing to sue state clerks or judges. Recall that the ultimate question in standing doctrine is not whether there is "adverseness," but whether the defendant has injured the plaintiff in a manner that a federal court can remedy. When a clerk dockets a case filed for the purpose of harassing an abortion provider, is there no injury in fact?

courts and clerks somehow qualify as "adverse litigants" for Article III purposes in the present case, when would they not? The petitioners offer no satisfactory answers.

Instead, only further questions follow. Under the petitioners' theory, would clerks have to assemble a blacklist of banned claims subject to immediate dismissal? What kind of inquiry would a state court have to apply to satisfy due process before dismissing those suits? How notorious would the alleged constitutional defects of a claim have to be before a state-court clerk would risk legal jeopardy merely for filing it? Would States have to hire independent legal counsel for their clerks—and would those advisers be the next target of suits seeking injunctive relief? When a party hales a state-court clerk into federal court for filing a complaint containing a purportedly unconstitutional claim, how would the clerk defend himself consistent with his ethical obligation of neutrality? . . . Could federal courts enjoin those who perform other ministerial tasks potentially related to litigation, like the postal carrier who delivers complaints to the courthouse? Many more questions than answers would present themselves if the Court journeyed this way. . . .

B

Perhaps recognizing the problems with their court-and-clerk theory, the petitioners briefly advance an alternative. They say they seek to enjoin the Texas attorney general from enforcing S. B. 8. . . . [But w]hile *Ex parte Young* authorizes federal courts to enjoin certain state officials from enforcing state laws, the petitioners do not direct this Court to any enforcement authority the attorney general possesses in connection with S. B. 8 that a federal court might enjoin him from exercising. . . .

[And even if] the attorney general did have some enforcement authority under S. B. 8, the petitioners have identified nothing that might allow a federal court to parlay that authority, or any defendant's enforcement authority, into an injunction against any and all unnamed private persons who might seek to bring their own S. B. 8 suits. The equitable powers of federal courts are limited by historical practice. *Atlas Life Ins. Co. v. W. I. Southern, Inc.*, 306 U. S. 563, 568 (1939). . . . Consistent with historical practice, a federal court exercising its equitable authority may enjoin named defendants from taking specified unlawful actions. But under traditional equitable principles, no court may "lawfully enjoin the world at large," *ibid.*, or purport to enjoin challenged "laws themselves." *Whole Woman's Health,* 594 U. S., at ___ (slip op., at 1). . . .[4]

[* * *]

While this should be enough to resolve the petitioners' appeal, a detour is required before we close. JUSTICE SOTOMAYOR charges this Court with "shrink[ing]" from the task of defending the supremacy of the Federal Constitution over state law. *Post,* at 10. That rhetoric bears no relation to reality.

The truth is, many paths exist to vindicate the supremacy of federal law in this area. . . . [Fourteen] state-court cases already seek to vindicate both federal and state constitutional claims against S. B. 8—and they have met with some success at the summary judgment stage. Separately, any individual sued under S. B. 8 may

[4] **Note:** After rejecting the plaintiffs' two primary theories—both of which are excerpted here—a majority of the Court concluded that a Texas law enacted before S.B. 8 could be read to permit certain state "licensing officials" to enforce any abortion law, including S.B. 8. This conclusion is not excerpted in this casebook for two reasons. First, these sorts of licensing officials were, at best, so peripheral to S.B. 8's enforcement scheme that enjoining them alone would have little effect on S.B. 8. Second, after this litigation, the U.S. Court of Appeals for the Fifth Circuit prevented a lawsuit against these licensing officials from going forward. Instead, the federal court asked a Texas court to clarify whether state law did, in fact, permit licensing officials to enforce S.B. 8 despite S.B. 8's attempt to prohibit all state executive officials from enforcing its terms. The Texas court answered no, effectively ending the litigation.

pursue state and federal constitutional arguments in his or her defense.[5] Still further viable avenues to contest the law's compliance with the Federal Constitution also may be possible; we do not prejudge the possibility. Given all this, JUSTICE SOTOMAYOR'S suggestion that the Court's ruling somehow "clears the way" for the "nullification" of federal law along the lines of what happened in the Jim Crow South not only wildly mischaracterizes the impact of today's decision, it cheapens the gravity of past wrongs. *Post,* at 11.

The truth is, too, that unlike the petitioners before us, those seeking to challenge the constitutionality of state laws are not always able to pick and choose the timing and preferred forum for their arguments. This Court has never recognized an unqualified right to pre-enforcement review of constitutional claims in federal court. In fact, general federal question jurisdiction did not even exist for much of this Nation's history. And pre-enforcement review under the statutory regime the petitioners invoke, 42 U. S. C. § 1983, was not prominent until the mid-20th century. See *Monroe v. Pape,* 365 U. S. 167, 180 (1961). To this day, many federal constitutional rights are as a practical matter asserted typically as defenses to state-law claims, not in federal preenforcement cases like this one. . . .

■ JUSTICE SOTOMAYOR, with whom JUSTICE BREYER and JUSTICE KAGAN join, . . . dissenting . . . .

For nearly three months, the Texas Legislature has substantially suspended a constitutional guarantee: a pregnant woman's right to control her own body. See *Roe v. Wade,* 410 U. S. 113 (1973); *Planned Parenthood of Southeastern Pa. v. Casey,* 505 U. S. 833 (1992). In open defiance of this Court's precedents, Texas enacted Senate Bill 8 (S.B. 8), which bans abortion starting approximately six weeks after a woman's last menstrual period, well before the point of fetal viability. Since S. B. 8 went into effect on September 1, 2021, the law has threatened abortion care providers with the prospect of essentially unlimited suits for damages, brought anywhere in Texas by private bounty hunters, for taking any action to assist women in exercising their constitutional right to choose. The chilling effect has been near total, depriving pregnant women in Texas of virtually all opportunity to seek abortion care within their home State after their sixth week of pregnancy. Some women have vindicated their rights by traveling out of State. For the many women who are unable to do so, their only alternatives are to carry unwanted pregnancies to term or attempt self-induced abortions outside of the medical system.[6]

The Court should have put an end to this madness months ago, before S. B. 8 first went into effect. It failed to do so then, and it fails again today. . . . I dissent . . . from the Court's dangerous departure from its precedents, which establish that federal courts can and should issue relief when a State enacts a law that chills the exercise of a constitutional right and aims to evade judicial review. By foreclosing suit against state-court officials and the state attorney general, the Court effectively invites other States to refine S. B. 8's model for nullifying federal rights. The Court thus betrays not only the citizens of Texas, but also our constitutional system of government. . . .

---

[5] **Question:** In *Ex parte Young* and the Court's recent standing decisions, like *Susan B. Anthony List v. Driehaus*, 573 U.S. 149 (2014), the Court refused to require the targets of allegedly unconstitutional enforcement actions to subject themselves to the costs and jeopardy of unfavorable state-court judgments. Why is this situation different?

[6] **Question:** Justice Sonia Sotomayor observes that the majority's decision will leave pregnant people in Texas with no recourse to vindicate their federally protected abortion rights in the state. Meanwhile, all five justices who joined the majority opinion in this case were widely suspected of being hostile to abortion rights. Do you think the procedural rules governing standing, sovereign immunity, and causes of action should change depending on the substantive issues at stake? For an analysis of this question, see Richard H. Fallon, Jr., *The Fragmentation of Standing*, 93 Tex. L. Rev. 1061 (2015).

II

This Court has confronted State attempts to evade federal constitutional commands before, including schemes that forced parties to expose themselves to catastrophic liability as state-court defendants in order to assert their rights. Until today, the Court had proven equal to those challenges.

In 1908, this Court decided *Ex parte Young,* 209 U. S. 123. In *Young,* the Court considered a Minnesota law fixing new rates for railroads and adopting high fines and penalties for failure to comply with the rates. *Id.,* at 128–129, 131. The law purported to provide no option to challenge the new rates other than disobeying the law and taking "the risk . . . of being subjected to such enormous penalties." *Id.,* at 145. Because the railroad officers and employees "could not be expected to disobey any of the provisions . . . at the risk of such fines and penalties," the law effectively resulted in "a denial of any hearing to the company." *Id.,* at 146.

The Court unequivocally rejected this design. Concluding that the legislature could not "preclude a resort to the courts . . . for the purpose of testing [the law's] validity," the Court decided the companies could obtain pre-enforcement relief by suing the Minnesota attorney general based on his "connection with the enforcement" of the challenged act. *Id.,* at 146, 157. The Court so held despite the fact that the attorney general's only such connection was the "general duty imposed upon him, which includes the right and the power to enforce the statutes of the State, including, of course, the act in question." *Id.,* at 161. Over the years, "the *Young* doctrine has been accepted as necessary to permit the federal courts to vindicate federal rights and hold state officials responsible to 'the supreme authority of the United States.' " *Pennhurst State School and Hospital v. Halderman,* 465 U. S. 89, 105 (1984) (quoting *Young,* 209 U. S., at 160).

Like the stockholders in *Young,* abortion providers face calamitous liability from a facially unconstitutional law. To be clear, the threat is not just the possibility of money judgments; it is also that, win or lose, providers may be forced to defend themselves against countless suits, all across the State, without any prospect of recovery for their losses or expenses. . . . In fact, the circumstances at hand present an even stronger need for preenforcement relief than in *Young,* given how S. B. 8 not only threatens a multiplicity of suits, but also turns state-court procedures against providers to ensure they cannot effectively defend their rights in a suit. . . .[7]

In addition, state-court clerks are proper defendants in this action. This Court has long recognized that "the action of state courts and judicial officers in their official capacities is to be regarded as action of the State." *Shelley v. Kraemer,* 334 U. S. 1, 14 (1948). In *Shelley,* private litigants sought to enforce restrictive racial covenants designed to preclude Black Americans from home ownership and to preserve residential segregation. The Court explained that these ostensibly private covenants involved state action because "but for the active intervention of the state courts, supported by the full panoply of state power," the covenants would be unenforceable. *Id.,* at 19. Here, there is more. S. B. 8's formidable chilling effect, even before suit, would be nonexistent if not for the state-court officials who docket S. B. 8 cases with

[7] **Question:** The "state-court procedures" that Sotomayor alludes to in this paragraph include the absence of issue preclusion, meaning one abortion provider could potentially be sued by an unlimited number of plaintiffs each seeking $10,000 bounties. Tex. Health & Safety Code Ann. § 171.208(e) And even if an abortion provider successfully defended itself, the provider would still be on the hook for court costs and attorney's fees. *Id.* § 171.208(*i*).

In light of these procedures, do you nevertheless agree with the majority that a federal injunction against state judges and clerks "would be a violation of the whole scheme of our Government?"

lopsided procedures and limited defenses. Because these state actors are necessary components of that chilling effect and play a clear role in the enforcement of S. B. 8, they are proper defendants.

These longstanding precedents establish how, and why, the Court should authorize relief against these officials as well. The Court instead hides behind a wooden reading of *Young,* stitching out-of-context quotations into a cover for its failure to act decisively. The Court relies on dicta in *Young* stating that "the right to enjoin an individual . . . does not include the power to restrain a court from acting in any case brought before it" and that "an injunction against a state court would be a violation of the whole scheme of our Government." 209 U. S., at 163. Modern cases, however, have recognized that suit may be proper even against state-court judges, including to enjoin state-court proceedings. See *Mitchum v. Foster,* 407 U. S. 225, 243 (1972); see also *Pulliam v. Allen,* 466 U. S. 522, 525 (1984). . . .

Moreover, the Court has emphasized that "the principles undergirding the *Ex parte Young* doctrine" may "support its application" to new circumstances, "novelty notwithstanding." *Stewart,* 563 U. S., at 261. No party has identified any prior circumstance in which a State has delegated an enforcement function to the populace, disclaimed official enforcement authority, and skewed state-court procedures to chill the exercise of constitutional rights. Because S. B. 8's architects designed this scheme to evade *Young* as historically applied, it is especially perverse for the Court to shield it from scrutiny based on its novelty.

Next, the Court claims that *Young* cannot apply because state-court clerks are not adverse to the petitioners. *Ante,* at 5–6. . . . [But with] S. B. 8's extreme alterations to court procedure and substantive defenses, the Texas court system no longer resembles a neutral forum for the adjudication of rights; S. B. 8 refashions that system into a weapon and points it directly at the petitioners. Under these circumstances, the parties are sufficiently adverse.

Finally, the Court raises "the question of remedy." *Ante,* at 6. For the Court, that question cascades into many others about the precise contours of an injunction against Texas court clerks in light of state procedural rules. *Ante,* at 6-7. Vexing though the Court may find these fact-intensive questions, they are exactly the sort of tailoring work that District Courts perform every day. The Court should have afforded the District Court an opportunity to craft appropriate relief before throwing up its hands and declaring the task unworkable. For today's purposes, the answer is simple: If, as our precedents make clear (and as the question presented presumes), S. B. 8 is unconstitutional, contrary state rules of civil procedure must give way. See U. S. Const., Art. VI, cl. 2 ("This Constitution, and the Laws of the United States which shall be made in Pursuance thereof . . . shall be the supreme Law of the Land"). . . .

III

My disagreement with the Court runs far deeper than a quibble over how many defendants these petitioners may sue. The dispute is over whether States may nullify federal constitutional rights by employing schemes like the one at hand. The Court indicates that they can, so long as they write their laws to more thoroughly disclaim all enforcement by state officials, including licensing officials. This choice to shrink from Texas' challenge to federal supremacy will have far-reaching repercussions. I doubt the Court, let alone the country, is prepared for them. . . .

This is a brazen challenge to our federal structure. It echoes the philosophy of John C. Calhoun, a virulent defender of the slaveholding South who insisted that States had the right to "veto" or "nullif[y]" any federal law with which they disagreed. Address of J. Calhoun, Speeches of John C. Calhoun 17-43 (1843). . . .

The Nation fought a Civil War over that proposition, but Calhoun's theories were not extinguished. They experienced a revival in the post-war South, and the violence that ensued led Congress to enact Rev. Stat. § 1979, 42 U. S. C. § 1983. "Proponents of the legislation noted that state courts were being used to harass and injure individuals, either because the state courts were powerless to stop deprivations or were in league with those who were bent upon abrogation of federally protected rights." *Mitchum,* 407 U. S., at 240. Thus, § 1983's "very purpose," consonant with the values that motivated the *Young* Court some decades later, was "to protect the people from unconstitutional action under color of state law, 'whether that action be executive, legislative, or judicial.' ", 407 U. S., at 242 (quoting *Ex parte Virginia,* 100 U. S. 339, 346 (1880)). . . .[8]

Federal constitutional violations and the APA

The law that provided the cause of action in *Whole Woman's Health v. Jackson*—42 U.S.C. § 1983—has long been interpreted to apply only when a *state* official violates federal law. The principal statute used to challenge *federal* violations of the law is the Administrative Procedure Act of 1946 (APA), Pub. L. No. 79–404, 60 Stat. 237 (codified at 5 U.S.C. § 702). The APA provides thus: "A person suffering legal wrong because of agency action, or adversely affected or aggrieved by agency action within the meaning of a relevant statute, is entitled to judicial review thereof." *Id.*

At the time the APA was enacted, *legal wrong* was defined as an injury to a right protected by the common law: "one of property, one arising out of contract, one protected against tortious invasion, or one founded on a statute which confers a privilege." *Tenn. Elec. Power Co. v. TVA*, 306 U.S. 118, 137 (1939). But in *Ass'n of Data Processing Service Organizations v. Camp*, 397 U.S. 150 (1970), the Court expanded the concept to include not only common-law injuries but also injuries to economic, aesthetic, conservational, and recreational interests. *See Camp*, 397 U.S. at 154. For example, if a federal agency issued an allegedly unconstitutional rule that contributed to increased pollution in a national park, plaintiffs might have suffered a legal wrong in the sense that their enjoyment of the park suffered.

To limit the scope of this broad interpretation of the APA, the *Camp* Court added a second requirement: a person seeking to challenge the action of a federal agency must be within the "zone of interests to be protected or regulated by the statute or constitutional guarantee in

[8] **Questions:** Justice Sotomayor concludes her opinion by arguing that the Court has undermined federal supremacy. She writes that when Congress enacted § 1983, it wanted federal courts to help it stop state officials from violating federal law. But she suggests that the majority has given states a model for how to avoid federal review. Do you agree? If Congress wanted to reverse this decision and reestablish federal supremacy, what options remain available?

Recall that the only reason the Eleventh Amendment was relevant to this case is because a 1979 decision held that Congress must use "clear language" when it intends to abrogate a state's sovereign immunity, and that such clear language was missing from § 1983 despite its purpose. *See Quern v. Jordan*, 440 U.S. 332, 343–44 (1979). If Congress amended § 1983 to more clearly abrogate state sovereign immunity, is there any reason to suspect that the Court would interpret such an amendment any less narrowly? Would standing remain an obstacle?

question." *Camp*, 397 U.S. at 153. For example, if an agency action allegedly violates the Free Speech Clause of the First Amendment, then the only people who may invoke the APA to challenge the action are people whose speech is arguably abridged. Similarly, if an agency action allegedly violates a statute, then the Court considers "whether Congress 'intended for [a particular] class [of plaintiffs] to be relied upon to challenge agency disregard of the law.'" *Clarke v. Sec. Indus. Ass'n*, 479 U.S. 388, 399 (1987) (quoting *Block v. Cmty. Nutrition Inst.*, 467 U.S. 340, 347 (1984)). For almost fifty years after *Camp*, the Court suggested that this "zone of interests" test was an element of standing required by Article III. But in *Lexmark International, Inc. v. Static Control Components, Inc.*, the Court emphasized that the "zone of interests" test has nothing to do with standing but is simply a question of statutory interpretation: "whether a legislatively conferred cause of action encompasses a particular plaintiff's claim." 572 U.S. 118, 126 (2014); *see also Bank of Am. Corp. v. City of Miami*, 137 S. Ct. 1296, 1302 (2017) (equating the "cause-of-action" and "prudential standing" requirements).

Another limit of the APA—a textual limit embedded in the statute—is that it applies only when an "agency" commits a legal wrong. The statute defines *agency* as "each authority of the Government of the United States . . . but does not include (A) the Congress; (B) the courts of the United States; (C) the governments of the territories or . . . (D) the government of the District of Columbia." 5 U.S.C. §§ 701(b)(1), 551(1). The statute, therefore, does not apply to individual federal officers, nor, according to the Court, does it apply to the president of the United States. *See Franklin v. Massachusetts*, 505 U.S. 788, 800–01 (1992). Challenges to actions by the president, FBI agents, border patrol officers, and other federal officials who are not themselves an "agency" therefore must rely on different causes of action.

Alternatives to § 1983 and the APA

One available alternative to § 1983 and the APA are other *express* causes of action like the Religious Freedom Restoration Act of 1993, which empowers anyone "whose religious exercise has been burdened in violation of [the act] . . . [to] assert that violation as a claim . . . in a judicial proceeding and obtain appropriate relief against a government." Pub. L. No. 103–141, 107 Stat. 1488, 1489. In *Tanzin v. Tanvir*, the Supreme Court held for the first time that this statute permitted Muslim plaintiffs to sue various FBI agents and seek damages for unconstitutionally placing the plaintiffs on the federal No Fly List. 141 S. Ct. 486, 491–93 (2020).

Other alternatives to § 1983 and the APA are *implied* causes of action. These will be discussed in the next section.

36.2 IMPLIED CAUSES OF ACTION FOR DAMAGES (*BIVENS*)

The Ku Klux Klan Act of 1871, ch. 22, 17 Stat. 13 (codified at 42 U.S.C. § 1983), and the Administrative Procedure Act of 1946 (APA), Pub. L. No. 79–404, 60 Stat. 237 (codified at 5 U.S.C. § 702), are examples of statutes that *expressly* confer causes of action upon individuals who want to go to court to enforce their terms. Many other statutes, by contrast, are silent or ambiguous about whether an individual can sue someone for a violation.

For example, the Securities Exchange Act of 1934, Pub. L. No. 73–291, 48 Stat. 881—which created the Securities and Exchange Commission (SEC)—prohibited certain companies from issuing false proxy statements about their financial information. But the act wasn't clear about whether the SEC was exclusively responsible for enforcing this prohibition or whether private individuals could also sue a company for issuing false statements. All the act said was that district courts have jurisdiction "of all suits in equity and actions at law brought to enforce any liability or duty created by this title." Securities Exchange Act, 48 Stat. at 902–03.

In *J. I. Case Co. v. Borak*, 377 U.S. 426 (1964), the Supreme Court announced that this language was sufficient to confer upon individuals an *implied* cause of action to enforce the statute. "Private enforcement of the proxy rules provides a necessary supplement to Commission action," the Court wrote, adding that the denial of a cause of action would be "tantamount to a denial of private relief." *J. I. Case Co.*, 377 U.S. at 432. In subsequent cases, the Court explained that the fact that Congress passes a statute to protect a class of people necessarily "implied a private right of action." *Allen v. State Bd. of Elections*, 393 U.S. 544, 557 (1969). In short, "The existence of a statutory right implies the existence of all necessary and appropriate remedies." *Sullivan v. Little Hunting Park*, 396 U.S. 229, 239 (1969).

The principle underlying these decisions was the same principle underlying *Marbury v. Madison*, 5 U.S. (1 Cranch) 137 (1803). As Chief Justice John Marshall repeatedly emphasized in that case, "it is a general and indisputable rule, that where there is a legal right, there is also a legal remedy by suit, or action at law, when ever that right is invaded." *Marbury*, 5 U.S. (1 Cranch) at 163.

In 1971, the Court read this every-right-deserves-a-remedy principle into the Constitution itself. As discussed in the previous section (section 36.1), § 1983 creates a cause of action when *state* officers violate the Constitution, and the APA creates a cause of action when federal *agencies* violate the Constitution, but neither creates a cause of action when *federal officers* violate the Constitution. This became a significant issue when agents of the federal Bureau of Narcotics raided the Brooklyn home of Webster Bivens, dragging him out of his bed, handcuffing him in front of his wife and children, and threatening to arrest his entire family. Bivens later sued the unknown agents for violating his Fourth Amendment right to be free from unreasonable searches and seizures. But government lawyers responded that no statute explicitly or implicitly gave Bivens a cause of action. In *Bivens v. Six Unknown Named Agents of the Federal Bureau of Narcotics*, 403 U.S. 388 (1971), the Court held that the Fourth Amendment itself provided Bivens with a cause of action. Citing *J.I. Case Co.* and *Marbury*, the Court declared that "where federally protected rights have been invaded, it has been the rule from the beginning that courts will be alert to adjust their remedies so as to grant the necessary relief." *Bivens*, 403 U.S. at 392. In Bivens's case, if the Fourth Amendment didn't provide a remedy for the federal agents' violation of his rights, then his only available remedy would have been "an action in tort, under state law, in the state court." *Id.* at 390. But the Court thought that state-law actions would be insufficient to remedy the federal constitutional violation, both because federal agents might violate the Fourth Amendment without also committing a trespass or battery and because states generally lack the power to limit federal agents from exercising federal authority. *Id.* at 393–95.

The *Bivens* Court therefore concluded that a federal cause of action for damages was necessary to remedy the Fourth Amendment violation: "For people in Bivens' shoes, it is damages or nothing." *Id.* at 410. The Court wrote that its conclusion was supported by the absence of any "special factors counselling hesitation in the absence of affirmative action by Congress." *Id.* at 396. Unless Congress provided "another remedy, equally effective in the view of Congress," the Court would find an implied cause of action in the Constitution itself. *Id.* at 397. Applying this standard, the Court soon found similar implied causes of action for damages against federal officers who violated the Fifth Amendment, *see Davis v. Passman*, 442 U.S. 228, 248–49 (1979); and federal officers who violated the Eighth Amendment, *see Carlson v. Green*, 446 U.S. 14, 19 (1980).

Bivens proved to be the high-water mark for implied causes of action. Shortly afterward, in *Cort v. Ash*, 422 U.S. 66 (1975), the Court began to retreat from finding implied causes of action in federal statutes. The Court explained that recognizing implied causes of action in every statute might interfere with Congress's purpose of giving the executive branch complete discretion over how and whether to enforce a statutory prohibition. *Cort*, 422 U.S. at 80. Moreover, if Congress really wanted to create causes of action, it could always do so explicitly. These considerations eventually led the Court to conclude that "[w]hen Congress intends private litigants to have a cause of action to support their statutory rights, the far better course is for it to specify as much when it creates those rights." *Cannon v. Univ. of Chi.*, 441 U.S. 677, 717 (1979). The Court fully abandoned the idea of implied statutory causes of action in *Alexander v. Sandoval*, in which it held that the "judicial task is to interpret the statute Congress has passed to determine whether it displays an intent to create not just a private right but also a private remedy." 532 U.S. 275, 286 (2001).

Just as the Court declined to recognize any more implied *statutory* causes of action, it also declined to recognize any more implied *constitutional* causes of action for damages. In *Bivens*, the Court had held that it would recognize an implied cause of action for damages to remedy a constitutional violation unless there existed "special factors counselling hesitation" such as "another remedy, equally effective in the view of Congress." 403 U.S. at 397. Since 1980, the Court has consistently found these sorts of special factors in every case that has come before it. *See, e.g., Hernandez v. Mesa*, 140 S. Ct. 735, 743 (2020); *Minneci v. Pollard*, 565 U.S. 118, 126 (2012).

The following case is an example of the Court considering whether to extend *Bivens* to a new situation.

36.2.1

Ziglar v. Abbasi

137 S. Ct. 1843 (2017)

On September 25, 2001, Ahmer Iqbal Abbasi, an undocumented immigrant from Pakistan and the owner of a small grocery store in New York City, was arrested by the Federal Bureau of Investigation (FBI). Although he wasn't told why he was being arrested, the FBI questioned him about his religious beliefs and his connections to terrorism. The arrest was part of an FBI dragnet, initiated after September 11, in which the FBI arrested over a thousand Arab, Muslim, and South Asian immigrants on the suspicion that they had some connection to the attacks. Without offering Abbasi the opportunity for bail, a hearing, or a consultation with a lawyer, federal agents sent Abbasi and one hundred other men to a maximum-security detention center in Brooklyn.

At the detention center, Abbasi and the other prisoners were subjected to harsh conditions. For weeks, the prisoners were kept in tiny cells for twenty-three hours a day, with the lights left on at all times. They were strip-searched often and at random, and they were denied basic hygiene products such as soap and toothbrushes. Guards slammed prisoners into walls, broke their bones, referred to them as terrorists, and subjected them to other humiliations. Eventually, Abbasi and the other prisoners were released, and Abbasi was deported to Pakistan.

After his release, Abbasi and a class of prisoners alleged a half-dozen different constitutional violations by several officials—including the attorney general, John Ashcroft; the FBI director, Robert Mueller; and the commissioner of the Immigration and Naturalization Service, James Ziglar. The Supreme Court dismissed their first complaint in *Ashcroft v. Iqbal*, 556 U.S. 662 (2009), a decision that declined to resolve the merits but instead announced a new, heightened pleading standard. After an amended complaint, the case again reached the Supreme Court in 2017. At issue this time was whether a cause of action permitted Abbasi to sue the officials.

The Court in *Ziglar v. Abbasi*, 137 S. Ct. 1843 (2017), declined to find a *Bivens* claim, punting to Congress to find a solution to the constitutional violations.

■ JUSTICE KENNEDY delivered the opinion of the Court.[9]

[The] question to be discussed is whether petitioners can be sued for damages under *Bivens* and the ensuing cases in this Court defining the reach and the limits of that precedent.

A

In 1871, Congress passed a statute that was later codified at 42 U.S.C. § 1983. It entitles an injured person to money damages if a state official violates his or her constitutional rights. Congress did not create an analogous statute for federal officials. Indeed, in the 100 years leading up to *Bivens,* Congress did not provide a specific damages remedy for plaintiffs whose constitutional rights were violated by agents of the Federal Government.

In 1971, and against this background, this Court decided *Bivens*. The Court held that, even absent statutory authorization, it would enforce a damages remedy to compensate persons injured by federal officers who violated the prohibition against unreasonable search and seizures. See 403 U.S., at 397. The Court acknowledged that the Fourth Amendment does not provide for money damages "in so many words." *Id.,* at 396. The Court noted, however, that Congress had not foreclosed a damages remedy in "explicit" terms and that no "special factors" suggested that the Judiciary should "hesitat[e]" in the face of congressional silence. *Id.,* at 396–397. The Court, accordingly, held that it could authorize a remedy under general principles of federal jurisdiction. See *id.,* at 392.

In the decade that followed, the Court recognized what has come to be called an implied cause of action in two cases involving other constitutional violations. In *Davis v. Passman,* 442 U.S. 228 (1979), an administrative assistant sued a Congressman for firing her because she was a woman. The Court held that the Fifth Amendment Due Process Clause gave her a damages remedy for gender discrimination. *Id.,* at 248–249. And in *Carlson v. Green,* 446 U.S. 14 (1980), a prisoner's estate sued federal jailers for failing to treat the prisoner's asthma. The Court held that the Eighth Amendment Cruel and Unusual Punishments Clause gave him a damages remedy for failure to provide adequate medical treatment. See *id.,* at 19. These three cases—*Bivens, Davis,* and *Carlson*—represent the only instances in which the Court has approved of an implied damages remedy under the Constitution itself.

B

To understand *Bivens* and the two other cases implying a damages remedy under the Constitution, it is necessary to understand the prevailing law when they were decided. In the mid-20th century, the Court followed a different approach to recognizing implied causes of action than it follows now. During this "*ancien regime,*" *Alexander v. Sandoval,* 532 U.S. 275, 287 (2001), the Court assumed it to be a proper judicial function to "provide such remedies as are necessary to make effective"

[9] **As You Read, Consider:** Justice Anthony Kennedy's opinion shows obvious reluctance about applying *Bivens* to allow Ahmer Iqbal Abbasi to sue the federal officials who horribly mistreated him. Why? What is Kennedy worried about?

a statute's purpose, *J.I. Case Co. v. Borak,* 377 U.S. 426, 433 (1964). Thus, as a routine matter with respect to statutes, the Court would imply causes of action not explicit in the statutory text itself. See, *e.g., id.,* at 430–432; *Allen v. State Bd. of Elections,* 393 U.S. 544, 557 (1969); *Sullivan v. Little Hunting Park, Inc.,* 396 U.S. 229, 239 (1969).

These statutory decisions were in place when *Bivens* recognized an implied cause of action to remedy a constitutional violation. Against that background, the *Bivens* decision held that courts must "adjust their remedies so as to grant the necessary relief" when "federally protected rights have been invaded." In light of this interpretive framework, there was a possibility that the Court would keep expanding *Bivens* until it became the substantial equivalent of [§]1983.

C

Later, the arguments for recognizing implied causes of action for damages began to lose their force. In cases decided after *Bivens,* and after the statutory implied cause-of-action cases that *Bivens* itself relied upon, the Court adopted a far more cautious course before finding implied causes of action. In two principal cases under other statutes, it declined to find an implied cause of action. See *Piper v. Chris-Craft Industries, Inc.,* 430 U.S. 1, 42, 45–46 (1977); *Cort v. Ash,* 422 U.S. 66, 68–69 (1975). Later, in *Cannon v. University of Chicago,* 441 U.S. 677 (1979), the Court did allow an implied cause of action; but it cautioned that, where Congress "intends private litigants to have a cause of action," the "far better course" is for Congress to confer that remedy in explicit terms. *Id.,* at 717.

Following this expressed caution, the Court clarified in a series of cases that, when deciding whether to recognize an implied cause of action, the "determinative" question is one of statutory intent. *Sandoval,* 532 U.S., at 286. If the statute itself does not "displa[y] an intent" to create "a private remedy," then "a cause of action does not exist and courts may not create one, no matter how desirable that might be as a policy matter, or how compatible with the statute." *Id.,* at 286–287. The Court held that the judicial task was instead "limited solely to determining whether Congress intended to create the private right of action asserted." *Touche Ross & Co. v. Redington,* 442 U.S. 560, 568 (1979). If the statute does not itself so provide, a private cause of action will not be created through judicial mandate.

The decision to recognize an implied cause of action under a statute involves somewhat different considerations than when the question is whether to recognize an implied cause of action to enforce a provision of the Constitution itself. When Congress enacts a statute, there are specific procedures and times for considering its terms and the proper means for its enforcement. It is logical, then, to assume that Congress will be explicit if it intends to create a private cause of action. With respect to the Constitution, however, there is no single, specific congressional action to consider and interpret.

Even so, it is a significant step under separation-of-powers principles for a court to determine that it has the authority, under the judicial power, to create and enforce a cause of action for damages against federal officials in order to remedy a constitutional violation. When determining whether traditional equitable powers suffice to give necessary constitutional protection—or whether, in addition, a damages remedy is necessary—there are a number of economic and governmental concerns to consider. Claims against federal officials often create substantial costs, in the form of defense and indemnification. Congress, then, has a substantial responsibility to determine whether, and the extent to which, monetary and other liabilities should be imposed upon individual officers and employees of the Federal Government. In addition, the time and administrative costs attendant upon intrusions resulting from the discovery and trial process are significant factors to be considered. In an analogous context, Congress, it is fair to assume, weighed those concerns in deciding not to substitute the Government as defendant in suits seeking damages for constitutional violations. See 28 U.S.C. § 2679(b)(2)(A) (providing that certain provisions of the Federal Tort Claims Act do not apply to any claim against a federal employee "which is brought for a violation of the Constitution").

For these and other reasons, the Court's expressed caution as to implied causes of actions under congressional statutes led to similar caution with respect to actions in the *Bivens* context, where the action is implied to enforce the Constitution itself. Indeed, in light of the changes to the Court's general approach to recognizing implied damages remedies, it is possible that the analysis in the Court's three *Bivens* cases might have been different if they were decided today. To be sure, no congressional enactment has disapproved of these decisions. And it must be understood that this opinion is not intended to cast doubt on the continued force, or even the necessity, of *Bivens* in the search-and-seizure context in which it arose. *Bivens* does vindicate the Constitution by allowing some redress for injuries, and it provides instruction and guidance to federal law enforcement officers going forward. The settled law of *Bivens* in this common and recurrent sphere of law enforcement, and the undoubted reliance upon it as a fixed principle in the law, are powerful reasons to retain it in that sphere.[10]

Given the notable change in the Court's approach to recognizing implied causes of action, however, the Court has made clear that expanding the *Bivens* remedy is now a "disfavored" judicial activity. *Iqbal,* 556 U.S., at 675. This is in accord with the Court's observation that it has "consistently refused to extend *Bivens* to any new context or new category of defendants." *Correctional Services Corp. v. Malesko,* 534 U.S. 61, 68 (2001). Indeed, the Court has refused to do so for the past 30 years.

For example, the Court declined to create an implied damages remedy in the following cases: a First Amendment suit against a federal employer, *Bush v. Lucas,* 462 U.S. 367, 390 (1983); a race-discrimination suit against military officers, *Chappell v. Wallace,* 462 U.S. 296, 297, 304–305 (1983); a substantive due process suit against military officers, *United States v. Stanley,* 483 U.S. 669, 671–672, 683–684 (1987); a procedural due process suit against Social Security officials, *Schweiker v. Chilicky,* 487 U.S. 412, 414 (1988); a procedural due process suit against a federal agency for wrongful termination, *FDIC v. Meyer,* 510 U.S. 471, 473–474 (1994); an Eighth Amendment suit against a private prison operator, *Malesko, supra,* at 63; a due process suit against officials from the Bureau of Land Management, *Wilkie v. Robbins,* 551 U.S. 537, 547–548, 562 (2007); and an Eighth Amendment suit against prison guards at a private prison, *Minneci v. Pollard,* 565 U.S. 118, 120 (2012).

When a party seeks to assert an implied cause of action under the Constitution itself, just as when a party seeks to assert an implied cause of action under a federal statute, separation-of-powers principles are or should be central to the analysis. The question is "who should decide" whether to provide for a damages remedy, Congress or the courts? *Bush,* 462 U.S., at 380.

The answer most often will be Congress. When an issue " 'involves a host of considerations that must be weighed and appraised,' " it should be committed to " 'those who write the laws' " rather than " 'those who interpret them.' " *Ibid.* In most instances, the Court's precedents now instruct, the Legislature is in the better position

[10] **Questions:** Do you agree with Kennedy that if the Court were to recognize additional implied causes of action under the Constitution, then the Court might interfere with Congress's role in determining how best to vindicate constitutional rights? Why, then, does Kennedy not overrule *Bivens* completely?

to consider if " 'the public interest would be served' " by imposing a " 'new substantive legal liability.' " *Schweiker, supra*, at 426–427. As a result, the Court has urged "caution" before "extending *Bivens* remedies into any new context." *Malesko, supra*, at 74. The Court's precedents now make clear that a *Bivens* remedy will not be available if there are " 'special factors counselling hesitation in the absence of affirmative action by Congress.' " *Carlson*, 446 U.S., at 18 (quoting *Bivens*, 403 U.S., at 396).[11]

This Court has not defined the phrase "special factors counselling hesitation." The necessary inference, though, is that the inquiry must concentrate on whether the Judiciary is well suited, absent congressional action or instruction, to consider and weigh the costs and benefits of allowing a damages action to proceed. Thus, to be a "special factor counselling hesitation," a factor must cause a court to hesitate before answering that question in the affirmative.

It is not necessarily a judicial function to establish whole categories of cases in which federal officers must defend against personal liability claims in the complex sphere of litigation, with all of its burdens on some and benefits to others. It is true that, if equitable remedies prove insufficient, a damages remedy might be necessary to redress past harm and deter future violations. Yet the decision to recognize a damages remedy requires an assessment of its impact on governmental operations systemwide. Those matters include the burdens on Government employees who are sued personally, as well as the projected costs and consequences to the Government itself when the tort and monetary liability mechanisms of the legal system are used to bring about the proper formulation and implementation of public policies. These and other considerations may make it less probable that Congress would want the Judiciary to entertain a damages suit in a given case.

Sometimes there will be doubt because the case arises in a context in which Congress has designed its regulatory authority in a guarded way, making it less likely that Congress would want the Judiciary to interfere. And sometimes there will be doubt because some other feature of a case—difficult to predict in advance—causes a court to pause before acting without express congressional authorization. In sum, if there are sound reasons to think Congress might doubt the efficacy or necessity of a damages remedy as part of the system for enforcing the law and correcting a wrong, the courts must refrain from creating the remedy in order to respect the role of Congress in determining the nature and extent of federal-court jurisdiction under Article III. . . .[12]

III

It is appropriate now to turn first to the *Bivens* claims challenging the conditions of confinement imposed on respondents pursuant to the formal policy adopted by the Executive Officials in the wake of the September 11 attacks. . . . [This is a two-part test: First, does this case present a new *Bivens* context? If so, do "special factors" counsel hesitation?]

The proper test for determining whether a case presents a new *Bivens* context is as follows. If the case is different in a meaningful way from previous *Bivens* cases decided by this Court, then the context is new. Without endeavoring to create an

---

11 **Question:** Kennedy here offers a two-part test: (1) if a plaintiff presents a situation that is a "new context" with respect to *Bivens*, then (2) the Court will decline to recognize an implied cause of action if any factor causes a court to "hesitate." In light of how Kennedy applies this test in Part III of this opinion, can you imagine any context in which the Court would recognize a new type of *Bivens* claim?

12 **Question:** Read charitably, Kennedy's opinion appears to be inviting Congress to enact a statute allowing individuals in Abbasi's position to sue federal officials for damages for violating the Constitution. Why do you think Congress has not yet done so?

exhaustive list of differences that are meaningful enough to make a given context a new one, some examples might prove instructive. A case might differ in a meaningful way because of the rank of the officers involved; the constitutional right at issue; the generality or specificity of the official action; the extent of judicial guidance as to how an officer should respond to the problem or emergency to be confronted; the statutory or other legal mandate under which the officer was operating; the risk of disruptive intrusion by the Judiciary into the functioning of other branches; or the presence of potential special factors that previous *Bivens* cases did not consider.

In the present suit, respondents' detention policy claims challenge the confinement conditions imposed on illegal aliens pursuant to a high-level executive policy created in the wake of a major terrorist attack on American soil. Those claims bear little resemblance to the three *Bivens* claims the Court has approved in the past: a claim against FBI agents for handcuffing a man in his own home without a warrant; a claim against a Congressman for firing his female secretary; and a claim against prison officials for failure to treat an inmate's asthma. . . . [This is therefore] a new *Bivens* context. [So] a special factors analysis [i]s required before allowing this damages suit to proceed.

After considering the special factors necessarily implicated by the detention policy claims, the Court now holds that those factors show that whether a damages action should be allowed is a decision for the Congress to make, not the courts.

With respect to the claims against the Executive Officials, it must be noted that a *Bivens* action . . . would call into question the formulation and implementation of a general policy. This, in turn, would necessarily require inquiry and discovery into the whole course of the discussions and deliberations that led to the policies and governmental acts being challenged. These consequences counsel against allowing a *Bivens* action against the Executive Officials, for the burden and demand of litigation might well prevent them—or, to be more precise, future officials like them—from devoting the time and effort required for the proper discharge of their duties. See *Cheney v. United States Dist. Court*, 542 U.S. 367, 382 (2004) (noting "the paramount necessity of protecting the Executive Branch from vexatious litigation that might distract it from the energetic performance of its constitutional duties"). . . .

In addition to this special factor, which applies to the claims against the Executive Officials, there are three other special factors that apply as well to the detention policy claims against all of the petitioners. First, respondents' detention policy claims challenge more than standard law enforcement operations. They challenge as well major elements of the Government's whole response to the September 11 attacks, thus of necessity requiring an inquiry into sensitive issues of national security. . . . National-security policy is the prerogative of the Congress and President. See U.S. Const. Art. I, § 8; Art. II, § 1, § 2. Judicial inquiry into the national-security realm raises concerns for the separation of powers in trenching on matters committed to the other branches. These concerns are even more pronounced when the judicial inquiry comes in the context of a claim seeking money damages rather than a claim seeking injunctive or other equitable relief. The risk of personal damages liability is more likely to cause an official to second-guess difficult but necessary decisions concerning national-security policy. . . .

[Second], in any inquiry respecting the likely or probable intent of Congress, the silence of Congress is relevant; and here that silence is telling. In the almost 16 years since September 11, the Federal Government's responses to that terrorist attack have been well documented. . . . Indeed, at Congress' behest, the Department of Justice's Office of the Inspector General compiled a 300-page report documenting the conditions in the MDC in great detail. Nevertheless, "[a]t no point did Congress choose to extend to any person the kind of remedies that respondents seek in this lawsuit." *Schweiker*, 487 U.S., at 426. . . . This silence is notable because it is likely that high-level policies will attract the attention of Congress. Thus, when Congress fails to provide a damages remedy in circumstances like these, it is much more difficult to believe that "congressional inaction" was "inadvertent." *Id.*, at 423.

It is of central importance, too, that this is not a case like *Bivens* or *Davis* in which "it is damages or nothing." Unlike the plaintiffs in those cases, respondents do not challenge individual instances of discrimination or law enforcement overreach, which due to their very nature are difficult to address except by way of damages actions after the fact. Respondents instead challenge large-scale policy decisions concerning the conditions of confinement imposed on hundreds of prisoners. To address those kinds of decisions, detainees may seek injunctive relief. And in addition to that, we have left open the question whether they might be able to challenge their confinement conditions via a petition for a writ of habeas corpus. . . . Indeed, the habeas remedy, if necessity required its use, would have provided a faster and more direct route to relief than a suit for money damages. A successful habeas petition would have required officials to place respondents in less-restrictive conditions immediately; yet this damages suit remains unresolved some 15 years later. . . . In sum, respondents had available to them other alternative forms of judicial relief. And when alternative methods of relief are available, a *Bivens* remedy usually is not.[13]

There is a persisting concern, of course, that absent a *Bivens* remedy there will be insufficient deterrence to prevent officers from violating the Constitution. In circumstances like those presented here, however, the stakes on both sides of the argument are far higher than in past cases the Court has considered. . . . The proper balance is one for the Congress, not the Judiciary, to undertake. For all of these reasons, the Court of Appeals erred by allowing respondents' detention policy claims to proceed under *Bivens*. . . .

NOTE: "NEW CONTEXTS" AND "SPECIAL FACTORS"

In *Abbasi*, the Supreme Court reaffirmed that courts should exercise " 'caution' before 'extending *Bivens* remedies into any new context.' " *Abbasi*, 137 S. Ct. at 1857. If the court does conclude that the claim arises in a "new context," the Court highlighted, *Bivens* will not be an available remedy "if there are 'special factors counselling hesitation in the absence of affirmative action by Congress.' " *Id.* The "new context" and "special factors" questions have since been seen as a two-step inquiry in determining whether a *Bivens* remedy is available.

The Court recently applied this two-step test in *Hernandez v. Mesa*, 140 S. Ct. 735 (2020). There, the Court held that the family of Sergio Hernandez, a fifteen-year-old boy killed on Mexican soil by a U.S. border patrol agent, could not recover under *Bivens* because this shooting occurred in a "new context" and "special factors" counseled hesitation. *Hernandez*, 140 S. Ct. at 743. Although the Court had previously recognized in *Bivens* itself that an implied cause of action existed for Fourth Amendment violations, Justice Samuel Alito wrote that "[t]here is a world of difference between those claims and petitioners' cross-border shooting claims, where 'the risk of disruptive

[13] **Question:** Kennedy here notes an important caveat to the Court's *Bivens* jurisprudence. As in this case, the Court looks unfavorably on implied causes of action for *damages*. At the same time, the Court has been quite willing to recognize implied causes of action for *injunctive relief*. This distinction will be discussed in more detail later (section 36.3), but can you think of any reason why damages might be more disruptive to the separation of powers than injunctions?

intrusion by the Judiciary into the functioning of other branches' is significant." *Id.* at 744 (quoting *Abbasi*, 137 S. Ct. at 1859–60). After determining that this "world of difference" represented a "new context," Alito applied the "special factors" prong and determined that there were multiple special factors counseling hesitation. These included (1) "the potential effect on foreign relations," *id.*; (2) "the risk of undermining border security," *id.* at 747; and (3) the Court's prior conclusions that § 1983 and other federal statutes typically do not extend remedies to victims of harm outside of the United States, *id.*

36.3 IMPLIED CAUSES OF ACTION FOR INJUNCTIVE RELIEF (§ 1331)

Bivens v. Six Unknown Named Agents of the Federal Bureau of Narcotics, 403 U.S. 388 (1971), and its follow-on cases, such as *Ziglar v. Abbasi*, 137 S. Ct. 1843 (2017), all address implied causes of action for *damages*. Had Ahmer Iqbal Abbasi been successful in his suit, John Ashcroft, the former attorney general, and other officials would have had to pay him and the other former prisoners money for their unconstitutional mistreatment. But as the *Abbasi* Court noted toward the end of its opinion, an implied cause of action for damages is distinct from an implied cause of action for *injunctive relief*. The Court contrasted *Bivens* actions with injunctions, approving of the latter as the typical method of challenging "large-scale policy decisions."

As law professor Steven Vladek has observed, there is a considerable amount of "tension" between the Supreme Court's hostility to implied causes of action for damages in *Abbasi* and the Court's approval in the same case of implied causes of action for injunctive relief. Stephen I. Vladeck, *The Inconsistent Originalism of Judge-Made Remedies Against Federal Officers*, 96 Notre Dame L. Rev. 1869, 1871 (2021). Regardless of the type of relief Abbasi wanted, he and others in his position were suing a federal officer for relief in a circumstance where no statute clearly and explicitly provides a cause of action. Yet the *Abbasi* Court narrowly interpreted Abbasi's ability to receive damages while keeping open his ability to receive an injunction. "The Supreme Court has never attempted to explain—or justify—the methodological (and historiographical) dichotomy between the propriety [or not] of judge-made prospective and retrospective relief against federal officers." *Id.*

One explanation for the Court's disapproval of implied actions for damages and approval of implied actions for injunctive relief is a historical one: actions for damages and actions for injunctive relief have very different histories.

In English and early American law, there were often two types of courts: common-law courts and courts of equity. If prospective plaintiffs wanted a court to compel another person to pay them money to remedy an injury, the plaintiffs went to a common-law court, where they had to prove each formal element of a particular action. But money cannot remedy all injuries. Money is particularly useless for remedying ongoing or future conduct by another person, where all the plaintiff wants is for the other person to stop. *See* Samuel L. Bray, *Equity: Notes on the American Reception*, *in Equity and Law* 32–37 (John C.P. Goldberg, Henry E. Smith & P.G. Turner eds., 2019).

In contrast with common-law courts, courts of equity were given flexible powers to basically tell people what to do—with the traditional limitation that they could act only to remedy an "irreparable injury" or an injury that could not be adequately remedied at law by an award of monetary damages. *See* Vladeck, *supra*, at 1881. A common form of relief issued by a court of equity was an *injunction*: an order to do things (e.g., perform your end of a contract) or not to do things (e.g., stop a nuisance). *Id.* Today, federal courts continue to award temporary or permanent injunctions frequently. *See* Fed. R. Civ. P. 65. To evaluate whether a preliminary injunction is warranted, federal courts today ask whether the plaintiff can establish "that he is likely to succeed on the merits, that he is likely to suffer irreparable harm in the absence of preliminary relief, that the balance of equities tips in his favor, and that an injunction is in the public interest." *Winter v. Nat. Res. Def. Council, Inc.*, 555 U.S. 7 (2008).

When Congress enacted the Judiciary Act of 1789, ch. 20, 1 Stat. 73, and the Judiciary Act of 1875, ch. 137, 18 Stat. 470, it didn't distinguish between common-law courts and courts of equity. It simply authorized federal courts to hear "all suits of a civil nature at common law or in equity"—an authorization that is now codified at 28 U.S.C. § 1331. *See* Judiciary Act of 1789, 1 Stat. at 78; Judiciary Act of 1875, 18 Stat. at 470; Bray, *supra*, at 37.

Even after the Supreme Court began the elimination of federal common law in *Erie Railroad Co. v. Tompkins*, 304 U.S. 64 (1938), litigants continued to cite § 1331's grant of equitable jurisdiction as a cause of action when seeking injunctions instead of damages. John F. Duffy, *Administrative Common Law in Judicial Review*, 77 Tex. L. Rev. 113, 122 (1998). From these litigants' perspective, "the 1875 grant of jurisdiction [was] best interpreted as an authorization for federal equity courts to engage in lawmaking." *Id.* Indeed, before Congress enacted the Administrative Procedure Act of 1946 (APA), Pub. L. No. 79–404, 60 Stat. 237 (codified at 5 U.S.C. § 702), these grants of equitable jurisdiction were the only statutes that authorized federal courts to engage in judicial review of federal agency action. Duffy, *supra*, at 122, 146–52. As law professor John F. Duffy writes,

> [t]he traditional equitable avenue of review remains and, because its pedigree can be traced back to a statute authorizing judge-made law, its survival should not be threatened by the demise of [federal common law]. Thus, a litigant having no other statutory authority for judicial review may unabashedly point to Section 1331 as the basis for injunctive relief.

Id. at 148.

36.3.1

Armstrong v. Exceptional Child Center, Inc.

575 U.S. 320 (2015)

Although the Supreme Court has been inconsistent about recognizing the effect of § 1331, the existence of federal equitable jurisdiction has led the Court to hear cases seeking injunctions even in areas where the causes of action created by 42 U.S.C. § 1983 or the APA don't apply. Neither statute, for example, creates a cause of action for injunctive relief against the president. Yet without commenting on the absence of an express cause of action, the Supreme Court has repeatedly heard cases seeking to enjoin a president's executive orders as unconstitutional. *See, e.g.*, *Trump v. Nat'l Ass'n for the Advancement of Colored People*, 140 S. Ct. 1891 (2020); *Trump v. Hawaii*, 138 S. Ct. 2392 (2018); *Clinton v. City of New York*, 524 U.S. 417 (1998); *Youngstown Sheet & Tube Co. v. Sawyer*, 343 U.S. 579 (1952). The Court granted certiorari to consider this question in *Trump v. Sierra Club*, 141 S. Ct. 618 (2020), a case involving President Donald Trump's dedication of funds to construct a border wall. But the inauguration of President Joe Biden rendered the case moot.

Because *Sierra Club* was never decided, the Supreme Court's most recent discussion of implied causes of action for injunctive relief was in *Armstrong v. Exceptional Child Center, Inc.*, 575 U.S. 320 (2015). As discussed earlier with regard to preemption (sections 2.1, 11.2), when a state law conflicts with a federal law, the Supremacy Clause of Article VI requires the federal law to control. Following the logic of *J.I. Case Co. v. Borak*, 377 U.S. 426 (1964), and *Bivens*, it was once common for plaintiffs to challenge preempted state laws by either invoking an implied cause of action under a federal statute or by invoking an implied cause of action under the Supremacy Clause itself. As the Supreme Court retreated from both options, the method for challenging these sorts of statutes became less obvious. The Supreme Court attempted to clarify where implied causes of action for equitable relief come from in *Armstrong*, which sought to enjoin the Idaho Department of Health and Welfare from violating Section 30(a) of the Medicaid Act of 1968, Pub. L. No. 90–248, 81 Stat. 821, 911. The act required states to reimburse in-home health-care providers at a rate higher than what Idaho was paying; and the plaintiffs, a group of in-home health-care providers, sued on the ground that the Supremacy Clause contained an implied cause of action.

The Supreme Court rejected their argument while recognizing the legitimacy of an implied cause of action for equitable relief.

■ JUSTICE SCALIA delivered the opinion of the Court.

We consider whether Medicaid providers can sue to enforce § (30)(A) of the Medicaid Act. 81 Stat. 911. . . .

II

The Supremacy Clause, Art. VI, cl. 2, reads:

> This Constitution, and the Laws of the United States which shall be made in Pursuance thereof; and all Treaties made, or which shall be made, under the Authority of the United States, shall be the supreme Law of the Land; and the Judges in every State shall be bound thereby, any Thing in the Constitution or Laws of any State to the Contrary notwithstanding.[14]

It is apparent that this Clause creates a rule of decision: Courts "shall" regard the "Constitution," and all laws "made in Pursuance thereof," as "the supreme Law of the Land." They must not give effect to state laws that conflict with federal laws. It is equally apparent that the Supremacy Clause is not the " 'source of any federal rights,' " *Golden State Transit Corp. v. Los Angeles*, 493 U.S. 103, 107 (1989), and certainly does not create a cause of action. It instructs courts what to do when state and federal law clash, but is silent regarding who may enforce federal laws in court, and in what circumstances they may do so.

Hamilton wrote that the Supremacy Clause "only declares a truth, which flows immediately and necessarily from the institution of a Federal Government." The Federalist No. 33, p. 207 (J. Cooke ed.1961). And Story described the Clause as "a positive affirmance of that, which is necessarily implied." 3 Commentaries on the Constitution of the United States § 1831, p. 693 (1833). These descriptions would have been grossly inapt if the Clause were understood to give affected parties a constitutional (and hence congressionally unalterable) right to enforce federal laws against the States. . . .

Additionally, it is important to read the Supremacy Clause in the context of the Constitution as a whole. Article I vests Congress with broad discretion over the manner of implementing its enumerated powers, giving it authority to "make all Laws which shall be necessary and proper for carrying [them] into Execution." Art. I, § 8. We have said that this confers upon the Legislature "that discretion, with respect to the means by which the powers [the Constitution] confers are to be carried into execution, which will enable that body to perform the high duties assigned to it," *McCulloch v. Maryland*, 4 Wheat. 316, 421 (1819). It is unlikely that the Constitution gave Congress such broad discretion with regard to the enactment of laws, while simultaneously limiting Congress's power over the manner of their implementation, making it impossible to leave the enforcement of federal law to federal actors. If the Supremacy Clause includes a private right of action, then the Constitution *requires* Congress to permit the enforcement of its laws by private actors, significantly curtailing its ability to guide the implementation of federal law. It would be strange indeed to give a clause that makes federal law supreme a reading that *limits* Congress's power to enforce that law, by imposing mandatory private enforcement—a limitation unheard-of with regard to state legislatures.

To say that the Supremacy Clause does not confer a right of action is not to diminish the significant role that courts play in assuring the supremacy of federal law. For once a case or controversy properly comes before a court, judges are bound by federal law. Thus, a court may not convict a criminal defendant of violating a state law that federal law prohibits. Similarly, a court may not hold a civil defendant liable under state law for conduct federal law requires. And, as we have long recognized, if an individual claims federal law immunizes him from state regulation, the court may

---

[14] **As You Read, Consider:** Even as Justice Antonin Scalia writes that the Constitution does not itself imply causes of action, he observes that American law has a long tradition of allowing courts of equity to create implied causes of action for equitable relief. What is the standard he uses to define when implied causes of action for equitable relief are appropriate?

issue an injunction upon finding the state regulatory actions preempted. *Ex parte Young*, 209 U.S. 123, 155–156 (1908).

Respondents contend that our preemption jurisprudence—specifically, the fact that we have regularly considered whether to enjoin the enforcement of state laws that are alleged to violate federal law—demonstrates that the Supremacy Clause creates a cause of action for its violation. They are incorrect. It is true enough that we have long held that federal courts may in some circumstances grant injunctive relief against state officers who are violating, or planning to violate, federal law. See, *e.g.*, *Osborn v. Bank of United States*, 9 Wheat. 738, 838–839, 844 (1824); *Ex parte Young, supra*, at 150–151. But that has been true not only with respect to violations of federal law by state officials, but also with respect to violations of federal law by federal officials. See *American School of Magnetic Healing v. McAnnulty*, 187 U.S. 94, 110 (1902). Thus, the Supremacy Clause need not be (and in light of our textual analysis above, cannot be) the explanation. What our cases demonstrate is that, "in a proper case, relief may be given in a court of equity . . . to prevent an injurious act by a public officer." *Carroll v. Safford*, 3 How. 441, 463 (1845).

The ability to sue to enjoin unconstitutional actions by state and federal officers is the creation of courts of equity, and reflects a long history of judicial review of illegal executive action, tracing back to England. See Jaffe & Henderson, Judicial Review and the Rule of Law: Historical Origins, 72 L.Q. Rev. 345 (1956). It is a judge-made remedy, and we have never held or even suggested that, in its application to state officers, it rests upon an implied right of action contained in the Supremacy Clause. . . .[15]

III

We turn next to respondents' contention that, quite apart from any cause of action conferred by the Supremacy Clause, this suit can proceed against Idaho in equity.

The power of federal courts of equity to enjoin unlawful executive action is subject to express and implied statutory limitations. See, *e.g.*, *Seminole Tribe of Fla. v. Florida*, 517 U.S. 44, 74 (1996). Courts of equity can no more disregard statutory and constitutional requirements and provisions than can courts of law. In our view the Medicaid Act implicitly precludes private enforcement of § 30(A), and respondents cannot, by invoking our equitable powers, circumvent Congress's exclusion of private enforcement.

Two aspects of § 30(A) establish Congress's intent to foreclose equitable relief. First, the sole remedy Congress provided for a State's failure to comply with Medicaid's requirements . . . is the withholding of Medicaid funds by the Secretary of Health and Human Services. 42 U.S.C. § 1396c. As we have elsewhere explained, the "express provision of one method of enforcing a substantive rule suggests that Congress intended to preclude others." *Alexander v. Sandoval*, 532 U.S. 275, 290 (2001). . . .

It is [also] difficult to imagine a requirement broader and less specific than § 30(A)'s mandate that state plans provide for payments that are "consistent with efficiency, economy, and quality of care," all the while "safeguard[ing] against unnecessary utilization of . . . care and services." Explicitly conferring enforcement of this judgment-laden standard upon the Secretary alone establishes, we think, that Congress "wanted to make the agency remedy that it provided exclusive," thereby

---

15 **Questions:** Scalia observes that the ability to sue to enjoin unconstitutional actions by federal officers is a creation of courts of equity, not a necessary implication of the Constitution. Why, then, does he proceed in Part III to hold that such equitable relief is unavailable in this case? What would have to change for equitable relief to be available?

achieving "the expertise, uniformity, widespread consultation, and resulting administrative guidance that can accompany agency decisionmaking," and avoiding "the comparative risk of inconsistent interpretations and misincentives that can arise out of an occasional inappropriate application of the statute in a private action." . . .

PART FOUR

THE STATES

CHAPTER 37

WHAT ARE THE POWERS "RESERVED TO THE STATES"?

ARTICLE I, SECTION 8, CLAUSE 3: The Congress shall have Power . . . To regulate Commerce with foreign Nations, and among the several States, and with the Indian Tribes. . . .

TENTH AMENDMENT (1791): The powers not delegated to the United States by the Constitution, nor prohibited by it to the States, are reserved to the States respectively, or to the people.

37.1 THE POLICE POWER

Whenever any branch of the federal government does anything, it typically must point to a clause of the Constitution that gives it express or implied powers to act. This is because the Constitution was designed principally to empower and limit a new federal government.

Things are different with states. Although several clauses of the federal Constitution give state legislatures specific powers over elections and amendments, states derive the vast majority of their powers from their own constitutions. As the Tenth Amendment declares, "[t]he powers not delegated to the United States by the Constitution, nor prohibited by it to the States, are reserved to the States respectively, or to the people."

States, in other words, can do far more than regulate commerce or levy indirect taxes. As the Supreme Court has observed many times over its history, the Tenth Amendment reserves to the states a general "police power." The Court most comprehensively defined this police power in *City of New York v. Miln*, considering the following positions "impregnable":

> That a state has the same undeniable and unlimited jurisdiction over all persons and things, within its territorial limits, as any foreign nation; where that jurisdiction is not surrendered or restrained by the constitution of the United States. That, by virtue of this, it is not only the right, but the bounden and solemn duty of a state, to advance the safety, happiness and prosperity of its people, and to provide for its general welfare, by any and every act of legislation, which it may deem to be conducive to these ends. . . . That all those powers which relate to merely municipal legislation, or what may perhaps, more properly be called internal police, are not thus surrendered or restrained; and that, consequently, in relation to these, the authority of a state is complete, unqualified, and exclusive.

36 U.S. (11 Pet.) 102, 139 (1837). In dozens of subsequent cases, the Court has reiterated that states have near-plenary authority to legislate for the health, welfare, and safety of their people—subject to the limits of the federal Constitution. *See, e.g.*, *Nebbia v. New York*, 291 U.S. 502, 523–29 (1934).

37.2 THE NEGATIVE COMMERCE CLAUSE AND REGULATION

In declaring that the powers not delegated to the United States are "reserved" to the states, the Tenth Amendment contains an important implication: the powers that *are* delegated to the United States are *not* necessarily reserved to the states. Even before the Tenth Amendment was adopted, the *dual sovereignty doctrine*, which we discussed in the context of the Taxing Clause and Commerce Clause, held that most of the powers delegated to Congress were "exclusive" and therefore couldn't be exercised by the states. *See The Federalist No. 32*, at 199–203 (Alexander Hamilton) (Jacob Cooke ed., 1961). During the ratification debates, Alexander Hamilton and James Madison repeatedly asserted that the principal aim of the Commerce Clause in particular was to protect a national market from economic discrimination or tariffs imposed by individual states against one another. *See, e.g.*, *id. No. 7*, at 39–41 (Alexander Hamilton); *id. No. 11*, at 65–73 (Alexander Hamilton); *id. No. 42*, at 283–84 (James Madison). And in *Gibbons v. Ogden*, the Supreme Court reiterated that while states could regulate the commerce within their borders as part of their "immense mass of legislation, which embraces every thing within the territory of a State," states could *not* necessarily regulate commerce with foreign nations or among the several states. 22 U.S. (9 Wheat.) 1, 203–04 (1824).

During the opening decades of the United States' history, the Court repeatedly considered whether to strike down state legislation for intruding on the power of Congress to regulate interstate and foreign commerce. *See, e.g.*, *Cooley v. Bd. of Wardens of the Port of Phila.*, 53 U.S. (12 How.) 299 (1851) (upholding a state law requiring ships to obtain pilots, or guides, to navigate the Port of Philadelphia); *The License Cases*, 46 U.S. (5 How.) 504 (1847) (upholding, in six separate opinions with no majority, state statutes that regulated the sale of alcoholic beverages brought in from other states); *Willson v. Black Bird Creek Marsh Co.*, 27 U.S. (2 Pet.) 245 (1829) (rejecting a challenge to a state dam across a navigable creek). The Court's most consequential opinion during this era was *The Passenger Cases*, in which it struck down a group of New York and Massachusetts laws that taxed and regulated the admission of new immigrants. But the decision drew eight separate opinions with no clear holding. Only a few of the justices agreed that the power to regulate foreign or interstate commerce was "exclusively vested in Congress." 48 U.S. (7 How.) 283, 400 (1849) (McLean, J.).

The negative implications of the Commerce Clause on state power finally crystallized in the 1850s when the states of Virginia and Ohio authorized the construction of the Wheeling Suspension Bridge. The bridge would have crossed the Ohio River near what is now the region separating West Virginia, Ohio, and Pennsylvania. The Pennsylvania state legislature sued to enjoin construction of the bridge for several reasons, including that it threatened to block steamboat traffic on the Ohio River. In *Pennsylvania v. Wheeling & Belmont Bridge Co.*, 54 U.S. (13 How.) 518 (1852), the Supreme Court agreed with Pennsylvania. It held that the bridge needed to be raised because its low height literally blocked the interstate commerce of ships that couldn't pass underneath. But after the decision, Virginia and Ohio successfully lobbied Congress to pass a statute declaring the bridge a lawful structure. In a second decision after Congress enacted the new federal statute, the Court held that the bridge could open as originally planned. *See Pennsylvania v. Wheeling & Belmont Bridge Co.*, 59 U.S. (18 How.) 421 (1856). The Court explained that even though the bridge originally intruded into Congress's exclusive power to regulate interstate commerce, the Commerce Clause gave Congress "the power to determine what shall or shall not be deemed in judgment of law an obstruction to navigation." *Id.* at 431.

After the *Wheeling Bridge* case, the Court's interpretation of the Commerce Clause's applicability to the states became a doctrine known as the "Negative Commerce Clause" (also called the "Dormant Commerce Clause"). The doctrine held that Congress had the exclusive power to regulate interstate commerce—a power that Congress could authorize the states to exercise. *See, e.g.*, *Prudential Ins. Co. v. Benjamin*, 328 U.S. 408 (1946) (discussing the effect of the McCarran-Ferguson Act of 1945, Pub. L. No. 79–15, 59 Stat. 33); Webb-Kenyon Act of 1913, Pub. L. No. 62–398, 37 Stat. 699 (authorizing states to regulate direct shipments of imports after *Bowman v. Chi. & Nw. Ry. Co.*, 125 U.S. 465 (1888)). But absent congressional authorization, the Court held that states typically had no power to "directly" regulate or interfere with interstate commerce, such as by setting rates on how much interstate railroads could charge. *Wabash, St. Louis & Pac. Ry. Co. v. Illinois*, 118 U.S. 557, 571 (1886).

Through the 1950s, the general prohibition on state regulation of interstate commerce had two exceptions. First, states could pass laws that "indirectly" regulated interstate commerce if their primary purpose was to regulate in-state activities. *See, e.g.*, *Ry. Express Agency v. Virginia* (*Ry. Express II*), 358 U.S. 434, 445 (1959) (upholding a state law that regulated the privilege of doing business in a corporate form within the state, even though it indirectly affected out-of-state businesses). Second, states could directly regulate interstate commerce or transportation networks to the extent necessary to protect the health or safety of their residents. *See, e.g.*, *Welch Co. v. New Hampshire*, 306 U.S. 79, 85 (1939) (upholding a law setting the maximum hours anyone could operate a motor vehicle); *Kane v. New Jersey*, 242 U.S. 160, 169 (1916) (upholding a car registration law).

But both exceptions were narrowly interpreted, and the Negative Commerce Clause became the most important limitation on state power next to the Contracts Clause and the Fourteenth Amendment. *See* Ezra Prentice & John Egan, *The Commerce Clause of the Federal Constitution* 14 (1898). Even when states argued that their regulations only indirectly affected interstate commerce or were designed to protect the health and safety of residents, the Supreme Court routinely struck down state laws regulating who could do business in the state. *See, e.g., Dahnke-Walker Co. v. Bondurant*, 257 U.S. 282, 303 (1921).

This interpretation of the Negative Commerce Clause began to change in *Southern Pacific Co. v. Arizona*, 325 U.S. 761 (1945), a case evaluating an Arizona law that restricted the length of trains. Rather than evaluate whether the law was motivated by health or safety, and rather than consider whether the burden on interstate commerce was direct or indirect, the Court instead adopted a balancing test. The Court explained that the purpose of its Negative Commerce Clause doctrine was to reconcile "the conflicting claims of state and national power," which could "be attained only by some appraisal and accommodation of the competing demands of the state and national interests involved." *S. Pac. Co.*, 325 U.S. at 769. To accommodate these competing demands, the Court considered

> the nature and extent of the burden which the state regulation of interstate trains, adopted as a safety measure, imposes on interstate commerce, and whether the relative weights of the state and national interests involved are such as to make inapplicable the rule, generally observed, that the free flow of interstate commerce and its freedom from local restraints . . . are interests safeguarded by the commerce clause from state interference.

Id. at 770–71. In this particular case, the Court concluded that the Arizona law was unjustified given the burden it imposed on railroads that passed through the state. *Id.* at 783.

37.2.1

Pike v. Bruce Church, Inc.

397 U.S. 137 (1970)

The Supreme Court adopted its modern interpretation of the Negative Commerce Clause, which evolved from the *Southern Pacific Co.* case, in another Arizona case—this one involving cantaloupes.

Under Arizona law, all cantaloupes grown in Arizona and offered for sale had to be packed in standardized crates. The crates indicated the cantaloupes' quality and their state of origin: Arizona. Bruce Church,

Inc., a commercial farming company in the exceptional growing environment of western Arizona, operated a cantaloupe farm that was nowhere near any packing facilities in the state. The company instead transported its uncrated, high-quality cantaloupes thirty miles across the border to a small town in California, where they could be packed in "California" crates and distributed elsewhere. But Loren Pike, the officer charged with enforcing the Arizona law, ordered the company to stop transporting uncrated cantaloupes across state lines. Pike argued that consumers might be confused and think that California cantaloupes were as good as Arizona cantaloupes.

The Arizona law didn't explicitly contemplate interstate commerce; it simply applied to all cantaloupes grown in the state. But Pike's order did have the effect of blocking the interstate travel of cantaloupes. Bruce Church claimed that if it had to build its own packing facility, it would cost $200,000.

In evaluating whether Pike's order violated the Negative Commerce Clause, the Court in *Pike v. Bruce Church, Inc.*, 397 U.S. 137 (1970), applied a new test to determine when incidental burdens on interstate commerce were constitutional. Arizona failed the test.

■ MR. JUSTICE STEWART delivered the opinion of the Court.[1]

The appellee is a company engaged in extensive commercial farming operations in Arizona and California. The appellant is the official charged with enforcing the Arizona Fruit and Vegetable Standardization Act. A provision of the Act requires that, with certain exceptions, all cantaloupes grown in Arizona and offered for sale must "be packed in regular compact arrangement in closed standard containers approved by the supervisor. . . ." Invoking his authority under that provision, the appellant issued an order prohibiting the appellee company from transporting uncrated cantaloupes from its Parker, Arizona, ranch to nearby Blythe, California, for packing and processing. The company then brought this action in a federal court to enjoin the order as unconstitutional. . . .

The appellant's threshold contention here is that even though the challenged order expressly forbids the interstate bulk shipment of the company's cantaloupes, it imposes no burden upon interstate commerce. If the Arizona Act is complied with, he argues, all that will be regulated will be the intrastate packing of goods destined for interstate commerce. Articles being made ready for interstate movement are not

---

1 **As You Read, Consider:** Where the first half of this casebook focused on constitutional provisions that gave the federal government *power* to act, the remainder focuses on provisions that *limit* the federal or state governments.

The Supreme Court typically evaluates whether laws are compatible with constitutional limits by applying one of three types of tests. First, a ***deferential means-ends test*** allows a government to overcome the limit as long as its law is "appropriate" or "rationally related" to a "legitimate" purpose. This sort of test is often called a ***rational-basis test*** and signifies that the Court thinks that the constitutional limit should be applied deferentially. Second, a ***least-restrictive-means test*** allows a government to overcome the limit only if the law is "necessary" or "narrowly tailored" to serve an "overriding" or "compelling" purpose. This sort of test is often called ***strict scrutiny*** and signifies that the Court thinks that the constitutional limit should be applied rigorously. Finally, a ***proportionality*** test allows a government to overcome the limit if the "benefit" or "state interest" served by the law outweighs the "burden" or "harm" that the law imposes. This sort of test is sometimes called a ***balancing test***.

Which of these three tests does Justice Potter Stewart use to evaluate the constitutionality of state laws whose interference with interstate commerce is "only incidental"? Why?

necessarily yet in interstate commerce, which, he says, begins only when the articles are delivered to the interstate shipper. . . .

Although the criteria for determining the validity of state statutes affecting interstate commerce have been variously stated, the general rule that emerges can be phrased as follows: Where the statute regulates evenhandedly to effectuate a legitimate local public interest, and its effects on interstate commerce are only incidental, it will be upheld unless the burden imposed on such commerce is clearly excessive in relation to the putative local benefits. If a legitimate local purpose is found, then the question becomes one of degree. And the extent of the burden that will be tolerated will of course depend on the nature of the local interest involved, and on whether it could be promoted as well with a lesser impact on interstate activities. Occasionally the Court has candidly undertaken a balancing approach in resolving these issues, *Southern Pacific Co. v. Arizona,* 325 U. S. 761, but more frequently it has spoken in terms of "direct" and "indirect" effects and burdens. See, *e.g., Shafer v. Farmers Grain Co., supra.*

At the core of the Arizona Fruit and Vegetable Standardization Act are the requirements that fruits and vegetables shipped from Arizona meet certain standards of wholesomeness and quality, and that they be packed in standard containers in such a way that the outer layer or exposed portion of the pack does not "materially misrepresent" the quality of the lot as a whole. The impetus for the Act was the fear that some growers were shipping inferior or deceptively packaged produce, with the result that the reputation of Arizona growers generally was being tarnished and their financial return concomitantly reduced. It was to prevent this that the Act was passed in 1929. The State has stipulated that its primary purpose is to promote and preserve the reputation of Arizona growers by prohibiting deceptive packaging.

We are not, then, dealing here with "state legislation in the field of safety where the propriety of local regulation has long been recognized," or with an Act designed to protect consumers in Arizona from contaminated or unfit goods. Its purpose and design are simply to protect and enhance the reputation of growers within the State. These are surely legitimate state interests. We have upheld a State's power to require that produce packaged in the State be packaged in a particular kind of receptacle, *Pacific States Box & Basket Co. v. White,* 296 U. S. 176. And we have recognized the legitimate interest of a State in maximizing the financial return to an industry within it. *Parker v. Brown,* 317 U. S. 341. Therefore, as applied to Arizona growers who package their produce in Arizona, we may assume the constitutional validity of the Act. We may further assume that Arizona has full constitutional power to forbid the misleading use of its name on produce that was grown or packed elsewhere. And, to the extent the Act forbids the shipment of contaminated or unfit produce, it clearly rests on sure footing. For, as the Court has said, such produce is "not the legitimate subject of trade or commerce, nor within the protection of the commerce clause of the Constitution." *Sligh v. Kirkwood, supra,* at 60.

But application of the Act through the appellant's order to the appellee company has a far different impact, and quite a different purpose.[2] The cantaloupes grown by the company at Parker are of exceptionally high quality. The company does not pack them in Arizona and cannot do so without making a capital expenditure of approximately $200,000. It transports them in bulk to nearby Blythe, California, where they are sorted, inspected, packed, and shipped in containers that do not identify them as Arizona cantaloupes, but bear the name of their California packer. The appellant's order would forbid the company to pack its cantaloupes outside

---

[2] **Question:** In the previous paragraph, Stewart wrote that the Arizona statute was constitutional in most of its applications. Why does it run into constitutional problems as applied to the Bruce Church company?

Arizona, not for the purpose of keeping the reputation of its growers unsullied, but to enhance their reputation through the reflected good will of the company's superior produce. The appellant, in other words, is not complaining because the company is putting the good name of Arizona on an inferior or deceptively packaged product, but because it is not putting that name on a product that is superior and well packaged. As the appellant's brief puts the matter, "It is within Arizona's legitimate interest to require that interstate cantaloupe purchasers be informed that this high-quality Parker fruit was grown in Arizona."

Although it is not easy to see why the other growers of Arizona are entitled to benefit at the company's expense from the fact that it produces superior crops, we may assume that the asserted state interest is a legitimate one. But the State's tenuous interest in having the company's cantaloupes identified as originating in Arizona cannot constitutionally justify the requirement that the company build and operate an unneeded $200,000 packing plant in the State. The nature of that burden is, constitutionally, more significant than its extent. For the Court has viewed with particular suspicion state statutes requiring business operations to be performed in the home State that could more efficiently be performed elsewhere. Even where the State is pursuing a clearly legitimate local interest, this particular burden on commerce has been declared to be virtually *per se* illegal. *Foster-Fountain Packing Co. v. Haydel*, 278 U. S. 1; *Johnson v. Haydel*, 278 U. S. 16; *Toomer v. Witsell*, 334 U. S. 385.[3]

The appellant argues that the above cases are different because they involved statutes whose express or concealed purpose was to preserve or secure employment for the home State, while here the statute is a regulatory one and there is no hint of such a purpose. But in *Toomer v. Witsell*, *supra*, the Court indicated that such a burden upon interstate commerce is unconstitutional even in the absence of such a purpose. In *Toomer* the Court held invalid a South Carolina statute requiring that owners of shrimp boats licensed by the State to fish in the maritime belt off South Carolina must unload and pack their catch in that State before "shipping or transporting it to another State." What we said there applies to this case as well:

> "There was also uncontradicted evidence that appellants' costs would be materially increased by the necessity of having their shrimp unloaded and packed in South Carolina ports rather than at their home bases in Georgia where they maintain their own docking, warehousing, refrigeration and packing facilities. In addition, an inevitable concomitant of a statute requiring that work be done in South Carolina, even though that be economically disadvantageous to the fishermen, is to divert to South Carolina employment and business which might otherwise go to Georgia; the necessary tendency of the statute is to impose an artificial rigidity on the economic pattern of the industry." 334 U. S., at 403.

While the order issued under the Arizona statute does not impose such rigidity on an entire industry, it does impose just such a straitjacket on the appellee company with respect to the allocation of its interstate resources. Such an incidental consequence of a regulatory scheme could perhaps be tolerated if a more compelling state interest were involved. But here the State's interest is minimal at best—certainly less substantial than a State's interest in securing employment for its people. If the Commerce Clause forbids a State to require work to be done within its jurisdiction to promote local employment, then surely it cannot permit a State to require a person

[3] **Question:** Bruce Church complained that if it were forced to comply with Arizona's law, it would have to pay $200,000 to build an in-state packing plant. But suppose the cost of construction were $200. Would Stewart's test come out the same way?

to go into a local packing business solely for the sake of enhancing the reputation of other producers within its borders.[4]

37.2.2
West Lynn Creamery, Inc. v. Healy
512 U.S. 186 (1994)

In *Pike*, the Supreme Court announced a new test to evaluate when a state could impose an "incidental" burden on interstate commerce: "Where the statute regulates evenhandedly to effectuate a legitimate local public interest, and its effects on interstate commerce are only incidental, it will be upheld unless the burden imposed on such commerce is clearly excessive in relation to the putative local benefits." 397 U.S. at 142. The Court has since observed that "state laws frequently survive this *Pike* scrutiny, though not always, as in *Pike* itself." *Dep't of Revenue v. Davis*, 553 U.S. 328, 339 (2008).

But the *Pike* test applies only where a statute regulates *evenhandedly*. Some state laws, by contrast, have a purpose of regulating or discriminating against activities from other states. *See, e.g., Great Atl. & Pac. Tea Co. v. Cottrell*, 424 U.S. 366, 381 (1976) (invalidating a Mississippi law that required states to sign reciprocity agreements in order for their companies to conduct business in Mississippi). And in that circumstance, the Court has applied a far more restrictive test.

The Court announced a version of this alternative, more restrictive test in *Hunt v. Washington State Apple Advertising Commission*, 432 U.S. 333, 353–54 (1977). In the 1970s, Washington employed a nationally recognized grading system to categorize the quality of its apples. The state grading system was, in many respects, superior to a similar system used by the U.S. Department of Agriculture (USDA). But North Carolina enacted a law that prohibited any apples from being sold in North Carolina if they were labeled with grades assigned by a state department of agriculture but not the USDA. Apple growers from Washington challenged this North Carolina law, complaining that the law made it more expensive for them to sell apples in North Carolina.

The Supreme Court in *Hunt* agreed with the growers that the North Carolina law had "the practical effect of not only burdening interstate sales of Washington apples, but also discriminating against them." 432 U.S. at 350. The Court explained that the law (1) required apple growers from Washington but not North Carolina to pay extra costs to adjust their labels, (2) "stripped the competitive and economic advantages" enjoyed by the Washington apple growers thanks to their superior grading system, and (3) imposed a "leveling effect which insidiously operates to

[4] **Question:** The Negative Commerce Clause is a negative implication of Article I's grant of power to *Congress* as opposed to *the states*. Indeed, if Congress were concerned that Arizona's law was intruding into the federal government's powers, Congress could enact a statute preempting the state law. Why, then, is the *Supreme Court*, as opposed to *Congress*, deciding whether this Arizona law intrudes on Congress's power?

the advantage of local apple growers" because it prevented Washington growers from distinguishing their apples from North Carolina apples. *Id.* at 351. The Court declared that "[w]hen discrimination against commerce of the type we have found is demonstrated, the burden falls on the State to justify it both in terms of the local benefits flowing from the statute and the unavailability of nondiscriminatory alternatives adequate to preserve the local interests at stake." *Id.* The Court found that North Carolina couldn't pass this least-restrictive-means test because the only "local benefit[ ] flowing from the statute" was an illegitimate desire to protect in-state growers from out-of-state competitors.

Over the next two decades, the Court continued to strike down laws under this restrictive *Hunt* test whenever it found that the state law had the purpose or effect of discriminating against interstate commerce and couldn't be justified by anything other than economic protectionism. For example, the Court repeatedly invalidated state laws that prohibited the importation of solid and liquid waste from other states. *See, e.g., Fort Gratiot Sanitary Landfill v. Mich. Nat. Res. Dep't*, 504 U.S. 353, 367 (1992); *City of Philadelphia v. New Jersey*, 437 U.S. 617, 629 (1978). It also struck down state laws that prevented the sale of energy to other states. *New Eng. Power Co. v. New Hampshire*, 455 U.S. 331, 344 (1982). And it struck down laws that created local monopolies, such as a town's ordinance that required companies to process their waste at a local private station instead of outside the state. *C & A Carbone, Inc. v. Town of Clarkstown*, 511 U.S. 383, 394 (1994). In each case, the Court held that a guiding purpose of the Negative Commerce Clause was to prevent economic discrimination among states.

But it is not always straightforward to predict when the Supreme Court will consider a state law "evenhanded," requiring the flexible *Pike* balancing test that weighs burdens against benefits, or "discriminatory," requiring the restrictive *Hunt* test that requires proof of no nondiscriminatory alternatives. *See, e.g., Davis*, 553 U.S. at 353 (applying *Pike* to uphold a Kentucky law that made public bonds tax-exempt when issued by Kentucky but not when issued by private institutions or other states); *United Haulers Ass'n, Inc. v. Oneida-Herkimer Solid Waste Mgmt. Auth.*, 550 U.S. 330 (2007) (upholding as evenhanded a New York law that required waste to go through publicly owned facilities because laws that favor the government aren't discriminatory); *Minnesota v. Clover Leaf Creamery Co.*, 449 U.S. 456, 460, 474 (1981) (upholding as evenhanded a state law banning the sale of milk in plastic containers despite evidence that the law's purpose was to benefit the local dairy and pulpwood industries).

The following case, *West Lynn Creamery, Inc. v. Healy*, 512 U.S. 186 (1994), is an illustration of how the Court determines whether a state law is discriminatory. It also highlights a long-standing puzzle of

Negative Commerce Clause cases: When can a state subsidy to in-state businesses constitute a burden on interstate commerce?

During the 1990s, milk prices in Massachusetts were so low that dairy officials in the state government worried that state dairy farms would go out of business. To "preserve our local industry," "protect the public health," and "ensure a continuous and adequate supply of fresh milk for our market," the state's commissioner of agriculture, Jonathan Healy, announced that the state would pay a subsidy to local dairy producers. But rather than draw this subsidy out of the state treasury, Healy proposed that the money should come from an "assessment" levied against all dairy farms that sold milk in Massachusetts. In other words, if a New York dairy farm sold milk in Massachusetts, it would pay the same assessment as a Massachusetts dairy farm—but only the Massachusetts dairy farm would receive the subsidy.

The West Lynn Creamery was a Massachusetts business that processed out-of-state milk for sale in Massachusetts. It sued Healy to enjoin the plan, complaining that the plan was the equivalent of a tariff on out-of-state milk. The state's supreme judicial court upheld the plan as an evenhanded regulation that only incidentally burdened interstate commerce.

The Supreme Court reached a different conclusion.

■ JUSTICE STEVENS, delivered the opinion of the Court.[5]

A Massachusetts pricing order imposes an assessment on all fluid milk sold by dealers to Massachusetts retailers. About two-thirds of that milk is produced out of State. The entire assessment, however, is distributed to Massachusetts dairy farmers. The question presented is whether the pricing order unconstitutionally discriminates against interstate commerce. We hold that it does. . . .

The Commerce Clause vests Congress with ample power to enact legislation providing for the regulation of prices paid to farmers for their products. *United States v. Darby*, 312 U. S. 100 (1941); *Wickard v. Filburn*, 317 U. S. 111 (1942). . . . The Commerce Clause also limits the power of the Commonwealth of Massachusetts to adopt regulations that discriminate against interstate commerce. "This 'negative' aspect of the Commerce Clause prohibits economic protectionism—that is, regulatory measures designed to benefit in-state economic interests by burdening out-of-state competitors. . . . Thus, state statutes that clearly discriminate against interstate commerce are routinely struck down . . . unless the discrimination is demonstrably justified by a valid factor unrelated to economic protectionism. . . ." *New Energy Co. of Ind. v. Limbach*, 486 U. S. 269, 273–274 (1988).

The paradigmatic example of a law discriminating against interstate commerce is the protective tariff or customs duty, which taxes goods imported from other States, but does not tax similar products produced in State. A tariff is an attractive measure because it simultaneously raises revenue and benefits local producers by burdening their out-of-state competitors. Nevertheless, it violates the principle of the unitary

---

[5] **As You Read, Consider:** In *Pike v. Bruce Church, Inc.*, the Supreme Court observed that a state burdens interstate commerce when it makes it difficult for out-of-state businesses to operate across state lines. Is the burden on interstate commerce equivalent when a state makes it *easier* for in-state businesses to operate within a single state? How do Justice John Paul Stevens and Justice Antonin Scalia answer this question?

national market by handicapping out-of-state competitors, thus artificially encouraging in-state production even when the same goods could be produced at lower cost in other States.

Because of their distorting effects on the geography of production, tariffs have long been recognized as violative of the Commerce Clause. In fact, tariffs against the products of other States are so patently unconstitutional that our cases reveal not a single attempt by any State to enact one. Instead, the cases are filled with state laws that aspire to reap some of the benefits of tariffs by other means. In *Baldwin v. G. A. F. Seelig, Inc.*, 294 U. S. 511 (1935), the State of New York attempted to protect its dairy farmers from the adverse effects of Vermont competition by establishing a single minimum price for all milk, whether produced in New York or elsewhere. This Court did not hesitate, however, to strike it down. Writing for a unanimous Court, Justice Cardozo reasoned:

> "Neither the power to tax nor the police power may be used by the state of destination with the aim and effect of establishing an economic barrier against competition with the products of another state or the labor of its residents. Restrictions so contrived are an unreasonable clog upon the mobility of commerce. They set up what is equivalent to a rampart of customs duties designed to neutralize advantages belonging to the place of origin." *Id.*, at 527.

Thus, because the minimum price regulation had the same effect as a tariff or customs duty—neutralizing the advantage possessed by lower cost out-of-state producers—it was held unconstitutional. . . . Other cases of this kind are legion. *Hunt v. Washington State Apple Advertising Comm'n*, 432 U. S. 333, 351 (1977) (invalidating statute, because it "has the effect of stripping away from the Washington apple industry the competitive and economic advantages it has earned").

Under these cases, Massachusetts' pricing order is clearly unconstitutional. Its avowed purpose and its undisputed effect are to enable higher cost Massachusetts dairy farmers to compete with lower cost dairy farmers in other States. The "premium payments" are effectively a tax which makes milk produced out of State more expensive. Although the tax also applies to milk produced in Massachusetts, its effect on Massachusetts producers is entirely (indeed more than) offset by the subsidy provided exclusively to Massachusetts dairy farmers. Like an ordinary tariff, the tax is thus effectively imposed only on out-of-state products. The pricing order thus allows Massachusetts dairy farmers who produce at higher cost to sell at or below the price charged by lower cost out-of-state producers. . . . The Massachusetts pricing order thus will almost certainly "cause local goods to constitute a larger share, and goods with an out-of-state source to constitute a smaller share, of the total sales in the market." *Exxon Corp. v. Governor of Maryland*, 437 U. S. 117, 126, n. 16 (1978). In fact, this effect was the motive behind the promulgation of the pricing order. This effect renders the program unconstitutional, because it, like a tariff, "neutraliz[es] advantages belonging to the place of origin." *Baldwin*, 294 U. S., at 527. . . .

III

[R]espondent's principal argument is that, because "the milk order achieves its goals through lawful means," the order as a whole is constitutional. Brief for Respondent 20. He argues that the payments to Massachusetts dairy farmers from the Dairy Equalization Fund are valid, because subsidies are constitutional exercises of state power, and that the order premium which provides money for the fund is valid, because it is a nondiscriminatory tax. Therefore the pricing order is constitutional, because it is merely the combination of two independently lawful regulations. In effect, respondent argues, if the State may impose a valid tax on dealers, it is free to use the proceeds of the tax as it chooses; and if it may independently subsidize its farmers, it is free to finance the subsidy by means of any legitimate tax.

Even granting respondent's assertion that both components of the pricing order would be constitutional standing alone,[15] the pricing order nevertheless must fall. A pure subsidy funded out of general revenue ordinarily imposes no burden on interstate commerce, but merely assists local business. The pricing order in this case, however, is funded principally from taxes on the sale of milk produced in other States. By so funding the subsidy, respondent not only assists local farmers, but burdens interstate commerce. The pricing order thus violates the cardinal principle that a State may not benefit in-state economic interests by burdening out-of-state competitors.[6]

More fundamentally, respondent errs in assuming that the constitutionality of the pricing order follows logically from the constitutionality of its component parts. By conjoining a tax and a subsidy, Massachusetts has created a program more dangerous to interstate commerce than either part alone. Nondiscriminatory measures, like the evenhanded tax at issue here, are generally upheld, in spite of any adverse effects on interstate commerce, in part because "[t]he existence of major in-state interests adversely affected . . . is a powerful safeguard against legislative abuse." *Minnesota v. Clover Leaf Creamery Co.*, 449 U. S. 456, 473, n. 17 (1981). However, when a nondiscriminatory tax is coupled with a subsidy to one of the groups hurt by the tax, a State's political processes can no longer be relied upon to prevent legislative abuse, because one of the in-state interests which would otherwise lobby against the tax has been mollified by the subsidy. So, in this case, one would ordinarily have expected at least three groups to lobby against the order premium, which, as a tax, raises the price (and hence lowers demand) for milk: dairy farmers, milk dealers, and consumers. But because the tax was coupled with a subsidy, one of the most powerful of these groups, Massachusetts dairy farmers, instead of exerting their influence against the tax, were in fact its primary supporters.[7]

Respondent's argument would require us to analyze separately two parts of an integrated regulation, but we cannot divorce the premium payments from the use to which the payments are put. It is the entire program—not just the contributions to the

---

[15] We have never squarely confronted the constitutionality of subsidies, and we need not do so now. We have, however, noted that "[d]irect subsidization of domestic industry does not ordinarily run afoul" of the negative Commerce Clause. In addition, it is undisputed that States may try to attract business by creating an environment conducive to economic activity, as by maintaining good roads, sound public education, or low taxes.

[6] **Questions:** Stevens observes in footnote 15 that state subsidies of in-state industries are presumptively OK. But he wrote earlier that state taxes on out-of-state industries—tariffs—are "patently unconstitutional." Why does the Court make this distinction? Suppose one state levied a $10 tax on out-of-state producers, and another state gave in-state producers a $10 subsidy. Wouldn't both of those laws have similar effects on interstate commerce?

For example, in 2018, Amazon facilitated a nationwide competition for where it would locate its second headquarters, "HQ2." Virginia, one of the winners, promised Amazon subsidies of $22,000 for each new job it created in the state. Doesn't such a subsidy obviously have the purpose and effect of influencing an interstate market?

[7] **Questions:** Stevens offers a political-process rationale for why states should not be allowed to pair nondiscriminatory taxes with subsidies. But doesn't his logic implicate *all* state subsidies of local businesses? For example, if a state raises in-state income taxes and spends some of the revenue on subsidizing in-state renewable-energy manufacturers, wouldn't such a subsidy compromise the political process as much as the Massachusetts law did in this case?

To understand why Stevens likely did not consider whether subsidies are unconstitutional, consider what it would mean if the Commerce Clause of the U.S. Constitution prohibited states from giving benefits to their own residents. Such an interpretation might compromise the ability of state governments to exercise a core function. Why, then, does the Court interpret the Commerce Clause to prohibit state tariffs?

fund or the distributions from that fund—that simultaneously burdens interstate commerce and discriminates in favor of local producers. The choice of constitutional means—nondiscriminatory tax and local subsidy—cannot guarantee the constitutionality of the program as a whole. New York's minimum price order also used constitutional means—a State's power to regulate prices—but was held unconstitutional because of its deleterious effects. *Baldwin v. G. A. F. Seelig, Inc.*, 294 U. S. 511 (1935). . . .

Our Commerce Clause jurisprudence is not so rigid as to be controlled by the form by which a State erects barriers to commerce. Rather our cases have eschewed formalism for a sensitive, case-by-case analysis of purposes and effects. As the Court declared over 50 years ago: "The commerce clause forbids discrimination, whether forthright or ingenious. In each case it is our duty to determine whether the statute under attack, whatever its name may be, will in its practical operation work discrimination against interstate commerce." *Best & Co. v. Maxwell*, 311 U. S. 454, 455–456 (1940). . . .

Finally, respondent argues that any incidental burden on interstate commerce "is outweighed by the 'local benefits' of preserving the Massachusetts dairy industry." Brief for Respondent 42. In a closely related argument, respondent urges that "the purpose of the order, to save an industry from collapse, is not protectionist." *Id.*, at 16. If we were to accept these arguments, we would make a virtue of the vice that the rule against discrimination condemns. Preservation of local industry by protecting it from the rigors of interstate competition is the hallmark of the economic protectionism that the Commerce Clause prohibits. In *Bacchus Imports, Ltd. v. Dias*, 468 U. S., at 272, we explicitly rejected any distinction "between thriving and struggling enterprises." Whether a State is attempting to " 'enhance thriving and substantial business enterprises' " or to " 'subsidize . . . financially troubled' " ones is irrelevant to Commerce Clause analysis. *Ibid*. . . .

■ JUSTICE SCALIA, with whom JUSTICE THOMAS joins, concurring in the judgment.[8]

[T]he purpose of the negative Commerce Clause, we have often said, is to create a national market. It does not follow from that, however, and we have never held, that every state law which obstructs a national market violates the Commerce Clause. Yet that is what the Court says today. It seems to have canvassed the entire corpus of negative-Commerce-Clause opinions, culled out every free-market snippet of reasoning, and melded them into the sweeping principle that the Constitution is violated by any state law or regulation that "artificially encourag[es] in-state production even when the same goods could be produced at lower cost in other States."

As the Court seems to appreciate by its eagerness expressly to reserve the question of the constitutionality of subsidies for in-state industry, *ante*, at n. 15, this expansive view of the Commerce Clause calls into question a wide variety of state laws that have hitherto been thought permissible. It seems to me that a state subsidy would *clearly* be invalid under any formulation of the Court's guiding principle identified above. The Court guardedly asserts that a "pure subsidy funded out of general revenue *ordinarily* imposes no burden on interstate commerce, but merely assists local business," but under its analysis that must be taken to be true only because most local businesses (*e.g.*, the local hardware store) are not competing with businesses out of State. The Court notes that, in funding this subsidy,

---

8 **Question:** Scalia points out many of the inconsistencies in the majority's opinion. But even he concurs in the judgment. Why do you think the entire Court supports an interpretation of the Commerce Clause that prohibits states from affecting interstate commerce in some (but not all) respects?

Massachusetts has taxed milk produced in other States, and thus "not only assists local farmers, but burdens interstate commerce." *Ibid.* But the same could be said of almost all subsidies funded from general state revenues, which almost invariably include moneys from use taxes on out-of-state products. And even where the funding does not come in any part from taxes on out-of-state goods, "merely assist[ing]" in-state businesses, *ibid.*, unquestionably neutralizes advantages possessed by out-of-state enterprises. Such subsidies, particularly where they are in the form of cash or (what comes to the same thing) tax forgiveness, are often admitted to have as their purpose—*indeed, are nationally advertised as having as their purpose*—making it more profitable to conduct business in State than elsewhere, *i.e.*, distorting normal market incentives.

The Court's guiding principle also appears to call into question many garden-variety state laws heretofore permissible under the negative Commerce Clause. A state law, for example, which requires, contrary to the industry practice, the use of recyclable packaging materials, favors local nonexporting producers, who do not have to establish an additional, separate packaging operation for in-state sales. If the Court's analysis is to be believed, such a law would be unconstitutional without regard to whether disruption of the "national market" is the real purpose of the restriction, and without the need to "balance" the importance of the state interests thereby pursued, see *Pike v. Bruce Church, Inc.*, 397 U. S. 137 (1970). These results would greatly extend the negative Commerce Clause beyond its current scope. If the Court does not intend these consequences, and does not want to foster needless litigation concerning them, it should not have adopted its expansive rationale. . . .

37.2.3

Hughes v. Alexandria Scrap Corp.

426 U.S. 794 (1976)

Pike and *Healy* represent the two tests that the Supreme Court uses to analyze regulations under the Negative Commerce Clause. If a regulation is "evenhanded" but imposes incidental burdens on interstate commerce, the Court balances the benefits against the harms. But if a regulation "discriminates against out-of-state goods"—as revealed by its effects or purpose—then the Court will uphold the regulation only if it is "narrowly tailored to advance a legitimate local purpose" besides economic protectionism. *Tenn. Wine & Spirits Retailers Ass'n v. Thomas*, 139 S. Ct. 2449, 2461 (2019). As the Court wrote in 2019, "it would be strange if the Constitution contained no provision curbing state protectionism, and at this point in the Court's history, no provision other than the Commerce Clause could easily do the job." *Id.* at 2460.

Yet, as the *Healy* Court observed, state subsidies have long been an important exception to the Supreme Court's Negative Commerce Clause analysis. One justification for subsidies—also called the "market-participant exception"—is illustrated in the following case, *Hughes v. Alexandria Scrap Corp.*, 426 U.S. 794 (1976).

In 1967, Maryland legislators began noticing a troubling trend in the state: people were increasingly abandoning their cars in public places. A state investigation concluded that the root of the problem was the existence of bottlenecks in the "scrap cycle," the course by which an abandoned vehicle is processed into scrap metal for reuse by steel mills. In 1969, the legislature passed a complicated law that, in effect, gave each junkyard in Maryland, Pennsylvania, or Virginia a subsidy for each vehicle, or "hulk," the junkyard destroyed. Junkyards in turn paid Marylanders to clean up the state's cars.

In 1974, after Maryland junkyards complained that the state was subsidizing its out-of-state competitors, the legislature amended its law to provide the subsidy only for Maryland junkyards. If an out-of-state junkyard wanted the subsidy, it first had to submit an onerous level of documentation to prove that it possessed the title to the scrapped car.

Alexandria Scrap Corp., a Virginia junkyard, sued Harry Hughes, Maryland's secretary of transportation, to challenge the constitutionality of the 1974 amendments. The junkyard claimed that the new law provided a major benefit to Maryland junkyards and discriminated on its face against Virginia junkyards.

Rather than apply the *Pike* or *Healy* tests, however, the Court adopted a third test for when a state "entered into the market itself" and found that Maryland, as a market-participant, did not act unconstitutionally. *Hughes*, 426 U.S. at 806.

■ MR. JUSTICE POWELL delivered the opinion of the Court.[9]

This case involves a two-pronged constitutional attack on a recent amendment to one part of a complex Maryland plan for ridding that State of abandoned automobiles. The three-judge District Court agreed with appellee, a Virginia scrap processor that participates in the plan, that the amendment violated the Commerce Clause. . . . We disagree. . . .

[The appellee's] argument starts from the premise, well established by the history of the Commerce Clause, that this Nation is a common market in which state lines cannot be made barriers to the free flow of both raw materials and finished goods in response to the economic laws of supply and demand. See *Great A&P Tea Co. v. Cottrell*, 424 U. S. 366, 370–371 (1976). Appellee concedes that until the 1974 amendment the Maryland system operated in conformity with the common-market principle. There was free competition among licensed processors for Maryland hulks from unlicensed suppliers and an unimpeded flow of such hulks out of Maryland to appellee and other non-Maryland processors. The only effect of the bounty was to enhance the value of hulks and thus make it more likely that they would be moved to processing plants.

The practical effect of the amendment, however, was to limit the enhanced price available to unlicensed suppliers to hulks that stayed inside Maryland, thus discouraging such suppliers from taking their hulks out of State for processing. The result was that the movement of hulks in interstate commerce was reduced. Appellee contends that this effect of the 1974 amendment is a "burden" on interstate commerce, the permissibility of which must be determined under the test of *Pike v. Bruce Church, Inc.*, 397 U. S. 137, 142 (1970). The Court there stated that "the extent of the burden that will be tolerated will . . . depend on the nature of the local

9 **As You Read, Consider:** Does Justice Lewis Powell's analysis persuade you that the Negative Commerce Clause categorically should not apply to situations in which a state subsidizes local businesses?

interest involved, and on whether it could be promoted as well with a lesser impact on interstate activities."

The District Court accepted appellee's analysis, and concluded that the 1974 amendment failed the *Pike* test. . . . [T]he court found that the amendment did impose "substantial burdens upon the free flow of interstate commerce." 391 F. Supp., at 62. . . .

This line of reasoning is not without force if its basic premise is accepted. That premise is that every action by a State that has the effect of reducing in some manner the flow of goods in interstate commerce is potentially an impermissible burden. But we are not persuaded that Maryland's action in amending its statute was the kind of action with which the Commerce Clause is concerned.

The situation presented by this statute and the 1974 amendment is quite unlike that found in the cases upon which appellee relies. In the most recent of those cases, *Pike v. Bruce Church, supra*, a burden was found to be imposed by an Arizona requirement that fresh fruit grown in the State be packed there before shipment interstate. The requirement prohibited the interstate shipment of fruit in bulk, no matter what the market demand for such shipments. . . . [T]he State [thus] interfered with the natural functioning of the interstate market either through prohibition or through burdensome regulation. . . .[10]

By contrast, Maryland has not sought to prohibit the flow of hulks, or to regulate the conditions under which it may occur. Instead, it has entered into the market itself to bid up their price. There has been an impact upon the interstate flow of hulks only because, since the 1974 amendment, Maryland effectively has made it more lucrative for unlicensed suppliers to dispose of their hulks in Maryland rather than take them outside the State. . . . [This is not] a burden which the Commerce Clause was intended to make suspect. The Clause was designed in part to prevent trade barriers that had undermined efforts of the fledgling States to form a cohesive whole following their victory in the Revolution. . . .

In realizing the Founders' vision this Court has adhered strictly to the principle "that the right to engage in interstate commerce is not the gift of a state, and that a state cannot regulate or restrain it." But until today the Court has not been asked to hold that the entry by the State itself into the market as a purchaser, in effect, of a potential article of interstate commerce creates a burden upon that commerce if the State restricts its trade to its own citizens or businesses within the State.

We do not believe the Commerce Clause was intended to require independent justification for such action. Maryland entered the market for the purpose, agreed by all to be commendable as well as legitimate, of protecting the State's environment. As the means of furthering this purpose, it elected the payment of state funds—in the form of bounties—to encourage the removal of automobile hulks from Maryland streets and junkyards. It is true that the state money initially was made available to licensed out-of-state processors as well as those located within Maryland, and not until the 1974 amendment was the financial benefit channeled, in practical effect, to domestic processors. But this chronology does not distinguish the case, for Commerce Clause purposes, from one in which a State offered bounties only to

---

[10] **Questions:** Powell distinguishes the Maryland subsidy from the *Pike* burden by observing that Maryland "has entered into the market itself." This statement would soon be expanded into a "market-participant exception": when a state acts as a *participant* in an interstate market instead of as a *regulator* of an interstate market, the Commerce Clause is not implicated.

Does this distinction make any sense? If the Court is accurate that a purpose of the Commerce Clause was to prevent states from erecting trade barriers, isn't an in-state subsidy as much of a barrier as an out-of-state tariff?

domestic processors from the start. Regardless of when the State's largesse is first confined to domestic processors, the effect upon the flow of hulks resting within the State is the same: they will tend to be processed inside the State rather than flowing to foreign processors. But no trade barrier of the type forbidden by the Commerce Clause, and involved in previous cases, impedes their movement out of State. They remain within Maryland in response to market forces, including that exerted by money from the State. Nothing in the purposes animating the Commerce Clause prohibits a State, in the absence of congressional action, from participating in the market and exercising the right to favor its own citizens over others.

NOTE: MARKET-PARTICIPANT EXCEPTION

It is not obvious why a state *burden* on out-of-state goods represents a threat to interstate commerce but a state *subsidy* to in-state goods represents no such threat—even though the two are functionally identical. Nevertheless, the Court has continued to maintain and even expand *Hughes*'s market-participant exception. In *White v. Massachusetts Council of Construction Employers*, 460 U.S. 204, 214–15 (1983), the Court upheld a Boston scheme in which the city favored its own residents in construction projects paid for with city funds. And in *McBurney v. Young*, 569 U.S. 221, 236–37 (2013), the Court upheld a Virginia scheme in which the state authorized only Virginia residents to inspect and copy public records under the Virginia Freedom of Information Act (FOIA).

NOTE: FOREIGN NEGATIVE COMMERCE CLAUSE AND REGULATION

Generally speaking, the Court applies the same analysis to state regulations of *foreign* commerce as it does to state regulations of *interstate* commerce. *See, e.g., City of New York v. Miln*, 36 U.S. (11 Pet.) 102 (1837). But, occasionally, the Court has suggested that states have even less discretion to regulate foreign commerce than interstate commerce because "federal power in the field affecting foreign relations [must] be left entirely free from local interference." *Hines v. Davidowitz*, 312 U.S. 52, 63 (1941). Most notably, in *Zschernig v. Miller*, 389 U.S. 429, 440–41 (1968), the Court invoked the Negative Commerce Clause to strike down an Oregon law that prevented citizens of communist countries from inheriting property. But instead of holding that the law literally burdened foreign commerce, the Court invalidated the law because it affected the United States's foreign policy. The Court explained that Oregon's law had "a direct impact upon foreign relations and may well adversely affect the power of the central government to deal with those problems." *Id.* at 441.

In the decades since *Zschernig*, the Court has declined to invalidate any further state laws on the sole ground that they might interfere with foreign policy. But the Court has suggested that state laws affecting foreign policy are very likely to be preempted by any federal law on the same topic. For example, in 1996, Massachusetts passed legislation prohibiting the state's agencies from purchasing goods or services from any companies that did business with the military junta in Burma. Reviewing this law, the Court found that the state law was preempted by a federal law that imposed federal sanctions on Burma. The Court wrote that the Massachusetts provisions "compromise the very capacity of the President to speak for the Nation with one voice in dealing with other governments." *Crosby v. Nat'l Foreign Trade Council*, 530 U.S. 363, 381 (2000).

37.3 THE NEGATIVE COMMERCE CLAUSE AND TAXATION

The Supreme Court's early Negative Commerce Clause cases didn't distinguish between state regulations and state taxes—both were unconstitutional if they unjustifiably burdened interstate or foreign commerce. *See, e.g., Reading R.R. Co. v. Pennsylvania* (*State Freight Tax Case*), 82 U.S. (15 Wall.) 232 (1872). But in the 1930s, as interstate business became far more common, the Court adopted a more deferential rule for state taxes, declaring that the Negative Commerce Clause invalidates only taxes that create a risk of "multiple taxation not borne by local commerce." *W. Live Stock v. Bureau of Revenue*, 303 U.S. 250, 257 (1938). This new rule allowed states to tax enterprises that did business in multiple states, provided that each state attempted to tax only the "business done within the state by a fair method of apportionment." *Id.* at 255. In other words, if an enterprise did 60 percent of its business in state A and 40 percent of its business in state B, then state A could tax only 60 percent of the company's income. *Id.*

In *Complete Auto Transit, Inc. v. Brady*, 430 U.S. 274 (1977), the Court refined this rule into a four-factor test. It declared that a state could tax a person or corporation doing business in multiple states only if the tax "[1] is applied to an activity with a substantial nexus with the taxing State, [2] is fairly apportioned, [3] does not discriminate against interstate commerce, and [4] is fairly related to the services provided by the State." *Complete Auto Transit*, 430 U.S. at 279.

The first factor, the *nexus test*, provides that a state has to have some minimum connection to any enterprise it taxes. This test is a slightly more restrictive version of the "minimum contacts" test used to evaluate whether an exercise of personal jurisdiction is appropriate under the Due Process Clause. *See Quill Corp. v. North Dakota ex rel. Heitkamp*, 504 U.S. 298 (1992). As long as an enterprise purposefully avails itself of a state's resources—making it fair for the state to ask for something in return—the state can apportion the share of the enterprise's business that is connected to the state. *See MeadWestvaco Corp. v. Ill. Dep't of Revenue*, 553 U.S. 16 (2008).

The second factor, the *apportionment test*, provides that a state may tax only an enterprise's business that is connected to the state. To satisfy this test, a tax must be *internally consistent* (structured so that if every state were to impose an identical tax, no multiple taxation would result), *Am. Trucking Ass'ns v. Scheiner*, 483 U.S. 266 (1987); and *externally consistent* (structured to tax only a portion of the revenues from the interstate activity that reasonably reflects the in-state component of the activity being taxed), *Goldberg v. Sweet*, 488 U.S. 252 (1989). For example, in *Comptroller of the Treasury v. Wynne*, 575 U.S. 542 (2015), the Court struck down a Maryland tax levied on the income of all people living in Maryland no matter where in the world they earned the income. The Court explained that the tax wasn't internally consistent because if every state adopted a similar tax, then all interstate income would be taxed multiple times. *Wynne*, 575 U.S. at 564–65.

The third factor, the *nondiscrimination test*, provides that a state cannot discriminate against interstate commerce by providing a direct commercial advantage to local business. *See Armco, Inc. v. Hardesty*, 467 U.S. 638 (1984). The Maryland tax at issue in *Wynne* failed both the apportionment test and this test because it "operate[d] as a tariff" on out-of-state income by making it more expensive for Marylanders to earn income in other states. *Wynne*, 575 U.S. at 565.

The fourth and final factor, the *benefits test*, provides that the tax has to be relatable to some benefit received by the enterprise. For example, in *American Trucking Ass'ns v. Michigan Public Service Commission*, 545 U.S. 429 (2005), the Court allowed Michigan to charge a fee on all trucks that picked up goods in the state, even if they conducted only a minor stop on an interstate trip. The Court held that given the costs Michigan had to pay to maintain the safety of the trucking industry, it was fair for the state to presume that all truck drivers received the same benefit no matter how many miles within the state they drove. *Am. Trucking Ass'ns*, 545 U.S. at 434–36.

37.3.1

South Dakota v. Wayfair, Inc.

138 S. Ct. 2080 (2018)

A recent illustration of *Complete Auto Transit*'s four-factor test involved commerce over the internet, which has presented its own problems for the Court's Negative Commerce Clause doctrine. In *Quill Corp. v. North Dakota*, 504 U.S. 298 (1992), a case decided only a few years after the invention of the World Wide Web, the Court considered the nexus factor of the *Complete Auto Transit* test and concluded that it was unconstitutional for a state to tax enterprises that were connected to the state only by selling goods through mail-order catalogs. *Quill* declared that an enterprise had to have a "physical presence" in a state before it was permissible for the state to tax it. *Quill*, 504 U.S. at 314. Over the next three decades, *Quill* became an enormous impediment to states because it prevented them from collecting sales taxes on goods sold over the internet unless the retailer had a presence in the state.

As Amazon, Apple, and other technology companies sold an increasing number of products online, *Quill* came under political pressure. In 2016, South Dakota directly challenged *Quill* by passing a law that required out-of-state retailers to collect and remit sales taxes for goods sold within the state. Three internet retailers with no presence in South Dakota—Wayfair, Overstock, and Newegg—challenged the state's attempt to collect sales taxes in light of *Quill*.

In *South Dakota v. Wayfair, Inc.*, 138 S. Ct. 2080 (2018), the Court abandoned *Quill* and reevaluated the nexus factor of its Negative Commerce Clause doctrine.

■ JUSTICE KENNEDY delivered the opinion of the Court.[11]

When a consumer purchases goods or services, the consumer's State often imposes a sales tax. This case requires the Court to determine when an out-of-state seller can be required to collect and remit that tax. All concede that taxing the sales in question here is lawful. The question is whether the out-of-state seller can be held responsible for its payment, and this turns on a proper interpretation of the Commerce Clause, U.S. Const., Art. I, § 8, cl. 3.

In two earlier cases the Court held that an out-of-state seller's liability to collect and remit the tax to the consumer's State depended on whether the seller had a physical presence in that State, but that mere shipment of goods into the consumer's State, following an order from a catalog, did not satisfy the physical presence requirement. *National Bellas Hess, Inc. v. Department of Revenue of Ill.*, 386 U.S. 753 (1967); *Quill Corp. v. North Dakota*, 504 U.S. 298 (1992). The Court granted certiorari here to reconsider the scope and validity of the physical presence rule mandated by those cases. . . .

II

The Constitution grants Congress the power "[t]o regulate Commerce. . . among the several States." Art. I, § 8, cl. 3. The Commerce Clause "reflect[s] a central concern of the Framers that was an immediate reason for calling the Constitutional Convention: the conviction that in order to succeed, the new Union would have to avoid the tendencies toward economic Balkanization that had plagued relations among the Colonies and later among the States under the Articles of Confederation." *Hughes v. Oklahoma*, 441 U.S. 322, 325–326 (1979). Although the Commerce Clause is written as an affirmative grant of authority to Congress, this Court has long held that in some instances it imposes limitations on the States absent congressional action. Of course, when Congress exercises its power to regulate commerce by enacting legislation, the legislation controls. *S. Pac. Co. v. Arizona ex rel. Sullivan*, 325 U.S. 761, 769 (1945). But this Court has observed that "in general Congress has left it to the courts to formulate the rules" to preserve "the free flow of interstate commerce." *Id.*, at 770.

To understand the issue presented in this case, it is instructive first to survey the general development of this Court's Commerce Clause principles and then to review the application of those principles to state taxes.

A

From early in its history, a central function of this Court has been to adjudicate disputes that require interpretation of the Commerce Clause in order to determine its meaning, its reach, and the extent to which it limits state regulations of commerce. *Gibbons v. Ogden*, 9 Wheat. 1 (1824), began setting the course by defining the

---

[11] **As You Read, Consider:** How does Justice Anthony Kennedy determine whether South Dakota's attempt to collect sales taxes from online retailers unconstitutionally burdens interstate commerce? Does his opinion require all businesses that sell things on the internet—no matter how small—to determine and remit sales taxes to each state in which they sell something?

meaning of commerce. Chief Justice Marshall explained that commerce included both "the interchange of commodities" and "commercial intercourse." *Id.*, at 189, 193. . . .

[Five years later,] in another opinion by Chief Justice Marshall, the Court sustained what in substance was a state regulation of interstate commerce. In *Willson v. Black-Bird Creek Marsh Co.*, 2 Pet. 245 (1829), the Court allowed a State to dam and bank a stream that was part of an interstate water system, an action that likely would have been an impermissible intrusion on the national power over commerce had it been the rule that only Congress could regulate in that sphere. See *id.*, at 252. Thus, by implication at least, the Court indicated that the power to regulate commerce in some circumstances was held by the States and Congress concurrently. And so both a broad interpretation of interstate commerce and the concurrent regulatory power of the States can be traced to *Gibbons* and *Willson*.

Over the next few decades, the Court refined the doctrine to accommodate the necessary balance between state and federal power. In *Cooley v. Board of Wardens of Port of Philadelphia ex rel. Soc. for Relief of Distressed Pilots*, 12 How. 299 (1852), the Court addressed local laws regulating river pilots who operated in interstate waters and guided many ships on interstate or foreign voyages. The Court held that, while Congress surely could regulate on this subject had it chosen to act, the State, too, could regulate. The Court distinguished between those subjects that by their nature "imperatively deman[d] a single uniform rule, operating equally on the commerce of the United States," and those that "deman[d] th[e] diversity, which alone can meet . . . local necessities." *Id.*, at 319. Though considerable uncertainties were yet to be overcome, these precedents still laid the groundwork for the analytical framework that now prevails for Commerce Clause cases.

This Court's doctrine has developed further with time. Modern precedents rest upon two primary principles that mark the boundaries of a State's authority to regulate interstate commerce. First, state regulations may not discriminate against interstate commerce; and second, States may not impose undue burdens on interstate commerce. State laws that discriminate against interstate commerce face "a virtually *per se* rule of invalidity." *Granholm v. Heald*, 544 U.S. 460, 476 (2005) (internal quotation marks omitted). State laws that "regulat[e] even-handedly to effectuate a legitimate local public interest. . . will be upheld unless the burden imposed on such commerce is clearly excessive in relation to the putative local benefits." *Pike v. Bruce Church, Inc.*, 397 U.S. 137, 142 (1970). Although subject to exceptions and variations, see, *e.g.*, *Hughes v. Alexandria Scrap Corp.*, 426 U.S. 794 (1976), these two principles guide the courts in adjudicating cases challenging state laws under the Commerce Clause.

B

These principles also animate the Court's Commerce Clause precedents addressing the validity of state taxes. The Court explained the now-accepted framework for state taxation in *Complete Auto Transit, Inc. v. Brady*, 430 U.S. 274 (1977). The Court held that a State "may tax exclusively interstate commerce so long as the tax does not create any effect forbidden by the Commerce Clause." *Id.*, at 285. After all, interstate commerce may be required to pay its fair share of state taxes. The Court will sustain a tax so long as it (1) applies to an activity with a substantial nexus with the taxing State, (2) is fairly apportioned, (3) does not discriminate against interstate commerce, and (4) is fairly related to the services the State provides. See *id.* at 279.

Before *Complete Auto*, the Court had addressed a challenge to an Illinois tax that required out-of-state retailers to collect and remit taxes on sales made to consumers who purchased goods for use within Illinois. *Bellas Hess*, 386 U.S., at

754–755. The Court held that a mail-order company "whose only connection with customers in the State is by common carrier or the United States mail" lacked the requisite minimum contacts with the State required by both the Due Process Clause and the Commerce Clause. *Id.*, at 758. Unless the retailer maintained a physical presence such as "retail outlets, solicitors, or property within a State," the State lacked the power to require that retailer to collect a local use tax. *Ibid.* The dissent disagreed: "There should be no doubt that this large-scale, systematic, continuous solicitation and exploitation of the Illinois consumer market is a sufficient 'nexus' to require Bellas Hess to collect from Illinois customers and to remit the use tax." *Id.*, at 761–762 (opinion of Fortas, J.).

In 1992, the Court reexamined the physical presence rule in *Quill*. That case presented a challenge to North Dakota's "attempt to require an out-of-state mail-order house that has neither outlets nor sales representatives in the State to collect and pay a use tax on goods purchased for use within the State." 504 U.S., at 301. Despite the fact that *Bellas Hess* linked due process and the Commerce Clause together, the Court in *Quill* overruled the due process holding, but not the Commerce Clause holding; and it thus reaffirmed the physical presence rule. 504 U.S., at 307–308, 317–318. . . .

III

The physical presence rule has "been the target of criticism over many years from many quarters." *Direct Marketing Assn. v. Brohl*, 814 F.3d 1129, 1148, 1150–1151 (C.A.10 2016) (Gorsuch, J., concurring). *Quill*, it has been said, was "premised on assumptions that are unfounded" and "riddled with internal inconsistencies." Rothfeld, *Quill*: Confusing the Commerce Clause, 56 Tax Notes 487, 488 (1992). *Quill* created an inefficient "online sales tax loophole" that gives out-of-state businesses an advantage. A. Laffer & D. Arduin, Pro-Growth Tax Reform and E-Fairness 1, 4 (July 2013). And "while nexus rules are clearly necessary," the Court "should focus on rules that are appropriate to the twenty-first century, not the nineteenth." Hellerstein, Deconstructing the Debate Over State Taxation of Electronic Commerce, 13 Harv. J.L. & Tech. 549, 553 (2000). Each year, the physical presence rule becomes further removed from economic reality and results in significant revenue losses to the States. These critiques underscore that the physical presence rule, both as first formulated and as applied today, is an incorrect interpretation of the Commerce Clause. . . .

Quill is flawed on its own terms. First, the physical presence rule is not a necessary interpretation of the requirement that a state tax must be "applied to an activity with a substantial nexus with the taxing State." *Complete Auto*, 430 U.S., at 279. Second, *Quill* creates rather than resolves market distortions. . . .

1

All agree that South Dakota has the authority to tax these transactions. . . . "It has long been settled" that the sale of goods or services "has a sufficient nexus to the State in which the sale is consummated to be treated as a local transaction taxable by that State." *Oklahoma Tax Comm'n v. Jefferson Lines, Inc.*, 514 U.S. 175, 184 (1995). . . .

The central dispute is whether South Dakota may require remote sellers to collect and remit the tax without some additional connection to the State. The Court has previously stated that "[t]he imposition on the seller of the duty to insure collection of the tax from the purchaser does not violate the [C]ommerce [C]lause." *McGoldrick v. Berwind-White Coal Mining Co.*, 309 U.S. 33, 50, n. 9 (1940). . . . There just must be "a substantial nexus with the taxing State." *Complete Auto, supra*, at 279.

This nexus requirement is "closely related," *Bellas Hess*, 386 U.S., at 756, to the due process requirement that there be "some definite link, some minimum connection, between a state and the person, property or transaction it seeks to tax," *Miller Brothers Co. v. Maryland*, 347 U.S. 340, 344–345 (1954). It is settled law that a business need not have a physical presence in a State to satisfy the demands of due process. *Burger King Corp. v. Rudzewicz*, 471 U.S. 462, 476 (1985). Although physical presence " 'frequently will enhance' " a business' connection with a State, " 'it is an inescapable fact of modern commercial life that a substantial amount of business is transacted . . . [with no] need for physical presence within a State in which business is conducted.' " *Quill*, 504 U.S., at 308. *Quill* itself recognized that "[t]he requirements of due process are met irrespective of a corporation's lack of physical presence in the taxing State." *Ibid.*

When considering whether a State may levy a tax, Due Process and Commerce Clause standards may not be identical or coterminous, but there are significant parallels. The reasons given in *Quill* for rejecting the physical presence rule for due process purposes apply as well to the question whether physical presence is a requisite for an out-of-state seller's liability to remit sales taxes. Physical presence is not necessary to create a substantial nexus.

The *Quill* majority expressed concern that without the physical presence rule "a state tax might unduly burden interstate commerce" by subjecting retailers to tax-collection obligations in thousands of different taxing jurisdictions. *Id.*, at 313, n.6. But the administrative costs of compliance, especially in the modern economy with its Internet technology, are largely unrelated to whether a company happens to have a physical presence in a State. For example, a business with one salesperson in each State must collect sales taxes in every jurisdiction in which goods are delivered; but a business with 500 salespersons in one central location and a website accessible in every State need not collect sales taxes on otherwise identical nationwide sales. In other words, under *Quill*, a small company with diverse physical presence might be equally or more burdened by compliance costs than a large remote seller. The physical presence rule is a poor proxy for the compliance costs faced by companies that do business in multiple States. Other aspects of the Court's doctrine can better and more accurately address any potential burdens on interstate commerce, whether or not *Quill*'s physical presence rule is satisfied.[12]

2

The Court has consistently explained that the Commerce Clause was designed to prevent States from engaging in economic discrimination so they would not divide into isolated, separable units. See *Philadelphia v. New Jersey*, 437 U.S. 617, 623 (1978). But it is "not the purpose of the [C]ommerce [C]lause to relieve those engaged in interstate commerce from their just share of state tax burden." *Complete Auto, supra*, at 288. . . .

Quill puts both local businesses and many interstate businesses with physical presence at a competitive disadvantage relative to remote sellers. Remote sellers can avoid the regulatory burdens of tax collection and can offer *de facto* lower prices caused by the widespread failure of consumers to pay the tax on their own. This "guarantees a competitive benefit to certain firms simply because of the organizational form they choose" while the rest of the Court's jurisprudence "is all about preventing discrimination between firms." *Direct Marketing*, 814 F.3d, at 1150–1151 (Gorsuch, J., concurring). In effect, *Quill* has come to serve as a judicially created tax shelter

[12] **Question:** Here, Kennedy recognizes that requiring online businesses to pay sales taxes in every state could impose an onerous burden on small businesses. What "[o]ther aspects of the Court's doctrine" might account for such a burden?

for businesses that decide to limit their physical presence and still sell their goods and services to a State's consumers—something that has become easier and more prevalent as technology has advanced.

Worse still, the rule produces an incentive to avoid physical presence in multiple States. Distortions caused by the desire of businesses to avoid tax collection mean that the market may currently lack storefronts, distribution points, and employment centers that otherwise would be efficient or desirable. The Commerce Clause must not prefer interstate commerce only to the point where a merchant physically crosses state borders. Rejecting the physical presence rule is necessary to ensure that artificial competitive advantages are not created by this Court's precedents. This Court should not prevent States from collecting lawful taxes through a physical presence rule that can be satisfied only if there is an employee or a building in the State. . . .

IV

"Although we approach the reconsideration of our decisions with the utmost caution, *stare decisis* is not an inexorable command." *Pearson v. Callahan*, 555 U.S. 223, 233 (2009). Here, *stare decisis* can no longer support the Court's prohibition of a valid exercise of the States' sovereign power.

If it becomes apparent that the Court's Commerce Clause decisions prohibit the States from exercising their lawful sovereign powers in our federal system, the Court should be vigilant in correcting the error. . . . Further, the real world implementation of Commerce Clause doctrines now makes it manifest that the physical presence rule as defined by *Quill* must give way to the "far-reaching systemic and structural changes in the economy" and "many other societal dimensions" caused by the Cyber Age. Though *Quill* was wrong on its own terms when it was decided in 1992, since then the Internet revolution has made its earlier error all the more egregious and harmful.

The *Quill* Court did not have before it the present realities of the interstate marketplace. In 1992, less than 2 percent of Americans had Internet access. See Brief for Retail Litigation Center, Inc., et al. as *Amici Curiae* 11, and n. 10. Today that number is about 89 percent. *Ibid.*, and n. 11. When it decided *Quill*, the Court could not have envisioned a world in which the world's largest retailer would be a remote seller. . . .

The Internet's prevalence and power have changed the dynamics of the national economy. In 1992, mail-order sales in the United States totaled $180 billion. 504 U.S., at 329 (opinion of White, J.). Last year, e-commerce retail sales alone were estimated at $453.5 billion. Dept. of Commerce, U.S. Census Bureau News, Quarterly Retail E-Commerce Sales: 4th Quarter 2017 (CB18–21, Feb. 16, 2018). Combined with traditional remote sellers, the total exceeds half a trillion dollars. Sales Taxes Report, at 9. . . . This expansion has also increased the revenue shortfall faced by States seeking to collect their sales and use taxes. In 1992, it was estimated that the States were losing between $694 million and $3 billion per year in sales tax revenues as a result of the physical presence rule. Brief for Law Professors et al. as *Amici Curiae* 11, n. 7. Now estimates range from $8 to $33 billion. Sales Taxes Report, at 11–12; Brief for Petitioner 34–35. The South Dakota Legislature has declared an emergency, S.B. 106, § 9, which again demonstrates urgency of overturning the physical presence rule.

The argument, moreover, that the physical presence rule is clear and easy to apply is unsound. Attempts to apply the physical presence rule to online retail sales are proving unworkable. States are already confronting the complexities of defining physical presence in the Cyber Age. For example, Massachusetts proposed a regulation that would have defined physical presence to include making apps available to be downloaded by in-state residents and placing cookies on in-state residents' web browsers. Ohio recently adopted a similar standard. . . .

Reliance interests are a legitimate consideration when the Court weighs adherence to an earlier but flawed precedent. But even on its own terms, the physical presence rule as defined by *Quill* is no longer a clear or easily applicable standard, so arguments for reliance based on its clarity are misplaced. And, importantly, *stare decisis* accommodates only "legitimate reliance interest[s]." *United States v. Ross,* 456 U.S. 798, 824 (1982). Here, the tax distortion created by *Quill* exists in large part because consumers regularly fail to comply with lawful use taxes. . . .

For these reasons, the Court concludes that the physical presence rule of *Quill* is unsound and incorrect. The Court's decisions in *Quill Corp. v. North Dakota*, 504 U.S. 298 (1992), and *National Bellas Hess, Inc. v. Department of Revenue of Ill.*, 386 U.S. 753 (1967), should be, and now are, overruled.

V

In the absence of *Quill* and *Bellas Hess*, the first prong of the *Complete Auto* test simply asks whether the tax applies to an activity with a substantial nexus with the taxing State. "[S]uch a nexus is established when the taxpayer [or collector] 'avails itself of the substantial privilege of carrying on business' in that jurisdiction." *Polar Tankers, Inc. v. City of Valdez*, 557 U.S. 1, 11 (2009).

Here, the nexus is clearly sufficient based on both the economic and virtual contacts respondents have with the State. The Act applies only to sellers that deliver more than $100,000 of goods or services into South Dakota or engage in 200 or more separate transactions for the delivery of goods and services into the State on an annual basis. S.B. 106, § 1. This quantity of business could not have occurred unless the seller availed itself of the substantial privilege of carrying on business in South Dakota. And respondents are large, national companies that undoubtedly maintain an extensive virtual presence. Thus, the substantial nexus requirement of *Complete Auto* is satisfied in this case. . . .

NOTE: THE FOREIGN NEGATIVE COMMERCE CLAUSE AND TAXATION

The Court has applied the *Complete Auto Transit* test not only to taxes of interstate commerce but also to taxes of foreign commerce. *See, e.g.*, *Japan Line, Ltd. v. County of Los Angeles*, 441 U.S. 434, 451–54 (1979). But in light of the additional foreign policy concerns presented by a state's taxation of foreign commerce, the Court has considered two more factors to the existing four-factor test: (5) whether a tax "may subject foreign commerce to the risk of a double tax burden to which domestic commerce is not exposed," leading to trade disputes, and (6) whether a tax "may impair federal uniformity in an area where federal uniformity is essential." *Id.* at 447–48 (internal quotation marks omitted). Applying these additional factors, the Court has struck down a county's property tax on cargo containers because it risked initiating a trade dispute with foreign countries that also taxed the cargo containers. *Id.* But the Court has upheld state taxes on the domestic sale of fuel to a foreign airline, *Container Corp. of Am. v. Franchise Tax Bd.*, 463 U.S. 159, 193 (1983); and state taxes on the domestic business of multinational corporations, *Barclays Bank v. Franchise Tax Bd.*, 512 U.S. 298, 314 (1994).

37.4 OTHER LIMITATIONS OF ARTICLE I, SECTION 8

Among the powers granted to Congress in Article I, Section 8, the Commerce Clause is the most important implied limit on state power. But many of the other powers granted to Congress in Article I, Section 8, have also been interpreted to impliedly or expressly preempt state exercises of the same power.

One source of preemption is the clause empowering Congress to "establish Post Offices and post Roads." For example, in *Johnson v. Maryland*, 254 U.S. 51, 56–57 (1920), the Supreme Court prohibited states from arresting postal workers who failed to obtain a driver's license. But as in the Negative Commerce Clause context, and as discussed earlier with regard to intergovernmental immunity (section 2.2), the Court has become more tolerant of state laws that are justified by a legitimate local purpose and that apply evenhandedly and don't discriminate against the federal government or federal mails. *See, e.g.*, *Railway Mail Ass'n v. Corsi*, 326 U.S. 88, 97 (1945) (upholding a state antidiscrimination law as applied to postal workers).

Another potential source of preemption is the clause that empowers Congress to establish "uniform Laws on the subject of Bankruptcies." Unlike with the Commerce Clause, the Supreme Court at first held that states could enact their own bankruptcy laws if Congress failed to do so itself. *See, e.g.*, *Ogden v. Saunders*, 25 U.S. (12 Wheat.) 213 (1827). Since 1898, when Congress first enacted the modern federal bankruptcy code, state insolvency laws have been evaluated under ordinary preemption standards. *See, e.g.*, *Ohio v. Kovacs*, 469 U.S. 274 (1985).

Finally, the Court has also held that states may not interfere with Congress's exclusive right to regulate patents and copyrights—except through evenhanded, nondiscriminatory laws that serve goals unrelated to patents and copyrights. *See Bonito Boats, Inc. v. Thunder Craft Boats, Inc.*, 489 U.S. 141, 168 (1989). But the Court has warned states not to use state laws to mimic federal patent or copyright law. For example, it has held that a state may not punish the copying of a product that isn't entitled to a patent, as such a scheme would interfere with Congress's ability to create a uniform national policy. *Sears, Roebuck & Co. v. Stiffel Co.*, 376 U.S. 225 (1964).

CHAPTER 38

WHAT LIMITATIONS DOES ARTICLE I, SECTION 10, IMPOSE ON THE STATES?

ARTICLE I, SECTION 10, CLAUSE 1: No State shall enter into any Treaty, Alliance, or Confederation; grant Letters of Marque and Reprisal; coin Money; emit Bills of Credit; make any Thing but gold and silver Coin a Tender in Payment of Debts; pass any Bill of Attainder, ex post facto Law, or Law impairing the Obligation of Contracts, or grant any Title of Nobility.

CLAUSE 2: No State shall, without the Consent of the Congress, lay any Imposts or Duties on Imports or Exports, except what may be absolutely necessary for executing it's inspection Laws: and the net Produce of all Duties and Imposts, laid by any State on Imports or Exports, shall be for the Use of the Treasury of the United States; and all such Laws shall be subject to the Revision and Controul of the Congress.

CLAUSE 3: No State shall, without the Consent of Congress, lay any Duty of Tonnage, keep Troops, or Ships of War in time of Peace, enter into any Agreement or Compact with another State, or with a foreign Power, or engage in War, unless actually invaded, or in such imminent Danger as will not admit of delay.

38.1 THE CONTRACTS CLAUSE

When the delegates assembled at the Constitutional Convention in 1787, one of their most widely shared goals was to end what they regarded as a pernicious form of state legislation: debt-relief laws. The end of the Revolutionary War brought with it a postwar recession, and nearly every state legislature responded by enacting legislation to lower taxes, forgive debts, or issue inflationary paper money. The one state that initially resisted pressure to enact one of these laws—Massachusetts—became the site of Shays' Rebellion, in which western farmers closed down local courts to prevent them from enforcing the farmers' outstanding debts. But even Massachusetts adopted its own debt-relief laws shortly after suppressing the rebellion by force. Michael Klarman, *The Framers' Coup: The Making of the United States Constitution* 74–92 (2017).

From the perspective of many farmers, these sorts of relief measures were reasonable responses to an economic depression. The laws eased oppressive tax burdens, loosened the money supply, and prevented mass foreclosures. *Id.* at 81. But from the perspective of the planters and financiers who attended the Philadelphia Convention, relief measures represented nothing less than a populist uprising whose goal was to undermine the property rights sanctified by the American Revolution.

Americans had just gone to war to protest the way in which Parliament had arbitrarily taken property from Americans without their consent; now, democratic majorities appeared to be taking property away from creditor minorities by making it difficult for creditors to collect the money that they had let other people borrow. *Id.* at 83–84.

James Madison and Alexander Hamilton interpreted debt-relief laws as a "disease which infects all our constitutions." *Id.* at 86. They were both leading advocates for inserting into Article I, Section 10, a dozen prohibitions on state laws. Many of these prohibitions clearly have debt-relief laws in mind. Section 10 declares that no state has the power to "coin Money; emit Bills of Credit; make any Thing but gold and silver Coin a Tender in Payment of Debts; [or] pass any . . . Law impairing the Obligation of Contracts. . . ."

The last of these prohibitions, the Contracts Clause, quickly became one of the most frequently litigated provisions of the federal Constitution. Not only did it suspend the operation of state debt-relief laws, but it also became the Constitution's main source of protection for the very idea of private property rights.

In *Chisholm v. Georgia*, 2 U.S. 419 (1793), the case in which the Supreme Court allowed a citizen of South Carolina to sue the State of Georgia, Alexander Chisholm's argument on the merits was that Georgia had violated the Contracts Clause by failing to pay him for services he had rendered during the American Revolution. Over the course of the next century, the Contracts Clause was at issue in 40 percent of all federal challenges to state laws. Benjamin F. Wright, *The Contract Clause of the Constitution* 95 (1938).

Chisholm's lawsuit revealed that while the Contracts Clause prohibits a state from impairing any "Obligation of Contract[,]" the clause doesn't define what a contract *is*. Theoretically, a contract could refer to any promise made by a state or person that is accepted or relied upon by someone else. But such a broad reading of the term *contract* would make it difficult for a state to amend its laws. For example, imagine that a state legislature granted land or a tax exemption to someone in 1800. If a different legislature in 1810 passed a law repealing either grant, did the 1810 legislature impair an obligation of contract?

In two cases in the 1810s, the Supreme Court answered yes. In *Fletcher v. Peck*, 10 U.S. (6 Cranch) 87 (1810), the Court considered a scandal in Georgia in which dozens of corrupt legislators were bribed to grant political associates cheap land by the Yazoo River. After the scandal broke, a subsequent legislature attempted to repeal the fraudulent land grants. But the Court said this repeal wasn't constitutional. "[A] grant is a contract executed," the Court wrote; once the legislature granted the land and extinguished Georgia's right to possess it, a future legislature couldn't reclaim the land without impairing the original grant. *Fletcher*, 10 U.S. (6 Cranch) at 123. Two years later, in *New Jersey v. Wilson*, 11 U.S. (7 Cranch) 164 (1812), the

Court reached an identical conclusion about a tax exemption, holding that an accepted promise not to tax a person was a contract that a future legislature couldn't repeal.

Both of these cases had enormous implications. Every benefit that a state awarded suddenly became the subject of federal constitutional law.

38.1.1

Trustees of Dartmouth College v. Woodward

17 U.S. (4 Wheat.) 518 (1819)

The Court's most far-reaching interpretation of the Contracts Clause, however, emerged in a case about Dartmouth College: *Trustees of Dartmouth College v. Woodward*, 17 U.S. (4 Wheat.) 518 (1819).

When Moor's Indian Charity School in Connecticut was founded in 1754, it struggled to attract students or funds. The school's founder, Eleazar Wheelock, wanted to convert Native Americans into Christian missionaries. But the closest tribes were far away and relatively uninterested in his goal. Wheelock appealed to philanthropists for help, and he received it from the Earl of Dartmouth. He also received a corporate charter from the Crown-appointed governor of New Hampshire, who offered to incorporate the school as "Dartmouth College" if Wheelock agreed to move his school to the colony. *See* Adam Winkler, *We the Corporations* 76–77 (2017).

At the time, the term *corporation* referred to any "agency of government, endowed with public attributes, exclusive privileges, and political power, and designed to serve a social function for the state." Oscar Handlin & Mary Handlin, *Origins of the American Business Corporation*, 5 J. Econ. Hist. 1, 22 (1945). The colony of Connecticut was a corporation chartered by the British Crown in 1662. Harvard College received a corporate charter in 1650 from the Massachusetts Bay Company, which itself was a corporation chartered in 1629 to govern New England. Philadelphia and New York City were municipal corporations chartered to provide local government for their respective cities. Other contemporary corporations included turnpike corporations, insurance corporations, pier-maintenance corporations, canal corporations, and manufacturing corporations.

Corporations, in other words, were institutions chartered by governments to perform some public function. So when the governor of New Hampshire issued a charter on behalf of the Crown to Dartmouth College in 1769, he was effectively chartering an eighteenth-century version of the University of New Hampshire: a public school whose chartered purpose was "the laudable and charitable design of spreading Christian knowledge among the savages of our American wilderness, and, also that the best means of education be established in our province of New Hampshire. . . ." The charter also established a government for the new corporation. Wheelock became the president of Dartmouth, and a board of trustees was formed as the corporation's legislature. Winkler, *supra*, at 77.

During the American Revolution, Wheelock died, and New Hampshire declared its independence. Years later, Wheelock's son, John, assumed the presidency of Dartmouth College. John quickly alienated several members of the board of trustees, who complained that John was turning Dartmouth into a "family dynasty." *Id.* After a high-profile fight over control of the college, the board fired John. But John had several friends in the legislature of the new state of New Hampshire, which enacted legislation to take control of the college. The legislature revised Dartmouth's charter to expand the board from twelve to twenty-one people, it created a new board of overseers to review the trustees' decisions, it authorized the governor to appoint new trustees, and it renamed the school "Dartmouth *University*." *Id.*

Several of Dartmouth's trustees challenged New Hampshire's revision of Dartmouth's charter. They sued the newly appointed secretary of the university, William H. Woodward. Their lawyer, a Dartmouth alum and member of Congress named Daniel Webster, delivered an oral argument that helped to launch his career as one of the United States' most successful corporate lawyers. Webster argued that the new law violated the Contracts Clause because it effectively nullified Dartmouth's 1769 corporate charter. Through tears, he added that Dartmouth was "a small college, . . . and yet there are those who love it." *Id.*

Woodward's lawyers responded to Webster's argument by contending that corporations were public agencies. Just as New Hampshire could pass a law reforming its department of the Treasury, its city governments, or its militia, the state also needed the authority to reform its educational institutions.

In *Dartmouth College*, Chief Justice John Marshall agreed that the Contracts Clause should not be interpreted to prohibit states from modifying their public institutions. But he famously declared that not all corporations are "public"—some are "private" and therefore protected by the Contracts Clause. 17 U.S. (4 Wheat.) at 638.

■ The opinion of the Court was delivered by MARSHALL, CH. J.[1]

The single question now to be considered is, [does the New Hampshire law] violate the constitution of the United States? . . .

---

[1] **As You Read, Consider:** *Dartmouth College* was decided the same year as *McCulloch v. Maryland*, a case in which Chief Justice John Marshall held that corporations were a necessary and proper means of achieving legitimate governmental ends. Just as Congress chartered the Bank of the United States to regulate the economy, New Hampshire chartered Dartmouth College to educate its residents. Why, then, does Marshall consider the law that chartered Dartmouth College a "contract" protected by the clause that prohibits states from "impairing the Obligation of Contracts"? Is it because Marshall thinks that *every* law creates a contract that a state cannot subsequently amend? Or does he think the Contracts Clause protects some institutions created by government but not all such institutions?

It can require no argument to prove, that the circumstances of this case constitute a contract. An application is made to the crown for a charter to incorporate a religious and literary institution. In the application, it is stated, that large contributions have been made for the object, which will be conferred on the corporation, as soon as it shall be created. The charter is granted, and on its faith the property is conveyed. Surely, in this transaction every ingredient of a complete and legitimate contract is to be found. The points for consideration are, 1. Is this contract protected by the constitution of the United States? 2. Is it impaired by the acts under which the defendant holds?

1. On the first point, is has been argued, that the word "contract," in its broadest sense, would comprehend the political relations between the government and its citizens, would extend to offices held within a state, for state purposes, and to many of those laws concerning civil institutions, which must change with circumstances, and be modified by ordinary legislation; which deeply concern the public, and which, to preserve good government, the public judgment must control. That even marriage is a contract, and its obligations are affected by the laws respecting divorces. That the clause in the constitution, if construed in its greatest latitude, would prohibit these laws. Taken in its broad, unlimited sense, the clause would be an unprofitable and vexatious interference with the internal concerns of a state, would unnecessarily and unwisely embarrass its legislation, and render immutable those civil institutions, which are established for purposes of internal government, and which, to subserve those purposes, ought to vary with varying circumstances. That as the framers of the constitution could never have intended to insert in that instrument, a provision so unnecessary, so mischievous, and so repugnant to its general spirit, the term "contract" must be understood in a more limited sense.[2] That it must be understood as intended to guard against a power, of at least doubtful utility, the abuse of which had been extensively felt; and to restrain the legislature in future from violating the right to property. That, anterior to the formation of the constitution, a course of legislation had prevailed in many, if not in all, of the states, which weakened the confidence of man in man, and embarrassed all transactions between individuals, by dispensing with a faithful performance of engagements. To correct this mischief, by restraining the power which produced it, the state legislatures were forbidden "to pass any law impairing the obligation of contracts," that is, of contracts respecting property, under which some individual could claim a right to something beneficial to himself; and that, since the clause in the constitution must in construction receive some limitation, it may be confined, and ought to be confined, to cases of this description; to cases within the mischief it was intended to remedy.

The general correctness of these observations cannot be controverted. That the framers of the constitution did not intend to restrain the states in the regulation of their civil institutions, adopted for internal government, and that the instrument they have given us, is not to be so construed, may be admitted. The provision of the constitution never has been understood to embrace other contracts, than those which respect property, or some object of value, and confer rights which may be asserted in a court of justice. It never has been understood to restrict the general right of the legislature to legislate on the subject of divorces. Those acts enable some tribunals, not to impair a marriage contract, but to liberate one of the parties, because it has been broken by the other. When any state legislature shall pass an act annulling all

[2] **Question:** Marshall begins by taking it for granted that (1) the charter creating Dartmouth College was a contract, but (2) it would be an "unprofitable and vexatious interference with the internal concerns of a state" if all contracts were protected by the Contracts Clause. In the next few paragraphs, how does he distinguish between contracts protected by the Contracts Clause and contracts that are not protected?

marriage contracts, or allowing either party to annul it, without the consent of the other, it will be time enough to inquire, whether such an act be constitutional.

The parties in this case differ less on general principles, less on the true construction of the constitution in the abstract, than on the application of those principles to this case, and on the true construction of the charter of 1769. This is the point on which the cause essentially depends. If the act of incorporation be a grant of political power, if it create a civil institution, to be employed in the administration of the government, or if the funds of the college be public property, or if the state of New Hampshire, as a government, be alone interested in its transactions, the subject is one in which the legislature of the state may act according to its own judgment, unrestrained by any limitation of its power imposed by the constitution of the United States.

But if this be a private eleemosynary [*i.e.*, charitable] institution, endowed with a capacity to take property, for objects unconnected with government, whose funds are bestowed by individuals, on the faith of the charter; if the donors have stipulated for the future disposition and management of those funds, in the manner prescribed by themselves; there may be more difficulty in the case, although neither the persons who have made these stipulations, nor those for whose benefit they were made, should be parties to the cause. . . .[3]

From the instrument itself, it appears, that about the year 1754, the Rev. Eleazer Wheelock established, at his own expense, and on his own estate, a charity school for the instruction of Indians in the Christian religion. The success of this institution inspired him with the design of soliciting contributions in England, for carrying on and extending his undertaking. In this pious work, he . . . appointed the Earl of Dartmouth and others, trustees of the money, which had been, and should be, contributed. . . . They determined to establish the school on Connecticut river, in the western part of New Hampshire; that situation being supposed favorable for carrying on the original design among the Indians, and also for promoting learning among the English; and the proprietors in the neighborhood having made large offers of land, on condition, that the college should there be placed. Dr. Wheelock then applied to the crown for an act of incorporation; and represented the expediency of appointing those whom he had, by his last will, named as trustees in America, to be members of the proposed corporation. "In consideration of the premises," "for the education and instruction of the youth of the Indian tribes," &c., "and also of English youth, and any others," the charter was granted, and the trustees of Dartmouth College were, by that name, created a body corporate, with power, for the use of the said college, to acquire real and personal property, and to pay the president, tutors and other officers of the college, such salaries as they shall allow. . . .

From this brief review of the most essential parts of the charter, it is apparent, that the funds of the college consisted entirely of private donations. . . . Dr. Wheelock was the founder of the college. . . . The charter of incorporation was granted at his instance. The persons named by him, in his last will, as the trustees of his charity-school, compose a part of the corporation, and he is declared to be the founder of the college, and its president for life. . . . Dartmouth College is really endowed by private individuals, who have bestowed their funds for the propagation of the Christian religion among the Indians, and for the promotion of piety and learning generally. From these funds, the salaries of the tutors are drawn; and these salaries lessen the expense of education to the students. It is then . . . a private corporation. . . .

---

[3] **Questions:** What is the basis for Marshall's distinction between a law that creates a "political" or public institution and one that creates a "private" institution? In which of these categories does he place Dartmouth's charter?

Whence, then, can be derived the idea, that Dartmouth College has become a public institution, and its trustees public officers, exercising powers conferred by the public for public objects? Not from the source whence its funds were drawn; for its foundation is purely private and eleemosynary—not from the application of those funds; for money may be given for education, and the persons receiving it do not, by being employed in the education of youth, become members of the civil government. Is it from the act of incorporation? Let this subject be considered.

A corporation is an artificial being, invisible, intangible, and existing only in contemplation of law. Being the mere creature of law, it possesses only those properties which the charter of its creation confers upon it, either expressly, or as incidental to its very existence. These are such as are supposed best calculated to effect the object for which it was created. Among the most important are immortality, and, if the expression may be allowed, individuality; properties, by which a perpetual succession of many persons are considered as the same, and may act as a single individual. They enable a corporation to manage its own affairs, and to hold property, without the perplexing intricacies, the hazardous and endless necessity, of perpetual conveyances for the purpose of transmitting it from hand to hand. It is chiefly for the purpose of clothing bodies of men, in succession, with these qualities and capacities, that corporations were invented, and are in use. By these means, a perpetual succession of individuals are capable of acting for the promotion of the particular object, like one immortal being. But this being does not share in the civil government of the country, unless that be the purpose for which it was created. Its immortality no more confers on it political power, or a political character, than immortality would confer such power or character on a natural person. It is no more a state instrument, than a natural person exercising the same powers would be. If, then, a natural person, employed by individuals in the education of youth, or for the government of a seminary in which youth is educated, would not become a public officer, or be considered as a member of the civil government, how is it, that this artificial being, created by law, for the purpose of being employed by the same individuals, for the same purposes, should become a part of the civil government of the country? Is it because its existence, its capacities, its powers, are given by law? Because the government has given it the power to take and to hold property, in a particular form, and for particular purposes, has the government a consequent right substantially to change that form, or to vary the purposes to which the property is to be applied? This principle has never been asserted or recognised, and is supported by no authority. . . .

From the fact, then, that a charter of incorporation has been granted, nothing can be inferred, which changes the character of the institution, or transfers to the government any new power over it. The character of civil institutions does not grow out of their incorporation, but out of the manner in which they are formed, and the objects for which they are created. The right to change them is not founded on their being incorporated, but on their being the instruments of government, created for its purposes. The same institutions, created for the same objects, though not incorporated, would be public institutions, and, of course, be controllable by the legislature. The incorporating act neither gives nor prevents this control. Neither, in reason, can the incorporating act change the character of a private eleemosynary institution.[4]

[4] **Questions:** Here, Marshall concludes that the mere fact that Dartmouth College is a corporation chartered by the state does not make it a public institution for which the Contracts Clause is inapplicable. Do you agree? New Hampshire gave the founders of Dartmouth the benefit of incorporation in exchange for Dartmouth's promise to educate Native Americans and New Hampshire residents. Does it make sense to conclude that this charter was a contract that New Hampshire should not be allowed to unilaterally amend?

We are next led to the inquiry, for whose benefit the property given to Dartmouth College was secured? The counsel for the defendant have insisted, that the beneficial interest is in the people of New Hampshire. . . . [But looking at the charter, the] particular interests of New Hampshire never entered into the mind of the donors, never constituted a motive for their donation. The propagation of the Christian religion among the savages, and the dissemination of useful knowledge among the youth of the country, were the avowed and the sole objects of their contributions. In these, New Hampshire would participate; but nothing particular or exclusive was intended for her. Even the site of the college was selected, not for the sake of New Hampshire, but because it was "most subservient to the great ends in view," and because liberal donations of land were offered by the proprietors, on condition that the institution should be there established. . . .

From this review of the charter, it appears, that Dartmouth College is [a private] institution, incorporated for the purpose of perpetuating the application of the bounty of the donors, to the specified objects of that bounty; that its trustees or governors were originally named by the founder, and invested with the power of perpetuating themselves; that they are not public officers, nor is it a civil institution, participating in the administration of government; but a charity-school, or a seminary of education, incorporated for the preservation of its property, and the perpetual application of that property to the objects of its creation. . . .

This is plainly a contract to which the donors, the trustees and the crown (to whose rights and obligations New Hampshire succeeds) were the original parties. It is a contract made on a valuable consideration. It is a contract for the security and disposition of property. It is a contract, on the faith of which, real and personal estate has been conveyed to the corporation. It is, then, a contract within the letter of the constitution, and within its spirit also. . . .

The opinion of the court, after mature deliberation, is, that this is a contract, the obligation of which cannot be impaired, without violating the constitution of the United States. . . .

2. We next proceed to the inquiry, whether its obligation has been impaired by those acts of the legislature of New Hampshire, to which the special verdict refers?[5]

From the review of this charter, which has been taken, it appears that the whole power of governing the college, of appointing and removing tutors, of fixing their salaries, of directing the course of study to be pursued by the students, and of filling up vacancies created in their own body, was vested in the trustees. On the part of the crown, it was expressly stipulated, that this corporation, thus constituted, should continue for ever; and that the number of trustees should for ever consist of twelve, and no more. By this contract, the crown was bound, and could have made no violent alteration in its essential terms, without impairing its obligation.

By the revolution, the duties, as well as the powers, of government devolved on the people of New Hampshire. . . . It has been already stated, that the act "to amend the charter, and enlarge and improve the corporation of Dartmouth College," increases the number of trustees to twenty-one, gives the appointment of the additional members to the executive of the state, and creates a board of overseers,

---

[5] **Questions:** So far, Marshall has concluded that (1) the Contracts Clause protects laws that create private institutions but not laws that create public institutions, and (2) the law chartering Dartmouth College created a private institution. Does this conclusion mean that New Hampshire is totally incapacitated from regulating Dartmouth College or any other private corporation? Applying the second half of Marshall's opinion (and Justice Joseph Story's concurring opinion), can you think of an example of a corporate regulation that the Contracts Clause might tolerate?

to consist of twenty-five persons, of whom twenty-one are also appointed by the executive of New Hampshire, who have power to inspect and control the most important acts of the trustees. . . .

The whole power of governing the college is transferred from trustees, appointed according to the will of the founder, expressed in the charter, to the executive of New Hampshire. The management and application of the funds of this eleemosynary institution, which are placed by the donors in the hands of trustees named in the charter, and empowered to perpetuate themselves, are placed by this act under the control of the government of the state. The will of the state is substituted for the will of the donors, in every essential operation of the college. This is not an immaterial change. The founders of the college contracted, not merely for the perpetual application of the funds which they gave, to the objects for which those funds were given; they contracted also, to secure that application by the constitution of the corporation. They contracted for a system, which should, so far as human foresight can provide, retain for ever the government of the literary institution they had formed, in the hands of persons approved by themselves. This system is totally changed. The charter of 1769 exists no longer. It is re-organized; and re-organized in such a manner, as to convert a literary institution, moulded according to the will of its founders, and placed under the control of private literary men, into a machine entirely subservient to the will of government. This may be for the advantage of this college in particular, and may be for the advantage of literature in general; but it is not according to the will of the donors, and is subversive of that contract, on the faith of which their property was given. . . .

It results from this opinion, that the acts of the legislature of New Hampshire, which are stated in the special verdict found in this cause, are repugnant to the constitution of the United States. . . .

■ STORY, JUSTICE.

Nothing seems better settled, at the common law, than the doctrine, that the crown cannot force upon a private corporation a new charter; or compel the old members to give up their own franchises, or to admit new members into the corporation. As little has it been supposed, that under our limited governments, the legislature possessed such transcendent authority. On one occasion, a very able court held, . . . that the rights legally vested in a corporation cannot be controlled or destroyed by any subsequent statute, unless a power for that purpose be reserved to the legislature in the act of incorporation. *Wales v. Stetson*, 2 Mass. 143, 146. These principles are so consonant with justice, sound policy and legal reasoning, that it is difficult to resist the impression of their perfect correctness. . . .[6]

NOTE: PUBLIC CORPORATIONS

Dartmouth College was the first major Supreme Court case to distinguish between "public" corporations and "private" corporations. According to Marshall, public corporations were civil institutions, like cities, that were (a) "employed in the administration of the government," (b) founded by "public property," or (c) intended to serve a state's interests above all others. *Dartmouth Coll.*, 17 U.S. (4 Wheat.) at 630. With these sorts of

[6] **Question:** Note Story's caveat: "[T]he rights legally vested in a corporation cannot be controlled or destroyed by any subsequent statute, unless a power for that purpose be reserved to the legislature in the act of incorporation." In other words, had Dartmouth's charter included the phrase *This charter may be unilaterally amended by the government*, there would be no Contracts Clause violation. How do you expect that states responded to the decision in *Dartmouth College* when they chartered new private corporations?

corporations, New Hampshire was "unrestrained by any limitation of its power imposed by the constitution of the United States." *Id.* But all other corporations were private corporations, whose charters were contracts protected by the Contracts Clause. According to Justice Joseph Story, unless a state "reserved to the legislature in the act of incorporation" some clause permitting the legislature to amend or control the charter, then the legislature had no power to impair the contract. *Id.* at 708.

Dartmouth College had profound effects on the development of public corporations and private corporations. The case gave states plenary authority to regulate their public corporations—cities, authorities, utilities, and state universities—free from oversight by the U.S. Constitution. This meant that as long as states didn't impair any contracts with private creditors, they could unilaterally change the powers, tenure, duties, charters, and boundaries of state institutions. *See, e.g., Mississippi ex rel. Robertson v. Miller*, 276 U.S. 174, 179 (1928). For example, in *Newton v. Commissioners*, the Court upheld a law that relocated a county seat even though citizens near the original seat relied on a statute that declared that the county seat would be "permanently established" there. 100 U.S. 548, 561 (1880). And most famously, in *Hunter v. City of Pittsburgh*, the Court declared that cities are "political subdivisions of the State" subject to the state's "absolute discretion. . . . [T]he State is supreme, and its legislative body, conforming its action to the state constitution, may do as it will, unrestrained by any provision of the Constitution of the United States." 207 U.S. 161, 178–79 (1907).

The Court later softened this language, suggesting that states are subject to some constitutional limits when they legislate with respect to local governments or public employees. *See, e.g., Romer v. Evans*, 517 U.S. 620 (1996) (states can't regulate local governments in violation of the Fourteenth Amendment); *Bd. of Educ. of Kiryas Joel Vill. Sch. Dist. v. Grumet*, 512 U.S. 687 (1994) (same in violation of Establishment Clause); *Gomillion v. Lightfoot*, 364 U.S. 339 (1960) (same in violation of the Fifteenth Amendment); *Indiana ex rel. Anderson v. Brand*, 303 U.S. 95 (1938) (state contracts with public employees are protected by the Contracts Clause).

38.1.2

Stone v. Mississippi

101 U.S. 814 (1880)

Although *Dartmouth College* allowed governments to regulate *public* corporations free from constitutional scrutiny, it offered a powerful weapon against regulations of *private* corporations, like Dartmouth itself. The opinion suggested that any modification of a corporation's charter could be an impairment of the obligation of contract. The opinion thus ratified the idea of a private sphere in which institutions created by governments were constitutionally protected from their governmental creators. This holding ushered in the rise of private business corporations. Within a few decades, railroads, manufacturing companies, banks, and other private enterprises dominated the American economy. *See* Morton J. Horwitz, *The Transformation of American Law, 1780–1860*, at 127–36 (1979).

But Story's concurring opinion in *Dartmouth College* included a critical caveat: when a state chartered a new corporation, it could "reserve" for itself the power to control or modify the corporation's charter in the future, thus insulating any future regulations from the charge that they "impair[ed]" the original contract. *Dartmouth Coll.*, 17 U.S. (4 Wheat.) at 675. After *Dartmouth College*, many states routinely adopted these sorts of reservation clauses when they chartered corporations, thus blunting *Dartmouth College*'s practical thrust. *See, e.g.*, *Louisville Water Co. v. Clark*, 143 U.S. 1, 12 (1892); *Pa. Coll. Cases*, 80 U.S. (13 Wall.) 190, 213 (1872); *Home of the Friendless v. Rouse*, 75 U.S. (8 Wall.) 430, 438 (1869).

Relatedly, after Marshall died in 1835, the Supreme Court began to hold that it would be inappropriate to interpret the Contracts Clause so broadly that one legislature could permanently disempower a future legislature by contracting away its own basic powers. Marshall's successor, Roger Taney, was a prominent member of President Andrew Jackson's cabinet and a populist opponent of corporate power.

One of the Taney Court's first cases involved the Charles River Bridge Company. In 1785, the Massachusetts legislature chartered the company to construct a toll bridge connecting Boston and Charlestown. Forty years later, the legislature chartered a second corporation, the Warren Bridge Company, to build a toll-free bridge nearby. The proprietors of the Charles River Bridge Company sued, complaining that this second corporation impaired their own charter because direct competition would reduce the profits that they could collect from tolls.

In *Proprietors of the Charles River Bridge v. Proprietors of the Warren Bridge*, the Taney Court refused to recognize the existence of any "implied contract" promising the Charles River Bridge Company a permanent monopoly on bridge traffic. 36 U.S. (11 Pet.) 420, 552 (1837). Taney explained that the Contracts Clause had to be narrowly interpreted in order to be compatible "with the rights reserved to the states." *Id.* at 510, 552. He would therefore decline to "take away from [the States] any portion of that power over their own internal police and improvement, which is so necessary to their well being and prosperity." *Id.* at 552. Applying this interpretation, the Court held that even though a new corporation might impair the value of the first corporation's charter, Massachusetts had never promised not to charter competing corporations.

In later cases, the Taney Court expanded the *Charles River Bridge* precedent into a new doctrine called the "reserved powers" doctrine: the Contracts Clause cannot be interpreted to prevent a state from exercising the most fundamental powers reserved to it by the Tenth Amendment. For example, unless a corporate charter explicitly gave a corporation a tax exemption, the Court refused to hold that the Contracts Clause prohibited a legislature from taxing a corporation that it had once exempted from taxation. *See, e.g.*, *Salt Co. v. East Saginaw*, 80 U.S. (13 Wall.) 373, 379 (1872); *State Bank v. Knoop*, 57 U.S. (16 How.) 369, 404 (1854). And even where a charter explicitly gave a corporation the exclusive exercise of the power of eminent domain, the Court allowed a state to withdraw this benefit on the theory that a state couldn't contract away its basic police powers, including the power of eminent domain. *W. River Bridge Co. v. Dix*, 47 U.S. (6 How.) 507, 535–36 (1848).

The following case, *Stone v. Mississippi*, 101 U.S. 814 (1880), provides a clear illustration of the reserved powers doctrine and the principles animating it. In 1867, Mississippi's Reconstruction-era legislature was desperate for funds. To earn some money, it decided to charter a lottery corporation. The charter authorized the deceptively named Mississippi Agricultural, Educational, and Manufacturing Aid Society to run a lottery for twenty-five years. In return, the society promised to pay the state $1,000 and a percentage of the lottery earnings every year. But only a year later, in 1868, the state adopted a new constitution that provided that "the legislature shall never authorize any lottery, nor shall the sale of lottery-tickets be allowed, nor shall any lottery heretofore authorized be permitted to be drawn, or tickets therein to be sold." Stone, 101 U.S. at 819 (quoting Miss. Const. art. 12, § 15 (1868)). The state then sued the society's representative, John B. Stone, for operating an illegal lottery. Stone responded that the new state constitution violated the Contracts Clause.

Although the *Stone* Court did find that a contract existed, it nevertheless ruled that the state cannot permanently bargain away the state's police power.

■ MR. CHIEF JUSTICE WAITE delivered the opinion of the Court.[7]

It is now too late to contend that any contract which a State actually enters into when granting a charter to a private corporation is not within the protection of the clause in the Constitution of the United States that prohibits States from passing laws impairing the obligation of contracts. Art. 1, sect. 10. The doctrines of *Trustees of Dartmouth College v. Woodward* (4 Wheat. 518), announced by this court more than sixty years ago, have become so imbedded in the jurisprudence of the United States as to make them to all intents and purposes a part of the Constitution itself. In this connection, however, it is to be kept in mind that it is not the charter which is protected, but only any contract the charter may contain. If there is no contract, there is nothing in the grant on which the Constitution can act. Consequently, the first inquiry in this class of cases always is, whether a contract has in fact been entered into, and if so, what its obligations are.

---

[7] **As You Read, Consider:** The Mississippi Constitution of 1868 clearly impaired a contract in roughly the same way that New Hampshire impaired Dartmouth College's corporate charter decades earlier. Before 1868, Mississippi promised the lottery corporation that it could operate a lottery for 25 years; after 1868, Mississippi made lotteries illegal. Why, then, does Chief Justice Morrison Waite decline to hold that the new constitution violates the Contracts Clause?

In the present case the question is whether the State of Mississippi, in its sovereign capacity, did by the charter now under consideration bind itself irrevocably by a contract to permit "the Mississippi Agricultural, Educational, and Manufacturing Aid Society," for twenty-five years, "to receive subscriptions, and sell and dispose of certificates of subscription which shall entitle the holders thereof to" "any lands, books, paintings, antiques, scientific instruments or apparatus, or any other property or thing that may be ornamental, valuable, or useful," "awarded to them" "by the casting of lots, or by lot, chance, or otherwise." There can be no dispute but that under this form of words the legislature of the State chartered a lottery company, having all the powers incident to such a corporation, for twenty-five years, and that in consideration thereof the company paid into the State treasury $5,000 for the use of a university, and agreed to pay, and until the commencement of this suit did pay, an annual tax of $1,000 and "one-half of one per cent on the amount of receipts derived from the sale of certificates or tickets." If the legislature that granted this charter had the power to bind the people of the State and all succeeding legislatures to allow the corporation to continue its corporate business during the whole term of its authorized existence, there is no doubt about the sufficiency of the language employed to effect that object, although there was an evident purpose to conceal the vice of the transaction by the phrases that were used. Whether the alleged contract exists, therefore, or not, depends on the authority of the legislature to bind the State and the people of the State in that way.

All agree that the legislature cannot bargain away the police power of a State.[8] Irrevocable grants of property and franchises may be made if they do not impair the supreme authority to make laws for the right government of the State; but no legislature can curtail the power of its successors to make such laws as they may deem proper in matters of police. Many attempts have been made in this court and elsewhere to define the police power, but never with entire success. It is always easier to determine whether a particular case comes within the general scope of the power, than to give an abstract definition of the power itself which will be in all respects accurate. No one denies, however, that it extends to all matters affecting the public health or the public morals. Neither can it be denied that lotteries are proper subjects for the exercise of this power. . . .

If lotteries are to be tolerated at all, it is no doubt better that they should be regulated by law, so that the people may be protected as far as possible against the inherent vices of the system; but that they are demoralizing in their effects, no matter how carefully regulated, cannot admit of a doubt. When the government is untrammelled by any claim of vested rights or chartered privileges, no one has ever supposed that lotteries could not lawfully be suppressed, and those who manage them punished severely as violators of the rules of social morality. From 1822 to 1867, without any constitutional requirement, they were prohibited by law in Mississippi, and those who conducted them punished as a kind of gamblers. During the provisional government of that State, in 1867, at the close of the late civil war, the present act of incorporation, with more of like character, was passed. The next year, 1868, the people, in adopting a new constitution with a view to the resumption of their political rights as one of the United States, provided that "the legislature shall never authorize any lottery, nor shall the sale of lottery-tickets be allowed, nor shall any lottery heretofore authorized be permitted to be drawn, or tickets therein to be

---

[8] **Questions:** Waite acknowledges that a contract has been made between Mississippi and the corporation—provided that the Mississippi legislature had the authority to make it. What does he mean when he says that "the legislature cannot bargain away the police power of a State"? What would be the consequence of an interpretation of the Contracts Clause that prohibited a state legislature from repealing its predecessor's legislation? For a related analysis, consider the *Chinese Exclusion Case*, which alludes to this opinion (section 10.3).

sold." Art. 12, sect. 15. There is now scarcely a State in the Union where lotteries are tolerated, and Congress has enacted a special statute, the object of which is to close the mails against them. . . .

The question is therefore directly presented, whether, in view of these facts, the legislature of a State can, by the charter of a lottery company, defeat the will of the people, authoritatively expressed, in relation to the further continuance of such business in their midst. We think it cannot. No legislature can bargain away the public health or the public morals. The people themselves cannot do it, much less their servants. The supervision of both these subjects of governmental power is continuing in its nature, and they are to be dealt with as the special exigencies of the moment may require. Government is organized with a view to their preservation, and cannot divest itself of the power to provide for them. For this purpose the largest legislative discretion is allowed, and the discretion cannot be parted with any more than the power itself.

In *Trustees of Dartmouth College v. Woodward* (4 Wheat. 518), it was argued that the contract clause of the Constitution, if given the effect contended for in respect to corporate franchises, "would be an unprofitable and vexatious interference with the internal concerns of a State, would unnecessarily and unwisely embarrass its legislation, and render immutable those civil institutions which are established for the purpose of internal government, and which, to subserve those purposes, ought to vary with varying circumstances" (p. 628); but Mr. Chief Justice Marshall, when he announced the opinion of the court, was careful to say (p. 629), "that the framers of the Constitution did not intend to restrain States in the regulation of their civil institutions, adopted for internal government, and that the instrument they have given us is not to be so construed." The present case, we think, comes within this limitation. . . .

[T]he power of governing is a trust committed by the people to the government, no part of which can be granted away. The people, in their sovereign capacity, have established their agencies for the preservation of the public health and the public morals, and the protection of public and private rights. These several agencies can govern according to their discretion, if within the scope of their general authority, while in power; but they cannot give away nor sell the discretion of those that are to come after them, in respect to matters the government of which, from the very nature of things, must "vary with varying circumstances." They may create corporations, and give them, so to speak, a limited citizenship; but as citizens, limited in their privileges, or otherwise, these creatures of the government creation are subject to such rules and regulations as may from time to time be ordained and established for the preservation of health and morality.

The contracts which the Constitution protects are those that relate to property rights, not governmental.[9] It is not always easy to tell on which side of the line which separates governmental from property rights a particular case is to be put; but in respect to lotteries there can be no difficulty. They are not, in the legal acceptation of the term, *mala in se* [*i.e.*, inherently wrong], but, as we have just seen, may properly be made *mala prohibita* [*i.e.*, made wrong by law]. They are a species of gambling, and wrong in their influences. They disturb the checks and balances of a well-ordered community. Society built on such a foundation would almost of necessity bring forth

---

[9] **Questions:** Waite concludes that the Contracts Clause has no application to a contract provision in which a state bargains away one of its "governmental" powers. Otherwise, the federal Constitution would prohibit state legislatures from repealing the work of their predecessors. But isn't such a prohibition the entire point of the Contracts Clause? What is the distinction between the Mississippi constitutional provision at issue here and an ordinary debt-relief law that the Contracts Clause was intended to prohibit?

a population of speculators and gamblers, living on the expectation of what, "by the casting of lots, or by lot, chance, or otherwise," might be "awarded" to them from the accumulations of others. Certainly the right to suppress them is governmental, to be exercised at all times by those in power, at their discretion. Any one, therefore, who accepts a lottery charter does so with the implied understanding that the people, in their sovereign capacity, and through their properly constituted agencies, may resume it at any time when the public good shall require, whether it be paid for or not. All that one can get by such a charter is a suspension of certain governmental rights in his favor, subject to withdrawal at will. He has in legal effect nothing more than a license to enjoy the privilege on the terms named for the specified time, unless it be sooner abrogated by the sovereign power of the State. It is a permit, good as against existing laws, but subject to future legislative and constitutional control or withdrawal. . . .

NOTE: POLICE POWER

The *Stone* Court didn't comprehensively define the scope of the reserved powers that a state may not permanently bargain away. But in later cases, the Supreme Court interpreted the reserved powers doctrine capaciously to allow states to regulate corporations for the purpose of preserving "the public health, the public morals, or the public safety" of their citizens—even when the regulations conflicted with existing corporate charters. *See, e.g.*, *Pa. Hosp. v. City of Philadelphia*, 245 U.S. 20, 23–24 (1917); *Butchers' Union Slaughter-House & Live-Stock Landing Co. v. Crescent City Live-Stock Landing & Slaughter-House Co.*, 111 U.S. 746, 754 (1884). The notable exception to this rule concerned state debt: where a state, city, or public corporation owed outstanding debt to a private creditor, the Court refused to allow the state to escape that debt by dissolving the corporation or transferring the debt to a less creditworthy institution. *Graham v. Folsom*, 200 U.S. 248, 254–55 (1906); *Mobile v. Watson*, 116 U.S. 289, 306 (1886).

38.1.3

Home Building & Loan Ass'n v. Blaisdell

290 U.S. 398 (1934)

Dartmouth College and *Stone* both addressed contracts in which the state contracted with a so-called private party. But as the Supreme Court acknowledged in both cases, the main purpose of the Contracts Clause wasn't to prevent a state from repudiating its *own* contracts but rather to prevent states from passing debt-relief laws that impaired contracts involving *two individuals*. Through the nineteenth century, the Supreme Court was considerably more aggressive about preventing states from helping indebted residents escape their debts than it was about regulating public contracts.

In *Sturges v. Crowninshield*, 17 U.S. (4 Wheat.) 122 (1819), the Court first considered a state debt-relief law that authorized debtors to declare bankruptcy if they couldn't pay all of their debts. The Court held that the state couldn't apply its law retroactively to affect existing contracts because those sorts of contracts were exactly what the Contracts Clause was intended to protect.

But in *Ogden v. Saunders*, the Court held that a state could apply its bankruptcy law prospectively to affect *future* contracts on the theory that a state could impliedly insert into any contract or charter the right to revise it, and that any such act became part of the contract itself. 25 U.S. (12 Wheat.) 213, 267 (1827). *Ogden* was the only case in which Chief Justice John Marshall dissented. He warned that its principle would allow states to declare all contracts subject to revision, nullifying the effectiveness of the Contracts Clause. *Id.* at 338–40 (Marshall, C.J., dissenting). The Court reconsidered Marshall's warning in *Oshkosh Waterworks Co. v. Oshkosh*, 187 U.S. 437 (1903). There, it upheld the power of states to prospectively change remedies available to creditors only as long as "a substantial or efficacious remedy" remained available for enforcing contract rights. *Oshkosh Waterworks Co.*, 187 U.S. at 438.

Despite *Sturges*'s ban on retroactive debt-relief laws, the Court didn't strike down all state legislation that happened to impair existing private contracts. One exception emerged based on the *type* of contract that the state law sought to regulate. For example, the Court held that *Sturges* did not apply when two private parties contracted to engage in cockfighting, horse racing, and other activities that were subsequently outlawed by the state. The Court was concerned that if the Contracts Clause prohibited the state from impairing the validity of such contracts, then individuals would be able to escape state legislation by forming private contracts legalizing their conduct. *See Hudson Water Co. v. McCarter,* 209 U.S. 349, 357 (1908). Additionally, in *Jackson v. Lamphire*, 28 U.S. (3 Pet.) 280, 290–91 (1830), the Court held that a state could apply a recording act to deeds dated before the passage of the act as such a law didn't implicate the same concerns as debt-relief laws. In later cases, the Court applied the reserved powers doctrine to hold that a state always has the power to protect the health, safety, and morals of its residents, even if its regulations impair preexisting contracts. *See, e.g., Manigault v. Springs*, 199 U.S. 473, 481 (1905).

A second—and more consequential—exception emerged during World War I: the Court allowed states to invalidate contracts to address public emergencies. For example, many states responded to housing shortages during the war by forbidding landlords from enforcing lease agreements that required tenants to surrender the premises at the expiration of the lease. In *Marcus Brown Co. v. Feldman*, 256 U.S. 170 (1921), the Court held that such an emergency could permit a state to temporarily impair the obligation of preexisting contracts. In later cases, the Court suggested that it would evaluate for itself whether an emergency justifying the impairment of contracts existed. *See, e.g., Chastleton Corp. v. Sinclair*, 264 U.S. 543 (1924).

But the precedent was set for the following case, *Home Building & Loan Ass'n v. Blaisdell*, 290 U.S. 398 (1934), in which the Court considered the greatest emergency for contracts that the United States had ever seen: the Great Depression.

Most homeowners don't own their homes outright. When people buy a home, they typically get the money for the purchase by signing a contract with a bank, which agrees to give them a loan. These loans are then typically repaid with interest over a thirty-year period. Contracts to purchase homes are usually secured by a "mortgage," or a lien against a home. If a homeowner (or "mortgagor") defaults on a monthly payment, then the bank (or "mortgagee") can attempt to collect the entire outstanding loan balance by selling the home to a third party without the homeowner's consent. The process by which a mortgagee takes over and sells a home is called *foreclosure*. To give homeowners the opportunity to stay in their home, the foreclosure process usually requires the bank to wait a year before selling the property, during which time the homeowners can pay off the loan balance and "redeem" their property.

In the early years of the Great Depression, millions of Americans lost their jobs and their only sources of income. Unable to make monthly mortgage payments, many families risked losing their homes through foreclosure. Minnesota was one of many states that responded to this crisis by passing a debt-relief law to assist jobless homeowners. The Minnesota Mortgage Moratorium Law provided that during the financial emergency, state courts could order the postponement of a foreclosure sale and extend the homeowner's redemption period. This law was quickly assailed as exactly the sort of state debt-relief law prohibited by the Contracts Clause.

After the Home Building and Loan Association foreclosed on the Minneapolis home of the Blaisdell family, the Blaisdells received a court-ordered extension. The extension allowed them to remain in their home in exchange for a monthly payment of the rental value of the home. The association challenged this extension in state court as unconstitutional under the Contracts Clause.

The Minnesota Supreme Court agreed with the association that the law impaired the Blaisdells' mortgage contract. But the court held that under the reserved powers doctrine of *Stone*, a state could validly impair a contract when an economic emergency required it to do so in order to protect the health and safety of its residents.

When the Supreme Court of the United States took up *Blaisdell*, the Court used it to reconsider its own Contracts Clause jurisprudence, finding that the Contracts Clause did not constrain state governmental action in the emergency at issue.

■ MR. CHIEF JUSTICE HUGHES delivered the opinion of the Court.[10]

Appellant contests the validity of Chapter 339 of the Laws of Minnesota of 1933, p. 514, approved April 18, 1933, called the Minnesota Mortgage Moratorium Law, as being repugnant to the contract clause (Art. I, § 10). . . .

[10] **As You Read, Consider:** The Minnesota law at issue in this case differed from the Mississippi law at issue in *Stone v. Mississippi* in that it was a debt-relief law—exactly the sort of law that the Contracts Clause was intended to prohibit. If the Contracts Clause allows a state

Emergency does not create power. Emergency does not increase granted power or remove or diminish the restrictions imposed upon power granted or reserved. The Constitution was adopted in a period of grave emergency. Its grants of power to the Federal Government and its limitations of the power of the States were determined in the light of emergency and they are not altered by emergency. What power was thus granted and what limitations were thus imposed are questions which have always been, and always will be, the subject of close examination under our constitutional system.

While emergency does not create power, emergency may furnish the occasion for the exercise of power. "Although an emergency may not call into life a power which has never lived, nevertheless emergency may afford a reason for the exertion of a living power already enjoyed." *Wilson v. New*, 243 U.S. 332, 348. The constitutional question presented in the light of an emergency is whether the power possessed embraces the particular exercise of it in response to particular conditions. Thus, the war power of the Federal Government is not created by the emergency of war, but it is a power given to meet that emergency. It is a power to wage war successfully, and thus it permits the harnessing of the entire energies of the people in a supreme cooperative effort to preserve the nation. But even the war power does not remove constitutional limitations safeguarding essential liberties. When the provisions of the Constitution, in grant or restriction, are specific, so particularized as not to admit of construction, no question is presented. Thus, emergency would not permit a State to have more than two Senators in the Congress, or permit the election of President by a general popular vote without regard to the number of electors to which the States are respectively entitled, or permit the States to "coin money" or to "make anything but gold and silver coin a tender in payment of debts." But where constitutional grants and limitations of power are set forth in general clauses, which afford a broad outline, the process of construction is essential to fill in the details. That is true of the contract clause. The necessity of construction is not obviated by the fact that the contract clause is associated in the same section with other and more specific prohibitions. Even the grouping of subjects in the same clause may not require the same application to each of the subjects, regardless of differences in their nature.

In the construction of the contract clause, the debates in the Constitutional Convention are of little aid. But the reasons which led to the adoption of that clause, are of the other prohibitions of Section 10 of Article I, are not left in doubt and have frequently been described with eloquent emphasis. The widespread distress following the revolutionary period, and the plight of debtors, had called forth in the States an ignoble array of legislative schemes for the defeat of creditors and the invasion of contractual obligations. Legislative interferences had been so numerous and extreme that the confidence essential to prosperous trade had been undermined and the utter destruction of credit was threatened. "The sober people of America" were convinced that some "thorough reform" was needed which would "inspire a general prudence and industry, and give a regular course to the business of society." *The Federalist*, No. 44. It was necessary to interpose the restraining power of a central authority in order to secure the foundations even of "private faith." . . .

But full recognition of the occasion and general purpose of the clause does not suffice to fix its precise scope. Nor does an examination of the details of prior legislation in the States yield criteria which can be considered controlling. To ascertain the scope of the constitutional prohibition we examine the course of judicial decisions

---

to impair these sorts of contracts, are there any laws that Chief Justice Charles Evans Hughes would invalidate under the clause?

in its application. These put it beyond question that the prohibition is not an absolute one and is not to be read with literal exactness like a mathematical formula. . . .

The inescapable problems of construction have been: What is a contract? What are the obligations of contracts? What constitutes impairment of these obligations? What residuum of power is there still in the States in relation to the operation of contracts, to protect the vital interests of the community? Questions of this character, "of no small nicety and intricacy, have vexed the legislative halls, as well as the judicial tribunals, with an uncounted variety and frequency of litigation and speculation." Story on the Constitution, § 1375.

The obligation of a contract is "the law which binds the parties to perform their agreement." *Sturges v. Crowninshield*, 4 Wheat. 122, 197. This Court has said that "the laws which subsist at the time and place of the making of a contract, and where it is to be performed, enter into and form a part of it, as if they were expressly referred to or incorporated in its terms. This principle embraces alike those which affect its validity, construction, discharge and enforcement. . . . Nothing can be more material to the obligation than the means of enforcement. . . . The ideas of validity and remedy are inseparable, and both are parts of the obligation, which is guaranteed by the Constitution against invasion." *Von Hoffman v. City of Quincy*, 4 Wall. 535, 550, 552. But this broad language cannot be taken without qualification. Chief Justice Marshall pointed out the distinction between obligation and remedy. *Sturges v. Crowninshield, supra*, p. 200. Said he: "The distinction between the obligation of a contract, and the remedy given by the legislature to enforce that obligation, has been taken at the bar, and exists in the nature of things. Without impairing the obligation of the contract, the remedy may certainly be modified as the wisdom of the nation shall direct." And in *Von Hoffman v. City of Quincy, supra*, pp. 553, 554, the general statement above quoted was limited by the further observation that "It is competent for the States to change the form of the remedy, or to modify it otherwise, as they may see fit, provided no substantial right secured by the contract is thereby impaired. No attempt has been made to fix definitely the line between alterations of the remedy, which are to be deemed legitimate, and those which, under the form of modifying the remedy, impair substantial rights. Every case must be determined upon its own circumstances." . . .

Not only is the constitutional provision qualified by the measure of control which the State retains over remedial processes, but the State also continues to possess authority to safeguard the vital interests of its people. It does not matter that legislation appropriate to that end "has the result of modifying or abrogating contracts already in effect." *Stephenson v. Binford*, 287 U.S. 251, 276. Not only are existing laws read into contracts in order to fix obligations as between the parties, but the reservation of essential attributes of sovereign power is also read into contracts as a postulate of the legal order. The policy of protecting contracts against impairment presupposes the maintenance of a government by virtue of which contractual relations are worth while,—a government which retains adequate authority to secure the peace and good order of society. This principle of harmonizing the constitutional prohibition with the necessary residuum of state power has had progressive recognition in the decisions of this Court.

While the charters of private corporations constitute contracts, a grant of exclusive privilege is not to be implied as against the State. *Charles River Bridge v. Warren Bridge*, 11 Pet. 420. And all contracts are subject to the right of eminent domain. *West River Bridge v. Dix*, 6 How. 507. The reservation of this necessary authority of the State is deemed to be a part of the contract. In the case last cited, the Court answered the forcible challenge of the State's power by the following statement of the controlling principle,—a statement reiterated by this Court speaking through Mr. Justice Brewer, nearly fifty years later, in *Long Island Water Supply Co. v. Brooklyn*, 166 U.S. 685, 692: "But into all contracts, whether made between States and individuals, or between individuals only, there enter conditions which arise not out of the literal terms of the contract itself; they are superinduced by the preexisting and higher authority of the laws of nature, of nations or of the community to which the parties belong; they are always presumed, and must be presumed, to be known and recognized by all, are binding upon all, and need never, therefore, be carried into express stipulation, for this could add nothing to their force. Every contract is made in subordination to them, and must yield to their control, as conditions inherent and paramount, wherever a necessity for their execution shall occur."

The legislature cannot "bargain away the public health or the public morals." Thus, the constitutional provision against the impairment of contracts was held not to be violated by an amendment of the state constitution which put an end to a lottery theretofore authorized by the legislature. *Stone v. Mississippi*, 101 U.S. 814, 819. The lottery was a valid enterprise when established under express state authority, but the legislature in the public interest could put a stop to it. A similar rule has been applied to the control by the State of the sale of intoxicating liquors. The States retain adequate power to protect the public health against the maintenance of nuisances despite insistence upon existing contracts. Legislation to protect the public safety comes within the same category of reserved power. . . .

Undoubtedly, whatever is reserved of state power must be consistent with the fair intent of the constitutional limitation of that power.[11] The reserved power cannot be construed so as to destroy the limitation, nor is the limitation to be construed to destroy the reserved power in its essential aspects. They must be construed in harmony with each other. This principle precludes a construction which would permit the State to adopt as its policy the repudiation of debts or the destruction of contracts or the denial of means to enforce them. But it does not follow that conditions may not arise in which a temporary restraint of enforcement may be consistent with the spirit and purpose of the constitutional provision and thus be found to be within the range of the reserved power of the State to protect the vital interests of the community. It cannot be maintained that the constitutional prohibition should be so construed as to prevent limited and temporary interpositions with respect to the enforcement of contracts if made necessary by a great public calamity such as fire, flood, or earthquake. The reservation of state power appropriate to such extraordinary conditions may be deemed to be as much a part of all contracts, as is the reservation of state power to protect the public interest in the other situations to which we have referred. And if state power exists to give temporary relief from the enforcement of contracts in the presence of disasters due to physical causes such as fire, flood or earthquake, that power cannot be said to be non-existent when the urgent public need demanding such relief is produced by other and economic causes. . . .

[T]here has been a growing appreciation of public needs and of the necessity of finding ground for a rational compromise between individual rights and public welfare. The settlement and consequent contraction of the public domain, the pressure of a constantly increasing density of population, the interrelation of the activities of our people and the complexity of our economic interests, have inevitably led to an increased use of the organization of society in order to protect the very

---

11 **Questions:** So far, Hughes has concluded that the Contracts Clause cannot be interpreted to interfere with a state's power (1) to provide *remedies* for contract violations and (2) to protect the public health, morals, or *public safety* of its residents, as in *Stone*. Does the Minnesota law fit within either exception? If a state declares that public safety requires it to prevent its courts from remedying contract violations, what protection is the Contracts Clause providing?

bases of individual opportunity. Where, in earlier days, it was thought that only the concerns of individuals or of classes were involved, and that those of the State itself were touched only remotely, it has later been found that the fundamental interests of the State are directly affected; and that the question is no longer merely that of one party to a contract as against another, but of the use of reasonable means to safeguard the economic structure upon which the good of all depends.

It is no answer to say that this public need was not apprehended a century ago, or to insist that what the provision of the Constitution meant to the vision of that day it must mean to the vision of our time. If by the statement that what the Constitution meant at the time of its adoption it means to-day, it is intended to say that the great clauses of the Constitution must be confined to the interpretation which the framers, with the conditions and outlook of their time, would have placed upon them, the statement carries its own refutation. It was to guard against such a narrow conception that Chief Justice Marshall uttered the memorable warning—"We must never forget that it is *a constitution* we are expounding" (*McCulloch v. Maryland*, 4 Wheat. 316, 407)—"a constitution intended to endure for ages to come, and consequently, to be adapted to the various *crises* of human affairs." *Id.*, p. 415. When we are dealing with the words of the Constitution, said this Court in *Missouri v. Holland*, 252 U.S. 416, 433, "we must realize that they have called into life a being the development of which could not have been foreseen completely by the most gifted of its begetters. . . . The case before us must be considered in the light of our whole experience and not merely in that of what was said a hundred years ago."

Nor is it helpful to attempt to draw a fine distinction between the intended meaning of the words of the Constitution and their intended application. When we consider the contract clause and the decisions which have expounded it in harmony with the essential reserved power of the States to protect the security of their peoples, we find no warrant for the conclusion that the clause has been warped by these decisions from its proper significance or that the founders of our Government would have interpreted the clause differently had they had occasion to assume that responsibility in the conditions of the later day. The vast body of law which has been developed was unknown to the fathers, but it is believed to have preserved the essential content and the spirit of the Constitution. With a growing recognition of public needs and the relation of individual right to public security, the court has sought to prevent the perversion of the clause through its use as an instrument to throttle the capacity of the States to protect their fundamental interests. This development is a growth from the seeds which the fathers planted. . . . The principle of this development is, as we have seen, that the reservation of the reasonable exercise of the protective power of the State is read into all contracts. . . .

Applying the criteria established by our decisions we conclude:

1. An emergency existed in Minnesota which furnished a proper occasion for the exercise of the reserved power of the State to protect the vital interests of the community. The declarations of the existence of this emergency by the legislature and by the Supreme Court of Minnesota cannot be regarded as a subterfuge or as lacking in adequate basis. . . .[12]

---

[12] **Question:** In 2020, at the beginning of the coronavirus pandemic, many states enacted eviction moratoria that temporarily prohibited landlords from using courts or local law enforcement to evict tenants. Several litigants challenged these moratoria, arguing that *Home Building & Loan Ass'n v. Blaisdell* should be overruled because it abandoned the original public meaning of the Contracts Clause in exchange for a narrow, modern interpretation. Considering the *Blaisdell* Court's interpretation of existing precedent—particularly its treatment of *Stone*—do you agree that Blaisdell represents a new doctrine and not merely a new application of existing doctrine?

2. The legislation was addressed to a legitimate end, that is, the legislation was not for the mere advantage of particular individuals but for the protection of a basic interest of society.

3. In view of the nature of the contracts in question—mortgages of unquestionable validity—the relief afforded and justified by the emergency, in order not to contravene the constitutional provision, could only be of a character appropriate to that emergency and could be granted only upon reasonable conditions.

4. The conditions upon which the period of redemption is extended do not appear to be unreasonable. . . . [T]he integrity of the mortgage indebtedness is not impaired; interest continues to run; the validity of the sale and the right of a mortgagee-purchaser to title or to obtain a deficiency judgment, if the mortgagor fails to redeem within the extended period, are maintained; and the conditions of redemption, if redemption there be, stand as they were under the prior law. . . .

5. The legislation is temporary in operation. It is limited to the exigency which called it forth. . . .

We are of the opinion that the Minnesota statute as here applied does not violate the contract clause of the Federal Constitution. Whether the legislation is wise or unwise as a matter of policy is a question with which we are not concerned.

38.1.4

United States Trust Co. v. New Jersey

431 U.S. 1 (1977)

The Supreme Court's *Blaisdell* decision insisted that it was applying existing precedent. Yet its application of that precedent transformed the Contracts Clause. By holding that all contracts impliedly recognize the reserved power of the state to take whatever actions are "reasonable" to respond to an economic emergency, the Court made it difficult to even conceive of a possible example in which the Contracts Clause could be enforced.

For the next forty years, the Court didn't once strike down another statute as a violation of the Contracts Clause. To the contrary, the Court appeared to go out of its way to uphold state laws that impaired contracts. For example, in *Faitoute Co. v. City of Asbury Park*, 316 U.S. 502 (1942), the Court upheld a New Jersey receivership law that authorized the state to reorganize and cancel a troubled municipality's debts. The Court explained that the practical value of the city's contracts with private creditors depended on the city's ability to raise revenue, so the state needed wide latitude to take reasonable actions to ensure that the contracts would be able to raise revenue. *Faitoute*, 316 U.S. at 509.

The Contracts Clause returned with a vengeance, however, in *United States Trust Co. v. New Jersey*, 431 U.S. 1 (1977).

In 1921, the legislatures of New York and New Jersey created a public corporation—the Port Authority of New York and New Jersey—to construct and manage infrastructure connecting the two states. Over the next three decades, the Port Authority accumulated power until it was responsible for managing virtually every bridge and tunnel out of New

York City. *See* Robert Caro, *The Power Broker: Robert Moses and the Fall of New York* 615–36 (1974). The Port Authority paid for new infrastructure projects by selling bonds, or long-term debt instruments, to banks and private creditors. It repaid these bonds by collecting tolls from its various bridges and tunnels. Each of these bonds was a contract protected by the Contracts Clause. *Id.* at 629.

In the late 1950s, the Port Authority was financially prosperous, but New York City's mass-transit systems were financially struggling. The New Jersey and New York legislatures therefore attempted to force the authority to take over the privately owned Hudson & Manhattan Railroad connecting New Jersey and New York City. The legislatures succeeded in 1962, when they passed a law placing the railroad under the Port Authority's control, renaming the railroad the Port Authority Trans-Hudson (PATH). In exchange, the states authorized the Port Authority (1) to construct what became the World Trade Center in Manhattan and (2) to borrow money from private creditors with a constitutionally protected "covenant," or promise, from the states. This 1962 covenant effectively declared that the states would never require the Port Authority to transfer revenues from its profitable tolls to the PATH system. By including this covenant in bonds that it used to borrow money, the Port Authority could reassure lenders that its acquisition of PATH would not harm its ability to repay its debts.

The states' 1962 covenant lasted until the early 1970s, at which point the PATH trains were an underfunded disaster. To compel the Port Authority to adequately maintain the PATH system, the New Jersey and New York legislatures repealed the 1962 covenant—rescinding their promise that they would never compel the Port Authority to transfer its revenues to the PATH system. Under the precedent of *Dartmouth College*, this repeal didn't violate the Contracts Clause with respect to the Port Authority because the Port Authority was a public corporation unprotected by the clause. But the Contracts Clause did protect the bonds issued by the Port Authority to its private creditors, including the United States Trust Company.

The United States Trust Company sued the states, claiming that the law impaired the value of its bonds by making it marginally less likely that the Port Authority would have enough money in its reserves to repay all of its debts. The states responded by emphasizing that the repeal of the 1962 covenant didn't impair any contracts. The evidence was on the states' side: the repeal didn't affect the enforceability of the Port Authority's bonds, it didn't affect their market price, and it didn't affect the Port Authority's credit rating.

Nevertheless, the Court in *United States Trust* found that the Contracts Clause was alive and well in this case.

■ MR. JUSTICE BLACKMUN delivered the opinion of the Court.[13]

This case presents a challenge to a New Jersey statute, 1974 N. J. Laws, c. 25, as violative of the Contract Clause of the United States Constitution. That statute, together with a concurrent and parallel New York statute, 1974 N. Y. Laws, c. 993, repealed a statutory covenant made by the two States in 1962 that had limited the ability of The Port Authority of New York and New Jersey to subsidize rail passenger transportation from revenues and reserves. . . .

II

At the time the Constitution was adopted, and for nearly a century thereafter, the Contract Clause was one of the few express limitations on state power. The many decisions of this Court involving the Contract Clause are evidence of its important place in our constitutional jurisprudence. Over the last century, however, the Fourteenth Amendment has assumed a far larger place in constitutional adjudication concerning the States. . . .

[T]he present role of the Contract Clause is largely illuminated by . . . *Home Building & Loan Assn. v. Blaisdell*, 290 U. S. 398 (1934), [which] is regarded as the leading case in the modern era of Contract Clause interpretation. At issue was the Minnesota Mortgage Moratorium Law, enacted in 1933, during the depth of the Depression and when that State was under severe economic stress, and appeared to have no effective alternative. The statute was a temporary measure that allowed judicial extension of the time for redemption; a mortgagor who remained in possession during the extension period was required to pay a reasonable income or rental value to the mortgagee. A closely divided Court, in an opinion by Mr. Chief Justice Hughes, observed that "emergency may furnish the occasion for the exercise of power" and that the "constitutional question presented in the light of an emergency is whether the power possessed embraces the particular exercise of it in response to particular conditions." *Id.*, at 426. . . .

[*Blaisdell*] eschewed a rigid application of the Contract Clause to invalidate state legislation. Yet [it didn't indicate] that the Contract Clause was without meaning in modern constitutional jurisprudence, or that its limitation on state power was illusory. Whether or not the protection of contract rights comports with current views of wise public policy, the Contract Clause remains a part of our written Constitution. We therefore must attempt to apply that constitutional provision to the instant case with due respect for its purpose and the prior decisions of this Court.

III

We first examine appellant's general claim that repeal of the 1962 covenant impaired the obligation of the States' contract with the bondholders. It long has been established that the Contract Clause limits the power of the States to modify their own contracts as well as to regulate those between private parties. *Dartmouth College v. Woodward*, 4 Wheat. 518 (1819). Yet the Contract Clause does not prohibit the States from repealing or amending statutes generally, or from enacting legislation with retroactive effects. Thus, as a preliminary matter, appellant's claim requires a determination that the repeal has the effect of impairing a contractual obligation.

In this case the obligation was itself created by a statute, the 1962 legislative covenant. . . . [T]he 1962 covenant constituted a contract between the two States

[13] **As You Read, Consider:** Like the contracts at issue in *Trustees of Dartmouth College v. Woodward* and *Stone v. Mississippi*, the contract at issue here was between states (New Jersey and New York, via the Port Authority) and private individuals (bondholders like the United States Trust Company). Why does the states' involvement in the contract matter so much to Justice Harry Blackmun? Does his opinion overrule *Home Building & Loan Ass'n v. Blaisdell* or distinguish it?

and the holders of the Consolidated Bonds issued between 1962 and the 1973 prospective repeal. The intent to make a contract is clear from the statutory language: "The 2 States covenant and agree with each other and with the holders of any affected bonds. . . ." 1962 N. J. Laws, c. 8, § 6; 1962 N. Y. Laws, c. 209, § 6 . . . . [T]he purpose of the covenant was to invoke the constitutional protection of the Contract Clause as security against repeal. In return for their promise, the States received the benefit they bargained for: public marketability of Port Authority bonds to finance construction of the World Trade Center and acquisition of the Hudson & Manhattan Railroad. We therefore have no doubt that the 1962 covenant has been properly characterized as a contractual obligation of the two States.

The parties sharply disagree about the value of the 1962 covenant to the bondholders. Appellant claims that after repeal the secondary market for affected bonds became "thin" and the price fell in relation to other formerly comparable bonds. . . . Appellees respond that the bonds nevertheless retained an "A" rating from the leading evaluating services and that after an initial adverse effect they regained a comparable price position in the market. . . . The fact is that no one can be sure precisely how much financial loss the bondholders suffered. Factors unrelated to repeal may have influenced price. In addition, the market may not have reacted fully, even as yet, to the covenant's repeal, because of the pending litigation and the possibility that the repeal would be nullified by the courts.

In any event, the question of valuation need not be resolved in the instant case because the State has made no effort to compensate the bondholders for any loss sustained by the repeal. As a security provision, the covenant was not superfluous; it limited the Port Authority's deficits and thus protected the general reserve fund from depletion. Nor was the covenant merely modified or replaced by an arguably comparable security provision. Its outright repeal totally eliminated an important security provision and thus impaired the obligation of the States' contract. . . .[14]

IV

Although the Contract Clause appears literally to proscribe "any" impairment, this Court observed in *Blaisdell* that "the prohibition is not an absolute one and is not to be read with literal exactness like a mathematical formula." 290 U. S., at 428. Thus, a finding that there has been a technical impairment is merely a preliminary step in resolving the more difficult question whether that impairment is permitted under the Constitution. In the instant case, as in *Blaisdell*, we must attempt to reconcile the strictures of the Contract Clause with the "essential attributes of sovereign power," *id.*, at 435, necessarily reserved by the States to safeguard the welfare of their citizens. *Id.*, at 434–440.

The trial court concluded that repeal of the 1962 covenant was a valid exercise of New Jersey's police power because repeal served important public interests in mass transportation, energy conservation, and environmental protection. Yet the Contract Clause limits otherwise legitimate exercises of state legislative authority, and the existence of an important public interest is not always sufficient to overcome that limitation. "Undoubtedly, whatever is reserved of state power must be consistent with the fair intent of the constitutional limitation of that power." *Blaisdell*, 290 U. S., at 439. Moreover, the scope of the State's reserved power depends on the nature of the contractual relationship with which the challenged law conflicts.

The States must possess broad power to adopt general regulatory measures without being concerned that private contracts will be impaired, or even destroyed,

---

14 **Questions:** Here, Blackmun concludes that New York and New Jersey's repeal of the 1962 covenant "impaired the obligation of the States' contract." How so? What, precisely, was impaired?

as a result.[15] Otherwise, one would be able to obtain immunity from state regulation by making private contractual arrangements. This principle is summarized in Mr. Justice Holmes' well-known dictum: "One whose rights, such as they are, are subject to state restriction, cannot remove them from the power of the State by making a contract about them." *Hudson Water Co. v. McCarter,* 209 U. S. 349, 357 (1908).

Yet private contracts are not subject to unlimited modification under the police power. The Court in *Blaisdell* recognized that laws intended to regulate existing contractual relationships must serve a legitimate public purpose. 290 U. S., at 444–445. A State could not "adopt as its policy the repudiation of debts or the destruction of contracts or the denial of means to enforce them." *Id.*, at 439. Legislation adjusting the rights and responsibilities of contracting parties must be upon reasonable conditions and of a character appropriate to the public purpose justifying its adoption. *Id.*, at 445–447. As is customary in reviewing economic and social regulation, however, courts properly defer to legislative judgment as to the necessity and reasonableness of a particular measure.

When a State impairs the obligation of its own contract, the reserved-powers doctrine has a different basis. The initial inquiry concerns the ability of the State to enter into an agreement that limits its power to act in the future. As early as *Fletcher v. Peck,* the Court considered the argument that "one legislature cannot abridge the powers of a succeeding legislature." 6 Cranch, at 135. It is often stated that "the legislature cannot bargain away the police power of a State." *Stone v. Mississippi,* 101 U. S. 814, 817 (1880). This doctrine requires a determination of the State's power to create irrevocable contract rights in the first place, rather than an inquiry into the purpose or reasonableness of the subsequent impairment. In short, the Contract Clause does not require a State to adhere to a contract that surrenders an essential attribute of its sovereignty.

In deciding whether a State's contract was invalid *ab initio* under the reserved-powers doctrine, earlier decisions relied on distinctions among the various powers of the State. Thus, the police power and the power of eminent domain were among those that could not be "contracted away," but the State could bind itself in the future exercise of the taxing and spending powers. Such formalistic distinctions perhaps cannot be dispositive, but they contain an important element of truth. Whatever the propriety of a State's binding itself to a future course of conduct in other contexts, the power to enter into effective financial contracts cannot be questioned. Any financial obligation could be regarded in theory as a relinquishment of the State's spending power, since money spent to repay debts is not available for other purposes. Similarly, the taxing power may have to be exercised if debts are to be repaid. Notwithstanding these effects, the Court has regularly held that the States are bound by their debt contracts.

---

[15] **Questions:** Over the next few paragraphs, Blackmun offers two different applications of the reserved powers doctrine from *Stone*.

With "private contracts," or contracts involving two individuals (as in *Blaisdell*), a state can enact any legislation that is rationally related to a legitimate purpose. This is a *deferential means-ends test*.

But with contracts in which a state is a party (as in *Dartmouth College*, *Stone*, and this case), Blackmun writes that the Court should ask two questions: First, does the contract "bargain away the police power of a State"? If so, the Contracts Clause does not protect the contract from future impairment. But if not, the second question arises: Is the law "reasonable and necessary to serve an important public purpose"? This is a *skeptical means-ends test*.

This decision invents the second test. Why does Blackmun think that such a test is necessary? Does it make sense for a court to be more skeptical of a state law that impairs its own contracts compared to a state law that impairs private contracts?

The instant case involves a financial obligation and thus as a threshold matter may not be said automatically to fall within the reserved powers that cannot be contracted away. Not every security provision, however, is necessarily financial. For example, a revenue bond might be secured by the State's promise to continue operating the facility in question; yet such a promise surely could not validly be construed to bind the State never to close the facility for health or safety reasons. The security provision at issue here, however, is different: The States promised that revenues and reserves securing the bonds would not be depleted by the Port Authority's operation of deficit-producing passenger railroads. . . . Such a promise is purely financial and thus not necessarily a compromise of the State's reserved powers.

Of course, to say that the financial restrictions of the 1962 covenant were valid when adopted does not finally resolve this case. The Contract Clause is not an absolute bar to subsequent modification of a State's own financial obligations. As with laws impairing the obligations of private contracts, an impairment may be constitutional if it is reasonable and necessary to serve an important public purpose. In applying this standard, however, complete deference to a legislative assessment of reasonableness and necessity is not appropriate because the State's self-interest is at stake. A governmental entity can always find a use for extra money, especially when taxes do not have to be raised. If a State could reduce its financial obligations whenever it wanted to spend the money for what it regarded as an important public purpose, the Contract Clause would provide no protection at all. . . .

The extent of impairment is certainly a relevant factor in determining its reasonableness. But we cannot sustain the repeal of the 1962 covenant simply because the bondholders' rights were not totally destroyed. . . .

V

Mass transportation, energy conservation, and environmental protection are goals that are important and of legitimate public concern. Appellees contend that these goals are so important that any harm to bondholders from repeal of the 1962 covenant is greatly outweighed by the public benefit. We do not accept this invitation to engage in a utilitarian comparison of public benefit and private loss. . . . [A] State cannot refuse to meet its legitimate financial obligations simply because it would prefer to spend the money to promote the public good rather than the private welfare of its creditors. We can only sustain the repeal of the 1962 covenant if that impairment was both reasonable and necessary to serve the admittedly important purposes claimed by the State.

The more specific justification offered for the repeal of the 1962 covenant was the States' plan for encouraging users of private automobiles to shift to public transportation. The States intended to discourage private automobile use by raising bridge and tunnel tolls and to use the extra revenue from those tolls to subsidize improved commuter railroad service. . . . We reject this justification because the repeal was neither necessary to achievement of the plan nor reasonable in light of the circumstances.

The determination of necessity can be considered on two levels. First, it cannot be said that total repeal of the covenant was essential; a less drastic modification would have permitted the contemplated plan without entirely removing the covenant's limitations on the use of Port Authority revenues and reserves to subsidize commuter railroads. Second, without modifying the covenant at all, the States could have adopted alternative means of achieving their twin goals of discouraging automobile use and improving mass transit. Appellees contend, however, that choosing among these alternatives is a matter for legislative discretion. But a State is not completely free to consider impairing the obligations of its own contracts on a par with other policy alternatives. Similarly, a State is not free to impose a drastic impairment when an evident and more moderate course would serve its purposes equally well. . . .

We also cannot conclude that repeal of the covenant was reasonable in light of the surrounding circumstances. . . . [T]he need for mass transportation in the New York metropolitan area was not a new development, and the likelihood that publicly owned commuter railroads would produce substantial deficits was well known. As early as 1922, over a half century ago, there were pressures to involve the Port Authority in mass transit. It was with full knowledge of these concerns that the 1962 covenant was adopted. Indeed, the covenant was specifically intended to protect the pledged revenues and reserves against the possibility that such concerns would lead the Port Authority into greater involvement in deficit mass transit.

During the 12-year period between adoption of the covenant and its repeal, public perception of the importance of mass transit undoubtedly grew because of increased general concern with environmental protection and energy conservation. But these concerns were not unknown in 1962, and the subsequent changes were of degree and not of kind. We cannot say that these changes caused the covenant to have a substantially different impact in 1974 than when it was adopted in 1962. And we cannot conclude that the repeal was reasonable in the light of changed circumstances.

We therefore hold that the Contract Clause of the United States Constitution prohibits the retroactive repeal of the 1962 covenant. . . .

NOTE: AFTERMATH OF *UNITED STATES TRUST*

The *United States Trust* Court completed the Supreme Court's modern approach to Contract Clause issues. Under *Dartmouth College*, the Contracts Clause prohibits a state government from "substantially" impairing the obligation of a contract involving an individual or private entity—regardless of whether the state is a party to the contract. *Trustees of Dartmouth College v. Woodward*, 17 U.S. (4 Wheat.) 518, 637 (1819). In *Stone*, however, the Court drew an exception to this obligation: the Contracts Clause doesn't protect contracts that infringe on a state's "police power" reserved by the Tenth Amendment—a state must always be able to enact reasonable protections of the health, safety, and welfare of its citizens despite the Contracts Clause. *Stone v. Mississippi*, 101 U.S. 814, 817 (1880). Under *Blaisdell*, the Court is deferential to a state's decision about when it is "reasonable" to substantially impair private contracts between two nonstate actors. *Home Bldg. & Loan Ass'n v. Blaisdell*, 290 U.S. 398, 444 (1934). But under *United States Trust*, the Court is less deferential to a state's decision about when it is reasonable to substantially impair contracts in which a state is a party. When a state substantially impairs *its own* contracts, the Court requires proof that the impairment was reasonable "in the light of changed circumstances" and that it was "necessary"—that is, the least restrictive means of serving important purposes. *U.S. Trust*, 431 U.S. at 31–32.

Since *United States Trust*, the Court has only considered the Contracts Clause in a handful of cases. Each time, it has declined to adjust the approach laid out in the previous paragraph, although it has supplemented its definitions. In *Sveen v. Melin*, for example, the Court summarized the above cases into a two-part test. 138 S. Ct. 1815, 1817 (2018). The Court explained that the Contracts Clause prohibits only (1) "substantial" impairments of contracts that (2) are not a "reasonable" method of advancing a purpose tied to the state's police powers. *Id.* at 1821–22. In *Sveen*, the Court defined a substantial impairment with reference to "the extent to which the law undermines the contractual bargain, interferes with a party's reasonable expectations, and prevents the party from safeguarding or reinstating his rights." *Id.* (upholding a Minnesota law for being an insubstantial impairment of contracts). And in another case, the Court defined a "reasonable" method of achieving a public purpose as one that (a) was "enacted to deal with a broad, generalized economic or social problem"; (b) "operate[d] in an area already subject to state regulation"; (c) imposed only "a temporary alteration"; or (d) operated on a broad class of issues and concerns. *Allied Structural Steel Co. v. Spannaus*, 438 U.S. 234, 250 (1978) (invalidating a different Minnesota law as unreasonable after finding that it substantially impaired preexisting contracts).

38.2 THE CONFEDERATION CLAUSE AND THE COMPACT CLAUSE

Although the most important clause of Article I, Section 10, prohibits states from *impairing* certain contracts, the section also prohibits states from *entering into* certain contracts. Two prohibitions for states stand out.

Confederation Clause

One, the Confederation Clause, prohibits any state from ever entering into any "Treaty, Alliance, or Confederation." Although the Supreme Court has never interpreted this clause so broadly as to prohibit states from passing laws or resolutions that apply extraterritorially, *Skiriotes v. Florida*, 313 U.S. 69, 79 (1941), the Court has held that a state may not enter into a formal, treaty-like agreement with a foreign state, *Holmes v. Jennison*, 39 U.S. (14 Pet.) 540, 574 (1840). The Court also wryly observed after the Civil War that the Confederate States of America, by definition, violated this clause. *Williams v. Bruffy*, 96 U.S. 176, 182–83 (1878).

Compact Clause

A second, related clause prohibits states from entering into "any Agreement or Compact with another State" without the "Consent of the Congress." One likely purpose of the Compact Clause was to prevent states from challenging Congress's authority by forming their own regional governments—something that the New England states threatened to do during the Revolutionary War. *See* 7 *Journals of the Continental Congress* 87–88 (Worthington Chauncey Ford ed., 1907). Because the Confederation Clause already bans *treaties*, the Supreme Court has interpreted the Compact Clause using "the broadest and most comprehensive terms." *Holmes*, 39 U.S. at 572. The phrase *agreement or compact* includes "every agreement, written or verbal, formal or informal, positive or implied, by the mutual understanding of the parties." *Id.*

Despite this broad interpretation of the Compact Clause, the Court has also recognized that the clause would be incapacitating if it required states to receive the consent of Congress every time two states happened to cooperate over, say, where to build an interstate road. The Court's first departure from a strict interpretation of the Compact Clause came in *Virginia v. West Virginia*, 78 U.S. (11 Wall.) 39, 59 (1871), when the Court held that "the Consent of the Congress" could in some circumstances be implied by Congress's inaction in the face of an ongoing agreement. The Court reached its modern interpretation of the clause in *Virginia v. Tennessee*, 148 U.S. 503 (1893), when Virginia and Tennessee wanted to make a minor boundary adjustment. The Court concluded that this sort of thing wasn't the "Agreement or Compact" that the Constitution was worried about. Instead, the Court concluded "that the prohibition is directed to the formation of any combination tending to the increase of political power in the states, which may encroach upon or interfere with the just supremacy of the United States." *Virginia*, 148 U.S. at 519. The Court observed that the only reason to require the consent of Congress for compacts and agreements was "to check any infringement of the rights of the national government" or to prevent some "permanent inconvenience or public mischief." *Id.* at 520–21. But where such checks were unnecessary, the Court wouldn't require Congress's consent. *See, e.g.*, *U.S. Steel Corp. v. Multistate Tax Comm'n*, 434 U.S. 452 (1978) (congressional consent not required for the Multistate Tax Compact, which created a multistate commission to propose nonbinding model legislation); *St. Louis & S.F. Ry. v. James*, 161 U.S. 545 (1896) (congressional consent not required for when two states granted a franchise to the same corporation).

Once Congress does consent to a valid interstate compact or agreement, the agreement becomes the equivalent of a treaty between sovereign powers and, according to the Court, has the same effect as any other federal law. *Kansas v. Nebraska*, 574 U.S. 445, 474–75 (2015); *Poole v. Fleeger*, 36 U.S. (11 Pet.) 185, 209–10 (1837). The Supreme Court has recognized its own power to enforce interstate compacts by applying general principles of contract law. *See Texas v. New Mexico*, 482 U.S. 124, 134 (1987). In addition, because interstate compacts are a type of contract, states may not breach a compact if doing so would violate the Contracts Clause. *See Virginia v. West Virginia*, 246 U.S. 565, 605 (1918). Absent a reservation clause in an interstate compact giving one state the power to modify its terms, states lack the power to unilaterally regulate an interstate entity such as the Port Authority of New York and New Jersey. *See Hess v. Port Auth. Trans-Hudson Corp.*, 513 U.S. 30, 52 (1994).

Additional limits of Section 10

In addition to the Confederation Clause and the Compact Clause, Section 10 also prohibits states from "keep[ing] Troops, or Ships of War in time of Peace." The Court has interpreted this final prohibition rarely but narrowly so as not to interfere with a state's organization and maintenance of a militia. *Presser v. Illinois*, 116 U.S. 252, 262–63 (1886).

38.3 THE BILL OF ATTAINDER CLAUSE AND THE EX POST FACTO CLAUSE

Section 10 also contains prohibitions on states that mirror prohibitions on the federal government. Just as Article I, Section 9, prohibits Congress from enacting a bill of attainder or an ex post facto law, Section 10 prohibits states from doing the same. Both sets of clauses have been interpreted identically.

Bill of Attainder Clause

Because states may not pass bills of attainder, they may not "punish" specified groups of people for conduct that wasn't criminal at the time it was done. *Cummings v. Missouri*, 71 U.S. (4 Wall.) 277, 287 (1867).

However, states may enact prophylactic qualifications for individuals in office, even if they target specific groups. Applying this distinction, the Supreme Court has upheld state laws that prohibit members of the Communist Party and people who have been convicted of a felony from holding certain offices. *See, e.g.*, *Konigsberg v. State Bar*, 366 U.S. 36, 47 n.9 (1961).

Ex Post Facto Clause

As for state ex post facto laws, the Court has applied this prohibition only to penal and criminal legislation, not to civil legislation. *Calder v. Bull*, 3 U.S. (3 Dall.) 386 (1798). Even then, the Court has held that the constitutional ban prohibits only laws that (1) punish an act that was innocent when it was done, (2) makes a punishment worse after an act was committed, (3) deprives the accused of a defense available at the time that the act was committed, or (4) changes the definition of a crime or makes it worse than when it was committed. *See, e.g.*, *Lindsey v. Washington*, 301 U.S. 397, 401 (1937).

Examples of ex post facto laws include a law that authorized the prosecution of a person after the statute of limitations had already expired, *Stogner v. California*, 539 U.S. 607 (2003); and a law that allowed the conviction of a person on less evidence than was required at the time of the act's commission, *Carmell v. Texas*, 529 U.S. 513 (2000).

Examples of state laws that have not violated the clause include laws that penalize the *continuance* of conduct that was lawful when it began, *Samuels v. McCurdy*, 267 U.S. 188 (1925); laws denying future privileges to people already convicted of crimes, *Lehmann v. State Bd. of Pub. Acct.*, 263 U.S. 394 (1923); and laws that enforce civil regulatory regimes, including in the immigration and sex-offender contexts, *Smith v. Doe*, 538 U.S. 84 (2003). In *Smith v. Doe*, 538 U.S. 84 (2003), the Court distinguished a "civil" law from a "criminal" law by evaluating whether the legislature intended for the law to be punitive, whether the adverse effect of the law was a traditional means of punishment, and whether there was any affirmative disability or restraint.

Although both the Bill of Attainder Clause and Ex Post Facto Clause traditionally apply only to legislation, the Supreme Court has held that an unforeseeable judicial enlargement of a criminal statute can operate as an ex post facto law if applied retroactively. *Bouie v. City of Columbia*, 378 U.S. 347 (1964).

38.4 THE BILLS OF CREDIT CLAUSE AND THE LEGAL TENDER CLAUSE

The Contracts Clause is not the only provision of Article I, Section 10, that prohibits certain debt-relief laws. The section also expressly prohibits states from coining money, emitting "Bills of Credit," and making "any Thing but gold and silver Coin a Tender in Payment of Debts."

Collectively, all of these clauses have the obvious purpose of prohibiting states from creating paper money—that is, any medium of exchange intended to circulate among individuals or between individuals and the government. *See Craig v. Missouri*, 29 U.S. (4 Pet.) 410 (1830). Accordingly, the Court struck down a Missouri scheme that established interest-bearing certificates, used the certificates to pay the salaries of state officers, and allowed anyone to pay their taxes with the certificates. *Byrne v. Missouri*, 33 U.S. (8 Pet.) 40 (1834).

But the Court hasn't extended these clauses much further. On their own, the clauses have never prohibited state-chartered *banks* from establishing their own paper currencies. *Curran v. Arkansas*, 56 U.S. (15 How.) 304, 317 (1854). Nor have they prohibited states from issuing bonds or coupons that for whatever reason are unfit "for general circulation in the community as a representative and substitute for money in the common transactions of business." *Poindexter v. Greenhow*, 114 U.S. 270, 284 (1885).

Today, the clauses are rarely litigated because the Federal Reserve Act of 1913, Pub. L. No. 63–43, 38 Stat. 251, largely displaced state banks. Still, the Court has interpreted the clauses to prohibit states from requiring creditors to accept anything in payment of debts other than gold, silver, or U.S. legal tender absent the creditor's prior consent. *Farmers & Merchants Bank v. Fed. Reserve Bank*, 262 U.S. 649 (1923).

38.5 THE IMPORT-EXPORT CLAUSE AND THE TONNAGE CLAUSE

The final provisions of Article I, Section 10, prohibit states, without the consent of Congress, from laying any "Duty of Tonnage" or "any Imposts or Duties on Imports or Exports, except what may be absolutely necessary for executing it's inspection Laws." The Supreme Court has interpreted the clauses similarly to the Negative Commerce Clause.

Import-Export Clause

The Import-Export Clause theoretically could be interpreted to prohibit states from taxing any goods that have at one point been imported. Acknowledging that possibility, in *Brown v. Maryland*, the Court under Chief Justice John Marshall limited the clause's application only to goods that remain in their "original form or package." 25 U.S. (12 Wheat.) 419, 441–42 (1827). Once a good is incorporated and mixed into the mass of property within a state, then a state is free to tax it—even if, in the future, the goods might one day be exported. Although the "original package" doctrine remains part of the interpretation of the Import-Export Clause, it applies only to goods imported from foreign countries, not to goods imported from other states. *Hooven & Allison Co. v. Evatt*, 324 U.S. 652, 673 (1945). The Court has also allowed states to levy nondiscriminatory taxes on all of a company's property—even imported goods still in their original package—provided that the tax isn't directed against imports or exports. *Michelin Tire Corp. v. Wages*, 423 U.S. 276, 302 (1976).

Even without the consent of Congress, the Constitution authorizes states to levy import and export duties when "absolutely necessary" for executing their inspection laws. *See Turner v. Maryland*, 107 U.S. 38, 53–54 (1883) (allowing states to levy reasonable duties to pay for the inspection of the "form, capacity, dimensions, and weight of packages").

Tonnage Clause

Finally, a purpose of the Tonnage Clause was to prevent states from evading the Import-Export Clause by taxing ships as opposed to the goods themselves. The Court has therefore applied the clause to prohibit all charges "for the privilege of entering, trading, or lying in a port." *Polar Tankers, Inc. v. City of Valdez*, 557 U.S. 1, 8 (2009).

CHAPTER 39

WHAT LIMITATIONS DO THE BILL OF RIGHTS, THE CITIZENSHIP CLAUSE, AND THE PRIVILEGES OR IMMUNITIES CLAUSE OF THE FOURTEENTH AMENDMENT IMPOSE ON THE STATES AND THE FEDERAL GOVERNMENT?

ARTICLE VI, PARAGRAPH 3: The Senators and Representatives before mentioned, and the Members of the several State Legislatures, and all executive and judicial Officers, both of the United States and of the several States, shall be bound by Oath or Affirmation, to support this Constitution; but no religious Test shall ever be required as a Qualification to any Office or public Trust under the United States.

FIRST AMENDMENT (1791): Congress shall make no law respecting an establishment of religion, or prohibiting the free exercise thereof; or abridging the freedom of speech, or of the press; or the right of the people peaceably to assemble, and to petition the Government for a redress of grievances.

SECOND AMENDMENT (1791): A well regulated Militia, being necessary to the security of a free State, the right of the people to keep and bear Arms, shall not be infringed.

THIRD AMENDMENT (1791): No Soldier shall, in time of peace be quartered in any house, without the consent of the Owner, nor in time of war, but in a manner to be prescribed by law.

FOURTH AMENDMENT (1791): The right of the people to be secure in their persons, houses, papers, and effects, against unreasonable searches and seizures, shall not be violated, and no Warrants shall issue, but upon probable cause, supported by Oath or affirmation, and particularly describing the place to be searched, and the persons or things to be seized.

FIFTH AMENDMENT (1791): No person shall be held to answer for a capital, or otherwise infamous crime, unless on a presentment or indictment of a Grand Jury, except in cases arising in the land or naval forces, or in the Militia, when in actual service in time of War or public danger; nor shall any person be subject for the same offence to be twice put in jeopardy of life or limb; nor shall be compelled in any criminal case to be a witness against himself, nor be deprived of life, liberty, or property, without due process of law; nor shall private property be taken for public use, without just compensation.

SIXTH AMENDMENT (1791): In all criminal prosecutions, the accused shall enjoy the right to a speedy and public trial, by an impartial jury of the State and district wherein the crime shall have been committed, which district shall have been previously ascertained by law, and to be informed of the nature and cause of the accusation; to be confronted with the witnesses against him; to have compulsory process for obtaining witnesses in his favor, and to have the Assistance of Counsel for his defence.

SEVENTH AMENDMENT (1791): In Suits at common law, where the value in controversy shall exceed twenty dollars, the right of trial by jury shall be preserved, and no fact tried by a jury, shall be otherwise re-examined in any Court of the United States, than according to the rules of the common law.

EIGHTH AMENDMENT (1791): Excessive bail shall not be required, nor excessive fines imposed, nor cruel and unusual punishments inflicted.

NINTH AMENDMENT (1791): The enumeration in the Constitution, of certain rights, shall not be construed to deny or disparage others retained by the people.

TENTH AMENDMENT (1791): The powers not delegated to the United States by the Constitution, nor prohibited by it to the States, are reserved to the States respectively, or to the people.

THIRTEENTH AMENDMENT (1865), SECTION 1: Neither slavery nor involuntary servitude, except as a punishment for crime whereof the party shall have been duly convicted, shall exist within the United States, or any place subject to their jurisdiction.

FOURTEENTH AMENDMENT (1868), SECTION 1: All persons born or naturalized in the United States, and subject to the jurisdiction thereof, are citizens of the United States and of the State wherein they reside. No State shall make or enforce any law which shall abridge the privileges or immunities of citizens of the United States; nor shall any State deprive any person of life, liberty, or property, without due process of law; nor deny to any person within its jurisdiction the equal protection of the laws.

39.1 THE BILL OF RIGHTS

For the first century of the United States' history, the Commerce Clause, the Contracts Clause, and other prohibitions in Article I, Section 10, represented the Constitution's principal limits on state power. Most other limits were imposed by preemptive federal laws, which the Supremacy Clause of Article VI made part of the "supreme Law of the Land."

Significantly, the principal limits on *Congress's* power—the first ten amendments—have always been interpreted to apply only to the federal government, not to the states. When James Madison first introduced his list of amendments in the summer of 1789, the House rejected what he considered his "most valuable" proposal: an amendment that would have declared that "[t]he equal rights of conscience, the freedom of speech or of the press, and the right of trial by jury in criminal cases shall not be infringed by any State." 1 Annals of Cong. 755 (1789). Most representatives thought it inappropriate to use the federal Constitution to protect individual rights from state governments when states already had declarations of rights in their own state constitutions. Accordingly, the First Amendment purposefully begins with *Congress shall make no law*.

That said, none of the other amendments specifically mentions Congress. For example, the Fifth Amendment declares, "No person shall be . . . deprived of life, liberty, or property, without due process of law; nor shall private property be taken for public use, without just compensation."

39.1.1

Barron ex rel. Tiernan v. Mayor of Baltimore

32 U.S. (7 Pet.) 243 (1833)

John Barron, the owner of a Baltimore wharf in the 1830s, interpreted the Fifth Amendment's language to protect a "person" like him from *all* deprivations, not just deprivations by the federal government. At the time, Baltimore was engaged in a municipal construction project that caused so much sand to accumulate in the harbor that ships couldn't dock at Barron's wharf. A frustrated Barron sued the city. He claimed that Baltimore had effectively "taken" his wharf without just compensation. When the case reached the Supreme Court, Chief Justice John Marshall therefore had to consider whether a city, or state, could violate the Fifth Amendment.

In *Barron ex rel. Tiernan v. Mayor of Baltimore*, 32 U.S. (7 Pet.) 243 (1833), the Court had no difficulty finding that the Fifth Amendment applied only to the federal government.

■ MR. CHIEF JUSTICE MARSHALL delivered the opinion of the Court.[1]

The plaintiff in error contends that [this case] comes within that clause in the fifth amendment to the constitution, which inhibits the taking of private property for public use, without just compensation. He insists that this amendment, being in favour of the liberty of the citizen, ought to be so construed as to restrain the legislative power of a state, as well as that of the United States. . . .

The question thus presented is, we think, of great importance, but not of much difficulty.

The constitution was ordained and established by the people of the United States for themselves, for their own government, and not for the government of the individual states. Each state established a constitution for itself, and, in that constitution, provided such limitations and restrictions on the powers of its particular government as its judgment dictated. The people of the United States framed such a government for the United States as they supposed best adapted to their situation, and best calculated to promote their interests. The powers they conferred on this government were to be exercised by itself; and the limitations on power, if expressed in general terms, are naturally, and, we think, necessarily applicable to the government created by the instrument. They are limitations of power granted in the

---

1 **As You Read, Consider:** Where some constitutional prohibitions specifically apply to "Congress," the text of the Fifth Amendment declares that it protects any "person" from unfair deprivations. Why, precisely, does Chief Justice John Marshall refuse to apply the amendment to Baltimore's or Maryland's conduct?

instrument itself; not of distinct governments, framed by different persons and for different purposes.[2]

If these propositions be correct, the fifth amendment must be understood as restraining the power of the general government, not as applicable to the states. In their several constitutions they have imposed such restrictions on their respective governments as their own wisdom suggested; such as they deemed most proper for themselves. It is a subject on which they judge exclusively, and with which others interfere no farther than they are supposed to have a common interest.

The counsel for the plaintiff in error insists that the constitution was intended to secure the people of the several states against the undue exercise of power by their respective state governments; as well as against that which might be attempted by their general government. In support of this argument he relies on the inhibitions contained in [Article I, Section 10].

We think that section affords a strong if not a conclusive argument in support of the opinion already indicated by the court.

The preceding section [Article I, Section 9] contains restrictions which are obviously intended for the exclusive purpose of restraining the exercise of power by the departments of the general government. Some of them use language applicable only to congress: others are expressed in general terms. The third clause, for example, declares that "no bill of attainder or ex post facto law shall be passed." No language can be more general; yet the demonstration is complete that it applies solely to the government of the United States. In addition to the general arguments furnished by the instrument itself, some of which have been already suggested, the succeeding section, [Article I, Section 10,] the avowed purpose of which is to restrain state legislation, contains in terms the very prohibition. It declares that "no state shall pass any bill of attainder or ex post facto law." This provision, then, of the ninth section, however comprehensive its language, contains no restriction on state legislation.

The ninth section having enumerated, in the nature of a bill of rights, the limitations intended to be imposed on the powers of the general government, the tenth proceeds to enumerate those which were to operate on the state legislatures. These restrictions are brought together in the same section, and are by express words applied to the states. "No state shall enter into any treaty," &c. Perceiving that in a constitution framed by the people of the United States for the government of all, no limitation of the action of government on the people would apply to the state government, unless expressed in terms; the restrictions contained in the tenth section are in direct words so applied to the states.

It is worthy of remark, too, that these inhibitions generally restrain state legislation on subjects entrusted to the general government, or in which the people of all the states feel an interest.

A state is forbidden to enter into any treaty, alliance or confederation. If these compacts are with foreign nations, they interfere with the treaty making power which is conferred entirely on the general government; if with each other, for political purposes, they can scarcely fail to interfere with the general purpose and intent of the constitution. To grant letters of marque and reprisal, would lead directly to war; the power of declaring which is expressly given to congress. To coin money is also the exercise of a power conferred on congress. It would be tedious to recapitulate the several limitations on the powers of the states which are contained in this section. They will be found, generally, to restrain state legislation on subjects entrusted to the

[2] **Questions:** Is this paragraph accurate? As the previous sections of this casebook discuss, Marshall himself participated in interpreting the Commerce Clause and the Contracts Clause to limit the powers of states. What makes the Fifth Amendment different?

government of the union, in which the citizens of all the states are interested. In these alone were the whole people concerned. The question of their application to states is not left to construction. It is averred in positive words.

If the original constitution, in the ninth and tenth sections of the first article, draws this plain and marked line of discrimination between the limitations it imposes on the powers of the general government, and on those of the states; if in every inhibition intended to act on state power, words are employed which directly express that intent; some strong reason must be assigned for departing from this safe and judicious course in framing the amendments, before that departure can be assumed.

We search in vain for that reason.

Had the people of the several states, or any of them, required changes in their constitutions; had they required additional safeguards to liberty from the apprehended encroachments of their particular governments: the remedy was in their own hands, and would have been applied by themselves. A convention would have been assembled by the discontented state, and the required improvements would have been made by itself. The unwieldy and cumbrous machinery of procuring a recommendation from two-thirds of congress, and the assent of three-fourths of their sister states, could never have occurred to any human being as a mode of doing that which might be effected by the state itself. Had the framers of these amendments intended them to be limitations on the powers of the state governments, they would have imitated the framers of the original constitution, and have expressed that intention. Had congress engaged in the extraordinary occupation of improving the constitutions of the several states by affording the people additional protection from the exercise of power by their own governments in matters which concerned themselves alone, they would have declared this purpose in plain and intelligible language.

But it is universally understood, it is a part of the history of the day, that the great revolution which established the constitution of the United States, was not effected without immense opposition. Serious fears were extensively entertained that those powers which the patriot statesmen, who then watched over the interests of our country, deemed essential to union, and to the attainment of those invaluable objects for which union was sought, might be exercised in a manner dangerous to liberty. In almost every convention by which the constitution was adopted, amendments to guard against the abuse of power were recommended. These amendments demanded security against the apprehended encroachments of the general government—not against those of the local governments.

In compliance with a sentiment thus generally expressed, to quiet fears thus extensively entertained, amendments were proposed by the required majority in congress, and adopted by the states. These amendments contain no expression indicating an intention to apply them to the state governments. This court cannot so apply them.

We are of opinion, that the provision in the fifth amendment to the constitution, declaring that private property shall not be taken for public use without just compensation, is intended solely as a limitation on the exercise of power by the government of the United States, and is not applicable to the legislation of the states. We are therefore of opinion that there is no repugnancy between the several acts of the general assembly of Maryland, given in evidence by the defendants at the trial of this cause, in the court of that state, and the constitution of the United States. . . .[3]

---

[3] **Question:** Marshall's opinion remains good law even to this day: no provision of the Bill of Rights directly limits the power of a state or local government. Yet even though the First Amendment begins with *Congress shall make no law*, the Bill of Rights *has* been interpreted to

39.2 THE PRIVILEGES OR IMMUNITIES CLAUSE

After the Court handed down its decision in *Barron ex rel. Tiernan v. Mayor of Baltimore*, 32 U.S. (7 Pet.) 243 (1833), *Barron*'s principle—i.e., the Bill of Rights applies only to the federal government, not to the states—was reaffirmed often until the end of the 1850s. *See, e.g.*, *Withers v. Buckley*, 61 U.S. (20 How.) 84, 90 (1858). But "[t]he constitutional Amendments adopted in the aftermath of the Civil War fundamentally altered our country's federal system." *McDonald v. City of Chicago*, 561 U.S. 742, 754 (2010). Many of the authors of the Reconstruction amendments were convinced that state legislatures and state constitutions couldn't be trusted to equally protect all residents of a state, particularly black residents. One of the principal objectives of the Reconstruction amendments, therefore, was to reverse *Barron*'s effect.

The Thirteenth Amendment was the first to depart from its predecessors' exclusive focus on the federal government. Section 1 declared, "Neither slavery nor involuntary servitude, except as a punishment for crime whereof the party shall have been duly convicted, shall exist within the United States, or any place subject to their jurisdiction."

Yet the amendment alone was not enough to prevent states from maintaining slavery. As discussed earlier in the section on Congress's power to enforce the Reconstruction amendments (section 20.1), several southern states reacted to the Thirteenth Amendment by adopting "black codes" that attempted to preserve a racialized system of forced labor. Congress responded by enacting the Civil Rights Act of 1866, which declared that "all persons born in the United States and not subject to any foreign power, excluding Indians not taxed, are . . . citizens of the United States." Civil Rights Act, ch. 31, 14 Stat. 27, 27. The act added that "such citizens, of every race and color, without regard to any previous condition of slavery or involuntary servitude," had the same right as white citizens to own property, to make and enforce contracts, to participate in court, and to enjoy the "full and equal benefit of all laws." *Id.*

Supporters of the Civil Rights Act maintained that Congress's power to pass the act flowed, in part, from the Privileges and Immunities Clause of Article IV. That clause declared, "The Citizens of each State shall be entitled to all Privileges and Immunities of Citizens in the several States." Justice Bushrod Washington had famously interpreted the Privileges and Immunities Clause to protect "those privileges and immunities which are, in their nature, fundamental." *Corfield v. Coryell*, 6 F. Cas. 546, 551–52 (C.C.E.D. Pa. 1823) (No. 3230). He thought that

---

apply to the conduct of the federal executive and judicial branches. *See, e.g.*, *Dep't of Homeland Sec. v. Regents of Univ. of Cal.*, 140 S. Ct. 1891, 1915–16 (2020) (applying the Fifth Amendment to unilateral action by the Trump administration). Does Marshall's opinion persuade you that the current regime makes sense?

these rights included the right to travel, "to claim the benefit of the writ of habeas corpus," to sue, to hold property, and to vote. *Id.*

But the Civil Rights Act was controversial, even among leading opponents of the black codes. Representative John Bingham of Ohio argued that Congress had no constitutional authority to "enforce by penal enactment these great canons of the supreme law, securing to all the citizens in every State the privileges and immunities of citizens." Cong. Globe, 39th Cong., 1st Sess. 1090 (1866). Bingham insisted that Congress should first adopt his Fourteenth Amendment, which would clearly authorize Congress to define the privileges and immunities of citizenship. Bingham's persistence eventually paid off. The same Congress that passed the Civil Rights Act over his objections also proposed a new constitutional amendment.

The opening sentences of the Fourteenth Amendment, which Bingham helped draft, constitutionalized the Civil Rights Act. It declared, "All persons born or naturalized in the United States and subject to the jurisdiction thereof, are citizens of the United States and of the State wherein they reside. No State shall make or enforce any law which shall abridge the privileges or immunities of citizens of the United States." Although Bingham didn't expressly define what the "privileges or immunities" of citizenship were, he emphasized that they definitely included the rights protected by the Bill of Rights. *See, e.g.*, Cong. Globe, 39th Cong., 1st Sess. at 1034, 1089–90, 1291–92, 2541–42. Pointing to the Civil Rights Act and Justice Washington's opinion in *Corfield*, he also suggested that Congress could define the privileges and immunities of U.S. citizenship in the future. *See* Note, *Congress's Power to Define the Privileges and Immunities of Citizenship*, 128 Harv. L. Rev. 1206, 1220–21 (2015).

39.2.1

The Slaughter-House Cases

83 U.S. (16 Wall.) 36 (1873)

When the Fourteenth Amendment was ratified in 1868, Bingham and other supporters fully anticipated that its Privileges or Immunities Clause had reversed *Barron*, ratified the Civil Rights Act, and applied the protections of the Bill of Rights to the states. Yet when the Supreme Court interpreted the amendment for the first time five years later in the *Slaughter-House Cases*, 83 U.S. (16 (Wall.) 36 (1873), its interpretation of the Privileges or Immunities Clause was so narrow that the Court effectively read the clause out of the Constitution.

Like many cities in the nineteenth century, New Orleans was filthy: the city had no public sewer system, toilets of homes and hotels emptied into gutters, and garbage filled the streets. *See* Michael A. Ross, *Justice of Shattered Dreams: Samuel Freeman Miller and the Supreme Court During the Civil War* 190 (2003). Worst of all, butchers and slaughterhouses filled the city's neighborhoods with the refuse of more than 300,000 animals each year. *Id.* These slaughterhouses unloaded barrels of entrails, blood, urine, and dung into New Orleans's streets, where they washed into the Mississippi River and collected around the intake pipes from which New Orleans drew its water supply. *Id.* at 190–91. The waste of slaughtered animals literally clogged the city's plumbing system. *Id.* at 191. The public health effects of the city's slaughterhouses were obvious: they contributed to contagious diseases, foul odors, and contaminated food.

In 1866, shortly after the Civil War ended, hundreds of New Orleans residents petitioned the state legislature to move the slaughterhouses out of the city to a place where they wouldn't poison the water supply. San Francisco, Boston, New York, and Philadelphia had recently passed similar ordinances centralizing those cities' slaughterhouses into single locations where meat could be inspected and the waste disposed of properly. In 1869, Louisiana's legislature passed a law similarly requiring the city's butchers to do their job in a central location. *Id.* at 191–92.

The Louisiana slaughterhouse law outraged the city's white butchers, who opposed it for a variety of reasons. For one thing, the law created a private monopoly. The law established a corporation to construct the "grand slaughterhouse," it required all butchers to use the slaughterhouse, and it authorized the corporation to collect user fees from the butchers. *Id.* at 192. But such measures were common at the time, particularly in places like postwar Louisiana that didn't have much money to finance new construction.

More galling to the white residents of New Orleans was the fact that the Louisiana legislature included large numbers of black representatives and Republicans for the first time in the state's history—thanks to the federal Reconstruction Acts. With the rallying cry "[T]he 'white man's flag' shall be upheld," New Orleans's newspapers vowed to oppose every law—good and bad—"brought upon us by ignorance, the incapacity, and the notorious corruption of our so-called representatives in the General Assembly." *Id.* at 196. Within weeks of passing the slaughterhouse law, the Reconstruction legislature further alienated these white reactionaries by integrating Louisiana's public schools and making it a crime to deny black people entry to hotels, railroad cars, and other public accommodations. *Id.* at 196–97.

The white opponents of the slaughterhouse and antidiscrimination laws hired as their lawyer John A. Campbell, a former Supreme Court justice who concurred with the majority in *Dred Scott v. Sandford*, 60 U.S. (19 How.) 393 (1857), before resigning to join the Confederacy. His case against the slaughterhouse reached the Supreme Court in 1873. Campbell raised virtually every argument he could think of, including that the law violated the Thirteenth Amendment because it forced the butchers to work in a central slaughterhouse against their will. But his most influential argument opposed the law for violating the Fourteenth Amendment's Privileges or Immunities Clause on the theory that the law denied the butchers the fundamental "right to exercise their trade." *The Slaughter-House Cases*, 83 U.S. (16 Wall.) 36, 60 (1873).

Campbell's "right to exercise their trade" argument might have been more persuasive had he been advocating to protect the rights of recently freed black people. Instead, he was defending white people from what he considered the excesses of multiracial democracy. Ross, *supra*, at 199. Yet the method by which the Court dismantled Campbell's argument in the *Slaughter-House Cases* took down any protection that the Privileges or Immunities Clause might have offered to white *or* black plaintiffs.

■ MR. JUSTICE MILLER delivered the opinion of the Court.[4]

These cases are brought here by writs of error to the Supreme Court of the State of Louisiana. They arise out of the efforts of the butchers of New Orleans to resist the Crescent City Live-Stock Landing and Slaughter-House Company in the exercise of certain powers conferred by the charter which created it, and which was granted by the legislature of that State. . . .

This statute is denounced not only as creating a monopoly and conferring odious and exclusive privileges upon a small number of persons at the expense of the great body of the community of New Orleans, but it is asserted that it deprives a large and meritorious class of citizens—the whole of the butchers of the city—of the right to exercise their trade, the business to which they have been trained and on which they depend for the support of themselves and their families; and that the unrestricted exercise of the business of butchering is necessary to the daily subsistence of the population of the city.

But a critical examination of the act hardly justifies these assertions. . . .

The power here exercised by the legislature of Louisiana is, in its essential nature, one which has been, up to the present period in the constitutional history of this country, always conceded to belong to the States, however it may now be questioned in some of its details. . . . This is called the police power. . . . This power is, and must be from its very nature, incapable of any very exact definition or limitation. Upon it depends the security of social order, the life and health of the citizen, the comfort of an existence in a thickly populated community, the enjoyment of private and social life, and the beneficial use of property. . . .

Unless, therefore, it can be maintained that the exclusive privilege granted by this charter to the corporation, is beyond the power of the legislature of Louisiana, there can be no just exception to the validity of the statute. And in this respect we are not able to see that these privileges are especially odious or objectionable. [The law authorizes the corporation to charge butchers a fee for using a sanitary slaughterhouse, and, in consideration, the corporation is obligated to allow all butchers to practice their trade within the slaughterhouse.] The prices or charges to be made by the company are limited by the statute, and we are not advised that they are on the whole exorbitant or unjust.

---

[4] **As You Read, Consider:** An incredibly unsympathetic group of white plaintiffs in this case offers a reasonable, race-neutral interpretation of the Thirteenth and Fourteenth Amendments: the amendments prohibit a state from depriving anyone of the right to labor under conditions of their own choice. Do you agree with the method by which Justice Samuel Miller disposes of the plaintiffs' case, or would you have adopted a different interpretation of the amendments?

The proposition is, therefore, reduced to these terms: Can any exclusive privileges be granted to any of its citizens, or to a corporation, by the legislature of a State? . . .

The plaintiffs in error accepting this issue, allege that the statute is a violation of the Constitution of the United States in these several particulars:

[1] That it creates an involuntary servitude forbidden by the thirteenth article of amendment; [2] That it abridges the privileges and immunities of citizens of the United States; [3] That it denies to the plaintiffs the equal protection of the laws; and, [4] That it deprives them of their property without due process of law; contrary to the provisions of the first section of the fourteenth article of amendment.

This court is thus called upon for the first time to give construction to these articles. . . .

The most cursory glance at these articles discloses a unity of purpose, when taken in connection with the history of the times, which cannot fail to have an important bearing on any question of doubt concerning their true meaning. Nor can such doubts, when any reasonably exist, be safely and rationally solved without a reference to that history; for in it is found the occasion and the necessity for recurring again to the great source of power in this country, the people of the States, for additional guarantees of human rights; additional powers to the Federal government; additional restraints upon those of the States. Fortunately that history is fresh within the memory of us all, and its leading features, as they bear upon the matter before us, free from doubt.

[History of the Reconstruction Amendments]

The institution of African slavery, as it existed in about half the States of the Union, and the contests pervading the public mind for many years, between those who desired its curtailment and ultimate extinction and those who desired additional safeguards for its security and perpetuation, culminated in the effort, on the part of most of the States in which slavery existed, to separate from the Federal government, and to resist its authority. This constituted the war of the rebellion, and whatever auxiliary causes may have contributed to bring about this war, undoubtedly the overshadowing and efficient cause was African slavery.

In that struggle slavery, as a legalized social relation, perished. . . . But the war being over, those who had succeeded in re-establishing the authority of the Federal government . . . determined to place this main and most valuable result in the Constitution of the restored Union as one of its fundamental articles. Hence the thirteenth article of amendment of that instrument. Its two short sections seem hardly to admit of construction, so vigorous is their expression and so appropriate to the purpose we have indicated.

> "1. Neither slavery nor involuntary servitude, except as a punishment for crime, whereof the party shall have been duly convicted, shall exist within the United States or any place subject to their jurisdiction.
>
> "2. Congress shall have power to enforce this article by appropriate legislation."

To withdraw the mind from the contemplation of this grand yet simple declaration of the personal freedom of all the human race within the jurisdiction of this government—a declaration designed to establish the freedom of four millions of slaves—and with a microscopic search endeavor to find in it a reference to servitudes, which may have been attached to property in certain localities, requires an effort, to say the least of it. . . .

The word servitude is of larger meaning than slavery, as the latter is popularly understood in this country, and the obvious purpose was to forbid all shades and conditions of African slavery. It was very well understood that in the form of apprenticeship for long terms, as it had been practiced in the West India Islands, on the abolition of slavery by the English government, or by reducing the slaves to the condition of serfs attached to the plantation, the purpose of the article might have been evaded, if only the word slavery had been used. . . . And it is all that we deem necessary to say on the application of that article to the statute of Louisiana, now under consideration.

The process of restoring to their proper relations with the Federal government and with the other States those which had sided with the rebellion, undertaken under the proclamation of President Johnson in 1865, and before the assembling of Congress, developed the fact that, notwithstanding the formal recognition by those States of the abolition of slavery, the condition of the slave race would, without further protection of the Federal government, be almost as bad as it was before. Among the first acts of legislation adopted by several of the States in the legislative bodies which claimed to be in their normal relations with the Federal government, were laws which imposed upon the colored race onerous disabilities and burdens, and curtailed their rights in the pursuit of life, liberty, and property to such an extent that their freedom was of little value, while they had lost the protection which they had received from their former owners from motives both of interest and humanity. . . .

These circumstances . . . forced upon the statesmen who had conducted the Federal government in safety through the crisis of the rebellion, and who supposed that by the thirteenth article of amendment they had secured the result of their labors, the conviction that something more was necessary in the way of constitutional protection to the unfortunate race who had suffered so much. They accordingly passed through Congress the proposition for the fourteenth amendment. . . .

Before we proceed to examine more critically the provisions of this amendment, on which the plaintiffs in error rely, let us complete and dismiss the history of the recent amendments, as that history relates to the general purpose which pervades them all. A few years' experience satisfied the thoughtful men who had been the authors of the other two amendments that, notwithstanding the restraints of those articles on the States, and the laws passed under the additional powers granted to Congress, these were inadequate for the protection of life, liberty, and property, without which freedom to the slave was no boon. They were in all those States denied the right of suffrage. The laws were administered by the white man alone. It was urged that a race of men distinctively marked as was the negro, living in the midst of another and dominant race, could never be fully secured in their person and their property without the right of suffrage.

Hence the fifteenth amendment, which declares that "the right of a citizen of the United States to vote shall not be denied or abridged by any State on account of race, color, or previous condition of servitude." The negro having, by the fourteenth amendment, been declared to be a citizen of the United States, is thus made a voter in every State of the Union.

We repeat, then, in the light of this recapitulation of events, almost too recent to be called history, but which are familiar to us all; and on the most casual examination of the language of these amendments, no one can fail to be impressed with the one pervading purpose found in them all . . .: we mean the freedom of the slave race, the security and firm establishment of that freedom, and the protection of the newly-made freeman and citizen from the oppressions of those who had formerly exercised unlimited dominion over him. . . . .[5]

We do not say that no one else but the negro can share in this protection. Both the language and spirit of these articles are to have their fair and just weight in any question of construction. Undoubtedly while negro slavery alone was in the mind of the Congress which proposed the thirteenth article, it forbids any other kind of slavery, now or hereafter. If Mexican peonage or the Chinese coolie labor system shall develop slavery of the Mexican or Chinese race within our territory, this amendment may safely be trusted to make it void. And so if other rights are assailed by the States which properly and necessarily fall within the protection of these articles, that protection will apply, though the party interested may not be of African descent. But what we do say, and what we wish to be understood is, that in any fair and just construction of any section or phrase of these amendments, it is necessary to look to the purpose which we have said was the pervading spirit of them all, the evil which they were designed to remedy, and the process of continued addition to the Constitution, until that purpose was supposed to be accomplished, as far as constitutional law can accomplish it.

[The Citizenship Clause of the Fourteenth Amendment]

The first section of the fourteenth article, to which our attention is more specially invited, opens with a definition of citizenship—not only citizenship of the United States, but citizenship of the States. No such definition was previously found in the Constitution, nor had any attempt been made to define it by act of Congress. . . . But it had been held by this court, in the celebrated *Dred Scott* case, only a few years before the outbreak of the civil war, that a man of African descent, whether a slave or not, was not and could not be a citizen of a State or of the United States. This decision, while it met the condemnation of some of the ablest statesmen and constitutional lawyers of the country, had never been overruled; and if it was to be accepted as a constitutional limitation of the right of citizenship, then all the negro race who had recently been made freemen, were still, not only not citizens, but were incapable of becoming so by anything short of an amendment to the Constitution.

To remove this difficulty primarily, and to establish a clear and comprehensive definition of citizenship which should declare what should constitute citizenship of the United States, and also citizenship of a State, the first clause of the first section was framed.

> "All persons born or naturalized in the United States, and subject to the jurisdiction thereof, are citizens of the United States and of the State wherein they reside."

The first observation we have to make on this clause is, that it . . . overturns the *Dred Scott* decision by making all persons born within the United States and subject to its jurisdiction citizens of the United States. That its main purpose was to establish the citizenship of the negro can admit of no doubt. The phrase, "subject to its jurisdiction" was intended to exclude from its operation children of ministers, consuls, and citizens or subjects of foreign States born within the United States.

---

[5] **Questions:** Here, Miller disposes of the Thirteenth Amendment argument by observing that the "pervading purpose" of the Reconstruction amendments was to protect the liberty of recently freed black people from the oppressions of white supremacy. Do you agree with him that the law requiring white butchers to work in a particular slaughterhouse is not "involuntary servitude" within the meaning of the Thirteenth Amendment? Based on this last paragraph, does the Thirteenth Amendment protect anything on its own beyond racial subordination approaching slavery?

The next observation is more important in view of the arguments of counsel in the present case. It is, that the distinction between citizenship of the United States and citizenship of a State is clearly recognized and established.[6] Not only may a man be a citizen of the United States without being a citizen of a State, but an important element is necessary to convert the former into the latter. He must reside within the State to make him a citizen of it, but it is only necessary that he should be born or naturalized in the United States to be a citizen of the Union.

It is quite clear, then, that there is a citizenship of the United States, and a citizenship of a State, which are distinct from each other, and which depend upon different characteristics or circumstances in the individual.

[The Privileges or Immunities Clause of the Fourteenth Amendment]

We think this distinction and its explicit recognition in this amendment of great weight in this argument, because the next paragraph of this same section, which is the one mainly relied on by the plaintiffs in error, speaks only of privileges and immunities of citizens of the United States, and does not speak of those of citizens of the several States. . . .

The language is, "No State shall make or enforce any law which shall abridge the privileges or immunities of citizens of the United States." It is a little remarkable, if this clause was intended as a protection to the citizen of a State against the legislative power of his own State, that the word citizen of the State should be left out when it is so carefully used, and used in contradistinction to citizens of the United States, in the very sentence which precedes it. It is too clear for argument that the change in phraseology was adopted understandingly and with a purpose.

Of the privileges and immunities of the citizen of the United States, and of the privileges and immunities of the citizen of the State, and what they respectively are, we will presently consider; but we wish to state here that it is only the former which are placed by this clause under the protection of the Federal Constitution, and that the latter, whatever they may be, are not intended to have any additional protection by this paragraph of the amendment. . . .

The first occurrence of the words "privileges and immunities" in our constitutional history, is to be found in the fourth of the articles of the old Confederation.[7]

It declares "that the better to secure and perpetuate mutual friendship and intercourse among the people of the different States in this Union, the free inhabitants of each of these States, paupers, vagabonds, and fugitives from justice excepted, shall be entitled to all the privileges and immunities of free citizens in the several States; and the people of each State shall have free ingress and regress to and from

---

6 **Questions:** Here, Miller takes a logical step in his argument that is easy to miss but crucial to his holding. In *Dred Scott v. Sandford*, Chief Justice Roger Taney emphasized that black people could not be citizens for purposes of the U.S. Constitution, even if some states like Massachusetts might call black residents of their state citizens. Here, Miller concludes that the Citizenship Clause reversed *Dred Scott*'s holding by declaring that people born within the United States were citizens of a state *and* of the United States. Why does it matter so much to him that a person might be a citizen of Massachusetts *and* a citizen of the United States? How might the rights of state citizenship be different from the rights of *U.S.* citizenship?

7 **Questions:** The butchers in this case are arguing that "the right to exercise their trade" is a privilege of U.S. citizenship protected by the Privileges *or* Immunities Clause of the Fourteenth Amendment. Here, Miller is addressing that argument by turning to the similarly named Privileges *and* Immunities Clause of Article IV. He is observing that the Article IV clause mentions "the privileges and immunities of citizens *of the several States*," while the Fourteenth Amendment mentions only "the privileges or immunities of citizens *of the United States*." Do you agree with him that these two clauses protect two different categories of rights? In which category does he place "the right to exercise their trade"? Does he consider it a right of state citizenship or a right of *U.S.* citizenship?

any other State, and shall enjoy therein all the privileges of trade and commerce, subject to the same duties, impositions, and restrictions as the inhabitants thereof respectively."

In the Constitution of the United States, which superseded the Articles of Confederation, the corresponding provision is found in section two of the fourth article, in the following words: "The citizens of each State shall be entitled to all the privileges and immunities of citizens of the several States."

There can be but little question that the purpose of both these provisions is the same, and that the privileges and immunities intended are the same in each. In the article of the Confederation we have some of these specifically mentioned, and enough perhaps to give some general idea of the class of civil rights meant by the phrase.

Fortunately we are not without judicial construction of this clause of the Constitution.[8] The first and the leading case on the subject is that of *Corfield v. Coryell*, decided by Mr. Justice Washington in the Circuit Court for the District of Pennsylvania in 1823.

"The inquiry," he says, "is, what are the privileges and immunities of citizens of the several States? We feel no hesitation in confining these expressions to those privileges and immunities which are fundamental; which belong of right to the citizens of all free governments, and which have at all times been enjoyed by citizens of the several States which compose this Union, from the time of their becoming free, independent, and sovereign. What these fundamental principles are, it would be more tedious than difficult to enumerate. They may all, however, be comprehended under the following general heads: protection by the government, with the right to acquire and possess property of every kind, and to pursue and obtain happiness and safety, subject, nevertheless, to such restraints as the government may prescribe for the general good of the whole." . . .

The constitutional provision there alluded to did not create those rights, which it called privileges and immunities of citizens of the States. It threw around them in that clause no security for the citizen of the State in which they were claimed or exercised. Nor did it profess to control the power of the State governments over the rights of its own citizens.

Its sole purpose was to declare to the several States, that whatever those rights, as you grant or establish them to your own citizens, or as you limit or qualify, or impose restrictions on their exercise, the same, neither more nor less, shall be the measure of the rights of citizens of other States within your jurisdiction.

---

[8] **Questions:** In the critical next few paragraphs, Miller makes four points.

First, quoting an 1823 interpretation of the Privileges and Immunities Clause of Article IV, Miller observes that the privileges and immunities of *state* citizenship include the right "to acquire and possess property of every kind, and to pursue and obtain happiness and safety."

Second, he concludes that the only protection that the Constitution offers for these rights is Article IV's Privileges and Immunities Clause. He writes that the "sole purpose" of the clause was to prohibit states from discriminating against citizens of other states in their exercise of these state-protected rights.

Third, he writes that the federal government was never thought to possess the power to protect these rights when a state discriminated against its citizens.

Finally, he concludes that the Fourteenth Amendment has not changed this arrangement.

Do you disagree with any of the above four points? Why is he so worried about interpreting the Fourteenth Amendment in a manner that would permit Congress or federal courts to protect the butchers' claimed "right to exercise their trade"? What does his conclusion say about the constitutionality of the Civil Rights Act of 1866?

It would be the vainest show of learning to attempt to prove by citations of authority, that up to the adoption of the recent amendments, no claim or pretence was set up that those rights depended on the Federal government for their existence or protection. . . . [T]he entire domain of the privileges and immunities of citizens of the States, as above defined, lay within the constitutional and legislative power of the States, and without that of the Federal government. Was it the purpose of the fourteenth amendment, by the simple declaration that no State should make or enforce any law which shall abridge the privileges and immunities of citizens of the United States, to transfer the security and protection of all the civil rights which we have mentioned, from the States to the Federal government? And where it is declared that Congress shall have the power to enforce that article, was it intended to bring within the power of Congress the entire domain of civil rights heretofore belonging exclusively to the States?

All this and more must follow, if the proposition of the plaintiffs in error be sound. For not only are these rights subject to the control of Congress whenever in its discretion any of them are supposed to be abridged by State legislation, but that body may also pass laws in advance, limiting and restricting the exercise of legislative power by the States, in their most ordinary and usual functions, as in its judgment it may think proper on all such subjects. . . . The argument we admit is not always the most conclusive which is drawn from the consequences urged against the adoption of a particular construction of an instrument. But when, as in the case before us, these consequences are so serious, so far-reaching and pervading, so great a departure from the structure and spirit of our institutions; when the effect is to fetter and degrade the State governments by subjecting them to the control of Congress, in the exercise of powers heretofore universally conceded to them of the most ordinary and fundamental character; when in fact it radically changes the whole theory of the relations of the State and Federal governments to each other and of both these governments to the people; the argument has a force that is irresistible, in the absence of language which expresses such a purpose too clearly to admit of doubt.

We are convinced that no such results were intended by the Congress which proposed these amendments, nor by the legislatures of the States which ratified them.

Having shown that the privileges and immunities relied on in the argument are those which belong to citizens of the States as such, and that they are left to the State governments for security and protection, and not by this article placed under the special care of the Federal government, we may hold ourselves excused from defining the privileges and immunities of citizens of the United States which no State can abridge, until some case involving those privileges may make it necessary to do so.

But lest it should be said that no such privileges and immunities are to be found if those we have been considering are excluded, we venture to suggest some which owe their existence to the Federal government, its National character, its Constitution, or its laws.

One of these is . . . the right of the citizen of this great country, protected by implied guarantees of its Constitution, to come to the seat of government to assert any claim he may have upon that government, to transact any business he may have with it, to seek its protection, to share its offices, to engage in administering its functions. He has the right of free access to its seaports, through which all operations of foreign commerce are conducted, to the subtreasuries, land offices, and courts of justice in the several States. . . .

Another privilege of a citizen of the United States is to demand the care and protection of the Federal government over his life, liberty, and property when on the high seas or within the jurisdiction of a foreign government. Of this there can be no doubt, nor that the right depends upon his character as a citizen of the United States. The right to peaceably assemble and petition for redress of grievances, the privilege of the writ of habeas corpus, are rights of the citizen guaranteed by the Federal Constitution. The right to use the navigable waters of the United States, however they may penetrate the territory of the several States, all rights secured to our citizens by treaties with foreign nations, are dependent upon citizenship of the United States, and not citizenship of a State. . . .

But it is useless to pursue this branch of the inquiry, since we are of opinion that the rights claimed by these plaintiffs in error, if they have any existence, are not privileges and immunities of citizens of the United States within the meaning of the clause of the fourteenth amendment under consideration.[9]

[The Due Process Clause of the Fourteenth Amendment]

"[N]or shall any State deprive any person of life, liberty, or property without due process of law. . . ."

The argument has not been much pressed in these cases that the defendant's charter deprives the plaintiffs of their property without due process of law. . . . [This language] has been in the Constitution since the adoption of the fifth amendment, as a restraint upon the Federal power. It is also to be found in some form of expression in the constitutions of nearly all the States, as a restraint upon the power of the States. This law, then, has practically been the same as it now is during the existence of the government, except so far as the present amendment may place the restraining power over the States in this matter in the hands of the Federal government.

We are not without judicial interpretation, therefore, both State and National of the meaning of this clause. And it is sufficient to say that under no construction of that provision that we have ever seen, or any that we deem admissible, can the restraint imposed by the State of Louisiana upon the exercise of their trade by the butchers of New Orleans be held to be a deprivation of property within the meaning of that provision.

[The Equal Protection Clause of the Fourteenth Amendment]

"Nor shall any State deny to any person within its jurisdiction the equal protection of the laws."

In the light of the history of these amendments, and the pervading purpose of them, which we have already discussed, it is not difficult to give a meaning to this clause. The existence of laws in the States where the newly emancipated negroes resided, which discriminated with gross injustice and hardship against them as a class, was the evil to be remedied by this clause, and by it such laws are forbidden.

If, however, the States did not conform their laws to its requirements, then by the fifth section of the article of amendment Congress was authorized to enforce it by suitable legislation. We doubt very much whether any action of a State not directed by way of discrimination against the negroes as a class, or on account of their race, will ever be held to come within the purview of this provision. . . . But as it is a State that is to be dealt with, and not alone the validity of its laws, we may safely leave that matter until Congress shall have exercised its power, or some case of State oppression, by denial of equal justice in its courts, shall have claimed a decision at our hands. . . .

---

9 **Question:** Miller concludes that the butchers' claimed "right to exercise their trade" is not a privilege or immunity of *U.S.* citizenship protected by the Fourteenth Amendment's Privileges or Immunities Clause. After his opinion (which remains good law), what, precisely, *does* the Privileges or Immunities Clause protect?

[* * *]

In the early history of the organization of the government, its statesmen seem to have divided on the line which should separate the powers of the National government from those of the State governments, and though this line has never been very well defined in public opinion, such a division has continued from that day to this.

The adoption of the first eleven amendments to the Constitution so soon after the original instrument was accepted, shows a prevailing sense of danger at that time from the Federal power. And it cannot be denied that such a jealousy continued to exist with many patriotic men until the breaking out of the late civil war. It was then discovered that the true danger to the perpetuity of the Union was in the capacity of the State organizations to combine and concentrate all the powers of the State, and of contiguous States, for a determined resistance to the General Government. . . .

But, however pervading this sentiment, and however it may have contributed to the adoption of the amendments we have been considering, we do not see in those amendments any purpose to destroy the main features of the general system.[10] Under the pressure of all the excited feeling growing out of the war, our statesmen have still believed that the existence of the States with powers for domestic and local government, including the regulation of civil rights—the rights of person and of property—was essential to the perfect working of our complex form of government, though they have thought proper to impose additional limitations on the States, and to confer additional power on that of the Nation. . . .

■ MR. JUSTICE FIELD, dissenting:[11]

[The] equality of right . . . in the lawful pursuits of life, throughout the whole country, is the distinguishing privilege of citizens of the United States. To them, everywhere, all pursuits, all professions, all avocations are open without other restrictions than such as are imposed equally upon all others of the same age, sex, and condition. The State may prescribe such regulations for every pursuit and calling of life as will promote the public health, secure the good order and advance the general prosperity of society, but when once prescribed, the pursuit or calling must be free to be followed by every citizen who is within the conditions designated, and will conform to the regulations. This is the fundamental idea upon which our institutions rest, and unless adhered to in the legislation of the country our government will be a republic only in name. The fourteenth amendment, in my judgment, makes it essential to the validity of the legislation of every State that this equality of right should be respected. . . . [T]his equality has been departed from [and] entirely rejected and trampled upon by the act of Louisiana. . . . And it is to me a matter of profound regret that its validity is recognized by a majority of this court, for by it the right of free labor, one of the most sacred and imprescriptible rights of man, is violated. . . . [G]rants of exclusive privileges, such as is made by the act in question, are opposed to the whole theory of free government, and it requires no aid from any bill of rights to render them void. That only is a free government, in the American sense of the term, under which the inalienable right of every citizen to pursue his happiness is unrestrained, except by just, equal, and impartial laws.

---

[10] **Question:** Referring to the antebellum belief that federalism was necessary to prevent the federal government from overreaching, Miller concludes his opinion by declaring that the Reconstruction amendments did not "destroy the main features of the general system." How does Miller's opinion compare with the *Civil Rights Cases*, which followed a decade later?

[11] **Question:** Justice Stephen Field (who will later author the *Chinese Exclusion Case*) and Justice Joseph Bradley (who will later author the *Civil Rights Cases*) each dissent on the ground that "the right of free labor" is a fundamental right with which states cannot unjustly interfere. Precisely why do they disagree with the majority opinion?

■ MR. JUSTICE BRADLEY, also dissenting:

[T]he right of a State to regulate the conduct of its citizens is undoubtedly a very broad and extensive one, and not to be lightly restricted. But there are certain fundamental rights which this right of regulation cannot infringe. . . .

The people of this country brought with them to its shores the rights of Englishmen; the rights which had been wrested from English sovereigns at various periods of the nation's history. One of these fundamental rights was expressed in these words, found in Magna Charta: "No freeman shall be taken or imprisoned, or be disseized of his freehold or liberties or free customs, or be outlawed or exiled, or any otherwise destroyed; nor will we pass upon him or condemn him but by lawful judgment of his peers or by the law of the land." English constitutional writers expound this article as rendering life, liberty, and property inviolable, except by due process of law. This is the very right which the plaintiffs in error claim in this case. . . .

[T]he Declaration of Independence[,] which was the first political act of the American people in their independent sovereign capacity, lays the foundation of our National existence upon this broad proposition: "That all men are created equal; that they are endowed by their Creator with certain inalienable rights; that among these are life, liberty, and the pursuit of happiness." Here again we have the great threefold division of the rights of freemen, asserted as the rights of man. Rights to life, liberty, and the pursuit of happiness are equivalent to the rights of life, liberty, and property. These are the fundamental rights which can only be taken away by due process of law, and which can only be interfered with, or the enjoyment of which can only be modified, by lawful regulations necessary or proper for the mutual good of all; and these rights, I contend, belong to the citizens of every free government.[12]

For the preservation, exercise, and enjoyment of these rights the individual citizen, as a necessity, must be left free to adopt such calling, profession, or trade as may seem to him most conducive to that end. Without this right he cannot be a freeman. This right to choose one's calling is an essential part of that liberty which it is the object of government to protect; and a calling, when chosen, is a man's property and right. Liberty and property are not protected where these rights are arbitrarily assailed.

I think sufficient has been said to show that citizenship is not an empty name, but that, in this country at least, it has connected with it certain incidental rights, privileges, and immunities of the greatest importance. And to say that these rights and immunities attach only to State citizenship, and not to citizenship of the United States, appears to me to evince a very narrow and insufficient estimate of constitutional history and the rights of men, not to say the rights of the American people. . . .

NOTE: THIRTEENTH AMENDMENT

The Thirteenth Amendment permanently freed more than four million enslaved people. As discussed earlier (section 20.2), Section 2 of the amendment, which empowered Congress to enforce its terms, has also remained an important source of civil rights legislation. But since the

[12] **Question:** Note Bradley's three-step analysis here: (1) the right to "life, liberty, and property" can be deprived only "by due process of law"; (2) the term *liberty* includes the "right to choose one's calling"; and (3) due process forbids a state from "arbitrarily" assailing that right. Within a few decades, this analysis would become the dominant interpretation of the Due Process Clause of the Fourteenth Amendment, illustrated most famously by *Lochner v. New York*. How does his analysis differ from the majority's brief discussion of the Due Process Clause?

Supreme Court first interpreted the amendment in the *Slaughter-House Cases*, the amendment itself has been infrequently invoked as a limit on state power.

Just as the *Slaughter-House Cases* interpreted the term *involuntary servitude* narrowly not to include the servitude at issue in the slaughterhouse law, the Supreme Court has since held that the amendment has no bearing on housing laws that require landlords to provide habitable apartments, *Marcus Brown Co. v. Feldman*, 265 U.S. 170, 199 (1921); injunctions requiring striking workers to return to work, *UAW v. WERB*, 336 U.S. 245, 252 (1949); or antidiscrimination laws requiring hotel owners to serve black customers, *Heart of Atlanta Motel, Inc. v. United States*, 379 U.S. 241, 276 (1964). The Court has also held that the amendment's prohibition on involuntary servitude doesn't apply to "services which have from time immemorial been treated as exceptional." *Robertson v. Baldwin*, 165 U.S. 275, 282 (1897). Such services principally include duties owed to the government such as the military draft, *Selective Draft Law Cases*, 245 U.S. 366, 390 (1918), and other "services in the army, militia, on the jury, etc." *Butler v. Perry*, 240 U.S. 328, 333 (1916).

The only laws that have been prohibited under the Thirteenth Amendment's own terms are those "akin to African slavery," *Butler*, 240 U.S. at 332, such as Alabama's peonage laws that made it a crime for anyone to refuse to work under an employment contract and punished the convicted person by requiring that person to work until all debts were repaid. *See United States v. Reynolds*, 235 U.S. 133, 150 (1914); *Bailey v. Alabama*, 219 U.S. 219, 245 (1911).

39.2.2

Minor v. Happersett

88 U.S. (21 Wall.) 162 (1875)

Bingham and other authors of the Fourteenth Amendment anticipated that the Privileges or Immunities Clause would protect all of the rights listed in the Bill of Rights and the Civil Rights Act of 1866—including the right to make contracts and own property. But the Supreme Court in the *Slaughter-House Cases* interpreted the clause exceptionally narrowly to protect only those privileges that a person could claim from the *federal* government exclusively, such as "the right to use the navigable waters of the United States." 83 U.S. (16 Wall.) at 79.

The Court reconfirmed its narrow interpretation of the Privileges or Immunities Clause only one day later in *Bradwell v. Illinois*, 83 U.S. (16 Wall.) 130 (1873). In its second-ever interpretation of the Fourteenth Amendment, the Court considered the claim of Myra Bradwell, a political activist from Illinois. When Bradwell moved for admission to the state bar, the Illinois Supreme Court denied her application on the ground that she was a woman. Bradwell appealed to the U.S. Supreme Court, arguing that this sex-based discrimination violated her privileges and immunities as a citizen of the United States. But the U.S. Supreme Court summarily rejected her argument in a paragraph:

> We agree with [Bradwell] that there are privileges and immunities belonging to citizens of the United States, in that relation and character, and that it is these and these alone which a State is forbidden to abridge. But the right to admission to practice in the courts of a State is not one of them. This right in no sense depends on citizenship of the United States. It has not, as far as we know, ever been made in any State, or in any case, to depend on citizenship at all. Certainly many prominent and distinguished lawyers have been admitted to practice, both in the State and Federal courts, who were not citizens of the United States or of any State. But, on whatever basis this right may be placed, so far as it can have any relation to citizenship at all, it would seem that, as to the courts of a State, it would relate to citizenship of the State, and as to Federal courts, it would relate to citizenship of the United States.

Bradwell, 83 U.S. (16 Wall.) at 139; *see also In re Lockwood*, 154 U.S. 116, 117 (1894) (same for Belva Ann Lockwood's application to the Virginia bar, despite being admitted by Congress to the Supreme Court bar).

Around the same time that Bradwell applied to become a lawyer in Illinois, another political activist, Virginia Minor, attempted to register to vote in Missouri. The local registrar, Reese Happersett, rejected her application because the Missouri Constitution specifically enfranchised only men. Minor sued Happersett, claiming that the right to vote for members of Congress was certainly a privilege or immunity of U.S. citizenship.

The Supreme Court was skeptical, as evidenced by its decision in *Minor v. Happersett*, 88 U.S. (21 Wall.) 162 (1875).

■ THE CHIEF JUSTICE delivered the opinion of the Court.[13]

The question is presented in this case, whether, since the adoption of the fourteenth amendment, a woman, who is a citizen of the United States and of the State of Missouri, is a voter in that State, notwithstanding the provision of the constitution and laws of the State, which confine the right of suffrage to men alone. . . . The argument is, that as a woman, born or naturalized in the United States and subject to the jurisdiction thereof, is a citizen of the United States and of the State in which she resides, she has the right of suffrage as one of the privileges and immunities of her citizenship, which the State cannot by its laws or constitution abridge.

There is no doubt that women may be citizens. They are persons, and by the fourteenth amendment "all persons born or naturalized in the United States and

[13] **As You Read, Consider:** The majority opinion in the *Slaughter-House Cases* interpreted the Fourteenth Amendment while relying heavily on principles of federalism and what it regarded as the amendment's purpose—ultimately dismissing the butchers' claims that Louisiana was treating them unequally or depriving them of their dignity. Does Chief Justice Morrison Waite adopt the same approach here? How, if at all, would you interpret the Privileges or Immunities Clause differently?

subject to the jurisdiction thereof" are expressly declared to be "citizens of the United States and of the State wherein they reside." . . . The direct question is, therefore, presented whether all citizens are necessarily voters.

The Constitution does not define the privileges and immunities of citizens. For that definition we must look elsewhere. In this case we need not determine what they are, but only whether suffrage is necessarily one of them.

It certainly is nowhere made so in express terms. The United States has no voters in the States of its own creation. The elective officers of the United States are all elected directly or indirectly by State voters. [For example, t]he members of the House of Representatives are to be chosen by the people of the States, and the electors in each State must have the qualifications requisite for electors of the most numerous branch of the State legislature. . . .

The [fourteenth] amendment did not add to the privileges and immunities of a citizen. It simply furnished an additional guaranty for the protection of such as he already had. No new voters were necessarily made by it. Indirectly it may have had that effect, because it may have increased the number of citizens entitled to suffrage under the constitution and laws of the States, but it operates for this purpose, if at all, through the States and the State laws, and not directly upon the citizen.

It is clear, therefore, we think, that the Constitution has not added the right of suffrage to the privileges and immunities of citizenship as they existed at the time it was adopted. This makes it proper to inquire whether suffrage was coextensive with the citizenship of the States at the time of its adoption. If it was, then it may with force be argued that suffrage was one of the rights which belonged to citizenship, and in the enjoyment of which every citizen must be protected. But if it was not, the contrary may with propriety be assumed.

When the Federal Constitution was adopted, all the States . . . had constitutions of their own. . . . Upon an examination of those constitutions we find that in no State were all citizens permitted to vote. Each State determined for itself who should have that power. Thus, in New Hampshire, "every male inhabitant of each town and parish with town privileges, and places unincorporated in the State, of twenty-one years of age and upwards, excepting paupers and persons excused from paying taxes at their own request," were its voters; . . . in New Jersey "all inhabitants . . . of full age who are worth fifty pounds, proclamation-money, clear estate in the same, and have resided in the county in which they claim a vote for twelve months immediately preceding the election." . . .

In this condition of the law in respect to suffrage in the several States it cannot for a moment be doubted that if it had been intended to make all citizens of the United States voters, the framers of the Constitution would not have left it to implication. So important a change in the condition of citizenship as it actually existed, if intended, would have been expressly declared.

And still again, after the adoption of the fourteenth amendment, it was deemed necessary to adopt a fifteenth, as follows: "The right of citizens of the United States to vote shall not be denied or abridged by the United States, or by any State, on account of race, color, or previous condition of servitude." The fourteenth amendment had already provided that no State should make or enforce any law which should abridge the privileges or immunities of citizens of the United States. If suffrage was one of these privileges or immunities, why amend the Constitution to prevent its being denied on account of race, &c.? Nothing is more evident than that the greater must include the less. . . .

Besides this, citizenship has not in all cases been made a condition precedent to the enjoyment of the right of suffrage. Thus, in Missouri, persons of foreign birth, who have declared their intention to become citizens of the United States, may under certain circumstances vote. The same provision is to be found in the constitutions of Alabama, Arkansas, Florida, Georgia, Indiana, Kansas, Minnesota, and Texas.[14]

Certainly, if the courts can consider any question settled, this is one. For nearly ninety years the people have acted upon the idea that the Constitution, when it conferred citizenship, did not necessarily confer the right of suffrage. If uniform practice long continued can settle the construction of so important an instrument as the Constitution of the United States confessedly is, most certainly it has been done here. Our province is to decide what the law is, not to declare what it should be. . . .

NOTE: PRIVILEGES OR IMMUNITIES CLAUSE

The holding of *Minor* was revised a decade later, when the Supreme Court held that the right to vote for national officers *was*, in fact, a privilege of U.S. citizenship—but only for people who met their state's qualifications. *Ex parte Yarbrough*, 110 U.S. 651, 664 (1884).

Modern interpretation of the Privileges or Immunities Clause. Nevertheless, for the next century, the Privileges or Immunities Clause remained a virtual dead letter—utterly failing to fulfill Bingham's goal of enforcing the Bill of Rights against the states. *See, e.g.*, *New York v. O'Neill*, 359 U.S. 1, 6 (1959) (Sixth Amendment); *Palko v. Connecticut*, 302 U.S. 319, 328–29 (1937) (Fifth Amendment); *Twining v. New Jersey*, 211 U.S. 78, 113 (1908) (Fifth Amendment); *Maxwell v. Dow*, 176 U.S. 581, 605 (1900) (Sixth Amendment); *In re Kemmler*, 136 U.S. 436, 449 (1890) (Eighth Amendment); *Walker v. Sauvinet*, 92 U.S. 90, 92 (1876) (Seventh Amendment).

That said, the clause has been successfully invoked to protect the modest list of items enumerated by the majority opinion in the *Slaughter-House Cases*. For example, because only Congress can "regulate Commerce . . . among the several States," the Court has held that being able to engage in interstate commerce is a privilege or immunity of U.S. citizenship. *Crutcher v. Kentucky*, 141 U.S. 47, 57 (1891).

More recently, the Privileges or Immunities Clause has also become a potential source of protection from discrimination on the basis of ancestry. In *Oyama v. California*, 332 U.S. 633 (1948), the Supreme Court struck down a California law that prohibited a U.S.-born citizen of Japanese descent from purchasing property. Unlike the Court in the *Slaughter-House Cases*, the Court in *Oyama* noted that the right to acquire and retain property was a privilege or immunity recognized by the Civil Rights Act of 1866. *Oyama*, 332 U.S. at 640. And in *Saenz v. Roe*, 526 U.S. 489 (1999), the Court struck down another California law that restricted the welfare benefits available for people who recently moved to California. The Court held that the Privileges or Immunities Clause protects the right to travel from one state to another and that this right is violated when a state treats newly arrived citizens differently than it does other citizens. *Saenz*, 526 U.S. at 502–03.

[14] **Question:** Waite observes that, as a matter of historical practice, citizenship has never been necessary nor sufficient for a person to vote: poor citizens were denied the right to vote, while noncitizen white men could vote in a dozen states in 1875. Along with his other arguments, does this one persuade you that the unqualified right to vote is not a privilege or immunity of U.S. citizenship protected by the Fourteenth Amendment?

The Court added that the Citizenship Clause of the Fourteenth Amendment made all U.S. citizens "citizens of the United States and of the State wherein they reside," further prohibiting California's disparate treatment of residents on the basis of their arrival in the state. *Id.*

Scope of the Privileges or Immunities Clause. The Privileges or Immunities Clause applies only to states—it isn't a restriction on Congress. It also applies only to *citizens*. In recent years, several justices and scholars have suggested that the *Slaughter-House Cases* should be overruled, interpreting the Privileges or Immunities Clause to apply the protections of the Bill of Rights to the states. *See, e.g.*, *Timbs v. Indiana*, 139 S. Ct. 682, 691 (2019) (Gorsuch, J., concurring) (citing Akhil Amar, *The Bill of Rights: Creation and Reconstruction* 163–214 (1998)); *id.* at 691–92 (Thomas, J., concurring in the judgment). As will be discussed shortly, a majority of the Court currently applies the Bill of Rights to the states by virtue of the Due Process Clause of the Fourteenth Amendment, which protects "persons," not just citizens. A new interpretation of the Privileges or Immunities Clause would therefore have the practical effect of allowing only U.S. citizens to invoke the Bill of Rights as a source of protection from state laws.

Beyond noncitizens, corporations are another group of legal persons who cannot invoke the Privileges or Immunities Clause. In *Paul v. Virginia*, 75 U.S. (8 Wall.) 168, 170 (1869), the Court invoked pre-Civil War precedents to hold that corporations are not "citizens" and are therefore not entitled to the protections of Article IV's Privileges *and* Immunities Clause or the Fourteenth Amendment's Privileges *or* Immunities Clause. The reasoning behind this decision has not since been revisited.

39.3 THE CITIZENSHIP CLAUSE

One of Congress's goals in enacting the Civil Rights Act of 1866, ch. 33, 14 Stat. 27, was to repudiate the Supreme Court's opinion in *Dred Scott v. Sandford*, 60 U.S. (19 How.) 393 (1857). In *Dred Scott*, the Court famously declared that black people "had no rights which the white man was bound to respect." 60 U.S. (19 How.) at 407. This holding repudiated a common-law principle known as *jus soli*, which provided that anyone born within a state automatically became a citizen of that state. For decades leading up to *Dred Scott*, lawyers in free black communities had published treatises and articles defending black people's claim to the same constitutional rights as their "white fellow-citizens" because they were all born in the United States. *See* Martha S. Jones, *Birthright Citizens* 1–13 (2018).

Embracing the perspective of these free black lawyers, the Civil Rights Act began by declaring that "all persons born in the United States and not subject to any foreign power, excluding Indians not taxed, are . . . citizens of the United States." 14 Stat. at 27. The Fourteenth Amendment, which constitutionalized the Civil Rights Act, was worded slightly differently. Section 1 of the amendment begins thus: "All persons born or naturalized in the United States and subject to the jurisdiction thereof, are citizens of the United States and of the State wherein they reside."

In contrast with the Civil Rights Act, the Citizenship Clause of the Fourteenth Amendment contained no language specifically exempting "Indians not taxed" from its terms. Citing this difference, John Elk, a Winnebago born on tribal land in Nebraska, attempted to register to vote in Nebraska on the ground that he was born in the United States and therefore a citizen of both the United States and Nebraska. But in *Elk v. Wilkins*, 112 U.S. 94 (1884), the Supreme Court held that the Fourteenth Amendment didn't modify the Court's earlier holding in *Cherokee Nation v. Georgia*, 30 U.S. (5 Pet.) 1 (1831), that a tribe was a "domestic dependent nation" and not formally part of the United States. The Court explained:

> Indians born within the territorial limits of the United States, members of, and owing immediate allegiance to, one of the Indian tribes (an alien, though dependent, power), although in a geographical sense born in the United States, are no more "born in the United States and subject to the jurisdiction thereof," within the meaning of the first section of the Fourteenth Amendment, than the children of subjects of any foreign government born within the domain of that government, or the children born within the United States, of ambassadors or other public ministers of foreign nations.

Elk, 112 U.S. at 102. To confirm this point, the Court cited the Civil Rights Act, several provisions of the original Constitution, and Section 2 of the Fourteenth Amendment, which penalized states that disenfranchised adult male citizens "excluding Indians not taxed." The Court therefore concluded that "Indians, then, not being citizens by birth, can only become citizens in the second way mentioned in the Fourteenth Amendment, by being 'naturalized in the United States,' by or under some treaty or statute." *Id.* at 103. It took decades before Congress passed the Indian Citizenship Act of 1924, Pub. L. No. 68–175, 43 Stat. 253. Even then, many states continued to discriminate against Native voters. *See, e.g.*, *Montoya v. Bolack*, 372 P.2d 387, 395 (N.M. 1962) (upholding, for the first time, the right of Navajos living on a reservation to vote).

39.3.1

United States v. Wong Kim Ark

169 U.S. 649 (1898)

In concluding that the Citizenship Clause didn't apply to American Indians, the Court in *Elk* equated Indians with "the children of subjects of any foreign government." But the Court didn't consider the applicability of the Fourteenth Amendment to the children of immigrants until a decade later in *United States v. Wong Kim Ark*, 169 U.S. 649 (1898).

Wong Kim Ark was born in San Francisco to two immigrant parents from China. At the time of his birth in 1873, federal law did not restrict immigration, but it did restrict eligibility for naturalization to white people and "persons of African descent." Naturalization Act of 1870, ch. 254, 16 Stat. 254, 256. Wong spent his entire childhood in California—watching as Congress enacted the Chinese Exclusion Act, ch. 126, 22 Stat. 58.

In 1894, five years after the Supreme Court decided the *Chinese Exclusion Case*, 130 U.S. 581 (1889), Wong decided to take a trip to China. When Wong returned to the United States in 1895, he showed the collector of customs a certification declaring that the Chinese Exclusion Act didn't apply to him because he had been born in the United States and was therefore a citizen. But the collector disagreed: Chinese immigrants routinely claimed to be U.S. citizens, and the federal government feared that if the Fourteenth Amendment granted birthright citizenship to the children of Chinese immigrants, then it would be impossible to enforce the Chinese Exclusion Act. *See* Amanda Frost, *You Are Not American: Citizenship Stripping from Dred Scott to the Dreamers* 58–63 (2021). When Wong challenged his exclusion in federal court, the solicitor general even suggested that the Fourteenth Amendment was invalid because it had been adopted against the will of California and southern states. *Id.*

In *Wong Kim Ark*, the Court rejected the solicitor general's arguments and found that birth in the United States automatically conferred citizenship.

■ MR. JUSTICE GRAY, after stating the case, delivered the opinion of the Court.[15]

The question presented by the record is whether a child born in the United States, of parents of Chinese descent, who, at the time of his birth, are subjects of the Emperor of China, but have a permanent domicil and residence in the United States, and are there carrying on business, and are not employed in any diplomatic or official capacity under the Emperor of China, becomes at the time of his birth a citizen of the United States, by virtue of the first clause of the Fourteenth Amendment of the Constitution, "All persons born or naturalized in the United States, and subject to the jurisdiction thereof, are citizens of the United States and of the State wherein they reside." . . .

I. [T]he Constitution of the United States, as originally adopted, uses the words "citizen of the United States," and "natural-born citizen of the United States." By the original Constitution, every representative in Congress is required to have been "seven years a citizen of the United States," and every Senator to have been "nine years a citizen of the United States;" and "no person except a natural-born citizen, or a citizen of the United States at the time of the adoption of this Constitution, shall be eligible to the office of President." The Fourteenth Article of Amendment,

---

[15] **As You Read, Consider:** Intuitively, the text of the Fourteenth Amendment's Citizenship Clause clearly applies to all persons born in the United States. Yet in *Elk v. Wilkins*, the Court held that the phrase "subject to its jurisdiction" excluded Indians. And in the *Slaughter-House Cases*, the Court held that the same phrase "was intended to exclude from its operation children of ministers, consuls, and citizens or subjects of foreign States born within the United States." 83 U.S. (16 Wall.) 36, 73 (1873). How, if at all, does Justice Horace Gray distinguish these precedents?

besides declaring that "all persons born or naturalized in the United States, and subject to the jurisdiction thereof, are citizens of the United States and of the State wherein they reside," also declares that "no State shall make or enforce any law which shall abridge the privileges or immunities of citizens of the United States. . . .["]

The Constitution nowhere defines the meaning of these words, either by way of inclusion or of exclusion, except in so far as this is done by the affirmative declaration that "all persons born or naturalized in the United States, and subject to the jurisdiction thereof, are citizens of the United States." In this, as in other respects, it must be interpreted in the light of the common law, the principles and history of which were familiarly known to the framers of the Constitution. . . .

II. The fundamental principle of the common law with regard to English nationality was birth within the allegiance, also called "legality," "obedience," "faith" or "power," of the King. The principle embraced all persons born within the King's allegiance and subject to his protection. Such allegiance and protection were mutual . . . and were not restricted to natural-born subjects and naturalized subjects, or to those who had taken an oath of allegiance; but were predicable of aliens in amity, so long as they were within the kingdom. Children, born in England, of such aliens, were therefore natural-born subjects. But the children, born within the realm, of foreign ambassadors, or the children of alien enemies, born during and within their hostile occupation of part of the King's dominions, were not natural-born subjects, because not born within the allegiance, the obedience, or the power, or, as would be said at this day, within the jurisdiction of the King. . . .

This fundamental principle, with these qualifications or explanations of it, was clearly, though quaintly, stated in the leading case, known as *Calvin's Case,* or the *Case of the Postnati,* decided in 1608. . . .[16]

III. The same rule was in force in all the English Colonies upon this continent . . . and in the United States [after the Declaration of Independence]. . . .

In the early case of *The Charming Betsy,* (1804) it appears to have been assumed by this court that all persons born in the United States were citizens of the United States; Chief Justice Marshall saying: "Whether a person born within the United States, or becoming a citizen according to the established laws of the country, can divest himself absolutely of that character otherwise than in such manner as may be prescribed by law, is a question which it is not necessary at present to decide." 2 Cranch, 64, 119. . . .

In *Dred Scott v. Sandford,* (1857) 19 How. 393, Mr. Justice Curtis said [in dissent]: "The first section of the second article of the Constitution uses the language, 'a natural-born citizen.' It thus assumes that citizenship may be acquired by birth. Undoubtedly, this language of the Constitution was used in reference to that principle of public law, well understood in this country at the time of the adoption of the Constitution, which referred citizenship to the place of birth." 19 How. 576. And to this extent no different opinion was expressed or intimated by any of the other judges. . . .

---

[16] **Note:** *Calvin's Case* [1608] 77 Eng. Rep. 377 (KB) was an English case that arose after King James VI of Scotland also became the king of England. The Court of the King's Bench declared that a child subsequently born in Scotland was—by virtue of his birth in the dominion of the king of England—an English subject with the same legal rights as other English subjects. *Calvin's Case* noted two exceptions to this rule of birthplace citizenship—children of ambassadors and children of enemy invaders—that Gray references throughout this opinion. As Gray also notes, English courts later extended this rule to children born in England's North American colonies.

The Supreme Judicial Court of Massachusetts [in 1805], . . . [t]he Supreme Court of North Carolina [in 1838], . . . [and] the Court of Chancery of New York [in 1844 all reached the same conclusion].

The same doctrine was repeatedly affirmed in the executive departments, as, for instance, by Mr. Marcy, Secretary of State, in 1854; by Attorney General Black in 1859; and by Attorney General Bates in 1862. . . .

IV. It was contended by one of the learned counsel for the United States that the rule of the Roman law, by which the citizenship of the child followed that of the parent, was the true rule of international law, as now recognized in most civilized countries, and had superseded the rule of the common law, depending on birth within the realm, originally founded on feudal considerations.

But at the time of the adoption of the Constitution of the United States in 1789, and long before, it would seem to have been the rule in Europe generally, as it certainly was in France, that, as said by Pothier, "citizens, true and native-born citizens, are those who are born within the extent of the dominion of France," and "mere birth within the realm gives the rights of a native-born citizen, independently of the origin of the father or mother, and of their domicil." . . . Pothier Traité des Personnes, pt. 1, tit. 2, sect. 1, nos. 43, 45. . . . The Code Napoleon of 1807 changed the law of France, and adopted, instead of the rule of country of birth, *jus soli,* the rule of descent or blood, *jus sanguinis,* as the leading principle; but an eminent commentator has observed that the framers of that code "appear not to have wholly freed themselves from the ancient rule of France, or rather, indeed, ancient rule of Europe . . . according to which nationality had always been, in former times, determined by the place of birth." 1 Demolombe Cours de Code Napoleon, (4th ed.) no. 146.[17]

The later modifications of the rule in Europe rest upon the constitutions, laws or ordinances of the various countries, and have no important bearing upon the interpretation and effect of the Constitution of the United States. . . .

There is, therefore, little ground for the theory that, at the time of the adoption of the Fourteenth Amendment of the Constitution of the United States, there was any settled and definite rule of international law, generally recognized by civilized nations, inconsistent with the ancient rule of citizenship by birth within the dominion.

Nor can it be doubted that it is the inherent right of every independent nation to determine for itself, and according to its own constitution and laws, what classes of persons shall be entitled to its citizenship. . . .

V. In the fore front, both of the Fourteenth Amendment of the Constitution, and of the Civil Rights Act of 1866, the fundamental principle of citizenship by birth within the dominion was reaffirmed in the most explicit and comprehensive terms.

The Civil Rights Act, passed at the first session of the Thirty-ninth Congress, began by enacting that "all persons born in the United States, and not subject to any foreign power, excluding Indians not taxed, are hereby declared to be citizens of the United States. . . ." Act of April 9, 1866, c. 31, § 1; 14 Stat. 27.

The same Congress, shortly afterwards, evidently thinking it unwise, and perhaps unsafe, to leave so important a declaration of rights to depend upon an ordinary act of legislation, which might be repealed by any subsequent Congress,

---

[17] **Question:** One of the solicitor general's strongest arguments was that few countries outside the British Empire recognized birthright citizenship by place of birth, or *jus soli*. Most recognized birthright citizenship by the nationality of the parents, or *jus sanguinis*. This distinction remains true today. Do you agree with the solicitor general that modern international practice can help a court understand the meaning of the U.S. Constitution?

framed the Fourteenth Amendment of the Constitution . . . with the words, "All persons born or naturalized in the United States, and subject to the jurisdiction thereof, are citizens of the United States and of the State wherein they reside." As appears upon the face of the amendment, as well as from the history of the times, this was not intended to impose any new restrictions upon citizenship. . . . It is declaratory in form, and enabling and extending in effect. Its main purpose doubtless was, as has been often recognized by this court, to establish the citizenship of free negroes, which had been denied in the opinion delivered by Chief Justice Taney in *Dred Scott v. Sandford,* (1857) 19 How. 393; and to put it beyond doubt that all blacks, as well as whites, born or naturalized within the jurisdiction of the United States, are citizens of the United States. . . .

The only adjudication that has been made by this court upon the meaning of the clause, "and subject to the jurisdiction thereof," in the leading provision of the Fourteenth Amendment, is *Elk v. Wilkins,* 112 U.S. 94, in which it was decided that an Indian born a member of one of the Indian tribes within the United States, which still existed and was recognized as an Indian tribe by the United States, who had voluntarily separated himself from his tribe, and taken up his residence among the white citizens of a State, but who did not appear to have been naturalized, or taxed, or in any way recognized or treated as a citizen, either by the United States or by the State, was not a citizen of the United States, as a person born in the United States, "and subject to the jurisdiction thereof," within the meaning of the clause in question.

That decision was placed upon the grounds, that the meaning of those words was, "not merely subject in some respect or degree to the jurisdiction of the United States, but completely subject to their political jurisdiction, and owing them direct and immediate allegiance"; . . . that the Indian tribes, being within the territorial limits of the United States, were not, strictly speaking, foreign States, but were alien nations, distinct political communities, the members of which owed immediate allegiance to their several tribes. . . .

The decision in *Elk v. Wilkins* concerned only members of the Indian tribes within the United States, and had no tendency to deny citizenship to children born in the United States of foreign parents of Caucasian, African or Mongolian descent, not in the diplomatic service of a foreign country.

The real object of the Fourteenth Amendment of the Constitution, in qualifying the words, "All persons born in the United States," by the addition, "and subject to the jurisdiction thereof," would appear to have been to exclude, by the fewest and fittest words, (besides children of members of the Indian tribes, standing in a peculiar relation to the National Government, unknown to the common law,) the two classes of cases—children born of alien enemies in hostile occupation, and children of diplomatic representatives of a foreign State—both of which, as has already been shown, by the law of England, and by our own law, from the time of the first settlement of the English colonies in America, had been recognized exceptions to the fundamental rule of citizenship by birth within the country. *Calvin's Case,* 7 Rep. 1, 18*b*. . . .[18]

From the first organization of the National Government under the Constitution, the naturalization acts of the United States, in providing for the admission of aliens to citizenship by judicial proceedings, uniformly required every applicant to have

---

18 **Questions:** Gray interprets the phrase *subject to the jurisdiction thereof* to exclude (1) Native Americans, (2) children of invading enemies, and (3) children of diplomats. Is this list as arbitrary as it appears, or does some common principle tie the categories together?

Today, conservative commentators have occasionally argued that this list should include a fourth category: (4) children of immigrants who live in the United States without federal authorization. Does anything in this opinion recognize or reject such a category?

resided for a certain time "within the limits and under the jurisdiction of the United States;" and thus applied the words "under the jurisdiction of the United States" to aliens residing here before they had taken an oath to support the Constitution of the United States, or had renounced allegiance to a foreign government. Acts of March 26, 1790, c. 3. And, from 1795, the provisions of those acts, which granted citizenship to foreign-born children of American parents, described such children as "born out of the limits and jurisdiction of the United States." Acts of January 29, 1795, c. 20, § 3. Thus Congress, when dealing with the question of citizenship in that aspect, treated aliens residing in this country as "under the jurisdiction of the United States," and American parents residing abroad as "out of the jurisdiction of the United States." . . .

These considerations confirm the view, already expressed in this opinion, that the opening sentence of the Fourteenth Amendment is throughout affirmative and declaratory, intended to allay doubts and to settle controversies which had arisen, and not to impose any new restrictions upon citizenship.

By the Civil Rights Act of 1866, "all persons born in the United States, and not subject to any foreign power, excluding Indians not taxed," were declared to be citizens of the United States. In the light of the law as previously established, and of the history of the times, it can hardly be doubted that the words of that act, "not subject to any foreign power," were not intended to exclude any children born in this country from the citizenship which would theretofore have been their birthright; or, for instance, for the first time in our history, to deny the right of citizenship to native-born children of foreign white parents not in the diplomatic service of their own country, nor in hostile occupation of part of our territory. But any possible doubt in this regard was removed when the negative words of the Civil Rights Act, "not subject to any foreign power," gave way, in the Fourteenth Amendment of the Constitution, to the affirmative words, "subject to the jurisdiction of the United States." . . .

The foregoing considerations and authorities irresistibly lead us to these conclusions: The Fourteenth Amendment affirms the ancient and fundamental rule of citizenship by birth within the territory, in the allegiance and under the protection of the country, including all children here born of resident aliens, with the exceptions or qualifications (as old as the rule itself) of children of foreign sovereigns or their ministers, or born on foreign public ships, or of enemies within and during a hostile occupation of part of our territory, and with the single additional exception of children of members of the Indian tribes owing direct allegiance to their several tribes. The Amendment, in clear words and in manifest intent, includes the children born, within the territory of the United States, of all other persons, of whatever race or color, domiciled within the United States. Every citizen or subject of another country, while domiciled here, is within the allegiance and the protection, and consequently subject to the jurisdiction, of the United States. His allegiance to the United States is direct and immediate, and, although but local and temporary, continuing only so long as he remains within our territory, is yet, in the words of Lord Coke, in *Calvin's Case*, 7 Rep. 6*a*, "strong enough to make a natural subject, for if he hath issue here, that issue is a natural-born subject." . . .

To hold that the Fourteenth Amendment of the Constitution excludes from citizenship the children, born in the United States, of citizens or subjects of other countries, would be to deny citizenship to thousands of persons of English, Scotch, Irish, German or other European parentage, who have always been considered and treated as citizens of the United States.[19]

---

[19] **Question:** *Wong Kim Ark* might seem like a surprising opinion in an era of virulent anti-Chinese sentiment. Does this paragraph explain what may have motivated it?

VI. [T]he acts of Congress, known as the Chinese Exclusion Acts, the earliest of which was passed some fourteen years after the adoption of the Constitutional Amendment, cannot control its meaning, or impair its effect, but must be construed and executed in subordination to its provisions. And the right of the United States, as exercised by and under those acts, to exclude or to expel from the country persons of the Chinese race, born in China, and continuing to be subjects of the Emperor of China, though having acquired a commercial domicil in the United States, has been upheld by this court, for reasons applicable to all aliens alike, and inapplicable to citizens, of whatever race or color. . . .[20]

The Fourteenth Amendment of the Constitution, in the declaration that "all persons born or naturalized in the United States, and subject to the jurisdiction thereof, are citizens of the United States and of the State wherein they reside," contemplates two sources of citizenship, and two only: birth and naturalization. Citizenship by naturalization can only be acquired by naturalization under the authority and in the forms of law. But citizenship by birth is established by the mere fact of birth under the circumstances defined in the Constitution. . . .

The power of naturalization, vested in Congress by the Constitution, is a power to confer citizenship, not a power to take it away. . . . The Fourteenth Amendment, while it leaves the power, where it was before, in Congress, to regulate naturalization, has conferred no authority upon Congress to restrict the effect of birth, declared by the Constitution to constitute a sufficient and complete right to citizenship. . . .

NOTE: PEOPLE BORN IN UNINCORPORATED TERRITORIES

As you may recall from the section on the *Insular Cases* (section 18.4), a few years after *Wong Kim Ark*, the Supreme Court declared that Puerto Rico and other "unincorporated" territories were territories "appurtenant and belonging to the United States, but not a part of the United States." *Downes v. Bidwell*, 182 U.S. 244, 287 (1901). The Court explained that a contrary rule would mean that anyone born in Puerto Rico—whether "civilized" or "savage"—would become a U.S. citizen. Since then, the federal government has operated as if the Citizenship Clause were inapplicable to unincorporated territories.

Although Congress has since passed statutes awarding citizenship to most people born in unincorporated territories, it has never done so for people born in the territory of American Samoa. People born there are instead considered "nationals, but not citizens, of the United States." 8 U.S.C. § 1408.

In 2015, a group of people born in American Samoa who fought in the U.S. military and lived on the U.S. mainland challenged their lack of U.S. citizenship in federal court. They were opposed, surprisingly, by the government of American Samoa, which worried that the application of the Fourteenth Amendment to the territory would endanger its customary laws that empowered chiefs to distribute land. In *Tuaua v. United States*, 788 F.3d 300 (D.C. Cir. 2015), the U.S. Court of Appeals for the D.C. Circuit declined to award them citizenship under the Fourteenth Amendment, holding that it would be improper for federal courts—as opposed to Congress—to decide

[20] **Questions:** Gray here notes that the logic of the *Chinese Exclusion Case* is not applicable to a law that excluded "citizens, of whatever race or color." Why not? Why, in other words, might Congress lack power over citizens that it possesses over noncitizens?

such a politically fraught question. *See also Fitisemanu v. United States*, 1 F.4th 862, 864 (10th Cir. 2021) (similar).

For more on Congress's power to naturalize or expatriate U.S. citizens in light of the Citizenship Clause, see the discussion of Congress's naturalization power (section 10.2).

CHAPTER 40

What Limitations Do the Due Process Clauses of the Fifth and Fourteenth Amendments Impose on the Procedure by Which a Person's Life, Liberty, or Property May Be Deprived?

FIFTH AMENDMENT (1791): No person shall be . . . deprived of life, liberty, or property, without due process of law. . . .

FOURTEENTH AMENDMENT (1868), SECTION 1: [N]o State shall . . . deprive any person of life, liberty, or property, without due process of law. . . .

The Overlap of the Due Process Clauses

Following the Privileges or Immunities Clause, the Fourteenth Amendment continues with the Due Process Clause: "[N]or shall any State deprive any person of life, liberty, or property without due process of law." As the Supreme Court dismissively observed in the *Slaughter-House Cases*, 83 U.S. (16 Wall.) 36 (1873), this language is nearly identical to the Due Process Clause of the Fifth Amendment, which says more broadly that "No person shall be . . . deprived of life, liberty, or property, without due process of law." In fact, although one clause deals with due process in terms of the state government and one clause deals with due process in terms of the federal government, both cover the same ground about due process—and the term *Due Process Clause* is typically used in a broad sense in discussions about due process. Thus, in the following sections (sections 40.1–40.5), the term *Due Process Clause* refers generally to either the Due Process Clause of the Fourteenth Amendment or the Due Process Clause of the Fifth Amendment or both, unless specified otherwise.

40.1 THE MEANING OF *DUE PROCESS OF LAW*

Read literally, the Due Process Clause requires a government to provide "due process of law" before it takes away a person's life, liberty, or property.

This phrase has its origin in the Magna Carta, a charter signed in 1215 by King John of England. King John was the leader of a fractious kingdom in which a group of rebellious barons offered to lay down their arms if the king signed a "great charter," or agreement, in which the king promised to respect legal limits on his otherwise absolute power. *See* Robert Tombs, *The English and Their History* 73–80 (2015). One of those limits was that

> [n]o free man shall be seized or imprisoned, or stripped of his rights or possessions, or outlawed or exiled, or deprived of his standing in any way, nor will we proceed with force against him, or send others to do so, except by the lawful judgment of his equals or by the law of the land.

Magna Carta ¶ 39 (British Library trans. 2014). As Justice Joseph Bradley wrote in his dissent in the *Slaughter-House Cases*, the phrase *by the lawful judgment of his equals or by the law of the land* has evolved into the modern phrase *due process of law*. 83 U.S. (16 Wall.) 36, 114–15 (1872).

As its origins suggest, the Due Process Clause was traditionally understood as a prohibition against depriving someone of something important without a trial ("lawful judgment of his equals") or an established and generally applicable law ("law of the land"). Both of these procedural requirements help ensure that deprivations are not mistaken or unfair. For example, if a law declares that anyone who commits robbery must be punished, a trial helps to ensure that the government doesn't mistakenly punish an innocent person. Relatedly, if a government wants to punish people who speed down the highway, a requirement that the speed limit be publicly posted as the "law of the land" ensures that drivers have fair notice of how to avoid losing their liberty or property.

In this respect, the Due Process Clause provides the basis for many of the most foundational elements of contemporary legal practice, including notice, the opportunity to be heard, the opportunity to confront and cross-examine witnesses, access to discovery, the availability of counsel, and a decision by an impartial tribunal.

That said, not every deprivation of life, liberty, or property requires *all* of these procedural protections. For example, imagine that a government wanted to fine a person for illegally parking in a loading zone. Such a fine might never be worth it if the Due Process Clause prohibited the government from forcing the parker to pay a fine without first holding a full-scale jury trial with counsel, witnesses, and discovery to prove that the parker was, in fact, in a loading zone.

The Supreme Court first confronted a similar situation in *Murray's Lessee v. Hoboken Land & Improvement Co.*, 59 U.S. (18 How.) 272 (1856), in which a statute authorized the federal government to seize delinquent taxpayers' property. A taxpayer objected to this statute, arguing that the Due Process Clause of the Fifth Amendment required the federal government to hold a jury trial before it could seize anyone's property. But the Supreme Court considered the history of how English and American state governments traditionally enforced their revenue laws. It found that most places considered it fair for an executive officer to determine whether a taxpayer was delinquent and to give the taxpayer an opportunity to challenge the executive officer's findings *after* the seizure. The Court concluded that such a course was "due process of law" and that a predeprivation trial wasn't required. *Murray's Lessee*, 59 U.S. (18 How.) at 280, 284–86.

Given the flexible nature of the Due Process Clause, litigants only rarely invoked the clause to challenge federal procedures. But after the ratification of the Fourteenth Amendment, the Court found it "remarkable" that "the docket of this court is crowded with cases in which we are asked to hold that State courts and State legislatures have deprived their own citizens of life, liberty, or property without due process of law." *Davidson v. New Orleans*, 96 U.S. 97, 103–04 (1878). The Court considered these challenges "[a] strange misconception of the scope of the provision." *Id.* at 104. It reiterated that the Due Process Clause could be satisfied by whatever procedures were "appropriate to the case, and just to the parties to be affected." *Hagar v. Reclamation Dist. No. 108*, 111 U.S. 701, 708 (1884). And it stressed that what process is "due" in a case might depend in part on "settled usage both in England and in this country"—although such usage could be updated by "the progressive development of legal ideas and institutions." *Hurtado v. California*, 110 U.S. 516, 528–29 (1884).

Procedural due process cases typically follow a basic formula. The challenge is not against the *substantive* rule (e.g., "anyone who does X shall be deprived of their life, liberty, or property"). Rather, the challenge is against the *procedure* by which the government determines whether someone fits within the substantive rule. A successful procedural due process claim typically argues that (1) the existing procedure creates an unreasonable risk of a mistaken or unfair deprivation (e.g., fining someone who has *not* done X), and (2) it would be reasonable for the government to introduce additional safeguards to decrease this risk.

The first two cases featured in this section, both out of Colorado, illustrate how such challenges work: *Londoner v. City of Denver*, 210 U.S. 373 (1908), and *Bi-Metallic Investment Co. v. State Board of Equalization*, 239 U.S. 441 (1915).

In the decades that followed *Londoner* and *Bi-Metallic*, the Supreme Court held that the Due Process Clause imposes various procedures on agencies like the Board of Immigration Appeals and the National Labor

Relations Board, which use judge-like procedures to establish whether certain immigrants are removable or whether certain employers have committed unfair labor practices. *Consol. Edison Co. v. NLRB*, 305 U.S. 197, 236 (1938). In addition to notice and an opportunity to be heard, the Court held that due process might also include things like a fair hearing before an impartial tribunal, *Wong Yang Sung v. McGrath*, 339 U.S. 33, 50 (1950); methods of assuring the underlying reliability and probative value of the evidence, *Richardson v. Perales*, 402 U.S. 389, 407–08 (1971); and sufficient notice to give each party an effective opportunity to present evidence, to know the claims of the opposing party, and to meet the opposing party, *NLRB v. Mackay Radio & Tel. Co.*, 304 U.S. 333, 350 (1938).

Despite these successive holdings, the Court did not attempt to systematically describe every safeguard that might be required by the Due Process Clause—until it heard the last two cases featured in this section, which addressed a government's deprivation of welfare benefits: *Goldberg v. Kelly*, 397 U.S. 254 (1970), and *Mathews v. Eldridge*, 424 U.S. 319 (1976).

40.1.1

Londoner v. City of Denver

210 U.S. 373 (1908)

When the City of Denver was chartered in 1893, Colorado gave it the power to make infrastructure improvements. To pay for these improvements, Colorado allowed Denver to assess any property owners who benefited from the improvements, regardless of whether they wanted them. Colorado required, however, that the assessment had to reasonably relate to the benefit—the city couldn't charge a landowner $1,000 for a sidewalk that improved the value of the landowner's home by $10. The substantive rule, therefore, was that anyone who benefits from an infrastructure improvement shall be assessed the value of that benefit.

Exercising its powers, Denver decided to pave a road. Following the procedures required by state law, the city first notified local landowners how much it planned to assess them for the improvement. The city also told the landowners that they could contest the value of their assessments if they submitted their complaints in writing. But after Wolfe Londoner and other landowners filed their written complaints, the city didn't hold a hearing or otherwise consider their objections. Instead, the city proceeded to pave the road and assess the landowners the original amount. Because Colorado law didn't permit Londoner to challenge the value of the assessment in state court, Londoner argued that the entire procedure violated the Due Process Clause of the Fourteenth Amendment.

In *Londoner v. City of Denver*, 210 U.S. 373 (1908), the Court agreed.

■ MR. JUSTICE MOODY delivered the opinion of the Court.[1]

The plaintiffs in error began this proceeding . . . to relieve lands owned by them from an assessment of a tax for the cost of paving a street upon which the lands abutted. . . .

The facts . . . may be compressed into small compass. The first step in the assessment proceedings was by the certificate of the board of public works of the cost of the improvement and a preliminary apportionment of it. The last step was the enactment of the assessment ordinance. From beginning to end of the proceedings the landowners, although allowed to formulate and file complaints and objections, were not afforded an opportunity to be heard upon them. Upon these facts was there a denial by the State of the due process of law guaranteed by the Fourteenth Amendment to the Constitution of the United States?

In the assessment, apportionment and collection of taxes upon property within their jurisdiction[,] the Constitution of the United States imposes few restrictions upon the States. In the enforcement of such restrictions as the Constitution does impose[,] this court has regarded substance and not form. But where the legislature of a State, instead of fixing the tax itself, commits to some subordinate body the duty of determining whether, in what amount, and upon whom it shall be levied, . . . due process of law requires that at some stage of the proceedings before the tax becomes irrevocably fixed, the taxpayer shall have an opportunity to be heard, of which he must have notice, either personal, by publication, or by a law fixing the time and place of the hearing. *Hager v. Reclamation District*, 111 U.S. 701. It must be remembered that the law of Colorado denies the landowner the right to object in the courts to the assessment, upon the ground that the objections are cognizable only by the board of equalization.

If it is enough that, under such circumstances, an opportunity is given to submit in writing all objections to and complaints of the tax to the board, then there was a hearing afforded in the case at bar. But we think that something more than that, even in proceedings for taxation, is required by due process of law. Many requirements essential in strictly judicial proceedings may be dispensed with in proceedings of this nature. But even here a hearing in its very essence demands that he who is entitled to it shall have the right to support his allegations by argument however brief, and, if need be, by proof, however informal. It is apparent that such a hearing was denied to the plaintiffs in error. . . .[2]

40.1.2

Bi-Metallic Investment Co. v. State Board of Equalization

239 U.S. 441 (1915)

Londoner established the basic principle that when a government takes property from a select group of people on the basis of specific fact-finding, the Due Process Clause requires the government to provide those people with notice and "an opportunity to be heard"—even if this hearing

[1] **As You Read, Consider:** Conceding the legitimacy of the substantive rule, does Justice William Moody think that Colorado's procedure creates an unreasonable risk of a mistaken or unfair deprivation? Does he think it reasonable for the state to introduce additional safeguards to decrease this risk?

[2] **Questions:** Why, precisely, was Colorado's procedure deficient here? How would the suggested safeguards reduce the risk of a mistaken or unfair deprivation?

lacks the requirements "essential in strictly judicial proceedings." 210 U.S. at 385–86. It was important to the Court that while Colorado law required Denver to tie any assessments to the value of a new improvement, Denver, representing Colorado, didn't give the assessed landowners *any* opportunity to provide argument or evidence that the assessment against them was too high. *See, e.g.*, *N. Am. Cold Storage Co. v. City of Chicago*, 211 U.S. 306 (1908) (upholding a city's order that seized contaminated food from a business because the order gave the business an opportunity to be heard *after* the seizure).

Londoner involved a situation in which a state, "instead of fixing the tax itself, commits to some subordinate body the duty of determining whether, in what amount, and upon whom it shall be levied." 210 U.S. at 385. Yet its holding could be read to suggest that whenever a city or state legislature enacts a new tax, the Due Process Clause requires that everyone in the city or state should receive notice and an opportunity to contest the tax. The Court confronted this latter situation in the following case, *Bi-Metallic Investment Co. v. State Board of Equalization*, 239 U.S. 441 (1915). There, a state board issued an order that increased the valuation of all taxable property in Denver—effectively increasing the tax rate for all of the city's landowners. The substantive rule, in other words, was, roughly, that everyone who owns property in Denver shall be deprived via the imposition of more taxes.

The Bi-Metallic Investment Company challenged this order under the Due Process Clause, arguing that it was surprised by the board's order and never received an opportunity to challenge it after it was issued.

The Court cursorily dismissed this argument.

■ MR. JUSTICE HOLMES delivered the opinion of the Court.[3]

This is a suit to enjoin the State Board of Equalization and the Colorado Tax Commission from putting in force, and the defendant Pitcher as assessor of Denver from obeying, an order of the boards increasing the valuation of all taxable property in Denver forty per cent. . . .

The question . . . is whether all individuals have a constitutional right to be heard before a matter can be decided in which all are equally concerned—here, for instance, before a superior board decides that the local taxing officers have adopted a system of undervaluation throughout a county, as notoriously often has been the case. . . .

Where a rule of conduct applies to more than a few people it is impracticable that every one should have a direct voice in its adoption. The Constitution does not require all public acts to be done in town meeting or an assembly of the whole. General statutes within the state power are passed that affect the person or property of individuals, sometimes to the point of ruin, without giving them a chance to be heard. Their rights are protected in the only way that they can be in a complex society, by their power, immediate or remote, over those who make the rule. If the result in

---

[3] **As You Read, Consider:** Conceding the legitimacy of the substantive rule, does Justice Oliver Wendell Holmes think that Colorado's procedure creates an unreasonable risk of a mistaken or unfair deprivation? Does he think it reasonable for the state to introduce additional safeguards to decrease this risk?

this case had been reached as it might have been by the State's doubling the rate of taxation, no one would suggest that the Fourteenth Amendment was violated unless every person affected had been allowed an opportunity to raise his voice against it before the body entrusted by the state constitution with the power. In considering this case in this court we must assume that the proper state machinery has been used, and the question is whether, if the state constitution had declared that Denver had been undervalued as compared with the rest of the State and had decreed that for the current year the valuation should be forty per cent higher, the objection now urged could prevail. It appears to us that to put the question is to answer it. There must be a limit to individual argument in such matters if government is to go on. In *Londoner v. Denver*, 210 U.S. 373, a local board had to determine 'whether, in what amount, and upon whom' a tax for paving a street should be levied for special benefits. A relatively small number of persons was concerned, who were exceptionally affected, in each case upon individual grounds, and it was held that they had a right to a hearing. But that decision is far from reaching a general determination dealing only with the principle upon which all the assessments in a county had been laid. . . .[4]

NOTE: DISTINCTION BETWEEN *LONDONER* AND *BI-METALLIC*

In contrast with *Londoner*, the Supreme Court in *Bi-Metallic* announced that the procedural elements of the Due Process Clause aren't required for *every* deprivation. Requiring the government to provide notice and a hearing to everyone affected by its decisions would be impossible, the Court observed—at least "if government is to go on." 239 U.S. at 445. Where a government rule is generally applicable, therefore, then the Court considers the process behind that rule fair as long as the people affected can exercise "their power, immediate or remote, over those who can make the rule." *Id.* Only where a government rule applies to a select group of people does the Due Process Clause require certain safeguards.

Another way of looking at the distinction between *Londoner* and *Bi-Metallic* is to consider the Due Process Clause's purpose of preventing a mistaken or unfair deprivation. In *Londoner*, there was a possibility that the City of Denver's assessment was mistaken: the road may have increased the value of a neighborhood by $1,000, yet the city may have assessed the landowners $1,500. In that case, notice and an opportunity to be heard would have allowed the landowners to prove that they were being overcharged, preventing a mistaken deprivation of their property. But in *Bi-Metallic*, there was no possibility of error: the assessed value of everyone's house was being increased by 40 percent, period. There would have been little benefit to allowing individual taxpayers to contest this increase because the rule didn't depend on certain facts being true.

This distinction between *Londoner*'s judge-like factual determination and *Bi-Metallic*'s generally applicable rule has become central to modern administrative law. Where legislatures, administrative agencies, or government officials issue prospective and generally applicable rules that

[4] **Questions:** Is Holmes's objection to the claim here simply that the substantive rule applies to many people? Or does something else distinguish the substantive rule in *Bi-Metallic Investment Co. v. State Board of Equalization* from the substantive rule in *Londoner v. City of Denver*? To answer these questions, consider a third: Conceding the legitimacy of the substantive rule—everyone who owns property in Denver shall pay 40 percent more in taxes—how, precisely, might a mistaken or unfair deprivation occur or be prevented in this setting?

depend on *legislative facts*—i.e., general knowledge of the world—then the Due Process Clause doesn't require that all people affected by those rules have notice and an opportunity to be heard. *R.R. Comm'n v. Rowan & Nichols Oil Co.*, 311 U.S. 570, 576–77 (1941). But where government officials issue retroactive and party-specific orders that depend on *adjudicative facts*—i.e., disputed facts that may be true or false—then the Due Process Clause requires that whatever procedures are used must be appropriate, just, and consistent with settled usage. *United States v. Fla. E. Coast Ry.*, 410 U.S. 224, 246 (1973).

40.1.3

Goldberg v. Kelly

397 U.S. 254 (1970)

The Due Process Clause doesn't require "due process of law" *every* time a government deprives a person of something. Rather, it applies only where a government deprives a person of "life, liberty, or property." With this in mind, courts after *Londoner* and *Bi-Metallic* typically held that a plaintiff could invoke the clause only after showing that the government was planning to execute the person (life), was confining the person (liberty), or was taking away the person's "vested property interest" in something (property). *Vested property interest* was defined as a legally protected property right—as opposed to a government benefit, or *privilege*, that the government could award or take away on a whim.

The author of *Bi-Metallic*, Holmes, famously described the distinction between a property right and a privilege in a case involving a New Bedford, Massachusetts, police officer. The officer, John McAuliffe, was fired after violating a rule that prohibited government officers from soliciting money for political purposes. McAuliffe complained that the firing deprived him of his free speech rights and his job without providing him with an opportunity to contest his firing. But the Massachusetts Supreme Judicial Court held that no constitutional protections were warranted because a government job was not a property interest—it was something that the City of New Bedford had complete discretion to withhold for whatever reason it chose. Writing for the court in *McAuliffe v. Mayor of New Bedford*, Holmes quipped, "The petitioner may have a constitutional right to talk politics, but he has no constitutional right to be a policeman." 29 N.E.2d 517, 522 (Mass. 1892).

For decades afterward, the Supreme Court agreed that if a government is under no obligation to provide a person with something, then it could choose to provide that thing subject to whatever conditions or procedures it found appropriate. *Barsky v. Bd. of Regents*, 347 U.S. 442, 451–52 (1954). Taken to the extreme, however, this rights-versus-privilege distinction would have allowed a government to award certain discretionary benefits only to people who were Christian, white, or Democrats. Opposed to this conclusion, in *Slochower v. Board of Higher Education*, 350 U.S. 551 (1956), and *Speiser v. Randall*, 357 U.S. 513

(1958), the Court began a two-decade retreat from the rights-versus-privilege distinction—now holding that even when a government may deny a person a benefit for any number of reasons, it may not do so on a basis that infringes a constitutionally protected interest.

The rights-versus-privilege distinction met its final end in the following case, *Goldberg v. Kelly*, 397 U.S. 254 (1970). New York, like many states, provided eligible residents with assistance payments from federal welfare programs, including Aid to Families with Dependent Children. When the state determined that a person was no longer eligible for a program—for example, if state officials determined that a once-eligible family no longer had dependent children—it terminated the payments immediately. Families who were denied payments could contest this termination only by appealing the denial after the fact and without the payments that they had once used for food and housing. Contesting this procedure under the Due Process Clause of the Fourteenth Amendment, several families sued the state commissioner of social services, Jack Goldberg.

■ MR. JUSTICE BRENNAN delivered the opinion of the Court.[5]

The question for decision is whether a State that terminates public assistance payments to a particular recipient without affording him the opportunity for an evidentiary hearing prior to termination denies the recipient procedural due process in violation of the Due Process Clause of the Fourteenth Amendment. . . .

[I]

The constitutional issue to be decided . . . is the narrow one whether the Due Process Clause requires that the recipient be afforded an evidentiary hearing *before* the termination of benefits. The District Court held that only a pre-termination evidentiary hearing would satisfy the constitutional command, and rejected the argument of the state and city officials that the combination of the post-termination "fair hearing" with the informal pre-termination review disposed of all due process claims. The court said: "While post-termination review is relevant, there is one overpowering fact which controls here. By hypothesis, a welfare recipient is destitute, without funds or assets. . . . Suffice it to say that to cut off a welfare recipient in the face of . . . 'brutal need' without a prior hearing of some sort is unconscionable, unless overwhelming considerations justify it." The court rejected the argument that the need to protect the public's tax revenues supplied the requisite "overwhelming consideration." . . .

Appellant does not contend that procedural due process is not applicable to the termination of welfare benefits. Such benefits are a matter of statutory entitlement for persons qualified to receive them. Their termination involves state action that adjudicates important rights. The constitutional challenge cannot be answered by an argument that public assistance benefits are a "privilege" and not a "right." Relevant constitutional restraints apply as much to the withdrawal of public assistance benefits as to disqualification for unemployment compensation, *Sherbert v. Verner*, 374 U. S. 398 (1963); or to denial of a tax exemption, *Speiser v. Randall*, 357 U. S. 513 (1958); or to discharge from public employment, *Slochower v. Board of Higher*

---

5 **As You Read, Consider:** Conceding the legitimacy of the substantive rule, does Justice William Brennan think that New York's procedure creates an unreasonable risk of a mistaken or unfair deprivation? Does he think it reasonable for the state to introduce additional safeguards to decrease this risk?

Education, 350 U. S. 551 (1956). The extent to which procedural due process must be afforded the recipient is influenced by the extent to which he may be condemned to suffer grievous loss, and depends upon whether the recipient's interest in avoiding that loss outweighs the governmental interest in summary adjudication. . . .

It is true, of course, that some governmental benefits may be administratively terminated without affording the recipient a pre-termination evidentiary hearing. But we agree with the District Court that when welfare is discontinued, only a pre-termination evidentiary hearing provides the recipient with procedural due process. For qualified recipients, welfare provides the means to obtain essential food, clothing, housing, and medical care. Thus the crucial factor in this context . . . is that termination of aid pending resolution of a controversy over eligibility may deprive an *eligible* recipient of the very means by which to live while he waits. . . .[6]

Moreover, important governmental interests are promoted by affording recipients a pre-termination evidentiary hearing. From its founding the Nation's basic commitment has been to foster the dignity and well-being of all persons within its borders. We have come to recognize that forces not within the control of the poor contribute to their poverty. . . . Welfare, by meeting the basic demands of subsistence, can help bring within the reach of the poor the same opportunities that are available to others to participate meaningfully in the life of the community. . . . The same governmental interests that counsel the provision of welfare, counsel as well its uninterrupted provision to those eligible to receive it; pre-termination evidentiary hearings are indispensable to that end.

Appellant does not challenge the force of these considerations but argues that they are outweighed by countervailing governmental interests in conserving fiscal and administrative resources. These interests, the argument goes, justify the delay of any evidentiary hearing until after discontinuance of the grants. . . . Since most terminations are accepted without challenge, summary adjudication . . . conserves both the fisc and administrative time and energy by reducing the number of evidentiary hearings actually held. . . .

[But] these governmental interests are not overriding in the welfare context. The requirement of a prior hearing doubtless involves some greater expense, and the benefits paid to ineligible recipients pending decision at the hearing probably cannot be recouped, since these recipients are likely to be judgment-proof. But . . . [m]uch of the drain on fiscal and administrative resources can be reduced by developing procedures for prompt pre-termination hearings and by skillful use of personnel and facilities. . . .

Thus, the interest of the eligible recipient in uninterrupted receipt of public assistance, coupled with the State's interest that his payments not be erroneously terminated, clearly outweighs the State's competing concern to prevent any increase in its fiscal and administrative burdens. As the District Court correctly concluded, "[t]he stakes are simply too high for the welfare recipient, and the possibility for honest error or irritable misjudgment too great, to allow termination of aid without

---

6 **Question:** Here, Brennan is observing that the consequences of a mistaken deprivation in this context are extremely severe, and the risk of a mistake could be reduced by a predeprivation evidentiary hearing. But the officials who ran New York's welfare programs presumably were aware of the trade-offs involved in holding a hearing before a deprivation rather than after. Suppose that New York officials concluded that predeprivation hearings were more expensive than postdeprivation hearings (because with predeprivation hearings, the state would have to continue providing welfare benefits while the hearing was pending). Suppose also that the officials decided that if they used postdeprivation hearings, they could use the money they saved to provide welfare benefits to a greater number of people. Does Brennan explain why the federal judiciary might be in a better position than state officials to evaluate this trade-off?

giving the recipient a chance, if he so desires, to be fully informed of the case against him so that he may contest its basis and produce evidence in rebuttal."

II

We also agree with the District Court, however, that the pre-termination hearing need not take the form of a judicial or quasi-judicial trial. . . . We recognize, too, that both welfare authorities and recipients have an interest in relatively speedy resolution of questions of eligibility, that they are used to dealing with one another informally, and that some welfare departments have very burdensome caseloads. These considerations justify the limitation of the pre-termination hearing to minimum procedural safeguards, adapted to the particular characteristics of welfare recipients, and to the limited nature of the controversies to be resolved. . . .[7]

"The fundamental requisite of due process of law is the opportunity to be heard." *Grannis v. Ordean*, 234 U. S. 385, 394 (1914). The hearing must be "at a meaningful time and in a meaningful manner." *Armstrong v. Manzo*, 380 U.S. 552 (1965). In the present context these principles require that a recipient have timely and adequate notice detailing the reasons for a proposed termination, and an effective opportunity to defend by confronting any adverse witnesses and by presenting his own arguments and evidence orally. These rights are important in cases such as those before us, where recipients have challenged proposed terminations as resting on incorrect or misleading factual premises or on misapplication of rules or policies to the facts of particular cases. . . .

The opportunity to be heard must be tailored to the capacities and circumstances of those who are to be heard. It is not enough that a welfare recipient may present his position to the decision maker in writing or secondhand through his caseworker. Written submissions are an unrealistic option for most recipients, who lack the educational attainment necessary to write effectively and who cannot obtain professional assistance. . . . Therefore a recipient must be allowed to state his position orally. . . .

In almost every setting where important decisions turn on questions of fact, due process requires an opportunity to confront and cross-examine adverse witnesses. *E.g., ICC v. Louisville & N. R. Co.*, 227 U. S. 88, 93–94 (1913). . . .

"The right to be heard would be, in many cases, of little avail if it did not comprehend the right to be heard by counsel." *Powell v. Alabama*, 287 U. S. 45, 68–69 (1932). We do not say that counsel must be provided at the pre-termination hearing, but only that the recipient must be allowed to retain an attorney if he so desires. Counsel can help delineate the issues, present the factual contentions in an orderly manner, conduct cross-examination, and generally safeguard the interests of the recipient. . . .

Finally, the decisionmaker's conclusion as to a recipient's eligibility must rest solely on the legal rules and evidence adduced at the hearing. *Ohio Bell Tel. Co. v. PUC*, 301 U. S. 292 (1937). To demonstrate compliance with this elementary requirement, the decision maker should state the reasons for his determination and indicate the evidence he relied on, though his statement need not amount to a full opinion or even formal findings of fact and conclusions of law. And, of course, an

7 **Question:** Brennan concludes in Part I that the Due Process Clause required New York to provide a predeprivation hearing. He now explains that such a hearing can employ "minimum procedural safeguards," which include (1) notice, (2) an opportunity to be heard, (3) an impartial decision maker, (4) confrontation of witnesses, (5) access to discovery, (6) access to counsel, and (7) a decision on the record. Do you agree that no fair deprivation can lack any of these elements? The note after this case discusses the seven elements in greater detail.

impartial decision maker is essential. Cf. *Wong Yang Sung v. McGrath*, 339 U. S. 33, 45–46 (1950). . . .

NOTE: ELEMENTS OF DUE PROCESS IN *GOLDBERG*

As *Goldberg* emphasized, the purpose of the Due Process Clause is to "protect persons not from the deprivation, but from the *mistaken* or *unjustified* deprivation of life, liberty, or property." *Carey v. Piphus*, 435 U.S. 247, 259 (1978) (emphasis added). In *Goldberg*, that meant that New York had to provide sufficient safeguards to protect *eligible* beneficiaries from mistakenly losing their assistance payments. The Court in *Goldberg* also defined the "minimum procedural safeguards" of due process to include seven elements, all of which must be satisfied before a government can deprive a person of that person's life, liberty, or property. 397 U.S. at 267.

First, the government must provide *notice* sufficient to enable a person to determine what deprivation is being proposed and what the person must do to prevent the deprivation. *See, e.g.*, *FCC v. Fox Television Stations, Inc.*, 567 U.S. 239, 253 (2012) (discussing fair notice in the context of laws and regulations); *Jones v. Flowers*, 547 U.S. 220, 226 (2006) (discussing fair notice in the context of service of process).

Second, the government must provide an *opportunity to be heard* sufficient to enable the person to prevent a mistaken or unjustified deprivation. *See, e.g.*, *Fuentes v. Shevin*, 407 U.S. 67, 80–81 (1972) (discussing the hearing requirement in the context of a pretrial seizure).

Third, the government must provide an *impartial tribunal* to guarantee that the deprivation will not be taken on the basis of an erroneous or distorted conception of the facts or law. *See, e.g.*, *Williams v. Pennsylvania*, 579 U.S. 1, 16 (2016) (discussing how a judge didn't appear sufficiently impartial when he participated in the same case as a district attorney); *Caperton v. A.T. Massey Coal Co.*, 556 U.S. 868, 873 (2009) (same when the judge accepted substantial donations from one of the parties).

Fourth, the government must provide the ability to *confront and cross-examine witnesses* to show that an individual's testimony is untrue, faulty, or biased. *See, e.g.*, *Greene v. McElroy*, 360 U.S. 474, 496–97 (1959) (discussing the importance of cross-examination after a suspected Communist was summarily denied a security clearance).

Fifth, the government must allow the person to *discover or see the adverse evidence* so that the person "has an opportunity to show that it is untrue." *Id.* at 496.

Sixth, the government must provide a *decision on the record* to ensure that the decision maker's conclusion rested solely on the legal rules and evidence adduced at the hearing. *See, e.g.*, *Dep't of Com. v. New York*, 139 S. Ct. 2551, 2574 (2019) (discussing a government decision that appeared pretextual in light of the record before the official).

Seventh, the government must allow the person to be *represented by counsel*. However, the government doesn't have to pay for counsel unless there aren't adequate alternative safeguards to preserve a person's "physical liberty." *See Turner v. Rogers*, 564 U.S. 431, 442, 448 (2011).

40.1.4

Mathews v. Eldridge

424 U.S. 319 (1976)

Goldberg's seven requirements are simply the *minimum* procedural safeguards required by the Due Process Clause. In some contexts, such as a criminal punishment, far more might be required, including appointed counsel, an impartial jury, and the right of appeal. To determine when more than the minimum is required, the *Goldberg* Court suggested that a court must weigh (1) "the extent to which [a person] may be condemned to suffer grievous loss," (2) "the recipient's interest in avoiding that loss," and (3) "the governmental interest in summary adjudication." 397 U.S. at 263. This three-factor test was both formalized and modified in *Mathews v. Eldridge*, 424 U.S. 319 (1976), a case that evaluated a Due Process Clause claim in the context of the Fifth Amendment.

Like the families in *Goldberg*, George Eldridge received assistance payments from the government. In his case, he received disability payments from the federal Social Security Administration due to his chronic anxiety and back pain. But in 1972, federal officials evaluated his annual doctor reports and concluded that Eldridge was no longer disabled. The administration sent Eldridge a letter informing him that his disability payments would cease unless he requested time to send additional information. The letter also told Eldridge that he would have an opportunity to contest the denial of benefits by filing a petition for reconsideration—a process that would take about one year.

Eldridge instead sued the Social Security Administration, arguing that it was constitutionally obligated to provide him with an in-person hearing before it could withhold welfare benefits. *Goldberg* had basically held as much—but *Goldberg* had been decided in 1970.

By the time Eldridge's case reached the Supreme Court in 1976, two members of the *Goldberg* majority had been replaced by appointees of President Richard Nixon. One of the new justices, Lewis Powell, offered a new test for evaluating whether additional procedural safeguards are due before a government can deprive a person of a protected interest.

The new test gave no relief to Eldridge as the Court in *Mathews* determined that no due process violation had occurred.

■ MR. JUSTICE POWELL delivered the opinion of the Court.[8]

The issue in this case is whether the Due Process Clause of the Fifth Amendment requires that prior to the termination of Social Security disability benefit payments the recipient be afforded an opportunity for an evidentiary hearing. . . .

Procedural due process imposes constraints on governmental decisions which deprive individuals of "liberty" or "property" interests within the meaning of the Due Process Clause of the Fifth or Fourteenth Amendment. The Secretary does not contend that procedural due process is inapplicable to terminations of Social Security disability benefits. He recognizes, as has been implicit in our prior decisions, that the interest of an individual in continued receipt of these benefits is a statutorily created "property" interest protected by the Fifth Amendment. Cf. *Goldberg v. Kelly*, 397 U. S., at 261–262. Rather, the Secretary contends that the existing administrative procedures, detailed below, provide all the process that is constitutionally due before a recipient can be deprived of that interest.

This Court consistently has held that some form of hearing is required before an individual is finally deprived of a property interest. *Wolff v. McDonnell*, 418 U. S. 539, 557–558 (1974). . . . The fundamental requirement of due process is the opportunity to be heard "at a meaningful time and in a meaningful manner." *Armstrong v. Manzo*, 380 U. S. 545, 552 (1965). Eldridge agrees that the review procedures available to a claimant before the initial determination of ineligibility becomes final would be adequate if disability benefits were not terminated until after the evidentiary hearing stage of the administrative process. The dispute centers upon what process is due prior to the initial termination of benefits, pending review.

In recent years this Court increasingly has had occasion to consider the extent to which due process requires an evidentiary hearing prior to the deprivation of some type of property interest even if such a hearing is provided thereafter. In only one case, *Goldberg v. Kelly*, 397 U. S., at 266–271, has the Court held that a hearing closely approximating a judicial trial is necessary. In other cases requiring some type of pretermination hearing as a matter of constitutional right the Court has spoken sparingly about the requisite procedures. . . .

These decisions underscore the truism that " '[d]ue process,' unlike some legal rules, is not a technical conception with a fixed content unrelated to time, place and circumstances." *Cafeteria Workers v. McElroy*, 367 U. S. 886, 895 (1961). "[D]ue process is flexible and calls for such procedural protections as the particular situation demands." *Morrissey v. Brewer*, 408 U. S. 471, 481 (1972). Accordingly, resolution of the issue whether the administrative procedures provided here are constitutionally sufficient requires analysis of the governmental and private interests that are affected. More precisely, our prior decisions indicate that identification of the specific dictates of due process generally requires consideration of three distinct factors: First, the private interest that will be affected by the official action; second, the risk of an erroneous deprivation of such interest through the procedures used, and the probable value, if any, of additional or substitute procedural safeguards; and finally, the Government's interest, including the function involved and the fiscal and

[8] **As You Read, Consider:** Conceding the legitimacy of the substantive rule, does Justice Lewis Powell think that the federal government's procedure creates an unreasonable risk of a mistaken or unfair deprivation? Does he think it reasonable for the state to introduce additional safeguards to decrease this risk?

administrative burdens that the additional or substitute procedural requirement would entail. See, *e.g.*, *Goldberg v. Kelly*, *supra*, at 263–271. . . .[9]

Despite the elaborate character of the administrative procedures provided by the Secretary, the courts below held them to be constitutionally inadequate, concluding that due process requires an evidentiary hearing prior to termination. In light of the private and governmental interests at stake here and the nature of the existing procedures, we think this was error.

[Factor One: The Private Interest]

Since a recipient whose benefits are terminated is awarded full retroactive relief if he ultimately prevails, his sole interest is in the uninterrupted receipt of this source of income pending final administrative decision on his claim. His potential injury is thus similar in nature to that of the welfare recipient in *Goldberg,* see 397 U. S., at 263–264. . . . [T]he Court held that due process requires an evidentiary hearing prior to a temporary deprivation. It was emphasized there that welfare assistance is given to persons on the very margin of subsistence. . . .

Eligibility for disability benefits, in contrast, is not based upon financial need. Indeed, it is wholly unrelated to the worker's income or support from many other sources, such as earnings of other family members. . . .

As *Goldberg* illustrates, the degree of potential deprivation that may be created by a particular decision is a factor to be considered in assessing the validity of any administrative decisionmaking process. The potential deprivation here is generally likely to be less than in *Goldberg*. . . .[10] In addition to the possibility of access to private resources, other forms of government assistance will become available where the termination of disability benefits places a worker or his family below the subsistence level. In view of these potential sources of temporary income, there is less reason here than in *Goldberg* to depart from the ordinary principle, established by our decisions, that something less than an evidentiary hearing is sufficient prior to adverse administrative action.

[Factor Two: The Value of Additional Safeguards in Preventing a Mistake]

An additional factor to be considered here is the fairness and reliability of the existing pretermination procedures, and the probable value, if any, of additional procedural safeguards. Central to the evaluation of any administrative process is the nature of the relevant inquiry. In order to remain eligible for benefits the disabled worker must demonstrate by means of "medically acceptable clinical and laboratory diagnostic techniques," 42 U. S. C. § 423(d)(3), that he is unable "to engage in any substantial gainful activity by reason of any *medically determinable* physical or mental impairment. . . ." § 423(d)(1)(A) (emphasis supplied). In short, a medical assessment of the worker's physical or mental condition is required. This is a more sharply focused and easily documented decision than the typical determination of welfare entitlement. In the latter case, a wide variety of information may be deemed relevant, and issues of witness credibility and veracity often are critical to the decisionmaking process. *Goldberg* noted that in such circumstances "written submissions are a wholly unsatisfactory basis for decision." 397 U. S., at 269.

---

[9] **Questions:** Powell here announces a three-part test to evaluate procedural due process questions—a test that remains in wide use. Are his three questions different from the questions asked by Justice William Brennan in *Goldberg v. Kelly*? Does he reach a similar result?

[10] **Questions:** On what basis does Powell conclude that the "private interest" in this case is "likely to be less than in *Goldberg*"? Is he assigning a numerical value to these interests? Do you agree with his intuition, or could it be contested? The same questions could be asked of the remaining two factors as well.

By contrast, the decision whether to discontinue disability benefits will turn, in most cases, upon routine, standard, and unbiased medical reports by physician specialists, concerning a subject whom they have personally examined. . . . To be sure, credibility and veracity may be a factor in the ultimate disability assessment in some cases. But procedural due process rules are shaped by the risk of error inherent in the truthfinding process as applied to the generality of cases, not the rare exceptions. The potential value of an evidentiary hearing, or even oral presentation to the decisionmaker, is substantially less in this context than in *Goldberg*.

The decision in *Goldberg* also was based on the Court's conclusion that written submissions were an inadequate substitute for oral presentation because they did not provide an effective means for the recipient to communicate his case to the decisionmaker. Written submissions were viewed as an unrealistic option, for most recipients lacked the "educational attainment necessary to write effectively" and could not afford professional assistance. . . .

The detailed questionnaire which the state agency periodically sends the recipient identifies with particularity the information relevant to the entitlement decision, and the recipient is invited to obtain assistance from the local SSA office in completing the questionnaire. More important, the information critical to the entitlement decision usually is derived from medical sources, such as the treating physician. Such sources are likely to be able to communicate more effectively through written documents than are welfare recipients or the lay witnesses supporting their cause. The conclusions of physicians often are supported by X-rays and the results of clinical or laboratory tests, information typically more amenable to written than to oral presentation. . . .

[Factor Three: The Costs to the Government of Additional Safeguards]

In striking the appropriate due process balance the final factor to be assessed is the public interest. This includes the administrative burden and other societal costs that would be associated with requiring, as a matter of constitutional right, an evidentiary hearing upon demand in all cases prior to the termination of disability benefits. The most visible burden would be the incremental cost resulting from the increased number of hearings and the expense of providing benefits to ineligible recipients pending decision. No one can predict the extent of the increase, but the fact that full benefits would continue until after such hearings would assure the exhaustion in most cases of this attractive option. Nor would the theoretical right of the Secretary to recover undeserved benefits result, as a practical matter, in any substantial offset to the added outlay of public funds. The parties submit widely varying estimates of the probable additional financial cost. We only need say that experience with the constitutionalizing of government procedures suggests that the ultimate additional cost in terms of money and administrative burden would not be insubstantial.

Financial cost alone is not a controlling weight in determining whether due process requires a particular procedural safeguard prior to some administrative decision. But the Government's interest, and hence that of the public, in conserving scarce fiscal and administrative resources is a factor that must be weighed. At some point the benefit of an additional safeguard to the individual affected by the administrative action and to society in terms of increased assurance that the action is just, may be outweighed by the cost. Significantly, the cost of protecting those whom the preliminary administrative process has identified as likely to be found undeserving may in the end come out of the pockets of the deserving since resources available for any particular program of social welfare are not unlimited.[11]

But more is implicated in cases of this type than ad hoc weighing of fiscal and administrative burdens against the interests of a particular category of claimants. The ultimate balance involves a determination as to when, under our constitutional system, judicial-type procedures must be imposed upon administrative action to assure fairness. . . . The judicial model of an evidentiary hearing is neither a required, nor even the most effective, method of decisionmaking in all circumstances. The essence of due process is the requirement that a person in jeopardy of serious loss [be given] notice of the case against him and opportunity to meet it. All that is necessary is that the procedures be tailored, in light of the decision to be made, to "the capacities and circumstances of those who are to be heard," *Goldberg v. Kelly,* 397 U. S., at 268–269, to insure that they are given a meaningful opportunity to present their case. In assessing what process is due in this case, substantial weight must be given to the good-faith judgments of the individuals charged by Congress with the administration of social welfare programs that the procedures they have provided assure fair consideration of the entitlement claims of individuals. This is especially so where, as here, the prescribed procedures not only provide the claimant with an effective process for asserting his claim prior to any administrative action, but also assure a right to an evidentiary hearing, as well as to subsequent judicial review, before the denial of his claim becomes final.

We conclude that an evidentiary hearing is not required prior to the termination of disability benefits and that the present administrative procedures fully comport with due process. . . .

NOTE: APPLICATION OF THE *MATHEWS* TEST TO STATE AND FEDERAL DEPRIVATIONS

State deprivations. The *Mathews* due process test can appear pretty abstract, requiring governments to prevent a mistaken or unfair deprivation by weighing an individual's interest in additional procedural safeguards against the government's own interest in maintaining existing safeguards. But the test rests on a basic intuition: some deprivations are far more consequential than others and therefore require far more safeguards to avoid a mistake. A mistaken parking ticket, for example, is not as bad as a mistaken prison sentence. So, while the Due Process Clause might require the minimal procedural safeguards before a government can deprive people by assessing a $25 parking fee, the clause might require many more procedural safeguards before the government can deprive people of their liberty, including appointed counsel, a jury trial, and the right to appeal.

Yet even in the criminal context, the cost of an additional procedural safeguard might eventually outweigh its marginal benefit. One appointed lawyer might make the difference between an innocent person going to prison and getting acquitted. A second appointed lawyer might also help. But a twentieth appointed lawyer would likely not help at all. Yet if the Due

---

11 **Questions:** A government's interest in conserving scarce fiscal and administrative resources is always a factor in procedural due process cases. *Goldberg* and *Mathews v. Eldridge* simply disagree about whether this interest is outweighed by the benefit of additional procedural safeguards in each case. But does either decision offer an explanation for why courts are better able to conduct this balancing test than administrative officials? Can you think of one?

Process Clause constitutionally required every possible procedural safeguard, such as twenty appointed lawyers, the clause might make trials so expensive that states would have to avoid them or pursue other techniques, such as plea bargaining. In this light, the *Mathews* test is the Supreme Court's attempt at finding an appropriate balance.

In the decades since *Mathews*, the Court has applied its test to a variety of contexts to determine the reasonable procedural safeguards needed to avoid a mistaken deprivation. In *Ingraham v. Wright*, 430 U.S. 651 (1977), the Court considered a child who was paddled by a teacher in a state that then authorized corporal punishment. The child's family wanted additional procedural safeguards, including a hearing before any paddling. Weighing the child's interest in avoiding a mistaken "deprivation" against the school's interest in quickly disciplining children, the Court disagreed that any safeguards were constitutionally necessary. *Id.* at 683. The Court noted that a mistaken punishment was unlikely given the ability of the teacher to directly witness the student's infraction, the visibility of the confrontation to other students and faculty, and the likelihood of parental reaction to an unreasonably harsh punishment. *Id.* at 677. In this light, the Court concluded that the Due Process Clause was satisfied by the child's ability to sue the teacher after the fact in state court if the punishment turned out to be wrong or excessive. *See also, e.g., City of Los Angeles v. David*, 538 U.S. 715, 717 (2003) (due process satisfied when city charged resident $134.50 to retrieve a towed car, as the car owner could challenge the fee afterward).

By contrast, in *Cleveland Board of Education v. Loudermill*, the Court held that a government must provide a public employee with "some kind of hearing" before it can discharge the employee. 470 U.S. 532, 542 (1985). Weighing the private interest of employees in keeping their job against the government's interest in removing unsatisfactory employees, the Court considered it constitutionally necessary that the government notify employees why they are being fired, giving them an opportunity to respond before they are deprived of their livelihood. *Id.* at 543.

Other cases have similarly required more procedural safeguards than a state was otherwise willing to provide. *See Nelson v. Colorado*, 137 S. Ct. 1249, 1257–58 (2017) (finding that all three *Mathews* factors cut against a state that deprived accused criminals by assessing fines and fees unless they could prove by clear and convincing evidence that they didn't commit a crime).

Federal deprivations. In the federal context, procedural due process issues most often arise in federal administrative proceedings, particularly immigration proceedings.

As discussed earlier with regard to Congress's power to exclude noncitizens (section 10.3), the Supreme Court has held that Congress has plenary power over noncitizens at the border. *See Shaughnessy v. United States ex rel. Mezei*, 345 U.S. 206, 215–16 (1953). Accordingly, when noncitizens attempt to enter the United States, the Court has held that the government's "sovereign prerogative" to exclude unwanted immigrants is so overwhelming that the Due Process Clause requires less than even the minimal procedural safeguards of *Goldberg*. *Dep't of Homeland Sec. v. Thuraissigiam*, 140 S. Ct. 1959, 1982 (2020). Instead, the Court has declared for over a century that "[w]hatever the procedure authorized by Congress is, it is due process as far as an alien denied entry is concerned." *Id.* (quoting *United States ex rel. Knauff v. Shaughnessy*, 338 U.S. 537, 544 (1950); *Ekiu v. United States*, 142 U.S. 651, 660 (1892)). Furthermore, the Court has held that an immigration officer's decision to exclude can be confidential and without any reasoning because "[d]enying entry to such a foreign national does not burden any American party" protected by the Due Process Clause. *Trump v. Int'l Refugee Assistance Project*, 137 S. Ct. 2080, 2088 (2017).

The calculus is different, however, when someone entering the country claims to be a U.S. citizen or has a close relationship with someone in the United States. In the case of someone who claims to be a U.S. citizen, the Court has required the government to provide a fair hearing at which all relevant and probative evidence is included. *Kwock Jan Fat v. White*, 253 U.S. 454, 464–65 (1920). In the case of someone who has a close relationship with a U.S. resident, the Court has suggested that the resident can challenge the exclusion of a noncitizen if the exclusion would violate a constitutional provision such as the First Amendment. *See, e.g.*, *Kleindienst v. Mandel*, 408 U.S. 753, 770 (1972). But even then, the Court has been extremely deferential, finding the Due Process Clause satisfied even if the government excludes a noncitizen spouse of a U.S. citizen with no explanation. *See Kerry v. Din*, 576 U.S. 86, 101 (2015).

The Supreme Court's approach to expulsion cases is marginally less deferential than its approach to exclusion cases. The Court has consistently distinguished deportation proceedings from criminal proceedings, holding that deportation is a civil proceeding drawn from Congress's power to regulate the entrance of noncitizens and to impose conditions upon their continued liberty to reside within the United States. *Harisiades v. Shaughnessy*, 342 U.S. 580, 595 (1952). So, while the Court recognizes the significant interest that a noncitizen has in avoiding being deported by mistake, the Court has never required the government to provide a deportee with the same protections of counsel or discovery to which a criminal defendant is entitled. Instead, the government may expel a person after providing "clear, unequivocal, and convincing evidence" that the person is removable. *Woodby v. INS*, 385 U.S. 276, 281 (1966). The Court has also held that when Congress so authorizes, noncitizens may be entitled to contest the legal grounds for their removal in federal court on a writ of habeas corpus. *Thuraissigiam*, 140 S. Ct. at 1978–81. The Court has allowed people who claim to be citizens to obtain a full civil trial before they can be deported. *Ng Fung Ho v. White*, 259 U.S. 276 (1981).

But the Court remains exceptionally deferential to the detention and removal of noncitizens. In *Demore v. Kim*, the Court upheld the indefinite detention without bail of a lawful permanent resident suspected of being removable, holding that the government had a strong interest in preventing the resident from "skipping their [removal] hearings and remaining at large in the United States unlawfully." 538 U.S. 510, 528 (2003). During wartime, the Court has also upheld the summary deportation of a noncitizen by executive action without judicial review. *Ludecke v. Watkins*, 335 U.S. 160, 183 (1948).

In a related line of cases, the Court has held that military commissions and courts-martial must provide defendants with minimal procedural safeguards. As discussed earlier with regard to Congress's power to wage war successfully (section 13.4), in *Hamdi v. Rumsfeld*, 542 U.S. 507 (2004), the Court held that U.S. citizens detained at Guantánamo Bay must be given a fair chance, with counsel before a neutral decision maker, to rebut the evidence that they were enemy combatants. And in *Boumediene v. Bush*, 553 U.S. 723 (2008), the Court cited *Mathews* to hold that Congress also may not provide noncitizen detainees on U.S.-controlled soil with fewer safeguards than would be available on a writ of habeas corpus. *Id.* at 783. But the *Boumediene* Court rejected the argument that military tribunals must provide the same protections as a federal *criminal* trial, *id.*, or that their decisions must always be subject to judicial review, *id.* at 786–87.

40.2 THE MEANING OF *LIFE, LIBERTY, OR PROPERTY*

The Due Process Clause doesn't protect against all deprivations—it only protects against deprivations of "life, liberty, or property." The Court has warned against interpreting these interests so expansively that the Due Process Clause would require notice and a hearing every time the government did something that a person didn't like. *See Bd. of Regents v. Roth*, 408 U.S. 564, 569–71 (1972).

Life

The deprivation of "life" is straightforward: it occurs when the government attempts to execute someone, and it has traditionally required every effective procedural safeguard necessary to prevent a mistaken deprivation. *See, e.g., Ring v. Arizona*, 536 U.S. 584, 609 (2002).

The deprivations of "property" and "liberty" require more elaboration.

Property

As discussed in the previous section, until *Goldberg v. Kelly*, 397 U.S. 254 (1970), the Supreme Court defined the term *property* narrowly to include only legally protected interests in land, chattels, and other things that could be owned. But *Goldberg* expanded the term to include not only vested rights but also "statutory entitlement[s]" from the government that had previously been described as "privilege[s]." Goldberg, 397 U.S. at 262. After *Goldberg*, the Court held that the Due Process Clause protected against the deprivation of any important benefit that a person possessed, including a driver's license, *Bell v. Burson*, 402 U.S. 535, 542 (1971); and household goods sold on an installment contract whose legal title was retained by the seller, *Fuentes v. Shevin*, 407 U.S. 67, 89 (1972).

The Court reversed course in *Board of Regents v. Roth*, 408 U.S. 564 (1972), a case involving a government's refusal to renew a nontenured professor's contract. Although the professor claimed to have a property interest in continuing to work, the Court held that the term *property* connoted "more than a unilateral expectation" of something. *Roth*, 408 U.S. at 577. Rather, it involved a "legitimate claim of entitlement to it, . . . defined by existing rules or understandings that stem from an independent source such as state law." *Id.* Absent an informal custom suggesting that the professor could expect to keep his job, the Court held that the Due Process Clause didn't require the university to hold a hearing before depriving the professor of another year of employment. Nevertheless, in a later case involving another untenured professor in which there *were* such "existing rules or understandings," the Court held that the Due Process Clause required a hearing before dismissing the professor. *See Perry v. Sindermann*, 408 U.S. 593, 601 (1972).

One complication of the Court's definition of a property interest is that some entitlements are granted with conditions. For example, a law might entitle public officers to keep their job as long as an administrative board thinks that they are performing it well. Such a case arose in *Arnett v. Kennedy*, 416 U.S. 134 (1974), when the federal government fired an employee who argued that he was entitled to more procedural protections than were provided by the statute governing his removal. Justice Lewis Powell wrote a controlling opinion in which he held that the Due Process Clause was a constitutional floor that states could not undermine by defining for themselves which safeguards were due. *Arnett*, 416 U.S. at 171. But Justice William Rehnquist argued for a plurality that the employee had no property interest in further protections than what the statute offered; he argued that the employee must "take the bitter with the sweet." *See id.* at 154.

The Court adopted and applied Rehnquist's theory in *Town of Castle Rock v. Gonzales*, 545 U.S. 748 (2005). There, it concluded that a person who obtains a state-law restraining order has no constitutionally protected property interest in having the police *enforce* the restraining order. The Court admitted that the facts of the case were "horrible." *Id.* at 751. A Colorado woman, Jessica Gonzales, obtained a restraining order against her estranged husband that required him to stay away from her and her children. After he violated the restraining order by picking up the children without warning, she called the police to demand that they find him and return the children. The police made no effort to enforce the restraining order for almost twelve hours, during which time the husband murdered the children. But the Court held that the police didn't violate the Due Process Clause because Gonzales's restraining order didn't mandate a precise means of enforcement. *Id.* at 764. Absent clear instructions, all Gonzales could expect was that the police would use their discretion in enforcing the order. The Court feared the consequences of recognizing a judicially enforceable property interest in having the government exercise its discretion in a particular manner. *Id.* at 766–68.

Liberty

In addition to "property," the Due Process Clause also protects "liberty" interests. At common law, *liberty* generally referred to a person's freedom from bodily restraint—an interest that continues to be recognized. *See, e.g.*, *Kansas v. Crane*, 534 U.S. 407, 409 (2002) (recognizing "liberty" interest in freedom from civil confinement); *Gagnon v. Scarpelli*, 411 U.S. 778, 791 (1973) (recognizing liberty interest in not having probation revoked); *Morrissey v. Brewer*, 408 U.S. 471, 482 (1972) (recognizing liberty interest in parole).

As we will discuss soon (section 42.1.1), the definition of *liberty* was dramatically expanded around the turn of the twentieth century to include

> not merely freedom from bodily restraint but also the right of the individual to contract, to engage in any of the common occupations of life, to acquire useful knowledge, to marry, establish a home and bring up children, to worship God according to the dictates of his own conscience, and generally to enjoy those privileges long recognized at common law as essential to the orderly pursuit of happiness by free men.

Meyer v. Nebraska, 262 U.S. 390, 399 (1923).

In recent decades, the Court has been ambivalent about expanding this list further. For instance, in *Wisconsin v. Constantineau*, 400 U.S. 433 (1971), the Court held that a person had a liberty interest in their reputation. *Id.* at 437. So when a state banned from bars certain people that it described as "excessive drink[ers]," the Court held that the Due Process Clause required the state to give the people a hearing at which they could rebut the claim. *Id.*; *see also Hampton v. Mow Sun Wong*, 426 U.S. 88, 102, n.23 (1976) (defining *liberty* to include personal, political, and social rights and privileges).

But this broad definition of a liberty interest in reputation lasted only until 1976. To combat shoplifting, Edgar Paul, the chief of police of Louisville, Kentucky, distributed posters with the photograph of Edward C. Davis III, accusing him of being an "active shoplifter[ ]." *Paul v. Davis*, 424 U.S. 693, 695 (1976). Davis challenged this circulation, contending that the Due Process Clause required the police to give him a prior opportunity to defend his reputation. *Id.* at 713. The Court disagreed, distinguishing *Constantineau* as a case in which a person's reputation was harmed *and* the person lost some tangible interest, such as the ability to enter a bar. *Id.* at 701. In Davis's case, the Court thought it enough that he could always sue Paul in state court for torts like defamation. The Court feared that if it recognized Davis's liberty interest, then it would "make of the Fourteenth Amendment a font of tort law to be superimposed upon whatever systems may already be administered by the States." *Id.* Since then, the Court has continued to decline to recognize constitutional interests in protecting against harms that could alternatively be remedied by suing a government official for tort damages. *See, e.g., County of Sacramento v. Lewis*, 523 U.S. 833, 854 (1998) (no due process life or liberty interest implicated by police officer who caused a person's death in a high-speed car chase); *DeShaney v. Winnebago Cnty. Soc. Servs. Dep't*, 489 U.S. 189, 203 (1989) (same where state failed to protect a child from his abusive parent).

40.3 THE MEANING OF PERSON

Just as the Due Process Clause only protects against deprivations of "life, liberty, or property," it also protects only "person[s]."

From an early date, the Supreme Court has held that this term means that the clause protects all human beings regardless of race or citizenship. *See, e.g., Wong Wing v. United States*, 163 U.S. 228, 237 (1896); *Yick Wo v. Hopkins*, 118 U.S. 356, 369 (1886).

The Court also quickly applied the term *person* to include corporations. *See, e.g., Sinking Fund Cases*, 99 U.S. 700, 722 (1879); *Munn v. Illinois*, 94 U.S. 113, 142 (1877). But while the Court held that a corporation might have recognizable *property* interests, *Smyth v. Ames*, 169 U.S. 466, 526 (1898), the Court at first held that a corporation cannot articulate *liberty* interests protected by the Due Process Clause as *liberty* is a term reserved for human beings. *See Pierce v. Soc'y of Sisters*, 268 U.S. 510, 535 (1925). As we will see, the Court implicitly reversed this conclusion when it began to interpret the Due Process Clause as a vehicle for incorporating the Bill of Rights, holding that newspapers and other corporations had liberty interests in free speech and a free press that were protected by the Due Process Clause. *See, e.g., Grosjean v. Am. Press Co.*, 297 U.S. 233, 244 (1936).

Today, therefore, the term *person* generally includes all private actors. It does not, however, include a *state*. *See South Carolina v. Katzenbach*, 383 U.S. 301, 323–24 (1966). Nor has the Court allowed municipal corporations—cities and local governments—to invoke the Due Process Clause in opposition to the state that chartered them. *See, e.g., Williams v. Mayor of Balt.*, 289 U.S. 36, 40 (1933); *City of Trenton v. New Jersey*, 262 U.S. 182, 187 (1923). The Court has similarly not allowed state officers to challenge state laws in order to avoid complying with them. *See, e.g., Columbus & Greenville Ry. v. Miller*, 283 U.S. 96, 101 (1931).

Finally, although the Fifth and Fourteenth Amendments don't include any limitations on *where* they apply, the Supreme Court has generally enforced them within the "United States," including incorporated territories and Washington, D.C. *See, e.g., Lovato v. New Mexico*, 242 U.S. 199, 202 (1916). The Court has not, by contrast, applied the amendments in unincorporated territories or military tribunals completely outside the jurisdiction of the United States. *See, e.g.*, *Boumediene v. Bush*, 553 U.S. 723, 766–67 (2008) (quoting *Johnson v. Eisentrager*, 339 U.S. 763 (1950)).

40.4 THE DUE PROCESS CLAUSE APPLIED TO CIVIL PROCEDURE

Perhaps the most obvious context in which a person's life, liberty, or property is subject to deprivation is in court. In the typical civil case, a government or private party files a complaint asking a court to deprive a person of his or her liberty (with an injunction) or property (with a claim for damages). Accordingly, the Due Process Clauses of the Fifth and Fourteenth Amendments define the minimum safeguards necessary to protect a person from mistakenly or unfairly suffering a deprivation. *See Ownbey v. Morgan*, 256 U.S. 94, 112 (1921).

Commencing an action

In the civil context, the Supreme Court has interpreted the Due Process Clause to require governments to provide all people with access to their courts. *Boddie v. Connecticut*, 401 U.S. 371, 382–83 (1971). Although governments can impose minimal conditions on the right to commence an action—requiring potential plaintiffs to pay a filing fee, for instance—they cannot enforce those conditions if they become obstacles that make it impossible for a person to remedy an important loss of liberty or property. *Id.* (striking down fees that denied a person the ability to obtain a divorce).

Personal jurisdiction

Once a suit is initiated, the Supreme Court has interpreted the Due Process Clause to prohibit courts from unfairly exercising jurisdiction over defendants—subjecting them to the potential loss of liberty or property. In the context of human defendants, the Court has considered the risk of a mistaken or unfair deprivation intolerably high if a state court were to proceed against people in a different state who received no notice of the case against them, who never interacted with anyone in the state, and who would find it difficult to adequately defend themselves in the state. *See Pennoyer v. Neff*, 95 U.S. 714, 737 (1878).

But the Court has considered it fair for a state court to exercise jurisdiction over someone who "consents" to the potential deprivation. *See McDonald v. Mabee*, 243 U.S. 90, 91 (1917); *Louisville & Nashville R.R. v. Schmidt*, 177 U.S. 230, 239 (1900). Under long-standing doctrine, people give their "implied consent" to a state's exercise of jurisdiction when they appear in the state, even temporarily, and receive notice of the case against them along with information about how they can defend themselves. *Hess v. Pawloski*, 274 U.S. 352, 356–57 (1927). A person also impliedly consents to a state's exercise of jurisdiction by becoming a citizen or domiciliary of the state, *Milliken v. Meyer*, 311 U.S. 457, 463 (1940), or by establishing "minimum contacts" with the state that are sufficient to ensure that a potential deprivation doesn't offend "traditional notions of fair play and substantial justice," *Int'l Shoe Co. v. Washington*, 326 U.S. 310, 316 (1945). Such minimum contacts may be established by doing business with people in the state, *id.*; by "purposefully avail[ing]" themselves of the privilege of conducting activities within a state, *Hanson v. Denckla*, 357 U.S. 235, 253 (1958); or by taking any other action that connects the person with the state "in a meaningful way," *Walden v. Fiore*, 571 U.S. 277, 288 (2014).

The Due Process Clause's requirements for exercising jurisdiction over out-of-state corporations are more complicated, in part because corporations don't literally live or exist anywhere. In light of this epistemological problem, the Supreme Court at first held that a corporation has no legal existence outside the boundaries of the state that charters it—meaning that the corporation could be sued only in the state in which it was incorporated. *Bank of Augusta v. Earle*, 38 U.S. (13 Pet.) 519, 597 (1839). Over time, the Court relaxed this rule as states required out-of-state corporations to consent to suit within the new states as a condition for operating within the new states' borders. *See, e.g.*, *Pa. Fire Ins. Co. v. Gold Issue Mining Co.*, 243 U.S. 93, 96 (1917). But this regime led the Court to worry that it was unfair for a corporation to have to defend itself for all of its activities in every state in which it did business—particularly when the subject of the lawsuit took place in a different state from the lawsuit itself. *See, e.g.*, *Old Wayne Life Ass'n v. McDonough*, 204 U.S. 8, 23 (1907).

The Court responded to this apparent unfairness by dividing a state's exercise of jurisdiction into two types: "specific" and "general."

The Court defined *specific jurisdiction* to include contexts in which a corporation does enough business with a particular state—establishing the same "minimum contacts" or "purposeful availment" as with a human defendant—that it is fair to expect that the corporation could adequately defend itself in that state's courts for situations arising from the corporation's activities in that particular state. *Bristol-Myers Squibb Co. v. Superior Court*, 137 S. Ct. 1773 (2017); *see, e.g.*, *Burger King Corp. v. Rudzewicz*, 471 U.S. 462 (1985); *Int'l Shoe Co.*, 326 U.S. at 316. One difference, however, is that the Court has also considered it fair for a state to exercise jurisdiction over a corporation that didn't purposefully do business with a particular state but that "delivered its products into the stream of commerce with the expectation that they will be purchased by consumers in the forum state," as in *World-Wide Volkswagen Corp. v. Woodson*, 444 U.S. 286, 298 (1980). Applying this "stream-of-commerce" test proved difficult, however. *See, e.g.*, *J. McIntyre Mach., Ltd. v. Nicastro*, 564 U.S. 873 (2011); *Asahi Metal Indus. Co. v. Superior Court*, 480 U.S. 102 (1987). In *Ford Motor Co. v. Montana Eighth Judicial*

District Court, 141 S. Ct. 1017 (2021), the Court recharacterized *World-Wide Volkswagen* as a "purposeful availment" case, emphasizing that car companies routinely urge people of every state to purchase their cars. *Id.* at 1027.

The Court defined *general jurisdiction* to include contexts in which a corporation has such a close relationship with a particular state that it would be fair to expect that the corporation could adequately defend itself in that state's courts for anything the corporation did anywhere in the world. *Perkins v. Benguet Consol. Mining Co.*, 342 U.S. 437 (1952). A state can exercise general jurisdiction over a corporation when the corporation's "continuous and systematic" affiliations with the state make them "essentially at home" there. *BNSF Ry. Co. v. Tyrrell*, 137 S. Ct. 1549, 1558 (2017) (quoting *Goodyear Dunlop Tires Operations, S.A. v. Brown*, 564 U.S. 915, 919 (2011) and *Daimler AG v. Bauman*, 571 U.S. 117, 137–38 (2014)). Typically, the only states that can exercise general jurisdiction over a particular corporation are the state that chartered the corporation and the state in which it has its "principal place of business." *Id.*

Notice

When an action is brought against a person over whom a court can exercise jurisdiction, the Supreme Court has interpreted the Due Process Clause to require the plaintiff to provide "notice reasonably calculated, under all the circumstances, to apprise interested parties of the pendency of the action and afford them an opportunity to present their objections." *Mullane v. Cent. Hanover Bank & Tr. Co.*, 339 U.S. 306, 314 (1950). This can usually be accomplished by delivering the complaint and a court summons either in person or via certified mail. Whatever the method, the Due Process Clause doesn't require that notice *actually* be accomplished so long as the method is reasonably calculated to deliver notice. *See Jones v. Flowers*, 547 U.S. 220, 226 (2006).

Defenses, costs, and damages

Once defendants are notified of an action, the Supreme Court has interpreted the Due Process Clause to require a court to give them the opportunity to defend themselves—but a court may limit the available defenses in a particular case or establish terms by which a defense may be raised. *See, e.g., Lindsey v. Normet*, 405 U.S. 56 (1972).

A court may then also regulate whether the losing side of a case must pay the other side's costs or attorney's fees. *See, e.g., Mo., Kan. & Tex. Ry. v. Cade*, 233 U.S. 642, 650–52 (1914). The Supreme Court has held that in some contexts in which courts don't provide a lawyer to an indigent party and also limit the attorney's fees available to a lawyer, the Due Process Clause might be violated—but only when the presence of an attorney would meaningfully reduce the probability of error. *See Walters v. Nat'l Ass'n of Radiation Survivors*, 473 U.S. 305, 326 (1985).

One context in which the Court has repeatedly invoked the Due Process Clause is as a limit on punitive damages. Traditionally, courts have long allowed juries to award punitive damages to deter a liable party from committing similar offenses in the future. *See, e.g., TXO Corp. v. Alliance Resources*, 509 U.S. 443, 462 (1993) (upholding a $10 million punitive damages award for $19,000 in compensatory damages). In more recent cases, however, the Court has repeatedly invalidated similar punitive damages awards as "grossly excessive" compared to what the Court considered reasonably necessary to vindicate a state's legitimate interest in punishing and deterring the actual defendant as opposed to all similar defendants. *See, e.g., Philip Morris USA v. Williams*, 549 U.S. 346, 349 (2007); *BMW of N. Am., Inc. v. Gore*, 517 U.S. 559, 583–86 (1996). The Court suggested that any punitive damages award more than ten times larger than the compensatory damages award would be unlikely to be consistent with due process. *State Farm Mut. Auto. Ins. Co. v. Campbell*, 538 U.S. 408, 425 (2003).

Burdens of proof and presumptions

Although the Supreme Court has not interpreted the Due Process Clause to require courts to adopt a particular burden of proof in civil cases, it has interpreted the clause to require a burden rigorous enough to "instruct the factfinder concerning the degree of confidence our society thinks he should have in the correctness of factual conclusions for a particular type of adjudication." *Addington v. Texas*, 441 U.S. 418, 423 (1979). In the civil context, this typically requires a "preponderance of the evidence" (more likely than not); but in contexts involving fundamental liberty interests, it can require at least "clear and convincing" evidence (more than just a preponderance). *Id.*

Legislatures can, consistent with this minimal requirement, create a presumption declaring that the proof of a fact can constitute prima facie evidence that an inference from that fact is true—for example, that an accident at a railroad crossing is the result of negligence. *See Atl. Coast Line R.R. v. Ford*, 287 U.S. 502, 509 (1933). But the Court has, at times, been hostile to "irrebuttable presumptions," for example, that every pregnant teacher who reaches a particular point in pregnancy becomes physically incapable of teaching. *Cleveland Bd. of Educ. v. LaFleur*, 414 U.S. 632, 651 (1974).

Trials, appeals, and judgments

In general, the Supreme Court has held that the Due Process Clause doesn't require that civil cases include jury trials, unanimous juries, twelve-member juries, or appellate review. *See Lindsey v. Normet*, 405 U.S. 56, 77 (1972). But if a jury trial or appeal is provided, the Court has held that a government may not impose fees or otherwise structure it in a manner that arbitrarily denies some people the privilege when it is granted to others. *Id.*

Taxation

The Supreme Court has applied a due process analysis to state tax procedure similar to that of state judicial procedure. In general, the Court has upheld a state's jurisdiction to tax people, property, and transactions anywhere in the world so long as there is "some definite link, some minimum connection, between a state and the person, property or transaction it seeks to tax." *South Dakota v. Wayfair, Inc.*, 138 S. Ct. 2080, 2093 (2018) (citing *Quill Corp. v. North Dakota*, 504 U.S. 298, 308 (1992) and *Burger King Corp. v. Rudzewicz*, 471 U.S. 462, 476 (1985)).

40.5 THE DUE PROCESS CLAUSE APPLIED TO CRIMINAL PROCEDURE

In the typical criminal case, a government files an indictment asking a court to punish a person by literally taking away that person's life, physical liberty, or property. In theory, the determination of what process is "due" in criminal cases could be said to follow from the process that is due in civil cases, which generally now depends on an application of the balancing test from *Mathews v. Eldridge*, 424 U.S. 319 (1976). But in practice, the Court's understanding of whether a criminal procedure is offensive to the concept of fundamental fairness has been heavily influenced by the U.S. Constitution's Fourth, Fifth, Sixth, and Eighth Amendments. *See Medina v. California*, 505 U.S. 437, 453 (1992). In applying the Due Process Clause to criminal trials, the Supreme Court has selectively "incorporated" the Bill of Rights to the states—something that the authors of the Fourteenth Amendment anticipated would happen under the Privileges or Immunities Clause.

Hurtado *and prosecution by information*

The development of selective incorporation began a decade after the *Slaughter-House Cases*, 83 U.S. (16 Wall.) 36 (1873), narrowed to insignificance the scope of the Privileges or Immunities Clause.

At the time, the federal government and most states initiated criminal prosecutions with an *indictment*, in which a prosecutor would summon a grand jury, provide the grand jury with evidence that a suspect has committed a crime, and request that the grand jury formally charge the suspect. For federal prosecutors, this procedure was mandated by the Fifth Amendment, which required an "indictment of a Grand Jury" for most offenses. But in sparsely populated western states, grand juries were expensive and difficult to maintain. In 1879, California adopted a new constitution that authorized prosecutions by *information*, in which a prosecutor could formally charge a suspect, bring the suspect before a magistrate, and then prove to the magistrate that sufficient evidence existed to jail the suspect until trial. *See* Cal. Const. of 1879, art. I, § 8.

California followed this new procedure to prosecute a man named Joseph Hurtado, who was arrested for allegedly murdering a man with whom his wife was having an affair. He challenged his prosecution in federal court, arguing that the Due Process Clause of the Fourteenth Amendment required California to provide him with the procedural protections of an indictment. But in *Hurtado v. California*, the Court held that the Due Process Clause didn't guarantee "particular forms of procedure," but only sufficient procedure to protect an individual's "rights to life, liberty, and property." 110 U.S. 516, 532 (1884). As in the civil context, the Court ascertained the meaning of the phrase *due process of law* by considering "those settled usages and modes of proceeding" in English and American history and asking whether departures from those settled usages remained consistent with "those fundamental principles of liberty and justice which lie at the base of all our civil and political institutions." *Id.* at 528, 535. While acknowledging that prosecutions traditionally were initiated by indictment, the Court held that the phrase *due process of law* was flexible enough to permit any procedure that provided a defendant with notice of the charges against him and an opportunity to defend himself: a procedure that "hears before it condemns, which proceeds upon inquiry, and renders judgment only after trial." *Id.* at 535–36. The Court thus upheld California's prosecution by information.

But the Court added an important exception, noting that the phrase *due process of law* wasn't flexible enough to include "partial and arbitrary exertions of power under the forms of legislation" such as "acts of attainder, bills of pains and penalties, acts of confiscation, acts reversing judgments, and acts directly transferring one man's estate to another." *Id.* at 536.

Twining *and self-incrimination*

Hurtado's exception proved important in subsequent cases as litigants continued to challenge state laws and criminal procedures for straying from the requirements of the Bill of Rights. For the most part, the Court emphasized the holding of *Barron ex rel. Tiernan v. Mayor & City Council of Baltimore*, 32 U.S. (7 Pet.) 243 (1833), "[t]hat the first ten Articles of Amendment were not intended to limit the powers of the state governments in respect to their own people, but to operate on the National Government alone." *Spies v. Illinois*, 123 U.S. 131, 166 (1887). But members of the Court also began to suggest that some state laws might be struck down for violating the principles of the Bill of Rights—even if the Bill of Rights didn't literally apply to states.

In one case in 1892, Justice John Harlan wrote in dissent that the "essential rights of life, liberty, and property which inhered in Anglo-Saxon freedom" were secured "by the Fourteenth Amendment against denial or abridgment by the States." *O'Neil v. Vermont*, 144 U.S. 323, 370 (1892) (Harlan, J., dissenting). And in another case five years later,

Harlan wrote for a majority that one of these essential rights was that a state could not deprive someone of property without just compensation. Rather than cite the Fifth Amendment's prohibition on taking "private property . . . for public use, without just compensation," Harlan wrote that such a deprivation could not comply with "due process of law" no matter what procedure was used. *Chi., Burlington & Quincy R.R. Co. v. City of Chicago*, 166 U.S. 226, 236–37 (1897).

During his tenure on the Court, which ended in 1911, Harlan never again convinced his colleagues that the Fourteenth Amendment's Due Process Clause protected a right listed in the Bill of Rights. Instead, the Court observed that it would be odd for the Fourteenth Amendment's Due Process Clause to include all of the protections of the Bill of Rights when the Fifth Amendment's identical Due Process Clause had never been interpreted as a substitute for all of the other amendments.

In *Twining v. New Jersey*, the Court did eventually agree with Harlan that "that some of the personal rights safeguarded by the first eight Amendments against National action may also be safeguarded against state action, because a denial of them would be a denial of due process of law." 211 U.S. 78, 99 (1908). Nevertheless, the Court emphasized that the test was not whether "those rights are enumerated in the first eight Amendments, but [whether] they are of such a nature that they are included in the conception of due process of law." *Id.* At issue in *Twining* was whether the Fifth Amendment's protection against self-incrimination was applicable to the states via the Fourteenth Amendment's Due Process Clause. To determine "whether the exemption from self-incrimination is of such a nature that it must be included in the conception of due process," the *Twining* Court asked a modified version of *Hurtado*'s question:

> Is it a fundamental principle of liberty and justice which inheres in the very idea of free government and is the inalienable right of a citizen of such government? If it is, and if it is of a nature that pertains to process of law, this court has declared it to be essential to due process of law.

Id. at 106. But the Court cautioned that in describing a procedural protection as "fundamental," it was not the judiciary's role to substitute its own conception of liberty and justice with that of a state legislature because "it must not be forgotten that in a free representative government nothing is more fundamental than the right of the people through their appointed servants to govern themselves in accordance with their own will." *Id.* at 106–07.

Asking whether the right against self-incrimination was so "fundamental" that it "inheres in the very idea of free government," *id.* at 106, the *Twining* Court concluded that it would "strain[ ] the meaning of due process of law to include this privilege within it." *id.* at 113. Even though the Court considered the right "of great value," the Court emphasized several examples in American, English, and European history where courts required certain defendants to testify against themselves. *Id.* Most importantly, most states already appeared willing and able to respect the right against self-incrimination without the Court's intervention. "The power of their people ought not to be fettered, their sense of responsibility lessened, and their capacity for sober and restrained self-government weakened by forced construction of the Federal Constitution," the Court wrote. *Id.* at 114.

40.5.1

Powell v. Alabama

287 U.S. 45 (1932)

The Court's faith in the ability of states to fairly administer their criminal procedure without its own intervention was severely tested in *Powell v. Alabama*, 287 U.S. 45 (1932).

In the early twentieth century, states throughout the South adopted dual forms of justice for criminal defendants: one process for white defendants and a far less protective process for black defendants. A dramatic illustration of this second process arose out of Alabama in 1931. There, a posse of fifty armed white men boarded a train near Scottsboro, Alabama, after a group of white boys claimed that a "bunch of Negroes" had started a fight on the train. *See* Dan T. Carter, *Scottsboro: Tragedy of the American South* 4 (1969). The posse seized all nine black boys on board. When the posse asked two white girls on the train whether the boys had bothered them, one of the girls falsely claimed that the boys had raped them. This sensational allegation was enough for the posse to drag the boys to a nearby jail. That night, a crowd of hundreds of white people gathered to lynch the "Scottsboro Boys." *Id.* at 4–9.

Although Alabama's governor sent National Guardsmen to Scottsboro in time to save the boys from being lynched, state prosecutors initiated four rapid-fire trials of the boys just twelve days after the arrest. Douglas O. Linder, *Without Fear or Favor*, 68 UMKC L. Rev. 549, 552 (2000). When the boys asked for an attorney, the trial judge asked two people in the audience to represent them—an alcoholic real estate attorney named Stephen Roddy and a "doddering, extremely unreliable, senile" co-counsel named Milo Moody. *Id.* The judge gave these lawyers half an hour to interview their clients before the trials began. *Id.* The attorneys provided virtually no defense as fifteen hundred white onlookers watched the two girls testify that they had been raped. As a brass band played outside the courthouse, three all-white juries successively convicted eight of the boys—aged thirteen to nineteen—and voted to impose the death penalty. *Id.*

National coverage of the show trials caught the attention of the Communist Party USA, which offered the Scottsboro Boys competent lawyers for their appeal. Before the Supreme Court, the new lawyers argued that Alabama was threatening to deprive the boys of their lives in violation of the Fourteenth Amendment's Due Process Clause. Citing *Hurtado* and *Twining*, the lawyers argued that the Sixth Amendment's "Assistance of Counsel" was an "immutable principle[ ] of justice which inhere[s] in the very idea of free government." *Powell*, 287 U.S. at 71–72. They also emphasized that competent attorneys clearly could have made a difference in preventing a mistaken deprivation of the boys' lives.

The Court agreed.

■ MR. JUSTICE SUTHERLAND delivered the opinion of the Court.[12]

The petitioners, hereinafter referred to as defendants, are negroes charged with the crime of rape, committed upon the persons of two white girls. The crime is said to have been committed on March 25, 1931. The indictment was returned in a state court of first instance on March 31, and the record recites that on the same day the defendants were arraigned and entered pleas of not guilty. . . . Each of the three trials was completed within a single day. Under the Alabama statute the punishment for rape is to be fixed by the jury, and in its discretion may be from ten years imprisonment to death. The juries found defendants guilty and imposed the death penalty upon all. The trial court . . . sentenced the defendants in accordance with the verdicts. The judgments were affirmed by the state supreme court. Chief Justice Anderson thought the defendants had not been accorded a fair trial and strongly dissented.

In this court the judgments are assailed upon the grounds that the defendants and each of them, were denied due process of law and the equal protection of the laws, in contravention of the Fourteenth Amendment, [because] . . . they were denied the right of counsel, with the accustomed incidents of consultation and opportunity of preparation for trial. . . .

The record shows that on the day when the offense is said to have been committed, these defendants, together with a number of other negroes, were upon a freight train on its way through Alabama. On the same train were seven white boys and the two white girls. A fight took place between the negroes and the white boys, in the course of which the white boys . . . were thrown off the train. A message was sent ahead, reporting the fight and asking that every negro be gotten off the train. The participants in the fight, and the two girls, were in an open gondola car. The two girls testified that each of them was assaulted by six different negroes in turn, and they identified the seven defendants as having been among the number. . . .

Before the train reached Scottsboro, Alabama, a sheriff's posse seized the defendants and two other negroes. Both girls and the negroes then were taken to Scottsboro, the county seat. Word of their coming and of the alleged assault had preceded them, and they were met at Scottsboro by a large crowd. It does not

---

[12] **As You Read, Consider:** In *Hurtado v. California*, the Supreme Court observed that it would be odd for the Fourteenth Amendment's Due Process Clause to require the same procedures in state criminal trials that the Bill of Rights required in federal criminal trials. The phrase *due process of law* appears in the Fifth Amendment, and it would therefore be redundant if the phrase were capacious enough to include everything else enumerated in the Fourth, Fifth, Sixth, and Eighth Amendments. The Court also thought that the best protectors of civil rights were not federal courts but the people of the various states, who had the capacity to decide democratically how to carry out criminal trials.

Here, the lawyers for the Scottsboro Boys nevertheless argue that the Due Process Clause requires states to comply with the same "Assistance of Counsel" guaranteed by the Sixth Amendment. Does Justice George Sutherland overrule *Barron ex rel. Tiernan v. Mayor of Baltimore* and hold that the Sixth Amendment applies to the states? Does he hold that the Due Process Clause protects all of the rights guaranteed by the Bill of Rights? Or does he hold something else?

sufficiently appear that the defendants were seriously threatened with, or that they were actually in danger of mob violence; but it does appear that the attitude of the community was one of great hostility. The sheriff thought it necessary to call for the militia to assist in safeguarding the prisoners. Chief Justice Anderson pointed out in his opinion that every step taken from the arrest and arraignment to the sentence was accompanied by the military. . . . It is perfectly apparent that the proceedings, from beginning to end, took place in an atmosphere of tense, hostile and excited public sentiment. During the entire time, the defendants were closely confined or were under military guard. The record does not disclose their ages, except that one of them was nineteen; but the record clearly indicates that most, if not all, of them were youthful, and they are constantly referred to as "the boys." They were ignorant and illiterate. All of them were residents of other states, where alone members of their families or friends resided.

However guilty defendants, upon due inquiry, might prove to have been, they were, until convicted, presumed to be innocent. It was the duty of the court having their cases in charge to see that they were denied no necessary incident of a fair trial. With any error of the state court involving alleged contravention of the state statutes or constitution we, of course, have nothing to do. The sole inquiry which we are permitted to make is whether the federal Constitution was contravened; and as to that, we confine ourselves, as already suggested, to the inquiry whether the defendants were in substance denied the right of counsel, and if so, whether such denial infringes the due process clause of the Fourteenth Amendment.

First. The record shows that immediately upon the return of the indictment defendants were arraigned and pleaded not guilty. Apparently they were not asked whether they had, or were able to employ, counsel, or wished to have counsel appointed; or whether they had friends or relatives who might assist in that regard if communicated with. . . . [As] Chief Justice Anderson [wrote] in the course of his dissenting opinion[:] "They were non-residents . . . and had little time or opportunity to get in touch with their families and friends who were scattered throughout two other states, and time has demonstrated that they could or would have been represented by able counsel had a better opportunity been given by a reasonable delay in the trial of the cases, judging from the number and activity of counsel that appeared immediately or shortly after their conviction."

It is hardly necessary to say that, the right to counsel being conceded, a defendant should be afforded a fair opportunity to secure counsel of his own choice. Not only was that not done here, but such designation of counsel as was attempted was either so indefinite or so close upon the trial as to amount to a denial of effective and substantial aid in that regard. This will be amply demonstrated by a brief review of the record.

April 6, six days after indictment, the trials began. When the first case was called, the court inquired whether the parties were ready for trial. The state's attorney replied that he was ready to proceed. No one answered for the defendants or appeared to represent or defend them. Mr. Roddy, a Tennessee lawyer not a member of the local bar, addressed the court, saying that he had not been employed, but that people who were interested had spoken to him about the case. He was asked by the court whether he intended to appear for the defendants, and answered that he would like to appear along with counsel that the court might appoint. . . . And in this casual fashion the matter of counsel in a capital case was disposed of. . . .

Nor do we think the situation was helped by what occurred on the morning of the trial. At that time, . . . Mr. Roddy stated to the court that he did not appear as counsel, but that he would like to appear along with counsel that the court might appoint; that he had not been given an opportunity to prepare the case; that he was not familiar with the procedure in Alabama, but merely came down as a friend of the people who were interested; that he thought the boys would be better off if he should step entirely out of the case. Mr. Moody, a member of the local bar, expressed a willingness to help Mr. Roddy in anything he could do under the circumstances. . . . With this dubious understanding, the trials immediately proceeded. The defendants, young, ignorant, illiterate, surrounded by hostile sentiment, haled back and forth under guard of soldiers, charged with an atrocious crime regarded with especial horror in the community where they were to be tried, were thus put in peril of their lives within a few moments after counsel for the first time charged with any degree of responsibility began to represent them.

It is not enough to assume that counsel thus precipitated into the case thought there was no defense, and exercised their best judgment in proceeding to trial without preparation. Neither they nor the court could say what a prompt and thoroughgoing investigation might disclose as to the facts. No attempt was made to investigate. No opportunity to do so was given. Defendants were immediately hurried to trial. Chief Justice Anderson, after disclaiming any intention to criticize harshly counsel who attempted to represent defendants at the trials, said: ". . . the record indicates that the appearance was rather *pro forma* than zealous and active . . ." Under the circumstances disclosed, we hold that defendants were not accorded the right of counsel in any substantial sense. To decide otherwise, would simply be to ignore actualities. . . .

It is true that great and inexcusable delay in the enforcement of our criminal law is one of the grave evils of our time. . . . The prompt disposition of criminal cases is to be commended and encouraged. But in reaching that result a defendant, charged with a serious crime, must not be stripped of his right to have sufficient time to advise with counsel and prepare his defense. To do that is not to proceed promptly in the calm spirit of regulated justice but to go forward with the haste of the mob. . . .

Second. The Constitution of Alabama provides that in all criminal prosecutions the accused shall enjoy the right to have the assistance of counsel; and a state statute requires the court in a capital case, where the defendant is unable to employ counsel, to appoint counsel for him. The state supreme court held that these provisions had not been infringed, and with that holding we are powerless to interfere. The question, however, which it is our duty, and within our power, to decide, is whether the denial of the assistance of counsel contravenes the due process clause of the Fourteenth Amendment to the federal Constitution.[13]

If recognition of the right of a defendant charged with a felony to have the aid of counsel depended upon the existence of a similar right at common law as it existed in England when our Constitution was adopted, there would be great difficulty in maintaining it as necessary to due process. Originally, in England, a person charged with treason or felony was denied the aid of counsel, except in respect of legal questions which the accused himself might suggest. At the same time parties in civil cases and persons accused of misdemeanors were entitled to the full assistance of counsel. . . .

An affirmation of the right to the aid of counsel in petty offenses, and its denial in the case of crimes of the gravest character, where such aid is most needed, is so outrageous and so obviously a perversion of all sense of proportion that the rule was

[13] **Questions:** After concluding that the Scottsboro Boys were effectively denied the right to have the assistance of counsel, Sutherland proceeds to ask whether such a right is protected by the Due Process Clause of the Fourteenth Amendment. How, precisely, does he pose this question—i.e., what test does he use? How does he answer this test?

constantly, vigorously and sometimes passionately assailed by English statesmen and lawyers. . . .

The rule was rejected by the colonies. Before the adoption of the federal Constitution, the Constitution of Maryland had declared "That, in all criminal prosecutions, every man hath a right . . . to be allowed counsel; . . ." (Art. XIX, Constitution of 1776). The Constitution of Massachusetts, adopted in 1780 (Part the First, Art. XII), the Constitution of New Hampshire, adopted in 1784 (Part I, Art. XV), the Constitution of New York of 1777 (Art. XXXIV), and the Constitution of Pennsylvania of 1776 (Art. IX), had also declared to the same effect. . . . [Indeed, it] appears that in at least twelve of the thirteen colonies the rule of the English common law, in the respect now under consideration, had been definitely rejected and the right to counsel fully recognized in all criminal prosecutions, save that in one or two instances the right was limited to capital offenses or to the more serious crimes. . . .

One test which has been applied to determine whether due process of law has been accorded in given instances is to ascertain what were the settled usages and modes of proceeding under the common and statute law of England before the Declaration of Independence, subject, however, to the qualification that they be shown not to have been unsuited to the civil and political conditions of our ancestors by having been followed in this country after it became a nation. *Murray's Lessee v. Hoboken Land* & *Improvement Co.*, 18 How. 272, 276–277; *Twining v. New Jersey*, 211 U.S. 78, 100–101. Plainly, as appears from the foregoing, this test, as thus qualified, has not been met in the present case.

We do not overlook the case of *Hurtado v. California*, 110 U.S. 516, where this court determined that due process of law does not require an indictment by a grand jury as a prerequisite to prosecution by a state for murder. In support of that conclusion the court (pp. 534–535) referred to the fact that the Fifth Amendment, in addition to containing the due process of law clause, provides in explicit terms that "No person shall be held to answer for a capital, or otherwise infamous crime, unless on a presentment or indictment of a grand jury, . . .", and said that since no part of this important amendment could be regarded as superfluous, the obvious inference is that in the sense of the Constitution due process of law was not intended to include, [by implication], the institution and procedure of a grand jury in any case; and that the same phrase, employed in the Fourteenth Amendment to restrain the action of the states, was to be interpreted as having been used in the same sense and with no greater extent; and that if it had been the purpose of that Amendment to perpetuate the institution of the grand jury in the states, it would have embodied, as did the Fifth Amendment, an express declaration to that effect.

The Sixth Amendment, in terms, provides that in all criminal prosecutions the accused shall enjoy the right "to have the assistance of counsel for his defense." In the face of the reasoning of the *Hurtado* case, if it stood alone, it would be difficult to justify the conclusion that the right to counsel, being thus specifically granted by the Sixth Amendment, was also within the intendment of the due process of law clause. But the *Hurtado* case does not stand alone. In the later case of *Chicago, Burlington & Quincy R. Co. v. Chicago*, 166 U.S. 226, 241, this court held that a judgment of a state court, even though authorized by statute, by which private property was taken for public use without just compensation, was in violation of the due process of law required by the Fourteenth Amendment, notwithstanding that the Fifth Amendment explicitly declares that private property shall not be taken for public use without just compensation. . . .

Likewise, this court has considered that freedom of speech and of the press are rights protected by the due process clause of the Fourteenth Amendment, although in the First Amendment, Congress is prohibited in specific terms from abridging the right. *Gitlow v. New York*, 268 U.S. 652, 666. . . .

These later cases establish that notwithstanding the sweeping character of the language in the *Hurtado* case, the rule laid down is not without exceptions. The rule is an aid to construction, and in some instances may be conclusive; but it must yield to more compelling considerations whenever such considerations exist. The fact that the right involved is of such a character that it cannot be denied without violating those "fundamental principles of liberty and justice which lie at the base of all our civil and political institutions" (*Hebert v. Louisiana*, 272 U.S. 312, 316), is obviously one of those compelling considerations which must prevail in determining whether it is embraced within the due process clause of the Fourteenth Amendment, although it be specifically dealt with in another part of the federal Constitution.[14] Evidently this court, in the later cases enumerated, regarded the rights there under consideration as of this fundamental character. That some such distinction must be observed is foreshadowed in *Twining v. New Jersey*, 211 U.S. 78, 99, where Mr. Justice Moody, speaking for the court, said that ". . . it is possible that some of the personal rights safeguarded by the first eight Amendments against National action may also be safeguarded against state action, because a denial of them would be a denial of due process of law. *Chicago, Burlington & Quincy R. Co. v. Chicago*, 166 U.S. 226. If this is so, it is not because those rights are enumerated in the first eight Amendments, but because they are of such a nature that they are included in the conception of due process of law." While the question has never been categorically determined by this court, a consideration of the nature of the right and a review of the expressions of this and other courts, makes it clear that the right to the aid of counsel is of this fundamental character.

It never has been doubted by this court, or any other so far as we know, that notice and hearing are preliminary steps essential to the passing of an enforceable judgment, and that they, together with a legally competent tribunal having jurisdiction of the case, constitute basic elements of the constitutional requirement of due process of law. The words of Webster, so often quoted, that by "the law of the land" is intended "a law which hears before it condemns," have been repeated in varying forms of expression in a multitude of decisions. In *Holden v. Hardy*, 169 U.S. 366, 389, the necessity of due notice and an opportunity of being heard is described as among the "immutable principles of justice which inhere in the very idea of free government which no member of the Union may disregard." . . .[15]

What, then, does a hearing include? Historically and in practice, in our own country at least, it has always included the right to the aid of counsel when desired and provided by the party asserting the right. The right to be heard would be, in many cases, of little avail if it did not comprehend the right to be heard by counsel. Even

---

[14] **Questions:** Recall the ultimate question Sutherland is asking here: Does the phrase *due process of law* require the assistance of counsel in a capital case? So far, Sutherland has written that such a right was *not* recognized in English history. He has also recognized that if such a right were included in the phrase *due process of law*, then the Sixth Amendment would be redundant because the Fifth Amendment includes a Due Process Clause yet the Sixth Amendment guarantees the right to counsel against the federal government.

Nevertheless, he writes here that the right might be required by the phrase *due process of law* when it is one of those "fundamental principles of liberty and justice which lie at the base of all our civil and political institutions." What does he mean by this test? How is anyone supposed to know what is "fundamental"?

[15] **Question:** Consider the Supreme Court's procedural due process cases in the civil context—particularly *Goldberg v. Kelly* and *Mathews v. Eldridge*. If Sutherland had lived long enough to be able to apply those tests, do you think he would have reached the same conclusion that the government must provide defendants with the assistance of counsel before depriving them of their lives?

the intelligent and educated layman has small and sometimes no skill in the science of law. If charged with crime, he is incapable, generally, of determining for himself whether the indictment is good or bad. He is unfamiliar with the rules of evidence. Left without the aid of counsel he may be put on trial without a proper charge, and convicted upon incompetent evidence, or evidence irrelevant to the issue or otherwise inadmissible. He lacks both the skill and knowledge adequately to prepare his defense, even though he have a perfect one. He requires the guiding hand of counsel at every step in the proceedings against him. Without it, though he be not guilty, he faces the danger of conviction because he does not know how to establish his innocence. If that be true of men of intelligence, how much more true is it of the ignorant and illiterate, or those of feeble intellect. If in any case, civil or criminal, a state or federal court were arbitrarily to refuse to hear a party by counsel, employed by and appearing for him, it reasonably may not be doubted that such a refusal would be a denial of a hearing, and, therefore, of due process in the constitutional sense.

In the light of the facts outlined in the forepart of this opinion—the ignorance and illiteracy of the defendants, their youth, the circumstances of public hostility, the imprisonment and the close surveillance of the defendants by the military forces, the fact that their friends and families were all in other states and communication with them necessarily difficult, and above all that they stood in deadly peril of their lives—we think the failure of the trial court to give them reasonable time and opportunity to secure counsel was a clear denial of due process.

But passing that, and assuming their inability, even if opportunity had been given, to employ counsel, as the trial court evidently did assume, we are of opinion that, under the circumstances just stated, the necessity of counsel was so vital and imperative that the failure of the trial court to make an effective appointment of counsel was likewise a denial of due process within the meaning of the Fourteenth Amendment. Whether this would be so in other criminal prosecutions, or under other circumstances, we need not determine. All that it is necessary now to decide, as we do decide, is that in a capital case, where the defendant is unable to employ counsel, and is incapable adequately of making his own defense because of ignorance, feeble mindedness, illiteracy, or the like, it is the duty of the court, whether requested or not, to assign counsel for him as a necessary requisite of due process of law; and that duty is not discharged by an assignment at such a time or under such circumstances as to preclude the giving of effective aid in the preparation and trial of the case. To hold otherwise would be to ignore the fundamental postulate, already adverted to, "that there are certain immutable principles of justice which inhere in the very idea of free government which no member of the Union may disregard." *Holden v. Hardy*, *supra*. In a case such as this, . . . the right to have counsel appointed, when necessary, is a logical corollary from the constitutional right to be heard by counsel. . . .

Let us suppose the extreme case of a prisoner charged with a capital offense, who is deaf and dumb, illiterate and feeble minded, unable to employ counsel, with the whole power of the state arrayed against him, prosecuted by counsel for the state without assignment of counsel for his defense, tried, convicted and sentenced to death. Such a result, which, if carried into execution, would be little short of judicial murder, it cannot be doubted would be a gross violation of the guarantee of due process of law; and we venture to think that no appellate court, state or federal, would hesitate so to decide. . . .

The United States by statute and every state in the Union by express provision of law, or by the determination of its courts, make it the duty of the trial judge, where the accused is unable to employ counsel, to appoint counsel for him. In most states the rule applies broadly to all criminal prosecutions, in others it is limited to the more serious crimes, and in a very limited number, to capital cases. A rule adopted with such unanimous accord reflects, if it does not establish, the inherent right to have counsel appointed, at least in cases like the present, and lends convincing support to the conclusion we have reached as to the fundamental nature of that right. . . .

NOTE: INCORPORATION OF THE BILL OF RIGHTS

Powell was one of the first Supreme Court decisions to hold that a protection guaranteed by the Bill of Rights was also guaranteed against the states by the Due Process Clause of the Fourteenth Amendment. The Court did not, however, hold that the Due Process Clause enforced a protection against the states simply because the protection was enumerated in the Bill of Rights. Instead, adopting a doctrine known as *selective incorporation*, the Court held that the Due Process Clause incorporates principles of justice "so rooted in the traditions and conscience of our people as to be ranked as fundamental." *Snyder v. Massachusetts*, 291 U.S. 97, 105 (1934). In subsequent cases, the Court continued to ask whether a particular protection was "implicit in the concept of ordered liberty" such that it was difficult to imagine a procedure being fair without it. *Palko v. Connecticut*, 302 U.S. 319, 325 (1937).

Significantly, the Court didn't just apply the *procedural* protections of the Bill of Rights to the states; it also applied the *substantive* protections such as the First Amendment's protection of free speech. The *Powell* Court alluded to this development in its opinion, citing *Chicago, Burlington & Quincy R.R. Co. v. Chicago*, 166 U.S. 226 (1897), which considered it a violation of due process to take property without just compensation. The *Powell* Court also cited *Gitlow v. New York*, which held that the "liberty" protected by the Fourteenth Amendment included "the liberty of speech and of the press." 268 U.S. 652, 664 (1925). As we will discuss in detail in the next section, these opinions considered no procedure fair if a state passed a law that was arbitrary, irrational, or inconsistent with "fundamental" principles of liberty and justice. *Id.* at 666. Along with *Powell*, they paved the way for the widespread incorporation of the Bill of Rights against the states—particularly after Justice Hugo Black, like Harlan before him, became convinced that the Fourteenth Amendment had been intended to incorporate the Bill of Rights against the states. *See Adamson v. California*, 332 U.S. 46, 68 (1947) (Black, J., dissenting).

When Chief Justice Earl Warren joined the Supreme Court in 1953, the Court systematically and individually began to make nearly every provision of the Bill of Rights "wholly applicable to the States" via the Fourteenth Amendment's Due Process Clause. *Abington Sch. Dist. v. Schempp*, 374 U.S. 203, 215 (1963). Instead of asking, as did *Powell*, whether a civilized system of justice could be imagined that didn't include a particular procedural safeguard, the Court began to simply look to the Bill of Rights to determine which criminal procedures counted as fundamental. *See Washington v. Texas*, 388 U.S. 14, 18 (1967). Once the Court imputed a provision of the Bill of Rights to the states, the Court applied the provision identically against state governments as against the federal government—meaning that the holdings of cases like *Powell* became as much a part of the Court's Sixth

Amendment jurisprudence as its Fourteenth Amendment jurisprudence. *See Malloy v. Hogan*, 378 U.S. 1, 10 (1964).

As we will see later (section 44.3), the Court also eventually engaged in the process of *reverse incorporation* by which it interpreted the Fifth Amendment's Due Process Clause as if it included language specific to the states, such as the clause of the Fourteenth Amendment that prohibits states from "deny[ing] to any person within its jurisdiction the equal protection of the laws." *See Bolling v. Sharpe*, 347 U.S. 497, 498–99 (1954).

Today, nearly every provision of the Bill of Rights has been incorporated against the states. For the First Amendment, see *Hamilton v. Regents*, 293 U.S. 245 (1934) (Free Exercise Clause); *Everson v. Bd. of Educ.*, 330 U.S. 1 (1947) (Establishment Clause); *Gitlow v. New York*, 268 U.S. 652 (1925) (Free Speech Clause); *Near v. Minnesota ex rel. Olson*, 283 U.S. 697 (1931) (Free Press Clause); *De Jonge v. Oregon*, 299 U.S. 353 (1937) (Assembly and Petition Clauses). For the Second Amendment, see *McDonald v. Chicago*, 561 U.S. 742 (2010). For the Fourth Amendment, see *Wolf v. Colorado*, 338 U.S. 25 (1949); *Mapp v. Ohio*, 367 U.S. 643 (1961) (exclusionary rule). For the Fifth Amendment, see *Benton v. Maryland*, 395 U.S. 784 (1969) (Double Jeopardy Clause); *Malloy v. Hogan*, 378 U.S. 1 (1964) (Self-Incrimination Clause) (overruling *Twining*, 211 U.S. 78); *Chi., Burlington & Quincy R.R. Co. v. City of Chicago*, 166 U.S. 226 (1897) (Takings Clause). For the Sixth Amendment, see *Klopfer v. North Carolina*, 386 U.S. 213 (1967) (Speedy Trial Clause); *In re Oliver*, 333 U.S. 257 (Notice of Accusation Clause); *Duncan v. Louisiana*, 391 U.S. 145 (1968) (Jury Trial Clause); *Irvin v. Dowd*, 366 U.S. 717 (1961) (Impartial Jury Clause); *Pointer v. Texas*, 380 U.S. 400 (1965) (Confrontation Clause); *Washington v. Texas*, 388 U.S. 14 (1967) (Compulsory Process Clause); *Powell v. Alabama*, 287 U.S. 45 (1932) (Counsel Clause). For the Eighth Amendment, see *Louisiana ex rel. Francis v. Resweber*, 329 U.S. 459 (1947) (Cruel and Unusual Punishment Clause); *Timbs v. Indiana*, 139 S. Ct. 682 (2019) (Excessive Fines Clause).

The only provisions that remain unincorporated include the Third Amendment, which has never been interpreted by the Supreme Court; the Fifth Amendment's Indictment Clause, which is still governed by *Hurtado*; the Seventh Amendment's requirement of a jury trial in civil cases, *see Minneapolis & St. Louis R.R. v. Bombolis*, 241 U.S. 211 (1916); and the Eighth Amendment's Excessive Bail Clause.

NOTE: ELEMENTS OF DUE PROCESS IN CRIMINAL CASES

Beyond the Bill of Rights, the Due Process Clauses of the Fifth and Fourteenth Amendments have been interpreted to require certain procedural safeguards to protect criminal defendants. In contrast with in the civil context, where *Mathews* focuses on reducing the risk of mistaken deprivations, procedural due process in the criminal context asks whether a defendant was "exposed to a procedure offensive to a fundamental principle of justice." *Nelson v. Colorado*, 137 S. Ct. 1249, 1255 (2017) (quoting *Medina v. California*, 505 U.S. 437, 445 (1992)).

Initiation of the prosecution. As the Supreme Court conclusively held in *Hurtado*, the Due Process Clause doesn't require a state to initiate a prosecution with a specific procedure, such as an indictment as opposed to information. But whatever procedure a state uses, it must give a defendant sufficient notice of the charged offense to adequately prepare a defense. *Smith v. O'Grady*, 312 U.S. 329, 334 (1941). For similar reasons, the Court has prohibited a state from changing a charge midway through a trial or during the appellate process. *See In re Ruffalo*, 390 U.S. 544, 551–52 (1968); *Cole v. Arkansas*, 333 U.S. 196, 201 (1948).

Pretrial detention. Because all criminal defendants are presumed innocent until proven guilty, the Court has held that "a detainee may not be punished prior to an adjudication of guilt in accordance with due process of law." *Bell v. Wolfish*, 441 U.S. 520, 536 (1979). Instead, "due process requires that the nature and duration of commitment bear some reasonable relation to the purpose for which the individual is committed." *Jackson v. Indiana*, 406 U.S. 715, 738 (1972). Applying this standard, the Court has allowed governments to impose restrictions that are "reasonably related to a legitimate governmental objective," including protecting society from the potential consequences of pretrial crime, *Schall v. Martin*, 467 U.S. 253, 271 (1984); and ensuring detainees' presence at trial, *Wolfish*, 441 U.S. at 539.

Clarity and vagueness. The Court has held that one of the core purposes of the Due Process Clause in the civil and criminal context is to ensure that every person is given sufficient notice of how to avoid being deprived of their life, liberty, or property. *Musser v. Utah*, 333 U.S. 95, 97 (1948). Accordingly, the Court has declared that a statute or conviction is *void for vagueness* if it violates this standard. Unconstitutionally vague statutes and convictions come in many forms. For example, the Court has invalidated statutes that have failed "to give adequate guidance to those who would be law-abiding." *Id.*; *see, e.g.*, *Papachristou v. City of Jacksonville*, 405 U.S. 156, 156 n.1 (1972) (invalidating a statute that made it a crime to "stroll[ ] around from place to place with no lawful purpose"). It has invalidated statutes that "impermissibly delegate[ ] basic policy matters to policemen, judges, and juries for resolution on an ad hoc and subjective basis, with the attendant dangers of arbitrary and discriminatory application." *Grayned v. City of Rockford*, 408 U.S. 104, 108–09 (1972). It has vacated convictions that were "unexpected and indefensible by reference to the law which had been express prior to the conduct in issue." *Bouie v. City of Columbia*, 378 U.S. 347, 354 (1964). And it has invalidated statutes whose terms are so indeterminate or difficult to define that they invite arbitrary enforcement by judges. *See Johnson v. United States*, 576 U.S. 591, 606 (2015).

Entrapment and false identification. The Supreme Court has long recognized the defense of "entrapment," calling it fundamentally unfair for government officials to "implant in the mind of an innocent person the disposition to commit [an] alleged offense and induce its commission in order that they may prosecute." *Sorrells v. United States*, 287 U.S. 435, 442 (1932). Relatedly, the Court has held that the Due Process Clause generally prohibits law enforcement officers from prompting a witness to identify a criminal suspect with procedures that create a "substantial likelihood of misidentification." *Perry v. New Hampshire*, 565 U.S. 228, 239 (2012).

Fair trials. As in the civil context, the Supreme Court has interpreted the Due Process Clause to require a trial before an impartial tribunal. This requirement is violated when "the probability of actual bias on the part of the judge or decisionmaker is too high to be constitutionally tolerable." *Withrow v. Larkin*, 421 U.S. 35, 47 (1975).

Applying this standard, the Court has vacated one conviction that was overseen by a trial judge who, at the time, was being investigated by the prosecutor. *Rippo v. Baker*, 137 S. Ct. 905, 907 (2017). It has also vacated another conviction that was overseen by a judge who was financially rewarded for convicting the defendants before him. *Tumey v. Ohio*, 273 U.S. 510, 535 (1927).

Prosecutorial misconduct. In *Brady v. Maryland*, 373 U.S. 83 (1963), the Supreme Court invalidated the conviction of a man for murder where the prosecution had withheld a written statement by another person who had confessed to committing the murder. Given the obvious risk of a mistaken deprivation of liberty in such a situation, the Court held that "the suppression by the prosecution of evidence favorable to an accused upon request violates due process where the evidence is material either to guilt or to punishment, irrespective of the good faith or bad faith of the prosecution." *Brady*, 373 U.S. at 87.

Burden of proof. For decades before the 1960s, the proper burden of proof for criminal trials was widely assumed to be proof "beyond a reasonable doubt." *See, e.g.*, *Speiser v. Randall*, 357 U.S. 513 (1958). The issue didn't reach the Supreme Court, however, until it decided in the late 1960s that due process standards applied to juvenile prosecutions that had previously employed a lower standard. *See In re Gault*, 387 U.S. 1 (1967). The Court ultimately concluded that in all criminal proceedings, "the Due Process Clause protects the accused against conviction except upon proof beyond a reasonable doubt of every fact necessary to constitute the crime with which he is charged." *In re Winship*, 397 U.S. 358, 364 (1970).

The holding of *In re Winship* had two important implications.

First, it established the standard by which appellate courts could review the sufficiency of the evidence to support a criminal conviction: "[T]he relevant question is whether, after viewing the evidence in the light most favorable to the prosecution, *any* rational trier of fact could have found the essential elements of the crime beyond a reasonable doubt." *Jackson v. Virginia*, 443 U.S. 307, 319 (1979). This standard replaced an earlier standard that turned on whether the jury was properly instructed. *See Musacchio v. United States*, 577 U.S. 237, 243 (2016).

Second, *In re Winship* also strongly suggested that it would be improper for a state to place the burden of proving any element of an offense on the defendant as opposed to the prosecution. In the decade afterward, the Court went back and forth about whether the Due Process Clause prohibited requiring a defendant to prove an "affirmative defense," such as an insanity defense or an allegation of "extreme emotional disturbance" that might reduce a homicide to manslaughter. *See, e.g.*, *Patterson v. New York*, 432 U.S. 197, 206 (1977); *Mullaney v. Wilbur*, 421 U.S. 684, 704 (1975). Eventually, the Court declared in *Apprendi v. New Jersey*, that any fact that contributes to an additional likelihood of punishment is an "essential element" that the prosecution must prove before a jury beyond a reasonable doubt. 530 U.S. 466, 490 (2000). But *Apprendi* did not disrupt an earlier line of cases that allowed states to create statutory presumptions by which proof of one fact might give a jury a rational basis for inferring the existence of a required element of an offense. *See Leary v. United States*, 395 U.S. 6, 36 (1969).

Competence and insanity. The Supreme Court has long considered it inconsistent with due process for a state to try or sentence a defendant who is insane or incompetent to stand trial. *See, e.g.*, *Pate v. Robinson*, 383 U.S. 375, 378 (1966). But as long as states are "informed by the medical community's diagnostic framework," *Moore v. Texas*, 137 S. Ct. 1039, 1048 (2017), states have wide discretion to define insanity and incompetence. *Kahler v. Kansas*, 140 S. Ct. 1021, 1037 (2020).

Guilty pleas and sentencing. The Supreme Court has interpreted the Due Process Clause to prohibit a government from coercing a guilty plea from a defendant. *United States v. Jackson*, 390 U.S. 570 (1968). Applying this standard, the Court has held that plea bargaining isn't inherently coercive. *Id.* at 583. But to provide some safeguards from coercive pleas, the Court has prohibited trial judges from accepting guilty pleas without first inquiring whether each defendant is pleading voluntarily, knowingly, and understandingly. *North Carolina v. Alford*, 400 U.S. 24, 37 (1971).

Yet the Court has held that a guilty plea, like a jury verdict, can provide the factual basis for a sentencing judge to impose a punishment consistent with the Due Process Clause. The Court has also held that a sentencing judge may also consider additional information from other sources as long as the information doesn't authorize the judge to increase the defendant's punishment beyond what the plea or verdict would allow. *See Hurst v. Florida*, 577 U.S. 92, 97–98 (2016).

Appeals. The Supreme Court has interpreted the Due Process Clause not to require a state to provide either appellate or postconviction review of a final judgment in a criminal case. *McKane v. Durston*, 153 U.S. 684, 687 (1894). But where a defendant alleges a federal constitutional violation, the Court has held that a state must provide *some* postconviction remedy. *Frank v. Mangum*, 237 U.S. 309, 345 (1915).

The Court has, however, allowed a state to exercise its discretion in choosing whatever postconviction remedy it wants to use. Such a remedy may lack ordinary procedural protections such as the right to counsel or the right to mitigating evidence. *See Dist. Att'y's Office for the Third Judicial Dist. v. Osborne*, 557 U.S. 52, 73 (2009). But when a state does choose to provide criminal defendants with the opportunity for appellate review, the Court has prohibited the state from conditioning this opportunity on the ability of defendants to pay. *Griffin v. Illinois*, 351 U.S. 12, 18 (1956).

NOTE: RIGHTS OF PRISONERS

Once a state has convicted a defendant, any subsequent deprivations of liberty are governed by the same *Mathews* standard that governs civil procedure. *See Nelson v. Colorado*, 137 S. Ct. 1249, 1255 (2017).

Existence of a liberty or property interest. The most basic "liberty" interest protected by the Due Process Clause is the liberty from bodily restraint. But because this liberty interest is necessarily sacrificed by a criminal conviction, the Supreme Court has held that a prisoner may challenge a further deprivation of liberty only if some form of positive entitlement guarantees a particular benefit. *See Meachum v. Fano*, 427 U.S. 215, 224 (1976). For example, the Court has held that a prisoner has no inherent right to parole or executive clemency absent a statute or some other entitlement protecting such a right—in which case the deprivation of that right can require notice, a hearing, and other procedural safeguards. *See, e.g.*, *Ohio Adult Parole Auth. v. Woodard*, 523 U.S. 272, 276 (1998).

Within the prison itself, the Court has occasionally defined *entitlement* narrowly to include mandatory regulations that substantially limit the exercise of discretion. *Ky. Dep't of Corr. v. Thompson*, 490 U.S. 454, 459–63 (1989). More recently, however, the Court has held that "the touchstone of the inquiry into the existence of a protected, state-created liberty interest in avoiding restrictive conditions of confinement is not the language of regulations regarding those conditions but the nature of those conditions themselves 'in relation to the ordinary incidents of prison life.' " *Wilkinson v. Austin*, 545 U.S. 209, 223 (2005). Applying this test, when a prisoner asked for due process protections before being assigned to segregated confinement for thirty days, the Court declined to intervene in such an "ordinary" assignment. *Sandin v. Conner*, 515 U.S. 472, 484–85 (1995). But when a prisoner asked for due process protections before being indefinitely assigned to a supermax prison, the Court agreed that such an atypical decision warranted some safeguards. *Wilkinson*, 545 U.S. at 224.

Negligent officers. Although the Supreme Court once applied procedural due process standards to avoid mistaken deprivations of property or liberty where prison officers acted negligently, *Parratt v. Taylor*, 451 U.S. 527, 542 (1981), the Court has since held that negligent acts by state officials do not implicate the Due Process Clause, *Daniels v. Williams*, 474 U.S. 327, 332 (1986).

Probation and parole. For a person who is in prison and eligible for parole or clemency, the Court has rejected the argument that even a high possibility of release is a liberty interest whose deprivation would implicate the Due Process Clause. *See, e.g.*, *Woodard*, 523 U.S. at 288. Instead, the Court has considered clemency and parole matters of discretion that are typically not subject to judicial review unless a positive entitlement requires that a prisoner receive certain benefits. *Bd. of Pardons v. Allen*, 482 U.S. 369, 381 (1987).

By contrast, when a prisoner is released from prison on probation or parole, any revocation of that status is a deprivation of liberty that implicates the Due Process Clause. *Gagnon v. Scarpelli*, 411 U.S. 778, 791 (1973).

Civil commitment. In the context of "protective commitment" for people who have a severe mental illness, addiction, or intellectual disability, the Supreme Court has held that "a State cannot constitutionally confine without more a nondangerous individual who is capable of surviving safely in freedom by himself or with the help of willing and responsible family members or friends." *O'Connor v. Donaldson*, 422 U.S. 563, 576 (1975). When a fact finder must determine whether involuntary commitment is warranted, the Court typically imposes a "clear and convincing" standard. *Addington v. Texas*, 441 U.S. 418, 433 (1979). Even when someone voluntarily commits themselves to a hospital, the Court has held that some sort of hearing may be necessary to prevent an incompetent person from mistakenly committing themselves. *See Zinermon v. Burch*, 494 U.S. 113, 139 (1990).

CHAPTER 41

What Limitations Do the Due Process Clauses of the Fifth and Fourteenth Amendments Impose on the Substantive Power of Government to Deprive People of Their Property or Liberty to Make Economic Decisions?

FIFTH AMENDMENT (1791): No person shall . . . be deprived of life, liberty, or property, without due process of law; nor shall private property be taken for public use, without just compensation.

FOURTEENTH AMENDMENT (1868), SECTION 1: No State shall . . . deprive any person of life, liberty, or property, without due process of law. . . .

41.1 The Origins of Substantive Due Process

As discussed in the previous section, the phrase *due process of law* was traditionally understood as a protection of certain *procedures*—a minimal set of safeguards necessary to prevent the government from mistakenly or unfairly depriving people of their life, liberty, or property. But the phrase also, historically, has been used in reference to certain *substantive laws* as well. As early as *Calder v. Bull*, 3 U.S. (3 Dall.) 386 (1798), members of the Supreme Court argued that some kinds of laws are so inherently unfair that no set of procedural safeguards could cure their arbitrary deprivation of life, liberty, or property. Such laws, wrote Justice Samuel Chase, included "[a] law that [retroactively] punished a citizen for an innocent action . . .; a law that destroys, or impairs, the lawful private contracts of citizens; a law that makes a man a Judge in his own cause; or a law that takes property from A. and gives it to B." *Calder*, 3 U.S. (3 Dall.) at 388.

When Daniel Webster represented his alma mater in *Trustees of Dartmouth College v. Woodward*, 17 U.S. (4 Wheat.) 518 (1819), the famous Contracts Clause case, he similarly argued that the phrase *due process of law* had to limit the substantive scope of a legislature's power.

Otherwise, "[t]he administration of justice would be an empty form, an idle ceremony." *Dartmouth Coll.*, 17 U.S. (4 Wheat.) at 582. Webster warned that if a legislature could pass "acts of attainder, bills of pains and penalties, acts of confiscation, acts reversing judgments, and acts directly transferring one man's estate to another," then individuals could be deprived of their life, liberty, and property without notice or an opportunity to protect themselves in court. *Id.* at 581–82.

Although the *Dartmouth College* Court had no occasion to adopt Webster's argument, the Court did adopt it three decades later. In *Murray's Lessee v. Hoboken Land & Improvement Co.*, the Court wrote that the Due Process Clause could not be interpreted to give Congress "power to enact any process which might be devised." 59 U.S. (18 How.) 272, 276 (1856). And in *Dred Scott v. Sandford*, 60 U.S. (19 How.) 393 (1857), the Supreme Court infamously interpreted the Fifth Amendment's Due Process Clause as a substantive limit on Congress's power to summarily deprive enslavers of their property interest in enslaved people. Writing for the majority, Chief Justice Roger Taney declared that a law depriving a slaveholder of his property, "merely because he came himself or brought his property into a particular Territory of the United States, and who had committed no offence against the laws, could hardly be dignified with the name of due process of law." *Dred Scott*, 60 U.S. (19 How.) at 450.

Although this particular holding was soon repudiated by the Civil War, *Dred Scott* reaffirmed a long-standing view that the Due Process Clause prohibited "a law that takes property from A. and gives it to B," *Calder*, 3 U.S. (3 Dall.) at 388, or a law that functioned as an "act[ ] of confiscation," *Dartmouth Coll.*, 17 U.S. (4 Wheat.) at 581.

41.1.1

Mugler v. Kansas

123 U.S. 623 (1887)

When the Supreme Court first interpreted the Fourteenth Amendment's Due Process Clause in the *Slaughter-House Cases*, 83 U.S. (16 Wall.) 36 (1873), the majority was dismissive of the argument that the clause had anything to do with Louisiana's requirement that butchers perform their work in a state-sanctioned monopoly. But Justices Stephen Field and Joseph Bradley, writing in dissent, forcefully declared that the "right to choose one's calling is an essential part of that liberty which it is the object of government to protect; and a calling, when chosen, is a man's property and right." *Slaughter-House Cases*, 83 U.S. (16 Wall.) at 51 (Bradley, J., dissenting). Bradley added that "[l]iberty and property are not protected where these rights are arbitrarily assailed." *Id.* He therefore argued that the Due Process Clause prohibited Louisiana or any other state from arbitrarily interfering with a person's liberty or property—regardless of what procedure it used to do so.

Two years later, these dissents effectively became the law. In *Citizens' Savings & Loan Ass'n v. City of Topeka*, 87 U.S. (20 Wall.) 655 (1875), the Supreme Court considered a Kansas law that authorized Topeka to use general tax revenue to subsidize the city's private manufacturing companies. A local financial institution objected that raising money from the public and donating that money to a private corporation "pervert[ed] the right of taxation." *Loan Ass'n*, 87 U.S. (20 Wall.) at 659. The Supreme Court agreed. "[T]here are such rights in every free government beyond the control of the State," the Court wrote. "A government which recognized no such rights, which held the lives, the liberty, and the property of its citizens subject at all times to the absolute disposition and unlimited control of even the most democratic depository of power, is after all but a despotism." *Id.* at 662. Invoking *Calder*, the Court emphasized that one of the limitations "which grow out of the essential nature of all free governments" was a prohibition on laws enacting that property "now owned by A. should no longer be his, but should henceforth be the property of B." *Id.* at 663. The Court conceded that states like Kansas could levy taxes in aid of "public purposes" but held that spending tax revenue "upon favored individuals to aid private enterprises and build up private fortunes, is none the less a robbery because it is done under the forms of law and is called taxation." *Id.* at 664. The *Loan Ass'n* decision was a watershed in the Supreme Court's history. For the first time, the Court held that the Constitution prohibited not only unfair state *procedures* but also state laws whose *substantive* effect was to "arbitrarily" deprive people of their property.

The following year, in *Munn v. Illinois*, 94 U.S. 113 (1876), the Court confirmed that this limit was grounded in the Fourteenth Amendment's Due Process Clause. The *Munn* Court held that a government had no power under the Due Process Clause to deprive people of their "purely and exclusively private" property by decree. *Munn*, 94 U.S. at 124. But the *Munn* Court added that when a person "devotes his property to a use in which the public has an interest, he, in effect, grants to the public an interest in that use, and must submit to be controlled by the public for the common good, to the extent of the interest he has thus created." *Id.* at 126. Such regulable property, the Court wrote, was "clothed with a public interest." *Id.* In distinguishing "exclusively private" property from property "clothed with a public interest," the *Munn* Court also announced that it would defer to the legislature: "[e]very statute is presumed to be constitutional." *Id.* at 123. On this basis, the Court upheld an Illinois law that required grain-storage companies to charge a reasonable rate to farmers, calling this law a regulation of private property "for the public good." *Id.* at 126. "We know that this is a power which may be abused," the Court conceded; "but that is no argument against its existence. For protection against abuses by legislatures the people must resort to the polls, not to the courts." *Id.* at 134.

Yet just two years later, in *Davidson v. City of New Orleans*, the Court added that a state could not "make anything due process of law which, by its own legislation, it chooses to declare such." 96 U.S. 97, 102 (1878). Otherwise, the Due Process Clause would be "of no avail, or ha[ve] no application where the invasion of private rights is effected under the forms of State legislation." *Id.*

Loan Ass'n, *Munn*, and *Davidson* planted the seeds of what became known as the doctrine of "substantive due process": the idea that the Due Process Clause imposed substantive limits on a legislature's power. This doctrine bloomed in the following opinion, *Mugler v. Kansas*, 123 U.S. 623 (1887), which also addressed another blossoming trend: Prohibition.

In 1880, Kansas became the first state in the Union to amend its constitution to prohibit the manufacture and sale of alcoholic beverages. This amendment had a predictably harmful effect on breweries throughout the state, whose business suddenly became worthless. One of the state's breweries belonged to a man named Peter Mugler, who had just spent thousands of dollars constructing a custom brewery. When Kansas passed statutes to enforce its new prohibition, the state indicted Mugler for continuing to brew beer.

In his defense, Mugler objected that Kansas's constitutional provision couldn't be enforced against him without violating the Fourteenth Amendment. By forcing him to close his brewery, Mugler argued, the state had effectively taken his private property without just compensation—an arbitrary and unfair deprivation. In response, state prosecutors argued that the regulation wasn't arbitrary but was instead motivated by the state's public purpose of protecting the health, morals, and safety of its residents.

In considering Mugler's challenge, the Supreme Court articulated a new test for evaluating whether a state law complied with the Due Process Clause's substantive requirements—a test that did not save Mugler.

■ MR. JUSTICE HARLAN delivered the opinion of the Court.[1]

These cases involve an inquiry into the validity of certain statutes of Kansas relating to the manufacture and sale of intoxicating liquors. . . . The general question in each case is, whether the [statutes] are in conflict with that clause of the Fourteenth Amendment, which provides that "no State shall . . . deprive any person of life, liberty, or property, without due process of law." . . .

[Has Kansas deprived Mugler of his right to manufacture his own property?]

[T]he States of the Union [have the right] to control their purely internal affairs, and, in so doing, to protect the health, morals, and safety of their people by regulations that do not interfere with the execution of the powers of the general

---

1 **As You Read, Consider:** Had Peter Mugler raised a *procedural* due process challenge to the Kansas law, he would have lost. There is no plausible argument that additional procedural safeguards would have reduced the risk of a mistaken or unfair deprivation of liberty or property. Why, then, is the Due *Process* Clause implicated by the Kansas law at all? Does Justice John Harlan agree that the clause is relevant here?

government, or violate rights secured by the Constitution of the United States. The power to establish such regulations, as was said in *Gibbons v. Ogden,* 9 Wheat. 1, 203, reaches everything within the territory of a State not surrendered to the national government.

It is, however, contended, that, although the State may prohibit the manufacture of intoxicating liquors for sale or barter within her limits, for general use as a beverage, "no convention or legislature has the right, under our form of government, to prohibit any citizen from manufacturing for his own use, or for export, or storage, any article of food or drink not endangering or affecting the rights of others." The argument made in support of the first branch of this proposition, briefly stated, is, that in the implied compact between the State and the citizen certain rights are reserved by the latter, which are guaranteed by the constitutional provision protecting persons against being deprived of life, liberty, or property, without due process of law, and with which the State cannot interfere; that among those rights is that of manufacturing for one's use either food or drink; and that while, according to the doctrines of the Commune, the State may control the tastes, appetites, habits, dress, food, and drink of the people, our system of government, based upon the individuality and intelligence of the citizen, does not claim to control him, except as to his conduct to others, leaving him the sole judge as to all that only affects himself.[2]

It will be observed that the proposition, and the argument made in support of it, equally concede that the right to manufacture drink for one's personal use is subject to the condition that such manufacture does not endanger or affect the rights of others. If such manufacture does prejudicially affect the rights and interests of the community, it follows, from the very premises stated, that society has the power to protect itself, by legislation, against the injurious consequences of that business. As was said in *Munn v. Illinois,* 94 U.S. 113, 124, while power does not exist with the whole people to control rights that are purely and exclusively private, government may require "each citizen to so conduct himself, and so use his own property, as not unnecessarily to injure another."

But by whom, or by what authority, is it to be determined whether the manufacture of particular articles of drink, either for general use or for the personal use of the maker, will injuriously affect the public? Power to determine such questions, so as to bind all, must exist somewhere; else society will be at the mercy of the few, who, regarding only their own appetites or passions, may be willing to imperil the peace and security of the many, provided only they are permitted to do as they please. Under our system that power is lodged with the legislative branch of the government. It belongs to that department to exert what are known as the police powers of the State, and to determine, primarily, what measures are appropriate or needful for the protection of the public morals, the public health, or the public safety.

It does not at all follow that every statute enacted ostensibly for the promotion of these ends, is to be accepted as a legitimate exertion of the police powers of the State. There are, of necessity, limits beyond which legislation cannot rightfully go. While every possible presumption is to be indulged in favor of the validity of a statute,

---

[2] **Questions:** Harlan here is alluding to the Paris Commune: a socialist, worker-led government that briefly ruled Paris in 1871. He is observing that *radical Parisians* might be willing to subordinate individual autonomy to the common good, but *Americans* adopt a classical liberal perspective. He paraphrases John Stuart Mill, who famously argued that "the only purpose for which power can be rightfully exercised over any member of a civilized community, against his will, is to prevent harm to others." John Stuart Mill, *On Liberty* 22 (1859).

Do you agree that a law that violates Mill's "harm principle" is so inherently unfair that no process could prevent its deprivations from being unconstitutionally arbitrary? How does Harlan decide whether Kansas's law violates the harm principle?

the courts must obey the Constitution rather than the law-making department of government, and must, upon their own responsibility, determine whether, in any particular case, these limits have been passed. . . . The courts are not bound by mere forms, nor are they to be misled by mere pretences. They are at liberty—indeed, are under a solemn duty—to look at the substance of things, whenever they enter upon the inquiry whether the legislature has transcended the limits of its authority. If, therefore, a statute purporting to have been enacted to protect the public health, the public morals, or the public safety, has no real or substantial relation to those objects, or is a palpable invasion of rights secured by the fundamental law, it is the duty of the courts to so adjudge, and thereby give effect to the Constitution.[3]

Keeping in view these principles, as governing the relations of the judicial and legislative departments of government with each other it is difficult to perceive any ground for the judiciary to declare that the prohibition by Kansas of the manufacture or sale, within her limits, of intoxicating liquors for general use there as a beverage, is not fairly adapted to the end of protecting the community against the evils which confessedly result from the excessive use of ardent spirits. There is no justification for holding that the State, under the guise merely of police regulations, is here aiming to deprive the citizen of his constitutional rights; for we cannot shut out of view the fact, within the knowledge of all, that the public health, the public morals, and the public safety, may be endangered by the general use of intoxicating drinks; nor the fact, established by statistics accessible to every one, that the idleness, disorder, pauperism, and crime existing in the country are, in some degree at least, traceable to this evil. If, therefore, a state deems the absolute prohibition of the manufacture and sale, within her limits, of intoxicating liquors . . ., to be necessary to the peace and security of society, the courts cannot, without usurping legislative functions, override the will of the people as thus expressed by their chosen representatives. They have nothing to do with the mere policy of legislation. Indeed, it is a fundamental principle in our institutions, indispensable to the preservation of public liberty, that one of the separate departments of government shall not usurp powers committed by the Constitution to another department. And so, if, in the judgment of the legislature, the manufacture of intoxicating liquors for the maker's own use, as a beverage, would tend to cripple, if it did not defeat, the effort to guard the community against the evils attending the excessive use of such liquors, it is not for the courts, upon their views as to what is best and safest for the community, to disregard the legislative determination of that question. So far from such a regulation having no relation to the general end sought to be accomplished, the entire scheme of prohibition, as embodied in the constitution and laws of Kansas, might fail, if the right of each citizen to manufacture intoxicating liquors for his own use as a beverage were recognized. Such a right does not inhere in citizenship. Nor can it be said that government interferes with or impairs any one's constitutional rights of liberty or of property, when it determines that the manufacture and sale of intoxicating drinks, for general or individual use, as a beverage, are, or may become, hurtful to society, and constitute, therefore, a business in which no one may lawfully engage. Those rights are best secured, in our government, by the observance, upon the part of all, of such regulations as are established by competent authority to promote the common good. No one may rightfully do that which the law-making power, upon reasonable grounds, declares to be prejudicial to the general welfare.

---

[3] **Questions:** Harlan writes that "every possible presumption is to be indulged in favor of the validity of a statute," yet it is the Court's role to determine whether a statute is *really* designed to prevent harm or whether the objectives of a statute are "mere pretences." Would you characterize this posture as deferential or skeptical? How, precisely, does Harlan determine whether Kansas's asserted purpose of preventing harm is pretextual?

This conclusion is unavoidable, unless the Fourteenth Amendment of the Constitution takes from the States of the Union those powers of police that were reserved at the time the original Constitution was adopted. But this court has declared, upon full consideration, in *Barbier v. Connolly*, 113 U.S. 27, 31, that the Fourteenth Amendment had no such effect. After observing, among other things, that that Amendment forbade the arbitrary deprivation of life or liberty, and the arbitrary spoliation of property . . ., the court said: "But neither the Amendment—broad and comprehensive as it is—nor any other amendment, was designed to interfere with the power of the State, sometimes termed its police power, to prescribe regulations to promote the health, peace, morals, education, and good order of the people, and to legislate so as to increase the industries of the State, develop its resources, and add to its wealth and prosperity."

[Has Kansas taken Mugler's property without just compensation?]

Undoubtedly the State, when providing, by legislation, for the protection of the public health, the public morals, or the public safety, is subject to the paramount authority of the Constitution of the United States, and may not violate rights secured or guaranteed by that instrument, or interfere with the execution of the powers confided to the general government.

Upon this ground—if we do not misapprehend the position of defendants—it is contended that, as the primary and principal use of beer is as a beverage; as their respective breweries were erected when it was lawful to engage in the manufacture of beer for every purpose; as such establishments will become of no value as property, or, at least, will be materially diminished in value, if not employed in the manufacture of beer for every purpose; the prohibition upon their being so employed is, in effect, a taking of property for public use without compensation, and depriving the citizen of his property without due process of law.[4] In other words, although the State, in the exercise of her police powers, may lawfully prohibit the manufacture and sale, within her limits, of intoxicating liquors to be used as a beverage, legislation having that object in view cannot be enforced against those who, at the time, happen to own property, the chief value of which consists in its fitness for such manufacturing purposes, unless compensation is first made for the diminution in the value of their property, resulting from such prohibitory enactments.

This interpretation of the Fourteenth Amendment is inadmissible. It cannot be supposed that the States intended, by adopting that Amendment, to impose restraints upon the exercise of their powers for the protection of the safety, health, or morals of the community. . . . "No legislature can bargain away the public health or the public morals. . . ." [*Stone v. Mississippi*, 101 U.S. 814, 816.]

The principle, that no person shall be deprived of life, liberty, or property, without due process of law, was embodied, in substance, in the constitutions of nearly all, if not all, of the States at the time of the adoption of the Fourteenth Amendment; and it has never been regarded as incompatible with the principle, equally vital, because essential to the peace and safety of society, that all property in this country is held

[4] **Question:** Mugler makes two arguments in this case. The first, rejected above, argues that the Kansas law violates the Fourteenth Amendment's Due Process Clause by depriving him of his *liberty* to manufacture his own food and drink without due process of law.

This second argument argues that the law deprives him of his *property*. The Fifth Amendment declares that "private property [shall not] be taken for public use, without just compensation." Mugler is arguing (1) that the Fourteenth Amendment's Due Process Clause applies this prohibition to the states, and (2) due process requires that Kansas pay him "just compensation" for taking away his property. How does Harlan evaluate each element of this argument?

under the implied obligation that the owner's use of it shall not be injurious to the community. . . .

[T]he present case must be governed by principles that do not involve the power of eminent domain, in the exercise of which property may not be taken for public use without compensation. A prohibition simply upon the use of property for purposes that are declared, by valid legislation, to be injurious to the health, morals, or safety of the community, cannot, in any just sense, be deemed a taking or an appropriation of property for the public benefit. Such legislation does not disturb the owner in the control or use of his property for lawful purposes, nor restrict his right to dispose of it, but is only a declaration by the State that its use by any one, for certain forbidden purposes, is prejudicial to the public interests. Nor can legislation of that character come within the Fourteenth Amendment, in any case, unless it is apparent that its real object is not to protect the community, or to promote the general well-being, but, under the guise of police regulation, to deprive the owner of his liberty and property, without due process of law. The power which the States have of prohibiting such use by individuals of their property as will be prejudicial to the health, the morals, or the safety of the public, is not—and, consistently with the existence and safety of organized society, cannot be—burdened with the condition that the State must compensate such individual owners for pecuniary losses they may sustain, by reason of their not being permitted, by a noxious use of their property, to inflict injury upon the community. . . .[5]

41.2 DEPRIVATIONS OF THE LIBERTY TO CONTRACT

The Court in *Mugler v. Kansas* upheld Kansas's power to protect "the public morals, the public health, or the public safety" of its residents—regardless of whether Kansas's exercise of that "police power" incidentally deprived its residents of their liberty or property. 123 U.S. 623, 661 (1887). But what made *Mugler* notable was that the Court held that Kansas's prohibition *would have* violated the Fourteenth Amendment had it been motivated by a different purpose. The Court strongly implied that it would have invalidated the prohibition had it believed "that the State, under the guise merely of police regulations, is here aiming to deprive the citizen of his constitutional rights," *id.* at 662, or that the state's "real object is not to protect the community, or to promote the general well-being, but, under the guise of police regulation, to deprive the owner of his liberty and property," *id.* at 669. The Court upheld the prohibition only after taking judicial notice of "statistics accessible to every one, that the idleness, disorder, pauperism, and crime existing in the country are, in some degree at least, traceable to [alcohol]." *Id.* at 662.

Also notable was *Mugler*'s capacious view of the "liberty" and "property" protected by the Due Process Clause. By these terms, the Court referred not only to people's physical freedom and real estate but also to their freedom to control their own occupation—not to mention their "tastes, appetites, habits, dress, food, and drink." *Id.* at 660. The Court's language echoed Justice Stephen Field's and Justice Joseph

[5] **Question:** On Harlan's reading of the Fourteenth Amendment, would any state actions other than the use of eminent domain require "just compensation," as Mugler demands?

Bradley's dissents in the *Slaughter-House Cases*, in which Bradley wrote that the "right to choose one's calling is an essential part of that liberty which it is the object of government to protect; and a calling, when chosen, is a man's property and right." 83 U.S. (16 Wall.) 36, 51 (1873) (Bradley, J., dissenting).

After *Mugler*, the Court began to evaluate deprivations of liberty and property by determining for itself whether the deprivation could be justified as a protection of the health, morals, and safety of a community. As a valid protection of public health, the Court upheld a Massachusetts law that required residents to be vaccinated for smallpox. *See Jacobson v. Massachusetts*, 197 U.S. 11, 35 (1905). As valid protections of public morality, the Court upheld laws that prohibited lotteries, prostitution, and gambling. *See, e.g., Ah Sin v. Wittman*, 198 U.S. 500, 506 (1905). And as a valid protection of public safety, the Court upheld a Utah law that prohibited anyone from working more than eight hours per day in a coal mine or manufacturing plant. *Holden v. Hardy*, 169 U.S. 366, 398 (1898). The Court explained that "it has been found that [mining and manufacturing] can no longer be carried on with due regard to the safety and health of those engaged in them without special protection against the dangers necessarily incident to these employments." *Id.* at 393; *see also Barbier v. Connolly*, 113 U.S. 27, 32 (1885) (same for public laundries).

At the same time, the Court invalidated laws that it considered insufficiently related to health, morals, or safety. One notable example was *Allgeyer v. Louisiana*, 165 U.S. 578 (1897), in which the Court struck down a Louisiana law that prohibited state residents from signing insurance contracts with certain out-of-state companies. The Court not only denied that the law had anything to do with health, morals, or safety, but it also held that the law interfered with residents' "liberty to contract." *Allgeyer*, 165 U.S. at 591. The Court defined this liberty broadly with reference to *Mugler* and the *Slaughter-House Cases*: "In the privilege of pursuing an ordinary calling or trade and of acquiring, holding and selling property must be embraced the right to make all proper contracts in relation thereto." *Id.* at 590.

41.2.1

Lochner v. New York

198 U.S. 45 (1905)

The liberty of contract became a defining feature of the Supreme Court's jurisprudence in the following case, *Lochner v. New York*, 198 U.S. 45 (1905), whose name also became a shorthand for describing the entire era.

In 1895, the New York legislature passed a law regulating the sanitation and working conditions in bakeries. At the time, 90 percent of the state's commercial bakeries were located in the basements of tenement buildings, which were disgusting places to make food. Walls and floors typically consisted of packed dirt. Sewer pipes leaked into rooms. And children worked long hours overnight to prepare food in time for customers at dawn. The new law responded to these concerns by setting minimum sanitary standards, prohibiting workers from sleeping in bakeries, and limiting work to ten hours per day and sixty hours per week. *See* Stephen Budiansky, *Oliver Wendell Holmes* 291 (2019).

Six years later, a state court convicted Joseph Lochner, the owner of a Utica bakery, for permitting one of his employees to work more than sixty hours in a single week. Lochner appealed his conviction on the ground that, like the statute in *Allgeyer*, the New York law violated his "liberty to contract" with employees on whatever terms he so chose. State prosecutors responded that the law was a valid health and safety law no different from the Utah law that prohibited miners from working more than eight hours per day, *Holden*, 169 U.S. 366, and the Massachusetts law that required people to get vaccinated, *Jacobson*, 197 U.S. 11.

The doctrinal issue in *Lochner*, therefore, was whether there was sufficient evidence that New York's "real object" was to protect health and safety. *Lochner*, 198 U.S. at 64. According to the Court, the evidence was insufficient.

■ MR. JUSTICE PECKHAM . . . delivered the opinion of the Court.[6]

The indictment . . . charges that the plaintiff in error violated . . . the labor law of the State of New York, in that he wrongfully and unlawfully required and permitted an employé working for him to work more than sixty hours in one week. . . . The mandate of the statute that "no employé shall be required or permitted to work," is the substantial equivalent of an enactment that "no employé shall contract or agree to work," more than ten hours per day . . . . It is not an act merely fixing the number of hours which shall constitute a legal day's work, but an absolute prohibition upon the employer, permitting, under any circumstances, more than ten hours work to be done in his establishment. The employé may desire to earn the extra money, which would arise from his working more than the prescribed time, but this statute forbids the employer from permitting the employé to earn it.

The statute necessarily interferes with the right of contract between the employer and employés, concerning the number of hours in which the latter may labor in the bakery of the employer. The general right to make a contract in relation to his business is part of the liberty of the individual protected by the Fourteenth Amendment of the Federal Constitution. *Allgeyer v. Louisiana,* 165 U.S. 578. Under that provision no State can deprive any person of life, liberty or property without due process of law. The right to purchase or to sell labor is part of the liberty protected by this amendment, unless there are circumstances which exclude the right. There are, however, certain powers, existing in the sovereignty of each State in the Union,

---

[6] **As You Read, Consider:** In *Mugler v. Kansas*, 123 U.S. 623 (1887), the Supreme Court held that the Due Process Clause embodies the harm principle and allows states to interfere with individual liberty only for the purpose of protecting others from harm. Justice John Harlan thought Kansas could deprive people of their liberty to manufacture liquor because it was "within the knowledge of all, that the public health, the public morals, and the public safety, may be endangered by the general use of intoxicating drinks." *Mugler*, 123 U.S. at 662. What does Justice Rufus Peckham think is the "liberty" at issue in this case? Does he agree with New York that the purpose of its maximum-hour law was to protect the health and safety of bakers?

somewhat vaguely termed police powers, the exact description and limitation of which have not been attempted by the courts. Those powers, broadly stated and without, at present, any attempt at a more specific limitation, relate to the safety, health, morals and general welfare of the public. Both property and liberty are held on such reasonable conditions as may be imposed by the governing power of the State in the exercise of those powers, and with such conditions the Fourteenth Amendment was not designed to interfere. *Mugler v. Kansas,* 123 U.S. 623.

The State, therefore, has power to prevent the individual from making certain kinds of contracts, and in regard to them the Federal Constitution offers no protection. If the contract be one which the State, in the legitimate exercise of its police power, has the right to prohibit, it is not prevented from prohibiting it by the Fourteenth Amendment. Contracts in violation of a statute, either of the Federal or state government, or a contract to let one's property for immoral purposes, or to do any other unlawful act, could obtain no protection from the Federal Constitution, as coming under the liberty of person or of free contract. Therefore, when the State, by its legislature, in the assumed exercise of its police powers, has passed an act which seriously limits the right to labor or the right of contract in regard to their means of livelihood between persons who are [legally competent] (both employer and employé), it becomes of great importance to determine which shall prevail—the right of the individual to labor for such time as he may choose, or the right of the State to prevent the individual from laboring or from entering into any contract to labor, beyond a certain time prescribed by the State.

This court has recognized the existence and upheld the exercise of the police powers of the States in many cases which might fairly be considered as border ones, and it has, in the course of its determination of questions regarding the asserted invalidity of such statutes, on the ground of their violation of the rights secured by the Federal Constitution, been guided by rules of a very liberal nature, the application of which has resulted, in numerous instances, in upholding the validity of state statutes thus assailed. Among the later cases where the state law has been upheld by this court is that of *Holden v. Hardy,* 169 U.S. 366. A provision in the act of the legislature of Utah was there under consideration, the act limiting the employment of workmen in all underground mines or [smelting institutions], to eight hours per day, "except in cases of emergency, where life or property is in imminent danger." . . . The act was held to be a valid exercise of the police powers of the State. . . . It was held that the kind of employment, mining, smelting, etc., and the character of the employés in such kinds of labor, were such as to make it reasonable and proper for the State to interfere to prevent the employés from being constrained by the rules laid down by the proprietors in regard to labor. . . . There is nothing in *Holden v. Hardy* which covers the case now before us. . . .

The latest case decided by this court, involving the police power, is that of *Jacobson v. Massachusetts*, decided at this term and reported in 197 U.S. 11. It related to compulsory vaccination, and the law was held valid as a proper exercise of the police powers with reference to the public health. It was stated in the opinion that it was a case "of an adult who, for aught that appears, was himself in perfect health and a fit subject for vaccination, and yet, while remaining in the community, refused to obey the statute and the regulation adopted in execution of its provisions for the protection of the public health and the public safety, confessedly endangered by the presence of a dangerous disease." That case is also far from covering the one now before the court. . . .

It must, of course, be conceded that there is a limit to the valid exercise of the police power by the State. There is no dispute concerning this general proposition. Otherwise the Fourteenth Amendment would have no efficacy and the legislatures of the States would have unbounded power, and it would be enough to say that any piece of legislation was enacted to conserve the morals, the health or the safety of the people; such legislation would be valid, no matter how absolutely without foundation the claim might be.[7] The claim of the police power would be a mere pretext—become another and delusive name for the supreme sovereignty of the State to be exercised free from constitutional restraint. This is not contended for. In every case that comes before this court, therefore, where legislation of this character is concerned and where the protection of the Federal Constitution is sought, the question necessarily arises: Is this a fair, reasonable and appropriate exercise of the police power of the State, or is it an unreasonable, unnecessary and arbitrary interference with the right of the individual to his personal liberty or to enter into those contracts in relation to labor which may seem to him appropriate or necessary for the support of himself and his family? Of course the liberty of contract relating to labor includes both parties to it. The one has as much right to purchase as the other to sell labor.

This is not a question of substituting the judgment of the court for that of the legislature. If the act be within the power of the State it is valid, although the judgment of the court might be totally opposed to the enactment of such a law. But the question would still remain: Is it within the police power of the State? and that question must be answered by the court.

The question whether this act is valid as a labor law, pure and simple, may be dismissed in a few words.[8] There is no reasonable ground for interfering with the liberty of person or the right of free contract, by determining the hours of labor, in the occupation of a baker. There is no contention that bakers as a class are not equal in intelligence and capacity to men in other trades or manual occupations, or that they are not able to assert their rights and care for themselves without the protecting arm of the State, interfering with their independence of judgment and of action. They are in no sense wards of the State. Viewed in the light of a purely labor law, with no reference whatever to the question of health, we think that a law like the one before us involves neither the safety, the morals nor the welfare of the public, and that the interest of the public is not in the slightest degree affected by such an act. The law must be upheld, if at all, as a law pertaining to the health of the individual engaged in the occupation of a baker. It does not affect any other portion of the public than those who are engaged in that occupation. Clean and wholesome bread does not depend upon whether the baker works but ten hours per day or only sixty hours a week. The limitation of the hours of labor does not come within the police power on that ground.

It is a question of which of two powers or rights shall prevail—the power of the State to legislate or the right of the individual to liberty of person and freedom of contract. The mere assertion that the subject relates though but in a remote degree to the public health does not necessarily render the enactment valid. The act must have a more direct relation, as a means to an end, and the end itself must be

---

[7] **Question:** New York insists that requiring maximum hours for *bakers* protects the public health and public safety at least as much as the previously upheld Utah law requiring maximum hours for *miners*. Yet Peckham here writes that the Fourteenth Amendment cannot tolerate every law that conceivably relates to health, safety, or morals, or else "the States would have unbounded power." Do you agree that such power is a problem that the Supreme Court has a duty to address?

[8] **Question:** In determining whether the New York law is a valid exercise of the state's police power, Peckham begins by dismissing the possibility that New York could justify its law for reasons other than protecting the health, safety, and welfare of others from harm. What, precisely, does he think is wrong with a state law whose *only* purpose is to enhance the bargaining power of laborers, regardless of their health, safety, or welfare?

appropriate and legitimate, before an act can be held to be valid which interferes with the general right of an individual to be free in his person and in his power to contract in relation to his own labor. . . .

We think the limit of the police power has been reached and passed in this case. There is, in our judgment, no reasonable foundation for holding this to be necessary or appropriate as a health law to safeguard the public health or the health of the individuals who are following the trade of a baker.[9] If this statute be valid, and if, therefore, a proper case is made out in which to deny the right of an individual, [legally competent], as employer or employé, to make contracts for the labor of the latter under the protection of the provisions of the Federal Constitution, there would seem to be no length to which legislation of this nature might not go. The case differs widely, as we have already stated, from the expressions of this court in regard to laws of this nature, as stated in *Holden v. Hardy* and *Jacobson v. Massachusetts, supra.*

We think that there can be no fair doubt that the trade of a baker, in and of itself, is not an unhealthy one to that degree which would authorize the legislature to interfere with the right to labor, and with the right of free contract on the part of the individual, either as employer or employé. In looking through statistics regarding all trades and occupations, it may be true that the trade of a baker does not appear to be as healthy as some other trades, and is also vastly more healthy than still others. To the common understanding the trade of a baker has never been regarded as an unhealthy one. Very likely physicians would not recommend the exercise of that or of any other trade as a remedy for ill health. Some occupations are more healthy than others, but we think there are none which might not come under the power of the legislature to supervise and control the hours of working therein, if the mere fact that the occupation is not absolutely and perfectly healthy is to confer that right upon the legislative department of the Government. It might be safely affirmed that almost all occupations more or less affect the health. There must be more than the mere fact of the possible existence of some small amount of unhealthiness to warrant legislative interference with liberty. It is unfortunately true that labor, even in any department, may possibly carry with it the seeds of unhealthiness. But are we all, on that account, at the mercy of legislative majorities? A printer, a tinsmith, a locksmith, a carpenter, a cabinetmaker, a dry goods clerk, a bank's, a lawyer's or a physician's clerk, or a clerk in almost any kind of business, would all come under the power of the legislature, on this assumption. No trade, no occupation, no mode of earning one's living, could escape this all-pervading power, and the acts of the legislature in limiting the hours of labor in all employments would be valid, although such limitation might seriously cripple the ability of the laborer to support himself and his family. In our large cities there are many buildings into which the sun penetrates for but a short time in each day, and these buildings are occupied by people carrying on the business of bankers, brokers, lawyers, real estate, and many other kinds of business, aided by many clerks, messengers, and other employés. Upon the assumption of the validity

---

[9] **Questions:** The test Peckham applies here is whether New York's maximum-hours-for-bakers law is reasonably related to protecting the public health, safety, or welfare. New York says it protects the health of bakers. Regardless of whether you agree with New York, do you agree with Peckham that the Court should not rely on New York's word alone?

For example, suppose a state enacted a law declaring that lawyers were overworked and harming their health, and therefore the state would prosecute any lawyer who worked for more than two hours per day. Or suppose a state declared that jogging harms runners' knees, and therefore anyone who jogs recreationally would be fined. Do you agree with Peckham that the Court has a responsibility to evaluate for itself whether such laws are reasonably related to health? Do you also agree that in conducting this evaluation, "[t]here must be more than the mere fact of the possible existence of some small amount of unhealthiness to warrant legislative interference with liberty?"

of this act under review, it is not possible to say that an act, prohibiting lawyers' or bank clerks, or others, from contracting to labor for their employers more than eight hours a day, would be invalid. It might be said that it is unhealthy to work more than that number of hours in an apartment lighted by artificial light during the working hours of the day; that the occupation of the bank clerk, the lawyer's clerk, the real estate clerk, or the broker's clerk in such offices is therefore unhealthy, and the legislature in its paternal wisdom must, therefore, have the right to legislate on the subject of and to limit the hours for such labor, and if it exercises that power and its validity be questioned, it is sufficient to say, it has reference to the public health; it has reference to the health of the employés condemned to labor day after day in buildings where the sun never shines; it is a health law, and therefore it is valid, and cannot be questioned by the courts.

It is also urged, pursuing the same line of argument, that it is to the interest of the State that its population should be strong and robust, and therefore any legislation which may be said to tend to make people healthy must be valid as health laws, enacted under the police power. If this be a valid argument and a justification for this kind of legislation, it follows that the protection of the Federal Constitution from undue interference with liberty of person and freedom of contract is visionary, wherever the law is sought to be justified as a valid exercise of the police power. Scarcely any law but might find shelter under such assumptions, and conduct, properly so called, as well as contract, would come under the restrictive sway of the legislature. Not only the hours of employés, but the hours of employers, could be regulated, and doctors, lawyers, scientists, all professional men, as well as athletes and artisans, could be forbidden to fatigue their brains and bodies by prolonged hours of exercise, lest the fighting strength of the State be impaired. We mention these extreme cases because the contention is extreme. We do not believe in the soundness of the views which uphold this law. On the contrary, we think that such a law as this, although passed in the assumed exercise of the police power, and as relating to the public health, or the health of the employés named, is not within that power, and is invalid. The act is not, within any fair meaning of the term, a health law, but is an illegal interference with the rights of individuals, both employers and employés, to make contracts regarding labor upon such terms as they may think best, or which they may agree upon with the other parties to such contracts. Statutes of the nature of that under review, limiting the hours in which grown and intelligent men may labor to earn their living, are mere meddlesome interferences with the rights of the individual, and they are not saved from condemnation by the claim that they are passed in the exercise of the police power and upon the subject of the health of the individual whose rights are interfered with, unless there be some fair ground, reasonable in and of itself, to say that there is material danger to the public health or to the health of the employés, if the hours of labor are not curtailed. If this be not clearly the case the individuals, whose rights are thus made the subject of legislative interference, are under the protection of the Federal Constitution regarding their liberty of contract as well as of person; and the legislature of the State has no power to limit their right as proposed in this statute. All that it could properly do has been done by it with regard to the conduct of bakeries, as provided for in the other sections of the act, above set forth. These several sections provide for the inspection of the premises where the bakery is carried on, with regard to furnishing proper wash-rooms and water-closets, apart from the bakeroom, also with regard to providing proper drainage, plumbing and painting; the sections, in addition, provide for the height of the ceiling, the cementing or tiling of floors, where necessary in the opinion of the factory inspector, and for other things of that nature; alterations are also provided for and are to be made where necessary in the opinion of the inspector, in order to comply with the provisions of the statute. These various sections may be wise and valid regulations, and they certainly go to the full extent of providing for the cleanliness and the healthiness, so far as possible, of the quarters in which bakeries are to be conducted. . . .

It was further urged on the argument that restricting the hours of labor in the case of bakers was valid because it tended to cleanliness on the part of the workers, as a man was more apt to be cleanly when not overworked, and if cleanly then his "output" was also more likely to be so. . . . In our judgment it is not possible in fact to discover the connection between the number of hours a baker may work in the bakery and the healthful quality of the bread made by the workman. The connection, if any exists, is too shadowy and thin to build any argument for the interference of the legislature. If the man works ten hours a day it is all right, but if ten and a half or eleven his health is in danger and his bread may be unhealthful, and, therefore, he shall not be permitted to do it. This, we think, is unreasonable and entirely arbitrary. When assertions such as we have adverted to become necessary in order to give, if possible, a plausible foundation for the contention that the law is a "health law," it gives rise to at least a suspicion that there was some other motive dominating the legislature than the purpose to subserve the public health or welfare. . . .

It is impossible for us to shut our eyes to the fact that many of the laws of this character, while passed under what is claimed to be the police power for the purpose of protecting the public health or welfare, are, in reality, passed from other motives. We are justified in saying so when, from the character of the law and the subject upon which it legislates, it is apparent that the public health or welfare bears but the most remote relation to the law. The purpose of a statute must be determined from the natural and legal effect of the language employed; and whether it is or is not repugnant to the Constitution of the United States must be determined from the natural effect of such statutes when put into operation, and not from their proclaimed purpose. . . .

It seems to us that the real object and purpose were simply to regulate the hours of labor between the master and his employés . . ., in a private business, not dangerous in any degree to morals or in any real and substantial degree, to the health of the employés. Under such circumstances the freedom of master and employé to contract with each other in relation to their employment, and in defining the same, cannot be prohibited or interfered with, without violating the Federal Constitution.

■ MR. JUSTICE HARLAN, with whom MR. JUSTICE WHITE and MR. JUSTICE DAY concurred, dissenting. . . .[10]

[L]iberty of contract is subject to such regulations as the State may reasonably prescribe for the common good and the well-being of society. . . . [T]he rule is universal that a legislative enactment, Federal or state, is never to be disregarded or held invalid unless it be, beyond question, plainly and palpably in excess of legislative power. . . . *Mugler v. Kansas,* 123 U.S. 623, 661. If there be doubt as to the validity of the statute, that doubt must therefore be resolved in favor of its validity, and the courts must keep their hands off, leaving the legislature to meet the responsibility for unwise legislation. . . .

It is plain that this statute was enacted in order to protect the physical well-being of those who work in bakery and confectionery establishments. It may be that the statute had its origin, in part, in the belief that employers and employés in such establishments were not upon an equal footing, and that the necessities of the latter often compelled them to submit to such exactions as unduly taxed their strength. Be this as it may, the statute must be taken as expressing the belief of the people of

---

[10] **Questions:** Harlan authored the opinion in *Mugler v. Kansas.* Why, precisely, does he disagree with the majority here? Does he reject the majority's doctrinal rule, or does he reject the majority's application of its rule?

New York that, as a general rule, and in the case of the average man, labor in excess of sixty hours during a week in such establishments may endanger the health of those who thus labor. Whether or not this be wise legislation it is not the province of the court to inquire. . . . I find it impossible, in view of common experience, to say that there is here no real or substantial relation between the means employed by the State and the end sought to be accomplished by its legislation. . . .[11]

[I]n bakery and confectionery establishments, . . . as all know, the air constantly breathed by workmen is not as pure and healthful as that to be found in some other establishments or out of doors. . . . Professor Hirt, in his treatise on the "Diseases of the Workers," has said: "The labor of the bakers is among the hardest and most laborious imaginable, because it has to be performed under conditions injurious to the health of those engaged in it.["] . . . In the Eighteenth Annual Report by the New York Bureau of Statistics of Labor it is stated that, among the occupations involving exposure to conditions that interfere with nutrition is that of a baker (p. 52). . . . Statistics show that the average daily working time among workingmen in different countries is, in Australia, 8 hours; in Great Britain, 9; in the United States, 9; in Denmark, 9; in Norway, 10; Sweden, France and Switzerland, 10; Germany, 10; Belgium, Italy and Austria, 11, and in Russia, 12 hours.

We judicially know that the question of the number of hours during which a workman should continuously labor has been, for a long period, and is yet, a subject of serious consideration among civilized peoples and by those having special knowledge of the laws of health. Suppose the statute prohibited labor in bakery and confectionery establishments in excess of eighteen hours each day. No one, I take it, could dispute the power of the State to enact such a statute. . . .

We also judicially know that the number of hours that should constitute a day's labor in particular occupations involving the physical strength and safety of workmen has been the subject of enactments by Congress and by nearly all of the States. Many if not most of those enactments fix eight hours as the proper basis of a day's labor.

I do not stop to consider whether any particular view of this economic question presents the sounder theory. What the precise facts are it may be difficult to say. It is enough for the determination of this case, and it is enough for this court to know, that the question is one about which there is room for debate and for an honest difference of opinion. There are many reasons of a weighty, substantial character, based upon the experience of mankind, in support of the theory that, all things considered, more than ten hours' steady work each day, from week to week, in a bakery or confectionery establishment, may endanger the health, and shorten the lives of the workmen, thereby diminishing their physical and mental capacity to serve the State, and to provide for those dependent upon them.

If such reasons exist, that ought to be the end of this case, for the State is not amenable to the judiciary in respect of its legislative enactments unless such

---

[11] **Question:** Harlan is attempting to demonstrate that the question of whether there should be limits on the maximum hours of bakers is a fact-specific question that requires a contextual balance between the liberty of contracting parties and the state's interest in protecting the public health. As in *Mugler*, Harlan conducts this balance by invoking "judicial notice"—a rule of evidence that permits a court to declare a fact to be common knowledge without formal presentation or briefing. The quotation from "Professor Hirt," for example, was drawn verbatim from a pamphlet published by the Bakery and Confectionery Workers' International Union of America. *See* Joseph Schmidt, *For Day Work and Eight Hours* 16 (1904).

Do you agree with Harlan's approach to this dispute? For a defense of Harlan's effort to "mediate rights rather than minimize or discriminate against them," see Jamal Greene, *How Rights Went Wrong* at xxxi, 44–57 (2021).

enactments are plainly, palpably, beyond all question, inconsistent with the Constitution of the United States. . . .

■ MR. JUSTICE HOLMES dissenting.

I regret sincerely that I am unable to agree with the judgment in this case, and that I think it my duty to express my dissent.[12]

This case is decided upon an economic theory which a large part of the country does not entertain. If it were a question whether I agreed with that theory, I should desire to study it further and long before making up my mind. But I do not conceive that to be my duty, because I strongly believe that my agreement or disagreement has nothing to do with the right of a majority to embody their opinions in law. It is settled by various decisions of this court that state constitutions and state laws may regulate life in many ways which we as legislators might think as injudicious or if you like as tyrannical as this, and which equally with this interfere with the liberty to contract. Sunday laws and usury laws are ancient examples. A more modern one is the prohibition of lotteries. The liberty of the citizen to do as he likes so long as he does not interfere with the liberty of others to do the same, which has been a shibboleth for some well-known writers, is interfered with by school laws, by the Post Office, by every state or municipal institution which takes his money for purposes thought desirable, whether he likes it or not. The Fourteenth Amendment does not enact Mr. Herbert Spencer's Social Statics. The other day we sustained the Massachusetts vaccination law. *Jacobson v. Massachusetts,* 197 U.S. 11. United States and state statutes and decisions cutting down the liberty to contract by way of combination are familiar to this court. *Northern Securities Co. v. United States,*193 U.S. 197. . . . The decision sustaining an eight hour law for miners is still recent. *Holden v. Hardy,* 169 U.S. 366. Some of these laws embody convictions or prejudices which judges are likely to share. Some may not. But a constitution is not intended to embody a particular economic theory, whether of paternalism and the organic relation of the citizen to the State or of *laissez faire*. It is made for people of fundamentally differing views, and the accident of our finding certain opinions natural and familiar or novel and even shocking ought not to conclude our judgment upon the question whether statutes embodying them conflict with the Constitution of the United States.

General propositions do not decide concrete cases. The decision will depend on a judgment or intuition more subtle than any articulate major premise. But I think that the proposition just stated, if it is accepted, will carry us far toward the end. Every opinion tends to become a law. I think that the word liberty in the Fourteenth Amendment is perverted when it is held to prevent the natural outcome of a dominant opinion, unless it can be said that a rational and fair man necessarily would admit that the statute proposed would infringe fundamental principles as they have been understood by the traditions of our people and our law.[13] It does not need research

---

12 **Questions:** Harlan's dissent was celebrated when *Lochner* was decided. But Justice Oliver Wendell Holmes's dissent has, since the 1930s, become one of the most famous in constitutional law. *See* Greene, *supra*, at 51. Where Harlan disagreed with the majority over the factual question of whether a maximum-hour law was reasonably related to public health, Holmes argues that courts should never interfere "with the right of a majority to embody their opinions in law." He emphasizes that the Fourteenth Amendment "does not enact Mr. Herbert Spencer's Social Statics," an 1851 defense of the harm principle by one of John Stuart Mill's contemporaries. (Spencer today is best remembered for coining the phrase *survival of the fittest.*)

If not courts, what else would Holmes rely on to ensure that legislators did not pass "injudicious" or "tyrannical" laws? Do you find his absolutist perspective more persuasive than Harlan's fact-specific approach?

13 **Questions:** Here, Holmes reconceptualizes the majority's test. Where the majority and Harlan would uphold only those laws reasonably related to public health, safety, or morals, Holmes would uphold all laws that do not necessarily infringe on "fundamental principles as they have been understood by the traditions of our people." Do you agree with his test? If so,

to show that no such sweeping condemnation can be passed upon the statute before us. A reasonable man might think it a proper measure on the score of health. Men whom I certainly could not pronounce unreasonable would uphold it as a first installment of a general regulation of the hours of work. Whether in the latter aspect it would be open to the charge of inequality I think it unnecessary to discuss.

NOTE: AFTERMATH OF *LOCHNER*

The dispute in *Lochner* is a classic illustration of a vexing question under the Fourteenth Amendment: How should courts resolve conflicts between competing interests?

In this instance, Lochner invoked an interest that goes to the heart of the Fourteenth Amendment: the liberty of people to choose their own calling and to make contracts "upon such terms as they may think best." *Lochner*, 198 U.S. at 61. The Congress that proposed the Fourteenth Amendment specifically protected this sort of liberty with the Civil Rights Act of 1866, which gave black people the same right "to make and enforce contracts . . . as is enjoyed by white citizens." Civil Rights Act of 1866, ch. 31, 14 Stat. 27, 27.

New York, by contrast, offered its own compelling interests. Its democratic legislature passed a law designed to protect the health of its residents—a law whose value was so widely shared that industrialized countries around the world enacted identical legislation. The law also supported the bargaining power of a subordinated class of residents: laborers whose poverty, immigration status, and other characteristics left them vulnerable to exploitation by employers who might fire them rather than treat them with dignity.

The three opinions in *Lochner* offer three ways of mediating this conflict.

Peckham's majority opinion adopted a skeptical means-ends test. Peckham treated certain interests as legitimate—Lochner's liberty to contract and the state's interest in public health—while disregarding all other interests as either inconsequential or tyrannically paternalistic. For him, New York's legitimate interests could outweigh Lochner's legitimate interests only if its law were *really* about serving such interests and was not, instead, pretextual. Skeptically evaluating the law, he concluded that a law limiting the working hours of bakers had nothing to do with New York's legitimate interest in public health. It warned that if this law could be justified as a public health measure, then "legislative majorities" might invoke health to justify virtually any regulation. Surely, the majority reasoned, the Constitution wouldn't permit a legislature to declare that excessive work is unhealthy and that therefore it is a crime for lawyers to work more than eight hours per day or for athletes to vigorously exercise.

Harlan, the author of *Mugler*, offered a test that looks more like a proportionality test. Harlan denied that New York's only legitimate interest was in protecting public health—he was willing to accept that New York might also be legitimately interested in promoting the bargaining power of

---

why isn't the liberty to choose one's calling a "fundamental" principle? And why should courts protect only those principles already protected by tradition?

workers. He also accepted the legitimacy of Lochner's liberty to contract. So, resolving this conflict was not a question of determining pretext but was instead a question of whether New York's legislature acted sensibly in adjudicating a compromise between the competing interests of employers and employees. Harlan answered this question by calling upon data, common sense, state records, and other fact-specific evidence that supported New York's conclusion. "He understood that not just laws but rights themselves often involve negotiation and compromise, even internal contradiction, not unlike the judges who interpret and apply them." Jamal Greene, *How Rights Went Wrong* 57 (2021).

Finally, Holmes offered a deferential means-ends test. Where the majority denied the legitimacy of New York's interest in a "a labor law, pure and simple," *Lochner*, 198 U.S. at 57, Holmes denied the legitimacy of Lochner's interest in a constitutionally protected liberty to contract. He thought the only individual interests worth protecting were "fundamental principles as they have been understood by the traditions of our people and our laws." *Lochner*, 198 U.S. at 75. He also embraced any interest that New York could possibly conceive for its legislation. He explained that the Fourteenth Amendment did not enact Herbert Spencer's *Social Statics* (1851) and its argument that state interference with liberty could be justified only when necessary to prevent harm. Holmes justified his minimization of Lochner's interest and his maximization of New York's interest with a popular sovereignty principle: he argued that judicial review of state laws should be avoided because it came at the expense of "the right of a majority to embody their opinions in law." *Id.* From his perspective, New York's interests should have prevailed because Lochner had articulated no "fundamental principles" that could justify second-guessing New York's majority rule. *Id.* at 76.

Invalidating laws insufficiently related to health, safety, or morals. For decades after *Lochner*, the Court ignored Holmes's proposed test and invalidated any law that it considered insufficiently related to health, safety, or morals.

For example, in *Adair v. United States*, 208 U.S. 161 (1908), the Court struck down a federal law that prohibited interstate railroad companies from demanding "yellow dog contracts," in which newly hired workers promised not to join a union. Extending *Lochner* to the Fifth Amendment's Due Process Clause, the Court held that Congress had "arbitrarily sanction[ed] an illegal invasion of the personal liberty" of a railroad manager, William Adair, "under the guise of regulating interstate commerce." *Adair*, 208 U.S. at 180.

For similar reasons, the Court struck down a segregation law that prohibited black people from living in predominantly white neighborhoods. In *Buchanan v. Warley*, 245 U.S. 60 (1917), the Court denied that racial segregation produced any health or safety benefits that could justify intruding into the right of black purchasers to contract with white sellers. *Buchanan*, 245 U.S. at 81–82. (This conclusion led cities and states to adopt color-blind "zoning" ordinances to accomplish the same purpose but with restrictions more directly tied to health and safety. *See* Richard Rothstein,

The Color of Law 48–54 (2017); *Vill. of Euclid v. Ambler Realty Co.*, 272 U.S. 365, 392 (1926)).

More controversially, in *Adkins v. Children's Hospital*, 261 U.S. 525 (1923), the Court struck down a federal law that established a minimum wage for women and children in the District of Columbia. Although Congress had accumulated statistics showing how women's health improved in the states that had already enacted minimum-wage laws, the Court found these statistics

> interesting but only mildly persuasive. That the earnings of women now are greater than they were formerly and that conditions affecting women have become better in other respects may be conceded, but convincing indications of the logical relation of these desirable changes to the law in question are significantly lacking.

Adkins, 261 U.S. at 560.

Conservatives on the Court defended their interpretation of the Due Process Clause "as a shield" for "the individual against the unjust demands of society," even if that meant "disregard[ing] the wishes and sentiments of a majority of the people." Jeff Shesol, *Supreme Power* 32–33 (2010).

Upholding laws sufficiently related to health, safety, or morals. But even at the height of the *Lochner* era, the Court upheld hundreds of laws from challenge that it thought *were* sufficiently related to health, safety, or morals.

The archetypical example was *Muller v. Oregon*, in which Louis Brandeis, then an attorney, defended a law regulating the number of hours that women could work in laundries. 208 U.S. 412, 423 (1908). Drawing inspiration from Harlan's dissenting opinion in *Lochner*, Brandeis wrote a 113-page brief that contained only two pages of law—citations to *Lochner*. All of the other pages cited thousands of factory reports, medical records, labor statistics, and other "facts of common knowledge" about how the working hours of women related to public health. *See* Brief for Appellant at 10, 208 U.S. 412 (1908) (No. 107). This new form of social science brief, later known as a "Brandeis brief," persuaded the Court that long working hours harmed the health of potential mothers, whose poor health might go on to harm the next generation of children. *See* Melvin I. Urofsky, *Louis D. Brandeis* 216–17 (2009).

These limited victories served to entrench paternalistic stereotypes about women's primary role as mothers and secondary role as workers—a point we will return to later in a discussion about the Equal Protection Clause and sex (section 48.2). They also did not satisfy progressive reformers, who unceasingly condemned the Supreme Court's approach to interpreting the Due Process Clauses. A developing field of legal realism charged the Court with manipulating the term *due process* far beyond its origins as a *procedural* protection and using it to strike down minimum-wage laws, price controls, collective bargaining laws, and other reforms favored by popular majorities. Law professor Felix Cohen memorably called the Due Process Clause "transcendental nonsense," or a circular legal concept without any definition independent of how the Court wanted to answer a particular empirical or ethical question. Felix Cohen, *Transcendental Nonsense and the Functional Approach*, 35 Colum. L. Rev. 809, 819–20 (1935).

41.2.2

West Coast Hotel Co. v. Parrish

300 U.S. 379 (1937)

By the dawn of the Great Depression in 1929, the Supreme Court was split into two wings: a progressive wing of four justices—including Holmes and the now-justice Brandeis—and a conservative wing pejoratively known as the Four Horsemen. Justice Owen Roberts carried the swing vote. As states aggressively responded to the Depression with attempts to regulate the economy, Roberts vacillated between upholding the laws and striking them down as deprivations of liberty.

For example, in *New State Ice Co. v. Liebmann*, 285 U.S. 262 (1932), Roberts joined the majority in striking down an Oklahoma law that regulated the sale of ice in the state. *New State Ice*, 285 U.S. at 277. Brandeis memorably dissented that the Court was using the Due Process Clause to interfere with America's "federal system [in which] a single courageous state may, if its citizens choose, serve as a laboratory; and try novel social and economic experiments without risk to the rest of the country." *Id.* at 311 (Brandeis, J., dissenting).

Yet only two years later, in *Nebbia v. New York*, 291 U.S. 502 (1934), Roberts wrote an opinion upholding a law that fixed the price at which milk could be sold. *Nebbia*, 291 U.S. at 531. Where *Lochner* held that a state had legitimate interests only in protecting public health, safety, or morals, Roberts held that states could also protect the "public welfare":

> So far as the requirement of due process is concerned, and in the absence of other constitutional restriction, a state is free to adopt whatever economic policy may reasonably be deemed to promote public welfare, and to enforce that policy by legislation adapted to its purpose. The courts are without authority either to declare such policy, or, when it is declared by the legislature, to override it. If the laws passed are seen to have a reasonable relation to a proper legislative purpose, and are neither arbitrary nor discriminatory, the requirements of due process are satisfied. . . .

Id. at 537.

Two years after *Nebbia*, Roberts switched again in *Morehead v. New York ex rel. Tipaldo*, 298 U.S. 587 (1936), joining an opinion that struck down New York's minimum-wage law. Even though the law fixed wages in an identical manner as the law in *Nebbia* had fixed prices, the majority opinion failed to acknowledge *Nebbia*'s existence. Over a dissent that repeatedly cited *Nebbia*, the majority held that it had already decided that minimum-wage laws were unconstitutional in *Adkins* and that the petitioners had not asked the Court to overturn *Adkins*.

Tipaldo enormously frustrated President Franklin D. Roosevelt, who interpreted it as part of a pattern of Supreme Court decisions that struck down state and federal redistributive legislation. As discussed earlier with regard to conditional spending (section 6.2) and regulate interstate commerce (section 8.2), Roosevelt responded to these cases with a plan to "pack" the Supreme Court with younger justices.

When he announced his plan in 1937, the Court had recently heard oral argument in yet another minimum-wage case out of Washington, *West Coast Hotel Co. v. Parrish*, 300 U.S. 379 (1937). Unlike *Tipaldo*, this new case asked the Court to overrule *Adkins*.

Even though Roberts had just voted to strike down New York's minimum-wage law in *Tipaldo*, he joined a 5–4 majority in *West Coast Hotel* to uphold Washington's minimum wage for women in what became known as the "switch in time that saved nine" (see section 6.2).

■ MR. CHIEF JUSTICE HUGHES delivered the opinion of the Court.[14]

This case presents the question of the constitutional validity of the minimum wage law of the State of Washington. . . .

The appellant conducts a hotel. The appellee Elsie Parrish was employed as a chambermaid and (with her husband) brought this suit to recover the difference between the wages paid her and the minimum wage fixed pursuant to the state law. The minimum wage was $14.50 per week of 48 hours. The appellant challenged the act as repugnant to the due process clause of the Fourteenth Amendment of the Constitution of the United States. . . . The appellant relies upon the decision of this Court in *Adkins v. Children's Hospital,* 261 U.S. 525, which held invalid the District of Columbia Minimum Wage Act, which was attacked under the due process clause of the Fifth Amendment. . . .

We are of the opinion that this ruling of the state court demands on our part a reexamination of the *Adkins* case. The importance of the question, in which many States having similar laws are concerned, the close division by which the decision in the *Adkins* case was reached, and the economic conditions which have supervened, and in the light of which the reasonableness of the exercise of the protective power of the State must be considered, make it not only appropriate, but we think imperative, that in deciding the present case the subject should receive fresh consideration. . . .

The principle which must control our decision is not in doubt. The constitutional provision invoked is the due process clause of the Fourteenth Amendment governing the States, as the due process clause invoked in the *Adkins* case governed Congress. In each case the violation alleged by those attacking minimum wage regulation for women is deprivation of freedom of contract. What is this freedom? The Constitution does not speak of freedom of contract. It speaks of liberty and prohibits the deprivation

---

[14] **As You Read, Consider:** As in *Lochner v. New York*, this case involves a conflict of interests. The employer here claims an interest in contracting on his own terms. Washington claims an interest in protecting female workers like Elsie Parrish from oppression. How does Chief Justice Charles Evans Hughes's resolution of this conflict compare with the three tests offered in *Lochner*? Does he maximize the employer's claimed interest and minimize the state's claimed interest, like the *Lochner* majority? Does he do the opposite, like Justice Oliver Wendell Holmes? Or does he determine whether the state appropriately mediated the two interests, like Justice John Harlan?

of liberty without due process of law. In prohibiting that deprivation the Constitution does not recognize an absolute and uncontrollable liberty. Liberty in each of its phases has its history and connotation. But the liberty safeguarded is liberty in a social organization which requires the protection of law against the evils which menace the health, safety, morals and welfare of the people. Liberty under the Constitution is thus necessarily subject to the restraints of due process, and regulation which is reasonable in relation to its subject and is adopted in the interests of the community is due process.[15]

This essential limitation of liberty in general governs freedom of contract in particular. More than twenty-five years ago we set forth the applicable principle in these words, after referring to the cases where the liberty guaranteed by the Fourteenth Amendment had been broadly described:

> "But it was recognized in the cases cited, as in many others, that freedom of contract is a qualified and not an absolute right. There is no absolute freedom to do as one wills or to contract as one chooses. The guaranty of liberty does not withdraw from legislative supervision that wide department of activity which consists of the making of contracts, or deny to government the power to provide restrictive safeguards. Liberty implies the absence of arbitrary restraint, not immunity from reasonable regulations and prohibitions imposed in the interests of the community." *Chicago, B. & Q.R. Co. v. McGuire,* 219 U.S. 549, 567.

This power under the Constitution to restrict freedom of contract has had many illustrations. That it may be exercised in the public interest with respect to contracts between employer and employee is undeniable. Thus statutes have been sustained limiting employment in underground mines and smelters to eight hours a day (*Holden v. Hardy,* 169 U.S. 366); in requiring redemption in cash of store orders or other evidences of indebtedness issued in the payment of wages (*Knoxville Iron Co. v. Harbison,* 183 U.S. 13); in forbidding the payment of seamen's wages in advance (*Patterson v. Bark Eudora,* 190 U.S. 169); in making it unlawful to contract to pay miners employed at quantity rates upon the basis of screened coal instead of the weight of the coal as originally produced in the mine (*McLean v. Arkansas,* 211 U.S. 539); in prohibiting contracts limiting liability for injuries to employees (*Chicago, B. & Q.R. Co. v. McGuire, supra*); in limiting hours of work of employees in manufacturing establishments (*Bunting v. Oregon,* 243 U.S. 426); and in maintaining workmen's compensation laws (*New York Central R. Co. v. White,* 243 U.S. 188; *Mountain Timber Co. v. Washington,* 243 U.S. 219). In dealing with the relation of employer and employed, the legislature has necessarily a wide field of discretion in order that there may be suitable protection of health and safety, and that peace and good order may be promoted through regulations designed to insure wholesome conditions of work and freedom from oppression. *Chicago, B. & Q.R. Co. v. McGuire, supra,* p. 570.

The point that has been strongly stressed that adult employees should be deemed competent to make their own contracts was decisively met nearly forty years ago in *Holden v. Hardy, supra,* where we pointed out the inequality in the footing of the parties. We said (*Id.,* 397):

---

[15] **Questions:** Hughes here treats the "freedom of contract" as a weak right that must be subordinated to any legislation "which is reasonable in relation to its subject." Does Hughes offer any consolation to adherents of *Lochner* who might be concerned about the possibility that states might act tyrannically? Under Hughes's test, did the Court correctly decide *Buchanan v. Warley*, in which it invalidated a racial segregation law for interfering with the freedom of contract?

> "The legislature has also recognized the fact, which the experience of legislators in many States has corroborated, that the proprietors of these establishments and their operatives do not stand upon an equality, and that their interests are, to a certain extent, conflicting. The former naturally desire to obtain as much labor as possible from their employes, while the latter are often induced by the fear of discharge to conform to regulations which their judgment, fairly exercised, would pronounce to be detrimental to their health or strength. In other words, the proprietors lay down the rules and the laborers are practically constrained to obey them. In such cases self-interest is often an unsafe guide, and the legislature may properly interpose its authority." . . .

It is manifest that this established principle is peculiarly applicable in relation to the employment of women in whose protection the State has a special interest. That phase of the subject received elaborate consideration in *Muller v. Oregon* (1908), 208 U.S. 412, where the constitutional authority of the State to limit the working hours of women was sustained. We emphasized the consideration that "woman's physical structure and the performance of maternal functions place her at a disadvantage in the struggle for subsistence" and that her physical well being "becomes an object of public interest and care in order to preserve the strength and vigor of the race." We emphasized the need of protecting women against oppression despite her possession of contractual rights. . . . Again, in *Quong Wing v. Kirkendall,* 223 U.S. 59, 63, in referring to a differentiation with respect to the employment of women, we said that the Fourteenth Amendment did not interfere with state power by creating a "fictitious equality." We referred to recognized classifications on the basis of sex with regard to hours of work and in other matters, and we observed that the particular points at which that difference shall be enforced by legislation were largely in the power of the State. . . .

The minimum wage to be paid under the Washington statute is fixed after full consideration by representatives of employers, employees and the public. It may be assumed that the minimum wage is fixed in consideration of the service that are performed in the particular occupations under normal conditions. Provision is made for special licenses at less wages in the case of women who are incapable of full service. The statement of Mr. Justice Holmes in the *Adkins* case is pertinent: "This statute does not compel anybody to pay anything. It simply forbids employment at rates below those fixed as the minimum requirement of health and right living. It is safe to assume that women will not be employed at even the lowest wages allowed unless they earn them, or unless the employer's business can sustain the burden. In short the law in its character and operation is like hundreds of so-called police laws that have been upheld." 261 U.S., p. 570. And Chief Justice Taft forcibly pointed out the consideration which is basic in a statute of this character: "Legislatures which adopt a requirement of maximum hours or minimum wages may be presumed to believe that when sweating employers are prevented from paying unduly low wages by positive law they will continue their business, abating that part of their profits, which were wrung from the necessities of their employees, and will concede the better terms required by the law; and that while in individual cases hardship may result, the restriction will enure to the benefit of the general class of employees in whose interest the law is passed and so to that of the community at large." *Id.,* p. 563. . . .

We think that the views thus expressed are sound and that the decision in the *Adkins* case was a departure from the true application of the principles governing the regulation by the State of the relation of employer and employed. Those principles have been reenforced by our subsequent decisions. Thus in . . . *Nebbia v. New York,* 291 U.S. 502, dealing with the New York statute providing for minimum prices for milk, the general subject of the regulation of the use of private property and of the making of private contracts received an exhaustive examination and we again declared that if such laws "have a reasonable relation to a proper legislative purpose, and are neither arbitrary nor discriminatory, the requirements of due process are satisfied"; that "with the wisdom of the policy adopted, with the adequacy or practicability of the law enacted to forward it, the courts are both incompetent and unauthorized to deal"; that "times without number we have said that the legislature is primarily the judge of the necessity of such an enactment, that every possible presumption is in favor of its validity, and that though the court may hold views inconsistent with the wisdom of the law, it may not be annulled unless palpably in excess of legislative power." *Id.*, pp. 537, 538.[16]

With full recognition of the earnestness and vigor which characterize the prevailing opinion in the *Adkins* case, we find it impossible to reconcile that ruling with these well-considered declarations. . . . The legislature of the State was clearly entitled to consider the situation of women in employment, the fact that they are in the class receiving the least pay, that their bargaining power is relatively weak, and that they are the ready victims of those who would take advantage of their necessitous circumstances. The legislature was entitled to adopt measures to reduce the evils of the "sweating system," the exploiting of workers at wages so low as to be insufficient to meet the bare cost of living, thus making their very helplessness the occasion of a most injurious competition. The legislature had the right to consider that its minimum wage requirements would be an important aid in carrying out its policy of protection. The adoption of similar requirements by many States evidences a deep-seated conviction both as to the presence of the evil and as to the means adapted to check it. Legislative response to that conviction cannot be regarded as arbitrary or capricious, and that is all we have to decide. Even if the wisdom of the policy be regarded as debatable and its effects uncertain, still the legislature is entitled to its judgment.

There is an additional and compelling consideration which recent economic experience has brought into a strong light. The exploitation of a class of workers who are in an unequal position with respect to bargaining power and are thus relatively defenceless against the denial of a living wage is not only detrimental to their health and well being but casts a direct burden for their support upon the community. What these workers lose in wages the taxpayers are called upon to pay. The bare cost of living must be met. We may take judicial notice of the unparalleled demands for relief which arose during the recent period of depression and still continue to an alarming extent despite the degree of economic recovery which has been achieved. It is unnecessary to cite official statistics to establish what is of common knowledge through the length and breadth of the land. While in the instant case no factual brief has been presented, there is no reason to doubt that the State of Washington has encountered the same social problem that is present elsewhere. The community is not bound to provide what is in effect a subsidy for unconscionable employers. The community may direct its law-making power to correct the abuse which springs from their selfish disregard of the public interest. . . .[17]

---

[16] **Questions:** In this paragraph, Hughes reaffirms a deferential ends-means test that has become known as the "rational-basis" test. What are the principles justifying his invocation of this test? What principles are sacrificed or harmed by this test?

[17] **Questions:** Like Harlan's dissenting opinion in *Lochner*, Hughes takes "judicial notice" of "common knowledge" and uses it as a basis for determining whether the state legislature acted reasonably. But like Holmes's dissenting opinion, Hughes appears to dismiss the legitimacy of the employer's interest in resisting this legislation. How would Hughes respond to the *Lochner* majority's nightmare scenario, in which state legislatures pass laws that prevent lawyers from working or prevent athletes from exercising? Or, more realistically, what remedy

Our conclusion is that the case of *Adkins* v. *Children's Hospital, supra,* should be, and it is, overruled. . . .

41.2.3

United States v. Carolene Products Co.

304 U.S. 144 (1938)

West Coast Hotel marked the end of the *Lochner* era—and the end of the Supreme Court's attempt to determine the reasonableness of federal and state economic regulations under the Due Process Clause. By the end of 1937, Roosevelt appointed the first of what would become nine appointments to the Supreme Court. Subsequent decisions consistently deferred to the will of legislative majorities instead of invalidating laws for interfering with property rights or the liberty to contract. *See, e.g., NLRB v. Jones & Laughlin Steel Corp.*, 301 U.S. 1, 30 (1937). Ever since 1937, the Court has analyzed economic regulations under the Due Process Clause by applying the test announced in *Nebbia*: if such laws "have a reasonable relation to a proper legislative purpose, and are neither arbitrary nor discriminatory, the requirements of due process are satisfied." 291 U.S. at 537. This test has become known as the "rational-basis" test and is significantly more deferential to legislatures than was *Lochner*.

Yet members of the Court were hesitant to completely abandon the Due Process Clause as a substantive restraint. The following opinion, *United States v. Carolene Products Co.*, 304 U.S. 144 (1938), contained a footnote that hinted at the sort of legislation of which the Court's liberal bloc remained wary.

■ MR. JUSTICE STONE delivered the opinion of the Court.[18]

The question for decision is whether the "Filled Milk Act" of Congress of March 4, 1923, which prohibits the shipment in interstate commerce of skimmed milk compounded with any fat or oil other than milk fat, so as to resemble milk or cream, . . . infringes the Fifth Amendment. . . .

The power of the legislature to secure a minimum of particular nutritive elements in a widely used article of food and to protect the public from fraudulent substitutions, [cannot be] doubted; and . . . there [is] ample scope for the legislative judgment that prohibition of the offending article [is] an appropriate means of preventing injury to the public. . . .

[A]ffirmative evidence also sustains the statute. . . . [E]vidence has steadily accumulated of the danger to the public health from the general consumption of foods which have been stripped of elements essential to the maintenance of health. . . .

---

does Hughes offer to black southerners who, at the time, were being disenfranchised, lynched, and subordinated by racist state legislatures?

[18] **As You Read, Consider:** In his dissenting opinion in *Lochner v. New York*, Justice Oliver Wendell Holmes argued that the only role for the Supreme Court was to protect "fundamental principles as they have been understood by the traditions of our people and our law." 198 U.S. 45, 76 (1905). Does Justice Harlan Stone embrace this view in his famous footnote 4?

[T]he statute itself declares, that the use of filled milk as a substitute for pure milk is . . . injurious to health and facilitates fraud on the public. . . .

We may assume for present purposes that no pronouncement of a legislature can forestall attack upon the constitutionality of the prohibition which it enacts by applying opprobrious epithets to the prohibited act, and that a statute would deny due process which precluded the disproof in judicial proceedings of all facts which would show or tend to show that a statute depriving the suitor of life, liberty or property had a rational basis.

But such we think is not the purpose or construction of the statutory characterization of filled milk as injurious to health and as a fraud upon the public. There is no need to consider it here as more than a declaration of the legislative findings deemed to support and justify the action taken as a constitutional exertion of the legislative power, aiding informed judicial review, . . . by revealing the rationale of the legislation. Even in the absence of such aids the existence of facts supporting the legislative judgment is to be presumed, for regulatory legislation affecting ordinary commercial transactions is not to be pronounced unconstitutional unless in the light of the facts made known or generally assumed it is of such a character as to preclude the assumption that it rests upon some rational basis within the knowledge and experience of the legislators.[4] . . .[19]

Where the existence of a rational basis for legislation whose constitutionality is attacked depends upon facts beyond the sphere of judicial notice, such facts may properly be made the subject of judicial inquiry, and the constitutionality of a statute predicated upon the existence of a particular state of facts may be challenged by showing to the court that those facts have ceased to exist. . . . But by their very nature such inquiries, where the legislative judgment is drawn in question, must be restricted to the issue whether any state of facts either known or which could reasonably be assumed affords support for it. Here . . . it is evident from all the considerations presented to Congress, and those of which we may take judicial notice, that the question is at least debatable whether commerce in filled milk should be left unregulated, or in some measure restricted, or wholly prohibited. As that

---

4 There may be narrower scope for operation of the presumption of constitutionality when legislation appears on its face to be within a specific prohibition of the Constitution, such as those of the first ten amendments, which are deemed equally specific when held to be embraced within the Fourteenth. *See Stromberg v. California*, 283 U. S. 359.

It is unnecessary to consider now whether legislation which restricts those political processes which can ordinarily be expected to bring about repeal of undesirable legislation, is to be subjected to more exacting judicial scrutiny under the general prohibitions of the Fourteenth Amendment than are most other types of legislation. On restrictions upon the right to vote, *see Nixon v. Herndon,* 273 U. S. 536; on restraints upon the dissemination of information, *see Near v. Minnesota,* 283 U. S. 697*;* on interferences with political organizations, *see Stromberg, supra*; as to prohibition of peaceable assembly, *see De Jonge v. Oregon,* 299 U. S. 353.

Nor need we enquire whether similar considerations enter into the review of statutes directed at particular religious, *Pierce v. Society of Sisters*, 268 U. S. 510, or national, *Meyer v. Nebraska*, 262 U. S. 390, or racial minorities, *Nixon v. Herndon, supra*: whether prejudice against discrete and insular minorities may be a special condition, which tends seriously to curtail the operation of those political processes ordinarily to be relied upon to protect minorities, and which may call for a correspondingly more searching judicial inquiry. [*Cf. McCulloch v.*] *Maryland*, 17 U. S. (4 Wheat.) 316, 428 (1819) [(observing that Maryland voters could trust themselves to repeal oppressive state taxation, but that the Bank of the United States required a different theory to defend it from oppressive state taxation)]

19 **Questions:** In the body text, Stone announces an incredibly deferential test for evaluating the substantive validity of legislation under the Due Process Clause: as long as the law is rationally related to any conceivable legitimate interest, the law is valid. But in footnote 4, Stone offers three exceptions to this test. What principles do these three exceptions advance? What common thread ties these exceptions together?

decision was for Congress, neither the finding of a court arrived at by weighing the evidence, nor the verdict of a jury can be substituted for it. . . .

NOTE: RATIONAL-BASIS TEST

Footnote 4 of *Carolene Products* is the most famous footnote in Supreme Court history. *See* John Hart Ely, *Democracy and Distrust* 75–76 (1980). Over time, it has become a blueprint for the sorts of statutes that the Supreme Court strictly scrutinized in the same way that the *Lochner* Court strictly scrutinized New York's baker law. But the text and actual holding of *Carolene Products* proved more immediately significant, as the Supreme Court declared that it would uphold any economic regulation as long as "any state of facts either known or which could reasonably be assumed affords support for it." *Carolene Prods.*, 304 U.S. at 154.

> Thus, a generation after *Carolene Products*, the Court wrote that [t]he doctrine that prevailed in *Lochner*, *Coppage*, *Adkins*, . . . and like cases—that due process authorizes courts to hold laws unconstitutional when they believe the legislature has acted unwisely—has long since been discarded. We have returned to the original constitutional proposition that courts do not substitute their social and economic beliefs for the judgment of legislative bodies, who are elected to pass laws.

Ferguson v. Skrupa, 372 U.S. 726, 730 (1963). Instead of employing "the 'vague contours' of the Due Process Clause to nullify laws which a majority of the Court believ[e] to be economically unwise," the Court declared that it would uphold any economic regulation that was rationally related to any imaginable legitimate purpose. *Id.*

41.3 DEPRIVATIONS OF PROPERTY (REGULATORY TAKINGS)

Even after *Nebbia v. New York*, 291 U.S. 502 (1934); *West Coast Hotel Co. v. Parrish*, 300 U.S. 379 (1937); and *United States v. Carolene Products Co.*, 304 U.S. 144 (1938), there remains a line of cases in which the Supreme Court carefully scrutinizes economic regulations. These regulations involve "takings": the functional equivalent of exercising eminent domain over property.

In *Mugler v. Kansas*, the second question decided was whether Kansas's prohibition on the manufacture of alcohol had effectively "taken," or destroyed, the value of Peter Mugler's brewery as if Kansas had physically condemned and seized the brewery via eminent domain. 123 U.S. 623, 667 (1887). In evaluating this question, the Supreme Court appeared to treat as a substantive element of due process the Fifth Amendment's Takings Clause—which declares that no "private property [shall] be taken for public use, without just compensation." For decades prior to *Mugler*, the Court had invoked the Takings Clause as a limit only on the federal government's exercise of eminent domain: the federal government could physically possess or occupy a person's land only for a public purpose and only if the government paid just compensation. *See The Legal Tender Cases*, 79 U.S. (12 Wall.) 457, 614 (1871); *see also Kohl v. United States*, 91 U.S. 367, 372 (1876); *Pumpelly v. Green Bay Co.*, 80 U.S. (13 Wall.) 166, 177 (1872) (discussing a state takings clause). Although *Mugler* emphasized that "the present case must be governed by principles that do not involve the power of eminent domain," 123 U.S. at 668, the opinion nevertheless suggested that some regulations of property might be so inherently unfair that they required just compensation as a remedy.

Shortly after *Mugler*, in *Chicago, Burlington & Quincy Railroad v. City of Chicago*, the Court definitively held that if a regulation effected the equivalent of seizing a person's property without just compensation, then the regulation would violate the Due Process Clause of the Fourteenth Amendment. 166 U.S. 226, 236 (1897). In retrospect, this decision became the first to incorporate a provision of the Bill of Rights—the Takings Clause of the Fifth Amendment—and apply it to the states.

Ever afterward, the Court evaluated the constitutionality of taxes, regulations, and other state deprivations of property under the Due Process Clause by asking (1) whether it effectively seized a person's property for something other than a "public use" or (2) whether it did so without "just compensation." *See, e.g.*, *Welch v. Swasey*, 214 U.S. 91, 105, 107 (1909).

Public use requirement

In deciding whether a deprivation of property was for a "public use" or a private use, the Court at first evaluated for itself the purpose of the deprivation. For example, it upheld as "public uses" the compelled transfer of property to build an irrigation ditch, *Clark v. Nash*, 198 U.S. 361 (1905); the government takeover of a privately owned water supply system, *Long Island Water Supply Co. v. Brooklyn*, 166 U.S. 685 (1897); and taxes to subsidize a bank, *Ottawa v. Carey*, 108 U.S. 110 (1883). But the Court struck down as "private uses" a law that paid a railroad to build a grain elevator for farmers, *Mo. Pac. Ry. Co. v. Nebraska*, 164 U.S. 403, 417 (1896); and taxes that subsidized various manufacturers, *Citizens' Sav. & Loan Ass'n v. City of Topeka*, 87 U.S. (20 Wall.) 655 (1875).

Eventually, however, the Court concluded that virtually any tax or regulation could be described as serving both a public use and a private use. For example, a government might tax its residents and offer the revenue to a railroad (a private use) to provide transportation (a public use); it might give bonds to a bank on favorable terms (a private use) to provide local farmers with access to credit (a public use); or it might condemn a person's land and give it to a private university (a private use) to provide education (a public use). *See* Nikolas Bowie, *The Government-Could-Not-Work Doctrine*, 105 Va. L. Rev. 1, 17, n. 71 (2019). By the beginning of the twentieth century, the Court stopped classifying any of these regulations as "private" transfers "from A. to B.," as it had in cases like *Citizens' Sav. & Loan Ass'n*, 87 U.S. (20 Wall.) at 655. Instead, the Court began to defer to state legislatures—and their "familiarity with local conditions"—to decide whether a deprivation's purpose was public or private. *Madden v. Kentucky*, 309 U.S. 83, 87–88 (1940).

Today, while the Court theoretically still asks whether a tax, regulation, or exercise of eminent domain is for a public use or a private use, it has long answered this question by deferring to the legislature. *See, e.g.*, *Brown v. Legal Found. of Wash.*, 538 U.S. 216, 231–32 (2003) (upholding as a "public use" an assessment on lawyers to finance legal services for the poor); *Haw. Hous. Auth. v. Midkiff*, 467 U.S. 229, 243 (1984) (upholding a law that transferred land from lessors to lessees to "correct deficiencies in the market"); *Berman v. Parker*, 348 U.S. 26, 32–33 (1954) (upholding use of eminent domain to eliminate "blight"); *United States ex rel. TVA v. Welch*, 327 U.S. 546, 552 (1946) (upholding use of eminent domain for agricultural and industrial development); *Helvering v. Davis*, 301 U.S. 619, 640 (1937) (deferring to legislature to determine whether tax was spent on general welfare).

The standard that the Court has employed asks simply whether a deprivation is "rationally related to a conceivable public purpose." *Midkiff*, 467 U.S. at 241. For example, in *Kelo v. City of New London*, 545 U.S. 469 (2005), the Court controversially upheld a Connecticut city's condemnation of a home to make room for a new campus for the pharmaceutical company Pfizer, Inc. Applying the same standards as the Fifth Amendment's Takings Clause and "reflecting our longstanding policy of deference to legislative judgments in this field," the Court upheld the use of eminent domain "to promote economic development." *Id.* at 489.

Just compensation requirement

The Supreme Court has employed a far more subjective and complicated test to evaluate when a deprivation of property is so unfair that it requires just compensation. In general, the more that a deprivation looks like a traditional exercise of eminent domain, the more likely it is that the Court will require just compensation. This is partly because, as discussed earlier in this section, the Court initially interpreted the Takings Clause of the Fifth Amendment to apply only to the federal government's use of eminent domain—that is, its physical possession or occupation of tangible property. It did not, by contrast, apply the Takings Clause to taxes, regulations, or other laws that allegedly deprived a person of their inchoate property interests.

The Court described this limited interpretation of the Takings Clause in the *Legal Tender Cases*, 79 U.S. (12 Wall.) 457 (1871). During the Civil War, Congress passed a law to finance the war by printing paper money and requiring creditors to accept the paper money as payment for all debts. Many creditors objected that this law unfairly took away their property interest in getting paid in gold and silver coin, which they considered far more valuable than inflationary paper currency. But the Court held that the Takings Clause was inapplicable:

> That provision has always been understood as referring only to a direct appropriation, and not to consequential injuries resulting from the exercise of lawful power. It has never been supposed to have any bearing upon, or to inhibit laws that indirectly work harm and loss to individuals. A new tariff, an embargo, a draft, or a war may inevitably bring upon individuals great losses; may, indeed, render valuable property almost valueless. They may destroy the worth of contracts. But whoever supposed that, because of this, a tariff could not be changed, or a non-intercourse act, or an embargo be enacted, or a war be declared?

The Legal Tender Cases, 79 U.S. (12 Wall.) at 551.

When the Court began interpreting the Due Process Clause of the Fourteenth Amendment to include the same standards as the Takings Clause, it continued to hold that the only laws requiring just compensation were direct appropriations of a person's land or personal property. *See Chi., Burlington & Quincy R.R. v. City of Chicago*, 166 U.S. 226, 236 (1897). The Court refused to require state and local governments to provide just compensation to property owners every time a regulation caused damage to their property. For example, when New York City authorized the construction of an elevated viaduct over a street, the Court held that the city wasn't responsible for compensating nearby property owners for lessening the circulation of light and air around their buildings. *Sauer v. City of New York*, 206 U.S. 536 (1907).

41.3.1

Pennsylvania Coal Co. v. Mahon

260 U.S. 393 (1922)

However, the Court announced a far different approach to evaluating the constitutionality of state regulations in *Pennsylvania Coal Co. v. Mahon*, 260 U.S. 393 (1922).

In the beginning of the twentieth century, Pennsylvania was one of the world's leading producers of oil, coal, and other natural resources from below the earth's surface. To extract these resources, mining companies typically contracted with landowners to purchase everything below the earth's surface. These contracts, usually expressed in deeds, also often held the mining companies harmless for any damage caused by their operations. As a result, many homes in western Pennsylvania sat above mine tunnels that could collapse and leave the homeowner without any remedy.

To address this situation, the Pennsylvania legislature passed a 1921 law that prohibited mining companies from extracting below-surface coal in places that might cause "subsidence," or sinking, of surface-level buildings. One of the companies affected was the Pennsylvania Coal Company, which in 1878 had entered into an agreement with a homeowner, H.J. Mahon, to extract the coal below his surface-level home. When the company told Mahon that it planned to ignore the 1921 law, Mahon sued to enforce its prohibition. In court, the company argued that the law violated the Fourteenth Amendment because due process required Pennsylvania to compensate the company for destroying the value of its coal and its contract with Mahon.

The Court in *Mahon* extended the principles underlying the Takings Clause to a more indirect appropriation than in the past.

■ MR. JUSTICE HOLMES delivered the opinion of the Court.[20]

This is a bill in equity brought by the [Mahons] to prevent the Pennsylvania Coal Company from mining under their property in such way as to remove the supports and cause a subsidence of the surface and of their house. . . . On appeal the Supreme Court of the State agreed that the defendant had contract and property rights protected by the Constitution of the United States, but held that the statute was a legitimate exercise of the police power and directed a decree for the plaintiffs. . . .

The statute forbids the mining of anthracite coal in such way as to cause the subsidence of . . . any structure used as a human habitation. . . . As applied to this case the statute is admitted to destroy previously existing rights of property and contract. The question is whether the police power can be stretched so far.

Government hardly could go on if to some extent values incident to property could not be diminished without paying for every such change in the general law. As long recognized, some values are enjoyed under an implied limitation and must yield to the police power. But obviously the implied limitation must have its limits, or the contract and due process clauses are gone. One fact for consideration in determining such limits is the extent of the diminution. When it reaches a certain magnitude, in most if not in all cases there must be an exercise of eminent domain and compensation to sustain the act. So the question depends upon the particular facts. The greatest weight is given to the judgment of the legislature, but it always is open to interested parties to contend that the legislature has gone beyond its constitutional power.

This is the case of a single private house. No doubt there is a public interest even in this, as there is in every purchase and sale and in all that happens within the commonwealth. Some existing rights may be modified even in such a case. But usually in ordinary private affairs the public interest does not warrant much of this kind of interference. A source of damage to such a house is not a public nuisance even if similar damage is inflicted on others in different places. The damage is not common or public. . . . Furthermore, it is not justified as a protection of personal safety. That could be provided for by notice. Indeed the very foundation of this bill is that the defendant gave timely notice of its intent to mine under the house. On the other hand the extent of the taking is great. It purports to abolish what is recognized in Pennsylvania as an estate in land—a very valuable estate—and what is declared by the Court below to be a contract hitherto binding the plaintiffs. . . . [W]e should

---

[20] **As You Read, Consider:** Justice Oliver Wendell Holmes dissented in *Lochner v. New York*. What do you think explains his lack of deference to state legislatures in this case, which is quite similar to *Mugler v. Kansas*?

think it clear that the statute does not disclose a public interest sufficient to warrant so extensive a destruction of the defendant's constitutionally protected rights. . . .

As said in a Pennsylvania case, "For practical purposes, the right to coal consists in the right to mine it." *Commonwealth v. Clearview Coal Co.*, 256 Pa. St. 328, 331. What makes the right to mine coal valuable is that it can be exercised with profit. To make it commercially impracticable to mine certain coal has very nearly the same effect for constitutional purposes as appropriating or destroying it. This we think that we are warranted in assuming that the statute does.

It is true that in *Plymouth Coal Co. v. Pennsylvania,* 232 U.S. 531, it was held competent for the legislature to require a pillar of coal to be left along the line of adjoining property, that, with the pillar on the other side of the line, would be a barrier sufficient for the safety of the employees of either mine in case the other should be abandoned and allowed to fill with water. But that was a requirement for the safety of employees invited into the mine, and secured an average reciprocity of advantage that has been recognized as a justification of various laws.

The rights of the public in a street purchased or laid out by eminent domain are those that it has paid for. If in any case its representatives have been so short sighted as to acquire only surface rights without the right of support, we see no more authority for supplying the latter without compensation than there was for taking the right of way in the first place and refusing to pay for it because the public wanted it very much. The protection of private property in the Fifth Amendment presupposes that it is wanted for public use, but provides that it shall not be taken for such use without compensation. A similar assumption is made in the decisions upon the Fourteenth Amendment. When this seemingly absolute protection is found to be qualified by the police power, the natural tendency of human nature is to extend the qualification more and more until at last private property disappears. But that cannot be accomplished in this way under the Constitution of the United States.

The general rule at least is, that while property may be regulated to a certain extent, if regulation goes too far it will be recognized as a taking.[21] It may be doubted how far exceptional cases, like the blowing up of a house to stop a conflagration, go—and if they go beyond the general rule, whether they do not stand as much upon tradition as upon principle. In general it is not plain that a man's misfortunes or necessities will justify his shifting the damages to his neighbor's shoulders. We are in danger of forgetting that a strong public desire to improve the public condition is not enough to warrant achieving the desire by a shorter cut than the constitutional way of paying for the change. As we already have said, this is a question of degree—and therefore cannot be disposed of by general propositions. But we regard this as going beyond any of the cases decided by this Court. . . .

[T]he question at bottom is upon whom the loss of the changes desired should fall. So far as private persons or communities have seen fit to take the risk of acquiring only surface rights, we cannot see that the fact that their risk has become a danger warrants the giving to them greater rights than they bought.

■ MR. JUSTICE BRANDEIS, dissenting. . . .[22]

[C]oal in place is land; and the right of the owner to use his land is not absolute. He may not so use it as to create a public nuisance; and uses, once harmless, may,

---

[21] **Questions:** In *Mugler*, the Court held that the Fourteenth Amendment required compensation for a "taking" only where a law was the functional equivalent of eminent domain. Here, Holmes writes that a taking occurs when a regulation "goes too far." What does *too far* mean? What principles can help a court determine when "too far" has been realized?

[22] **Question:** Justice Louis Brandeis treats this case as the equivalent of any other Due Process Clause case in the *Lochner* era: legislatures can pass any law that is reasonably related

owing to changed conditions, seriously threaten the public welfare. Whenever they do, the legislature has power to prohibit such uses without paying compensation; and the power to prohibit extends alike to the manner, the character and the purpose of the use. Are we justified in declaring that the Legislature of Pennsylvania has, in restricting the right to mine anthracite, exercised this power so arbitrarily as to violate the Fourteenth Amendment?

Every restriction upon the use of property imposed in the exercise of the police power deprives the owner of some right theretofore enjoyed, and is, in that sense, an abridgment by the State of rights in property without making compensation. But restriction imposed to protect the public health, safety or morals from dangers threatened is not a taking. The restriction here in question is merely the prohibition of a noxious use. The property so restricted remains in the possession of its owner. The State does not appropriate it or make any use of it. The State merely prevents the owner from making a use which interferes with paramount rights of the public. . . .

The restriction upon the use of this property can not, of course, be lawfully imposed, unless its purpose is to protect the public. But the purpose of a restriction does not cease to be public, because incidentally some private persons may thereby receive gratuitously valuable special benefits. Thus, owners of low buildings may obtain, through statutory restrictions upon the height of neighboring structures, benefits equivalent to an easement of light and air. *Welch v. Swasey,* 214 U.S. 91. Furthermore, a restriction, though imposed for a public purpose, will not be lawful, unless the restriction is an appropriate means to the public end. But to keep coal in place is surely an appropriate means of preventing subsidence of the surface; and ordinarily it is the only available means. Restriction upon use does not become inappropriate as a means, merely because it deprives the owner of the only use to which the property can then be profitably put. The liquor and the oleomargarine cases settled that. *Mugler v. Kansas,* 123 U.S. 623, 668, 669; *Powell v. Pennsylvania,* 127 U.S. 678, 682. Nor is a restriction imposed through exercise of the police power inappropriate as a means, merely because the same end might be affected through exercise of the power of eminent domain, or otherwise at public expense. Every restriction upon the height of buildings might be secured through acquiring by eminent domain the right of each owner to build above the limiting height; but it is settled that the State need not resort to that power. If by mining anthracite coal the owner would necessarily unloose poisonous gasses, I suppose no one would doubt the power of the State to prevent the mining, without buying his coal fields. And why may not the State, likewise, without paying compensation, prohibit one from digging so deep or excavating so near the surface, as to expose the community to like dangers? In the latter case, as in the former, carrying on the business would be a public nuisance.

It is said that one fact for consideration in determining whether the limits of the police power have been exceeded is the extent of the resulting diminution in value; and that here the restriction destroys existing rights of property and contract. But values are relative. If we are to consider the value of the coal kept in place by the restriction, we should compare it with the value of all other parts of the land. That is, with the value not of the coal alone, but with the value of the whole property. The rights of an owner as against the public are not increased by dividing the interests in his property into surface and subsoil. The sum of the rights in the parts can not be greater than the rights in the whole. . . . For aught that appears the value of the coal kept in place by the restriction may be negligible as compared with the value of the

---

to public health, safety, or morals. Why does Brandeis object to Holmes's new test, which holds that legislatures are prohibited from enacting any regulation that "goes too far"?

whole property, or even as compared with that part of it which is represented by the coal remaining in place and which may be extracted despite the statute. . . .[23]

[T]he statute should, in my opinion, be upheld in this case. For the defendant has failed to adduce any evidence from which it appears that to restrict its mining operations was an unreasonable exercise of the police power. . . .

NOTE: FOUR TYPES OF REGULATORY TAKINGS

In a brief opinion, Justice Oliver Wendell Holmes transformed the law of takings by striking down a law that didn't literally seize anyone's property but merely made a portion of the mining company's property—some of the coal in its subsurface estate—less valuable. Consider the contrast with *Mugler*, in which the Supreme Court upheld a prohibition on the manufacture of alcohol even though the prohibition made Mugler's brewery worthless. Consider also the contrast with *Lochner v. New York*, 198 U.S. 45 (1905), in which Holmes famously urged the Court to defer to legislative majorities. Now, Holmes wrote that when a regulation resembled the use of eminent domain, whether just compensation was required was "a question of degree." *Mahon*, 260 U.S. at 416. As a general rule, he offered merely that "while property may be regulated to a certain extent, if regulation goes too far it will be recognized as a taking." *Id.* at 415.

Holmes's opinion drew a dissent from his closest ally on the Court, Brandeis, who objected that this new rule marked a significant departure from the Court's other due process cases. Even in *Lochner*, the Court asked merely whether a regulation promoted health, morals, or safety—not whether it went "too far." Brandeis was right. Even after the Court ended the *Lochner* era and adopted an extremely deferential approach toward most economic regulations in *West Coast Hotel*, the Court has continued to closely scrutinize regulations that resemble the use of eminent domain.

In the century since *Mahon*, the Court has had predictable difficulty coming up with clear guidelines to determine whether a regulation goes too far, requiring just compensation, or whether it is just an ordinary regulation. In fact, the Court has applied different guidelines for different categories of deprivation: (1) physical invasions; (2) prohibitions of economically viable uses of land; (3) regulations that decrease a property's value; and (4) *exactions*, or conditions on how property may be used. These tests apply to deprivations of all kinds of "property," including easements on land, *United States v. Welch*, 217 U.S. 333 (1910); tangible personal property, *Horne v. Dep't of Agric.*, 576 U.S. 350 (2015); intangible property such as contract rights and corporate franchises, *Ruckelshaus v. Monsanto Co.*, 467 U.S. 986 (1984); and even, perhaps, money, *E. Enters. v. Apfel*, 524 U.S. 498 (1998).

Whenever a government takes any of these property interests, the "question at bottom" is the same as that in *Mahon*: "upon whom [should] the

[23] **Question:** Brandeis and Holmes disagree about what, precisely, has been taken in this case. Holmes characterizes the law as completely prohibiting the mining company from taking the coal it contracted for. Brandeis writes that the level of generality is expanded slightly: the mining company still has lots of coal—it is just prohibited from taking more than is necessary to keep houses above the mine shafts from sinking. Does Holmes's "too far" test resolve this level-of-generality problem?

loss . . . fall." *Mahon*, 260 U.S. at 416. Where the Court thinks that a regulation "force[s] some people alone to bear public burdens which, in all fairness and justice, should be borne by the public as a whole," then the Court requires the government to pay just compensation. *Armstrong v. United States*, 364 U.S. 40, 49 (1960).

Option 1: Physical invasions. The most straightforward category of deprivation involves contexts in which the government physically invades a person's property. Because eminent domain is defined by the government's physical appropriation of land, the Supreme Court has generally considered all similar appropriations "takings" that require just compensation, even if the compensation required is minimal. For example, in *Loretto v. Teleprompter Manhattan CATV Corp.*, 458 U.S. 419 (1982), the Court considered it a taking when New York City required landlords to permit cable companies to install television wires on the exterior of apartment buildings—even though the wires took up very little space and had no economic impact on any building. Other examples in which the Court held that a government had conducted an "actual physical invasion" include when a government required a property owner to allow public access to its pond, *Kaiser Aetna v. United States*, 444 U.S. 164 (1979); when a government dam induced temporary flooding of downstream land, *Ark. Game & Fishing Comm'n v. United States*, 568 U.S. 23 (2012); when a government fort fired guns across a person's land, *Portsmouth Harbor Land & Hotel Co. v. United States*, 260 U.S. 327 (1922); and when government airports made nearby land unfit for use because planes taking off and landing had to loudly fly over the land, *United States v. Causby*, 328 U.S. 256 (1946).

For decades, the Court distinguished this categorical rule from contexts in which a government prohibited an employer or landlord from excluding certain *people* from their property. *See, e.g.*, *Yee v. City of Escondido*, 503 U.S. 519 (1992) (no physical possession where city prohibited trailer park from setting rents or discriminating against certain tenants); *PruneYard Shopping Ctr. v. Robins*, 447 U.S. 74, 84 (1980) (distinguishing *Aetna* to hold that there was no physical possession where California required a shopping mall to admit certain protestors temporarily).

But in *Cedar Point Nursery v. Hassid*, 141 S. Ct. 2063 (2021), the Court modified its rule to hold that with some exceptions, the government conducts a *per se* physical taking whenever it interferes with a property owner's "right to exclude"—as when California required agricultural employers to admit union organizers temporarily on company property. *Cedar Point*, 141 S. Ct. at 2072. The Court's four exceptions, which did not save California's regulation, included contexts in which (1) the government allows someone to enter property only once, (2) there are "longstanding background restrictions" against excluding certain people, (3) the property owner gives up the right to exclude "as a condition of receiving certain benefits," or (4) the property is already open to the general public. *Id.* at 2078–80. Despite these exceptions, the decision cast doubt on the constitutionality of many other laws that prohibit employers or landlords from excluding workers or tenants from their property for discriminatory or retaliatory reasons. *See* Nikolas Bowie, *Antidemocracy*, 135 Harv. L. Rev. 160, 162 (2021).

Option 2: Prohibitions of economic viability. Closely related to physical occupations of land are regulations like the law in *Mahon*, in which the government denies a property owner "economically viable use of his land." *Agins v. City of Tiburon*, 447 U.S. 255, 260 (1980). When a regulation requires a landowner "to leave his property economically idle," the Court has held that the regulation is valid only if it "inhere[s] in the title itself, in the restrictions that background principles of the State's law of property and nuisance already place upon land ownership." *Lucas v. S.C. Coastal Council*, 505 U.S. 1003, 1019 (1992). For example, the Court has considered it a taking where a government prohibits or severely restricts people from alienating their land or passing it on to heirs. *See Hodel v. Irving*, 481 U.S. 704 (1987). Even where a government notifies future landowners that certain parcels of land cannot be used in an economically viable way, that alone is not enough to prevent the government from having to provide just compensation. *See Tahoe-Sierra Pres. Council v. Tahoe Reg. Plann. Agency*, 535 U.S. 302 (2002); *Palazzolo v. Rhode Island*, 533 U.S. 606 (2001).

One complication with this category of taking is that whether a regulation denies property owners the economically viable use of their "land" depends on how *land* is defined. In *Mahon*, Holmes emphasized that the Pennsylvania law had denied the mining company the economically viable use of the land containing coal: "the right to coal consists in the right to mine it." *Mahon*, 260 U.S. at 414. But Brandeis emphasized that Holmes was taking too narrow a view of the mining company's land: the company owned an enormous estate of subsurface land that it could still make use of, and it could still mine as much coal as it could from that land until further mining would cause homes on the surface to collapse.

In more recent cases, the Court has taken Brandeis's view. In evaluating the effect of a regulation, it now considers the "parcel as a whole," which includes a *spatial dimension* (a court must consider the entire relevant tract), a *functional dimension* (a court must consider the plaintiff's full bundle of property rights), and a *temporal dimension* (a court must consider the entire time span of a property interest). *Tahoe-Sierra Pres. Council*, 535 U.S. at 327. Moreover, the spatial dimension is defined with reference to "[1] the treatment of the land under state and local law; [2] the physical characteristics of the land; and [3] the prospective value of the regulated land." *Murr v. Wisconsin*, 137 S. Ct. 1933, 1945 (2017). So, in a case where plaintiffs owned two parcels of land, A and B, and claimed that the government deprived them of the economically viable use of parcel B, the Court applied its three-factor test and determined that it was more appropriate to consider both parcels as if they were a single parcel in which the government could regulate a fraction of the total land without needing to provide just compensation. *Id.*

Option 3: Regulations that decrease a property's value. Before the 1970s, the Supreme Court generally held that the government could regulate property without just compensation as long as it regulated it such that it didn't physically occupy the property or deprive the owner of all economically viable uses of the property. *See Goldblatt v. Town of Hempstead*, 369 U.S. 590 (1962). In *Mugler*, for example, the Court upheld Kansas's prohibition on the sale of alcohol even though this regulation effectively ruined the state's breweries.

But in *Penn Central Transportation Co. v. City of New York*, 438 U.S. 104 (1978), the Court reaffirmed Holmes's statement in *Mahon* that while all regulations of property might decrease a property's value, some regulations nevertheless go too far. The Court suggested that a regulatory taking might occur when a government's interest in prohibiting harmful uses of property are outweighed by the property owner's reasonable "investment-backed expectations" in being able to use its property without restraint. *Penn Cent.*, 438 U.S. at 124.

The *Penn Central* decision analyzed New York City's landmarks preservation law. The law prohibited the owner of Grand Central Terminal from constructing a fifty-three-story office building above its property. Like the coal company in *Mahon*, which claimed that Pennsylvania had effectively appropriated the coal underneath its land, the developer in *Penn Central* claimed that New York had effectively appropriated the air above its terminal. But the Court disagreed after considering the "parcel as a whole" and determining that New York's prohibition on developing the air was part of a reasonable and unsurprising policy that was expected to produce a widespread public benefit applicable to all similarly situated property. *Penn Cent.*, 438 U.S. at 133, n.30.

Examples of laws that have survived *Penn Central*'s "investment-backed expectations" test include a federal ban on the sale of eagle feathers because the substantial public purpose in protecting the eagle from extinction outweighed the owner's inability to sell the feathers—especially considering that the owner could continue to possess the feathers. *See Andrus v. Allard*, 444 U.S. 51 (1979). The Court also upheld a restriction on mining that was nearly identical to the restriction in *Mahon* because the state had apparently offered a more substantial public purpose in protecting all structures from sinking. *See Keystone Bituminous Coal Ass'n v. DeBenedictis*, 480 U.S. 470 (1987).

By contrast, the Court has been relatively hostile to laws that retroactively impose liabilities. The most notable example is *Eastern Enterprises v. Apfel*, 524 U.S. 498 (1998), in which the Court struck down a federal law that required all companies formerly engaged in mining to pay health benefits to retirees. The federal government applied this law to Eastern Enterprises, a company that had spun off its mining operations thirty years earlier—long before any collective bargaining agreements promised to pay lifetime pensions to miners. In light of Eastern Enterprises' reasonable investment-backed expectations, four justices wrote that to retroactively require Eastern Enterprises to pay hundreds of millions of dollars would be a taking without just compensation. *E. Enters.*, 524 U.S. at 537 (plurality opinion).

The plurality opinion of *Eastern Enterprises* wasn't the controlling opinion, however. In a concurrence, Justice Anthony Kennedy joined four dissenting justices in holding that the Court's takings jurisprudence should apply only to deprivations of real or personal property, not to deprivations of money alone. *Id.* at 541–42 (Kennedy, J., concurring in the judgment and dissenting in part). Kennedy and the dissenters warned that if the Court considered the deprivation of money a taking, then the Court might invalidate all taxes—which, by definition, take or deprive a person of property without just compensation. *Id.* Kennedy therefore argued that the law had to be evaluated under the Court's ordinary due process jurisprudence: the rational-basis test of *West Coast Hotel* and *Carolene Products. Id.* at 547. In the years after *Carolene Products*, the Court had consistently upheld the power of legislatures to impose taxes and other regulations retroactively as long as "the retroactive application of the legislation is itself justified by a rational legislative purpose." *United States v. Carlton*, 512 U.S. 26, 31 (1994) (quoting *Usery v. Turner Elkhorn Mining Co.*, 428 U.S. 1, 16–17 (1976)). Applying this test in *Eastern Enterprises*, Kennedy held that the law was arbitrary. 524 U.S. at 547–50.

Option 4: Exactions. The final type of regulation that the Court has struck down as a taking involves *exactions*, or conditions on how property may be used. The Court first developed this category in *Nollan v. California Coastal Commission*, 483 U.S. 825 (1987), in which the Nollan family wanted to develop their beachfront bungalow into a multistory building. A state agency determined that a larger building would block the public's view of the beach; thus, the commission offered the Nollans a permit only if they gave the state an easement allowing members of the public to walk across their property to access the beach. Calling this "an out-and-out plan of extortion," the Court held that a state had to offer just compensation for conditions on development unless there was an "essential nexus" that was currently missing between the condition (public access to the beach) and the cost to the public caused by the development (the public's lost view). *Nollan*, 483 U.S. at 837.

The Court amended the *Nollan* test in *Dolan v. City of Tigard*, 512 U.S. 374 (1994), in which an Oregon city allowed an electrical supply store to pave a parking lot as long as the store (1) dedicated land to a public greenway (to mitigate flooding caused by the paved parking lot) and (2) developed a pedestrian and bike pathway (to relieve congestion). These proposals satisfied *Nollan* because there was an essential nexus, or reasonable relationship, between the conditions and the costs to the public. But the Court nevertheless held that for a condition not to be a taking, the condition must be related to a proposed development not only in *nature* but also in *degree*. The Court explained that there must be a "rough proportionality" between the burden imposed by the conditions on the property owner and the impact of the proposed development on the community. *Dolan*, 512 U.S. at 391–92. In other words, the city was asking for far more than the property owner was getting in return.

The *Nollan/Dolan* "essential nexus"/"rough proportionality" test exists uneasily alongside the Court's approach to most economic regulations, in which the Court upholds any law for which there is a rational basis. But the Court has explained that a government may not directly appropriate property without just compensation, and therefore a government may not indirectly accomplish the same end by offering unrelated and coercive conditions. *Lingle v. Chevron U.S.A. Inc.*, 544 U.S. 528, 546 (2005). The Court therefore applies *Nollan/Dolan* whenever a government introduces a condition as an alternative to the use of eminent domain—including where the condition demanded comes in the form of money or fees. *Koontz v. St. Johns River Water Mgmt. Dist.*, 570 U.S. 595 (2013).

NOTE: RIPENESS AND REMEDIES

For almost a century, when individuals challenged regulations as uncompensated takings, the Court held that no constitutional violation occurred until (1) the government issued a "final, definitive position" regarding how it would apply a regulation to the individual's property and (2) the government denied the individual just compensation. *Williamson Cnty. Reg'l Plan. Comm'n v. Hamilton Bank*, 473 U.S. 172, 191 (1985). But in *Knick v. Township of Scott*, 139 S. Ct. 2162, 2179 (2019), the Court overruled its precedent and held that an individual could challenge an alleged taking in federal court as soon as it happened.

Because of the unstable relationship between alleged takings and economic regulations, the Supreme Court's modern takings jurisprudence has the potential to return the Court to the *Lochner* era, in which federal courts regularly struck down economic legislation as unconstitutional deprivations of property and liberty. One potential difference between the *Lochner* era and now, however, is the relief available to a person challenging the law. When a person successfully challenges a law as "arbitrary" under the *Lochner-West Coast Hotel* line of cases, the law is invalid and cannot be enforced. *See, e.g., E. Enters.*, 524 U.S. 498. But when a person successfully challenges a law as an uncompensated taking under the *Mahon* line of cases, the law may stand if the government can effectively provide "just compensation," or the fair market value of the regulation to the property owner. *See Knick*, 139 S. Ct. at 2179 ("As long as just compensation remedies are available . . . injunctive relief will be foreclosed.").

CHAPTER 42

WHAT LIMITATIONS DO THE DUE PROCESS CLAUSES OF THE FIFTH AND FOURTEENTH AMENDMENTS IMPOSE ON THE SUBSTANTIVE POWER OF GOVERNMENT TO DEPRIVE PEOPLE OF THEIR LIBERTY TO MAKE PRIVATE DECISIONS?

FIRST AMENDMENT (1791): Congress shall make no law respecting an establishment of religion, or prohibiting the free exercise thereof; or abridging the freedom of speech, or of the press; or the right of the people peaceably to assemble, and to petition the Government for a redress of grievances.

THIRD AMENDMENT (1791): No Soldier shall, in time of peace be quartered in any house, without the consent of the Owner, nor in time of war, but in a manner to be prescribed by law.

FOURTH AMENDMENT (1791): The right of the people to be secure in their persons, houses, papers, and effects, against unreasonable searches and seizures, shall not be violated. . . .

FIFTH AMENDMENT (1791): No person shall be . . . deprived of life, liberty, or property, without due process of law. . . .

NINTH AMENDMENT (1791): The enumeration in the Constitution, of certain rights, shall not be construed to deny or disparage others retained by the people.

FOURTEENTH AMENDMENT (1868), SECTION 1: No State shall . . . deprive any person of life, liberty, or property, without due process of law. . . .

42.1 THE RIGHT OF PRIVACY

The era of *Lochner v. New York*, 198 U.S. 45 (1905), is best remembered for its recognition of a "liberty to contract"—a broadly defined right to choose one's own calling; to freely make contracts; and to acquire, use, and sell property. But the Court during this period claimed to protect more than just property rights. As early as *Mugler v. Kansas*, the Court declared that the American system of government, "based upon the individuality and intelligence of the citizen, does not claim to control" the "tastes, appetites, habits, dress, food, and drink of the people." 123 U.S. 623, 660 (1887). Over time, this broad declaration of individual autonomy in social and cultural matters evolved into a second liberty interest: the right of privacy.

Louis Brandeis and his law partner, Samuel Warren, developed one of the earliest articulations of this liberty interest in a law review article titled "The Right to Privacy." Samuel Warren & Louis Brandeis, *The Right to Privacy*, 4 Harv. L. Rev. 193 (1890). "Political, social, and economic changes entail the recognition of new rights," the article began, "and the common law, in its eternal youth, grows to meet the demands of society." *Id.* at 193. English and state courts that once defined *liberty* to mean "freedom from actual restraint" had begun to protect "man's spiritual nature, . . . his feelings and his intellect[,] . . . [and] the exercise of extensive civil privileges." *Id.* Discussing recent developments in the common law of nuisance, copyright, contract, and libel, Brandeis and Warren concluded that courts were expanding existing doctrines into "[a] general right of the individual to be let alone." *Id.* at 206. A person whose photograph was taken, for example, had recently persuaded a court to prevent the photographer from publishing the photograph—providing "a principle which may be invoked to protect the privacy of the individual from invasion either by the too enterprising press, the photographer, or the possessor of any other modern device for recording." *Id.* Brandeis and Warren described this "right to privacy" as a new tort—invasion of privacy—that courts around the country soon recognized and enforced. *See* Restatement (First) of Torts § 867 (1939).

When Brandeis joined the Supreme Court in 1916, he became a consistent opponent of the Court's use of the Due Process Clause to strike down legislation. *See, e.g.*, *Truax v. Corrigan*, 257 U.S. 312, 373–76 (1921) (Brandeis, J., dissenting). But as long as the Court was interpreting the Due Process Clause broadly, Brandeis argued that the Court should invoke the clause to protect more than only liberty to acquire and enjoy property. Years before the Supreme Court incorporated the First Amendment against the states, Brandeis dissented in a case, *Gilbert v. Minnesota*, in which the Court upheld the conviction of a pacifist under a World War I-era statute that prohibited interfering with military enlistment:

> I have difficulty in believing that the liberty guaranteed by the Constitution, which has been held to protect against state denial the right of an employer to discriminate against a workman because he is a member of a trade union . . . does not include liberty to teach, either in the privacy of the home or publicly, the doctrine of pacifism.

254 U.S. 325, 343 (1920) (Brandeis, J., dissenting).

42.1.1

Meyer v. Nebraska

262 U.S. 390 (1923)

Three years later, one of the most conservative justices on the Supreme Court—James McReynolds—turned Brandeis's *Gilbert* dissent into a majority opinion in *Meyer v. Nebraska*, 262 U.S. 390 (1923).

McReynolds was Brandeis's opposite: Where Brandeis opposed substantive due process, McReynolds defended it until his retirement in 1941. And where Brandeis was a leader of the American Zionist movement, McReynolds was so anti-Semitic that there was no official portrait of the Supreme Court in 1924 because McReynolds wouldn't sit next to Brandeis, as protocol required. Melvin I. Urofsky, *Louis D. Brandeis* 479 (2009). But the two men's judicial philosophies converged when the Court interpreted another World War I-era statute, this one from Nebraska, in *Meyer*.

Like many states during the war, Nebraska was captivated by anti-German hysteria. Nebraska had a large German-speaking population, and the legislature feared that the state's German communities would undermine the war effort. In 1918, the legislature passed a law that banned all foreign-language classes. Later that year, the Americanization Division of the U.S. Bureau of Education proposed that states increase "race assimilation" among immigrants by teaching them classes only in English. *See* P. P. Claxton, *Americanization*, 1 Americanization Bull. 1–5 (1918). In 1919, Nebraska's legislature complied by making it a crime for any person "in any private, denominational, parochial or public school, [to] teach any subject to any person in any language other than the English language." *Meyer*, 262 U.S. at 397 (quoting Nebraska law).

State prosecutors soon tried and convicted a teacher, Robert T. Meyer, of knowingly teaching in German during an after-hours religion class at a Lutheran parochial school. Rejecting a *Lochner* challenge, the Nebraska Supreme Court affirmed Meyer's conviction on the ground that "[t]he legislature had seen the baneful effects of permitting foreigners, who had taken residence in this country, to rear and educate their children in the language of their native land. The result of that condition was found to be inimical to our own safety." *Meyer v. State*, 187 N.W. 100, 102 (Neb. 1922).

In *Meyer*, the U.S. Supreme Court ruled that although "[t]he desire of the legislature to foster a homogeneous people with American ideals prepared readily to understand current discussions of civic matters is easy to appreciate[,] . . . the means adopted . . . exceed the limitations upon the power of the State." *Meyer*, 262 U.S. at 402.

■ MR. JUSTICE MCREYNOLDS delivered the opinion of the Court.[1]

Plaintiff in error was tried and convicted in the District Court for Hamilton County, Nebraska, under an information which charged that on May 25, 1920, while an instructor in Zion Parochial School, he unlawfully taught the subject of reading in the German language to Raymond Parpart, a child of ten years . . . .

The problem for our determination is whether the statute as construed and applied unreasonably infringes the liberty guaranteed to the plaintiff in error by the Fourteenth Amendment. . . .

While this Court has not attempted to define with exactness the liberty thus guaranteed, the term has received much consideration and some of the included things have been definitely stated. Without doubt, it denotes not merely freedom from bodily restraint but also the right of the individual to contract, to engage in any of the common occupations of life, to acquire useful knowledge, to marry, establish a home and bring up children, to worship God according to the dictates of his own conscience, and generally to enjoy those privileges long recognized at common law as essential to the orderly pursuit of happiness by free men. *Slaughter-House Cases,* 16 Wall. 36; *Lochner v. New York,* 198 U.S. 45; *Adkins v. Children's Hospital,* 261 U.S. 525. The established doctrine is that this liberty may not be interfered with, under the guise of protecting the public interest, by legislative action which is arbitrary or without reasonable relation to some purpose within the competency of the State to effect. Determination by the legislature of what constitutes proper exercise of police power is not final or conclusive but is subject to supervision by the courts.

The American people have always regarded education and acquisition of knowledge as matters of supreme importance which should be diligently promoted. . . . Corresponding to the right of control, it is the natural duty of the parent to give his children education suitable to their station in life; and nearly all the States, including Nebraska, enforce this obligation by compulsory laws.

Practically, education of the young is only possible in schools conducted by especially qualified persons who devote themselves thereto. The calling always has been regarded as useful and honorable, essential, indeed, to the public welfare. Mere knowledge of the German language cannot reasonably be regarded as harmful. Heretofore it has been commonly looked upon as helpful and desirable. Plaintiff in error taught this language in school as part of his occupation. His right thus to teach and the right of parents to engage him so to instruct their children, we think, are within the liberty of the Amendment.

The challenged statute forbids the teaching in school of any subject except in English; also the teaching of any other language until the pupil has attained and successfully passed the eighth grade, which is not usually accomplished before the age of twelve. . . . Evidently the legislature has attempted materially to interfere with . . . the opportunities of pupils to acquire knowledge, and with the power of parents to control the education of their own.

It is said the purpose of the legislation was to promote civic development by inhibiting training and education of the immature in foreign tongues and ideals before they could learn English and acquire American ideals; and "that the English language

[1] **As You Read, Consider:** *Lochner v. New York* and its follow-on cases, like *Adkins v. Children's Hospital* (striking down a minimum-wage law), were derided by progressives as antidemocratic efforts by the Supreme Court to impose its will on legislative majorities. *Meyer v. Nebraska,* by contrast, escaped this condemnation. What, if anything, is the difference between *Lochner* and Justice James McReynolds's opinion in this case? As you answer this question, note how McReynolds supportively cites *Lochner* and *Adkins* in his opening paragraphs.

should be and become the mother tongue of all children reared in this State." It is also affirmed that the foreign born population is very large, that certain communities commonly use foreign words, follow foreign leaders, move in a foreign atmosphere, and that the children are thereby hindered from becoming citizens of the most useful type and the public safety is imperiled.

That the State may do much, go very far, indeed, in order to improve the quality of its citizens, physically, mentally and morally, is clear; but the individual has certain fundamental rights which must be respected. The protection of the Constitution extends to all, to those who speak other languages as well as to those born with English on the tongue. Perhaps it would be highly advantageous if all had ready understanding of our ordinary speech, but this cannot be coerced by methods which conflict with the Constitution—a desirable end cannot be promoted by prohibited means. . . .

The desire of the legislature to foster a homogeneous people with American ideals prepared readily to understand current discussions of civic matters is easy to appreciate. Unfortunate experiences during the late war and aversion toward every characteristic of truculent adversaries were certainly enough to quicken that aspiration. But the means adopted, we think, exceed the limitations upon the power of the State and conflict with rights assured to plaintiff in error. . . .

We are constrained to conclude that the statute as applied is arbitrary and without reasonable relation to any end within the competency of the State. . . . It is well known that proficiency in a foreign language seldom comes to one not instructed at an early age, and experience shows that this is not injurious to the health, morals or understanding of the ordinary child. . . .[2]

42.1.2

Griswold v. Connecticut

381 U.S. 479 (1965)

To prove that the Due Process Clause's definition of *liberty* included not just "freedom from bodily restraint" but also the right to marry, to raise children, and to pursue happiness, McReynolds cited *Lochner* and *Adkins v. Children's Hospital*, 261 U.S. 525 (1923). *Meyer*, 262 U.S. at 399. But both cases concerned the liberty to contract—not broader protections of noneconomic autonomy. Nevertheless, after *Meyer*, McReynolds and Brandeis proceeded to invoke the Constitution to protect broader interests than mere property.

In *Pierce v. Society of Sisters*, 268 U.S. 510 (1925), McReynolds wrote a majority opinion that struck down an Oregon law, sponsored by the Ku Klux Klan, that prohibited families from sending their children to Catholic or other parochial schools. Invoking *Meyer*, he wrote that the law

---

[2] **Questions:** McReynolds concedes that states have a legitimate interest in compelling all children to go to school to "learn English and acquire American ideals." What, therefore, is wrong with Nebraska's law? When he calls the law "arbitrary," is he concluding that Nebraska irrationally mediated this particular conflict between its interest in homogeneity and Meyer's interest in teaching German? Or is he concluding that the right of parents to "bring up children" and the right of teachers to pursue their calling are "fundamental rights" with which virtually no law could, with reason, interfere?

> unreasonably interferes with the liberty of parents and guardians to direct the upbringing and education of children under their control. . . . The fundamental theory of liberty upon which all governments in this Union repose excludes any general power of the State to standardize its children by forcing them to accept instruction from public teachers only.

Pierce, 268 U.S. at 534–35.

Relatedly, in *Olmstead v. United States*, 277 U.S. 438 (1928), Brandeis dissented from an opinion that upheld the federal government's use of warrantless wiretaps to collect evidence for criminal trials. Interpreting the Bill of Rights in light of his *Harvard Law Review* article about the right to privacy, he maintained that "the right to be let alone" was "the most comprehensive of rights and the right most valued by civilized men." *Olmstead*, 277 U.S. at 478 (Brandeis, J., dissenting).

McReynolds's and Brandeis's broad embrace of individual autonomy led both to participate in using the Due Process Clause to treat the protections of the Bill of Rights as "among the fundamental personal rights and 'liberties' protected by the due process clause of the Fourteenth Amendment from impairment by the States." *Gitlow v. New York*, 268 U.S. 652, 666 (1925). As discussed earlier with regard to the incorporation of the Bill of Rights against the states (section 40.4), the Court began to hold that the Due Process Clause prohibited state interference in rights "implicit in the concept of ordered liberty" or "so rooted in the traditions and conscience of our people as to be ranked as fundamental." *Palko v. Connecticut*, 302 U.S. 319, 325 (1937) (quoting *Snyder v. Massachusetts*, 291 U.S. 97, 105 (1934)).

But as this rhetoric implied, not every claim of individual autonomy was "fundamental" enough to be vindicated by the Court. In *Jacobson v. Massachusetts*, the Court upheld a Massachusetts law that compelled all residents to receive smallpox vaccinations—even without their consent. 197 U.S. 11, 35 (1905). And in *Buck v. Bell*, the Court invoked *Jacobson* to uphold Virginia's involuntary sterilization of "mental defectives." 274 U.S. 200, 205 (1927). In an infamous passage, Justice Oliver Wendell Holmes concluded that "[t]he principle that sustains compulsory vaccination is broad enough to cover cutting the Fallopian tubes. Three generations of imbeciles are enough." *Id.* at 207.

After the Supreme Court repudiated *Lochner* in 1937, a new generation of progressive justices joined Holmes in committing themselves to upholding state laws, no matter how obnoxious they were to individual autonomy. Justice Felix Frankfurter, a protégé of Holmes and Brandeis who joined the Court in 1939, was particularly adamant that "[e]ven where the social undesirability of a law may be convincingly urged, invalidation of the law by a court debilitates democratic government." *Am. Fed'n of Labor v. Am. Sash & Door Co.*, 335 U.S. 538, 553 (1949) (Frankfurter, J., concurring). "[T]o the legislature no less than to courts is committed the guardianship of deeply-cherished liberties,"

Frankfurter wrote in *Minersville School District v. Gobitis*, 310 U.S. 586, 600 (1940). "To fight out the wise use of legislative authority in the forum of public opinion and before legislative assemblies rather than to transfer such a contest to the judicial arena, serves to vindicate the self-confidence of a free people." *Id.*

At the same time, the same group of justices continued to incorporate the Bill of Rights against the states through the Due Process Clause. *See, e.g.*, *De Jonge v. Oregon*, 299 U.S. 353 (1937). Incorporation reflected the continued, if uninvited, influence of *Lochner*. Before the *Lochner* era, the Bill of Rights had rarely been invoked to strike down legislation; instead, the amendments mainly guided juries and legislatures in interpreting their own responsibilities. *See* Jamal Greene, *How Rights Went Wrong* 8–31 (2021). But the post-*Lochner* Court followed Brandeis in reinterpreting the Bill of Rights as if it had always been designed to insulate certain rights from the legislative process. *Id.* at 66–69. Justice Robert Jackson famously made this point in a 1943 case striking down a state law that required children with religious objections to stand for the pledge of allegiance:

> The very purpose of a Bill of Rights was to withdraw certain subjects from the vicissitudes of political controversy, to place them beyond the reach of majorities and officials and to establish them as legal principles to be applied by the courts. One's right to life, liberty, and property, to free speech, a free press, freedom of worship and assembly, and other fundamental rights may not be submitted to vote; they depend on the outcome of no elections.

W. Va. State Bd. of Educ. v. Barnette, 319 U.S. 624, 642 (1943).

Complicating and completing this messy picture was race. Although the post-*Lochner* justices were committed to deferring to state legislative judgments, they could all see how state legislatures abused their autonomy to violently entrench racial caste systems throughout the country. In *United States v. Carolene Products Co.*, the Court suggested that it could counteract this trend by applying "more exacting judicial scrutiny" to laws that subjected "discrete and insular minorities" to burdens that could not be removed by "those political process ordinarily to be relied upon to protect minorities." 304 U.S. 144, 154–55 n.4 (1938). But carrying out this suggestion required the Court to do more than merely incorporate the Bill of Rights against the states, as in *Powell v. Alabama*, 287 U.S. 45 (1932). For example, in *National Ass'n for the Advancement of Colored People v. Alabama ex rel. Patterson* (*NAACP*), 357 U.S. 449 (1958), the Court considered an Alabama law that would have required the nation's largest civil rights organization to disclose the names of its Alabama members. The disclosure would have subjected the members to violent reprisals. The Court invalidated the law for violating the members' "freedom to associate"—an unenumerated right that the

Court considered implied by the First Amendment's protections of speech and assembly. *NAACP*, 357 U.S. at 460, 463.

By the 1960s, the justices of the Supreme Court were uniform in their rejection of *Lochner*. They repeatedly declared that it was not the Court's role "to sit as a 'superlegislature to weigh the wisdom of legislation.'" *Ferguson v. Skrupa*, 372 U.S. 726, 731 (1963) (quoting *Day-Brite Lighting, Inc. v. Missouri*, 342 U.S. 421, 423 (1952)). Yet they were equally committed to weighing the wisdom of legislation that violated the prohibitions of the Bill of Rights or that subordinated racial minorities. This tension eventually forced the justices to address why, precisely, they thought that *Lochner* was wrong.

The Court began this reevaluation of *Lochner* during the sexual revolution of the mid-twentieth century, as sympathetic plaintiffs challenged the constitutionality of state laws that had been adopted decades earlier during an intensely moralistic period of the nineteenth century. *See* Geoffrey R. Stone, *Sex and the Constitution* 351–55 (2017). In *Tileston v. Ullman*, 318 U.S. 44 (1943), a doctor challenged a Connecticut law that banned all uses of contraception—even among married couples—and also prohibited doctors from advising patients about their use. In an unsigned opinion, the Court employed tortured reasoning to conclude that the doctor lacked standing to challenge the law. *Tileston*, 318 U.S. at 46. A second set of plaintiffs—a married couple—challenged the same law in *Poe v. Ullman*, 367 U.S. 497 (1961). Frankfurter, the justice most inclined to defer to state legislatures, wrote an opinion for four justices dismissing the suit as unripe because there was no evidence that the statute had ever been enforced. *Poe*, 367 U.S. at 509 (plurality opinion). This time, however, the challenge attracted dissenting opinions from Justices William O. Douglas and John Harlan. Both justices wrote that the law violated the liberty interests of married couples: "an invasion of the privacy that is implicit in a free society." *Id.* at 519–21 (Douglas, J., dissenting); *see id.* at 549–51 (Harlan, J., dissenting). But both justices also felt the need to offer lengthy explanations for why invalidating this law would be different from what the *Lochner* Court did to New York's maximum-hour law. Douglas was particularly blunt: "The error of the old Court, as I see it, was not in entertaining inquiries concerning the constitutionality of social legislation but in applying the standards that it did." *Id.* at 517 (Douglas, J., dissenting).

Months after *Poe* was decided in June 1961, the executive director of the Planned Parenthood League of Connecticut, Estelle Griswold, opened a birth control clinic in New Haven. Connecticut prosecutors tried Griswold and convicted her of giving medical advice to married patients about contraception.

Four years later, Griswold's appeal reached the Supreme Court, where a fractured majority in *Griswold v. Connecticut*, 381 U.S. 479 (1965), considered how to reconcile their deep distaste of the Connecticut law with their fear of returning the Court to the *Lochner* era. Notably, Frankfurter had recently been replaced by Justice Arthur Goldberg, a labor lawyer who shared none of Frankfurter's deference to legislative majorities.

■ MR. JUSTICE DOUGLAS delivered the opinion of the Court.[3]

Appellant Griswold is Executive Director of the Planned Parenthood League of Connecticut. . . . [She and her codefendant, a doctor, were convicted of giving] information, instruction, and medical advice to *married persons* as to the means of preventing conception. . . .

[W]e are met with a wide range of questions that implicate the Due Process Clause of the Fourteenth Amendment. Overtones of some arguments suggest that *Lochner v. New York,* 198 U. S. 45, should be our guide. But we decline that invitation as we did in *West Coast Hotel Co. v. Parrish,* 300 U. S. 379. We do not sit as a super-legislature to determine the wisdom, need, and propriety of laws that touch economic problems, business affairs, or social conditions. This law, however, operates directly on an intimate relation of husband and wife and their physician's role in one aspect of that relation.

The association of people is not mentioned in the Constitution nor in the Bill of Rights. The right to educate a child in a school of the parents' choice—whether public or private or parochial—is also not mentioned. Nor is the right to study any particular subject or any foreign language. Yet the First Amendment has been construed to include certain of those rights.

By *Pierce v. Society of Sisters, supra,* the right to educate one's children as one chooses is made applicable to the States by the force of the First and Fourteenth Amendments. By *Meyer v. Nebraska, supra,* the same dignity is given the right to study the German language in a private school. In other words, the State may not, consistently with the spirit of the First Amendment, contract the spectrum of available knowledge. The right of freedom of speech and press includes not only the right to utter or to print, but the right to distribute, the right to receive, the right to read, and freedom of inquiry, freedom of thought, and freedom to teach—indeed the freedom of the entire university community. Without those peripheral rights the specific rights would be less secure. . . .

In *NAACP v. Alabama,* 357 U. S. 449, 462, we protected the "freedom to associate and privacy in one's associations," noting that freedom of association was a peripheral First Amendment right. Disclosure of membership lists of a constitutionally valid association, we held, was invalid "as entailing the likelihood of a substantial restraint upon the exercise by petitioner's members of their right to freedom of association." *Ibid.* In other words, the First Amendment has a penumbra where privacy is protected from governmental intrusion. . . .[4]

---

[3] **As You Read, Consider:** Each of the opinions here offers a different approach toward evaluating the substantive reasonableness of state legislation. One calls for a deferential means-ends test unless the law can be interpreted to violate the textual prohibitions of the Bill of Rights. Another calls for the same test unless the law interferes with a "fundamental" right, a label that includes unenumerated rights. Still another interprets the lesson of *Lochner v. New York* to require deference in all contexts. And one calls for the judiciary to engage in a context-specific evaluation of the interests on both sides of a dispute to determine whether the legislature mediated the interests appropriately.

Which approach do you find most attractive?

[4] **Questions:** Justice William O. Douglas—perhaps the most liberal member of the Supreme Court—is arguing that Connecticut's law here differs from New York's law in *Lochner* because it interferes with a right of privacy implied by the text of the Bill of Rights.

[That case] involved more than the "right of assembly" . . . . The right of "association," like the right of belief (*Board of Education v. Barnette,* 319 U. S. 624), is more than the right to attend a meeting; it includes the right to express one's attitudes or philosophies by membership in a group or by affiliation with it or by other lawful means. Association in that context is a form of expression of opinion; and while it is not expressly included in the First Amendment its existence is necessary in making the express guarantees fully meaningful.

The foregoing cases suggest that specific guarantees in the Bill of Rights have penumbras, formed by emanations from those guarantees that help give them life and substance. Various guarantees create zones of privacy. The right of association contained in the penumbra of the First Amendment is one, as we have seen. The Third Amendment in its prohibition against the quartering of soldiers "in any house" in time of peace without the consent of the owner is another facet of that privacy. The Fourth Amendment explicitly affirms the "right of the people to be secure in their persons, houses, papers, and effects, against unreasonable searches and seizures." The Fifth Amendment in its Self-Incrimination Clause enables the citizen to create a zone of privacy which government may not force him to surrender to his detriment. The Ninth Amendment provides: "The enumeration in the Constitution, of certain rights, shall not be construed to deny or disparage others retained by the people." . . .

The present case, then, concerns a relationship lying within the zone of privacy created by several fundamental constitutional guarantees. And it concerns a law which, in forbidding the *use* of contraceptives rather than regulating their manufacture or sale, seeks to achieve its goals by means having a maximum destructive impact upon that relationship. Such a law cannot stand in light of the familiar principle, so often applied by this Court, that a "governmental purpose to control or prevent activities constitutionally subject to state regulation may not be achieved by means which sweep unnecessarily broadly and thereby invade the area of protected freedoms." *NAACP v. Alabama,* 377 U. S. 288, 307. Would we allow the police to search the sacred precincts of marital bedrooms for telltale signs of the use of contraceptives? The very idea is repulsive to the notions of privacy surrounding the marriage relationship.

We deal with a right of privacy older than the Bill of Rights—older than our political parties, older than our school system. Marriage is a coming together for better or for worse, hopefully enduring, and intimate to the degree of being sacred. It is an association that promotes a way of life, not causes; a harmony in living, not political faiths; a bilateral loyalty, not commercial or social projects. Yet it is an association for as noble a purpose as any involved in our prior decisions. . . .

He reaches this conclusion by explaining that each amendment in the Bill of Rights protects more than its literal text would suggest. The First Amendment, for example, had already been interpreted by the Court to protect not only the express rights of speech and assembly but also the implied right of "association," whose "existence is necessary in making the express guarantees fully meaningful." Using this as an analogy, he argues that other amendments similarly cast "emanations" whose "penumbras" imply the existence of other implied rights, such as the right of privacy.

Douglas is therefore making two claims here. First, courts should generally defer to legislatures but assess for themselves the reasonableness of laws that interfere with rights protected by the Bill of Rights. Second, the Bill of Rights protects more than its literal text. Do you agree with either argument? If a state law causes harm, why should it matter whether it also interferes with the text of various amendments, ratified in 1791, that don't even apply directly to states? Why, in other words, should only particular types of legislative harm warrant judicial scrutiny?

■ MR. JUSTICE GOLDBERG, whom THE CHIEF JUSTICE and MR. JUSTICE BRENNAN join, concurring. . . .

[I]n reaching the conclusion that the right of marital privacy is protected, as being within the protected penumbra of specific guarantees of the Bill of Rights, the Court refers to the Ninth Amendment. I add these words to emphasize the relevance of that Amendment to the Court's holding. . . .

The Court stated many years ago that the Due Process Clause protects those liberties that are "so rooted in the traditions and conscience of our people as to be ranked as fundamental." *Snyder v. Massachusetts,* 291 U. S. 97, 105.

This Court, in a series of decisions, has held that the Fourteenth Amendment absorbs and applies to the States those specifics of the first eight amendments which express fundamental personal rights. The language and history of the Ninth Amendment reveal that the Framers of the Constitution believed that there are additional fundamental rights, protected from governmental infringement, which exist alongside those fundamental rights specifically mentioned in the first eight constitutional amendments.

The Ninth Amendment reads, "The enumeration in the Constitution, of certain rights, shall not be construed to deny or disparage others retained by the people." The Amendment is almost entirely the work of James Madison. It was introduced in Congress by him and passed the House and Senate with little or no debate and virtually no change in language. It was proffered to quiet expressed fears that a bill of specifically enumerated rights could not be sufficiently broad to cover all essential rights and that the specific mention of certain rights would be interpreted as a denial that others were protected. . . . [*See*] I Annals of Congress 439 (Gales and Seaton ed. 1834). . . .

The Ninth Amendment to the Constitution may be regarded by some as a recent discovery and may be forgotten by others, but since 1791 it has been a basic part of the Constitution which we are sworn to uphold. To hold that a right so basic and fundamental and so deep-rooted in our society as the right of privacy in marriage may be infringed because that right is not guaranteed in so many words by the first eight amendments to the Constitution . . . would violate the Ninth Amendment, which specifically states that "[t]he enumeration in the Constitution, of certain rights, shall not be *construed* to deny or disparage others retained by the people." (Emphasis added.) . . .[5]

I do not mean to imply that the Ninth Amendment is applied against the States by the Fourteenth. Nor do I mean to state that the Ninth Amendment constitutes an independent source of rights protected from infringement by either the States or the Federal Government. Rather, . . . the Ninth Amendment simply lends strong support to the view that the "liberty" protected by the Fifth and Fourteenth Amendments from infringement by the Federal Government or the States is not restricted to rights specifically mentioned in the first eight amendments.

---

[5] **Questions:** Justice Arthur Goldberg agrees with Douglas's opinion. But he adds that the Ninth Amendment makes it difficult to conclude that the Bill of Rights is a comprehensive catalog of rights that warrant judicial protection. He would defer to most state laws but assess the reasonableness of laws that interfere with "fundamental" liberty interests as determined by the "traditions and [collective] conscience of our people."

Do you find this view more persuasive than Douglas's argument? If so, why should the judiciary protect only those interests *traditionally* regarded as important? What about state laws that harm interests that new generations regard as important?

On the flip side, what justifies the judicial reevaluation of laws that infringe on traditionally important interests? Wouldn't you expect a state legislature to be pretty solicitous about protecting these sorts of interests?

In determining which rights are fundamental, judges are not left at large to decide cases in light of their personal and private notions. Rather, they must look to the "traditions and [collective] conscience of our people" to determine whether a principle is "so rooted [there] . . . as to be ranked as fundamental." *Snyder v. Massachusetts,* 291 U. S. 97, 105. The inquiry is whether a right involved "is of such a character that it cannot be denied without violating those 'fundamental principles of liberty and justice which lie at the base of all our civil and political institutions' . . . ." *Powell v. Alabama,* 287 U. S. 45, 67. . . .

I agree fully with the Court that, applying these tests, the right of privacy is a fundamental personal right, emanating from the totality of the constitutional scheme under which we live. [*See Olmstead* v. *United States,* 277 U. S. 438, 478 (Brandeis, J., dissenting) (describing "the right to be let alone"). . . .]

The Connecticut statutes here involved deal with a particularly important and sensitive area of privacy—that of the marital relation and the marital home. This Court recognized in *Meyer v. Nebraska, supra,* that the right "to marry, establish a home and bring up children" was an essential part of the liberty guaranteed by the Fourteenth Amendment. 262 U. S., at 399. [*See also Pierce v. Society of Sisters,* 268 U. S. 510; *Prince v. Massachusetts,* 321 U. S. 158.]

The entire fabric of the Constitution and the purposes that clearly underlie its specific guarantees demonstrate that the rights to marital privacy and to marry and raise a family are of similar order and magnitude as the fundamental rights specifically protected. . . .

My Brother STEWART, while characterizing the Connecticut birth control law as "an uncommonly silly law," would nevertheless let it stand on the ground that it is not for the courts to " 'substitute their social and economic beliefs for the judgment of legislative bodies, who are elected to pass laws.' " . . . [W]hile I quite agree with Mr. Justice Brandeis that ["]a . . . State may . . . serve as a laboratory; and try novel social and economic experiments,["] *New State Ice Co. v. Liebmann,* 285 U. S. 262, 280, 311 (dissenting opinion), I do not believe that this includes the power to experiment with the fundamental liberties of citizens. . . . The vice of the dissenters' views is that it would permit such experimentation by the States in the area [of] fundamental personal rights. . . .

The logic of the dissents would sanction federal or state legislation that seems to me even more plainly unconstitutional than the statute before us. Surely the Government, absent a showing of a compelling subordinating state interest, could not decree that all husbands and wives must be sterilized after two children have been born to them. Yet by their reasoning such an invasion of marital privacy would not be subject to constitutional challenge because, while it might be "silly," no provision of the Constitution specifically prevents the Government from curtailing the marital right to bear children and raise a family. While it may shock some of my Brethren that the Court today holds that the Constitution protects the right of marital privacy, in my view it is far more shocking to believe that the personal liberty guaranteed by the Constitution does not include protection against such totalitarian limitation of family size, which is at complete variance with our constitutional concepts. . . .

In a long series of cases this Court has held that where fundamental personal liberties are involved, they may not be abridged by the States simply on a showing that a regulatory statute has some rational relationship to the effectuation of a proper state purpose. "Where there is a significant encroachment upon personal liberty, the State may prevail only upon showing a subordinating interest which is compelling," *Bates v. Little Rock,* 361 U. S. 516, 524. The law must be shown "necessary, and not merely rationally related, to the accomplishment of a permissible state policy." *McLaughlin v. Florida,* 379 U. S. 184, 196.[6]

Although the Connecticut birth-control law obviously encroaches upon a fundamental personal liberty, the State does not show that the law serves any "subordinating [state] interest which is compelling" or that it is "necessary . . . to the accomplishment of a permissible state policy." The State, at most, argues that there is some rational relation between this statute and what is admittedly a legitimate subject of state concern—the discouraging of extra-marital relations. It says that preventing the use of birth-control devices by married persons helps prevent the indulgence by some in such extramarital relations. The rationality of this justification is dubious. . . . But, in any event, it is clear that the state interest in safeguarding marital fidelity can be served by a more discriminately tailored statute, which does not, like the present one, sweep unnecessarily broadly, reaching far beyond the evil sought to be dealt with and intruding upon the privacy of all married couples. . . . The State of Connecticut does have statutes, the constitutionality of which is beyond doubt, which prohibit adultery and fornication. See Conn. Gen. Stat. §§ 53–218, 53–219 *et seq.* These statutes demonstrate that means for achieving the same basic purpose of protecting marital fidelity are available to Connecticut without the need to "invade the area of protected freedoms." *NAACP v. Alabama, supra,* at 307. . . .

In sum, I believe that the right of privacy in the marital relation is fundamental and basic—a personal right "retained by the people" within the meaning of the Ninth Amendment. Connecticut cannot constitutionally abridge this fundamental right, which is protected by the Fourteenth Amendment from infringement by the States. . . .

■ MR. JUSTICE HARLAN, concurring in the judgment.[7]

I fully agree with the judgment of reversal, but find myself unable to join the Court's opinion. The reason is that it seems to me to evince an approach . . . [that] the Due Process Clause of the Fourteenth Amendment does not touch this Connecticut statute unless the enactment is found to violate some right assured by the letter or penumbra of the Bill of Rights. . . .

---

[6] **Questions:** In contrast with Douglas, Goldberg doesn't argue that the Court should evaluate for itself the reasonableness of state laws that infringe on protected interests. Rather, he would apply a skeptical means-ends test and ask whether the law is "necessary" to achieve a "compelling" state interest. Goldberg is borrowing this test from the Supreme Court's interpretation of the Equal Protection Clause. As will be discussed later (section 45.3), the Court in *McLaughlin v. Florida* began applying this "strict scrutiny" to laws that discriminated on the basis of race.

Does this sort of test affirm your intuition about how courts should mediate conflicts between competing interests? If so, why should the Court reserve such a test only for when "fundamental" interests are at stake, leaving all other interests to the political process? Is such a categorical approach preferable to Justice John Harlan's dissent in *Lochner*, in which he accepted the legitimacy of all interests on both sides of a dispute and attempted to evaluate, in a fact-specific manner, whether the legislature acted reasonably in mediating the various interests?

[7] **Questions:** The John Harlan who dissented in *Lochner* had a grandson with the same name who authored this brief concurring opinion. The younger Harlan elaborated on this opinion in *Poe v. Ullman*, in which he argued that the Due Process Clause "represented the balance which our Nation, built upon postulates of respect for the liberty of the individual, has struck between that liberty and the demands of organized society. . . . No formula could serve as a substitute, in this area, for judgment and restraint." 367 U.S. 497, 542 (1961).

Rather than categorically protect only those rights listed in the Bill of Rights, Harlan appears to call for a more contextual evaluation of whether a legislature has transgressed a "fundamental" limit on its power. Do you think that a fact-specific proportionality approach untethered to formalistic rules would better guide "[j]udicial self-restraint" than Douglas or Goldberg's categorical tests? If so, how is a court supposed to act consistently and predictably when evaluating the legitimacy of legislation?

In my view, the proper constitutional inquiry in this case is whether this Connecticut statute infringes the Due Process Clause of the Fourteenth Amendment because the enactment violates basic values "implicit in the concept of ordered liberty," *Palko v. Connecticut,* 302 U. S. 319, 325. . . . I believe that it does. While the relevant inquiry may be aided by resort to one or more of the provisions of the Bill of Rights, it is not dependent on them or any of their radiations. The Due Process Clause of the Fourteenth Amendment stands, in my opinion, on its own bottom.

Judicial self-restraint . . . will be achieved in this area, as in other constitutional areas, only by continual insistence upon respect for the teachings of history, solid recognition of the basic values that underlie our society, and wise appreciation of the great roles that the doctrines of federalism and separation of powers have played in establishing and preserving American freedoms. See *Adamson v. California,* 332 U. S. 46, 59 (Mr. Justice Frankfurter, concurring). Adherence to these principles will not, of course, obviate all constitutional differences of opinion among judges, nor should it. Their continued recognition will, however, go farther toward keeping most judges from roaming at large in the constitutional field than will the interpolation into the Constitution of an artificial and largely illusory restriction on the content of the Due Process Clause.

■ MR. JUSTICE WHITE, concurring in the judgment. . . .

[I]t would be unduly repetitious, and belaboring the obvious, to expound on the impact of this statute on the liberty guaranteed by the Fourteenth Amendment against arbitrary or capricious denials or on the nature of this liberty. Suffice it to say that this is not the first time this Court has had occasion to articulate that the liberty entitled to protection under the Fourteenth Amendment includes the right "to marry, establish a home and bring up children," *Meyer v. Nebraska,* 262 U. S. 390, 399. . . . Surely the right invoked in this case, to be free of regulation of the intimacies of the marriage relationship, "come[s] to this Court with a momentum for respect lacking when appeal is made to liberties which derive merely from shifting economic arrangements." *Kovacs v. Cooper,* 336 U. S. 77, 95 (opinion of Frankfurter, J.). . . .

[S]tatutes regulating sensitive areas of liberty[,] under the cases of this Court, require "strict scrutiny," *Skinner v. Oklahoma,* 316 U. S. 535, 541, and "must be viewed in the light of less drastic means for achieving the same basic purpose." *Shelton v. Tucker,* 364 U. S. 479, 488. "Where there is a significant encroachment upon personal liberty, the State may prevail only upon showing a subordinating interest which is compelling." *Bates v. Little Rock,* 361 U. S. 516, 524. But such statutes, if reasonably necessary for the effectuation of a legitimate and substantial state interest, and not arbitrary or capricious in application, are not invalid under the Due Process Clause. . . .[8]

[T]his statute is said to serve the State's policy against all forms of promiscuous or illicit sexual relationships, be they premarital or extramarital, concededly a permissible and legitimate legislative goal. . . . [But] one is rather hard pressed to explain how the ban on use by married persons in any way prevents use of such devices by persons engaging in illicit sexual relations and thereby contributes to the State's policy against such relationships. . . . I find nothing in this record justifying the sweeping scope of this statute, with its telling effect on the freedoms of married

---

[8] **Questions:** Like most of the other justices, Justice Byron White would apply the rational-basis test to protect "economic" interests but apply "strict scrutiny" to protect more intimate interests. What justifies this distinction? Why should economic interests—the same basic interests first protected by the Civil Rights Act of 1866—deserve less judicial protection than novel interests like the right to obtain birth control?

persons, and therefore conclude that it deprives such persons of liberty without due process of law.

■ MR. JUSTICE BLACK, with whom MR. JUSTICE STEWART joins, dissenting. . . .

The Court talks about a constitutional "right of privacy" as though there is some constitutional provision or provisions forbidding any law ever to be passed which might abridge the "privacy" of individuals. But there is not. There are, of course, guarantees in certain specific constitutional provisions which are designed in part to protect privacy at certain times and places with respect to certain activities. Such, for example, is the Fourth Amendment's guarantee against "unreasonable searches and seizures." But I think it belittles that Amendment to talk about it as though it protects nothing but "privacy." . . . The average man would very likely not have his feelings soothed any more by having his property seized openly than by having it seized privately and by stealth. He simply wants his property left alone. And a person can be just as much, if not more, irritated, annoyed and injured by an unceremonious public arrest by a policeman as he is by a seizure in the privacy of his office or home.[9]

One of the most effective ways of diluting or expanding a constitutionally guaranteed right is to substitute for the crucial word or words of a constitutional guarantee another word or words, more or less flexible and more or less restricted in meaning. This fact is well illustrated by the use of the term "right of privacy" as a comprehensive substitute for the Fourth Amendment's guarantee against "unreasonable searches and seizures." "Privacy" is a broad, abstract and ambiguous concept which can easily be shrunken in meaning but which can also, on the other hand, easily be interpreted as a constitutional ban against many things other than searches and seizures. . . . For these reasons I get nowhere in this case by talk about a constitutional "right of privacy" as an emanation from one or more constitutional provisions. I like my privacy as well as the next one, but I am nevertheless compelled to admit that government has a right to invade it unless prohibited by some specific constitutional provision. . . .

While I completely subscribe to the holding of *Marbury v. Madison,* 1 Cranch 137, and subsequent cases, that our Court has constitutional power to strike down statutes, state or federal, that violate commands of the Federal Constitution, I do not believe that we are granted power by the Due Process Clause or any other constitutional provision or provisions to measure constitutionality by our belief that legislation is arbitrary, capricious or unreasonable. . . . Such an appraisal of the wisdom of legislation is an attribute of the power to make laws, not of the power to interpret them. The use by federal courts of such a formula or doctrine or whatnot to veto federal or state laws simply takes away from Congress and States the power to make laws based on their own judgment of fairness and wisdom and transfers that power to this Court for ultimate determination—a power which was specifically denied to federal courts by the convention that framed the Constitution.

Of the cases on which my Brothers WHITE and GOLDBERG rely so heavily, undoubtedly the reasoning of two of them supports their result here. . . . [But] *Meyer v. Nebraska,* 262 U. S. 390, and *Pierce v. Society of Sisters,* 268 U. S. 510, were both decided in opinions by Mr. Justice McReynolds which elaborated the same

[9] **Questions:** Justice Hugo Black, dissenting, appears to apply a similar test as Douglas's majority opinion, which would skeptically evaluate only those laws that interfere with rights protected by the Bill of Rights. He merely disagrees about whether the Bill of Rights protects the right of privacy.

Do you find his textualist approach persuasive? If so, recall that *none* of the amendments in the Bill of Rights applies to the states. Assuming that the Fourteenth Amendment permits judicial scrutiny of state laws, why should such scrutiny depend on the text of the Bill of Rights?

natural law due process philosophy found in *Lochner v. New York, supra,* one of the cases on which he relied in *Meyer*. . . .[10]

My Brother GOLDBERG has adopted the recent discovery that the Ninth Amendment as well as the Due Process Clause can be used by this Court as authority to strike down all state legislation which this Court thinks . . . is contrary to the "traditions and [collective] conscience of our people." He also states, without proof satisfactory to me, that in making decisions on this basis judges will not consider "their personal and private notions." One may ask how they can avoid considering them. Our Court certainly has no machinery with which to take a Gallup Poll. And the scientific miracles of this age have not yet produced a gadget which the Court can use to determine what traditions are rooted in the "[collective] conscience of our people."

Moreover, one would certainly have to look far beyond the language of the Ninth Amendment to find that the Framers vested in this Court any such awesome veto powers over lawmaking, either by the States or by the Congress. Nor does anything in the history of the Amendment offer any support for such a shocking doctrine. . . . That Amendment was passed, not to broaden the powers of this Court or any other department of "the General Government," but, as every student of history knows, to assure the people that the Constitution in all its provisions was intended to limit the Federal Government to the powers granted expressly or by necessary implication. If any broad, unlimited power to hold laws unconstitutional because they offend what this Court conceives to be the "[collective] conscience of our people" is vested in this Court by the Ninth Amendment, the Fourteenth Amendment, or any other provision of the Constitution, it was not given by the Framers, but rather has been bestowed on the Court by the Court. . . . Use of any such broad, unbounded judicial authority would make of this Court's members a day-to-day constitutional convention. . . .

I realize that many good and able men have eloquently spoken and written, sometimes in rhapsodical strains, about the duty of this Court to keep the Constitution in tune with the times. The idea is that the Constitution must be changed from time to time and that this Court is charged with a duty to make those changes. For myself, I must with all deference reject that philosophy. The Constitution makers knew the need for change and provided for it. Amendments suggested by the people's elected representatives can be submitted to the people or their selected agents for ratification. That method of change was good for our Fathers, and being somewhat old-fashioned I must add it is good enough for me. And so, I cannot rely on the Due Process Clause or the Ninth Amendment or any mysterious and uncertain natural law concept as a reason for striking down this state law. The Due Process Clause with an "arbitrary and capricious" or "shocking to the conscience" formula was liberally used by this Court to strike down economic legislation in the early decades of this century, threatening, many people thought, the tranquility and stability of the Nation. See, *e. g., Lochner v. New York,* 198 U. S. 45. That formula, based on subjective considerations of "natural justice," is no less dangerous when used to enforce this Court's views about personal rights than those about economic rights. I had thought that we had laid that formula, as a means for striking down state legislation, to rest once and for all in cases like *West Coast Hotel Co. v. Parrish,* 300 U. S. 379. . . .

---

[10] **Questions:** Black accuses the justices in the majority of revitalizing *Lochner*, with its unbridled power to strike down "unreasonable" legislation. Regardless of whether you accept Black's textualism, do you agree with him that any of the majority's tests risks allowing an unelected federal judiciary to unjustifiably roam the American landscape looking for laws to invalidate? How, if at all, would Black respond to Goldberg's concern that judicial nonenforcement of the Due Process Clause would lead to "totalitarian" legislation?

■ MR. JUSTICE STEWART, whom MR. JUSTICE BLACK joins, dissenting.

Since 1879 Connecticut has had on its books a law which forbids the use of contraceptives by anyone. I think this is an uncommonly silly law. . . . But we are not asked in this case to say whether we think this law is unwise, or even asinine. We are asked to hold that it violates the United States Constitution. And that I cannot do.

In the course of its opinion the Court refers to no less than six Amendments to the Constitution: the First, the Third, the Fourth, the Fifth, the Ninth, and the Fourteenth. But the Court does not say which of these Amendments, if any, it thinks is infringed by this Connecticut law.

We *are* told that the Due Process Clause of the Fourteenth Amendment is not, as such, the "guide" in this case. With that much I agree. There is no claim that this law, duly enacted by the Connecticut Legislature is unconstitutionally vague. There is no claim that the appellants were denied any of the elements of procedural due process at their trial, so as to make their convictions constitutionally invalid. And, as the Court says, the day has long passed since the Due Process Clause was regarded as a proper instrument for determining "the wisdom, need, and propriety" of state laws. Compare *Lochner v. New York,* 198 U. S. 45, with *Ferguson v. Skrupa,* 372 U. S. 726. . . .[11]

What provision of the Constitution, then, does make this state law invalid? The Court says it is the right of privacy "created by several fundamental constitutional guarantees." With all deference, I can find no such general right of privacy in the Bill of Rights, in any other part of the Constitution, or in any case ever before decided by this Court. . . .

If, as I should surely hope, the law before us does not reflect the standards of the people of Connecticut, the people of Connecticut can freely exercise their true Ninth and Tenth Amendment rights to persuade their elected representatives to repeal it. That is the constitutional way to take this law off the books.

42.2 THE TEST FOR EVALUATING UNCONSTITUTIONAL INVASIONS OF PRIVACY

Although Justice William O. Douglas wrote for a 7–2 majority in *Griswold v. Connecticut*, 381 U.S. 479 (1965), the three concurrences and two dissents illustrate that the justices were deeply uncertain about the scope of the "right of privacy." Specifically, two questions bothered the justices: First, what exactly *was* the right of privacy, and what in the Constitution protected it? Second, what should be the test for evaluating claims that the right of privacy had been infringed?

To answer the first question, Douglas wrote that the right of privacy was one of the fundamental liberty interests protected by the Due Process Clause, which could be deciphered by interpreting the guarantees of the Bill of Rights at a high level of generality. To Douglas, the First Amendment didn't protect just the literal right to speak—it also protected the right to associate, which in turn protected intimate relationships like marriage. Douglas described the other amendments as

---

[11] **Question:** Like Black, Justice Potter Stewart would interpret the Due Process Clause as a protection of *procedural,* not *substantive,* limitations. What, then, justifies incorporating the First Amendment and other substantive protections of the Bill of Rights against the states?

emitting similarly broad "emanations" that formed "penumbras," or shadows, that covered unenumerated rights. *Griswold*, 381 U.S. at 484. Presumably, future litigants could attract his vote by explaining how the broadly defined principles underlying the Bill of Rights protected their conduct.

Justice Arthur Goldberg emphasized the importance of the Ninth Amendment as a justification for Douglas's interpretation of the Bill of Rights. To Goldberg, it seemed obvious that if one of the amendments had expressly protected a right to use contraception with a spouse, then all nine justices would have struck down Connecticut's law. The Ninth Amendment confirmed that such an express protection was unnecessary: the Due Process Clause and the Bill of Rights had to be "construed" to protect more than just what was literally written in their text. *Id.* at 490–91 (Goldberg, J., concurring). As a guide for what other rights might be protected by the Constitution, Goldberg employed the same formula that the Court had used in incorporation cases: looking at the "traditions and collective conscience of our people" to determine whether it was possible to imagine a just society without the right. *Id.* at 487 (quoting *Snyder v. Massachusetts,* 291 U.S. 97, 105 (1934)).

Justices John Harlan and Byron White employed a more contextual test without reference to the Ninth Amendment, interpreting the Due Process Clause as standing "on its own bottom." *Id.* at 500 (Harlan, J., concurring). Harlan would require judges to exercise their own judgment when balancing competing interests.

Justices Hugo Black and Potter Stewart mocked all of these interpretations, writing that Connecticut's "uncommonly silly law" was nevertheless constitutional. *Id.* at 527 (Stewart, J., dissenting). Both dissenting justices argued that there was no functional difference between *Griswold* and *Lochner v. New York*, 198 U.S. 45 (1905): each case involved a bunch of judges determining for themselves whether they thought a legislature had acted wisely. *See id.* at 523–24. The dissenting justices urged the members of the majority to support a constitutional amendment if they wanted to recognize a right to marital intimacy. *Id.* at 522. They were clearly unpersuaded by Goldberg's attempt to anchor the Due Process Clause to the Ninth Amendment, "traditions," or any other untethered source.

After each justice in the *Griswold* majority resolved for himself how to determine what the right of privacy entailed, the justices also had to determine what test the Court would use to determine when a legislature had unconstitutionally invaded the right.

Writing for the majority, Douglas offered little guidance: he wrote simply that a " 'governmental purpose to control or prevent activities constitutionally subject to state regulation may not be achieved by means which sweep unnecessarily broadly and thereby invade the area of protected freedoms.' " *Griswold,* 381 U.S. at 485 (quoting *Nat'l Ass'n for the Advancement of Colored People v. Alabama ex rel. Flowers*, 377 U.S. 288, 307 (1964)).

Goldberg and White found a different test in the Equal Protection Clause cases of *Skinner* v. *Oklahoma ex rel. Williamson,* 316 U.S. 535 (1942), and *McLaughlin v. Florida*, 379 U.S. 184 (1964). In *Skinner*, the Supreme Court applied what it called *strict scrutiny* when it invalidated a law that required the sterilization of certain criminals. 316 U.S. at 541. And in *McLaughlin*, the Court cited *Skinner* to strike down a Florida law that prohibited interracial couples from occupying the same bedroom at night. The *McLaughlin* Court explained that a law that "trenches upon the constitutionally protected freedom from invidious official discrimination based on race" must be shown "necessary, and not merely rationally related, to the accomplishment of a permissible state policy." 379 U.S. at 196.

This idea of strict scrutiny had indirectly evolved from the "more exacting judicial scrutiny" that the Supreme Court had called for in footnote 4 of *United States v. Carolene Products Co.*, 304 U.S. 144 (1938). There, the Court had suggested that the presumption of constitutionality in *West Coast Hotel Co. v. Parrish*, 300 U.S. 379 (1937), shouldn't apply if a law (1) "appears on its face to be within a specific prohibition of the Constitution, such as those of the first ten amendments," (2) "restricts those political processes which can ordinarily be expected to bring about repeal of undesirable legislation," or (3) "curtail[s] the operation of those political processes ordinarily to be relied upon" to protect "discrete and insular minorities." *Carolene Products*, 304 U.S. at 152–53 n.4 (1938). But *Carolene Products* hadn't defined what *more exacting . . . scrutiny* meant, nor had the Court ever applied such scrutiny to cases under the Due Process Clause.

42.2.1

Loving v. Virginia

388 U.S. 1 (1967)

Although *Griswold* resolved that states had no power to ban the use of contraception among married couples, the various opinions did not resolve (1) what constitutional provision was violated by Connecticut's law or (2) which of the various proposed tests the Court would use to evaluate the constitutionality of similar laws going forward. The Court went a long way toward answering those questions two years later in the following case: *Loving v. Virginia*, 388 U.S. 1 (1967).

In 1924, Virginia's legislature passed the Racial Integrity Act, which made it a crime for "any white person in this State to marry any save a white person." *Loving*, 388 U.S. at n.4 (quoting Virginia law). The law defined a white person as someone who "has no trace whatever of any blood other than Caucasian," although it made an exception for the descendants of John Rolfe and Pocahontas. The law also made it a crime for an interracial couple to return to Virginia after getting married outside the state. The legislature passed this law the same year it required the compulsory sterilization of the "feeble minded"—a practice that the Supreme Court upheld in *Buck v. Bell*, 274 U.S. 200, 205 (1927) (see section 42.1).

Mildred and Richard Loving, an interracial couple from Virginia, were married in the District of Columbia in 1958. When they returned to Virginia, they were convicted of violating the Racial Integrity Act. The court that convicted them stated in its opinion that "Almighty God created the races white, black, yellow, malay and red, and he placed them on separate continents. . . . The fact that he separated the races shows that he did not intend for the races to mix." *Loving*, 388 U.S. at 3 (quoting trial court judge).

The Lovings eventually challenged their convictions before the Supreme Court, which issued a brief and remarkable opinion in favor of the plaintiffs.

■ MR. CHIEF JUSTICE WARREN delivered the opinion of the Court.[12]

This case presents a constitutional question never addressed by this Court: whether a statutory scheme adopted by the State of Virginia to prevent marriages between persons solely on the basis of racial classifications violates the Equal Protection and Due Process Clauses of the Fourteenth Amendment. For reasons which seem to us to reflect the central meaning of those constitutional commands, we conclude that these statutes cannot stand consistently with the Fourteenth Amendment. . . .

[I]

Virginia is now one of 16 States which prohibit and punish marriages on the basis of racial classifications. Penalties for miscegenation arose as an incident to slavery and have been common in Virginia since the colonial period. The present statutory scheme dates from the adoption of the Racial Integrity Act of 1924, passed during the period of extreme nativism which followed the end of the First World War. The central features of this Act, and current Virginia law, are the absolute prohibition of a "white person" marrying other than another "white person," a prohibition against issuing marriage licenses until the issuing official is satisfied that the applicants' statements as to their race are correct, certificates of "racial composition" to be kept by both local and state registrars, and the carrying forward of earlier prohibitions against racial intermarriage. . . .

There can be no question but that Virginia's miscegenation statutes rest solely upon distinctions drawn according to race. The statutes proscribe generally accepted conduct if engaged in by members of different races. Over the years, this Court has consistently repudiated "[d]istinctions between citizens solely because of their ancestry" as being "odious to a free people whose institutions are founded upon the doctrine of equality." *Hirabayashi v. United States,* 320 U. S. 81, 100 (1943). At the very least, the Equal Protection Clause demands that racial classifications, especially suspect in criminal statutes, be subjected to the "most rigid scrutiny," *Korematsu v. United States,* 323 U. S. 214, 216 (1944), and, if they are ever to be upheld, they

[12] **As You Read, Consider:** Chief Justice Earl Warren joined two opinions in *Griswold v. Connecticut*: Justice William O. Douglas's majority opinion and Justice Arthur Goldberg's concurring opinion. How does Warren's opinion in this case compare with the tests employed in *Griswold*?

must be shown to be necessary to the accomplishment of some permissible state objective, independent of the racial discrimination which it was the object of the Fourteenth Amendment to eliminate. . . .

There is patently no legitimate overriding purpose independent of invidious racial discrimination which justifies this classification. The fact that Virginia prohibits only interracial marriages involving white persons demonstrates that the racial classifications must stand on their own justification, as measures designed to maintain White Supremacy. We have consistently denied the constitutionality of measures which restrict the rights of citizens on account of race. There can be no doubt that restricting the freedom to marry solely because of racial classifications violates the central meaning of the Equal Protection Clause.[13]

II.

These statutes also deprive the Lovings of liberty without due process of law in violation of the Due Process Clause of the Fourteenth Amendment. The freedom to marry has long been recognized as one of the vital personal rights essential to the orderly pursuit of happiness by free men.

Marriage is one of the "basic civil rights of man," fundamental to our very existence and survival. *Skinner v. Oklahoma,* 316 U. S. 535, 541 (1942). To deny this fundamental freedom on so unsupportable a basis as the racial classifications embodied in these statutes, classifications so directly subversive of the principle of equality at the heart of the Fourteenth Amendment, is surely to deprive all the State's citizens of liberty without due process of law. The Fourteenth Amendment requires that the freedom of choice to marry not be restricted by invidious racial discriminations. Under our Constitution, the freedom to marry, or not marry, a person of another race resides with the individual and cannot be infringed by the State.[14]

---

[13] **Question:** Most of Warren's opinion interprets the Equal Protection Clause. We will describe this clause in much further detail later (section 44). For now, observe how Warren cites two cases upholding the curfew and exclusion of Japanese Americans—*Hirabayashi v. United States* and *Korematsu v. United States*—to conclude that the Equal Protection Clause tolerates racial classifications only where the classifications satisfy "the most rigid scrutiny." Such scrutiny asks whether the classifications are "necessary" to achieve a "compelling" race-neutral interest.

Before becoming chief justice, Warren was governor of California. During World War II, he encouraged the federal government to intern Japanese Americans, and he publicly defended *Hirabayashi* and *Korematsu*. Why might he have believed that the internment of Japanese Americans was necessary to achieve a compelling race-neutral interest, while the Virginia classifications at issue in this decision were unconstitutional "measures designed to maintain White Supremacy"?

[14] **Questions:** In evaluating the constitutionality of Virginia's law under the Due Process Clause, Warren cites another decision interpreting the Equal Protection Clause: *Skinner v. Oklahoma*, 316 U.S. 535 (1942). In that decision, the Court called for the same "strict scrutiny" when evaluating classifications that affect "fundamental" rights. *Skinner*, 316 U.S. at 541. By embracing this test, Warren follows Justice Arthur Goldberg's opinion in *Griswold v. Connecticut*, 381 U.S. 479 (1965). Recall that Goldberg argued that when a law infringes on rights "so rooted in the traditions and conscience of our people as to be ranked as fundamental," the Court should uphold the law only if it is "necessary" to serve a "compelling" state interest. *Griswold*, 381 U.S. at 487, 497 (Goldberg, J., concurring).

But how does Warren know that this case presents a "fundamental" right? Surely the right to *interracial* marriage is not "rooted in the traditions . . . of our people," right? For example, in *Dred Scott v. Sandford*, Chief Justice Roger Taney could point to several colonial laws that banned interracial marriage. 60 U.S. (19 How.) 393, 413 (1857).

What, then, justifies Warren's use of the less specific language *freedom to marry* for his description of the right at issue in this case? Why not the even less specific freedom of personal autonomy or freedom of choice? When the level of generality is flexible, is there any conduct that cannot be described as involving "fundamental" rights?

NOTE: STRICT SCRUTINY AND THE RATIONAL-BASIS TEST

Although *Loving*'s analysis of the Due Process Clause was only two paragraphs long, it implicitly resolved the two questions left outstanding by *Griswold*. First, the opinion firmly based the right to privacy—or, at least, the "freedom of choice to marry"—in the Due Process Clause of the Fourteenth Amendment, without reference to the Bill of Rights or the Ninth Amendment. *See Loving*, 388 U.S. at 12. Second, the opinion strongly suggested that when certain "fundamental" rights are at stake, the Court's analysis under the Equal Protection Clause would inform its analysis under the Due Process Clause. *Id.* (quoting *Skinner v. Oklahoma*, 316 U.S. 535, 541 (1942)).

The Court confirmed this second implication of *Loving* in a series of cases involving contraception and abortion.

Five years after *Loving*, a reproductive-rights activist named William Baird purposefully distributed contraceptive foam and a condom to a 19-year-old Boston University student in violation of Massachusetts law. Although *Griswold* had struck down Connecticut's prohibition on the use of contraception by *married* people, many heavily Catholic states, including Massachusetts, retained laws that made it a crime to distribute contraception to *unmarried* people. *See* Geoffrey R. Stone, *Sex and the Constitution* 363–66 (2017). When state prosecutors charged and convicted Baird of violating Massachusetts's ban, state courts distinguished *Griswold* and *Loving* on the ground that those opinions both emphasized the "marital relationship." *Eisenstadt v. Baird*, 405 U.S. 438, 454 (1972). But a 6–1 Supreme Court majority held that the liberty interest at stake was broader than marriage. "If the right of privacy means anything," the Court wrote, "it is the right of the individual, married or single, to be free from unwarranted governmental intrusion into matters so fundamentally affecting a person as the decision whether to bear or beget a child." *Id.* at 453.

The following year, the Supreme Court decided *Roe v. Wade*, 410 U.S. 113 (1973), a decision that we will discuss in detail later (section 43.1). Although *Roe* is best known for its conclusion "that the right of personal privacy includes the abortion decision," *Roe*, 410 U.S. at 154, the opinion was also notable as one of the first times that the Court formally applied the Court's most rigid scrutiny to the deprivation of a fundamental liberty interest. Citing *Eisenstadt*; *Loving*; *Griswold*; *Skinner*; *Pierce v. Society of Sisters*, 268 U.S. 510 (1925); *Meyer v. Nebraska*, 262 U.S. 390 (1923); and a series of equal-protection cases, the Court wrote that "[w]here certain 'fundamental rights' are involved, the Court has held that regulation limiting these rights may be justified only by a 'compelling state interest,' and that legislative enactments must be narrowly drawn to express only the legitimate state interests at stake." *Roe*, 410 U.S. at 155. Applying this exacting standard, the Court held that while Texas had compelling state interests in protecting the health of pregnant women and in "fetal life after viability," a criminal prohibition on first-trimester or pre-viability abortions "sweeps too broadly." *Id.* at 162–64.

42.3 THE TEST FOR EVALUATING WHEN A LIBERTY INTEREST IS "FUNDAMENTAL"

In cases since *Loving v. Virginia*, 388 U.S. 1 (1967), the Supreme Court has consistently held that "the Fifth and Fourteenth Amendments' guarantee of 'due process of law' . . . forbids the government to infringe certain 'fundamental' liberty interests *at all*, no matter what process is provided, unless the infringement is narrowly tailored to serve a compelling state interest." *Reno v. Flores*, 507 U.S. 292, 302 (1993). This is today called *strict scrutiny*. By contrast, the Court interprets the Due Process Clauses to permit the government to interfere with any nonfundamental liberty interests—including the liberty to contract—as long as the law meets "the (unexacting) standard of rationally advancing some legitimate government purpose." *Id.* at 306. This is the *rational-basis test* from *West Coast Hotel Co. v. Parrish*, 300 U.S. 379 (1937).

In a *Harvard Law Review* article from 1972, Professor Gerald Gunther famously described the Supreme Court's "new interventionist stance" as applying either "scrutiny that was 'strict' in theory and fatal in fact" or "minimal scrutiny in theory and virtually none in fact." Gerald Gunther, *Foreword—In Search of Evolving Doctrine on a Changing Court*, 86 Harv. L. Rev. 1, 8 (1972). Because strict scrutiny is so much more difficult for the government to satisfy than the rational-basis test, the Court's determination of whether a liberty interest is "fundamental" has become nearly determinative in whether it invalidates a law under the Due Process Clause.

This categorical framework has made the United States unique in the international community. Most courts around the world evaluate the reasonableness of legislation using a proportionality test similar to Justice John Harlan's *Lochner* dissent. Contextually balancing all of the interests burdened by a law against all of the interests it serves, courts from Germany to South Africa employ a fact-specific approach to determine whether a legislature has appropriately mediated any conflicts. *See* Jamal Greene, *How Rights Went Wrong* 92–113 (2021). In the United States, by contrast, challenges to the reasonableness of legislation turn on whether a litigant's claim of individual autonomy involves a "fundamental" liberty interest that would trigger strict scrutiny. The result is an all-or-nothing approach in which "fundamental" rights cannot be infringed by the political process, while nonfundamental rights are meaningless. *See, e.g.*, *Eisenstadt v. Baird*, 405 U.S. 438, 453 (1972) (recognizing "the decision whether to bear or beget a child" as fundamental); *Roe v. Wade*, 410 U.S. 113, 154 (1973) (recognizing "the abortion decision" as fundamental); *Carey v. Pop. Servs. Int'l*, 431 U.S. 678, 686–87 (1977) (recognizing the "right of access to contraceptives" as fundamental); *Moore v. City of East Cleveland*, 431 U.S. 494, 499 (1977) (recognizing the "choices concerning family living arrangements" as fundamental); *Zablocki v. Redhail*, 434 U.S. 374, 384 (1978) (reaffirming "the right to marry" as fundamental).

As more conservative justices joined the Supreme Court in the 1970s and 1980s, the Court began to impose limits on its recognition of fundamental rights in new factual situations. The most notable example was in *Bowers v. Hardwick*, in which the Court considered a Georgia law that criminalized "sodomy," defined as "any sexual act involving the sex organs of one person and the mouth or anus of another." 478 U.S. 186, 188 n.1 (1986). Michael Hardwick was charged with violating this statute for having consensual sex with another man inside his own home. His attorney, law professor Laurence Tribe, argued that the fundamental right of privacy recognized in *Griswold v. Connecticut*, 381 U.S. 479 (1965), included the right of individuals "to decide for themselves whether to engage in particular forms of private, consensual sexual activity." *See Bowers*, 478 U.S. at 199 (Blackmun, J., dissenting). But the majority disagreed, defining the right at issue with a lower level of generality.

Summarizing due process cases since *Meyer v. Nebraska*, 262 U.S. 390 (1923), Justice Byron White saw "[n]o connection between family, marriage, and procreation on the one hand and homosexual activity on the other." *Bowers*, 478 U.S. at 191. "[R]espondent would have us announce . . . a fundamental right to engage in homosexual sodomy," Justice White wrote. "This we are quite unwilling to do." *Id.* Although White had written a concurring opinion in *Griswold*, in *Bowers* he was contemptuous of *Griswold* and other cases for "recognizing rights that have little or no textual support in the constitutional language." *Id.* Alluding to the era of *Lochner v. New York*, 198 U.S. 45 (1905), White warned in *Bowers* that "announcing rights not readily identifiable in the Constitution's text involves . . . the imposition of the Justices' own choice of values on the States and the Federal Government." *Id.* at 191. To protect the Court from the "illegitimacy" of "discover[ing] new fundamental rights," White wrote that the only rights that should be understood as "fundamental" were those " 'implicit in the concept of ordered liberty,' such that 'neither liberty nor justice would exist if [they] were sacrificed.' " *Id.* at 191–92 (quoting *Palko v. Connecticut*, 302 U.S. 319, 325, 326 (1937)). Applying this test—the same test that the Court used in the incorporation context—White called it "facetious" to claim that the "right [of] homosexuals to engage in acts of consensual sodomy" was "deeply rooted in this Nation's history and tradition." *Id.* at 194.

After *Bowers*, conservative members of the Court insisted that when litigants claimed that their conduct involved a fundamental liberty interest, the Court should "refer to the most specific level at which a relevant tradition protecting, or denying protection to, the asserted right can be identified." *Michael H. v. Gerald D.*, 491 U.S. 110, 127 n.6 (1989) (plurality opinion of Scalia, J.). For instance, in *Michael H. v. Gerald D.*, a man challenged the constitutionality of a California law that denied his paternity of a child born out of wedlock. He claimed that the law interfered with his fundamental right of "parenthood." *Id.* A plurality of the Court disagreed, reframing the question to be whether there existed a fundamental right of "the natural father to assert parental rights over a child born into a woman's existing marriage with another man." *Id.* at 125. It answered no.

42.3.1

Washington v. Glucksberg

521 U.S. 702 (1997)

In the following 1997 case, *Washington v. Glucksberg*, 521 U.S. 702 (1997), a Washington physician named Harold Glucksberg challenged the constitutionality of a state law that made it a felony for a physician to knowingly assist another person in attempting suicide. In support of his challenge, Glucksberg argued that Washington patients had a fundamental "liberty to choose how to die." *Glucksberg*, 521 U.S. at 722.

In considering whether to recognize Glucksberg's claim, the Court established a new, two-part test for when it would consider a liberty interest "fundamental." Under this test, the Court did not recognize Glucksberg's claim.

■ CHIEF JUSTICE REHNQUIST delivered the opinion of the Court.[15]

The question presented in this case is whether Washington's prohibition against "caus[ing]" or "aid[ing]" a suicide offends the Fourteenth Amendment to the United States Constitution. We hold that it does not. . . .

I

We begin, as we do in all due process cases, by examining our Nation's history, legal traditions, and practices. In almost every State—indeed, in almost every western democracy—it is a crime to assist a suicide. The States' assisted-suicide bans are not innovations. Rather, they are longstanding expressions of the States' commitment to the protection and preservation of all human life. . . .

More specifically, for over 700 years, the Anglo-American common-law tradition has punished or otherwise disapproved of both suicide and assisting suicide. . . .

Though deeply rooted, the States' assisted-suicide bans have in recent years been reexamined and, generally, reaffirmed. Because of advances in medicine and technology, Americans today are increasingly likely to die in institutions, from chronic illnesses. Public concern and democratic action are therefore sharply focused on how best to protect dignity and independence at the end of life, with the result that there have been many significant changes in state laws and in the attitudes these laws reflect. Many States, for example, now permit "living wills," surrogate health-care decisionmaking, and the withdrawal or refusal of life-sustaining medical treatment. See *People v. Kevorkian,* 447 Mich. 436, 478–480. At the same time, however, voters and legislators continue for the most part to reaffirm their States' prohibitions on assisting suicide.

[15] **As You Read, Consider:** Recall Chief Justice Earl Warren's approach to the due process question in *Loving v. Virginia*, 388 U.S. 1 (1967). Rather than describe the right at issue narrowly as a "right to interracial marriage," and rather than ask whether a relevant "tradition" protected such a right, he simply declared that the freedom to marry was both fundamental and infringed by Virginia's law. *Loving*, 388 U.S. at 12. Why does Chief Justice William Rehnquist reject Warren's approach here? What principles does Rehnquist's two-part test serve?

The Washington statute at issue in this case was enacted in 1975 as part of a revision of that State's criminal code. . . . In 1991, Washington voters rejected a ballot initiative which, had it passed, would have permitted a form of physician-assisted suicide. . . .

On the other hand, in 1994, voters in Oregon enacted, also through ballot initiative, that State's "Death With Dignity Act," which legalized physician-assisted suicide for competent, terminally ill adults. Since the Oregon vote, many proposals to legalize assisted-suicide have been and continue to be introduced in the States' legislatures, but none has been enacted. . . .

Thus, the States are currently engaged in serious, thoughtful examinations of physician-assisted suicide. . . . Against this backdrop of history, tradition, and practice, we now turn to respondents' constitutional claim.[16]

II

The Due Process Clause guarantees more than fair process, and the "liberty" it protects includes more than the absence of physical restraint. The Clause also provides heightened protection against government interference with certain fundamental rights and liberty interests. *Reno v. Flores,* 507 U. S. 292, 301–302 (1993). In a long line of cases, we have held that, in addition to the specific freedoms protected by the Bill of Rights, the "liberty" specially protected by the Due Process Clause includes the rights to marry, *Loving v. Virginia,* 388 U. S. 1 (1967); to have children, *Skinner v. Oklahoma ex rel. Williamson,* 316 U. S. 535 (1942); to direct the education and upbringing of one's children, *Meyer v. Nebraska,* 262 U. S. 390 (1923); *Pierce v. Society of Sisters,* 268 U. S. 510 (1925); to marital privacy, *Griswold v. Connecticut,* 381 U. S. 479 (1965); to use contraception, *Eisenstadt v. Baird,*405 U. S. 438 (1972); to bodily integrity, *Rochin v. California,* 342 U. S. 165 (1952), and to abortion, *Casey, supra.* . . .

But we have always been reluctant to expand the concept of substantive due process because guide posts for responsible decision making in this unchartered area are scarce and open-ended. By extending constitutional protection to an asserted right or liberty interest, we, to a great extent, place the matter outside the arena of public debate and legislative action. We must therefore exercise the utmost care whenever we are asked to break new ground in this field, lest the liberty protected by the Due Process Clause be subtly transformed into the policy preferences of the Members of this Court.

Our established method of substantive-due-process analysis has two primary features: First, we have regularly observed that the Due Process Clause specially protects those fundamental rights and liberties which are, objectively, "deeply rooted in this Nation's history and tradition," *Snyder v. Massachusetts,* 291 U. S. 97, 105 (1934), and "implicit in the concept of ordered liberty," such that "neither liberty nor justice would exist if they were sacrificed," *Palko v. Connecticut,* 302 U. S. 319, 325, 326 (1937). Second, we have required in substantive-due-process cases a careful description of the asserted fundamental liberty interest. Our Nation's history, legal traditions, and practices thus provide the crucial guide posts for responsible decisionmaking, that direct and restrain our exposition of the Due Process Clause. . . .[17]

---

[16] **Question:** Rehnquist here emphasizes that the claimed right at issue in this case—a right to death with dignity—is the subject of "serious, thoughtful examinations" in the political process. Why does he think such examinations should be relevant to whether the Supreme Court treats the right as "fundamental" and therefore protected by strict scrutiny?

[17] **Questions:** Is the two-part test that Rehnquist announces here consistent with *Loving*? Do you agree with him about the principles served by a test that emphasizes "history" and "legal

[T]he development of this Court's substantive-due-process jurisprudence, described briefly, has been a process whereby the outlines of the "liberty" specially protected by the Fourteenth Amendment—never fully clarified, to be sure, and perhaps not capable of being fully clarified—have at least been carefully refined by concrete examples involving fundamental rights found to be deeply rooted in our legal tradition. This approach tends to rein in the subjective elements that are necessarily present in due process judicial review. In addition, by establishing a threshold requirement—that a challenged state action implicate a fundamental right—before requiring more than a reasonable relation to a legitimate state interest to justify the action, it avoids the need for complex balancing of competing interests in every case.

Turning to the claim at issue here, . . . respondents assert a "liberty to choose how to die" and a right to "control of one's final days," Brief for Respondents 7, and describe the asserted liberty as "the right to choose a humane, dignified death," *id.*, at 15, and "the liberty to shape death," *id.*, at 18. As noted above, we have a tradition of carefully formulating the interest at stake in substantive-due-process cases. . . . The Washington statute at issue in this case prohibits "aid[ing] another person to attempt suicide," Wash. Rev. Code § 9A.36.060(1) (1994), and, thus, the question before us is whether the "liberty" specially protected by the Due Process Clause includes a right to commit suicide which itself includes a right to assistance in doing so.

We now inquire whether this asserted right has any place in our Nation's traditions. Here, as discussed [above], we are confronted with a consistent and almost universal tradition that has long rejected the asserted right, and continues explicitly to reject it today. . . . To hold for respondents, we would have to reverse centuries of legal doctrine and practice, and strike down the considered policy choice of almost every State. . . . That being the case, our decisions lead us to conclude that the asserted "right" to assistance in committing suicide is not a fundamental liberty interest protected by the Due Process Clause.

[III]

The Constitution also requires, however, that Washington's assisted-suicide ban be rationally related to legitimate government interests. This requirement is unquestionably met here. As the court below recognized, Washington's assisted-suicide ban implicates a number of state interests.

First, Washington has an unqualified interest in the preservation of human life. . . . The State also has an interest in protecting the integrity and ethics of the medical profession. . . . Next, the State has an interest in protecting vulnerable groups—including the poor, the elderly, and disabled persons—from abuse, neglect, and mistakes. . . . Finally, the State may fear that permitting assisted suicide will start it down the path to voluntary and perhaps even involuntary euthanasia. . . .

We need not weigh exactingly the relative strengths of these various interests. They are unquestionably important and legitimate, and Washington's ban on assisted suicide is at least reasonably related to their promotion and protection. . . . [The ban therefore] does not violate the Fourteenth Amendment . . . .

Throughout the Nation, Americans are engaged in an earnest and profound debate about the morality, legality, and practicality of physician-assisted suicide. Our holding permits this debate to continue, as it should in a democratic society. . . .

---

traditions" to determine whether a liberty interest should be insulated from the political process? Do you agree with him about the principles served by a categorical test that insulates only certain interests in contrast with a balancing test that weighs all interests?

42.3.2

Lawrence v. Texas

539 U.S. 558 (2003)

Glucksberg articulated a two-part test for when a liberty interest is "fundamental" and therefore protected by strict scrutiny: (1) a "carefully described" version of the liberty interest (2) is "deeply rooted" in the nation's history and tradition. This test was purposefully narrow and designed to prevent the Court from constitutionalizing claims of individual autonomy. Using language less inflammatory than White's opinion in *Bowers*, Chief Justice William Rehnquist wrote for a unanimous Court that when the Supreme Court recognizes something as a fundamental liberty interest, its recognition has the potential to end democratic debate. *See Glucksberg*, 521 U.S. at 720. For example, where voters in Oregon, Washington, and elsewhere were deciding whether to adopt "death with dignity" laws, an opinion in favor of Glucksberg would have had the effect of constitutionalizing similar laws for the entire country.

Yet it immediately became unclear whether the Court would continue to apply *Glucksberg*'s test to new situations. In particular, *Glucksberg* played no role in the following opinion, *Lawrence v. Texas*, 539 U.S. 558 (2003), which rigorously (and surprisingly) applied the Court's rational-basis test to strike down a law without first recognizing a fundamental liberty interest.

The facts of *Lawrence* are as follows: In 1998, police officers in Houston, Texas, were dispatched to the home of John Geddes Lawrence. Entering his apartment, the officers observed Lawrence having sex with another man. Like Michael Hardwick years earlier, Lawrence was arrested and charged with a crime: "deviate sexual intercourse, namely anal sex, with a member of the same sex (man)." *Lawrence*, 539 U.S. at 563.

Although *Bowers* had sanctioned Georgia's similar prohibition, a new 6–3 majority in *Lawrence* held that *Bowers* had been wrongly decided.

■ JUSTICE KENNEDY delivered the opinion of the Court.[18]

Liberty protects the person from unwarranted government intrusions into a dwelling or other private places. . . . Liberty [also] presumes an autonomy of self that includes freedom of thought, belief, expression, and certain intimate conduct. The instant case involves liberty of the person both in its spatial and more transcendent dimensions. . . .

---

[18] **As You Read, Consider:** Doctrinally, Justice Anthony Kennedy never reaches the question of whether the liberty interest at issue in this case is "fundamental" enough to warrant strict scrutiny. Instead, he asks the same question as in *West Coast Hotel Co. v. Parrish*: Is the law rationally related to a legitimate interest? Do you agree with him that it is impossible to *conceive of* a legitimate interest served by the law? Or do you suspect that he is really applying a different test that weighs the harms imposed by the law against its alleged benefits?

The question before the Court is the validity of a Texas statute making it a crime for two persons of the same sex to engage in certain intimate sexual conduct. . . . For this inquiry we deem it necessary to reconsider the Court's holding in *Bowers*. . . .

The Court began its substantive discussion in *Bowers* as follows: "The issue presented is whether the Federal Constitution confers a fundamental right upon homosexuals to engage in sodomy and hence invalidates the laws of the many States that still make such conduct illegal and have done so for a very long time." *Id.*, at 190. That statement, we now conclude, discloses the Court's own failure to appreciate the extent of the liberty at stake. To say that the issue in *Bowers* was simply the right to engage in certain sexual conduct demeans the claim the individual put forward, just as it would demean a married couple were it to be said marriage is simply about the right to have sexual intercourse. The laws involved in *Bowers* and here are, to be sure, statutes that purport to do no more than prohibit a particular sexual act. Their penalties and purposes, though, have more far-reaching consequences, touching upon the most private human conduct, sexual behavior, and in the most private of places, the home. The statutes do seek to control a personal relationship that, whether or not entitled to formal recognition in the law, is within the liberty of persons to choose without being punished as criminals.

This, as a general rule, should counsel against attempts by the State, or a court, to define the meaning of the relationship or to set its boundaries absent injury to a person or abuse of an institution the law protects. It suffices for us to acknowledge that adults may choose to enter upon this relationship in the confines of their homes and their own private lives and still retain their dignity as free persons. When sexuality finds overt expression in intimate conduct with another person, the conduct can be but one element in a personal bond that is more enduring. The liberty protected by the Constitution allows homosexual persons the right to make this choice.

Having misapprehended the claim of liberty there presented to it, and thus stating the claim to be whether there is a fundamental right to engage in consensual sodomy, the *Bowers* Court said: "Proscriptions against that conduct have ancient roots." *Id.*, at 192. . . . [T]he Court in *Bowers* was making the broader point that for centuries there have been powerful voices to condemn homosexual conduct as immoral. The condemnation has been shaped by religious beliefs, conceptions of right and acceptable behavior, and respect for the traditional family. For many persons these are not trivial concerns but profound and deep convictions accepted as ethical and moral principles to which they aspire and which thus determine the course of their lives. These considerations do not answer the question before us, however. The issue is whether the majority may use the power of the State to enforce these views on the whole society through operation of the criminal law. . . .

In all events we think that our laws and traditions in the past half century are of most relevance here. These references show an emerging awareness that liberty gives substantial protection to adult persons in deciding how to conduct their private lives in matters pertaining to sex. History and tradition are the starting point but not in all cases the ending point of the substantive due process inquiry.[19]

---

[19] **Questions:** Kennedy does not hold that the liberty interest at issue in this case is "fundamental." Yet his claim that "[h]istory and tradition" are not "the ending point of the substantive due process inquiry" is a clear departure from *Washington v. Glucksberg*.

What does his evaluation of *recent* history in the next few paragraphs reveal about the principles served by *Glucksberg*'s emphasis on tradition when deciding whether a liberty interest warrants strict scrutiny? What does his evaluation of the "stigma" and "demean[ing]" nature of Texas's law reveal about the principles served by the Court's categorical approach to the Due Process Clause, which subjects laws to either a skeptical or deferential means-ends test rather than the "complex balancing of competing interests" rejected by *Glucksberg*?

This emerging recognition should have been apparent when *Bowers* was decided. In 1955 the American Law Institute promulgated the Model Penal Code and made clear that it did not recommend or provide for "criminal penalties for consensual sexual relations conducted in private." ALI, Model Penal Code § 213.2, Comment 2, p. 372 (1980). . . .

In *Bowers* the Court referred to the fact that before 1961 all 50 States had outlawed sodomy, and that at the time of the Court's decision 24 States and the District of Columbia had sodomy laws. Justice Powell pointed out that these prohibitions often were being ignored, however. Georgia, for instance, had not sought to enforce its law for decades. . . .

The sweeping references by Chief Justice Burger to the history of Western civilization and to Judeo-Christian moral and ethical standards did not take account of other authorities pointing in an opposite direction. A committee advising the British Parliament recommended in 1957 repeal of laws punishing homosexual conduct. . . . Parliament enacted the substance of those recommendations 10 years later. Sexual Offences Act 1967, § 1.

Of even more importance, almost five years before *Bowers* was decided the European Court of Human Rights considered a case with parallels to *Bowers* and to today's case. . . . The court held that the laws proscribing [consensual homosexual] conduct were invalid under the European Convention on Human Rights. *Dudgeon v. United Kingdom,* 45 Eur. Ct. H. R. (1981) ¶ 52. Authoritative in all countries that are members of the Council of Europe (21 nations then, 45 nations now), the decision is at odds with the premise in *Bowers* that the claim put forward was insubstantial in our Western civilization.

In our own constitutional system the deficiencies in *Bowers* became even more apparent in the years following its announcement. The 25 States with laws prohibiting the relevant conduct referenced in the *Bowers* decision are reduced now to 13, of which 4 enforce their laws only against homosexual conduct. . . .

When homosexual conduct is made criminal by the law of the State, that declaration in and of itself is an invitation to subject homosexual persons to discrimination both in the public and in the private spheres. The central holding of *Bowers* . . . demeans the lives of homosexual persons.

The stigma this criminal statute imposes, moreover, is not trivial. The offense, to be sure, is but a class C misdemeanor, a minor offense in the Texas legal system. Still, it remains a criminal offense with all that imports for the dignity of the persons charged. The petitioners will bear on their record the history of their criminal convictions. . . . Furthermore, the Texas criminal conviction carries with it the other collateral consequences always following a conviction, such as notations on job application forms, to mention but one example. . . .

The doctrine of *stare decisis* is essential to the respect accorded to the judgments of the Court and to the stability of the law. It is not, however, an inexorable command. In [*Planned Parenthood v.*] *Casey* we noted that when a court is asked to overrule a precedent recognizing a constitutional liberty interest, individual or societal reliance on the existence of that liberty cautions with particular strength against reversing course. . . . [But] there has been no individual or societal reliance on *Bowers* of the sort that could counsel against overturning its holding once there are compelling reasons to do so. . . .

The rationale of *Bowers* does not withstand careful analysis. . . . ["T]he fact that the governing majority in a State has traditionally viewed a particular practice as immoral is not a sufficient reason for upholding a law prohibiting the practice; neither history nor tradition could save a law prohibiting miscegenation from constitutional attack. . . .["] [*Bowers*, 478 U. S., at 216 (Stevens, J., dissenting).][20]

Bowers was not correct when it was decided, and it is not correct today. It ought not to remain binding precedent. *Bowers v. Hardwick* should be and now is overruled. . . .

[This case involves] two adults who, with full and mutual consent from each other, engaged in sexual practices common to a homosexual lifestyle. The petitioners are entitled to respect for their private lives. The State cannot demean their existence or control their destiny by making their private sexual conduct a crime. Their right to liberty under the Due Process Clause gives them the full right to engage in their conduct without intervention of the government. . . . The Texas statute furthers no legitimate state interest which can justify its intrusion into the personal and private life of the individual.

Had those who drew and ratified the Due Process Clauses of the Fifth Amendment or the Fourteenth Amendment known the components of liberty in its manifold possibilities, they might have been more specific. They did not presume to have this insight. They knew times can blind us to certain truths and later generations can see that laws once thought necessary and proper in fact serve only to oppress. As the Constitution endures, persons in every generation can invoke its principles in their own search for greater freedom. . . .

■ JUSTICE SCALIA, with whom THE CHIEF JUSTICE and JUSTICE THOMAS join, dissenting. . . .

[Most] of today's opinion has no relevance to its actual holding—that the Texas statute "furthers no legitimate state interest which can justify" its application to petitioners under rational-basis review. . . . [The Court's] unheard-of form of rational-basis review . . . will have far-reaching implications beyond this case. . . .

The Texas statute undeniably seeks to further the belief of its citizens that certain forms of sexual behavior are "immoral and unacceptable"—the same interest furthered by criminal laws against fornication, bigamy, adultery, adult incest, bestiality, and obscenity. *Bowers* held that this *was* a legitimate state interest. The Court today reaches the opposite conclusion. . . . This effectively decrees the end of all morals legislation. If, as the Court asserts, the promotion of majoritarian sexual morality is not even a *legitimate* state interest, none of the above-mentioned laws can survive rational-basis review. . . .

Let me be clear that I have nothing against homosexuals, or any other group, promoting their agenda through normal democratic means. Social perceptions of sexual and other morality change over time, and every group has the right to persuade its fellow citizens that its view of such matters is the best. . . . What Texas has chosen to do is well within the range of traditional democratic action, and its hand should not be stayed through the invention of a brand-new "constitutional right" by a Court that is impatient of democratic change. It is indeed true that "later generations can see that laws once thought necessary and proper in fact serve only to oppress"; and when

---

[20] **Questions:** Doctrinally, this is the most important paragraph of Kennedy's opinion. Quoting Justice John Paul Stevens's dissent in *Bowers v. Hardwick*, Kennedy holds that a history or tradition of viewing a particular practice as immoral is not a legitimate interest that could *ever* justify a law on its own—even under the rational-basis test.

Do you agree? Consider the role that morality plays in virtually all legislation. A governing majority might consider it immoral to allow people to go hungry, for example. Or the majority might consider it immoral to allow certain people to die, to be discriminated against, or to be subjugated. Are Kennedy and Stevens nevertheless correct that laws acting on these moral judgments must be justified with reference to other legitimate interests? Are no such legitimate interests involved in this case?

that happens, later generations can repeal those laws. But it is the premise of our system that those judgments are to be made by the people, and not imposed by a governing caste that knows best. . . .

If moral disapprobation of homosexual conduct is "no legitimate state interest" for purposes of proscribing that conduct[,] . . . what justification could there possibly be for denying the benefits of marriage to homosexual couples exercising "[t]he liberty protected by the Constitution"? Surely not the encouragement of procreation, since the sterile and the elderly are allowed to marry. This case "does not involve" the issue of homosexual marriage only if one entertains the belief that principle and logic have nothing to do with the decisions of this Court. . . .

NOTE: MORALS LEGISLATION AND SAME-SEX MARRIAGE

Lawrence had far-reaching doctrinal implications for the Supreme Court's interpretation of the Due Process Clause. While saying nothing about *Glucksberg*'s test for determining whether a liberty interest was fundamental and therefore subject to strict scrutiny, the majority held that Texas's law was rationally related to no legitimate state interest and therefore failed even the deferential rational-basis test. More significantly, the majority explicitly declared that Texas's interest in enforcing a historically and widely held disapproval of conduct was not alone a legitimate state purpose. In other words, the majority held that regardless of whether a fundamental liberty interest is at stake, a state cannot infringe on a person's private conduct simply because most people regard the conduct as immoral.

As Justice Antonin Scalia predicted in his dissent, eliminating traditional views of morality as a legitimate state interest undermined the strongest argument in favor of laws that prohibited same-sex couples from getting married. Five months after *Lawrence*, the Supreme Judicial Court of Massachusetts held that the denial of marriage licenses to same-sex couples violated Massachusetts's state constitution because the denial wasn't rationally related to any legitimate state interest. *Goodridge v. Dep't of Pub. Health*, 798 N.E.2d 941, 968 (Mass. 2003). Over the next decade, numerous state supreme courts reached the same conclusion under their own constitutions. These decisions galvanized the public in dozens of states to campaign for repealing prohibitions against same-sex marriage through legislation or by amending their constitutions. And when the issue reached federal courts of appeals, most followed *Loving* in treating marriage as a fundamental liberty interest, or *Lawrence* in deciding that states had no legitimate interest in defining *marriage* as a relationship between one man and one woman.

In *Obergefell v. Hodges*, 576 U.S. 644 (2015), the Court invalidated the remaining state bans on same-sex marriage under the Due Process Clause and Equal Protection Clause. The opinion will be discussed in more detail later with regard to the Equal Protection Clause (section 48.3) because of that clause's centrality to the Court's holding. For now, the opinion is notable for its departure from *Glucksberg*'s two-part test for evaluating whether a liberty interest is fundamental. In considering whether the right at issue was the "right to marry" rather than a "right to same-sex marriage," Justice

Anthony Kennedy observed that "*Loving* did not ask about a 'right to interracial marriage.' . . . Rather, [it] inquired about the right to marry in its comprehensive sense, asking if there was a sufficient justification for excluding the relevant class from the right." *Obergefell*, 576 U.S. at 671. And in considering whether history and tradition recognized such a right, Kennedy cited *Loving* and *Lawrence* to note that "[i]f rights were defined by who exercised them in the past, then received practices could serve as their own continued justification and new groups could not invoke rights once denied. . . . [R]ights come not from ancient sources alone." *Id.*

42.4 OTHER CONCEPTIONS OF THE RIGHT OF PRIVACY

As *Loving v. Virginia*, 388 U.S. 1 (1967); *Lawrence v. Texas*, 539 U.S. 558 (2003); and *Obergefell v. Hodges*, 576 U.S. 644 (2015), indicate, the right of privacy has evolved into a right of dignity and individual autonomy protected by the Due Process Clause, which prohibits unnecessary deprivations of "fundamental" liberty interests and irrational deprivations of all other liberty interests. But individual autonomy isn't the only constitutionally protected conception of "privacy"—or even the most intuitive. Other conceptions of privacy include informational secrecy, protected personal space, and physical liberty.

Informational secrecy

When Louis Brandeis and Samuel Warren used the term *privacy* in their 1890 *Harvard Law Review* article, they didn't use the term to connote a right of individuals to make personal choices. Samuel Warren & Louis Brandeis, *The Right to Privacy,* 4 Harv. L. Rev. 193 (1890). Rather, they invoked privacy to connote the "right to be let alone" and to keep secret information hidden. In *Griswold v. Connecticut*, 381 U.S. 479 (1965), Justice William O. Douglas had the same idea in mind when he rhetorically asked for the majority, "Would we allow the police to search the sacred precincts of marital bedrooms for telltale signs of the use of contraceptives?" 381 U.S. 479, 485 (1965). Douglas and the concurring justices also invoked the Fourth Amendment's protection against unlawful searches and seizures as a basis for recognizing the right of privacy.

In contrast with *Loving*, which protected a right of individual autonomy under the Fourteenth Amendment, decisions protecting a right of informational secrecy have generally done so under the Fourth and Fifth Amendments. *See, e.g.*, *Zurcher v. Stanford Daily*, 436 U.S. 547, 567 (1978); *Cal. Bankers Ass'n v. Shultz*, 416 U.S. 21, 77 (1974). For example, to determine whether a government official has committed a "search" for purposes of the Fourth Amendment, the Court today asks whether the government has infringed on a person's "reasonable expectation of privacy"—a test developed two years after *Griswold. See Katz v. United States*, 389 U.S. 347, 360 (1967) (Harlan, J., concurring);

see, e.g., *Carpenter v. United States*, 138 S. Ct. 2206 (2018) (recognizing an expectation of privacy in cell phone location records). Because the Court has tied this conception of privacy to the text of specific amendments, however, the Court hasn't engaged in the same *Washington v. Glucksberg*-style analysis, 521 U.S. 702 (1997), to protect all invasions of informational secrecy. The Fifth Amendment, for instance, has not been interpreted to protect against the compelled testimony of *private* information, but only against the compelled testimony of *incriminating* information. *See Fisher v. United States*, 425 U.S. 391, 401 (1976).

That said, the Court has occasionally suggested that the Fourteenth Amendment itself protects a liberty interest in informational secrecy. For example, in *NASA v. Nelson*, the Court assumed without deciding that a liberty interest in informational secrecy existed, but applied the rational-basis test to a regulation that required extensive background checks before a person could work at National Aeronautics and Space Administration (NASA) facilities. 562 U.S. 134, 147–48, 159 (2011).

Protected personal space

Another conception of privacy that animated the opinions in *Griswold* was the idea that some spaces, particularly the home, should remain free from government intrusion regardless of the conduct at issue. In *Stanley v. Georgia*, 394 U.S. 557 (1969), the Court elaborated on this conception of privacy. At issue was a Georgia statute that prohibited the possession of "obscene matter." *Stanley*, 394 U.S. at 558. After Georgia police raided the home of Robert Stanley, prosecutors convicted Stanley of possessing pornographic films.

Invoking *Griswold* and the First Amendment, the Supreme Court invalidated the statute as an invasion of privacy. Stanley, the Court wrote, "is asserting the right to read or observe what he pleases—the right to satisfy his intellectual and emotional needs in the privacy of his own home." *Id.* at 565. The Court emphasized that "a State has no business telling a man, sitting alone in his own house, what books he may read or what films he may watch." *Id.* Conceding that "the States retain broad power to regulate obscenity[,] that power simply does not extend to mere possession by the individual in the privacy of his own home." *Id.* at 568.

As an illustration of Fourteenth Amendment doctrine, however, *Stanley* didn't last long. Within a few years, the Court repeatedly held that individuals don't have free license to use drugs, possess contraband, view child pornography, or do whatever they want just because they do it in the home. *See, e.g., Osborne v. Ohio*, 495 U.S. 103 (1990). By the time the Court decided *Bowers v. Hardwick*, the Court had an easy time declaring that *Stanley* "was firmly grounded in the First Amendment" but that "otherwise illegal conduct is not always immunized whenever it occurs in the home." 478 U.S. 186, 195 (1986). In *Lawrence*, the opening paragraph emphasized that "[l]iberty protects the person from unwarranted government intrusions into a dwelling or other private places." 539 U.S. at 562. But it isn't clear how that sentence affected the rest of the opinion's holding.

Physical liberty

One final conception of privacy—closely related to the right of individual autonomy recognized by *Loving* and *Lawrence*—is the right of physical liberty. As the Court emphasized in *Meyer v. Nebraska*, the liberty protected by the Due Process Clause includes not only abstract liberties but also the literal "freedom from bodily restraint." 262 U.S. 390, 399 (1923). We discussed deprivations of physical liberty earlier in the context of procedural due process (section 40.5) as governments may not confine people without giving them notice and an opportunity to be heard. But deprivations of physical liberty also present a puzzle for the Supreme Court's *substantive* due process doctrine.

As we've just seen, since 1973, when a law interferes with a person's fundamental liberty interest, that law violates the Due Process Clause unless the deprivation can be justified under strict scrutiny. Physical liberty has "always" been regarded as a fundamental liberty interest. *Greenholtz v. Inmates of Neb. Penal Complex*, 442 U.S. 1, 18 (1979) (Powell, J., concurring). Therefore, one would expect that when a government confines a person, the government would have to justify that confinement under strict scrutiny—that is, confinement would have to be "narrowly tailored" to serve a compelling interest. Thus, before punishing shoplifting with a one-year prison sentence, the government would have to explain why a year of prison is necessary to serve the government's interest in preventing theft when a fine or some other punishment could also serve that interest.

What makes this a puzzle is that the Supreme Court has never suggested that confinement must be justified by strict scrutiny. Instead, the Court has taken the opposite approach, applying a lenient standard when evaluating state regulations that infringe on a person's liberty interest in being free from bodily restraint. In *Bell v. Wolfish*, the Court explained that when a government has sufficient evidence to confine a person for purposes of *procedural* due process, the government may *substantively*

> employ devices that are calculated to effectuate this detention. Traditionally, this has meant confinement in a facility which, no matter how modern or how antiquated, results in restricting the movement of a detainee in a manner in which he would not be restricted if he simply were free to walk the streets.

441 U.S. 520, 537 (1979).

The Court has applied a variation of the rational-basis test when evaluating challenges to government regulations of confined people who have not been convicted of a crime. For such pretrial detainees, people in immigration detention, or involuntarily committed people, the Court has prohibited any "expressed intent to punish" but upheld any "condition or restriction" that is "reasonably related to a legitimate governmental objective." *Id.* at 538–39. Applying this test, the Court has held that a person who is confined continues to enjoy "constitutionally protected interests" in "adequate food, shelter, clothing[,] medical care . . . and safety[;] reasonably nonrestrictive confinement conditions[;] and such training as may be required by these interests." *Youngberg v. Romeo*, 457 U.S. 307, 324 (1982). The Court has also held that such a person has a liberty interest in being protected from objectively unreasonable uses of force. *Kingsley v. Hendrickson*, 576 U.S. 389, 392 (2015).

The Court applies a similar test to evaluate regulations that affect people who have been convicted of a crime, except that the Court applies this test even when other fundamental rights, such as marriage, are at stake. Once a person has been convicted, the Court held in *Turner v. Safley*, the government may take any action that is " 'reasonably related' to legitimate penological objectives" as long as the action isn't an " 'exaggerated response' to those concerns." 482 U.S. 78, 87 (1987). In *Turner*, the Court applied this test to uphold a prison rule that prohibited inmates from corresponding with one another, but it struck down a separate prison rule that prohibited inmates from marrying one another. The Court ruled that the marriage prohibition "represented an exaggerated response" to the state's interest in preventing "love triangles" that might lead to violent confrontations. *Id.* at 97–98.

CHAPTER 43

WHAT LIMITATIONS DO THE DUE PROCESS CLAUSES OF THE FIFTH AND FOURTEENTH AMENDMENTS IMPOSE ON THE SUBSTANTIVE POWER OF GOVERNMENT TO DEPRIVE SOMEONE OF THEIR LIBERTY TO ABORT A PREGNANCY?

FIFTH AMENDMENT (1791): No person shall . . . be deprived of life, liberty, or property, without due process of law. . . .

FOURTEENTH AMENDMENT (1868), SECTION 1: No State shall . . . deprive any person of life, liberty, or property, without due process of law. . . .

43.1 THE RIGHT OF PRIVACY APPLIED TO ABORTION

On January 22, 1973, the "right of privacy" transitioned from an obscure legal theory into one of the central issues of American politics. In *Roe v. Wade*, the Supreme Court held for the first time that the "fundamental" right of privacy "includes the abortion decision," and states therefore could not restrict access to an abortion without satisfying strict scrutiny. 410 U.S. 113, 154 (1973). Yet cultural and legal debates over abortion had already been simmering for decades.

Genesis of antiabortion laws

At the beginning of the nineteenth century, no law in the United States prohibited either contraception or abortion before "quickening": the moment during a pregnancy, usually after four months, when a pregnant person first feels fetal movement. Geoffrey R. Stone, *Sex and the Constitution* 180 (2017). As late as the 1870s, advertisements for condoms, diaphragms, IUDs, and abortions were commonplace and unregulated, and approximately 20 percent of all pregnancies were purposefully terminated. *Id.* at 181, 189.

This began to change in the middle of the century, when crusaders affiliated with the temperance movement pushed state legislatures to pass a range of laws to combat alcoholism and illicit sex. Mary Ziegler,

After Roe 2 (2015). New York set a novel precedent in 1845 with a law that made it unlawful for anyone, including a pregnant person, to induce "a miscarriage" before or after quickening. Stone, *supra*, at 185–86.

After the Civil War, the newly created American Medical Association launched a campaign to nationalize New York's antiabortion law. Ziegler, *supra*, at 2–3. Male physicians argued that their superior medical understanding of fetal life gave them license to wrest decisions over contraception away from female midwives and pregnant people, whose minds were prone "to temporary actual derangement, under the stimulus of uterine excitement." Stone, *supra*, at 188. They joined a religious anti-vice campaign led by Anthony Comstock, who considered information about contraception "obscene" because it encouraged immoral thoughts. *Id.* at 190. Congress eventually enacted the Comstock Act of 1873, which made it a crime to send "indecent" or "immoral" material in the mail, including information about "where, how, . . . or by what means" a person could obtain "any article or thing designed or intended for the prevention of conception or procuring of abortion." Comstock Act, ch. 258, 17 Stat. 598, 599; *see* Stone, *supra*, at 190–93. By 1900, nearly every state had passed an antiabortion law that typically allowed abortions only when necessary to save the life of the pregnant person. Ziegler, *supra*, at 3.

These laws did little to actually end abortions. In light of prevailing societal attitudes toward unwed mothers, approximately 90 percent of premarital pregnancies in the early twentieth century ended in illegal abortions. Stone, *supra*, at 208–09. People who performed illegal abortions included licensed physicians, dentists, nurses, barbers, prostitutes, doormen, and the pregnant people themselves. *Id.* at 209. By the 1950s, approximately one million people were obtaining an illegal abortion each year—representing the same 20 percent of all pregnancies as in the mid-nineteenth century. *Id.*

Advocates' arguments against antiabortion laws

In light of the health risks and difficulty of obtaining safe abortions, Margaret Sanger, Mary Ware Dennett, and other advocates of "family planning" began to promote contraception as a method of helping women assert their independence. *Id.* at 195–97. Influenced by her background as a socialist in the labor movement, Sanger argued that "birth control" would help poor women escape poverty. David M. Kennedy, *Birth Control in America* 10–13 (1970). Sanger was also influenced by the parallel eugenics movement, leading her to conclude that birth control could also check the spread of undesirable heritable traits, including alcoholism and intellectual disabilities. *Id.* at 115–19. The birth control movement and eugenics movement were remarkably successful in state legislatures, securing the passage of dozens of compulsory sterilization laws. Ziegler, *supra*, at 3; *see* Adam Cohen, *Imbeciles: The Supreme Court, American Eugenics, and the Sterilization of Carrie Buck* 56–57 (2017).

World War II and press coverage of the Nazi sterilization regime ended the eugenics movement in the United States. In its place, a diverse group of activists formed a social movement focused on the dangers of population growth. Ziegler, *supra*, at 4–5. Led by organizations like the Population Council and the Association for Voluntary Sterilization, the population-control movement emphasized the need for contraception to help poor urban and rural communities conserve already insufficient supplies of adequate food, housing, sanitation, and health care. *Id.* at 5. This movement, along with changing generational attitudes toward respectable sexual behavior, eroded much of the religious and cultural opposition toward birth control. In a 1968 Gallup poll, 76 percent of Catholics responded that birth control should be "available to anyone who wants it." *Id.* By the time the Supreme Court decided *Griswold v. Connecticut*, 381 U.S. 479 (1965), millions of women were using the birth control pill, and nearly one half of unmarried women reported that they had been sexually active before age nineteen. Ziegler, *supra*, at 5.

Challenges of state bans, legal abortion, and backlash

Although most states continued to criminalize abortions, nearly one million pregnant people continued to obtain illegal abortions every year. Stone, *supra*, at 209; Leslie J. Reagan, *When Abortion Was a Crime* 23–24 (1997). Some of these people had the connections or wealth necessary to find a physician willing to perform a safe, illegal abortion. Stone, *supra*, at 372. The going rate was more than $8,000 in today's dollars. *Id.* But the vast majority of people seeking an abortion could not find a doctor or afford this expense, forcing them to turn to unreliable back-alley practitioners or dangerous self-abortions. *Id.* at 373. Approximately 30 percent of illegal abortions were self-induced in the 1960s, typically with bleach, coat hangers, knitting needles, or other risky methods. *Id.* On average, more than two hundred women died each year as a result of botched abortions. *Id.*

A broad coalition emerged after *Griswold* to challenge state bans on birth control. Feminist organizations, including the National Organization for Women and New York Radical Women, argued that access to safe abortion was essential to securing more opportunities for women. *Id.* Legal scholars affiliated with the American Law Institute proposed a model statute that would legalize abortion in cases of rape, incest, fetal deformity, or threats to the physical or mental health of the pregnant person. Ziegler, *supra*, at 6. And public fears about fetal defects—galvanized by a 1964 rubella epidemic—convinced many middle-class white people to question existing abortion restrictions. *Id.* In 1962, a children's television host named Sherri Finkbine famously traveled to Sweden to obtain an abortion after discovering she had inadvertently taken thalidomide, a drug known to cause severe birth defects. Sara Dubow, *Ourselves Unborn* 64–65 (2010). A Gallup poll taken shortly afterward revealed that 52 percent of Americans supported her decision to obtain an abortion, while only 32 percent opposed it. *Id.* Finkbine's story also illustrated how abortion was legally available for some people—but only if they could afford to travel elsewhere. Ziegler, *supra*, at 7.

By 1970, this newly energized coalition successfully convinced four states, including New York, to eliminate all meaningful legal restrictions on abortion access. *Id.* at 8. A dozen other states adopted the American Law Institute's model statute—despite criticism that the statute meant "[y]ou have to be rich, crazy, or a victim of rape to get an abortion legally." *Id.* at 7.

These new laws drew fierce backlash from the Catholic Church, which established the National Right to Life Committee in response. *See* Stone, *supra*, at 380. In legislatures and courts, Catholic activists argued that laws permitting abortions unconstitutionally deprived "unborn children" of their "life . . . without due process of law." *Id.* In 1972, the antiabortion movement even convinced New York's legislature to reinstate its abortion ban. *Id.* at 381–82. Republican governor Nelson Rockefeller vetoed the legislature's action, but no state liberalized its abortion restrictions between 1970 and 1973. *Id.* at 382.

43.1.1

Roe v. Wade

410 U.S. 113 (1973)

Facing legislative inertia at the state level, supporters of contraception and abortion access turned to federal courts. In 1972, the Supreme Court decided *Eisenstadt v. Baird*, 405 U.S. 438 (1972), striking down Massachusetts's prohibition on distributing contraception to unmarried people. "If the right of privacy means anything," Justice William Brennan wrote for the 6–1 Court, "it is the right of the individual, married or single, to be free from unwarranted governmental intrusion into matters so fundamentally affecting a person as the decision whether to bear or beget a child." *Baird*, 405 U.S. at 453.

That same year, a Gallup poll reported that 64 percent of Americans agreed "that abortion should be a decision between a woman and her physician." Ziegler, *supra*, at 10. Justice Harry Blackmun kept a news clipping of this poll in his files when he authored the following decision, *Roe v. Wade*, 410 U.S. 113 (1973). *Id.*

Like most states in 1973, Texas prohibited abortion except "for the purpose of saving the life of the mother." *Roe*, 410 U.S. at 118. Norma McCorvey, a single woman living in Texas, wanted to terminate her pregnancy by an abortion "performed by a competent, licensed physician, under safe, clinical conditions." *Id.* at 120. But McCorvey couldn't afford to travel to one of the four states in which such abortions were legal. Represented by two women who recently graduated from law school, McCorvey—calling herself "Jane Roe"—sued her local district attorney,

Henry Wade. She argued that Texas's prohibition "abridged her right of personal privacy,. protected by the First, Fourth, Fifth, Ninth, and Fourteenth Amendments." *Id.*

The *Roe* Court, in a 7–2 decision, affirmed McCorvey's right of privacy with regard to her choice whether to have an abortion.

■ MR. JUSTICE BLACKMUN delivered the opinion of the Court.[1]

This Texas federal appeal and its Georgia companion, *Doe v. Bolton,* present constitutional challenges to state criminal abortion legislation. . . .

We forthwith acknowledge our awareness of the sensitive and emotional nature of the abortion controversy, of the vigorous opposing views, even among physicians, and of the deep and seemingly absolute convictions that the subject inspires. One's philosophy, one's experiences, one's exposure to the raw edges of human existence, one's religious training, one's attitudes toward life and family and their values, and the moral standards one establishes and seeks to observe, are all likely to influence and to color one's thinking and conclusions about abortion. . . .

We bear in mind, too, Mr. Justice Holmes' admonition in his now-vindicated dissent in *Lochner v. New York*, 198 U. S. 45, 76 (1905): "[The Constitution] is made for people of fundamentally differing views, and the accident of our finding certain opinions natural and familiar or novel and even shocking ought not to conclude our judgment upon the question whether statutes embodying them conflict with the Constitution of the United States." . . .

V

The principal thrust of appellant's attack on the Texas statutes is that they improperly invade a right, said to be possessed by the pregnant woman, to choose to terminate her pregnancy. . . . Before addressing this claim, we feel it desirable briefly to survey, in several aspects, the history of abortion, for such insight as that history may afford us, and then to examine the state purposes and interests behind the criminal abortion laws.

VI

It perhaps is not generally appreciated that the restrictive criminal abortion laws in effect in a majority of States today are of relatively recent vintage. Those laws, generally proscribing abortion or its attempt at any time during pregnancy except when necessary to preserve the pregnant woman's life, are not of ancient or even of common-law origin. Instead, they derive from statutory changes effected, for the most part, in the latter half of the 19th century. . . .

VII

Three reasons have been advanced to explain historically the enactment of criminal abortion laws in the 19th century and to justify their continued existence.

It has been argued occasionally that these laws were the product of a Victorian social concern to discourage illicit sexual conduct. Texas, however, does not advance

---

1 **As You Read, Consider:** Justice Harry Blackmun could have analyzed Texas's abortion ban in a number of ways. He could have evaluated whether it discriminated on the basis of sex or wealth. He could have analyzed whether the Texas legislature appropriately balanced Norma McCorvey's interest in bodily integrity and self-fulfillment against the state's interest in promoting certain morals and child-rearing. He could have deferred to the democratic process.

What do you think of the path he took, i.e., asking whether McCorvey's alleged right was "fundamental" and whether Texas's law was "necessary" to serve a "compelling" interest? Does it affirm your intuition about the justice or injustice of abortion restrictions?

this justification in the present case, and it appears that no court or commentator has taken the argument seriously. . . .

A second reason is concerned with abortion as a medical procedure. When most criminal abortion laws were first enacted, the procedure was a hazardous one for the woman. . . . Modern medical techniques have altered this situation. . . . Mortality rates for women undergoing early abortions, where the procedure is legal, appear to be as low as or lower than the rates for normal childbirth. . . . Of course, important state interests in the areas of health and medical standards do remain. The State has a legitimate interest in seeing to it that abortion, like any other medical procedure, is performed under circumstances that insure maximum safety for the patient. . . . Moreover, the risk to the woman increases as her pregnancy continues. Thus, the State retains a definite interest in protecting the woman's own health and safety when an abortion is proposed at a late stage of pregnancy.[2]

The third reason is the State's interest—some phrase it in terms of duty—in protecting prenatal life. Some of the argument for this justification rests on the theory that a new human life is present from the moment of conception. The State's interest and general obligation to protect life then extends, it is argued, to prenatal life. Only when the life of the pregnant mother herself is at stake, balanced against the life she carries within her, should the interest of the embryo or fetus not prevail. Logically, of course, a legitimate state interest in this area need not stand or fall on acceptance of the belief that life begins at conception or at some other point prior to live birth. In assessing the State's interest, recognition may be given to the less rigid claim that as long as at least *potential* life is involved, the State may assert interests beyond the protection of the pregnant woman alone. . . .

It is with these interests, and the weight to be attached to them, that this case is concerned.

VIII

The Constitution does not explicitly mention any right of privacy. In a line of decisions, however, going back perhaps as far as *Union Pacific R. Co. v. Botsford*, 141 U. S. 250, 251 (1891), the Court has recognized that a right of personal privacy, or a guarantee of certain areas or zones of privacy, does exist under the Constitution. In varying contexts, the Court or individual Justices have, indeed, found at least the roots of that right in the First Amendment, *Stanley v. Georgia,* 394 U. S. 557, 564 (1969); in the Fourth and Fifth Amendments, *Katz v. United States,* 389 U. S. 347, 350 (1967); in the penumbras of the Bill of Rights, *Griswold v. Connecticut,* 381 U. S., at 484–485; in the Ninth Amendment, *id.,* at 486 (Goldberg, J., concurring); or in the concept of liberty guaranteed by the first section of the Fourteenth Amendment, see *Meyer v. Nebraska,* 262 U. S. 390, 399 (1923). These decisions make it clear that only personal rights that can be deemed "fundamental" or "implicit in the concept of ordered liberty," *Palko v. Connecticut,* 302 U. S. 319, 325 (1937), are included in this guarantee of personal privacy. They also make it clear that the right has some extension to activities relating to marriage, *Loving v. Virginia,* 388 U. S. 1, 12 (1967); procreation, *Skinner v. Oklahoma,* 316 U. S. 535, 541–542 (1942); contraception, *Eisenstadt v. Baird,* 405 U. S., at 453–454; family relationships, *Prince v.*

---

[2] **Question:** Before he became a justice, Blackmun served as in-house counsel for the Mayo Clinic. This opinion reflects his self-identity as a medical professional. While writing the opinion, he was struck by an observation in the *American Journal of Public Health* that the health risk of "legal abortion in the first trimester" was less than the risk of "carrying pregnancy to term." Geoffrey R. Stone, *Sex and the Constitution* 387 (2017). What role, if any, do you think such health risks should play in evaluating the constitutionality of Texas's law?

Massachusetts, 321 U. S. 158, 166 (1944); and child rearing and education, *Pierce v. Society of Sisters,* 268 U. S. 510, 535 (1925).

This right of privacy, whether it be founded in the Fourteenth Amendment's concept of personal liberty and restrictions upon state action, as we feel it is, or, as the District Court determined, in the Ninth Amendment's reservation of rights to the people, is broad enough to encompass a woman's decision whether or not to terminate her pregnancy.[3] The detriment that the State would impose upon the pregnant woman by denying this choice altogether is apparent. Specific and direct harm medically diagnosable even in early pregnancy may be involved. Maternity, or additional offspring, may force upon the woman a distressful life and future. Psychological harm may be imminent. Mental and physical health may be taxed by child care. There is also the distress, for all concerned, associated with the unwanted child, and there is the problem of bringing a child into a family already unable, psychologically and otherwise, to care for it. In other cases, as in this one, the additional difficulties and continuing stigma of unwed motherhood may be involved. All these are factors the woman and her responsible physician necessarily will consider in consultation.

On the basis of elements such as these, appellant and some *amici* argue that the woman's right is absolute and that she is entitled to terminate her pregnancy at whatever time, in whatever way, and for whatever reason she alone chooses. With this we do not agree. . . . As noted above, a State may properly assert important interests in safeguarding health, in maintaining medical standards, and in protecting potential life. At some point in pregnancy, these respective interests become sufficiently compelling to sustain regulation of the factors that govern the abortion decision. The privacy right involved, therefore, cannot be said to be absolute. In fact, it is not clear to us that the claim asserted by some *amici* that one has an unlimited right to do with one's body as one pleases bears a close relationship to the right of privacy previously articulated in the Court's decisions. The Court has refused to recognize an unlimited right of this kind in the past. *Jacobson v. Massachusetts,* 197 U. S. 11 (1905) (vaccination); *Buck v. Bell,* 274 U. S. 200 (1927) (sterilization).

We, therefore, conclude that the right of personal privacy includes the abortion decision, but that this right is not unqualified and must be considered against important state interests in regulation. . . . Where certain "fundamental rights" are involved, the Court has held that regulation limiting these rights may be justified only by a "compelling state interest," *Kramer v. Union Free School District,* 395 U. S. 621, 627 (1969), and that legislative enactments must be narrowly drawn to express only

---

[3] **Questions:** Note how Blackmun characterizes the right at issue in this case: "a woman's decision whether or not to terminate her pregnancy." He does not characterize it as a right to *obtain* or *have access to* an abortion. He does not even characterize it as a right that a woman possesses alone. Instead, throughout the opinion, he emphasizes that the "privacy" at issue here is the private relationship between "the woman and her responsible physician."

Texas's criminalization of virtually all abortions obviously interferes with Blackmun's description of the right. Accordingly, after calling the right *fundamental*, Blackmun spends the rest of his opinion evaluating under what circumstances a complete ban can satisfy strict scrutiny.

But what is the benefit of such a right to the millions of women who lack access to a physician or who have difficulty paying for either an abortion or childcare? Does a state infringe on Blackmun's description of the right when it encourages pregnant women to give birth? What about when a state refuses to subsidize abortions, contraception, or childcare? What about when it forces the closure of abortion providers so that some but not all women are prohibitively far from a "responsible physician"? As these hypothetical questions suggest, Blackmun's description of the right would soon have major consequences.

the legitimate state interests at stake. *Griswold v. Connecticut*, 381 U. S., at 485. . . .[4]

IX

[A.] The appellee and certain *amici* argue that the fetus is a "person" within the language and meaning of the Fourteenth Amendment. In support of this, they outline at length and in detail the well-known facts of fetal development. If this suggestion of personhood is established, the appellant's case, of course, collapses, for the fetus' right to life would then be guaranteed specifically by the Amendment. . . .

The Constitution does not define "person" in so many words. Section 1 of the Fourteenth Amendment contains three references to "person." The first, in defining "citizens," speaks of "persons born or naturalized in the United States." The word also appears both in the Due Process Clause and in the Equal Protection Clause. "Person" is used in other places in the Constitution. . . . But in nearly all these instances, the use of the word is such that it has application only postnatally. None indicates, with any assurance, that it has any possible pre-natal application.

All this, together with our observation that throughout the major portion of the 19th century prevailing legal abortion practices were far freer than they are today, persuades us that the word "person," as used in the Fourteenth Amendment, does not include the unborn. . . .

[B.] Texas urges that, apart from the Fourteenth Amendment, life begins at conception and is present throughout pregnancy, and that, therefore, the State has a compelling interest in protecting that life from and after conception. We need not resolve the difficult question of when life begins. When those trained in the respective disciplines of medicine, philosophy, and theology are unable to arrive at any consensus, the judiciary, at this point in the development of man's knowledge, is not in a position to speculate as to the answer. . . .

There has always been strong support for the view that life does not begin until live birth. . . . As we have noted, the common law found greater significance in quickening. Physicians and their scientific colleagues have regarded that event with less interest and have tended to focus either upon conception, upon live birth, or upon the interim point at which the fetus becomes "viable," that is, potentially able to live outside the mother's womb, albeit with artificial aid. Viability is usually placed at about seven months (28 weeks) but may occur earlier, even at 24 weeks. . . . In short, the unborn have never been recognized in the law as persons in the whole sense.

X

In view of all this, we do not agree that, by adopting one theory of life, Texas may override the rights of the pregnant woman that are at stake. We repeat, however, that the State does have an important and legitimate interest in preserving and protecting the health of the pregnant woman . . . and that it has still *another* important and legitimate interest in protecting the potentiality of human life. These interests are

---

[4] **Questions:** *Roe v. Wade* is a classic example of how the modern Supreme Court typically applies strict scrutiny. After finding that a "fundamental" right is at stake, the Court next determines whether a state has any "sufficiently compelling" interests that would justify its infringement on that right. The Court finally determines whether the state law is the least-restrictive means of achieving those compelling interests.

Why, precisely, does Blackmun disagree that Texas has a compelling interest in protecting "the fetus' right to life"? Which of Texas's several stated interests *does* Blackmun think is compelling enough to infringe upon "a woman's decision whether or not to terminate her pregnancy"?

separate and distinct. Each grows in substantiality as the woman approaches term and, at a point during pregnancy, each becomes "compelling."[5]

With respect to the State's important and legitimate interest in the health of the mother, the "compelling" point, in the light of present medical knowledge, is at approximately the end of the first trimester. This is so because of the now-established medical fact . . . that until the end of the first trimester mortality in abortion may be less than mortality in normal childbirth. It follows that, from and after this point, a State may regulate the abortion procedure to the extent that the regulation reasonably relates to the preservation and protection of maternal health. . . .

This means, on the other hand, that, for the period of pregnancy prior to this "compelling" point, the attending physician, in consultation with his patient, is free to determine, without regulation by the State, that, in his medical judgment, the patient's pregnancy should be terminated. If that decision is reached, the judgment may be effectuated by an abortion free of interference by the State.

With respect to the State's important and legitimate interest in potential life, the "compelling" point is at viability. This is so because the fetus then presumably has the capability of meaningful life outside the mother's womb. State regulation protective of fetal life after viability thus has both logical and biological justifications. If the State is interested in protecting fetal life after viability, it may go so far as to proscribe abortion during that period, except when it is necessary to preserve the life or health of the mother.

Measured against these standards, Art. 1196 of the Texas Penal Code, in restricting legal abortions to those "procured or attempted by medical advice for the purpose of saving the life of the mother," sweeps too broadly. The statute makes no distinction between abortions performed early in pregnancy and those performed later, and it limits to a single reason, "saving" the mother's life, the legal justification for the procedure. The statute, therefore, cannot survive the constitutional attack made upon it here. . . .

■ MR. JUSTICE REHNQUIST, dissenting. . . .[6]

[I] have difficulty in concluding, as the Court does, that the right of "privacy" is involved in this case. Texas, by the statute here challenged, bars the performance of a medical abortion by a licensed physician on a plaintiff such as Roe. A transaction resulting in an operation such as this is not "private" in the ordinary usage of that word. . . .

While the Court's opinion quotes from the dissent of Mr. Justice Holmes in *Lochner v. New York*, 198 U. S. 45, 74 (1905), the result it reaches is more closely attuned to the majority opinion of Mr. Justice Peckham in that case. As in *Lochner* and similar cases applying substantive due process standards to economic and social welfare legislation, the adoption of the compelling state interest standard will inevitably require this Court to examine the legislative policies and pass on the

---

5 **Questions:** Recall Blackmun's earlier observation that childbirth is more dangerous to a woman's mortality than a first-trimester abortion. Why should that "now-established medical fact" have anything to do with whether a state can "regulate the abortion procedure"? If a state determines that women's mental health is always better served by childbirth than by an abortion, does this opinion allow the state to restrict abortion access after the first trimester?

Similarly, how does Blackmun determine that a state's interest in sustaining the life of a "viable" fetus *categorically* outweighs a woman's interest in terminating her pregnancy? Does this opinion require a state to subsidize obstetric services, childcare, or adoption services if it forces a woman to carry a viable pregnancy to term?

6 **Question:** Justice William Rehnquist offers two points of disagreement with the majority opinion. Are either of his objections compatible with the Court's due process holding in *Loving v. Virginia*—decided before he joined the Court?

wisdom of these policies in the very process of deciding whether a particular state interest put forward may or may not be "compelling." The decision here to break pregnancy into three distinct terms and to outline the permissible restrictions the State may impose in each one, for example, partakes more of judicial legislation than it does of a determination of the intent of the drafters of the Fourteenth Amendment.

The fact that a majority of the States reflecting, after all, the majority sentiment in those States, have had restrictions on abortions for at least a century is a strong indication, it seems to me, that the asserted right to an abortion is not "so rooted in the traditions and conscience of our people as to be ranked as fundamental," *Snyder v. Massachusetts*, 291 U. S. 97, 105 (1934). . . .

To reach its result, the Court necessarily has had to find within the scope of the Fourteenth Amendment a right that was apparently completely unknown to the drafters of the Amendment. . . . By the time of the adoption of the Fourteenth Amendment in 1868, there were at least 36 laws enacted by state or territorial legislatures limiting abortion. . . . Indeed, the Texas statute struck down today was, as the majority notes, first enacted in 1857, and has remained substantially unchanged to the present time. There apparently was no question concerning the validity of this provision or of any of the other state statutes when the Fourteenth Amendment was adopted. The only conclusion possible from this history is that the drafters did not intend to have the Fourteenth Amendment withdraw from the States the power to legislate with respect to this matter. . . .

■ MR. JUSTICE WHITE, with whom MR. JUSTICE REHNQUIST joins, dissenting. . . .[7]

[W]ith all due respect, I dissent. I find nothing in the language or history of the Constitution to support the Court's judgment. The Court simply fashions and announces a new constitutional right for pregnant mothers and, with scarcely any reason or authority for its action, invests that right with sufficient substance to override most existing state abortion statutes. . . . As an exercise of raw judicial power, the Court perhaps has authority to do what it does today; but in my view its judgment is an improvident and extravagant exercise of the power of judicial review that the Constitution extends to this Court.

The Court apparently values the convenience of the pregnant mother more than the continued existence and development of the life or potential life that she carries. Whether or not I might agree with that marshaling of values, I can in no event join the Court's judgment because I find no constitutional warrant for imposing such an order of priorities on the people and legislatures of the States. In a sensitive area such as this, involving as it does issues over which reasonable men may easily and heatedly differ, I cannot accept the Court's exercise of its clear power of choice by interposing a constitutional barrier to state efforts to protect human life and by investing mothers and doctors with the constitutionally protected right to exterminate it. This issue, for the most part, should be left with the people and to the political processes the people have devised to govern their affairs.

NOTE: *DOE V. BOLTON*

Roe was one of two companion cases. The second case, *Doe v. Bolton*, 410 U.S. 179 (1973), considered a Georgia law similar to many promoted by the American Law Institute. It prohibited abortion unless continued pregnancy would endanger a pregnant woman's life and the procedure (1) was

[7] **Question:** Justice Byron White concurred in *Griswold v. Connecticut*, in which the Supreme Court invalidated Connecticut's contraception prohibition. Based on his objection here, what do you think distinguishes this decision from that one?

performed in an accredited hospital, (2) had the approval of a "hospital staff abortion committee," and (3) was confirmed in its necessity by independent examinations by two licensed physicians. *Doe*, 410 U.S. at 192.

When *Roe* struck down Texas's more restrictive law, Justice Blackmun preserved Texas's power (1) to regulate abortion after the first trimester with any law that "reasonably relates to the preservation and protection of maternal health" and (2) to proscribe abortion after the fetal "viability" date "except when it is necessary to preserve the life or health of the mother." *Roe*, 410 U.S. at 164–65. In *Doe*, the Court elaborated that the definition of *maternal health* depended upon the "medical judgment" of a pregnant person's physician: "the medical judgment may be exercised in the light of all factors—physical, emotional, psychological, familial, and the woman's age—relevant to the wellbeing of the patient." *Doe*, 410 U.S. at 192. Applying this definition to Georgia's restrictions, the Court concluded that each was "unduly restrictive of the patient's rights and needs" as determined by her personal physician. *Id.* at 198.

With such a broad definition of *health*, *Roe* and *Doe* effectively legalized abortion nationwide for the first two trimesters.

43.2 THE UNDUE BURDEN TEST

When *Roe v. Wade*, 410 U.S. 113 (1973), and *Doe v. Bolton*, 410 U.S. 179 (1973), were decided in 1973, abortion was a major political issue but not a major partisan issue. Both cases were 7–2 decisions in which five of the six Republican-appointed justices were in the majority and one of the three Democratic-appointed justices was in the dissent. Justice Potter Stewart, an Eisenhower appointee who dissented in *Griswold v. Connecticut*, 381 U.S. 479 (1965), joined the majority. Justice Byron White, a Kennedy appointee who concurred in *Griswold*, dissented.

At the same time, abortion was already contributing to party polarization. After a close primary battle with antichoice candidate Ronald Reagan in 1976, President Gerald Ford announced support for a constitutional amendment to prohibit abortion. Democratic candidate Jimmy Carter responded by supporting funding restrictions and family planning initiatives but not a constitutional amendment. Moderate positions began to be synonymous with losing positions, as centrist Republicans lost seats to conservative counterparts and southern Democrats left the Democratic Party. *See* Mary Ziegler, *Abortion and the Law in America* 42 (2020).

Yet activists on the left and the right responded to *Roe* very differently. The response from the right eventually culminated in a case that led to the undue burden test.

Response to Roe *from the left*

On the left, *Roe* was one of several examples illustrating that the women's liberation movement had become mainstream. Under pressure from activists such as Pauli Murray and organizations such as the

National Organization for Women, Congress had already passed the Civil Rights Act of 1964, the Equal Rights Amendment, and the Education Amendments Act of 1972, Title IX of which prohibited sex discrimination in federally funded education programs. *See* Rosalind Rosenberg, *Jane Crow: The Life of Pauli Murray* 277–81, 335–40 (2017). After *Roe*, the National Association for the Repeal of Abortion Laws changed its name to the National Abortion Rights Action League (NARAL) and celebrated *Roe*'s protection of women's autonomy. The ACLU's Sexual Privacy Project, the National Gay and Lesbian Task Force, and members of the gay liberation movement also framed *Roe* as a decision about adults' sexual liberty, invoking it as an argument that no government had the authority to restrict what a person did with his or her own body. Mary Ziegler, *After Roe* 233–34 (2015).

At the same time, the coalition on the left that promoted abortion rights in the 1960s fractured and evolved in the wake of *Roe*. The first paragraphs of *Roe* itself acknowledged the social, racial, and economic controversies that made abortion a complex issue. Scandals about the forced sterilization of women of color undermined the once-powerful population-control movement, which supported abortion rights as a mechanism to slow demographic change domestically and overseas. *Id.* at 15; *see* Dorothy Roberts, *Killing the Black Body* 90–103 (2017 ed.) (1997). Feminists of color, such as Angela Davis, also sharply criticized the historical ties between the birth control movement, eugenics, and concerns about welfare costs and illegitimacy rates. Ziegler, *After Roe*, *supra*, at 16–17; *see* Angela Davis, *Women, Race, and Class* 202–15 (1981). A decade after *Roe*, the Democratic Party and the mainstream women's liberation movement tended to emphasize equal rights and antidiscrimination over reproductive rights. Ziegler, *After Roe*, *supra*, at 18–19.

Response to Roe *from the right*

Meanwhile, in the wake of *Roe* and the Watergate scandal, conservative activists seeking to reshape the Republican Party used abortion as a rallying cry to build a movement around social and political conservatism. Paul Weyrich, one of the cofounders of the Heritage Foundation, described *Roe* as one of several modern threats to the survival of the American family—along with women in the workplace and the decline of religion in public life. Ziegler, *After Roe*, *supra*, at 13–14. Phyllis Schlafly and other prominent conservatives tied opposition to abortion with opposition to the proposed Equal Rights Amendment (ERA), a tactic that helped block the ERA's ratification. *See* Marjorie J. Spruill, *Divided We Stand: The Battle over Women's Rights and Family Values That Polarized American Politics* (2017). New Right leaders also deliberately recruited clergymen such as Reverend Jerry Falwell to found new organizations like Moral Majority to help attract evangelical Protestant voters to conservative politics. *Id.* at 298–99.

While lobbying for a constitutional amendment to criminalize abortion in the long term, conservative organizations found short-term success in state legislatures by highlighting the perceived cost of abortions and underscoring the benefits of limiting access to the procedure. This framing contrasted with the rights-based justifications that the pro-choice movement embraced following *Roe*. *See* Ziegler, *Abortion and the Law in America*, *supra*, at 12, 22. It also marked a shift in strategy for conservative groups, which in the years before *Roe* had adopted secular rights-based arguments grounded in the Fourteenth Amendment to appeal to those unmoved by faith-based arguments. *Id.* at 17. The wave of state laws passed at the behest of conservative groups raised issues of access beyond *Roe*'s finding that a woman's right to privacy encompassed a decision to terminate her pregnancy.

Supreme Court's response to state laws targeting Roe

As these new state laws reached the Supreme Court, the Court amended its approach to *Roe*, developing a new rubric for abortion restrictions quite different from its approach to other "fundamental" rights. In the first case to reach the Court, *Planned Parenthood of Central Missouri v. Danforth*, the Court heard and addressed what it considered the "logical and anticipated corollary to *Roe*": a series of provisions adopted by the Missouri legislature in 1974 to regulate abortions during all stages of pregnancy. 428 U.S. 52, 56 (1976).

The first two provisions, a "spousal consent" requirement and a "parental consent" requirement, prohibited a pregnant person from seeking an abortion without the consent of their spouse or parent. *Id.* at 58–59. The Court considered the spousal-consent provision an unconstitutional attempt "to delegate to the husband a power it itself could not exercise": a "veto power exercisable for any reason whatsoever or for no reason at all." *Id.* at 71. The Court struck down the parental-consent provision for the same reason, noting that "[c]onstitutional rights do not mature and come into being magically only when one attains the state-defined age of majority." *Id.* at 74.

A third provision, a "standard of care" requirement, made it a crime for a physician to perform an abortion without exercising care to "preserve the life and health of any fetus." *Id.* at 58–59. The Court found this provision inconsistent with *Roe* because it made it a crime for a physician to abort a fetus before viability. *Id.* at 82.

A fourth provision, a "saline amniocentesis" prohibition, banned a method employed by 70 percent of abortions effected after the first trimester. The legislature found that the saline method was "deleterious to maternal health." *Id.* at 59. The Court struck down this prohibition after considering the trial court's evidence that saline was not only safer than any available alternative method of abortion but also safer than childbirth. In this light, the Court considered the ban less of "a reasonable regulation for the protection of maternal health" and more of "an unreasonable or arbitrary regulation designed to inhibit . . . the vast majority of abortions after the first 12 weeks." *Id.* at 79.

Finally, the Court upheld a fifth provision that required any pregnant person seeking an abortion during the first trimester to certify in writing "that her consent is informed and freely given." *Id.* at 58–59. "Despite the fact that apparently no other Missouri statute . . . requires a patient's prior written consent to a surgical procedure," and even though this requirement could deter pregnant people from obtaining an abortion, the Court considered it "desirable and imperative that [the decision to abort] be made with full knowledge of its nature and consequences." *Id.* at 66–67.

For similar reasons, the Court upheld a sixth provision that imposed record-keeping requirements on health facilities that performed abortions, considering this provision "reasonably directed to the preservation of maternal health." *Id.* at 80. But the Court warned that it was assuming that the "burden" of these requirements wouldn't rise to the level of an unconstitutional restriction. *Id.* at 81.

Evolution of the undue burden test and reaction against it

Danforth gave rise to what the Court later called the *undue burden test*: the Court would uphold facially neutral regulations of abortion access unless they restricted "the *decision* of the patient and her physician regarding abortion." *Id.* at 66 (emphasis added). This test was sharply criticized by *Roe*'s critics from the left, who warned that the Court was focusing too much on the individual autonomy of a pregnant person and too little on the ways in which the "decision" was available only to people who could afford it.

For example, the lead attorney of the American Civil Liberties Union (ACLU) Women's Rights Project, Ruth Bader Ginsburg, criticized *Roe* for its "concentration on a medically approved autonomy idea, to the exclusion of a constitutionally based sex-equality perspective." Ruth Bader Ginsburg, *Some Thoughts on Autonomy and Equality in Relation to* Roe v. Wade, 63 N.C. L. Rev. 375, 386 (1985). Ginsburg added that in light of the quickly moving political process in the early 1970s, *Roe*'s "[h]eavy-handed judicial intervention was difficult to justify and appears to have provoked, not resolved, conflict." *Id.* at 385–86.

Feminists of color offered a parallel criticism later captured by the term *reproductive justice*, a framework that included "not only the human right not to have a child, but also the right to have children and to raise them with dignity in safe, healthy, and supportive environments." Roberts, *supra*, at xix–xxi. On the theory that reproductive freedom meant not only freedom from government oversight but also freedom to meaningfully choose among alternatives, reproductive-justice activists responded to the conservative backlash against *Roe* by campaigning for governments to provide poor women with the resources that they needed to access contraception, childcare, work, housing, and essential medical services, including abortions. Ziegler, *After Roe*, *supra*, at 231, 236–39. Against the backdrop of growing and racialized criticism of the welfare state, reproductive-justice activists emphasized the overlap among human rights, reproductive rights, and the provision of adequate resources. *See* Ziegler, *Abortion and the Law in America*, *supra*, at 28–29, 130.

But the Supreme Court was not receptive to arguments grounded in the idea that the government had an affirmative obligation to provide women with reproductive health services. In *Maher v. Roe*, the Court rejected an argument that Connecticut violated the Fourteenth Amendment when it prohibited the use of Medicaid benefits for abortions unless "medically necessary." 432 U.S. 464, 474 (1977). The Court explained that "*Roe* did not declare an unqualified 'constitutional right to an abortion.' " *Id.* at 473. "Rather, the right protects the woman from unduly burdensome interference with her freedom to decide whether to terminate her pregnancy." *Id.* at 473–74. The Court didn't think that this right was implicated by a law that "places no obstacles—absolute or otherwise—in the pregnant woman's path to an abortion." *Id.* at 474. The only obstacle in the Court's view was poverty—which was "neither created nor in any way affected by the Connecticut regulation." *Id.*; *see also Poelker v. Doe*, 432 U.S. 519, 521 (1977) (upholding the constitutionality of a city policy that barred nontherapeutic abortions in public hospitals but funded childbirth services).

43.2.1

Harris v. McRae

448 U.S. 297 (1980)

In 1977, Representative Henry J. Hyde of Illinois sponsored an amendment to a congressional appropriations bill that prohibited the use of federal funds to pay for abortions. Before 1976, federally funded Medicaid programs paid for approximately 300,000 abortions annually. The Hyde Amendment prohibited the federal government from reimbursing states for the cost of any abortion-related services except "where the life of the mother would be endangered if the fetus were carried to term." *See* Maris A. Vinovskis, *The Politics of Abortion in the House of Representatives in 1976*, 77 Mich. L. Rev. 1790, 1795, 1798 (1979). This meant that while the federal government would continue providing pregnant people with access to childbirth services, it would not provide them with access to abortion services.

Cora McRae, a pregnant woman in New York, challenged the constitutionality of the Hyde Amendment. She argued that the amendment violated her freedom of being able to choose whether to have an abortion as she could not afford private services. In this respect, McRae's argument was similar to that of the defendant in *Gideon v. Wainwright*, 372 U.S. 335 (1963), who successfully argued that the right to counsel included not only the right to choose a lawyer but also the right to have a lawyer provided by the government.

But in *Harris v. McRae*, 448 U.S. 297 (1980), the Court responded that the right articulated in *Roe* was a right of individual autonomy, not one of equal access to services.

■ MR. JUSTICE STEWART delivered the opinion of the Court.[8]

This case presents statutory and constitutional questions concerning the public funding of abortions under . . . recent annual Appropriations Acts containing the so-called "Hyde Amendment." . . . The constitutional question . . . is whether the Hyde Amendment, by denying public funding for certain medically necessary abortions, . . . impinges on the "liberty" protected by the Due Process Clause as recognized in *Roe v. Wade,* 410 U. S. 113, and its progeny.

In the *Wade* case, this Court held unconstitutional a Texas statute making it a crime to procure or attempt an abortion except on medical advice for the purpose of saving the mother's life. The constitutional underpinning of *Wade* was a recognition that the "liberty" protected by the Due Process Clause of the Fourteenth Amendment includes not only the freedoms explicitly mentioned in the Bill of Rights, but also a freedom of personal choice in certain matters of marriage and family life. This implicit constitutional liberty, the Court in *Wade* held, includes the freedom of a woman to decide whether to terminate a pregnancy. . . . But the Court in *Wade* also recognized that a State has legitimate interests during a pregnancy in both ensuring the health of the mother and protecting potential human life. . . .

The doctrine of *Roe v. Wade* . . . protects the woman from unduly burdensome interference with her freedom to decide whether to terminate her pregnancy, such as the severe criminal sanctions at issue in *Roe v. Wade, supra,* or the absolute requirement of spousal consent for an abortion challenged in *Planned Parenthood of Central Missouri v. Danforth,* 428 U. S. 52.

But [as we explained in *Maher v. Roe,* 432 U. S. 464,] the constitutional freedom recognized in *Wade* and its progeny. . . [does not prevent a State] from making "a value judgment favoring childbirth over abortion, and . . . implement[ing] that judgment by the allocation of public funds." [*Id.* at 474.] . . . An indigent woman who desires an abortion suffers no disadvantage as a consequence of [a State's] decision to fund childbirth; she continues as before to be dependent on private sources for the service she desires. The State may have made childbirth a more attractive alternative, thereby influencing the woman's decision, but it has imposed no restriction on access to abortions that was not already there. The indigency that may make it difficult—and in some cases, perhaps, impossible—for some women to have abortions is neither created nor in any way affected by [such a] regulation. . . .

The Hyde Amendment, like the Connecticut welfare regulation at issue in *Maher,* places no governmental obstacle in the path of a woman who chooses to terminate her pregnancy, but rather, by means of unequal subsidization of abortion and other medical services, encourages alternative activity deemed in the public interest. . . .

[A] woman's freedom of choice [does not carry] with it a constitutional entitlement to the financial resources to avail herself of the full range of protected choices. . . . [A]lthough government may not place obstacles in the path of a woman's exercise of her freedom of choice, it need not remove those not of its own creation. Indigency falls in the latter category. The financial constraints that restrict

[8] **As You Read, Consider:** How does Justice Potter Stewart characterize the right protected by *Roe v. Wade*? Does it matter to him whether everyone equally possesses this "fundamental" right?

an indigent woman's ability to enjoy the full range of constitutionally protected freedom of choice are the product not of governmental restrictions on access to abortions, but rather of her indigency. Although Congress has opted to subsidize medically necessary services generally, but not certain medically necessary abortions, the fact remains that the Hyde Amendment leaves an indigent woman with at least the same range of choice in deciding whether to obtain a medically necessary abortion as she would have had if Congress had chosen to subsidize no health care costs at all. We are thus not persuaded that the Hyde Amendment impinges on the constitutionally protected freedom of choice recognized in *Wade*.[9]

Although the liberty protected by the Due Process Clause affords protection against unwarranted government interference with freedom of choice in the context of certain personal decisions, it does not confer an entitlement to such funds as may be necessary to realize all the advantages of that freedom. To hold otherwise would mark a drastic change in our understanding of the Constitution. It cannot be that because government may not prohibit the use of contraceptives, *Griswold v. Connecticut*, 381 U. S. 479, or prevent parents from sending their child to a private school, *Pierce v. Society of Sisters*, 268 U. S. 510, government, therefore, has an affirmative constitutional obligation to ensure that all persons have the financial resources to obtain contraceptives or send their children to private schools. To translate the limitation on governmental power implicit in the Due Process Clause into an affirmative funding obligation would require Congress to subsidize the medically necessary abortion of an indigent woman even if Congress had not enacted a Medicaid program to subsidize other medically necessary services. Nothing in the Due Process Clause supports such an extraordinary result. Whether freedom of choice that is constitutionally protected warrants federal subsidization is a question for Congress to answer, not a matter of constitutional entitlement. . . .

NOTE: RESTRICTIONS ON ABORTION FUNDING

The *Harris* Court's rejection of Cora McRae's claim illustrated how the Supreme Court responded to criticisms of *Roe* from the left: the Court would not interpret the liberty to decide whether to have a child as if it imposed a corresponding duty on the government to provide equal access to reproductive health services or to respect the dignity and situation of poor women. Even if a government's decision to no longer fund abortions burdened poor women, the Court would not consider this an "undue burden" as long as the women still retained the right to choose in the abstract. The Court's decision in *Harris* validated arguments from an emerging coalition of antichoice attorneys that framed lack of abortion access as the product of the imprudent behavior of women, not the outcome of restrictive laws and regulations. *See* Ziegler, *Abortion and the Law in America*, *supra*, at 29.

The Court reaffirmed *Harris* in *Webster v. Reproductive Health Services*, 492 U.S. 490 (1989), and *Rust v. Sullivan*, 500 U.S. 173 (1991). In *Webster*, the Court invoked *Harris* to uphold a Missouri statute that prohibited the

[9] **Question:** In General Welfare Clause cases like *United States v. Butler* and *National Federation of Independent* Business (*NFIB*) *v. Sebelius*, the Supreme Court held that Congress lacked the power to "coerce" people into accepting grant conditions. In *Butler*, for instance, the Court called conditional payments for impoverished farmers "coercion by economic pressure" in which "[t]he asserted power of choice is illusory." 297 U.S. 1, 71 (1936). In this case, Congress once provided Medicaid funding for abortions, but it now requires recipients to use the funds only for childbirth services. Why doesn't Stewart cite *Butler*, much less treat the situation as similar?

use of state facilities, funds, or employees to perform abortions unless necessary to save the life of the pregnant woman. 492 U.S. at 508. The Court explained that "Missouri's refusal to allow public employees to perform abortions in public hospitals leaves a pregnant woman with the same choices as if the State had chosen not to operate any public hospitals at all." *Id.* at 509. And in *Rust*, the Court upheld the Family Planning Services and Population Research Act of 1970, Pub. L. No. 91–572, 84 Stat. 1504, commonly known as "Title X." Title X had been interpreted to prohibit employees of any family-planning facility from even counseling a patient on abortion if the facility received federal funds. Rejecting a challenge to this law under the General Welfare Clause, the Court held that Congress had not denied anyone "the right to engage in abortion-related activities. Congress ha[d] merely refused to fund such activities out of the public fisc, and . . . required a certain degree of separation from the project in order to ensure the integrity of the federally funded program." *Rust*, 500 U.S. at 198.

43.2.2

Planned Parenthood of Southeastern Pennsylvania v. Casey

505 U.S. 833 (1992)

By 1992, the campaign to overrule *Roe* appeared to have reached its climax. President Ronald Reagan campaigned for president in 1980 and 1984 on a platform of overturning *Roe*. The three justices he appointed—Sandra Day O'Connor, Antonin Scalia, and Anthony Kennedy—each replaced a justice who had been in the *Roe* majority. President George H. W. Bush followed by appointing two more justices—David Souter and Clarence Thomas—who replaced the two most liberal members of the Court. The year that the following case, *Planned Parenthood of Southeastern Pennsylvania v. Casey*, 505 U.S. 833 (1992), was argued before the Supreme Court, a half-million people marched on the nation's capital to demand that *Roe* be overturned. Geoffrey R. Stone, *Sex and the Constitution* 415–16 (2017). There was a widespread expectation that the Court would comply with the Bush administration's request to overrule *Roe*. *Id.* at 416.

Casey involved a series of laws promoted by Pennsylvania's governor, Bob Casey Sr., who was one of the leading opponents of abortion within the Democratic Party. Building on the success of Missouri's abortion regulations in the 1970s and 1980s, the Pennsylvania legislature amended its abortion law to impose three requirements. The first required that a pregnant person seeking an abortion give their "informed consent" by receiving information about alternatives to abortion and waiting twenty-four hours before obtaining an abortion. *Casey*, 505 U.S. at 844. The second required that a minor seeking an abortion first obtain the consent of one of their parents or a juvenile court. *Id.* The third required any married woman seeking an abortion to first notify her spouse. *Id.* All three requirements could be waived in a "medical emergency." *Id.*

The transparent purpose of all three requirements was to dissuade women from obtaining abortions. Nevertheless, when Planned Parenthood of Southeastern Pennsylvania sued Governor Casey, Judge Samuel Alito of the U.S. Court of Appeals for the Third Circuit concluded that all of the provisions were constitutional. 947 F.2d 682, 726–27 (1991) (Alito, J., concurring in part and dissenting in part).

Initially, Kennedy and four other justices agreed. But after reading Chief Justice William Rehnquist's draft majority opinion, Kennedy revised his position and joined an unusual opinion coauthored by three of the justices appointed by Reagan and Bush. *See* Stone, *supra*, at 416. The new plurality opinion in *Casey* reevaluated *Roe* and articulated a new, "undue burden" test.

■ JUSTICE O'CONNOR, JUSTICE KENNEDY, and JUSTICE SOUTER announced the judgment of the Court and delivered the opinion of the Court with respect to Parts I, II, III, V-A, V-C, and VI. . . .[10]

I

Liberty finds no refuge in a jurisprudence of doubt. Yet 19 years after our holding that the Constitution protects a woman's right to terminate her pregnancy in its early stages, *Roe v. Wade,* 410 U. S. 113 (1973), that definition of liberty is still questioned. . . .

After considering the fundamental constitutional questions resolved by *Roe,* principles of institutional integrity, and the rule of *stare decisis,* we are led to conclude this: the essential holding of *Roe v. Wade* should be retained and once again reaffirmed.

It must be stated at the outset and with clarity that *Roe*'s essential holding, the holding we reaffirm, has three parts. First is a recognition of the right of the woman to choose to have an abortion before viability and to obtain it without undue interference from the State. Before viability, the State's interests are not strong enough to support a prohibition of abortion or the imposition of a substantial obstacle to the woman's effective right to elect the procedure. Second is a confirmation of the State's power to restrict abortions after fetal viability, if the law contains exceptions for pregnancies which endanger the woman's life or health. And third is the principle that the State has legitimate interests from the outset of the pregnancy in protecting the health of the woman and the life of the fetus that may become a child. . . .

II

Constitutional protection of the woman's decision to terminate her pregnancy derives from the Due Process Clause of the Fourteenth Amendment. It declares that no State shall "deprive any person of life, liberty, or property, without due process of law." The controlling word in the cases before us is "liberty." Although a literal reading of the Clause might suggest that it governs only the procedures by which a State may deprive persons of liberty, for at least 105 years, since *Mugler v. Kansas,* 123 U. S.

---

[10] **As You Read, Consider:** The *Planned Parenthood of Southeastern Pennsylvania v. Casey* plurality purports to reaffirm *Roe*'s "essential holding." But the right it describes and the test it applies are remarkably different from *Roe v. Wade*. How, precisely, does the plurality's approach to abortion restrictions differ from *Roe*'s approach? Why doesn't the plurality simply overrule *Roe* and start over?

623 (1887), the Clause has been understood to contain a substantive component as well, one barring certain government actions regardless of the fairness of the procedures used to implement them. . . .

Neither the Bill of Rights nor the specific practices of States at the time of the adoption of the Fourteenth Amendment marks the outer limits of the substantive sphere of liberty which the Fourteenth Amendment protects. See U. S. Const., Amdt. 9. . . . Our law affords constitutional protection to personal decisions relating to marriage, procreation, contraception, family relationships, child rearing, and education. . . . At the heart of liberty is the right to define one's own concept of existence, of meaning, of the universe, and of the mystery of human life. Beliefs about these matters could not define the attributes of personhood were they formed under compulsion of the State. . . .

III

[W]hen this Court reexamines a prior holding, its judgment is customarily informed by a series of prudential and pragmatic considerations designed to test the consistency of overruling a prior decision with the ideal of the rule of law, and to gauge the respective costs of reaffirming and overruling a prior case. Thus, for example, we may ask [1] whether the rule has proven to be intolerable simply in defying practical workability; [2] whether the rule is subject to a kind of reliance that would lend a special hardship to the consequences of overruling and add inequity to the cost of repudiation; [3] whether related principles of law have so far developed as to have left the old rule no more than a remnant of abandoned doctrine; or [4] whether facts have so changed, or come to be seen so differently, as to have robbed the old rule of significant application or justification. . . .

[All four of these factors confirm that while *Roe* has] engendered disapproval, . . . the stronger argument is for affirming *Roe*'s central holding, with whatever degree of personal reluctance any of us have, not for overruling it. . . .

Our analysis would not be complete, however, without explaining why overruling *Roe*'s central holding . . . would seriously weaken the Court's capacity to exercise the judicial power and to function as the Supreme Court of a Nation dedicated to the rule of law. . . .[11]

The root of American governmental power is revealed most clearly in the instance of the power conferred by the Constitution upon the Judiciary of the United States and specifically upon this Court. As Americans of each succeeding generation are rightly told, the Court cannot buy support for its decisions by spending money and, except to a minor degree, it cannot independently coerce obedience to its decrees. The Court's power lies, rather, in its legitimacy, a product of substance and perception that shows itself in the people's acceptance of the Judiciary as fit to determine what the Nation's law means and to declare what it demands.

The underlying substance of this legitimacy is of course the warrant for the Court's decisions in the Constitution and the lesser sources of legal principle on which the Court draws. That substance is expressed in the Court's opinions, and our

---

[11] **Questions:** The paragraphs that follow contain some of the most self-aware language in Supreme Court history. The plurality bluntly acknowledges that the Court's power derives not from the text of the Constitution or even the correctness of its interpretations but rather from the "legitimacy" produced by "the people's acceptance of the Judiciary as fit to determine what the Nation's law means." The plurality then identifies two threats to this legitimacy posed by overruling *Roe*.

Do you agree with the plurality about the nature of the Court's legitimacy and how it might be threatened? What might be the consequences of the Court's loss of legitimacy? For one recent possibility, see Astead W. Herndon & Maggie Astor, *Ruth Bader Ginsburg's Death Revives Calls for Court Packing*, N.Y. Times, Sept. 19, 2020.

contemporary understanding is such that a decision without principled justification would be no judicial act at all. But even when justification is furnished by apposite legal principle, something more is required. Because not every conscientious claim of principled justification will be accepted as such, the justification claimed must be beyond dispute. The Court must take care to speak and act in ways that allow people to accept its decisions on the terms the Court claims for them, as grounded truly in principle, not as compromises with social and political pressures having, as such, no bearing on the principled choices that the Court is obliged to make. Thus, the Court's legitimacy depends on making legally principled decisions under circumstances in which their principled character is sufficiently plausible to be accepted by the Nation.

The need for principled action to be perceived as such is implicated to some degree whenever this, or any other appellate court, overrules a prior case. . . . In two circumstances, however, the Court would almost certainly fail to receive the benefit of the doubt in overruling prior cases. There is, first, a point beyond which frequent overruling would overtax the country's belief in the Court's good faith. . . . There is a limit to the amount of error that can plausibly be imputed to prior Courts. If that limit should be exceeded, disturbance of prior rulings would be taken as evidence that justifiable reexamination of principle had given way to drives for particular results in the short term. The legitimacy of the Court would fade with the frequency of its vacillation.

[Second, when] the Court decides a case in such a way as to resolve the sort of intensely divisive controversy reflected in *Roe* and those rare, comparable cases, . . . only the most convincing justification under accepted standards of precedent could suffice to demonstrate that a later decision overruling the first was anything but a surrender to political pressure, and an unjustified repudiation of the principle on which the Court staked its authority in the first instance. So to overrule under fire in the absence of the most compelling reason to reexamine a watershed decision would subvert the Court's legitimacy beyond any serious question. Cf. *Brown v. Board of Education,* 349 U.S. 294, 300 (1955) (*Brown II*) ("[I]t should go without saying that the vitality of th[e] constitutional principles [announced in *Brown I,*] cannot be allowed to yield simply because of disagreement with them").

IV

From what we have said so far it follows that it is a constitutional liberty of the woman to have some freedom to terminate her pregnancy. We conclude that the basic decision in *Roe* was based on a constitutional analysis which we cannot now repudiate. The woman's liberty is not so unlimited, however, that from the outset the State cannot show its concern for the life of the unborn, and at a later point in fetal development the State's interest in life has sufficient force so that the right of the woman to terminate the pregnancy can be restricted. . . .

The woman's right to terminate her pregnancy before viability is the most central principle of *Roe v. Wade*. It is a rule of law and a component of liberty we cannot renounce.[12]

On the other side of the equation is the interest of the State in the protection of potential life. The *Roe* Court recognized the State's "important and legitimate interest

[12] **Questions:** *Roe* described "a woman's decision whether or not to terminate her pregnancy . . . [in consultation with] her responsible physician" as a "fundamental" right. It held that such a right could be infringed only by a law that satisfied strict scrutiny. Applying strict scrutiny, it held that a state could not regulate abortion in the first trimester, and it could do so before "viability" only to protect a woman's health.

How does the *Casey* plurality describe the right at issue here? What test does the *Casey* plurality use to evaluate whether a law interferes with this right?

in protecting the potentiality of human life." *Roe, supra,* at 162. . . . That portion of the decision in *Roe* has been given too little acknowledgment and implementation by the Court in its subsequent cases. Those cases decided that any regulation touching upon the abortion decision must survive strict scrutiny, to be sustained only if drawn in narrow terms to further a compelling state interest. See, *e. g., Akron I, supra,* at 427. . . .

Roe established a trimester framework to govern abortion regulations. Under this elaborate but rigid construct, almost no regulation at all is permitted during the first trimester of pregnancy; regulations designed to protect the woman's health, but not to further the State's interest in potential life, are permitted during the second trimester; and during the third trimester, when the fetus is viable, prohibitions are permitted provided the life or health of the mother is not at stake. *Roe, supra,* at 163–166. . .

We reject the trimester framework, which we do not consider to be part of the essential holding of *Roe*. . . .

As our jurisprudence relating to all liberties save perhaps abortion has recognized, not every law which makes a right more difficult to exercise is, *ipso facto*, an infringement of that right. . . . Numerous forms of state regulation might have the incidental effect of increasing the cost or decreasing the availability of medical care, whether for abortion or any other medical procedure. The fact that a law which serves a valid purpose, one not designed to strike at the right itself, has the incidental effect of making it more difficult or more expensive to procure an abortion cannot be enough to invalidate it. Only where state regulation imposes an undue burden on a woman's ability to make this decision does the power of the State reach into the heart of the liberty protected by the Due Process Clause. . . .[13]

A finding of an undue burden is a shorthand for the conclusion that a state regulation has the purpose or effect of placing a substantial obstacle in the path of a woman seeking an abortion of a nonviable fetus. A statute with this purpose is invalid because the means chosen by the State to further the interest in potential life must be calculated to inform the woman's free choice, not hinder it. And a statute which, while furthering the interest in potential life or some other valid state interest, has the effect of placing a substantial obstacle in the path of a woman's choice cannot be considered a permissible means of serving its legitimate ends. . .

Some guiding principles should emerge. What is at stake is the woman's right to make the ultimate decision, not a right to be insulated from all others in doing so. Regulations which do no more than create a structural mechanism by which the State, or the parent or guardian of a minor, may express profound respect for the life of the

[13] **Questions:** Is the "undue burden" test described here a deferential means-ends test or a proportionality test? To illustrate the distinction, how does the plurality expect someone to evaluate whether a statute has the "purpose or effect" of placing a "substantial" obstacle in the path of a woman seeking an abortion?

Some of the plurality's language suggests that the evaluator should consider whether the statute is "reasonably related" to a "legitimate" state interest, such as promoting childbirth or protecting the woman's health. This sort of test sounds like a deferential means-ends test. But such a test would fail to account for the plurality's hypothetical statute that "further[s] . . . [a] valid state interest [but] has the effect of placing a substantial obstacle in the path of a woman's choice."

In this respect, the plurality's language instead suggests that the evaluator should determine whether the burdens imposed by an "obstacle in the path of a woman seeking an abortion" are so "substantial" that they outweigh whatever legitimate interests the statute allegedly serves. This sort of test sounds like a proportionality test. But if balancing is what the plurality intends, why does the plurality explicitly use means . . . ends language?

unborn are permitted, if they are not a substantial obstacle to the woman's exercise of the right to choose.

Unless it has that effect on her right of choice, a state measure designed to persuade her to choose childbirth over abortion will be upheld if reasonably related to that goal. Regulations designed to foster the health of a woman seeking an abortion are valid if they do not constitute an undue burden. . . .

These principles control our assessment of the Pennsylvania statute, and we now turn to the issue of the validity of its challenged provisions. . . .

V

[B. The Informed-Consent Requirement]

[E]xcept in a medical emergency, the statute requires that at least 24 hours before performing an abortion a physician inform the woman of the nature of the procedure, the health risks of the abortion and of childbirth[,] the "probable gestational age of the unborn child[,]" . . . information about child support from the father, and a list of agencies which provide adoption and other services as alternatives to abortion. . . . Petitioners challenge the statute's definition of informed consent because it includes the provision of specific information by the doctor and the mandatory 24-hour waiting period. . . .

The findings of fact by the District Court indicate that because of the distances many women must travel to reach an abortion provider, the practical effect will often be a delay of much more than a day because the waiting period requires that a woman seeking an abortion make at least two visits to the doctor. The District Court also found that in many instances this will increase the exposure of women seeking abortions to "the harassment and hostility of antiabortion protestors demonstrating outside a clinic." 744 F. Supp., at 1351. As a result, the District Court found that for those women who have the fewest financial resources, those who must travel long distances, and those who have difficulty explaining their whereabouts to husbands, employers, or others, the 24-hour waiting period will be "particularly burdensome." *Id.,* at 1352.

These findings are troubling in some respects, but they do not demonstrate that the waiting period constitutes an undue burden. We do not doubt that, as the District Court held, the waiting period has the effect of "increasing the cost and risk of delay of abortions." . . . Yet, as we have stated, under the undue burden standard a State is permitted to enact persuasive measures which favor childbirth over abortion, even if those measures do not further a health interest. . . .

We also disagree . . . that the "particularly burdensome" effects of the waiting period on some women require its invalidation. . . . Even the broadest reading of *Roe* . . . has not suggested that there is a constitutional right to abortion on demand. Rather, the right protected by *Roe* is a right to decide to terminate a pregnancy free of undue interference by the State. . . . [T]he informed consent requirement facilitates the wise exercise of that right. . . .[14]

[C. The Spousal-Consent Requirement]

Section 3209 of Pennsylvania's abortion law provides, except in cases of medical emergency, that no physician shall perform an abortion on a married woman without receiving a signed statement from the woman that she has notified her spouse

[14] **Questions:** The plurality here upholds the constitutionality of a twenty-four-hour waiting period that has "particularly burdensome" effects on poor women's abortion access but that also serves the state's legitimate interest in promoting childbirth. Does this holding offer evidence regarding whether the undue burden test is a proportionality test or a deferential means-ends test? Do any of the other holdings point one way or the other?

that she is about to undergo an abortion. The woman has the option of providing an alternative signed statement certifying . . . that the woman believes that notifying her husband will cause him or someone else to inflict bodily injury upon her. A physician who performs an abortion on a married woman without receiving the appropriate signed statement will have his or her license revoked, and is liable to the husband for damages. . . .

The District Court heard the testimony of numerous expert witnesses, and made detailed findings of fact regarding the effect of this statute. . . . In well-functioning marriages, spouses discuss important intimate decisions such as whether to bear a child. But there are millions of women in this country who are the victims of regular physical and psychological abuse at the hands of their husbands. Should these women become pregnant, they may have very good reasons for not wishing to inform their husbands of their decision to obtain an abortion. Many may have justifiable fears of physical abuse, but may be no less fearful of the consequences of reporting prior abuse to the Commonwealth of Pennsylvania. Many may have a reasonable fear that notifying their husbands will provoke further instances of child abuse; these women are not exempt from § 3209's notification requirement. Many may fear devastating forms of psychological abuse from their husbands, including verbal harassment, threats of future violence, the destruction of possessions, physical confinement to the home, the withdrawal of financial support, or the disclosure of the abortion to family and friends. These methods of psychological abuse may act as even more of a deterrent to notification than the possibility of physical violence, but women who are the victims of the abuse are not exempt from [the] notification requirement. . . .

The spousal notification requirement is thus likely to prevent a significant number of women from obtaining an abortion. It does not merely make abortions a little more difficult or expensive to obtain; for many women, it will impose a substantial obstacle. We must not blind ourselves to the fact that the significant number of women who fear for their safety and the safety of their children are likely to be deterred from procuring an abortion as surely as if the Commonwealth had outlawed abortion in all cases.

Respondents attempt to avoid the conclusion that § 3209 is invalid by pointing out that it imposes almost no burden at all for the vast majority of women seeking abortions. They begin by noting that only about 20 percent of the women who obtain abortions are married. They then note that of these women about 95 percent notify their husbands of their own volition. Thus, respondents argue, the effects of § 3209 are felt by only one percent of the women who obtain abortions. Respondents argue that since some of these women will be able to notify their husbands without adverse consequences or will qualify for one of the exceptions, the statute affects fewer than one percent of women seeking abortions. . . . We disagree with respondents' basic method of analysis.

The analysis does not end with the one percent of women upon whom the statute operates; it begins there. . . .[15] The proper focus of constitutional inquiry is

---

[15] **Question:** When the plurality evaluated the twenty-four-hour waiting period, it held that the waiting period was valid even with respect to poor women for whom it had "particularly burdensome" effects.

Here, the plurality notes that the spousal-consent provision will impose a "substantial obstacle" on approximately 1 percent of women seeking an abortion, but that is enough to invalidate it. The plurality reaches its conclusion because in the cases where the provision does impose a burden, that burden will likely be greater than making abortions "a little more difficult or expensive to obtain." Does this evaluation of the quality of the burden offer evidence of whether the undue burden test is a deferential means-ends test or a proportionality test?

the group for whom the law is a restriction, not the group for whom the law is irrelevant.

[Section] 3209's real target is narrower even than the class of women seeking abortions identified by the State: it is married women seeking abortions who do not wish to notify their husbands of their intentions and who do not qualify for one of the statutory exceptions to the notice requirement. The unfortunate yet persisting conditions we document above will mean that in a large fraction of the cases in which § 3209 is relevant, it will operate as a substantial obstacle to a woman's choice to undergo an abortion. It is an undue burden, and therefore invalid. . . .

[D. The Parental-Consent Requirement]

We next consider the parental consent provision. . . . Our cases establish, and we reaffirm today, that a State may require a minor seeking an abortion to obtain the consent of a parent or guardian, provided that there is an adequate judicial bypass procedure. . . .

[E. The Record-Keeping Requirement]

Under the recordkeeping and reporting requirements of the statute, every facility which performs abortions is required to file a report stating its name and address . . . For each abortion performed, a report must be filed identifying [information about the woman, her physician, and the fetus]. . . . In all events, the identity of each woman who has had an abortion remains confidential. . . .

The collection of information with respect to actual patients is a vital element of medical research, and so it cannot be said that the requirements serve no purpose other than to make abortions more difficult. Nor do we find that the requirements impose a substantial obstacle to a woman's choice. At most they might increase the cost of some abortions by a slight amount. While at some point increased cost could become a substantial obstacle, there is no such showing on the record before us. . . .

■ JUSTICE SCALIA, with whom THE CHIEF JUSTICE, JUSTICE WHITE, and JUSTICE THOMAS join, concurring in the judgment in part and dissenting in part.

My views on this matter are unchanged from those I set forth in [earlier] opinions. . . . The States may, if they wish, permit abortion on demand, but the Constitution does not *require* them to do so. The permissibility of abortion, and the limitations upon it, are to be resolved like most important questions in our democracy: by citizens trying to persuade one another and then voting. . . .

[T]he issue in these cases [is] not whether the power of a woman to abort her unborn child is a "liberty" in the absolute sense; or even whether it is a liberty of great importance to many women. Of course it is both. The issue is whether it is a liberty protected by the Constitution of the United States. I am sure it is not. I reach that conclusion not because of anything so exalted as my views concerning the "concept of existence, of meaning, of the universe, and of the mystery of human life." Rather, I reach it for the same reason I reach the conclusion that bigamy is not constitutionally protected—because of two simple facts: (1) the Constitution says absolutely nothing about it, and (2) the longstanding traditions of American society have permitted it to be legally proscribed. . . . [A]pplying the rational basis test, I would uphold the Pennsylvania statute in its entirety. . . .

* * *

There is a poignant aspect to today's opinion. Its length, and what might be called its epic tone, suggest that its authors believe they are bringing to an end a troublesome era in the history of our Nation and of our Court. . . .

There comes vividly to mind a portrait by Emanuel Leutze that hangs in the Harvard Law School: Roger Brooke Taney, painted in 1859, the 82d year of his life, the 24th of his Chief Justiceship, the second after his opinion in *Dred Scott*. He is all in black, sitting in a shadowed red armchair, left hand resting upon a pad of paper in his lap, right hand hanging limply, almost lifelessly, beside the inner arm of the chair. He sits facing the viewer and staring straight out. There seems to be on his face, and in his deep-set eyes, an expression of profound sadness and disillusionment. Perhaps he always looked that way, even when dwelling upon the happiest of thoughts. But those of us who know how the lustre of his great Chief Justiceship came to be eclipsed by *Dred Scott* cannot help believing that he had that case—its already apparent consequences for the Court and its soon-to-be played-out consequences for the Nation—burning on his mind. I expect that two years earlier he, too, had thought himself "call[ing] the contending sides of national controversy to end their national division by accepting a common mandate rooted in the Constitution." . . .

It is no more realistic for us in this litigation, than it was for him in that, to think that an issue of the sort they both involved—an issue involving life and death, freedom and subjugation—can be "speedily and finally settled" by the Supreme Court, as President James Buchanan in his inaugural address said the issue of slavery in the territories would be. Quite to the contrary, by foreclosing all democratic outlet for the deep passions this issue arouses, by banishing the issue from the political forum that gives all participants, even the losers, the satisfaction of a fair hearing and an honest fight, by continuing the imposition of a rigid national rule instead of allowing for regional differences, the Court merely prolongs and intensifies the anguish.

We should get out of this area, where we have no right to be, and where we do neither ourselves nor the country any good by remaining.[16]

NOTE: UNDUE BURDEN STANDARD AS APPLIED TO METHODS OF ABORTION

Although a majority of the *Casey* Court emphatically declared that it was reaffirming the "essential holding of *Roe*," 505 U.S. at 846, the plurality also overruled part of *Roe* and adopted a new test to evaluate regulations of abortion before a fetus's viability: the undue burden test. This test was purposefully more deferential to legislatures than the strict scrutiny that the Court had previously applied to all regulations that interfered with a fundamental right. Instead of requiring that a law be narrowly tailored to serve a compelling state interest, the undue burden test required simply that a law not impose "a substantial obstacle to the woman's exercise of the right to choose." *Casey*, 505 U.S. at 877. Significantly, the test distinguished between a law that *influenced a woman's choice*, which the plurality considered valid, and a law that *prevented a woman from making a choice*, which the plurality considered invalid.

Undue burden standard and methods of abortion. In the wake of *Casey*, states around the country adopted Pennsylvania's waiting periods,

---

16 **Questions:** Setting aside whether you believe that the *Casey* plurality reached the correct result, do you agree with Justice Antonin Scalia that *Casey* "foreclos[es] all democratic outlet for the deep passions this issue arouses"? Is Scalia's provocative reference to *Dred Scott v. Sandford* correct that the likely consequence of decisions like *Casey* will be to radicalize partisans and relocate national debates away from legislatures and toward violence (or, at the very least, toward judicial nominations)?

informed-consent provisions, and other methods of attempting to persuade pregnant women to choose not to obtain an abortion. States also introduced new laws to regulate the *method* of abortion—a type of regulation that the *Casey* Court had not evaluated.

Decades before *Casey*, in *Planned Parenthood of Central Missouri v. Danforth*, 428 U.S. 52 (1976), the Court struck down a law that made it illegal to use saline amniocentesis. At the time, saline was the most common method of aborting a pregnancy after the first trimester. But by the 1990s, the medical profession had largely switched to using surgical procedures for most second-trimester abortions. The most commonly used surgical procedure was "dilation and evacuation," which involved dilating a woman's cervix and using surgical instruments inside her uterus to dismember and remove parts of the fetus. This procedure could be risky for a woman's health late in her pregnancy, however, which led some physicians to develop alternatives. The main alternative involved removing the fetus from a woman's uterus "intact" before dismembering it. Depending on the positioning of the fetus in the uterus, this procedure was known either as *dilation and extraction* or *intact dilation and evacuation*.

In 1997, Nebraska and other states passed laws banning this alternative procedure, which they pejoratively called *partial-birth abortion*. Nebraska made it a crime to "partially deliver[ ] vaginally a living unborn child before killing the unborn child and completing the delivery"—unless the method was necessary to preserve the life of the pregnant person. In *Stenberg v. Carhart*, 530 U.S. 914 (2000), the Court invalidated the law under the undue burden test. Explaining that the law had nothing to do with preserving the health of a pregnant woman or the potential life of the fetus, the Court held that a ban on "the most commonly used method for performing previability second trimester abortions" resulted in "an undue burden upon a woman's right to make an abortion decision." *Stenberg*, 530 U.S. at 945–46.

Stenberg was a 5–4 decision whose majority included two of the three members of the *Casey* plurality: O'Connor and Souter. But when O'Connor retired in 2006, she was replaced by Samuel Alito, the circuit judge who had earlier voted to uphold all of the provisions at issue in *Casey*. Immediately, Congress enacted a federal law nearly identical to Nebraska's ban: Congress made it a crime to "kill" a fetus after it had been partially delivered. And when the same physician in *Stenberg* challenged the law in *Gonzales v. Carhart*, 550 U.S. 124 (2007), the Court upheld the new ban. Writing for a new majority that included all of the *Stenberg* dissenters, Kennedy wrote that the purpose of the ban wasn't to place "a substantial obstacle in the path of a woman seeking an abortion" but to serve the federal government's interest in the mental health of the pregnant woman. *Gonzales*, 550 U.S. at 156, 159. "While we find no reliable data to measure the phenomenon," Kennedy wrote, "it seems unexceptionable to conclude some women come to regret their choice to abort the infant life they once created and sustained." *Id.* at 159. He also wrote that the effect of the ban didn't impose an undue burden either because the Court considered it a matter of "medical and scientific uncertainty" whether dilation and extraction was a safer method of aborting a pregnancy than dilation and evacuation, which remained the most common method early in a pregnancy and which the law did not affect. *Id.* at 163.

Undue burden standard and people affected. The only provision of Pennsylvania's abortion law that the *Casey* Court invalidated was the provision that required a married woman to notify her husband that she was seeking an abortion. Pennsylvania's defense of the provision was that very few women would be affected. Among the total population of women seeking abortions in Pennsylvania, only 20 percent were married. Among that 20 percent, only 5 percent would not voluntarily notify their husbands. And among that 5 percent, not all would face adverse consequences.

But the *Casey* plurality responded that this was the wrong way to approach the question. The plurality explained that "[t]he proper focus of constitutional inquiry is the group for whom the law is a restriction, not the group for whom the law is irrelevant." *Casey*, 505 U.S. at 894. So, rather than treat the provision as applying to less than 1 percent of Pennsylvania women, the Court evaluated the provision's effect on the women seeking an abortion who would not otherwise voluntarily notify their husbands. Considering this population, the Court concluded that "in a large fraction of the cases in which § 3209 is relevant, it will operate as a substantial obstacle to a woman's choice to undergo an abortion." *Id.* at 895.

43.2.3

Whole Woman's Health v. Hellerstedt

579 U.S. 582 (2016)

An essential question left open by *Casey* was whether its undue burden test was a deferential means-ends test or a proportionality test. The plurality opinion employed language that supported both interpretations. On the one hand, the opinion instructed future courts to consider whether a restriction on abortion was "reasonably related" to a "legitimate state interest"—an archetypical rational-basis test. *Casey*, 505 U.S. at 878, On the other hand, as Scalia observed in his dissent, the opinion's invalidation of Pennsylvania's spousal-consent provision indicated that it was doing something other than applying the rational-basis test. *Id.* at 988–99 (Scalia, J., dissenting). With language that appeared to evaluate the burden imposed by the provision, the plurality wrote that the spousal-consent provision "does not merely make abortions a little more difficult or expensive to obtain; for many women, it will impose a substantial obstacle." *Id.* at 893–94.

The Court temporarily offered an answer to the "test" question in *Whole Woman's Health v. Hellerstedt*, 136 S. Ct 2292 (2016).

In 2013, over a filibuster that attracted nationwide attention, Texas's governor Rick Perry signed into law House Bill 2 (H.B. 2), a bill that imposed strict restrictions on how abortion clinics could operate in the state. Among other things, the law included an *admitting-privileges requirement* that required any physician performing an abortion to "have active admitting privileges at a hospital that . . . is located not further than 30 miles from the location at which the abortion is performed." *Whole Woman's Health*, 136 S. Ct at 2300 (quoting H.B. 2). It also included a *surgical-center requirement* that imposed the same minimum health and safety standards for abortion facilities that existed for "ambulatory surgical centers." *Id.* (quoting H.B. 2). Texas was one of many Republican-controlled states after the 2010 elections to enact these sorts of targeted regulations of abortion providers (TRAP laws), whose goal was to shut down abortion clinics. *See* Stone, *supra*, at 434–35.

H.B. 2 threatened to close all but seven of Texas's forty abortion clinics, leaving clinics only in the state's major metropolitan areas. *See* Manny Fernandez & Erik Eckholm, *Texas House Restricts Abortions in a Move That Could Force Clinics to Shut*, N.Y. Times, June 24, 2013, at A11. Whole Woman's Health, an abortion provider, challenged H.B. 2 as a law whose purpose and effect had nothing to do with the health of women and everything to do with closing the state's abortion clinics. Although the district court agreed, the U.S. Court of Appeals for the Fifth Circuit held that the purpose of the law was to protect the health of patients. The court also didn't think that a "large fraction" of women seeking abortions would be affected by the mass closures. *Whole Woman's Health v. Cole*, 790 F.3d 563, 590 (5th Cir. 2015). Women who lived in West Texas, for example, could use abortion providers in nearby New Mexico.

Interpreting *Casey*'s holding as a proportionality test, the Supreme Court in *Whole Woman's Health* determined that the law was an unconstitutionally undue burden.

■ JUSTICE BREYER delivered the opinion of the Court.[17]

We must here decide whether two provisions of Texas' House Bill 2 violate the Federal Constitution as interpreted in [*Planned Parenthood v. Casey,* 505 U.S. 833 (1992)]. . . . We conclude that neither of these provisions confers medical benefits sufficient to justify the burdens upon access that each imposes. . . .

III. *Undue Burden—Legal Standard*

We begin with the standard, as described in *Casey*. We recognize that the "State has a legitimate interest in seeing to it that abortion, like any other medical procedure, is performed under circumstances that insure maximum safety for the patient." *Roe v. Wade*, 410 U.S. 113, 150 (1973). But, we added, "a statute which, while furthering [a] valid state interest, has the effect of placing a substantial obstacle in the path of a woman's choice cannot be considered a permissible means of serving its legitimate ends." *Casey*, 505 U.S., at 877. Moreover, "[u]nnecessary health regulations that have the purpose or effect of presenting a substantial obstacle to a woman seeking an abortion impose an undue burden on the right." *Id.*, at 878.

The Court of Appeals wrote that a state law is "constitutional if: (1) it does not have the purpose or effect of placing a substantial obstacle in the path of a woman

[17] **As You Read, Consider:** How does Justice Stephen Breyer characterize the undue burden test: as a deferential means-ends test or a proportionality test? Would the two tests lead to different results here?

seeking an abortion of a nonviable fetus; and (2) it is reasonably related to (or designed to further) a legitimate state interest." 790 F.3d, at 572. . . .

The Court of Appeals' articulation of the relevant standard is incorrect. The first part of the Court of Appeals' test may be read to imply that a district court should not consider the existence or non-existence of medical benefits when considering whether a regulation of abortion constitutes an undue burden. The rule announced in *Casey,* however, requires that courts consider the burdens a law imposes on abortion access together with the benefits those laws confer. And the second part of the test is wrong to equate the judicial review applicable to the regulation of a constitutionally protected personal liberty with the less strict review applicable where, for example, economic legislation is at issue. The Court of Appeals' approach simply does not match the standard that this Court laid out in *Casey,* which asks courts to consider whether any burden imposed on abortion access is "undue." . . . [This standard requires placing] considerable weight upon evidence and argument presented in judicial proceedings. . . .

IV. *Undue Burden—Admitting-Privileges Requirement*

[H.B. 2 requires] that a "physician performing or inducing an abortion . . . [must] have active admitting privileges at a hospital that . . . is located not further than 30 miles from the location at which the abortion is performed or induced." [*Id.*] § 171.0031(a). The District Court held that the legislative change imposed an "undue burden" on a woman's right to have an abortion. We [agree]. . . .

The purpose of the admitting-privileges requirement is to help ensure that women have easy access to a hospital should complications arise during an abortion procedure. But the District Court found that it brought about no such health-related benefit. The court found that "[t]he great weight of evidence demonstrates that, before the act's passage, abortion in Texas was extremely safe with particularly low rates of serious complications and virtually no deaths occurring on account of the procedure." 46 F.Supp.3d, at 684. Thus, there was no significant health-related problem that the new law helped to cure. . . .

[W]hen directly asked at oral argument whether Texas knew of a single instance in which the new requirement would have helped even one woman obtain better treatment, Texas admitted that there was no evidence in the record of such a case. See Tr. of Oral Arg. 47. . . .

At the same time, the record evidence indicates that the admitting-privileges requirement places a "substantial obstacle in the path of a woman's choice." *Casey,* 505 U.S., at 877 (plurality opinion). The District Court found, as of the time the admitting-privileges requirement began to be enforced, the number of facilities providing abortions dropped in half, from about 40 to about 20. . . .

Other evidence helps to explain why the new requirement led to the closure of clinics. "[H]ospitals often condition admitting privileges on reaching a certain number of admissions per year." Brief for Society of Hospital Medicine et al. as *Amici Curiae* 11. . . . [I]t would be difficult for doctors regularly performing abortions at the El Paso clinic to obtain admitting privileges at nearby hospitals because "[d]uring the past 10 years, over 17,000 abortion procedures were performed at the El Paso clinic [and n]ot a single one of those patients had to be transferred to a hospital for emergency treatment, much less admitted to the hospital." App. 730. In a word, doctors would be unable to maintain admitting privileges or obtain those privileges for the future, because the fact that abortions are so safe meant that providers were unlikely to have any patients to admit. . . .

In our view, the record contains sufficient evidence that the admitting-privileges requirement led to the closure of half of Texas' clinics, or thereabouts. Those closures meant fewer doctors, longer waiting times, and increased crowding. [Also,] after the admitting-privileges provision went into effect, the "number of women of reproductive age living in a county . . . more than 150 miles from a provider increased from approximately 86,000 to 400,000 . . . and the number of women living in a county more than 200 miles from a provider from approximately 10,000 to 290,000." 46 F.Supp.3d, at 681. We recognize that increased driving distances do not always constitute an "undue burden." See *Casey,* 505 U.S., at 885–887. But here, those increases are but one additional burden, which, when taken together with others that the closings brought about, and when viewed in light of the virtual absence of any health benefit, lead us to conclude that the record adequately supports the District Court's "undue burden" conclusion. . . .

V. *Undue Burden—Surgical-Center Requirement*

The second challenged provision of Texas' new law sets forth the surgical-center requirement. Prior to enactment of the new requirement, Texas law required abortion facilities to meet a host of health and safety requirements. . . . H.B. 2 added the requirement that an "abortion facility" meet the "minimum standards . . . for ambulatory surgical centers" under Texas law. § 245.010(a). The surgical-center regulations include, among other things, detailed specifications relating to the size of the nursing staff, building dimensions, and other building requirements. . . . Facilities must include a full surgical suite with an operating room that has "a clear floor area of at least 240 square feet" in which "[t]he minimum clear dimension between built-in cabinets, counters, and shelves shall be 14 feet." § 135.52(d)(15)(A). There must be a preoperative patient holding room and a postoperative recovery suite. . . . Surgical centers must meet numerous other spatial requirements, including specific corridor widths. . . .

There is considerable evidence in the record supporting the District Court's findings indicating that the statutory provision requiring all abortion facilities to meet all surgical-center standards does not benefit patients and is not necessary. . . .

The record makes clear . . . that abortions taking place in an abortion facility are safe—indeed, safer than numerous procedures that take place outside hospitals and to which Texas does not apply its surgical-center requirements. The total number of deaths in Texas from abortions was five in the period from 2001 to 2012, or about one every two years (that is to say, one out of about 120,000 to 144,000 abortions). Nationwide, childbirth is 14 times more likely than abortion to result in death, but Texas law allows a midwife to oversee childbirth in the patient's own home. Colonoscopy, a procedure that typically takes place outside a hospital (or surgical center) setting, has a mortality rate 10 times higher than an abortion. [App.] 276–277; see ACOG Brief 15 (the mortality rate for liposuction, another outpatient procedure, is 28 times higher than the mortality rate for abortion). . . . These facts indicate that the surgical-center provision imposes "a requirement that simply is not based on differences" between abortion and other surgical procedures "that are reasonably related to" preserving women's health. . . . *Doe,* 410 U.S., at 194.[18]

---

[18] **Questions:** Recall that Justice Harry Blackmun's opinion in *Roe v. Wade* recognized that Texas had a compelling interest in protecting a woman's health after the first trimester, when legal abortions no longer appeared to be safer than childbirth. Abortion procedures have, in the fifty years since, become far safer than childbirth. Under Breyer's version of the undue burden test, will it *ever* be appropriate for a government to restrict access to abortion in the name of maternal health? For example, suppose a scientist develops a novel abortion pill that is safer and more effective than virtually any other medical procedure. Could the federal government constitutionally delay or block the distribution of the pill? *See FDA v. Am. Coll. of Obstetricians & Gynecologists*, 141 S. Ct. 578, 579 (2021) (suggesting that the answer to this question is yes).

Moreover, many surgical-center requirements are inappropriate as applied to surgical abortions. Requiring scrub facilities; maintaining a one-way traffic pattern through the facility; having ceiling, wall, and floor finishes; separating soiled utility and sterilization rooms; and regulating air pressure, filtration, and humidity control can help reduce infection where doctors conduct procedures that penetrate the skin. App. 304. But abortions typically involve either the administration of medicines or procedures performed through the natural opening of the birth canal, which is itself not sterile. See *id.,* at 302–303. Nor do provisions designed to safeguard heavily sedated patients . . . provide any help to abortion patients, as abortion facilities do not use general anesthesia or deep sedation, *id.,* at 304–305. . . .

At the same time, the record provides adequate evidentiary support for the District Court's conclusion that the surgical-center requirement places a substantial obstacle in the path of women seeking an abortion. The parties stipulated that the requirement would further reduce the number of abortion facilities available to seven or eight facilities, located in Houston, Austin, San Antonio, and Dallas/Fort Worth. See App. 182–183. In the District Court's view, the proposition that these "seven or eight providers could meet the demand of the entire State stretches credulity." 46 F.Supp.3d, at 682. . . .

[I]n the face of no threat to women's health, Texas seeks to force women to travel long distances to get abortions in crammed-to-capacity superfacilities. Patients seeking these services are less likely to get the kind of individualized attention, serious conversation, and emotional support that doctors at less taxed facilities may have offered. . . . We agree with the District Court that the surgical-center requirement, like the admitting-privileges requirement, provides few, if any, health benefits for women, poses a substantial obstacle to women seeking abortions, and constitutes an "undue burden" on their constitutional right to do so.

VI

[T]exas claims that the provisions at issue here do not impose a substantial obstacle because the women affected by those laws are not a "large fraction" of Texan women "of reproductive age," which Texas reads *Casey* to have required. See Brief for Respondents 45, 48. But *Casey* used the language "large fraction" to refer to "a large fraction of cases in which [the provision at issue] is *relevant,*" a class narrower than "all women," "pregnant women," or even "the class of *women seeking abortions* identified by the State." 505 U.S., at 894–895 (opinion of the Court) (emphasis added). Here, as in *Casey,* the relevant denominator is "those [women] for whom [the provision] is an actual rather than an irrelevant restriction." *Id.,* at 895. . . .

43.2.4

June Medical Services L.L.C. v. Russo

140 S. Ct. 2103 (2020)

Whole Woman's Health reinvigorated *Roe* and *Casey* by confirming that the undue burden test was a proportionality test, not a deferential means-ends test. Under *Whole Woman's Health*, the undue burden test required courts to determine whether the burdens that a law imposed on abortion access outweighed the law's benefits for women's health and its respect for childbirth. If so, the law imposed an unconstitutionally "substantial burden." *Whole Woman's Health*, 133 S. Ct. at 2333.

But *Whole Woman's Health* was a 5–3 decision in which Justice Anthony Kennedy joined the four justices appointed by Democrats. The election of President Donald Trump cast doubt on the decision as the new president ultimately replaced two of the justices in the *Whole Woman's Health* majority. Daring the new Court to reconsider *Whole Woman's Health*, Louisiana and other states quickly enacted laws that were virtually identical to the Texas law invalidated in 2016.

In the following decision, *June Medical Services L.L.C. v. Russo*, 140 S. Ct. 2103 (2020), the Supreme Court evaluated the constitutionality of Louisiana's abortion restrictions. Writing for a four-justice plurality that included Justice Ruth Bader Ginsburg, Justice Stephen Breyer reaffirmed *Whole Woman's Health* and reached an identical conclusion. Significantly, Chief Justice John Roberts provided the crucial fifth vote in a decision that was "nonetheless selective about which aspects of the 2016 decision demanded deference." Melissa Murray, *The Symbiosis of Abortion and Precedent,* 134 Harv. L. Rev. 308, 312 (2020).

■ CHIEF JUSTICE ROBERTS, concurring in the judgment. . . .[19]

I joined the dissent in *Whole Woman's Health* and continue to believe that the case was wrongly decided. The question today however is not whether *Whole Woman's Health* was right or wrong, but whether to adhere to it in deciding the present case. . . .

The legal doctrine of *stare decisis* requires us, absent special circumstances, to treat like cases alike. The Louisiana law imposes a burden on access to abortion just as severe as that imposed by the Texas law, for the same reasons. Therefore Louisiana's law cannot stand under our precedents. . . .

II

Both Louisiana and the providers agree that the undue burden standard announced in *Casey* provides the appropriate framework to analyze Louisiana's law. Neither party has asked us to reassess the constitutional validity of that standard. . . .

Under *Casey*, [a] State may not impose an undue burden on [a] woman's ability to obtain an abortion. "A finding of an undue burden is a shorthand for the conclusion that a state regulation has the purpose or effect of placing a substantial obstacle in the path of a woman seeking an abortion of a nonviable fetus." *Id.*, at 877. Laws that do not pose a substantial obstacle to abortion access are permissible, so long as they are "reasonably related" to a legitimate state interest. *Id.*, at 878.

After faithfully reciting this standard, the Court in *Whole Woman's Health* added the following observation: "The rule announced in *Casey* . . . requires that courts consider the burdens a law imposes on abortion access together with the benefits those laws confer." 579 U. S., at ___. . . .

Read in isolation from *Casey*, such an inquiry could invite a grand "balancing test in which unweighted factors mysteriously are weighed." *Marrs v. Motorola, Inc.*, 577 F.3d 783, 788 (CA7 2009). Under such tests, "equality of treatment is . . . impossible to achieve; predictability is destroyed; judicial arbitrariness is facilitated;

[19] **As You Read, Consider:** What, precisely, is the difference between Chief Justice John Roberts's interpretation of *Planned Parenthood of Southeastern Pennsylvania v. Casey*'s undue burden test and Justice Stephen Breyer's interpretation of the test? Considering that Roberts dissented in *Whole Woman's Health v. Hellerstedt*, in which situations might the two interpretations lead to different results?

judicial courage is impaired." Scalia, The Rule of Law as a Law of Rules, 56 U. Chi. L. Rev. 1175, 1182 (1989).

In this context, courts applying a balancing test would be asked in essence to weigh the State's interests in "protecting the potentiality of human life" and the health of the woman, on the one hand, against the woman's liberty interest in defining her "own concept of existence, of meaning, of the universe, and of the mystery of human life" on the other. *Casey*, 505 U.S. at 851. There is no plausible sense in which anyone, let alone this Court, could objectively assign weight to such imponderable values and no meaningful way to compare them if there were. Attempting to do so would be like "judging whether a particular line is longer than a particular rock is heavy," *Bendix Autolite Corp. v. Midwesco Enterprises, Inc.*, 486 U.S. 888, 897 (1988) (Scalia, J., concurring in judgment). Pretending that we could pull that off would require us to act as legislators, not judges, and would result in nothing other than an "unanalyzed exercise of judicial will" in the guise of a "neutral utilitarian calculus." *New Jersey v. T. L. O.*, 469 U.S. 325, 369 (1985) (Brennan, J., concurring in part and dissenting in part).

Nothing about *Casey* suggested that a weighing of costs and benefits of an abortion regulation was a job for the courts. . . . *Casey* instead focuses on the existence of a substantial obstacle, the sort of inquiry familiar to judges across a variety of contexts. See, *e.g., Burwell v. Hobby Lobby Stores, Inc.*, 573 U.S. 682, 694–695 (2014) (asking whether the government "substantially burdens a person's exercise of religion" under the Religious Freedom Restoration Act); *Arizona Free Enterprise Club's Freedom Club PAC v. Bennett*, 564 U.S. 721, 748 (2011) (asking whether a law "imposes a substantial burden on the speech of privately financed candidates and independent expenditure groups"); *Murphy v. United Parcel Service, Inc.*, 527 U.S. 516, 521 (1999) (asking, in the context of the Americans with Disabilities Act, whether an individual's impairment "substantially limits one or more major life activities").[20]

Casey's analysis of the various restrictions that were at issue in that case is illustrative. For example, the opinion recognized that Pennsylvania's 24-hour waiting period for abortions "has the effect of increasing the cost and risk of delay of abortions," but observed that the District Court did not find that the "increased costs and potential delays amount to substantial obstacles." 505 U.S. at 886. . . . Because the law did not impose a substantial obstacle, *Casey* upheld it. And it did so notwithstanding the District Court's finding that the law did "not further the state interest in maternal health." *Ibid.* (internal quotation marks omitted). . . .

The only restriction *Casey* found unconstitutional was Pennsylvania's spousal notification requirement. On that score, the Court recited a bevy of social science evidence demonstrating that "millions of women in this country . . . may have justifiable fears of physical abuse" or "devastating forms of psychological abuse from their husbands." *Id.*, at 893. . . . The spousal notification requirement was "thus likely to prevent a significant number of women from obtaining an abortion." *Ibid.* It did not "merely make abortions a little more difficult or expensive to obtain; for many women, it [imposed] a substantial obstacle." *Id.*, at 893–894. The Court emphasized that it would not "blind [itself] to the fact that the significant number of women who fear for their safety and the safety of their children are likely to be deterred from procuring an

---

[20] **Questions:** Roberts is pretty emphatic here that the undue burden test is *not* a proportionality test. What, then, is it? If the substantialness of a law's obstacle to abortion access is not at all related to the benefits that the law provides, how should an evaluator determine when an obstacle is so substantial that it imposes an undue burden?

abortion as surely as if the Commonwealth had outlawed abortion in all cases." *Id.*, at 894.

The upshot of *Casey* is clear: The several restrictions that did not impose a substantial obstacle were constitutional, while the restriction that did impose a substantial obstacle was unconstitutional.

To be sure, the Court at times discussed the benefits of the regulations, including when it distinguished spousal notification from parental consent. See *Whole Woman's Health*, 579 U. S., at ___. But in the context of *Casey*'s governing standard, these benefits were not placed on a scale opposite the law's burdens. Rather, *Casey* discussed benefits in considering the threshold requirement that the State have a "legitimate purpose" and that the law be "reasonably related to that goal." 505 U. S., at 878.[21]

So long as that showing is made, the only question for a court is whether a law has the "effect of placing a substantial obstacle in the path of a woman seeking an abortion of a nonviable fetus." *Id.*, at 877 (plurality opinion). *Casey* repeats that "substantial obstacle" standard nearly verbatim no less than 15 times. . . .

We should respect the statement in *Whole Woman's Health* that it was applying the undue burden standard of *Casey*. . . . In this case, *Casey*'s requirement of finding a substantial obstacle before invalidating an abortion regulation is therefore a sufficient basis for the decision, as it was in *Whole Woman's Health*. In neither case, nor in *Casey* itself, was there call for consideration of a regulation's benefits, and nothing in *Casey* commands such consideration. Under principles of *stare decisis*, I agree with the plurality that the determination in *Whole Woman's Health* that Texas's law imposed a substantial obstacle requires the same determination about Louisiana's law. . . .

NOTE: AFTERMATH OF *JUNE MEDICAL SERVICES*

The precedential value of *June Medical Services* is unclear. Although Justice Breyer's four-justice plurality opinion and Chief Justice Roberts's single-justice concurring opinion treated *Whole Woman's Health* as controlling precedent, the concurrence expressed doubt about the test employed by *Whole Woman's Health*. Then, only months after the Court decided *June Medical Services*, one of the justices in the plurality, Ruth Bader Ginsburg, died. President Donald Trump replaced her by nominating Amy Coney Barrett, a conservative whose confirmation put the future of *Roe* in jeopardy.

Many states responded to Justice Barrett's confirmation by enacting laws that effectively repealed *Roe*. Texas, for instance, enacted a law known as S.B. 8 that effectively banned all abortions in the state after six weeks of pregnancy, even in cases of rape or sexual abuse. In this respect, S.B. 8 was even more restrictive than the Texas law invalidated in *Roe*. But Texas adopted a creative scheme to evade judicial review: S.B. 8 prohibited state

---

[21] **Questions:** Under Roberts's interpretation, *Planned Parenthood of Southeastern Pennsylvania v. Casey* presents a two-step inquiry for evaluating abortion restrictions. First, is the law "reasonably related" to a state's "legitimate purpose"? If a law passes this deferential means-ends test, then the second question is whether the obstacle that the law imposes on abortion access is "substantial."

Presumably, Roberts thinks that Louisiana and Texas would satisfy this two-part test if not for *stare decisis*. How do you think he reaches the conclusion that the obstacle at issue here is not substantial?

officials from seeking enforcement of the ban. Instead, the law authorized ordinary people to sue in state court anyone they suspected of violating S.B. 8's provisions. If the state court concluded that S.B. 8 had been violated, then the law required the state court to order the violator to pay the plaintiff at least $10,000 for each illegal abortion.

Whole Woman's Health and other abortion providers in Texas attempted to block S.B. 8 from taking effect by suing the state's judges in their official capacity. Invoking the Ku Klux Klan Act of 1871, 42 U.S.C. § 1983, they argued that S.B. 8 illegally required the state judges to deprive pregnant people of their constitutional rights. Although a district court agreed with the abortion providers that an injunction was warranted, the Supreme Court did not. In a 5–4 decision in which Justice Barrett was in the majority and Chief Justice Roberts was in the dissent, the Court held that it was not clear "whether, under existing precedent, this Court can issue an injunction against state judges asked to decide a lawsuit under Texas's law." *Whole Woman's Health v. Jackson*, 141 S. Ct. 2494, 2495 (2021). *But see, e.g.*, *Pulliam v. Allen*, 466 U.S. 522, 539 (1984) (upholding the use of § 1983 to secure injunctive relief against a state judge); *Ex parte Virginia*, 100 U.S. 339, 346–47 (1880) (upholding the federal prosecution of a state judge for violating another Reconstruction-era statute, because if Congress could not compel state judges to comply with the Fourteenth Amendment, then "the constitutional prohibition has no meaning").

Whole Woman's Health v. Jackson allowed the Texas law to take effect without expressly deciding its constitutionality. Future decisions may end up invalidating the Texas law. But by allowing such an obvious violation of *June*, *Casey*, and *Roe* to stand even temporarily, the Court signaled that these precedents likely lack five votes to sustain them. *See United States v. Texas*, 142 S. Ct. 14 (Oct. 22, 2021) (Sotomayor, J., concurring in part and dissenting in part) ("The State's gambit has worked. The impact is catastrophic."); *see also, e.g.*, *FDA v. Am. Coll. of Obstetricians & Gynecologists*, 141 S. Ct. 578, 579 (2021) (refusing to enjoin the FDA's decision to prohibit the distribution of a safe and effective abortion pill by mail during the COVID-19 pandemic).

CHAPTER 44

WHAT MINIMUM LIMITATIONS DO THE EQUAL-PROTECTION PRINCIPLES OF THE FIFTH AND FOURTEENTH AMENDMENTS IMPOSE ON THE POWER OF GOVERNMENT TO TREAT PEOPLE DIFFERENTLY?

FIFTH AMENDMENT (1791): No person shall be . . . deprived of life, liberty, or property, without due process of law. . . .

FOURTEENTH AMENDMENT (1868), SECTION 1: No State shall . . . deprive any person of life, liberty, or property, without due process of law; nor deny to any person within its jurisdiction the equal protection of the laws.

44.1 THE ORIGINS OF THE RATIONAL-BASIS TEST

For almost the entire first century of the Fourteenth Amendment's existence, the Equal Protection Clause was overshadowed by the other clauses in Section 1. For example, in the *Slaughter-House Cases*, 83 U.S. (16 Wall.) 36 (1873), the majority dismissed the white butchers' equal-protection challenge to Louisiana's slaughterhouse law in a few paragraphs. *Id.* at 81. The Court was equally dismissive when black people later began bringing claims of racial discrimination to the justices' attention. *See, e.g., Plessy v. Ferguson*, 163 U.S. 537 (1896).

There are many reasons why the nineteenth-century Supreme Court may have been so dismissive of equal-protection challenges. One explanation offered by the Court during this period was that all laws, by necessity, treat some people differently from others. Graduated taxes treat wealthy people differently from poor people. Traffic laws treat drivers differently from pedestrians. Business regulations treat butchers differently from lawyers. And so on. If this differential treatment were enough to invalidate a law, then government could scarcely function. "Indeed, the very idea of classification is that of inequality," the Court wrote in *Atchison, Topeka & Santa Fe Rail Road Co. v. Matthews*. 174 U.S. 96, 106 (1899). "[I]t goes without saying that the fact of inequality in no manner determines the matter of constitutionality." *Id.*

In light of the risk that a broad reading of the Equal Protection Clause might invalidate all legislation that treated people differently, the Court instead interpreted the clause by applying a deferential means-ends test. For example, in *Barbier v. Connolly*, 113 U.S. 27 (1885), the Court upheld a San Francisco ordinance that prohibited public laundry facilities from operating at night. Even though this ordinance applied only to laundries (and not, say, to slaughterhouses), the Court considered the classification reasonable. It explained that laundry facilities typically used fires to clean clothing, and San Francisco was "a city composed largely of wooden buildings." *Barbier*, 113 U.S. at 30. "Regulations for these purposes may press with more or less weight upon one than upon another," the Court continued, "but they are designed, not to impose unequal or unnecessary restrictions upon any one, but to promote, with as little individual inconvenience as possible, the general good." *Id.* at 31–32. The Court therefore concluded that it was constitutional for states to adopt "legislation which, in carrying out a public purpose, . . . affects alike all persons similarly situated." *Id.* at 32. The only legislation prohibited by the Equal Protection Clause, according to the Court, was "[c]lass legislation, discriminating against some and favoring others." *Id.*

Surprisingly, only one year after *Barbier*, the Court employed this same deferential test to invalidate a different San Francisco laundry ordinance. The following decision was one of a handful of cases before the 1940s in which the Court used the Equal Protection Clause to invalidate a state law.

44.1.1
Yick Wo v. Hopkins

118 U.S. 356 (1886)

Like many large cities in the 1880s, San Francisco had a white population that was violently xenophobic toward residents from China. As discussed earlier with regard to Congress's power to regulate immigration (section 10.3), white workers were generally hostile to Chinese laborers and called for legislation to restrict their residence. In addition to passing blatantly anti-Chinese measures to expel and punish people "of the Chinese or Mongolian races," 1858 Cal. Stat. 295, western states also restricted where Chinese people could work and live. So-called Chinatowns emerged in the slums of western cities, while Chinese workers concentrated in dangerous and undesirable jobs like operating public laundries. *See* Charles J. McClain, *In Search of Equality* 47 (1996).

Many white San Franciscans eventually objected even to these "Chinese laundries" on the ground that "the Chinese were as a race careless in the use of fire, that fires were more frequent in Chinatown than anywhere else, and that Chinese washhouses, scattered as they were throughout the city, were a general menace to the community's fire safety." *Id.* at 99. Preferring "French laundries," which they regarded as cleaner and safer, the city's leaders proposed an ordinance to prohibit anyone in the city from operating a laundry in a wooden building without a permit from the city's board of supervisors. *Id.* Because nearly every laundry in the city was operated from a wooden building, nearly everyone operating a laundry had to apply for a permit. But without providing an explanation, the supervisors refused to grant permits to Chinese laundry operators.

When one Chinese operator, named Yick Wo, continued to operate his wooden laundry despite not having a permit, he was imprisoned. He appealed to the Supreme Court.

In *Yick Wo v. Hopkins*, 118 U.S. 356 (1886), the Court, using an early version of what became known as the "rational-basis test," found that the law, as applied, violated the Equal Protection Clause of the Fourteenth Amendment.

■ MR. JUSTICE MATTHEWS delivered the opinion of the Court.[1]

In the case of the petitioner, brought here by writ of error to the Supreme Court of California, our jurisdiction is limited to the question, whether the plaintiff in error has been denied a right in violation of the Constitution, laws, or treaties of the United States. . . .

We are consequently constrained, at the outset, to differ from the Supreme Court of California upon the real meaning of the ordinances in question. That court considered these ordinances as vesting in the board of supervisors a not unusual discretion in granting or withholding their assent to the use of wooden buildings as laundries, to be exercised in reference to the circumstances of each case, with a view to the protection of the public against the dangers of fire. We are not able to concur in that interpretation of the power conferred upon the supervisors. There is nothing in the ordinances which points to such a regulation of the business of keeping and conducting laundries. They seem intended to confer, and actually do confer, not a discretion to be exercised upon a consideration of the circumstances of each case, but a naked and arbitrary power to give or withhold consent, not only as to places, but as to persons. So that, if an applicant for such consent, being in every way a competent and qualified person, and having complied with every reasonable condition demanded by any public interest, should, failing to obtain the requisite consent of the supervisors to the prosecution of his business, apply for redress by the judicial process of *mandamus,* to require the supervisors to consider and act upon his case, it would be a sufficient answer for them to say that the law had conferred upon them authority to withhold their assent, without reason and without responsibility. The power given to them is not confided to their discretion in the legal sense of that term, but is granted to their mere will. It is purely arbitrary, and acknowledges neither guidance nor restraint.

This erroneous view of the ordinances in question led the Supreme Court of California into the further error of holding that they were justified by the decisions of this court in the case[ ] of *Barbier* v. *Connolly,* 113 U.S. 27. In [that case] the

1 **As You Read, Consider:** A year earlier, in *Barbier v. Connolly*, the Supreme Court upheld an ordinance that prohibited laundries (but not other businesses) from operating at night. The Court accepted San Francisco's argument that the disparate treatment of businesses was reasonably related to the legitimate purpose of reducing fire hazards. Here, San Francisco has adopted another ordinance—requiring laundry operators in wooden buildings to obtain a permit—for the same stated purpose of reducing fire hazards. What, precisely, does Justice Stanley Matthews think distinguishes this second ordinance from the Barbier ordinance?

ordinance involved was simply a prohibition to carry on the washing and ironing of clothes in public laundries and washhouses, within certain prescribed limits of the city and county of San Francisco, from ten o'clock at night until six o'clock in the morning of the following day. This provision was held to be purely a police regulation, within the competency of any municipality possessed of the ordinary powers belonging to such bodies; a necessary measure of precaution in a city composed largely of wooden buildings like San Francisco, in the application of which there was no invidious discrimination against any one within the prescribed limits, all persons engaged in the same business being treated alike, and subject to the same restrictions, and entitled to the same privileges, under similar conditions.

For these reasons, that ordinance was adjudged not to be within the prohibitions of the Fourteenth Amendment to the Constitution of the United States, which, it was said, . . . "undoubtedly intended . . . that equal protection and security should be given to all under like circumstances in the enjoyment of their personal and civil rights; that all persons should be equally entitled to pursue their happiness and acquire and enjoy property; that they should have like access to the courts of the country for the protection of their persons and property, the prevention and redress of wrongs, and the enforcement of contracts; that no impediment should be interposed to the pursuits of any one, except as applied to the same pursuits by others under like circumstances; that no greater burdens should be laid upon one than are laid upon others in the same calling and condition; and that in the administration of criminal justice no different or higher punishment should be imposed upon one than such as is prescribed to all for like offences." "Class legislation, discriminating against some and favoring others, is prohibited, but legislation which, in carrying out a public purpose, is limited in its application, if within the sphere of its operation it affects alike all persons similarly situated, is not within the amendment."

The ordinance drawn in question in the present case is of a very different character. It does not prescribe a rule and conditions for the regulation of the use of property for laundry purposes, to which all similarly situated may conform. It allows without restriction the use for such purposes of buildings of brick or stone; but, as to wooden buildings, constituting nearly all those in previous use, it divides the owners or occupiers into two classes, not having respect to their personal character and qualifications for the business, nor the situation and nature and adaptation of the buildings themselves, but merely by an arbitrary line, on one side of which are those who are permitted to pursue their industry by the mere will and consent of the supervisors, and on the other those from whom that consent is withheld, at their mere will and pleasure. And both classes are alike only in this, that they are tenants at will, under the supervisors, of their means of living. The ordinance, therefore, also differs from the not unusual case, where discretion is lodged by law in public officers or bodies to grant or withhold licenses to keep taverns, . . . when one of the conditions is that the applicant shall be a fit person for the exercise of the privilege, because in such cases the fact of fitness is submitted to the judgment of the officer, and calls for the exercise of a discretion of a judicial nature.[2]

The rights of the petitioners, as affected by the proceedings of which they complain, are not less, because they are aliens and subjects of the Emperor of

---

[2] **Questions:** Here, Matthews is rejecting San Francisco's argument that its ordinance is reasonably related to preventing fires. He observes that the ordinance offers literally no guidance to the city's board of supervisors for how to exercise their discretion in granting permits. Instead, it allows them to erect "an arbitrary line" permitting some laundry operators to conduct business while depriving others "of their means of living."

Given this conclusion, what does he think was the "real meaning" of the ordinance? Does he think that such a meaning was legitimate?

China. . . . The Fourteenth Amendment to the Constitution is not confined to the protection of citizens. It says: "Nor shall any State deprive any person of life, liberty, or property without due process of law; nor deny to any person within its jurisdiction the equal protection of the laws." These provisions are universal in their application, to all persons within the territorial jurisdiction, without regard to any differences of race, of color, or of nationality; and the equal protection of the laws is a pledge of the protection of equal laws. . . .[3]

When we consider the nature and the theory of our institutions of government, the principles upon which they are supposed to rest, and review the history of their development, we are constrained to conclude that they do not mean to leave room for the play and action of purely personal and arbitrary power. Sovereignty itself is, of course, not subject to law, for it is the author and source of law; but in our system, while sovereign powers are delegated to the agencies of government, sovereignty itself remains with the people, by whom and for whom all government exists and acts. And the law is the definition and limitation of power. It is, indeed, quite true, that there must always be lodged somewhere, and in some person or body, the authority of final decision; and in many cases of mere administration the responsibility is purely political, no appeal lying except to the ultimate tribunal of the public judgment, exercised either in the pressure of opinion or by means of the suffrage. But the fundamental rights to life, liberty, and the pursuit of happiness, considered as individual possessions, are secured by those maxims of constitutional law which are the monuments showing the victorious progress of the race in securing to men the blessings of civilization under the reign of just and equal laws, so that, in the famous language of the Massachusetts Bill of Rights, the government of the commonwealth "may be a government of laws and not of men." For, the very idea that one man may be compelled to hold his life, or the means of living, or any material right essential to the enjoyment of life, at the mere will of another, seems to be intolerable in any country where freedom prevails, as being the essence of slavery itself. . . .

This conclusion, and the reasoning on which it is based, are deductions from the face of the ordinance, as to its necessary tendency and ultimate actual operation. In the present cases we are not obliged to reason from the probable to the actual, and pass upon the validity of the ordinances complained of, as tried merely by the opportunities which their terms afford, of unequal and unjust discrimination in their administration. For the cases present the ordinances in actual operation, and the facts shown establish an administration directed so exclusively against a particular class of persons as to warrant and require the conclusion, that, whatever may have been the intent of the ordinances as adopted, they are applied by the public authorities charged with their administration, and thus representing the State itself, with a mind so unequal and oppressive as to amount to a practical denial by the State of that equal protection of the laws which is secured to the petitioners, as to all other persons, by the broad and benign provisions of the Fourteenth Amendment to the Constitution of the United States. Though the law itself be fair on its face and impartial in appearance, yet, if it is applied and administered by public authority with an evil eye and an unequal hand, so as practically to make unjust and illegal discriminations between persons in similar circumstances, material to their rights, the denial of equal justice is still within the prohibition of the Constitution. . . .

[3] **Question:** Note here that Matthews rejects the claim that the Fourteenth Amendment is applicable only to U.S. citizens. He writes that it protects "any person." Yet only three years after this decision, in the *Chinese Exclusion Case*, the Court upheld the federal government's power to discriminate on the basis of race and nationality without even considering the Fourteenth Amendment. Why do you think the *Chinese Exclusion Case* Court considered the Fourteenth Amendment inapplicable?

The present cases, as shown by the facts disclosed in the record, are within this class. It appears that both petitioners have complied with every requisite, deemed by the law or by the public officers charged with its administration, necessary for the protection of neighboring property from fire, or as a precaution against injury to the public health. No reason whatever, except the will of the supervisors, is assigned why they should not be permitted to carry on, in the accustomed manner, their harmless and useful occupation, on which they depend for a livelihood. And while this consent of the supervisors is withheld from them and from two hundred others who have also petitioned, all of whom happen to be Chinese subjects, eighty others, not Chinese subjects, are permitted to carry on the same business under similar conditions. The fact of this discrimination is admitted. No reason for it is shown, and the conclusion cannot be resisted, that no reason for it exists except hostility to the race and nationality to which the petitioners belong, and which in the eye of the law is not justified. The discrimination is, therefore, illegal, and the public administration which enforces it is a denial of the equal protection of the laws and a violation of the Fourteenth Amendment of the Constitution. . . .[4]

44.2 THE RATIONAL-BASIS TEST APPLIED

Yick Wo v. Hopkins emphatically declared that the Equal Protection Clause protected all people, citizens and noncitizens, from what the Court called "invidious discrimination." 118 U.S. 356, 367 (1886). But the Court's reasoning was subtle and far narrower than its tone might suggest. The Court's problem with San Francisco's ordinance wasn't that the ordinance had the purpose or effect of discriminating against Chinese people—although the Court was clearly bothered by the fact that San Francisco permitted eighty white people to operate laundries while denying permits to two hundred Chinese laundry operators. Rather, the problem was that the ordinance authorized the board of supervisors to distinguish between who could and could not receive a permit for "[n]o reason whatever, except the will of the supervisors." *Id.* at 374.

The Court, in other words, objected that the ordinance had created a classification "without reason"—an "arbitrary line, on one side of which are those who are permitted to pursue their industry by the mere will and consent of the supervisors, and on the other those from whom that consent is withheld, at their mere will and pleasure." *Id.* at 366, 368. The Court strongly suggested that had the ordinance offered some rational guidance for the classification, it would have upheld the ordinance.

Shortly after *Yick Wo*, the Court confirmed as much. In case after case, the Court held that

> [t]he equal protection clause of the Fourteenth Amendment does not take from the state the power to classify in the adoption of

---

[4] **Questions:** The Supreme Court of 1886 was not a racially progressive institution. In context, this decision invalidating a racially discriminatory ordinance is surprising. As Matthews alludes to here, San Francisco's lawyers "admitted" that lots of Chinese laundry operators were being denied permits but argued that the denials were meant to induce them to move from wooden buildings into safer, brick buildings.

Taking the aberrational nature of this decision into account, what, precisely, is Matthew's objection to the ordinance? In light of his objection, what is the minimum that San Francisco would need to do to fix its ordinance?

> police laws, but admits of the exercise of a wide scope of discretion in that regard, and avoids what is done only when it is without any reasonable basis and therefore is purely arbitrary.

Lindsley v. Nat. Carbonic Gas Co., 220 U.S. 61, 78 (1911).

The standard the Court announced in *Lindsley v. Natural Carbonic Gas Co.*, 220 U.S. 61 (1911), has become known as the "rational-basis test." And it is significant that during a period when the Court in *Lochner v. New York*, 198 U.S. 45 (1905), routinely struck down laws under the Due Process Clause, the same Court upheld virtually all legislation under the Equal Protection Clause. *See, e.g.*, *Hadacheck v. Sebastian*, 239 U.S. 394, 413 (1915) (law prohibiting brickyards from operating only in certain sections of a city). As the *Lindsley* Court elaborated in 1911, six years after *Lochner*, "[a] classification having some reasonable basis does not offend against that clause merely because it is not made with mathematical nicety or because in practice it results in some inequality." 220 U.S. at 78. Moreover, the Court didn't even care whether the rational basis for a law was included in the law's legislative history: "[I]f any state of facts reasonably can be conceived that would sustain it, the existence of that state of facts at the time the law was enacted must be assumed." *Id.*

By 1927, the Supreme Court had rejected so many claims under the Equal Protection Clause that Justice Oliver Wendell Holmes could summarily dismiss equal-protection challenges as "the usual last resort of constitutional arguments." *Buck v. Bell*, 274 U.S. 200, 208 (1927). But the Supreme Court's narrow interpretation of the Equal Protection Clause didn't stop people from invoking the clause to challenge state laws. Ironically, the most frequent litigants under the clause have always been white businesspeople as opposed to black freed people. In *Santa Clara County v. Southern Pacific Railroad*, members of the Court even assumed during oral argument that "the provision in the Fourteenth Amendment to the Constitution, which forbids a State to deny to any *person* within its jurisdiction the equal protection of the laws, applies to . . . corporations." 118 U.S. 394, 396 (1886) (emphasis added). After the Supreme Court's reporter took note of this remark in his summary of one of the Court's opinions, future cases cited the summary as if the Court had held that corporations were "persons" who could invoke the Equal Protection Clause. *See, e.g.*, *Minneapolis & St. Louis Ry. v. Beckwith*, 129 U.S. 26, 28 (1889). This precedent remains good law today. *See* Adam Winkler, *We the Corporations* 155 (2018).

When the *Lochner* era ended with *West Coast Hotel Co. v. Parrish*, 300 U.S. 379 (1937), the Supreme Court declared that it would uphold all laws under the Due Process Clause provided that such laws "have a reasonable relation to a proper legislative purpose, and are neither arbitrary nor discriminatory." *Id.* at 398 (quoting *Nebbia v. New York*, 291 U.S. 502, 537–38 (1934)). In this respect, the Court adopted the same rational-basis test that it had used to evaluate equal-protection challenges since *Yick Wo*. As long as the Court could imagine any legitimate reason to justify a state's classification, the Court would uphold the classification under any clause of the Fourteenth Amendment.

For example, when Michigan prohibited women from bartending unless they worked for a family member, the Court conjectured that the legislature might have reasonably concluded that women bartenders give rise to "moral and social problems" absent "the oversight assured through ownership of a bar by a barmaid's husband or father." *Goesaert v. Cleary*, 335 U.S. 464, 466 (1948). When New York prohibited anyone from advertising on the side of delivery trucks—unless the advertiser was employing the truck—the Court conjectured that the legislature may have wanted to reduce roadside distractions and "may well have concluded that those who advertised their own wares on their trucks do not present the same traffic problem in view of the nature or extent of the advertising which they use." *Ry. Express Agency v. New York*, 336 U.S. 106, 110 (1949). And when Louisiana prohibited from working as a river pilot anyone who hadn't received an apprenticeship—something that typically was available only to friends and relatives of existing river pilots—the Court conjectured "that the Louisiana legislature weighed the obvious possibility of [nepotism] against whatever useful function a closely knit pilotage system may serve." *Kotch v. Bd. of River Port Pilot Comm'rs*, 330 U.S. 552, 563 (1947).

44.2.1
Williamson v. Lee Optical of Oklahoma, Inc.

348 U.S. 483 (1955)

At issue in the following case, *Williamson v. Lee Optical of Oklahoma, Inc.*, 348 U.S. 483 (1955), was an Oklahoma law, Section 2 of which made it unlawful for *opticians* to duplicate or fit custom eyeglass lenses without a prescription from an *ophthalmologist* or *optometrist*. Section 3 exempted from this prohibition anyone who sold ready-to-wear eyeglasses. Lee Optical, a company of opticians who fit and replaced custom eyeglasses for years without incident, challenged the law as an arbitrary restriction of its business.

Williamson is a typical illustration of the Supreme Court's approach to the Equal Protection Clause (and the Due Process Clause) in the decades after *West Coast Hotel*.

■ MR. JUSTICE DOUGLAS delivered the opinion of the Court.[5]

This suit was instituted in the District Court to have an Oklahoma law declared unconstitutional and to enjoin state officials from enforcing it for the reason that it allegedly violated various provisions of the Federal Constitution. . . .

The District Court held unconstitutional portions of . . . the Act. First, it held invalid under the Due Process Clause of the Fourteenth Amendment the portions of § 2 which make it unlawful for any person not a licensed optometrist or ophthalmologist to fit lenses to a face or to duplicate or replace into frames lenses or other optical appliances, except upon written prescriptive authority of an Oklahoma licensed ophthalmologist or optometrist.

An ophthalmologist is a duly licensed physician who specializes in the care of the eyes. An optometrist examines eyes for refractive error, recognizes (but does not treat) diseases of the eye, and fills prescriptions for eyeglasses. The optician is an artisan qualified to grind lenses, fill prescriptions, and fit frames.

The effect of § 2 is to forbid the optician from fitting or duplicating lenses without a prescription from an ophthalmologist or optometrist. In practical effect, it means that no optician can fit old glasses into new frames or supply a lens, whether it be a new lens or one to duplicate a lost or broken lens, without a prescription. The District Court conceded that it was in the competence of the police power of a State to regulate the examination of the eyes. But it rebelled at the notion that a State could require a prescription from an optometrist or ophthalmologist "to take old lenses and place them in new frames and then fit the completed spectacles to the *face* of the eyeglass wearer." 120 F. Supp., at 135. It held that such a requirement was not "reasonably and rationally related to the health and welfare of the people." *Id.,* at 136. The court found that through mechanical devices and ordinary skills the optician could take a broken lens or a fragment thereof, measure its power, and reduce it to prescriptive terms. The court held that "Although on this precise issue of duplication, the legislature in the instant regulation was dealing with a matter of public interest, the particular means chosen are neither reasonably necessary nor reasonably related to the end sought to be achieved." *Id.,* at 137. It was, accordingly, the opinion of the court that this provision of the law violated the Due Process Clause by arbitrarily interfering with the optician's right to do business. . . .

The Oklahoma law may exact a needless, wasteful requirement in many cases. But it is for the legislature, not the courts, to balance the advantages and disadvantages of the new requirement. It appears that in many cases the optician can easily supply the new frames or new lenses without reference to the old written prescription. It also appears that many written prescriptions contain no directive data in regard to fitting spectacles to the face. But in some cases the directions contained in the prescription are essential, if the glasses are to be fitted so as to correct the particular defects of vision or alleviate the eye condition. The legislature might have concluded that the frequency of occasions when a prescription is necessary was sufficient to justify this regulation of the fitting of eyeglasses. Likewise, when it is necessary to duplicate a lens, a written prescription may or may not be necessary. But the legislature might have concluded that one was needed often enough to require one in every case. Or the legislature may have concluded that eye examinations were

---

[5] **As You Read, Consider:** The district court in this case invalidated Oklahoma's law on the theory that its prohibition was ridiculous. The court couldn't conceive of a reason for a state to demand a prescription before someone could take old eyeglass lenses, put them in new frames, and fit the frames to a person's face. It also couldn't conceive of why this prohibition would apply only to opticians, like Lee Optical, and not to sellers of ready-to-wear eyeglasses. Does Justice William O. Douglas agree with the lower court that the law has led to an unreasonable result in this case? What does he think the Court should do about it?

so critical, not only for correction of vision but also for detection of latent ailments or diseases, that every change in frames and every duplication of a lens should be accompanied by a prescription from a medical expert. To be sure, the present law does not require a new examination of the eyes every time the frames are changed or the lenses duplicated. For if the old prescription is on file with the optician, he can go ahead and make the new fitting or duplicate the lenses. But the law need not be in every respect logically consistent with its aims to be constitutional. It is enough that there is an evil at hand for correction, and that it might be thought that the particular legislative measure was a rational way to correct it.

The day is gone when this Court uses the Due Process Clause of the Fourteenth Amendment to strike down state laws, regulatory of business and industrial conditions, because they may be unwise, improvident, or out of harmony with a particular school of thought. See *Nebbia* v. *New York,* 291 U. S. 502; *West Coast Hotel Co.* v. *Parrish,* 300 U. S. 379. We emphasize again what Chief Justice Waite said in *Munn* v. *Illinois,* 94 U. S. 113, 134, "For protection against abuses by legislatures the people must resort to the polls, not to the courts."

Secondly, the District Court held that it violated the Equal Protection Clause of the Fourteenth Amendment to subject opticians to this regulatory system and to exempt, as § 3 of the Act does, all sellers of ready-to-wear glasses. The problem of legislative classification is a perennial one, admitting of no doctrinaire definition. Evils in the same field may be of different dimensions and proportions, requiring different remedies. Or so the legislature may think. Or the reform may take one step at a time, addressing itself to the phase of the problem which seems most acute to the legislative mind. The legislature may select one phase of one field and apply a remedy there, neglecting the others. The prohibition of the Equal Protection Clause goes no further than the invidious discrimination. We cannot say that that point has been reached here. For all this record shows, the ready-to-wear branch of this business may not loom large in Oklahoma or may present problems of regulation distinct from the other branch.

NOTE: OTHER ECONOMIC CLASSIFICATIONS UPHELD UNDER THE EQUAL PROTECTION CLAUSE

To this day, the vast majority of economic regulation to reach the Supreme Court has been upheld under the rational-basis test.

For example, in 1972, New Orleans adopted an ordinance that prohibited all pushcart vendors from operating in the French Quarter—except for those that had continuously operated in the French Quarter for at least eight years. A vendor who had recently started selling in the French Quarter challenged this "grandfather clause" as an arbitrary protection of two of her identifiable competitors.

But in *City of New Orleans v. Dukes*, the Court issued a per curiam opinion rejecting the challenge in emphatic language:

> When local economic regulation is challenged solely as violating the Equal Protection Clause, this Court consistently defers to legislative determinations as to the desirability of particular statutory discriminations . . . and require[s] only that the classification challenged be rationally related to a legitimate state interest. States are accorded wide latitude in the regulation of their local economies under their police powers, and rational distinctions

> may be made with substantially less than mathematical exactitude. Legislatures may implement their program step by step in such economic areas, adopting regulations that only partially ameliorate a perceived evil and deferring complete elimination of the evil to future regulations. See, *e.g., Williamson* v. *Lee Optical Co.,* 348 U. S. 483, 488–489 (1955). In short, the judiciary may not sit as a superlegislature to judge the wisdom or desirability of legislative policy determinations . . .; in the local economic sphere, it is only the invidious discrimination, the wholly arbitrary act, which cannot stand consistently with the Fourteenth Amendment.

427 U.S. 297, 303–04 (1976).

Applying this standard, the Court had no difficulty upholding the general ban on pushcart vendors:

> The City Council plainly could . . . [make] the reasoned judgment that street peddlers and hawkers tend to interfere with the charm and beauty of a historic area and disturb tourists and disrupt their enjoyment of that charm and beauty, and that such vendors in the [French Quarter], the heart of the city's tourist industry, might thus have a deleterious effect on the economy of the city.

Id. at 304–05.

And it also had no difficulty upholding the grandfather clause even though it effectively singled out for protection two specific vendors:

> The city could reasonably decide that newer businesses were less likely to have built up substantial reliance interests in continued operation in the [French Quarter] and that the two vendors who qualified under the "grandfather clause" . . . had themselves become part of the distinctive character and charm that distinguishes the [French Quarter].

Id. at 305.

Rational-basis test and expanded deference. The Court extended the deference of the rational-basis test even further in *Minnesota v. Clover Leaf Creamery Co.*, 449 U.S. 456 (1981), in which the Court evaluated a Minnesota law that banned the use of nonreturnable plastic for milk cartons in order to conserve resources and promote recycling. A milk company challenged the law as irrational because the legislature prohibited the use of nonreturnable *plastic* while continuing to permit the use of nonreturnable *paper* for milk cartons. But rather than evaluate "[w]hether *in fact* the Act will promote more environmentally desirable milk packaging," the Court emphasized that "the Equal Protection Clause is satisfied by our conclusion that the Minnesota Legislature *could rationally have decided* that its ban on plastic nonreturnable milk jugs might foster greater use of environmentally desirable alternatives." *Clover Leaf Creamery*, 449 U.S. at 466. The Court saw nothing in the Equal Protection Clause that required Minnesota to "strike at all evils at the same time or in the same way." *Id.* Instead, the legislature could "implement [its] program step by step." *Id.*

Applying this extremely deferential test, the Court has upheld hundreds of economic regulations. The Court has also upheld hundreds of tax classifications, including classifications whose unequal application is obvious. For example, in 1978, California adopted Proposition 13, which changed the method by which the state and local governments would assess property taxes. Instead of assessing property based on its current fair market value, the state would assess property based on the fair market value at the time the property was acquired. This distinction quickly created a two-tier system of property taxes: longtime residents paid very little taxes relative to new residents, whose high taxes reflected the rapidly rising fair market value of California real estate in the 1970s and 1980s. But in *Nordlinger v. Hahn*, the Court upheld this scheme as reflecting a reasonable value judgment: Proposition 13 rationally promoted the state's legitimate interests in "local neighborhood preservation, continuity, and stability." 505 U.S. 1, 12 (1992); *see also, e.g., Fitzgerald v. Racing Ass'n of Cent. Iowa*, 539 U.S. 103, 108 (2003) (law that taxes racetrack slot machines at a higher rate than riverboat slot machines is rationally related to the state's interest in helping the riverboat industry).

44.3 THE EQUAL-PROTECTION PRINCIPLE OF THE FIFTH AMENDMENT

The Equal Protection Clause of the Fourteenth Amendment applies only to states and their local governments: "No State shall . . . deny to any person within its jurisdiction the equal protection of the laws." But the development of the rational-basis test illustrates how the Equal Protection Clause has long been "associated in the Amendment with the due process clause and it is customary to consider them together." *Truax v. Corrigan*, 257 U.S. 312, 332 (1921). Indeed, the two clauses "overlap": Where the Equal Protection Clause requires a government to demonstrate that its differential treatment of people is reasonable and fair, the Due Process Clause requires a government to demonstrate that its deprivation of life, liberty, or property also is both substantively reasonable and procedurally fair. *Id.*

During the era of *Lochner v. New York*, 198 U.S. 45 (1905), when the Supreme Court typically struck down legislation under the Due Process Clause while upholding legislation under the Equal Protection Clause, the Court held that the Due Process Clause prohibited not only *unfair* deprivations but also *discriminatory* deprivations. *E.g., Buchanan v. Warley*, 245 U.S. 60, 76 (1917). The Due Process Clause, the Court wrote,

> tends to secure equality of law in the sense that it makes a required minimum of protection for every one's right of life, liberty and property, which the Congress or the legislature may not withhold. Our whole system of law is predicated on the general, fundamental principle of equality of application of the law.

Truax, 257 U.S. at 332. In other words, the Court considered the Due Process Clause to contain an *equal-protection principle*, one embodied in phrases like "All men are equal before the law," "This is a government of laws and not of men," "No man is above the law," and other "maxims showing the spirit in which legislatures, executives and courts are expected to make, execute and apply the laws." *Id.*

This equal-protection principle proved to be significant when the Court first considered equal-protection challenges to federal legislation. At first, the Court repeatedly declared that "[t]he Fifth Amendment unlike the Fourteenth has no equal protection clause." *Steward Mach. Co. v. Davis*, 301 U.S. 548, 584 (1937); *see also, e.g., Detroit Bank v. United States*, 317 U.S. 329, 337 (1943); *Helvering v. Lerner Stores Corp.*, 314 U.S. 463, 468 (1941). But the Court also recognized "that there might be discrimination of such an injurious character as to bring into operation the due process clause of the Fifth Amendment." *Currin v. Wallace*, 306 U.S. 1, 14 (1939); *see, e.g., Korematsu v. United States*, 323 U.S. 214, 216 (1944); *Hirabayashi v. United States*, 320 U.S. 81, 100 (1943).

The Court finally encountered an example of federal discrimination that amounted to a violation of the Fifth Amendment's Due Process Clause in a case decided the same day as *Brown v. Board of Education*, 347 U.S. 483 (1954). As will be discussed in detail later (section 45.2), the Court in *Brown* held that the Equal Protection Clause of the Fourteenth Amendment prohibited states from maintaining racially segregated public schools. But one of the consolidated challenges in *Brown* involved the segregated schools of the District of Columbia, which were operated by the federal government. In *Bolling v. Sharpe*, the Court explained that while the Fifth Amendment doesn't contain an equal-protection clause, it would be "unthinkable" that the same Constitution that prohibited racial segregation in the states "would impose a lesser duty on the Federal Government":

> The Fifth Amendment, which is applicable in the District of Columbia, does not contain an equal protection clause as does the Fourteenth Amendment which applies only to the states. But the concepts of equal protection and due process, both stemming from our American ideal of fairness, are not mutually exclusive. The "equal protection of the laws" is a more explicit safeguard of prohibited unfairness than "due process of law," and, therefore, we do not imply that the two are always interchangeable phrases. But, as this Court has recognized, discrimination may be so unjustifiable as to be violative of due process. . . .

347 U.S. 497, 499–500 (1954).

The Court has since held that, absent "overriding national interests which justify selective federal legislation that would be unacceptable for an individual State," *Hampton v. Mow Sun Wong*, 426 U.S. 88, 100 (1976), the Due Process Clause of the Fifth Amendment imposes "precisely the same" requirements on the federal government that the Equal Protection Clause imposes on states, *Weinberger v. Wiesenfeld*, 420 U.S. 636, 638 n.2 (1975).

44.4 RATIONAL BASIS WITH BITE

Applying the rational-basis test, the Supreme Court has upheld the vast majority of legislation challenged under the Equal Protection Clause. But as *Yick Wo v. Hopkins* makes clear, the Court has also occasionally struck down classifications on the ground that they are completely "arbitrary" or utterly unrelated to any legitimate state interest. 118 U.S. 356, 367 (1886). These invalidations under the rational-basis test—called *rational basis with bite*—have been few and far between. Gerald Gunther, *The Supreme Court: 1971 Term—Foreword: In Search of Evolving Doctrine on a Changing Court*, 86 Harv. L. Rev. 1, 21 (1972). Yet the contexts in which the Court has applied rational basis with bite have followed a somewhat predictable pattern. In each context, the Court has held (1) that the main interest served by a classification is not a "legitimate" interest and (2) that the law's relationship to other concededly legitimate interests is too attenuated to be "rational."

The interest that the Court has most often considered illegitimate is *hostility* or *animus* toward a disfavored person or group. *Yick Wo* is the archetypical example, as the Court there objected not only that the law vested in San Francisco's board of supervisors the discretion to make "arbitrary" decisions but also that the only explanation the Court could fathom for the supervisors' exercise of discretion was "hostility to the race and nationality to which the petitioners belong, and which in the eye of the law is not justified." 118 U.S. at 374. Such hostility, in other words, was not a legitimate interest. But the illegitimacy of this interest extended beyond discrimination on the basis of nationality.

The next case in which the Court struck down an economic regulation under the Equal Protection Clause involved what the Court regarded as hostility to out-of-state business. In 1916, the Virginia legislature amended its income tax law to grant an exemption to Virginia corporations that earned all of their income outside the state. But the legislature failed to exempt the foreign income from Virginia corporations that happened to earn at least a dollar of income in Virginia. The F.S. Royster Guano Company, which did business in Virginia and abroad, challenged Virginia's refusal to grant it the exemption for its foreign income that it would have received had it done no business in Virginia. Applying the rational-basis test, the Supreme Court agreed that "no ground is suggested, nor can we conceive of any," for why Virginia would tax the foreign income of companies that did some business in the state when Virginia exempted the foreign income of companies that did no business in the state. *F.S. Royster Guano Co. v. Virginia*, 253 U.S. 412, 415 (1920). Assuming that the purpose of the tax exemption was to reflect Virginia's recognition that it was unfair for Virginia to tax income acquired elsewhere, the Court held that for Virginia to tax F.S. Royster's foreign income "has the effect of discriminating against them for that which ought to operate if at all in their favor. It is obvious that the ground of difference upon which the discrimination is rested has no fair or substantial relation to the proper object sought to be accomplished by legislation." *Id.* at 416. The law was therefore "arbitrary in effect; and none the less because it is probable that the unequal operation of the taxing system was due to inadvertence rather than design." *Id.*

In later cases, the Court elaborated on *F.S. Royster Guano* to hold that while the rational-basis test authorizes a state to impose any regulation that is rationally related to a legitimate interest, a state has no legitimate interest in "parochial discrimination": favoring domestic businesses within the state "no matter what the cost to foreign corporations also seeking to do business there." *Metro. Life Ins. Co. v. Ward*, 470 U.S. 869, 878 (1985).

In the cases in which the Court has found that the main purpose of a classification is to serve an illegitimate interest, the Court has tended to be more skeptical than usual of claims that the classification is rationally related to other interests. Ordinarily, the Court has long emphasized that a government doesn't bear the burden of proving that its law has a rational relationship with a legitimate state interest: "[I]f any state of facts reasonably can be conceived that would sustain it, the existence of that state of facts at the time the law was enacted must be assumed." *Lindsley v. Nat. Carbonic Gas Co.*, 220 U.S. 61, 78 (1911). But the Court has often rejected alleged connections between a classification and any legitimate interests as resting "wholly upon prophecy" when the classification appears targeted at a disfavored group. *Thomas v. Kan. City S. Ry. Co.*, 261 U.S. 481, 485 (1923). For example, in early twentieth-century cases, the Court invalidated assessments levied on property owned by railroads when (1) similar assessments weren't levied on property owned by individuals or similar corporations and (2) the Court couldn't imagine any reason for the differential treatment other than that the legislature was hostile toward railroads. *See Rd. Improvement Dist. No. 1 v. Mo. Pac. R.R. Co.*, 274 U.S. 188, 194 (1927); *Kan. City S. Ry. Co. v. Rd. Improvement Dist. No. 6*, 256 U.S. 658, 661 (1921). And the Court has also expressed disbelief about the rationality of classifications that are so full of exceptions that any alleged connection between the law and a legitimate interest seems like a pretextual cover for animus toward the targeted group. *See, e.g., Hartford Steam Boiler Inspection & Ins. Co. v. Harrison*, 301 U.S. 459, 462–63 (1937).

The Court attempted to repudiate this line of cases in the 1970s and 1980s, reiterating that the rational-basis test asks not whether a classification is *actually* related to a legitimate interest, but rather whether a state "*could rationally have decided*" that there was a relationship. *Minnesota v. Clover Leaf Creamery Co.*, 449 U.S. 456, 466 (1981). But in contexts where the Court suspects that a person or group has been the target of governmental hostility, the Court continues to carefully scrutinize the relationship between the classification and interests other than hostility toward a targeted group. For example, in *Allegheny Pittsburgh Coal Co. v. Webster County Commission*, the Court struck down a tax assessment scheme that formally required the equal treatment of all property owners but that in practice resulted in local tax assessors intentionally favoring and disfavoring particular properties. 488 U.S. 336, 343 (1989). And in *Village of Willowbrook v. Olech*, the Court held that an individual targeted by the ill will of a local government could bring a "class of one" claim by alleging that she had been "intentionally treated differently from others similarly situated and that there is no rational basis for the difference in treatment." 528 U.S. 562, 564 (2000).

44.4.1

U.S. Department of Agriculture v. Moreno

413 U.S. 528 (1973)

However, in *U.S. Department of Agriculture v. Moreno*, 413 U.S. 528 (1973), the Court applied its rational-basis-with-bite analysis to inaugurate a successful line of challenges with lasting ramifications.

After *Griswold v. Connecticut*, 381 U.S. 479 (1965), and *Loving v. Virginia*, 388 U.S. 1 (1967), when the Supreme Court once again invoked the Due Process Clause to strike down legislation, the Court distinguished between *economic* regulations and *social welfare* regulations. For economic regulations for which no fundamental right was at stake, the Court evaluated laws under the Due Process Clause by applying the rational-basis test. But for social welfare regulations for which a fundamental right was at stake, the Court steadily applied a stricter standard of scrutiny. *See, e.g., Roe v. Wade*, 410 U.S. 113, 155 (1973).

As will be discussed later (section 48.1), the Equal Protection Clause followed the same pattern: where a classification infringed upon a "fundamental right," the Court applied a stricter standard of scrutiny than the rational-basis test. *See, e.g., Eisenstadt v. Baird*, 405 U.S. 438, 447 n.7 (1972) (invalidating a classification that allowed the distribution of contraception to married people but not unmarried people); *Stanley v. Illinois*, 405 U.S. 645, 657–58 (1972) (invalidating a classification that allowed unmarried mothers but not unmarried fathers to contest their unfitness to take custody of a child). But where no fundamental right was implicated, the Court continued to apply the rational-basis test to social welfare legislation. *See, e.g., Dandridge v. Williams*, 397 U.S. 471, 485 (1970).

Nevertheless, challenges to social welfare legislation have become the main area in which the Supreme Court continues to apply rational basis with bite, evaluating for itself whether an alleged interest is legitimate and whether the classification's relationship to legitimate interests is rational. One such challenge, *Moreno*, involved the Food Stamp Act of 1964, Pub. L. 88–525, 84 Stat. 2048.

The Food Stamp Act formally established a program to distribute food stamps to households in need. But the act excluded from participation any household containing a person who was unrelated to any other member of the household. Jacinta Moreno, a woman who lived with an unrelated caregiver and her three children, challenged the law's constitutionality. She claimed that its classification—dividing all households into those in which everyone was related and those in which that wasn't true—was not rationally related to any legitimate interest.

As discussed earlier, in the context of economic regulations, the Court from an early date held that states have no legitimate interest in (1) parochial discrimination, *see F.S. Royster Guano Co.*, 253 U.S. at 415, or (2) hostility or animus toward a disfavored group, *see Thomas*, 261 U.S. at 483–84. In *Moreno*, the Court reached a similar conclusion to strike down part of the Food Stamp Act.

■ MR. JUSTICE BRENNAN delivered the opinion of the Court.[6]

This case requires us to consider the constitutionality of § 3(e) of the Food Stamp Act of 1964, which, with certain exceptions, excludes from participation in the food stamp program any household containing an individual who is unrelated to any other member of the household. . . .

I

The federal food stamp program was established in 1964 in an effort to alleviate hunger and malnutrition among the more needy segments of our society. Eligibility for participation in the program is determined on a household rather than an individual basis. An eligible household purchases sufficient food stamps to provide that household with a nutritionally adequate diet. The household pays for the stamps at a reduced rate based upon its size and cumulative income. The food stamps are then used to purchase food at retail stores, and the Government redeems the stamps at

---

6 **As You Read, Consider:** In cases applying the rational-basis test, the Supreme Court has held that a legislature may enact any classification that is rationally related to any *conceivable* legitimate interest. *Williamson v. Lee Optical, Inc.*, 348 U.S. 483, 487 (1955). The Court has upheld classifications even when they are overbroad or underinclusive, *Ry. Express Agency v. New York*, 336 U.S. 106, 110 (1949); even when the legislature's rational beliefs are factually wrong, *Minnesota v. Clover Leaf Creamery Co.*, 449 U.S. 456, 466 (1981); and even when the Court thinks that the law serves a legitimate interest that is different from the legislature's actual motivation, *City of New Orleans v. Dukes*, 427 U.S. 297, 305 (1976). The Court has recognized that this test can lead to abusive results. But it has insisted that "[f]or protection against abuses by legislatures, the people must resort to the polls, not to the courts." *Williamson*, 348 U.S. at 488.

In light of this very, very deferential test, why does Justice William Brennan invalidate the federal classification under the rational-basis test?

Note that Brennan is interpreting the Due Process Clause of the Fifth Amendment, not the Equal Protection Clause of the Fourteenth Amendment. For more on why the Court interprets the two clauses identically in cases alleging discrimination by the federal government, see the discussion in section 44.3.

face value, thereby paying the difference between the actual cost of the food and the amount paid by the household for the stamps. See 7 U. S. C. §§ 2013(a), 2016, 2025(a).

As initially enacted, § 3(e) defined a "household" as "a group of *related or non-related* individuals, who are not residents of an institution or boarding house, but are living as one economic unit sharing common cooking facilities and for whom food is customarily purchased in common." In January 1971, however, Congress redefined the term "household" so as to include only groups of *related* individuals. Pursuant to this amendment, the Secretary of Agriculture promulgated regulations rendering ineligible for participation in the program any "household" whose members are not "all related to each other."

Appellees in this case consist of several groups of individuals who allege that, although they satisfy the income eligibility requirements for federal food assistance, they have nevertheless been excluded from the program solely because the persons in each group are not "all related to each other." . . . In essence, appellees contend, and the District Court held, that the "unrelated person" provision of § 3(e) creates an irrational classification in violation of the equal protection component of the Due Process Clause of the Fifth Amendment. We agree.

II

Under traditional equal protection analysis, a legislative classification must be sustained if the classification itself is rationally related to a legitimate governmental interest. See *Dandridge* v. *Williams,* 397 U. S. 471, 485 (1970); *McGowan* v. *Maryland,* 366 U. S. 420, 426 (1961). The purposes of the Food Stamp Act were expressly set forth in the congressional "declaration of policy":

> "It is hereby declared to be the policy of Congress . . . to safeguard the health and well-being of the Nation's population and raise levels of nutrition among low-income households. The Congress hereby finds that the limited food purchasing power of low-income households contributes to hunger and malnutrition among members of such households. The Congress further finds that increased utilization of food in establishing and maintaining adequate national levels of nutrition will promote the distribution in a beneficial manner of our agricultural abundances and will strengthen our agricultural economy, as well as result in more orderly marketing and distribution of food. To alleviate such hunger and malnutrition, a food stamp program is herein authorized which will permit low-income households to purchase a nutritionally adequate diet through normal channels of trade." 7 U. S. C. § 2011.

The challenged statutory classification (households of related persons versus households containing one or more unrelated persons) is clearly irrelevant to the stated purposes of the Act. As the District Court recognized, "[t]he relationships among persons constituting one economic unit and sharing cooking facilities have nothing to do with their abilities to stimulate the agricultural economy by purchasing farm surpluses, or with their personal nutritional requirements." 345 F. Supp., at 313.

Thus, if it is to be sustained, the challenged classification must rationally further some legitimate governmental interest other than those specifically stated in the congressional "declaration of policy." Regrettably, there is little legislative history to illuminate the purposes of the 1971 amendment of § 3(e). The legislative history that does exist, however, indicates that that amendment was intended to prevent so-called "hippies" and "hippie communes" from participating in the food stamp program. See H. R. Conf. Rep. No. 91–1793, p. 8; 116 Cong. Rec. 44439 (1970) (Sen. Holland). The challenged classification clearly cannot be sustained by reference to this congressional purpose. For if the constitutional conception of "equal protection of the laws" means anything, it must at the very least mean that a bare congressional desire to harm a politically unpopular group cannot constitute a *legitimate* governmental interest. . . .

Although apparently conceding this point, the Government maintains that the challenged classification should nevertheless be upheld as rationally related to the clearly legitimate governmental interest in minimizing fraud in the administration of the food stamp program. In essence, the Government contends that, in adopting the 1971 amendment, Congress might rationally have thought (1) that households with one or more unrelated members are more likely than "fully related" households to contain individuals who abuse the program by fraudulently failing to report sources of income or by voluntarily remaining poor; and (2) that such households are "relatively unstable," thereby increasing the difficulty of detecting such abuses. But even if we were to accept as rational the Government's wholly unsubstantiated assumptions concerning the differences between "related" and "unrelated" households, we still could not agree with the Government's conclusion that the denial of essential federal food assistance to *all* otherwise eligible households containing unrelated members constitutes a rational effort to deal with these concerns.

At the outset, it is important to note that the Food Stamp Act itself contains provisions, wholly independent of § 3(e), aimed specifically at the problems of fraud and of the voluntarily poor. For example, with certain exceptions, § 5(c) of the Act renders ineligible for assistance any household containing "an able-bodied adult person between the ages of eighteen and sixty-five" who fails to register for, and accept, offered employment. . . .

Moreover, in practical effect, the challenged classification simply does not operate so as rationally to further the prevention of fraud. As previously noted, § 3(e) defines an eligible "household" as "a group of related individuals . . . [1] living as one economic unit [2] sharing common cooking facilities [and 3] for whom food is customarily purchased in common." Thus, two *unrelated* persons living together and meeting all three of these conditions would constitute a single household ineligible for assistance. If financially feasible, however, these same two individuals can legally avoid the "unrelated person" exclusion simply by altering their living arrangements so as to eliminate any one of the three conditions. By so doing, they effectively create two separate "households," both of which are eligible for assistance. Indeed, as the California Director of Social Welfare has explained:

> "The 'related household' limitations will eliminate many households from eligibility in the Food Stamp Program. It is my understanding that the Congressional intent of the new regulations are specifically aimed at the 'hippies' and 'hippie communes.' Most people in this category can and will alter their living arrangements in order to remain eligible for food stamps. However, the AFDC mothers who try to raise their standard of living by sharing housing will be affected. They will not be able to utilize the altered living patterns in order to continue to be eligible without giving up their advantage of shared housing costs."

Thus, in practical operation, the 1971 amendment excludes from participation in the food stamp program, *not* those persons who are "likely to abuse the program" but, rather, *only* those persons who are so desperately in need of aid that they cannot even afford to alter their living arrangements so as to retain their eligibility. Traditional equal protection analysis does not require that every classification be drawn with precise " 'mathematical nicety.' " *Dandridge* v. *Williams,* 397 U. S., at 485. But the classification here in issue is not only "imprecise," it is wholly without any rational basis. . . .

■ MR. JUSTICE REHNQUIST, with whom THE CHIEF JUSTICE concurs, dissenting. . . .

[I] am unable to agree with the Court's disposition of this case. Here appellees challenged a provision in the Federal Food Stamp Act, 7 U. S. C. § 2011 *et seq.,* which limited food stamps to related people living in one "household." The result of this provision is that unrelated persons who live under the same roof and pool their resources may not obtain food stamps even though otherwise eligible.

The Court's opinion would make a very persuasive congressional committee report arguing against the adoption of the limitation in question. Undoubtedly, Congress attacked the problem with a rather blunt instrument and, just as undoubtedly, persuasive arguments may be made that what we conceive to be its purpose will not be significantly advanced by the enactment of the limitation. But questions such as this are for Congress, rather than for this Court; our role is limited to the determination of whether there is any rational basis on which Congress could decide that public funds made available under the food stamp program should not go to a household containing an individual who is unrelated to any other member of the household.[7]

I do not believe that asserted congressional concern with the fraudulent use of food stamps is, when interpreted in the light most favorable to sustaining the limitation, quite as irrational as the Court seems to believe. A basic unit which Congress has chosen for determination of availability for food stamps is the "household," a determination which is not criticized by the Court. By the limitation here challenged, it has singled out households which contain unrelated persons and made such households ineligible. I do not think it is unreasonable for Congress to conclude that the basic unit which it was willing to support with federal funding through food stamps is some variation on the family as we know it—a household consisting of related individuals. This unit provides a guarantee which is not provided by households containing unrelated individuals that the household exists for some purpose other than to collect federal food stamps.

Admittedly, as the Court points out, the limitation will make ineligible many households which have not been formed for the purpose of collecting federal food stamps, and will at the same time not wholly deny food stamps to those households which may have been formed in large part to take advantage of the program. But, as the Court concedes, "[t]raditional equal protection analysis does not require that every classification be drawn with precise 'mathematical nicety.' " . . .

The limitation which Congress enacted could, in the judgment of reasonable men, conceivably deny food stamps to members of households which have been formed solely for the purpose of taking advantage of the food stamp program. Since the food stamp program is not intended to be a subsidy for every individual who desires low-cost food, this was a permissible congressional decision quite consistent

---

7 **Questions:** As Justice William Rehnquist correctly observes, the majority opinion appears to depart from *Williamson* and other traditional applications of the rational-basis test. Rehnquist's opinion is more aligned with the Court's typical approach to economic regulations after *Lochner v. New York*: it is up to democratic legislatures and the political process to allocate scarce resources, and all classifications will inevitably result in "unfortunate and perhaps unintended consequences."

Yet the majority opinion was clearly bothered by what it regarded as a "bare congressional desire to harm a politically unpopular group." The majority considers this animus to be an illegitimate purpose. What role does this finding of animus play in how the majority proceeds to conduct the rational-basis test? Does it signal that the allegedly legitimate interests served by the classification should be evaluated skeptically? Or does it signal that a court should reject the means-ends analysis and balance the benefits of the classification against the harms imposed by the classification?

with the underlying policy of the Act. The fact that the limitation will have unfortunate and perhaps unintended consequences beyond this does not make it unconstitutional.

44.4.2

Romer v. Evans

517 U.S. 620 (1996)

The *Moreno* majority emphasized that the rational-basis test may be a deferential test, but it is, in fact, a test. To satisfy the test, (1) a law must serve a *legitimate* interest, and (2) it must be *rationally related* to that interest. The *Moreno* Court found that the Food Stamp Act was rationally related to Congress's interest in preventing hippies from participating in the food stamp program. But the Court held that this interest failed the first prong of the rational-basis test because "a bare congressional desire to harm a politically unpopular group" isn't a *legitimate* interest. 413 U.S. at 534. By contrast, the Court considered the "prevention of fraud" to be a legitimate interest. *Id.* at 537. But it held that this interest failed the second prong of the rational-basis test because it wasn't *rationally related* to the classification.

In fact, the Court's treatment of the second prong—its evaluation of the relationship between the food stamp classification and the government's interest in preventing fraud—was far more skeptical than normal. Nearly every other rational-basis case has applied an analysis similar to that of Justice William Rehnquist's dissent, upholding even admittedly overbroad classifications. For example, in *Massachusetts Board of Retirement v. Murgia*, 427 U.S. 307 (1976), the Court upheld a state law that required police officers to retire at age fifty. Employing "a relatively relaxed standard reflecting the Court's awareness that the drawing of lines that create distinctions is peculiarly a legislative task and an unavoidable one," the Court noted that "physical ability generally declines with age" and therefore Massachusetts's mandatory retirement age was a rational means of "assuring physical preparedness of its uniformed police." *Murgia*, 427 U.S. at 314. The *Murgia* Court recognized that many people over the age of fifty are physically fit to serve as police officers, but the Court didn't think that the law's overbreadth rendered the classification unconstitutional. *Id.* at 316.

Although the Court has never formally declared that its rational-basis test is really two tests—one with bite, like *Moreno*; and one without, like *Murgia*—in practice, it has used a signal to distinguish between the two tests. In particular, the Court often applies a *Moreno*-like test after announcing that the *real* interest served by the classification is illegitimate. For example, in *City of Cleburne v. Cleburne Living Center*, 473 U.S. 432 (1985), the Court considered a zoning ordinance that prohibited the construction of a group home for people with intellectual disabilities. The same ordinance permitted the construction of an identical building for people without disabilities. As in *Moreno*, the Court found that the ordinance was motivated by an "irrational prejudice" against people with disabilities. *Cleburne*, 473 U.S. at 451. After noting that "mere negative attitudes, or fear, . . . are not permissible bases" for a classification, it proceeded to skeptically evaluate other legitimate interests allegedly served by the ordinance. *Id.* at 448, 450. The city argued that it had an interest in regulating the size of buildings and in protecting residents from neighbors who might engage in irresponsible conduct. But the Court found these interests "difficult to believe" in light of the ordinance's permission of identical boarding and fraternity houses. *Id.* at 449. It therefore invalidated the ordinance.

The Supreme Court has since upheld the vast majority of classifications under the rational-basis test; but in *Romer v. Evans*, 517 U.S. 620 (1996), a case litigating an antidiscrimination ordinance protecting sexual orientation, the Court bucked that trend.

In 1977, Aspen, Colorado, and Dade County, Florida, became two of the first places in the country to legally prohibit discrimination on the basis of sexual orientation. Reflecting their relatively large lesbian, gay, and bisexual (LGB) populations, the local governments prohibited employers, public accommodations, and landlords from discriminating against anyone on the basis of sexual orientation. William N. Eskridge Jr., *Dishonorable Passions* 279 (2008). These ordinances generated enormous opposition among religious and cultural traditionalists. In Dade County, the singer Anita Bryant led an infamous campaign called "Save Our Children," which passed a local referendum to revoke the county's antidiscrimination ordinance. Anti-gay rights campaigns around the country were similarly successful, achieving a 79 percent success rate through the 1970s and 1980s. *Id.*

By the 1990s, however, as more openly LGB voters concentrated in urban areas, Colorado cities including Denver and Boulder joined Aspen in passing antidiscrimination ordinances and resisting attempts to repeal them. Opponents of these ordinances therefore turned to state referenda, where they could appeal to rural and suburban voters. Eskridge, *supra*, at 279–80.

James Dobson, the founder of the nationally influential Focus on the Family, sponsored one such referendum in his home state of Colorado. Forming a new organization called Colorado for Family Values, Dobson placed on the 1992 fall ballot an amendment to the Colorado Constitution—Amendment 2—which read:

> No Protected Status Based on Homosexual, Lesbian or Bisexual Orientation. Neither the State of Colorado, through any of its branches or departments, nor any of its agencies, political subdivisions, municipalities or school districts, shall enact, adopt or enforce any statute, regulation, ordinance or policy whereby homosexual, lesbian or bisexual orientation, conduct, practices or relationships shall constitute or otherwise be the basis of or entitle any person or class of persons to have or claim

any minority status, quota preferences, protected status or claim of discrimination.

During the fall campaign, Colorado for Family Values accused the state's gay men of being AIDS-infected "monsters" who "try and convince children—maybe even your own—that they should consider homosexuality!" *Id.* at 280. Dobson's organization also accused LGB activists of seeking "special rights" that so-called normal people lacked. *Id.* That fall, Colorado voters approved Amendment 2 by a 53.4 to 46.6 percent margin, with suburbs and rural areas outvoting the more LGB-friendly cities. *Id.*

Although Governor Roy Romer opposed the amendment, civil rights lawyers representing Colorado cities and LGB state workers sued Romer in his official capacity. They alleged that the amendment violated the Equal Protection Clause not only because it prohibited cities from adopting antidiscrimination ordinances but also because it effectively permitted the state to engage in discrimination by prohibiting people from legally challenging their exclusion under any "policy whereby homosexual . . . orientation . . . [shall] be the basis of . . . discrimination." *Romer*, 517 U.S. at 624.

The Court in *Romer* notably repeated the pattern from *Moreno* and *Cleburne*, opting for a rational-basis-with-bite analysis.

■ JUSTICE KENNEDY delivered the opinion of the Court. . . .[8]

I

The enactment challenged in this case is an amendment to the Constitution of the State of Colorado, adopted in a 1992 statewide referendum. The parties and the state courts refer to it as "Amendment 2," its designation when submitted to the voters. The impetus for the amendment and the contentious campaign that preceded its adoption came in large part from ordinances that had been passed in various Colorado municipalities. For example, the cities of Aspen and Boulder and the city and County of Denver each had enacted ordinances which banned discrimination in many transactions and activities, including housing, employment, education, public accommodations, and health and welfare services. What gave rise to the statewide controversy was the protection the ordinances afforded to persons discriminated against by reason of their sexual orientation. Amendment 2 repeals these ordinances to the extent they prohibit discrimination on the basis of "homosexual, lesbian or bisexual orientation, conduct, practices or relationships." Colo. Const., Art. II, § 30b.

Yet Amendment 2, in explicit terms, does more than repeal or rescind these provisions. It prohibits all legislative, executive or judicial action at any level of state or local government designed to protect the named class, a class we shall refer to as homosexual persons or gays and lesbians. . . .

---

[8] **As You Read, Consider:** As in *U.S. Department of Agriculture v. Moreno* and *City of Cleburne v. Cleburne Living Center*, Justice Anthony Kennedy finds that Colorado's Amendment 2 reflects illegitimate animus toward an unpopular group and then proceeds to apply a skeptical version of the rational-basis test. How does he know what role animus played among the thousands of people who supported the amendment? And how, precisely, would you describe the test he employs? In other words, is it a skeptical means-ends test or a proportionality test?

II

The State's principal argument in defense of Amendment 2 is that it puts gays and lesbians in the same position as all other persons. So, the State says, the measure does no more than deny homosexuals special rights. This reading of the amendment's language is implausible. We rely not upon our own interpretation of the amendment but upon the authoritative construction of Colorado's Supreme Court . . .: "The immediate objective of Amendment 2 is, at a minimum, to repeal existing statutes, regulations, ordinances, and policies of state and local entities that barred discrimination based on sexual orientation. . . . The 'ultimate effect' of Amendment 2 is to prohibit any governmental entity from adopting similar, or more protective . . . policies in the future unless the state constitution is first amended to permit such measures."

Sweeping and comprehensive is the change in legal status effected by this law. . . . Homosexuals, by state decree, are put in a solitary class with respect to transactions and relations in both the private and governmental spheres. The amendment withdraws from homosexuals, but no others, specific legal protection from the injuries caused by discrimination, and it forbids reinstatement of these laws and policies.

The change Amendment 2 works in the legal status of gays and lesbians in the private sphere is far reaching, both on its own terms and when considered in light of the structure and operation of modern antidiscrimination laws. That structure is well illustrated by contemporary statutes and ordinances prohibiting discrimination by providers of public accommodations. "At common law, innkeepers, smiths, and others who 'made profession of a public employment,' were prohibited from refusing, without good reason, to serve a customer." *Hurley* v. *Irish-American Gay, Lesbian and Bisexual Group of Boston, Inc.,* 515 U. S. 557, 571 (1995). The duty was a general one and did not specify protection for particular groups. The common-law rules, however, proved insufficient in many instances, and it was settled early that the Fourteenth Amendment did not give Congress a general power to prohibit discrimination in public accommodations, *Civil Rights Cases,* 109 U. S. 3, 25 (1883). In consequence, most States have chosen to counter discrimination by enacting detailed statutory schemes.

Colorado's state and municipal laws typify this emerging tradition of statutory protection and follow a consistent pattern. The laws first enumerate the persons or entities subject to a duty not to discriminate. The list goes well beyond the entities covered by the common law. The Boulder ordinance, for example, has a comprehensive definition of entities deemed places of "public accommodation." They include "any place of business engaged in any sales to the general public and any place that offers services, facilities, privileges, or advantages to the general public or that receives financial support through solicitation of the general public or through governmental subsidy of any kind." Boulder Rev. Code § 12–1–1(j) (1987). . . .

These statutes and ordinances also depart from the common law by enumerating the groups or persons within their ambit of protection. Enumeration is the essential device used to make the duty not to discriminate concrete and to provide guidance for those who must comply. In following this approach, Colorado's state and local governments have . . . set forth an extensive catalog of traits which cannot be the basis for discrimination, including age, military status, marital status, pregnancy, parenthood, custody of a minor child, political affiliation, physical or mental disability of an individual or of his or her associates—and, in recent times, sexual orientation.

Amendment 2 bars homosexuals from securing protection against the injuries that these public-accommodations laws address. That in itself is a severe consequence, but there is more. Amendment 2, in addition, nullifies specific legal protections for this targeted class in all transactions in housing, sale of real estate, insurance, health and welfare services, private education, and employment.

Not confined to the private sphere, Amendment 2 also operates to repeal and forbid all laws or policies providing specific protection for gays or lesbians from discrimination by every level of Colorado government. The State Supreme Court cited two examples of protections in the governmental sphere that are now rescinded and may not be reintroduced. The first is Colorado Executive Order D0035 (1990), which forbids employment discrimination against " 'all state employees, classified and exempt' on the basis of sexual orientation." 854 P. 2d, at 1284. Also repealed, and now forbidden, are "various provisions prohibiting discrimination based on sexual orientation at state colleges." *Id.*, at 1284. . . .

Amendment 2's reach may not be limited to specific laws passed for the benefit of gays and lesbians. It is a fair, if not necessary, inference from the broad language of the amendment that it deprives gays and lesbians even of the protection of general laws and policies that prohibit arbitrary discrimination in governmental and private settings. At some point in the systematic administration of these laws, an official must determine whether homosexuality is an arbitrary and, thus, forbidden basis for decision. Yet a decision to that effect would itself amount to a policy prohibiting discrimination on the basis of homosexuality, and so would appear to be no more valid under Amendment 2 than the specific prohibitions against discrimination the state court held invalid.

If this consequence follows from Amendment 2, as its broad language suggests, it would compound the constitutional difficulties the law creates. . . . [T]he amendment imposes a special disability upon [certain] persons alone. Homosexuals are forbidden the safeguards that others enjoy or may seek without constraint. They can obtain specific protection against discrimination only by enlisting the citizenry of Colorado to amend the State Constitution. . . . We find nothing special in the protections Amendment 2 withholds. These are protections taken for granted by most people either because they already have them or do not need them; these are protections against exclusion from an almost limitless number of transactions and endeavors that constitute ordinary civic life in a free society.

III

The Fourteenth Amendment's promise that no person shall be denied the equal protection of the laws must coexist with the practical necessity that most legislation classifies for one purpose or another, with resulting disadvantage to various groups or persons. *F. S. Royster Guano Co.* v. *Virginia,* 253 U. S. 412 (1920). We have attempted to reconcile the principle with the reality by stating that, if a law neither burdens a fundamental right nor targets a suspect class, we will uphold the legislative classification so long as it bears a rational relation to some legitimate end. See, *e. g., Heller* v. *Doe,* 509 U. S. 312, 319–320 (1993).

Amendment 2 fails, indeed defies, even this conventional inquiry. First, the amendment has the peculiar property of imposing a broad and undifferentiated disability on a single named group, an exceptional and, as we shall explain, invalid form of legislation. Second, its sheer breadth is so discontinuous with the reasons offered for it that the amendment seems inexplicable by anything but animus toward the class it affects; it lacks a rational relationship to legitimate state interests.

Taking the first point, even in the ordinary equal protection case calling for the most deferential of standards, we insist on knowing the relation between the classification adopted and the object to be attained. The search for the link between classification and objective gives substance to the Equal Protection Clause; it provides guidance and discipline for the legislature, which is entitled to know what sorts of laws it can pass; and it marks the limits of our own authority. In the ordinary case, a law will be sustained if it can be said to advance a legitimate government interest, even if the law seems unwise or works to the disadvantage of a particular group, or if the rationale for it seems tenuous. See *New Orleans* v. *Dukes,* 427 U. S. 297 (1976) (tourism benefits justified classification favoring pushcart vendors of certain longevity); *Williamson* v. *Lee Optical of Okla., Inc.,* 348 U. S. 483 (1955) (assumed health concerns justified law favoring optometrists over opticians); *Railway Express Agency, Inc.* v. *New York,* 336 U. S. 106 (1949) (potential traffic hazards justified exemption of vehicles advertising the owner's products from general advertising ban); *Kotch* v. *Board of River Port Pilot Comm'rs for Port of New Orleans,* 330 U. S. 552 (1947) (licensing scheme that disfavored persons unrelated to current river boat pilots justified by possible efficiency and safety benefits of a closely knit pilotage system). The laws challenged in the cases just cited were narrow enough in scope and grounded in a sufficient factual context for us to ascertain some relation between the classification and the purpose it served. By requiring that the classification bear a rational relationship to an independent and legitimate legislative end, we ensure that classifications are not drawn for the purpose of disadvantaging the group burdened by the law. See *Railroad Retirement Bd.* v. *Fritz,* 449 U. S. 166, 181 (1980) (Stevens, J., concurring) ("If the adverse impact on the disfavored class is an apparent aim of the legislature, its impartiality would be suspect").

Amendment 2 confounds this normal process of judicial review. It is at once too narrow and too broad. It identifies persons by a single trait and then denies them protection across the board. The resulting disqualification of a class of persons from the right to seek specific protection from the law is unprecedented in our jurisprudence. The absence of precedent for Amendment 2 is itself instructive; "[d]iscriminations of an unusual character especially suggest careful consideration to determine whether they are obnoxious to the constitutional provision." *Louisville Gas & Elec. Co.* v. *Coleman,* 277 U. S. 32, 37–38 (1928).

It is not within our constitutional tradition to enact laws of this sort. Central both to the idea of the rule of law and to our own Constitution's guarantee of equal protection is the principle that government and each of its parts remain open on impartial terms to all who seek its assistance. . . . Respect for this principle explains why laws singling out a certain class of citizens for disfavored legal status or general hardships are rare. A law declaring that in general it shall be more difficult for one group of citizens than for all others to seek aid from the government is itself a denial of equal protection of the laws in the most literal sense. "The guaranty of 'equal protection of the laws is a pledge of the protect-ion of equal laws.' " *Skinner* v. *Oklahoma ex rel. Williamson,* 316 U. S. 535, 541 (1942) (quoting *Yick Wo* v. *Hopkins,* 118 U. S. 356, 369 (1886)). . . .

A second and related point is that laws of the kind now before us raise the inevitable inference that the disadvantage imposed is born of animosity toward the class of persons affected. "[I]f the constitutional conception of 'equal protection of the laws' means anything, it must at the very least mean that a bare . . . desire to harm a politically unpopular group cannot constitute a *legitimate* governmental interest." *Department of Agriculture* v. *Moreno,* 413 U. S. 528, 534 (1973). Even laws enacted for broad and ambitious purposes often can be explained by reference to legitimate public policies which justify the incidental disadvantages they impose on certain persons. Amendment 2, however, in making a general announcement that gays and lesbians shall not have any particular protections from the law, inflicts on them immediate, continuing, and real injuries that outrun and belie any legitimate justifications that may be claimed for it. We conclude that, in addition to the far-reaching deficiencies of Amendment 2 that we have noted, the principles it offends, in another sense, are conventional and venerable; a law must bear a rational relationship to a legitimate governmental purpose, and Amendment 2 does not.[9]

The primary rationale the State offers for Amendment 2 is respect for other citizens' freedom of association, and in particular the liberties of landlords or employers who have personal or religious objections to homosexuality. Colorado also cites its interest in conserving resources to fight discrimination against other groups. The breadth of the amendment is so far removed from these particular justifications that we find it impossible to credit them. We cannot say that Amendment 2 is directed to any identifiable legitimate purpose or discrete objective. It is a status-based enactment divorced from any factual context from which we could discern a relationship to legitimate state interests; it is a classification of persons undertaken for its own sake, something the Equal Protection Clause does not permit. . . .

We must conclude that Amendment 2 classifies homosexuals not to further a proper legislative end but to make them unequal to everyone else. This Colorado cannot do. A State cannot so deem a class of persons a stranger to its laws. . . .

■ JUSTICE SCALIA, with whom THE CHIEF JUSTICE and JUSTICE THOMAS join, dissenting.

The Court has mistaken a Kulturkampf for a fit of spite. The constitutional amendment before us here is not the manifestation of a " 'bare . . . desire to harm' " homosexuals, but is rather a modest attempt by seemingly tolerant Coloradans to preserve traditional sexual mores against the efforts of a politically powerful minority to revise those mores through use of the laws. That objective, and the means chosen to achieve it, are not only unimpeachable under any constitutional doctrine hitherto pronounced (hence the opinion's heavy reliance upon principles of righteousness rather than judicial holdings); they have been specifically approved by the Congress of the United States and by this Court.

In holding that homosexuality cannot be singled out for disfavorable treatment, the Court contradicts a decision, unchallenged here, pronounced only 10 years ago, see *Bowers* v. *Hardwick,* 478 U. S. 186 (1986), and places the prestige of this institution behind the proposition that opposition to homosexuality is as reprehensible as racial or religious bias. Whether it is or not is *precisely* the cultural debate that gave rise to the Colorado constitutional amendment (and to the preferential laws against which the amendment was directed). Since the Constitution of the United States says nothing about this subject, it is left to be resolved by normal democratic means, including the democratic adoption of provisions in state constitutions. This Court has no business imposing upon all Americans the resolution favored by the elite class from which the Members of this institution are selected, pronouncing that "animosity" toward homosexuality is evil. I vigorously dissent.[10]

---

9 **Questions:** The rational-basis test is a means-ends test. In applying it, the Court typically asks only whether the law is rationally related to a legitimate end. It typically disregards any harm that the law might impose on certain groups, like the opticians in *Williamson v. Lee Optical of Oklahoma, Inc.*

Kennedy *says* that he is applying this test. Yet, in these last few paragraphs, he describes the "immediate, continuing, and real injuries that *outrun and belie* any legitimate justifications that may be claimed for it" (emphasis added). What role is this language playing in his test? Is he conducting a means-ends test or a proportionality test that weighs the classification's burdens against its benefits? Which test would you prefer?

10 **Questions:** Like Justice William Rehnquist's dissent in *Moreno*, Justice Antonin Scalia emphasizes that a fundamental principle underlying the rational-basis test is democratic majoritarianism. By deferring to legislatures (and, in this case, popular referenda), the ordinary rational-basis test allows majorities to decide challenging questions of morality and justice for themselves.

NOTE: LEGITIMATE AND ILLEGITIMATE INTERESTS AFTER *ROMER*

More than any case before it, *Romer* illustrated that *animus* toward a particular group was an illegitimate interest for any classification to promote. Animus alone didn't mean that the law was invalid—it just meant that the law had to be justified by an alternative interest and that the Court would apply "careful consideration" toward ensuring that the law was rationally related to this alternative. *Romer*, 517 U.S. at 633. The *Romer* Court also offered a new explanation for this pattern. It explained that the very purpose of the rational-basis test was to "ensure that classifications are not drawn for the purpose of disadvantaging the group burdened by the law." *Id.* While ordinary applications of the rational-basis test would generally defer to legislative judgments about the interests that the law promoted, those interests had to be legitimate or else the Court would view the law with suspicion.

Moral disapproval. In the due process case of *Lawrence v. Texas*, 539 U.S. 558 (2003), excerpted earlier (section 42.3), the Court added a second illegitimate interest: *moral disapproval*. Adopting Justice John Paul Stevens's dissent from *Bowers v. Hardwick*, 478 U.S. 186, 216 (1986), the Court wrote that "[t]he fact that the governing majority in a State has traditionally viewed a particular practice as immoral is not a sufficient reason for upholding a law prohibiting the practice; neither history nor tradition could save a law prohibiting miscegenation from constitutional attack." *Lawrence*, 539 U.S. at 577–78.

Defense of Marriage Act. *Romer* and *Lawrence* were both cases in which the Court struck down anti-LGB laws under the rational-basis test. Soon, the Court also applied the rational-basis test to the Defense of Marriage Act of 1996, Pub. L. No. 104–199, 110 Stat. 2419, a law passed in the wake of *Romer*. The act declared that, for purposes of federal law, "the word 'marriage' means only a legal union between one man and one woman." Defense of Marriage Act § 3(a). This definition controlled over one thousand federal laws in which marital status was relevant.

Edith Windsor, a New York woman, married her partner, Thea Spyer, in Canada in 2007. When they returned home to New York, the state not only recognized their marriage but also later authorized same-sex couples to get married in the state. But when Spyer died, the federal Defense of Marriage Act required Windsor to pay federal estate taxes even though she would have received a spousal exemption had she been a man. Invoking *Romer* and *Lawrence*, Windsor challenged the Defense of Marriage Act as irrational under the equal-protection principle of the Fifth Amendment.

In *United States v. Windsor*, 570 U.S. 744 (2013), the Supreme Court agreed with Windsor that the law couldn't survive the rational-basis test. Quoting *Romer*, the Court observed that "in determining whether a law is motived by an improper animus or purpose, '[d]iscriminations of an unusual

---

Do you agree with Scalia that Kennedy's majority opinion is antidemocratic? If not, why not? Are there alternatives to Kennedy's approach that might vindicate the equality and dignity of lesbian, gay, and bisexual Coloradans while also addressing Scalia's professed concern for the democratic process?

character' especially require careful consideration." *Windsor*, 570 U.S. at 770. When the Court considered the text, legislative history, and arguments presented to defend the law, the Court concluded that the law's "unusual deviation from the [federal government's] usual tradition of recognizing and accepting state definitions of marriage . . . is strong evidence of a law having the purpose and effect of disapproval of that class." *Id.* The Court added that "animus" against a particular group—one whose effect imposed a "stigma upon all who enter into same-sex marriages"—was illegitimate. *Id.*

Significantly, the Court didn't then consider whether the law was rationally related to alternative legitimate interests. The Court wrote that because the law's "principal" purpose was to "impose inequality," the Court was "require[d]" to invalidate the law. *Id.* at 772, 774. Supporting the Court's conclusion were the harms that the law imposed: it placed "same-sex couples in an unstable position of being in a second-tier marriage," which "demean[ed] the couple" and "humiliate[d] tens of thousands of children now being raised by same-sex couples." *Id.* at 772. The Court concluded, "[T]he principal purpose and the necessary effect of this law are to demean those persons who are in a lawful same-sex marriage. . . . The federal statute is invalid, for no legitimate purpose overcomes th[is] purpose and effect." *Id.* at 774–75.

CHAPTER 45

WHAT LIMITATIONS DO THE EQUAL-PROTECTION PRINCIPLES OF THE FIFTH AND FOURTEENTH AMENDMENTS IMPOSE ON THE POWER OF GOVERNMENT TO TREAT PEOPLE DIFFERENTLY BECAUSE OF THEIR RACE?

FIFTH AMENDMENT (1791): No person shall . . . be deprived of life, liberty, or property, without due process of law. . . .

FOURTEENTH AMENDMENT (1868), SECTION 1: No State shall . . . deny to any person within its jurisdiction the equal protection of the laws.

45.1 SEPARATE BUT EQUAL

When the Supreme Court first interpreted the Equal Protection Clause of the Fourteenth Amendment, it applied the same rational-basis analysis from *Yick Wo v. Hopkins*, 118 U.S. 356 (1886), to all classifications, including classifications on the basis of race. At the same time, the Court understood the purpose of the Equal Protection Clause to be the elimination of "laws in the States where the newly emancipated negroes resided which discriminated with gross injustice and hardship against them as a class." *Slaughter-House Cases*, 83 U.S. (16 Wall.) 36, 81 (1872). Accordingly, when Congress exercised its power under Section 5 of the Fourteenth Amendment to enforce the Equal Protection Clause, the Court initially upheld federal laws that required states to protect the civil rights of black people in juries and other official proceedings. *See, e.g., Strauder v. West Virginia*, 100 U.S. 303, 308 (1880); *Ex parte Virginia*, 100 U.S. 339, 346 (1880).

At the time the Fourteenth Amendment was ratified, however, many American lawyers had an archaically narrow understanding of the term *civil rights*, which meant something different than *political rights* or *social rights. See, e.g.,* Cong. Globe, 39th Cong., 1st Sess. 599 (1866) (statement of Sen. Lyman Trumbull). The phrase *civil rights* was often used to describe fundamental rights that governments had an obligation to protect, including the right to own property, to contract, and to access courts and juries. *See id.* *Political rights*, by contrast, included discretionary rights that a government could withhold from women, children, and other citizens, including the right to vote and run for office. *See id.* And *social rights* included rights that legislatures traditionally didn't protect at all, such as the right to determine with whom to socialize.

In the *Civil Rights Cases*, the Supreme Court applied this formal distinction when it stated that the Reconstruction amendments "did not assume . . . to adjust what may be called the social rights of men and races in the community, but only to declare and vindicate those fundamental rights which appertain to the essence of citizenship." 109 U.S. 3, 22 (1883). Partly on this ground, the Court struck down the Civil Rights Act of 1875, ch. 114, 18 Stat. 335, the federal law sponsored by Senator Charles Sumner of Massachusetts to prohibit racial discrimination in public accommodations and on public transportation.

In the wake of the *Civil Rights Cases*, dozens of states adopted laws that both authorized and required racial discrimination in public places. *See* Steve Luxenberg, *Separate* 355–59 (2019). The model for many of these laws, ironically, was Massachusetts. In 1849, when Sumner was still a practicing attorney in Boston, he lost a case before the Massachusetts Supreme Judicial Court that had lasting repercussions, *Roberts v. City of Boston*, 59 Mass. (5 Cush.) 198 (1849).

In the 1830s, Massachusetts was a national leader in adopting new technologies and social policies, from the railroad to compulsory public education. But Massachusetts was also a national leader in racial segregation. Several of Massachusetts's first railroad companies required black patrons to ride in poorly furnished "Jim Crow" cars, named after a local blackface performer who popularized the song, "Jump Jim Crow." *Id.* at 9–10. Similarly, Massachusetts towns and cities assigned black students to separate schools on the basis of their race.

Civil rights activists, led by a recently escaped fugitive from slavery named Frederick Douglass, used boycotts and public shaming to pressure Massachusetts's railroad companies to abolish their Jim Crow cars in the early 1840s. *Id.* at 13–22; David W. Blight, *Frederick Douglass* 109–16 (2018). But these activists had a difficult time persuading local schools to integrate their students.

In 1849, the family of a five-year-old black girl named Sarah Roberts hired Sumner, then a local attorney, to challenge Boston's school segregation policy under the Massachusetts Constitution. In state court, Sumner argued that "[t]he separation of children in the public schools of Boston, on account of color or race, is in the nature of caste, and is a violation of equality." *See* Goodwin Liu, *State Courts and Constitutional Structure*, 128 Yale L.J. 1304, 1342 (2019).

Sumner made his argument twenty years before the adoption of the Fourteenth Amendment. But he observed that "Equality before the Law" was embedded throughout Massachusetts's state constitution. *See* David Herbert Donald, *Charles Sumner and the Coming of the Civil War* 151 (2009). He argued that Boston's policy violated this principle of equality because it required black students to walk past well-furnished public schools to attend physically inferior and poorly resourced separate schools. *Id.* "[T]he separate school is not an equivalent," he argued. "The matters taught in the two schools may be precisely the same, but a school devoted to one class must differ essentially in spirit and character from that Common School known to the law, where all classes meet together in Equality." *Id.* In response, the city's attorneys maintained that racial separation was no different from separation by age or sex, both of which were concededly permissible.

In *Roberts*, the Massachusetts Supreme Judicial Court upheld the city's policy of racial segregation in schools. In an opinion written by Chief Justice Lemuel Shaw, one of the most influential judges of the nineteenth century, the court agreed with Sumner that the Massachusetts Constitution embodied the "great principle" that all persons were "equal before the law." *Roberts*, 59 Mass. (5 Cush.) at 206. But the Court disagreed about what *legal equality* meant. The court wrote that it did not mean that men and women, children and adults must be "legally clothed with the same civil and political powers" and be "subject to the same treatment." *Id. Legal equality* meant only that "the rights of all, as they are settled and regulated by law, are equally entitled to the paternal consideration and protection of the law, for their maintenance and security." *Id.*

Applying this definition of *equality* to Boston's public schools, the Supreme Judicial Court held that the city could appropriately determine that separating students on the basis of race would serve "the good of both classes of children." *Id.* at 209. Roberts still "had access to a school" that was as "well conducted . . . and as well fitted . . . as the other primary schools," the court wrote. *Id.* at 205. In response to Sumner's argument that Boston's racial segregation was perpetuating a "caste, founded in a deep-rooted prejudice in public opinion," the court wrote that "[t]his prejudice, if it exists, is not created by law, and probably cannot be changed by law." *Id.* at 209.

Sumner's argument failed to convince the state court, but it did convince the state legislature. By 1855, the legislature abolished racial segregation in public schools and elected Sumner to the U.S. Senate, where he later became instrumental in passing federal Reconstruction legislation.

But as the Supreme Court struck down this federal legislation in decisions like the *Civil Rights Cases*, officials around the country quoted the *Roberts* decision as evidence that the Equal Protection Clause was consistent with racial segregation. Liu, *supra*, at 1343–44; *see, e.g.*, *Ward v. Flood*, 48 Cal. 36, 52 (1874); *Lehew v. Brummell*, 15 S.W. 765, 767 (Mo. 1891); *People ex rel. King v. Gallagher*, 93 N.Y. 438, 453 (1883). By the 1890s, many states passed new Jim Crow laws that prohibited interracial gatherings, marriages, and other interactions on the theory that "[t]he punishment of each offending person, whether white or black, is the same." *Pace v. Alabama*, 106 U.S. 583, 585 (1883). One of these states was Louisiana.

45.1.1

Plessy v. Ferguson

163 U.S. 537 (1896)

Before the Civil War, New Orleans was home to a large population of prosperous, French-speaking black people known as the *gens de couleur libres*, or free people of color. *See* Luxenberg, *supra*, at 91–103. Although the *gens de couleur libres* were frequently discriminated against by New Orleans's white population, they attempted to fully participate in the city's social and economic life. *Id.* After the Union army occupied New Orleans during the Civil War, the *gens de couleur libres* asserted their political rights, reluctantly allying themselves with formerly enslaved people. During Reconstruction, representatives of the *gens de couleur* incorporated dozens of long-desired clauses into Louisiana's 1868 constitution, including an article declaring, "All persons shall enjoy equal rights and privileges upon any conveyance of a public character; and all places of business, or of public resort . . . without discrimination on account of race or color." La. Const. of 1868, art. 13.

Between 1868 and 1877, the *gens de couleur libres* literally battled the Ku Klux Klan and white Democrats for control of the state's government. They lost in 1877, and Democrats quickly drafted a new state constitution that repealed the antidiscrimination provision of 1868. After the *Civil Rights Cases*, when the Supreme Court declared that the Fourteenth Amendment did not empower Congress to enact a federal antidiscrimination law, Louisiana's Democratic legislature adopted the Separate Car Act of 1890, 1890 La. Acts 152. The act required all railroad cars to have "equal but separate accommodations for the white and colored races." *Id.* To enforce this provision, the law made it a crime for passengers to sit anywhere other than their racially appropriate car. *Id.*

The Separate Car Act infuriated the *gens de couleur libres*, who established a new organization, the *Comité des Citoyens*, to test the law's constitutionality. The *Comité* complained not only that the law was racially discriminatory but also that the law's enforcement would be "arbitrary" in violation of the analysis set forth in *Yick Wo*. Louisiana law didn't define the term *colored*, yet the law penalized railroad employees who failed to seat passengers in the car of their race. This was a problem for the *gens de couleur libres*, many of whom were light-skinned. *See* Luxenberg, *supra*, at 471–72.

In the *Comité*'s first test case, a *gen de couleur libre* boarded a whites-only car on an interstate train bound for Alabama. The man was arrested, but the judge in his case, John Howard Ferguson, released him after the Louisiana Supreme Court decided that the Separate Car Act's application to interstate railroads violated the Negative Commerce Clause. *Louisiana ex rel. Abbott v. Hicks*, 11 So. 74, 76 (La. 1892).

For its second test case, the *Comité* recruited Homer Plessy, a *gen de couleur libre* who so easily passed for white that he later described himself as "white" on the federal census. Luxenberg, *supra*, at 489–90. Collaborating with a sympathetic intrastate railroad, Plessy sat in a compartment reserved for white passengers, where he refused to leave after announcing that he was "one eighth African blood." *Plessy v. Ferguson*, 163 U.S. 537, 541 (1896). After Plessy was arrested for violating the Separate Car Act, the *Comité* sued the same Judge Ferguson to invalidate Plessy's conviction.

The case eventually reached the Supreme Court, and the Court in *Plessy v. Ferguson*, 163 U.S. 537 (1896), handed down its infamous separate-but-equal ruling.

■ MR. JUSTICE BROWN, after stating the case, delivered the opinion of the Court.[1]

This case turns upon the constitutionality of an act of the General Assembly of the State of Louisiana, passed in 1890, providing for separate railway carriages for the white and colored races. Acts 1890, No. 111, p. 152. . . .

The petition for the writ of prohibition averred that petitioner was seven eighths Caucasian and one eighth African blood; that the mixture of colored blood was not discernible in him, and that he was entitled to every right, privilege and immunity secured to citizens of the United States of the white race; and that, upon such theory, he took possession of a vacant seat in a coach where passengers of the white race were accommodated, and was ordered by the conductor to vacate coach and take a seat in another assigned to persons of the colored race, and having refused to comply with such demand he was forcibly ejected with the aid of a police officer, and imprisoned in the parish jail to answer a charge of having violated the above act.

The constitutionality of this act is attacked upon the ground that it conflicts both with the Thirteenth Amendment of the Constitution, abolishing slavery, and the Fourteenth Amendment, which prohibits certain restrictive legislation on the part of the States.

1. That it does not conflict with the Thirteenth Amendment, which abolished slavery and involuntary servitude, except as a punishment for crime, is too clear for

---

[1] **As You Read, Consider:** During the Civil War, Congress established the Freedmen's Bureau to assist refugees and recently freed black people in the South. Among other things, the bureau established the first southern schools to educate black children. In 1866, Congress reauthorized the bureau to take all actions necessary to enable black people "to become self-supporting citizens of the United States, and to aid them in making the freedom conferred . . . by [the Thirteenth Amendment], available to them." Act of July 16, 1866, ch. 200, 14 Stat. 173, 174. Congress enacted this reauthorization over President Andrew Johnson's veto. He objected that the bureau's race-conscious activities discriminated against "millions, of the white race, who are honestly toiling from day to day for their subsistence." Cong. Globe, 39th Cong., 1st Sess. 916 (1866).

To the extent that the bureau engaged in race-conscious activities, do you think that it violated the principle of equality underlying the Equal Protection Clause? Precisely how, if at all, was Louisiana's Separate Car Act different?

argument. Slavery implies involuntary servitude—a state of bondage; the ownership of mankind as a chattel. . . . This amendment was said in the *Slaughter-house cases,* 16 Wall. 36, to have been intended primarily to abolish slavery, as it had been previously known in this country. . . .

A statute which implies merely a legal distinction between the white and colored races—a distinction which is founded in the color of the two races, and which must always exist so long as white men are distinguished from the other race by color—has no tendency to destroy the legal equality of the two races, or reëstablish a state of involuntary servitude. Indeed, we do not understand that the Thirteenth Amendment is strenuously relied upon by the plaintiff in error . . . .

2. By the Fourteenth Amendment, . . . the States are forbidden from making or enforcing any law which shall . . . deprive any person of life, liberty, or property without due process of law, or deny to any person within their jurisdiction the equal protection of the laws. . . .

The object of the amendment was undoubtedly to enforce the absolute equality of the two races before the law, but in the nature of things it could not have been intended to abolish distinctions based upon color, or to enforce social, as distinguished from political equality, or a commingling of the two races upon terms unsatisfactory to either. Laws permitting, and even requiring, their separation in places where they are liable to be brought into contact do not necessarily imply the inferiority of either race to the other, and have been generally, if not universally, recognized as within the competency of the state legislatures in the exercise of their police power. The most common instance of this is connected with the establishment of separate schools for white and colored children, which has been held to be a valid exercise of the legislative power even by courts of States where the political rights of the colored race have been longest and most earnestly enforced.

One of the earliest of these cases is that of *Roberts* v. *City of Boston,* 5 Cush. 198, in which the Supreme Judicial Court of Massachusetts held that the general school committee of Boston had power to make provision for the instruction of colored children in separate schools established exclusively for them, and to prohibit their attendance upon the other schools. "The great principle," said Chief Justice Shaw, p. 206, "advanced by the learned and eloquent advocate for the plaintiff," (Mr. Charles Sumner,) "is, that by the constitution and laws of Massachusetts, all persons without distinction of age or sex, birth or color, origin or condition, are equal before the law. . . . But, when this great principle comes to be applied to the actual and various conditions of persons in society, it will not warrant the assertion, that men and women are legally clothed with the same civil and political powers, and that children and adults are legally to have the same functions and be subject to the same treatment; but only that the rights of all, as they are settled and regulated by law, are equally entitled to the paternal consideration and protection of the law for their maintenance and security." It was held that the powers of the committee extended to the establishment of separate schools for children of different ages, sexes and colors, and that they might also establish special schools for poor and neglected children, who have become too old to attend the primary school, and yet have not acquired the rudiments of learning, to enable them to enter the ordinary schools. Similar laws have been enacted by Congress under its general power of legislation over the District of Columbia, Rev. Stat. D.C. §§ 281, 282, 283, 310, 319, as well as by the legislatures of many of the States, and have been generally, if not uniformly, sustained by the courts. . . .[2]

---

[2] **Questions:** Justice Henry Brown here is arguing that the enforcement of racial separation does not imply the enforcement of racial inequality. Do you agree that a law requiring

Laws forbidding the intermarriage of the two races may be said in a technical sense to interfere with the freedom of contract, and yet have been universally recognized as within the police power of the State. . . .

The distinction between laws interfering with the political equality of the negro and those requiring the separation of the two races in schools, theatres and railway carriages has been frequently drawn by this court. Thus in *Strauder* v. *West Virginia,* 100 U.S. 303, it was held that a law of West Virginia limiting to white male persons, 21 years of age and citizens of the State, the right to sit upon juries, was a discrimination which implied a legal inferiority in civil society, which lessened the security of the right of the colored race, and was a step toward reducing them to a condition of servility. . . . [But in] the *Civil Rights case,* 109 U.S. 3, it was held that an act of Congress, entitling all persons within the jurisdiction of the United States to the full and equal enjoyment of [public accommodations and public conveyances] . . ., was unconstitutional and void . . . .

[W]e think the enforced separation of the races, as applied to the internal commerce of the State, neither . . . deprives him of his property without due process of law, nor denies him the equal protection of the laws. . . .

It is claimed by the plaintiff in error that, in any mixed community, the reputation of belonging to the dominant race, in this instance the white race, is *property,* in the same sense that a right of action, or of inheritance, is property. Conceding this to be so, for the purposes of this case, we are unable to see how this statute deprives him of, or in any way affects his right to, such property. If he be a white man and assigned to a colored coach, he may have his action for damages against the company for being deprived of his so called property. Upon the other hand, if he be a colored man and be so assigned, he has been deprived of no property, since he is not lawfully entitled to the reputation of being a white man.

In this connection, it is also suggested by the learned counsel for the plaintiff in error that the same argument that will justify the state legislature in requiring railways to provide separate accommodations for the two races will also authorize them to require separate cars to be provided for people whose hair is of a certain color, or who are aliens, or who belong to certain nationalities, or to enact laws requiring colored people to walk upon one side of the street, and white people upon the other, or requiring white men's houses to be painted white, and colored men's black, or their vehicles or business signs to be of different colors, upon the theory that one side of the street is as good as the other, or that a house or vehicle of one color is as good as one of another color. The reply to all this is that every exercise of the police power must be reasonable, and extend only to such laws as are enacted in good faith for the promotion for the public good, and not for the annoyance or oppression of a particular class. Thus in *Yick Wo* v. *Hopkins,* 118 U.S. 356, it was held by this court that a municipal ordinance of the city of San Francisco, to regulate the carrying on of public laundries within the limits of the municipality, violated the provisions of the Constitution of the United States, if it conferred upon the municipal authorities arbitrary power, at their own will, and without regard to discretion, in the legal sense of the term, to give or withhold consent as to persons or places, without regard to the competency of the persons applying, or the propriety of the places selected for the carrying on of the business. It was held to be a covert attempt on the part of the municipality to make an arbitrary and unjust discrimination against the Chinese race. . . .

---

young children to go to elementary school and old children to go to high school does not treat them unequally? Is such a law distinguishable from this one?

So far, then, as a conflict with the Fourteenth Amendment is concerned, the case reduces itself to the question whether the statute of Louisiana is a reasonable regulation, and with respect to this there must necessarily be a large discretion on the part of the legislature. In determining the question of reasonableness it is at liberty to act with reference to the established usages, customs and traditions of the people, and with a view to the promotion of their comfort, and the preservation of the public peace and good order. Gauged by this standard, we cannot say that a law which authorizes or even requires the separation of the two races in public conveyances is unreasonable, or more obnoxious to the Fourteenth Amendment than the acts of Congress requiring separate schools for colored children in the District of Columbia, the constitutionality of which does not seem to have been questioned, or the corresponding acts of state legislatures.[3]

We consider the underlying fallacy of the plaintiff's argument to consist in the assumption that the enforced separation of the two races stamps the colored race with a badge of inferiority. If this be so, it is not by reason of anything found in the act, but solely because the colored race chooses to put that construction upon it.[4] The argument necessarily assumes that if, as has been more than once the case, and is not unlikely to be so again, the colored race should become the dominant power in the state legislature, and should enact a law in precisely similar terms, it would thereby relegate the white race to an inferior position. We imagine that the white race, at least, would not acquiesce in this assumption. The argument also assumes that social prejudices may be overcome by legislation, and that equal rights cannot be secured to the negro except by an enforced commingling of the two races. We cannot accept this proposition. If the two races are to meet upon terms of social equality, it must be the result of natural affinities, a mutual appreciation of each other's merits and a voluntary consent of individuals. . . . Legislation is powerless to eradicate racial instincts or to abolish distinctions based upon physical differences, and the attempt to do so can only result in accentuating the difficulties of the present situation. If the civil and political rights of both races be equal one cannot be inferior to the other civilly or politically. If one race be inferior to the other socially, the Constitution of the United States cannot put them upon the same plane.

It is true that the question of the proportion of colored blood necessary to constitute a colored person, as distinguished from a white person, is one upon which there is a difference of opinion in the different States, some holding that any visible admixture of black blood stamps the person as belonging to the colored race, others

---

[3] **Questions:** A central theme of Homer Plessy's argument was that the Separate Car Act humiliated him. He appeared white, yet the law irrationally prohibited him from sitting among white passengers. He argued that Louisiana's white legislature was enforcing a racial hierarchy in which he was at the bottom.

Brown responds by invoking the Court's formal, deferential tests for interpreting the Fourteenth Amendment. Interpreting the Due Process Clause, he writes that no property interest has been "deprived" because Plessy never had a legal interest in being treated as white. Interpreting the Equal Protection Clause, he writes that this law survives the test of *Yick Wo* because the law is rationally related to the legitimate interest of promoting "the public peace and good order."

Does Brown make any analytical errors here? If not, then do you think that the rational-basis test is the appropriate method of interpreting the Fourteenth Amendment?

[4] **Question:** In an infamous passage, Brown disputes Plessy's "assumption" that the Separate Car Act necessarily subordinates black people. He alludes to Reconstruction, when "the colored race" was "the dominant power in the state legislature." He imagines that if such a legislature had enacted this law, no one would think that the law "relegate[d] the white race to an inferior position."

Is Brown correct that legally enforced separation can be consistent with a commitment to equality—at least if the separate facilities are truly equal in physical quality?

that it depends upon the preponderance of blood, and still others that the predominance of white blood must only be in the proportion of three fourths. But these are questions to be determined under the laws of each State and are not properly put in issue in this case. Under the allegations of his petition it may undoubtedly become a question of importance whether, under the laws of Louisiana, the petitioner belongs to the white or colored race. . . .

■ MR. JUSTICE HARLAN, dissenting. . . .[5]

[I]n respect of civil rights, common to all citizens, the Constitution of the United States does not, I think, permit any public authority to know the race of those entitled to be protected in the enjoyment of such rights. Every true man has pride of race, and under appropriate circumstances when the rights of others, his equals before the law, are not to be affected, it is his privilege to express such pride and to take such action based upon it as to him seems proper. But I deny that any legislative body or judicial tribunal may have regard to the race of citizens when the civil rights of those citizens are involved. Indeed, such legislation, as that here in question, is inconsistent not only with that equality of rights which pertains to citizenship, National and State, but with the personal liberty enjoyed by every one within the United States. . . .

[The Thirteenth, Fourteenth, and Fifteenth Amendments] removed the race line from our governmental systems. They had, as this court has said, a common purpose, namely, . . . "that all persons, whether colored or white, shall stand equal before the laws of the States, and, in regard to the colored race, for whose protection the amendment was primarily designed, that no discrimination shall be made against them by law because of their color." . . .

It was said in argument that the statute of Louisiana does not discriminate against either race, but prescribes a rule applicable alike to white and colored citizens. But this argument does not meet the difficulty. Every one knows that the statute in question had its origin in the purpose, not so much to exclude white persons from railroad cars occupied by blacks, as to exclude colored people from coaches occupied by or assigned to white persons. . . . The thing to accomplish was, under the guise of giving equal accommodation for whites and blacks, to compel the latter to keep to themselves while travelling in railroad passenger coaches. No one would be so wanting in candor as to assert the contrary. The fundamental objection, therefore, to the statute is that it interferes with the personal freedom of citizens. . . . If a white man and a black man choose to occupy the same public conveyance on a public highway, it is their right to do so, and no government, proceeding alone on grounds of race, can prevent it without infringing the personal liberty of each.

It is one thing for railroad carriers to furnish, or to be required by law to furnish, equal accommodations for all whom they are under a legal duty to carry. It is quite

[5] **Questions:** A generation after Justice John Harlan wrote the below dissent, civil rights litigators rallied around it as the correct interpretation of the Equal Protection Clause. A generation after that, the dissent was also embraced by these litigators' opponents. This legacy illustrates how the dissent—and the Equal Protection Clause itself—is subject to competing interpretations.

One dispute is over what the clause prohibits. An *anti-race-consciousness* view argues that the clause prohibits governments from taking race into account. By contrast, an *antisubordination* view argues that the clause allows governments to take race into account but prohibits them from creating a superior caste.

A second dispute is over how someone should determine whether the clause has been violated. One view argues that the clause prohibits only laws with illegitimate *purposes*. By contrast, another view argues that a law's *effect* or *significance in context* can also violate the clause.

Does Harlan object to Louisiana's law because it is *race-conscious* or because it *subordinates* black people? Does he object only to the law's *purpose* or also its *effect*?

another thing for government to forbid citizens of the white and black races from travelling in the same public conveyance, and to punish officers of railroad companies for permitting persons of the two races to occupy the same passenger coach. If a State can prescribe, as a rule of civil conduct, that whites and blacks shall not travel as passengers in the same railroad coach, why may it not so regulate the use of the streets of its cities and towns as to compel white citizens to keep on one side of a street and black citizens to keep on the other? Why may it not, upon like grounds, punish whites and blacks who ride together in street cars or in open vehicles on a public road or street? Why may it not require sheriffs to assign whites to one side of a court-room and blacks to the other? And why may it not also prohibit the commingling of the two races in the galleries of legislative halls or in public assemblages convened for the consideration of the political questions of the day? Further, if this statute of Louisiana is consistent with the personal liberty of citizens, why may not the State require the separation in railroad coaches of native and naturalized citizens of the United States, or of Protestants and Roman Catholics? . . .

The white race deems itself to be the dominant race in this country. And so it is, in prestige, in achievements, in education, in wealth and in power. So, I doubt not, it will continue to be for all time, if it remains true to its great heritage and holds fast to the principles of constitutional liberty. But in view of the Constitution, in the eye of the law, there is in this country no superior, dominant, ruling class of citizens. There is no caste here. Our Constitution is color-blind, and neither knows nor tolerates classes among citizens.[6] In respect of civil rights, all citizens are equal before the law. The humblest is the peer of the most powerful. The law regards man as man, and takes no account of his surroundings or of his color when his civil rights as guaranteed by the supreme law of the land are involved. It is, therefore, to be regretted that this high tribunal, the final expositor of the fundamental law of the land, has reached the conclusion that it is competent for a State to regulate the enjoyment by citizens of their civil rights solely upon the basis of race.

In my opinion, the judgment this day rendered will, in time, prove to be quite as pernicious as the decision made by this tribunal in the *Dred Scott case*. It was adjudged in that case that the descendants of Africans who were imported into this country and sold as slaves were not included nor intended to be included under the word "citizens" in the Constitution, and could not claim any of the rights and privileges which that instrument provided for and secured to citizens of the United States. . . . The recent amendments of the Constitution, it was supposed, had eradicated these principles from our institutions. But it seems that we have yet, in some of the States, a dominant race—a superior class of citizens, which assumes to regulate the enjoyment of civil rights, common to all citizens, upon the basis of race. The present decision, it may well be apprehended, will not only stimulate aggressions, more or less brutal and irritating, upon the admitted rights of colored citizens, but will encourage the belief that it is possible, by means of state enactments, to defeat the beneficent purposes which the people of the United States had in view when they adopted the recent amendments of the Constitution. . . . Sixty millions of whites are in no danger from the presence here of eight millions of blacks. The destinies of the two races, in this country, are indissolubly linked together, and the interests of both require that the common government of all shall not permit the seeds of race hate to be planted under the sanction of law. What can more certainly arouse race hate, what more certainly create and perpetuate a feeling of distrust between these races, than

[6] **Questions:** In this famous passage, Harlan declares, "There is no caste here. Our Constitution is color-blind, and neither knows nor tolerates classes among citizens." What does he mean? Is he announcing an anti-race-consciousness perspective or an antisubordination perspective?

state enactments, which, in fact, proceed on the ground that colored citizens are so inferior and degraded that they cannot be allowed to sit in public coaches occupied by white citizens? That, as all will admit, is the real meaning of such legislation as was enacted in Louisiana. . . .[7]

There is a race so different from our own that we do not permit those belonging to it to become citizens of the United States. Persons belonging to it are, with few exceptions, absolutely excluded from our country. I allude to the Chinese race. But by the statute in question, a Chinaman can ride in the same passenger coach with white citizens of the United States, while citizens of the black race in Louisiana, many of whom, perhaps, risked their lives for the preservation of the Union, who are entitled, by law, to participate in the political control of the State and nation, who are not excluded, by law or by reason of their race, from public stations of any kind, and who have all the legal rights that belong to white citizens, are yet declared to be criminals, liable to imprisonment, if they ride in a public coach occupied by citizens of the white race. It is scarcely just to say that a colored citizen should not object to occupying a public coach assigned to his own race. He does not object, nor, perhaps, would he object to separate coaches for his race, if his rights under the law were recognized. But he objects, and ought never to cease objecting to the proposition, that citizens of the white and black races can be adjudged criminals because they sit, or claim the right to sit, in the same public coach on a public highway.

The arbitrary separation of citizens, on the basis of race, while they are on a public highway, is a badge of servitude wholly inconsistent with the civil freedom and the equality before the law established by the Constitution. It cannot be justified upon any legal grounds. . . .

NOTE: SEPARATE-BUT-EQUAL DOCTRINE

In upholding Louisiana's "equal but separate" railroad car law, the *Plessy* Court distinguished *Yick Wo* by concluding that Louisiana's classification was rationally related to a legitimate interest. 163 U.S. at 540, 550. That interest was "the preservation of the public peace and good order," as determined by "the established usages, customs and traditions of the people." *Id.* at 550. In response to the argument that there was nothing legitimate about preserving public peace by stamping black people with a "badge of inferiority," the Court responded with an infamous passage dismissing this argument as based on a "fallacy." *Id.* at 551. Mere racial separation didn't imply the inferiority of either race, the Court wrote; and if it did, "it is not by reason of anything found in the act, but solely because the colored race chooses to put that construction upon it." *Id.*

Justice John Harlan, the Kentucky scion of a prominent family that enslaved people, dissented in *Plessy* as he had earlier in the *Civil Rights Cases*. As he predicted, states around the country responded to *Plessy* by adopting racial segregation laws to govern every aspect of social and political life, from where people could sit on streetcars to where people could stand "in the galleries of legislative halls or in public assemblages." *Id.* at 558 (Harlan, J., dissenting). The decision gave rise to the doctrine of "separate

---

[7] **Question:** Harlan joined the majority in the Chinese Exclusion Case. And he seems appalled that Louisiana 's law treats Chinese immigrants better than it treats black U.S. citizens who fought in the Civil War. How do his anti—Chinese views—not to mention his earlier declaration that the white race is "the dominant race in this country"—square with his interpretation of the Equal Protection Clause?

but equal," which allowed states to provide segregated facilities of equivalent quality.

Almost immediately, however, the Supreme Court—with Harlan's approval—authorized states to provide segregated facilities that lacked the same quality in practice. In *Cumming v. Richmond County Board of Education*, 175 U.S. 528 (1899), Harlan wrote a unanimous opinion for the Court that upheld a Georgia school district's decision to close its only high school for black children while maintaining a high school for white children. The district complained that it lacked the funds to operate two high schools. Harlan took the district at its word. "The colored school children of the county would not be advanced in the matter of their education by a decree compelling the defendant board to cease giving support to a high-school for white children," Harlan wrote. *Cumming*, 175 U.S. at 544. "[W]hile all admit that the benefits and burdens of public taxation must be shared by citizens without discrimination against any class on account of their race, the education of the people in schools maintained by state taxation is a matter belonging to the respective states." *Id.* at 545; *see also Berea Coll. v. Kentucky*, 211 U.S. 45 (1908) (upholding a law that prohibited integrated private colleges).

The Court quoted Harlan's words three decades later in *Lum v. Rice*, 275 U.S. 78 (1927), when it formally applied *Plessy*'s doctrine to racially segregated public schools. Martha Lum, "a child of Chinese blood" living in Mississippi, wanted to attend a local high school that was reserved exclusively for white children. *Lum*, 275 U.S. at 85. Her case presented the question of whether "a Chinese citizen of the United States is denied equal protection of the laws when he is classed among the colored races and furnished facilities for education equal to that offered to all, whether white, brown, yellow, or black." *Id.* Quoting the Supreme Court's opinions in *Plessy* and *Cumming*, the Court concluded that no "different result can be reached." *Id.* at 87

Separate but equal was the law of the land.

45.2 THE ORIGINS OF STRICT SCRUTINY

Through the 1930s, the Supreme Court formalized the rational-basis test into a doctrine to govern all questions under the Equal Protection Clause (as well as all questions under the Due Process Clause after *West Coast Hotel Co. v. Parrish*, 300 U.S. 379 (1937)). Applying this deferential test, the Court generally upheld racial classifications by invoking *Plessy v. Ferguson*, 168 U.S. 537 (1896), and *Lum v. Rice*, 275 U.S. 78 (1927): a law was rationally related to the legitimate interest of preserving "public peace and good order" provided that the facilities furnished to people of color were as equal as practicable to those furnished to white people. *Plessy*, 163 U.S. at 551. Yet in a dozen or so cases, the Court invalidated legislation for failing even this permissive separate-but-equal standard. These examples slowly persuaded members of the Court to adopt a less deferential standard of review when race was involved.

In the context of train and bus transportation, for example, the Supreme Court invalidated state laws that departed from *Plessy* by imposing segregation without offering black customers *any* separate accommodations. *See, e.g., McCabe v. Atchison, Topeka & Santa Fe Railway*, 235 U.S. 151, 161–62 (1914). Eventually, the Court reaffirmed a pre-*Plessy* ruling that state laws requiring or banning segregation in interstate travel violated the Negative Commerce Clause. *See Morgan v. Virginia*, 328 U.S. 373, 383 (1946). Southern states, however, simply defied these rulings throughout the 1960s. *See* Taylor Branch, *Parting the Waters* 451–91 (1988).

The Court similarly invalidated housing laws that facially prohibited people of color from living in certain areas. *See Buchanan v. Warley*, 245 U.S. 60, 79 (1917). In *Shelley v. Kraemer*, 334 U.S. 1 (1948), the Court went even further and held that the Equal Protection Clause prohibited a state court from enforcing a racially restrictive covenant—that is, a clause in a deed that prohibited the homeowner from selling the property to someone of a different race. The Court cited a recent decision in which members of the Court had written that "a rational basis is completely lacking where, as here, the discrimination stems directly from racial hatred and intolerance." *Oyama v. California*, 332 U.S. 633, 663 (1948) (Murphy, J., concurring).

45.2.1

Korematsu v. United States

323 U.S. 214 (1944)

Although the Court continued to apply the rational-basis test to racial classifications through the 1950s, several members of the Court began searching for an alternative approach. In *United States v. Carolene Products Co.*, a due process decision (section 41.2), Chief Justice Harlan Stone proposed that the Court apply "more exacting judicial scrutiny" to "legislation which restricts those political processes which can ordinarily be expected to bring about the repeal of undesirable legislation." 304 U.S. 144, 152–53 n.4 (1938). Stone had in mind not only laws that infringed on the first ten amendments or the right to vote but also any statute that reflected "prejudice against discrete and insular minorities . . . [and] which tends seriously to curtail the operation of those political processes ordinarily to be relied upon to protect minorities." *Id.* But Stone didn't explain what this "more searching judicial inquiry" might look like. *Id.*

The Court offered a hint in *Skinner v. Oklahoma ex rel. Williamson*, 316 U.S. 535 (1942) (see section 48.1). There, it evaluated a law that required the sterilization of anyone convicted two or more times for crimes "amounting to felonies involving moral turpitude." *Skinner*, 316 U.S. at 536. This definition included larceny—a crime committed predominantly by poor people—but specifically exempted "embezzlement, or political offenses." *Id.* at 537. Although the Court announced that it would interpret the law with "that large deference which the rule of [its earlier] cases requires," the Court added that "strict scrutiny of the classification which a State makes in a sterilization law is essential, lest unwittingly, or otherwise, invidious discriminations are made against groups or types of individuals in violation of the constitutional guaranty of just and equal laws." *Id.* at 541 (citing *Yick Wo. v. Hopkins*, 118 U.S. 356 (1886)). Applying this strict scrutiny, the Court wrote that the sterilization of people who committed larceny, with immunity for (presumably well-off) people who committed embezzlement, "is a clear, pointed, unmistakable discrimination." *Id.* Strict scrutiny, in practice, therefore appeared to be a term for when the Court suspected that the *real* purpose of a law was "to perpetuate . . . discrimination." *Id.* at 542.

In the following case, *Korematsu v. United States*, 323 U.S. 214 (1944), the Court formally applied this strict scrutiny to racial classifications—and federal legislation—for the first time. As discussed earlier in the context of Congress's power to wage war successfully (section 13.4), the federal government responded to the 1941 attack on Pearl Harbor by imposing restrictions on Japanese Americans who lived on the West Coast. In *Hirabayashi v. United States*, the Court condemned "[d]istinctions between citizens solely because of their ancestry," but it nevertheless upheld a federal curfew that applied only to Gordon Hirabayashi and other Americans of Japanese ancestry. 320 U.S. 81, 100 (1943).

In *Korematsu*, the Court considered a similar federal law that excluded Japanese Americans from large geographic areas—the prelude to their forced imprisonment in the country's interior. Like Hirabayashi, Fred Korematsu was a college-age activist who defied the law and challenged its constitutionality.

Despite applying what it called "the most rigid scrutiny," the *Korematsu* Court was no more ready to do away with race-based discrimination than was the *Hirabayashi* Court.

■ MR. JUSTICE BLACK delivered the opinion of the Court.[8]

The petitioner, an American citizen of Japanese descent, was convicted in a federal district court for remaining in San Leandro, California, a "Military Area," contrary to Civilian Exclusion Order No. 34 . . ., which directed that after May 9, 1942, all persons of Japanese ancestry should be excluded from that area. No question was raised as to petitioner's loyalty to the United States. . . .

---

8 **As You Read, Consider:** In *Plessy v. Ferguson*, the Supreme Court upheld Louisiana's segregation law after concluding that it satisfied the rational—basis test. Here, Justice Hugo Black applies "the most rigid scrutiny" to a law he regards as "immediately suspect"—yet he still upholds the law. Why?

Given the injustice of the outcome here, does Black's opinion reflect an analytical error in his application of a skeptical means-ends test? Or do *Korematsu v. United States and Plessy* reflect a flaw inherent in using any means-ends test to evaluate whether a law is unconstitutionally discriminatory?

It should be noted, to begin with, that all legal restrictions which curtail the civil rights of a single racial group are immediately suspect. That is not to say that all such restrictions are unconstitutional. It is to say that courts must subject them to the most rigid scrutiny. Pressing public necessity may sometimes justify the existence of such restrictions; racial antagonism never can. . . .

Nothing short of apprehension by the proper military authorities of the gravest imminent danger to the public safety can constitutionally justify [exclusion from the area in which one's home is located]. But exclusion from a threatened area, no less than curfew, has a definite and close relationship to the prevention of espionage and sabotage. The military authorities, charged with the primary responsibility of defending our shores, concluded that curfew provided inadequate protection and ordered exclusion. They did so, as pointed out in our *Hirabayashi* opinion, in accordance with Congressional authority to the military to say who should, and who should not, remain in the threatened areas. . . .

Here, as in the *Hirabayashi* case, . . . exclusion of those of Japanese origin was deemed necessary because of the presence of an unascertained number of disloyal members of the group, most whom we have no doubt were loyal to this country. It was because we could not reject the finding of the military authorities that it was impossible to bring about an immediate segregation of the disloyal from the loyal that we sustained the validity of the curfew order as applying to the whole group. In the instant case, temporary exclusion of the entire group was rested by the military on the same ground. The judgment that exclusion of the whole group was for the same reason a military imperative answers the contention that the exclusion was in the nature of group punishment based on antagonism to those of Japanese origin. That there were members of the group who retained loyalties to Japan has been confirmed by investigations made subsequent to the exclusion. Approximately five thousand American citizens of Japanese ancestry refused to swear unqualified allegiance to the United States and to renounce allegiance to the Japanese Emperor, and several thousand evacuees requested repatriation to Japan. . . .

It is said that we are dealing here with the case of imprisonment of a citizen in a concentration camp solely because of his ancestry, without evidence or inquiry concerning his loyalty and good disposition towards the United States. Our task would be simple, our duty clear, were this a case involving the imprisonment of a loyal citizen in a concentration camp because of racial prejudice. Regardless of the true nature of the assembly and relocation centers—and we deem it unjustifiable to call them concentration camps with all the ugly connotations that term implies—we are dealing specifically with nothing but an exclusion order. To cast this case into outlines of racial prejudice, without reference to the real military dangers which were presented, merely confuses the issue. Korematsu was not excluded from the Military Area because of hostility to him or his race. He *was* excluded because we are at war with the Japanese Empire, because the properly constituted military authorities feared an invasion of our West Coast and felt constrained to take proper security measures, because they decided that the military urgency of the situation demanded that all citizens of Japanese ancestry be segregated from the West Coast temporarily, and finally, because Congress, reposing its confidence in this time of war in our military leaders—as inevitably it must—determined that they should have the power to do just this. There was evidence of disloyalty on the part of some, the military authorities considered that the need for action was great, and time was short. We cannot—by availing ourselves of the calm perspective of hindsight—now say that at that time these actions were unjustified. . . .[9]

---

[9] **Questions:** Black agrees with the military that the blanket exclusion of Japanese Americans from the West Coast was "necessary" to prevent "the gravest imminent danger to the

■ MR. JUSTICE MURPHY, dissenting.

This exclusion of "all persons of Japanese ancestry, both alien and non-alien," from the Pacific Coast area on a plea of military necessity in the absence of martial law ought not to be approved. Such exclusion goes over "the very brink of constitutional power" and falls into the ugly abyss of racism.

In dealing with matters relating to the prosecution and progress of a war, we must accord great respect and consideration to the judgments of the military authorities who are on the scene and who have full knowledge of the military facts. . . . At the same time, however, it is essential that there be definite limits to military discretion, especially where martial law has not been declared. Individuals must not be left impoverished of their constitutional rights on a plea of military necessity that has neither substance nor support. . . .

The judicial test of whether the Government, on a plea of military necessity, can validly deprive an individual of any of his constitutional rights is whether the deprivation is reasonably related to a public danger that is so "immediate, imminent, and impending" as not to admit of delay and not to permit the intervention of ordinary constitutional processes to alleviate the danger. *United States* v. *Russell,* 13 Wall. 623, 627–8. Civilian Exclusion Order No. 34, banishing from a prescribed area of the Pacific Coast "all persons of Japanese ancestry, both alien and non-alien," clearly does not meet that test. Being an obvious racial discrimination, the order deprives all those within its scope of the equal protection of the laws as guaranteed by the Fifth Amendment. . . .

The military necessity which is essential to the validity of the evacuation order [is based on nothing more than an inference] that the entire group of Japanese Americans could not be trusted to be or remain loyal to the United States. No one denies, of course, that there were some disloyal persons of Japanese descent on the Pacific Coast who did all in their power to aid their ancestral land. Similar disloyal activities have been engaged in by many persons of German, Italian and even more pioneer stock in our country. But to infer that examples of individual disloyalty prove group disloyalty and justify discriminatory action against the entire group is to deny that under our system of law individual guilt is the sole basis for deprivation of rights. Moreover, this inference, which is at the very heart of the evacuation orders, has been used in support of the abhorrent and despicable treatment of minority groups by the dictatorial tyrannies which this nation is now pledged to destroy. To give constitutional sanction to that inference in this case, however well-intentioned may have been the military command on the Pacific Coast, is to adopt one of the cruelest of the rationales used by our enemies to destroy the dignity of the individual and to encourage and open the door to discriminatory actions against other minority groups in the passions of tomorrow.

No adequate reason is given for the failure to treat these Japanese Americans on an individual basis by holding investigations and hearings to separate the loyal from the disloyal, as was done in the case of persons of German and Italian ancestry. It is asserted merely that the loyalties of this group "were unknown and time was of the essence." Yet nearly four months elapsed after Pearl Harbor before the first exclusion order was issued; nearly eight months went by until the last order was

---

public safety." Because the law satisfies his skeptical means-ends test, he upholds the law without regard to whether it was racist. In fact, he insists that it was not.

But suppose Korematsu was correct that the law inflicted racial subordination and the military was correct that the law was necessary to serve a compelling interest. Should such a law be constitutional? If so, is this opinion at all distinguishable from the *Plessy* Court's insistence that if the law was racist, "it is not by reason of anything found in the act, but solely because the colored race chooses to put that construction upon it"? 163 U.S. at 551.

issued; and the last of these "subversive" persons was not actually removed until almost eleven months had elapsed. Leisure and deliberation seem to have been more of the essence than speed. And the fact that conditions were not such as to warrant a declaration of martial law adds strength to the belief that the factors of time and military necessity were not as urgent as they have been represented to be.

Moreover, there was no adequate proof that the Federal Bureau of Investigation and the military and naval intelligence services did not have the espionage and sabotage situation well in hand during this long period. Nor is there any denial of the fact that not one person of Japanese ancestry was accused or convicted of espionage or sabotage after Pearl Harbor while they were still free, a fact which is some evidence of the loyalty of the vast majority of these individuals and of the effectiveness of the established methods of combatting these evils. It seems incredible that under these circumstances it would have been impossible to hold loyalty hearings for the mere 112,000 persons involved—or at least for the 70,000 American citizens—especially when a large part of this number represented children and elderly men and women. . . .[10]

I dissent, therefore, from this legalization of racism. Racial discrimination in any form and in any degree has no justifiable part whatever in our democratic way of life. It is unattractive in any setting but it is utterly revolting among a free people who have embraced the principles set forth in the Constitution of the United States. All residents of this nation are kin in some way by blood or culture to a foreign land. Yet they are primarily and necessarily a part of the new and distinct civilization of the United States. They must accordingly be treated at all times as the heirs of the American experiment and as entitled to all the rights and freedoms guaranteed by the Constitution.

45.2.2

Brown v. Board of Education (Brown I)

347 U.S. 483 (1954)

Korematsu was the first time that the Supreme Court applied strict scrutiny to a racial classification. Both the majority opinion and Murphy's dissent asked whether the racial classification was, in fact, necessary to serve a *compelling interest* (e.g., "military necessity") or whether the classification could have been more *narrowly tailored* to serve the same interest (e.g., "holding investigations and hearings to separate the loyal from the disloyal, as was done in the case of persons of German and Italian ancestry"). 323 U.S. at 241. But even though this test was less deferential to the government than *Plessy*'s rational-basis test, the result was the same. The Court upheld the classification.

Today, both *Plessy* and *Korematsu* are widely understood as decisions that are emphatically wrong. As law professor Jamal Greene has written, *Plessy*, *Korematsu*, *Lochner v. New York*, 198 U.S. 45 (1905),

---

[10] **Questions:** Here, Justice Frank Murphy contests the majority's application of a skeptical means-ends test. He writes that the exclusion was not the least-restrictive means of accomplishing the military's goal. And he also forcefully writes that this opinion reflects the "legalization of racism."

Again, is the problem with this law that it should have failed a skeptical means-ends test? Or does the test itself fail to capture what made this law unjust?

and *Dred Scott v. Sandford*, 60 U.S. (19 How.) 393 (1857), are "the American anticanon. Each case embodies a set of propositions that all legitimate constitutional decisions must be prepared to refute." Jamal Greene, *The Anticanon*, 125 Harv. L. Rev. 379, 380 (2011).

However, there is little consensus regarding *why*, precisely, the decisions were wrong. *See, e.g., Trump v. Hawaii*, 138 S. Ct. 2392, 2423 (2018) (declaring *Korematsu* "gravely wrong the day it was decided" in an opinion upholding the president's ban on the admission of immigrants from specified Muslim-majority countries). The decisions do not contain obvious "analytic errors." Greene, *supra*, at 381. Nor are they distinguishable "by unusually poor reasoning, by special moral failings, or because these problems exist in tandem." *Id.* at 383. Indeed, while many observers have argued that the decisions applied their means-ends tests incorrectly, Murphy's forceful dissent—the first opinion in Supreme Court history to use the word *racism*—illustrates in an understated manner how the problem with racial segregation and Japanese internment was not merely that the projects could have been more narrowly tailored.

The following decision, *Brown v. Board of Education* (*Brown I*), 347 U.S. 483 (1954)—a consolidated opinion considering a series of related cases—offers an alternative approach to evaluating the constitutionality of racial classifications. Instead of applying strict scrutiny, the Court overruled *Plessy* after contextually evaluating the ways in which certain racial classifications had been used to enforce racial subordination. Yet in contrast with *Plessy* and *Korematsu*, contemporary law professors found the decision difficult to justify with respect to "neutral principles" that "transcend any immediate result that is involved." Herbert Wechsler, *Toward Neutral Principles of Constitutional Law*, 73 Harv. L. Rev. 1, 19 (1959). "*Brown* was inconsistent with longstanding precedent, was in tension with the original expected application of the Fourteenth Amendment, was not compelled by the text of the Equal Protection Clause, and has required a Herculean effort—one well beyond the Court's competence—to implement comprehensively." Greene, *supra*, at 381–82.

Marshall, Houston, and social enlightenment. The effort began in 1933, when a law student named Thurgood Marshall graduated at the top of his class at Howard University School of Law, one of the few law schools in the South that accepted black students. Marshall had thrived under the mentorship of the law school's dean, Charles Hamilton Houston, whose rigorous classes on constitutional law trained students to do three things. First, learn the law *as it existed*. Second, learn *to apply that law* to a multitude of hypothetical fact patterns. And the third step was the most critical:

> In order to give meaning to steps one and two—if they were to be anything but 'parasites' on their society—African American lawyers were obligated to know what the law *should be*. They had to know the Constitution better than the Supreme Court

had allowed it to be known and trust its precepts more than the framers had themselves.

See Rawn James Jr., *Root and Branch* 52–53 (2009). One student remembered, "He kept hammering at us all those years that, as lawyers, we had to be social engineers or else we were parasites." *Id.* at 54.

Marshall and Houston's work on integrating law and grad schools. Nearly as soon as Marshall graduated, he began collaborating with Houston on a case that sought to integrate the University of Maryland School of Law. Although Marshall was from Baltimore, he hadn't applied to his home state's law school because of its informal policy of denying admission to all black students. *Id.* at 81. Yet the state also failed to establish any alternative law school—meaning that there was no public law school in the state for black students to attend. Instead, when a well-qualified black applicant named Donald Gaines Murray sought admission to the law school, the rejection letter told him that Maryland would pay for him to attend a law school in another state. *Id.* at 68–69.

Houston and Marshall represented Murray in a lawsuit seeking his admission under the Fourteenth Amendment. Invoking the separate-but-equal standard of *Plessy*, the lawyers argued that Maryland prohibited Murray from entering its law school solely because of his race yet had unconstitutionally failed to provide Murray with equal accommodations. *Id.* at 69–70. In response to Maryland's argument that Murray could attend a school of equal caliber outside the state, Houston and Marshall introduced evidence that the University of Maryland had the preeminent law school for lawyers who wanted to practice in Maryland. Its curriculum was unique in that it focused on Maryland state law, and its faculty and alumni were prominent Maryland attorneys. *Id.* at 72–73.

In *Murray v. Pearson*, 182 A. 590 (Md. 1936), the Maryland Court of Appeals agreed with Houston and Marshall that the doctrine of *Plessy* required the state to admit Murray as a student. Because this was a state decision, however, it applied only to Maryland. But Houston and Marshall realized that they had a winning argument: in states with graduate and professional schools that admitted only white students, they could invoke *Plessy* to force the states to integrate.

In a nearly identical case two years later, they persuaded the Supreme Court that the Equal Protection Clause prohibited Missouri from excluding black students from its flagship law school even though Missouri offered to pay for black students to attend school elsewhere. *Missouri ex rel. Gaines v. Canada*, 305 U.S. 337, 346 (1938); *see also Sipuel v. Bd. of Regents*, 332 U.S. 631, 633 (1948) (similar for Oklahoma).

Fresh from this success, Marshall founded the National Association for the Advancement of Colored People (NAACP) Legal Defense Fund (LDF), whose lawyers brought a second case against Missouri to seek the integration of its prestigious journalism school. But the state simply closed its school rather than integrate. *See State ex rel. Bluford v. Canada*, 153 S.W.2d 12, 18 (Mo. 1941).

A decade later, Constance Baker Motley, another LDF lawyer, brought similar lawsuits against Texas and Oklahoma, which adopted farcical tactics in defense. To prevent a black student named Heman Sweatt from attending the University of Texas Law School, Texas authorized the Texas State University for Negroes to hire five full-time professors to begin teaching law. Oklahoma, meanwhile, admitted a black student named George W. McLaurin to the University of Oklahoma graduate school but physically separated him from the rest of the student body. During lunch, the state required McLaurin to sit alone in the cafeteria. During class, it forced him to sit at a desk immediately outside the classroom door.

The Supreme Court struck down both states' policies. In *Sweatt v. Painter*, the Court explained that there was no "substantial equality" between Texas's flagship law school and the black law school that it established three years earlier. 339 U.S. 629, 633 (1950). Not only did the University of Texas have far more resources, but it also possessed "to a far greater degree those qualities which are incapable of objective measurement but which make for greatness in a school." *Id.* at 634. Considering the "reputation of the faculty, experience of the administration, position and influence of the alumni, standing in the community, traditions and prestige," the Court found it "difficult to believe that one who had a free choice between these law schools would consider the question close." *Id.* In *McLaurin v. Oklahoma State Regents for Higher Education*, the Court added that physically separating a black student from his classmates would "impair and inhibit his ability to study, to engage in discussions and exchange views with other students, and, in general, to learn his profession." 339 U.S. 637, 641 (1950). The Court concluded, "State-imposed restrictions which produce such inequalities cannot be sustained." *Id.*

Targeting *Plessy*. After their victories in Texas and Oklahoma, Marshall, Motley, and other lawyers from LDF trained their attack on *Plessy* itself. *Sweatt* and *McLaurin* established that racial segregation in graduate and professional schools was inherently unequal. When given the opportunity, states would dedicate enormous resources toward building the prestige, academic quality, and facilities of its flagship schools for white students while dedicating far fewer resources toward educating black students. The cases also established that even when black students were taught identical material as white students, forcing black students to sit outside a classroom—literally and figuratively—harmed and humiliated them. As a graduate of Howard University Law School, Marshall never argued that all-black schools were necessarily inferior to all-white schools. Far from it: Howard was producing the country's most exceptional constitutional lawyers, and all-black schools throughout the South were led by incredible teachers and administrators. The problems with segregation as Marshall saw it were that it stigmatized black students and, in practice, denied them access to tangible and intangible resources that states reserved for white students. James, *supra*, at 211–14.

Segregated elementary schools and the doll test. For their next case, Marshall and the LDF lawyers worked with plaintiffs from four states and the District of Columbia to amass a record demonstrating how segregated elementary schools violated the Equal Protection Clause. Most of their evidence described how states had, for decades, brazenly underfunded black schools and underpaid black teachers—denying students the basic textbooks, school buses, and heating equipment necessary to learn. But some of the plaintiffs, notably Linda Brown of Topeka, Kansas, attended black schools that were as well resourced as white schools.

To demonstrate how even students like Brown were harmed by segregation, the lawyers introduced evidence known to history as the "doll test." *See* Richard Kluger, *Simple Justice* 315–21 (2004). Two black social psychologists, Kenneth and Mamie Clark, conducted a series of experiments in which they gave four dolls—two painted brown, two painted pink—to children aged three and up. When the children were asked which dolls were "good," which dolls "looked nice," or which dolls they preferred, even the black children pointed toward the pink dolls. *Id.* Yet when the black children were asked which dolls were most like them, they pointed toward the brown dolls—or they cried and ran out of the room. *Id.* The Clarks testified that these tests illustrated how even truly separate but equal schools could impose a "badge of inferiority" that *Plessy* had insisted did not exist. *Plessy*, 163 U.S. at 551.

The tests also illustrated how white children were harmed by racial segregation. Because white children were "being taught to gain personal status in an unrealistic and non-adaptive way," the Clarks found that they "often develop patterns of guilt feelings, rationalizations, and other mechanisms which they must use in an attempt to protect themselves from recognizing the essential injustice of their unrealistic fears and hatreds of minority groups." Heather McGhee, *The Sum of Us* 182–83 (2021).

When the *Brown* cases were argued before the Supreme Court in 1952, the justices deadlocked in conference over whether to overturn *Plessy*. Chief Justice Fred Vinson indicated that he would vote with a 5–4 majority to sustain the precedent. Michael Klarman, *From Jim Crow to Civil Rights* 298 (2004). Worried about the "catastrophic" impact of such a decision, Justice Felix Frankfurter suggested that the cases should be reargued on the pretext that the justices required further briefing on the original understanding of the Fourteenth Amendment and the remedial options that would be available if the Court invalidated segregation. *Id.* at 301. The Court agreed, and reargument was set for December 1953. That September, Vinson died. Frankfurter recorded

Vinson's death as "the first indication I have ever had that there is a God." *Id.* at 302.

President Dwight D. Eisenhower replaced Vinson with Earl Warren, the governor of California who had presided over the World War II internment of Japanese Americans. As chief justice, however, Warren established himself as one of the most racially progressive justices in the Court's history. Not only did he cast the deciding vote in favor of overruling *Plessy*, but he also persuaded the Court to do so unanimously. Aware that white southerners would violently resist the Court's declaration that racial segregation was unconstitutional, the Court presented a united front in a brief opinion.

■ MR. CHIEF JUSTICE WARREN delivered the opinion of the Court.[11]

These cases come to us from the States of Kansas, South Carolina, Virginia, and Delaware. They are premised on different facts and different local conditions, but a common legal question justifies their consideration together in this consolidated opinion.

In each of the cases, minors of the Negro race, through their legal representatives, seek the aid of the courts in obtaining admission to the public schools of their community on a nonsegregated basis. In each instance, they had been denied admission to schools attended by white children under laws requiring or permitting segregation according to race. This segregation was alleged to deprive the plaintiffs of the equal protection of the laws under the Fourteenth Amendment. In each of the cases other than the Delaware case, a three-judge federal district court denied relief to the plaintiffs on the so-called "separate but equal" doctrine announced by this Court in *Plessy* v. *Ferguson,* 163 U. S. 537. Under that doctrine, equality of treatment is accorded when the races are provided substantially equal facilities, even though these facilities be separate. In the Delaware case, the Supreme Court of Delaware adhered to that doctrine, but ordered that the plaintiffs be admitted to the white schools because of their superiority to the Negro schools.

The plaintiffs contend that segregated public schools are not "equal" and cannot be made "equal," and that hence they are deprived of the equal protection of the laws. Because of the obvious importance of the question presented, the Court took jurisdiction. Argument was heard in the 1952 Term, and reargument was heard this Term on certain questions propounded by the Court.

Reargument was largely devoted to the circumstances surrounding the adoption of the Fourteenth Amendment in 1868. It covered exhaustively consideration of the Amendment in Congress, ratification by the states, then existing practices in racial segregation, and the views of proponents and opponents of the Amendment. This

---

[11] **As You Read, Consider:** *Brown v. Board of Education* is correctly recognized as one of the Supreme Court's greatest decisions. It is also cited as the primary illustration of the need for the judicial review of all legislation, state and federal. Yet the Supreme Court decided Brown 71 years after the Civil Rights Cases, in which it held that Congress had no power to enact an antidiscrimination law. By disabling Congress from preempting state laws in this field, the Civil Rights Cases encouraged states to adopt Jim Crow laws—a practice that the Court then upheld in *Plessy v. Ferguson*. Combined, the Civil Rights Cases and Plessy meant that the only institution capable of overturning racial segregation on a nationwide basis in 1954 was the Supreme Court, not Congress.

In light of this background, does Chief Justice Earl Warren's opinion represent the best possible accommodation between majoritarianism on the one hand and the equality and dignity of a subordinated group on the other? What else might the Court have done to vindicate these dueling principles?

discussion and our own investigation convince us that, although these sources cast some light, it is not enough to resolve the problem with which we are faced. At best, they are inconclusive. The most avid proponents of the post-War Amendments undoubtedly intended them to remove all legal distinctions among "all persons born or naturalized in the United States." Their opponents, just as certainly, were antagonistic to both the letter and the spirit of the Amendments and wished them to have the most limited effect. What others in Congress and the state legislatures had in mind cannot be determined with any degree of certainty.

An additional reason for the inconclusive nature of the Amendment's history, with respect to segregated schools, is the status of public education at that time. In the South, the movement toward free common schools, supported by general taxation, had not yet taken hold. Education of white children was largely in the hands of private groups. Education of Negroes was almost nonexistent, and practically all of the race were illiterate. In fact, any education of Negroes was forbidden by law in some states. Today, in contrast, many Negroes have achieved outstanding success in the arts and sciences as well as in the business and professional world. It is true that public school education at the time of the Amendment had advanced further in the North, but the effect of the Amendment on Northern States was generally ignored in the congressional debates. Even in the North, the conditions of public education did not approximate those existing today. The curriculum was usually rudimentary; ungraded schools were common in rural areas; the school term was but three months a year in many states; and compulsory school attendance was virtually unknown. As a consequence, it is not surprising that there should be so little in the history of the Fourteenth Amendment relating to its intended effect on public education.

In the first cases in this Court construing the Fourteenth Amendment, decided shortly after its adoption, the Court interpreted it as proscribing all state-imposed discriminations against the Negro race.[5] The doctrine of "separate but equal" did not make its appearance in this Court until 1896 in the case of *Plessy* v. *Ferguson, supra,* involving not education but transportation. American courts have since labored with the doctrine for over half a century. In this Court, there have been six cases involving the "separate but equal" doctrine in the field of public education. In *Cumming* v. *County Board of Education,* 175 U. S. 528, and *Gong Lum* v. *Rice,* 275 U. S. 78, the validity of the doctrine itself was not challenged. In more recent cases, all on the graduate school level, inequality was found in that specific benefits enjoyed by white students were denied to Negro students of the same educational qualifications. *Missouri ex rel. Gaines* v. *Canada,* 305 U. S. 337; *Sipuel* v. *Oklahoma,* 332 U. S. 631; *Sweatt* v. *Painter,* 339 U. S. 629; *McLaurin* v. *Oklahoma State Regents,* 339 U. S. 637. In none of these cases was it necessary to re-examine the doctrine to grant relief to the Negro plaintiff. And in *Sweatt* v. *Painter,* the Court expressly reserved decision on the question whether *Plessy* v. *Ferguson* should be held inapplicable to public education.

In the instant cases, that question is directly presented. Here, unlike *Sweatt* v. *Painter,* there are findings below that the Negro and white schools involved have been equalized, or are being equalized, with respect to buildings, curricula, qualifications and salaries of teachers, and other "tangible" factors. Our decision, therefore, cannot turn on merely a comparison of these tangible factors in the Negro and white schools involved in each of the cases. We must look instead to the effect of segregation itself on public education.

---

[5] *Slaughter-House Cases,* 16 Wall. 36, 67–72 (1873); *Strauder* v. *West Virginia,* 100 U. S. 303, 307–308 (1880). . . .

In approaching this problem, we cannot turn the clock back to 1868 when the Amendment was adopted, or even to 1896 when *Plessy* v. *Ferguson* was written. We must consider public education in the light of its full development and its present place in American life throughout the Nation. Only in this way can it be determined if segregation in public schools deprives these plaintiffs of the equal protection of the laws.[12]

Today, education is perhaps the most important function of state and local governments. Compulsory school attendance laws and the great expenditures for education both demonstrate our recognition of the importance of education to our democratic society. It is required in the performance of our most basic public responsibilities, even service in the armed forces. It is the very foundation of good citizenship. Today it is a principal instrument in awakening the child to cultural values, in preparing him for later professional training, and in helping him to adjust normally to his environment. In these days, it is doubtful that any child may reasonably be expected to succeed in life if he is denied the opportunity of an education. Such an opportunity, where the state has undertaken to provide it, is a right which must be made available to all on equal terms.

We come then to the question presented: Does segregation of children in public schools solely on the basis of race, even though the physical facilities and other "tangible" factors may be equal, deprive the children of the minority group of equal educational opportunities? We believe that it does.

In *Sweatt* v. *Painter*, in finding that a segregated law school for Negroes could not provide them equal educational opportunities, this Court relied in large part on "those qualities which are incapable of objective measurement but which make for greatness in a law school." In *McLaurin* v. *Oklahoma State Regents*, the Court, in requiring that a Negro admitted to a white graduate school be treated like all other students, again resorted to intangible considerations: ". . . his ability to study, to engage in discussions and exchange views with other students, and, in general, to learn his profession." Such considerations apply with added force to children in grade and high schools. To separate them from others of similar age and qualifications solely because of their race generates a feeling of inferiority as to their status in the community that may affect their hearts and minds in a way unlikely ever to be undone. The effect of this separation on their educational opportunities was well stated by a finding in the Kansas case by a court which nevertheless felt compelled to rule against the Negro plaintiffs:

"Segregation of white and colored children in public schools has a detrimental effect upon the colored children. The impact is greater when it has the sanction of the law; for the policy of separating the races is usually interpreted as denoting the inferiority of the negro group. A sense of inferiority affects the motivation of a child to learn. Segregation with the sanction of law, therefore, has a tendency to [retard] the educational and mental development of negro children and to deprive them of some of the benefits they would receive in a racial[ly] integrated school system."

---

12 **Question:** Warren here explicitly rejects the need to interpret the Fourteenth Amendment in light of the intentions of its ratifiers. One scholar has recently observed that conservative critics of racial integration attempted to "delegitimize *Brown*" in the 1960s by arguing that the Constitution should always be interpreted as its authors originally intended. Calvin TerBeek, "*Clocks Must Always Be Turned Back*": Brown v. Board of Education *and the Racial Origins of Constitutional Originalism*, 115 Am. Pol. Sci. Rev. 821, 822 (2021). Assuming for the sake of argument that *Brown I* is inconsistent with originalism, does that suggest that *Brown I* was wrongly decided or that originalism may sometimes be incompatible with just results?

Whatever may have been the extent of psychological knowledge at the time of *Plessy* v. *Ferguson,* this finding is amply supported by modern authority.[11] Any language in *Plessy* v. *Ferguson* contrary to this finding is rejected.

We conclude that in the field of public education the doctrine of "separate but equal" has no place. Separate educational facilities are inherently unequal.[13] Therefore, we hold that the plaintiffs and others similarly situated for whom the actions have been brought are, by reason of the segregation complained of, deprived of the equal protection of the laws guaranteed by the Fourteenth Amendment. This disposition makes unnecessary any discussion whether such segregation also violates the Due Process Clause of the Fourteenth Amendment.

Because these are class actions, because of the wide applicability of this decision, and because of the great variety of local conditions, the formulation of decrees in these cases presents problems of considerable complexity. On reargument, the consideration of appropriate relief was necessarily subordinated to the primary question—the constitutionality of segregation in public education. We have now announced that such segregation is a denial of the equal protection of the laws. In order that we may have the full assistance of the parties in formulating decrees, the cases will be restored to the docket, and the parties are requested to present further argument [on what should be the appropriate remedy].[14]

NOTE: DISTRICT OF COLUMBIA

Brown addressed challenges to racial segregation in state public schools and held that such segregation violated the Fourteenth Amendment. But there was also a challenge to racial segregation in the District of Columbia, which the Fourteenth Amendment doesn't cover. As discussed earlier with regard to the equal-protection principle of the Fifth Amendment (section 44.3), the Court thought it would be "unthinkable" that the Constitution "would impose a lesser duty on the Federal Government." *Bolling v. Sharpe*, 347 U.S. 497, 500 (1954).

In *Bolling v. Sharpe*, 347 U.S. 497 (1954), decided the same day as *Brown I*, the Court therefore interpreted the Due Process Clause of the Fifth Amendment to embody the same equal-protection principles as the Fourteenth Amendment. As in *Korematsu*, the *Bolling* Court declared that "[c]lassifications based solely upon race must be scrutinized with particular care, since they are contrary to our traditions and hence constitutionally suspect." 347 U.S. at 499. Applying a version of the rational-basis-with-bite test, the Court concluded, "Segregation in public education is not reasonably related to any proper governmental objective, and thus it imposes on Negro children of the District of Columbia a burden that constitutes an arbitrary deprivation of their liberty in violation of the Due Process Clause." *Id.* at 500.

---

11 K. B. Clark, Effect of Prejudice and Discrimination on Personality Development (Midcentury White House Conference on Children and Youth, 1950). . . . And see generally Myrdal, An American Dilemma (1944).

13 **Questions:** Warren repeatedly emphasizes that the constitutional violation in this case does not depend on the unequal distribution of resources among schools. Why, then, does he think that racial segregation in education is *inherently* unequal? Do you agree with him that the harm caused by segregation is inevitable?

14 **Note:** Warren and the rest of the *Brown I* Court correctly predicted that the decision would generate massive resistance. Sections 46.1–46.2 discuss how the Supreme Court attempted to enforce its holding in the South and, later, in the North.

45.3 STRICT SCRUTINY APPLIED

Brown v. Board of Education, 347 U.S. 483 (1954), worked a revolution in American society. It also generated an enormous backlash in the South. We will discuss the Court's response to this "massive resistance" shortly, in the context of the power of federal courts to remedy equal-protection violations (section 46.1). But southern segregationists were not the only people who objected to *Brown*. One of the nation's leading constitutional scholars, Columbia law professor Herbert Wechsler, famously and controversially criticized *Brown* as an unprincipled decision—criticism that led to the Court's embrace of strict scrutiny.

Wechsler argued that for judicial review to be legitimate, a decision must rest on principles "that in their generality and their neutrality transcend any immediate result that is involved." Herbert Wechsler, *Toward Neutral Principles of Constitutional Law*, 73 Harv. L. Rev. 1, 19 (1959). Wechsler claimed that such "neutral principles" were absent from *Brown*. He charged *Brown* with (1) failing to adhere to judicial precedent, (2) failing to interpret the Constitution consistently with historical practice, (3) failing to respect the intentions of the Fourteenth Amendment's authors, (4) failing to consider the consequences of its ruling—and also, most importantly, (5) failing to explain its reasoning. *Id.* at 31–32. Wechsler observed that *Brown* held that segregated schools were "inherently unequal" in light of the stigma that they imposed on black children, but the only supporting evidence that the Court offered was a footnote containing "modern authority." *Id.* at 32. Wechsler wrote that as an empirical matter, this holding was untested: "Suppose that more Negroes in a community preferred separation than opposed it? Would that be relevant to whether they were hurt or aided by segregation as opposed to integration?" *Id.* at 33. And Wechsler wrote that as an ideological matter, *Plessy v. Ferguson*, 163 U.S. 537 (1896), had a point when it reasoned that truly equal but separate facilities weren't inherently discriminatory. He asked, "Is a prohibition of miscegenation a discrimination against the colored member of the couple who would like to marry?" *Id.* at 34.

Wechsler concluded that the only neutral principle that could justify *Brown* was that segregation was "the denial by the state of freedom to associate, a denial that impinges in the same way on any groups or races that may be involved." *Id.* But, he added, "if the freedom of association is denied by segregation, integration forces an association upon those for whom it is unpleasant or repugnant." *Id.* The Court, therefore, had denied the right of association to segregationists while granting it to integrationists without any external basis in "neutral" principles." *Id.*

Later scholars heavily criticized Wechsler's conclusions because they saw no difference between his so-called neutral principle (people should be free to associate) and the principle he criticized (political majorities should not stigmatize minorities). *See, e.g.*, Ronald Turner, *On Neutral and Preferred Principles of Constitutional Law*, 74 U. Pitt. L. Rev. 433 (2013). These scholars have observed that when "'neutral' (taking no sides or position) modifies 'principle' (taking a side and declaring a substantive position), 'neutral principle' (distinguishable from a principle of neutrality) is incoherent, indeterminate, and oxymoronic." *Id.* at 471. "To put it more bluntly, there simply cannot *be* a neutral principle." Frederick Schauer, *Neutrality and Judicial Review*, 22 L. & Phil. 217, 234 (2003). In this respect, *Brown*'s interpretation of the Equal Protection Clause may have departed from precedent while still being principled.

Other scholars took issue with Wechsler's claim that *Brown* had favored the associational interests of integrationists at the expense of the associational interests of segregationists. In 1980, Harvard law professor Derrick Bell analyzed the history of Supreme Court cases involving black people and announced that the neutral principle of *Brown* was the principle of "interest convergence": "The interest of blacks in achieving racial equality will be accommodated only when it converges with the interests of whites." Derrick A. Bell Jr., Brown v. Board of Education *and the Interest-Convergence Dilemma*, 93 Harv. L. Rev. 518, 523 (1980). That is, "the availability of fourteenth amendment protection in racial cases may not actually be determined by the character of harm suffered by blacks or the quantum of liability proved against whites" but is instead dependent upon "perhaps subconscious judicial conclusions that the remedies, if granted, will secure, advance, or at least not harm societal interests deemed important by middle and upper class whites." *Id.* Bell observed that before *Brown*, the Court had no reason to think that ending segregation would advance the goals of the justices' social acquaintances. But in *Brown*, the State Department filed an amicus brief complaining that racial segregation was interfering with the United States' efforts to compete with the Soviet Union in Africa and Latin America. *Id.* at 524–25. Other institutions that catered to white interests, including *Time* magazine, accordingly predicted that "[i]n many countries, where U.S. prestige and leadership have been damaged by the fact of U.S. segregation," a decision in favor of the NAACP "will come as a timely reassertion of the basic American principle that 'all men are created equal.'" *Id.* at 524.

Despite these criticisms of Wechsler's position, Wechsler's own criticism of *Brown* profoundly influenced the manner by which the Supreme Court approached future questions of racial discrimination. In later cases, members of the Court attempted to avoid directly weighing the principles in favor of a racial classification against the burdens that such a classification imposed. Instead, the Court embraced what it regarded as another neutral principle: it is illegitimate for a state to treat people differently because of their race. To apply this principle, the Court turned to the "most rigid scrutiny," *Korematsu v. United States*, 323 U.S.

214, 216 (1944), or "strict scrutiny," *Skinner v. Oklahoma ex rel. Williamson*, 316 U.S. 535, 541 (1942), of earlier cases. In this respect, strict scrutiny became a method by which the Court determined whether a law was *really* motivated by race or whether it was motivated instead by an innocuous purpose.

45.3.1

McLaughlin v. Florida

379 U.S. 184 (1964)

The Court first formally applied strict scrutiny in its modern sense in the following case, *McLaughlin v. Florida*, 379 U.S. 184 (1964)—decided one year before *Griswold v. Connecticut*, 381 U.S. 479 (1965), and three years before *Loving v. Virginia*, 388 U.S. 1 (1967). Like many southern states, Florida made it a crime for "[a]ny negro man and white woman, or any white man and negro woman, who are not married to each other, [to] habitually live in and occupy in the nighttime the same room." Fla. Stat. § 798.05. This sort of law had been upheld by the *Plessy*-era case of *Pace v. Alabama* because it treated white people and black people equally. 106 U.S. 583, 585 (1883). As noted, Wechsler referenced this point in his criticism of *Brown*, as he found it difficult to understand how the equal application of a law like this was *discriminatory* against only the black person in the relationship.

In striking down Florida's law, the Supreme Court in *McLaughlin* embraced its own neutral principle: any reference to race is presumptively motivated by a purpose of discriminating against black people unless the law can be proven to be necessary to serve a compelling purpose.

■ MR. JUSTICE WHITE delivered the opinion of the Court. . . .[15]

Appellants were charged with a violation of § 798.05[, part of a chapter entitled "Adultery and Fornication."] The elements of the offense as described by the trial judge are the (1) habitual occupation of a room at night, (2) by a Negro and a white person (3) who are not married. The State presented evidence going to each factor, appellants' constitutional contentions were overruled and the jury returned a verdict of guilty. . . .

It is readily apparent that § 798.05 treats the interracial couple made up of a white person and a Negro differently than it does any other couple. No couple other than a Negro and a white person can be convicted under § 798.05 and no other section proscribes the precise conduct banned by § 798.05. Florida makes no claim to the contrary in this Court. However, all whites and Negroes who engage in the forbidden conduct are covered by the section and each member of the interracial couple is subject to the same penalty.

---

[15] **As You Read, Consider:** Why, precisely, does Justice Byron White think that Florida's law violates the Equal Protection Clause when it treats white people and black people equally? Does he embrace an anti-race-consciousness interpretation of the clause or an antisubordination interpretation? Does he emphasize the law's illegitimate purpose or its illegitimate effect in context?

In this situation, *Pace* v. *Alabama* is relied upon as controlling authority. In our view, however, *Pace* represents a limited view of the Equal Protection Clause which has not withstood analysis in the subsequent decisions of this Court. In that case, the Court let stand a conviction under an Alabama statute forbidding adultery or fornication between a white person and a Negro and imposing a greater penalty than allowed under another Alabama statute of general application and proscribing the same conduct whatever the race of the participants. The opinion acknowledged that the purpose of the Equal Protection Clause "was to prevent hostile and discriminating State legislation against any person or class of persons" and that equality of protection under the laws implies that any person, "whatever his race . . . shall not be subjected, for the same offence, to any greater or different punishment." 106 U. S., at 584. But taking quite literally its own words, "for the same *offence*" (emphasis supplied), the Court pointed out that Alabama had designated as a separate offense the commission by a white person and a Negro of the identical acts forbidden by the general provisions. There was, therefore, no impermissible discrimination because the difference in punishment was "directed against the offense designated" and because in the case of each offense all who committed it, white and Negro, were treated alike. Under *Pace* the Alabama law regulating the conduct of both Negroes and whites satisfied the Equal Protection Clause since it applied equally to and among the members of the class which it reached without regard to the fact that the statute did not reach other types of couples performing the identical conduct and without any necessity to justify the difference in penalty established for the two offenses. Because each of the Alabama laws applied equally to those to whom it was applicable, the different treatment accorded interracial and intraracial couples was irrelevant.

This narrow view of the Equal Protection Clause was soon swept away. While acknowledging the currency of the view that "if the law deals alike with all of a certain class" it is not obnoxious to the Equal Protection Clause and that "as a general proposition, this is undeniably true," the Court in *Gulf, C. & S. F. R. Co.* v. *Ellis,* 165 U. S. 150, 155, said that it was "equally true that such classification cannot be made arbitrarily. . . ." Classification "must always rest upon some difference which bears a reasonable and just relation to the act in respect to which the classification is proposed, and can never be made arbitrarily and without any such basis." *Ibid.* "[A]rbitrary selection can never be justified by calling it classification." *Id.,* at 159. . . .

Judicial inquiry under the Equal Protection Clause, therefore, does not end with a showing of equal application among the members of the class defined by the legislation. The courts must reach and determine the question whether the classifications drawn in a statute are reasonable in light of its purpose—in this case, whether there is an arbitrary or invidious discrimination between those classes covered by Florida's cohabitation law and those excluded. That question is what *Pace* ignored and what must be faced here.

Normally, the widest discretion is allowed the legislative judgment in determining whether to attack some, rather than all, of the manifestations of the evil aimed at; and normally that judgment is given the benefit of every conceivable circumstance which might suffice to characterize the classification as reasonable rather than arbitrary and invidious. See, *e. g., Railway Express Agency, Inc.* v. *New York,* 336 U. S. 106, 110; *Lindsley* v. *Natural Carbonic Gas Co.,* 220 U. S. 61, 78–79. But we deal here with a classification based upon the race of the participants, which must be viewed in light of the historical fact that the central purpose of the Fourteenth Amendment was to eliminate racial discrimination emanating from official sources in the States. This strong policy renders racial classifications "constitutionally suspect," *Bolling* v. *Sharpe,* 347 U. S. 497, 499; and subject to the "most rigid scrutiny," *Korematsu* v. *United States,* 323 U. S. 214, 216; and "in most circumstances irrelevant" to any constitutionally acceptable legislative purpose, *Hirabayashi* v. *United States,* 320 U. S. 81, 100. Thus it is that racial classifications have been held invalid in a variety of contexts. See, *e. g., Watson* v. *City of Memphis,* 373 U. S. 526 (segregation in public parks and playgrounds); *Brown* v. *Board of Education,* 349 U. S. 294 (segregation in public schools).

We deal here with a racial classification embodied in a criminal statute. In this context, where the power of the State weighs most heavily upon the individual or the group, we must be especially sensitive to the policies of the Equal Protection Clause which, as reflected in congressional enactments dating from 1870, were intended to secure "the full and equal benefit of all laws and proceedings for the security of persons and property" and to subject all persons "to like punishment, pains, penalties, taxes, licenses, and exactions of every kind, and to no other." R. S. § 1977, 42 U. S. C. § 1981 (1958 ed.).

Our inquiry, therefore, is whether there clearly appears in the relevant materials some overriding statutory purpose requiring the proscription of the specified conduct when engaged in by a white person and a Negro, but not otherwise. Without such justification the racial classification contained in § 798.05 is reduced to an invidious discrimination forbidden by the Equal Protection Clause.

The State in its brief in this Court . . . says that the legislative purpose of § 798.05, like the other sections of chapter 798, was to prevent breaches of the basic concepts of sexual decency; and we see no reason to quarrel with the State's characterization of this statute, dealing as it does with illicit extramarital and premarital promiscuity.

We find nothing in this suggested legislative purpose, however, which makes it essential to punish promiscuity of one racial group and not that of another. There is no suggestion that a white person and a Negro are any more likely habitually to occupy the same room together than the white or the Negro couple or to engage in illicit intercourse if they do. Sections 798.01–798.05 indicate no legislative conviction that promiscuity by the interracial couple presents any particular problems requiring separate or different treatment if the suggested over-all policy of the chapter is to be adequately served. . . . This is not, therefore, a case . . . where the "[e]vils in the same field may be of different dimensions and proportions, requiring different remedies," *Williamson* v. *Lee Optical Co.,* 348 U. S. 483, 489. . . . That a general evil will be partially corrected may at times, and without more, serve to justify the limited application of a criminal law; but legislative discretion to employ the piecemeal approach stops short of permitting a State to narrow statutory coverage to focus on a racial group. . . .

There is involved here an exercise of the state police power which trenches upon the constitutionally protected freedom from invidious official discrimination based on race. Such a law, even though enacted pursuant to a valid state interest, bears a heavy burden of justification . . ., and will be upheld only if it is necessary, and not merely rationally related, to the accomplishment of a permissible state policy. . . .

NOTE: OTHER APPLICATIONS OF STRICT SCRUTINY

The "strict scrutiny" test of *McLaughlin* held that a law involving a "suspect" classification such as race is constitutional only where it is "necessary" to serve some "overriding statutory purpose." 379 U.S. at 192, 196. *McLaughlin*'s test was soon cited in *Griswold* and *Loving* as appropriate not only for equal-protection violations involving suspect classifications but also for due process violations involving "fundamental rights." *Griswold*, 381

U.S. at 497 (Goldberg, J., concurring); *Loving*, 388 U.S. at 12. Since 1965, therefore, the Supreme Court has applied roughly the same tests to analyze claims under the Due Process Clause and the Equal Protection Clause: rational-basis review for ordinary legislation, and strict scrutiny when suspect classes and fundamental rights are involved.

Applying strict scrutiny, the Court in the 1950s and 1960s invalidated virtually every racial classification it encountered. As *McLaughlin* noted, in cases like *Watson v. City of Memphis*, the Court prohibited states and local governments from operating racially segregated parks, golf courses, beaches, and other facilities. *Watson*, 373 U.S. 526, 533 (1963). In *Bailey v. Patterson*, the Court prohibited states from requiring racial segregation interstate transportation facilities. 369 U.S. 31, 33 (1962). And in cases arising under the criminal legal system, the Court invalidated racial segregation in places such as courtrooms. *See, e.g.*, *Johnson v. Virginia*, 373 U.S. 61, 62 (1963) (per curiam).

The biggest problem for the Court during this era was no longer which standard of scrutiny to apply to racial classifications, but rather whether a racial classification could be attributed to the "State" for purposes of the Fourteenth Amendment. *See, e.g.*, *Burton v. Wilmington Parking Auth.*, 365 U.S. 715, 721–22 (1961). This problem is the subject of the next section (section 45.4).

45.4 THE STATE-ACTION DOCTRINE

As discussed earlier with regard to Congress's power to enforce the Reconstruction amendments against personal violations (section 20.3), the Supreme Court has long interpreted the Fourteenth Amendment to apply only to states, not to individuals. As the Court wrote in the *Civil Rights Cases*, the Fourteenth Amendment declares only that "No State" shall deny anyone the equal protection of the laws: "It is State action of a particular character that is prohibited." 109 U.S. 3, 11 (1883). The *Civil Rights Cases* invoked this principle to strike down the Civil Rights Act of 1875, ignoring the argument that such "State action" is satisfied when a state breaches its duty to equally protect all of its residents. But while the *Civil Rights Cases* concerned Congress's power to enforce Section 5 of the Fourteenth Amendment, the Court has applied its state-action requirement to claims arising directly under the Fourteenth Amendment itself.

In general, under this state-action doctrine, the Court has held that the Fourteenth Amendment inarguably applies to state laws and regulations (as in *McLaughlin v. Florida*, 379 U.S. 184 (1964)) and local ordinances (as in *Yick Wo v. Hopkins*, 118 U.S. 356 (1886)). Although the Court held that state officers acting contrary to the law are not the "State" for purposes of the Eleventh Amendment, *see Ex parte Young*, 209 U.S. 123 (1908), the Court has also held that "[w]hen a state official, acting under color of state authority, invades, in the course of his duties, a private right secured by the Federal Constitution, that right is violated, even if the state officer not only exceeded his authority but disregarded special commands of the state law." *Iowa-Des Moines Nat'l Bank v. Bennett*, 284 U.S. 239, 246 (1931). Applying this logic, the Court has applied the Fourteenth Amendment to the acts of state governors, *Cooper v. Aaron*, 358 U.S. 1, 18–19 (1958); prosecutors, *Flowers v. Mississippi*, 139 S. Ct. 2228, 2251 (2019); judges, *Pulliam v. Allen*, 466 U.S. 522, 524–25 (1984); and law enforcement officers, *Graham v. Connor*, 490 U.S. 386, 399 (1989). As the Court wrote in *United States v. Classic*, "Misuse of power, possessed by virtue of state law and made possible only because the wrongdoer is clothed with the authority of the state law, is action taken 'under color of' state law." 313 U.S. 299, 326 (1941).

The state-action doctrine presented an enormous problem for Thurgood Marshall, legal counsel for the National Association for the Advancement of Colored People (NAACP), and the NAACP Legal Defense Fund (LDF) as they sought to attack segregation in settings outside of education. For example, for nearly a century before the 1960s, southern political elections were dominated by the Democratic Party, a private organization, which refused to allow black voters to participate in primary elections. When a black voter named R. R. Grovey challenged his exclusion from the Democratic primary, the Supreme Court applied the state-action doctrine and held that Grovey had not been "discriminated against or denied any right to vote by the state of Texas." *Grovey v. Townsend*, 295 U.S. 45, 55 (1935).

But as the Court became more progressive after 1937, it expanded the scope of the state-action doctrine to include private political organizations like the Democratic Party. In *Smith v. Allwright*, 321 U.S. 649 (1944)—a case argued by Marshall in his role as NAACP counsel—the Court overruled *Grovey* and declared the "white primary" unconstitutional. The Court explained that the Fifteenth Amendment "is not to be nullified by a state through casting its electoral process in a form which permits a private organization to practice racial discrimination in the election." *Id.* at 664.

The Court expanded the state-action doctrine still further in *Shelley v. Kraemer*, 334 U.S. 1 (1948). When J. D. Shelley and his family purchased a home in St. Louis, Missouri, a white neighbor who lived ten blocks away, Louis Kraemer, sued to enforce a racially restrictive covenant in Shelley's deed. Shelley was black, yet the deed prohibited anyone who belonged to "the Negro or Mongolian Race" from occupying the home. *Shelley*, 334 U.S. at 5. When Shelley's case reached the Supreme Court, it was consolidated with a similar case brought by Marshall and the NAACP LDF. Marshall argued that while a discriminatory private contract between a home buyer and seller might not involve any state action, Kraemer's lawsuit to *enforce* the covenant introduced a court—a state actor—into the discrimination.

The Supreme Court agreed, writing that the "purposes of the agreements were secured only by judicial enforcement by state courts of the restrictive terms of the agreements." *Id.* at 13–14. The Court wrote that "from the time of the adoption of the Fourteenth Amendment until the present, it has been the consistent ruling of this Court that the action of the States to which the Amendment has reference includes action of state courts and state judicial officials." *Id.* at 18. It explained that the states had not merely allowed private individuals to discriminate, but had "made available to such individuals the full coercive power of government to deny to petitioners, on the grounds of race or color, the enjoyment of property rights . . . ." *Id.* at 19. Therefore, "[t]he judicial action in each case bears the clear and unmistakable imprimatur of the State." *Id.*; *see Hurd v. Hodge*, 334 U.S. 24, 33–34 (1948) (holding that a similar racial covenant in the District of Columbia violated the Civil Rights Act of 1866).

After the Supreme Court began applying strict scrutiny to all racial classifications, states and local governments sought to take advantage of the state-action requirement by closing public schools and facilitating the opening of private schools known derisively as "segregation academies." *See* J. Todd Moye, *Let the People Decide* 177–79 (2004). Southern governments similarly transferred ownership of parks, playgrounds, and pools to private hands—or closed them. *Id.* In light of this obvious attempt to evade *Brown*, LDF lawyers successfully invoked the Fourteenth Amendment to challenge discrimination by privately owned restaurants, department stores, parks, and other gathering places.

In one of the first of these cases, *Burton v. Wilmington Parking Authority*, 365 U.S. 715 (1961), the Court applied the Equal Protection Clause to the Eagle Coffee Shoppe, a privately owned restaurant leased from the City of Wilmington's public parking authority. The Court reaffirmed "that private conduct abridging individual rights does no violence to the Equal Protection Clause unless to some significant extent the State in any of its manifestations has been found to become involved in it." *Burton*, 365 U.S. at 722. But the Court held that the State of Delaware had become sufficiently "involved" in the discrimination by the coffee shop: the parking authority had built and owned the building, the restaurant was "operated as an integral part of a public building devoted to a public parking service," the funds from the restaurant financed the rest of the building, and the state had the authority to regulate the restaurant. *Id.* at 724. The Court concluded:

> It is irony amounting to grave injustice that in one part of a single building, erected and maintained with public funds by an agency of the State to serve a public purpose, all persons have equal rights, while in another portion, also serving the public, a Negro is a second-class citizen.

Id.

But while *Burton* considered discrimination by a privately owned restaurant within a public building to be state action, the Court fractured when presented with sit-in cases involving privately owned restaurants.

In 1960, several black students conducted a sit-in at a segregated restaurant in downtown Baltimore, where they were arrested and convicted of criminal trespass. The students challenged their conviction under the Fourteenth Amendment: either the state was sufficiently involved in regulating the restaurant to constitute state action, as in *Burton*, or the arrest and conviction by a police officer and judge constituted state action, as in *Shelley*.

In *Bell v. Maryland*, 378 U.S. 226 (1964), the Supreme Court ultimately dodged the question by observing that Maryland had changed its state law to prohibit racial segregation. But in dueling separate opinions, Justice William O. Douglas and Justice Hugo Black sharply disagreed about whether state action was involved. Douglas cited *Shelley* to maintain that "Maryland's actions against these Negroes was as authoritative as any case where the State in one way or another puts its full force behind a policy. The policy here was segregation in places of public accommodation; and Maryland enforced that policy with her police, her prosecutors, and her courts." *Bell*, 378 U.S. at 257 (Douglas, J., concurring). But Black observed that if the restaurant owner had removed the protestors by force instead of by calling the police, then no state action would have been involved. "None of our past cases justifies reading the Fourteenth Amendment in a way that might well penalize citizens who are law-abiding enough to call upon the law and its officers for protection instead of using their own physical strength or dangerous weapons to preserve their rights," Black wrote. *Id.* at 328 (Black, J., dissenting). "Nor can whatever prejudice and bigotry the victim of a crime may have be automatically attributed to the State that prosecutes. *Id.* at 327 (Black, J., dissenting). *But see N.Y. Times Co. v. Sullivan*, 376 U.S. 254, 266 (1964) (finding state action where an individual sued the *New York Times* for publishing an allegedly defamatory advertisement).

45.4.1

Moose Lodge No. 107 v. Irvis

407 U.S. 163 (1972)

By the time Chief Justice Earl Warren retired from the Supreme Court in 1969, the Supreme Court still had not conclusively determined when a private restaurant or other business could violate the Fourteenth Amendment. But in many cases challenging discrimination by individuals, the Warren Court found state action. In *United States v. Guest*, 383 U.S. 745 (1966), discussed earlier with respect to Congress's power to enforce the Reconstruction amendments against personal violations (section 20.3), the most liberal members of the Warren Court wrote that Congress could enforce the Fourteenth Amendment directly against private individuals, while the moderates were willing to interpret the state-action doctrine very loosely. Similarly, in cases involving segregated parks, lunch counters, and restrooms, the Court held that a state official could trigger the state-action requirement merely by encouraging a business to maintain segregation, *Lombard v. Louisiana*, 373 U.S. 267, 273 (1963), or by allowing private parties to arrest trespassers, *Griffin v. Maryland*, 378 U.S. 130, 135 (1964).

This expansive view of state action abruptly came to an end in 1969, when President Richard Nixon replaced Warren with Warren Burger. Chief Justice Burger and other Nixon appointees, notably William Rehnquist, restored the narrow reading of the state-action doctrine in their first opportunity to do so: *Moose Lodge No. 107 v. Irvis*, 407 U.S. 163 (1972).

The Loyal Order of Moose is one of the country's many fraternal and service organizations, along with the Freemasons, the Rotary Club, and the Lions Club. Local "lodges" of the Moose typically operate bars and dining rooms for use by members and their guests. Through the 1970s, the Moose maintained an exclusive membership policy—one that "restrict[ed] membership to the Caucasian race and permitt[ed] members to bring only Caucasian guests on lodge premises, particularly to the dining room and bar." *Moose Lodge*, 407 U.S. at 166. When a white member brought a black guest named K. Leroy Irvis to the Moose Lodge No. 107 in Pennsylvania, the dining room refused to serve Irvis because of his race.

In *Daniel v. Paul,* the Warren Court had held that a similar segregation policy violated the Civil Rights Act of 1964 because the private club in that case served food and drinks whose ingredients had traveled in interstate commerce. 395 U.S. 298, 313 (1969). But in this case, Irvis brought his challenge directly under the Fourteenth Amendment. Irvis argued that because the Pennsylvania liquor board issued the Moose Lodge a license that authorized the sale of alcoholic beverages on its premises, the refusal of service to him was state action for purposes of the Equal Protection Clause.

The *Moose Lodge* Court found no Fourteenth Amendment violation.

■ MR. JUSTICE REHNQUIST delivered the opinion of the Court. . . .[16]

Moose Lodge is a private club in the ordinary meaning of that term. It is a local chapter of a national fraternal organization having well-defined requirements for membership. It conducts all of its activities in a building that is owned by it. It is not publicly funded. Only members and guests are permitted in any lodge of the order; one may become a guest only by invitation of a member or upon invitation of the house committee.

[Appellee Leroy Irvis], while conceding the right of private clubs to choose members upon a discriminatory basis, asserts that the licensing of Moose Lodge to serve liquor by the Pennsylvania Liquor Control Board amounts to such state involvement with the club's activities as to make its discriminatory practices forbidden

[16] **As You Read, Consider:** Pennsylvania has authorized Moose Lodge No. 107 to sell alcoholic beverages to white people without also requiring Moose Lodge to sell alcoholic beverages to black people. Why does Justice William Rehnquist think that this authorization is not enough to implicate Pennsylvania under the Fourteenth Amendment? How does he define *state action*?

by the Equal Protection Clause of the Fourteenth Amendment. The relief sought and obtained by appellee in the District Court was an injunction forbidding the licensing by the liquor authority of Moose Lodge until it ceased its discriminatory practices. We conclude that Moose Lodge's refusal to serve food and beverages to a guest by reason of the fact that he was a Negro does not, under the circumstances here presented, violate the Fourteenth Amendment.

In 1883, this Court in *The Civil Rights Cases,* 109 U. S. 3, set forth the essential dichotomy between discriminatory action by the State, which is prohibited by the Equal Protection Clause, and private conduct, "however discriminatory or wrongful," against which that clause "erects no shield," *Shelley* v. *Kraemer,* 334 U. S. 1, 13 (1948). That dichotomy has been subsequently reaffirmed in *Shelley* and in *Burton* v. *Wilmington Parking Authority,* 365 U. S. 715 (1961).

While the principle is easily stated, the question of whether particular discriminatory conduct is private, on the one hand, or amounts to "state action," on the other hand, frequently admits of no easy answer. "Only by sifting facts and weighing circumstances can the non-obvious involvement of the State in private conduct be attributed its true significance." *Burton* v. *Wilmington Parking Authority, supra,* at 722. . . .

The Court has never held, of course, that discrimination by an otherwise private entity would be violative of the Equal Protection Clause if the private entity receives any sort of benefit or service at all from the State, or if it is subject to state regulation in any degree whatever. Since state-furnished services include such necessities of life as electricity, water, and police and fire protection, such a holding would utterly emasculate the distinction between private as distinguished from state conduct set forth in *The Civil Rights Cases,* and adhered to in subsequent decisions. Our holdings indicate that where the impetus for the discrimination is private, the State must have "significantly involved itself with invidious discriminations," *Reitman* v. *Mulkey,* 387 U. S. 369, 380 (1967), in order for the discriminatory action to fall within the ambit of the constitutional prohibition.

Our prior decisions dealing with discriminatory refusal of service in public eating places are significantly different factually from the case now before us. *Peterson* v. *City of Greenville,* 373 U. S. 244 (1963), dealt with the trespass prosecution of persons who "sat in" at a restaurant to protest its refusal of service to Negroes. There the Court held that although the ostensible initiative for the trespass prosecution came from the proprietor, the existence of a local ordinance requiring segregation of races in such places was tantamount to the State having "commanded a particular result," 373 U. S., at 248. . . . [T]here is no suggestion in this record that the Pennsylvania statutes and regulations governing the sale of liquor are intended either overtly or covertly to encourage discrimination. . . .

[T]here is [also] nothing approaching the symbiotic relationship between lessor and lessee that was present in *Burton,* where the private lessee obtained the benefit of locating in a building owned by the state-created parking authority, and the parking authority was enabled to carry out its primary public purpose of furnishing parking space by advantageously leasing portions of the building constructed for that purpose to commercial lessees such as the owner of the Eagle Restaurant. Unlike *Burton,* the Moose Lodge building is located on land owned by it, not by any public authority. Far from apparently holding itself out as a place of public accommodation, Moose Lodge quite ostentatiously proclaims the fact that it is not open to the public at large. Nor is it located and operated in such surroundings that although private in name, it discharges a function or performs a service that would otherwise in all likelihood be performed by the State. In short, while Eagle was a public restaurant in a public building, Moose Lodge is a private social club in a private building. . . .

[T]he Pennsylvania Liquor Control Board plays absolutely no part in establishing or enforcing the membership or guest policies of the club that it licenses to serve liquor. There is no suggestion in this record that Pennsylvania law, either as written or as applied, discriminates against minority groups either in their right to apply for club licenses themselves or in their right to purchase and be served liquor in places of public accommodation. . . .

The District Court was at pains to point out in its opinion what it considered to be the "pervasive" nature of the regulation of private clubs by the Pennsylvania Liquor Control Board. As that court noted, an applicant for a club license must make such physical alterations in its premises as the board may require, must file a list of the names and addresses of its members and employees, and must keep extensive financial records. The board is granted the right to inspect the licensed premises at any time when patrons, guests, or members are present.

However detailed this type of regulation may be in some particulars, it cannot be said to in any way foster or encourage racial discrimination. Nor can it be said to make the State in any realistic sense a partner or even a joint venturer in the club's enterprise. . . . We therefore hold that . . . the operation of the regulatory scheme enforced by the Pennsylvania Liquor Control Board does not sufficiently implicate the State in the discriminatory guest policies of Moose Lodge to make the latter "state action" within the ambit of the Equal Protection Clause of the Fourteenth Amendment. . . .

■ MR. JUSTICE BRENNAN, with whom MR. JUSTICE MARSHALL joins, dissenting.

When Moose Lodge obtained its liquor license, the State of Pennsylvania became an active participant in the operation of the Lodge bar. Liquor licensing laws are only incidentally revenue measures; they are primarily pervasive regulatory schemes under which the State dictates and continually supervises virtually every detail of the operation of the licensee's business. Very few, if any, other licensed businesses experience such complete state involvement. Yet the Court holds that such involvement does not constitute "state action" making the Lodge's refusal to serve a guest liquor solely because of his race a violation of the Fourteenth Amendment. . . .

Plainly, the State of Pennsylvania's liquor regulations intertwine the State with the operation of the Lodge bar in a "significant way [and] lend [the State's] authority to the sordid business of racial discrimination." . . . [T]he decisive factor is the uniqueness and the all-pervasiveness of the regulation by the Commonwealth of Pennsylvania of the dispensing of liquor under licenses granted by the state. The regulation inherent in the grant of a state liquor license is so different in nature and extent from the ordinary licenses issued by the state that it is different in quality.

[It has] always been held in Pennsylvania . . . that the exercise of the power to grant licenses for the sale of intoxicating liquor was an exercise of the highest governmental power, one in which the state had the fullest freedom inhering in the police power of the sovereign. . . . [O]nce a license has been issued the license must comply with many detailed requirements or risk its suspension or revocation. He must in any event have it renewed periodically. Liquor licenses have been employed in Pennsylvania to regulate a wide variety of moral conduct, such as the presence and activities of homosexuals, performance by a topless dancer, lewd dancing, swearing, being noisy or disorderly. So broad is the state's power that the courts of Pennsylvania have upheld its restriction of freedom of expression of a licensee on the ground that in doing so it merely exercises its plenary power to attach conditions to the privilege of dispensing liquor which a licensee holds at the sufferance of the state. . . .

> This is thus a case requiring application of the principle that until today has governed our determinations of the existence of "state action": Our prior decisions leave no doubt that the mere existence of efforts by the State, through legislation or otherwise, to authorize, encourage, or otherwise support racial discrimination in a particular facet of life constitutes illegal state involvement in those pertinent private acts of discrimination that subsequently occur. See, *e. g., Peterson* v. *City of Greenville,* 373 U. S. 244 (1963); *Burton* v. *Wilmington Parking Authority,* 365 U. S. 715 (1961) . . . .

NOTE: STATE-ACTION DOCTRINE AFTER *MOOSE LODGE*

Since *Moose Lodge*, the Court has generally applied the Fourteenth Amendment's Equal Protection and Due Process Clauses only where someone employed by a state or local government (1) directly engages in unconstitutional activity, (2) fosters or encourages such activity, or (3) is a partner or joint venture in an enterprise that engages in unconstitutional activity. *See, e.g., Lugar v. Edmondson Oil Co.*, 457 U.S. 922 (1982). Everything else is "private" action. As we will see in the next question (section 46.2), the Court applied this framework in the context of school desegregation to distinguish between de jure racial segregation, which it considered unconstitutional, and de facto racial segregation, which it considered constitutional because it arises from actions not associated with the state.

Moose Lodge has had the effect of insulating much modern discrimination from Fourteenth Amendment review, even where states and local governments cooperate with the discriminatory entity. For example, in *Rendell-Baker v. Kohn*, the Court considered discrimination by a private school in Brookline, Massachusetts, that received students with special needs referred to it by the Boston and Brookline school committees. 457 U.S. 830, 832 (1982). Even though students graduated from the school with a diploma certified by the Brookline School Committee, and even though public funds accounted for 99 percent of the school's operating budget, the Court held that Brookline couldn't be held liable for the school's conduct. *Id.* at 840. The Court reiterated that "a State normally can be held responsible for a private decision only when it has exercised coercive power or has provided such significant encouragement, either overt or covert, that the choice must in law be deemed to be that of the State." *Id.*

In nearly every recent case to present the question, the Court has held that conduct by a business or other actor that the Court considers distinct from the state cannot be attributed to a state or local government. *Compare, e.g., Manhattan Cmty. Access Corp. v. Halleck*, 139 S. Ct. 1921, 1926 (2019) (heavily regulated operator of public-access cable channel isn't a state actor), *with Brentwood Academy v. Tennessee Secondary School Athletic Ass'n*, 531 U.S. 288, 299 (2001) (association "overwhelmingly composed of public school officials who select representatives" is a state actor).

NOTE: INCORPORATION OF THE BILL OF RIGHTS

The state-action doctrine isn't limited to the Equal Protection Clause. The doctrine derives from the text of Section 1 of the Fourteenth

Amendment—"No State shall . . ."—and it therefore applies to the Due Process Clause as well. As discussed earlier (section 39.2), the Due Process Clause is the mechanism by which the Supreme Court selectively incorporated the Bill of Rights against the states. In practice, this means that the First Amendment and other limitations of the Bill of Rights also apply only to federal and state actors and not to private individuals. *See, e.g.*, *Halleck*, 139 S. Ct. at 1921.

The Court announced an important exception to this principle in a case arising out of Chickasaw, Alabama—a suburb of Mobile whose buildings, streets, sewers, and homes were all owned by the Gulf Shipbuilding Corporation. With the exception of its private ownership structure, this "company town" otherwise looked like any other town in Alabama. But when Grace Marsh, a Jehovah's Witness, walked on the town's sidewalks to distribute religious literature, she was told that the town prohibited such distribution. When Marsh refused to leave the town, an Alabama deputy sheriff arrested her for trespassing on private property.

In *Marsh v. Alabama*, 326 U.S. 501 (1946), the Supreme Court held that Alabama had violated the First Amendment as applied to the states via the Fourteenth Amendment's Due Process Clause. Rather than focus on the identity of the deputy sheriff who arrested Marsh, the Court emphasized that the corporation itself had sufficiently exercised public functions to trigger the state-action doctrine. "The more an owner, for his advantage, opens up his property for use by the public in general, the more do his rights become circumscribed by the statutory and constitutional rights of those who use it," the Court wrote. *Marsh*, 326 U.S. at 506.

Marsh's public-function principle remains good law. The Court has invoked it, for example, to hold that private litigants can be "state actors" for Fourteenth Amendment purposes while in court. In *Edmonson v. Leesville Concrete Co.*, the Court explained that a civil litigant may not use peremptory challenges in a racially discriminatory way because such challenges have their "source in state authority." 500 U.S. 614, 620 (1991). And in *Georgia v. McCollum*, the Court reached a similar conclusion about a criminal defendant (as opposed to a state prosecutor) who used peremptory challenges to racially discriminate against potential jurors. 505 U.S. 42, 59 (1992).

Moreover, the state-action doctrine doesn't apply to every provision of the Constitution. The Thirteenth Amendment notably applies to private actors as well as state actors. *See, e.g.*, *Runyon v. McCrary*, 427 U.S. 160, 170–71 (1976) (invalidating a segregation academy's discriminatory policy under the Civil Rights Act of 1866, which the Court interpreted as a congressional exercise of Section 2 of the Thirteenth Amendment). Nor does the state-action doctrine apply to state constitutions, whose clauses don't necessarily include the same *no state shall* language as the Fourteenth Amendment. California's constitution, for example, declares, "Every person may freely speak, write and publish his or her sentiments on all subjects." Cal. Const. art. I, § 2. Applying this clause, the California Supreme Court held that a private shopping mall's prohibition on distributing literature violated the state constitution. In *PruneYard Shopping Center v. Robins*, 447

U.S. 74 (1980), the Supreme Court held that states could interpret their own constitutional state-action doctrines more broadly than the Fourteenth Amendment—although the Court warned that such doctrines had to be balanced against owners' own First Amendment liberty of expression and Fifth Amendment protection from takings without just compensation. *PruneYard*, 447 U.S. at 81–88. Since *PruneYard*, several states have joined California in applying their own free speech clauses in a manner similar to *Marsh*. *See, e.g.*, *Dublirer v. 2000 Linwood Ave. Owners, Inc.*, 103 A.3d 249, 254 (N.J. 2014).

CHAPTER 46

WHAT IS THE SCOPE OF THE FEDERAL JUDICIARY'S POWER TO REMEDY EQUAL-PROTECTION VIOLATIONS?

FIFTH AMENDMENT (1791): No person shall . . . be deprived of life, liberty, or property, without due process of law. . . .

FOURTEENTH AMENDMENT (1868), SECTION 1: No State shall . . . deprive any person of life, liberty, or property, without due process of law; nor deny to any person within its jurisdiction the equal protection of the laws.

46.1 MASSIVE RESISTANCE IN THE SOUTH

When the Supreme Court decided *Brown v. Board of Education* (*Brown I*) in 1954, it correctly anticipated that white people would respond harshly to a court decision declaring segregation "inherently unequal." 347 U.S. 483, 495 (1954). The justices therefore ordered the parties to return the following term and present arguments regarding what should be the appropriate remedy.

The Court announced its decision a year later, in May 1955. The decision was not well received by many white people, spawning a movement known as "massive resistance."

46.1.1

Brown v. Board of Education (Brown II)

349 U.S. 294 (1955)

The Court's decision, *Brown v. Board of Education*, 349 U.S. 294 (1955)—today known as *Brown II*—explained how it wanted lower courts to apply its earlier ruling.

■ MR. CHIEF JUSTICE WARREN delivered the opinion of the Court.[1]

These cases were decided on May 17, 1954. The opinions of that date, declaring the fundamental principle that racial discrimination in public education is

[1] **As You Read, Consider:** In *Giles v. Harris*, 189 U.S. 475 (1903), the Supreme Court refused to remedy Alabama's disenfranchisement of its black population. The Court explained that equitable relief is characterized by contextually balancing competing considerations, and nothing the Court could do would stop "the great mass of the white population [that] intends to keep the blacks from voting." *Giles*, 189 U.S. at 488.

Here, Chief Justice Earl Warren does attempt to craft an equitable balancing test for determining how to remedy segregation—not just in Alabama, but nationwide. In "reconciling public and private needs," what interests does he place on either side of the scales? How would unconstitutional, are incorporated herein by reference. All provisions of federal, state, or local law requiring or permitting such discrimination must yield to this principle. There remains for consideration the manner in which relief is to be accorded. . . .

Full implementation of these constitutional principles may require solution of varied local school problems. School authorities have the primary responsibility for elucidating, assessing, and solving these problems; courts will have to consider whether the action of school authorities constitutes good faith implementation of the governing constitutional principles. Because of their proximity to local conditions and the possible need for further hearings, the courts which originally heard these cases can best perform this judicial appraisal. Accordingly, we believe it appropriate to remand the cases to those courts.

In fashioning and effectuating the decrees, the courts will be guided by equitable principles. Traditionally, equity has been characterized by a practical flexibility in shaping its remedies and by a facility for adjusting and reconciling public and private needs. These cases call for the exercise of these traditional attributes of equity power. At stake is the personal interest of the plaintiffs in admission to public schools as soon as practicable on a nondiscriminatory basis. To effectuate this interest may call for elimination of a variety of obstacles in making the transition to school systems operated in accordance with the constitutional principles set forth in our May 17, 1954, decision. Courts of equity may properly take into account the public interest in the elimination of such obstacles in a systematic and effective manner. But it should go without saying that the vitality of these constitutional principles cannot be allowed to yield simply because of disagreement with them.

While giving weight to these public and private considerations, the courts will require that the defendants make a prompt and reasonable start toward full compliance with our May 17, 1954, ruling. Once such a start has been made, the courts may find that additional time is necessary to carry out the ruling in an effective manner. The burden rests upon the defendants to establish that such time is necessary in the public interest and is consistent with good faith compliance at the earliest practicable date. To that end, the courts may consider problems related to administration, arising from the physical condition of the school plant, the school transportation system, personnel, revision of school districts and attendance areas into compact units to achieve a system of determining admission to the public schools on a nonracial basis, and revision of local laws and regulations which may be necessary in solving the foregoing problems. They will also consider the adequacy of any plans the defendants may propose to meet these problems and to effectuate a transition to a racially nondiscriminatory school system. During this period of transition, the courts will retain jurisdiction of these cases.

The judgments below, except that in the Delaware case, are accordingly reversed and the cases are remanded to the District Courts to take such proceedings and enter such orders and decrees consistent with this opinion as are necessary and proper to admit to public schools on a racially nondiscriminatory basis with all deliberate speed the parties to these cases. . . .

NOTE: AFTERMATH OF *BROWN II*

White people's reaction to *Brown II*. *Brown II* did not order the immediate desegregation of southern schools. It instead ordered the parties in the case to "make a prompt and reasonable start." 349 U.S. at 300. But if

---

you weigh those interests in deciding whether a school district must integrate despite massive white opposition?

this language was intended to placate white southerners, it failed. Instead, southern politicians seized on the Court's final sentence—calling for states to act "with all deliberate speed," *id.* at 301—as an excuse to move slowly, if at all.

Shortly afterward, Virginia Senator Harry F. Byrd announced a plan to "organize the Southern States for massive resistance to this order" so that "the rest of the country will realize that racial integration is not going to be accepted in the South." *Byrd Calls on South to Challenge Court*, N.Y. Times, Feb. 26, 1956, at 1. Following his lead, several counties in Virginia shut down their public schools for all children. *See Harrison v. Day*, 106 S.E.2d 636, 640–41 (Va. 1959). And in Congress, nineteen senators and eighty-two representatives—nearly the entire southern delegation—signed the "Southern Manifesto," in which they condemned *Brown II* as a "clear abuse of judicial power":

> The original Constitution does not mention education. Neither does the Fourteenth Amendment nor any other amendment. The debates preceding the submission of the Fourteenth Amendment clearly show that there was no intent that it should affect the systems of education maintained by the states. . . .
>
> [The "separate but equal" principle of *Plessy v. Ferguson*], restated time and again, became a part of the life of the people of many of the states and confirmed their habits, customs, tradition and way of life. It is founded on elemental humanity and common sense, for parents should not be deprived by government of the right to direct the lives and education of their own children.
>
> Though there has been no constitutional amendment or act of Congress changing this established legal principle almost a century old, the Supreme Court of the United States, with no legal basis for such action, undertook to exercise their naked judicial power and substituted their personal political and social ideas for the established law of the land. This unwarranted exercise of power by the court, contrary to the Constitution, is creating chaos and confusion in the states principally affected. It is destroying the amicable relations between the white and Negro races that have been created through 90 years of patient effort by the good people of both races. It has planted hatred and suspicion where there has been heretofore friendship and understanding.

102 Cong. Rec. 4459 (1956).

In the face of this backlash, the Court itself acted slowly. In 1956, for example, it declined to review a Virginia law forbidding interracial marriage out of fear that "[o]ne bombshell at a time is enough." Richard Delgado, Naim v. Naim, 12 Nev. L.J. 525, 526 (2012) (discussing and criticizing the Court's decision in *Naim v. Naim*, 350 U.S. 985 (1956)).

Black people's reaction to *Brown*. Where many southern white people were opposed to desegregation, the hedge words of *Brown II* couldn't undermine the revelation that was *Brown I.* In sharp contrast with earlier decisions like *Giles v. Harris*, in which the Supreme Court had refused to intervene against "the great mass of the white population [that] intends to keep the blacks from voting," 189 U.S. 475, 488 (1903), the Court had now announced its intention to enforce the Constitution, however deliberately.

Months after the Court delivered *Brown II*, a young black preacher invoked the Court in his first speech at the Holt Street Baptist Church in Montgomery, Alabama, to protest the arraignment of a black woman who refused to give up her seat on a segregated bus. The Rev. Dr. Martin Luther King Jr. told the congregation:

> [Y]ou know, my friends, there comes a time when people get tired of being trampled over by the iron feet of oppression. . . . If we are wrong, the Supreme Court of this nation is wrong. If we are wrong, the Constitution of the United States is wrong. If we are wrong, God Almighty is wrong. If we are wrong, Jesus of Nazareth was merely a utopian dreamer that never came down to Earth. If we are wrong, justice is a lie.

Gerald Torres & Lani Guinier, *The Constitutional Imaginary: Just Stories About We the People*, 71 Md. L. Rev. 1053, 1070 n.112 (2012).

Yet even King was wary of the *Brown* decisions' effects. In 1960, nearly half of southern black people with a postsecondary education were teachers—and these black teachers risked being fired by white administrators as schools integrated. *See* Owen Thompson, *School Desegregation and Black Teacher Employment* 1, 2 (2019). Losing black teachers also risked harming black students, King noted in 1959:

> I favor integration on buses and in all areas of public accommodation and travel. . . . I am for equality. However, I think integration in our public schools is different. In that setting, you are dealing with one of the most important assets of an individual—the mind. White people view black people as inferior. A large percentage of them have a very low opinion of our race. People with such a low view of the black race cannot be given free rein and put in charge of the intellectual care and development of our boys and girls.

Samuel G. Freedman, *Still Separate, Still Unequal*, N.Y. Times, May 16, 2004, at 8.

Political defiance of desegregation. Despite King's concerns, the *Brown* decisions had little immediate effect on school segregation. Rather than comply with the decisions, white politicians preached "segregation now, segregation tomorrow, segregation forever." *The Inaugural Address of Governor George Wallace* 2 (1963).

Repudiation of the Supreme Court became a winning electoral strategy for otherwise unpopular politicians like Arkansas Governor Orval Faubus. Facing a tough reelection campaign in the fall of 1957, Faubus dispatched the Arkansas National Guard to prevent nine black students from entering Little Rock's Central High School. Jean Edward Smith, *Eisenhower in War and Peace* 717 (2012).

Faubus's blatant defiance of a federal court's desegregation order led President Dwight D. Eisenhower to issue an official proclamation ordering the governor to cease or face federal intervention. *Id.* at 722. By the end of September 1957, Eisenhower federalized the Arkansas National Guard and dispatched the famed 101st Airborne Division of the U.S. Army to escort the "Little Rock Nine" into Central High School. *Id.* at 723. Even then, the Little Rock Nine faced overwhelming hostility from their white classmates, who taunted them and even threw acid in the face of one of the black students. Melba Pattillo Beals, *Warriors Don't Cry* 122 (1994).

Cooper. By the end of the 1957–58 school year, the local school board, led by William Cooper, announced that the school district would have to delay desegregation because "the legislative, executive, and judicial departments of the state government opposed the desegregation of Little Rock schools by enacting laws, calling out troops, making statements vilifying federal law and federal courts, and failing to utilize state law enforcement agencies and judicial processes to maintain public peace." *Cooper v. Aaron*, 358 U.S. 1, 15 (1958). In *Cooper v. Aaron*, 358 U.S. 1, 15 (1958), the Supreme Court unanimously coauthored a joint opinion ordering the school board to continue desegregating Little Rock High. As noted in the discussion on alternatives to judicial review (section 3.2), the *Cooper* Court invoked *Marbury v. Madison*, 5 U.S. (1 Cranch) 137 (1803), to hold that "the federal judiciary is supreme in the exposition of the law of the Constitution." *Cooper*, 358 U.S. at 18. Following this principle, the Court wrote that "the interpretation of the Fourteenth Amendment enunciated by this Court in the *Brown* case is the supreme law of the land." *Id.* The Court therefore ordered Arkansas's state officials to cease their "war against the Constitution." *Id.*

Court handling of desegregation-avoidance strategies. Despite *Cooper*'s emphatic rhetoric, the Supreme Court declined to weigh in on any further desegregation cases for another five years, leaving it to lower federal courts to administer remedies consistent with *Brown II*'s mandate. In the meantime, southern states embraced a variety of strategies to avoid desegregating their public schools. When the Supreme Court again intervened a decade after the *Brown* rulings, its impatience with southern school desegregation led the Court to empower lower federal courts to take increasingly comprehensive administrative responsibilities over segregated school districts.

For example, in Virginia, as noted earlier, counties simply stopped funding their public schools and instead paid tuition grants and retirement benefits to children and teachers in segregated private schools. Other states, including Louisiana, followed Virginia's lead, spawning "segregation academies" across the South. When J. Skelly Wright, John Minor Wisdom, and other southern federal judges ordered these states to reopen their schools, they were personally ostracized and officially ignored. *See* Jack Bass, *Unlikely Heroes* 112–35 (1981); *see, e.g.*, *Orleans Parish Sch. Bd. v. Bush* 365 U.S. 569 (1961). After over a decade of litigation, in *Griffin v. County School Board of Prince Edward County*, the Supreme Court held that "under the circumstances," Virginia's approach violated the Equal Protection Clause. 377 U.S. 218, 255 (1964). To ensure that southern states actually complied with the ruling, the Supreme Court authorized district courts to "require [local officials] to exercise the power that is theirs to levy taxes to raise funds adequate to reopen, operate, and maintain without racial discrimination a public school system." *Id.* at 233. "The time for mere 'deliberate speed' has run out," the Court wrote. *Id.* at 234.

Other plans that the Supreme Court and lower courts invalidated included "pupil placement laws," through which officials assigned each student to a school based on formally nondiscriminatory criteria, and "minority transfer plans," in which school districts gave students the right to transfer to another school if they were placed in a school in which students of their race were in the minority. *See, e.g., Goss v. Knoxville Bd. of Educ.*, 373 U.S. 683, 685 (1963); *McNeese v. Cahokia Board of Education*, 373 U.S. 668, 674 (1963). The rezoning of school district boundaries often suffered the same fate.

46.1.2

Swann v. Charlotte-Mecklenburg Board of Education

402 U.S. 1 (1971)

Despite *Brown II* and the nationwide litigation that followed, federal courts had little immediate effect on school segregation. When *Brown II* was decided, virtually no black students in the South attended schools with white students. Reed Sarratt, *The Ordeal of Desegregation* 362 (1966). After ten years, that number rose to just 1.2 percent. Michael J. Klarman, Brown, *Racial Change, and the Civil Rights Movement*, 80 Va. L. Rev. 7, 9 (1994).

Desegregation didn't meaningfully advance until Congress passed the Civil Rights Act of 1964, Pub. L. No. 88–352, 78 Stat. 241. Title VI of the act, an exercise of the General Welfare Clause, prohibited discrimination in "any program or activity receiving Federal financial assistance." Civil Rights Act, 78 Stat. at 252. Because every state heavily relied on grants under the National Defense Education Act of 1958, Pub. L. No. 85–864, 72 Stat. 1580, school districts finally took steps to desegregate their schools. *See* Thompson, *supra*, at 2.

In the wake of the Civil Rights Act, the Supreme Court abandoned the *all deliberate speed* rhetoric of *Brown II* and became more assertive. *See, e.g., Bradley v. School Board of the City of Richmond*, 382 U.S. 103, 105 (1965). In *Green v. School Board of New Kent County*, the Court declared that the only sort of desegregation plan it would tolerate was "a plan that promises realistically to work, and promises realistically to work *now*." 391 U.S. 430, 439 (1968). The *Green* Court held that school boards must take "whatever steps might be necessary to convert to a unitary system in which racial discrimination would be eliminated root and branch." *Id.* at 437–38.

The Supreme Court soon offered two illustrations of what *Green* meant by *whatever steps might be necessary*. In *United States v.*

Montgomery County Board of Education, the Supreme Court authorized a district court in Alabama to require a school board to assign faculty so that "in each school the ratio of white to Negro faculty members is substantially the same as it is throughout the system." 395 U.S. 225, 232 (1969). And in the following case, *Swann v. Charlotte-Mecklenburg Board of Education*, 402 U.S. 1 (1971), the Court offered guidance for how district courts going forward might remedy racial segregation.

Like many southern states, North Carolina organized its school districts by county. The state's largest school district, surrounding Charlotte, was large: 550 square miles. In 1969, it included approximately 84,000 students, of whom 29 percent were black and 71 percent were white. Of the district's 24,000 black students, 21,000 attended school in the city of Charlotte itself. And of those 21,000 black students in Charlotte, two-thirds attended schools in which the student body was nearly exclusively black.

In April 1969, a federal district court ordered the school board to propose a desegregation plan. When the school board failed to do so, the district court adopted its own plan that required the county to bus students to different schools to ensure that each school had a similar ratio of white and black students. In a case that made its way to the Supreme Court, the school board challenged aspects of the plan as unreasonable.

The *Swann* Court, however, found nothing unreasonable about the plan.

■ MR. CHIEF JUSTICE BURGER delivered the opinion of the Court.[2]

We granted certiorari in this case to review important issues as to the duties of school authorities and the scope of powers of federal courts under this Court's mandates to eliminate racially separate public schools established and maintained by state action. *Brown* v. *Board of Education,* 347 U. S. 483 (1954). . . .

Nearly 17 years ago this Court held, in explicit terms, that state-imposed segregation by race in public schools denies equal protection of the laws. At no time has the Court deviated in the slightest degree from that holding or its constitutional underpinnings. . . .

[But over] the 16 years since *Brown II,* many difficulties were encountered in implementation of the basic constitutional requirement that the State not discriminate between public school children on the basis of their race. Nothing in our national experience prior to 1955 prepared anyone for dealing with changes and adjustments of the magnitude and complexity encountered since then. Deliberate resistance of some to the Court's mandates has impeded the good-faith efforts of others to bring school systems into compliance. . . .

The problems encountered by the district courts and courts of appeals make plain that we should now try to amplify guidelines, however incomplete and imperfect, for the assistance of school authorities and courts. The failure of local authorities to

[2] **As You Read, Consider:** At issue in this case is whether a federal district court appropriately exercised its power to remedy a constitutional violation. What, precisely, does Chief Justice Warren Burger think is the scope of the remedial power of a federal court? Does he think that a federal court has the power to order a state or local government to bus students, raise taxes, adhere to racial quotas, and exercise other police powers despite federalism and so-called states' rights?

meet their constitutional obligations aggravated the massive problem of converting from the state-enforced discrimination of racially separate school systems. This process has been rendered more difficult by changes since 1954 in the structure and patterns of communities, the growth of student population, movement of families, and other changes, some of which had marked impact on school planning, sometimes neutralizing or negating remedial action before it was fully implemented. . . .

[III. What standards should courts use to remedy constitutional violations?]

The objective today remains to eliminate from the public schools all vestiges of state-imposed segregation. Segregation was the evil struck down by *Brown I* as contrary to the equal protection guarantees of the Constitution. That was the violation sought to be corrected by the remedial measures of *Brown II*. That was the basis for the holding in *Green* that school authorities are "clearly charged with the affirmative duty to take whatever steps might be necessary to convert to a unitary system in which racial discrimination would be eliminated root and branch." 391 U. S., at 437–438.

If school authorities fail in their affirmative obligations under these holdings, judicial authority may be invoked. Once a right and a violation have been shown, the scope of a district court's equitable powers to remedy past wrongs is broad, for breadth and flexibility are inherent in equitable remedies. . . .

This allocation of responsibility once made, the Court attempted from time to time to provide some guidelines for the exercise of the district judge's discretion and for the reviewing function of the courts of appeals. However, a school desegregation case does not differ fundamentally from other cases involving the framing of equitable remedies to repair the denial of a constitutional right. The task is to correct, by a balancing of the individual and collective interests, the condition that offends the Constitution.

In seeking to define even in broad and general terms how far this remedial power extends it is important to remember that judicial powers may be exercised only on the basis of a constitutional violation. Remedial judicial authority does not put judges automatically in the shoes of school authorities whose powers are plenary. Judicial authority enters only when local authority defaults.

School authorities are traditionally charged with broad power to formulate and implement educational policy and might well conclude, for example, that in order to prepare students to live in a pluralistic society each school should have a prescribed ratio of Negro to white students reflecting the proportion for the district as a whole. To do this as an educational policy is within the broad discretionary powers of school authorities; absent a finding of a constitutional violation, however, that would not be within the authority of a federal court. As with any equity case, the nature of the violation determines the scope of the remedy.[3] In default by the school authorities of their obligation to proffer acceptable remedies, a district court has broad power to fashion a remedy that will assure a unitary school system. . . .

[IV. What kind of school systems violate the Constitution?]

We turn now to the problem of defining with more particularity the responsibilities of school authorities in desegregating a state-enforced dual school system in light of the Equal Protection Clause. Although the several related cases before us are

[3] **Questions:** What does Burger mean when he says that "the nature of the violation determines the scope of the remedy"? Is he suggesting that an extensive violation allows for extraordinary exercises of judicial power? That a geographically limited violation allows for geographically limited exercises of power? Something else?

primarily concerned with problems of student assignment, it may be helpful to begin with a brief discussion of other aspects of the process.

In *Green,* we pointed out that existing policy and practice with regard to faculty, staff, transportation, extra-curricular activities, and facilities were among the most important indicia of a segregated system. Independent of student assignment, where it is possible to identify a "white school" or a "Negro school" simply by reference to the racial composition of teachers and staff, the quality of school buildings and equipment, or the organization of sports activities, a *prima facie* case of violation of substantive constitutional rights under the Equal Protection Clause is shown. . . .

The construction of new schools and the closing of old ones are two of the most important functions of local school authorities and also two of the most complex. They must decide questions of location and capacity in light of population growth, finances, land values, site availability, through an almost endless list of factors to be considered. The result of this will be a decision which, when combined with one technique or another of student assignment, will determine the racial composition of the student body in each school in the system. Over the long run, the consequences of the choices will be far reaching. People gravitate toward school facilities, just as schools are located in response to the needs of people. The location of schools may thus influence the patterns of residential development of a metropolitan area and have important impact on composition of inner-city neighborhoods.

In the past, choices in this respect have been used as a potent weapon for creating or maintaining a state-segregated school system. In addition to the classic pattern of building schools specifically intended for Negro or white students, school authorities have sometimes, since *Brown,* closed schools which appeared likely to become racially mixed through changes in neighborhood residential patterns. This was sometimes accompanied by building new schools in the areas of white suburban expansion farthest from Negro population centers in order to maintain the separation of the races with a minimum departure from the formal principles of "neighborhood zoning." Such a policy does more than simply influence the short-run composition of the student body of a new school. It may well promote segregated residential patterns which, when combined with "neighborhood zoning," further lock the school system into the mold of separation of the races. . . . In ascertaining the existence of legally imposed school segregation, the existence of a pattern of school construction and abandonment is thus a factor of great weight. . . .

[V. What options are available for remedying a segregated school system?]

The central issue in this case is that of student assignment, and there are essentially four problem areas: (1) to what extent racial balance or racial quotas may be used as an implement in a remedial order to correct a previously segregated system; (2) whether every all-Negro and all-white school must be eliminated as an indispensable part of a remedial process of desegregation; (3) what the limits are, if any, on the rearrangement of school districts and attendance zones, as a remedial measure; and (4) what the limits are, if any, on the use of transportation facilities to correct state-enforced racial school segregation.

(1) *Racial Balances or Racial Quotas. . . .*

In this case it is urged that the District Court has imposed a racial balance requirement of 71%–29% on individual schools. . . . [The District Court directed:] "that efforts should be made to reach a 71–29 ratio in the various schools so that there will be no basis for contending that one school is racially different from the others . . ., [t]hat no school [should] be operated with an all-black or predominantly black student body, [and] [t]hat pupils of all grades [should] be assigned in such a way that as nearly as practicable the various schools at various grade levels have about the same proportion of black and white students." . . .

If we were to read the holding of the District Court to require, as a matter of substantive constitutional right, any particular degree of racial balance or mixing, that approach would be disapproved and we would be obliged to reverse. The constitutional command to desegregate schools does not mean that every school in every community must always reflect the racial composition of the school system as a whole.[4]

[But as] the voluminous record in this case shows, the predicate for the District Court's use of the 71%–29% ratio was twofold: first, its express finding . . . that a dual school system had been maintained by the school authorities at least until 1969; second, its finding . . . that the school board had totally defaulted in its acknowledged duty to come forward with an acceptable plan of its own. . . .

We see therefore that the use made of mathematical ratios was no more than a starting point in the process of shaping a remedy, rather than an inflexible requirement. From that starting point the District Court proceeded to frame a decree that was within its discretionary powers, as an equitable remedy for the particular circumstances. As we said in *Green,* a school authority's remedial plan or a district court's remedial decree is to be judged by its effectiveness. Awareness of the racial composition of the whole school system is likely to be a useful starting point in shaping a remedy to correct past constitutional violations. In sum, the very limited use made of mathematical ratios was within the equitable remedial discretion of the District Court.

(2) *One-race Schools.*

The record in this case reveals the familiar phenomenon that in metropolitan areas minority groups are often found concentrated in one part of the city. . . . Schools all or predominately of one race in a district of mixed population will require close scrutiny to determine that school assignments are not part of state-enforced segregation. . . .

An optional majority-to-minority transfer provision has long been recognized as a useful part of every desegregation plan. Provision for optional transfer of those in the majority racial group of a particular school to other schools where they will be in the minority is an indispensable remedy for those students willing to transfer to other schools in order to lessen the impact on them of the state-imposed stigma of segregation. In order to be effective, such a transfer arrangement must grant transferring student free transportation and space must be made available in the school to which he desires to move. . . .

(3) *Remedial Altering of Attendance Zones.*

The maps submitted in these cases graphically demonstrate that one of the principal tools employed by school planners and by courts to break up the dual school system has been a frank—and sometimes drastic—gerry-mandering of school districts and attendance zones. An additional step was pairing, "clustering," or "grouping" of schools with attendance assignments made deliberately to accomplish the transfer of Negro students out of formerly segregated Negro schools and transfer of white students to formerly all-Negro schools. . . .

---

[4] **Question:** Burger here is observing that the Equal Protection Clause does not require school districts to ensure that all schools are proportionally representative by race given the school districts' racial demographics. Does he therefore conclude that it is inappropriate for a district court to require proportional representation (or "racial quotas") to remedy an intentionally segregated school district?

Absent a constitutional violation there would be no basis for judicially ordering assignment of students on a racial basis. All things being equal, with no history of discrimination, it might well be desirable to assign pupils to schools nearest their homes. But all things are not equal in a system that has been deliberately constructed and maintained to enforce racial segregation. The remedy for such segregation may be administratively awkward, inconvenient, and even bizarre in some situations and may impose burdens on some; but all awkwardness and inconvenience cannot be avoided in the interim period when remedial adjustments are being made to eliminate the dual school systems.

No fixed or even substantially fixed guidelines can be established as to how far a court can go, but it must be recognized that there are limits. The objective is to dismantle the dual school system. "Racially neutral" assignment plans proposed by school authorities to a district court may be inadequate; such plans may fail to counteract the continuing effects of past school segregation resulting from discriminatory location of school sites or distortion of school size in order to achieve or maintain an artificial racial separation. When school authorities present a district court with a "loaded game board," affirmative action in the form of remedial altering of attendance zones is proper to achieve truly nondiscriminatory assignments. In short, an assignment plan is not acceptable simply because it appears to be neutral. . . .[5]

(4) ***Transportation of Students. . . .***

Bus transportation has been an integral part of the public education system for years, and was perhaps the single most important factor in the transition from the one-room schoolhouse to the consolidated school. Eighteen million of the Nation's public school children, approximately 39%, were transported to their schools by bus in 1969–1970 in all parts of the country. . . .

The District Court's conclusion that assignment of children to the school nearest their home serving their grade would not produce an effective dismantling of the dual system is supported by the record. Thus the remedial techniques used in the District Court's order were within that court's power to provide equitable relief. . . .

The decree provided that the buses used to implement the plan would operate on direct routes. Students would be picked up at schools near their homes and transported to the schools they were to attend. The trips for elementary school pupils average about seven miles and the District Court found that they would take "not over 35 minutes at the most." . . . In these circumstances, we find no basis for holding that the local school authorities may not be required to employ bus transportation as one tool of school desegregation. Desegregation plans cannot be limited to the walk-in school.

An objection to transportation of students may have validity when the time or distance of travel is so great as to either risk the health of the children or significantly impinge on the educational process. . . . The reconciliation of competing values in a desegregation case is, of course, a difficult task with many sensitive facets but fundamentally no more so than remedial measures courts of equity have traditionally employed.

---

5 **Question:** Note that Burger expressly authorizes federal courts to adopt race-conscious "affirmative action" to remedy racially segregated schools. Is this sort of race consciousness consistent with John Harlan's dissent in *Plessy v. Ferguson* and Earl Warren's opinion in *Brown I*?

VI

The Court of Appeals, searching for a term to define the equitable remedial power of the district courts, used the term "reasonableness." In *Green*, this Court used the term "feasible" and by implication, "workable," "effective," and "realistic" in the mandate to develop "a plan that promises realistically to work, and . . . to work *now*." On the facts of this case, we are unable to conclude that the order of the District Court is not reasonable, feasible and workable. However, in seeking to define the scope of remedial power or the limits on remedial power of courts in an area as sensitive as we deal with here, words are poor instruments to convey the sense of basic fairness inherent in equity. Substance, not semantics, must govern, and we have sought to suggest the nature of limitations without frustrating the appropriate scope of equity. . . .

NOTE: POWER OF FEDERAL COURTS AND CONGRESS TO REMEDY CONSTITUTIONAL VIOLATIONS

As *Swann* emphasized, the Court in 1971 was no longer tolerant of delays in implementing *Brown II*'s mandate. The "continued operation of segregated schools under a standard of allowing 'all deliberate speed' for desegregation is no longer constitutionally permissible," the Court wrote in *Alexander v. Holmes County Board of Education,* 396 U.S. 19, 20 (1969). "Under explicit holdings of this Court the obligation of every school district is to terminate dual school systems at once and to operate now and hereafter only unitary schools." *Id.*

Thanks in part to this impatience—and thanks even more to the financial incentives of the Civil Rights Act of 1964, Pub. L. No. 88–352, 78 Stat. 241—southern states actually began to desegregate. Where the number of southern black students attending school with white students rose from 0 percent in 1954 to 1.2 percent in 1964, it climbed to 91.3 percent by 1974. Klarman, *supra*, at 9.

Swann contributed to this trend by definitively confirming that federal courts had powers to remedy constitutional violations that they may have lacked absent a constitutional violation. These powers included anything that would effectively remedy constitutional wrongs, including the power to order the busing of children for the purpose of balancing the racial composition of schools. Later decisions would go even further, authorizing federal courts to order states and local governments to levy tax increases to pay for remedial programs. *See, e.g., Missouri v. Jenkins* (*Jenkins II*), 495 U.S. 33 (1990). These decisions even authorized federal courts to enjoin the operation of state constitutional provisions that otherwise limited the government's power to levy the taxes. *Id.* at 52.

By contrast, as noted in the discussion on the anticommandeering doctrine (section 12.1), the Court later interpreted Article I not to give Congress any power to direct states or local governments to enforce federal law. In *New York v. United States*, the Court attempted to reconcile the anticommandeering doctrine with "the power of federal *courts* to order state officials to comply with federal law." 505 U.S. 144, 179 (1992). The Court explained that "the Supremacy Clause makes federal law paramount over the contrary positions of state officials; the power of federal courts to enforce federal law thus presupposes some authority to order state officials to comply." *Id.*

Nevertheless, as discussed earlier with regard to Congress's power to enforce the Reconstruction amendments (sections 21.2, 21.3), the Court has upheld Congress's exercise of the same *remedial* power that federal courts possess to amend state laws—at least as long as there is "a congruence and proportionality between the injury to be prevented or remedied and the means adopted to that end." *City of Boerne v. Flores*, 521 U.S. 507, 520 (1997).

46.2 DE FACTO SEGREGATION IN THE NORTH

As racial integration in southern states progressed, racial integration in northern states stalled. Unlike southern states, northern states didn't have a recent history of segregating their school systems by law. Massachusetts, for instance, abolished its policy of school segregation in 1855—a century before *Brown v. Board of Education* (*Brown II*), 349 U.S. 294 (1955). Yet even in the absence of officially separate schools, northern public schools were nearly as segregated as those in the South. Thomas Sugrue, *Sweet Land of Liberty: The Forgotten Struggle for Civil Rights in the North* 183 (2009). The causes were just more complex.

A principal cause of racial segregation in schools, in both the North and the South, was racial segregation in housing. In many places, white people lived in neighborhoods in which a majority of their neighbors were white, and black people lived in neighborhoods in which a majority of their neighbors were black—meaning that local schools also tended to be racially segregated. The Court in *Swann v. Charlotte-Mecklenburg Board of Education* implicitly distinguished this sort of residential segregation from "state action," which it defined as "discriminatory action *by the school authorities.*" 402 U.S. at 23 (emphasis added). Like many observers, the *Swann* Court was careful not to attribute residential segregation to any particular cause, observing only "the familiar phenomenon that in metropolitan areas minority groups are often found concentrated in one part of the city." *Id.* at 25.

This "familiar phenomenon" of residential segregation was often misleadingly called *de facto segregation* (segregation by practice) in contrast with *de jure segregation* (segregation by law). As historian Thomas Sugrue has written, "[a]t the heart of the analysis of de facto segregation was an erasure of intention: Northern schools were segregated because of the natural forces of the market, of individuals making choices about where to live, ostensibly unaffected by government policy and unshaped by considerations of race." Sugrue, *supra*, at 183–84. On the basis of this assumption, federal courts—including the *Swann* Court—treated residential segregation as a problem beyond the remedial powers of federal courts. Absent state action, the Fourteenth Amendment didn't apply.

But while residential segregation in the North didn't always include the public manifestations of Jim Crow in the South—with "Colored Only" signs, lynch mobs, and white-only elections—it was largely the consequence of federal and state policy. *Id.*

Before World War I, over 90 percent of black Americans lived in the former Confederacy. In most northern cities, from Oakland and Detroit to New York City and Boston, black people made up less than 3 percent of the population. But as the two World Wars produced labor shortages in the North, a "Great Migration" of over six million black people poured north in the largest movement of people in American history. *See* Isabel Wilkerson, *The Warmth of Other Suns* 9 (2010). By 1970, black people represented 20–50 percent of the populations of those same large northern cities. *See* Campbell Gibson & Kay Jung, *Historical Census Statistics on Population Totals by Race, 1790 to 1990* (2005).

Northern state governments and the federal government responded to the Great Migration in a number of ways that were purposefully designed to ferry black newcomers into undesirable neighborhoods. One technique was zoning, in which cities prohibited black people from purchasing homes in particular places. When the city council of Louisville, Kentucky, literally prohibited black people from purchasing homes in majority-white neighborhoods, the Supreme Court in *Buchanan v. Warley* struck down the ordinance as a violation of the Due Process Clause. 245 U.S. 60, 80 (1917). But other cities circumvented this decision in numerous ways. *See* Richard Rothstein, *The Color of Law: A Forgotten History of How Our Government Segregated America* 49–50 (2017). In particular, many cities and suburbs adopted facially neutral zoning ordinances that prohibited the construction of affordable homes—particularly multifamily homes and apartment buildings—that they expected would attract black people. To live in certain neighborhoods, potential residents had to have the wealth to purchase a single-family house. *Id.* at 56–57, 83.

The federal government exacerbated the effect of these ordinances with the National Housing Act of 1934, Pub. L. No. 73–479, 48 Stat. 1246, which created the Federal Housing Administration (FHA). For white people, the FHA made home mortgages more affordable. When a bank applied to the FHA for insurance on a prospective loan, the agency conducted an appraisal of the property and the buyer. If it deemed the loan safe, the agency would guarantee the loan. But the southern legislators who passed the National Housing Act permitted the FHA to deny black people access to what became the major vehicle for homeownership in the 1940s and 1950s. *Id.* at 64–65.

Even worse for black people, the FHA also refused to insure loans for properties in racially mixed neighborhoods on the theory that "[a] change in social or racial occupancy generally leads to instability and a reduction in values." *Id.* at 65. In a practice known as *redlining*, appraisers for the FHA discouraged banks from making loans in neighborhoods whose homes were at risk of losing value. The FHA considered places risky if children might be "compelled to attend school where the majority or a considerable number of the pupils represent a far lower level of society or an incompatible racial element." *Id.* at 64–65. By contrast, the FHA favored neighborhoods in which highways or train tracks separated white neighborhoods from black neighborhoods, stating that "[n]atural or artificially established barriers will prove effective in protecting a neighborhood and the locations within it from adverse influences . . . includ[ing] prevention of the infiltration of . . . lower class occupancy, and inharmonious racial groups." *Id.*

As redlining and zoning ordinances effectively prohibited people of color from living in certain neighborhoods, states licensed real estate agents and prohibited the agents from showing certain homes to black buyers. *Id.* at 102. States also enforced racially restrictive covenants that blanketed cities and suburbs and prohibited homeowners from selling their property to black purchasers. *Id.* at 82. These racial covenants weren't outlawed until thirty years after *Buchanan*, in *Shelley v. Kraemer*, 334 U.S. 1 (1948). Yet even after *Shelley*, housing developers used state and federal aid to construct racially exclusive housing projects like Levittown, New York, while state-licensed realtors continued to blatantly discriminate. When black homeowners did manage to purchase or rent a home in predominantly white neighborhoods, realtors engaged in "blockbusting," where they persuaded white residents that the economic value of their homes would soon collapse under the weight of integration. White residents responded either by violently intimidating black homeowners—burning crosses on their lawns and throwing rocks through their windows—or by fleeing to the exclusionary-zoned suburbs. Sugrue, *supra*, at 225–59.

It wasn't until Congress passed the Fair Housing Act of 1968, Pub. L. No. 90–284, 82 Stat. 73, that all of these discriminatory practices were made illegal. *See also Jones v. Alfred H. Mayer Co.*, 392 U.S. 409, 436 (1968) (interpreting the Civil Rights Act of 1866 also to prohibit racial discrimination in housing). Yet school districts continued to contribute to residential segregation in the North. As the racial composition of neighborhoods shifted, school administrators carefully mapped the boundaries of attendance districts to ensure that children attended racially homogenous schools. Sugrue, *supra*, at 186. And as *Swann* itself recognized, school administrators after *Brown II* shuttered schools in racially integrated neighborhoods while authorizing the construction of schools far away from neighborhood boundaries.

The National Association for the Advancement of Colored People (NAACP) Legal Defense Fund (LDF) responded to northern discrimination by focusing its attention on schools. But its lawyers faced two challenges. First, it was not clear whether federal courts would recognize racial segregation in northern schools as a result of state action, or whether they would treat it as the consequence of individual decisions about where to live and send children to school. Second, it was also not clear what the appropriate remedy should be. *Swann* offered a narrow answer to the first question, suggesting that "state action" for school desegregation purposes referred only to "discriminatory action by the school authorities." 402 U.S. at 23. But it offered a broad answer to the second question, authorizing school districts to bus students for the purpose of meeting demographic targets.

The first major application of *Swann* to a northern school district, *Keyes v. School District No. 1*, 413 U.S. 189 (1973), arose in Denver. Unlike most southern school districts, Denver had never formally enforced a "dual system" in which it ordered the racial segregation of its schools. *Keyes*, 413 U.S. at 198. But the LDF attorneys introduced evidence that the school district had deliberately isolated 38 percent of its black students in a neighborhood of northeast Denver called Park Hill. *Id.* The Denver school district assigned black students and teachers to the Park Hill schools, it structured attendance zones to keep white students out, and it built a new school in the neighborhood "with conscious knowledge that it would be a segregated school." *Id.* at 201.

The school district responded by arguing that any evidence of segregation was limited to the Park Hill neighborhood. Therefore, the school district argued, any judicial remedy must be limited to desegregating the schools of Park Hill, not all of Denver. The district court agreed, ruling that the evidence in the rest of Denver was insufficient to "dictate the conclusion that this is *de jure* segregation which calls for an all-out effort to desegregate. It is more like *de facto* segregation, with respect to which the rule is that the court cannot order desegregation in order to provide a better balance." *Id.* at 193.

In *Keyes*, the Supreme Court sided with the LDF, holding that the district court had the power to remedy segregation in all of Denver's schools, not just in Park Hill. But in a significant concession to the government, the Court accepted the distinction "between *de jure* segregation and so-called *de facto* segregation," emphasizing that federal courts had the power to remedy only the former. *Id.* at 208. To prove that de jure segregation existed, the Court held that a plaintiff like the LDF must produce evidence of a government's "*purpose* or *intent* to segregate." *Id.* The Court sided with the LDF only because it had demonstrated "intentionally segregative school board actions in a meaningful portion of a school system," which the Court held was enough to establish "a prima facie case of unlawful segregative design on the part of school authorities" in the entire school district. *Id.* In other words, because the LDF had proved that the Denver school district had intentionally segregated in Park Hill, that was enough to establish the inference that it had intentionally segregated elsewhere. The Court held that the school district could rebut this inference only by "proving that other segregated schools within the system are not also the result of intentionally segregative actions." *Id.*

The *Keyes* Court's distinction between de jure segregation and de facto segregation would make it significantly more difficult for future plaintiffs to prove racial segregation in northern school districts as school administrators in the North rarely revealed their "intention" to engage in racial segregation. Moreover, the Court's remedy was limited to a single school district: Denver's school district. This remedy would prove ineffective elsewhere as white families fled the desegregation of urban school districts for the suburbs, where school-district lines paralleled town borders. In places where the racial separation of cities and suburbs resulted in segregated school systems—including Baltimore, Dallas, Houston, Los Angeles, Miami, Memphis, New York, Philadelphia, and, in the following case, Detroit—*inter*district remedies would prove necessary. *See* Erwin Chemerinsky, *The Segregation and Resegregation of American Public Education: The Court's Role*, 81 N.C. L. Rev. 1597, 1605–06 (2003).

46.2.1

Milliken v. Bradley (Milliken I)

418 U.S. 717 (1974)

Detroit in the 1940s was what Silicon Valley was in the 2010s: the technological capital of the United States. With a booming auto industry, the city was a magnet for black southerners seeking to escape Jim Crow and poverty. Yet Detroit and its suburbs used every legal tool available to quarantine the new black migrants in undesirable neighborhoods. Exclusionary zoning ordinances prohibited the construction of multifamily residences in white neighborhoods, the FHA refused to insure mortgages if the buyer was black or in a racially mixed neighborhood, racially restrictive covenants and realtors prohibited black home buyers from living in certain areas, and the eighty-six school districts in metropolitan Detroit mapped attendance zones to segregate schools. *See* Thomas Sugrue, *The Origins of the Urban Crisis* 64 (1996). In 1941, the city even built a six-foot-high wall to physically separate a white and black neighborhood and make the white neighborhood more attractive for FHA funding. *Id.*

Despite these figurative and literal walls, black residents arrived and thrived. Through the 1960s, many white Detroiters therefore fled the city in a pattern known as "white flight," selling their homes at bargain prices and moving to exclusionary-zoned suburbs where they could continue sending their children to all-white schools. Because most cities, including Detroit, relied on property taxes to finance services, the rapid departure of middle-class residents sapped the city's income stream. Sugrue, *Sweet Land of Liberty*, *supra*, at 449–50.

Like many black Detroiters, Verda Bradley arrived in the city as part of the Great Migration and eventually had children. Working in the auto industry, Bradley hoped her children would have a better future in the

North than they ever could have had in Tennessee. But the school to which Bradley sent her two children, the DeWitt Clinton School, represented Detroit's schools in miniature. Where one in ten students at the school were black in 1960, 97 percent of the students were black in 1970. And where the school district in 1960 earned enough in property taxes to properly finance its schools, the tax base by 1970 had plummeted. The DeWitt Clinton School became "hopelessly overcrowded," with out-of-date textbooks, a building in need of repair, and classes of forty to fifty students held in shabby portable trailers in the schoolyard. *Id.* at 450.

When Bradley contacted the NAACP to challenge the segregation of Detroit's public schools, she didn't make the same argument that Thurgood Marshall had made twenty-five years earlier in *Brown v. Board of Education* (*Brown I*), 347 U.S. 483 (1954), i.e., that her children's self-esteem was at stake in Detroit's segregated school system. Nor did she argue that going to school with white children would help her own children overcome their educational deficiencies. Instead, she cared simply about quality. As she later recalled, "We were upset because they weren't getting as many materials as some other schools. . . . We figured if it was desegregated, we would get the same." *Id.*

Bradley's lawsuit against Governor William Milliken began in 1970 after the Michigan legislature passed a law, Act 48, to prohibit the Detroit school district from attempting to integrate its public schools in which there remained a few white enclaves. After a forty-one-day trial in 1971, federal judge Stephen J. Roth found that "[g]overnmental actions and inaction at all levels, federal, state and local, have combined, with those of private organizations, such as loaning institutions and real estate associations and brokerage firms, to establish and to maintain the pattern of residential segregation throughout the Detroit metropolitan area." *Milliken v. Bradley* (*Milliken I*), 418 U.S. 717, 724 (1974). At the local level, Roth found that the Detroit school district had purposefully used attendance zones, busing programs, and school construction practices to segregate black students from white students. And at the state level, Roth found that the governor and legislature had contributed to segregated schools in three ways. First, he found that through Act 48, the state had acted to "impede, delay and minimize racial integration in Detroit schools." *Id.* at 727. Second, he found that the state had funded programs in white suburban districts that the state refused to fund within Detroit itself. And third, he found that the acts of the Detroit school district, "as a subordinate entity of the State, were attributable to the State of Michigan, thus creating a vicarious liability on the part of the State." *Id.*

In light of these findings, Roth proposed a novel remedy: he ordered the state to desegregate not only the school district of Detroit but also the eighty-five school districts in the three-county metropolitan area. In subsequent rulings, Roth rejected the state's arguments that interdistrict relief was inappropriate absent evidence that the suburban districts themselves had committed violations. The court concluded that a Detroit-only plan "would make the Detroit school system more identifiably Black . . . thereby increasing the flight of Whites from the city and the system." *Id.* at 732. Accordingly, he held that he "must look beyond the limits of the Detroit school district for a solution to the problem" and that "[s]chool district lines are simply matters of political convenience and may not be used to deny constitutional rights." *Id.* at 732–33. Roth's final ruling ordered the state to purchase at least 295 school buses for the purpose of integrating schools across a large "desegregation area" that included fifty-three of the school districts surrounding Detroit.

As white parents put bumper stickers on their cars declaring "Roth is a four-letter word," his ruling wound its way to the Supreme Court. By the time the Court heard argument, federal judges in other northern cities—notably Boston—were also authorizing busing programs in the face of a cresting white backlash. *See, e.g.*, *Morgan v. Hennigan*, 379 F. Supp. 410 (D. Mass 1974).

The following decision, *Milliken v. Bradley* (*Milliken I*), 418 U.S. 717 (1974), became the Court's opportunity to reinforce *Brown*—or to retreat. Proponents hoping for reinforcement were disappointed.

■ MR. CHIEF JUSTICE BURGER delivered the opinion of the Court.[6]

We granted certiorari in these consolidated cases to determine whether a federal court may impose a multidistrict, areawide remedy to a single-district *de jure* segregation problem absent any finding that the other included school districts have failed to operate unitary school systems within their districts, absent any claim or finding that the boundary lines of any affected school district were established with the purpose of fostering racial segregation in public schools, [and] absent any finding that the included districts committed acts which effected segregation within the other districts. . . .

II

Ever since *Brown* v. *Board of Education,* 347 U. S. 483 (1954), judicial consideration of school desegregation cases has begun with the standard: "[I]n the field of public education the doctrine of 'separate but equal' has no place. Separate educational facilities are inherently unequal." *Id.,* at 495. This has been reaffirmed time and again as the meaning of the Constitution and the controlling rule of law. . . .

In *Brown* v. *Board of Education,* 349 U. S. 294 (1955) (*Brown II*), the Court's first encounter with the problem of remedies in school desegregation cases, the Court noted: "In fashioning and effectuating the decrees, the courts will be guided by equitable principles. Traditionally, equity has been characterized by a practical flexibility in shaping its remedies and by a facility for adjusting and reconciling public and private needs." *Id.,* at 300 (footnotes omitted).

In further refining the remedial process, *Swann* [v. *Charlotte-Mecklenburg Board of Education,* 402 U. S. 1 (1971)] held, the task is to correct, by a balancing of the

---

6 **As You Read, Consider:** In *Swann v. Charlotte-Mecklenburg Board of Education*, Chief Justice Warren Burger upheld the power of a district court to remedy racially segregated schools by requiring busing and altering school attendance zones. Why is he more skeptical of the remedy in this case? In addition, what is the source of the limits he introduces on the remedial power of district courts: the Constitution, federalism, or something else?

individual and collective interests, "the condition that offends the Constitution." A federal remedial power may be exercised "only on the basis of a constitutional violation" and, "[a]s with any equity case, the nature of the violation determines the scope of the remedy." 402 U. S., at 16.

Proceeding from these basic principles, we first note that in the District Court the complainants sought a remedy aimed at the *condition* alleged to offend the Constitution—the segregation within the Detroit City School District. The court acted on this theory of the case and in its initial ruling on the "Desegregation Area" stated: "The task before this court, therefore, is . . . how to desegregate the Detroit public schools." 345 F. Supp., at 921.

Thereafter, however, the District Court abruptly rejected the proposed Detroit-only plans on the ground that "while [they] would provide a racial mix more in keeping with the Black-White proportions of the student population [they] would accentuate the racial identifiability of the [Detroit] district as a Black school system, and would not accomplish desegregation." "[T]he racial composition of the student body is such," said the court, "that the plan's implementation would clearly make the entire Detroit public school system racially identifiable," "leav[ing] many of its schools 75 to 90 per cent Black." Consequently, the court reasoned, it was imperative to "look beyond the limits of the Detroit school district for a solution to the problem of segregation in the Detroit public schools . . ." since "[s]chool district lines are simply matters of political convenience and may not be used to deny constitutional rights." Accordingly, the District Court proceeded to redefine the relevant area to include areas of predominantly white pupil population in order to ensure that "upon implementation, no school, grade or classroom [would be] substantially disproportionate to the overall pupil racial composition" of the entire metropolitan area. . . .

Viewing the record as a whole, it seems clear that the District Court . . . shifted the primary focus from a Detroit remedy to the metropolitan area only because of [its] conclusion that total desegregation of Detroit would not produce the racial balance which [it] perceived as desirable. [It] proceeded on an assumption that the Detroit schools could not be truly desegregated . . . unless the racial composition of the student body of each school substantially reflected the racial composition of the population of the metropolitan area as a whole. . . .

[But in] *Swann,* which arose in the context of a single independent school district, the Court held: "If we were to read the holding of the District Court to require, as a matter of substantive constitutional right, any particular degree of racial balance or mixing, that approach would be disapproved and we would be obliged to reverse." 402 U. S., at 24. The clear import of this language . . . is that desegregation, in the sense of dismantling a dual school system, does not require any particular racial balance in each "school, grade or classroom."

Here the District Court's approach to what constituted "actual desegregation" raises the fundamental question, not presented in *Swann,* as to the circumstances in which a federal court may order desegregation relief that embraces more than a single school district. The court's analytical starting point was its conclusion that school district lines are no more than arbitrary lines on a map drawn "for political convenience." Boundary lines may be bridged where there has been a constitutional violation calling for interdistrict relief, but the notion that school district lines may be casually ignored or treated as a mere administrative convenience is contrary to the history of public education in our country. No single tradition in public education is more deeply rooted than local control over the operation of schools; local autonomy has long been thought essential both to the maintenance of community concern and support for public schools and to quality of the educational process. . . .[7]

The Michigan educational structure involved in this case, in common with most States, provides for a large measure of local control, and a review of the scope and character of these local powers indicates the extent to which the interdistrict remedy approved by the two courts could disrupt and alter the structure of public education in Michigan. The metropolitan remedy would require, in effect, consolidation of 54 independent school districts historically administered as separate units into a vast new super school district. Entirely apart from the logistical and other serious problems attending large-scale transportation of students, the consolidation would give rise to an array of other problems in financing and operating this new school system. Some of the more obvious questions would be: What would be the status and authority of the present popularly elected school boards? Would the children of Detroit be within the jurisdiction and operating control of a school board elected by the parents and residents of other districts? What board or boards would levy taxes for school operations in these 54 districts constituting the consolidated metropolitan area? What provisions could be made for assuring substantial equality in tax levies among the 54 districts, if this were deemed requisite? . . . Who would establish attendance zones, purchase school equipment, locate and construct new schools, and indeed attend to all the myriad day-to-day decisions that are necessary to school operations affecting potentially more than three-quarters of a million pupils?

It may be suggested that all of these vital operational problems are yet to be resolved by the District Court. . . . But it is obvious from the scope of the interdistrict remedy itself that absent a complete restructuring of the laws of Michigan relating to school districts the District Court will become first, a *de facto* "legislative authority" to resolve these complex questions, and then the "school superintendent" for the entire area. This is a task which few, if any, judges are qualified to perform and one which would deprive the people of control of schools through their elected representatives.

Of course, no state law is above the Constitution. School district lines and the present laws with respect to local control, are not sacrosanct and if they conflict with the Fourteenth Amendment federal courts have a duty to prescribe appropriate remedies. But our prior holdings have been confined to violations and remedies within a single school district. We therefore turn to address, for the first time, the validity of a remedy mandating cross-district or interdistrict consolidation to remedy a condition of segregation found to exist in only one district.

The controlling principle consistently expounded in our holdings is that the scope of the remedy is determined by the nature and extent of the constitutional violation. *Swann,* 402 U. S., at 16. Before the boundaries of separate and autonomous school districts may be set aside by consolidating the separate units for remedial purposes or by imposing a cross-district remedy, it must first be shown that there has been a constitutional violation within one district that produces a significant segregative effect in another district. Specifically, it must be shown that racially discriminatory acts of the state or local school districts, or of a single school district have been a substantial cause of interdistrict segregation. Thus an interdistrict remedy might be in order where the racially discriminatory acts of one or more school districts caused racial segregation in an adjacent district, or where district lines have been deliberately

---

[7] **Question:** Recall the constitutional violation at issue here. Detroit segregated its schools; the State of Michigan prohibited Detroit from integrating its schools; and the district court found that local, state, and federal officials were all responsible for the fact that Detroit's schools were nearly all black while suburban schools were nearly all white. Why, then, does Burger think it exceeded the district court's equitable powers to craft a remedy that incorporated Detroit and suburban school districts?

drawn on the basis of race. In such circumstances an interdistrict remedy would be appropriate to eliminate the interdistrict segregation directly caused by the constitutional violation. Conversely, without an interdistrict violation and interdistrict effect, there is no constitutional wrong calling for an interdistrict remedy.[8]

The record before us, voluminous as it is, contains evidence of *de jure* segregated conditions only in the Detroit schools. . . . With no showing of significant violation by the 53 outlying school districts and no evidence of any interdistrict violation or effect, the court went beyond the original theory of the case . . . and mandated a metropolitan area remedy. To approve the remedy ordered by the court would impose on the outlying districts, not shown to have committed any constitutional violation, a wholly impermissible remedy based on a standard not hinted at in *Brown I* and *II* or any holding of this Court.

[The dissents in this case] undertake to demonstrate that agencies having statewide authority participated in maintaining the dual school system found to exist in Detroit. They are apparently of the view that once such participation is shown, the District Court should have a relatively free hand to reconstruct school districts outside of Detroit in fashioning relief. Our assumption . . . that state agencies did participate in the maintenance of the Detroit system, should make it clear that it is not on this point that we part company. The difference between us arises instead from established doctrine laid down by our cases. *Brown*, *Green*, [and] *Swann* . . . each addressed the issue of constitutional wrong in terms of an established geographic and administrative school system populated by both Negro and white children. In such a context, terms such as "unitary" and "dual" systems, and "racially identifiable schools," have meaning, and the necessary federal authority to remedy the constitutional wrong is firmly established. But the remedy is necessarily designed, as all remedies are, to restore the victims of discriminatory conduct to the position they would have occupied in the absence of such conduct. Disparate treatment of white and Negro students occurred within the Detroit school system, and not elsewhere, and on this record the remedy must be limited to that system. *Swann, supra,* at 16.

The constitutional right of the Negro respondents residing in Detroit is to attend a unitary school system in that district. Unless petitioners drew the district lines in a discriminatory fashion, or arranged for white students residing in the Detroit District to attend schools in Oakland and Macomb Counties, they were under no constitutional duty to make provisions for Negro students to do so. The view of the dissenters, that the existence of a dual system in *Detroit* can be made the basis for a decree requiring cross-district transportation of pupils, cannot be supported on the grounds that it represents merely the devising of a suitably flexible remedy for the violation of rights already established by our prior decisions. It can be supported only by drastic expansion of the constitutional right itself, an expansion without any support in either constitutional principle or precedent. . . .

■ MR. JUSTICE MARSHALL, with whom MR. JUSTICE DOUGLAS, MR. JUSTICE BRENNAN, and MR. JUSTICE WHITE join, dissenting.[9]

---

[8] **Questions:** In *Swann*, Burger held that Charlotte-Mecklenburg County had a segregated school district that required a district-wide remedy. But suppose Charlotte had divided its single school district into dozens of districts, one for each school. Does Burger's opinion in this case suggest that interdistrict busing would have been inappropriate in such a situation? If so, is there anything in Burger's opinion that would prevent metropolitan areas from maintaining segregated schools by adopting multiple school districts or by concentrating white students in suburbs and students of color in urban cores?

[9] **Questions:** Justice Thurgood Marshall was the lead attorney in *Brown I*. Is his prediction of how school districts will respond to this decision reasonable? What does this decision suggest about the limits of using constitutional litigation to effect lasting change?

In *Brown* v. *Board of Education,* 347 U. S. 483 (1954), this Court held that segregation of children in public schools on the basis of race deprives minority group children of equal educational opportunities and therefore denies them the equal protection of the laws under the Fourteenth Amendment. This Court recognized then that remedying decades of segregation in public education would not be an easy task. Subsequent events, unfortunately, have seen that prediction bear bitter fruit. But however imbedded old ways, however ingrained old prejudices, this Court has not been diverted from its appointed task of making "a living truth" of our constitutional ideal of equal justice under law. *Cooper* v. *Aaron,* 358 U. S. 1, 20 (1958).

After 20 years of small, often difficult steps toward that great end, the Court today takes a giant step backwards. Notwithstanding a record showing widespread and pervasive racial segregation in the educational system provided by the State of Michigan for children in Detroit, this Court holds that the District Court was powerless to require the State to remedy its constitutional violation in any meaningful fashion. Ironically purporting to base its result on the principle that the scope of the remedy in a desegregation case should be determined by the nature and the extent of the constitutional violation, the Court's answer is to provide no remedy at all for the violation proved in this case, thereby guaranteeing that Negro children in Detroit will receive the same separate and inherently unequal education in the future as they have been unconstitutionally afforded in the past.

I cannot subscribe to this emasculation of our constitutional guarantee of equal protection of the laws and must respectfully dissent. Our precedents . . . firmly establish that where, as here, state-imposed segregation has been demonstrated, it becomes the duty of the State to eliminate root and branch all vestiges of racial discrimination and to achieve the greatest possible degree of actual desegregation. I agree with both the District Court and the Court of Appeals that, under the facts of this case, this duty cannot be fulfilled unless the State of Michigan involves outlying metropolitan area school districts in its desegregation remedy. Furthermore, I perceive no basis either in law or in the practicalities of the situation justifying the State's interposition of school district boundaries as absolute barriers to the implementation of an effective desegregation remedy. . . .

Under a Detroit-only decree, Detroit's schools will clearly remain racially identifiable in comparison with neighboring schools in the metropolitan community. Schools with 65% and more Negro students will stand in sharp and obvious contrast to schools in neighboring districts with less than 2% Negro enrollment. Negro students will continue to perceive their schools as segregated educational facilities and this perception will only be increased when whites react to a Detroit-only decree by fleeing to the suburbs to avoid integration. School district lines, however innocently drawn, will surely be perceived as fences to separate the races when, under a Detroit-only decree, white parents withdraw their children from the Detroit city schools and move to the suburbs in order to continue them in all-white schools. The message of this action will not escape the Negro children in the city of Detroit. It will be of scant significance to Negro children who have for years been confined by *de jure* acts of segregation to a growing core of all-Negro schools surrounded by a ring of all-white schools that the new dividing line between the races is the school district boundary. . . .

NOTE: AFTERMATH OF *MILLIKEN I*

Milliken I didn't mark the end of federal court involvement in desegregating northern schools. Indeed, the decision didn't mark the end of

Verda Bradley's litigation. *See, e.g.*, *Milliken v. Bradley* (*Milliken II*), 433 U.S. 267 (1977) (upholding a subsequent order).

But *Milliken I* did make it practically impossible for federal courts to overcome white flight. As Justice Thurgood Marshall—the lawyer who litigated the *Brown* decisions—predicted in his dissent, "[s]chool district lines, however innocently drawn, will surely be perceived as fences to separate the races when, under a Detroit-only decree, white parents withdraw their children from the Detroit city schools and move to the suburbs in order to continue them in all-white schools." *Milliken I*, 418 U.S. at 804–05. This is precisely what happened in Detroit and other cities across the country. A decade after *Milliken I*, in 1987, 90 percent of the students in Detroit schools were black. *See* Robert A. Sedler, *The Profound Impact of* Milliken v. Bradley, 33 Wayne L. Rev. 1693, 1695 (1987).

Busing after *Milliken I*. Subsequent cases reinforced the inability of federal courts to desegregate northern school districts through busing. On the one hand, the Court continued to hold that, under *Swann* and *Keyes*, once a federal court found proof of de jure segregation throughout an entire school district, it could order the district to eliminate it. *See, e.g.*, *Columbus Bd. of Educ. v. Penick*, 443 U.S. 449, 459 (1979).

On the other hand, the Court serially disapproved of lower-court findings that a school district had, in fact, engaged in de jure segregation. For example, in *Pasadena City Board of Education v. Spangler*, a case out of Southern California, the Court held that after a school district has complied with a federal court's desegregation plan, the court could not continue to exercise jurisdiction to respond to shifting residential patterns. 427 U.S. 424, 433 (1976). As in *Swann*, the Court held that the equitable power of federal courts doesn't extend to demographic shifts "not attributed to any segregative actions on the part of the petitioners." *Id.* at 436.

The Court's antagonism toward busing wasn't unique to the justices. Across the country, white parents and politicians, liberal and conservative, complained that court-ordered desegregation put "the races at war" by benefiting black children at the expense of white children. Astead W. Herndon & Sheryl Gay Stolberg, *How Joe Biden Became the Democrats' Anti-Busing Crusader*, N.Y. Times, July 15, 2019, at A1. "This is the real problem with busing," Senator Joe Biden of Delaware said in a 1975 television interview. "You take people who aren't racist, people who are good citizens, who believe in equal education and opportunity, and you stunt their children's intellectual growth by busing them to an inferior school, and you're going to fill them with hatred." *Id.*

Many black families also objected to busing—but for far different reasons. Like Bradley, the black plaintiffs in desegregation suits typically cared less about sending their children to school with white children and more about ensuring that their children received an equal education with access to all available resources. Yet the mission of the NAACP LDF, since its founding, had been to pursue integration even if the litigation lasted so long that the children themselves never benefited. And as Harvard law professor Derrick Bell wrote in a famous 1976 article, "Now that traditional racial balance remedies are becoming increasingly difficult to achieve or maintain, there is tardy concern that racial balance may not be the relief actually desired by the victims of segregated schools." Derrick A. Bell Jr., *Serving Two Masters: Integration Ideals and Client Interest in School Desegregation Litigation*, 85 Yale L.J. 470, 471–72 (1976). Encouraging civil rights lawyers to negotiate with school boards and petition courts for educational improvements in black schools, Bell wrote:

> The tactics that worked for civil rights lawyers in the first decade of school desegregation—the careful selection and filing of class action suits seeking standardized relief in accordance with set, uncompromising national goals—are no longer unfailingly effective. In recent years, the relief sought and obtained in these suits has helped to precipitate a rise in militant white opposition and has seriously eroded carefully cultivated judicial support. Opposition to any civil rights program can be expected, but the hoped-for improvement in schooling for black children that might have justified the sacrifice and risk has proven minimal at best. It has been virtually nonexistent for the great mass of urban black children locked in all-black schools, many of which are today as separate and unequal as they were before 1954. . . .

Id. at 515–16.

Despite these criticisms, where busing was implemented, it successfully closed various achievement gaps between black and white students without harming white students. For example, between 1971, the year of *Swann*, and 1990, when busing was phased out as a remedy nationwide, the gap between the average reading scores of black and white students was cut in half. *See* U.S. Dep't of Educ., Nat'l Ctr. for Educ. Stat., *Trends in Academic Progress: 1971–2012*, at 18 (2013). Since 1990, that gap has remained largely consistent. *Id.* In light of these statistics, a reporter for the *New York Times*, Nikole Hannah-Jones, has recently taken issue with the claim that busing "failed." Nikole Hannah-Jones, *It Was Never About Busing*, N.Y. Times, July 14, 2019, at 6. "[It] is an incredible sleight of hand to argue that mandatory school desegregation failed, while ignoring that the past three decades of reforms promising to make separate schools equal have produced dismal results for black children," she wrote. *Id.*

Beyond busing. In addition to ordering busing, federal courts after *Swann* and *Milliken I* also ordered states and local governments to remedy de jure segregation in other ways, including by spending money to equalize educational opportunities among schools. Indeed, on remand from the Supreme Court's decision in *Milliken I*, the district court in Verda Bradley's case ordered the Detroit school board and the State of Michigan to fund remedial educational programs for schoolchildren who had been subjected to past acts of de jure segregation.

The state objected that federal courts have no power to require states to raise taxes and pay for services. But in *Milliken II*, the Supreme Court rejected Michigan's three arguments. First, the Court rejected the argument that ordering states and local governments to pay for programs is beyond the equitable powers of federal courts. 433 U.S. at 289. Second, the Court rejected the claim that the Eleventh Amendment stood in the way of such an order, noting that its Eleventh Amendment precedents already authorized the subordination of sovereign immunity "as a necessary consequence of compliance in the future with a substantive federal question determination." *Id.* at 289 (quoting *Edelman v. Jordan*, 415 U.S. 651 (1974)). Third, the Court rejected the argument that the Tenth Amendment prohibited federal courts from interfering with a state's reserved powers. The Court wrote that the Tenth Amendment "is not implicated by a federal-court judgment enforcing the express prohibitions of unlawful state conduct enacted by the Fourteenth Amendment." *Id.* at 291 (citing *Fitzpatrick v. Bitzer*, 427 U.S. 445 (1976)).

But even if federal courts have the power to force states to raise taxes, the Court has cautioned courts to exercise this power only to the extent necessary to remedy a constitutional violation. For example, in *Missouri v. Jenkins* (*Jenkins II*), 495 U.S. 33 (1990), a district court raised taxes to fund a desegregation program in Kansas City after finding that the Missouri constitution made it difficult for school districts to raise taxes on their own. The Supreme Court invalidated the district court's order, holding that before ordering the increase in taxes itself, the district court should have first "authorized or required [the school district] to levy property taxes at a rate adequate to fund the desegregation remedy and [should] have enjoined the operation of state laws that would have prevented [the school district] from exercising this power." *Id.* at 51. On remand, the district court issued a new ruling that ordered the state and school district to raise taxes and annually spend $200 million on an ambitious series of educational improvements designed to attract white families from the suburbs to voluntarily bus their children to Kansas City schools, helping them desegregate. The Supreme Court reversed this ruling in *Missouri v. Jenkins* (*Jenkins III*), 515 U.S. 70 (1995), holding that the ruling improperly attempted to remedy de facto segregation as opposed to a constitutional violation. *Id.* at 74–75.

Termination of court supervision. When the Supreme Court decided *Jenkins III* in 1995, the *Jenkins* litigation had proceeded before the same district judge since 1977—eighteen years. Other desegregation cases lasted a similarly long time. But beginning in the 1980s, the Department of Justice under President Ronald Reagan began opposing the continuation of existing desegregation plans, arguing that desegregation had failed and that existing desegregation orders should be canceled. *See* Erica Frankenberg, Chungmei Lee & Gary Orfield, Harv. Univ. Civil Rights Project, *A Multiracial Society with Segregated Schools: Are We Losing the Dream?* 18 (2003). Professor Bell agreed, writing that white resistance to desegregation had left the *Brown* rulings practically valueless "to millions of black children who have not experienced the decision's promise of equal educational opportunity." Derrick A. Bell Jr., Brown v. Board of Education *and the Interest-Convergence Dilemma*, 93 Harv. L. Rev. 518, 519 (1980). To Bell, it was preferable to "focus on obtaining real educational effectiveness which may entail the improvement of presently desegregated schools as well as the creation or preservation of model black schools." *Id.* at 532.

In the 1990s, the Supreme Court began prodding district courts to lift their desegregation decrees and end their decades-long cases. In a case closing the thirty-year litigation to desegregate Oklahoma City's public schools, *Board of Education of Oklahoma City Public Schools v. Dowell*, the Court declared that a desegregation decree should be dissolved "after the local authorities have operated in compliance with it"—eliminating all vestiges of de jure segregation—"for a reasonable period of time." 498 U.S. 237, 248 (1991). *Dowell* prompted many school districts and white parents to return to court to seek the end of their desegregation orders, leading judges to employ "considerable speed" in terminating desegregation orders. Frankenberg, Lee & Orfield, *supra*, at 19.

CHAPTER 47

WHEN DOES A FACIALLY NEUTRAL LAW CLASSIFY WITH RESPECT TO RACE?

FIFTH AMENDMENT (1791): No person shall . . . be deprived of life, liberty, or property, without due process of law. . . .

FOURTEENTH AMENDMENT (1868), SECTION 1: No State shall . . . deprive any person of life, liberty, or property, without due process of law; nor deny to any person within its jurisdiction the equal protection of the laws.

47.1 DISPARATE IMPACT VERSUS DISCRIMINATORY PURPOSE

A major theme of the Supreme Court's desegregation cases after *Swann v. Charlotte-Mecklenburg Board of Education*, 402 U.S. 1 (1971), was the Court's distinction between de jure segregation and de facto segregation. The Court employed the distinction to maintain that the Fourteenth Amendment didn't prohibit all racial segregation—only segregation that resulted from a school district's "*purpose* or *intent* to segregate." *Keyes v. School Dist. No. 1*, 413 U.S. 189, 208–09 (1973). Later decisions, including *Milliken v. Bradley* (*Milliken I*), 418 U.S. 717, 745 (1974), relied on this distinction to explain why it was inappropriate for a federal court to remedy de jure segregation in a single school district by seeking to eliminate de facto segregation in the metropolitan region.

Yet as early as *Yick Wo v. Hopkins*, 118 U.S. 356 (1886), the Court also recognized that a state could violate the Constitution with laws that, on their face, did not demonstrate a discriminatory purpose. "Though the law itself be fair on its face, and impartial in appearance," the Court wrote, it could still violate the Fourteenth Amendment "if it is applied and administered by public authority with an evil eye and an unequal hand." *Id.* at 373–74.

In the decades after *Yick Wo*, as the Supreme Court began applying strict scrutiny to laws that discriminated on the basis of race, it soon became critical for the Court to determine when facially neutral laws like the ordinance in *Yick Wo* were racially discriminatory. Under the rational-basis test reserved for most legislation, the Court typically upheld classifications as long as they were rationally related to a legitimate state interest. *See, e.g.*, *Williamson v. Lee Optical Co.*, 348 U.S. 483, 487 (1955). But under the strict scrutiny reserved for racial classifications, the Court typically struck down classifications unless they were necessary to serve a compelling state interest. *See, e.g.*, *McLaughlin v. Florida*, 379 U.S. 184 (1964). Determining whether a law discriminated on the basis of race therefore determined whether the rational-basis test or strict scrutiny would apply.

At times, the Supreme Court held that it would apply strict scrutiny to facially neutral laws only if they had a racially discriminatory *effect*, not just a racially discriminatory *purpose*. For example, in 1962, a group of black residents of Jackson, Mississippi, sued the city for racially segregating five public parks that each had swimming pools. In response to the lawsuit, the city desegregated all of its facilities except for its swimming pools—which the city council decided to close to everyone rather than open on a desegregated basis. *See* Heather McGhee, *The Sum of Us* 27 (2021) (noting that the nationwide closure of pools by defiant white communities illustrates how racism harms all people, including white people). The black residents of Jackson initiated another lawsuit to force the city to reopen its pools. But in *Palmer v. Thompson*, the Court held that there was nothing racially discriminatory about the city's pool closures as all residents, white and black, were equally affected. 403 U.S. 217, 220–21 (1971). In response to the black petitioners' argument that the decision to close the pools was motivated by a desire to avoid racial integration, the Court responded that none of its cases had ever held "that a legislative act may violate equal protection solely because of the motivations of the men who voted for it." *Id.* at 224. The Court emphasized "the hazards of declaring a law unconstitutional because of the motivations of its sponsors":

> First, it is extremely difficult for a court to ascertain the motivation, or collection of different motivations, that lie behind a legislative enactment. Here, for example, petitioners have argued that the Jackson pools were closed because of ideological opposition to racial integration in swimming pools. Some evidence in the record appears to support this argument. On the other hand the courts below found that the pools were closed because the city council felt they could not be operated safely and economically on an integrated basis. . . . It is difficult or impossible for any court to determine the "sole" or "dominant" motivation behind the choices of a group of legislators. Furthermore, there is an element of futility in a judicial attempt to invalidate a law because of the bad motives of its supporters. If the law is struck down for this reason, rather than because of its facial content or effect, it would presumably be valid as soon as the legislature or relevant governing body repassed it for different reasons.

Id. at 224–25. In light of these hazards, the Court held that it would treat Jackson's ordinance as racially discriminatory only if its "actual effect" was discriminatory. *Id.* at 225. It added that the black petitioners had shown "no state action affecting blacks differently from whites." *Id.*

The Court applied similar logic—although with a different result—in *Griggs v. Duke Power Co.*, 401 U.S. 424 (1971), a case that interpreted

Title VII of the Civil Rights Act of 1964, Pub. L. No. 88–352, 78 Stat. 255. In the years before Congress passed the Civil Rights Act, the Duke Power Company in Draper, North Carolina, engaged in overt racial discrimination against its black employees. After the Civil Rights Act prohibited employers from "depriv[ing] any individual of employment opportunities . . . because of such individual's race, color, religion, sex, or national origin," Duke Power imposed a series of educational requirements that an employee must meet before transferring out of an undesirable "labor" department historically staffed by black workers. *Griggs*, 401 U.S. at 427. When black workers sued, a lower federal court held that Duke Power's actions couldn't have violated the Civil Rights Act because there was no evidence that it had imposed the new requirements with a discriminatory purpose. *Id.* at 428. But the Supreme Court reversed, holding that proof of a "discriminatory purpose" was unnecessary to prove a violation of the Civil Rights Act. *Id.* at 431. "Discriminatory preference for any group, minority or majority, is precisely and only what Congress has proscribed," the Court declared. *Id.* "What is required by Congress is the removal of artificial, arbitrary, and unnecessary barriers to employment when the barriers operate invidiously to discriminate on the basis of racial or other impermissible classification." *Id.* The Court concluded that Title VII forbids the use of employment tests that are discriminatory in effect unless the employer meets "the burden of showing that any given requirement [has] . . . a manifest relationship to the employment in question." *Id.* at 432. In other words, Duke Power's actions were illegal unless it could prove that its educational requirements had some nondiscriminatory relationship to job performance outside the "labor" department.

47.1.1

Washington v. Davis

426 U.S. 229 (1976)

Palmer and *Griggs* both established that a racially discriminatory *effect*, not a racially discriminatory *purpose*, was relevant for determining whether a facially neutral action was, in fact, racial discrimination. Shortly afterward, however, in a case out of the District of Columbia—*Washington v. Davis*, 426 U.S. 229 (1976)—the Court announced a new test to evaluate whether racial segregation was the product of unconstitutional discrimination.

Like many police departments in the 1960s, the D.C. Metropolitan Police Department was almost exclusively white. This proved to be a liability during the so-called long, hot summer of 1967, when black people in dozens of cities protested police violence and racial discrimination in housing, employment, and education. To identify the cause of what were widely termed *race riots*, President Lyndon Johnson appointed Illinois Governor Otto Kerner Jr. to chair the National Advisory Commission on

Civil Disorders. Among other conclusions, the Kerner Commission found that the overwhelmingly white makeup of police departments contributed to police harassment of black people, who viewed the police as "an occupying force." *Report of the National Advisory Commission on Civil Disorders* 158 (1968). The Kerner Commission recommended that "[p]olice departments should intensify their efforts to recruit more Negroes . . . and review promotion policies to ensure that Negroes have full opportunity to be rapidly and fairly promoted." *Id.* at 166.

When two black officers in the District of Columbia reviewed their department's recruitment and promotion policies, they found that the department discriminated against new black applicants with a written personnel test that excluded a disproportionately high number of black applicants. This test, known as "Test 21," was administered before an applicant could take an intensive, seventeen-week training program to become a police officer. It was designed to test verbal ability, vocabulary, reading and comprehension. But the officers found that the test results had virtually no relationship to an officer's later job performance. The following question was typical:

> 3. Laws restricting hunting to certain regions and to a specific time of the year were passed chiefly to
>
> (A) prevent people from endangering their lives by hunting
>
> (B) keep our forests more beautiful
>
> (C) raise funds from the sale of hunting licenses
>
> (D) prevent complete destruction of certain kinds of animals
>
> (E) preserve certain game for eating purposes

Davis v. Washington, 512 F.2d 956, 968 (D.C. Cir. 1975).

In a lawsuit against D.C.'s black mayor, Walter Washington, the black police officers argued that the test's questions were irrelevant to becoming a good police officer yet were excluding black applicants from joining the force. The officers introduced evidence that (1) the police department was disproportionately white relative to the population of the District of Columbia, (2) four times as many black applicants failed the test as white applicants, and (3) the department had never established that its test was a reliable measurement of a person's job performance. But the district court treated this evidence as insufficient to apply strict scrutiny because there was no racially discriminatory *purpose*: it was undisputed that the department was affirmatively seeking to enroll more black officers. Under the rational-basis test, the court thought it enough that the test had a rational relationship to the training program.

The court of appeals reversed on the ground that the test had a racially discriminatory *effect*. Applying the disparate-impact standard that the Supreme Court had used in *Griggs* to interpret the Civil Rights

Act of 1964, the court of appeals struck down the test because the department couldn't prove that the test was needed to predict how well applicants would perform as police officers.

The Supreme Court determined that although disparate impact was important, it was not enough, by itself, to trigger strict scrutiny.

■ MR. JUSTICE WHITE delivered the opinion of the Court.[1]

This case involves the validity of a qualifying test administered to applicants for positions as police officers in the [D.C.] Metropolitan Police Department. . . .

[T]he central purpose of the Equal Protection Clause of the Fourteenth Amendment is the prevention of official conduct discriminating on the basis of race. It is also true that the Due Process Clause of the Fifth Amendment contains an equal protection component prohibiting the United States from invidiously discriminating between individuals or groups. *Bolling* v. *Sharpe,* 347 U. S. 497 (1954). But our cases have not embraced the proposition that a law or other official act, without regard to whether it reflects a racially discriminatory purpose, is unconstitutional *solely* because it has a racially disproportionate impact.

Almost 100 years ago, *Strauder* v. *West Virginia,* 100 U. S. 303 (1880), established that the exclusion of Negroes from grand and petit juries in criminal proceedings violated the Equal Protection Clause, but the fact that a particular jury or a series of juries does not statistically reflect the racial composition of the community does not in itself make out an invidious discrimination forbidden by the Clause. "A purpose to discriminate must be present which may be proven by systematic exclusion of eligible jurymen of the proscribed race or by unequal application of the law to such an extent as to show intentional discrimination." *Akins* v. *Texas,* 325 U. S. 398, 403–404 (1945). A defendant in a criminal case is entitled "to require that the State not deliberately and systematically deny to members of his race the right to participate as jurors in the administration of justice." *Alexander* v. *Louisiana,* 405 U. S. 625, 628–629 (1972). . . .

The school desegregation cases have also adhered to the basic equal protection principle that the invidious quality of a law claimed to be racially discriminatory must ultimately be traced to a racially discriminatory purpose. That there are both predominantly black and predominantly white schools in a community is not alone violative of the Equal Protection Clause. The essential element of *de jure* segregation is "a current condition of segregation resulting from intentional state action." *Keyes* v. *School Dist. No. 1,* 413 U. S. 189, 205 (1973). "The differentiating factor between *de jure* segregation and so-called *de facto* segregation . . . is *purpose* or *intent* to segregate." *Id.,* at 208. . . .

This is not to say that the necessary discriminatory racial purpose must be express or appear on the face of the statute, or that a law's disproportionate impact is irrelevant in cases involving Constitution-based claims of racial discrimination. A

[1] **As You Read, Consider:** One way of describing the difference between a discriminatory-purpose standard and a disproportionate-impact standard is as a burden of proof. Under a discriminatory-purpose standard, the *plaintiff* has the burden of *proving* that the government acted with a "suspect" purpose. If the plaintiff fails to carry this burden, then the court applies the rational-basis test. Under a disproportionate- or disparate-impact standard, the *government* has the burden of *disproving* that it acted with a "suspect" purpose, at least when its actions disproportionately harm a particular group. If the government fails to carry this burden, then the court applies a higher level of scrutiny.

In other words, both standards can be framed as attempts to prove whether the government's purpose was illegitimate. Why does Justice Byron White think that the burden of proof is better placed on a plaintiff rather than on the government?

statute, otherwise neutral on its face, must not be applied so as invidiously to discriminate on the basis of race. *Yick Wo* v. *Hopkins,* 118 U. S. 356 (1886). It is also clear from the cases dealing with racial discrimination in the selection of juries that the systematic exclusion of Negroes is itself such an "unequal application of the law . . . as to show intentional discrimination." *Akins* v. *Texas,* at 404. . . .

Necessarily, an invidious discriminatory purpose may often be inferred from the totality of the relevant facts, including the fact, if it is true, that the law bears more heavily on one race than another. It is also not infrequently true that the discriminatory impact—in the jury cases for example, the total or seriously disproportionate exclusion of Negroes from jury venires—may for all practical purposes demonstrate unconstitutionality because in various circumstances the discrimination is very difficult to explain on nonracial grounds. Nevertheless, we have not held that a law, neutral on its face and serving ends otherwise within the power of government to pursue, is invalid under the Equal Protection Clause simply because it may affect a greater proportion of one race than of another. Disproportionate impact is not irrelevant, but it is not the sole touchstone of an invidious racial discrimination forbidden by the Constitution. Standing alone, it does not trigger the rule, *McLaughlin* v. *Florida,* 379 U. S. 184 (1964), that racial classifications are to be subjected to the strictest scrutiny and are justifiable only by the weightiest of considerations.

There are some indications to the contrary in our cases. [See *Palmer* v. *Thompson,* 403 U. S. 217 (1971)]. [But] . . . the prevailing rule . . . is apparent from *Keyes* v. *School Dist. No. 1,* where the principal issue in litigation was whether and to what extent there had been purposeful discrimination resulting in a partially or wholly segregated school system. . . .

As an initial matter, we have difficulty understanding how a law establishing a racially neutral qualification for employment is nevertheless racially discriminatory and denies "any person . . . equal protection of the laws" simply because a greater proportion of Negroes fail to qualify than members of other racial or ethnic groups. . . . Test 21, which is administered generally to prospective Government employees, concededly seeks to ascertain whether those who take it have acquired a particular level of verbal skill; and it is untenable that the Constitution prevents the Government from seeking modestly to upgrade the communicative abilities of its employees rather than to be satisfied with some lower level of competence, particularly where the job requires special ability to communicate orally and in writing. Respondents, as Negroes, could no more successfully claim that the test denied them equal protection than could white applicants who also failed. The conclusion would not be different in the face of proof that more Negroes than whites had been disqualified by Test 21. That other Negroes also failed to score well would, alone, not demonstrate that respondents individually were being denied equal protection of the laws by the application of an otherwise valid qualifying test being administered to prospective police recruits.[2]

Nor on the facts of the case before us would the disproportionate impact of Test 21 warrant the conclusion that it is a purposeful device to discriminate against Negroes and hence an infringement of the constitutional rights of respondents as well as other black applicants. As we have said, the test is neutral on its face and rationally may be said to serve a purpose the Government is constitutionally empowered to

---

[2] **Questions:** White here frames the police officers' challenge as a conflict between merit and diversity. He writes that it cannot possibly violate the Constitution for a government to increase the standards of its job applicants, even if its higher standards disproportionately harm black people. Is this framing accurate? If the challengers are correct and the test is irrelevant to predicting a person's performance as a police officer but relevant to predicting a person's race, what "merit" is the test evaluating?

pursue. Even agreeing with the District Court that the differential racial effect of Test 21 called for further inquiry, we think the District Court correctly held that the affirmative efforts of the Metropolitan Police Department to recruit black officers, the changing racial composition of the recruit classes and of the force in general, and the relationship of the test to the training program negated any inference that the Department discriminated on the basis of race or that a police officer qualifies on the color of his skin rather than ability.

Under Title VII, Congress provided that when hiring and promotion practices disqualifying substantially disproportionate numbers of blacks are challenged, discriminatory purpose need not be proved, and that it is an insufficient response to demonstrate some rational basis for the challenged practices. It is necessary, in addition, that they be "validated" in terms of job performance in any one of several ways, perhaps by ascertaining the minimum skill, ability, or potential necessary for the position at issue and determining whether the qualifying tests are appropriate for the selection of qualified applicants for the job in question. However this process proceeds, it involves a more probing judicial review of, and less deference to, the seemingly reasonable acts of administrators and executives than is appropriate under the Constitution where special racial impact, without discriminatory purpose, is claimed. We are not disposed to adopt this more rigorous standard for the purposes of applying the Fifth and the Fourteenth Amendments in cases such as this.

A rule that a statute designed to serve neutral ends is nevertheless invalid, absent compelling justification, if in practice it benefits or burdens one race more than another would be far reaching and would raise serious questions about, and perhaps invalidate, a whole range of tax, welfare, public service, regulatory, and licensing statutes that may be more burdensome to the poor and to the average black than to the more affluent white.[3]

Given that rule, such consequences would perhaps be likely to follow. However, in our view, extension of the rule beyond those areas where it is already applicable by reason of statute, such as in the field of public employment, should await legislative prescription. . . .

47.1.2

Village of Arlington Heights v. Metropolitan Housing Development Corp.

429 U.S. 252 (1977)

Davis announced that before a federal court should apply strict scrutiny to a facially neutral law, the plaintiff must establish that the law's "purpose" was to implicate a suspect classification such as race. No justice dissented from this point. The Supreme Court continues to use this test in a variety of contexts, from cases alleging violations of the

3 **Questions:** White ultimately rejects placing the burden of proof on the government in these sorts of cases because the consequences would be "far reaching." In *McCleskey v. Kemp*, a later decision that relied heavily on White's opinion in this case, the Court applied similar logic to reject a well-documented claim that all aspects of the criminal legal system were racially discriminatory. 481 U.S. 279, 316–19 (1987). "Taken on its face, such a statement seems to suggest a fear of too much justice," Justice William Brennan wrote in dissent. *Id.* at 339. Is Brennan right? If the majority is willing to concede that a wide range of activities produces structural disadvantages for black people, why does it follow that black people—and not the government—should bear the burden of proving in each individual case that each statute has a discriminatory purpose? How is a challenger supposed to uncover that information?

Equal Protection Clause to cases alleging violations of the voting-rights amendments.

But *Davis* provided only ambiguous hints for how to determine a law's purpose, suggesting that "an invidious discriminatory purpose may often be inferred from the totality of the relevant facts, including the fact, if it is true, that the law bears more heavily on one race than another." 426 U.S. at 242.

In theory, a totality-of-the-relevant-facts approach to determining a law's purpose could yield the same results as an approach that focused on a law's disparate impact. For example, the public schools of the District of Columbia were segregated until the Supreme Court's decision in *Bolling v. Sharpe*, 347 U.S. 497 (1954). The purpose of that school segregation was undoubtedly discriminatory, and it resulted in black children attending poorly resourced schools. Twenty-two years later, those children were the same young adults applying to become police officers in the District of Columbia—which could explain part of the divergence in the police department's test scores. So, in theory at least, the disparate impact of Test 21 could be explained in part by the government's racially discriminatory purpose.

In light of this possibility, the Supreme Court added more limits to its totality-of-the-relevant-facts approach in the following case, *Village of Arlington Heights v. Metropolitan Housing Development Corp.*, 429 U.S. 252 (1977).

During the Great Migration, when black people streamed to northern cities like Detroit and Chicago, suburbs of affluent white people adopted exclusionary zoning laws that prohibited the construction of multifamily apartment buildings. One of those suburbs was the village of Arlington Heights, twenty-six miles outside Chicago, which adopted an exclusionary zoning ordinance in 1959. In 1971, the Metropolitan Housing Development Corporation (MHDC) applied to the village to request that it rezone a parcel for the construction of Lincoln Green, a development of multifamily townhouses for low- and moderate-income tenants. The village refused.

The MHDC sued the village in federal court, claiming that the denial was racially discriminatory. Among other evidence, the MHDC proved at trial that (1) only twenty-seven of the village's 64,000 residents were black; (2) black people constituted 40 percent of Chicago-area residents who would be eligible tenants of Lincoln Green; (3) the MHDC's rezoning application indicated that Lincoln Green would probably be racially integrated; and (4) during public comment sessions, local residents and members of the planning commission complained about what they called the "social issue"—i.e., that the development would decrease nearby property values.

When the case reached the Supreme Court, the Court used the case as an opportunity to further limit when a facially neutral law implicates race.

■ MR. JUSTICE POWELL delivered the opinion of the Court.[4]

In 1971 respondent Metropolitan Housing Development Corporation (MHDC) applied to petitioner, the Village of Arlington Heights, Ill., for the rezoning of a 15-acre parcel from single-family to multiple-family classification. Using federal financial assistance, MHDC planned to build 190 clustered townhouse units for low- and moderate-income tenants. The Village denied the rezoning request. MHDC . . . alleged that the denial was racially discriminatory and that it violated . . . the Fourteenth Amendment. . . .

III

Our decision last Term in *Washington* v. *Davis,* 426 U. S. 229 (1976), made it clear that official action will not be held unconstitutional solely because it results in a racially disproportionate impact. "Disproportionate impact is not irrelevant, but it is not the sole touchstone of an invidious racial discrimination." *Id.,* at 242. Proof of racially discriminatory intent or purpose is required to show a violation of the Equal Protection Clause. . . .

Davis does not require a plaintiff to prove that the challenged action rested solely on racially discriminatory purposes. Rarely can it be said that a legislature or administrative body operating under a broad mandate made a decision motivated solely by a single concern, or even that a particular purpose was the "dominant" or "primary" one. In fact, it is because legislators and administrators are properly concerned with balancing numerous competing considerations that courts refrain from reviewing the merits of their decisions, absent a showing of arbitrariness or irrationality. But racial discrimination is not just another competing consideration. When there is a proof that a discriminatory purpose has been a motivating factor in the decision, this judicial deference is no longer justified.

Determining whether invidious discriminatory purpose was a motivating factor demands a sensitive inquiry into such circumstantial and direct evidence of intent as may be available. The impact of the official action—whether it "bears more heavily on one race than another," *Washington* v. *Davis, supra,* at 242—may provide an important starting point. Sometimes a clear pattern, unexplainable on grounds other than race, emerges from the effect of the state action even when the governing legislation appears neutral on its face. *Yick Wo* v. *Hopkins,* 118 U. S. 356 (1886). The evidentiary inquiry is then relatively easy. But such cases are rare. Absent a pattern as stark as that in . . . *Yick Wo,* impact alone is not determinative, and the Court must look to other evidence.

The historical background of the decision is one evidentiary source, particularly if it reveals a series of official actions taken for invidious purposes. The specific sequence of events leading up to the challenged decision also may shed some light on the decisionmaker's purposes. *Reitman* v. *Mulkey,* 387 U. S. 369, 373–376 (1967). For example, if the property involved here always had been zoned [for high density] but suddenly was changed to [single-family housing] when the town learned

[4] **As You Read, Consider:** Justice Lewis Powell formalizes the discriminatory purpose standard of *Washington v. Davis* into a multifactor test. Before the Court will apply strict scrutiny to a facially neutral law, plaintiffs must use his test to satisfy their burden of proving that a suspect purpose was a "motivating factor" in the government's decision.

If the plaintiffs in this case fail to satisfy Powell's test, is it conceivable to imagine a situation in which a plaintiff will be successful absent government officials announcing that they're racist?

of MHDC's plans to erect integrated housing, we would have a far different case. Departures from the normal procedural sequence also might afford evidence that improper purposes are playing a role. Substantive departures too may be relevant, particularly if the factors usually considered important by the decisionmaker strongly favor a decision contrary to the one reached.

The legislative or administrative history may be highly relevant, especially where there are contemporary statements by members of the decisionmaking body, minutes of its meetings, or reports. In some extraordinary instances the members might be called to the stand at trial to testify concerning the purpose of the official action, although even then such testimony frequently will be barred by privilege.

The foregoing summary identifies, without purporting to be exhaustive, subjects of proper inquiry in determining whether racially discriminatory intent existed. With these in mind, we now address the case before us.

IV

[T]he impact of the Village's decision does arguably bear more heavily on racial minorities. Minorities constitute 18% of the Chicago area population, and 40% of the income groups said to be eligible for Lincoln Green. But there is little about the sequence of events leading up to the decision that would spark suspicion. The area around the [parcel] has been zoned [for single-family housing] since 1959, the year when Arlington Heights first adopted a zoning map. Single-family homes surround the 80-acre site, and the Village is undeniably committed to single-family homes as its dominant residential land use. The rezoning request progressed according to the usual procedures. . . .[5]

The statements by the Plan Commission and Village Board members, as reflected in the official minutes, focused almost exclusively on the zoning aspects of the MHDC petition, and the zoning factors on which they relied are not novel criteria in the Village's rezoning decisions. There is no reason to doubt that there has been reliance by some neighboring property owners on the maintenance of single-family zoning in the vicinity. . . . Finally, MHDC called one member of the Village Board to the stand at trial. Nothing in her testimony supports an inference of invidious purpose.

In sum, . . . Respondents simply failed to carry their burden of proving that discriminatory purpose was a motivating factor in the Village's decision. . . . The Court of Appeals' further finding that the Village's decision carried a discriminatory "ultimate effect" is without independent constitutional significance. . . .

NOTE: APPLYING THE *DAVIS-ARLINGTON HEIGHTS* TEST

Considered together, *Davis* and *Arlington Heights* formalized the test that a plaintiff must satisfy before a federal court will treat a facially neutral action as discriminatory and therefore subject to strict scrutiny. Under *Davis*, a court will apply strict scrutiny only if the "purpose" of the action was to discriminate on the basis of a suspect classification, such as race. 426 U.S. at 242. Under *Arlington Heights*, the discriminatory purpose need not be the sole or primary purpose of the law, but it must be a "motivating

[5] **Question:** Powell treats the age of Arlington Heights's zoning map—dating back to 1959—as if it demonstrates that racial discrimination was not a motivating factor in its decision-making. But in the 1940s and 1950s, cities and suburbs around the country adopted facially neutral zoning laws to insulate themselves from the Great Migration of black people out of the South. Do you think that Powell was unaware of this history, or rather that he doesn't think such history demonstrates that Arlington Heights acted with a discriminatory purpose in *this particular* case?

factor." 429 U.S. at 265. The Court added, "Determining whether invidious discriminatory purpose was a motivating factor demands a sensitive inquiry into such circumstantial and direct evidence of intent as may be available." *Id.* at 266. This inquiry may consider, among other evidence, (1) the "impact of the official action," (2) the "historical background of the decision," (3) the "specific sequence of events leading up to the challenged decision," (4) "[d]epartures from the normal procedural sequence," (5) "[s]ubstantive departures" from considerations relied on in the past, and (6) "contemporary statements by members of the decisionmaking body." *Id.* at 266–68.

Upping the challenges of meeting the *Davis-Arlington Heights* test. *Davis* and *Arlington Heights* were quickly followed by a series of cases that made this already demanding test even more difficult for a plaintiff to satisfy.

In *Mt. Healthy City School District v. Doyle*, an employment case alleging unconstitutional retaliation in violation of the Due Process Clause, the Court held that the *Arlington Heights* motivating-factor analysis merely establishes a prima facie case of discriminatory purpose that shifts the burden to the government. 429 U.S. 274, 287 (1977). The Court held that the government may then rebut this evidence if it can show "by a preponderance of the evidence that it would have reached the same decision . . . even in the absence of the" discriminatory purpose. *Id.*

The Court thereafter held that it would apply strict scrutiny to a facially neutral law only when the government cannot carry this burden and it is clear that the government would not have made its decision but for a purpose of discriminating on the basis of a suspect classification. In an oft-cited case, the Court explained that a discriminatory purpose means the decisionmaker "selected or reaffirmed a particular course of action at least in part 'because of,' not merely 'in spite of,' its adverse effects upon an identifiable group." *Pers. Adm'r* v. *Feeney*, 442 U.S. 256, 279 (1979).

Satisfying the *Davis-Arlington Heights* test. Supreme Court cases in which a plaintiff satisfies the *Davis-Arlington Heights* test are rare. *Hunter v. Underwood*, 471 U.S. 222 (1985), was one exception.

In *Hunter*, the Court considered a provision of the Alabama Constitution of 1901 that provided for the disenfranchisement of anyone convicted of a "crime involving moral turpitude." 471 U.S. at 226. The plaintiffs—two men disenfranchised after being convicted of presenting a worthless check—alleged that the entire state constitution had been adopted with the discriminatory purpose of preventing black people from voting. *Hunter*, 471 U.S. at 226–27. The Alabama Constitution was the same constitution at issue in *Giles v. Harris*, in which the Supreme Court had declined to reenfranchise a black man on the ground that the Court could not effectively stop "the great mass of the white population [that] intends to keep the blacks from voting." 189 U.S. 475 (1903).

In *Hunter*, the Court agreed with the plaintiffs that, applying the *Davis-Arlington Heights* test, the constitutional provision would not have been passed but for the purpose of discriminating against black people. 471 U.S. at 232. Specifically, the Court emphasized the contemporary statements of the constitution's framers—who asserted that their purpose was "to establish white supremacy in this State"—as well as the provision's disparate impact on black voters. *Id.* at 229, 232. "Without deciding whether [the provision] would be valid if enacted today without any impermissible motivation," the Court noted, "we simply observe that its original enactment was motivated by a desire to discriminate against blacks on account of race, and the section continues to this day to have that effect." *Id.* at 233; *see also Rogers v. Lodge*, 458 U.S. 613 (1982) (striking down the creation of an at-large electoral district after inferring an invidious purpose from the totality of relevant facts, including a disparate impact).

Individualizing the need for strict scrutiny. More common are decisions like *McCleskey v. Kemp*, 481 U.S. 279 (1987), in which the Court considered the constitutionality of the death penalty as applied to black defendants.

The lawyers for Warren McCleskey, a black man convicted of murdering a white police officer, introduced into evidence a report conducted by law professor David C. Baldus and other scholars that studied 2,500 murder cases in Georgia. *McCleskey*, 481 U.S. at 286. The Baldus study found that, even after controlling for thirty-nine nonracial variables, a defendant in Georgia was 4.3 times more likely to be sentenced to death if the victim was white than if the victim was black. *Id.* at 287. In addition, black defendants were 1.1 times more likely to receive a death sentence as other defendants. *Id.* McCleskey argued that this study compelled the inference that his own sentence—as a black defendant whose victim was white—rested on purposeful discrimination.

But the Supreme Court rejected his claim, holding that even assuming that the study was accurate, McCleskey hadn't proved "that the decisionmakers in *his* case acted with discriminatory purpose." *Id.* at 292. "Each jury is unique in its composition, and the Constitution requires that its decision rest on consideration of innumerable factors that vary according to the characteristics of the individual defendant and the facts of the particular capital offense," the Court wrote. *Id.* at 294. "Because discretion is essential to the criminal justice process," the Court added, "we would demand exceptionally clear proof before we would infer that the discretion has been abused. The unique nature of the decisions at issue in this case also counsels against adopting such an inference from the disparities indicated by the Baldus study." *Id.* at 297.

The Court also added that recognizing McCleskey's claim would open the door to widespread challenges to all aspects of criminal sentencing, *id.* at 316–19, a point that Justice William Brennan cogently criticized in dissent. "Taken on its face, such a statement seems to suggest a fear of too much justice," he wrote. *Id.* at 339 (Brennan, J., dissenting). "The prospect that there may be more widespread abuse than McCleskey documents may be dismaying, but it does not justify complete abdication of our judicial role." *Id.*; *see also City of Mobile v. Bolden*, 446 U.S. 55 (1980) (applying the *Davis-Arlington Heights* discriminatory-purpose test to uphold a multimember electoral district with a racially discriminatory impact).

McCleskey has had the effect of making it nearly impossible to challenge racial discrimination in the criminal legal system despite widespread evidence that such discrimination is rampant. "[T]he Court's opinion was driven by a desire to immunize the entire criminal justice system from claims of racial bias," wrote law professor Michelle Alexander. Michelle Alexander, *The New Jim Crow: Mass Incarceration in the Age of Colorblindness* 111 (2010). "In the years following *McCleskey*, lower courts consistently rejected claims of race discrimination in the criminal justice system, finding that gross racial disparities do not merit strict scrutiny in the absence of evidence of explicit race discrimination—the very evidence unavailable in the era of colorblindness." *Id.* at 113.

Rejecting strict scrutiny in the face of explicit discrimination. Indeed, even when "explicit race discrimination" exists, the modern Supreme Court has invoked *Davis* and *Arlington Heights* to reject applications of strict scrutiny.

In *Department of Homeland Security v. Regents of the University of California*, several plaintiffs challenged, on statutory and constitutional grounds, the Trump administration's decision to rescind the Deferred Action for Childhood Arrivals program (DACA). 140 S. Ct. 1891, 1901 (2020).

Although Chief Justice John Roberts agreed with the statutory challenge, he went out of his way to reject the constitutional challenge. In their complaint, the plaintiffs cataloged President Donald Trump's declarations that Mexican immigrants are "people that have lots of problems"; "the bad ones"; and "criminals, drug dealers, [and] rapists." *Id.* at 1917 (Sotomayor, J., dissenting in part). They also quoted the president's 2017 statement comparing undocumented immigrants to "animals" responsible for "the drugs, the gangs, the cartels, the crisis of smuggling and trafficking." *Id.* But Roberts insisted that the statements were "unilluminating," "remote in time," and "made in unrelated contexts." *Id.* at 1916 (majority opinion). Walking through the *Davis-Arlington Heights* factors, Roberts wrote that the complaints failed to allege that the attorney general or secretary of homeland security made similar public statements even though they, not the president, were the "relevant actors" for rescinding DACA. *Id.* Therefore, he wrote, the complaint should have been dismissed from the outset because the president's statements "fail to raise a plausible inference that the rescission was motivated by animus." *Id.*

Such a holding—on a motion to dismiss—prohibited the plaintiffs from using discovery to determine whether Trump's publicly stated beliefs were passed along to subordinates. *Id.*

NOTE: *DAVIS-ARLINGTON HEIGHTS* TEST AND JURIES

In adopting the discriminatory-purpose test, *Davis* heavily relied on previous decisions involving jury selection. These earlier cases emerged after *Strauder v. West Virginia*, when the Court held that it violated the Fourteenth Amendment for states to discriminate against potential jurors because of their race. 100 U.S. 303, 312 (1880). But the same day that it decided *Strauder*, the Court also held that the Fourteenth Amendment didn't require a state to provide every defendant with a "mixed" jury of white and black jurors. *Virginia v. Rives*, 100 U.S. 313, 323 (1880). Accordingly, because an all-white jury alone didn't violate the Fourteenth Amendment, in subsequent cases the Court had to determine whether particular all-white juries were caused by racial discrimination.

After the 1970s, the Court used the test from *Davis* and *Arlington Heights* to apply strict scrutiny to the actions of prosecutors only if they engaged in "purposeful racial discrimination." *Batson v. Kentucky*, 476 U.S. 79, 95 (1986). Today, the Court uses a similar burden-shifting approach as in the civil context: once a defendant makes a prima facie showing of racial discrimination, the prosecutor "must articulate a neutral explanation related to the particular case to be tried." *Id.* at 98. "The trial court then will have the duty to determine if the defendant has established purposeful discrimination." *Id.*

As in other contexts, proving that a prosecutor acted with a discriminatory purpose is very difficult. *See, e.g.*, *Felkner v. Jackson*, 562 U.S. 594, 598 (2011). Nevertheless, the Court has occasionally reversed trial court decisions on the ground that the prosecutor's race-neutral explanation for a peremptory challenge was implausible. For example, in *Foster v. Chatman*, 578 U.S. 488 (2016), a black prisoner filed a freedom-of-information request for records from his 1986 murder trial, in which prosecutors struck all four black prospective jurors. Among the records were handwritten copies of the jury list in which the names of the black jurors were highlighted in bright green. *Foster*, 578 U.S. at 493–96. A legend in the corner indicated that the highlighting "represents Blacks." *Id.* Three of the black prospective jurors were also denoted as "B#1," "B#2," and "B#3." *Id.* In light of this new evidence, the Court held that the trial court's conclusion that the defendant had failed to show purposeful discrimination was "clearly erroneous." *Id.* at 1741.

47.2 THE POLITICAL PROCESS DOCTRINE

Around the same time that the Supreme Court announced one approach to evaluating facially neutral laws in *Washington v. Davis*, 426 U.S. 229 (1976), and *Village of Arlington Heights v. Metropolitan Housing Development Corp.*, 429 U.S. 252 (1977), it adopted an alternative approach to evaluating facially neutral popular referenda. In a series of cases beginning in the late 1960s, the Court held that when voters adopt laws that make it more difficult for racial minorities to implement new policies to desegregate schools and housing, they may violate the Equal Protection Clause by virtue of the laws' effect on the political process.

This "political process" doctrine lasted for almost fifty years and may become viable again in the future. But in 2014, the Court radically narrowed the scope of the doctrine until it was indistinguishable from the *Davis-Arlington Heights* test.

Court cases striking down racially discriminatory amendments

Reitman v. Mulkey. Although Congress and the Supreme Court in the 1960s led the way toward desegregating schools and housing across the country, many state and local governments voluntarily adopted their own desegregation policies without a federal order. In California, for example, the legislature passed several laws between 1959 and 1963 that prohibited racial discrimination in housing.

In response to these laws, white voters took advantage of the state constitution's "initiative" power—a Progressive Era reform adopted in two dozen states that allows voters to amend the state constitution by popular vote. In 1964, these voters won a ballot question that amended the California Constitution to prohibit the state legislature from abridging "the right of any person, . . . to decline to sell, lease, or rent [his] property to such person or persons as he, in his absolute discretion, chooses." Cal. Const. art. I, § 26 (1964).

In *Reitman v. Mulkey*, 387 U.S. 369 (1967), the Supreme Court struck down this amendment as a violation of the Equal Protection Clause. Although the Court rejected the notion that "our cases or the Fourteenth Amendment [establish] an automatic constitutional barrier to the repeal of an existing law prohibiting racial discrimination in housing," it affirmed the state supreme court's holding that "the intent of [the provision] was to authorize private racial discriminations in the housing market . . . and to create a constitutional right to discriminate on racial grounds in the sale and leasing of real property." *Reitman*, 387 U.S. at 376.

The *Reitman* decision was later described in *Arlington Heights* as an example of where "[t]he specific sequence of events leading up to the challenged decision also may shed some light on the decisionmaker's purposes." 429 U.S. at 267. But *Reitman* soon evolved into its own doctrine independent of *Arlington Heights*.

Hunter v. Erickson. The fact pattern of *Reitman* repeated itself in the city of Akron, Ohio, where the city council adopted a fair housing ordinance in 1964 that was repealed by a local ballot initiative to amend the city's charter. The charter amendment required that any future ordinance regulating property transactions on the basis of "race, color, religion, national origin or ancestry" must be submitted to a popular vote before it could become effective.

In *Hunter v. Erickson*, the Court invoked *Reitman* to invalidate the charter amendment—not because the amendment's intent was to discriminate on the basis of race but because "the reality is that the law's impact falls on the minority." 393 U.S. 385, 391 (1969). The Court wrote that the amendment placed "special burdens on racial minorities within the governmental process," adding that the "majority needs no protection against discrimination and if it did, a referendum might be bothersome but no more than that." *Id.*

Washington v. Seattle School District No. 1. The Supreme Court crystallized the political process doctrine in *Washington v. Seattle School District No. 1*, 458 U.S. 457 (1982).

Like many western cities, Seattle was a hostile place for people of color for most of its history: Chinese immigrants were forcibly expelled from the city in 1886, and Japanese Americans were marched into internment camps in the 1940s. Persistent housing segregation contributed to school segregation, and the local school district systematically underfunded schools attended by Asian American and black students.

In 1977, after the Urban League and other civil rights groups threatened a lawsuit, the school board of directors voted 6–1 for a mandatory busing program to desegregate the district. The plan was immediately attacked by white parents, who in 1978 won a statewide ballot initiative that had the effect of prohibiting the Seattle school district from busing students within the district for the purpose of desegregating its schools.

After the Seattle school district challenged the referendum in federal court, the Supreme Court held that the referendum violated the Equal Protection Clause. That clause, the Court wrote, prohibits "a political structure that treats all individuals as equals yet more subtly distorts governmental processes in such a way as to place special burdens on the ability of minority groups to achieve beneficial legislation." *Seattle*, 458 U.S. at 467. The Court explained that it was fine for a state to structure political institutions "according to 'neutral principles'—such as the executive veto, or the typically burdensome requirements for amending state constitutions—. . . [b]ecause such laws make it more difficult for *every* group in the community to enact comparable laws." *Id.* at 470. But the Court would apply strict scrutiny "when the State allocates governmental power nonneutrally, by explicitly using the *racial* nature of a decision to determine the decisionmaking process." *Id.* In Washington's case, the statewide initiative had "remove[d] the authority to address a racial problem—and only a racial problem—from the existing decisionmaking body, in such a way as to burden minority interests." *Id.* at 474. The Court therefore applied strict scrutiny and found the initiative overbroad to address any compelling state interests. *Id.* at 487.

Narrowing the political process doctrine in Schuette

The vitality of the *Seattle* decision lasted until *Schuette v. Coalition to Defend Affirmative Action*, 572 U.S. 291 (2014), where the Court severely narrowed the reach of the political process doctrine. There, Michigan voters adopted an amendment to their constitution forbidding the practice of affirmative action in public employment and public education. The plurality opinion, written by Justice Anthony Kennedy for two justices, held that "*Seattle* is best understood as a case in which the state action in question . . . had the serious risk, if not purpose, of causing specific injuries on account of race, just as had been the case in *Mulkey* and *Hunter*." *Schuette*, 572 U.S. at 305. An additional concurring opinion of two justices—representing a majority—dismissed as dicta everything in *Seattle* that appeared to contradict the Court's approach toward facially neutral laws in *Davis* and *Arlington Heights*. *Id.* at 330 (Scalia, J., concurring in the judgment). Justice Stephen Breyer also criticized "the principle underlying *Hunter* and *Seattle*" for "run[ning] up against a competing principle favoring decisionmaking through the democratic process." *Id.* at 337 (Breyer, J., concurring in the judgment).

Only Justice Sonia Sotomayor, joined by Justice Ruth Bader Ginsburg, defended the political process doctrine, arguing that unlike *Davis* and *Arlington Heights*, the doctrine required courts to consider in a race-conscious way how facially neutral laws "burden minority interests":

> My colleagues are of the view that we should leave race out of the picture entirely and let the voters sort it out. . . . It is a sentiment out of touch with reality, one not required by the Constitution, and one that has properly been rejected as "not sufficient" to resolve cases of this nature. . . .
>
> Race matters. Race matters in part because of the long history of racial minorities' being denied access to the political process. . . . Race also matters because of persistent racial inequality in society—inequality that cannot be ignored and that has produced stark socioeconomic disparities. . . . And race matters for reasons that really are only skin deep, that cannot be discussed any other way, and that cannot be wished away. . . . Race matters because of the slights, the snickers, the silent judgments that reinforce that most crippling of thoughts: "I do not belong here."
>
> In my colleagues' view, examining the racial impact of legislation only perpetuates racial discrimination. This refusal to accept the stark reality that race matters is regrettable. The way to stop discrimination on the basis of race is to speak openly and candidly on the subject of race, and to apply the Constitution with eyes open to the unfortunate effects of centuries of racial discrimination. As members of the judiciary tasked with intervening to carry out the guarantee of equal protection, we ought not sit back and wish away, rather than confront, the racial inequality that exists in our society. It is this view that works harm, by perpetuating the facile notion that what makes race matter is acknowledging the simple truth that race *does* matter.

Id. at 380–81 (Sotomayor, J., dissenting).

CHAPTER 48

WHAT OTHER CLASSIFICATIONS ARE STRICTLY SCRUTINIZED?

FIFTH AMENDMENT (1791): No person shall . . . be deprived of life, liberty, or property, without due process of law. . . .

FOURTEENTH AMENDMENT (1868), SECTION 1: No State shall . . . deprive any person of life, liberty, or property, without due process of law; nor deny to any person within its jurisdiction the equal protection of the laws.

48.1 WEALTH

Although the Supreme Court's equal-protection jurisprudence developed primarily in the context of racial classifications, the Court never suggested that race was the only classification to which it would apply strict scrutiny. As discussed earlier (sections 41.2.3, 45.2.1), in *United States v. Carolene Products Co.*, Chief Justice Harlan Stone proposed that the Court would defer to most legislation but apply "more exacting judicial scrutiny" to "legislation which restricts those political processes which can ordinarily be expected to bring about repeal of undesirable legislation." 304 U.S. 144, 152–53 n.4 (1938). Stone's footnote referenced any law that infringed on the first ten amendments, interfered with the right to vote, or reflected "prejudice against discrete and insular minorities." *Id.* Stone's call to protect "discrete and insular" minorities—in contrast with "all" minorities or even "racial" minorities—suggests that he thought courts after *Lochner v. New York*, 198 U.S. 45 (1905), should ordinarily allow the legislative process to run its course. Only when a minority group was systematically unable to form a winning political coalition did the chief justice think that the Court should intervene in "those political processes ordinarily to be relied upon to protect minorities." *Id.*

Shortly afterward, in *Edwards v. California*, the Court invalidated a California law that made it a crime to bring into the state "any indigent person who is not a resident of the State, knowing him to be an indigent person." 314 U.S. 160, 171 (1941). The Court held that the statute failed "any known test of the validity of State interference with interstate commerce" because "the indigent non-residents who are the real victims of the statute are deprived of the opportunity to exert political pressure upon the California legislature in order to obtain a change in policy." *Id.* at 174. Although the Court didn't indicate what level of scrutiny it was applying, concurring opinions explained that the statute interfered with the "fundamental" right "to move freely from State to State." *Id.* at 178

(Douglas, J., concurring); *see also id.* at 184–85 (Jackson, J., concurring). These justices argued that the Court shouldn't apply its deferential standard of review.

Relatedly, the first time the Court ever applied strict scrutiny was in a case involving not race, but wealth. In *Skinner v. Oklahoma ex rel. Williamson*, 316 U.S. 535 (1942), the Court struck down a law that required the sterilization of people convicted multiple times of specified crimes (see section 45.2). The list of crimes requiring sterilization included petty larceny but exempted embezzlement and political offenses. The Court applied "strict scrutiny" because the law affected "one of the basic civil rights"—procreation—and also because of the law's "clear, pointed, unmistakable discrimination." *Skinner*, 316 U.S. at 541. Presumably, the Court thought that the law discriminated on the basis of wealth: poor defendants were more likely than white-collar defendants to commit larceny and less likely to commit embezzlement or political offenses.

The Court continued this pattern of skeptically evaluating wealth-based classifications in *Griffin v. Illinois*, 351 U.S. 12 (1956). Illinois law entitled all criminal defendants to direct appellate review of their convictions, but the state conditioned such review on the defendant's payment of a fee to obtain a transcript of the trial proceedings. *Griffin*, 351 U.S. at 13. This law made it impossible for many poor defendants to obtain access to a procedural safeguard—appellate review—that wealthy defendants could afford. In a plurality opinion, Justice Hugo Black declared the law invalid after writing that in criminal trials, "a State can no more discriminate on account of poverty than on account of religion, race, or color." *Id.* at 17. Applying an enhanced version of the rational-basis test, Black observed that "the ability to pay . . . bears no rational relationship to a defendant's guilt or innocence and could not be used as an excuse to deprive a defendant of a fair trial." *Id.* at 17–18.

Cases in the 1960s repeatedly expanded on *Griffin*'s holding that it was unconstitutional for a state to discriminate on the basis of poverty when allocating procedural safeguards in criminal trials or appeals. Most famously, in *Gideon v. Wainwright*, the Court held that the Due Process Clause and the Sixth Amendment required governments to provide indigent criminal defendants with court-appointed counsel during trial. 372 U.S. 335, 342 (1963).

During the same decade that it protected equal access to the courts, the Court also protected equal access to the ballot. Although the Supreme Court's voting cases will be discussed in detail later (section 50.1), the decisions announced a broad principle that "any alleged infringement of the right of citizens to vote must be carefully and meticulously scrutinized." *Reynolds v. Sims*, 377 U.S. 533, 562 (1964). In *Harper v. Virginia Board of Elections*, the Court invalidated a poll tax after citing its criminal-procedure cases to equate wealth with race. 383 U.S. 663, 668 (1966). "To introduce wealth or payment of a fee as a measure of a voter's qualifications is to introduce a capricious or irrelevant factor," the Court insisted. *Id*

Distilling these decisions in *Shapiro v. Thompson*, the Court announced that when a classification "touches on [a] fundamental right . . ., its constitutionality must be judged by the stricter standard of whether it promotes a *compelling* state interest." 394 U.S. 618, 638 (1969). The *Shapiro* Court evaluated several state laws that conditioned eligibility for welfare benefits on an applicant's residency in the state for one year. The states explained that the laws were rationally related to their legitimate interest in preventing poor people from fraudulently obtaining welfare payments from multiple states. Agreeing that the laws could survive the rational-basis test, the Court nevertheless applied strict scrutiny because the laws infringed on the same "freedom to travel" that it earlier recognized in *Edwards*. *Shapiro*, 394 U.S. at 631. Under this more demanding standard, the Court held that the interest wasn't "compelling" enough to justify granting welfare benefits to longtime residents but denying them to recent arrivals. *Id.* at 627.

The Supreme Court ultimately merged this "fundamental right" analysis in equal-protection cases with its "fundamental liberty interest" analysis in due process cases. *See, e.g.*, *Eisenstadt v. Baird*, 405 U.S. 438, 443 (1972). The Court formally applied strict scrutiny to a due process case for the first time in *Roe v. Wade*, 410 U.S. 113 (1973).

The merger of the Court's equal-protection and due process analyses provided an elegant explanation for the Court's earlier criminal-procedure, voting-rights, and right-to-travel decisions, as all of them arguably involved fundamental rights. Yet it left unclear whether wealth, like race, was a "suspect classification" that could trigger strict scrutiny even if a law didn't violate a fundamental right. In cases leading up to 1973, the Court wavered on whether to apply strict scrutiny to laws that discriminated with respect to the allegedly fundamental right to housing, *Lindsey v. Normet*, 405 U.S. 56, 73 (1972), or with the allegedly suspect classification of sex, *Reed v. Reed*, 404 U.S. 71, 74 (1971).

48.1.1

San Antonio Independent School District v. Rodriguez

411 U.S. 1 (1973)

In the following case, *San Antonio Independent School District v. Rodriguez*, 411 U.S. 1 (1973), the Court formalized its test for determining which classifications besides race were constitutionally suspect and which contexts besides voting, travel, and criminal procedure involved fundamental interests.

In the late 1960s, as federal courts ordered the racial desegregation of schools with all deliberate speed, civil rights attorneys developed a new strategy to attack persistent educational inequalities. Rather than challenge the racial composition of individual schools, they would challenge the method by which states funded schools. In most states, school districts received funding from two sources: (1) local taxes on property within each district and (2) grants from the state and federal government. Although the 1960s saw dramatic increases in school spending by states and the federal government, in practice most school districts' budgets depended on how much they could raise from local property taxes.

Texas provided a stark example of the inequalities caused by this "dual" method of funding schools. *San Antonio Indep. Sch. Dist. v. Rodriguez*, 411 U.S. 1, 6 (1973). In 1968, the city of San Antonio was served by seven school districts, each of which was governed by a fiscally independent school board. The Edgewood Independent School District, the poorest in the area, contained twenty-five schools that served 22,000 students, 96 percent of whom were Mexican American or black. The total value of the assessed property in the district averaged about $6,000 per student. With a tax rate of over 1 percent—the highest in the metropolitan area—the district raised about $60 per pupil. Thanks to state and federal grants, the district's total budget was about $350 per pupil.

By contrast, in the wealthy Alamo Heights Independent School District, six schools served 5,000 students, 81 percent of whom were white. The assessed property value in the district exceeded $49,000 per student. With a tax rate considerably lower than that of Edgewood, the district raised considerably more: $450 per pupil. Coupled with aid from the state and federal government, its total budget was $600 per pupil.

In the face of this massive disparity, Mexican American parents of children in Edgewood schools challenged Texas's system of funding schools primarily through local property taxes. They argued that strict scrutiny should apply because the system discriminated on the basis of a suspect classification (wealth) or with respect to a fundamental interest (education).

The Supreme Court disagreed.

■ MR. JUSTICE POWELL delivered the opinion of the Court.[1]

This suit attacking the Texas system of financing public education was initiated by Mexican-American parents whose children attend the elementary and secondary schools in the Edgewood Independent School District, an urban school district in San Antonio, Texas. They brought a class action on behalf of schoolchildren throughout the State who are members of minority groups or who are poor and reside in school districts having a low property tax base. . . . [The District Court found] substantial interdistrict disparities in school expenditures . . . in San Antonio and in varying

---

[1] **As You Read, Consider:** How does Justice Lewis Powell determine which classifications, beyond race, are suspect and therefore subject to strict scrutiny? How does he determine which interests, beyond privacy, are fundamental and therefore also subject to strict scrutiny? Do you think that the constitutionality of Texas's decision to fund schools with local property taxes should turn on the answer to those two questions?

degrees throughout the State. . . . [T]hese disparities, largely attributable to differences in the amounts of money collected through local property taxation, . . . led the District Court to conclude that Texas' dual system of . . . school financing violated the Equal Protection Clause.

We must decide, first, whether the Texas system of financing public education operates to the disadvantage of some suspect class or impinges upon a fundamental right explicitly or implicitly protected by the Constitution, thereby requiring strict judicial scrutiny. If so, the judgment of the District Court should be affirmed. If not, the Texas scheme must still be examined to determine whether it rationally furthers some legitimate, articulated state purpose. . . .

II

[A. Is Wealth a Suspect Classification?]

The wealth discrimination discovered by the District Court in this case, and by several other courts that have recently struck down school-financing laws in other States, is quite unlike any of the forms of wealth discrimination heretofore reviewed by this Court. Rather than focusing on the unique features of the alleged discrimination, the courts in these cases have virtually assumed their findings of a suspect classification through a simplistic process of analysis: since, under the traditional systems of financing public schools, some poorer people receive less expensive educations than other more affluent people, these systems discriminate on the basis of wealth. This approach largely ignores the hard threshold questions, including whether it makes a difference for purposes of consideration under the Constitution that the class of disadvantaged "poor" cannot be identified or defined in customary equal protection terms, and whether the relative—rather than absolute—nature of the asserted deprivation is of significant consequence. . . .

The precedents of this Court provide the proper starting point. The individuals, or groups of individuals, who constituted the class discriminated against in our prior cases shared two distinguishing characteristics: because of their impecunity they were completely unable to pay for some desired benefit, and as a consequence, they sustained an absolute deprivation of a meaningful opportunity to enjoy that benefit. In *Griffin* v. *Illinois,* 351 U. S. 12 (1956), and its progeny, the Court invalidated state laws that prevented an indigent criminal defendant from acquiring a transcript, or an adequate substitute for a transcript, for use at several stages of the trial and appeal process. The payment requirements in each case were found to occasion *de facto* discrimination against those who, because of their indigency, were totally unable to pay for transcripts. . . .

Even a cursory examination, however, demonstrates that neither of the two distinguishing characteristics of wealth classifications can be found here. First, in support of their charge that the system discriminates against the "poor," appellees have made no effort to demonstrate that it operates to the peculiar disadvantage of any class fairly definable as indigent, or as composed of persons whose incomes are beneath any designated poverty level. Indeed, there is reason to believe that the poorest families are not necessarily clustered in the poorest property districts. . . .

Second, . . . lack of personal resources has not occasioned an absolute deprivation of the desired benefit. The argument here is not that the children in districts having relatively low assessable property values are receiving no public education; rather, it is that they are receiving a poorer quality education than that available to children in districts having more assessable wealth. Apart from the unsettled and disputed question whether the quality of education may be determined by the amount of money expended for it, a sufficient answer to appellees' argument is that, at least where wealth is involved, the Equal Protection Clause does not require absolute equality or precisely equal advantages. . . .

This brings us, then, to [a second] way in which the classification scheme might be defined—*district* wealth discrimination. Since the only correlation indicated by the evidence is between district property wealth and expenditures, it may be argued that discrimination might be found without regard to the individual income characteristics of district residents. Assuming a perfect correlation between district property wealth and expenditures from top to bottom, the disadvantaged class might be viewed as encompassing every child in every district except the district that has the most assessable wealth and spends the most on education. . . .

However described, it is clear that appellees' suit asks this Court to extend its most exacting scrutiny to review a system that allegedly discriminates against a large, diverse, and amorphous class, unified only by the common factor of residence in districts that happen to have less taxable wealth than other districts. The system of alleged discrimination and the class it defines have none of the traditional indicia of suspectness: the class is not saddled with such disabilities, or subjected to such a history of purposeful unequal treatment, or relegated to such a position of political powerlessness as to command extraordinary protection from the majoritarian political process.[2]

We thus conclude that the Texas system does not operate to the peculiar disadvantage of any suspect class. But . . . appellees have not relied solely on this contention. They also assert that the State's system impermissibly interferes with the exercise of a "fundamental" right and that accordingly the prior decisions of this Court require the application of the strict standard of judicial review. *Shapiro* v. *Thompson,* 394 U. S. 618 (1969). . . .

[B. Is Education a Fundamental Right?]

In *Brown* v. *Board of Education,* 347 U. S. 483 (1954), a unanimous Court recognized that "education is perhaps the most important function of state and local governments." *Id.,* at 493. . . . Nothing this Court holds today in any way detracts from our historic dedication to public education. . . . But the importance of a service performed by the State does not determine whether it must be regarded as fundamental for purposes of examination under the Equal Protection Clause. . . . "[V]irtually every state statute affects important rights." *Shapiro* v. *Thompson,* 394 U. S., at 655, 661 [(Harlan, J., dissenting)]. . . . [I]f the degree of judicial scrutiny of state legislation fluctuated, depending on a majority's view of the importance of the interest affected, we would have gone "far toward making this Court a 'super-legislature.' " *Ibid.* . . .

Lindsey v. *Normet,* 405 U. S. 56 (1972), decided only last Term, firmly reiterates that social importance is not the critical determinant for subjecting state legislation to strict scrutiny. The complainants in that case, involving a challenge to the procedural limitations imposed on tenants in suits brought by landlords . . ., argued that the statutory limitations implicated "fundamental interests which are particularly important to the poor," such as the " 'need for decent shelter' " and the

---

[2] **Questions:** When the Supreme Court first developed the idea of strict scrutiny, it explained that "[t]his strong policy renders racial classifications 'constitutionally suspect' and subject to the 'most rigid scrutiny' " because race was " 'in most circumstances irrelevant' to any constitutionally acceptable legislative purpose." *McLaughlin v. Florida,* 379 U.S. 184, 192 (1964). In other words, it was the racial *classification* that was suspect. Here, Powell holds that strict scrutiny is inappropriate because there is no *class of people* with the "traditional indicia of suspectness." Why does he focus on whether the plaintiffs are members of a defined *class* rather than whether Texas has enacted a *classification* on the basis of wealth? What principles does this distinction serve?

" 'right to retain peaceful possession of one's home.' " *Ibid.* [We responded]: "We do not denigrate the importance of decent, safe, and sanitary housing. But the Constitution does not provide judicial remedies for every social and economic ill. We are unable to perceive in that document any constitutional guarantee of access to dwellings of a particular quality or any recognition of the right of a tenant to occupy the real property of his landlord beyond the term of his lease, without the payment of rent. . . ." *Id.,* at 74.

Similarly, in *Dandridge* v. *Williams,* 397 U. S. 471 (1970), the Court's explicit recognition of the fact that the "administration of public welfare assistance . . . involves the most basic economic needs of impoverished human beings" provided no basis for departing from the settled mode of [analyzing] classifications involving questions of economic and social policy. . . .

The lesson of these cases in addressing the question now before the Court is plain. It is not the province of this Court to create substantive constitutional rights in the name of guaranteeing equal protection of the laws. Thus, the key to discovering whether education is "fundamental" is not to be found in comparisons of the relative societal significance of education as opposed to subsistence or housing. . . . Rather, the answer lies in assessing whether there is a right to education explicitly or implicitly guaranteed by the Constitution. *Eisenstadt* v. *Baird,* 405 U. S. 438 (1972); *Skinner* v. *Oklahoma,* 316 U. S. 535 (1942).[3]

Education, of course, is not among the rights afforded explicit protection under our Federal Constitution. Nor do we find any basis for saying it is implicitly so protected. . . . It is appellees' contention, however, that education is distinguishable from other services and benefits provided by the State because it bears a peculiarly close relationship to other rights and liberties accorded protection under the Constitution. Specifically, they insist that education is itself a fundamental personal right because it is essential to the effective exercise of First Amendment freedoms and to intelligent utilization of the right to vote. . . . The "marketplace of ideas" is an empty forum for those lacking basic communicative tools. Likewise, . . . [t]he electoral process, if reality is to conform to the democratic ideal, depends on an informed electorate: a voter cannot cast his ballot intelligently unless his reading skills and thought processes have been adequately developed. . . .

Even if it were conceded that some identifiable quantum of education is a constitutionally protected prerequisite to the meaningful exercise of either right, we have no indication that the present levels of educational expenditures in Texas provide an education that falls short. Whatever merit appellees' argument might have if a State's financing system occasioned an absolute denial of educational opportunities to any of its children, that argument provides no basis for finding an interference with fundamental rights where only relative differences in spending levels are involved and where—as is true in the present case—no charge fairly could be made that the system fails to provide each child with an opportunity to acquire the basic minimal skills necessary for the enjoyment of the rights of speech and of full participation in the political process.

Furthermore, the logical limitations on appellees' nexus theory are difficult to perceive. How, for instance, is education to be distinguished from the significant personal interests in the basics of decent food and shelter? Empirical examination

---

3 **Questions:** Here, Powell cites recent precedents in which the post-Warren Court held that "social importance is not the critical determinant for subjecting state legislation to strict scrutiny." Why not? Does it make sense to apply precisely the same rational-basis test to issues of housing, education, or welfare assistance as if the state were merely regulating opticians? Shouldn't the importance of these issues matter in determining whether a state has acted reasonably in denying equal access to these services?

might well buttress an assumption that the ill-fed, ill-clothed, and ill-housed are among the most ineffective participants in the political process. . . . If so, appellees' thesis would cast serious doubt on the authority of *Dandridge* v. *Williams* and *Lindsey* v. *Normet*. . . .[4]

In one further respect we find this a particularly inappropriate case in which to subject state action to strict judicial scrutiny. . . . Each of our prior cases involved legislation which "deprived," "infringed," or "interfered" with the free exercise of some such fundamental personal right or liberty. A critical distinction between those cases and the one now before us lies in what Texas is endeavoring to do with respect to education. . . .

Every step leading to the establishment of the system Texas utilizes today—including the decisions permitting localities to tax and expend locally, and creating and continuously expanding state aid—was implemented in an effort to *extend* public education and to improve its quality. . . . [T]he thrust of the Texas system is affirmative and reformatory and, therefore, should be scrutinized under judicial principles sensitive to the nature of the State's efforts and to the rights reserved to the States under the Constitution. . . .

It must be remembered, also, that . . . [q]uestions of federalism are always inherent in the process of determining whether a State's laws are to be accorded the traditional presumption of constitutionality, or are to be subjected instead to rigorous judicial scrutiny. . . . [I]t would be difficult to imagine a case having a greater potential impact on our federal system than the one now before us, in which we are urged to abrogate systems of financing public education presently in existence in virtually every State.

The foregoing considerations buttress our conclusion that Texas' system of public school finance is an inappropriate candidate for strict judicial scrutiny. These same considerations are relevant to the determination whether that system, with its conceded imperfections, nevertheless bears some rational relationship to a legitimate state purpose. It is to this question that we next turn our attention.

[III. Applying the Rational-Basis Test][5]

[T]he history of education since the industrial revolution shows a continual struggle between two forces: the desire by members of society to have educational opportunity for all children, and the desire of each family to provide the best education it can afford for its own children.

The Texas system of school finance is responsive to these two forces. While assuring a basic education for every child in the State, it permits and encourages a large measure of participation in and control of each district's schools at the local level. In an era that has witnessed a consistent trend toward centralization of the functions of government, local sharing of responsibility for public education has survived. . . .

---

[4] **Question:** Powell concludes that education cannot be a fundamental right because if it were, then the Constitution would also demand close scrutiny when states fail to guarantee equal access to food, clothing, and shelter. This sounds like another example in which the Court fears "too much justice." *McCleskey v. Kemp*, 481 U.S. 279, 339 (1987) (Brennan, J., dissenting). Why might Powell be concerned about empowering federal courts to ensure that states are adequately guaranteeing these basic and extremely important provisions?

[5] **Question:** In the final part of his opinion, Powell applies the rational-basis test to evaluate Texas's decision to fund its schools with local property taxes. Texas doesn't *have* to fund its schools this way; instead, it could fund all of its schools equally on a per capita basis so that every Texan had equal access to the same financial resources. In light of the relative inequality of the current system, what legitimate interests does Powell think it serves?

The persistence of attachment to government at the lowest level where education is concerned reflects the depth of commitment of its supporters. In part, local control means . . . the freedom to devote more money to the education of one's children. Equally important, however, is the opportunity it offers for participation in the decisionmaking process that determines how those local tax dollars will be spent. . . . An analogy to the Nation-State relationship in our federal system seems uniquely appropriate. Mr. Justice Brandeis identified as one of the peculiar strengths of our form of government each State's freedom to "serve as a laboratory; and try novel social and economic experiments." No area of social concern stands to profit more from a multiplicity of viewpoints and from a diversity of approaches than does public education. . . .

Appellees . . . urge that the Texas system is unconstitutionally arbitrary because it allows the availability of local taxable resources to turn on "happenstance." They see no justification for a system that allows . . . the quality of education to fluctuate on the basis of the fortuitous positioning of the boundary lines of political subdivisions and the location of valuable commercial and industrial property. But any scheme of local taxation—indeed the very existence of identifiable local governmental units—requires the establishment of jurisdictional boundaries that are inevitably arbitrary. It is equally inevitable that some localities are going to be blessed with more taxable assets than others. . . . It has simply never been within the constitutional prerogative of this Court to nullify statewide measures for financing public services merely because the burdens or benefits thereof fall unevenly depending upon the relative wealth of the political subdivisions in which citizens live.

In sum, to the extent that the Texas system of school financing results in unequal expenditures between children who happen to reside in different districts, we cannot say that such disparities are the product of a system that is so irrational as to be invidiously discriminatory. . . . One also must remember that the system here challenged is not peculiar to Texas or to any other State. . . . We are unwilling to assume for ourselves a level of wisdom superior to that of legislators, scholars, and educational authorities in 50 States, especially where the alternatives proposed are only recently conceived and nowhere yet tested. The constitutional standard under the Equal Protection Clause is whether the challenged state action rationally furthers a legitimate state purpose or interest. We hold that the Texas plan abundantly satisfies this standard. . . .

■ MR. JUSTICE MARSHALL, with whom MR. JUSTICE DOUGLAS concurs, dissenting.[6]

The Court today decides, in effect, that a State may constitutionally vary the quality of education which it offers its children in accordance with the amount of taxable wealth located in the school districts within which they reside. The majority's decision . . . can only be seen as a retreat from our historic commitment to equality of educational opportunity and as unsupportable acquiescence in a system which deprives children in their earliest years of the chance to reach their full potential as citizens. . . . *Brown* v. *Board of Education,* 347 U. S. 483, 494 (1954). I must therefore respectfully dissent. . . .

[In addition], I must once more voice my disagreement with the Court's rigidified approach to equal protection analysis. The Court apparently seeks to establish today that equal protection cases fall into one of two neat categories which dictate the appropriate standard of review—strict scrutiny or mere rationality. But this Court's

---

6 **Questions:** Justice Thurgood Marshall's dissenting opinion sharply disagrees with Powell's definition of *suspect classifications* and *fundamental interests.* He also calls for a completely different test than the majority's categorical bifurcation between the rational-basis test and strict scrutiny. Do you find Marshall's alternative test compelling? What might be the downsides of his balancing approach?

decisions in the field of equal protection defy such easy categorization. A principled reading of what this Court has done reveals that it has applied a spectrum of standards in reviewing discrimination allegedly violative of the Equal Protection Clause. This spectrum clearly comprehends variations in the degree of care with which the Court will scrutinize particular classifications, depending, I believe, on the constitutional and societal importance of the interest adversely affected and the recognized invidiousness of the basis upon which the particular classification is drawn. I find in fact that many of the Court's recent decisions embody the very sort of reasoned approach to equal protection analysis for which I previously argued—that is, an approach in which "concentration [is] placed upon the character of the classification in question, the relative importance to individuals in the class discriminated against of the governmental benefits that they do not receive, and the asserted state interests in support of the classification." *Dandridge*, at 520–521 (dissenting opinion).

I therefore cannot accept the majority's labored efforts to demonstrate that fundamental interests, which call for strict scrutiny of the challenged classification, encompass only established rights which we are somehow bound to recognize from the text of the Constitution itself. To be sure, some interests which the Court has deemed to be fundamental for purposes of equal protection analysis are themselves constitutionally protected rights. . . . But it will not do to suggest that the "answer" to whether an interest is fundamental for purposes of equal protection analysis is *always* determined by whether that interest "is a right . . . explicitly or implicitly guaranteed by the Constitution."

I would like to know where the Constitution guarantees the right to procreate, *Skinner* v. *Oklahoma,* 316 U. S. 535, 541 (1942), or the right to vote in state elections, *e. g., Reynolds* v. *Sims,* 377 U. S. 533 (1964), or the right to an appeal from a criminal conviction, *e. g., Griffin* v. *Illinois,* 351 U. S. 12 (1956). These are instances in which, due to the importance of the interests at stake, the Court has displayed a strong concern with the existence of discriminatory state treatment. . . .

The majority is, of course, correct when it suggests that the process of determining which interests are fundamental is a difficult one. But I do not think the problem is insurmountable. And I certainly do not accept the view that the process need necessarily degenerate into an unprincipled, subjective "picking-and-choosing" between various interests or that it must involve this Court in creating "substantive constitutional rights in the name of guaranteeing equal protection of the laws." . . . [T]he determination of which interests are fundamental should be firmly rooted in the text of the Constitution. The task in every case should be to determine the extent to which constitutionally guaranteed rights are dependent on interests not mentioned in the Constitution. As the nexus between the specific constitutional guarantee and the nonconstitutional interest draws closer, the nonconstitutional interest becomes more fundamental and the degree of judicial scrutiny applied when the interest is infringed on a discriminatory basis must be adjusted accordingly. . . . Only if we closely protect the related interests from state discrimination do we ultimately ensure the integrity of the constitutional guarantee itself. . . .

A similar process of analysis with respect to the invidiousness of the basis on which a particular classification is drawn has also influenced the Court as to the appropriate degree of scrutiny to be accorded any particular case. The highly suspect character of classifications based on race, nationality, or alienage is well established. The reasons why such classifications call for close judicial scrutiny are manifold. Certain racial and ethnic groups have frequently been recognized as "discrete and insular minorities" who are relatively powerless to protect their interests in the political process. Cf. *United States* v. *Carolene Products Co.,* 304 U. S. 144, 152–153, n. 4

(1938). Moreover, race, nationality, or alienage is " 'in most circumstances irrelevant' to any constitutionally acceptable legislative purpose." *McLaughlin* v. *Florida,* 379 U. S., at 192. Instead, lines drawn on such bases are frequently the reflection of historic prejudices rather than legislative rationality. . . . [T]hese considerations have undoubtedly influenced the care with which the Court has scrutinized other forms of discrimination. . . .

[For example], in *Reed* v. *Reed,* 404 U. S. 71 (1971), the Court, in striking down a state statute which gave men preference over women when persons of equal entitlement apply for assignment as an administrator of a particular estate, resorted to a more stringent standard of equal protection review than that employed in cases involving commercial matters. . . . *Reed* can only be understood as [an instance] in which the particularly invidious character of the classification caused the Court to pause and scrutinize with more than traditional care the rationality of state discrimination. Discrimination . . . on the basis of sex posed for the Court the specter of forms of discrimination which it implicitly recognized to have deep social and legal roots without necessarily having any basis in actual differences. . . .

In summary, . . . this Court has consistently adjusted the care with which it will review state discrimination in light of the constitutional significance of the interests affected and the invidiousness of the particular classification. In the context of economic interests, we find that discriminatory state action is almost always sustained, for such interests are generally far removed from constitutional guarantees. . . . But the situation differs markedly when discrimination against important individual interests with constitutional implications and against particularly disadvantaged or powerless classes is involved. The majority suggests, however, that a variable standard of review would give this Court the appearance of a "superlegislature." I cannot agree. Such an approach seems to me a part of the guarantees of our Constitution and of the historic experiences with oppression of and discrimination against discrete, powerless minorities which underlie that document. In truth, the Court itself will be open to the criticism raised by the majority so long as it continues on its present course of effectively selecting in private which cases will be afforded special consideration without acknowledging the true basis of its action. . . .

NOTE: AFTERMATH OF *RODRIGUEZ*

Tiers of scrutiny. As Justice Thurgood Marshall observed in his dissent, the *Rodriguez* majority formalized the Supreme Court's approach toward evaluating most constitutional claims of discrimination into "two neat categories": rational basis and strict scrutiny. *Rodriguez*, 411 U.S. at 98.

For most legislation since *Rodriguez*, the Court has applied the rational-basis test, in which the Court upholds the law as long as it is "rationally related" to any conceivable legitimate state interest. *See Williamson v. Lee Optical of Okla., Inc.*, 348 U.S. 483, 489 (1955). And the Court has considered virtually every interest *legitimate* with a few notable exceptions. These exceptions include "a bare . . . desire to harm a politically unpopular group." *U.S. Dep't of Agric. v. Moreno*, 413 U.S. 528, 534 (1973).

But for laws whose purpose is to discriminate on the basis of a constitutionally suspect classification such as race, ancestry, or nationality, the Court has applied strict scrutiny, in which the Court strikes down the law unless it is necessary to serve a compelling state interest. *See McLaughlin v. Florida*, 379 U.S. 184, 195–96 (1964). To determine a law's *purpose*, the Court uses a "totality-of-the-circumstances" test to evaluate whether the law was passed because of, not merely in spite of, its discriminatory effect. *See Vill. of Arlington Heights v. Metro. Hous. Dev. Corp.*, 429 U.S. 252, 266 (1977); *Washington v. Davis*, 426 U.S. 229, 242 (1976). And to determine whether a classification is *suspect*, *Rodriguez* considered whether the class was "saddled with such disabilities, or subjected to such a history of purposeful unequal treatment, or relegated to such a position of political powerlessness as to command extraordinary protection from the majoritarian political process." 411 U.S. at 28.

Rodriguez added that the Court will also apply strict scrutiny to laws that infringe on the exercise of a "fundamental right," such as the right to vote, the right of interstate travel, or the right of privacy. *Id.* at 29. This approach is virtually identical to the approach that the Court uses in its substantive-due-process cases. In that context, the Court has also applied the rational-basis test to most legislation, *see W. Coast Hotel Co. v. Parrish*, 300 U.S. 379, 391 (1937); and has also applied strict scrutiny to laws that infringe on a "fundamental" liberty interest, *Roe*, 410 U.S. at 152. Today, as discussed in an earlier section on the Due Process Clause (section 42.3), the Court typically considers an interest "fundamental" after asking whether a "careful description" of the interest is "deeply rooted in this Nation's history and tradition." *Washington v. Glucksberg*, 521 U.S. 702, 703 (1997). *But see Lawrence v. Texas*, 539 U.S. 558, 572 (2003) ("History and tradition are the starting point but not in all cases the ending point of the . . . inquiry.").

This "tiers-of-scrutiny" approach to equal-protection and due process cases has been heavily criticized for its rigid formalism. *See, e.g.*, Jamal Greene, *How Rights Went Wrong* 94–98 (2021). As Marshall wrote in his *Rodriguez* dissent, the approach made winning a Fourteenth Amendment claim turn on whether the plaintiffs could allege that they were members of a suspect class or were engaged in a fundamental right. Contemporaries of the *Rodriguez* Court agreed that the approach forced the Court to apply either "scrutiny that was 'strict' in theory and fatal in fact" or "minimal scrutiny in theory and virtually none in fact." Gerald Gunther, *Foreword—In Search of Evolving Doctrine on a Changing Court*, 1 Harv. L. Rev. 1, 8 (1972). In his *Rodriguez* dissent, Marshall preferred that the Court abandon the tiers of scrutiny in favor of a flexible balancing test—one that would weigh, on the one hand, the interests of "individuals in the class discriminated against" and, on the other hand, "the asserted state interests in support of the classification." 411 U.S. at 99. Marshall added that the Court was already engaged in a covert form of this balancing in its sex-discrimination cases—to which we will turn in a moment.

As we will also see, when Justice John Stevens joined the Court in 1975, he joined Marshall in complaining that there is only "one Equal Protection Clause." *Craig v. Boren*, 429 U.S. 190, 211 (1976) (Stevens, J., concurring). Stevens agreed with Marshall that the role of the Court was to ask not about suspect classifications and fundamental rights, but only whether the "justification put forward by the State is sufficient to make an otherwise offensive classification acceptable." *Id.* at 213. This proportionality approach may explain the Court's rational-basis-with-bite decisions in cases like

United States Department of Agriculture v. Moreno, 413 U.S. 528 (1973); *Romer v. Evans*, 517 U.S. 620 (1996); and *Lawrence v. Texas*, 539 U.S. 558 (2003). But the Court has never explicitly embraced the idea of balancing as an alternative to the tiers of scrutiny.

School funding. By shutting the door to Fourteenth Amendment claims challenging school-finance systems, *Rodriguez* ended most federal litigation over school funding. But school-funding litigation surged in the wake of *Rodriguez*—in state courts. Although the federal Constitution doesn't mention education, Texas and most other states contain provisions in their state constitutions that require the state to provide all students with an "adequate" or "efficient" or "equal" education. Invoking these provisions, litigants over the past five decades have successfully argued that Texas's school-finance system and others like it were unconstitutional. *See* Jeffrey S. Sutton, San Antonio Independent School District v. Rodriguez *and Its Aftermath*, 94 Va. L. Rev. 1963 (2008); *see, e.g., DeRolph v. State*, 677 N.E.2d 733, 740 (Ohio 1997); *Edgewood Indep. Sch. Dist. v. Kirby*, 777 S.W.2d 391, 392 (Tex. 1989).

Although these state courts have had some difficulty evaluating whether a state is providing an equal or adequate education, the larger challenge—as in the school desegregation cases—has been remedying the constitutional violation.

One approach is to provide all school districts with identical levels of funding—an approach that requires "the politically unpalatable recapture and redistribution of local tax revenue from wealthy districts." J. Steven Farr & Mark Trachtenberg, *The Edgewood Drama: An Epic Quest for Education Equity*, 17 Yale & Pol'y Rev. 607, 720 (1999). In practice, it has proved difficult for state courts or state legislatures to prohibit parents in wealthy districts from voluntarily supplementing their local school budgets—perpetuating the interdistrict inequality. *Id.*

Another approach is to define the specific standards and learning outcomes of a constitutionally "adequate" education at each grade level and to require the legislature to provide sufficient funding for all school districts to meet those standards. *See, e.g., Seattle Sch. Dist. No. 1 v. State*, 585 P.2d 71 (Wash. 1978). But this approach can also run into problems of enforcement. In *McCleary v. State*, the Washington Supreme Court held that the state was failing to provide its school districts with enough money to provide all students with a "basic education" as the state constitution required. 269 P.3d 227, 261 (Wash. 2012). But the legislature—still reeling from the Great Recession—ignored this holding. The state supreme court therefore held the state legislature in contempt and imposed sanctions on the legislature of $100,000 per day. *McCleary v. State*, No. 84362-7 (Wash. Sept. 11, 2014). The legislature finally purged the contempt four years later, in 2018, after which the state supreme court donated the sanction proceeds that it had collected to the state's education budget. *McCleary v. State*, No. 84362-7 (Wash. June 7, 2018). By that point, however, forty years had passed since the court's initial ruling that the state had a duty to provide all students with a basic education.

Wealth-based classifications. The Court after *Rodriguez* consistently held that because wealth wasn't a suspect classification, laws denying financial assistance for the exercise of fundamental interests didn't violate the Equal Protection Clause. *See, e.g., Jiminez v. Weinberger*, 417 U.S. 628 (1974). As discussed earlier with regard to the undue burden test (section 43.2), the Court explained that the Fourteenth Amendment "affords protection against unwarranted government interference with freedom of choice in the context of certain personal decisions, [but] it does not confer an entitlement to such funds as may be necessary to realize all the advantages of that freedom." *Harris v. McRae*, 448 U.S. 297, 317–18 (1980). Applying this logic, the Court upheld laws that denied public funding for a woman's choice to seek an abortion as opposed to adoption services. *Id.*

The one area where the Court has continued to strike down wealth-based classifications as it had earlier is with respect to the fundamental right to travel recognized in *Edwards v. California*, 314 U.S. 160 (1941), and *Shapiro v. Thompson*, 394 U.S. 618 (1969). Applying the Equal Protection Clause, the Court after *Rodriguez* has continued to invalidate state laws that withhold public benefits from recent arrivals, such as the right to receive free medical care. *Mem'l Hosp. v. Maricopa County*, 415 U.S. 250, 269 (1974).

The Court elaborated on this "right to travel" in *Saenz v. Roe*, 526 U.S. 489 (1999), where the Court invalidated a California law that limited the welfare benefits available to new residents for the first year that they lived in the state. Locating the source of the right in the Equal Protection Clause, the Privileges and Immunities Clause of Article IV, and the Privileges or Immunities Clause of the Fourteenth Amendment, the Court called the right "fundamental" and disaggregated it into three component parts: (1) the right of travelers to cross state borders, (2) the right of visitors to obtain the same privileges and immunities as citizens, and (3) the right of newly arrived citizens to enjoy the same privileges and immunities as long-term citizens. *Saenz*, 526 U.S. at 500–01. The *Saenz* Court concluded that the California law infringed on the third component of the right to travel. It held that "the State's legitimate interest in saving money provides no justification for its decision to discriminate among equally eligible citizens." *Id.* at 507.

Yet the *Saenz* Court did not hold that all laws that interfered with the right to travel would be invalidated under strict scrutiny. The Court specifically distinguished a situation in which there was a "danger that recognition of [a] claim will encourage citizens of other states to establish residency for just long enough to acquire some readily portable benefit, such as a divorce or a college education, that will be enjoyed after they return to their original domicile." *Id.* at 505. In such a case, the Court suggested that it would evaluate the state law with more deference.

48.2 SEX

When *Brown v. Board of Education* (*Brown I*) declared that "in the field of public education, the doctrine of 'separate but equal' has no place," the Supreme Court was talking about race, not sex. 347 U.S. 483, 495 (1954). When it came to distinctions on the basis of sex, the Court would long continue to apply the rational-basis test to uphold laws that treated women differently from men. Many of these laws had a long pedigree, one infused with sexist stereotypes and paternalistic attitudes about the proper role of women in society. By the time civil rights lawyers systematically challenged these laws in the 1970s, members of the Court were as unwilling as the *Plessy v. Ferguson* Court had been to think of separate-but-equal facilities as implying a "badge of inferiority." *Plessy*, 163 U.S. 537, 551 (1896).

When women first invoked the Fourteenth Amendment to challenge laws that discriminated on the basis of sex, they typically invoked the Privileges or Immunities Clause or Due Process Clause. However, as discussed earlier in the section on the Privileges or Immunities Clause (section 39.2), the Supreme Court was utterly unwilling to treat sex-based discrimination in voting, the right to contract, or any other context as inconsistent with the fundamental rights of citizenship. *See, e.g.*, *Minor v. Happersett*, 88 U.S. (21 Wall.) 162 (1875). In *Bradwell v. Illinois*, 83 U.S. (16 Wall.) 130 (1873), the Court rejected a challenge to an Illinois law that prohibited women from practicing law. In an infamous concurring opinion, Justice Joseph Bradley explained that "the civil law, as well as nature itself, has always recognized a wide difference in the respective spheres and destinies of man and woman." *Bradwell*, 83 U.S. (16 Wall.) at 141 (Bradley, J., concurring). He added,

> The natural and proper timidity and delicacy which belongs to the female sex evidently unfits it for many of the occupations of civil life. The Constitution of the family organization, which is founded in the divine ordinance as well as in the nature of things, indicates the domestic sphere as that which properly belongs to the domain and functions of womanhood.

Id.

During the era of *Lochner v. New York*, 198 U.S. 45 (1905), when Louis Brandeis wrote his famous "Brandeis brief" to defend the constitutionality of Oregon's labor law (see section 41.2), he invoked similar stereotypes about women to explain how a maximum-hour law served states' legitimate interests in health, safety, and morals. *See* Melvin I. Urofsky, *Louis D. Brandeis* 216–17 (2009). In *Muller v. Oregon*, the Supreme Court agreed, writing that it was "obvious" that because "healthy mothers are essential to vigorous offspring, the physical well-being of woman becomes an object of public interest and care in order to preserve the strength and vigor of the race." 208 U.S. 412, 421 (1908). Setting a precedent that loomed well beyond the close of the *Lochner* era, the Court added that "woman has always been dependent upon man" because of her physical and mental infirmities. *Id.* Therefore "some legislation to protect her seems necessary to secure a real equality of right . . ., even when like legislation is not necessary for men and could not be sustained." *Id.*

When the Supreme Court began applying the rational-basis test to all economic regulations after 1937, it continued to consider a state's paternalistic protection of women to be a legitimate interest—even where such "protection" deprived women of legal rights. In *Goesaert v. Cleary*, the Court upheld a law that prohibited women from bartending absent the protection of a nearby husband or father. 335 U.S. 464, 466–67 (1948). And in *Hoyt v. Florida*, the Court upheld a state law that "relieved" women "from the civic duty of jury service unless she herself determines that such service is consistent with her own special responsibilities." 368 U.S. 57, 62 (1961).

In a widely circulated 1962 memo that criticized these precedents, Pauli Murray—a black civil rights lawyer who self-identified as queer and "in between" genders—accused the Court of entrenching what she later called "Jane Crow." *See* Rosalind Rosenberg, *Jane Crow: The Life of Pauli Murray* 1 (2017). Earlier in her career, Murray had contributed to the National Association for the Advancement of Colored People Legal Defense Fund's litigation strategy in *Brown*. *Id.* at 4. She now argued that the legal subordination of women was analogous to the legal subordination of black people. *See* Pauli Murray, *The Autobiography of a Black Activist, Feminist, Lawyer, Priest, and Poet* 238–55 (1987). Conceding that women were "numerically more than one-half of the adult population," Murray argued that women were nevertheless comparable to other discrete and insular minorities in three respects:

> (1) They are an easily identifiable group, to a large degree unrepresented in the formal decision-making process, and thus easy targets of both public and private discrimination; (2) their legal history is one of slow progress against considerable resistance from the dominant (male) group toward an approximation of equality with the dominant group; (3) because of the first two factors and the cultural lag which results, legal distinctions based upon sex are particularly susceptible to an application which prolongs women's inferior status and may, in fact, reinforce it.

Pauli Murray, *A Proposal to Reexamine the Applicability of the Fourteenth Amendment to State Laws and Practices Which Discriminate on the Basis of Sex Per Se* 10 (Dec. 1962). Murray ultimately proposed an influential two-prong legal strategy for attacking Jane Crow. First, she proposed lobbying Congress for an Equal Rights Amendment to the Constitution. Second, she urged litigators to invoke the Fourteenth Amendment to "shift [the] emphasis from [women's] *class* attributes (sex *per se*) to their functional attributes and to redelineate the boundaries between social policies that are genuinely protective of the family and maternal functions and those which are unjustly discriminatory against women as individuals." *Id.* at 8–9; *see* Rosenberg, *supra*, at 253–57.

Two years later, Murray wrote a second widely circulated memo while the House of Representatives debated the bill that would become the Civil Rights Act of 1964. The original bill prohibited discrimination on the basis of "race," "religion," and "national origin." In a half-hearted effort to ensure that the bill would not itself discriminate against "a *White Woman*, a *Woman of the Christian Religion*, or a *Woman of United States Origin*," Representative Howard Smith of Virginia introduced an amendment to add "sex" to the bill. Rosenberg, *supra*, at 275. Civil rights advocates worried that the amendment was a last-ditch, surprise move to kill the bill. *Id.* But Murray persuasively argued that the amendment was, indeed, necessary to protect black women from discrimination. *See* Pauli Murray, *Memorandum in Support of Retaining the Amendment to H.R. 7152, Title VII (Equal Employment Opportunity) to Prohibit Discrimination in Employment Because of Sex* (Apr. 14, 1964). Murray's memo convinced the bill's supporters to call the Virginian's bluff and prohibit sex discrimination in the workplace. Rosenberg, *supra*, at 276–80.

In the wake of her success, Murray joined the board of the American Civil Liberties Union (ACLU) and helped to found the National Organization for Women. She persuaded both organizations to adopt her strategy of pursuing equal-protection litigation alongside an Equal Rights Amendment. *Id.* at 260.

48.2.1

Craig v. Boren

429 U.S. 190 (1976)

Murray's memoranda and strategy influenced a young law professor at Rutgers named Ruth Bader Ginsburg. *Id.* at 361. A brilliant law student who graduated at the top of the Columbia Law School class of 1959, Ginsburg was scarred when judges and lawyers refused to hire her as a clerk or associate because of her sex. *See* Jane Sherron De Hart, *Ruth Bader Ginsburg* 78–80 (2018). Ginsburg eventually became a professor of comparative law and civil procedure, but she retained an interest in antidiscrimination law. *Id.* at 106–09.

In 1970, on behalf of the ACLU's New Jersey affiliate, she and her husband, Marty, a tax lawyer, began investigating a fateful tax case involving sex discrimination. A bachelor named Charles E. Moritz had paid a nurse to take care of his eighty-nine-year-old mother, and he wanted a tax deduction that was available for women in his situation. *Id.* at 124–25. But the Internal Revenue Code prohibited him from receiving the deduction on the theory that caring for parents was not a bachelor's role. *Id.* The Ginsburgs reached out to Moritz, who agreed to hire them as his counsel before the U.S. Court of Appeals for the Tenth Circuit.

In researching their brief, Ginsburg drew heavily on Murray's earlier arguments analogizing sex discrimination with race discrimination. She argued that the Internal Revenue Code's discrimination on the basis of sex was as irrational as if Congress had specified that a white person but not a black person could qualify for the deduction. *Id.* at 128–33. This argument persuaded the Tenth Circuit, which ruled in Moritz's favor. *See Moritz v. Comm'r of Internal Revenue*, 469 F.2d 466 (10th Cir. 1972). It also persuaded the ACLU that similar arguments could advance Murray's strategy of using the Fourteenth Amendment to combat sex discrimination. On the strength of her *Moritz* brief, Ginsburg was recruited to direct the ACLU's new Women's Rights Project, which she led for much of the next decade. De Hart, *supra*, at 134–39.

Ginsburg's first case with the project was a probate case out of Idaho. In the 1960s, Sally Reed and her husband Cecil Reed separated, leaving Sally with custody of their son Richard. When Richard died, Sally and Cecil filed competing petitions in Idaho probate court to administer his estate. Under Idaho law, a father and mother were equally entitled to serve as estate administrator. But the law added that, to break ties, "males must be preferred to females." *Reed v. Reed*, 465 P.2d 635, 637 (Idaho 1970). Sally challenged the constitutionality of this tiebreaker. But the Idaho Supreme Court affirmed it on the ground that it was rationally related to the legitimate purpose of eliminating an issue "that would otherwise require a hearing as to the relative merits . . . of the two or more petitioning relatives." *Id.* at 638.

In *Reed v. Reed*, 404 U.S. 71 (1971), the Supreme Court reversed. Applying the rational-basis test, the Court held that Idaho's interest was not legitimate:

> To give a mandatory preference to members of either sex over members of the other, merely to accomplish the elimination of hearings on the merits, is to make the very kind of arbitrary legislative choice forbidden by the Equal Protection Clause of the Fourteenth Amendment; and whatever may be said as to the positive values of avoiding intrafamily controversy, the choice in this context may not lawfully be mandated solely on the basis of sex.

Reed, 404 U.S. at 76–77. It was the first Supreme Court decision ever to declare that a law was unconstitutional sex discrimination. But as Justice Thurgood Marshall observed in his dissent in *San Antonio Independent School District v. Rodriguez*, 411 U.S. 1 (1973), the decision left open whether the Court would apply a heightened standard of scrutiny to sex discrimination in the future.

Ginsburg tried to answer this open question in another case two years after *Reed*. Sharron Frontiero, a female lieutenant in the U.S. Air Force, sought housing and medical allowances for her husband on the ground that he was her "dependent." *See* De Hart, *supra*, at 201–03. But while federal law entitled any serviceman to claim his wife as a dependent, it prohibited a servicewoman from claiming her husband as a dependent unless he was, in fact, dependent on her for over one-half of his support. Ginsburg wrote an amicus brief on behalf of Frontiero arguing that the Court should treat sex as a suspect classification subject to strict scrutiny. *See id.*

And in *Frontiero v. Richardson*, Justice William Brennan and three other justices agreed that "classifications based upon sex, like classifications based upon race, alienage, or national origin, are inherently suspect, and must therefore be subjected to strict judicial scrutiny." 411 U.S. 677, 688 (1973). However, Brennan couldn't attract a fifth vote. In a concurring opinion, Justice Lewis Powell accused the plurality of "acting prematurely and unnecessarily" because one year earlier, in 1972, Congress had proposed the Equal Rights Amendment. *Id.* at 692 (Powell, J., concurring in the judgment). Like the plurality opinion, the amendment would require "[e]quality of rights under the law . . . on account of sex." *Id.* at 687. Powell therefore thought "that this reaching out to pre-empt by judicial action a major political decision which is currently in process of resolution does not reflect appropriate respect for duly prescribed legislative processes." *Id.* at 692 (Powell, J., concurring in the judgment).

As ratification of the Equal Rights Amendment stalled in the years after *Frontiero*, Ginsburg brought more cases urging the Court to treat sex as a suspect classification. But even in cases that Ginsburg won, the Court persistently declined to apply strict scrutiny. *See, e.g.*, *Weinberger v. Wiesenfeld*, 420 U.S. 636, 651 (1975) (applying the rational-basis test to strike a provision of the Social Security Act that gave survivors benefits to a surviving mother but not a surviving father). Even worse for Ginsburg, a member of the *Frontiero* plurality later reconsidered his position and voted to uphold a sex-based classification on the ground that it helped women. *Kahn v. Shevin*, 416 U.S. 351, 353 (1974) (Douglas, J.) (upholding a Florida law that awarded a tax exemption to widows but not to widowers because "[t]here can be no dispute that the financial difficulties confronting the lone woman in Florida or in any other State exceed those facing the man").

Facing a stalemate over the appropriate standard of scrutiny for evaluating sex discrimination, Ginsburg adopted a new approach in the following case, *Craig v. Boren*, 429 U.S. 190 (1976). Rather than argue that sex-based classifications were inherently suspect and deserved to be struck down under strict scrutiny, Ginsburg instead argued that *Reed* had adopted an alternative form of "heightened scrutiny" that called for a more flexible test. De Hart, *supra*, at 254–55.

The Court found this new approach more compelling.

■ MR. JUSTICE BRENNAN delivered the opinion of the Court.[7]

[A]n Oklahoma statute prohibits the sale of "nonintoxicating" 3.2% beer to males under the age of 21 and to females under the age of 18. The question to be

[7] **As You Read, Consider:** In evaluating this sex-based classification, Justice William Brennan asks whether the classification is "substantially related" to "important governmental objectives." What kind of test is this? Is it a means-ends test in between strict scrutiny and the

decided is whether such a gender-based differential constitutes a denial to males 18–20 years of age of the equal protection of the laws. . . .

[T]o withstand constitutional challenge, previous cases establish that classifications by gender must serve important governmental objectives and must be substantially related to achievement of those objectives. Thus, in *Reed* [v. *Reed,* 404 U. S. 71, 76–77 (1971)], the objectives of "reducing the workload on probate courts" and "avoiding intrafamily controversy" were deemed of insufficient importance to sustain use of an overt gender criterion in the appointment of administrators of intestate decedents' estates. Decisions following *Reed* similarly have rejected administrative ease and convenience as sufficiently important objectives to justify gender-based classifications. See, *e. g., Frontiero* v. *Richardson,* 411 U. S. 677, 690 (1973). . . .[8]

Reed v. *Reed* has also provided the underpinning for decisions that have invalidated statutes employing gender as an inaccurate proxy for other, more germane bases of classification. Hence, "archaic and overbroad" generalizations, *Schlesinger* v. *Ballard, supra,* at 508, concerning the financial position of servicewomen, *Frontiero* v. *Richardson, supra,* at 689 n. 23, and working women, *Weinberger* v. *Wiesenfeld,* 420 U. S. 636, 643 (1975), could not justify use of a gender line in determining eligibility for certain governmental entitlements. Similarly, increasingly outdated misconceptions concerning the role of females in the home rather than in the "marketplace and world of ideas" were rejected as loose-fitting characterizations incapable of supporting state statutory schemes that were premised upon their accuracy. *Taylor* v. *Louisiana,* 419 U. S. 522, 535 n. 17 (1975). In light of the weak congruence between gender and the characteristic or trait that gender purported to represent, it was necessary that the legislatures choose either to realign their substantive laws in a gender-neutral fashion, or to adopt procedures for identifying those instances where the sex-centered generalization actually comported with fact. . . .

We turn then to the question whether, under *Reed,* the difference between males and females with respect to the purchase of 3.2% beer warrants the differential in age drawn by the Oklahoma statute. We conclude that it does not. . . .

We accept for purposes of discussion the District Court's identification of the objective underlying [the classification] as the enhancement of traffic safety. Clearly, the protection of public health and safety represents an important function of state and local governments. However, appellees' statistics in our view cannot support the conclusion that the gender-based distinction closely serves to achieve that objective and therefore the distinction cannot under *Reed* withstand equal protection challenge.

The appellees introduced a variety of statistical surveys . . ., [including] an analysis of arrest statistics for 1973 demonstrated that 18–20-year-old male arrests for "driving under the influence" and "drunkenness" substantially exceeded female arrests for that same age period. Similarly, youths aged 17–21 were found to be overrepresented among those killed or injured in traffic accidents, with males again numerically exceeding females in this regard. . . .

Even were this statistical evidence accepted as accurate, it nevertheless offers only a weak answer to the equal protection question presented here. . . . Viewed in terms of the correlation between sex and the actual activity that Oklahoma seeks to

---

rational-basis test? Or is it more like the proportionality test called for by Justice Thurgood Marshall in *San Antonio Independent School District v. Rodriguez*, 411 U.S. 1, 106–07 (1973)?

[8] **Note:** Many people distinguish between *sex* and *gender*, using sex to describe a set of physical characteristics and gender to describe social values associated with those characteristics. The Court, by contrast, has typically used the terms interchangeably.

regulate—driving while under the influence of alcohol—the statistics broadly establish that .18% of females and 2% of males in [the 18–20] age group were arrested for that offense. While such a disparity is not trivial in a statistical sense, it hardly can form the basis for employment of a gender line as a classifying device. Certainly if maleness is to serve as a proxy for drinking and driving, a correlation of 2% must be considered an unduly tenuous "fit." . . .

Moreover, . . . the surveys do not adequately justify the salient features of Oklahoma's gender-based traffic-safety law. None purports to measure the use and dangerousness of 3.2% beer as opposed to alcohol generally, a detail that is of particular importance since, in light of its low alcohol lever, Oklahoma apparently considers the 3.2% beverage to be "nonintoxicating." [T]he studies, while graphically documenting the unfortunate increase in driving while under the influence of alcohol, make no effort to relate their findings to age-sex differential as involved here. . . .

There is no reason to belabor this line of analysis. It is unrealistic to expect either members of the judiciary or state officials to be well versed in the rigors of experimental or statistical technique. But this merely illustrates that proving broad sociological propositions by statistics is a dubious business, and one that inevitably is in tension with the normative philosophy that underlies the Equal Protection Clause. Suffice to say that the showing offered by the appellees does not satisfy us that sex represents a legitimate, accurate proxy for the regulation of drinking and driving. In fact, when it is further recognized that Oklahoma's statute prohibits only the selling of 3.2% beer to young males and not their drinking the beverage once acquired (even after purchase by their 18–20-year-old female companions), the relationship between gender and traffic safety becomes far too tenuous to satisfy *Reed*'s requirement that the gender-based difference be substantially related to achievement of the statutory objective. . . .

■ MR. JUSTICE STEVENS, concurring.

There is only one Equal Protection Clause. It requires every State to govern impartially. It does not direct the courts to apply one standard of review in some cases and a different standard in other cases. . . .

I am inclined to believe that what has become known as the two-tiered analysis of equal protection claims does not describe a completely logical method of deciding cases, but rather is a method the Court has employed to explain decisions that actually apply a single standard in a reasonably consistent fashion. I also suspect that a careful explanation of the reasons motivating particular decisions may contribute more to an identification of that standard than an attempt to articulate it in all-encompassing terms. . . .

In this case, the classification is not as obnoxious as some the Court has condemned, nor as inoffensive as some the Court has accepted. It is objectionable because it is based on an accident of birth, because it is a mere remnant of the now almost universally rejected tradition of discriminating against males in this age bracket, and because, to the extent it reflects any physical difference between males and females, it is actually perverse. The question then is whether the traffic safety justification put forward by the State is sufficient to make an otherwise offensive classification acceptable.[9]

The classification is not totally irrational. For the evidence does indicate that there are more males than females in this age bracket who drive and also more who drink. Nevertheless, there are several reasons why I regard the justification as

[9] **Questions:** Like Marshall in *Rodriguez*, Justice John Paul Stevens calls for proportionality review rather than the tiers of scrutiny. Again, what principles does such an approach serve? What are the difficulties?

unacceptable. It is difficult to believe that the statute was actually intended to cope with the problem of traffic safety, since it has only a minimal effect on access to a not very intoxicating beverage and does not prohibit its consumption. Moreover, the empirical data submitted by the State accentuate the unfairness of treating all 18–20-year-old males as inferior to their female counterparts. . . . [I]t does not seem to me that an insult to all of the young men of the State can be justified by visiting the sins of the 2% on the 98%.

NOTE: INTERMEDIATE SCRUTINY

Although the discrimination at issue in *Craig* was relatively innocuous, the decision announced a new standard for evaluating all forms of sex discrimination: intermediate scrutiny. *See Califano v. Goldfarb*, 430 U.S. 199, 210 (1977). *Craig* provided that "[t]o withstand constitutional challenge, . . . classifications by gender must serve important governmental objectives and must be substantially related to achievement of those objectives." 429 U.S. at 197. On its face, this two-pronged test appeared like a means-ends test in which the means must be "substantially related" (rather than "rationally related" or "necessary") and the end must be "important" (rather than "legitimate" or "compelling").

Like Marshall in *Rodriguez*, Justice John Paul Stevens criticized the use of means-ends tests as a formalistic alternative to what he thought the Court was in fact doing in all equal-protection cases: weighing whether the "justification put forward by the State is sufficient to make an otherwise offensive classification acceptable." *Id.* at 213. From Stevens's perspective, the fact that "[t]here is only one Equal Protection Clause" meant that the Court should transparently apply the same balancing test to all claims of discrimination rather than hide the ball with three different means-ends tests that attempted to determine the legislature's true purpose. *Id.* at 211.

Nevertheless, to varying degrees of success, the Court attempted to apply intermediate scrutiny in the years after *Craig*. Even after the decision, though, it remained unclear (1) which facially neutral classifications would count as sex-based classification (2) what relationship might count as "rationally related" but not "substantially related," and (3) what ends might count as "legitimate" but not "important."

Facially neutral classifications. Shortly after *Craig*, the Supreme Court answered the first question by announcing that intermediate scrutiny would apply only where the government acted with a "discriminatory purpose"—the same test for evaluating facially neutral laws that the Court employed in *Washington v. Davis*, 426 U.S. 229 (1976), and *Village of Arlington Heights v. Metropolitan Housing Development Corp.*, 429 U.S. 252 (1977).

In the 1970s, Massachusetts granted hiring preferences to veterans by placing them at the top of an "eligible list" of job candidates for vacant civil service positions. *Personnel Administrator v. Feeney*, 442 U.S. 256, 263 (1979). Because so few veterans were women, this preference had the practical effect of excluding qualified women, including Helen Feeney, from government jobs. But when Feeney challenged the preference as a violation of the Equal Protection Clause, the Supreme Court applied the rational-basis test because it didn't see the hiring preference as a gender-based classification. In *Personnel Administrator v. Feeney*, the Court cited *Davis* and *Arlington Heights* to explain that it wouldn't apply intermediate scrutiny to all laws that had a disparate impact on men and women, but only laws that were "based upon gender" or that reflected "invidious gender-based discrimination." 442 U.S. 256, 274 (1979). "The dispositive question," the Court continued, "is whether the appellee has shown that a gender-based discriminatory purpose has, at least in some measure, shaped the Massachusetts veterans' preference." *Id.* at 276. Running through the totality-of-the-circumstances factors of *Arlington Heights*, the Court concluded that Feeney hadn't proved "that the decisionmaker, in this case a state legislature, selected or reaffirmed a particular course of action at least in part 'because of,' not merely 'in spite of,' its adverse effects upon an identifiable group." *Id.* at 279. The Court therefore upheld the preference as "a preference for veterans of either sex over nonveterans of either sex, not for men over women." *Id.* at 280.

The Court's emphasis on purpose over impact has occasionally yielded bizarre results. In *Geduldig v. Aiello*, 417 U.S. 484 (1974), the Court held that a program that provided insurance for workplace disabilities did not involve "discrimination based upon gender" even though the program specifically excluded pregnancy-related disabilities. *Geduldig*, 417 U.S. at 496 n.20. The Court denied that "every legislative classification concerning pregnancy is a sex-based classification" because women, like men, could receive benefits for non-pregnancy-related disabilities. *Id.*; *see also Gen. Elec. Co. v. Gilbert*, 429 U.S. 125, 145–46 (1976) (reaching same conclusion under Civil Rights Act of 1964); *Cleveland Bd. of Educ. v. LaFleur*, 414 U.S. 632, 643 (1974) (applying the rational-basis test, not intermediate scrutiny, to strike down a school's policy of requiring pregnant women to leave work months before their expected childbirth).

Congress responded to the Court's formalism by passing the Pregnancy Discrimination Act of 1978, Pub. L. No. 95–555, 92 Stat. 2076. The act authorized pregnant employees to bring disparate-impact claims where their employers refused to provide them with accommodations provided to other employees with similar restrictions. *See Young v. United Parcel Serv.*, 575 U.S. 206 (2015).

"Substantially related" prong. In contrast with the rational-basis test—where the Court upholds a law as long as the justices can conceive of any possible legitimate interest that the law could rationally relate to—when the Court initially applied intermediate scrutiny, it skeptically evaluated the relationship between the law and the "actual purposes" of the classification. *See Califano v. Goldfarb*, 430 U.S. 199, 212–13 (1977) (plurality opinion); *Wengler v. Druggists Mut. Ins. Co.*, 446 U.S. 142 (1980).

"Important" prong. The Court similarly departed from the rational-basis test by requiring any interests served by a law to be "important" and not merely legitimate. For example, the Court held that a government's interest in "administrative convenience" was insufficiently important to treat men and women differently. *Goldfarb*, 430 U.S. at 205. The Court also repeatedly held that a state's preference for men and women to play traditional or stereotypical gender roles "can no longer justify a statute that discriminates on the basis of gender." *Orr v. Orr*, 440 U.S. 268, 279–80 (1979).

Nevertheless, the Court has declared many governmental interests important. Most significantly, in *Rostker v. Goldberg*, the Court upheld an act of Congress that required the registration of men but not women for a future military draft. 453 U.S. 57, 78–79 (1981). Even though a presidential investigation concluded that women should be drafted, the Court deferred to Congress's extensive deliberations over the law and emphasized that, at the time, women were ineligible for combat duty. *Id.* at 76. In light of this unchallenged ineligibility, the Court found that the law served Congress's important purpose "to develop a pool of potential combat troops." *Id.* at 79. In light of *Rostker*'s distinction, when the Department of Justice announced in 2013 that it would open all combat positions to women, male litigants raised a second sex-discrimination challenge seeking to overrule *Rostker* and extend the draft-registration requirement to women. The Supreme Court declined to take the case, however, citing its "longstanding deference to Congress on matters of national defense and military affairs." *Nat'l Coal. for Men v. Selective Serv. Sys.*, 141 S. Ct. 1815, 1816 (2021) (Sotomayor, J., respecting the denial of certiorari).

Remedial purposes. Before and after *Craig*, perhaps the most common justification for sex-based classifications was the "compensatory," or "remedial," purpose of remedying sex discrimination. *See, e.g.*, *Weinberger v. Wiesenfeld*, 420 U.S. 636, 653 (1975).

Yet after Sandra Day O'Connor became the first woman to join the Supreme Court in 1981, the Court reconsidered its earlier willingness to indiscriminately accept any claim that the purpose of a sex-based classification was remedial. In one of her first opinions for the Court, O'Connor evaluated the Mississippi University for Women's school of nursing, which the university established in 1971 to admit only women. When Joe Hogan, a registered nurse, applied to the school's baccalaureate program, he was denied admission solely because of his sex. Hogan's only alternative was a nursing school over one hundred miles away—so he challenged the single-sex admissions policy in court.

In *Mississippi University for Women v. Hogan*, 458 U.S. 718 (1982), O'Connor wrote the majority opinion invalidating the school of nursing's admissions policy under intermediate scrutiny. Considering the state's asserted interest in providing "a unique educational opportunity for females," she responded that such a remedial purpose was "important" only where it was, in fact, remedial. *Hogan*, 458 U.S. at 721–22. "It is readily apparent that a State can evoke a compensatory purpose to justify an otherwise discriminatory classification only if members of the gender benefited by the classification actually suffer a disadvantage related to the classification," she wrote. *Id.* at 728. But, she added,

> Mississippi ha[d] made no showing that women lacked opportunities to obtain training in the field of nursing or to attain positions of leadership in that field. . . . In fact, in 1970, the year

> before the School of Nursing's first class enrolled, women earned 94 percent of the nursing baccalaureate degrees conferred in Mississippi.

Id. at 729.

In light of this statistic, the Court wrote that the single-sex admission policy was an invalid perpetuation of "the old view that women, not men, should become nurses, and makes the assumption that nursing is a field for women a self-fulfilling prophecy." *Id.* at 730.

In an important conclusion, the Court summarized the intermediate scrutiny test with a new phrase: "we conclude that the State has fallen far short of establishing the 'exceedingly persuasive justification' needed to sustain the gender-based classification." *Id.*

48.2.2

United States v. Virginia

518 U.S. 515 (1996)

By 1996, most public colleges in the United States had become coeducational. But the Virginia Military Institute (VMI) resisted this trend, offering its all-male students a unique "adversative" experience grounded in military tradition, male-bonding rituals, and Lost Cause defiance. De Hart, *supra*, at 332. Freshman "rats" spent their first year serving in a boot-camp atmosphere at the whim of unsupervised upperclassmen, who hazed them, raided their communal bathrooms, and stripped them of their individuality. *Id.* at 333. At the end of the year during "breakout," the rats would attempt to crawl up a muddy hill as the upperclassmen kicked them and smeared them with mud. *Id.* Those who survived this experience graduated as "VMI men." *Id.* at 334. Although VMI had been unable to resist when the federal government forced it to racially integrate in 1968, its alumni in Congress and the military argued that admitting women would "dilute the strength of the 'adversative' method" and "distract male students from their studies." *Id.* at 334–37.

The Department of Justice under President Bill Clinton successfully challenged VMI's admission policy in federal court. In response, Virginia created the Virginia Women's Institute for Leadership (VWIL) at the private Mary Baldwin College. But rather than replicate VMI, the new program "deemphasized" military education and used a "cooperative method" to "reinforce[ ] self-esteem." *United States v. Virginia*, 518 U.S. 515, 548 (1996). The district court accepted this alternative, ruling that "[i]f VMI marches to the beat of a drum, then Mary Baldwin marches to the melody of a fife and when the march is over, both will have arrived at the same destination." *Id.* at 528 (quoting district court decision).

By the time the Supreme Court considered VMI's program, Clinton had appointed Ruth Bader Ginsburg as a justice to the Court. Two decades after leading the litigation strategy that created intermediate scrutiny in *Craig*, Ginsburg in *United States v. Virginia*, 518 U.S. 515 (1996), developed the test into its modern form, under which VMI's exclusionary policy was found unconstitutional.

■ JUSTICE GINSBURG delivered the opinion of the Court.[10]

Virginia's public institutions of higher learning include an incomparable military college, Virginia Military Institute (VMI). The United States maintains that the Constitution's equal protection guarantee precludes Virginia from reserving exclusively to men the unique educational opportunities VMI affords. We agree. . . .

[IV]

Today's skeptical scrutiny of official action denying rights or opportunities based on sex responds to volumes of history. As a plurality of this Court acknowledged a generation ago, "our Nation has had a long and unfortunate history of sex discrimination." *Frontiero* v. *Richardson,* 411 U. S. 677, 684 (1973). Through a century plus three decades and more of that history, women did not count among voters composing "We the People"; not until 1920 did women gain a constitutional right to the franchise. And for a half century thereafter, it remained the prevailing doctrine that government, both federal and state, could withhold from women opportunities accorded men so long as any "basis in reason" could be conceived for the discrimination. See, *e. g., Goesaert* v. *Cleary,* 335 U. S. 464, 467 (1948).

In 1971, for the first time in our Nation's history, this Court ruled in favor of a woman who complained that her State had denied her the equal protection of its laws. *Reed* v. *Reed,* 404 U. S. 71, 73. Since *Reed,* the Court has repeatedly recognized that neither federal nor state government acts compatibly with the equal protection principle when a law or official policy denies to women, simply because they are women, full citizenship stature. . . .[11]

Without equating gender classifications, for all purposes, to classifications based on race or national origin, the Court, in post-*Reed* decisions, has carefully inspected official action that closes a door or denies opportunity to women (or to men). See *J. E. B.,* 511 U. S., at 152. To summarize the Court's current directions for cases of official classification based on gender: Focusing on the differential treatment or denial of opportunity for which relief is sought, the reviewing court must determine whether the proffered justification is "exceedingly persuasive." The burden of justification is demanding and it rests entirely on the State. See *Mississippi Univ. for Women,* 458 U. S., at 724. The State must show "at least that the [challenged] classification serves 'important governmental objectives and that the discriminatory means employed' are 'substantially related to the achievement of those objectives.' " *Ibid.* The justification must be genuine, not hypothesized or invented *post hoc* in response to litigation. And it must not rely on overbroad generalizations about the different talents, capacities, or preferences of males and females.

The heightened review standard our precedent establishes does not make sex a proscribed classification. Supposed "inherent differences" are no longer accepted as a ground for race or national origin classifications. See *Loving* v. *Virginia,* 388 U. S. 1 (1967). Physical differences between men and women, however, are enduring: "[T]he two sexes are not fungible; a community made up exclusively of

---

[10] **As You Read, Consider:** In evaluating this sex-based classification, what kind of test does Justice Ruth Bader Ginsburg use? Is it a means-ends test in between strict scrutiny and the rational-basis test? Or is it more like a proportionality test?

[11] **Question:** In the next few paragraphs, Ginsburg summarizes the transition from *Reed v. Reed* and *Craig v. Boren* to the modern "exceedingly persuasive justification" test. Formally, how does this test differ from strict scrutiny?

one [sex] is different from a community composed of both." *Ballard* v. *United States,* 329 U. S. 187, 193 (1946).

"Inherent differences" between men and women, we have come to appreciate, remain cause for celebration, but not for denigration of the members of either sex or for artificial constraints on an individual's opportunity. Sex classifications may be used to compensate women "for particular economic disabilities [they have] suffered," *Califano* v. *Webster,* 430 U. S. 313, 320 (1977) *(per curiam),* to promote equal employment opportunity, to advance full development of the talent and capacities of our Nation's people. But such classifications may not be used, as they once were, see *Goesaert,* 335 U. S., at 467, to create or perpetuate the legal, social, and economic inferiority of women.

Measuring the record in this case against the review standard just described, we conclude that Virginia has shown no "exceedingly persuasive justification" for excluding all women from the citizen-soldier training afforded by VMI. . . .

V

[Virginia] asserts two justifications in defense of VMI's exclusion of women. First, the Commonwealth contends, "single-sex education provides important educational benefits," and the option of single-sex education contributes to "diversity in educational approaches." Second, the Commonwealth argues, "the unique VMI method of character development and leadership training," the school's adversative approach, would have to be modified were VMI to admit women. We consider these two justifications in turn.

A

Single-sex education affords pedagogical benefits to at least some students. . . . Similarly, it is not disputed that diversity among public educational institutions can serve the public good. But Virginia has not shown that VMI was established, or has been maintained, with a view to diversifying, by its categorical exclusion of women, educational opportunities within the Commonwealth. In cases of this genre, our precedent instructs that "benign" justifications proffered in defense of categorical exclusions will not be accepted automatically; a tenable justification must describe actual state purposes, not rationalizations for actions in fact differently grounded. . . .

Neither recent nor distant history bears out Virginia's alleged pursuit of diversity through single-sex educational options. In 1839, when the Commonwealth established VMI, a range of educational opportunities for men and women was scarcely contemplated. Higher education at the time was considered dangerous for women; reflecting widely held views about women's proper place, the Nation's first universities and colleges—for example, Harvard in Massachusetts, William and Mary in Virginia—admitted only men. See E. Farello, A History of the Education of Women in the United States 163 (1970). VMI was not at all novel in this respect: In admitting no women, VMI followed the lead of the Commonwealth's flagship school, the University of Virginia, founded in 1819. . . . [The University of Virginia did not admit women until 1970, when it was under threat of litigation.]

Virginia describes the current absence of public single-sex higher education for women as an historical anomaly. But the historical record indicates action more deliberate than anomalous: First, protection of women against higher education; next, schools for women far from equal in resources and stature to schools for men; finally, conversion of the separate schools to coeducation. . . .

In sum, we find no persuasive evidence in this record that VMI's male-only admission policy "is in furtherance of a state policy of 'diversity.' " . . . However "liberally" this plan serves the Commonwealth's sons, it makes no provision whatever for her daughters. That is not *equal* protection.

B

Virginia next argues that VMI's adversative method of training provides educational benefits that cannot be made available, unmodified, to women. Alterations to accommodate women would necessarily be "radical," so "drastic," Virginia asserts, as to transform, indeed "destroy," VMI's program. See Brief for Cross-Petitioners 34–36. Neither sex would be favored by the transformation, Virginia maintains: Men would be deprived of the unique opportunity currently available to them; women would not gain that opportunity because their participation would "eliminat[e] the very aspects of [the] program that distinguish [VMI] from . . . other institutions of higher education in Virginia." *Id.* . . .[12]

It may be assumed, for purposes of this decision, that most women would not choose VMI's adversative method. . . . [I]t is also probable that many men would not want to be educated in such an environment. . . . Education, to be sure, is not a "one size fits all" business. The issue, however, is not whether "women—or men—should be forced to attend VMI"; rather, the question is whether the Commonwealth can constitutionally deny to women who have the will and capacity, the training and attendant opportunities that VMI uniquely affords.

The notion that admission of women would downgrade VMI's stature, destroy the adversative system and, with it, even the school, is a judgment hardly proved, a prediction hardly different from other self-fulfilling prophecies once routinely used to deny rights or opportunities.

When women first sought admission to the bar and access to legal education, concerns of the same order were expressed. . . . A like fear. . . . accounted for Columbia Law School's resistance to women's admission. . . . ["]If women were admitted to the Columbia Law School, [the faculty] said, then the choicer, more manly and red-blooded graduates of our great universities would go to the Harvard Law School!" The Nation, Feb. 18, 1925, p. 173.

Medical faculties similarly resisted men and women as partners in the study of medicine. . . . More recently, women seeking careers in policing encountered resistance based on fears that their presence would "undermine male solidarity," deprive male partners of adequate assistance, and lead to sexual misconduct. Field studies did not confirm these fears. See P. Bloch & D. Anderson, Policewomen on Patrol: Final Report (1974).

Women's successful entry into the federal military academies, and their participation in the Nation's military forces, indicate that Virginia's fears for the future of VMI may not be solidly grounded. . . .

[In any event,] Virginia and VMI trained their argument on "means" rather than "end," and thus misperceived our precedent. Single-sex education at VMI serves an "important governmental objective," they maintained, and exclusion of women is not only "substantially related," it is essential to that objective. By this notably circular

---

[12] **Question:** Virginia's second argument here is different in kind from its first argument. With the first argument, Virginia contended that the Virginia Military Institute's (VMI's) policy was substantially related to helping *all Virginians* by offering a diverse array of higher-education options. With this second argument, Virginia contends that VMI's policy is substantially related to helping *men* by offering them a world-class, single-sex education. There does appear to be a close (indeed, obvious) relationship between a male-only policy and single-sex education. Does Ginsburg agree that providing a single-sex education is an "important" interest?

argument, the "straightforward" test *Mississippi Univ. for Women* described, see 458 U. S., at 724–725, was bent and bowed.

The Commonwealth's misunderstanding . . . is apparent from VMI's mission: to produce "citizen-soldiers," individuals " 'imbued with love of learning, confident in the functions and attitudes of leadership, possessing a high sense of public service, advocates of the American democracy and free enterprise system, and ready . . . to defend their country in time of national peril.' " Mission Study Committee of the VMI Board of Visitors, Report, May 16, 1986.

Surely that goal is great enough to accommodate women, who today count as citizens in our American democracy equal in stature to men. Just as surely, the Commonwealth's great goal is not substantially advanced by women's categorical exclusion, in total disregard of their individual merit, from the Commonwealth's premier "citizen-soldier" corps. Virginia, in sum, "has fallen far short of establishing the 'exceedingly persuasive justification' " that must be the solid base for any gender-defined classification.[13]

VI . . .

Virginia chose not to eliminate, but to leave untouched, VMI's exclusionary policy. For women only, however, Virginia proposed a separate program, different in kind from VMI and unequal in tangible and intangible facilities. . . . VWIL affords women no opportunity to experience the rigorous military training for which VMI is famed. Instead, the VWIL program "deemphasize[s]" military education, and uses a "cooperative method" of education "which reinforces self-esteem." . . .

Virginia maintains that these methodological differences are "justified pedagogically," based on . . . "psychological and sociological differences" Virginia describes as "real" and "not stereotypes." The Task Force charged with developing the leadership program for women . . . "determined that a military model and, especially VMI's adversative method, would be wholly inappropriate for educating and training *most women*." . . . [But] estimates of what is appropriate for *most women* no longer justify denying opportunity to women whose talent and capacity place them outside the average description. Notably, Virginia never asserted that VMI's method of education suits *most men*. . . .

In contrast to the generalizations about women on which Virginia rests, we note again [that] . . . "some women, at least, would want to attend [VMI] if they had the opportunity," . . . and "can meet the physical standards [VMI] now impose[s] on men." . . . [I]t is for them that a remedy must be crafted. . . .

A prime part of the history of our Constitution . . . is the story of the extension of constitutional rights and protections to people once ignored or excluded. VMI's story continued as our comprehension of "We the People" expanded. There is no reason to believe that the admission of women capable of all the activities required of VMI cadets would destroy the Institute rather than enhance its capacity to serve the "more perfect Union."

---

13 **Questions:** Rather than address whether single-sex education is an important interest, Ginsburg uses VMI's mission statement to reframe the interest at a higher level of generality: producing "citizen-soldiers." Once framed at this higher level of generality, it seems clear that excluding women is no longer substantially related to the interest. But what justifies changing the level of generality like this? Is Ginsburg saying that providing a single-sex education is not the *real* interest involved in this case? Or is she saying that whatever benefits Virginia gains from single-sex education are outweighed by the harm of excluding women from accessing those benefits?

NOTE: "EXCEEDINGLY PERSUASIVE JUSTIFICATION" TEST

Since *Virginia*, the Court has called intermediate scrutiny the "exceedingly persuasive justification" test. Ginsburg's opinion applied the means-ends test in an unusually rigorous way. For one thing, she skeptically analyzed Virginia's means (e.g., disagreeing with Virginia that the policy was, in fact, designed to promote diversity). For another, she analyzed Virginia's ends at a high level of generality (e.g., asking whether the policy was substantially related to creating "citizen-soldiers" rather than "single-sex education").

But Ginsburg's rephrasing of the test didn't provide the Court with consistent guidance for evaluating sex discrimination going forward. In *Nguyen v. INS*, 533 U.S. 53 (2001), and *Sessions v. Morales-Santana*, 137 S. Ct. 1678 (2017), the Court evaluated two federal naturalization statutes that governed how a child born abroad to unwed parents could apply for U.S. citizenship if only one parent was a U.S. citizen.

The first statute, upheld in *Nguyen*, required the child to obtain the U.S. citizen father's acknowledgment of paternity—even though there was no similar requirement for U.S. citizen mothers. 533 U.S. at 71. Although the Court cited *Virginia*, it offered its own justification for the law that the federal government didn't provide: ensuring that a parental relationship exists and, presumably, preventing fraudulent conveyances of citizenship. *Id.*

By contrast, the second statute, struck down in *Morales-Santana*, required the child of a U.S. citizen father to prove that the father was physically present in the United States for ten years before the child's birth—even though the child of a U.S. citizen mother needed to prove only that the mother was present just for one year. 137 S. Ct. at 1686. Dissenting in *Nguyen* and writing the majority opinion in *Morales-Santana*, Ginsburg emphasized that sex-based classifications "must substantially serve an important governmental interest *today*," and not further whatever traditional stereotypes may have justified the classification at its inception. *Id.* at 1690.

48.3 SEXUAL ORIENTATION

On June 28, 1969, New York City police officers raided the Stonewall Inn in Greenwich Village, a popular bar for New York's lesbian, gay, bisexual, transgender, and queer (LGBTQ+) community. At the time, it was illegal in most states for people who identified as LGBTQ+ to express their identity in public or private. Police raids on gay bars were routine. This time, however, crowds spontaneously gathered outside the bar yelling "gay power" and "enough is enough." *See* David Carter, *Stonewall* 164 (2004). As police officers within Stonewall violently harassed and handcuffed its patrons, the crowd outside fought back, slashing the police cars' tires, throwing bricks at the building, and barricading the officers inside. The next night, thousands of people protested in the streets of

Greenwich Village calling for the "liberation" of the neighborhood from police oppression. *Id.* at 147–49, 174–78, 205.

Within six months of the Stonewall riots, activists around the country formed the Gay Liberation Front, which called for "Gay Power to Gay People" and encouraging "all Gay men and women in the homosexual community" to embrace one another with pride. *Id.* at 225–27. Similarly militant organizations formed across the country, employing tactics used by the Black Power and women's liberation movements to overturn established cultural and sexual hierarchies. Many of these organizations, including the Gay Liberation Front, fractured into dissident organizations whose goal was to use politics and litigation to win civil rights for LGBTQ+ people. The breakaway Gay Activists Alliance formed in December 1969 to demand "the freedom for expression of our dignity and value as human beings . . . and the immediate unconditional recognition of . . . basic rights." *Id.* at 235. These included "[t]he right to our own feelings. . . . The right to love . . . . The right to our own bodies. . . . [And] the right freely to express our own individuality under the governance of laws justly made and executed." *Id.*

In the decade after Stonewall, activists affiliated with the legal wing of the gay liberation movement formed several advocacy organizations including Lambda Legal, Gay & Lesbian Advocates & Defenders (GLAD), and the Human Rights Campaign. These organizations embarked on a litigation strategy similar to that of the National Association for the Advancement of Colored People Legal Defense Fund in the 1950s and the ACLU Women's Rights Project in the 1970s. Through lobbying, LGBTQ+ activists encouraged state governments to repeal sodomy laws and other harmful legislation while encouraging local governments to adopt antidiscrimination ordinances. They also challenged discriminatory policies in court under the Equal Protection Clause.

Marriage licenses for gay couples

In an early challenge from 1971, two gay activists from the University of Minnesota, Michael McConnell and Jack Baker, applied for a marriage license in Minneapolis. The local clerk, Gerald Nelson, denied the request on the ground that McConnell and Baker were both men. Baker and McConnell sued Nelson, arguing that Minnesota's marriage law imposed no requirements regarding the sex of the couple—and if it did, that would violate the Due Process Clause and the Equal Protection Clause of the Fourteenth Amendment.

In *Baker v. Nelson*, 191 N.W.2d 185 (1971), the Supreme Court of Minnesota disagreed. Acknowledging that the right to marry had been described as "fundamental" in *Loving v. Virginia*, 388 U.S. 1 (1967), the state supreme court wrote that the *Loving* Court could only have thought of marriage "as a union of man and woman, uniquely involving the procreation and rearing of children within a family." *Nelson*, 191 N.W.2d at 186. "[I]n commonsense and in a constitutional sense, there is a clear distinction between a marital restriction based merely upon race and one based upon the fundamental difference in sex," it added. *Id.* at 313–15.

Baker and McConnell appealed to the Supreme Court, which summarily affirmed the Minnesota supreme court by dismissing the case for "want of a substantial federal question." *Baker v. Nelson*, 409 U.S. 810, 810 (1972). The Court issued a similar decision in *Doe v. Commonwealth's Attorney of Richmond*, 425 U.S. 901 (1976), in which it upheld Virginia's sodomy law from an equal-protection challenge.

Avoidance of equal-protection arguments

In the wake of *Nelson* and *Doe*, Lambda Legal and GLAD avoided equal-protection arguments—although their tactics enjoyed only mixed success.

For example, in *Fricke v. Lynch*, GLAD lawyers argued before a federal district court that gay and lesbian students had a First Amendment right to bring same-sex dates to their proms—but the lawyers "conceded that homosexuals are not a suspect class sufficient to trigger a higher standard of scrutiny." 491 F. Supp. 381, 388 (D.R.I. 1980). Instead, they argued—and the district court agreed—that the students had a First Amendment right to express themselves. *Id.* at 389.

Similarly, in *Bowers v. Hardwick*, the lawyers for Michael Hardwick didn't press an equal-protection argument before the Supreme Court. 478 U.S. 186, 198 n.8 (1986). Instead, they pursued a due process argument, which the Court rejected. *Id.* at 189. And in *Hurley v. Irish-American Gay, Lesbian, and Bisexual Group of Boston*, 515 U.S. 557 (1995), another GLAD case, the lawyers argued that the organizers of Boston's St. Patrick's Day parade were required to admit an LGB organization to the parade. Rather than raise an equal-protection claim, the lawyers argued that the parade organizers violated a state antidiscrimination statute. *Hurley*, 515 U.S. at 561. The Supreme Court rejected the argument, holding that the statute itself violated the First Amendment rights of the parade organizers to choose with whom to associate. *Id.* at 566.

The LGBTQ+ legal movement finally won its first major Supreme Court victory in *Romer v. Evans*, 517 U.S. 620 (1996). As discussed earlier with regard to rational basis with bite (section 44.4), the decision applied the rational-basis test to strike down Colorado's Amendment 2, which the Court held wasn't rationally related to any interests other than illegitimate "animus." *Romer*, 517 U.S. at 632. But, as in earlier cases, the Lambda Legal lawyers challenging Amendment 2 declined to argue "that homosexuals constitute a 'suspect' or 'quasi-suspect class.' " *Id.* at 640 n.1 (Scalia, J., dissenting). For its part, the Supreme Court declined to evaluate Colorado's Amendment 2 under strict scrutiny.

Defense of same-sex marriage in state courts

Lambda Legal and GLAD had more consistent success in state court. Adopting a legal strategy of challenging state bans on same-sex marriage, the two organizations hoped to demonstrate that state marriage laws were as separate and unequal as state racial segregation laws fifty years earlier. They focused on marriage because of two Supreme Court decisions—*Zablocki v. Redhail*, 434 U.S. 374 (1978), and *Turner v. Safley*, 482 U.S. 78 (1987)—in which the Court reaffirmed *Loving*'s holding that the right to marry was fundamental and subject to strict scrutiny.

The first victory arrived in *Baehr v. Lewin*, 852 P.2d 44 (Haw. 1993). Adopting the analysis of the plurality in the sex-discrimination case of *Frontiero v. Richardson*, 411 U.S. 677 (1973), the Hawaii Supreme Court held that "sex is a 'suspect category' for purposes of equal protection analysis under article I, section 5 of the Hawaii Constitution," and a statutory ban on same-sex marriage "is subject to the 'strict scrutiny' test." *Baehr*, 852 P.2d at 67. The decision did not go further and actually strike down Hawaii's marriage ban. But it did spark a nationwide reaction. Hawaii and dozens of other states amended their constitutions to define *marriage* as a relationship between one man and one woman. Congress did the same for federal purposes with the Defense of Marriage Act of 1996, Pub. L. No. 104–199, 110 Stat. 2419.

Few states followed Hawaii in treating same-sex marriage bans as sex discrimination. For example, in *Baker v. State*, Lambda Legal persuaded the Vermont Supreme Court that the Vermont Constitution prohibited the state from denying same-sex couples "the same benefits and protections afforded by Vermont law to married opposite-sex couples." 744 A.2d 864, 866 (Vt. 1999). But the Vermont court claimed that its standard of review didn't track "the federal rational-basis/strict-scrutiny tests." *Id.* at 872.

Two years later, GLAD represented a Massachusetts couple, Hillary and Julie Goodridge, in their challenge to Massachusetts's ban on same-sex marriage. By the time the Supreme Judicial Court of Massachusetts reached a decision, however, the Supreme Court of the United States decided *Lawrence v. Texas*, 539 U.S. 558, 578 (2003), in which the Court invalidated Texas's sodomy law under the rational-basis test. The Massachusetts court followed with *Goodridge v. Department of Public Health*, 798 N.E.2d 941 (2003), becoming the first court in the country to rule that it was unconstitutional to withhold marriage licenses from same-sex couples. Like *Romer* and *Lawrence*, however, the state court declined to decide whether the case involved a suspect classification or a fundamental right. *Goodridge*, 798 N.E.2d at 961. Instead, the court declared that "[t]he marriage ban works a deep and scarring hardship on a very real segment of the community for no rational reason." *Id.* at 966–68.

Goodridge inaugurated a decade of litigation around the country in which state courts issued sweeping decisions striking down bans on same-sex marriage. *See, e.g., In re Marriage Cases*, 183 P.3d 384, 401 (Cal. 2008); *Kerrigan v. Comm'r of Pub. Health*, 957 A.2d 407, 469, 481 (Conn. 2008). Although many states responded by adopting state constitutional amendments banning same-sex marriage, a dozen state legislatures and ballot initiatives legalized same-sex marriage without a court order. *See, e.g.*, Del. Code Ann., tit. 13, § 129 (Supp. 2014); 2009 Vt. Acts & Resolves 33. Furthermore, in the states with constitutional amendments banning same-sex marriage, federal courts almost uniformly invalidated the amendments under rational-basis review or strict scrutiny. *See, e.g., Latta v. Otter*, 771 F. 3d 456, 468, 472 (9th Cir. 2014); *Perry v. Schwarzenegger*, 704 F. Supp. 2d 921, 995 (N.D. Cal. 2010).

48.3.1

Obergefell v. Hodges

576 U.S. 644 (2015)

The only court of appeals case that didn't follow this pattern, *DeBoer v. Snyder*, 772 F. 3d 388, 413 (6th Cir. 2014), led the Supreme Court to intervene.

The Sixth Circuit case involved Jim Obergefell, who married his partner, John Arthur, in Maryland. But when the couple returned home to Ohio, they learned that the state wouldn't recognize their out-of-state marriage. While their lawsuit was pending, Arthur died. Yet Ohio refused to list Arthur as "married" on his death certificate or Obergefell as his "surviving spouse."

By the time the Supreme Court heard argument in Obergefell's case, thirty-six states and the District of Columbia were already issuing marriage licenses to same-sex couples. But courts continued to inconsistently evaluate whether sexual orientation was a suspect classification, whether marriage was a fundamental right, and whether a prohibition on same-sex marriage could survive the rational-basis test.

The Court's ruling in *Obergefell v. Hodges*, 576 U.S. 644 (2015), clarified that marriage was a fundamental right and invalidated Ohio's prohibition on same-sex marriage, yet did not apply strict scrutiny to do so.

■ JUSTICE KENNEDY, delivered the opinion of the Court.[14]

The Constitution promises liberty to all within its reach, a liberty that includes certain specific rights that allow persons, within a lawful realm, to define and express their identity. The petitioners in these cases seek to find that liberty by marrying

[14] **As You Read, Consider:** What test does Justice Anthony Kennedy use to determine whether a state ban on same-sex marriage is constitutional? Does he employ strict scrutiny, intermediate scrutiny, the rational-basis test, or something else?

someone of the same sex and having their marriages deemed lawful on the same terms and conditions as marriages between persons of the opposite sex.

[II]

[T]he history of marriage is one of both continuity and change. That institution—even as confined to opposite-sex relations—has evolved over time.

For example, marriage was once viewed as an arrangement by the couple's parents based on political, religious, and financial concerns; but by the time of the Nation's founding it was understood to be a voluntary contract between a man and a woman. See N. Cott, Public Vows: A History of Marriage and the Nation 9–17 (2000). As the role and status of women changed, the institution further evolved. Under the centuries-old doctrine of coverture, a married man and woman were treated by the State as a single, male-dominated legal entity. As women gained legal, political, and property rights, and as society began to understand that women have their own equal dignity, the law of coverture was abandoned. These and other developments in the institution of marriage over the past centuries were not mere superficial changes. Rather, they worked deep transformations in its structure, affecting aspects of marriage long viewed by many as essential. . . .

These new insights have strengthened, not weakened, the institution of marriage. Indeed, changed understandings of marriage are characteristic of a Nation where new dimensions of freedom become apparent to new generations, often through perspectives that begin in pleas or protests and then are considered in the political sphere and the judicial process.

This dynamic can be seen in the Nation's experiences with the rights of gays and lesbians. Until the mid-20th century, same-sex intimacy long had been condemned as immoral by the state itself in most Western nations, a belief often embodied in the criminal law. For this reason, among others, many persons did not deem homosexuals to have dignity in their own distinct identity. . . .

For much of the 20th century, moreover, homosexuality was treated as an illness. When the American Psychiatric Association published the first Diagnostic and Statistical Manual of Mental Disorders in 1952, homosexuality was classified as a mental disorder, a position adhered to until 1973. . . .

In the late 20th century, following substantial cultural and political developments, same-sex couples began to lead more open and public lives and to establish families. This development was followed by a quite extensive discussion of the issue in both governmental and private sectors and by a shift in public attitudes toward greater tolerance. As a result, questions about the rights of gays and lesbians soon reached the courts, where the issue could be discussed in the formal discourse of the law. . . .

After years of litigation, legislation, referenda, and the discussions that attended these public acts, the States are now divided on the issue of same-sex marriage.

III

Under the Due Process Clause of the Fourteenth Amendment, no State shall "deprive any person of life, liberty, or property, without due process of law." The fundamental liberties protected by this Clause include most of the rights enumerated in the Bill of Rights. In addition these liberties extend to certain personal choices central to individual dignity and autonomy, including intimate choices that define personal identity and beliefs. See, *e.g.*, *Griswold* v. *Connecticut,* 381 U. S. 479, 484–486 (1965).

The identification and protection of fundamental rights is an enduring part of the judicial duty to interpret the Constitution. That responsibility, however, "has not been reduced to any formula." *Poe* v. *Ullman,* 367 U. S. 497, 542 (1961) (Harlan, J., dissenting). Rather, it requires courts to exercise reasoned judgment in identifying interests of the person so fundamental that the State must accord them its respect. That process is guided by many of the same considerations relevant to analysis of other constitutional provisions that set forth broad principles rather than specific requirements. History and tradition guide and discipline this inquiry but do not set its outer boundaries. See *Lawrence, supra,* at 572. That method respects our history and learns from it without allowing the past alone to rule the present.[15]

The nature of injustice is that we may not always see it in our own times. The generations that wrote and ratified the Bill of Rights and the Fourteenth Amendment did not presume to know the extent of freedom in all of its dimensions, and so they entrusted to future generations a charter protecting the right of all persons to enjoy liberty as we learn its meaning. When new insight reveals discord between the Constitution's central protections and a received legal stricture, a claim to liberty must be addressed.

Applying these established tenets, the Court has long held the right to marry is protected by the Constitution. In *Loving* v. *Virginia,* 388 U. S. 1, 12 (1967), which invalidated bans on interracial unions, a unanimous Court held marriage is "one of the vital personal rights essential to the orderly pursuit of happiness by free men." The Court reaffirmed that holding in *Zablocki* v. *Redhail,* 434 U. S. 374, 384 (1978), which held the right to marry is burdened by a law prohibiting fathers who were behind on child support from marrying. The Court again applied this principle in *Turner* v. *Safley,* 482 U. S. 78, 95 (1987), which held the right to marry was abridged by regulations limiting the privilege of prison inmates to marry. Over time and in other contexts, the Court has reiterated that the right to marry is fundamental under the Due Process Clause. . . .

It cannot be denied that this Court's cases describing the right to marry presumed a relationship involving opposite-sex partners. . . . Still, there are other, more instructive precedents. This Court's cases have expressed constitutional principles of broader reach. . . . The four principles and traditions to be discussed demonstrate that the reasons marriage is fundamental under the Constitution apply with equal force to same-sex couples.

A first premise of the Court's relevant precedents is that the right to personal choice regarding marriage is inherent in the concept of individual autonomy. This abiding connection between marriage and liberty is why *Loving* invalidated interracial marriage bans under the Due Process Clause. Like choices concerning contraception, family relationships, procreation, and childrearing, all of which are protected by the Constitution, decisions concerning marriage are among the most intimate that an individual can make. . . .

A second principle in this Court's jurisprudence is that the right to marry is fundamental because it supports a two-person union unlike any other in its importance to the committed individuals. This point was central to *Griswold,* which held the Constitution protects the right of married couples to use contraception. . . . [And a]s this Court held in *Lawrence,* same-sex couples have the same right as opposite-sex couples to enjoy intimate association. . . .

---

[15] **Question:** Note that in identifying whether this case involves a fundamental right, Kennedy does not invoke the two-part "tradition" test of *Washington v. Glucksberg.* Instead, as in *Lawrence v. Texas,* he writes that "[h]istory and tradition guide and discipline this inquiry but do not set its outer boundaries." He also cites a *Griswold v. Connecticut*-era opinion in which Justice John Harlan called for a context-specific proportionality inquiry into the constitutionality of legislation. Does Kennedy employ a similar proportionality test and evaluate the harms and benefits of a ban on same-sex marriage?

A third basis for protecting the right to marry is that it safeguards children and families and thus draws meaning from related rights of childrearing, procreation, and education. See *Meyer,* 262 U. S., at 399. . . . Marriage also affords the permanency and stability important to children's best interests. . . .

Fourth and finally, this Court's cases and the Nation's traditions make clear that marriage is a keystone of our social order. . . . [J]ust as a couple vows to support each other, so does society pledge to support the couple, offering symbolic recognition and material benefits to protect and nourish the union. . . . Yet by virtue of their exclusion from that institution, same-sex couples are denied the constellation of benefits that the States have linked to marriage. . . . Same-sex couples are consigned to an instability many opposite-sex couples would deem intolerable in their own lives. . . . It demeans gays and lesbians for the State to lock them out of a central institution of the Nation's society. . . .

The limitation of marriage to opposite-sex couples may long have seemed natural and just, but its inconsistency with the central meaning of the fundamental right to marry is now manifest. With that knowledge must come the recognition that laws excluding same-sex couples from the marriage right impose stigma and injury of the kind prohibited by our basic charter.

Objecting that this does not reflect an appropriate framing of the issue, the respondents refer to *Washington* v. *Glucksberg,* 521 U. S. 702, 721 (1997), which called for a " 'careful description' " of fundamental rights. They assert the petitioners do not seek to exercise the right to marry but rather a new and nonexistent "right to same-sex marriage." *Glucksberg* did insist that liberty under the Due Process Clause must be defined in a most circumscribed manner, with central reference to specific historical practices. Yet while that approach may have been appropriate for the asserted right there involved (physician-assisted suicide), it is inconsistent with the approach this Court has used in discussing other fundamental rights, including marriage and intimacy. *Loving* did not ask about a "right to interracial marriage"; *Turner* did not ask about a "right of inmates to marry"; and *Zablocki* did not ask about a "right of fathers with unpaid child support duties to marry." Rather, each case inquired about the right to marry in its comprehensive sense, asking if there was a sufficient justification for excluding the relevant class from the right.

That principle applies here. If rights were defined by who exercised them in the past, then received practices could serve as their own continued justification and new groups could not invoke rights once denied. This Court has rejected that approach, both with respect to the right to marry and the rights of gays and lesbians. See *Loving* 388 U. S., at 12; *Lawrence,* 539 U. S., at 566–567.

The right to marry is fundamental as a matter of history and tradition, but rights come not from ancient sources alone. They rise, too, from a better informed understanding of how constitutional imperatives define a liberty that remains urgent in our own era. Many who deem same-sex marriage to be wrong reach that conclusion based on decent and honorable religious or philosophical premises, and neither they nor their beliefs are disparaged here. But when that sincere, personal opposition becomes enacted law and public policy, the necessary consequence is to put the imprimatur of the State itself on an exclusion that soon demeans or stigmatizes those whose own liberty is then denied. Under the Constitution, same-sex couples seek in marriage the same legal treatment as opposite-sex couples, and it would disparage their choices and diminish their personhood to deny them this right.

The right of same-sex couples to marry that is part of the liberty promised by the Fourteenth Amendment is derived, too, from that Amendment's guarantee of the equal protection of the laws.[16] The Due Process Clause and the Equal Protection Clause are connected in a profound way, though they set forth independent principles. Rights implicit in liberty and rights secured by equal protection may rest on different precepts and are not always coextensive, yet in some instances each may be instructive as to the meaning and reach of the other. In any particular case one Clause may be thought to capture the essence of the right in a more accurate and comprehensive way, even as the two Clauses may converge in the identification and definition of the right. . . .

The Court's cases touching upon the right to marry reflect this dynamic. In *Loving* the Court invalidated a prohibition on interracial marriage under both the Equal Protection Clause and the Due Process Clause. The Court first declared the prohibition invalid because of its unequal treatment of interracial couples. . . . With this link to equal protection the Court proceeded to hold the prohibition offended central precepts of liberty: "To deny this fundamental freedom on so unsupportable a basis as the racial classifications embodied in these statutes, classifications so directly subversive of the principle of equality at the heart of the Fourteenth Amendment, is surely to deprive all the State's citizens of liberty without due process of law." *Ibid.* The reasons why marriage is a fundamental right became more clear and compelling from a full awareness and understanding of the hurt that resulted from laws barring interracial unions. . . .

Indeed, in interpreting the Equal Protection Clause, the Court has recognized that new insights and societal understandings can reveal unjustified inequality within our most fundamental institutions that once passed unnoticed and unchallenged. To take but one period, this occurred with respect to marriage in the 1970's and 1980's. Notwithstanding the gradual erosion of the doctrine of coverture, invidious sex-based classifications in marriage remained common through the mid-20th century. See App. to Brief for Appellant in *Reed* v. *Reed,* O. T. 1971, No. 70-4, pp. 69–88. These classifications denied the equal dignity of men and women. One State's law, for example, provided in 1971 that "the husband is the head of the family and the wife is subject to him; her legal civil existence is merged in the husband, except so far as the law recognizes her separately, either for her own protection, or for her benefit." Ga. Code Ann. § 53–501 (1935). Responding to a new awareness, the Court invoked equal protection principles to invalidate laws imposing sex-based inequality on marriage. See, *e.g., Califano* v. *Goldfarb,* 430 U. S. 199 (1977); *Weinberger* v. *Wiesenfeld,* 420 U. S. 636 (1975); *Frontiero* v. *Richardson,* 411 U. S. 677 (1973). Like *Loving* . . ., these precedents show the Equal Protection Clause can help to identify and correct inequalities in the institution of marriage, vindicating precepts of liberty and equality under the Constitution. . . .

This dynamic also applies to same-sex marriage. It is now clear that the challenged laws burden the liberty of same-sex couples, and it must be further acknowledged that they abridge central precepts of equality. Here the marriage laws enforced by the respondents are in essence unequal: same-sex couples are denied all the benefits afforded to opposite-sex couples and are barred from exercising a fundamental right. Especially against a long history of disapproval of their relationships, this denial to same-sex couples of the right to marry works a grave and continuing harm. The imposition of this disability on gays and lesbians serves to disrespect and subordinate them. And the Equal Protection Clause, like the Due Process Clause, prohibits this unjustified infringement of the fundamental right to marry.

---

[16] **Question:** So far, Kennedy has evaluated this case under the Due Process Clause. How does his due process analysis differ, if at all, from his equal-protection analysis that follows?

These considerations lead to the conclusion that the right to marry is a fundamental right inherent in the liberty of the person, and under the Due Process and Equal Protection Clauses of the Fourteenth Amendment couples of the same-sex may not be deprived of that right and that liberty. The Court now holds that same-sex couples may exercise the fundamental right to marry. No longer may this liberty be denied to them. *Baker* v. *Nelson* must be and now is overruled, and the State laws challenged by Petitioners in these cases are now held invalid to the extent they exclude same-sex couples from civil marriage on the same terms and conditions as opposite-sex couples. . . .

NOTE: STANDARD OF SCRUTINY FOR SEXUAL ORIENTATION

When *Obergefell* declared that "rights come not from ancient sources alone," the Court marked a radical departure from some of its prior interpretations of fundamental rights under the Due Process Clause. 576 U.S. at 671. In contrast with *Washington v. Glucksberg,* which asked whether a "careful description" of a liberty interest was "deeply rooted" in the nation's history and tradition, 521 U.S. 702, 721 (1997), *Obergefell* recognized that the fundamental nature of a liberty interest could change over time. "When new insight reveals discord between the Constitution's central protections and a received legal stricture, a claim to liberty must be addressed," the Court wrote, disparaging *Glucksberg*'s analysis as one that would allow "the past alone to rule the present." *Obergefell*, 576 U.S. at 664.

Obergefell also marked a radical departure from the past with its equal-protection analysis, which is difficult to square with the tiers of scrutiny articulated in *San Antonio Independent School District v. Rodriguez*, 411 U.S. 1 (1973). On a superficial level, the opinion simply decided that the right to marry was fundamental and therefore, under *Rodriguez*, subject to strict scrutiny. But the term *strict scrutiny* doesn't appear anywhere in *Obergefell*'s analysis—nor did the Court ask whether the states' prohibitions on marriage were narrowly tailored to serve a compelling state interest. Instead, the Court emphasized the harm imposed by a state's prohibition on same-sex marriage, writing that such a prohibition "demeans gays and lesbians" and "would disparage their choices and diminish their personhood." *Obergefell*, 576 U.S. at 672. The Court strongly suggested that it was unconstitutional "to put the imprimatur of the State itself on an exclusion that soon demeans or stigmatizes those whose own liberty is then denied." *Id.*

The decision actually looks most like Justice Thurgood Marshall's dissent in *Rodriguez* and Justice John Stevens's concurrence in *Craig v. Boren*, 429 U.S. 190 (1976), both of which called for an approach to the Equal Protection Clause that would balance "the constitutional and societal importance of the interest adversely affected and the recognized invidiousness of the basis upon which the particular classification is drawn" against "the asserted state interests in support of the classification." *Rodriguez*, 411 U.S. at 99 (Marshall, J., dissenting). The balancing test proposed by the two justices had the virtue of allowing the Court to directly weigh the burdens imposed by a classification against its objectives—avoiding an indirect inquiry into determining whether the law was truly necessary to serve a compelling purpose. Indeed, the purpose of the laws at issue in *Obergefell* was almost beside the point: what mattered to the majority was the effect of the laws on gay and lesbian couples.

The author of *Obergefell*, Kennedy, resigned from the Court three years after the decision and was replaced by President Donald Trump's second appointment, Brett Kavanaugh. As of 2021, the Court's commitment to *Obergefell*'s equal-protection analysis remains an open question. This question is particularly important because even after *Obergefell*, the Court has never considered sexual orientation or gender identity to be a suspect classification. In fact, the Court hasn't considered a new classification to be "suspect" or "quasi-suspect" since 1977. *See* Kenji Yoshino, *The New Equal Protection*, 124 Harv. L. Rev. 747, 757 (2011).

The only hint that the Court has yet provided about its interpretation of *Obergefell* came in *Pavan v. Smith*, 137 S. Ct. 2075 (2017). A 6–3 majority, including Kennedy, applied *Obergefell* to invalidate an Arkansas law that required birth certificates to list the name of a married mother's "husband." *Pavan*, 137 S. Ct. at 2079. The Court explained that Arkansas had

> chosen to make its birth certificates more than a mere marker of biological relationships: The State uses those certificates to give married parents a form of legal recognition that is not available to unmarried parents. Having made that choice, Arkansas may not, consistent with *Obergefell*, deny married same-sex couples that recognition.

Id. at 2078–79. Justice Neil Gorsuch and two other justices dissented, applying the rational-basis test to conclude that "[t]he statute in question establishes a set of rules designed to ensure that the biological parents of a child are listed on the child's birth certificate." *Id.* at 2079 (Gorsuch, J., dissenting, joined by Thomas and Alito, JJ.).

48.4 ALIENAGE

Although the Supreme Court has not decided one way or another whether sexual orientation or gender identity are suspect classifications, it has long considered distinctions on the basis of alienage, nationality, and ancestry to be equivalent to racial classifications. Indeed, in *Yick Wo v. Hopkins*, the Court invalidated San Francisco's application of its laundry ordinance to Chinese nationals because "no reason for it exists except hostility to the race *and nationality* to which the petitioners belong." 118 U.S. 356, 374 (1886) (emphasis added). And in *Truax v. Raich*, the Court struck down an Arizona law that imposed a quota on the number of noncitizens that any business could hire. 239 U.S. 33, 43 (1915). The Court explained that the Equal Protection Clause applied to "any person within [a state's] jurisdiction," which, "as it has frequently been held, includes aliens." *Id.* at 39 (citing *Yick Wo*, 118 U.S. at 369; *United States v. Wong Kim Ark*, 169 U.S. 649, 695 (1898)). The Court therefore held that a state had no "authority to deny to aliens, upon the mere fact of their alienage, the right to obtain support in the ordinary fields of labor." *Id.* at 41–42.

Special-public-interest exception

Truax did, however, emphasize that

> [t]he discrimination defined by the act does not pertain to the regulation or distribution of the public domain, or of the common property or resources of the people of the State, the enjoyment of which may be limited to its citizens as against both aliens and the citizens of other States.

Id. at 39–40. And the same month that the Court struck down the Arizona law, the Court upheld a New York law prohibiting the employment of noncitizens on public works projects. That decision, *Crane v. New York*, 239 U.S. 195 (1915), affirmed an opinion by Judge Benjamin Cardozo, who thought that a state, in spending its own money, "may legitimately consult the welfare of its own citizens rather than that of aliens." *People v. Crane*, 108 N.E. 427, 429–30 (N.Y. 1915); *see also, e.g.*, *Webb v. O'Brien*, 263 U.S. 313, 322 (1923) (upholding a state law prohibiting Japanese noncitizens from buying land).

But this exception for so-called special public interests didn't survive the dawn of strict scrutiny. In *Korematsu v. United States*, 323 U.S. 214, 214 (1944), the Court upheld a law targeting Japanese immigrants and Japanese Americans while declaring that "all legal restrictions which curtail the civil rights of a single racial group are immediately suspect." And in *Takahashi v. Fish & Game Commission*, the Court reiterated that the protections of the Equal Protection Clause "extend to aliens as well as to citizens." 334 U.S. 410, 419 (1948). The *Takahashi* Court struck down a California law that prohibited certain noncitizens from engaging in commercial fishing. *Id.* at 422. The Court declared, "The Fourteenth Amendment and the laws adopted under its authority . . . embody a general policy that all persons lawfully in this country shall abide 'in any state' on an equality of legal privileges with all citizens under non-discriminatory law." *Id.* at 420; *see also Graham v. Richardson*, 403 U.S. 365, 372 (1971) (applying "close judicial scrutiny" to invalidate an Arizona law that prohibited noncitizens from receiving welfare benefits).

Political function doctrine

Despite the Supreme Court's application of strict scrutiny to laws that discriminate against noncitizens, the Court has upheld a wide range of discriminatory state laws after a decision in 1973.

Like many states in the early 1970s, New York's constitution declared that only U.S. citizens could vote or serve as governor, in the legislature, or in other public offices. By statute, the state also banned noncitizens from serving in civil service positions for which there was a competitive examination, including positions as administrative assistants or typists in state agencies.

Applying strict scrutiny to this exclusion in *Sugarman v. Dougall*, the Court held that a state had two compelling interests that might justify discriminating against noncitizens: (1) the "State's interest in establishing its own form of government, and in limiting participation in that government to those who are within 'the basic conception of a political community,'" and (2) the "State's broad power to define its political community." 413 U.S. 634, 642–43 (1973). But, the Court added, in seeking to serve these compelling interests, "with discrimination against aliens, the means the State employs must be precisely drawn in light of the acknowledged purpose." *Id.* at 643.

These compelling interests were enough for the Court to uphold New York's laws that banned noncitizens from "holding state elective or important nonelective executive, legislative, and judicial positions." *Id.* It also allowed states to ban noncitizens from performing "public policy . . . functions that go to the heart of representative government." *Id.* Although the question of noncitizen voting was not before the Court, the Court also emphasized that it had "never held that aliens have a constitutional right to vote or to hold high public office under the Equal Protection Clause." *Id.* at 648–49.

In subsequent cases, the Court expanded the political function doctrine to rationalize almost every state discrimination on the basis of citizenship. In *Foley v. Connelie*, the Court reinterpreted *Sugarman* to hold that where the political function doctrine applies, a state need only justify its exclusion of noncitizens under the rational-basis test, not the narrow tailoring prong of strict scrutiny. 435 U.S. 291, 296 (1978). The Court explained that "[t]o require every statutory exclusion of aliens to clear the high hurdle of 'strict scrutiny' . . . would 'obliterate all the distinctions between citizens and aliens, and thus depreciate the historic values of citizenship.'" *Id.* at 295.

Applying this more-deferential version of the political function doctrine, the Court upheld another New York law that prohibited noncitizens from serving as police officers—asserting that "it would be as anomalous to conclude that citizens may be subjected to the broad discretionary powers of noncitizen police officers as it would be to say that judicial officers and jurors with power to judge citizens can be aliens." *Id.* at 299. The Court even upheld a California law that prohibited noncitizens from serving as furniture and bedding inspectors, toll workers, and other "peace officers." *Cabell v. Chavez-Salido*, 454 U.S. 432, 442 (1982). Connecting these decisions—and distinguishing them from contexts in which the Court continued to apply strict scrutiny—was the Court's sense that the particular form of discrimination was tied not to the receipt of government benefits but rather a broad conception of "a State's constitutional prerogatives [and] constitutional responsibility for the establishment and operation of its own government." *Cabell*, 454 U.S. at 439.

Mixture of strict scrutiny and rational basis

In addition to strict scrutiny (for laws that discriminate on the basis of nationality or alienage) and the rational-basis test (for laws that discriminate on the basis of citizenship with respect to offices covered by the political function doctrine), the Court has also applied a mixture of intermediate scrutiny and rational basis in two other alienage contexts.

Undocumented immigrants. The first context is with undocumented migrants.

In *Plyler v. Doe*, 457 U.S. 202 (1982), the Court struck down a Texas law that excluded undocumented children from attending public school. Although the law discriminated on the basis of alienage with respect to a benefit not covered by the political function doctrine, the Court explained that a lesser standard than strict scrutiny was required. While "illegal aliens . . . may claim the benefit of the Fourteenth Amendment's guarantee of equal protection," the Court wrote, they "cannot be treated as a suspect class because their presence in this country in violation of federal law is not a 'constitutional irrelevancy.' " *Plyler*, 457 U.S. at 215, 223. The Court therefore applied what it called the "technique of 'intermediate' scrutiny," which it said would permit it "to evaluate the rationality of the legislative judgment with reference to well-settled constitutional principles." *Id.* at 218 n.16 (citing *Craig v. Boren*, 429 U.S. 190 (1976)).

In practice, the *Plyler* Court's version of intermediate scrutiny looked a lot like the rational-basis-with-bite approach of *United States Department of Agriculture v. Moreno*, 413 U.S. 528 (1973). The *Plyler* Court wrote that Texas's exclusion of undocumented schoolchildren imposed the "stigma of illiteracy" on "a discrete class of children not accountable for their disabling status." *Plyler*, 457 U.S. at 223. And it concluded that Texas had no legitimate interest in imposing this stigma: "a concern for the preservation of resources standing alone can hardly justify the classification used in allocating those resources. The State must do more than justify its classification with a concise expression of an intention to discriminate." *Id.* at 227.

Cases since *Plyler* have expressly declined to apply its version of intermediate scrutiny "beyond the unique circumstances that provoked [the case's] unique confluence of theories and rationales." *Kadrmas v. Dickinson Pub. Schs.*, 487 U.S. 450, 459 (1988). Instead, the Court has tended to apply the rational-basis-with-bite approach to similarly discriminatory laws. *See, e.g., Lawrence v. Texas*, 539 U.S. 558, 579 (O'Connor, J., concurring in the judgment) (classifying *Plyler* with *Moreno* and *Romer v. Evans*, 517 U.S. 620 (1996)).

Federal legislation. The second context in which the Court has declined to apply strict scrutiny to discrimination on the basis of citizenship is with acts of Congress.

In *Mathews v. Diaz*, the Court upheld a federal statute that denied Medicare benefits to most noncitizens—even though the Court in *Graham v. Richardson*, 403 U.S. 365 (1971), had invalidated a similar state statute. *Diaz*, 426 U.S. 67, 87 (1976). The *Diaz* Court considered the federal law distinguished by Congress's "broad power over naturalization and immigration," which authorized Congress to "make[ ] rules that would be unacceptable if applied to citizens." *Id.* at 79. Where Arizona had "little, if any, basis for treating persons who are citizens of another State differently from persons who are citizens of another country," the federal government, according to the Court, routinely distinguished between aliens on the basis of nationality, residency, and purpose for entering the country. *Id.* at 85. "In short, it is unquestionably reasonable for Congress to make an alien's eligibility depend on both the character and duration of his residence. The fact that an Act of Congress treats aliens differently from citizens does not in itself imply that such disparate treatment is 'invidious.' " *Id.* at 79–83.

The Court impliedly modified *Diaz* in *Sessions v. Morales-Santana*, which applied intermediate scrutiny to a naturalization law that discriminated on the basis of sex. 137 S. Ct. 1678, 1690 (2017). Even though the law implicated the same "broad power over naturalization and immigration" as was at issue in *Diaz*, the Court considered the case no different from any other sex-discrimination case. *Morales-Santana* suggests that to the extent *Diaz* remains good law, its deferential test applies to immigration or naturalization classifications that discriminate only on the basis of alienage or national origin, and not some other suspect classification.

48.5 ILLEGITIMACY

In addition to applying intermediate scrutiny to sex-discrimination challenges emanating from state discrimination on the basis of undocumented status, the Supreme Court has also applied intermediate scrutiny to classifications on the basis of "legitimacy"—that is, whether a child was born to married or unmarried parents.

This standard of review has not always been fixed, however. In a number of cases beginning in the late 1960s, the Court toggled between various levels of scrutiny in evaluating legitimacy-based classifications. *See, e.g., Glona v. Am. Guar. & Liab. Ins. Co.*, 391 U.S. 73, 75 (1968) (applying rational basis with bite to invalidate a law that prohibited a parent from bringing a wrongful death action on behalf of her illegitimate son); *Levy v. Louisiana*, 391 U.S. 68, 72 (1968) (same while invoking strict scrutiny decisions).

After *Craig v. Boren*, 429 U.S. 190 (1976), however, the Court settled on a level of scrutiny that was "less than strictest scrutiny" but not "toothless." *Trimble v. Gordon*, 430 U.S. 762, 767 (1977). The Court explained that "the roots of the discrimination rest in the conduct of the parents rather than the child," and "illegitimacy does not carry an obvious badge, as race or sex do." *Mathews v. Lucas*, 427 U.S. 495, 506 (1976). The Court therefore thought it inappropriate for distinctions on the basis of legitimacy to " 'command extraordinary protection from the majoritarian political process,' which our most exacting scrutiny would entail." *Id.*

48.6 AGE AND DISABILITY

Unlike classifications such as race, nationality, alienage, sex, and legitimacy, the Supreme Court has decisively rejected the argument that classifications based on age or disability should be treated as suspect.

Age-based discrimination

Many of the Supreme Court's decisions regarding age emerged in the context of mandatory retirement laws. In *Massachusetts Board of Retirement v. Murgia*, a decision that applied the rational-basis test to uphold a mandatory retirement age for police officers, the Court explained that

> [w]hile the treatment of the aged in this Nation has not been wholly free of discrimination, such persons, unlike, say, those who have been discriminated against on the basis of race or national origin, have not experienced a 'history of purposeful unequal treatment' or been subjected to unique disabilities on the basis of stereotyped characteristics not truly indicative of their abilities.

427 U.S. 307, 313 (1976).

The life-tenured justices of the Supreme Court also upheld a state law requiring state-court judges to retire at age seventy. *See Gregory v. Ashcroft*, 501 U.S. 452 (1991). The Court wrote that the people of Missouri "rationally could conclude that the threat of deterioration at age [seventy] is sufficiently great, and the alternatives for removal sufficiently inadequate, that they will require all judges to step aside at age [seventy]." *Id.* at 472.

Disability-based discrimination

With respect to classifications on the basis of disability, the Court has also rejected stricter levels of scrutiny in favor of the rational-basis test.

In *City of Cleburne v. Cleburne Living Ctr.*, 473 U.S. 432 (1985), discussed earlier in the section on rational basis with bite (section 44.4), the Court described the "lesson of *Murgia*," writing

> that where individuals in the group affected by a law have distinguishing characteristics relevant to interests the State has the authority to implement, the courts have been very

> reluctant, as they should be in our federal system and with our respect for the separation of powers, to closely scrutinize legislative choices as to whether, how, and to what extent those interests should be pursued.

Id. at 441–42.

The Court followed this summary by offering four reasons why it wouldn't consider people with intellectual disabilities as members of a suspect class: First, "those who are mentally retarded have a reduced ability to cope with and function in the everyday world. . . . They are thus different, immutably so, in relevant respects, and the States' interest in dealing with and providing for them is plainly a legitimate one." *Id.* at 442. Second, state and federal "lawmakers have been addressing their difficulties in a manner that belies a continuing antipathy or prejudice and a corresponding need for more intrusive oversight by the judiciary." *Id.* at 443. Third, "the legislative response, which could hardly have occurred and survived without public support, negates any claim that the mentally retarded are politically powerless in the sense that they have no ability to attract the attention of the lawmakers." *Id.* at 445. Finally, the class was too "large and amorphous" to distinguish it from other groups with "immutable disabilities setting them off from others, who cannot themselves mandate the desired legislative responses, and who can claim some degree of prejudice from at least part of the public at large." *Id.* at 445 (citing "the aging, the disabled, the mentally ill, and the infirm").

So, while the Court recognized that individuals living with intellectual disabilities experience discrimination, it found the ordinary political process more appropriate than its elevation of this classification to a suspect status for addressing such discrimination.

CHAPTER 49

ARE RACIAL CLASSIFICATIONS ALWAYS STRICTLY SCRUTINIZED?

FIFTH AMENDMENT (1791): No person shall . . . be deprived of life, liberty, or property, without due process of law. . . .

FOURTEENTH AMENDMENT (1868), SECTION 1: No State shall . . . deprive any person of life, liberty, or property, without due process of law.

49.1 THE ORIGINS OF AFFIRMATIVE ACTION

When Congress passed the Civil Rights Act of 1866, ch. 31, 14 Stat. 27, it extended citizenship and basic civil rights to recently freed black people. Congress enacted the law over the veto of President Andrew Johnson, who offered a variety of arguments against the act's constitutionality. One of his boldest arguments was that the act—passed only a year after the abolition of slavery—discriminated against white people. The president complained that the law established "for the security of the colored race safeguards which go indefinitely beyond any that the General Government has ever adopted for the white race. In fact, the distinction of race and color is by the bill made to operate in favor of the colored race against the white race." 6 *The Compilation of the Messages and Papers of the Presidents* 405 (James D. Richardson ed., 1911). Johnson would not be the last person to argue that government action to remedy racial injustice inherently discriminated on the basis of race.

At the same time as it passed the Civil Rights Act, Congress rechartered the Freedmen's Bureau to provide relief services, health care, schooling, labor mediation, land redistribution, and legal assistance to recently freed black people in the South. Act of July 16, 1866, ch. 200, 14 Stat. 173, 174. But the bureau was effectively abolished after three years, its presence deemed an expensive "humiliation" for white southerners and "an experiment in social policy that did not belong to the America of its day." Eric Foner, *Reconstruction* 142, 168 (2014).

Shortly afterward, the Supreme Court grumbled that it was time for black people to cease being "the special favorite of the laws." *Civil Rights Cases*, 109 U.S. 3, 24–25 (1883). "We certainly hope that the time will come when the colored man in America shall cease to require special attention," agreed the most influential black man of the nineteenth century, Frederick Douglass. Melvin I. Urofsky, *The Affirmative Action Puzzle* 6 (2020). "But that time has not yet come, and is not even at the door." *Id.*

Government-imposed racial subordination

For most of the century that followed the end of Reconstruction, government programs that took race into account almost universally harmed people of color. Redeemed southern states passed Jim Crow laws that subordinated people of color in the name of formal equality. In *Plessy v. Ferguson*, 163 U.S. 537 (1896), the Supreme Court sanctioned this practice over the dissent of Justice John Harlan, who famously objected, "Our Constitution is color-blind, and neither knows nor tolerates classes among citizens." *Id.* at 559 (Harlan, J., dissenting).

While Jim Crow laws grew increasingly repressive after *Plessy*, racial subordination wasn't limited to the South. In 1913, President Woodrow Wilson infamously segregated most federal civil service positions so that white employees around the country would never have to work under black supervisors. A. Scott Berg, *Wilson* 409 (2013). And in the 1930s, when the New Deal Congress enacted social welfare programs that launched millions of Americans into the middle class, it authorized the programs' administrators to exclude people of color. *See* Ira Katznelson, *When Affirmative Action Was White* 33–34 (2005).

For instance, the G.I. Bill of 1944, Pub. L. No. 78–346, 58 Stat. 284, was "arguably the most massive affirmative action program in U.S. history." Urofsky, *supra*, at 23–24. It provided soldiers returning home from World War II with a variety of critical benefits, including small-business loans, private-sector hiring preferences, educational expenses, and low-interest home loans. But, as historian Melvin Urofsky wrote, "[b]ecause local white officials directed the programs, many black veterans did not benefit. Of the first sixty-seven thousand mortgages insured by the G.I. Bill, for example, fewer than a hundred had been taken out by nonwhites. In addition, many banks and mortgage companies simply refused loans to black applicants." *Id.* at 24. Along with similar laws, the G.I. Bill widened racial gaps in wealth and education that persisted across generations. Katznelson, *supra*, at 161–65.

Government action to address racial subordination

One of the principal goals of civil rights activists like Thurgood Marshall was not only the desegregation of schools and universities but also equal access to the same public- and private-sector jobs that white men were receiving. The federal government responded to the activists' demands slowly. In 1940, President Franklin D. Roosevelt issued an executive order effectively reversing the Wilson administration's segregation policy by prohibiting racial discrimination among federal agencies. *See* Exec. Order No. 8587 (1940). But this order was not enforced—leading A. Phillip Randolph, the leader of the country's largest black union, to threaten a massive march on the capital for equitable participation in federal jobs and contracts. Roosevelt capitulated by issuing a second executive order that declared, "There shall be no discrimination in the employment of workers in defense industries and in Government, because of race, creed, color, or national origin." Exec. Order No. 8802 (1941). But existing, white-dominated labor unions effectively neutralized this order by claiming seniority benefits, thereby concentrating new black hires in low-paying, unskilled jobs. Urofsky, *supra*, at 16–17.

Roosevelt's successors nevertheless built on his second order with increasingly assertive calls for private-sector employers with federal contracts to provide people of color with an equal opportunity to work in all jobs. In 1946, President Harry Truman commissioned the President's Committee on Civil Rights to investigate, among other things, racial discrimination in employment. Exec. Order No. 9808, 11 Fed. Reg. 14,153 (Dec. 5, 1946). On the basis of the committee's landmark 1947 report, *To Secure These Rights*, Truman ordered the immediate desegregation of the U.S. armed forces and federal civil service. Exec. Order Nos. 9980, 9981, 13 Fed. Reg. 4311, 4313 (Jul. 26, 1948). President Dwight D. Eisenhower continued this policy through his own administration. Exec. Order No. 10479, 18 Fed. Reg. 4899 (Aug. 13, 1953). And when President John F. Kennedy assumed office in 1961, he issued an order creating a similar committee, chaired by Vice President Lyndon Johnson, "to promote and ensure equal opportunity for all qualified persons . . . employed or seeking employment with the Federal Government and on government contracts." Exec. Order No. 10925, 26 Fed. Reg. 1977 (Mar. 6, 1961). In a phrase that would soon become pervasive, Kennedy's order declared that all future government contracts would require employers to "take *affirmative action* to ensure that applicants are employed, and that employees are treated during employment, without regard to their race, creed, color, or national origin." *Id.* (emphasis added).

When Lyndon Johnson became president, he pushed for and signed into law the Civil Rights Act of 1964, which prohibited employment discrimination on the basis of "race, color, religion, sex, or national origin." Pub. L. No. 88–352, 78 Stat. 241, 243. He hoped that the act would address persistent inequalities in access to well-paying jobs. At the time, only 8 percent of black families had an annual income of over $12,000, compared to 24 percent of white families. On the other end of the income spectrum, 57 percent of black families had an annual income of less than $5,000, compared to 25 percent of white families. Urofsky, *supra*, at 38. Civil rights activists such as James Farmer of the Congress of Racial Equality demanded that the federal government address this inequality by instituting "compensatory preferential hiring," where federal contractors would be obligated to hire and promote people of color to high-paying positions regardless of their seniority. *Id.* at 31. Johnson agreed but advised, "[D]on't call it compensatory. Call it 'affirmative action.' It's moving the nation forward! It is going out of our way to bring minorities in that have been excluded! That is positive affirmative action!" *Id.* Shortly afterward, the president reaffirmed that federal contractors must take "affirmative action" to ensure that all job applicants and employees, regardless of their race or sex, have an equal opportunity to succeed in the workplace. Exec. Order No. 11246, 30 Fed. Reg. 12,319 (Sep. 24, 1965).

When the Equal Employment Opportunity Commission (EEOC) enforced the president's order, it threatened to terminate federal contracts with employers in which women or people of color were underrepresented relative to their population in the workforce. Urofsky, *supra*, at 75–80. On the insistence of the EEOC, private employers that depended on federal contracts adopted affirmative-action plans with specific hiring and promotion targets. These plans resulted in millions of women and people of color ascending to positions from which they had long been excluded. *Id.* at 113. In 1972, for example, after the EEOC began investigating sex discrimination among universities with federal contracts, Columbia Law School hired its first tenured female professor, Ruth Bader Ginsburg. *See* Jane Sherron De Hart, *Ruth Bader Ginsburg* 137–39 (2018).

Opposition to affirmative action

As with the earlier Civil Rights Act of 1866, these antidiscrimination and preferential hiring programs were assailed as discriminatory against white men. *See, e.g.*, Nathan Glazer, *Affirmative Discrimination* 220 (1975). James J. Kilpatrick, one of the champions of "massive resistance," an anti-desegregation policy in Virginia, condemned the Civil Rights Act of 1964 by arguing that "the Negro race, as a race, is in fact an inferior race." Urofsky, *supra*, at 198. But as time passed, Kilpatrick and other critics of the act began to selectively quote Harlan's dissent in *Plessy*, in which the justice wrote that the Constitution was "color-blind." Kilpatrick found this facially neutral criticism of race- and sex-conscious proposals to be an effective indictment of the proposals while ignoring the injustices that led to them. By the mid-1970s, Kilpatrick began saying that "if it is wrong to discriminate by reason of race or sex, well, then, it is wrong to discriminate by reason of race or sex." *Id.* at 198–99.

The proponents of affirmative action anticipated this criticism. "Whenever this issue of compensatory or preferential treatment for the Negro is raised, some of our friends recoil in horror," wrote Rev. Martin Luther King Jr. in 1964. *Why We Can't Wait* 147 (1964). King acknowledged that the criticism was superficially "reasonable, but it is not realistic. For it is obvious that if a man enters the starting line of a race 300 years after another man, the first would have to perform some incredible feat in order to catch up." *Id.* "This is the next and more profound stage of the battle for civil rights," President Johnson added in a speech at Howard University. *Public Papers of the Presidents, Lyndon B. Johnson, 1965*, at 636 (1966). "Freedom is not enough. . . . We seek not just freedom but opportunity. We seek not just legal equity but human ability, not just equality as a right and a theory but equality as a fact and as a result." *Id.*

Court rulings on affirmative action

The Supreme Court first considered race-conscious proposals to remedy societal inequalities in the context of desegregating schools. As discussed earlier with regard to massive resistance (section 46.1), federal district courts routinely remedied de jure segregation by ordering school districts to reallocate teachers and students on the basis of race. In *Swann v. Charlotte-Mecklenburg Board of Education*, the Supreme Court affirmed that "[a]wareness of the racial composition of the whole school system is likely to be a useful starting point in shaping a remedy to correct past constitutional violations." 402 U.S. 1, 25 (1971). But the Court added that "[t]he constitutional command to desegregate schools does not mean that every school in every community must always reflect the racial composition of the school system as a whole." *Id.* at 24.

Shortly after *Swann*, lower courts upheld affirmative-action programs mandated by the federal government to desegregate private-sector construction employers. Labor unions in the construction trades had long opposed affirmative action because it conflicted with hiring on the basis of seniority. When President Richard Nixon, a Republican, succeeded Johnson, he saw affirmative action as a wedge issue that could divide the Democratic base. In 1969, his administration threatened to withhold federal contracts from construction contractors in the Philadelphia area unless they set "goals" for hiring members of groups that were underrepresented relative to their population in the workforce. Urofsky, *supra*, at 95–96. The contractors challenged the legality of this "Philadelphia Plan," arguing that the federal government had no authority to hold individual contractors liable for the discrimination of an entire industry. But a court of appeals upheld the plan as a valid remedial program. *Contractors Ass'n of E. Pa. v. Sec'y of Lab.*, 442 F.2d 159, 177 (3d Cir. 1971).

On the basis of the Philadelphia Plan, the federal government issued similar orders around the country, penalizing employers who failed to hire sufficient numbers of women and people of color. The government's biggest victory came in 1973, when the EEOC successfully forced AT&T, the nation's largest private employer, to sign a consent decree in which it promised to hire, train, and promote tens of thousands of women and people of color into high-paying jobs in which the company had long permitted only white men to work. Alice Kessler-Harris, *Out to Work* 333–34 (2003). Although the Supreme Court didn't review this consent decree, it consistently held that governments had an important interest in compensating women "for past economic discrimination . . . [,] [w]hether from overt discrimination or from the socialization process of a male-dominated culture," *Califano v. Webster*, 430 U.S. 313, 318 (1977).

49.1.1

Regents of the University of California v. Bakke

438 U.S. 265 (1978)

Elementary schools and private employers were not the only entities to initiate affirmative-action programs on the insistence of government. The 1970s also saw a nationwide trend in which previously all-male and predominantly white universities—from Harvard University to the University of Virginia—opened their doors to large numbers of women and people of color for the first time.

In 1970, four years after the University of California, Davis, founded its medical school, only 3 percent of its applications came from people of color. At the time, only eight hundred students of color attended medical school anywhere in the United States. Urofsky, *supra*, at 140. To "counter[ ] the effects of societal discrimination" and "obtain[ ] the educational benefits that flow from an ethnically diverse student body," the Davis faculty established a program that gave students of color two paths to admission. *Regents of the Univ. of Cal. v. Bakke*, 438 U.S. 265, 306 (1978).

First, under the "regular admissions procedure," an admissions committee considered all applicants' college grade-point averages, standardized-test scores, letters of recommendation, and similar information; the committee rejected applicants whose grade-point averages fell below 2.5 out of 4.0. *Id.* at 273–74. Second, under a "special admissions program," a separate committee reviewed applications of students who self-identified as "economically and/or educationally disadvantaged" and as members of a "minority group." *Id.* at 274. The school authorized this committee to select 16 students to be admitted as part of the 100 total admitted students.

Allan Bakke, a white man, applied to several medical schools but was rejected by every one. When Bakke found out that U.C. Davis was reserving 16 percent of its seats for a program for which he was racially ineligible, he sued, arguing that the school had a racial quota that violated the Equal Protection Clause and the Civil Rights Act of 1964.

Justice Lewis Powell, writing only for himself, wrote a controlling opinion for a fractured Court in *Regents of the University of California v. Bakke*, 438 U.S. 265 (1978). Four conservative justices agreed with him that the medical school had to admit Bakke, and four liberal justices agreed with him that universities could consider race in some contexts.

■ MR. JUSTICE POWELL announced the judgment of the Court.[1]

This case presents a challenge to the special admissions program of the petitioner, the Medical School of the University of California at Davis, which is

---

[1] **As You Read, Consider:** In *San Antonio Independent School District v. Rodriguez*, 411 U.S. 1 (1973), Justice Lewis Powell declined to apply strict scrutiny to Texas's system of unequally funding schools with local property taxes. One of his explanations was that "the

designed to assure the admission of a specified number of students from certain minority groups. . . .

[II. Title VI of the Civil Rights Act of 1964]

[Because Bakke raised a challenge under Title VI of the Civil Rights Act of 1964, we must first consider whether Title VI imposed a different legal standard than did the Equal Protection Clause. Title VI declares: "No person in the United States shall, on the ground of race, color, or national origin, be excluded from participation in, be denied the benefits of, or be subjected to discrimination under any program or activity receiving Federal financial assistance." Bakke argued that this language should be interpreted to require recipients of federal financial assistance, such as the Medical School, to engage in "colorblind" programs and activities. But the legislative history of the act leads to the conclusion that "Title VI must be held to proscribe only those racial classifications that would violate the Equal Protection Clause." We therefore turn to the Equal Protection Clause next.]

[III. Determining the Standard of Scrutiny]

A

The guarantees of the Fourteenth Amendment extend to all persons. Its language is explicit: "No State shall . . . deny to any person within its jurisdiction the equal protection of the laws." It is settled beyond question that the "rights created by the first section of the Fourteenth Amendment are, by its terms, guaranteed to the individual. The rights established are personal rights," *Shelley* v. *Kraemer, supra,* at 22. The guarantee of equal protection cannot mean one thing when applied to one individual and something else when applied to a person of another color. If both are not accorded the same protection, then it is not equal.

Nevertheless, petitioner argues that the court below erred in applying strict scrutiny to the special admissions program because white males, such as respondent, are not a "discrete and insular minority" requiring extraordinary protection from the majoritarian political process. *Carolene Products Co., supra,* at 152–153, n. 4. This rationale, however, has never been invoked in our decisions as a prerequisite to subjecting racial or ethnic distinctions to strict scrutiny. Nor has this Court held that discreteness and insularity constitute necessary preconditions to a holding that a particular classification is invidious. See, *e. g., Skinner* v. *Oklahoma ex rel. Williamson,* 316 U. S. 535, 541 (1942). These characteristics may be relevant in deciding whether or not to add new types of classifications to the list of "suspect" categories or whether a particular classification survives close examination. See, *e. g., Massachusetts Board of Retirement* v. *Murgia,* 427 U. S. 307 (1976) (age); *San Antonio Indep. School Dist.* v. *Rodriguez,* 411 U. S. 1 (1973) (wealth); *Graham* v. *Richardson,* 403 U. S. 365 (1971) (aliens). Racial and ethnic classifications, however, are subject to stringent examination without regard to these additional characteristics. We declared as much in the first cases explicitly to recognize racial distinctions as suspect: "[A]ll legal restrictions which curtail the civil rights of a single racial group are immediately suspect. That is not to say that all such restrictions are unconstitutional. It is to say that courts must subject them to the most rigid scrutiny." *Korematsu,* 323 U. S., at 216. . . .[2]

---

thrust of the Texas system is affirmative and reformatory and, therefore, should be scrutinized under judicial principles sensitive to the nature of the State's efforts." *Rodriguez,* 411 U.S. at 39. Does he apply similar deference in this case?

2 **Questions:** In *Rodriguez,* Powell wrote that wealth is not a "suspect classification" because poor people are not a "suspect class." 411 U.S. at 28. He wrote that the *Rodriguez* plaintiffs had not been "subjected to such a history of purposeful unequal treatment, or relegated to such a position of political powerlessness as to command extraordinary protection from the

B

This perception of racial and ethnic distinctions is rooted in our Nation's constitutional and demographic history. The Court's initial view of the Fourteenth Amendment was that its "one pervading purpose" was "the freedom of the slave race. . . ." *Slaughter-House Cases,* 16 Wall. 36, 71 (1873). The Equal Protection Clause, however, was "[v]irtually strangled in infancy by post-civil-war judicial reactionism." It was relegated to decades of relative desuetude while the Due Process Clause of the Fourteenth Amendment, after a short germinal period, flourished as a cornerstone in the Court's defense of property and liberty of contract. See, *e. g., Mugler* v. *Kansas,* 123 U. S. 623, 661 (1887); *Lochner* v. *New York,* 198 U. S. 45 (1905). In that cause, the Fourteenth Amendment's "one pervading purpose" was displaced. See, *e. g., Plessy* v. *Ferguson,* 163 U. S. 537 (1896). It was only as the era of substantive due process came to a close, see, *e. g., West Coast Hotel Co.* v. *Parrish,* 300 U. S. 379 (1937), that the Equal Protection Clause began to attain a genuine measure of vitality. . . .

By that time it was no longer possible to peg the guarantees of the Fourteenth Amendment to the struggle for equality of one racial minority. During the dormancy of the Equal Protection Clause, the United States had become a Nation of minorities. . . . As the Nation filled with the stock of many lands, the reach of the Clause was gradually extended to all ethnic groups seeking protection from official discrimination. . . . The guarantees of equal protection, said the Court in *Yick Wo,* "are universal in their application, to all persons within the territorial jurisdiction, without regard to any differences of race, of color, or of nationality. . . ."

Petitioner urges us to adopt for the first time a more restrictive view of the Equal Protection Clause and hold that discrimination against members of the white "majority" cannot be suspect if its purpose can be characterized as "benign." The clock of our liberties, however, cannot be turned back to 1868. *Brown, supra,* at 492. It is far too late to argue that the guarantee of equal protection to *all* persons permits the recognition of special wards entitled to a degree of protection greater than that accorded others. "The Fourteenth Amendment is not directed solely against discrimination due to a 'two-class theory'—that is, based upon differences between 'white' and Negro." *Hernandez,* 347 U. S., at 478.

Once the artificial line of a "two-class theory" of the Fourteenth Amendment is put aside, the difficulties entailed in varying the level of judicial review according to a perceived "preferred" status of a particular racial or ethnic minority are intractable. The concepts of "majority" and "minority" necessarily reflect temporary arrangements and political judgments. . . . Courts would be asked to evaluate the extent of the prejudice and consequent harm suffered by various minority groups. Those whose societal injury is thought to exceed some arbitrary level of tolerability then would be entitled to preferential classifications at the expense of individuals belonging to other groups. . . . The kind of variable sociological and political analysis necessary to produce such rankings simply does not lie within the judicial competence. . . .[3]

---

majoritarian political process." *Id.* at 28. In other words, he reserved strict scrutiny for legislation that he would not expect the political process alone to repeal if it were unreasonable.

In this case, what justifies applying strict scrutiny to a law that allegedly discriminates against white men? Is there any logic behind his choices to focus on suspect classes (as in *Rodriguez*) versus suspect classifications (as here)?

[3] **Questions:** To the extent that this sort of analysis requires "political judgments," why doesn't Powell defer to political institutions regarding the need for affirmative-action programs? The alternative to this sort of "sociological and political analysis" is a categorical rule that treats all invocations of race as presumptively unconstitutional. Is such formalism superior to *Plessy*

Moreover, there are serious problems of justice connected with the idea of preference itself. First, it may not always be clear that a so-called preference is in fact benign. Courts may be asked to validate burdens imposed upon individual members of a particular group in order to advance the group's general interest. Nothing in the Constitution supports the notion that individuals may be asked to suffer otherwise impermissible burdens in order to enhance the societal standing of their ethnic groups. Second, preferential programs may only reinforce common stereotypes holding that certain groups are unable to achieve success without special protection based on a factor having no relationship to individual worth. Third, there is a measure of inequity in forcing innocent persons in respondent's position to bear the burdens of redressing grievances not of their making. . . .

C

Petitioner contends that on several occasions this Court has approved preferential classifications without applying the most exacting scrutiny. Most of the cases upon which petitioner relies are drawn from three areas: school desegregation, employment discrimination, and sex discrimination. Each of the cases cited presented a situation materially different from the facts of this case.

The school desegregation cases are inapposite. Each involved remedies for clearly determined constitutional violations. *E. g., Swann* v. *Charlotte-Mecklenburg Board of Education,* 402 U. S. 1 (1971). Racial classifications thus were designed as remedies for the vindication of constitutional entitlement. Moreover, the scope of the remedies was not permitted to exceed the extent of the violations. *E. g., Milliken* v. *Bradley,* 418 U. S. 717 (1974). Here, there was no judicial determination of constitutional violation as a predicate for the formulation of a remedial classification.

The employment discrimination cases also do not advance petitioner's cause. . . . The Courts of Appeals have fashioned various types of racial preferences as remedies for constitutional or statutory violations resulting in identified, race-based injuries to individuals held entitled to the preference. . . . *E. g., Contractors Association of Eastern Pennsylvania* v. *Secretary of Labor,* 442 F. 2d 159 (CA3 1971). But we have never approved preferential classifications in the absence of proved constitutional or statutory violations.

Nor is petitioner's view as to the applicable standard supported by the fact that gender-based classifications are not subjected to this level of scrutiny. *E. g., Craig* v. *Boren,* 429 U. S. 190, 211 n. (1976). Gender-based distinctions are less likely to create the analytical and practical problems present in preferential programs premised on racial or ethnic criteria. With respect to gender there are only two possible classifications. The incidence of the burdens imposed by preferential classifications is clear. There are no rival groups which can claim that they, too, are entitled to preferential treatment. . . . More importantly, the perception of racial classifications as inherently odious stems from a lengthy and tragic history that gender-based classifications do not share. . . .[4]

[IV. Determining Which Interests Are Compelling]

We have held that in order to justify the use of a suspect classification, a State must show that its [interest is compelling] . . . and that its use of the classification is

---

v. Ferguson, in which the Court refused to analyze how "separate but equal" was understood in context?

[4] **Questions:** Setting aside Powell's declaration that there are only two genders, are you persuaded by his explanation as to why courts should defer to sex-based affirmative-action programs even if they skeptically scrutinize race-based affirmative-action programs? If the admission slots at issue in this case were reserved for women rather than for people of color, does it make sense to apply intermediate scrutiny rather than strict scrutiny?

"necessary . . . [to] the safeguarding of its interest." [See] *McLaughlin* v. *Florida,* 379 U. S. 184, 196 (1964). The special admissions program purports to serve the purposes of: (i) "reducing the historic deficit of traditionally disfavored minorities in medical schools and in the medical profession," (ii) countering the effects of societal discrimination; (iii) increasing the number of physicians who will practice in communities currently underserved; and (iv) obtaining the educational benefits that flow from an ethnically diverse student body. It is necessary to decide which, if any, of these purposes is substantial enough to support the use of a suspect classification.

A

If petitioner's purpose is to assure within its student body some specified percentage of a particular group merely because of its race or ethnic origin, such a preferential purpose must be rejected not as insubstantial but as facially invalid. Preferring members of any one group for no reason other than race or ethnic origin is discrimination for its own sake. This the Constitution forbids. *E. g., Brown* v. *Board of Education,* 347 U. S. 483 (1954).

B

The State certainly has a legitimate and substantial interest in ameliorating . . . the disabling effects of identified discrimination. The line of school desegregation cases, commencing with *Brown,* attests to the importance of this state goal and the commitment of the judiciary to affirm all lawful means toward its attainment. In the school cases, the States were required by court order to redress the wrongs worked by specific instances of racial discrimination. That goal was far more focused than the remedying of the effects of "societal discrimination," an amorphous concept of injury that may be ageless in its reach into the past.

We have never approved a classification that aids persons perceived as members of relatively victimized groups at the expense of other innocent individuals in the absence of judicial, legislative, or administrative findings of constitutional or statutory violations. See, *e. g., South Carolina* v. *Katzenbach,* 383 U. S. 301 (1966). After such findings have been made, the governmental interest in preferring members of the injured groups at the expense of others is substantial, since the legal rights of the victims must be vindicated. In such a case, the extent of the injury and the consequent remedy will have been judicially, legislatively, or administrative[ly] defined. . . . Without such findings of constitutional or statutory violations, it cannot be said that the government has any greater interest in helping one individual than in refraining from harming another. Thus, the government has no compelling justification for inflicting such harm.[5]

Petitioner does not purport to have made, and is in no position to make, such findings. Its broad mission is education, not the formulation of any legislative policy or the adjudication of particular claims of illegality. . . . Before relying upon these sorts of findings in establishing a racial classification, a governmental body must have the authority and capability to establish, in the record, that the classification is responsive to identified discrimination. . . .

---

[5] **Question:** Here, Powell writes that a government may not use racial classifications to remedy "societal discrimination" because such a concept is "amorphous" and "may be ageless in its reach into the past." But he distinguishes the Voting Rights Act of 1965, upheld in *South Carolina v. Katzenbach*, by writing that it *is* compelling for a government to use racial classifications to remedy "judicially, legislatively, or administrative[ly] defined . . . constitutional or statutory violations."

How does his fear of remedying societal discrimination compare with the *Civil Rights Cases*, in which the Court prohibited Congress from enacting an antidiscrimination law because there must be some point when black people "cease[ ] to be the special favorite of the laws"? 109 U.S. 3, 25 (1883).

Hence, the purpose of helping certain groups whom the faculty of the Davis Medical School perceived as victims of "societal discrimination" does not justify a classification that imposes disadvantages upon persons like respondent, who bear no responsibility for whatever harm the beneficiaries of the special admissions program are thought to have suffered. To hold otherwise would be to convert a remedy heretofore reserved for violations of legal rights into a privilege that all institutions throughout the Nation could grant at their pleasure to whatever groups are perceived as victims of societal discrimination. . . .

C

Petitioner identifies, as another purpose of its program, improving the delivery of health-care services to communities currently underserved. . . . But there is virtually no evidence in the record indicating that petitioner's special admissions program is either needed or geared to promote that goal. . . .

D

The fourth goal asserted by petitioner is the attainment of a diverse student body. This clearly is a constitutionally permissible goal for an institution of higher education.[6] Academic freedom, though not a specifically enumerated constitutional right, long has been viewed as a special concern of the First Amendment. . . .

The atmosphere of "speculation, experiment and creation"—so essential to the quality of higher education—is widely believed to be promoted by a diverse student body. . . . [I]t is not too much to say that the "nation's future depends upon leaders trained through wide exposure" to the ideas and mores of students as diverse as this Nation of many peoples. . . . Thus, in arguing that its universities must be accorded the right to select those students who will contribute the most to the "robust exchange of ideas," petitioner invokes a countervailing constitutional interest, that of the First Amendment. In this light, petitioner must be viewed as seeking to achieve a goal that is of paramount importance in the fulfillment of its mission. . . .

Physicians serve a heterogeneous population. . . . [A] medical student with a particular background—whether it be ethnic, geographic, culturally advantaged or disadvantaged—may bring to a professional school of medicine experiences, outlooks, and ideas that enrich the training of its student body and better equip its graduates to render with understanding their vital service to humanity. . . .

As the interest of diversity is compelling in the context of a university's admissions program, the question remains whether the program's racial classification is necessary to promote this interest.

[V. Determining Whether the Program Is Necessary or Narrowly Tailored]

It may be assumed that the reservation of a specified number of seats in each class for individuals from the preferred ethnic groups would contribute to the attainment of considerable ethnic diversity in the student body. But petitioner's argument that this is the only effective means of serving the interest of diversity is seriously flawed. . . . The diversity that furthers a compelling state interest encompasses a far broader array of qualifications and characteristics of which racial or ethnic origin is but a single though important element. . . .

The experience of other university admissions programs, which take race into account in achieving the educational diversity valued by the First Amendment,

6 **Questions:** In addition to allowing governments to use racial classifications to remedy specific findings of constitutional violations, Powell adds that a government may use racial classifications to attain "a diverse student body." Why? Is such an interest necessarily consistent with the decades of demand for affirmative-action programs to equitably provide women and people of color with access to previously denied economic opportunities?

demonstrates that the assignment of a fixed number of places to a minority group is not a necessary means toward that end. An illuminating example is found in the Harvard College program:

> "In recent years Harvard College has expanded the concept of diversity to include students from disadvantaged economic, racial and ethnic groups. Harvard College now recruits not only Californians or Louisianans but also blacks and Chicanos and other minority students. . . .
>
> "In practice, this new definition of diversity has meant that race has been a factor in some admission decisions. When the Committee on Admissions reviews the large middle group of applicants who are 'admissible' and deemed capable of doing good work in their courses, the race of an applicant may tip the balance in his favor just as geographic origin or a life spent on a farm may tip the balance in other candidates' cases. A farm boy from Idaho can bring something to Harvard College that a Bostonian cannot offer. Similarly, a black student can usually bring something that a white person cannot offer. . . ." App. to Brief for Columbia University, Harvard University, Stanford University, and the University of Pennsylvania, as *Amici Curiae* 2–3.

In such an admissions program, race or ethnic background may be deemed a "plus" in a particular applicant's file, yet it does not insulate the individual from comparison with all other candidates for the available seats. . . .

This kind of program treats each applicant as an individual in the admissions process. The applicant who loses out on the last available seat to another candidate receiving a "plus" on the basis of ethnic background will not have been foreclosed from all consideration for that seat simply because he was not the right color or had the wrong surname. It would mean only that his combined qualifications, which may have included similar nonobjective factors, did not outweigh those of the other applicant. His qualifications would have been weighed fairly and competitively, and he would have no basis to complain of unequal treatment under the Fourteenth Amendment. . . .

In summary, it is evident that the Davis special admissions program involves the use of an explicit racial classification never before countenanced by this Court. . . . [But] the State has a substantial interest that legitimately may be served by a properly devised admissions program involving the competitive consideration of race and ethnic origin. . . .

■ Opinion of MR. JUSTICE BRENNAN, MR. JUSTICE WHITE, MR. JUSTICE MARSHALL, and MR. JUSTICE BLACKMUN, concurring in the judgment in part and dissenting in part.

The Court today . . . affirms the constitutional power of Federal and State Governments to act affirmatively to achieve equal opportunity for all.[7] The difficulty of the issue presented—whether government may use race-conscious programs to redress the continuing effects of past discrimination—and the mature consideration which each of our Brethren has brought to it have resulted in many opinions, no single one speaking for the Court. But this should not and must not mask the central meaning of today's opinions: Government may take race into account when it acts not to demean or insult any racial group, but to remedy disadvantages cast on minorities by past racial prejudice, at least when appropriate findings have been made

---

[7] **Questions:** At the end of the day, Powell allows universities to use racial classifications as a "plus" in the admissions process in order to achieve a diverse student body. But he was the only justice to join his controlling opinion. What test would these four relatively liberal justices apply to the admissions program at the University of California, Davis? Do you find their analysis more or less persuasive than Powell's analysis?

by judicial, legislative, or administrative bodies with competence to act in this area. . . .

[C]laims that law must be "color-blind" or that the datum of race is no longer relevant to public policy must be seen as aspiration rather than as description of reality. . . . [W]e cannot . . . let color blindness become myopia which masks the reality that many "created equal" have been treated within our lifetimes as inferior both by the law and by their fellow citizens. . . .

[T]his is not a case where racial classifications are "irrelevant and therefore prohibited." *Hirabayashi, supra,* at 100. Nor has anyone suggested that the University's purposes contravene the cardinal principle that racial classifications that stigmatize—because they are drawn on the presumption that one race is inferior to another or because they put the weight of government behind racial hatred and separatism—are invalid without more.

On the other hand, the fact that this case does not fit neatly into our prior analytic framework for race cases does not mean that it should be analyzed by applying the very loose rational-basis standard of review that is the very least that is always applied in equal protection cases. " '[T]he mere recitation of a benign, compensatory purpose is not an automatic shield which protects against any inquiry into the actual purposes underlying a statutory scheme.' " *Califano* v. *Webster,* 430 U. S. 313, 317 (1977). Instead, a number of considerations—developed in gender-discrimination cases but which carry even more force when applied to racial classifications—lead us to conclude that racial classifications designed to further remedial purposes "must serve important governmental objectives and must be substantially related to achievement of those objectives." *Craig* v. *Boren,* 429 U. S. 190, 197 (1976).[8]

First, race, like, "gender-based classifications too often [have] been inexcusably utilized to stereotype and stigmatize politically powerless segments of society." While a carefully tailored statute designed to remedy past discrimination could avoid these vices, we nonetheless have recognized that the line between honest and thoughtful appraisal of the effects of past discrimination and paternalistic stereotyping is not so clear and that a statute based on the latter is patently capable of stigmatizing all women with a badge of inferiority. State programs designed ostensibly to ameliorate the effects of past racial discrimination obviously create the same hazard of stigma, since they may . . . reinforce the views of those who believe that members of racial minorities are inherently incapable of succeeding on their own.

Second, race, like gender and illegitimacy, is an immutable characteristic which its possessors are powerless to escape or set aside. . . . [L]egal burdens should bear some relationship to individual responsibility or wrongdoing, and . . . [advancement] approved by the State should ideally be based on individual merit or achievement, or at the least on factors within the control of an individual. . . .

In sum, because of the significant risk that racial classifications established for ostensibly benign purposes can be misused, causing effects not unlike those created by invidious classifications, it is inappropriate to inquire only whether there is any conceivable basis that might sustain such a classification. Instead, to justify such a classification an important and articulated purpose for its use must be shown. In addition, any statute must be stricken that stigmatizes any group or that singles out

---

[8] **Questions:** The liberal justices spend the next several paragraphs defending the application of intermediate scrutiny to "classifications designed to further remedial purposes." Do they explain how a court is supposed to determine when a classification is "remedial"? What if a black student complains that an affirmative-action program harmfully imposes a "racial stigma" by encouraging white students to assume that all black students are unqualified? *See* Corey Robin, *The Enigma of Clarence Thomas* 56–58 (2019).

those least well represented in the political process to bear the brunt of a benign program. . . .

Davis' articulated purpose of remedying the effects of past societal discrimination is, under our cases, sufficiently important to justify the use of race-conscious admissions programs where there is a sound basis for concluding that minority underrepresentation is substantial and chronic, and that the handicap of past discrimination is impeding access of minorities to the Medical School. . . .

■ MR. JUSTICE BLACKMUN.

[I]t is gratifying to know that the Court at least finds it constitutional for an academic institution to take race and ethnic background into consideration as one factor, among many, in the administration of its admissions program. . . . I suspect that it would be impossible to arrange an affirmative-action program in a racially neutral way and have it successful. To ask that this be so is to demand the impossible. In order to get beyond racism, we must first take account of race. There is no other way. And in order to treat some persons equally, we must treat them differently. We cannot—we dare not—let the Equal Protection Clause perpetuate racial supremacy. . . .[9]

■ MR. JUSTICE STEVENS, with whom THE CHIEF JUSTICE, MR. JUSTICE STEWART, and MR. JUSTICE REHNQUIST join, concurring in the judgment . . . and dissenting in part.

[T]he University's special admissions program violated Title VI of the Civil Rights Act of 1964 by excluding Bakke from the Medical School because of his race. It is therefore our duty to affirm the judgment ordering Bakke admitted to the University. . . .

49.2 THE STANDARD OF REVIEW FOR AFFIRMATIVE ACTION

Regents of the University of California v. Bakke, 438 U.S. 265 (1978), was a disappointing decision for both sides of the emerging debate over affirmative action.

Critics on the right lambasted *Bakke*'s split decision as the expected consequence of abandoning Justice John Harlan's *Plessy v. Ferguson* dissent that the "Constitution is color-blind." *Plessy*, 163 U.S. 537, 559 (1896). In a 1979 essay titled *The Disease as Cure*, Antonin Scalia, then a law professor, wrote that *Bakke* was "an embarrassment to teach. Here, as in some other fields of constitutional law, it is increasingly difficult to pretend to one's students that the decisions of the Supreme Court are tied together by threads of logic and analysis." Antonin Scalia, *The Disease as Cure*, 1979 Wash. Univ. L.Q. 147, 147 (1979). The "disease" that his essay's title referred to was a line from Justice Harry Blackmun's concurrence: "In order to get beyond racism, we must first take account of race." *Bakke*, 438 U.S. at 407. Scalia mocked this line along with

---

[9] **Question:** When the racist firebrand James J. Kilpatrick opposed federal attempts to promote women and black people in workplaces that previously excluded them, he complained that "if it is wrong to discriminate by reason of race or sex, well, then, it is wrong to discriminate by reason of race or sex." Nancy MacLean, *Freedom Is Not Enough* 236 (2006). Justice Harry Blackmun offers an alternative formulation of that aphorism—one based in equality of outcome rather than equality of treatment. Which do you find to be a more persuasive account of "equal protection of the laws"?

Justice Lewis Powell's controlling opinion, which he paraphrased as holding that

> the "compelling" interest at issue in *Bakke* is the enormously important goal of assuring that in medical school ... impressionable youngsters ... [will] work and play with pianists, maybe flute players. . . . And, oh yes, . . . some racial minorities, too. If that is all it takes to overcome the presumption against discrimination by race, we have witnessed an historic trivialization of the Constitution.

Scalia, *supra*, at 147–48.

Proponents of race-conscious remedial policies were no kinder to Powell's opinion. Although Powell held out Harvard's affirmative-action program as a model that other universities and governments could properly follow, Harvard took race into account not for the purpose of remedying societal discrimination but to enhance the educational experience of its predominantly white student body. And while Powell suggested that governments could, in theory, use race to remedy discrimination, his model for such a remedy was *South Carolina* v. *Katzenbach,* 383 U.S. 301 (1966), which upheld the Voting Rights Act of 1965. His opinion therefore suggested that a government could remedy the effects of "identified discrimination" only when an appropriate governmental institution developed a factual record analogous to Congress's legislative hearings in 1965. *Bakke*, 438 U.S. at 309.

Given the 4–1–4 nature of the *Bakke* decision, it is perhaps unsurprising that, over the next decade, the Court was unable to coalesce around a single standard for evaluating affirmative-action programs. *See, e.g., Fullilove v. Klutznick*, 448 U.S. 448, 492 (1980) (3–3–3 decision applying deferential scrutiny to a federal statute that required states and local governments to dedicate 10 percent of federal grants to "minority business enterprises"); *Wygant v. Jackson Bd. of Educ.*, 476 U.S. 267, 276 (1986) (4–1–4 decision applying strict scrutiny to invalidate a school district's attempt to protect teachers of color from layoffs).

By 1995, the Court was applying one rule for *state and local* affirmative-action programs and a different rule for *federal* programs.

For *states and local governments*, the Court applied strict scrutiny to all race-conscious programs. In *City of Richmond v. J. A. Croson Co.*, 488 U.S. 469 (1989)—a case involving an affirmative-action program initiated by the majority-black city council of Richmond, Virginia—Justice Sandra Day O'Connor explained that strict scrutiny was necessary to ensure that race-conscious programs were, in fact, remedial. "Indeed, the purpose of strict scrutiny is to 'smoke out' illegitimate uses of race by assuring that the legislative body is pursuing a goal important enough to warrant use of a highly suspect tool," she wrote. *J. A. Croson*, 488 U.S. at 493–94. The result of this opinion, however, was to apply the same skeptical test to affirmative-action programs that the Court applied to Jim Crow-era miscegenation laws.

For the *federal government*, by contrast, the Court applied intermediate scrutiny to race-conscious programs. In *Metro Broadcasting, Inc. v. FCC*, 497 U.S. 547 (1990), Justice William Brennan explained why Congress deserved more deference than states and local governments in its interpretation of the Constitution. Congress, he wrote, was "a co-equal branch charged by the Constitution with the power to 'provide for the . . . general Welfare of the United States' and 'to enforce, by appropriate legislation,' the equal protection guarantees of the Fourteenth Amendment." *Metro Broad.*, 497 U.S. at 563. Even Powell agreed that Section 5 of the Fourteenth Amendment—along with Congress's Reconstruction-era legislation—confirmed that Congress had broad power to enact race-conscious programs to address societal discrimination. *Fullilove*, 448 U.S. at 509–10 (Powell, J., concurring). Applying this reasoning, the *Metro Broadcasting* Court held that "benign race-conscious measures mandated by Congress . . . are constitutionally permissible to the extent that they serve important governmental objectives within the power of Congress and are substantially related to achievement of those objectives." 497 U.S. at 564–65. In this respect, the 5–4 Court adopted the deferential standard articulated by the liberal justices in *Bakke*.

49.2.1

Adarand Constructors, Inc. v. Peña

515 U.S. 200 (1995)

Metro Broadcasting was the final opinion of Brennan's career. Within two years, he and Justice Thurgood Marshall were replaced by far more conservative justices. In the meantime, Congress continued to enact affirmative-action programs, including one that paid federal contractors to hire subcontractors controlled by "socially and economically disadvantaged individuals." *Adarand Constructors, Inc. v. Peña*, 515 U.S. 200, 204 (1995). Although this language was facially race-neutral, Congress instructed federal contractors to "presume that socially and economically disadvantaged individuals include Black Americans, Hispanic Americans, Native Americans, Asian Pacific Americans, and other minorities." *Id.* at 205.

When a federal contractor in Colorado solicited bids for a subcontract to build guardrails along a new highway, Adarand Constructors submitted the lowest bid. But the contractor selected a higher bid from Gonzales Construction because that company was a "disadvantaged" business and therefore eligible for federal financial incentives. Adarand sued the secretary of transportation, Federico Peña, to challenge these race-based incentives.

The Court in *Adarand Constructors, Inc. v. Peña*, 515 U.S. 200 (1995), found that federal race-based classifications warranted strict scrutiny.

■ JUSTICE O'CONNOR announced the judgment of the Court and delivered an opinion with respect to Parts I, II, III-A, III-B, III-D, and IV. . . .[10]

Petitioner Adarand Constructors, Inc., claims that the Federal Government's practice of giving general contractors on Government projects a financial incentive to hire subcontractors controlled by "socially and economically disadvantaged individuals," and in particular, the Government's use of race-based presumptions in identifying such individuals, violates the equal protection component of the Fifth Amendment's Due Process Clause. . . .

[III-A]

[A]darand's claim arises under the Fifth Amendment to the Constitution, which provides that "No person shall . . . be deprived of life, liberty, or property, without due process of law." . . . Through the 1940's, this Court had routinely taken the view in non-race-related cases that, "[u]nlike the Fourteenth Amendment, the Fifth contains no equal protection clause and it provides no guaranty against discriminatory legislation by Congress." *Detroit Bank* v. *United States,* 317 U. S. 329, 337 (1943). When the Court first faced a Fifth Amendment equal protection challenge to a federal racial classification, it adopted a similar approach, with most unfortunate results. [See] *Hirabayashi* v. *United States,* 320 U. S. 81 (1943). . . .

In *Bolling* v. *Sharpe,* 347 U. S. 497 (1954), the Court for the first time explicitly questioned the existence of any difference between the obligations of the Federal Government and the States to avoid racial classifications. . . . [It] concluded[:] "In view of [the] decision that the Constitution prohibits the states from maintaining racially segregated public schools, it would be unthinkable that the same Constitution would impose a lesser duty on the Federal Government." [*Ibid.*] . . .

Later cases in contexts other than school desegregation did not distinguish between the duties of the States and the Federal Government to avoid racial classifications. [See, e.g.,] *McLaughlin* v. *Florida,* 379 U. S. 184 [(1964) (quoting *Bolling*, *Hirabayashi*, and *Korematsu* v. *United States,* 323 U. S. 214)]. . . . Cases decided after *McLaughlin* continued to treat the equal protection obligations imposed by the Fifth and the Fourteenth Amendments as indistinguishable. . . .

[III-B]

Most of the cases discussed above involved classifications burdening groups that have suffered discrimination in our society. In 1978, the Court confronted the question whether race-based governmental action designed to *benefit* such groups should also be subject to "the most rigid scrutiny." *Regents of Univ. of Cal.* v. *Bakke,* 438 U. S. 265. . . . Justice Powell's opinion announcing the Court's judgment [answered yes]. . . .

Two years after *Bakke,* the Court faced another challenge to remedial race-based action, this time involving action undertaken by the Federal Government. In *Fullilove* v. *Klutznick,* 448 U. S. 448 (1980), the Court upheld Congress' inclusion

---

10 **As You Read, Consider:** Since at least the Civil Rights Act of 1866, Congress has enacted race-conscious remedies for societal discrimination. Even though the Fourteenth Amendment prohibited racial discrimination by states, Section 5 empowered Congress to enforce the amendment's terms. Why, then, does Justice Sandra Day O'Connor think that federal affirmative-action programs must be subject to the same strict scrutiny that the Court applied to state Jim Crow laws?

of a 10% set-aside for minority-owned businesses in the Public Works Employment Act of 1977. As in *Bakke,* there was no opinion for the Court. . . .

The Court's failure to produce a majority opinion in *Bakke* [and] *Fullilove* . . . left unresolved the proper analysis for remedial race-based governmental action. . . . The Court resolved the issue, at least in part, in 1989. *Richmond* v. *J. A. Croson Co.,* 488 U. S. 469 (1989), concerned a city's determination that 30% of its contracting work should go to minority-owned businesses. A majority of the Court in *Croson* held that "the standard of review under the Equal Protection Clause is not dependent on the race of those burdened or benefited by a particular classification," and that the single standard of review for racial classifications should be "strict scrutiny." *Id.,* at 493–494. . . .

With *Croson,* the Court finally agreed that the Fourteenth Amendment requires strict scrutiny of all race-based action by state and local governments. But *Croson* of course had no occasion to declare what standard of review the Fifth Amendment requires for such action taken by the Federal Government. . . .

Despite lingering uncertainty in the details, however, the Court's cases through *Croson* had established three general propositions with respect to governmental racial classifications. First, skepticism: " 'Any preference based on racial or ethnic criteria must necessarily receive a most searching examination.' " *Wygant,* 476 U. S., at 273. . . . Second, consistency: "[T]he standard of review under the Equal Protection Clause is not dependent on the race of those burdened or benefited by a particular classification," *Croson,* 488 U. S., at 494. . . . And third, congruence: "Equal protection analysis in the Fifth Amendment area is the same as that under the Fourteenth Amendment," *Buckley* v. *Valeo,* 424 U. S., at 93. Taken together, these three propositions lead to the conclusion that any person, of whatever race, has the right to demand that any governmental actor subject to the Constitution justify any racial classification subjecting that person to unequal treatment under the strictest judicial scrutiny. . . .

A year later, however, the Court took a surprising turn. *Metro Broadcasting, Inc.* v. *FCC, supra,* involved a Fifth Amendment challenge to two race-based policies of the Federal Communications Commission. . . . [The Court held] that "benign" federal racial classifications need only satisfy intermediate scrutiny, even though *Croson* had recently concluded that such classifications enacted by a State must satisfy strict scrutiny. . . .

Metro Broadcasting departed from prior cases in two significant respects. First, it turned its back on *Croson*'s explanation of why strict scrutiny of all governmental racial classifications is essential:

> "Absent searching judicial inquiry into the justification for such race-based measures, there is simply no way of determining what classifications are 'benign' or 'remedial' and what classifications are in fact motivated by illegitimate notions of racial inferiority or simple racial politics. Indeed, the purpose of strict scrutiny is to 'smoke out' illegitimate uses of race by assuring that the legislative body is pursuing a goal important enough to warrant use of a highly suspect tool. The test also ensures that the means chosen 'fit' this compelling goal so closely that there is little or no possibility that the motive for the classification was illegitimate racial prejudice or stereotype." *Croson, supra,* at 493.

Second, *Metro Broadcasting* squarely rejected one of the three propositions established by the Court's earlier equal protection cases, namely, congruence between the standards applicable to federal and state racial classifications, and in so doing also undermined the other two—skepticism of all racial classifications and consistency of treatment irrespective of the race of the burdened or benefited group. . . .

The three propositions undermined by *Metro Broadcasting* all derive from the basic principle that the Fifth and Fourteenth Amendments to the Constitution protect *persons,* not *groups*. It follows from that principle that all governmental action based on race—a *group* classification long recognized as "in most circumstances irrelevant and therefore prohibited," *Hirabayashi,* 320 U. S., at 100—should be subjected to detailed judicial inquiry to ensure that the *personal* right to equal protection of the laws has not been infringed. . . . [W]e hold today that all racial classifications, imposed by whatever federal, state, or local governmental actor, must be analyzed by a reviewing court under strict scrutiny. In other words, such classifications are constitutional only if they are narrowly tailored measures that further compelling governmental interests. To the extent that *Metro Broadcasting* is inconsistent with that holding, it is overruled. . . .

[III-C]

"Although adherence to precedent is not rigidly required in constitutional cases, any departure from the doctrine of *stare decisis* demands special justification." *Arizona* v. *Rumsey,* 467 U. S. 203, 212 (1984). In deciding whether this case presents such justification, we recall Justice Frankfurter's admonition that "*stare decisis* is a principle of policy and not a mechanical formula of adherence to the latest decision, however recent and questionable, when such adherence involves collision with a prior doctrine more embracing in its scope, intrinsically sounder, and verified by experience." *Helvering* v. *Hallock,* 309 U. S. 106, 119 (1940). Remaining true to an "intrinsically sounder" doctrine established in prior cases better serves the values of *stare decisis* than would following a more recently decided case inconsistent with the decisions that came before it; the latter course would simply compound the recent error and would likely make the unjustified break from previously established doctrine complete. In such a situation, "special justification" exists to depart from the recently decided case. . . .[11]

[III-D]

[W]e think that requiring strict scrutiny is the best way to ensure that courts will consistently give racial classifications that kind of detailed examination, both as to ends and as to means. *Korematsu* demonstrates vividly that even "the most rigid scrutiny" can sometimes fail to detect an illegitimate racial classification. Any retreat from the most searching judicial inquiry can only increase the risk of another such error. . . .

Finally, we wish to dispel the notion that strict scrutiny is "strict in theory, but fatal in fact." *Fullilove, supra,* at 519 (Marshall, J., concurring in judgment). The unhappy persistence of both the practice and the lingering effects of racial discrimination against minority groups in this country is an unfortunate reality, and government is not disqualified from acting in response to it. As recently as 1987, for example, every Justice of this Court agreed that the Alabama Department of Public Safety's "pervasive, systematic, and obstinate discriminatory conduct" justified a narrowly tailored race-based remedy. See *United States* v. *Paradise,* 480 U. S., at 167. When race-based action is necessary to further a compelling interest, such action is within constitutional constraints if it satisfies the "narrow tailoring" test this Court has set out in previous cases.

---

[11] **Question:** Three years before this opinion, in *Planned Parenthood of Southeastern Pennsylvania v. Casey*, O'Connor coauthored an extended explanation of why *stare decisis* compelled the Court to reaffirm the essential holding of *Roe v. Wade*. Why is that explanation inapplicable in this case?

IV

Because our decision today alters the playing field in some important respects, we think it best to remand the case to the lower courts for further consideration in light of the principles we have announced. . . .

■ JUSTICE THOMAS, concurring in part. . . .

I agree with the majority's conclusion that strict scrutiny applies to *all* government classifications based on race. I write separately, however, to express my disagreement with the premise underlying Justice Stevens' . . . dissent[:] that there is a racial paternalism exception to the principle of equal protection. I believe that there is a "moral [and] constitutional equivalence" between laws designed to subjugate a race and those that distribute benefits on the basis of race in order to foster some current notion of equality. Government cannot make us equal; it can only recognize, respect, and protect us as equal before the law. . . .[12]

[T]here can be no doubt that racial paternalism and its unintended consequences can be as poisonous and pernicious as any other form of discrimination. So-called "benign" discrimination teaches many that because of chronic and apparently immutable handicaps, minorities cannot compete with them without their patronizing indulgence. Inevitably, such programs engender attitudes of superiority or, alternatively, provoke resentment among those who believe that they have been wronged by the government's use of race. These programs stamp minorities with a badge of inferiority and may cause them to develop dependencies or to adopt an attitude that they are "entitled" to preferences. . . .

In my mind, government-sponsored racial discrimination based on benign prejudice is just as noxious as discrimination inspired by malicious prejudice. In each instance, it is racial discrimination, plain and simple.

■ JUSTICE STEVENS, with whom JUSTICE GINSBURG joins, dissenting.

Instead of deciding this case in accordance with controlling precedent, the Court today delivers a disconcerting lecture about the evils of governmental racial classifications. For its text the Court has selected three propositions, represented by the bywords "skepticism," "consistency," and "congruence." . . .

The Court's concept of "consistency" assumes that there is no significant difference between a decision by the majority to impose a special burden on the members of a minority race and a decision by the majority to provide a benefit to certain members of that minority notwithstanding its incidental burden on some members of the majority. In my opinion that assumption is untenable. There is no moral or constitutional equivalence between a policy that is designed to perpetuate a caste system and one that seeks to eradicate racial subordination. Invidious discrimination is an engine of oppression, subjugating a disfavored group to enhance or maintain the power of the majority. Remedial race-based preferences reflect the opposite impulse: a desire to foster equality in society. No sensible conception of the Government's constitutional obligation to govern impartially, should ignore this distinction. . . .

---

12 **Questions:** Justice Clarence Thomas—the second black justice in U.S. history after the person he replaced, Thurgood Marshall—supplied the fifth vote in support of this 5–4 opinion overruling *Metro Broadcasting, Inc. v. FCC.* His disagreement with Justice John Stevens is over whether "benign" or "remedial" racial classifications are as pernicious as the racial classification in *Korematsu v. United States*. Does he persuade you that "racial paternalism" is so harmful that it should be presumptively unconstitutional? For example, is Stevens wrong to observe that Marshall was likely nominated as a Supreme Court justice after President Lyndon Johnson evaluated "his nominee's race as a positive factor"?

The consistency that the Court espouses would disregard the difference between a "No Trespassing" sign and a welcome mat. It would treat a Dixiecrat Senator's decision to vote against Thurgood Marshall's confirmation in order to keep African-Americans off the Supreme Court as on a par with President Johnson's evaluation of his nominee's race as a positive factor. It would equate a law that made black citizens ineligible for military service with a program aimed at recruiting black soldiers. An attempt by the majority to exclude members of a minority race from a regulated market is fundamentally different from a subsidy that enables a relatively small group of newcomers to enter that market. . . .

Moreover, the Court may find that its new "consistency" approach to race-based classifications is difficult to square with its insistence upon rigidly separate categories for discrimination against different classes of individuals. For example, as the law currently stands, the Court will apply "intermediate scrutiny" to cases of invidious gender discrimination and "strict scrutiny" to cases of invidious race discrimination, while applying the same standard for benign classifications as for invidious ones. If this remains the law, then today's lecture about "consistency" will produce the anomalous result that the Government can more easily enact affirmative-action programs to remedy discrimination against women than it can enact affirmative-action programs to remedy discrimination against African-Americans—even though the primary purpose of the Equal Protection Clause was to end discrimination against the former slaves. . . .

The Court's concept of "congruence" assumes that there is no significant difference between a decision by the Congress of the United States to adopt an affirmative-action program and such a decision by a State or a municipality. In my opinion that assumption is untenable. . . .

The Fourteenth Amendment directly empowers Congress at the same time it expressly limits the States. This is no accident. It represents our Nation's consensus, achieved after hard experience throughout our sorry history of race relations, that the Federal Government must be the primary defender of racial minorities against the States, some of which may be inclined to oppress such minorities. A rule of "congruence" that ignores a purposeful "incongruity" so fundamental to our system of government is unacceptable. . . .

NOTE: STANDARD OF REVIEW FOR SEX-BASED AFFIRMATIVE-ACTION PROGRAMS

Adarand conclusively established that the Court would evaluate all racial classifications under strict scrutiny—regardless of whether the classification was "subordinating" or "benign." As Justice John Stevens observed in his dissent, however, the Court's emphasis on "consistency" ironically meant that the Court would apply one standard of review for race-based affirmative-action programs (strict scrutiny) and another standard of review for sex-based affirmative-action programs (intermediate scrutiny). 515 U.S. at 247. The Court confirmed Stevens's observation the following year in *United States v. Virginia*, 518 U.S. 515 (1996) (see section 48.2). There, Justice Ruth Bader Ginsburg—who joined Stevens's *Adarand* dissent—wrote that

> "[i]nherent differences" between men and women . . . remain cause for celebration, but not for denigration of the members of either sex or for artificial constraints on an individual's opportunity. Sex classifications may be used to compensate women "for particular

> economic disabilities [they have] suffered," to "promot[e] equal employment opportunity," to advance full development of the talent and capacities of our Nation's people. But such classifications may not be used, as they once were, to create or perpetuate the legal, social, and economic inferiority of women.

Virginia, 518 U.S. at 533–34.

49.3 STRICT SCRUTINY APPLIED TO AFFIRMATIVE ACTION

When the Supreme Court decided *Adarand Constructors, Inc. v. Peña*, 515 U.S. 200, 204 (1995), affirmative action had become one of the major battlegrounds in the so-called culture wars of the 1990s. *See* James Davidson Hunter, *Culture Wars: The Struggle to Define America* 42 (1991). By declaring that it would analyze all race-based affirmative-action programs using strict scrutiny—the test the Court used for presumptively unconstitutional laws—the Court gave conservative critics of affirmative action a new weapon to discredit the practice. Although Justice Sandra Day O'Connor tried to "dispel the notion that strict scrutiny is 'strict in theory, but fatal in fact,' the only racial classifications that had ever survived strict scrutiny were the products of federal court orders or the World War II-era decisions upholding the internment of Japanese Americans. In the face of this antagonism, President Bill Clinton ambivalently defended affirmative action, asking the American people to "mend it, don't end it." *See Excerpts from Clinton Talk on Affirmative Action*, N.Y. Times, July 20, 1995, at B10.

Ballot initiative to address affirmative action

The Republican governor of California, Pete Wilson, denounced the president's entreaty as "trying to keep in place a system that will contain the virus that threatens to tribalize America, and to divide us." Melvin I. Urofsky, *The Affirmative Action Puzzle* 315 (2020). On the governor's order, the regents of the University of California met a month after *Adarand* and adopted a policy, "Ensuring Equal Treatment of Admissions," that formally prohibited the university from considering race, sex, religion, or ethnicity in its admissions decisions. *Id.* at 315–16.

One year later, opponents of affirmative action in California sought to constitutionalize this policy. A ballot initiative, Proposition 209 (Prop 209), proposed that "[t]he state shall not discriminate against, or grant preferential treatment to, any individual or group on the basis of race, sex, color, ethnicity, or national origin in the operation of public employment, public education, or public contracting." In the 1996 elections, California voters adopted Prop 209 by a margin of 55 to 45 percent. *Id.* at 317–319. Prop 209's immediate effect was to discourage black and Hispanic students from applying to the University of California's various schools; in 1997, only one of the seventeen black students admitted to the law school at Berkeley chose to attend. *Id.* at

320. Its long-term effect is harder to gauge. Although black enrollment in the University of California system hovered around 4 percent between 1997 and 2010, white enrollment dropped from 40 percent to 27 percent, and Hispanic and Asian-American enrollment increased to 21 percent and 40 percent, respectively. *Id.*

Litigation to address affirmative action

Where activists in California ended affirmative action at the ballot, activists in Texas (and, later, Michigan) turned to the courts.

In 1992, the University of Texas School of Law rejected the application of a white woman named Cheryl Hopwood, whose combined standardized-test scores and grade-point average were higher than those of most of the admitted black and Hispanic students. Hopwood sued, complaining that "the law school discriminated against me. It gave my spot to a minority student because I happened to be white." Nat Hentoff, *Cheryl Hopwood vs. State of Texas*, Vill. Voice, Nov. 25, 1997, at 22.

In *Hopwood v. Texas*, 78 F.3d 932 (5th Cir. 1996), the U.S. Court of Appeals for the Fifth Circuit applied strict scrutiny to strike down the law school's admission policy—the first invalidation of a university's affirmative-action program since *Regents of the University of California v. Bakke*, 438 U.S. 265 (1978).

The Supreme Court declined to review the decision, in part because the university announced that it would abandon its consideration of race in admissions. *Texas v. Hopwood*, 518 U.S. 1033 (1996) (Ginsburg, J., respecting the denial of certiorari).

Study of university affirmative-action policies

Sensing that affirmative action was in trouble, a former president of Princeton, William Bowen, and a former president of Harvard, Derek Bok, published a landmark study of university affirmative-action policies: *The Shape of the River: Long-Term Consequences of Considering Race in College and University Admissions*. William Bowen & Derek Bok, *The Shape of the River: Long-Term Consequences of Considering Race in College and University Admissions* (1998). The book observed that most universities now embraced Justice Lewis Powell's "diversity" rationale for affirmative action. Rather than seek to remedy past discrimination, universities now considered race and sex in their admissions policies because of the educational and societal benefits of assembling a student body of diverse backgrounds. *Id.* at 8. The central finding of the book was that there was no conflict between admitting a diverse student body and admitting the most meritorious students. Instead, Bowen and Bok found that students of color who entered elite institutions with lower grade-point averages and test scores than white students were, in fact, more likely than their white classmates to earn advanced degrees, participate in civic activities, and receive higher salaries after graduation. *Id.* at 109,

156, 370. The authors also found that employers at the highest levels of business and government craved a diverse pool of future leaders to help them navigate a multicultural society. *Id.* at 11–12. In other words, the students who were the most "qualified" to advance universities' public missions were not necessarily the students with the highest test scores.

49.3.1

Grutter v. Bollinger

539 U.S. 306 (2003)

The Shape of the River marked a profound shift in the debate over affirmative action: five years later, as two major affirmative-action cases reached the Supreme Court, the justices cited *The Shape of the River* as evidence that student body diversity was a compelling interest that could still survive strict scrutiny. The two cases arose out of the University of Michigan: *Grutter v. Bollinger*, 539 U.S. 306 (2003), and *Gratz v. Bollinger*, 539 U.S. 244 (2003).

Grutter—featured below—involved Barbara Grutter (pronounced GROO-ter), a white applicant who was rejected from the university's law school. The law school's race-conscious admissions program survived strict scrutiny based on the Court's finding that student body diversity was a compelling interest.

In contrast, in *Gratz*—discussed in the note after the *Grutter* case—the Court found that the strong favoritism toward racial and ethnic minorities in a point-based admissions policy for matriculating undergrads at the University of Michigan lacked the individualized decision making necessary to survive the means prong of strict scrutiny's means-ends test.

■ JUSTICE O'CONNOR delivered the opinion of the Court.[13]

This case requires us to decide whether the use of race as a factor in student admissions by the University of Michigan Law School . . . is unlawful. . . .

The Law School ranks among the Nation's top law schools. It receives more than 3,500 applications each year for a class of around 350 students. Seeking to "admit a group of students who individually and collectively are among the most capable," the Law School looks for individuals with "substantial promise for success in law school" and "a strong likelihood of succeeding in the practice of law and contributing in diverse ways to the well-being of others." . . .

In reviewing an applicant's file, admissions officials must consider the applicant's undergraduate grade point average (GPA) and Law School Admission Test (LSAT) score because they are important (if imperfect) predictors of academic success in law school. The policy stresses that "no applicant should be admitted unless we expect that applicant to do well enough to graduate with no serious academic problems." . . . [But] the policy requires admissions officials to look beyond grades

---

13 **As You Read, Consider:** Justice Sandra Day O'Connor applies strict scrutiny to the University of Michigan Law School's race-conscious admissions program, yet she upholds the program. Why? What, precisely, does she find compelling about Michigan's interest in obtaining the benefits of student-body diversity?

and test scores to other criteria that are important to the Law School's educational objectives. So-called " 'soft' variables" such as "the enthusiasm of recommenders, the quality of the undergraduate institution, the quality of the applicant's essay, and the areas and difficulty of undergraduate course selection" are all brought to bear in assessing an "applicant's likely contributions to the intellectual and social life of the institution." . . .

The policy does not restrict the types of diversity contributions eligible for "substantial weight" in the admissions process, but instead recognizes "many possible bases for diversity admissions." The policy does, however, reaffirm the Law School's longstanding commitment to . . . "racial and ethnic diversity with special reference to the inclusion of students from groups which have been historically discriminated against. . . .["] By enrolling a " 'critical mass' of [underrepresented] minority students," the Law School seeks to "ensur[e] their ability to make unique contributions to the character of the Law School."

We have held that all racial classifications imposed by government "must be analyzed by a reviewing court under strict scrutiny." *Ibid.* This means that such classifications are constitutional only if they are narrowly tailored to further compelling governmental interests. . . .

[III-A Determining Which Interests Are Compelling]

With these principles in mind, we turn to the question whether the Law School's use of race is justified by a compelling state interest. Before this Court, as they have throughout this litigation, respondents assert only one justification for their use of race in the admissions process: obtaining "the educational benefits that flow from a diverse student body." . . .

As part of its goal of "assembling a class that is both exceptionally academically qualified and broadly diverse," the Law School seeks to "enroll a 'critical mass' of minority students." The Law School's interest is not simply "to assure within its student body some specified percentage of a particular group merely because of its race or ethnic origin." *Bakke,* 438 U. S., at 307 (opinion of Powell, J.). That would amount to outright racial balancing, which is patently unconstitutional. *Ibid.* Rather, the Law School's concept of critical mass is defined by reference to the educational benefits that diversity is designed to produce.

These benefits are substantial. As the District Court emphasized, the Law School's admissions policy promotes "cross-racial understanding," helps to break down racial stereotypes, and "enables [students] to better understand persons of different races." These benefits are "important and laudable," because "classroom discussion is livelier, more spirited, and simply more enlightening and interesting" when the students have "the greatest possible variety of backgrounds." *Id.,* at 246a, 244a.

The Law School's claim of a compelling interest is further bolstered by its *amici,* who point to the educational benefits that flow from student body diversity. In addition to the expert studies and reports entered into evidence at trial, numerous studies show that student body diversity promotes learning outcomes, and "better prepares students for an increasingly diverse workforce and society, and better prepares them as professionals." [S]ee, *e. g.,* W. Bowen & D. Bok, The Shape of the River (1998). . . .

These benefits are not theoretical but real, as major American businesses have made clear that the skills needed in today's increasingly global marketplace can only be developed through exposure to widely diverse people, cultures, ideas, and viewpoints. Brief for 3M et al. as *Amici Curiae* 5; Brief for General Motors Corp. as *Amicus Curiae* 3–4. What is more, high-ranking retired officers and civilian leaders of the United States military assert that, "[b]ased on [their] decades of experience," a "highly qualified, racially diverse officer corps . . . is essential to the military's ability to fulfill its principle mission to provide national security." Brief for Julius W. Becton, Jr., et al. as *Amici Curiae* 5. The primary sources for the Nation's officer corps are the service academies and the Reserve Officers Training Corps (ROTC), the latter comprising students already admitted to participating colleges and universities. *Ibid.* At present, "the military cannot achieve an officer corps that is *both* highly qualified *and* racially diverse unless the service academies and the ROTC used limited race-conscious recruiting and admissions policies." *Ibid.*(emphasis in original). . . . We agree that "[i]t requires only a small step from this analysis to conclude that our country's other most selective institutions must remain both diverse and selective." *Ibid.* . . .

[U]niversities, and in particular, law schools, represent the training ground for a large number of our Nation's leaders. Individuals with law degrees occupy roughly half the state governorships, more than half the seats in the United States Senate, and more than a third of the seats in the United States House of Representatives. The pattern is even more striking when it comes to highly selective law schools. A handful of these schools accounts for 25 of the 100 United States Senators, 74 United States Courts of Appeals judges, and nearly 200 of the more than 600 United States District Court judges.

In order to cultivate a set of leaders with legitimacy in the eyes of the citizenry, it is necessary that the path to leadership be visibly open to talented and qualified individuals of every race and ethnicity. All members of our heterogeneous society must have confidence in the openness and integrity of the educational institutions that provide this training. As we have recognized, law schools "cannot be effective in isolation from the individuals and institutions with which the law interacts." See *Sweatt* v. *Painter, supra,* at 634. Access to legal education (and thus the legal profession) must be inclusive of talented and qualified individuals of every race and ethnicity, so that all members of our heterogeneous society may participate in the educational institutions that provide the training and education necessary to succeed in America.[14]

The Law School does not premise its need for critical mass on "any belief that minority students always (or even consistently) express some characteristic minority viewpoint on any issue." To the contrary, diminishing the force of such stereotypes is both a crucial part of the Law School's mission, and one that it cannot accomplish with only token numbers of minority students. Just as growing up in a particular region or having particular professional experiences is likely to affect an individual's views, so too is one's own, unique experience of being a racial minority in a society, like our own, in which race unfortunately still matters. The Law School has determined, based on its experience and expertise, that a "critical mass" of underrepresented minorities is necessary to further its compelling interest in securing the educational benefits of a diverse student body.

---

14 **Questions:** In *Planned Parenthood of Southeastern Pennsylvania v. Casey*, O'Connor's coauthored opinion emphasized that the Supreme Court draws its power from its legitimacy: "a product of substance and perception that shows itself in the people's acceptance of the judiciary as fit to determine what the Nation's law means and to declare what it demands." 505 U.S. 833, 865 (1992). Here, she applies a similar analysis to the legitimacy of what Justice Clarence Thomas calls "the country's leadership caste." Do you agree with her that the State of Michigan has a compelling interest in helping to ensure that the nation's leadership appears diverse "in the eyes of the citizenry"? Is such an interest distinct from the interest in remedying "societal discrimination," which was rejected in *Regents of the University of California v. Bakke*?

[III-B Determining Whether the Program Is Necessary or Narrowly Tailored]

Even in the limited circumstance when drawing racial distinctions is permissible to further a compelling state interest, . . . "[t]he means chosen to accomplish the [government's] asserted purpose must be specifically and narrowly framed to accomplish that purpose." *Shaw* v. *Hunt,* 517 U. S. 899, 908 (1996). . . .

To be narrowly tailored, a race-conscious admissions program cannot use a quota system—it cannot "insulat[e] each category of applicants with certain desired qualifications from competition with all other applicants." *Bakke,* 438 U. S., at 315. Instead, a university may consider race or ethnicity only as a " 'plus' in a particular applicant's file," . . .

We are satisfied that the Law School's admissions program, like the Harvard plan described by Justice Powell, does not operate as a quota. Properly understood, a "quota" is a program in which a certain fixed number or proportion of opportunities are "reserved exclusively for certain minority groups." *Richmond* v. *J. A. Croson Co., supra,* at 496 . . . . In contrast, . . . the Law School engages in a highly individualized, holistic review of each applicant's file, giving serious consideration to all the ways an applicant might contribute to a diverse educational environment. . . . Unlike the program at issue in *Gratz* v. *Bollinger, ante,* p. 244, the Law School awards no mechanical, predetermined diversity "bonuses" based on race or ethnicity. . . .

Petitioner and the United States argue that the Law School's plan is not narrowly tailored because race-neutral means exist to obtain the educational benefits of student body diversity that the Law School seeks. We disagree. Narrow tailoring does not require exhaustion of every conceivable race-neutral alternative. Nor does it require a university to choose between maintaining a reputation for excellence or fulfilling a commitment to provide educational opportunities to members of all racial groups. Narrow tailoring does, however, require serious, good faith consideration of workable race-neutral alternatives that will achieve the diversity the university seeks.

We agree with the Court of Appeals that the Law School sufficiently considered workable race-neutral alternatives. The District Court took the Law School to task for failing to consider race-neutral alternatives such as "using a lottery system" or "decreasing the emphasis for all applicants on undergraduate GPA and LSAT scores." App. to Pet. for Cert. 251a. But these alternatives would require a dramatic sacrifice of diversity, the academic quality of all admitted students, or both.

The Law School's current admissions program considers race as one factor among many, in an effort to assemble a student body that is diverse in ways broader than race. Because a lottery would make that kind of nuanced judgment impossible, it would effectively sacrifice all other educational values, not to mention every other kind of diversity. So too with the suggestion that the Law School simply lower admissions standards for all students, a drastic remedy that would require the Law School to become a much different institution and sacrifice a vital component of its educational mission. . . .

We are mindful, however, that "[a] core purpose of the Fourteenth Amendment was to do away with all governmentally imposed discrimination based on race." Accordingly, race-conscious admissions policies must be limited in time. This requirement reflects that racial classifications, however compelling their goals, are potentially so dangerous that they may be employed no more broadly than the interest demands. Enshrining a permanent justification for racial preferences would offend this fundamental equal protection principle. . . .

It has been 25 years since Justice Powell first approved the use of race to further an interest in student body diversity in the context of public higher education. Since that time, the number of minority applicants with high grades and test scores has indeed increased. We expect that 25 years from now, the use of racial preferences will no longer be necessary to further the interest approved today. . . .[15]

■ JUSTICE THOMAS, . . . dissenting. . . .

Frederick Douglass, speaking to a group of abolitionists almost 140 years ago, delivered a message lost on today's majority:

> "[I]n regard to the colored people, there is always more that is benevolent, I perceive, than just, manifested towards us. What I ask for the negro is not benevolence, not pity, not sympathy, but simply *justice*. The American people have always been anxious to know what they shall do with us. . . . I have had but one answer from the beginning. Do nothing with us! Your doing with us has already played the mischief with us. . . . [I]f the negro cannot stand on his own legs, let him fall. . . . All I ask is, give him a chance to stand on his own legs! Let him alone! . . . [Y]our interference is doing him positive injury." What the Black Man Wants: An Address Delivered in Boston, Massachusetts, on 26 January 1865, reprinted in 4 The Frederick Douglass Papers 59, 68 (J. Blassingame & J. McKivigan eds. 1991).

Like Douglass, I believe blacks can achieve in every avenue of American life without the meddling of university administrators. . . . No one would argue that a university could set up a lower general admissions standard and then impose heightened requirements only on black applicants. Similarly, a university may not maintain a high admissions standard and grant exemptions to favored races. The Law School, of its own choosing, and for its own purposes, maintains an exclusionary admissions system that it knows produces racially disproportionate results. Racial discrimination is not a permissible solution to the self-inflicted wounds of this elitist admissions policy. . . .

[T]he Law School's racial discrimination . . . stamp[s] minorities with a badge of inferiority. . . . [I]t is uncontested that each year, the Law School admits a handful of blacks who would be admitted in the absence of racial discrimination. Who can differentiate between those who belong and those who do not? The majority of blacks are admitted to the Law School because of discrimination, and because of this policy all are tarred as undeserving. . . . When blacks take positions in the highest places of government, industry, or academia, it is an open question today whether their skin color played a part in their advancement. The question itself is the stigma—because either racial discrimination did play a role, in which case the person may be deemed "otherwise unqualified," or it did not, in which case asking the question itself unfairly marks those blacks who would succeed without discrimination. . . .

[T]he Court has soundly rejected the remedying of societal discrimination as a justification for governmental use of race. For those who believe that every racial disproportionality in our society is caused by some kind of racial discrimination, there can be no distinction between remedying societal discrimination and erasing racial disproportionalities in the country's leadership caste.

The majority appears to believe that broader utopian goals justify the Law School's use of race, but "[t]he Equal Protection Clause commands the elimination of racial barriers, not their creation in order to satisfy our theory as to how society ought to be organized." . . .

---

[15] **Questions:** O'Connor ends her opinion by predicting that Michigan's affirmative-action policy will no longer be narrowly tailored in 2028. What is she expecting to happen in the meantime? The University of Michigan is not responsible for producing "minority applicants with high grades and test scores." So why should the predicted number of such applicants affect the constitutionality of its program under the Equal Protection Clause?

NOTE: *GRATZ*

In her opinion for a 5–4 Court, Justice Sandra Day O'Connor reaffirmed Justice Lewis Powell's position in *Bakke* that maintaining student body diversity was a compelling state interest. Because Michigan Law School's consideration of applicants was "truly individualized" and used race in a "flexible, nonmechanical way," she also wrote that the plan was narrow enough to survive strict scrutiny. *Grutter*, 539 U.S. at 334. But in a notable sign of O'Connor's discomfort with affirmative-action programs, she concluded her opinion with a prediction that "25 years from now, the use of racial preferences will no longer be necessary to further the interest approved today." *Id.* at 343. In a concurring opinion, Justice Ruth Bader Ginsburg noted that "it was only 25 years before *Bakke* that this Court declared public school segregation unconstitutional, a declaration that, after prolonged resistance, yielded an end to a law-enforced racial caste system, itself the legacy of centuries of slavery." *Id.* at 345.

O'Connor joined a different majority in *Gratz v. Bollinger*, 539 U.S. 244 (2003). That second case out of the University of Michigan involved a high school student, Jennifer Gratz, who was rejected when she applied to the college in 1995. Through a freedom-of-information request, her attorneys discovered that the college admitted students using a 150-point scale based on a number of factors—including grade-point average, test scores, having alumni as parents, and having "extraordinary artistic talent." *Gratz*, 539 U.S. at 272. One of these factors, "membership in an underrepresented racial or ethnic minority group," counted for 20 points. *Id.* at 255. This boost was enough to get many students close to the 100 points needed for admission. Gratz sued, complaining that this policy was the equivalent of a quota.

A 5–1–3 Court agreed that the college's point system was insufficiently tailored to achieve the purpose of diversity. *Id.* at 258–59. Citing Powell's opinion in *Bakke*, the *Gratz* Court emphasized "the importance of considering each particular applicant as an individual." *Id.* at 271–72. The college's policy, the Court wrote, failed to "provide such individualized consideration" when it automatically distributed twenty points "to every single applicant from an 'underrepresented minority' group." *Id.* at 271. To the Court, this distribution had "the effect of making 'the factor of race . . . decisive' for virtually every minimally qualified underrepresented minority applicant." *Id.* at 272.

49.3.2

Parents Involved in Community Schools v. Seattle School District No. 1

551 U.S. 701 (2007)

After *Grutter*, the use of "holistic" race-conscious programs in higher education, 539 U.S. at 337, appeared secure, at least for the twenty-five-year period predicted by O'Connor. But O'Connor announced her retirement two years later, in 2005. The person nominated to replace her, John Roberts, ended up becoming chief justice. In his first decision evaluating a race-conscious program, *Parents Involved in Community Schools v. Seattle School District No. 1*, 551 U.S. 701 (2007), Roberts determined how far *Grutter*'s holding would reach outside the context of academia.

Jefferson County, Kentucky, which includes Louisville, maintained a racially segregated dual school system for most of the twentieth century. When a federal court ordered the county to desegregate its schools in 1975, white protestors reacted so violently that armed guards had to accompany students on buses. William Griffin, *Two Cities Await Day of the Buses*, Chi. Trib., Sept. 8, 1975, at 1. Federal oversight lasted for twenty-five years, after which the court determined that the county had eliminated the vestiges of its dual system "[t]o the greatest extent practicable." *Hampton v. Jefferson Cnty. Bd. of Educ.*, 102 F. Supp. 2d 358, 360 (W.D. Ky. 2000). By that point, most residents of Louisville had become so committed to integration that the county voluntarily continued a desegregation program that took students' race into account to ensure that its schools would remain integrated.

During the same period, Seattle, Washington, had a long history of legalized racial segregation in *housing* but no formally segregated *school system*. Nevertheless, its schools had long been segregated in practice, leading civil rights activists to threaten a lawsuit in 1977. In response, Seattle's school district adopted a busing program to desegregate the district. As discussed earlier in the section on the political process doctrine (section 47.2), a statewide referendum overturned the busing program before the Supreme Court reinstated it in *Washington v. Seattle School District No. 1*, 458 U.S. 457 (1982). By the 2000s, even though white people represented 65 percent of Seattle's population, they made up only 41 percent of its public-school children. Students of color remained confined to the city's southern schools. Seattle modified its desegregation policy to allow anyone to choose which school to attend. But if too many students wanted to attend the same school, the district employed a series of "tiebreakers" to allocate the slots. *Parents Involved*, 551 U.S. at 711. One of these tiebreakers—for schools that were less than 31 percent white or more than 51 percent white—admitted the student if the student's race would help "bring the school into balance." *Id.* at 712.

Plaintiffs from cases involving both school districts (Jefferson County and Seattle)—which were consolidated in *Parents Involved*—sued, claiming that "allocating children to different public schools based solely on their race violates the Fourteenth Amendment guarantee of equal protection." *Id.* at 711. The Court agreed.

■ CHIEF JUSTICE ROBERTS . . . delivered the opinion of the Court with respect to Parts I, II, III-A, and III-C. . . .[16]

The school districts in these cases voluntarily adopted student assignment plans that rely upon race to determine which public schools certain children may attend.

[16] **As You Read, Consider:** In *Swann v. Charlotte-Mecklenburg Board of Education*, the Supreme Court upheld the use of busing and racial quotas to remedy unconstitutional racial

The Seattle school district classifies children as white or nonwhite; the Jefferson County school district as black or "other." In Seattle, this racial classification is used to allocate slots in oversubscribed high schools. In Jefferson County, it is used to make certain elementary school assignments and to rule on transfer requests. In each case, the school district relies upon an individual student's race in assigning that student to a particular school, so that the racial balance at the school falls within a predetermined range based on the racial composition of the school district as a whole. . . .

[III-A Determining Which Interests Are Compelling]

It is well established that when the government distributes burdens or benefits on the basis of individual racial classifications, that action is reviewed under strict scrutiny. *Grutter v. Bollinger,* 539 U.S. 306 (2003); *Adarand, supra,* at 224. . . . In order to satisfy this searching standard of review, the school districts must demonstrate that the use of individual racial classifications in the assignment plans here under review is "narrowly tailored" to achieve a "compelling" government interest. *Adarand, supra,* at 227.

Without attempting in these cases to set forth all the interests a school district might assert, it suffices to note that our prior cases, in evaluating the use of racial classifications in the school context, have recognized two interests that qualify as compelling. The first is the compelling interest of remedying the effects of past intentional discrimination. See *Freeman v. Pitts,* 503 U.S. 467, 494 (1992). Yet the Seattle public schools have not shown that they were ever segregated by law, and were not subject to court-ordered desegregation decrees. The Jefferson County public schools were previously segregated by law and were subject to a desegregation decree entered in 1975. In 2000, the District Court that entered that decree dissolved it, finding that Jefferson County had "eliminated the vestiges associated with the former policy of segregation and its pernicious effects[.]" . . . Jefferson County accordingly does not rely upon an interest in remedying the effects of past intentional discrimination in defending its present use of race in assigning students.

Nor could it. We have emphasized that the harm being remedied by mandatory desegregation plans is the harm that is traceable to segregation, and that "the Constitution is not violated by racial imbalance in the schools, without more." *Milliken v. Bradley,* 433 U.S. 267, 280, n. 14 (1977). Once Jefferson County achieved unitary [*i.e.,* desegregated] status, it had remedied the constitutional wrong that allowed race-based assignments. Any continued use of race must be justified on some other basis.

The second government interest we have recognized as compelling for purposes of strict scrutiny is the interest in diversity in higher education upheld in *Grutter,* 539 U.S., at 328. The specific interest found compelling in *Grutter* was student body diversity "in the context of higher education." *Ibid.* . . . We described the various types of diversity that the law school sought:

> "[The law school's] policy makes clear there are many possible bases for diversity admissions, and provides examples of admittees who have lived or traveled widely abroad, are fluent in several languages, have overcome personal adversity and family hardship, have exceptional records of

segregation. But these remedies were instituted after a federal court found that Charlotte-Mecklenburg had violated the Constitution. Here, Seattle has attempted to remedy racial segregation caused by widespread housing discrimination, while Jefferson County has attempted to remedy the long-term effects of past segregation. Why does Chief Justice John Roberts think that Swann and other busing cases are inapplicable?

extensive community service, and have had successful careers in other fields." *Id.,* at 338. . . .

In the present cases, by contrast, race is not considered as part of a broader effort to achieve "exposure to widely diverse people, cultures, ideas, and viewpoints"; race, for some students, is determinative standing alone. The districts argue that other factors, such as student preferences, affect assignment decisions under their plans, but under each plan when race comes into play, it is decisive by itself. It is not simply one factor weighed with others in reaching a decision, as in *Grutter*; it is *the* factor. . . .

In upholding the admissions plan in *Grutter*, . . . this Court relied upon considerations unique to institutions of higher education, noting that in light of "the expansive freedoms of speech and thought associated with the university environment, universities occupy a special niche in our constitutional tradition." 539 U.S., at 329. . . . The present cases are not governed by *Grutter*. . . .

[III-C Determining Whether the Program Is Necessary or Narrowly Tailored]

The districts assert, as they must, that the way in which they have employed individual racial classifications is necessary to achieve their stated ends. The minimal effect these classifications have on student assignments, however, suggests that other means would be effective. Seattle's racial tiebreaker results, in the end, only in shifting a small number of students between schools. Approximately 307 student assignments were affected by the racial tie-breaker in 2000–2001. . . . In over one-third of the assignments affected by the racial tiebreaker, . . . the use of race in the end made no difference, and the district could identify only 52 students who were ultimately affected adversely by the racial tiebreaker in that it resulted in assignment to a school they had not listed as a preference and to which they would not otherwise have been assigned. . . .

Similarly, Jefferson County's use of racial classifications has only a minimal effect on the assignment of students. . . .

While we do not suggest that *greater* use of race would be preferable, the minimal impact of the districts' racial classifications on school enrollment casts doubt on the necessity of using racial classifications. In *Grutter,* the consideration of race was viewed as indispensable in more than tripling minority representation at the law school—from 4 to 14.5 percent. Here the most Jefferson County itself claims is that "because the guidelines provide a firm definition of the Board's goal of racially integrated schools, they 'provide administrators with the authority to facilitate, negotiate and collaborate with principals and staff to maintain schools within the 15–50% range.' " Classifying and assigning school-children according to a binary conception of race is an extreme approach in light of our precedents and our Nation's history of using race in public schools, and requires more than such an amorphous end to justify it.

The districts have also failed to show that they considered methods other than explicit racial classifications to achieve their stated goals. Narrow tailoring requires "serious, good faith consideration of workable race-neutral alternatives," *Grutter, supra,* at 339, and yet in Seattle several alternative assignment plans—many of which would not have used express racial classifications—were rejected with little or no consideration. Jefferson County has failed to present any evidence that it considered alternatives, even though the district already claims that its goals are achieved primarily through means other than the racial classifications. . . .

[* * *]

In *Brown v. Board of Education,* 347 U.S. 483 (1954) (*Brown I*), we held that segregation deprived black children of equal educational opportunities regardless of whether school facilities and other tangible factors were equal, because government classification and separation on grounds of race themselves denoted inferiority. *Id.,* at 493–494. . . . The next Term, we accordingly stated that "full compliance" with *Brown I* required school districts "to achieve a system of determining admission to the public schools *on a nonracial basis.*" *Brown II,* 349 U.S., at 300–301 (emphasis added).

The parties and their *amici* debate which side is more faithful to the heritage of *Brown,* but the position of the plaintiffs in *Brown* . . . could not have been clearer: "[T]he Fourteenth Amendment prevents states from according differential treatment to American children on the basis of their color or race." Brief for Appellants in *Brown I,* O.T. 1953, p. 15. What do the racial classifications at issue here do, if not accord differential treatment on the basis of race? . . .

Before *Brown,* schoolchildren were told where they could and could not go to school based on the color of their skin. The school districts in these cases have not carried the heavy burden of demonstrating that we should allow this once again—even for very different reasons. For schools that never segregated on the basis of race, such as Seattle, or that have removed the vestiges of past segregation, such as Jefferson County, the way "to achieve a system of determining admission to the public schools on a nonracial basis," *Brown II, supra,* at 300–301, is to stop assigning students on a racial basis. The way to stop discrimination on the basis of race is to stop discriminating on the basis of race.[17]

■ JUSTICE KENNEDY, concurring in part and concurring in the judgment.[18]

[P]arts of the opinion by THE CHIEF JUSTICE imply an all-too-unyielding insistence that race cannot be a factor in instances when, in my view, it may be taken into account. The plurality opinion is too dismissive of the legitimate interest government has in ensuring all people have equal opportunity regardless of their race. The plurality's postulate that "[t]he way to stop discrimination on the basis of race is to stop discriminating on the basis of race," is not sufficient to decide these cases.

---

17 **Questions:** Roberts ends his opinion with an infamous aphorism: "The way to stop discriminating on the basis of race is to stop discriminating on the basis of race." Yet unlike James J. Kilpatrick, who used a similar phrase to oppose enforcement of the Civil Rights Act of 1964, Roberts attributes it to Thurgood Marshall and the lawyers who argued *Brown v. Board of Education* (*Brown II*). Is he correct that the principles underlying *Brown II* should prohibit any government from using race-conscious remedies to address racial segregation? What about Justice Harry Blackmun's argument in *Regents of the University of California v. Bakke* that "[i]n order to get beyond racism, we must first take account of race"? 438 U.S. 265, 407 (1978).

18 **Question:** In this controlling opinion for a 5–4 majority, Justice Anthony Kennedy writes that governments may adopt individualized, race-based policies to achieve diverse student bodies only if such diversity cannot be achieved by "facially race neutral" approaches. He defines a facially race-neutral approach as one that does not *tell* each student that "he or she is to be defined by race." Yet such an approach may still be "race conscious" in the sense that it *affects* students of different races differently.

In other words, when a government is remedying violations of constitutional or statutory rights, it may candidly use a race-based tiebreaker. But if it wants to desegregate schools absent such a violation, it must first assess whether it can achieve its goal by taking advantage of facially neutral proxies for race, like segregated neighborhoods. Governments can get away with these plans, Kennedy writes, because *Washington v. Davis* and *Village of Arlington Heights v. Metropolitan Housing Development Corp.* make it so difficult to prove that a government's purpose is to classify on the basis of race.

Kennedy's opinion has encouraged governments to become secretive and pretextual about adopting race-conscious policies to achieve the benefits of diversity. Is this world preferable to one in which governments are candid about their use of race?

Fifty years of experience since *Brown v. Board of Education,* 347 U.S. 483 (1954), should teach us that the problem before us defies so easy a solution. . . . The plurality opinion is at least open to the interpretation that the Constitution requires school districts to ignore the problem of *de facto* resegregation in schooling. I cannot endorse that conclusion. . . .

The statement by Justice Harlan that "[o]ur Constitution is color-blind" was most certainly justified in the context of his dissent in *Plessy v. Ferguson,* 163 U.S. 537, 559 (1896). . . . In the real world, it is regrettable to say, it cannot be a universal constitutional principle.

In the administration of public schools by the state and local authorities it is permissible to consider the racial makeup of schools and to adopt general policies to encourage a diverse student body, one aspect of which is its racial composition. Cf. *Grutter v. Bollinger,* 539 U.S. 306 (2003). If school authorities are concerned that the student-body compositions of certain schools interfere with the objective of offering an equal educational opportunity to all of their students, they are free to devise race-conscious measures to address the problem in a general way and without treating each student in different fashion solely on the basis of a systematic, individual typing by race.

School boards may pursue the goal of bringing together students of diverse backgrounds and races through other means, including strategic site selection of new schools; drawing attendance zones with general recognition of the demographics of neighborhoods; allocating resources for special programs; recruiting students and faculty in a targeted fashion; and tracking enrollments, performance, and other statistics by race. These mechanisms are race conscious but do not lead to different treatment based on a classification that tells each student he or she is to be defined by race, so it is unlikely any of them would demand strict scrutiny to be found permissible. See *Bush v. Vera,* 517 U.S. 952, 958 (1996) ("[Government action] performed with consciousness of race . . . [may still be] 'facially race neutral,' so a more searching inquiry is necessary [under *Davis* and *Arlington Heights*] before strict scrutiny can be found applicable[."]). Executive and legislative branches, which for generations now have considered these types of policies and procedures, should be permitted to employ them with candor and with confidence that a constitutional violation does not occur whenever a decisionmaker considers the impact a given approach might have on students of different races. . . .

Each respondent has asserted that its assignment of individual students by race is permissible because there is no other way to avoid racial isolation in the school districts. Yet, as explained, each has failed to provide the support necessary for that proposition. And individual racial classifications employed in this manner may be considered legitimate only if they are a last resort to achieve a compelling interest.

In the cases before us it is noteworthy that the number of students whose assignment depends on express racial classifications is limited. I join Part III-C of the Court's opinion because I agree that in the context of these plans, the small number of assignments affected suggests that the schools could have achieved their stated ends through different means. These include the facially race-neutral means set forth above or, if necessary, a more nuanced, individual evaluation of school needs and student characteristics that might include race as a component. . . .

NOTE: RACIALLY CONSCIOUS BUT FACIALLY NEUTRAL POLICIES

Justice Anthony Kennedy provided the fifth vote for the judgment in *Parents Involved*, so his concurring opinion explaining his disagreement with Roberts has been interpreted as controlling. During the administration of

President Barack Obama, the Department of Education and Department of Justice attempted to explain Kennedy's position in a guidance document, *Guidance on the Voluntary Use of Race to Achieve Diversity and Avoid Racial Isolation in Elementary and Secondary Schools*. U.S. Dep't of Justice & U.S. Dep't of Educ., *Guidance on the Voluntary Use of Race to Achieve Diversity and Avoid Racial Isolation in Elementary and Secondary Schools* (2011). The document emphasized Kennedy's praise of "race-conscious measures to address [a] problem in a general way . . . but [that] do not lead to different treatment based on a classification that tells each student he or she is to be defined by race." *Id.* at 4. The document noted that by writing that it would be "unlikely" that the Court would evaluate such measures under strict scrutiny—*even if one of the goals of the measures was to "bring[ ] together students of diverse backgrounds"*—Kennedy suggested that school districts could take advantage of the difficult-to-satisfy discriminatory-purpose test of *Washington v. Davis*, 426 U.S. 229 (1976), and *Village of Arlington Heights v. Metropolitan Housing Development Corp.*, 429 U.S. 252 (1977). *Id.* (emphasis added). As long as school districts could argue that they took an action in spite of, not because of, its racial effects, the document concluded, then they could theoretically employ race in a covert way without needing to satisfy strict scrutiny.

The Obama administration's guidance document divided Kennedy's concurring opinion into three "approaches to achieve diversity or avoid racial isolation": (1) "race-neutral approaches," (2) "generalized race-based approaches," and (3) "approaches that rely on individual racial classifications." *Id.* at 5. Where the first two would likely be evaluated under the rational-basis test, the third would be evaluated under strict scrutiny:

> Examples of race-neutral approaches include—but are not limited to—the use of criteria such as: students' socioeconomic status; parental education (e.g., highest degree attained or years of education); students' household status (e.g., dual or single-parent household); neighborhood socioeconomic status; geography (e.g., existing neighborhood lines); and composition of area housing (e.g., subsidized housing, single-family home, high-density public housing, or rental housing). . . .
>
> Generalized race-based approaches employ expressly racial criteria, such as the overall racial composition of neighborhoods, but do not involve decision-making on the basis of any individual student's race. For example, a school district could draw attendance zones based on the racial composition of particular neighborhoods, as well as on race-neutral factors such as the average household income and average parental education level of particular neighborhoods within the school district. . . .
>
> [A] school district may only consider the race of individual students if it does so in a manner that is narrowly tailored to meet a compelling interest. . . . A district may consider a student's race as a "plus factor" (among other, non-racial considerations) to achieve its compelling interests. But . . . a school district should not evaluate student applicants in a way that makes a student's race

> his or her defining feature. School districts should consider how the range of student attributes, including both non-racial characteristics . . . and racial characteristics, contribute to meeting the district's compelling interest in achieving diversity. . . .

Id. at 6–7.

Following Kennedy's analysis, the administration instructed states and local governments seeking to achieve diversity or avoid racial isolation to start with the first approach and to turn to the second or third only if the more race-neutral approach proved "unworkable." *Id.* at 6. Citing *Grutter* and *Parents Involved*, the administration defined an unworkable approach as one that would be "ineffective to achieve the diversity that the [government] seeks" or "would require the [government] to sacrifice a component of [its] educational mission or priorities (*e.g.*, academic selectivity)." *Id.* As for the third approach, which uses individual racial classifications, the administration instructed states and local governments to "periodically review the program to determine whether such racial classifications remain necessary." *Id.* at 7.

49.3.3

Fisher v. University of Texas at Austin (Fisher II)

579 U.S. 365 (2016)

One state that continued to employ a facially race-neutral admissions program to achieve diversity after *Parents Involved* was Texas. In 1997, a year after a federal court struck down the University of Texas's race-conscious admissions policy, Governor George W. Bush signed into law the "Top Ten Percent Plan." Tex. Educ. Code Ann. § 51.803. The plan granted all students graduating in the top 10 percent of their public high school class automatic admission to the University of Texas at Austin. Because Texas's schools remained racially and economically segregated after *San Antonio Independent School District v. Rodriguez*, 411 U.S. 1 (1973), the plan cleverly ensured that students from predominantly Hispanic or black schools would be admitted to the flagship university—in a facially race-neutral way.

The university soon admitted the vast majority of its students from the Top Ten Percent Plan, with the rest of its admissions determined by a race-neutral holistic review process. Yet through 2003, the few students of color who chose to attend the university reported feeling isolated on campus. After *Grutter*, the university adjusted its admissions program. While continuing to admit most students via the Top Ten Percent Plan, the university began considering applicants' race as a "plus" factor in its holistic review process.

Abigail Fisher was a white Texan whose high-school standing was too low to make her eligible for the Top Ten Percent Plan. When she applied to the University of Texas in 2008, the holistic review process rejected her application. Although Fisher could provide no evidence that she would have been more likely to have been admitted had she been black or Hispanic, she challenged the university's consideration of race as a constitutional violation.

In *Fisher v. University of Texas at Austin* (*Fisher I*), 570 U.S. 297 (2013), the Supreme Court initially planned to side with Fisher. But Justice Sonia Sotomayor circulated a draft dissent that was so scathing of the majority opinion that several justices negotiated a compromise. *See* Joan Biskupic, *Breaking In* 206–08 (2015); *Schuette v. Coal. to Defend Affirmative Action*, 572 U.S. 291, 381 (2014) (Sotomayor, J., dissenting) ("The way to stop discrimination on the basis of race is to speak openly and candidly on the subject of race. . . ."). In the end, a 7–1 Court voted to remand the case for lower courts to reapply strict scrutiny. On remand, the Fifth Circuit applied strict scrutiny and concluded that the University of Texas's admissions policy was narrowly tailored to its interest in achieving a "critical mass." *Fisher v. University of Texas at Austin*, 758 F.3d 633, 660 (5th Cir. 2014).

When the case returned to the Supreme Court, Justice Antonin Scalia suggested at oral argument that "it does not benefit African Americans to—to get them into the University of Texas where they do not do well, as opposed to having them go to a less-advanced school, a less—a slower-track school where they do well." Transcript of Oral Argument at 67, *Fisher v. University of Texas at Austin* (*Fisher II*), 136 S. Ct. 2198 (2016). Chief Justice Roberts, meanwhile, expressed his skepticism of the educational benefits of diversity, rhetorically asking, "What unique perspective does a minority student bring to a physics class?" *Id.* at 55.

Justice Anthony Kennedy wrote the opinion for a 4–3 Court in *Fisher*, which affirmed the admissions policy of the university.

■ JUSTICE KENNEDY delivered the opinion of the Court.[19]

The Court is asked once again to consider whether the race-conscious admissions program at the University of Texas is lawful under the Equal Protection Clause. . . .

Fisher I set forth three controlling principles relevant to assessing the constitutionality of a public university's affirmative-action program. First, . . . "[r]ace may not be considered [by a university] unless the admissions process can withstand strict scrutiny," *Fisher I*, 570 U.S., at ___. Strict scrutiny requires the university to demonstrate with clarity that its " 'purpose or interest is both constitutionally permissible and substantial, and that its use of the classification is necessary . . . to the accomplishment of its purpose.' " *Ibid.*

Second, *Fisher I* confirmed that "the decision to pursue 'the educational benefits that flow from student body diversity' . . . is, in substantial measure, an academic judgment to which some, but not complete, judicial deference is proper." A university cannot impose a fixed quota or otherwise "define diversity as 'some specified

19 **As You Read, Consider:** Justice Anthony Kennedy dissented in *Grutter v. Bollinger*. Yet he upholds Texas's use of a similar holistic review program here. Why? Consider whether he consistently applies the "narrow tailoring" factors that he outlined in *Parents Involved in Community Schools v. Seattle School District No. 1*, 551 U.S. 701 (2007).

percentage of a particular group merely because of its race or ethnic origin.' " *Ibid.* Once, however, a university gives "a reasoned, principled explanation" for its decision, deference must be given "to the University's conclusion, based on its experience and expertise, that a diverse student body would serve its educational goals."

Third, *Fisher I* clarified that no deference is owed when determining whether the use of race is narrowly tailored to achieve the university's permissible goals. A university, *Fisher I* explained, bears the burden of proving a "nonracial approach" would not promote its interest in the educational benefits of diversity "about as well and at tolerable administrative expense." Though "[n]arrow tailoring does not require exhaustion of every conceivable race-neutral alternative" or "require a university to choose between maintaining a reputation for excellence [and] fulfilling a commitment to provide educational opportunities to members of all racial groups," *Grutter,* 539 U.S., at 339, it does impose "on the university the ultimate burden of demonstrating" that "race-neutral alternatives" that are both "available" and "workable" "do not suffice."

In seeking to reverse the judgment of the Court of Appeals, petitioner makes four arguments. First, she argues that the University has not articulated its compelling interest with sufficient clarity. According to petitioner, the University must set forth more precisely the level of minority enrollment that would constitute a "critical mass." Without a clearer sense of what the University's ultimate goal is, petitioner argues, a reviewing court cannot assess whether the University's admissions program is narrowly tailored to that goal.

As this Court's cases have made clear, however, the compelling interest that justifies consideration of race in college admissions is not an interest in enrolling a certain number of minority students. Rather, a university may institute a race-conscious admissions program as a means of obtaining "the educational benefits that flow from student body diversity." *Grutter,* 539 U.S., at [330]. As this Court has said, enrolling a diverse student body "promotes cross-racial understanding, helps to break down racial stereotypes, and enables students to better understand persons of different races." [*Ibid.*]. Equally important, "student body diversity promotes learning outcomes, and better prepares students for an increasingly diverse workforce and society." *Ibid.* . . .

The record reveals that in first setting forth its current admissions policy, the University articulated concrete and precise goals . . . [which], as a general matter, mirror the "compelling interest" this Court has approved in its prior cases. . . . The University has provided in addition a "reasoned, principled explanation" for its decision to pursue these goals. The University's 39-page proposal was written following a year-long study, which concluded that "[t]he use of race-neutral policies and programs ha[d] not been successful" in "provid[ing] an educational setting that fosters cross-racial understanding, provid[ing] enlightened discussion and learning, [or] prepar[ing] students to function in an increasingly diverse workforce and society." . . . Petitioner's contention that the University's goal was insufficiently concrete is rebutted by the record.

Second, petitioner argues that the University has no need to consider race because it had already "achieved critical mass" by 2003 using the Top Ten Percent Plan and race-neutral holistic review. Petitioner is correct that a university bears a heavy burden in showing that it had not obtained the educational benefits of diversity before it turned to a race-conscious plan. . . . [But] the University conducted "months of study and deliberation, including retreats, interviews, [and] review of data," and concluded that "[t]he use of race-neutral policies and programs ha[d] not been successful in achieving" sufficient racial diversity at the University. . . . [The demographic data] show consistent stagnation in terms of the percentage of minority students enrolling at the University from 1996 to 2002. . . . [And] the University put forward evidence that minority students admitted under the *Hopwood* regime experienced feelings of loneliness and isolation. . . . Though a college must continually reassess its need for race-conscious review, here that assessment appears to have been done with care. . . .

Third, petitioner argues that considering race was not necessary because such consideration has had only a " 'minimal impact' in advancing the [University's] compelling interest." Again, the record does not support this assertion. In 2003, 11 percent of the Texas residents enrolled through holistic review were Hispanic and 3.5 percent were African-American. In 2007, by contrast, 16.9 percent of the Texas holistic-review freshmen were Hispanic and 6.8 percent were African-American. Those increases—of 54 percent and 94 percent, respectively—show that consideration of race has had a meaningful, if still limited, effect on the diversity of the University's freshman class. . . . In any event, it is not a failure of narrow tailoring for the impact of racial consideration to be minor. The fact that race consciousness played a role in only a small portion of admissions decisions should be a hallmark of narrow tailoring, not evidence of unconstitutionality.

Petitioner's final argument is that "there are numerous other available race-neutral means of achieving" the University's compelling interest. A review of the record reveals, however, that . . . none of her proposed alternatives was a workable means for the University to attain the benefits of diversity it sought. For example, petitioner suggests that the University could intensify its outreach efforts to African-American and Hispanic applicants. But the University submitted extensive evidence of the many ways in which it already had intensified its outreach efforts to those students. . . . None of these efforts succeeded, and petitioner fails to offer any meaningful way in which the University could have improved upon them at the time of her application. . . .

Petitioner's final suggestion is to uncap the Top Ten Percent Plan, and admit more—if not all—the University's students through a percentage plan. As an initial matter, petitioner overlooks the fact that the Top Ten Percent Plan, though facially neutral, cannot be understood apart from its basic purpose, which is to boost minority enrollment. Percentage plans are "adopted with racially segregated neighborhoods and schools front and center stage." *Fisher I,* 570 U.S., at ___ (Ginsburg, J., dissenting). "It is race consciousness, not blindness to race, that drives such plans." *Ibid.* Consequently, petitioner cannot assert simply that increasing the University's reliance on a percentage plan would make its admissions policy more race neutral. . . .

In short, none of petitioner's suggested alternatives—nor other proposals considered or discussed in the course of this litigation—have been shown to be "available" and "workable" means through which the University could have met its educational goals, as it understood and defined them in 2008. The University has thus met its burden of showing that the admissions policy it used at the time it rejected petitioner's application was narrowly tailored. . . .

CHAPTER 50

WHAT LIMITATIONS DO THE FOURTEENTH AMENDMENT AND VOTING-RIGHTS AMENDMENTS IMPOSE ON THE POWER OF STATES TO REGULATE THE POLITICAL PROCESS?

FIFTH AMENDMENT (1791): No person shall . . . be deprived of life, liberty, or property, without due process of law. . . .

FOURTEENTH AMENDMENT (1868), SECTION 1: All persons born or naturalized in the United States, and subject to the jurisdiction thereof, are citizens of the United States and of the State wherein they reside. No State shall make or enforce any law which shall abridge the privileges or immunities of citizens of the United States; nor shall any State deprive any person of life, liberty, or property, without due process of law; nor deny to any person within its jurisdiction the equal protection of the laws.

> **SECTION 2:** Representatives shall be apportioned among the several States according to their respective numbers, counting the whole number of persons in each State, excluding Indians not taxed. But when the right to vote at any election for the choice of electors for President and Vice-President of the United States, Representatives in Congress, the Executive and Judicial officers of a State, or the members of the Legislature thereof, is denied to any of the male inhabitants of such State, being twenty-one years of age, and citizens of the United States, or in any way abridged, except for participation in rebellion, or other crime, the basis of representation therein shall be reduced in the proportion which the number of such male citizens shall bear to the whole number of male citizens twenty-one years of age in such State.

FIFTEENTH AMENDMENT (1870), SECTION 1: The right of citizens of the United States to vote shall not be denied or abridged by the United States or by any State on account of race, color, or previous condition of servitude. . . .

NINETEENTH AMENDMENT (1920), CLAUSE 1: The right of citizens of the United States to vote shall not be denied or abridged by the United States or by any State on account of sex.

TWENTY-FOURTH AMENDMENT (1964), SECTION 1: The right of citizens of the United States to vote in any primary or other election for President or Vice President, for electors for President or Vice President, or for Senator or Representative in Congress, shall not be denied or abridged by the United States or any State by reason of failure to pay any poll tax or other tax.

TWENTY-SIXTH AMENDMENT (1971), SECTION 1: The right of citizens of the United States, who are eighteen years of age or older, to vote shall not be denied or abridged by the United States or by any State on account of age.

50.1 VOTER QUALIFICATIONS

Fourteenth Amendment's Section 2

Section 1 of the Fourteenth Amendment has become the most litigated provision of the Fourteenth Amendment, if not the entire Constitution. But when Congress proposed the Fourteenth Amendment in 1866, its members intended to do more than extend to formerly enslaved people the privileges and immunities of citizenship, the due process of law, and the equal protection of the laws. As discussed earlier in the section on the origin of the Reconstruction amendments (section 20.1), Congress included in Section 2 of the amendment a convoluted scheme in which it hoped to extend the franchise to black southerners. *See* Eric Foner, *The Second Founding* 81–83 (2019).

The northern-dominated Congress was worried about the political threat posed by the Thirteenth Amendment's effective abolition of the Three-Fifths Clause. Before the Civil War, southern states counted only three-fifths of their enslaved people for purposes of congressional representation and electoral votes. Now that slavery was no longer legal, southern states could count their entire black populations and send even more representatives and electoral votes to Washington. This struck Congress as patently unfair when southern states continued to disenfranchise their black populations. *See generally* Gabriel J. Chin, *Reconstruction, Felon Disenfranchisement, and the Right to Vote: Did the Fifteenth Amendment Repeal Section 2 of the Fourteenth Amendment?*, 92 Geo. L.J. 259, 264–68 (2004) (overviewing briefly the history of black suffrage in the years following the end of the Civil War).

Congress addressed this dilemma with Section 2 of the Fourteenth Amendment. That section declared that "when the right to vote at any election" for any federal or state officer "is denied to any of the male inhabitants of such State, being twenty-one years of age, and citizens of the United States, or in any way abridged, except for participation in rebellion, or other crime," then a state would lose its representation in Congress by a number equal to the number of disenfranchised adult male citizens divided by the total number of adult male citizens. In other words, for every 70,000 or so adult male citizens that a state prevented from voting in a state or federal election, the state would lose one representative. Congress hoped that states would fear losing representation and therefore extend the franchise to all citizens, not just white citizens.

Section 2 proved to be an ineffective procedure for encouraging states to enfranchise black men. Although the National Association for the Advancement of Colored People (NAACP) campaigned to implement the provision in the 1920s, neither courts nor Congress has ever imposed a penalty on offending states. Franita Tolson, *What Is Abridgement?: A Critique of Two Section Twos*, 67 Ala. L. Rev. 433, 434 (2015); *see Saunders v. Wilkins*, 152 F.2d 235, 238 (4th Cir. 1945), *cert. denied*, 328 U.S. 870 (1946) (rejecting an attempt to enforce Section 2 by litigation). As the 1866 Congress feared, nonenforcement contributed to the disenfranchisement of black southerners, the fall of the Republican Party in the South, and the rise of the all-white Democratic Party. Tolson, *supra*, at 434–35. Between 1903 and 1953, southern states sent approximately twenty-five more representatives to Congress than they deserved under Section 2's terms. *Id.*

Section 2 was not the only voting-rights provision that the thirty-sixth Congress proposed. That Congress also extended the right to vote to black men in the District of Columbia, Act of Jan. 8, 1867, ch. 6, 14 Stat. 375, and in the territories, Act of Jan. 25, 1867, ch. 15, 14 Stat. 379 (1867). When Congress admitted Nebraska as a state, it did so on the condition that Nebraska enshrine in its state constitution a guarantee against racial qualifications in voting—a condition discussed earlier in the section on the equal-footing doctrine (section 18.5). *See* Act of Feb. 9, 1867, ch. 36, 14 Stat. 391 (1867). And with the first Reconstruction Act of 1867, ch. 153, 14 Stat. 428, Congress prohibited ex-Confederate states from sending representatives to Congress until they guaranteed the right to vote to all black men.

Fifteenth Amendment

Many members of Congress hoped that the Fifteenth Amendment—which prohibited states from denying or abridging the right to vote "on account of race, color, or previous condition of servitude"—would constitutionalize these gains for black male suffrage. But as discussed earlier in the section on the origin of the Fifteenth Amendment (section 20.1), the amendment's spartan language was a compromised version of a proposed amendment that would have enfranchised all people, men and women. Even the amendment's supporters recognized that its focus on race would be easily evaded. As the Supreme Court declared in its first opinion interpreting the amendment, "[t]he Fifteenth Amendment does not confer the right of suffrage upon any one." *United States v. Reese*, 92 U.S. 214, 217 (1876). The amendment merely "invested the citizens of the United States with a new constitutional right which is within the protecting power of Congress. That right is exemption from discrimination in the exercise of the elective franchise on account of race, color, or previous condition of servitude." *Id.* at 218.

The Court's narrow interpretation of the Fifteenth Amendment would prove ineffective when "redeemed" southern states adopted race-neutral methods of disenfranchising black voters, such as literacy tests, poll taxes, voter-registration requirements, and other devices. *See* J. Morgan Kousser, *The Shaping of Southern Politics: Suffrage Restriction and the Establishment of the One-Party South, 1880–1910*, at 56–59 (1974); *see, e.g.*, *Giles v. Harris*, 189 U.S. 475, 488 (1903) (failing to remedy the effects of the Alabama Constitution of 1901, which disenfranchised thousands of black men); *Williams v. Mississippi*, 170 U.S. 213, 225 (1898) (upholding a literacy test).

Nineteenth Amendment

As northern states enfranchised black men and southern states disenfranchised them, western states during the late nineteenth century began enfranchising women. When New Jersey adopted its first constitution in 1776, it authorized "all inhabitants" of the state who could meet certain wealth and residency qualifications to vote for all public officers. *See* N.J. Const. of 1776, art. IV. It thus became the first state to extend the franchise to women—not to mention black people and noncitizens. In 1807, however, New Jersey also became one of the first states to restrict the franchise when its legislature passed a law prohibiting anyone from voting "unless such person be a free, white male citizen." Alexander Keyssar, *The Right to Vote* 43–44 (2009). In the decades afterward, few states even debated enfranchising women. In 1838, Kentucky authorized widows and unmarried women to vote in school elections. *Id.* at 141. But most references to women in constitutional discussions of suffrage were designed to demonstrate that voting was a privilege, not a right. *Id.*

Women's suffrage became a major national issue after Elizabeth Cady Stanton, a prominent abolitionist, helped to organize a women's rights convention in Seneca Falls, New York, in 1848. At the convention, Stanton presented the Declaration of Sentiments, modeled off the Declaration of Independence, which included the line, "We hold these truths to be self-evident: that all men *and women* are created equal." *See Declaration of Sentiments, reprinted in The Liberator*, Aug. 25, 1848, at 136. Where the Declaration of Independence included a list of grievances against King George III, the Declaration of Sentiments included a list of "repeated injuries and usurpation on the part of man toward woman," including that "he has not ever permitted her to exercise her inalienable right to the elective franchise." *Id.* Among the signers were Lucretia Mott, Frederick Douglass, and other abolitionists.

For the next twenty years, abolitionists and suffragists collaborated in a joint campaign to end slavery and expand the franchise to all people. Stanton was therefore bitterly disappointed when Section 2 of the Fourteenth Amendment not only failed to enfranchise black people but also included the word *male* in the Constitution for the first time. Foner, *supra*, at 81–83. "[I]t will take us a century at least to get it out," Stanton warned. *Id.* Stanton was even more disturbed by the final version of the Fifteenth Amendment, which also failed to enfranchise women. Douglass paternalistically urged Stanton to accept that this was "the Negro's hour" and that the woman's hour would come next. *Id.* But Stanton and her ally, Susan B. Anthony, led a racist campaign against the Fifteenth Amendment. "Think of Patrick and Sambo and Hans and Yung Tung, . . . who cannot read the Declaration of Independence or Webster's spelling book, making laws for Lucretia Mott," Stanton said at an 1869 equal-rights convention. " 'Manhood suffrage' creates an antagonism everywhere between educated, refined women and the lower orders of men, especially at the South, where the slaves of yesterday are the lawmakers of to-day." *Equal Rights*, N.Y. Times, May 13, 1869, at 1. Less inflammatory speakers replied to Douglass by observing that "the Government could consider two questions at the same time." *Id.*

Although Stanton and Anthony lost the battle over the Fifteenth Amendment, their second-generation movement for women's suffrage won notable successes in western states and territories. In 1869, Wyoming became the first territory to allow women to vote on the same terms as men. *See* Keyssar, *supra,* at 150. Kansas and other states granted women the right to vote in municipal elections. *Id.*

However, over the next thirty years, the movement for women's suffrage met little success on the campaign trail or in the courts. As discussed earlier in the section on the Privileges or Immunities Clause (section 39.2), the Supreme Court rejected a constitutional claim of equal suffrage in *Minor v. Happersett,* 88 U.S. (21 Wall.) 162, 178 (1875). By 1914, only ten states joined Wyoming in equally enfranchising women. *See* Keyssar, *supra*, at 368.

World War I galvanized a third-generation suffrage movement, as millions of women joined the domestic workforce to support the war effort. Carrie Chapman Catt's National American Woman Suffrage Association led legislative campaigns in dozens of states to earn the right of women to vote in state and federal elections. Alice Paul's National Woman's Party employed civil disobedience and demonstrations outside the White House to contrast President Woodrow Wilson's democratic rhetoric against his position on women's suffrage. *Id.* at 172–74. The joint pressure convinced Wilson to announce his support for women's suffrage "as a war measure." *Id.* at 174–75. After Congress proposed the Nineteenth Amendment in 1919, states ratified it within a year. *Id.* at 175. Modeled after the Fifteenth Amendment, the Nineteenth Amendment prohibited states from denying the right of citizens to vote "on account of sex."

The Nineteenth Amendment, like the Fifteenth Amendment, broadly expanded the franchise throughout the United States. But it was just as ineffective as the Fifteenth Amendment for stopping the widespread disenfranchisement of black men and women in the South. For example, in *Breedlove v. Suttles*, 302 U.S. 277 (1937), the Supreme Court needed only five pages to uphold a Georgia poll tax from a challenge under the Privileges or Immunities Clause and the Nineteenth Amendment. Like most poll taxes, Georgia's tax effectively penalized people who wished to vote because the state collected the tax at the polls.

Yet Georgia's tax was unique in that it exempted unregistered women—heightening its penalizing effect. Nevertheless, the Court held that it was rational for the state to exempt unregistered women from the poll tax "on the basis of special considerations to which they are naturally entitled," namely, "burdens necessarily borne by them for the preservation of the race" and the extra "burden" that the tax would place on their husbands. *Id.* at 282.

Fourteenth Amendment's Section 1 and the Texas white primary

By the 1930s, the three amendments to the Constitution that explicitly addressed voting rights—Section 2 of the Fourteenth Amendment, the Fifteenth Amendment, and the Nineteenth Amendment—were relatively useless in litigation. In this hopeless context, litigants challenging southern disenfranchisement turned to Section 1 of the Fourteenth Amendment, even though the authors of the Fourteenth Amendment purposefully failed to mention voting rights in Section 1. Yet in a series of cases challenging Texas's "white primary," a state-condoned primary election operated by a political party instead of by the state and open only to whites, the Supreme Court demonstrated that the scope of the Equal Protection Clause was broad enough to protect the right to vote. By the 1960s, the Texas primary cases convinced the Court to begin intervening in southern disenfranchisement.

***Nixon* cases.** The first two cases involved Dr. Lawrence A. Nixon, a black physician in El Paso, Texas, and a member of the Democratic Party.

When Nixon tried to vote in the party primary in 1924, he was denied because Texas law declared that "in no event shall a negro be eligible to participate in a Democratic party primary election held in the State of Texas." *Nixon v. Herndon*, 273 U.S. 536, 540 (1927). In the one-party South, the Democratic primary was the only election that mattered. Recognizing this fact, the Court wrote in *Nixon v. Herndon* that "it seems to us hard to imagine a more direct and obvious infringement of the Fourteenth [Amendment]." *Id.* at 541.

Texas promptly modified its law to declare that "every political party in this State through its State Executive Committee . . . shall in its own way determine who shall be qualified to vote." *Nixon v. Condon*, 286 U.S. 73, 82 (1932). The Democratic Party's executive committee then adopted a resolution authorizing only "white democrats" to vote. *Id.* When Nixon again tried to vote, he was rejected. Invoking *Herndon*, the Supreme Court again struck down Texas's law, writing that the Equal Protection Clause prohibited a state from delegating its powers to officials "in such a way as to discriminate invidiously between white citizens and black." *Id.* at 89.

Grovey. The Texas Democratic Party responded to this second bench slap by adopting a resolution at its 1932 convention resolving that "white citizens" could vote in its primary. When R. R. Grovey, another black Texan, attempted to cast a ballot in the 1934 primary, a county clerk refused because Grovey was black. This time, the Supreme Court refused to intervene. In *Grovey v. Townsend*, 295 U.S. 45 (1935), the Court invoked the state-action doctrine, writing, "We are not prepared to hold that in Texas the state convention of a party has become a mere instrumentality or agency for expressing the voice or will of the state." *Id.* at 54.

Classic. *Grovey* appeared to secure the future of the Texas white primary until federal prosecutors won a surprising conviction in the neighboring state of Louisiana. When Patrick B. Classic and five other election commissioners corruptly altered dozens of ballots in Louisiana's Democratic primary, federal prosecutors charged them under a Reconstruction-era statute that criminalized depriving people of their constitutional rights. Classic's defense was that no one had a constitutional right to participate in a primary election. But in *United States v. Classic*, the Court disagreed, invoking *Ex parte Yarbrough*, 110 U.S. 651 (1884), for the principle that voters had a constitutional right under Article I, Section 2, to participate in a congressional election. 313 U.S. 299, 315 (1941). The Court explained that the right to participate in congressional elections was meaningless if the right to vote in primaries is abridged—at least "where the primary is by law made an integral part of the election machinery." *Id.* at 318.

Smith. By describing the right to participate in a primary election as constitutionally protected, *Classic* set in motion a fourth challenge to Texas's white primary, this one led by Thurgood Marshall as NAACP legal counsel. In *Smith v. Allwright*, a case functionally identical to *Grovey*, the Court accepted Marshall's argument that *Classic*'s "recognition of the place of the primary in the electoral scheme makes clear that state delegation to a party of the power to fix the qualifications of primary elections is delegation of a state function that may make the party's action the action of the State." 321 U.S. 649, 660 (1944). The Court added: "The United States is a constitutional democracy," and the right to vote "is not to be nullified by a State through casting its electoral process in a form which permits a private organization to practice racial discrimination in the election." *Id.* at 664. After describing the many ways in which Texas law regulated primary elections, the Court overruled *Grovey*. *Id.* at 662–66.

Terry. States throughout the South responded to *Smith* by repealing their laws regulating primary elections and political parties and by adopting alternative methods of excluding black voters. In Texas, unregulated clubs continued holding preprimary nominating contests in which only white voters decided whom the clubs would support in the upcoming state primary. The winners of these preprimary elections invariably won the subsequent Democratic Party primary. The NAACP Legal Defense Fund challenged the constitutionality of one such preprimary election organized by the Jaybird Democratic Association of Fort Bend County. The Jaybird Democratic Association argued in defense that it was a "mere private group" with no formal ties to the state or the Democratic Party.

But in *Terry v. Adams*, 345 U.S. 461 (1953), the Court rejected the distinction. "For a state to permit such a duplication of its election processes is to permit a flagrant abuse of those processes to defeat the purposes of the Fifteenth Amendment," the Court wrote. *Terry*, 345 U.S. at 469. "It violates the Fifteenth Amendment for a state, by such circumvention, to permit within its borders the use of any device that produces an equivalent of the prohibited election." *Id.*

50.1.1

Harper v. Virginia Board of Elections

383 U.S. 663 (1966)

By the 1950s, the Supreme Court finally began prohibiting voter qualifications that were discriminatory on their face. After decades of failing to enforce the Fourteenth Amendment's Section 2, the Fifteenth Amendment, and the Nineteenth Amendment, the Court now held that the Equal Protection Clause banned southern practices that prohibited black people from voting, including primaries maintained by the Democratic Party and other nonstate actors.

At the same time, the Court declined to reevaluate its prior decisions upholding facially neutral voter qualifications. *Breedlove*, the five-page 1937 decision mentioned earlier in this section that upheld Georgia's poll tax as a "familiar form of taxation," 302 U.S. at 281, continued to authorize states to penalize poor people for the privilege of voting. *See, e.g., Butler v. Thompson*, 97 F. Supp. 17 (E.D. Va.), *aff'd*, 341 U.S. 937 (1951) (upholding a Virginia poll tax). And in 1959, a unanimous Court reaffirmed the constitutionality of southern literacy tests despite their widespread use in preventing black people from registering to vote. "States have long been held to have broad powers to determine the conditions under which the right of suffrage may be exercised," Justice William O. Douglas wrote in *Lassiter v. Northampton County Board of Elections*. 360 U.S. 45, 50 (1959). Douglas feebly cautioned states that they couldn't use literacy tests as "merely a device to make racial discrimination easy." *Id.* But he observed that "in our society where newspapers, periodicals, books, and other printed matter canvass and debate campaign issues, a State might conclude that only those who are literate should exercise the franchise." *Id.*

Much changed over the next seven years. In 1962, Congress proposed a constitutional amendment to overturn *Breedlove* and abolish the poll tax. *See* H.R. Rep. No. 1821, at 3, 5 (1962). In 1964, the states ratified the Twenty-Fourth Amendment, which prohibited governments from abridging the right to vote in federal primary or general elections "by reason of failure to pay any poll tax or other tax." In 1965, the Court interpreted this amendment to nullify "sophisticated as well as simple-minded" schemes to evade its words, including Virginia's attempt to impose a "material requirement solely upon those who refuse to surrender their constitutional right to vote in federal elections without paying a poll tax." *Harman v. Forssenius*, 380 U.S. 528, 540–41 (1965). And later that same year, Congress also passed the Voting Rights Act of 1965, Pub. L. No. 89–110, 79 Stat. 437, which outlawed literacy tests. Without overruling *Lassiter*, the Court upheld this ban on literacy tests in *South Carolina v. Katzenbach*, ruling that Congress's power to enforce the Fifteenth Amendment authorized Congress to remedy racial discrimination in voting even if literacy tests were not inherently flawed. 383 U.S. 301, 333–34 (1966).

Despite this revolution in federal voting rights, poll taxes in *state* elections survived. Annie Harper, a poor resident of Virginia unable to afford the $1.50 that the state continued to collect before voters could participate in state elections, challenged the tax under the Fourteenth Amendment.

Douglas, the author of *Lassiter*, wrote this opinion as well. However, Douglas found that *Lassiter* did not apply in *Harper v. Virginia Board of Elections*, 383 U.S. 663 (1966).

■ MR. JUSTICE DOUGLAS delivered the opinion of the Court.[1]

These are suits by Virginia residents to have declared unconstitutional Virginia's poll tax. . . .

While the right to vote in federal elections is conferred by Art. I, § 2, of the Constitution (*United States* v. *Classic,* 313 U. S. 299, 314–315), the right to vote in state elections is nowhere expressly mentioned. . . . [But] it is enough to say that once the franchise is granted to the electorate, lines may not be drawn which are inconsistent with the Equal Protection Clause of the Fourteenth Amendment. That is to say, the right of suffrage "is subject to the imposition of state standards which are not discriminatory and which do not contravene any restriction that Congress, acting pursuant to its constitutional powers, has imposed." *Lassiter* v. *Northampton Election Board,* 360 U. S. 45, 51. We were speaking there of a state literacy test which we sustained, warning that the result would be different if a literacy test, fair on its face, were used to discriminate against a class. *Id.,* at 53. But the *Lassiter* case does not govern the result here, because, unlike a poll tax, the "ability to read and write . . . has some relation to standards designed to promote intelligent use of the ballot." *Id.,* at 51.

We conclude that a State violates the Equal Protection Clause of the Fourteenth Amendment whenever it makes the affluence of the voter or payment of any fee an electoral standard. Voter qualifications have no relation to wealth nor to paying or not paying this or any other tax. Our cases demonstrate that the Equal Protection Clause of the Fourteenth Amendment restrains the States from fixing voter qualifications which invidiously discriminate. Thus without questioning the power of a State to impose reasonable residence restrictions on the availability of the ballot, we held in *Carrington* v. *Rash,* 380 U. S. 89, that a State may not deny the opportunity to vote

[1] **As You Read, Consider:** Virginia's state poll tax survived decades of scrutiny by federal courts as well as the ratification of the Twenty-Fourth Amendment, which banned poll taxes in federal elections. Yet Justice William O. Douglas invalidates the tax here anyway. What kind of test does he use to evaluate the tax's constitutionality: the rational-basis test, strict scrutiny, or something else?

to a bona fide resident merely because he is a member of the armed services. "By forbidding a soldier ever to controvert the presumption of non-residence, the Texas Constitution imposes an invidious discrimination in violation of the Fourteenth Amendment." *Id.,* at 96. Previously we had said that neither homesite nor occupation "affords a permissible basis for distinguishing between qualified voters within the State." *Gray* v. *Sanders,* 372 U. S. 368, 380. We think the same must be true of requirements of wealth or affluence or payment of a fee.

Long ago in *Yick Wo* v. *Hopkins,* 118 U. S. 356, 370, the Court referred to "the political franchise of voting" as a "fundamental political right, because preservative of all rights." Recently in *Reynolds* v. *Sims,* 377 U. S. 533, 561–562, we said, "The Equal Protection Clause demands no less than substantially equal state legislative representation for all citizens, of all places as well as of all races." *Id.,* at 568.

We say the same whether the citizen, otherwise qualified to vote, has $1.50 in his pocket or nothing at all, pays the fee or fails to pay it. The principle that denies the State the right to dilute a citizen's vote on account of his economic status or other such factors by analogy bars a system which excludes those unable to pay a fee to vote or who fail to pay.

It is argued that a State may exact fees from citizens for many different kinds of licenses; that if it can demand from all an equal fee for a driver's license, it can demand from all an equal poll tax for voting. But we must remember that the interest of the State, when it comes to voting, is limited to the power to fix qualifications. Wealth, like race, creed, or color, is not germane to one's ability to participate intelligently in the electoral process. Lines drawn on the basis of wealth or property, like those of race (*Korematsu* v. *United States,* 323 U. S. 214, 216), are traditionally disfavored. See *Edwards* v. *California,* 314 U. S. 160, 184–185 (Jackson, J., concurring); *Griffin* v. *Illinois,* 351 U. S. 12; *Douglas* v. *California,* 372 U. S. 353. To introduce wealth or payment of a fee as a measure of a voter's qualifications is to introduce a capricious or irrelevant factor. The degree of the discrimination is irrelevant. In this context—that is, as a condition of obtaining a ballot—the requirement of fee paying causes an "invidious" discrimination (*Skinner* v. *Oklahoma,* 316 U. S. 535, 541) that runs afoul of the Equal Protection Clause. Levy "by the poll," as stated in *Breedlove* v. *Suttles, supra,* at 281, is an old familiar form of taxation; and we say nothing to impair its validity so long as it is not made a condition to the exercise of the franchise. *Breedlove* v. *Suttles* sanctioned its use as "a prerequisite of voting." *Id.,* at 283. To that extent the *Breedlove* case is overruled. . . .

We have long been mindful that where fundamental rights and liberties are asserted under the Equal Protection Clause, classifications which might invade or restrain them must be closely scrutinized and carefully confined. See, *e. g., Skinner* v. *Oklahoma,* 316 U. S. 535, 541.

Those principles apply here. For to repeat, wealth or fee paying has, in our view, no relation to voting qualifications; the right to vote is too precious, too fundamental to be so burdened or conditioned.

NOTE: WEALTH AS A SUSPECT CLASSIFICATION

Harper strongly implied that the Supreme Court regarded wealth as a suspect classification, observing that "[l]ines drawn on the basis of wealth or property, like those of race, are traditionally disfavored." 383 U.S. at 668.

But later opinions emphasized *Harper*'s voting-rights context, not wealth, and applied strict scrutiny to all "statutes which deny some residents the right to vote." *Kramer v. Union Free Sch. Dist. No. 15*, 395 U.S. 621, 626–

28 (1969). As discussed above (section 48.1), in *San Antonio Independent School District v. Rodriguez*, 411 U.S. 1 (1973), the Court explicitly declined to hold that all classifications on the basis of wealth would be evaluated under strict scrutiny if the classifications did not also involve a fundamental right like voting.

NOTE: EDUCATIONAL AND AGE QUALIFICATIONS

Although the Supreme Court in *Harper* declined to reevaluate its decision in *Lassiter* that upheld state literacy tests, Congress did. With the Voting Rights Act of 1965, Congress prohibited states from imposing English literacy requirements on Puerto Rican voters—a prohibition the Court soon upheld in *Katzenbach v. Morgan*, discussed earlier in the section on Congress's power to enforce the Reconstruction amendments (section 21.3). 384 U.S. 641, 657–59 (1966). When Congress enacted the Voting Rights Act Amendments of 1970, it extended its abolition of literacy tests to all elections nationwide. Pub. L. No. 91–285, 84 Stat. 314, 315. The Court upheld this abolition in *Oregon v. Mitchell*, although the fractured Court could not arrive at a single explanation for why Congress had this power. 400 U.S. 112, 118 (1970).

A majority of the Court in *Mitchell* did, however, think that Congress went too far when it lowered the voting age in all elections to eighteen years old. *Id.* Although one majority of the Court thought that Congress could lower the age qualification in *federal* elections, a separate majority of the Court thought that Congress could not lower the age qualifications in *state or local* elections. *Id.* Congress immediately responded by proposing the Twenty-Sixth Amendment, which declared, "The right of citizens of the United States, who are eighteen years of age or older, to vote shall not be denied or abridged by the United States or by any State on account of age." The amendment was ratified by the end of 1971.

NOTE: RESIDENCY QUALIFICATIONS

Harper did not declare that *all* laws that burden the ability to vote would be evaluated under strict scrutiny. Rather, it favorably cited an earlier decision, *Carrington v. Rash*, which acknowledged the "unquestioned power [of a state] to impose reasonable residence restrictions on the availability of the ballot." 380 U.S. 89, 91 (1965). *Carrington* struck down a Texas law that prohibited soldiers on military bases from voting in local elections. Yet it also suggested that some less discriminatory residence restrictions might be tolerable. Over the next decade, the Court slowly moved from applying strict scrutiny to all voting restrictions to applying a balancing approach.

At first, the Court applied strict scrutiny to most residence requirements. For instance, in *Dunn v. Blumstein*, 405 U.S. 330 (1972), the Court applied strict scrutiny to a Tennessee law that imposed a three-month residency requirement for citizens to vote in certain state and county elections. The effect of the law prohibited students at Vanderbilt and other universities from voting in November elections, and the Court held that burdening the right to vote of newly arrived residents was not narrowly tailored to meet a compelling interest in "the prevention of . . . fraud." *Dunn*, 405 U.S. at 345. The Court also emphasized that the state's alternative interest in having "knowledgeable voters" with a "common interest in all matters pertaining to [the community's] government" was not compelling. *Id.* at 355.

But the following year, in *Marston v. Lewis*, the Court added that "[s]tates have valid and sufficient interests in providing for *some* period of time—prior to an election—in order to prepare adequate voter records and protect its electoral processes from possible frauds." 410 U.S. 679, 680 (1973). The Court upheld Arizona's fifty-day residency requirement because the state closed its voter-registration process at fifty days prior to elections and because the administrative work involved in voter registrations is time-consuming. *Id.*

NOTE: REGULATIONS OF POLITICAL PARTIES AND THE END OF STRICT SCRUTINY

The Court moved even further from applying strict scrutiny in cases involving the qualifications of candidates and the regulation of political parties. By the 1980s, the Court replaced *Harper*'s tiers-of-scrutiny approach with a formal balancing test.

When the Court first confronted laws that prohibited certain candidates from accessing a ballot, in *Williams v. Rhodes*, the Court held that such laws were analogous to poll taxes because they abridged "the right of qualified voters, regardless of their political persuasion, to cast their votes effectively." 393 U.S. 23, 30 (1968). The Court therefore applied strict scrutiny to strike down laws that made it difficult for third parties to put candidates on the ballot. *Id.* at 31–34; *see also, e.g.*, *Bullock v. Carter*, 405 U.S. 134, 144 (1972) (invalidating an expensive filing fee); *Moore v. Ogilvie*, 394 U.S. 814, 819 (1969) (invalidating a law that required certain candidates for office to obtain signatures from unpopulated areas of the state).

But in *Rosario v. Rockefeller*, 410 U.S. 752 (1973), the Court suggested that strict scrutiny would not always be appropriate for regulations of political parties. *Rosario* considered a challenge to a New York law that prohibited people from voting in a primary election unless they had enrolled in the political party at least thirty days before the election. Distinguishing *Harper*, *Dunn*, and other strict scrutiny cases as examples where "the State totally denied the electoral franchise to a particular class of residents," *Rosario*, 410 U.S. at 757, the *Rosario* Court instead asked whether the thirty-day time limitation was "so severe as itself to constitute an unconstitutionally onerous burden on the petitioners' exercise of the franchise," *id.* at 760. Applying a relatively deferential test, the Court concluded that this thirty-day limit was reasonably related to a "legitimate and valid state goal" of inhibiting "party 'raiding,' whereby voters in sympathy with one party designate themselves as voters of another party so as to influence or determine the results of the other party's primary." *Id.*

The Court later explained that "as a practical matter, there must be a substantial regulation of elections if they are to be fair and honest and if some sort of order, rather than chaos, is to accompany the democratic processes." In *Storer v. Brown*, 415 U.S. 724, 730 (1974). The Court therefore concluded that it would be inappropriate to apply strict scrutiny to *all* state election laws as opposed to only those that impose "severe" or "invidious" burdens on the right to vote. *Id.* at 729. For "reasonable, nondiscriminatory" election regulations, the Court announced a balancing test in *Anderson v. Celebrezze*, 460 U.S. 780 (1983):

> Constitutional challenges to specific provisions of a State's election laws . . . cannot be resolved by any "litmus-paper test" that will separate valid from invalid restrictions. *Storer,* 415 U.S. at 730. Instead, a court . . . must first consider the character and magnitude of the asserted injury to the rights protected by the First and Fourteenth Amendments that the plaintiff seeks to vindicate. It then must identify and evaluate the precise interests put forward by the State as justifications for the burden imposed by its rule. In passing judgment, the Court must not only determine the legitimacy and strength of each of those interests; it also must consider the extent to which those interests make it necessary to burden the plaintiff's rights. Only after weighing all these factors is the reviewing court in a position to decide whether the challenged provision is unconstitutional. The results of this evaluation will not be automatic; as we have recognized, there is "no substitute for the hard judgments that must be made." *Storer,* 415 U.S. at 730.

Id. at 789–90.

By declining to apply strict scrutiny to all laws that burdened the right to vote, *Anderson* opened the door for the Court to uphold laws whose burdens it subjectively regarded as not "severe." For example, in *Burdick v. Takushi*, 504 U.S. 428 (1992), the Court invoked *Anderson* to uphold Hawaii's prohibition on write-in voting—even though such a prohibition directly burdened the rights of voters to cast ballots. "[T]o subject every voting regulation to strict scrutiny and to require that the regulation be narrowly tailored to advance a compelling state interest . . . would tie the hands of States seeking to assure that elections are operated equitably and efficiently," the Court wrote. *Burdick*, 504 U.S. at 433–34. The Court distinguished *Harper*, *Dunn*, and earlier cases as examples of " 'severe' restrictions" on the right to vote. *Id.* at 434. Only in such cases would the Court continue to apply strict scrutiny. *Id.*; *see, e.g.*, *Norman v. Reed*, 502 U.S. 279 (1992).

50.1.2

Crawford v. Marion County Election Board

553 U.S. 181 (2008)

In 2002, two years after 537 votes in Florida and one vote on the Supreme Court decided the presidential election, Attorney General John Ashcroft announced a campaign against voting fraud. Ari Berman, *Give Us the Ballot* 219 (2015). The 2000 election had demonstrated that national elections could turn on a handful of votes—an issue that the two major parties interpreted very differently. Democrats focused on the twelve thousand eligible voters whom Florida had purged from its voter rolls because they had names similar to those in the state's database of disenfranchised felons. *Id.* at 209–10. But Republicans, led by Ashcroft, focused on the possibility that future close elections could be decided by people who showed up to vote under false pretenses. *See id.* at 218.

Ashcroft could point to no evidence of in-person voter fraud anywhere in the country. But Republican state officials—as well as a bipartisan commission led by former president Jimmy Carter and former secretary of state James A. Baker—agreed that "[t]he potential for . . . fraudulent registrations to produce fraudulent votes at the ballot box is very real." *Id.* at 218–20.

In 2005, Georgia and Indiana became the first states to require government-issued photo identification to cast a ballot. Representative John Lewis, who in 1965 had marched in Selma for the Voting Rights Act, called Georgia's voter ID law "a modern-day poll tax" and an obvious plan to disenfranchise Democratic-leaning poor voters. *Id.* A 2006 study found that 10 percent of eligible voters in the United States didn't have government-issued photo IDs, including 25 percent of black people, 18 percent of seniors, and 15 percent of people making less than $35,000 a year. *Id.* at 254. Yet Georgia planned to charge $20 for a new ID card—far more than the present-day value of *Harper*'s $1.50 poll tax. *Id.* Indiana, by contrast, offered free voter IDs—but only to people who could afford to drive to a Bureau of Motor Vehicles with a birth certificate and similar documents, each of which would still cost a fee to reproduce.

State representative William Crawford challenged Indiana's law in court as a violation of the Equal Protection Clause. The U.S. Court of Appeals for the Seventh Circuit sustained the law over the dissent of Judge Terence Evans, who complained, "Let's not beat around the bush: The Indiana voter photo ID law is a not-too-thinly-veiled attempt to discourage election-day turnout by certain folks believed to skew Democratic." *Crawford v. Marion Cnty. Election Bd.*, 472 F.3d 949, 954 (7th Cir. 2007) (Evans, J., dissenting).

Reviewing the law in *Crawford v. Marion County Election Board*, 553 U.S. 181 (2008), the Supreme Court applied the balancing test that it had developed in the decades after *Harper* to uphold the law.

■ JUSTICE STEVENS . . . delivered an opinion, in which THE CHIEF JUSTICE and JUSTICE KENNEDY join.[2]

At issue in these cases is the constitutionality of an Indiana statute requiring citizens voting in person on election day . . . to present photo identification issued by the government. . . .

---

2 **As You Read, Consider:** As Justice John Paul Stevens's plurality opinion explains, the Supreme Court followed its decision in *Harper v. Virginia Board of Elections* by announcing that it would apply a proportionality test—not strict scrutiny—to any "reasonable, nondiscriminatory" law that incidentally made it more difficult to vote. *See Anderson v.*

I

In *Harper v. Virginia Bd. of Elections,* 383 U.S. 663 (1966), the Court held that Virginia could not condition the right to vote in a state election on the payment of a poll tax of $1.50. . . . [W]e concluded that a State "violates the Equal Protection Clause of the Fourteenth Amendment whenever it makes the affluence of the voter or payment of any fee an electoral standard." *Id.,* at 666. We used the term "invidiously discriminate" to describe conduct prohibited under that standard, noting that we had previously held that while a State may obviously impose "reasonable residence restrictions on the availability of the ballot," it "may not deny the opportunity to vote to a bona fide resident merely because he is a member of the armed services." *Id.,* at 666–667 (citing *Carrington v. Rash,* 380 U.S. 89, 96 (1965)). Although the State's justification for the tax was rational, it was invidious because it was irrelevant to the voter's qualifications.

Thus, under the standard applied in *Harper,* even rational restrictions on the right to vote are invidious if they are unrelated to voter qualifications. In *Anderson v. Celebrezze,* 460 U.S. 780 (1983), however, we confirmed the general rule that "evenhanded restrictions that protect the integrity and reliability of the electoral process itself" are not invidious and satisfy the standard set forth in *Harper.* Rather than applying any "litmus test" that would neatly separate valid from invalid restrictions, we concluded that a court must identify and evaluate the interests put forward by the State as justifications for the burden imposed by its rule, and then make the "hard judgment" that our adversary system demands.

In later election cases we have followed *Anderson*'s balancing approach. Thus, in *Norman v. Reed,* 502 U.S. 279, 288–289 (1992), after identifying the burden Illinois imposed on a political party's access to the ballot, we "called for the demonstration of a corresponding interest sufficiently weighty to justify the limitation," and concluded that the "severe restriction" was not justified by a narrowly drawn state interest of compelling importance. Later, in *Burdick v. Takushi,* 504 U.S. 428 (1992), we applied *Anderson*'s standard for " 'reasonable, nondiscriminatory restrictions,' " 504 U.S., at 434, and upheld Hawaii's prohibition on write-in voting despite the fact that it prevented a significant number of "voters from participating in Hawaii elections in a meaningful manner." We reaffirmed *Anderson*'s requirement that a court evaluating a constitutional challenge to an election regulation weigh the asserted injury to the right to vote against the " 'precise interests put forward by the State as justifications for the burden imposed by its rule.' " [*Ibid.*]

In neither *Norman* nor *Burdick* did we identify any litmus test for measuring the severity of a burden that a state law imposes on a political party, an individual voter, or a discrete class of voters. However slight that burden may appear, as *Harper* demonstrates, it must be justified by relevant and legitimate state interests "sufficiently weighty to justify the limitation." . . .

II

The State has identified several state interests that arguably justify the burdens that [the Voter ID law] imposes on voters and potential voters. . . .

The first is the interest in deterring and detecting voter fraud. . . . Two recently enacted federal statutes[, the National Voter Registration Act of 1993, 107 Stat. 77, and the Help America Vote Act of 2002, 116 Stat. 1666,] . . . indicate that Congress believes that photo identification is one effective method of establishing a voter's qualification to vote . . . . That conclusion is also supported by a report issued . . .

Celebrezze, 460 U.S. 780, 789–90 (1983). Do you agree that laws that burden the right to vote should be subject to a more deferential standard of scrutiny than laws that burden other fundamental rights, such as the right to obtain contraception?

by the Commission on Federal Election Reform chaired by former President Jimmy Carter and former Secretary of State James A. Baker III[:]

> "There is no evidence of extensive fraud in U.S. elections or of multiple voting, but both occur, and it could affect the outcome of a close election. The electoral system cannot inspire public confidence if no safeguards exist to deter or detect fraud or to confirm the identity of voters. Photo [identification cards] currently are needed to board a plane, enter federal buildings, and cash a check. Voting is equally important." Building Confidence in U.S. Elections § 2.5 (Sept. 2005). . . .

The only kind of voter fraud that [the Indiana law] addresses is in-person voter impersonation at polling places. The record contains no evidence of any such fraud actually occurring in Indiana at any time in its history. Moreover, petitioners argue that provisions of the Indiana Criminal Code punishing such conduct as a felony provide adequate protection against the risk that such conduct will occur in the future. It remains true, however, that flagrant examples of such fraud in other parts of the country have been documented throughout this Nation's history by respected historians and journalists, that occasional examples have surfaced in recent years, and that Indiana's own experience with fraudulent voting in the 2003 Democratic primary for East Chicago Mayor—though perpetrated using absentee ballots and not in-person fraud—demonstrate that not only is the risk of voter fraud real but that it could affect the outcome of a close election.[3]

There is no question about the legitimacy or importance of the State's interest in counting only the votes of eligible voters. Moreover, the interest in orderly administration and accurate recordkeeping provides a sufficient justification for carefully identifying all voters participating in the election process. While the most effective method of preventing election fraud may well be debatable, the propriety of doing so is perfectly clear.

In its brief, the State argues that the inflation of its voter rolls provides further support for its enactment of [its law]. The record contains a November 5, 2000, newspaper article asserting that as a result of . . . "sloppy record-keeping," Indiana's lists of registered voters included the names of thousands of persons who had either moved, died, or were not eligible to vote because they had been convicted of felonies. . . . Even though Indiana's own negligence may have contributed to the serious inflation of its registration lists . . ., the fact of inflated voter rolls does provide a neutral and nondiscriminatory reason supporting the State's decision to require photo identification. . . .

[T]he State [also] contends that it has an interest in protecting public confidence "in the integrity and legitimacy of representative government." . . . [This interest] has independent significance, because it encourages citizen participation in the democratic process. . . .

III

[T]he burdens that are relevant to the issue before us are those imposed on persons who are eligible to vote but do not possess a current photo identification that complies with the requirements of [the Indiana law]. The fact that most voters already possess a valid driver's license, or some other form of acceptable identification, would

---

3 **Question:** When the Supreme Court has applied a proportionality test in cases like *Whole Woman's Health v. Hellerstedt*, the absence of real-life evidence supporting the state-interest side of the scales is usually pretty damning. *See Hellerstedt*, 136 S. Ct. 2292, 2311–12 (2016) (noting "no evidence in the record" that a Texas abortion regulation "would have helped even one woman obtain better treatment"). Why doesn't the lack of evidence of in-person fraud in Indiana doom the voter ID law here?

not save the statute under our reasoning in *Harper,* if the State required voters to pay a tax or a fee to obtain a new photo identification. But just as other States provide free voter registration cards, the photo identification cards issued by Indiana's BMV are also free. For most voters who need them, the inconvenience of making a trip to the BMV, gathering the required documents, and posing for a photograph surely does not qualify as a substantial burden on the right to vote, or even represent a significant increase over the usual burdens of voting.[4]

Both evidence in the record and facts of which we may take judicial notice, however, indicate that a somewhat heavier burden may be placed on a limited number of persons. They include elderly persons born out of State, who may have difficulty obtaining a birth certificate; persons who because of economic or other personal limitations may find it difficult either to secure a copy of their birth certificate or to assemble the other required documentation to obtain a state-issued identification; homeless persons; and persons with a religious objection to being photographed. . . .

The severity of that burden is, of course, mitigated by the fact that, if eligible, voters without photo identification may cast provisional ballots that will ultimately be counted. To do so, however, they must travel to the circuit court clerk's office within 10 days to execute the required affidavit. It is unlikely that such a requirement would pose a constitutional problem unless it is wholly unjustified. And even assuming that the burden may not be justified as to a few voters, that conclusion is by no means sufficient to establish petitioners' right to the relief they seek in this litigation. . . .

The record says virtually nothing about the difficulties faced by either indigent voters or voters with religious objections to being photographed. While one elderly man stated that he did not have the money to pay for a birth certificate, when asked if he did not have the money or did not wish to spend it, he replied, "both." From this limited evidence we do not know the magnitude of the impact [the law] will have on indigent voters in Indiana. . . .

In sum, on the basis of the record that has been made in this litigation, we cannot conclude that the statute imposes "excessively burdensome requirements" on any class of voters. . . . When we consider only the statute's broad application to all Indiana voters we conclude that it "imposes only a limited burden on voters' rights." *Burdick,* 504 U.S., at 439. The " 'precise interests' " advanced by the State are therefore sufficient to defeat petitioners' facial challenge. . . .

In their briefs, petitioners stress the fact that all of the Republicans in the General Assembly voted in favor of [the Indiana voter ID law] and the Democrats were unanimous in opposing it. . . . It is fair to infer that partisan considerations may have played a significant role in the decision to enact [the law]. If such considerations had provided the only justification for a photo identification requirement, we may also assume that [the law] would suffer the same fate as the poll tax at issue in *Harper.*

But if a nondiscriminatory law is supported by valid neutral justifications, those justifications should not be disregarded simply because partisan interests may have provided one motivation for the votes of individual legislators. . . . The application of the statute to the vast majority of Indiana voters is amply justified by the valid interest in protecting "the integrity and reliability of the electoral process." *Anderson,* 460 U.S., at 788, n. 9. . . .

---

4 **Question:** Stevens observes that Indiana provides free photo ID cards to drivers who can gather "the required documents." Yet as Justice David Souter observes in his dissent, those documents can cost more to obtain than the $1.50 at issue in *Harper*. To the extent that a person has to either (1) pay $12 for a birth certificate and obtain an ID or (2) cast a provisional ballot and travel to a different circuit court to execute an affidavit, isn't this a pretty substantial—undue, even—burden on the right to vote?

■ JUSTICE SCALIA, with whom JUSTICE THOMAS and JUSTICE ALITO join, concurring in the judgment.

[T]o evaluate a law respecting the right to vote—whether it governs voter qualifications, candidate selection, or the voting process—we use the approach set out in *Burdick v. Takushi,* 504 U.S. 428 (1992). This calls for application of a deferential "important regulatory interests" standard for nonsevere, nondiscriminatory restrictions, reserving strict scrutiny for laws that severely restrict the right to vote. *Id.,* at 433–434. . . . Thus, the first step is to decide whether a challenged law severely burdens the right to vote. Ordinary and widespread burdens, such as those requiring "nominal effort" of everyone, are not severe. Burdens are severe if they go beyond the merely inconvenient. . . .[5]

Of course, we have to identify a burden before we can weigh it. The Indiana law affects different voters differently, but what petitioners view as the law's several light and heavy burdens are no more than the different *impacts* of the single burden that the law uniformly imposes on all voters. To vote in person in Indiana, *everyone* must have and present a photo identification that can be obtained for free. . . . The Indiana photo-identification law is [therefore] a generally applicable, nondiscriminatory voting regulation, and our precedents refute the view that individual impacts are relevant to determining the severity of the burden it imposes. . . .

■ JUSTICE SOUTER, with whom JUSTICE GINSBURG joins, dissenting.

Indiana's "Voter ID Law" threatens to impose nontrivial burdens on the voting right of tens of thousands of the State's citizens and a significant percentage of those individuals are likely to be deterred from voting. . . .

The first set of burdens shown in these cases is the travel costs and fees necessary to get one of the limited variety of federal or state photo identifications needed to cast a regular ballot under the Voter ID Law. The travel is required for the personal visit to a license branch of the Indiana Bureau of Motor Vehicles (BMV), which is demanded of anyone applying for a driver's license or nondriver photo identification. . . . Poor, old, and disabled voters who do not drive a car . . . may find the trip prohibitive. . . . [T]he BMV has far fewer license branches in each county than there are voting precincts. Marion County, for example, has over 900 active voting precincts, yet only 12 BMV license branches. . . .

The burden of traveling to a more distant BMV office rather than a conveniently located polling place is probably serious for many of the individuals who lack photo identification. They almost certainly will not own cars, and public transportation in Indiana is fairly limited. According to a report published by Indiana's Department of Transportation in August 2007, 21 of Indiana's 92 counties have no public transportation system at all, and as of 2000, nearly 1 in every 10 voters lived within 1 of these 21 counties. . . .

For those voters who can afford the round trip, a second financial hurdle appears: in order to get photo identification for the first time, they need to present "a birth certificate, certificate of naturalization, U.S. veterans photo identification, U.S. military photo identification, or a U.S. passport.'" . . . [T]he two most common of these documents come at a price: Indiana counties charge anywhere from $3 to $12 for a birth certificate (and in some other States the fee is significantly higher). . . . The total fees for a passport, moreover, are up to about $100. So most voters must pay at least one fee to get the ID necessary to cast a regular ballot. As with the travel

[5] **Questions:** Justice Antonin Scalia's concurring opinion would have gone further than Stevens's plurality opinion in deferring to Indiana's interests. Applying Scalia's standard, was *Harper* correctly decided? If a state required everyone to pay a "nominal" poll tax of $12 to vote in state elections, would he consider it valid?

costs, . . . it matters that both the travel costs and the fees are disproportionately heavy for, and thus disproportionately likely to deter, the poor, the old, and the immobile. . . .

The State says that it adopted the ID law principally to combat voter fraud. . . . There is no denying the abstract importance, the compelling nature, of combating voter fraud. . . . [But] requiring a voter to show photo identification before casting a regular ballot addresses only one form of voter fraud: in-person voter impersonation. The photo identification requirement leaves untouched the problems of absentee-ballot fraud, which (unlike in-person voter impersonation) is a documented problem in Indiana. . . .

And even the State's interest in deterring a voter from showing up at the polls and claiming to be someone he is not must, in turn, be discounted for the fact that the State has not come across a single instance of in-person voter impersonation fraud in all of Indiana's history. . . . [There is a similar] dearth of evidence of in-person voter impersonation in any other part of the country.

The State responds to the want of evidence with the assertion that in-person voter impersonation fraud is hard to detect. But this is like saying the "man who wasn't there" is hard to spot, and to know whether difficulty in detection accounts for the lack of evidence one at least has to ask whether in-person voter impersonation is (or would be) relatively harder to ferret out than other kinds of fraud (*e.g.,* by absentee ballot) which the State has had no trouble documenting. The answer seems to be no; there is reason to think that "impersonation of voters is . . . the most likely type of fraud to be discovered." U.S. Election Assistance Commission, Election Crimes: An Initial Review and Recommendations for Future Study 9 (Dec.2006). This is in part because an individual who impersonates another at the polls commits his fraud in the open, under the scrutiny of local pollworkers who may well recognize a fraudulent voter when they hear who he claims to be. . . .

Without a shred of evidence that in-person voter impersonation is a problem in the State, much less a crisis, Indiana has adopted one of the most restrictive photo identification requirements in the country. The State recognizes that tens of thousands of qualified voters lack the necessary federally issued or state-issued identification, but it insists on implementing the requirement immediately, without allowing a transition period for targeted efforts to distribute the required identification to individuals who need it. . . . It is impossible to say, on this record, that the State's interest in adopting its signally inhibiting photo identification requirement has been shown to outweigh the serious burdens it imposes on the right to vote. . . .

If the Court's decision in *Harper v. Virginia Bd. of Elections,* 383 U.S. 663 (1966), stands for anything, it is that being poor has nothing to do with being qualified to vote. *Harper* made clear that "[t]o introduce wealth or payment of a fee as a measure of a voter's qualifications is to introduce a capricious or irrelevant factor." *Id.,* at 668. The State's requirements here, that people without cars travel to a motor vehicle registry and that the poor who fail to do that get to their county seats within 10 days of every election, likewise translate into unjustified economic burdens uncomfortably close to the outright $1.50 fee we struck down 42 years ago. Like that fee, the onus of the Indiana law is illegitimate just because it correlates with no state interest so well as it does with the object of deterring poorer residents from exercising the franchise. . . .[6]

[6] **Question:** Again, after reading Souter's dissenting opinion, has *Harper* been silently overruled?

NOTE: CRIMINAL-RECORD AND RACIAL QUALIFICATIONS

Criminal-record qualifications. One of the state interests that the *Crawford* Court recognized in applying its balancing test was Indiana's interest in excluding people who were "not eligible to vote because they had been convicted of felonies." 553 U.S. at 196. Like many states, Indiana disenfranchised people who were in prison or "otherwise subject to lawful detention." *See* Ind. Code 3–7–13–4 (1995).

When the Supreme Court in the 1960s and 1970s first evaluated laws that made it difficult or impossible for incarcerated people to vote, the Court fit the laws within its emerging balancing test that weighed the burden that the laws imposed against the state's various interests in passing the laws. *See, e.g., O'Brien v. Skinner*, 414 U.S. 524, 530 (1974) (invalidating a New York law that provided no ability for inmates awaiting trial or serving misdemeanor sentences to vote).

But in *Richardson v. Ramirez*, 418 U.S. 24 (1974), a 7–2 Court categorically upheld the power of states to disqualify people convicted of a felony from ever voting again. The Court explained that the Congress that proposed the Equal Protection Clause also proposed Section 2 of the Fourteenth Amendment. As discussed above, Section 2 reduced the congressional representation of any state in which the right to vote "is denied to any of the male inhabitants of such State, being twenty-one years of age, and citizens of the United States, or in any way abridged, *except for participation in rebellion, or other crime*" (emphasis added). In light of this language, the Court held that "the exclusion of felons from the vote has an affirmative sanction in § 2 of the Fourteenth Amendment," and therefore "the understanding of those who adopted the Fourteenth Amendment, as reflected in the express language of § 2 . . ., is of controlling significance." *Richardson*, 418 U.S. at 54–55. Writing in dissent, Justice Thurgood Marshall argued that the "historical purpose" and "political motivation behind § 2" made it clear that "§ 2 was not intended and should not be construed to be a limitation on the other sections of the Fourteenth Amendment." *Id.* at 73–74.

Racial qualifications. The *Crawford* Court didn't evaluate whether Indiana's voter ID law should be subjected to strict scrutiny as discrimination on the basis of race. This is likely because—since *Washington v. Davis*, 426 U.S. 229 (1976), and *Village of Arlington Heights v. Metropolitan Housing Development Corp.*, 429 U.S. 252 (1977)—a plaintiff who wants to attack a facially neutral law as racially discriminatory under the Equal Protection Clause must prove that the law was passed with a discriminatory purpose. This is an incredibly difficult standard to meet. Yet there are a handful of cases since the 1960s in which plaintiffs have met it.

One is *Hunter v. Underwood*, 471 U.S. 222 (1985), a case evaluating a provision of Alabama's constitution that prohibited people convicted of a felony from voting. The provision dated back to 1901, when Alabama's constitution was drafted by an all-white constitutional convention in the wake of Reconstruction. In his opening address, the president of the convention declared that the convention's purpose was "to establish white supremacy in this State" and to disenfranchise as many black people as possible. *Hunter*, 471 U.S. at 229–30. As the Court recognized in *Giles v. Harris*, 189 U.S. 475 (1903), the convention was successful. In light of this unusually explicit evidence of a discriminatory purpose, the Court in *Hunter* accepted that *Arlington Heights* required strict scrutiny. 471 U.S. at 231–32.

A second, and more controversial, application of strict scrutiny to an allegedly facially neutral law emerged from Hawaii. By the time western explorers visited Hawaii for the first time in 1778, over one hundred thousand people lived on the archipelago. Over the next century, many of these native Hawaiians were displaced or colonized by white settlers, particularly after the United States annexed Hawaii in 1898. *See* Julia Flynn Siler, *Lost Kingdom* 289–96 (2012). Treating the native population analogously to American Indians, Congress eventually set aside enormous tracts of public land as a trust for the benefit of statutorily defined "native Hawaiians." Act of July 9, 1921, ch. 42, 42 Stat. 108. After Hawaii was admitted as a state in 1959, the state established an elected agency to oversee this trust land. State law limited the right to vote for this agency only to "descendant[s] of the aboriginal peoples inhabiting the Hawaiian Islands which exercised sovereignty and subsisted in the Hawaiian Islands in 1778." Haw. Rev. Stat. § 10–2 (1993).

The authors of this state law drew support from a Supreme Court decision, *Morton v. Mancari*, 417 U.S. 535 (1974), in which the Court had held that an affirmative action program that benefitted American Indians didn't violate equal-protection principles because tribal status was "political rather than racial in nature." *Id.* at 553 n.24. But in *Rice v. Cayetano*, 528 U.S. 495 (2000), the Court disagreed that *Mancari* insulated Hawaii's voting scheme from Fifteenth Amendment scrutiny. The Court explained that "[a]ncestry can be a proxy for race. It is that proxy here." *Id.* at 516–17. By allowing only the descendants of certain "peoples" to vote in the election for a state agency, the Court continued, the state had demeaned other races in violation of the Fifteenth Amendment. *Id.* The Court distinguished *Mancari* as a case involving hiring preferences rather than voting. "It does not follow from *Mancari*," the Court wrote, "that Congress may authorize a State to establish a voting scheme that limits the electorate for its public officials to a class of tribal Indians, to the exclusion of all non-Indian citizens." *Id.* at 520.

50.2 RACIAL GERRYMANDERING

In 1957, shortly after the Supreme Court effectively abolished the white primary in *Terry v. Adams*, 345 U.S. 461 (1953), Congress passed the first civil rights statute since Reconstruction. The Civil Rights Act of 1957, Pub. L. No. 85–315, 71 Stat. 634, was a limited measure that established a civil rights division within the Department of Justice and empowered the division to obtain court injunctions against local governments that interfered with anyone seeking the right to vote.

Although the act was relatively toothless in the face of widespread disenfranchisement, voter-registration campaigns were successful in a few southern cities, including Tuskegee, Alabama. Home of the famous Tuskegee Institute, black students and faculty registered in large enough numbers to begin influencing local politics.

The leader of the local white citizens' council was also a state senator. He prompted the Alabama legislature to redraw the city of Tuskegee's boundaries to remove all but five of its four hundred black voters. Where the city's shape had once been a square, in 1957 the city's borders were reshaped into what the Supreme Court later called "an uncouth twenty-eight-sided figure." *Gomillion v. Lightfoot*, 364 U.S. 339, 340 (1960). C. G. Gomillion, the dean of students at the Tuskegee Institute, sued Mayor Phil M. Lightfoot and other local officials to enjoin them from "fencing Negro citizens out of town so as to deprive them of their pre-existing municipal vote." *Id.* at 341. But the federal district court held that states had plenary authority to redraw local boundaries notwithstanding any limits of the federal Constitution.

In *Gomillion v. Lightfoot*, 364 U.S. 339 (1960), the Supreme Court reversed, holding that the change in Tuskegee's boundaries violated the Fifteenth Amendment because it was intended to deprive black citizens of the right to vote. Conceding that Alabama had the power to change the boundaries of local governments, the Court declared that "Acts generally lawful may become unlawful when done to accomplish an unlawful end, and a constitutional power cannot be used by way of condition to attain an unconstitutional result." *Gomillion*, 364 U.S. at 347–48. In an influential concurring opinion, the otherwise unremarkable Justice Charles Whittaker argued that the decision should rest not on the Fifteenth Amendment but rather on the Equal Protection Clause of the Fourteenth Amendment. He observed that Gomillion and other excluded citizens still had the right to vote—in county elections as opposed to city elections—and therefore the harm of the changed borders was that it segregated Alabama citizens on the basis of race. *See id.* at 349 (Whittaker, J., concurring).

The Court decided *Gomillion* in 1960, a census year after which most states redrew the boundaries of their congressional and state legislative districts. As the Court evaluated these boundaries, the Court cited *Gomillion* for the principle that states had no power to redraw districts "on racial lines" or in a manner "motivated by racial considerations." *Wright v. Rockefeller*, 376 U.S. 52, 56 (1964). The Court also cited *Gomillion* to prohibit states from evading the Voting Rights Act of 1965 by adopting novel voting schemes such as at-large or multimember districts in which 50 percent of voters could elect two or more representatives. *Id.* Although the Court upheld the constitutionality of multimember districts in the abstract, it warned that states could not use such districts "invidiously to cancel out or minimize the voting strength of racial groups." *White v. Regester*, 412 U.S. 755 (1973).

Discriminatory purpose

Determining precisely when a state drew district boundaries to "minimize the voting strength of racial groups" proved to be difficult in practice. At first, the Court applied a disparate-impact test—one that looked at the history of racial discrimination and the effect of district lines on voting patterns—to evaluate whether racial groups were effectively shut out of the political process. *See, e.g.*, *Whitcomb v. Chavis*, 403 U.S. 124 (1971).

But after *Washington v. Davis*, 426 U.S. 229 (1976), the Court began to hold that future plaintiffs who challenged district boundaries were required to prove that the districting body acted with a discriminatory purpose. *See, e.g.*, *Rogers v. Lodge*, 458 U.S. 613 (1982); *City of Mobile v. Bolden*, 446 U.S. 55 (1980).

Disparate impact and majority-minority districts

Congress responded to this situation with the Voting Rights Act Amendments of 1982, Pub. L. No. 97–205, 96 Stat. 131. It Congress amended Section 2 of the Voting Rights Act to clarify that statutory violations could be proved by showing that a voting regulation had a disparate impact on the right of protected classes to vote. Voting Rights Act Amendments, 96 Stat. at 134.

Interpreting the amended Voting Rights Act in *Thornburg v. Gingles*, the court held that it is illegal for a state to "dilute [a minority group's] votes by submerging them in a white majority, thus impairing their ability to elect representatives of their choice." 478 U.S. 30, 46 (1986). The Court held that such dilution occurs when (1) a minority group is "sufficiently large and geographically compact to constitute a majority in a single-member district," (2) the minority group is "politically cohesive," and (3) the white majority votes sufficiently as a bloc . . . usually to defeat the minority's preferred candidate." *Id.* at 50–56.

Gingles involved a lawsuit against North Carolina, a state with a large black population that had failed to elect any black members to Congress since 1898. After the decision, the counsel for the Republican National Committee (RNC), Ben Ginsberg, gave a presentation to the Congressional Black Caucus in which he observed that "the Voting Rights Act now requires the drawing of majority-minority districts wherever possible." Ari Berman, *Give Us the Ballot* 188 (2015).

The RNC liked majority-minority districts because they concentrated Democratic-leaning black voters into very safe districts while making all neighboring districts whiter and safer for Republican candidates. Representative John Lewis endorsed this "unholy alliance" between black Democrats and the GOP because while it would decrease the number of Democratic representatives in Congress, it would increase the number of representatives of color. *Id.*

The Twelfth District

After the 1990 census, the North Carolina legislature—led by its first-ever black speaker of the house—drew two majority-minority districts, one contiguous district in the eastern part of the state and one unusually shaped district, the Twelfth, that snaked throughout the state to connect black neighborhoods in Durham, Greensboro, and Charlotte. Because these three cities were so far away from one another and separated by largely white communities, state legislators drew the connections between the three cities as narrowly as possible along swamps and highways. One state legislator remarked that "[i]f you drove down the interstate with both car doors open, you'd kill most of the people in the district." *Shaw v. Reno*, 509 U.S. 630, 636 (1993). The district even inspired poetry: "Ask not for whom the line is drawn; it is drawn to avoid thee." *Id.*

A white resident of North Carolina, Ruth Shaw, challenged Attorney General Janet Reno's approval of the Twelfth District as an unconstitutional racial gerrymander that violated the rights of white voters to "participate in a 'color-blind' electoral process." *Id.* at 641. In a 5–4 opinion, the Supreme Court in *Shaw v. Reno* agreed that the Voting Rights Act did not give states "*carte blanche* to engage in racial gerrymandering." *Id.* at 655. Citing the Court's earlier affirmative-action cases alongside *Gomillion*, Justice Sandra Day O'Connor wrote that where "a reapportionment plan rationally cannot be understood as anything other than an effort to segregate citizens into separate voting districts on the basis of race," the Court would strictly scrutinize the plan regardless of whether the intentions behind it were "benign." *Id.* at 652–53.

The lesson that the Court drew from North Carolina's Twelfth District was that all districting maps should be subject to strict scrutiny if "race was the predominant factor motivating the legislature's decision to place a significant number of voters within or without a particular district." *Miller v. Johnson*, 515 U.S. 900, 916 (1995). Shortly after *Shaw*, the Court announced that it would determine "predominance" with evidence that the legislature "subordinated traditional race-neutral districting principles, including but not limited to compactness, contiguity, and respect for political subdivisions or communities defined by actual shared interests, to racial considerations." *Id.* Once it applied strict scrutiny, the Court would then demand that the use of race be narrowly tailored to meet a compelling purpose, such as complying with the Voting Rights Act or remedying de jure discrimination. *See Bush v. Vera*, 517 U.S. 952, 979 (1996).

But this entire test quickly evolved into the Court declining to apply strict scrutiny when a legislature's purpose was to engage in *partisan* gerrymandering—even though voters of color in most states overwhelmingly vote Democratic. *See Rucho v. Common Cause*, 139 S. Ct. 2484 (2019); *Vieth v. Jubelirer*, 541 U.S. 267 (2004). Many racial gerrymandering cases therefore have turned on whether the Court thinks that the state was predominantly motivated by race or by partisanship when it drew the boundaries of a particular district.

North Carolina's Twelfth District illustrated the difficulties posed by the race/party distinction as the district returned to the Court four times over the next two decades. *See, e.g.*, *Shaw v. Hunt* (*Shaw II*), 517 U.S. 899, 902–07 (1996) (holding in the second case that race, not partisanship, was the predominant factor); *Hunt v. Cromartie*, 526 U.S. 541, 550 (1999) (holding in the third case that partisanship, not race, could have been the predominant factor); *Easley v. Cromartie*, 532 U.S. 234, 258 (2001) (holding in the fourth case that partisanship, not race, was the predominant factor). In *Cooper v. Harris*, the Twelfth District's "fifth(!) appearance" before the Supreme Court, the Court agreed with the district court "that race, not politics, accounted for the district's reconfiguration." 137 S. Ct. 1455, 1472–74 (2017). The Court then invalidated the district's boundaries because the state had made no attempt to justify the district under strict scrutiny by showing that "(to meet the 'narrow tailoring' requirement) . . . it had 'a strong basis in evidence' for concluding that the [Voting Rights Act or need to remedy de jure discrimination] required its action." *Id.* at 1464.

50.3 ONE PERSON, ONE VOTE

In addition to limiting a state's use of race in the political process, the Equal Protection Clause has also been interpreted to limit racially neutral methods by which states count and weigh ballots. In this respect, the Supreme Court's interpretation of the clause has paralleled its interpretation of Article I, Section 2, which declares that members of the House of Representatives shall be chosen "by the People of the several States."

50.3.1

Reynolds v. Sims

377 U.S. 533 (1964)

In *Wesberry v. Sanders*, the Supreme Court interpreted Article I, Section 2, of the U.S. Constitution to mean that "one man's vote in a congressional election is to be worth as much as another's." 376 U.S. 1, 8 (1964). *Wesberry* rebuked Georgia's failure to redraw its congressional districts to ensure that each of its members of Congress represented an equal number of constituents. Because Georgia's rural congressional districts had fewer people than its urban districts, rural voters had relatively more influence with their representatives. The Court held that this inequality violated a long-standing principle of "one person, one vote," adding, "To say that a vote is worth more in one district than in another would not only run counter to our fundamental ideas of democratic government, it would cast aside the principle of a House of Representatives elected 'by the People.' " *Id.*

Wesberry invalidated Georgia's *congressional* districts. Simultaneously, the Court also considered a challenge to Alabama's *state legislative* districts. As in Georgia, Alabama's urban districts for its house of representatives had ballooned in population, yet the state hadn't changed the boundaries of its districts since 1900. This inequality between rural and urban areas was magnified in the state senate, as Alabama proposed to give each county one senator regardless of its population. The result effectively diluted the political power of the state's cities.

M. O. Sims and other voters in Alabama's most populous county challenged Alabama's districting scheme under the Equal Protection Clause. They sued probate judge B. A. Reynolds and other officials, seeking an order to compel the state to redraw its legislative boundaries in compliance with the principle of one person, one vote.

Agreeing with Sims, the Court in *Reynolds v. Sims*, 377 U.S. 533 (1964), found that Alabama's districting scheme was unconstitutionally unequal in its treatment of voters.

■ MR. CHIEF JUSTICE WARREN delivered the opinion of the Court.[7]

Involved in these cases are an appeal and two cross-appeals from a decision of the Federal District Court for the Middle District of Alabama holding invalid, under the Equal Protection Clause of the Federal Constitution, the existing and two legislatively proposed plans for the apportionment of seats in the two houses of the Alabama Legislature. . . .

II.

Undeniably the Constitution of the United States protects the right of all qualified citizens to vote, in state as well as in federal elections. A consistent line of decisions by this Court in cases involving attempts to deny or restrict the right of suffrage has made this indelibly clear. It has been repeatedly recognized that all qualified voters have a constitutionally protected right to vote, *Ex parte Yarbrough,* 110 U. S. 651, and to have their votes counted, *United States* v. *Mosley,* 238 U. S. 383. . . . The right to vote can neither be denied outright, *Guinn* v. *United States,* 238 U. S. 347, nor destroyed by alteration of ballots, *United States* v. *Classic,* 313 U. S. 299, 315, nor diluted by ballot-box stuffing, *Ex parte Siebold,* 100 U. S. 371. . . . Racially based gerrymandering, *Gomillion* v. *Lightfoot,* 364 U. S. 339, and the conducting of white primaries, *Nixon* v. *Herndon,* 273 U. S. 536, *Nixon* v. *Condon,* 286 U. S. 73, *Smith* v. *Allwright,* 321 U. S. 649, *Terry* v. *Adams,* 345 U. S. 461, both of which result in denying to some citizens their right to vote, have been held to be constitutionally impermissible. And history has seen a continuing expansion of the scope of the right of suffrage in this country. The right to vote freely for the candidate of one's choice is of the essence of a democratic society, and any restrictions on that right strike at the heart of representative government. And the right of suffrage can be denied by a

---

7 **As You Read, Consider:** Alabama has proposed to structure its state senate identically to the U.S. Senate, in which senators represent formally equal political communities instead of mathematically equal populations. Why, precisely, does Chief Justice Earl Warren think that such an arrangement harms someone? To the extent that he invalidates Alabama's senate, does he also suggest that the U.S. Senate is unconstitutional?

debasement or dilution of the weight of a citizen's vote just as effectively as by wholly prohibiting the free exercise of the franchise. . . .

In *Baker* v. *Carr,* 369 U. S. 186, we held that a claim asserted under the Equal Protection Clause challenging the constitutionality of a State's apportionment of seats in its legislature, . . . in effect presented a justiciable controversy subject to adjudication by federal courts. . . .

In *Gray* v. *Sanders,* 372 U. S. 368, we held that the Georgia county unit system, applicable in statewide primary elections, was unconstitutional since it resulted in a dilution of the weight of the votes of certain Georgia voters merely because of where they resided. . . .

In *Wesberry* v. *Sanders,* 376 U. S. 1, decided earlier this Term, we held that . . . the constitutional test for the validity of congressional districting schemes was one of substantial equality of population among the various districts established by a state legislature for the election of members of the Federal House of Representatives. . . . We found further, in *Wesberry,* that "our Constitution's plain objective" was that "of making equal representation for equal numbers of people the fundamental goal[."] . . . [O]ur decision in *Wesberry* was of course grounded on that language of the Constitution which prescribes that members of the Federal House of Representatives are to be chosen "by the People," while attacks on state legislative apportionment schemes, such as that involved in the instant cases, are principally based on the Equal Protection Clause of the Fourteenth Amendment. Nevertheless, *Wesberry* clearly established that the fundamental principle of representative government in this country is one of equal representation for equal numbers of people, without regard to race, sex, economic status, or place of residence within a State. . . .

III.

A predominant consideration in determining whether a State's legislative apportionment scheme constitutes an invidious discrimination violative of rights asserted under the Equal Protection Clause is . . . whether there has been any discrimination against certain of the State's citizens which constitutes an impermissible impairment of their constitutionally protected right to vote. Like *Skinner* v. *Oklahoma,* 316 U. S. 535, such a case "touches a sensitive and important area of human rights," and "involves one of the basic civil rights of man[."] . . . Undoubtedly, the right of suffrage is a fundamental matter in a free and democratic society. Especially since the right to exercise the franchise in a free and unimpaired manner is preservative of other basic civil and political rights, any alleged infringement of the right of citizens to vote must be carefully and meticulously scrutinized. Almost a century ago, in *Yick Wo* v. *Hopkins,* 118 U. S. 356, the Court referred to "the political franchise of voting" as "a fundamental political right, because preservative of all rights." 118 U. S., at 370.

Legislators represent people, not trees or acres. Legislators are elected by voters, not farms or cities or economic interests. As long as ours is a representative form of government, and our legislatures are those instruments of government elected directly by and directly representative of the people, the right to elect legislators in a free and unimpaired fashion is a bedrock of our political system. It could hardly be gainsaid that a constitutional claim had been asserted by an allegation that certain otherwise qualified voters had been entirely prohibited from voting for members of their state legislature. And, if a State should provide that the votes of citizens in one part of the State should be given two times, or five times, or 10 times the weight of votes of citizens in another part of the State, it could hardly be contended that the right to vote of those residing in the disfavored areas had not been effectively diluted. . . . And it is inconceivable that a state law to the effect that, in counting votes for legislators, the votes of citizens in one part of the State would be multiplied by two, five, or 10, while the votes of persons in another area would be counted only at face value, could be constitutionally sustainable. . . .

Of course, the effect of state legislative districting schemes which give the same number of representatives to unequal numbers of constituents is identical. Overweighting and overvaluation of the votes of those living here has the certain effect of dilution and undervaluation of the votes of those living there. The resulting discrimination against those individual voters living in disfavored areas is easily demonstrable mathematically. Their right to vote is simply not the same right to vote as that of those living in a favored part of the State. Two, five, or 10 of them must vote before the effect of their voting is equivalent to that of their favored neighbor. Weighting the votes of citizens differently, by any method or means, merely because of where they happen to reside, hardly seems justifiable. One must be ever aware that the Constitution forbids "sophisticated as well as simple-minded modes of discrimination." . . .

Logically, in a society ostensibly grounded on representative government, it would seem reasonable that a majority of the people of a State could elect a majority of that State's legislators. To conclude differently, and to sanction minority control of state legislative bodies, would appear to deny majority rights in a way that far surpasses any possible denial of minority rights that might otherwise be thought to result. Since legislatures are responsible for enacting laws by which all citizens are to be governed, they should be bodies which are collectively responsive to the popular will. And the concept of equal protection has been traditionally viewed as requiring the uniform treatment of persons standing in the same relation to the governmental action questioned or challenged. With respect to the allocation of legislative representation, all voters, as citizens of a State, stand in the same relation regardless of where they live. Any suggested criteria for the differentiation of citizens are insufficient to justify any discrimination, as to the weight of their votes, unless relevant to the permissible purposes of legislative apportionment. . . .

Since the achieving of fair and effective representation for all citizens is concededly the basic aim of legislative apportionment, we conclude that the Equal Protection Clause guarantees the opportunity for equal participation by all voters in the election of state legislators. Diluting the weight of votes because of place of residence impairs basic constitutional rights under the Fourteenth Amendment just as much as invidious discriminations based upon factors such as race, *Brown* v. *Board of Education,* 347 U. S. 483, or economic status, *Griffin* v. *Illinois,* 351 U. S. 12. Our constitutional system amply provides for the protection of minorities by means other than giving them majority control of state legislatures. And the democratic ideals of equality and majority rule, which have served this Nation so well in the past, are hardly of any less significance for the present and the future. . . .

We are cautioned about the dangers of entering into political thickets and mathematical quagmires. Our answer is this: a denial of constitutionally protected rights demands judicial protection; our oath and our office require no less. . . .

To the extent that a citizen's right to vote is debased, he is that much less a citizen. The fact that an individual lives here or there is not a legitimate reason for overweighting or diluting the efficacy of his vote. The complexions of societies and civilizations change, often with amazing rapidity. A nation once primarily rural in character becomes predominantly urban. Representation schemes once fair and equitable become archaic and outdated. But the basic principle of representative government remains, and must remain, unchanged—the weight of a citizen's vote cannot be made to depend on where he lives. Population is, of necessity, the starting point for consideration and the controlling criterion for judgment in legislative apportionment controversies. A citizen, a qualified voter, is no more nor no less so because he lives in the city or on the farm. This is the clear and strong command of our Constitution's Equal Protection Clause. This is an essential part of the concept of a government of laws and not men. This is at the heart of Lincoln's vision of "government of the people, by the people, [and] for the people." The Equal Protection Clause demands no less than substantially equal state legislative representation for all citizens, of all places as well as of all races.

IV.

We hold that, as a basic constitutional standard, the Equal Protection Clause requires that the seats in both houses of a bicameral state legislature must be apportioned on a population basis. Simply stated, an individual's right to vote for state legislators is unconstitutionally impaired when its weight is in a substantial fashion diluted when compared with votes of citizens living in other parts of the State. Since, under neither the existing apportionment provisions nor either of the proposed plans was either of the houses of the Alabama Legislature apportioned on a population basis, the District Court correctly held that all three of these schemes were constitutionally invalid. . . .

V.

Since neither of the houses of the Alabama Legislature, under any of the three plans considered by the District Court, was apportioned on a population basis, we would be justified in proceeding no further. However, one of the proposed plans, that contained in the so-called 67-Senator Amendment, at least superficially resembles the scheme of legislative representation followed in the Federal Congress. Under this plan, each of Alabama's 67 counties is allotted one senator. . . . Arguably, this is analogous to the allocation of two Senate seats, in the Federal Congress, to each of the 50 States, regardless of population. Seats in the Alabama House, under the proposed constitutional amendment, are distributed by giving each of the 67 counties at least one, with the remaining 39 seats being allotted among the more populous counties on a population basis. This scheme, at least at first glance, appears to resemble that prescribed for the Federal House of Representatives, where the 435 seats are distributed among the States on a population basis, although each State, regardless of its population, is given at least one Congressman. Thus, . . . [the plan] proposed by the Alabama Legislature, at least arguably presents for consideration a scheme analogous to that used for apportioning seats in Congress. . . .

Attempted reliance on the federal analogy appears often to be little more than an after-the-fact rationalization offered in defense of maladjusted state apportionment arrangements. The original constitutions of 36 of our States provided that representation in both houses of the state legislatures would be based completely, or predominantly, on population. And the Founding Fathers clearly had no intention of establishing a pattern or model for the apportionment of seats in state legislatures when the system of representation in the Federal Congress was adopted. . . .

The system of representation in the two Houses of the Federal Congress is one ingrained in our Constitution, as part of the law of the land. It is one conceived out of compromise and concession indispensable to the establishment of our federal republic. Arising from unique historical circumstances, it is based on the consideration that . . . at the time of the inception of the system of representation in the Federal Congress, a compromise between the larger and smaller States on this matter averted a deadlock in the Constitutional Convention which had threatened to abort the birth of our Nation. . . .

Political subdivisions of States—counties, cities, or whatever—never were and never have been considered as sovereign entities. . . . As stated by the Court in

Hunter v. *City of Pittsburgh,* 207 U. S. 161, 178, these governmental units are "created as convenient agencies for exercising such of the governmental powers of the State as may be entrusted to them," and the "number, nature and duration of the powers conferred upon [them] . . . and the territory over which they shall be exercised rests in the absolute discretion of the State." The relationship of the States to the Federal Government could hardly be less analogous.

Thus, we conclude that the plan contained in the 67-Senator Amendment for apportioning seats in the Alabama Legislature cannot be sustained by recourse to the so-called federal analogy. . . .[8]

VI.

By holding that as a federal constitutional requisite both houses of a state legislature must be apportioned on a population basis, we mean that the Equal Protection Clause requires that a State make an honest and good faith effort to construct districts, in both houses of its legislature, as nearly of equal population as is practicable. We realize that it is a practical impossibility to arrange legislative districts so that each one has an identical number of residents, or citizens, or voters. Mathematical exactness or precision is hardly a workable constitutional requirement. . . .

[S]ome distinctions may well be made between congressional and state legislative representation. Since, almost invariably, there is a significantly larger number of seats in state legislative bodies to be distributed within a State than congressional seats, . . . [s]omewhat more flexibility may therefore be constitutionally permissible with respect to state legislative apportionment than in congressional districting. . . .

A State may legitimately desire to maintain the integrity of various political subdivisions, insofar as possible, and provide for compact districts of contiguous territory. . . . Indiscriminate districting, without any regard for political subdivision or natural or historical boundary lines, may be little more than an open invitation to partisan gerrymandering. Single-member districts may be the rule in one State, while another State might desire to achieve some flexibility by creating multimember or floterial districts. Whatever the means of accomplishment, the overriding objective must be substantial equality of population among the various districts, so that the vote of any citizen is approximately equal in weight to that of any other citizen in the State. . . .[9]

NOTE: GOVERNMENTS COVERED BY THE ONE PERSON, ONE VOTE PRINCIPLE

Reynolds launched a revolution in how elected state and local governments structured themselves. In an immediate illustration of *Reynolds*'s wide applicability, the Court issued five decisions alongside *Reynolds* that applied its one person, one vote principle to strike down the

---

[8] **Questions:** What do you make of Warren's distinction between the U.S. Senate and the Alabama senate? Are you persuaded that the principles that render the Alabama senate invalid should not apply to the U.S. Senate because of the historical "compromise" that gave rise to the structure of Congress?

[9] **Questions:** In *Rucho v. Common Cause,* Chief Justice John Roberts acknowledged the possibility that a voter could be harmed by partisan gerrymandering but held that the issue was a political question because of the absence of any "judicially manageable" standards. 139 S. Ct. 2484, 2505 (2019). Does Warren provide such standards for the geographic discrimination of this case? How is a court supposed to figure out whether, say, "natural or historical boundary lines" justify a deviation from equally populated districts?

state legislative districts of Colorado, Delaware, Maryland, New York, and Virginia. *See, e.g., Lucas v. Forty-Fourth Gen. Assembly of Colo.*, 377 U.S. 713 (1964).

County and city governments. And in the years after *Reynolds*, the Court invoked the one person, one vote principle to strictly scrutinize how other governments structured elections as well. For example, in *Avery v. Midland County*, the Court applied the one person, one vote principle to a county government, holding that a state could not allow unpopulated rural areas of a county to elect the same number of county commissioners as heavily populated towns and cities. 390 U.S. 474, 485–86 (1968). And in *New York City Board of Estimate v. Morris*, the Court applied the one person, one vote principle to New York City's government, holding that New York could not give each of the city's five boroughs the same number of votes in the municipal government when the largest borough of Brooklyn had vastly more people than the smallest borough of Staten Island. 489 U.S. 688, 703 (1989); *see also Hadley v. Junior Coll. Dist.*, 397 U.S. 50 (1970) (applying one person, one vote principle to a junior college district); *Kramer v. Union Free Sch. Dist. No. 15*, 395 U.S. 621 (1969) (same to a school district).

Ballot initiatives and referenda. The Court also applied the one person, one vote principle to invalidate ballot initiatives and referenda in which affected residents were excluded from participating. As discussed earlier with regard to voter qualifications (section 50.1), the Court held that the principle required the application of strict scrutiny to states and local governments that allowed only taxpayers or certain classes of residents to vote on decisions that generally affected the whole community. *See, e.g., Hill v. Stone*, 421 U.S. 289 (1975) (general obligation bonds); *City of Phoenix v. Kolodziejski*, 399 U.S. 204 (1970) (similar); *Cipriano v. City of Houma*, 395 U.S. 701 (1969) (revenue bonds).

Exceptions to one person, one vote principle. But the Court declined to apply the one person, one vote principle to every situation. Three exceptions stand out.

Exception 1: Appointed offices. First, the Court held that the principle applies only to *elected* offices, not to offices that are appointed by an officer whose own election complies with the one person, one vote principle—such as a state governor. *See Rodriguez v. Popular Democratic Party*, 457 U.S. 1 (1982); *Sailors v. Bd. of Educ.*, 387 U.S. 105 (1967).

Exception 2: Nonresidents. Second, the Court held that the principle applies only to *residents* who live within the relevant government's jurisdiction. In *Holt Civic Club v. City of Tuscaloosa*, the Court rejected the argument that the principle required Alabama to allow people in the suburbs of Tuscaloosa to vote in Tuscaloosa elections—even though the state allowed the city to enforce its own laws extraterritorially in the suburbs. 439 U.S. 60, 73–74 (1978).

And in *Town of Lockport v. Citizens for Community Action at the Local Level, Inc.*, the Court held that in situations where two constituencies would be affected very differently by a change in boundaries—for example, where two cities vote on whether to merge—a state could condition the change on a vote of both constituencies, even if they have different populations. 430 U.S. 259, 271–72 (1977) (upholding a New York law that authorized a change in county government only if concurrent majorities of the numerous city residents and the less numerous county residents voted to approve the change). *Cf. Hunter v. City of Pittsburgh*, 207 U.S. 161, 181 (1907) (allowing a state to take the opposite approach and authorize two cities to merge where an absolute majority of all voters approve, even if most voters in the smaller city disapprove).

Exception 3: Special-purpose governments. Third, and most significantly, the Court held that the one person, one vote principle applies only to *general-purpose* governments whose purpose and activities affect most people equally, not to *special-purpose* governments whose purpose and activities disproportionately affect a particular group.

The Court first explained this exception in *Salyer Land Co. v. Tulare Lake Basin Water Storage District*, a case involving a water-storage district whose primary purpose was to manage water in an agricultural region. 410 U.S. 719, 721 (1973). California authorized only landowners to vote for the district's board of directors. It also gave each landowner voting power in proportion to the assessed value of the landowner's land. The Court applied the rational-basis test—not strict scrutiny—to this voting scheme because of the district's "special limited purpose and [because] of the disproportionate effect of its activities on landowners as a group." *Id.* at 728. In other words, the Court held that the one person, one vote principle doesn't apply to governments whose purpose "is sufficiently specialized and narrow" and whose "activities bear on [a particular group] so disproportionately as to distinguish the [government] from those public entities whose more general governmental functions demand application of the *Reynolds* principle." *Ball v. James*, 451 U.S. 355, 362 (1981).

In practice, the nonresident and special-purpose exceptions—both developed in 1973 or thereafter—have threatened the viability of the Supreme Court's earlier cases in which the Court applied the one person, one vote principle to strike down elections in which only property owners could vote. For example, in the earlier decision of *City of Phoenix v. Kolodziejski*, the Court applied the one person, one vote principle to a law that allowed only property owners to vote on Phoenix's decision to take on debt. 399 U.S. 204, 215 (1970). The Court rejected the city's argument that municipal debt disproportionately affected people who paid property taxes, declaring that "all residents of Phoenix, property owners and nonproperty owners alike, have a substantial interest in the public facilities and the services available in the city and will be substantially affected by the ultimate outcome of the bond election at issue in this case." *Id.* at 209.

But in *Ball v. James*, the Court declined to apply the one person, one vote principle to an Arizona water reclamation district that was responsible for supplying electric power to the entire metropolitan Phoenix area, even though the residents of Phoenix had a substantial interest in the district. 451 U.S. at 370. The Court emphasized the district's primary purpose of managing water for agricultural uses, and distinguished *Kolodziejski* as a case "concern[ing] the operations of traditional municipalities exercising the full range of normal governmental powers, . . . [not] a special-purpose governmental entity." *Id.* at 366 n.11. The Court deepened the incompatibility between *Ball* and *Kolodziejski* in a later case, *Quinn v. Millsap*, in which the Court distinguished "the three water-district cases" from a Missouri "board of freeholders" empowered to propose a revision of local government. 491 U.S. 95, 109 (1989). Even though the board of freeholders was not a traditional municipality or even a general-purpose government, the Court applied the one person, one vote principle because "the scope of its mandate is far more encompassing" than land-use issues and because its work "affects all citizens of the city and county, regardless of land ownership." *Id.*

NOTE: EXACTNESS REQUIRED BY THE ONE PERSON, ONE VOTE PRINCIPLE

Although *Reynolds* struck down Alabama's districting scheme for violating the one person, one vote principle, the Court did not hold that all voting schemes are automatically invalid if some voters have more voting power than others. Rather, in contexts where the one person, one vote principle applies, the Court has applied strict scrutiny to evaluate a state's departure from "substantially equal . . . representation for all citizens." *Reynolds*, 377 U.S. at 568. *Reynolds* added that what counted as "substantially equal" might depend on the context. The Court recognized that "more flexibility may . . . be constitutionally permissible with respect to state legislative apportionment than in congressional districting." *Id.* at 578.

Applying these principles, in the context of congressional districting, the Court held that it would apply strict scrutiny to any departure from "precise mathematical equality." *Kirkpatrick v. Preisler*, 394 U.S. 526, 530–31 (1969). For example, where the difference in population between New Jersey's largest and smallest congressional districts was a mere 0.7 percent, the Court applied strict scrutiny because, given "rapid advances in computer technology," the state could have drawn contiguous districts of equal population. *Karcher v. Daggett*, 462 U.S. 725, 733 (1983).

But in the context of state legislative districting, the Court reaffirmed that "mathematical exactness is not required in state apportionment plans. De minimis deviations are unavoidable." *Swann v. Adams*, 384 U.S. 440 (1967); *see also Gaffney v. Cummings*, 412 U.S. 735, 745 (1973).

In the decades after *Reynolds*, the Court eventually settled on a 10 percent deviation between the smallest and largest district as its definition of a de minimus deviation. *See, e.g.*, *Chapman v. Meier*, 420 U.S. 1, 22 (1975) (20 percent); *White v. Regester*, 412 U.S. 755, 761 (1973) (9.9 percent). In *Harris v. Arizona Independent Redistricting Commission*, the Court explained that for deviations of more than 10 percent, it would apply strict scrutiny; and for all other deviations it would apply a version of the rational-basis test: "[T]hose attacking a state-approved plan must show that it is more probable than not that a deviation of less than 10% reflects the predominance of illegitimate reapportionment factors rather than the 'legitimate considerations' to which we have referred in *Reynolds* and later cases." 578

U.S. 253, 259 (2016). The *Harris* Court added, "Given the inherent difficulty of measuring and comparing factors that may legitimately account for small deviations from strict mathematical equality, we believe that attacks on deviations under 10% will succeed only rarely, in unusual cases." *Id.*

The factors to which the *Harris* Court referred that could theoretically justify departures from substantial equality include a state's interest in maintaining the integrity of political subdivisions, maintaining the competitive balance among political parties, assuring each county at least one representative, preserving compactness and contiguity, and complying with the requirements of the Voting Rights Act. *See, e.g., League of United Latin Am. Citizens v. Perry*, 548 U.S. 399 (2006); *Brown v. Thomson*, 462 U.S. 835 (1983).

NOTE: DEFINITION OF *PERSON* IN *ONE PERSON, ONE VOTE*

A year before *Reynolds*, in *Gray v. Sanders*, the Court held that the Equal Protection Clause prohibited a state from diluting a person's vote by legally weighing some people's ballots more heavily than others. 372 U.S. 368, 380 (1963). Extending this holding, *Reynolds* added that a state worked an equivalent harm when a state diluted the effect of a person's vote by putting the person in an overpopulated legislative district. People in overpopulated districts had more competition electing representatives of their choice than people in less populated districts, and therefore their vote effectively counted for less. The *Reynolds* Court's description of the harm therefore could be interpreted as vote dilution.

Although the remedy that *Reynolds* offered for this harm was to require states to put a substantially equal number of *people* in each legislative district, the harm would arguably be remedied even further by putting a substantially equal number of *voters* in each legislative district. To illustrate with an extreme example, if Alabama redrew its legislative districts so that a First District had 10,000 people but only 100 eligible voters and a Second District had 10,000 people and 10,000 eligible voters, then the voters in the Second District would arguably suffer the same kind of vote dilution as existed before *Reynolds*. Some states therefore responded to *Reynolds* by equalizing the population of *registered voters*, not just the total population. In *Burns v. Richardson*, the Court rejected a challenge to Hawaii's use of the registered-voter population. 384 U.S. 73, 94–97 (1966).

More recently, campaign strategists affiliated with the Republican Party have argued that less extreme versions of the above hypothetical may exist in districts with large populations of people ineligible to vote, such as noncitizens and children. Because such districts tend to vote Democratic, one prominent Republican redistricting specialist wrote in 2015 that equalizing districts on the basis of citizens or registered voters rather than total population "would be advantageous to Republicans and Non-Hispanic Whites," "would clearly be a disadvantage for the Democrats," and would "provoke a high degree of resistance from Democrats and the major minority groups in the nation." Plaintiffs' Motion for an Order to Show Cause at 2, *New York v. U.S. Dep't of Com.*, No. 18-CV-2921 (S.D.N.Y. May 30, 2019).

That same year, Texas Republicans challenged Texas's legislative districts on the ground that the one person, one vote principle requires states to use voting population rather than total population to determine legislative districts. But in *Evenwel v. Abbott*, 578 U.S. 54 (2016), the Supreme Court disagreed. Without deciding whether states could optionally choose to equalize districts on the basis of voting population rather than total population, the Court held that the history of the Fourteenth Amendment, precedent since *Reynolds*, and historical practice all confirmed the constitutionality of equalizing districts on the basis of total population. *Evenwel*, 136 S. Ct. at 1132–33. The Court also explained that the harm identified by *Reynolds* was not only vote dilution but the lack of "equal representation for equal numbers of people"—that is, in overpopulated districts, a resident could less easily get a representative's attention. *Id.* at 1131 (quoting *Reynolds*, 377 U.S. at 560–61).

50.4 THE JUDICIARY'S POWER TO REMEDY VOTING-RIGHTS VIOLATIONS

As discussed earlier in the context of the Supreme Court's school-desegregation cases (section 46.1), once a federal court concludes that a government has violated the Constitution, "the scope of [the] court's equitable powers to remedy past wrongs is broad, for breadth and flexibility are inherent in equitable remedies." *Swann v. Charlotte-Mecklenburg Bd. of Educ.*, 402 U.S. 1, 15 (1971). This is true in the voting-rights context as well, as the Supreme Court has upheld the power of district courts to redraw legislative boundaries and order other relief in voter-qualification; racial gerrymandering; and one person, one vote cases. *See, e.g.*, *Reynolds v. Sims*, 377 U.S. 533, 586–87 (1964) (upholding a district court's order that reapportioned the Alabama legislature as "an appropriate and well-considered exercise of judicial power").

But, as in the desegregation case of *Milliken v. Bradley*, 418 U.S. 717 (1974), the Court in voting-rights cases has warned that "[t]he remedial powers of an equity court must be adequate to the task, but they are not unlimited." *Whitcomb v. Chavis*, 403 U.S. 124, 161 (1971). For instance, in *Sixty-Seventh Minnesota State Senate v. Beens*, the Court invalidated a district court's order that remedied Minnesota's violation of the one person, one vote principle by "slash[ing] [the] state senate's size almost in half." 406 U.S. 187, 199 (1972). The Court explained that remedial courts should attempt to accommodate state constitutions and state legislative decisions as much as possible when remedying federal constitutional violations. *Id.* at 197. As the Court added in a later case, "a federal court, lacking the political authoritativeness that the legislature can bring to the task, must act circumspectly, and in a manner free from any taint of arbitrariness or discrimination." *Wise v. Lipscomb*, 437 U.S. 535, 539–41 (1978) (internal quotation marks omitted).

50.4.1
Bush v. Gore
531 U.S. 98 (2000)

In the following case, *Bush v. Gore*, 531 U.S. 98 (2000), the Supreme Court offered unique interpretations of the concern of *Harper v. Virginia Board of Elections*, 383 U.S. 663 (1966), with arbitrary voter qualifications; the concern of *Reynolds v. Sims*, 377 U.S. 533 (1964), with vote dilution; and the scope of its own power to remedy constitutional violations.

On the night of the 2000 presidential election, Vice President Al Gore led Texas Governor George W. Bush in the electoral vote, 255 to 246. But the results from Florida—with its 25 electoral votes—remained unclear. Bush led Gore in Florida by 1,784 votes. This margin was close enough to trigger a machine recount in each of Florida's sixty-seven counties.

The national media that descended on Florida revealed three enormous election problems.

First, Florida was one of eight states that prohibited formerly incarcerated people from voting. Enacted as part of the state's so-called black codes in the aftermath of the Civil War (see section 20.1), this disenfranchisement was racially discriminatory in purpose and effect. Black people, who largely voted Democratic, made up a sixth of the state population but nearly half of its disenfranchised population. *See* Ari Berman, *Give Us the Ballot* 208–10 (2015).

Second, the state's disenfranchisement of so many people had collateral effects. Before the election, Florida's secretary of state distributed to its counties a list of 58,000 people who recently had been disenfranchised. This "purge list" was littered with errors: a fifth of the list—12,000 people—were names of people who remained eligible to vote, including the elections supervisor of Madison County. *Id.* These numerous errors led twenty of Florida's counties to disregard the list. But the remaining counties prohibited people named on the list from voting. *Id.*

Third, and more comically, each of Florida's counties had the discretion to use different ballots, some of which were disastrously designed. Palm Beach County infamously used a "butterfly ballot," on which the names of various candidates appeared on both sides of a punch card like wings on a butterfly. Voters chose their candidate by dislodging a "chad," or perforation, on the part of the card that corresponded to a candidate's name. Bush's name appeared at the top of the left wing; to vote for Bush, voters had to punch the first chad. Gore's name appeared immediately below Bush's name; but to vote for Gore, voters had to punch the *third* chad, rather than the second. The second chad corresponded to Reform Party candidate Pat Buchanan, whose name appeared on the right wing of the ballot. This design caused an estimated 3,000

Democratic voters to vote by mistake for Buchanan. *See* Jonathan N. Wand et al., *The Butterfly Did It: The Aberrant Vote for Buchanan in Palm Beach County, Florida*, 95 Am. Pol. Sci. Rev. 793, 797 (2001).

The conclusion of the automatic machine recount resulted in a much smaller margin of victory for Bush but reaffirmed the result. *See Bush v. Palm Beach Cnty. Canvassing Bd.*, 531 U.S. 70, 73–74 (2000).

The Gore campaign then requested manual recounts in four counties, including Miami-Dade and Palm Beach. A Florida state court allowed the recount but ruled that the counties had to submit final results before a statutory deadline of November 14. The court added that Florida's secretary of state, Katherine Harris, could decide whether to allow for late filings. *Id.* Harris—the person responsible for Florida's error-filled purge list—also was the cochair of Bush's Florida campaign. Despite the obvious appearance of bias, Harris declined to extend the statutory deadline.

In light of the enormous political stakes, Florida became what the chief counsel for the Bush campaign called "Woodstock for constitutional lawyers." Berman, *supra*, at 210. Among the lawyers that the Bush campaign recruited were Ted Cruz, then a twenty-nine-year-old campaign adviser and recent clerk to Chief Justice William Rehnquist; John Roberts, another former Rehnquist clerk then in private practice; Amy Coney Barrett, a recent clerk to Justice Antonin Scalia also in private practice; Brett Kavanaugh, a former member of Kenneth Starr's investigation of President Bill Clinton; Theodore Olson, a former assistant attorney general; and John Manning, a law professor at Columbia. *Id.*; *see* Joan Biskupic, *Supreme Court Is About to Have 3 Bush v. Gore Alumni Sitting on the Bench*, CNN, Oct. 17, 2020. The Gore campaign's lawyers included Larry Tribe, a Harvard law professor; Kathleen Sullivan, dean of Stanford Law School; and David Boies, a notable trial lawyer.

The Gore campaign sued Harris in state court, seeking an order compelling her to accept late-filed results of the manual recount. The Florida Supreme Court—a majority of which had been appointed by a Democratic governor—agreed that the Florida Constitution required Harris to accept manual counts after the statutory deadline, until at least November 26. The Bush campaign appealed to the U.S. Supreme Court, alleging that the Florida court's extension of the statutory deadline violated Article II of the U.S. Constitution, which provides that "[e]ach State shall appoint, in such Manner as the *Legislature* thereof may direct, a Number of Electors" (emphasis added). In *Bush v. Palm Beach County Canvassing Board*, the Supreme Court vacated the Florida court's order and remanded the case for the Florida court to determine whether its extension conflicted with Article II. 531 U.S. at 75–78.

On remand, the Florida court reaffirmed its extension of the deadline.

Meanwhile, on November 26, Harris certified the election results and declared Bush the winner by a margin of 537 votes. The Gore campaign challenged this certification in state court, arguing that Miami-Dade County had failed to manually recount 9,000 "undervotes" in which voter machines failed to detect a vote for president. These undervotes revealed another quirk of Florida's various ballot designs: thousands of voters across Florida had marked their punch-card ballots insufficiently to completely dislodge the chads. The entire country soon became familiar with "hanging chads" (where one or more corners were still attached to the ballot) and "dimpled chads."

On December 8, the Florida Supreme Court agreed with Gore that "there are legal votes within the 9,000 uncounted votes sufficient to place the results of this election in doubt." *Gore v. Harris*, 772 So. 2d 1243, 1261 (Fla. 2000). The court defined *legal vote* as "one in which there is a 'clear indication of the intent of the voter.'" *Id.* at 1257. Observing that Florida law vested broad discretion in trial judges to "provide any relief appropriate under such circumstances," the court held that the trial judge could order every Florida county—including those that had not conducted a manual recount—to manually recount all undervotes. *Id.* at 1262. The court added that Harris was required to accept results after the November 26 deadline it had previously set as it had not intended to exclude votes identified through ongoing manual recounts. *Id.* at 1260.

A federal statute, 3 U.S.C. § 7, required electors to meet ten days later, on December 18. Another statute, 3 U.S.C. § 5, provided that if a state made "its final determination of any controversy . . . by judicial or other methods . . . at least six days before the time fixed for the meeting of the electors, such determination . . . shall be conclusive." Racing against this § 5 deadline of December 12, the Bush campaign filed an emergency application for a stay in the U.S. Supreme Court, complaining that the Florida court's December 8 order changed state law in violation of Article II. The campaign also argued that the order violated the Equal Protection Clause because the Florida court failed to provide a precise standard by which each county would determine whether a ballot physically contained a "clear indication of the intent of the voter." After issuing a weekend stay, the U.S. Supreme Court heard argument on December 11.

The Court issued its opinion in *Bush v. Gore* the next day—and, thus, Bush became the forty-third president of the United States.

■ PER CURIAM.[10]

[This] petition presents the following questions: whether the Florida Supreme Court established new standards for resolving Presidential election contests, thereby violating Art. II, § 1, cl. 2, of the United States Constitution and failing to comply with 3 U. S. C. § 5, and whether the use of standardless manual recounts violates the

[10] **As You Read, Consider:** A majority of the Court holds that the Florida Supreme Court violated the Equal Protection Clause. Who, precisely, was treated unequally? Is someone's vote being valued more than another person's vote, as in *Reynolds v. Sims*?

Equal Protection and Due Process Clauses. . . . [W]e find a violation of the Equal Protection Clause. . . .

[T]he individual citizen has no federal constitutional right to vote for electors for the President of the United States unless and until the state legislature chooses a statewide election as the means to implement its power to appoint members of the electoral college. U. S. Const., Art. II, § 1. This is the source for the statement in *McPherson* v. *Blacker,* 146 U. S. 1, 35 (1892), that the state legislature's power to select the manner for appointing electors is plenary; it may, if it so chooses, select the electors itself, which indeed was the manner used by state legislatures in several States for many years after the framing of our Constitution. *Id.,* at 28–33. History has now favored the voter, and in each of the several States the citizens themselves vote for Presidential electors. When the state legislature vests the right to vote for President in its people, the right to vote as the legislature has prescribed is fundamental; and one source of its fundamental nature lies in the equal weight accorded to each vote and the equal dignity owed to each voter. The State, of course, after granting the franchise in the special context of Article II, can take back the power to appoint electors. See *id.,* at 35 (" '[T]here is no doubt of the right of the legislature to resume the power at any time, for it can neither be taken away nor abdicated' ").

The right to vote is protected in more than the initial allocation of the franchise. Equal protection applies as well to the manner of its exercise. Having once granted the right to vote on equal terms, the State may not, by later arbitrary and disparate treatment, value one person's vote over that of another. See, *e. g., Harper* v. *Virginia Bd. of Elections,* 383 U. S. 663, 665 (1966). It must be remembered that "the right of suffrage can be denied by a debasement or dilution of the weight of a citizen's vote just as effectively as by wholly prohibiting the free exercise of the franchise." *Reynolds* v. *Sims,* 377 U. S. 533, 555 (1964).

There is no difference between the two sides of the present controversy on these basic propositions. Respondents say that the very purpose of vindicating the right to vote justifies the recount procedures now at issue. The question before us, however, is whether the recount procedures the Florida Supreme Court has adopted are consistent with its obligation to avoid arbitrary and disparate treatment of the members of its electorate.

Much of the controversy seems to revolve around ballot cards designed to be perforated by a stylus but which, either through error or deliberate omission, have not been perforated with sufficient precision for a machine to register the perforations. In some cases a piece of the card—a chad—is hanging, say, by two corners. In other cases there is no separation at all, just an indentation.

The Florida Supreme Court has ordered that the intent of the voter be discerned from such ballots. . . . [But t]he recount mechanisms implemented in response to the decisions of the Florida Supreme Court do not satisfy the minimum requirement for nonarbitrary treatment of voters. . . . Florida's basic command for the count of legally cast votes is to consider the "intent of the voter." 772 So. 2d, at 1262. This is unobjectionable as an abstract proposition and a starting principle. The problem inheres in the absence of specific standards to ensure its equal application. The formulation of uniform rules to determine intent based on these recurring circumstances is practicable and, we conclude, necessary.

The law does not refrain from searching for the intent of the actor in a multitude of circumstances; and in some cases the general command to ascertain intent is not susceptible to much further refinement. In this instance, however, the question is not whether to believe a witness but how to interpret the marks or holes or scratches on an inanimate object, a piece of cardboard or paper which, it is said, might not have registered as a vote during the machine count. The factfinder confronts a thing, not a person. The search for intent can be confined by specific rules designed to ensure uniform treatment.

The want of those rules here has led to unequal evaluation of ballots in various respects. See *id.,* at 1267 (Wells, C. J., dissenting) ("Should a county canvassing board count or not count a 'dimpled chad' where the voter is able to successfully dislodge the chad in every other contest on that ballot? Here, the county canvassing boards disagree"). As seems to have been acknowledged at oral argument, the standards for accepting or rejecting contested ballots might vary not only from county to county but indeed within a single county from one recount team to another.

The record provides some examples. A monitor in Miami-Dade County testified at trial that he observed that three members of the county canvassing board applied different standards in defining a legal vote. And testimony at trial also revealed that at least one county changed its evaluative standards during the counting process. Palm Beach County, for example, began the process with a 1990 guideline which precluded counting completely attached chads, switched to a rule that considered a vote to be legal if any light could be seen through a chad, changed back to the 1990 rule, and then abandoned any pretense of a *per se* rule, only to have a court order that the county consider dimpled chads legal. This is not a process with sufficient guarantees of equal treatment.

An early case in our one-person, one-vote jurisprudence arose when a State accorded arbitrary and disparate treatment to voters in its different counties. *Gray* v. *Sanders,* 372 U. S. 368 (1963). The Court found a constitutional violation. We relied on these principles in the context of the Presidential selection process in *Moore* v. *Ogilvie,* 394 U. S. 814 (1969), where we invalidated a county-based procedure that diluted the influence of citizens in larger counties in the nominating process. There we observed that "[t]he idea that one group can be granted greater voting strength than another is hostile to the one man, one vote basis of our representative government." *Id.,* at 819.

The State Supreme Court ratified this uneven treatment. It mandated that the recount totals from two counties, Miami-Dade and Palm Beach, be included in the certified total. . . . Yet each of the counties used varying standards to determine what was a legal vote. Broward County used a more forgiving standard than Palm Beach County, and uncovered almost three times as many new votes, a result markedly disproportionate to the difference in population between the counties.[11]

In addition, the recounts in these three counties were not limited to so-called undervotes but extended to all of the ballots. The distinction has real consequences. A manual recount of all ballots identifies not only those ballots which show no vote but also those which contain more than one, the so-called overvotes. Neither category will be counted by the machine. This is not a trivial concern. At oral argument, respondents estimated there are as many as 110,000 overvotes statewide. As a result, the citizen whose ballot was not read by a machine because he failed to vote for a candidate in a way readable by a machine may still have his vote counted in a manual recount; on the other hand, the citizen who marks two candidates in a way discernible by the machine will not have the same opportunity to have his vote count, even if a manual examination of the ballot would reveal the requisite indicia of intent. Furthermore, the citizen who marks two candidates, only one of which is discernible

11 **Question:** The plurality here suggests that it violates the Equal Protection Clause when different counties apply different procedures for counting ballots. Yet every state in the Union has different methods of counting ballots in federal elections, and most states join Florida in allowing local governments or precincts to develop their own standards. Does this discussion cast into doubt all of U.S. election law?

by the machine, will have his vote counted even though it should have been read as an invalid ballot. . . .

That brings [up] yet a further equal protection problem. The votes certified by the court included a partial total from one county, Miami-Dade. The Florida Supreme Court's decision thus gives no assurance that the recounts included in a final certification must be complete. Indeed, it is respondents' submission that it would be consistent with the rules of the recount procedures to include whatever partial counts are done by the time of final certification, and we interpret the Florida Supreme Court's decision to permit this. This accommodation no doubt results from the truncated contest period established by the Florida Supreme Court in *Palm Beach County Canvassing Bd.* v. *Harris,* at respondents' own urging. The press of time does not diminish the constitutional concern. A desire for speed is not a general excuse for ignoring equal protection guarantees.

In addition to these difficulties the actual process by which the votes were to be counted under the Florida Supreme Court's decision raises further concerns. That order did not specify who would recount the ballots. The county canvassing boards were forced to pull together ad hoc teams of judges from various Circuits who had no previous training in handling and interpreting ballots. . . .

The recount process, in its features here described, is inconsistent with the minimum procedures necessary to protect the fundamental right of each voter in the special instance of a statewide recount under the authority of a single state judicial officer. Our consideration is limited to the present circumstances, for the problem of equal protection in election processes generally presents many complexities.[12]

The question before the Court is not whether local entities, in the exercise of their expertise, may develop different systems for implementing elections. Instead, we are presented with a situation where a state court with the power to assure uniformity has ordered a statewide recount with minimal procedural safeguards. When a court orders a statewide remedy, there must be at least some assurance that the rudimentary requirements of equal treatment and fundamental fairness are satisfied. . . .

Upon due consideration of the difficulties identified to this point, it is obvious that the recount cannot be conducted in compliance with the requirements of equal protection and due process without substantial additional work. It would require not only the adoption (after opportunity for argument) of adequate statewide standards for determining what is a legal vote, and practicable procedures to implement them, but also orderly judicial review of any disputed matters that might arise. . . .

The Supreme Court of Florida has said that the legislature intended the State's electors to "participat[e] fully in the federal electoral process," as provided in 3 U. S. C. § 5. That statute, in turn, requires that any controversy or contest that is designed to lead to a conclusive selection of electors be completed by December 12. That date is upon us, and there is no recount procedure in place under the State Supreme Court's order that comports with minimal constitutional standards. Because it is evident that any recount seeking to meet the December 12 date will be

---

12 **Questions:** The plurality here writes that "[o]ur consideration is limited to the present circumstances." It then distinguishes the many divergent election procedures in other states by observing that *this* case involves "a situation where a state court with the power to assure uniformity has ordered a statewide recount with minimal procedural safeguards." In other words, the plurality appears to suggest that this opinion should not be taken as precedent outside the context of the 2000 Florida recount. As it happens, the Supreme Court has never cited *Bush v. Gore* again in a majority opinion.

Is this one-time-only analysis a principled method of judicial interpretation? If so, what principles does it serve?

unconstitutional for the reasons we have discussed, we reverse the judgment of the Supreme Court of Florida ordering a recount to proceed.[13]

Seven Justices of the Court agree that there are constitutional problems with the recount ordered by the Florida Supreme Court that demand a remedy. See *post* (Souter, J., dissenting); (Breyer, J., dissenting). The only disagreement is as to the remedy. . . .

None are more conscious of the vital limits on judicial authority than are the Members of this Court, and none stand more in admiration of the Constitution's design to leave the selection of the President to the people, through their legislatures, and to the political sphere. When contending parties invoke the process of the courts, however, it becomes our unsought responsibility to resolve the federal and constitutional issues the judicial system has been forced to confront. . . .

■ CHIEF JUSTICE REHNQUIST, with whom JUSTICE SCALIA and JUSTICE THOMAS join, concurring.

We join the *per curiam* opinion. We write separately because we believe there are additional grounds that require us to reverse . . . .

In most cases, comity and respect for federalism compel us to defer to the decisions of state courts on issues of state law. . . . Cf. *Erie R. Co.* v. *Tompkins,* 304 U. S. 64 (1938). Of course, in ordinary cases, the distribution of powers among the branches of a State's government raises no questions of federal constitutional law, subject to the requirement that the government be republican in character. See U. S. Const., Art. IV, § 4. But there are a few exceptional cases in which the Constitution imposes a duty or confers a power on a particular branch of a State's government. This is one of them. Article II, § 1, cl. 2, provides that "[e]ach State shall appoint, in such Manner as the *Legislature* thereof may direct," electors for President and Vice President. (Emphasis added.) Thus, the text of the election law itself, and not just its interpretation by the courts of the States, takes on independent significance. . . .[14]

In Florida, the legislature has chosen to hold statewide elections to appoint the State's 25 electors. Importantly, the legislature has delegated the authority to run the elections and to oversee election disputes to the Secretary of State, Fla. Stat. Ann. § 97.012(1), and to state circuit courts, §§ 102.168(1), 102.168(8). Isolated sections of the code may well admit of more than one interpretation, but the general coherence of the legislative scheme may not be altered by judicial interpretation so as to wholly change the statutorily provided apportionment of responsibility among these various bodies. In any election but a Presidential election, the Florida Supreme Court can give as little or as much deference to Florida's executives as it chooses, so far as

---

[13] **Questions:** A safe-harbor provision, 3 U.S.C. § 5, provides that if a state resolves any election-related controversies by December 12, then the state's electoral votes cannot be challenged when Congress counts them the following January. Critically, § 5 does not say that all controversies must be resolved by December 12. Why, then, does the plurality not remand this case for the Florida Supreme Court to fix its order and extend the recount beyond December 12? Does Chief Justice William Rehnquist's concurring opinion offer more persuasive reasoning?

[14] **Questions:** Rehnquist here writes that Article II requires a state's "Legislature" alone to determine how the state will appoint its electors. In this case, the Florida legislature has, by statute, declared that "[n]o vote shall be declared invalid or void if there is a clear indication of the intent of the voter." Fla. Stat. Ann. § 101.5614. The legislature has also empowered Florida circuit courts to "provide any relief appropriate" to correct any alleged wrongs in how ballots are counted. *Id.* § 102.168(8).

In light of the legislature's actions, why does Rehnquist believe that it violates the federal Constitution for the Florida Supreme Court to direct Florida circuit courts to provide "appropriate" relief? Rehnquist spent his entire judicial career advocating for federalism; is he now suggesting that the U.S. Supreme Court has the power to reverse a state court's interpretation of state law?

Article II is concerned . . . . But, with respect to a Presidential election, the court must be both mindful of the legislature's role under Article II in choosing the manner of appointing electors and deferential to those bodies expressly empowered by the legislature to carry out its constitutional mandate. . . .

The scope and nature of the remedy ordered by the Florida Supreme Court jeopardizes the "legislative wish" to take advantage of the safe harbor provided by 3 U. S. C. § 5. December 12, 2000, is the last date for a final determination of the Florida electors that will satisfy § 5. Yet in the late afternoon of December 8th—four days before this deadline—the Supreme Court of Florida ordered recounts of tens of thousands of so-called "undervotes" spread through 64 of the State's 67 counties. This was done in a search for elusive—perhaps delusive—certainty as to the exact count of 6 million votes. . . . The Supreme Court of Florida ordered this additional recount under the provision of the Election Code giving the circuit judge the authority to provide relief that is "appropriate under such circumstances." Fla. Stat. Ann. § 102.168(8).

Surely when the Florida Legislature empowered the courts of the State to grant "appropriate" relief, it must have meant relief that would have become final by the cutoff date of 3 U. S. C. § 5. In light of the inevitable legal challenges and ensuing appeals to the Supreme Court of Florida and petitions for certiorari to this Court, the entire recounting process could not possibly be completed by that date. . . . Given all these factors, . . . the remedy prescribed by the Supreme Court of Florida cannot be deemed an "appropriate" one as of December 8. . . .

■ JUSTICE STEVENS, with whom JUSTICE GINSBURG and JUSTICE BREYER join, dissenting.[15]

The Constitution assigns to the States the primary responsibility for determining the manner of selecting the Presidential electors. See Art. II, § 1, cl. 2. When questions arise about the meaning of state laws, including election laws, it is our settled practice to accept the opinions of the highest courts of the States as providing the final answers. On rare occasions, however, either federal statutes or the Federal Constitution may require federal judicial intervention in state elections. This is not such an occasion.

The federal questions that ultimately emerged in this case are not substantial. Article II provides that "[e]ach *State* shall appoint, in such Manner as the Legislature *thereof* may direct, a Number of Electors." *Ibid.* (emphasis added). It does not create state legislatures out of whole cloth, but rather takes them as they come—as creatures born of, and constrained by, their state constitutions. Lest there be any doubt, we stated over 100 years ago in *McPherson* v. *Blacker,* 146 U. S. 1, 25 (1892), that . . . "[t]he [State's] legislative power is the supreme authority except as limited by the constitution of the State." The legislative power in Florida is subject to judicial review pursuant to Article V of the Florida Constitution, and nothing in Article II of the Federal Constitution frees the state legislature from the constraints in the State Constitution that created it. . . .

It hardly needs stating that Congress, pursuant to 3 U. S. C. § 5, did not impose any affirmative duties upon the States that their governmental branches could "violate." Rather, § 5 provides a safe harbor for States to select electors in contested elections "by judicial or other methods" established by laws prior to the election day.

15 **Questions:** Are Justice John Paul Stevens's criticisms of the plurality and concurring opinions persuasive? If they are, does the majority's interpretation of the Constitution—a one-time-only interpretation offered by Republican-appointed justices that has the practical effect of deciding an election in favor of a Republican presidential candidate—nevertheless deserve respect because it was reached by a majority of the Court?

Section 5, like Article II, assumes the involvement of the state judiciary in interpreting state election laws and resolving election disputes under those laws. Neither § 5 nor Article II grants federal judges any special authority to substitute their views for those of the state judiciary on matters of state law.

Nor are petitioners correct in asserting that the failure of the Florida Supreme Court to specify in detail the precise manner in which the "intent of the voter," Fla. Stat. Ann. § 101.5614(5), is to be determined rises to the level of a constitutional violation. We found such a violation when individual votes within the same State were weighted unequally, see, *e. g., Reynolds* v. *Sims,* 377 U. S. 533, 568 (1964), but we have never before called into question the substantive standard by which a State determines that a vote has been legally cast. And there is no reason to think that the guidance provided to the fact finders, specifically the various canvassing boards, by the "intent of the voter" standard is any less sufficient—or will lead to results any less uniform—than, for example, the "beyond a reasonable doubt" standard employed every day by ordinary citizens in courtrooms across this country.

Admittedly, the use of differing substandards for determining voter intent in different counties employing similar voting systems may raise serious concerns. Those concerns are alleviated—if not eliminated—by the fact that a single impartial magistrate will ultimately adjudicate all objections arising from the recount process. . . . If it were otherwise, Florida's decision to leave to each county the determination of what balloting system to employ—despite enormous differences in accuracy—might run afoul of equal protection. So, too, might the similar decisions of the vast majority of state legislatures to delegate to local authorities certain decisions with respect to voting systems and ballot design.

Even assuming that aspects of the remedial scheme might ultimately be found to violate the Equal Protection Clause, I could not subscribe to the majority's disposition of the case. As the majority explicitly holds, once a state legislature determines to select electors through a popular vote, the right to have one's vote counted is of constitutional stature. As the majority further acknowledges, Florida law holds that all ballots that reveal the intent of the voter constitute valid votes. Recognizing these principles, the majority nonetheless orders the termination of the contest proceeding before all such votes have been tabulated. Under their own reasoning, the appropriate course of action would be to remand to allow more specific procedures for implementing the legislature's uniform general standard to be established.

In the interest of finality, however, the majority effectively orders the disenfranchisement of an unknown number of voters whose ballots reveal their intent—and are therefore legal votes under state law—but were for some reason rejected by ballot-counting machines. It does so on the basis of the deadlines set forth in Title 3 of the United States Code. But . . . those provisions merely provide rules of decision for Congress to follow when selecting among conflicting slates of electors. They do not prohibit a State from counting what the majority concedes to be legal votes until a bona fide winner is determined. Indeed, in 1960, Hawaii appointed two slates of electors and Congress chose to count the one appointed on January 4, 1961, well after the Title 3 deadlines. See Josephson & Ross, Repairing the Electoral College, 22 J. Legis. 145 (1996). Thus, nothing prevents the majority, even if it properly found an equal protection violation, from ordering relief appropriate to remedy that violation without depriving Florida voters of their right to have their votes counted. As the majority notes, "[a] desire for speed is not a general excuse for ignoring equal protection guarantees." . . .

What must underlie petitioners' entire federal assault on the Florida election procedures is an unstated lack of confidence in the impartiality and capacity of the state judges who would make the critical decisions if the vote count were to proceed. Otherwise, their position is wholly without merit. The endorsement of that position by the majority of this Court can only lend credence to the most cynical appraisal of the work of judges throughout the land. It is confidence in the men and women who administer the judicial system that is the true backbone of the rule of law. Time will one day heal the wound to that confidence that will be inflicted by today's decision. One thing, however, is certain. Although we may never know with complete certainty the identity of the winner of this year's Presidential election, the identity of the loser is perfectly clear. It is the Nation's confidence in the judge as an impartial guardian of the rule of law. . . .

■ JUSTICE SOUTER, with whom JUSTICE BREYER joins, . . . dissenting.

[I] am in substantial agreement with the dissenting opinion[ ] of Justice Stevens . . . . [But] there is a meritorious argument for relief, as this Court's *per curiam* opinion recognizes. . . . Petitioners have raised an equal protection claim (or, alternatively, a due process claim), in the charge that unjustifiably disparate standards are applied in different electoral jurisdictions to otherwise identical facts. It is true that the Equal Protection Clause does not forbid the use of a variety of voting mechanisms within a jurisdiction, even though different mechanisms will have different levels of effectiveness in recording voters' intentions; local variety can be justified by concerns about cost, the potential value of innovation, and so on. But evidence in the record here suggests that a different order of disparity obtains under rules for determining a voter's intent that have been applied (and could continue to be applied) to identical types of ballots used in identical brands of machines and exhibiting identical physical characteristics (such as "hanging" or "dimpled" chads). I can conceive of no legitimate state interest served by these differing treatments of the expressions of voters' fundamental rights. The differences appear wholly arbitrary.

In deciding what to do about this, we should take account of the fact that electoral votes are due to be cast in six days. I would therefore remand the case to the courts of Florida with instructions to establish uniform standards for evaluating the several types of ballots that have prompted differing treatments, to be applied within and among counties when passing on such identical ballots in any further recounting (or successive recounting) that the courts might order.

Unlike the majority, I see no warrant for this Court to assume that Florida could not possibly comply with this requirement before the date set for the meeting of electors, December 18. . . . There is no justification for denying the State the opportunity to try to count all disputed ballots now.

NOTE: PRECEDENTIAL VALUE OF *BUSH V. GORE*

Bush v. Gore was a surprising decision for many reasons. For one thing, a Supreme Court that had recently and repeatedly reaffirmed the value of federalism—in decisions such as *United States v. Lopez*, 514 U.S. 549 (1995); *City of Boerne v. Flores*, 521 U.S. 507 (1997); *Printz v. United States*, 521 U.S. 898 (1997); and *United States v. Morrison*, 529 U.S. 598 (2000)—overruled a state court's application of state law. Three justices—Rehnquist, Scalia, and Clarence Thomas—also wrote that they would have gone further and overruled the state court's *interpretation* of state law. And rather than remand for the Florida Supreme Court to amend its opinion in light of the Court's complaints, five Republican-appointed justices voted to simply end the recount. Florida certified Bush the winner by 537 votes.

Equally surprising was what the per curiam opinion held: the Florida Supreme Court violated the Equal Protection Clause by failing to provide precise standards for how its counties should determine "legal votes." *Bush*, 531 U.S. at 102. A hallmark of American elections is their lack of uniformity; every state in the country delegates enormous amounts of discretion for local governments to determine how to count votes. As Justice Ruth Bader Ginsburg observed at oral argument, in Florida itself "[t]here are machines, there's the optical scanning. . . . There is the butterfly ballot that we've heard about. . . . How can you have one standard when there are so many varieties of ballots?" Jane Sherron De Hart, *Ruth Bader Ginsburg* 370 (2018). In a draft dissent, Ginsburg emphasized that if there were any violation of equal protection in Florida, it was by the state and local authorities that disenfranchised and excluded black voters with its purge list. But when Scalia accused Ginsburg of engaging in "Al Sharpton" tactics, she withheld her criticism. *Id.* at 371.

Yet even Scalia privately scoffed that the per curiam opinion's equal-protection rationale was, "as we say in Brooklyn, a piece of shit." Evan Thomas, *First: Sandra Day O'Connor* 332 (2019). Indeed, the per curiam opinion didn't suggest that the lack of uniformity in the administration of national elections or in Florida's general election was objectionable. To the contrary, the opinion's principal author, Justice Sandra Day O'Connor, insisted on an unusual and telling sentence: "Our consideration is limited to the present circumstances, for the problem of equal protection in election processes generally presents many complexities." *Bush*, 531 U.S. at 109. In other words, the opinion was a one-time ticket that would apply only to "a situation where a state court with the power to assure uniformity has ordered a statewide recount with minimal procedural safeguards." *Id.*

In the decades since *Bush v. Gore*, the only justices who have ever cited the decision are Thomas and Brett Kavanaugh, the latter of whom worked on Bush's legal team. During the 2020 election campaign, for example, Kavanaugh argued that *federal courts* have the power to alter a state's election laws, but *state courts* cannot, because "as Chief Justice Rehnquist persuasively explained in *Bush v. Gore*, . . . the text of the Constitution requires federal courts to ensure that state courts do not rewrite state election laws." *Democratic Nat'l Comm. v. Wis. State Legis.*, 141 S. Ct. 28, 34 n.1 (2020) (Kavanaugh, J., concurring in denial of application to vacate stay); *see also, e.g.*, *Republican Party of Pa. v. Degraffenreid*, 141 S. Ct. 732 (2021) (Thomas, J., dissenting from the denial of certiorari) ("[P]etitioners presented a strong argument that the Pennsylvania Supreme Court's decision [to extend the deadline for absentee ballots in the 2020 election] violated the Constitution by overriding 'the clearly expressed intent of the legislature.' " (citing *Bush*, 531 U.S. at 120 (Rehnquist, C.J., concurring))).

But the Supreme Court as a whole has not once cited *Bush v. Gore* in the last two decades. The Court therefore has had no opportunity to reconcile its holding with those of earlier opinions that upheld disuniform state standards, such as *San Antonio Independent School District v. Rodriguez*, 411 U.S. 1 (1973), or *North v. Russell*, 427 U.S. 328, 339 (1976) (applying the rational-basis test to uphold a Kentucky system of criminal courts in which defendants in some districts were tried before legally trained judges and defendants in other districts were tried before coal miners with no legal training).

But at a more fundamental level, *Bush v. Gore* is also the archetypical opinion interpreting the Constitution, one of a piece with *McCulloch v. Maryland*, 17 U.S. (4 Wheat.) 159 (1819), and *Marbury v. Madison*, 5 U.S. (1 Cranch) 137 (1803). Like *McCulloch*, *Bush v. Gore* exercised the power of federal courts to achieve the partisan goals of the justices by appealing to broad, abstract principles that could never be expressly enumerated in any constitution. Like *Marbury*, *Bush v. Gore* also asserted the Court's power to invalidate the decisions of democratic governments despite lacking the power to enforce its orders. All three decisions illustrate what the Court expressed in *Planned Parenthood of Southeastern Pennsylvania v. Casey*: the judicial power lies not in its objective capacity to say what the law is but "in its legitimacy, a product of substance and perception that shows itself in the people's *acceptance* of the Judiciary as fit to determine what the Nation's law means and to declare what it demands." 505 U.S. 833, 865 (1992) (emphasis added). As James Madison wrote in 1791, "[p]ublic opinion sets bounds to every government, and is the real sovereign in every free one." 14 *The Papers of James Madison* 170 (Robert A. Rutland & Thomas A. Mason eds., 1983).

Of course, this is not to say that judicial interpretations lack principle whenever they conflict with public opinion. The Supreme Court's interpretations of the Constitution have done much to change the public's understanding of how principles of equality, dignity, and fairness should be prioritized with reference to competing principles. But these interpretations are not merely abstract ideas; in the words of law professor Robert Cover, they take place "in a field of pain and death." Robert Cover, *Violence and the Word*, 95 Yale L.J. 1601, 1601 (1986). When "[a] judge articulates her understanding of a text, . . . somebody loses his freedom, his property, his children, even his life." *Id.* In this respect, no judicial interpretation should be accepted in isolation from how it is enforced by the coercive authority of the state. All judicial interpretation—even constitutional interpretation—is political. Ultimately, the only thing that sanctions it is our acceptance of the principles used to justify its commands.

INDEX

References are to Pages

COMPACT CLAUSE

COMPETENCE AND INSANITY

CONFEDERATION CLAUSE

CONGRESS

CONSTITUTIONAL AMENDMENTS

CONSTITUTIONAL DOCUMENTS

CONSTRUCTION AND INTERPRETATION

CONTEMPT

CONTRACEPTION

CONTRACT RIGHTS

CONTRACTS CLAUSE

COPYRIGHTS

LIBERTY TO CONTRACT, DEPRIVATION OF

MARRIAGE

MILITARY FORCE

MOOTNESS